In the
beginning
God created
the heavens
and
the earth.

Genesis 1:1

PRESENTED

TO

_____

_____

FROM

_____

_____

ON

_____

_____

GOD'S LITTLE DEVOTIONAL BIBLE FOR WOMEN

GOD'S LITTLE
DEVOTIONAL BIBLE
FOR WOMEN

HONOR BOOKS
TULSA, OKLAHOMA

CONTENTS

Beginning Page for Each Bible Book

Old Testament

New Testament

Dear Reader,

We at Honor Books are excited to introduce you to *God's Little Devotional Bible For Women*, the newest and most complete devotional Bible on the market today.

This new devotional Bible is unique because:

- It combines one of today's most popular Bible translations (NKJV) with the best-selling "*God's Little Devotional Book*" series (more than 1.2 million sold in 1996 alone!) to create a powerful 1600-page volume.

- Every day contains a Scripture passage from the Old Testament, The New Testament, Psalms, and Proverbs, along with a devotional reading for each day of the year (no skimping on the weekends!)

- This user-friendly plan allows you to read through the **entire** Bible in 365 days, digesting realistic, bite-sized portions while enjoying dynamic devotional stories that illustrate the timeless truths of Scripture.

- It includes a topical table of contents (beginning on page 1575) that allows readers to quickly find the devotional subject that meets their immediate needs!

Whether it's a deeper relationship with God, fresh inspiration to help you fulfill your God-given potential, or practical encouragement for overcoming the daily challenges of life, you'll find the answers you need in this **ultimate** devotional book—*God's Little Devotional Bible For Women*.

May God bless you as you discover the insights and inspiration that can help you become the woman God has created you to be.

In Christ,

The Publisher

PREFACE
TO
THE NEW KING JAMES VERSION

Purpose

In the preface to the 1611 edition, the translators of the Authorized Version, known popularly as the King James Bible, state that it was not their purpose "to make a new translation . . . but to make a good one better." Indebted to the earlier work of William Tyndale and others, they saw their best contribution to consist in revising and enhancing the excellence of the English versions which had sprung from the Reformation of the sixteenth century. In harmony with the purpose of the King James scholars, the translators and editors of the present work have not pursued a goal of innovation. They have perceived the Holy Bible, New King James Version, as a continuation of the labors of the earlier translators, thus unlocking for today's readers the spiritual treasures found especially in the Authorized Version of the Holy Scriptures.

A Living Legacy

For nearly four hundred years, and throughout several revisions of its English form, the King James Bible has been deeply revered among the English-speaking peoples of the world. The precision of translation for which it is historically renowned, and its majesty of style, have enabled that monumental version of the Word of God to become the mainspring of the religion, language, and legal foundations of our civilization.

Although the Elizabethan period and our own era share in zeal for technical advance, the former period was more aggressively devoted to classical learning. Along with this awakened concern for the classics came a flourishing companion interest in the Scriptures, an interest that was enlivened by the conviction that the manuscripts were providentially handed down and were a trustworthy record of the inspired Word of God. The King James translators were committed to producing an English Bible that would be a precise translation, and by no means a paraphrase or a broadly approximate rendering. On the one hand, the scholars were almost as familiar with the original languages of the Bible as with their native English. On the other hand, their reverence for the divine Author and His Word assured a translation of the Scriptures in which only a principle of utmost accuracy could be accepted.

In 1786 Catholic scholar Alexander Geddes said of the King James Bible, "If accuracy and strictest attention to the letter of the text be supposed to constitute an excellent version, this is of all versions the most excellent." George Bernard Shaw became a literary legend in our century because of his severe and often humorous criticisms of our most cherished values. Surprisingly, however, Shaw pays the following tribute to the scholars commissioned by King James: "The translation was extraordinarily well done because to the translators what they were translating was not merely a curious collection of ancient books written by different authors in different stages of culture, but the Word of God divinely revealed through His chosen and expressly inspired scribes. In this conviction they carried out their work with boundless reverence and care and achieved a beautifully artistic result." History agrees with these estimates. Therefore, while seeking to unveil the excellent *form* of the traditional English Bible, special care has also been taken in the present edition to preserve the work of *precision* which is the legacy of the 1611 translators.

Complete Equivalence in Translation

Where new translation has been necessary in the New King James Version, the most complete representation of the original has been rendered by considering the history of usage and etymology of words in their contexts. This principle of complete equivalence seeks to preserve *all* of the information in the text, while presenting it in good literary form. Dynamic equivalence, a recent procedure in Bible translation, commonly results in paraphrasing where a more literal rendering is needed to reflect a specific and vital sense. For example, complete equivalence truly renders the original text in expressions such as "lifted her voice and wept" (Gen. 21:16); "I gave you cleanness of teeth" (Amos 4:6); "Jesus met them, saying, 'Rejoice!' " (Matt. 28:9); and " 'Woman, what does your concern have to do with Me?' " (John 2:4). Complete equivalence translates fully, in order to provide an English text that is both accurate and readable.

In keeping with the principle of complete equivalence, it is the policy to translate interjections which are commonly omitted in modern language renderings of the Bible. As an example, the interjection *behold,* in the older King James editions, continues to have a place in English usage, especially in dramatically calling attention to a spectacular scene, or an event of profound importance such as the Immanuel prophecy of Isaiah 7:14. Consequently, *behold* is retained for these occasions in the present edition. However, the Hebrew and Greek originals for this word can be translated variously, depending on the circumstances in the passage. Therefore, in addition to *behold,* words such as *indeed, look, see,* and *surely* are also rendered to convey the appropriate sense suggested by the context in each case.

In faithfulness to God and to our readers, it was deemed appropriate that all participating scholars sign a statement affirming their belief in the verbal and plenary inspiration of Scripture, and in the inerrancy of the original autographs.

Devotional Quality

The King James scholars readily appreciated the intrinsic beauty of divine revelation. They accordingly disciplined their talents to render well-chosen English words of their time, as well as a graceful, often musical arrangement of language, which has stirred the hearts of Bible readers through the years. The translators,

the committees, and the editors of the present edition, while sensitive to the late-twentieth-century English idiom, and while adhering faithfully to the Hebrew, Aramaic, and Greek texts, have sought to maintain those lyrical and devotional qualities that are so highly regarded in the Authorized Version. This devotional quality is especially apparent in the poetic and prophetic books, although even the relatively plain style of the Gospels and Epistles cannot strictly be likened, as sometimes suggested, to modern newspaper style. The Koine Greek of the New Testament is influenced by the Hebrew background of the writers, for whom even the Gospel narratives were not merely flat utterance, but often song in various degrees of rhythm.

The Style

Students of the Bible applaud the timeless devotional character of our historic Bible. Yet it is also universally understood that our language, like all living languages, has undergone profound change since 1611. Subsequent revisions of the King James Bible have sought to keep abreast of changes in English speech. The present work is a further step toward this objective. Where obsolescence and other reading difficulties exist, present-day vocabulary, punctuation, and grammar have been carefully integrated. Words representing ancient objects, such as *chariot* and *phylactery,* have no modern substitutes and are therefore retained.

A special feature of the New King James Version is its conformity to the thought flow of the 1611 Bible. The reader discovers that the sequence and selection of words, phrases, and clauses of the new edition, while much clearer, are so close to the traditional that there is remarkable ease in listening to the reading of either edition while following with the other.

In the discipline of translating biblical and other ancient languages, a standard method of transliteration, that is, the English spelling of untranslated words, such as names of persons and places, has never been commonly adopted. In keeping with the design of the present work, the King James spelling of untranslated words is retained, although made uniform throughout. For example, instead of the spellings *Isaiah* and *Elijah* in the Old Testament, and *Esaias* and *Elias* in the New Testament, *Isaiah* and *Elijah* now appear in both Testaments.

King James doctrinal and theological terms, for example, *propitiation, justification,* and *sanctification,* are generally familiar to English-speaking peoples. Such terms have been retained except where the original language indicates need for a more precise translation.

Readers of the Authorized Version will immediately be struck by the absence of several pronouns: *thee, thou,* and *ye* are replaced by the simple *you,* while *your* and *yours* are substituted for *thy* and *thine* as applicable. *Thee, thou, thy,* and *thine* were once forms of address to express a special relationship to human as well as divine persons. These pronouns are no longer part of our language. However, reverence for God in the present work is preserved by capitalizing pronouns, including *You, Your,* and *Yours,* which refer to Him. Additionally, capitalization of these pronouns benefits the reader by clearly distinguishing divine and human persons referred to in a passage. Without such capitalization the distinction is often obscure, because the antecedent of a pronoun is not always clear in the English translation.

In addition to the pronoun usages of the seventeenth century, the *-eth* and *-est* verb endings, so familiar in the earlier King James editions, are now obsolete. Unless a speaker is schooled in these verb endings, there is common difficulty in selecting the correct form to be used with a given subject of the verb in vocal prayer. That is, should we use *love, loveth,* or *lovest? do, doeth, doest,* or *dost? have, hath,* or *hast?* Because these forms are obsolete, contemporary English usage has been substituted for the previous verb endings.

In older editions of the King James Version, the frequency of the connective *and* far exceeded the limits of present English usage. Also, biblical linguists agree that the Hebrew and Greek original words for this conjunction may commonly be translated otherwise, depending on the immediate context. Therefore, instead of *and,* alternatives such as *also, but, however, now, so, then,* and *thus* are accordingly rendered in the present edition, when the original language permits.

The real character of the Authorized Version does not reside in its archaic pronouns or verbs or other grammatical forms of the seventeenth century, but rather in the care taken by its scholars to impart the letter and spirit of the original text in a majestic and reverent style.

The Format

The format of the New King James Version is designed to enhance the vividness and devotional quality of the Holy Scriptures:

—Words or phrases in *italics* indicate expressions in the original language which require clarification by additional English words, as also done throughout the history of the King James Bible.
—Poetry is structured as contemporary verse to reflect the poetic form and beauty of the passage in the original language.
—The covenant name of God was usually translated from the Hebrew as "LORD" or "GOD" (using capital letters as shown) in the King James Old Testament. This tradition is maintained. In the present edition the name is so capitalized whenever the covenant name is quoted in the New Testament from a passage in the Old Testament.

The Old Testament Text

The Hebrew Bible has come down to us through the scrupulous care of ancient scribes who copied the original text in successive generations. By the sixth century A.D. the scribes were succeeded by a group known as the Masoretes, who continued to preserve the sacred Scriptures for another five hundred years in a form known as the Masoretic Text. Babylonia, Palestine, and Tiberias were the main centers of Masoretic activity; but by the tenth century A.D. the Masoretes of Tiberias, led by the family of ben Asher, gained the ascendancy. Through subsequent editions, the ben Asher text became in the twelfth century the only recognized form of the Hebrew Scriptures.

Daniel Bomberg printed the first Rabbinic Bible in 1516–17; that work was followed in 1524–25 by a second edition prepared by Jacob ben Chayyim and also published by Bomberg. The text of ben Chayyim was adopted in most subsequent Hebrew Bibles, including those used by the King James translators. The ben Chayyim text was also used for the first two editions of Rudolph Kittel's *Biblia Hebraica* of 1906 and 1912. In 1937 Paul Kahle published a third edition of *Biblia Hebraica*. This edition was based on the oldest dated manuscript of the ben Asher text, the Leningrad Manuscript B19a (A.D. 1008), which Kahle regarded as superior to that used by ben Chayyim.

For the New King James Version the text used was the 1967/1977 Stuttgart edition of the *Biblia Hebraica*, with frequent comparisons being made with the Bomberg edition of 1524–25. The Septuagint (Greek) Version of the Old Testament and the Latin Vulgate also were consulted. In addition to referring to a variety of ancient versions of the Hebrew Scriptures, the New King James Version draws on the resources of relevant manuscripts from the Dead Sea caves. In the few places where the Hebrew was so obscure that the 1611 King James was compelled to follow one of the versions, but where information is now available to resolve the problems, the New King James Version follows the Hebrew text.

The New Testament Text

There is more manuscript support for the New Testament than for any other body of ancient literature. Over five thousand Greek, eight thousand Latin, and many more manuscripts in other languages attest the integrity of the New Testament. There is only one basic New Testament used by Protestants, Roman Catholics, and Orthodox, by conservatives and liberals. Minor variations in hand copying have appeared through the centuries, before mechanical printing began about A.D. 1450.

Some variations exist in the spelling of Greek words, in word order, and in similar details. These ordinarily do not show up in translation and do not affect the sense of the text in any way.

Other manuscript differences such as omission or inclusion of a word or a clause, and two paragraphs in the Gospels, should not overshadow the overwhelming degree of *agreement* which exists among the ancient records. Bible readers may be assured that the most important differences in English New Testaments of today are due, not to manuscript divergence, but to the way in which translators view the task of translation: How literally should the text be rendered? How does the translator view the matter of biblical inspiration? Does the translator adopt a paraphrase when a literal rendering would be quite clear and more to the point? The New King James Version follows the historic precedent of the Authorized Version in maintaining a literal approach to translation, except where the idiom of the original language cannot be translated directly into our tongue.

The King James New Testament was based on the traditional text of the Greek-speaking churches, first published in 1516, and later called the Textus Receptus or Received Text. Although based on the relatively few available manuscripts, these were representative of many more which existed at the time but only became known later. In the late nineteenth century, B. Westcott and F. Hort taught that this text had been officially edited by the fourth-century church, but a total lack of historical evidence for this event has forced a revision of the theory. It is now widely held that the Byzantine Text that largely supports the Textus Receptus has as much right as the Alexandrian or any other tradition to be weighed in determining the text of the New Testament.

Since the 1880s most contemporary translations of the New Testament have relied upon a relatively few manuscripts discovered chiefly in the late nineteenth and early twentieth centuries. Such translations depend primarily on two manuscripts, Codex Vaticanus and Codex Sinaiticus, because of their greater age. The Greek text obtained by using these sources and the related papyri (our most ancient manuscripts) is known as the Alexandrian Text. However, some scholars have grounds for doubting the faithfulness of Vaticanus and Sinaiticus, since they often disagree with one another, and Sinaiticus exhibits excessive omission.

A third viewpoint of New Testament scholarship holds that the best text is based on the consensus of the majority of existing Greek manuscripts. The text is called the Majority Text. Most of these manuscripts are in substantial agreement. Even though many are late, and none is earlier than the fifth century, usually their readings are verified by papyri, ancient versions, quotations from the early church fathers, or a combination of these. The Majority Text is similar to the Textus Receptus, but it corrects those readings which have little or no support in the Greek manuscript tradition.

Today, scholars agree that the science of New Testament textual criticism is in a state of flux. Very few scholars still favor the Textus Receptus as such, and then often for its historical prestige as the text of Luther, Calvin, Tyndale, and the King James Version. For about a century most have followed a Critical Text (so called because it is edited according to specific principles of textual criticism) which depends heavily upon the Alexandrian type of text. More recently many have abandoned this Critical Text (which is quite similar to the one edited by Westcott and Hort) for one that is more eclectic. Finally, a small but growing number of scholars prefer the Majority Text, which is close to the traditional text except in the Revelation.

In light of these facts, and also because the New King James Version is the fifth revision of a historic document translated from specific Greek texts, the editors decided to retain the traditional text in the body of the New Testament. It is most important to emphasize that fully eighty-five percent of the New Testament text is the same in the Textus Receptus, the Alexandrian Text, and the Majority Text.

∾ GENESIS 1:1—2:25 ∾

In the beginning God created the heavens and the earth. ² The earth was without form, and void; and darkness *was* on the face of the deep. And the Spirit of God was hovering over the face of the waters.

³ Then God said, "Let there be light"; and there was light. ⁴ And God saw the light, that *it was* good; and God divided the light from the darkness. ⁵ God called the light Day, and the darkness He called Night. So the evening and the morning were the first day.

⁶ Then God said, "Let there be a firmament in the midst of the waters, and let it divide the waters from the waters." ⁷ Thus God made the firmament, and divided the waters which *were* under the firmament from the waters which *were* above the firmament; and it was so. ⁸ And God called the firmament Heaven. So the evening and the morning were the second day.

⁹ Then God said, "Let the waters under the heavens be gathered together into one place, and let the dry *land* appear"; and it was so. ¹⁰ And God called the dry *land* Earth, and the gathering together of the waters He called Seas. And God saw that *it was* good.

¹¹ Then God said, "Let the earth bring forth grass, the herb *that* yields seed, *and* the fruit tree *that* yields fruit according to its kind, whose seed *is* in itself, on the earth"; and it was so. ¹² And the earth brought forth grass, the herb *that* yields seed according to its kind, and the tree *that* yields fruit, whose seed *is* in itself according to its kind. And God saw that *it was* good. ¹³ So the evening and the morning were the third day.

¹⁴ Then God said, "Let there be lights in the firmament of the heavens to divide the day from the night; and let them be for signs and seasons, and for days and years; ¹⁵ and let them be for lights in the firmament of the heavens to give light on the earth"; and it was so. ¹⁶ Then God made two great lights: the greater light to rule the day, and the lesser light to rule the night. *He made* the stars also. ¹⁷ God set them in the firmament of the heavens to give light on the earth, ¹⁸ and to rule over the day and over the night, and to divide the light from the darkness. And God saw that *it was* good. ¹⁹ So the evening and the morning were the fourth day.

²⁰ Then God said, "Let the waters abound with an abundance of living creatures, and let birds fly above the earth across the face of the firmament of the heavens." ²¹ So God created great sea creatures and every living thing that moves, with which the waters abounded, according to their kind, and every winged bird according to its kind. And God saw that *it was* good. ²² And God blessed them, saying, "Be fruitful and multiply, and fill the waters in the seas, and let birds multiply on the earth." ²³ So the evening and the morning were the fifth day.

²⁴ Then God said, "Let the earth bring forth the living creature according to its kind: cattle and creeping thing and beast of the earth, *each* according to its kind"; and it was so. ²⁵ And God made the beast of the earth according to its kind, cattle according to its kind, and everything that creeps on the earth according to its kind. And God saw that *it was* good.

²⁶ Then God said, "Let Us make man in Our image, according to Our likeness; let them have dominion over the fish of the sea, over the birds of the air, and over the cattle, over all the earth and over every creeping thing that creeps on the earth." ²⁷ So God created man in His *own* image; in the image of God He created him; male and female He created them. ²⁸ Then God blessed them, and God said to them, "Be fruitful and multiply; fill the earth and subdue it; have dominion over the fish of the sea, over the birds of the air, and over every living thing that moves on the earth."

²⁹ And God said, "See, I have given you every herb *that* yields seed which *is* on the face of all the earth, and every tree whose fruit yields seed; to you it shall be for food. ³⁰ Also, to every beast of the earth, to every bird of the air, and to everything that creeps on the earth, in which *there is* life, *I have given* every green herb for food"; and it was so. ³¹ Then God saw everything that He had made, and indeed

it was very good. So the evening and the morning were the sixth day.

2 Thus the heavens and the earth, and all the host of them, were finished. ² And on the seventh day God ended His work which He had done, and He rested on the seventh day from all His work which He had done. ³ Then God blessed the seventh day and sanctified it, because in it He rested from all His work which God had created and made.

⁴ This *is* the history of the heavens and the earth when they were created, in the day that the LORD God made the earth and the heavens, ⁵ before any plant of the field was in the earth and before any herb of the field had grown. For the LORD God had not caused it to rain on the earth, and *there was* no man to till the ground; ⁶ but a mist went up from the earth and watered the whole face of the ground.

⁷ And the LORD God formed man *of* the dust of the ground, and breathed into his nostrils the breath of life; and man became a living being.

⁸ The LORD God planted a garden eastward in Eden, and there He put the man whom He had formed. ⁹ And out of the ground the LORD God made every tree grow that is pleasant to the sight and good for food. The tree of life *was* also in the midst of the garden, and the tree of the knowledge of good and evil.

¹⁰ Now a river went out of Eden to water the garden, and from there it parted and became four riverheads. ¹¹ The name of the first *is* Pishon; it *is* the one which skirts the whole land of Havilah, where *there is* gold. ¹² And the gold of that land *is* good. Bdellium and the onyx stone *are* there. ¹³ The name of the second river *is* Gihon; it *is* the one which goes around the whole land of Cush. ¹⁴ The name of the third river *is* Hiddekel; it *is* the one which goes toward the east of Assyria. The fourth river *is* the Euphrates.

¹⁵ Then the LORD God took the man and put him in the garden of Eden to tend and keep it. ¹⁶ And the LORD God commanded the man, saying, "Of every tree of the garden you may freely eat; ¹⁷ but of the tree of the knowledge of good and evil you shall not eat, for in the day that you eat of it you shall surely die."

¹⁸ And the LORD God said, "It is not good that man should be alone; I will make him a helper comparable to him." ¹⁹ Out of the ground the LORD God formed every beast of the field and every bird of the air, and brought *them* to Adam to see what he would call them. And whatever Adam called each living creature, that *was* its name. ²⁰ So Adam gave names to all cattle, to the birds of the air, and to every beast of the field. But for Adam there was not found a helper comparable to him.

²¹ And the LORD God caused a deep sleep to fall on Adam, and he slept; and He took one of his ribs, and closed up the flesh in its place. ²² Then the rib which the LORD God had taken from man He made into a woman, and He brought her to the man.

²³ And Adam said:

"This *is* now bone of my bones
    And flesh of my flesh;
She shall be called Woman,
    Because she was taken out of
        Man."

²⁴ Therefore a man shall leave his father and mother and be joined to his wife, and they shall become one flesh.

²⁵ And they were both naked, the man and his wife, and were not ashamed.

～ PSALM 1:1–6 ～

¹   Blessed *is* the man
    Who walks not in the counsel of the
        ungodly,
        Nor stands in the path of sinners,
        Nor sits in the seat of the scornful;
²   But his delight *is* in the law of the
        LORD,
        And in His law he meditates day
            and night.
³   He shall be like a tree
        Planted by the rivers of water,
        That brings forth its fruit in its
            season,
        Whose leaf also shall not wither;
    And whatever he does shall prosper.

⁴   The ungodly *are* not so,
    But *are* like the chaff which the wind
        drives away.

Bending Low

As a young man Carlos Romulo, the former president of the Philippines, won an oratorical contest in the Manila high school he attended. His father was puzzled, however, when he noticed his son ignoring the congratulations of one of the other contestants. As they left the auditorium he asked Carlos, "Why didn't you shake hands with Julio?"

"I have no use for Julio," Carlos replied. "He was speaking ill of me before the contest." The father put his arm around his son and said, "Your grandfather used to tell me that the taller the bamboo grows, the lower it bends. Remember that always, my boy. The taller the bamboo grows, the lower it bends."

A woman once advised a new employee: "Fifty percent of the people in this organization will teach you what to do and the other 50 percent what not to do. It's your challenge to figure out which percent goes with which person." Even if a person doesn't provide a good example, you can always learn from him or her what not to do.

Every person has something to teach us — not only those who are experts in their fields or those who just tell us what we want to hear. Every human being is a living encyclopedia of ideas, insights, facts, experiences, and opinions. If we are wise we will keep our eyes and ears open, and learn from everyone around us.

> A wise man will hear and increase learning, and a man of understanding will attain wise counsel.
>
> *Proverbs 1:5*

5 Therefore the ungodly shall not
stand in the judgment,
Nor sinners in the congregation of
the righteous.

6 For the LORD knows the way of the
righteous,
But the way of the ungodly shall
perish.

~ PROVERBS 1:1-7 ~

The proverbs of Solomon the son of David, king of Israel:

2 To know wisdom and instruction,
To perceive the words of
understanding,
3 To receive the instruction of wisdom,
Justice, judgment, and equity;
4 To give prudence to the simple,
To the young man knowledge and
discretion—
5 A wise *man* will hear and increase
learning,
And a man of understanding will
attain wise counsel,
6 To understand a proverb and an
enigma,
The words of the wise and their
riddles.

7 The fear of the LORD *is* the
beginning of knowledge,
But fools despise wisdom and
instruction.

~ MATTHEW 1:1-25 ~

The book of the genealogy of Jesus Christ,
the Son of David, the Son of Abraham:
2 Abraham begot Isaac, Isaac begot
Jacob, and Jacob begot Judah and his
brothers. 3 Judah begot Perez and Zerah
by Tamar, Perez begot Hezron, and
Hezron begot Ram. 4 Ram begot Amminadab, Amminadab begot Nahshon, and
Nahshon begot Salmon. 5 Salmon begot
Boaz by Rahab, Boaz begot Obed by Ruth,
Obed begot Jesse, 6 and Jesse begot David
the king.

David the king begot Solomon by her
who had been the wife of Uriah. 7 Solomon
begot Rehoboam, Rehoboam begot
Abijah, and Abijah begot Asa. 8 Asa begot
Jehoshaphat, Jehoshaphat begot Joram,
and Joram begot Uzziah. 9 Uzziah begot
Jotham, Jotham begot Ahaz, and Ahaz
begot Hezekiah. 10 Hezekiah begot
Manasseh, Manasseh begot Amon, and
Amon begot Josiah. 11 Josiah begot
Jeconiah and his brothers about the time
they were carried away to Babylon.

12 And after they were brought to
Babylon, Jeconiah begot Shealtiel, and
Shealtiel begot Zerubbabel. 13 Zerubbabel
begot Abiud, Abiud begot Eliakim, and
Eliakim begot Azor. 14 Azor begot Zadok,
Zadok begot Achim, and Achim begot
Eliud. 15 Eliud begot Eleazar, Eleazar begot Matthan, and Matthan begot Jacob.
16 And Jacob begot Joseph the husband
of Mary, of whom was born Jesus who is
called Christ.

17 So all the generations from Abraham
to David *are* fourteen generations, from
David until the captivity in Babylon *are*
fourteen generations, and from the captivity in Babylon until the Christ *are* fourteen generations.

18 Now the birth of Jesus Christ was as
follows: After His mother Mary was betrothed to Joseph, before they came together, she was found with child of the
Holy Spirit. 19 Then Joseph her husband,
being a just *man,* and not wanting to make
her a public example, was minded to put
her away secretly. 20 But while he thought
about these things, behold, an angel of
the Lord appeared to him in a dream, saying, "Joseph, son of David, do not be
afraid to take to you Mary your wife, for
that which is conceived in her is of the
Holy Spirit. 21 And she will bring forth a
Son, and you shall call His name JESUS,
for He will save His people from their
sins."

22 So all this was done that it might be
fulfilled which was spoken by the Lord
through the prophet, saying: 23 "Behold,
the virgin shall be with child, and bear a
Son, and they shall call His name
Immanuel," which is translated, "God
with us."

24 Then Joseph, being aroused from
sleep, did as the angel of the Lord commanded him and took to him his wife,
25 and did not know her till she had
brought forth her firstborn Son. And he
called His name JESUS.

～ GENESIS 3:1—4:26 ～

Now the serpent was more cunning than any beast of the field which the LORD God had made. And he said to the woman, "Has God indeed said, 'You shall not eat of every tree of the garden'?"

2 And the woman said to the serpent, "We may eat the fruit of the trees of the garden; 3 but of the fruit of the tree which *is* in the midst of the garden, God has said, 'You shall not eat it, nor shall you touch it, lest you die.' "

4 Then the serpent said to the woman, "You will not surely die. 5 For God knows that in the day you eat of it your eyes will be opened, and you will be like God, knowing good and evil."

6 So when the woman saw that the tree *was* good for food, that it *was* pleasant to the eyes, and a tree desirable to make *one* wise, she took of its fruit and ate. She also gave to her husband with her, and he ate. 7 Then the eyes of both of them were opened, and they knew that they *were* naked; and they sewed fig leaves together and made themselves coverings.

8 And they heard the sound of the LORD God walking in the garden in the cool of the day, and Adam and his wife hid themselves from the presence of the LORD God among the trees of the garden. 9 Then the LORD God called to Adam and said to him, "Where *are* you?"

10 So he said, "I heard Your voice in the garden, and I was afraid because I was naked; and I hid myself."

11 And He said, "Who told you that you *were* naked? Have you eaten from the tree of which I commanded you that you should not eat?"

12 Then the man said, "The woman whom You gave *to be* with me, she gave me of the tree, and I ate."

13 And the LORD God said to the woman, "What *is* this you have done?"

The woman said, "The serpent deceived me, and I ate."

14 So the LORD God said to the serpent:

"Because you have done this,
  You *are* cursed more than all
    cattle,
And more than every beast of the
    field;
On your belly you shall go,
  And you shall eat dust
  All the days of your life.
15 And I will put enmity
  Between you and the woman,
  And between your seed and her
    Seed;
  He shall bruise your head,
  And you shall bruise His heel."

16 To the woman He said:

"I will greatly multiply your sorrow
    and your conception;
  In pain you shall bring forth
    children;
  Your desire *shall be* for your
    husband,
  And he shall rule over you."

17 Then to Adam He said, "Because you have heeded the voice of your wife, and have eaten from the tree of which I commanded you, saying, 'You shall not eat of it':

"Cursed *is* the ground for your
    sake;
  In toil you shall eat *of* it
  All the days of your life.
18 Both thorns and thistles it shall
    bring forth for you,
  And you shall eat the herb of the
    field.
19 In the sweat of your face you shall
    eat bread
  Till you return to the ground,
  For out of it you were taken;
  For dust you *are*,
  And to dust you shall return."

20 And Adam called his wife's name Eve, because she was the mother of all living.

21 Also for Adam and his wife the LORD God made tunics of skin, and clothed them.

22 Then the LORD God said, "Behold, the man has become like one of Us, to know good and evil. And now, lest he put out his hand and take also of the tree of

life, and eat, and live forever"— ²³ therefore the LORD God sent him out of the garden of Eden to till the ground from which he was taken. ²⁴ So He drove out the man; and He placed cherubim at the east of the garden of Eden, and a flaming sword which turned every way, to guard the way to the tree of life.

4 Now Adam knew Eve his wife, and she conceived and bore Cain, and said, "I have acquired a man from the LORD." ² Then she bore again, this time his brother Abel. Now Abel was a keeper of sheep, but Cain was a tiller of the ground. ³ And in the process of time it came to pass that Cain brought an offering of the fruit of the ground to the LORD. ⁴ Abel also brought of the firstborn of his flock and of their fat. And the LORD respected Abel and his offering, ⁵ but He did not respect Cain and his offering. And Cain was very angry, and his countenance fell.

⁶ So the LORD said to Cain, "Why are you angry? And why has your countenance fallen? ⁷ If you do well, will you not be accepted? And if you do not do well, sin lies at the door. And its desire *is* for you, but you should rule over it."

⁸ Now Cain talked with Abel his brother; and it came to pass, when they were in the field, that Cain rose up against Abel his brother and killed him.

⁹ Then the LORD said to Cain, "Where *is* Abel your brother?"

He said, "I do not know. *Am* I my brother's keeper?"

¹⁰ And He said, "What have you done? The voice of your brother's blood cries out to Me from the ground. ¹¹ So now you *are* cursed from the earth, which has opened its mouth to receive your brother's blood from your hand. ¹² When you till the ground, it shall no longer yield its strength to you. A fugitive and a vagabond you shall be on the earth."

¹³ And Cain said to the LORD, "My punishment *is* greater than I can bear! ¹⁴ Surely You have driven me out this day from the face of the ground; I shall be hidden from Your face; I shall be a fugitive and a vagabond on the earth, and it will happen *that* anyone who finds me will kill me."

¹⁵ And the LORD said to him, "Therefore, whoever kills Cain, vengeance shall be taken on him sevenfold." And the LORD set a mark on Cain, lest anyone finding him should kill him.

¹⁶ Then Cain went out from the presence of the LORD and dwelt in the land of Nod on the east of Eden. ¹⁷ And Cain knew his wife, and she conceived and bore Enoch. And he built a city, and called the name of the city after the name of his son—Enoch. ¹⁸ To Enoch was born Irad; and Irad begot Mehujael, and Mehujael begot Methushael, and Methushael begot Lamech.

¹⁹ Then Lamech took for himself two wives: the name of one *was* Adah, and the name of the second *was* Zillah. ²⁰ And Adah bore Jabal. He was the father of those who dwell in tents and have livestock. ²¹ His brother's name *was* Jubal. He was the father of all those who play the harp and flute. ²² And as for Zillah, she also bore Tubal-Cain, an instructor of every craftsman in bronze and iron. And the sister of Tubal-Cain *was* Naamah.

²³ Then Lamech said to his wives:

"Adah and Zillah, hear my voice;
Wives of Lamech, listen to my
speech!
For I have killed a man for
wounding me,
Even a young man for hurting me.
²⁴ If Cain shall be avenged sevenfold,
Then Lamech seventy-sevenfold."

²⁵ And Adam knew his wife again, and she bore a son and named him Seth, "For God has appointed another seed for me instead of Abel, whom Cain killed." ²⁶ And as for Seth, to him also a son was born; and he named him Enosh. Then *men* began to call on the name of the LORD.

～ PSALM 2:1–6 ～

1 Why do the nations rage,
And the people plot a vain thing?
2 The kings of the earth set
themselves,
And the rulers take counsel together,
Against the LORD and against His
Anointed, *saying,*
3 "Let us break Their bonds in pieces
And cast away Their cords from us."

Loving the Unlovable

When both of Susie's parents died, she had no other relatives to care for her so she was placed into foster care. Eventually, she came to live with the Weavers. Mrs. Weaver found Susie sullen, withdrawn, and uncommunicative. When she asked to see Susie's records she found that other families agreed. The first foster family wrote, "Susie is a quiet, shy girl." The second family wrote, "She obeys, but she doesn't participate much in the family." *I doubt if Susie will be with us long,* Mrs. Weaver thought. Still, she decided to keep Susie through the Christmas holiday and then talk to her social worker about a transfer to another home.

At Christmas, the Weavers exchanged a number of lovely presents, including gifts for Susie. Then Susie handed Mrs. Weaver a brown paper sack decorated with a rough drawing of a Christmas scene. Inside, she found a rhinestone necklace with a couple of stones missing and a little bottle of perfume, half empty. As she put on the necklace and dabbed perfume behind her ear, Susie said, "Mom's necklace looks good on you. You smell good like she did, too." Mrs. Weaver's heart melted. She vowed to renew her efforts to love Susie, and she succeeded! By the following Christmas, Susie had become her adopted daughter.

When we come across someone in need, sometimes our first inclination is to send them on to someone who can help them. Often, however, the someone who can help them is standing right in front of them — you. Just as Mrs. Weaver experienced, when we make the decision to help, God supplies the strength and the wisdom we need to make a difference in someone's life.

⁴ He who sits in the heavens shall laugh;
   The LORD shall hold them in
      derision.
⁵ Then He shall speak to them in His
      wrath,
   And distress them in His deep
      displeasure:
⁶ "Yet I have set My King
   On My holy hill of Zion."

∼ PROVERBS 1:8, 9 ∼

⁸ My son, hear the instruction of your
      father,
   And do not forsake the law of your
      mother;
⁹ For they *will be* a graceful ornament
      on your head,
   And chains about your neck.

∼ MATTHEW 2:1–23 ∼

Now after Jesus was born in Bethlehem of Judea in the days of Herod the king, behold, wise men from the East came to Jerusalem, ² saying, "Where is He who has been born King of the Jews? For we have seen His star in the East and have come to worship Him."

³ When Herod the king heard *this,* he was troubled, and all Jerusalem with him. ⁴ And when he had gathered all the chief priests and scribes of the people together, he inquired of them where the Christ was to be born.

⁵ So they said to him, "In Bethlehem of Judea, for thus it is written by the prophet:

⁶ 'But you, Bethlehem, *in* the land of
      Judah,
   Are not the least among the rulers
      of Judah;
   For out of you shall come a Ruler
   Who will shepherd My people
      Israel.' "

⁷ Then Herod, when he had secretly called the wise men, determined from them what time the star appeared. ⁸ And he sent them to Bethlehem and said, "Go and search carefully for the young Child, and when you have found *Him,* bring back word to me, that I may come and worship Him also."

⁹ When they heard the king, they departed; and behold, the star which they had seen in the East went before them, till it came and stood over where the young Child was. ¹⁰ When they saw the star, they rejoiced with exceedingly great joy. ¹¹ And when they had come into the house, they saw the young Child with Mary His mother, and fell down and worshiped Him. And when they had opened their treasures, they presented gifts to Him: gold, frankincense, and myrrh.

¹² Then, being divinely warned in a dream that they should not return to Herod, they departed for their own country another way.

¹³ Now when they had departed, behold, an angel of the Lord appeared to Joseph in a dream, saying, "Arise, take the young Child and His mother, flee to Egypt, and stay there until I bring you word; for Herod will seek the young Child to destroy Him."

¹⁴ When he arose, he took the young Child and His mother by night and departed for Egypt, ¹⁵ and was there until the death of Herod, that it might be fulfilled which was spoken by the Lord through the prophet, saying, "Out of Egypt I called My Son."

¹⁶ Then Herod, when he saw that he was deceived by the wise men, was exceedingly angry; and he sent forth and put to death all the male children who were in Bethlehem and in all its districts, from two years old and under, according to the time which he had determined from the wise men. ¹⁷ Then was fulfilled what was spoken by Jeremiah the prophet, saying:

¹⁸ "A voice was heard in Ramah,
   Lamentation, weeping, and great
      mourning,
   Rachel weeping *for* her children,
   Refusing to be comforted,
   Because they are no more."

¹⁹ Now when Herod was dead, behold, an angel of the Lord appeared in a dream to Joseph in Egypt, ²⁰ saying, "Arise, take the young Child and His mother, and go to the land of Israel, for those who sought the young Child's life are dead." ²¹ Then he arose, took the young Child and His

mother, and came into the land of Israel. ²² But when he heard that Archelaus was reigning over Judea instead of his father Herod, he was afraid to go there. And being warned by God in a dream, he turned aside into the region of Galilee. ²³ And he came and dwelt in a city called Nazareth, that it might be fulfilled which was spoken by the prophets, "He shall be called a Nazarene."

∼ GENESIS 5:1—6:22 ∼

This is the book of the genealogy of Adam. In the day that God created man, He made him in the likeness of God. ² He created them male and female, and blessed them and called them Mankind in the day they were created. ³ And Adam lived one hundred and thirty years, and begot *a son* in his own likeness, after his image, and named him Seth. ⁴ After he begot Seth, the days of Adam were eight hundred years; and he had sons and daughters. ⁵ So all the days that Adam lived were nine hundred and thirty years; and he died.

⁶ Seth lived one hundred and five years, and begot Enosh. ⁷ After he begot Enosh, Seth lived eight hundred and seven years, and had sons and daughters. ⁸ So all the days of Seth were nine hundred and twelve years; and he died.

⁹ Enosh lived ninety years, and begot Cainan. ¹⁰ After he begot Cainan, Enosh lived eight hundred and fifteen years, and had sons and daughters. ¹¹ So all the days of Enosh were nine hundred and five years; and he died.

¹² Cainan lived seventy years, and begot Mahalalel. ¹³ After he begot Mahalalel, Cainan lived eight hundred and forty years, and had sons and daughters. ¹⁴ So all the days of Cainan were nine hundred and ten years; and he died.

¹⁵ Mahalalel lived sixty-five years, and begot Jared. ¹⁶ After he begot Jared, Mahalalel lived eight hundred and thirty years, and had sons and daughters. ¹⁷ So all the days of Mahalalel were eight hundred and ninety-five years; and he died.

¹⁸ Jared lived one hundred and sixty-two years, and begot Enoch. ¹⁹ After he begot Enoch, Jared lived eight hundred years, and had sons and daughters. ²⁰ So all the days of Jared were nine hundred and sixty-two years; and he died.

²¹ Enoch lived sixty-five years, and begot Methuselah. ²² After he begot Methuselah, Enoch walked with God three hundred years, and had sons and daughters. ²³ So all the days of Enoch were three hundred and sixty-five years. ²⁴ And Enoch walked with God; and he *was* not, for God took him.

²⁵ Methuselah lived one hundred and eighty-seven years, and begot Lamech. ²⁶ After he begot Lamech, Methuselah lived seven hundred and eighty-two years, and had sons and daughters. ²⁷ So all the days of Methuselah were nine hundred and sixty-nine years; and he died.

²⁸ Lamech lived one hundred and eighty-two years, and had a son. ²⁹ And he called his name Noah, saying, "This *one* will comfort us concerning our work and the toil of our hands, because of the ground which the LORD has cursed." ³⁰ After he begot Noah, Lamech lived five hundred and ninety-five years, and had sons and daughters. ³¹ So all the days of Lamech were seven hundred and seventy-seven years; and he died.

³² And Noah was five hundred years old, and Noah begot Shem, Ham, and Japheth.

6 Now it came to pass, when men began to multiply on the face of the earth, and daughters were born to them, ² that the sons of God saw the daughters of men, that they *were* beautiful; and they took wives for themselves of all whom they chose.

³ And the LORD said, "My Spirit shall not strive with man forever, for he *is* indeed flesh; yet his days shall be one hundred and twenty years." ⁴ There were giants on the earth in those days, and also afterward, when the sons of God came in to the daughters of men and they bore

children to them. Those *were* the mighty men who *were* of old, men of renown.

⁵ Then the LORD saw that the wickedness of man *was* great in the earth, and *that* every intent of the thoughts of his heart *was* only evil continually. ⁶ And the LORD was sorry that He had made man on the earth, and He was grieved in His heart. ⁷ So the LORD said, "I will destroy man whom I have created from the face of the earth, both man and beast, creeping thing and birds of the air, for I am sorry that I have made them." ⁸ But Noah found grace in the eyes of the LORD.

⁹ This is the genealogy of Noah. Noah was a just man, perfect in his generations. Noah walked with God. ¹⁰ And Noah begot three sons: Shem, Ham, and Japheth.

¹¹ The earth also was corrupt before God, and the earth was filled with violence. ¹² So God looked upon the earth, and indeed it was corrupt; for all flesh had corrupted their way on the earth.

¹³ And God said to Noah, "The end of all flesh has come before Me, for the earth is filled with violence through them; and behold, I will destroy them with the earth. ¹⁴ Make yourself an ark of gopherwood; make rooms in the ark, and cover it inside and outside with pitch. ¹⁵ And this is how you shall make it: The length of the ark *shall be* three hundred cubits, its width fifty cubits, and its height thirty cubits. ¹⁶ You shall make a window for the ark, and you shall finish it to a cubit from above; and set the door of the ark in its side. You shall make it *with* lower, second, and third *decks*. ¹⁷ And behold, I Myself am bringing floodwaters on the earth, to destroy from under heaven all flesh in which *is* the breath of life; everything that *is* on the earth shall die. ¹⁸ But I will establish My covenant with you; and you shall go into the ark—you, your sons, your wife, and your sons' wives with you. ¹⁹ And of every living thing of all flesh you shall bring two of every *sort* into the ark, to keep *them* alive with you; they shall be male and female. ²⁰ Of the birds after their kind, of animals after their kind, and of every creeping thing of the earth after its kind, two of every *kind* will come to you to keep *them* alive. ²¹ And you shall take for yourself of all food that is eaten, and

you shall gather *it* to yourself; and it shall be food for you and for them."

²² Thus Noah did; according to all that God commanded him, so he did.

∼ PSALM 2:7–12 ∼

⁷ "I will declare the decree:
   The LORD has said to Me,
 'You *are* My Son,
   Today I have begotten You.
⁸ Ask of Me, and I will give *You*
   The nations *for* Your inheritance,
   And the ends of the earth *for* Your
      possession.
⁹ You shall break them with a rod of
      iron;
   You shall dash them to pieces like a
      potter's vessel.' "

¹⁰ Now therefore, be wise, O kings;
   Be instructed, you judges of the
      earth.
¹¹ Serve the LORD with fear,
   And rejoice with trembling.
¹² Kiss the Son, lest He be angry,
   And you perish *in* the way,
   When His wrath is kindled but a
      little.
   Blessed *are* all those who put their
      trust in Him.

∼ PROVERBS 1:10–19 ∼

¹⁰ My son, if sinners entice you,
   Do not consent.
¹¹ If they say, "Come with us,
   Let us lie in wait to *shed* blood;
   Let us lurk secretly for the innocent
      without cause;
¹² Let us swallow them alive like Sheol,
   And whole, like those who go down
      to the Pit;
¹³ We shall find all *kinds* of precious
      possessions,
   We shall fill our houses with spoil;
¹⁴ Cast in your lot among us,
   Let us all have one purse"—
¹⁵ My son, do not walk in the way with
      them,
   Keep your foot from their path;
¹⁶ For their feet run to evil,
   And they make haste to shed blood.
¹⁷ Surely, in vain the net is spread
   In the sight of any bird;

Helplessness

A man once asked Dwight L. Moody, "How can you accept the Bible with all its mysteries and contradictions, you with your fine mind?"

Moody replied, "I don't explain it. I don't understand it. I don't make anything of it. I simply believe it."

In his classic book, *Prayer*, Dr. O. Hallesby echoed this attitude. He wrote, "Prayer and helplessness are inseparable. Only he who is helpless can truly pray. . . . Prayer [therefore] consists simply in telling God day by day in what ways we feel helpless. We are moved to pray every time the Spirit of God, which is the spirit of prayer, emphasizes anew to us our helplessness, and we realize how impotent we are by nature to believe, to love, to hope, to serve, to sacrifice, to suffer, to read the Bible, to pray, and to struggle against our sinful desires."

God isn't looking for your perfection and your strength today. He is looking for you to trust in His perfection and His strength.

18 But they lie in wait for their *own*
blood,
They lurk secretly for their *own*
lives.
19 So *are* the ways of everyone who is
greedy for gain;
It takes away the life of its owners.

∼ MATTHEW 3:1–17 ∼

In those days John the Baptist came preaching in the wilderness of Judea, 2 and saying, "Repent, for the kingdom of heaven is at hand!" 3 For this is he who was spoken of by the prophet Isaiah, saying:

"The voice of one crying in the
wilderness:
'Prepare the way of the LORD;
Make His paths straight.' "

4 Now John himself was clothed in camel's hair, with a leather belt around his waist; and his food was locusts and wild honey. 5 Then Jerusalem, all Judea, and all the region around the Jordan went out to him 6 and were baptized by him in the Jordan, confessing their sins.

7 But when he saw many of the Pharisees and Sadducees coming to his baptism, he said to them, "Brood of vipers! Who warned you to flee from the wrath to come? 8 Therefore bear fruits worthy of repentance, 9 and do not think to say to yourselves, 'We have Abraham as *our* father.' For I say to you that God is able to raise up children to Abraham from these stones. 10 And even now the ax is laid to the root of the trees. Therefore every tree which does not bear good fruit is cut down and thrown into the fire. 11 I indeed baptize you with water unto repentance, but He who is coming after me is mightier than I, whose sandals I am not worthy to carry. He will baptize you with the Holy Spirit and fire. 12 His winnowing fan *is* in His hand, and He will thoroughly clean out His threshing floor, and gather His wheat into the barn; but He will burn up the chaff with unquenchable fire."

13 Then Jesus came from Galilee to John at the Jordan to be baptized by him. 14 And John *tried to* prevent Him, saying, "I need to be baptized by You, and are You coming to me?"

15 But Jesus answered and said to him, "Permit *it to be so* now, for thus it is fitting for us to fulfill all righteousness." Then he allowed Him.

16 When He had been baptized, Jesus came up immediately from the water; and behold, the heavens were opened to Him, and He saw the Spirit of God descending like a dove and alighting upon Him. 17 And suddenly a voice *came* from heaven, saying, "This is My beloved Son, in whom I am well pleased."

READING 4 · JANUARY 4

∼ GENESIS 7:1—8:22 ∼

Then the LORD said to Noah, "Come into the ark, you and all your household, because I have seen *that* you *are* righteous before Me in this generation. 2 You shall take with you seven each of every clean animal, a male and his female; two each of animals that *are* unclean, a male and his female; 3 also seven each of birds of the air, male and female, to keep the species alive on the face of all the earth. 4 For after seven more days I will cause it to rain on the earth forty days and forty nights, and I will destroy from the face of the earth all living things that I have made." 5 And Noah did according to all that the LORD commanded him. 6 Noah *was* six hundred years old when the floodwaters were on the earth.

7 So Noah, with his sons, his wife, and his sons' wives, went into the ark because of the waters of the flood. 8 Of clean animals, of animals that *are* unclean, of birds, and of everything that creeps on the earth, 9 two by two they went into the ark to Noah, male and female, as God had commanded Noah. 10 And it came to pass after seven days that the waters of the flood were on the earth. 11 In the six hundredth year of Noah's life, in the second month, the seventeenth day of the month, on that day all the fountains of the great deep were

It's How High You Bounce

Max Cleland was a typical All-American boy, who starred in sports and was voted his high school's most outstanding senior. At age twenty-four, he volunteered for combat duty in Vietnam as a first lieutenant in the Army. One month before his return home, Cleland noticed a grenade that had been accidentally dropped. Moving to retrieve it, he was thrown backward by its explosion. He looked down to find his right hand and leg were missing and his left leg was badly mangled. He tried to cry out, but shrapnel had ripped his throat.

No one expected Cleland to survive. But as he recovered from a triple amputation, he recalled two things: Paul the apostle had said that hope did not disappoint, and General George Patton had said, "Success is how high you bounce after you hit bottom."

Upon his return to civilian life, Cleland entered politics, learned to drive a special car, and traveled extensively mobilizing support for veterans' causes. At age thirty-four, he became the youngest man ever to head the Veterans Administration, and was later elected Georgia's secretary of state. Max says, "Life doesn't revolve around an arm and a leg. People look at you the way you look at yourself."

broken up, and the windows of heaven were opened. [12] And the rain was on the earth forty days and forty nights.

[13] On the very same day Noah and Noah's sons, Shem, Ham, and Japheth, and Noah's wife and the three wives of his sons with them, entered the ark— [14] they and every beast after its kind, all cattle after their kind, every creeping thing that creeps on the earth after its kind, and every bird after its kind, every bird of every sort. [15] And they went into the ark to Noah, two by two, of all flesh in which *is* the breath of life. [16] So those that entered, male and female of all flesh, went in as God had commanded him; and the LORD shut him in.

[17] Now the flood was on the earth forty days. The waters increased and lifted up the ark, and it rose high above the earth. [18] The waters prevailed and greatly increased on the earth, and the ark moved about on the surface of the waters. [19] And the waters prevailed exceedingly on the earth, and all the high hills under the whole heaven were covered. [20] The waters prevailed fifteen cubits upward, and the mountains were covered. [21] And all flesh died that moved on the earth: birds and cattle and beasts and every creeping thing that creeps on the earth, and every man. [22] All in whose nostrils *was* the breath of the spirit of life, all that *was* on the dry *land*, died. [23] So He destroyed all living things which were on the face of the ground: both man and cattle, creeping thing and bird of the air. They were destroyed from the earth. Only Noah and those who *were* with him in the ark remained *alive*. [24] And the waters prevailed on the earth one hundred and fifty days.

8 Then God remembered Noah, and every living thing, and all the animals that *were* with him in the ark. And God made a wind to pass over the earth, and the waters subsided. [2] The fountains of the deep and the windows of heaven were also stopped, and the rain from heaven was restrained. [3] And the waters receded continually from the earth. At the end of the hundred and fifty days the waters decreased. [4] Then the ark rested in the seventh month, the seventeenth day of the month, on the mountains of Ararat.

[5] And the waters decreased continually until the tenth month. In the tenth *month*, on the first *day* of the month, the tops of the mountains were seen.

[6] So it came to pass, at the end of forty days, that Noah opened the window of the ark which he had made. [7] Then he sent out a raven, which kept going to and fro until the waters had dried up from the earth. [8] He also sent out from himself a dove, to see if the waters had receded from the face of the ground. [9] But the dove found no resting place for the sole of her foot, and she returned into the ark to him, for the waters *were* on the face of the whole earth. So he put out his hand and took her, and drew her into the ark to himself. [10] And he waited yet another seven days, and again he sent the dove out from the ark. [11] Then the dove came to him in the evening, and behold, a freshly plucked olive leaf *was* in her mouth; and Noah knew that the waters had receded from the earth. [12] So he waited yet another seven days and sent out the dove, which did not return again to him anymore.

[13] And it came to pass in the six hundred and first year, in the first *month*, the first *day* of the month, that the waters were dried up from the earth; and Noah removed the covering of the ark and looked, and indeed the surface of the ground was dry. [14] And in the second month, on the twenty-seventh day of the month, the earth was dried.

[15] Then God spoke to Noah, saying, [16] "Go out of the ark, you and your wife, and your sons and your sons' wives with you. [17] Bring out with you every living thing of all flesh that *is* with you: birds and cattle and every creeping thing that creeps on the earth, so that they may abound on the earth, and be fruitful and multiply on the earth." [18] So Noah went out, and his sons and his wife and his sons' wives with him. [19] Every animal, every creeping thing, every bird, *and* whatever creeps on the earth, according to their families, went out of the ark.

[20] Then Noah built an altar to the LORD, and took of every clean animal and of every clean bird, and offered burnt offerings on the altar. [21] And the LORD smelled a soothing aroma. Then the LORD said in

His heart, "I will never again curse the ground for man's sake, although the imagination of man's heart *is* evil from his youth; nor will I again destroy every living thing as I have done.

22 "While the earth remains,
Seedtime and harvest,
Cold and heat,
Winter and summer,
And day and night
Shall not cease."

~ PSALM 3:1–4 ~

1 LORD, how they have increased who
trouble me!
Many *are* they who rise up against
me.
2 Many *are* they who say of me,
"*There is* no help for him in God."
Selah

3 But You, O LORD, *are* a shield for me,
My glory and the One who lifts up
my head.
4 I cried to the LORD with my voice,
And He heard me from His holy hill.
Selah

~ PROVERBS 1:20–22 ~

20 Wisdom calls aloud outside;
She raises her voice in the open
squares.
21 She cries out in the chief concourses,
At the openings of the gates in the
city
She speaks her words:
22 "How long, you simple ones, will you
love simplicity?
For scorners delight in their
scorning,
And fools hate knowledge.

~ MATTHEW 4:1–25 ~

Then Jesus was led up by the Spirit into the wilderness to be tempted by the devil. 2 And when He had fasted forty days and forty nights, afterward He was hungry. 3 Now when the tempter came to Him, he said, "If You are the Son of God, command that these stones become bread."
4 But He answered and said, "It is writ-

ten, 'Man shall not live by bread alone, but by every word that proceeds from the mouth of God.' "
5 Then the devil took Him up into the holy city, set Him on the pinnacle of the temple, 6 and said to Him, "If You are the Son of God, throw Yourself down. For it is written:

'He shall give His angels charge
over you,'

and,

'In *their* hands they shall bear you
up,
Lest you dash your foot against a
stone.' "

7 Jesus said to him, "It is written again, 'You shall not tempt the LORD your God.' "
8 Again, the devil took Him up on an exceedingly high mountain, and showed Him all the kingdoms of the world and their glory. 9 And he said to Him, "All these things I will give You if You will fall down and worship me."
10 Then Jesus said to him, "Away with you, Satan! For it is written, 'You shall worship the LORD your God, and Him only you shall serve.' "
11 Then the devil left Him, and behold, angels came and ministered to Him.
12 Now when Jesus heard that John had been put in prison, He departed to Galilee. 13 And leaving Nazareth, He came and dwelt in Capernaum, which is by the sea, in the regions of Zebulun and Naphtali, 14 that it might be fulfilled which was spoken by Isaiah the prophet, saying:

15 "The land of Zebulun and the land
of Naphtali,
By the way of the sea, beyond the
Jordan,
Galilee of the Gentiles:
16 The people who sat in darkness
have seen a great light,
And upon those who sat in the
region and shadow of death
Light has dawned."

17 From that time Jesus began to preach and to say, "Repent, for the kingdom of heaven is at hand."

[18] And Jesus, walking by the Sea of Galilee, saw two brothers, Simon called Peter, and Andrew his brother, casting a net into the sea; for they were fishermen. [19] Then He said to them, "Follow Me, and I will make you fishers of men." [20] They immediately left *their* nets and followed Him.

[21] Going on from there, He saw two other brothers, James *the son* of Zebedee, and John his brother, in the boat with Zebedee their father, mending their nets. He called them, [22] and immediately they left the boat and their father, and followed Him.

[23] And Jesus went about all Galilee, teaching in their synagogues, preaching the gospel of the kingdom, and healing all kinds of sickness and all kinds of disease among the people. [24] Then His fame went throughout all Syria; and they brought to Him all sick people who were afflicted with various diseases and torments, and those who were demon-possessed, epileptics, and paralytics; and He healed them. [25] Great multitudes followed Him—from Galilee, and *from* Decapolis, Jerusalem, Judea, and beyond the Jordan.

READING 5 · JANUARY 5

～ GENESIS 9:1—10:32 ～

So God blessed Noah and his sons, and said to them: "Be fruitful and multiply, and fill the earth. [2] And the fear of you and the dread of you shall be on every beast of the earth, on every bird of the air, on all that move *on* the earth, and on all the fish of the sea. They are given into your hand. [3] Every moving thing that lives shall be food for you. I have given you all things, even as the green herbs. [4] But you shall not eat flesh with its life, *that is*, its blood. [5] Surely for your lifeblood I will demand *a reckoning*; from the hand of every beast I will require it, and from the hand of man. From the hand of every man's brother I will require the life of man.

[6] "Whoever sheds man's blood,
By man his blood shall be shed;
For in the image of God
He made man.
[7] And as for you, be fruitful and
multiply;
Bring forth abundantly in the
earth
And multiply in it."

[8] Then God spoke to Noah and to his sons with him, saying: [9] "And as for Me, behold, I establish My covenant with you and with your descendants after you, [10] and with every living creature that *is* with you: the birds, the cattle, and every beast of the earth with you, of all that go out of the ark, every beast of the earth. [11] Thus I establish My covenant with you: Never again shall all flesh be cut off by the waters of the flood; never again shall there be a flood to destroy the earth."

[12] And God said: "This *is* the sign of the covenant which I make between Me and you, and every living creature that *is* with you, for perpetual generations: [13] I set My rainbow in the cloud, and it shall be for the sign of the covenant between Me and the earth. [14] It shall be, when I bring a cloud over the earth, that the rainbow shall be seen in the cloud; [15] and I will remember My covenant which *is* between Me and you and every living creature of all flesh; the waters shall never again become a flood to destroy all flesh. [16] The rainbow shall be in the cloud, and I will look on it to remember the everlasting covenant between God and every living creature of all flesh that *is* on the earth." [17] And God said to Noah, "This *is* the sign of the covenant which I have established between Me and all flesh that *is* on the earth."

[18] Now the sons of Noah who went out of the ark were Shem, Ham, and Japheth. And Ham *was* the father of Canaan. [19] These three *were* the sons of Noah, and from these the whole earth was populated.

[20] And Noah began *to be* a farmer, and he planted a vineyard. [21] Then he drank of the wine and was drunk, and became uncovered in his tent. [22] And Ham, the

Forgiveness and Trust

Lisa was shocked when she discovered that David had run up thousands of dollars on every one of their credit cards. Not only was she furious about the mountain of debt, she was frustrated with herself for not recognizing David's compulsive spending habits.

In the days that followed, she wondered if she could ever trust her husband again and whether they would ever be able to get out of debt.

Rather than wait for something to happen, she took two bold steps. The first was to convince David he needed help, and the second was to seek out a financial planner. She learned if she carefully monitored the family funds, they could be out of debt in a few years. This brought hope for their financial future, and for the future of their marriage.

Another turnaround in their marriage came when David asked Lisa to forgive him. She found that forgiving David freed her to turn away from the matter of money and to focus on their relationship. She decided it was possible to love someone even though they had "messed up." Forgiving made trust possible again, and once trust was reestablished their marriage began to be healed.

Forgiveness turns the heart away from what was and is, to what can be. Is it time for you to take some bold steps? If love is your motive, be encouraged! When you replace frustration and fear with forgiveness and trust, situations and circumstances are subject to change.

father of Canaan, saw the nakedness of his father, and told his two brothers outside. ²³ But Shem and Japheth took a garment, laid *it* on both their shoulders, and went backward and covered the nakedness of their father. Their faces *were* turned away, and they did not see their father's nakedness.

²⁴ So Noah awoke from his wine, and knew what his younger son had done to him. ²⁵ Then he said:

"Cursed *be* Canaan;
A servant of servants
He shall be to his brethren."

²⁶ And he said:

"Blessed *be* the LORD,
The God of Shem,
And may Canaan be his servant.
²⁷ May God enlarge Japheth,
And may he dwell in the tents of
    Shem;
And may Canaan be his servant."

²⁸ And Noah lived after the flood three hundred and fifty years. ²⁹ So all the days of Noah were nine hundred and fifty years; and he died.

10 Now this *is* the genealogy of the sons of Noah: Shem, Ham, and Japheth. And sons were born to them after the flood.
² The sons of Japheth *were* Gomer, Magog, Madai, Javan, Tubal, Meshech, and Tiras. ³ The sons of Gomer *were* Ashkenaz, Riphath, and Togarmah. ⁴ The sons of Javan *were* Elishah, Tarshish, Kittim, and Dodanim. ⁵ From these the coastland *peoples* of the Gentiles were separated into their lands, everyone according to his language, according to their families, into their nations.
⁶ The sons of Ham *were* Cush, Mizraim, Put, and Canaan. ⁷ The sons of Cush *were* Seba, Havilah, Sabtah, Raamah, and Sabtechah; and the sons of Raamah *were* Sheba and Dedan.
⁸ Cush begot Nimrod; he began to be a mighty one on the earth. ⁹ He was a mighty hunter before the LORD; therefore it is said, "Like Nimrod the mighty hunter before the LORD." ¹⁰ And the beginning of his kingdom was Babel, Erech, Accad,

and Calneh, in the land of Shinar. ¹¹ From that land he went to Assyria and built Nineveh, Rehoboth Ir, Calah, ¹² and Resen between Nineveh and Calah (that *is* the principal city).
¹³ Mizraim begot Ludim, Anamim, Lehabim, Naphtuhim, ¹⁴ Pathrusim, and Casluhim (from whom came the Philistines and Caphtorim).
¹⁵ Canaan begot Sidon his firstborn, and Heth; ¹⁶ the Jebusite, the Amorite, and the Girgashite; ¹⁷ the Hivite, the Arkite, and the Sinite; ¹⁸ the Arvadite, the Zemarite, and the Hamathite. Afterward the families of the Canaanites were dispersed. ¹⁹ And the border of the Canaanites was from Sidon as you go toward Gerar, as far as Gaza; then as you go toward Sodom, Gomorrah, Admah, and Zeboiim, as far as Lasha. ²⁰ These *were* the sons of Ham, according to their families, according to their languages, in their lands and in their nations.
²¹ And *children* were born also to Shem, the father of all the children of Eber, the brother of Japheth the elder. ²² The sons of Shem *were* Elam, Asshur, Arphaxad, Lud, and Aram. ²³ The sons of Aram *were* Uz, Hul, Gether, and Mash. ²⁴ Arphaxad begot Salah, and Salah begot Eber. ²⁵ To Eber were born two sons: the name of one *was* Peleg, for in his days the earth was divided; and his brother's name *was* Joktan. ²⁶ Joktan begot Almodad, Sheleph, Hazarmaveth, Jerah, ²⁷ Hadoram, Uzal, Diklah, ²⁸ Obal, Abimael, Sheba, ²⁹ Ophir, Havilah, and Jobab. All these *were* the sons of Joktan. ³⁰ And their dwelling place was from Mesha as you go toward Sephar, the mountain of the east. ³¹ These *were* the sons of Shem, according to their families, according to their languages, in their lands, according to their nations.
³² These *were* the families of the sons of Noah, according to their generations, in their nations; and from these the nations were divided on the earth after the flood.

~ PSALM 3:5–8 ~

⁵ I lay down and slept;
    I awoke, for the LORD sustained me.
⁶ I will not be afraid of ten thousands
        of people

Who have set *themselves* against me
all around.

7 Arise, O LORD;
Save me, O my God!
For You have struck all my enemies
on the cheekbone;
You have broken the teeth of the
ungodly.
8 Salvation *belongs* to the LORD.
Your blessing *is* upon Your people.
Selah

~ PROVERBS 1:23-27 ~

23 Turn at my rebuke;
Surely I will pour out my spirit on
you;
I will make my words known to you.
24 Because I have called and you
refused,
I have stretched out my hand and no
one regarded,
25 Because you disdained all my counsel,
And would have none of my rebuke,
26 I also will laugh at your calamity;
I will mock when your terror comes,
27 When your terror comes like a storm,
And your destruction comes like a
whirlwind,
When distress and anguish come
upon you.

~ MATTHEW 5:1-26 ~

And seeing the multitudes, He went up on
a mountain, and when He was seated His
disciples came to Him. 2 Then He opened
His mouth and taught them, saying:

3 "Blessed *are* the poor in spirit,
For theirs is the kingdom of
heaven.
4 Blessed *are* those who mourn,
For they shall be comforted.
5 Blessed *are* the meek,
For they shall inherit the earth.
6 Blessed *are* those who hunger and
thirst for righteousness,
For they shall be filled.
7 Blessed *are* the merciful,
For they shall obtain mercy.
8 Blessed *are* the pure in heart,
For they shall see God.
9 Blessed *are* the peacemakers,
For they shall be called sons of
God.
10 Blessed *are* those who are
persecuted for righteousness'
sake,
For theirs is the kingdom of
heaven.

11 "Blessed are you when they revile and
persecute you, and say all kinds of evil
against you falsely for My sake. 12 Rejoice
and be exceedingly glad, for great *is* your
reward in heaven, for so they persecuted
the prophets who were before you.
13 "You are the salt of the earth; but if
the salt loses its flavor, how shall it be seasoned? It is then good for nothing but to
be thrown out and trampled underfoot
by men.
14 "You are the light of the world. A city
that is set on a hill cannot be hidden.
15 Nor do they light a lamp and put it under a basket, but on a lampstand, and it
gives light to all *who are* in the house.
16 Let your light so shine before men, that
they may see your good works and glorify your Father in heaven.
17 "Do not think that I came to destroy
the Law or the Prophets. I did not come
to destroy but to fulfill. 18 For assuredly, I
say to you, till heaven and earth pass away,
one jot or one tittle will by no means pass
from the law till all is fulfilled. 19 Whoever therefore breaks one of the least of
these commandments, and teaches men
so, shall be called least in the kingdom of
heaven; but whoever does and teaches
them, he shall be called great in the kingdom of heaven. 20 For I say to you, that
unless your righteousness exceeds *the righteousness* of the scribes and Pharisees, you
will by no means enter the kingdom of
heaven.
21 "You have heard that it was said to
those of old, 'You shall not murder, and
whoever murders will be in danger of the
judgment.' 22 But I say to you that whoever is angry with his brother without a
cause shall be in danger of the judgment.
And whoever says to his brother, 'Raca!'
shall be in danger of the council. But whoever says, 'You fool!' shall be in danger of
hell fire. 23 Therefore if you bring your
gift to the altar, and there remember that

your brother has something against you, ²⁴ leave your gift there before the altar, and go your way. First be reconciled to your brother, and then come and offer your gift. ²⁵ Agree with your adversary quickly, while you are on the way with

him, lest your adversary deliver you to the judge, the judge hand you over to the officer, and you be thrown into prison. ²⁶ Assuredly, I say to you, you will by no means get out of there till you have paid the last penny.

∼ GENESIS 11:1—12:20 ∼

Now the whole earth had one language and one speech. ² And it came to pass, as they journeyed from the east, that they found a plain in the land of Shinar, and they dwelt there. ³ Then they said to one another, "Come, let us make bricks and bake *them* thoroughly." They had brick for stone, and they had asphalt for mortar. ⁴ And they said, "Come, let us build ourselves a city, and a tower whose top *is* in the heavens; let us make a name for ourselves, lest we be scattered abroad over the face of the whole earth."

⁵ But the LORD came down to see the city and the tower which the sons of men had built. ⁶ And the LORD said, "Indeed the people *are* one and they all have one language, and this is what they begin to do; now nothing that they propose to do will be withheld from them. ⁷ Come, let Us go down and there confuse their language, that they may not understand one another's speech." ⁸ So the LORD scattered them abroad from there over the face of all the earth, and they ceased building the city. ⁹ Therefore its name is called Babel, because there the LORD confused the language of all the earth; and from there the LORD scattered them abroad over the face of all the earth.

¹⁰ This *is* the genealogy of Shem: Shem *was* one hundred years old, and begot Arphaxad two years after the flood. ¹¹ After he begot Arphaxad, Shem lived five hundred years, and begot sons and daughters.

¹² Arphaxad lived thirty-five years, and begot Salah. ¹³ After he begot Salah, Arphaxad lived four hundred and three years, and begot sons and daughters.

¹⁴ Salah lived thirty years, and begot Eber. ¹⁵ After he begot Eber, Salah lived

four hundred and three years, and begot sons and daughters.

¹⁶ Eber lived thirty-four years, and begot Peleg. ¹⁷ After he begot Peleg, Eber lived four hundred and thirty years, and begot sons and daughters.

¹⁸ Peleg lived thirty years, and begot Reu. ¹⁹ After he begot Reu, Peleg lived two hundred and nine years, and begot sons and daughters.

²⁰ Reu lived thirty-two years, and begot Serug. ²¹ After he begot Serug, Reu lived two hundred and seven years, and begot sons and daughters.

²² Serug lived thirty years, and begot Nahor. ²³ After he begot Nahor, Serug lived two hundred years, and begot sons and daughters.

²⁴ Nahor lived twenty-nine years, and begot Terah. ²⁵ After he begot Terah, Nahor lived one hundred and nineteen years, and begot sons and daughters.

²⁶ Now Terah lived seventy years, and begot Abram, Nahor, and Haran.

²⁷ This *is* the genealogy of Terah: Terah begot Abram, Nahor, and Haran. Haran begot Lot. ²⁸ And Haran died before his father Terah in his native land, in Ur of the Chaldeans. ²⁹ Then Abram and Nahor took wives: the name of Abram's wife *was* Sarai, and the name of Nahor's wife, Milcah, the daughter of Haran the father of Milcah and the father of Iscah. ³⁰ But Sarai was barren; she had no child.

³¹ And Terah took his son Abram and his grandson Lot, the son of Haran, and his daughter-in-law Sarai, his son Abram's wife, and they went out with them from Ur of the Chaldeans to go to the land of Canaan; and they came to Haran and dwelt there. ³² So the days of Terah were two hundred and five years, and Terah died in Haran.

Right Words

While in training, surgeons are encouraged to weigh the importance and potential impact of each word spoken during an operation. As the anesthetic is administered, fear may strike a patient if she hears someone say, "I'm going to shoot her now." Even a phrase such as "hook up the monitor" may be interpreted by a drugged patient as: "shake up the monster." Can you imagine the impact on a half-dazed patient if she heard a doctor say, "This just isn't my day!"

> But let your "Yes" be "Yes," and your "No," "No." For whatever is more than these is from the evil one.
>
> *Matthew 5:37*

The same directions given by two different physicians could encourage or discourage a patient, simply by their tone of voice. One doctor's voice might suggest a prescription will work, while another's might convey reservations. These sometimes subtle differences can drastically affect the morale of a patient.

Theodore Roosevelt popularized an expression about the need for clear, precise communication. He called words with several possible meanings "weasel words" — by using them a speaker might weasel out of any commitment, claiming a different interpretation of the word.

The Bible also tells us again and again to remember the importance of our words. We are to always speak words of encouragement, hope, and faith to those around us. Even if we aren't operating on the person we're talking to, we should choose our words, and our tone of voice, carefully. Our words do have an impact on those who hear them. Let's make it a positive one!

12

Now the LORD had said to Abram:

"Get out of your country,
From your family
And from your father's house,
To a land that I will show you.
2 I will make you a great nation;
I will bless you
And make your name great;
And you shall be a blessing.
3 I will bless those who bless you,
And I will curse him who curses
you;
And in you all the families of the
earth shall be blessed."

4 So Abram departed as the LORD had spoken to him, and Lot went with him. And Abram *was* seventy-five years old when he departed from Haran. 5 Then Abram took Sarai his wife and Lot his brother's son, and all their possessions that they had gathered, and the people whom they had acquired in Haran, and they departed to go to the land of Canaan. So they came to the land of Canaan. 6 Abram passed through the land to the place of Shechem, as far as the terebinth tree of Moreh. And the Canaanites *were* then in the land. 7 Then the LORD appeared to Abram and said, "To your descendants I will give this land." And there he built an altar to the LORD, who had appeared to him. 8 And he moved from there to the mountain east of Bethel, and he pitched his tent *with* Bethel on the west and Ai on the east; there he built an altar to the LORD and called on the name of the LORD. 9 So Abram journeyed, going on still toward the South.

10 Now there was a famine in the land, and Abram went down to Egypt to dwell there, for the famine *was* severe in the land. 11 And it came to pass, when he was close to entering Egypt, that he said to Sarai his wife, "Indeed I know that you *are* a woman of beautiful countenance. 12 Therefore it will happen, when the Egyptians see you, that they will say, 'This *is* his wife'; and they will kill me, but they will let you live. 13 Please say you *are* my sister, that it may be well with me for your sake, and that I may live because of you."

14 So it was, when Abram came into Egypt, that the Egyptians saw the woman, that she *was* very beautiful. 15 The princes of Pharaoh also saw her and commended her to Pharaoh. And the woman was taken to Pharaoh's house. 16 He treated Abram well for her sake. He had sheep, oxen, male donkeys, male and female servants, female donkeys, and camels.

17 But the LORD plagued Pharaoh and his house with great plagues because of Sarai, Abram's wife. 18 And Pharaoh called Abram and said, "What *is* this you have done to me? Why did you not tell me that she *was* your wife? 19 Why did you say, 'She *is* my sister'? I might have taken her as my wife. Now therefore, here is your wife; take *her* and go your way." 20 So Pharaoh commanded *his* men concerning him; and they sent him away, with his wife and all that he had.

~ PSALM 4:1–3 ~

1 Hear me when I call, O God of my
righteousness!
You have relieved me in *my* distress;
Have mercy on me, and hear my
prayer.

2 How long, O you sons of men,
Will you turn my glory to shame?
How long will you love
worthlessness
And seek falsehood?   Selah
3 But know that the LORD has set
apart for Himself him who is
godly;
The LORD will hear when I call to
Him.

~ PROVERBS 1:28–33 ~

28 "Then they will call on me, but I will
not answer;
They will seek me diligently, but they
will not find me.
29 Because they hated knowledge
And did not choose the fear of the
LORD,
30 They would have none of my
counsel
And despised my every rebuke.
31 Therefore they shall eat the fruit of
their own way,

And be filled to the full with their own fancies.

32　For the turning away of the simple will slay them,
And the complacency of fools will destroy them;

33　But whoever listens to me will dwell safely,
And will be secure, without fear of evil."

~ MATTHEW 5:27–48 ~

"You have heard that it was said to those of old, 'You shall not commit adultery.' 28 But I say to you that whoever looks at a woman to lust for her has already committed adultery with her in his heart. 29 If your right eye causes you to sin, pluck it out and cast *it* from you; for it is more profitable for you that one of your members perish, than for your whole body to be cast into hell. 30 And if your right hand causes you to sin, cut it off and cast *it* from you; for it is more profitable for you that one of your members perish, than for your whole body to be cast into hell.

31 "Furthermore it has been said, 'Whoever divorces his wife, let him give her a certificate of divorce.' 32 But I say to you that whoever divorces his wife for any reason except sexual immorality causes her to commit adultery; and whoever marries a woman who is divorced commits adultery.

33 "Again you have heard that it was said to those of old, 'You shall not swear falsely, but shall perform your oaths to the Lord.' 34 But I say to you, do not swear at all: neither by heaven, for it is God's throne; 35 nor by the earth, for it is His footstool; nor by Jerusalem, for it is the city of the great King. 36 Nor shall you swear by your head, because you cannot make one hair white or black. 37 But let your 'Yes' be 'Yes,' and your 'No,' 'No.' For whatever is more than these is from the evil one.

38 "You have heard that it was said, 'An eye for an eye and a tooth for a tooth.' 39 But I tell you not to resist an evil person. But whoever slaps you on your right cheek, turn the other to him also. 40 If anyone wants to sue you and take away your tunic, let him have *your* cloak also. 41 And whoever compels you to go one mile, go with him two. 42 Give to him who asks you, and from him who wants to borrow from you do not turn away.

43 "You have heard that it was said, 'You shall love your neighbor and hate your enemy.' 44 But I say to you, love your enemies, bless those who curse you, do good to those who hate you, and pray for those who spitefully use you and persecute you, 45 that you may be sons of your Father in heaven; for He makes His sun rise on the evil and on the good, and sends rain on the just and on the unjust. 46 For if you love those who love you, what reward have you? Do not even the tax collectors do the same? 47 And if you greet your brethren only, what do you do more *than others?* Do not even the tax collectors do so? 48 Therefore you shall be perfect, just as your Father in heaven is perfect.

READING 7 · JANUARY 7

~ GENESIS 13:1—14:24 ~

Then Abram went up from Egypt, he and his wife and all that he had, and Lot with him, to the South. 2 Abram *was* very rich in livestock, in silver, and in gold. 3 And he went on his journey from the South as far as Bethel, to the place where his tent had been at the beginning, between Bethel and Ai, 4 to the place of the altar which he had made there at first. And there Abram called on the name of the LORD.

5 Lot also, who went with Abram, had flocks and herds and tents. 6 Now the land was not able to support them, that they might dwell together, for their possessions were so great that they could not dwell together. 7 And there was strife between the herdsmen of Abram's livestock and the herdsmen of Lot's livestock. The Canaanites and the Perizzites then dwelt in the land.

8 So Abram said to Lot, "Please let there

be no strife between you and me, and between my herdsmen and your herdsmen; for we *are* brethren. ⁹ *Is* not the whole land before you? Please separate from me. If *you take* the left, then I will go to the right; or, if *you go* to the right, then I will go to the left."

¹⁰ And Lot lifted his eyes and saw all the plain of Jordan, that it *was* well watered everywhere (before the LORD destroyed Sodom and Gomorrah) like the garden of the LORD, like the land of Egypt as you go toward Zoar. ¹¹ Then Lot chose for himself all the plain of Jordan, and Lot journeyed east. And they separated from each other. ¹² Abram dwelt in the land of Canaan, and Lot dwelt in the cities of the plain and pitched *his* tent even as far as Sodom. ¹³ But the men of Sodom *were* exceedingly wicked and sinful against the LORD.

¹⁴ And the LORD said to Abram, after Lot had separated from him: "Lift your eyes now and look from the place where you are—northward, southward, eastward, and westward; ¹⁵ for all the land which you see I give to you and your descendants forever. ¹⁶ And I will make your descendants as the dust of the earth; so that if a man could number the dust of the earth, *then* your descendants also could be numbered. ¹⁷ Arise, walk in the land through its length and its width, for I give it to you."

¹⁸ Then Abram moved *his* tent, and went and dwelt by the terebinth trees of Mamre, which *are* in Hebron, and built an altar there to the LORD.

14 And it came to pass in the days of Amraphel king of Shinar, Arioch king of Ellasar, Chedorlaomer king of Elam, and Tidal king of nations, ² *that* they made war with Bera king of Sodom, Birsha king of Gomorrah, Shinab king of Admah, Shemeber king of Zeboiim, and the king of Bela (that is, Zoar). ³ All these joined together in the Valley of Siddim (that is, the Salt Sea). ⁴ Twelve years they served Chedorlaomer, and in the thirteenth year they rebelled.

⁵ In the fourteenth year Chedorlaomer and the kings that *were* with him came and attacked the Rephaim in Ashteroth Karnaim, the Zuzim in Ham, the Emim

in Shaveh Kiriathaim, ⁶ and the Horites in their mountain of Seir, as far as El Paran, which *is* by the wilderness. ⁷ Then they turned back and came to En Mishpat (that *is*, Kadesh), and attacked all the country of the Amalekites, and also the Amorites who dwelt in Hazezon Tamar.

⁸ And the king of Sodom, the king of Gomorrah, the king of Admah, the king of Zeboiim, and the king of Bela (that *is*, Zoar) went out and joined together in battle in the Valley of Siddim ⁹ against Chedorlaomer king of Elam, Tidal king of nations, Amraphel king of Shinar, and Arioch king of Ellasar—four kings against five. ¹⁰ Now the Valley of Siddim *was full of* asphalt pits; and the kings of Sodom and Gomorrah fled; *some* fell there, and the remainder fled to the mountains. ¹¹ Then they took all the goods of Sodom and Gomorrah, and all their provisions, and went their way. ¹² They also took Lot, Abram's brother's son who dwelt in Sodom, and his goods, and departed.

¹³ Then one who had escaped came and told Abram the Hebrew, for he dwelt by the terebinth trees of Mamre the Amorite, brother of Eshcol and brother of Aner; and they *were* allies with Abram. ¹⁴ Now when Abram heard that his brother was taken captive, he armed his three hundred and eighteen trained *servants* who were born in his own house, and went in pursuit as far as Dan. ¹⁵ He divided his forces against them by night, and he and his servants attacked them and pursued them as far as Hobah, which *is* north of Damascus. ¹⁶ So he brought back all the goods, and also brought back his brother Lot and his goods, as well as the women and the people.

¹⁷ And the king of Sodom went out to meet him at the Valley of Shaveh (that *is*, the King's Valley), after his return from the defeat of Chedorlaomer and the kings who *were* with him.

¹⁸ Then Melchizedek king of Salem brought out bread and wine; he *was* the priest of God Most High. ¹⁹ And he blessed him and said:

"Blessed be Abram of God Most
    High,
    Possessor of heaven and earth;
²⁰   And blessed be God Most High,

Broken Silence

Meredith was surprised to find a letter in the mailbox from her brother, Tim. It had been three years since she had spoken to him, even though they lived in the same town. In the letter, Tim told her he and his wife were expecting twins and he hoped she would come to visit the babies after they were born. He expressed his sorrow that they had not communicated more, and apologized for whatever it was he had done to cause them to become estranged.

Meredith's initial reaction was one of anger. "Whatever it was?" Didn't he know? She immediately sat down and wrote a five-page letter detailing all the things Tim had done to hurt her. Before she could put the letter in an envelope the phone rang, and it was several hours before she returned to her writing desk. Upon rereading her letter, she was horrified by what she found.

She had thought she was being very matter-of-fact, but her words were full of anger and pain. Tears of forgiveness filled her eyes. Perhaps it wasn't all Tim's fault.

She called him the next day to say, "I can hardly wait to be the aunt of twins!"

You may not even realize you're harboring past hurts until something comes along to expose your pain. But when you forgive and release your hurts into God's hands, He can cleanse your heart and mind with His love and forgiveness and give you the power to forgive.

Who has delivered your enemies
    into your hand."

And he gave him a tithe of all.

²¹ Now the king of Sodom said to
Abram, "Give me the persons, and take
the goods for yourself."

²² But Abram said to the king of Sodom,
"I have raised my hand to the LORD, God
Most High, the Possessor of heaven and
earth, ²³ that I *will take* nothing, from a
thread to a sandal strap, and that I will
not take anything that *is* yours, lest you
should say, 'I have made Abram rich'—
²⁴ except only what the young men have
eaten, and the portion of the men who
went with me: Aner, Eshcol, and Mamre;
let them take their portion."

∼ PSALM 4:4–8 ∼

⁴ Be angry, and do not sin.
    Meditate within your heart on your
        bed, and be still.   Selah
⁵ Offer the sacrifices of righteousness,
    And put your trust in the LORD.

⁶ *There are* many who say,
    "Who will show us *any* good?"
    LORD, lift up the light of Your
        countenance upon us.
⁷ You have put gladness in my heart,
    More than in the season that their
        grain and wine increased.
⁸ I will both lie down in peace, and
        sleep;
    For You alone, O LORD, make me
        dwell in safety.

∼ PROVERBS 2:1–5 ∼

¹ My son, if you receive my words,
    And treasure my commands within
        you,
² So that you incline your ear to
        wisdom,
    And apply your heart to
        understanding;
³ Yes, if you cry out for discernment,
    And lift up your voice for
        understanding,
⁴ If you seek her as silver,
    And search for her as *for* hidden
        treasures;

⁵ Then you will understand the fear of
        the LORD,
    And find the knowledge of God.

∼ MATTHEW 6:1–18 ∼

"Take heed that you do not do your charitable deeds before men, to be seen by
them. Otherwise you have no reward
from your Father in heaven. ² Therefore,
when you do a charitable deed, do not
sound a trumpet before you as the hypocrites do in the synagogues and in the
streets, that they may have glory from
men. Assuredly, I say to you, they have
their reward. ³ But when you do a charitable deed, do not let your left hand know
what your right hand is doing, ⁴ that your
charitable deed may be in secret; and your
Father who sees in secret will Himself reward you openly.

⁵ "And when you pray, you shall not be
like the hypocrites. For they love to pray
standing in the synagogues and on the
corners of the streets, that they may be
seen by men. Assuredly, I say to you, they
have their reward. ⁶ But you, when you
pray, go into your room, and when you
have shut your door, pray to your Father
who *is* in the secret *place;* and your Father who sees in secret will reward you
openly. ⁷ And when you pray, do not use
vain repetitions as the heathen *do.* For
they think that they will be heard for their
many words.

⁸ "Therefore do not be like them. For
your Father knows the things you have
need of before you ask Him. ⁹ In this manner, therefore, pray:

    Our Father in heaven,
    Hallowed be Your name.
¹⁰ Your kingdom come.
    Your will be done
    On earth as *it is* in heaven.
¹¹ Give us this day our daily bread.
¹² And forgive us our debts,
    As we forgive our debtors.
¹³ And do not lead us into
        temptation,
    But deliver us from the evil one.
    For Yours is the kingdom and the
        power and the glory forever.
    Amen.

¹⁴ "For if you forgive men their trespasses, your heavenly Father will also forgive you. ¹⁵ But if you do not forgive men their trespasses, neither will your Father forgive your trespasses.

¹⁶ "Moreover, when you fast, do not be like the hypocrites, with a sad countenance. For they disfigure their faces that they may appear to men to be fasting. Assuredly, I say to you, they have their reward. ¹⁷ But you, when you fast, anoint your head and wash your face, ¹⁸ so that you do not appear to men to be fasting, but to your Father who *is* in the secret *place;* and your Father who sees in secret will reward you openly.

READING 8 · JANUARY 8

~ GENESIS 15:1—16:16 ~

After these things the word of the LORD came to Abram in a vision, saying, "Do not be afraid, Abram. I *am* your shield, your exceedingly great reward."

² But Abram said, "Lord GOD, what will You give me, seeing I go childless, and the heir of my house *is* Eliezer of Damascus?" ³ Then Abram said, "Look, You have given me no offspring; indeed one born in my house is my heir!"

⁴ And behold, the word of the LORD *came* to him, saying, "This one shall not be your heir, but one who will come from your own body shall be your heir." ⁵ Then He brought him outside and said, "Look now toward heaven, and count the stars if you are able to number them." And He said to him, "So shall your descendants be."

⁶ And he believed in the LORD, and He accounted it to him for righteousness.

⁷ Then He said to him, "I *am* the LORD, who brought you out of Ur of the Chaldeans, to give you this land to inherit it."

⁸ And he said, "Lord GOD, how shall I know that I will inherit it?"

⁹ So He said to him, "Bring Me a three-year-old heifer, a three-year-old female goat, a three-year-old ram, a turtledove, and a young pigeon." ¹⁰ Then he brought all these to Him and cut them in two, down the middle, and placed each piece opposite the other; but he did not cut the birds in two. ¹¹ And when the vultures came down on the carcasses, Abram drove them away.

¹² Now when the sun was going down, a deep sleep fell upon Abram; and behold, horror *and* great darkness fell upon him.

¹³ Then He said to Abram: "Know certainly that your descendants will be strangers in a land *that is* not theirs, and will serve them, and they will afflict them four hundred years. ¹⁴ And also the nation whom they serve I will judge; afterward they shall come out with great possessions. ¹⁵ Now as for you, you shall go to your fathers in peace; you shall be buried at a good old age. ¹⁶ But in the fourth generation they shall return here, for the iniquity of the Amorites *is* not yet complete."

¹⁷ And it came to pass, when the sun went down and it was dark, that behold, there appeared a smoking oven and a burning torch that passed between those pieces. ¹⁸ On the same day the LORD made a covenant with Abram, saying:

"To your descendants I have given this land, from the river of Egypt to the great river, the River Euphrates— ¹⁹ the Kenites, the Kenezzites, the Kadmonites, ²⁰ the Hittites, the Perizzites, the Rephaim, ²¹ the Amorites, the Canaanites, the Girgashites, and the Jebusites."

16 Now Sarai, Abram's wife, had borne him no *children.* And she had an Egyptian maidservant whose name was Hagar. ² So Sarai said to Abram, "See now, the LORD has restrained me from bearing *children.* Please, go in to my maid; perhaps I shall obtain children by her." And Abram heeded the voice of Sarai. ³ Then Sarai, Abram's wife, took Hagar her maid, the Egyptian, and gave her to her husband Abram to be his wife, after Abram had dwelt ten years in the land of Canaan. ⁴ So he went in to Hagar, and she conceived. And when she saw that she had conceived, her mistress became despised in her eyes.

⁵ Then Sarai said to Abram, "My wrong *be* upon you! I gave my maid into your embrace; and when she saw that she had conceived, I became despised in her eyes. The LORD judge between you and me."

⁶ So Abram said to Sarai, "Indeed your maid *is* in your hand; do to her as you please." And when Sarai dealt harshly with her, she fled from her presence.

⁷ Now the Angel of the LORD found her by a spring of water in the wilderness, by the spring on the way to Shur. ⁸ And He said, "Hagar, Sarai's maid, where have you come from, and where are you going?"

She said, "I am fleeing from the presence of my mistress Sarai."

⁹ The Angel of the LORD said to her, "Return to your mistress, and submit yourself under her hand." ¹⁰ Then the Angel of the LORD said to her, "I will multiply your descendants exceedingly, so that they shall not be counted for multitude." ¹¹ And the Angel of the LORD said to her:

> "Behold, you *are* with child,
> And you shall bear a son.
> You shall call his name Ishmael,
> Because the LORD has heard your affliction.
> ¹² He shall be a wild man;
> His hand *shall be* against every man,
> And every man's hand against him.
> And he shall dwell in the presence of all his brethren."

¹³ Then she called the name of the LORD who spoke to her, You-Are-the-God-Who-Sees; for she said, "Have I also here seen Him who sees me?" ¹⁴ Therefore the well was called Beer Lahai Roi; observe, *it is* between Kadesh and Bered.

¹⁵ So Hagar bore Abram a son; and Abram named his son, whom Hagar bore, Ishmael. ¹⁶ Abram *was* eighty-six years old when Hagar bore Ishmael to Abram.

∾ PSALM 5:1–7 ∾

¹ Give ear to my words, O LORD,
  Consider my meditation.
² Give heed to the voice of my cry,
  My King and my God,
  For to You I will pray.

³ My voice You shall hear in the morning, O LORD;
  In the morning I will direct *it* to You,
  And I will look up.

⁴ For You *are* not a God who takes pleasure in wickedness,
  Nor shall evil dwell with You.
⁵ The boastful shall not stand in Your sight;
  You hate all workers of iniquity.
⁶ You shall destroy those who speak falsehood;
  The LORD abhors the bloodthirsty and deceitful man.

⁷ But as for me, I will come into Your house in the multitude of Your mercy;
  In fear of You I will worship toward Your holy temple.

∾ PROVERBS 2:6–9 ∾

⁶ For the LORD gives wisdom;
  From His mouth *come* knowledge and understanding;
⁷ He stores up sound wisdom for the upright;
  He is a shield to those who walk uprightly;
⁸ He guards the paths of justice,
  And preserves the way of His saints.
⁹ Then you will understand righteousness and justice,
  Equity *and* every good path.

∾ MATTHEW 6:19–34 ∾

"Do not lay up for yourselves treasures on earth, where moth and rust destroy and where thieves break in and steal; ²⁰ but lay up for yourselves treasures in heaven, where neither moth nor rust destroys and where thieves do not break in and steal. ²¹ For where your treasure is, there your heart will be also.

²² "The lamp of the body is the eye. If therefore your eye is good, your whole body will be full of light. ²³ But if your eye is bad, your whole body will be full of darkness. If therefore the light that is in you is darkness, how great *is* that darkness!

Pleasing One

The story is told of a painter who desired to produce one work that would please the entire world. Marshaling all her skills, she drew a picture and took it to the marketplace. At the bottom of the piece, she posted directions for spectators to mark each portion of the picture that didn't meet their approval. The spectators came and, in general, applauded her work. However, eager to make a personal critique, each person marked a small portion of the picture. By evening, the painter was mortified to find the entire picture had become a blot.

The next day, the painter returned with a copy of the original picture. This time she asked the spectators to mark the portions of the work they admired. The spectators again complied. When the artist returned several hours later, she found every stroke that had been panned the day before had received praise by this day's critics.

The artist concluded, "I now believe the best way to please one-half of the world is not to mind what the other half says."

People will always have an opinion about what we say or do. That is why we must live our lives according to the words of the Bible — God's opinion. When we do, we will not fret over the opinions of others, because God's opinion is the only one that merits our efforts.

> No one can serve two masters; for either he will hate the one and love the other, or else he will be loyal to the one and despise the other. You cannot serve God and mammon.
>
> *Matthew 6:24*

²⁴ "No one can serve two masters; for either he will hate the one and love the other, or else he will be loyal to the one and despise the other. You cannot serve God and mammon.

²⁵ "Therefore I say to you, do not worry about your life, what you will eat or what you will drink; nor about your body, what you will put on. Is not life more than food and the body more than clothing? ²⁶ Look at the birds of the air, for they neither sow nor reap nor gather into barns; yet your heavenly Father feeds them. Are you not of more value than they? ²⁷ Which of you by worrying can add one cubit to his stature?

²⁸ "So why do you worry about clothing? Consider the lilies of the field, how they grow: they neither toil nor spin; ²⁹ and yet I say to you that even Solomon in all his glory was not arrayed like one of these. ³⁰ Now if God so clothes the grass of the field, which today is, and tomorrow is thrown into the oven, *will He* not much more *clothe* you, O you of little faith?

³¹ "Therefore do not worry, saying, 'What shall we eat?' or 'What shall we drink?' or 'What shall we wear?' ³² For after all these things the Gentiles seek. For your heavenly Father knows that you need all these things. ³³ But seek first the kingdom of God and His righteousness, and all these things shall be added to you. ³⁴ Therefore do not worry about tomorrow, for tomorrow will worry about its own things. Sufficient for the day *is* its own trouble.

READING 9 · JANUARY 9

∼ GENESIS 17:1—18:33 ∼

When Abram was ninety-nine years old, the LORD appeared to Abram and said to him, "I *am* Almighty God; walk before Me and be blameless. ² And I will make My covenant between Me and you, and will multiply you exceedingly." ³ Then Abram fell on his face, and God talked with him, saying: ⁴ "As for Me, behold, My covenant is with you, and you shall be a father of many nations. ⁵ No longer shall your name be called Abram, but your name shall be Abraham; for I have made you a father of many nations. ⁶ I will make you exceedingly fruitful; and I will make nations of you, and kings shall come from you. ⁷ And I will establish My covenant between Me and you and your descendants after you in their generations, for an everlasting covenant, to be God to you and your descendants after you. ⁸ Also I give to you and your descendants after you the land in which you are a stranger, all the land of Canaan, as an everlasting possession; and I will be their God."

⁹ And God said to Abraham: "As for you, you shall keep My covenant, you and your descendants after you throughout their generations. ¹⁰ This *is* My covenant which you shall keep, between Me and you and your descendants after you: Every male child among you shall be circumcised; ¹¹ and you shall be circumcised in the flesh of your foreskins, and it shall be a sign of the covenant between Me and you. ¹² He who is eight days old among you shall be circumcised, every male child in your generations, he who is born in your house or bought with money from any foreigner who is not your descendant. ¹³ He who is born in your house and he who is bought with your money must be circumcised, and My covenant shall be in your flesh for an everlasting covenant. ¹⁴ And the uncircumcised male child, who is not circumcised in the flesh of his foreskin, that person shall be cut off from his people; he has broken My covenant."

¹⁵ Then God said to Abraham, "As for Sarai your wife, you shall not call her name Sarai, but Sarah *shall be* her name. ¹⁶ And I will bless her and also give you a son by her; then I will bless her, and she shall be *a mother of* nations; kings of peoples shall be from her." ¹⁷ Then Abraham fell on his face and laughed, and said in his heart, "Shall *a child* be born to a man who is one hundred years old? And shall Sarah, who is ninety years old, bear *a child*?" ¹⁸ And

Small Kindnesses

Millie was a mentally retarded adult who lived with her mother in a small town. She was well-known for her "green thumb." Lawns, hedges, and flower beds flourished under her loving attention. Millie also volunteered by cutting grass and weeds, raking leaves, and planting flowers in vacant lots throughout the town.

As Millie went from place to place working in gardens and yards, she always carried an oil can with her. She applied a dose of oil to any squeaky door, hinge, or gate she encountered.

On Sundays, Millie went to church with her mother. When teased, she always responded with good humor and unflappable cheer.

When Millie died, everyone in town showed up for her funeral. There were scores who traveled from distant places to attend, including many of those who had once teased her.

Without consciously attempting to do so, Millie exemplified good citizenship. She worked hard, was an optimist, eased tensions, and was a faithful church member.

The Bible's admonition to "Do unto others as you would have them do unto you," calls us to live our lives as Millie did. It doesn't mean those you "do unto" will ever "do unto you the way you've done unto them," but every small kindness you perform is noticed — by people, and most importantly, by God.

Abraham said to God, "Oh, that Ishmael might live before You!"

[19] Then God said: "No, Sarah your wife shall bear you a son, and you shall call his name Isaac; I will establish My covenant with him for an everlasting covenant, *and* with his descendants after him. [20] And as for Ishmael, I have heard you. Behold, I have blessed him, and will make him fruitful, and will multiply him exceedingly. He shall beget twelve princes, and I will make him a great nation. [21] But My covenant I will establish with Isaac, whom Sarah shall bear to you at this set time next year." [22] Then He finished talking with him, and God went up from Abraham.

[23] So Abraham took Ishmael his son, all who were born in his house and all who were bought with his money, every male among the men of Abraham's house, and circumcised the flesh of their foreskins that very same day, as God had said to him. [24] Abraham *was* ninety-nine years old when he was circumcised in the flesh of his foreskin. [25] And Ishmael his son *was* thirteen years old when he was circumcised in the flesh of his foreskin. [26] That very same day Abraham was circumcised, and his son Ishmael; [27] and all the men of his house, born in the house or bought with money from a foreigner, were circumcised with him.

18 Then the LORD appeared to him by the terebinth trees of Mamre, as he was sitting in the tent door in the heat of the day. [2] So he lifted his eyes and looked, and behold, three men were standing by him; and when he saw *them,* he ran from the tent door to meet them, and bowed himself to the ground, [3] and said, "My Lord, if I have now found favor in Your sight, do not pass on by Your servant. [4] Please let a little water be brought, and wash your feet, and rest yourselves under the tree. [5] And I will bring a morsel of bread, that you may refresh your hearts. After that you may pass by, inasmuch as you have come to your servant."

They said, "Do as you have said."

[6] So Abraham hurried into the tent to Sarah and said, "Quickly, make ready three measures of fine meal; knead *it* and make cakes." [7] And Abraham ran to the herd, took a tender and good calf, gave *it*

to a young man, and he hastened to prepare it. [8] So he took butter and milk and the calf which he had prepared, and set *it* before them; and he stood by them under the tree as they ate.

[9] Then they said to him, "Where *is* Sarah your wife?"

So he said, "Here, in the tent."

[10] And He said, "I will certainly return to you according to the time of life, and behold, Sarah your wife shall have a son."

(Sarah was listening in the tent door which *was* behind him.) [11] Now Abraham and Sarah were old, well advanced in age; *and* Sarah had passed the age of childbearing. [12] Therefore Sarah laughed within herself, saying, "After I have grown old, shall I have pleasure, my lord being old also?"

[13] And the LORD said to Abraham, "Why did Sarah laugh, saying, 'Shall I surely bear *a child,* since I am old?' [14] Is anything too hard for the LORD? At the appointed time I will return to you, according to the time of life, and Sarah shall have a son."

[15] But Sarah denied *it,* saying, "I did not laugh," for she was afraid.

And He said, "No, but you did laugh!"

[16] Then the men rose from there and looked toward Sodom, and Abraham went with them to send them on the way. [17] And the LORD said, "Shall I hide from Abraham what I am doing, [18] since Abraham shall surely become a great and mighty nation, and all the nations of the earth shall be blessed in him? [19] For I have known him, in order that he may command his children and his household after him, that they keep the way of the LORD, to do righteousness and justice, that the LORD may bring to Abraham what He has spoken to him." [20] And the LORD said, "Because the outcry against Sodom and Gomorrah is great, and because their sin is very grave, [21] I will go down now and see whether they have done altogether according to the outcry against it that has come to Me; and if not, I will know."

[22] Then the men turned away from there and went toward Sodom, but Abraham still stood before the LORD. [23] And Abraham came near and said, "Would You also destroy the righteous with the wicked? [24] Suppose there were

fifty righteous within the city; would You also destroy the place and not spare *it* for the fifty righteous that were in it? ²⁵ Far be it from You to do such a thing as this, to slay the righteous with the wicked, so that the righteous should be as the wicked; far be it from You! Shall not the Judge of all the earth do right?"

²⁶ So the LORD said, "If I find in Sodom fifty righteous within the city, then I will spare all the place for their sakes."

²⁷ Then Abraham answered and said, "Indeed now, I who *am but* dust and ashes have taken it upon myself to speak to the Lord: ²⁸ Suppose there were five less than the fifty righteous; would You destroy all of the city for *lack of* five?"

So He said, "If I find there forty-five, I will not destroy *it*."

²⁹ And he spoke to Him yet again and said, "Suppose there should be forty found there?"

So He said, "I will not do *it* for the sake of forty."

³⁰ Then he said, "Let not the Lord be angry, and I will speak: Suppose thirty should be found there?"

So He said, "I will not do *it* if I find thirty there."

³¹ And he said, "Indeed now, I have taken it upon myself to speak to the Lord: Suppose twenty should be found there?"

So He said, "I will not destroy *it* for the sake of twenty."

³² Then he said, "Let not the Lord be angry, and I will speak but once more: Suppose ten should be found there?"

And He said, "I will not destroy *it* for the sake of ten." ³³ So the LORD went His way as soon as He had finished speaking with Abraham; and Abraham returned to his place.

∼ PSALM 5:8–12 ∼

8 Lead me, O LORD, in Your
      righteousness because of my
      enemies;
   Make Your way straight before my
      face.

9 For *there is* no faithfulness in their
      mouth;
   Their inward part *is* destruction;
   Their throat *is* an open tomb;

They flatter with their tongue.
10 Pronounce them guilty, O God!
   Let them fall by their own counsels;
   Cast them out in the multitude of
      their transgressions,
   For they have rebelled against You.

11 But let all those rejoice who put their
      trust in You;
   Let them ever shout for joy, because
      You defend them;
   Let those also who love Your name
   Be joyful in You.
12 For You, O LORD, will bless the
      righteous;
   With favor You will surround him as
      with a shield.

∼ PROVERBS 2:10–22 ∼

10 When wisdom enters your heart,
   And knowledge is pleasant to your
      soul,
11 Discretion will preserve you;
   Understanding will keep you,
12 To deliver you from the way of evil,
   From the man who speaks perverse
      things,
13 From those who leave the paths of
      uprightness
   To walk in the ways of darkness;
14 Who rejoice in doing evil,
   And delight in the perversity of the
      wicked;
15 Whose ways *are* crooked,
   And *who are* devious in their paths;
16 To deliver you from the immoral
      woman,
   From the seductress *who* flatters
      with her words,
17 Who forsakes the companion of her
      youth,
   And forgets the covenant of her
      God.
18 For her house leads down to death,
   And her paths to the dead;
19 None who go to her return,
   Nor do they regain the paths of
      life—
20 So you may walk in the way of
      goodness,
   And keep *to* the paths of
      righteousness.
21 For the upright will dwell in the
      land,

And the blameless will remain in it;
22 But the wicked will be cut off from
    the earth,
And the unfaithful will be uprooted
    from it.

∼ MATTHEW 7:1–29 ∼

"Judge not, that you be not judged. ² For
with what judgment you judge, you will
be judged; and with the measure you use,
it will be measured back to you. ³ And why
do you look at the speck in your brother's
eye, but do not consider the plank in your
own eye? ⁴ Or how can you say to your
brother, 'Let me remove the speck from
your eye'; and look, a plank is in your
own eye? ⁵ Hypocrite! First remove the
plank from your own eye, and then you
will see clearly to remove the speck from
your brother's eye.

⁶ "Do not give what is holy to the dogs;
nor cast your pearls before swine, lest they
trample them under their feet, and turn
and tear you in pieces.

⁷ "Ask, and it will be given to you; seek,
and you will find; knock, and it will be
opened to you. ⁸ For everyone who asks
receives, and he who seeks finds, and to
him who knocks it will be opened. ⁹ Or
what man is there among you who, if his
son asks for bread, will give him a stone?
¹⁰ Or if he asks for a fish, will he give him
a serpent? ¹¹ If you then, being evil, know
how to give good gifts to your children,
how much more will your Father who is
in heaven give good things to those who
ask Him! ¹² Therefore, whatever you want
men to do to you, do also to them, for
this is the Law and the Prophets.

¹³ "Enter by the narrow gate; for wide
is the gate and broad is the way that leads
to destruction, and there are many who

go in by it. ¹⁴ Because narrow is the gate
and difficult is the way which leads to life,
and there are few who find it.

¹⁵ "Beware of false prophets, who come
to you in sheep's clothing, but inwardly
they are ravenous wolves. ¹⁶ You will know
them by their fruits. Do men gather grapes
from thornbushes or figs from thistles?
¹⁷ Even so, every good tree bears good
fruit, but a bad tree bears bad fruit. ¹⁸ A
good tree cannot bear bad fruit, nor can a
bad tree bear good fruit. ¹⁹ Every tree that
does not bear good fruit is cut down and
thrown into the fire. ²⁰ Therefore by their
fruits you will know them.

²¹ "Not everyone who says to Me,
'Lord, Lord,' shall enter the kingdom of
heaven, but he who does the will of My
Father in heaven. ²² Many will say to Me
in that day, 'Lord, Lord, have we not
prophesied in Your name, cast out demons
in Your name, and done many wonders
in Your name?' ²³ And then I will declare
to them, 'I never knew you; depart from
Me, you who practice lawlessness!'

²⁴ "Therefore whoever hears these sayings of Mine, and does them, I will liken
him to a wise man who built his house on
the rock: ²⁵ and the rain descended, the
floods came, and the winds blew and beat
on that house; and it did not fall, for it
was founded on the rock.

²⁶ "But everyone who hears these sayings of Mine, and does not do them, will
be like a foolish man who built his house
on the sand: ²⁷ and the rain descended,
the floods came, and the winds blew and
beat on that house; and it fell. And great
was its fall."

²⁸ And so it was, when Jesus had ended
these sayings, that the people were astonished at His teaching, ²⁹ for He taught
them as one having authority, and not as
the scribes.

READING 10 · JANUARY 10

∼ GENESIS 19:1—20:18 ∼

Now the two angels came to Sodom
in the evening, and Lot was sitting in the gate of Sodom. When
Lot saw them, he rose to meet them, and
he bowed himself with his face toward

the ground. ² And he said, "Here now, my
lords, please turn in to your servant's
house and spend the night, and wash your
feet; then you may rise early and go on
your way."

The Law of Christ

Andrew Davison had a rare and life-impacting opportunity to visit Dr. Albert Schweitzer at his jungle hospital on the banks of the Ogowe River. For three days, he engaged in leisurely conversation with the great humanitarian, theologian, musician, and physician. He reported later that his three-day visit had a deep and profound effect on him. In writing of his visit, however, Davison didn't relay the content of their conversations, only this incident:

"It was about eleven in the morning. The equatorial sun was beating down mercilessly, and we were walking up a hill with Dr. Schweitzer. Suddenly he left us and strode across the slope of the hill to a place where an African woman was struggling upward with a huge armload of wood for the cookfires. I watched with both admiration and concern as the eighty-five-year-old man took the entire load of wood and carried it on up the hill for the relieved woman. When we all reached the top of the hill, one of the members of our group asked Dr. Schweitzer why he did things like that, implying that in that heat and at his age he should not. Albert Schweitzer, looking right at all of us and pointing to the woman, said simply, 'No one should ever have to carry a burden like that alone.'"

God has not called us to carry our burdens alone, but to bear one another's burdens. When we do so, we are fulfilling the law of Christ — the law of love.

And they said, "No, but we will spend the night in the open square."

³ But he insisted strongly; so they turned in to him and entered his house. Then he made them a feast, and baked unleavened bread, and they ate.

⁴ Now before they lay down, the men of the city, the men of Sodom, both old and young, all the people from every quarter, surrounded the house. ⁵ And they called to Lot and said to him, "Where are the men who came to you tonight? Bring them out to us that we may know them *carnally*."

⁶ So Lot went out to them through the doorway, shut the door behind him, ⁷ and said, "Please, my brethren, do not do so wickedly! ⁸ See now, I have two daughters who have not known a man; please, let me bring them out to you, and you may do to them as you wish; only do nothing to these men, since this is the reason they have come under the shadow of my roof."

⁹ And they said, "Stand back!" Then they said, "This one came in to stay *here*, and he keeps acting as a judge; now we will deal worse with you than with them." So they pressed hard against the man Lot, and came near to break down the door. ¹⁰ But the men reached out their hands and pulled Lot into the house with them, and shut the door. ¹¹ And they struck the men who *were* at the doorway of the house with blindness, both small and great, so that they became weary *trying* to find the door.

¹² Then the men said to Lot, "Have you anyone else here? Son-in-law, your sons, your daughters, and whomever you have in the city—take *them* out of this place! ¹³ For we will destroy this place, because the outcry against them has grown great before the face of the LORD, and the LORD has sent us to destroy it."

¹⁴ So Lot went out and spoke to his sons-in-law, who had married his daughters, and said, "Get up, get out of this place; for the LORD will destroy this city!" But to his sons-in-law he seemed to be joking.

¹⁵ When the morning dawned, the angels urged Lot to hurry, saying, "Arise, take your wife and your two daughters who are here, lest you be consumed in the pun-ishment of the city." ¹⁶ And while he lingered, the men took hold of his hand, his wife's hand, and the hands of his two daughters, the LORD being merciful to him, and they brought him out and set him outside the city. ¹⁷ So it came to pass, when they had brought them outside, that he said, "Escape for your life! Do not look behind you nor stay anywhere in the plain. Escape to the mountains, lest you be destroyed."

¹⁸ Then Lot said to them, "Please, no, my lords! ¹⁹ Indeed now, your servant has found favor in your sight, and you have increased your mercy which you have shown me by saving my life; but I cannot escape to the mountains, lest some evil overtake me and I die. ²⁰ See now, this city *is* near *enough* to flee to, and it *is* a little one; please let me escape there (*is* it not a little one?) and my soul shall live."

²¹ And he said to him, "See, I have favored you concerning this thing also, in that I will not overthrow this city for which you have spoken. ²² Hurry, escape there. For I cannot do anything until you arrive there."

Therefore the name of the city was called Zoar.

²³ The sun had risen upon the earth when Lot entered Zoar. ²⁴ Then the LORD rained brimstone and fire on Sodom and Gomorrah, from the LORD out of the heavens. ²⁵ So He overthrew those cities, all the plain, all the inhabitants of the cities, and what grew on the ground.

²⁶ But his wife looked back behind him, and she became a pillar of salt.

²⁷ And Abraham went early in the morning to the place where he had stood before the LORD. ²⁸ Then he looked toward Sodom and Gomorrah, and toward all the land of the plain; and he saw, and behold, the smoke of the land which went up like the smoke of a furnace. ²⁹ And it came to pass, when God destroyed the cities of the plain, that God remembered Abraham, and sent Lot out of the midst of the overthrow, when He overthrew the cities in which Lot had dwelt.

³⁰ Then Lot went up out of Zoar and dwelt in the mountains, and his two daughters were with him; for he was afraid to dwell in Zoar. And he and his two daughters dwelt in a cave. ³¹ Now the

firstborn said to the younger, "Our father *is* old, and *there is* no man on the earth to come in to us as is the custom of all the earth. [32] Come, let us make our father drink wine, and we will lie with him, that we may preserve the lineage of our father." [33] So they made their father drink wine that night. And the firstborn went in and lay with her father, and he did not know when she lay down or when she arose.

[34] It happened on the next day that the firstborn said to the younger, "Indeed I lay with my father last night; let us make him drink wine tonight also, and you go in *and* lie with him, that we may preserve the lineage of our father." [35] Then they made their father drink wine that night also. And the younger arose and lay with him, and he did not know when she lay down or when she arose.

[36] Thus both the daughters of Lot were with child by their father. [37] The firstborn bore a son and called his name Moab; he *is* the father of the Moabites to this day. [38] And the younger, she also bore a son and called his name Ben-Ammi; he *is* the father of the people of Ammon to this day.

20 And Abraham journeyed from there to the South, and dwelt between Kadesh and Shur, and stayed in Gerar. [2] Now Abraham said of Sarah his wife, "She *is* my sister." And Abimelech king of Gerar sent and took Sarah.

[3] But God came to Abimelech in a dream by night, and said to him, "Indeed you *are* a dead man because of the woman whom you have taken, for she *is* a man's wife."

[4] But Abimelech had not come near her; and he said, "Lord, will You slay a righteous nation also? [5] Did he not say to me, 'She *is* my sister'? And she, even she herself said, 'He *is* my brother.' In the integrity of my heart and innocence of my hands I have done this."

[6] And God said to him in a dream, "Yes, I know that you did this in the integrity of your heart. For I also withheld you from sinning against Me; therefore I did not let you touch her. [7] Now therefore, restore the man's wife; for he *is* a prophet, and he will pray for you and you shall live. But if you do not restore *her,* know that you shall surely die, you and all who *are* yours."

[8] So Abimelech rose early in the morning, called all his servants, and told all these things in their hearing; and the men were very much afraid. [9] And Abimelech called Abraham and said to him, "What have you done to us? How have I offended you, that you have brought on me and on my kingdom a great sin? You have done deeds to me that ought not to be done." [10] Then Abimelech said to Abraham, "What did you have in view, that you have done this thing?"

[11] And Abraham said, "Because I thought, surely the fear of God *is* not in this place; and they will kill me on account of my wife. [12] But indeed *she is* truly my sister. She *is* the daughter of my father, but not the daughter of my mother; and she became my wife. [13] And it came to pass, when God caused me to wander from my father's house, that I said to her, 'This *is* your kindness that you should do for me: in every place, wherever we go, say of me, "He *is* my brother." ' "

[14] Then Abimelech took sheep, oxen, and male and female servants, and gave *them* to Abraham; and he restored Sarah his wife to him. [15] And Abimelech said, "See, my land *is* before you; dwell where it pleases you." [16] Then to Sarah he said, "Behold, I have given your brother a thousand *pieces* of silver; indeed this vindicates you before all who *are* with you and before everybody." Thus she was rebuked.

[17] So Abraham prayed to God; and God healed Abimelech, his wife, and his female servants. Then they bore *children;* [18] for the LORD had closed up all the wombs of the house of Abimelech because of Sarah, Abraham's wife.

~ PSALM 6:1–5 ~

1   O LORD, do not rebuke me in Your
        anger,
    Nor chasten me in Your hot
        displeasure.
2   Have mercy on me, O LORD, for I
    am weak;
    O LORD, heal me, for my bones are
        troubled.

3 My soul also is greatly troubled;
  But You, O LORD—how long?

4 Return, O LORD, deliver me!
  Oh, save me for Your mercies' sake!
5 For in death *there is* no
    remembrance of You;
  In the grave who will give You
    thanks?

~ PROVERBS 3:1–4 ~

1 My son, do not forget my law,
  But let your heart keep my
    commands;
2 For length of days and long life
  And peace they will add to you.

3 Let not mercy and truth forsake you;
  Bind them around your neck,
  Write them on the tablet of your
    heart,
4 *And* so find favor and high esteem
  In the sight of God and man.

~ MATTHEW 8:1–17 ~

When He had come down from the mountain, great multitudes followed Him. 2 And behold, a leper came and worshiped Him, saying, "Lord, if You are willing, You can make me clean."

3 Then Jesus put out *His* hand and touched him, saying, "I am willing; be cleansed." Immediately his leprosy was cleansed.

4 And Jesus said to him, "See that you tell no one; but go your way, show yourself to the priest, and offer the gift that Moses commanded, as a testimony to them."

5 Now when Jesus had entered Caper-naum, a centurion came to Him, pleading with Him, 6 saying, "Lord, my servant is lying at home paralyzed, dreadfully tormented."

7 And Jesus said to him, "I will come and heal him."

8 The centurion answered and said, "Lord, I am not worthy that You should come under my roof. But only speak a word, and my servant will be healed. 9 For I also am a man under authority, having soldiers under me. And I say to this *one,* 'Go,' and he goes; and to another, 'Come,' and he comes; and to my servant, 'Do this,' and he does *it.*"

10 When Jesus heard *it,* He marveled, and said to those who followed, "Assuredly, I say to you, I have not found such great faith, not even in Israel! 11 And I say to you that many will come from east and west, and sit down with Abraham, Isaac, and Jacob in the kingdom of heaven. 12 But the sons of the kingdom will be cast out into outer darkness. There will be weeping and gnashing of teeth." 13 Then Jesus said to the centurion, "Go your way; and as you have believed, *so* let it be done for you." And his servant was healed that same hour.

14 Now when Jesus had come into Peter's house, He saw his wife's mother lying sick with a fever. 15 So He touched her hand, and the fever left her. And she arose and served them.

16 When evening had come, they brought to Him many who were demon-possessed. And He cast out the spirits with a word, and healed all who were sick, 17 that it might be fulfilled which was spoken by Isaiah the prophet, saying:

"He Himself took our infirmities
  And bore *our* sicknesses."

READING 11 · JANUARY 11

~ GENESIS 21:1—22:24 ~

And the LORD visited Sarah as He had said, and the LORD did for Sarah as He had spoken. 2 For Sarah conceived and bore Abraham a son in his old age, at the set time of which God had spoken to him. 3 And Abraham called the name of his son who was born to him—whom Sarah bore to him—Isaac. 4 Then Abraham circumcised his son Isaac when he was eight days old, as God had commanded him. 5 Now Abraham was one hundred years old when his son Isaac

Misdirected?

A church once sent a man to spend two months as a volunteer at Mother Teresa's mission in Calcutta, caring for India's sick, poor, and dying. He left on his mission with great joy — the trip was a dream come true.

Standing by a luggage carousel in Bangkok forty hours later, he felt anything but elation. Somewhere between South Korea and Thailand his luggage had been "misdirected." Nerves worn raw by sleeplessness, he collapsed into a nearby chair and wondered, *Was this trip a mistake?* He felt as lost as his bags.

As his eyes wandered around the walls of the lobby, which was mostly empty owing to the late hour, he noticed a row of clocks on one wall. They displayed the time in London, New York, Sydney, and Bangkok. He quickly noted that it was noon at his home church — and it was Sunday.

His church had promised to pray for him at noon services that day. *They're praying for me right now*, he thought. And with that realization came a tremendous peace. *I'm not alone now. And I won't be alone in the months ahead!*

Luggage may often be misdirected, but not our prayers. God knows your need and He knows right where you are.

> Trust in the Lord with all your heart, and lean not on your own understanding; in all your ways acknowledge Him, and He shall direct your paths.
>
> *Proverbs 3:5-6*

was born to him. ⁶ And Sarah said, "God has made me laugh, *and* all who hear will laugh with me." ⁷ She also said, "Who would have said to Abraham that Sarah would nurse children? For I have borne *him* a son in his old age."

⁸ So the child grew and was weaned. And Abraham made a great feast on the same day that Isaac was weaned.

⁹ And Sarah saw the son of Hagar the Egyptian, whom she had borne to Abraham, scoffing. ¹⁰ Therefore she said to Abraham, "Cast out this bondwoman and her son; for the son of this bondwoman shall not be heir with my son, *namely* with Isaac." ¹¹ And the matter was very displeasing in Abraham's sight because of his son.

¹² But God said to Abraham, "Do not let it be displeasing in your sight because of the lad or because of your bondwoman. Whatever Sarah has said to you, listen to her voice; for in Isaac your seed shall be called. ¹³ Yet I will also make a nation of the son of the bondwoman, because he *is* your seed."

¹⁴ So Abraham rose early in the morning, and took bread and a skin of water; and putting *it* on her shoulder, he gave *it* and the boy to Hagar, and sent her away. Then she departed and wandered in the Wilderness of Beersheba. ¹⁵ And the water in the skin was used up, and she placed the boy under one of the shrubs. ¹⁶ Then she went and sat down across from *him* at a distance of about a bowshot; for she said to herself, "Let me not see the death of the boy." So she sat opposite *him*, and lifted her voice and wept.

¹⁷ And God heard the voice of the lad. Then the angel of God called to Hagar out of heaven, and said to her, "What ails you, Hagar? Fear not, for God has heard the voice of the lad where he *is*. ¹⁸ Arise, lift up the lad and hold him with your hand, for I will make him a great nation." ¹⁹ Then God opened her eyes, and she saw a well of water. And she went and filled the skin with water, and gave the lad a drink. ²⁰ So God was with the lad; and he grew and dwelt in the wilderness, and became an archer. ²¹ He dwelt in the Wilderness of Paran; and his mother took a wife for him from the land of Egypt.

²² And it came to pass at that time that Abimelech and Phichol, the commander of his army, spoke to Abraham, saying, "God *is* with you in all that you do. ²³ Now therefore, swear to me by God that you will not deal falsely with me, with my offspring, or with my posterity; but that according to the kindness that I have done to you, you will do to me and to the land in which you have dwelt."

²⁴ And Abraham said, "I will swear."

²⁵ Then Abraham rebuked Abimelech because of a well of water which Abimelech's servants had seized. ²⁶ And Abimelech said, "I do not know who has done this thing; you did not tell me, nor had I heard *of it* until today." ²⁷ So Abraham took sheep and oxen and gave them to Abimelech, and the two of them made a covenant. ²⁸ And Abraham set seven ewe lambs of the flock by themselves.

²⁹ Then Abimelech asked Abraham, "What *is the meaning of* these seven ewe lambs which you have set by themselves?"

³⁰ And he said, "You will take *these* seven ewe lambs from my hand, that they may be my witness that I have dug this well." ³¹ Therefore he called that place Beersheba, because the two of them swore an oath there.

³² Thus they made a covenant at Beersheba. So Abimelech rose with Phichol, the commander of his army, and they returned to the land of the Philistines. ³³ Then *Abraham* planted a tamarisk tree in Beersheba, and there called on the name of the LORD, the Everlasting God. ³⁴ And Abraham stayed in the land of the Philistines many days.

22 Now it came to pass after these things that God tested Abraham, and said to him, "Abraham!"

And he said, "Here I am."

² Then He said, "Take now your son, your only *son* Isaac, whom you love, and go to the land of Moriah, and offer him there as a burnt offering on one of the mountains of which I shall tell you."

³ So Abraham rose early in the morning and saddled his donkey, and took two of his young men with him, and Isaac his son; and he split the wood for the burnt offering, and arose and went to the place of which God had told him. ⁴ Then on the third day Abraham lifted his eyes and

saw the place afar off. [5] And Abraham said to his young men, "Stay here with the donkey; the lad and I will go yonder and worship, and we will come back to you."

[6] So Abraham took the wood of the burnt offering and laid *it* on Isaac his son; and he took the fire in his hand, and a knife, and the two of them went together. [7] But Isaac spoke to Abraham his father and said, "My father!"

And he said, "Here I am, my son."

Then he said, "Look, the fire and the wood, but where *is* the lamb for a burnt offering?"

[8] And Abraham said, "My son, God will provide for Himself the lamb for a burnt offering." So the two of them went together.

[9] Then they came to the place of which God had told him. And Abraham built an altar there and placed the wood in order; and he bound Isaac his son and laid him on the altar, upon the wood. [10] And Abraham stretched out his hand and took the knife to slay his son.

[11] But the Angel of the LORD called to him from heaven and said, "Abraham, Abraham!"

So he said, "Here I am."

[12] And He said, "Do not lay your hand on the lad, or do anything to him; for now I know that you fear God, since you have not withheld your son, your only *son*, from Me."

[13] Then Abraham lifted his eyes and looked, and there behind *him was* a ram caught in a thicket by its horns. So Abraham went and took the ram, and offered it up for a burnt offering instead of his son. [14] And Abraham called the name of the place, The-LORD-Will-Provide; as it is said *to* this day, "In the Mount of the LORD it shall be provided."

[15] Then the Angel of the LORD called to Abraham a second time out of heaven, [16] and said: "By Myself I have sworn, says the LORD, because you have done this thing, and have not withheld your son, your only *son*— [17] blessing I will bless you, and multiplying I will multiply your descendants as the stars of the heaven and as the sand which *is* on the seashore; and your descendants shall possess the gate of their enemies. [18] In your seed all the nations of the earth shall be blessed, because

you have obeyed My voice." [19] So Abraham returned to his young men, and they rose and went together to Beersheba; and Abraham dwelt at Beersheba.

[20] Now it came to pass after these things that it was told Abraham, saying, "Indeed Milcah also has borne children to your brother Nahor: [21] Huz his firstborn, Buz his brother, Kemuel the father of Aram, [22] Chesed, Hazo, Pildash, Jidlaph, and Bethuel." [23] And Bethuel begot Rebekah. These eight Milcah bore to Nahor, Abraham's brother. [24] His concubine, whose name was Reumah, also bore Tebah, Gaham, Thahash, and Maachah.

~ PSALM 6:6–10 ~

[6] I am weary with my groaning;
All night I make my bed swim;
I drench my couch with my tears.

[7] My eye wastes away because of grief;
It grows old because of all my enemies.

[8] Depart from me, all you workers of iniquity;
For the LORD has heard the voice of my weeping.

[9] The LORD has heard my supplication;
The LORD will receive my prayer.

[10] Let all my enemies be ashamed and greatly troubled;
Let them turn back *and* be ashamed suddenly.

~ PROVERBS 3:5, 6 ~

[5] Trust in the LORD with all your heart,
And lean not on your own understanding;

[6] In all your ways acknowledge Him,
And He shall direct your paths.

~ MATTHEW 8:18–34 ~

And when Jesus saw great multitudes about Him, He gave a command to depart to the other side. [19] Then a certain scribe came and said to Him, "Teacher, I will follow You wherever You go."

[20] And Jesus said to him, "Foxes have

holes and birds of the air *have* nests, but the Son of Man has nowhere to lay *His* head."

²¹ Then another of His disciples said to Him, "Lord, let me first go and bury my father."

²² But Jesus said to him, "Follow Me, and let the dead bury their own dead."

²³ Now when He got into a boat, His disciples followed Him. ²⁴ And suddenly a great tempest arose on the sea, so that the boat was covered with the waves. But He was asleep. ²⁵ Then His disciples came to *Him* and awoke Him, saying, "Lord, save us! We are perishing!"

²⁶ But He said to them, "Why are you fearful, O you of little faith?" Then He arose and rebuked the winds and the sea, and there was a great calm. ²⁷ So the men marveled, saying, "Who can this be, that even the winds and the sea obey Him?"

²⁸ When He had come to the other side, to the country of the Gergesenes, there met Him two demon-possessed *men,* coming out of the tombs, exceedingly fierce, so that no one could pass that way. ²⁹ And suddenly they cried out, saying, "What have we to do with You, Jesus, You Son of God? Have You come here to torment us before the time?"

³⁰ Now a good way off from them there was a herd of many swine feeding. ³¹ So the demons begged Him, saying, "If You cast us out, permit us to go away into the herd of swine."

³² And He said to them, "Go." So when they had come out, they went into the herd of swine. And suddenly the whole herd of swine ran violently down the steep place into the sea, and perished in the water.

³³ Then those who kept *them* fled; and they went away into the city and told everything, including what *had happened* to the demon-possessed *men.* ³⁴ And behold, the whole city came out to meet Jesus. And when they saw Him, they begged *Him* to depart from their region.

READING 12 · JANUARY 12

~ GENESIS 23:1—24:67 ~

S arah lived one hundred and twenty-seven years; *these were* the years of the life of Sarah. ² So Sarah died in Kirjath Arba (that *is,* Hebron) in the land of Canaan, and Abraham came to mourn for Sarah and to weep for her.

³ Then Abraham stood up from before his dead, and spoke to the sons of Heth, saying, ⁴ "I *am* a foreigner and a visitor among you. Give me property for a burial place among you, that I may bury my dead out of my sight."

⁵ And the sons of Heth answered Abraham, saying to him, ⁶ "Hear us, my lord: You *are* a mighty prince among us; bury your dead in the choicest of our burial places. None of us will withhold from you his burial place, that you may bury your dead."

⁷ Then Abraham stood up and bowed himself to the people of the land, the sons of Heth. ⁸ And he spoke with them, saying, "If it is your wish that I bury my dead out of my sight, hear me, and meet with Ephron the son of Zohar for me, ⁹ that he may give me the cave of Machpelah which he has, which *is* at the end of his field. Let him give it to me at the full price, as property for a burial place among you."

¹⁰ Now Ephron dwelt among the sons of Heth; and Ephron the Hittite answered Abraham in the presence of the sons of Heth, all who entered at the gate of his city, saying, ¹¹ "No, my lord, hear me: I give you the field and the cave that *is* in it; I give it to you in the presence of the sons of my people. I give it to you. Bury your dead!"

¹² Then Abraham bowed himself down before the people of the land; ¹³ and he spoke to Ephron in the hearing of the people of the land, saying, "If you *will* give it, please hear me. I will give you money for the field; take *it* from me and I will bury my dead there."

¹⁴ And Ephron answered Abraham, saying to him, ¹⁵ "My lord, listen to me; the land *is worth* four hundred shekels of silver. What *is* that between you and me? So bury your dead." ¹⁶ And Abraham

Nothin' Outside Can Lick Us

In *Gone With the Wind*, at the funeral of Gerald O'Hara — a heavy drinker who dies in an alcohol-related accident — his prospective son-in-law gives this eulogy: "There warn't nothin' that come to him from the outside that could lick him. He warn't scared of the English government when they wanted to hang him. He just lit out and left home. And when he come to this country . . . he warn't scared to tackle this section when it was part wild and the Injuns had just been run out of it. He made a big plantation out of a wilderness. And when the war come on and his money begun to go, he warn't scared to be poor again. And when the Yankees came through Tara and might of burnt him out or killed him, he warn't fazed a bit and he warn't licked neither. . . . That's why I say he had our good points. . . .

"All you all and me, too, are like him. We got the same weakness and failin'. There ain't nothin' that walks can lick us, any more than it could lick him, not Yankees nor Carpetbaggers nor hard times nor high taxes nor even downright starvation. But that weakness that's in our hearts can lick us in the time it takes to bat your eye."

The world of "self" is truly the toughest frontier, but with humility and patience we can conquer it!

listened to Ephron; and Abraham weighed out the silver for Ephron which he had named in the hearing of the sons of Heth, four hundred shekels of silver, currency of the merchants.

¹⁷ So the field of Ephron which *was* in Machpelah, which *was* before Mamre, the field and the cave which *was* in it, and all the trees that *were* in the field, which *were* within all the surrounding borders, were deeded ¹⁸ to Abraham as a possession in the presence of the sons of Heth, before all who went in at the gate of his city.

¹⁹ And after this, Abraham buried Sarah his wife in the cave of the field of Machpelah, before Mamre (that *is*, Hebron) in the land of Canaan. ²⁰ So the field and the cave that *is* in it were deeded to Abraham by the sons of Heth as property for a burial place.

24 Now Abraham was old, well advanced in age; and the LORD had blessed Abraham in all things. ² So Abraham said to the oldest servant of his house, who ruled over all that he had, "Please, put your hand under my thigh, ³ and I will make you swear by the LORD, the God of heaven and the God of the earth, that you will not take a wife for my son from the daughters of the Canaanites, among whom I dwell; ⁴ but you shall go to my country and to my family, and take a wife for my son Isaac."

⁵ And the servant said to him, "Perhaps the woman will not be willing to follow me to this land. Must I take your son back to the land from which you came?"

⁶ But Abraham said to him, "Beware that you do not take my son back there. ⁷ The LORD God of heaven, who took me from my father's house and from the land of my family, and who spoke to me and swore to me, saying, 'To your descendants I give this land,' He will send His angel before you, and you shall take a wife for my son from there. ⁸ And if the woman is not willing to follow you, then you will be released from this oath; only do not take my son back there." ⁹ So the servant put his hand under the thigh of Abraham his master, and swore to him concerning this matter.

¹⁰ Then the servant took ten of his master's camels and departed, for all his master's goods *were in* his hand. And he arose and went to Mesopotamia, to the city of Nahor. ¹¹ And he made his camels kneel down outside the city by a well of water at evening time, the time when women go out to draw *water*. ¹² Then he said, "O LORD God of my master Abraham, please give me success this day, and show kindness to my master Abraham. ¹³ Behold, *here* I stand by the well of water, and the daughters of the men of the city are coming out to draw water. ¹⁴ Now let it be that the young woman to whom I say, 'Please let down your pitcher that I may drink,' and she says, 'Drink, and I will also give your camels a drink'—*let her be the one* You have appointed for Your servant Isaac. And by this I will know that You have shown kindness to my master."

¹⁵ And it happened, before he had finished speaking, that behold, Rebekah, who was born to Bethuel, son of Milcah, the wife of Nahor, Abraham's brother, came out with her pitcher on her shoulder. ¹⁶ Now the young woman *was* very beautiful to behold, a virgin; no man had known her. And she went down to the well, filled her pitcher, and came up. ¹⁷ And the servant ran to meet her and said, "Please let me drink a little water from your pitcher."

¹⁸ So she said, "Drink, my lord." Then she quickly let her pitcher down to her hand, and gave him a drink. ¹⁹ And when she had finished giving him a drink, she said, "I will draw *water* for your camels also, until they have finished drinking." ²⁰ Then she quickly emptied her pitcher into the trough, ran back to the well to draw *water*, and drew for all his camels. ²¹ And the man, wondering at her, remained silent so as to know whether the LORD had made his journey prosperous or not.

²² So it was, when the camels had finished drinking, that the man took a golden nose ring weighing half a shekel, and two bracelets for her wrists weighing ten *shekels* of gold, ²³ and said, "Whose daughter *are* you? Tell me, please, is there room *in* your father's house for us to lodge?"

²⁴ So she said to him, "I *am* the daughter of Bethuel, Milcah's son, whom she bore to Nahor." ²⁵ Moreover she said to

him, "We have both straw and feed enough, and room to lodge."

²⁶ Then the man bowed down his head and worshiped the LORD. ²⁷ And he said, "Blessed *be* the LORD God of my master Abraham, who has not forsaken His mercy and His truth toward my master. As for me, being on the way, the LORD led me to the house of my master's brethren." ²⁸ So the young woman ran and told her mother's household these things.

²⁹ Now Rebekah had a brother whose name *was* Laban, and Laban ran out to the man by the well. ³⁰ So it came to pass, when he saw the nose ring, and the bracelets on his sister's wrists, and when he heard the words of his sister Rebekah, saying, "Thus the man spoke to me," that he went to the man. And there he stood by the camels at the well. ³¹ And he said, "Come in, O blessed of the LORD! Why do you stand outside? For I have prepared the house, and a place for the camels."

³² Then the man came to the house. And he unloaded the camels, and provided straw and feed for the camels, and water to wash his feet and the feet of the men who *were* with him. ³³ *Food* was set before him to eat, but he said, "I will not eat until I have told about my errand."

And he said, "Speak on."

³⁴ So he said, "I *am* Abraham's servant. ³⁵ The LORD has blessed my master greatly, and he has become great; and He has given him flocks and herds, silver and gold, male and female servants, and camels and donkeys. ³⁶ And Sarah my master's wife bore a son to my master when she was old; and to him he has given all that he has. ³⁷ Now my master made me swear, saying, 'You shall not take a wife for my son from the daughters of the Canaanites, in whose land I dwell; ³⁸ but you shall go to my father's house and to my family, and take a wife for my son.' ³⁹ And I said to my master, 'Perhaps the woman will not follow me.' ⁴⁰ But he said to me, 'The LORD, before whom I walk, will send His angel with you and prosper your way; and you shall take a wife for my son from my family and from my father's house. ⁴¹ You will be clear from this oath when you arrive among my family; for if they will not give *her* to you, then you will be released from my oath.'

⁴² "And this day I came to the well and said, 'O LORD God of my master Abraham, if You will now prosper the way in which I go, ⁴³ behold, I stand by the well of water; and it shall come to pass that when the virgin comes out to draw *water*, and I say to her, "Please give me a little water from your pitcher to drink," ⁴⁴ and she says to me, "Drink, and I will draw for your camels also,"—*let* her *be* the woman whom the LORD has appointed for my master's son.'

⁴⁵ "But before I had finished speaking in my heart, there was Rebekah, coming out with her pitcher on her shoulder; and she went down to the well and drew *water*. And I said to her, 'Please let me drink.' ⁴⁶ And she made haste and let her pitcher down from her *shoulder*, and said, 'Drink, and I will give your camels a drink also.' So I drank, and she gave the camels a drink also. ⁴⁷ Then I asked her, and said, 'Whose daughter *are* you?' And she said, 'The daughter of Bethuel, Nahor's son, whom Milcah bore to him.' So I put the nose ring on her nose and the bracelets on her wrists. ⁴⁸ And I bowed my head and worshiped the LORD, and blessed the LORD God of my master Abraham, who had led me in the way of truth to take the daughter of my master's brother for his son. ⁴⁹ Now if you will deal kindly and truly with my master, tell me. And if not, tell me, that I may turn to the right hand or to the left."

⁵⁰ Then Laban and Bethuel answered and said, "The thing comes from the LORD; we cannot speak to you either bad or good. ⁵¹ Here *is* Rebekah before you; take *her* and go, and let her be your master's son's wife, as the LORD has spoken."

⁵² And it came to pass, when Abraham's servant heard their words, that he worshiped the LORD, *bowing himself* to the earth. ⁵³ Then the servant brought out jewelry of silver, jewelry of gold, and clothing, and gave *them* to Rebekah. He also gave precious things to her brother and to her mother.

⁵⁴ And he and the men who *were* with him ate and drank and stayed all night. Then they arose in the morning, and he said, "Send me away to my master."

⁵⁵ But her brother and her mother said,

"Let the young woman stay with us *a few* days, at least ten; after that she may go."

⁵⁶ And he said to them, "Do not hinder me, since the LORD has prospered my way; send me away so that I may go to my master."

⁵⁷ So they said, "We will call the young woman and ask her personally." ⁵⁸ Then they called Rebekah and said to her, "Will you go with this man?"

And she said, "I will go."

⁵⁹ So they sent away Rebekah their sister and her nurse, and Abraham's servant and his men. ⁶⁰ And they blessed Rebekah and said to her:

> "Our sister, *may* you *become*
> *The mother of* thousands of ten
>   thousands;
> And may your descendants possess
> The gates of those who hate
>   them."

⁶¹ Then Rebekah and her maids arose, and they rode on the camels and followed the man. So the servant took Rebekah and departed.

⁶² Now Isaac came from the way of Beer Lahai Roi, for he dwelt in the South. ⁶³ And Isaac went out to meditate in the field in the evening; and he lifted his eyes and looked, and there, the camels *were* coming. ⁶⁴ Then Rebekah lifted her eyes, and when she saw Isaac she dismounted from her camel; ⁶⁵ for she had said to the servant, "Who *is* this man walking in the field to meet us?"

The servant said, "It *is* my master." So she took a veil and covered herself.

⁶⁶ And the servant told Isaac all the things that he had done. ⁶⁷ Then Isaac brought her into his mother Sarah's tent; and he took Rebekah and she became his wife, and he loved her. So Isaac was comforted after his mother's *death*.

∼ PSALM 7:1–5 ∼

1   O LORD my God, in You I put my
       trust;
    Save me from all those who
       persecute me;
    And deliver me,
2   Lest they tear me like a lion,

Rending *me* in pieces, while *there is*
   none to deliver.
3   O LORD my God, if I have done this:
    If there is iniquity in my hands,
4   If I have repaid evil to him who was
       at peace with me,
    Or have plundered my enemy
       without cause,
5   Let the enemy pursue me and
       overtake *me*;
    Yes, let him trample my life to the
       earth,
    And lay my honor in the dust.   Selah

∼ PROVERBS 3:7, 8 ∼

7   Do not be wise in your own eyes;
    Fear the LORD and depart from evil.
8   It will be health to your flesh,
    And strength to your bones.

∼ MATTHEW 9:1–17 ∼

So He got into a boat, crossed over, and came to His own city. ² Then behold, they brought to Him a paralytic lying on a bed. When Jesus saw their faith, He said to the paralytic, "Son, be of good cheer; your sins are forgiven you."

³ And at once some of the scribes said within themselves, "This Man blasphemes!"

⁴ But Jesus, knowing their thoughts, said, "Why do you think evil in your hearts? ⁵ For which is easier, to say, 'Your sins are forgiven you,' or to say, 'Arise and walk'? ⁶ But that you may know that the Son of Man has power on earth to forgive sins"—then He said to the paralytic, "Arise, take up your bed, and go to your house." ⁷ And he arose and departed to his house.

⁸ Now when the multitudes saw *it,* they marveled and glorified God, who had given such power to men.

⁹ As Jesus passed on from there, He saw a man named Matthew sitting at the tax office. And He said to him, "Follow Me." So he arose and followed Him.

¹⁰ Now it happened, as Jesus sat at the table in the house, *that* behold, many tax collectors and sinners came and sat down with Him and His disciples. ¹¹ And when

the Pharisees saw *it*, they said to His disciples, "Why does your Teacher eat with tax collectors and sinners?"

¹² When Jesus heard *that*, He said to them, "Those who are well have no need of a physician, but those who are sick. ¹³ But go and learn what *this* means: 'I desire mercy and not sacrifice.' For I did not come to call the righteous, but sinners, to repentance."

¹⁴ Then the disciples of John came to Him, saying, "Why do we and the Pharisees fast often, but Your disciples do not fast?"

¹⁵ And Jesus said to them, "Can the friends of the bridegroom mourn as long as the bridegroom is with them? But the days will come when the bridegroom will be taken away from them, and then they will fast. ¹⁶ No one puts a piece of unshrunk cloth on an old garment; for the patch pulls away from the garment, and the tear is made worse. ¹⁷ Nor do they put new wine into old wineskins, or else the wineskins break, the wine is spilled, and the wineskins are ruined. But they put new wine into new wineskins, and both are preserved."

READING 13 · JANUARY 13

∼ GENESIS 25:1—26:35 ∼

Abraham again took a wife, and her name *was* Keturah. ² And she bore him Zimran, Jokshan, Medan, Midian, Ishbak, and Shuah. ³ Jokshan begot Sheba and Dedan. And the sons of Dedan were Asshurim, Letushim, and Leummim. ⁴ And the sons of Midian *were* Ephah, Epher, Hanoch, Abidah, and Eldaah. All these *were* the children of Keturah.

⁵ And Abraham gave all that he had to Isaac. ⁶ But Abraham gave gifts to the sons of the concubines which Abraham had; and while he was still living he sent them eastward, away from Isaac his son, to the country of the east.

⁷ This *is* the sum of the years of Abraham's life which he lived: one hundred and seventy-five years. ⁸ Then Abraham breathed his last and died in a good old age, an old man and full *of years*, and was gathered to his people. ⁹ And his sons Isaac and Ishmael buried him in the cave of Machpelah, which *is* before Mamre, in the field of Ephron the son of Zohar the Hittite, ¹⁰ the field which Abraham purchased from the sons of Heth. There Abraham was buried, and Sarah his wife. ¹¹ And it came to pass, after the death of Abraham, that God blessed his son Isaac. And Isaac dwelt at Beer Lahai Roi.

¹² Now this *is* the genealogy of Ishmael, Abraham's son, whom Hagar the Egyptian, Sarah's maidservant, bore to Abraham. ¹³ And these *were* the names of the sons of Ishmael, by their names, according to their generations: The firstborn of Ishmael, Nebajoth; then Kedar, Adbeel, Mibsam, ¹⁴ Mishma, Dumah, Massa, ¹⁵ Hadar, Tema, Jetur, Naphish, and Kedemah. ¹⁶ These *were* the sons of Ishmael and these *were* their names, by their towns and their settlements, twelve princes according to their nations. ¹⁷ These *were* the years of the life of Ishmael: one hundred and thirty-seven years; and he breathed his last and died, and was gathered to his people. ¹⁸(They dwelt from Havilah as far as Shur, which *is* east of Egypt as you go toward Assyria.) He died in the presence of all his brethren.

¹⁹ This *is* the genealogy of Isaac, Abraham's son. Abraham begot Isaac. ²⁰ Isaac was forty years old when he took Rebekah as wife, the daughter of Bethuel the Syrian of Padan Aram, the sister of Laban the Syrian. ²¹ Now Isaac pleaded with the LORD for his wife, because she *was* barren; and the LORD granted his plea, and Rebekah his wife conceived. ²² But the children struggled together within her; and she said, "If *all is* well, why *am I like* this? " So she went to inquire of the LORD.

²³ And the LORD said to her:

"Two nations *are* in your womb,
Two peoples shall be separated
     from your body;

One people shall be stronger than
   the other,
And the older shall serve the
   younger."

24 So when her days were fulfilled *for her* to give birth, indeed *there were* twins in her womb. 25 And the first came out red. *He was* like a hairy garment all over; so they called his name Esau. 26 Afterward his brother came out, and his hand took hold of Esau's heel; so his name was called Jacob. Isaac *was* sixty years old when she bore them.

27 So the boys grew. And Esau was a skillful hunter, a man of the field; but Jacob was a mild man, dwelling in tents. 28 And Isaac loved Esau because he ate *of his* game, but Rebekah loved Jacob.

29 Now Jacob cooked a stew; and Esau came in from the field, and he *was* weary. 30 And Esau said to Jacob, "Please feed me with that same red *stew,* for I *am* weary." Therefore his name was called Edom.

31 But Jacob said, "Sell me your birthright as of this day."

32 And Esau said, "Look, I *am* about to die; so what *is* this birthright to me?"

33 Then Jacob said, "Swear to me as of this day."

So he swore to him, and sold his birthright to Jacob. 34 And Jacob gave Esau bread and stew of lentils; then he ate and drank, arose, and went his way. Thus Esau despised *his* birthright.

26 There was a famine in the land, besides the first famine that was in the days of Abraham. And Isaac went to Abimelech king of the Philistines, in Gerar.

2 Then the LORD appeared to him and said: "Do not go down to Egypt; live in the land of which I shall tell you. 3 Dwell in this land, and I will be with you and bless you; for to you and your descendants I give all these lands, and I will perform the oath which I swore to Abraham your father. 4 And I will make your descendants multiply as the stars of heaven; I will give to your descendants all these lands; and in your seed all the nations of the earth shall be blessed; 5 because Abraham obeyed My voice and kept My charge, My commandments, My statutes, and My laws."

6 So Isaac dwelt in Gerar. 7 And the men of the place asked about his wife. And he said, "She *is* my sister"; for he was afraid to say, "She *is* my wife," *because he thought,* "lest the men of the place kill me for Rebekah, because she *is* beautiful to behold." 8 Now it came to pass, when he had been there a long time, that Abimelech king of the Philistines looked through a window, and saw, and there was Isaac, showing endearment to Rebekah his wife. 9 Then Abimelech called Isaac and said, "Quite obviously she *is* your wife; so how could you say, 'She *is* my sister'?"

Isaac said to him, "Because I said, 'Lest I die on account of her.' "

10 And Abimelech said, "What *is* this you have done to us? One of the people might soon have lain with your wife, and you would have brought guilt on us." 11 So Abimelech charged all *his* people, saying, "He who touches this man or his wife shall surely be put to death."

12 Then Isaac sowed in that land, and reaped in the same year a hundredfold; and the LORD blessed him. 13 The man began to prosper, and continued prospering until he became very prosperous; 14 for he had possessions of flocks and possessions of herds and a great number of servants. So the Philistines envied him. 15 Now the Philistines had stopped up all the wells which his father's servants had dug in the days of Abraham his father, and they had filled them with earth. 16 And Abimelech said to Isaac, "Go away from us, for you are much mightier than we."

17 Then Isaac departed from there and pitched his tent in the Valley of Gerar, and dwelt there. 18 And Isaac dug again the wells of water which they had dug in the days of Abraham his father, for the Philistines had stopped them up after the death of Abraham. He called them by the names which his father had called them.

19 Also Isaac's servants dug in the valley, and found a well of running water there. 20 But the herdsmen of Gerar quarreled with Isaac's herdsmen, saying, "The water *is* ours." So he called the name of the well Esek, because they quarreled with him. 21 Then they dug another well, and they quarreled over that *one* also. So he called its name Sitnah. 22 And he moved from there and dug another well, and they

Honor
the Lord

Honor the Lord with your possessions, and with the firstfruits of all your increase.

Proverbs 3:9

A businessman was once very concerned about selling a warehouse property he owned. Since he had last surveyed the building, vandals had damaged the doors, smashed the windows, and strewn trash throughout it. The building had been empty for several months and needed additional repairs due to weather and general lack of maintenance. As the man showed a prospective buyer the building, he took great pains to assure him that he would replace the broken windows, correct any structural damage, mend the roof, and clean out the garbage. He felt as if he was apologizing for the condition of the building at every turn, but he wanted to present the building in the best possible light.

To his surprise, the buyer finally said to him, "Forget about the repairs. I'm going to build something completely different on this land. I don't want the building. I want the site."

So often, we attempt to present to our Creator what we think is good — justifying our actions, promising to do better, trying to put the best spin on the state of our souls. In the end, what God wants is us. When we honor Him by giving our whole self, He gives us the very best He has.

did not quarrel over it. So he called its name Rehoboth, because he said, "For now the LORD has made room for us, and we shall be fruitful in the land."

²³ Then he went up from there to Beersheba. ²⁴ And the LORD appeared to him the same night and said, "I *am* the God of your father Abraham; do not fear, for I *am* with you. I will bless you and multiply your descendants for My servant Abraham's sake." ²⁵ So he built an altar there and called on the name of the LORD, and he pitched his tent there; and there Isaac's servants dug a well.

²⁶ Then Abimelech came to him from Gerar with Ahuzzath, one of his friends, and Phichol the commander of his army. ²⁷ And Isaac said to them, "Why have you come to me, since you hate me and have sent me away from you?"

²⁸ But they said, "We have certainly seen that the LORD is with you. So we said, 'Let there now be an oath between us, between you and us; and let us make a covenant with you, ²⁹ that you will do us no harm, since we have not touched you, and since we have done nothing to you but good and have sent you away in peace. You *are* now the blessed of the LORD.' "

³⁰ So he made them a feast, and they ate and drank. ³¹ Then they arose early in the morning and swore an oath with one another; and Isaac sent them away, and they departed from him in peace.

³² It came to pass the same day that Isaac's servants came and told him about the well which they had dug, and said to him, "We have found water." ³³ So he called it Shebah. Therefore the name of the city *is* Beersheba to this day.

³⁴ When Esau was forty years old, he took as wives Judith the daughter of Beeri the Hittite, and Basemath the daughter of Elon the Hittite. ³⁵ And they were a grief of mind to Isaac and Rebekah.

∼ PSALM 7:6–8 ∼

⁶ Arise, O LORD, in Your anger;
  Lift Yourself up because of the rage
    of my enemies;
  Rise up for me *to* the judgment You
    have commanded!
⁷ So the congregation of the peoples
    shall surround You;

For their sakes, therefore, return on
    high.
⁸ The LORD shall judge the peoples;
  Judge me, O LORD, according to my
    righteousness,
  And according to my integrity within
    me.

∼ PROVERBS 3:9, 10 ∼

⁹ Honor the LORD with your
    possessions,
  And with the firstfruits of all your
    increase;
¹⁰ So your barns will be filled with
    plenty,
  And your vats will overflow with
    new wine.

∼ MATTHEW 9:18–38 ∼

While He spoke these things to them, behold, a ruler came and worshiped Him, saying, "My daughter has just died, but come and lay Your hand on her and she will live." ¹⁹ So Jesus arose and followed him, and so *did* His disciples.

²⁰ And suddenly, a woman who had a flow of blood for twelve years came from behind and touched the hem of His garment. ²¹ For she said to herself, "If only I may touch His garment, I shall be made well." ²² But Jesus turned around, and when He saw her He said, "Be of good cheer, daughter; your faith has made you well." And the woman was made well from that hour.

²³ When Jesus came into the ruler's house, and saw the flute players and the noisy crowd wailing, ²⁴ He said to them, "Make room, for the girl is not dead, but sleeping." And they ridiculed Him. ²⁵ But when the crowd was put outside, He went in and took her by the hand, and the girl arose. ²⁶ And the report of this went out into all that land.

²⁷ When Jesus departed from there, two blind men followed Him, crying out and saying, "Son of David, have mercy on us!" ²⁸ And when He had come into the house, the blind men came to Him. And Jesus said to them, "Do you believe that I am able to do this?"

They said to Him, "Yes, Lord."

²⁹ Then He touched their eyes, saying, "According to your faith let it be to you." ³⁰ And their eyes were opened. And Jesus sternly warned them, saying, "See *that* no one knows *it.*" ³¹ But when they had departed, they spread the news about Him in all that country.

³² As they went out, behold, they brought to Him a man, mute and demon-possessed. ³³ And when the demon was cast out, the mute spoke. And the multitudes marveled, saying, "It was never seen like this in Israel!"

³⁴ But the Pharisees said, "He casts out demons by the ruler of the demons."

³⁵ Then Jesus went about all the cities and villages, teaching in their synagogues, preaching the gospel of the kingdom, and healing every sickness and every disease among the people. ³⁶ But when He saw the multitudes, He was moved with compassion for them, because they were weary and scattered, like sheep having no shepherd. ³⁷ Then He said to His disciples, "The harvest truly *is* plentiful, but the laborers *are* few. ³⁸ Therefore pray the Lord of the harvest to send out laborers into His harvest."

READING 14 · JANUARY 14

～ GENESIS 27:1—28:22 ～

Now it came to pass, when Isaac was old and his eyes were so dim that he could not see, that he called Esau his older son and said to him, "My son."

And he answered him, "Here I am."

² Then he said, "Behold now, I am old. I do not know the day of my death. ³ Now therefore, please take your weapons, your quiver and your bow, and go out to the field and hunt game for me. ⁴ And make me savory food, such as I love, and bring *it* to me that I may eat, that my soul may bless you before I die."

⁵ Now Rebekah was listening when Isaac spoke to Esau his son. And Esau went to the field to hunt game and to bring *it*. ⁶ So Rebekah spoke to Jacob her son, saying, "Indeed I heard your father speak to Esau your brother, saying, ⁷ 'Bring me game and make savory food for me, that I may eat it and bless you in the presence of the LORD before my death.' ⁸ Now therefore, my son, obey my voice according to what I command you. ⁹ Go now to the flock and bring me from there two choice kids of the goats, and I will make savory food from them for your father, such as he loves. ¹⁰ Then you shall take *it* to your father, that he may eat *it,* and that he may bless you before his death."

¹¹ And Jacob said to Rebekah his mother, "Look, Esau my brother *is* a hairy man, and I *am* a smooth-*skinned* man.

¹² Perhaps my father will feel me, and I shall seem to be a deceiver to him; and I shall bring a curse on myself and not a blessing."

¹³ But his mother said to him, "*Let* your curse *be* on me, my son; only obey my voice, and go, get *them* for me." ¹⁴ And he went and got *them* and brought *them* to his mother, and his mother made savory food, such as his father loved. ¹⁵ Then Rebekah took the choice clothes of her elder son Esau, which *were* with her in the house, and put them on Jacob her younger son. ¹⁶ And she put the skins of the kids of the goats on his hands and on the smooth part of his neck. ¹⁷ Then she gave the savory food and the bread, which she had prepared, into the hand of her son Jacob.

¹⁸ So he went to his father and said, "My father."

And he said, "Here I am. Who *are* you, my son?"

¹⁹ Jacob said to his father, "I *am* Esau your firstborn; I have done just as you told me; please arise, sit and eat of my game, that your soul may bless me."

²⁰ But Isaac said to his son, "How *is it* that you have found *it* so quickly, my son?"

And he said, "Because the LORD your God brought *it* to me."

²¹ Isaac said to Jacob, "Please come near, that I may feel you, my son, whether you *are* really my son Esau or not." ²² So Jacob

went near to Isaac his father, and he felt him and said, "The voice *is* Jacob's voice, but the hands *are* the hands of Esau." ²³ And he did not recognize him, because his hands were hairy like his brother Esau's hands; so he blessed him.

²⁴ Then he said, "*Are* you really my son Esau?"

He said, "I *am*."

²⁵ He said, "Bring *it* near to me, and I will eat of my son's game, so that my soul may bless you." So he brought *it* near to him, and he ate; and he brought him wine, and he drank. ²⁶ Then his father Isaac said to him, "Come near now and kiss me, my son." ²⁷ And he came near and kissed him; and he smelled the smell of his clothing, and blessed him and said:

"Surely, the smell of my son
Is like the smell of a field
Which the LORD has blessed.
²⁸ Therefore may God give you
Of the dew of heaven,
Of the fatness of the earth,
And plenty of grain and wine.
²⁹ Let peoples serve you,
And nations bow down to you.
Be master over your brethren,
And let your mother's sons bow
down to you.
Cursed *be* everyone who curses
you,
And blessed *be* those who bless
you!"

³⁰ Now it happened, as soon as Isaac had finished blessing Jacob, and Jacob had scarcely gone out from the presence of Isaac his father, that Esau his brother came in from his hunting. ³¹ He also had made savory food, and brought it to his father, and said to his father, "Let my father arise and eat of his son's game, that your soul may bless me."

³² And his father Isaac said to him, "Who *are* you?"

So he said, "I *am* your son, your first-born, Esau."

³³ Then Isaac trembled exceedingly, and said, "Who? Where *is* the one who hunted game and brought *it* to me? I ate all *of it* before you came, and I have blessed him—*and* indeed he shall be blessed."

³⁴ When Esau heard the words of his father, he cried with an exceedingly great and bitter cry, and said to his father, "Bless me—me also, O my father!"

³⁵ But he said, "Your brother came with deceit and has taken away your blessing."

³⁶ And *Esau* said, "Is he not rightly named Jacob? For he has supplanted me these two times. He took away my birthright, and now look, he has taken away my blessing!" And he said, "Have you not reserved a blessing for me?"

³⁷ Then Isaac answered and said to Esau, "Indeed I have made him your master, and all his brethren I have given to him as servants; with grain and wine I have sustained him. What shall I do now for you, my son?"

³⁸ And Esau said to his father, "Have you only one blessing, my father? Bless me—me also, O my father!" And Esau lifted up his voice and wept.

³⁹ Then Isaac his father answered and said to him:

"Behold, your dwelling shall be of
the fatness of the earth,
And of the dew of heaven from
above.
⁴⁰ By your sword you shall live,
And you shall serve your brother;
And it shall come to pass, when
you become restless,
That you shall break his yoke
from your neck."

⁴¹ So Esau hated Jacob because of the blessing with which his father blessed him, and Esau said in his heart, "The days of mourning for my father are at hand; then I will kill my brother Jacob."

⁴² And the words of Esau her older son were told to Rebekah. So she sent and called Jacob her younger son, and said to him, "Surely your brother Esau comforts himself concerning you *by intending* to kill you. ⁴³ Now therefore, my son, obey my voice: arise, flee to my brother Laban in Haran. ⁴⁴ And stay with him a few days, until your brother's fury turns away, ⁴⁵ until your brother's anger turns away from you, and he forgets what you have done to him; then I will send and bring you from there. Why should I be bereaved also of you both in one day?"

⁴⁶ And Rebekah said to Isaac, "I am

Discipline Pays Off in the End

In *Dare to Discipline*, Dr. James Dobson tells about his own mother's approach to discipline: "I found her reasonable on most issues. If I was late coming home from school, I could just explain what had caused the delay. . . . If I didn't get my work done, we could sit down and come to some kind of agreement for future action. But there was one matter on which she was absolutely rigid: She did not tolerate 'sassiness.'

"She knew that backtalk and 'lip' are the child's most potent weapons of defiance and they must be discouraged." Through the years, Dobson recalls having been spanked with a shoe, and often with a handy belt. He vividly recalls, however, one particular spanking. He made the costly mistake of sassing his mother when the only object nearby for a spanking was her girdle. He says, "Now those were the days when a girdle was a weapon. It weighed about sixteen pounds and was lined with lead and steel . . . with a multitude of straps and buckles. . . . She gave me an entire thrashing with one massive blow!"

While Jim may not have appreciated her principles about discipline at the time, he certainly did in later years. His book, *The Strong-Willed Child,* is dedicated to her!

Disciplining our children shows them how much we love them. It may not seem that way at the time, but a child feels more secure and loved when he's been given boundaries and they're enforced.

weary of my life because of the daughters of Heth; if Jacob takes a wife of the daughters of Heth, like these *who are* the daughters of the land, what good will my life be to me?"

28

Then Isaac called Jacob and blessed him, and charged him, and said to him: "You shall not take a wife from the daughters of Canaan. ² Arise, go to Padan Aram, to the house of Bethuel your mother's father; and take yourself a wife from there of the daughters of Laban your mother's brother.

³ "May God Almighty bless you,
    And make you fruitful and
       multiply you,
    That you may be an assembly of
       peoples;
⁴ And give you the blessing of
    Abraham,
    To you and your descendants with
       you,
    That you may inherit the land
    In which you are a stranger,
    Which God gave to Abraham."

⁵ So Isaac sent Jacob away, and he went to Padan Aram, to Laban the son of Bethuel the Syrian, the brother of Rebekah, the mother of Jacob and Esau.

⁶ Esau saw that Isaac had blessed Jacob and sent him away to Padan Aram to take himself a wife from there, *and that* as he blessed him he gave him a charge, saying, "You shall not take a wife from the daughters of Canaan," ⁷ and that Jacob had obeyed his father and his mother and had gone to Padan Aram. ⁸ Also Esau saw that the daughters of Canaan did not please his father Isaac. ⁹ So Esau went to Ishmael and took Mahalath the daughter of Ishmael, Abraham's son, the sister of Nebajoth, to be his wife in addition to the wives he had.

¹⁰ Now Jacob went out from Beersheba and went toward Haran. ¹¹ So he came to a certain place and stayed there all night, because the sun had set. And he took one of the stones of that place and put it at his head, and he lay down in that place to sleep. ¹² Then he dreamed, and behold, a ladder *was* set up on the earth, and its top reached to heaven; and there the an-

gels of God were ascending and descending on it.

¹³ And behold, the LORD stood above it and said: "I *am* the LORD God of Abraham your father and the God of Isaac; the land on which you lie I will give to you and your descendants. ¹⁴ Also your descendants shall be as the dust of the earth; you shall spread abroad to the west and the east, to the north and the south; and in you and in your seed all the families of the earth shall be blessed. ¹⁵ Behold, I *am* with you and will keep you wherever you go, and will bring you back to this land; for I will not leave you until I have done what I have spoken to you."

¹⁶ Then Jacob awoke from his sleep and said, "Surely the LORD is in this place, and I did not know *it.*" ¹⁷ And he was afraid and said, "How awesome *is* this place! This *is* none other than the house of God, and this *is* the gate of heaven!"

¹⁸ Then Jacob rose early in the morning, and took the stone that he had put at his head, set it up as a pillar, and poured oil on top of it. ¹⁹ And he called the name of that place Bethel; but the name of that city had been Luz previously. ²⁰ Then Jacob made a vow, saying, "If God will be with me, and keep me in this way that I am going, and give me bread to eat and clothing to put on, ²¹ so that I come back to my father's house in peace, then the LORD shall be my God. ²² And this stone which I have set as a pillar shall be God's house, and of all that You give me I will surely give a tenth to You."

∽ PSALM 7:9–17 ∽

⁹ Oh, let the wickedness of the wicked
      come to an end,
    But establish the just;
    For the righteous God tests the
       hearts and minds.
¹⁰ My defense *is* of God,
    Who saves the upright in heart.

¹¹ God *is* a just judge,
    And God is angry *with the wicked*
       every day.
¹² If he does not turn back,
    He will sharpen His sword;
    He bends His bow and makes it
       ready.

13 He also prepares for Himself
    instruments of death;
    He makes His arrows into fiery
    shafts.

14 Behold, *the wicked* brings forth
    iniquity;
    Yes, he conceives trouble and brings
    forth falsehood.
15 He made a pit and dug it out,
    And has fallen into the ditch *which*
    he made.
16 His trouble shall return upon his
    own head,
    And his violent dealing shall come
    down on his own crown.

17 I will praise the LORD according to
    His righteousness,
    And will sing praise to the name of
    the LORD Most High.

~ PROVERBS 3:11, 12 ~

11 My son, do not despise the
    chastening of the LORD,
    Nor detest His correction;
12 For whom the LORD loves He
    corrects,
    Just as a father the son *in whom* he
    delights.

~ MATTHEW 10:1–20 ~

And when He had called His twelve disciples to *Him,* He gave them power *over*
unclean spirits, to cast them out, and to
heal all kinds of sickness and all kinds of
disease. 2 Now the names of the twelve
apostles are these: first, Simon, who is
called Peter, and Andrew his brother;
James the *son* of Zebedee, and John his
brother; 3 Philip and Bartholomew; Thomas and Matthew the tax collector; James

the *son* of Alphaeus, and Lebbaeus, whose
surname was Thaddaeus; 4 Simon the
Cananite, and Judas Iscariot, who also
betrayed Him.
5 These twelve Jesus sent out and commanded them, saying: "Do not go into
the way of the Gentiles, and do not enter
a city of the Samaritans. 6 But go rather
to the lost sheep of the house of Israel.
7 And as you go, preach, saying, 'The kingdom of heaven is at hand.' 8 Heal the sick,
cleanse the lepers, raise the dead, cast out
demons. Freely you have received, freely
give. 9 Provide neither gold nor silver nor
copper in your money belts, 10 nor bag for
your journey, nor two tunics, nor sandals,
nor staffs; for a worker is worthy of his
food.
11 "Now whatever city or town you
enter, inquire who in it is worthy, and stay
there till you go out. 12 And when you go
into a household, greet it. 13 If the household is worthy, let your peace come upon
it. But if it is not worthy, let your peace
return to you. 14 And whoever will not
receive you nor hear your words, when
you depart from that house or city, shake
off the dust from your feet. 15 Assuredly, I
say to you, it will be more tolerable for
the land of Sodom and Gomorrah in the
day of judgment than for that city!
16 "Behold, I send you out as sheep in
the midst of wolves. Therefore be wise as
serpents and harmless as doves. 17 But beware of men, for they will deliver you up
to councils and scourge you in their synagogues. 18 You will be brought before governors and kings for My sake, as a
testimony to them and to the Gentiles.
19 But when they deliver you up, do not
worry about how or what you should
speak. For it will be given to you in that
hour what you should speak; 20 for it is
not you who speak, but the Spirit of your
Father who speaks in you.

~ GENESIS 29:1—30:43 ~

So Jacob went on his journey and
came to the land of the people of
the East. 2 And he looked, and saw a

well in the field; and behold, there *were*
three flocks of sheep lying by it; for out of
that well they watered the flocks. A large

stone *was* on the well's mouth. ³ Now all the flocks would be gathered there; and they would roll the stone from the well's mouth, water the sheep, and put the stone back in its place on the well's mouth.

⁴ And Jacob said to them, "My brethren, where *are* you from?"

And they said, "We *are* from Haran."

⁵ Then he said to them, "Do you know Laban the son of Nahor?"

And they said, "We know him."

⁶ So he said to them, "Is he well?"

And they said, "*He is* well. And look, his daughter Rachel is coming with the sheep."

⁷ Then he said, "Look, *it is* still high day; *it is* not time for the cattle to be gathered together. Water the sheep, and go and feed *them*."

⁸ But they said, "We cannot until all the flocks are gathered together, and they have rolled the stone from the well's mouth; then we water the sheep."

⁹ Now while he was still speaking with them, Rachel came with her father's sheep, for she was a shepherdess. ¹⁰ And it came to pass, when Jacob saw Rachel the daughter of Laban his mother's brother, and the sheep of Laban his mother's brother, that Jacob went near and rolled the stone from the well's mouth, and watered the flock of Laban his mother's brother. ¹¹ Then Jacob kissed Rachel, and lifted up his voice and wept. ¹² And Jacob told Rachel that he *was* her father's relative and that he *was* Rebekah's son. So she ran and told her father.

¹³ Then it came to pass, when Laban heard the report about Jacob his sister's son, that he ran to meet him, and embraced him and kissed him, and brought him to his house. So he told Laban all these things. ¹⁴ And Laban said to him, "Surely you *are* my bone and my flesh." And he stayed with him for a month.

¹⁵ Then Laban said to Jacob, "Because you *are* my relative, should you therefore serve me for nothing? Tell me, what *should* your wages *be?*" ¹⁶ Now Laban had two daughters: the name of the elder *was* Leah, and the name of the younger *was* Rachel. ¹⁷ Leah's eyes *were* delicate, but Rachel was beautiful of form and appearance.

¹⁸ Now Jacob loved Rachel; so he said,

"I will serve you seven years for Rachel your younger daughter."

¹⁹ And Laban said, "*It is* better that I give her to you than that I should give her to another man. Stay with me." ²⁰ So Jacob served seven years for Rachel, and they seemed *only* a few days to him because of the love he had for her.

²¹ Then Jacob said to Laban, "Give *me* my wife, for my days are fulfilled, that I may go in to her." ²² And Laban gathered together all the men of the place and made a feast. ²³ Now it came to pass in the evening, that he took Leah his daughter and brought her to Jacob; and he went in to her. ²⁴ And Laban gave his maid Zilpah to his daughter Leah *as* a maid. ²⁵ So it came to pass in the morning, that behold, it *was* Leah. And he said to Laban, "What is this you have done to me? Was it not for Rachel that I served you? Why then have you deceived me?"

²⁶ And Laban said, "It must not be done so in our country, to give the younger before the firstborn. ²⁷ Fulfill her week, and we will give you this one also for the service which you will serve with me still another seven years."

²⁸ Then Jacob did so and fulfilled her week. So he gave him his daughter Rachel as wife also. ²⁹ And Laban gave his maid Bilhah to his daughter Rachel as a maid. ³⁰ Then *Jacob* also went in to Rachel, and he also loved Rachel more than Leah. And he served with Laban still another seven years.

³¹ When the LORD saw that Leah *was* unloved, He opened her womb; but Rachel *was* barren. ³² So Leah conceived and bore a son, and she called his name Reuben; for she said, "The LORD has surely looked on my affliction. Now therefore, my husband will love me." ³³ Then she conceived again and bore a son, and said, "Because the LORD has heard that I *am* unloved, He has therefore given me this *son* also." And she called his name Simeon. ³⁴ She conceived again and bore a son, and said, "Now this time my husband will become attached to me, because I have borne him three sons." Therefore his name was called Levi. ³⁵ And she conceived again and bore a son, and said, "Now I will praise the LORD." Therefore she called his name Judah. Then she stopped bearing.

Today

Psychologist William Marston once asked three thousand people, "What have you to live for?" He was shocked to discover that 94 percent of the people he polled were simply enduring the present while they waited for the future. Some indicated they were waiting for something to happen — waiting for children to grow up and leave home, waiting for next year, waiting to take a trip, waiting for someone to die, or waiting for tomorrow. They had hope, but no ongoing purpose for their lives!

Only 6 percent of the people identified relationships and activities in the present tense of their lives as valuable reasons for living!

The 94 percent would be wise to recall the words of this poem by an unknown author:

> During all the years since time began,
> Today has been the friend of man;
> But in his blindness and his sorrow,
> He looks to yesterday and tomorrow.
> Forget past trials and your sorrow.
> There was, but is, no yesterday,
> And there may be no tomorrow.

30 Now when Rachel saw that she bore Jacob no children, Rachel envied her sister, and said to Jacob, "Give me children, or else I die!"

2 And Jacob's anger was aroused against Rachel, and he said, "*Am* I in the place of God, who has withheld from you the fruit of the womb?"

3 So she said, "Here is my maid Bilhah; go in to her, and she will bear *a child* on my knees, that I also may have children by her." 4 Then she gave him Bilhah her maid as wife, and Jacob went in to her. 5 And Bilhah conceived and bore Jacob a son. 6 Then Rachel said, "God has judged my case; and He has also heard my voice and given me a son." Therefore she called his name Dan. 7 And Rachel's maid Bilhah conceived again and bore Jacob a second son. 8 Then Rachel said, "With great wrestlings I have wrestled with my sister, *and* indeed I have prevailed." So she called his name Naphtali.

9 When Leah saw that she had stopped bearing, she took Zilpah her maid and gave her to Jacob as wife. 10 And Leah's maid Zilpah bore Jacob a son. 11 Then Leah said, "A troop comes!" So she called his name Gad. 12 And Leah's maid Zilpah bore Jacob a second son. 13 Then Leah said, "I am happy, for the daughters will call me blessed." So she called his name Asher.

14 Now Reuben went in the days of wheat harvest and found mandrakes in the field, and brought them to his mother Leah. Then Rachel said to Leah, "Please give me *some* of your son's mandrakes."

15 But she said to her, "*Is it* a small matter that you have taken away my husband? Would you take away my son's mandrakes also?"

And Rachel said, "Therefore he will lie with you tonight for your son's mandrakes."

16 When Jacob came out of the field in the evening, Leah went out to meet him and said, "You must come in to me, for I have surely hired you with my son's mandrakes." And he lay with her that night.

17 And God listened to Leah, and she conceived and bore Jacob a fifth son. 18 Leah said, "God has given me my wages, because I have given my maid to my hus-

band." So she called his name Issachar. 19 Then Leah conceived again and bore Jacob a sixth son. 20 And Leah said, "God has endowed me *with* a good endowment; now my husband will dwell with me, because I have borne him six sons." So she called his name Zebulun. 21 Afterward she bore a daughter, and called her name Dinah.

22 Then God remembered Rachel, and God listened to her and opened her womb. 23 And she conceived and bore a son, and said, "God has taken away my reproach." 24 So she called his name Joseph, and said, "The LORD shall add to me another son."

25 And it came to pass, when Rachel had borne Joseph, that Jacob said to Laban, "Send me away, that I may go to my own place and to my country. 26 Give *me* my wives and my children for whom I have served you, and let me go; for you know my service which I have done for you."

27 And Laban said to him, "Please *stay,* if I have found favor in your eyes, *for* I have learned by experience that the LORD has blessed me for your sake." 28 Then he said, "Name me your wages, and I will give *it.*"

29 So *Jacob* said to him, "You know how I have served you and how your livestock has been with me. 30 For what you had before I *came was* little, and it has increased to a great amount; the LORD has blessed you since my coming. And now, when shall I also provide for my own house?"

31 So he said, "What shall I give you?"

And Jacob said, "You shall not give me anything. If you will do this thing for me, I will again feed and keep your flocks: 32 Let me pass through all your flock today, removing from there all the speckled and spotted sheep, and all the brown ones among the lambs, and the spotted and speckled among the goats; and *these* shall be my wages. 33 So my righteousness will answer for me in time to come, when the subject of my wages comes before you: every one that *is* not speckled and spotted among the goats, and brown among the lambs, will be considered stolen, if *it is* with me."

34 And Laban said, "Oh, that it were according to your word!" 35 So he

removed that day the male goats that were speckled and spotted, all the female goats that were speckled and spotted, every one that had *some* white in it, and all the brown ones among the lambs, and gave *them* into the hand of his sons. ³⁶ Then he put three days' journey between himself and Jacob, and Jacob fed the rest of Laban's flocks.

³⁷ Now Jacob took for himself rods of green poplar and of the almond and chestnut trees, peeled white strips in them, and exposed the white which *was* in the rods. ³⁸ And the rods which he had peeled, he set before the flocks in the gutters, in the watering troughs where the flocks came to drink, so that they should conceive when they came to drink. ³⁹ So the flocks conceived before the rods, and the flocks brought forth streaked, speckled, and spotted. ⁴⁰ Then Jacob separated the lambs, and made the flocks face toward the streaked and all the brown in the flock of Laban; but he put his own flocks by themselves and did not put them with Laban's flock.

⁴¹ And it came to pass, whenever the stronger livestock conceived, that Jacob placed the rods before the eyes of the livestock in the gutters, that they might conceive among the rods. ⁴² But when the flocks were feeble, he did not put *them* in; so the feebler were Laban's and the stronger Jacob's. ⁴³ Thus the man became exceedingly prosperous, and had large flocks, female and male servants, and camels and donkeys.

∼ PSALM 8:1–5 ∼

¹ O LORD, our Lord,
How excellent *is* Your name in all the earth,
Who have set Your glory above the heavens!

² Out of the mouth of babes and nursing infants
You have ordained strength,
Because of Your enemies,
That You may silence the enemy and the avenger.

³ When I consider Your heavens, the work of Your fingers,

The moon and the stars, which You have ordained,
⁴ What is man that You are mindful of him,
And the son of man that You visit him?
⁵ For You have made him a little lower than the angels,
And You have crowned him with glory and honor.

∼ PROVERBS 3:13–18 ∼

¹³ Happy *is* the man *who* finds wisdom,
And the man *who* gains understanding;
¹⁴ For her proceeds *are* better than the profits of silver,
And her gain than fine gold.
¹⁵ She *is* more precious than rubies,
And all the things you may desire cannot compare with her.
¹⁶ Length of days *is* in her right hand,
In her left hand riches and honor.
¹⁷ Her ways *are* ways of pleasantness,
And all her paths *are* peace.
¹⁸ She *is* a tree of life to those who take hold of her,
And happy *are* all who retain her.

∼ MATTHEW 10:21–42 ∼

"Now brother will deliver up brother to death, and a father *his* child; and children will rise up against parents and cause them to be put to death. ²² And you will be hated by all for My name's sake. But he who endures to the end will be saved. ²³ When they persecute you in this city, flee to another. For assuredly, I say to you, you will not have gone through the cities of Israel before the Son of Man comes.

²⁴ "A disciple is not above *his* teacher, nor a servant above his master. ²⁵ It is enough for a disciple that he be like his teacher, and a servant like his master. If they have called the master of the house Beelzebub, how much more *will they call* those of his household! ²⁶ Therefore do not fear them. For there is nothing covered that will not be revealed, and hidden that will not be known.

²⁷ "Whatever I tell you in the dark, speak in the light; and what you hear in

the ear, preach on the housetops. ²⁸ And do not fear those who kill the body but cannot kill the soul. But rather fear Him who is able to destroy both soul and body in hell. ²⁹ Are not two sparrows sold for a copper coin? And not one of them falls to the ground apart from your Father's will. ³⁰ But the very hairs of your head are all numbered. ³¹ Do not fear therefore; you are of more value than many sparrows.

³² "Therefore whoever confesses Me before men, him I will also confess before My Father who is in heaven. ³³ But whoever denies Me before men, him I will also deny before My Father who is in heaven.

³⁴ "Do not think that I came to bring peace on earth. I did not come to bring peace but a sword. ³⁵ For I have come to 'set a man against his father, a daughter against her mother, and a daughter-in-law against her mother-in-law'; ³⁶ and 'a man's enemies will be those of his *own* household.' ³⁷ He who loves father or mother more than Me is not worthy of Me. And he who loves son or daughter more than Me is not worthy of Me. ³⁸ And he who does not take his cross and follow after Me is not worthy of Me. ³⁹ He who finds his life will lose it, and he who loses his life for My sake will find it.

⁴⁰ "He who receives you receives Me, and he who receives Me receives Him who sent Me. ⁴¹ He who receives a prophet in the name of a prophet shall receive a prophet's reward. And he who receives a righteous man in the name of a righteous man shall receive a righteous man's reward. ⁴² And whoever gives one of these little ones only a cup of cold *water* in the name of a disciple, assuredly, I say to you, he shall by no means lose his reward."

READING 16 · JANUARY 16

∼ GENESIS 31:1—32:32 ∼

Now *Jacob* heard the words of Laban's sons, saying, "Jacob has taken away all that was our father's, and from what was our father's he has acquired all this wealth." ² And Jacob saw the countenance of Laban, and indeed it *was* not *favorable* toward him as before. ³ Then the LORD said to Jacob, "Return to the land of your fathers and to your family, and I will be with you."

⁴ So Jacob sent and called Rachel and Leah to the field, to his flock, ⁵ and said to them, "I see your father's countenance, that it *is* not *favorable* toward me as before; but the God of my father has been with me. ⁶ And you know that with all my might I have served your father. ⁷ Yet your father has deceived me and changed my wages ten times, but God did not allow him to hurt me. ⁸ If he said thus: 'The speckled shall be your wages,' then all the flocks bore speckled. And if he said thus: 'The streaked shall be your wages,' then all the flocks bore streaked. ⁹ So God has taken away the livestock of your father and given *them* to me.

¹⁰ "And it happened, at the time when the flocks conceived, that I lifted my eyes and saw in a dream, and behold, the rams which leaped upon the flocks *were* streaked, speckled, and gray-spotted. ¹¹ Then the Angel of God spoke to me in a dream, saying, 'Jacob.' And I said, 'Here I am.' ¹² And He said, 'Lift your eyes now and see, all the rams which leap on the flocks *are* streaked, speckled, and gray-spotted; for I have seen all that Laban is doing to you. ¹³ I *am* the God of Bethel, where you anointed the pillar *and* where you made a vow to Me. Now arise, get out of this land, and return to the land of your family.' "

¹⁴ Then Rachel and Leah answered and said to him, "Is there still any portion or inheritance for us in our father's house? ¹⁵ Are we not considered strangers by him? For he has sold us, and also completely consumed our money. ¹⁶ For all these riches which God has taken from our father are *really* ours and our children's; now then, whatever God has said to you, do it."

¹⁷ Then Jacob rose and set his sons and his wives on camels. ¹⁸ And he carried away all his livestock and all his possessions which he had gained, his acquired

O God, Help!

"Dad," a little boy once asked, "does the Lord know everything?"

"Yes, son," the father replied. The boy nodded, but didn't look very convinced, prompting the father to ask a question of his own, "Why do you ask?"

"Because," the boy replied, "when the preacher prays, he prays so long telling God everything, that I thought maybe God wasn't clued in on what's happening to folks around here."

God is much more concerned about our motives than the type, amount, or form of the words we use in prayer. He looks on the heart. Sometimes a simple SOS is all that is required.

One Sunday morning as the great preacher Charles H. Spurgeon passed through the door on his way to the pulpit, he was overwhelmed by the great crowd of people who had already gathered for the service. As strong in faith and as profound and experienced a preacher as he was, an assistant overheard him pray simply, "O God, help!" Spurgeon's prayer needed no elaboration. And often, ours don't either.

livestock which he had gained in Padan Aram, to go to his father Isaac in the land of Canaan. ¹⁹ Now Laban had gone to shear his sheep, and Rachel had stolen the household idols that were her father's. ²⁰ And Jacob stole away, unknown to Laban the Syrian, in that he did not tell him that he intended to flee. ²¹ So he fled with all that he had. He arose and crossed the river, and headed toward the mountains of Gilead.

²² And Laban was told on the third day that Jacob had fled. ²³ Then he took his brethren with him and pursued him for seven days' journey, and he overtook him in the mountains of Gilead. ²⁴ But God had come to Laban the Syrian in a dream by night, and said to him, "Be careful that you speak to Jacob neither good nor bad."

²⁵ So Laban overtook Jacob. Now Jacob had pitched his tent in the mountains, and Laban with his brethren pitched in the mountains of Gilead.

²⁶ And Laban said to Jacob: "What have you done, that you have stolen away unknown to me, and carried away my daughters like captives *taken* with the sword? ²⁷ Why did you flee away secretly, and steal away from me, and not tell me; for I might have sent you away with joy and songs, with timbrel and harp? ²⁸ And you did not allow me to kiss my sons and my daughters. Now you have done foolishly in *so* doing. ²⁹ It is in my power to do you harm, but the God of your father spoke to me last night, saying, 'Be careful that you speak to Jacob neither good nor bad.' ³⁰ And now you have surely gone because you greatly long for your father's house, *but* why did you steal my gods?"

³¹ Then Jacob answered and said to Laban, "Because I was afraid, for I said, 'Perhaps you would take your daughters from me by force.' ³² With whomever you find your gods, do not let him live. In the presence of our brethren, identify what I have of yours and take *it* with you." For Jacob did not know that Rachel had stolen them.

³³ And Laban went into Jacob's tent, into Leah's tent, and into the two maids' tents, but he did not find *them*. Then he went out of Leah's tent and entered Rachel's tent. ³⁴ Now Rachel had taken the household idols, put them in the camel's saddle, and sat on them. And Laban searched all about the tent but did not find *them*. ³⁵ And she said to her father, "Let it not displease my lord that I cannot rise before you, for the manner of women *is* with me." And he searched but did not find the household idols.

³⁶ Then Jacob was angry and rebuked Laban, and Jacob answered and said to Laban: "What *is* my trespass? What *is* my sin, that you have so hotly pursued me? ³⁷ Although you have searched all my things, what part of your household things have you found? Set *it* here before my brethren and your brethren, that they may judge between us both! ³⁸ These twenty years I *have been* with you; your ewes and your female goats have not miscarried their young, and I have not eaten the rams of your flock. ³⁹ That which was torn *by beasts* I did not bring to you; I bore the loss of it. You required it from my hand, *whether* stolen by day or stolen by night. ⁴⁰ *There* I was! In the day the drought consumed me, and the frost by night, and my sleep departed from my eyes. ⁴¹ Thus I have been in your house twenty years; I served you fourteen years for your two daughters, and six years for your flock, and you have changed my wages ten times. ⁴² Unless the God of my father, the God of Abraham and the Fear of Isaac, had been with me, surely now you would have sent me away empty-handed. God has seen my affliction and the labor of my hands, and rebuked *you* last night."

⁴³ And Laban answered and said to Jacob, "*These* daughters *are* my daughters, and *these* children *are* my children, and *this* flock *is* my flock; all that you see *is* mine. But what can I do this day to these my daughters or to their children whom they have borne? ⁴⁴ Now therefore, come, let us make a covenant, you and I, and let it be a witness between you and me."

⁴⁵ So Jacob took a stone and set it up *as* a pillar. ⁴⁶ Then Jacob said to his brethren, "Gather stones." And they took stones and made a heap, and they ate there on the heap. ⁴⁷ Laban called it Jegar Sahadutha, but Jacob called it Galeed. ⁴⁸ And Laban said, "This heap *is* a witness between you and me this day." Therefore its name was called Galeed, ⁴⁹ also Mizpah, because he said, "May the LORD watch

between you and me when we are absent one from another. ⁵⁰ If you afflict my daughters, or if you take *other* wives besides my daughters, *although* no man *is* with us—see, God *is* witness between you and me!"

⁵¹ Then Laban said to Jacob, "Here is this heap and here is *this* pillar, which I have placed between you and me. ⁵² This heap *is* a witness, and *this* pillar *is* a witness, that I will not pass beyond this heap to you, and you will not pass beyond this heap and this pillar to me, for harm. ⁵³ The God of Abraham, the God of Nahor, and the God of their father judge between us." And Jacob swore by the Fear of his father Isaac. ⁵⁴ Then Jacob offered a sacrifice on the mountain, and called his brethren to eat bread. And they ate bread and stayed all night on the mountain. ⁵⁵ And early in the morning Laban arose, and kissed his sons and daughters and blessed them. Then Laban departed and returned to his place.

32 So Jacob went on his way, and the angels of God met him. ² When Jacob saw them, he said, "This *is* God's camp." And he called the name of that place Mahanaim.

³ Then Jacob sent messengers before him to Esau his brother in the land of Seir, the country of Edom. ⁴ And he commanded them, saying, "Speak thus to my lord Esau, 'Thus your servant Jacob says: "I have dwelt with Laban and stayed there until now. ⁵ I have oxen, donkeys, flocks, and male and female servants; and I have sent to tell my lord, that I may find favor in your sight." ' "

⁶ Then the messengers returned to Jacob, saying, "We came to your brother Esau, and he also is coming to meet you, and four hundred men *are* with him." ⁷ So Jacob was greatly afraid and distressed; and he divided the people that *were* with him, and the flocks and herds and camels, into two companies. ⁸ And he said, "If Esau comes to the one company and attacks it, then the other company which is left will escape."

⁹ Then Jacob said, "O God of my father Abraham and God of my father Isaac, the LORD who said to me, 'Return to your country and to your family, and I will deal well with you': ¹⁰ I am not worthy of the least of all the mercies and of all the truth which You have shown Your servant; for I crossed over this Jordan with my staff, and now I have become two companies. ¹¹ Deliver me, I pray, from the hand of my brother, from the hand of Esau; for I fear him, lest he come and attack me *and* the mother with the children. ¹² For You said, 'I will surely treat you well, and make your descendants as the sand of the sea, which cannot be numbered for multitude.' "

¹³ So he lodged there that same night, and took what came to his hand as a present for Esau his brother: ¹⁴ two hundred female goats and twenty male goats, two hundred ewes and twenty rams, ¹⁵ thirty milk camels with their colts, forty cows and ten bulls, twenty female donkeys and ten foals. ¹⁶ Then he delivered *them* to the hand of his servants, every drove by itself, and said to his servants, "Pass over before me, and put some distance between successive droves." ¹⁷ And he commanded the first one, saying, "When Esau my brother meets you and asks you, saying, 'To whom do you belong, and where are you going? Whose *are* these in front of you?' ¹⁸ then you shall say, 'They *are* your servant Jacob's. It *is* a present sent to my lord Esau; and behold, he also *is* behind us.' " ¹⁹ So he commanded the second, the third, and all who followed the droves, saying, "In this manner you shall speak to Esau when you find him; ²⁰ and also say, 'Behold, your servant Jacob *is* behind us.' " For he said, "I will appease him with the present that goes before me, and afterward I will see his face; perhaps he will accept me." ²¹ So the present went on over before him, but he himself lodged that night in the camp.

²² And he arose that night and took his two wives, his two female servants, and his eleven sons, and crossed over the ford of Jabbok. ²³ He took them, sent them over the brook, and sent over what he had. ²⁴ Then Jacob was left alone; and a Man wrestled with him until the breaking of day. ²⁵ Now when He saw that He did not prevail against him, He touched the socket of his hip; and the socket of Jacob's hip was out of joint as He wrestled

with him. ²⁶ And He said, "Let Me go, for the day breaks."

But he said, "I will not let You go unless You bless me!"

²⁷ So He said to him, "What *is* your name?"

He said, "Jacob."

²⁸ And He said, "Your name shall no longer be called Jacob, but Israel; for you have struggled with God and with men, and have prevailed."

²⁹ Then Jacob asked, saying, "Tell *me* Your name, I pray."

And He said, "Why *is* it *that* you ask about My name?" And He blessed him there.

³⁰ So Jacob called the name of the place Peniel: "For I have seen God face to face, and my life is preserved." ³¹ Just as he crossed over Penuel the sun rose on him, and he limped on his hip. ³² Therefore to this day the children of Israel do not eat the muscle that shrank, which *is* on the hip socket, because He touched the socket of Jacob's hip in the muscle that shrank.

~ PSALM 8:6–9 ~

⁶ You have made him to have
       dominion over the works of Your
       hands;
    You have put all *things* under his
       feet,
⁷ All sheep and oxen—
    Even the beasts of the field,
⁸ The birds of the air,
    And the fish of the sea
    That pass through the paths of the
       seas.

⁹ O LORD, our Lord,
    How excellent *is* Your name in all
       the earth!

~ PROVERBS 3:19, 20 ~

¹⁹ The LORD by wisdom founded the
        earth;
     By understanding He established the
        heavens;
²⁰ By His knowledge the depths were
        broken up,
     And clouds drop down the dew.

~ MATTHEW 11:1–30 ~

Now it came to pass, when Jesus finished commanding His twelve disciples, that He departed from there to teach and to preach in their cities.

² And when John had heard in prison about the works of Christ, he sent two of his disciples ³ and said to Him, "Are You the Coming One, or do we look for another?"

⁴ Jesus answered and said to them, "Go and tell John the things which you hear and see: ⁵ *The* blind see and *the* lame walk; *the* lepers are cleansed and *the* deaf hear; *the* dead are raised up and *the* poor have the gospel preached to them. ⁶ And blessed is he who is not offended because of Me."

⁷ As they departed, Jesus began to say to the multitudes concerning John: "What did you go out into the wilderness to see? A reed shaken by the wind? ⁸ But what did you go out to see? A man clothed in soft garments? Indeed, those who wear soft *clothing* are in kings' houses. ⁹ But what did you go out to see? A prophet? Yes, I say to you, and more than a prophet. ¹⁰ For this is *he* of whom it is written:

'Behold, I send My messenger
    before Your face,
  Who will prepare Your way before
    You.'

¹¹ "Assuredly, I say to you, among those born of women there has not risen one greater than John the Baptist; but he who is least in the kingdom of heaven is greater than he. ¹² And from the days of John the Baptist until now the kingdom of heaven suffers violence, and the violent take it by force. ¹³ For all the prophets and the law prophesied until John. ¹⁴ And if you are willing to receive *it*, he is Elijah who is to come. ¹⁵ He who has ears to hear, let him hear!

¹⁶ "But to what shall I liken this generation? It is like children sitting in the marketplaces and calling to their companions, ¹⁷ and saying:

'We played the flute for you,
    And you did not dance;

We mourned to you,
    And you did not lament.'

¹⁸ For John came neither eating nor drinking, and they say, 'He has a demon.' ¹⁹ The Son of Man came eating and drinking, and they say, 'Look, a glutton and a winebibber, a friend of tax collectors and sinners!' But wisdom is justified by her children."

²⁰ Then He began to rebuke the cities in which most of His mighty works had been done, because they did not repent: ²¹ "Woe to you, Chorazin! Woe to you, Bethsaida! For if the mighty works which were done in you had been done in Tyre and Sidon, they would have repented long ago in sackcloth and ashes. ²² But I say to you, it will be more tolerable for Tyre and Sidon in the day of judgment than for you. ²³ And you, Capernaum, who are exalted to heaven, will be brought down to Hades; for if the mighty works which were done in you had been done in Sodom, it would have remained until this day. ²⁴ But I say to you that it shall be more tolerable for the land of Sodom in the day of judgment than for you."

²⁵ At that time Jesus answered and said, "I thank You, Father, Lord of heaven and earth, that You have hidden these things from *the* wise and prudent and have revealed them to babes. ²⁶ Even so, Father, for so it seemed good in Your sight. ²⁷ All things have been delivered to Me by My Father, and no one knows the Son except the Father. Nor does anyone know the Father except the Son, and *the one* to whom the Son wills to reveal *Him*. ²⁸ Come to Me, all *you* who labor and are heavy laden, and I will give you rest. ²⁹ Take My yoke upon you and learn from Me, for I am gentle and lowly in heart, and you will find rest for your souls. ³⁰ For My yoke *is* easy and My burden is light."

～ GENESIS 33:1—34:31 ～

Now Jacob lifted his eyes and looked, and there, Esau was coming, and with him were four hundred men. So he divided the children among Leah, Rachel, and the two maidservants. ² And he put the maidservants and their children in front, Leah and her children behind, and Rachel and Joseph last. ³ Then he crossed over before them and bowed himself to the ground seven times, until he came near to his brother.

⁴ But Esau ran to meet him, and embraced him, and fell on his neck and kissed him, and they wept. ⁵ And he lifted his eyes and saw the women and children, and said, "Who *are* these with you?"

So he said, "The children whom God has graciously given your servant." ⁶ Then the maidservants came near, they and their children, and bowed down. ⁷ And Leah also came near with her children, and they bowed down. Afterward Joseph and Rachel came near, and they bowed down.

⁸ Then Esau said, "What *do* you *mean* by all this company which I met?"

And he said, "*These are* to find favor in the sight of my lord."

⁹ But Esau said, "I have enough, my brother; keep what you have for yourself."

¹⁰ And Jacob said, "No, please, if I have now found favor in your sight, then receive my present from my hand, inasmuch as I have seen your face as though I had seen the face of God, and you were pleased with me. ¹¹ Please, take my blessing that is brought to you, because God has dealt graciously with me, and because I have enough." So he urged him, and he took *it*.

¹² Then Esau said, "Let us take our journey; let us go, and I will go before you."

¹³ But Jacob said to him, "My lord knows that the children *are* weak, and the flocks and herds which are nursing *are* with me. And if the men should drive them hard one day, all the flock will die. ¹⁴ Please let my lord go on ahead before his servant. I will lead on slowly at a pace which the livestock that go before me, and the children, are able to endure, until I come to my lord in Seir."

¹⁵ And Esau said, "Now let me leave with you *some* of the people who *are* with me."

But he said, "What need is there? Let me find favor in the sight of my lord." ¹⁶ So Esau returned that day on his way to Seir. ¹⁷ And Jacob journeyed to Succoth, built himself a house, and made booths for his livestock. Therefore the name of the place is called Succoth.

¹⁸ Then Jacob came safely to the city of Shechem, which *is* in the land of Canaan, when he came from Padan Aram; and he pitched his tent before the city. ¹⁹ And he bought the parcel of land, where he had pitched his tent, from the children of Hamor, Shechem's father, for one hundred pieces of money. ²⁰ Then he erected an altar there and called it El Elohe Israel.

34 Now Dinah the daughter of Leah, whom she had borne to Jacob, went out to see the daughters of the land. ² And when Shechem the son of Hamor the Hivite, prince of the country, saw her, he took her and lay with her, and violated her. ³ His soul was strongly attracted to Dinah the daughter of Jacob, and he loved the young woman and spoke kindly to the young woman. ⁴ So Shechem spoke to his father Hamor, saying, "Get me this young woman as a wife."

⁵ And Jacob heard that he had defiled Dinah his daughter. Now his sons were with his livestock in the field; so Jacob held his peace until they came. ⁶ Then Hamor the father of Shechem went out to Jacob to speak with him. ⁷ And the sons of Jacob came in from the field when they heard *it*; and the men were grieved and very angry, because he had done a disgraceful thing in Israel by lying with Jacob's daughter, a thing which ought not to be done. ⁸ But Hamor spoke with them, saying, "The soul of my son Shechem longs for your daughter. Please give her to him as a wife. ⁹ And make marriages with us; give your daughters to us, and take our daughters to yourselves. ¹⁰ So you shall dwell with us, and the land shall be before you. Dwell and trade in it, and acquire possessions for yourselves in it."

¹¹ Then Shechem said to her father and her brothers, "Let me find favor in your eyes, and whatever you say to me I will give. ¹² Ask me ever so much dowry and gift, and I will give according to what you say to me; but give me the young woman as a wife."

¹³ But the sons of Jacob answered Shechem and Hamor his father, and spoke deceitfully, because he had defiled Dinah their sister. ¹⁴ And they said to them, "We cannot do this thing, to give our sister to one who is uncircumcised, for that *would be* a reproach to us. ¹⁵ But on this *condition* we will consent to you: If you will become as we *are*, if every male of you is circumcised, ¹⁶ then we will give our daughters to you, and we will take your daughters to us; and we will dwell with you, and we will become one people. ¹⁷ But if you will not heed us and be circumcised, then we will take our daughter and be gone."

¹⁸ And their words pleased Hamor and Shechem, Hamor's son. ¹⁹ So the young man did not delay to do the thing, because he delighted in Jacob's daughter. He *was* more honorable than all the household of his father.

²⁰ And Hamor and Shechem his son came to the gate of their city, and spoke with the men of their city, saying: ²¹ "These men *are* at peace with us. Therefore let them dwell in the land and trade in it. For indeed the land *is* large enough for them. Let us take their daughters to us as wives, and let us give them our daughters. ²² Only on this *condition* will the men consent to dwell with us, to be one people: if every male among us is circumcised as they *are* circumcised. ²³ *Will* not their livestock, their property, and every animal of theirs *be* ours? Only let us consent to them, and they will dwell with us." ²⁴ And all who went out of the gate of his city heeded Hamor and Shechem his son; every male was circumcised, all who went out of the gate of his city.

²⁵ Now it came to pass on the third day, when they were in pain, that two of the sons of Jacob, Simeon and Levi, Dinah's brothers, each took his sword and came boldly upon the city and killed all the males. ²⁶ And they killed Hamor and Shechem his son with the edge of the sword, and took Dinah from Shechem's house, and went out. ²⁷ The sons of Jacob

Opportunity

Are you waiting for the perfect conditions before you set out to pursue your dreams? This poem by Edward Rowland Sill challenges that mindset.

Opportunity

This I beheld, or dreamed it in a
    dream:
There spread a cloud of dust along a plain;
And underneath the cloud, or in it, raged
A furious battle, and men yelled, and swords
Shocked upon swords and shields. A prince's banner
Wavered, then staggered backward, hemmed by foes.
A craven hung along the battle's edge
And thought, "Had I a sword of keener steel —
That blue blade that the king's son bears — but this
Blunt thing — !" He snapt and flung it from his hand,
And lowering, crept away and left the field.
Then came the king's son, wounded, sore bestead,
And weaponless, and saw the broken sword,
Hilt-buried in the dry and trodden sand,
And ran and snatched it, and with battle-shout
Lifted afresh, he hewed his enemy down,
And saved a great cause that heroic day.

Don't overlook the potential of what you already hold in your hand.

came upon the slain, and plundered the city, because their sister had been defiled. ²⁸ They took their sheep, their oxen, and their donkeys, what *was* in the city and what *was* in the field, ²⁹ and all their wealth. All their little ones and their wives they took captive; and they plundered even all that *was* in the houses.

³⁰ Then Jacob said to Simeon and Levi, "You have troubled me by making me obnoxious among the inhabitants of the land, among the Canaanites and the Perizzites; and since I *am* few in number, they will gather themselves together against me and kill me. I shall be destroyed, my household and I."

³¹ But they said, "Should he treat our sister like a harlot?"

∼ PSALM 9:1-5 ∼

¹ I will praise *You*, O LORD, with my
whole heart;
I will tell of all Your marvelous
works.
² I will be glad and rejoice in You;
I will sing praise to Your name,
O Most High.

³ When my enemies turn back,
They shall fall and perish at Your
presence.
⁴ For You have maintained my right
and my cause;
You sat on the throne judging in
righteousness.
⁵ You have rebuked the nations,
You have destroyed the wicked;
You have blotted out their name
forever and ever.

∼ PROVERBS 3:21-26 ∼

²¹ My son, let them not depart from
your eyes—
Keep sound wisdom and discretion;
²² So they will be life to your soul
And grace to your neck.
²³ Then you will walk safely in your
way,
And your foot will not stumble.
²⁴ When you lie down, you will not be
afraid;
Yes, you will lie down and your sleep
will be sweet.

²⁵ Do not be afraid of sudden terror,
Nor of trouble from the wicked
when it comes;
²⁶ For the LORD will be your
confidence,
And will keep your foot from being
caught.

∼ MATTHEW 12:1-21 ∼

At that time Jesus went through the grainfields on the Sabbath. And His disciples were hungry, and began to pluck heads of grain and to eat. ² And when the Pharisees saw *it*, they said to Him, "Look, Your disciples are doing what is not lawful to do on the Sabbath!"

³ But He said to them, "Have you not read what David did when he was hungry, he and those who were with him: ⁴ how he entered the house of God and ate the showbread which was not lawful for him to eat, nor for those who were with him, but only for the priests? ⁵ Or have you not read in the law that on the Sabbath the priests in the temple profane the Sabbath, and are blameless? ⁶ Yet I say to you that in this place there is *One* greater than the temple. ⁷ But if you had known what *this* means, 'I desire mercy and not sacrifice,' you would not have condemned the guiltless. ⁸ For the Son of Man is Lord even of the Sabbath."

⁹ Now when He had departed from there, He went into their synagogue. ¹⁰ And behold, there was a man who had a withered hand. And they asked Him, saying, "Is it lawful to heal on the Sabbath?"—that they might accuse Him. ¹¹ Then He said to them, "What man is there among you who has one sheep, and if it falls into a pit on the Sabbath, will not lay hold of it and lift *it* out? ¹² Of how much more value then is a man than a sheep? Therefore it is lawful to do good on the Sabbath." ¹³ Then He said to the man, "Stretch out your hand." And he stretched *it* out, and it was restored as whole as the other. ¹⁴ Then the Pharisees went out and plotted against Him, how they might destroy Him.

¹⁵ But when Jesus knew *it*, He withdrew from there. And great multitudes followed Him, and He healed them all. ¹⁶ Yet He

warned them not to make Him known, [17] that it might be fulfilled which was spoken by Isaiah the prophet, saying:

[18] "Behold! My Servant whom I have
    chosen,
My Beloved in whom My soul is
    well pleased!
I will put My Spirit upon Him,
And He will declare justice to the
    Gentiles.

[19] He will not quarrel
    nor cry out,
Nor will anyone hear His voice in
    the streets.
[20] A bruised reed He will not break,
And smoking flax He will not
    quench,
Till He sends forth justice to
    victory;
[21] And in His name Gentiles will
    trust."

READING 18 · JANUARY 18

~ GENESIS 35:1—36:43 ~

Then God said to Jacob, "Arise, go up to Bethel and dwell there; and make an altar there to God, who appeared to you when you fled from the face of Esau your brother."

[2] And Jacob said to his household and to all who *were* with him, "Put away the foreign gods that *are* among you, purify yourselves, and change your garments. [3] Then let us arise and go up to Bethel; and I will make an altar there to God, who answered me in the day of my distress and has been with me in the way which I have gone." [4] So they gave Jacob all the foreign gods which *were* in their hands, and the earrings which *were* in their ears; and Jacob hid them under the terebinth tree which *was* by Shechem.

[5] And they journeyed, and the terror of God was upon the cities that *were* all around them, and they did not pursue the sons of Jacob. [6] So Jacob came to Luz (that *is*, Bethel), which *is* in the land of Canaan, he and all the people who *were* with him. [7] And he built an altar there and called the place El Bethel, because there God appeared to him when he fled from the face of his brother.

[8] Now Deborah, Rebekah's nurse, died, and she was buried below Bethel under the terebinth tree. So the name of it was called Allon Bachuth.

[9] Then God appeared to Jacob again, when he came from Padan Aram, and blessed him. [10] And God said to him, "Your name *is* Jacob; your name shall not be called Jacob anymore, but Israel shall be your name." So He called his name Israel. [11] Also God said to him: "I *am* God Almighty. Be fruitful and multiply; a nation and a company of nations shall proceed from you, and kings shall come from your body. [12] The land which I gave Abraham and Isaac I give to you; and to your descendants after you I give this land." [13] Then God went up from him in the place where He talked with him. [14] So Jacob set up a pillar in the place where He talked with him, a pillar of stone; and he poured a drink offering on it, and he poured oil on it. [15] And Jacob called the name of the place where God spoke with him, Bethel.

[16] Then they journeyed from Bethel. And when there was but a little distance to go to Ephrath, Rachel labored *in childbirth*, and she had hard labor. [17] Now it came to pass, when she was in hard labor, that the midwife said to her, "Do not fear; you will have this son also." [18] And so it was, as her soul was departing (for she died), that she called his name Ben-Oni; but his father called him Benjamin. [19] So Rachel died and was buried on the way to Ephrath (that *is*, Bethlehem). [20] And Jacob set a pillar on her grave, which *is* the pillar of Rachel's grave to this day.

[21] Then Israel journeyed and pitched his tent beyond the tower of Eder. [22] And it happened, when Israel dwelt in that land, that Reuben went and lay with Bilhah his father's concubine; and Israel heard *about it*.

Now the sons of Jacob were twelve: [23] the sons of Leah *were* Reuben, Jacob's firstborn, and Simeon, Levi, Judah,

Issachar, and Zebulun; ²⁴ the sons of Rachel *were* Joseph and Benjamin; ²⁵ the sons of Bilhah, Rachel's maidservant, *were* Dan and Naphtali; ²⁶ and the sons of Zilpah, Leah's maidservant, *were* Gad and Asher. These *were* the sons of Jacob who were born to him in Padan Aram.

²⁷ Then Jacob came to his father Isaac at Mamre, or Kirjath Arba (that *is*, Hebron), where Abraham and Isaac had dwelt. ²⁸ Now the days of Isaac were one hundred and eighty years. ²⁹ So Isaac breathed his last and died, and was gathered to his people, *being* old and full of days. And his sons Esau and Jacob buried him.

36 Now this *is* the genealogy of Esau, who is Edom. ² Esau took his wives from the daughters of Canaan: Adah the daughter of Elon the Hittite; Aholibamah the daughter of Anah, the daughter of Zibeon the Hivite; ³ and Basemath, Ishmael's daughter, sister of Nebajoth. ⁴ Now Adah bore Eliphaz to Esau, and Basemath bore Reuel. ⁵ And Aholibamah bore Jeush, Jaalam, and Korah. These *were* the sons of Esau who were born to him in the land of Canaan.

⁶ Then Esau took his wives, his sons, his daughters, and all the persons of his household, his cattle and all his animals, and all his goods which he had gained in the land of Canaan, and went to a country away from the presence of his brother Jacob. ⁷ For their possessions were too great for them to dwell together, and the land where they were strangers could not support them because of their livestock. ⁸ So Esau dwelt in Mount Seir. Esau *is* Edom.

⁹ And this *is* the genealogy of Esau the father of the Edomites in Mount Seir. ¹⁰ These *were* the names of Esau's sons: Eliphaz the son of Adah the wife of Esau, and Reuel the son of Basemath the wife of Esau. ¹¹ And the sons of Eliphaz were Teman, Omar, Zepho, Gatam, and Kenaz. ¹² Now Timna was the concubine of Eliphaz, Esau's son, and she bore Amalek to Eliphaz. These *were* the sons of Adah, Esau's wife. ¹³ These *were* the sons of Reuel: Nahath, Zerah, Shammah, and Mizzah.

These were the sons of Basemath, Esau's wife.

¹⁴ These were the sons of Aholibamah, Esau's wife, the daughter of Anah, the daughter of Zibeon. And she bore to Esau: Jeush, Jaalam, and Korah.

¹⁵ These *were* the chiefs of the sons of Esau. The sons of Eliphaz, the firstborn *son* of Esau, were Chief Teman, Chief Omar, Chief Zepho, Chief Kenaz, ¹⁶ Chief Korah, Chief Gatam, *and* Chief Amalek. These *were* the chiefs of Eliphaz in the land of Edom. They *were* the sons of Adah.

¹⁷ These *were* the sons of Reuel, Esau's son: Chief Nahath, Chief Zerah, Chief Shammah, and Chief Mizzah. These *were* the chiefs of Reuel in the land of Edom. These *were* the sons of Basemath, Esau's wife.

¹⁸ And these *were* the sons of Aholibamah, Esau's wife: Chief Jeush, Chief Jaalam, and Chief Korah. These *were* the chiefs *who descended* from Aholibamah, Esau's wife, the daughter of Anah. ¹⁹ These *were* the sons of Esau, who is Edom, and these *were* their chiefs.

²⁰ These *were* the sons of Seir the Horite who inhabited the land: Lotan, Shobal, Zibeon, Anah, ²¹ Dishon, Ezer, and Dishan. These *were* the chiefs of the Horites, the sons of Seir, in the land of Edom. ²² And the sons of Lotan were Hori and Hemam. Lotan's sister *was* Timna. ²³ These *were* the sons of Shobal: Alvan, Manahath, Ebal, Shepho, and Onam. ²⁴ These *were* the sons of Zibeon: both Ajah and Anah. This *was the* Anah who found the water in the wilderness as he pastured the donkeys of his father Zibeon. ²⁵ These *were* the children of Anah: Dishon and Aholibamah the daughter of Anah. ²⁶ These *were* the sons of Dishon: Hemdan, Eshban, Ithran, and Cheran. ²⁷ These *were* the sons of Ezer: Bilhan, Zaavan, and Akan. ²⁸ These *were* the sons of Dishan: Uz and Aran.

²⁹ These *were* the chiefs of the Horites: Chief Lotan, Chief Shobal, Chief Zibeon, Chief Anah, ³⁰ Chief Dishon, Chief Ezer, and Chief Dishan. These *were* the chiefs of the Horites, according to their chiefs in the land of Seir.

The Charity of Happiness

His mother, Eliza, was an intelligent woman with strong common sense and straitlaced conduct. A disciplinarian, she was devoutly religious, and a believer in hard work and thrift. Her strong will and deep piety gave her a remarkable serenity, which she transmitted to her son, John. A diligent and serious student, John was trained by his mother in matters of piety, neatness, and industry. Attendance at church and Sunday school was weekly.

His father was full of the joy of life and loved song, talk, and sociability. He taught John to develop his innate gift for business. William was as anxious as Eliza that all their children grow up self-reliant, honest, keen-witted, and dependable. John recalled later that both of his parents were examples of courtesy and patience. He said, "I cannot remember to have heard the voices of either Father or Mother raised in anger or complaint in speaking to any of us."

William and Eliza also instilled in their son a rich heritage of giving to church and charities, the gifts being made from their childhood earnings. In all, William and Eliza gave their son, John D. Rockefeller, a happy childhood — a gift he valued throughout his life far more than the millions of dollars he made.

³¹ Now these *were* the kings who reigned in the land of Edom before any king reigned over the children of Israel: ³² Bela the son of Beor reigned in Edom, and the name of his city *was* Dinhabah. ³³ And when Bela died, Jobab the son of Zerah of Bozrah reigned in his place. ³⁴ When Jobab died, Husham of the land of the Temanites reigned in his place. ³⁵ And when Husham died, Hadad the son of Bedad, who attacked Midian in the field of Moab, reigned in his place. And the name of his city *was* Avith. ³⁶ When Hadad died, Samlah of Masrekah reigned in his place. ³⁷ And when Samlah died, Saul of Rehoboth-*by*-the-River reigned in his place. ³⁸ When Saul died, Baal-Hanan the son of Achbor reigned in his place. ³⁹ And when Baal-Hanan the son of Achbor died, Hadar reigned in his place; and the name of his city *was* Pau. His wife's name *was* Mehetabel, the daughter of Matred, the daughter of Mezahab.

⁴⁰ And these *were* the names of the chiefs of Esau, according to their families and their places, by their names: Chief Timnah, Chief Alvah, Chief Jetheth, ⁴¹ Chief Aholibamah, Chief Elah, Chief Pinon, ⁴² Chief Kenaz, Chief Teman, Chief Mibzar, ⁴³ Chief Magdiel, and Chief Iram. These *were* the chiefs of Edom, according to their dwelling places in the land of their possession. Esau *was* the father of the Edomites.

∼ PSALM 9:6–10 ∼

⁶ O enemy, destructions are finished forever!
And you have destroyed cities;
Even their memory has perished.
⁷ But the LORD shall endure forever;
He has prepared His throne for judgment.
⁸ He shall judge the world in righteousness,
And He shall administer judgment for the peoples in uprightness.

⁹ The LORD also will be a refuge for the oppressed,
A refuge in times of trouble.
¹⁰ And those who know Your name will put their trust in You;

For You, LORD, have not forsaken those who seek You.

∼ PROVERBS 3:27–30 ∼

²⁷ Do not withhold good from those to whom it is due,
When it is in the power of your hand to do *so*.
²⁸ Do not say to your neighbor,
"Go, and come back,
And tomorrow I will give *it*,"
When *you have* it with you.
²⁹ Do not devise evil against your neighbor,
For he dwells by you for safety's sake.
³⁰ Do not strive with a man without cause,
If he has done you no harm.

∼ MATTHEW 12:22–50 ∼

Then one was brought to Him who was demon-possessed, blind and mute; and He healed him, so that the blind and mute man both spoke and saw. ²³ And all the multitudes were amazed and said, "Could this be the Son of David?"

²⁴ Now when the Pharisees heard *it* they said, "This *fellow* does not cast out demons except by Beelzebub, the ruler of the demons."

²⁵ But Jesus knew their thoughts, and said to them: "Every kingdom divided against itself is brought to desolation, and every city or house divided against itself will not stand. ²⁶ If Satan casts out Satan, he is divided against himself. How then will his kingdom stand? ²⁷ And if I cast out demons by Beelzebub, by whom do your sons cast *them* out? Therefore they shall be your judges. ²⁸ But if I cast out demons by the Spirit of God, surely the kingdom of God has come upon you. ²⁹ Or how can one enter a strong man's house and plunder his goods, unless he first binds the strong man? And then he will plunder his house. ³⁰ He who is not with Me is against Me, and he who does not gather with Me scatters abroad.

³¹ "Therefore I say to you, every sin and blasphemy will be forgiven men, but the blasphemy *against* the Spirit will not be

forgiven men. [32] Anyone who speaks a word against the Son of Man, it will be forgiven him; but whoever speaks against the Holy Spirit, it will not be forgiven him, either in this age or in the *age* to come.

[33] "Either make the tree good and its fruit good, or else make the tree bad and its fruit bad; for a tree is known by *its* fruit. [34] Brood of vipers! How can you, being evil, speak good things? For out of the abundance of the heart the mouth speaks. [35] A good man out of the good treasure of his heart brings forth good things, and an evil man out of the evil treasure brings forth evil things. [36] But I say to you that for every idle word men may speak, they will give account of it in the day of judgment. [37] For by your words you will be justified, and by your words you will be condemned."

[38] Then some of the scribes and Pharisees answered, saying, "Teacher, we want to see a sign from You."

[39] But He answered and said to them, "An evil and adulterous generation seeks after a sign, and no sign will be given to it except the sign of the prophet Jonah. [40] For as Jonah was three days and three nights in the belly of the great fish, so will the Son of Man be three days and three nights in the heart of the earth. [41] The men of Nineveh will rise up in the judgment with this generation and condemn it, because they repented at the preaching of Jonah; and indeed a greater than Jonah *is* here. [42] The queen of the South will rise up in the judgment with this generation and condemn it, for she came from the ends of the earth to hear the wisdom of Solomon; and indeed a greater than Solomon *is* here.

[43] "When an unclean spirit goes out of a man, he goes through dry places, seeking rest, and finds none. [44] Then he says, 'I will return to my house from which I came.' And when he comes, he finds *it* empty, swept, and put in order. [45] Then he goes and takes with him seven other spirits more wicked than himself, and they enter and dwell there; and the last *state* of that man is worse than the first. So shall it also be with this wicked generation."

[46] While He was still talking to the multitudes, behold, His mother and brothers stood outside, seeking to speak with Him. [47] Then one said to Him, "Look, Your mother and Your brothers are standing outside, seeking to speak with You."

[48] But He answered and said to the one who told Him, "Who is My mother and who are My brothers?" [49] And He stretched out His hand toward His disciples and said, "Here are My mother and My brothers! [50] For whoever does the will of My Father in heaven is My brother and sister and mother."

READING 19 · JANUARY 19

~ GENESIS 37:1—38:30 ~

Now Jacob dwelt in the land where his father was a stranger, in the land of Canaan. [2] This *is* the history of Jacob.

Joseph, *being* seventeen years old, was feeding the flock with his brothers. And the lad *was* with the sons of Bilhah and the sons of Zilpah, his father's wives; and Joseph brought a bad report of them to his father.

[3] Now Israel loved Joseph more than all his children, because he *was* the son of his old age. Also he made him a tunic of *many* colors. [4] But when his brothers saw that their father loved him more than all his brothers, they hated him and could not speak peaceably to him.

[5] Now Joseph had a dream, and he told *it* to his brothers; and they hated him even more. [6] So he said to them, "Please hear this dream which I have dreamed: [7] There we were, binding sheaves in the field. Then behold, my sheaf arose and also stood upright; and indeed your sheaves stood all around and bowed down to my sheaf."

[8] And his brothers said to him, "Shall you indeed reign over us? Or shall you indeed have dominion over us?" So they hated him even more for his dreams and for his words.

⁹ Then he dreamed still another dream and told it to his brothers, and said, "Look, I have dreamed another dream. And this time, the sun, the moon, and the eleven stars bowed down to me."

¹⁰ So he told *it* to his father and his brothers; and his father rebuked him and said to him, "What *is* this dream that you have dreamed? Shall your mother and I and your brothers indeed come to bow down to the earth before you?" ¹¹ And his brothers envied him, but his father kept the matter *in mind*.

¹² Then his brothers went to feed their father's flock in Shechem. ¹³ And Israel said to Joseph, "Are not your brothers feeding *the flock* in Shechem? Come, I will send you to them."

So he said to him, "Here I am."

¹⁴ Then he said to him, "Please go and see if it is well with your brothers and well with the flocks, and bring back word to me." So he sent him out of the Valley of Hebron, and he went to Shechem.

¹⁵ Now a certain man found him, and there he was, wandering in the field. And the man asked him, saying, "What are you seeking?"

¹⁶ So he said, "I am seeking my brothers. Please tell me where they are feeding *their flocks*."

¹⁷ And the man said, "They have departed from here, for I heard them say, 'Let us go to Dothan.' " So Joseph went after his brothers and found them in Dothan.

¹⁸ Now when they saw him afar off, even before he came near them, they conspired against him to kill him. ¹⁹ Then they said to one another, "Look, this dreamer is coming! ²⁰ Come therefore, let us now kill him and cast him into some pit; and we shall say, 'Some wild beast has devoured him.' We shall see what will become of his dreams!"

²¹ But Reuben heard *it*, and he delivered him out of their hands, and said, "Let us not kill him." ²² And Reuben said to them, "Shed no blood, *but* cast him into this pit which *is* in the wilderness, and do not lay a hand on him"—that he might deliver him out of their hands, and bring him back to his father.

²³ So it came to pass, when Joseph had come to his brothers, that they stripped Joseph *of* his tunic, the tunic of *many* colors that *was* on him. ²⁴ Then they took him and cast him into a pit. And the pit *was* empty; *there was* no water in it.

²⁵ And they sat down to eat a meal. Then they lifted their eyes and looked, and there was a company of Ishmaelites, coming from Gilead with their camels, bearing spices, balm, and myrrh, on their way to carry *them* down to Egypt. ²⁶ So Judah said to his brothers, "What profit *is there* if we kill our brother and conceal his blood? ²⁷ Come and let us sell him to the Ishmaelites, and let not our hand be upon him, for he *is* our brother *and* our flesh." And his brothers listened. ²⁸ Then Midianite traders passed by; so *the brothers* pulled Joseph up and lifted him out of the pit, and sold him to the Ishmaelites for twenty *shekels* of silver. And they took Joseph to Egypt.

²⁹ Then Reuben returned to the pit, and indeed Joseph *was* not in the pit; and he tore his clothes. ³⁰ And he returned to his brothers and said, "The lad *is* no *more*; and I, where shall I go?"

³¹ So they took Joseph's tunic, killed a kid of the goats, and dipped the tunic in the blood. ³² Then they sent the tunic of *many* colors, and they brought *it* to their father and said, "We have found this. Do you know whether it *is* your son's tunic or not?"

³³ And he recognized it and said, "*It is* my son's tunic. A wild beast has devoured him. Without doubt Joseph is torn to pieces." ³⁴ Then Jacob tore his clothes, put sackcloth on his waist, and mourned for his son many days. ³⁵ And all his sons and all his daughters arose to comfort him; but he refused to be comforted, and he said, "For I shall go down into the grave to my son in mourning." Thus his father wept for him.

³⁶ Now the Midianites had sold him in Egypt to Potiphar, an officer of Pharaoh *and* captain of the guard.

38

It came to pass at that time that Judah departed from his brothers, and visited a certain Adullamite whose name *was* Hirah. ² And Judah saw there a daughter of a certain Canaanite whose name *was* Shua, and he married her and went in to her. ³ So she conceived and bore a son,

Heavenly Home

Home has been called "heaven's fallen sister." Our homes can't help but bear at least a partial imprint of our fallen world. And yet, home holds the greatest potential for being like heaven of any place on earth. A godly home, built upon heaven's principles, can be the sweetest, best, happiest, and most perfect place to be!

> The curse of the Lord is on the house of the wicked, but He blesses the home of the just.
>
> *Proverbs 3:33*

When we think of our earthly homes as being a reflection of our heavenly home, we must ask ourselves, "What must God's home be like?"

Surely it is a place where there are no harsh or unkind words, no prolonged silence born of anger. It must be a place where each person is made to feel special, important, and valued beyond measure. It is a place of laughter and gladness, a place each person would desire to return to at the end of a difficult day. It must be a place of nourishment and growth, a place of total acceptance and unconditional love. Every person in God's home would surely be willing to be vulnerable and to share his or her innermost secrets, dreams, and hopes. Communication flows freely, as do hugs and kisses.

The good news is that we have the privilege of creating our homes to mirror heaven. It is within our power — with God's help — to do so!

and he called his name Er. ⁴ She conceived again and bore a son, and she called his name Onan. ⁵ And she conceived yet again and bore a son, and called his name Shelah. He was at Chezib when she bore him.

⁶ Then Judah took a wife for Er his first-born, and her name *was* Tamar. ⁷ But Er, Judah's firstborn, was wicked in the sight of the LORD, and the LORD killed him. ⁸ And Judah said to Onan, "Go in to your brother's wife and marry her, and raise up an heir to your brother." ⁹ But Onan knew that the heir would not be his; and it came to pass, when he went in to his brother's wife, that he emitted on the ground, lest he should give an heir to his brother. ¹⁰ And the thing which he did displeased the LORD; therefore He killed him also.

¹¹ Then Judah said to Tamar his daughter-in-law, "Remain a widow in your father's house till my son Shelah is grown." For he said, "Lest he also die like his brothers." And Tamar went and dwelt in her father's house.

¹² Now in the process of time the daughter of Shua, Judah's wife, died; and Judah was comforted, and went up to his sheepshearers at Timnah, he and his friend Hirah the Adullamite. ¹³ And it was told Tamar, saying, "Look, your father-in-law is going up to Timnah to shear his sheep." ¹⁴ So she took off her widow's garments, covered *herself* with a veil and wrapped herself, and sat in an open place which *was* on the way to Timnah; for she saw that Shelah was grown, and she was not given to him as a wife. ¹⁵ When Judah saw her, he thought she *was* a harlot, because she had covered her face. ¹⁶ Then he turned to her by the way, and said, "Please let me come in to you"; for he did not know that she *was* his daughter-in-law.

So she said, "What will you give me, that you may come in to me?"

¹⁷ And he said, "I will send a young goat from the flock."

So she said, "Will you give *me* a pledge till you send *it*?"

¹⁸ Then he said, "What pledge shall I give you?"

So she said, "Your signet and cord, and your staff that *is* in your hand." Then he gave *them* to her, and went in to her, and

she conceived by him. ¹⁹ So she arose and went away, and laid aside her veil and put on the garments of her widowhood.

²⁰ And Judah sent the young goat by the hand of his friend the Adullamite, to receive *his* pledge from the woman's hand, but he did not find her. ²¹ Then he asked the men of that place, saying, "Where is the harlot who *was* openly by the road-side?"

And they said, "There was no harlot in this *place*."

²² So he returned to Judah and said, "I cannot find her. Also, the men of the place said there was no harlot in this *place*."

²³ Then Judah said, "Let her take *them* for herself, lest we be shamed; for I sent this young goat and you have not found her."

²⁴ And it came to pass, about three months after, that Judah was told, saying, "Tamar your daughter-in-law has played the harlot; furthermore she *is* with child by harlotry."

So Judah said, "Bring her out and let her be burned!"

²⁵ When she *was* brought out, she sent to her father-in-law, saying, "By the man to whom these belong, I *am* with child." And she said, "Please determine whose these *are*—the signet and cord, and staff."

²⁶ So Judah acknowledged *them* and said, "She has been more righteous than I, because I did not give her to Shelah my son." And he never knew her again.

²⁷ Now it came to pass, at the time for giving birth, that behold, twins *were* in her womb. ²⁸ And so it was, when she was giving birth, that *the one* put out *his* hand; and the midwife took a scarlet *thread* and bound it on his hand, saying, "This one came out first." ²⁹ Then it happened, as he drew back his hand, that his brother came out unexpectedly; and she said, "How did you break through? *This* breach *be* upon you!" Therefore his name was called Perez. ³⁰ Afterward his brother came out who had the scarlet *thread* on his hand. And his name was called Zerah.

∼ PSALM 9:11–20 ∼

¹¹ Sing praises to the LORD, who dwells in Zion!

Declare His deeds among the people.
¹² When He avenges blood, He
  remembers them;
He does not forget the cry of the
  humble.

¹³ Have mercy on me, O LORD!
Consider my trouble from those who
  hate me,
You who lift me up from the gates of
  death,
¹⁴ That I may tell of all Your praise
In the gates of the daughter of
  Zion.
I will rejoice in Your salvation.

¹⁵ The nations have sunk down in the
  pit *which* they made;
In the net which they hid, their own
  foot is caught.
¹⁶ The LORD is known *by* the judgment
  He executes;
The wicked is snared in the work of
  his own hands.
                    Meditation.   Selah

¹⁷ The wicked shall be turned into hell,
And all the nations that forget God.
¹⁸ For the needy shall not always be
  forgotten;
The expectation of the poor shall
  not perish forever.

¹⁹ Arise, O LORD,
Do not let man prevail;
Let the nations be judged in Your
  sight.
²⁰ Put them in fear, O LORD,
That the nations may know
  themselves *to be but* men.   Selah

∼ PROVERBS 3:31–35 ∼

³¹ Do not envy the oppressor,
And choose none of his ways;
³² For the perverse *person* is an
  abomination to the LORD,
But His secret counsel *is* with the
  upright.
³³ The curse of the LORD *is* on the
  house of the wicked,
But He blesses the home of the just.
³⁴ Surely He scorns the scornful,
But gives grace to the humble.

³⁵ The wise shall inherit glory,
But shame shall be the legacy of
  fools.

∼ MATTHEW 13:1–30 ∼

On the same day Jesus went out of the house and sat by the sea. ² And great multitudes were gathered together to Him, so that He got into a boat and sat; and the whole multitude stood on the shore.

³ Then He spoke many things to them in parables, saying: "Behold, a sower went out to sow. ⁴ And as he sowed, some *seed* fell by the wayside; and the birds came and devoured them. ⁵ Some fell on stony places, where they did not have much earth; and they immediately sprang up because they had no depth of earth. ⁶ But when the sun was up they were scorched, and because they had no root they withered away. ⁷ And some fell among thorns, and the thorns sprang up and choked them. ⁸ But others fell on good ground and yielded a crop: some a hundredfold, some sixty, some thirty. ⁹ He who has ears to hear, let him hear!"

¹⁰ And the disciples came and said to Him, "Why do You speak to them in parables?"

¹¹ He answered and said to them, "Because it has been given to you to know the mysteries of the kingdom of heaven, but to them it has not been given. ¹² For whoever has, to him more will be given, and he will have abundance; but whoever does not have, even what he has will be taken away from him. ¹³ Therefore I speak to them in parables, because seeing they do not see, and hearing they do not hear, nor do they understand. ¹⁴ And in them the prophecy of Isaiah is fulfilled, which says:

'Hearing you will hear and shall
  not understand,
And seeing you will see and not
  perceive;
¹⁵ For the hearts of this people have
  grown dull.
Their ears are hard of hearing,
And their eyes they have closed,
Lest they should see with *their*
  eyes and hear with *their* ears,

Lest they should understand with
their hearts and turn,
So that I should heal them.'

16 But blessed *are* your eyes for they see,
and your ears for they hear; 17 for assuredly, I say to you that many prophets and
righteous *men* desired to see what you see,
and did not see *it*, and to hear what you
hear, and did not hear *it*.
18 "Therefore hear the parable of the
sower: 19 When anyone hears the word
of the kingdom, and does not understand
it, then the wicked *one* comes and snatches
away what was sown in his heart. This is
he who received seed by the wayside.
20 But he who received the seed on stony
places, this is he who hears the word and
immediately receives it with joy; 21 yet he
has no root in himself, but endures only
for a while. For when tribulation or persecution arises because of the word, immediately he stumbles. 22 Now he who
received seed among the thorns is he who
hears the word, and the cares of this world
and the deceitfulness of riches choke the
word, and he becomes unfruitful. 23 But

he who received seed on the good ground
is he who hears the word and understands
it, who indeed bears fruit and produces:
some a hundredfold, some sixty, some
thirty."
24 Another parable He put forth to
them, saying: "The kingdom of heaven is
like a man who sowed good seed in his
field; 25 but while men slept, his enemy
came and sowed tares among the wheat
and went his way. 26 But when the grain
had sprouted and produced a crop, then
the tares also appeared. 27 So the servants
of the owner came and said to him, 'Sir,
did you not sow good seed in your field?
How then does it have tares?' 28 He said
to them, 'An enemy has done this.' The
servants said to him, 'Do you want us then
to go and gather them up?' 29 But he said,
'No, lest while you gather up the tares
you also uproot the wheat with them.
30 Let both grow together until the harvest, and at the time of harvest I will say
to the reapers, "First gather together the
tares and bind them in bundles to burn
them, but gather the wheat into my
barn." ' "

READING 20 · JANUARY 20

∼ GENESIS 39:1—40:23 ∼

Now Joseph had been taken down
to Egypt. And Potiphar, an officer
of Pharaoh, captain of the guard,
an Egyptian, bought him from the Ishmaelites who had taken him down there.
2 The LORD was with Joseph, and he was
a successful man; and he was in the house
of his master the Egyptian. 3 And his master saw that the LORD *was* with him and
that the LORD made all he did to prosper
in his hand. 4 So Joseph found favor in
his sight, and served him. Then he made
him overseer of his house, and all *that* he
had he put under his authority. 5 So it was,
from the time *that* he had made him overseer of his house and all that he had, that
the LORD blessed the Egyptian's house for
Joseph's sake; and the blessing of the
LORD was on all that he had in the house
and in the field. 6 Thus he left all that he
had in Joseph's hand, and he did not know

what he had except for the bread which
he ate.
Now Joseph was handsome in form and
appearance.
7 And it came to pass after these things
that his master's wife cast longing eyes
on Joseph, and she said, "Lie with me."
8 But he refused and said to his master's
wife, "Look, my master does not know
what *is* with me in the house, and he has
committed all that he has to my hand.
9 *There is* no one greater in this house than
I, nor has he kept back anything from me
but you, because you *are* his wife. How
then can I do this great wickedness, and
sin against God?"
10 So it was, as she spoke to Joseph day
by day, that he did not heed her, to lie
with her *or* to be with her.
11 But it happened about this time, when
Joseph went into the house to do his work,

Hop for It

An author once sought to escape city life by moving to a little house in the country. His house was located across the street from a farm, and he often looked up from his writing to watch from his library window as his neighbor engaged in a wide variety of farm chores. He was intrigued to the point of distraction.

He watched as the man mended the fence after his cattle had broken through it. He marveled as the man replanted a field after a heavy deluge washed out a new planting. He observed as the farmer made repairs to his tractor and removed several large stones from his field after a tractor blade broke. The farmer seemed to work from sunup to sundown, battling against the elements and facing one problem after another with unlimited energy and enthusiasm. The author began to wonder about the man's optimism.

One day the author strolled from his cottage to talk to the farmer. "You amaze me," he said after greeting his neighbor. "You never seem to lose heart. Do you always hope for the best?"

The farmer thought for a moment and then, eyes flashing, he replied, "No, I don't hope for it — I hop for it!"

and none of the men of the house was inside, [12] that she caught him by his garment, saying, "Lie with me." But he left his garment in her hand, and fled and ran outside. [13] And so it was, when she saw that he had left his garment in her hand and fled outside, [14] that she called to the men of her house and spoke to them, saying, "See, he has brought in to us a Hebrew to mock us. He came in to me to lie with me, and I cried out with a loud voice. [15] And it happened, when he heard that I lifted my voice and cried out, that he left his garment with me, and fled and went outside."

[16] So she kept his garment with her until his master came home. [17] Then she spoke to him with words like these, saying, "The Hebrew servant whom you brought to us came in to me to mock me; [18] so it happened, as I lifted my voice and cried out, that he left his garment with me and fled outside."

[19] So it was, when his master heard the words which his wife spoke to him, saying, "Your servant did to me after this manner," that his anger was aroused. [20] Then Joseph's master took him and put him into the prison, a place where the king's prisoners *were* confined. And he was there in the prison. [21] But the LORD was with Joseph and showed him mercy, and He gave him favor in the sight of the keeper of the prison. [22] And the keeper of the prison committed to Joseph's hand all the prisoners who *were* in the prison; whatever they did there, it was his doing. [23] The keeper of the prison did not look into anything *that was* under *Joseph's* authority, because the LORD was with him; and whatever he did, the LORD made *it* prosper.

40 It came to pass after these things *that* the butler and the baker of the king of Egypt offended their lord, the king of Egypt. [2] And Pharaoh was angry with his two officers, the chief butler and the chief baker. [3] So he put them in custody in the house of the captain of the guard, in the prison, the place where Joseph *was* confined. [4] And the captain of the guard charged Joseph with them, and he served them; so they were in custody for a while.

[5] Then the butler and the baker of the king of Egypt, who *were* confined in the prison, had a dream, both of them, each man's dream in one night *and* each man's dream with its *own* interpretation. [6] And Joseph came in to them in the morning and looked at them, and saw that they *were* sad. [7] So he asked Pharaoh's officers who *were* with him in the custody of his lord's house, saying, "Why do you look *so* sad today?"

[8] And they said to him, "We each have had a dream, and *there is* no interpreter of it."

So Joseph said to them, "Do not interpretations belong to God? Tell *them* to me, please."

[9] Then the chief butler told his dream to Joseph, and said to him, "Behold, in my dream a vine *was* before me, [10] and in the vine *were* three branches; it *was* as though it budded, its blossoms shot forth, and its clusters brought forth ripe grapes. [11] Then Pharaoh's cup *was* in my hand; and I took the grapes and pressed them into Pharaoh's cup, and placed the cup in Pharaoh's hand."

[12] And Joseph said to him, "This *is* the interpretation of it: The three branches *are* three days. [13] Now within three days Pharaoh will lift up your head and restore you to your place, and you will put Pharaoh's cup in his hand according to the former manner, when you were his butler. [14] But remember me when it is well with you, and please show kindness to me; make mention of me to Pharaoh, and get me out of this house. [15] For indeed I was stolen away from the land of the Hebrews; and also I have done nothing here that they should put me into the dungeon."

[16] When the chief baker saw that the interpretation was good, he said to Joseph, "I also *was* in my dream, and there *were* three white baskets on my head. [17] In the uppermost basket *were* all kinds of baked goods for Pharaoh, and the birds ate them out of the basket on my head."

[18] So Joseph answered and said, "This *is* the interpretation of it: The three baskets *are* three days. [19] Within three days Pharaoh will lift off your head from you and hang you on a tree; and the birds will eat your flesh from you."

[20] Now it came to pass on the third day, *which was* Pharaoh's birthday, that he

made a feast for all his servants; and he lifted up the head of the chief butler and of the chief baker among his servants. ²¹ Then he restored the chief butler to his butlership again, and he placed the cup in Pharaoh's hand. ²² But he hanged the chief baker, as Joseph had interpreted to them. ²³ Yet the chief butler did not remember Joseph, but forgot him.

～ PSALM 10:1–11 ～

1 Why do You stand afar off, O LORD?
   Why do You hide in times of
        trouble?
2 The wicked in *his* pride persecutes
        the poor;
   Let them be caught in the plots
        which they have devised.

3 For the wicked boasts of his heart's
        desire;
   He blesses the greedy *and* renounces
        the LORD.
4 The wicked in his proud
        countenance does not seek *God*;
   God *is* in none of his thoughts.

5 His ways are always prospering;
   Your judgments *are* far above, out of
        his sight;
   As *for* all his enemies, he sneers at
        them.
6 He has said in his heart, "I shall not
        be moved;
   I shall never be in adversity."
7 His mouth is full of cursing and
        deceit and oppression;
   Under his tongue *is* trouble and
        iniquity.

8 He sits in the lurking places of the
        villages;
   In the secret places he murders the
        innocent;
   His eyes are secretly fixed on the
        helpless.
9 He lies in wait secretly, as a lion in
        his den;
   He lies in wait to catch the poor;
   He catches the poor when he draws
        him into his net.
10 So he crouches, he lies low,
   That the helpless may fall by his
        strength.

11 He has said in his heart,
   "God has forgotten;
   He hides His face;
   He will never see."

～ PROVERBS 4:1–6 ～

1 Hear, *my* children, the instruction of
        a father,
   And give attention to know
        understanding;
2 For I give you good doctrine:
   Do not forsake my law.
3 When I was my father's son,
   Tender and the only one in the sight
        of my mother,
4 He also taught me, and said to me:
   "Let your heart retain my words;
   Keep my commands, and live.
5 Get wisdom! Get understanding!
   Do not forget, nor turn away from
        the words of my mouth.
6 Do not forsake her, and she will
        preserve you;
   Love her, and she will keep you.

～ MATTHEW 13:31–58 ～

Another parable He put forth to them, saying: "The kingdom of heaven is like a mustard seed, which a man took and sowed in his field, ³² which indeed is the least of all the seeds; but when it is grown it is greater than the herbs and becomes a tree, so that the birds of the air come and nest in its branches."

³³ Another parable He spoke to them: "The kingdom of heaven is like leaven, which a woman took and hid in three measures of meal till it was all leavened."

³⁴ All these things Jesus spoke to the multitude in parables; and without a parable He did not speak to them, ³⁵ that it might be fulfilled which was spoken by the prophet, saying:

"I will open My mouth in parables;
   I will utter things kept secret from
        the foundation of the world."

³⁶ Then Jesus sent the multitude away and went into the house. And His disciples came to Him, saying, "Explain to us the parable of the tares of the field."

³⁷ He answered and said to them: "He

who sows the good seed is the Son of Man. [38] The field is the world, the good seeds are the sons of the kingdom, but the tares are the sons of the wicked *one*. [39] The enemy who sowed them is the devil, the harvest is the end of the age, and the reapers are the angels. [40] Therefore as the tares are gathered and burned in the fire, so it will be at the end of this age. [41] The Son of Man will send out His angels, and they will gather out of His kingdom all things that offend, and those who practice lawlessness, [42] and will cast them into the furnace of fire. There will be wailing and gnashing of teeth. [43] Then the righteous will shine forth as the sun in the kingdom of their Father. He who has ears to hear, let him hear!

[44] "Again, the kingdom of heaven is like treasure hidden in a field, which a man found and hid; and for joy over it he goes and sells all that he has and buys that field.

[45] "Again, the kingdom of heaven is like a merchant seeking beautiful pearls, [46] who, when he had found one pearl of great price, went and sold all that he had and bought it.

[47] "Again, the kingdom of heaven is like a dragnet that was cast into the sea and gathered some of every kind, [48] which, when it was full, they drew to shore; and they sat down and gathered the good into vessels, but threw the bad away. [49] So it will be at the end of the age. The angels will come forth, separate the wicked from among the just, [50] and cast them into the furnace of fire. There will be wailing and gnashing of teeth."

[51] Jesus said to them, "Have you understood all these things?"

They said to Him, "Yes, Lord."

[52] Then He said to them, "Therefore every scribe instructed concerning the kingdom of heaven is like a householder who brings out of his treasure *things* new and old."

[53] Now it came to pass, when Jesus had finished these parables, that He departed from there. [54] When He had come to His own country, He taught them in their synagogue, so that they were astonished and said, "Where did this *Man* get this wisdom and *these* mighty works? [55] Is this not the carpenter's son? Is not His mother called Mary? And His brothers James, Joses, Simon, and Judas? [56] And His sisters, are they not all with us? Where then did this *Man* get all these things?" [57] So they were offended at Him.

But Jesus said to them, "A prophet is not without honor except in his own country and in his own house." [58] Now He did not do many mighty works there because of their unbelief.

READING 21 · JANUARY 21

~ GENESIS 41:1—42:38 ~

Then it came to pass, at the end of two full years, that Pharaoh had a dream; and behold, he stood by the river. [2] Suddenly there came up out of the river seven cows, fine looking and fat; and they fed in the meadow. [3] Then behold, seven other cows came up after them out of the river, ugly and gaunt, and stood by the *other* cows on the bank of the river. [4] And the ugly and gaunt cows ate up the seven fine looking and fat cows. So Pharaoh awoke. [5] He slept and dreamed a second time; and suddenly seven heads of grain came up on one stalk, plump and good. [6] Then behold, seven thin heads, blighted by the east wind, sprang up after them. [7] And the seven thin heads devoured the seven plump and full heads. So Pharaoh awoke, and indeed, *it was* a dream. [8] Now it came to pass in the morning that his spirit was troubled, and he sent and called for all the magicians of Egypt and all its wise men. And Pharaoh told them his dreams, but *there was* no one who could interpret them for Pharaoh.

[9] Then the chief butler spoke to Pharaoh, saying: "I remember my faults this day. [10] When Pharaoh was angry with his servants, and put me in custody in the house of the captain of the guard, *both* me and the chief baker, [11] we each had a dream in one night, he and I. Each of us dreamed according to the interpretation of his *own* dream. [12] Now there *was* a

Christmas in December

Two lifelong friends in their early fifties began to argue over the forthcoming marriage of one of them to a man who was only in his thirties.

"I just don't believe in May-December marriages," the friend said. "After all, December is going to find in May the strength and virility of springtime, but whatever is May going to find in December?"

The bride-to-be thought for a moment and then replied with a twinkle in her eye, "Christmas."

Many couples who claim they "fell in love at first sight" look back after years of marriage and adjust their opinions, saying, "I was infatuated," or "We felt an immediate attraction," or "There was electricity between us when we first met." "Love," however, is a word they have come to cherish — it is something they now share that is far richer and more meaningful than the emotions they felt "at first sight."

One of the great qualities about genuine love is that it grows and deepens over time. Time is life's nursery for love. Tend to it as you would your most cherished plant, and love's fragrance will continually remain.

young Hebrew man with us there, a servant of the captain of the guard. And we told him, and he interpreted our dreams for us; to each man he interpreted according to his *own* dream. ¹³ And it came to pass, just as he interpreted for us, so it happened. He restored me to my office, and he hanged him."

¹⁴ Then Pharaoh sent and called Joseph, and they brought him quickly out of the dungeon; and he shaved, changed his clothing, and came to Pharaoh. ¹⁵ And Pharaoh said to Joseph, "I have had a dream, and *there is* no one who can interpret it. But I have heard it said of you *that* you can understand a dream, to interpret it."

¹⁶ So Joseph answered Pharaoh, saying, "*It is* not in me; God will give Pharaoh an answer of peace."

¹⁷ Then Pharaoh said to Joseph: "Behold, in my dream I stood on the bank of the river. ¹⁸ Suddenly seven cows came up out of the river, fine looking and fat; and they fed in the meadow. ¹⁹ Then behold, seven other cows came up after them, poor and very ugly and gaunt, such ugliness as I have never seen in all the land of Egypt. ²⁰ And the gaunt and ugly cows ate up the first seven, the fat cows. ²¹ When they had eaten them up, no one would have known that they had eaten them, for they *were* just as ugly as at the beginning. So I awoke. ²² Also I saw in my dream, and suddenly seven heads came up on one stalk, full and good. ²³ Then behold, seven heads, withered, thin, *and* blighted by the east wind, sprang up after them. ²⁴ And the thin heads devoured the seven good heads. So I told *this* to the magicians, but *there was* no one who could explain *it* to me."

²⁵ Then Joseph said to Pharaoh, "The dreams of Pharaoh *are* one; God has shown Pharaoh what He *is* about to do: ²⁶ The seven good cows *are* seven years, and the seven good heads *are* seven years; the dreams *are* one. ²⁷ And the seven thin and ugly cows which came up after them *are* seven years, and the seven empty heads blighted by the east wind are seven years of famine. ²⁸ This *is* the thing which I have spoken to Pharaoh. God has shown Pharaoh what He *is* about to do. ²⁹ Indeed seven years of great plenty will come

throughout all the land of Egypt; ³⁰ but after them seven years of famine will arise, and all the plenty will be forgotten in the land of Egypt; and the famine will deplete the land. ³¹ So the plenty will not be known in the land because of the famine following, for it *will be* very severe. ³² And the dream was repeated to Pharaoh twice because the thing *is* established by God, and God will shortly bring it to pass.

³³ "Now therefore, let Pharaoh select a discerning and wise man, and set him over the land of Egypt. ³⁴ Let Pharaoh do *this*, and let him appoint officers over the land, to collect one-fifth *of the produce* of the land of Egypt in the seven plentiful years. ³⁵ And let them gather all the food of those good years that are coming, and store up grain under the authority of Pharaoh, and let them keep food in the cities. ³⁶ Then that food shall be as a reserve for the land for the seven years of famine which shall be in the land of Egypt, that the land may not perish during the famine."

³⁷ So the advice was good in the eyes of Pharaoh and in the eyes of all his servants. ³⁸ And Pharaoh said to his servants, "Can we find *such a one* as this, a man in whom *is* the Spirit of God?"

³⁹ Then Pharaoh said to Joseph, "Inasmuch as God has shown you all this, *there is* no one as discerning and wise as you. ⁴⁰ You shall be over my house, and all my people shall be ruled according to your word; only in regard to the throne will I be greater than you." ⁴¹ And Pharaoh said to Joseph, "See, I have set you over all the land of Egypt."

⁴² Then Pharaoh took his signet ring off his hand and put it on Joseph's hand; and he clothed him in garments of fine linen and put a gold chain around his neck. ⁴³ And he had him ride in the second chariot which he had; and they cried out before him, "Bow the knee!" So he set him over all the land of Egypt. ⁴⁴ Pharaoh also said to Joseph, "I *am* Pharaoh, and without your consent no man may lift his hand or foot in all the land of Egypt." ⁴⁵ And Pharaoh called Joseph's name Zaphnath-Paaneah. And he gave him as a wife Asenath, the daughter of Poti-Pherah priest of On. So Joseph went out over *all* the land of Egypt.

⁴⁶ Joseph was thirty years old when he

stood before Pharaoh king of Egypt. And Joseph went out from the presence of Pharaoh, and went throughout all the land of Egypt. [47] Now in the seven plentiful years the ground brought forth abundantly. [48] So he gathered up all the food of the seven years which were in the land of Egypt, and laid up the food in the cities; he laid up in every city the food of the fields which surrounded them. [49] Joseph gathered very much grain, as the sand of the sea, until he stopped counting, for *it was* immeasurable.

[50] And to Joseph were born two sons before the years of famine came, whom Asenath, the daughter of Poti-Pherah priest of On, bore to him. [51] Joseph called the name of the firstborn Manasseh: "For God has made me forget all my toil and all my father's house." [52] And the name of the second he called Ephraim: "For God has caused me to be fruitful in the land of my affliction."

[53] Then the seven years of plenty which were in the land of Egypt ended, [54] and the seven years of famine began to come, as Joseph had said. The famine was in all lands, but in all the land of Egypt there was bread. [55] So when all the land of Egypt was famished, the people cried to Pharaoh for bread. Then Pharaoh said to all the Egyptians, "Go to Joseph; whatever he says to you, do." [56] The famine was over all the face of the earth, and Joseph opened all the storehouses and sold to the Egyptians. And the famine became severe in the land of Egypt. [57] So all countries came to Joseph in Egypt to buy *grain*, because the famine was severe in all lands.

42 When Jacob saw that there was grain in Egypt, Jacob said to his sons, "Why do you look at one another?" [2] And he said, "Indeed I have heard that there is grain in Egypt; go down to that place and buy for us there, that we may live and not die."

[3] So Joseph's ten brothers went down to buy grain in Egypt. [4] But Jacob did not send Joseph's brother Benjamin with his brothers, for he said, "Lest some calamity befall him." [5] And the sons of Israel went to buy *grain* among those who journeyed, for the famine was in the land of Canaan.

[6] Now Joseph *was* governor over the land; and it was he who sold to all the people of the land. And Joseph's brothers came and bowed down before him with *their* faces to the earth. [7] Joseph saw his brothers and recognized them, but he acted as a stranger to them and spoke roughly to them. Then he said to them, "Where do you come from?"

And they said, "From the land of Canaan to buy food."

[8] So Joseph recognized his brothers, but they did not recognize him. [9] Then Joseph remembered the dreams which he had dreamed about them, and said to them, "You *are* spies! You have come to see the nakedness of the land!"

[10] And they said to him, "No, my lord, but your servants have come to buy food. [11] We *are* all one man's sons; we *are* honest *men*; your servants are not spies."

[12] But he said to them, "No, but you have come to see the nakedness of the land."

[13] And they said, "Your servants *are* twelve brothers, the sons of one man in the land of Canaan; and in fact, the youngest *is* with our father today, and one *is* no more."

[14] But Joseph said to them, "It *is* as I spoke to you, saying, 'You *are* spies!' [15] In this *manner* you shall be tested: By the life of Pharaoh, you shall not leave this place unless your youngest brother comes here. [16] Send one of you, and let him bring your brother; and you shall be kept in prison, that your words may be tested to see whether *there is* any truth in you; or else, by the life of Pharaoh, surely you *are* spies!" [17] So he put them all together in prison three days.

[18] Then Joseph said to them the third day, "Do this and live, *for* I fear God: [19] If you *are* honest *men*, let one of your brothers be confined to your prison house; but you, go and carry grain for the famine of your houses. [20] And bring your youngest brother to me; so your words will be verified, and you shall not die."

And they did so. [21] Then they said to one another, "We *are* truly guilty concerning our brother, for we saw the anguish of his soul when he pleaded with us, and we would not hear; therefore this distress has come upon us."

[22] And Reuben answered them, saying, "Did I not speak to you, saying, 'Do not

sin against the boy'; and you would not listen? Therefore behold, his blood is now required of us." ²³ But they did not know that Joseph understood *them*, for he spoke to them through an interpreter. ²⁴ And he turned himself away from them and wept. Then he returned to them again, and talked with them. And he took Simeon from them and bound him before their eyes.

²⁵ Then Joseph gave a command to fill their sacks with grain, to restore every man's money to his sack, and to give them provisions for the journey. Thus he did for them. ²⁶ So they loaded their donkeys with the grain and departed from there. ²⁷ But as one *of them* opened his sack to give his donkey feed at the encampment, he saw his money; and there it was, in the mouth of his sack. ²⁸ So he said to his brothers, "My money has been restored, and there it is, in my sack!" Then their hearts failed *them* and they were afraid, saying to one another, "What *is* this *that* God has done to us?"

²⁹ Then they went to Jacob their father in the land of Canaan and told him all that had happened to them, saying: ³⁰ "The man *who is* lord of the land spoke roughly to us, and took us for spies of the country. ³¹ But we said to him, 'We *are* honest *men*; we are not spies. ³² We *are* twelve brothers, sons of our father; one *is* no *more*, and the youngest *is* with our father this day in the land of Canaan.' ³³ Then the man, the lord of the country, said to us, 'By this I will know that you *are* honest *men*: Leave one of your brothers *here* with me, take *food for* the famine of your households, and be gone. ³⁴ And bring your youngest brother to me; so I shall know that you *are* not spies, but *that* you *are* honest *men*. I will grant your brother to you, and you may trade in the land.' "

³⁵ Then it happened as they emptied their sacks, that surprisingly each man's bundle of money *was* in his sack; and when they and their father saw the bundles of money, they were afraid. ³⁶ And Jacob their father said to them, "You have bereaved me: Joseph is no *more*, Simeon is no *more*, and you want to take Benjamin. All these things are against me."

³⁷ Then Reuben spoke to his father, saying, "Kill my two sons if I do not bring him *back* to you; put him in my hands, and I will bring him back to you."

³⁸ But he said, "My son shall not go down with you, for his brother is dead, and he is left alone. If any calamity should befall him along the way in which you go, then you would bring down my gray hair with sorrow to the grave."

∼ PSALM 10:12–18 ∼

¹² Arise, O LORD!
O God, lift up Your hand!
Do not forget the humble.
¹³ Why do the wicked renounce God?
He has said in his heart,
"You will not require *an account*."

¹⁴ But You have seen, for You observe
    trouble and grief,
To repay *it* by Your hand.
The helpless commits himself to You;
You are the helper of the fatherless.
¹⁵ Break the arm of the wicked and the
    evil *man*;
Seek out his wickedness *until* You
    find none.

¹⁶ The LORD *is* King forever and ever;
The nations have perished out of His
    land.
¹⁷ LORD, You have heard the desire of
    the humble;
You will prepare their heart;
You will cause Your ear to hear,
¹⁸ To do justice to the fatherless and
    the oppressed,
That the man of the earth may
    oppress no more.

∼ PROVERBS 4:7–9 ∼

⁷ Wisdom *is* the principal thing;
Therefore get wisdom.
And in all your getting, get
    understanding.
⁸ Exalt her, and she will promote you;
She will bring you honor, when you
    embrace her.
⁹ She will place on your head an
    ornament of grace;
A crown of glory she will deliver to
    you."

∼ Matthew 14:1–21 ∼

At that time Herod the tetrarch heard the report about Jesus [2] and said to his servants, "This is John the Baptist; he is risen from the dead, and therefore these powers are at work in him." [3] For Herod had laid hold of John and bound him, and put *him* in prison for the sake of Herodias, his brother Philip's wife. [4] Because John had said to him, "It is not lawful for you to have her." [5] And although he wanted to put him to death, he feared the multitude, because they counted him as a prophet.

[6] But when Herod's birthday was celebrated, the daughter of Herodias danced before them and pleased Herod. [7] Therefore he promised with an oath to give her whatever she might ask.

[8] So she, having been prompted by her mother, said, "Give me John the Baptist's head here on a platter."

[9] And the king was sorry; nevertheless, because of the oaths and because of those who sat with him, he commanded *it* to be given to *her*. [10] So he sent and had John beheaded in prison. [11] And his head was brought on a platter and given to the girl, and she brought *it* to her mother. [12] Then his disciples came and took away the body and buried it, and went and told Jesus.

[13] When Jesus heard *it*, He departed from there by boat to a deserted place by Himself. But when the multitudes heard it, they followed Him on foot from the cities. [14] And when Jesus went out He saw a great multitude; and He was moved with compassion for them, and healed their sick. [15] When it was evening, His disciples came to Him, saying, "This is a deserted place, and the hour is already late. Send the multitudes away, that they may go into the villages and buy themselves food."

[16] But Jesus said to them, "They do not need to go away. You give them something to eat."

[17] And they said to Him, "We have here only five loaves and two fish."

[18] He said, "Bring them here to Me." [19] Then He commanded the multitudes to sit down on the grass. And He took the five loaves and the two fish, and looking up to heaven, He blessed and broke and gave the loaves to the disciples; and the disciples gave to the multitudes. [20] So they all ate and were filled, and they took up twelve baskets full of the fragments that remained. [21] Now those who had eaten were about five thousand men, besides women and children.

∼ Genesis 43:1—44:34 ∼

Now the famine *was* severe in the land. [2] And it came to pass, when they had eaten up the grain which they had brought from Egypt, that their father said to them, "Go back, buy us a little food."

[3] But Judah spoke to him, saying, "The man solemnly warned us, saying, 'You shall not see my face unless your brother *is* with you.' [4] If you send our brother with us, we will go down and buy you food. [5] But if you will not send *him*, we will not go down; for the man said to us, 'You shall not see my face unless your brother *is* with you.' "

[6] And Israel said, "Why did you deal *so* wrongfully with me *as* to tell the man whether you had still *another* brother?"

[7] But they said, "The man asked us pointedly about ourselves and our family, saying, '*Is* your father still alive? Have you *another* brother?' And we told him according to these words. Could we possibly have known that he would say, 'Bring your brother down'?"

[8] Then Judah said to Israel his father, "Send the lad with me, and we will arise and go, that we may live and not die, both we and you *and* also our little ones. [9] I myself will be surety for him; from my hand you shall require him. If I do not bring him *back* to you and set him before you, then let me bear the blame forever. [10] For if we had not lingered, surely by now we would have returned this second time."

¹¹ And their father Israel said to them, "If *it must be* so, then do this: Take some of the best fruits of the land in your vessels and carry down a present for the man—a little balm and a little honey, spices and myrrh, pistachio nuts and almonds. ¹² Take double money in your hand, and take back in your hand the money that was returned in the mouth of your sacks; perhaps it was an oversight. ¹³ Take your brother also, and arise, go back to the man. ¹⁴ And may God Almighty give you mercy before the man, that he may release your other brother and Benjamin. If I am bereaved, I am bereaved!"

¹⁵ So the men took that present and Benjamin, and they took double money in their hand, and arose and went down to Egypt; and they stood before Joseph. ¹⁶ When Joseph saw Benjamin with them, he said to the steward of his house, "Take *these* men to my home, and slaughter an animal and make ready; for *these* men will dine with me at noon." ¹⁷ Then the man did as Joseph ordered, and the man brought the men into Joseph's house.

¹⁸ Now the men were afraid because they were brought into Joseph's house; and they said, "*It is* because of the money, which was returned in our sacks the first time, that we are brought in, so that he may make a case against us and seize us, to take us as slaves with our donkeys."

¹⁹ When they drew near to the steward of Joseph's house, they talked with him at the door of the house, ²⁰ and said, "O sir, we indeed came down the first time to buy food; ²¹ but it happened, when we came to the encampment, that we opened our sacks, and there, *each* man's money *was* in the mouth of his sack, our money in full weight; so we have brought it back in our hand. ²² And we have brought down other money in our hands to buy food. We do not know who put our money in our sacks."

²³ But he said, "Peace *be* with you, do not be afraid. Your God and the God of your father has given you treasure in your sacks; I had your money." Then he brought Simeon out to them.

²⁴ So the man brought the men into Joseph's house and gave *them* water, and they washed their feet; and he gave their donkeys feed. ²⁵ Then they made the present ready for Joseph's coming at noon, for they heard that they would eat bread there.

²⁶ And when Joseph came home, they brought him the present which *was* in their hand into the house, and bowed down before him to the earth. ²⁷ Then he asked them about *their* well-being, and said, "*Is* your father well, the old man of whom you spoke? *Is* he still alive?"

²⁸ And they answered, "Your servant our father *is* in good health; he *is* still alive." And they bowed their heads down and prostrated themselves.

²⁹ Then he lifted his eyes and saw his brother Benjamin, his mother's son, and said, "*Is* this your younger brother of whom you spoke to me?" And he said, "God be gracious to you, my son." ³⁰ Now his heart yearned for his brother; so Joseph made haste and sought *somewhere* to weep. And he went into *his* chamber and wept there. ³¹ Then he washed his face and came out; and he restrained himself, and said, "Serve the bread."

³² So they set him a place by himself, and them by themselves, and the Egyptians who ate with him by themselves; because the Egyptians could not eat food with the Hebrews, for that *is* an abomination to the Egyptians. ³³ And they sat before him, the firstborn according to his birthright and the youngest according to his youth; and the men looked in astonishment at one another. ³⁴ Then he took servings to them from before him, but Benjamin's serving was five times as much as any of theirs. So they drank and were merry with him.

44 And he commanded the steward of his house, saying, "Fill the men's sacks with food, as much as they can carry, and put each man's money in the mouth of his sack. ² Also put my cup, the silver cup, in the mouth of the sack of the youngest, and his grain money." So he did according to the word that Joseph had spoken. ³ As soon as the morning dawned, the men were sent away, they and their donkeys. ⁴ When they had gone out of the city, *and* were not *yet* far off, Joseph said to his steward, "Get up, follow the men; and when you overtake them, say to them,

Try and Try Again

Franklin D. Roosevelt said, "It is common sense to take a method and try it. If it fails, admit it frankly. But above all, try something."

In *The Pursuit of Excellence*, Ted W. Engstrom gives this advice about the importance of trying: "Starting today, you can begin to enjoy using and developing your gifts. For a start, you may want to risk something small — like a toe rather than a neck.

"For example, if you've always wanted to write, then write something, a short article, a poem, an account of your vacation. Write it as if it were going to be published; then submit it somewhere. If you're a photographer, gather your best pictures together and submit them as entries in a contest. If you think you're a fair tennis player or golfer, enter some tournaments and see how you do. You may not win the top prize, but think how much you'll learn and experience just by trying."

The first step in trying may be taking a course at a local college, getting some private lessons, or conducting your own simple experiments. Trying is perfected by practice.

The only true failure is the failure to try.

'Why have you repaid evil for good? [5] *Is* not this *the one* from which my lord drinks, and with which he indeed practices divination? You have done evil in so doing.' "

[6] So he overtook them, and he spoke to them these same words. [7] And they said to him, "Why does my lord say these words? Far be it from us that your servants should do such a thing. [8] Look, we brought back to you from the land of Canaan the money which we found in the mouth of our sacks. How then could we steal silver or gold from your lord's house? [9] With whomever of your servants it is found, let him die, and we also will be my lord's slaves."

[10] And he said, "Now also *let* it *be* according to your words; he with whom it is found shall be my slave, and you shall be blameless." [11] Then each man speedily let down his sack to the ground, and each opened his sack. [12] So he searched. He began with the oldest and left off with the youngest; and the cup was found in Benjamin's sack. [13] Then they tore their clothes, and each man loaded his donkey and returned to the city.

[14] So Judah and his brothers came to Joseph's house, and he *was* still there; and they fell before him on the ground. [15] And Joseph said to them, "What deed *is* this you have done? Did you not know that such a man as I can certainly practice divination?"

[16] Then Judah said, "What shall we say to my lord? What shall we speak? Or how shall we clear ourselves? God has found out the iniquity of your servants; here we are, my lord's slaves, both we and *he* also with whom the cup was found."

[17] But he said, "Far be it from me that I should do so; the man in whose hand the cup was found, he shall be my slave. And as for you, go up in peace to your father."

[18] Then Judah came near to him and said: "O my lord, please let your servant speak a word in my lord's hearing, and do not let your anger burn against your servant; for you *are* even like Pharaoh. [19] My lord asked his servants, saying, 'Have you a father or a brother?' [20] And we said to my lord, 'We have a father, an old man, and a child of *his* old age, *who is* young; his brother is dead, and he alone

is left of his mother's children, and his father loves him.' [21] Then you said to your servants, 'Bring him down to me, that I may set my eyes on him.' [22] And we said to my lord, 'The lad cannot leave his father, for *if* he should leave his father, *his father* would die.' [23] But you said to your servants, 'Unless your youngest brother comes down with you, you shall see my face no more.'

[24] "So it was, when we went up to your servant my father, that we told him the words of my lord. [25] And our father said, 'Go back *and* buy us a little food.' [26] But we said, 'We cannot go down; if our youngest brother is with us, then we will go down; for we may not see the man's face unless our youngest brother *is* with us.' [27] Then your servant my father said to us, 'You know that my wife bore me two sons; [28] and the one went out from me, and I said, "Surely he is torn to pieces"; and I have not seen him since. [29] But if you take this one also from me, and calamity befalls him, you shall bring down my gray hair with sorrow to the grave.'

[30] "Now therefore, when I come to your servant my father, and the lad *is* not with us, since his life is bound up in the lad's life, [31] it will happen, when he sees that the lad *is* not *with us*, that he will die. So your servants will bring down the gray hair of your servant our father with sorrow to the grave. [32] For your servant became surety for the lad to my father, saying, 'If I do not bring him *back* to you, then I shall bear the blame before my father forever.' [33] Now therefore, please let your servant remain instead of the lad as a slave to my lord, and let the lad go up with his brothers. [34] For how shall I go up to my father if the lad is not with me, lest perhaps I see the evil that would come upon my father?"

~ PSALM 11:1–7 ~

[1]   In the LORD I put my trust;
     How can you say to my soul,
     "Flee *as* a bird to your mountain"?
[2]   For look! The wicked bend *their*
         bow,
     They make ready their arrow on the
         string,

That they may shoot secretly at the
upright in heart.
3 If the foundations are destroyed,
What can the righteous do?

4 The LORD *is* in His holy temple,
The LORD's throne *is* in heaven;
His eyes behold,
His eyelids test the sons of men.
5 The LORD tests the righteous,
But the wicked and the one who
loves violence His soul hates.
6 Upon the wicked He will rain coals;
Fire and brimstone and a burning
wind
Shall be the portion of their cup.

7 For the LORD *is* righteous,
He loves righteousness;
His countenance beholds the
upright.

∼ PROVERBS 4:10–13 ∼

10 Hear, my son, and receive my
sayings,
And the years of your life will be
many.
11 I have taught you in the way of
wisdom;
I have led you in right paths.
12 When you walk, your steps will not
be hindered,
And when you run, you will not
stumble.
13 Take firm hold of instruction, do not
let go;
Keep her, for she *is* your life.

∼ MATTHEW 14:22–36 ∼

Immediately Jesus made His disciples get
into the boat and go before Him to the
other side, while He sent the multitudes away. 23 And when He had sent the
multitudes away, He went up on the
mountain by Himself to pray. Now when
evening came, He was alone there. 24 But
the boat was now in the middle of the
sea, tossed by the waves, for the wind was
contrary.
25 Now in the fourth watch of the night
Jesus went to them, walking on the sea.
26 And when the disciples saw Him walking on the sea, they were troubled, saying, "It is a ghost!" And they cried out for
fear.
27 But immediately Jesus spoke to them,
saying, "Be of good cheer! It is I; do not
be afraid."
28 And Peter answered Him and said,
"Lord, if it is You, command me to come
to You on the water."
29 So He said, "Come." And when Peter had come down out of the boat, he
walked on the water to go to Jesus. 30 But
when he saw that the wind *was* boister-
ous, he was afraid; and beginning to sink
he cried out, saying, "Lord, save me!"
31 And immediately Jesus stretched out
His hand and caught him, and said to him,
"O you of little faith, why did you doubt?"
32 And when they got into the boat, the
wind ceased.
33 Then those who were in the boat
came and worshiped Him, saying, "Truly
You are the Son of God."
34 When they had crossed over, they
came to the land of Gennesaret. 35 And
when the men of that place recognized
Him, they sent out into all that surrounding region, brought to Him all who were
sick, 36 and begged Him that they might
only touch the hem of His garment. And
as many as touched *it* were made perfectly
well.

∼ GENESIS 45:1—46:34 ∼

Then Joseph could not restrain himself before all those who stood by
him, and he cried out, "Make everyone go out from me!" So no one stood
with him while Joseph made himself
known to his brothers. 2 And he wept
aloud, and the
of Pharaoh hea
3 Then Josep
am Joseph; does
his brothers cou
they were dismay

Joseph said to his brothers, "Please come near to me." So they came near. Then he said: "I *am* Joseph your brother, whom you sold into Egypt. ⁵ But now, do not therefore be grieved or angry with yourselves because you sold me here; for God sent me before you to preserve life. ⁶ For these two years the famine *has been* in the land, and *there are* still five years in which *there will be* neither plowing nor harvesting. ⁷ And God sent me before you to preserve a posterity for you in the earth, and to save your lives by a great deliverance. ⁸ So now *it was* not you *who* sent me here, but God; and He has made me a father to Pharaoh, and lord of all his house, and a ruler throughout all the land of Egypt.

⁹ "Hurry and go up to my father, and say to him, 'Thus says your son Joseph: "God has made me lord of all Egypt; come down to me, do not tarry. ¹⁰ You shall dwell in the land of Goshen, and you shall be near to me, you and your children, your children's children, your flocks and your herds, and all that you have. ¹¹ There I will provide for you, lest you and your household, and all that you have, come to poverty; for *there are* still five years of famine." '

¹² "And behold, your eyes and the eyes of my brother Benjamin see that *it is* my mouth that speaks to you. ¹³ So you shall tell my father of all my glory in Egypt, and of all that you have seen; and you shall hurry and bring my father down here."

¹⁴ Then he fell on his brother Benjamin's neck and wept, and Benjamin wept on his neck. ¹⁵ Moreover he kissed all his brothers and wept over them, and after that his brothers talked with him.

¹⁶ Now the report of it was heard in Pharaoh's house, saying, "Joseph's brothers have come." So it pleased Pharaoh and his servants well. ¹⁷ And Pharaoh said to Joseph, "Say to your brothers, 'Do this: Load your animals and depart; go to the ˻la˼nd of Canaan. ¹⁸ Bring your father and ˻your˼ households and come to me; I will ˻give y˼ou the best of the land of Egypt, ˻and you˼ will eat the fat of the land. ¹⁹ Now ˻you are co˼mmanded—do this: Take carts ˻out of the˼ land of Egypt for your little ˻ones and you˼r wives; bring your father

and come. ²⁰ Also do not be concerned about your goods, for the best of all the land of Egypt *is* yours.' "

²¹ Then the sons of Israel did so; and Joseph gave them carts, according to the command of Pharaoh, and he gave them provisions for the journey. ²² He gave to all of them, to each man, changes of garments; but to Benjamin he gave three hundred *pieces* of silver and five changes of garments. ²³ And he sent to his father these *things*: ten donkeys loaded with the good things of Egypt, and ten female donkeys loaded with grain, bread, and food for his father for the journey. ²⁴ So he sent his brothers away, and they departed; and he said to them, "See that you do not become troubled along the way."

²⁵ Then they went up out of Egypt, and came to the land of Canaan to Jacob their father. ²⁶ And they told him, saying, "Joseph *is* still alive, and he *is* governor over all the land of Egypt." And Jacob's heart stood still, because he did not believe them. ²⁷ But when they told him all the words which Joseph had said to them, and when he saw the carts which Joseph had sent to carry him, the spirit of Jacob their father revived. ²⁸ Then Israel said, "*It is* enough. Joseph my son *is* still alive. I will go and see him before I die."

46

So Israel took his journey with all that he had, and came to Beersheba, and offered sacrifices to the God of his father Isaac. ² Then God spoke to Israel in the visions of the night, and said, "Jacob, Jacob!"

And he said, "Here I am."

³ So He said, "I *am* God, the God of your father; do not fear to go down to Egypt, for I will make of you a great nation there. ⁴ I will go down with you to Egypt, and I will also surely bring you up *again*; and Joseph will put his hand on your eyes."

⁵ Then Jacob arose from Beersheba; and the sons of Israel carried their father Jacob, their little ones, and their wives, in the carts which Pharaoh had sent to carry him. ⁶ So they took their livestock and their goods, which they had acquired in the land of Canaan, and went to Egypt, Jacob and all his descendants with him. ⁷ His sons and his sons' sons, his daughters and

Hope for the Homeless

Some thought Les Goldberg was crazy when he cashed in his personal investments to buy a home to lease to the homeless. Goldberg, a retired engineer, felt it was the only right decision he could make.

Since his retirement, Goldberg has been a busy volunteer, serving on six service boards and leading a crew of homeless people at odd jobs and charity work. He spends at least an hour a day with his homeless friends and has helped renovate several properties on their behalf. In all his efforts, Goldberg never regarded the homeless as irresponsible or unreliable. He only saw them as people. He figured the house he purchased could be used as both a temporary shelter and a drop-in center, a place where homeless people might pick up mail, make phone calls, follow up job leads, and receive donated commodities. Four homeless men live at the house, paying minimal rent to offset expenses. House rules are strict — no alcohol, no drugs, no loitering.

Goldberg has never been rich. For twenty years he ran his own business, making about $25,000 a year designing and installing fire sprinklers. He simply saw a need and found a way to help meet it. What can you do today to help meet the needs of those around you?

> "For the oppression of the poor, for the sighing of the needy, now I will arise," says the Lord; "I will set him in the safety for which he yearns."
>
> *Psalm 12:5*

his sons' daughters, and all his descendants he brought with him to Egypt.

8 Now these *were* the names of the children of Israel, Jacob and his sons, who went to Egypt: Reuben *was* Jacob's firstborn. 9 The sons of Reuben *were* Hanoch, Pallu, Hezron, and Carmi. 10 The sons of Simeon *were* Jemuel, Jamin, Ohad, Jachin, Zohar, and Shaul, the son of a Canaanite woman. 11 The sons of Levi *were* Gershon, Kohath, and Merari. 12 The sons of Judah *were* Er, Onan, Shelah, Perez, and Zerah (but Er and Onan died in the land of Canaan). The sons of Perez were Hezron and Hamul. 13 The sons of Issachar *were* Tola, Puvah, Job, and Shimron. 14 The sons of Zebulun *were* Sered, Elon, and Jahleel. 15 These *were* the sons of Leah, whom she bore to Jacob in Padan Aram, with his daughter Dinah. All the persons, his sons and his daughters, *were* thirty-three.

16 The sons of Gad *were* Ziphion, Haggi, Shuni, Ezbon, Eri, Arodi, and Areli. 17 The sons of Asher *were* Jimnah, Ishuah, Isui, Beriah, and Serah, their sister. And the sons of Beriah *were* Heber and Malchiel. 18 These *were* the sons of Zilpah, whom Laban gave to Leah his daughter; and these she bore to Jacob: sixteen persons.

19 The sons of Rachel, Jacob's wife, *were* Joseph and Benjamin. 20 And to Joseph in the land of Egypt were born Manasseh and Ephraim, whom Asenath, the daughter of Poti-Pherah priest of On, bore to him. 21 The sons of Benjamin *were* Belah, Becher, Ashbel, Gera, Naaman, Ehi, Rosh, Muppim, Huppim, and Ard. 22 These *were* the sons of Rachel, who were born to Jacob: fourteen persons in all.

23 The son of Dan *was* Hushim. 24 The sons of Naphtali *were* Jahzeel, Guni, Jezer, and Shillem. 25 These *were* the sons of Bilhah, whom Laban gave to Rachel his daughter, and she bore these to Jacob: seven persons in all.

26 All the persons who went with Jacob to Egypt, who came from his body, besides Jacob's sons' wives, *were* sixty-six persons in all. 27 And the sons of Joseph who were born to him in Egypt *were* two persons. All the persons of the house of Jacob who went to Egypt were seventy.

28 Then he sent Judah before him to Joseph, to point out before him *the way* to Goshen. And they came to the land of Goshen. 29 So Joseph made ready his chariot and went up to Goshen to meet his father Israel; and he presented himself to him, and fell on his neck and wept on his neck a good while.

30 And Israel said to Joseph, "Now let me die, since I have seen your face, because you *are* still alive."

31 Then Joseph said to his brothers and to his father's household, "I will go up and tell Pharaoh, and say to him, 'My brothers and those of my father's house, who *were* in the land of Canaan, have come to me. 32 And the men *are* shepherds, for their occupation has been to feed livestock; and they have brought their flocks, their herds, and all that they have.' 33 So it shall be, when Pharaoh calls you and says, 'What is your occupation?' 34 that you shall say, 'Your servants' occupation has been with livestock from our youth even till now, both we *and* also our fathers,' that you may dwell in the land of Goshen; for every shepherd *is* an abomination to the Egyptians."

~ PSALM 12:1-8 ~

1   Help, LORD, for the godly man
        ceases!
    For the faithful disappear from
        among the sons of men.
2   They speak idly everyone with his
        neighbor;
    With flattering lips *and* a double
        heart they speak.

3   May the LORD cut off all flattering
        lips,
    And the tongue that speaks proud
        things,
4   Who have said,
    "With our tongue we will prevail;
    Our lips *are* our own;
    Who *is* lord over us?"

5   "For the oppression of the poor, for
        the sighing of the needy,
    Now I will arise," says the LORD;
    "I will set *him* in the safety for which
        he yearns."

⁶ The words of the LORD *are* pure
    words,
    Like silver tried in a furnace of earth,
    Purified seven times.
⁷ You shall keep them, O LORD,
    You shall preserve them from this
    generation forever.

⁸ The wicked prowl on every side,
    When vileness is exalted among the
    sons of men.

∼ PROVERBS 4:14–17 ∼

¹⁴ Do not enter the path of the wicked,
    And do not walk in the way of evil.
¹⁵ Avoid it, do not travel on it;
    Turn away from it and pass on.
¹⁶ For they do not sleep unless they
    have done evil;
    And their sleep is taken away unless
    they make *someone* fall.
¹⁷ For they eat the bread of wickedness,
    And drink the wine of violence.

∼ MATTHEW 15:1–20 ∼

Then the scribes and Pharisees who were
from Jerusalem came to Jesus, saying,
² "Why do Your disciples transgress the
tradition of the elders? For they do not
wash their hands when they eat bread."

³ He answered and said to them, "Why
do you also transgress the commandment
of God because of your tradition? ⁴ For
God commanded, saying, 'Honor your
father and your mother'; and, 'He who
curses father or mother, let him be put to
death.' ⁵ But you say, 'Whoever says to his
father or mother, "Whatever profit you
might have received from me *is* a gift *to*
God"— ⁶ then he need not honor his fa-

ther or mother.' Thus you have made the
commandment of God of no effect by
your tradition. ⁷ Hypocrites! Well did Isaiah prophesy about you, saying:

⁸ 'These people draw near to Me
    with their mouth,
    And honor Me with *their* lips,
    But their heart is far from Me.
⁹ And in vain they worship Me,
    Teaching *as* doctrines the
    commandments of men.' "

¹⁰ When He had called the multitude
to *Himself*, He said to them, "Hear and
understand: ¹¹ Not what goes into the
mouth defiles a man; but what comes out
of the mouth, this defiles a man."

¹² Then His disciples came and said to
Him, "Do You know that the Pharisees
were offended when they heard this saying?"

¹³ But He answered and said, "Every
plant which My heavenly Father has not
planted will be uprooted. ¹⁴ Let them
alone. They are blind leaders of the blind.
And if the blind leads the blind, both will
fall into a ditch."

¹⁵ Then Peter answered and said to
Him, "Explain this parable to us."

¹⁶ So Jesus said, "Are you also still without understanding? ¹⁷ Do you not yet understand that whatever enters the mouth
goes into the stomach and is eliminated?
¹⁸ But those things which proceed out of
the mouth come from the heart, and they
defile a man. ¹⁹ For out of the heart proceed evil thoughts, murders, adulteries,
fornications, thefts, false witness, blasphemies. ²⁰ These are *the things* which defile
a man, but to eat with unwashed hands
does not defile a man."

∼ GENESIS 47:1—48:22 ∼

Then Joseph went and told Pharaoh,
and said, "My father and my brothers, their flocks and their herds and
all that they possess, have come from the
land of Canaan; and indeed they *are* in
the land of Goshen." ² And he took five
men from among his brothers and pre-

sented them to Pharaoh. ³ Then Pharaoh
said to his brothers, "What *is* your occupation?"

And they said to Pharaoh, "Your servants *are* shepherds, both we *and* also our
fathers." ⁴ And they said to Pharaoh, "We
have come to dwell in the land, because

your servants have no pasture for their flocks, for the famine *is* severe in the land of Canaan. Now therefore, please let your servants dwell in the land of Goshen."

⁵ Then Pharaoh spoke to Joseph, saying, "Your father and your brothers have come to you. ⁶ The land of Egypt *is* before you. Have your father and brothers dwell in the best of the land; let them dwell in the land of Goshen. And if you know *any* competent men among them, then make them chief herdsmen over my livestock."

⁷ Then Joseph brought in his father Jacob and set him before Pharaoh; and Jacob blessed Pharaoh. ⁸ Pharaoh said to Jacob, "How old *are* you?"

⁹ And Jacob said to Pharaoh, "The days of the years of my pilgrimage *are* one hundred and thirty years; few and evil have been the days of the years of my life, and they have not attained to the days of the years of the life of my fathers in the days of their pilgrimage." ¹⁰ So Jacob blessed Pharaoh, and went out from before Pharaoh.

¹¹ And Joseph situated his father and his brothers, and gave them a possession in the land of Egypt, in the best of the land, in the land of Rameses, as Pharaoh had commanded. ¹² Then Joseph provided his father, his brothers, and all his father's household with bread, according to the number in *their* families.

¹³ Now *there was* no bread in all the land; for the famine *was* very severe, so that the land of Egypt and the land of Canaan languished because of the famine. ¹⁴ And Joseph gathered up all the money that was found in the land of Egypt and in the land of Canaan, for the grain which they bought; and Joseph brought the money into Pharaoh's house. ¹⁵ So when the money failed in the land of Egypt and in the land of Canaan, all the Egyptians came to Joseph and said, "Give us bread, for why should we die in your presence? For the money has failed." ¹⁶ Then Joseph said, "Give your livestock, and I will give you *bread* for your livestock, if the money is gone." ¹⁷ So they brought their livestock to Joseph, and Joseph gave them bread *in exchange* for the horses, the flocks, the cattle of the herds, and for the donkeys. Thus he fed them with bread *in exchange* for all their livestock that year.

¹⁸ When that year had ended, they came to him the next year and said to him, "We will not hide from my lord that our money is gone; my lord also has our herds of livestock. There is nothing left in the sight of my lord but our bodies and our lands. ¹⁹ Why should we die before your eyes, both we and our land? Buy us and our land for bread, and we and our land will be servants of Pharaoh; give *us* seed, that we may live and not die, that the land may not be desolate."

²⁰ Then Joseph bought all the land of Egypt for Pharaoh; for every man of the Egyptians sold his field, because the famine was severe upon them. So the land became Pharaoh's. ²¹ And as for the people, he moved them into the cities, from *one* end of the borders of Egypt to the *other* end. ²² Only the land of the priests he did not buy; for the priests had rations *allotted to them* by Pharaoh, and they ate their rations which Pharaoh gave them; therefore they did not sell their lands.

²³ Then Joseph said to the people, "Indeed I have bought you and your land this day for Pharaoh. Look, *here is* seed for you, and you shall sow the land. ²⁴ And it shall come to pass in the harvest that you shall give one-fifth to Pharaoh. Four-fifths shall be your own, as seed for the field and for your food, for those of your households and as food for your little ones."

²⁵ So they said, "You have saved our lives; let us find favor in the sight of my lord, and we will be Pharaoh's servants." ²⁶ And Joseph made it a law over the land of Egypt to this day, *that* Pharaoh should have one-fifth, except for the land of the priests only, *which* did not become Pharaoh's.

²⁷ So Israel dwelt in the land of Egypt, in the country of Goshen; and they had possessions there and grew and multiplied exceedingly. ²⁸ And Jacob lived in the land of Egypt seventeen years. So the length of Jacob's life was one hundred and forty-seven years. ²⁹ When the time drew near that Israel must die, he called his son Joseph and said to him, "Now if I have found favor in your sight, please put your hand

From a Dump to a Meadow

> **But He answered her not a word.**
> *Matthew 15:23*

A bus driver became annoyed with what he saw. At the end of his run lay an open field which local "litterbugs" had turned into an unofficial dump. The driver had at least a seven-minute layover there several times a day. One day, he decided to get out of his bus and spend his few minutes of waiting time picking up a few of the bottles and cans.

The next day he took along a little bigger sack and some gloves, and during each layover he gathered up a little more of the trash. After a week of doing this, he was so encouraged by the change he had made in the field that he decided to spend all his free moments cleaning up the site. He worked all through the winter months, and when spring came he decided to sow some flower seeds on the land.

By the end of the summer, some of his regular riders actually began riding with him to the end of the line just to see what the driver had accomplished. He had turned a dump into a meadow, just a few minutes at a time, and the entire community benefited.

Our neighborhoods are only as good as those who live in them. One step, one minute, one day at a time, you can make yours an even better place for you and your neighbors to call home!

under my thigh, and deal kindly and truly with me. Please do not bury me in Egypt, [30] but let me lie with my fathers; you shall carry me out of Egypt and bury me in their burial place."

And he said, "I will do as you have said." [31] Then he said, "Swear to me." And he swore to him. So Israel bowed himself on the head of the bed.

48 Now it came to pass after these things that Joseph was told, "Indeed your father is sick"; and he took with him his two sons, Manasseh and Ephraim. [2] And Jacob was told, "Look, your son Joseph is coming to you"; and Israel strengthened himself and sat up on the bed. [3] Then Jacob said to Joseph: "God Almighty appeared to me at Luz in the land of Canaan and blessed me, [4] and said to me, 'Behold, I will make you fruitful and multiply you, and I will make of you a multitude of people, and give this land to your descendants after you as an everlasting possession.' [5] And now your two sons, Ephraim and Manasseh, who were born to you in the land of Egypt before I came to you in Egypt, are mine; as Reuben and Simeon, they shall be mine. [6] Your offspring whom you beget after them shall be yours; they will be called by the name of their brothers in their inheritance. [7] But as for me, when I came from Padan, Rachel died beside me in the land of Canaan on the way, when there was but a little distance to go to Ephrath; and I buried her there on the way to Ephrath (that is, Bethlehem)."

[8] Then Israel saw Joseph's sons, and said, "Who are these?"

[9] Joseph said to his father, "They are my sons, whom God has given me in this place."

And he said, "Please bring them to me, and I will bless them." [10] Now the eyes of Israel were dim with age, so that he could not see. Then Joseph brought them near him, and he kissed them and embraced them. [11] And Israel said to Joseph, "I had not thought to see your face; but in fact, God has also shown me your offspring!"

[12] So Joseph brought them from beside his knees, and he bowed down with his face to the earth. [13] And Joseph took them both, Ephraim with his right hand toward Israel's left hand, and Manasseh with his left hand toward Israel's right hand, and brought them near him. [14] Then Israel stretched out his right hand and laid it on Ephraim's head, who was the younger, and his left hand on Manasseh's head, guiding his hands knowingly, for Manasseh was the firstborn. [15] And he blessed Joseph, and said:

"God, before whom my fathers
    Abraham and Isaac walked,
The God who has fed me all my
    life long to this day,
[16] The Angel who has redeemed me
    from all evil,
Bless the lads;
Let my name be named upon
    them,
And the name of my fathers
    Abraham and Isaac;
And let them grow into a
    multitude in the midst of the
    earth."

[17] Now when Joseph saw that his father laid his right hand on the head of Ephraim, it displeased him; so he took hold of his father's hand to remove it from Ephraim's head to Manasseh's head. [18] And Joseph said to his father, "Not so, my father, for this one is the firstborn; put your right hand on his head." [19] But his father refused and said, "I know, my son, I know. He also shall become a people, and he also shall be great; but truly his younger brother shall be greater than he, and his descendants shall become a multitude of nations." [20] So he blessed them that day, saying, "By you Israel will bless, saying, 'May God make you as Ephraim and as Manasseh!' " And thus he set Ephraim before Manasseh.

[21] Then Israel said to Joseph, "Behold, I am dying, but God will be with you and bring you back to the land of your fathers. [22] Moreover I have given to you one portion above your brothers, which I took from the hand of the Amorite with my sword and my bow."

~ PSALM 13:1-6 ~

[1] How long, O LORD? Will You forget me forever?

How long will You hide Your face
   from me?
2 How long shall I take counsel in my
   soul,
   Having sorrow in my heart daily?
   How long will my enemy be exalted
   over me?

3 Consider *and* hear me, O LORD my
   God;
   Enlighten my eyes,
   Lest I sleep the *sleep of* death;
4 Lest my enemy say,
   "I have prevailed against him";
   Lest those who trouble me rejoice
   when I am moved.

5 But I have trusted in Your mercy;
   My heart shall rejoice in Your
   salvation.
6 I will sing to the LORD,
   Because He has dealt bountifully
   with me.

~ PROVERBS 4:18, 19 ~

18 But the path of the just *is* like the
   shining sun,
   That shines ever brighter unto the
   perfect day.
19 The way of the wicked *is* like
   darkness;
   They do not know what makes them
   stumble.

~ MATTHEW 15:21–39 ~

Then Jesus went out from there and departed to the region of Tyre and Sidon.
22 And behold, a woman of Canaan came
from that region and cried out to Him,
saying, "Have mercy on me, O Lord, Son
of David! My daughter is severely demon-
possessed."
23 But He answered her not a word.
And His disciples came and urged Him,
saying, "Send her away, for she cries out
after us."
24 But He answered and said, "I was not
sent except to the lost sheep of the house
of Israel."
25 Then she came and worshiped Him,
saying, "Lord, help me!"
26 But He answered and said, "It is not
good to take the children's bread and
throw *it* to the little dogs."
27 And she said, "Yes, Lord, yet even the
little dogs eat the crumbs which fall from
their masters' table."
28 Then Jesus answered and said to her,
"O woman, great *is* your faith! Let it be
to you as you desire." And her daughter
was healed from that very hour.
29 Jesus departed from there, skirted the
Sea of Galilee, and went up on the mountain and sat down there. 30 Then great
multitudes came to Him, having with
them *the* lame, blind, mute, maimed, and
many others; and they laid them down at
Jesus' feet, and He healed them. 31 So the
multitude marveled when they saw *the*
mute speaking, *the* maimed made whole,
the lame walking, and *the* blind seeing;
and they glorified the God of Israel.
32 Now Jesus called His disciples to
Himself and said, "I have compassion on
the multitude, because they have now continued with Me three days and have nothing to eat. And I do not want to send them
away hungry, lest they faint on the way."
33 Then His disciples said to Him,
"Where could we get enough bread in the
wilderness to fill such a great multitude?"
34 Jesus said to them, "How many loaves
do you have?"
And they said, "Seven, and a few little
fish."
35 So He commanded the multitude to
sit down on the ground. 36 And He took
the seven loaves and the fish and gave
thanks, broke *them* and gave *them* to His
disciples; and the disciples *gave* to the
multitude. 37 So they all ate and were filled,
and they took up seven large baskets full
of the fragments that were left. 38 Now
those who ate were four thousand men,
besides women and children. 39 And He
sent away the multitude, got into the boat,
and came to the region of Magdala.

∼ GENESIS 49:1—50:26 ∼

And Jacob called his sons and said, "Gather together, that I may tell you what shall befall you in the last days:

2 "Gather together and hear, you sons of Jacob,
And listen to Israel your father.

3 "Reuben, you are my firstborn,
My might and the beginning of my strength,
The excellency of dignity and the excellency of power.
4 Unstable as water, you shall not excel,
Because you went up to your father's bed;
Then you defiled *it*—
He went up to my couch.

5 "Simeon and Levi *are* brothers;
Instruments of cruelty *are in* their dwelling place.
6 Let not my soul enter their council;
Let not my honor be united to their assembly;
For in their anger they slew a man,
And in their self-will they hamstrung an ox.
7 Cursed *be* their anger, for *it is* fierce;
And their wrath, for it is cruel!
I will divide them in Jacob
And scatter them in Israel.

8 "Judah, you *are he* whom your brothers shall praise;
Your hand *shall be* on the neck of your enemies;
Your father's children shall bow down before you.
9 Judah *is* a lion's whelp;
From the prey, my son, you have gone up.
He bows down, he lies down as a lion;
And as a lion, who shall rouse him?
10 The scepter shall not depart from Judah,

Nor a lawgiver from between his feet,
Until Shiloh comes;
And to Him *shall be* the obedience of the people.
11 Binding his donkey to the vine,
And his donkey's colt to the choice vine,
He washed his garments in wine,
And his clothes in the blood of grapes.
12 His eyes *are* darker than wine,
And his teeth whiter than milk.

13 "Zebulun shall dwell by the haven of the sea;
He *shall become* a haven for ships,
And his border shall adjoin Sidon.

14 "Issachar is a strong donkey,
Lying down between two burdens;
15 He saw that rest *was* good,
And that the land *was* pleasant;
He bowed his shoulder to bear *a burden,*
And became a band of slaves.

16 "Dan shall judge his people
As one of the tribes of Israel.
17 Dan shall be a serpent by the way,
A viper by the path,
That bites the horse's heels
So that its rider shall fall backward.
18 I have waited for your salvation,
O LORD!

19 "Gad, a troop shall tramp upon him,
But he shall triumph at last.

20 "Bread from Asher *shall be* rich,
And he shall yield royal dainties.

21 "Naphtali *is* a deer let loose;
He uses beautiful words.

22 "Joseph *is* a fruitful bough,
A fruitful bough by a well;
His branches run over the wall.

An Upstretched Hand

> The Lord looks down from heaven upon the children of men, to see if there are any who understand, who seek God.
>
> *Psalm 14:2*

Matthew Huffman, the son of missionaries in Salvador, Brazil, awoke one morning complaining of a fever. As his temperature soared, he began to lose his eyesight. His mother and father put him in the car and raced to the nearest hospital. As they drove, the boy lay in his mother's lap, listless. Then suddenly, he put one hand into the air. His mother took it gently and pulled it down to his body, but he extended it again. Again, she pulled it down. He reached into the air a third time. Confused at this unusual behavior, the mother asked her son, "What are you reaching for?" "I'm reaching for Jesus' hand," he answered.

With those words, Matthew closed his eyes and slid into a coma from which he never awakened. He died two days later, a victim of bacterial meningitis.

Matthew did not have a long life, but he learned the most important lesson a person can learn before he or she dies: He learned whom to reach for in the hour of death.

Matthew's upstretched hand was more eloquent than any prayer he might have made. It said in action what words could never fully convey.

Reaching for God is not only for the dying, it is for the living. Reaching for God's hand, we find the strength to live every day.

Are you looking to God with an upstretched hand today? He is always reaching down to you.

²³ The archers have bitterly grieved
   him,
   Shot *at him* and hated him.
²⁴ But his bow remained in strength,
   And the arms of his hands were
   made strong
   By the hands of the Mighty *God*
   of Jacob
   (From there *is* the Shepherd, the
   Stone of Israel),
²⁵ By the God of your father who
   will help you,
   And by the Almighty who will
   bless you
   With blessings of heaven above,
   Blessings of the deep that lies
   beneath,
   Blessings of the breasts and of the
   womb.
²⁶ The blessings of your father
   Have excelled the blessings of my
   ancestors,
   Up to the utmost bound of the
   everlasting hills.
   They shall be on the head of
   Joseph,
   And on the crown of the head of
   him who was separate from his
   brothers.

²⁷ "Benjamin is a ravenous wolf;
   In the morning he shall devour the
   prey,
   And at night he shall divide the
   spoil."

²⁸ All these *are* the twelve tribes of Israel, and this *is* what their father spoke to
them. And he blessed them; he blessed
each one according to his own blessing.
²⁹ Then he charged them and said to
them: "I am to be gathered to my people;
bury me with my fathers in the cave that
is in the field of Ephron the Hittite, ³⁰ in
the cave that *is* in the field of Machpelah,
which *is* before Mamre in the land of
Canaan, which Abraham bought with the
field of Ephron the Hittite as a possession for a burial place. ³¹ There they buried Abraham and Sarah his wife, there they
buried Isaac and Rebekah his wife, and
there I buried Leah. ³² The field and the
cave that *is* there *were* purchased from
the sons of Heth." ³³ And when Jacob had
finished commanding his sons, he drew

his feet up into the bed and breathed his
last, and was gathered to his people.

50 Then Joseph fell on his father's face
and wept over him, and kissed him. ² And
Joseph commanded his servants the physicians to embalm his father. So the
physicians embalmed Israel. ³ Forty days
were required for him, for such are the
days required for those who are embalmed; and the Egyptians mourned for
him seventy days.
⁴ Now when the days of his mourning
were past, Joseph spoke to the household
of Pharaoh, saying, "If now I have found
favor in your eyes, please speak in the
hearing of Pharaoh, saying, ⁵ 'My father
made me swear, saying, "Behold, I am dying; in my grave which I dug for myself in
the land of Canaan, there you shall bury
me." Now therefore, please let me go up
and bury my father, and I will come back.' "
⁶ And Pharaoh said, "Go up and bury
your father, as he made you swear."
⁷ So Joseph went up to bury his father;
and with him went up all the servants of
Pharaoh, the elders of his house, and all
the elders of the land of Egypt, ⁸ as well
as all the house of Joseph, his brothers,
and his father's house. Only their little
ones, their flocks, and their herds they left
in the land of Goshen. ⁹ And there went
up with him both chariots and horsemen,
and it was a very great gathering.
¹⁰ Then they came to the threshing floor
of Atad, which *is* beyond the Jordan, and
they mourned there with a great and very
solemn lamentation. He observed seven
days of mourning for his father. ¹¹ And
when the inhabitants of the land, the
Canaanites, saw the mourning at the
threshing floor of Atad, they said, "This
is a deep mourning of the Egyptians."
Therefore its name was called Abel
Mizraim, which *is* beyond the Jordan.
¹² So his sons did for him just as he had
commanded them. ¹³ For his sons carried
him to the land of Canaan, and buried
him in the cave of the field of Machpelah,
before Mamre, which Abraham bought
with the field from Ephron the Hittite as
property for a burial place. ¹⁴ And after
he had buried his father, Joseph returned
to Egypt, he and his brothers and all who
went up with him to bury his father.

¹⁵ When Joseph's brothers saw that their father was dead, they said, "Perhaps Joseph will hate us, and may actually repay us for all the evil which we did to him." ¹⁶ So they sent *messengers* to Joseph, saying, "Before your father died he commanded, saying, ¹⁷ 'Thus you shall say to Joseph: "I beg you, please forgive the trespass of your brothers and their sin; for they did evil to you." ' Now, please, forgive the trespass of the servants of the God of your father." And Joseph wept when they spoke to him.

¹⁸ Then his brothers also went and fell down before his face, and they said, "Behold, we *are* your servants."

¹⁹ Joseph said to them, "Do not be afraid, for *am* I in the place of God? ²⁰ But as for you, you meant evil against me; *but* God meant it for good, in order to bring it about as *it is* this day, to save many people alive. ²¹ Now therefore, do not be afraid; I will provide for you and your little ones." And he comforted them and spoke kindly to them.

²² So Joseph dwelt in Egypt, he and his father's household. And Joseph lived one hundred and ten years. ²³ Joseph saw Ephraim's children to the third *generation*. The children of Machir, the son of Manasseh, were also brought up on Joseph's knees.

²⁴ And Joseph said to his brethren, "I am dying; but God will surely visit you, and bring you out of this land to the land of which He swore to Abraham, to Isaac, and to Jacob." ²⁵ Then Joseph took an oath from the children of Israel, saying, "God will surely visit you, and you shall carry up my bones from here." ²⁶ So Joseph died, *being* one hundred and ten years old; and they embalmed him, and he was put in a coffin in Egypt.

~ PSALM 14:1-7 ~

¹ The fool has said in his heart,
   "*There is* no God."
   They are corrupt,
   They have done abominable works,
   There is none who does good.

² The LORD looks down from heaven
   upon the children of men,

To see if there are any who
   understand, who seek God.
³ They have all turned aside,
   They have together become corrupt;
   There is none who does good,
   No, not one.

⁴ Have all the workers of iniquity no
   knowledge,
   Who eat up my people *as* they eat
   bread,
   And do not call on the LORD?
⁵ There they are in great fear,
   For God *is* with the generation of
   the righteous.
⁶ You shame the counsel of the poor,
   But the LORD *is* his refuge.

⁷ Oh, that the salvation of Israel
   would come out of Zion!
   When the LORD brings back the
   captivity of His people,
   Let Jacob rejoice *and* Israel be glad.

~ PROVERBS 4:20-24 ~

²⁰ My son, give attention to my words;
   Incline your ear to my sayings.
²¹ Do not let them depart from your
   eyes;
   Keep them in the midst of your
   heart;
²² For they *are* life to those who find
   them,
   And health to all their flesh.
²³ Keep your heart with all diligence,
   For out of it *spring* the issues of life.
²⁴ Put away from you a deceitful
   mouth,
   And put perverse lips far from you.

~ MATTHEW 16:1-28 ~

Then the Pharisees and Sadducees came, and testing Him asked that He would show them a sign from heaven. ² He answered and said to them, "When it is evening you say, '*It will be* fair weather, for the sky is red'; ³ and in the morning, '*It will be* foul weather today, for the sky is red and threatening.' Hypocrites! You know how to discern the face of the sky, but you cannot *discern* the signs of the times. ⁴ A wicked and adulterous generation seeks after a sign, and no sign shall be given to it except the sign of the prophet Jonah." And He left them and departed.

⁵ Now when His disciples had come to the other side, they had forgotten to take bread. ⁶ Then Jesus said to them, "Take heed and beware of the leaven of the Pharisees and the Sadducees."

⁷ And they reasoned among themselves, saying, "*It is* because we have taken no bread."

⁸ But Jesus, being aware of *it*, said to them, "O you of little faith, why do you reason among yourselves because you have brought no bread? ⁹ Do you not yet understand, or remember the five loaves of the five thousand and how many baskets you took up? ¹⁰ Nor the seven loaves of the four thousand and how many large baskets you took up? ¹¹ How is it you do not understand that I did not speak to you concerning bread?—*but* to beware of the leaven of the Pharisees and Sadducees." ¹² Then they understood that He did not tell *them* to beware of the leaven of bread, but of the doctrine of the Pharisees and Sadducees.

¹³ When Jesus came into the region of Caesarea Philippi, He asked His disciples, saying, "Who do men say that I, the Son of Man, am?"

¹⁴ So they said, "Some *say* John the Baptist, some Elijah, and others Jeremiah or one of the prophets."

¹⁵ He said to them, "But who do you say that I am?"

¹⁶ Simon Peter answered and said, "You are the Christ, the Son of the living God."

¹⁷ Jesus answered and said to him, "Blessed are you, Simon Bar-Jonah, for flesh and blood has not revealed *this* to you, but My Father who is in heaven. ¹⁸ And I also say to you that you are Peter, and on this rock I will build My church, and the gates of Hades shall not prevail against it. ¹⁹ And I will give you the keys of the kingdom of heaven, and whatever you bind on earth will be bound in heaven, and whatever you loose on earth will be loosed in heaven."

²⁰ Then He commanded His disciples that they should tell no one that He was Jesus the Christ.

²¹ From that time Jesus began to show to His disciples that He must go to Jerusalem, and suffer many things from the elders and chief priests and scribes, and be killed, and be raised the third day.

²² Then Peter took Him aside and began to rebuke Him, saying, "Far be it from You, Lord; this shall not happen to You!"

²³ But He turned and said to Peter, "Get behind Me, Satan! You are an offense to Me, for you are not mindful of the things of God, but the things of men."

²⁴ Then Jesus said to His disciples, "If anyone desires to come after Me, let him deny himself, and take up his cross, and follow Me. ²⁵ For whoever desires to save his life will lose it, but whoever loses his life for My sake will find it. ²⁶ For what profit is it to a man if he gains the whole world, and loses his own soul? Or what will a man give in exchange for his soul? ²⁷ For the Son of Man will come in the glory of His Father with His angels, and then He will reward each according to his works. ²⁸ Assuredly, I say to you, there are some standing here who shall not taste death till they see the Son of Man coming in His kingdom."

READING 26 · JANUARY 26

~ EXODUS 1:1—2:25 ~

Now these *are* the names of the children of Israel who came to Egypt; each man and his household came with Jacob: ² Reuben, Simeon, Levi, and Judah; ³ Issachar, Zebulun, and Benjamin; ⁴ Dan, Naphtali, Gad, and Asher. ⁵ All those who were descendants of Jacob were seventy persons (for Joseph was in Egypt already). ⁶ And Joseph died, all his brothers, and all that generation. ⁷ But the children of Israel were fruitful and increased abundantly, multiplied and grew exceedingly mighty; and the land was filled with them.

⁸ Now there arose a new king over Egypt, who did not know Joseph. ⁹ And

Weep With the Weeping

A young girl was very late coming home from school. With growing concern, her mother watched the clock nervously. Finally she arrived. Her mother, nearly frantic at that point, hugged her daughter, and after giving her a thorough appraisal and realizing nothing appeared to be wrong, demanded, "Where were you? What took you so long? Haven't I told you to be home by four o'clock?"

The girl answered her mother's first question, "I was at Mary's house." "And what was so important that you couldn't get home on time?" her mother scolded. The daughter replied, "Her favorite doll got broken."

"Did you break it?" the mother asked. When her daughter shook her head "no," she then asked, "Could the doll be fixed?" Again, the girl replied with a "no." Both bewildered and frustrated, the mother asked a third time, "So what was the point of staying so long?"

Tears began to well up in the little girl's eyes and stream down her face under her mother's inquisition. "I helped her cry," she said softly.

The Scriptures tell us to "rejoice with those who rejoice, and weep with those who weep" (Romans 12:15). Mothers may not be able to do everything for their children, but we can all do that!

> And when she opened it, she saw the child, and behold, the baby wept. So she had compassion on him, and said, "This is one of the Hebrews' children."
>
> *Exodus 2:6*

he said to his people, "Look, the people of the children of Israel *are* more and mightier than we; ¹⁰ come, let us deal shrewdly with them, lest they multiply, and it happen, in the event of war, that they also join our enemies and fight against us, and *so* go up out of the land." ¹¹ Therefore they set taskmasters over them to afflict them with their burdens. And they built for Pharaoh supply cities, Pithom and Raamses. ¹² But the more they afflicted them, the more they multiplied and grew. And they were in dread of the children of Israel. ¹³ So the Egyptians made the children of Israel serve with rigor. ¹⁴ And they made their lives bitter with hard bondage—in mortar, in brick, and in all manner of service in the field. All their service in which they made them serve *was* with rigor.

¹⁵ Then the king of Egypt spoke to the Hebrew midwives, of whom the name of one *was* Shiphrah and the name of the other Puah; ¹⁶ and he said, "When you do the duties of a midwife for the Hebrew women, and see *them* on the birthstools, if it *is* a son, then you shall kill him; but if it *is* a daughter, then she shall live." ¹⁷ But the midwives feared God, and did not do as the king of Egypt commanded them, but saved the male children alive. ¹⁸ So the king of Egypt called for the midwives and said to them, "Why have you done this thing, and saved the male children alive?"

¹⁹ And the midwives said to Pharaoh, "Because the Hebrew women *are* not like the Egyptian women; for they *are* lively and give birth before the midwives come to them."

²⁰ Therefore God dealt well with the midwives, and the people multiplied and grew very mighty. ²¹ And so it was, because the midwives feared God, that He provided households for them.

²² So Pharaoh commanded all his people, saying, "Every son who is born you shall cast into the river, and every daughter you shall save alive."

2 And a man of the house of Levi went and took *as wife* a daughter of Levi. ² So the woman conceived and bore a son. And when she saw that he *was* a beautiful *child*, she hid him three months. ³ But when she could no longer hide him, she took an ark of bulrushes for him, daubed it with asphalt and pitch, put the child in it, and laid *it* in the reeds by the river's bank. ⁴ And his sister stood afar off, to know what would be done to him.

⁵ Then the daughter of Pharaoh came down to bathe at the river. And her maidens walked along the riverside; and when she saw the ark among the reeds, she sent her maid to get it. ⁶ And when she opened *it*, she saw the child, and behold, the baby wept. So she had compassion on him, and said, "This is one of the Hebrews' children."

⁷ Then his sister said to Pharaoh's daughter, "Shall I go and call a nurse for you from the Hebrew women, that she may nurse the child for you?"

⁸ And Pharaoh's daughter said to her, "Go." So the maiden went and called the child's mother. ⁹ Then Pharaoh's daughter said to her, "Take this child away and nurse him for me, and I will give *you* your wages." So the woman took the child and nursed him. ¹⁰ And the child grew, and she brought him to Pharaoh's daughter, and he became her son. So she called his name Moses, saying, "Because I drew him out of the water."

¹¹ Now it came to pass in those days, when Moses was grown, that he went out to his brethren and looked at their burdens. And he saw an Egyptian beating a Hebrew, one of his brethren. ¹² So he looked this way and that way, and when he saw no one, he killed the Egyptian and hid him in the sand. ¹³ And when he went out the second day, behold, two Hebrew men were fighting, and he said to the one who did the wrong, "Why are you striking your companion?"

¹⁴ Then he said, "Who made you a prince and a judge over us? Do you intend to kill me as you killed the Egyptian?"

So Moses feared and said, "Surely this thing is known!" ¹⁵ When Pharaoh heard of this matter, he sought to kill Moses. But Moses fled from the face of Pharaoh and dwelt in the land of Midian; and he sat down by a well.

¹⁶ Now the priest of Midian had seven daughters. And they came and drew water, and they filled the troughs to water

their father's flock. ¹⁷ Then the shepherds came and drove them away; but Moses stood up and helped them, and watered their flock.

¹⁸ When they came to Reuel their father, he said, "How *is it that* you have come so soon today?"

¹⁹ And they said, "An Egyptian delivered us from the hand of the shepherds, and he also drew enough water for us and watered the flock."

²⁰ So he said to his daughters, "And where *is* he? Why *is it that* you have left the man? Call him, that he may eat bread."

²¹ Then Moses was content to live with the man, and he gave Zipporah his daughter to Moses. ²² And she bore *him* a son. He called his name Gershom, for he said, "I have been a stranger in a foreign land."

²³ Now it happened in the process of time that the king of Egypt died. Then the children of Israel groaned because of the bondage, and they cried out; and their cry came up to God because of the bondage. ²⁴ So God heard their groaning, and God remembered His covenant with Abraham, with Isaac, and with Jacob. ²⁵ And God looked upon the children of Israel, and God acknowledged *them*.

∼ PSALM 15:1–5 ∼

1   Lord, who may abide in Your
        tabernacle?
    Who may dwell in Your holy hill?

2   He who walks uprightly,
        And works righteousness,
        And speaks the truth in his heart;

3   He *who* does not backbite with his
            tongue,
        Nor does evil to his neighbor,
        Nor does he take up a reproach
            against his friend;

4   In whose eyes a vile person is
            despised,
        But he honors those who fear the
            Lord;
    He *who* swears to his own hurt and
        does not change;

5   He *who* does not put out his money
        at usury,
        Nor does he take a bribe against
            the innocent.

He who does these *things* shall never be moved.

∼ PROVERBS 4:25–27 ∼

25 Let your eyes look straight ahead,
        And your eyelids look right before you.
26 Ponder the path of your feet,
        And let all your ways be established.
27 Do not turn to the right or the left;
        Remove your foot from evil.

∼ MATTHEW 17:1–27 ∼

Now after six days Jesus took Peter, James, and John his brother, led them up on a high mountain by themselves; ² and He was transfigured before them. His face shone like the sun, and His clothes became as white as the light. ³ And behold, Moses and Elijah appeared to them, talking with Him. ⁴ Then Peter answered and said to Jesus, "Lord, it is good for us to be here; if You wish, let us make here three tabernacles: one for You, one for Moses, and one for Elijah."

⁵ While he was still speaking, behold, a bright cloud overshadowed them; and suddenly a voice came out of the cloud, saying, "This is My beloved Son, in whom I am well pleased. Hear Him!" ⁶ And when the disciples heard *it*, they fell on their faces and were greatly afraid. ⁷ But Jesus came and touched them and said, "Arise, and do not be afraid." ⁸ When they had lifted up their eyes, they saw no one but Jesus only.

⁹ Now as they came down from the mountain, Jesus commanded them, saying, "Tell the vision to no one until the Son of Man is risen from the dead."

¹⁰ And His disciples asked Him, saying, "Why then do the scribes say that Elijah must come first?"

¹¹ Jesus answered and said to them, "Indeed, Elijah is coming first and will restore all things. ¹² But I say to you that Elijah has come already, and they did not know him but did to him whatever they wished. Likewise the Son of Man is also about to suffer at their hands." ¹³ Then the disciples understood that He spoke to them of John the Baptist.

¹⁴ And when they had come to the multitude, a man came to Him, kneeling down

to Him and saying, [15] "Lord, have mercy on my son, for he is an epileptic and suffers severely; for he often falls into the fire and often into the water. [16] So I brought him to Your disciples, but they could not cure him."

[17] Then Jesus answered and said, "O faithless and perverse generation, how long shall I be with you? How long shall I bear with you? Bring him here to Me." [18] And Jesus rebuked the demon, and it came out of him; and the child was cured from that very hour.

[19] Then the disciples came to Jesus privately and said, "Why could we not cast it out?"

[20] So Jesus said to them, "Because of your unbelief; for assuredly, I say to you, if you have faith as a mustard seed, you will say to this mountain, 'Move from here to there,' and it will move; and nothing will be impossible for you. [21] However, this kind does not go out except by prayer and fasting."

[22] Now while they were staying in Galilee, Jesus said to them, "The Son of Man is about to be betrayed into the hands of men, [23] and they will kill Him, and the third day He will be raised up." And they were exceedingly sorrowful.

[24] When they had come to Capernaum, those who received the *temple* tax came to Peter and said, "Does your Teacher not pay the *temple* tax?"

[25] He said, "Yes."

And when he had come into the house, Jesus anticipated him, saying, "What do you think, Simon? From whom do the kings of the earth take customs or taxes, from their sons or from strangers?"

[26] Peter said to Him, "From strangers."

Jesus said to him, "Then the sons are free. [27] Nevertheless, lest we offend them, go to the sea, cast in a hook, and take the fish that comes up first. And when you have opened its mouth, you will find a piece of money; take that and give it to them for Me and you."

∼ EXODUS 3:1—4:31 ∼

Now Moses was tending the flock of Jethro his father-in-law, the priest of Midian. And he led the flock to the back of the desert, and came to Horeb, the mountain of God. [2] And the Angel of the LORD appeared to him in a flame of fire from the midst of a bush. So he looked, and behold, the bush was burning with fire, but the bush *was* not consumed. [3] Then Moses said, "I will now turn aside and see this great sight, why the bush does not burn."

[4] So when the LORD saw that he turned aside to look, God called to him from the midst of the bush and said, "Moses, Moses!"

And he said, "Here I am."

[5] Then He said, "Do not draw near this place. Take your sandals off your feet, for the place where you stand *is* holy ground." [6] Moreover He said, "I *am* the God of your father—the God of Abraham, the God of Isaac, and the God of Jacob." And Moses hid his face, for he was afraid to look upon God.

[7] And the LORD said: "I have surely seen the oppression of My people who *are* in Egypt, and have heard their cry because of their taskmasters, for I know their sorrows. [8] So I have come down to deliver them out of the hand of the Egyptians, and to bring them up from that land to a good and large land, to a land flowing with milk and honey, to the place of the Canaanites and the Hittites and the Amorites and the Perizzites and the Hivites and the Jebusites. [9] Now therefore, behold, the cry of the children of Israel has come to Me, and I have also seen the oppression with which the Egyptians oppress them. [10] Come now, therefore, and I will send you to Pharaoh that you may bring My people, the children of Israel, out of Egypt."

[11] But Moses said to God, "Who *am* I that I should go to Pharaoh, and that I should bring the children of Israel out of Egypt?"

[12] So He said, "I will certainly be with you. And this *shall be* a sign to you that I have sent you: When you have brought

The Power of Teamwork

Debora Dempsey, captain of the transport ship *Lyra*, was glad to be home. The storm that raged off Cape Fear on January 26, 1993, was a sailor's nightmare. She thought she had seen her 634-ton ship for the last time the day it left Chesapeake Bay on its way to a buyer in New Orleans. Then Dempsey received a call. Northeast of Cape Fear, the *Lyra* had broken loose from its towline. The crewless ship — with 387,000 gallons of oil on board to run its engines — was being pushed toward land by the strong winds. An ecological disaster was in the making, not to mention the loss of the $22-million vessel. Dempsey and four volunteer crew members were called upon to save the ship and avert disaster.

Lowered from a helicopter onto the pitching deck, they immediately began to lower the two 5½-ton anchors. After they got the first anchor safely down, the generator failed. Without the aid of a power winch and only flashlights to see by, they finally got the second anchor down, stopping the ship's deadly drift. It was a dangerous mission, accomplished only by a strong team effort. Dempsey received the Admiralty of the Ocean Sea award, a high honor, for her leadership and courage.

Effort may be self-rewarding, but it is the accomplishment of a goal that brings recognition. Often the best way to *complete* the task is teamwork.

> For where two or three are gathered together in My name, I am there in the midst of them.
>
> *Matthew 18:20*

the people out of Egypt, you shall serve God on this mountain."

[13] Then Moses said to God, "Indeed, *when* I come to the children of Israel and say to them, 'The God of your fathers has sent me to you,' and they say to me, 'What *is* His name?' what shall I say to them?"

[14] And God said to Moses, "I AM WHO I AM." And He said, "Thus you shall say to the children of Israel, 'I AM has sent me to you.' " [15] Moreover God said to Moses, "Thus you shall say to the children of Israel: 'The LORD God of your fathers, the God of Abraham, the God of Isaac, and the God of Jacob, has sent me to you. This *is* My name forever, and this *is* My memorial to all generations.' [16] Go and gather the elders of Israel together, and say to them, 'The LORD God of your fathers, the God of Abraham, of Isaac, and of Jacob, appeared to me, saying, "I have surely visited you and *seen* what is done to you in Egypt; [17] and I have said I will bring you up out of the affliction of Egypt to the land of the Canaanites and the Hittites and the Amorites and the Perizzites and the Hivites and the Jebusites, to a land flowing with milk and honey." ' [18] Then they will heed your voice; and you shall come, you and the elders of Israel, to the king of Egypt; and you shall say to him, 'The LORD God of the Hebrews has met with us; and now, please, let us go three days' journey into the wilderness, that we may sacrifice to the LORD our God.' [19] But I am sure that the king of Egypt will not let you go, no, not even by a mighty hand. [20] So I will stretch out My hand and strike Egypt with all My wonders which I will do in its midst; and after that he will let you go. [21] And I will give this people favor in the sight of the Egyptians; and it shall be, when you go, that you shall not go empty-handed. [22] But every woman shall ask of her neighbor, namely, of her who dwells near her house, articles of silver, articles of gold, and clothing; and you shall put *them* on your sons and on your daughters. So you shall plunder the Egyptians."

4 Then Moses answered and said, "But suppose they will not believe me or listen to my voice; suppose they say, 'The LORD has not appeared to you.' "

[2] So the LORD said to him, "What *is* that in your hand?"

He said, "A rod."

[3] And He said, "Cast it on the ground." So he cast it on the ground, and it became a serpent; and Moses fled from it. [4] Then the LORD said to Moses, "Reach out your hand and take *it* by the tail" (and he reached out his hand and caught it, and it became a rod in his hand), [5] "that they may believe that the LORD God of their fathers, the God of Abraham, the God of Isaac, and the God of Jacob, has appeared to you."

[6] Furthermore the LORD said to him, "Now put your hand in your bosom." And he put his hand in his bosom, and when he took it out, behold, his hand *was* leprous, like snow. [7] And He said, "Put your hand in your bosom again." So he put his hand in his bosom again, and drew it out of his bosom, and behold, it was restored like his *other* flesh. [8] "Then it will be, if they do not believe you, nor heed the message of the first sign, that they may believe the message of the latter sign. [9] And it shall be, if they do not believe even these two signs, or listen to your voice, that you shall take water from the river and pour *it* on the dry *land*. The water which you take from the river will become blood on the dry *land*."

[10] Then Moses said to the LORD, "O my Lord, I *am* not eloquent, neither before nor since You have spoken to Your servant; but I *am* slow of speech and slow of tongue."

[11] So the LORD said to him, "Who has made man's mouth? Or who makes the mute, the deaf, the seeing, or the blind? *Have* not I, the LORD? [12] Now therefore, go, and I will be with your mouth and teach you what you shall say."

[13] But he said, "O my Lord, please send by the hand of whomever *else* You may send."

[14] So the anger of the LORD was kindled against Moses, and He said: "Is not Aaron the Levite your brother? I know that he can speak well. And look, he is also coming out to meet you. When he sees you, he will be glad in his heart. [15] Now you shall speak to him and put the words in his mouth. And I will be with your mouth and with his mouth, and I will teach you

what you shall do. ¹⁶ So he shall be your spokesman to the people. And he himself shall be as a mouth for you, and you shall be to him as God. ¹⁷ And you shall take this rod in your hand, with which you shall do the signs."

¹⁸ So Moses went and returned to Jethro his father-in-law, and said to him, "Please let me go and return to my brethren who *are* in Egypt, and see whether they are still alive."

And Jethro said to Moses, "Go in peace."

¹⁹ Now the LORD said to Moses in Midian, "Go, return to Egypt; for all the men who sought your life are dead." ²⁰ Then Moses took his wife and his sons and set them on a donkey, and he returned to the land of Egypt. And Moses took the rod of God in his hand.

²¹ And the LORD said to Moses, "When you go back to Egypt, see that you do all those wonders before Pharaoh which I have put in your hand. But I will harden his heart, so that he will not let the people go. ²² Then you shall say to Pharaoh, 'Thus says the LORD: "Israel *is* My son, My firstborn. ²³ So I say to you, let My son go that he may serve Me. But if you refuse to let him go, indeed I will kill your son, your firstborn." ' "

²⁴ And it came to pass on the way, at the encampment, that the LORD met him and sought to kill him. ²⁵ Then Zipporah took a sharp stone and cut off the foreskin of her son and cast *it* at *Moses'* feet, and said, "Surely you *are* a husband of blood to me!" ²⁶ So He let him go. Then she said, "*You are* a husband of blood!"— because of the circumcision.

²⁷ And the LORD said to Aaron, "Go into the wilderness to meet Moses." So he went and met him on the mountain of God, and kissed him. ²⁸ So Moses told Aaron all the words of the LORD who had sent him, and all the signs which He had commanded him. ²⁹ Then Moses and Aaron went and gathered together all the elders of the children of Israel. ³⁰ And Aaron spoke all the words which the LORD had spoken to Moses. Then he did the signs in the sight of the people. ³¹ So the people believed; and when they heard that the LORD had visited the children of Israel and that He had looked on their affliction,

then they bowed their heads and worshiped.

∼ PSALM 16:1–6 ∼

1   Preserve me, O God, for in You I put
    my trust.

2   *O my soul*, you have said to the
        LORD,
    "You *are* my Lord,
    My goodness is nothing apart from
        You."
3   As for the saints who *are* on the
        earth,
    "They are the excellent ones, in
        whom is all my delight."

4   Their sorrows shall be multiplied
        who hasten *after* another *god*;
    Their drink offerings of blood I will
        not offer,
    Nor take up their names on my lips.

5   O LORD, *You are* the portion of my
        inheritance and my cup;
    You maintain my lot.
6   The lines have fallen to me in
        pleasant *places*;
    Yes, I have a good inheritance.

∼ PROVERBS 5:1–6 ∼

1   My son, pay attention to my
        wisdom;
    Lend your ear to my understanding,
2   That you may preserve discretion,
    And your lips may keep knowledge.
3   For the lips of an immoral woman
        drip honey,
    And her mouth *is* smoother than oil;
4   But in the end she is bitter as
        wormwood,
    Sharp as a two-edged sword.
5   Her feet go down to death,
    Her steps lay hold of hell.
6   Lest you ponder *her* path of life—
    Her ways are unstable;
    You do not know *them*.

∼ MATTHEW 18:1–20 ∼

At that time the disciples came to Jesus, saying, "Who then is greatest in the kingdom of heaven?"

2 Then Jesus called a little child to Him, set him in the midst of them, 3 and said, "Assuredly, I say to you, unless you are converted and become as little children, you will by no means enter the kingdom of heaven. 4 Therefore whoever humbles himself as this little child is the greatest in the kingdom of heaven. 5 Whoever receives one little child like this in My name receives Me.

6 "Whoever causes one of these little ones who believe in Me to sin, it would be better for him if a millstone were hung around his neck, and he were drowned in the depth of the sea. 7 Woe to the world because of offenses! For offenses must come, but woe to that man by whom the offense comes!

8 "If your hand or foot causes you to sin, cut it off and cast *it* from you. It is better for you to enter into life lame or maimed, rather than having two hands or two feet, to be cast into the everlasting fire. 9 And if your eye causes you to sin, pluck it out and cast *it* from you. It is better for you to enter into life with one eye, rather than having two eyes, to be cast into hell fire.

10 "Take heed that you do not despise one of these little ones, for I say to you that in heaven their angels always see the face of My Father who is in heaven. 11 For the Son of Man has come to save that which was lost.

12 "What do you think? If a man has a hundred sheep, and one of them goes astray, does he not leave the ninety-nine and go to the mountains to seek the one that is straying? 13 And if he should find it, assuredly, I say to you, he rejoices more over that *sheep* than over the ninety-nine that did not go astray. 14 Even so it is not the will of your Father who is in heaven that one of these little ones should perish.

15 "Moreover if your brother sins against you, go and tell him his fault between you and him alone. If he hears you, you have gained your brother. 16 But if he will not hear, take with you one or two more, that 'by the mouth of two or three witnesses every word may be established.' 17 And if he refuses to hear them, tell *it* to the church. But if he refuses even to hear the church, let him be to you like a heathen and a tax collector.

18 "Assuredly, I say to you, whatever you bind on earth will be bound in heaven, and whatever you loose on earth will be loosed in heaven.

19 "Again I say to you that if two of you agree on earth concerning anything that they ask, it will be done for them by My Father in heaven. 20 For where two or three are gathered together in My name, I am there in the midst of them."

READING 28 · JANUARY 28

~ EXODUS 5:1—6:30 ~

Afterward Moses and Aaron went in and told Pharaoh, "Thus says the LORD God of Israel: 'Let My people go, that they may hold a feast to Me in the wilderness.'"

2 And Pharaoh said, "Who *is* the LORD, that I should obey His voice to let Israel go? I do not know the LORD, nor will I let Israel go."

3 So they said, "The God of the Hebrews has met with us. Please, let us go three days' journey into the desert and sacrifice to the LORD our God, lest He fall upon us with pestilence or with the sword."

4 Then the king of Egypt said to them, "Moses and Aaron, why do you take the people from their work? Get *back* to your labor." 5 And Pharaoh said, "Look, the people of the land *are* many now, and you make them rest from their labor!"

6 So the same day Pharaoh commanded the taskmasters of the people and their officers, saying, 7 "You shall no longer give the people straw to make brick as before. Let them go and gather straw for themselves. 8 And you shall lay on them the quota of bricks which they made before. You shall not reduce it. For they are idle; therefore they cry out, saying, 'Let us go *and* sacrifice to our God.' 9 Let more work be laid on the men, that they may labor in it, and let them not regard false words."

10 And the taskmasters of the people and

The Guide

In *A Slow and Certain Light*, Elisabeth Elliot writes: "When I lived in the forest of Ecuador I usually traveled on foot. . . . Trails often led through streams and rivers which we had to wade, but sometimes there was a log high above the water which we had to cross.

"I dreaded those logs and was always tempted to take the steep, hard way down into the ravine and up the other side. But the Indians would say, 'Just walk across, señorita,' and over they would go, light-footed and confident. I was barefoot as they were, but it was not enough. On the log, I couldn't keep from looking down at the river below. I knew I would slip. I had never been any good at balancing myself . . . so my guide would stretch out a hand, and the touch of it was all I needed. I stopped worrying about slipping. I stopped looking down at the river or even at the log and looked at the guide, who held my hand with only the lightest touch. When I reached the other side, I realized that if I had slipped he could not have held me. But his being there and his touch were all I needed."

A major source of comfort in prayer is simply realizing that God *is* present, gently guiding us along our way. Any fear of falling vanishes if we but keep our eyes on Him.

> You will show me the path of life; in Your presence is fullness of joy; at Your right hand are pleasures forevermore.
>
> *Psalm 16:11*

their officers went out and spoke to the people, saying, "Thus says Pharaoh: 'I will not give you straw. [11] Go, get yourselves straw where you can find it; yet none of your work will be reduced.'" [12] So the people were scattered abroad throughout all the land of Egypt to gather stubble instead of straw. [13] And the taskmasters forced *them* to hurry, saying, "Fulfill your work, *your* daily quota, as when there was straw." [14] Also the officers of the children of Israel, whom Pharaoh's taskmasters had set over them, were beaten *and* were asked, "Why have you not fulfilled your task in making brick both yesterday and today, as before?"

[15] Then the officers of the children of Israel came and cried out to Pharaoh, saying, "Why are you dealing thus with your servants? [16] There is no straw given to your servants, and they say to us, 'Make brick!' And indeed your servants *are* beaten, but the fault *is* in your *own* people."

[17] But he said, "You *are* idle! Idle! Therefore you say, 'Let us go *and* sacrifice to the LORD.' [18] Therefore go now *and* work; for no straw shall be given you, yet you shall deliver the quota of bricks." [19] And the officers of the children of Israel saw *that* they *were* in trouble after it was said, "You shall not reduce *any* bricks from your daily quota."

[20] Then, as they came out from Pharaoh, they met Moses and Aaron who stood there to meet them. [21] And they said to them, "Let the LORD look on you and judge, because you have made us abhorrent in the sight of Pharaoh and in the sight of his servants, to put a sword in their hand to kill us."

[22] So Moses returned to the LORD and said, "Lord, why have You brought trouble on this people? Why *is* it You have sent me? [23] For since I came to Pharaoh to speak in Your name, he has done evil to this people; neither have You delivered Your people at all."

6 Then the LORD said to Moses, "Now you shall see what I will do to Pharaoh. For with a strong hand he will let them go, and with a strong hand he will drive them out of his land."

[2] And God spoke to Moses and said to him: "I *am* the LORD. [3] I appeared to Abraham, to Isaac, and to Jacob, as God Almighty, but *by* My name LORD I was not known to them. [4] I have also established My covenant with them, to give them the land of Canaan, the land of their pilgrimage, in which they were strangers. [5] And I have also heard the groaning of the children of Israel whom the Egyptians keep in bondage, and I have remembered My covenant. [6] Therefore say to the children of Israel: 'I *am* the LORD; I will bring you out from under the burdens of the Egyptians, I will rescue you from their bondage, and I will redeem you with an outstretched arm and with great judgments. [7] I will take you as My people, and I will be your God. Then you shall know that I *am* the LORD your God who brings you out from under the burdens of the Egyptians. [8] And I will bring you into the land which I swore to give to Abraham, Isaac, and Jacob; and I will give it to you *as* a heritage: I *am* the LORD.'" [9] So Moses spoke thus to the children of Israel; but they did not heed Moses, because of anguish of spirit and cruel bondage.

[10] And the LORD spoke to Moses, saying, [11] "Go in, tell Pharaoh king of Egypt to let the children of Israel go out of his land."

[12] And Moses spoke before the LORD, saying, "The children of Israel have not heeded me. How then shall Pharaoh heed me, for I *am* of uncircumcised lips?"

[13] Then the LORD spoke to Moses and Aaron, and gave them a command for the children of Israel and for Pharaoh king of Egypt, to bring the children of Israel out of the land of Egypt.

[14] These *are* the heads of their fathers' houses: The sons of Reuben, the firstborn of Israel, *were* Hanoch, Pallu, Hezron, and Carmi. These are the families of Reuben. [15] And the sons of Simeon *were* Jemuel, Jamin, Ohad, Jachin, Zohar, and Shaul the son of a Canaanite woman. These *are* the families of Simeon. [16] These *are* the names of the sons of Levi according to their generations: Gershon, Kohath, and Merari. And the years of the life of Levi *were* one hundred and thirty-seven. [17] The sons of Gershon *were* Libni and Shimi according to their families. [18] And the sons of Kohath *were* Amram, Izhar, Hebron, and Uzziel. And the years of the life of

Kohath *were* one hundred and thirty-three. ¹⁹ The sons of Merari *were* Mahli and Mushi. These *are* the families of Levi according to their generations.

²⁰ Now Amram took for himself Jochebed, his father's sister, as wife; and she bore him Aaron and Moses. And the years of the life of Amram *were* one hundred and thirty-seven. ²¹ The sons of Izhar *were* Korah, Nepheg, and Zichri. ²² And the sons of Uzziel *were* Mishael, Elzaphan, and Zithri. ²³ Aaron took to himself Elisheba, daughter of Amminadab, sister of Nahshon, as wife; and she bore him Nadab, Abihu, Eleazar, and Ithamar. ²⁴ And the sons of Korah *were* Assir, Elkanah, and Abiasaph. These are the families of the Korahites. ²⁵ Eleazar, Aaron's son, took for himself one of the daughters of Putiel as wife; and she bore him Phinehas. These *are* the heads of the fathers' houses of the Levites according to their families.

²⁶ These *are the same* Aaron and Moses to whom the LORD said, "Bring out the children of Israel from the land of Egypt according to their armies." ²⁷ These *are* the ones who spoke to Pharaoh king of Egypt, to bring out the children of Israel from Egypt. These *are the same* Moses and Aaron.

²⁸ And it came to pass, on the day the LORD spoke to Moses in the land of Egypt, ²⁹ that the LORD spoke to Moses, saying, "I *am* the LORD. Speak to Pharaoh king of Egypt all that I say to you." ³⁰ But Moses said before the LORD, "Behold, I *am* of uncircumcised lips, and how shall Pharaoh heed me?"

~ PSALM 16:7–11 ~

⁷ I will bless the LORD who has given me counsel;
   My heart also instructs me in the night seasons.
⁸ I have set the LORD always before me;
   Because *He is* at my right hand I shall not be moved.

⁹ Therefore my heart is glad, and my glory rejoices;
   My flesh also will rest in hope.

¹⁰ For You will not leave my soul in Sheol,
   Nor will You allow Your Holy One to see corruption.
¹¹ You will show me the path of life;
   In Your presence *is* fullness of joy;
   At Your right hand *are* pleasures forevermore.

~ PROVERBS 5:7–14 ~

⁷ Therefore hear me now, *my* children,
   And do not depart from the words of my mouth.
⁸ Remove your way far from her,
   And do not go near the door of her house,
⁹ Lest you give your honor to others,
   And your years to the cruel *one;*
¹⁰ Lest aliens be filled with your wealth,
   And your labors *go* to the house of a foreigner;
¹¹ And you mourn at last,
   When your flesh and your body are consumed,
¹² And say:
   "How I have hated instruction,
   And my heart despised correction!
¹³ I have not obeyed the voice of my teachers,
   Nor inclined my ear to those who instructed me!
¹⁴ I was on the verge of total ruin,
   In the midst of the assembly and congregation."

~ MATTHEW 18:21–35 ~

Then Peter came to Him and said, "Lord, how often shall my brother sin against me, and I forgive him? Up to seven times?" ²² Jesus said to him, "I do not say to you, up to seven times, but up to seventy times seven. ²³ Therefore the kingdom of heaven is like a certain king who wanted to settle accounts with his servants. ²⁴ And when he had begun to settle accounts, one was brought to him who owed him ten thousand talents. ²⁵ But as he was not able to pay, his master commanded that he be sold, with his wife and children and all that he had, and that payment be made. ²⁶ The servant therefore fell down before him, saying, 'Master, have patience with me, and I will pay you all.' ²⁷ Then the master of that servant was moved with compassion, released him, and forgave him the debt.

²⁸ "But that servant went out and found one of his fellow servants who owed him a hundred denarii; and he laid hands on him and took *him* by the throat, saying, 'Pay me what you owe!' ²⁹ So his fellow servant fell down at his feet and begged him, saying, 'Have patience with me, and I will pay you all.' ³⁰ And he would not, but went and threw him into prison till he should pay the debt. ³¹ So when his fellow servants saw what had been done, they were very grieved, and came and told their master all that had been done. ³² Then his master, after he had called him, said to him, 'You wicked servant! I forgave you all that debt because you begged me. ³³ Should you not also have had compassion on your fellow servant, just as I had pity on you?' ³⁴ And his master was angry, and delivered him to the torturers until he should pay all that was due to him.

³⁵ "So My heavenly Father also will do to you if each of you, from his heart, does not forgive his brother his trespasses."

READING 29 · JANUARY 29

~ EXODUS 7:1—8:32 ~

So the LORD said to Moses: "See, I have made you *as* God to Pharaoh, and Aaron your brother shall be your prophet. ² You shall speak all that I command you. And Aaron your brother shall tell Pharaoh to send the children of Israel out of his land. ³ And I will harden Pharaoh's heart, and multiply My signs and My wonders in the land of Egypt. ⁴ But Pharaoh will not heed you, so that I may lay My hand on Egypt and bring My armies *and* My people, the children of Israel, out of the land of Egypt by great judgments. ⁵ And the Egyptians shall know that I *am* the LORD, when I stretch out My hand on Egypt and bring out the children of Israel from among them."

⁶ Then Moses and Aaron did *so;* just as the LORD commanded them, so they did. ⁷ And Moses *was* eighty years old and Aaron eighty-three years old when they spoke to Pharaoh.

⁸ Then the LORD spoke to Moses and Aaron, saying, ⁹ "When Pharaoh speaks to you, saying, 'Show a miracle for yourselves,' then you shall say to Aaron, 'Take your rod and cast *it* before Pharaoh, *and* let it become a serpent.' " ¹⁰ So Moses and Aaron went in to Pharaoh, and they did so, just as the LORD commanded. And Aaron cast down his rod before Pharaoh and before his servants, and it became a serpent. ¹¹ But Pharaoh also called the wise men and the sorcerers; so the magicians of Egypt, they also did in like manner with their enchantments. ¹² For every man threw down his rod, and they became serpents. But Aaron's rod swallowed up their rods. ¹³ And Pharaoh's heart grew hard, and he did not heed them, as the LORD had said.

¹⁴ So the LORD said to Moses: "Pharaoh's heart *is* hard; he refuses to let the people go. ¹⁵ Go to Pharaoh in the morning, when he goes out to the water, and you shall stand by the river's bank to meet him; and the rod which was turned to a serpent you shall take in your hand. ¹⁶ And you shall say to him, 'The LORD God of the Hebrews has sent me to you, saying, "Let My people go, that they may serve Me in the wilderness"; but indeed, until now you would not hear! ¹⁷ Thus says the LORD: "By this you shall know that I *am* the LORD. Behold, I will strike the waters which *are* in the river with the rod that *is* in my hand, and they shall be turned to blood. ¹⁸ And the fish that *are* in the river shall die, the river shall stink, and the Egyptians will loathe to drink the water of the river." ' "

¹⁹ Then the LORD spoke to Moses, "Say to Aaron, 'Take your rod and stretch out your hand over the waters of Egypt, over their streams, over their rivers, over their ponds, and over all their pools of water, that they may become blood. And there

Complaining Against God

In *The Pursuit of Holiness*, Jerry Bridges has written: "I still vividly recall how God first dealt with me over twenty-five years ago about complaining against Him. In response to His will, I had settled in San Diego, California, and had begun to look for a job. When several weeks went by without success, I mentally began to accuse God. 'After all, I gave up my plans to do His will and now He has let me down.' God graciously directed my attention to Job 34:18-19: 'Is it fitting to say to a king, "You are worthless," And to nobles, "You are wicked"? Yet He is not partial to princes, Nor does He regard the rich more than the poor; For they are all the work of His hands.'

"As soon as I read that passage I immediately fell to my knees, confessing to Him my terrible sin of complaining and questioning His holiness. God mercifully forgave and the next day I received two job offers."

God graciously directs our paths. The One Who placed you on the path is the One Who steadies your steps upon it.

If your life is not turning out the way you had planned . . .

If your day seems to be haphazard and out of control . . .

If your hour isn't as productive as you had desired . . .

If you can't seem to find peace . . .

It's time to pray.

shall be blood throughout all the land of Egypt, both in *buckets of* wood and *pitchers of* stone.' " ²⁰ And Moses and Aaron did so, just as the LORD commanded. So he lifted up the rod and struck the waters that *were* in the river, in the sight of Pharaoh and in the sight of his servants. And all the waters that *were* in the river were turned to blood. ²¹ The fish that *were* in the river died, the river stank, and the Egyptians could not drink the water of the river. So there was blood throughout all the land of Egypt.

²² Then the magicians of Egypt did so with their enchantments; and Pharaoh's heart grew hard, and he did not heed them, as the LORD had said. ²³ And Pharaoh turned and went into his house. Neither was his heart moved by this. ²⁴ So all the Egyptians dug all around the river for water to drink, because they could not drink the water of the river. ²⁵ And seven days passed after the LORD had struck the river.

8 And the LORD spoke to Moses, "Go to Pharaoh and say to him, 'Thus says the LORD: "Let My people go, that they may serve Me. ² But if you refuse to let *them* go, behold, I will smite all your territory with frogs. ³ So the river shall bring forth frogs abundantly, which shall go up and come into your house, into your bedroom, on your bed, into the houses of your servants, on your people, into your ovens, and into your kneading bowls. ⁴ And the frogs shall come up on you, on your people, and on all your servants." ' "

⁵ Then the LORD spoke to Moses, "Say to Aaron, 'Stretch out your hand with your rod over the streams, over the rivers, and over the ponds, and cause frogs to come up on the land of Egypt.' " ⁶ So Aaron stretched out his hand over the waters of Egypt, and the frogs came up and covered the land of Egypt. ⁷ And the magicians did so with their enchantments, and brought up frogs on the land of Egypt.

⁸ Then Pharaoh called for Moses and Aaron, and said, "Entreat the LORD that He may take away the frogs from me and from my people; and I will let the people go, that they may sacrifice to the LORD."

⁹ And Moses said to Pharaoh, "Accept the honor of saying when I shall inter-cede for you, for your servants, and for your people, to destroy the frogs from you and your houses, *that* they may remain in the river only."

¹⁰ So he said, "Tomorrow." And he said, "*Let it be* according to your word, that you may know that *there is* no one like the LORD our God. ¹¹ And the frogs shall depart from you, from your houses, from your servants, and from your people. They shall remain in the river only."

¹² Then Moses and Aaron went out from Pharaoh. And Moses cried out to the LORD concerning the frogs which He had brought against Pharaoh. ¹³ So the LORD did according to the word of Moses. And the frogs died out of the houses, out of the courtyards, and out of the fields. ¹⁴ They gathered them together in heaps, and the land stank. ¹⁵ But when Pharaoh saw that there was relief, he hardened his heart and did not heed them, as the LORD had said.

¹⁶ So the LORD said to Moses, "Say to Aaron, 'Stretch out your rod, and strike the dust of the land, so that it may become lice throughout all the land of Egypt.' " ¹⁷ And they did so. For Aaron stretched out his hand with his rod and struck the dust of the earth, and it became lice on man and beast. All the dust of the land became lice throughout all the land of Egypt.

¹⁸ Now the magicians so worked with their enchantments to bring forth lice, but they could not. So there were lice on man and beast. ¹⁹ Then the magicians said to Pharaoh, "This *is* the finger of God." But Pharaoh's heart grew hard, and he did not heed them, just as the LORD had said.

²⁰ And the LORD said to Moses, "Rise early in the morning and stand before Pharaoh as he comes out to the water. Then say to him, 'Thus says the LORD: "Let My people go, that they may serve Me. ²¹ Or else, if you will not let My people go, behold, I will send swarms *of flies* on you and your servants, on your people and into your houses. The houses of the Egyptians shall be full of swarms *of flies,* and also the ground on which they *stand.* ²² And in that day I will set apart the land of Goshen, in which My people dwell, that no swarms *of flies* shall be there, in order that you may know that I

am the LORD in the midst of the land. ²³ I will make a difference between My people and your people. Tomorrow this sign shall be." ' " ²⁴ And the LORD did so. Thick swarms *of flies* came into the house of Pharaoh, *into* his servants' houses, and into all the land of Egypt. The land was corrupted because of the swarms *of flies*.

²⁵ Then Pharaoh called for Moses and Aaron, and said, "Go, sacrifice to your God in the land."

²⁶ And Moses said, "It is not right to do so, for we would be sacrificing the abomination of the Egyptians to the LORD our God. If we sacrifice the abomination of the Egyptians before their eyes, then will they not stone us? ²⁷ We will go three days' journey into the wilderness and sacrifice to the LORD our God as He will command us."

²⁸ So Pharaoh said, "I will let you go, that you may sacrifice to the LORD your God in the wilderness; only you shall not go very far away. Intercede for me."

²⁹ Then Moses said, "Indeed I am going out from you, and I will entreat the LORD, that the swarms *of flies* may depart tomorrow from Pharaoh, from his servants, and from his people. But let Pharaoh not deal deceitfully anymore in not letting the people go to sacrifice to the LORD."

³⁰ So Moses went out from Pharaoh and entreated the LORD. ³¹ And the LORD did according to the word of Moses; He removed the swarms *of flies* from Pharaoh, from his servants, and from his people. Not one remained. ³² But Pharaoh hardened his heart at this time also; neither would he let the people go.

∼ PSALM 17:1–7 ∼

1 Hear a just cause, O LORD,
   Attend to my cry;
   Give ear to my prayer *which is* not
   from deceitful lips.
2 Let my vindication come from Your
   presence;
   Let Your eyes look on the things that
   are upright.

3 You have tested my heart;
   You have visited *me* in the night;
   You have tried me and have found
   nothing;
   I have purposed that my mouth shall
   not transgress.
4 Concerning the works of men,
   By the word of Your lips,
   I have kept away from the paths of
   the destroyer.
5 Uphold my steps in Your paths,
   That my footsteps may not slip.

6 I have called upon You, for You will
   hear me, O God;
   Incline Your ear to me, *and* hear my
   speech.
7 Show Your marvelous lovingkindness
   by Your right hand,
   O You who save those who trust *in
   You*
   From those who rise up *against
   them.*

∼ PROVERBS 5:15–20 ∼

15 Drink water from your own cistern,
    And running water from your own
    well.
16 Should your fountains be dispersed
    abroad,
    Streams of water in the streets?
17 Let them be only your own,
    And not for strangers with you.
18 Let your fountain be blessed,
    And rejoice with the wife of your
    youth.
19 *As a* loving deer and a graceful doe,
    Let her breasts satisfy you at all
    times;
    And always be enraptured with her
    love.
20 For why should you, my son, be
    enraptured by an immoral
    woman,
    And be embraced in the arms of a
    seductress?

∼ MATTHEW 19:1–30 ∼

Now it came to pass, when Jesus had finished these sayings, *that* He departed from Galilee and came to the region of Judea beyond the Jordan. ² And great multitudes followed Him, and He healed them there.

³ The Pharisees also came to Him, testing Him, and saying to Him, "Is it lawful

for a man to divorce his wife for *just* any reason?"

⁴ And He answered and said to them, "Have you not read that He who made *them* at the beginning 'made them male and female,' ⁵ and said, 'For this reason a man shall leave his father and mother and be joined to his wife, and the two shall become one flesh' ? ⁶ So then, they are no longer two but one flesh. Therefore what God has joined together, let not man separate."

⁷ They said to Him, "Why then did Moses command to give a certificate of divorce, and to put her away?"

⁸ He said to them, "Moses, because of the hardness of your hearts, permitted you to divorce your wives, but from the beginning it was not so. ⁹ And I say to you, whoever divorces his wife, except for sexual immorality, and marries another, commits adultery; and whoever marries her who is divorced commits adultery."

¹⁰ His disciples said to Him, "If such is the case of the man with *his* wife, it is better not to marry."

¹¹ But He said to them, "All cannot accept this saying, but only *those* to whom it has been given: ¹² For there are eunuchs who were born thus from *their* mother's womb, and there are eunuchs who were made eunuchs by men, and there are eunuchs who have made themselves eunuchs for the kingdom of heaven's sake. He who is able to accept *it,* let him accept *it."*

¹³ Then little children were brought to Him that He might put *His* hands on them and pray, but the disciples rebuked them. ¹⁴ But Jesus said, "Let the little children come to Me, and do not forbid them; for of such is the kingdom of heaven." ¹⁵ And He laid *His* hands on them and departed from there.

¹⁶ Now behold, one came and said to Him, "Good Teacher, what good thing shall I do that I may have eternal life?"

¹⁷ So He said to him, "Why do you call Me good? No one *is* good but One, *that is,* God. But if you want to enter into life, keep the commandments."

¹⁸ He said to Him, "Which ones?"

Jesus said, " 'You shall not murder,' 'You shall not commit adultery,' 'You shall not steal,' 'You shall not bear false witness,' ¹⁹ 'Honor your father and your mother,' and, 'You shall love your neighbor as yourself.' "

²⁰ The young man said to Him, "All these things I have kept from my youth. What do I still lack?"

²¹ Jesus said to him, "If you want to be perfect, go, sell what you have and give to the poor, and you will have treasure in heaven; and come, follow Me."

²² But when the young man heard that saying, he went away sorrowful, for he had great possessions.

²³ Then Jesus said to His disciples, "Assuredly, I say to you that it is hard for a rich man to enter the kingdom of heaven. ²⁴ And again I say to you, it is easier for a camel to go through the eye of a needle than for a rich man to enter the kingdom of God."

²⁵ When His disciples heard *it,* they were greatly astonished, saying, "Who then can be saved?"

²⁶ But Jesus looked at *them* and said to them, "With men this is impossible, but with God all things are possible."

²⁷ Then Peter answered and said to Him, "See, we have left all and followed You. Therefore what shall we have?"

²⁸ So Jesus said to them, "Assuredly I say to you, that in the regeneration, when the Son of Man sits on the throne of His glory, you who have followed Me will also sit on twelve thrones, judging the twelve tribes of Israel. ²⁹ And everyone who has left houses or brothers or sisters or father or mother or wife or children or lands, for My name's sake, shall receive a hundredfold, and inherit eternal life. ³⁰ But many *who are* first will be last, and the last first.

~ EXODUS 9:1—10:29 ~

Then the LORD said to Moses, "Go in to Pharaoh and tell him, 'Thus says the LORD God of the Hebrews: "Let My people go, that they may serve Me. ² For if you refuse to let *them* go, and still hold them, ³ behold, the hand of the LORD will be on your cattle in the field, on the horses, on the donkeys, on the camels, on the oxen, and on the sheep—a very severe pestilence. ⁴ And the LORD will make a difference between the livestock of Israel and the livestock of Egypt. So nothing shall die of all *that* belongs to the children of Israel." ' " ⁵ Then the LORD appointed a set time, saying, "Tomorrow the LORD will do this thing in the land."

⁶ So the LORD did this thing on the next day, and all the livestock of Egypt died; but of the livestock of the children of Israel, not one died. ⁷ Then Pharaoh sent, and indeed, not even one of the livestock of the Israelites was dead. But the heart of Pharaoh became hard, and he did not let the people go.

⁸ So the LORD said to Moses and Aaron, "Take for yourselves handfuls of ashes from a furnace, and let Moses scatter it toward the heavens in the sight of Pharaoh. ⁹ And it will become fine dust in all the land of Egypt, and it will cause boils that break out in sores on man and beast throughout all the land of Egypt." ¹⁰ Then they took ashes from the furnace and stood before Pharaoh, and Moses scattered *them* toward heaven. And *they* caused boils that break out in sores on man and beast. ¹¹ And the magicians could not stand before Moses because of the boils, for the boils were on the magicians and on all the Egyptians. ¹² But the LORD hardened the heart of Pharaoh; and he did not heed them, just as the LORD had spoken to Moses.

¹³ Then the LORD said to Moses, "Rise early in the morning and stand before Pharaoh, and say to him, 'Thus says the LORD God of the Hebrews: "Let My people go, that they may serve Me, ¹⁴ for at this time I will send all My plagues to your very heart, and on your servants and on your people, that you may know that

there is none like Me in all the earth. ¹⁵ Now if I had stretched out My hand and struck you and your people with pestilence, then you would have been cut off from the earth. ¹⁶ But indeed for this *purpose* I have raised you up, that I may show My power *in* you, and that My name may be declared in all the earth. ¹⁷ As yet you exalt yourself against My people in that you will not let them go. ¹⁸ Behold, tomorrow about this time I will cause very heavy hail to rain down, such as has not been in Egypt since its founding until now. ¹⁹ Therefore send now *and* gather your livestock and all that you have in the field, for the hail shall come down on every man and every animal which is found in the field and is not brought home; and they shall die." ' "

²⁰ He who feared the word of the LORD among the servants of Pharaoh made his servants and his livestock flee to the houses. ²¹ But he who did not regard the word of the LORD left his servants and his livestock in the field.

²² Then the LORD said to Moses, "Stretch out your hand toward heaven, that there may be hail in all the land of Egypt—on man, on beast, and on every herb of the field, throughout the land of Egypt." ²³ And Moses stretched out his rod toward heaven; and the LORD sent thunder and hail, and fire darted to the ground. And the LORD rained hail on the land of Egypt. ²⁴ So there was hail, and fire mingled with the hail, so very heavy that there was none like it in all the land of Egypt since it became a nation. ²⁵ And the hail struck throughout the whole land of Egypt, all that *was* in the field, both man and beast; and the hail struck every herb of the field and broke every tree of the field. ²⁶ Only in the land of Goshen, where the children of Israel *were,* there was no hail.

²⁷ And Pharaoh sent and called for Moses and Aaron, and said to them, "I have sinned this time. The LORD *is* righteous, and my people and I *are* wicked. ²⁸ Entreat the LORD, that there may be no *more* mighty thundering and hail, for *it is* enough. I will let you go, and you shall stay no longer."

²⁹ So Moses said to him, "As soon as I have gone out of the city, I will spread out my hands to the LORD; the thunder will cease, and there will be no more hail, that you may know that the earth *is* the LORD's. ³⁰ But as for you and your servants, I know that you will not yet fear the LORD God."

³¹ Now the flax and the barley were struck, for the barley *was* in the head and the flax *was* in bud. ³² But the wheat and the spelt were not struck, for they *are* late crops.

³³ So Moses went out of the city from Pharaoh and spread out his hands to the LORD; then the thunder and the hail ceased, and the rain was not poured on the earth. ³⁴ And when Pharaoh saw that the rain, the hail, and the thunder had ceased, he sinned yet more; and he hardened his heart, he and his servants. ³⁵ So the heart of Pharaoh was hard; neither would he let the children of Israel go, as the LORD had spoken by Moses.

10 Now the LORD said to Moses, "Go in to Pharaoh; for I have hardened his heart and the hearts of his servants, that I may show these signs of Mine before him, ² and that you may tell in the hearing of your son and your son's son the mighty things I have done in Egypt, and My signs which I have done among them, that you may know that I *am* the LORD."

³ So Moses and Aaron came in to Pharaoh and said to him, "Thus says the LORD God of the Hebrews: 'How long will you refuse to humble yourself before Me? Let My people go, that they may serve Me. ⁴ Or else, if you refuse to let My people go, behold, tomorrow I will bring locusts into your territory. ⁵ And they shall cover the face of the earth, so that no one will be able to see the earth; and they shall eat the residue of what is left, which remains to you from the hail, and they shall eat every tree which grows up for you out of the field. ⁶ They shall fill your houses, the houses of all your servants, and the houses of all the Egyptians—which neither your fathers nor your fathers' fathers have seen, since the day that they were on the earth to this day.' " And he turned and went out from Pharaoh.

⁷ Then Pharaoh's servants said to him, "How long shall this man be a snare to us? Let the men go, that they may serve the LORD their God. Do you not yet know that Egypt is destroyed?"

⁸ So Moses and Aaron were brought again to Pharaoh, and he said to them, "Go, serve the LORD your God. Who *are* the ones that are going?"

⁹ And Moses said, "We will go with our young and our old; with our sons and our daughters, with our flocks and our herds we will go, for we must hold a feast to the LORD."

¹⁰ Then he said to them, "The LORD had better be with you when I let you and your little ones go! Beware, for evil is ahead of you. ¹¹ Not so! Go now, you *who are* men, and serve the LORD, for that is what you desired." And they were driven out from Pharaoh's presence.

¹² Then the LORD said to Moses, "Stretch out your hand over the land of Egypt for the locusts, that they may come upon the land of Egypt, and eat every herb of the land—all that the hail has left." ¹³ So Moses stretched out his rod over the land of Egypt, and the LORD brought an east wind on the land all that day and all *that* night. When it was morning, the east wind brought the locusts. ¹⁴ And the locusts went up over all the land of Egypt and rested on all the territory of Egypt. *They were* very severe; previously there had been no such locusts as they, nor shall there be such after them. ¹⁵ For they covered the face of the whole earth, so that the land was darkened; and they ate every herb of the land and all the fruit of the trees which the hail had left. So there remained nothing green on the trees or on the plants of the field throughout all the land of Egypt.

¹⁶ Then Pharaoh called for Moses and Aaron in haste, and said, "I have sinned against the LORD your God and against you. ¹⁷ Now therefore, please forgive my sin only this once, and entreat the LORD your God, that He may take away from me this death only." ¹⁸ So he went out from Pharaoh and entreated the LORD. ¹⁹ And the LORD turned a very strong west wind, which took the locusts away and blew them into the Red Sea. There remained not one locust in all the territory

Making our Best Better

Johann Olav Koss was a star at the 1994 Winter Olympic Games at Lillehammer, Norway. A hometown favorite, he skated his way to three gold medals and three world records in the 1,500-, 5,000-, and 10,000-meter races. Perhaps no one was as surprised as Koss when he won his first medal. He said, "There was so much joy over this gold medal that it made me think a little bit before the next race . . . I decided, if this will happen to me again, I want to give the bonus that I get to Olympic Aid. . . . It made me strong, I think, to be skating for someone else."

At a press conference after winning the second gold medal, Koss made his announcement: He would donate all his bonus money from equipment sponsors and the Norwegian Olympic Committee to Olympic Aid — a gift of more than $175,000. Koss challenged his countrymen to donate 10 kroner ($1.37US) for every Norwegian gold medal. The response was tremendous, more than $200,000 was raised during the games and up to a million dollars came in afterward.

Koss, who entered medical school after the Olympics, was surprised by all the fuss he had caused. Helping children and the less fortunate was not only his future career, it was his nature.

Our best efforts become even better when we perform for the benefit of others, rather than for our own gain.

of Egypt. ²⁰ But the LORD hardened Pharaoh's heart, and he did not let the children of Israel go.

²¹ Then the LORD said to Moses, "Stretch out your hand toward heaven, that there may be darkness over the land of Egypt, darkness *which* may even be felt." ²² So Moses stretched out his hand toward heaven, and there was thick darkness in all the land of Egypt three days. ²³ They did not see one another; nor did anyone rise from his place for three days. But all the children of Israel had light in their dwellings.

²⁴ Then Pharaoh called to Moses and said, "Go, serve the LORD; only let your flocks and your herds be kept back. Let your little ones also go with you."

²⁵ But Moses said, "You must also give us sacrifices and burnt offerings, that we may sacrifice to the LORD our God. ²⁶ Our livestock also shall go with us; not a hoof shall be left behind. For we must take some of them to serve the LORD our God, and even we do not know with what we must serve the LORD until we arrive there."

²⁷ But the LORD hardened Pharaoh's heart, and he would not let them go. ²⁸ Then Pharaoh said to him, "Get away from me! Take heed to yourself and see my face no more! For in the day you see my face you shall die!"

²⁹ So Moses said, "You have spoken well. I will never see your face again."

∼ PSALM 17:8–15 ∼

⁸ Keep me as the apple of Your eye;
   Hide me under the shadow of Your wings,
⁹ From the wicked who oppress me,
   From my deadly enemies who surround me.

¹⁰ They have closed up their fat *hearts;*
   With their mouths they speak proudly.
¹¹ They have now surrounded us in our steps;
   They have set their eyes, crouching down to the earth,
¹² As a lion is eager to tear his prey,
   And like a young lion lurking in secret places.

¹³ Arise, O LORD,
   Confront him, cast him down;
   Deliver my life from the wicked with Your sword,
¹⁴ With Your hand from men, O LORD,
   From men of the world *who have* their portion in *this* life,
   And whose belly You fill with Your hidden treasure.
   They are satisfied with children,
   And leave the rest of their *possession* for their babes.

¹⁵ As for me, I will see Your face in righteousness;
   I shall be satisfied when I awake in Your likeness.

∼ PROVERBS 5:21–23 ∼

²¹ For the ways of man *are* before the eyes of the LORD,
   And He ponders all his paths.
²² His own iniquities entrap the wicked *man,*
   And he is caught in the cords of his sin.
²³ He shall die for lack of instruction,
   And in the greatness of his folly he shall go astray.

∼ MATTHEW 20:1–16 ∼

"For the kingdom of heaven is like a landowner who went out early in the morning to hire laborers for his vineyard. ² Now when he had agreed with the laborers for a denarius a day, he sent them into his vineyard. ³ And he went out about the third hour and saw others standing idle in the marketplace, ⁴ and said to them, 'You also go into the vineyard, and whatever is right I will give you.' So they went. ⁵ Again he went out about the sixth and the ninth hour, and did likewise. ⁶ And about the eleventh hour he went out and found others standing idle, and said to them, 'Why have you been standing here idle all day?' ⁷ They said to him, 'Because no one hired us.' He said to them, 'You also go into the vineyard, and whatever is right you will receive.'

⁸ "So when evening had come, the owner of the vineyard said to his steward, 'Call the laborers and give them *their* wages,

beginning with the last to the first.' ⁹ And when those came who *were hired* about the eleventh hour, they each received a denarius. ¹⁰ But when the first came, they supposed that they would receive more; and they likewise received each a denarius. ¹¹ And when they had received *it*, they complained against the landowner, ¹² saying, 'These last *men* have worked *only* one hour, and you made them equal to us who have borne the burden and the heat of the day.' ¹³ But he answered one of them and said, 'Friend, I am doing you no wrong. Did you not agree with me for a denarius? ¹⁴ Take *what is* yours and go your way. I wish to give to this last man *the same* as to you. ¹⁵ Is it not lawful for me to do what I wish with my own things? Or is your eye evil because I am good?' ¹⁶ So the last will be first, and the first last. For many are called, but few chosen."

~ EXODUS 11:1—12:51 ~

And the LORD said to Moses, "I will bring one more plague on Pharaoh and on Egypt. Afterward he will let you go from here. When he lets *you* go, he will surely drive you out of here altogether. ² Speak now in the hearing of the people, and let every man ask from his neighbor and every woman from her neighbor, articles of silver and articles of gold." ³ And the LORD gave the people favor in the sight of the Egyptians. Moreover the man Moses *was* very great in the land of Egypt, in the sight of Pharaoh's servants and in the sight of the people.

⁴ Then Moses said, "Thus says the LORD: 'About midnight I will go out into the midst of Egypt; ⁵ and all the firstborn in the land of Egypt shall die, from the firstborn of Pharaoh who sits on his throne, even to the firstborn of the female servant who *is* behind the handmill, and all the firstborn of the animals. ⁶ Then there shall be a great cry throughout all the land of Egypt, such as was not like it *before,* nor shall be like it again. ⁷ But against none of the children of Israel shall a dog move its tongue, against man or beast, that you may know that the LORD does make a difference between the Egyptians and Israel.' ⁸ And all these your servants shall come down to me and bow down to me, saying, 'Get out, and all the people who follow you!' After that I will go out." Then he went out from Pharaoh in great anger.

⁹ But the LORD said to Moses, "Pharaoh will not heed you, so that My wonders may be multiplied in the land of Egypt." ¹⁰ So Moses and Aaron did all these wonders before Pharaoh; and the LORD hardened Pharaoh's heart, and he did not let the children of Israel go out of his land.

12 Now the LORD spoke to Moses and Aaron in the land of Egypt, saying, ² "This month *shall be* your beginning of months; it *shall be* the first month of the year to you. ³ Speak to all the congregation of Israel, saying: 'On the tenth of this month every man shall take for himself a lamb, according to the house of *his* father, a lamb for a household. ⁴ And if the household is too small for the lamb, let him and his neighbor next to his house take *it* according to the number of the persons; according to each man's need you shall make your count for the lamb. ⁵ Your lamb shall be without blemish, a male of the first year. You may take *it* from the sheep or from the goats. ⁶ Now you shall keep it until the fourteenth day of the same month. Then the whole assembly of the congregation of Israel shall kill it at twilight. ⁷ And they shall take *some* of the blood and put *it* on the two doorposts and on the lintel of the houses where they eat it. ⁸ Then they shall eat the flesh on that night; roasted in fire, with unleavened bread *and* with bitter *herbs* they shall eat it. ⁹ Do not eat it raw, nor boiled at all with water, but roasted in fire—its head with its legs and its entrails. ¹⁰ You shall let none of it remain until morning, and what remains of it until morning you shall burn with fire. ¹¹ And thus you shall eat

it: *with* a belt on your waist, your sandals on your feet, and your staff in your hand. So you shall eat it in haste. It *is* the LORD's Passover.

¹² 'For I will pass through the land of Egypt on that night, and will strike all the firstborn in the land of Egypt, both man and beast; and against all the gods of Egypt I will execute judgment: I *am* the LORD. ¹³ Now the blood shall be a sign for you on the houses where you *are*. And when I see the blood, I will pass over you; and the plague shall not be on you to destroy *you* when I strike the land of Egypt.

¹⁴ "So this day shall be to you a memorial; and you shall keep it as a feast to the LORD throughout your generations. You shall keep it as a feast by an everlasting ordinance. ¹⁵ Seven days you shall eat unleavened bread. On the first day you shall remove leaven from your houses. For whoever eats leavened bread from the first day until the seventh day, that person shall be cut off from Israel. ¹⁶ On the first day *there shall be* a holy convocation, and on the seventh day there shall be a holy convocation for you. No manner of work shall be done on them; but *that* which everyone must eat—that only may be prepared by you. ¹⁷ So you shall observe *the Feast of* Unleavened Bread, for on this same day I will have brought your armies out of the land of Egypt. Therefore you shall observe this day throughout your generations as an everlasting ordinance. ¹⁸ In the first *month,* on the fourteenth day of the month at evening, you shall eat unleavened bread, until the twenty-first day of the month at evening. ¹⁹ For seven days no leaven shall be found in your houses, since whoever eats what is leavened, that same person shall be cut off from the congregation of Israel, whether *he is* a stranger or a native of the land. ²⁰ You shall eat nothing leavened; in all your dwellings you shall eat unleavened bread.' "

²¹ Then Moses called for all the elders of Israel and said to them, "Pick out and take lambs for yourselves according to your families, and kill the Passover *lamb.* ²² And you shall take a bunch of hyssop, dip *it* in the blood that *is* in the basin, and strike the lintel and the two doorposts with the blood that *is* in the basin. And

none of you shall go out of the door of his house until morning. ²³ For the LORD will pass through to strike the Egyptians; and when He sees the blood on the lintel and on the two doorposts, the LORD will pass over the door and not allow the destroyer to come into your houses to strike *you.* ²⁴ And you shall observe this thing as an ordinance for you and your sons forever. ²⁵ It will come to pass when you come to the land which the LORD will give you, just as He promised, that you shall keep this service. ²⁶ And it shall be, when your children say to you, 'What do you mean by this service?' ²⁷ that you shall say, 'It *is* the Passover sacrifice of the LORD, who passed over the houses of the children of Israel in Egypt when He struck the Egyptians and delivered our households.' " So the people bowed their heads and worshiped. ²⁸ Then the children of Israel went away and did *so;* just as the LORD had commanded Moses and Aaron, so they did.

²⁹ And it came to pass at midnight that the LORD struck all the firstborn in the land of Egypt, from the firstborn of Pharaoh who sat on his throne to the firstborn of the captive who *was* in the dungeon, and all the firstborn of livestock. ³⁰ So Pharaoh rose in the night, he, all his servants, and all the Egyptians; and there was a great cry in Egypt, for *there was* not a house where *there was* not one dead.

³¹ Then he called for Moses and Aaron by night, and said, "Rise, go out from among my people, both you and the children of Israel. And go, serve the LORD as you have said. ³² Also take your flocks and your herds, as you have said, and be gone; and bless me also."

³³ And the Egyptians urged the people, that they might send them out of the land in haste. For they said, "We *shall* all *be* dead." ³⁴ So the people took their dough before it was leavened, having their kneading bowls bound up in their clothes on their shoulders. ³⁵ Now the children of Israel had done according to the word of Moses, and they had asked from the Egyptians articles of silver, articles of gold, and clothing. ³⁶ And the LORD had given the people favor in the sight of the Egyptians, so that they granted them *what they requested.* Thus they plundered the Egyptians.

"Heave!"

Many years ago, a rider on horseback came across a squad of soldiers who were trying to move a heavy piece of timber. The rider noticed that a well-dressed corporal was standing by, commanding the men to "heave." The piece of timber was just a little too heavy for the group of men to move, however.

"Why don't you help them?" the rider quietly asked the corporal.

"Me?" the corporal responded with shock in his voice. "Why, I'm a corporal, sir!"

The rider then dismounted and took his place with the soldiers. Smiling at them he said encouragingly, "Now, all together boys — heave!" The big piece of timber moved easily with the help of one more man. The stranger then mounted his horse. As he prepared to ride on, he said to the corporal, "The next time you have a piece of timber for your men to handle corporal, send for the commander in chief." It was only then that the corporal and his men realized that the helpful stranger was none other than George Washington.

No person is too great to help others. In truth, only a little person fails to do so.

> And whoever desires to be first among you, let him be your slave.
>
> *Matthew 20:27*

37 Then the children of Israel journeyed from Rameses to Succoth, about six hundred thousand men on foot, besides children. 38 A mixed multitude went up with them also, and flocks and herds—a great deal of livestock. 39 And they baked unleavened cakes of the dough which they had brought out of Egypt; for it was not leavened, because they were driven out of Egypt and could not wait, nor had they prepared provisions for themselves.

40 Now the sojourn of the children of Israel who lived in Egypt *was* four hundred and thirty years. 41 And it came to pass at the end of the four hundred and thirty years—on that very same day—it came to pass that all the armies of the LORD went out from the land of Egypt. 42 It *is* a night of solemn observance to the LORD for bringing them out of the land of Egypt. This *is* that night of the LORD, a solemn observance for all the children of Israel throughout their generations.

43 And the LORD said to Moses and Aaron, "This *is* the ordinance of the Passover: No foreigner shall eat it. 44 But every man's servant who is bought for money, when you have circumcised him, then he may eat it. 45 A sojourner and a hired servant shall not eat it. 46 In one house it shall be eaten; you shall not carry any of the flesh outside the house, nor shall you break one of its bones. 47 All the congregation of Israel shall keep it. 48 And when a stranger dwells with you *and wants* to keep the Passover to the LORD, let all his males be circumcised, and then let him come near and keep it; and he shall be as a native of the land. For no uncircumcised person shall eat it. 49 One law shall be for the native-born and for the stranger who dwells among you."

50 Thus all the children of Israel did; as the LORD commanded Moses and Aaron, so they did. 51 And it came to pass, on that very same day, that the LORD brought the children of Israel out of the land of Egypt according to their armies.

~ PSALM 18:1-12 ~

1 I will love You, O LORD, my strength.
2 The LORD is my rock and my fortress and my deliverer;

My God, my strength, in whom I will trust;
My shield and the horn of my salvation, my stronghold.
3 I will call upon the LORD, *who is worthy* to be praised;
So shall I be saved from my enemies.

4 The pangs of death surrounded me,
And the floods of ungodliness made me afraid.
5 The sorrows of Sheol surrounded me;
The snares of death confronted me.
6 In my distress I called upon the LORD,
And cried out to my God;
He heard my voice from His temple,
And my cry came before Him, *even* to His ears.

7 Then the earth shook and trembled;
The foundations of the hills also quaked and were shaken,
Because He was angry.
8 Smoke went up from His nostrils,
And devouring fire from His mouth;
Coals were kindled by it.
9 He bowed the heavens also, and came down
With darkness under His feet.
10 And He rode upon a cherub, and flew;
He flew upon the wings of the wind.
11 He made darkness His secret place;
His canopy around Him *was* dark waters
And thick clouds of the skies.
12 From the brightness before Him,
His thick clouds passed with hailstones and coals of fire.

~ PROVERBS 6:1-5 ~

1 My son, if you become surety for your friend,
If you have shaken hands in pledge for a stranger,
2 You are snared by the words of your mouth;
You are taken by the words of your mouth.
3 So do this, my son, and deliver yourself;

For you have come into the hand of
    your friend:
Go and humble yourself;
Plead with your friend.
4 Give no sleep to your eyes,
    Nor slumber to your eyelids.
5 Deliver yourself like a gazelle from
    the hand *of the hunter,*
And like a bird from the hand of the
    fowler.

∼ MATTHEW 20:17–34 ∼

Now Jesus, going up to Jerusalem, took
the twelve disciples aside on the road and
said to them, 18 "Behold, we are going up
to Jerusalem, and the Son of Man will be
betrayed to the chief priests and to the
scribes; and they will condemn Him to
death, 19 and deliver Him to the Gentiles
to mock and to scourge and to crucify.
And the third day He will rise again."

20 Then the mother of Zebedee's sons
came to Him with her sons, kneeling
down and asking something from Him.

21 And He said to her, "What do you
wish?"

She said to Him, "Grant that these two
sons of mine may sit, one on Your right
hand and the other on the left, in Your
kingdom."

22 But Jesus answered and said, "You do
not know what you ask. Are you able to
drink the cup that I am about to drink,
and be baptized with the baptism that I
am baptized with?"

They said to Him, "We are able."

23 So He said to them, "You will indeed
drink My cup, and be baptized with the
baptism that I am baptized with; but to
sit on My right hand and on My left is
not Mine to give, but *it is for those* for
whom it is prepared by My Father."

24 And when the ten heard *it,* they were
greatly displeased with the two brothers.
25 But Jesus called them to *Himself* and
said, "You know that the rulers of the
Gentiles lord it over them, and those who
are great exercise authority over them.
26 Yet it shall not be so among you; but
whoever desires to become great among
you, let him be your servant. 27 And whoever desires to be first among you, let him
be your slave— 28 just as the Son of Man
did not come to be served, but to serve,
and to give His life a ransom for many."

29 Now as they went out of Jericho, a
great multitude followed Him. 30 And
behold, two blind men sitting by the road,
when they heard that Jesus was passing
by, cried out, saying, "Have mercy on us,
O Lord, Son of David!"

31 Then the multitude warned them that
they should be quiet; but they cried out
all the more, saying, "Have mercy on us,
O Lord, Son of David!"

32 So Jesus stood still and called them,
and said, "What do you want Me to do
for you?"

33 They said to Him, "Lord, that our
eyes may be opened." 34 So Jesus had compassion and touched their eyes. And immediately their eyes received sight, and
they followed Him.

∼ EXODUS 13:1—14:31 ∼

Then the LORD spoke to Moses, saying, 2 "Consecrate to Me all the
firstborn, whatever opens the
womb among the children of Israel, *both*
of man and beast; it is Mine."

3 And Moses said to the people: "Remember this day in which you went out
of Egypt, out of the house of bondage;
for by strength of hand the LORD brought
you out of this *place.* No leavened bread
shall be eaten. 4 On this day you are going out, in the month Abib. 5 And it shall

be, when the LORD brings you into the
land of the Canaanites and the Hittites
and the Amorites and the Hivites and the
Jebusites, which He swore to your fathers
to give you, a land flowing with milk
and honey, that you shall keep this service in this month. 6 Seven days you shall
eat unleavened bread, and on the seventh
day *there shall be* a feast to the LORD.
7 Unleavened bread shall be eaten seven
days. And no leavened bread shall be
seen among you, nor shall leaven be seen

among you in all your quarters. [8] And you shall tell your son in that day, saying, 'This is done because of what the LORD did for me when I came up from Egypt.' [9] It shall be as a sign to you on your hand and as a memorial between your eyes, that the LORD's law may be in your mouth; for with a strong hand the LORD has brought you out of Egypt. [10] You shall therefore keep this ordinance in its season from year to year.

[11] "And it shall be, when the LORD brings you into the land of the Canaanites, as He swore to you and your fathers, and gives it to you, [12] that you shall set apart to the LORD all that open the womb, that is, every firstborn that comes from an animal which you have; the males *shall be* the LORD's. [13] But every firstborn of a donkey you shall redeem with a lamb; and if you will not redeem *it*, then you shall break its neck. And all the firstborn of man among your sons you shall redeem. [14] So it shall be, when your son asks you in time to come, saying, 'What *is* this?' that you shall say to him, 'By strength of hand the LORD brought us out of Egypt, out of the house of bondage. [15] And it came to pass, when Pharaoh was stubborn about letting us go, that the LORD killed all the firstborn in the land of Egypt, both the firstborn of man and the firstborn of beast. Therefore I sacrifice to the LORD all males that open the womb, but all the firstborn of my sons I redeem.' [16] It shall be as a sign on your hand and as frontlets between your eyes, for by strength of hand the LORD brought us out of Egypt."

[17] Then it came to pass, when Pharaoh had let the people go, that God did not lead them *by* way of the land of the Philistines, although that *was* near; for God said, "Lest perhaps the people change their minds when they see war, and return to Egypt." [18] So God led the people around *by* way of the wilderness of the Red Sea. And the children of Israel went up in orderly ranks out of the land of Egypt.

[19] And Moses took the bones of Joseph with him, for he had placed the children of Israel under solemn oath, saying, "God will surely visit you, and you shall carry up my bones from here with you."

[20] So they took their journey from Succoth and camped in Etham at the edge of the wilderness. [21] And the LORD went before them by day in a pillar of cloud to lead the way, and by night in a pillar of fire to give them light, so as to go by day and night. [22] He did not take away the pillar of cloud by day or the pillar of fire by night *from* before the people.

14 Now the LORD spoke to Moses, saying: [2] "Speak to the children of Israel, that they turn and camp before Pi Hahiroth, between Migdol and the sea, opposite Baal Zephon; you shall camp before it by the sea. [3] For Pharaoh will say of the children of Israel, 'They *are* bewildered by the land; the wilderness has closed them in.' [4] Then I will harden Pharaoh's heart, so that he will pursue them; and I will gain honor over Pharaoh and over all his army, that the Egyptians may know that I *am* the LORD." And they did so.

[5] Now it was told the king of Egypt that the people had fled, and the heart of Pharaoh and his servants was turned against the people; and they said, "Why have we done this, that we have let Israel go from serving us?" [6] So he made ready his chariot and took his people with him. [7] Also, he took six hundred choice chariots, and all the chariots of Egypt with captains over every one of them. [8] And the LORD hardened the heart of Pharaoh king of Egypt, and he pursued the children of Israel; and the children of Israel went out with boldness. [9] So the Egyptians pursued them, all the horses *and* chariots of Pharaoh, his horsemen and his army, and overtook them camping by the sea beside Pi Hahiroth, before Baal Zephon.

[10] And when Pharaoh drew near, the children of Israel lifted their eyes, and behold, the Egyptians marched after them. So they were very afraid, and the children of Israel cried out to the LORD. [11] Then they said to Moses, "Because *there were* no graves in Egypt, have you taken us away to die in the wilderness? Why have you so dealt with us, to bring us up out of Egypt? [12] *Is* this not the word that we told you in Egypt, saying, 'Let us alone that we may serve the Egyptians'? For *it would have been* better for us to serve the Egyptians than that we should die in the wilderness."

No Shortcuts

Award-winning figure skater Erin Sutton, thirteen, and world-class figure skater Brian Boitano have something in common: a love for ice skating and an intense dedication to their sport. They both know a great deal about getting up before dawn in order to put in hours of practice on the ice.

Erin has been skating since she was four years old. As an eighth-grader, her "workday" on the ice began at 5:30 AM. Even on Saturday mornings she was usually at the rink by 6:30. Boitano also knew that schedule as a young skater. For years, he skated from 5 to 10 AM before going to school. His dedication paid off. In 1988 he won Olympic gold, and in 1995 he was the professional world champion.

Being a champion hasn't changed Boitano's schedule a great deal. He is still at the ice rink before sunrise each day to practice for the competitive figure-skating season. Whether a skater is a veteran or a novice, it takes months of work to produce the three to five minute routines of leaps, spins, and intricate footwork that keep fans on the edge of their seats, and judges awarding high scores.

If you want to be a champion, there are no shortcuts.

A little sleep, a little slumber, a little folding of the hands to sleep— so shall your poverty come on you like a prowler, and your need like an armed man.

Proverbs 6:10-11

[13] And Moses said to the people, "Do not be afraid. Stand still, and see the salvation of the LORD, which He will accomplish for you today. For the Egyptians whom you see today, you shall see again no more forever. [14] The LORD will fight for you, and you shall hold your peace."

[15] And the LORD said to Moses, "Why do you cry to Me? Tell the children of Israel to go forward. [16] "But lift up your rod, and stretch out your hand over the sea and divide it. And the children of Israel shall go on dry *ground* through the midst of the sea. [17] And I indeed will harden the hearts of the Egyptians, and they shall follow them. So I will gain honor over Pharaoh and over all his army, his chariots, and his horsemen. [18] Then the Egyptians shall know that I *am* the LORD, when I have gained honor for Myself over Pharaoh, his chariots, and his horsemen."

[19] And the Angel of God, who went before the camp of Israel, moved and went behind them; and the pillar of cloud went from before them and stood behind them. [20] So it came between the camp of the Egyptians and the camp of Israel. Thus it was a cloud and darkness *to the one,* and it gave light by night *to the other,* so that the one did not come near the other all that night.

[21] Then Moses stretched out his hand over the sea; and the LORD caused the sea to go *back* by a strong east wind all that night, and made the sea into dry *land,* and the waters were divided. [22] So the children of Israel went into the midst of the sea on the dry *ground,* and the waters *were* a wall to them on their right hand and on their left. [23] And the Egyptians pursued and went after them into the midst of the sea, all Pharaoh's horses, his chariots, and his horsemen.

[24] Now it came to pass, in the morning watch, that the LORD looked down upon the army of the Egyptians through the pillar of fire and cloud, and He troubled the army of the Egyptians. [25] And He took off their chariot wheels, so that they drove them with difficulty; and the Egyptians said, "Let us flee from the face of Israel, for the LORD fights for them against the Egyptians."

[26] Then the LORD said to Moses, "Stretch out your hand over the sea, that the waters may come back upon the Egyptians, on their chariots, and on their horsemen." [27] And Moses stretched out his hand over the sea; and when the morning appeared, the sea returned to its full depth, while the Egyptians were fleeing into it. So the LORD overthrew the Egyptians in the midst of the sea. [28] Then the waters returned and covered the chariots, the horsemen, *and* all the army of Pharaoh that came into the sea after them. Not so much as one of them remained. [29] But the children of Israel had walked on dry *land* in the midst of the sea, and the waters *were* a wall to them on their right hand and on their left.

[30] So the LORD saved Israel that day out of the hand of the Egyptians, and Israel saw the Egyptians dead on the seashore. [31] Thus Israel saw the great work which the LORD had done in Egypt; so the people feared the LORD, and believed the LORD and His servant Moses.

～ PSALM 18:13–19 ～

[13] The LORD thundered from heaven,
And the Most High uttered His voice,
Hailstones and coals of fire.
[14] He sent out His arrows and scattered the foe,
Lightnings in abundance, and He vanquished them.
[15] Then the channels of the sea were seen,
The foundations of the world were uncovered
At Your rebuke, O LORD,
At the blast of the breath of Your nostrils.

[16] He sent from above, He took me;
He drew me out of many waters.
[17] He delivered me from my strong enemy,
From those who hated me,
For they were too strong for me.
[18] They confronted me in the day of my calamity,
But the LORD was my support.
[19] He also brought me out into a broad place;

He delivered me because He
delighted in me.

~ PROVERBS 6:6–11 ~

6 Go to the ant, you sluggard!
   Consider her ways and be wise,
7 Which, having no captain,
   Overseer or ruler,
8 Provides her supplies in the summer,
   And gathers her food in the harvest.
9 How long will you slumber,
   O sluggard?
   When will you rise from your sleep?
10 A little sleep, a little slumber,
   A little folding of the hands to
   sleep—
11 So shall your poverty come on you
   like a prowler,
   And your need like an armed man.

~ MATTHEW 21:1–22 ~

Now when they drew near Jerusalem, and
came to Bethphage, at the Mount of Olives, then Jesus sent two disciples, ² saying to them, "Go into the village opposite
you, and immediately you will find a donkey tied, and a colt with her. Loose *them*
and bring *them* to Me. ³ And if anyone
says anything to you, you shall say, 'The
Lord has need of them,' and immediately
he will send them."

⁴ All this was done that it might be fulfilled which was spoken by the prophet,
saying:

5 "Tell the daughter of Zion,
   'Behold, your King is coming to
   you,
   Lowly, and sitting on a donkey,
   A colt, the foal of a donkey.' "

⁶ So the disciples went and did as Jesus
commanded them. ⁷ They brought the
donkey and the colt, laid their clothes on
them, and set *Him* on them. ⁸ And a very
great multitude spread their clothes on the
road; others cut down branches from the
trees and spread *them* on the road. ⁹ Then
the multitudes who went before and those
who followed cried out, saying:

"Hosanna to the Son of David!
'Blessed *is* He who comes in the
name of the LORD!'
Hosanna in the highest!"

¹⁰ And when He had come into Jerusalem, all the city was moved, saying, "Who
is this?"

¹¹ So the multitudes said, "This is Jesus,
the prophet from Nazareth of Galilee."

¹² Then Jesus went into the temple of
God and drove out all those who bought
and sold in the temple, and overturned
the tables of the money changers and the
seats of those who sold doves. ¹³ And He
said to them, "It is written, 'My house
shall be called a house of prayer,' but you
have made it a 'den of thieves.' "

¹⁴ Then *the* blind and *the* lame came to
Him in the temple, and He healed them.
¹⁵ But when the chief priests and scribes
saw the wonderful things that He did, and
the children crying out in the temple and
saying, "Hosanna to the Son of David!"
they were indignant ¹⁶ and said to Him,
"Do You hear what these are saying?"

And Jesus said to them, "Yes. Have you
never read,

'Out of the mouth of babes and
nursing infants
You have perfected praise'? "

¹⁷ Then He left them and went out of
the city to Bethany, and He lodged there.

¹⁸ Now in the morning, as He returned
to the city, He was hungry. ¹⁹ And seeing
a fig tree by the road, He came to it and
found nothing on it but leaves, and said
to it, "Let no fruit grow on you ever
again." Immediately the fig tree withered
away.

²⁰ And when the disciples saw *it*, they
marveled, saying, "How did the fig tree
wither away so soon?"

²¹ So Jesus answered and said to them,
"Assuredly, I say to you, if you have faith
and do not doubt, you will not only do
what was done to the fig tree, but also if
you say to this mountain, 'Be removed
and be cast into the sea,' it will be done.
²² And whatever things you ask in prayer,
believing, you will receive."

∼ EXODUS 15:1—16:36 ∼

Then Moses and the children of Israel sang this song to the LORD, and spoke, saying:

"I will sing to the LORD,
   For He has triumphed gloriously!
   The horse and its rider
   He has thrown into the sea!
2 The LORD is my strength and song,
   And He has become my salvation;
   He is my God, and I will praise Him;
   My father's God, and I will exalt Him.
3 The LORD is a man of war;
   The LORD is His name.
4 Pharaoh's chariots and his army
   He has cast into the sea;
   His chosen captains also are drowned in the Red Sea.
5 The depths have covered them;
   They sank to the bottom like a stone.

6 "Your right hand, O LORD, has become glorious in power;
   Your right hand, O LORD, has dashed the enemy in pieces.
7 And in the greatness of Your excellence
   You have overthrown those who rose against You;
   You sent forth Your wrath;
   It consumed them like stubble.
8 And with the blast of Your nostrils
   The waters were gathered together;
   The floods stood upright like a heap;
   The depths congealed in the heart of the sea.
9 The enemy said, 'I will pursue,
   I will overtake,
   I will divide the spoil;
   My desire shall be satisfied on them.
   I will draw my sword,
   My hand shall destroy them.'
10 You blew with Your wind,
   The sea covered them;

They sank like lead in the mighty waters.

11 "Who is like You, O LORD, among the gods?
   Who is like You, glorious in holiness,
   Fearful in praises, doing wonders?
12 You stretched out Your right hand;
   The earth swallowed them.
13 You in Your mercy have led forth
   The people whom You have redeemed;
   You have guided them in Your strength
   To Your holy habitation.

14 "The people will hear and be afraid;
   Sorrow will take hold of the inhabitants of Philistia.
15 Then the chiefs of Edom will be dismayed;
   The mighty men of Moab,
   Trembling will take hold of them;
   All the inhabitants of Canaan will melt away.
16 Fear and dread will fall on them;
   By the greatness of Your arm
   They will be as still as a stone,
   Till Your people pass over,
      O LORD,
   Till the people pass over
   Whom You have purchased.
17 You will bring them in and plant them
   In the mountain of Your inheritance,
   In the place, O LORD, which You have made
   For Your own dwelling,
   The sanctuary, O LORD, which Your hands have established.

18 "The LORD shall reign forever and ever."

19 For the horses of Pharaoh went with his chariots and his horsemen into the sea, and the LORD brought back the waters of the sea upon them. But the children of

God is Always Near

In *Love and Duty*, Anne Purcell writes about seeing Major Jim Statler standing with her pastor outside his study after a Sunday service. She knew instantly that he was there with news about her husband, Ben, who was on active duty in Vietnam. As she had feared, Jim had chilling news: "He was on a helicopter that was shot down . . . he's missing in action."

Anne recalls, "Somewhere in the back of my mind, a little candle flame flickered. This tiny flame was the vestige of my faith." Days passed without word. To her, being the wife of an MIA was like being caught in limbo. She found herself able to pray only one thing: "Help me, dear Father." She says, "I hung onto this important truth — that He would help me — and the flickering flame of my candle of faith began to grow." Then one day, she noticed a white dove sitting in her yard. It was particularly beautiful, very still and quiet, and a highly uncommon sight in her neighborhood. She took it as a sign from God that He was, indeed, always near.

For five years, Anne Purcell clung to the fact that God was near. Little did she know that during those years before she was reunited with her husband, he was whispering to her from a POW cell, "Anne, find solace and strength in the Lord."

Remember, God *is* always near. In the good times and bad. Rest in His strength and your faith in Him will grow into a blazing fire.

> The Lord is my strength and song, and He has become my salvation; He is my God, and I will praise Him; my father's God, and I will exalt Him.
>
> *Exodus 15:2*

Israel went on dry *land* in the midst of the sea.

²⁰ Then Miriam the prophetess, the sister of Aaron, took the timbrel in her hand; and all the women went out after her with timbrels and with dances. ²¹ And Miriam answered them:

> "Sing to the LORD,
> For He has triumphed gloriously!
> The horse and its rider
> He has thrown into the sea!"

²² So Moses brought Israel from the Red Sea; then they went out into the Wilderness of Shur. And they went three days in the wilderness and found no water. ²³ Now when they came to Marah, they could not drink the waters of Marah, for they *were* bitter. Therefore the name of it was called Marah. ²⁴ And the people complained against Moses, saying, "What shall we drink?" ²⁵ So he cried out to the LORD, and the LORD showed him a tree. When he cast *it* into the waters, the waters were made sweet.

There He made a statute and an ordinance for them, and there He tested them, ²⁶ and said, "If you diligently heed the voice of the LORD your God and do what is right in His sight, give ear to His commandments and keep all His statutes, I will put none of the diseases on you which I have brought on the Egyptians. For I *am* the LORD who heals you."

²⁷ Then they came to Elim, where there *were* twelve wells of water and seventy palm trees; so they camped there by the waters.

16 And they journeyed from Elim, and all the congregation of the children of Israel came to the Wilderness of Sin, which is between Elim and Sinai, on the fifteenth day of the second month after they departed from the land of Egypt. ² Then the whole congregation of the children of Israel complained against Moses and Aaron in the wilderness. ³ And the children of Israel said to them, "Oh, that we had died by the hand of the LORD in the land of Egypt, when we sat by the pots of meat *and* when we ate bread to the full! For you have brought us out into this wilderness to kill this whole assembly with hunger."

⁴ Then the LORD said to Moses, "Behold, I will rain bread from heaven for you. And the people shall go out and gather a certain quota every day, that I may test them, whether they will walk in My law or not. ⁵ And it shall be on the sixth day that they shall prepare what they bring in, and it shall be twice as much as they gather daily."

⁶ Then Moses and Aaron said to all the children of Israel, "At evening you shall know that the LORD has brought you out of the land of Egypt. ⁷ And in the morning you shall see the glory of the LORD; for He hears your complaints against the LORD. But what *are* we, that you complain against us?" ⁸ Also Moses said, "*This shall be seen* when the LORD gives you meat to eat in the evening, and in the morning bread to the full; for the LORD hears your complaints which you make against Him. And what *are* we? Your complaints *are* not against us but against the LORD."

⁹ Then Moses spoke to Aaron, "Say to all the congregation of the children of Israel, 'Come near before the LORD, for He has heard your complaints.' " ¹⁰ Now it came to pass, as Aaron spoke to the whole congregation of the children of Israel, that they looked toward the wilderness, and behold, the glory of the LORD appeared in the cloud.

¹¹ And the LORD spoke to Moses, saying, ¹² "I have heard the complaints of the children of Israel. Speak to them, saying, 'At twilight you shall eat meat, and in the morning you shall be filled with bread. And you shall know that I *am* the LORD your God.' "

¹³ So it was that quails came up at evening and covered the camp, and in the morning the dew lay all around the camp. ¹⁴ And when the layer of dew lifted, there, on the surface of the wilderness, was a small round substance, *as* fine as frost on the ground. ¹⁵ So when the children of Israel saw *it*, they said to one another, "What is it?" For they did not know what it *was*.

And Moses said to them, "This *is* the bread which the LORD has given you to eat. ¹⁶ This is the thing which the LORD has commanded: 'Let every man gather it according to each one's need, one omer for each person, *according to the* number of persons; let every man take for *those* who *are* in his tent.' "

¹⁷ Then the children of Israel did so and gathered, some more, some less. ¹⁸ So when they measured *it* by omers, he who gathered much had nothing left over, and he who gathered little had no lack. Every man had gathered according to each one's need. ¹⁹ And Moses said, "Let no one leave any of it till morning." ²⁰ Notwithstanding they did not heed Moses. But some of them left part of it until morning, and it bred worms and stank. And Moses was angry with them. ²¹ So they gathered it every morning, every man according to his need. And when the sun became hot, it melted.

²² And so it was, on the sixth day, *that* they gathered twice as much bread, two omers for each one. And all the rulers of the congregation came and told Moses. ²³ Then he said to them, "This *is what* the LORD has said: 'Tomorrow *is* a Sabbath rest, a holy Sabbath to the LORD. Bake what you will bake *today,* and boil what you will boil; and lay up for yourselves all that remains, to be kept until morning.' " ²⁴ So they laid it up till morning, as Moses commanded; and it did not stink, nor were there any worms in it. ²⁵ Then Moses said, "Eat that today, for today *is* a Sabbath to the LORD; today you will not find it in the field. ²⁶ Six days you shall gather it, but on the seventh day, the Sabbath, there will be none."

²⁷ Now it happened *that some* of the people went out on the seventh day to gather, but they found none. ²⁸ And the LORD said to Moses, "How long do you refuse to keep My commandments and My laws? ²⁹ See! For the LORD has given you the Sabbath; therefore He gives you on the sixth day bread for two days. Let every man remain in his place; let no man go out of his place on the seventh day." ³⁰ So the people rested on the seventh day.

³¹ And the house of Israel called its name Manna. And it *was* like white coriander seed, and the taste of it *was* like wafers *made* with honey. ³² Then Moses said, "This *is* the thing which the LORD has commanded: 'Fill an omer with it, to be kept for your generations, that they may see the bread with which I fed you in the wilderness, when I brought you out of the land of Egypt.' " ³³ And Moses said to Aaron, "Take a pot and put an omer of manna in it, and lay it up before the LORD, to be kept for your generations." ³⁴ As the LORD commanded Moses, so Aaron laid it up before the Testimony, to be kept. ³⁵ And the children of Israel ate manna forty years, until they came to an inhabited land; they ate manna until they came to the border of the land of Canaan. ³⁶ Now an omer *is* one-tenth of an ephah.

~ PSALM 18:20–27 ~

²⁰ The LORD rewarded me according to
     my righteousness;
   According to the cleanness of my
     hands
   He has recompensed me.
²¹ For I have kept the ways of the
     LORD,
   And have not wickedly departed
     from my God.
²² For all His judgments *were* before
     me,
   And I did not put away His statutes
     from me.
²³ I was also blameless before Him,
   And I kept myself from my iniquity.
²⁴ Therefore the LORD has
     recompensed me according to my
     righteousness,
   According to the cleanness of my
     hands in His sight.

²⁵ With the merciful You will show
     Yourself merciful;
   With a blameless man You will show
     Yourself blameless;
²⁶ With the pure You will show Yourself
     pure;
   And with the devious You will show
     Yourself shrewd.
²⁷ For You will save the humble
   But will bring down haug

~ PROVERB

¹² A worthless pe
   Walks with a pe
¹³ He winks with his

He shuffles his feet,
He points with his fingers;
¹⁴ Perversity *is* in his heart,
He devises evil continually,
He sows discord.
¹⁵ Therefore his calamity shall come suddenly;
Suddenly he shall be broken without remedy.

~ MATTHEW 21:23–46 ~

Now when He came into the temple, the chief priests and the elders of the people confronted Him as He was teaching, and said, "By what authority are You doing these things? And who gave You this authority?"

²⁴ But Jesus answered and said to them, "I also will ask you one thing, which if you tell Me, I likewise will tell you by what authority I do these things: ²⁵ The baptism of John—where was it from? From heaven or from men?"

And they reasoned among themselves, saying, "If we say, 'From heaven,' He will say to us, 'Why then did you not believe him?' ²⁶ But if we say, 'From men,' we fear the multitude, for all count John as a prophet." ²⁷ So they answered Jesus and said, "We do not know."

And He said to them, "Neither will I tell you by what authority I do these things.

²⁸ "But what do you think? A man had two sons, and he came to the first and said, 'Son, go, work today in my vineyard.' ²⁹ He answered and said, 'I will not,' but afterward he regretted it and went. ³⁰ Then he came to the second and said likewise. And he answered and said, 'I *go,* sir,' but he did not go. ³¹ Which of the two did the will of *his* father?"

They said to Him, "The first."

Jesus said to them, "Assuredly, I say to you that tax collectors and harlots enter the kingdom of God before you. ³² For ohn came to you in the way of righteous- ₃ss, and you did not believe him; but tax collectors and harlots believed him; and when you saw *it,* you did not afterward relent and believe him.

³³ "Hear another parable: There was a certain landowner who planted a vineyard and set a hedge around it, dug a winepress in it and built a tower. And he leased it to vinedressers and went into a far country. ³⁴ Now when vintage-time drew near, he sent his servants to the vinedressers, that they might receive its fruit. ³⁵ And the vinedressers took his servants, beat one, killed one, and stoned another. ³⁶ Again he sent other servants, more than the first, and they did likewise to them. ³⁷ Then last of all he sent his son to them, saying, 'They will respect my son.' ³⁸ But when the vinedressers saw the son, they said among themselves, 'This is the heir. Come, let us kill him and seize his inheritance.' ³⁹ So they took him and cast *him* out of the vineyard and killed *him.*

⁴⁰ "Therefore, when the owner of the vineyard comes, what will he do to those vinedressers?"

⁴¹ They said to Him, "He will destroy those wicked men miserably, and lease *his* vineyard to other vinedressers who will render to him the fruits in their seasons."

⁴² Jesus said to them, "Have you never read in the Scriptures:

'The stone which the builders rejected
Has become the chief cornerstone.
This was the LORD's doing,
And it is marvelous in our eyes' ?

⁴³ "Therefore I say to you, the kingdom of God will be taken from you and given to a nation bearing the fruits of it. ⁴⁴ And whoever falls on this stone will be broken; but on whomever it falls, it will grind him to powder."

⁴⁵ Now when the chief priests and Pharisees heard His parables, they perceived that He was speaking of them. ⁴⁶ But when they sought to lay hands on Him, they feared the multitudes, because they took Him for a prophet.

∼ EXODUS 17:1—18:27 ∼

Then all the congregation of the children of Israel set out on their journey from the Wilderness of Sin, according to the commandment of the LORD, and camped in Rephidim; but *there was* no water for the people to drink. [2] Therefore the people contended with Moses, and said, "Give us water, that we may drink."

So Moses said to them, "Why do you contend with me? Why do you tempt the LORD?"

[3] And the people thirsted there for water, and the people complained against Moses, and said, "Why *is* it you have brought us up out of Egypt, to kill us and our children and our livestock with thirst?"

[4] So Moses cried out to the LORD, saying, "What shall I do with this people? They are almost ready to stone me!"

[5] And the LORD said to Moses, "Go on before the people, and take with you some of the elders of Israel. Also take in your hand your rod with which you struck the river, and go. [6] Behold, I will stand before you there on the rock in Horeb; and you shall strike the rock, and water will come out of it, that the people may drink."

And Moses did so in the sight of the elders of Israel. [7] So he called the name of the place Massah and Meribah, because of the contention of the children of Israel, and because they tempted the LORD, saying, "Is the LORD among us or not?"

[8] Now Amalek came and fought with Israel in Rephidim. [9] And Moses said to Joshua, "Choose us some men and go out, fight with Amalek. Tomorrow I will stand on the top of the hill with the rod of God in my hand." [10] So Joshua did as Moses said to him, and fought with Amalek. And Moses, Aaron, and Hur went up to the top of the hill. [11] And so it was, when Moses held up his hand, that Israel prevailed; and when he let down his hand, Amalek prevailed. [12] But Moses' hands *became* heavy; so they took a stone and put *it* under him, and he sat on it. And Aaron and Hur supported his hands, one on one side, and the other on the other side; and his hands were steady until the going down of the sun. [13] So Joshua defeated Amalek and his people with the edge of the sword.

[14] Then the LORD said to Moses, "Write this *for* a memorial in the book and recount *it* in the hearing of Joshua, that I will utterly blot out the remembrance of Amalek from under heaven." [15] And Moses built an altar and called its name, The-LORD-Is-My-Banner; [16] for he said, "Because the LORD has sworn: the LORD *will have* war with Amalek from generation to generation."

18 And Jethro, the priest of Midian, Moses' father-in-law, heard of all that God had done for Moses and for Israel His people—that the LORD had brought Israel out of Egypt. [2] Then Jethro, Moses' father-in-law, took Zipporah, Moses' wife, after he had sent her back, [3] with her two sons, of whom the name of one *was* Gershom (for he said, "I have been a stranger in a foreign land") [4] and the name of the other *was* Eliezer (for *he said,* "The God of my father *was* my help, and delivered me from the sword of Pharaoh"); [5] and Jethro, Moses' father-in-law, came with his sons and his wife to Moses in the wilderness, where he was encamped at the mountain of God. [6] Now he had said to Moses, "I, your father-in-law Jethro, am coming to you with your wife and her two sons with her."

[7] So Moses went out to meet his father-in-law, bowed down, and kissed him. And they asked each other about *their* well-being, and they went into the tent. [8] And Moses told his father-in-law all that the LORD had done to Pharaoh and to the Egyptians for Israel's sake, all the hardship that had come upon them on the way, and *how* the LORD had delivered them. [9] Then Jethro rejoiced for all the good which the LORD had done for Israel, whom He had delivered out of the hand of the Egyptians. [10] And Jethro said, "Blessed *be* the LORD, who has delivered you out of the hand of the Egyptians and out of the hand of Pharaoh, *and* who has delivered the people from under the hand of the Egyptians. [11] Now I know that the LORD *is* greater than all the gods; for in

the very thing in which they behaved proudly, *He was* above them." ¹² Then Jethro, Moses' father-in-law, took a burnt offering and *other* sacrifices *to offer* to God. And Aaron came with all the elders of Israel to eat bread with Moses' father-in-law before God.

¹³ And so it was, on the next day, that Moses sat to judge the people; and the people stood before Moses from morning until evening. ¹⁴ So when Moses' father-in-law saw all that he did for the people, he said, "What *is* this thing that you are doing for the people? Why do you alone sit, and all the people stand before you from morning until evening?" ¹⁵ And Moses said to his father-in-law, "Because the people come to me to inquire of God. ¹⁶ When they have a difficulty, they come to me, and I judge between one and another; and I make known the statutes of God and His laws."

¹⁷ So Moses' father-in-law said to him, "The thing that you do *is* not good. ¹⁸ Both you and these people who *are* with you will surely wear yourselves out. For this thing *is* too much for you; you are not able to perform it by yourself. ¹⁹ Listen now to my voice; I will give you counsel, and God will be with you: Stand before God for the people, so that you may bring the difficulties to God. ²⁰ And you shall teach them the statutes and the laws, and show them the way in which they must walk and the work they must do. ²¹ Moreover you shall select from all the people able men, such as fear God, men of truth, hating covetousness; and place *such* over them *to be* rulers of thousands, rulers of hundreds, rulers of fifties, and rulers of tens. ²² And let them judge the people at all times. Then it will be *that* every great matter they shall bring to you, but every small matter they themselves shall judge. So it will be easier for you, for they will bear *the burden* with you. ²³ If you do this thing, and God *so* commands you, then you will be able to endure, and all this people will also go to their place in peace."

²⁴ So Moses heeded the voice of his father-in-law and did all that he had said. ²⁵ And Moses chose able men out of all Israel, and made them heads over the people: rulers of thousands, rulers of hundreds, rulers of fifties, and rulers of tens.

²⁶ So they judged the people at all times; the hard cases they brought to Moses, but they judged every small case themselves. ²⁷ Then Moses let his father-in-law depart, and he went his way to his own land.

∼ PSALM 18:28–36 ∼

²⁸ For You will light my lamp;
The LORD my God will enlighten my darkness.
²⁹ For by You I can run against a troop,
By my God I can leap over a wall.
³⁰ *As for* God, His way *is* perfect;
The word of the LORD is proven;
He *is* a shield to all who trust in Him.

³¹ For who *is* God, except the LORD?
And who *is* a rock, except our God?
³² *It is* God who arms me with strength,
And makes my way perfect.
³³ He makes my feet like the *feet of* deer,
And sets me on my high places.
³⁴ He teaches my hands to make war,
So that my arms can bend a bow of bronze.

³⁵ You have also given me the shield of Your salvation;
Your right hand has held me up,
Your gentleness has made me great.
³⁶ You enlarged my path under me,
So my feet did not slip.

∼ PROVERBS 6:16–19 ∼

¹⁶ These six *things* the LORD hates,
Yes, seven *are* an abomination to Him:
¹⁷ A proud look,
A lying tongue,
Hands that shed innocent blood,
¹⁸ A heart that devises wicked plans,
Feet that are swift in running to evil,
¹⁹ A false witness *who* speaks lies,
And one who sows discord among brethren.

∼ MATTHEW 22:1–22 ∼

And Jesus answered and spoke to them again by parables and said: ² "The

A Gentle Answer

You have also given me the shield of Your salvation; Your right hand has held me up, Your gentleness has made me great.

Psalm 18:35

Mentor Graham was so absorbed in evaluating assignments he failed to notice the youthful giant who slouched into his Illinois schoolroom one day after school. The brightness of the late-afternoon sunshine, silhouetted the husky young man before him. When his eyes adjusted, he recognized the youth as a newcomer to the community. The lad already had a reputation for "whipping the daylights" out of all the local tough guys.

Graham would have been justified in thinking, *What does he want? Am I in danger?* But instead, he looked up and down the six-foot-four-inches of muscle and ignorance before him and offered to help the lad with his reading. When the young man left the schoolroom an hour later, he had several books under his arm — a loan from Mentor Graham, with a promise of more in the future.

Few people remember Graham. He was a quiet man, simply willing to do his best for any student who came his way. His pupil, however, is well-remembered. His name was Abraham Lincoln.

A kind, helpful response to others is often perceived as strength. It is this gentle strength to which we are drawn. When you find yourself in a sensitive situation, try a gentle touch!

kingdom of heaven is like a certain king who arranged a marriage for his son, ³ and sent out his servants to call those who were invited to the wedding; and they were not willing to come. ⁴ Again, he sent out other servants, saying, 'Tell those who are invited, "See, I have prepared my dinner; my oxen and fatted cattle *are* killed, and all things *are* ready. Come to the wedding." ' ⁵ But they made light of it and went their ways, one to his own farm, another to his business. ⁶ And the rest seized his servants, treated *them* spitefully, and killed *them*. ⁷ But when the king heard *about it,* he was furious. And he sent out his armies, destroyed those murderers, and burned up their city. ⁸ Then he said to his servants, 'The wedding is ready, but those who were invited were not worthy. ⁹ Therefore go into the highways, and as many as you find, invite to the wedding.' ¹⁰ So those servants went out into the highways and gathered together all whom they found, both bad and good. And the wedding *hall* was filled with guests.

¹¹ "But when the king came in to see the guests, he saw a man there who did not have on a wedding garment. ¹² So he said to him, 'Friend, how did you come in here without a wedding garment?' And he was speechless. ¹³ Then the king said to the servants, 'Bind him hand and foot, take him away, and cast *him* into outer darkness; there will be weeping and gnashing of teeth.'

¹⁴ "For many are called, but few *are* chosen."

¹⁵ Then the Pharisees went and plotted how they might entangle Him in *His* talk. ¹⁶ And they sent to Him their disciples with the Herodians, saying, "Teacher, we know that You are true, and teach the way of God in truth; nor do You care about anyone, for You do not regard the person of men. ¹⁷ Tell us, therefore, what do You think? Is it lawful to pay taxes to Caesar, or not?"

¹⁸ But Jesus perceived their wickedness, and said, "Why do you test Me, *you* hypocrites? ¹⁹ Show Me the tax money."

So they brought Him a denarius.

²⁰ And He said to them, "Whose image and inscription *is* this?"

²¹ They said to Him, "Caesar's."

And He said to them, "Render therefore to Caesar the things that are Caesar's, and to God the things that are God's."

²² When they had heard *these words,* they marveled, and left Him and went their way.

READING 35 · FEBRUARY 4

～ Exodus 19:1—20:26 ～

In the third month after the children of Israel had gone out of the land of Egypt, on the same day, they came *to* the Wilderness of Sinai. ² For they had departed from Rephidim, had come *to* the Wilderness of Sinai, and camped in the wilderness. So Israel camped there before the mountain.

³ And Moses went up to God, and the LORD called to him from the mountain, saying, "Thus you shall say to the house of Jacob, and tell the children of Israel: ⁴ 'You have seen what I did to the Egyptians, and *how* I bore you on eagles' wings and brought you to Myself. ⁵ Now therefore, if you will indeed obey My voice and keep My covenant, then you shall be a special treasure to Me above all people; for all the earth *is* Mine. ⁶ And you shall be to Me a kingdom of priests and a holy nation.' These *are* the words which you shall speak to the children of Israel."

⁷ So Moses came and called for the elders of the people, and laid before them all these words which the LORD commanded him. ⁸ Then all the people answered together and said, "All that the LORD has spoken we will do." So Moses brought back the words of the people to the LORD. ⁹ And the LORD said to Moses, "Behold, I come to you in the thick cloud, that the people may hear when I speak with you, and believe you forever."

So Moses told the words of the people to the LORD.

¹⁰ Then the LORD said to Moses, "Go to the people and consecrate them today and tomorrow, and let them wash their

Bargaining with God

Janette Oke, a best-selling novelist with more than forty books to her credit, is considered the modern-day "pioneer author" for Christian fiction. Since her first novel was published in 1979, her books have sold millions of copies.

When she first decided to write, she said to God, "Lord, I'm going to write this book. If it works, and if I discover I have talent, I'll give it all to You."

Janette sensed God was not pleased with the bargain she was trying to strike with Him. She felt in her heart as if He was responding, "If you're serious about this, then I want everything before you start." Thus she gave Him her ambitions and dreams, and trusted Him with the outcome of her efforts. She left it up to Him to teach her, whether she was successful or not.

Out of that resolve came a secondary resolve. She refused to compromise her principles. Although she would write realistically, her stories would be "wholesome and good and encouraging." Many thought that approach was doomed to failure at the outset, but a shelf of novels later, Janette Oke has proven "God can teach spiritual truths through fictional characters."

The greatest step of faith is to trust God *before* we see the results of our efforts. Whether we fail or succeed, God will still be with us. God doesn't ask for our best, He asks us for our selves. When we give Him everything He can take our best and make it better!

clothes. ¹¹ And let them be ready for the third day. For on the third day the LORD will come down upon Mount Sinai in the sight of all the people. ¹² You shall set bounds for the people all around, saying, 'Take heed to yourselves *that* you do *not* go up to the mountain or touch its base. Whoever touches the mountain shall surely be put to death. ¹³ Not a hand shall touch him, but he shall surely be stoned or shot *with an arrow;* whether man or beast, he shall not live.' When the trumpet sounds long, they shall come near the mountain."

¹⁴ So Moses went down from the mountain to the people and sanctified the people, and they washed their clothes. ¹⁵ And he said to the people, "Be ready for the third day; do not come near *your* wives."

¹⁶ Then it came to pass on the third day, in the morning, that there were thunderings and lightnings, and a thick cloud on the mountain; and the sound of the trumpet was very loud, so that all the people who *were* in the camp trembled. ¹⁷ And Moses brought the people out of the camp to meet with God, and they stood at the foot of the mountain. ¹⁸ Now Mount Sinai *was* completely in smoke, because the LORD descended upon it in fire. Its smoke ascended like the smoke of a furnace, and the whole mountain quaked greatly. ¹⁹ And when the blast of the trumpet sounded long and became louder and louder, Moses spoke, and God answered him by voice. ²⁰ Then the LORD came down upon Mount Sinai, on the top of the mountain. And the LORD called Moses to the top of the mountain, and Moses went up.

²¹ And the LORD said to Moses, "Go down and warn the people, lest they break through to gaze at the LORD, and many of them perish. ²² Also let the priests who come near the LORD consecrate themselves, lest the LORD break out against them."

²³ But Moses said to the LORD, "The people cannot come up to Mount Sinai; for You warned us, saying, 'Set bounds around the mountain and consecrate it.' "

²⁴ Then the LORD said to him, "Away! Get down and then come up, you and Aaron with you. But do not let the priests and the people break through to come up to the LORD, lest He break out against them." ²⁵ So Moses went down to the people and spoke to them.

20 And God spoke all these words, saying:

² "I *am* the LORD your God, who brought you out of the land of Egypt, out of the house of bondage.

³ "You shall have no other gods before Me.

⁴ "You shall not make for yourself a carved image—any likeness *of anything* that *is* in heaven above, or that *is* in the earth beneath, or that *is* in the water under the earth; ⁵ you shall not bow down to them nor serve them. For I, the LORD your God, *am* a jealous God, visiting the iniquity of the fathers upon the children to the third and fourth *generations* of those who hate Me, ⁶ but showing mercy to thousands, to those who love Me and keep My commandments.

⁷ "You shall not take the name of the LORD your God in vain, for the LORD will not hold *him* guiltless who takes His name in vain.

⁸ "Remember the Sabbath day, to keep it holy. ⁹ Six days you shall labor and do all your work, ¹⁰ but the seventh day *is* the Sabbath of the LORD your God. *In it* you shall do no work: you, nor your son, nor your daughter, nor your male servant, nor your female servant, nor your cattle, nor your stranger who *is* within your gates. ¹¹ For *in* six days the LORD made the heavens and the earth, the sea, and all that *is* in them, and rested the seventh day. Therefore the LORD blessed the Sabbath day and hallowed it.

¹² "Honor your father and your mother, that your days may be long upon the land which the LORD your God is giving you.

¹³ "You shall not murder.

14 "You shall not commit adultery.
15 "You shall not steal.
16 "You shall not bear false witness against your neighbor.
17 "You shall not covet your neighbor's house; you shall not covet your neighbor's wife, nor his male servant, nor his female servant, nor his ox, nor his donkey, nor anything that *is* your neighbor's."

18 Now all the people witnessed the thunderings, the lightning flashes, the sound of the trumpet, and the mountain smoking; and when the people saw *it*, they trembled and stood afar off. 19 Then they said to Moses, "You speak with us, and we will hear; but let not God speak with us, lest we die."

20 And Moses said to the people, "Do not fear; for God has come to test you, and that His fear may be before you, so that you may not sin." 21 So the people stood afar off, but Moses drew near the thick darkness where God *was*.

22 Then the LORD said to Moses, "Thus you shall say to the children of Israel: 'You have seen that I have talked with you from heaven. 23 You shall not make *anything to be* with Me—gods of silver or gods of gold you shall not make for yourselves. 24 An altar of earth you shall make for Me, and you shall sacrifice on it your burnt offerings and your peace offerings, your sheep and your oxen. In every place where I record My name I will come to you, and I will bless you. 25 And if you make Me an altar of stone, you shall not build it of hewn stone; for if you use your tool on it, you have profaned it. 26 Nor shall you go up by steps to My altar, that your nakedness may not be exposed on it.'

∽ PSALM 18:37–45 ∽

37 I have pursued my enemies and overtaken them;
Neither did I turn back again till they were destroyed.
38 I have wounded them,
So that they could not rise;
They have fallen under my feet.
39 For You have armed me with strength for the battle;
You have subdued under me those who rose up against me.

40 You have also given me the necks of my enemies,
So that I destroyed those who hated me.
41 They cried out, but *there was* none to save;
Even to the LORD, but He did not answer them.
42 Then I beat them as fine as the dust before the wind;
I cast them out like dirt in the streets.

43 You have delivered me from the strivings of the people;
You have made me the head of the nations;
A people I have not known shall serve me.
44 As soon as they hear of me they obey me;
The foreigners submit to me.
45 The foreigners fade away,
And come frightened from their hideouts.

∽ PROVERBS 6:20–25 ∽

20 My son, keep your father's command,
And do not forsake the law of your mother.
21 Bind them continually upon your heart;
Tie them around your neck.
22 When you roam, they will lead you;
When you sleep, they will keep you;
And *when* you awake, they will speak with you.
23 For the commandment *is* a lamp,
And the law a light;
Reproofs of instruction *are* the way of life,
24 To keep you from the evil woman,
From the flattering tongue of a seductress.
25 Do not lust after her beauty in your heart,
Nor let her allure you with her eyelids.

∽ MATTHEW 22:23–46 ∽

The same day the Sadducees, who say there is no resurrection, came to Him and asked Him, [24] saying: "Teacher, Moses said that if a man dies, having no children, his brother shall marry his wife and raise up offspring for his brother. [25] Now there were with us seven brothers. The first died after he had married, and having no offspring, left his wife to his brother. [26] Likewise the second also, and the third, even to the seventh. [27] Last of all the woman died also. [28] Therefore, in the resurrection, whose wife of the seven will she be? For they all had her."

[29] Jesus answered and said to them, "You are mistaken, not knowing the Scriptures nor the power of God. [30] For in the resurrection they neither marry nor are given in marriage, but are like angels of God in heaven. [31] But concerning the resurrection of the dead, have you not read what was spoken to you by God, saying, [32] 'I am the God of Abraham, the God of Isaac, and the God of Jacob'? God is not the God of the dead, but of the living." [33] And when the multitudes heard this, they were astonished at His teaching.

[34] But when the Pharisees heard that He had silenced the Sadducees, they gathered together. [35] Then one of them, a lawyer, asked Him a question, testing Him, and saying, [36] "Teacher, which is the great commandment in the law?"

[37] Jesus said to him, " 'You shall love the LORD your God with all your heart, with all your soul, and with all your mind.' [38] This is the first and great commandment. [39] And the second is like it: 'You shall love your neighbor as yourself.' [40] On these two commandments hang all the Law and the Prophets."

[41] While the Pharisees were gathered together, Jesus asked them, [42] saying, "What do you think about the Christ? Whose Son is He?"

They said to Him, "The Son of David."

[43] He said to them, "How then does David in the Spirit call Him 'Lord,' saying:

[44] 'The LORD said to my Lord,
   "Sit at My right hand,
    Till I make Your enemies Your
       footstool" ' ?

[45] If David then calls Him 'Lord,' how is He his Son?" [46] And no one was able to answer Him a word, nor from that day on did anyone dare question Him anymore.

READING 36 · FEBRUARY 5

~ EXODUS 21:1—22:31 ~

"Now these are the judgments which you shall set before them: [2] If you buy a Hebrew servant, he shall serve six years; and in the seventh he shall go out free and pay nothing. [3] If he comes in by himself, he shall go out by himself; if he comes in married, then his wife shall go out with him. [4] If his master has given him a wife, and she has borne him sons or daughters, the wife and her children shall be her master's, and he shall go out by himself. [5] But if the servant plainly says, 'I love my master, my wife, and my children; I will not go out free,' [6] then his master shall bring him to the judges. He shall also bring him to the door, or to the doorpost, and his master shall pierce his ear with an awl; and he shall serve him forever.

[7] "And if a man sells his daughter to be a female slave, she shall not go out as the male slaves do. [8] If she does not please her master, who has betrothed her to himself, then he shall let her be redeemed. He shall have no right to sell her to a foreign people, since he has dealt deceitfully with her. [9] And if he has betrothed her to his son, he shall deal with her according to the custom of daughters. [10] If he takes another wife, he shall not diminish her food, her clothing, and her marriage rights. [11] And if he does not do these three for her, then she shall go out free, without paying money.

[12] "He who strikes a man so that he dies shall surely be put to death. [13] However,

True Rewards

> But he who is greatest among you shall be your servant.
>
> *Matthew 23:11*

A recent plot of the soap opera *All My Children* called for high-society philanthropist Brooke English to move into a homeless shelter in order to better understand their plight. Julia Barr, who plays Brooke, felt prompted to take some real-life action of her own. She became a participant in First Step, a New York City job-readiness program for homeless and formerly homeless women. The eight-week session included one-on-one mentoring, resume advice, access to job internships, interview clothing, and pep talks from people such as herself.

Says Julia, "I know how it feels to lack motivation and self-esteem. I tend to procrastinate, I'm rarely on time, I'm rather bossy, I'm very stubborn — we all have things that hold us back and so I share mine."

Julia is not only giving her time, but her money as well. When her maternal grandmother, Myrtle, died at the age of 104, she left Julia "a nice amount of money." It was all donated to First Step.

Julia Barr has one Emmy award and six nominations, but those in First Step will remember her, not for those accolades she's received as an actress, but for the care she showed to them.

You have something to give someone around you today— a word of encouragement, a gentle hug, a bit of advice. Those are the eternal things that will not pass away. Awards will eventually crumble and accolades will be forgotten, but those little things you do in service to others will remain.

if he did not lie in wait, but God delivered *him* into his hand, then I will appoint for you a place where he may flee.

¹⁴ "But if a man acts with premeditation against his neighbor, to kill him by treachery, you shall take him from My altar, that he may die.

¹⁵ "And he who strikes his father or his mother shall surely be put to death.

¹⁶ "He who kidnaps a man and sells him, or if he is found in his hand, shall surely be put to death.

¹⁷ "And he who curses his father or his mother shall surely be put to death.

¹⁸ "If men contend with each other, and one strikes the other with a stone or with *his* fist, and he does not die but is confined to *his* bed, ¹⁹ if he rises again and walks about outside with his staff, then he who struck *him* shall be acquitted. He shall only pay *for* the loss of his time, and shall provide *for him* to be thoroughly healed.

²⁰ "And if a man beats his male or female servant with a rod, so that he dies under his hand, he shall surely be punished. ²¹ Notwithstanding, if he remains alive a day or two, he shall not be punished; for he *is* his property.

²² "If men fight, and hurt a woman with child, so that she gives birth prematurely, yet no harm follows, he shall surely be punished accordingly as the woman's husband imposes on him; and he shall pay as the judges *determine*. ²³ But if *any* harm follows, then you shall give life for life, ²⁴ eye for eye, tooth for tooth, hand for hand, foot for foot, ²⁵ burn for burn, wound for wound, stripe for stripe.

²⁶ "If a man strikes the eye of his male or female servant, and destroys it, he shall let him go free for the sake of his eye. ²⁷ And if he knocks out the tooth of his male or female servant, he shall let him go free for the sake of his tooth.

²⁸ "If an ox gores a man or a woman to death, then the ox shall surely be stoned, and its flesh shall not be eaten; but the owner of the ox *shall be* acquitted. ²⁹ But if the ox tended to thrust with its horn in times past, and it has been made known to his owner, and he has not kept it confined, so that it has killed a man or a woman, the ox shall be stoned and its owner also shall be put to death. ³⁰ If there

is imposed on him a sum of money, then he shall pay to redeem his life, whatever is imposed on him. ³¹ Whether it has gored a son or gored a daughter, according to this judgment it shall be done to him. ³² If the ox gores a male or female servant, he shall give to their master thirty shekels of silver, and the ox shall be stoned.

³³ "And if a man opens a pit, or if a man digs a pit and does not cover it, and an ox or a donkey falls in it, ³⁴ the owner of the pit shall make *it* good; he shall give money to their owner, but the dead *animal* shall be his.

³⁵ "If one man's ox hurts another's, so that it dies, then they shall sell the live ox and divide the money from it; and the dead *ox* they shall also divide. ³⁶ Or if it was known that the ox tended to thrust in time past, and its owner has not kept it confined, he shall surely pay ox for ox, and the dead animal shall be his own.

22 "If a man steals an ox or a sheep, and slaughters it or sells it, he shall restore five oxen for an ox and four sheep for a sheep. ² If the thief is found breaking in, and he is struck so that he dies, *there shall be* no guilt for his bloodshed. ³ If the sun has risen on him, *there shall be* guilt for his bloodshed. He should make full restitution; if he has nothing, then he shall be sold for his theft. ⁴ If the theft is certainly found alive in his hand, whether it is an ox or donkey or sheep, he shall restore double.

⁵ "If a man causes a field or vineyard to be grazed, and lets loose his animal, and it feeds in another man's field, he shall make restitution from the best of his own field and the best of his own vineyard.

⁶ "If fire breaks out and catches in thorns, so that stacked grain, standing grain, or the field is consumed, he who kindled the fire shall surely make restitution.

⁷ "If a man delivers to his neighbor money or articles to keep, and it is stolen out of the man's house, if the thief is found, he shall pay double. ⁸ If the thief is not found, then the master of the house shall be brought to the judges *to see* whether he has put his hand into his neighbor's goods.

⁹ "For any kind of trespass, *whether it*

concerns an ox, a donkey, a sheep, or clothing, *or* for any kind of lost thing which *another* claims to be his, the cause of both parties shall come before the judges; *and* whomever the judges condemn shall pay double to his neighbor. ¹⁰ If a man delivers to his neighbor a donkey, an ox, a sheep, or any animal to keep, and it dies, is hurt, or driven away, no one seeing *it,* ¹¹ *then* an oath of the LORD shall be between them both, that he has not put his hand into his neighbor's goods; and the owner of it shall accept *that,* and he shall not make *it* good. ¹² But if, in fact, it is stolen from him, he shall make restitution to the owner of it. ¹³ If it is torn to pieces *by a beast, then* he shall bring it as evidence, *and* he shall not make good what was torn.

¹⁴ "And if a man borrows *anything* from his neighbor, and it becomes injured or dies, the owner of it not *being* with it, he shall surely make *it* good. ¹⁵ If its owner *was* with it, he shall not make *it* good; if it *was* hired, it came for its hire.

¹⁶ "If a man entices a virgin who is not betrothed, and lies with her, he shall surely pay the bride-price for her *to be* his wife. ¹⁷ If her father utterly refuses to give her to him, he shall pay money according to the bride-price of virgins.

¹⁸ "You shall not permit a sorceress to live.

¹⁹ "Whoever lies with an animal shall surely be put to death.

²⁰ "He who sacrifices to *any* god, except to the LORD only, he shall be utterly destroyed.

²¹ "You shall neither mistreat a stranger nor oppress him, for you were strangers in the land of Egypt.

²² "You shall not afflict any widow or fatherless child. ²³ If you afflict them in any way, *and* they cry at all to Me, I will surely hear their cry; ²⁴ and My wrath will become hot, and I will kill you with the sword; your wives shall be widows, and your children fatherless.

²⁵ "If you lend money to *any of* My people *who are* poor among you, you shall not be like a moneylender to him; you shall not charge him interest. ²⁶ If you ever take your neighbor's garment as a pledge, you shall return it to him before the sun goes down. ²⁷ For that *is* his only

covering, it *is* his garment for his skin. What will he sleep in? And it will be that when he cries to Me, I will hear, for I *am* gracious.

²⁸ "You shall not revile God, nor curse a ruler of your people.

²⁹ "You shall not delay *to offer* the first of your ripe produce and your juices. The firstborn of your sons you shall give to Me. ³⁰ Likewise you shall do with your oxen *and* your sheep. It shall be with its mother seven days; on the eighth day you shall give it to Me.

³¹ "And you shall be holy men to Me: you shall not eat meat torn *by beasts* in the field; you shall throw it to the dogs.

∼ PSALM 18:46–50 ∼

⁴⁶ The LORD lives!
Blessed *be* my Rock!
Let the God of my salvation be exalted.
⁴⁷ *It is* God who avenges me,
And subdues the peoples under me;
⁴⁸ He delivers me from my enemies.
You also lift me up above those who rise against me;
You have delivered me from the violent man.
⁴⁹ Therefore I will give thanks to You, O LORD, among the Gentiles,
And sing praises to Your name.

⁵⁰ Great deliverance He gives to His king,
And shows mercy to His anointed,
To David and his descendants forevermore.

∼ PROVERBS 6:26–29 ∼

²⁶ For by means of a harlot
A man is reduced to a crust of bread;
And an adulteress will prey upon his precious life.
²⁷ Can a man take fire to his bosom,
And his clothes not be burned?
²⁸ Can one walk on hot coals,
And his feet not be seared?
²⁹ So *is* he who goes in to his neighbor's wife;
Whoever touches her shall not be innocent.

∼ MATTHEW 23:1–22 ∼

Then Jesus spoke to the multitudes and to His disciples, ² saying: "The scribes and the Pharisees sit in Moses' seat. ³ Therefore whatever they tell you to observe, *that* observe and do, but do not do according to their works; for they say, and do not do. ⁴ For they bind heavy burdens, hard to bear, and lay *them* on men's shoulders; but they *themselves* will not move them with one of their fingers. ⁵ But all their works they do to be seen by men. They make their phylacteries broad and enlarge the borders of their garments. ⁶ They love the best places at feasts, the best seats in the synagogues, ⁷ greetings in the marketplaces, and to be called by men, 'Rabbi, Rabbi.' ⁸ But you, do not be called 'Rabbi'; for One is your Teacher, the Christ, and you are all brethren. ⁹ Do not call anyone on earth your father; for One is your Father, He who is in heaven. ¹⁰ And do not be called teachers; for One is your Teacher, the Christ. ¹¹ But he who is greatest among you shall be your servant. ¹² And whoever exalts himself will be humbled, and he who humbles himself will be exalted.

¹³ "But woe to you, scribes and Pharisees, hypocrites! For you shut up the kingdom of heaven against men; for you neither go in *yourselves,* nor do you allow those who are entering to go in. ¹⁴ Woe to you, scribes and Pharisees, hypocrites! For you devour widows' houses, and for a pretense make long prayers. Therefore you will receive greater condemnation.

¹⁵ "Woe to you, scribes and Pharisees, hypocrites! For you travel land and sea to win one proselyte, and when he is won, you make him twice as much a son of hell as yourselves.

¹⁶ "Woe to you, blind guides, who say, 'Whoever swears by the temple, it is nothing; but whoever swears by the gold of the temple, he is obliged *to perform it.*' ¹⁷ Fools and blind! For which is greater, the gold or the temple that sanctifies the gold? ¹⁸ And, 'Whoever swears by the altar, it is nothing; but whoever swears by the gift that is on it, he is obliged *to perform it.*' ¹⁹ Fools and blind! For which is greater, the gift or the altar that sanctifies the gift? ²⁰ Therefore he who swears by the altar, swears by it and by all things on it. ²¹ He who swears by the temple, swears by it and by Him who dwells in it. ²² And he who swears by heaven, swears by the throne of God and by Him who sits on it.

∼ EXODUS 23:1—24:18 ∼

"You shall not circulate a false report. Do not put your hand with the wicked to be an unrighteous witness. ² You shall not follow a crowd to do evil; nor shall you testify in a dispute so as to turn aside after many to pervert *justice.* ³ You shall not show partiality to a poor man in his dispute.

⁴ "If you meet your enemy's ox or his donkey going astray, you shall surely bring it back to him again. ⁵ If you see the donkey of one who hates you lying under its burden, and you would refrain from helping it, you shall surely help him with it.

⁶ "You shall not pervert the judgment of your poor in his dispute. ⁷ Keep yourself far from a false matter; do not kill the innocent and righteous. For I will not justify the wicked. ⁸ And you shall take no bribe, for a bribe blinds the discerning and perverts the words of the righteous.

⁹ "Also you shall not oppress a stranger, for you know the heart of a stranger, because you were strangers in the land of Egypt.

¹⁰ "Six years you shall sow your land and gather in its produce, ¹¹ but the seventh *year* you shall let it rest and lie fallow, that the poor of your people may eat; and what they leave, the beasts of the field may eat. In like manner you shall do with your vineyard *and* your olive grove. ¹² Six days you shall do your work, and on the seventh day you shall rest, that your ox

A Time for Rest

Our grandparents may have worked hard, with less sophisticated technology, but most analysts today agree that at the day's end, our grandparents gave themselves a chance to unwind. In today's world, there seems to be no downtime. The home has become a branch office — with cell phones in cars, beepers in pockets, and home offices complete with e-mail, fax machines, and answering machines waiting to be attended to. Some have estimated that more than 80 percent of all white-collar employees are in the habit of taking work home on a daily basis.

A report in *Newsweek* magazine quoted Dr. Mark Moskowitz of Boston University Medical Center as saying, "A lot of people are working 24 hours a day, seven days a week, even when they're not technically at work." Moskowitz sees this as a classic formula for first-class exhaustion. Stewart Noyce would probably agree. He is reported in the same magazine to have slept on his couch for an entire week, in a fit of exhaustion after graduating from business school. Noyce concluded, "It's really important to have some balance. Otherwise, it won't be fun anymore."

The writer of Ecclesiastes would no doubt say today, "There's a time for work . . . and for rest!"

> Six days you shall do your work, and on the seventh day you shall rest, that your ox and your donkey may rest, and the son of your female servant and the stranger may be refreshed.
>
> *Exodus 23:12*

and your donkey may rest, and the son of your female servant and the stranger may be refreshed.

[13] "And in all that I have said to you, be circumspect and make no mention of the name of other gods, nor let it be heard from your mouth.

[14] "Three times you shall keep a feast to Me in the year: [15] You shall keep the Feast of Unleavened Bread (you shall eat unleavened bread seven days, as I commanded you, at the time appointed in the month of Abib, for in it you came out of Egypt; none shall appear before Me empty); [16] and the Feast of Harvest, the firstfruits of your labors which you have sown in the field; and the Feast of Ingathering at the end of the year, when you have gathered in *the fruit of* your labors from the field.

[17] "Three times in the year all your males shall appear before the Lord GOD.

[18] "You shall not offer the blood of My sacrifice with leavened bread; nor shall the fat of My sacrifice remain until morning. [19] The first of the firstfruits of your land you shall bring into the house of the LORD your God. You shall not boil a young goat in its mother's milk.

[20] "Behold, I send an Angel before you to keep you in the way and to bring you into the place which I have prepared. [21] Beware of Him and obey His voice; do not provoke Him, for He will not pardon your transgressions; for My name *is* in Him. [22] But if you indeed obey His voice and do all that I speak, then I will be an enemy to your enemies and an adversary to your adversaries. [23] For My Angel will go before you and bring you in to the Amorites and the Hittites and the Perizzites and the Canaanites and the Hivites and the Jebusites; and I will cut them off. [24] You shall not bow down to their gods, nor serve them, nor do according to their works; but you shall utterly overthrow them and completely break down their *sacred* pillars.

[25] "So you shall serve the LORD your God, and He will bless your bread and your water. And I will take sickness away from the midst of you. [26] No one shall suffer miscarriage or be barren in your land; I will fulfill the number of your days. [27] "I will send My fear before you, I will cause confusion among all the people to whom you come, and will make all your enemies turn *their* backs to you. [28] And I will send hornets before you, which shall drive out the Hivite, the Canaanite, and the Hittite from before you. [29] I will not drive them out from before you in one year, lest the land become desolate and the beasts of the field become too numerous for you. [30] Little by little I will drive them out from before you, until you have increased, and you inherit the land. [31] And I will set your bounds from the Red Sea to the sea, Philistia, and from the desert to the River. For I will deliver the inhabitants of the land into your hand, and you shall drive them out before you. [32] You shall make no covenant with them, nor with their gods. [33] They shall not dwell in your land, lest they make you sin against Me. For *if* you serve their gods, it will surely be a snare to you."

24

Now He said to Moses, "Come up to the LORD, you and Aaron, Nadab and Abihu, and seventy of the elders of Israel, and worship from afar. [2] And Moses alone shall come near the LORD, but they shall not come near; nor shall the people go up with him."

[3] So Moses came and told the people all the words of the LORD and all the judgments. And all the people answered with one voice and said, "All the words which the LORD has said we will do." [4] And Moses wrote all the words of the LORD. And he rose early in the morning, and built an altar at the foot of the mountain, and twelve pillars according to the twelve tribes of Israel. [5] Then he sent young men of the children of Israel, who offered burnt offerings and sacrificed peace offerings of oxen to the LORD. [6] And Moses took half the blood and put *it* in basins, and half the blood he sprinkled on the altar. [7] Then he took the Book of the Covenant and read in the hearing of the people. And they said, "All that the LORD has said we will do, and be obedient." [8] And Moses took the blood, sprinkled *it* on the people, and said, "This is the blood of the covenant which the LORD has made with you according to all these words."

[9] Then Moses went up, also Aaron, Nadab, and Abihu, and seventy of the

elders of Israel, [10] and they saw the God of Israel. And *there was* under His feet as it were a paved work of sapphire stone, and it was like the very heavens in *its* clarity. [11] But on the nobles of the children of Israel He did not lay His hand. So they saw God, and they ate and drank.

[12] Then the LORD said to Moses, "Come up to Me on the mountain and be there; and I will give you tablets of stone, and the law and commandments which I have written, that you may teach them."

[13] So Moses arose with his assistant Joshua, and Moses went up to the mountain of God. [14] And he said to the elders, "Wait here for us until we come back to you. Indeed, Aaron and Hur *are* with you. If any man has a difficulty, let him go to them." [15] Then Moses went up into the mountain, and a cloud covered the mountain.

[16] Now the glory of the LORD rested on Mount Sinai, and the cloud covered it six days. And on the seventh day He called to Moses out of the midst of the cloud. [17] The sight of the glory of the LORD *was* like a consuming fire on the top of the mountain in the eyes of the children of Israel. [18] So Moses went into the midst of the cloud and went up into the mountain. And Moses was on the mountain forty days and forty nights.

~ PSALM 19:1–6 ~

[1] The heavens declare the glory of
        God;
      And the firmament shows His
        handiwork.
[2] Day unto day utters speech,
      And night unto night reveals
        knowledge.
[3] *There is* no speech nor language
      Where their voice is not heard.
[4] Their line has gone out through all
        the earth,
      And their words to the end of the
        world.

      In them He has set a tabernacle for
        the sun,
[5] Which *is* like a bridegroom coming
        out of his chamber,
      And rejoices like a strong man to run
        its race.

[6] Its rising *is* from one end of heaven,
      And its circuit to the other end;
      And there is nothing hidden from its
        heat.

~ PROVERBS 6:30, 31 ~

[30] *People* do not despise a thief
       If he steals to satisfy himself when he
         is starving.
[31] Yet *when* he is found, he must
         restore sevenfold;
       He may have to give up all the
         substance of his house.

~ MATTHEW 23:23–39 ~

"Woe to you, scribes and Pharisees, hypocrites! For you pay tithe of mint and anise and cummin, and have neglected the weightier *matters* of the law: justice and mercy and faith. These you ought to have done, without leaving the others undone. [24] Blind guides, who strain out a gnat and swallow a camel!

[25] "Woe to you, scribes and Pharisees, hypocrites! For you cleanse the outside of the cup and dish, but inside they are full of extortion and self-indulgence. [26] Blind Pharisee, first cleanse the inside of the cup and dish, that the outside of them may be clean also.

[27] "Woe to you, scribes and Pharisees, hypocrites! For you are like whitewashed tombs which indeed appear beautiful outwardly, but inside are full of dead *men's* bones and all uncleanness. [28] Even so you also outwardly appear righteous to men, but inside you are full of hypocrisy and lawlessness.

[29] "Woe to you, scribes and Pharisees, hypocrites! Because you build the tombs of the prophets and adorn the monuments of the righteous, [30] and say, 'If we had lived in the days of our fathers, we would not have been partakers with them in the blood of the prophets.'

[31] "Therefore you are witnesses against yourselves that you are sons of those who murdered the prophets. [32] Fill up, then, the measure of your fathers' *guilt.* [33] Serpents, brood of vipers! How can you escape the condemnation of hell? [34] Therefore, indeed, I send you prophets, wise men, and scribes: *some* of them you will

kill and crucify, and *some* of them you will scourge in your synagogues and persecute from city to city, ³⁵ that on you may come all the righteous blood shed on the earth, from the blood of righteous Abel to the blood of Zechariah, son of Berechiah, whom you murdered between the temple and the altar. ³⁶ Assuredly, I say to you, all these things will come upon this generation.

³⁷ "O Jerusalem, Jerusalem, the one who kills the prophets and stones those who are sent to her! How often I wanted to gather your children together, as a hen gathers her chicks under *her* wings, but you were not willing! ³⁸ See! Your house is left to you desolate; ³⁹ for I say to you, you shall see Me no more till you say, 'Blessed is He who comes in the name of the LORD!' "

READING 38 · FEBRUARY 7

~ Exodus 25:1—26:37 ~

Then the LORD spoke to Moses, saying: ² "Speak to the children of Israel, that they bring Me an offering. From everyone who gives it willingly with his heart you shall take My offering. ³ And this *is* the offering which you shall take from them: gold, silver, and bronze; ⁴ blue, purple, and scarlet *thread*, fine linen, and goats' *hair*; ⁵ ram skins dyed red, badger skins, and acacia wood; ⁶ oil for the light, and spices for the anointing oil and for the sweet incense; ⁷ onyx stones, and stones to be set in the ephod and in the breastplate. ⁸ And let them make Me a sanctuary, that I may dwell among them. ⁹ According to all that I show you, *that is*, the pattern of the tabernacle and the pattern of all its furnishings, just so you shall make *it*.

¹⁰ "And they shall make an ark of acacia wood; two and a half cubits *shall be* its length, a cubit and a half its width, and a cubit and a half its height. ¹¹ And you shall overlay it with pure gold, inside and out you shall overlay it, and shall make on it a molding of gold all around. ¹² You shall cast four rings of gold for it, and put *them* in its four corners; two rings *shall be* on one side, and two rings on the other side. ¹³ And you shall make poles *of* acacia wood, and overlay them with gold. ¹⁴ You shall put the poles into the rings on the sides of the ark, that the ark may be carried by them. ¹⁵ The poles shall be in the rings of the ark; they shall not be taken from it. ¹⁶ And you shall put into the ark the Testimony which I will give you.

¹⁷ "You shall make a mercy seat of pure gold; two and a half cubits *shall be* its length and a cubit and a half its width. ¹⁸ And you shall make two cherubim of gold; of hammered work you shall make them at the two ends of the mercy seat. ¹⁹ Make one cherub at one end, and the other cherub at the other end; you shall make the cherubim at the two ends of it *of one piece* with the mercy seat. ²⁰ And the cherubim shall stretch out *their* wings above, covering the mercy seat with their wings, and they shall face one another; the faces of the cherubim *shall be* toward the mercy seat. ²¹ You shall put the mercy seat on top of the ark, and in the ark you shall put the Testimony that I will give you. ²² And there I will meet with you, and I will speak with you from above the mercy seat, from between the two cherubim which *are* on the ark of the Testimony, about everything which I will give you in commandment to the children of Israel.

²³ "You shall also make a table of acacia wood; two cubits *shall be* its length, a cubit its width, and a cubit and a half its height. ²⁴ And you shall overlay it with pure gold, and make a molding of gold all around. ²⁵ You shall make for it a frame of a handbreadth all around, and you shall make a gold molding for the frame all around. ²⁶ And you shall make for it four rings of gold, and put the rings on the four corners that *are* at its four legs. ²⁷ The rings shall be close to the frame, as holders for the poles to bear the table. ²⁸ And

Praying through the Window

> And this gospel of the kingdom will be preached in all the world as a witness to all the nations, and then the end will come.
>
> *Matthew 24:14*

Back in 1993, a group called AD 2000 United Prayer Track came up with an innovative idea. In order to help realize their goal of "a church for every people and the gospel for every person by AD 2000," they established a program called "Praying through the Window."

The "window" refers to an area on the globe from 10 degrees to 40 degrees north of the equator, from North Africa and southern Spain eastward to Japan and the northern Philippines. More than 2.5 billion people live in this area, where the most prominent religions are Buddhism, Islam, and Hinduism. For the entire month of October 1993, and again in 1995, millions of Christians from around the world prayed for the people in the 10/40 window.

The goal was that new churches might be established and new missionaries sent to these areas. In 1993 alone, the number of churches in Albania grew from 50 to more than 300, and the number of Christian fellowship groups formed daily in India rose from an average of three to seventeen.

In praying for people around the world, we are called to remember not only those who already *are* believers, that they might grow in their faith and be equipped to endure persecution and hardships, but we are called to pray for *new* believers to enter the Kingdom!

you shall make the poles of acacia wood, and overlay them with gold, that the table may be carried with them. ²⁹ You shall make its dishes, its pans, its pitchers, and its bowls for pouring. You shall make them of pure gold. ³⁰ And you shall set the showbread on the table before Me always.

³¹ "You shall also make a lampstand of pure gold; the lampstand shall be of hammered work. Its shaft, its branches, its bowls, its *ornamental* knobs, and flowers shall be *of one piece*. ³² And six branches shall come out of its sides: three branches of the lampstand out of one side, and three branches of the lampstand out of the other side. ³³ Three bowls *shall be* made like almond *blossoms* on one branch, *with* an *ornamental* knob and a flower, and three bowls made like almond *blossoms* on the other branch, *with* an *ornamental* knob and a flower—and so for the six branches that come out of the lampstand. ³⁴ On the lampstand itself four bowls *shall be* made like almond *blossoms, each with* its *ornamental* knob and flower. ³⁵ And *there shall be* a knob under the *first* two branches of the same, a knob under the *second* two branches of the same, and a knob under the *third* two branches of the same, according to the six branches that extend from the lampstand. ³⁶ Their knobs and their branches *shall be of one piece*; all of it *shall be* one hammered piece of pure gold. ³⁷ You shall make seven lamps for it, and they shall arrange its lamps so that they give light in front of it. ³⁸ And its wick-trimmers and their trays *shall be* of pure gold. ³⁹ It shall be made of a talent of pure gold, with all these utensils. ⁴⁰ And see to it that you make *them* according to the pattern which was shown you on the mountain.

26

"Moreover you shall make the tabernacle *with* ten curtains *of* fine woven linen and blue, purple, and scarlet *thread*; with artistic designs of cherubim you shall weave them. ² The length of each curtain *shall be* twenty-eight cubits, and the width of each curtain four cubits. And every one of the curtains shall have the same measurements. ³ Five curtains shall be coupled to one another, and *the other* five curtains *shall be* coupled to one another. ⁴ And you shall make loops of blue *yarn* on the edge of the curtain on the selvedge of *one* set, and likewise you shall do on the outer edge of *the other* curtain of the second set. ⁵ Fifty loops you shall make in the one curtain, and fifty loops you shall make on the edge of the curtain that *is* on the end of the second set, that the loops may be clasped to one another. ⁶ And you shall make fifty clasps of gold, and couple the curtains together with the clasps, so that it may be one tabernacle.

⁷ "You shall also make curtains of goats' *hair*, to be a tent over the tabernacle. You shall make eleven curtains. ⁸ The length of each curtain *shall be* thirty cubits, and the width of each curtain four cubits; and the eleven curtains shall all have the same measurements. ⁹ And you shall couple five curtains by themselves and six curtains by themselves, and you shall double over the sixth curtain at the forefront of the tent. ¹⁰ You shall make fifty loops on the edge of the curtain that is outermost in *one* set, and fifty loops on the edge of the curtain of the second set. ¹¹ And you shall make fifty bronze clasps, put the clasps into the loops, and couple the tent together, that it may be one. ¹² The remnant that remains of the curtains of the tent, the half curtain that remains, shall hang over the back of the tabernacle. ¹³ And a cubit on one side and a cubit on the other side, of what remains of the length of the curtains of the tent, shall hang over the sides of the tabernacle, on this side and on that side, to cover it.

¹⁴ "You shall also make a covering of ram skins dyed red for the tent, and a covering of badger skins above that.

¹⁵ "And for the tabernacle you shall make the boards of acacia wood, standing upright. ¹⁶ Ten cubits *shall be* the length of a board, and a cubit and a half *shall be* the width of each board. ¹⁷ Two tenons *shall be* in each board for binding one to another. Thus you shall make for all the boards of the tabernacle. ¹⁸ And you shall make the boards for the tabernacle, twenty boards for the south side. ¹⁹ You shall make forty sockets of silver under the twenty boards: two sockets under each of the boards for its two tenons. ²⁰ And for the second side of the tabernacle, the north side, *there shall be*

twenty boards ²¹ and their forty sockets of silver: two sockets under each of the boards. ²² For the far side of the tabernacle, westward, you shall make six boards. ²³ And you shall also make two boards for the two back corners of the tabernacle. ²⁴ They shall be coupled together at the bottom and they shall be coupled together at the top by one ring. Thus it shall be for both of them. They shall be for the two corners. ²⁵ So there shall be eight boards with their sockets of silver—sixteen sockets—two sockets under each of the boards.

²⁶ "And you shall make bars of acacia wood: five for the boards on one side of the tabernacle, ²⁷ five bars for the boards on the other side of the tabernacle, and five bars for the boards of the side of the tabernacle, for the far side westward. ²⁸ The middle bar shall pass through the midst of the boards from end to end. ²⁹ You shall overlay the boards with gold, make their rings of gold as holders for the bars, and overlay the bars with gold. ³⁰ And you shall raise up the tabernacle according to its pattern which you were shown on the mountain.

³¹ "You shall make a veil woven of blue, purple, and scarlet *thread*, and fine woven linen. It shall be woven with an artistic design of cherubim. ³² You shall hang it upon the four pillars of acacia *wood* overlaid with gold. Their hooks *shall be* gold, upon four sockets of silver. ³³ And you shall hang the veil from the clasps. Then you shall bring the ark of the Testimony in there, behind the veil. The veil shall be a divider for you between the holy *place* and the Most Holy. ³⁴ You shall put the mercy seat upon the ark of the Testimony in the Most Holy. ³⁵ You shall set the table outside the veil, and the lampstand across from the table on the side of the tabernacle toward the south; and you shall put the table on the north side.

³⁶ "You shall make a screen for the door of the tabernacle, *woven of* blue, purple, and scarlet *thread*, and fine woven linen, made by a weaver. ³⁷ And you shall make for the screen five pillars of acacia *wood*, and overlay them with gold; their hooks *shall be* gold, and you shall cast five sockets of bronze for them.

∼ PSALM 19:7–14 ∼

7 The law of the LORD *is* perfect,
      converting the soul;
   The testimony of the LORD *is* sure,
      making wise the simple;
8 The statutes of the LORD *are* right,
      rejoicing the heart;
   The commandment of the LORD *is*
      pure, enlightening the eyes;
9 The fear of the LORD *is* clean,
      enduring forever;
   The judgments of the LORD *are* true
      and righteous altogether.
10 More to be desired *are they* than
      gold,
   Yea, than much fine gold;
   Sweeter also than honey and the
      honeycomb.
11 Moreover by them Your servant is
      warned,
   And in keeping them *there is* great
      reward.

12 Who can understand *his* errors?
   Cleanse me from secret *faults*.
13 Keep back Your servant also from
      presumptuous *sins*;
   Let them not have dominion over
      me.
   Then I shall be blameless,
   And I shall be innocent of great
      transgression.

14 Let the words of my mouth and the
      meditation of my heart
   Be acceptable in Your sight,
   O LORD, my strength and my
      Redeemer.

∼ PROVERBS 6:32–35 ∼

32 Whoever commits adultery with a
      woman lacks understanding;
   He *who* does so destroys his own
      soul.
33 Wounds and dishonor he will get,
   And his reproach will not be wiped
      away.
34 For jealousy *is* a husband's fury;
   Therefore he will not spare in the
      day of vengeance.
35 He will accept no recompense,

Nor will he be appeased though you give many gifts.

~ MATTHEW 24:1–28 ~

Then Jesus went out and departed from the temple, and His disciples came up to show Him the buildings of the temple. [2] And Jesus said to them, "Do you not see all these things? Assuredly, I say to you, not *one* stone shall be left here upon another, that shall not be thrown down."

[3] Now as He sat on the Mount of Olives, the disciples came to Him privately, saying, "Tell us, when will these things be? And what *will be* the sign of Your coming, and of the end of the age?"

[4] And Jesus answered and said to them: "Take heed that no one deceives you. [5] For many will come in My name, saying, 'I am the Christ,' and will deceive many. [6] And you will hear of wars and rumors of wars. See that you are not troubled; for all *these things* must come to pass, but the end is not yet. [7] For nation will rise against nation, and kingdom against kingdom. And there will be famines, pestilences, and earthquakes in various places. [8] All these *are* the beginning of sorrows.

[9] "Then they will deliver you up to tribulation and kill you, and you will be hated by all nations for My name's sake. [10] And then many will be offended, will betray one another, and will hate one another. [11] Then many false prophets will rise up and deceive many. [12] And because lawlessness will abound, the love of many will grow cold. [13] But he who endures to the end shall be saved. [14] And this gospel of the kingdom will be preached in all the world as a witness to all the nations, and then the end will come.

[15] "Therefore when you see the 'abomination of desolation,' spoken of by Daniel the prophet, standing in the holy place" (whoever reads, let him understand), [16] "then let those who are in Judea flee to the mountains. [17] Let him who is on the housetop not go down to take anything out of his house. [18] And let him who is in the field not go back to get his clothes. [19] But woe to those who are pregnant and to those who are nursing babies in those days! [20] And pray that your flight may not be in winter or on the Sabbath. [21] For then there will be great tribulation, such as has not been since the beginning of the world until this time, no, nor ever shall be. [22] And unless those days were shortened, no flesh would be saved; but for the elect's sake those days will be shortened.

[23] "Then if anyone says to you, 'Look, here *is* the Christ!' or 'There!' do not believe *it*. [24] For false christs and false prophets will rise and show great signs and wonders to deceive, if possible, even the elect. [25] See, I have told you beforehand. [26] "Therefore if they say to you, 'Look, He is in the desert!' do not go out; *or* 'Look, *He is* in the inner rooms!' do not believe *it*. [27] For as the lightning comes from the east and flashes to the west, so also will the coming of the Son of Man be. [28] For wherever the carcass is, there the eagles will be gathered together.

READING 39 · FEBRUARY 8

~ EXODUS 27:1—28:43 ~

"You shall make an altar of acacia wood, five cubits long and five cubits wide—the altar shall be square—and its height *shall be* three cubits. [2] You shall make its horns on its four corners; its horns shall be of one piece with it. And you shall overlay it with bronze. [3] Also you shall make its pans to receive its ashes, and its shovels and its basins and its forks and its firepans; you shall make all its utensils of bronze. [4] You shall make a grate for it, a network of bronze; and on the network you shall make four bronze rings at its four corners. [5] You shall put it under the rim of the altar beneath, that the network may be midway up the altar. [6] And you shall make poles for the altar, poles of acacia wood, and overlay them with bronze. [7] The poles shall be put in the rings, and the poles shall be on the two sides of the altar to bear it. [8] You shall make it hollow

Fulfilling Your Purpose

At forty-three, Lenny felt the time had come to give something back to his community, so he volunteered at a feeding program for homeless people. Soon he was counseling the families who came for food, directing them to places that provided shelter and helping several of the men find jobs. The director of the program told him he had a talent for working with people and encouraged him to develop it.

Lenny had been working in a semi-clerical position as an administrative aid to a corporate executive. There wasn't any higher place he could go in his field or within the company. His one regret had been that he had never gone to college. Armed with the encouraging words of his fellow volunteers, he and his wife sold their home and went back to school. They both eventually earned doctoral degrees and became full-time family therapists. They opened a clinic together and rebuilt their lives, this time enjoying a much greater sense of personal fulfillment.

It's never too late to start a new career. And it's never too late to make a new start in your spiritual life. Genuine success is found in establishing a relationship with God, discovering who He created you to be, then developing talents and gifts He has given you!

with boards; as it was shown you on the mountain, so shall they make it.

⁹ "You shall also make the court of the tabernacle. For the south side *there shall be* hangings for the court *made of* fine woven linen, one hundred cubits long for one side. ¹⁰ And its twenty pillars and their twenty sockets *shall be* bronze. The hooks of the pillars and their bands *shall be* silver. ¹¹ Likewise along the length of the north side *there shall be* hangings one hundred *cubits* long, with its twenty pillars and their twenty sockets of bronze, and the hooks of the pillars and their bands of silver.

¹² "And along the width of the court on the west side *shall be* hangings of fifty cubits, with their ten pillars and their ten sockets. ¹³ The width of the court on the east side *shall be* fifty cubits. ¹⁴ The hangings on *one* side *of the gate shall be* fifteen cubits, *with* their three pillars and their three sockets. ¹⁵ And on the other side *shall be* hangings of fifteen *cubits,* *with* their three pillars and their three sockets.

¹⁶ "For the gate of the court *there shall be* a screen twenty cubits long, *woven of* blue, purple, and scarlet *thread,* and fine woven linen, made by a weaver. It *shall have* four pillars and four sockets. ¹⁷ All the pillars around the court shall have bands of silver; their hooks *shall be* of silver and their sockets of bronze. ¹⁸ The length of the court *shall be* one hundred cubits, the width fifty throughout, and the height five cubits, *made of* fine woven linen, and its sockets of bronze. ¹⁹ All the utensils of the tabernacle for all its service, all its pegs, and all the pegs of the court, *shall be* of bronze.

²⁰ "And you shall command the children of Israel that they bring you pure oil of pressed olives for the light, to cause the lamp to burn continually. ²¹ In the tabernacle of meeting, outside the veil which *is* before the Testimony, Aaron and his sons shall tend it from evening until morning before the LORD. *It shall be* a statute forever to their generations on behalf of the children of Israel.

28 "Now take Aaron your brother, and his sons with him, from among the children of Israel, that he may minister to Me

as priest, Aaron *and* Aaron's sons: Nadab, Abihu, Eleazar, and Ithamar. ² And you shall make holy garments for Aaron your brother, for glory and for beauty. ³ So you shall speak to all *who are* gifted artisans, whom I have filled with the spirit of wisdom, that they may make Aaron's garments, to consecrate him, that he may minister to Me as priest. ⁴ And these *are* the garments which they shall make: a breastplate, an ephod, a robe, a skillfully woven tunic, a turban, and a sash. So they shall make holy garments for Aaron your brother and his sons, that he may minister to Me as priest.

⁵ "They shall take the gold, blue, purple, and scarlet *thread,* and the fine linen, ⁶ and they shall make the ephod of gold, blue, purple, *and* scarlet *thread,* and fine woven linen, artistically worked. ⁷ It shall have two shoulder straps joined at its two edges, and *so* it shall be joined together. ⁸ And the intricately woven band of the ephod, which *is* on it, shall be of the same workmanship, *made of* gold, blue, purple, and scarlet *thread,* and fine woven linen.

⁹ "Then you shall take two onyx stones and engrave on them the names of the sons of Israel: ¹⁰ six of their names on one stone and six names on the other stone, in order of their birth. ¹¹ With the work of an engraver in stone, *like* the engravings of a signet, you shall engrave the two stones with the names of the sons of Israel. You shall set them in settings of gold. ¹² And you shall put the two stones on the shoulders of the ephod *as* memorial stones for the sons of Israel. So Aaron shall bear their names before the LORD on his two shoulders as a memorial. ¹³ You shall also make settings of gold, ¹⁴ and you shall make two chains of pure gold like braided cords, and fasten the braided chains to the settings.

¹⁵ "You shall make the breastplate of judgment. Artistically woven according to the workmanship of the ephod you shall make it: of gold, blue, purple, and scarlet *thread,* and fine woven linen, you shall make it. ¹⁶ It shall be doubled into a square: a span *shall be* its length, and a span *shall be* its width. ¹⁷ And you shall put settings of stones in it, four rows of stones: *The first* row *shall be* a sardius, a topaz, and an emerald; *this shall be* the

first row; [18] the second row *shall be* a turquoise, a sapphire, and a diamond; [19] the third row, a jacinth, an agate, and an amethyst; [20] and the fourth row, a beryl, an onyx, and a jasper. They shall be set in gold settings. [21] And the stones shall have the names of the sons of Israel, twelve according to their names, *like* the engravings of a signet, each one with its own name; they shall be according to the twelve tribes.

[22] "You shall make chains for the breastplate at the end, like braided cords of pure gold. [23] And you shall make two rings of gold for the breastplate, and put the two rings on the two ends of the breastplate. [24] Then you shall put the two braided *chains* of gold in the two rings which are on the ends of the breastplate; [25] and the *other* two ends of the two braided *chains* you shall fasten to the two settings, and put them on the shoulder straps of the ephod in the front.

[26] "You shall make two rings of gold, and put them on the two ends of the breastplate, on the edge of it, which is on the inner side of the ephod. [27] And two *other* rings of gold you shall make, and put them on the two shoulder straps, underneath the ephod toward its front, right at the seam above the intricately woven band of the ephod. [28] They shall bind the breastplate by means of its rings to the rings of the ephod, using a blue cord, so that it is above the intricately woven band of the ephod, and so that the breastplate does not come loose from the ephod.

[29] "So Aaron shall bear the names of the sons of Israel on the breastplate of judgment over his heart, when he goes into the holy *place,* as a memorial before the LORD continually. [30] And you shall put in the breastplate of judgment the Urim and the Thummim, and they shall be over Aaron's heart when he goes in before the LORD. So Aaron shall bear the judgment of the children of Israel over his heart before the LORD continually.

[31] "You shall make the robe of the ephod all of blue. [32] There shall be an opening for his head in the middle of it; it shall have a woven binding all around its opening, like the opening in a coat of mail, so that it does not tear. [33] And upon its hem you shall make pomegranates of blue,

purple, and scarlet, all around its hem, and bells of gold between them all around: [34] a golden bell and a pomegranate, a golden bell and a pomegranate, upon the hem of the robe all around. [35] And it shall be upon Aaron when he ministers, and its sound will be heard when he goes into the holy *place* before the LORD and when he comes out, that he may not die.

[36] "You shall also make a plate of pure gold and engrave on it, *like* the engraving of a signet:

HOLINESS TO THE LORD.

[37] And you shall put it on a blue cord, that it may be on the turban; it shall be on the front of the turban. [38] So it shall be on Aaron's forehead, that Aaron may bear the iniquity of the holy things which the children of Israel hallow in all their holy gifts; and it shall always be on his forehead, that they may be accepted before the LORD.

[39] "You shall skillfully weave the tunic of fine linen *thread,* you shall make the turban of fine linen, and you shall make the sash of woven work.

[40] "For Aaron's sons you shall make tunics, and you shall make sashes for them. And you shall make hats for them, for glory and beauty. [41] So you shall put them on Aaron your brother and on his sons with him. You shall anoint them, consecrate them, and sanctify them, that they may minister to Me as priests. [42] And you shall make for them linen trousers to cover their nakedness; they shall reach from the waist to the thighs. [43] They shall be on Aaron and on his sons when they come into the tabernacle of meeting, or when they come near the altar to minister in the holy *place,* that they do not incur iniquity and die. *It shall be* a statute forever to him and his descendants after him.

～ PSALM 20:1–5 ～

1   May the LORD answer you in the
      day of trouble;
    May the name of the God of Jacob
      defend you;
2   May He send you help from the
      sanctuary,
    And strengthen you out of Zion;

³ May He remember all your
   offerings,
   And accept your burnt sacrifice.
                              Selah

⁴ May He grant you according to your
   heart's *desire*,
   And fulfill all your purpose.

⁵ We will rejoice in your salvation,
   And in the name of our God we will
   set up *our* banners!
   May the LORD fulfill all your
   petitions.

～ PROVERBS 7:1–5 ～

¹ My son, keep my words,
   And treasure my commands within
   you.

² Keep my commands and live,
   And my law as the apple of your eye.

³ Bind them on your fingers;
   Write them on the tablet of your
   heart.

⁴ Say to wisdom, "You *are* my sister,"
   And call understanding *your* nearest
   kin,

⁵ That they may keep you from the
   immoral woman,
   From the seductress *who* flatters
   with her words.

～ MATTHEW 24:29–51 ～

"Immediately after the tribulation of those days the sun will be darkened, and the moon will not give its light; the stars will fall from heaven, and the powers of the heavens will be shaken. ³⁰ Then the sign of the Son of Man will appear in heaven, and then all the tribes of the earth will mourn, and they will see the Son of Man coming on the clouds of heaven with power and great glory. ³¹ And He will send His angels with a great sound of a trumpet, and they will gather together His elect from the four winds, from one end of heaven to the other.

³² "Now learn this parable from the fig tree: When its branch has already become tender and puts forth leaves, you know that summer *is* near. ³³ So you also, when you see all these things, know that it is near—at the doors! ³⁴ Assuredly, I say to you, this generation will by no means pass away till all these things take place. ³⁵ Heaven and earth will pass away, but My words will by no means pass away.

³⁶ "But of that day and hour no one knows, not even the angels of heaven, but My Father only. ³⁷ But as the days of Noah *were,* so also will the coming of the Son of Man be. ³⁸ For as in the days before the flood, they were eating and drinking, marrying and giving in marriage, until the day that Noah entered the ark, ³⁹ and did not know until the flood came and took them all away, so also will the coming of the Son of Man be. ⁴⁰ Then two *men* will be in the field: one will be taken and the other left. ⁴¹ Two *women will be* grinding at the mill: one will be taken and the other left. ⁴² Watch therefore, for you do not know what hour your Lord is coming. ⁴³ But know this, that if the master of the house had known what hour the thief would come, he would have watched and not allowed his house to be broken into. ⁴⁴ Therefore you also be ready, for the Son of Man is coming at an hour you do not expect.

⁴⁵ "Who then is a faithful and wise servant, whom his master made ruler over his household, to give them food in due season? ⁴⁶ Blessed *is* that servant whom his master, when he comes, will find so doing. ⁴⁷ Assuredly, I say to you that he will make him ruler over all his goods. ⁴⁸ But if that evil servant says in his heart, 'My master is delaying his coming,' ⁴⁹ and begins to beat *his* fellow servants, and to eat and drink with the drunkards, ⁵⁰ the master of that servant will come on a day when he is not looking for *him* and at an hour that he is not aware of, ⁵¹ and will cut him in two and appoint *him* his portion with the hypocrites. There shall be weeping and gnashing of teeth.

~ EXODUS 29:1—30:38 ~

"And this is what you shall do to them to hallow them for ministering to Me as priests: Take one young bull and two rams without blemish, [2] and unleavened bread, unleavened cakes mixed with oil, and unleavened wafers anointed with oil (you shall make them of wheat flour). [3] You shall put them in one basket and bring them in the basket, with the bull and the two rams.

[4] "And Aaron and his sons you shall bring to the door of the tabernacle of meeting, and you shall wash them with water. [5] Then you shall take the garments, put the tunic on Aaron, and the robe of the ephod, the ephod, and the breastplate, and gird him with the intricately woven band of the ephod. [6] You shall put the turban on his head, and put the holy crown on the turban. [7] And you shall take the anointing oil, pour *it* on his head, and anoint him. [8] Then you shall bring his sons and put tunics on them. [9] And you shall gird them with sashes, Aaron and his sons, and put the hats on them. The priesthood shall be theirs for a perpetual statute. So you shall consecrate Aaron and his sons.

[10] "You shall also have the bull brought before the tabernacle of meeting, and Aaron and his sons shall put their hands on the head of the bull. [11] Then you shall kill the bull before the LORD, *by* the door of the tabernacle of meeting. [12] You shall take *some* of the blood of the bull and put *it* on the horns of the altar with your finger, and pour all the blood beside the base of the altar. [13] And you shall take all the fat that covers the entrails, the fatty lobe *attached* to the liver, and the two kidneys and the fat that *is* on them, and burn *them* on the altar. [14] But the flesh of the bull, with its skin and its offal, you shall burn with fire outside the camp. It *is* a sin offering.

[15] "You shall also take one ram, and Aaron and his sons shall put their hands on the head of the ram; [16] and you shall kill the ram, and you shall take its blood and sprinkle *it* all around on the altar. [17] Then you shall cut the ram in pieces, wash its entrails and its legs, and put *them* with its pieces and with its head. [18] And you shall burn the whole ram on the altar. It *is* a burnt offering to the LORD; it *is* a sweet aroma, an offering made by fire to the LORD.

[19] "You shall also take the other ram, and Aaron and his sons shall put their hands on the head of the ram. [20] Then you shall kill the ram, and take some of its blood and put *it* on the tip of the right ear of Aaron and on the tip of the right ear of his sons, on the thumb of their right hand and on the big toe of their right foot, and sprinkle the blood all around on the altar. [21] And you shall take some of the blood that is on the altar, and some of the anointing oil, and sprinkle *it* on Aaron and on his garments, on his sons and on the garments of his sons with him; and he and his garments shall be hallowed, and his sons and his sons' garments with him.

[22] "Also you shall take the fat of the ram, the fat tail, the fat that covers the entrails, the fatty lobe *attached to* the liver, the two kidneys and the fat on them, the right thigh (for it *is* a ram of consecration), [23] one loaf of bread, one cake *made with* oil, and one wafer from the basket of the unleavened bread that *is* before the LORD; [24] and you shall put all these in the hands of Aaron and in the hands of his sons, and you shall wave them *as* a wave offering before the LORD. [25] You shall receive them back from their hands and burn *them* on the altar as a burnt offering, as a sweet aroma before the LORD. It *is* an offering made by fire to the LORD.

[26] "Then you shall take the breast of the ram of Aaron's consecration and wave it *as* a wave offering before the LORD; and it shall be your portion. [27] And from the ram of the consecration you shall consecrate the breast of the wave offering which is waved, and the thigh of the heave offering which is raised, of *that* which *is* for Aaron and of *that* which is for his sons. [28] It shall be from the children of Israel *for* Aaron and his sons by a statute forever. For it is a heave offering; it shall be a heave offering from the children of Israel from the sacrifices of their peace offerings, *that is,* their heave offering to the LORD.

29 "And the holy garments of Aaron shall be his sons' after him, to be anointed in them and to be consecrated in them. 30 That son who becomes priest in his place shall put them on for seven days, when he enters the tabernacle of meeting to minister in the holy *place.*

31 "And you shall take the ram of the consecration and boil its flesh in the holy place. 32 Then Aaron and his sons shall eat the flesh of the ram, and the bread that *is* in the basket, *by* the door of the tabernacle of meeting. 33 They shall eat those things with which the atonement was made, to consecrate *and* to sanctify them; but an outsider shall not eat *them,* because they *are* holy. 34 And if any of the flesh of the consecration offerings, or of the bread, remains until the morning, then you shall burn the remainder with fire. It shall not be eaten, because it *is* holy.

35 "Thus you shall do to Aaron and his sons, according to all that I have commanded you. Seven days you shall consecrate them. 36 And you shall offer a bull every day *as* a sin offering for atonement. You shall cleanse the altar when you make atonement for it, and you shall anoint it to sanctify it. 37 Seven days you shall make atonement for the altar and sanctify it. And the altar shall be most holy. Whatever touches the altar must be holy.

38 "Now this *is* what you shall offer on the altar: two lambs of the first year, day by day continually. 39 One lamb you shall offer in the morning, and the other lamb you shall offer at twilight. 40 With the one lamb shall be one-tenth *of an ephah* of flour mixed with one-fourth of a hin of pressed oil, and one-fourth of a hin of wine *as* a drink offering. 41 And the other lamb you shall offer at twilight; and you shall offer with it the grain offering and the drink offering, as in the morning, for a sweet aroma, an offering made by fire to the LORD. 42 *This shall be* a continual burnt offering throughout your generations *at* the door of the tabernacle of meeting before the LORD, where I will meet you to speak with you. 43 And there I will meet with the children of Israel, and *the tabernacle* shall be sanctified by My glory. 44 So I will consecrate the tabernacle of meeting and the altar. I will also consecrate both Aaron and his sons to minister to Me as priests. 45 I will dwell among the children of Israel and will be their God. 46 And they shall know that I *am* the LORD their God, who brought them up out of the land of Egypt, that I may dwell among them. I *am* the LORD their God.

30 "You shall make an altar to burn incense on; you shall make it of acacia wood. 2 A cubit *shall be* its length and a cubit its width—it shall be square—and two cubits *shall be* its height. Its horns *shall be* of one piece with it. 3 And you shall overlay its top, its sides all around, and its horns with pure gold; and you shall make for it a molding of gold all around. 4 Two gold rings you shall make for it, under the molding on both its sides. You shall place *them* on its two sides, and they will be holders for the poles with which to bear it. 5 You shall make the poles of acacia wood, and overlay them with gold. 6 And you shall put it before the veil that *is* before the ark of the Testimony, before the mercy seat that *is* over the Testimony, where I will meet with you.

7 "Aaron shall burn on it sweet incense every morning; when he tends the lamps, he shall burn incense on it. 8 And when Aaron lights the lamps at twilight, he shall burn incense on it, a perpetual incense before the LORD throughout your generations. 9 You shall not offer strange incense on it, or a burnt offering, or a grain offering; nor shall you pour a drink offering on it. 10 And Aaron shall make atonement upon its horns once a year with the blood of the sin offering of atonement; once a year he shall make atonement upon it throughout your generations. It *is* most holy to the LORD."

11 Then the LORD spoke to Moses, saying: 12 "When you take the census of the children of Israel for their number, then every man shall give a ransom for himself to the LORD, when you number them, that there may be no plague among them when *you* number them. 13 This is what everyone among those who are numbered shall give: half a shekel according to the shekel of the sanctuary (a shekel *is* twenty gerahs). The half-shekel *shall be* an offering to the LORD. 14 Everyone included among those who are numbered, from twenty years old and above, shall give an

He is Risen

When British minister W. E. Sangster first noticed an uneasiness in his throat and a dragging in his leg, he went to his physician. It was found that he had an incurable muscle disease that would result in gradual muscular atrophy, until he died. Rather than retreat in dismay, Sangster threw himself into his work in British home missions. He figured he could still write and that he would have even more time for prayer. He prayed, "Lord, let me stay in the struggle. . . . I don't mind if I can no longer be a general." He wrote articles and books, and helped organize prayer cells throughout England. When people came to him with words of pity, he insisted, "I'm only in the kindergarten of suffering."

Over time, Sangster's legs became useless. He completely lost his voice. However, at that point he could still hold a pen and write, although shakily. On Easter morning just a few weeks before he died, he wrote a letter to his daughter, saying, "It is terrible to wake up on Easter morning and have no voice to shout, 'He is risen!' — but it would be still more terrible to have a voice and not want to shout."

Are you using all of your capabilities to serve God today? In spite of the circumstances you may be in, there is something you can do. You can choose to have the proper attitude toward your suffering and go on in God's grace, shouting, "He is risen!"

offering to the LORD. ¹⁵ The rich shall not give more and the poor shall not give less than half a shekel, when *you* give an offering to the LORD, to make atonement for yourselves. ¹⁶ And you shall take the atonement money of the children of Israel, and shall appoint it for the service of the tabernacle of meeting, that it may be a memorial for the children of Israel before the LORD, to make atonement for yourselves."

¹⁷ Then the LORD spoke to Moses, saying: ¹⁸ "You shall also make a laver of bronze, with its base also of bronze, for washing. You shall put it between the tabernacle of meeting and the altar. And you shall put water in it, ¹⁹ for Aaron and his sons shall wash their hands and their feet in water from it. ²⁰ When they go into the tabernacle of meeting, or when they come near the altar to minister, to burn an offering made by fire to the LORD, they shall wash with water, lest they die. ²¹ So they shall wash their hands and their feet, lest they die. And it shall be a statute forever to them—to him and his descendants throughout their generations."

²² Moreover the LORD spoke to Moses, saying: ²³ "Also take for yourself quality spices—five hundred *shekels* of liquid myrrh, half as much sweet-smelling cinnamon (two hundred and fifty *shekels*), two hundred and fifty *shekels* of sweet-smelling cane, ²⁴ five hundred *shekels* of cassia, according to the shekel of the sanctuary, and a hin of olive oil. ²⁵ And you shall make from these a holy anointing oil, an ointment compounded according to the art of the perfumer. It shall be a holy anointing oil. ²⁶ With it you shall anoint the tabernacle of meeting and the ark of the Testimony; ²⁷ the table and all its utensils, the lampstand and its utensils, and the altar of incense; ²⁸ the altar of burnt offering with all its utensils, and the laver and its base. ²⁹ You shall consecrate them, that they may be most holy; whatever touches them must be holy. ³⁰ And you shall anoint Aaron and his sons, and consecrate them, that *they* may minister to Me as priests.

³¹ "And you shall speak to the children of Israel, saying: 'This shall be a holy anointing oil to Me throughout your generations. ³² It shall not be poured on man's flesh; nor shall you make *any other* like it, according to its composition. It *is* holy, *and* it shall be holy to you. ³³ Whoever compounds *any* like it, or whoever puts *any* of it on an outsider, shall be cut off from his people.' "

³⁴ And the LORD said to Moses: "Take sweet spices, stacte and onycha and galbanum, and pure frankincense with *these* sweet spices; there shall be equal amounts of each. ³⁵ You shall make of these an incense, a compound according to the art of the perfumer, salted, pure, *and* holy. ³⁶ And you shall beat *some* of it very fine, and put some of it before the Testimony in the tabernacle of meeting where I will meet with you. It shall be most holy to you. ³⁷ But *as for* the incense which you shall make, you shall not make any for yourselves, according to its composition. It shall be to you holy for the LORD. ³⁸ Whoever makes *any* like it, to smell it, he shall be cut off from his people."

∼ PSALM 20:6–9 ∼

⁶ Now I know that the LORD saves His anointed;
He will answer him from His holy heaven
With the saving strength of His right hand.

⁷ Some *trust* in chariots, and some in horses;
But we will remember the name of the LORD our God.
⁸ They have bowed down and fallen;
But we have risen and stand upright.

⁹ Save, LORD!
May the King answer us when we call.

∼ PROVERBS 7:6–23 ∼

⁶ For at the window of my house
I looked through my lattice,
⁷ And saw among the simple,
I perceived among the youths,
A young man devoid of understanding,
⁸ Passing along the street near her corner;
And he took the path to her house

9 In the twilight, in the evening,
   In the black and dark night.

10 And there a woman met him,
   With the attire of a harlot, and a
      crafty heart.

11 She *was* loud and rebellious,
   Her feet would not stay at home.

12 At times *she was* outside, at times in
      the open square,
   Lurking at every corner.

13 So she caught him and kissed him;
   With an impudent face she said to
      him:

14 "*I have* peace offerings with me;
   Today I have paid my vows.

15 So I came out to meet you,
   Diligently to seek your face,
   And I have found you.

16 I have spread my bed with tapestry,
   Colored coverings of Egyptian linen.

17 I have perfumed my bed
   With myrrh, aloes, and cinnamon.

18 Come, let us take our fill of love
      until morning;
   Let us delight ourselves with love.

19 For my husband *is* not at home;
   He has gone on a long journey;

20 He has taken a bag of money with
      him,
   And will come home on the
      appointed day."

21 With her enticing speech she caused
      him to yield,
   With her flattering lips she seduced
      him.

22 Immediately he went after her, as an
      ox goes to the slaughter,
   Or as a fool to the correction of the
      stocks,

23 Till an arrow struck his liver.
   As a bird hastens to the snare,
   He did not know it *would cost* his
      life.

~ MATTHEW 25:1–30 ~

"Then the kingdom of heaven shall be likened to ten virgins who took their lamps and went out to meet the bridegroom. [2] Now five of them were wise, and five *were* foolish. [3] Those who *were* foolish took their lamps and took no oil with them, [4] but the wise took oil in their vessels with their lamps. [5] But while the bridegroom was delayed, they all slumbered and slept.

[6] "And at midnight a cry was *heard:* 'Behold, the bridegroom is coming; go out to meet him!' [7] Then all those virgins arose and trimmed their lamps. [8] And the foolish said to the wise, 'Give us *some* of your oil, for our lamps are going out.' [9] But the wise answered, saying, 'No, lest there should not be enough for us and you; but go rather to those who sell, and buy for yourselves.' [10] And while they went to buy, the bridegroom came, and those who were ready went in with him to the wedding; and the door was shut.

[11] "Afterward the other virgins came also, saying, 'Lord, Lord, open to us!' [12] But he answered and said, 'Assuredly, I say to you, I do not know you.'

[13] "Watch therefore, for you know neither the day nor the hour in which the Son of Man is coming.

[14] "For *the kingdom of heaven is* like a man traveling to a far country, *who* called his own servants and delivered his goods to them. [15] And to one he gave five talents, to another two, and to another one, to each according to his own ability; and immediately he went on a journey. [16] Then he who had received the five talents went and traded with them, and made another five talents. [17] And likewise he who *had received* two gained two more also. [18] But he who had received one went and dug in the ground, and hid his lord's money. [19] After a long time the lord of those servants came and settled accounts with them.

[20] "So he who had received five talents came and brought five other talents, saying, 'Lord, you delivered to me five talents; look, I have gained five more talents besides them.' [21] His lord said to him, 'Well *done,* good and faithful servant; you were faithful over a few things, I will make you ruler over many things. Enter into the joy of your lord.' [22] He also who had received two talents came and said, 'Lord, you delivered to me two talents; look, I have gained two more talents besides them.' [23] His lord said to him, 'Well *done,* good and faithful servant; you have been faithful over a few things, I will make you ruler over many things. Enter into the joy of your lord.'

24 "Then he who had received the one talent came and said, 'Lord, I knew you to be a hard man, reaping where you have not sown, and gathering where you have not scattered seed. 25 And I was afraid, and went and hid your talent in the ground. Look, *there* you have *what is* yours.'

26 "But his lord answered and said to him, 'You wicked and lazy servant, you knew that I reap where I have not sown, and gather where I have not scattered seed. 27 So you ought to have deposited my money with the bankers, and at my coming I would have received back my own with interest. 28 So take the talent from him, and give *it* to him who has ten talents.

29 'For to everyone who has, more will be given, and he will have abundance; but from him who does not have, even what he has will be taken away. 30 And cast the unprofitable servant into the outer darkness. There will be weeping and gnashing of teeth.'

READING 41 · FEBRUARY 10

~ EXODUS 31:1—32:35 ~

Then the LORD spoke to Moses, saying: 2 "See, I have called by name Bezalel the son of Uri, the son of Hur, of the tribe of Judah. 3 And I have filled him with the Spirit of God, in wisdom, in understanding, in knowledge, and in all *manner of* workmanship, 4 to design artistic works, to work in gold, in silver, in bronze, 5 in cutting jewels for setting, in carving wood, and to work in all *manner of* workmanship.

6 "And I, indeed I, have appointed with him Aholiab the son of Ahisamach, of the tribe of Dan; and I have put wisdom in the hearts of all the gifted artisans, that they may make all that I have commanded you: 7 the tabernacle of meeting, the ark of the Testimony and the mercy seat that *is* on it, and all the furniture of the tabernacle— 8 the table and its utensils, the pure *gold* lampstand with all its utensils, the altar of incense, 9 the altar of burnt offering with all its utensils, and the laver and its base— 10 the garments of ministry, the holy garments for Aaron the priest and the garments of his sons, to minister as priests, 11 and the anointing oil and sweet incense for the holy *place.* According to all that I have commanded you they shall do."

12 And the LORD spoke to Moses, saying, 13 "Speak also to the children of Israel, saying: 'Surely My Sabbaths you shall keep, for it *is* a sign between Me and you throughout your generations, that *you* may know that I *am* the LORD who sanctifies you. 14 You shall keep the Sabbath, therefore, for *it is* holy to you. Everyone who profanes it shall surely be put to death; for whoever does *any* work on it, that person shall be cut off from among his people. 15 Work shall be done for six days, but the seventh *is* the Sabbath of rest, holy to the LORD. Whoever does *any* work on the Sabbath day, he shall surely be put to death. 16 Therefore the children of Israel shall keep the Sabbath, to observe the Sabbath throughout their generations *as* a perpetual covenant. 17 It *is* a sign between Me and the children of Israel forever; for *in* six days the LORD made the heavens and the earth, and on the seventh day He rested and was refreshed.' "

18 And when He had made an end of speaking with him on Mount Sinai, He gave Moses two tablets of the Testimony, tablets of stone, written with the finger of God.

32 Now when the people saw that Moses delayed coming down from the mountain, the people gathered together to Aaron, and said to him, "Come, make us gods that shall go before us; for *as for* this Moses, the man who brought us up out of the land of Egypt, we do not know what has become of him."

2 And Aaron said to them, "Break off the golden earrings which *are* in the ears of your wives, your sons, and your daughters, and bring *them* to me." 3 So all the people broke off the golden earrings

Honoring the Sabbath

For months, Eric Liddell trained with his heart set on winning the 100-meter race at the Olympics of 1924. Many sportswriters predicted that he would win. When he arrived at the games, however, Liddell learned that the 100-meter race was scheduled to be run on a Sunday. This posed a major problem for him, because Liddell did not believe he could honor God by running on the Sabbath. He bowed out of the race, and fans were stunned. Some who had praised him in the past now called him a fool. He came under intense pressure to change his mind, but Liddell stood firm.

Then a runner dropped out of the 400-meter race which was scheduled on a week day, and Liddell offered to fill the slot. This was not really his race — the distance was four times as long as the race for which he had diligently trained. Even so, Liddell crossed the tape as victor and set a record of 47.6 seconds in the process. He had earned an Olympic gold medal and made an uncompromising stand for his faith.

Liddell went on to become a missionary in China, where he died in a war camp in 1945. He lives in history as a man known more for his inner mettle than for his gold medal.

When we stand firm in our convictions, God will always reward us. It may not always be as quickly as in this case, maybe not even in our lifetime on earth, but the reward is inevitable. God always desires to bless us!

> You shall keep the Sabbath, therefore, for it is holy to you. Everyone who profanes it shall surely be put to death; for whoever does any work on it, that person shall be cut off from among his people.
>
> *Exodus 31:14*

which *were* in their ears, and brought *them* to Aaron. ⁴ And he received *the gold* from their hand, and he fashioned it with an engraving tool, and made a molded calf.

Then they said, "This *is* your god, O Israel, that brought you out of the land of Egypt!"

⁵ So when Aaron saw *it*, he built an altar before it. And Aaron made a proclamation and said, "Tomorrow *is* a feast to the LORD." ⁶ Then they rose early on the next day, offered burnt offerings, and brought peace offerings; and the people sat down to eat and drink, and rose up to play.

⁷ And the LORD said to Moses, "Go, get down! For your people whom you brought out of the land of Egypt have corrupted *themselves*. ⁸ They have turned aside quickly out of the way which I commanded them. They have made themselves a molded calf, and worshiped it and sacrificed to it, and said, 'This *is* your god, O Israel, that brought you out of the land of Egypt!' " ⁹ And the LORD said to Moses, "I have seen this people, and indeed it *is* a stiff-necked people! ¹⁰ Now therefore, let Me alone, that My wrath may burn hot against them and I may consume them. And I will make of you a great nation."

¹¹ Then Moses pleaded with the LORD his God, and said: "LORD, why does Your wrath burn hot against Your people whom You have brought out of the land of Egypt with great power and with a mighty hand? ¹² Why should the Egyptians speak, and say, 'He brought them out to harm them, to kill them in the mountains, and to consume them from the face of the earth'? Turn from Your fierce wrath, and relent from this harm to Your people. ¹³ Remember Abraham, Isaac, and Israel, Your servants, to whom You swore by Your own self, and said to them, 'I will multiply your descendants as the stars of heaven; and all this land that I have spoken of I give to your descendants, and they shall inherit *it* forever.' " ¹⁴ So the LORD relented from the harm which He said He would do to His people.

¹⁵ And Moses turned and went down from the mountain, and the two tablets of the Testimony *were* in his hand. The tablets *were* written on both sides; on the one *side* and on the other they were written. ¹⁶ Now the tablets *were* the work of God, and the writing *was* the writing of God engraved on the tablets.

¹⁷ And when Joshua heard the noise of the people as they shouted, he said to Moses, "*There is* a noise of war in the camp."

¹⁸ But he said:

"*It is* not the noise of the shout of victory,
Nor the noise of the cry of defeat,
But the sound of singing I hear."

¹⁹ So it was, as soon as he came near the camp, that he saw the calf *and* the dancing. So Moses' anger became hot, and he cast the tablets out of his hands and broke them at the foot of the mountain. ²⁰ Then he took the calf which they had made, burned *it* in the fire, and ground *it* to powder; and he scattered *it* on the water and made the children of Israel drink *it*. ²¹ And Moses said to Aaron, "What did this people do to you that you have brought *so* great a sin upon them?"

²² So Aaron said, "Do not let the anger of my lord become hot. You know the people, that they *are set* on evil. ²³ For they said to me, 'Make us gods that shall go before us; *as for* this Moses, the man who brought us out of the land of Egypt, we do not know what has become of him.' ²⁴ And I said to them, 'Whoever has any gold, let them break *it* off.' So they gave *it* to me, and I cast it into the fire, and this calf came out."

²⁵ Now when Moses saw that the people *were* unrestrained (for Aaron had not restrained them, to *their* shame among their enemies), ²⁶ then Moses stood in the entrance of the camp, and said, "Whoever *is* on the LORD's side—*come* to me!" And all the sons of Levi gathered themselves together to him. ²⁷ And he said to them, "Thus says the LORD God of Israel: 'Let every man put his sword on his side, and go in and out from entrance to entrance throughout the camp, and let every man kill his brother, every man his companion, and every man his neighbor.' " ²⁸ So the sons of Levi did according to the word of Moses. And about three thousand men of the people fell that day. ²⁹ Then Moses said, "Consecrate

yourselves today to the LORD, that He may bestow on you a blessing this day, for every man has opposed his son and his brother."

³⁰ Now it came to pass on the next day that Moses said to the people, "You have committed a great sin. So now I will go up to the LORD; perhaps I can make atonement for your sin." ³¹ Then Moses returned to the LORD and said, "Oh, these people have committed a great sin, and have made for themselves a god of gold! ³² Yet now, if You will forgive their sin— but if not, I pray, blot me out of Your book which You have written."

³³ And the LORD said to Moses, "Whoever has sinned against Me, I will blot him out of My book. ³⁴ Now therefore, go, lead the people to *the place* of which I have spoken to you. Behold, My Angel shall go before you. Nevertheless, in the day when I visit for punishment, I will visit punishment upon them for their sin."

³⁵ So the LORD plagued the people because of what they did with the calf which Aaron made.

∽ PSALM 21:1-7 ∽

¹ The king shall have joy in Your
        strength, O LORD;
    And in Your salvation how greatly
        shall he rejoice!
² You have given him his heart's
        desire,
    And have not withheld the request
        of his lips.   Selah

³ For You meet him with the blessings
        of goodness;
    You set a crown of pure gold upon
        his head.
⁴ He asked life from You, *and* You
        gave *it* to him—
    Length of days forever and ever.
⁵ His glory *is* great in Your salvation;
    Honor and majesty You have placed
        upon him.
⁶ For You have made him most blessed
        forever;
    You have made him exceedingly glad
        with Your presence.
⁷ For the king trusts in the LORD,
    And through the mercy of the Most
        High he shall not be moved.

∽ PROVERBS 7:24-27 ∽

²⁴ Now therefore, listen to me, *my*
        children;
    Pay attention to the words of my
        mouth:
²⁵ Do not let your heart turn aside to
        her ways,
    Do not stray into her paths;
²⁶ For she has cast down many
        wounded,
    And all who were slain by her were
        strong *men.*
²⁷ Her house *is* the way to hell,
    Descending to the chambers of
        death.

∽ MATTHEW 25:31-46 ∽

"When the Son of Man comes in His glory, and all the holy angels with Him, then He will sit on the throne of His glory. ³² All the nations will be gathered before Him, and He will separate them one from another, as a shepherd divides *his* sheep from the goats. ³³ And He will set the sheep on His right hand, but the goats on the left. ³⁴ Then the King will say to those on His right hand, 'Come, you blessed of My Father, inherit the kingdom prepared for you from the foundation of the world: ³⁵ for I was hungry and you gave Me food; I was thirsty and you gave Me drink; I was a stranger and you took Me in; ³⁶ I *was* naked and you clothed Me; I was sick and you visited Me; I was in prison and you came to Me.'

³⁷ "Then the righteous will answer Him, saying, 'Lord, when did we see You hungry and feed *You,* or thirsty and give *You* drink? ³⁸ When did we see You a stranger and take *You* in, or naked and clothe *You?* ³⁹ Or when did we see You sick, or in prison, and come to You?' ⁴⁰ And the King will answer and say to them, 'Assuredly, I say to you, inasmuch as you did *it* to one of the least of these My brethren, you did *it* to Me.'

⁴¹ "Then He will also say to those on the left hand, 'Depart from Me, you cursed, into the everlasting fire prepared for the devil and his angels: ⁴² for I was hungry and you gave Me no food; I was thirsty and you gave Me no drink;

⁴³ I was a stranger and you did not take Me in, naked and you did not clothe Me, sick and in prison and you did not visit Me.'

⁴⁴ "Then they also will answer Him, saying, 'Lord, when did we see You hungry or thirsty or a stranger or naked or sick or in prison, and did not minister to You?' ⁴⁵ Then He will answer them, saying, 'Assuredly, I say to you, inasmuch as you did not do *it* to one of the least of these, you did not do *it* to Me.' ⁴⁶ And these will go away into everlasting punishment, but the righteous into eternal life."

READING 42 · FEBRUARY 11

~ EXODUS 33:1—34:35 ~

Then the LORD said to Moses, "Depart *and* go up from here, you and the people whom you have brought out of the land of Egypt, to the land of which I swore to Abraham, Isaac, and Jacob, saying, 'To your descendants I will give it.' ² And I will send *My* Angel before you, and I will drive out the Canaanite and the Amorite and the Hittite and the Perizzite and the Hivite and the Jebusite. ³ *Go up* to a land flowing with milk and honey; for I will not go up in your midst, lest I consume you on the way, for you *are* a stiff-necked people."

⁴ And when the people heard this bad news, they mourned, and no one put on his ornaments. ⁵ For the LORD had said to Moses, "Say to the children of Israel, 'You *are* a stiff-necked people. I could come up into your midst in one moment and consume you. Now therefore, take off your ornaments, that I may know what to do to you.' " ⁶ So the children of Israel stripped themselves of their ornaments by Mount Horeb.

⁷ Moses took his tent and pitched it outside the camp, far from the camp, and called it the tabernacle of meeting. And it came to pass *that* everyone who sought the LORD went out to the tabernacle of meeting which *was* outside the camp. ⁸ So it was, whenever Moses went out to the tabernacle, *that* all the people rose, and each man stood *at* his tent door and watched Moses until he had gone into the tabernacle. ⁹ And it came to pass, when Moses entered the tabernacle, that the pillar of cloud descended and stood *at* the door of the tabernacle, and *the* LORD talked with Moses. ¹⁰ All the people saw the pillar of cloud standing *at* the tabernacle door, and all the people rose and worshiped, each man *in* his tent door. ¹¹ So the LORD spoke to Moses face to face, as a man speaks to his friend. And he would return to the camp, but his servant Joshua the son of Nun, a young man, did not depart from the tabernacle.

¹² Then Moses said to the LORD, "See, You say to me, 'Bring up this people.' But You have not let me know whom You will send with me. Yet You have said, 'I know you by name, and you have also found grace in My sight.' ¹³ Now therefore, I pray, if I have found grace in Your sight, show me now Your way, that I may know You and that I may find grace in Your sight. And consider that this nation *is* Your people."

¹⁴ And He said, "My Presence will go *with you,* and I will give you rest."

¹⁵ Then he said to Him, "If Your Presence does not go *with us,* do not bring us up from here. ¹⁶ For how then will it be known that Your people and I have found grace in Your sight, except You go with us? So we shall be separate, Your people and I, from all the people who *are* upon the face of the earth."

¹⁷ So the LORD said to Moses, "I will also do this thing that you have spoken; for you have found grace in My sight, and I know you by name."

¹⁸ And he said, "Please, show me Your glory."

¹⁹ Then He said, "I will make all My goodness pass before you, and I will proclaim the name of the LORD before you. I will be gracious to whom I will be gracious, and I will have compassion on whom I will have compassion." ²⁰ But He said, "You cannot see My face; for no man

Teaching Responsibility

Some have theorized that it is a fear of taking responsibility that led to the development of "errorless" machines — ones that allow for work to be done in a repetitive way so that it is "perfect" every time. Columbia University psychologist Herbert Terrace argues this approach. He contends that errorless machines fail to help people deal with the real world, where "you have to cope when you make a mistake."

In support of his view, he cites a study in which pigeons were taught to distinguish green from red. If they pecked a green light, they received no food. If they pecked a red light—half got food every time, but the other half received food on an erratic basis. When the pigeons that got a "reward" every time they pecked the right light were switched over to the group that received rewards irregularly, they hit their heads against the wall, flapped their wings, and pecked at everything in sight. The birds trained on the intermittent system didn't go wild when a correct peck failed to produce food. Instead, they remained calm and just continued pecking only at the red light until they were rewarded with a snack.

Responsibility is built as we take life in stride and acknowledge failures, disappointments, and faults. That's a valuable lesson we can teach our children. When we let them take responsibility for their own mistakes, rather than always trying to fix things, they become responsible people who won't end up directionless, hitting their heads against the wall.

shall see Me, and live." ²¹ And the LORD said, "Here is a place by Me, and you shall stand on the rock. ²² So it shall be, while My glory passes by, that I will put you in the cleft of the rock, and will cover you with My hand while I pass by. ²³ Then I will take away My hand, and you shall see My back; but My face shall not be seen."

34 And the LORD said to Moses, "Cut two tablets of stone like the first *ones,* and I will write on *these* tablets the words that were on the first tablets which you broke. ² So be ready in the morning, and come up in the morning to Mount Sinai, and present yourself to Me there on the top of the mountain. ³ And no man shall come up with you, and let no man be seen throughout all the mountain; let neither flocks nor herds feed before that mountain."

⁴ So he cut two tablets of stone like the first *ones.* Then Moses rose early in the morning and went up Mount Sinai, as the LORD had commanded him; and he took in his hand the two tablets of stone.

⁵ Now the LORD descended in the cloud and stood with him there, and proclaimed the name of the LORD. ⁶ And the LORD passed before him and proclaimed, "The LORD, the LORD God, merciful and gracious, longsuffering, and abounding in goodness and truth, ⁷ keeping mercy for thousands, forgiving iniquity and transgression and sin, by no means clearing *the guilty,* visiting the iniquity of the fathers upon the children and the children's children to the third and the fourth generation."

⁸ So Moses made haste and bowed his head toward the earth, and worshiped. ⁹ Then he said, "If now I have found grace in Your sight, O Lord, let my Lord, I pray, go among us, even though we *are* a stiff-necked people; and pardon our iniquity and our sin, and take us as Your inheritance."

¹⁰ And He said: "Behold, I make a covenant. Before all your people I will do marvels such as have not been done in all the earth, nor in any nation; and all the people among whom you *are* shall see the work of the LORD. For it *is* an awesome thing that I will do with you. ¹¹ Observe what I command you this day. Behold, I

am driving out from before you the Amorite and the Canaanite and the Hittite and the Perizzite and the Hivite and the Jebusite. ¹² Take heed to yourself, lest you make a covenant with the inhabitants of the land where you are going, lest it be a snare in your midst. ¹³ But you shall destroy their altars, break their *sacred* pillars, and cut down their wooden images ¹⁴(for you shall worship no other god, for the LORD, whose name *is* Jealous, *is* a jealous God), ¹⁵ lest you make a covenant with the inhabitants of the land, and they play the harlot with their gods and make sacrifice to their gods, and *one of them* invites you and you eat of his sacrifice, ¹⁶ and you take of his daughters for your sons, and his daughters play the harlot with their gods and make your sons play the harlot with their gods.

¹⁷ "You shall make no molded gods for yourselves.

¹⁸ "The Feast of Unleavened Bread you shall keep. Seven days you shall eat unleavened bread, as I commanded you, in the appointed time of the month of Abib; for in the month of Abib you came out from Egypt.

¹⁹ "All that open the womb *are* Mine, and every male firstborn among your livestock, *whether* ox or sheep. ²⁰ But the firstborn of a donkey you shall redeem with a lamb. And if you will not redeem *him,* then you shall break his neck. All the firstborn of your sons you shall redeem.

"And none shall appear before Me empty-handed.

²¹ "Six days you shall work, but on the seventh day you shall rest; in plowing time and in harvest you shall rest.

²² "And you shall observe the Feast of Weeks, of the firstfruits of wheat harvest, and the Feast of Ingathering at the year's end.

²³ "Three times in the year all your men shall appear before the Lord, the LORD God of Israel. ²⁴ For I will cast out the nations before you and enlarge your borders; neither will any man covet your land when you go up to appear before the LORD your God three times in the year.

²⁵ "You shall not offer the blood of My sacrifice with leaven, nor shall the sacrifice of the Feast of the Passover be left until morning.

²⁶ "The first of the firstfruits of your land you shall bring to the house of the LORD your God. You shall not boil a young goat in its mother's milk."

²⁷ Then the LORD said to Moses, "Write these words, for according to the tenor of these words I have made a covenant with you and with Israel." ²⁸ So he was there with the LORD forty days and forty nights; he neither ate bread nor drank water. And He wrote on the tablets the words of the covenant, the Ten Commandments.

²⁹ Now it was so, when Moses came down from Mount Sinai (and the two tablets of the Testimony *were* in Moses' hand when he came down from the mountain), that Moses did not know that the skin of his face shone while he talked with Him. ³⁰ So when Aaron and all the children of Israel saw Moses, behold, the skin of his face shone, and they were afraid to come near him. ³¹ Then Moses called to them, and Aaron and all the rulers of the congregation returned to him; and Moses talked with them. ³² Afterward all the children of Israel came near, and he gave them as commandments all that the LORD had spoken with him on Mount Sinai. ³³ And when Moses had finished speaking with them, he put a veil on his face. ³⁴ But whenever Moses went in before the LORD to speak with Him, he would take the veil off until he came out; and he would come out and speak to the children of Israel whatever he had been commanded. ³⁵ And whenever the children of Israel saw the face of Moses, that the skin of Moses' face shone, then Moses would put the veil on his face again, until he went in to speak with Him.

~ PSALM 21:8–13 ~

⁸ Your hand will find all Your
   enemies;
Your right hand will find those who
   hate You.
⁹ You shall make them as a fiery oven
   in the time of Your anger;
The LORD shall swallow them up in
   His wrath,
And the fire shall devour them.
¹⁰ Their offspring You shall destroy
   from the earth,

And their descendants from among
   the sons of men.
¹¹ For they intended evil against You;
They devised a plot *which* they are
   not able *to perform.*
¹² Therefore You will make them turn
   their back;
You will make ready *Your arrows* on
   Your string toward their faces.

¹³ Be exalted, O LORD, in Your own
   strength!
We will sing and praise Your power.

~ PROVERBS 8:1–5 ~

¹ Does not wisdom cry out,
And understanding lift up her voice?
² She takes her stand on the top of the
   high hill,
Beside the way, where the paths
   meet.
³ She cries out by the gates, at the
   entry of the city,
At the entrance of the doors:
⁴ "To you, O men, I call,
And my voice *is* to the sons of men.
⁵ O you simple ones, understand
   prudence,
And you fools, be of an
   understanding heart.

~ MATTHEW 26:1–25 ~

Now it came to pass, when Jesus had finished all these sayings, *that* He said to His disciples, ² "You know that after two days is the Passover, and the Son of Man will be delivered up to be crucified."

³ Then the chief priests, the scribes, and the elders of the people assembled at the palace of the high priest, who was called Caiaphas, ⁴ and plotted to take Jesus by trickery and kill *Him.* ⁵ But they said, "Not during the feast, lest there be an uproar among the people."

⁶ And when Jesus was in Bethany at the house of Simon the leper, ⁷ a woman came to Him having an alabaster flask of very costly fragrant oil, and she poured *it* on His head as He sat *at the table.* ⁸ But when His disciples saw *it,* they were indignant, saying, "Why this waste? ⁹ For this fragrant oil might have been sold for much and given to *the* poor."

¹⁰ But when Jesus was aware of *it,* He said to them, "Why do you trouble the woman? For she has done a good work for Me. ¹¹ For you have the poor with you always, but Me you do not have always. ¹² For in pouring this fragrant oil on My body, she did *it* for My burial. ¹³ Assuredly, I say to you, wherever this gospel is preached in the whole world, what this woman has done will also be told as a memorial to her."

¹⁴ Then one of the twelve, called Judas Iscariot, went to the chief priests ¹⁵ and said, "What are you willing to give me if I deliver Him to you?" And they counted out to him thirty pieces of silver. ¹⁶ So from that time he sought opportunity to betray Him.

¹⁷ Now on the first *day of the Feast* of Unleavened Bread the disciples came to Jesus, saying to Him, "Where do You want us to prepare for You to eat the Passover?"

¹⁸ And He said, "Go into the city to a certain man, and say to him, 'The Teacher says, "My time is at hand; I will keep the Passover at your house with My disciples." ' "

¹⁹ So the disciples did as Jesus had directed them; and they prepared the Passover.

²⁰ When evening had come, He sat down with the twelve. ²¹ Now as they were eating, He said, "Assuredly, I say to you, one of you will betray Me."

²² And they were exceedingly sorrowful, and each of them began to say to Him, "Lord, is it I?"

²³ He answered and said, "He who dipped *his* hand with Me in the dish will betray Me. ²⁴ The Son of Man indeed goes just as it is written of Him, but woe to that man by whom the Son of Man is betrayed! It would have been good for that man if he had not been born."

²⁵ Then Judas, who was betraying Him, answered and said, "Rabbi, is it I?"

He said to him, "You have said it."

READING 43 · FEBRUARY 12

~ EXODUS 35:1—36:38 ~

Then Moses gathered all the congregation of the children of Israel together, and said to them, "These *are* the words which the LORD has commanded *you* to do: ² Work shall be done for six days, but the seventh day shall be a holy day for you, a Sabbath of rest to the LORD. Whoever does any work on it shall be put to death. ³ You shall kindle no fire throughout your dwellings on the Sabbath day."

⁴ And Moses spoke to all the congregation of the children of Israel, saying, "This *is* the thing which the LORD commanded, saying: ⁵ 'Take from among you an offering to the LORD. Whoever *is* of a willing heart, let him bring it as an offering to the LORD: gold, silver, and bronze; ⁶ blue, purple, and scarlet *thread,* fine linen, and goats' *hair;* ⁷ ram skins dyed red, badger skins, and acacia wood; ⁸ oil for the light, and spices for the anointing oil and for the sweet incense; ⁹ onyx stones, and stones to be set in the ephod and in the breastplate.

¹⁰ 'All *who are* gifted artisans among you shall come and make all that the LORD has commanded: ¹¹ the tabernacle, its tent, its covering, its clasps, its boards, its bars, its pillars, and its sockets; ¹² the ark and its poles, *with* the mercy seat, and the veil of the covering; ¹³ the table and its poles, all its utensils, and the showbread; ¹⁴ also the lampstand for the light, its utensils, its lamps, and the oil for the light; ¹⁵ the incense altar, its poles, the anointing oil, the sweet incense, and the screen for the door at the entrance of the tabernacle; ¹⁶ the altar of burnt offering with its bronze grating, its poles, all its utensils, *and* the laver and its base; ¹⁷ the hangings of the court, its pillars, their sockets, and the screen for the gate of the court; ¹⁸ the pegs of the tabernacle, the pegs of the court, and their cords; ¹⁹ the garments of ministry, for ministering in the holy *place*—the holy

The Vigil

In the Middle Ages, an elaborate ceremony surrounded the conferring of knighthood. After certain rites had been performed, the candidate was conducted into his lord's chapel, where he was told to keep a vigil until sunrise. He was to pass the night by "bestowing himself in visions and prayer."

This ritual was vividly captured by artist John Pettie, in a painting he entitled "The Vigil." In it, a young armor-clad knight is seen kneeling before an altar. The light of dawn illuminates the dim aisles of the chapel behind him, but the knight doesn't seem to notice that his vigil is over. His noble but weary young face is still turned to the altar. His eyes have the look of one who has meditated at length on divine and holy things. His helmet and armor are laid on the steps leading to the altar, but he holds his sword in front of him. Its silhouette is the shape of a cross.

It is the cross that speaks to us of complete surrender to God's will, and compels us to follow Christ wherever He leads. It is the cross that unites us to God.

What is it that compels you to keep a prayer vigil? Are you holding the cross before you as you pray?

He went a little farther and fell on His face, and prayed, saying, "O My Father, if it is possible, let this cup pass from Me; nevertheless, not as I will, but as You will."

Matthew 26:39

garments for Aaron the priest and the garments of his sons, to minister as priests.' "

20 And all the congregation of the children of Israel departed from the presence of Moses. 21 Then everyone came whose heart was stirred, and everyone whose spirit was willing, *and* they brought the LORD's offering for the work of the tabernacle of meeting, for all its service, and for the holy garments. 22 They came, both men and women, as many as had a willing heart, *and* brought earrings and nose rings, rings and necklaces, all jewelry of gold, that is, every man who *made* an offering of gold to the LORD. 23 And every man, with whom was found blue, purple, and scarlet *thread,* fine linen, and goats' *hair,* red skins of rams, and badger skins, brought *them.* 24 Everyone who offered an offering of silver or bronze brought the LORD's offering. And everyone with whom was found acacia wood for any work of the service, brought *it.* 25 All the women *who were* gifted artisans spun yarn with their hands, and brought what they had spun, of blue, purple, *and* scarlet, and fine linen. 26 And all the women whose hearts stirred with wisdom spun yarn of goats' *hair.* 27 The rulers brought onyx stones, and the stones to be set in the ephod and in the breastplate, 28 and spices and oil for the light, for the anointing oil, and for the sweet incense. 29 The children of Israel brought a freewill offering to the LORD, all the men and women whose hearts were willing to bring *material* for all kinds of work which the LORD, by the hand of Moses, had commanded to be done.

30 And Moses said to the children of Israel, "See, the LORD has called by name Bezalel the son of Uri, the son of Hur, of the tribe of Judah; 31 and He has filled him with the Spirit of God, in wisdom and understanding, in knowledge and all manner of workmanship, 32 to design artistic works, to work in gold and silver and bronze, 33 in cutting jewels for setting, in carving wood, and to work in all manner of artistic workmanship.

34 "And He has put in his heart the ability to teach, *in* him and Aholiab the son of Ahisamach, of the tribe of Dan. 35 He has filled them with skill to do all manner of work of the engraver and the designer and the tapestry maker, in blue, purple, and scarlet *thread,* and fine linen, and of the weaver—those who do every work and those who design artistic works.

36 "And Bezalel and Aholiab, and every gifted artisan in whom the LORD has put wisdom and understanding, to know how to do all manner of work for the service of the sanctuary, shall do according to all that the LORD has commanded."

2 Then Moses called Bezalel and Aholiab, and every gifted artisan in whose heart the LORD had put wisdom, everyone whose heart was stirred, to come and do the work. 3 And they received from Moses all the offering which the children of Israel had brought for the work of the service of making the sanctuary. So they continued bringing to him freewill offerings every morning. 4 Then all the craftsmen who were doing all the work of the sanctuary came, each from the work he was doing, 5 and they spoke to Moses, saying, "The people bring much more than enough for the service of the work which the LORD commanded *us* to do."

6 So Moses gave a commandment, and they caused it to be proclaimed throughout the camp, saying, "Let neither man nor woman do any more work for the offering of the sanctuary." And the people were restrained from bringing, 7 for the material they had was sufficient for all the work to be done—indeed too much.

8 Then all the gifted artisans among them who worked on the tabernacle made ten curtains woven of fine linen, and of blue, purple, and scarlet thread; *with* artistic designs of cherubim they made them. 9 The length of each curtain *was* twenty-eight cubits, and the width of each curtain four cubits; the curtains *were* all the same size. 10 And he coupled five curtains to one another, and *the other* five curtains he coupled to one another. 11 He made loops of blue *yarn* on the edge of the curtain on the selvedge of one set; likewise he did on the outer edge of *the other* curtain of the second set. 12 Fifty loops he made on one curtain, and fifty loops he made on the edge of the curtain on the end of the second set; the loops held one *curtain* to another. 13 And he made fifty

clasps of gold, and coupled the curtains to one another with the clasps, that it might be one tabernacle.

¹⁴ He made curtains of goats' *hair* for the tent over the tabernacle; he made eleven curtains. ¹⁵ The length of each curtain *was* thirty cubits, and the width of each curtain four cubits; the eleven curtains *were* the same size. ¹⁶ He coupled five curtains by themselves and six curtains by themselves. ¹⁷ And he made fifty loops on the edge of the curtain that is outermost in one set, and fifty loops he made on the edge of the curtain of the second set. ¹⁸ He also made fifty bronze clasps to couple the tent together, that it might be one. ¹⁹ Then he made a covering for the tent of ram skins dyed red, and a covering of badger skins above *that.*

²⁰ For the tabernacle he made boards of acacia wood, standing upright. ²¹ The length of each board *was* ten cubits, and the width of each board a cubit and a half. ²² Each board had two tenons for binding one to another. Thus he made for all the boards of the tabernacle. ²³ And he made boards for the tabernacle, twenty boards for the south side. ²⁴ Forty sockets of silver he made to go under the twenty boards: two sockets under each of the boards for its two tenons. ²⁵ And for the other side of the tabernacle, the north side, he made twenty boards ²⁶ and their forty sockets of silver: two sockets under each of the boards. ²⁷ For the west side of the tabernacle he made six boards. ²⁸ He also made two boards for the two back corners of the tabernacle. ²⁹ And they were coupled at the bottom and coupled together at the top by one ring. Thus he made both of them for the two corners. ³⁰ So there were eight boards and their sockets—sixteen sockets of silver—two sockets under each of the boards.

³¹ And he made bars of acacia wood: five for the boards on one side of the tabernacle, ³² five bars for the boards on the other side of the tabernacle, and five bars for the boards of the tabernacle on the far side westward. ³³ And he made the middle bar to pass through the boards from one end to the other. ³⁴ He overlaid the boards with gold, made their rings of gold *to be* holders for the bars, and overlaid the bars with gold.

³⁵ And he made a veil of blue, purple, and scarlet *thread,* and fine woven linen; it was worked *with* an artistic design of cherubim. ³⁶ He made for it four pillars of acacia *wood,* and overlaid them with gold, with their hooks of gold; and he cast four sockets of silver for them.

³⁷ He also made a screen for the tabernacle door, of blue, purple, and scarlet *thread,* and fine woven linen, made by a weaver, ³⁸ and its five pillars with their hooks. And he overlaid their capitals and their rings with gold, but their five sockets *were* bronze.

∼ PSALM 22:1–8 ∼

1 My God, My God, why have You
     forsaken Me?
   Why are You so far from helping Me,
   And from the words of My
     groaning?
2 O My God, I cry in the daytime, but
     You do not hear;
   And in the night season, and am not
     silent.

3 But You *are* holy,
   Enthroned in the praises of Israel.
4 Our fathers trusted in You;
   They trusted, and You delivered
     them.
5 They cried to You, and were
     delivered;
   They trusted in You, and were not
     ashamed.

6 But I *am* a worm, and no man;
   A reproach of men, and despised by
     the people.
7 All those who see Me ridicule Me;
   They shoot out the lip, they shake
     the head, *saying,*
8 "He trusted in the LORD, let Him
     rescue Him;
   Let Him deliver Him, since He
     delights in Him!"

∼ PROVERBS 8:6–11 ∼

6 Listen, for I will speak of excellent
     things,
   And from the opening of my lips
     will come right things;
7 For my mouth will speak truth;

Wickedness *is* an abomination to my
lips.
8 All the words of my mouth *are* with
righteousness;
Nothing crooked or perverse *is* in
them.
9 They *are* all plain to him who
understands,
And right to those who find
knowledge.
10 Receive my instruction, and not
silver,
And knowledge rather than choice
gold;
11 For wisdom *is* better than rubies,
And all the things one may desire
cannot be compared with her.

~ MATTHEW 26:26–50 ~

And as they were eating, Jesus took bread,
blessed and broke *it,* and gave *it* to the
disciples and said, "Take, eat; this is My
body."
27 Then He took the cup, and gave
thanks, and gave *it* to them, saying, "Drink
from it, all of you. 28 For this is My blood
of the new covenant, which is shed for
many for the remission of sins. 29 But I
say to you, I will not drink of this fruit of
the vine from now on until that day when
I drink it new with you in My Father's
kingdom."
30 And when they had sung a hymn, they
went out to the Mount of Olives.
31 Then Jesus said to them, "All of you
will be made to stumble because of Me
this night, for it is written:

'I will strike the Shepherd,
And the sheep of the flock will be
scattered.'

32 But after I have been raised, I will go
before you to Galilee."
33 Peter answered and said to Him,
"Even if all are made to stumble because
of You, I will never be made to stumble."
34 Jesus said to him, "Assuredly, I say to
you that this night, before the rooster
crows, you will deny Me three times."

35 Peter said to Him, "Even if I have to
die with You, I will not deny You!"
And so said all the disciples.
36 Then Jesus came with them to a place
called Gethsemane, and said to the disciples, "Sit here while I go and pray over
there." 37 And He took with Him Peter
and the two sons of Zebedee, and He began to be sorrowful and deeply distressed.
38 Then He said to them, "My soul is exceedingly sorrowful, even to death. Stay
here and watch with Me."
39 He went a little farther and fell on
His face, and prayed, saying, "O My
Father, if it is possible, let this cup pass
from Me; nevertheless, not as I will, but
as You *will*."
40 Then He came to the disciples and
found them sleeping, and said to Peter,
"What! Could you not watch with Me
one hour? 41 Watch and pray, lest you enter into temptation. The spirit indeed *is*
willing, but the flesh *is* weak."
42 Again, a second time, He went away
and prayed, saying, "O My Father, if this
cup cannot pass away from Me unless I
drink it, Your will be done." 43 And He
came and found them asleep again, for
their eyes were heavy.
44 So He left them, went away again,
and prayed the third time, saying the same
words. 45 Then He came to His disciples
and said to them, "Are *you* still sleeping and
resting? Behold, the hour is at hand, and
the Son of Man is being betrayed into the
hands of sinners. 46 Rise, let us be going.
See, My betrayer is at hand."
47 And while He was still speaking, behold, Judas, one of the twelve, with a great
multitude with swords and clubs, came
from the chief priests and elders of the
people.
48 Now His betrayer had given them a
sign, saying, "Whomever I kiss, He is the
One; seize Him." 49 Immediately he went
up to Jesus and said, "Greetings, Rabbi!"
and kissed Him.
50 But Jesus said to him, "Friend, why
have you come?"
Then they came and laid hands on Jesus
and took Him.

~ EXODUS 37:1—38:31 ~

Then Bezalel made the ark of acacia wood; two and a half cubits *was* its length, a cubit and a half its width, and a cubit and a half its height. ² He overlaid it with pure gold inside and outside, and made a molding of gold all around it. ³ And he cast for it four rings of gold *to be set* in its four corners: two rings on one side, and two rings on the other side of it. ⁴ He made poles of acacia wood, and overlaid them with gold. ⁵ And he put the poles into the rings at the sides of the ark, to bear the ark. ⁶ He also made the mercy seat of pure gold; two and a half cubits *was* its length and a cubit and a half its width. ⁷ He made two cherubim of beaten gold; he made them of one piece at the two ends of the mercy seat: ⁸ one cherub at one end on this side, and the other cherub at the *other* end on that side. He made the cherubim at the two ends *of one piece* with the mercy seat. ⁹ The cherubim spread out *their* wings above, *and* covered the mercy seat with their wings. They faced one another; the faces of the cherubim were toward the mercy seat.

¹⁰ He made the table of acacia wood; two cubits *was* its length, a cubit its width, and a cubit and a half its height. ¹¹ And he overlaid it with pure gold, and made a molding of gold all around it. ¹² Also he made a frame of a handbreadth all around it, and made a molding of gold for the frame all around it. ¹³ And he cast for it four rings of gold, and put the rings on the four corners that *were* at its four legs. ¹⁴ The rings were close to the frame, as holders for the poles to bear the table. ¹⁵ And he made the poles of acacia wood to bear the table, and overlaid them with gold. ¹⁶ He made of pure gold the utensils which were on the table: its dishes, its cups, its bowls, and its pitchers for pouring.

¹⁷ He also made the lampstand of pure gold; of hammered work he made the lampstand. Its shaft, its branches, its bowls, its *ornamental* knobs, and its flowers were of the same piece. ¹⁸ And six branches came out of its sides: three branches of the lampstand out of one side, and three branches of the lampstand out of the other side. ¹⁹ There were three bowls made like almond *blossoms* on one branch, with an *ornamental* knob and a flower, and three bowls made like almond *blossoms* on the other branch, with an *ornamental* knob and a flower—and so for the six branches coming out of the lampstand. ²⁰ And on the lampstand itself *were* four bowls made like almond *blossoms, each with* its *ornamental* knob and flower. ²¹ *There was* a knob under the *first* two branches of the same, a knob under the *second* two branches of the same, and a knob under the *third* two branches of the same, according to the six branches extending from it. ²² Their knobs and their branches were of one piece; all of it *was* one hammered piece of pure gold. ²³ And he made its seven lamps, its wick-trimmers, and its trays of pure gold. ²⁴ Of a talent of pure gold he made it, with all its utensils.

²⁵ He made the incense altar of acacia wood. Its length *was* a cubit and its width a cubit—*it was* square—and two cubits *was* its height. Its horns were *of one piece* with it. ²⁶ And he overlaid it with pure gold: its top, its sides all around, and its horns. He also made for it a molding of gold all around it. ²⁷ He made two rings of gold for it under its molding, by its two corners on both sides, as holders for the poles with which to bear it. ²⁸ And he made the poles of acacia wood, and overlaid them with gold.

²⁹ He also made the holy anointing oil and the pure incense of sweet spices, according to the work of the perfumer.

38 He made the altar of burnt offering of acacia wood; five cubits *was* its length and five cubits its width—*it was* square—and its height *was* three cubits. ² He made its horns on its four corners; the horns were *of one piece* with it. And he overlaid it with bronze. ³ He made all the utensils for the altar: the pans, the shovels, the basins, the forks, and the firepans; all its utensils he made of bronze. ⁴ And he made a grate of bronze network for the altar, under its rim, midway from the bottom. ⁵ He cast four rings for the four corners of the bronze grating, *as* holders for the

poles. ⁶ And he made the poles of acacia wood, and overlaid them with bronze. ⁷ Then he put the poles into the rings on the sides of the altar, with which to bear it. He made the altar hollow with boards.

⁸ He made the laver of bronze and its base of bronze, from the bronze mirrors of the serving women who assembled at the door of the tabernacle of meeting.

⁹ Then he made the court on the south side; the hangings of the court *were of* fine linen, one hundred cubits long. ¹⁰ There *were* twenty pillars for them, with twenty bronze sockets. The hooks of the pillars and their bands *were* silver. ¹¹ On the north side *the hangings were* one hundred cubits *long*, with twenty pillars and their twenty bronze sockets. The hooks of the pillars and their bands *were* silver. ¹² And on the west side *there were* hangings of fifty cubits, with ten pillars and their ten sockets. The hooks of the pillars and their bands *were* silver. ¹³ For the east side *the hangings were* fifty cubits. ¹⁴ The hangings of one side *of the gate were* fifteen cubits *long, with* their three pillars and their three sockets, ¹⁵ and the same for the other side of the court gate; on this side and that *were* hangings of fifteen cubits, *with* their three pillars and their three sockets. ¹⁶ All the hangings of the court all around *were of* fine woven linen. ¹⁷ The sockets for the pillars *were* bronze, the hooks of the pillars and their bands *were* silver, and the overlay of their capitals *was* silver; and all the pillars of the court had bands of silver. ¹⁸ The screen for the gate of the court *was* woven of blue, purple, and scarlet *thread*, and of fine woven linen. The length *was* twenty cubits, and the height along its width *was* five cubits, corresponding to the hangings of the court. ¹⁹ And *there were* four pillars *with* their four sockets of bronze; their hooks *were* silver, and the overlay of their capitals and their bands *was* silver. ²⁰ All the pegs of the tabernacle, and of the court all around, *were* bronze.

²¹ This is the inventory of the tabernacle, the tabernacle of the Testimony, which was counted according to the commandment of Moses, for the service of the Levites, by the hand of Ithamar, son of Aaron the priest.

²² Bezalel the son of Uri, the son of Hur, of the tribe of Judah, made all that the LORD had commanded Moses. ²³ And with him *was* Aholiab the son of Ahisamach, of the tribe of Dan, an engraver and designer, a weaver of blue, purple, and scarlet *thread*, and of fine linen.

²⁴ All the gold that was used in all the work of the holy *place*, that is, the gold of the offering, was twenty-nine talents and seven hundred and thirty shekels, according to the shekel of the sanctuary. ²⁵ And the silver from those who were numbered of the congregation *was* one hundred talents and one thousand seven hundred and seventy-five shekels, according to the shekel of the sanctuary: ²⁶ a bekah for each man (*that is*, half a shekel, according to the shekel of the sanctuary), for everyone included in the numbering from twenty years old and above, for six hundred and three thousand, five hundred and fifty *men*. ²⁷ And from the hundred talents of silver were cast the sockets of the sanctuary and the bases of the veil: one hundred sockets from the hundred talents, one talent for each socket. ²⁸ Then from the one thousand seven hundred and seventy-five *shekels* he made hooks for the pillars, overlaid their capitals, and made bands for them.

²⁹ The offering of bronze *was* seventy talents and two thousand four hundred shekels. ³⁰ And with it he made the sockets for the door of the tabernacle of meeting, the bronze altar, the bronze grating for it, and all the utensils for the altar, ³¹ the sockets for the court all around, the bases for the court gate, all the pegs for the tabernacle, and all the pegs for the court all around.

∼ PSALM 22:9–15 ∼

⁹   But You *are* He who took Me out of
     the womb;
    You made Me trust *while* on My
     mother's breasts.
¹⁰ I was cast upon You from birth.
    From My mother's womb
    You *have been* My God.
¹¹ Be not far from Me,
    For trouble is near;
    For *there is* none to help.

O Rugged Land of Gold

> I, wisdom, dwell with prudence, and find out knowledge and discretion.
>
> *Proverbs 8:12*

Many a woman has felt alone during and after childbirth, but consider the true story of Martha Martin, the wife of an Alaskan prospector in the 1920s.

While she was pregnant, her husband left her at their camp and went to a neighboring island to run an errand. A series of disasters struck almost immediately. First, an avalanche pinned her under a rock on the mountainside, where she laid unconscious for several days. She finally managed to crawl back to their cabin and reset the broken bones she had suffered, making a splint for her leg and a cast for her arm. Then, a storm prevented her husband's return. Stranded, injured, alone, and with supplies almost gone, she quickly learned to be self-sufficient — killing animals for food and using their fur to make coverings for the coming baby. Bit by bit, she began burning pieces of the cabin for heat.

Martha had never seen a child born before, but when she went into two days of hard labor she kept her head and helped herself after her daughter finally arrived. She later baptized the infant Dannas. Several weeks later, some Indians appeared and she finally had help until her husband, who had been caught on the other island, arrived. Her published diary was appropriately titled, *O Rugged Land of Gold*.

When you feel alone, the Word of God and the wisdom you gain from reading it will sustain you through any trial.

12 Many bulls have surrounded Me;
   Strong *bulls* of Bashan have
   encircled Me.
13 They gape at Me *with* their mouths,
   Like a raging and roaring lion.

14 I am poured out like water,
   And all My bones are out of joint;
   My heart is like wax;
   It has melted within Me.
15 My strength is dried up like a
   potsherd,
   And My tongue clings to My jaws;
   You have brought Me to the dust of
   death.

∼ PROVERBS 8:12–21 ∼

12 "I, wisdom, dwell with prudence,
   And find out knowledge *and*
   discretion.
13 The fear of the LORD is to hate evil;
   Pride and arrogance and the evil way
   And the perverse mouth I hate.
14 Counsel is mine, and sound wisdom;
   I *am* understanding, I have strength.
15 By me kings reign,
   And rulers decree justice.
16 By me princes rule, and nobles,
   All the judges of the earth.
17 I love those who love me,
   And those who seek me diligently
   will find me.
18 Riches and honor *are* with me,
   Enduring riches and righteousness.
19 My fruit *is* better than gold, yes,
   than fine gold,
   And my revenue than choice silver.
20 I traverse the way of righteousness,
   In the midst of the paths of justice,
21 That I may cause those who love me
   to inherit wealth,
   That I may fill their treasuries.

∼ MATTHEW 26:51–75 ∼

And suddenly, one of those *who were* with
Jesus stretched out *his* hand and drew his
sword, struck the servant of the high
priest, and cut off his ear. 52 But Jesus said to him, "Put your
sword in its place, for all who take the
sword will perish by the sword. 53 Or do
you think that I cannot now pray to My
Father, and He will provide Me with more
than twelve legions of angels? 54 How then
could the Scriptures be fulfilled, that it
must happen thus?"

55 In that hour Jesus said to the multitudes, "Have you come out, as against a
robber, with swords and clubs to take Me?
I sat daily with you, teaching in the temple,
and you did not seize Me. 56 But all this
was done that the Scriptures of the prophets might be fulfilled."

Then all the disciples forsook Him and
fled.

57 And those who had laid hold of Jesus
led *Him* away to Caiaphas the high priest,
where the scribes and the elders were assembled. 58 But Peter followed Him at a
distance to the high priest's courtyard.
And he went in and sat with the servants
to see the end.

59 Now the chief priests, the elders, and
all the council sought false testimony
against Jesus to put Him to death, 60 but
found none. Even though many false witnesses came forward, they found none.
But at last two false witnesses came forward 61 and said, "This *fellow* said, 'I am
able to destroy the temple of God and to
build it in three days.' "

62 And the high priest arose and said to
Him, "Do You answer nothing? What *is
it* these men testify against You?" 63 But
Jesus kept silent. And the high priest
answered and said to Him, "I put You under oath by the living God: Tell us if You
are the Christ, the Son of God!"

64 Jesus said to him, "*It is as* you said.
Nevertheless, I say to you, hereafter you
will see the Son of Man sitting at the right
hand of the Power, and coming on the
clouds of heaven."

65 Then the high priest tore his clothes,
saying, "He has spoken blasphemy! What
further need do we have of witnesses?
Look, now you have heard His blasphemy! 66 What do you think?"

They answered and said, "He is deserving of death."

67 Then they spat in His face and beat
Him; and others struck *Him* with the
palms of their hands, 68 saying, "Prophesy to us, Christ! Who is the one who
struck You?"

69 Now Peter sat outside in the

courtyard. And a servant girl came to him, saying, "You also were with Jesus of Galilee."

70 But he denied it before *them* all, saying, "I do not know what you are saying."

71 And when he had gone out to the gateway, another *girl* saw him and said to those *who were* there, "This *fellow* also was with Jesus of Nazareth."

72 But again he denied with an oath, "I do not know the Man!"

73 And a little later those who stood by came up and said to Peter, "Surely you also are *one* of them, for your speech betrays you."

74 Then he began to curse and swear, *saying,* "I do not know the Man!"

Immediately a rooster crowed. 75 And Peter remembered the word of Jesus who had said to him, "Before the rooster crows, you will deny Me three times." So he went out and wept bitterly.

READING 45 · FEBRUARY 14

~ EXODUS 39:1—40:38 ~

O f the blue, purple, and scarlet *thread* they made garments of ministry, for ministering in the holy *place,* and made the holy garments for Aaron, as the LORD had commanded Moses.

2 He made the ephod of gold, blue, purple, and scarlet *thread,* and of fine woven linen. 3 And they beat the gold into thin sheets and cut *it into* threads, to work *it in with* the blue, purple, and scarlet *thread,* and the fine linen, *into* artistic designs. 4 They made shoulder straps for it to couple *it* together; it was coupled together at its two edges. 5 And the intricately woven band of his ephod that *was* on it *was* of the same workmanship, *woven* of gold, blue, purple, and scarlet *thread,* and of fine woven linen, as the LORD had commanded Moses.

6 And they set onyx stones, enclosed in settings of gold; they were engraved, as signets are engraved, with the names of the sons of Israel. 7 He put them on the shoulders of the ephod *as* memorial stones for the sons of Israel, as the LORD had commanded Moses.

8 And he made the breastplate, artistically woven like the workmanship of the ephod, of gold, blue, purple, and scarlet *thread,* and of fine woven linen. 9 They made the breastplate square by doubling it; a span *was* its length and a span its width when doubled. 10 And they set in it four rows of stones: a row with a sardius, a topaz, and an emerald *was* the first row; 11 the second row, a turquoise, a sapphire, and a diamond; 12 the third row, a jacinth,

an agate, and an amethyst; 13 the fourth row, a beryl, an onyx, and a jasper. *They were* enclosed in settings of gold in their mountings. 14 *There were* twelve stones according to the names of the sons of Israel: according to their names, *engraved like* a signet, each one with its own name according to the twelve tribes. 15 And they made chains for the breastplate at the ends, like braided cords of pure gold. 16 They also made two settings of gold and two gold rings, and put the two rings on the two ends of the breastplate. 17 And they put the two braided *chains* of gold in the two rings on the ends of the breastplate. 18 The two ends of the two braided *chains* they fastened in the two settings, and put them on the shoulder straps of the ephod in the front. 19 And they made two rings of gold and put *them* on the two ends of the breastplate, on the edge of it, which *was* on the inward side of the ephod. 20 They made two *other* gold rings and put them on the two shoulder straps, underneath the ephod toward its front, right at the seam above the intricately woven band of the ephod. 21 And they bound the breastplate by means of its rings to the rings of the ephod with a blue cord, so that it would be above the intricately woven band of the ephod, and that the breastplate would not come loose from the ephod, as the LORD had commanded Moses.

22 He made the robe of the ephod of woven work, all of blue. 23 And *there was* an opening in the middle of the robe, like the opening in a coat of mail, *with a*

woven binding all around the opening, so that it would not tear. [24] They made on the hem of the robe pomegranates of blue, purple, and scarlet, and of fine woven *linen*. [25] And they made bells of pure gold, and put the bells between the pomegranates on the hem of the robe all around between the pomegranates: [26] a bell and a pomegranate, a bell and a pomegranate, all around the hem of the robe to minister in, as the LORD had commanded Moses.

[27] They made tunics, artistically woven of fine linen, for Aaron and his sons, [28] a turban of fine linen, exquisite hats of fine linen, short trousers of fine woven linen, [29] and a sash of fine woven linen with blue, purple, and scarlet *thread*, made by a weaver, as the LORD had commanded Moses.

[30] Then they made the plate of the holy crown of pure gold, and wrote on it an inscription like the engraving of a signet:

HOLINESS TO THE LORD.

[31] And they tied to it a blue cord, to fasten *it* above on the turban, as the LORD had commanded Moses.

[32] Thus all the work of the tabernacle of the tent of meeting was finished. And the children of Israel did according to all that the LORD had commanded Moses; so they did. [33] And they brought the tabernacle to Moses, the tent and all its furnishings: its clasps, its boards, its bars, its pillars, and its sockets; [34] the covering of ram skins dyed red, the covering of badger skins, and the veil of the covering; [35] the ark of the Testimony with its poles, and the mercy seat; [36] the table, all its utensils, and the showbread; [37] the pure *gold* lampstand with its lamps (the lamps set in order), all its utensils, and the oil for light; [38] the gold altar, the anointing oil, and the sweet incense; the screen for the tabernacle door; [39] the bronze altar, its grate of bronze, its poles, and all its utensils; the laver with its base; [40] the hangings of the court, its pillars and its sockets, the screen for the court gate, its cords, and its pegs; all the utensils for the service of the tabernacle, for the tent of meeting; [41] and the garments of ministry, to minister in the holy *place*: the holy garments for Aaron the priest, and his sons' garments, to minister as priests.

[42] According to all that the LORD had commanded Moses, so the children of Israel did all the work. [43] Then Moses looked over all the work, and indeed they had done it; as the LORD had commanded, just so they had done it. And Moses blessed them.

40 Then the LORD spoke to Moses, saying: [2] "On the first day of the first month you shall set up the tabernacle of the tent of meeting. [3] You shall put in it the ark of the Testimony, and partition off the ark with the veil. [4] You shall bring in the table and arrange the things that are to be set in order on it; and you shall bring in the lampstand and light its lamps. [5] You shall also set the altar of gold for the incense before the ark of the Testimony, and put up the screen for the door of the tabernacle. [6] Then you shall set the altar of the burnt offering before the door of the tabernacle of the tent of meeting. [7] And you shall set the laver between the tabernacle of meeting and the altar, and put water in it. [8] You shall set up the court all around, and hang up the screen at the court gate.

[9] "And you shall take the anointing oil, and anoint the tabernacle and all that *is* in it; and you shall hallow it and all its utensils, and it shall be holy. [10] You shall anoint the altar of the burnt offering and all its utensils, and consecrate the altar. The altar shall be most holy. [11] And you shall anoint the laver and its base, and consecrate it.

[12] "Then you shall bring Aaron and his sons to the door of the tabernacle of meeting and wash them with water. [13] You shall put the holy garments on Aaron, and anoint him and consecrate him, that he may minister to Me as priest. [14] And you shall bring his sons and clothe them with tunics. [15] You shall anoint them, as you anointed their father, that they may minister to Me as priests; for their anointing shall surely be an everlasting priesthood throughout their generations."

[16] Thus Moses did; according to all that the LORD had commanded him, so he did.

[17] And it came to pass in the first month of the second year, on the first *day* of the

Coming Clean

> Thus Moses did; according to all that the Lord had commanded him, so he did.
>
> *Exodus 40:16*

As a professional stock-car racer, Darrell Waltrip was once proud of his image as "the guy folks loved to hate." When the crowds booed, he'd just kick the dirt and smile. Then things began to change. After miraculously surviving a crash in the Daytona 500, he began going to church with his wife, Stevie. They began trying to have a family, but Stevie suffered four miscarriages.

One day their pastor came to visit. He asked, "Your car is sponsored by a beer company. Is that the image you want?" Darrell had never thought about it. He had always loved watching kids admire his car, but the more he thought about it, he discovered that he did care about his image. He thought, *If our prayers were answered for a child, what kind of dad would I be?* He remembered his pastor's admonition to "walk the walk, not just talk the talk."

He didn't know what to do to convince his car's owner to change sponsors, but amazingly, an opportunity opened for him to sign with a new racing team sponsored by a laundry detergent company! After much thought and more prayer, he switched teams. Two years later, daughter Jessica was born, and a few years later, daughter Sarah. In 1989, he won Daytona.

Obedience to God and His Word opens up the doors for God to rain down blessings on our lives.

month, *that* the tabernacle was raised up. [18] So Moses raised up the tabernacle, fastened its sockets, set up its boards, put in its bars, and raised up its pillars. [19] And he spread out the tent over the tabernacle and put the covering of the tent on top of it, as the LORD had commanded Moses. [20] He took the Testimony and put *it* into the ark, inserted the poles through the rings of the ark, and put the mercy seat on top of the ark. [21] And he brought the ark into the tabernacle, hung up the veil of the covering, and partitioned off the ark of the Testimony, as the LORD had commanded Moses.

[22] He put the table in the tabernacle of meeting, on the north side of the tabernacle, outside the veil; [23] and he set the bread in order upon it before the LORD, as the LORD had commanded Moses. [24] He put the lampstand in the tabernacle of meeting, across from the table, on the south side of the tabernacle; [25] and he lit the lamps before the LORD, as the LORD had commanded Moses. [26] He put the gold altar in the tabernacle of meeting in front of the veil; [27] and he burned sweet incense on it, as the LORD had commanded Moses. [28] He hung up the screen *at* the door of the tabernacle. [29] And he put the altar of burnt offering *before* the door of the tabernacle of the tent of meeting, and offered upon it the burnt offering and the grain offering, as the LORD had commanded Moses. [30] He set the laver between the tabernacle of meeting and the altar, and put water there for washing; [31] and Moses, Aaron, and his sons would wash their hands and their feet *with water* from it. [32] Whenever they went into the tabernacle of meeting, and when they came near the altar, they washed, as the LORD had commanded Moses. [33] And he raised up the court all around the tabernacle and the altar, and hung up the screen of the court gate. So Moses finished the work.

[34] Then the cloud covered the tabernacle of meeting, and the glory of the LORD filled the tabernacle. [35] And Moses was not able to enter the tabernacle of meeting, because the cloud rested above it, and the glory of the LORD filled the tabernacle. [36] Whenever the cloud was taken up from above the tabernacle, the children of Israel would go onward in all their journeys. [37] But if the cloud was not taken up, then they did not journey till the day that it was taken up. [38] For the cloud of the LORD *was* above the tabernacle by day, and fire was over it by night, in the sight of all the house of Israel, throughout all their journeys.

∼ PSALM 22:16–21 ∼

[16] For dogs have surrounded Me;
The congregation of the wicked has enclosed Me.
They pierced My hands and My feet;
[17] I can count all My bones.
They look *and* stare at Me.
[18] They divide My garments among them,
And for My clothing they cast lots.

[19] But You, O LORD, do not be far from Me;
O My Strength, hasten to help Me!
[20] Deliver Me from the sword,
My precious *life* from the power of the dog.
[21] Save Me from the lion's mouth
And from the horns of the wild oxen!

You have answered Me.

∼ PROVERBS 8:22–31 ∼

[22] "The LORD possessed me at the beginning of His way,
Before His works of old.
[23] I have been established from everlasting,
From the beginning, before there was ever an earth.
[24] When *there were* no depths I was brought forth,
When *there were* no fountains abounding with water.
[25] Before the mountains were settled,
Before the hills, I was brought forth;
[26] While as yet He had not made the earth or the fields,
Or the primal dust of the world.
[27] When He prepared the heavens, I *was* there,
When He drew a circle on the face of the deep,

28 When He established the clouds
  above,
  When He strengthened the fountains
  of the deep,
29 When He assigned to the sea its
  limit,
  So that the waters would not
  transgress His command,
  When He marked out the
  foundations of the earth,
30 Then I was beside Him *as* a master
  craftsman;
  And I was daily *His* delight,
  Rejoicing always before Him,
31 Rejoicing in His inhabited world,
  And my delight *was* with the sons of
  men.

~ MATTHEW 27:1–26 ~

When morning came, all the chief priests and elders of the people plotted against Jesus to put Him to death. 2 And when they had bound Him, they led Him away and delivered Him to Pontius Pilate the governor.

3 Then Judas, His betrayer, seeing that He had been condemned, was remorseful and brought back the thirty pieces of silver to the chief priests and elders, 4 saying, "I have sinned by betraying innocent blood."

And they said, "What *is that* to us? You see *to it*!"

5 Then he threw down the pieces of silver in the temple and departed, and went and hanged himself.

6 But the chief priests took the silver pieces and said, "It is not lawful to put them into the treasury, because they are the price of blood." 7 And they consulted together and bought with them the potter's field, to bury strangers in. 8 Therefore that field has been called the Field of Blood to this day.

9 Then was fulfilled what was spoken by Jeremiah the prophet, saying, "And they took the thirty pieces of silver, the value of Him who was priced, whom they of the children of Israel priced, 10 and gave them for the potter's field, as the LORD directed me."

11 Now Jesus stood before the governor. And the governor asked Him, saying, "Are You the King of the Jews?"

Jesus said to him, "*It is as* you say."
12 And while He was being accused by the chief priests and elders, He answered nothing.

13 Then Pilate said to Him, "Do You not hear how many things they testify against You?" 14 But He answered him not one word, so that the governor marveled greatly.

15 Now at the feast the governor was accustomed to releasing to the multitude one prisoner whom they wished. 16 And at that time they had a notorious prisoner called Barabbas. 17 Therefore, when they had gathered together, Pilate said to them, "Whom do you want me to release to you? Barabbas, or Jesus who is called Christ?" 18 For he knew that they had handed Him over because of envy.

19 While he was sitting on the judgment seat, his wife sent to him, saying, "Have nothing to do with that just Man, for I have suffered many things today in a dream because of Him."

20 But the chief priests and elders persuaded the multitudes that they should ask for Barabbas and destroy Jesus. 21 The governor answered and said to them, "Which of the two do you want me to release to you?"

They said, "Barabbas!"
22 Pilate said to them, "What then shall I do with Jesus who is called Christ?"

They all said to him, "Let Him be crucified!"

23 Then the governor said, "Why, what evil has He done?"

But they cried out all the more, saying, "Let Him be crucified!"

24 When Pilate saw that he could not prevail at all, but rather *that* a tumult was rising, he took water and washed *his* hands before the multitude, saying, "I am innocent of the blood of this just Person. You see *to it*."

25 And all the people answered and said, "His blood *be* on us and on our children."

26 Then he released Barabbas to them; and when he had scourged Jesus, he delivered *Him* to be crucified.

～ LEVITICUS 1:1—2:16 ～

Now the LORD called to Moses, and spoke to him from the tabernacle of meeting, saying, [2] "Speak to the children of Israel, and say to them: 'When any one of you brings an offering to the LORD, you shall bring your offering of the livestock—of the herd and of the flock.

[3] 'If his offering is a burnt sacrifice of the herd, let him offer a male without blemish; he shall offer it of his own free will at the door of the tabernacle of meeting before the LORD. [4] Then he shall put his hand on the head of the burnt offering, and it will be accepted on his behalf to make atonement for him. [5] He shall kill the bull before the LORD; and the priests, Aaron's sons, shall bring the blood and sprinkle the blood all around on the altar that is by the door of the tabernacle of meeting. [6] And he shall skin the burnt offering and cut it into its pieces. [7] The sons of Aaron the priest shall put fire on the altar, and lay the wood in order on the fire. [8] Then the priests, Aaron's sons, shall lay the parts, the head, and the fat in order on the wood that is on the fire upon the altar; [9] but he shall wash its entrails and its legs with water. And the priest shall burn all on the altar as a burnt sacrifice, an offering made by fire, a sweet aroma to the LORD.

[10] 'If his offering is of the flocks—of the sheep or of the goats—as a burnt sacrifice, he shall bring a male without blemish. [11] He shall kill it on the north side of the altar before the LORD; and the priests, Aaron's sons, shall sprinkle its blood all around on the altar. [12] And he shall cut it into its pieces, with its head and its fat; and the priest shall lay them in order on the wood that is on the fire upon the altar; [13] but he shall wash the entrails and the legs with water. Then the priest shall bring it all and burn it on the altar; it is a burnt sacrifice, an offering made by fire, a sweet aroma to the LORD.

[14] 'And if the burnt sacrifice of his offering to the LORD is of birds, then he shall bring his offering of turtledoves or young pigeons. [15] The priest shall bring it to the altar, wring off its head, and burn it on the altar; its blood shall be drained out at the side of the altar. [16] And he shall remove its crop with its feathers and cast it beside the altar on the east side, into the place for ashes. [17] Then he shall split it at its wings, but shall not divide it completely; and the priest shall burn it on the altar, on the wood that is on the fire. It is a burnt sacrifice, an offering made by fire, a sweet aroma to the LORD.

2 'When anyone offers a grain offering to the LORD, his offering shall be of fine flour. And he shall pour oil on it, and put frankincense on it. [2] He shall bring it to Aaron's sons, the priests, one of whom shall take from it his handful of fine flour and oil with all the frankincense. And the priest shall burn it as a memorial on the altar, an offering made by fire, a sweet aroma to the LORD. [3] The rest of the grain offering shall be Aaron's and his sons'. It is most holy of the offerings to the LORD made by fire.

[4] 'And if you bring as an offering a grain offering baked in the oven, it shall be unleavened cakes of fine flour mixed with oil, or unleavened wafers anointed with oil. [5] But if your offering is a grain offering baked in a pan, it shall be of fine flour, unleavened, mixed with oil. [6] You shall break it in pieces and pour oil on it; it is a grain offering.

[7] 'If your offering is a grain offering baked in a covered pan, it shall be made of fine flour with oil. [8] You shall bring the grain offering that is made of these things to the LORD. And when it is presented to the priest, he shall bring it to the altar. [9] Then the priest shall take from the grain offering a memorial portion, and burn it on the altar. It is an offering made by fire, a sweet aroma to the LORD. [10] And what is left of the grain offering shall be Aaron's and his sons'. It is most holy of the offerings to the LORD made by fire.

[11] 'No grain offering which you bring to the LORD shall be made with leaven, for you shall burn no leaven nor any honey in any offering to the LORD made by fire. [12] As for the offering of the firstfruits, you shall offer them to the LORD, but they shall not be burned on the altar for a sweet

Talk to God

In the midst of her intense grief, Betty found it very difficult to pray. She was drowning in a sea of turbulent emotions and hardly knew her own name, much less what to request from God.

One afternoon, a friend of Betty's came by and soon, Betty was pouring all of her hurts, fears, and struggles out to her. She admitted she was angry with God, and disappointed that her prayers for her husband's healing weren't answered. She admitted she was having difficulty believing God would do anything for her — in the present or the future. Finally, as the well of her emotions began to run dry, Betty's friend said quietly, "I have only one piece of advice to give you. Let's talk to God."

Betty's friend put her arms around her and prayed a simple, heartfelt prayer, claiming Christ's promise to heal her broken heart and restore her soul. After she had finished, she said, "Christ is with you. He is in you. And where He is, because of Who He is, He heals."

No matter what you may be going through today, your best recourse is to invite Jesus Christ to manifest Himself in you and through you. He knows the answer — He *is* the answer. He gives you Himself, and in Him is all the power, strength, encouragement, love, and comfort you need.

> Blessed is the man who listens to me, watching daily at my gates, waiting at the posts of my doors. For whoever finds me finds life, and obtains favor from the Lord.
>
> *Proverbs 8:34-35*

aroma. [13] And every offering of your grain offering you shall season with salt; you shall not allow the salt of the covenant of your God to be lacking from your grain offering. With all your offerings you shall offer salt.

[14] 'If you offer a grain offering of your firstfruits to the LORD, you shall offer for the grain offering of your firstfruits green heads of grain roasted on the fire, grain beaten from full heads. [15] And you shall put oil on it, and lay frankincense on it. It *is* a grain offering. [16] Then the priest shall burn the memorial portion: *part* of its beaten grain and *part* of its oil, with all the frankincense, as an offering made by fire to the LORD.

~ PSALM 22:22–31 ~

[22] I will declare Your name to My brethren;
In the midst of the assembly I will praise You.
[23] You who fear the LORD, praise Him!
All you descendants of Jacob, glorify Him,
And fear Him, all you offspring of Israel!
[24] For He has not despised nor abhorred the affliction of the afflicted;
Nor has He hidden His face from Him;
But when He cried to Him, He heard.

[25] My praise *shall be* of You in the great assembly;
I will pay My vows before those who fear Him.
[26] The poor shall eat and be satisfied;
Those who seek Him will praise the LORD.
Let your heart live forever!

[27] All the ends of the world
Shall remember and turn to the LORD,
And all the families of the nations
Shall worship before You.
[28] For the kingdom *is* the LORD's,
And He rules over the nations.

[29] All the prosperous of the earth
Shall eat and worship;

All those who go down to the dust
Shall bow before Him,
Even he who cannot keep himself alive.

[30] A posterity shall serve Him.
It will be recounted of the Lord to the *next* generation,
[31] They will come and declare His righteousness to a people who will be born,
That He has done *this*.

~ PROVERBS 8:32–36 ~

[32] "Now therefore, listen to me, *my* children,
For blessed *are those who* keep my ways.
[33] Hear instruction and be wise,
And do not disdain *it*.
[34] Blessed is the man who listens to me,
Watching daily at my gates,
Waiting at the posts of my doors.
[35] For whoever finds me finds life,
And obtains favor from the LORD;
[36] But he who sins against me wrongs his own soul;
All those who hate me love death."

~ MATTHEW 27:27–54 ~

Then the soldiers of the governor took Jesus into the Praetorium and gathered the whole garrison around Him. [28] And they stripped Him and put a scarlet robe on Him. [29] When they had twisted a crown of thorns, they put *it* on His head, and a reed in His right hand. And they bowed the knee before Him and mocked Him, saying, "Hail, King of the Jews!" [30] Then they spat on Him, and took the reed and struck Him on the head. [31] And when they had mocked Him, they took the robe off Him, put His *own* clothes on Him, and led Him away to be crucified.

[32] Now as they came out, they found a man of Cyrene, Simon by name. Him they compelled to bear His cross. [33] And when they had come to a place called Golgotha, that is to say, Place of a Skull, [34] they gave Him sour wine mingled with gall to drink.

But when He had tasted *it,* He would not drink.

³⁵ Then they crucified Him, and divided His garments, casting lots, that it might be fulfilled which was spoken by the prophet:

> "They divided My garments among them,
> And for My clothing they cast lots."

³⁶ Sitting down, they kept watch over Him there. ³⁷ And they put up over His head the accusation written against Him:

THIS IS JESUS
THE KING OF THE JEWS.

³⁸ Then two robbers were crucified with Him, one on the right and another on the left.

³⁹ And those who passed by blasphemed Him, wagging their heads ⁴⁰ and saying, "You who destroy the temple and build *it* in three days, save Yourself! If You are the Son of God, come down from the cross."

⁴¹ Likewise the chief priests also, mocking with the scribes and elders, said, ⁴² "He saved others; Himself He cannot save. If He is the King of Israel, let Him now come down from the cross, and we will believe Him. ⁴³ He trusted in God; let Him deliver Him now if He will have Him; for He said, 'I am the Son of God.' "

⁴⁴ Even the robbers who were crucified with Him reviled Him with the same thing.

⁴⁵ Now from the sixth hour until the ninth hour there was darkness over all the land. ⁴⁶ And about the ninth hour Jesus cried out with a loud voice, saying, "Eli, Eli, lama sabachthani?" that is, "My God, My God, why have You forsaken Me?"

⁴⁷ Some of those who stood there, when they heard *that,* said, "This Man is calling for Elijah!" ⁴⁸ Immediately one of them ran and took a sponge, filled *it* with sour wine and put *it* on a reed, and offered it to Him to drink.

⁴⁹ The rest said, "Let Him alone; let us see if Elijah will come to save Him."

⁵⁰ And Jesus cried out again with a loud voice, and yielded up His spirit.

⁵¹ Then, behold, the veil of the temple was torn in two from top to bottom; and the earth quaked, and the rocks were split, ⁵² and the graves were opened; and many bodies of the saints who had fallen asleep were raised; ⁵³ and coming out of the graves after His resurrection, they went into the holy city and appeared to many.

⁵⁴ So when the centurion and those with him, who were guarding Jesus, saw the earthquake and the things that had happened, they feared greatly, saying, "Truly this was the Son of God!"

READING 47 · FEBRUARY 16

~ LEVITICUS 3:1—4:35 ~

'When his offering *is* a sacrifice of a peace offering, if he offers *it* of the herd, whether male or female, he shall offer it without blemish before the LORD. ² And he shall lay his hand on the head of his offering, and kill it *at* the door of the tabernacle of meeting; and Aaron's sons, the priests, shall sprinkle the blood all around on the altar. ³ Then he shall offer from the sacrifice of the peace offering an offering made by fire to the LORD. The fat that covers the entrails and all the fat that *is* on the entrails, ⁴ the two kidneys and the fat that is on them by the flanks, and the fatty lobe *attached* to the liver above the kidneys, he shall remove; ⁵ and Aaron's sons shall burn it on the altar upon the burnt sacrifice, which *is* on the wood that *is* on the fire, *as* an offering made by fire, a sweet aroma to the LORD.

⁶ 'If his offering as a sacrifice of a peace offering to the LORD *is* of the flock, *whether* male or female, he shall offer it without blemish. ⁷ If he offers a lamb as his offering, then he shall offer it before the LORD. ⁸ And he shall lay his hand on the head of his offering, and kill it before

the tabernacle of meeting; and Aaron's sons shall sprinkle its blood all around on the altar.

9 'Then he shall offer from the sacrifice of the peace offering, as an offering made by fire to the LORD, its fat *and* the whole fat tail which he shall remove close to the backbone. And the fat that covers the entrails and all the fat that *is* on the entrails, 10 the two kidneys and the fat that *is* on them by the flanks, and the fatty lobe *attached* to the liver above the kidneys, he shall remove; 11 and the priest shall burn *them* on the altar *as* food, an offering made by fire to the LORD.

12 'And if his offering *is* a goat, then he shall offer it before the LORD. 13 He shall lay his hand on its head and kill it before the tabernacle of meeting; and the sons of Aaron shall sprinkle its blood all around on the altar. 14 Then he shall offer from it his offering, as an offering made by fire to the LORD. The fat that covers the entrails and all the fat that *is* on the entrails, 15 the two kidneys and the fat that *is* on them by the flanks, and the fatty lobe *attached* to the liver above the kidneys, he shall remove; 16 and the priest shall burn them on the altar *as* food, an offering made by fire for a sweet aroma; all the fat *is* the LORD's.

17 '*This shall be* a perpetual statute throughout your generations in all your dwellings: you shall eat neither fat nor blood.' "

4 Now the LORD spoke to Moses, saying, 2 "Speak to the children of Israel, saying: 'If a person sins unintentionally against any of the commandments of the LORD *in anything* which ought not to be done, and does any of them, 3 if the anointed priest sins, bringing guilt on the people, then let him offer to the LORD for his sin which he has sinned a young bull without blemish as a sin offering. 4 He shall bring the bull to the door of the tabernacle of meeting before the LORD, lay his hand on the bull's head, and kill the bull before the LORD. 5 Then the anointed priest shall take some of the bull's blood and bring it to the tabernacle of meeting. 6 The priest shall dip his finger in the blood and sprinkle some of the blood seven times before the LORD, in front of the veil

of the sanctuary. 7 And the priest shall put some of the blood on the horns of the altar of sweet incense before the LORD, which is in the tabernacle of meeting; and he shall pour the remaining blood of the bull at the base of the altar of the burnt offering, which is at the door of the tabernacle of meeting. 8 He shall take from it all the fat of the bull as the sin offering. The fat that covers the entrails and all the fat which *is* on the entrails, 9 the two kidneys and the fat that *is* on them by the flanks, and the fatty lobe *attached* to the liver above the kidneys, he shall remove, 10 as it was taken from the bull of the sacrifice of the peace offering; and the priest shall burn them on the altar of the burnt offering. 11 But the bull's hide and all its flesh, with its head and legs, its entrails and offal— 12 the whole bull he shall carry outside the camp to a clean place, where the ashes are poured out, and burn it on wood with fire; where the ashes are poured out it shall be burned.

13 'Now if the whole congregation of Israel sins unintentionally, and the thing is hidden from the eyes of the assembly, and they have done *something against* any of the commandments of the LORD *in anything* which should not be done, and are guilty; 14 when the sin which they have committed becomes known, then the assembly shall offer a young bull for the sin, and bring it before the tabernacle of meeting. 15 And the elders of the congregation shall lay their hands on the head of the bull before the LORD. Then the bull shall be killed before the LORD. 16 The anointed priest shall bring some of the bull's blood to the tabernacle of meeting. 17 Then the priest shall dip his finger in the blood and sprinkle *it* seven times before the LORD, in front of the veil. 18 And he shall put *some* of the blood on the horns of the altar which *is* before the LORD, which *is* in the tabernacle of meeting; and he shall pour the remaining blood at the base of the altar of burnt offering, which is at the door of the tabernacle of meeting. 19 He shall take all the fat from it and burn *it* on the altar. 20 And he shall do with the bull as he did with the bull as a sin offering; thus he shall do with it. So the priest shall make atonement for them, and it shall be forgiven them. 21 Then he shall carry the

Worry is Worthless

Opera star Marguerite Piazza was at the height of her career, married to a devoted husband, and the mother of six healthy children. Then, her world seemed to turn upside down. Her husband died suddenly and soon after, a spot on her cheek was diagnosed as melanoma, a deadly type of cancer. She was told that a disfiguring surgery to remove her cheek was her only hope for survival. The same day she received that news, she was scheduled to sing to a sell-out audience.

She says, "What do you do at a time like that? You do what you are paid to do, and I was paid to lift people with my talent. So, as I stood in the wings of the opera house, I prayed. Then I hung my troubles on a hanger and left them in the closet." She performed her heart out and even after her surgery, she kept her beauty, raised her family, and continued to sing!

Rather than hang his worries in a closet, one man took another approach. He put them in a box. Each time he had a worry, he'd write it down and deposit it. Then, on Worry Wednesday, he read the contents of his box. To his amazement, most of the things he had worried about had already been resolved. He soon discarded the box!

Worry doesn't produce anything, it only slows you down. When you give your worries to God, you have the freedom to accomplish more in life.

> Yea, though I walk through the valley of the shadow of death, I will fear no evil; for You are with me; Your rod and Your staff, they comfort me.
>
> *Psalm 23:4*

bull outside the camp, and burn it as he burned the first bull. It *is* a sin offering for the assembly.

22 'When a ruler has sinned, and done *something* unintentionally *against* any of the commandments of the LORD his God *in anything* which should not be done, and is guilty, 23 or if his sin which he has committed comes to his knowledge, he shall bring as his offering a kid of the goats, a male without blemish. 24 And he shall lay his hand on the head of the goat, and kill it at the place where they kill the burnt offering before the LORD. It *is* a sin offering. 25 The priest shall take some of the blood of the sin offering with his finger, put *it* on the horns of the altar of burnt offering, and pour its blood at the base of the altar of burnt offering. 26 And he shall burn all its fat on the altar, like the fat of the sacrifice of the peace offering. So the priest shall make atonement for him concerning his sin, and it shall be forgiven him.

27 'If anyone of the common people sins unintentionally by doing *something against* any of the commandments of the LORD *in anything* which ought not to be done, and is guilty, 28 or if his sin which he has committed comes to his knowledge, then he shall bring as his offering a kid of the goats, a female without blemish, for his sin which he has committed. 29 And he shall lay his hand on the head of the sin offering, and kill the sin offering at the place of the burnt offering. 30 Then the priest shall take *some* of its blood with his finger, put *it* on the horns of the altar of burnt offering, and pour all *the remaining* blood at the base of the altar. 31 He shall remove all its fat, as fat is removed from the sacrifice of the peace offering; and the priest shall burn it on the altar for a sweet aroma to the LORD. So the priest shall make atonement for him, and it shall be forgiven him.

32 'If he brings a lamb as his sin offering, he shall bring a female without blemish. 33 Then he shall lay his hand on the head of the sin offering, and kill it as a sin offering at the place where they kill the burnt offering. 34 The priest shall take *some* of the blood of the sin offering with his finger, put *it* on the horns of the altar of burnt offering, and pour all *the remain-*

ing blood at the base of the altar. 35 He shall remove all its fat, as the fat of the lamb is removed from the sacrifice of the peace offering. Then the priest shall burn it on the altar, according to the offerings made by fire to the LORD. So the priest shall make atonement for his sin that he has committed, and it shall be forgiven him.

～ PSALM 23:1–6 ～

1 The LORD *is* my shepherd;
   I shall not want.
2 He makes me to lie down in green
     pastures;
   He leads me beside the still waters.
3 He restores my soul;
   He leads me in the paths of
     righteousness
   For His name's sake.

4 Yea, though I walk through the
     valley of the shadow of death,
   I will fear no evil;
   For You *are* with me;
   Your rod and Your staff, they
     comfort me.

5 You prepare a table before me in the
     presence of my enemies;
   You anoint my head with oil;
   My cup runs over.
6 Surely goodness and mercy shall
     follow me
   All the days of my life;
   And I will dwell in the house of the
     LORD
   Forever.

～ PROVERBS 9:1–6 ～

1 Wisdom has built her house,
   She has hewn out her seven pillars;
2 She has slaughtered her meat,
   She has mixed her wine,
   She has also furnished her table.
3 She has sent out her maidens,
   She cries out from the highest places
     of the city,
4 "Whoever *is* simple, let him turn in
     here!"
   As for him who lacks understanding,
     she says to him,
5 "Come, eat of my bread

And drink of the wine I have mixed.
6   Forsake foolishness and live,
    And go in the way of understanding.

~ MATTHEW 27:55–66 ~

And many women who followed Jesus from Galilee, ministering to Him, were there looking on from afar, ⁵⁶ among whom were Mary Magdalene, Mary the mother of James and Joses, and the mother of Zebedee's sons.

⁵⁷ Now when evening had come, there came a rich man from Arimathea, named Joseph, who himself had also become a disciple of Jesus. ⁵⁸ This man went to Pilate and asked for the body of Jesus. Then Pilate commanded the body to be given to him. ⁵⁹ When Joseph had taken the body, he wrapped it in a clean linen cloth, ⁶⁰ and laid it in his new tomb which he had hewn out of the rock; and he rolled a large stone against the door of the tomb, and departed. ⁶¹ And Mary Magdalene was there, and the other Mary, sitting opposite the tomb.

⁶² On the next day, which followed the Day of Preparation, the chief priests and Pharisees gathered together to Pilate, ⁶³ saying, "Sir, we remember, while He was still alive, how that deceiver said, 'After three days I will rise.' ⁶⁴ Therefore command that the tomb be made secure until the third day, lest His disciples come by night and steal Him *away,* and say to the people, 'He has risen from the dead.' So the last deception will be worse than the first."

⁶⁵ Pilate said to them, "You have a guard; go your way, make *it* as secure as you know how." ⁶⁶ So they went and made the tomb secure, sealing the stone and setting the guard.

~ LEVITICUS 5:1—6:30 ~

'If a person sins in hearing the utterance of an oath, and *is* a witness, whether he has seen or known *of the matter*—if he does not tell *it,* he bears guilt.

² 'Or if a person touches any unclean thing, whether *it is* the carcass of an unclean beast, or the carcass of unclean livestock, or the carcass of unclean creeping things, and he is unaware of it, he also shall be unclean and guilty. ³ Or if he touches human uncleanness—whatever uncleanness with which a man may be defiled, and he is unaware of it—when he realizes *it,* then he shall be guilty.

⁴ 'Or if a person swears, speaking thoughtlessly with *his* lips to do evil or to do good, whatever *it is* that a man may pronounce by an oath, and he is unaware of it—when he realizes *it,* then he shall be guilty in any of these *matters.*

⁵ 'And it shall be, when he is guilty in any of these *matters,* that he shall confess that he has sinned in that *thing;* ⁶ and he shall bring his trespass offering to the LORD for his sin which he has committed, a female from the flock, a lamb or a kid of the goats as a sin offering. So the priest shall make atonement for him concerning his sin.

⁷ 'If he is not able to bring a lamb, then he shall bring to the LORD, for his trespass which he has committed, two turtledoves or two young pigeons: one as a sin offering and the other as a burnt offering. ⁸ And he shall bring them to the priest, who shall offer *that* which *is* for the sin offering first, and wring off its head from its neck, but shall not divide *it* completely. ⁹ Then he shall sprinkle *some* of the blood of the sin offering on the side of the altar, and the rest of the blood shall be drained out at the base of the altar. It *is* a sin offering. ¹⁰ And he shall offer the second *as* a burnt offering according to the prescribed manner. So the priest shall make atonement on his behalf for his sin which he has committed, and it shall be forgiven him.

¹¹ 'But if he is not able to bring two turtledoves or two young pigeons, then he who sinned shall bring for his offering one-tenth of an ephah of fine flour as a sin offering. He shall put no oil on it, nor shall he put frankincense on it, for it *is* a

sin offering. [12] Then he shall bring it to the priest, and the priest shall take his handful of it as a memorial portion, and burn *it* on the altar according to the offerings made by fire to the LORD. It *is* a sin offering. [13] The priest shall make atonement for him, for his sin that he has committed in any of these matters; and it shall be forgiven him. *The rest* shall be the priest's as a grain offering.' "

[14] Then the LORD spoke to Moses, saying: [15] "If a person commits a trespass, and sins unintentionally in regard to the holy things of the LORD, then he shall bring to the LORD as his trespass offering a ram without blemish from the flocks, with your valuation in shekels of silver according to the shekel of the sanctuary, as a trespass offering. [16] And he shall make restitution for the harm that he has done in regard to the holy thing, and shall add one-fifth to it and give it to the priest. So the priest shall make atonement for him with the ram of the trespass offering, and it shall be forgiven him.

[17] "If a person sins, and commits any of these things which are forbidden to be done by the commandments of the LORD, though he does not know *it,* yet he is guilty and shall bear his iniquity. [18] And he shall bring to the priest a ram without blemish from the flock, with your valuation, as a trespass offering. So the priest shall make atonement for him regarding his ignorance in which he erred and did not know *it,* and it shall be forgiven him. [19] It is a trespass offering; he has certainly trespassed against the LORD."

6 And the LORD spoke to Moses, saying: [2] "If a person sins and commits a trespass against the LORD by lying to his neighbor about what was delivered to him for safekeeping, or about a pledge, or about a robbery, or if he has extorted from his neighbor, [3] or if he has found what was lost and lies concerning it, and swears falsely—in any one of these things that a man may do in which he sins: [4] then it shall be, because he has sinned and is guilty, that he shall restore what he has stolen, or the thing which he has extorted, or what was delivered to him for safekeeping, or the lost thing which he found, [5] or all that about which he has sworn falsely.

He shall restore its full value, add one-fifth more to it, *and* give it to whomever it belongs, on the day of his trespass offering. [6] And he shall bring his trespass offering to the LORD, a ram without blemish from the flock, with your valuation, as a trespass offering, to the priest. [7] So the priest shall make atonement for him before the LORD, and he shall be forgiven for any one of these things that he may have done in which he trespasses."

[8] Then the LORD spoke to Moses, saying, [9] "Command Aaron and his sons, saying, 'This *is* the law of the burnt offering: The burnt offering *shall be* on the hearth upon the altar all night until morning, and the fire of the altar shall be kept burning on it. [10] And the priest shall put on his linen garment, and his linen trousers he shall put on his body, and take up the ashes of the burnt offering which the fire has consumed on the altar, and he shall put them beside the altar. [11] Then he shall take off his garments, put on other garments, and carry the ashes outside the camp to a clean place. [12] And the fire on the altar shall be kept burning on it; it shall not be put out. And the priest shall burn wood on it every morning, and lay the burnt offering in order on it; and he shall burn on it the fat of the peace offerings. [13] A fire shall always be burning on the altar; it shall never go out.

[14] 'This *is* the law of the grain offering: The sons of Aaron shall offer it on the altar before the LORD. [15] He shall take from it his handful of the fine flour of the grain offering, with its oil, and all the frankincense which *is* on the grain offering, and shall burn *it* on the altar *for* a sweet aroma, as a memorial to the LORD. [16] And the remainder of it Aaron and his sons shall eat; with unleavened bread it shall be eaten in a holy place; in the court of the tabernacle of meeting they shall eat it. [17] It shall not be baked with leaven. I have given it *as* their portion of My offerings made by fire; it *is* most holy, like the sin offering and the trespass offering. [18] All the males among the children of Aaron may eat it. *It shall be* a statute forever in your generations concerning the offerings made by fire to the LORD. Everyone who touches them must be holy.' "

[19] And the LORD spoke to Moses,

Just Visiting

> The earth is the Lord's, and all its fullness, the world and those who dwell therein.
>
> *Psalm 24:1*

In the last century, an American tourist heard that a renowned Polish rabbi, Hofetz Chaim, lived in the area where he was traveling. A great admirer of Rabbi Chaim, he asked if he might be able to visit him at his home. Word came back from the rabbi that he was welcome to stop by at any time.

The excited young tourist arrived at the rabbi's home and was invited to take off his knapsack and come inside. He entered the doorway and found a simple one-room lodging, filled with books. The furnishings were limited to a table, a lamp, and a cot.

The tourist asked in amazement, "Rabbi, where is the rest of your furniture?" Hofetz Chaim replied, "Where is yours?"

The puzzled American replied, glancing out the door at his knapsack, "My furniture? But I'm only a visitor here." The rabbi responded, "So am I."

Very often it is when we empty ourselves not only of our pride, but of the possessions we pride ourselves in, that we truly can find those things which will last for all eternity. It is impossible to grasp hold of Heaven and earth with the same outstretched hand.

saying, 20 "This *is* the offering of Aaron and his sons, which they shall offer to the LORD, *beginning* on the day when he is anointed: one-tenth of an ephah of fine flour as a daily grain offering, half of it in the morning and half of it at night. 21 It shall be made in a pan with oil. *When it is* mixed, you shall bring it in. The baked pieces of the grain offering you shall offer *for* a sweet aroma to the LORD. 22 The priest from among his sons, who is anointed in his place, shall offer it. *It is* a statute forever to the LORD. It shall be wholly burned. 23 For every grain offering for the priest shall be wholly burned. It shall not be eaten."

24 Also the LORD spoke to Moses, saying, 25 "Speak to Aaron and to his sons, saying, 'This *is* the law of the sin offering: In the place where the burnt offering is killed, the sin offering shall be killed before the LORD. It *is* most holy. 26 The priest who offers it for sin shall eat it. In a holy place it shall be eaten, in the court of the tabernacle of meeting. 27 Everyone who touches its flesh must be holy. And when its blood is sprinkled on any garment, you shall wash that on which it was sprinkled, in a holy place. 28 But the earthen vessel in which it is boiled shall be broken. And if it is boiled in a bronze pot, it shall be both scoured and rinsed in water. 29 All the males among the priests may eat it. It *is* most holy. 30 But no sin offering from which *any* of the blood is brought into the tabernacle of meeting, to make atonement in the holy *place*, shall be eaten. It shall be burned in the fire.

~ PSALM 24:1–6 ~

1 The earth *is* the LORD's, and all its
  fullness,
  The world and those who dwell
  therein.
2 For He has founded it upon the seas,
  And established it upon the waters.

3 Who may ascend into the hill of the
  LORD?
  Or who may stand in His holy place?
4 He who has clean hands and a pure
  heart,
  Who has not lifted up his soul to an
  idol,

Nor sworn deceitfully.
5 He shall receive blessing from the
  LORD,
  And righteousness from the God of
  his salvation.
6 This *is* Jacob, the generation of those
  who seek Him,
  Who seek Your face.   Selah

~ PROVERBS 9:7–9 ~

7 "He who corrects a scoffer gets shame
  for himself,
  And he who rebukes a wicked *man*
  only harms himself.
8 Do not correct a scoffer, lest he hate
  you;
  Rebuke a wise *man*, and he will love
  you.
9 Give *instruction* to a wise *man*, and
  he will be still wiser;
  Teach a just *man*, and he will
  increase in learning.

~ MATTHEW 28:1–20 ~

Now after the Sabbath, as the first *day* of the week began to dawn, Mary Magdalene and the other Mary came to see the tomb. 2 And behold, there was a great earthquake; for an angel of the Lord descended from heaven, and came and rolled back the stone from the door, and sat on it. 3 His countenance was like lightning, and his clothing as white as snow. 4 And the guards shook for fear of him, and became like dead *men*.

5 But the angel answered and said to the women, "Do not be afraid, for I know that you seek Jesus who was crucified. 6 He is not here; for He is risen, as He said. Come, see the place where the Lord lay. 7 And go quickly and tell His disciples that He is risen from the dead, and indeed He is going before you into Galilee; there you will see Him. Behold, I have told you."

8 So they went out quickly from the tomb with fear and great joy, and ran to bring His disciples word.

9 And as they went to tell His disciples, behold, Jesus met them, saying, "Rejoice!" So they came and held Him by the feet and worshiped Him. 10 Then Jesus said to

them, "Do not be afraid. Go *and* tell My brethren to go to Galilee, and there they will see Me."

¹¹ Now while they were going, behold, some of the guard came into the city and reported to the chief priests all the things that had happened. ¹² When they had assembled with the elders and consulted together, they gave a large sum of money to the soldiers, ¹³ saying, "Tell them, 'His disciples came at night and stole Him *away* while we slept.' ¹⁴ And if this comes to the governor's ears, we will appease him and make you secure." ¹⁵ So they took the money and did as they were instructed; and this saying is commonly reported among the Jews until this day.

¹⁶ Then the eleven disciples went away into Galilee, to the mountain which Jesus had appointed for them. ¹⁷ When they saw Him, they worshiped Him; but some doubted.

¹⁸ And Jesus came and spoke to them, saying, "All authority has been given to Me in heaven and on earth. ¹⁹ Go therefore and make disciples of all the nations, baptizing them in the name of the Father and of the Son and of the Holy Spirit, ²⁰ teaching them to observe all things that I have commanded you; and lo, I am with you always, *even* to the end of the age." Amen.

READING 49 · FEBRUARY 18

～ LEVITICUS 7:1—8:36 ～

'Likewise this *is* the law of the trespass offering (it *is* most holy): ² In the place where they kill the burnt offering they shall kill the trespass offering. And its blood he shall sprinkle all around on the altar. ³ And he shall offer from it all its fat. The fat tail and the fat that covers the entrails, ⁴ the two kidneys and the fat that *is* on them by the flanks, and the fatty lobe *attached* to the liver above the kidneys, he shall remove; ⁵ and the priest shall burn them on the altar *as* an offering made by fire to the LORD. It *is* a trespass offering. ⁶ Every male among the priests may eat it. It shall be eaten in a holy place. It *is* most holy. ⁷ The trespass offering *is* like the sin offering; *there is* one law for them both: the priest who makes atonement with it shall have *it*. ⁸ And the priest who offers anyone's burnt offering, that priest shall have for himself the skin of the burnt offering which he has offered. ⁹ Also every grain offering that is baked in the oven and all that is prepared in the covered pan, or in a pan, shall be the priest's who offers it. ¹⁰ Every grain offering, *whether* mixed with oil or dry, shall belong to all the sons of Aaron, to one *as much* as the other.

¹¹ 'This *is* the law of the sacrifice of peace offerings which he shall offer to the LORD: ¹² If he offers it for a thanksgiving, then he shall offer, with the sacrifice of thanksgiving, unleavened cakes mixed with oil, unleavened wafers anointed with oil, or cakes of blended flour mixed with oil. ¹³ Besides the cakes, *as* his offering he shall offer leavened bread with the sacrifice of thanksgiving of his peace offering. ¹⁴ And from it he shall offer one cake from each offering *as* a heave offering to the LORD. It shall belong to the priest who sprinkles the blood of the peace offering.

¹⁵ 'The flesh of the sacrifice of his peace offering for thanksgiving shall be eaten the same day it is offered. He shall not leave any of it until morning. ¹⁶ But if the sacrifice of his offering *is* a vow or a voluntary offering, it shall be eaten the same day that he offers his sacrifice; but on the next day the remainder of it also may be eaten; ¹⁷ the remainder of the flesh of the sacrifice on the third day must be burned with fire. ¹⁸ And if *any* of the flesh of the sacrifice of his peace offering is eaten at all on the third day, it shall not be accepted, nor shall it be imputed to him; it shall be an abomination *to* him who offers it, and the person who eats of it shall bear guilt.

¹⁹ 'The flesh that touches any unclean thing shall not be eaten. It shall be burned with fire. And as for the *clean* flesh, all who are clean may eat of it. ²⁰ But the

person who eats the flesh of the sacrifice of the peace offering that *belongs* to the LORD, while he is unclean, that person shall be cut off from his people. [21] Moreover the person who touches any unclean thing, *such as* human uncleanness, *an* unclean animal, or any abominable unclean thing, and who eats the flesh of the sacrifice of the peace offering that *belongs* to the LORD, that person shall be cut off from his people.' "

[22] And the LORD spoke to Moses, saying, [23] "Speak to the children of Israel, saying: 'You shall not eat any fat, of ox or sheep or goat. [24] And the fat of an animal that dies *naturally,* and the fat of what is torn by wild beasts, may be used in any other way; but you shall by no means eat it. [25] For whoever eats the fat of the animal of which men offer an offering made by fire to the LORD, the person who eats *it* shall be cut off from his people. [26] Moreover you shall not eat any blood in any of your dwellings, *whether* of bird or beast. [27] Whoever eats any blood, that person shall be cut off from his people.' "

[28] Then the LORD spoke to Moses, saying, [29] "Speak to the children of Israel, saying: 'He who offers the sacrifice of his peace offering to the LORD shall bring his offering to the LORD from the sacrifice of his peace offering. [30] His own hands shall bring the offerings made by fire to the LORD. The fat with the breast he shall bring, that the breast may be waved *as* a wave offering before the LORD. [31] And the priest shall burn the fat on the altar, but the breast shall be Aaron's and his sons'. [32] Also the right thigh you shall give to the priest *as* a heave offering from the sacrifices of your peace offerings. [33] He among the sons of Aaron, who offers the blood of the peace offering and the fat, shall have the right thigh for *his* part. [34] For the breast of the wave offering and the thigh of the heave offering I have taken from the children of Israel, from the sacrifices of their peace offerings, and I have given them to Aaron the priest and to his sons from the children of Israel by a statute forever.' "

[35] This *is* the consecrated portion for Aaron and his sons, from the offerings made by fire to the LORD, on the day when *Moses* presented them to minister to the LORD as priests. [36] The LORD commanded this to be given to them by the children of Israel, on the day that He anointed them, *by* a statute forever throughout their generations.

[37] This *is* the law of the burnt offering, the grain offering, the sin offering, the trespass offering, the consecrations, and the sacrifice of the peace offering, [38] which the LORD commanded Moses on Mount Sinai, on the day when He commanded the children of Israel to offer their offerings to the LORD in the Wilderness of Sinai.

8 And the LORD spoke to Moses, saying: [2] "Take Aaron and his sons with him, and the garments, the anointing oil, a bull as the sin offering, two rams, and a basket of unleavened bread; [3] and gather all the congregation together at the door of the tabernacle of meeting."

[4] So Moses did as the LORD commanded him. And the congregation was gathered together at the door of the tabernacle of meeting. [5] And Moses said to the congregation, "This *is* what the LORD commanded to be done."

[6] Then Moses brought Aaron and his sons and washed them with water. [7] And he put the tunic on him, girded him with the sash, clothed him with the robe, and put the ephod on him; and he girded him with the intricately woven band of the ephod, and with it tied *the ephod* on him. [8] Then he put the breastplate on him, and he put the Urim and the Thummim in the breastplate. [9] And he put the turban on his head. Also on the turban, on its front, he put the golden plate, the holy crown, as the LORD had commanded Moses.

[10] Also Moses took the anointing oil, and anointed the tabernacle and all that *was* in it, and consecrated them. [11] He sprinkled some of it on the altar seven times, anointed the altar and all its utensils, and the laver and its base, to consecrate them. [12] And he poured some of the anointing oil on Aaron's head and anointed him, to consecrate him.

[13] Then Moses brought Aaron's sons and put tunics on them, girded them with sashes, and put hats on them, as the LORD had commanded Moses.

[14] And he brought the bull for the sin

Alone with the Eternal

Dr. Alexander Maclaren is considered one of the clearest Bible expositors of his time. He attributed becoming such a great Bible scholar to a habit he had, which he never broke: spending one hour a day "alone with the Eternal."

The hour which Dr. Maclaren designated was from nine to ten in the morning. At times, he allowed others into his prayer closet, but they were never allowed to utter a word. Maclaren would sit in his well-worn armchair, with his big Bible laying across his knees. Sometimes he would read its pages, but most often he would just sit with his hand over his face.

During that hour he did not allow himself to read the Bible as a student, or to search for texts to use in sermons or lessons. One of his assistants noted, "He read the Bible as a child would read a letter from an absent father, as a loving heart would drink in again the message from a loved one far away."

When we pray, we open our hearts to a clearer and deeper understanding of God's Word. As we read His Word, we open our minds to a greater understanding of how and for what to pray.

> The fear of the Lord is the beginning of wisdom, and the knowledge of the Holy One is understanding.
>
> *Proverbs 9:10*

offering. Then Aaron and his sons laid their hands on the head of the bull for the sin offering, [15] and Moses killed *it*. Then he took the blood, and put *some* on the horns of the altar all around with his finger, and purified the altar. And he poured the blood at the base of the altar, and consecrated it, to make atonement for it. [16] Then he took all the fat that *was* on the entrails, the fatty lobe *attached to* the liver, and the two kidneys with their fat, and Moses burned *them* on the altar. [17] But the bull, its hide, its flesh, and its offal, he burned with fire outside the camp, as the LORD had commanded Moses.

[18] Then he brought the ram as the burnt offering. And Aaron and his sons laid their hands on the head of the ram, [19] and Moses killed *it*. Then he sprinkled the blood all around on the altar. [20] And he cut the ram into pieces; and Moses burned the head, the pieces, and the fat. [21] Then he washed the entrails and the legs in water. And Moses burned the whole ram on the altar. It *was* a burnt sacrifice for a sweet aroma, an offering made by fire to the LORD, as the LORD had commanded Moses.

[22] And he brought the second ram, the ram of consecration. Then Aaron and his sons laid their hands on the head of the ram, [23] and Moses killed *it*. Also he took *some* of its blood and put it on the tip of Aaron's right ear, on the thumb of his right hand, and on the big toe of his right foot. [24] Then he brought Aaron's sons. And Moses put *some* of the blood on the tips of their right ears, on the thumbs of their right hands, and on the big toes of their right feet. And Moses sprinkled the blood all around on the altar. [25] Then he took the fat and the fat tail, all the fat that *was* on the entrails, the fatty lobe *attached to* the liver, the two kidneys and their fat, and the right thigh; [26] and from the basket of unleavened bread that was before the LORD he took one unleavened cake, a cake of bread *anointed with* oil, and one wafer, and put *them* on the fat and on the right thigh; [27] and he put all *these* in Aaron's hands and in his sons' hands, and waved *them as* a wave offering before the LORD. [28] Then Moses took them from their hands and burned *them* on the altar, on the burnt offering. They *were* conse-

cration offerings for a sweet aroma. That *was* an offering made by fire to the LORD. [29] And Moses took the breast and waved it *as* a wave offering before the LORD. It was Moses' part of the ram of consecration, as the LORD had commanded Moses.

[30] Then Moses took some of the anointing oil and some of the blood which *was* on the altar, and sprinkled *it* on Aaron, on his garments, on his sons, and on the garments of his sons with him; and he consecrated Aaron, his garments, his sons, and the garments of his sons with him.

[31] And Moses said to Aaron and his sons, "Boil the flesh *at* the door of the tabernacle of meeting, and eat it there with the bread that *is* in the basket of consecration offerings, as I commanded, saying, 'Aaron and his sons shall eat it.' [32] What remains of the flesh and of the bread you shall burn with fire. [33] And you shall not go outside the door of the tabernacle of meeting *for* seven days, until the days of your consecration are ended. For seven days he shall consecrate you. [34] As he has done this day, *so* the LORD has commanded to do, to make atonement for you. [35] Therefore you shall stay *at* the door of the tabernacle of meeting day and night for seven days, and keep the charge of the LORD, so that you may not die; for so I have been commanded." [36] So Aaron and his sons did all the things that the LORD had commanded by the hand of Moses.

~ PSALM 24:7–10 ~

[7] Lift up your heads, O you gates!
  And be lifted up, you everlasting
    doors!
  And the King of glory shall come in.
[8] Who *is* this King of glory?
  The LORD strong and mighty,
  The LORD mighty in battle.
[9] Lift up your heads, O you gates!
  Lift up, you everlasting doors!
  And the King of glory shall come in.
[10] Who is this King of glory?
  The LORD of hosts,
  He *is* the King of glory.   Selah

~ PROVERBS 9:10–12 ~

[10] "The fear of the LORD *is* the
    beginning of wisdom,

And the knowledge of the Holy One
is understanding.
11 For by me your days will be
multiplied,
And years of life will be added to
you.
12 If you are wise, you are wise for
yourself,
And *if* you scoff, you will bear *it*
alone."

~ MARK 1:1–22 ~

The beginning of the gospel of Jesus
Christ, the Son of God. 2 As it is written
in the Prophets:

"Behold, I send My messenger
before Your face,
Who will prepare Your way
before You."
3 "The voice of one crying in the
wilderness:
'Prepare the way of the LORD;
Make His paths straight.' "

4 John came baptizing in the wilderness
and preaching a baptism of repentance
for the remission of sins. 5 Then all the
land of Judea, and those from Jerusalem,
went out to him and were all baptized by
him in the Jordan River, confessing their
sins.
6 Now John was clothed with camel's
hair and with a leather belt around his
waist, and he ate locusts and wild honey.
7 And he preached, saying, "There comes
One after me who is mightier than I,
whose sandal strap I am not worthy to
stoop down and loose. 8 I indeed baptized

you with water, but He will baptize you
with the Holy Spirit."
9 It came to pass in those days *that* Jesus
came from Nazareth of Galilee, and was
baptized by John in the Jordan. 10 And
immediately, coming up from the water,
He saw the heavens parting and the Spirit
descending upon Him like a dove. 11 Then
a voice came from heaven, "You are My
beloved Son, in whom I am well pleased."
12 Immediately the Spirit drove Him
into the wilderness. 13 And He was there
in the wilderness forty days, tempted by
Satan, and was with the wild beasts; and
the angels ministered to Him.
14 Now after John was put in prison,
Jesus came to Galilee, preaching the gospel of the kingdom of God, 15 and saying,
"The time is fulfilled, and the kingdom
of God is at hand. Repent, and believe in
the gospel."
16 And as He walked by the Sea of Galilee, He saw Simon and Andrew his
brother casting a net into the sea; for they
were fishermen. 17 Then Jesus said to
them, "Follow Me, and I will make you
become fishers of men." 18 They immediately left their nets and followed Him.
19 When He had gone a little farther
from there, He saw James the *son* of
Zebedee, and John his brother, who also
were in the boat mending their nets. 20 And
immediately He called them, and they left
their father Zebedee in the boat with the
hired servants, and went after Him.
21 Then they went into Capernaum, and
immediately on the Sabbath He entered
the synagogue and taught. 22 And they
were astonished at His teaching, for He
taught them as one having authority, and
not as the scribes.

READING 50 · FEBRUARY 19

~ LEVITICUS 9:1—10:20 ~

It came to pass on the eighth day that
Moses called Aaron and his sons and
the elders of Israel. 2 And he said to
Aaron, "Take for yourself a young bull as
a sin offering and a ram as a burnt offering, without blemish, and offer *them*
before the LORD. 3 And to the children of
Israel you shall speak, saying, 'Take a kid

of the goats as a sin offering, and a calf
and a lamb, *both* of the first year, without
blemish, as a burnt offering, 4 also a bull
and a ram as peace offerings, to sacrifice
before the LORD, and a grain offering
mixed with oil; for today the LORD will
appear to you.' "
5 So they brought what Moses

commanded before the tabernacle of meeting. And all the congregation drew near and stood before the LORD. ⁶ Then Moses said, "This *is* the thing which the LORD commanded you to do, and the glory of the LORD will appear to you." ⁷ And Moses said to Aaron, "Go to the altar, offer your sin offering and your burnt offering, and make atonement for yourself and for the people. Offer the offering of the people, and make atonement for them, as the LORD commanded."

⁸ Aaron therefore went to the altar and killed the calf of the sin offering, which *was* for himself. ⁹ Then the sons of Aaron brought the blood to him. And he dipped his finger in the blood, put *it* on the horns of the altar, and poured the blood at the base of the altar. ¹⁰ But the fat, the kidneys, and the fatty lobe from the liver of the sin offering he burned on the altar, as the LORD had commanded Moses. ¹¹ The flesh and the hide he burned with fire outside the camp.

¹² And he killed the burnt offering; and Aaron's sons presented to him the blood, which he sprinkled all around on the altar. ¹³ Then they presented the burnt offering to him, with its pieces and head, and he burned *them* on the altar. ¹⁴ And he washed the entrails and the legs, and burned *them* with the burnt offering on the altar.

¹⁵ Then he brought the people's offering, and took the goat, which *was* the sin offering for the people, and killed it and offered it for sin, like the first one. ¹⁶ And he brought the burnt offering and offered it according to the prescribed manner. ¹⁷ Then he brought the grain offering, took a handful of it, and burned *it* on the altar, besides the burnt sacrifice of the morning.

¹⁸ He also killed the bull and the ram *as* sacrifices of peace offerings, which *were* for the people. And Aaron's sons presented to him the blood, which he sprinkled all around on the altar, ¹⁹ and the fat from the bull and the ram—the fatty tail, what covers *the entrails* and the kidneys, and the fatty lobe *attached to* the liver; ²⁰ and they put the fat on the breasts. Then he burned the fat on the altar; ²¹ but the breasts and the right thigh Aaron waved *as* a wave offering before the LORD, as Moses had commanded.

²² Then Aaron lifted his hand toward the people, blessed them, and came down from offering the sin offering, the burnt offering, and peace offerings. ²³ And Moses and Aaron went into the tabernacle of meeting, and came out and blessed the people. Then the glory of the LORD appeared to all the people, ²⁴ and fire came out from before the LORD and consumed the burnt offering and the fat on the altar. When all the people saw *it*, they shouted and fell on their faces.

10 Then Nadab and Abihu, the sons of Aaron, each took his censer and put fire in it, put incense on it, and offered profane fire before the LORD, which He had not commanded them. ² So fire went out from the LORD and devoured them, and they died before the LORD. ³ And Moses said to Aaron, "This is what the LORD spoke, saying:

'By those who come near Me
　I must be regarded as holy;
And before all the people
　I must be glorified.' "

So Aaron held his peace.

⁴ Then Moses called Mishael and Elzaphan, the sons of Uzziel the uncle of Aaron, and said to them, "Come near, carry your brethren from before the sanctuary out of the camp." ⁵ So they went near and carried them by their tunics out of the camp, as Moses had said.

⁶ And Moses said to Aaron, and to Eleazar and Ithamar, his sons, "Do not uncover your heads nor tear your clothes, lest you die, and wrath come upon all the people. But let your brethren, the whole house of Israel, bewail the burning which the LORD has kindled. ⁷ You shall not go out from the door of the tabernacle of meeting, lest you die, for the anointing oil of the LORD *is* upon you." And they did according to the word of Moses.

⁸ Then the LORD spoke to Aaron, saying: ⁹ "Do not drink wine or intoxicating drink, you, nor your sons with you, when you go into the tabernacle of meeting, lest you die. *It shall be* a statute forever throughout your generations, ¹⁰ that you

A Real Role Model

His name conjures up memories of booming home runs, tremendous speed, and enormous natural ability. Mickey Mantle was a baseball giant. And yet, just a month after receiving a liver transplant, Mantle had the graciousness to say, "You talk about your role models. This is your role model: Don't be like me." Mantle squarely faced the fact that while he was a superstar on the field, his personal life was not worthy of emulation.

Nevertheless, in the ninth inning of his life, with two outs and a full count, Mantle hit a personal home run. With humility, humor, and no self-pity, he eloquently pleaded with others to take heed of his mistakes. In return, his final days were marked by a great outpouring of love — not only in response to the great memories he had made on the baseball fields of America, but in response to his honest self-appraisal.

Because of his pleas, organ donations increased all across America virtually overnight, giving countless people what Mantle himself did not enjoy: extra innings.

> Do not remember the sins of my youth, nor my transgressions; according to Your mercy remember me, for Your goodness' sake, O Lord.
>
> *Psalm 25:7*

may distinguish between holy and unholy, and between unclean and clean, [11] and that you may teach the children of Israel all the statutes which the LORD has spoken to them by the hand of Moses."

[12] And Moses spoke to Aaron, and to Eleazar and Ithamar, his sons who were left: "Take the grain offering that remains of the offerings made by fire to the LORD, and eat it without leaven beside the altar; for it *is* most holy. [13] You shall eat it in a holy place, because it *is* your due and your sons' due, of the sacrifices made by fire to the LORD; for so I have been commanded. [14] The breast of the wave offering and the thigh of the heave offering you shall eat in a clean place, you, your sons, and your daughters with you; for *they are* your due and your sons' due, *which* are given from the sacrifices of peace offerings of the children of Israel. [15] The thigh of the heave offering and the breast of the wave offering they shall bring with the offerings of fat made by fire, to offer *as* a wave offering before the LORD. And it shall be yours and your sons' with you, by a statute forever, as the LORD has commanded."

[16] Then Moses made careful inquiry about the goat of the sin offering, and there it was—burned up. And he was angry with Eleazar and Ithamar, the sons of Aaron *who were* left, saying, [17] "Why have you not eaten the sin offering in a holy place, since it *is* most holy, and *God* has given it to you to bear the guilt of the congregation, to make atonement for them before the LORD? [18] See! Its blood was not brought inside the holy *place;* indeed you should have eaten it in a holy *place,* as I commanded."

[19] And Aaron said to Moses, "Look, this day they have offered their sin offering and their burnt offering before the LORD, and such things have befallen me! *If* I had eaten the sin offering today, would it have been accepted in the sight of the LORD?" [20] So when Moses heard *that,* he was content.

∼ PSALM 25:1–7 ∼

[1]   To You, O LORD, I lift up my soul.
[2]   O my God, I trust in You;
      Let me not be ashamed;

Let not my enemies triumph over me.
[3]   Indeed, let no one who waits on You be ashamed;
      Let those be ashamed who deal treacherously without cause.

[4]   Show me Your ways, O LORD;
      Teach me Your paths.
[5]   Lead me in Your truth and teach me,
      For You *are* the God of my salvation;
      On You I wait all the day.

[6]   Remember, O LORD, Your tender mercies and Your lovingkindnesses,
      For they *are* from of old.
[7]   Do not remember the sins of my youth, nor my transgressions;
      According to Your mercy remember me,
      For Your goodness' sake, O LORD.

∼ PROVERBS 9:13–18 ∼

[13] A foolish woman is clamorous;
      She is simple, and knows nothing.
[14] For she sits at the door of her house,
      On a seat *by* the highest places of the city,
[15] To call to those who pass by,
      Who go straight on their way:
[16] "Whoever *is* simple, let him turn in here";
      And *as for* him who lacks understanding, she says to him,
[17] "Stolen water is sweet,
      And bread *eaten* in secret is pleasant."
[18] But he does not know that the dead *are* there,
      That her guests *are* in the depths of hell.

∼ MARK 1:23–45 ∼

Now there was a man in their synagogue with an unclean spirit. And he cried out, [24] saying, "Let *us* alone! What have we to do with You, Jesus of Nazareth? Did You come to destroy us? I know who You are— the Holy One of God!"

[25] But Jesus rebuked him, saying, "Be quiet, and come out of him!" [26] And when the unclean spirit had convulsed him and

cried out with a loud voice, he came out of him. [27] Then they were all amazed, so that they questioned among themselves, saying, "What is this? What new doctrine *is* this? For with authority He commands even the unclean spirits, and they obey Him." [28] And immediately His fame spread throughout all the region around Galilee.

[29] Now as soon as they had come out of the synagogue, they entered the house of Simon and Andrew, with James and John. [30] But Simon's wife's mother lay sick with a fever, and they told Him about her at once. [31] So He came and took her by the hand and lifted her up, and immediately the fever left her. And she served them.

[32] At evening, when the sun had set, they brought to Him all who were sick and those who were demon-possessed. [33] And the whole city was gathered together at the door. [34] Then He healed many who were sick with various diseases, and cast out many demons; and He did not allow the demons to speak, because they knew Him.

[35] Now in the morning, having risen a long while before daylight, He went out and departed to a solitary place; and there He prayed. [36] And Simon and those *who were* with Him searched for Him. [37] When they found Him, they said to Him, "Everyone is looking for You."

[38] But He said to them, "Let us go into the next towns, that I may preach there also, because for this purpose I have come forth." [39] And He was preaching in their synagogues throughout all Galilee, and casting out demons.

[40] Now a leper came to Him, imploring Him, kneeling down to Him and saying to Him, "If You are willing, You can make me clean." [41] Then Jesus, moved with compassion, stretched out *His* hand and touched him, and said to him, "I am willing; be cleansed." [42] As soon as He had spoken, immediately the leprosy left him, and he was cleansed. [43] And He strictly warned him and sent him away at once, [44] and said to him, "See that you say nothing to anyone; but go your way, show yourself to the priest, and offer for your cleansing those things which Moses commanded, as a testimony to them."

[45] However, he went out and began to proclaim *it* freely, and to spread the matter, so that Jesus could no longer openly enter the city, but was outside in deserted places; and they came to Him from every direction.

~ LEVITICUS 11:1—12:8 ~

Now the LORD spoke to Moses and Aaron, saying to them, [2] "Speak to the children of Israel, saying, 'These *are* the animals which you may eat among all the animals that *are* on the earth: [3] Among the animals, whatever divides the hoof, having cloven hooves *and* chewing the cud—that you may eat. [4] Nevertheless these you shall not eat among those that chew the cud or those that have cloven hooves: the camel, because it chews the cud but does not have cloven hooves, is unclean to you; [5] the rock hyrax, because it chews the cud but does not have cloven hooves, *is* unclean to you; [6] the hare, because it chews the cud but does not have cloven hooves, *is* unclean to you; [7] and the swine, though it divides the hoof, having cloven hooves, yet does not chew the cud, *is* unclean to you. [8] Their flesh you shall not eat, and their carcasses you shall not touch. They *are* unclean to you.

[9] 'These you may eat of all that *are* in the water: whatever in the water has fins and scales, whether in the seas or in the rivers—that you may eat. [10] But all in the seas or in the rivers that do not have fins and scales, all that move in the water or any living thing which *is* in the water, they *are* an abomination to you. [11] They shall be an abomination to you; you shall not eat their flesh, but you shall regard their carcasses as an abomination. [12] Whatever in the water does not have fins or scales— that *shall be* an abomination to you.

¹³ 'And these you shall regard as an abomination among the birds; they shall not be eaten, they *are* an abomination: the eagle, the vulture, the buzzard, ¹⁴ the kite, and the falcon after its kind; ¹⁵ every raven after its kind, ¹⁶ the ostrich, the short-eared owl, the sea gull, and the hawk after its kind; ¹⁷ the little owl, the fisher owl, and the screech owl; ¹⁸ the white owl, the jackdaw, and the carrion vulture; ¹⁹ the stork, the heron after its kind, the hoopoe, and the bat.

²⁰ 'All flying insects that creep on *all* fours *shall be* an abomination to you. ²¹ Yet these you may eat of every flying insect that creeps on *all* fours: those which have jointed legs above their feet with which to leap on the earth. ²² These you may eat: the locust after its kind, the destroying locust after its kind, the cricket after its kind, and the grasshopper after its kind. ²³ But all *other* flying insects which have four feet *shall be* an abomination to you.

²⁴ 'By these you shall become unclean; whoever touches the carcass of any of them shall be unclean until evening; ²⁵ whoever carries part of the carcass of any of them shall wash his clothes and be unclean until evening: ²⁶ *The carcass* of any animal which divides the foot, but is not cloven-hoofed or does not chew the cud, *is* unclean to you. Everyone who touches it shall be unclean. ²⁷ And whatever goes on its paws, among all kinds of animals that go on *all* fours, those *are* unclean to you. Whoever touches any such carcass shall be unclean until evening. ²⁸ Whoever carries *any such* carcass shall wash his clothes and be unclean until evening. It *is* unclean to you.

²⁹ 'These also *shall be* unclean to you among the creeping things that creep on the earth: the mole, the mouse, and the large lizard after its kind; ³⁰ the gecko, the monitor lizard, the sand reptile, the sand lizard, and the chameleon. ³¹ These *are* unclean to you among all that creep. Whoever touches them when they are dead shall be unclean until evening. ³² Anything on which *any* of them falls, when they are dead shall be unclean, whether *it is* any item of wood or clothing or skin or sack, whatever item *it is*, in which *any* work is done, it must be put in water. And

it shall be unclean until evening; then it shall be clean. ³³ Any earthen vessel into which *any* of them falls you shall break; and whatever *is* in it shall be unclean: ³⁴ in such a vessel, any edible food upon which water falls becomes unclean, and any drink that may be drunk from it becomes unclean. ³⁵ And everything on which *a part* of *any such* carcass falls shall be unclean; *whether it is* an oven or cooking stove, it shall be broken down; *for* they *are* unclean, and shall be unclean to you. ³⁶ Nevertheless a spring or a cistern, *in which there is* plenty of water, shall be clean, but whatever touches any such carcass becomes unclean. ³⁷ And if a part of *any such* carcass falls on any planting seed which is to be sown, it *remains* clean. ³⁸ But if water is put on the seed, and if *a part* of *any such* carcass falls on it, it *becomes* unclean to you.

³⁹ 'And if any animal which you may eat dies, he who touches its carcass shall be unclean until evening. ⁴⁰ He who eats of its carcass shall wash his clothes and be unclean until evening. He also who carries its carcass shall wash his clothes and be unclean until evening.

⁴¹ 'And every creeping thing that creeps on the earth *shall be* an abomination. It shall not be eaten. ⁴² Whatever crawls on its belly, whatever goes on *all* fours, or whatever has many feet among all creeping things that creep on the earth—these you shall not eat, for they *are* an abomination. ⁴³ You shall not make yourselves abominable with any creeping thing that creeps; nor shall you make yourselves unclean with them, lest you be defiled by them. ⁴⁴ For I *am* the LORD your God. You shall therefore consecrate yourselves, and you shall be holy; for I *am* holy. Neither shall you defile yourselves with any creeping thing that creeps on the earth. ⁴⁵ For I *am* the LORD who brings you up out of the land of Egypt, to be your God. You shall therefore be holy, for I *am* holy.

⁴⁶ 'This *is* the law of the animals and the birds and every living creature that moves in the waters, and of every creature that creeps on the earth, ⁴⁷ to distinguish between the unclean and the clean, and between the animal that may be eaten and the animal that may not be eaten.' "

Paths of Mercy and Truth

Many people have thrilled to the voice of the opera great Beverly Sills. Few know, however, that her natural daughter was born deaf and that she has a step-daughter who is also severely handi-capped.

She writes in her autobiography, *Bubbles*:

"I was now only thirty-four, but a very mature thirty-four. In a strange way my children had brought me an inner peace. The first question I had when I learned of their tragedies was self-pitying 'Why me?' Then gradually it changed to a much more important 'Why them?' Despite their handicaps they were showing enormous strength in continuing to live as normal and constructive lives as possible. How could Peter and I show any less strength?"

Oscar Wilde once wrote: "In this world there are only two tragedies. One is not getting what one wants, and the other is getting it." A third tragedy may be added: the tragedy of not being able to go forward after tragedy has occurred. When a tragedy strikes, our first tendency is to ask, "Why?" We may never know "why," but God promises to be with us always. When we make the decision to go on with life, He leads us in His paths of mercy and truth.

12 Then the LORD spoke to Moses, saying, ² "Speak to the children of Israel, saying: 'If a woman has conceived, and borne a male child, then she shall be unclean seven days; as in the days of her customary impurity she shall be unclean. ³ And on the eighth day the flesh of his foreskin shall be circumcised. ⁴ She shall then continue in the blood of *her* purification thirty-three days. She shall not touch any hallowed thing, nor come into the sanctuary until the days of her purification are fulfilled.

⁵ 'But if she bears a female child, then she shall be unclean two weeks, as in her customary impurity, and she shall continue in the blood of *her* purification sixty-six days.

⁶ 'When the days of her purification are fulfilled, whether for a son or a daughter, she shall bring to the priest a lamb of the first year as a burnt offering, and a young pigeon or a turtledove as a sin offering, to the door of the tabernacle of meeting. ⁷ Then he shall offer it before the LORD, and make atonement for her. And she shall be clean from the flow of her blood. This *is* the law for her who has borne a male or a female.

⁸ 'And if she is not able to bring a lamb, then she may bring two turtledoves or two young pigeons—one as a burnt offering and the other as a sin offering. So the priest shall make atonement for her, and she will be clean.' "

∼ PSALM 25:8–15 ∼

⁸ Good and upright *is* the LORD;
   Therefore He teaches sinners in the way.
⁹ The humble He guides in justice,
   And the humble He teaches His way.
¹⁰ All the paths of the LORD *are* mercy and truth,
   To such as keep His covenant and His testimonies.
¹¹ For Your name's sake, O LORD,
   Pardon my iniquity, for it *is* great.

¹² Who *is* the man that fears the LORD?
   Him shall He teach in the way He chooses.
¹³ He himself shall dwell in prosperity,

And his descendants shall inherit the earth.
¹⁴ The secret of the LORD *is* with those who fear Him,
   And He will show them His covenant.
¹⁵ My eyes *are* ever toward the LORD,
   For He shall pluck my feet out of the net.

∼ PROVERBS 10:1–3 ∼

The proverbs of Solomon:

A wise son makes a glad father,
   But a foolish son *is* the grief of his mother.

² Treasures of wickedness profit nothing,
   But righteousness delivers from death.
³ The LORD will not allow the righteous soul to famish,
   But He casts away the desire of the wicked.

∼ MARK 2:1–28 ∼

And again He entered Capernaum after *some* days, and it was heard that He was in the house. ² Immediately many gathered together, so that there was no longer room to receive *them*, not even near the door. And He preached the word to them. ³ Then they came to Him, bringing a paralytic who was carried by four *men*. ⁴ And when they could not come near Him because of the crowd, they uncovered the roof where He was. So when they had broken through, they let down the bed on which the paralytic was lying. ⁵ When Jesus saw their faith, He said to the paralytic, "Son, your sins are forgiven you."

⁶ And some of the scribes were sitting there and reasoning in their hearts, ⁷ "Why does this *Man* speak blasphemies like this? Who can forgive sins but God alone?"

⁸ But immediately, when Jesus perceived in His spirit that they reasoned thus within themselves, He said to them, "Why do you reason about these things in your hearts? ⁹ Which is easier, to say to

the paralytic, 'Your sins are forgiven you,' or to say, 'Arise, take up your bed and walk'? [10] But that you may know that the Son of Man has power on earth to forgive sins"—He said to the paralytic, [11] "I say to you, arise, take up your bed, and go to your house." [12] Immediately he arose, took up the bed, and went out in the presence of them all, so that all were amazed and glorified God, saying, "We never saw *anything* like this!"

[13] Then He went out again by the sea; and all the multitude came to Him, and He taught them. [14] As He passed by, He saw Levi the *son* of Alphaeus sitting at the tax office. And He said to him, "Follow Me." So he arose and followed Him.

[15] Now it happened, as He was dining in *Levi's* house, that many tax collectors and sinners also sat together with Jesus and His disciples; for there were many, and they followed Him. [16] And when the scribes and Pharisees saw Him eating with the tax collectors and sinners, they said to His disciples, "How *is it* that He eats and drinks with tax collectors and sinners?"

[17] When Jesus heard *it,* He said to them, "Those who are well have no need of a physician, but those who are sick. I did not come to call *the* righteous, but sinners, to repentance."

[18] The disciples of John and of the Pharisees were fasting. Then they came and said to Him, "Why do the disciples of John and of the Pharisees fast, but Your disciples do not fast?"

[19] And Jesus said to them, "Can the friends of the bridegroom fast while the bridegroom is with them? As long as they have the bridegroom with them they cannot fast. [20] But the days will come when the bridegroom will be taken away from them, and then they will fast in those days. [21] No one sews a piece of unshrunk cloth on an old garment; or else the new piece pulls away from the old, and the tear is made worse. [22] And no one puts new wine into old wineskins; or else the new wine bursts the wineskins, the wine is spilled, and the wineskins are ruined. But new wine must be put into new wineskins."

[23] Now it happened that He went through the grainfields on the Sabbath; and as they went His disciples began to pluck the heads of grain. [24] And the Pharisees said to Him, "Look, why do they do what is not lawful on the Sabbath?"

[25] But He said to them, "Have you never read what David did when he was in need and hungry, he and those with him: [26] how he went into the house of God *in the days* of Abiathar the high priest, and ate the showbread, which is not lawful to eat except for the priests, and also gave some to those who were with him?"

[27] And He said to them, "The Sabbath was made for man, and not man for the Sabbath. [28] Therefore the Son of Man is also Lord of the Sabbath."

READING 52 · FEBRUARY 21

~ LEVITICUS 13:1–59 ~

And the LORD spoke to Moses and Aaron, saying: [2] "When a man has on the skin of his body a swelling, a scab, or a bright spot, and it becomes on the skin of his body *like* a leprous sore, then he shall be brought to Aaron the priest or to one of his sons the priests. [3] The priest shall examine the sore on the skin of the body; and if the hair on the sore has turned white, and the sore appears *to be* deeper than the skin of his body, it *is* a leprous sore. Then the priest shall examine him, and pronounce him unclean. [4] But if the bright spot *is* white on the skin of his body, and does not appear *to be* deeper than the skin, and its hair has not turned white, then the priest shall isolate *the one who has* the sore seven days. [5] And the priest shall examine him on the seventh day; and indeed *if* the sore appears to be as it was, *and* the sore has not spread on the skin, then the priest shall isolate him another seven days. [6] Then the priest shall examine him again on the seventh day; and indeed *if* the sore has faded, *and* the sore has not spread on the skin, then the priest shall pronounce him clean; it *is only* a scab, and he shall wash his clothes and be clean. [7] But if the scab should at all spread over the skin, after he has been seen by the priest for his cleansing, he shall be seen by the priest again. [8] And *if* the priest sees that the scab has indeed spread on the skin, then the priest shall pronounce him unclean. It *is* leprosy.

[9] "When the leprous sore is on a person, then he shall be brought to the priest. [10] And the priest shall examine *him;* and indeed *if* the swelling on the skin *is* white, and it has turned the hair white, and *there is* a spot of raw flesh in the swelling, [11] it *is* an old leprosy on the skin of his body. The priest shall pronounce him unclean, and shall not isolate him, for he *is* unclean.

[12] "And if leprosy breaks out all over the skin, and the leprosy covers all the skin of *the one who has* the sore, from his head to his foot, wherever the priest looks, [13] then the priest shall consider; and indeed *if* the leprosy has covered all his body, he shall pronounce *him* clean *who has* the sore. It has all turned white. He *is* clean. [14] But when raw flesh appears on him, he shall be unclean. [15] And the priest shall examine the raw flesh and pronounce him to be unclean; *for* the raw flesh *is* unclean. It *is* leprosy. [16] Or if the raw flesh changes and turns white again, he shall come to the priest. [17] And the priest shall examine him; and indeed *if* the sore has turned white, then the priest shall pronounce *him* clean *who has* the sore. He *is* clean.

[18] "If the body develops a boil in the skin, and it is healed, [19] and in the place of the boil there comes a white swelling or a bright spot, reddish-white, then it shall be shown to the priest; [20] and *if,* when the priest sees it, it indeed *appears* deeper than the skin, and its hair has turned white, the priest shall pronounce him unclean. It *is* a leprous sore which has broken out of the boil. [21] But if the priest examines it, and indeed *there are* no white hairs in it, and it *is* not deeper than the skin, but has faded, then the priest shall isolate him seven days; [22] and if it should at all spread over the skin, then the priest shall pronounce him unclean. It *is* a leprous sore. [23] But if the bright spot stays in one place, *and* has not spread, it *is* the

scar of the boil; and the priest shall pronounce him clean.

[24] "Or if the body receives a burn on its skin by fire, and the raw *flesh* of the burn becomes a bright spot, reddish-white or white, [25] then the priest shall examine it; and indeed *if* the hair of the bright spot has turned white, and it appears deeper than the skin, it *is* leprosy broken out in the burn. Therefore the priest shall pronounce him unclean. It *is* a leprous sore. [26] But if the priest examines it, and indeed *there are* no white hairs in the bright spot, and it *is* not deeper than the skin, but has faded, then the priest shall isolate him seven days. [27] And the priest shall examine him on the seventh day. If it has at all spread over the skin, then the priest shall pronounce him unclean. It *is* a leprous sore. [28] But if the bright spot stays in one place, *and* has not spread on the skin, but has faded, it *is* a swelling from the burn. The priest shall pronounce him clean, for it *is* the scar from the burn.

[29] "If a man or woman has a sore on the head or the beard, [30] then the priest shall examine the sore; and indeed if it appears deeper than the skin, *and there is* in it thin yellow hair, then the priest shall pronounce him unclean. It *is* a scaly leprosy of the head or beard. [31] But if the priest examines the scaly sore, and indeed it does not appear deeper than the skin, and *there is* no black hair in it, then the priest shall isolate *the one who has* the scale seven days. [32] And on the seventh day the priest shall examine the sore; and indeed *if* the scale has not spread, and there is no yellow hair in it, and the scale does not appear deeper than the skin, [33] he shall shave himself, but the scale he shall not shave. And the priest shall isolate *the one who has* the scale another seven days. [34] On the seventh day the priest shall examine the scale; and indeed *if* the scale has not spread over the skin, and does not appear deeper than the skin, then the priest shall pronounce him clean. He shall wash his clothes and be clean. [35] But if the scale should at all spread over the skin after his cleansing, [36] then the priest shall examine him; and indeed *if* the scale has spread over the skin, the priest need not seek for yellow hair. He *is* unclean. [37] But if the scale appears to be at a standstill,

Unseen Details

On a shelf sits a beautiful and expensive carving from the Orient. It is a statue of a woman wearing a tall headdress, and balanced atop the headdress is an intricately carved ball. Inside that seamless sphere is another slightly smaller sphere of equal intricacy — and inside that still another, and then another — until one can no longer see through the tiny carved holes to see how many more balls there actually are.

Several things make this orb truly remarkable. Each of the nested balls is seamless, completely free from the one outside it and inside it, and magnificent in its airy, lacy design. The orb was carved from a single piece of ivory over 100 years ago, before the days of electronic magnifying instruments.

Why did the artist carve so many layers with such precision? The smallest orbs would not be clearly seen by most people, yet each one was finished with as much skill and artistry as was applied to the larger, outer ones.

The small details of a job may not always remain unnoticed or unseen. Like this artist, your excellence in small things can bring you prosperity in this life and make you a legend for future generations to follow.

and there is black hair grown up in it, the scale has healed. He *is* clean, and the priest shall pronounce him clean.

38 "If a man or a woman has bright spots on the skin of the body, *specifically* white bright spots, 39 then the priest shall look; and indeed *if* the bright spots on the skin of the body *are* dull white, it *is* a white spot *that* grows on the skin. He *is* clean.

40 "As for the man whose hair has fallen from his head, he *is* bald, *but* he *is* clean. 41 He whose hair has fallen from his forehead, he *is* bald on the forehead, *but* he *is* clean. 42 And if there is on the bald head or bald forehead a reddish-white sore, it *is* leprosy breaking out on his bald head or his bald forehead. 43 Then the priest shall examine it; and indeed *if* the swelling of the sore *is* reddish-white on his bald head or on his bald forehead, as the appearance of leprosy on the skin of the body, 44 he is a leprous man. He *is* unclean. The priest shall surely pronounce him unclean; his sore *is* on his head.

45 "Now the leper on whom the sore *is,* his clothes shall be torn and his head bare; and he shall cover his mustache, and cry, 'Unclean! Unclean!' 46 He shall be unclean. All the days he has the sore he shall be unclean. He *is* unclean, and he shall dwell alone; his dwelling *shall be* outside the camp.

47 "Also, if a garment has a leprous plague in it, *whether it is* a woolen garment or a linen garment, 48 whether *it is* in the warp or woof of linen or wool, whether in leather or in anything made of leather, 49 and if the plague is greenish or reddish in the garment or in the leather, whether in the warp or in the woof, or in anything made of leather, it *is* a leprous plague and shall be shown to the priest. 50 The priest shall examine the plague and isolate *that which has* the plague seven days. 51 And he shall examine the plague on the seventh day. If the plague has spread in the garment, either in the warp or in the woof, in the leather *or* in anything made of leather, the plague *is* an active leprosy. It *is* unclean. 52 He shall therefore burn that garment in which is the plague, whether warp or woof, in wool or in linen, or anything of leather, for it *is* an active leprosy; *the garment* shall be burned in the fire.

53 "But if the priest examines *it,* and indeed the plague has not spread in the garment, either in the warp or in the woof, or in anything made of leather, 54 then the priest shall command that they wash *the thing* in which *is* the plague; and he shall isolate it another seven days. 55 Then the priest shall examine the plague after it has been washed; and indeed *if* the plague has not changed its color, though the plague has not spread, it *is* unclean, and you shall burn it in the fire; it continues eating away, *whether* the damage *is* outside or inside. 56 If the priest examines *it,* and indeed the plague has faded after washing it, then he shall tear it out of the garment, whether out of the warp or out of the woof, or out of the leather. 57 But if it appears again in the garment, either in the warp or in the woof, or in anything made of leather, it *is* a spreading *plague;* you shall burn with fire that which is the plague. 58 And if you wash the garment, either warp or woof, or whatever is made of leather, if the plague has disappeared from it, then it shall be washed a second time, and shall be clean.

59 "This *is* the law of the leprous plague in a garment of wool or linen, either in the warp or woof, or in anything made of leather, to pronounce it clean or to pronounce it unclean."

~ PSALM 25:16–22 ~

16 Turn Yourself to me, and have mercy
        on me,
     For I *am* desolate and afflicted.
17 The troubles of my heart have
        enlarged;
     Bring me out of my distresses!
18 Look on my affliction and my pain,
     And forgive all my sins.
19 Consider my enemies, for they are
        many;
     And they hate me with cruel hatred.
20 Keep my soul, and deliver me;
     Let me not be ashamed, for I put my
        trust in You.
21 Let integrity and uprightness
        preserve me,
     For I wait for You.

22 Redeem Israel, O God,
     Out of all their troubles!

PROVERBS 10:4, 5 ~

4　He who has a slack hand becomes
　　poor,
　　But the hand of the diligent makes
　　rich.
5　He who gathers in summer *is* a wise
　　son;
　　He who sleeps in harvest *is* a son
　　who causes shame.

~ MARK 3:1–19 ~

And He entered the synagogue again, and a man was there who had a withered hand. 2 So they watched Him closely, whether He would heal him on the Sabbath, so that they might accuse Him. 3 And He said to the man who had the withered hand, "Step forward." 4 Then He said to them, "Is it lawful on the Sabbath to do good or to do evil, to save life or to kill?" But they kept silent. 5 And when He had looked around at them with anger, being grieved by the hardness of their hearts, He said to the man, "Stretch out your hand." And he stretched *it* out, and his hand was restored as whole as the other. 6 Then the Pharisees went out and immediately plotted with the Herodians against Him, how they might destroy Him.

7 But Jesus withdrew with His disciples to the sea. And a great multitude from Galilee followed Him, and from Judea 8 and Jerusalem and Idumea and beyond the Jordan; and those from Tyre and Sidon, a great multitude, when they heard how many things He was doing, came to Him. 9 So He told His disciples that a small boat should be kept ready for Him because of the multitude, lest they should crush Him. 10 For He healed many, so that as many as had afflictions pressed about Him to touch Him. 11 And the unclean spirits, whenever they saw Him, fell down before Him and cried out, saying, "You are the Son of God." 12 But He sternly warned them that they should not make Him known.

13 And He went up on the mountain and called to *Him* those He Himself wanted. And they came to Him. 14 Then He appointed twelve, that they might be with Him and that He might send them out to preach, 15 and to have power to heal sicknesses and to cast out demons: 16 Simon, to whom He gave the name Peter; 17 James the *son* of Zebedee and John the brother of James, to whom He gave the name Boanerges, that is, "Sons of Thunder"; 18 Andrew, Philip, Bartholomew, Matthew, Thomas, James the *son* of Alphaeus, Thaddaeus, Simon the Cananite; 19 and Judas Iscariot, who also betrayed Him. And they went into a house.

~ LEVITICUS 14:1–57 ~

Then the LORD spoke to Moses, saying, 2 "This shall be the law of the leper for the day of his cleansing: He shall be brought to the priest. 3 And the priest shall go out of the camp, and the priest shall examine *him*; and indeed, *if* the leprosy is healed in the leper, 4 then the priest shall command to take for him who is to be cleansed two living *and* clean birds, cedar wood, scarlet, and hyssop. 5 And the priest shall command that one of the birds be killed in an earthen vessel over running water. 6 As for the living bird, he shall take it, the cedar wood and the scarlet and the hyssop, and dip them and the living bird in the blood of the bird *that was* killed over the running water. 7 And he shall sprinkle it seven times on him who is to be cleansed from the leprosy, and shall pronounce him clean, and shall let the living bird loose in the open field. 8 He who is to be cleansed shall wash his clothes, shave off all his hair, and wash himself in water, that he may be clean. After that he shall come into the camp, and shall stay outside his tent seven days. 9 But on the seventh day he shall shave all the hair off his head and his beard and his eyebrows—all his hair he shall shave off. He shall wash his clothes and wash his body in water, and he shall be clean.

¹⁰ "And on the eighth day he shall take two male lambs without blemish, one ewe lamb of the first year without blemish, three-tenths *of an ephah* of fine flour mixed with oil as a grain offering, and one log of oil. ¹¹ Then the priest who makes *him* clean shall present the man who is to be made clean, and those things, before the LORD, *at* the door of the tabernacle of meeting. ¹² And the priest shall take one male lamb and offer it as a trespass offering, and the log of oil, and wave them *as* a wave offering before the LORD. ¹³ Then he shall kill the lamb in the place where he kills the sin offering and the burnt offering, in a holy place; for as the sin offering *is* the priest's, so *is* the trespass offering. It *is* most holy. ¹⁴ The priest shall take *some* of the blood of the trespass offering, and the priest shall put *it* on the tip of the right ear of him who is to be cleansed, on the thumb of his right hand, and on the big toe of his right foot. ¹⁵ And the priest shall take *some* of the log of oil, and pour *it* into the palm of his own left hand. ¹⁶ Then the priest shall dip his right finger in the oil that *is* in his left hand, and shall sprinkle some of the oil with his finger seven times before the LORD. ¹⁷ And of the rest of the oil in his hand, the priest shall put *some* on the tip of the right ear of him who is to be cleansed, on the thumb of his right hand, and on the big toe of his right foot, on the blood of the trespass offering. ¹⁸ The rest of the oil that *is* in the priest's hand he shall put on the head of him who is to be cleansed. So the priest shall make atonement for him before the LORD.

¹⁹ "Then the priest shall offer the sin offering, and make atonement for him who is to be cleansed from his uncleanness. Afterward he shall kill the burnt offering. ²⁰ And the priest shall offer the burnt offering and the grain offering on the altar. So the priest shall make atonement for him, and he shall be clean.

²¹ "But if he *is* poor and cannot afford it, then he shall take one male lamb *as* a trespass offering to be waved, to make atonement for him, one-tenth *of an ephah* of fine flour mixed with oil as a grain offering, a log of oil, ²² and two turtledoves or two young pigeons, such as he is able to afford: one shall be a sin offering and the other a burnt offering. ²³ He shall bring them to the priest on the eighth day for his cleansing, to the door of the tabernacle of meeting, before the LORD. ²⁴ And the priest shall take the lamb of the trespass offering and the log of oil, and the priest shall wave them *as* a wave offering before the LORD. ²⁵ Then he shall kill the lamb of the trespass offering, and the priest shall take *some* of the blood of the trespass offering and put *it* on the tip of the right ear of him who is to be cleansed, on the thumb of his right hand, and on the big toe of his right foot. ²⁶ And the priest shall pour some of the oil into the palm of his own left hand. ²⁷ Then the priest shall sprinkle with his right finger *some* of the oil that *is* in his left hand seven times before the LORD. ²⁸ And the priest shall put *some* of the oil that *is* in his hand on the tip of the right ear of him who is to be cleansed, on the thumb of the right hand, and on the big toe of his right foot, on the place of the blood of the trespass offering. ²⁹ The rest of the oil that *is* in the priest's hand he shall put on the head of him who is to be cleansed, to make atonement for him before the LORD. ³⁰ And he shall offer one of the turtledoves or young pigeons, such as he can afford— ³¹ such as he is able to afford, the one *as* a sin offering and the other *as* a burnt offering, with the grain offering. So the priest shall make atonement for him who is to be cleansed before the LORD. ³² This *is* the law *for one* who had a leprous sore, who cannot afford the usual cleansing."

³³ And the LORD spoke to Moses and Aaron, saying: ³⁴ "When you have come into the land of Canaan, which I give you as a possession, and I put the leprous plague in a house in the land of your possession, ³⁵ and he who owns the house comes and tells the priest, saying, 'It seems to me that *there is* some plague in the house,' ³⁶ then the priest shall command that they empty the house, before the priest goes *into it* to examine the plague, that all that *is* in the house may not be made unclean; and afterward the priest shall go in to examine the house. ³⁷ And he shall examine the plague; and indeed *if* the plague *is* on the walls of the house with ingrained streaks, greenish or reddish, which appear to be deep in the wall,

The Headboard Diary

The bed was about forty-five years old when Elaine's mother offered it to her. Elaine decided to refinish it for her daughter's room. However, as she prepared to strip the wood, she noticed that the headboard was full of scratches. She realized one scratch was the date her parents were married. Above another date was a name she didn't recognize. A call to her mother revealed the details of a miscarriage that occurred before Elaine was born.

Elaine suddenly realized the headboard had been something of a diary for her parents! She wrote down all the scratches she could decipher and over lunch with her mother, she heard stories about the times when her mother lost her purse at a department store; a rattlesnake was shot just as it was poised to strike her brother; a man saved her brother's life in Vietnam; her sister nearly died after falling from a swing; a stranger broke up a potential mugging.

Elaine couldn't strip and sand away so many memories — so she moved the headboard into her own bedroom. She and her husband began to carve their own dates and names. "Someday," she says, "we'll tell our daughter the stories from her grandparents' lives and the stories from her parents' lives. And someday the bed will pass on to her."

Memories are a powerful tool we can use in teaching our children. They tell our children of trust in God's faithfulness, patience with His timing, and reliance on His goodness.

[38] then the priest shall go out of the house, to the door of the house, and shut up the house seven days. [39] And the priest shall come again on the seventh day and look; and indeed *if* the plague has spread on the walls of the house, [40] then the priest shall command that they take away the stones in which *is* the plague, and they shall cast them into an unclean place outside the city. [41] And he shall cause the house to be scraped inside, all around, and the dust that they scrape off they shall pour out in an unclean place outside the city. [42] Then they shall take other stones and put *them* in the place of *those* stones, and he shall take other mortar and plaster the house.

[43] "Now if the plague comes back and breaks out in the house, after he has taken away the stones, after he has scraped the house, and after it is plastered, [44] then the priest shall come and look; and indeed *if* the plague has spread in the house, it *is* an active leprosy in the house. It *is* unclean. [45] And he shall break down the house, its stones, its timber, and all the plaster of the house, and he shall carry *them* outside the city to an unclean place. [46] Moreover he who goes into the house at all while it is shut up shall be unclean until evening. [47] And he who lies down in the house shall wash his clothes, and he who eats in the house shall wash his clothes.

[48] "But if the priest comes in and examines *it,* and indeed the plague has not spread in the house after the house was plastered, then the priest shall pronounce the house clean, because the plague is healed. [49] And he shall take, to cleanse the house, two birds, cedar wood, scarlet, and hyssop. [50] Then he shall kill one of the birds in an earthen vessel over running water; [51] and he shall take the cedar wood, the hyssop, the scarlet, and the living bird, and dip them in the blood of the slain bird and in the running water, and sprinkle the house seven times. [52] And he shall cleanse the house with the blood of the bird and the running water and the living bird, with the cedar wood, the hyssop, and the scarlet. [53] Then he shall let the living bird loose outside the city in the open field, and make atonement for the house, and it shall be clean.

[54] "This *is* the law for any leprous sore and scale, [55] for the leprosy of a garment and of a house, [56] for a swelling and a scab and a bright spot, [57] to teach when *it is* unclean and when *it is* clean. This *is* the law of leprosy."

～ PSALM 26:1-5 ～

1 Vindicate me, O LORD,
For I have walked in my integrity.
I have also trusted in the LORD;
I shall not slip.
2 Examine me, O LORD, and prove me;
Try my mind and my heart.
3 For Your lovingkindness *is* before my eyes,
And I have walked in Your truth.
4 I have not sat with idolatrous mortals,
Nor will I go in with hypocrites.
5 I have hated the assembly of evildoers,
And will not sit with the wicked.

～ PROVERBS 10:6, 7 ～

6 Blessings *are* on the head of the righteous,
But violence covers the mouth of the wicked.
7 The memory of the righteous *is* blessed,
But the name of the wicked will rot.

～ MARK 3:20-35 ～

Then the multitude came together again, so that they could not so much as eat bread. [21] But when His own people heard *about this,* they went out to lay hold of Him, for they said, "He is out of His mind."

[22] And the scribes who came down from Jerusalem said, "He has Beelzebub," and, "By the ruler of the demons He casts out demons."

[23] So He called them to *Himself* and said to them in parables: "How can Satan cast out Satan? [24] If a kingdom is divided against itself, that kingdom cannot stand. [25] And if a house is divided against itself, that house cannot stand. [26] And if Satan

has risen up against himself, and is divided, he cannot stand, but has an end. ²⁷ No one can enter a strong man's house and plunder his goods, unless he first binds the strong man. And then he will plunder his house.

²⁸ "Assuredly, I say to you, all sins will be forgiven the sons of men, and whatever blasphemies they may utter; ²⁹ but he who blasphemes against the Holy Spirit never has forgiveness, but is subject to eternal condemnation"— ³⁰ because they said, "He has an unclean spirit."

³¹ Then His brothers and His mother came, and standing outside they sent to Him, calling Him. ³² And a multitude was sitting around Him; and they said to Him, "Look, Your mother and Your brothers are outside seeking You."

³³ But He answered them, saying, "Who is My mother, or My brothers?" ³⁴ And He looked around in a circle at those who sat about Him, and said, "Here are My mother and My brothers! ³⁵ For whoever does the will of God is My brother and My sister and mother."

∼ LEVITICUS 15:1—16:34 ∼

And the LORD spoke to Moses and Aaron, saying, ² "Speak to the children of Israel, and say to them: 'When any man has a discharge from his body, his discharge is unclean. ³ And this shall be his uncleanness in regard to his discharge—whether his body runs with his discharge, or his body is stopped up by his discharge, it is his uncleanness. ⁴ Every bed is unclean on which he who has the discharge lies, and everything on which he sits shall be unclean. ⁵ And whoever touches his bed shall wash his clothes and bathe in water, and be unclean until evening. ⁶ He who sits on anything on which he who has the discharge sat shall wash his clothes and bathe in water, and be unclean until evening. ⁷ And he who touches the body of him who has the discharge shall wash his clothes and bathe in water, and be unclean until evening. ⁸ If he who has the discharge spits on him who is clean, then he shall wash his clothes and bathe in water, and be unclean until evening. ⁹ Any saddle on which he who has the discharge rides shall be unclean. ¹⁰ Whoever touches anything that was under him shall be unclean until evening. He who carries any of those things shall wash his clothes and bathe in water, and be unclean until evening. ¹¹ And whomever the one who has the discharge touches, and has not rinsed his hands in water, he shall wash his clothes and bathe in water, and be unclean until evening. ¹² The vessel of earth that he who has the discharge touches shall be broken, and every vessel of wood shall be rinsed in water.

¹³ 'And when he who has a discharge is cleansed of his discharge, then he shall count for himself seven days for his cleansing, wash his clothes, and bathe his body in running water; then he shall be clean. ¹⁴ On the eighth day he shall take for himself two turtledoves or two young pigeons, and come before the LORD, to the door of the tabernacle of meeting, and give them to the priest. ¹⁵ Then the priest shall offer them, the one as a sin offering and the other as a burnt offering. So the priest shall make atonement for him before the LORD because of his discharge.

¹⁶ 'If any man has an emission of semen, then he shall wash all his body in water, and be unclean until evening. ¹⁷ And any garment and any leather on which there is semen, it shall be washed with water, and be unclean until evening. ¹⁸ Also, when a woman lies with a man, and there is an emission of semen, they shall bathe in water, and be unclean until evening.

¹⁹ 'If a woman has a discharge, and the discharge from her body is blood, she shall be set apart seven days; and whoever touches her shall be unclean until evening. ²⁰ Everything that she lies on during her impurity shall be unclean; also everything that she sits on shall be unclean. ²¹ Whoever touches her bed shall wash his clothes and bathe in water, and be unclean until evening. ²² And whoever touches anything

that she sat on shall wash his clothes and bathe in water, and be unclean until evening. ²³ If *anything* is on *her* bed or on anything on which she sits, when he touches it, he shall be unclean until evening. ²⁴ And if any man lies with her at all, so that her impurity is on him, he shall be unclean seven days; and every bed on which he lies shall be unclean.

²⁵ 'If a woman has a discharge of blood for many days, other than at the time of her *customary* impurity, or if it runs beyond her *usual time of* impurity, all the days of her unclean discharge shall be as the days of her *customary* impurity. She *shall be* unclean. ²⁶ Every bed on which she lies all the days of her discharge shall be to her as the bed of her impurity; and whatever she sits on shall be unclean, as the uncleanness of her impurity. ²⁷ Whoever touches those things shall be unclean; he shall wash his clothes and bathe in water, and be unclean until evening.

²⁸ 'But if she is cleansed of her discharge, then she shall count for herself seven days, and after that she shall be clean. ²⁹ And on the eighth day she shall take for herself two turtledoves or two young pigeons, and bring them to the priest, to the door of the tabernacle of meeting. ³⁰ Then the priest shall offer the one *as* a sin offering and the other *as* a burnt offering, and the priest shall make atonement for her before the LORD for the discharge of her uncleanness.

³¹ 'Thus you shall separate the children of Israel from their uncleanness, lest they die in their uncleanness when they defile My tabernacle that *is* among them. ³² This *is* the law for one who has a discharge, and *for him* who emits semen and is unclean thereby, ³³ and for her who is indisposed because of her *customary* impurity, and for one who has a discharge, either man or woman, and for him who lies with her who is unclean.' "

16 Now the LORD spoke to Moses after the death of the two sons of Aaron, when they offered *profane fire* before the LORD, and died; ² and the LORD said to Moses: "Tell Aaron your brother not to come at *just* any time into the Holy *Place* inside the veil, before the mercy seat which

is on the ark, lest he die; for I will appear in the cloud above the mercy seat.

³ "Thus Aaron shall come into the Holy *Place:* with *the blood of* a young bull as a sin offering, and *of* a ram as a burnt offering. ⁴ He shall put the holy linen tunic and the linen trousers on his body; he shall be girded with a linen sash, and with the linen turban he shall be attired. These *are* holy garments. Therefore he shall wash his body in water, and put them on. ⁵ And he shall take from the congregation of the children of Israel two kids of the goats as a sin offering, and one ram as a burnt offering.

⁶ "Aaron shall offer the bull as a sin offering, which *is* for himself, and make atonement for himself and for his house. ⁷ He shall take the two goats and present them before the LORD *at* the door of the tabernacle of meeting. ⁸ Then Aaron shall cast lots for the two goats: one lot for the LORD and the other lot for the scapegoat. ⁹ And Aaron shall bring the goat on which the LORD's lot fell, and offer it *as* a sin offering. ¹⁰ But the goat on which the lot fell to be the scapegoat shall be presented alive before the LORD, to make atonement upon it, *and* to let it go as the scapegoat into the wilderness.

¹¹ "And Aaron shall bring the bull of the sin offering, which is for himself, and make atonement for himself and for his house, and shall kill the bull as the sin offering which *is* for himself. ¹² Then he shall take a censer full of burning coals of fire from the altar before the LORD, with his hands full of sweet incense beaten fine, and bring *it* inside the veil. ¹³ And he shall put the incense on the fire before the LORD, that the cloud of incense may cover the mercy seat that *is* on the Testimony, lest he die. ¹⁴ He shall take some of the blood of the bull and sprinkle *it* with his finger on the mercy seat on the east *side;* and before the mercy seat he shall sprinkle some of the blood with his finger seven times.

¹⁵ "Then he shall kill the goat of the sin offering, which *is* for the people, bring its blood inside the veil, do with that blood as he did with the blood of the bull, and sprinkle it on the mercy seat and before the mercy seat. ¹⁶ So he shall make atonement for the Holy *Place,* because of the

Listen and Obey

While skiing in Colorado one day, a man noticed some people on the slope wearing red vests. Moving closer, he could read these words on their vests: BLIND SKIER. He couldn't believe it. He had difficulty skiing with 20/20 vision! How could people without sight manage to ski?

He watched the skiers for awhile, and discovered their secret. Each skier had a guide who skied beside, behind, or in front of him, always in a position where the two could easily communicate. The guide used two basic forms of communication. First, tapping his ski poles together to assure the blind person that he was there, and second, speaking simple, specific directions: "Go right. Turn left. Slow. Stop. Skier on your right."

The skier's responsibility was to trust the guide to give good instructions, and to immediately and completely obey those instructions.

We can't see even five seconds into the future. We cannot see the struggles to come. Other people may run into us, or we into them, like errant skiers on a crowded slope. But God has given us the Holy Spirit to be our Guide through life — to walk before and behind us, and to dwell in us. Our role is to listen and to obey.

uncleanness of the children of Israel, and because of their transgressions, for all their sins; and so he shall do for the tabernacle of meeting which remains among them in the midst of their uncleanness. ¹⁷ There shall be no man in the tabernacle of meeting when he goes in to make atonement in the Holy *Place,* until he comes out, that he may make atonement for himself, for his household, and for all the assembly of Israel. ¹⁸ And he shall go out to the altar that *is* before the LORD, and make atonement for it, and shall take some of the blood of the bull and some of the blood of the goat, and put it on the horns of the altar all around. ¹⁹ Then he shall sprinkle some of the blood on it with his finger seven times, cleanse it, and consecrate it from the uncleanness of the children of Israel.

²⁰ "And when he has made an end of atoning for the Holy *Place,* the tabernacle of meeting, and the altar, he shall bring the live goat. ²¹ Aaron shall lay both his hands on the head of the live goat, confess over it all the iniquities of the children of Israel, and all their transgressions, concerning all their sins, putting them on the head of the goat, and shall send *it* away into the wilderness by the hand of a suitable man. ²² The goat shall bear on itself all their iniquities to an uninhabited land; and he shall release the goat in the wilderness.

²³ "Then Aaron shall come into the tabernacle of meeting, shall take off the linen garments which he put on when he went into the Holy *Place,* and shall leave them there. ²⁴ And he shall wash his body with water in a holy place, put on his garments, come out and offer his burnt offering and the burnt offering of the people, and make atonement for himself and for the people. ²⁵ The fat of the sin offering he shall burn on the altar. ²⁶ And he who released the goat as the scapegoat shall wash his clothes and bathe his body in water, and afterward he may come into the camp. ²⁷ The bull *for* the sin offering and the goat *for* the sin offering, whose blood was brought in to make atonement in the Holy *Place,* shall be carried outside the camp. And they shall burn in the fire their skins, their flesh, and their offal. ²⁸ Then he who burns them shall wash his clothes and bathe his

body in water, and afterward he may come into the camp.

²⁹ "*This* shall be a statute forever for you: In the seventh month, on the tenth *day* of the month, you shall afflict your souls, and do no work at all, *whether* a native of your own country or a stranger who dwells among you. ³⁰ For on that day *the priest* shall make atonement for you, to cleanse you, *that* you may be clean from all your sins before the LORD. ³¹ It *is* a sabbath of solemn rest for you, and you shall afflict your souls. *It is* a statute forever. ³² And the priest, who is anointed and consecrated to minister as priest in his father's place, shall make atonement, and put on the linen clothes, the holy garments; ³³ then he shall make atonement for the Holy Sanctuary, and he shall make atonement for the tabernacle of meeting and for the altar, and he shall make atonement for the priests and for all the people of the assembly. ³⁴ This shall be an everlasting statute for you, to make atonement for the children of Israel, for all their sins, once a year." And he did as the LORD commanded Moses.

∼ PSALM 26:6–12 ∼

⁶ I will wash my hands in innocence;
   So I will go about Your altar,
       O LORD,
⁷ That I may proclaim with the voice
       of thanksgiving,
   And tell of all Your wondrous works.
⁸ LORD, I have loved the habitation of
       Your house,
   And the place where Your glory
       dwells.

⁹ Do not gather my soul with sinners,
   Nor my life with bloodthirsty men,
¹⁰ In whose hands *is* a sinister scheme,
   And whose right hand is full of
       bribes.

¹¹ But as for me, I will walk in my
       integrity;
   Redeem me and be merciful to me.
¹² My foot stands in an even place;
   In the congregations I will bless the
       LORD.

∼ PROVERBS 10:8 ∼

⁸ The wise in heart will receive
   commands,
   But a prating fool will fall.

∼ MARK 4:1–20 ∼

And again He began to teach by the sea.
And a great multitude was gathered to
Him, so that He got into a boat and sat *in
it* on the sea; and the whole multitude
was on the land facing the sea. ² Then He
taught them many things by parables, and
said to them in His teaching:

³ "Listen! Behold, a sower went out to
sow. ⁴ And it happened, as he sowed, *that*
some *seed* fell by the wayside; and the
birds of the air came and devoured it.
⁵ Some fell on stony ground, where it did
not have much earth; and immediately it
sprang up because it had no depth of
earth. ⁶ But when the sun was up it was
scorched, and because it had no root it
withered away. ⁷ And some *seed* fell
among thorns; and the thorns grew up
and choked it, and it yielded no crop. ⁸ But
other *seed* fell on good ground and yielded
a crop that sprang up, increased and produced: some thirtyfold, some sixty, and
some a hundred."

⁹ And He said to them, "He who has
ears to hear, let him hear!"

¹⁰ But when He was alone, those around
Him with the twelve asked Him about the
parable. ¹¹ And He said to them, "To you

it has been given to know the mystery of
the kingdom of God; but to those who
are outside, all things come in parables,
¹² so that

'Seeing they may see and not
   perceive,
And hearing they may hear and
   not understand;
Lest they should turn,
And their sins be forgiven them.' "

¹³ And He said to them, "Do you not
understand this parable? How then will
you understand all the parables? ¹⁴ The
sower sows the word. ¹⁵ And these are
the ones by the wayside where the word
is sown. When they hear, Satan comes immediately and takes away the word that
was sown in their hearts. ¹⁶ These likewise
are the ones sown on stony ground who,
when they hear the word, immediately
receive it with gladness; ¹⁷ and they have
no root in themselves, and so endure only
for a time. Afterward, when tribulation
or persecution arises for the word's sake,
immediately they stumble. ¹⁸ Now these
are the ones sown among thorns; *they are*
the ones who hear the word, ¹⁹ and the
cares of this world, the deceitfulness of
riches, and the desires for other things
entering in choke the word, and it becomes unfruitful. ²⁰ But these are the ones
sown on good ground, those who hear
the word, accept *it*, and bear fruit: some
thirtyfold, some sixty, and some a hundred."

READING 55 · FEBRUARY 24

∼ LEVITICUS 17:1—18:30 ∼

And the LORD spoke to Moses, saying, ² "Speak to Aaron, to his sons,
and to all the children of Israel,
and say to them, 'This *is* the thing which
the LORD has commanded, saying:
³ "Whatever man of the house of Israel
who kills an ox or lamb or goat in the
camp, or who kills *it* outside the camp,
⁴ and does not bring it to the door of the
tabernacle of meeting to offer an offering
to the LORD before the tabernacle of the
LORD, the guilt of bloodshed shall be im-

puted to that man. He has shed blood;
and that man shall be cut off from among
his people, ⁵ to the end that the children
of Israel may bring their sacrifices which
they offer in the open field, that they may
bring them to the LORD at the door of
the tabernacle of meeting, to the priest,
and offer them *as* peace offerings to the
LORD. ⁶ And the priest shall sprinkle the
blood on the altar of the LORD *at* the door
of the tabernacle of meeting, and burn the
fat for a sweet aroma to the LORD. ⁷ They

shall no more offer their sacrifices to demons, after whom they have played the harlot. This shall be a statute forever for them throughout their generations." '

8 "Also you shall say to them: 'Whatever man of the house of Israel, or of the strangers who dwell among you, who offers a burnt offering or sacrifice, 9 and does not bring it to the door of the tabernacle of meeting, to offer it to the LORD, that man shall be cut off from among his people.

10 'And whatever man of the house of Israel, or of the strangers who dwell among you, who eats any blood, I will set My face against that person who eats blood, and will cut him off from among his people. 11 For the life of the flesh *is* in the blood, and I have given it to you upon the altar to make atonement for your souls; for it *is* the blood *that* makes atonement for the soul.' 12 Therefore I said to the children of Israel, 'No one among you shall eat blood, nor shall any stranger who dwells among you eat blood.'

13 "Whatever man of the children of Israel, or of the strangers who dwell among you, who hunts and catches any animal or bird that may be eaten, he shall pour out its blood and cover it with dust; 14 for *it is* the life of all flesh. Its blood sustains its life. Therefore I said to the children of Israel, 'You shall not eat the blood of any flesh, for the life of all flesh is its blood. Whoever eats it shall be cut off.'

15 "And every person who eats what died *naturally* or what was torn *by beasts, whether he is* a native of your own country or a stranger, he shall both wash his clothes and bathe in water, and be unclean until evening. Then he shall be clean. 16 But if he does not wash *them* or bathe his body, then he shall bear his guilt."

18 Then the LORD spoke to Moses, saying, 2 "Speak to the children of Israel, and say to them: 'I am the LORD your God. 3 According to the doings of the land of Egypt, where you dwelt, you shall not do; and according to the doings of the land of Canaan, where I am bringing you, you shall not do; nor shall you walk in their ordinances. 4 You shall observe My judgments and keep My ordinances, to walk in them: I *am* the LORD your God. 5 You shall therefore keep My statutes and My judgments, which if a man does, he shall live by them: I *am* the LORD.

6 'None of you shall approach anyone who is near of kin to him, to uncover his nakedness: I *am* the LORD. 7 The nakedness of your father or the nakedness of your mother you shall not uncover. She *is* your mother; you shall not uncover her nakedness. 8 The nakedness of your father's wife you shall not uncover; it *is* your father's nakedness. 9 The nakedness of your sister, the daughter of your father, or the daughter of your mother, *whether* born at home or elsewhere, their nakedness you shall not uncover. 10 The nakedness of your son's daughter or your daughter's daughter, their nakedness you shall not uncover; for theirs *is* your own nakedness. 11 The nakedness of your father's wife's daughter, begotten by your father—she *is* your sister—you shall not uncover her nakedness. 12 You shall not uncover the nakedness of your father's sister; she *is* near of kin to your father. 13 You shall not uncover the nakedness of your mother's sister, for she *is* near of kin to your mother. 14 You shall not uncover the nakedness of your father's brother. You shall not approach his wife; she *is* your aunt. 15 You shall not uncover the nakedness of your daughter-in-law—she *is* your son's wife—you shall not uncover her nakedness. 16 You shall not uncover the nakedness of your brother's wife; it *is* your brother's nakedness. 17 You shall not uncover the nakedness of a woman and her daughter, nor shall you take her son's daughter or her daughter's daughter, to uncover her nakedness. They *are* near of kin to her. It *is* wickedness. 18 Nor shall you take a woman as a rival to her sister, to uncover her nakedness while the other is alive.

19 'Also you shall not approach a woman to uncover her nakedness as long as she is in her *customary* impurity. 20 Moreover you shall not lie carnally with your neighbor's wife, to defile yourself with her. 21 And you shall not let any of your descendants pass through *the fire* to Molech, nor shall you profane the name of your God: I *am* the LORD. 22 You shall not lie with a male as with a woman. It *is* an

Integrity, Not for Sale

> He who walks with integrity walks securely.
>
> *Proverbs 10:9*

When Orv Krieger, a hotel broker, received a call about a property for sale in Spokane, Washington, he decided to take the plunge and buy it himself rather than list it for sale. He knew the 140-unit Holiday Inn — minutes from the airport and located on thirteen acres of fir-covered hillside overlooking the city — was a prime property.

Krieger quickly discovered that the Inn's restaurant was the big moneymaker. The bar grossed an average of $10,000 a month. However, Krieger's Christian principles were incompatible with running a business subsidized by alcohol sales. The motel manager argued that if guests couldn't get a drink at the Inn, they'd be off to other hotels in a flash. He had convincing statistics for his argument, but Krieger closed the bar anyway. The manager resigned.

Krieger remodeled the hotel lobby, and replaced the bar area with a cozy coffee shop filled with greenery. In the first five years of business, food sales went up 20 percent and bookings were up 30 percent. Profits might not have been what they *could* have, but they were substantial enough to satisfy Krieger. He has said, "Beliefs aren't worth much if a fella's not ready to live by them."

When you walk in integrity, God will reward you and people will respect you.

abomination. ²³ Nor shall you mate with any animal, to defile yourself with it. Nor shall any woman stand before an animal to mate with it. It *is* perversion.

²⁴ 'Do not defile yourselves with any of these things; for by all these the nations are defiled, which I am casting out before you. ²⁵ For the land is defiled; therefore I visit the punishment of its iniquity upon it, and the land vomits out its inhabitants. ²⁶ You shall therefore keep My statutes and My judgments, and shall not commit *any* of these abominations, *either* any of your own nation or any stranger who dwells among you ²⁷(for all these abominations the men of the land have done, who *were* before you, and thus the land is defiled); ²⁸ lest the land vomit you out also when you defile it, as it vomited out the nations that *were* before you. ²⁹ For whoever commits any of these abominations, the persons who commit *them* shall be cut off from among their people.

³⁰ 'Therefore you shall keep My ordinance, so that *you* do not commit *any* of these abominable customs which were committed before you, and that you do not defile yourselves by them: I *am* the LORD your God.' "

∾ PSALM 27:1–3 ∾

¹   The LORD *is* my light and my
         salvation;
     Whom shall I fear?
     The LORD *is* the strength of my
         life;
     Of whom shall I be afraid?
²   When the wicked came against me
     To eat up my flesh,
     My enemies and foes,
     They stumbled and fell.
³   Though an army may encamp
         against me,
     My heart shall not fear;
     Though war may rise against me,
     In this I *will* be confident.

∾ PROVERBS 10:9 ∾

⁹   He who walks with integrity walks
         securely,

But he who perverts his ways will
     become known.

∾ MARK 4:21–41 ∾

Also He said to them, "Is a lamp brought to be put under a basket or under a bed? Is it not to be set on a lampstand? ²² For there is nothing hidden which will not be revealed, nor has anything been kept secret but that it should come to light. ²³ If anyone has ears to hear, let him hear."

²⁴ Then He said to them, "Take heed what you hear. With the same measure you use, it will be measured to you; and to you who hear, more will be given. ²⁵ For whoever has, to him more will be given; but whoever does not have, even what he has will be taken away from him."

²⁶ And He said, "The kingdom of God is as if a man should scatter seed on the ground, ²⁷ and should sleep by night and rise by day, and the seed should sprout and grow, he himself does not know how. ²⁸ For the earth yields crops by itself: first the blade, then the head, after that the full grain in the head. ²⁹ But when the grain ripens, immediately he puts in the sickle, because the harvest has come."

³⁰ Then He said, "To what shall we liken the kingdom of God? Or with what parable shall we picture it? ³¹ *It is* like a mustard seed which, when it is sown on the ground, is smaller than all the seeds on earth; ³² but when it is sown, it grows up and becomes greater than all herbs, and shoots out large branches, so that the birds of the air may nest under its shade."

³³ And with many such parables He spoke the word to them as they were able to hear it. ³⁴ But without a parable He did not speak to them. And when they were alone, He explained all things to His disciples.

³⁵ On the same day, when evening had come, He said to them, "Let us cross over to the other side." ³⁶ Now when they had left the multitude, they took Him along in the boat as He was. And other little boats were also with Him. ³⁷ And a great windstorm arose, and the waves beat into the boat, so that it was already filling. ³⁸ But He was in the stern, asleep on a

pillow. And they awoke Him and said to Him, "Teacher, do You not care that we are perishing?"

³⁹ Then He arose and rebuked the wind, and said to the sea, "Peace, be still!" And the wind ceased and there was a great calm. ⁴⁰ But He said to them, "Why are you so fearful? How *is it* that you have no faith?"⁴¹ And they feared exceedingly, and said to one another, "Who can this be, that even the wind and the sea obey Him!"

READING 56 · FEBRUARY 25

∼ LEVITICUS 19:1—20:27 ∼

And the LORD spoke to Moses, saying, ² "Speak to all the congregation of the children of Israel, and say to them: 'You shall be holy, for I the LORD your God *am* holy.

³ 'Every one of you shall revere his mother and his father, and keep My Sabbaths: I *am* the LORD your God.

⁴ 'Do not turn to idols, nor make for yourselves molded gods: I *am* the LORD your God.

⁵ 'And if you offer a sacrifice of a peace offering to the LORD, you shall offer it of your own free will. ⁶ It shall be eaten the same day you offer *it*, and on the next day. And if any remains until the third day, it shall be burned in the fire. ⁷ And if it is eaten at all on the third day, it *is* an abomination. It shall not be accepted. ⁸ Therefore *everyone* who eats it shall bear his iniquity, because he has profaned the hallowed *offering* of the LORD; and that person shall be cut off from his people.

⁹ 'When you reap the harvest of your land, you shall not wholly reap the corners of your field, nor shall you gather the gleanings of your harvest. ¹⁰ And you shall not glean your vineyard, nor shall you gather *every* grape of your vineyard; you shall leave them for the poor and the stranger: I *am* the LORD your God.

¹¹ 'You shall not steal, nor deal falsely, nor lie to one another. ¹² And you shall not swear by My name falsely, nor shall you profane the name of your God: I *am* the LORD.

¹³ 'You shall not cheat your neighbor, nor rob *him*. The wages of him who is hired shall not remain with you all night until morning. ¹⁴ You shall not curse the deaf, nor put a stumbling block before the blind, but shall fear your God: I *am* the LORD.

¹⁵ 'You shall do no injustice in judgment. You shall not be partial to the poor, nor honor the person of the mighty. In righteousness you shall judge your neighbor. ¹⁶ You shall not go about *as* a talebearer among your people; nor shall you take a stand against the life of your neighbor: I *am* the LORD.

¹⁷ 'You shall not hate your brother in your heart. You shall surely rebuke your neighbor, and not bear sin because of him. ¹⁸ You shall not take vengeance, nor bear any grudge against the children of your people, but you shall love your neighbor as yourself: I *am* the LORD.

¹⁹ 'You shall keep My statutes. You shall not let your livestock breed with another kind. You shall not sow your field with mixed seed. Nor shall a garment of mixed linen and wool come upon you.

²⁰ 'Whoever lies carnally with a woman who *is* betrothed to a man as a concubine, and who has not at all been redeemed nor given her freedom, for this there shall be scourging; *but* they shall not be put to death, because she was not free. ²¹ And he shall bring his trespass offering to the LORD, to the door of the tabernacle of meeting, a ram as a trespass offering. ²² The priest shall make atonement for him with the ram of the trespass offering before the LORD for his sin which he has committed. And the sin which he has committed shall be forgiven him.

²³ 'When you come into the land, and have planted all kinds of trees for food, then you shall count their fruit as uncircumcised. Three years it shall be as uncircumcised to you. *It* shall not be eaten. ²⁴ But in the fourth year all its fruit shall be holy, a praise to the LORD. ²⁵ And in

the fifth year you may eat its fruit, that it may yield to you its increase: I *am* the LORD your God.

²⁶ 'You shall not eat *anything* with the blood, nor shall you practice divination or soothsaying. ²⁷ You shall not shave around the sides of your head, nor shall you disfigure the edges of your beard. ²⁸ You shall not make any cuttings in your flesh for the dead, nor tattoo any marks on you: I *am* the LORD.

²⁹ 'Do not prostitute your daughter, to cause her to be a harlot, lest the land fall into harlotry, and the land become full of wickedness.

³⁰ 'You shall keep My Sabbaths and reverence My sanctuary: I *am* the LORD.

³¹ 'Give no regard to mediums and familiar spirits; do not seek after them, to be defiled by them: I *am* the LORD your God.

³² 'You shall rise before the gray headed and honor the presence of an old man, and fear your God: I *am* the LORD.

³³ 'And if a stranger dwells with you in your land, you shall not mistreat him. ³⁴ The stranger who dwells among you shall be to you as one born among you, and you shall love him as yourself; for you were strangers in the land of Egypt: I *am* the LORD your God.

³⁵ 'You shall do no injustice in judgment, in measurement of length, weight, or volume. ³⁶ You shall have honest scales, honest weights, an honest ephah, and an honest hin: I *am* the LORD your God, who brought you out of the land of Egypt.

³⁷ 'Therefore you shall observe all My statutes and all My judgments, and perform them: I *am* the LORD.' "

20 Then the LORD spoke to Moses, saying, ² "Again, you shall say to the children of Israel: 'Whoever of the children of Israel, or of the strangers who dwell in Israel, who gives *any* of his descendants to Molech, he shall surely be put to death. The people of the land shall stone him with stones. ³ I will set My face against that man, and will cut him off from his people, because he has given *some* of his descendants to Molech, to defile My sanctuary and profane My holy name. ⁴ And if the people of the land should in any way hide their eyes from the man,

when he gives *some* of his descendants to Molech, and they do not kill him, ⁵ then I will set My face against that man and against his family; and I will cut him off from his people, and all who prostitute themselves with him to commit harlotry with Molech.

⁶ 'And the person who turns to mediums and familiar spirits, to prostitute himself with them, I will set My face against that person and cut him off from his people. ⁷ Consecrate yourselves therefore, and be holy, for I *am* the LORD your God. ⁸ And you shall keep My statutes, and perform them: I *am* the LORD who sanctifies you.

⁹ 'For everyone who curses his father or his mother shall surely be put to death. He has cursed his father or his mother. His blood *shall be* upon him.

¹⁰ 'The man who commits adultery with *another* man's wife, *he* who commits adultery with his neighbor's wife, the adulterer and the adulteress, shall surely be put to death. ¹¹ The man who lies with his father's wife has uncovered his father's nakedness; both of them shall surely be put to death. Their blood *shall be* upon them. ¹² If a man lies with his daughter-in-law, both of them shall surely be put to death. They have committed perversion. Their blood *shall be* upon them. ¹³ If a man lies with a male as he lies with a woman, both of them have committed an abomination. They shall surely be put to death. Their blood *shall be* upon them. ¹⁴ If a man marries a woman and her mother, it *is* wickedness. They shall be burned with fire, both he and they, that there may be no wickedness among you. ¹⁵ If a man mates with an animal, he shall surely be put to death, and you shall kill the animal. ¹⁶ If a woman approaches any animal and mates with it, you shall kill the woman and the animal. They shall surely be put to death. Their blood *is* upon them.

¹⁷ 'If a man takes his sister, his father's daughter or his mother's daughter, and sees her nakedness and she sees his nakedness, it *is* a wicked thing. And they shall be cut off in the sight of their people. He has uncovered his sister's nakedness. He shall bear his guilt. ¹⁸ If a man lies with a woman during her sickness and

Adequate Enough

On a bitterly cold night in February of 1943, occurred one of the great maritime losses of World War II — the sinking of the *SS Dorchester* in the North Atlantic. Of the 904 men aboard, 678 lost their lives.

Clark Poling was a young chaplain assigned to the ship. Before going to sea he asked his father, Daniel A. Poling, to pray for him, but with this stipulation: pray not for his safety, but that he would be adequate for any situation. Poling prayed as his son had requested.

When the enemy's torpedo struck the Dorchester and the ship began to sink, many of the men became paralyzed with fear. Young Poling, along with three other chaplains, strapped their own life belts to the fear-stricken men. They helped load the lifeboats, and then joined hands in a circle of prayer as they sank to their watery graves. Poling's prayer had been answered. Although his son had not remained in safety, he had been more than adequate for the situation.

Ultimately, our adequacy for any situation is found only in the Lord. He provides what we need to remain true to Him and to be His brightest light in the darkest of circumstances.

> When You said, "Seek My face," My heart said to You, "Your face, Lord, I will seek."
>
> *Psalm 27:8*

uncovers her nakedness, he has exposed her flow, and she has uncovered the flow of her blood. Both of them shall be cut off from their people.

19 'You shall not uncover the nakedness of your mother's sister nor of your father's sister, for that would uncover his near of kin. They shall bear their guilt. 20 If a man lies with his uncle's wife, he has uncovered his uncle's nakedness. They shall bear their sin; they shall die childless. 21 If a man takes his brother's wife, it *is* an unclean thing. He has uncovered his brother's nakedness. They shall be childless.

22 'You shall therefore keep all My statutes and all My judgments, and perform them, that the land where I am bringing you to dwell may not vomit you out. 23 And you shall not walk in the statutes of the nation which I am casting out before you; for they commit all these things, and therefore I abhor them. 24 But I have said to you, "You shall inherit their land, and I will give it to you to possess, a land flowing with milk and honey." I *am* the LORD your God, who has separated you from the peoples. 25 You shall therefore distinguish between clean animals and unclean, between unclean birds and clean, and you shall not make yourselves abominable by beast or by bird, or by any kind of living thing that creeps on the ground, which I have separated from you as unclean. 26 And you shall be holy to Me, for I the LORD *am* holy, and have separated you from the peoples, that you should be Mine.

27 'A man or a woman who is a medium, or who has familiar spirits, shall surely be put to death; they shall stone them with stones. Their blood *shall be* upon them.' "

∼ PSALM 27:4–10 ∼

4 One *thing* I have desired of the LORD,
That will I seek:
That I may dwell in the house of the LORD
All the days of my life,
To behold the beauty of the LORD,
And to inquire in His temple.

5 For in the time of trouble
He shall hide me in His pavilion;

In the secret place of His tabernacle
He shall hide me;
He shall set me high upon a rock.

6 And now my head shall be lifted up
above my enemies all around me;
Therefore I will offer sacrifices of joy
in His tabernacle;
I will sing, yes, I will sing praises to
the LORD.

7 Hear, O LORD, *when* I cry with my
voice!
Have mercy also upon me, and
answer me.

8 *When You said*, "Seek My face,"
My heart said to You, "Your face,
LORD, I will seek."

9 Do not hide Your face from me;
Do not turn Your servant away in
anger;
You have been my help;
Do not leave me nor forsake me,
O God of my salvation.

10 When my father and my mother
forsake me,
Then the LORD will take care of me.

∼ PROVERBS 10:10–12 ∼

10 He who winks with the eye causes
trouble,
But a prating fool will fall.

11 The mouth of the righteous is a well
of life,
But violence covers the mouth of the
wicked.

12 Hatred stirs up strife,
But love covers all sins.

∼ MARK 5:1–20 ∼

Then they came to the other side of the sea, to the country of the Gadarenes. 2 And when He had come out of the boat, immediately there met Him out of the tombs a man with an unclean spirit, 3 who had *his* dwelling among the tombs; and no one could bind him, not even with chains, 4 because he had often been bound with shackles and chains. And the chains had been pulled apart by him, and the shackles broken in pieces; neither could anyone tame him. [5] And always, night and day, he was in the mountains and in the tombs, crying out and cutting himself with stones.

[6] When he saw Jesus from afar, he ran and worshiped Him. [7] And he cried out with a loud voice and said, "What have I to do with You, Jesus, Son of the Most High God? I implore You by God that You do not torment me."

[8] For He said to him, "Come out of the man, unclean spirit!" [9] Then He asked him, "What *is* your name?"

And he answered, saying, "My name *is* Legion; for we are many." [10] Also he begged Him earnestly that He would not send them out of the country.

[11] Now a large herd of swine was feeding there near the mountains. [12] So all the demons begged Him, saying, "Send us to the swine, that we may enter them." [13] And at once Jesus gave them permission. Then the unclean spirits went out and entered the swine (there were about two thousand); and the herd ran violently down the steep place into the sea, and drowned in the sea.

[14] So those who fed the swine fled, and they told *it* in the city and in the country. And they went out to see what it was that had happened. [15] Then they came to Jesus, and saw the one *who had been* demon-possessed and had the legion, sitting and clothed and in his right mind. And they were afraid. [16] And those who saw it told them how it happened to him *who had been* demon-possessed, and about the swine. [17] Then they began to plead with Him to depart from their region.

[18] And when He got into the boat, he who had been demon-possessed begged Him that he might be with Him. [19] However, Jesus did not permit him, but said to him, "Go home to your friends, and tell them what great things the Lord has done for you, and how He has had compassion on you." [20] And he departed and began to proclaim in Decapolis all that Jesus had done for him; and all marveled.

~ LEVITICUS 21:1—22:33 ~

And the LORD said to Moses, "Speak to the priests, the sons of Aaron, and say to them: 'None shall defile himself for the dead among his people, [2] except for his relatives who are nearest to him: his mother, his father, his son, his daughter, and his brother; [3] also his virgin sister who is near to him, who has had no husband, for her he may defile himself. [4] *Otherwise* he shall not defile himself, *being* a chief man among his people, to profane himself.

[5] 'They shall not make any bald *place* on their heads, nor shall they shave the edges of their beards nor make any cuttings in their flesh. [6] They shall be holy to their God and not profane the name of their God, for they offer the offerings of the LORD made by fire, *and* the bread of their God; therefore they shall be holy. [7] They shall not take a wife *who is* a harlot or a defiled woman, nor shall they take a woman divorced from her husband; for *the priest* is holy to his God. [8] Therefore you shall consecrate him, for he offers the bread of your God. He shall be holy to you, for I the LORD, who sanctify you, *am* holy. [9] The daughter of any priest, if she profanes herself by playing the harlot, she profanes her father. She shall be burned with fire.

[10] 'He who is the high priest among his brethren, on whose head the anointing oil was poured and who is consecrated to wear the garments, shall not uncover his head nor tear his clothes; [11] nor shall he go near any dead body, nor defile himself for his father or his mother; [12] nor shall he go out of the sanctuary, nor profane the sanctuary of his God; for the consecration of the anointing oil of his God *is* upon him: I *am* the LORD. [13] And he shall take a wife in her virginity. [14] A widow or a divorced woman or a defiled woman *or* a harlot—these he shall not marry; but he shall take a virgin of his own people as

wife. ¹⁵ Nor shall he profane his posterity among his people, for I the LORD sanctify him.' "

¹⁶ And the LORD spoke to Moses, saying, ¹⁷ "Speak to Aaron, saying: 'No man of your descendants in *succeeding* generations, who has *any* defect, may approach to offer the bread of his God. ¹⁸ For any man who has a defect shall not approach: a man blind or lame, who has a marred *face* or any *limb* too long, ¹⁹ a man who has a broken foot or broken hand, ²⁰ or is a hunchback or a dwarf, or *a man* who has a defect in his eye, or eczema or scab, or is a eunuch. ²¹ No man of the descendants of Aaron the priest, who has a defect, shall come near to offer the offerings made by fire to the LORD. He has a defect; he shall not come near to offer the bread of his God. ²² He may eat the bread of his God, *both* the most holy and the holy; ²³ only he shall not go near the veil or approach the altar, because he has a defect, lest he profane My sanctuaries; for I the LORD sanctify them.' "

²⁴ And Moses told *it* to Aaron and his sons, and to all the children of Israel.

22 Then the LORD spoke to Moses, saying, ² "Speak to Aaron and his sons, that they separate themselves from the holy things of the children of Israel, and that they do not profane My holy name *by* what they dedicate to Me: I *am* the LORD. ³ Say to them: 'Whoever of all your descendants throughout your generations, who goes near the holy things which the children of Israel dedicate to the LORD, while he has uncleanness upon him, that person shall be cut off from My presence: I *am* the LORD.

⁴ 'Whatever man of the descendants of Aaron, who *is* a leper or has a discharge, shall not eat the holy offerings until he is clean. And whoever touches anything made unclean *by* a corpse, or a man who has had an emission of semen, ⁵ or whoever touches any creeping thing by which he would be made unclean, or any person by whom he would become unclean, whatever his uncleanness may be— ⁶ the person who has touched any such thing shall be unclean until evening, and shall not eat the holy *offerings* unless

he washes his body with water. ⁷ And when the sun goes down he shall be clean; and afterward he may eat the holy *offerings*, because it *is* his food. ⁸ Whatever dies *naturally* or is torn *by beasts* he shall not eat, to defile himself with it: I *am* the LORD.

⁹ 'They shall therefore keep My ordinance, lest they bear sin for it and die thereby, if they profane it: I the LORD sanctify them.

¹⁰ 'No outsider shall eat the holy *offering*; one who dwells with the priest, or a hired servant, shall not eat the holy thing. ¹¹ But if the priest buys a person with his money, he may eat it; and one who is born in his house may eat his food. ¹² If the priest's daughter is married to an outsider, she may not eat of the holy offerings. ¹³ But if the priest's daughter is a widow or divorced, and has no child, and has returned to her father's house as in her youth, she may eat her father's food; but no outsider shall eat it.

¹⁴ 'And if a man eats the holy *offering* unintentionally, then he shall restore a holy *offering* to the priest, and add one-fifth to it. ¹⁵ They shall not profane the holy *offerings* of the children of Israel, which they offer to the LORD, ¹⁶ or allow them to bear the guilt of trespass when they eat their holy *offerings*; for I the LORD sanctify them.' "

¹⁷ And the LORD spoke to Moses, saying, ¹⁸ "Speak to Aaron and his sons, and to all the children of Israel, and say to them: 'Whatever man of the house of Israel, or of the strangers in Israel, who offers his sacrifice for any of his vows or for any of his freewill offerings, which they offer to the LORD as a burnt offering— ¹⁹ you *shall offer* of your own free will a male without blemish from the cattle, from the sheep, or from the goats. ²⁰ Whatever has a defect, you shall not offer, for it shall not be acceptable on your behalf. ²¹ And whoever offers a sacrifice of a peace offering to the LORD, to fulfill *his* vow, or a freewill offering from the cattle or the sheep, it must be perfect to be accepted; there shall be no defect in it. ²² Those *that are* blind or broken or maimed, or have an ulcer or eczema or scabs, you shall not offer to the LORD, nor make an offering by fire of them on

Thy Will Be Done

An overweight man decided it was time to shed a few pounds. One morning, however, he arrived at work carrying a gigantic coffee cake. His coworkers scolded him, but he smiled and said, "This is a very *special* coffee cake. I drove by the bakery this morning and there in the window were a host of goodies. I felt this was no accident, so I prayed, 'Lord, if You want me to have one of these delicious coffee cakes, let me have a parking place directly in front of the bakery.' And sure enough, the eighth time around the block, there it was!"

In *A Lamp for My Feet*, Elisabeth Elliot writes about the relationship in prayer between our will and God's will: "Does prayer work? The answer to that depends on one's definition of work. It is necessary to know what a thing is for in order to judge whether it works. It would be senseless, for example, to say that if a screwdriver fails to drive nails into a board it doesn't 'work.' A screwdriver works very well for driving screws. Often we expect to arrange things according to our whims by praying about them, and when the arrangement fails to materialize we conclude that prayer doesn't work. God wants our willing cooperation in the bringing in of His kingdom. If 'Thy kingdom come' is an honest prayer, we will seek to ask for whatever contributes to that end."

Indeed. When we go to God in prayer, we should ever be mindful of surrendering our will to His. His will, His plan for our life, is far better than anything we can dream up. When we pray "Thy will be done," we're opening the way for God's best to pour into our lives.

the altar to the LORD. ²³ Either a bull or a lamb that has any limb too long or too short you may offer *as* a freewill offering, but for a vow it shall not be accepted.

²⁴ 'You shall not offer to the LORD what is bruised or crushed, or torn or cut; nor shall you make *any offering of them* in your land. ²⁵ Nor from a foreigner's hand shall you offer any of these as the bread of your God, because their corruption *is* in them, *and* defects *are* in them. They shall not be accepted on your behalf.' "

²⁶ And the LORD spoke to Moses, saying: ²⁷ "When a bull or a sheep or a goat is born, it shall be seven days with its mother; and from the eighth day and thereafter it shall be accepted as an offering made by fire to the LORD. ²⁸ *Whether it is* a cow or ewe, do not kill both her and her young on the same day. ²⁹ And when you offer a sacrifice of thanksgiving to the LORD, offer *it* of your own free will. ³⁰ On the same day it shall be eaten; you shall leave none of it until morning: I *am* the LORD.

³¹ "Therefore you shall keep My commandments, and perform them: I *am* the LORD. ³² You shall not profane My holy name, but I will be hallowed among the children of Israel. I *am* the LORD who sanctifies you, ³³ who brought you out of the land of Egypt, to be your God: I *am* the LORD."

~ PSALM 27:11–14 ~

¹¹ Teach me Your way, O LORD,
    And lead me in a smooth path,
        because of my enemies.
¹² Do not deliver me to the will of my
        adversaries;
    For false witnesses have risen against
        me,
    And such as breathe out violence.
¹³ *I would have lost heart*, unless I had
        believed
    That I would see the goodness of the
        LORD
    In the land of the living.

¹⁴ Wait on the LORD;
    Be of good courage,
    And He shall strengthen your heart;
    Wait, I say, on the LORD!

~ PROVERBS 10:13–16 ~

¹³ Wisdom is found on the lips of him
        who has understanding,
    But a rod *is* for the back of him who
        is devoid of understanding.

¹⁴ Wise *people* store up knowledge,
    But the mouth of the foolish *is* near
        destruction.

¹⁵ The rich man's wealth *is* his strong
        city;
    The destruction of the poor *is* their
        poverty.

¹⁶ The labor of the righteous *leads* to
        life,
    The wages of the wicked to sin.

~ MARK 5:21–43 ~

Now when Jesus had crossed over again by boat to the other side, a great multitude gathered to Him; and He was by the sea. ²² And behold, one of the rulers of the synagogue came, Jairus by name. And when he saw Him, he fell at His feet ²³ and begged Him earnestly, saying, "My little daughter lies at the point of death. Come and lay Your hands on her, that she may be healed, and she will live." ²⁴ So Jesus went with him, and a great multitude followed Him and thronged Him.

²⁵ Now a certain woman had a flow of blood for twelve years, ²⁶ and had suffered many things from many physicians. She had spent all that she had and was no better, but rather grew worse. ²⁷ When she heard about Jesus, she came behind *Him* in the crowd and touched His garment. ²⁸ For she said, "If only I may touch His clothes, I shall be made well." ²⁹ Immediately the fountain of her blood was dried up, and she felt in *her* body that she was healed of the affliction. ³⁰ And Jesus, immediately knowing in Himself that power had gone out of Him, turned around in the crowd and said, "Who touched My clothes?" ³¹ But His disciples said to Him, "You see the multitude thronging You, and You say, 'Who touched Me?' " ³² And He looked around to see her

who had done this thing. [33] But the woman, fearing and trembling, knowing what had happened to her, came and fell down before Him and told Him the whole truth. [34] And He said to her, "Daughter, your faith has made you well. Go in peace, and be healed of your affliction."

[35] While He was still speaking, *some* came from the ruler of the synagogue's *house* who said, "Your daughter is dead. Why trouble the Teacher any further?"

[36] As soon as Jesus heard the word that was spoken, He said to the ruler of the synagogue, "Do not be afraid; only believe." [37] And He permitted no one to follow Him except Peter, James, and John the brother of James. [38] Then He came to the house of the ruler of the synagogue, and saw a tumult and those who wept and wailed loudly. [39] When He came in, He said to them, "Why make this commotion and weep? The child is not dead, but sleeping."

[40] And they ridiculed Him. But when He had put them all outside, He took the father and the mother of the child, and those *who were* with Him, and entered where the child was lying. [41] Then He took the child by the hand, and said to her, "Talitha, cumi," which is translated, "Little girl, I say to you, arise." [42] Immediately the girl arose and walked, for she was twelve years *of age*. And they were overcome with great amazement. [43] But He commanded them strictly that no one should know it, and said that *something* should be given her to eat.

∼ LEVITICUS 23:1—24:23 ∼

And the LORD spoke to Moses, saying, [2] "Speak to the children of Israel, and say to them: 'The feasts of the LORD, which you shall proclaim *to be* holy convocations, these *are* My feasts.

[3] 'Six days shall work be done, but the seventh day *is* a Sabbath of solemn rest, a holy convocation. You shall do no work on it; it *is* the Sabbath of the LORD in all your dwellings.

[4] 'These *are* the feasts of the LORD, holy convocations which you shall proclaim at their appointed times. [5] On the fourteenth *day* of the first month at twilight *is* the LORD's Passover. [6] And on the fifteenth day of the same month *is* the Feast of Unleavened Bread to the LORD; seven days you must eat unleavened bread. [7] On the first day you shall have a holy convocation; you shall do no customary work on it. [8] But you shall offer an offering made by fire to the LORD for seven days. The seventh day *shall be* a holy convocation; you shall do no customary work *on it*.' "

[9] And the LORD spoke to Moses, saying, [10] "Speak to the children of Israel, and say to them: 'When you come into the land which I give to you, and reap its harvest, then you shall bring a sheaf of the firstfruits of your harvest to the priest.

[11] He shall wave the sheaf before the LORD, to be accepted on your behalf; on the day after the Sabbath the priest shall wave it. [12] And you shall offer on that day, when you wave the sheaf, a male lamb of the first year, without blemish, as a burnt offering to the LORD. [13] Its grain offering *shall be* two-tenths *of an ephah* of fine flour mixed with oil, an offering made by fire to the LORD, for a sweet aroma; and its drink offering *shall be* of wine, one-fourth of a hin. [14] You shall eat neither bread nor parched grain nor fresh grain until the same day that you have brought an offering to your God; *it shall be* a statute forever throughout your generations in all your dwellings.

[15] 'And you shall count for yourselves from the day after the Sabbath, from the day that you brought the sheaf of the wave offering: seven Sabbaths shall be completed. [16] Count fifty days to the day after the seventh Sabbath; then you shall offer a new grain offering to the LORD. [17] You shall bring from your dwellings two wave *loaves* of two-tenths *of an ephah*. They shall be of fine flour; they shall be baked with leaven. *They are* the firstfruits to the LORD. [18] And you shall offer with the bread seven lambs of the first year,

without blemish, one young bull, and two rams. They shall be *as* a burnt offering to the LORD, with their grain offering and their drink offerings, an offering made by fire for a sweet aroma to the LORD. ¹⁹ Then you shall sacrifice one kid of the goats as a sin offering, and two male lambs of the first year as a sacrifice of a peace offering. ²⁰ The priest shall wave them with the bread of the firstfruits *as* a wave offering before the LORD, with the two lambs. They shall be holy to the LORD for the priest. ²¹ And you shall proclaim on the same day *that* it is a holy convocation to you. You shall do no customary work *on it. It shall be* a statute forever in all your dwellings throughout your generations.

²² 'When you reap the harvest of your land, you shall not wholly reap the corners of your field when you reap, nor shall you gather any gleaning from your harvest. You shall leave them for the poor and for the stranger: I *am* the LORD your God.' "

²³ Then the LORD spoke to Moses, saying, ²⁴ "Speak to the children of Israel, saying: 'In the seventh month, on the first *day* of the month, you shall have a sabbath-*rest*, a memorial of blowing of trumpets, a holy convocation. ²⁵ You shall do no customary work *on it*; and you shall offer an offering made by fire to the LORD.' "

²⁶ And the LORD spoke to Moses, saying: ²⁷ "Also the tenth *day* of this seventh month *shall be* the Day of Atonement. It shall be a holy convocation for you; you shall afflict your souls, and offer an offering made by fire to the LORD. ²⁸ And you shall do no work on that same day, for it *is* the Day of Atonement, to make atonement for you before the LORD your God. ²⁹ For any person who is not afflicted *in soul* on that same day shall be cut off from his people. ³⁰ And any person who does any work on that same day, that person I will destroy from among his people. ³¹ You shall do no manner of work; *it shall be* a statute forever throughout your generations in all your dwellings. ³² It *shall be* to you a sabbath of *solemn* rest, and you shall afflict your souls; on the ninth *day* of the month at evening, from evening to evening, you shall celebrate your sabbath."

³³ Then the LORD spoke to Moses, saying, ³⁴ "Speak to the children of Israel, saying: 'The fifteenth day of this seventh month *shall be* the Feast of Tabernacles *for* seven days to the LORD. ³⁵ On the first day *there shall be* a holy convocation. You shall do no customary work *on it*. ³⁶ For seven days you shall offer an offering made by fire to the LORD. On the eighth day you shall have a holy convocation, and you shall offer an offering made by fire to the LORD. It *is* a sacred assembly, *and* you shall do no customary work *on it*.

³⁷ 'These *are* the feasts of the LORD which you shall proclaim *to be* holy convocations, to offer an offering made by fire to the LORD, a burnt offering and a grain offering, a sacrifice and drink offerings, everything on its day— ³⁸ besides the Sabbaths of the LORD, besides your gifts, besides all your vows, and besides all your freewill offerings which you give to the LORD.

³⁹ 'Also on the fifteenth day of the seventh month, when you have gathered in the fruit of the land, you shall keep the feast of the LORD *for* seven days; on the first day *there shall be* a sabbath-*rest*, and on the eighth day a sabbath-*rest*. ⁴⁰ And you shall take for yourselves on the first day the fruit of beautiful trees, branches of palm trees, the boughs of leafy trees, and willows of the brook; and you shall rejoice before the LORD your God for seven days. ⁴¹ You shall keep it as a feast to the LORD for seven days in the year. *It shall be* a statute forever in your generations. You shall celebrate it in the seventh month. ⁴² You shall dwell in booths for seven days. All who are native Israelites shall dwell in booths, ⁴³ that your generations may know that I made the children of Israel dwell in booths when I brought them out of the land of Egypt: I *am* the LORD your God.' "

⁴⁴ So Moses declared to the children of Israel the feasts of the LORD.

24 Then the LORD spoke to Moses, saying: ² "Command the children of Israel that they bring to you pure oil of pressed olives for the light, to make the lamps burn continually. ³ Outside the veil of the Testimony, in the tabernacle of

Grateful Giving

The story is told of a man and woman who gave a sizable contribution to their church to honor the memory of their son, who lost his life in the war. When the generous donation was announced to the congregation, a woman whispered to her husband, "Let's give the same amount in honor of each of our boys."

The husband replied, "What are you talking about? Neither one of our sons was killed in the war."

"Exactly," said the woman. "Let's give it as an expression of our gratitude to God for sparing their lives!"

All of our charitable giving in life produces benefits in three ways: (l) it helps those in need, (2) it inspires others to give, and (3) it builds character in us — selflessness, temperance, generosity, and compassion.

Keep in mind that when you give, you are ultimately giving to people, even though your gift might be made to an institution or organization. Churches and other charitable organizations are comprised of people. Your giving not only brings sunshine to the lives of others, but to your life as well.

> Besides the Sabbaths of the Lord, besides your gifts, besides all your vows, and besides all your freewill offerings which you give to the Lord.
>
> *Leviticus 23:38*

meeting, Aaron shall be in charge of it from evening until morning before the LORD continually; *it shall be* a statute forever in your generations. ⁴ He shall be in charge of the lamps on the pure *gold* lampstand before the LORD continually.

⁵ "And you shall take fine flour and bake twelve cakes with it. Two-tenths *of an ephah* shall be in each cake. ⁶ You shall set them in two rows, six in a row, on the pure *gold* table before the LORD. ⁷ And you shall put pure frankincense on *each* row, that it may be on the bread for a memorial, an offering made by fire to the LORD. ⁸ Every Sabbath he shall set it in order before the LORD continually, *being taken* from the children of Israel by an everlasting covenant. ⁹ And it shall be for Aaron and his sons, and they shall eat it in a holy place; for it *is* most holy to him from the offerings of the LORD made by fire, by a perpetual statute."

¹⁰ Now the son of an Israelite woman, whose father *was* an Egyptian, went out among the children of Israel; and this Israelite *woman's* son and a man of Israel fought each other in the camp. ¹¹ And the Israelite woman's son blasphemed the name *of the* LORD and cursed; and so they brought him to Moses. (His mother's name *was* Shelomith the daughter of Dibri, of the tribe of Dan.) ¹² Then they put him in custody, that the mind of the LORD might be shown to them.

¹³ And the LORD spoke to Moses, saying, ¹⁴ "Take outside the camp him who has cursed; then let all who heard *him* lay their hands on his head, and let all the congregation stone him.

¹⁵ "Then you shall speak to the children of Israel, saying: 'Whoever curses his God shall bear his sin. ¹⁶ And whoever blasphemes the name of the LORD shall surely be put to death. All the congregation shall certainly stone him, the stranger as well as him who is born in the land. When he blasphemes the name *of the* LORD, he shall be put to death.

¹⁷ 'Whoever kills any man shall surely be put to death. ¹⁸ Whoever kills an animal shall make it good, animal for animal.

¹⁹ 'If a man causes disfigurement of his neighbor, as he has done, so shall it be done to him— ²⁰ fracture for fracture, eye for eye, tooth for tooth; as he has caused disfigurement of a man, so shall it be done to him. ²¹ And whoever kills an animal shall restore it; but whoever kills a man shall be put to death. ²² You shall have the same law for the stranger and for one from your own country; for I *am* the LORD your God.' "

²³ Then Moses spoke to the children of Israel; and they took outside the camp him who had cursed, and stoned him with stones. So the children of Israel did as the LORD commanded Moses.

∼ PSALM 28:1–5 ∼

¹ To You I will cry, O LORD my Rock:
Do not be silent to me,
Lest, if You *are* silent to me,
I become like those who go down to
the pit.
² Hear the voice of my supplications
When I cry to You,
When I lift up my hands toward
Your holy sanctuary.

³ Do not take me away with the
wicked
And with the workers of iniquity,
Who speak peace to their neighbors,
But evil *is* in their hearts.
⁴ Give them according to their deeds,
And according to the wickedness of
their endeavors;
Give them according to the work of
their hands;
Render to them what they deserve.
⁵ Because they do not regard the
works of the LORD,
Nor the operation of His hands,
He shall destroy them
And not build them up.

∼ PROVERBS 10:17, 18 ∼

¹⁷ He who keeps instruction *is in* the
way of life,
But he who refuses correction goes
astray.

¹⁸ Whoever hides hatred *has* lying lips,
And whoever spreads slander *is* a
fool.

～ MARK 6:1–29 ～

Then He went out from there and came to His own country, and His disciples followed Him. [2] And when the Sabbath had come, He began to teach in the synagogue. And many hearing *Him* were astonished, saying, "Where *did* this Man *get* these things? And what wisdom *is* this which is given to Him, that such mighty works are performed by His hands! [3] Is this not the carpenter, the Son of Mary, and brother of James, Joses, Judas, and Simon? And are not His sisters here with us?" So they were offended at Him.

[4] But Jesus said to them, "A prophet is not without honor except in his own country, among his own relatives, and in his own house." [5] Now He could do no mighty work there, except that He laid His hands on a few sick people and healed *them.* [6] And He marveled because of their unbelief. Then He went about the villages in a circuit, teaching.

[7] And He called the twelve to *Himself,* and began to send them out two *by* two, and gave them power over unclean spirits. [8] He commanded them to take nothing for the journey except a staff— no bag, no bread, no copper in *their* money belts— [9] but to wear sandals, and not to put on two tunics.

[10] Also He said to them, "In whatever place you enter a house, stay there till you depart from that place. [11] And whoever will not receive you nor hear you, when you depart from there, shake off the dust under your feet as a testimony against them. Assuredly, I say to you, it will be more tolerable for Sodom and Gomorrah in the day of judgment than for that city!"

[12] So they went out and preached that *people* should repent. [13] And they cast out many demons, and anointed with oil many who were sick, and healed *them.*

[14] Now King Herod heard *of Him,* for His name had become well known. And he said, "John the Baptist is risen from the dead, and therefore these powers are at work in him."

[15] Others said, "It is Elijah."

And others said, "It is the Prophet, or like one of the prophets."

[16] But when Herod heard, he said, "This is John, whom I beheaded; he has been raised from the dead!" [17] For Herod himself had sent and laid hold of John, and bound him in prison for the sake of Herodias, his brother Philip's wife; for he had married her. [18] Because John had said to Herod, "It is not lawful for you to have your brother's wife."

[19] Therefore Herodias held it against him and wanted to kill him, but she could not; [20] for Herod feared John, knowing that he *was* a just and holy man, and he protected him. And when he heard him, he did many things, and heard him gladly.

[21] Then an opportune day came when Herod on his birthday gave a feast for his nobles, the high officers, and the chief *men* of Galilee. [22] And when Herodias' daughter herself came in and danced, and pleased Herod and those who sat with him, the king said to the girl, "Ask me whatever you want, and I will give *it* to you." [23] He also swore to her, "Whatever you ask me, I will give you, up to half my kingdom."

[24] So she went out and said to her mother, "What shall I ask?"

And she said, "The head of John the Baptist!"

[25] Immediately she came in with haste to the king and asked, saying, "I want you to give me at once the head of John the Baptist on a platter."

[26] And the king was exceedingly sorry; *yet,* because of the oaths and because of those who sat with him, he did not want to refuse her. [27] Immediately the king sent an executioner and commanded his head to be brought. And he went and beheaded him in prison, [28] brought his head on a platter, and gave it to the girl; and the girl gave it to her mother. [29] When his disciples heard *of it,* they came and took away his corpse and laid it in a tomb.

∼ LEVITICUS 25:1–55 ∼

And the LORD spoke to Moses on Mount Sinai, saying, [2] "Speak to the children of Israel, and say to them: 'When you come into the land which I give you, then the land shall keep a sabbath to the LORD. [3] Six years you shall sow your field, and six years you shall prune your vineyard, and gather its fruit; [4] but in the seventh year there shall be a sabbath of solemn rest for the land, a sabbath to the LORD. You shall neither sow your field nor prune your vineyard. [5] What grows of its own accord of your harvest you shall not reap, nor gather the grapes of your untended vine, *for* it is a year of rest for the land. [6] And the sabbath *produce* of the land shall be food for you: for you, your male and female servants, your hired man, and the stranger who dwells with you, [7] for your livestock and the beasts that *are* in your land—all its produce shall be for food.

[8] 'And you shall count seven sabbaths of years for yourself, seven times seven years; and the time of the seven sabbaths of years shall be to you forty-nine years. [9] Then you shall cause the trumpet of the Jubilee to sound on the tenth *day* of the seventh month; on the Day of Atonement you shall make the trumpet to sound throughout all your land. [10] And you shall consecrate the fiftieth year, and proclaim liberty throughout *all* the land to all its inhabitants. It shall be a Jubilee for you; and each of you shall return to his possession, and each of you shall return to his family. [11] That fiftieth year shall be a Jubilee to you; in it you shall neither sow nor reap what grows of its own accord, nor gather *the grapes* of your untended vine. [12] For it *is* the Jubilee; it shall be holy to you; you shall eat its produce from the field.

[13] 'In this Year of Jubilee, each of you shall return to his possession. [14] And if you sell anything to your neighbor or buy from your neighbor's hand, you shall not oppress one another. [15] According to the number of years after the Jubilee you shall buy from your neighbor, and according to the number of years of crops he shall sell to you. [16] According to the multitude of years you shall increase its price, and according to the fewer number of years you shall diminish its price; for he sells to you *according* to the number *of the years* of the crops. [17] Therefore you shall not oppress one another, but you shall fear your God; for I *am* the LORD your God.

[18] 'So you shall observe My statutes and keep My judgments, and perform them; and you will dwell in the land in safety. [19] Then the land will yield its fruit, and you will eat your fill, and dwell there in safety.

[20] 'And if you say, "What shall we eat in the seventh year, since we shall not sow nor gather in our produce?" [21] Then I will command My blessing on you in the sixth year, and it will bring forth produce enough for three years. [22] And you shall sow in the eighth year, and eat old produce until the ninth year; until its produce comes in, you shall eat *of* the old *harvest*.

[23] 'The land shall not be sold permanently, for the land *is* Mine; for you *are* strangers and sojourners with Me. [24] And in all the land of your possession you shall grant redemption of the land.

[25] 'If one of your brethren becomes poor, and has sold *some* of his possession, and if his redeeming relative comes to redeem it, then he may redeem what his brother sold. [26] Or if the man has no one to redeem it, but he himself becomes able to redeem it, [27] then let him count the years since its sale, and restore the remainder to the man to whom he sold it, that he may return to his possession. [28] But if he is not able to have *it* restored to himself, then what was sold shall remain in the hand of him who bought it until the Year of Jubilee; and in the Jubilee it shall be released, and he shall return to his possession.

[29] 'If a man sells a house in a walled city, then he may redeem it within a whole year after it is sold; *within* a full year he may redeem it. [30] But if it is not redeemed within the space of a full year, then the house in the walled city shall belong permanently to him who bought it, throughout his generations. It shall not

Conserving Words

During World War I, Eleanor Roosevelt made a valiant effort to conserve food, but things didn't turn out exactly as she had planned. In July 1917, the Food Administration picked their household as "a model for other large households." The New York Times sent a newswoman to interview Mrs. Roosevelt about her food-saving methods, and she later wrote: "Mrs. Roosevelt does the shopping, the cooks see that there is no food wasted, the laundress is sparing in her use of soap, each servant has a watchful eye . . . and all are encouraged to make helpful suggestions in the use of leftovers." The article ended with a quote from Mrs. Roosevelt: "Making ten servants help me do my saving has not only been possible but also highly profitable."

As might be expected, the story created a great deal of mirth in Washington. FDR joined in teasing his wife, saying, "Please have a photo taken showing the family, the ten cooperating servants, the scraps saved from the table, and the handbook." To which Mrs. Roosevelt moaned in reply, "I feel dreadfully about it because so much is not true and yet some of it I did say. I will never be caught again, that's sure, and I'd like to crawl away for shame."

The book of proverbs tells us even a fool is thought wise when he holds his tongue. When in doubt about what to say — don't say anything!

be released in the Jubilee. [31] However the houses of villages which have no wall around them shall be counted as the fields of the country. They may be redeemed, and they shall be released in the Jubilee. [32] Nevertheless the cities of the Levites, *and* the houses in the cities of their possession, the Levites may redeem at any time. [33] And if a man purchases a house from the Levites, then the house that was sold in the city of his possession shall be released in the Jubilee; for the houses in the cities of the Levites *are* their possession among the children of Israel. [34] But the field of the common-land of their cities may not be sold, for it is their perpetual possession.

[35] 'If one of your brethren becomes poor, and falls into poverty among you, then you shall help him, like a stranger or a sojourner, that he may live with you. [36] Take no usury or interest from him; but fear your God, that your brother may live with you. [37] You shall not lend him your money for usury, nor lend him your food at a profit. [38] I *am* the LORD your God, who brought you out of the land of Egypt, to give you the land of Canaan *and* to be your God.

[39] 'And if *one of* your brethren *who dwells* by you becomes poor, and sells himself to you, you shall not compel him to serve as a slave. [40] As a hired servant *and* a sojourner he shall be with you, *and* shall serve you until the Year of Jubilee. [41] And *then* he shall depart from you—he and his children with him—and shall return to his own family. He shall return to the possession of his fathers. [42] For they *are* My servants, whom I brought out of the land of Egypt; they shall not be sold as slaves. [43] You shall not rule over him with rigor, but you shall fear your God. [44] And as for your male and female slaves whom you may have—from the nations that are around you, from them you may buy male and female slaves. [45] Moreover you may buy the children of the strangers who dwell among you, and their families who are with you, which they beget in your land; and they shall become your property. [46] And you may take them as an inheritance for your children after you, to inherit *them as* a possession; they shall be your permanent slaves. But regarding your brethren, the children of Israel, you shall not rule over one another with rigor.

[47] 'Now if a sojourner or stranger close to you becomes rich, and *one of* your brethren *who dwells* by him becomes poor, and sells himself to the stranger *or* sojourner close to you, or to a member of the stranger's family, [48] after he is sold he may be redeemed again. One of his brothers may redeem him; [49] or his uncle or his uncle's son may redeem him; or *anyone* who is near of kin to him in his family may redeem him; or if he is able he may redeem himself. [50] Thus he shall reckon with him who bought him: The price of his release shall be according to the number of years, from the year that he was sold to him until the Year of Jubilee; *it shall be* according to the time of a hired servant for him. [51] If *there are* still many years *remaining*, according to them he shall repay the price of his redemption from the money with which he was bought. [52] And if there remain but a few years until the Year of Jubilee, then he shall reckon with him, *and* according to his years he shall repay him the price of his redemption. [53] He shall be with him as a yearly hired servant, and he shall not rule with rigor over him in your sight. [54] And if he is not redeemed in these *years*, then he shall be released in the Year of Jubilee—he and his children with him. [55] For the children of Israel *are* servants to Me; they *are* My servants whom I brought out of the land of Egypt: I *am* the LORD your God.

∼ PSALM 28:6–9 ∼

[6] Blessed *be* the LORD,
   Because He has heard the voice of
      my supplications!
[7] The LORD *is* my strength and my
      shield;
   My heart trusted in Him, and I am
      helped;
   Therefore my heart greatly rejoices,
   And with my song I will praise Him.

[8] The LORD *is* their strength,
   And He *is* the saving refuge of His
      anointed.
[9] Save Your people,
   And bless Your inheritance;

Shepherd them also,
And bear them up forever.

~ PROVERBS 10:19–21 ~

19 In the multitude of words sin is not
lacking,
But he who restrains his lips *is* wise.
20 The tongue of the righteous *is* choice
silver;
The heart of the wicked *is worth*
little.
21 The lips of the righteous feed many,
But fools die for lack of wisdom.

~ MARK 6:30–56 ~

Then the apostles gathered to Jesus and
told Him all things, both what they had
done and what they had taught. 31 And
He said to them, "Come aside by yourselves to a deserted place and rest a while."
For there were many coming and going,
and they did not even have time to eat.
32 So they departed to a deserted place in
the boat by themselves.

33 But the multitudes saw them departing, and many knew Him and ran there
on foot from all the cities. They arrived
before them and came together to Him.
34 And Jesus, when He came out, saw a
great multitude and was moved with compassion for them, because they were like
sheep not having a shepherd. So He began to teach them many things. 35 When
the day was now far spent, His disciples
came to Him and said, "This is a deserted
place, and already the hour *is* late. 36 Send
them away, that they may go into the surrounding country and villages and buy
themselves bread; for they have nothing
to eat."

37 But He answered and said to them,
"You give them something to eat."

And they said to Him, "Shall we go and
buy two hundred denarii worth of bread
and give them *something* to eat?"

38 But He said to them, "How many
loaves do you have? Go and see."

And when they found out they said,
"Five, and two fish."

39 Then He commanded them to make
them all sit down in groups on the green
grass. 40 So they sat down in ranks, in hundreds and in fifties. 41 And when He had
taken the five loaves and the two fish, He
looked up to heaven, blessed and broke
the loaves, and gave *them* to His disciples
to set before them; and the two fish He
divided among *them* all. 42 So they all ate
and were filled. 43 And they took up twelve
baskets full of fragments and of the fish.
44 Now those who had eaten the loaves
were about five thousand men.

45 Immediately He made His disciples
get into the boat and go before Him to
the other side, to Bethsaida, while He sent
the multitude away. 46 And when He had
sent them away, He departed to the mountain to pray. 47 Now when evening came,
the boat was in the middle of the sea; and
He *was* alone on the land. 48 Then He saw
them straining at rowing, for the wind was
against them. Now about the fourth watch
of the night He came to them, walking
on the sea, and would have passed them
by. 49 And when they saw Him walking
on the sea, they supposed it was a ghost,
and cried out; 50 for they all saw Him and
were troubled. But immediately He talked
with them and said to them, "Be of good
cheer! It is I; do not be afraid." 51 Then
He went up into the boat to them, and
the wind ceased. And they were greatly
amazed in themselves beyond measure,
and marveled. 52 For they had not understood about the loaves, because their heart
was hardened.

53 When they had crossed over, they
came to the land of Gennesaret and an-
chored there. 54 And when they came
out of the boat, immediately the people
recognized Him, 55 ran through that
whole surrounding region, and began to
carry about on beds those who were
sick to wherever they heard He was.
56 Wherever He entered, into villages, cities, or the country, they laid the sick in
the marketplaces, and begged Him that
they might just touch the hem of His garment. And as many as touched Him were
made well.

~ LEVITICUS 26:1—27:34 ~

1 'You shall not make idols for yourselves;
neither a carved image nor a *sacred* pillar shall you rear up for yourselves;
nor shall you set up an engraved stone in your land, to bow down to it;
for I *am* the LORD your God.

2 You shall keep My Sabbaths and reverence My sanctuary:
I *am* the LORD.

3 'If you walk in My statutes and keep My commandments, and perform them,

4 then I will give you rain in its season,
the land shall yield its produce, and the trees of the field shall yield their fruit.

5 Your threshing shall last till the time of vintage, and the vintage shall last till the time of sowing;
you shall eat your bread to the full, and dwell in your land safely.

6 I will give peace in the land, and you shall lie down, and none will make *you* afraid;
I will rid the land of evil beasts, and the sword will not go through your land.

7 You will chase your enemies, and they shall fall by the sword before you.

8 Five of you shall chase a hundred, and a hundred of you shall put ten thousand to flight;
your enemies shall fall by the sword before you.

9 'For I will look on you favorably and make you fruitful, multiply you and confirm My covenant with you.

10 You shall eat the old harvest, and clear out the old because of the new.

11 I will set My tabernacle among you, and My soul shall not abhor you.

12 I will walk among you and be your God, and you shall be My people.

13 I *am* the LORD your God, who brought you out of the land of Egypt, that *you* should not be their slaves;
I have broken the bands of your yoke and made you walk upright.

14 'But if you do not obey Me, and do not observe all these commandments,

15 and if you despise My statutes, or if your soul abhors My judgments, so that you do not perform all My commandments, *but* break My covenant,

16 I also will do this to you:
I will even appoint terror over you, wasting disease and fever which shall consume the eyes and cause sorrow of heart.
And you shall sow your seed in vain, for your enemies shall eat it.

17 I will set My face against you, and you shall be defeated by your enemies.
Those who hate you shall reign over you, and you shall flee when no one pursues you.

18 'And after all this, if you do not obey Me, then I will punish you seven times more for your sins.

19 I will break the pride of your power;
I will make your heavens like iron and your earth like bronze.

20 And your strength shall be spent in vain;
for your land shall not yield its produce, nor shall the trees of the land yield their fruit.

21 'Then, if you walk contrary to Me, and are not willing to obey Me, I will bring on you seven times more plagues, according to your sins.

Holding On

Tracy's grandmother was a survivor of a prison camp. Tracy often spent her time after school at Gram's house but had never heard her grandmother's stories. She decided that she would write about Gram for her English assignment, a paper on "Modern Day Heroes."

After explaining to Gram what she wanted to do, Tracy sat down with Gram to work on the report. Tracy's heart almost broke as Gram told story after story of the suffering of her friends and the deaths of so many she loved. Tracy made some notes and asked some questions along the way, but finally she put down her pen and paper and asked Gram, "How did you do it? How did you live through such an awful experience?"

After thinking a moment, Gram answered honestly, "I don't think all of me did live through it. You lose part of yourself in the face of so much evil. But there was a part of me that believed this was the evil of men, not of God. Part of me never forgot there was a power greater than this evil and only love would help me find that power to make it through."

"You ARE a hero, Gram," Tracy said.

"Maybe to you I am," Gram said with a smile, "but to me I am someone who was fortunate enough to have something to hold on to when the storm came by."

> When the storm has swept by, the wicked are gone, but the righteous stand firm forever.
>
> *Proverbs 10:25*

22 I will also send wild beasts among
   you, which shall rob you of
   your children, destroy your
   livestock, and make you few in
   number;
   and your highways shall be desolate.

23 'And if by these things you are not
   reformed by Me, but walk contrary to Me,
24 then I also will walk contrary to you,
   and I will punish you yet seven
   times for your sins.
25 And I will bring a sword against you
   that will execute the vengeance
   of the covenant;
   when you are gathered together
   within your cities I will send
   pestilence among you;
   and you shall be delivered into the
   hand of the enemy.
26 When I have cut off your supply of
   bread, ten women shall bake your
   bread in one oven, and they shall
   bring back your bread by weight,
   and you shall eat and not be
   satisfied.

27 'And after all this, if you do not obey
   Me, but walk contrary to Me,
28 then I also will walk contrary to you
   in fury;
   and I, even I, will chastise you seven
   times for your sins.
29 You shall eat the flesh of your sons,
   and you shall eat the flesh of your
   daughters.
30 I will destroy your high places, cut
   down your incense altars, and cast
   your carcasses on the lifeless
   forms of your idols;
   and My soul shall abhor you.
31 I will lay your cities waste and bring
   your sanctuaries to desolation,
   and I will not smell the fragrance
   of your sweet aromas.
32 I will bring the land to desolation,
   and your enemies who dwell in it
   shall be astonished at it.
33 I will scatter you among the nations
   and draw out a sword after you;
   your land shall be desolate and your
   cities waste.

34 Then the land shall enjoy its sabbaths
   as long as it lies desolate and you
   are in your enemies' land;
   then the land shall rest and enjoy its
   sabbaths.
35 As long as it lies desolate it shall
   rest—
   for the time it did not rest on your
   sabbaths when you dwelt in it.

36 'And as for those of you who are left,
   I will send faintness into their
   hearts in the lands of their
   enemies;
   the sound of a shaken leaf shall cause
   them to flee;
   they shall flee as though fleeing from
   a sword, and they shall fall when
   no one pursues.
37 They shall stumble over one
   another, as it were before a sword,
   when no one pursues;
   and you shall have no *power* to stand
   before your enemies.
38 You shall perish among the nations,
   and the land of your enemies shall
   eat you up.
39 And those of you who are left shall
   waste away in their iniquity in
   your enemies' lands;
   also in their fathers' iniquities, which
   are with them, they shall waste
   away.

40 '*But* if they confess their iniquity and
   the iniquity of their fathers, with
   their unfaithfulness in which they
   were unfaithful to Me, and that
   they also have walked contrary to
   Me,
41 and *that* I also have walked contrary
   to them and have brought them
   into the land of their enemies;
   if their uncircumcised hearts are
   humbled, and they accept their
   guilt—
42 then I will remember My covenant
   with Jacob, and My covenant
   with Isaac and My covenant with
   Abraham I will remember;
   I will remember the land.
43 The land also shall be left empty by
   them, and will enjoy its sabbaths

while it lies desolate without them;

they will accept their guilt, because they despised My judgments and because their soul abhorred My statutes.

44 Yet for all that, when they are in the land of their enemies, I will not cast them away, nor shall I abhor them, to utterly destroy them and break My covenant with them;

for I *am* the LORD their God.

45 But for their sake I will remember the covenant of their ancestors, whom I brought out of the land of Egypt in the sight of the nations, that I might be their God:

I *am* the LORD.' "

46 These *are* the statutes and judgments and laws which the LORD made between Himself and the children of Israel on Mount Sinai by the hand of Moses.

27 Now the LORD spoke to Moses, saying, 2 "Speak to the children of Israel, and say to them: 'When a man consecrates by a vow certain persons to the LORD, according to your valuation, 3 if your valuation is of a male from twenty years old up to sixty years old, then your valuation shall be fifty shekels of silver, according to the shekel of the sanctuary. 4 If it *is* a female, then your valuation shall be thirty shekels; 5 and if from five years old up to twenty years old, then your valuation for a male shall be twenty shekels, and for a female ten shekels; 6 and if from a month old up to five years old, then your valuation for a male shall be five shekels of silver, and for a female your valuation shall be three shekels of silver; 7 and if from sixty years old and above, if *it is* a male, then your valuation shall be fifteen shekels, and for a female ten shekels.

8 'But if he is too poor to pay your valuation, then he shall present himself before the priest, and the priest shall set a value for him; according to the ability of him who vowed, the priest shall value him.

9 'If *it is* an animal that men may bring as an offering to the LORD, all that *anyone* gives to the LORD shall be holy. 10 He shall not substitute it or exchange it, good for bad or bad for good; and if he at all exchanges animal for animal, then both it and the one exchanged for it shall be holy. 11 If *it is* an unclean animal which they do not offer as a sacrifice to the LORD, then he shall present the animal before the priest; 12 and the priest shall set a value for it, whether it is good or bad; as you, the priest, value it, so it shall be. 13 But if he *wants* at all *to* redeem it, then he must add one-fifth to your valuation.

14 'And when a man dedicates his house *to be* holy to the LORD, then the priest shall set a value for it, whether it is good or bad; as the priest values it, so it shall stand. 15 If he who dedicated it *wants* to redeem his house, then he must add one-fifth of the money of your valuation to it, and it shall be his.

16 'If a man dedicates to the LORD *part* of a field of his possession, then your valuation shall be according to the seed for it. A homer of barley seed *shall be valued* at fifty shekels of silver. 17 If he dedicates his field from the Year of Jubilee, according to your valuation it shall stand. 18 But if he dedicates his field after the Jubilee, then the priest shall reckon to him the money due according to the years that remain till the Year of Jubilee, and it shall be deducted from your valuation. 19 And if he who dedicates the field ever wishes to redeem it, then he must add one-fifth of the money of your valuation to it, and it shall belong to him. 20 But if he does not want to redeem the field, or if he has sold the field to another man, it shall not be redeemed anymore; 21 but the field, when it is released in the Jubilee, shall be holy to the LORD, as a devoted field; it shall be the possession of the priest.

22 'And if a man dedicates to the LORD a field which he has bought, which is not the field of his possession, 23 then the priest shall reckon to him the worth of your valuation, up to the Year of Jubilee, and he shall give your valuation on that day *as* a holy *offering* to the LORD. 24 In the Year of Jubilee the field shall return to him from whom it was bought, to the one who *owned* the land as a possession. 25 And all your valuations shall be according to the

shekel of the sanctuary: twenty gerahs to the shekel.

²⁶ 'But the firstborn of the animals, which should be the LORD's firstborn, no man shall dedicate; whether *it is* an ox or sheep, it *is* the LORD's. ²⁷ And if *it is* an unclean animal, then he shall redeem *it* according to your valuation, and shall add one-fifth to it; or if it is not redeemed, then it shall be sold according to your valuation.

²⁸ 'Nevertheless no devoted *offering* that a man may devote to the LORD of all that he has, *both* man and beast, or the field of his possession, shall be sold or redeemed; every devoted *offering* is most holy to the LORD. ²⁹ No person under the ban, who may become doomed to destruction among men, shall be redeemed, *but* shall surely be put to death. ³⁰ And all the tithe of the land, *whether* of the seed of the land *or* of the fruit of the tree, *is* the LORD's. It is holy to the LORD. ³¹ If a man wants at all to redeem *any* of his tithes, he shall add one-fifth to it. ³² And concerning the tithe of the herd or the flock, of whatever passes under the rod, the tenth one shall be holy to the LORD. ³³ He shall not inquire whether it is good or bad, nor shall he exchange it; and if he exchanges it at all, then both it and the one exchanged for it shall be holy; it shall not be redeemed.' "

³⁴ These *are* the commandments which the LORD commanded Moses for the children of Israel on Mount Sinai.

~ PSALM 29:1–6 ~

¹ Give unto the LORD, O you mighty ones,
  Give unto the LORD glory and strength.
² Give unto the LORD the glory due to His name;
  Worship the LORD in the beauty of holiness.

³ The voice of the LORD *is* over the waters;
  The God of glory thunders;
  The LORD *is* over many waters.
⁴ The voice of the LORD *is* powerful;
  The voice of the LORD *is* full of majesty.

⁵ The voice of the LORD breaks the cedars,
  Yes, the LORD splinters the cedars of Lebanon.
⁶ He makes them also skip like a calf,
  Lebanon and Sirion like a young wild ox.

~ PROVERBS 10:22–25 ~

²² The blessing of the LORD makes *one* rich,
  And He adds no sorrow with it.

²³ To do evil *is* like sport to a fool,
  But a man of understanding has wisdom.
²⁴ The fear of the wicked will come upon him,
  And the desire of the righteous will be granted.
²⁵ When the whirlwind passes by, the wicked *is* no *more*,
  But the righteous *has* an everlasting foundation.

~ MARK 7:1–13 ~

Then the Pharisees and some of the scribes came together to Him, having come from Jerusalem. ² Now when they saw some of His disciples eat bread with defiled, that is, with unwashed hands, they found fault. ³ For the Pharisees and all the Jews do not eat unless they wash *their* hands in a special way, holding the tradition of the elders. ⁴ *When they come* from the marketplace, they do not eat unless they wash. And there are many other things which they have received and hold, *like* the washing of cups, pitchers, copper vessels, and couches.

⁵ Then the Pharisees and scribes asked Him, "Why do Your disciples not walk according to the tradition of the elders, but eat bread with unwashed hands?"

⁶ He answered and said to them, "Well did Isaiah prophesy of you hypocrites, as it is written:

  'This people honors Me with their lips,
    But their heart is far from Me.

7 And in vain they worship Me,
Teaching as doctrines the
    commandments of men.'

8 For laying aside the commandment of God, you hold the tradition of men—the washing of pitchers and cups, and many other such things you do."

9 He said to them, "*All too* well you reject the commandment of God, that you may keep your tradition. 10 For Moses said,

'Honor your father and your mother'; and, 'He who curses father or mother, let him be put to death.' 11 But you say, 'If a man says to his father or mother, "Whatever profit you might have received from me *is* Corban"—' (that is, a gift *to God*), 12 then you no longer let him do anything for his father or his mother, 13 making the word of God of no effect through your tradition which you have handed down. And many such things you do."

∽ NUMBERS 1:1—2:34 ∽

Now the LORD spoke to Moses in the Wilderness of Sinai, in the tabernacle of meeting, on the first *day* of the second month, in the second year after they had come out of the land of Egypt, saying: 2 "Take a census of all the congregation of the children of Israel, by their families, by their fathers' houses, according to the number of names, every male individually, 3 from twenty years old and above—all who *are able to* go to war in Israel. You and Aaron shall number them by their armies. 4 And with you there shall be a man from every tribe, each one the head of his father's house.

5 "These are the names of the men who shall stand with you: from Reuben, Elizur the son of Shedeur; 6 from Simeon, Shelumiel the son of Zurishaddai; 7 from Judah, Nahshon the son of Amminadab; 8 from Issachar, Nethanel the son of Zuar; 9 from Zebulun, Eliab the son of Helon; 10 from the sons of Joseph: from Ephraim, Elishama the son of Ammihud; from Manasseh, Gamaliel the son of Pedahzur; 11 from Benjamin, Abidan the son of Gideoni; 12 from Dan, Ahiezer the son of Ammishaddai; 13 from Asher, Pagiel the son of Ocran; 14 from Gad, Eliasaph the son of Deuel; 15 from Naphtali, Ahira the son of Enan." 16 These *were* chosen from the congregation, leaders of their fathers' tribes, heads of the divisions in Israel.

17 Then Moses and Aaron took these men who had been mentioned by name, 18 and they assembled all the congregation together on the first *day* of the second month; and they recited their ancestry by families, by their fathers' houses, according to the number of names, from twenty years old and above, each one individually. 19 As the LORD commanded Moses, so he numbered them in the Wilderness of Sinai.

20 Now the children of Reuben, Israel's oldest son, their genealogies by their families, by their fathers' house, according to the number of names, every male individually, from twenty years old and above, all who *were able to* go to war: 21 those who were numbered of the tribe of Reuben *were* forty-six thousand five hundred.

22 From the children of Simeon, their genealogies by their families, by their fathers' house, of those who were numbered, according to the number of names, every male individually, from twenty years old and above, all who *were able to* go to war: 23 those who were numbered of the tribe of Simeon *were* fifty-nine thousand three hundred.

24 From the children of Gad, their genealogies by their families, by their fathers' house, according to the number of names, from twenty years old and above, all who *were able to* go to war: 25 those who were numbered of the tribe of Gad *were* forty-five thousand six hundred and fifty.

26 From the children of Judah, their genealogies by their families, by their fathers' house, according to the number of names, from twenty years old and above, all who *were able to* go to war: 27 those

who were numbered of the tribe of Judah *were* seventy-four thousand six hundred.

28 From the children of Issachar, their genealogies by their families, by their fathers' house, according to the number of names, from twenty years old and above, all who *were able to* go to war: 29 those who were numbered of the tribe of Issachar *were* fifty-four thousand four hundred.

30 From the children of Zebulun, their genealogies by their families, by their fathers' house, according to the number of names, from twenty years old and above, all who *were able to* go to war: 31 those who were numbered of the tribe of Zebulun *were* fifty-seven thousand four hundred.

32 From the sons of Joseph, the children of Ephraim, their genealogies by their families, by their fathers' house, according to the number of names, from twenty years old and above, all who *were able to* go to war: 33 those who were numbered of the tribe of Ephraim *were* forty thousand five hundred.

34 From the children of Manasseh, their genealogies by their families, by their fathers' house, according to the number of names, from twenty years old and above, all who *were able to* go to war: 35 those who were numbered of the tribe of Manasseh *were* thirty-two thousand two hundred.

36 From the children of Benjamin, their genealogies by their families, by their fathers' house, according to the number of names, from twenty years old and above, all who *were able to* go to war: 37 those who were numbered of the tribe of Benjamin *were* thirty-five thousand four hundred.

38 From the children of Dan, their genealogies by their families, by their fathers' house, according to the number of names, from twenty years old and above, all who *were able to* go to war: 39 those who were numbered of the tribe of Dan *were* sixty-two thousand seven hundred.

40 From the children of Asher, their genealogies by their families, by their fathers' house, according to the number of names, from twenty years old and above, all who *were able to* go to war: 41 those who were numbered of the tribe of Asher *were* forty-one thousand five hundred.

42 From the children of Naphtali, their genealogies by their families, by their fathers' house, according to the number of names, from twenty years old and above, all who *were able to* go to war: 43 those who were numbered of the tribe of Naphtali *were* fifty-three thousand four hundred.

44 These are the ones who were numbered, whom Moses and Aaron numbered, with the leaders of Israel, twelve men, each one representing his father's house. 45 So all who were numbered of the children of Israel, by their fathers' houses, from twenty years old and above, all who *were able to* go to war in Israel— 46 all who were numbered were six hundred and three thousand five hundred and fifty.

47 But the Levites were not numbered among them by their fathers' tribe; 48 for the LORD had spoken to Moses, saying: 49 "Only the tribe of Levi you shall not number, nor take a census of them among the children of Israel; 50 but you shall appoint the Levites over the tabernacle of the Testimony, over all its furnishings, and over all things that belong to it; they shall carry the tabernacle and all its furnishings; they shall attend to it and camp around the tabernacle. 51 And when the tabernacle is to go forward, the Levites shall take it down; and when the tabernacle is to be set up, the Levites shall set it up. The outsider who comes near shall be put to death. 52 The children of Israel shall pitch their tents, everyone by his own camp, everyone by his own standard, according to their armies; 53 but the Levites shall camp around the tabernacle of the Testimony, that there may be no wrath on the congregation of the children of Israel; and the Levites shall keep charge of the tabernacle of the Testimony."

54 Thus the children of Israel did; according to all that the LORD commanded Moses, so they did.

2 And the LORD spoke to Moses and Aaron, saying: 2 "Everyone of the children of Israel shall camp by his own standard, beside the emblems of his father's house; they shall camp some distance from the

From Catching Footballs to Flipping Burgers

In 1961, Jerry Richardson faced an important decision. As a wide receiver for the Baltimore Colts, he had a job that was considered glamorous and secure. But when the raise he had requested was turned down, he felt the time had come to take a risk and do what he had always wanted to do: He would start his own business.

Richardson and his family moved back to South Carolina, where an old college buddy invited him to buy into a hamburger stand. Richardson took the plunge and bought Hardee's first franchise. He went from catching footballs to flipping hamburgers twelve hours a day. After hours, he scrubbed stoves and mopped floors. His reward? $417 a month. Some would have thought, *It's time to punt.*

Tired and frustrated as he was, Richardson refused to give up. He employed the same discipline he had used on the football field to focus on making his restaurant more efficient, his employees the friendliest in town, and his prices affordable. Before long, his business boomed.

Today, Richardson heads one of the largest food-service companies in the United States with $3.7 billion a year in sales and owns a NFL team!

God gives us the dreams and desires in our hearts. He will help us achieve them, but we must still apply discipline and diligence to get there. When it looks like you're not getting anywhere, turn up the heat and keep going. Hard work gets results!

tabernacle of meeting. ³ On the east side, toward the rising of the sun, those of the standard of the forces with Judah shall camp according to their armies; and Nahshon the son of Amminadab *shall be* the leader of the children of Judah." ⁴ And his army was numbered at seventy-four thousand six hundred.

⁵ "Those who camp next to him *shall be* the tribe of Issachar, and Nethanel the son of Zuar *shall be* the leader of the children of Issachar." ⁶ And his army was numbered at fifty-four thousand four hundred.

⁷ "Then *comes* the tribe of Zebulun, and Eliab the son of Helon *shall be* the leader of the children of Zebulun." ⁸ And his army was numbered at fifty-seven thousand four hundred. ⁹ "All who were numbered according to their armies of the forces with Judah, one hundred and eighty-six thousand four hundred—these shall break camp first.

¹⁰ "On the south side *shall be* the standard of the forces with Reuben according to their armies, and the leader of the children of Reuben *shall be* Elizur the son of Shedeur." ¹¹ And his army was numbered at forty-six thousand five hundred.

¹² "Those who camp next to him *shall be* the tribe of Simeon, and the leader of the children of Simeon *shall be* Shelumiel the son of Zurishaddai." ¹³ And his army was numbered at fifty-nine thousand three hundred.

¹⁴ "Then *comes* the tribe of Gad, and the leader of the children of Gad *shall be* Eliasaph the son of Reuel." ¹⁵ And his army was numbered at forty-five thousand six hundred and fifty. ¹⁶ "All who were numbered according to their armies of the forces with Reuben, one hundred and fifty-one thousand four hundred and fifty—they shall be the second to break camp.

¹⁷ "And the tabernacle of meeting shall move out with the camp of the Levites in the middle of the camps; as they camp, so they shall move out, everyone in his place, by their standards.

¹⁸ "On the west side *shall be* the standard of the forces with Ephraim according to their armies, and the leader of the children of Ephraim *shall be* Elishama the son of Ammihud." ¹⁹ And

his army was numbered at forty thousand five hundred.

²⁰ "Next to him *comes* the tribe of Manasseh, and the leader of the children of Manasseh *shall be* Gamaliel the son of Pedahzur." ²¹ And his army was numbered at thirty-two thousand two hundred.

²² "Then *comes* the tribe of Benjamin, and the leader of the children of Benjamin *shall be* Abidan the son of Gideoni." ²³ And his army was numbered at thirty-five thousand four hundred. ²⁴ "All who were numbered according to their armies of the forces with Ephraim, one hundred and eight thousand one hundred—they shall be the third to break camp.

²⁵ "The standard of the forces with Dan *shall be* on the north side according to their armies, and the leader of the children of Dan *shall be* Ahiezer the son of Ammishaddai." ²⁶ And his army was numbered at sixty-two thousand seven hundred.

²⁷ "Those who camp next to him *shall be* the tribe of Asher, and the leader of the children of Asher *shall be* Pagiel the son of Ocran." ²⁸ And his army was numbered at forty-one thousand five hundred.

²⁹ "Then *comes* the tribe of Naphtali, and the leader of the children of Naphtali *shall be* Ahira the son of Enan." ³⁰ And his army was numbered at fifty-three thousand four hundred. ³¹ "All who were numbered of the forces with Dan, one hundred and fifty-seven thousand six hundred—they shall break camp last, with their standards."

³² These *are* the ones who were numbered of the children of Israel by their fathers' houses. All who were numbered according to their armies of the forces *were* six hundred and three thousand five hundred and fifty. ³³ But the Levites were not numbered among the children of Israel, just as the LORD commanded Moses.

³⁴ Thus the children of Israel did according to all that the LORD commanded Moses; so they camped by their standards and so they broke camp, each one by his family, according to their fathers' houses.

~ PSALM 29:7–11 ~

⁷   The voice of the LORD divides the
      flames of fire.

8 The voice of the LORD shakes the
    wilderness;
    The LORD shakes the Wilderness of
    Kadesh.
9 The voice of the LORD makes the
    deer give birth,
    And strips the forests bare;
    And in His temple everyone says,
    "Glory!"

10 The LORD sat *enthroned* at the
    Flood,
    And the LORD sits as King forever.
11 The LORD will give strength to His
    people;
    The LORD will bless His people with
    peace.

∼ PROVERBS 10:26–29 ∼

26 As vinegar to the teeth and smoke to
    the eyes,
    So *is* the lazy *man* to those who send
    him.

27 The fear of the LORD prolongs days,
    But the years of the wicked will be
    shortened.
28 The hope of the righteous *will be*
    gladness,
    But the expectation of the wicked
    will perish.
29 The way of the LORD *is* strength for
    the upright,
    But destruction *will come* to the
    workers of iniquity.

∼ MARK 7:14–37 ∼

When He had called all the multitude to
Himself, He said to them, "Hear Me,
everyone, and understand: 15 There is
nothing that enters a man from outside
which can defile him; but the things which
come out of him, those are the things that
defile a man. 16 If anyone has ears to hear,
let him hear!"

17 When He had entered a house away
from the crowd, His disciples asked Him
concerning the parable. 18 So He said to
them, "Are you thus without understanding
also? Do you not perceive that
whatever enters a man from outside cannot
defile him, 19 because it does not enter

his heart but his stomach, and is eliminated,
thus purifying all foods?" 20 And
He said, "What comes out of a man, that
defiles a man. 21 For from within, out of
the heart of men, proceed evil thoughts,
adulteries, fornications, murders, 22 thefts,
covetousness, wickedness, deceit, lewdness,
an evil eye, blasphemy, pride,
foolishness. 23 All these evil things come
from within and defile a man."

24 From there He arose and went to the
region of Tyre and Sidon. And He entered
a house and wanted no one to know *it,*
but He could not be hidden. 25 For a
woman whose young daughter had an
unclean spirit heard about Him, and she
came and fell at His feet. 26 The woman
was a Greek, a Syro-Phoenician by birth,
and she kept asking Him to cast the demon
out of her daughter. 27 But Jesus said
to her, "Let the children be filled first, for
it is not good to take the children's bread
and throw *it* to the little dogs."

28 And she answered and said to Him,
"Yes, Lord, yet even the little dogs under
the table eat from the children's crumbs."

29 Then He said to her, "For this saying
go your way; the demon has gone out of
your daughter."

30 And when she had come to her house,
she found the demon gone out, and her
daughter lying on the bed.

31 Again, departing from the region of
Tyre and Sidon, He came through the
midst of the region of Decapolis to
the Sea of Galilee. 32 Then they brought
to Him one who was deaf and had an impediment
in his speech, and they begged
Him to put His hand on him. 33 And He
took him aside from the multitude, and
put His fingers in his ears, and He spat
and touched his tongue. 34 Then, looking
up to heaven, He sighed, and said to him,
"Ephphatha," that is, "Be opened."

35 Immediately his ears were opened,
and the impediment of his tongue was
loosed, and he spoke plainly. 36 Then He
commanded them that they should tell no
one; but the more He commanded them,
the more widely they proclaimed *it.* 37 And
they were astonished beyond measure,
saying, "He has done all things well. He
makes both the deaf to hear and the mute
to speak."

∼ NUMBERS 3:1—4:49 ∼

Now these *are* the records of Aaron and Moses when the LORD spoke with Moses on Mount Sinai. ² And these *are* the names of the sons of Aaron: Nadab, the firstborn, and Abihu, Eleazar, and Ithamar. ³ These *are* the names of the sons of Aaron, the anointed priests, whom he consecrated to minister as priests. ⁴ Nadab and Abihu had died before the LORD when they offered profane fire before the LORD in the Wilderness of Sinai; and they had no children. So Eleazar and Ithamar ministered as priests in the presence of Aaron their father.

⁵ And the LORD spoke to Moses, saying: ⁶ "Bring the tribe of Levi near, and present them before Aaron the priest, that they may serve him. ⁷ And they shall attend to his needs and the needs of the whole congregation before the tabernacle of meeting, to do the work of the tabernacle. ⁸ Also they shall attend to all the furnishings of the tabernacle of meeting, and to the needs of the children of Israel, to do the work of the tabernacle. ⁹ And you shall give the Levites to Aaron and his sons; they *are* given entirely to him from among the children of Israel. ¹⁰ So you shall appoint Aaron and his sons, and they shall attend to their priesthood; but the outsider who comes near shall be put to death."

¹¹ Then the LORD spoke to Moses, saying: ¹² "Now behold, I Myself have taken the Levites from among the children of Israel instead of every firstborn who opens the womb among the children of Israel. Therefore the Levites shall be Mine, ¹³ because all the firstborn *are* Mine. On the day that I struck all the firstborn in the land of Egypt, I sanctified to Myself all the firstborn in Israel, both man and beast. They shall be Mine: I *am* the LORD."

¹⁴ Then the LORD spoke to Moses in the Wilderness of Sinai, saying: ¹⁵ "Number the children of Levi by their fathers' houses, by their families; you shall number every male from a month old and above."

¹⁶ So Moses numbered them according to the word of the LORD, as he was commanded. ¹⁷ These were the sons of Levi by their names: Gershon, Kohath, and Merari. ¹⁸ And these *are* the names of the sons of Gershon by their families: Libni and Shimei. ¹⁹ And the sons of Kohath by their families: Amram, Izehar, Hebron, and Uzziel. ²⁰ And the sons of Merari by their families: Mahli and Mushi. These *are* the families of the Levites by their fathers' houses.

²¹ From Gershon *came* the family of the Libnites and the family of the Shimites; these *were* the families of the Gershonites. ²² Those who were numbered, according to the number of all the males from a month old and above—of those who were numbered *there were* seven thousand five hundred. ²³ The families of the Gershonites were to camp behind the tabernacle westward. ²⁴ And the leader of the father's house of the Gershonites *was* Eliasaph the son of Lael. ²⁵ The duties of the children of Gershon in the tabernacle of meeting *included* the tabernacle, the tent with its covering, the screen for the door of the tabernacle of meeting, ²⁶ the screen for the door of the court, the hangings of the court which *are* around the tabernacle and the altar, and their cords, according to all the work relating to them.

²⁷ From Kohath *came* the family of the Amramites, the family of the Izharites, the family of the Hebronites, and the family of the Uzzielites; these *were* the families of the Kohathites. ²⁸ According to the number of all the males, from a month old and above, *there were* eight thousand six hundred keeping charge of the sanctuary. ²⁹ The families of the children of Kohath were to camp on the south side of the tabernacle. ³⁰ And the leader of the fathers' house of the families of the Kohathites *was* Elizaphan the son of Uzziel. ³¹ Their duty *included* the ark, the table, the lampstand, the altars, the utensils of the sanctuary with which they ministered, the screen, and all the work relating to them.

³² And Eleazar the son of Aaron the priest *was to be* chief over the leaders of

Forgiveness Heals

In his book, *With Justice for All*, John Perkins tells how God gave him a real compassion for white people.

The incident began when a van load of students who had participated in a civil rights march were pulled over by a highway patrolman and taken to jail. The driver of a second van called Perkins, who went to post bail for the students. No sooner had Perkins arrived at the jailhouse than he was beaten by the sheriff and tortured by several other officers.

He later testified in court that, although he was unconscious most of the night, he had ample opportunity to see the faces of those who had beaten him. They were faces "twisted with hate," the "victims of their own racism." Rather than hate them back, though, Perkins felt pity for them. He prayed, "God . . . I really want to preach a gospel that will heal these people, too."

In the months that followed, God brought the faces of numerous white people to Perkins' mind, and one by one, he forgave them. Forgiveness healed the wounds that had long kept him from loving whites. He wrote, "How sweet God's forgiveness and healing was!"

Are you at odds with someone today? Pray for that person, so that you *both* might be healed.

the Levites, *with* oversight of those who kept charge of the sanctuary.

³³ From Merari *came* the family of the Mahlites and the family of the Mushites; these *were* the families of Merari. ³⁴ And those who were numbered, according to the number of all the males from a month old and above, *were* six thousand two hundred. ³⁵ The leader of the fathers' house of the families of Merari *was* Zuriel the son of Abihail. These *were* to camp on the north side of the tabernacle. ³⁶ And the appointed duty of the children of Merari *included* the boards of the tabernacle, its bars, its pillars, its sockets, its utensils, all the work relating to them, ³⁷ and the pillars of the court all around, with their sockets, their pegs, and their cords.

³⁸ Moreover those who were to camp before the tabernacle on the east, before the tabernacle of meeting, *were* Moses, Aaron, and his sons, keeping charge of the sanctuary, to meet the needs of the children of Israel; but the outsider who came near was to be put to death. ³⁹ All who were numbered of the Levites, whom Moses and Aaron numbered at the commandment of the LORD, by their families, all the males from a month old and above, *were* twenty-two thousand.

⁴⁰ Then the LORD said to Moses: "Number all the firstborn males of the children of Israel from a month old and above, and take the number of their names. ⁴¹ And you shall take the Levites for Me— I *am* the LORD—instead of all the firstborn among the children of Israel, and the livestock of the Levites instead of all the firstborn among the livestock of the children of Israel." ⁴² So Moses numbered all the firstborn among the children of Israel, as the LORD commanded him. ⁴³ And all the firstborn males, according to the number of names from a month old and above, of those who were numbered of them, were twenty-two thousand two hundred and seventy-three.

⁴⁴ Then the LORD spoke to Moses, saying: ⁴⁵ "Take the Levites instead of all the firstborn among the children of Israel, and the livestock of the Levites instead of their livestock. The Levites shall be Mine: I *am* the LORD. ⁴⁶ And for the redemption of the two hundred and seventy-three of the firstborn of the children of Israel, who are more than the number of the Levites, ⁴⁷ you shall take five shekels for each one individually; you shall take *them* in the currency of the shekel of the sanctuary, the shekel of twenty gerahs. ⁴⁸ And you shall give the money, with which the excess number of them is redeemed, to Aaron and his sons."

⁴⁹ So Moses took the redemption money from those who were over and above those who were redeemed by the Levites. ⁵⁰ From the firstborn of the children of Israel he took the money, one thousand three hundred and sixty-five *shekels,* according to the shekel of the sanctuary. ⁵¹ And Moses gave their redemption money to Aaron and his sons, according to the word of the LORD, as the LORD commanded Moses.

4 Then the LORD spoke to Moses and Aaron, saying: ² "Take a census of the sons of Kohath from among the children of Levi, by their families, by their fathers' house, ³ from thirty years old and above, even to fifty years old, all who enter the service to do the work in the tabernacle of meeting.

⁴ "This *is* the service of the sons of Kohath in the tabernacle of meeting, *relating to* the most holy things: ⁵ When the camp prepares to journey, Aaron and his sons shall come, and they shall take down the covering veil and cover the ark of the Testimony with it. ⁶ Then they shall put on it a covering of badger skins, and spread over *that* a cloth entirely of blue; and they shall insert its poles.

⁷ "On the table of showbread they shall spread a blue cloth, and put on it the dishes, the pans, the bowls, and the pitchers for pouring; and the showbread shall be on it. ⁸ They shall spread over them a scarlet cloth, and cover the same with a covering of badger skins; and they shall insert its poles. ⁹ And they shall take a blue cloth and cover the lampstand of the light, with its lamps, its wick-trimmers, its trays, and all its oil vessels, with which they service it. ¹⁰ Then they shall put it with all its utensils in a covering of badger skins, and put *it* on a carrying beam.

¹¹ "Over the golden altar they shall spread a blue cloth, and cover it with a

covering of badger skins; and they shall insert its poles. ¹² Then they shall take all the utensils of service with which they minister in the sanctuary, put *them* in a blue cloth, cover them with a covering of badger skins, and put *them* on a carrying beam. ¹³ Also they shall take away the ashes from the altar, and spread a purple cloth over it. ¹⁴ They shall put on it all its implements with which they minister there—the firepans, the forks, the shovels, the basins, and all the utensils of the altar—and they shall spread on it a covering of badger skins, and insert its poles. ¹⁵ And when Aaron and his sons have finished covering the sanctuary and all the furnishings of the sanctuary, when the camp is set to go, then the sons of Kohath shall come to carry *them;* but they shall not touch any holy thing, lest they die.

"These *are* the things in the tabernacle of meeting which the sons of Kohath are to carry.

¹⁶ "The appointed duty of Eleazar the son of Aaron the priest *is* the oil for the light, the sweet incense, the daily grain offering, the anointing oil, the oversight of all the tabernacle, of all that *is* in it, with the sanctuary and its furnishings."

¹⁷ Then the LORD spoke to Moses and Aaron, saying: ¹⁸ "Do not cut off the tribe of the families of the Kohathites from among the Levites; ¹⁹ but do this in regard to them, that they may live and not die when they approach the most holy things: Aaron and his sons shall go in and appoint each of them to his service and his task. ²⁰ But they shall not go in to watch while the holy things are being covered, lest they die."

²¹ Then the LORD spoke to Moses, saying: ²² "Also take a census of the sons of Gershon, by their fathers' house, by their families. ²³ From thirty years old and above, even to fifty years old, you shall number them, all who enter to perform the service, to do the work in the tabernacle of meeting. ²⁴ This *is* the service of the families of the Gershonites, in serving and carrying: ²⁵ They shall carry the curtains of the tabernacle and the tabernacle of meeting *with* its covering, the covering of badger skins that *is* on it, the screen for the door of the tabernacle of meeting, ²⁶ the screen for the door of the gate of the court, the hangings of the court which *are* around the tabernacle and altar, and their cords, all the furnishings for their service and all that is made for these things: so shall they serve.

²⁷ "Aaron and his sons shall assign all the service of the sons of the Gershonites, all their tasks and all their service. And you shall appoint to them all their tasks as their duty. ²⁸ This *is* the service of the families of the sons of Gershon in the tabernacle of meeting. And their duties *shall be* under the authority of Ithamar the son of Aaron the priest.

²⁹ "*As for* the sons of Merari, you shall number them by their families and by their fathers' house. ³⁰ From thirty years old and above, even to fifty years old, you shall number them, everyone who enters the service to do the work of the tabernacle of meeting. ³¹ And this *is* what they must carry as all their service for the tabernacle of meeting: the boards of the tabernacle, its bars, its pillars, its sockets, ³² and the pillars around the court with their sockets, pegs, and cords, with all their furnishings and all their service; and you shall assign *to each man* by name the items he must carry. ³³ This *is* the service of the families of the sons of Merari, as all their service for the tabernacle of meeting, under the authority of Ithamar the son of Aaron the priest."

³⁴ And Moses, Aaron, and the leaders of the congregation numbered the sons of the Kohathites by their families and by their fathers' house, ³⁵ from thirty years old and above, even to fifty years old, everyone who entered the service for work in the tabernacle of meeting; ³⁶ and those who were numbered by their families were two thousand seven hundred and fifty. ³⁷ These *were* the ones who were numbered of the families of the Kohathites, all who might serve in the tabernacle of meeting, whom Moses and Aaron numbered according to the commandment of the LORD by the hand of Moses.

³⁸ And those who were numbered of the sons of Gershon, by their families and by their fathers' house, ³⁹ from thirty years old and above, even to fifty years old, everyone who entered the service for work in the tabernacle of meeting—

⁴⁰ those who were numbered by their families, by their fathers' house, were two thousand six hundred and thirty. ⁴¹ These *are* the ones who were numbered of the families of the sons of Gershon, of all who might serve in the tabernacle of meeting, whom Moses and Aaron numbered according to the commandment of the LORD.

⁴² Those of the families of the sons of Merari who were numbered, by their families, by their fathers' house, ⁴³ from thirty years old and above, even to fifty years old, everyone who entered the service for work in the tabernacle of meeting— ⁴⁴ those who were numbered by their families were three thousand two hundred. ⁴⁵ These *are* the ones who were numbered of the families of the sons of Merari, whom Moses and Aaron numbered according to the word of the LORD by the hand of Moses.

⁴⁶ All who were numbered of the Levites, whom Moses, Aaron, and the leaders of Israel numbered, by their families and by their fathers' houses, ⁴⁷ from thirty years old and above, even to fifty years old, everyone who came to do the work of service and the work of bearing burdens in the tabernacle of meeting— ⁴⁸ those who were numbered were eight thousand five hundred and eighty.

⁴⁹ According to the commandment of the LORD they were numbered by the hand of Moses, each according to his service and according to his task; thus were they numbered by him, as the LORD commanded Moses.

~ PSALM 30:1–7 ~

¹ I will extol You, O LORD, for You have lifted me up,
And have not let my foes rejoice over me.
² O LORD my God, I cried out to You,
And You healed me.
³ O LORD, You brought my soul up from the grave;
You have kept me alive, that I should not go down to the pit.

⁴ Sing praise to the LORD, you saints of His,
And give thanks at the remembrance of His holy name.
⁵ For His anger *is but for* a moment,
His favor *is for* life;
Weeping may endure for a night,
But joy *comes* in the morning.

⁶ Now in my prosperity I said,
"I shall never be moved."
⁷ LORD, by Your favor You have made my mountain stand strong;
You hid Your face, *and* I was troubled.

~ PROVERBS 10:30–32 ~

³⁰ The righteous will never be removed,
But the wicked will not inhabit the earth.
³¹ The mouth of the righteous brings forth wisdom,
But the perverse tongue will be cut out.
³² The lips of the righteous know what is acceptable,
But the mouth of the wicked *what is* perverse.

~ MARK 8:1–21 ~

In those days, the multitude being very great and having nothing to eat, Jesus called His disciples *to Him* and said to them, ² "I have compassion on the multitude, because they have now continued with Me three days and have nothing to eat. ³ And if I send them away hungry to their own houses, they will faint on the way; for some of them have come from afar."

⁴ Then His disciples answered Him, "How can one satisfy these people with bread here in the wilderness?"

⁵ He asked them, "How many loaves do you have?"

And they said, "Seven."

⁶ So He commanded the multitude to sit down on the ground. And He took the seven loaves and gave thanks, broke *them* and gave *them* to His disciples to set before *them;* and they set *them* before the multitude. ⁷ They also had a few small fish;

and having blessed them, He said to set them also before *them*. [8] So they ate and were filled, and they took up seven large baskets of leftover fragments. [9] Now those who had eaten were about four thousand. And He sent them away, [10] immediately got into the boat with His disciples, and came to the region of Dalmanutha.

[11] Then the Pharisees came out and began to dispute with Him, seeking from Him a sign from heaven, testing Him. [12] But He sighed deeply in His spirit, and said, "Why does this generation seek a sign? Assuredly, I say to you, no sign shall be given to this generation."

[13] And He left them, and getting into the boat again, departed to the other side. [14] Now the disciples had forgotten to take bread, and they did not have more than one loaf with them in the boat. [15] Then He charged them, saying, "Take heed, beware of the leaven of the Pharisees and the leaven of Herod."

[16] And they reasoned among themselves, saying, "It is because we have no bread."

[17] But Jesus, being aware of *it,* said to them, "Why do you reason because you have no bread? Do you not yet perceive nor understand? Is your heart still hardened? [18] Having eyes, do you not see? And having ears, do you not hear? And do you not remember? [19] When I broke the five loaves for the five thousand, how many baskets full of fragments did you take up?"

They said to Him, "Twelve."

[20] "Also, when I broke the seven for the four thousand, how many large baskets full of fragments did you take up?"

And they said, "Seven."

[21] So He said to them, "How *is it* you do not understand?"

~ Numbers 5:1—6:27 ~

And the LORD spoke to Moses, saying: [2] "Command the children of Israel that they put out of the camp every leper, everyone who has a discharge, and whoever becomes defiled by a corpse. [3] You shall put out both male and female; you shall put them outside the camp, that they may not defile their camps in the midst of which I dwell." [4] And the children of Israel did so, and put them outside the camp; as the LORD spoke to Moses, so the children of Israel did.

[5] Then the LORD spoke to Moses, saying, [6] "Speak to the children of Israel: 'When a man or woman commits any sin that men commit in unfaithfulness against the LORD, and that person is guilty, [7] then he shall confess the sin which he has committed. He shall make restitution for his trespass in full, plus one-fifth of it, and give *it* to the one he has wronged. [8] But if the man has no relative to whom restitution may be made for the wrong, the restitution for the wrong *must go* to the LORD for the priest, in addition to the ram of the atonement with which atonement is made for him. [9] Every offering of all the holy things of the children of Is-rael, which they bring to the priest, shall be his. [10] And every man's holy things shall be his; whatever any man gives the priest shall be his.' "

[11] And the LORD spoke to Moses, saying, [12] "Speak to the children of Israel, and say to them: 'If any man's wife goes astray and behaves unfaithfully toward him, [13] and a man lies with her carnally, and it is hidden from the eyes of her husband, and it is concealed that she has defiled herself, and *there was* no witness against her, nor was she caught— [14] if the spirit of jealousy comes upon him and he becomes jealous of his wife, who has defiled herself; or if the spirit of jealousy comes upon him and he becomes jealous of his wife, although she has not defiled herself— [15] then the man shall bring his wife to the priest. He shall bring the offering required for her, one-tenth of an ephah of barley meal; he shall pour no oil on it and put no frankincense on it, because it *is* a grain offering of jealousy, an offering for remembering, for bringing iniquity to remembrance.

[16] 'And the priest shall bring her near, and set her before the LORD. [17] The priest

shall take holy water in an earthen vessel, and take some of the dust that is on the floor of the tabernacle and put *it* into the water. ¹⁸ Then the priest shall stand the woman before the LORD, uncover the woman's head, and put the offering for remembering in her hands, which *is* the grain offering of jealousy. And the priest shall have in his hand the bitter water that brings a curse. ¹⁹ And the priest shall put her under oath, and say to the woman, "If no man has lain with you, and if you have not gone astray to uncleanness *while* under your husband's *authority*, be free from this bitter water that brings a curse. ²⁰ But if you have gone astray *while* under your husband's *authority*, and if you have defiled yourself and some man other than your husband has lain with you"— ²¹ then the priest shall put the woman under the oath of the curse, and he shall say to the woman—"the LORD make you a curse and an oath among your people, when the LORD makes your thigh rot and your belly swell; ²² and may this water that causes the curse go into your stomach, and make *your* belly swell and *your* thigh rot."

'Then the woman shall say, "Amen, so be it."

²³ 'Then the priest shall write these curses in a book, and he shall scrape *them* off into the bitter water. ²⁴ And he shall make the woman drink the bitter water that brings a curse, and the water that brings the curse shall enter her *to become* bitter. ²⁵ Then the priest shall take the grain offering of jealousy from the woman's hand, shall wave the offering before the LORD, and bring it to the altar; ²⁶ and the priest shall take a handful of the offering, as its memorial portion, burn *it* on the altar, and afterward make the woman drink the water. ²⁷ When he has made her drink the water, then it shall be, if she has defiled herself and behaved unfaithfully toward her husband, that the water that brings a curse will enter her *and become* bitter, and her belly will swell, her thigh will rot, and the woman will become a curse among her people. ²⁸ But if the woman has not defiled herself, and is clean, then she shall be free and may conceive children.

²⁹ 'This *is* the law of jealousy, when a wife, *while* under her husband's *author-*

ity, goes astray and defiles herself, ³⁰ or when the spirit of jealousy comes upon a man, and he becomes jealous of his wife; then he shall stand the woman before the LORD, and the priest shall execute all this law upon her. ³¹ Then the man shall be free from iniquity, but that woman shall bear her guilt.' "

6 Then the LORD spoke to Moses, saying, ² "Speak to the children of Israel, and say to them: 'When either a man or woman consecrates an offering to take the vow of a Nazirite, to separate himself to the LORD, ³ he shall separate himself from wine and *similar* drink; he shall drink neither vinegar made from wine nor vinegar made from *similar* drink; neither shall he drink any grape juice, nor eat fresh grapes or raisins. ⁴ All the days of his separation he shall eat nothing that is produced by the grapevine, from seed to skin.

⁵ 'All the days of the vow of his separation no razor shall come upon his head; until the days are fulfilled for which he separated himself to the LORD, he shall be holy. *Then* he shall let the locks of the hair of his head grow. ⁶ All the days that he separates himself to the LORD he shall not go near a dead body. ⁷ He shall not make himself unclean even for his father or his mother, for his brother or his sister, when they die, because his separation to God *is* on his head. ⁸ All the days of his separation he shall be holy to the LORD.

⁹ 'And if anyone dies very suddenly beside him, and he defiles his consecrated head, then he shall shave his head on the day of his cleansing; on the seventh day he shall shave it. ¹⁰ Then on the eighth day he shall bring two turtledoves or two young pigeons to the priest, to the door of the tabernacle of meeting; ¹¹ and the priest shall offer one as a sin offering and *the* other as a burnt offering, and make atonement for him, because he sinned in regard to the corpse; and he shall sanctify his head that same day. ¹² He shall consecrate to the LORD the days of his separation, and bring a male lamb in its first year as a trespass offering; but the former days shall be lost, because his separation was defiled.

¹³ 'Now this *is* the law of the Nazirite: When the days of his separation are

Scientific Selflessness

Everybody knows of Isaac Newton's famed encounter with a falling apple, and how he introduced the law of gravity and revolutionized the study of astronomy. But few know that if it weren't for Edmund Halley, the world may never have heard of Isaac Newton.

Halley challenged Newton to think through his original theories. He corrected Newton's mathematical errors and prepared geometrical figures to support his discoveries. It was Halley who coaxed the hesitant Newton to write his great work, *Mathematical Principles of Natural Philosophy*. And it was Halley who edited and supervised its publication. He even financed its printing, although Newton was wealthier and could better afford the cost.

Historians have called Halley's relationship with Newton one of the most selfless in science. Newton began almost immediately to reap the rewards of prominence; Halley received little credit. He did use the principles Newton developed to predict the orbit of a comet that would later bear his name, but since Halley's Comet only returns every seventy-six years, few hear his name. Still, Halley didn't care who received the credit as long as the cause of science was advanced. He was content to live without fame.

Sometimes the reward of what we are doing far outweighs any recognition we may or may not receive. Though no one else may see or hear of our efforts, the God Who sees what is done in secret, will reward us openly. And His rewards are always far better than any accolades of man.

fulfilled, he shall be brought to the door of the tabernacle of meeting. ¹⁴ And he shall present his offering to the LORD: one male lamb in its first year without blemish as a burnt offering, one ewe lamb in its first year without blemish as a sin offering, one ram without blemish as a peace offering, ¹⁵ a basket of unleavened bread, cakes of fine flour mixed with oil, unleavened wafers anointed with oil, and their grain offering with their drink offerings.

¹⁶ 'Then the priest shall bring *them* before the LORD and offer his sin offering and his burnt offering; ¹⁷ and he shall offer the ram as a sacrifice of a peace offering to the LORD, with the basket of unleavened bread; the priest shall also offer its grain offering and its drink offering. ¹⁸ Then the Nazirite shall shave his consecrated head *at* the door of the tabernacle of meeting, and shall take the hair from his consecrated head and put *it* on the fire which is under the sacrifice of the peace offering.

¹⁹ 'And the priest shall take the boiled shoulder of the ram, one unleavened cake from the basket, and one unleavened wafer, and put *them* upon the hands of the Nazirite after he has shaved his consecrated *hair,* ²⁰ and the priest shall wave them as a wave offering before the LORD; they *are* holy for the priest, together with the breast of the wave offering and the thigh of the heave offering. After that the Nazirite may drink wine.'

²¹ "This is the law of the Nazirite who vows to the LORD the offering for his separation, and besides that, whatever else his hand is able to provide; according to the vow which he takes, so he must do according to the law of his separation."

²² And the LORD spoke to Moses, saying: ²³ "Speak to Aaron and his sons, saying, 'This is the way you shall bless the children of Israel. Say to them:

²⁴ "The LORD bless you and keep you;
²⁵ The LORD make His face shine upon you,
And be gracious to you;
²⁶ The LORD lift up His countenance upon you,
And give you peace." '

²⁷ "So they shall put My name on the children of Israel, and I will bless them."

~ PSALM 30:8–12 ~

⁸ I cried out to You, O LORD;
And to the LORD I made supplication:
⁹ "What profit *is there* in my blood,
When I go down to the pit?
Will the dust praise You?
Will it declare Your truth?
¹⁰ Hear, O LORD, and have mercy on me;
LORD, be my helper!"

¹¹ You have turned for me my mourning into dancing;
You have put off my sackcloth and clothed me with gladness,
¹² To the end that *my* glory may sing praise to You and not be silent.
O LORD my God, I will give thanks to You forever.

~ PROVERBS 11:1–3 ~

¹ Dishonest scales *are* an abomination to the LORD,
But a just weight *is* His delight.

² When pride comes, then comes shame;
But with the humble *is* wisdom.

³ The integrity of the upright will guide them,
But the perversity of the unfaithful will destroy them.

~ MARK 8:22–38 ~

Then He came to Bethsaida; and they brought a blind man to Him, and begged Him to touch him. ²³ So He took the blind man by the hand and led him out of the town. And when He had spit on his eyes and put His hands on him, He asked him if he saw anything.

²⁴ And he looked up and said, "I see men like trees, walking."

²⁵ Then He put *His* hands on his eyes again and made him look up. And he was restored and saw everyone clearly. ²⁶ Then He sent him away to his house, saying,

"Neither go into the town, nor tell anyone in the town."

²⁷ Now Jesus and His disciples went out to the towns of Caesarea Philippi; and on the road He asked His disciples, saying to them, "Who do men say that I am?"

²⁸ So they answered, "John the Baptist; but some *say*, Elijah; and others, one of the prophets."

²⁹ He said to them, "But who do you say that I am?"

Peter answered and said to Him, "You are the Christ."

³⁰ Then He strictly warned them that they should tell no one about Him.

³¹ And He began to teach them that the Son of Man must suffer many things, and be rejected by the elders and chief priests and scribes, and be killed, and after three days rise again. ³² He spoke this word openly. Then Peter took Him aside and began to rebuke Him. ³³ But when He had turned around and looked at His disciples, He rebuked Peter, saying, "Get behind Me, Satan! For you are not mindful of the things of God, but the things of men."

³⁴ When He had called the people to *Himself*, with His disciples also, He said to them, "Whoever desires to come after Me, let him deny himself, and take up his cross, and follow Me. ³⁵ For whoever desires to save his life will lose it, but whoever loses his life for My sake and the gospel's will save it. ³⁶ For what will it profit a man if he gains the whole world, and loses his own soul? ³⁷ Or what will a man give in exchange for his soul? ³⁸ For whoever is ashamed of Me and My words in this adulterous and sinful generation, of him the Son of Man also will be ashamed when He comes in the glory of His Father with the holy angels."

READING 64 · MARCH 5

～ NUMBERS 7:1—8:26 ～

Now it came to pass, when Moses had finished setting up the tabernacle, that he anointed it and consecrated it and all its furnishings, and the altar and all its utensils; so he anointed them and consecrated them. ² Then the leaders of Israel, the heads of their fathers' houses, who *were* the leaders of the tribes and over those who were numbered, made an offering. ³ And they brought their offering before the LORD, six covered carts and twelve oxen, a cart for *every* two of the leaders, and for each one an ox; and they presented them before the tabernacle.

⁴ Then the LORD spoke to Moses, saying, ⁵ "Accept *these* from them, that they may be used in doing the work of the tabernacle of meeting; and you shall give them to the Levites, *to* every man according to his service." ⁶ So Moses took the carts and the oxen, and gave them to the Levites. ⁷ Two carts and four oxen he gave to the sons of Gershon, according to their service; ⁸ and four carts and eight oxen he gave to the sons of Merari, according to their service, under the authority of Ithamar the son of Aaron the priest. ⁹ But to the sons of Kohath he gave none, because theirs *was* the service of the holy things, *which* they carried on their shoulders.

¹⁰ Now the leaders offered the dedication *offering* for the altar when it was anointed; so the leaders offered their offering before the altar. ¹¹ For the LORD said to Moses, "They shall offer their offering, one leader each day, for the dedication of the altar."

¹² And the one who offered his offering on the first day *was* Nahshon the son of Amminadab, from the tribe of Judah. ¹³ His offering *was* one silver platter, the weight of which *was* one hundred and thirty *shekels,* and one silver bowl of seventy shekels, according to the shekel of the sanctuary, both of them full of fine flour mixed with oil as a grain offering; ¹⁴ one gold pan of ten *shekels,* full of incense; ¹⁵ one young bull, one ram, and one male lamb in its first year, as a burnt offering; ¹⁶ one kid of the goats as a sin offering; ¹⁷ and for the sacrifice of peace offerings: two oxen, five rams, five

male goats, and five male lambs in their first year. This *was* the offering of Nahshon the son of Amminadab.

[18] On the second day Nethanel the son of Zuar, leader of Issachar, presented *an offering.* [19] *For* his offering he offered one silver platter, the weight of which *was* one hundred and thirty *shekels,* and one silver bowl of seventy shekels, according to the shekel of the sanctuary, both of them full of fine flour mixed with oil as a grain offering; [20] one gold pan of ten *shekels,* full of incense; [21] one young bull, one ram, and one male lamb in its first year, as a burnt offering; [22] one kid of the goats as a sin offering; [23] and as the sacrifice of peace offerings: two oxen, five rams, five male goats, and five male lambs in their first year. This *was* the offering of Nethanel the son of Zuar.

[24] On the third day Eliab the son of Helon, leader of the children of Zebulun, *presented an offering.* [25] His offering *was* one silver platter, the weight of which *was* one hundred and thirty *shekels,* and one silver bowl of seventy shekels, according to the shekel of the sanctuary, both of them full of fine flour mixed with oil as a grain offering; [26] one gold pan of ten *shekels,* full of incense; [27] one young bull, one ram, and one male lamb in its first year, as a burnt offering; [28] one kid of the goats as a sin offering; [29] and for the sacrifice of peace offerings: two oxen, five rams, five male goats, and five male lambs in their first year. This *was* the offering of Eliab the son of Helon.

[30] On the fourth day Elizur the son of Shedeur, leader of the children of Reuben, *presented an offering.* [31] His offering *was* one silver platter, the weight of which *was* one hundred and thirty *shekels,* and one silver bowl of seventy shekels, according to the shekel of the sanctuary, both of them full of fine flour mixed with oil as a grain offering; [32] one gold pan of ten *shekels,* full of incense; [33] one young bull, one ram, and one male lamb in its first year, as a burnt offering; [34] one kid of the goats as a sin offering; [35] and as the sacrifice of peace offerings: two oxen, five rams, five male goats, and five male lambs in their first year. This *was* the offering of Elizur the son of Shedeur.

[36] On the fifth day Shelumiel the son of Zurishaddai, leader of the children of Simeon, *presented an offering.* [37] His offering *was* one silver platter, the weight of which *was* one hundred and thirty *shekels,* and one silver bowl of seventy shekels, according to the shekel of the sanctuary, both of them full of fine flour mixed with oil as a grain offering; [38] one gold pan of ten *shekels,* full of incense; [39] one young bull, one ram, and one male lamb in its first year, as a burnt offering; [40] one kid of the goats as a sin offering; [41] and as the sacrifice of peace offerings: two oxen, five rams, five male goats, and five male lambs in their first year. This *was* the offering of Shelumiel the son of Zurishaddai.

[42] On the sixth day Eliasaph the son of Deuel, leader of the children of Gad, *presented an offering.* [43] His offering *was* one silver platter, the weight of which *was* one hundred and thirty *shekels,* and one silver bowl of seventy shekels, according to the shekel of the sanctuary, both of them full of fine flour mixed with oil as a grain offering; [44] one gold pan of ten *shekels,* full of incense; [45] one young bull, one ram, and one male lamb in its first year, as a burnt offering; [46] one kid of the goats as a sin offering; [47] and as the sacrifice of peace offerings: two oxen, five rams, five male goats, and five male lambs in their first year. This *was* the offering of Eliasaph the son of Deuel.

[48] On the seventh day Elishama the son of Ammihud, leader of the children of Ephraim, *presented an offering.* [49] His offering *was* one silver platter, the weight of which *was* one hundred and thirty *shekels,* and one silver bowl of seventy shekels, according to the shekel of the sanctuary, both of them full of fine flour mixed with oil as a grain offering; [50] one gold pan of ten *shekels,* full of incense; [51] one young bull, one ram, and one male lamb in its first year, as a burnt offering; [52] one kid of the goats as a sin offering; [53] and as the sacrifice of peace offerings: two oxen, five rams, five male goats, and five male lambs in their first year. This *was* the offering of Elishama the son of Ammihud.

[54] On the eighth day Gamaliel the son of Pedahzur, leader of the children of Manasseh, *presented an offering.* [55] His

Good Advice

A woman once accepted a job in a field for which she had a college degree and past experience. She had community contacts, she enjoyed this type of work, and her family could use the extra income — the job seemed to be a perfect fit! Almost immediately however, problems emerged. As the weeks wore on, she wore out. Being a die-hard, she held on, trying to force the job to work for her, and to be successful in the job. "God, please show me what I should do!" she prayed.

One cold winter day, her phone rang and a young woman said, "You probably don't remember me, but I was in a seminar group you taught about a year ago. Could I come talk to you today?" Although her schedule was full, she made an appointment with the young woman. She discovered that the young woman was in despair about her job, and was yearning to enter a field where she could express her strengths and gifts. The woman urged her to do what was right for her, to move away from what had kept her imprisoned, to choose excellence and quality, and to recognize that her gifts were from God.

It was only after the young woman left that the woman realized, "That advice I gave was for my benefit!"

Don't be surprised at how God may answer your prayers today. It may even come through something you say to help someone else.

> Immediately the father of the child cried out and said with tears, "Lord, I believe; help my unbelief!"
>
> *Mark 9:24*

offering *was* one silver platter, the weight of which *was* one hundred and thirty *shekels,* and one silver bowl of seventy shekels, according to the shekel of the sanctuary, both of them full of fine flour mixed with oil as a grain offering; [56] one gold pan of ten *shekels,* full of incense; [57] one young bull, one ram, and one male lamb in its first year, as a burnt offering; [58] one kid of the goats as a sin offering; [59] and as the sacrifice of peace offerings: two oxen, five rams, five male goats, and five male lambs in their first year. This *was* the offering of Gamaliel the son of Pedahzur.

[60] On the ninth day Abidan the son of Gideoni, leader of the children of Benjamin, *presented an offering.* [61] His offering *was* one silver platter, the weight of which *was* one hundred and thirty *shekels,* and one silver bowl of seventy shekels, according to the shekel of the sanctuary, both of them full of fine flour mixed with oil as a grain offering; [62] one gold pan of ten *shekels,* full of incense; [63] one young bull, one ram, and one male lamb in its first year, as a burnt offering; [64] one kid of the goats as a sin offering; [65] and as the sacrifice of peace offerings: two oxen, five rams, five male goats, and five male lambs in their first year. This *was* the offering of Abidan the son of Gideoni.

[66] On the tenth day Ahiezer the son of Ammishaddai, leader of the children of Dan, *presented an offering.* [67] His offering *was* one silver platter, the weight of which *was* one hundred and thirty *shekels,* and one silver bowl of seventy shekels, according to the shekel of the sanctuary, both of them full of fine flour mixed with oil as a grain offering; [68] one gold pan of ten *shekels,* full of incense; [69] one young bull, one ram, and one male lamb in its first year, as a burnt offering; [70] one kid of the goats as a sin offering; [71] and as the sacrifice of peace offerings: two oxen, five rams, five male goats, and five male lambs in their first year. This *was* the offering of Ahiezer the son of Ammishaddai.

[72] On the eleventh day Pagiel the son of Ocran, leader of the children of Asher, *presented an offering.* [73] His offering *was* one silver platter, the weight of which *was* one hundred and thirty *shekels,* and one silver bowl of seventy shekels, according to the shekel of the sanctuary, both of

them full of fine flour mixed with oil as a grain offering; [74] one gold pan of ten *shekels,* full of incense; [75] one young bull, one ram, and one male lamb in its first year, as a burnt offering; [76] one kid of the goats as a sin offering; [77] and as the sacrifice of peace offerings: two oxen, five rams, five male goats, and five male lambs in their first year. This *was* the offering of Pagiel the son of Ocran.

[78] On the twelfth day Ahira the son of Enan, leader of the children of Naphtali, *presented an offering.* [79] His offering *was* one silver platter, the weight of which *was* one hundred and thirty *shekels,* and one silver bowl of seventy shekels, according to the shekel of the sanctuary, both of them full of fine flour mixed with oil as a grain offering; [80] one gold pan of ten *shekels,* full of incense; [81] one young bull, one ram, and one male lamb in its first year, as a burnt offering; [82] one kid of the goats as a sin offering; [83] and as the sacrifice of peace offerings: two oxen, five rams, five male goats, and five male lambs in their first year. This *was* the offering of Ahira the son of Enan.

[84] This *was* the dedication *offering* for the altar from the leaders of Israel, when it was anointed: twelve silver platters, twelve silver bowls, and twelve gold pans. [85] Each silver platter *weighed* one hundred and thirty *shekels* and each bowl seventy *shekels.* All the silver of the vessels *weighed* two thousand four hundred *shekels,* according to the shekel of the sanctuary. [86] The twelve gold pans full of incense *weighed* ten *shekels* apiece, according to the shekel of the sanctuary; all the gold of the pans *weighed* one hundred and twenty *shekels.* [87] All the oxen for the burnt offering *were* twelve young bulls, the rams twelve, the male lambs in their first year twelve, with their grain offering, and the kids of the goats as a sin offering twelve. [88] And all the oxen for the sacrifice of peace offerings were twenty-four bulls, the rams sixty, the male goats sixty, and the lambs in their first year sixty. This *was* the dedication *offering* for the altar after it was anointed.

[89] Now when Moses went into the tabernacle of meeting to speak with Him, he heard the voice of One speaking to him from above the mercy seat that *was* on

the ark of the Testimony, from between the two cherubim; thus He spoke to him.

8 And the LORD spoke to Moses, saying: ² "Speak to Aaron, and say to him, 'When you arrange the lamps, the seven lamps shall give light in front of the lampstand.' " ³ And Aaron did so; he arranged the lamps to face toward the front of the lampstand, as the LORD commanded Moses. ⁴ Now this workmanship of the lampstand *was* hammered gold; from its shaft to its flowers it *was* hammered work. According to the pattern which the LORD had shown Moses, so he made the lampstand.

⁵ Then the LORD spoke to Moses, saying: ⁶ "Take the Levites from among the children of Israel and cleanse them *ceremonially*. ⁷ Thus you shall do to them to cleanse them: Sprinkle water of purification on them, and let them shave all their body, and let them wash their clothes, and *so* make themselves clean. ⁸ Then let them take a young bull with its grain offering of fine flour mixed with oil, and you shall take another young bull as a sin offering. ⁹ And you shall bring the Levites before the tabernacle of meeting, and you shall gather together the whole congregation of the children of Israel. ¹⁰ So you shall bring the Levites before the LORD, and the children of Israel shall lay their hands on the Levites; ¹¹ and Aaron shall offer the Levites before the LORD *like* a wave offering from the children of Israel, that they may perform the work of the LORD. ¹² Then the Levites shall lay their hands on the heads of the young bulls, and you shall offer one as a sin offering and the other as a burnt offering to the LORD, to make atonement for the Levites.

¹³ "And you shall stand the Levites before Aaron and his sons, and then offer them *like* a wave offering to the LORD. ¹⁴ Thus you shall separate the Levites from among the children of Israel, and the Levites shall be Mine. ¹⁵ After that the Levites shall go in to service the tabernacle of meeting. So you shall cleanse them and offer them *like* a wave offering. ¹⁶ For they *are* wholly given to Me from among the children of Israel; I have taken them for Myself instead of all who open the womb, the firstborn of all the children of Israel.

¹⁷ For all the firstborn among the children of Israel *are* Mine, *both* man and beast; on the day that I struck all the firstborn in the land of Egypt I sanctified them to Myself. ¹⁸ I have taken the Levites instead of all the firstborn of the children of Israel. ¹⁹ And I have given the Levites as a gift to Aaron and his sons from among the children of Israel, to do the work for the children of Israel in the tabernacle of meeting, and to make atonement for the children of Israel, that there be no plague among the children of Israel when the children of Israel come near the sanctuary."

²⁰ Thus Moses and Aaron and all the congregation of the children of Israel did to the Levites; according to all that the LORD commanded Moses concerning the Levites, so the children of Israel did to them. ²¹ And the Levites purified themselves and washed their clothes; then Aaron presented them *like* a wave offering before the LORD, and Aaron made atonement for them to cleanse them. ²² After that the Levites went in to do their work in the tabernacle of meeting before Aaron and his sons; as the LORD commanded Moses concerning the Levites, so they did to them.

²³ Then the LORD spoke to Moses, saying, ²⁴ "This *is* what *pertains* to the Levites: From twenty-five years old and above one may enter to perform service in the work of the tabernacle of meeting; ²⁵ and at the age of fifty years they must cease performing this work, and shall work no more. ²⁶ They may minister with their brethren in the tabernacle of meeting, to attend to needs, but they *themselves* shall do no work. Thus you shall do to the Levites regarding their duties."

～ PSALM 31:1–5 ～

¹ In You, O LORD, I put my trust;
   Let me never be ashamed;
   Deliver me in Your righteousness.
² Bow down Your ear to me,
   Deliver me speedily;
   Be my rock of refuge,
   A fortress of defense to save me.

³ For You *are* my rock and my fortress;
   Therefore, for Your name's sake,

Lead me and guide me.
4 Pull me out of the net which they
  have secretly laid for me,
  For You *are* my strength.
5 Into Your hand I commit my spirit;
  You have redeemed me, O LORD
  God of truth.

~ PROVERBS 11:4–6 ~

4 Riches do not profit in the day of
  wrath,
  But righteousness delivers from
  death.
5 The righteousness of the blameless
  will direct his way aright,
  But the wicked will fall by his own
  wickedness.
6 The righteousness of the upright will
  deliver them,
  But the unfaithful will be caught by
  their lust.

~ MARK 9:1–29 ~

And He said to them, "Assuredly, I say to
you that there are some standing here who
will not taste death till they see the kingdom of God present with power."

2 Now after six days Jesus took Peter,
James, and John, and led them up on a
high mountain apart by themselves; and
He was transfigured before them. 3 His
clothes became shining, exceedingly
white, like snow, such as no launderer on
earth can whiten them. 4 And Elijah appeared to them with Moses, and they were
talking with Jesus. 5 Then Peter answered
and said to Jesus, "Rabbi, it is good for us
to be here; and let us make three tabernacles: one for You, one for Moses, and
one for Elijah"— 6 because he did not
know what to say, for they were greatly
afraid.

7 And a cloud came and overshadowed
them; and a voice came out of the cloud,
saying, "This is My beloved Son. Hear
Him!" 8 Suddenly, when they had looked
around, they saw no one anymore, but
only Jesus with themselves.

9 Now as they came down from the
mountain, He commanded them that they
should tell no one the things they had
seen, till the Son of Man had risen from
the dead. 10 So they kept this word to

themselves, questioning what the rising
from the dead meant.

11 And they asked Him, saying, "Why
do the scribes say that Elijah must come
first?"

12 Then He answered and told them,
"Indeed, Elijah is coming first and restores
all things. And how is it written concerning the Son of Man, that He must suffer
many things and be treated with contempt? 13 But I say to you that Elijah has
also come, and they did to him whatever
they wished, as it is written of him."

14 And when He came to the disciples,
He saw a great multitude around them,
and scribes disputing with them. 15 Immediately, when they saw Him, all the people
were greatly amazed, and running to *Him*,
greeted Him. 16 And He asked the scribes,
"What are you discussing with them?"

17 Then one of the crowd answered and
said, "Teacher, I brought You my son, who
has a mute spirit. 18 And wherever it seizes
him, it throws him down; he foams at the
mouth, gnashes his teeth, and becomes
rigid. So I spoke to Your disciples, that
they should cast it out, but they could
not."

19 He answered him and said, "O faithless generation, how long shall I be with
you? How long shall I bear with you?
Bring him to Me." 20 Then they brought
him to Him. And when he saw Him, immediately the spirit convulsed him, and
he fell on the ground and wallowed, foaming at the mouth.

21 So He asked his father, "How long
has this been happening to him?"

And he said, "From childhood. 22 And
often he has thrown him both into the
fire and into the water to destroy him.
But if You can do anything, have compassion on us and help us."

23 Jesus said to him, "If you can believe,
all things *are* possible to him who believes."

24 Immediately the father of the child
cried out and said with tears, "Lord, I
believe; help my unbelief!"

25 When Jesus saw that the people came
running together, He rebuked the unclean
spirit, saying to it, "Deaf and dumb spirit,
I command you, come out of him and
enter him no more!" 26 Then *the spirit*
cried out, convulsed him greatly, and came

out of him. And he became as one dead, so that many said, "He is dead." ²⁷ But Jesus took him by the hand and lifted him up, and he arose.

²⁸ And when He had come into the house, His disciples asked Him privately, "Why could we not cast it out?"

²⁹ So He said to them, "This kind can come out by nothing but prayer and fasting."

READING 65 · MARCH 6

∼ NUMBERS 9:1—10:36 ∼

Now the LORD spoke to Moses in the Wilderness of Sinai, in the first month of the second year after they had come out of the land of Egypt, saying: ² "Let the children of Israel keep the Passover at its appointed time. ³ On the fourteenth day of this month, at twilight, you shall keep it at its appointed time. According to all its rites and ceremonies you shall keep it." ⁴ So Moses told the children of Israel that they should keep the Passover. ⁵ And they kept the Passover on the fourteenth day of the first month, at twilight, in the Wilderness of Sinai; according to all that the LORD commanded Moses, so the children of Israel did.

⁶ Now there were *certain* men who were defiled by a human corpse, so that they could not keep the Passover on that day; and they came before Moses and Aaron that day. ⁷ And those men said to him, "We *became* defiled by a human corpse. Why are we kept from presenting the offering of the LORD at its appointed time among the children of Israel?"

⁸ And Moses said to them, "Stand still, that I may hear what the LORD will command concerning you."

⁹ Then the LORD spoke to Moses, saying, ¹⁰ "Speak to the children of Israel, saying: 'If anyone of you or your posterity is unclean because of a corpse, or *is* far away on a journey, he may still keep the LORD's Passover. ¹¹ On the fourteenth day of the second month, at twilight, they may keep it. They shall eat it with unleavened bread and bitter herbs. ¹² They shall leave none of it until morning, nor break one of its bones. According to all the ordinances of the Passover they shall keep it. ¹³ But the man who *is* clean and is not on a journey, and ceases to keep the Passover, that same person shall be cut off from

among his people, because he did not bring the offering of the LORD at its appointed time; that man shall bear his sin.

¹⁴ 'And if a stranger dwells among you, and would keep the LORD's Passover, he must do so according to the rite of the Passover and according to its ceremony; you shall have one ordinance, both for the stranger and the native of the land.' "

¹⁵ Now on the day that the tabernacle was raised up, the cloud covered the tabernacle, the tent of the Testimony; from evening until morning it was above the tabernacle like the appearance of fire. ¹⁶ So it was always: the cloud covered it *by day,* and the appearance of fire by night. ¹⁷ Whenever the cloud was taken up from above the tabernacle, after that the children of Israel would journey; and in the place where the cloud settled, there the children of Israel would pitch their tents. ¹⁸ At the command of the LORD the children of Israel would journey, and at the command of the LORD they would camp; as long as the cloud stayed above the tabernacle they remained encamped. ¹⁹ Even when the cloud continued long, many days above the tabernacle, the children of Israel kept the charge of the LORD and did not journey. ²⁰ So it was, when the cloud was above the tabernacle a few days: according to the command of the LORD they would remain encamped, and according to the command of the LORD they would journey. ²¹ So it was, when the cloud remained only from evening until morning: when the cloud was taken up in the morning, then they would journey; whether by day or by night, whenever the cloud was taken up, they would journey. ²² *Whether it was* two days, a month, or a year that the cloud remained above the tabernacle, the children of Israel would remain encamped and not journey; but

when it was taken up, they would journey. [23] At the command of the LORD they remained encamped, and at the command of the LORD they journeyed; they kept the charge of the LORD, at the command of the LORD by the hand of Moses.

10 And the LORD spoke to Moses, saying: [2] "Make two silver trumpets for yourself; you shall make them of hammered work; you shall use them for calling the congregation and for directing the movement of the camps. [3] When they blow both of them, all the congregation shall gather before you at the door of the tabernacle of meeting. [4] But if they blow *only* one, then the leaders, the heads of the divisions of Israel, shall gather to you. [5] When you sound the advance, the camps that lie on the east side shall then begin their journey. [6] When you sound the advance the second time, then the camps that lie on the south side shall begin their journey; they shall sound the call for them to begin their journeys. [7] And when the assembly is to be gathered together, you shall blow, but not sound the advance. [8] The sons of Aaron, the priests, shall blow the trumpets; and these shall be to you as an ordinance forever throughout your generations.

[9] "When you go to war in your land against the enemy who oppresses you, then you shall sound an alarm with the trumpets, and you will be remembered before the LORD your God, and you will be saved from your enemies. [10] Also in the day of your gladness, in your appointed feasts, and at the beginning of your months, you shall blow the trumpets over your burnt offerings and over the sacrifices of your peace offerings; and they shall be a memorial for you before your God: I *am* the LORD your God."

[11] Now it came to pass on the twentieth *day* of the second month, in the second year, that the cloud was taken up from above the tabernacle of the Testimony. [12] And the children of Israel set out from the Wilderness of Sinai on their journeys; then the cloud settled down in the Wilderness of Paran. [13] So they started out for the first time according to the command of the LORD by the hand of Moses.

[14] The standard of the camp of the chil-

dren of Judah set out first according to their armies; over their army was Nahshon the son of Amminadab. [15] Over the army of the tribe of the children of Issachar *was* Nethanel the son of Zuar. [16] And over the army of the tribe of the children of Zebulun *was* Eliab the son of Helon.

[17] Then the tabernacle was taken down; and the sons of Gershon and the sons of Merari set out, carrying the tabernacle.

[18] And the standard of the camp of Reuben set out according to their armies; over their army *was* Elizur the son of Shedeur. [19] Over the army of the tribe of the children of Simeon *was* Shelumiel the son of Zurishaddai. [20] And over the army of the tribe of the children of Gad *was* Eliasaph the son of Deuel.

[21] Then the Kohathites set out, carrying the holy things. (The tabernacle would be prepared for their arrival.)

[22] And the standard of the camp of the children of Ephraim set out according to their armies; over their army *was* Elishama the son of Ammihud. [23] Over the army of the tribe of the children of Manasseh *was* Gamaliel the son of Pedahzur. [24] And over the army of the tribe of the children of Benjamin *was* Abidan the son of Gideoni.

[25] Then the standard of the camp of the children of Dan (the rear guard of all the camps) set out according to their armies; over their army *was* Ahiezer the son of Ammishaddai. [26] Over the army of the tribe of the children of Asher *was* Pagiel the son of Ocran. [27] And over the army of the tribe of the children of Naphtali *was* Ahira the son of Enan.

[28] Thus *was* the order of march of the children of Israel, according to their armies, when they began their journey.

[29] Now Moses said to Hobab the son of Reuel the Midianite, Moses' father-in-law, "We are setting out for the place of which the LORD said, 'I will give it to you.' Come with us, and we will treat you well; for the LORD has promised good things to Israel."

[30] And he said to him, "I will not go, but I will depart to my *own* land and to my relatives."

[31] So *Moses* said, "Please do not leave, inasmuch as you know how we are to camp in the wilderness, and you can be

Are You a Slave or a Servant?

For more than a quarter of a century, Arnold Billie was a rural mail carrier in southern New Jersey. His daily route took him sixty-three miles through two counties and five municipalities. Mr. Billie, as he was affectionately known, did more than deliver the mail. He provided "personal service." Anything a person might need to purchase from the post office, Mr. Billie provided — stamps, money orders, pickup service. All a customer needed to do to let Mr. Billie know they needed something was leave the flag up on their mailbox.

One elderly woman had trouble starting her lawn mower, so whenever she desired to use it, she would simply leave it by her mailbox, raise the flag, and when Mr. Billie came by, he would start it for her! Mr. Billie added a new dimension to the phrase "public servant."

True Christian servants rarely think of themselves as doing anything out of the ordinary, when what they do is actually quite extraordinary! The apostle Paul called himself a slave to Christ, yet he was too concerned about being a good servant to ever worry about being a real slave. Why? Because true servants are motivated by love. It is love they know they have received from Christ. And it is love they give.

As women and mothers, we are called upon to serve in many areas of life. Sometimes all at once! Let us always remember that the difference between a slave and a servant is love.

our eyes. ³² And it shall be, if you go with us—indeed it shall be—that whatever good the LORD will do to us, the same we will do to you."

³³ So they departed from the mountain of the LORD on a journey of three days; and the ark of the covenant of the LORD went before them for the three days' journey, to search out a resting place for them. ³⁴ And the cloud of the LORD *was* above them by day when they went out from the camp.

³⁵ So it was, whenever the ark set out, that Moses said:

"Rise up, O LORD!
Let Your enemies be scattered,
And let those who hate You flee
before You."

³⁶ And when it rested, he said:

"Return, O LORD,
To the many thousands of
Israel."

∼ PSALM 31:6–14 ∼

⁶ I have hated those who regard
useless idols;
But I trust in the LORD.
⁷ I will be glad and rejoice in Your
mercy,
For You have considered my trouble;
You have known my soul in
adversities,
⁸ And have not shut me up into the
hand of the enemy;
You have set my feet in a wide place.

⁹ Have mercy on me, O LORD, for I
am in trouble;
My eye wastes away with grief,
Yes, my soul and my body!
¹⁰ For my life is spent with grief,
And my years with sighing;
My strength fails because of my
iniquity,
And my bones waste away.
¹¹ I am a reproach among all my
enemies,
But especially among my neighbors,
And *am* repulsive to my
acquaintances;

Those who see me outside flee from
me.
¹² I am forgotten like a dead man, out
of mind;
I am like a broken vessel.
¹³ For I hear the slander of many;
Fear *is* on every side;
While they take counsel together
against me,
They scheme to take away my life.

¹⁴ But as for me, I trust in You,
O LORD;
I say, "You *are* my God."

∼ PROVERBS 11:7–11 ∼

⁷ When a wicked man dies, *his*
expectation will perish,
And the hope of the unjust perishes.
⁸ The righteous is delivered from
trouble,
And it comes to the wicked instead.
⁹ The hypocrite with *his* mouth
destroys his neighbor,
But through knowledge the
righteous will be delivered.
¹⁰ When it goes well with the
righteous, the city rejoices;
And when the wicked perish, *there
is* jubilation.
¹¹ By the blessing of the upright the
city is exalted,
But it is overthrown by the mouth of
the wicked.

∼ MARK 9:30–50 ∼

Then they departed from there and passed through Galilee, and He did not want anyone to know *it*. ³¹ For He taught His disciples and said to them, "The Son of Man is being betrayed into the hands of men, and they will kill Him. And after He is killed, He will rise the third day." ³² But they did not understand this saying, and were afraid to ask Him.

³³ Then He came to Capernaum. And when He was in the house He asked them, "What was it you disputed among yourselves on the road?" ³⁴ But they kept silent, for on the road they had disputed among themselves who *would be the* greatest.

35 And He sat down, called the twelve, and said to them, "If anyone desires to be first, he shall be last of all and servant of all." 36 Then He took a little child and set him in the midst of them. And when He had taken him in His arms, He said to them, 37 "Whoever receives one of these little children in My name receives Me; and whoever receives Me, receives not Me but Him who sent Me."

38 Now John answered Him, saying, "Teacher, we saw someone who does not follow us casting out demons in Your name, and we forbade him because he does not follow us."

39 But Jesus said, "Do not forbid him, for no one who works a miracle in My name can soon afterward speak evil of Me. 40 For he who is not against us is on our side. 41 For whoever gives you a cup of water to drink in My name, because you belong to Christ, assuredly, I say to you, he will by no means lose his reward.

42 "But whoever causes one of these little ones who believe in Me to stumble, it would be better for him if a millstone were hung around his neck, and he were thrown into the sea. 43 If your hand causes you to sin, cut it off. It is better for you to enter into life maimed, rather than hav-ing two hands, to go to hell, into the fire that shall never be quenched— 44 where

> 'Their worm does not die
> And the fire is not quenched.'

45 And if your foot causes you to sin, cut it off. It is better for you to enter life lame, rather than having two feet, to be cast into hell, into the fire that shall never be quenched— 46 where

> 'Their worm does not die
> And the fire is not quenched.'

47 And if your eye causes you to sin, pluck it out. It is better for you to enter the king-dom of God with one eye, rather than having two eyes, to be cast into hell fire— 48 where

> 'Their worm does not die
> And the fire is not quenched.'

49 "For everyone will be seasoned with fire, and every sacrifice will be seasoned with salt. 50 Salt is good, but if the salt loses its flavor, how will you season it? Have salt in yourselves, and have peace with one another."

READING 66 · MARCH 7

~ Numbers 11:1—12:16 ~

Now *when* the people complained, it displeased the LORD; for the LORD heard *it*, and His anger was aroused. So the fire of the LORD burned among them, and consumed *some* in the outskirts of the camp. 2 Then the people cried out to Moses, and when Moses prayed to the LORD, the fire was quenched. 3 So he called the name of the place Taberah, because the fire of the LORD had burned among them.

4 Now the mixed multitude who were among them yielded to intense craving; so the children of Israel also wept again and said: "Who will give us meat to eat? 5 We remember the fish which we ate freely in Egypt, the cucumbers, the mel-ons, the leeks, the onions, and the garlic; 6 but now our whole being *is* dried up; *there is* nothing at all except this manna *before* our eyes!"

7 Now the manna *was* like coriander seed, and its color like the color of bdel-lium. 8 The people went about and gathered *it*, ground *it* on millstones or beat *it* in the mortar, cooked *it* in pans, and made cakes of it; and its taste was like the taste of pastry prepared with oil. 9 And when the dew fell on the camp in the night, the manna fell on it.

10 Then Moses heard the people weep-ing throughout their families, everyone at the door of his tent; and the anger of the LORD was greatly aroused; Moses also was displeased. 11 So Moses said to the LORD, "Why have You afflicted Your servant?

And why have I not found favor in Your sight, that You have laid the burden of all these people on me? ¹² Did I conceive all these people? Did I beget them, that You should say to me, 'Carry them in your bosom, as a guardian carries a nursing child,' to the land which You swore to their fathers? ¹³ Where am I to get meat to give to all these people? For they weep all over me, saying, 'Give us meat, that we may eat.' ¹⁴ I am not able to bear all these people alone, because the burden is too heavy for me. ¹⁵ If You treat me like this, please kill me here and now—if I have found favor in Your sight—and do not let me see my wretchedness!"

¹⁶ So the LORD said to Moses: "Gather to Me seventy men of the elders of Israel, whom you know to be the elders of the people and officers over them; bring them to the tabernacle of meeting, that they may stand there with you. ¹⁷ Then I will come down and talk with you there. I will take of the Spirit that is upon you and will put the same upon them; and they shall bear the burden of the people with you, that you may not bear it yourself alone. ¹⁸ Then you shall say to the people, 'Consecrate yourselves for tomorrow, and you shall eat meat; for you have wept in the hearing of the LORD, saying, "Who will give us meat to eat? For it was well with us in Egypt." Therefore the LORD will give you meat, and you shall eat. ¹⁹ You shall eat, not one day, nor two days, nor five days, nor ten days, nor twenty days, ²⁰ but for a whole month, until it comes out of your nostrils and becomes loathsome to you, because you have despised the LORD who is among you, and have wept before Him, saying, "Why did we ever come up out of Egypt?" ' "

²¹ And Moses said, "The people whom I am among are six hundred thousand men on foot; yet You have said, 'I will give them meat, that they may eat for a whole month.' ²² Shall flocks and herds be slaughtered for them, to provide enough for them? Or shall all the fish of the sea be gathered together for them, to provide enough for them?"

²³ And the LORD said to Moses, "Has the LORD's arm been shortened? Now you shall see whether what I say will happen to you or not."

²⁴ So Moses went out and told the people the words of the LORD, and he gathered the seventy men of the elders of the people and placed them around the tabernacle. ²⁵ Then the LORD came down in the cloud, and spoke to him, and took of the Spirit that was upon him, and placed the same upon the seventy elders; and it happened, when the Spirit rested upon them, that they prophesied, although they never did so again.

²⁶ But two men had remained in the camp: the name of one was Eldad, and the name of the other Medad. And the Spirit rested upon them. Now they were among those listed, but who had not gone out to the tabernacle; yet they prophesied in the camp. ²⁷ And a young man ran and told Moses, and said, "Eldad and Medad are prophesying in the camp." ²⁸ So Joshua the son of Nun, Moses' assistant, one of his choice men, answered and said, "Moses my lord, forbid them!" ²⁹ Then Moses said to him, "Are you zealous for my sake? Oh, that all the LORD's people were prophets and that the LORD would put His Spirit upon them!" ³⁰ And Moses returned to the camp, he and the elders of Israel.

³¹ Now a wind went out from the LORD, and it brought quail from the sea and left them fluttering near the camp, about a day's journey on this side and about a day's journey on the other side, all around the camp, and about two cubits above the surface of the ground. ³² And the people stayed up all that day, all night, and all the next day, and gathered the quail (he who gathered least gathered ten homers); and they spread them out for themselves all around the camp. ³³ But while the meat was still between their teeth, before it was chewed, the wrath of the LORD was aroused against the people, and the LORD struck the people with a very great plague. ³⁴ So he called the name of that place Kibroth Hattaavah, because there they buried the people who had yielded to craving.

³⁵ From Kibroth Hattaavah the people moved to Hazeroth, and camped at Hazeroth.

12 Then Miriam and Aaron spoke against Moses because of the Ethiopian

From Local to Long-Distance

In order to communicate among themselves, Serbian shepherd boys developed an ingenious system. They would stick the blades of their long knives into the ground of a pasture, and when one of the boys sensed an approaching cattle thief, he would strike the handle of his knife. The vibration created a signal that could be picked up by other shepherd boys, their ears pressed tightly against the ground. It was by using this unique system that they outwitted thieves who tried to creep up on their flocks and herds under the cover of darkness and tall corn.

Most of the shepherd boys grew up and forgot about their ground signals, but one boy remembered. Twenty-five years after he left the pastures, he developed one of the greatest inventions of the modern era. Michael Pupin expanded the use of the telephone from speaking only across a city, to a long-distance instrument that could be heard across an entire continent.

Something you take for granted today, something others may consider insignificant or ordinary, may actually become your key to greatness. Look around you. What has God placed at your disposal?

woman whom he had married; for he had married an Ethiopian woman. ² So they said, "Has the LORD indeed spoken only through Moses? Has He not spoken through us also?" And the LORD heard *it*. ³(Now the man Moses *was* very humble, more than all men who *were* on the face of the earth.)

⁴ Suddenly the LORD said to Moses, Aaron, and Miriam, "Come out, you three, to the tabernacle of meeting!" So the three came out. ⁵ Then the LORD came down in the pillar of cloud and stood *in* the door of the tabernacle, and called Aaron and Miriam. And they both went forward. ⁶ Then He said,

> "Hear now My words:
> If there is a prophet among you,
> *I*, the LORD, make Myself known
>   to him in a vision;
> I speak to him in a dream.
> ⁷ Not so with My servant Moses;
> He *is* faithful in all My house.
> ⁸ I speak with him face to face,
> Even plainly, and not in dark
>   sayings;
> And he sees the form of the LORD.
> Why then were you not afraid
> To speak against My servant
>   Moses?"

⁹ So the anger of the LORD was aroused against them, and He departed. ¹⁰ And when the cloud departed from above the tabernacle, suddenly Miriam *became* leprous, as *white as* snow. Then Aaron turned toward Miriam, and there she was, a leper. ¹¹ So Aaron said to Moses, "Oh, my lord! Please do not lay *this* sin on us, in which we have done foolishly and in which we have sinned. ¹² Please do not let her be as one dead, whose flesh is half consumed when he comes out of his mother's womb!"

¹³ So Moses cried out to the LORD, saying, "Please heal her, O God, I pray!"

¹⁴ Then the LORD said to Moses, "If her father had but spit in her face, would she not be shamed seven days? Let her be shut out of the camp seven days, and afterward she may be received *again*." ¹⁵ So Miriam was shut out of the camp seven days, and the people did not journey till Miriam was brought in *again*. ¹⁶ And afterward the people moved from Hazeroth and camped in the Wilderness of Paran.

～ PSALM 31:15–18 ～

¹⁵ My times *are* in Your hand;
Deliver me from the hand of my
    enemies,
And from those who persecute me.
¹⁶ Make Your face shine upon Your
    servant;
Save me for Your mercies' sake.
¹⁷ Do not let me be ashamed, O LORD,
    for I have called upon You;
Let the wicked be ashamed;
Let them be silent in the grave.
¹⁸ Let the lying lips be put to silence,
Which speak insolent things proudly
    and contemptuously against the
    righteous.

～ PROVERBS 11:12–14 ～

¹² He who is devoid of wisdom
    despises his neighbor,
But a man of understanding holds
    his peace.

¹³ A talebearer reveals secrets,
But he who is of a faithful spirit
    conceals a matter.

¹⁴ Where *there is* no counsel, the
    people fall;
But in the multitude of counselors
    there is safety.

～ MARK 10:1–31 ～

Then He arose from there and came to the region of Judea by the other side of the Jordan. And multitudes gathered to Him again, and as He was accustomed, He taught them again.

² The Pharisees came and asked Him, "Is it lawful for a man to divorce *his* wife?" testing Him.

³ And He answered and said to them, "What did Moses command you?"

⁴ They said, "Moses permitted *a man* to write a certificate of divorce, and to dismiss *her*."

⁵ And Jesus answered and said to them, "Because of the hardness of your heart he wrote you this precept. ⁶ But from the

beginning of the creation, God 'made them male and female.' ⁷ 'For this reason a man shall leave his father and mother and be joined to his wife, ⁸ and the two shall become one flesh'; so then they are no longer two, but one flesh. ⁹ Therefore what God has joined together, let not man separate."

¹⁰ In the house His disciples also asked Him again about the same *matter.* ¹¹ So He said to them, "Whoever divorces his wife and marries another commits adultery against her. ¹² And if a woman divorces her husband and marries another, she commits adultery."

¹³ Then they brought little children to Him, that He might touch them; but the disciples rebuked those who brought *them.* ¹⁴ But when Jesus saw *it,* He was greatly displeased and said to them, "Let the little children come to Me, and do not forbid them; for of such is the kingdom of God. ¹⁵ Assuredly, I say to you, whoever does not receive the kingdom of God as a little child will by no means enter it." ¹⁶ And He took them up in His arms, laid *His* hands on them, and blessed them.

¹⁷ Now as He was going out on the road, one came running, knelt before Him, and asked Him, "Good Teacher, what shall I do that I may inherit eternal life?"

¹⁸ So Jesus said to him, "Why do you call Me good? No one *is* good but One, *that is,* God. ¹⁹ You know the commandments: 'Do not commit adultery,' 'Do not murder,' 'Do not steal,' 'Do not bear false witness,' 'Do not defraud,' 'Honor your father and your mother.' "

²⁰ And he answered and said to Him, "Teacher, all these things I have kept from my youth."

²¹ Then Jesus, looking at him, loved him, and said to him, "One thing you lack: Go your way, sell whatever you have and give to the poor, and you will have treasure in heaven; and come, take up the cross, and follow Me."

²² But he was sad at this word, and went away sorrowful, for he had great possessions.

²³ Then Jesus looked around and said to His disciples, "How hard it is for those who have riches to enter the kingdom of God!" ²⁴ And the disciples were astonished at His words. But Jesus answered again and said to them, "Children, how hard it is for those who trust in riches to enter the kingdom of God! ²⁵ It is easier for a camel to go through the eye of a needle than for a rich man to enter the kingdom of God."

²⁶ And they were greatly astonished, saying among themselves, "Who then can be saved?"

²⁷ But Jesus looked at them and said, "With men *it is* impossible, but not with God; for with God all things are possible."

²⁸ Then Peter began to say to Him, "See, we have left all and followed You."

²⁹ So Jesus answered and said, "Assuredly, I say to you, there is no one who has left house or brothers or sisters or father or mother or wife or children or lands, for My sake and the gospel's, ³⁰ who shall not receive a hundredfold now in this time—houses and brothers and sisters and mothers and children and lands, with persecutions—and in the age to come, eternal life. ³¹ But many *who are* first will be last, and the last first."

READING 67 · MARCH 8

∼ Numbers 13:1—14:45 ∼

And the LORD spoke to Moses, saying, ² "Send men to spy out the land of Canaan, which I am giving to the children of Israel; from each tribe of their fathers you shall send a man, every one a leader among them."

³ So Moses sent them from the Wilderness of Paran according to the command of the LORD, all of them men who *were* heads of the children of Israel. ⁴ Now these *were* their names: from the tribe of Reuben, Shammua the son of Zaccur; ⁵ from the tribe of Simeon, Shaphat the son of Hori; ⁶ from the tribe of Judah, Caleb the son of Jephunneh; ⁷ from the tribe of Issachar, Igal the son of Joseph;

⁸ from the tribe of Ephraim, Hoshea the son of Nun; ⁹ from the tribe of Benjamin, Palti the son of Raphu; ¹⁰ from the tribe of Zebulun, Gaddiel the son of Sodi; ¹¹ from the tribe of Joseph, *that is,* from the tribe of Manasseh, Gaddi the son of Susi; ¹² from the tribe of Dan, Ammiel the son of Gemalli; ¹³ from the tribe of Asher, Sethur the son of Michael; ¹⁴ from the tribe of Naphtali, Nahbi the son of Vophsi; ¹⁵ from the tribe of Gad, Geuel the son of Machi.

¹⁶ These *are* the names of the men whom Moses sent to spy out the land. And Moses called Hoshea the son of Nun, Joshua.

¹⁷ Then Moses sent them to spy out the land of Canaan, and said to them, "Go up this *way* into the South, and go up to the mountains, ¹⁸ and see what the land is like: whether the people who dwell in it *are* strong or weak, few or many; ¹⁹ whether the land they dwell in *is* good or bad; whether the cities they inhabit *are* like camps or strongholds; ²⁰ whether the land *is* rich or poor; and whether there are forests there or not. Be of good courage. And bring some of the fruit of the land." Now the time *was* the season of the first ripe grapes.

²¹ So they went up and spied out the land from the Wilderness of Zin as far as Rehob, near the entrance of Hamath. ²² And they went up through the South and came to Hebron; Ahiman, Sheshai, and Talmai, the descendants of Anak, *were* there. (Now Hebron was built seven years before Zoan in Egypt.) ²³ Then they came to the Valley of Eshcol, and there cut down a branch with one cluster of grapes; they carried it between two of them on a pole. *They* also *brought* some of the pomegranates and figs. ²⁴ The place was called the Valley of Eshcol, because of the cluster which the men of Israel cut down there. ²⁵ And they returned from spying out the land after forty days.

²⁶ Now they departed and came back to Moses and Aaron and all the congregation of the children of Israel in the Wilderness of Paran, at Kadesh; they brought back word to them and to all the congregation, and showed them the fruit of the land. ²⁷ Then they told him, and said: "We went to the land where you sent us. It truly flows with milk and honey, and this *is* its fruit. ²⁸ Nevertheless the people who dwell in the land *are* strong; the cities *are* fortified *and* very large; moreover we saw the descendants of Anak there. ²⁹ The Amalekites dwell in the land of the South; the Hittites, the Jebusites, and the Amorites dwell in the mountains; and the Canaanites dwell by the sea and along the banks of the Jordan."

³⁰ Then Caleb quieted the people before Moses, and said, "Let us go up at once and take possession, for we are well able to overcome it."

³¹ But the men who had gone up with him said, "We are not able to go up against the people, for they *are* stronger than we." ³² And they gave the children of Israel a bad report of the land which they had spied out, saying, "The land through which we have gone as spies *is* a land that devours its inhabitants, and all the people whom we saw in it *are* men of *great* stature. ³³ There we saw the giants (the descendants of Anak came from the giants); and we were like grasshoppers in our own sight, and so we were in their sight."

14 So all the congregation lifted up their voices and cried, and the people wept that night. ² And all the children of Israel complained against Moses and Aaron, and the whole congregation said to them, "If only we had died in the land of Egypt! Or if only we had died in this wilderness! ³ Why has the LORD brought us to this land to fall by the sword, that our wives and children should become victims? Would it not be better for us to return to Egypt?" ⁴ So they said to one another, "Let us select a leader and return to Egypt."

⁵ Then Moses and Aaron fell on their faces before all the assembly of the congregation of the children of Israel.

⁶ But Joshua the son of Nun and Caleb the son of Jephunneh, *who were* among those who had spied out the land, tore their clothes; ⁷ and they spoke to all the congregation of the children of Israel, saying: "The land we passed through to spy out *is* an exceedingly good land. ⁸ If the LORD delights in us, then He will bring us into this land and give it to us, 'a land which flows with milk and honey.' ⁹ Only

Speak Out and Stand Up

Be of good courage, and He shall strengthen your heart, all you who hope in the Lord.

Psalm 31:24

While he was a pastor in Indianapolis, Henry Ward Beecher preached a series of sermons about gambling and drunkenness. He soundly denounced the men of the community who profited by these sins.

The next week, Beecher was accosted on the street by a would-be assailant. Brandishing a pistol, the man demanded that Beecher make some kind of retraction about what he had said the previous Sunday.

"Take it back, right here!" he demanded with an oath, "Or I will shoot you on the spot!"

Beecher calmly replied, "Shoot away!" The man was taken aback by his response. Beecher just walked away, saying over his shoulder as he left the scene, "I don't believe you can hit the mark as well as I did!"

Courage is more than just having convictions. It requires being willing to speak and to act in order to bring about change — in individual lives, in families, in neighborhoods, in cities, and in nations. It's not enough to "just believe" in something. In order to be a truly courageous person, you must be willing to speak out and stand up. Your voice can make a difference.

do not rebel against the LORD, nor fear the people of the land, for they *are* our bread; their protection has departed from them, and the LORD *is* with us. Do not fear them."

¹⁰ And all the congregation said to stone them with stones. Now the glory of the LORD appeared in the tabernacle of meeting before all the children of Israel.

¹¹ Then the LORD said to Moses: "How long will these people reject Me? And how long will they not believe Me, with all the signs which I have performed among them? ¹² I will strike them with the pestilence and disinherit them, and I will make of you a nation greater and mightier than they."

¹³ And Moses said to the LORD: "Then the Egyptians will hear *it,* for by Your might You brought these people up from among them, ¹⁴ and they will tell *it* to the inhabitants of this land. They have heard that You, LORD, *are* among these people; that You, LORD, are seen face to face and Your cloud stands above them, and You go before them in a pillar of cloud by day and in a pillar of fire by night. ¹⁵ Now *if* You kill these people as one man, then the nations which have heard of Your fame will speak, saying, ¹⁶ 'Because the LORD was not able to bring this people to the land which He swore to give them, therefore He killed them in the wilderness.' ¹⁷ And now, I pray, let the power of my Lord be great, just as You have spoken, saying, ¹⁸ 'The LORD is longsuffering and abundant in mercy, forgiving iniquity and transgression; but He by no means clears *the guilty,* visiting the iniquity of the fathers on the children to the third and fourth *generation.*' ¹⁹ Pardon the iniquity of this people, I pray, according to the greatness of Your mercy, just as You have forgiven this people, from Egypt even until now."

²⁰ Then the LORD said: "I have pardoned, according to your word; ²¹ but truly, as I live, all the earth shall be filled with the glory of the LORD— ²² because all these men who have seen My glory and the signs which I did in Egypt and in the wilderness, and have put Me to the test now these ten times, and have not heeded My voice, ²³ they certainly shall not see the land of which I swore to their

fathers, nor shall any of those who rejected Me see it. ²⁴ But My servant Caleb, because he has a different spirit in him and has followed Me fully, I will bring into the land where he went, and his descendants shall inherit it. ²⁵ Now the Amalekites and the Canaanites dwell in the valley; tomorrow turn and move out into the wilderness by the Way of the Red Sea."

²⁶ And the LORD spoke to Moses and Aaron, saying, ²⁷ "How long *shall I bear with* this evil congregation who complain against Me? I have heard the complaints which the children of Israel make against Me. ²⁸ Say to them, 'As I live,' says the LORD, 'just as you have spoken in My hearing, so I will do to you: ²⁹ The carcasses of you who have complained against Me shall fall in this wilderness, all of you who were numbered, according to your entire number, from twenty years old and above. ³⁰ Except for Caleb the son of Jephunneh and Joshua the son of Nun, you shall by no means enter the land which I swore I would make you dwell in. ³¹ But your little ones, whom you said would be victims, I will bring in, and they shall know the land which you have despised. ³² But *as for* you, your carcasses shall fall in this wilderness. ³³ And your sons shall be shepherds in the wilderness forty years, and bear the brunt of your infidelity, until your carcasses are consumed in the wilderness. ³⁴ According to the number of the days in which you spied out the land, forty days, for each day you shall bear your guilt one year, *namely* forty years, and you shall know My rejection. ³⁵ I the LORD have spoken this. I will surely do so to all this evil congregation who are gathered together against Me. In this wilderness they shall be consumed, and there they shall die.' "

³⁶ Now the men whom Moses sent to spy out the land, who returned and made all the congregation complain against him by bringing a bad report of the land, ³⁷ those very men who brought the evil report about the land, died by the plague before the LORD. ³⁸ But Joshua the son of Nun and Caleb the son of Jephunneh remained alive, of the men who went to spy out the land.

³⁹ Then Moses told these words to all

the children of Israel, and the people mourned greatly. [40] And they rose early in the morning and went up to the top of the mountain, saying, "Here we are, and we will go up to the place which the LORD has promised, for we have sinned!"

[41] And Moses said, "Now why do you transgress the command of the LORD? For this will not succeed. [42] Do not go up, lest you be defeated by your enemies, for the LORD *is* not among you. [43] For the Amalekites and the Canaanites *are* there before you, and you shall fall by the sword; because you have turned away from the LORD, the LORD will not be with you."

[44] But they presumed to go up to the mountaintop. Nevertheless, neither the ark of the covenant of the LORD nor Moses departed from the camp. [45] Then the Amalekites and the Canaanites who dwelt in that mountain came down and attacked them, and drove them back as far as Hormah.

~ PSALM 31:19–24 ~

[19] Oh, how great *is* Your goodness,
　　Which You have laid up for those
　　　who fear You,
　　Which You have prepared for those
　　　who trust in You
　　In the presence of the sons of men!
[20] You shall hide them in the secret
　　　place of Your presence
　　From the plots of man;
　　You shall keep them secretly in a
　　　pavilion
　　From the strife of tongues.

[21] Blessed *be* the LORD,
　　For He has shown me His marvelous
　　　kindness in a strong city!
[22] For I said in my haste,
　　"I am cut off from before Your eyes";
　　Nevertheless You heard the voice of
　　　my supplications
　　When I cried out to You.

[23] Oh, love the LORD, all you His
　　　saints!
　　For the LORD preserves the faithful,
　　And fully repays the proud person.
[24] Be of good courage,

And He shall strengthen your heart,
All you who hope in the LORD.

~ PROVERBS 11:15 ~

[15] He who is surety for a stranger will
　　suffer,
　　But one who hates being surety is
　　secure.

~ MARK 10:32–52 ~

Now they were on the road, going up to Jerusalem, and Jesus was going before them; and they were amazed. And as they followed they were afraid. Then He took the twelve aside again and began to tell them the things that would happen to Him: [33] "Behold, we are going up to Jerusalem, and the Son of Man will be betrayed to the chief priests and to the scribes; and they will condemn Him to death and deliver Him to the Gentiles; [34] and they will mock Him, and scourge Him, and spit on Him, and kill Him. And the third day He will rise again."

[35] Then James and John, the sons of Zebedee, came to Him, saying, "Teacher, we want You to do for us whatever we ask."

[36] And He said to them, "What do you want Me to do for you?"

[37] They said to Him, "Grant us that we may sit, one on Your right hand and the other on Your left, in Your glory."

[38] But Jesus said to them, "You do not know what you ask. Are you able to drink the cup that I drink, and be baptized with the baptism that I am baptized with?"

[39] They said to Him, "We are able."

So Jesus said to them, "You will indeed drink the cup that I drink, and with the baptism I am baptized with you will be baptized; [40] but to sit on My right hand and on My left is not Mine to give, but *it is for those* for whom it is prepared."

[41] And when the ten heard *it*, they began to be greatly displeased with James and John. [42] But Jesus called them to *Himself* and said to them, "You know that those who are considered rulers over the Gentiles lord it over them, and their great ones exercise authority over them. [43] Yet it shall not be so among you; but whoever desires to become great among you

shall be your servant. ⁴⁴ And whoever of you desires to be first shall be slave of all. ⁴⁵ For even the Son of Man did not come to be served, but to serve, and to give His life a ransom for many."

⁴⁶ Now they came to Jericho. As He went out of Jericho with His disciples and a great multitude, blind Bartimaeus, the son of Timaeus, sat by the road begging. ⁴⁷ And when he heard that it was Jesus of Nazareth, he began to cry out and say, "Jesus, Son of David, have mercy on me!" ⁴⁸ Then many warned him to be quiet; but he cried out all the more, "Son of David, have mercy on me!"

⁴⁹ So Jesus stood still and commanded him to be called.

Then they called the blind man, saying to him, "Be of good cheer. Rise, He is calling you."

⁵⁰ And throwing aside his garment, he rose and came to Jesus.

⁵¹ So Jesus answered and said to him, "What do you want Me to do for you?"

The blind man said to Him, "Rabboni, that I may receive my sight."

⁵² Then Jesus said to him, "Go your way; your faith has made you well." And immediately he received his sight and followed Jesus on the road.

READING 68 · MARCH 9

∼ NUMBERS 15:1—16:50 ∼

And the LORD spoke to Moses, saying, ² "Speak to the children of Israel, and say to them: 'When you have come into the land you are to inhabit, which I am giving to you, ³ and you make an offering by fire to the LORD, a burnt offering or a sacrifice, to fulfill a vow or as a freewill offering or in your appointed feasts, to make a sweet aroma to the LORD, from the herd or the flock, ⁴ then he who presents his offering to the LORD shall bring a grain offering of one-tenth *of an ephah* of fine flour mixed with one-fourth of a hin of oil; ⁵ and one-fourth of a hin of wine as a drink offering you shall prepare with the burnt offering or the sacrifice, for each lamb. ⁶ Or for a ram you shall prepare as a grain offering two-tenths *of an ephah* of fine flour mixed with one-third of a hin of oil; ⁷ and as a drink offering you shall offer one-third of a hin of wine as a sweet aroma to the LORD. ⁸ And when you prepare a young bull as a burnt offering, or as a sacrifice to fulfill a vow, or as a peace offering to the LORD, ⁹ then shall be offered with the young bull a grain offering of three-tenths *of an ephah* of fine flour mixed with half a hin of oil; ¹⁰ and you shall bring as the drink offering half a hin of wine as an offering made by fire, a sweet aroma to the LORD.

¹¹ 'Thus it shall be done for each young bull, for each ram, or for each lamb or young goat. ¹² According to the number that you prepare, so you shall do with everyone according to their number. ¹³ All who are native-born shall do these things in this manner, in presenting an offering made by fire, a sweet aroma to the LORD. ¹⁴ And if a stranger dwells with you, or whoever *is* among you throughout your generations, and would present an offering made by fire, a sweet aroma to the LORD, just as you do, so shall he do. ¹⁵ One ordinance *shall be* for you of the assembly and for the stranger who dwells *with you*, an ordinance forever throughout your generations; as you are, so shall the stranger be before the LORD. ¹⁶ One law and one custom shall be for you and for the stranger who dwells with you.' "

¹⁷ Again the LORD spoke to Moses, saying, ¹⁸ "Speak to the children of Israel, and say to them: 'When you come into the land to which I bring you, ¹⁹ then it will be, when you eat of the bread of the land, that you shall offer up a heave offering to the LORD. ²⁰ You shall offer up a cake of the first of your ground meal *as* a heave offering; as a heave offering of the threshing floor, so shall you offer it up. ²¹ Of the first of your ground meal you shall give to the LORD a heave offering throughout your generations.

²² 'If you sin unintentionally, and do not observe all these commandments which the LORD has spoken to Moses— ²³ all that the LORD has commanded you

Don't Cut Corners

Joe Smith was a loyal carpenter who worked nearly two decades for a very successful contractor. One day, the contractor called him into his office and said, "Joe, I'm putting you in charge of the next house we build. I want you to order all the materials and oversee the job from the ground up." Joe accepted the assignment with great enthusiasm. He studied the blueprints, checked every measurement and specification. Suddenly, he had a thought, *If I am really in charge, why couldn't I cut a few corners, use less expensive materials, and put the extra money in my pocket? Who will know? Once the house is painted, it will look great*.

So Joe went about his scheme. He ordered second-grade lumber and inexpensive concrete, put in cheap wiring, and cut every corner he could. When the home was finished, the contractor came to see it.

"What a fine job you have done!" he said. "You have been such a faithful carpenter to me all these years that I have decided to show you my gratitude by giving to you this very house which you have built."

Build well today. You may have to live with the reputation you create.

> **The wicked man does deceptive work, but he who sows righteousness will have a sure reward.**
>
> *Proverbs 11:18*

by the hand of Moses, from the day the LORD gave commandment and onward throughout your generations— ²⁴ then it will be, if it is unintentionally committed, without the knowledge of the congregation, that the whole congregation shall offer one young bull as a burnt offering, as a sweet aroma to the LORD, with its grain offering and its drink offering, according to the ordinance, and one kid of the goats as a sin offering. ²⁵ So the priest shall make atonement for the whole congregation of the children of Israel, and it shall be forgiven them, for it was unintentional; they shall bring their offering, an offering made by fire to the LORD, and their sin offering before the LORD, for their unintended sin. ²⁶ It shall be forgiven the whole congregation of the children of Israel and the stranger who dwells among them, because all the people *did it* unintentionally.

²⁷ 'And if a person sins unintentionally, then he shall bring a female goat in its first year as a sin offering. ²⁸ So the priest shall make atonement for the person who sins unintentionally, when he sins unintentionally before the LORD, to make atonement for him; and it shall be forgiven him. ²⁹ You shall have one law for him who sins unintentionally, *for* him who is native-born among the children of Israel and for the stranger who dwells among them.

³⁰ 'But the person who does *anything* presumptuously, *whether he is* native-born or a stranger, that one brings reproach on the LORD, and he shall be cut off from among his people. ³¹ Because he has despised the word of the LORD, and has broken His commandment, that person shall be completely cut off; his guilt *shall be* upon him.' "

³² Now while the children of Israel were in the wilderness, they found a man gathering sticks on the Sabbath day. ³³ And those who found him gathering sticks brought him to Moses and Aaron, and to all the congregation. ³⁴ They put him under guard, because it had not been explained what should be done to him. ³⁵ Then the LORD said to Moses, "The man must surely be put to death; all the congregation shall stone him with stones outside the camp." ³⁶ So, as the LORD commanded Moses, all the congregation brought him outside the camp and stoned him with stones, and he died.

³⁷ Again the LORD spoke to Moses, saying, ³⁸ "Speak to the children of Israel: Tell them to make tassels on the corners of their garments throughout their generations, and to put a blue thread in the tassels of the corners. ³⁹ And you shall have the tassel, that you may look upon it and remember all the commandments of the LORD and do them, and that you *may* not follow the harlotry to which your own heart and your own eyes are inclined, ⁴⁰ and that you may remember and do all My commandments, and be holy for your God. ⁴¹ I *am* the LORD your God, who brought you out of the land of Egypt, to be your God: I *am* the LORD your God."

16 Now Korah the son of Izhar, the son of Kohath, the son of Levi, with Dathan and Abiram the sons of Eliab, and On the son of Peleth, sons of Reuben, took *men;* ² and they rose up before Moses with some of the children of Israel, two hundred and fifty leaders of the congregation, representatives of the congregation, men of renown. ³ They gathered together against Moses and Aaron, and said to them, "*You take* too much upon yourselves, for all the congregation *is* holy, every one of them, and the LORD *is* among them. Why then do you exalt yourselves above the assembly of the LORD?"

⁴ So when Moses heard *it,* he fell on his face; ⁵ and he spoke to Korah and all his company, saying, "Tomorrow morning the LORD will show who *is* His and *who is* holy, and will cause *him* to come near to Him. That one whom He chooses He will cause to come near to Him. ⁶ Do this: Take censers, Korah and all your company; ⁷ put fire in them and put incense in them before the LORD tomorrow, and it shall be *that* the man whom the LORD chooses *is* the holy one. *You take* too much upon yourselves, you sons of Levi!"

⁸ Then Moses said to Korah, "Hear now, you sons of Levi: ⁹ *Is it* a small thing to you that the God of Israel has separated you from the congregation of Israel, to bring you near to Himself, to do the work of the tabernacle of the LORD, and

to stand before the congregation to serve them; [10] and that He has brought you near *to Himself,* you and all your brethren, the sons of Levi, with you? And are you seeking the priesthood also? [11] Therefore you and all your company *are* gathered together against the LORD. And what *is* Aaron that you complain against him?"

[12] And Moses sent to call Dathan and Abiram the sons of Eliab, but they said, "We will not come up! [13] *Is it* a small thing that you have brought us up out of a land flowing with milk and honey, to kill us in the wilderness, that you should keep acting like a prince over us? [14] Moreover you have not brought us into a land flowing with milk and honey, nor given us inheritance of fields and vineyards. Will you put out the eyes of these men? We will not come up!"

[15] Then Moses was very angry, and said to the LORD, "Do not respect their offering. I have not taken one donkey from them, nor have I hurt one of them."

[16] And Moses said to Korah, "Tomorrow, you and all your company be present before the LORD—you and they, as well as Aaron. [17] Let each take his censer and put incense in it, and each of you bring his censer before the LORD, two hundred and fifty censers; both you and Aaron, each *with* his censer." [18] So every man took his censer, put fire in it, laid incense on it, and stood at the door of the tabernacle of meeting with Moses and Aaron. [19] And Korah gathered all the congregation against them at the door of the tabernacle of meeting. Then the glory of the LORD appeared to all the congregation.

[20] And the LORD spoke to Moses and Aaron, saying, [21] "Separate yourselves from among this congregation, that I may consume them in a moment."

[22] Then they fell on their faces, and said, "O God, the God of the spirits of all flesh, shall one man sin, and You be angry with all the congregation?"

[23] So the LORD spoke to Moses, saying, [24] "Speak to the congregation, saying, 'Get away from the tents of Korah, Dathan, and Abiram.' "

[25] Then Moses rose and went to Dathan and Abiram, and the elders of Israel followed him. [26] And he spoke to the congregation, saying, "Depart now from the tents of these wicked men! Touch nothing of theirs, lest you be consumed in all their sins." [27] So they got away from around the tents of Korah, Dathan, and Abiram; and Dathan and Abiram came out and stood at the door of their tents, with their wives, their sons, and their little children.

[28] And Moses said: "By this you shall know that the LORD has sent me to do all these works, for I *have* not *done them* of my own will. [29] If these men die naturally like all men, or if they are visited by the common fate of all men, *then* the LORD has not sent me. [30] But if the LORD creates a new thing, and the earth opens its mouth and swallows them up with all that belongs to them, and they go down alive into the pit, then you will understand that these men have rejected the LORD."

[31] Now it came to pass, as he finished speaking all these words, that the ground split apart under them, [32] and the earth opened its mouth and swallowed them up, with their households and all the men with Korah, with all *their* goods. [33] So they and all those with them went down alive into the pit; the earth closed over them, and they perished from among the assembly. [34] Then all Israel who *were* around them fled at their cry, for they said, "Lest the earth swallow us up *also!*"

[35] And a fire came out from the LORD and consumed the two hundred and fifty men who were offering incense.

[36] Then the LORD spoke to Moses, saying: [37] "Tell Eleazar, the son of Aaron the priest, to pick up the censers out of the blaze, for they are holy, and scatter the fire some distance away. [38] The censers of these men who sinned against their own souls, let them be made into hammered plates as a covering for the altar. Because they presented them before the LORD, therefore they are holy; and they shall be a sign to the children of Israel." [39] So Eleazar the priest took the bronze censers, which those who were burned up had presented, and they were hammered out as a covering on the altar, [40] *to be* a memorial to the children of Israel that no outsider, who *is* not a descendant of Aaron, should come near to offer incense before the LORD, that he might not become like Korah and his companions, just

as the LORD had said to him through Moses.

⁴¹ On the next day all the congregation of the children of Israel complained against Moses and Aaron, saying, "You have killed the people of the LORD." ⁴² Now it happened, when the congregation had gathered against Moses and Aaron, that they turned toward the tabernacle of meeting; and suddenly the cloud covered it, and the glory of the LORD appeared. ⁴³ Then Moses and Aaron came before the tabernacle of meeting.

⁴⁴ And the LORD spoke to Moses, saying, ⁴⁵ "Get away from among this congregation, that I may consume them in a moment."

And they fell on their faces.

⁴⁶ So Moses said to Aaron, "Take a censer and put fire in it from the altar, put incense *on it,* and take it quickly to the congregation and make atonement for them; for wrath has gone out from the LORD. The plague has begun." ⁴⁷ Then Aaron took *it* as Moses commanded, and ran into the midst of the assembly; and already the plague had begun among the people. So he put in the incense and made atonement for the people. ⁴⁸ And he stood between the dead and the living; so the plague was stopped. ⁴⁹ Now those who died in the plague were fourteen thousand seven hundred, besides those who died in the Korah incident. ⁵⁰ So Aaron returned to Moses at the door of the tabernacle of meeting, for the plague had stopped.

∼ PSALM 32:1–5 ∼

¹ Blessed *is he whose* transgression *is* forgiven,
　Whose sin *is* covered.
² Blessed *is* the man to whom the
　LORD does not impute iniquity,
　And in whose spirit *there is* no
　　deceit.

³ When I kept silent, my bones grew
　old
　Through my groaning all the day
　　long.
⁴ For day and night Your hand was
　heavy upon me;

My vitality was turned into the
　drought of summer.　　　Selah
⁵ I acknowledged my sin to You,
　And my iniquity I have not hidden.
　I said, "I will confess my
　　transgressions to the LORD,"
　And You forgave the iniquity of my
　　sin.　　　　　　　　　　　Selah

∼ PROVERBS 11:16–18 ∼

¹⁶ A gracious woman retains honor,
　But ruthless *men* retain riches.
¹⁷ The merciful man does good for his
　own soul,
　But *he who is* cruel troubles his own
　　flesh.
¹⁸ The wicked *man* does deceptive
　work,
　But he who sows righteousness *will
　have* a sure reward.

∼ MARK 11:1–19 ∼

Now when they drew near Jerusalem, to Bethphage and Bethany, at the Mount of Olives, He sent two of His disciples; ² and He said to them, "Go into the village opposite you; and as soon as you have entered it you will find a colt tied, on which no one has sat. Loose it and bring *it.* ³ And if anyone says to you, 'Why are you doing this?' say, 'The Lord has need of it,' and immediately he will send it here."

⁴ So they went their way, and found the colt tied by the door outside on the street, and they loosed it. ⁵ But some of those who stood there said to them, "What are you doing, loosing the colt?" ⁶ And they spoke to them just as Jesus had commanded. So they let them go. ⁷ Then they brought the colt to Jesus and threw their clothes on it, and He sat on it. ⁸ And many spread their clothes on the road, and others cut down leafy branches from the trees and spread *them* on the road. ⁹ Then those who went before and those who followed cried out, saying:

　"Hosanna!
　'Blessed is He who comes in the
　　name of the LORD!'
¹⁰ Blessed *is* the kingdom of our
　father David

That comes in the name of the
Lord!
Hosanna in the highest!"

¹¹ And Jesus went into Jerusalem and into the temple. So when He had looked around at all things, as the hour was already late, He went out to Bethany with the twelve.

¹² Now the next day, when they had come out from Bethany, He was hungry. ¹³ And seeing from afar a fig tree having leaves, He went to see if perhaps He would find something on it. When He came to it, He found nothing but leaves, for it was not the season for figs. ¹⁴ In response Jesus said to it, "Let no one eat fruit from you ever again."

And His disciples heard it.
¹⁵ So they came to Jerusalem. Then Jesus went into the temple and began to drive out those who bought and sold in the temple, and overturned the tables of the money changers and the seats of those who sold doves. ¹⁶ And He would not allow anyone to carry wares through the temple. ¹⁷ Then He taught, saying to them, "Is it not written, 'My house shall be called a house of prayer for all nations'? But you have made it a 'den of thieves.'"

¹⁸ And the scribes and chief priests heard it and sought how they might destroy Him; for they feared Him, because all the people were astonished at His teaching. ¹⁹ When evening had come, He went out of the city.

READING 69 · MARCH 10

∼ NUMBERS 17:1—18:32 ∼

And the LORD spoke to Moses, saying: ² "Speak to the children of Israel, and get from them a rod from each father's house, all their leaders according to their fathers' houses—twelve rods. Write each man's name on his rod. ³ And you shall write Aaron's name on the rod of Levi. For there shall be one rod for the head of *each* father's house. ⁴ Then you shall place them in the tabernacle of meeting before the Testimony, where I meet with you. ⁵ And it shall be *that* the rod of the man whom I choose will blossom; thus I will rid Myself of the complaints of the children of Israel, which they make against you."

⁶ So Moses spoke to the children of Israel, and each of their leaders gave him a rod apiece, for each leader according to their fathers' houses, twelve rods; and the rod of Aaron *was* among their rods. ⁷ And Moses placed the rods before the LORD in the tabernacle of witness.

⁸ Now it came to pass on the next day that Moses went into the tabernacle of witness, and behold, the rod of Aaron, of the house of Levi, had sprouted and put forth buds, had produced blossoms and yielded ripe almonds. ⁹ Then Moses brought out all the rods from before the

LORD to all the children of Israel; and they looked, and each man took his rod.

¹⁰ And the LORD said to Moses, "Bring Aaron's rod back before the Testimony, to be kept as a sign against the rebels, that you may put their complaints away from Me, lest they die." ¹¹ Thus did Moses; just as the LORD had commanded him, so he did.

¹² So the children of Israel spoke to Moses, saying, "Surely we die, we perish, we all perish! ¹³ Whoever even comes near the tabernacle of the LORD must die. Shall we all utterly die?"

18 Then the LORD said to Aaron: "You and your sons and your father's house with you shall bear the iniquity *related to* the sanctuary, and you and your sons with you shall bear the iniquity *associated with* your priesthood. ² Also bring with you your brethren of the tribe of Levi, the tribe of your father, that they may be joined with you and serve you while you and your sons *are* with you before the tabernacle of witness. ³ They shall attend to your needs and all the needs of the tabernacle; but they shall not come near the articles of the sanctuary and the altar, lest they die—they and you also. ⁴ They shall

be joined with you and attend to the needs of the tabernacle of meeting, for all the work of the tabernacle; but an outsider shall not come near you. [5] And you shall attend to the duties of the sanctuary and the duties of the altar, that there *may* be no more wrath on the children of Israel. [6] Behold, I Myself have taken your brethren the Levites from among the children of Israel; *they are* a gift to you, given by the LORD, to do the work of the tabernacle of meeting. [7] Therefore you and your sons with you shall attend to your priesthood for everything at the altar and behind the veil; and you shall serve. I give your priesthood *to you* as a gift for service, but the outsider who comes near shall be put to death."

[8] And the LORD spoke to Aaron: "Here, I Myself have also given you charge of My heave offerings, all the holy gifts of the children of Israel; I have given them as a portion to you and your sons, as an ordinance forever. [9] This shall be yours of the most holy things *reserved* from the fire: every offering of theirs, every grain offering and every sin offering and every trespass offering which they render to Me, *shall be* most holy for you and your sons. [10] In a most holy *place* you shall eat it; every male shall eat it. It shall be holy to you.

[11] "This also *is* yours: the heave offering of their gift, with all the wave offerings of the children of Israel; I have given them to you, and your sons and daughters with you, as an ordinance forever. Everyone who is clean in your house may eat it.

[12] "All the best of the oil, all the best of the new wine and the grain, their firstfruits which they offer to the LORD, I have given them to you. [13] Whatever first ripe fruit is in their land, which they bring to the LORD, shall be yours. Everyone who is clean in your house may eat it.

[14] "Every devoted thing in Israel shall be yours.

[15] "Everything that first opens the womb of all flesh, which they bring to the LORD, whether man or beast, shall be yours; nevertheless the firstborn of man you shall surely redeem, and the firstborn of unclean animals you shall redeem. [16] And those redeemed of the devoted things you shall redeem when one month old, according to your valuation, for five

shekels of silver, according to the shekel of the sanctuary, which *is* twenty gerahs. [17] But the firstborn of a cow, the firstborn of a sheep, or the firstborn of a goat you shall not redeem; they *are* holy. You shall sprinkle their blood on the altar, and burn their fat *as* an offering made by fire for a sweet aroma to the LORD. [18] And their flesh shall be yours, just as the wave breast and the right thigh are yours.

[19] "All the heave offerings of the holy things, which the children of Israel offer to the LORD, I have given to you and your sons and daughters with you as an ordinance forever; it *is* a covenant of salt forever before the LORD with you and your descendants with you."

[20] Then the LORD said to Aaron: "You shall have no inheritance in their land, nor shall you have any portion among them; I *am* your portion and your inheritance among the children of Israel.

[21] "Behold, I have given the children of Levi all the tithes in Israel as an inheritance in return for the work which they perform, the work of the tabernacle of meeting. [22] Hereafter the children of Israel shall not come near the tabernacle of meeting, lest they bear sin and die. [23] But the Levites shall perform the work of the tabernacle of meeting, and they shall bear their iniquity; *it shall be* a statute forever, throughout your generations, that among the children of Israel they shall have no inheritance. [24] For the tithes of the children of Israel, which they offer up *as* a heave offering to the LORD, I have given to the Levites as an inheritance; therefore I have said to them, 'Among the children of Israel they shall have no inheritance.' "

[25] Then the LORD spoke to Moses, saying, [26] "Speak thus to the Levites, and say to them: 'When you take from the children of Israel the tithes which I have given you from them as your inheritance, then you shall offer up a heave offering of it to the LORD, a tenth of the tithe. [27] And your heave offering shall be reckoned to you as though *it were* the grain of the threshing floor and as the fullness of the winepress. [28] Thus you shall also offer a heave offering to the LORD from all your tithes which you receive from the children of Israel, and you shall give the LORD's heave offering from it to Aaron

Small Beginnings

Near the top of one of the highest peaks in the Rocky Mountain range — more than 10,000 feet above sea level — are two natural springs. They are so close together and level in height, that it would not take a great deal of effort to divert one streamlet toward the other. Yet if you follow the course of one of these streams, you will find that it travels easterly, and after traversing plateaus and valleys and receiving water from countless tributaries, it becomes part of the great Mississippi River and empties into the Gulf of Mexico.

If you follow the water from the other fountain, you will find that it gradually descends in a westerly direction, also combining with other tributaries, until it becomes part of the Columbia River, which empties into the Pacific Ocean.

The terminal points of the two streams are more than five thousand miles apart, separated by one of the highest ranges of mountains in the world. And yet at their onset, the two streams were close neighbors. Very little effort would be required to make the easterly stream run west, or the westerly stream run east.

The direction of any person, project, or plan is determined at the very beginning. Our greatest opportunity to impact the lives of our children for the long haul is to teach them while they're young. It's never too early to start!

the priest. 29 Of all your gifts you shall offer up every heave offering due to the LORD, from all the best of them, the consecrated part of them.' 30 Therefore you shall say to them: 'When you have lifted up the best of it, then *the rest* shall be accounted to the Levites as the produce of the threshing floor and as the produce of the winepress. 31 You may eat it in any place, you and your households, for it *is* your reward for your work in the tabernacle of meeting. 32 And you shall bear no sin because of it, when you have lifted up the best of it. But you shall not profane the holy gifts of the children of Israel, lest you die.' "

～ PSALM 32:6–11 ～

6 For this cause everyone who is godly
    shall pray to You
  In a time when You may be found;
  Surely in a flood of great waters
  They shall not come near him.
7 You *are* my hiding place;
  You shall preserve me from trouble;
  You shall surround me with songs of
    deliverance.   Selah

8 I will instruct you and teach you in
    the way you should go;
  I will guide you with My eye.
9 Do not be like the horse *or* like the
    mule,
  Which have no understanding,
  Which must be harnessed with bit
    and bridle,
  Else they will not come near you.

10 Many sorrows *shall be* to the
    wicked;
  But he who trusts in the LORD,
    mercy shall surround him.
11 Be glad in the LORD and rejoice, you
    righteous;
  And shout for joy, all *you* upright in
    heart!

～ PROVERBS 11:19–21 ～

19 As righteousness *leads* to life,
  So he who pursues evil *pursues it* to
    his own death.
20 Those who are of a perverse heart
    are an abomination to the LORD,

But *the* blameless in their ways *are*
    His delight.
21 *Though they join* forces, the wicked
    will not go unpunished;
  But the posterity of the righteous
    will be delivered.

～ MARK 11:20–33 ～

Now in the morning, as they passed by, they saw the fig tree dried up from the roots. 21 And Peter, remembering, said to Him, "Rabbi, look! The fig tree which You cursed has withered away."

22 So Jesus answered and said to them, "Have faith in God. 23 For assuredly, I say to you, whoever says to this mountain, 'Be removed and be cast into the sea,' and does not doubt in his heart, but believes that those things he says will be done, he will have whatever he says. 24 Therefore I say to you, whatever things you ask when you pray, believe that you receive *them,* and you will have *them.*

25 "And whenever you stand praying, if you have anything against anyone, forgive him, that your Father in heaven may also forgive you your trespasses. 26 But if you do not forgive, neither will your Father in heaven forgive your trespasses."

27 Then they came again to Jerusalem. And as He was walking in the temple, the chief priests, the scribes, and the elders came to Him. 28 And they said to Him, "By what authority are You doing these things? And who gave You this authority to do these things?"

29 But Jesus answered and said to them, "I also will ask you one question; then answer Me, and I will tell you by what authority I do these things: 30 The baptism of John—was it from heaven or from men? Answer Me."

31 And they reasoned among themselves, saying, "If we say, 'From heaven,' He will say, 'Why then did you not believe him?' 32 But if we say, 'From men' "— they feared the people, for all counted John to have been a prophet indeed. 33 So they answered and said to Jesus, "We do not know."

And Jesus answered and said to them, "Neither will I tell you by what authority I do these things."

Now the LORD spoke to Moses and Aaron, saying, ² "This *is* the ordinance of the law which the LORD has commanded, saying: 'Speak to the children of Israel, that they bring you a red heifer without blemish, in which there *is* no defect *and* on which a yoke has never come. ³ You shall give it to Eleazar the priest, that he may take it outside the camp, and it shall be slaughtered before him; ⁴ and Eleazar the priest shall take some of its blood with his finger, and sprinkle some of its blood seven times directly in front of the tabernacle of meeting. ⁵ Then the heifer shall be burned in his sight: its hide, its flesh, its blood, and its offal shall be burned. ⁶ And the priest shall take cedar wood and hyssop and scarlet, and cast *them* into the midst of the fire burning the heifer. ⁷ Then the priest shall wash his clothes, he shall bathe in water, and afterward he shall come into the camp; the priest shall be unclean until evening. ⁸ And the one who burns it shall wash his clothes in water, bathe in water, and shall be unclean until evening. ⁹ Then a man *who is* clean shall gather up the ashes of the heifer, and store *them* outside the camp in a clean place; and they shall be kept for the congregation of the children of Israel for the water of purification; it *is* for purifying from sin. ¹⁰ And the one who gathers the ashes of the heifer shall wash his clothes, and be unclean until evening. It shall be a statute forever to the children of Israel and to the stranger who dwells among them.

¹¹ 'He who touches the dead body of anyone shall be unclean seven days. ¹² He shall purify himself with the water on the third day and on the seventh day; *then* he will be clean. But if he does not purify himself on the third day and on the seventh day, he will not be clean. ¹³ Whoever touches the body of anyone who has died, and does not purify himself, defiles the tabernacle of the LORD. That person shall be cut off from Israel. He shall be unclean, because the water of purification was not sprinkled on him; his uncleanness *is* still on him.

¹⁴ 'This *is* the law when a man dies in a tent: All who come into the tent and all who *are* in the tent shall be unclean seven days; ¹⁵ and every open vessel, which has no cover fastened on it, *is* unclean. ¹⁶ Whoever in the open field touches one who is slain by a sword or who has died, or a bone of a man, or a grave, shall be unclean seven days.

¹⁷ 'And for an unclean *person* they shall take some of the ashes of the heifer burnt for purification from sin, and running water shall be put on them in a vessel. ¹⁸ A clean person shall take hyssop and dip *it* in the water, sprinkle *it* on the tent, on all the vessels, on the persons who were there, or on the one who touched a bone, the slain, the dead, or a grave. ¹⁹ The clean *person* shall sprinkle the unclean on the third day and on the seventh day; and on the seventh day he shall purify himself, wash his clothes, and bathe in water; and at evening he shall be clean.

²⁰ 'But the man who is unclean and does not purify himself, that person shall be cut off from among the assembly, because he has defiled the sanctuary of the LORD. The water of purification has not been sprinkled on him; he *is* unclean. ²¹ It shall be a perpetual statute for them. He who sprinkles the water of purification shall wash his clothes; and he who touches the water of purification shall be unclean until evening. ²² Whatever the unclean *person* touches shall be unclean; and the person who touches *it* shall be unclean until evening.' "

20 Then the children of Israel, the whole congregation, came into the Wilderness of Zin in the first month, and the people stayed in Kadesh; and Miriam died there and was buried there.

² Now there was no water for the congregation; so they gathered together against Moses and Aaron. ³ And the people contended with Moses and spoke, saying: "If only we had died when our brethren died before the LORD! ⁴ Why have you brought up the assembly of the LORD into this wilderness, that we and our animals should die here? ⁵ And why have you made us come up out of Egypt,

to bring us to this evil place? It *is* not a place of grain or figs or vines or pomegranates; nor *is* there any water to drink."

⁶ So Moses and Aaron went from the presence of the assembly to the door of the tabernacle of meeting, and they fell on their faces. And the glory of the LORD appeared to them.

⁷ Then the LORD spoke to Moses, saying, ⁸ "Take the rod; you and your brother Aaron gather the congregation together. Speak to the rock before their eyes, and it will yield its water; thus you shall bring water for them out of the rock, and give drink to the congregation and their animals." ⁹ So Moses took the rod from before the LORD as He commanded him.

¹⁰ And Moses and Aaron gathered the assembly together before the rock; and he said to them, "Hear now, you rebels! Must we bring water for you out of this rock?" ¹¹ Then Moses lifted his hand and struck the rock twice with his rod; and water came out abundantly, and the congregation and their animals drank.

¹² Then the LORD spoke to Moses and Aaron, "Because you did not believe Me, to hallow Me in the eyes of the children of Israel, therefore you shall not bring this assembly into the land which I have given them."

¹³ This *was* the water of Meribah, because the children of Israel contended with the LORD, and He was hallowed among them.

¹⁴ Now Moses sent messengers from Kadesh to the king of Edom. "Thus says your brother Israel: 'You know all the hardship that has befallen us, ¹⁵ how our fathers went down to Egypt, and we dwelt in Egypt a long time, and the Egyptians afflicted us and our fathers. ¹⁶ When we cried out to the LORD, He heard our voice and sent the Angel and brought us up out of Egypt; now here we are in Kadesh, a city on the edge of your border. ¹⁷ Please let us pass through your country. We will not pass through fields or vineyards, nor will we drink water from wells; we will go along the King's Highway; we will not turn aside to the right hand or to the left until we have passed through your territory.' "

¹⁸ Then Edom said to him, "You shall not pass through my *land,* lest I come out against you with the sword."

¹⁹ So the children of Israel said to him, "We will go by the Highway, and if I or my livestock drink any of your water, then I will pay for it; let me only pass through on foot, nothing *more.*"

²⁰ Then he said, "You shall not pass through." So Edom came out against them with many men and with a strong hand. ²¹ Thus Edom refused to give Israel passage through his territory; so Israel turned away from him.

²² Now the children of Israel, the whole congregation, journeyed from Kadesh and came to Mount Hor. ²³ And the LORD spoke to Moses and Aaron in Mount Hor by the border of the land of Edom, saying: ²⁴ "Aaron shall be gathered to his people, for he shall not enter the land which I have given to the children of Israel, because you rebelled against My word at the water of Meribah. ²⁵ Take Aaron and Eleazar his son, and bring them up to Mount Hor; ²⁶ and strip Aaron of his garments and put them on Eleazar his son; for Aaron shall be gathered *to his people* and die there." ²⁷ So Moses did just as the LORD commanded, and they went up to Mount Hor in the sight of all the congregation. ²⁸ Moses stripped Aaron of his garments and put them on Eleazar his son; and Aaron died there on the top of the mountain. Then Moses and Eleazar came down from the mountain. ²⁹ Now when all the congregation saw that Aaron was dead, all the house of Israel mourned for Aaron thirty days.

～ PSALM 33:1–9 ～

1 Rejoice in the LORD, O you
       righteous!
     For praise from the upright is
       beautiful.
2 Praise the LORD with the harp;
     Make melody to Him with an
       instrument of ten strings.
3 Sing to Him a new song;
     Play skillfully with a shout of joy.

4 For the word of the LORD *is* right,
     And all His work *is done* in truth.
5 He loves righteousness and justice;

The Worry Table

A military chaplain once drew up a "Worry Table" based upon the problems men and women had brought to him through his years of service. He found their worries fit into the following categories:

Worries about things that never happened—40 percent.

Worries about past, unchangeable decisions—30 percent.

Worries about illness that never happened—12 percent.

Worries about adult children and friends (who were able to take care of themselves)—10 percent.

Worries about real problems—8 percent.

According to his chart, 92 percent of all our worries are about things we can't control, things which are better left to God. The truth is, anxiety is rooted in a failure to trust God.

We simply don't believe He is big enough, or cares enough, to help with our problems, give us the desires of our hearts, and keep us and our loved ones from harm.

Once we know God's character, we can easily see how we worry for nothing most of the time. God is more than big enough, and cares more than enough to help us, bless us, and protect us. Give your worries to Him and He will replace them with His peace.

The earth is full of the goodness of
the LORD.

6 By the word of the LORD the
    heavens were made,
And all the host of them by the
    breath of His mouth.
7 He gathers the waters of the sea
    together as a heap;
He lays up the deep in storehouses.

8 Let all the earth fear the LORD;
Let all the inhabitants of the world
    stand in awe of Him.
9 For He spoke, and it was *done;*
He commanded, and it stood fast.

~ PROVERBS 11:22–24 ~

22 *As* a ring of gold in a swine's snout,
    So is a lovely woman who lacks
    discretion.

23 The desire of the righteous *is* only
    good,
But the expectation of the wicked *is*
    wrath.

24 There is *one* who scatters, yet
    increases more;
And there is *one* who withholds
    more than is right,
But it *leads* to poverty.

~ MARK 12:1–27 ~

Then He began to speak to them in
parables: "A man planted a vineyard and
set a hedge around *it,* dug *a place for* the
wine vat and built a tower. And he leased
it to vinedressers and went into a far
country. 2 Now at vintage-time he sent a
servant to the vinedressers, that he might
receive some of the fruit of the vineyard
from the vinedressers. 3 And they took *him*
and beat him and sent *him* away empty-
handed. 4 Again he sent them another
servant, and at him they threw stones,
wounded *him* in the head, and sent *him*
away shamefully treated. 5 And again he
sent another, and him they killed; and
many others, beating some and killing
some. 6 Therefore still having one son, his
beloved, he also sent him to them last,
saying, 'They will respect my son.' 7 But

those vinedressers said among themselves,
'This is the heir. Come, let us kill him,
and the inheritance will be ours.' 8 So they
took him and killed *him* and cast *him* out
of the vineyard.

9 "Therefore what will the owner of the
vineyard do? He will come and destroy
the vinedressers, and give the vineyard to
others. 10 Have you not even read this
Scripture:

'The stone which the builders
    rejected
Has become the chief cornerstone.
11 This was the LORD's doing,
And it is marvelous in our eyes'? "

12 And they sought to lay hands on Him,
but feared the multitude, for they knew
He had spoken the parable against them.
So they left Him and went away.

13 Then they sent to Him some of the
Pharisees and the Herodians, to catch Him
in *His* words. 14 When they had come, they
said to Him, "Teacher, we know that You
are true, and care about no one; for
You do not regard the person of men, but
teach the way of God in truth. Is it lawful
to pay taxes to Caesar, or not? 15 Shall we
pay, or shall we not pay?"

But He, knowing their hypocrisy, said
to them, "Why do you test Me? Bring Me
a denarius that I may see *it.*" 16 So they
brought *it.*

And He said to them, "Whose image
and inscription *is* this?" They said to Him,
"Caesar's."

17 And Jesus answered and said to them,
"Render to Caesar the things that are
Caesar's, and to God the things that
are God's."

And they marveled at Him.

18 Then *some* Sadducees, who say there
is no resurrection, came to Him; and they
asked Him, saying: 19 "Teacher, Moses
wrote to us that if a man's brother dies,
and leaves *his* wife behind, and leaves no
children, his brother should take his wife
and raise up offspring for his brother.
20 Now there were seven brothers. The
first took a wife; and dying, he left no
offspring. 21 And the second took her, and
he died; nor did he leave any offspring.
And the third likewise. 22 So the seven had

her and left no offspring. Last of all the woman died also. [23] Therefore, in the resurrection, when they rise, whose wife will she be? For all seven had her as wife."

[24] Jesus answered and said to them, "Are you not therefore mistaken, because you do not know the Scriptures nor the power of God? [25] For when they rise from the dead, they neither marry nor are given in marriage, but are like angels in heaven. [26] But concerning the dead, that they rise, have you not read in the book of Moses, in the *burning* bush *passage,* how God spoke to him, saying, '*I am* the God of Abraham, the God of Isaac, and the God of Jacob'? [27] He is not the God of the dead, but the God of the living. You are therefore greatly mistaken."

READING 71 · MARCH 12

∼ Numbers 21:1—22:41 ∼

The king of Arad, the Canaanite, who dwelt in the South, heard that Israel was coming on the road to Atharim. Then he fought against Israel and took *some* of them prisoners. [2] So Israel made a vow to the LORD, and said, "If You will indeed deliver this people into my hand, then I will utterly destroy their cities." [3] And the LORD listened to the voice of Israel and delivered up the Canaanites, and they utterly destroyed them and their cities. So the name of that place was called Hormah.

[4] Then they journeyed from Mount Hor by the Way of the Red Sea, to go around the land of Edom; and the soul of the people became very discouraged on the way. [5] And the people spoke against God and against Moses: "Why have you brought us up out of Egypt to die in the wilderness? For *there is* no food and no water, and our soul loathes this worthless bread." [6] So the LORD sent fiery serpents among the people, and they bit the people; and many of the people of Israel died. [7] Therefore the people came to Moses, and said, "We have sinned, for we have spoken against the LORD and against you; pray to the LORD that He take away the serpents from us." So Moses prayed for the people. [8] Then the LORD said to Moses, "Make a fiery *serpent,* and set it on a pole; and it shall be that everyone who is bitten, when he looks at it, shall live." [9] So Moses made a bronze serpent, and put it on a pole; and so it was, if a serpent had bitten anyone, when he looked at the bronze serpent, he lived.

[10] Now the children of Israel moved on and camped in Oboth. [11] And they journeyed from Oboth and camped at Ije Abarim, in the wilderness which *is* east of Moab, toward the sunrise. [12] From there they moved and camped in the Valley of Zered. [13] From there they moved and camped on the other side of the Arnon, which *is* in the wilderness that extends from the border of the Amorites; for the Arnon *is* the border of Moab, between Moab and the Amorites. [14] Therefore it is said in the Book of the Wars of the LORD:

"Waheb in Suphah,
    The brooks of the Arnon,
[15]   And the slope of the brooks
    That reaches to the dwelling of Ar,
    And lies on the border of Moab."

[16] From there *they went* to Beer, which *is* the well where the LORD said to Moses, "Gather the people together, and I will give them water." [17] Then Israel sang this song:

"Spring up, O well!
    All of you sing to it—
[18]   The well the leaders sank,
    Dug by the nation's nobles,
    By the lawgiver, with their staves."

And from the wilderness *they went* to Mattanah, [19] from Mattanah to Nahaliel, from Nahaliel to Bamoth, [20] and from Bamoth, *in* the valley that *is* in the country of Moab, to the top of Pisgah which looks down on the wasteland.

[21] Then Israel sent messengers to Sihon king of the Amorites, saying, [22] "Let me pass through your land. We will not turn

aside into fields or vineyards; we will not drink water from wells. We will go by the King's Highway until we have passed through your territory." ²³ But Sihon would not allow Israel to pass through his territory. So Sihon gathered all his people together and went out against Israel in the wilderness, and he came to Jahaz and fought against Israel. ²⁴ Then Israel defeated him with the edge of the sword, and took possession of his land from the Arnon to the Jabbok, as far as the people of Ammon; for the border of the people of Ammon *was* fortified. ²⁵ So Israel took all these cities, and Israel dwelt in all the cities of the Amorites, in Heshbon and in all its villages. ²⁶ For Heshbon *was* the city of Sihon king of the Amorites, who had fought against the former king of Moab, and had taken all his land from his hand as far as the Arnon. ²⁷ Therefore those who speak in proverbs say:

"Come to Heshbon, let it be built;
Let the city of Sihon be repaired.

²⁸ "For fire went out from Heshbon,
A flame from the city of Sihon;
It consumed Ar of Moab,
The lords of the heights of the Arnon.
²⁹ Woe to you, Moab!
You have perished, O people of Chemosh!
He has given his sons as fugitives,
And his daughters into captivity,
To Sihon king of the Amorites.

³⁰ "But we have shot at them;
Heshbon has perished as far as Dibon.
Then we laid waste as far as Nophah,
Which *reaches* to Medeba."

³¹ Thus Israel dwelt in the land of the Amorites. ³² Then Moses sent to spy out Jazer; and they took its villages and drove out the Amorites who *were* there.
³³ And they turned and went up by the way to Bashan. So Og king of Bashan went out against them, he and all his people, to battle at Edrei. ³⁴ Then the LORD said to Moses, "Do not fear him, for I have delivered him into your hand, with all his people and his land; and you shall do to him as you did to Sihon king of the Amorites, who dwelt at Heshbon." ³⁵ So they defeated him, his sons, and all his people, until there was no survivor left him; and they took possession of his land.

22 Then the children of Israel moved, and camped in the plains of Moab on the side of the Jordan *across from* Jericho.
² Now Balak the son of Zippor saw all that Israel had done to the Amorites. ³ And Moab was exceedingly afraid of the people because they *were* many, and Moab was sick with dread because of the children of Israel. ⁴ So Moab said to the elders of Midian, "Now this company will lick up everything around us, as an ox licks up the grass of the field." And Balak the son of Zippor *was* king of the Moabites at that time. ⁵ Then he sent messengers to Balaam the son of Beor at Pethor, which *is* near the River in the land of the sons of his people, to call him, saying: "Look, a people has come from Egypt. See, they cover the face of the earth, and are settling next to me! ⁶ Therefore please come at once, curse this people for me, for they *are* too mighty for me. Perhaps I shall be able to defeat them and drive them out of the land, for I know that he whom you bless *is* blessed, and he whom you curse is cursed."
⁷ So the elders of Moab and the elders of Midian departed with the diviner's fee in their hand, and they came to Balaam and spoke to him the words of Balak. ⁸ And he said to them, "Lodge here tonight, and I will bring back word to you, as the LORD speaks to me." So the princes of Moab stayed with Balaam.
⁹ Then God came to Balaam and said, "Who *are* these men with you?"
¹⁰ So Balaam said to God, "Balak the son of Zippor, king of Moab, has sent to me, *saying,* ¹¹ 'Look, a people has come out of Egypt, and they cover the face of the earth. Come now, curse them for me; perhaps I shall be able to overpower them and drive them out.' "
¹² And God said to Balaam, "You shall

Kindness Returns

The generous soul will be made rich, and he who waters will also be watered himself.

Proverbs 11:25

Many years ago, an elderly man and his wife entered the lobby of a small Philadelphia hotel. "All the big places are filled," the man said. "Can you give us a room?" The clerk replied that with three conventions in town, no accommodations were available anywhere. "Every guest room is taken," he said, but then added, "I can't send a nice couple like you out into the rain at one o'clock in the morning, though. Would you be willing to sleep in my room?"

The next morning as he paid his bill, the elderly man said to the clerk, "You are the kind of manager who should be the boss of the best hotel in the United States. Maybe someday I'll build one for you." The clerk laughed and forgot about the incident. About two years later, however, he received a letter containing a round-trip ticket to New York and a request that he be the guest of the elderly couple he had befriended.

Once in New York, the old man led the clerk to the corner of Fifth Avenue and Thirty-fourth Street, where he pointed to an incredible new building and declared, "That is the hotel I have just built for you to manage." The young man, George C. Boldt, accepted the offer of William Waldorf Astor to become the manager of the original Waldorf-Astoria, considered the finest hotel in the world in its time.

When you go out of your way to help someone, they often return the favor. Even if they don't, someone else will, and most importantly — God will.

not go with them; you shall not curse the people, for they *are* blessed."

¹³ So Balaam rose in the morning and said to the princes of Balak, "Go back to your land, for the LORD has refused to give me permission to go with you."

¹⁴ And the princes of Moab rose and went to Balak, and said, "Balaam refuses to come with us."

¹⁵ Then Balak again sent princes, more numerous and more honorable than they. ¹⁶ And they came to Balaam and said to him, "Thus says Balak the son of Zippor: 'Please let nothing hinder you from coming to me; ¹⁷ for I will certainly honor you greatly, and I will do whatever you say to me. Therefore please come, curse this people for me.' "

¹⁸ Then Balaam answered and said to the servants of Balak, "Though Balak were to give me his house full of silver and gold, I could not go beyond the word of the LORD my God, to do less or more. ¹⁹ Now therefore, please, you also stay here tonight, that I may know what more the LORD will say to me."

²⁰ And God came to Balaam at night and said to him, "If the men come to call you, rise *and* go with them; but only the word which I speak to you—that you shall do." ²¹ So Balaam rose in the morning, saddled his donkey, and went with the princes of Moab.

²² Then God's anger was aroused because he went, and the Angel of the LORD took His stand in the way as an adversary against him. And he was riding on his donkey, and his two servants *were* with him. ²³ Now the donkey saw the Angel of the LORD standing in the way with His drawn sword in His hand, and the donkey turned aside out of the way and went into the field. So Balaam struck the donkey to turn her back onto the road. ²⁴ Then the Angel of the LORD stood in a narrow path between the vineyards, *with* a wall on this side and a wall on that side. ²⁵ And when the donkey saw the Angel of the LORD, she pushed herself against the wall and crushed Balaam's foot against the wall; so he struck her again. ²⁶ Then the Angel of the LORD went further, and stood in a narrow place where there *was* no way to turn either to the right hand or to the left. ²⁷ And when the donkey saw

the Angel of the LORD, she lay down under Balaam; so Balaam's anger was aroused, and he struck the donkey with his staff.

²⁸ Then the LORD opened the mouth of the donkey, and she said to Balaam, "What have I done to you, that you have struck me these three times?"

²⁹ And Balaam said to the donkey, "Because you have abused me. I wish there were a sword in my hand, for now I would kill you!"

³⁰ So the donkey said to Balaam, "*Am* I not your donkey on which you have ridden, ever since *I became* yours, to this day? Was I ever disposed to do this to you?"

And he said, "No."

³¹ Then the LORD opened Balaam's eyes, and he saw the Angel of the LORD standing in the way with His drawn sword in His hand; and he bowed his head and fell flat on his face. ³² And the Angel of the LORD said to him, "Why have you struck your donkey these three times? Behold, I have come out to stand against you, because *your* way is perverse before Me. ³³ The donkey saw Me and turned aside from Me these three times. If she had not turned aside from Me, surely I would also have killed you by now, and let her live."

³⁴ And Balaam said to the Angel of the LORD, "I have sinned, for I did not know You stood in the way against me. Now therefore, if it displeases You, I will turn back."

³⁵ Then the Angel of the LORD said to Balaam, "Go with the men, but only the word that I speak to you, that you shall speak." So Balaam went with the princes of Balak.

³⁶ Now when Balak heard that Balaam was coming, he went out to meet him at the city of Moab, which *is* on the border at the Arnon, the boundary of the territory. ³⁷ Then Balak said to Balaam, "Did I not earnestly send to you, calling for you? Why did you not come to me? Am I not able to honor you?"

³⁸ And Balaam said to Balak, "Look, I have come to you! Now, have I any power at all to say anything? The word that God puts in my mouth, that I must speak." ³⁹ So Balaam went with Balak, and they came to Kirjath Huzoth. ⁴⁰ Then Balak offered

oxen and sheep, and he sent *some* to Balaam and to the princes who *were* with him.

⁴¹ So it was, the next day, that Balak took Balaam and brought him up to the high places of Baal, that from there he might observe the extent of the people.

~ PSALM 33:10–17 ~

¹⁰ The LORD brings the counsel of the
nations to nothing;
He makes the plans of the peoples of
no effect.
¹¹ The counsel of the LORD stands
forever,
The plans of His heart to all
generations.
¹² Blessed *is* the nation whose God *is*
the LORD,
The people He has chosen as His
own inheritance.

¹³ The LORD looks from heaven;
He sees all the sons of men.
¹⁴ From the place of His dwelling He
looks
On all the inhabitants of the earth;
¹⁵ He fashions their hearts individually;
He considers all their works.

¹⁶ No king *is* saved by the multitude of
an army;
A mighty man is not delivered by
great strength.
¹⁷ A horse *is* a vain hope for safety;
Neither shall it deliver *any* by its
great strength.

~ PROVERBS 11:25, 26 ~

²⁵ The generous soul will be made rich,
And he who waters will also be
watered himself.
²⁶ The people will curse him who
withholds grain,
But blessing *will be* on the head of
him who sells *it*.

~ MARK 12:28–44 ~

Then one of the scribes came, and having heard them reasoning together, perceiv-

ing that He had answered them well, asked Him, "Which is the first commandment of all?"

²⁹ Jesus answered him, "The first of all the commandments *is:* 'Hear, O Israel, the LORD our God, the LORD is one. ³⁰ And you shall love the LORD your God with all your heart, with all your soul, with all your mind, and with all your strength.' This *is* the first commandment. ³¹ And the second, like *it, is* this: 'You shall love your neighbor as yourself.' There is no other commandment greater than these."

³² So the scribe said to Him, "Well *said,* Teacher. You have spoken the truth, for there is one God, and there is no other but He. ³³ And to love Him with all the heart, with all the understanding, with all the soul, and with all the strength, and to love one's neighbor as oneself, is more than all the whole burnt offerings and sacrifices."

³⁴ Now when Jesus saw that he answered wisely, He said to him, "You are not far from the kingdom of God."

But after that no one dared question Him.

³⁵ Then Jesus answered and said, while He taught in the temple, "How *is it* that the scribes say that the Christ is the Son of David? ³⁶ For David himself said by the Holy Spirit:

'The LORD said to my Lord,
"Sit at My right hand,
Till I make Your enemies Your
footstool." '

³⁷ Therefore David himself calls Him 'Lord'; how is He *then* his Son?"

And the common people heard Him gladly.

³⁸ Then He said to them in His teaching, "Beware of the scribes, who desire to go around in long robes, *love* greetings in the marketplaces, ³⁹ the best seats in the synagogues, and the best places at feasts, ⁴⁰ who devour widows' houses, and for a pretense make long prayers. These will receive greater condemnation."

⁴¹ Now Jesus sat opposite the treasury and saw how the people put money into the treasury. And many *who were* rich put in much. ⁴² Then one poor widow came and threw in two mites, which make a

quadrans. ⁴³ So He called His disciples to *Himself* and said to them, "Assuredly, I say to you that this poor widow has put in more than all those who have given to the treasury; ⁴⁴ for they all put in out of their abundance, but she out of her poverty put in all that she had, her whole livelihood."

∼ NUMBERS 23:1—24:25 ∼

Then Balaam said to Balak, "Build seven altars for me here, and prepare for me here seven bulls and seven rams."

² And Balak did just as Balaam had spoken, and Balak and Balaam offered a bull and a ram on *each* altar. ³ Then Balaam said to Balak, "Stand by your burnt offering, and I will go; perhaps the LORD will come to meet me, and whatever He shows me I will tell you." So he went to a desolate height. ⁴ And God met Balaam, and he said to Him, "I have prepared the seven altars, and I have offered on *each* altar a bull and a ram."

⁵ Then the LORD put a word in Balaam's mouth, and said, "Return to Balak, and thus you shall speak." ⁶ So he returned to him, and there he was, standing by his burnt offering, he and all the princes of Moab.

⁷ And he took up his oracle and said:

"Balak the king of Moab has
brought me from Aram,
From the mountains of the east.
'Come, curse Jacob for me,
And come, denounce Israel!'

⁸ "How shall I curse whom God has
not cursed?
And how shall I denounce *whom*
the LORD has not denounced?
⁹ For from the top of the rocks I see
him,
And from the hills I behold him;
There! A people dwelling alone,
Not reckoning itself among the
nations.

¹⁰ "Who can count the dust of Jacob,
Or number one-fourth of Israel?
Let me die the death of the
righteous,
And let my end be like his!"

¹¹ Then Balak said to Balaam, "What have you done to me? I took you to curse my enemies, and look, you have blessed *them* bountifully!"

¹² So he answered and said, "Must I not take heed to speak what the LORD has put in my mouth?"

¹³ Then Balak said to him, "Please come with me to another place from which you may see them; you shall see only the outer part of them, and shall not see them all; curse them for me from there." ¹⁴ So he brought him to the field of Zophim, to the top of Pisgah, and built seven altars, and offered a bull and a ram on *each* altar.

¹⁵ And he said to Balak, "Stand here by your burnt offering while I meet *the* LORD over there."

¹⁶ Then the LORD met Balaam, and put a word in his mouth, and said, "Go back to Balak, and thus you shall speak." ¹⁷ So he came to him, and there he was, standing by his burnt offering, and the princes of Moab were with him. And Balak said to him, "What has the LORD spoken?"

¹⁸ Then he took up his oracle and said:

"Rise up, Balak, and hear!
Listen to me, son of Zippor!

¹⁹ "God *is* not a man, that He should
lie,
Nor a son of man, that He should
repent.
Has He said, and will He not do?
Or has He spoken, and will He
not make it good?
²⁰ Behold, I have received *a
command* to bless;
He has blessed, and I cannot
reverse it.

²¹ "He has not observed iniquity in
Jacob,

A Warm Heart and Willing Hands

Bob Richie, a former truck driver and Marine "no longer on active duty," found that the idleness of early retirement got on his nerves. So he created an unusual full-time "volunteer job" for himself at St. Christopher's Hospital for Children in Philadelphia. He makes beds, picks up toys, changes diapers — whatever needs to be done. But the activities he enjoys most are sitting for hours rocking irritable babies or walking toddlers up and down the hall all afternoon.

Richie came to his volunteer work after his own experience in a hospital. A three-packs-a-day smoker for thirty years, he'd lost a lung to cancer. He said, "My wife stayed with me the whole time. That's when I realized how important it was to have somebody there." A ward full of children fighting devastating diseases may seem like the last place that a man battling cancer would want to be. Richie sees it differently. "Being here keeps my mind off it. One reason I've done so well with the cancer is seeing how the children fight. These kids — they're the real heroes."

It doesn't take great talent, exhaustive energy, or huge chunks of time to do good. All it takes is a warm heart and willing hands. If you have those, you'll find all the time, energy, and ability that you need.

Nor has He seen wickedness in
Israel.
The LORD his God *is* with him,
And the shout of a King *is* among
them.
²² God brings them out of Egypt;
He has strength like a wild ox.

²³ "For *there is* no sorcery against
Jacob,
Nor any divination against Israel.
It now must be said of Jacob
And of Israel, 'Oh, what God has
done!'
²⁴ Look, a people rises like a lioness,
And lifts itself up like a lion;
It shall not lie down until it
devours the prey,
And drinks the blood of the
slain."

²⁵ Then Balak said to Balaam, "Neither
curse them at all, nor bless them at all!"

²⁶ So Balaam answered and said to
Balak, "Did I not tell you, saying, 'All that
the LORD speaks, that I must do'?"

²⁷ Then Balak said to Balaam, "Please
come, I will take you to another place;
perhaps it will please God that you may
curse them for me from there." ²⁸ So Balak
took Balaam to the top of Peor, that overlooks the wasteland. ²⁹ Then Balaam said
to Balak, "Build for me here seven altars,
and prepare for me here seven bulls and
seven rams." ³⁰ And Balak did as Balaam
had said, and offered a bull and a ram on
every altar.

24 Now when Balaam saw that it
pleased the LORD to bless Israel, he did
not go as at other times, to seek to use
sorcery, but he set his face toward the
wilderness. ² And Balaam raised his eyes,
and saw Israel encamped according to
their tribes; and the Spirit of God came
upon him.
³ Then he took up his oracle and said:

"The utterance of Balaam the son
of Beor,
The utterance of the man whose
eyes are opened,
⁴ The utterance of him who hears
the words of God,

Who sees the vision of the
Almighty,
Who falls down, with eyes wide
open:

⁵ "How lovely are your tents,
O Jacob!
Your dwellings, O Israel!
⁶ Like valleys that stretch out,
Like gardens by the riverside,
Like aloes planted by the LORD,
Like cedars beside the waters.
⁷ He shall pour water from his
buckets,
And his seed *shall be* in many
waters.

"His king shall be higher than
Agag,
And his kingdom shall be exalted.

⁸ "God brings him out of Egypt;
He has strength like a wild ox;
He shall consume the nations, his
enemies;
He shall break their bones
And pierce *them* with his arrows.
⁹ 'He bows down, he lies down as a
lion;
And as a lion, who shall rouse
him?'

"Blessed *is* he who blesses you,
And cursed *is* he who curses you."

¹⁰ Then Balak's anger was aroused
against Balaam, and he struck his hands
together; and Balak said to Balaam, "I
called you to curse my enemies, and look,
you have bountifully blessed *them* these
three times! ¹¹ Now therefore, flee to your
place. I said I would greatly honor you,
but in fact, the LORD has kept you back
from honor."

¹² So Balaam said to Balak, "Did I not
also speak to your messengers whom you
sent to me, saying, ¹³ 'If Balak were to give
me his house full of silver and gold, I could
not go beyond the word of the LORD, to
do good or bad of my own will. What the
LORD says, that I must speak'? ¹⁴ And now,
indeed, I am going to my people. Come, I
will advise you what this people will do
to your people in the latter days."

¹⁵ So he took up his oracle and said:

"The utterance of Balaam the son
   of Beor,
And the utterance of the man
   whose eyes are opened;
¹⁶ The utterance of him who hears
   the words of God,
And has the knowledge of the
   Most High,
Who sees the vision of the
   Almighty,
Who falls down, with eyes wide
   open:

¹⁷ "I see Him, but not now;
I behold Him, but not near;
A Star shall come out of Jacob;
A Scepter shall rise out of Israel,
And batter the brow of Moab,
And destroy all the sons of tumult.

¹⁸ "And Edom shall be a possession;
Seir also, his enemies, shall be a
   possession,
While Israel does valiantly.
¹⁹ Out of Jacob One shall have
   dominion,
And destroy the remains of the
   city."

²⁰ Then he looked on Amalek, and he took up his oracle and said:

"Amalek *was* first among the
   nations,
But *shall be* last until he perishes."

²¹ Then he looked on the Kenites, and he took up his oracle and said:

"Firm is your dwelling place,
And your nest is set in the rock;
²² Nevertheless Kain shall be burned.
How long until Asshur carries you
   away captive?"

²³ Then he took up his oracle and said:

"Alas! Who shall live when God
   does this?
²⁴ But ships *shall come* from the
   coasts of Cyprus,
And they shall afflict Asshur and
   afflict Eber,
And so shall *Amalek*, until he
   perishes."

²⁵ So Balaam rose and departed and returned to his place; Balak also went his way.

～ PSALM 33:18–22 ～

¹⁸ Behold, the eye of the LORD *is* on
   those who fear Him,
On those who hope in His mercy,
¹⁹ To deliver their soul from death,
And to keep them alive in famine.

²⁰ Our soul waits for the LORD;
He *is* our help and our shield.
²¹ For our heart shall rejoice in Him,
Because we have trusted in His holy
   name.
²² Let Your mercy, O LORD, be upon
   us,
Just as we hope in You.

～ PROVERBS 11:27 ～

²⁷ He who earnestly seeks good finds
   favor,
But trouble will come to him who
   seeks *evil*.

～ MARK 13:1–20 ～

Then as He went out of the temple, one of His disciples said to Him, "Teacher, see what manner of stones and what buildings *are here*!"
² And Jesus answered and said to him, "Do you see these great buildings? Not *one* stone shall be left upon another, that shall not be thrown down."
³ Now as He sat on the Mount of Olives opposite the temple, Peter, James, John, and Andrew asked Him privately, ⁴ "Tell us, when will these things be? And what *will be* the sign when all these things will be fulfilled?"
⁵ And Jesus, answering them, began to say: "Take heed that no one deceives you. ⁶ For many will come in My name, saying, 'I am *He*,' and will deceive many. ⁷ But when you hear of wars and rumors of wars, do not be troubled; for *such things* must happen, but the end *is* not yet. ⁸ For nation will rise against nation, and kingdom against kingdom. And there will be earthquakes in various places, and there

will be famines and troubles. These *are* the beginnings of sorrows. ⁹ "But watch out for yourselves, for they will deliver you up to councils, and you will be beaten in the synagogues. You will be brought before rulers and kings for My sake, for a testimony to them. ¹⁰ And the gospel must first be preached to all the nations. ¹¹ But when they arrest *you* and deliver you up, do not worry beforehand, or premeditate what you will speak. But whatever is given you in that hour, speak that; for it is not you who speak, but the Holy Spirit. ¹² Now brother will betray brother to death, and a father *his* child; and children will rise up against parents and cause them to be put to death. ¹³ And you will be hated by all for My name's sake. But he who endures to the end shall be saved.

¹⁴ "So when you see the 'abomination of desolation,' spoken of by Daniel the prophet, standing where it ought not" (let the reader understand), "then let those who are in Judea flee to the mountains. ¹⁵ Let him who is on the housetop not go down into the house, nor enter to take anything out of his house. ¹⁶ And let him who is in the field not go back to get his clothes. ¹⁷ But woe to those who are pregnant and to those who are nursing babies in those days! ¹⁸ And pray that your flight may not be in winter. ¹⁹ For *in* those days there will be tribulation, such as has not been since the beginning of the creation which God created until this time, nor ever shall be. ²⁰ And unless the Lord had shortened those days, no flesh would be saved; but for the elect's sake, whom He chose, He shortened the days.

READING 73 · MARCH 14

～ NUMBERS 25:1—26:65 ～

Now Israel remained in Acacia Grove, and the people began to commit harlotry with the women of Moab. ² They invited the people to the sacrifices of their gods, and the people ate and bowed down to their gods. ³ So Israel was joined to Baal of Peor, and the anger of the LORD was aroused against Israel.

⁴ Then the LORD said to Moses, "Take all the leaders of the people and hang the offenders before the LORD, out in the sun, that the fierce anger of the LORD may turn away from Israel."

⁵ So Moses said to the judges of Israel, "Every one of you kill his men who were joined to Baal of Peor."

⁶ And indeed, one of the children of Israel came and presented to his brethren a Midianite woman in the sight of Moses and in the sight of all the congregation of the children of Israel, who *were* weeping at the door of the tabernacle of meeting. ⁷ Now when Phinehas the son of Eleazar, the son of Aaron the priest, saw *it,* he rose from among the congregation and took a javelin in his hand; ⁸ and he went after the man of Israel into the tent and thrust both of them through, the man of Israel,

and the woman through her body. So the plague was stopped among the children of Israel. ⁹ And those who died in the plague were twenty-four thousand.

¹⁰ Then the LORD spoke to Moses, saying: ¹¹ "Phinehas the son of Eleazar, the son of Aaron the priest, has turned back My wrath from the children of Israel, because he was zealous with My zeal among them, so that I did not consume the children of Israel in My zeal. ¹² Therefore say, 'Behold, I give to him My covenant of peace; ¹³ and it shall be to him and his descendants after him a covenant of an everlasting priesthood, because he was zealous for his God, and made atonement for the children of Israel.' "

¹⁴ Now the name of the Israelite who was killed, who was killed with the Midianite woman, *was* Zimri the son of Salu, a leader of a father's house among the Simeonites. ¹⁵ And the name of the Midianite woman who was killed *was* Cozbi the daughter of Zur; he *was* head of the people of a father's house in Midian.

¹⁶ Then the LORD spoke to Moses, saying: ¹⁷ "Harass the Midianites, and attack them; ¹⁸ for they harassed you with their

Watch and Pray

Lawrence Cunningham sometimes visits a nearby Trappist monastery. For him, the best part of the monastic day comes in the two hours between 3:15 and 5:15 AM, a time set aside for vigilance: "O Watchman, what of the night?" He writes:

"I think of those who lie awake staring at the ceiling, worrying about money or children or the nagging pain in the belly that keeps them from sleep. I think of those who work in all-night diners or convenience stores. . . . Have the bars closed? . . . Have the street hustlers and the young-but-so-old hookers quit the streets yet? Have the dopers found some rest? Are the street people now snoring in wine-drenched quiet? Is it easy for the cops in their patrol cars and the firemen in their stations and the nurses in the ER room? Have the sirens silenced a bit? Do the people on death row sleep easily amid the coughs and groans of the prison population? . . . Is it now too late for the rapist and housebreaker? . . . Are the milkers and produce buyers and long-haul truckers at work? . . . Are my kids and wife and friends and students safe?"

Each question becomes a prayer to Cunningham, who agrees with what Thomas Merton wrote: "The more we are alone with God, the more we are with one another in darkness." It is always a good time to watch and pray!

schemes by which they seduced you in the matter of Peor and in the matter of Cozbi, the daughter of a leader of Midian, their sister, who was killed in the day of the plague because of Peor."

26 And it came to pass, after the plague, that the LORD spoke to Moses and Eleazar the son of Aaron the priest, saying: ² "Take a census of all the congregation of the children of Israel from twenty years old and above, by their fathers' houses, all who are able to go to war in Israel." ³ So Moses and Eleazar the priest spoke with them in the plains of Moab by the Jordan, *across from* Jericho, saying: ⁴ *"Take a census of the people* from twenty years old and above, just as the LORD commanded Moses and the children of Israel who came out of the land of Egypt."

⁵ Reuben *was* the firstborn of Israel. The children of Reuben *were: of* Hanoch, the family of the Hanochites; *of* Pallu, the family of the Palluites; ⁶ *of* Hezron, the family of the Hezronites; *of* Carmi,the family of the Carmites. ⁷ These *are* the families of the Reubenites: those who were numbered of them were forty-three thousand seven hundred and thirty. ⁸ And the son of Pallu *was* Eliab. ⁹ The sons of Eliab *were* Nemuel, Dathan, and Abiram. These *are* the Dathan and Abiram, representatives of the congregation, who contended against Moses and Aaron in the company of Korah, when they contended against the LORD; ¹⁰ and the earth opened its mouth and swallowed them up together with Korah when that company died, when the fire devoured two hundred and fifty men; and they became a sign. ¹¹ Nevertheless the children of Korah did not die.

¹² The sons of Simeon according to their families *were: of* Nemuel, the family of the Nemuelites; *of* Jamin, the family of the Jaminites; *of* Jachin, the family of the Jachinites; ¹³ *of* Zerah, the family of the Zarhites; *of* Shaul, the family of the Shaulites. ¹⁴ These *are* the families of the Simeonites: twenty-two thousand two hundred.

¹⁵ The sons of Gad according to their families *were: of* Zephon, the family of the Zephonites; *of* Haggi, the family of the Haggites; *of* Shuni, the family of the Shunites; ¹⁶ *of* Ozni, the family of the Oznites; *of* Eri, the family of the Erites; ¹⁷ *of* Arod, the family of the Arodites; *of* Areli, the family of the Arelites. ¹⁸ These *are* the families of the sons of Gad according to those who were numbered of them: forty thousand five hundred.

¹⁹ The sons of Judah *were* Er and Onan; and Er and Onan died in the land of Canaan. ²⁰ And the sons of Judah according to their families were: *of* Shelah, the family of the Shelanites; *of* Perez, the family of the Parzites; *of* Zerah, the family of the Zarhites. ²¹ And the sons of Perez were: *of* Hezron, the family of the Hezronites; *of* Hamul, the family of the Hamulites. ²² These *are* the families of Judah according to those who were numbered of them: seventy-six thousand five hundred.

²³ The sons of Issachar according to their families *were: of* Tola, the family of the Tolaites; *of* Puah, the family of the Punites; ²⁴ *of* Jashub, the family of the Jashubites; *of* Shimron, the family of the Shimronites. ²⁵ These *are* the families of Issachar according to those who were numbered of them: sixty-four thousand three hundred.

²⁶ The sons of Zebulun according to their families *were: of* Sered, the family of the Sardites; *of* Elon, the family of the Elonites; *of* Jahleel, the family of the Jahleelites. ²⁷ These *are* the families of the Zebulunites according to those who were numbered of them: sixty thousand five hundred.

²⁸ The sons of Joseph according to their families, by Manasseh and Ephraim, *were:* ²⁹ The sons of Manasseh: of Machir, the family of the Machirites; and Machir begot Gilead; of Gilead, the family of the Gileadites. ³⁰ These *are* the sons of Gilead: *of* Jeezer, the family of the Jeezerites; of Helek, the family of the Helekites; ³¹ *of* Asriel, the family of the Asrielites; *of* Shechem, the family of the Shechemites; ³² *of* Shemida, the family of the Shemidaites; *of* Hepher, the family of the Hepherites. ³³ Now Zelophehad the son of Hepher had no sons, but daughters; and the names of the daughters of Zelophehad *were* Mahlah, Noah, Hoglah, Milcah, and Tirzah. ³⁴ These *are* the families of Manasseh; and those who were

numbered of them *were* fifty-two thousand seven hundred.

³⁵ These *are* the sons of Ephraim according to their families: of Shuthelah, the family of the Shuthalhites; of Becher, the family of the Bachrites; of Tahan, the family of the Tahanites. ³⁶ And these *are* the sons of Shuthelah: of Eran, the family of the Eranites. ³⁷ These *are* the families of the sons of Ephraim according to those who were numbered of them: thirty-two thousand five hundred.

These *are* the sons of Joseph according to their families.

³⁸ The sons of Benjamin according to their families were: of Bela, the family of the Belaites; of Ashbel, the family of the Ashbelites; of Ahiram, the family of the Ahiramites; ³⁹ of Shupham, the family of the Shuphamites; of Hupham, the family of the Huphamites. ⁴⁰ And the sons of Bela were Ard and Naaman: *of Ard,* the family of the Ardites; *of Naaman,* the family of the Naamites. ⁴¹ These *are* the sons of Benjamin according to their families; and those who were numbered of them *were* forty-five thousand six hundred.

⁴² These *are* the sons of Dan according to their families: of Shuham, the family of the Shuhamites. These *are* the families of Dan according to their families. ⁴³ All the families of the Shuhamites, according to those who were numbered of them, *were* sixty-four thousand four hundred.

⁴⁴ The sons of Asher according to their families *were:* of Jimna, the family of the Jimnites; of Jesui, the family of the Jesuites; of Beriah, the family of the Beriites. ⁴⁵ Of the sons of Beriah: of Heber, the family of the Heberites; of Malchiel, the family of the Malchielites. ⁴⁶ And the name of the daughter of Asher *was* Serah. ⁴⁷ These *are* the families of the sons of Asher according to those who were numbered of them: fifty-three thousand four hundred.

⁴⁸ The sons of Naphtali according to their families *were:* of Jahzeel, the family of the Jahzeelites; of Guni, the family of the Gunites; ⁴⁹ of Jezer, the family of the Jezerites; of Shillem, the family of the Shillemites. ⁵⁰ These *are* the families of Naphtali according to their families; and those who were numbered of them *were* forty-five thousand four hundred.

⁵¹ These *are* those who were numbered of the children of Israel: six hundred and one thousand seven hundred and thirty.

⁵² Then the LORD spoke to Moses, saying: ⁵³ "To these the land shall be divided as an inheritance, according to the number of names. ⁵⁴ To a large *tribe* you shall give a larger inheritance, and to a small *tribe* you shall give a smaller inheritance. Each shall be given its inheritance according to those who were numbered of them. ⁵⁵ But the land shall be divided by lot; they shall inherit according to the names of the tribes of their fathers. ⁵⁶ According to the lot their inheritance shall be divided between the larger and the smaller."

⁵⁷ And these *are* those who were numbered of the Levites according to their families: of Gershon, the family of the Gershonites; of Kohath, the family of the Kohathites; of Merari, the family of the Merarites. ⁵⁸ These *are* the families of the Levites: the family of the Libnites, the family of the Hebronites, the family of the Mahlites, the family of the Mushites, and the family of the Korathites. And Kohath begot Amram. ⁵⁹ The name of Amram's wife *was* Jochebed the daughter of Levi, who was born to Levi in Egypt; and to Amram she bore Aaron and Moses and their sister Miriam. ⁶⁰ To Aaron were born Nadab and Abihu, Eleazar and Ithamar. ⁶¹ And Nadab and Abihu died when they offered profane fire before the LORD.

⁶² Now those who were numbered of them were twenty-three thousand, every male from a month old and above; for they were not numbered among the other children of Israel, because there was no inheritance given to them among the children of Israel.

⁶³ These *are* those who were numbered by Moses and Eleazar the priest, who numbered the children of Israel in the plains of Moab by the Jordan, *across from* Jericho. ⁶⁴ But among these there was not a man of those who were numbered by Moses and Aaron the priest when they numbered the children of Israel in the Wilderness of Sinai. ⁶⁵ For the LORD had said of them, "They shall surely die in the wilderness." So there was not left a man of them, except Caleb the son of Jephunneh and Joshua the son of Nun.

~ PSALM 34:1–7 ~

1 I will bless the LORD at all times;
   His praise *shall* continually *be* in my
      mouth.
2 My soul shall make its boast in the
      LORD;
   The humble shall hear *of it* and be
      glad.
3 Oh, magnify the LORD with me,
   And let us exalt His name together.

4 I sought the LORD, and He heard
      me,
   And delivered me from all my fears.
5 They looked to Him and were
      radiant,
   And their faces were not ashamed.
6 This poor man cried out, and the
      LORD heard *him,*
   And saved him out of all his
      troubles.
7 The angel of the LORD encamps all
      around those who fear Him,
   And delivers them.

~ PROVERBS 11:28 ~

28 He who trusts in his riches will fall,
   But the righteous will flourish like
      foliage.

~ MARK 13:21–37 ~

"Then if anyone says to you, 'Look, here
is the Christ!' or, 'Look, *He is* there!' do
not believe it. 22 For false christs and false
prophets will rise and show signs and
wonders to deceive, if possible, even the
elect. 23 But take heed; see, I have told you
all things beforehand.

24 "But in those days, after that tribulation, the sun will be darkened, and the
moon will not give its light; 25 the stars of
heaven will fall, and the powers in the
heavens will be shaken. 26 Then they will
see the Son of Man coming in the clouds
with great power and glory. 27 And then
He will send His angels, and gather together His elect from the four winds, from
the farthest part of earth to the farthest
part of heaven.

28 "Now learn this parable from the fig
tree: When its branch has already become
tender, and puts forth leaves, you know
that summer is near. 29 So you also, when
you see these things happening, know that
it is near—at the doors! 30 Assuredly, I say
to you, this generation will by no means
pass away till all these things take place.
31 Heaven and earth will pass away, but
My words will by no means pass away.

32 "But of that day and hour no one
knows, not even the angels in heaven, nor
the Son, but only the Father. 33 Take heed,
watch and pray; for you do not know
when the time is. 34 *It is* like a man going
to a far country, who left his house and
gave authority to his servants, and to each
his work, and commanded the doorkeeper
to watch. 35 Watch therefore, for you do
not know when the master of the house
is coming—in the evening, at midnight,
at the crowing of the rooster, or in the
morning— 36 lest, coming suddenly, he
find you sleeping. 37 And what I say to you,
I say to all: Watch!"

~ NUMBERS 27:1—28:31 ~

Then came the daughters of
Zelophehad the son of Hepher, the
son of Gilead, the son of Machir,
the son of Manasseh, from the families of
Manasseh the son of Joseph; and these
were the names of his daughters: Mahlah,
Noah, Hoglah, Milcah, and Tirzah. 2 And
they stood before Moses, before Eleazar
the priest, and before the leaders and all
the congregation, *by* the doorway of the
tabernacle of meeting, saying: 3 "Our father died in the wilderness; but he was
not in the company of those who gathered
together against the LORD, in company
with Korah, but he died in his own sin;
and he had no sons. 4 Why should the
name of our father be removed from
among his family because he had no son?

What Was Lincoln Doing?

Abraham Lincoln is often held up to children as a model of achievement, the embodiment of "The American Dream." He is regarded by many as the greatest President the United States has ever seen. His second Inaugural Address is one of the noblest political speeches ever given, and his Gettysburg Address is still studied and memorized by many a student. Amazingly, Lincoln had only four months of formal education, and that in a one-room country schoolhouse where the students ranged from age five to twenty-five.

One day a father was reciting all of Lincoln's achievements to his son. "Where else but in America could this happen?" he mused. And then, hoping to motivate his son to study, he asked, "Do you know what Abe Lincoln was doing when he was your age?"

The boy answered, "No, but I do know what he was doing when he was your age."

We nearly always err when we suggest to someone, especially our children, that they be like anybody other than their own best selves. While we can urge our children to look to good examples, we should always encourage them to be just who God created them to be.

Give us a possession among our father's brothers."

[5] So Moses brought their case before the LORD.

[6] And the LORD spoke to Moses, saying: [7] "The daughters of Zelophehad speak *what is* right; you shall surely give them a possession of inheritance among their father's brothers, and cause the inheritance of their father to pass to them. [8] And you shall speak to the children of Israel, saying: 'If a man dies and has no son, then you shall cause his inheritance to pass to his daughter. [9] If he has no daughter, then you shall give his inheritance to his brothers. [10] If he has no brothers, then you shall give his inheritance to his father's brothers. [11] And if his father has no brothers, then you shall give his inheritance to the relative closest to him in his family, and he shall possess it.' " And it shall be to the children of Israel a statute of judgment, just as the LORD commanded Moses.

[12] Now the LORD said to Moses: "Go up into this Mount Abarim, and see the land which I have given to the children of Israel. [13] And when you have seen it, you also shall be gathered to your people, as Aaron your brother was gathered. [14] For in the Wilderness of Zin, during the strife of the congregation, you rebelled against My command to hallow Me at the waters before their eyes." (These *are* the waters of Meribah, at Kadesh in the Wilderness of Zin.)

[15] Then Moses spoke to the LORD, saying: [16] "Let the LORD, the God of the spirits of all flesh, set a man over the congregation, [17] who may go out before them and go in before them, who may lead them out and bring them in, that the congregation of the LORD may not be like sheep which have no shepherd."

[18] And the LORD said to Moses: "Take Joshua the son of Nun with you, a man in whom *is* the Spirit, and lay your hand on him; [19] set him before Eleazar the priest and before all the congregation, and inaugurate him in their sight. [20] And you shall give *some* of your authority to him, that all the congregation of the children of Israel may be obedient. [21] He shall stand before Eleazar the priest, who shall inquire before the LORD for him by the judgment of the Urim. At his word they shall go out, and at his word they shall come in, he and all the children of Israel with him—all the congregation."

[22] So Moses did as the LORD commanded him. He took Joshua and set him before Eleazar the priest and before all the congregation. [23] And he laid his hands on him and inaugurated him, just as the LORD commanded by the hand of Moses.

28

Now the LORD spoke to Moses, saying, [2] "Command the children of Israel, and say to them, 'My offering, My food for My offerings made by fire as a sweet aroma to Me, you shall be careful to offer to Me at their appointed time.'

[3] "And you shall say to them, 'This *is* the offering made by fire which you shall offer to the LORD: two male lambs in their first year without blemish, day by day, as a regular burnt offering. [4] The one lamb you shall offer in the morning, the other lamb you shall offer in the evening, [5] and one-tenth of an ephah of fine flour as a grain offering mixed with one-fourth of a hin of pressed oil. [6] *It is* a regular burnt offering which was ordained at Mount Sinai for a sweet aroma, an offering made by fire to the LORD. [7] And its drink offering *shall be* one-fourth of a hin for each lamb; in a holy *place* you shall pour out the drink to the LORD as an offering. [8] The other lamb you shall offer in the evening; as the morning grain offering and its drink offering, you shall offer *it* as an offering made by fire, a sweet aroma to the LORD.

[9] 'And on the Sabbath day two lambs in their first year, without blemish, and two-tenths *of an ephah* of fine flour as a grain offering, mixed with oil, with its drink offering— [10] *this is* the burnt offering for every Sabbath, besides the regular burnt offering with its drink offering.

[11] 'At the beginnings of your months you shall present a burnt offering to the LORD: two young bulls, one ram, and seven lambs in their first year, without blemish; [12] three-tenths *of an ephah* of fine flour as a grain offering, mixed with oil, for each bull; two-tenths *of an ephah* of fine flour as a grain offering, mixed with oil, for the one ram; [13] and one-tenth *of an ephah* of

fine flour, mixed with oil, as a grain offering for each lamb, as a burnt offering of sweet aroma, an offering made by fire to the LORD. ¹⁴ Their drink offering shall be half a hin of wine for a bull, one-third of a hin for a ram, and one-fourth of a hin for a lamb; this *is* the burnt offering for each month throughout the months of the year. ¹⁵ Also one kid of the goats as a sin offering to the LORD shall be offered, besides the regular burnt offering and its drink offering.

¹⁶ 'On the fourteenth day of the first month *is* the Passover of the LORD. ¹⁷ And on the fifteenth day of this month *is* the feast; unleavened bread shall be eaten for seven days. ¹⁸ On the first day *you shall have* a holy convocation. You shall do no customary work. ¹⁹ And you shall present an offering made by fire as a burnt offering to the LORD: two young bulls, one ram, and seven lambs in their first year. Be sure they are without blemish. ²⁰ Their grain offering shall be of fine flour mixed with oil: three-tenths *of an ephah* you shall offer for a bull, and two-tenths for a ram; ²¹ you shall offer one-tenth *of an ephah* for each of the seven lambs; ²² also one goat *as* a sin offering, to make atonement for you. ²³ You shall offer these besides the burnt offering of the morning, which *is* for a regular burnt offering. ²⁴ In this manner you shall offer the food of the offering made by fire daily for seven days, as a sweet aroma to the LORD; it shall be offered besides the regular burnt offering and its drink offering. ²⁵ And on the seventh day you shall have a holy convocation. You shall do no customary work.

²⁶ 'Also on the day of the firstfruits, when you bring a new grain offering to the LORD at your *Feast of* Weeks, you shall have a holy convocation. You shall do no customary work. ²⁷ You shall present a burnt offering as a sweet aroma to the LORD: two young bulls, one ram, and seven lambs in their first year, ²⁸ with their grain offering of fine flour mixed with oil: three-tenths *of an ephah* for each bull, two-tenths for the one ram, ²⁹ and one-tenth for each of the seven lambs; ³⁰ *also* one kid of the goats, to make atonement for you. ³¹ Be sure they are without blemish. You shall present *them* with their drink

offerings, besides the regular burnt offering with its grain offering.

∼ PSALM 34:8–14 ∼

⁸ Oh, taste and see that the LORD *is* good;
Blessed *is* the man *who* trusts in Him!
⁹ Oh, fear the LORD, you His saints!
There is no want to those who fear Him.
¹⁰ The young lions lack and suffer hunger;
But those who seek the LORD shall not lack any good *thing.*

¹¹ Come, you children, listen to me;
I will teach you the fear of the LORD.
¹² Who *is* the man *who* desires life,
And loves *many* days, that he may see good?
¹³ Keep your tongue from evil,
And your lips from speaking deceit.
¹⁴ Depart from evil and do good;
Seek peace and pursue it.

∼ PROVERBS 11:29 ∼

²⁹ He who troubles his own house will inherit the wind,
And the fool *will be* servant to the wise of heart.

∼ MARK 14:1–26 ∼

After two days it was the Passover and *the Feast* of Unleavened Bread. And the chief priests and the scribes sought how they might take Him by trickery and put *Him* to death. ² But they said, "Not during the feast, lest there be an uproar of the people."

³ And being in Bethany at the house of Simon the leper, as He sat at the table, a woman came having an alabaster flask of very costly oil of spikenard. Then she broke the flask and poured *it* on His head. ⁴ But there were some who were indignant among themselves, and said, "Why was this fragrant oil wasted? ⁵ For it might have been sold for more than three hundred denarii and given to the poor." And they criticized her sharply.

⁶ But Jesus said, "Let her alone. Why

do you trouble her? She has done a good work for Me. 7 For you have the poor with you always, and whenever you wish you may do them good; but Me you do not have always. 8 She has done what she could. She has come beforehand to anoint My body for burial. 9 Assuredly, I say to you, wherever this gospel is preached in the whole world, what this woman has done will also be told as a memorial to her."

10 Then Judas Iscariot, one of the twelve, went to the chief priests to betray Him to them. 11 And when they heard *it,* they were glad, and promised to give him money. So he sought how he might conveniently betray Him.

12 Now on the first day of Unleavened Bread, when they killed the Passover *lamb,* His disciples said to Him, "Where do You want us to go and prepare, that You may eat the Passover?"

13 And He sent out two of His disciples and said to them, "Go into the city, and a man will meet you carrying a pitcher of water; follow him. 14 Wherever he goes in, say to the master of the house, 'The Teacher says, "Where is the guest room in which I may eat the Passover with My disciples?" ' 15 Then he will show you a large upper room, furnished *and* prepared; there make ready for us."

16 So His disciples went out, and came into the city, and found it just as He had said to them; and they prepared the Passover.

17 In the evening He came with the twelve. 18 Now as they sat and ate, Jesus said, "Assuredly, I say to you, one of you who eats with Me will betray Me."

19 And they began to be sorrowful, and to say to Him one by one, "*Is* it I?" And another *said,* "*Is* it I?"

20 He answered and said to them, "*It is* one of the twelve, who dips with Me in the dish. 21 The Son of Man indeed goes just as it is written of Him, but woe to that man by whom the Son of Man is betrayed! It would have been good for that man if he had never been born."

22 And as they were eating, Jesus took bread, blessed and broke *it,* and gave *it* to them and said, "Take, eat; this is My body."

23 Then He took the cup, and when He had given thanks He gave *it* to them, and they all drank from it. 24 And He said to them, "This is My blood of the new covenant, which is shed for many. 25 Assuredly, I say to you, I will no longer drink of the fruit of the vine until that day when I drink it new in the kingdom of God."

26 And when they had sung a hymn, they went out to the Mount of Olives.

READING 75 · MARCH 16

~ NUMBERS 29:1—30:16 ~

'And in the seventh month, on the first *day* of the month, you shall have a holy convocation. You shall do no customary work. For you it is a day of blowing the trumpets. 2 You shall offer a burnt offering as a sweet aroma to the LORD: one young bull, one ram, *and* seven lambs in their first year, without blemish. 3 Their grain offering *shall be* fine flour mixed with oil: three-tenths *of an ephah* for the bull, two-tenths for the ram, 4 and one-tenth for each of the seven lambs; 5 also one kid of the goats *as* a sin offering, to make atonement for you; 6 besides the burnt offering with its grain offering for the New Moon, the regular

burnt offering with its grain offering, and their drink offerings, according to their ordinance, as a sweet aroma, an offering made by fire to the LORD.

7 'On the tenth *day* of this seventh month you shall have a holy convocation. You shall afflict your souls; you shall not do any work. 8 You shall present a burnt offering to the LORD *as* a sweet aroma: one young bull, one ram, *and* seven lambs in their first year. Be sure they are without blemish. 9 Their grain offering *shall be of* fine flour mixed with oil: three-tenths *of an ephah* for the bull, two-tenths for the one ram, 10 and one-tenth for each of the seven lambs; 11 also one kid of the

Staying Together

> Watch and pray, lest you enter into temptation. The spirit indeed is willing, but the flesh is weak.
>
> *Mark 14:38*

Mike and Teri had one major thing in common: They both wanted to make their first million dollars by the age of thirty. Teri wasn't a Christian when they met, but Mike was, and after attending church with Mike and reading Christian books he gave to her, she accepted the Lord. They were married a short while later, and for the next two years lived what both called an ideal life.

Their focus on financial success, however, caused their dreams to unravel. They began to drift apart, and to drift away from Jesus Christ. Eventually, they separated and divorced. A year after the divorce, Teri went to a conference and came away believing that God could restore their marriage. She began to pray earnestly for Mike.

Not long after, Mike began to recognize that God was not finished with him. He set his heart toward God, walked away from the life he had been leading, and made contact with Teri. They remarried and reordered the focus of their lives.

Can prayer keep a marriage together? Mike and Teri believe it can, and so did Rev. and Mrs. Robert Newton. They met twice a day to pray with and for each other, every day of their more than fifty years of marriage. At their jubilee wedding anniversary, Rev. Newton said, "I know not that an unkind look or an unkind word has ever passed between us."

The old saying is still true: "The family that prays together, stays together."

goats *as* a sin offering, besides the sin offering for atonement, the regular burnt offering with its grain offering, and their drink offerings.

¹² 'On the fifteenth day of the seventh month you shall have a holy convocation. You shall do no customary work, and you shall keep a feast to the LORD seven days. ¹³ You shall present a burnt offering, an offering made by fire as a sweet aroma to the LORD: thirteen young bulls, two rams, *and* fourteen lambs in their first year. They shall be without blemish. ¹⁴ Their grain offering *shall be of* fine flour mixed with oil: three-tenths *of an ephah* for each of the thirteen bulls, two-tenths for each of the two rams, ¹⁵ and one-tenth for each of the fourteen lambs; ¹⁶ also one kid of the goats *as* a sin offering, besides the regular burnt offering, its grain offering, and its drink offering.

¹⁷ 'On the second day *present* twelve young bulls, two rams, fourteen lambs in their first year without blemish, ¹⁸ and their grain offering and their drink offerings for the bulls, for the rams, and for the lambs, by their number, according to the ordinance; ¹⁹ also one kid of the goats *as* a sin offering, besides the regular burnt offering with its grain offering, and their drink offerings.

²⁰ 'On the third day *present* eleven bulls, two rams, fourteen lambs in their first year without blemish, ²¹ and their grain offering and their drink offerings for the bulls, for the rams, and for the lambs, by their number, according to the ordinance; ²² also one goat *as* a sin offering, besides the regular burnt offering, its grain offering, and its drink offering.

²³ 'On the fourth day *present* ten bulls, two rams, *and* fourteen lambs in their first year, without blemish, ²⁴ and their grain offering and their drink offerings for the bulls, for the rams, and for the lambs, by their number, according to the ordinance; ²⁵ also one kid of the goats *as* a sin offering, besides the regular burnt offering, its grain offering, and its drink offering.

²⁶ 'On the fifth day *present* nine bulls, two rams, *and* fourteen lambs in their first year without blemish, ²⁷ and their grain offering and their drink offerings for the bulls, for the rams, and for the lambs, by their number, according to the ordinance;

²⁸ also one goat *as* a sin offering, besides the regular burnt offering, its grain offering, and its drink offering.

²⁹ 'On the sixth day *present* eight bulls, two rams, *and* fourteen lambs in their first year without blemish, ³⁰ and their grain offering and their drink offerings for the bulls, for the rams, and for the lambs, by their number, according to the ordinance; ³¹ also one goat *as* a sin offering, besides the regular burnt offering, its grain offering, and its drink offering.

³² 'On the seventh day *present* seven bulls, two rams, *and* fourteen lambs in their first year without blemish, ³³ and their grain offering and their drink offerings for the bulls, for the rams, and for the lambs, by their number, according to the ordinance; ³⁴ also one goat *as* a sin offering, besides the regular burnt offering, its grain offering, and its drink offering.

³⁵ 'On the eighth day you shall have a sacred assembly. You shall do no customary work. ³⁶ You shall present a burnt offering, an offering made by fire as a sweet aroma to the LORD: one bull, one ram, seven lambs in their first year without blemish, ³⁷ and their grain offering and their drink offerings for the bull, for the ram, and for the lambs, by their number, according to the ordinance; ³⁸ also one goat *as* a sin offering, besides the regular burnt offering, its grain offering, and its drink offering.

³⁹ 'These you shall present to the LORD at your appointed feasts (besides your vowed offerings and your freewill offerings) as your burnt offerings and your grain offerings, as your drink offerings and your peace offerings.' "

⁴⁰ So Moses told the children of Israel everything, just as the LORD commanded Moses.

30 Then Moses spoke to the heads of the tribes concerning the children of Israel, saying, "This *is* the thing which the LORD has commanded: ² If a man makes a vow to the LORD, or swears an oath to bind himself by some agreement, he shall not break his word; he shall do according to all that proceeds out of his mouth.

³ "Or if a woman makes a vow to the LORD, and binds *herself* by some

agreement while in her father's house in her youth, ⁴ and her father hears her vow and the agreement by which she has bound herself, and her father holds his peace, then all her vows shall stand, and every agreement with which she has bound herself shall stand. ⁵ But if her father overrules her on the day that he hears, then none of her vows nor her agreements by which she has bound herself shall stand; and the LORD will release her, because her father overruled her.

⁶ "If indeed she takes a husband, while bound by her vows or by a rash utterance from her lips by which she bound herself, ⁷ and her husband hears *it,* and makes no response to her on the day that he hears, then her vows shall stand, and her agreements by which she bound herself shall stand. ⁸ But if her husband overrules her on the day that he hears *it,* he shall make void her vow which she took and what she uttered with her lips, by which she bound herself, and the LORD will release her.

⁹ "Also any vow of a widow or a divorced woman, by which she has bound herself, shall stand against her.

¹⁰ "If she vowed in her husband's house, or bound herself by an agreement with an oath, ¹¹ and her husband heard *it,* and made no response to her *and* did not overrule her, then all her vows shall stand, and every agreement by which she bound herself shall stand. ¹² But if her husband truly made them void on the day he heard *them,* then whatever proceeded from her lips concerning her vows or concerning the agreement binding her, it shall not stand; her husband has made them void, and the LORD will release her. ¹³ Every vow and every binding oath to afflict her soul, her husband may confirm it, or her husband may make it void. ¹⁴ Now if her husband makes no response whatever to her from day to day, then he confirms all her vows or all the agreements that bind her; he confirms them, because he made no response to her on the day that he heard *them.* ¹⁵ But if he does make them void after he has heard *them,* then he shall bear her guilt."

¹⁶ These *are* the statutes which the LORD commanded Moses, between a man and his wife, and between a father and his daughter in her youth in her father's house.

∼ PSALM 34:15–22 ∼

¹⁵ The eyes of the LORD *are* on the righteous,
And His ears *are open* to their cry.
¹⁶ The face of the LORD *is* against those who do evil,
To cut off the remembrance of them from the earth.

¹⁷ *The righteous* cry out, and the LORD hears,
And delivers them out of all their troubles.
¹⁸ The LORD *is* near to those who have a broken heart,
And saves such as have a contrite spirit.

¹⁹ Many *are* the afflictions of the righteous,
But the LORD delivers him out of them all.
²⁰ He guards all his bones;
Not one of them is broken.
²¹ Evil shall slay the wicked,
And those who hate the righteous shall be condemned.
²² The LORD redeems the soul of His servants,
And none of those who trust in Him shall be condemned.

∼ PROVERBS 11:30, 31 ∼

³⁰ The fruit of the righteous *is a* tree of life,
And he who wins souls *is* wise.

³¹ If the righteous will be recompensed on the earth,
How much more the ungodly and the sinner.

∼ MARK 14:27–54 ∼

Then Jesus said to them, "All of you will be made to stumble because of Me this night, for it is written:

'I will strike the Shepherd,
And the sheep will be scattered.'

²⁸ "But after I have been raised, I will go before you to Galilee."

²⁹ Peter said to Him, "Even if all are made to stumble, yet I *will* not *be*."

³⁰ Jesus said to him, "Assuredly, I say to you that today, *even* this night, before the rooster crows twice, you will deny Me three times."

³¹ But he spoke more vehemently, "If I have to die with You, I will not deny You!" And they all said likewise.

³² Then they came to a place which was named Gethsemane; and He said to His disciples, "Sit here while I pray." ³³ And He took Peter, James, and John with Him, and He began to be troubled and deeply distressed. ³⁴ Then He said to them, "My soul is exceedingly sorrowful, *even* to death. Stay here and watch."

³⁵ He went a little farther, and fell on the ground, and prayed that if it were possible, the hour might pass from Him. ³⁶ And He said, "Abba, Father, all things *are* possible for You. Take this cup away from Me; nevertheless, not what I will, but what You *will*."

³⁷ Then He came and found them sleeping, and said to Peter, "Simon, are you sleeping? Could you not watch one hour? ³⁸ Watch and pray, lest you enter into temptation. The spirit indeed *is* willing, but the flesh *is* weak."

³⁹ Again He went away and prayed, and spoke the same words. ⁴⁰ And when He returned, He found them asleep again, for their eyes were heavy; and they did not know what to answer Him.

⁴¹ Then He came the third time and said to them, "Are you still sleeping and resting? It is enough! The hour has come; behold, the Son of Man is being betrayed into the hands of sinners. ⁴² Rise, let us be going. See, My betrayer is at hand."

⁴³ And immediately, while He was still speaking, Judas, one of the twelve, with a great multitude with swords and clubs, came from the chief priests and the scribes and the elders. ⁴⁴ Now His betrayer had given them a signal, saying, "Whomever I kiss, He is the One; seize Him and lead *Him* away safely."

⁴⁵ As soon as he had come, immediately he went up to Him and said to Him, "Rabbi, Rabbi!" and kissed Him.

⁴⁶ Then they laid their hands on Him and took Him. ⁴⁷ And one of those who stood by drew his sword and struck the servant of the high priest, and cut off his ear.

⁴⁸ Then Jesus answered and said to them, "Have you come out, as against a robber, with swords and clubs to take Me? ⁴⁹ I was daily with you in the temple teaching, and you did not seize Me. But the Scriptures must be fulfilled."

⁵⁰ Then they all forsook Him and fled.

⁵¹ Now a certain young man followed Him, having a linen cloth thrown around *his* naked *body*. And the young men laid hold of him, ⁵² and he left the linen cloth and fled from them naked.

⁵³ And they led Jesus away to the high priest; and with him were assembled all the chief priests, the elders, and the scribes. ⁵⁴ But Peter followed Him at a distance, right into the courtyard of the high priest. And he sat with the servants and warmed himself at the fire.

READING 76 · MARCH 17

～ NUMBERS 31:1—32:42 ～

And the LORD spoke to Moses, saying: ² "Take vengeance on the Midianites for the children of Israel. Afterward you shall be gathered to your people."

³ So Moses spoke to the people, saying, "Arm some of yourselves for war, and let them go against the Midianites to take vengeance for the LORD on Midian. ⁴ A thousand from each tribe of all the tribes of Israel you shall send to the war."

⁵ So there were recruited from the divisions of Israel one thousand from *each* tribe, twelve thousand armed for war. ⁶ Then Moses sent them to the war, one thousand from *each* tribe; he sent them

Five More Minutes

But he who
follows frivolity
is devoid of
understanding.

Proverbs 12:11

While at the park one day, a woman sat down next to a man on a bench near a playground. "That's my son over there," she said, pointing to a little boy in a red sweater who was gliding down the slide. "He's a fine looking boy," the man said. "That's my son on the swing in the blue sweater." Then, looking at his watch, he called to his son, "What do you say we go, Sam?"

Sam pleaded, "Just five more minutes, Dad. Please? Just five more minutes." The man nodded and Sam continued to swing to his heart's content.

Minutes passed and the father stood and called again to his son, "Time to go now." Again Sam pleaded, "Five more minutes, Dad. Just five more minutes." The man smiled and said, "Okay."

"My, you certainly are a patient father," the woman responded.

The man smiled and then said, "My older son Tommy was killed by a drunk driver last year while he was riding his bike near here. I never spent much time with Tommy and now I'd give anything for just five more minutes with him. I've vowed not to make the same mistake with Sam. He thinks he has five more minutes to swing. The truth is, I get five more minutes to watch him play."

to the war with Phinehas the son of Eleazar the priest, with the holy articles and the signal trumpets in his hand. [7] And they warred against the Midianites, just as the LORD commanded Moses, and they killed all the males. [8] They killed the kings of Midian with *the rest of* those who were killed—Evi, Rekem, Zur, Hur, and Reba, the five kings of Midian. Balaam the son of Beor they also killed with the sword.

[9] And the children of Israel took the women of Midian captive, with their little ones, and took as spoil all their cattle, all their flocks, and all their goods. [10] They also burned with fire all the cities where they dwelt, and all their forts. [11] And they took all the spoil and all the booty—of man and beast.

[12] Then they brought the captives, the booty, and the spoil to Moses, to Eleazar the priest, and to the congregation of the children of Israel, to the camp in the plains of Moab by the Jordan, *across from* Jericho. [13] And Moses, Eleazar the priest, and all the leaders of the congregation, went to meet them outside the camp. [14] But Moses was angry with the officers of the army, *with* the captains over thousands and captains over hundreds, who had come from the battle.

[15] And Moses said to them: "Have you kept all the women alive? [16] Look, these *women* caused the children of Israel, through the counsel of Balaam, to trespass against the LORD in the incident of Peor, and there was a plague among the congregation of the LORD. [17] Now therefore, kill every male among the little ones, and kill every woman who has known a man intimately. [18] But keep alive for yourselves all the young girls who have not known a man intimately. [19] And as for you, remain outside the camp seven days; whoever has killed any person, and whoever has touched any slain, purify yourselves and your captives on the third day and on the seventh day. [20] Purify every garment, everything made of leather, everything woven of goats' *hair,* and everything made of wood."

[21] Then Eleazar the priest said to the men of war who had gone to the battle, "This *is* the ordinance of the law which the LORD commanded Moses:

[22] "Only the gold, the silver, the bronze, the iron, the tin, and the lead, [23] everything that can endure fire, you shall put through the fire, and it shall be clean; and it shall be purified with the water of purification. But all that cannot endure fire you shall put through water. [24] And you shall wash your clothes on the seventh day and be clean, and afterward you may come into the camp."

[25] Now the LORD spoke to Moses, saying: [26] "Count up the plunder that was taken—of man and beast—you and Eleazar the priest and the chief fathers of the congregation; [27] and divide the plunder into two parts, between those who took part in the war, who went out to battle, and all the congregation. [28] And levy a tribute for the LORD on the men of war who went out to battle: one of every five hundred of the persons, the cattle, the donkeys, and the sheep; [29] take *it* from their half, and give *it* to Eleazar the priest as a heave offering to the LORD. [30] And from the children of Israel's half you shall take one of every fifty, drawn from the persons, the cattle, the donkeys, and the sheep, from all the livestock, and give them to the Levites who keep charge of the tabernacle of the LORD." [31] So Moses and Eleazar the priest did as the LORD commanded Moses.

[32] The booty remaining from the plunder, which the men of war had taken, was six hundred and seventy-five thousand sheep, [33] seventy-two thousand cattle, [34] sixty-one thousand donkeys, [35] and thirty-two thousand persons in all, of women who had not known a man intimately. [36] And the half, the portion for those who had gone out to war, was in number three hundred and thirty-seven thousand five hundred sheep; [37] and the LORD's tribute of the sheep was six hundred and seventy-five. [38] The cattle *were* thirty-six thousand, of which the LORD's tribute *was* seventy-two. [39] The donkeys *were* thirty thousand five hundred, of which the LORD's tribute *was* sixty-one. [40] The persons *were* sixteen thousand, of which the LORD's tribute *was* thirty-two persons. [41] So Moses gave the tribute *which was* the LORD's heave offering to Eleazar the priest, as the LORD commanded Moses.

⁴² And from the children of Israel's half, which Moses separated from the men who fought— ⁴³ now the half belonging to the congregation was three hundred and thirty-seven thousand five hundred sheep, ⁴⁴ thirty-six thousand cattle, ⁴⁵ thirty thousand five hundred donkeys, ⁴⁶ and sixteen thousand persons— ⁴⁷ and from the children of Israel's half Moses took one of every fifty, drawn from man and beast, and gave them to the Levites, who kept charge of the tabernacle of the LORD, as the LORD commanded Moses.

⁴⁸ Then the officers who *were* over thousands of the army, the captains of thousands and captains of hundreds, came near to Moses; ⁴⁹ and they said to Moses, "Your servants have taken a count of the men of war who *are* under our command, and not a man of us is missing. ⁵⁰ Therefore we have brought an offering for the LORD, what every man found of ornaments of gold: armlets and bracelets and signet rings and earrings and necklaces, to make atonement for ourselves before the LORD." ⁵¹ So Moses and Eleazar the priest received the gold from them, all the fashioned ornaments. ⁵² And all the gold of the offering that they offered to the LORD, from the captains of thousands and captains of hundreds, was sixteen thousand seven hundred and fifty shekels. ⁵³(The men of war had taken spoil, every man for himself.) ⁵⁴ And Moses and Eleazar the priest received the gold from the captains of thousands and of hundreds, and brought it into the tabernacle of meeting as a memorial for the children of Israel before the LORD.

32 Now the children of Reuben and the children of Gad had a very great multitude of livestock; and when they saw the land of Jazer and the land of Gilead, that indeed the region *was* a place for livestock, ² the children of Gad and the children of Reuben came and spoke to Moses, to Eleazar the priest, and to the leaders of the congregation, saying, ³ "Ataroth, Dibon, Jazer, Nimrah, Heshbon, Elealeh, Shebam, Nebo, and Beon, ⁴ the country which the LORD defeated before the congregation of Israel, *is* a land for livestock, and your servants have livestock." ⁵ Therefore they said, "If we have found favor in your sight, let this land be given to your servants as a possession. Do not take us over the Jordan."

⁶ And Moses said to the children of Gad and to the children of Reuben: "Shall your brethren go to war while you sit here? ⁷ Now why will you discourage the heart of the children of Israel from going over into the land which the LORD has given them? ⁸ Thus your fathers did when I sent them away from Kadesh Barnea to see the land. ⁹ For when they went up to the Valley of Eshcol and saw the land, they discouraged the heart of the children of Israel, so that they did not go into the land which the LORD had given them. ¹⁰ So the LORD's anger was aroused on that day, and He swore an oath, saying, ¹¹ 'Surely none of the men who came up from Egypt, from twenty years old and above, shall see the land of which I swore to Abraham, Isaac, and Jacob, because they have not wholly followed Me, ¹² except Caleb the son of Jephunneh, the Kenizzite, and Joshua the son of Nun, for they have wholly followed the LORD.' ¹³ So the LORD's anger was aroused against Israel, and He made them wander in the wilderness forty years, until all the generation that had done evil in the sight of the LORD was gone. ¹⁴ And look! You have risen in your fathers' place, a brood of sinful men, to increase still more the fierce anger of the LORD against Israel. ¹⁵ For if you turn away from following Him, He will once again leave them in the wilderness, and you will destroy all these people."

¹⁶ Then they came near to him and said: "We will build sheepfolds here for our livestock, and cities for our little ones; ¹⁷ but we ourselves will be armed, ready *to go* before the children of Israel until we have brought them to their place; and our little ones will dwell in the fortified cities because of the inhabitants of the land. ¹⁸ We will not return to our homes until every one of the children of Israel has received his inheritance. ¹⁹ For we will not inherit with them on the other side of the Jordan and beyond, because our inheritance has fallen to us on this eastern side of the Jordan."

²⁰ Then Moses said to them: "If you do this thing, if you arm yourselves before

the LORD for the war, [21] and all your armed men cross over the Jordan before the LORD until He has driven out His enemies from before Him, [22] and the land is subdued before the LORD, then afterward you may return and be blameless before the LORD and before Israel; and this land shall be your possession before the LORD. [23] But if you do not do so, then take note, you have sinned against the LORD; and be sure your sin will find you out. [24] Build cities for your little ones and folds for your sheep, and do what has proceeded out of your mouth."

[25] And the children of Gad and the children of Reuben spoke to Moses, saying: "Your servants will do as my lord commands. [26] Our little ones, our wives, our flocks, and all our livestock will be there in the cities of Gilead; [27] but your servants will cross over, every man armed for war, before the LORD to battle, just as my lord says."

[28] So Moses gave command concerning them to Eleazar the priest, to Joshua the son of Nun, and to the chief fathers of the tribes of the children of Israel. [29] And Moses said to them: "If the children of Gad and the children of Reuben cross over the Jordan with you, every man armed for battle before the LORD, and the land is subdued before you, then you shall give them the land of Gilead as a possession. [30] But if they do not cross over armed with you, they shall have possessions among you in the land of Canaan."

[31] Then the children of Gad and the children of Reuben answered, saying: "As the LORD has said to your servants, so we will do. [32] We will cross over armed before the LORD into the land of Canaan, but the possession of our inheritance *shall remain* with us on this side of the Jordan."

[33] So Moses gave to the children of Gad, to the children of Reuben, and to half the tribe of Manasseh the son of Joseph, the kingdom of Sihon king of the Amorites and the kingdom of Og king of Bashan, the land with its cities within the borders, the cities of the surrounding country. [34] And the children of Gad built Dibon and Ataroth and Aroer, [35] Atroth and Shophan and Jazer and Jogbehah, [36] Beth

Nimrah and Beth Haran, fortified cities, and folds for sheep. [37] And the children of Reuben built Heshbon and Elealeh and Kirjathaim, [38] Nebo and Baal Meon (*their* names being changed) and Shibmah; and they gave *other* names to the cities which they built.

[39] And the children of Machir the son of Manasseh went to Gilead and took it, and dispossessed the Amorites who *were* in it. [40] So Moses gave Gilead to Machir the son of Manasseh, and he dwelt in it. [41] Also Jair the son of Manasseh went and took its small towns, and called them Havoth Jair. [42] Then Nobah went and took Kenath and its villages, and he called it Nobah, after his own name.

∼ PSALM 35:1–8 ∼

[1] Plead *my cause,* O LORD, with those
    who strive with me;
    Fight against those who fight against
    me.
[2] Take hold of shield and buckler,
    And stand up for my help.
[3] Also draw out the spear,
    And stop those who pursue me.
    Say to my soul,
    "I *am* your salvation."

[4] Let those be put to shame and
    brought to dishonor
    Who seek after my life;
    Let those be turned back and
    brought to confusion
    Who plot my hurt.
[5] Let them be like chaff before the
    wind,
    And let the angel of the LORD chase
    them.
[6] Let their way be dark and slippery,
    And let the angel of the LORD pursue
    them.
[7] For without cause they have hidden
    their net for me *in* a pit,
    Which they have dug without cause
    for my life.
[8] Let destruction come upon him
    unexpectedly,
    And let his net that he has hidden
    catch himself;
    Into that very destruction let him
    fall.

∼ PROVERBS 12:1 ∼

1 Whoever loves instruction loves
     knowledge,
   But he who hates correction *is*
     stupid.

∼ MARK 14:55–72 ∼

Now the chief priests and all the council sought testimony against Jesus to put Him to death, but found none. ⁵⁶ For many bore false witness against Him, but their testimonies did not agree.

⁵⁷ Then some rose up and bore false witness against Him, saying, ⁵⁸ "We heard Him say, 'I will destroy this temple made with hands, and within three days I will build another made without hands.' " ⁵⁹ But not even then did their testimony agree.

⁶⁰ And the high priest stood up in the midst and asked Jesus, saying, "Do You answer nothing? What *is it* these men testify against You?" ⁶¹ But He kept silent and answered nothing.

Again the high priest asked Him, saying to Him, "Are You the Christ, the Son of the Blessed?"

⁶² Jesus said, "I am. And you will see the Son of Man sitting at the right hand of the Power, and coming with the clouds of heaven."

⁶³ Then the high priest tore his clothes and said, "What further need do we have

of witnesses? ⁶⁴ You have heard the blasphemy! What do you think?"

And they all condemned Him to be deserving of death.

⁶⁵ Then some began to spit on Him, and to blindfold Him, and to beat Him, and to say to Him, "Prophesy!" And the officers struck Him with the palms of their hands.

⁶⁶ Now as Peter was below in the courtyard, one of the servant girls of the high priest came. ⁶⁷ And when she saw Peter warming himself, she looked at him and said, "You also were with Jesus of Nazareth."

⁶⁸ But he denied it, saying, "I neither know nor understand what you are saying." And he went out on the porch, and a rooster crowed.

⁶⁹ And the servant girl saw him again, and began to say to those who stood by, "This is one of them." ⁷⁰ But he denied it again.

And a little later those who stood by said to Peter again, "Surely you are *one* of them; for you are a Galilean, and your speech shows *it*."

⁷¹ Then he began to curse and swear, "I do not know this Man of whom you speak!"

⁷² A second time *the* rooster crowed. Then Peter called to mind the word that Jesus had said to him, "Before the rooster crows twice, you will deny Me three times." And when he thought about it, he wept.

READING 77 · MARCH 18

∼ NUMBERS 33:1—34:29 ∼

These *are* the journeys of the children of Israel, who went out of the land of Egypt by their armies under the hand of Moses and Aaron. ² Now Moses wrote down the starting points of their journeys at the command of the LORD. And these *are* their journeys according to their starting points: ³ They departed from Rameses in the first month, on the fifteenth day of the first month; on the day after the Passover the children of Israel went out with boldness in the sight of all the Egyptians.

⁴ For the Egyptians were burying all *their* firstborn, whom the LORD had killed among them. Also on their gods the LORD had executed judgments.

⁵ Then the children of Israel moved from Rameses and camped at Succoth. ⁶ They departed from Succoth and camped at Etham, which *is* on the edge of the wilderness. ⁷ They moved from Etham and turned back to Pi Hahiroth, which *is* east of Baal Zephon; and they camped near Migdol. ⁸ They departed from before Hahiroth and passed through

the midst of the sea into the wilderness, went three days' journey in the Wilderness of Etham, and camped at Marah. [9] They moved from Marah and came to Elim. At Elim *were* twelve springs of water and seventy palm trees; so they camped there.

[10] They moved from Elim and camped by the Red Sea. [11] They moved from the Red Sea and camped in the Wilderness of Sin. [12] They journeyed from the Wilderness of Sin and camped at Dophkah. [13] They departed from Dophkah and camped at Alush. [14] They moved from Alush and camped at Rephidim, where there was no water for the people to drink.

[15] They departed from Rephidim and camped in the Wilderness of Sinai. [16] They moved from the Wilderness of Sinai and camped at Kibroth Hattaavah. [17] They departed from Kibroth Hattaavah and camped at Hazeroth. [18] They departed from Hazeroth and camped at Rithmah. [19] They departed from Rithmah and camped at Rimmon Perez. [20] They departed from Rimmon Perez and camped at Libnah. [21] They moved from Libnah and camped at Rissah. [22] They journeyed from Rissah and camped at Kehelathah. [23] They went from Kehelathah and camped at Mount Shepher. [24] They moved from Mount Shepher and camped at Haradah. [25] They moved from Haradah and camped at Makheloth. [26] They moved from Makheloth and camped at Tahath. [27] They departed from Tahath and camped at Terah. [28] They moved from Terah and camped at Mithkah. [29] They went from Mithkah and camped at Hashmonah. [30] They departed from Hashmonah and camped at Moseroth. [31] They departed from Moseroth and camped at Bene Jaakan. [32] They moved from Bene Jaakan and camped at Hor Hagidgad. [33] They went from Hor Hagidgad and camped at Jotbathah. [34] They moved from Jotbathah and camped at Abronah. [35] They departed from Abronah and camped at Ezion Geber. [36] They moved from Ezion Geber and camped in the Wilderness of Zin, which *is* Kadesh. [37] They moved from Kadesh and camped at Mount Hor, on the boundary of the land of Edom.

[38] Then Aaron the priest went up to Mount Hor at the command of the LORD, and died there in the fortieth year after the children of Israel had come out of the land of Egypt, on the first *day* of the fifth month. [39] Aaron *was* one hundred and twenty-three years old when he died on Mount Hor.

[40] Now the king of Arad, the Canaanite, who dwelt in the South in the land of Canaan, heard of the coming of the children of Israel.

[41] So they departed from Mount Hor and camped at Zalmonah. [42] They departed from Zalmonah and camped at Punon. [43] They departed from Punon and camped at Oboth. [44] They departed from Oboth and camped at Ije Abarim, at the border of Moab. [45] They departed from Ijim and camped at Dibon Gad. [46] They moved from Dibon Gad and camped at Almon Diblathaim. [47] They moved from Almon Diblathaim and camped in the mountains of Abarim, before Nebo. [48] They departed from the mountains of Abarim and camped in the plains of Moab by the Jordan, *across from* Jericho. [49] They camped by the Jordan, from Beth Jesimoth as far as the Abel Acacia Grove in the plains of Moab.

[50] Now the LORD spoke to Moses in the plains of Moab by the Jordan, *across from* Jericho, saying, [51] "Speak to the children of Israel, and say to them: 'When you have crossed the Jordan into the land of Canaan, [52] then you shall drive out all the inhabitants of the land from before you, destroy all their engraved stones, destroy all their molded images, and demolish all their high places; [53] you shall dispossess *the inhabitants of* the land and dwell in it, for I have given you the land to possess. [54] And you shall divide the land by lot as an inheritance among your families; to the larger you shall give a larger inheritance, and to the smaller you shall give a smaller inheritance; there everyone's *inheritance* shall be whatever falls to him by lot. You shall inherit according to the tribes of your fathers. [55] But if you do not drive out the inhabitants of the land from before you, then it shall be that those whom you let remain *shall be* irritants in your eyes and thorns in your sides, and they shall harass you in the land where you dwell. [56] Moreover it shall be

Deep in the Earth

When England needed to increase its coal production during World War II, Winston Churchill called labor leaders together to enlist their support. He asked them to picture in their minds a parade in Piccadilly Circus after the war. First, he said, would come the sailors who had kept the critical sea lanes open. Then would come the soldiers who had returned from Dunkirk after defeating Rommel in Africa. Then would come the pilots who had wiped the Luftwaffe from the skies.

Next would come a long line of sweat-stained, soot-streaked men in miner's caps. As Churchill painted the scene for the labor leaders, he depicted someone crying out from the crowd, " 'And where were you during the critical days of our struggle?' And from ten thousand throats would come the answer, 'We were deep in the earth with our faces to the coal.' "

Whatever your profession, not every person can be number one. Not everyone can be "the star." But anyone can be a hero. Nothing worthwhile is ever accomplished by one person alone. Every person can make a significant contribution, whatever they do — whether it's behind the scenes or on the front lines, each person plays an important part in the success of the whole.

that I will do to you as I thought to do to them.' "

34 Then the LORD spoke to Moses, saying, ² "Command the children of Israel, and say to them: 'When you come into the land of Canaan, this *is* the land that shall fall to you as an inheritance—the land of Canaan to its boundaries. ³ Your southern border shall be from the Wilderness of Zin along the border of Edom; then your southern border shall extend eastward to the end of the Salt Sea; ⁴ your border shall turn from the southern side of the Ascent of Akrabbim, continue to Zin, and be on the south of Kadesh Barnea; then it shall go on to Hazar Addar, and continue to Azmon; ⁵ the border shall turn from Azmon to the Brook of Egypt, and it shall end at the Sea.

⁶ 'As for the western border, you shall have the Great Sea for a border; this shall be your western border.

⁷ 'And this shall be your northern border: From the Great Sea you shall mark out your *border* line to Mount Hor; ⁸ from Mount Hor you shall mark out *your border* to the entrance of Hamath; then the direction of the border shall be toward Zedad; ⁹ the border shall proceed to Ziphron, and it shall end at Hazar Enan. This shall be your northern border.

¹⁰ 'You shall mark out your eastern border from Hazar Enan to Shepham; ¹¹ the border shall go down from Shepham to Riblah on the east side of Ain; the border shall go down and reach to the eastern side of the Sea of Chinnereth; ¹² the border shall go down along the Jordan, and it shall end at the Salt Sea. This shall be your land with its surrounding boundaries.' "

¹³ Then Moses commanded the children of Israel, saying: "This *is* the land which you shall inherit by lot, which the LORD has commanded to give to the nine tribes and to the half-tribe. ¹⁴ For the tribe of the children of Reuben according to the house of their fathers, and the tribe of the children of Gad according to the house of their fathers, have received *their inheritance;* and the half-tribe of Manasseh has received its inheritance. ¹⁵ The two tribes and the half-tribe have received their inheritance on this side of the Jordan, *across from* Jericho eastward, toward the sunrise."

¹⁶ And the LORD spoke to Moses, saying, ¹⁷ "These *are* the names of the men who shall divide the land among you as an inheritance: Eleazar the priest and Joshua the son of Nun. ¹⁸ And you shall take one leader of every tribe to divide the land for the inheritance. ¹⁹ These *are* the names of the men: from the tribe of Judah, Caleb the son of Jephunneh; ²⁰ from the tribe of the children of Simeon, Shemuel the son of Ammihud; ²¹ from the tribe of Benjamin, Elidad the son of Chislon; ²² a leader from the tribe of the children of Dan, Bukki the son of Jogli; ²³ from the sons of Joseph: a leader from the tribe of the children of Manasseh, Hanniel the son of Ephod, ²⁴ and a leader from the tribe of the children of Ephraim, Kemuel the son of Shiphtan; ²⁵ a leader from the tribe of the children of Zebulun, Elizaphan the son of Parnach; ²⁶ a leader from the tribe of the children of Issachar, Paltiel the son of Azzan; ²⁷ a leader from the tribe of the children of Asher, Ahihud the son of Shelomi; ²⁸ and a leader from the tribe of the children of Naphtali, Pedahel the son of Ammihud."

²⁹ These *are* the ones the LORD commanded to divide the inheritance among the children of Israel in the land of Canaan.

∼ PSALM 35:9–16 ∼

⁹ And my soul shall be joyful in the
      LORD;
    It shall rejoice in His salvation.
¹⁰ All my bones shall say,
    "LORD, who *is* like You,
      Delivering the poor from him who is
        too strong for him,
      Yes, the poor and the needy from
        him who plunders him?"

¹¹ Fierce witnesses rise up;
    They ask me *things* that I do not
      know.
¹² They reward me evil for good,
    To the sorrow of my soul.
¹³ But as for me, when they were sick,
    My clothing *was* sackcloth;
    I humbled myself with fasting;

And my prayer would return to my
own heart.
[14] I paced about as though *he were* my
friend *or* brother;
I bowed down heavily, as one who
mourns *for his* mother.

[15] But in my adversity they rejoiced
And gathered together;
Attackers gathered against me,
And I did not know *it;*
They tore *at me* and did not cease;
[16] With ungodly mockers at feasts
They gnashed at me with their teeth.

∼ PROVERBS 12:2 ∼

[2] A good *man* obtains favor from the
LORD,
But a man of wicked intentions He
will condemn.

∼ MARK 15:1–24 ∼

Immediately, in the morning, the chief
priests held a consultation with the elders
and scribes and the whole council; and
they bound Jesus, led *Him* away, and delivered *Him* to Pilate. [2] Then Pilate asked
Him, "Are You the King of the Jews?"

He answered and said to him, "*It is as*
you say."

[3] And the chief priests accused Him of
many things, but He answered nothing.
[4] Then Pilate asked Him again, saying,
"Do You answer nothing? See how many
things they testify against You!" [5] But Jesus
still answered nothing, so that Pilate marveled.

[6] Now at the feast he was accustomed
to releasing one prisoner to them, whomever they requested. [7] And there was one
named Barabbas, *who was* chained with
his fellow rebels; they had committed
murder in the rebellion. [8] Then the multitude, crying aloud, began to ask *him to*

do just as he had always done for them.
[9] But Pilate answered them, saying, "Do
you want me to release to you the King
of the Jews?" [10] For he knew that the chief
priests had handed Him over because of
envy.

[11] But the chief priests stirred up the
crowd, so that he should rather release
Barabbas to them. [12] Pilate answered and
said to them again, "What then do you
want me to do *with Him* whom you call
the King of the Jews?"

[13] So they cried out again, "Crucify
Him!"

[14] Then Pilate said to them, "Why, what
evil has He done?"

But they cried out all the more, "Crucify Him!"

[15] So Pilate, wanting to gratify the
crowd, released Barabbas to them; and
he delivered Jesus, after he had scourged
Him, to be crucified.

[16] Then the soldiers led Him away into
the hall called Praetorium, and they called
together the whole garrison. [17] And they
clothed Him with purple; and they twisted
a crown of thorns, put it on His *head,*
[18] and began to salute Him, "Hail, King
of the Jews!" [19] Then they struck Him on
the head with a reed and spat on Him;
and bowing the knee, they worshiped
Him. [20] And when they had mocked Him,
they took the purple off Him, put His own
clothes on Him, and led Him out to crucify Him.

[21] Then they compelled a certain man,
Simon a Cyrenian, the father of Alexander
and Rufus, as he was coming out of the
country and passing by, to bear His cross.
[22] And they brought Him to the place
Golgotha, which is translated, Place of a
Skull. [23] Then they gave Him wine
mingled with myrrh to drink, but He did
not take *it.* [24] And when they crucified
Him, they divided His garments, casting
lots for them to determine what every man
should take.

~ NUMBERS 35:1—36:13 ~

And the LORD spoke to Moses in the plains of Moab by the Jordan *across from* Jericho, saying: ² "Command the children of Israel that they give the Levites cities to dwell in from the inheritance of their possession, and you shall *also* give the Levites common-land around the cities. ³ They shall have the cities to dwell in; and their common-land shall be for their cattle, for their herds, and for all their animals. ⁴ The common-land of the cities which you will give the Levites *shall extend* from the wall of the city outward a thousand cubits all around. ⁵ And you shall measure outside the city on the east side two thousand cubits, on the south side two thousand cubits, on the west side two thousand cubits, and on the north side two thousand cubits. The city *shall be* in the middle. This shall belong to them as common-land for the cities.

⁶ "Now among the cities which you will give to the Levites *you shall appoint* six cities of refuge, to which a manslayer may flee. And to these you shall add forty-two cities. ⁷ So all the cities you will give to the Levites *shall be* forty-eight; these *you shall give* with their common-land. ⁸ And the cities which you will give *shall be* from the possession of the children of Israel; from the larger *tribe* you shall give many, from the smaller you shall give few. Each shall give some of its cities to the Levites, in proportion to the inheritance that each receives."

⁹ Then the LORD spoke to Moses, saying, ¹⁰ "Speak to the children of Israel, and say to them: 'When you cross the Jordan into the land of Canaan, ¹¹ then you shall appoint cities to be cities of refuge for you, that the manslayer who kills any person accidentally may flee there. ¹² They shall be cities of refuge for you from the avenger, that the manslayer may not die until he stands before the congregation in judgment. ¹³ And of the cities which you give, you shall have six cities of refuge. ¹⁴ You shall appoint three cities on this side of the Jordan, and three cities you shall appoint in the land of Canaan, *which* will be cities of refuge. ¹⁵ These six cities shall be for refuge for the children of Israel, for the stranger, and for the sojourner among them, that anyone who kills a person accidentally may flee there.

¹⁶ 'But if he strikes him with an iron implement, so that he dies, he *is* a murderer; the murderer shall surely be put to death. ¹⁷ And if he strikes him with a stone in the hand, by which one could die, and he does die, he *is* a murderer; the murderer shall surely be put to death. ¹⁸ Or *if* he strikes him with a wooden hand weapon, by which one could die, and he does die, he *is* a murderer; the murderer shall surely be put to death. ¹⁹ The avenger of blood himself shall put the murderer to death; when he meets him, he shall put him to death. ²⁰ If he pushes him out of hatred or, while lying in wait, hurls something at him so that he dies, ²¹ or in enmity he strikes him with his hand so that he dies, the one who struck *him* shall surely be put to death. He *is* a murderer. The avenger of blood shall put the murderer to death when he meets him.

²² 'However, if he pushes him suddenly without enmity, or throws anything at him without lying in wait, ²³ or uses a stone, by which a man could die, throwing *it* at him without seeing *him,* so that he dies, while he was not his enemy or seeking his harm, ²⁴ then the congregation shall judge between the manslayer and the avenger of blood according to these judgments. ²⁵ So the congregation shall deliver the manslayer from the hand of the avenger of blood, and the congregation shall return him to the city of refuge where he had fled, and he shall remain there until the death of the high priest who was anointed with the holy oil. ²⁶ But if the manslayer at any time goes outside the limits of the city of refuge where he fled, ²⁷ and the avenger of blood finds him outside the limits of his city of refuge, and the avenger of blood kills the manslayer, he shall not be guilty of blood, ²⁸ because he should have remained in his city of refuge until the death of the high priest. But after the death of the high priest the manslayer may return to the land of his possession.

De Forest's Worthless Glass Bulb

Years ago in a federal courtroom in New York, a sarcastic district attorney presented to a jury a glass gadget which looked something like a small electric light bulb. With great scorn and ridicule, the attorney accused the defendant of claiming that this "worthless device" might be used to transmit the human voice across the Atlantic! He alleged that gullible investors had been persuaded by preposterous claims to buy stock in the company — an obvious act of fraud. He urged the jury to give the defendant and his two partners stiff prison terms. Ultimately, the two associates were convicted, but the defendant was given his freedom after he received a severe scolding from the judge.

The defendant was inventor Lee de Forest. The "worthless glass bulb" that was also on trial was the audion tube he had developed — perhaps the single greatest invention of the twentieth century. It was the foundation for what has become a multibillion-dollar electronics industry.

No matter how harsh the criticism or how stinging the sarcasm aimed at your original ideas — pursue them further. Take them to their logical end, either convincing yourself that you were indeed wrong, or creating something new and beneficial!

> And those who passed by blasphemed Him, wagging their heads and saying, "Aha! You who destroy the temple and build it in three days, save Yourself, and come down from the cross!"
>
> *Mark 15:29-30*

²⁹ 'And these *things* shall be a statute of judgment to you throughout your generations in all your dwellings. ³⁰ Whoever kills a person, the murderer shall be put to death on the testimony of witnesses; but one witness is not *sufficient* testimony against a person for the death *penalty.* ³¹ Moreover you shall take no ransom for the life of a murderer who *is* guilty of death, but he shall surely be put to death. ³² And you shall take no ransom for him who has fled to his city of refuge, that he may return to dwell in the land before the death of the priest. ³³ So you shall not pollute the land where you *are;* for blood defiles the land, and no atonement can be made for the land, for the blood that is shed on it, except by the blood of him who shed it. ³⁴ Therefore do not defile the land which you inhabit, in the midst of which I dwell; for I the LORD dwell among the children of Israel.' "

36 Now the chief fathers of the families of the children of Gilead the son of Machir, the son of Manasseh, of the families of the sons of Joseph, came near and spoke before Moses and before the leaders, the chief fathers of the children of Israel. ² And they said: "The LORD commanded my lord *Moses* to give the land as an inheritance by lot to the children of Israel, and my lord was commanded by the LORD to give the inheritance of our brother Zelophehad to his daughters. ³ Now if they are married to any of the sons of the *other* tribes of the children of Israel, then their inheritance will be taken from the inheritance of our fathers, and it will be added to the inheritance of the tribe into which they marry; so it will be taken from the lot of our inheritance. ⁴ And when the Jubilee of the children of Israel comes, then their inheritance will be added to the inheritance of the tribe into which they marry; so their inheritance will be taken away from the inheritance of the tribe of our fathers."

⁵ Then Moses commanded the children of Israel according to the word of the LORD, saying: "What the tribe of the sons of Joseph speaks is right. ⁶ This *is* what the LORD commands concerning the daughters of Zelophehad, saying, 'Let them marry whom they think best, but they may marry only within the family of their father's tribe.' ⁷ So the inheritance of the children of Israel shall not change hands from tribe to tribe, for every one of the children of Israel shall keep the inheritance of the tribe of his fathers. ⁸ And every daughter who possesses an inheritance in any tribe of the children of Israel shall be the wife of one of the family of her father's tribe, so that the children of Israel each may possess the inheritance of his fathers. ⁹ Thus no inheritance shall change hands from *one* tribe to another, but every tribe of the children of Israel shall keep its own inheritance."

¹⁰ Just as the LORD commanded Moses, so did the daughters of Zelophehad; ¹¹ for Mahlah, Tirzah, Hoglah, Milcah, and Noah, the daughters of Zelophehad, were married to the sons of their father's brothers. ¹² They were married into the families of the children of Manasseh the son of Joseph, and their inheritance remained in the tribe of their father's family.

¹³ These *are* the commandments and the judgments which the LORD commanded the children of Israel by the hand of Moses in the plains of Moab by the Jordan, *across from* Jericho.

∽ PSALM 35:17–28 ∽

¹⁷ Lord, how long will You look on?
   Rescue me from their destructions,
   My precious *life* from the lions.
¹⁸ I will give You thanks in the great
      assembly;
   I will praise You among many
      people.

¹⁹ Let them not rejoice over me who
      are wrongfully my enemies;
   Nor let them wink with the eye who
      hate me without a cause.
²⁰ For they do not speak peace,
   But they devise deceitful matters
   Against *the* quiet ones in the land.
²¹ They also opened their mouth wide
      against me,
   And said, "Aha, aha!
   Our eyes have seen *it.*"

²² *This* You have seen, O LORD;
   Do not keep silence.
   O Lord, do not be far from me.

23 Stir up Yourself, and awake to my
      vindication,
   To my cause, my God and my Lord.
24 Vindicate me, O LORD my God,
      according to Your righteousness;
   And let them not rejoice over me.
25 Let them not say in their hearts, "Ah,
      so we would have it!"
   Let them not say, "We have
      swallowed him up."

26 Let them be ashamed and brought to
      mutual confusion
   Who rejoice at my hurt;
   Let them be clothed with shame and
      dishonor
   Who exalt themselves against me.

27 Let them shout for joy and be glad,
   Who favor my righteous cause;
   And let them say continually,
   "Let the LORD be magnified,
   Who has pleasure in the prosperity
      of His servant."
28 And my tongue shall speak of Your
      righteousness
   And of Your praise all the day long.

～ PROVERBS 12:3 ～

3 A man is not established by
      wickedness,
   But the root of the righteous cannot
      be moved.

～ MARK 15:25–47 ～

Now it was the third hour, and they crucified Him. 26 And the inscription of His
accusation was written above:

THE KING OF THE JEWS.

27 With Him they also crucified two robbers, one on His right and the other on
His left. 28 So the Scripture was fulfilled
which says, "And He was numbered with
the transgressors."
   29 And those who passed by blasphemed
Him, wagging their heads and saying,
"Aha! *You* who destroy the temple and
build *it* in three days, 30 save Yourself,
and come down from the cross!"
   31 Likewise the chief priests also, mocking among themselves with the scribes,

said, "He saved others; Himself He cannot save. 32 Let the Christ, the King of Israel, descend now from the cross, that we
may see and believe."
   Even those who were crucified with
Him reviled Him.
   33 Now when the sixth hour had come,
there was darkness over the whole land
until the ninth hour. 34 And at the ninth
hour Jesus cried out with a loud voice,
saying, "Eloi, Eloi, lama sabachthani?"
which is translated, "My God, My God,
why have You forsaken Me?"
   35 Some of those who stood by, when
they heard *that,* said, "Look, He is calling for Elijah!" 36 Then someone ran and
filled a sponge full of sour wine, put *it* on
a reed, and offered *it* to Him to drink,
saying, "Let Him alone; let us see if Elijah
will come to take Him down."
   37 And Jesus cried out with a loud voice,
and breathed His last.
   38 Then the veil of the temple was torn
in two from top to bottom. 39 So when
the centurion, who stood opposite Him,
saw that He cried out like this and
breathed His last, he said, "Truly this Man
was the Son of God!"
   40 There were also women looking on
from afar, among whom were Mary
Magdalene, Mary the mother of James
the Less and of Joses, and Salome, 41 who
also followed Him and ministered to Him
when He was in Galilee, and many other
women who came up with Him to Jerusalem.
   42 Now when evening had come, because it was the Preparation Day, that is,
the day before the Sabbath, 43 Joseph of
Arimathea, a prominent council member,
who was himself waiting for the kingdom
of God, coming and taking courage, went
in to Pilate and asked for the body of Jesus.
44 Pilate marveled that He was already
dead; and summoning the centurion, he
asked him if He had been dead for some
time. 45 So when he found out from the
centurion, he granted the body to Joseph.
46 Then he bought fine linen, took Him
down, and wrapped Him in the linen. And
he laid Him in a tomb which had been
hewn out of the rock, and rolled a stone
against the door of the tomb. 47 And Mary
Magdalene and Mary *the mother* of Joses
observed where He was laid.

~ Deuteronomy 1:1—2:37 ~

These *are* the words which Moses spoke to all Israel on this side of the Jordan in the wilderness, in the plain opposite Suph, between Paran, Tophel, Laban, Hazeroth, and Dizahab. ² *It is* eleven days' *journey* from Horeb by way of Mount Seir to Kadesh Barnea. ³ Now it came to pass in the fortieth year, in the eleventh month, on the first *day* of the month, *that* Moses spoke to the children of Israel according to all that the LORD had given him as commandments to them, ⁴ after he had killed Sihon king of the Amorites, who dwelt in Heshbon, and Og king of Bashan, who dwelt at Ashtaroth in Edrei.

⁵ On this side of the Jordan in the land of Moab, Moses began to explain this law, saying, ⁶ "The LORD our God spoke to us in Horeb, saying: 'You have dwelt long enough at this mountain. ⁷ Turn and take your journey, and go to the mountains of the Amorites, to all the neighboring *places* in the plain, in the mountains and in the lowland, in the South and on the seacoast, to the land of the Canaanites and to Lebanon, as far as the great river, the River Euphrates. ⁸ See, I have set the land before you; go in and possess the land which the LORD swore to your fathers—to Abraham, Isaac, and Jacob—to give to them and their descendants after them.'

⁹ "And I spoke to you at that time, saying: 'I alone am not able to bear you. ¹⁰ The LORD your God has multiplied you, and here you *are* today, as the stars of heaven in multitude. ¹¹ May the LORD God of your fathers make you a thousand times more numerous than you are, and bless you as He has promised you! ¹² How can I alone bear your problems and your burdens and your complaints? ¹³ Choose wise, understanding, and knowledgeable men from among your tribes, and I will make them heads over you.' ¹⁴ And you answered me and said, 'The thing which you have told *us* to do *is* good.' ¹⁵ So I took the heads of your tribes, wise and knowledgeable men, and made them heads over you, leaders of thousands, leaders of hundreds, leaders of fifties, leaders of tens, and officers for your tribes.

¹⁶ "Then I commanded your judges at that time, saying, 'Hear *the cases* between your brethren, and judge righteously between a man and his brother or the stranger who is with him. ¹⁷ You shall not show partiality in judgment; you shall hear the small as well as the great; you shall not be afraid in any man's presence, for the judgment *is* God's. The case that is too hard for you, bring to me, and I will hear it.' ¹⁸ And I commanded you at that time all the things which you should do.

¹⁹ "So we departed from Horeb, and went through all that great and terrible wilderness which you saw on the way to the mountains of the Amorites, as the LORD our God had commanded us. Then we came to Kadesh Barnea. ²⁰ And I said to you, 'You have come to the mountains of the Amorites, which the LORD our God is giving us. ²¹ Look, the LORD your God has set the land before you; go up *and* possess *it,* as the LORD God of your fathers has spoken to you; do not fear or be discouraged.'

²² "And every one of you came near to me and said, 'Let us send men before us, and let them search out the land for us, and bring back word to us of the way by which we should go up, and of the cities into which we shall come.'

²³ "The plan pleased me well; so I took twelve of your men, one man from *each* tribe. ²⁴ And they departed and went up into the mountains, and came to the Valley of Eshcol, and spied it out. ²⁵ They also took *some* of the fruit of the land in their hands and brought *it* down to us; and they brought back word to us, saying, '*It is* a good land which the LORD our God is giving us.'

²⁶ "Nevertheless you would not go up, but rebelled against the command of the LORD your God; ²⁷ and you complained in your tents, and said, 'Because the LORD hates us, He has brought us out of the land of Egypt to deliver us into the hand of the Amorites, to destroy us. ²⁸ Where can we go up? Our brethren have discouraged our hearts, saying, "The people *are* greater and taller than we; the cities *are* great and fortified up to heaven;

An Audience with the King

Long ago, a band of minstrels traveled from town to town performing music to make a living. They were not very financially successful however. Times were hard and there was little money for common folk to spend on entertainment. Attendance was sparse.

One night, the troupe met to discuss their plight. One said, "I see no reason for singing tonight. It's starting to snow. Who will venture out on a night like this?" Another said, "I agree. Last night we performed for only a handful. Fewer will come tonight. Why not give back the price of their tickets and cancel." A third added, "It's hard to do one's best for so few."

Then an older man rose, and looking straight at the group as a whole, he said, "I know you are discouraged. I am too. It's not the fault of those who come that others do not. They should not be punished with less than the best we can give. We will go on and we will do our best."

Heartened by his words, the minstrels went on with their show. Even though the audience was small, they had never performed better. After the concert, the old man called the troupe together. "Listen to this," he said as he began to read a note he held in his hand: 'Thank you for a beautiful performance.'" The note was signed simply, "Your King."

There are always at least two people who see what you do and how well you do it — you, and God.

moreover we have seen the sons of the Anakim there." '

²⁹ "Then I said to you, 'Do not be terrified, or afraid of them. ³⁰ The LORD your God, who goes before you, He will fight for you, according to all He did for you in Egypt before your eyes, ³¹ and in the wilderness where you saw how the LORD your God carried you, as a man carries his son, in all the way that you went until you came to this place.' ³² Yet, for all that, you did not believe the LORD your God, ³³ who went in the way before you to search out a place for you to pitch your tents, to show you the way you should go, in the fire by night and in the cloud by day.

³⁴ "And the LORD heard the sound of your words, and was angry, and took an oath, saying, ³⁵ 'Surely not one of these men of this evil generation shall see that good land of which I swore to give to your fathers, ³⁶ except Caleb the son of Jephunneh; he shall see it, and to him and his children I am giving the land on which he walked, because he wholly followed the LORD.' ³⁷ The LORD was also angry with me for your sakes, saying, 'Even you shall not go in there. ³⁸ Joshua the son of Nun, who stands before you, he shall go in there. Encourage him, for he shall cause Israel to inherit it.

³⁹ 'Moreover your little ones and your children, who you say will be victims, who today have no knowledge of good and evil, they shall go in there; to them I will give it, and they shall possess it. ⁴⁰ But *as for* you, turn and take your journey into the wilderness by the Way of the Red Sea.'

⁴¹ "Then you answered and said to me, 'We have sinned against the LORD; we will go up and fight, just as the LORD our God commanded us.' And when everyone of you had girded on his weapons of war, you were ready to go up into the mountain.

⁴² "And the LORD said to me, 'Tell them, "Do not go up nor fight, for I *am* not among you; lest you be defeated before your enemies." ' ⁴³ So I spoke to you; yet you would not listen, but rebelled against the command of the LORD, and presumptuously went up into the mountain. ⁴⁴ And the Amorites who dwelt in that mountain came out against you and chased you

as bees do, and drove you back from Seir to Hormah. ⁴⁵ Then you returned and wept before the LORD, but the LORD would not listen to your voice nor give ear to you.

⁴⁶ "So you remained in Kadesh many days, according to the days that you spent *there*.

2 "Then we turned and journeyed into the wilderness of the Way of the Red Sea, as the LORD spoke to me, and we skirted Mount Seir for many days.

² "And the LORD spoke to me, saying: ³ 'You have skirted this mountain long enough; turn northward. ⁴ And command the people, saying, "You *are about to* pass through the territory of your brethren, the descendants of Esau, who live in Seir; and they will be afraid of you. Therefore watch yourselves carefully. ⁵ Do not meddle with them, for I will not give you *any* of their land, no, not so much as one footstep, because I have given Mount Seir to Esau *as* a possession. ⁶ You shall buy food from them with money, that you may eat; and you shall also buy water from them with money, that you may drink.

⁷ "For the LORD your God has blessed you in all the work of your hand. He knows your trudging through this great wilderness. These forty years the LORD your God *has been* with you; you have lacked nothing." '

⁸ "And when we passed beyond our brethren, the descendants of Esau who dwell in Seir, away from the road of the plain, away from Elath and Ezion Geber, we turned and passed by way of the Wilderness of Moab. ⁹ Then the LORD said to me, 'Do not harass Moab, nor contend with them in battle, for I will not give you *any* of their land *as* a possession, because I have given Ar to the descendants of Lot *as* a possession.' "

¹⁰(The Emim had dwelt there in times past, a people as great and numerous and tall as the Anakim. ¹¹ They were also regarded as giants, like the Anakim, but the Moabites call them Emim. ¹² The Horites formerly dwelt in Seir, but the descendants of Esau dispossessed them and destroyed them from before them, and dwelt in their place, just as Israel did to the land of their possession which the LORD gave them.)

[13] " 'Now rise and cross over the Valley of the Zered.' So we crossed over the Valley of the Zered. [14] And the time we took to come from Kadesh Barnea until we crossed over the Valley of the Zered *was* thirty-eight years, until all the generation of the men of war was consumed from the midst of the camp, just as the LORD had sworn to them. [15] For indeed the hand of the LORD was against them, to destroy them from the midst of the camp until they were consumed.

[16] "So it was, when all the men of war had finally perished from among the people, [17] that the LORD spoke to me, saying: [18] 'This day you are to cross over at Ar, the boundary of Moab. [19] And *when* you come near the people of Ammon, do not harass them or meddle with them, for I will not give you *any* of the land of the people of Ammon *as* a possession, because I have given it to the descendants of Lot *as* a possession.' "

[20] (That was also regarded as a land of giants; giants formerly dwelt there. But the Ammonites call them Zamzummim, [21] a people as great and numerous and tall as the Anakim. But the LORD destroyed them before them, and they dispossessed them and dwelt in their place, [22] just as He had done for the descendants of Esau, who dwelt in Seir, when He destroyed the Horites from before them. They dispossessed them and dwelt in their place, even to this day. [23] And the Avim, who dwelt in villages as far as Gaza—the Caphtorim, who came from Caphtor, destroyed them and dwelt in their place.)

[24] " 'Rise, take your journey, and cross over the River Arnon. Look, I have given into your hand Sihon the Amorite, king of Heshbon, and his land. Begin to possess *it,* and engage him in battle. [25] This day I will begin to put the dread and fear of you upon the nations under the whole heaven, who shall hear the report of you, and shall tremble and be in anguish because of you.'

[26] "And I sent messengers from the Wilderness of Kedemoth to Sihon king of Heshbon, with words of peace, saying, [27] 'Let me pass through your land; I will keep strictly to the road, and I will turn neither to the right nor to the left. [28] You shall sell me food for money, that I may eat, and give me water for money, that I may drink; only let me pass through on foot, [29] just as the descendants of Esau who dwell in Seir and the Moabites who dwell in Ar did for me, until I cross the Jordan to the land which the LORD our God is giving us.'

[30] "But Sihon king of Heshbon would not let us pass through, for the LORD your God hardened his spirit and made his heart obstinate, that He might deliver him into your hand, as *it is* this day.

[31] "And the LORD said to me, 'See, I have begun to give Sihon and his land over to you. Begin to possess *it,* that you may inherit his land.' [32] Then Sihon and all his people came out against us to fight at Jahaz. [33] And the LORD our God delivered him over to us; so we defeated him, his sons, and all his people. [34] We took all his cities at that time, and we utterly destroyed the men, women, and little ones of every city; we left none remaining. [35] We took only the livestock as plunder for ourselves, with the spoil of the cities which we took. [36] From Aroer, which *is* on the bank of the River Arnon, and *from* the city that *is* in the ravine, as far as Gilead, there was not one city too strong for us; the LORD our God delivered all to us. [37] Only you did not go near the land of the people of Ammon—anywhere along the River Jabbok, or to the cities of the mountains, or wherever the LORD our God had forbidden us.

∼ PSALM 36:1–6 ∼

1   An oracle within my heart
        concerning the transgression of
        the wicked:
    There is no fear of God before his
        eyes.
2   For he flatters himself in his own
        eyes,
    When he finds out his iniquity *and*
        when he hates.
3   The words of his mouth *are*
        wickedness and deceit;
    He has ceased to be wise *and* to do
        good.
4   He devises wickedness on his bed;
    He sets himself in a way *that is* not
        good;
    He does not abhor evil.

5 Your mercy, O LORD, *is* in the
      heavens;
   Your faithfulness *reaches* to the
      clouds.
6 Your righteousness *is* like the great
      mountains;
   Your judgments *are* a great deep;
   O LORD, You preserve man and
      beast.

~ PROVERBS 12:4–6 ~

4 An excellent wife *is* the crown of her
      husband,
   But she who causes shame *is* like
      rottenness in his bones.

5 The thoughts of the righteous *are*
      right,
   But the counsels of the wicked *are*
      deceitful.
6 The words of the wicked *are*, "Lie in
      wait for blood,"
   But the mouth of the upright will
      deliver them.

~ MARK 16:1–20 ~

Now when the Sabbath was past, Mary
Magdalene, Mary *the mother* of James,
and Salome bought spices, that they might
come and anoint Him. 2 Very early in the
morning, on the first *day* of the week, they
came to the tomb when the sun had risen.
3 And they said among themselves, "Who
will roll away the stone from the door of
the tomb for us?" 4 But when they looked
up, they saw that the stone had been rolled
away—for it was very large. 5 And entering the tomb, they saw a young man
clothed in a long white robe sitting on
the right side; and they were alarmed.
6 But he said to them, "Do not be
alarmed. You seek Jesus of Nazareth, who

was crucified. He is risen! He is not here.
See the place where they laid Him. 7 But
go, tell His disciples—and Peter—that He
is going before you into Galilee; there you
will see Him, as He said to you."
8 So they went out quickly and fled from
the tomb, for they trembled and were
amazed. And they said nothing to anyone, for they were afraid.
9 Now when *He* rose early on the first
day of the week, He appeared first to
Mary Magdalene, out of whom He
had cast seven demons. 10 She went and
told those who had been with Him, as
they mourned and wept. 11 And when they
heard that He was alive and had been seen
by her, they did not believe.
12 After that, He appeared in another
form to two of them as they walked and
went into the country. 13 And they went
and told *it* to the rest, *but* they did not
believe them either.
14 Later He appeared to the eleven as
they sat at the table; and He rebuked their
unbelief and hardness of heart, because
they did not believe those who had seen
Him after He had risen. 15 And He said to
them, "Go into all the world and preach
the gospel to every creature. 16 He who
believes and is baptized will be saved; but
he who does not believe will be condemned. 17 And these signs will follow
those who believe: In My name they will
cast out demons; they will speak with new
tongues; 18 they will take up serpents; and
if they drink anything deadly, it will by
no means hurt them; they will lay hands
on the sick, and they will recover."
19 So then, after the Lord had spoken
to them, He was received up into heaven,
and sat down at the right hand of God.
20 And they went out and preached everywhere, the Lord working with *them* and
confirming the word through the accompanying signs. Amen.

READING 80 · MARCH 21

~ DEUTERONOMY 3:1—4:49 ~

"Then we turned and went up
the road to Bashan; and Og
king of Bashan came out
against us, he and all his people, to battle

at Edrei. 2 And the LORD said to me, 'Do
not fear him, for I have delivered him and
all his people and his land into your hand;
you shall do to him as you did to Sihon

"You're Special!"

While on vacation in New England the year after they were married, Sue and Kevin purchased two red "You're Special" plates at an outlet mall. They liked them so much they decided to use them as their "everyday dishes." Then one day, one of the plates broke. That night, Kevin said, "You should get the special plate tonight." "Why?" Sue asked. "Because you finished that big project that you were working on."

The next night, Sue insisted that Kevin dine from the "You're Special" plate, in honor of the help he had given to a neighbor in need. Thereafter, Sue and Kevin vied nightly for the "You're Special" plate honors — not to receive the plate, but for the privilege of awarding it to the other!

When the plate finally broke, Sue said sadly, "I had never been affirmed as much in my entire life as I was those eight months that Kevin and I bestowed upon each other the 'You're Special' honors. What seemed like courtesy the first night Kevin gave me the plate actually set a precedent for our encouraging each other on a daily basis. We're looking for another set of plates now — including one for the baby that's on the way!"

There are many little things you can do every day to make your family feel special. Encouraging them on a daily basis sets a tone of warmth, peace, and comfort in your home. Think of ways to make each member of your family feel special today.

> But command Joshua, and encourage him and strengthen him; for he shall go over before this people.
>
> *Deuteronomy 3:28*

king of the Amorites, who dwelt at Heshbon.'

³ "So the LORD our God also delivered into our hands Og king of Bashan, with all his people, and we attacked him until he had no survivors remaining. ⁴ And we took all his cities at that time; there was not a city which we did not take from them: sixty cities, all the region of Argob, the kingdom of Og in Bashan. ⁵ All these cities *were* fortified with high walls, gates, and bars, besides a great many rural towns. ⁶ And we utterly destroyed them, as we did to Sihon king of Heshbon, utterly destroying the men, women, and children of every city. ⁷ But all the livestock and the spoil of the cities we took as booty for ourselves.

⁸ "And at that time we took the land from the hand of the two kings of the Amorites who *were* on this side of the Jordan, from the River Arnon to Mount Hermon ⁹(the Sidonians call Hermon Sirion, and the Amorites call it Senir), ¹⁰ all the cities of the plain, all Gilead, and all Bashan, as far as Salcah and Edrei, cities of the kingdom of Og in Bashan.

¹¹ "For only Og king of Bashan remained of the remnant of the giants. Indeed his bedstead *was* an iron bedstead. (*Is* it not in Rabbah of the people of Ammon?) Nine cubits *is* its length and four cubits its width, according to the standard cubit.

¹² "And this land, *which* we possessed at that time, from Aroer, which *is* by the River Arnon, and half the mountains of Gilead and its cities, I gave to the Reubenites and the Gadites. ¹³ The rest of Gilead, and all Bashan, the kingdom of Og, I gave to half the tribe of Manasseh. (All the region of Argob, with all Bashan, was called the land of the giants. ¹⁴ Jair the son of Manasseh took all the region of Argob, as far as the border of the Geshurites and the Maachathites, and called Bashan after his own name, Havoth Jair, to this day.)

¹⁵ "Also I gave Gilead to Machir. ¹⁶ And to the Reubenites and the Gadites I gave from Gilead as far as the River Arnon, the middle of the river as *the* border, as far as the River Jabbok, the border of the people of Ammon; ¹⁷ the plain also, with the Jordan as *the* border, from Chinnereth as far as the east side of the Sea of the Arabah (the Salt Sea), below the slopes of Pisgah.

¹⁸ "Then I commanded you at that time, saying: 'The LORD your God has given you this land to possess. All you men of valor shall cross over armed before your brethren, the children of Israel. ¹⁹ But your wives, your little ones, and your livestock (I know that you have much livestock) shall stay in your cities which I have given you, ²⁰ until the LORD has given rest to your brethren as to you, and they also possess the land which the LORD your God is giving them beyond the Jordan. Then each of you may return to his possession which I have given you.'

²¹ "And I commanded Joshua at that time, saying, 'Your eyes have seen all that the LORD your God has done to these two kings; so will the LORD do to all the kingdoms through which you pass. ²² You must not fear them, for the LORD your God Himself fights for you.'

²³ "Then I pleaded with the LORD at that time, saying: ²⁴ 'O Lord GOD, You have begun to show Your servant Your greatness and Your mighty hand, for what god *is there* in heaven or on earth who can do *anything* like Your works and Your mighty *deeds?* ²⁵ I pray, let me cross over and see the good land beyond the Jordan, those pleasant mountains, and Lebanon.'

²⁶ "But the LORD was angry with me on your account, and would not listen to me. So the LORD said to me: 'Enough of that! Speak no more to Me of this matter. ²⁷ Go up to the top of Pisgah, and lift your eyes toward the west, the north, the south, and the east; behold *it* with your eyes, for you shall not cross over this Jordan. ²⁸ But command Joshua, and encourage him and strengthen him; for he shall go over before this people, and he shall cause them to inherit the land which you will see.'

²⁹ "So we stayed in the valley opposite Beth Peor.

4 "Now, O Israel, listen to the statutes and the judgments which I teach you to observe, that you may live, and go in and possess the land which the LORD God of your fathers is giving you. ² You shall not add to the word which I command you,

nor take from it, that you may keep the commandments of the LORD your God which I command you. ³ Your eyes have seen what the LORD did at Baal Peor; for the LORD your God has destroyed from among you all the men who followed Baal of Peor. ⁴ But you who held fast to the LORD your God *are* alive today, every one of you.

⁵ "Surely I have taught you statutes and judgments, just as the LORD my God commanded me, that you should act according *to them* in the land which you go to possess. ⁶ Therefore be careful to observe *them;* for this *is* your wisdom and your understanding in the sight of the peoples who will hear all these statutes, and say, 'Surely this great nation *is* a wise and understanding people.'

⁷ "For what great nation *is there* that has God *so* near to it, as the LORD our God *is* to us, for whatever *reason* we may call upon Him? ⁸ And what great nation *is there* that has *such* statutes and righteous judgments as are in all this law which I set before you this day? ⁹ Only take heed to yourself, and diligently keep yourself, lest you forget the things your eyes have seen, and lest they depart from your heart all the days of your life. And teach them to your children and your grandchildren, ¹⁰ *especially concerning* the day you stood before the LORD your God in Horeb, when the LORD said to me, 'Gather the people to Me, and I will let them hear My words, that they may learn to fear Me all the days they live on the earth, and *that* they may teach their children.'

¹¹ "Then you came near and stood at the foot of the mountain, and the mountain burned with fire to the midst of heaven, with darkness, cloud, and thick darkness. ¹² And the LORD spoke to you out of the midst of the fire. You heard the sound of the words, but saw no form; *you* only *heard* a voice. ¹³ So He declared to you His covenant which He commanded you to perform, the Ten Commandments; and He wrote them on two tablets of stone. ¹⁴ And the LORD commanded me at that time to teach you statutes and judgments, that you might observe them in the land which you cross over to possess.

¹⁵ "Take careful heed to yourselves, for you saw no form when the LORD spoke to you at Horeb out of the midst of the fire, ¹⁶ lest you act corruptly and make for yourselves a carved image in the form of any figure: the likeness of male or female, ¹⁷ the likeness of any animal that *is* on the earth or the likeness of any winged bird that flies in the air, ¹⁸ the likeness of anything that creeps on the ground or the likeness of any fish that *is* in the water beneath the earth. ¹⁹ And *take heed,* lest you lift your eyes to heaven, and *when* you see the sun, the moon, and the stars, all the host of heaven, you feel driven to worship them and serve them, which the LORD your God has given to all the peoples under the whole heaven as a heritage. ²⁰ But the LORD has taken you and brought you out of the iron furnace, out of Egypt, to be His people, an inheritance, as you are this day. ²¹ Furthermore the LORD was angry with me for your sakes, and swore that I would not cross over the Jordan, and that I would not enter the good land which the LORD your God is giving you as an inheritance. ²² But I must die in this land, I must not cross over the Jordan; but you shall cross over and possess that good land. ²³ Take heed to yourselves, lest you forget the covenant of the LORD your God which He made with you, and make for yourselves a carved image in the form of anything which the LORD your God has forbidden you. ²⁴ For the LORD your God *is* a consuming fire, a jealous God.

²⁵ "When you beget children and grandchildren and have grown old in the land, and act corruptly and make a carved image in the form of anything, and do evil in the sight of the LORD your God to provoke Him to anger, ²⁶ I call heaven and earth to witness against you this day, that you will soon utterly perish from the land which you cross over the Jordan to possess; you will not prolong *your* days in it, but will be utterly destroyed. ²⁷ And the LORD will scatter you among the peoples, and you will be left few in number among the nations where the LORD will drive you. ²⁸ And there you will serve gods, the work of men's hands, wood and stone, which neither see nor hear nor eat nor smell. ²⁹ But from there you will seek the LORD your God, and you will find *Him* if you seek Him with all your heart and with all

your soul. [30] When you are in distress, and all these things come upon you in the latter days, when you turn to the LORD your God and obey His voice [31](for the LORD your God is a merciful God), He will not forsake you nor destroy you, nor forget the covenant of your fathers which He swore to them.

[32] "For ask now concerning the days that are past, which were before you, since the day that God created man on the earth, and ask from one end of heaven to the other, whether any great thing like this has happened, or anything like it has been heard. [33] Did any people ever hear the voice of God speaking out of the midst of the fire, as you have heard, and live? [34] Or did God ever try to go and take for Himself a nation from the midst of another nation, by trials, by signs, by wonders, by war, by a mighty hand and an outstretched arm, and by great terrors, according to all that the LORD your God did for you in Egypt before your eyes? [35] To you it was shown, that you might know that the LORD Himself is God; there is none other besides Him. [36] Out of heaven He let you hear His voice, that He might instruct you; on earth He showed you His great fire, and you heard His words out of the midst of the fire. [37] And because He loved your fathers, therefore He chose their descendants after them; and He brought you out of Egypt with His Presence, with His mighty power, [38] driving out from before you nations greater and mightier than you, to bring you in, to give you their land as an inheritance, as it is this day. [39] Therefore know this day, and consider it in your heart, that the LORD Himself is God in heaven above and on the earth beneath; there is no other. [40] You shall therefore keep His statutes and His commandments which I command you today, that it may go well with you and with your children after you, and that you may prolong your days in the land which the LORD your God is giving you for all time."

[41] Then Moses set apart three cities on this side of the Jordan, toward the rising of the sun, [42] that the manslayer might flee there, who kills his neighbor unintentionally, without having hated him in time past, and that by fleeing to one of these cities he might live: [43] Bezer in the wilderness on the plateau for the Reubenites, Ramoth in Gilead for the Gadites, and Golan in Bashan for the Manassites.

[44] Now this is the law which Moses set before the children of Israel. [45] These are the testimonies, the statutes, and the judgments which Moses spoke to the children of Israel after they came out of Egypt, [46] on this side of the Jordan, in the valley opposite Beth Peor, in the land of Sihon king of the Amorites, who dwelt at Heshbon, whom Moses and the children of Israel defeated after they came out of Egypt. [47] And they took possession of his land and the land of Og king of Bashan, two kings of the Amorites, who were on this side of the Jordan, toward the rising of the sun, [48] from Aroer, which is on the bank of the River Arnon, even to Mount Sion (that is, Hermon), [49] and all the plain on the east side of the Jordan as far as the Sea of the Arabah, below the slopes of Pisgah.

∼ PSALM 36:7–12 ∼

7 How precious is Your
    lovingkindness, O God!
   Therefore the children of men put
    their trust under the shadow of
    Your wings.
8 They are abundantly satisfied with
    the fullness of Your house,
   And You give them drink from the
    river of Your pleasures.
9 For with You is the fountain of life;
   In Your light we see light.

10 Oh, continue Your lovingkindness to
     those who know You,
    And Your righteousness to the
     upright in heart.
11 Let not the foot of pride come
     against me,
    And let not the hand of the wicked
     drive me away.
12 There the workers of iniquity have
     fallen;
    They have been cast down and are
     not able to rise.

∼ PROVERBS 12:7 ∼

7 The wicked are overthrown and are
    no more,

But the house of the righteous will stand.

~ LUKE 1:1-20 ~

Inasmuch as many have taken in hand to set in order a narrative of those things which have been fulfilled among us, ² just as those who from the beginning were eyewitnesses and ministers of the word delivered them to us, ³ it seemed good to me also, having had perfect understanding of all things from the very first, to write to you an orderly account, most excellent Theophilus, ⁴ that you may know the certainty of those things in which you were instructed.

⁵ There was in the days of Herod, the king of Judea, a certain priest named Zacharias, of the division of Abijah. His wife *was* of the daughters of Aaron, and her name *was* Elizabeth. ⁶ And they were both righteous before God, walking in all the commandments and ordinances of the Lord blameless. ⁷ But they had no child, because Elizabeth was barren, and they were both well advanced in years.

⁸ So it was, that while he was serving as priest before God in the order of his division, ⁹ according to the custom of the priesthood, his lot fell to burn incense when he went into the temple of the Lord. ¹⁰ And the whole multitude of the people was praying outside at the hour of incense. ¹¹ Then an angel of the Lord appeared to him, standing on the right side of the altar of incense. ¹² And when Zacharias saw *him,* he was troubled, and fear fell upon him.

¹³ But the angel said to him, "Do not be afraid, Zacharias, for your prayer is heard; and your wife Elizabeth will bear you a son, and you shall call his name John. ¹⁴ And you will have joy and gladness, and many will rejoice at his birth. ¹⁵ For he will be great in the sight of the Lord, and shall drink neither wine nor strong drink. He will also be filled with the Holy Spirit, even from his mother's womb. ¹⁶ And he will turn many of the children of Israel to the Lord their God. ¹⁷ He will also go before Him in the spirit and power of Elijah, 'to turn the hearts of the fathers to the children,' and the disobedient to the wisdom of the just, to make ready a people prepared for the Lord."

¹⁸ And Zacharias said to the angel, "How shall I know this? For I am an old man, and my wife is well advanced in years."

¹⁹ And the angel answered and said to him, "I am Gabriel, who stands in the presence of God, and was sent to speak to you and bring you these glad tidings. ²⁰ But behold, you will be mute and not able to speak until the day these things take place, because you did not believe my words which will be fulfilled in their own time."

~ DEUTERONOMY 5:1—6:25 ~

And Moses called all Israel, and said to them: "Hear, O Israel, the statutes and judgments which I speak in your hearing today, that you may learn them and be careful to observe them. ² The LORD our God made a covenant with us in Horeb. ³ The LORD did not make this covenant with our fathers, but with us, those who *are* here today, all of us who *are* alive. ⁴ The LORD talked with you face to face on the mountain from the midst of the fire. ⁵ I stood between the LORD and you at that time, to declare to you the word of the LORD; for you were afraid because of the fire, and you did not go up the mountain. *He* said:

⁶ 'I *am* the LORD your God who brought you out of the land of Egypt, out of the house of bondage.

⁷ 'You shall have no other gods before Me.

⁸ 'You shall not make for yourself a carved image—any likeness *of anything* that *is* in heaven above, or that *is* in the earth beneath, or that *is* in the water under the earth; ⁹ you shall not bow down

to them nor serve them. For I, the LORD your God, *am* a jealous God, visiting the iniquity of the fathers upon the children to the third and fourth *generations* of those who hate Me, ¹⁰ but showing mercy to thousands, to those who love Me and keep My commandments.

¹¹ 'You shall not take the name of the LORD your God in vain, for the LORD will not hold *him* guiltless who takes His name in vain.

¹² 'Observe the Sabbath day, to keep it holy, as the LORD your God commanded you. ¹³ Six days you shall labor and do all your work, ¹⁴ but the seventh day *is* the Sabbath of the LORD your God. *In it* you shall do no work: you, nor your son, nor your daughter, nor your male servant, nor your female servant, nor your ox, nor your donkey, nor any of your cattle, nor your stranger who *is* within your gates, that your male servant and your female servant may rest as well as you. ¹⁵ And remember that you were a slave in the land of Egypt, and the LORD your God brought you out from there by a mighty hand and by an outstretched arm; therefore the LORD your God commanded you to keep the Sabbath day.

¹⁶ 'Honor your father and your mother, as the LORD your God has commanded you, that your days may be long, and that it may be well with you in the land which the LORD your God is giving you.

¹⁷ 'You shall not murder.

¹⁸ 'You shall not commit adultery.

¹⁹ 'You shall not steal.

²⁰ 'You shall not bear false witness against your neighbor.

²¹ 'You shall not covet your neighbor's wife; and you shall not desire your neighbor's house, his field, his male servant, his female servant, his ox, his donkey, or anything that *is* your neighbor's.'

²² "These words the LORD spoke to all your assembly, in the mountain from the midst of the fire, the cloud, and the thick darkness, with a loud voice; and He added no more. And He wrote them on two tablets of stone and gave them to me.

²³ "So it was, when you heard the voice from the midst of the darkness, while the mountain was burning with fire, that you came near to me, all the heads of your tribes and your elders. ²⁴ And you said: 'Surely the LORD our God has shown us His glory and His greatness, and we have heard His voice from the midst of the fire. We have seen this day that God speaks with man; yet he *still* lives. ²⁵ Now therefore, why should we die? For this great fire will consume us; if we hear the voice of the LORD our God anymore, then we shall die. ²⁶ For who *is there* of all flesh who has heard the voice of the living God speaking from the midst of the fire, as we *have,* and lived? ²⁷ You go near and hear all that the LORD our God may say, and tell us all that the LORD our God says to you, and we will hear and do *it.*'

²⁸ "Then the LORD heard the voice of your words when you spoke to me, and the LORD said to me: 'I have heard the voice of the words of this people which they have spoken to you. They are right *in* all that they have spoken. ²⁹ Oh, that they had such a heart in them that they would fear Me and always keep all My commandments, that it might be well with them and with their children forever! ³⁰ Go and say to them, "Return to your tents." ³¹ But as for you, stand here by Me, and I will speak to you all the commandments, the statutes, and the judgments which you shall teach them, that they may observe *them* in the land which I am giving them to possess.'

³² "Therefore you shall be careful to do as the LORD your God has commanded you; you shall not turn aside to the right hand or to the left. ³³ You shall walk in all the ways which the LORD your God has commanded you, that you may live and *that it may be* well with you, and *that* you may prolong *your* days in the land which you shall possess.

6 "Now this *is* the commandment, *and these are* the statutes and judgments which

Courage Under Fire

Many years ago, a huge oil refinery caught fire. Flames shot hundreds of feet into the air and the sky filled with grimy smoke. The heat was so intense that firefighters parked a block away, hoping for the heat to die down. Instead, the fire raged ever closer to a nearby row of oil tanks.

Suddenly, a fire truck came careening down the street. Brakes screeching, it hit the curb directly in front of the blaze. The firefighters jumped out and began to battle the blaze. Inspired by this courageous act, the other firefighters drove closer and joined in the fight. As a result of their cooperative effort, the fire was brought under control in the nick of time.

Those who witnessed these events decided to honor the man who had driven the lead fire truck to the brink of the blaze. In preparing for the awards ceremony, the mayor said, "Captain, we want to honor you for your fantastic act. You prevented the loss of property, perhaps even the loss of life. Is there something we can give you as a token of our appreciation?" The captain replied without hesitation, "Your Honor, a new set of brakes would be dandy!"

Acts of heroism all begin the same way: one person is willing to try when others are not.

the LORD your God has commanded to teach you, that you may observe *them* in the land which you are crossing over to possess, [2] that you may fear the LORD your God, to keep all His statutes and His commandments which I command you, you and your son and your grandson, all the days of your life, and that your days may be prolonged. [3] Therefore hear, O Israel, and be careful to observe *it,* that it may be well with you, and that you may multiply greatly as the LORD God of your fathers has promised you—'a land flowing with milk and honey.'

[4] "Hear, O Israel: The LORD our God, the LORD *is* one! [5] You shall love the LORD your God with all your heart, with all your soul, and with all your strength.

[6] "And these words which I command you today shall be in your heart. [7] You shall teach them diligently to your children, and shall talk of them when you sit in your house, when you walk by the way, when you lie down, and when you rise up. [8] You shall bind them as a sign on your hand, and they shall be as frontlets between your eyes. [9] You shall write them on the doorposts of your house and on your gates.

[10] "So it shall be, when the LORD your God brings you into the land of which He swore to your fathers, to Abraham, Isaac, and Jacob, to give you large and beautiful cities which you did not build, [11] houses full of all good things, which you did not fill, hewn-out wells which you did not dig, vineyards and olive trees which you did not plant—when you have eaten and are full— [12] then beware, lest you forget the LORD who brought you out of the land of Egypt, from the house of bondage. [13] You shall fear the LORD your God and serve Him, and shall take oaths in His name. [14] You shall not go after other gods, the gods of the peoples who *are* all around you [15] (for the LORD your God *is* a jealous God among you), lest the anger of the LORD your God be aroused against you and destroy you from the face of the earth.

[16] "You shall not tempt the LORD your God as you tempted *Him* in Massah. [17] You shall diligently keep the commandments of the LORD your God, His testimonies, and His statutes which He has commanded you. [18] And you shall do *what is* right and good in the sight of the

LORD, that it may be well with you, and that you may go in and possess the good land of which the LORD swore to your fathers, [19] to cast out all your enemies from before you, as the LORD has spoken.

[20] "When your son asks you in time to come, saying, 'What *is the meaning of* the testimonies, the statutes, and the judgments which the LORD our God has commanded you?' [21] then you shall say to your son: 'We were slaves of Pharaoh in Egypt, and the LORD brought us out of Egypt with a mighty hand; [22] and the LORD showed signs and wonders before our eyes, great and severe, against Egypt, Pharaoh, and all his household. [23] Then He brought us out from there, that He might bring us in, to give us the land of which He swore to our fathers. [24] And the LORD commanded us to observe all these statutes, to fear the LORD our God, for our good always, that He might preserve us alive, as *it is* this day. [25] Then it will be righteousness for us, if we are careful to observe all these commandments before the LORD our God, as He has commanded us.'

~ PSALM 37:1-4 ~

[1] Do not fret because of evildoers,
    Nor be envious of the workers of
        iniquity.
[2] For they shall soon be cut down like
        the grass,
    And wither as the green herb.

[3] Trust in the LORD, and do good;
    Dwell in the land, and feed on His
        faithfulness.
[4] Delight yourself also in the LORD,
    And He shall give you the desires of
        your heart.

~ PROVERBS 12:8 ~

[8] A man will be commended according
        to his wisdom,
    But he who is of a perverse heart
        will be despised.

~ LUKE 1:21-38 ~

And the people waited for Zacharias, and marveled that he lingered so long in the temple. [22] But when he came out, he could not speak to them; and they perceived that he had seen a vision in the temple, for he beckoned to them and remained speechless.

[23] So it was, as soon as the days of his service were completed, that he departed to his own house. [24] Now after those days his wife Elizabeth conceived; and she hid herself five months, saying, [25] "Thus the Lord has dealt with me, in the days when He looked on *me,* to take away my reproach among people."

[26] Now in the sixth month the angel Gabriel was sent by God to a city of Galilee named Nazareth, [27] to a virgin betrothed to a man whose name was Joseph, of the house of David. The virgin's name *was* Mary. [28] And having come in, the angel said to her, "Rejoice, highly favored *one,* the Lord *is* with you; blessed *are* you among women!"

[29] But when she saw *him,* she was troubled at his saying, and considered what manner of greeting this was. [30] Then the angel said to her, "Do not be afraid, Mary, for you have found favor with God. [31] And behold, you will conceive in your womb and bring forth a Son, and shall call His name JESUS. [32] He will be great, and will be called the Son of the Highest; and the Lord God will give Him the throne of His father David. [33] And He will reign over the house of Jacob forever, and of His kingdom there will be no end."

[34] Then Mary said to the angel, "How can this be, since I do not know a man?"

[35] And the angel answered and said to her, "*The* Holy Spirit will come upon you, and the power of the Highest will overshadow you; therefore, also, that Holy One who is to be born will be called the Son of God. [36] Now indeed, Elizabeth your relative has also conceived a son in her old age; and this is now the sixth month for her who was called barren. [37] For with God nothing will be impossible."

[38] Then Mary said, "Behold the maidservant of the Lord! Let it be to me according to your word." And the angel departed from her.

~ DEUTERONOMY 7:1—8:20 ~

"**W**hen the LORD your God brings you into the land which you go to possess, and has cast out many nations before you, the Hittites and the Girgashites and the Amorites and the Canaanites and the Perizzites and the Hivites and the Jebusites, seven nations greater and mightier than you, [2] and when the LORD your God delivers them over to you, you shall conquer them *and* utterly destroy them. You shall make no covenant with them nor show mercy to them. [3] Nor shall you make marriages with them. You shall not give your daughter to their son, nor take their daughter for your son. [4] For they will turn your sons away from following Me, to serve other gods; so the anger of the LORD will be aroused against you and destroy you suddenly. [5] But thus you shall deal with them: you shall destroy their altars, and break down their *sacred* pillars, and cut down their wooden images, and burn their carved images with fire.

[6] "For you *are* a holy people to the LORD your God; the LORD your God has chosen you to be a people for Himself, a special treasure above all the peoples on the face of the earth. [7] The LORD did not set His love on you nor choose you because you were more in number than any other people, for you were the least of all peoples; [8] but because the LORD loves you, and because He would keep the oath which He swore to your fathers, the LORD has brought you out with a mighty hand, and redeemed you from the house of bondage, from the hand of Pharaoh king of Egypt.

[9] "Therefore know that the LORD your God, He *is* God, the faithful God who keeps covenant and mercy for a thousand generations with those who love Him and

keep His commandments; [10] and He repays those who hate Him to their face, to destroy them. He will not be slack with him who hates Him; He will repay him to his face. [11] Therefore you shall keep the commandment, the statutes, and the judgments which I command you today, to observe them.

[12] "Then it shall come to pass, because you listen to these judgments, and keep and do them, that the LORD your God will keep with you the covenant and the mercy which He swore to your fathers. [13] And He will love you and bless you and multiply you; He will also bless the fruit of your womb and the fruit of your land, your grain and your new wine and your oil, the increase of your cattle and the offspring of your flock, in the land of which He swore to your fathers to give you. [14] You shall be blessed above all peoples; there shall not be a male or female barren among you or among your livestock. [15] And the LORD will take away from you all sickness, and will afflict you with none of the terrible diseases of Egypt which you have known, but will lay *them* on all those who hate you. [16] Also you shall destroy all the peoples whom the LORD your God delivers over to you; your eye shall have no pity on them; nor shall you serve their gods, for that *will be* a snare to you.

[17] "If you should say in your heart, 'These nations are greater than I; how can I dispossess them?'— [18] you shall not be afraid of them, *but* you shall remember well what the LORD your God did to Pharaoh and to all Egypt: [19] the great trials which your eyes saw, the signs and the wonders, the mighty hand and the outstretched arm, by which the LORD your God brought you out. So shall the LORD your God do to all the peoples of whom you are afraid. [20] Moreover the LORD your God will send the hornet among them until those who are left, who hide themselves from you, are destroyed. [21] You shall not be terrified of them; for the LORD your God, the great and awesome God, *is* among you. [22] And the LORD your God will drive out those nations before you little by little; you will be unable to destroy them at once, lest the beasts of the field become *too* numerous for you. [23] But the LORD your God will deliver them over to you, and will inflict defeat upon them until they are destroyed. [24] And He will deliver their kings into your hand, and you will destroy their name from under heaven; no one shall be able to stand against you until you have destroyed them. [25] You shall burn the carved images of their gods with fire; you shall not covet the silver or gold *that is* on them, nor take *it* for yourselves, lest you be snared by it; for it *is* an abomination to the LORD your God. [26] Nor shall you bring an abomination into your house, lest you be doomed to destruction like it. You shall utterly detest it and utterly abhor it, for it *is* an accursed thing.

8 "Every commandment which I command you today you must be careful to observe, that you may live and multiply, and go in and possess the land of which the LORD swore to your fathers. [2] And you shall remember that the LORD your God led you all the way these forty years in the wilderness, to humble you *and* test you, to know what *was* in your heart, whether you would keep His commandments or not. [3] So He humbled you, allowed you to hunger, and fed you with manna which you did not know nor did your fathers know, that He might make you know that man shall not live by bread alone; but man lives by every *word* that proceeds from the mouth of the LORD. [4] Your garments did not wear out on you, nor did your foot swell these forty years. [5] You should know in your heart that as a man chastens his son, *so* the LORD your God chastens you.

[6] "Therefore you shall keep the commandments of the LORD your God, to walk in His ways and to fear Him. [7] For the LORD your God is bringing you into a good land, a land of brooks of water, of fountains and springs, that flow out of valleys and hills; [8] a land of wheat and barley, of vines and fig trees and pomegranates, a land of olive oil and honey; [9] a land in which you will eat bread without scarcity, in which you will lack nothing; a land whose stones *are* iron and out of whose hills you can dig copper. [10] When you have eaten and are full, then you shall bless the LORD your God for the good land which He has given you.

A Gardener's Prayer

This prayer from *The Gardener's Year*, reminds us that when we tell God what to do in prayer, we are speaking from our limited, finite point of view. We are much better off when we simply state our requests, and then trust Him to respond from His eternal storehouse with His great generosity and unquestionable wisdom.

"O Lord, grant that in some way it may rain every day, say from about midnight until three o'clock in the morning, but you see, it must be gentle and warm so that it can soak in; grant that at the same time it would not rain on campion, alyssum, helianthemum, lavender, and the others which you . . . know are drought-loving plants — I will write their names on a bit of paper if you like — and grant that the sun may shine the whole day long, but not everywhere (not, for instance, on spiraea or on gentian, platain lily and rhododendron) and not too much; that there may be plenty of dew and little wind, enough worms, no plant lice and snails, no mildew, and that once a week thin liquid manure and guano may fall from heaven. Amen."

11 "Beware that you do not forget the LORD your God by not keeping His commandments, His judgments, and His statutes which I command you today, 12 lest—*when* you have eaten and are full, and have built beautiful houses and dwell *in them;* 13 and *when* your herds and your flocks multiply, and your silver and your gold are multiplied, and all that you have is multiplied; 14 when your heart is lifted up, and you forget the LORD your God who brought you out of the land of Egypt, from the house of bondage; 15 who led you through that great and terrible wilderness, *in which were* fiery serpents and scorpions and thirsty land where there was no water; who brought water for you out of the flinty rock; 16 who fed you in the wilderness with manna, which your fathers did not know, that He might humble you and that He might test you, to do you good in the end— 17 then you say in your heart, 'My power and the might of my hand have gained me this wealth.'

18 "And you shall remember the LORD your God, for *it is* He who gives you power to get wealth, that He may establish His covenant which He swore to your fathers, as *it is* this day. 19 Then it shall be, if you by any means forget the LORD your God, and follow other gods, and serve them and worship them, I testify against you this day that you shall surely perish. 20 As the nations which the LORD destroys before you, so you shall perish, because you would not be obedient to the voice of the LORD your God.

~ PSALM 37:5–11 ~

5 Commit your way to the LORD,
   Trust also in Him,
   And He shall bring *it* to pass.
6 He shall bring forth your
      righteousness as the light,
   And your justice as the noonday.

7 Rest in the LORD, and wait patiently
      for Him;
   Do not fret because of him who
      prospers in his way,
   Because of the man who brings
      wicked schemes to pass.

8 Cease from anger, and forsake
      wrath;
   Do not fret—*it* only *causes* harm.

9 For evildoers shall be cut off;
   But those who wait on the LORD,
   They shall inherit the earth.
10 For yet a little while and the wicked
      shall be no *more;*
   Indeed, you will look carefully for
      his place,
   But it *shall be* no *more.*
11 But the meek shall inherit the
      earth,
   And shall delight themselves in the
      abundance of peace.

~ PROVERBS 12:9, 10 ~

9 Better *is the one* who is slighted but
      has a servant,
   Than he who honors himself but
      lacks bread.

10 A righteous *man* regards the life of
      his animal,
   But the tender mercies of the wicked
      are cruel.

~ LUKE 1:39–56 ~

Now Mary arose in those days and went into the hill country with haste, to a city of Judah, 40 and entered the house of Zacharias and greeted Elizabeth. 41 And it happened, when Elizabeth heard the greeting of Mary, that the babe leaped in her womb; and Elizabeth was filled with the Holy Spirit. 42 Then she spoke out with a loud voice and said, "Blessed *are* you among women, and blessed *is* the fruit of your womb! 43 But why *is* this *granted* to me, that the mother of my Lord should come to me? 44 For indeed, as soon as the voice of your greeting sounded in my ears, the babe leaped in my womb for joy. 45 Blessed *is* she who believed, for there will be a fulfillment of those things which were told her from the Lord."
46 And Mary said:

   "My soul magnifies the Lord,
47 And my spirit has rejoiced in God
      my Savior.

⁴⁸ For He has regarded the lowly
state of His maidservant;
For behold, henceforth all
generations will call me
blessed.
⁴⁹ For He who is mighty has done
great things for me,
And holy *is* His name.
⁵⁰ And His mercy *is* on those who
fear Him
From generation to generation.
⁵¹ He has shown strength with His
arm;
He has scattered *the* proud in the
imagination of their hearts.

⁵² He has put down the mighty from
their thrones,
And exalted *the* lowly.
⁵³ He has filled *the* hungry with
good things,
And *the* rich He has sent away
empty.
⁵⁴ He has helped His servant Israel,
In remembrance of *His* mercy,
⁵⁵ As He spoke to our fathers,
To Abraham and to his seed
forever."

⁵⁶ And Mary remained with her about
three months, and returned to her house.

READING 83 · MARCH 24

∼ DEUTERONOMY 9:1—10:22 ∼

"Hear, O Israel: You *are* to cross over the Jordan today, and go in to dispossess nations greater and mightier than yourself, cities great and fortified up to heaven, ² a people great and tall, the descendants of the Anakim, whom you know, and *of whom* you heard *it said,* 'Who can stand before the descendants of Anak?' ³ Therefore understand today that the LORD your God *is* He who goes over before you *as* a consuming fire. He will destroy them and bring them down before you; so you shall drive them out and destroy them quickly, as the LORD has said to you.

⁴ "Do not think in your heart, after the LORD your God has cast them out before you, saying, 'Because of my righteousness the LORD has brought me in to possess this land'; but *it is* because of the wickedness of these nations *that* the LORD is driving them out from before you. ⁵ *It is* not because of your righteousness or the uprightness of your heart *that* you go in to possess their land, but because of the wickedness of these nations *that* the LORD your God drives them out from before you, and that He may fulfill the word which the LORD swore to your fathers, to Abraham, Isaac, and Jacob. ⁶ Therefore understand that the LORD your God is not giving you this good land to possess because of your righteousness, for you *are* a stiff-necked people.

⁷ "Remember! Do not forget how you provoked the LORD your God to wrath in the wilderness. From the day that you departed from the land of Egypt until you came to this place, you have been rebellious against the LORD. ⁸ Also in Horeb you provoked the LORD to wrath, so that the LORD was angry *enough* with you to have destroyed you. ⁹ When I went up into the mountain to receive the tablets of stone, the tablets of the covenant which the LORD made with you, then I stayed on the mountain forty days and forty nights. I neither ate bread nor drank water. ¹⁰ Then the LORD delivered to me two tablets of stone written with the finger of God, and on them *were* all the words which the LORD had spoken to you on the mountain from the midst of the fire in the day of the assembly. ¹¹ And it came to pass, at the end of forty days and forty nights, *that* the LORD gave me the two tablets of stone, the tablets of the covenant.

¹² "Then the LORD said to me, 'Arise, go down quickly from here, for your people whom you brought out of Egypt have acted corruptly; they have quickly turned aside from the way which I commanded them; they have made themselves a molded image.'

¹³ "Furthermore the LORD spoke to me, saying, 'I have seen this people, and indeed they are a stiff-necked people. ¹⁴ Let Me

alone, that I may destroy them and blot out their name from under heaven; and I will make of you a nation mightier and greater than they.'

¹⁵ "So I turned and came down from the mountain, and the mountain burned with fire; and the two tablets of the covenant *were* in my two hands. ¹⁶ And I looked, and behold, you had sinned against the LORD your God—had made for yourselves a molded calf! You had turned aside quickly from the way which the LORD had commanded you. ¹⁷ Then I took the two tablets and threw them out of my two hands and broke them before your eyes. ¹⁸ And I fell down before the LORD, as at the first, forty days and forty nights; I neither ate bread nor drank water, because of all your sin which you committed in doing wickedly in the sight of the LORD, to provoke Him to anger. ¹⁹ For I was afraid of the anger and hot displeasure with which the LORD was angry with you, to destroy you. But the LORD listened to me at that time also. ²⁰ And the LORD was very angry with Aaron *and* would have destroyed him; so I prayed for Aaron also at the same time. ²¹ Then I took your sin, the calf which you had made, and burned it with fire and crushed it *and* ground *it* very small, until it was as fine as dust; and I threw its dust into the brook that descended from the mountain.

²² "Also at Taberah and Massah and Kibroth Hattaavah you provoked the LORD to wrath. ²³ Likewise, when the LORD sent you from Kadesh Barnea, saying, 'Go up and possess the land which I have given you,' then you rebelled against the commandment of the LORD your God, and you did not believe Him nor obey His voice. ²⁴ You have been rebellious against the LORD from the day that I knew you.

²⁵ "Thus I prostrated myself before the LORD; forty days and forty nights I kept prostrating myself, because the LORD had said He would destroy you. ²⁶ Therefore I prayed to the LORD, and said: 'O Lord GOD, do not destroy Your people and Your inheritance whom You have redeemed through Your greatness, whom You have brought out of Egypt with a mighty hand. ²⁷ Remember Your servants, Abraham, Isaac, and Jacob; do not look on the stubbornness of this people, or on their wickedness or their sin, ²⁸ lest the land from which You brought us should say, "Because the LORD was not able to bring them to the land which He promised them, and because He hated them, He has brought them out to kill them in the wilderness." ²⁹ Yet they *are* Your people and Your inheritance, whom You brought out by Your mighty power and by Your outstretched arm.'

10 "At that time the LORD said to me, 'Hew for yourself two tablets of stone like the first, and come up to Me on the mountain and make yourself an ark of wood. ² And I will write on the tablets the words that were on the first tablets, which you broke; and you shall put them in the ark.'

³ "So I made an ark of acacia wood, hewed two tablets of stone like the first, and went up the mountain, having the two tablets in my hand. ⁴ And He wrote on the tablets according to the first writing, the Ten Commandments, which the LORD had spoken to you in the mountain from the midst of the fire in the day of the assembly; and the LORD gave them to me. ⁵ Then I turned and came down from the mountain, and put the tablets in the ark which I had made; and there they are, just as the LORD commanded me."

⁶(Now the children of Israel journeyed from the wells of Bene Jaakan to Moserah, where Aaron died, and where he was buried; and Eleazar his son ministered as priest in his stead. ⁷ From there they journeyed to Gudgodah, and from Gudgodah to Jotbathah, a land of rivers of water. ⁸ At that time the LORD separated the tribe of Levi to bear the ark of the covenant of the LORD, to stand before the LORD to minister to Him and to bless in His name, to this day. ⁹ Therefore Levi has no portion nor inheritance with his brethren; the LORD *is* his inheritance, just as the LORD your God promised him.)

¹⁰ "As at the first time, I stayed in the mountain forty days and forty nights; the LORD also heard me at that time, *and* the LORD chose not to destroy you. ¹¹ Then the LORD said to me, 'Arise, begin *your* journey before the people, that they may go in and possess the land which I swore to their fathers to give them.'

Somebody's Mother

She stood at the crossing and waited long,
Alone, uncared for, amid the throng.
Past the woman so old and gray
Hastened the children on their way.
No one offered a helping hand to her —
So meek, so timid, afraid to stir
Lest the carriage wheels or the horses' feet
Should crowd her down in the slippery street.
He paused beside her and whispered low,
"I'll help you cross, if you wish to go."
Her aged hand on his strong young arm
She placed, and so, without hurt or harm,
He guided the trembling feet along,
Proud that his own were firm and strong.
Then back again to his friends he went,
His young heart happy and well content.
"She's somebody's mother, boys, you know.
For all she's aged and poor and slow.
And I hope some fellow will lend a hand
To help my mother, you understand,
If ever she's poor and old and gray,
When her own dear boy is far away."

12 "And now, Israel, what does the LORD your God require of you, but to fear the LORD your God, to walk in all His ways and to love Him, to serve the LORD your God with all your heart and with all your soul, 13 *and* to keep the commandments of the LORD and His statutes which I command you today for your good? 14 Indeed heaven and the highest heavens belong to the LORD your God, *also* the earth with all that *is* in it. 15 The LORD delighted only in your fathers, to love them; and He chose their descendants after them, you above all peoples, as *it is* this day. 16 Therefore circumcise the foreskin of your heart, and be stiff-necked no longer. 17 For the LORD your God *is* God of gods and Lord of lords, the great God, mighty and awesome, who shows no partiality nor takes a bribe. 18 He administers justice for the fatherless and the widow, and loves the stranger, giving him food and clothing. 19 Therefore love the stranger, for you were strangers in the land of Egypt. 20 You shall fear the LORD your God; you shall serve Him, and to Him you shall hold fast, and take oaths in His name. 21 He *is* your praise, and He *is* your God, who has done for you these great and awesome things which your eyes have seen. 22 Your fathers went down to Egypt with seventy persons, and now the LORD your God has made you as the stars of heaven in multitude.

∾ PSALM 37:12–17 ∾

12 The wicked plots against the just,
　And gnashes at him with his teeth.
13 The Lord laughs at him,
　For He sees that his day is coming.
14 The wicked have drawn the sword
　And have bent their bow,
　To cast down the poor and needy,
　To slay those who are of upright
　　conduct.
15 Their sword shall enter their own
　　heart,
　And their bows shall be broken.

16 A little that a righteous man has
　Is better than the riches of many
　　wicked.
17 For the arms of the wicked shall be
　　broken,
　But the LORD upholds the righteous.

∾ PROVERBS 12:11 ∾

11 He who tills his land will be satisfied
　　with bread,
　But he who follows frivolity *is*
　　devoid of understanding.

∾ LUKE 1:57–80 ∾

Now Elizabeth's full time came for her to be delivered, and she brought forth a son. 58 When her neighbors and relatives heard how the Lord had shown great mercy to her, they rejoiced with her.

59 So it was, on the eighth day, that they came to circumcise the child; and they would have called him by the name of his father, Zacharias. 60 His mother answered and said, "No; he shall be called John."

61 But they said to her, "There is no one among your relatives who is called by this name." 62 So they made signs to his father—what he would have him called.

63 And he asked for a writing tablet, and wrote, saying, "His name is John." So they all marveled. 64 Immediately his mouth was opened and his tongue *loosed,* and he spoke, praising God. 65 Then fear came on all who dwelt around them; and all these sayings were discussed throughout all the hill country of Judea. 66 And all those who heard *them* kept *them* in their hearts, saying, "What kind of child will this be?" And the hand of the Lord was with him.

67 Now his father Zacharias was filled with the Holy Spirit, and prophesied, saying:

68 "Blessed *is* the Lord God of Israel,
　For He has visited and redeemed
　　His people,
69 And has raised up a horn of
　　salvation for us
　In the house of His servant
　　David,
70 As He spoke by the mouth of His
　　holy prophets,
　Who *have been* since the world
　　began,
71 That we should be saved from our
　　enemies

And from the hand of all who hate us,

72 To perform the mercy *promised* to our fathers
And to remember His holy covenant,

73 The oath which He swore to our father Abraham:

74 To grant us that we,
Being delivered from the hand of our enemies,
Might serve Him without fear,

75 In holiness and righteousness before Him all the days of our life.

76 "And you, child, will be called the prophet of the Highest;

For you will go before the face of the Lord to prepare His ways,

77 To give knowledge of salvation to His people
By the remission of their sins,

78 Through the tender mercy of our God,
With which the Dayspring from on high has visited us;

79 To give light to those who sit in darkness and the shadow of death,
To guide our feet into the way of peace."

80 So the child grew and became strong in spirit, and was in the deserts till the day of his manifestation to Israel.

READING 84 · MARCH 25

∼ DEUTERONOMY 11:1—12:32 ∼

"Therefore you shall love the LORD your God, and keep His charge, His statutes, His judgments, and His commandments always. ² Know today that *I do* not *speak* with your children, who have not known and who have not seen the chastening of the LORD your God, His greatness and His mighty hand and His outstretched arm— ³ His signs and His acts which He did in the midst of Egypt, to Pharaoh king of Egypt, and to all his land; ⁴ what He did to the army of Egypt, to their horses and their chariots: how He made the waters of the Red Sea overflow them as they pursued you, and *how* the LORD has destroyed them to this day; ⁵ what He did for you in the wilderness until you came to this place; ⁶ and what He did to Dathan and Abiram the sons of Eliab, the son of Reuben: how the earth opened its mouth and swallowed them up, their households, their tents, and all the substance that *was* in their possession, in the midst of all Israel— ⁷ but your eyes have seen every great act of the LORD which He did.

⁸ "Therefore you shall keep every commandment which I command you today, that you may be strong, and go in and possess the land which you cross over to possess, ⁹ and that you may prolong *your* days in the land which the LORD swore to give your fathers, to them and their descendants, 'a land flowing with milk and honey.' ¹⁰ For the land which you go to possess *is* not like the land of Egypt from which you have come, where you sowed your seed and watered *it* by foot, as a vegetable garden; ¹¹ but the land which you cross over to possess *is* a land of hills and valleys, which drinks water from the rain of heaven, ¹² a land for which the LORD your God cares; the eyes of the LORD your God *are* always on it, from the beginning of the year to the very end of the year.

¹³ 'And it shall be that if you earnestly obey My commandments which I command you today, to love the LORD your God and serve Him with all your heart and with all your soul, ¹⁴ then I will give *you* the rain for your land in its season, the early rain and the latter rain, that you may gather in your grain, your new wine, and your oil. ¹⁵ And I will send grass in your fields for your livestock, that you may eat and be filled.' ¹⁶ Take heed to yourselves, lest your heart be deceived, and you turn aside and serve other gods and worship them, ¹⁷ lest the LORD's anger be aroused against you, and He shut up the heavens so that there be no rain,

and the land yield no produce, and you perish quickly from the good land which the LORD is giving you.

¹⁸ "Therefore you shall lay up these words of mine in your heart and in your soul, and bind them as a sign on your hand, and they shall be as frontlets between your eyes. ¹⁹ You shall teach them to your children, speaking of them when you sit in your house, when you walk by the way, when you lie down, and when you rise up. ²⁰ And you shall write them on the doorposts of your house and on your gates, ²¹ that your days and the days of your children may be multiplied in the land of which the LORD swore to your fathers to give them, like the days of the heavens above the earth.

²² "For if you carefully keep all these commandments which I command you to do—to love the LORD your God, to walk in all His ways, and to hold fast to Him— ²³ then the LORD will drive out all these nations from before you, and you will dispossess greater and mightier nations than yourselves. ²⁴ Every place on which the sole of your foot treads shall be yours: from the wilderness and Lebanon, from the river, the River Euphrates, even to the Western Sea, shall be your territory. ²⁵ No man shall be able to stand against you; the LORD your God will put the dread of you and the fear of you upon all the land where you tread, just as He has said to you.

²⁶ "Behold, I set before you today a blessing and a curse: ²⁷ the blessing, if you obey the commandments of the LORD your God which I command you today; ²⁸ and the curse, if you do not obey the commandments of the LORD your God, but turn aside from the way which I command you today, to go after other gods which you have not known. ²⁹ Now it shall be, when the LORD your God has brought you into the land which you go to possess, that you shall put the blessing on Mount Gerizim and the curse on Mount Ebal. ³⁰ *Are* they not on the other side of the Jordan, toward the setting sun, in the land of the Canaanites who dwell in the plain opposite Gilgal, beside the terebinth trees of Moreh? ³¹ For you will cross over the Jordan and go in to possess the land which the LORD your God is giving

you, and you will possess it and dwell in it. ³² And you shall be careful to observe all the statutes and judgments which I set before you today.

12 "These *are* the statutes and judgments which you shall be careful to observe in the land which the LORD God of your fathers is giving you to possess, all the days that you live on the earth. ² You shall utterly destroy all the places where the nations which you shall dispossess served their gods, on the high mountains and on the hills and under every green tree. ³ And you shall destroy their altars, break their *sacred* pillars, and burn their wooden images with fire; you shall cut down the carved images of their gods and destroy their names from that place. ⁴ You shall not worship the LORD your God *with* such *things*.

⁵ "But you shall seek the place where the LORD your God chooses, out of all your tribes, to put His name for His dwelling place; and there you shall go. ⁶ There you shall take your burnt offerings, your sacrifices, your tithes, the heave offerings of your hand, your vowed offerings, your freewill offerings, and the firstborn of your herds and flocks. ⁷ And there you shall eat before the LORD your God, and you shall rejoice in all to which you have put your hand, you and your households, in which the LORD your God has blessed you.

⁸ "You shall not at all do as we are doing here today—every man doing whatever *is* right in his own eyes— ⁹ for as yet you have not come to the rest and the inheritance which the LORD your God is giving you. ¹⁰ But *when* you cross over the Jordan and dwell in the land which the LORD your God is giving you to inherit, and He gives you rest from all your enemies round about, so that you dwell in safety, ¹¹ then there will be the place where the LORD your God chooses to make His name abide. There you shall bring all that I command you: your burnt offerings, your sacrifices, your tithes, the heave offerings of your hand, and all your choice offerings which you vow to the LORD. ¹² And you shall rejoice before the LORD your God, you and your sons and your daughters, your male and female servants, and

The Teacher

A king once decided to honor the greatest of his subjects. Word spread throughout the kingdom and various nominations were immediately forthcoming. A man of wealth and property was singled out. One person was lauded for her healing skills, another for his fair practice of the law. Still another was praised for his honesty in business and yet another for his bravery as a soldier. Each candidate was brought to the palace and presented to the king. He admitted to his counselors that this choice was going to be very difficult.

As the last day before the ceremony arrived, the last candidate was finally brought before the king — a white-haired woman whose eyes sparkled with the light of knowledge, love, and understanding.

"Who is this?" the king asked. "What has she accomplished of note?" An aide replied, "You have seen and heard all the other candidates. This woman is their teacher." The king's court erupted into applause and the king immediately stepped from his throne to honor her.

Virtues do not happen by accident or as a natural part of growth. As with any skill or means of success, they must be taught.

Therefore you shall lay up these words of mine in your heart and in your soul, and bind them as a sign on your hand, and they shall be as frontlets between your eyes. You shall teach them to your children, speaking of them when you sit in your house, when you walk by the way, when you lie down, and when you rise up.

Deuteronomy 11:18-19

the Levite who *is* within your gates, since he has no portion nor inheritance with you. [13] Take heed to yourself that you do not offer your burnt offerings in every place that you see; [14] but in the place which the LORD chooses, in one of your tribes, there you shall offer your burnt offerings, and there you shall do all that I command you.

[15] "However, you may slaughter and eat meat within all your gates, whatever your heart desires, according to the blessing of the LORD your God which He has given you; the unclean and the clean may eat of it, of the gazelle and the deer alike. [16] Only you shall not eat the blood; you shall pour it on the earth like water. [17] You may not eat within your gates the tithe of your grain or your new wine or your oil, of the firstborn of your herd or your flock, of any of your offerings which you vow, of your freewill offerings, or of the heave offering of your hand. [18] But you must eat them before the LORD your God in the place which the LORD your God chooses, you and your son and your daughter, your male servant and your female servant, and the Levite who *is* within your gates; and you shall rejoice before the LORD your God in all to which you put your hands. [19] Take heed to yourself that you do not forsake the Levite as long as you live in your land.

[20] "When the LORD your God enlarges your border as He has promised you, and you say, 'Let me eat meat,' because you long to eat meat, you may eat as much meat as your heart desires. [21] If the place where the LORD your God chooses to put His name is too far from you, then you may slaughter from your herd and from your flock which the LORD has given you, just as I have commanded you, and you may eat within your gates as much as your heart desires. [22] Just as the gazelle and the deer are eaten, so you may eat them; the unclean and the clean alike may eat them. [23] Only be sure that you do not eat the blood, for the blood *is* the life; you may not eat the life with the meat. [24] You shall not eat it; you shall pour it on the earth like water. [25] You shall not eat it, that it may go well with you and your children after you, when you do *what is* right in the sight of the LORD. [26] Only the

holy things which you have, and your vowed offerings, you shall take and go to the place which the LORD chooses. [27] And you shall offer your burnt offerings, the meat and the blood, on the altar of the LORD your God; and the blood of your sacrifices shall be poured out on the altar of the LORD your God, and you shall eat the meat. [28] Observe and obey all these words which I command you, that it may go well with you and your children after you forever, when you do *what is* good and right in the sight of the LORD your God.

[29] "When the LORD your God cuts off from before you the nations which you go to dispossess, and you displace them and dwell in their land, [30] take heed to yourself that you are not ensnared to follow them, after they are destroyed from before you, and that you do not inquire after their gods, saying, 'How did these nations serve their gods? I also will do likewise.' [31] You shall not worship the LORD your God in that way; for every abomination to the LORD which He hates they have done to their gods; for they burn even their sons and daughters in the fire to their gods.

[32] "Whatever I command you, be careful to observe it; you shall not add to it nor take away from it.

~ PSALM 37:18–22 ~

[18] The LORD knows the days of the upright,
   And their inheritance shall be forever.
[19] They shall not be ashamed in the evil time,
   And in the days of famine they shall be satisfied.
[20] But the wicked shall perish;
   And the enemies of the LORD,
   Like the splendor of the meadows, shall vanish.
   Into smoke they shall vanish away.

[21] The wicked borrows and does not repay,
   But the righteous shows mercy and gives.
[22] For *those* blessed by Him shall inherit the earth,

But *those* cursed by Him shall be cut off.

～ PROVERBS 12:12–14 ～

12 The wicked covet the catch of evil
    men,
    But the root of the righteous yields
    fruit.
13 The wicked is ensnared by the
    transgression of *his* lips,
    But the righteous will come through
    trouble.
14 A man will be satisfied with good by
    the fruit of *his* mouth,
    And the recompense of a man's
    hands will be rendered to him.

～ LUKE 2:1–24 ～

And it came to pass in those days *that* a decree went out from Caesar Augustus that all the world should be registered. ² This census first took place while Quirinius was governing Syria. ³ So all went to be registered, everyone to his own city.

⁴ Joseph also went up from Galilee, out of the city of Nazareth, into Judea, to the city of David, which is called Bethlehem, because he was of the house and lineage of David, ⁵ to be registered with Mary, his betrothed wife, who was with child. ⁶ So it was, that while they were there, the days were completed for her to be delivered. ⁷ And she brought forth her firstborn Son, and wrapped Him in swaddling cloths, and laid Him in a manger, because there was no room for them in the inn.

⁸ Now there were in the same country shepherds living out in the fields, keeping watch over their flock by night. ⁹ And behold, an angel of the Lord stood before them, and the glory of the Lord shone around them, and they were greatly afraid. ¹⁰ Then the angel said to them, "Do not be afraid, for behold, I bring you good tidings of great joy which will be to all people. ¹¹ For there is born to you this day in the city of David a Savior, who is Christ the Lord. ¹² And this *will be* the sign to you: You will find a Babe wrapped in swaddling cloths, lying in a manger."

¹³ And suddenly there was with the angel a multitude of the heavenly host praising God and saying:

¹⁴ "Glory to God in the highest,
    And on earth peace, goodwill
        toward men!"

¹⁵ So it was, when the angels had gone away from them into heaven, that the shepherds said to one another, "Let us now go to Bethlehem and see this thing that has come to pass, which the Lord has made known to us." ¹⁶ And they came with haste and found Mary and Joseph, and the Babe lying in a manger. ¹⁷ Now when they had seen *Him,* they made widely known the saying which was told them concerning this Child. ¹⁸ And all those who heard *it* marveled at those things which were told them by the shepherds. ¹⁹ But Mary kept all these things and pondered *them* in her heart. ²⁰ Then the shepherds returned, glorifying and praising God for all the things that they had heard and seen, as it was told them.

²¹ And when eight days were completed for the circumcision of the Child, His name was called JESUS, the name given by the angel before He was conceived in the womb.

²² Now when the days of her purification according to the law of Moses were completed, they brought Him to Jerusalem to present *Him* to the Lord ²³(as it is written in the law of the Lord, "Every male who opens the womb shall be called holy to the LORD"), ²⁴ and to offer a sacrifice according to what is said in the law of the Lord, "A pair of turtledoves or two young pigeons."

~ DEUTERONOMY 13:1—14:29 ~

"If there arises among you a prophet or a dreamer of dreams, and he gives you a sign or a wonder, ² and the sign or the wonder comes to pass, of which he spoke to you, saying, 'Let us go after other gods'—which you have not known—'and let us serve them,' ³ you shall not listen to the words of that prophet or that dreamer of dreams, for the LORD your God is testing you to know whether you love the LORD your God with all your heart and with all your soul. ⁴ You shall walk after the LORD your God and fear Him, and keep His commandments and obey His voice; you shall serve Him and hold fast to Him. ⁵ But that prophet or that dreamer of dreams shall be put to death, because he has spoken in order to turn *you* away from the LORD your God, who brought you out of the land of Egypt and redeemed you from the house of bondage, to entice you from the way in which the LORD your God commanded you to walk. So you shall put away the evil from your midst.

⁶ "If your brother, the son of your mother, your son or your daughter, the wife of your bosom, or your friend who is as your own soul, secretly entices you, saying, 'Let us go and serve other gods,' which you have not known, neither you nor your fathers, ⁷ of the gods of the people which *are* all around you, near to you or far off from you, from *one* end of the earth to the *other* end of the earth, ⁸ you shall not consent to him or listen to him, nor shall your eye pity him, nor shall you spare him or conceal him; ⁹ but you shall surely kill him; your hand shall be first against him to put him to death, and afterward the hand of all the people. ¹⁰ And you shall stone him with stones until he dies, because he sought to entice you away from the LORD your God, who brought you out of the land of Egypt, from the house of bondage. ¹¹ So all Israel shall hear and fear, and not again do such wickedness as this among you.

¹² "If you hear someone in one of your cities, which the LORD your God gives you to dwell in, saying, ¹³ 'Corrupt men have gone out from among you and enticed the inhabitants of their city, saying, "Let us go and serve other gods" '—which you have not known— ¹⁴ then you shall inquire, search out, and ask diligently. And *if it is* indeed true *and* certain *that* such an abomination was committed among you, ¹⁵ you shall surely strike the inhabitants of that city with the edge of the sword, utterly destroying it, all that is in it and its livestock—with the edge of the sword. ¹⁶ And you shall gather all its plunder into the middle of the street, and completely burn with fire the city and all its plunder, for the LORD your God. It shall be a heap forever; it shall not be built again. ¹⁷ So none of the accursed things shall remain in your hand, that the LORD may turn from the fierceness of His anger and show you mercy, have compassion on you and multiply you, just as He swore to your fathers, ¹⁸ because you have listened to the voice of the LORD your God, to keep all His commandments which I command you today, to do *what is* right in the eyes of the LORD your God.

14 "You *are* the children of the LORD your God; you shall not cut yourselves nor shave the front of your head for the dead. ² For you *are* a holy people to the LORD your God, and the LORD has chosen you to be a people for Himself, a special treasure above all the peoples who *are* on the face of the earth.

³ "You shall not eat any detestable thing. ⁴ These *are* the animals which you may eat: the ox, the sheep, the goat, ⁵ the deer, the gazelle, the roe deer, the wild goat, the mountain goat, the antelope, and the mountain sheep. ⁶ And you may eat every animal with cloven hooves, having the hoof split into two parts, *and that* chews the cud, among the animals. ⁷ Nevertheless, of those that chew the cud or have cloven hooves, you shall not eat, *such as* these: the camel, the hare, and the rock hyrax; for they chew the cud but do not have cloven hooves; they *are* unclean for you. ⁸ Also the swine is unclean for you, because it has cloven hooves, yet *does* not *chew* the cud; you shall not eat their flesh or touch their dead carcasses.

Caution: Watch for Falling Eggs!

In his autobiography, Lee Iacocca gives us an opportunity to learn from a mistake he once made. In 1956, the Ford Motor Company emphasized auto safety, rather than performance and horsepower. The company introduced crash padding for dashboards and sent out a film to dealers explaining how much safer the new dashboards were. The narrator on the film claimed the padding was so thick a person could drop an egg on it from a two-story building and it would bounce right off without breaking. As a district assistant sales manager for Ford, Iacocca decided he'd demonstrate!

With 1,100 salesmen watching him, he climbed a high ladder and proceeded to drop an egg on a strip of the dash padding he had placed on the floor of the stage. The egg missed the padding and splattered on the floor. A second egg bounced off his assistant's shoulder. Eggs three and four landed on target, but broke on impact. Finally, with the fifth egg, he got the desired result. Iacocca writes, "I learned two lessons that day. First, never use eggs at a sales rally. And second, never go before your customers without rehearsing what you want to say — as well as what you're going to do — to help sell your product."

In other words, think before you speak!

⁹ "These you may eat of all that *are* in the waters: you may eat all that have fins and scales. ¹⁰ And whatever does not have fins and scales you shall not eat; it *is* unclean for you.

¹¹ "All clean birds you may eat. ¹² But these you shall not eat: the eagle, the vulture, the buzzard, ¹³ the red kite, the falcon, and the kite after their kinds; ¹⁴ every raven after its kind; ¹⁵ the ostrich, the short-eared owl, the sea gull, and the hawk after their kinds; ¹⁶ the little owl, the screech owl, the white owl, ¹⁷ the jackdaw, the carrion vulture, the fisher owl, ¹⁸ the stork, the heron after its kind, and the hoopoe and the bat.

¹⁹ "Also every creeping thing that flies is unclean for you; they shall not be eaten.

²⁰ "You may eat all clean birds.

²¹ "You shall not eat anything that dies *of itself;* you may give it to the alien who *is* within your gates, that he may eat it, or you may sell it to a foreigner; for you *are* a holy people to the LORD your God.

"You shall not boil a young goat in its mother's milk.

²² "You shall truly tithe all the increase of your grain that the field produces year by year. ²³ And you shall eat before the LORD your God, in the place where He chooses to make His name abide, the tithe of your grain and your new wine and your oil, of the firstborn of your herds and your flocks, that you may learn to fear the LORD your God always. ²⁴ But if the journey is too long for you, so that you are not able to carry *the tithe, or* if the place where the LORD your God chooses to put His name is too far from you, when the LORD your God has blessed you, ²⁵ then you shall exchange *it* for money, take the money in your hand, and go to the place which the LORD your God chooses. ²⁶ And you shall spend that money for whatever your heart desires: for oxen or sheep, for wine or similar drink, for whatever your heart desires; you shall eat there before the LORD your God, and you shall rejoice, you and your household. ²⁷ You shall not forsake the Levite who *is* within your gates, for he has no part nor inheritance with you.

²⁸ "At the end of *every* third year you shall bring out the tithe of your produce of that year and store *it* up within your gates. ²⁹ And the Levite, because he has no portion nor inheritance with you, and the stranger and the fatherless and the widow who *are* within your gates, may come and eat and be satisfied, that the LORD your God may bless you in all the work of your hand which you do.

～ PSALM 37:23–29 ～

²³ The steps of a *good* man are ordered
    by the LORD,
And He delights in his way.
²⁴ Though he fall, he shall not be
    utterly cast down;
For the LORD upholds *him with* His
    hand.

²⁵ I have been young, and *now* am old;
Yet I have not seen the righteous
    forsaken,
Nor his descendants begging bread.
²⁶ *He is* ever merciful, and lends;
And his descendants *are* blessed.

²⁷ Depart from evil, and do good;
And dwell forevermore.
²⁸ For the LORD loves justice,
And does not forsake His saints;
They are preserved forever,
But the descendants of the wicked
    shall be cut off.
²⁹ The righteous shall inherit the land,
And dwell in it forever.

～ PROVERBS 12:15, 16 ～

¹⁵ The way of a fool *is* right in his own
    eyes,
But he who heeds counsel *is* wise.
¹⁶ A fool's wrath is known at once,
But a prudent *man* covers shame.

～ LUKE 2:25–52 ～

And behold, there was a man in Jerusalem whose name was Simeon, and this man was just and devout, waiting for the Consolation of Israel, and the Holy Spirit was upon him. ²⁶ And it had been revealed to him by the Holy Spirit that he would not see death before he had seen the Lord's Christ. ²⁷ So he came by the Spirit into the temple. And when the parents brought in the Child Jesus, to do for Him according to the custom of the law, [28] he took Him up in his arms and blessed God and said:

[29] "Lord, now You are letting Your
    servant depart in peace,
    According to Your word;
[30] For my eyes have seen Your
    salvation
[31] Which You have prepared before
    the face of all peoples,
[32] A light to *bring* revelation to the
    Gentiles,
    And the glory of Your people
    Israel."

[33] And Joseph and His mother marveled at those things which were spoken of Him. [34] Then Simeon blessed them, and said to Mary His mother, "Behold, this *Child* is destined for the fall and rising of many in Israel, and for a sign which will be spoken against [35](yes, a sword will pierce through your own soul also), that the thoughts of many hearts may be revealed."

[36] Now there was one, Anna, a prophetess, the daughter of Phanuel, of the tribe of Asher. She was of a great age, and had lived with a husband seven years from her virginity; [37] and this woman *was* a widow of about eighty-four years, who did not depart from the temple, but served *God* with fastings and prayers night and day. [38] And coming in that instant she gave thanks to the Lord, and spoke of Him to all those who looked for redemption in Jerusalem.

[39] So when they had performed all things according to the law of the Lord, they returned to Galilee, to their *own* city, Nazareth. [40] And the Child grew and became strong in spirit, filled with wisdom; and the grace of God was upon Him.

[41] His parents went to Jerusalem every year at the Feast of the Passover. [42] And when He was twelve years old, they went up to Jerusalem according to the custom of the feast. [43] When they had finished the days, as they returned, the Boy Jesus lingered behind in Jerusalem. And Joseph and His mother did not know *it;* [44] but supposing Him to have been in the company, they went a day's journey, and sought Him among *their* relatives and acquaintances. [45] So when they did not find Him, they returned to Jerusalem, seeking Him. [46] Now so it was *that* after three days they found Him in the temple, sitting in the midst of the teachers, both listening to them and asking them questions. [47] And all who heard Him were astonished at His understanding and answers. [48] So when they saw Him, they were amazed; and His mother said to Him, "Son, why have You done this to us? Look, Your father and I have sought You anxiously."

[49] And He said to them, "Why did you seek Me? Did you not know that I must be about My Father's business?" [50] But they did not understand the statement which He spoke to them.

[51] Then He went down with them and came to Nazareth, and was subject to them, but His mother kept all these things in her heart. [52] And Jesus increased in wisdom and stature, and in favor with God and men.

~ DEUTERONOMY 15:1—16:22 ~

"**A**t the end of *every* seven years you shall grant a release *of debts.* [2] And this *is* the form of the release: Every creditor who has lent *anything* to his neighbor shall release *it;* he shall not require *it* of his neighbor or his brother, because it is called the LORD's release. [3] Of a foreigner you may require *it;* but you shall give up your claim to what is owed by your brother, [4] except when there may be no poor among you; for the LORD will greatly bless you in the land which the LORD your God is giving you to possess *as* an inheritance— [5] only if you carefully obey the voice of the LORD your God, to observe with care all these commandments which I command you today. [6] For the LORD your God will bless you just as He promised you; you shall lend to many nations, but you shall not borrow; you shall reign over many nations, but they shall not reign over you.

[7] "If there is among you a poor man of your brethren, within any of the gates in your land which the LORD your God is giving you, you shall not harden your heart nor shut your hand from your poor brother, [8] but you shall open your hand wide to him and willingly lend him sufficient for his need, whatever he needs. [9] Beware lest there be a wicked thought in your heart, saying, 'The seventh year, the year of release, is at hand,' and your eye be evil against your poor brother and you give him nothing, and he cry out to the LORD against you, and it become sin among you. [10] You shall surely give to him, and your heart should not be grieved when you give to him, because for this thing the LORD your God will bless you in all your works and in all to which you put your hand. [11] For the poor will never cease from the land; therefore I command you, saying, 'You shall open your hand wide to your brother, to your poor and your needy, in your land.'

[12] "If your brother, a Hebrew man, or a Hebrew woman, is sold to you and serves you six years, then in the seventh year you shall let him go free from you. [13] And when you send him away free from you, you shall not let him go away empty-handed; [14] you shall supply him liberally from your flock, from your threshing floor, and from your winepress. *From what* the LORD has blessed you with, you shall give to him. [15] You shall remember that you were a slave in the land of Egypt, and the LORD your God redeemed you; therefore I command you this thing today. [16] And if it happens that he says to you, 'I will not go away from you,' because he loves you and your house, since he prospers with you, [17] then you shall take an awl and thrust *it* through his ear to the door, and he shall be your servant forever. Also to your female servant you shall do likewise. [18] It shall not seem hard to you when you send him away free from you; for he has been worth a double hired servant in serving you six years. Then the LORD your God will bless you in all that you do.

[19] "All the firstborn males that come from your herd and your flock you shall sanctify to the LORD your God; you shall do no work with the firstborn of your herd, nor shear the firstborn of your flock. [20] You and your household shall eat *it* before the LORD your God year by year in the place which the LORD chooses. [21] But if there is a defect in it, *if it is* lame or blind *or has* any serious defect, you shall not sacrifice it to the LORD your God. [22] You may eat it within your gates; the unclean and the clean *person* alike *may eat it,* as *if it were* a gazelle or a deer. [23] Only you shall not eat its blood; you shall pour it on the ground like water.

16 "Observe the month of Abib, and keep the Passover to the LORD your God, for in the month of Abib the LORD your God brought you out of Egypt by night. [2] Therefore you shall sacrifice the Passover to the LORD your God, from the flock and the herd, in the place where the LORD chooses to put His name. [3] You shall eat no leavened bread with it; seven days you shall eat unleavened bread with it, *that is,* the bread of affliction (for you came out of the land of Egypt in haste), that you may remember the day in which you came out of the land of Egypt all the days of your life. [4] And no leaven shall be seen among you in all your territory for seven days, nor shall *any* of the meat which you sacrifice the first day at twilight remain overnight until morning.

[5] "You may not sacrifice the Passover within any of your gates which the LORD your God gives you; [6] but at the place where the LORD your God chooses to make His name abide, there you shall sacrifice the Passover at twilight, at the going down of the sun, at the time you came out of Egypt. [7] And you shall roast and eat *it* in the place which the LORD your God chooses, and in the morning you shall turn and go to your tents. [8] Six days you shall eat unleavened bread, and on the seventh day there *shall be* a sacred assembly to the LORD your God. You shall do no work *on it.*

[9] "You shall count seven weeks for yourself; begin to count the seven weeks from *the time* you begin *to put* the sickle to the grain. [10] Then you shall keep the Feast of

Blessed in All Your Works

In *The Seven Habits of Highly Successful People*, Stephen Covey tells about a small computer software company that had developed a new program, which it sold on a five-year contract to a bank. The bank president was excited about the product and his people were highly supportive. A month later, though, the bank changed presidents. The new president said he wanted to back out of the deal.

The computer company was in financial trouble. The president knew he had every legal right to enforce the contract, but he also knew the right thing to do. He told the bank president, "We have a contract. Your bank has secured our products and services to convert you to this new software program. But we understand that you're not happy about it. So what we'd like to do is give you back the contract, give you back your deposit, and if you are ever looking for a software solution in the future, come back and see us."

Just like that, he walked away from an $84,000 contract. It was nearly financial suicide for his company. However, three months later, the new bank president called to say, "I'm now going to make changes in my data processing, and I want to do business with you." They signed a contract worth $240,000.

Who says nice guys always finish last?

———◦◦◦———

You shall surely give to him, and your heart should not be grieved when you give to him, because for this thing the Lord your God will bless you in all your works and in all to which you put your hand.

Deuteronomy 15:10

Weeks to the LORD your God with the tribute of a freewill offering from your hand, which you shall give as the LORD your God blesses you. [11] You shall rejoice before the LORD your God, you and your son and your daughter, your male servant and your female servant, the Levite who *is* within your gates, the stranger and the fatherless and the widow who *are* among you, at the place where the LORD your God chooses to make His name abide. [12] And you shall remember that you were a slave in Egypt, and you shall be careful to observe these statutes.

[13] "You shall observe the Feast of Tabernacles seven days, when you have gathered from your threshing floor and from your winepress. [14] And you shall rejoice in your feast, you and your son and your daughter, your male servant and your female servant and the Levite, the stranger and the fatherless and the widow, who *are* within your gates. [15] Seven days you shall keep a sacred feast to the LORD your God in the place which the LORD chooses, because the LORD your God will bless you in all your produce and in all the work of your hands, so that you surely rejoice.

[16] "Three times a year all your males shall appear before the LORD your God in the place which He chooses: at the Feast of Unleavened Bread, at the Feast of Weeks, and at the Feast of Tabernacles; and they shall not appear before the LORD empty-handed. [17] Every man *shall give* as he is able, according to the blessing of the LORD your God which He has given you.

[18] "You shall appoint judges and officers in all your gates, which the LORD your God gives you, according to your tribes, and they shall judge the people with just judgment. [19] You shall not pervert justice; you shall not show partiality, nor take a bribe, for a bribe blinds the eyes of the wise and twists the words of the righteous. [20] You shall follow what is altogether just, that you may live and inherit the land which the LORD your God is giving you.

[21] "You shall not plant for yourself any tree, as a wooden image, near the altar which you build for yourself to the LORD your God. [22] You shall not set up a sacred pillar, which the LORD your God hates.

~ PSALM 37:30–36 ~

[30] The mouth of the righteous speaks wisdom,
And his tongue talks of justice.
[31] The law of his God *is* in his heart;
None of his steps shall slide.

[32] The wicked watches the righteous,
And seeks to slay him.
[33] The LORD will not leave him in his hand,
Nor condemn him when he is judged.

[34] Wait on the LORD,
And keep His way,
And He shall exalt you to inherit the land;
When the wicked are cut off, you shall see *it*.
[35] I have seen the wicked in great power,
And spreading himself like a native green tree.
[36] Yet he passed away, and behold, he *was* no *more;*
Indeed I sought him, but he could not be found.

~ PROVERBS 12:17–19 ~

[17] He *who* speaks truth declares righteousness,
But a false witness,
deceit.
[18] There is one who speaks like the piercings of a sword,
But the tongue of the wise *promotes* health.
[19] The truthful lip shall be established forever,
But a lying tongue *is* but for a moment.

~ LUKE 3:1–38 ~

Now in the fifteenth year of the reign of Tiberius Caesar, Pontius Pilate being governor of Judea, Herod being tetrarch of Galilee, his brother Philip tetrarch of Iturea and the region of Trachonitis, and

Lysanias tetrarch of Abilene, [2] while Annas and Caiaphas were high priests, the word of God came to John the son of Zacharias in the wilderness. [3] And he went into all the region around the Jordan, preaching a baptism of repentance for the remission of sins, [4] as it is written in the book of the words of Isaiah the prophet, saying:

> "The voice of one crying in the
>   wilderness:
> 'Prepare the way of the LORD;
>   Make His paths straight.
> [5] Every valley shall be filled
>   And every mountain and hill
>   brought low;
>   The crooked places shall be made
>   straight
>   And the rough ways smooth;
> [6] And all flesh shall see the salvation
>   of God.' "

[7] Then he said to the multitudes that came out to be baptized by him, "Brood of vipers! Who warned you to flee from the wrath to come? [8] Therefore bear fruits worthy of repentance, and do not begin to say to yourselves, 'We have Abraham as *our* father.' For I say to you that God is able to raise up children to Abraham from these stones. [9] And even now the ax is laid to the root of the trees. Therefore every tree which does not bear good fruit is cut down and thrown into the fire."

[10] So the people asked him, saying, "What shall we do then?"

[11] He answered and said to them, "He who has two tunics, let him give to him who has none; and he who has food, let him do likewise."

[12] Then tax collectors also came to be baptized, and said to him, "Teacher, what shall we do?"

[13] And he said to them, "Collect no more than what is appointed for you."

[14] Likewise the soldiers asked him, saying, "And what shall we do?"

So he said to them, "Do not intimidate anyone or accuse falsely, and be content with your wages."

[15] Now as the people were in expectation, and all reasoned in their hearts about John, whether he was the Christ *or* not, [16] John answered, saying to all, "I indeed baptize you with water; but One mightier than I is coming, whose sandal strap I am not worthy to loose. He will baptize you with the Holy Spirit and fire. [17] His winnowing fan *is* in His hand, and He will thoroughly clean out His threshing floor, and gather the wheat into His barn; but the chaff He will burn with unquenchable fire."

[18] And with many other exhortations he preached to the people. [19] But Herod the tetrarch, being rebuked by him concerning Herodias, his brother Philip's wife, and for all the evils which Herod had done, [20] also added this, above all, that he shut John up in prison.

[21] When all the people were baptized, it came to pass that Jesus also was baptized; and while He prayed, the heaven was opened. [22] And the Holy Spirit descended in bodily form like a dove upon Him, and a voice came from heaven which said, "You are My beloved Son; in You I am well pleased."

[23] Now Jesus Himself began *His ministry at* about thirty years of age, being (as was supposed) *the* son of Joseph, *the son* of Heli, [24] *the son* of Matthat, *the son* of Levi, *the son* of Melchi, *the son* of Janna, *the son* of Joseph, [25] *the son* of Mattathiah, *the son* of Amos, *the son* of Nahum, *the son* of Esli, *the son* of Naggai, [26] *the son* of Maath, *the son* of Mattathiah, *the son* of Semei, *the son* of Joseph, *the son* of Judah, [27] *the son* of Joannas, *the son* of Rhesa, *the son* of Zerubbabel, *the son* of Shealtiel, *the son* of Neri, [28] *the son* of Melchi, *the son* of Addi, *the son* of Cosam, *the son* of Elmodam, *the son* of Er, [29] *the son* of Jose, *the son* of Eliezer, *the son* of Jorim, *the son* of Matthat, *the son* of Levi, [30] *the son* of Simeon, *the son* of Judah, *the son* of Joseph, *the son* of Jonan, *the son* of Eliakim, [31] *the son* of Melea, *the son* of Menan, *the son* of Mattathah, *the son* of Nathan, *the son* of David, [32] *the son* of Jesse, *the son* of Obed, *the son* of Boaz, *the son* of Salmon, *the son* of Nahshon, [33] *the son* of Amminadab, *the son* of Ram, *the son* of Hezron, *the son* of Perez, *the son* of Judah, [34] *the son* of Jacob, *the son* of Isaac, *the son* of Abraham, *the son* of Terah, *the son* of Nahor, [35] *the son* of Serug, *the son* of Reu, *the son* of Peleg, *the son* of Eber, *the son* of Shelah, [36] *the son* of Cainan, *the son* of Arphaxad,

the son of Shem, *the son* of Noah, *the son* of Lamech, [37] *the son* of Methuselah, *the son* of Enoch, *the son* of Jared, *the son* of Mahalalel, *the son* of Cainan, [38] *the son* of Enosh, *the son* of Seth, *the son* of Adam, *the son* of God.

∼ DEUTERONOMY 17:1—18:22 ∼

"You shall not sacrifice to the LORD your God a bull or sheep which has any blemish *or* defect, for that *is* an abomination to the LORD your God.

[2] "If there is found among you, within any of your gates which the LORD your God gives you, a man or a woman who has been wicked in the sight of the LORD your God, in transgressing His covenant, [3] who has gone and served other gods and worshiped them, either the sun or moon or any of the host of heaven, which I have not commanded, [4] and it is told you, and you hear *of it,* then you shall inquire diligently. And if *it is* indeed true *and* certain that such an abomination has been committed in Israel, [5] then you shall bring out to your gates that man or woman who has committed that wicked thing, and shall stone to death that man or woman with stones. [6] Whoever is deserving of death shall be put to death on the testimony of two or three witnesses; he shall not be put to death on the testimony of one witness. [7] The hands of the witnesses shall be the first against him to put him to death, and afterward the hands of all the people. So you shall put away the evil from among you.

[8] "If a matter arises which is too hard for you to judge, between degrees of guilt for bloodshed, between one judgment or another, or between one punishment or another, matters of controversy within your gates, then you shall arise and go up to the place which the LORD your God chooses. [9] And you shall come to the priests, the Levites, and to the judge *there* in those days, and inquire *of them;* they shall pronounce upon you the sentence of judgment. [10] You shall do according to the sentence which they pronounce upon you in that place which the LORD chooses. And you shall be careful to do according to all that they order you. [11] According to the sentence of the law in which they instruct you, according to the judgment which they tell you, you shall do; you shall not turn aside *to* the right hand or *to* the left from the sentence which they pronounce upon you. [12] Now the man who acts presumptuously and will not heed the priest who stands to minister there before the LORD your God, or the judge, that man shall die. So you shall put away the evil from Israel. [13] And all the people shall hear and fear, and no longer act presumptuously.

[14] "When you come to the land which the LORD your God is giving you, and possess it and dwell in it, and say, 'I will set a king over me like all the nations that *are* around me,' [15] you shall surely set a king over you whom the LORD your God chooses; *one* from among your brethren you shall set as king over you; you may not set a foreigner over you, who *is* not your brother. [16] But he shall not multiply horses for himself, nor cause the people to return to Egypt to multiply horses, for the LORD has said to you, 'You shall not return that way again.' [17] Neither shall he multiply wives for himself, lest his heart turn away; nor shall he greatly multiply silver and gold for himself.

[18] "Also it shall be, when he sits on the throne of his kingdom, that he shall write for himself a copy of this law in a book, from *the one* before the priests, the Levites. [19] And it shall be with him, and he shall read it all the days of his life, that he may learn to fear the LORD his God and be careful to observe all the words of this law and these statutes, [20] that his heart may not be lifted above his brethren, that he may not turn aside from the commandment *to* the right hand or *to* the left, and

Turning the Other Cheek

Ruth Bell Graham tells a humorous story about her daughters, Anne and Bunny. One day Ruth was in another room in the house when she heard some loud cries coming from the kitchen. When she ran to the kitchen to investigate, she found three-year-old Bunny holding her hand to her cheek, looking very disapprovingly at her sister. "Mommy," explained five-year-old Anne, "I'm teaching Bunny the Bible. I'm slapping her on one cheek and teaching her to turn the other one so I can slap it, too."

When we are wronged, our first response is more likely to fight back than to turn the other cheek. But many have found that fighting back is usually counterproductive.

Missionary E. Stanley Jones found himself being publicly slandered by someone he had once helped. Jones' first response was to write his accuser a letter he says was, "the kind of reply you are proud of the first five minutes, the second five minutes you're not so certain, and the third five minutes you know you're wrong."

Jones knew his comments would win the argument, but lose the person. "The Christian," he said, "is not in the business of winning arguments, but of winning people," and he tore up the letter. A few weeks later — without having said a word — Jones received a letter of apology from the one who had turned on him.

When we turn the other cheek and let God fight the battle, He can bring about a greater victory than we can imagine.

that he may prolong *his* days in his kingdom, he and his children in the midst of Israel.

18 "The priests, the Levites—all the tribe of Levi—shall have no part nor inheritance with Israel; they shall eat the offerings of the LORD made by fire, and His portion. ² Therefore they shall have no inheritance among their brethren; the LORD is their inheritance, as He said to them.

³ "And this shall be the priest's due from the people, from those who offer a sacrifice, whether *it is* bull or sheep: they shall give to the priest the shoulder, the cheeks, and the stomach. ⁴ The firstfruits of your grain and your new wine and your oil, and the first of the fleece of your sheep, you shall give him. ⁵ For the LORD your God has chosen him out of all your tribes to stand to minister in the name of the LORD, him and his sons forever.

⁶ "So if a Levite comes from any of your gates, from where he dwells among all Israel, and comes with all the desire of his mind to the place which the LORD chooses, ⁷ then he may serve in the name of the LORD his God as all his brethren the Levites *do,* who stand there before the LORD. ⁸ They shall have equal portions to eat, besides what comes from the sale of his inheritance.

⁹ "When you come into the land which the LORD your God is giving you, you shall not learn to follow the abominations of those nations. ¹⁰ There shall not be found among you *anyone* who makes his son or his daughter pass through the fire, *or one* who practices witchcraft, *or* a soothsayer, or one who interprets omens, or a sorcerer, ¹¹ or one who conjures spells, or a medium, or a spiritist, or one who calls up the dead. ¹² For all who do these things *are* an abomination to the LORD, and because of these abominations the LORD your God drives them out from before you. ¹³ You shall be blameless before the LORD your God. ¹⁴ For these nations which you will dispossess listened to soothsayers and diviners; but as for you, the LORD your God has not appointed such for you.

¹⁵ "The LORD your God will raise up for you a Prophet like me from your midst, from your brethren. Him you shall hear, ¹⁶ according to all you desired of the LORD your God in Horeb in the day of the assembly, saying, 'Let me not hear again the voice of the LORD my God, nor let me see this great fire anymore, lest I die.'

¹⁷ "And the LORD said to me: 'What they have spoken is good. ¹⁸ I will raise up for them a Prophet like you from among their brethren, and will put My words in His mouth, and He shall speak to them all that I command Him. ¹⁹ And it shall be *that* whoever will not hear My words, which He speaks in My name, I will require *it* of him. ²⁰ But the prophet who presumes to speak a word in My name, which I have not commanded him to speak, or who speaks in the name of other gods, that prophet shall die.' ²¹ And if you say in your heart, 'How shall we know the word which the LORD has not spoken?'— ²² when a prophet speaks in the name of the LORD, if the thing does not happen or come to pass, that *is* the thing which the LORD has not spoken; the prophet has spoken it presumptuously; you shall not be afraid of him.

~ PSALM 37:37–40 ~

³⁷ Mark the blameless *man,* and
    observe the upright;
For the future of *that* man *is* peace.
³⁸ But the transgressors shall be
    destroyed together;
The future of the wicked shall be cut off.

³⁹ But the salvation of the righteous *is*
    from the LORD;
He is their strength in the time of
    trouble.
⁴⁰ And the LORD shall help them and
    deliver them;
He shall deliver them from the wicked,
And save them,
Because they trust in Him.

~ PROVERBS 12:20–22 ~

²⁰ Deceit is in the heart of those who
    devise evil,

But counselors of peace have joy.
21 No grave trouble will overtake the
   righteous,
   But the wicked shall be filled with
   evil.
22 Lying lips *are* an abomination to the
   LORD,
   But those who deal truthfully *are* His
   delight.

∼ LUKE 4:1–30 ∼

Then Jesus, being filled with the Holy
Spirit, returned from the Jordan and was
led by the Spirit into the wilderness, 2 being tempted for forty days by the devil.
And in those days He ate nothing, and
afterward, when they had ended, He was
hungry.
3 And the devil said to Him, "If You are
the Son of God, command this stone to
become bread."
4 But Jesus answered him, saying, "It is
written, 'Man shall not live by bread alone,
but by every word of God.' "
5 Then the devil, taking Him up on a
high mountain, showed Him all the kingdoms of the world in a moment of time.
6 And the devil said to Him, "All this authority I will give You, and their glory;
for *this* has been delivered to me, and I
give it to whomever I wish. 7 Therefore,
if You will worship before me, all will be
Yours."
8 And Jesus answered and said to him,
"Get behind Me, Satan! For it is written,
'You shall worship the LORD your God,
and Him only you shall serve.' "
9 Then he brought Him to Jerusalem,
set Him on the pinnacle of the temple,
and said to Him, "If You are the Son of
God, throw Yourself down from here.
10 For it is written:

'He shall give His angels charge
    over you,
  To keep you,'

11 and,

'In their hands they shall bear you
    up,
  Lest you dash your foot against a
    stone.' "

12 And Jesus answered and said to him,
"It has been said, 'You shall not tempt the
LORD your God.' "
13 Now when the devil had ended every temptation, he departed from Him
until an opportune time.
14 Then Jesus returned in the power of
the Spirit to Galilee, and news of Him
went out through all the surrounding
region. 15 And He taught in their synagogues, being glorified by all.
16 So He came to Nazareth, where He
had been brought up. And as His custom
was, He went into the synagogue on the
Sabbath day, and stood up to read. 17 And
He was handed the book of the prophet
Isaiah. And when He had opened the
book, He found the place where it was
written:

18 "The Spirit of the LORD is upon
      Me,
   Because He has anointed Me
   To preach the gospel to the poor;
   He has sent Me to heal the
      brokenhearted,
   To proclaim liberty to the captives
   And recovery of sight to the blind,
   To set at liberty those who are
      oppressed;
19 To proclaim the acceptable year of
   the LORD."

20 Then He closed the book, and gave *it*
back to the attendant and sat down. And
the eyes of all who were in the synagogue
were fixed on Him. 21 And He began to
say to them, "Today this Scripture is fulfilled in your hearing." 22 So all bore witness to Him, and marveled at the gracious
words which proceeded out of His mouth.
And they said, "Is this not Joseph's son?"
23 He said to them, "You will surely say
this proverb to Me, 'Physician, heal yourself! Whatever we have heard done in
Capernaum, do also here in Your country.' " 24 Then He said, "Assuredly, I say to
you, no prophet is accepted in his own
country. 25 But I tell you truly, many widows were in Israel in the days of Elijah,
when the heaven was shut up three years
and six months, and there was a great famine throughout all the land; 26 but to none
of them was Elijah sent except to Zarephath, *in the region* of Sidon, to a woman

who was a widow. ²⁷ And many lepers were in Israel in the time of Elisha the prophet, and none of them was cleansed except Naaman the Syrian."

²⁸ So all those in the synagogue, when they heard these things, were filled with wrath, ²⁹ and rose up and thrust Him out of the city; and they led Him to the brow of the hill on which their city was built, that they might throw Him down over the cliff. ³⁰ Then passing through the midst of them, He went His way.

READING 88 · MARCH 29

∽ DEUTERONOMY 19:1—20:20 ∽

"When the LORD your God has cut off the nations whose land the LORD your God is giving you, and you dispossess them and dwell in their cities and in their houses, ² you shall separate three cities for yourself in the midst of your land which the LORD your God is giving you to possess. ³ You shall prepare roads for yourself, and divide into three parts the territory of your land which the LORD your God is giving you to inherit, that any manslayer may flee there.

⁴ "And this is the case of the manslayer who flees there, that he may live: Whoever kills his neighbor unintentionally, not having hated him in time past— ⁵ as when a man goes to the woods with his neighbor to cut timber, and his hand swings a stroke with the ax to cut down the tree, and the head slips from the handle and strikes his neighbor so that he dies—he shall flee to one of these cities and live; ⁶ lest the avenger of blood, while his anger is hot, pursue the manslayer and overtake him, because the way is long, and kill him, though he was not deserving of death, since he had not hated the victim in time past. ⁷ Therefore I command you, saying, 'You shall separate three cities for yourself.'

⁸ "Now if the LORD your God enlarges your territory, as He swore to your fathers, and gives you the land which He promised to give to your fathers, ⁹ and if you keep all these commandments and do them, which I command you today, to love the LORD your God and to walk always in His ways, then you shall add three more cities for yourself besides these three,

¹⁰ lest innocent blood be shed in the midst of your land which the LORD your God is giving you as an inheritance, and thus guilt of bloodshed be upon you.

¹¹ "But if anyone hates his neighbor, lies in wait for him, rises against him and strikes him mortally, so that he dies, and he flees to one of these cities, ¹² then the elders of his city shall send and bring him from there, and deliver him over to the hand of the avenger of blood, that he may die. ¹³ Your eye shall not pity him, but you shall put away the guilt of innocent blood from Israel, that it may go well with you.

¹⁴ "You shall not remove your neighbor's landmark, which the men of old have set, in your inheritance which you will inherit in the land that the LORD your God is giving you to possess.

¹⁵ "One witness shall not rise against a man concerning any iniquity or any sin that he commits; by the mouth of two or three witnesses the matter shall be established. ¹⁶ If a false witness rises against any man to testify against him of wrongdoing, ¹⁷ then both men in the controversy shall stand before the LORD, before the priests and the judges who serve in those days. ¹⁸ And the judges shall make careful inquiry, and indeed, if the witness is a false witness, who has testified falsely against his brother, ¹⁹ then you shall do to him as he thought to have done to his brother; so you shall put away the evil from among you. ²⁰ And those who remain shall hear and fear, and hereafter they shall not again commit such evil among you. ²¹ Your eye shall not pity: life shall be for life, eye for eye, tooth for tooth, hand for hand, foot for foot.

A Basic Survival Skill

Business consultant C. W. Metcalf tells how he once signed up for a hospice training program to work with terminally ill patients. He was assigned to Roy, an elderly man with colon cancer. Offering to assist Roy one day, Metcalf said, "Maybe you want me to help you out of those Mickey Mouse pajamas and into something more respectable." Despite his great pain, Roy whispered back, "I like these pj's. Mickey reminds me that I can still laugh a little, which is more than the doctor has ever done. Maybe you should get some Goofy pj's." Roy laughed, but Metcalf didn't. "Young man," Roy continued, "you're one of the most depressing people I've ever met. I'm sure you're a nice person, but if you're here to help, it ain't working." Such blunt truth made Metcalf angry.

On the last day of his training, Metcalf learned that Roy had died. His instructor handed him a paper bag that Roy had left for him. Inside, he found a T-shirt with the grinning face of Goofy and a note that read: "Put on this shirt at the first sign you're taking yourself too seriously. In other words, wear it all the time." Metcalf finally laughed. Roy had taught him one of the best lessons he ever learned: Humor isn't an occasional joke. It's a basic survival skill for living life to the fullest!

20 "When you go out to battle against your enemies, and see horses and chariots *and* people more numerous than you, do not be afraid of them; for the LORD your God *is* with you, who brought you up from the land of Egypt. ² So it shall be, when you are on the verge of battle, that the priest shall approach and speak to the people. ³ And he shall say to them, 'Hear, O Israel: Today you are on the verge of battle with your enemies. Do not let your heart faint, do not be afraid, and do not tremble or be terrified because of them; ⁴ for the LORD your God *is* He who goes with you, to fight for you against your enemies, to save you.'

⁵ "Then the officers shall speak to the people, saying: 'What man *is there* who has built a new house and has not dedicated it? Let him go and return to his house, lest he die in the battle and another man dedicate it. ⁶ Also what man *is there* who has planted a vineyard and has not eaten of it? Let him go and return to his house, lest he die in the battle and another man eat of it. ⁷ And what man *is there* who is betrothed to a woman and has not married her? Let him go and return to his house, lest he die in the battle and another man marry her.'

⁸ "The officers shall speak further to the people, and say, 'What man *is there who is* fearful and fainthearted? Let him go and return to his house, lest the heart of his brethren faint like his heart.' ⁹ And so it shall be, when the officers have finished speaking to the people, that they shall make captains of the armies to lead the people.

¹⁰ "When you go near a city to fight against it, then proclaim an offer of peace to it. ¹¹ And it shall be that if they accept your offer of peace, and open to you, then all the people *who are* found in it shall be placed under tribute to you, and serve you. ¹² Now if *the city* will not make peace with you, but war against you, then you shall besiege it. ¹³ And when the LORD your God delivers it into your hands, you shall strike every male in it with the edge of the sword. ¹⁴ But the women, the little ones, the livestock, and all that is in the city, all its spoil, you shall plunder for yourself; and you shall eat the enemies' plunder which the LORD your God gives you. ¹⁵ Thus you shall do to all the cities *which are* very far from you, which *are* not of the cities of these nations.

¹⁶ "But of the cities of these peoples which the LORD your God gives you *as* an inheritance, you shall let nothing that breathes remain alive, ¹⁷ but you shall utterly destroy them: the Hittite and the Amorite and the Canaanite and the Perizzite and the Hivite and the Jebusite, just as the LORD your God has commanded you, ¹⁸ lest they teach you to do according to all their abominations which they have done for their gods, and you sin against the LORD your God.

¹⁹ "When you besiege a city for a long time, while making war against it to take it, you shall not destroy its trees by wielding an ax against them; if you can eat of them, do not cut them down to use in the siege, for the tree of the field *is* man's *food.* ²⁰ Only the trees which you know *are* not trees for food you may destroy and cut down, to build siegeworks against the city that makes war with you, until it is subdued.

~ PSALM 38:1–8 ~

1 O LORD, do not rebuke me in Your wrath,
  Nor chasten me in Your hot displeasure!
2 For Your arrows pierce me deeply,
  And Your hand presses me down.

3 *There is* no soundness in my flesh
  Because of Your anger,
  Nor *any* health in my bones
  Because of my sin.
4 For my iniquities have gone over my head;
  Like a heavy burden they are too heavy for me.
5 My wounds are foul *and* festering
  Because of my foolishness.

6 I am troubled, I am bowed down greatly;
  I go mourning all the day long.
7 For my loins are full of inflammation,
  And *there is* no soundness in my flesh.

8   I am feeble and severely broken;
    I groan because of the turmoil of my
    heart.

~ PROVERBS 12:23–25 ~

23   A prudent man conceals knowledge,
    But the heart of fools proclaims
    foolishness.

24   The hand of the diligent will rule,
    But the lazy *man* will be put to
    forced labor.

25   Anxiety in the heart of man causes
    depression,
    But a good word makes it glad.

~ LUKE 4:31–44 ~

Then He went down to Capernaum, a city of Galilee, and was teaching them on the Sabbaths. 32 And they were astonished at His teaching, for His word was with authority. 33 Now in the synagogue there was a man who had a spirit of an unclean demon. And he cried out with a loud voice, 34 saying, "Let *us* alone! What have we to do with You, Jesus of Nazareth? Did You come to destroy us? I know who You are— the Holy One of God!"

35 But Jesus rebuked him, saying, "Be quiet, and come out of him!" And when the demon had thrown him in *their* midst, it came out of him and did not hurt him. 36 Then they were all amazed and spoke among themselves, saying, "What a word this *is*! For with authority and power He commands the unclean spirits, and they come out." 37 And the report about Him went out into every place in the surrounding region.

38 Now He arose from the synagogue and entered Simon's house. But Simon's wife's mother was sick with a high fever, and they made request of Him concerning her. 39 So He stood over her and rebuked the fever, and it left her. And immediately she arose and served them.

40 When the sun was setting, all those who had any that were sick with various diseases brought them to Him; and He laid His hands on every one of them and healed them. 41 And demons also came out of many, crying out and saying, "You are the Christ, the Son of God!"

And He, rebuking *them,* did not allow them to speak, for they knew that He was the Christ.

42 Now when it was day, He departed and went into a deserted place. And the crowd sought Him and came to Him, and tried to keep Him from leaving them; 43 but He said to them, "I must preach the kingdom of God to the other cities also, because for this purpose I have been sent." 44 And He was preaching in the synagogues of Galilee.

READING 89 · MARCH 30

~ DEUTERONOMY 21:1—22:30 ~

"If *anyone* is found slain, lying in the field in the land which the LORD your God is giving you to possess, *and* it is not known who killed him, 2 then your elders and your judges shall go out and measure *the distance* from the slain man to the surrounding cities. 3 And it shall be *that* the elders of the city nearest to the slain man will take a heifer which has not been worked *and* which has not pulled with a yoke. 4 The elders of that city shall bring the heifer down to a valley with flowing water, which is neither plowed nor sown, and they shall break the heifer's neck there in the valley.

5 Then the priests, the sons of Levi, shall come near, for the LORD your God has chosen them to minister to Him and to bless in the name of the LORD; by their word every controversy and every assault shall be *settled.* 6 And all the elders of that city nearest to the slain *man* shall wash their hands over the heifer whose neck was broken in the valley. 7 Then they shall answer and say, 'Our hands have not shed this blood, nor have our eyes seen *it.* 8 Provide atonement, O LORD, for Your people Israel, whom You have redeemed, and do not lay innocent blood to the charge of Your people Israel.' And atonement shall

be provided on their behalf for the blood. [9] So you shall put away the *guilt of* innocent blood from among you when you do *what is* right in the sight of the LORD.

[10] "When you go out to war against your enemies, and the LORD your God delivers them into your hand, and you take them captive, [11] and you see among the captives a beautiful woman, and desire her and would take her for your wife, [12] then you shall bring her home to your house, and she shall shave her head and trim her nails. [13] She shall put off the clothes of her captivity, remain in your house, and mourn her father and her mother a full month; after that you may go in to her and be her husband, and she shall be your wife. [14] And it shall be, if you have no delight in her, then you shall set her free, but you certainly shall not sell her for money; you shall not treat her brutally, because you have humbled her.

[15] "If a man has two wives, one loved and the other unloved, and they have borne him children, *both* the loved and the unloved, and *if* the firstborn son is of her who is unloved, [16] then it shall be, on the day he bequeaths his possessions to his sons, *that* he must not bestow firstborn status on the son of the loved wife in preference to the son of the unloved, the *true* firstborn. [17] But he shall acknowledge the son of the unloved wife *as* the firstborn by giving him a double portion of all that he has, for he *is* the beginning of his strength; the right of the firstborn *is* his.

[18] "If a man has a stubborn and rebellious son who will not obey the voice of his father or the voice of his mother, and *who,* when they have chastened him, will not heed them, [19] then his father and his mother shall take hold of him and bring him out to the elders of his city, to the gate of his city. [20] And they shall say to the elders of his city, 'This son of ours is stubborn and rebellious; he will not obey our voice; he is a glutton and a drunkard.' [21] Then all the men of his city shall stone him to death with stones; so you shall put away the evil from among you, and all Israel shall hear and fear.

[22] "If a man has committed a sin deserving of death, and he is put to death, and you hang him on a tree, [23] his body shall not remain overnight on the tree, but you shall surely bury him that day, so that you do not defile the land which the LORD your God is giving you *as* an inheritance; for he who is hanged *is* accursed of God.

22 "You shall not see your brother's ox or his sheep going astray, and hide yourself from them; you shall certainly bring them back to your brother. [2] And if your brother *is* not near you, or if you do not know him, then you shall bring it to your own house, and it shall remain with you until your brother seeks it; then you shall restore it to him. [3] You shall do the same with his donkey, and so shall you do with his garment; with any lost thing of your brother's, which he has lost and you have found, you shall do likewise; you must not hide yourself.

[4] "You shall not see your brother's donkey or his ox fall down along the road, and hide yourself from them; you shall surely help him lift *them* up again.

[5] "A woman shall not wear anything that pertains to a man, nor shall a man put on a woman's garment, for all who do so *are* an abomination to the LORD your God.

[6] "If a bird's nest happens to be before you along the way, in any tree or on the ground, with young ones or eggs, with the mother sitting on the young or on the eggs, you shall not take the mother with the young; [7] you shall surely let the mother go, and take the young for yourself, that it may be well with you and *that* you may prolong *your* days.

[8] "When you build a new house, then you shall make a parapet for your roof, that you may not bring guilt of bloodshed on your household if anyone falls from it.

[9] "You shall not sow your vineyard with different kinds of seed, lest the yield of the seed which you have sown and the fruit of your vineyard be defiled.

[10] "You shall not plow with an ox and a donkey together.

[11] "You shall not wear a garment of different sorts, *such as* wool and linen mixed together.

[12] "You shall make tassels on the four corners of the clothing with which you cover *yourself.*

Pedal Faster!

Success in business is often closely associated with a person's courage and ability to recover from his or her most recent failure.

In 1928, a thirty-three-year-old man by the name of Paul Galvin, found himself staring at failure — again. He had failed in business twice at this point, his competitors having forced him to fold his latest venture in the storage-battery business. Convinced, however, that he still had a marketable idea, Galvin attended the auction of his own business. With $750 he had managed to raise, he bought back the battery eliminator portion of the inventory. With it, he built a new company — one in which he succeeded. He eventually retired from his company, but not before it became a household name: Motorola. Upon his retirement, Galvin advised others: "Do not fear mistakes. You will know failure — continue to reach out."

A failure isn't truly a failure until you quit trying. If a venture begins to slow down, try speeding up your efforts. Consider the child who quits pedaling his bike. Eventually the bicycle wobbles to the point where the child falls off. The key to avoiding the crash? Faster peddling! The same holds true for many an enterprise. Don't give up, just pedal faster!

> The lazy man does not roast what he took in hunting, but diligence is man's precious possession.
>
> *Proverbs 12:27*

¹³ "If any man takes a wife, and goes in to her, and detests her, ¹⁴ and charges her with shameful conduct, and brings a bad name on her, and says, 'I took this woman, and when I came to her I found she *was* not a virgin,' ¹⁵ then the father and mother of the young woman shall take and bring out *the evidence of* the young woman's virginity to the elders of the city at the gate. ¹⁶ And the young woman's father shall say to the elders, 'I gave my daughter to this man as wife, and he detests her. ¹⁷ Now he has charged her with shameful conduct, saying, "I found your daughter *was* not a virgin," and yet these *are the evidences of* my daughter's virginity.' And they shall spread the cloth before the elders of the city. ¹⁸ Then the elders of that city shall take that man and punish him; ¹⁹ and they shall fine him one hundred *shekels* of silver and give *them* to the father of the young woman, because he has brought a bad name on a virgin of Israel. And she shall be his wife; he cannot divorce her all his days.

²⁰ "But if the thing is true, *and evidences of* virginity are not found for the young woman, ²¹ then they shall bring out the young woman to the door of her father's house, and the men of her city shall stone her to death with stones, because she has done a disgraceful thing in Israel, to play the harlot in her father's house. So you shall put away the evil from among you.

²² "If a man is found lying with a woman married to a husband, then both of them shall die—the man that lay with the woman, and the woman; so you shall put away the evil from Israel.

²³ "If a young woman *who is* a virgin is betrothed to a husband, and a man finds her in the city and lies with her, ²⁴ then you shall bring them both out to the gate of that city, and you shall stone them to death with stones, the young woman because she did not cry out in the city, and the man because he humbled his neighbor's wife; so you shall put away the evil from among you.

²⁵ "But if a man finds a betrothed young woman in the countryside, and the man forces her and lies with her, then only the man who lay with her shall die. ²⁶ But you shall do nothing to the young woman; *there is* in the young woman no sin *deserving* of death, for just as when a man rises against his neighbor and kills him, even so *is* this matter. ²⁷ For he found her in the countryside, *and* the betrothed young woman cried out, but *there was* no one to save her.

²⁸ "If a man finds a young woman *who is* a virgin, who is not betrothed, and he seizes her and lies with her, and they are found out, ²⁹ then the man who lay with her shall give to the young woman's father fifty *shekels* of silver, and she shall be his wife because he has humbled her; he shall not be permitted to divorce her all his days.

³⁰ "A man shall not take his father's wife, nor uncover his father's bed.

～ PSALM 38:9–22 ～

⁹ LORD, all my desire *is* before You;
  And my sighing is not hidden from You.
¹⁰ My heart pants, my strength fails me;
  As for the light of my eyes, it also has gone from me.

¹¹ My loved ones and my friends stand aloof from my plague,
  And my relatives stand afar off.
¹² Those also who seek my life lay snares *for me;*
  Those who seek my hurt speak of destruction,
  And plan deception all the day long.

¹³ But I, like a deaf *man,* do not hear;
  And *I am* like a mute *who* does not open his mouth.
¹⁴ Thus I am like a man who does not hear,
  And in whose mouth *is* no response.

¹⁵ For in You, O LORD, I hope;
  You will hear, O Lord my God.
¹⁶ For I said, "*Hear me,* lest they rejoice over me,
  Lest, when my foot slips, they exalt *themselves* against me."

¹⁷ For I *am* ready to fall,
  And my sorrow *is* continually before me.
¹⁸ For I will declare my iniquity;

I will be in anguish over my sin.
19 But my enemies *are* vigorous, *and*
    they are strong;
    And those who hate me wrongfully
    have multiplied.
20 Those also who render evil for good,
    They are my adversaries, because I
    follow *what is* good.

21 Do not forsake me, O LORD;
    O my God, be not far from me!
22 Make haste to help me,
    O Lord, my salvation!

~ PROVERBS 12:26–28 ~

26 The righteous should choose his
    friends carefully,
    For the way of the wicked leads
    them astray.

27 The lazy *man* does not roast what he
    took in hunting,
    But diligence *is* man's precious
    possession.

28 In the way of righteousness *is* life,
    And in *its* pathway *there is* no death.

~ LUKE 5:1–16 ~

So it was, as the multitude pressed about
Him to hear the word of God, that He
stood by the Lake of Gennesaret, 2 and
saw two boats standing by the lake; but
the fishermen had gone from them and
were washing *their* nets. 3 Then He got
into one of the boats, which was Simon's,
and asked him to put out a little from the
land. And He sat down and taught
the multitudes from the boat.
4 When He had stopped speaking, He
said to Simon, "Launch out into the deep
and let down your nets for a catch."
5 But Simon answered and said to Him,
"Master, we have toiled all night and
caught nothing; nevertheless at Your word
I will let down the net." 6 And when they
had done this, they caught a great number of fish, and their net was breaking.
7 So they signaled to *their* partners in the
other boat to come and help them. And
they came and filled both the boats, so
that they began to sink. 8 When Simon
Peter saw *it,* he fell down at Jesus' knees,
saying, "Depart from me, for I am a sinful man, O Lord!"
9 For he and all who were with him
were astonished at the catch of fish which
they had taken; 10 and so also *were* James
and John, the sons of Zebedee, who were
partners with Simon. And Jesus said to
Simon, "Do not be afraid. From now on
you will catch men." 11 So when they had
brought their boats to land, they forsook
all and followed Him.
12 And it happened when He was in a
certain city, that behold, a man who was
full of leprosy saw Jesus; and he fell on
his face and implored Him, saying, "Lord,
if You are willing, You can make me clean."
13 Then He put out *His* hand and
touched him, saying, "I am willing; be
cleansed." Immediately the leprosy left
him. 14 And He charged him to tell no one,
"But go and show yourself to the priest,
and make an offering for your cleansing,
as a testimony to them, just as Moses commanded."
15 However, the report went around
concerning Him all the more; and great
multitudes came together to hear, and to
be healed by Him of their infirmities. 16 So
He Himself *often* withdrew into the wilderness and prayed.

READING 90 · MARCH 31

~ DEUTERONOMY 23:1—24:22 ~

"He who is emasculated by
crushing or mutilation shall
not enter the assembly of the
LORD.
2 "One of illegitimate birth shall not
enter the assembly of the LORD; even to
the tenth generation none of his *descendants* shall enter the assembly of the LORD.
3 "An Ammonite or Moabite shall not
enter the assembly of the LORD; even to
the tenth generation none of his *descendants* shall enter the assembly of the LORD

forever, [4] because they did not meet you with bread and water on the road when you came out of Egypt, and because they hired against you Balaam the son of Beor from Pethor of Mesopotamia, to curse you. [5] Nevertheless the LORD your God would not listen to Balaam, but the LORD your God turned the curse into a blessing for you, because the LORD your God loves you. [6] You shall not seek their peace nor their prosperity all your days forever.

[7] "You shall not abhor an Edomite, for he is your brother. You shall not abhor an Egyptian, because you were an alien in his land. [8] The children of the third generation born to them may enter the assembly of the LORD.

[9] "When the army goes out against your enemies, then keep yourself from every wicked thing. [10] If there is any man among you who becomes unclean by some occurrence in the night, then he shall go outside the camp; he shall not come inside the camp. [11] But it shall be, when evening comes, that he shall wash with water; and when the sun sets, he may come into the camp.

[12] "Also you shall have a place outside the camp, where you may go out; [13] and you shall have an implement among your equipment, and when you sit down outside, you shall dig with it and turn and cover your refuse. [14] For the LORD your God walks in the midst of your camp, to deliver you and give your enemies over to you; therefore your camp shall be holy, that He may see no unclean thing among you, and turn away from you.

[15] "You shall not give back to his master the slave who has escaped from his master to you. [16] He may dwell with you in your midst, in the place which he chooses within one of your gates, where it seems best to him; you shall not oppress him.

[17] "There shall be no ritual harlot of the daughters of Israel, or a perverted one of the sons of Israel. [18] You shall not bring the wages of a harlot or the price of a dog to the house of the LORD your God for any vowed offering, for both of these are an abomination to the LORD your God.

[19] "You shall not charge interest to your brother—interest on money or food or anything that is lent out at interest. [20] To a foreigner you may charge interest, but to your brother you shall not charge interest, that the LORD your God may bless you in all to which you set your hand in the land which you are entering to possess.

[21] "When you make a vow to the LORD your God, you shall not delay to pay it; for the LORD your God will surely require it of you, and it would be sin to you. [22] But if you abstain from vowing, it shall not be sin to you. [23] That which has gone from your lips you shall keep and perform, for you voluntarily vowed to the LORD your God what you have promised with your mouth.

[24] "When you come into your neighbor's vineyard, you may eat your fill of grapes at your pleasure, but you shall not put any in your container. [25] When you come into your neighbor's standing grain, you may pluck the heads with your hand, but you shall not use a sickle on your neighbor's standing grain.

24

"When a man takes a wife and marries her, and it happens that she finds no favor in his eyes because he has found some uncleanness in her, and he writes her a certificate of divorce, puts it in her hand, and sends her out of his house, [2] when she has departed from his house, and goes and becomes another man's wife, [3] if the latter husband detests her and writes her a certificate of divorce, puts it in her hand, and sends her out of his house, or if the latter husband dies who took her as his wife, [4] then her former husband who divorced her must not take her back to be his wife after she has been defiled; for that is an abomination before the LORD, and you shall not bring sin on the land which the LORD your God is giving you as an inheritance.

[5] "When a man has taken a new wife, he shall not go out to war or be charged with any business; he shall be free at home one year, and bring happiness to his wife whom he has taken.

[6] "No man shall take the lower or the upper millstone in pledge, for he takes one's living in pledge.

[7] "If a man is found kidnapping any of his brethren of the children of Israel, and mistreats him or sells him, then that

Encouraging Your Children

> He who guards his mouth preserves his life, but he who opens wide his lips shall have destruction.
>
> *Proverbs 13:3*

Glenn Van Ekeren tells about an experience he had with his son one summer vacation. For the first couple of days, his son Matt seemed to misbehave constantly. Glenn seemed to be continually rebuking and correcting him. Thinking, *No son of mine is going to act this way*, he made it clear to his son in no uncertain terms that he expected him to start behaving.

Matt tried very hard to live up to his father's standards. In fact, later in the week a day went by in which he hadn't done a single thing that called for correction. That night, after Matt had said his prayers and jumped into bed, Glenn noticed that his bottom lip began to quiver. "What's the matter, buddy?" he asked his son. Barely able to speak, Matt looked up at his father with tear-puddled eyes and asked, "Daddy, haven't I been a good boy today?"

Glenn said, "Those words cut through my parental arrogance like a knife. I had been quick to criticize and correct his misbehavior, but failed to mention my pleasure with his attempt to be a good boy. My son taught me never to put my children to bed without a word of appreciation and encouragement."

Statistics show that most parents make ten negative statements to their children for every one positive. Furthermore, studies have concluded that it takes four positive statements to overcome one negative statement. Take a moment and check yourself. Do you need to play catch-up with your children today?

kidnapper shall die; and you shall put away the evil from among you.

8 "Take heed in an outbreak of leprosy, that you carefully observe and do according to all that the priests, the Levites, shall teach you; just as I commanded them, *so* you shall be careful to do. 9 Remember what the LORD your God did to Miriam on the way when you came out of Egypt!

10 "When you lend your brother anything, you shall not go into his house to get his pledge. 11 You shall stand outside, and the man to whom you lend shall bring the pledge out to you. 12 And if the man *is* poor, you shall not keep his pledge overnight. 13 You shall in any case return the pledge to him again when the sun goes down, that he may sleep in his own garment and bless you; and it shall be righteousness to you before the LORD your God.

14 "You shall not oppress a hired servant *who is* poor and needy, *whether* one of your brethren or one of the aliens who *is* in your land within your gates. 15 Each day you shall give *him* his wages, and not let the sun go down on it, for he *is* poor and has set his heart on it; lest he cry out against you to the LORD, and it be sin to you.

16 "Fathers shall not be put to death for *their* children, nor shall children be put to death for *their* fathers; a person shall be put to death for his own sin.

17 "You shall not pervert justice due the stranger or the fatherless, nor take a widow's garment as a pledge. 18 But you shall remember that you were a slave in Egypt, and the LORD your God redeemed you from there; therefore I command you to do this thing.

19 "When you reap your harvest in your field, and forget a sheaf in the field, you shall not go back to get it; it shall be for the stranger, the fatherless, and the widow, that the LORD your God may bless you in all the work of your hands. 20 When you beat your olive trees, you shall not go over the boughs again; it shall be for the stranger, the fatherless, and the widow. 21 When you gather the grapes of your vineyard, you shall not glean *it* afterward; it shall be for the stranger, the fatherless, and the widow. 22 And you shall remember that you were a slave in the land of Egypt; therefore I command you to do this thing.

~ PSALM 39:1–6 ~

1 I said, "I will guard my ways,
   Lest I sin with my tongue;
   I will restrain my mouth with a
      muzzle,
   While the wicked are before me."
2 I was mute with silence,
   I held my peace *even* from good;
   And my sorrow was stirred up.
3 My heart was hot within me;
   While I was musing, the fire burned.
   Then I spoke with my tongue:

4 "LORD, make me to know my end,
   And what *is* the measure of my days,
   That I may know how frail I *am*.
5 Indeed, You have made my days *as*
      handbreadths,
   And my age *is* as nothing before You;
   Certainly every man at his best state
      is but vapor.   Selah
6 Surely every man walks about like a
      shadow;
   Surely they busy themselves in vain;
   He heaps up *riches,*
   And does not know who will gather
      them.

~ PROVERBS 13:1–3 ~

1 A wise son *heeds* his father's
      instruction,
   But a scoffer does not listen to
      rebuke.

2 A man shall eat well by the fruit of
      his mouth,
   But the soul of the unfaithful feeds
      on violence.
3 He who guards his mouth preserves
      his life,
   But he who opens wide his lips shall
      have destruction.

~ LUKE 5:17–39 ~

Now it happened on a certain day, as He was teaching, that there were Pharisees and teachers of the law sitting by, who had come out of every town of Galilee, Judea, and Jerusalem. And the power of the Lord was *present* to heal them. ¹⁸ Then behold, men brought on a bed a man who was paralyzed, whom they sought to bring in and lay before Him. ¹⁹ And when they could not find how they might bring him in, because of the crowd, they went up on the housetop and let him down with *his* bed through the tiling into the midst before Jesus.

²⁰ When He saw their faith, He said to him, "Man, your sins are forgiven you."

²¹ And the scribes and the Pharisees began to reason, saying, "Who is this who speaks blasphemies? Who can forgive sins but God alone?"

²² But when Jesus perceived their thoughts, He answered and said to them, "Why are you reasoning in your hearts? ²³ Which is easier, to say, 'Your sins are forgiven you,' or to say, 'Rise up and walk'? ²⁴ But that you may know that the Son of Man has power on earth to forgive sins"—He said to the man who was paralyzed, "I say to you, arise, take up your bed, and go to your house."

²⁵ Immediately he rose up before them, took up what he had been lying on, and departed to his own house, glorifying God. ²⁶ And they were all amazed, and they glorified God and were filled with fear, saying, "We have seen strange things today!"

²⁷ After these things He went out and saw a tax collector named Levi, sitting at the tax office. And He said to him, "Fol-

low Me." ²⁸ So he left all, rose up, and followed Him.

²⁹ Then Levi gave Him a great feast in his own house. And there were a great number of tax collectors and others who sat down with them. ³⁰ And their scribes and the Pharisees complained against His disciples, saying, "Why do You eat and drink with tax collectors and sinners?"

³¹ Jesus answered and said to them, "Those who are well have no need of a physician, but those who are sick. ³² I have not come to call *the* righteous, but sinners, to repentance."

³³ Then they said to Him, "Why do the disciples of John fast often and make prayers, and likewise those of the Pharisees, but Yours eat and drink?"

³⁴ And He said to them, "Can you make the friends of the bridegroom fast while the bridegroom is with them? ³⁵ But the days will come when the bridegroom will be taken away from them; then they will fast in those days."

³⁶ Then He spoke a parable to them: "No one puts a piece from a new garment on an old one; otherwise the new makes a tear, and also the piece that was *taken* out of the new does not match the old. ³⁷ And no one puts new wine into old wineskins; or else the new wine will burst the wineskins and be spilled, and the wineskins will be ruined. ³⁸ But new wine must be put into new wineskins, and both are preserved. ³⁹ And no one, having drunk old *wine,* immediately desires new; for he says, 'The old is better.'"

~ DEUTERONOMY 25:1—26:19 ~

"If there is a dispute between men, and they come to court, that *the judges* may judge them, and they justify the righteous and condemn the wicked, ² then it shall be, if the wicked man deserves to be beaten, that the judge will cause him to lie down and be beaten in his presence, according to his guilt, with a certain number of blows. ³ Forty blows he may give him *and* no more, lest he should exceed this and beat him with

many blows above these, and your brother be humiliated in your sight.

⁴ "You shall not muzzle an ox while it treads out *the grain.*

⁵ "If brothers dwell together, and one of them dies and has no son, the widow of the dead man shall not be *married* to a stranger outside *the family;* her husband's brother shall go in to her, take her as his wife, and perform the duty of a husband's brother to her. ⁶ And it shall be *that* the

firstborn son which she bears will succeed to the name of his dead brother, that his name may not be blotted out of Israel. [7] But if the man does not want to take his brother's wife, then let his brother's wife go up to the gate to the elders, and say, 'My husband's brother refuses to raise up a name to his brother in Israel; he will not perform the duty of my husband's brother.' [8] Then the elders of his city shall call him and speak to him. But *if* he stands firm and says, 'I do not want to take her,' [9] then his brother's wife shall come to him in the presence of the elders, remove his sandal from his foot, spit in his face, and answer and say, 'So shall it be done to the man who will not build up his brother's house.' [10] And his name shall be called in Israel, 'The house of him who had his sandal removed.'

[11] "If *two* men fight together, and the wife of one draws near to rescue her husband from the hand of the one attacking him, and puts out her hand and seizes him by the genitals, [12] then you shall cut off her hand; your eye shall not pity *her.*

[13] "You shall not have in your bag differing weights, a heavy and a light. [14] You shall not have in your house differing measures, a large and a small. [15] You shall have a perfect and just weight, a perfect and just measure, that your days may be lengthened in the land which the LORD your God is giving you. [16] For all who do such things, all who behave unrighteously, *are* an abomination to the LORD your God.

[17] "Remember what Amalek did to you on the way as you were coming out of Egypt, [18] how he met you on the way and attacked your rear ranks, all the stragglers at your rear, when you *were* tired and weary; and he did not fear God. [19] Therefore it shall be, when the LORD your God has given you rest from your enemies all around, in the land which the LORD your God is giving you to possess *as* an inheritance, *that* you will blot out the remembrance of Amalek from under heaven. You shall not forget.

26 "And it shall be, when you come into the land which the LORD your God is giving you *as* an inheritance, and you possess it and dwell in it, [2] that you shall take some of the first of all the produce of the ground, which you shall bring from your land that the LORD your God is giving you, and put *it* in a basket and go to the place where the LORD your God chooses to make His name abide. [3] And you shall go to the one who is priest in those days, and say to him, 'I declare today to the LORD your God that I have come to the country which the LORD swore to our fathers to give us.'

[4] "Then the priest shall take the basket out of your hand and set it down before the altar of the LORD your God. [5] And you shall answer and say before the LORD your God: 'My father *was* a Syrian, about to perish, and he went down to Egypt and dwelt there, few in number; and there he became a nation, great, mighty, and populous. [6] But the Egyptians mistreated us, afflicted us, and laid hard bondage on us. [7] Then we cried out to the LORD God of our fathers, and the LORD heard our voice and looked on our affliction and our labor and our oppression. [8] So the LORD brought us out of Egypt with a mighty hand and with an outstretched arm, with great terror and with signs and wonders. [9] He has brought us to this place and has given us this land, "a land flowing with milk and honey"; [10] and now, behold, I have brought the firstfruits of the land which you, O LORD, have given me.'

"Then you shall set it before the LORD your God, and worship before the LORD your God. [11] So you shall rejoice in every good *thing* which the LORD your God has given to you and your house, you and the Levite and the stranger who *is* among you.

[12] "When you have finished laying aside all the tithe of your increase in the third year—the year of tithing—and have given *it* to the Levite, the stranger, the fatherless, and the widow, so that they may eat within your gates and be filled, [13] then you shall say before the LORD your God: 'I have removed the holy *tithe* from *my* house, and also have given them to the Levite, the stranger, the fatherless, and the widow, according to all Your commandments which You have commanded me; I have not transgressed Your commandments, nor have I forgotten *them.*

Transplanting

Japanese bonsai trees are tiny, perfectly formed miniatures. They remain small no matter how old they get. Most are only fifteen to eighteen inches tall. To make a bonsai tree, a young sapling is pulled from the soil. Then, its taproot and some of the feeder roots are tied off. Thus, the growth of the bonsai is deliberately stunted.

In sharp contrast, California sequoia trees grow extremely large. The General Sherman stands 272 feet and measures 79 feet in circumference. If felled, this giant tree would provide enough lumber to build 35 five-room homes! The sequoia begins life as a small seed, no larger than the seed of the bonsai. However, its sapling is allowed to be nourished in the rich California soil and sunshine.

Neither the bonsai nor the giant sequoia has a choice in determining how large it will become. But we human beings do! We cannot blame others — including our parents — for what they have done or are doing to us. We have the opportunity to transplant ourselves into a nurturing, positive environment.

If others are trying to whittle you down today, get away from their shears! Rejoice in who you are and who you can be. Find a new place to put down roots.

Blessed are you when men hate you, and when they exclude you, and revile you, and cast out your name as evil, for the Son of Man's sake. Rejoice in that day and leap for joy! For indeed your reward is great in heaven, for in like manner their fathers did to the prophets.

Luke 6:22-23

[14] I have not eaten any of it when in mourning, nor have I removed *any* of it for an unclean *use,* nor given *any* of it for the dead. I have obeyed the voice of the LORD my God, and have done according to all that You have commanded me. [15] Look down from Your holy habitation, from heaven, and bless Your people Israel and the land which You have given us, just as You swore to our fathers, "a land flowing with milk and honey." '

[16] "This day the LORD your God commands you to observe these statutes and judgments; therefore you shall be careful to observe them with all your heart and with all your soul. [17] Today you have proclaimed the LORD to be your God, and that you will walk in His ways and keep His statutes, His commandments, and His judgments, and that you will obey His voice. [18] Also today the LORD has proclaimed you to be His special people, just as He promised you, that *you* should keep all His commandments, [19] and that He will set you high above all nations which He has made, in praise, in name, and in honor, and that you may be a holy people to the LORD your God, just as He has spoken."

∼ PSALM 39:7–11 ∼

[7] "And now, Lord, what do I wait for?
   My hope *is* in You.
[8] Deliver me from all my
     transgressions;
   Do not make me the reproach of the
     foolish.
[9] I was mute, I did not open my
     mouth,
   Because it was You who did *it.*
[10] Remove Your plague from me;
   I am consumed by the blow of Your
     hand.
[11] When with rebukes You correct man
     for iniquity,
   You make his beauty melt away like a
     moth;
   Surely every man *is* vapor.   Selah

∼ PROVERBS 13:4–6 ∼

[4] The soul of a lazy *man* desires, and
   has nothing;
   But the soul of the diligent shall be
     made rich.

[5] A righteous *man* hates lying,
   But a wicked *man* is loathsome and
     comes to shame.
[6] Righteousness guards *him whose*
     way is blameless,
   But wickedness overthrows the
     sinner.

∼ LUKE 6:1–26 ∼

Now it happened on the second Sabbath after the first that He went through the grainfields. And His disciples plucked the heads of grain and ate *them,* rubbing *them* in *their* hands. [2] And some of the Pharisees said to them, "Why are you doing what is not lawful to do on the Sabbath?"

[3] But Jesus answering them said, "Have you not even read this, what David did when he was hungry, he and those who were with him: [4] how he went into the house of God, took and ate the showbread, and also gave some to those with him, which is not lawful for any but the priests to eat?" [5] And He said to them, "The Son of Man is also Lord of the Sabbath."

[6] Now it happened on another Sabbath, also, that He entered the synagogue and taught. And a man was there whose right hand was withered. [7] So the scribes and Pharisees watched Him closely, whether He would heal on the Sabbath, that they might find an accusation against Him. [8] But He knew their thoughts, and said to the man who had the withered hand, "Arise and stand here." And he arose and stood. [9] Then Jesus said to them, "I will ask you one thing: Is it lawful on the Sabbath to do good or to do evil, to save life or to destroy?" [10] And when He had looked around at them all, He said to the man, "Stretch out your hand." And he did so, and his hand was restored as whole as the other. [11] But they were filled with rage, and discussed with one another what they might do to Jesus.

[12] Now it came to pass in those days that He went out to the mountain to pray, and continued all night in prayer to God. [13] And when it was day, He called His disciples to *Himself;* and from them He chose twelve whom He also named

apostles: [14] Simon, whom He also named Peter, and Andrew his brother; James and John; Philip and Bartholomew; [15] Matthew and Thomas; James the *son* of Alphaeus, and Simon called the Zealot; [16] Judas *the son* of James, and Judas Iscariot who also became a traitor.

[17] And He came down with them and stood on a level place with a crowd of His disciples and a great multitude of people from all Judea and Jerusalem, and from the seacoast of Tyre and Sidon, who came to hear Him and be healed of their diseases, [18] as well as those who were tormented with unclean spirits. And they were healed. [19] And the whole multitude sought to touch Him, for power went out from Him and healed *them* all.

[20] Then He lifted up His eyes toward His disciples, and said:

> "Blessed *are you* poor,
>> For yours is the kingdom of God.
> [21] Blessed *are you* who hunger now,
>> For you shall be filled.

> Blessed *are you* who weep now,
>> For you shall laugh.
> [22] Blessed are you when men hate you,
>> And when they exclude you,
>> And revile *you,* and cast out your name as evil,
>> For the Son of Man's sake.
> [23] Rejoice in that day and leap for joy!
>> For indeed your reward *is* great in heaven,
>> For in like manner their fathers did to the prophets.

> [24] "But woe to you who are rich,
>> For you have received your consolation.
> [25] Woe to you who are full,
>> For you shall hunger.
> Woe to you who laugh now,
>> For you shall mourn and weep.
> [26] Woe to you when all men speak well of you,
>> For so did their fathers to the false prophets.

~ DEUTERONOMY 27:1—28:68 ~

Now Moses, with the elders of Israel, commanded the people, saying: "Keep all the commandments which I command you today. [2] And it shall be, on the day when you cross over the Jordan to the land which the LORD your God is giving you, that you shall set up for yourselves large stones, and whitewash them with lime. [3] You shall write on them all the words of this law, when you have crossed over, that you may enter the land which the LORD your God is giving you, 'a land flowing with milk and honey,' just as the LORD God of your fathers promised you. [4] Therefore it shall be, when you have crossed over the Jordan, *that* on Mount Ebal you shall set up these stones, which I command you today, and you shall whitewash them with lime. [5] And there you shall build an altar to the LORD your God, an altar of stones; you shall not use an iron *tool* on them. [6] You shall build with whole stones the altar of the LORD your God, and offer burnt offerings on it to the LORD your God. [7] You shall offer peace offerings, and shall eat there, and rejoice before the LORD your God. [8] And you shall write very plainly on the stones all the words of this law."

[9] Then Moses and the priests, the Levites, spoke to all Israel, saying, "Take heed and listen, O Israel: This day you have become the people of the LORD your God. [10] Therefore you shall obey the voice of the LORD your God, and observe His commandments and His statutes which I command you today."

[11] And Moses commanded the people on the same day, saying, [12] "These shall stand on Mount Gerizim to bless the people, when you have crossed over the Jordan: Simeon, Levi, Judah, Issachar, Joseph, and Benjamin; [13] and these shall stand on Mount Ebal to curse: Reuben, Gad, Asher, Zebulun, Dan, and Naphtali. [14] "And the Levites shall speak with a

loud voice and say to all the men of Israel: [15] 'Cursed *is* the one who makes a carved or molded image, an abomination to the LORD, the work of the hands of the craftsman, and sets *it* up in secret.'

"And all the people shall answer and say, 'Amen!'

[16] 'Cursed *is* the one who treats his father or his mother with contempt.'

"And all the people shall say, 'Amen!'

[17] 'Cursed *is* the one who moves his neighbor's landmark.'

"And all the people shall say, 'Amen!'

[18] 'Cursed *is* the one who makes the blind to wander off the road.'

"And all the people shall say, 'Amen!'

[19] 'Cursed *is* the one who perverts the justice due the stranger, the fatherless, and widow.'

"And all the people shall say, 'Amen!'

[20] 'Cursed *is* the one who lies with his father's wife, because he has uncovered his father's bed.'

"And all the people shall say, 'Amen!'

[21] 'Cursed *is* the one who lies with any kind of animal.'

"And all the people shall say, 'Amen!'

[22] 'Cursed *is* the one who lies with his sister, the daughter of his father or the daughter of his mother.'

"And all the people shall say, 'Amen!'

[23] 'Cursed *is* the one who lies with his mother-in-law.'

"And all the people shall say, 'Amen!'

[24] 'Cursed *is* the one who attacks his neighbor secretly.'

"And all the people shall say, 'Amen!'

[25] 'Cursed *is* the one who takes a bribe to slay an innocent person.'

"And all the people shall say, 'Amen!'

[26] 'Cursed *is* the one who does not confirm *all* the words of this law.'

"And all the people shall say, 'Amen!' "

28

"Now it shall come to pass, if you diligently obey the voice of the LORD your God, to observe carefully all His commandments which I command you today, that the LORD your God will set you high above all nations of the earth. [2] And all these blessings shall come upon you and overtake you, because you obey the voice of the LORD your God:

[3] "Blessed *shall* you *be* in the city, and blessed *shall* you *be* in the country.

[4] "Blessed *shall be* the fruit of your body, the produce of your ground and the increase of your herds, the increase of your cattle and the offspring of your flocks.

[5] "Blessed *shall be* your basket and your kneading bowl.

[6] "Blessed *shall* you *be* when you come in, and blessed *shall* you *be* when you go out.

[7] "The LORD will cause your enemies who rise against you to be defeated before your face; they shall come out against you one way and flee before you seven ways.

[8] "The LORD will command the blessing on you in your storehouses and in all to which you set your hand, and He will bless you in the land which the LORD your God is giving you.

[9] "The LORD will establish you as a holy people to Himself, just as He has sworn to you, if you keep the commandments of the LORD your God and walk in His ways. [10] Then all peoples of the earth shall see that you are called by the name of the LORD, and they shall be afraid of you. [11] And the LORD will grant you plenty of goods, in the fruit of your body, in the increase of your livestock, and in the produce of your ground, in the land of which the LORD swore to your fathers to give you. [12] The LORD will open to you His good treasure, the heavens, to give the rain to your land in its season, and to bless all the work of your hand. You shall lend to many nations, but you shall not borrow. [13] And the LORD will make you the head and not the tail; you shall be above only, and not be beneath, if you heed the commandments of the LORD your God, which I command you today, and are careful to observe *them*. [14] So you shall not turn aside from any of the words which I command you this day, *to* the right or the left, to go after other gods to serve them.

[15] "But it shall come to pass, if you do not obey the voice of the LORD your God, to observe carefully all His commandments and His statutes which I command you today, that all these curses will come upon you and overtake you:

[16] "Cursed *shall* you *be* in the city, and cursed *shall* you *be* in the country.

Give, and It Shall Be Given

The grief-stricken mother sat in a hospital room in stunned silence, tears slipping down her cheeks. She had just lost her only child. As she gazed into space the head nurse asked her, "Did you notice the little boy sitting in the hall just outside?" The woman shook her head no.

The nurse continued. "His mother was brought here by ambulance from their poor one-room apartment. The two of them came to this country only three months ago, because all their family members had been killed in war. They don't know anyone here.

"That little boy has been sitting outside his mother's room every day for a week in hopes his mother would come out of her coma and speak to him."

By now the woman was listening intently. The nurse continued, "Fifteen minutes ago his mother died. It's my job to tell him that at age seven, he is all alone in the world — no one even knows his name." The nurse paused and then asked, "I don't suppose you would tell him for me?" The woman stood, dried her tears, and went out to the boy.

She put her arms around the homeless child and invited him to come to her childless home. In the darkest hour of both their lives, they became lights to one another.

God's law of sowing and reaping works in every area of life, not just finances. When you need a friend, be a friend. When you need comfort, be a comforter. When you need light, be a light. Even in your darkest hour, you have something to give. In return, you'll receive from God exactly what you need.

> Give, and it will be given to you: good measure, pressed down, shaken together, and running over will be put into your bosom. For with the same measure that you use, it will be measured back to you.
>
> *Luke 6:38*

[17] "Cursed *shall be* your basket and your kneading bowl.

[18] "Cursed *shall be* the fruit of your body and the produce of your land, the increase of your cattle and the offspring of your flocks.

[19] "Cursed *shall* you *be* when you come in, and cursed *shall* you *be* when you go out.

[20] "The LORD will send on you cursing, confusion, and rebuke in all that you set your hand to do, until you are destroyed and until you perish quickly, because of the wickedness of your doings in which you have forsaken Me. [21] The LORD will make the plague cling to you until He has consumed you from the land which you are going to possess. [22] The LORD will strike you with consumption, with fever, with inflammation, with severe burning fever, with the sword, with scorching, and with mildew; they shall pursue you until you perish. [23] And your heavens which *are* over your head shall be bronze, and the earth which is under you *shall be* iron. [24] The LORD will change the rain of your land to powder and dust; from the heaven it shall come down on you until you are destroyed.

[25] "The LORD will cause you to be defeated before your enemies; you shall go out one way against them and flee seven ways before them; and you shall become troublesome to all the kingdoms of the earth. [26] Your carcasses shall be food for all the birds of the air and the beasts of the earth, and no one shall frighten *them* away. [27] The LORD will strike you with the boils of Egypt, with tumors, with the scab, and with the itch, from which you cannot be healed. [28] The LORD will strike you with madness and blindness and confusion of heart. [29] And you shall grope at noonday, as a blind man gropes in darkness; you shall not prosper in your ways; you shall be only oppressed and plundered continually, and no one shall save *you.*

[30] "You shall betroth a wife, but another man shall lie with her; you shall build a house, but you shall not dwell in it; you shall plant a vineyard, but shall not gather its grapes. [31] Your ox *shall be* slaughtered before your eyes, but you shall not eat of it; your donkey *shall be* violently taken away from before you, and shall not be restored to you; your sheep *shall be* given to your enemies, and you shall have no one to rescue *them.* [32] Your sons and your daughters *shall be* given to another people, and your eyes shall look and fail *with longing* for them all day long; and *there shall be* no strength in your hand. [33] A nation whom you have not known shall eat the fruit of your land and the produce of your labor, and you shall be only oppressed and crushed continually. [34] So you shall be driven mad because of the sight which your eyes see. [35] The LORD will strike you in the knees and on the legs with severe boils which cannot be healed, and from the sole of your foot to the top of your head.

[36] "The LORD will bring you and the king whom you set over you to a nation which neither you nor your fathers have known, and there you shall serve other gods—wood and stone. [37] And you shall become an astonishment, a proverb, and a byword among all nations where the LORD will drive you.

[38] "You shall carry much seed out to the field but gather little in, for the locust shall consume it. [39] You shall plant vineyards and tend *them,* but you shall neither drink *of* the wine nor gather the *grapes;* for the worms shall eat them. [40] You shall have olive trees throughout all your territory, but you shall not anoint *yourself* with the oil; for your olives shall drop off. [41] You shall beget sons and daughters, but they shall not be yours; for they shall go into captivity. [42] Locusts shall consume all your trees and the produce of your land.

[43] "The alien who *is* among you shall rise higher and higher above you, and you shall come down lower and lower. [44] He shall lend to you, but you shall not lend to him; he shall be the head, and you shall be the tail.

[45] "Moreover all these curses shall come upon you and pursue and overtake you, until you are destroyed, because you did not obey the voice of the LORD your God, to keep His commandments and His statutes which He commanded you. [46] And they shall be upon you for a sign and a wonder, and on your descendants forever.

[47] "Because you did not serve the LORD your God with joy and gladness of heart, for the abundance of everything,

⁴⁸ therefore you shall serve your enemies, whom the LORD will send against you, in hunger, in thirst, in nakedness, and in need of everything; and He will put a yoke of iron on your neck until He has destroyed you. ⁴⁹ The LORD will bring a nation against you from afar, from the end of the earth, *as swift* as the eagle flies, a nation whose language you will not understand, ⁵⁰ a nation of fierce countenance, which does not respect the elderly nor show favor to the young. ⁵¹ And they shall eat the increase of your livestock and the produce of your land, until you are destroyed; they shall not leave you grain or new wine or oil, *or* the increase of your cattle or the offspring of your flocks, until they have destroyed you.

⁵² "They shall besiege you at all your gates until your high and fortified walls, in which you trust, come down throughout all your land; and they shall besiege you at all your gates throughout all your land which the LORD your God has given you. ⁵³ You shall eat the fruit of your own body, the flesh of your sons and your daughters whom the LORD your God has given you, in the siege and desperate straits in which your enemy shall distress you. ⁵⁴ The sensitive and very refined man among you will be hostile toward his brother, toward the wife of his bosom, and toward the rest of his children whom he leaves behind, ⁵⁵ so that he will not give any of them the flesh of his children whom he will eat, because he has nothing left in the siege and desperate straits in which your enemy shall distress you at all your gates. ⁵⁶ The tender and delicate woman among you, who would not venture to set the sole of her foot on the ground because of her delicateness and sensitivity, will refuse to the husband of her bosom, and to her son and her daughter, ⁵⁷ her placenta which comes out from between her feet and her children whom she bears; for she will eat them secretly for lack of everything in the siege and desperate straits in which your enemy shall distress you at all your gates.

⁵⁸ "If you do not carefully observe all the words of this law that are written in this book, that you may fear this glorious and awesome name, THE LORD YOUR GOD, ⁵⁹ then the LORD will bring upon you and your descendants extraordinary plagues—great and prolonged plagues—and serious and prolonged sicknesses. ⁶⁰ Moreover He will bring back on you all the diseases of Egypt, of which you were afraid, and they shall cling to you. ⁶¹ Also every sickness and every plague, which *is* not written in this Book of the Law, will the LORD bring upon you until you are destroyed. ⁶² You shall be left few in number, whereas you were as the stars of heaven in multitude, because you would not obey the voice of the LORD your God. ⁶³ And it shall be, *that* just as the LORD rejoiced over you to do you good and multiply you, so the LORD will rejoice over you to destroy you and bring you to nothing; and you shall be plucked from off the land which you go to possess.

⁶⁴ "Then the LORD will scatter you among all peoples, from one end of the earth to the other, and there you shall serve other gods, which neither you nor your fathers have known—wood and stone. ⁶⁵ And among those nations you shall find no rest, nor shall the sole of your foot have a resting place; but there the LORD will give you a trembling heart, failing eyes, and anguish of soul. ⁶⁶ Your life shall hang in doubt before you; you shall fear day and night, and have no assurance of life. ⁶⁷ In the morning you shall say, 'Oh, that it were evening!' And at evening you shall say, 'Oh, that it were morning!' because of the fear which terrifies your heart, and because of the sight which your eyes see.

⁶⁸ "And the LORD will take you back to Egypt in ships, by the way of which I said to you, 'You shall never see it again.' And there you shall be offered for sale to your enemies as male and female slaves, but no one will buy *you*."

∽ PSALM 39:12, 13 ∽

¹² "Hear my prayer, O LORD,
    And give ear to my cry;
    Do not be silent at my tears;
    For I *am* a stranger with You,
    A sojourner, as all my fathers *were*.
¹³ Remove Your gaze from me, that I
        may regain strength,
    Before I go away and am no more."

~ PROVERBS 13:7, 8 ~

7 There is one who makes himself
    rich, yet *has* nothing;
    And one who makes himself poor,
    yet *has* great riches.

8 The ransom of a man's life *is* his
    riches,
    But the poor does not hear rebuke.

~ LUKE 6:27–49 ~

"But I say to you who hear: Love your
enemies, do good to those who hate you,
28 bless those who curse you, and pray for
those who spitefully use you. 29 To him
who strikes you on the *one* cheek, offer
the other also. And from him who takes
away your cloak, do not withhold *your*
tunic either. 30 Give to everyone who asks
of you. And from him who takes away
your goods do not ask *them* back. 31 And
just as you want men to do to you, you
also do to them likewise.

32 "But if you love those who love you,
what credit is that to you? For even sinners love those who love them. 33 And if
you do good to those who do good
to you, what credit is that to you? For
even sinners do the same. 34 And if you
lend *to those* from whom you hope to
receive back, what credit is that to you?
For even sinners lend to sinners to receive
as much back. 35 But love your enemies,
do good, and lend, hoping for nothing in
return; and your reward will be great, and
you will be sons of the Most High. For
He is kind to the unthankful and evil.
36 Therefore be merciful, just as your Father also is merciful.

37 "Judge not, and you shall not be
judged. Condemn not, and you shall not
be condemned. Forgive, and you will be
forgiven. 38 Give, and it will be given to
you: good measure, pressed down, shaken

together, and running over will be put into
your bosom. For with the same measure
that you use, it will be measured back
to you."

39 And He spoke a parable to them:
"Can the blind lead the blind? Will they
not both fall into the ditch? 40 A disciple
is not above his teacher, but everyone
who is perfectly trained will be like his
teacher. 41 And why do you look at the
speck in your brother's eye, but do not
perceive the plank in your own eye? 42 Or
how can you say to your brother, 'Brother,
let me remove the speck that *is* in your
eye,' when you yourself do not see the
plank that *is* in your own eye? Hypocrite!
First remove the plank from your own
eye, and then you will see clearly to
remove the speck that is in your brother's eye.

43 "For a good tree does not bear bad
fruit, nor does a bad tree bear good fruit.
44 For every tree is known by its own
fruit. For *men* do not gather figs from
thorns, nor do they gather grapes from a
bramble bush. 45 A good man out of
the good treasure of his heart brings forth
good; and an evil man out of the evil treasure of his heart brings forth evil. For out
of the abundance of the heart his mouth
speaks.

46 "But why do you call Me 'Lord,
Lord,' and not do the things which I say?
47 Whoever comes to Me, and hears My
sayings and does them, I will show you
whom he is like: 48 He is like a man building a house, who dug deep and laid the
foundation on the rock. And when
the flood arose, the stream beat vehemently against that house, and could not
shake it, for it was founded on the rock.
49 But he who heard and did nothing is
like a man who built a house on the earth
without a foundation, against which the
stream beat vehemently; and immediately
it fell. And the ruin of that house was
great."

~ DEUTERONOMY 29:1—30:20 ~

These *are* the words of the covenant which the LORD commanded Moses to make with the children of Israel in the land of Moab, besides the covenant which He made with them in Horeb.

2 Now Moses called all Israel and said to them: "You have seen all that the LORD did before your eyes in the land of Egypt, to Pharaoh and to all his servants and to all his land— 3 the great trials which your eyes have seen, the signs, and those great wonders. 4 Yet the LORD has not given you a heart to perceive and eyes to see and ears to hear, to this *very* day. 5 And I have led you forty years in the wilderness. Your clothes have not worn out on you, and your sandals have not worn out on your feet. 6 You have not eaten bread, nor have you drunk wine or *similar* drink, that you may know that I *am* the LORD your God. 7 And when you came to this place, Sihon king of Heshbon and Og king of Bashan came out against us to battle, and we conquered them. 8 We took their land and gave it as an inheritance to the Reubenites, to the Gadites, and to half the tribe of Manasseh. 9 Therefore keep the words of this covenant, and do them, that you may prosper in all that you do.

10 "All of you stand today before the LORD your God: your leaders and your tribes and your elders and your officers, all the men of Israel, 11 your little ones and your wives—also the stranger who *is* in your camp, from the one who cuts your wood to the one who draws your water— 12 that you may enter into covenant with the LORD your God, and into His oath, which the LORD your God makes with you today, 13 that He may establish you today as a people for Himself, and *that* He may be God to you, just as He has spoken to you, and just as He has sworn to your fathers, to Abraham, Isaac, and Jacob.

14 "I make this covenant and this oath, not with you alone, 15 but with *him* who stands here with us today before the LORD our God, as well as with *him* who *is* not here with us today 16 (for you know that we dwelt in the land of Egypt and that we came through the nations which you passed by, 17 and you saw their abominations and their idols which *were* among them—wood and stone and silver and gold); 18 so that there may not be among you man or woman or family or tribe, whose heart turns away today from the LORD our God, to go *and* serve the gods of these nations, and that there may not be among you a root bearing bitterness or wormwood; 19 and so it may not happen, when he hears the words of this curse, that he blesses himself in his heart, saying, 'I shall have peace, even though I follow the dictates of my heart'—as though the drunkard could be included with the sober.

20 "The LORD would not spare him; for then the anger of the LORD and His jealousy would burn against that man, and every curse that is written in this book would settle on him, and the LORD would blot out his name from under heaven. 21 And the LORD would separate him from all the tribes of Israel for adversity, according to all the curses of the covenant that are written in this Book of the Law, 22 so that the coming generation of your children who rise up after you, and the foreigner who comes from a far land, would say, when they see the plagues of that land and the sicknesses which the LORD has laid on it:

23 'The whole land *is* brimstone, salt, and burning; it is not sown, nor does it bear, nor does any grass grow there, like the overthrow of Sodom and Gomorrah, Admah, and Zeboiim, which the LORD overthrew in His anger and His wrath.' 24 All nations would say, 'Why has the LORD done so to this land? What does the heat of this great anger mean?' 25 Then *people* would say: 'Because they have forsaken the covenant of the LORD God of their fathers, which He made with them when He brought them out of the land of Egypt; 26 for they went and served other gods and worshiped them, gods that they did not know and that He had not given to them. 27 Then the anger of the LORD was aroused against this land, to bring on it every curse that is written in this book.

[28] And the LORD uprooted them from their land in anger, in wrath, and in great indignation, and cast them into another land, as *it is* this day.'

[29] "The secret *things belong* to the LORD our God, but those *things which are* revealed *belong* to us and to our children forever, that *we* may do all the words of this law.

30 "Now it shall come to pass, when all these things come upon you, the blessing and the curse which I have set before you, and you call *them* to mind among all the nations where the LORD your God drives you, [2] and you return to the LORD your God and obey His voice, according to all that I command you today, you and your children, with all your heart and with all your soul, [3] that the LORD your God will bring you back from captivity, and have compassion on you, and gather you again from all the nations where the LORD your God has scattered you. [4] If *any* of you are driven out to the farthest *parts* under heaven, from there the LORD your God will gather you, and from there He will bring you. [5] Then the LORD your God will bring you to the land which your fathers possessed, and you shall possess it. He will prosper you and multiply you more than your fathers. [6] And the LORD your God will circumcise your heart and the heart of your descendants, to love the LORD your God with all your heart and with all your soul, that you may live. [7] "Also the LORD your God will put all these curses on your enemies and on those who hate you, who persecuted you. [8] And you will again obey the voice of the LORD and do all His commandments which I command you today. [9] The LORD your God will make you abound in all the work of your hand, in the fruit of your body, in the increase of your livestock, and in the produce of your land for good. For the LORD will again rejoice over you for good as He rejoiced over your fathers, [10] if you obey the voice of the LORD your God, to keep His commandments and His statutes which are written in this Book of the Law, *and* if you turn to the LORD your God with all your heart and with all your soul.

[11] "For this commandment which I command you today *is* not *too* mysterious for you, nor *is* it far off. [12] It *is* not in heaven, that you should say, 'Who will ascend into heaven for us and bring it to us, that we may hear it and do it?' [13] Nor *is* it beyond the sea, that you should say, 'Who will go over the sea for us and bring it to us, that we may hear it and do it?' [14] But the word *is* very near you, in your mouth and in your heart, that you may do it.

[15] "See, I have set before you today life and good, death and evil, [16] in that I command you today to love the LORD your God, to walk in His ways, and to keep His commandments, His statutes, and His judgments, that you may live and multiply; and the LORD your God will bless you in the land which you go to possess. [17] But if your heart turns away so that you do not hear, and are drawn away, and worship other gods and serve them, [18] I announce to you today that you shall surely perish; you shall not prolong *your* days in the land which you cross over the Jordan to go in and possess. [19] I call heaven and earth as witnesses today against you, *that* I have set before you life and death, blessing and cursing; therefore choose life, that both you and your descendants may live; [20] that you may love the LORD your God, that you may obey His voice, and that you may cling to Him, for He *is* your life and the length of your days; and that you may dwell in the land which the LORD swore to your fathers, to Abraham, Isaac, and Jacob, to give them."

~ PSALM 40:1–5 ~

[1] I waited patiently for the LORD;
And He inclined to me,
And heard my cry.
[2] He also brought me up out of a
horrible pit,
Out of the miry clay,
And set my feet upon a rock,
And established my steps.
[3] He has put a new song in my
mouth—
Praise to our God;
Many will see *it* and fear,
And will trust in the LORD.

God's Work — God's Pay

As a young man, J. C. Penney ran a butcher shop. He was told that if he gave a fifth of Scotch to the head chef in a popular hotel, the business of that hotel would be his. Penney did this for some time. Then he felt convicted that what he was doing was wrong. He discontinued the gifts of liquor and sure enough, lost the hotel's business, causing him to go broke. God, however, had better things planned for him. In time, he began a merchandise business that grew into a nationwide enterprise.

Unsuccessful years alone don't create success. Remaining true to principles and doing the right thing — even when you seem to be failing — produce success in time. A poem by an unknown writer says it well:

> Who does God's work will get God's pay,
> However long may seem the day,
> However weary be the way;
> Though powers and princes thunder "Nay,"
> Who does God's work will get God's pay.
> He does not pay as others pay,
> In gold or land or raiment gay;
> In goods that vanish and decay;
> But God in wisdom knows a way,
> And that is sure, let come what may,
> Who does God's work will get God's pay.

> He also brought me up out of a horrible pit, out of the miry clay, and set my feet upon a rock, and established my steps.
>
> *Psalm 40:2*

⁴ Blessed *is* that man who makes the
LORD his trust,
And does not respect the proud, nor
such as turn aside to lies.
⁵ Many, O LORD my God, *are* Your
wonderful works
Which You have done;
And Your thoughts toward us
Cannot be recounted to You in
order;
If I would declare and speak *of them,*
They are more than can be
numbered.

∼ PROVERBS 13:9, 10 ∼

⁹ The light of the righteous rejoices,
But the lamp of the wicked will be
put out.

¹⁰ By pride comes nothing but strife,
But with the well-advised *is* wisdom.

∼ LUKE 7:1–30 ∼

Now when He concluded all His sayings
in the hearing of the people, He entered
Capernaum. ² And a certain centurion's
servant, who was dear to him, was sick
and ready to die. ³ So when he heard about
Jesus, he sent elders of the Jews to Him,
pleading with Him to come and heal his
servant. ⁴ And when they came to Jesus,
they begged Him earnestly, saying that the
one for whom He should do this was deserving, ⁵ "for he loves our nation, and
has built us a synagogue."

⁶ Then Jesus went with them. And when
He was already not far from the house,
the centurion sent friends to Him, saying
to Him, "Lord, do not trouble Yourself,
for I am not worthy that You should enter under my roof. ⁷ Therefore I did not
even think myself worthy to come to You.
But say the word, and my servant will be
healed. ⁸ For I also am a man placed under authority, having soldiers under me.
And I say to one, 'Go,' and he goes; and
to another, 'Come,' and he comes; and to
my servant, 'Do this,' and he does *it*."

⁹ When Jesus heard these things, He
marveled at him, and turned around and
said to the crowd that followed Him, "I
say to you, I have not found such great
faith, not even in Israel!" ¹⁰ And those who

were sent, returning to the house, found
the servant well who had been sick.

¹¹ Now it happened, the day after, *that*
He went into a city called Nain; and many
of His disciples went with Him, and a
large crowd. ¹² And when He came near
the gate of the city, behold, a dead man
was being carried out, the only son of his
mother; and she was a widow. And a large
crowd from the city was with her. ¹³ When
the Lord saw her, He had compassion on
her and said to her, "Do not weep."
¹⁴ Then He came and touched the open
coffin, and those who carried *him* stood
still. And He said, "Young man, I say to
you, arise." ¹⁵ So he who was dead sat up
and began to speak. And He presented
him to his mother.

¹⁶ Then fear came upon all, and they
glorified God, saying, "A great prophet
has risen up among us"; and, "God has
visited His people." ¹⁷ And this report
about Him went throughout all Judea and
all the surrounding region.

¹⁸ Then the disciples of John reported
to him concerning all these things. ¹⁹ And
John, calling two of his disciples to *him*,
sent *them* to Jesus, saying, "Are You the
Coming One, or do we look for another?"

²⁰ When the men had come to Him,
they said, "John the Baptist has sent us to
You, saying, 'Are You the Coming One,
or do we look for another?' " ²¹ And that
very hour He cured many of infirmities,
afflictions, and evil spirits; and to many
blind He gave sight.

²² Jesus answered and said to them, "Go
and tell John the things you have seen and
heard: that *the* blind see, *the* lame walk,
the lepers are cleansed, *the* deaf hear, *the*
dead are raised, *the* poor have the gospel
preached to them. ²³ And blessed is *he* who
is not offended because of Me."

²⁴ When the messengers of John had
departed, He began to speak to the multitudes concerning John: "What did you
go out into the wilderness to see? A reed
shaken by the wind? ²⁵ But what did you
go out to see? A man clothed in soft garments? Indeed those who are gorgeously
appareled and live in luxury are in kings'
courts. ²⁶ But what did you go out to see?
A prophet? Yes, I say to you, and more
than a prophet. ²⁷ This is *he* of whom it is
written:

'Behold, I send My messenger
before Your face,
Who will prepare Your way before
You.'

28 For I say to you, among those born
of women there is not a greater prophet
than John the Baptist; but he who is
least in the kingdom of God is greater
than he."

29 And when all the people heard *Him*,
even the tax collectors justified God,
having been baptized with the baptism of
John. 30 But the Pharisees and lawyers
rejected the will of God for themselves,
not having been baptized by him.

∼ DEUTERONOMY 31:1—32:52 ∼

Then Moses went and spoke these
words to all Israel. 2 And he said
to them: "I *am* one hundred and
twenty years old today. I can no longer
go out and come in. Also the LORD has
said to me, 'You shall not cross over this
Jordan.' 3 The LORD your God Himself
crosses over before you; He will destroy
these nations from before you, and you
shall dispossess them. Joshua himself
crosses over before you, just as the LORD
has said. 4 And the LORD will do to them
as He did to Sihon and Og, the kings of
the Amorites and their land, when He
destroyed them. 5 The LORD will give
them over to you, that you may do
to them according to every commandment which I have commanded you. 6 Be
strong and of good courage, do not fear
nor be afraid of them; for the LORD your
God, He *is* the One who goes with you.
He will not leave you nor forsake you."

7 Then Moses called Joshua and said to
him in the sight of all Israel, "Be strong
and of good courage, for you must go with
this people to the land which the LORD
has sworn to their fathers to give them,
and you shall cause them to inherit it.
8 And the LORD, He *is* the One who goes
before you. He will be with you, He will
not leave you nor forsake you; do not fear
nor be dismayed."

9 So Moses wrote this law and delivered it to the priests, the sons of Levi, who
bore the ark of the covenant of the LORD,
and to all the elders of Israel. 10 And Moses
commanded them, saying: "At the end of
every seven years, at the appointed time
in the year of release, at the Feast of
Tabernacles, 11 when all Israel comes to
appear before the LORD your God in the
place which He chooses, you shall read
this law before all Israel in their hearing.
12 Gather the people together, men and
women and little ones, and the stranger
who *is* within your gates, that they may
hear and that they may learn to fear the
LORD your God and carefully observe all
the words of this law, 13 and *that* their
children, who have not known it, may
hear and learn to fear the LORD your God
as long as you live in the land which you
cross the Jordan to possess."

14 Then the LORD said to Moses, "Behold, the days approach when you must
die; call Joshua, and present yourselves
in the tabernacle of meeting, that I may
inaugurate him."

So Moses and Joshua went and presented themselves in the tabernacle of
meeting. 15 Now the LORD appeared at
the tabernacle in a pillar of cloud, and the
pillar of cloud stood above the door of
the tabernacle.

16 And the LORD said to Moses: "Behold, you will rest with your fathers; and
this people will rise and play the harlot
with the gods of the foreigners of the land,
where they go *to be* among them, and they
will forsake Me and break My covenant
which I have made with them. 17 Then My
anger shall be aroused against them in that
day, and I will forsake them, and I will
hide My face from them, and they shall
be devoured. And many evils and troubles
shall befall them, so that they will say in
that day, 'Have not these evils come upon
us because our God *is* not among us?'
18 And I will surely hide My face in that
day because of all the evil which they have
done, in that they have turned to other
gods.

¹⁹ "Now therefore, write down this song for yourselves, and teach it to the children of Israel; put it in their mouths, that this song may be a witness for Me against the children of Israel. ²⁰ When I have brought them to the land flowing with milk and honey, of which I swore to their fathers, and they have eaten and filled themselves and grown fat, then they will turn to other gods and serve them; and they will provoke Me and break My covenant. ²¹ Then it shall be, when many evils and troubles have come upon them, that this song will testify against them as a witness; for it will not be forgotten in the mouths of their descendants, for I know the inclination of their behavior today, even before I have brought them to the land of which I swore *to give them.*"

²² Therefore Moses wrote this song the same day, and taught it to the children of Israel. ²³ Then He inaugurated Joshua the son of Nun, and said, "Be strong and of good courage; for you shall bring the children of Israel into the land of which I swore to them, and I will be with you."

²⁴ So it was, when Moses had completed writing the words of this law in a book, when they were finished, ²⁵ that Moses commanded the Levites, who bore the ark of the covenant of the LORD, saying: ²⁶ "Take this Book of the Law, and put it beside the ark of the covenant of the LORD your God, that it may be there as a witness against you; ²⁷ for I know your rebellion and your stiff neck. *If* today, while I am yet alive with you, you have been rebellious against the LORD, then how much more after my death? ²⁸ Gather to me all the elders of your tribes, and your officers, that I may speak these words in their hearing and call heaven and earth to witness against them. ²⁹ For I know that after my death you will become utterly corrupt, and turn aside from the way which I have commanded you. And evil will befall you in the latter days, because you will do evil in the sight of the LORD, to provoke Him to anger through the work of your hands."

³⁰ Then Moses spoke in the hearing of all the assembly of Israel the words of this song until they were ended:

32 "Give ear, O heavens, and I will speak;
And hear, O earth, the words of my mouth.
² Let my teaching drop as the rain,
My speech distill as the dew,
As raindrops on the tender herb,
And as showers on the grass.
³ For I proclaim the name of the LORD:
Ascribe greatness to our God.
⁴ *He is* the Rock, His work *is* perfect;
For all His ways *are* justice,
A God of truth and without injustice;
Righteous and upright *is* He.

⁵ "They have corrupted themselves;
They are not His children,
Because of their blemish:
A perverse and crooked generation.
⁶ Do you thus deal with the LORD,
O foolish and unwise people?
Is He not your Father, *who* bought you?
Has He not made you and established you?

⁷ "Remember the days of old,
Consider the years of many generations.
Ask your father, and he will show you;
Your elders, and they will tell you:
⁸ When the Most High divided their inheritance to the nations,
When He separated the sons of Adam,
He set the boundaries of the peoples
According to the number of the children of Israel.
⁹ For the LORD's portion *is* His people;
Jacob *is* the place of His inheritance.

¹⁰ "He found him in a desert land
And in the wasteland, a howling wilderness;
He encircled him, He instructed him,

Repent and Remit

A woman in a fancy luxury car waited patiently in a crowded mall parking lot for a space to open up. She drove up and down between rows until finally, she saw a man with a load of packages heading for his car. She followed him and parked behind him, waiting while he opened his trunk and loaded it. Finally he got into his car and backed out. Just as she was preparing to pull forward into the space, a young man in a little sports car — coming from the opposite direction — zipped into the space, got out of his car, and walked away. The woman was livid. She shouted from her big luxury car, "Hey, young man! I was waiting for that parking place."

The teenager responded, "Sorry, lady, but that's how it is when you're young and quick." She instantly put her car in gear, floorboarded it, and crashed into the little sports car, crushing its right rear fender. Now it was the young man's turn to get angry. He jumped up and down shouting, "What are you doing?" The woman in the luxury car calmly responded, "Well, son, that's how it is when you're old and rich."

Most of the world's problems and conflicts could probably be resolved if, instead of retaliation and revenge, we opted more often for repentance and remission.

He kept him as the apple of His eye.

11 As an eagle stirs up its nest,
Hovers over its young,
Spreading out its wings, taking them up,
Carrying them on its wings,

12 So the LORD alone led him,
And there was no foreign god with him.

13 "He made him ride in the heights of the earth,
That he might eat the produce of the fields;
He made him draw honey from the rock,
And oil from the flinty rock;

14 Curds from the cattle, and milk of the flock,
With fat of lambs;
And rams of the breed of Bashan, and goats,
With the choicest wheat;
And you drank wine, the blood of the grapes.

15 "But Jeshurun grew fat and kicked;
You grew fat, you grew thick,
You are obese!
Then he forsook God who made him,
And scornfully esteemed the Rock of his salvation.

16 They provoked Him to jealousy with foreign gods;
With abominations they provoked Him to anger.

17 They sacrificed to demons, not to God,
To gods they did not know,
To new gods, new arrivals
That your fathers did not fear.

18 Of the Rock who begot you, you are unmindful,
And have forgotten the God who fathered you.

19 "And when the LORD saw it, He spurned them,
Because of the provocation of His sons and His daughters.

20 And He said: 'I will hide My face from them,
I will see what their end will be,

For they are a perverse generation,
Children in whom is no faith.

21 They have provoked Me to jealousy by what is not God;
They have moved Me to anger by their foolish idols.
But I will provoke them to jealousy by those who are not a nation;
I will move them to anger by a foolish nation.

22 For a fire is kindled in My anger,
And shall burn to the lowest hell;
It shall consume the earth with her increase,
And set on fire the foundations of the mountains.

23 'I will heap disasters on them;
I will spend My arrows on them.

24 They shall be wasted with hunger,
Devoured by pestilence and bitter destruction;
I will also send against them the teeth of beasts,
With the poison of serpents of the dust.

25 The sword shall destroy outside;
There shall be terror within
For the young man and virgin,
The nursing child with the man of gray hairs.

26 I would have said, "I will dash them in pieces,
I will make the memory of them to cease from among men,"

27 Had I not feared the wrath of the enemy,
Lest their adversaries should misunderstand,
Lest they should say, "Our hand is high;
And it is not the LORD who has done all this." '

28 "For they are a nation void of counsel,
Nor is there any understanding in them.

29 Oh, that they were wise, that they understood this,
That they would consider their latter end!

30 How could one chase a thousand,

And two put ten thousand to
    flight,
Unless their Rock had sold them,
And the LORD had surrendered
    them?
³¹ For their rock *is* not like our
    Rock,
Even our enemies themselves
    being judges.
³² For their vine *is* of the vine of
    Sodom
And of the fields of Gomorrah;
Their grapes *are* grapes of gall,
Their clusters *are* bitter.
³³ Their wine *is* the poison of
    serpents,
And the cruel venom of cobras.

³⁴ '*Is* this not laid up in store with
    Me,
Sealed up among My treasures?
³⁵ Vengeance is Mine, and
    recompense;
Their foot shall slip in *due* time;
For the day of their calamity *is* at
    hand,
And the things to come hasten
    upon them.'

³⁶ "For the LORD will judge His
    people
And have compassion on His
    servants,
When He sees that *their* power is
    gone,
And *there is* no one *remaining*,
    bond or free.
³⁷ He will say: 'Where *are* their gods,
The rock in which they sought
    refuge?
³⁸ Who ate the fat of their sacrifices,
And drank the wine of their drink
    offering?
Let them rise and help you,
And be your refuge.

³⁹ 'Now see that I, *even* I, *am* He,
And *there is* no God besides Me;
I kill and I make alive;
I wound and I heal;
Nor *is there any* who can deliver
    from My hand.
⁴⁰ For I raise My hand to heaven,
And say, "*As* I live forever,

⁴¹ If I whet My glittering sword,
And My hand takes hold on
    judgment,
I will render vengeance to My
    enemies,
And repay those who hate Me.
⁴² I will make My arrows drunk with
    blood,
And My sword shall devour flesh,
With the blood of the slain and
    the captives,
From the heads of the leaders of
    the enemy." '

⁴³ "Rejoice, O Gentiles, *with* His
    people;
For He will avenge the blood of
    His servants,
And render vengeance to His
    adversaries;
He will provide atonement for His
    land *and* His people."

⁴⁴ So Moses came with Joshua the son
of Nun and spoke all the words of this
song in the hearing of the people. ⁴⁵ Moses
finished speaking all these words to all
Israel, ⁴⁶ and he said to them: "Set your
hearts on all the words which I testify
among you today, which you shall command your children to be careful to
observe—all the words of this law. ⁴⁷ For
it *is* not a futile thing for you, because it *is*
your life, and by this word you shall prolong *your* days in the land which you cross
over the Jordan to possess."

⁴⁸ Then the LORD spoke to Moses that
very same day, saying: ⁴⁹ "Go up this
mountain of the Abarim, Mount Nebo,
which *is* in the land of Moab, across from
Jericho; view the land of Canaan, which
I give to the children of Israel as a possession; ⁵⁰ and die on the mountain which
you ascend, and be gathered to your
people, just as Aaron your brother died
on Mount Hor and was gathered to his
people; ⁵¹ because you trespassed against
Me among the children of Israel at the
waters of Meribah Kadesh, in the Wilderness of Zin, because you did not hallow
Me in the midst of the children of Israel.
⁵² Yet you shall see the land before *you*,
though you shall not go there, into the
land which I am giving to the children of
Israel."

∼ Psalm 40:6–12 ∼

6 Sacrifice and offering You did not
      desire;
   My ears You have opened.
   Burnt offering and sin offering You
      did not require.
7 Then I said, "Behold, I come;
   In the scroll of the book *it is* written
      of me.
8 I delight to do Your will, O my God,
   And Your law *is* within my heart."

9 I have proclaimed the good news of
      righteousness
   In the great assembly;
   Indeed, I do not restrain my lips,
   O LORD, You Yourself know.
10 I have not hidden Your righteousness
      within my heart;
   I have declared Your faithfulness and
      Your salvation;
   I have not concealed Your
      lovingkindness and Your truth
   From the great assembly.

11 Do not withhold Your tender
      mercies from me, O LORD;
   Let Your lovingkindness and Your
      truth continually preserve me.
12 For innumerable evils have
      surrounded me;
   My iniquities have overtaken me, so
      that I am not able to look up;
   They are more than the hairs of my
      head;
   Therefore my heart fails me.

∼ Proverbs 13:11, 12 ∼

11 Wealth *gained by* dishonesty will be
      diminished,
   But he who gathers by labor will
      increase.

12 Hope deferred makes the heart sick,
   But *when* the desire comes, *it is* a
      tree of life.

∼ Luke 7:31–50 ∼

And the Lord said, "To what then shall I
liken the men of this generation, and what
are they like? 32 They are like children sitting in the marketplace and calling to one
another, saying:

   'We played the flute for you,
      And you did not dance;
   We mourned to you,
      And you did not weep.'

33 For John the Baptist came neither eating bread nor drinking wine, and you say,
'He has a demon.' 34 The Son of Man
has come eating and drinking, and you
say, 'Look, a glutton and a winebibber,
a friend of tax collectors and sinners!'
35 But wisdom is justified by all her children."
   36 Then one of the Pharisees asked Him
to eat with him. And He went to the
Pharisee's house, and sat down to eat.
37 And behold, a woman in the city who
was a sinner, when she knew that *Jesus*
sat at the table in the Pharisee's house,
brought an alabaster flask of fragrant oil,
38 and stood at His feet behind *Him* weeping; and she began to wash His feet with
her tears, and wiped *them* with the hair
of her head; and she kissed His feet and
anointed *them* with the fragrant oil.
39 Now when the Pharisee who had invited Him saw *this,* he spoke to himself,
saying, "This Man, if He were a prophet,
would know who and what manner of
woman *this is* who is touching Him, for
she is a sinner."
   40 And Jesus answered and said to him,
"Simon, I have something to say to you."
   So he said, "Teacher, say it."
   41 "There was a certain creditor who
had two debtors. One owed five hundred
denarii, and the other fifty. 42 And when
they had nothing with which to repay, he
freely forgave them both. Tell Me, therefore, which of them will love him more?"
   43 Simon answered and said, "I suppose
the *one* whom he forgave more."
   And He said to him, "You have rightly
judged." 44 Then He turned to the woman
and said to Simon, "Do you see this
woman? I entered your house; you gave
Me no water for My feet, but she has
washed My feet with her tears and wiped
them with the hair of her head. 45 You gave
Me no kiss, but this woman has not ceased

to kiss My feet since the time I came in. [46] You did not anoint My head with oil, but this woman has anointed My feet with fragrant oil. [47] Therefore I say to you, her sins, *which are* many, are forgiven, for she loved much. But to whom little is forgiven, *the same* loves little."

[48] Then He said to her, "Your sins are forgiven."

[49] And those who sat at the table with Him began to say to themselves, "Who is this who even forgives sins?"

[50] Then He said to the woman, "Your faith has saved you. Go in peace."

READING 95 · APRIL 5

∼ DEUTERONOMY 33:1—34:12 ∼

Now this *is* the blessing with which Moses the man of God blessed the children of Israel before his death. [2] And he said:

"The LORD came from Sinai,
And dawned on them from Seir;
He shone forth from Mount Paran,
And He came with ten thousands
    of saints;
From His right hand
Came a fiery law for them.
[3] Yes, He loves the people;
All His saints *are* in Your hand;
They sit down at Your feet;
Everyone receives Your words.
[4] Moses commanded a law for us,
A heritage of the congregation of
    Jacob.
[5] And He was King in Jeshurun,
When the leaders of the people
    were gathered,
All the tribes of Israel together.

[6] "Let Reuben live, and not die,
Nor let his men be few."

[7] And this he said of Judah:

"Hear, LORD, the voice of Judah,
And bring him to his people;
Let his hands be sufficient for him,
And may You be a help against his
    enemies."

[8] And of Levi he said:

"*Let* Your Thummim and Your
    Urim *be* with Your holy one,
Whom You tested at Massah,
And with whom You contended at
    the waters of Meribah,

[9] Who says of his father and
    mother,
'I have not seen them';
Nor did he acknowledge his
    brothers,
Or know his own children;
For they have observed Your word
And kept Your covenant.
[10] They shall teach Jacob Your
    judgments,
And Israel Your law.
They shall put incense before You,
And a whole burnt sacrifice on
    Your altar.
[11] Bless his substance, LORD,
And accept the work of his hands;
Strike the loins of those who rise
    against him,
And of those who hate him, that
    they rise not again."

[12] Of Benjamin he said:

"The beloved of the LORD shall
    dwell in safety by Him,
Who shelters him all the day long;
And he shall dwell between His
    shoulders."

[13] And of Joseph he said:

"Blessed of the LORD *is* his land,
With the precious things of
    heaven, with the dew,
And the deep lying beneath,
[14] With the precious fruits of the sun,
With the precious produce of the
    months,
[15] With the best things of the ancient
    mountains,
With the precious things of the
    everlasting hills,

16 With the precious things of the
    earth and its fullness,
    And the favor of Him who dwelt
    in the bush.
    Let *the blessing* come 'on the head
    of Joseph,
    And on the crown of the head of
    him *who was* separate from his
    brothers.'
17 His glory *is like* a firstborn bull,
    And his horns *like* the horns of the
    wild ox;
    Together with them
    He shall push the peoples
    To the ends of the earth;
    They *are* the ten thousands of
    Ephraim,
    And they *are* the thousands of
    Manasseh."

18 And of Zebulun he said:

    "Rejoice, Zebulun, in your going
    out,
    And Issachar in your tents!
19 They shall call the peoples *to* the
    mountain;
    There they shall offer sacrifices of
    righteousness;
    For they shall partake *of* the
    abundance of the seas
    And *of* treasures hidden in the
    sand."

20 And of Gad he said:

    "Blessed *is* he who enlarges Gad;
    He dwells as a lion,
    And tears the arm and the crown
    of his head.
21 He provided the first *part* for
    himself,
    Because a lawgiver's portion was
    reserved there.
    He came *with* the heads of the
    people;
    He administered the justice of the
    LORD,
    And His judgments with
    Israel."

22 And of Dan he said:

    "Dan *is* a lion's whelp;
    He shall leap from Bashan."

23 And of Naphtali he said:

    "O Naphtali, satisfied with favor,
    And full of the blessing of the
    LORD,
    Possess the west and the south."

24 And of Asher he said:

    "Asher *is* most blessed of sons;
    Let him be favored by his
    brothers,
    And let him dip his foot in oil.
25 Your sandals *shall be* iron and
    bronze;
    As your days, *so shall* your
    strength *be.*

26 "*There is* no one like the God of
    Jeshurun,
    Who rides the heavens to help
    you,
    And in His excellency on the
    clouds.
27 The eternal God *is your* refuge,
    And underneath *are* the
    everlasting arms;
    He will thrust out the enemy from
    before you,
    And will say, 'Destroy!'
28 Then Israel shall dwell in safety,
    The fountain of Jacob alone,
    In a land of grain and new wine;
    His heavens shall also drop dew.
29 Happy *are* you, O Israel!
    Who *is* like you, a people saved by
    the LORD,
    The shield of your help
    And the sword of your majesty!
    Your enemies shall submit to you,
    And you shall tread down their
    high places."

34 Then Moses went up from the plains
of Moab to Mount Nebo, to the top of
Pisgah, which is across from Jericho. And
the LORD showed him all the land of
Gilead as far as Dan, 2 all Naphtali and
the land of Ephraim and Manasseh,
all the land of Judah as far as the Western
Sea, 3 the South, and the plain of the Valley of Jericho, the city of palm trees, as
far as Zoar. 4 Then the LORD said to him,
"This *is* the land of which I swore to give
Abraham, Isaac, and Jacob, saying, 'I will

Where to Go

Mary George, known to her friends as "the girl of prayer," tells of a time when she, her six sisters, and her brother were facing eviction. Mary's parents had died, and the owners of the house in which she and her siblings were living wanted to convert the home into an apartment house. The house itself was in dire need of repair. The roof leaked, the water heater was broken, and the ceilings were about to cave in. Mary wasn't at all sorry at the prospect of leaving the old house, but finding a house large enough for a family of eight, and more importantly, one they could afford, wasn't easy. They prayed and prayed, both individually and as a family.

> The eternal God is your refuge, and underneath are the everlasting arms; He will thrust out the enemy from before you, and will say, "Destroy!"
>
> *Deuteronomy 33:27*

Then, Mary felt led to ask about a house just a block away. She was told that a buyer was closing on the sale the next day. But later that same week, the owner phoned her to tell her that the buyer had backed out. The house was theirs. Unfortunately, it was in an equal state of disrepair to the house they were vacating. Mary recalled, "The next day we signed the lease, and word got around the neighborhood how God took care of the Georges. Immediately, neighbors and friends volunteered to help us clean and do repairs, and make the house livable."

When you think you have nowhere to turn, the best place to go is the throne room of Heaven.

give it to your descendants.' I have caused you to see *it* with your eyes, but you shall not cross over there."

⁵ So Moses the servant of the LORD died there in the land of Moab, according to the word of the LORD. ⁶ And He buried him in a valley in the land of Moab, opposite Beth Peor; but no one knows his grave to this day. ⁷ Moses *was* one hundred and twenty years old when he died. His eyes were not dim nor his natural vigor diminished. ⁸ And the children of Israel wept for Moses in the plains of Moab thirty days. So the days of weeping *and* mourning for Moses ended.

⁹ Now Joshua the son of Nun was full of the spirit of wisdom, for Moses had laid his hands on him; so the children of Israel heeded him, and did as the LORD had commanded Moses.

¹⁰ But since then there has not arisen in Israel a prophet like Moses, whom the LORD knew face to face, ¹¹ in all the signs and wonders which the LORD sent him to do in the land of Egypt, before Pharaoh, before all his servants, and in all his land, ¹² and by all that mighty power and all the great terror which Moses performed in the sight of all Israel.

∼ PSALM 40:13–17 ∼

¹³ Be pleased, O LORD, to deliver me;
    O LORD, make haste to help me!
¹⁴ Let them be ashamed and brought to
        mutual confusion
    Who seek to destroy my life;
    Let them be driven backward and
        brought to dishonor
    Who wish me evil.
¹⁵ Let them be confounded because of
        their shame,
    Who say to me, "Aha, aha!"

¹⁶ Let all those who seek You rejoice
        and be glad in You;
    Let such as love Your salvation say
        continually,
    "The LORD be magnified!"
¹⁷ But I *am* poor and needy;
    Yet the LORD thinks upon me.
    You *are* my help and my
        deliverer;
    Do not delay, O my God.

∼ PROVERBS 13:13, 14 ∼

¹³ He who despises the word will be
        destroyed,
    But he who fears the commandment
        will be rewarded.
¹⁴ The law of the wise *is* a fountain of
        life,
    To turn *one* away from the snares of
        death.

∼ LUKE 8:1–25 ∼

Now it came to pass, afterward, that He went through every city and village, preaching and bringing the glad tidings of the kingdom of God. And the twelve *were* with Him, ² and certain women who had been healed of evil spirits and infirmities—Mary called Magdalene, out of whom had come seven demons, ³ and Joanna the wife of Chuza, Herod's steward, and Susanna, and many others who provided for Him from their substance.

⁴ And when a great multitude had gathered, and they had come to Him from every city, He spoke by a parable: ⁵ "A sower went out to sow his seed. And as he sowed, some fell by the wayside; and it was trampled down, and the birds of the air devoured it. ⁶ Some fell on rock; and as soon as it sprang up, it withered away because it lacked moisture. ⁷ And some fell among thorns, and the thorns sprang up with it and choked it. ⁸ But others fell on good ground, sprang up, and yielded a crop a hundredfold." When He had said these things He cried, "He who has ears to hear, let him hear!"

⁹ Then His disciples asked Him, saying, "What does this parable mean?"

¹⁰ And He said, "To you it has been given to know the mysteries of the kingdom of God, but to the rest *it is given* in parables, that

'Seeing they may not see,
    And hearing they may not
        understand.'

¹¹ "Now the parable is this: The seed is the word of God. ¹² Those by the wayside are the ones who hear; then the devil comes and takes away the word out of

their hearts, lest they should believe and be saved. ¹³ But the ones on the rock *are those* who, when they hear, receive the word with joy; and these have no root, who believe for a while and in time of temptation fall away. ¹⁴ Now the ones *that* fell among thorns are those who, when they have heard, go out and are choked with cares, riches, and pleasures of life, and bring no fruit to maturity. ¹⁵ But the ones *that* fell on the good ground are those who, having heard the word with a noble and good heart, keep *it* and bear fruit with patience.

¹⁶ "No one, when he has lit a lamp, covers it with a vessel or puts *it* under a bed, but sets *it* on a lampstand, that those who enter may see the light. ¹⁷ For nothing is secret that will not be revealed, nor *anything* hidden that will not be known and come to light. ¹⁸ Therefore take heed how you hear. For whoever has, to him *more* will be given; and whoever does not have, even what he seems to have will be taken from him."

¹⁹ Then His mother and brothers came to Him, and could not approach Him because of the crowd. ²⁰ And it was told Him *by some,* who said, "Your mother and Your brothers are standing outside, desiring to see You."

²¹ But He answered and said to them, "My mother and My brothers are these who hear the word of God and do it."

²² Now it happened, on a certain day, that He got into a boat with His disciples. And He said to them, "Let us cross over to the other side of the lake." And they launched out. ²³ But as they sailed He fell asleep. And a windstorm came down on the lake, and they were filling *with water,* and were in jeopardy. ²⁴ And they came to Him and awoke Him, saying, "Master, Master, we are perishing!"

Then He arose and rebuked the wind and the raging of the water. And they ceased, and there was a calm. ²⁵ But He said to them, "Where is your faith?"

And they were afraid, and marveled, saying to one another, "Who can this be? For He commands even the winds and water, and they obey Him!"

READING 96 · APRIL 6

~ JOSHUA 1:1—2:24 ~

After the death of Moses the servant of the LORD, it came to pass that the LORD spoke to Joshua the son of Nun, Moses' assistant, saying: ² "Moses My servant is dead. Now therefore, arise, go over this Jordan, you and all this people, to the land which I am giving to them—the children of Israel. ³ Every place that the sole of your foot will tread upon I have given you, as I said to Moses. ⁴ From the wilderness and this Lebanon as far as the great river, the River Euphrates, all the land of the Hittites, and to the Great Sea toward the going down of the sun, shall be your territory. ⁵ No man shall *be able to* stand before you all the days of your life; as I was with Moses, *so* I will be with you. I will not leave you nor forsake you. ⁶ Be strong and of good courage, for to this people you shall divide as an inheritance the land which I swore to their fathers to give them. ⁷ Only be strong and

very courageous, that you may observe to do according to all the law which Moses My servant commanded you; do not turn from it to the right hand or to the left, that you may prosper wherever you go. ⁸ This Book of the Law shall not depart from your mouth, but you shall meditate in it day and night, that you may observe to do according to all that is written in it. For then you will make your way prosperous, and then you will have good success. ⁹ Have I not commanded you? Be strong and of good courage; do not be afraid, nor be dismayed, for the LORD your God *is* with you wherever you go."

¹⁰ Then Joshua commanded the officers of the people, saying, ¹¹ "Pass through the camp and command the people, saying, 'Prepare provisions for yourselves, for within three days you will cross over this Jordan, to go in to possess the land which

the LORD your God is giving you to possess.' "

¹² And to the Reubenites, the Gadites, and half the tribe of Manasseh Joshua spoke, saying, ¹³ "Remember the word which Moses the servant of the LORD commanded you, saying, 'The LORD your God is giving you rest and is giving you this land.' ¹⁴ Your wives, your little ones, and your livestock shall remain in the land which Moses gave you on this side of the Jordan. But you shall pass before your brethren armed, all your mighty men of valor, and help them, ¹⁵ until the LORD has given your brethren rest, as He *gave* you, and they also have taken possession of the land which the LORD your God is giving them. Then you shall return to the land of your possession and enjoy it, which Moses the LORD's servant gave you on this side of the Jordan toward the sunrise."

¹⁶ So they answered Joshua, saying, "All that you command us we will do, and wherever you send us we will go. ¹⁷ Just as we heeded Moses in all things, so we will heed you. Only the LORD your God be with you, as He was with Moses. ¹⁸ Whoever rebels against your command and does not heed your words, in all that you command him, shall be put to death. Only be strong and of good courage."

2 Now Joshua the son of Nun sent out two men from Acacia Grove to spy secretly, saying, "Go, view the land, especially Jericho."

So they went, and came to the house of a harlot named Rahab, and lodged there. ² And it was told the king of Jericho, saying, "Behold, men have come here tonight from the children of Israel to search out the country."

³ So the king of Jericho sent to Rahab, saying, "Bring out the men who have come to you, who have entered your house, for they have come to search out all the country."

⁴ Then the woman took the two men and hid them. So she said, "Yes, the men came to me, but I did not know where they *were* from. ⁵ And it happened as the gate was being shut, when it was dark, that the men went out. Where the men went I do not know; pursue them

quickly, for you may overtake them." ⁶(But she had brought them up to the roof and hidden them with the stalks of flax, which she had laid in order on the roof.) ⁷ Then the men pursued them by the road to the Jordan, to the fords. And as soon as those who pursued them had gone out, they shut the gate.

⁸ Now before they lay down, she came up to them on the roof, ⁹ and said to the men: "I know that the LORD has given you the land, that the terror of you has fallen on us, and that all the inhabitants of the land are fainthearted because of you. ¹⁰ For we have heard how the LORD dried up the water of the Red Sea for you when you came out of Egypt, and what you did to the two kings of the Amorites who *were* on the other side of the Jordan, Sihon and Og, whom you utterly destroyed. ¹¹ And as soon as we heard *these things,* our hearts melted; neither did there remain any more courage in anyone because of you, for the LORD your God, He *is* God in heaven above and on earth beneath. ¹² Now therefore, I beg you, swear to me by the LORD, since I have shown you kindness, that you also will show kindness to my father's house, and give me a true token, ¹³ and spare my father, my mother, my brothers, my sisters, and all that they have, and deliver our lives from death."

¹⁴ So the men answered her, "Our lives for yours, if none of you tell this business of ours. And it shall be, when the LORD has given us the land, that we will deal kindly and truly with you."

¹⁵ Then she let them down by a rope through the window, for her house *was* on the city wall; she dwelt on the wall. ¹⁶ And she said to them, "Get to the mountain, lest the pursuers meet you. Hide there three days, until the pursuers have returned. Afterward you may go your way."

¹⁷ So the men said to her: "We *will be* blameless of this oath of yours which you have made us swear, ¹⁸ unless, *when* we come into the land, you bind this line of scarlet cord in the window through which you let us down, and unless you bring your father, your mother, your brothers, and all your father's household to your own home. ¹⁹ So it shall be *that* whoever goes

Then What?

Early one morning Charles G. Finney, a young apprentice lawyer, was sitting in a small-town law office in the state of New York. He was all alone when he sensed the Lord speaking to him.

"Finney, what are you going to do when you finish your course?" He said, "Put out a shingle and practice law."

"Then what?" "Get rich," he replied.

"Then what?" "Retire," he said.

"Then what?" "Die."

"Then what?" And as he spoke his next words his voice trembled, "The judgment."

Finney immediately left the office and ran for the woods a half mile away. He prayed there all day and vowed that he would not leave until he had made peace with God. He had studied law for four years, but he emerged from the woods that evening with the high purpose of living to the glory of God and enjoying Him forever. God began to use him in a mighty way, not as a lawyer, but as a preacher. He brought thousands of people to a personal relationship with Jesus Christ over the next fifty years of his life.

Any career can bring glory to God, as long as you know you are working to further His kingdom, and not simply to build one of your own.

This Book of the Law shall not depart from your mouth, but you shall meditate in it day and night, that you may observe to do according to all that is written in it. For then you will make your way prosperous, and then you will have good success.

Joshua 1:8

outside the doors of your house into the street, his blood *shall be* on his own head, and we *will be* guiltless. And whoever is with you in the house, his blood *shall be* on our head if a hand is laid on him. ²⁰ And if you tell this business of ours, then we will be free from your oath which you made us swear."

²¹ Then she said, "According to your words, so *be* it." And she sent them away, and they departed. And she bound the scarlet cord in the window.

²² They departed and went to the mountain, and stayed there three days until the pursuers returned. The pursuers sought *them* all along the way, but did not find *them.* ²³ So the two men returned, descended from the mountain, and crossed over; and they came to Joshua the son of Nun, and told him all that had befallen them. ²⁴ And they said to Joshua, "Truly the LORD has delivered all the land into our hands, for indeed all the inhabitants of the country are fainthearted because of us."

~ PSALM 41:1–13 ~

¹ Blessed *is* he who considers the
    poor;
  The LORD will deliver him in time of
    trouble.
² The LORD will preserve him and
    keep him alive,
  And he will be blessed on the earth;
  You will not deliver him to the will
    of his enemies.
³ The LORD will strengthen him on his
    bed of illness;
  You will sustain him on his sickbed.

⁴ I said, "LORD, be merciful to me;
  Heal my soul, for I have sinned
    against You."
⁵ My enemies speak evil of me:
  "When will he die, and his name
    perish?"
⁶ And if he comes to see *me,* he speaks
    lies;
  His heart gathers iniquity to itself;
  When he goes out, he tells *it.*

⁷ All who hate me whisper together
    against me;
  Against me they devise my hurt.

⁸ "An evil disease," *they say,* "clings to
    him.
  And *now* that he lies down, he will
    rise up no more."
⁹ Even my own familiar friend in
    whom I trusted,
  Who ate my bread,
  Has lifted up *his* heel against me.

¹⁰ But You, O LORD, be merciful to me,
    and raise me up,
  That I may repay them.
¹¹ By this I know that You are well
    pleased with me,
  Because my enemy does not triumph
    over me.
¹² As for me, You uphold me in my
    integrity,
  And set me before Your face forever.

¹³ Blessed *be* the LORD God of Israel
  From everlasting to everlasting!
  Amen and Amen.

~ PROVERBS 13:15, 16 ~

¹⁵ Good understanding gains favor,
  But the way of the unfaithful *is* hard.
¹⁶ Every prudent *man* acts with
    knowledge,
  But a fool lays open *his* folly.

~ LUKE 8:26–56 ~

Then they sailed to the country of the Gadarenes, which is opposite Galilee. ²⁷ And when He stepped out on the land, there met Him a certain man from the city who had demons for a long time. And he wore no clothes, nor did he live in a house but in the tombs. ²⁸ When he saw Jesus, he cried out, fell down before Him, and with a loud voice said, "What have I to do with You, Jesus, Son of the Most High God? I beg You, do not torment me!" ²⁹ For He had commanded the unclean spirit to come out of the man. For it had often seized him, and he was kept under guard, bound with chains and shackles; and he broke the bonds and was driven by the demon into the wilderness. ³⁰ Jesus asked him, saying, "What is your name?"

And he said, "Legion," because many

demons had entered him. [31] And they begged Him that He would not command them to go out into the abyss.

[32] Now a herd of many swine was feeding there on the mountain. So they begged Him that He would permit them to enter them. And He permitted them. [33] Then the demons went out of the man and entered the swine, and the herd ran violently down the steep place into the lake and drowned.

[34] When those who fed *them* saw what had happened, they fled and told *it* in the city and in the country. [35] Then they went out to see what had happened, and came to Jesus, and found the man from whom the demons had departed, sitting at the feet of Jesus, clothed and in his right mind. And they were afraid. [36] They also who had seen *it* told them by what means he who had been demon-possessed was healed. [37] Then the whole multitude of the surrounding region of the Gadarenes asked Him to depart from them, for they were seized with great fear. And He got into the boat and returned.

[38] Now the man from whom the demons had departed begged Him that he might be with Him. But Jesus sent him away, saying, [39] "Return to your own house, and tell what great things God has done for you." And he went his way and proclaimed throughout the whole city what great things Jesus had done for him.

[40] So it was, when Jesus returned, that the multitude welcomed Him, for they were all waiting for Him. [41] And behold, there came a man named Jairus, and he was a ruler of the synagogue. And he fell down at Jesus' feet and begged Him to come to his house, [42] for he had an only daughter about twelve years of age, and she was dying.

But as He went, the multitudes thronged Him. [43] Now a woman, having a flow of blood for twelve years, who had spent all her livelihood on physicians and could not be healed by any, [44] came from behind and touched the border of His garment. And immediately her flow of blood stopped.

[45] And Jesus said, "Who touched Me?"

When all denied it, Peter and those with him said, "Master, the multitudes throng and press You, and You say, 'Who touched Me?'"

[46] But Jesus said, "Somebody touched Me, for I perceived power going out from Me." [47] Now when the woman saw that she was not hidden, she came trembling; and falling down before Him, she declared to Him in the presence of all the people the reason she had touched Him and how she was healed immediately.

[48] And He said to her, "Daughter, be of good cheer; your faith has made you well. Go in peace."

[49] While He was still speaking, someone came from the ruler of the synagogue's *house,* saying to him, "Your daughter is dead. Do not trouble the Teacher."

[50] But when Jesus heard *it,* He answered him, saying, "Do not be afraid; only believe, and she will be made well." [51] When He came into the house, He permitted no one to go in except Peter, James, and John, and the father and mother of the girl. [52] Now all wept and mourned for her; but He said, "Do not weep; she is not dead, but sleeping." [53] And they ridiculed Him, knowing that she was dead.

[54] But He put them all outside, took her by the hand and called, saying, "Little girl, arise." [55] Then her spirit returned, and she arose immediately. And He commanded that she be given *something* to eat. [56] And her parents were astonished, but He charged them to tell no one what had happened.

~ JOSHUA 3:1—4:24 ~

Then Joshua rose early in the morning; and they set out from Acacia Grove and came to the Jordan, he and all the children of Israel, and lodged there before they crossed over. [2] So it was, after three days, that the officers went through the camp; [3] and they commanded the people, saying, "When you see the ark of the covenant of the LORD your God, and the priests, the Levites, bearing it, then you shall set out from your place and go after it. ⁴ Yet there shall be a space between you and it, about two thousand cubits by measure. Do not come near it, that you may know the way by which you must go, for you have not passed *this* way before."

⁵ And Joshua said to the people, "Sanctify yourselves, for tomorrow the LORD will do wonders among you." ⁶ Then Joshua spoke to the priests, saying, "Take up the ark of the covenant and cross over before the people."

So they took up the ark of the covenant and went before the people.

⁷ And the LORD said to Joshua, "This day I will begin to exalt you in the sight of all Israel, that they may know that, as I was with Moses, *so* I will be with you. ⁸ You shall command the priests who bear the ark of the covenant, saying, 'When you have come to the edge of the water of the Jordan, you shall stand in the Jordan.' "

⁹ So Joshua said to the children of Israel, "Come here, and hear the words of the LORD your God." ¹⁰ And Joshua said, "By this you shall know that the living God *is* among you, and *that* He will without fail drive out from before you the Canaanites and the Hittites and the Hivites and the Perizzites and the Girgashites and the Amorites and the Jebusites: ¹¹ Behold, the ark of the covenant of the Lord of all the earth is crossing over before you into the Jordan. ¹² Now therefore, take for yourselves twelve men from the tribes of Israel, one man from every tribe. ¹³ And it shall come to pass, as soon as the soles of the feet of the priests who bear the ark of the LORD, the Lord of all the earth, shall rest in the waters of the Jordan, *that* the waters of the Jordan shall be cut off, the waters that come down from upstream, and they shall stand as a heap."

¹⁴ So it was, when the people set out from their camp to cross over the Jordan, with the priests bearing the ark of the covenant before the people, ¹⁵ and as those who bore the ark came to the Jordan, and the feet of the priests who bore the ark dipped in the edge of the water (for the Jordan overflows all its banks during the whole time of harvest), ¹⁶ that the waters which came down from upstream stood *still, and* rose in a heap very far away at Adam, the city that *is* beside Zaretan. So the waters that went down into the Sea of the Arabah, the Salt Sea, failed, *and* were cut off; and the people crossed over opposite Jericho. ¹⁷ Then the priests who bore the ark of the covenant of the LORD stood firm on dry ground in the midst of the Jordan; and all Israel crossed over on dry ground, until all the people had crossed completely over the Jordan.

4 And it came to pass, when all the people had completely crossed over the Jordan, that the LORD spoke to Joshua, saying: ² "Take for yourselves twelve men from the people, one man from every tribe, ³ and command them, saying, 'Take for yourselves twelve stones from here, out of the midst of the Jordan, from the place where the priests' feet stood firm. You shall carry them over with you and leave them in the lodging place where you lodge tonight.' "

⁴ Then Joshua called the twelve men whom he had appointed from the children of Israel, one man from every tribe; ⁵ and Joshua said to them: "Cross over before the ark of the LORD your God into the midst of the Jordan, and each one of you take up a stone on his shoulder, according to the number of the tribes of the children of Israel, ⁶ that this may be a sign among you when your children ask in time to come, saying, 'What do these stones *mean* to you?' ⁷ Then you shall answer them that the waters of the Jordan were cut off before the ark of the covenant of the LORD; when it crossed over the Jordan, the waters of the Jordan were cut off. And these stones shall be for a memorial to the children of Israel forever."

⁸ And the children of Israel did so, just as Joshua commanded, and took up twelve stones from the midst of the Jordan, as the LORD had spoken to Joshua, according to the number of the tribes of the children of Israel, and carried them over with them to the place where they lodged, and laid them down there. ⁹ Then Joshua set up twelve stones in the midst of the Jordan, in the place where the feet

Perfect Timing

Carolyn, a preacher's wife, had just found evidence that her daughter was involved in activities that Carolyn knew were not only sinful, but potentially deadly. Because of her position, however, Carolyn felt that to tell anyone this family secret might expose her husband and his ministry to ridicule or shame. To keep the secret was painful — she needed a friend. In near desperation, she cried out to God, "I've got to talk to *someone*! Can't You send me somebody I can trust?"

Almost before she had finished praying, the doorbell rang. When she opened the door, there stood another preacher's wife. She was new to the city and had come to make her acquaintance. Almost immediately the women developed a rapport as they discussed their lives, their many moves, and the difficulties of raising children.

Carolyn discovered her newfound friend had also gone through the struggle of raising a rebellious teenager. She poured out her problem to her new friend, who offered, "Would you mind if I prayed for you before I go?" Within minutes, Carolyn felt a profound peace fill her heart. She realized God had sent her help the very *minute* she needed it. In that, she felt confident she could trust Him to begin a healing in her daughter's heart, and in her own heart, just as quickly!

Hope in God is never misplaced. He always comes through. The very minute we pray the answer is sent — and sometimes it arrives before we even finish.

> Why are you cast down, O my soul? And why are you disquieted within me? Hope in God, for I shall yet praise Him for the help of His countenance.
>
> *Psalm 42:5*

----◦◦◦----

of the priests who bore the ark of the covenant stood; and they are there to this day.

[10] So the priests who bore the ark stood in the midst of the Jordan until everything was finished that the LORD had commanded Joshua to speak to the people, according to all that Moses had commanded Joshua; and the people hurried and crossed over. [11] Then it came to pass, when all the people had completely crossed over, that the ark of the LORD and the priests crossed over in the presence of the people. [12] And the men of Reuben, the men of Gad, and half the tribe of Manasseh crossed over armed before the children of Israel, as Moses had spoken to them. [13] About forty thousand prepared for war crossed over before the LORD for battle, to the plains of Jericho. [14] On that day the LORD exalted Joshua in the sight of all Israel; and they feared him, as they had feared Moses, all the days of his life.

[15] Then the LORD spoke to Joshua, saying, [16] "Command the priests who bear the ark of the Testimony to come up from the Jordan." [17] Joshua therefore commanded the priests, saying, "Come up from the Jordan." [18] And it came to pass, when the priests who bore the ark of the covenant of the LORD had come from the midst of the Jordan, *and* the soles of the priests' feet touched the dry land, that the waters of the Jordan returned to their place and overflowed all its banks as before.

[19] Now the people came up from the Jordan on the tenth *day* of the first month, and they camped in Gilgal on the east border of Jericho. [20] And those twelve stones which they took out of the Jordan, Joshua set up in Gilgal. [21] Then he spoke to the children of Israel, saying: "When your children ask their fathers in time to come, saying, 'What *are* these stones?' [22] then you shall let your children know, saying, 'Israel crossed over this Jordan on dry land'; [23] for the LORD your God dried up the waters of the Jordan before you until you had crossed over, as the LORD your God did to the Red Sea, which He dried up before us until we had crossed over, [24] that all the peoples of the earth may know the hand of the LORD, that it

is mighty, that you may fear the LORD your God forever."

~ PSALM 42:1–5 ~

[1] As the deer pants for the water brooks,
So pants my soul for You, O God.
[2] My soul thirsts for God, for the living God.
When shall I come and appear before God?
[3] My tears have been my food day and night,
While they continually say to me, "Where *is* your God?"

[4] When I remember these *things,*
I pour out my soul within me.
For I used to go with the multitude;
I went with them to the house of God,
With the voice of joy and praise,
With a multitude that kept a pilgrim feast.

[5] Why are you cast down, O my soul?
And *why* are you disquieted within me?
Hope in God, for I shall yet praise Him
For the help of His countenance.

~ PROVERBS 13:17, 18 ~

[17] A wicked messenger falls into trouble,
But a faithful ambassador *brings* health.

[18] Poverty and shame *will come* to him who disdains correction,
But he who regards a rebuke will be honored.

~ LUKE 9:1–17 ~

Then He called His twelve disciples together and gave them power and authority over all demons, and to cure diseases. [2] He sent them to preach the kingdom of God and to heal the sick. [3] And He said to them, "Take nothing for the journey, neither staffs nor bag nor bread nor money; and do not have two tunics apiece.

⁴ "Whatever house you enter, stay there, and from there depart. ⁵ And whoever will not receive you, when you go out of that city, shake off the very dust from your feet as a testimony against them."

⁶ So they departed and went through the towns, preaching the gospel and healing everywhere.

⁷ Now Herod the tetrarch heard of all that was done by Him; and he was perplexed, because it was said by some that John had risen from the dead, ⁸ and by some that Elijah had appeared, and by others that one of the old prophets had risen again. ⁹ Herod said, "John I have beheaded, but who is this of whom I hear such things?" So he sought to see Him.

¹⁰ And the apostles, when they had returned, told Him all that they had done. Then He took them and went aside privately into a deserted place belonging to the city called Bethsaida. ¹¹ But when the multitudes knew *it*, they followed Him;

and He received them and spoke to them about the kingdom of God, and healed those who had need of healing. ¹² When the day began to wear away, the twelve came and said to Him, "Send the multitude away, that they may go into the surrounding towns and country, and lodge and get provisions; for we are in a deserted place here."

¹³ But He said to them, "You give them something to eat."

And they said, "We have no more than five loaves and two fish, unless we go and buy food for all these people." ¹⁴ For there were about five thousand men.

Then He said to His disciples, "Make them sit down in groups of fifty." ¹⁵ And they did so, and made them all sit down. ¹⁶ Then He took the five loaves and the two fish, and looking up to heaven, He blessed and broke *them*, and gave *them* to the disciples to set before the multitude. ¹⁷ So they all ate and were filled, and twelve baskets of the leftover fragments were taken up by them.

～ JOSHUA 5:1—6:27 ～

S o it was, when all the kings of the Amorites who *were* on the west side of the Jordan, and all the kings of the Canaanites who *were* by the sea, heard that the LORD had dried up the waters of the Jordan from before the children of Israel until we had crossed over, that their heart melted; and there was no spirit in them any longer because of the children of Israel.

² At that time the LORD said to Joshua, "Make flint knives for yourself, and circumcise the sons of Israel again the second time." ³ So Joshua made flint knives for himself, and circumcised the sons of Israel at the hill of the foreskins. ⁴ And this *is* the reason why Joshua circumcised them: All the people who came out of Egypt *who were* males, all the men of war, had died in the wilderness on the way, after they had come out of Egypt. ⁵ For all the people who came out had been circumcised, but all the people born in the

wilderness, on the way as they came out of Egypt, had not been circumcised. ⁶ For the children of Israel walked forty years in the wilderness, till all the people *who were* men of war, who came out of Egypt, were consumed, because they did not obey the voice of the LORD—to whom the LORD swore that He would not show them the land which the LORD had sworn to their fathers that He would give us, "a land flowing with milk and honey." ⁷ Then Joshua circumcised their sons *whom* He raised up in their place; for they were uncircumcised, because they had not been circumcised on the way.

⁸ So it was, when they had finished circumcising all the people, that they stayed in their places in the camp till they were healed. ⁹ Then the LORD said to Joshua, "This day I have rolled away the reproach of Egypt from you." Therefore the name of the place is called Gilgal to this day.

[10] Now the children of Israel camped in Gilgal, and kept the Passover on the fourteenth day of the month at twilight on the plains of Jericho. [11] And they ate of the produce of the land on the day after the Passover, unleavened bread and parched grain, on the very same day. [12] Then the manna ceased on the day after they had eaten the produce of the land; and the children of Israel no longer had manna, but they ate the food of the land of Canaan that year.

[13] And it came to pass, when Joshua was by Jericho, that he lifted his eyes and looked, and behold, a Man stood opposite him with His sword drawn in His hand. And Joshua went to Him and said to Him, "*Are* You for us or for our adversaries?"

[14] So He said, "No, but *as* Commander of the army of the LORD I have now come."

And Joshua fell on his face to the earth and worshiped, and said to Him, "What does my Lord say to His servant?"

[15] Then the Commander of the LORD's army said to Joshua, "Take your sandal off your foot, for the place where you stand *is* holy." And Joshua did so.

6 Now Jericho was securely shut up because of the children of Israel; none went out, and none came in. [2] And the LORD said to Joshua: "See! I have given Jericho into your hand, its king, *and* the mighty men of valor. [3] You shall march around the city, all *you* men of war; you shall go all around the city once. This you shall do six days. [4] And seven priests shall bear seven trumpets of rams' horns before the ark. But the seventh day you shall march around the city seven times, and the priests shall blow the trumpets. [5] It shall come to pass, when they make a long *blast* with the ram's horn, *and* when you hear the sound of the trumpet, that all the people shall shout with a great shout; then the wall of the city will fall down flat. And the people shall go up every man straight before him."

[6] Then Joshua the son of Nun called the priests and said to them, "Take up the ark of the covenant, and let seven priests bear seven trumpets of rams' horns before the ark of the LORD." [7] And he said to the people, "Proceed, and march around the city, and let him who is armed advance before the ark of the LORD."

[8] So it was, when Joshua had spoken to the people, that the seven priests bearing the seven trumpets of rams' horns before the LORD advanced and blew the trumpets, and the ark of the covenant of the LORD followed them. [9] The armed men went before the priests who blew the trumpets, and the rear guard came after the ark, while *the priests* continued blowing the trumpets. [10] Now Joshua had commanded the people, saying, "You shall not shout or make any noise with your voice, nor shall a word proceed out of your mouth, until the day I say to you, 'Shout!' Then you shall shout." [11] So he had the ark of the LORD circle the city, going around *it* once. Then they came into the camp and lodged in the camp.

[12] And Joshua rose early in the morning, and the priests took up the ark of the LORD. [13] Then seven priests bearing seven trumpets of rams' horns before the ark of the LORD went on continually and blew with the trumpets. And the armed men went before them. But the rear guard came after the ark of the LORD, while *the priests* continued blowing the trumpets. [14] And the second day they marched around the city once and returned to the camp. So they did six days.

[15] But it came to pass on the seventh day that they rose early, about the dawning of the day, and marched around the city seven times in the same manner. On that day only they marched around the city seven times. [16] And the seventh time it happened, when the priests blew the trumpets, that Joshua said to the people: "Shout, for the LORD has given you the city! [17] Now the city shall be doomed by the LORD to destruction, it and all who *are* in it. Only Rahab the harlot shall live, she and all who *are* with her in the house, because she hid the messengers that we sent. [18] And you, by all means abstain from the accursed things, lest you become accursed when you take of the accursed things, and make the camp of Israel a curse, and trouble it. [19] But all the silver and gold, and vessels of bronze and iron, *are* consecrated to the LORD; they shall come into the treasury of the LORD."

The Loudest Message

Dorothy Canfield Fisher has written a poignant story about a physically powerful, but dimwitted farmhand named Lem who lived in a Vermont valley. His mother resented him from the day he was born. She often ridiculed him with harsh and demeaning words. Even so, the boy served her faithfully until she died.

Lem was the brunt of many village jokes. But then, he came upon a huge dog killing some farmer's sheep one night. Using his bare hands as his only weapon, he strangled the dog to death. When morning came, the villagers discovered the dog was really a giant timber wolf. Lem quickly earned the villagers' silent admiration.

Later, an unwed village girl falsely accused Lem of being the father of her baby. Even though he was innocent, he married the girl so the baby would have a father. Unfortunately, the mother died within a year, so Lem raised the little girl by himself. After she was grown and married, her own baby became desperately ill and Lem sold all his sheep to pay for the baby's medical care.

Confronted with meanness, misunderstanding, and loneliness all his life, Lem had no recourse in professing the true nature of his own life except to live it out in serving others. And that he did!

The way you live your life is the loudest message you will ever speak.

> Then He said to them all, "If anyone desires to come after Me, let him deny himself, and take up his cross daily, and follow Me."
>
> *Luke 9:23*

²⁰ So the people shouted when *the priests* blew the trumpets. And it happened when the people heard the sound of the trumpet, and the people shouted with a great shout, that the wall fell down flat. Then the people went up into the city, every man straight before him, and they took the city. ²¹ And they utterly destroyed all that *was* in the city, both man and woman, young and old, ox and sheep and donkey, with the edge of the sword. ²² But Joshua had said to the two men who had spied out the country, "Go into the harlot's house, and from there bring out the woman and all that she has, as you swore to her." ²³ And the young men who had been spies went in and brought out Rahab, her father, her mother, her brothers, and all that she had. So they brought out all her relatives and left them outside the camp of Israel. ²⁴ But they burned the city and all that *was* in it with fire. Only the silver and gold, and the vessels of bronze and iron, they put into the treasury of the house of the LORD. ²⁵ And Joshua spared Rahab the harlot, her father's household, and all that she had. So she dwells in Israel to this day, because she hid the messengers whom Joshua sent to spy out Jericho.

²⁶ Then Joshua charged *them* at that time, saying, "Cursed *be* the man before the LORD who rises up and builds this city Jericho; he shall lay its foundation with his firstborn, and with his youngest he shall set up its gates."

²⁷ So the LORD was with Joshua, and his fame spread throughout all the country.

~ PSALM 42:6–11 ~

⁶ O my God, my soul is cast down within me;
  Therefore I will remember You from the land of the Jordan,
  And from the heights of Hermon, From the Hill Mizar.
⁷ Deep calls unto deep at the noise of Your waterfalls;
  All Your waves and billows have gone over me.
⁸ The LORD will command His lovingkindness in the daytime,

And in the night His song *shall be* with me—
  A prayer to the God of my life.

⁹ I will say to God my Rock, "Why have You forgotten me?
  Why do I go mourning because of the oppression of the enemy?"
¹⁰ *As* with a breaking of my bones, My enemies reproach me,
  While they say to me all day long, "Where *is* your God?"

¹¹ Why are you cast down, O my soul? And why are you disquieted within me?
  Hope in God;
  For I shall yet praise Him,
  The help of my countenance and my God.

~ PROVERBS 13:19–21 ~

¹⁹ A desire accomplished is sweet to the soul,
  But *it is* an abomination to fools to depart from evil.

²⁰ He who walks with wise *men* will be wise,
  But the companion of fools will be destroyed.

²¹ Evil pursues sinners,
  But to the righteous, good shall be repaid.

~ LUKE 9:18–36 ~

And it happened, as He was alone praying, *that* His disciples joined Him, and He asked them, saying, "Who do the crowds say that I am?"

¹⁹ So they answered and said, "John the Baptist, but some *say* Elijah; and others *say* that one of the old prophets has risen again."

²⁰ He said to them, "But who do you say that I am?"

Peter answered and said, "The Christ of God."

²¹ And He strictly warned and commanded them to tell this to no one, ²² saying, "The Son of Man must suffer many things, and be rejected by the elders

and chief priests and scribes, and be killed, and be raised the third day."

²³ Then He said to *them* all, "If anyone desires to come after Me, let him deny himself, and take up his cross daily, and follow Me. ²⁴ For whoever desires to save his life will lose it, but whoever loses his life for My sake will save it. ²⁵ For what profit is it to a man if he gains the whole world, and is himself destroyed or lost? ²⁶ For whoever is ashamed of Me and My words, of him the Son of Man will be ashamed when He comes in His *own* glory, and *in His* Father's, and of the holy angels. ²⁷ But I tell you truly, there are some standing here who shall not taste death till they see the kingdom of God."

²⁸ Now it came to pass, about eight days after these sayings, that He took Peter, John, and James and went up on the mountain to pray. ²⁹ As He prayed, the appearance of His face was altered, and His robe *became* white *and* glisten-

ing. ³⁰ And behold, two men talked with Him, who were Moses and Elijah, ³¹ who appeared in glory and spoke of His decease which He was about to accomplish at Jerusalem. ³² But Peter and those with him were heavy with sleep; and when they were fully awake, they saw His glory and the two men who stood with Him. ³³ Then it happened, as they were parting from Him, *that* Peter said to Jesus, "Master, it is good for us to be here; and let us make three tabernacles: one for You, one for Moses, and one for Elijah"—not knowing what he said.

³⁴ While he was saying this, a cloud came and overshadowed them; and they were fearful as they entered the cloud. ³⁵ And a voice came out of the cloud, saying, "This is My beloved Son. Hear Him!" ³⁶ When the voice had ceased, Jesus was found alone. But they kept quiet, and told no one in those days any of the things they had seen.

∼ JOSHUA 7:1—8:35 ∼

But the children of Israel committed a trespass regarding the accursed things, for Achan the son of Carmi, the son of Zabdi, the son of Zerah, of the tribe of Judah, took of the accursed things; so the anger of the LORD burned against the children of Israel.

² Now Joshua sent men from Jericho to Ai, which *is* beside Beth Aven, on the east side of Bethel, and spoke to them, saying, "Go up and spy out the country." So the men went up and spied out Ai. ³ And they returned to Joshua and said to him, "Do not let all the people go up, but let about two or three thousand men go up and attack Ai. Do not weary all the people there, for *the people of Ai are* few." ⁴ So about three thousand men went up there from the people, but they fled before the men of Ai. ⁵ And the men of Ai struck down about thirty-six men, for they chased them *from* before the gate as far as Shebarim, and struck them down on the descent; therefore the hearts of the people melted and became like water.

⁶ Then Joshua tore his clothes, and fell

to the earth on his face before the ark of the LORD until evening, he and the elders of Israel; and they put dust on their heads. ⁷ And Joshua said, "Alas, Lord GOD, why have You brought this people over the Jordan at all—to deliver us into the hand of the Amorites, to destroy us? Oh, that we had been content, and dwelt on the other side of the Jordan! ⁸ O Lord, what shall I say when Israel turns its back before its enemies? ⁹ For the Canaanites and all the inhabitants of the land will hear *it*, and surround us, and cut off our name from the earth. Then what will You do for Your great name?"

¹⁰ So the LORD said to Joshua: "Get up! Why do you lie thus on your face? ¹¹ Israel has sinned, and they have also transgressed My covenant which I commanded them. For they have even taken some of the accursed things, and have both stolen and deceived; and they have also put *it* among their own stuff. ¹² Therefore the children of Israel could not stand before their enemies, *but* turned *their* backs before their enemies, because they have become

doomed to destruction. Neither will I be with you anymore, unless you destroy the accursed from among you. [13] Get up, sanctify the people, and say, 'Sanctify yourselves for tomorrow, because thus says the LORD God of Israel: "*There is* an accursed thing in your midst, O Israel; you cannot stand before your enemies until you take away the accursed thing from among you." [14] In the morning therefore you shall be brought according to your tribes. And it shall be *that* the tribe which the LORD takes shall come according to families; and the family which the LORD takes shall come by households; and the household which the LORD takes shall come man by man. [15] Then it shall be *that* he who is taken with the accursed thing shall be burned with fire, he and all that he has, because he has transgressed the covenant of the LORD, and because he has done a disgraceful thing in Israel.' "

[16] So Joshua rose early in the morning and brought Israel by their tribes, and the tribe of Judah was taken. [17] He brought the clan of Judah, and he took the family of the Zarhites; and he brought the family of the Zarhites man by man, and Zabdi was taken. [18] Then he brought his household man by man, and Achan the son of Carmi, the son of Zabdi, the son of Zerah, of the tribe of Judah, was taken.

[19] Now Joshua said to Achan, "My son, I beg you, give glory to the LORD God of Israel, and make confession to Him, and tell me now what you have done; do not hide *it* from me."

[20] And Achan answered Joshua and said, "Indeed I have sinned against the LORD God of Israel, and this is what I have done: [21] When I saw among the spoils a beautiful Babylonian garment, two hundred shekels of silver, and a wedge of gold weighing fifty shekels, I coveted them and took them. And there they are, hidden in the earth in the midst of my tent, with the silver under it."

[22] So Joshua sent messengers, and they ran to the tent; and there it was, hidden in his tent, with the silver under it. [23] And they took them from the midst of the tent, brought them to Joshua and to all the children of Israel, and laid them out before the LORD. [24] Then Joshua, and all Israel with him, took Achan the son of Zerah, the silver, the garment, the wedge of gold, his sons, his daughters, his oxen, his donkeys, his sheep, his tent, and all that he had, and they brought them to the Valley of Achor. [25] And Joshua said, "Why have you troubled us? The LORD will trouble you this day." So all Israel stoned him with stones; and they burned them with fire after they had stoned them with stones.

[26] Then they raised over him a great heap of stones, still there to this day. So the LORD turned from the fierceness of His anger. Therefore the name of that place has been called the Valley of Achor to this day.

8 Now the LORD said to Joshua: "Do not be afraid, nor be dismayed; take all the people of war with you, and arise, go up to Ai. See, I have given into your hand the king of Ai, his people, his city, and his land. [2] And you shall do to Ai and its king as you did to Jericho and its king. Only its spoil and its cattle you shall take as booty for yourselves. Lay an ambush for the city behind it."

[3] So Joshua arose, and all the people of war, to go up against Ai; and Joshua chose thirty thousand mighty men of valor and sent them away by night. [4] And he commanded them, saying: "Behold, you shall lie in ambush against the city, behind the city. Do not go very far from the city, but all of you be ready. [5] Then I and all the people who *are* with me will approach the city; and it will come about, when they come out against us as at the first, that we shall flee before them. [6] For they will come out after us till we have drawn them from the city, for they will say, '*They are* fleeing before us as at the first.' Therefore we will flee before them. [7] Then you shall rise from the ambush and seize the city, for the LORD your God will deliver it into your hand. [8] And it will be, when you have taken the city, *that* you shall set the city on fire. According to the commandment of the LORD you shall do. See, I have commanded you."

[9] Joshua therefore sent them out; and they went to lie in ambush, and stayed between Bethel and Ai, on the west side of Ai; but Joshua lodged that night among the people. [10] Then Joshua rose up early

A Good Name

The first major movie star to wear a uniform in World War II was Jimmy Stewart. Unlike so many other prominent people who sought excuses not to serve, Jimmy willingly accepted the draft and tried to get into the Army Air Corps, since he already had a pilot's license. The corps, however, had a strict weight requirement — for Jimmy's height, a minimum of 153 pounds. He weighed 143. When he suggested that they forget to weigh him, the officer responded, "That would be highly irregular." Jimmy replied, "Wars are highly irregular, too." Without weighing in, Jimmy won his new role, one in which he often prayed, not for himself, but that he "wouldn't make a mistake."

Over the course of the War, Stewart worked his way up from buck private to full-fledged pilot, and completed twenty-five missions over enemy territory, many of them as command pilot of a B-24 bomber wing. By the time he returned to Hollywood, he was a full colonel with the Air Medal, Croix de Guerre, Distinguished Flying Cross, and seven battle stars. He remained in the Air Force Reserve and was promoted to brigadier general in 1959. He once said, "There's a tremendous difference between a warmonger and a patriot."

Although he was a general, Jimmy Stewart was better known as "the nice guy." When we are more concerned with our character than our reputation, we will leave a good name for our children and our children's children.

> A good man leaves an inheritance to his children's children, but the wealth of the sinner is stored up for the righteous.
>
> *Proverbs 13:22*

in the morning and mustered the people, and went up, he and the elders of Israel, before the people to Ai. [11] And all the people of war who *were* with him went up and drew near; and they came before the city and camped on the north side of Ai. Now a valley *lay* between them and Ai. [12] So he took about five thousand men and set them in ambush between Bethel and Ai, on the west side of the city. [13] And when they had set the people, all the army that *was* on the north of the city, and its rear guard on the west of the city, Joshua went that night into the midst of the valley.

[14] Now it happened, when the king of Ai saw *it,* that the men of the city hurried and rose early and went out against Israel to battle, he and all his people, at an appointed place before the plain. But he did not know that *there was* an ambush against him behind the city. [15] And Joshua and all Israel made as if they were beaten before them, and fled by the way of the wilderness. [16] So all the people who *were* in Ai were called together to pursue them. And they pursued Joshua and were drawn away from the city. [17] There was not a man left in Ai or Bethel who did not go out after Israel. So they left the city open and pursued Israel.

[18] Then the LORD said to Joshua, "Stretch out the spear that *is* in your hand toward Ai, for I will give it into your hand." And Joshua stretched out the spear that *was* in his hand toward the city. [19] So *those in* ambush arose quickly out of their place; they ran as soon as he had stretched out his hand, and they entered the city and took it, and hurried to set the city on fire. [20] And when the men of Ai looked behind them, they saw, and behold, the smoke of the city ascended to heaven. So they had no power to flee this way or that way, and the people who had fled to the wilderness turned back on the pursuers. [21] Now when Joshua and all Israel saw that the ambush had taken the city and that the smoke of the city ascended, they turned back and struck down the men of Ai. [22] Then the others came out of the city against them; so they were *caught* in the midst of Israel, some on this side and some on that side. And they struck them down, so that they let none of them

remain or escape. [23] But the king of Ai they took alive, and brought him to Joshua.

[24] And it came to pass when Israel had made an end of slaying all the inhabitants of Ai in the field, in the wilderness where they pursued them, and when they all had fallen by the edge of the sword until they were consumed, that all the Israelites returned to Ai and struck it with the edge of the sword. [25] So it was *that* all who fell that day, both men and women, *were* twelve thousand—all the people of Ai. [26] For Joshua did not draw back his hand, with which he stretched out the spear, until he had utterly destroyed all the inhabitants of Ai. [27] Only the livestock and the spoil of that city Israel took as booty for themselves, according to the word of the LORD which He had commanded Joshua. [28] So Joshua burned Ai and made it a heap forever, a desolation to this day. [29] And the king of Ai he hanged on a tree until evening. And as soon as the sun was down, Joshua commanded that they should take his corpse down from the tree, cast it at the entrance of the gate of the city, and raise over it a great heap of stones *that remains* to this day.

[30] Now Joshua built an altar to the LORD God of Israel in Mount Ebal, [31] as Moses the servant of the LORD had commanded the children of Israel, as it is written in the Book of the Law of Moses: "an altar of whole stones over which no man has wielded an iron *tool."* And they offered on it burnt offerings to the LORD, and sacrificed peace offerings. [32] And there, in the presence of the children of Israel, he wrote on the stones a copy of the law of Moses, which he had written. [33] Then all Israel, with their elders and officers and judges, stood on either side of the ark before the priests, the Levites, who bore the ark of the covenant of the LORD, the stranger as well as he who was born among them. Half of them *were* in front of Mount Gerizim and half of them in front of Mount Ebal, as Moses the servant of the LORD had commanded before, that they should bless the people of Israel. [34] And afterward he read all the words of the law, the blessings and the cursings, according to all that is written in the Book of the Law. [35] There was not a word of all that Moses had commanded which Joshua

did not read before all the assembly of
Israel, with the women, the little ones, and
the strangers who were living among
them.

~ PSALM 43:1–5 ~

1   Vindicate me, O God,
    And plead my cause against an
        ungodly nation;
    Oh, deliver me from the deceitful
        and unjust man!
2   For You *are* the God of my strength;
    Why do You cast me off?
    Why do I go mourning because of
        the oppression of the enemy?

3   Oh, send out Your light and Your
        truth!
    Let them lead me;
    Let them bring me to Your holy hill
    And to Your tabernacle.
4   Then I will go to the altar of God,
    To God my exceeding joy;
    And on the harp I will praise You,
    O God, my God.

5   Why are you cast down, O my soul?
    And why are you disquieted within
        me?
    Hope in God;
    For I shall yet praise Him,
    The help of my countenance and my
        God.

~ PROVERBS 13:22, 23 ~

22 A good *man* leaves an inheritance to
        his children's children,
    But the wealth of the sinner is stored
        up for the righteous.

23 Much food *is in* the fallow *ground* of
        the poor,
    And for lack of justice there is waste.

~ LUKE 9:37–62 ~

Now it happened on the next day, when
they had come down from the mountain,
that a great multitude met Him. 38 Suddenly a man from the multitude cried out,
saying, "Teacher, I implore You, look on
my son, for he is my only child. 39 And
behold, a spirit seizes him, and he sud-

denly cries out; it convulses him so that
he foams *at the mouth;* and it departs from
him with great difficulty, bruising him.
40 So I implored Your disciples to cast it
out, but they could not."
41 Then Jesus answered and said, "O
faithless and perverse generation, how
long shall I be with you and bear with
you? Bring your son here." 42 And as he
was still coming, the demon threw him
down and convulsed *him.* Then Jesus rebuked the unclean spirit, healed the child,
and gave him back to his father.
43 And they were all amazed at the majesty of God.
But while everyone marveled at all the
things which Jesus did, He said to His
disciples, 44 "Let these words sink down
into your ears, for the Son of Man is about
to be betrayed into the hands of men."
45 But they did not understand this saying, and it was hidden from them so that
they did not perceive it; and they were
afraid to ask Him about this saying.
46 Then a dispute arose among them as
to which of them would be greatest. 47 And
Jesus, perceiving the thought of their
heart, took a little child and set him by
Him, 48 and said to them, "Whoever
receives this little child in My name receives Me; and whoever receives Me
receives Him who sent Me. For he who is
least among you all will be great."
49 Now John answered and said, "Master, we saw someone casting out demons
in Your name, and we forbade him because he does not follow with us."
50 But Jesus said to him, "Do not forbid *him,* for he who is not against us is on
our side."
51 Now it came to pass, when the time
had come for Him to be received up, that
He steadfastly set His face to go to Jerusalem, 52 and sent messengers before His
face. And as they went, they entered a village of the Samaritans, to prepare for
Him. 53 But they did not receive Him,
because His face was *set* for the journey
to Jerusalem. 54 And when His disciples
James and John saw *this,* they said, "Lord,
do You want us to command fire to come
down from heaven and consume them,
just as Elijah did?"
55 But He turned and rebuked them, and
said, "You do not know what manner of

spirit you are of. [56] For the Son of Man did not come to destroy men's lives but to save *them*." And they went to another village.

[57] Now it happened as they journeyed on the road, *that* someone said to Him, "Lord, I will follow You wherever You go."

[58] And Jesus said to him, "Foxes have holes and birds of the air *have* nests, but the Son of Man has nowhere to lay His head."

[59] Then He said to another, "Follow Me." But he said, "Lord, let me first go and bury my father."

[60] Jesus said to him, "Let the dead bury their own dead, but you go and preach the kingdom of God."

[61] And another also said, "Lord, I will follow You, but let me first go *and* bid them farewell who are at my house."

[62] But Jesus said to him, "No one, having put his hand to the plow, and looking back, is fit for the kingdom of God."

READING 100 · APRIL 10

~ JOSHUA 9:1—10:43 ~

And it came to pass when all the kings who *were* on this side of the Jordan, in the hills and in the lowland and in all the coasts of the Great Sea toward Lebanon—the Hittite, the Amorite, the Canaanite, the Perizzite, the Hivite, and the Jebusite—heard *about it,* [2] that they gathered together to fight with Joshua and Israel with one accord.

[3] But when the inhabitants of Gibeon heard what Joshua had done to Jericho and Ai, [4] they worked craftily, and went and pretended to be ambassadors. And they took old sacks on their donkeys, old wineskins torn and mended, [5] old and patched sandals on their feet, and old garments on themselves; and all the bread of their provision was dry *and* moldy. [6] And they went to Joshua, to the camp at Gilgal, and said to him and to the men of Israel, "We have come from a far country; now therefore, make a covenant with us."

[7] Then the men of Israel said to the Hivites, "Perhaps you dwell among us; so how can we make a covenant with you?"

[8] But they said to Joshua, "We *are* your servants."

And Joshua said to them, "Who *are* you, and where do you come from?"

[9] So they said to him: "From a very far country your servants have come, because of the name of the LORD your God; for we have heard of His fame, and all that He did in Egypt, [10] and all that He did to the two kings of the Amorites who *were* beyond the Jordan—to Sihon king of Heshbon, and Og king of Bashan, who was at Ashtaroth. [11] Therefore our elders and all the inhabitants of our country spoke to us, saying, 'Take provisions with you for the journey, and go to meet them, and say to them, "We *are* your servants; now therefore, make a covenant with us." ' [12] This bread of ours we took hot *for* our provision from our houses on the day we departed to come to you. But now look, it is dry and moldy. [13] And these wineskins which we filled *were* new, and see, they are torn; and these our garments and our sandals have become old because of the very long journey."

[14] Then the men of Israel took some of their provisions; but they did not ask counsel of the LORD. [15] So Joshua made peace with them, and made a covenant with them to let them live; and the rulers of the congregation swore to them.

[16] And it happened at the end of three days, after they had made a covenant with them, that they heard that they *were* their neighbors who dwelt near them. [17] Then the children of Israel journeyed and came to their cities on the third day. Now their cities *were* Gibeon, Chephirah, Beeroth, and Kirjath Jearim. [18] But the children of Israel did not attack them, because the rulers of the congregation had sworn to them by the LORD God of Israel. And all the congregation complained against the rulers.

[19] Then all the rulers said to all the congregation, "We have sworn to them by the LORD God of Israel; now therefore,

In the Very Hour

During World War II, a missionary family lived near a place where the Japanese tortured and killed their captives. The family was often awakened by the screams of the tormented. Twice, the missionary was taken captive, then released unharmed. The third time the officer said to the missionary's wife, "He has been returned to you two times — don't think he will be spared a third time. This time he dies."

After she had put her five children to bed, the wife began a prayer vigil. At four o'clock, she awoke her family to join her, saying, "The burden has become so heavy I cannot bear it alone." A short while later, they heard footsteps approaching — ones she recognized as those of her husband!

Safely inside their home, he told her what had happened. He had been the last in a row of ten men. A Japanese soldier had gone down the row, slashing off the head of each man with a sword. Just as he raised his sword to kill the missionary, the officer shouted, "Stop!" Then he roared to the missionary, "Go home. Quick, get out of here!" He pushed the missionary past the guard and toward the gate. "I looked at my watch," the missionary said. "It was 4 AM."

Nothing impacts the impossible like prayer.

Then Joshua spoke to the Lord in the day when the Lord delivered up the Amorites before the children of Israel, and he said in the sight of Israel: "Sun, stand still over Gibeon; and Moon, in the Valley of Aijalon." So the sun stood still, and the moon stopped, till the people had revenge upon their enemies. Is this not written in the Book of Jasher? So the sun stood still in the midst of heaven, and did not hasten to go down for about a whole day.

Joshua 10:12-13

we may not touch them. ²⁰ This we will do to them: We will let them live, lest wrath be upon us because of the oath which we swore to them." ²¹ And the rulers said to them, "Let them live, but let them be woodcutters and water carriers for all the congregation, as the rulers had promised them."

²² Then Joshua called for them, and he spoke to them, saying, "Why have you deceived us, saying, 'We *are* very far from you,' when you dwell near us? ²³ Now therefore, you *are* cursed, and none of you shall be freed from being slaves—woodcutters and water carriers for the house of my God."

²⁴ So they answered Joshua and said, "Because your servants were clearly told that the LORD your God commanded His servant Moses to give you all the land, and to destroy all the inhabitants of the land from before you; therefore we were very much afraid for our lives because of you, and have done this thing. ²⁵ And now, here we are, in your hands; do with us as it seems good and right to do to us." ²⁶ So he did to them, and delivered them out of the hand of the children of Israel, so that they did not kill them. ²⁷ And that day Joshua made them woodcutters and water carriers for the congregation and for the altar of the LORD, in the place which He would choose, even to this day.

10 Now it came to pass when Adoni-Zedek king of Jerusalem heard how Joshua had taken Ai and had utterly destroyed it—as he had done to Jericho and its king, so he had done to Ai and its king—and how the inhabitants of Gibeon had made peace with Israel and were among them, ² that they feared greatly, because Gibeon *was* a great city, like one of the royal cities, and because it *was* greater than Ai, and all its men *were* mighty. ³ Therefore Adoni-Zedek king of Jerusalem sent to Hoham king of Hebron, Piram king of Jarmuth, Japhia king of Lachish, and Debir king of Eglon, saying, ⁴ "Come up to me and help me, that we may attack Gibeon, for it has made peace with Joshua and with the children of Israel." ⁵ Therefore the five kings of the Amorites, the king of Jerusalem, the king of Hebron, the king of Jarmuth, the king of Lachish, *and* the king of Eglon, gathered together and went up, they and all their armies, and camped before Gibeon and made war against it.

⁶ And the men of Gibeon sent to Joshua at the camp at Gilgal, saying, "Do not forsake your servants; come up to us quickly, save us and help us, for all the kings of the Amorites who dwell in the mountains have gathered together against us."

⁷ So Joshua ascended from Gilgal, he and all the people of war with him, and all the mighty men of valor. ⁸ And the LORD said to Joshua, "Do not fear them, for I have delivered them into your hand; not a man of them shall stand before you." ⁹ Joshua therefore came upon them suddenly, having marched all night from Gilgal. ¹⁰ So the LORD routed them before Israel, killed them with a great slaughter at Gibeon, chased them along the road that goes to Beth Horon, and struck them down as far as Azekah and Makkedah. ¹¹ And it happened, as they fled before Israel *and* were on the descent of Beth Horon, that the LORD cast down large hailstones from heaven on them as far as Azekah, and they died. *There were* more who died from the hailstones than the children of Israel killed with the sword.

¹² Then Joshua spoke to the LORD in the day when the LORD delivered up the Amorites before the children of Israel, and he said in the sight of Israel:

"Sun, stand still over Gibeon;
    And Moon, in the Valley of
        Aijalon."
¹³ So the sun stood still,
    And the moon stopped,
    Till the people had revenge
    Upon their enemies.

Is this not written in the Book of Jasher? So the sun stood still in the midst of heaven, and did not hasten to go *down* for about a whole day. ¹⁴ And there has been no day like that, before it or after it, that the LORD heeded the voice of a man; for the LORD fought for Israel.

¹⁵ Then Joshua returned, and all Israel with him, to the camp at Gilgal.

¹⁶ But these five kings had fled and hidden themselves in a cave at Makkedah.

¹⁷ And it was told Joshua, saying, "The five kings have been found hidden in the cave at Makkedah."

¹⁸ So Joshua said, "Roll large stones against the mouth of the cave, and set men by it to guard them. ¹⁹ And do not stay *there* yourselves, *but* pursue your enemies, and attack their rear *guard*. Do not allow them to enter their cities, for the LORD your God has delivered them into your hand." ²⁰ Then it happened, while Joshua and the children of Israel made an end of slaying them with a very great slaughter, till they had finished, that those who escaped entered fortified cities. ²¹ And all the people returned to the camp, to Joshua at Makkedah, in peace.

No one moved his tongue against any of the children of Israel.

²² Then Joshua said, "Open the mouth of the cave, and bring out those five kings to me from the cave." ²³ And they did so, and brought out those five kings to him from the cave: the king of Jerusalem, the king of Hebron, the king of Jarmuth, the king of Lachish, *and* the king of Eglon.

²⁴ So it was, when they brought out those kings to Joshua, that Joshua called for all the men of Israel, and said to the captains of the men of war who went with him, "Come near, put your feet on the necks of these kings." And they drew near and put their feet on their necks. ²⁵ Then Joshua said to them, "Do not be afraid, nor be dismayed; be strong and of good courage, for thus the LORD will do to all your enemies against whom you fight." ²⁶ And afterward Joshua struck them and killed them, and hanged them on five trees; and they were hanging on the trees until evening. ²⁷ So it was at the time of the going down of the sun *that* Joshua commanded, and they took them down from the trees, cast them into the cave where they had been hidden, and laid large stones against the cave's mouth, *which remain* until this very day.

²⁸ On that day Joshua took Makkedah, and struck it and its king with the edge of the sword. He utterly destroyed them— all the people who *were* in it. He let none remain. He also did to the king of Makkedah as he had done to the king of Jericho.

²⁹ Then Joshua passed from Makkedah, and all Israel with him, to Libnah; and they fought against Libnah. ³⁰ And the LORD also delivered it and its king into the hand of Israel; he struck it and all the people who *were* in it with the edge of the sword. He let none remain in it, but did to its king as he had done to the king of Jericho.

³¹ Then Joshua passed from Libnah, and all Israel with him, to Lachish; and they encamped against it and fought against it. ³² And the LORD delivered Lachish into the hand of Israel, who took it on the second day, and struck it and all the people who *were* in it with the edge of the sword, according to all that he had done to Libnah. ³³ Then Horam king of Gezer came up to help Lachish; and Joshua struck him and his people, until he left him none remaining.

³⁴ From Lachish Joshua passed to Eglon, and all Israel with him; and they encamped against it and fought against it. ³⁵ They took it on that day and struck it with the edge of the sword; all the people who *were* in it he utterly destroyed that day, according to all that he had done to Lachish.

³⁶ So Joshua went up from Eglon, and all Israel with him, to Hebron; and they fought against it. ³⁷ And they took it and struck it with the edge of the sword—its king, all its cities, and all the people who *were* in it; he left none remaining, according to all that he had done to Eglon, but utterly destroyed it and all the people who *were* in it.

³⁸ Then Joshua returned, and all Israel with him, to Debir; and they fought against it. ³⁹ And he took it and its king and all its cities; they struck them with the edge of the sword and utterly destroyed all the people who *were* in it. He left none remaining; as he had done to Hebron, so he did to Debir and its king, as he had done also to Libnah and its king.

⁴⁰ So Joshua conquered all the land: the mountain country and the South and the lowland and the wilderness slopes, and all their kings; he left none remaining, but utterly destroyed all that breathed, as the LORD God of Israel had commanded. ⁴¹ And Joshua conquered them from Kadesh Barnea as far as Gaza, and

all the country of Goshen, even as far as Gibeon. 42 All these kings and their land Joshua took at one time, because the LORD God of Israel fought for Israel. 43 Then Joshua returned, and all Israel with him, to the camp at Gilgal.

~ PSALM 44:1–3 ~

1 We have heard with our ears,
   O God,
   Our fathers have told us,
   The deeds You did in their days,
   In days of old:
2 You drove out the nations with Your
   hand,
   But them You planted;
   You afflicted the peoples, and cast
   them out.
3 For they did not gain possession of
   the land by their own sword,
   Nor did their own arm save them;
   But it was Your right hand, Your
   arm, and the light of Your
   countenance,
   Because You favored them.

~ PROVERBS 13:24, 25 ~

24 He who spares his rod hates his son,
   But he who loves him disciplines him
   promptly.

25 The righteous eats to the satisfying
   of his soul,
   But the stomach of the wicked shall
   be in want.

~ LUKE 10:1–24 ~

After these things the Lord appointed seventy others also, and sent them two by two before His face into every city and place where He Himself was about to go. 2 Then He said to them, "The harvest truly is great, but the laborers are few; therefore pray the Lord of the harvest to send out laborers into His harvest. 3 Go your way; behold, I send you out as lambs among wolves. 4 Carry neither money bag, knapsack, nor sandals; and greet no one along the road. 5 But whatever house you enter, first say, 'Peace to this house.' 6 And if a son of peace is there, your peace will rest on it; if not, it will return to you. 7 And remain in the same house, eating and drinking such things as they give, for the laborer is worthy of his wages. Do not go from house to house. 8 Whatever city you enter, and they receive you, eat such things as are set before you. 9 And heal the sick there, and say to them, 'The kingdom of God has come near to you.' 10 But whatever city you enter, and they do not receive you, go out into its streets and say, 11 'The very dust of your city which clings to us we wipe off against you. Nevertheless know this, that the kingdom of God has come near you.' 12 But I say to you that it will be more tolerable in that Day for Sodom than for that city.

13 "Woe to you, Chorazin! Woe to you, Bethsaida! For if the mighty works which were done in you had been done in Tyre and Sidon, they would have repented long ago, sitting in sackcloth and ashes. 14 But it will be more tolerable for Tyre and Sidon at the judgment than for you. 15 And you, Capernaum, who are exalted to heaven, will be brought down to Hades. 16 He who hears you hears Me, he who rejects you rejects Me, and he who rejects Me rejects Him who sent Me."

17 Then the seventy returned with joy, saying, "Lord, even the demons are subject to us in Your name."

18 And He said to them, "I saw Satan fall like lightning from heaven. 19 Behold, I give you the authority to trample on serpents and scorpions, and over all the power of the enemy, and nothing shall by any means hurt you. 20 Nevertheless do not rejoice in this, that the spirits are subject to you, but rather rejoice because your names are written in heaven."

21 In that hour Jesus rejoiced in the Spirit and said, "I thank You, Father, Lord of heaven and earth, that You have hidden these things from the wise and prudent and revealed them to babes. Even so, Father, for so it seemed good in Your sight. 22 All things have been delivered to Me by My Father, and no one knows who the Son is except the Father, and who the Father is except the Son, and the one to whom the Son wills to reveal Him."

23 Then He turned to His disciples and

said privately, "Blessed *are* the eyes which see the things you see; ²⁴ for I tell you that many prophets and kings have desired to see what you see, and have not seen *it,* and to hear what you hear, and have not heard *it.*"

~ Joshua 11:1—12:24 ~

And it came to pass, when Jabin king of Hazor heard *these things,* that he sent to Jobab king of Madon, to the king of Shimron, to the king of Achshaph, ² and to the kings who *were* from the north, in the mountains, in the plain south of Chinneroth, in the lowland, and in the heights of Dor on the west, ³ to the Canaanites in the east and in the west, the Amorite, the Hittite, the Perizzite, the Jebusite in the mountains, and the Hivite below Hermon in the land of Mizpah. ⁴ So they went out, they and all their armies with them, *as* many people *as* the sand that *is* on the seashore in multitude, with very many horses and chariots. ⁵ And when all these kings had met together, they came and camped together at the waters of Merom to fight against Israel.

⁶ But the LORD said to Joshua, "Do not be afraid because of them, for tomorrow about this time I will deliver all of them slain before Israel. You shall hamstring their horses and burn their chariots with fire." ⁷ So Joshua and all the people of war with him came against them suddenly by the waters of Merom, and they attacked them. ⁸ And the LORD delivered them into the hand of Israel, who defeated them and chased them to Greater Sidon, to the Brook Misrephoth, and to the Valley of Mizpah eastward; they attacked them until they left none of them remaining. ⁹ So Joshua did to them as the LORD had told him: he hamstrung their horses and burned their chariots with fire.

¹⁰ Joshua turned back at that time and took Hazor, and struck its king with the sword; for Hazor was formerly the head of all those kingdoms. ¹¹ And they struck all the people who *were* in it with the edge of the sword, utterly destroying *them.* There was none left breathing. Then he burned Hazor with fire.

¹² So all the cities of those kings, and all their kings, Joshua took and struck with the edge of the sword. He utterly destroyed them, as Moses the servant of the LORD had commanded. ¹³ But *as for* the cities that stood on their mounds, Israel burned none of them, except Hazor only, *which* Joshua burned. ¹⁴ And all the spoil of these cities and the livestock, the children of Israel took as booty for themselves; but they struck every man with the edge of the sword until they had destroyed them, and they left none breathing. ¹⁵ As the LORD had commanded Moses his servant, so Moses commanded Joshua, and so Joshua did. He left nothing undone of all that the LORD had commanded Moses.

¹⁶ Thus Joshua took all this land: the mountain country, all the South, all the land of Goshen, the lowland, and the Jordan plain—the mountains of Israel and its lowlands, ¹⁷ from Mount Halak and the ascent to Seir, even as far as Baal Gad in the Valley of Lebanon below Mount Hermon. He captured all their kings, and struck them down and killed them. ¹⁸ Joshua made war a long time with all those kings. ¹⁹ There was not a city that made peace with the children of Israel, except the Hivites, the inhabitants of Gibeon. All *the others* they took in battle. ²⁰ For it was of the LORD to harden their hearts, that they should come against Israel in battle, that He might utterly destroy them, *and* that they might receive no mercy, but that He might destroy them, as the LORD had commanded Moses.

²¹ And at that time Joshua came and cut off the Anakim from the mountains: from Hebron, from Debir, from Anab, from all the mountains of Judah, and from all the mountains of Israel; Joshua utterly destroyed them with their cities. ²² None of the Anakim were left in the land of the children of Israel; they remained only in Gaza, in Gath, and in Ashdod.

²³ So Joshua took the whole land, according to all that the LORD had said to Moses; and Joshua gave it as an inheritance to Israel according to their divisions by their tribes. Then the land rested from war.

12 These *are* the kings of the land whom the children of Israel defeated, and whose land they possessed on the other side of the Jordan toward the rising of the sun, from the River Arnon to Mount Hermon, and all the eastern Jordan plain: ² *One king was* Sihon king of the Amorites, who dwelt in Heshbon *and* ruled half of Gilead, from Aroer, which is on the bank of the River Arnon, from the middle of that river, even as far as the River Jabbok, *which is* the border of the Ammonites, ³ and the eastern Jordan plain from the Sea of Chinneroth as far as the Sea of the Arabah (the Salt Sea), the road to Beth Jeshimoth, and southward below the slopes of Pisgah. ⁴ *The other king was* Og king of Bashan and his territory, *who was* of the remnant of the giants, who dwelt at Ashtaroth and at Edrei, ⁵ and reigned over Mount Hermon, over Salcah, over all Bashan, as far as the border of the Geshurites and the Maachathites, and over half of Gilead *to* the border of Sihon king of Heshbon.

⁶ These Moses the servant of the LORD and the children of Israel had conquered; and Moses the servant of the LORD had given it *as* a possession to the Reubenites, the Gadites, and half the tribe of Manasseh.

⁷ And these *are* the kings of the country which Joshua and the children of Israel conquered on this side of the Jordan, on the west, from Baal Gad in the Valley of Lebanon as far as Mount Halak and the ascent to Seir, which Joshua gave to the tribes of Israel *as* a possession according to their divisions, ⁸ in the mountain country, in the lowlands, in the *Jordan* plain, in the slopes, in the wilderness, and in the South—the Hittites, the Amorites, the Canaanites, the Perizzites, the Hivites, and the Jebusites: ⁹ the king of Jericho, one; the king of Ai, which *is* beside Bethel, one; ¹⁰ the king of Jerusalem, one; the king of Hebron, one; ¹¹ the king of Jarmuth, one; the king of Lachish, one; ¹² the king of Eglon, one; the king of Gezer, one; ¹³ the king of Debir, one; the king of Geder, one; ¹⁴ the king of Hormah, one; the king of Arad, one; ¹⁵ the king of Libnah, one; the king of Adullam, one; ¹⁶ the king of Makkedah, one; the king of Bethel, one; ¹⁷ the king of Tappuah, one; the king of Hepher, one; ¹⁸ the king of Aphek, one; the king of Lasharon, one; ¹⁹ the king of Madon, one; the king of Hazor, one; ²⁰ the king of Shimron Meron, one; the king of Achshaph, one; ²¹ the king of Taanach, one; the king of Megiddo, one; ²² the king of Kedesh, one; the king of Jokneam in Carmel, one; ²³ the king of Dor in the heights of Dor, one; the king of the people of Gilgal, one; ²⁴ the king of Tirzah, one—all the kings, thirty-one.

~ PSALM 44:4–19 ~

⁴ You are my King, O God;
  Command victories for Jacob.
⁵ Through You we will push down our
    enemies;
  Through Your name we will trample
    those who rise up against us.
⁶ For I will not trust in my bow,
  Nor shall my sword save me.
⁷ But You have saved us from our
    enemies,
  And have put to shame those who
    hated us.
⁸ In God we boast all day long,
  And praise Your name forever.
                              Selah

⁹ But You have cast *us* off and put us
    to shame,
  And You do not go out with our
    armies.
¹⁰ You make us turn back from the
    enemy,
  And those who hate us have taken
    spoil for themselves.
¹¹ You have given us up like sheep
    intended for food,
  And have scattered us among the
    nations.
¹² You sell Your people for *next to*
    nothing,
  And are not enriched by selling
    them.

Jesus Loves Me

A woman minister received a call from a friend she had not seen in two years. The friend said, "My husband is leaving me for another woman. I need for you to pray with me." The minister said, "Come quickly."

When her friend arrived, the minister could not help but notice that her friend was carelessly dressed, had gained weight, and had not combed her hair or put on makeup. As they began to converse, the friend admitted to being an uninteresting, nagging wife and a sloppy housekeeper. The minister quickly concluded to herself, *My friend has grown to hate herself!*

When her friend paused to ask for her advice, the minister said only, "Will you join me in a song?" Surprised, her friend agreed. The minister began to sing, "Jesus loves me, this I know." Her friend joined in, tears flooding her eyes. "If Jesus loves me, I must love myself, too," she concluded.

Amazing changes followed. Because she felt loved and lovable, this woman was transformed into the confident woman she once had been. In the process, she recaptured her husband's heart.

We can never accept God's love beyond the degree to which we are willing to love ourselves. We rarely receive more than we are willing to believe God has for us. Our part is to believe, to receive, and to give.

So he answered and said, "You shall love the Lord your God with all your heart, with all your soul, with all your strength, and with all your mind," and "your neighbor as yourself."

Luke 10:27

13 You make us a reproach to our
        neighbors,
    A scorn and a derision to those all
        around us.
14 You make us a byword among the
        nations,
    A shaking of the head among the
        peoples.
15 My dishonor *is* continually before
        me,
    And the shame of my face has
        covered me,
16 Because of the voice of him who
        reproaches and reviles,
    Because of the enemy and the
        avenger.

17 All this has come upon us;
    But we have not forgotten You,
    Nor have we dealt falsely with Your
        covenant.
18 Our heart has not turned back,
    Nor have our steps departed from
        Your way;
19 But You have severely broken us in
        the place of jackals,
    And covered us with the shadow of
        death.

∼ PROVERBS 14:1, 2 ∼

1   The wise woman builds her house,
    But the foolish pulls it down with
        her hands.

2   He who walks in his uprightness
        fears the LORD,
    But *he who is* perverse in his ways
        despises Him.

∼ LUKE 10:25–42 ∼

And behold, a certain lawyer stood up and
tested Him, saying, "Teacher, what shall I
do to inherit eternal life?"
    26 He said to him, "What is written in
the law? What is your reading *of it?*"
    27 So he answered and said, " 'You
shall love the LORD your God with all
your heart, with all your soul, with all your
strength, and with all your mind,' and
'your neighbor as yourself.' "
    28 And He said to him, "You have an-
swered rightly; do this and you will live."
    29 But he, wanting to justify himself, said
to Jesus, "And who is my neighbor?"
    30 Then Jesus answered and said: "A
certain *man* went down from Jerusalem
to Jericho, and fell among thieves, who
stripped him of his clothing, wounded
him, and departed, leaving *him* half dead.
31 Now by chance a certain priest came
down that road. And when he saw him,
he passed by on the other side. 32 Likewise a Levite, when he arrived at the place,
came and looked, and passed by on the
other side. 33 But a certain Samaritan, as
he journeyed, came where he was. And
when he saw him, he had compassion.
34 So he went to *him* and bandaged his
wounds, pouring on oil and wine; and he
set him on his own animal, brought him
to an inn, and took care of him. 35 On the
next day, when he departed, he took out
two denarii, gave *them* to the innkeeper,
and said to him, 'Take care of him; and
whatever more you spend, when I come
again, I will repay you.' 36 So which of
these three do you think was neighbor to
him who fell among the thieves?"
    37 And he said, "He who showed mercy
on him."
    Then Jesus said to him, "Go and do
likewise."
    38 Now it happened as they went that
He entered a certain village; and a certain woman named Martha welcomed
Him into her house. 39 And she had a sister called Mary, who also sat at Jesus' feet
and heard His word. 40 But Martha was
distracted with much serving, and she
approached Him and said, "Lord, do You
not care that my sister has left me to serve
alone? Therefore tell her to help me."
    41 And Jesus answered and said to her,
"Martha, Martha, you are worried and
troubled about many things. 42 But one
thing is needed, and Mary has chosen that
good part, which will not be taken away
from her."

～ JOSHUA 13:1—14:15 ～

Now Joshua was old, advanced in years. And the LORD said to him: "You are old, advanced in years, and there remains very much land yet to be possessed. ² This is the land that yet remains: all the territory of the Philistines and all *that of* the Geshurites, ³ from Sihor, which *is* east of Egypt, as far as the border of Ekron northward (*which* is counted as Canaanite); the five lords of the Philistines—the Gazites, the Ashdodites, the Ashkelonites, the Gittites, and the Ekronites; also the Avites; ⁴ from the south, all the land of the Canaanites, and Mearah that belongs to the Sidonians as far as Aphek, to the border of the Amorites; ⁵ the land of the Gebalites, and all Lebanon, toward the sunrise, from Baal Gad below Mount Hermon as far as the entrance to Hamath; ⁶ all the inhabitants of the mountains from Lebanon as far as the Brook Misrephoth, *and* all the Sidonians—them I will drive out from before the children of Israel; only divide it by lot to Israel as an inheritance, as I have commanded you. ⁷ Now therefore, divide this land as an inheritance to the nine tribes and half the tribe of Manasseh."

⁸ With the other half-tribe the Reubenites and the Gadites received their inheritance, which Moses had given them, beyond the Jordan eastward, as Moses the servant of the LORD had given them: ⁹ from Aroer which *is* on the bank of the River Arnon, and the town that *is* in the midst of the ravine, and all the plain of Medeba as far as Dibon; ¹⁰ all the cities of Sihon king of the Amorites, who reigned in Heshbon, as far as the border of the children of Ammon; ¹¹ Gilead, and the border of the Geshurites and Maachathites, all Mount Hermon, and all Bashan as far as Salcah; ¹² all the kingdom of Og in Bashan, who reigned in Ashtaroth and Edrei, who remained of the remnant of the giants; for Moses had defeated and cast out these.

¹³ Nevertheless the children of Israel did not drive out the Geshurites or the Maachathites, but the Geshurites and the Maachathites dwell among the Israelites until this day.

¹⁴ Only to the tribe of Levi he had given no inheritance; the sacrifices of the LORD God of Israel made by fire *are* their inheritance, as He said to them.

¹⁵ And Moses had given to the tribe of the children of Reuben *an inheritance* according to their families. ¹⁶ Their territory was from Aroer, which *is* on the bank of the River Arnon, and the city that *is* in the midst of the ravine, and all the plain by Medeba; ¹⁷ Heshbon and all its cities that *are* in the plain: Dibon, Bamoth Baal, Beth Baal Meon, ¹⁸ Jahaza, Kedemoth, Mephaath, ¹⁹ Kirjathaim, Sibmah, Zereth Shahar on the mountain of the valley, ²⁰ Beth Peor, the slopes of Pisgah, and Beth Jeshimoth— ²¹ all the cities of the plain and all the kingdom of Sihon king of the Amorites, who reigned in Heshbon, whom Moses had struck with the princes of Midian: Evi, Rekem, Zur, Hur, and Reba, who *were* princes of Sihon dwelling in the country. ²² The children of Israel also killed with the sword Balaam the son of Beor, the soothsayer, among those who were killed by them. ²³ And the border of the children of Reuben was the bank of the Jordan. This *was* the inheritance of the children of Reuben according to their families, the cities and their villages.

²⁴ Moses also had given *an inheritance* to the tribe of Gad, to the children of Gad according to their families. ²⁵ Their territory was Jazer, and all the cities of Gilead, and half the land of the Ammonites as far as Aroer, which *is* before Rabbah, ²⁶ and from Heshbon to Ramath Mizpah and Betonim, and from Mahanaim to the border of Debir, ²⁷ and in the valley Beth Haram, Beth Nimrah, Succoth, and Zaphon, the rest of the kingdom of Sihon king of Heshbon, with the Jordan as *its* border, as far as the edge of the Sea of Chinnereth, on the other side of the Jordan eastward. ²⁸ This *is* the inheritance of the children of Gad according to their families, the cities and their villages.

²⁹ Moses also had given *an inheritance* to half the tribe of Manasseh; it was for half the tribe of the children of Manasseh according to their families: ³⁰ Their territory was from Mahanaim, all Bashan, all

the kingdom of Og king of Bashan, and all the towns of Jair which are in Bashan, sixty cities; [31] half of Gilead, and Ashtaroth and Edrei, cities of the kingdom of Og in Bashan, *were* for the children of Machir the son of Manasseh, for half of the children of Machir according to their families.

[32] These *are the areas* which Moses had distributed as an inheritance in the plains of Moab on the other side of the Jordan, by Jericho eastward. [33] But to the tribe of Levi Moses had given no inheritance; the LORD God of Israel *was* their inheritance, as He had said to them.

14 These *are the areas* which the children of Israel inherited in the land of Canaan, which Eleazar the priest, Joshua the son of Nun, and the heads of the fathers of the tribes of the children of Israel distributed as an inheritance to them. [2] Their inheritance *was* by lot, as the LORD had commanded by the hand of Moses, for the nine tribes and the half-tribe. [3] For Moses had given the inheritance of the two tribes and the half-tribe on the other side of the Jordan; but to the Levites he had given no inheritance among them. [4] For the children of Joseph were two tribes: Manasseh and Ephraim. And they gave no part to the Levites in the land, except cities to dwell *in*, with their common-lands for their livestock and their property. [5] As the LORD had commanded Moses, so the children of Israel did; and they divided the land.

[6] Then the children of Judah came to Joshua in Gilgal. And Caleb the son of Jephunneh the Kenizzite said to him: "You know the word which the LORD said to Moses the man of God concerning you and me in Kadesh Barnea. [7] I *was* forty years old when Moses the servant of the LORD sent me from Kadesh Barnea to spy out the land, and I brought back word to him as *it was* in my heart. [8] Nevertheless my brethren who went up with me made the heart of the people melt, but I wholly followed the LORD my God. [9] So Moses swore on that day, saying, 'Surely the land where your foot has trodden shall be your inheritance and your children's forever, because you have wholly followed the LORD my God.' [10] And now, behold, the LORD has kept me alive, as He said, these forty-five years, ever since the LORD spoke this word to Moses while Israel wandered in the wilderness; and now, here I am this day, eighty-five years old. [11] As yet I *am as* strong this day as on the day that Moses sent me; just as my strength *was* then, so now *is* my strength for war, both for going out and for coming in. [12] Now therefore, give me this mountain of which the LORD spoke in that day; for you heard in that day how the Anakim *were* there, and *that* the cities *were* great *and* fortified. It may be that the LORD *will be* with me, and I shall be able to drive them out as the LORD said."

[13] And Joshua blessed him, and gave Hebron to Caleb the son of Jephunneh as an inheritance. [14] Hebron therefore became the inheritance of Caleb the son of Jephunneh the Kenizzite to this day, because he wholly followed the LORD God of Israel. [15] And the name of Hebron formerly was Kirjath Arba (*Arba was* the greatest man among the Anakim).

Then the land had rest from war.

~ PSALM 44:20–26 ~

[20] If we had forgotten the name of our God,
Or stretched out our hands to a foreign god,
[21] Would not God search this out?
For He knows the secrets of the heart.
[22] Yet for Your sake we are killed all day long;
We are accounted as sheep for the slaughter.

[23] Awake! Why do You sleep, O Lord?
Arise! Do not cast *us* off forever.
[24] Why do You hide Your face,
And forget our affliction and our oppression?
[25] For our soul is bowed down to the dust;
Our body clings to the ground.
[26] Arise for our help,
And redeem us for Your mercies' sake.

Teach Us How to Pray

The story is told of a monk who overheard two people from the nearby village praising the virtues of a holy man. The monk felt certain that they must be talking about him. To his surprise, he discovered they were talking about a humble farmer who lived a life of uncompromising virtue and profound prayer.

The monk was determined to meet this man for himself to discover what it was that had motivated such great admiration. He found the farmer selling vegetables and asked him for overnight shelter. The farmer, overjoyed to be of service, welcomed the monk into his home.

After supper, the monk suggested to his host that they pray. Almost immediately, the monk heard the sound of vulgar songs coming from a group of drunks as they passed along the road outside the farmer's home. With great annoyance the monk exclaimed, "Tell me, what kind of prayer can be made with such noise and vulgarity!" The farmer replied, "A prayer that they travel safely on their way to the kingdom of God."

The old monk marveled. He returned to his monastery, aware that he had never prayed a prayer as noble as that of the humble farmer.

The key to profound prayer is to first let go of the prideful notion that you know how to pray. Like the disciples, we should ask Jesus, "Teach us how to pray," and never cease listening or asking.

> Now it came to pass, as He was praying in a certain place, when He ceased, that one of His disciples said to Him, "Lord, teach us to pray, as John also taught his disciples."
>
> *Luke 11:1*

~ PROVERBS 14:3 ~

3 In the mouth of a fool *is* a rod of
      pride,
   But the lips of the wise will preserve
      them.

~ LUKE 11:1–28 ~

Now it came to pass, as He was praying
in a certain place, when He ceased, *that*
one of His disciples said to Him, "Lord,
teach us to pray, as John also taught his
disciples."

² So He said to them, "When you
pray, say:

> Our Father in heaven,
> Hallowed be Your name.
> Your kingdom come.
> Your will be done
> On earth as *it is* in heaven.
> 3 Give us day by day our daily
>   bread.
> 4 And forgive us our sins,
>   For we also forgive everyone who
>   is indebted to us.
>   And do not lead us into
>   temptation,
>   But deliver us from the evil one."

⁵ And He said to them, "Which of you
shall have a friend, and go to him at midnight and say to him, 'Friend, lend me
three loaves; ⁶ for a friend of mine has
come to me on his journey, and I have
nothing to set before him'; ⁷ and he will
answer from within and say, 'Do not
trouble me; the door is now shut, and my
children are with me in bed; I cannot rise
and give to you'? ⁸ I say to you, though he
will not rise and give to him because he
is his friend, yet because of his persistence
he will rise and give him as many as he
needs.
⁹ "So I say to you, ask, and it will be
given to you; seek, and you will find;
knock, and it will be opened to you. ¹⁰ For
everyone who asks receives, and he who
seeks finds, and to him who knocks it will
be opened. ¹¹ If a son asks for bread from
any father among you, will he give him a
stone? Or if *he asks* for a fish, will he give
him a serpent instead of a fish? ¹² Or if he
asks for an egg, will he offer him a scorpion? ¹³ If you then, being evil, know how
to give good gifts to your children,
how much more will *your* heavenly Father give the Holy Spirit to those who ask
Him!"

¹⁴ And He was casting out a demon, and
it was mute. So it was, when the demon
had gone out, that the mute spoke; and
the multitudes marveled. ¹⁵ But some of
them said, "He casts out demons by
Beelzebub, the ruler of the demons."
¹⁶ Others, testing *Him,* sought from
Him a sign from heaven. ¹⁷ But He, knowing their thoughts, said to them: "Every
kingdom divided against itself is brought
to desolation, and a house *divided* against
a house falls. ¹⁸ If Satan also is divided
against himself, how will his kingdom
stand? Because you say I cast out demons
by Beelzebub. ¹⁹ And if I cast out demons by Beelzebub, by whom do your
sons cast *them* out? Therefore they will
be your judges. ²⁰ But if I cast out demons
with the finger of God, surely the kingdom of God has come upon you. ²¹ When
a strong man, fully armed, guards his own
palace, his goods are in peace. ²² But when
a stronger than he comes upon him and
overcomes him, he takes from him all his
armor in which he trusted, and divides
his spoils. ²³ He who is not with Me is
against Me, and he who does not gather
with Me scatters.
²⁴ "When an unclean spirit goes out of
a man, he goes through dry places, seeking rest; and finding none, he says, 'I will
return to my house from which I came.'
²⁵ And when he comes, he finds *it* swept
and put in order. ²⁶ Then he goes and takes
with *him* seven other spirits more wicked
than himself, and they enter and dwell
there; and the last *state* of that man is
worse than the first."
²⁷ And it happened, as He spoke these
things, that a certain woman from the
crowd raised her voice and said to Him,
"Blessed *is* the womb that bore You, and
the breasts which nursed You!"
²⁸ But He said, "More than that, blessed
are those who hear the word of God and
keep it!"

～ JOSHUA 15:1—16:10 ～

So *this* was the lot of the tribe of the children of Judah according to their families:

The border of Edom at the Wilderness of Zin southward *was* the extreme southern boundary. ² And their southern border began at the shore of the Salt Sea, from the bay that faces southward. ³ Then it went out to the southern side of the Ascent of Akrabbim, passed along to Zin, ascended on the south side of Kadesh Barnea, passed along to Hezron, went up to Adar, and went around to Karkaa. ⁴ *From there* it passed toward Azmon and went out to the Brook of Egypt; and the border ended at the sea. This shall be your southern border.

⁵ The east border *was* the Salt Sea as far as the mouth of the Jordan.

And the border on the northern quarter *began* at the bay of the sea at the mouth of the Jordan. ⁶ The border went up to Beth Hoglah and passed north of Beth Arabah; and the border went up to the stone of Bohan the son of Reuben. ⁷ Then the border went up toward Debir from the Valley of Achor, and it turned northward toward Gilgal, which *is* before the Ascent of Adummim, which *is* on the south side of the valley. The border continued toward the waters of En Shemesh and ended at En Rogel. ⁸ And the border went up by the Valley of the Son of Hinnom to the southern slope of the Jebusite *city* (which *is* Jerusalem). The border went up to the top of the mountain that *lies* before the Valley of Hinnom westward, which *is* at the end of the Valley of Rephaim northward. ⁹ Then the border went around from the top of the hill to the fountain of the water of Nephtoah, and extended to the cities of Mount Ephron. And the border went around to Baalah (which *is* Kirjath Jearim). ¹⁰ Then the border turned westward from Baalah to Mount Seir, passed along to the side of Mount Jearim on the north (which *is* Chesalon), went down to Beth Shemesh, and passed on to Timnah. ¹¹ And the border went out to the side of Ekron northward. Then the border went around to Shicron, passed along to Mount Baalah, and extended to Jabneel; and the border ended at the sea.

¹² The west border *was* the coastline of the Great Sea. This *is* the boundary of the children of Judah all around according to their families.

¹³ Now to Caleb the son of Jephunneh he gave a share among the children of Judah, according to the commandment of the LORD to Joshua, *namely*, Kirjath Arba, which *is* Hebron (*Arba was* the father of Anak). ¹⁴ Caleb drove out the three sons of Anak from there: Sheshai, Ahiman, and Talmai, the children of Anak. ¹⁵ Then he went up from there to the inhabitants of Debir (formerly the name of Debir *was* Kirjath Sepher).

¹⁶ And Caleb said, "He who attacks Kirjath Sepher and takes it, to him I will give Achsah my daughter as wife." ¹⁷ So Othniel the son of Kenaz, the brother of Caleb, took it; and he gave him Achsah his daughter as wife. ¹⁸ Now it was so, when she came *to him,* that she persuaded him to ask her father for a field. So she dismounted from *her* donkey, and Caleb said to her, "What do you wish?" ¹⁹ She answered, "Give me a blessing; since you have given me land in the South, give me also springs of water." So he gave her the upper springs and the lower springs.

²⁰ This *was* the inheritance of the tribe of the children of Judah according to their families:

²¹ The cities at the limits of the tribe of the children of Judah, toward the border of Edom in the South, were Kabzeel, Eder, Jagur, ²² Kinah, Dimonah, Adadah, ²³ Kedesh, Hazor, Ithnan, ²⁴ Ziph, Telem, Bealoth, ²⁵ Hazor, Hadattah, Kerioth, Hezron (which *is* Hazor), ²⁶ Amam, Shema, Moladah, ²⁷ Hazar Gaddah, Heshmon, Beth Pelet, ²⁸ Hazar Shual, Beersheba, Bizjothjah, ²⁹ Baalah, Ijim, Ezem, ³⁰ Eltolad, Chesil, Hormah, ³¹ Ziklag, Madmannah, Sansannah, ³² Lebaoth, Shilhim, Ain, and Rimmon: all the cities *are* twenty-nine, with their villages.

³³ In the lowland: Eshtaol, Zorah, Ashnah, ³⁴ Zanoah, En Gannim, Tappuah, Enam, ³⁵ Jarmuth, Adullam, Socoh, Azekah, ³⁶ Sharaim, Adithaim, Gederah, and

Gederothaim: fourteen cities with their villages; ³⁷ Zenan, Hadashah, Migdal Gad, ³⁸ Dilean, Mizpah, Joktheel, ³⁹ Lachish, Bozkath, Eglon, ⁴⁰ Cabbon, Lahmas, Kithlish, ⁴¹ Gederoth, Beth Dagon, Naamah, and Makkedah: sixteen cities with their villages; ⁴² Libnah, Ether, Ashan, ⁴³ Jiphtah, Ashnah, Nezib, ⁴⁴ Keilah, Achzib, and Mareshah: nine cities with their villages; ⁴⁵ Ekron, with its towns and villages; ⁴⁶ from Ekron to the sea, all that *lay* near Ashdod, with their villages; ⁴⁷ Ashdod with its towns and villages, Gaza with its towns and villages—as far as the Brook of Egypt and the Great Sea with *its* coastline.

⁴⁸ And in the mountain country: Shamir, Jattir, Sochoh, ⁴⁹ Dannah, Kirjath Sannah (which *is* Debir), ⁵⁰ Anab, Eshtemoh, Anim, ⁵¹ Goshen, Holon, and Giloh: eleven cities with their villages; ⁵² Arab, Dumah, Eshean, ⁵³ Janum, Beth Tappuah, Aphekah, ⁵⁴ Humtah, Kirjath Arba (which *is* Hebron), and Zior: nine cities with their villages; ⁵⁵ Maon, Carmel, Ziph, Juttah, ⁵⁶ Jezreel, Jokdeam, Zanoah, ⁵⁷ Kain, Gibeah, and Timnah: ten cities with their villages; ⁵⁸ Halhul, Beth Zur, Gedor, ⁵⁹ Maarath, Beth Anoth, and Eltekon: six cities with their villages; ⁶⁰ Kirjath Baal (which *is* Kirjath Jearim) and Rabbah: two cities with their villages.

⁶¹ In the wilderness: Beth Arabah, Middin, Secacah, ⁶² Nibshan, the City of Salt, and En Gedi: six cities with their villages.

⁶³ As for the Jebusites, the inhabitants of Jerusalem, the children of Judah could not drive them out; but the Jebusites dwell with the children of Judah at Jerusalem to this day.

16 The lot fell to the children of Joseph from the Jordan, by Jericho, to the waters of Jericho on the east, to the wilderness that goes up from Jericho through the mountains to Bethel, ² then went out from Bethel to Luz, passed along to the border of the Archites at Ataroth, ³ and went down westward to the boundary of the Japhletites, as far as the boundary of Lower Beth Horon to Gezer; and it ended at the sea.

⁴ So the children of Joseph, Manasseh and Ephraim, took their inheritance.

⁵ The border of the children of Ephra-im, according to their families, was *thus:* The border of their inheritance on the east side was Ataroth Addar as far as Upper Beth Horon.

⁶ And the border went out toward the sea on the north side of Michmethath; then the border went around eastward to Taanath Shiloh, and passed by it on the east of Janohah. ⁷ Then it went down from Janohah to Ataroth and Naarah, reached to Jericho, and came out at the Jordan.

⁸ The border went out from Tappuah westward to the Brook Kanah, and it ended at the sea. This *was* the inheritance of the tribe of the children of Ephraim according to their families. ⁹ The separate cities for the children of Ephraim *were* among the inheritance of the children of Manasseh, all the cities with their villages.

¹⁰ And they did not drive out the Canaanites who dwelt in Gezer; but the Canaanites dwell among the Ephraimites to this day and have become forced laborers.

∼ PSALM 45:1–5 ∼

1   My heart is overflowing with a good theme;
    I recite my composition concerning the King;
    My tongue *is* the pen of a ready writer.

2   You are fairer than the sons of men;
    Grace is poured upon Your lips;
    Therefore God has blessed You forever.

3   Gird Your sword upon *Your* thigh, O Mighty One,
    With Your glory and Your majesty.

4   And in Your majesty ride prosperously because of truth, humility, *and* righteousness;
    And Your right hand shall teach You awesome things.

5   Your arrows *are* sharp in the heart of the King's enemies;
    The peoples fall under You.

∼ PROVERBS 14:4, 5 ∼

4   Where no oxen *are*, the trough *is* clean;

A Small Piece of Butter

When the elderly head of the trust department at a bank retired, four very competent young men competed to fill the vacancy. After considering the merits of each applicant, the board of directors made its decision. They decided to notify the young man of his promotion, which included a substantial raise in salary, at a meeting already scheduled for after lunch.

During the noon hour, the young man they had selected went to the cafeteria for lunch. One of the directors was a few spots behind him in the line. The director saw the young man select his food, including a small piece of butter. As soon as he flipped the butter onto his plate, he shuffled some food on top of it to hide it from the cashier. Thus, he avoided paying for it.

That afternoon the directors met to notify the young man of his promotion, but prior to bringing him into the room, the entire board was told of the incident. Rather than giving the young man the promotion, they called him in to discharge him from the bank. They had concluded that if he was willing to lie to a cashier about what was on his plate, he would be just as willing to lie about what was in the bank's accounts.

Lying isn't a matter of degrees. A lie is a lie. And truth is the truth. You can bank on it!

But much increase *comes* by the strength of an ox.

5 A faithful witness does not lie,
But a false witness will utter lies.

∼ LUKE 11:29–54 ∼

And while the crowds were thickly gathered together, He began to say, "This is an evil generation. It seeks a sign, and no sign will be given to it except the sign of Jonah the prophet. ³⁰ For as Jonah became a sign to the Ninevites, so also the Son of Man will be to this generation. ³¹ The queen of the South will rise up in the judgment with the men of this generation and condemn them, for she came from the ends of the earth to hear the wisdom of Solomon; and indeed a greater than Solomon *is* here. ³² The men of Nineveh will rise up in the judgment with this generation and condemn it, for they repented at the preaching of Jonah; and indeed a greater than Jonah *is* here.

³³ "No one, when he has lit a lamp, puts *it* in a secret place or under a basket, but on a lampstand, that those who come in may see the light. ³⁴ The lamp of the body is the eye. Therefore, when your eye is good, your whole body also is full of light. But when *your eye* is bad, your body also *is* full of darkness. ³⁵ Therefore take heed that the light which is in you is not darkness. ³⁶ If then your whole body *is* full of light, having no part dark, *the* whole *body* will be full of light, as when the bright shining of a lamp gives you light."

³⁷ And as He spoke, a certain Pharisee asked Him to dine with him. So He went in and sat down to eat. ³⁸ When the Pharisee saw *it,* he marveled that He had not first washed before dinner. ³⁹ Then the Lord said to him, "Now you Pharisees make the outside of the cup and dish clean, but your inward part is full of greed and wickedness. ⁴⁰ Foolish ones! Did not He who made the outside make the inside also? ⁴¹ But rather give alms of such things as you have; then indeed all things are clean to you.

⁴² "But woe to you Pharisees! For you tithe the mint and rue and all manner of herbs, and pass by justice and the love of God. These you ought to have done, without leaving the others undone. ⁴³ Woe to you Pharisees! For you love the best seats in the synagogues and greetings in the marketplaces. ⁴⁴ Woe to you, scribes and Pharisees, hypocrites! For you are like graves which are not seen, and the men who walk over *them* are not aware *of them.*"

⁴⁵ Then one of the lawyers answered and said to Him, "Teacher, by saying these things You reproach us also."

⁴⁶ And He said, "Woe to you also, lawyers! For you load men with burdens hard to bear, and you yourselves do not touch the burdens with one of your fingers. ⁴⁷ Woe to you! For you build the tombs of the prophets, and your fathers killed them. ⁴⁸ In fact, you bear witness that you approve the deeds of your fathers; for they indeed killed them, and you build their tombs. ⁴⁹ Therefore the wisdom of God also said, 'I will send them prophets and apostles, and *some* of them they will kill and persecute,' ⁵⁰ that the blood of all the prophets which was shed from the foundation of the world may be required of this generation, ⁵¹ from the blood of Abel to the blood of Zechariah who perished between the altar and the temple. Yes, I say to you, it shall be required of this generation.

⁵² "Woe to you lawyers! For you have taken away the key of knowledge. You did not enter in yourselves, and those who were entering in you hindered."

⁵³ And as He said these things to them, the scribes and the Pharisees began to assail *Him* vehemently, and to cross-examine Him about many things, ⁵⁴ lying in wait for Him, and seeking to catch Him in something He might say, that they might accuse Him.

~ JOSHUA 17:1—18:28 ~

There was also a lot for the tribe of Manasseh, for he *was* the firstborn of Joseph: *namely* for Machir the firstborn of Manasseh, the father of Gilead, because he was a man of war; therefore he was given Gilead and Bashan. ² And there was *a lot* for the rest of the children of Manasseh according to their families: for the children of Abiezer, the children of Helek, the children of Asriel, the children of Shechem, the children of Hepher, and the children of Shemida; these *were* the male children of Manasseh the son of Joseph according to their families.

³ But Zelophehad the son of Hepher, the son of Gilead, the son of Machir, the son of Manasseh, had no sons, but only daughters. And these *are* the names of his daughters: Mahlah, Noah, Hoglah, Milcah, and Tirzah. ⁴ And they came near before Eleazar the priest, before Joshua the son of Nun, and before the rulers, saying, "The LORD commanded Moses to give us an inheritance among our brothers." Therefore, according to the commandment of the LORD, he gave them an inheritance among their father's brothers. ⁵ Ten shares fell to Manasseh, besides the land of Gilead and Bashan, which *were* on the other side of the Jordan, ⁶ because the daughters of Manasseh received an inheritance among his sons; and the rest of Manasseh's sons had the land of Gilead.

⁷ And the territory of Manasseh was from Asher to Michmethath, that *lies* east of Shechem; and the border went along south to the inhabitants of En Tappuah. ⁸ Manasseh had the land of Tappuah, but Tappuah on the border of Manasseh *belonged* to the children of Ephraim. ⁹ And the border descended to the Brook Kanah, southward to the brook. These cities of Ephraim *are* among the cities of Manasseh. The border of Manasseh *was* on the north side of the brook; and it ended at the sea. ¹⁰ Southward it *was* Ephraim's, northward it *was* Manasseh's, and the sea was its border. Manasseh's territory was adjoining Asher on the north and Issachar on the east. ¹¹ And in Issachar and in Asher,

Manasseh had Beth Shean and its towns, Ibleam and its towns, the inhabitants of Dor and its towns, the inhabitants of En Dor and its towns, the inhabitants of Taanach and its towns, and the inhabitants of Megiddo and its towns—three hilly regions. ¹² Yet the children of Manasseh could not drive out *the inhabitants of* those cities, but the Canaanites were determined to dwell in that land. ¹³ And it happened, when the children of Israel grew strong, that they put the Canaanites to forced labor, but did not utterly drive them out.

¹⁴ Then the children of Joseph spoke to Joshua, saying, "Why have you given us *only* one lot and one share to inherit, since we *are* a great people, inasmuch as the LORD has blessed us until now?"

¹⁵ So Joshua answered them, "If you *are* a great people, *then* go up to the forest *country* and clear a place for yourself there in the land of the Perizzites and the giants, since the mountains of Ephraim are too confined for you."

¹⁶ But the children of Joseph said, "The mountain country is not enough for us; and all the Canaanites who dwell in the land of the valley have chariots of iron, *both those* who *are* of Beth Shean and its towns and *those* who *are* of the Valley of Jezreel."

¹⁷ And Joshua spoke to the house of Joseph—to Ephraim and Manasseh—saying, "You *are* a great people and have great power; you shall not have *only* one lot, ¹⁸ but the mountain country shall be yours. Although it *is* wooded, you shall cut it down, and its farthest extent shall be yours; for you shall drive out the Canaanites, though they have iron chariots *and* are strong."

18 Now the whole congregation of the children of Israel assembled together at Shiloh, and set up the tabernacle of meeting there. And the land was subdued before them. ² But there remained among the children of Israel seven tribes which had not yet received their inheritance.

³ Then Joshua said to the children of Israel: "How long will you neglect to go

and possess the land which the LORD God of your fathers has given you? ⁴ Pick out from among you three men for *each* tribe, and I will send them; they shall rise and go through the land, survey it according to their inheritance, and come *back* to me. ⁵ And they shall divide it into seven parts. Judah shall remain in their territory on the south, and the house of Joseph shall remain in their territory on the north. ⁶ You shall therefore survey the land in seven parts and bring *the survey* here to me, that I may cast lots for you here before the LORD our God. ⁷ But the Levites have no part among you, for the priesthood of the LORD *is* their inheritance. And Gad, Reuben, and half the tribe of Manasseh have received their inheritance beyond the Jordan on the east, which Moses the servant of the LORD gave them."

⁸ Then the men arose to go away; and Joshua charged those who went to survey the land, saying, "Go, walk through the land, survey it, and come back to me, that I may cast lots for you here before the LORD in Shiloh." ⁹ So the men went, passed through the land, and wrote the survey in a book in seven parts by cities; and they came to Joshua at the camp in Shiloh. ¹⁰ Then Joshua cast lots for them in Shiloh before the LORD, and there Joshua divided the land to the children of Israel according to their divisions.

¹¹ Now the lot of the tribe of the children of Benjamin came up according to their families, and the territory of their lot came out between the children of Judah and the children of Joseph. ¹² Their border on the north side began at the Jordan, and the border went up to the side of Jericho on the north, and went up through the mountains westward; it ended at the Wilderness of Beth Aven. ¹³ The border went over from there toward Luz, to the side of Luz (which *is* Bethel) southward; and the border descended to Ataroth Addar, near the hill that *lies* on the south side of Lower Beth Horon.

¹⁴ Then the border extended around the west side to the south, from the hill that *lies* before Beth Horon southward; and it ended at Kirjath Baal (which *is* Kirjath Jearim), a city of the children of Judah. This *was* the west side.

¹⁵ The south side *began* at the end of Kirjath Jearim, and the border extended on the west and went out to the spring of the waters of Nephtoah. ¹⁶ Then the border came down to the end of the mountain that *lies* before the Valley of the Son of Hinnom, which *is* in the Valley of the Rephaim on the north, descended to the Valley of Hinnom, to the side of the Jebusite *city* on the south, and descended to En Rogel. ¹⁷ And it went around from the north, went out to En Shemesh, and extended toward Geliloth, which is before the Ascent of Adummim, and descended to the stone of Bohan the son of Reuben. ¹⁸ Then it passed along toward the north side of Arabah, and went down to Arabah. ¹⁹ And the border passed along to the north side of Beth Hoglah; then the border ended at the north bay at the Salt Sea, at the south end of the Jordan. This *was* the southern boundary.

²⁰ The Jordan was its border on the east side. This *was* the inheritance of the children of Benjamin, according to its boundaries all around, according to their families.

²¹ Now the cities of the tribe of the children of Benjamin, according to their families, were Jericho, Beth Hoglah, Emek Keziz, ²² Beth Arabah, Zemaraim, Bethel, ²³ Avim, Parah, Ophrah, ²⁴ Chephar Haammoni, Ophni, and Gaba: twelve cities with their villages; ²⁵ Gibeon, Ramah, Beeroth, ²⁶ Mizpah, Chephirah, Mozah, ²⁷ Rekem, Irpeel, Taralah, ²⁸ Zelah, Eleph, Jebus (which *is* Jerusalem), Gibeath, *and* Kirjath: fourteen cities with their villages. This was the inheritance of the children of Benjamin according to their families.

∼ PSALM 45:6–17 ∼

⁶ Your throne, O God, *is* forever and ever;
A scepter of righteousness *is* the scepter of Your kingdom.
⁷ You love righteousness and hate wickedness;
Therefore God, Your God, has anointed You
With the oil of gladness more than Your companions.
⁸ All Your garments are scented with myrrh and aloes *and* cassia,

Procrastination

How long will you neglect to go and possess the land which the Lord God of your fathers has given you?

Joshua 18:3

When Beth's boss asked her to take on an extra project, Beth saw the opportunity to prove she could handle greater responsibility. She immediately began to think how she might approach the task and her enthusiasm ran high. But when the time came to start the project, Beth found herself telling her boss she was too busy to do it justice. The project was given to someone else, who earned a promotion for completing it successfully. Beth didn't receive any new opportunities and eventually took a position with another firm.

What had kept Beth from doing the project? Simple procrastination. She put off getting started on the job until she was paralyzed with fear — fear that she might not be able to do the job or that her performance would not meet her boss' expectations. In the end, Beth didn't move ahead and thus reinforced her fears with a bigger sense of insecurity about her own ability.

If you find yourself procrastinating, ask God to show you how to overcome your fear, then do what He says. He wants you to succeed and live a fulfilled life, but you must step out in faith — He's waiting to bless you!

Out of the ivory palaces, by which
   they have made You glad.
9 Kings' daughters *are* among Your
   honorable women;
   At Your right hand stands the queen
   in gold from Ophir.

10 Listen, O daughter,
   Consider and incline your ear;
   Forget your own people also, and
   your father's house;
11 So the King will greatly desire your
   beauty;
   Because He *is* your Lord, worship
   Him.
12 And the daughter of Tyre *will come*
   with a gift;
   The rich among the people will seek
   your favor.

13 The royal daughter *is* all glorious
   within *the palace;*
   Her clothing *is* woven with gold.
14 She shall be brought to the King in
   robes of many colors;
   The virgins, her companions who
   follow her, shall be brought to
   You.
15 With gladness and rejoicing they
   shall be brought;
   They shall enter the King's palace.

16 Instead of Your fathers shall be Your
   sons,
   Whom You shall make princes in all
   the earth.
17 I will make Your name to be
   remembered in all generations;
   Therefore the people shall praise You
   forever and ever.

∼ PROVERBS 14:6 ∼

6 A scoffer seeks wisdom and does not
   find it,
   But knowledge *is* easy to him who
   understands.

∼ LUKE 12:1–31 ∼

In the meantime, when an innumerable
multitude of people had gathered together, so that they trampled one another,
He began to say to His disciples first *of
all,* "Beware of the leaven of the Pharisees, which is hypocrisy. 2 For there is
nothing covered that will not be revealed,
nor hidden that will not be known.
3 Therefore whatever you have spoken
in the dark will be heard in the light,
and what you have spoken in the ear in
inner rooms will be proclaimed on the
housetops.

4 "And I say to you, My friends, do not
be afraid of those who kill the body, and
after that have no more that they can do.
5 But I will show you whom you should
fear: Fear Him who, after He has killed,
has power to cast into hell; yes, I say to
you, fear Him!

6 "Are not five sparrows sold for two
copper coins? And not one of them is forgotten before God. 7 But the very hairs of
your head are all numbered. Do not fear
therefore; you are of more value than
many sparrows.

8 "Also I say to you, whoever confesses
Me before men, him the Son of Man also
will confess before the angels of God. 9 But
he who denies Me before men will be
denied before the angels of God.

10 "And anyone who speaks a word
against the Son of Man, it will be forgiven
him; but to him who blasphemes against
the Holy Spirit, it will not be forgiven.

11 "Now when they bring you to the
synagogues and magistrates and authorities, do not worry about how or what you
should answer, or what you should say.
12 For the Holy Spirit will teach you in
that very hour what you ought to say."

13 Then one from the crowd said to
Him, "Teacher, tell my brother to divide
the inheritance with me."

14 But He said to him, "Man, who made
Me a judge or an arbitrator over you?"
15 And He said to them, "Take heed and
beware of covetousness, for one's life does
not consist in the abundance of the things
he possesses."

16 Then He spoke a parable to them,
saying: "The ground of a certain rich man
yielded plentifully. 17 And he thought
within himself, saying, 'What shall I do,
since I have no room to store my crops?'
18 So he said, 'I will do this: I will pull
down my barns and build greater, and
there I will store all my crops and my
goods. 19 And I will say to my soul, "Soul,
you have many goods laid up for many

years; take your ease; eat, drink, *and* be merry." ' [20] But God said to him, 'Fool! This night your soul will be required of you; then whose will those things be which you have provided?'

[21] "So *is* he who lays up treasure for himself, and is not rich toward God."

[22] Then He said to His disciples, "Therefore I say to you, do not worry about your life, what you will eat; nor about the body, what you will put on. [23] Life is more than food, and the body *is more* than clothing. [24] Consider the ravens, for they neither sow nor reap, which have neither storehouse nor barn; and God feeds them. Of how much more value are you than the birds? [25] And which of you by worrying can add one cubit to his stature? [26] If you then are not able to do *the* least, why are you anxious for the rest? [27] Consider the lilies, how they grow: they neither toil nor spin; and yet I say to you, even Solomon in all his glory was not arrayed like one of these. [28] If then God so clothes the grass, which today is in the field and tomorrow is thrown into the oven, how much more *will He clothe* you, O *you* of little faith?

[29] "And do not seek what you should eat or what you should drink, nor have an anxious mind. [30] For all these things the nations of the world seek after, and your Father knows that you need these things. [31] But seek the kingdom of God, and all these things shall be added to you.

READING 105 · APRIL 15

~ JOSHUA 19:1—20:9 ~

The second lot came out for Simeon, for the tribe of the children of Simeon according to their families. And their inheritance was within the inheritance of the children of Judah. [2] They had in their inheritance Beersheba (Sheba), Moladah, [3] Hazar Shual, Balah, Ezem, [4] Eltolad, Bethul, Hormah, [5] Ziklag, Beth Marcaboth, Hazar Susah, [6] Beth Lebaoth, and Sharuhen: thirteen cities and their villages; [7] Ain, Rimmon, Ether, and Ashan: four cities and their villages; [8] and all the villages that *were* all around these cities as far as Baalath Beer, Ramah of the South. This *was* the inheritance of the tribe of the children of Simeon according to their families.

[9] The inheritance of the children of Simeon *was included* in the share of the children of Judah, for the share of the children of Judah was too much for them. Therefore the children of Simeon had *their* inheritance within the inheritance of that people.

[10] The third lot came out for the children of Zebulun according to their families, and the border of their inheritance was as far as Sarid. [11] Their border went toward the west and to Maralah, went to Dabbasheth, and extended along the brook that is east of Jokneam. [12] Then from Sarid it went eastward toward the sunrise along the border of Chisloth Tabor, and went out toward Daberath, bypassing Japhia. [13] And from there it passed along on the east of Gath Hepher, toward Eth Kazin, and extended to Rimmon, which borders on Neah. [14] Then the border went around it on the north side of Hannathon, and it ended in the Valley of Jiphthah El. [15] Included were Kattath, Nahallal, Shimron, Idalah, and Bethlehem: twelve cities with their villages. [16] This *was* the inheritance of the children of Zebulun according to their families, these cities with their villages.

[17] The fourth lot came out to Issachar, for the children of Issachar according to their families. [18] And their territory went to Jezreel, and *included* Chesulloth, Shunem, [19] Haphraim, Shion, Anaharath, [20] Rabbith, Kishion, Abez, [21] Remeth, En Gannim, En Haddah, and Beth Pazzez. [22] And the border reached to Tabor, Shahazimah, and Beth Shemesh; their border ended at the Jordan: sixteen cities with their villages. [23] This *was* the inheritance of the tribe of the children of Issachar according to their families, the cities and their villages.

[24] The fifth lot came out for the tribe of the children of Asher according to their families. [25] And their territory includ-

ed Helkath, Hali, Beten, Achshaph, [26] Alammelech, Amad, and Mishal; it reached to Mount Carmel westward, along *the Brook* Shihor Libnath. [27] It turned toward the sunrise to Beth Dagon; and it reached to Zebulun and to the Valley of Jiphthah El, then northward beyond Beth Emek and Neiel, bypassing Cabul *which was* on the left, [28] including Ebron, Rehob, Hammon, and Kanah, as far as Greater Sidon. [29] And the border turned to Ramah and to the fortified city of Tyre; then the border turned to Hosah, and ended at the sea by the region of Achzib. [30] Also Ummah, Aphek, and Rehob *were included:* twenty-two cities with their villages. [31] This *was* the inheritance of the tribe of the children of Asher according to their families, these cities with their villages.

[32] The sixth lot came out to the children of Naphtali, for the children of Naphtali according to their families. [33] And their border began at Heleph, enclosing the territory from the terebinth tree in Zaanannim, Adami Nekeb, and Jabneel, as far as Lakkum; it ended at the Jordan. [34] From Heleph the border extended westward to Aznoth Tabor, and went out from there toward Hukkok; it adjoined Zebulun on the south side and Asher on the west side, and ended at Judah by the Jordan toward the sunrise. [35] And the fortified cities *are* Ziddim, Zer, Hammath, Rakkath, Chinnereth, [36] Adamah, Ramah, Hazor, [37] Kedesh, Edrei, En Hazor, [38] Iron, Migdal El, Horem, Beth Anath, and Beth Shemesh: nineteen cities with their villages. [39] This *was* the inheritance of the tribe of the children of Naphtali according to their families, the cities and their villages.

[40] The seventh lot came out for the tribe of the children of Dan according to their families. [41] And the territory of their inheritance was Zorah, Eshtaol, Ir Shemesh, [42] Shaalabbin, Aijalon, Jethlah, [43] Elon, Timnah, Ekron, [44] Eltekeh, Gibbethon, Baalath, [45] Jehud, Bene Berak, Gath Rimmon, [46] Me Jarkon, and Rakkon, with the region near Joppa. [47] And the border of the children of Dan went beyond these, because the children of Dan went up to fight against Leshem and took it; and they struck it with the edge of the sword, took

possession of it, and dwelt in it. They called Leshem, Dan, after the name of Dan their father. [48] This *is* the inheritance of the tribe of the children of Dan according to their families, these cities with their villages.

[49] When they had made an end of dividing the land as an inheritance according to their borders, the children of Israel gave an inheritance among them to Joshua the son of Nun. [50] According to the word of the LORD they gave him the city which he asked for, Timnath Serah in the mountains of Ephraim; and he built the city and dwelt in it.

[51] These *were* the inheritances which Eleazar the priest, Joshua the son of Nun, and the heads of the fathers of the tribes of the children of Israel divided as an inheritance by lot in Shiloh before the LORD, at the door of the tabernacle of meeting. So they made an end of dividing the country.

20 The LORD also spoke to Joshua, saying, [2] "Speak to the children of Israel, saying: 'Appoint for yourselves cities of refuge, of which I spoke to you through Moses, [3] that the slayer who kills a person accidentally *or* unintentionally may flee there; and they shall be your refuge from the avenger of blood. [4] And when he flees to one of those cities, and stands at the entrance of the gate of the city, and declares his case in the hearing of the elders of that city, they shall take him into the city as one of them, and give him a place, that he may dwell among them. [5] Then if the avenger of blood pursues him, they shall not deliver the slayer into his hand, because he struck his neighbor unintentionally, but did not hate him beforehand. [6] And he shall dwell in that city until he stands before the congregation for judgment, *and* until the death of the one who is high priest in those days. Then the slayer may return and come to his own city and his own house, to the city from which he fled.' "

[7] So they appointed Kedesh in Galilee, in the mountains of Naphtali, Shechem in the mountains of Ephraim, and Kirjath Arba (which *is* Hebron) in the mountains of Judah. [8] And on the other side of the Jordan, by Jericho eastward, they assigned

One Percent

A philosophical clock — one capable of deep pondering and meditation — once spent a great deal of time thinking about its own future. It noticed that it had to tick twice each second. *How much ticking might that be?* the clock questioned.

The clock calculated that it ticked 120 times each minute, which was 7,200 times every hour. In the twenty-four hours of a day it would tick 172,800 times. This meant 63,072,000 ticks every year. At that point in his calculations, the clock had begun to perspire profusely at the very thought.

Finally, the clock calculated that in a ten-year period it would have to tick 630,720,000 times! At that point, the clock collapsed from nervous exhaustion!

An equally scientific and philosophical person has concluded that ninety-five percent of everything that we worry about doesn't happen. Of the five percent that does happen, four out of five times, things turn out much better than anticipated. In the end, only about one percent of all the bad that we think might happen actually does, and of this it's rarely as bad as we imagine. Therefore, what profit is there in worry? Enjoy life!

> Do not fear, little flock, for it is your Father's good pleasure to give you the kingdom.
>
> *Luke 12:32*

Bezer in the wilderness on the plain, from the tribe of Reuben, Ramoth in Gilead, from the tribe of Gad, and Golan in Bashan, from the tribe of Manasseh. [9] These were the cities appointed for all the children of Israel and for the stranger who dwelt among them, that whoever killed a person accidentally might flee there, and not die by the hand of the avenger of blood until he stood before the congregation.

~ PSALM 46:1–6 ~

[1] God *is* our refuge and strength,
    A very present help in trouble.
[2] Therefore we will not fear,
    Even though the earth be removed,
    And though the mountains be
        carried into the midst of the sea;
[3] *Though* its waters roar *and* be
        troubled,
    Though the mountains shake with its
        swelling.   Selah

[4] *There is* a river whose streams shall
        make glad the city of God,
    The holy *place* of the tabernacle of
        the Most High.
[5] God *is* in the midst of her, she shall
        not be moved;
    God shall help her, just at the break
        of dawn.
[6] The nations raged, the kingdoms
        were moved;
    He uttered His voice, the earth
        melted.

~ PROVERBS 14:7–11 ~

[7] Go from the presence of a foolish
        man,
    When you do not perceive *in him*
        the lips of knowledge.
[8] The wisdom of the prudent *is* to
        understand his way,
    But the folly of fools *is* deceit.

[9] Fools mock at sin,
    But among the upright *there is*
        favor.

[10] The heart knows its own bitterness,
    And a stranger does not share its joy.

[11] The house of the wicked will be
        overthrown,
    But the tent of the upright will
        flourish.

~ LUKE 12:32–59 ~

"Do not fear, little flock, for it is your Father's good pleasure to give you the kingdom. [33] Sell what you have and give alms; provide yourselves money bags which do not grow old, a treasure in the heavens that does not fail, where no thief approaches nor moth destroys. [34] For where your treasure is, there your heart will be also.

[35] "Let your waist be girded and *your* lamps burning; [36] and you yourselves be like men who wait for their master, when he will return from the wedding, that when he comes and knocks they may open to him immediately. [37] Blessed *are* those servants whom the master, when he comes, will find watching. Assuredly, I say to you that he will gird himself and have them sit down *to eat,* and will come and serve them. [38] And if he should come in the second watch, or come in the third watch, and find *them* so, blessed are those servants. [39] But know this, that if the master of the house had known what hour the thief would come, he would have watched and not allowed his house to be broken into. [40] Therefore you also be ready, for the Son of Man is coming at an hour you do not expect."

[41] Then Peter said to Him, "Lord, do You speak this parable *only* to us, or to all *people?*"

[42] And the Lord said, "Who then is that faithful and wise steward, whom *his* master will make ruler over his household, to give *them their* portion of food in due season? [43] Blessed *is* that servant whom his master will find so doing when he comes. [44] Truly, I say to you that he will make him ruler over all that he has. [45] But if that servant says in his heart, 'My master is delaying his coming,' and begins to beat the male and female servants, and to eat and drink and be drunk, [46] the master of that servant will come on a day when he is not looking for *him,* and at an hour when he is not aware, and will cut him in two and appoint *him* his portion with the

unbelievers. ⁴⁷ And that servant who knew his master's will, and did not prepare *himself* or do according to his will, shall be beaten with many *stripes.* ⁴⁸ But he who did not know, yet committed things deserving of stripes, shall be beaten with few. For everyone to whom much is given, from him much will be required; and to whom much has been committed, of him they will ask the more.

⁴⁹ "I came to send fire on the earth, and how I wish it were already kindled! ⁵⁰ But I have a baptism to be baptized with, and how distressed I am till it is accomplished! ⁵¹ Do *you* suppose that I came to give peace on earth? I tell you, not at all, but rather division. ⁵² For from now on five in one house will be divided: three against two, and two against three. ⁵³ Father will be divided against son and son against father, mother against daughter and

daughter against mother, mother-in-law against her daughter-in-law and daughter-in-law against her mother-in-law."

⁵⁴ Then He also said to the multitudes, "Whenever *you see* a cloud rising out of the west, immediately you say, 'A shower is coming'; and so it is. ⁵⁵ And when you see the south wind blow, you say, 'There will be hot weather'; and there is. ⁵⁶ Hypocrites! You can discern the face of the sky and of the earth, but how *is it* you do not discern this time?

⁵⁷ "Yes, and why, even of yourselves, do you not judge what is right? ⁵⁸ When you go with your adversary to the magistrate, make every effort along the way to settle with him, lest he drag you to the judge, the judge deliver you to the officer, and the officer throw you into prison. ⁵⁹ I tell you, you shall not depart from there till you have paid the very last mite."

READING 106 · APRIL 16

～ JOSHUA 21:1—22:34 ～

Then the heads of the fathers' *houses* of the Levites came near to Eleazar the priest, to Joshua the son of Nun, and to the heads of the fathers' *houses* of the tribes of the children of Israel. ² And they spoke to them at Shiloh in the land of Canaan, saying, "The LORD commanded through Moses to give us cities to dwell in, with their common-lands for our livestock." ³ So the children of Israel gave to the Levites from their inheritance, at the commandment of the LORD, these cities and their common-lands:

⁴ Now the lot came out for the families of the Kohathites. And the children of Aaron the priest, *who were* of the Levites, had thirteen cities by lot from the tribe of Judah, from the tribe of Simeon, and from the tribe of Benjamin. ⁵ The rest of the children of Kohath had ten cities by lot from the families of the tribe of Ephraim, from the tribe of Dan, and from the half-tribe of Manasseh.

⁶ And the children of Gershon had thirteen cities by lot from the families of the tribe of Issachar, from the tribe of Asher,

from the tribe of Naphtali, and from the half-tribe of Manasseh in Bashan.

⁷ The children of Merari according to their families had twelve cities from the tribe of Reuben, from the tribe of Gad, and from the tribe of Zebulun.

⁸ And the children of Israel gave these cities with their common-lands by lot to the Levites, as the LORD had commanded by the hand of Moses.

⁹ So they gave from the tribe of the children of Judah and from the tribe of the children of Simeon these cities which are designated by name, ¹⁰ which were for the children of Aaron, one of the families of the Kohathites, *who were* of the children of Levi; for the lot was theirs first. ¹¹ And they gave them Kirjath Arba (*Arba was* the father of Anak), which *is* Hebron, in the mountains of Judah, with the common-land surrounding it. ¹² But the fields of the city and its villages they gave to Caleb the son of Jephunneh as his possession.

¹³ Thus to the children of Aaron the priest they gave Hebron with its common-land (a city of refuge for the slayer),

Libnah with its common-land, ¹⁴ Jattir with its common-land, Eshtemoa with its common-land, ¹⁵ Holon with its common-land, Debir with its common-land, ¹⁶ Ain with its common-land, Juttah with its common-land, and Beth Shemesh with its common-land: nine cities from those two tribes; ¹⁷ and from the tribe of Benjamin, Gibeon with its common-land, Geba with its common-land, ¹⁸ Anathoth with its common-land, and Almon with its common-land: four cities. ¹⁹ All the cities of the children of Aaron, the priests, *were* thirteen cities with their common-lands.

²⁰ And the families of the children of Kohath, the Levites, the rest of the children of Kohath, even they had the cities of their lot from the tribe of Ephraim. ²¹ For they gave them Shechem with its common-land in the mountains of Ephraim (a city of refuge for the slayer), Gezer with its common-land, ²² Kibzaim with its common-land, and Beth Horon with its common-land: four cities; ²³ and from the tribe of Dan, Eltekeh with its common-land, Gibbethon with its common-land, ²⁴ Aijalon with its common-land, *and* Gath Rimmon with its common-land: four cities; ²⁵ and from the half-tribe of Manasseh, Tanach with its common-land and Gath Rimmon with its common-land: two cities. ²⁶ All the ten cities with their common-lands were for the rest of the families of the children of Kohath.

²⁷ Also to the children of Gershon, of the families of the Levites, from the *other* half-tribe of Manasseh, *they gave* Golan in Bashan with its common-land (a city of refuge for the slayer), and Be Eshterah with its common-land: two cities; ²⁸ and from the tribe of Issachar, Kishion with its common-land, Daberath with its common-land, ²⁹ Jarmuth with its common-land, *and* En Gannim with its common-land: four cities; ³⁰ and from the tribe of Asher, Mishal with its common-land, Abdon with its common-land, ³¹ Helkath with its common-land, and Rehob with its common-land: four cities; ³² and from the tribe of Naphtali, Kedesh in Galilee with its common-land (a city of refuge for the slayer), Hammoth Dor with its common-land, and Kartan with its common-land: three cities. ³³ All

the cities of the Gershonites according to their families *were* thirteen cities with their common-lands.

³⁴ And to the families of the children of Merari, the rest of the Levites, from the tribe of Zebulun, Jokneam with its common-land, Kartah with its common-land, ³⁵ Dimnah with its common-land, *and* Nahalal with its common-land: four cities; ³⁶ and from the tribe of Reuben, Bezer with its common-land, Jahaz with its common-land, ³⁷ Kedemoth with its common-land, and Mephaath with its common-land: four cities; ³⁸ and from the tribe of Gad, Ramoth in Gilead with its common-land (a city of refuge for the slayer), Mahanaim with its common-land, ³⁹ Heshbon with its common-land, *and* Jazer with its common-land: four cities in all. ⁴⁰ So all the cities for the children of Merari according to their families, the rest of the families of the Levites, were *by* their lot twelve cities.

⁴¹ All the cities of the Levites within the possession of the children of Israel *were* forty-eight cities with their common-lands. ⁴² Every one of these cities had its common-land surrounding it; thus *were* all these cities.

⁴³ So the LORD gave to Israel all the land of which He had sworn to give to their fathers, and they took possession of it and dwelt in it. ⁴⁴ The LORD gave them rest all around, according to all that He had sworn to their fathers. And not a man of all their enemies stood against them; the LORD delivered all their enemies into their hand. ⁴⁵ Not a word failed of any good thing which the LORD had spoken to the house of Israel. All came to pass.

22 Then Joshua called the Reubenites, the Gadites, and half the tribe of Manasseh, ² and said to them: "You have kept all that Moses the servant of the LORD commanded you, and have obeyed my voice in all that I commanded you. ³ You have not left your brethren these many days, up to this day, but have kept the charge of the commandment of the LORD your God. ⁴ And now the LORD your God has given rest to your brethren, as He promised them; now therefore, return and go to your tents *and* to the land of your possession, which Moses the

Something Better

A little girl had been playing with a neighbor who had a new bicycle and wanted more than anything to trade in her "baby bike" for a real "big girl" model like the one her friend rode. When she asked her parents for a new bike, they both said, "Wait until your birthday."

Two weeks later, the little girl saw a picture of a bicycle in the newspaper. She stared at it in awe. The ad read, "Three speeds. Gear shifts. Light and easy to handle. Hand brakes. In many colors. The works!" She asked her parents if they might visit the store where the bike was for sale, and they agreed. To her delight, she found the bicycle came in hot pink! "But don't you want a bike just like your friend has?" Mom asked with a smile. "No way," the little girl replied. "I've got something better in mind!"

Very often, we can look back with thanksgiving that God did *not* answer our prayers the way we thought they should be answered. His answer reflects something better that we didn't know about or think to request!

When God's answer to our prayer is not what we expect, we can have confidence in His loving wisdom, recognizing He always knows what's best!

servant of the LORD gave you on the other side of the Jordan. 5 But take careful heed to do the commandment and the law which Moses the servant of the LORD commanded you, to love the LORD your God, to walk in all His ways, to keep His commandments, to hold fast to Him, and to serve Him with all your heart and with all your soul." 6 So Joshua blessed them and sent them away, and they went to their tents.

7 Now to half the tribe of Manasseh Moses had given a possession in Bashan, but to the other half of it Joshua gave a possession among their brethren on this side of the Jordan, westward. And indeed, when Joshua sent them away to their tents, he blessed them, 8 and spoke to them, saying, "Return with much riches to your tents, with very much livestock, with silver, with gold, with bronze, with iron, and with very much clothing. Divide the spoil of your enemies with your brethren."

9 So the children of Reuben, the children of Gad, and half the tribe of Manasseh returned, and departed from the children of Israel at Shiloh, which is in the land of Canaan, to go to the country of Gilead, to the land of their possession, which they had obtained according to the word of the LORD by the hand of Moses.

10 And when they came to the region of the Jordan which is in the land of Canaan, the children of Reuben, the children of Gad, and half the tribe of Manasseh built an altar there by the Jordan—a great, impressive altar. 11 Now the children of Israel heard someone say, "Behold, the children of Reuben, the children of Gad, and half the tribe of Manasseh have built an altar on the frontier of the land of Canaan, in the region of the Jordan—on the children of Israel's side." 12 And when the children of Israel heard of it, the whole congregation of the children of Israel gathered together at Shiloh to go to war against them.

13 Then the children of Israel sent Phinehas the son of Eleazar the priest to the children of Reuben, to the children of Gad, and to half the tribe of Manasseh, into the land of Gilead, 14 and with him ten rulers, one ruler each from the chief house of every tribe of Israel; and each one was the head of the house of his father among the divisions of Israel. 15 Then they came to the children of Reuben, to the children of Gad, and to half the tribe of Manasseh, to the land of Gilead, and they spoke with them, saying, 16 "Thus says the whole congregation of the LORD: 'What treachery is this that you have committed against the God of Israel, to turn away this day from following the LORD, in that you have built for yourselves an altar, that you might rebel this day against the LORD? 17 Is the iniquity of Peor not enough for us, from which we are not cleansed till this day, although there was a plague in the congregation of the LORD, 18 but that you must turn away this day from following the LORD? And it shall be, if you rebel today against the LORD, that tomorrow He will be angry with the whole congregation of Israel. 19 Nevertheless, if the land of your possession is unclean, then cross over to the land of the possession of the LORD, where the LORD's tabernacle stands, and take possession among us; but do not rebel against the LORD, nor rebel against us, by building yourselves an altar besides the altar of the LORD our God. 20 Did not Achan the son of Zerah commit a trespass in the accursed thing, and wrath fell on all the congregation of Israel? And that man did not perish alone in his iniquity.' "

21 Then the children of Reuben, the children of Gad, and half the tribe of Manasseh answered and said to the heads of the divisions of Israel: 22 "The LORD God of gods, the LORD God of gods, He knows, and let Israel itself know—if it is in rebellion, or if in treachery against the LORD, do not save us this day. 23 If we have built ourselves an altar to turn from following the LORD, or if to offer on it burnt offerings or grain offerings, or if to offer peace offerings on it, let the LORD Himself require an account. 24 But in fact we have done it for fear, for a reason, saying, 'In time to come your descendants may speak to our descendants, saying, "What have you to do with the LORD God of Israel? 25 For the LORD has made the Jordan a border between you and us, you children of Reuben and children of Gad. You have no part in the LORD." So your

descendants would make our descendants cease fearing the LORD.' ²⁶ Therefore we said, 'Let us now prepare to build ourselves an altar, not for burnt offering nor for sacrifice, ²⁷ but *that* it *may be* a witness between you and us and our generations after us, that we may perform the service of the LORD before Him with our burnt offerings, with our sacrifices, and with our peace offerings; that your descendants may not say to our descendants in time to come, "You have no part in the LORD." ' ²⁸ Therefore we said that it will be, when they say *this* to us or to our generations in time to come, that we may say, 'Here is the replica of the altar of the LORD which our fathers made, though not for burnt offerings nor for sacrifices; but it *is* a witness between you and us.' ²⁹ Far be it from us that we should rebel against the LORD, and turn from following the LORD this day, to build an altar for burnt offerings, for grain offerings, or for sacrifices, besides the altar of the LORD our God which *is* before His tabernacle."

³⁰ Now when Phinehas the priest and the rulers of the congregation, the heads of the divisions of Israel who *were* with him, heard the words that the children of Reuben, the children of Gad, and the children of Manasseh spoke, it pleased them. ³¹ Then Phinehas the son of Eleazar the priest said to the children of Reuben, the children of Gad, and the children of Manasseh, "This day we perceive that the LORD *is* among us, because you have not committed this treachery against the LORD. Now you have delivered the children of Israel out of the hand of the LORD."

³² And Phinehas the son of Eleazar the priest, and the rulers, returned from the children of Reuben and the children of Gad, from the land of Gilead to the land of Canaan, to the children of Israel, and brought back word to them. ³³ So the thing pleased the children of Israel, and the children of Israel blessed God; they spoke no more of going against them in battle, to destroy the land where the children of Reuben and Gad dwelt.

³⁴ The children of Reuben and the children of Gad called the altar, *Witness,* "For *it is* a witness between us that the LORD *is* God."

∼ PSALM 46:7-11 ∼

⁷ The LORD of hosts *is* with us;
The God of Jacob *is* our refuge.
                                    Selah

⁸ Come, behold the works of the
    LORD,
Who has made desolations in the
    earth.
⁹ He makes wars cease to the end of
    the earth;
He breaks the bow and cuts the
    spear in two;
He burns the chariot in the fire.

¹⁰ Be still, and know that I *am* God;
I will be exalted among the nations,
I will be exalted in the earth!

¹¹ The LORD of hosts *is* with us;
The God of Jacob *is* our refuge.
                                    Selah

∼ PROVERBS 14:12, 13 ∼

¹² There is a way *that seems* right to a
    man,
But its end *is* the way of death.

¹³ Even in laughter the heart may
    sorrow,
And the end of mirth *may be* grief.

∼ LUKE 13:1-23 ∼

There were present at that season some who told Him about the Galileans whose blood Pilate had mingled with their sacrifices. ² And Jesus answered and said to them, "Do you suppose that these Galileans were worse sinners than all *other* Galileans, because they suffered such things? ³ I tell you, no; but unless you repent you will all likewise perish. ⁴ Or those eighteen on whom the tower in Siloam fell and killed them, do you think that they were worse sinners than all *other* men who dwelt in Jerusalem? ⁵ I tell you, no; but unless you repent you will all likewise perish."

⁶ He also spoke this parable: "A certain *man* had a fig tree planted in his vineyard, and he came seeking fruit on it and

found none. [7] Then he said to the keeper of his vineyard, 'Look, for three years I have come seeking fruit on this fig tree and find none. Cut it down; why does it use up the ground?' [8] But he answered and said to him, 'Sir, let it alone this year also, until I dig around it and fertilize *it*. [9] And if it bears fruit, *well*. But if not, after that you can cut it down.' "

[10] Now He was teaching in one of the synagogues on the Sabbath. [11] And behold, there was a woman who had a spirit of infirmity eighteen years, and was bent over and could in no way raise *herself* up. [12] But when Jesus saw her, He called *her* to *Him* and said to her, "Woman, you are loosed from your infirmity." [13] And He laid *His* hands on her, and immediately she was made straight, and glorified God.

[14] But the ruler of the synagogue answered with indignation, because Jesus had healed on the Sabbath; and he said to the crowd, "There are six days on which men ought to work; therefore come and be healed on them, and not on the Sabbath day."

[15] The Lord then answered him and said, "Hypocrite! Does not each one of you on the Sabbath loose his ox or donkey from the stall, and lead *it* away to water it? [16] So ought not this woman, being a daughter of Abraham, whom Satan has bound—think of it—for eighteen years, be loosed from this bond on the Sabbath?" [17] And when He said these things, all His adversaries were put to shame; and all the multitude rejoiced for all the glorious things that were done by Him.

[18] Then He said, "What is the kingdom of God like? And to what shall I compare it? [19] It is like a mustard seed, which a man took and put in his garden; and it grew and became a large tree, and the birds of the air nested in its branches."

[20] And again He said, "To what shall I liken the kingdom of God? [21] It is like leaven, which a woman took and hid in three measures of meal till it was all leavened."

[22] And He went through the cities and villages, teaching, and journeying toward Jerusalem. [23] Then one said to Him, "Lord, are there few who are saved?"

READING 107 · APRIL 17

~ JOSHUA 23:1—24:33 ~

Now it came to pass, a long time after the LORD had given rest to Israel from all their enemies round about, that Joshua was old, advanced in age. [2] And Joshua called for all Israel, for their elders, for their heads, for their judges, and for their officers, and said to them:

"I am old, advanced in age. [3] You have seen all that the LORD your God has done to all these nations because of you, for the LORD your God *is* He who has fought for you. [4] See, I have divided to you by lot these nations that remain, to be an inheritance for your tribes, from the Jordan, with all the nations that I have cut off, as far as the Great Sea westward. [5] And the LORD your God will expel them from before you and drive them out of your sight. So you shall possess their land, as the LORD your God promised you. [6] Therefore be very courageous to keep and to do all that is written in the Book of the Law of Moses, lest you turn aside from it to the right hand or to the left, [7] *and* lest you go among these nations, these who remain among you. You shall not make mention of the name of their gods, nor cause *anyone* to swear *by them;* you shall not serve them nor bow down to them, [8] but you shall hold fast to the LORD your God, as you have done to this day. [9] For the LORD has driven out from before you great and strong nations; but *as for* you, no one has been able to stand against you to this day. [10] One man of you shall chase a thousand, for the LORD your God *is* He who fights for you, as He promised you. [11] Therefore take careful heed to yourselves, that you love the LORD your God. [12] Or else, if indeed you do go back, and cling to the remnant of these nations—these that remain among you—and make marriages with

The Importance of Agreement

Choose for yourselves this day whom you will serve. . . . As for me and my house, we will serve the Lord.

Joshua 24:15

As Train 8017 made its way through Salerno, Italy, on March 2, 1944, it gave no sign that disaster was in the making. The chugging train didn't collide with anything on that rain-soaked evening. It didn't derail or burn. But shortly after 1:00 AM, the train loaded with 600 passengers lumbered into the Galleria delle Armi.

When the two locomotives pulling the train reached mid-tunnel, its drivewheels began to slip. Sand was sprayed on the tracks but to no avail. The wheels lost traction and the train stopped. Any other details are pure speculation since both engineers died. Carbon monoxide snuffed out the lives of nearly 500 people.

As analysts surveyed the wreckage, they found that the leading locomotive was unbraked, its controls set in reverse. The second locomotive was also unbraked, but its throttle was positioned "full ahead." The two locomotives had pulled and pushed against each other, their engineers obviously having fatally different ideas about what to do! Some have speculated that no lives would have been lost if the engineers had only been in agreement about which direction to go.

Today, make a decision with your spouse that you will both move your thought life in the direction of God — then stay ready by the controls of your minds.

them, and go in to them and they to you, [13] know for certain that the LORD your God will no longer drive out these nations from before you. But they shall be snares and traps to you, and scourges on your sides and thorns in your eyes, until you perish from this good land which the LORD your God has given you.

[14] "Behold, this day I *am* going the way of all the earth. And you know in all your hearts and in all your souls that not one thing has failed of all the good things which the LORD your God spoke concerning you. All have come to pass for you; not one word of them has failed. [15] Therefore it shall come to pass, that as all the good things have come upon you which the LORD your God promised you, so the LORD will bring upon you all harmful things, until He has destroyed you from this good land which the LORD your God has given you. [16] When you have transgressed the covenant of the LORD your God, which He commanded you, and have gone and served other gods, and bowed down to them, then the anger of the LORD will burn against you, and you shall perish quickly from the good land which He has given you."

24 Then Joshua gathered all the tribes of Israel to Shechem and called for the elders of Israel, for their heads, for their judges, and for their officers; and they presented themselves before God. [2] And Joshua said to all the people, "Thus says the LORD God of Israel: 'Your fathers, *including* Terah, the father of Abraham and the father of Nahor, dwelt on the other side of the River in old times; and they served other gods. [3] Then I took your father Abraham from the other side of the River, led him throughout all the land of Canaan, and multiplied his descendants and gave him Isaac. [4] To Isaac I gave Jacob and Esau. To Esau I gave the mountains of Seir to possess, but Jacob and his children went down to Egypt. [5] Also I sent Moses and Aaron, and I plagued Egypt, according to what I did among them. Afterward I brought you out.

[6] 'Then I brought your fathers out of Egypt, and you came to the sea; and the Egyptians pursued your fathers with chariots and horsemen to the Red Sea. [7] So they cried out to the LORD; and He put darkness between you and the Egyptians, brought the sea upon them, and covered them. And your eyes saw what I did in Egypt. Then you dwelt in the wilderness a long time. [8] And I brought you into the land of the Amorites, who dwelt on the other side of the Jordan, and they fought with you. But I gave them into your hand, that you might possess their land, and I destroyed them from before you. [9] Then Balak the son of Zippor, king of Moab, arose to make war against Israel, and sent and called Balaam the son of Beor to curse you. [10] But I would not listen to Balaam; therefore he continued to bless you. So I delivered you out of his hand. [11] Then you went over the Jordan and came to Jericho. And the men of Jericho fought against you—*also* the Amorites, the Perizzites, the Canaanites, the Hittites, the Girgashites, the Hivites, and the Jebusites. But I delivered them into your hand. [12] I sent the hornet before you which drove them out from before you, *also* the two kings of the Amorites, *but* not with your sword or with your bow. [13] I have given you a land for which you did not labor, and cities which you did not build, and you dwell in them; you eat of the vineyards and olive groves which you did not plant.'

[14] "Now therefore, fear the LORD, serve Him in sincerity and in truth, and put away the gods which your fathers served on the other side of the River and in Egypt. Serve the LORD! [15] And if it seems evil to you to serve the LORD, choose for yourselves this day whom you will serve, whether the gods which your fathers served that *were* on the other side of the River, or the gods of the Amorites, in whose land you dwell. But as for me and my house, we will serve the LORD."

[16] So the people answered and said: "Far be it from us that we should forsake the LORD to serve other gods; [17] for the LORD our God *is* He who brought us and our fathers up out of the land of Egypt, from the house of bondage, who did those great signs in our sight, and preserved us in all the way that we went and among all the people through whom we passed. [18] And the LORD drove out from before us all the people, including the Amorites who

dwelt in the land. We also will serve the LORD, for He *is* our God."

¹⁹ But Joshua said to the people, "You cannot serve the LORD, for He *is* a holy God. He *is* a jealous God; He will not forgive your transgressions nor your sins. ²⁰ If you forsake the LORD and serve foreign gods, then He will turn and do you harm and consume you, after He has done you good."

²¹ And the people said to Joshua, "No, but we will serve the LORD!"

²² So Joshua said to the people, "You *are* witnesses against yourselves that you have chosen the LORD for yourselves, to serve Him."

And they said, "*We are* witnesses!"

²³ "Now therefore," *he said,* "put away the foreign gods which *are* among you, and incline your heart to the LORD God of Israel."

²⁴ And the people said to Joshua, "The LORD our God we will serve, and His voice we will obey!"

²⁵ So Joshua made a covenant with the people that day, and made for them a statute and an ordinance in Shechem.

²⁶ Then Joshua wrote these words in the Book of the Law of God. And he took a large stone, and set it up there under the oak that *was* by the sanctuary of the LORD. ²⁷ And Joshua said to all the people, "Behold, this stone shall be a witness to us, for it has heard all the words of the LORD which He spoke to us. It shall therefore be a witness to you, lest you deny your God." ²⁸ So Joshua let the people depart, each to his own inheritance.

²⁹ Now it came to pass after these things that Joshua the son of Nun, the servant of the LORD, died, *being* one hundred and ten years old. ³⁰ And they buried him within the border of his inheritance at Timnath Serah, which *is* in the mountains of Ephraim, on the north side of Mount Gaash.

³¹ Israel served the LORD all the days of Joshua, and all the days of the elders who outlived Joshua, who had known all the works of the LORD which He had done for Israel.

³² The bones of Joseph, which the children of Israel had brought up out of Egypt, they buried at Shechem, in the plot of ground which Jacob had bought from the sons of Hamor the father of Shechem for one hundred pieces of silver, and which had become an inheritance of the children of Joseph.

³³ And Eleazar the son of Aaron died. They buried him in a hill *belonging to* Phinehas his son, which was given to him in the mountains of Ephraim.

∼ PSALM 47:1–9 ∼

¹ Oh, clap your hands, all you peoples!
   Shout to God with the voice of triumph!
² For the LORD Most High *is* awesome;
   He is a great King over all the earth.
³ He will subdue the peoples under us,
   And the nations under our feet.
⁴ He will choose our inheritance for us,
   The excellence of Jacob whom He loves.   Selah

⁵ God has gone up with a shout,
   The LORD with the sound of a trumpet.
⁶ Sing praises to God, sing praises!
   Sing praises to our King, sing praises!
⁷ For God *is* the King of all the earth;
   Sing praises with understanding.

⁸ God reigns over the nations;
   God sits on His holy throne.
⁹ The princes of the people have gathered together,
   The people of the God of Abraham.
   For the shields of the earth *belong* to God;
   He is greatly exalted.

∼ PROVERBS 14:14 ∼

¹⁴ The backslider in heart will be filled with his own ways,
   But a good man *will be satisfied* from above.

∼ LUKE 13:23–35 ∼

And He said to them, ²⁴ "Strive to enter through the narrow gate, for many, I say to you, will seek to enter and will not be able. ²⁵ When once the Master of the house has risen up and shut the door, and you begin to stand outside and knock at the door, saying, 'Lord, Lord, open for us,' and He will answer and say to you, 'I do not know you, where you are from,' ²⁶ then you will begin to say, 'We ate and drank in Your presence, and You taught in our streets.' ²⁷ But He will say, 'I tell you I do not know you, where you are from. Depart from Me, all you workers of iniquity.' ²⁸ There will be weeping and gnashing of teeth, when you see Abraham and Isaac and Jacob and all the prophets in the kingdom of God, and yourselves thrust out. ²⁹ They will come from the east and the west, from the north and the south, and sit down in the kingdom of God. ³⁰ And indeed there are last who will be first, and there are first who will be last."

³¹ On that very day some Pharisees came, saying to Him, "Get out and depart from here, for Herod wants to kill You."

³² And He said to them, "Go, tell that fox, 'Behold, I cast out demons and perform cures today and tomorrow, and the third *day* I shall be perfected.' ³³ Nevertheless I must journey today, tomorrow, and the *day* following; for it cannot be that a prophet should perish outside of Jerusalem.

³⁴ "O Jerusalem, Jerusalem, the one who kills the prophets and stones those who are sent to her! How often I wanted to gather your children together, as a hen *gathers* her brood under *her* wings, but you were not willing! ³⁵ See! Your house is left to you desolate; and assuredly, I say to you, you shall not see Me until *the time* comes when you say, 'Blessed is He who comes in the name of the LORD!' "

READING 108 · APRIL 18

～ JUDGES 1:1—2:23 ～

Now after the death of Joshua it came to pass that the children of Israel asked the LORD, saying, "Who shall be first to go up for us against the Canaanites to fight against them?"

² And the LORD said, "Judah shall go up. Indeed I have delivered the land into his hand."

³ So Judah said to Simeon his brother, "Come up with me to my allotted territory, that we may fight against the Canaanites; and I will likewise go with you to your allotted territory." And Simeon went with him. ⁴ Then Judah went up, and the LORD delivered the Canaanites and the Perizzites into their hand; and they killed ten thousand men at Bezek. ⁵ And they found Adoni-Bezek in Bezek, and fought against him; and they defeated the Canaanites and the Perizzites. ⁶ Then Adoni-Bezek fled, and they pursued him and caught him and cut off his thumbs and big toes. ⁷ And Adoni-Bezek said, "Seventy kings with their thumbs and big toes cut off used to gather *scraps* under my table; as I have done, so God has re-

paid me." Then they brought him to Jerusalem, and there he died.

⁸ Now the children of Judah fought against Jerusalem and took it; they struck it with the edge of the sword and set the city on fire. ⁹ And afterward the children of Judah went down to fight against the Canaanites who dwelt in the mountains, in the South, and in the lowland. ¹⁰ Then Judah went against the Canaanites who dwelt in Hebron. (Now the name of Hebron *was* formerly Kirjath Arba.) And they killed Sheshai, Ahiman, and Talmai.

¹¹ From there they went against the inhabitants of Debir. (The name of Debir *was* formerly Kirjath Sepher.)

¹² Then Caleb said, "Whoever attacks Kirjath Sepher and takes it, to him I will give my daughter Achsah as wife." ¹³ And Othniel the son of Kenaz, Caleb's younger brother, took it; so he gave him his daughter Achsah as wife. ¹⁴ Now it happened, when she came *to him,* that she urged him to ask her father for a field. And she dismounted from *her* donkey, and Caleb said to her, "What do you wish?" ¹⁵ So she

Silence Beyond Words

Marie Louise de La Ramee says in *Ouida*, "There are many moments in friendship, as in love, when silence is beyond words. The faults of our friend may be clear to us, but it is well to seem to shut our eyes to them.

"Friendship is usually treated by the majority of mankind as a tough and everlasting thing which will survive all manner of bad treatment. But this is an exceedingly great and foolish error; it may die in an hour of a single unwise word."

If the words "I love you" are the most important three words in a marriage, the words "I'm sorry" are probably the most important two! The more a spouse is willing to admit fault, the greater the likelihood the other spouse will also grow to be vulnerable enough to admit error. That doesn't mean a person should apologize for an error that has not been made; to do so would be to become a doormat or to manifest a false humility. When one is standing in the right, although the other cannot see it, the better approach is silence. Not saying, "I'm not speaking to you until you apologize," but saying nothing more about the issue. Remember, silence is golden.

said to him, "Give me a blessing; since you have given me land in the South, give me also springs of water."

And Caleb gave her the upper springs and the lower springs.

[16] Now the children of the Kenite, Moses' father-in-law, went up from the City of Palms with the children of Judah into the Wilderness of Judah, which *lies* in the South *near* Arad; and they went and dwelt among the people. [17] And Judah went with his brother Simeon, and they attacked the Canaanites who inhabited Zephath, and utterly destroyed it. So the name of the city was called Hormah. [18] Also Judah took Gaza with its territory, Ashkelon with its territory, and Ekron with its territory. [19] So the LORD was with Judah. And they drove out the mountaineers, but they could not drive out the inhabitants of the lowland, because they had chariots of iron. [20] And they gave Hebron to Caleb, as Moses had said. Then he expelled from there the three sons of Anak. [21] But the children of Benjamin did not drive out the Jebusites who inhabited Jerusalem; so the Jebusites dwell with the children of Benjamin in Jerusalem to this day.

[22] And the house of Joseph also went up against Bethel, and the LORD *was* with them. [23] So the house of Joseph sent men to spy out Bethel. (The name of the city *was* formerly Luz.) [24] And when the spies saw a man coming out of the city, they said to him, "Please show us the entrance to the city, and we will show you mercy." [25] So he showed them the entrance to the city, and they struck the city with the edge of the sword; but they let the man and all his family go. [26] And the man went to the land of the Hittites, built a city, and called its name Luz, which *is* its name to this day.

[27] However, Manasseh did not drive out *the inhabitants of* Beth Shean and its villages, or Taanach and its villages, or the inhabitants of Dor and its villages, or the inhabitants of Ibleam and its villages, or the inhabitants of Megiddo and its villages; for the Canaanites were determined to dwell in that land. [28] And it came to pass, when Israel was strong, that they put the Canaanites under tribute, but did not completely drive them out.

[29] Nor did Ephraim drive out the Canaanites who dwelt in Gezer; so the Canaanites dwelt in Gezer among them.

[30] Nor did Zebulun drive out the inhabitants of Kitron or the inhabitants of Nahalol; so the Canaanites dwelt among them, and were put under tribute.

[31] Nor did Asher drive out the inhabitants of Acco or the inhabitants of Sidon, or of Ahlab, Achzib, Helbah, Aphik, or Rehob. [32] So the Asherites dwelt among the Canaanites, the inhabitants of the land; for they did not drive them out.

[33] Nor did Naphtali drive out the inhabitants of Beth Shemesh or the inhabitants of Beth Anath; but they dwelt among the Canaanites, the inhabitants of the land. Nevertheless the inhabitants of Beth Shemesh and Beth Anath were put under tribute to them.

[34] And the Amorites forced the children of Dan into the mountains, for they would not allow them to come down to the valley; [35] and the Amorites were determined to dwell in Mount Heres, in Aijalon, and in Shaalbim; yet when the strength of the house of Joseph became greater, they were put under tribute.

[36] Now the boundary of the Amorites *was* from the Ascent of Akrabbim, from Sela, and upward.

2 Then the Angel of the LORD came up from Gilgal to Bochim, and said: "I led you up from Egypt and brought you to the land of which I swore to your fathers; and I said, 'I will never break My covenant with you. [2] And you shall make no covenant with the inhabitants of this land; you shall tear down their altars.' But you have not obeyed My voice. Why have you done this? [3] Therefore I also said, 'I will not drive them out before you; but they shall be *thorns* in your side, and their gods shall be a snare to you.' " [4] So it was, when the Angel of the LORD spoke these words to all the children of Israel, that the people lifted up their voices and wept.

[5] Then they called the name of that place Bochim; and they sacrificed there to the LORD. [6] And when Joshua had dismissed the people, the children of Israel went each to his own inheritance to possess the land.

[7] So the people served the LORD all the days of Joshua, and all the days of the elders who outlived Joshua, who had seen all the great works of the LORD which He had done for Israel. [8] Now Joshua the son of Nun, the servant of the LORD, died *when he was* one hundred and ten years old. [9] And they buried him within the border of his inheritance at Timnath Heres, in the mountains of Ephraim, on the north side of Mount Gaash. [10] When all that generation had been gathered to their fathers, another generation arose after them who did not know the LORD nor the work which He had done for Israel.

[11] Then the children of Israel did evil in the sight of the LORD, and served the Baals; [12] and they forsook the LORD God of their fathers, who had brought them out of the land of Egypt; and they followed other gods from *among* the gods of the people who *were* all around them, and they bowed down to them; and they provoked the LORD to anger. [13] They forsook the LORD and served Baal and the Ashtoreths. [14] And the anger of the LORD was hot against Israel. So He delivered them into the hands of plunderers who despoiled them; and He sold them into the hands of their enemies all around, so that they could no longer stand before their enemies. [15] Wherever they went out, the hand of the LORD was against them for calamity, as the LORD had said, and as the LORD had sworn to them. And they were greatly distressed.

[16] Nevertheless, the LORD raised up judges who delivered them out of the hand of those who plundered them. [17] Yet they would not listen to their judges, but they played the harlot with other gods, and bowed down to them. They turned quickly from the way in which their fathers walked, in obeying the commandments of the LORD; they did not do so. [18] And when the LORD raised up judges for them, the LORD was with the judge and delivered them out of the hand of their enemies all the days of the judge; for the LORD was moved to pity by their groaning because of those who oppressed them and harassed them. [19] And it came to pass, when the judge was dead, that they reverted and behaved more corruptly than their fathers, by following other gods, to serve them and bow down to them. They did not cease from their own doings nor from their stubborn way.

[20] Then the anger of the LORD was hot against Israel; and He said, "Because this nation has transgressed My covenant which I commanded their fathers, and has not heeded My voice, [21] I also will no longer drive out before them any of the nations which Joshua left when he died, [22] so that through them I may test Israel, whether they will keep the ways of the LORD, to walk in them as their fathers kept *them,* or not." [23] Therefore the LORD left those nations, without driving them out immediately; nor did He deliver them into the hand of Joshua.

～ PSALM 48:1–8 ～

[1] Great *is* the LORD, and greatly to be praised
In the city of our God,
In His holy mountain.
[2] Beautiful in elevation,
The joy of the whole earth,
Is Mount Zion *on* the sides of the north,
The city of the great King.
[3] God *is* in her palaces;
He is known as her refuge.

[4] For behold, the kings assembled,
They passed by together.
[5] They saw *it, and* so they marveled;
They were troubled, they hastened away.
[6] Fear took hold of them there,
And pain, as of a woman in birth pangs,
[7] *As when* You break the ships of Tarshish
With an east wind.

[8] As we have heard,
So we have seen
In the city of the LORD of hosts,
In the city of our God:
God will establish it forever.　　Selah

～ PROVERBS 14:15–17 ～

[15] The simple believes every word,
But the prudent considers well his steps.

16 A wise *man* fears and departs from evil,
But a fool rages and is self-confident.
17 A quick-tempered *man* acts foolishly,
And a man of wicked intentions is hated.

~ LUKE 14:1–24 ~

Now it happened, as He went into the house of one of the rulers of the Pharisees to eat bread on the Sabbath, that they watched Him closely. 2 And behold, there was a certain man before Him who had dropsy. 3 And Jesus, answering, spoke to the lawyers and Pharisees, saying, "Is it lawful to heal on the Sabbath?"

4 But they kept silent. And He took *him* and healed him, and let him go. 5 Then He answered them, saying, "Which of you, having a donkey or an ox that has fallen into a pit, will not immediately pull him out on the Sabbath day?" 6 And they could not answer Him regarding these things.

7 So He told a parable to those who were invited, when He noted how they chose the best places, saying to them: 8 "When you are invited by anyone to a wedding feast, do not sit down in the best place, lest one more honorable than you be invited by him; 9 and he who invited you and him come and say to you, 'Give place to this man,' and then you begin with shame to take the lowest place. 10 But when you are invited, go and sit down in the lowest place, so that when he who invited you comes he may say to you, 'Friend, go up higher.' Then you will have glory in the presence of those who sit at the table with you. 11 For whoever exalts himself will be humbled, and he who humbles himself will be exalted."

12 Then He also said to him who invited Him, "When you give a dinner or a supper, do not ask your friends, your brothers, your relatives, nor rich neighbors, lest they also invite you back, and you be repaid. 13 But when you give a feast, invite *the* poor, *the* maimed, *the* lame, *the* blind. 14 And you will be blessed, because they cannot repay you; for you shall be repaid at the resurrection of the just."

15 Now when one of those who sat at the table with Him heard these things, he said to Him, "Blessed *is* he who shall eat bread in the kingdom of God!"

16 Then He said to him, "A certain man gave a great supper and invited many, 17 and sent his servant at supper time to say to those who were invited, 'Come, for all things are now ready.' 18 But they all with one *accord* began to make excuses. The first said to him, 'I have bought a piece of ground, and I must go and see it. I ask you to have me excused.' 19 And another said, 'I have bought five yoke of oxen, and I am going to test them. I ask you to have me excused.' 20 Still another said, 'I have married a wife, and therefore I cannot come.' 21 So that servant came and reported these things to his master. Then the master of the house, being angry, said to his servant, 'Go out quickly into the streets and lanes of the city, and bring in here *the* poor and *the* maimed and *the* lame and *the* blind.' 22 And the servant said, 'Master, it is done as you commanded, and still there is room.' 23 Then the master said to the servant, 'Go out into the highways and hedges, and compel *them* to come in, that my house may be filled. 24 For I say to you that none of those men who were invited shall taste my supper.' "

READING 109 · APRIL 19

~ JUDGES 3:1—4:24 ~

Now these *are* the nations which the LORD left, that He might test Israel by them, *that is,* all who had not known any of the wars in Canaan 2(this *was* only so that the generations of the children of Israel might be taught to know war, at least those who had not formerly known it), 3 *namely,* five lords of the Philistines, all the Canaanites, the Sidonians, and the Hivites who dwelt in Mount Lebanon, from Mount Baal Hermon to the entrance of Hamath. 4 And

Allowed to Serve

When British prime minister William E. Gladstone was facing one of the greatest crises of his political life, he sat down at two o'clock one morning to write a speech he hoped would help him win a great political victory in Parliament the following day.

At that hour, the mother of a poor, dying cripple saw the light on in his home and knocked at the door. She asked him to come and bring a message of hope to her son.

Without hesitation, Gladstone left his half-finished speech on his desk and spent the remainder of the night with the child, leading him to Christ before he died. As morning light was breaking, he went back to his study and faced his own day with a smile of confidence and peace. Later that morning he said to a friend, "I am the happiest man in the world today." When asked why, he replied that the previous night he had been allowed to serve a child in the name of the Master.

Later in the day Gladstone made the greatest speech of his life in the House of Commons and carried his cause to a triumphant success. Were the two events related? Gladstone could never be convinced that they weren't.

they were *left, that He might* test Israel by them, to know whether they would obey the commandments of the LORD, which He had commanded their fathers by the hand of Moses.

⁵ Thus the children of Israel dwelt among the Canaanites, the Hittites, the Amorites, the Perizzites, the Hivites, and the Jebusites. ⁶ And they took their daughters to be their wives, and gave their daughters to their sons; and they served their gods.

⁷ So the children of Israel did evil in the sight of the LORD. They forgot the LORD their God, and served the Baals and Asherahs. ⁸ Therefore the anger of the LORD was hot against Israel, and He sold them into the hand of Cushan-Rishathaim king of Mesopotamia; and the children of Israel served Cushan-Rishathaim eight years. ⁹ When the children of Israel cried out to the LORD, the LORD raised up a deliverer for the children of Israel, who delivered them: Othniel the son of Kenaz, Caleb's younger brother. ¹⁰ The Spirit of the LORD came upon him, and he judged Israel. He went out to war, and the LORD delivered Cushan-Rishathaim king of Mesopotamia into his hand; and his hand prevailed over Cushan-Rishathaim. ¹¹ So the land had rest for forty years. Then Othniel the son of Kenaz died.

¹² And the children of Israel again did evil in the sight of the LORD. So the LORD strengthened Eglon king of Moab against Israel, because they had done evil in the sight of the LORD. ¹³ Then he gathered to himself the people of Ammon and Amalek, went and defeated Israel, and took possession of the City of Palms. ¹⁴ So the children of Israel served Eglon king of Moab eighteen years.

¹⁵ But when the children of Israel cried out to the LORD, the LORD raised up a deliverer for them: Ehud the son of Gera, the Benjamite, a left-handed man. By him the children of Israel sent tribute to Eglon king of Moab. ¹⁶ Now Ehud made himself a dagger (it was double-edged and a cubit in length) and fastened it under his clothes on his right thigh. ¹⁷ So he brought the tribute to Eglon king of Moab. (Now Eglon *was* a very fat man.) ¹⁸ And when he had finished presenting the tribute, he sent away the people who

had carried the tribute. ¹⁹ But he himself turned back from the stone images that *were* at Gilgal, and said, "I have a secret message for you, O king."

He said, "Keep silence!" And all who attended him went out from him.

²⁰ So Ehud came to him (now he was sitting upstairs in his cool private chamber). Then Ehud said, "I have a message from God for you." So he arose from *his* seat. ²¹ Then Ehud reached with his left hand, took the dagger from his right thigh, and thrust it into his belly. ²² Even the hilt went in after the blade, and the fat closed over the blade, for he did not draw the dagger out of his belly; and his entrails came out. ²³ Then Ehud went out through the porch and shut the doors of the upper room behind him and locked them.

²⁴ When he had gone out, *Eglon's* servants came to look, and *to their* surprise, the doors of the upper room were locked. So they said, "He is probably attending to his needs in the cool chamber." ²⁵ So they waited till they were embarrassed, and still he had not opened the doors of the upper room. Therefore they took the key and opened *them*. And there was their master, fallen dead on the floor.

²⁶ But Ehud had escaped while they delayed, and passed beyond the stone images and escaped to Seirah. ²⁷ And it happened, when he arrived, that he blew the trumpet in the mountains of Ephraim, and the children of Israel went down with him from the mountains; and he led them. ²⁸ Then he said to them, "Follow *me*, for the LORD has delivered your enemies the Moabites into your hand." So they went down after him, seized the fords of the Jordan leading to Moab, and did not allow anyone to cross over. ²⁹ And at that time they killed about ten thousand men of Moab, all stout men of valor; not a man escaped. ³⁰ So Moab was subdued that day under the hand of Israel. And the land had rest for eighty years.

³¹ After him was Shamgar the son of Anath, who killed six hundred men of the Philistines with an ox goad; and he also delivered Israel.

4 When Ehud was dead, the children of Israel again did evil in the sight of the LORD. ² So the LORD sold them into

the hand of Jabin king of Canaan, who reigned in Hazor. The commander of his army *was* Sisera, who dwelt in Harosheth Hagoyim. ³ And the children of Israel cried out to the LORD; for Jabin had nine hundred chariots of iron, and for twenty years he had harshly oppressed the children of Israel.

⁴ Now Deborah, a prophetess, the wife of Lapidoth, was judging Israel at that time. ⁵ And she would sit under the palm tree of Deborah between Ramah and Bethel in the mountains of Ephraim. And the children of Israel came up to her for judgment. ⁶ Then she sent and called for Barak the son of Abinoam from Kedesh in Naphtali, and said to him, "Has not the LORD God of Israel commanded, 'Go and deploy *troops* at Mount Tabor; take with you ten thousand men of the sons of Naphtali and of the sons of Zebulun; ⁷ and against you I will deploy Sisera, the commander of Jabin's army, with his chariots and his multitude at the River Kishon; and I will deliver him into your hand'?"

⁸ And Barak said to her, "If you will go with me, then I will go; but if you will not go with me, I will not go!"

⁹ So she said, "I will surely go with you; nevertheless there will be no glory for you in the journey you are taking, for the LORD will sell Sisera into the hand of a woman." Then Deborah arose and went with Barak to Kedesh. ¹⁰ And Barak called Zebulun and Naphtali to Kedesh; he went up with ten thousand men under his command, and Deborah went up with him.

¹¹ Now Heber the Kenite, of the children of Hobab the father-in-law of Moses, had separated himself from the Kenites and pitched his tent near the terebinth tree at Zaanaim, which *is* beside Kedesh.

¹² And they reported to Sisera that Barak the son of Abinoam had gone up to Mount Tabor. ¹³ So Sisera gathered together all his chariots, nine hundred chariots of iron, and all the people who *were* with him, from Harosheth Hagoyim to the River Kishon.

¹⁴ Then Deborah said to Barak, "Up! For this *is* the day in which the LORD has delivered Sisera into your hand. Has not the LORD gone out before you?" So Barak went down from Mount Tabor with ten thousand men following him. ¹⁵ And the LORD routed Sisera and all *his* chariots and all *his* army with the edge of the sword before Barak; and Sisera alighted from *his* chariot and fled away on foot. ¹⁶ But Barak pursued the chariots and the army as far as Harosheth Hagoyim, and all the army of Sisera fell by the edge of the sword; not a man was left.

¹⁷ However, Sisera had fled away on foot to the tent of Jael, the wife of Heber the Kenite; for *there was* peace between Jabin king of Hazor and the house of Heber the Kenite. ¹⁸ And Jael went out to meet Sisera, and said to him, "Turn aside, my lord, turn aside to me; do not fear." And when he had turned aside with her into the tent, she covered him with a blanket. ¹⁹ Then he said to her, "Please give me a little water to drink, for I am thirsty." So she opened a jug of milk, gave him a drink, and covered him. ²⁰ And he said to her, "Stand at the door of the tent, and if any man comes and inquires of you, and says, 'Is there any man here?' you shall say, 'No.' "

²¹ Then Jael, Heber's wife, took a tent peg and took a hammer in her hand, and went softly to him and drove the peg into his temple, and it went down into the ground; for he was fast asleep and weary. So he died. ²² And then, as Barak pursued Sisera, Jael came out to meet him, and said to him, "Come, I will show you the man whom you seek." And when he went into her *tent*, there lay Sisera, dead with the peg in his temple.

²³ So on that day God subdued Jabin king of Canaan in the presence of the children of Israel. ²⁴ And the hand of the children of Israel grew stronger and stronger against Jabin king of Canaan, until they had destroyed Jabin king of Canaan.

～ PSALM 48:9–14 ～

⁹ We have thought, O God, on Your
     lovingkindness,
   In the midst of Your temple.
¹⁰ According to Your name, O God,
   So *is* Your praise to the ends of the
     earth;
   Your right hand is full of
     righteousness.
¹¹ Let Mount Zion rejoice,

Let the daughters of Judah be glad,
Because of Your judgments.

12 Walk about Zion,
And go all around her.
Count her towers;
13 Mark well her bulwarks;
Consider her palaces;
That you may tell *it* to the
generation following.
14 For this *is* God,
Our God forever and ever;
He will be our guide
Even to death.

～ PROVERBS 14:18, 19 ～

18 The simple inherit folly,
But the prudent are crowned with
knowledge.
19 The evil will bow before the good,
And the wicked at the gates of the
righteous.

～ LUKE 14:25–35 ～

Now great multitudes went with Him.
And He turned and said to them, 26 "If
anyone comes to Me and does not hate
his father and mother, wife and children,
brothers and sisters, yes, and his own life
also, he cannot be My disciple. 27 And
whoever does not bear his cross and come
after Me cannot be My disciple. 28 For
which of you, intending to build a tower,
does not sit down first and count the cost,
whether he has *enough* to finish *it*— 29 lest,
after he has laid the foundation, and is
not able to finish, all who see *it* begin to
mock him, 30 saying, 'This man began to
build and was not able to finish.' 31 Or
what king, going to make war against
another king, does not sit down first and
consider whether he is able with ten thousand to meet him who comes against him
with twenty thousand? 32 Or else, while
the other is still a great way off, he sends
a delegation and asks conditions of peace.
33 So likewise, whoever of you does not
forsake all that he has cannot be My disciple.
34 "Salt *is* good; but if the salt has lost
its flavor, how shall it be seasoned? 35 It is
neither fit for the land nor for the dung-
hill, *but* men throw it out. He who has
ears to hear, let him hear!"

READING 110 · APRIL 20

～ JUDGES 5:1—6:40 ～

Then Deborah and Barak the son of
Abinoam sang on that day, saying:

2 "When leaders lead in Israel,
When the people willingly offer
themselves,
Bless the LORD!

3 "Hear, O kings! Give ear,
O princes!
I, *even* I, will sing to the LORD;
I will sing praise to the LORD God
of Israel.

4 "LORD, when You went out from
Seir,
When You marched from the field
of Edom,
The earth trembled and the
heavens poured,
The clouds also poured water;

5 The mountains gushed before the
LORD,
This Sinai, before the LORD God
of Israel.

6 "In the days of Shamgar, son of
Anath,
In the days of Jael,
The highways were deserted,
And the travelers walked along the
byways.
7 Village life ceased, it ceased in
Israel,
Until I, Deborah, arose,
Arose a mother in Israel.
8 They chose new gods;
Then *there was* war in the gates;
Not a shield or spear was seen
among forty thousand in Israel.
9 My heart *is* with the rulers of
Israel

Reaching Out

When thirteen-year-old Bobby Hill, the son of a U.S. Army sergeant stationed in Italy, read a book about the work of Nobel Prize winner Albert Schweitzer, he decided to do something to help the medical missionary. He sent a bottle of aspirin to Lieutenant General Richard C. Lindsay, Commander of the Allied air forces in Southern Europe, asking if any of his airplanes could parachute the bottle of aspirin to Dr. Schweitzer's jungle hospital in Africa.

Upon hearing of the letter, an Italian radio station issued an appeal which resulted in more than $400,000 worth of donated medical supplies. The French and Italian governments each supplied a plane to fly the medicines and the boy to Dr. Schweitzer. The grateful doctor responded, "I never thought a child could do so much for my hospital."

Not one of us can solve all the problems in the world, but we can feed a hungry family in a nearby neighborhood, clothe the homeless person who has just arrived at a local shelter, or give a blanket to a street person who sleeps near our office building. It's amazing what can happen when just one person reaches out to help those in need. Inevitably, they are joined by many others who want to help as well.

Who offered themselves willingly
with the people.
Bless the LORD!

10 "Speak, you who ride on white
donkeys,
Who sit in judges' attire,
And who walk along the road.
11 Far from the noise of the archers,
among the watering places,
There they shall recount the
righteous acts of the LORD,
The righteous acts *for* His villagers
in Israel;
Then the people of the LORD shall
go down to the gates.

12 "Awake, awake, Deborah!
Awake, awake, sing a song!
Arise, Barak, and lead your
captives away,
O son of Abinoam!

13 "Then the survivors came down,
the people against the nobles;
The LORD came down for me
against the mighty.
14 From Ephraim *were* those whose
roots were in Amalek.
After you, Benjamin, with your
peoples,
From Machir rulers came down,
And from Zebulun those who bear
the recruiter's staff.
15 And the princes of Issachar *were*
with Deborah;
As Issachar, so *was* Barak
Sent into the valley under his
command;
Among the divisions of Reuben
There were great resolves of heart.
16 Why did you sit among the
sheepfolds,
To hear the pipings for the flocks?
The divisions of Reuben have
great searchings of heart.
17 Gilead stayed beyond the Jordan,
And why did Dan remain on
ships?
Asher continued at the seashore,
And stayed by his inlets.
18 Zebulun *is* a people *who*
jeopardized their lives to the
point of death,

Naphtali also, on the heights of
the battlefield.

19 "The kings came *and* fought,
Then the kings of Canaan fought
In Taanach, by the waters of
Megiddo;
They took no spoils of silver.
20 They fought from the heavens;
The stars from their courses
fought against Sisera.
21 The torrent of Kishon swept them
away,
That ancient torrent, the torrent
of Kishon.
O my soul, march on in strength!
22 Then the horses' hooves pounded,
The galloping, galloping of his
steeds.
23 'Curse Meroz,' said the angel of
the LORD,
'Curse its inhabitants bitterly,
Because they did not come to the
help of the LORD,
To the help of the LORD against
the mighty.'

24 "Most blessed among women is
Jael,
The wife of Heber the Kenite;
Blessed is she among women in
tents.
25 He asked for water, she gave milk;
She brought out cream in a lordly
bowl.
26 She stretched her hand to the tent
peg,
Her right hand to the workmen's
hammer;
She pounded Sisera, she pierced
his head,
She split and struck through his
temple.
27 At her feet he sank, he fell, he lay
still;
At her feet he sank, he fell;
Where he sank, there he fell dead.

28 "The mother of Sisera looked
through the window,
And cried out through the lattice,
'Why is his chariot *so* long in
coming?
Why tarries the clatter of his
chariots?'

²⁹ Her wisest ladies answered her,
Yes, she answered herself,
³⁰ 'Are they not finding and dividing
the spoil:
To every man a girl *or* two;
For Sisera, plunder of dyed
garments,
Plunder of garments embroidered
and dyed,
Two pieces of dyed embroidery
for the neck of the looter?'

³¹ "Thus let all Your enemies perish,
O LORD!
But *let* those who love Him *be* like
the sun
When it comes out in full
strength."

So the land had rest for forty years.

6 Then the children of Israel did evil in
the sight of the LORD. So the LORD delivered them into the hand of Midian for
seven years, ² and the hand of Midian prevailed against Israel. Because of the
Midianites, the children of Israel made for
themselves the dens, the caves, and the
strongholds which *are* in the mountains.
³ So it was, whenever Israel had sown,
Midianites would come up; also
Amalekites and the people of the East
would come up against them. ⁴ Then
they would encamp against them and destroy the produce of the earth as far as
Gaza, and leave no sustenance for Israel,
neither sheep nor ox nor donkey. ⁵ For
they would come up with their livestock
and their tents, coming in as numerous as
locusts; both they and their camels were
without number; and they would enter
the land to destroy it. ⁶ So Israel was
greatly impoverished because of the
Midianites, and the children of Israel cried
out to the LORD.
⁷ And it came to pass, when the children of Israel cried out to the LORD because of the Midianites, ⁸ that the LORD
sent a prophet to the children of Israel,
who said to them, "Thus says the LORD
God of Israel: 'I brought you up from
Egypt and brought you out of the house
of bondage; ⁹ and I delivered you out of
the hand of the Egyptians and out of the
hand of all who oppressed you, and drove

them out before you and gave you their
land. ¹⁰ Also I said to you, "I *am* the LORD
your God; do not fear the gods of the
Amorites, in whose land you dwell." But
you have not obeyed My voice.' "
¹¹ Now the Angel of the LORD came and
sat under the terebinth tree which *was* in
Ophrah, which *belonged* to Joash the
Abiezrite, while his son Gideon threshed
wheat in the winepress, in order to hide
it from the Midianites. ¹² And the Angel
of the LORD appeared to him, and said to
him, "The LORD *is* with you, you mighty
man of valor!"
¹³ Gideon said to Him, "O my lord, if
the LORD is with us, why then has all this
happened to us? And where *are* all His
miracles which our fathers told us about,
saying, 'Did not the LORD bring us up
from Egypt?' But now the LORD has forsaken us and delivered us into the hands
of the Midianites."
¹⁴ Then the LORD turned to him and
said, "Go in this might of yours, and you
shall save Israel from the hand of the
Midianites. Have I not sent you?"
¹⁵ So he said to Him, "O my Lord, how
can I save Israel? Indeed my clan *is* the
weakest in Manasseh, and I *am* the least
in my father's house."
¹⁶ And the LORD said to him, "Surely I
will be with you, and you shall defeat the
Midianites as one man."
¹⁷ Then he said to Him, "If now I have
found favor in Your sight, then show me
a sign that it is You who talk with me.
¹⁸ Do not depart from here, I pray, until I
come to You and bring out my offering
and set *it* before You."
And He said, "I will wait until you come
back."
¹⁹ So Gideon went in and prepared a
young goat, and unleavened bread from
an ephah of flour. The meat he put in a
basket, and he put the broth in a pot; and
he brought *them* out to Him under
the terebinth tree and presented *them*.
²⁰ The Angel of God said to him, "Take
the meat and the unleavened bread and
lay *them* on this rock, and pour out the
broth." And he did so.
²¹ Then the Angel of the LORD put out
the end of the staff that *was* in His hand,
and touched the meat and the unleavened
bread; and fire rose out of the rock and

consumed the meat and the unleavened bread. And the Angel of the LORD departed out of his sight.

²² Now Gideon perceived that He *was* the Angel of the LORD. So Gideon said, "Alas, O Lord GOD! For I have seen the Angel of the LORD face to face." ²³ Then the LORD said to him, "Peace *be* with you; do not fear, you shall not die." ²⁴ So Gideon built an altar there to the LORD, and called it The-LORD-*Is*-Peace. To this day it *is* still in Ophrah of the Abiezrites.

²⁵ Now it came to pass the same night that the LORD said to him, "Take your father's young bull, the second bull of seven years old, and tear down the altar of Baal that your father has, and cut down the wooden image that *is* beside it; ²⁶ and build an altar to the LORD your God on top of this rock in the proper arrangement, and take the second bull and offer a burnt sacrifice with the wood of the image which you shall cut down." ²⁷ So Gideon took ten men from among his servants and did as the LORD had said to him. But because he feared his father's household and the men of the city too much to do *it* by day, he did *it* by night.

²⁸ And when the men of the city arose early in the morning, there was the altar of Baal, torn down; and the wooden image that *was* beside it was cut down, and the second bull was being offered on the altar *which had been* built. ²⁹ So they said to one another, "Who has done this thing?" And when they had inquired and asked, they said, "Gideon the son of Joash has done this thing." ³⁰ Then the men of the city said to Joash, "Bring out your son, that he may die, because he has torn down the altar of Baal, and because he has cut down the wooden image that *was* beside it."

³¹ But Joash said to all who stood against him, "Would you plead for Baal? Would you save him? Let the one who would plead for him be put to death by morning! If he *is* a god, let him plead for himself, because his altar has been torn down!" ³² Therefore on that day he called him Jerubbaal, saying, "Let Baal plead against him, because he has torn down his altar."

³³ Then all the Midianites and Ama-lekites, the people of the East, gathered together; and they crossed over and encamped in the Valley of Jezreel. ³⁴ But the Spirit of the LORD came upon Gideon; then he blew the trumpet, and the Abiezrites gathered behind him. ³⁵ And he sent messengers throughout all Manasseh, who also gathered behind him. He also sent messengers to Asher, Zebulun, and Naphtali; and they came up to meet them.

³⁶ So Gideon said to God, "If You will save Israel by my hand as You have said— ³⁷ look, I shall put a fleece of wool on the threshing floor; if there is dew on the fleece only, and *it is* dry on all the ground, then I shall know that You will save Israel by my hand, as You have said." ³⁸ And it was so. When he rose early the next morning and squeezed the fleece together, he wrung the dew out of the fleece, a bowlful of water. ³⁹ Then Gideon said to God, "Do not be angry with me, but let me speak just once more: Let me test, I pray, just once more with the fleece; let it now be dry only on the fleece, but on all the ground let there be dew." ⁴⁰ And God did so that night. It was dry on the fleece only, but there was dew on all the ground.

∼ PSALM 49:1–9 ∼

¹ Hear this, all peoples;
  Give ear, all inhabitants of the world,
² Both low and high,
  Rich and poor together.
³ My mouth shall speak wisdom,
  And the meditation of my heart *shall give* understanding.
⁴ I will incline my ear to a proverb;
  I will disclose my dark saying on the harp.

⁵ Why should I fear in the days of evil,
  When the iniquity at my heels surrounds me?
⁶ Those who trust in their wealth
  And boast in the multitude of their riches,
⁷ None *of them* can by any means redeem *his* brother,
  Nor give to God a ransom for him—
⁸ For the redemption of their souls *is* costly,

And it shall cease forever—
9 That he should continue to live
    eternally,
And not see the Pit.

∼ PROVERBS 14:20, 21 ∼

20 The poor *man* is hated even by his
    own neighbor,
    But the rich *has* many friends.
21 He who despises his neighbor sins;
    But he who has mercy on the poor,
    happy *is* he.

∼ LUKE 15:1–10 ∼

Then all the tax collectors and the sinners drew near to Him to hear Him. ² And the Pharisees and scribes complained, saying, "This Man receives sinners and eats with them." ³ So He spoke this parable to them, saying:
    ⁴ "What man of you, having a hundred sheep, if he loses one of them, does not leave the ninety-nine in the wilderness, and go after the one which is lost until he finds it? ⁵ And when he has found *it*, he lays *it* on his shoulders, rejoicing. ⁶ And when he comes home, he calls together *his* friends and neighbors, saying to them, 'Rejoice with me, for I have found my sheep which was lost!' ⁷ I say to you that likewise there will be more joy in heaven over one sinner who repents than over ninety-nine just persons who need no repentance.
    ⁸ "Or what woman, having ten silver coins, if she loses one coin, does not light a lamp, sweep the house, and search carefully until she finds *it?* ⁹ And when she has found *it*, she calls *her* friends and neighbors together, saying, 'Rejoice with me, for I have found the piece which I lost!' ¹⁰ Likewise, I say to you, there is joy in the presence of the angels of God over one sinner who repents."

∼ JUDGES 7:1—8:35 ∼

Then Jerubbaal (that *is,* Gideon) and all the people who *were* with him rose early and encamped beside the well of Harod, so that the camp of the Midianites was on the north side of them by the hill of Moreh in the valley.
    ² And the LORD said to Gideon, "The people who *are* with you *are* too many for Me to give the Midianites into their hands, lest Israel claim glory for itself against Me, saying, 'My own hand has saved me.' ³ Now therefore, proclaim in the hearing of the people, saying, 'Whoever *is* fearful and afraid, let him turn and depart at once from Mount Gilead.' " And twenty-two thousand of the people returned, and ten thousand remained.
    ⁴ But the LORD said to Gideon, "The people *are* still *too* many; bring them down to the water, and I will test them for you there. Then it will be, *that* of whom I say to you, 'This one shall go with you,' the same shall go with you; and of whomever I say to you, 'This one shall not go with you,' the same shall not go."
    ⁵ So he brought the people down to the water. And the LORD said to Gideon, "Everyone who laps from the water with his tongue, as a dog laps, you shall set apart by himself; likewise everyone who gets down on his knees to drink." ⁶ And the number of those who lapped, *putting* their hand to their mouth, was three hundred men; but all the rest of the people got down on their knees to drink water. ⁷ Then the LORD said to Gideon, "By the three hundred men who lapped I will save you, and deliver the Midianites into your hand. Let all the *other* people go, every man to his place." ⁸ So the people took provisions and their trumpets in their hands. And he sent away all *the rest of* Israel, every man to his tent, and retained those three hundred men. Now the camp of Midian was below him in the valley.
    ⁹ It happened on the same night that the LORD said to him, "Arise, go down against the camp, for I have delivered it into your hand. ¹⁰ But if you are afraid to go down, go down to the camp with Purah your servant, ¹¹ and you shall hear what they say; and afterward your hands shall

be strengthened to go down against the camp." Then he went down with Purah his servant to the outpost of the armed men who *were* in the camp. [12] Now the Midianites and Amalekites, all the people of the East, were lying in the valley as numerous as locusts; and their camels *were* without number, as the sand by the seashore in multitude.

[13] And when Gideon had come, there was a man telling a dream to his companion. He said, "I have had a dream: *To my* surprise, a loaf of barley bread tumbled into the camp of Midian; it came to a tent and struck it so that it fell and overturned, and the tent collapsed."

[14] Then his companion answered and said, "This *is* nothing else but the sword of Gideon the son of Joash, a man of Israel! Into his hand God has delivered Midian and the whole camp."

[15] And so it was, when Gideon heard the telling of the dream and its interpretation, that he worshiped. He returned to the camp of Israel, and said, "Arise, for the LORD has delivered the camp of Midian into your hand." [16] Then he divided the three hundred men *into* three companies, and he put a trumpet into every man's hand, with empty pitchers, and torches inside the pitchers. [17] And he said to them, "Look at me and do likewise; watch, and when I come to the edge of the camp you shall do as I do: [18] When I blow the trumpet, I and all who *are* with me, then you also blow the trumpets on every side of the whole camp, and say, 'The sword of the LORD and of Gideon!' "

[19] So Gideon and the hundred men who *were* with him came to the outpost of the camp at the beginning of the middle watch, just as they had posted the watch; and they blew the trumpets and broke the pitchers that *were* in their hands. [20] Then the three companies blew the trumpets and broke the pitchers—they held the torches in their left hands and the trumpets in their right hands for blowing—and they cried, "The sword of the LORD and of Gideon!" [21] And every man stood in his place all around the camp; and the whole army ran and cried out and fled. [22] When the three hundred blew the trumpets, the LORD set every man's sword against his companion throughout the whole camp; and the army fled to Beth Acacia, toward Zererah, as far as the border of Abel Meholah, by Tabbath.

[23] And the men of Israel gathered together from Naphtali, Asher, and all Manasseh, and pursued the Midianites. [24] Then Gideon sent messengers throughout all the mountains of Ephraim, saying, "Come down against the Midianites, and seize from them the watering places as far as Beth Barah and the Jordan." Then all the men of Ephraim gathered together and seized the watering places as far as Beth Barah and the Jordan. [25] And they captured two princes of the Midianites, Oreb and Zeeb. They killed Oreb at the rock of Oreb, and Zeeb they killed at the winepress of Zeeb. They pursued Midian and brought the heads of Oreb and Zeeb to Gideon on the other side of the Jordan.

8 Now the men of Ephraim said to him, "Why have you done this to us by not calling us when you went to fight with the Midianites?" And they reprimanded him sharply.

[2] So he said to them, "What have I done now in comparison with you? *Is* not the gleaning *of the grapes* of Ephraim better than the vintage of Abiezer? [3] God has delivered into your hands the princes of Midian, Oreb and Zeeb. And what was I able to do in comparison with you?" Then their anger toward him subsided when he said that.

[4] When Gideon came to the Jordan, he and the three hundred men who *were* with him crossed over, exhausted but still in pursuit. [5] Then he said to the men of Succoth, "Please give loaves of bread to the people who follow me, for they are exhausted, and I am pursuing Zebah and Zalmunna, kings of Midian."

[6] And the leaders of Succoth said, "*Are* the hands of Zebah and Zalmunna now in your hand, that we should give bread to your army?"

[7] So Gideon said, "For this cause, when the LORD has delivered Zebah and Zalmunna into my hand, then I will tear your flesh with the thorns of the wilderness and with briers!" [8] Then he went up from there to Penuel and spoke to them in the same way. And the men of Penuel

The Examen

Dennis Hamm has noted the "examen," or examination of conscience, is an ancient practice among Christians. In the early days of the Church, the examen was a time for confession. Specifically, it was a process of examining one's daily behavior against the criteria of the Ten Commandments.

Hamm proposes five practices that can help a person examine his or her day in prayer:

1. *Pray for light*. Ask God to give you illumination to help you see His plan in the buzzing confusion of your day.
2. *Review the day in thanksgiving*. Think of the past 24 hours as a beautiful gift from the Lord. Walk through your day, hour by hour, thanking God for each task He gave you, each person He allowed you to encounter.
3. *Review the feelings that surface as you replay your day*. Both positive and negative feelings are signals to you about your own spiritual state. Let all of your feelings flow to the surface of your conscious mind.
4. *Take one of the feelings that surfaces (positive or negative) and pray from it*. You may be led to praise, petition, repentance, or a cry for helping or healing.
5. *Finally, look toward tomorrow*. What feelings do you have about the tasks and appointments that lie ahead? Whatever you are feeling, ask for God's help.

Any one of the five prayer practices listed above will enhance your prayer time, all five can revolutionize it. You can implement them gradually, one at a time, or all at once. Either way, you'll find your prayers becoming more effective and meaningful in your life. Remember, the only wrong way to pray is not to pray at all.

> In all labor there is profit, but idle chatter leads only to poverty.
>
> *Proverbs 14:23*

answered him as the men of Succoth had answered. ⁹ So he also spoke to the men of Penuel, saying, "When I come back in peace, I will tear down this tower!"

¹⁰ Now Zebah and Zalmunna *were* at Karkor, and their armies with them, about fifteen thousand, all who were left of all the army of the people of the East; for one hundred and twenty thousand men who drew the sword had fallen. ¹¹ Then Gideon went up by the road of those who dwell in tents on the east of Nobah and Jogbehah; and he attacked the army while the camp felt secure. ¹² When Zebah and Zalmunna fled, he pursued them; and he took the two kings of Midian, Zebah and Zalmunna, and routed the whole army.

¹³ Then Gideon the son of Joash returned from battle, from the Ascent of Heres. ¹⁴ And he caught a young man of the men of Succoth and interrogated him; and he wrote down for him the leaders of Succoth and its elders, seventy-seven men. ¹⁵ Then he came to the men of Succoth and said, "Here are Zebah and Zalmunna, about whom you ridiculed me, saying, '*Are* the hands of Zebah and Zalmunna now in your hand, that we should give bread to your weary men?' " ¹⁶ And he took the elders of the city, and thorns of the wilderness and briers, and with them he taught the men of Succoth. ¹⁷ Then he tore down the tower of Penuel and killed the men of the city.

¹⁸ And he said to Zebah and Zalmunna, "What kind of men *were they* whom you killed at Tabor?"

So they answered, "As you *are,* so *were* they; each one resembled the son of a king."

¹⁹ Then he said, "They *were* my brothers, the sons of my mother. *As* the LORD lives, if you had let them live, I would not kill you." ²⁰ And he said to Jether his firstborn, "Rise, kill them!" But the youth would not draw his sword; for he was afraid, because he *was* still a youth.

²¹ So Zebah and Zalmunna said, "Rise yourself, and kill us; for as a man *is, so is* his strength." So Gideon arose and killed Zebah and Zalmunna, and took the crescent ornaments that *were* on their camels' necks.

²² Then the men of Israel said to Gideon, "Rule over us, both you and your son, and your grandson also; for you have delivered us from the hand of Midian."

²³ But Gideon said to them, "I will not rule over you, nor shall my son rule over you; the LORD shall rule over you." ²⁴ Then Gideon said to them, "I would like to make a request of you, that each of you would give me the earrings from his plunder." For they had golden earrings, because they *were* Ishmaelites.

²⁵ So they answered, "We will gladly give *them.*" And they spread out a garment, and each man threw into it the earrings from his plunder. ²⁶ Now the weight of the gold earrings that he requested was one thousand seven hundred *shekels* of gold, besides the crescent ornaments, pendants, and purple robes which *were* on the kings of Midian, and besides the chains that *were* around their camels' necks. ²⁷ Then Gideon made it into an ephod and set it up in his city, Ophrah. And all Israel played the harlot with it there. It became a snare to Gideon and to his house.

²⁸ Thus Midian was subdued before the children of Israel, so that they lifted their heads no more. And the country was quiet for forty years in the days of Gideon.

²⁹ Then Jerubbaal the son of Joash went and dwelt in his own house. ³⁰ Gideon had seventy sons who were his own offspring, for he had many wives. ³¹ And his concubine who *was* in Shechem also bore him a son, whose name he called Abimelech. ³² Now Gideon the son of Joash died at a good old age, and was buried in the tomb of Joash his father, in Ophrah of the Abiezrites.

³³ So it was, as soon as Gideon was dead, that the children of Israel again played the harlot with the Baals, and made Baal-Berith their god. ³⁴ Thus the children of Israel did not remember the LORD their God, who had delivered them from the hands of all their enemies on every side; ³⁵ nor did they show kindness to the house of Jerubbaal (Gideon) in accordance with the good he had done for Israel.

≈ PSALM 49:10–20 ≈

¹⁰ For he sees wise men die;
Likewise the fool and the senseless
     person perish,

And leave their wealth to others.
11 Their inner thought *is that* their
houses *will last* forever,
Their dwelling places to all
generations;
They call *their* lands after their own
names.
12 Nevertheless man, *though* in honor,
does not remain;
He is like the beasts *that* perish.

13 This is the way of those who *are*
foolish,
And of their posterity who approve
their sayings.   Selah
14 Like sheep they are laid in the grave;
Death shall feed on them;
The upright shall have dominion
over them in the morning;
And their beauty shall be consumed
in the grave, far from their
dwelling.
15 But God will redeem my soul from
the power of the grave,
For He shall receive me.   Selah

16 Do not be afraid when one becomes
rich,
When the glory of his house is
increased;
17 For when he dies he shall carry
nothing away;
His glory shall not descend after
him.
18 Though while he lives he blesses
himself
(For *men* will praise you when you
do well for yourself),
19 He shall go to the generation of his
fathers;
They shall never see light.
20 A man *who is* in honor, yet does not
understand,
Is like the beasts *that* perish.

∼ PROVERBS 14:22-24 ∼

22 Do they not go astray who devise
evil?
But mercy and truth *belong* to those
who devise good.

23 In all labor there is profit,
But idle chatter *leads* only to
poverty.

24 The crown of the wise is their riches,
But the foolishness of fools *is* folly.

∼ LUKE 15:11-32 ∼

Then He said: "A certain man had two
sons. 12 And the younger of them said to
his father, 'Father, give me the portion of
goods that falls *to me.*' So he divided to
them *his* livelihood. 13 And not many days
after, the younger son gathered all together, journeyed to a far country, and
there wasted his possessions with prodi-
gal living. 14 But when he had spent all,
there arose a severe famine in that land,
and he began to be in want. 15 Then he
went and joined himself to a citizen of
that country, and he sent him into his fields
to feed swine. 16 And he would gladly have
filled his stomach with the pods that the
swine ate, and no one gave him *anything*.

17 "But when he came to himself, he
said, 'How many of my father's hired servants have bread enough and to spare, and
I perish with hunger! 18 I will arise and go
to my father, and will say to him, "Father,
I have sinned against heaven and before
you, 19 and I am no longer worthy to be
called your son. Make me like one of your
hired servants." '

20 "And he arose and came to his father.
But when he was still a great way off, his
father saw him and had compassion,
and ran and fell on his neck and kissed
him. 21 And the son said to him, 'Father, I
have sinned against heaven and in your
sight, and am no longer worthy to be
called your son.'

22 "But the father said to his servants,
'Bring out the best robe and put *it* on him,
and put a ring on his hand and sandals on
his feet. 23 And bring the fatted calf here
and kill *it,* and let us eat and be merry;
24 for this my son was dead and is alive
again; he was lost and is found.' And they
began to be merry.

25 "Now his older son was in the field.
And as he came and drew near to the
house, he heard music and dancing. 26 So
he called one of the servants and asked
what these things meant. 27 And he said
to him, 'Your brother has come, and because he has received him safe and sound,
your father has killed the fatted calf.'

²⁸ "But he was angry and would not go in. Therefore his father came out and pleaded with him. ²⁹ So he answered and said to *his* father, 'Lo, these many years I have been serving you; I never transgressed your commandment at any time; and yet you never gave me a young goat, that I might make merry with my friends. ³⁰ But as soon as this son of yours came, who has devoured your livelihood with harlots, you killed the fatted calf for him.'

³¹ "And he said to him, 'Son, you are always with me, and all that I have is yours. ³² It was right that we should make merry and be glad, for your brother was dead and is alive again, and was lost and is found.' "

READING 112 · APRIL 22

～ JUDGES 9:1—10:18 ～

Then Abimelech the son of Jerubbaal went to Shechem, to his mother's brothers, and spoke with them and with all the family of the house of his mother's father, saying, ² "Please speak in the hearing of all the men of Shechem: 'Which is better for you, that all seventy of the sons of Jerubbaal reign over you, or that one reign over you?' Remember that I *am* your own flesh and bone."

³ And his mother's brothers spoke all these words concerning him in the hearing of all the men of Shechem; and their heart was inclined to follow Abimelech, for they said, "He is our brother." ⁴ So they gave him seventy *shekels* of silver from the temple of Baal-Berith, with which Abimelech hired worthless and reckless men; and they followed him. ⁵ Then he went to his father's house at Ophrah and killed his brothers, the seventy sons of Jerubbaal, on one stone. But Jotham the youngest son of Jerubbaal was left, because he hid himself. ⁶ And all the men of Shechem gathered together, all of Beth Millo, and they went and made Abimelech king beside the terebinth tree at the pillar that *was* in Shechem.

⁷ Now when they told Jotham, he went and stood on top of Mount Gerizim, and lifted his voice and cried out. And he said to them:

"Listen to me, you men of Shechem,
That God may listen to you!

⁸ "The trees once went forth to anoint a king over them.

And they said to the olive tree,
'Reign over us!'
⁹ But the olive tree said to them,
'Should I cease giving my oil,
With which they honor God and men,
And go to sway over trees?'

¹⁰ "Then the trees said to the fig tree,
'You come *and* reign over us!'
¹¹ But the fig tree said to them,
'Should I cease my sweetness and my good fruit,
And go to sway over trees?'

¹² "Then the trees said to the vine,
'You come *and* reign over us!'
¹³ But the vine said to them,
'Should I cease my new wine,
Which cheers *both* God and men,
And go to sway over trees?'

¹⁴ "Then all the trees said to the bramble,
'You come *and* reign over us!'
¹⁵ And the bramble said to the trees,
'If in truth you anoint me as king over you,
Then come *and* take shelter in my shade;
But if not, let fire come out of the bramble
And devour the cedars of Lebanon!'

¹⁶ "Now therefore, if you have acted in truth and sincerity in making Abimelech king, and if you have dealt well with Jerubbaal and his house, and have done to him as he deserves— ¹⁷ for my father

More Than All Right

A mother was awakened one night to hear the news that her son, who was away at college, had fallen and was seriously injured. As she and her husband raced to the hospital, she prayed over and over again, "Dear God, please let our son be all right." The doctor greeted them with grim news. Their son had injured his spinal cord in the fall and would be permanently paralyzed from the neck down.

The mother thought it would be impossible for her son to finish college, but he remained determined to do so. Within three months after his hospitalization and rehabilitation at a spinal center, he enrolled at a college near home.

His mother was concerned about how he would get around campus in a wheelchair, or take notes with the special brace he had just begun learning to use. But four years later, her son graduated with his bachelor's degree. He then went on to law school, and within three years, received his law degree. He passed the bar exam and began to work for a law firm.

She has said about her experience, "No, God didn't answer my prayers in the way I had thought He would . . . [my son] had to struggle, but . . . he has done more than all right!"

fought for you, risked his life, and delivered you out of the hand of Midian; ¹⁸ but you have risen up against my father's house this day, and killed his seventy sons on one stone, and made Abimelech, the son of his female servant, king over the men of Shechem, because he is your brother— ¹⁹ if then you have acted in truth and sincerity with Jerubbaal and with his house this day, *then* rejoice in Abimelech, and let him also rejoice in you. ²⁰ But if not, let fire come from Abimelech and devour the men of Shechem and Beth Millo; and let fire come from the men of Shechem and from Beth Millo and devour Abimelech!" ²¹ And Jotham ran away and fled; and he went to Beer and dwelt there, for fear of Abimelech his brother.

²² After Abimelech had reigned over Israel three years, ²³ God sent a spirit of ill will between Abimelech and the men of Shechem; and the men of Shechem dealt treacherously with Abimelech, ²⁴ that the crime *done* to the seventy sons of Jerubbaal might be settled and their blood be laid on Abimelech their brother, who killed them, and on the men of Shechem, who aided him in the killing of his brothers. ²⁵ And the men of Shechem set men in ambush against him on the tops of the mountains, and they robbed all who passed by them along that way; and it was told Abimelech.

²⁶ Now Gaal the son of Ebed came with his brothers and went over to Shechem; and the men of Shechem put their confidence in him. ²⁷ So they went out into the fields, and gathered *grapes* from their vineyards and trod *them,* and made merry. And they went into the house of their god, and ate and drank, and cursed Abimelech. ²⁸ Then Gaal the son of Ebed said, "Who *is* Abimelech, and who *is* Shechem, that we should serve him? *Is he* not the son of Jerubbaal, and *is not* Zebul his officer? Serve the men of Hamor the father of Shechem; but why should we serve him? ²⁹ If only this people were under my authority! Then I would remove Abimelech." So he said to Abimelech, "Increase your army and come out!"

³⁰ When Zebul, the ruler of the city, heard the words of Gaal the son of Ebed, his anger was aroused. ³¹ And he sent messengers to Abimelech secretly, saying,

"Take note! Gaal the son of Ebed and his brothers have come to Shechem; and here they are, fortifying the city against you. ³² Now therefore, get up by night, you and the people who *are* with you, and lie in wait in the field. ³³ And it shall be, as soon as the sun is up in the morning, *that* you shall rise early and rush upon the city; and *when* he and the people who are with him come out against you, you may then do to them as you find opportunity."

³⁴ So Abimelech and all the people who *were* with him rose by night, and lay in wait against Shechem in four companies. ³⁵ When Gaal the son of Ebed went out and stood in the entrance to the city gate, Abimelech and the people who *were* with him rose from lying in wait. ³⁶ And when Gaal saw the people, he said to Zebul, "Look, people are coming down from the tops of the mountains!"

But Zebul said to him, "You see the shadows of the mountains as *if they were* men."

³⁷ So Gaal spoke again and said, "See, people are coming down from the center of the land, and another company is coming from the Diviners' Terebinth Tree."

³⁸ Then Zebul said to him, "Where indeed *is* your mouth now, with which you said, 'Who is Abimelech, that we should serve him?' *Are* not these the people whom you despised? Go out, if you will, and fight with them now."

³⁹ So Gaal went out, leading the men of Shechem, and fought with Abimelech. ⁴⁰ And Abimelech chased him, and he fled from him; and many fell wounded, to the *very* entrance of the gate. ⁴¹ Then Abimelech dwelt at Arumah, and Zebul drove out Gaal and his brothers, so that they would not dwell in Shechem.

⁴² And it came about on the next day that the people went out into the field, and they told Abimelech. ⁴³ So he took his people, divided them into three companies, and lay in wait in the field. And he looked, and there were the people, coming out of the city; and he rose against them and attacked them. ⁴⁴ Then Abimelech and the company that *was* with him rushed forward and stood at the entrance of the gate of the city; and the *other* two companies rushed upon all who *were* in the fields and killed them. ⁴⁵ So

Abimelech fought against the city all that day; he took the city and killed the people who *were* in it; and he demolished the city and sowed it with salt.

⁴⁶ Now when all the men of the tower of Shechem had heard *that,* they entered the stronghold of the temple of the god Berith. ⁴⁷ And it was told Abimelech that all the men of the tower of Shechem were gathered together. ⁴⁸ Then Abimelech went up to Mount Zalmon, he and all the people who *were* with him. And Abimelech took an ax in his hand and cut down a bough from the trees, and took it and laid *it* on his shoulder; then he said to the people who were with him, "What you have seen me do, make haste *and* do as I *have done.*" ⁴⁹ So each of the people likewise cut down his own bough and followed Abimelech, put *them* against the stronghold, and set the stronghold on fire above them, so that all the people of the tower of Shechem died, about a thousand men and women.

⁵⁰ Then Abimelech went to Thebez, and he encamped against Thebez and took it. ⁵¹ But there was a strong tower in the city, and all the men and women—all the people of the city—fled there and shut themselves in; then they went up to the top of the tower. ⁵² So Abimelech came as far as the tower and fought against it; and he drew near the door of the tower to burn it with fire. ⁵³ But a certain woman dropped an upper millstone on Abimelech's head and crushed his skull. ⁵⁴ Then he called quickly to the young man, his armorbearer, and said to him, "Draw your sword and kill me, lest men say of me, 'A woman killed him.'" So his young man thrust him through, and he died. ⁵⁵ And when the men of Israel saw that Abimelech was dead, they departed, every man to his place.

⁵⁶ Thus God repaid the wickedness of Abimelech, which he had done to his father by killing his seventy brothers. ⁵⁷ And all the evil of the men of Shechem God returned on their own heads, and on them came the curse of Jotham the son of Jerubbaal.

10 After Abimelech there arose to save Israel Tola the son of Puah, the son of Dodo, a man of Issachar; and he dwelt in Shamir in the mountains of Ephraim. ² He judged Israel twenty-three years; and he died and was buried in Shamir.

³ After him arose Jair, a Gileadite; and he judged Israel twenty-two years. ⁴ Now he had thirty sons who rode on thirty donkeys; they also had thirty towns, which are called "Havoth Jair" to this day, which *are* in the land of Gilead. ⁵ And Jair died and was buried in Camon.

⁶ Then the children of Israel again did evil in the sight of the LORD, and served the Baals and the Ashtoreths, the gods of Syria, the gods of Sidon, the gods of Moab, the gods of the people of Ammon, and the gods of the Philistines; and they forsook the LORD and did not serve Him. ⁷ So the anger of the LORD was hot against Israel; and He sold them into the hands of the Philistines and into the hands of the people of Ammon. ⁸ From that year they harassed and oppressed the children of Israel for eighteen years—all the children of Israel who *were* on the other side of the Jordan in the land of the Amorites, in Gilead. ⁹ Moreover the people of Ammon crossed over the Jordan to fight against Judah also, against Benjamin, and against the house of Ephraim, so that Israel was severely distressed.

¹⁰ And the children of Israel cried out to the LORD, saying, "We have sinned against You, because we have both forsaken our God and served the Baals!"

¹¹ So the LORD said to the children of Israel, "*Did I* not *deliver you* from the Egyptians and from the Amorites and from the people of Ammon and from the Philistines? ¹² Also the Sidonians and Amalekites and Maonites oppressed you; and you cried out to Me, and I delivered you from their hand. ¹³ Yet you have forsaken Me and served other gods. Therefore I will deliver you no more. ¹⁴ Go and cry out to the gods which you have chosen; let them deliver you in your time of distress."

¹⁵ And the children of Israel said to the LORD, "We have sinned! Do to us whatever seems best to You; only deliver us this day, we pray." ¹⁶ So they put away the foreign gods from among them and served the LORD. And His soul could no longer endure the misery of Israel.

¹⁷ Then the people of Ammon gathered

together and encamped in Gilead. And the children of Israel assembled together and encamped in Mizpah. ¹⁸ And the people, the leaders of Gilead, said to one another, "Who *is* the man who will begin the fight against the people of Ammon? He shall be head over all the inhabitants of Gilead."

~ PSALM 50:1–6 ~

¹ The Mighty One, God the LORD,
  Has spoken and called the earth
  From the rising of the sun to its
    going down.
² Out of Zion, the perfection of
    beauty,
  God will shine forth.
³ Our God shall come, and shall not
    keep silent;
  A fire shall devour before Him,
  And it shall be very tempestuous all
    around Him.
⁴ He shall call to the heavens from
    above,
  And to the earth, that He may judge
    His people:
⁵ "Gather My saints together to Me,
  Those who have made a covenant
    with Me by sacrifice."
⁶ Let the heavens declare His
    righteousness,
  For God Himself *is* Judge.   Selah

~ PROVERBS 14:25–27 ~

²⁵ A true witness delivers souls,
   But a deceitful *witness* speaks lies.
²⁶ In the fear of the LORD *there is*
     strong confidence,
   And His children will have a place of
     refuge.
²⁷ The fear of the LORD *is* a fountain of
     life,
   To turn *one* away from the snares of
     death.

~ LUKE 16:1–31 ~

He also said to His disciples: "There was a certain rich man who had a steward, and an accusation was brought to him that this man was wasting his goods. ² So he called him and said to him, 'What is this I hear about you? Give an account of your stewardship, for you can no longer be steward.'

³ "Then the steward said within himself, 'What shall I do? For my master is taking the stewardship away from me. I cannot dig; I am ashamed to beg. ⁴ I have resolved what to do, that when I am put out of the stewardship, they may receive me into their houses.'

⁵ "So he called every one of his master's debtors to *him,* and said to the first, 'How much do you owe my master?' ⁶ And he said, 'A hundred measures of oil.' So he said to him, 'Take your bill, and sit down quickly and write fifty.' ⁷ Then he said to another, 'And how much do you owe?' So he said, 'A hundred measures of wheat.' And he said to him, 'Take your bill, and write eighty.' ⁸ So the master commended the unjust steward because he had dealt shrewdly. For the sons of this world are more shrewd in their generation than the sons of light.

⁹ "And I say to you, make friends for yourselves by unrighteous mammon, that when you fail, they may receive you into an everlasting home. ¹⁰ He who *is* faithful in *what is* least is faithful also in much; and he who is unjust in *what is* least is unjust also in much. ¹¹ Therefore if you have not been faithful in the unrighteous mammon, who will commit to your trust the true *riches?* ¹² And if you have not been faithful in what is another man's, who will give you what is your own?

¹³ "No servant can serve two masters; for either he will hate the one and love the other, or else he will be loyal to the one and despise the other. You cannot serve God and mammon."

¹⁴ Now the Pharisees, who were lovers of money, also heard all these things, and they derided Him. ¹⁵ And He said to them, "You are those who justify yourselves before men, but God knows your hearts. For what is highly esteemed among men is an abomination in the sight of God.

¹⁶ "The law and the prophets *were* until John. Since that time the kingdom of God has been preached, and everyone is pressing into it. ¹⁷ And it is easier for heaven and earth to pass away than for one tittle of the law to fail.

[18] "Whoever divorces his wife and marries another commits adultery; and whoever marries her who is divorced from *her* husband commits adultery.

[19] "There was a certain rich man who was clothed in purple and fine linen and fared sumptuously every day. [20] But there was a certain beggar named Lazarus, full of sores, who was laid at his gate, [21] desiring to be fed with the crumbs which fell from the rich man's table. Moreover the dogs came and licked his sores. [22] So it was that the beggar died, and was carried by the angels to Abraham's bosom. The rich man also died and was buried. [23] And being in torments in Hades, he lifted up his eyes and saw Abraham afar off, and Lazarus in his bosom.

[24] "Then he cried and said, 'Father Abraham, have mercy on me, and send Lazarus that he may dip the tip of his finger in water and cool my tongue; for I am tormented in this flame.' [25] But Abraham said, 'Son, remember that in your lifetime you received your good things, and likewise Lazarus evil things; but now he is comforted and you are tormented. [26] And besides all this, between us and you there is a great gulf fixed, so that those who want to pass from here to you cannot, nor can those from there pass to us.'

[27] "Then he said, 'I beg you therefore, father, that you would send him to my father's house, [28] for I have five brothers, that he may testify to them, lest they also come to this place of torment.' [29] Abraham said to him, 'They have Moses and the prophets; let them hear them.' [30] And he said, 'No, father Abraham; but if one goes to them from the dead, they will repent.' [31] But he said to him, 'If they do not hear Moses and the prophets, neither will they be persuaded though one rise from the dead.' "

READING 113 · APRIL 23

~ JUDGES 11:1—12:15 ~

Now Jephthah the Gileadite was a mighty man of valor, but he *was* the son of a harlot; and Gilead begot Jephthah. [2] Gilead's wife bore sons; and when his wife's sons grew up, they drove Jephthah out, and said to him, "You shall have no inheritance in our father's house, for you *are* the son of another woman." [3] Then Jephthah fled from his brothers and dwelt in the land of Tob; and worthless men banded together with Jephthah and went out *raiding* with him.

[4] It came to pass after a time that the people of Ammon made war against Israel. [5] And so it was, when the people of Ammon made war against Israel, that the elders of Gilead went to get Jephthah from the land of Tob. [6] Then they said to Jephthah, "Come and be our commander, that we may fight against the people of Ammon."

[7] So Jephthah said to the elders of Gilead, "Did you not hate me, and expel me from my father's house? Why have you come to me now when you are in distress?"

[8] And the elders of Gilead said to Jephthah, "That is why we have turned again to you now, that you may go with us and fight against the people of Ammon, and be our head over all the inhabitants of Gilead."

[9] So Jephthah said to the elders of Gilead, "If you take me back home to fight against the people of Ammon, and the LORD delivers them to me, shall I be your head?"

[10] And the elders of Gilead said to Jephthah, "The LORD will be a witness between us, if we do not do according to your words." [11] Then Jephthah went with the elders of Gilead, and the people made him head and commander over them; and Jephthah spoke all his words before the LORD in Mizpah.

[12] Now Jephthah sent messengers to the king of the people of Ammon, saying, "What do you have against me, that you have come to fight against me in my land?"

[13] And the king of the people of Ammon answered the messengers of Jephthah, "Because Israel took away my land when they came up out of Egypt, from the

Arnon as far as the Jabbok, and to the Jordan. Now therefore, restore those *lands* peaceably."

¹⁴ So Jephthah again sent messengers to the king of the people of Ammon, ¹⁵ and said to him, "Thus says Jephthah: 'Israel did not take away the land of Moab, nor the land of the people of Ammon; ¹⁶ for when Israel came up from Egypt, they walked through the wilderness as far as the Red Sea and came to Kadesh. ¹⁷ Then Israel sent messengers to the king of Edom, saying, "Please let me pass through your land." But the king of Edom would not heed. And in like manner they sent to the king of Moab, but he would not *consent.* So Israel remained in Kadesh. ¹⁸ And they went along through the wilderness and bypassed the land of Edom and the land of Moab, came to the east side of the land of Moab, and encamped on the other side of the Arnon. But they did not enter the border of Moab, for the Arnon *was* the border of Moab. ¹⁹ Then Israel sent messengers to Sihon king of the Amorites, king of Heshbon; and Israel said to him, "Please let us pass through your land into our place." ²⁰ But Sihon did not trust Israel to pass through his territory. So Sihon gathered all his people together, encamped in Jahaz, and fought against Israel. ²¹ And the LORD God of Israel delivered Sihon and all his people into the hand of Israel, and they defeated them. Thus Israel gained possession of all the land of the Amorites, who inhabited that country. ²² They took possession of all the territory of the Amorites, from the Arnon to the Jabbok and from the wilderness to the Jordan.

²³ 'And now the LORD God of Israel has dispossessed the Amorites from before His people Israel; should you then possess it? ²⁴ Will you not possess whatever Chemosh your god gives you to possess? So whatever the LORD our God takes possession of before us, we will possess. ²⁵ And now, *are* you any better than Balak the son of Zippor, king of Moab? Did he ever strive against Israel? Did he ever fight against them? ²⁶ While Israel dwelt in Heshbon and its villages, in Aroer and its villages, and in all the cities along the banks of the Arnon, for three hundred years, why did you not recover *them* within that

time? ²⁷ Therefore I have not sinned against you, but you wronged me by fighting against me. May the LORD, the Judge, render judgment this day between the children of Israel and the people of Ammon.' " ²⁸ However, the king of the people of Ammon did not heed the words which Jephthah sent him.

²⁹ Then the Spirit of the LORD came upon Jephthah, and he passed through Gilead and Manasseh, and passed through Mizpah of Gilead; and from Mizpah of Gilead he advanced *toward* the people of Ammon. ³⁰ And Jephthah made a vow to the LORD, and said, "If You will indeed deliver the people of Ammon into my hands, ³¹ then it will be that whatever comes out of the doors of my house to meet me, when I return in peace from the people of Ammon, shall surely be the LORD's, and I will offer it up as a burnt offering."

³² So Jephthah advanced toward the people of Ammon to fight against them, and the LORD delivered them into his hands. ³³ And he defeated them from Aroer as far as Minnith—twenty cities— and to Abel Keramim, with a very great slaughter. Thus the people of Ammon were subdued before the children of Israel.

³⁴ When Jephthah came to his house at Mizpah, there was his daughter, coming out to meet him with timbrels and dancing; and she *was his* only child. Besides her he had neither son nor daughter. ³⁵ And it came to pass, when he saw her, that he tore his clothes, and said, "Alas, my daughter! You have brought me very low! You are among those who trouble me! For I have given my word to the LORD, and I cannot go back on it."

³⁶ So she said to him, "My father, *if* you have given your word to the LORD, do to me according to what has gone out of your mouth, because the LORD has avenged you of your enemies, the people of Ammon." ³⁷ Then she said to her father, "Let this thing be done for me: let me alone for two months, that I may go and wander on the mountains and bewail my virginity, my friends and I."

³⁸ So he said, "Go." And he sent her away *for* two months; and she went with her friends, and bewailed her virginity on the mountains. ³⁹ And it was so at the end

Shattered

One Sunday afternoon, Doris Louise Seger opened the door of her office at the church to practice a violin solo she was to play that night, only to find her violin in pieces, scattered across the floor. Doris was crushed. She had received the violin as a high school graduation present from her parents — fifty years ago. She thought, *Who? Why? How can I forgive the person who did this?*

A week later, police found the vandal and Doris went to his home. When she saw the skinny, blond eleven-year-old sitting next to his father, she understood that the real tragedy was not her shattered violin, but a young life that seemed headed for a shattered future. She explained to the family what the violin had meant to her life and then she found herself saying, "I forgive you, and God will, too, if you ask Him."

A few days later, the boy came to the pastor's office, asking hesitantly, "Is there any work that I can do at the church to pay for the violin?" At the sign of his repentant heart, the pastor shared the Gospel with him and the boy received Jesus as his Savior that day.

Doris purchased a new violin, but she later wrote, "It would never compare with this 'new creature' in Christ Jesus. I learned anew that God's grace is sufficient enough to give me a forgiving heart."

His grace is sufficient for you too.

> Take heed to yourselves. If your brother sins against you, rebuke him; and if he repents, forgive him.
>
> *Luke 17:3*

of two months that she returned to her father, and he carried out his vow with her which he had vowed. She knew no man.

And it became a custom in Israel [40] *that* the daughters of Israel went four days each year to lament the daughter of Jephthah the Gileadite.

12 Then the men of Ephraim gathered together, crossed over toward Zaphon, and said to Jephthah, "Why did you cross over to fight against the people of Ammon, and did not call us to go with you? We will burn your house down on you with fire!"

[2] And Jephthah said to them, "My people and I were in a great struggle with the people of Ammon; and when I called you, you did not deliver me out of their hands. [3] So when I saw that you would not deliver *me*, I took my life in my hands and crossed over against the people of Ammon; and the LORD delivered them into my hand. Why then have you come up to me this day to fight against me?" [4] Now Jephthah gathered together all the men of Gilead and fought against Ephraim. And the men of Gilead defeated Ephraim, because they said, "You Gileadites *are* fugitives of Ephraim among the Ephraimites *and* among the Manassites." [5] The Gileadites seized the fords of the Jordan before the Ephraimites *arrived*. And when *any* Ephraimite who escaped said, "Let me cross over," the men of Gilead would say to him, "*Are* you an Ephraimite?" If he said, "No," [6] then they would say to him, "Then say, 'Shibboleth'!" And he would say, "Sibboleth," for he could not pronounce *it* right. Then they would take him and kill him at the fords of the Jordan. There fell at that time forty-two thousand Ephraimites.

[7] And Jephthah judged Israel six years. Then Jephthah the Gileadite died and was buried among the cities of Gilead.

[8] After him, Ibzan of Bethlehem judged Israel. [9] He had thirty sons. And he gave away thirty daughters in marriage, and brought in thirty daughters from elsewhere for his sons. He judged Israel seven years. [10] Then Ibzan died and was buried at Bethlehem.

[11] After him, Elon the Zebulunite judged Israel. He judged Israel ten years. [12] And Elon the Zebulunite died and was buried at Aijalon in the country of Zebulun.

[13] After him, Abdon the son of Hillel the Pirathonite judged Israel. [14] He had forty sons and thirty grandsons, who rode on seventy young donkeys. He judged Israel eight years. [15] Then Abdon the son of Hillel the Pirathonite died and was buried in Pirathon in the land of Ephraim, in the mountains of the Amalekites.

~ PSALM 50:7–15 ~

[7] "Hear, O My people, and I will speak,
O Israel, and I will testify against
    you;
I *am* God, your God!
[8] I will not rebuke you for your
    sacrifices
Or your burnt offerings,
Which are continually before Me.
[9] I will not take a bull from your
    house,
Nor goats out of your folds.
[10] For every beast of the forest *is* Mine,
And the cattle on a thousand hills.
[11] I know all the birds of the
    mountains,
And the wild beasts of the field *are*
    Mine.

[12] "If I were hungry, I would not tell
    you;
For the world *is* Mine, and all its
    fullness.
[13] Will I eat the flesh of bulls,
Or drink the blood of goats?
[14] Offer to God thanksgiving,
And pay your vows to the Most
    High.
[15] Call upon Me in the day of trouble;
I will deliver you, and you shall
    glorify Me."

~ PROVERBS 14:28 ~

[28] In a multitude of people *is* a king's
    honor,
But in the lack of people *is* the
    downfall of a prince.

～ LUKE 17:1–19 ～

Then He said to the disciples, "It is impossible that no offenses should come, but woe *to him* through whom they do come! ² It would be better for him if a millstone were hung around his neck, and he were thrown into the sea, than that he should offend one of these little ones. ³ Take heed to yourselves. If your brother sins against you, rebuke him; and if he repents, forgive him. ⁴ And if he sins against you seven times in a day, and seven times in a day returns to you, saying, 'I repent,' you shall forgive him."

⁵ And the apostles said to the Lord, "Increase our faith."

⁶ So the Lord said, "If you have faith as a mustard seed, you can say to this mulberry tree, 'Be pulled up by the roots and be planted in the sea,' and it would obey you. ⁷ And which of you, having a servant plowing or tending sheep, will say to him when he has come in from the field, 'Come at once and sit down to eat'? ⁸ But will he not rather say to him, 'Prepare something for my supper, and gird yourself and serve me till I have eaten and drunk, and afterward you will eat and drink'? ⁹ Does he thank that servant because he did the things that were commanded him? I think not. ¹⁰ So likewise you, when you have done all those things which you are commanded, say, 'We are unprofitable servants. We have done what was our duty to do.' "

¹¹ Now it happened as He went to Jerusalem that He passed through the midst of Samaria and Galilee. ¹² Then as He entered a certain village, there met Him ten men who were lepers, who stood afar off. ¹³ And they lifted up *their* voices and said, "Jesus, Master, have mercy on us!" ¹⁴ So when He saw *them,* He said to them, "Go, show yourselves to the priests." And so it was that as they went, they were cleansed.

¹⁵ And one of them, when he saw that he was healed, returned, and with a loud voice glorified God, ¹⁶ and fell down on *his* face at His feet, giving Him thanks. And he was a Samaritan.

¹⁷ So Jesus answered and said, "Were there not ten cleansed? But where *are* the nine? ¹⁸ Were there not any found who returned to give glory to God except this foreigner?" ¹⁹ And He said to him, "Arise, go your way. Your faith has made you well."

READING 114 · APRIL 24

～ JUDGES 13:1—14:20 ～

Again the children of Israel did evil in the sight of the LORD, and the LORD delivered them into the hand of the Philistines for forty years.

² Now there was a certain man from Zorah, of the family of the Danites, whose name *was* Manoah; and his wife *was* barren and had no children. ³ And the Angel of the LORD appeared to the woman and said to her, "Indeed now, you are barren and have borne no children, but you shall conceive and bear a son. ⁴ Now therefore, please be careful not to drink wine or *similar* drink, and not to eat anything unclean. ⁵ For behold, you shall conceive and bear a son. And no razor shall come upon his head, for the child shall be a Nazirite to God from the womb; and he shall begin to deliver Israel out of the hand of the Philistines."

⁶ So the woman came and told her husband, saying, "A Man of God came to me, and His countenance *was* like the countenance of the Angel of God, very awesome; but I did not ask Him where He *was* from, and He did not tell me His name. ⁷ And He said to me, 'Behold, you shall conceive and bear a son. Now drink no wine or *similar* drink, nor eat anything unclean, for the child shall be a Nazirite to God from the womb to the day of his death.' "

⁸ Then Manoah prayed to the LORD, and said, "O my Lord, please let the Man

of God whom You sent come to us again and teach us what we shall do for the child who will be born."

⁹ And God listened to the voice of Manoah, and the Angel of God came to the woman again as she was sitting in the field; but Manoah her husband *was* not with her. ¹⁰ Then the woman ran in haste and told her husband, and said to him, "Look, the Man who came to me the *other* day has just now appeared to me!"

¹¹ So Manoah arose and followed his wife. When he came to the Man, he said to Him, "Are You the Man who spoke to this woman?"

And He said, "I *am*."

¹² Manoah said, "Now let Your words come *to pass*! What will be the boy's rule of life, and his work?"

¹³ So the Angel of the LORD said to Manoah, "Of all that I said to the woman let her be careful. ¹⁴ She may not eat anything that comes from the vine, nor may she drink wine or *similar* drink, nor eat anything unclean. All that I commanded her let her observe."

¹⁵ Then Manoah said to the Angel of the LORD, "Please let us detain You, and we will prepare a young goat for You."

¹⁶ And the Angel of the LORD said to Manoah, "Though you detain Me, I will not eat your food. But if you offer a burnt offering, you must offer it to the LORD." (For Manoah did not know He *was* the Angel of the LORD.)

¹⁷ Then Manoah said to the Angel of the LORD, "What *is* Your name, that when Your words come *to pass* we may honor You?"

¹⁸ And the Angel of the LORD said to him, "Why do you ask My name, seeing it *is* wonderful?"

¹⁹ So Manoah took the young goat with the grain offering, and offered it upon the rock to the LORD. And He did a wondrous thing while Manoah and his wife looked on— ²⁰ it happened as the flame went up toward heaven from the altar— the Angel of the LORD ascended in the flame of the altar! When Manoah and his wife saw *this*, they fell on their faces to the ground. ²¹ When the Angel of the LORD appeared no more to Manoah and his wife, then Manoah knew that He *was* the Angel of the LORD.

²² And Manoah said to his wife, "We shall surely die, because we have seen God!"

²³ But his wife said to him, "If the LORD had desired to kill us, He would not have accepted a burnt offering and a grain offering from our hands, nor would He have shown us all these *things*, nor would He have told us *such things* as these at this time."

²⁴ So the woman bore a son and called his name Samson; and the child grew, and the LORD blessed him. ²⁵ And the Spirit of the LORD began to move upon him at Mahaneh Dan between Zorah and Eshtaol.

14 Now Samson went down to Timnah, and saw a woman in Timnah of the daughters of the Philistines. ² So he went up and told his father and mother, saying, "I have seen a woman in Timnah of the daughters of the Philistines; now therefore, get her for me as a wife."

³ Then his father and mother said to him, "*Is there* no woman among the daughters of your brethren, or among all my people, that you must go and get a wife from the uncircumcised Philistines?"

And Samson said to his father, "Get her for me, for she pleases me well."

⁴ But his father and mother did not know that it was of the LORD—that He was seeking an occasion to move against the Philistines. For at that time the Philistines had dominion over Israel.

⁵ So Samson went down to Timnah with his father and mother, and came to the vineyards of Timnah.

Now *to his* surprise, a young lion *came* roaring against him. ⁶ And the Spirit of the LORD came mightily upon him, and he tore the lion apart as one would have torn apart a young goat, though *he had* nothing in his hand. But he did not tell his father or his mother what he had done.

⁷ Then he went down and talked with the woman; and she pleased Samson well. ⁸ After some time, when he returned to get her, he turned aside to see the carcass of the lion. And behold, a swarm of bees and honey *were* in the carcass of the lion. ⁹ He took some of it in his hands and went along, eating. When he came to his father and mother, he gave *some* to them, and

Following Orders

One of the favorite stories of Arturo Toscanini, the great symphony conductor, was this:

An orchestra was playing Beethoven's *Leonore* overture, which has two great musical climaxes. Each of these musical high points is followed by a trumpet passage, which the composer intended to be played offstage.

The first climax arrived, but no sound came from the trumpet offstage. The conductor, annoyed, went on to the second musical high point. But again — no trumpet was heard.

This time, the conductor rushed, fuming, into the wings, with every intention of demanding a full explanation. There he found the trumpet player struggling with the house security man who was insisting as he held onto the man's trumpet for dear life, "I tell you, you can't play that trumpet back here! You'll disturb the rehearsal!"

Like the security man, we often jump to conclusions when we try to judge the actions of others. The trumpet player knew what the conductor had directed him to do; the security man did not. We are not called to be God's security men, we are called to obey the Conductor, and allow, even help, others to as well.

they also ate. But he did not tell them that he had taken the honey out of the carcass of the lion.

10 So his father went down to the woman. And Samson gave a feast there, for young men used to do so. 11 And it happened, when they saw him, that they brought thirty companions to be with him.

12 Then Samson said to them, "Let me pose a riddle to you. If you can correctly solve and explain it to me within the seven days of the feast, then I will give you thirty linen garments and thirty changes of clothing. 13 But if you cannot explain *it* to me, then you shall give me thirty linen garments and thirty changes of clothing."

And they said to him, "Pose your riddle, that we may hear it."

14 So he said to them:

> "Out of the eater came something to eat,
> And out of the strong came something sweet."

Now for three days they could not explain the riddle.

15 But it came to pass on the seventh day that they said to Samson's wife, "Entice your husband, that he may explain the riddle to us, or else we will burn you and your father's house with fire. Have you invited us in order to take what is ours? *Is that* not *so?*"

16 Then Samson's wife wept on him, and said, "You only hate me! You do not love me! You have posed a riddle to the sons of my people, but you have not explained *it* to me."

And he said to her, "Look, I have not explained *it* to my father or my mother; so should I explain *it* to you?" 17 Now she had wept on him the seven days while their feast lasted. And it happened on the seventh day that he told her, because she pressed him so much. Then she explained the riddle to the sons of her people. 18 So the men of the city said to him on the seventh day before the sun went down:

> "What *is* sweeter than honey?
> And what *is* stronger than a lion?"

And he said to them:

> "If you had not plowed with my heifer,
> You would not have solved my riddle!"

19 Then the Spirit of the LORD came upon him mightily, and he went down to Ashkelon and killed thirty of their men, took their apparel, and gave the changes *of clothing* to those who had explained the riddle. So his anger was aroused, and he went back up to his father's house. 20 And Samson's wife was *given* to his companion, who had been his best man.

~ PSALM 50:16–23 ~

16 But to the wicked God says:
"What *right* have you to declare My statutes,
Or take My covenant in your mouth,
17 Seeing you hate instruction
And cast My words behind you?
18 When you saw a thief, you consented with him,
And have been a partaker with adulterers.
19 You give your mouth to evil,
And your tongue frames deceit.
20 You sit *and* speak against your brother;
You slander your own mother's son.
21 These *things* you have done, and I kept silent;
You thought that I was altogether like you;
But I will rebuke you,
And set *them* in order before your eyes.

22 "Now consider this, you who forget God,
Lest I tear *you* in pieces,
And *there be* none to deliver:
23 Whoever offers praise glorifies Me;
And to him who orders *his* conduct *aright*
I will show the salvation of God."

~ PROVERBS 14:29, 30 ~

29 *He who is* slow to wrath has great understanding,
But *he who is* impulsive exalts folly.

[30] A sound heart *is* life to the body,
But envy *is* rottenness to the bones.

∼ LUKE 17:20–37 ∼

Now when He was asked by the Pharisees when the kingdom of God would come, He answered them and said, "The kingdom of God does not come with observation; [21] nor will they say, 'See here!' or 'See there!' For indeed, the kingdom of God is within you."

[22] Then He said to the disciples, "The days will come when you will desire to see one of the days of the Son of Man, and you will not see *it*. [23] And they will say to you, 'Look here!' or 'Look there!' Do not go after *them* or follow *them*. [24] For as the lightning that flashes out of one *part* under heaven shines to the other *part* under heaven, so also the Son of Man will be in His day. [25] But first He must suffer many things and be rejected by this generation. [26] And as it was in the days of Noah, so it will be also in the days of the Son of Man: [27] They ate, they drank, they married wives, they were given in marriage, until the day that Noah entered the ark, and the flood came and destroyed them all. [28] Likewise as it was also in the days of Lot: They ate, they drank, they bought, they sold, they planted, they built; [29] but on the day that Lot went out of Sodom it rained fire and brimstone from heaven and destroyed *them* all. [30] Even so will it be in the day when the Son of Man is revealed.

[31] "In that day, he who is on the housetop, and his goods *are* in the house, let him not come down to take them away. And likewise the one who is in the field, let him not turn back. [32] Remember Lot's wife. [33] Whoever seeks to save his life will lose it, and whoever loses his life will preserve it. [34] I tell you, in that night there will be two *men* in one bed: the one will be taken and the other will be left. [35] Two *women* will be grinding together: the one will be taken and the other left. [36] Two *men* will be in the field: the one will be taken and the other left."

[37] And they answered and said to Him, "Where, Lord?"

So He said to them, "Wherever the body is, there the eagles will be gathered together."

∼ JUDGES 15:1—16:31 ∼

After a while, in the time of wheat harvest, it happened that Samson visited his wife with a young goat. And he said, "Let me go in to my wife, into *her* room." But her father would not permit him to go in.

[2] Her father said, "I really thought that you thoroughly hated her; therefore I gave her to your companion. *Is* not her younger sister better than she? Please, take her instead."

[3] And Samson said to them, "This time I shall be blameless regarding the Philistines if I harm them!" [4] Then Samson went and caught three hundred foxes; and he took torches, turned *the foxes* tail to tail, and put a torch between each pair of tails. [5] When he had set the torches on fire, he let *the foxes* go into the standing grain of the Philistines, and burned up both the shocks and the standing grain, as well as the vineyards *and* olive groves.

[6] Then the Philistines said, "Who has done this?"

And they answered, "Samson, the son-in-law of the Timnite, because he has taken his wife and given her to his companion." So the Philistines came up and burned her and her father with fire.

[7] Samson said to them, "Since you would do a thing like this, I will surely take revenge on you, and after that I will cease." [8] So he attacked them hip and thigh with a great slaughter; then he went down and dwelt in the cleft of the rock of Etam.

[9] Now the Philistines went up, encamped in Judah, and deployed themselves against Lehi. [10] And the men of Judah said, "Why have you come up against us?"

So they answered, "We have come up

to arrest Samson, to do to him as he has done to us."

[11] Then three thousand men of Judah went down to the cleft of the rock of Etam, and said to Samson, "Do you not know that the Philistines rule over us? What *is* this you have done to us?"

And he said to them, "As they did to me, so I have done to them."

[12] But they said to him, "We have come down to arrest you, that we may deliver you into the hand of the Philistines."

Then Samson said to them, "Swear to me that you will not kill me yourselves."

[13] So they spoke to him, saying, "No, but we will tie you securely and deliver you into their hand; but we will surely not kill you." And they bound him with two new ropes and brought him up from the rock.

[14] When he came to Lehi, the Philistines came shouting against him. Then the Spirit of the LORD came mightily upon him; and the ropes that *were* on his arms became like flax that is burned with fire, and his bonds broke loose from his hands. [15] He found a fresh jawbone of a donkey, reached out his hand and took it, and killed a thousand men with it. [16] Then Samson said:

> "With the jawbone of a donkey,
> Heaps upon heaps,
> With the jawbone of a donkey
> I have slain a thousand men!"

[17] And so it was, when he had finished speaking, that he threw the jawbone from his hand, and called that place Ramath Lehi.

[18] Then he became very thirsty; so he cried out to the LORD and said, "You have given this great deliverance by the hand of Your servant; and now shall I die of thirst and fall into the hand of the uncircumcised?" [19] So God split the hollow place that *is* in Lehi, and water came out, and he drank; and his spirit returned, and he revived. Therefore he called its name En Hakkore, which is in Lehi to this day. [20] And he judged Israel twenty years in the days of the Philistines.

16 Now Samson went to Gaza and saw a harlot there, and went in to her. [2] When the Gazites *were told*, "Samson has come here!" they surrounded *the place* and lay in wait for him all night at the gate of the city. They were quiet all night, saying, "In the morning, when it is daylight, we will kill him." [3] And Samson lay *low* till midnight; then he arose at midnight, took hold of the doors of the gate of the city and the two gateposts, pulled them up, bar and all, put *them* on his shoulders, and carried them to the top of the hill that faces Hebron.

[4] Afterward it happened that he loved a woman in the Valley of Sorek, whose name *was* Delilah. [5] And the lords of the Philistines came up to her and said to her, "Entice him, and find out where his great strength *lies,* and by what *means* we may overpower him, that we may bind him to afflict him; and every one of us will give you eleven hundred *pieces* of silver."

[6] So Delilah said to Samson, "Please tell me where your great strength *lies,* and with what you may be bound to afflict you."

[7] And Samson said to her, "If they bind me with seven fresh bowstrings, not yet dried, then I shall become weak, and be like any *other* man."

[8] So the lords of the Philistines brought up to her seven fresh bowstrings, not yet dried, and she bound him with them. [9] Now *men were* lying in wait, staying with her in the room. And she said to him, "The Philistines *are* upon you, Samson!" But he broke the bowstrings as a strand of yarn breaks when it touches fire. So the secret of his strength was not known.

[10] Then Delilah said to Samson, "Look, you have mocked me and told me lies. Now, please tell me what you may be bound with."

[11] So he said to her, "If they bind me securely with new ropes that have never been used, then I shall become weak, and be like any *other* man."

[12] Therefore Delilah took new ropes and bound him with them, and said to him, "The Philistines *are* upon you, Samson!" And *men were* lying in wait, staying in the room. But he broke them off his arms like a thread.

[13] Delilah said to Samson, "Until now you have mocked me and told me lies. Tell me what you may be bound with."

Mother's Anchor

Henry Ward Beecher, considered by many to be one of the most effective and powerful pulpit orators in the history of the United States, not only had a reputation for having an extremely sensitive heart, but also for having a great love of the sea. Many of his sermons were laced with loving anecdotes with a seafaring flavor.

Beecher once said, "Children are the hands by which we take hold of heaven." And he had this to say about a mother's relationship with her child:

> A babe is a mother's anchor. She cannot swing far from her moorings. And yet a true mother never lives so little in the present as when by the side of the cradle. Her thoughts follow the imagined future of her child. That babe is the boldest of pilots, and guides her fearless thoughts down through scenes of coming years. The old ark never made such voyages as the cradle daily makes.

What a wonderful image to think of a child as being on a voyage from Heaven, through life, to return to Heaven's port one day. What a challenge to think that our children have not come along to join us in our sail through life, but we are to join in their voyage!

Assuredly, I say to you, whoever does not receive the kingdom of God as a little child will by no means enter it.

Luke 18:17

And he said to her, "If you weave the seven locks of my head into the web of the loom"—

¹⁴ So she wove *it* tightly with the batten of the loom, and said to him, "The Philistines *are* upon you, Samson!" But he awoke from his sleep, and pulled out the batten and the web from the loom.

¹⁵ Then she said to him, "How can you say, 'I love you,' when your heart *is* not with me? You have mocked me these three times, and have not told me where your great strength *lies.*" ¹⁶ And it came to pass, when she pestered him daily with her words and pressed him, *so* that his soul was vexed to death, ¹⁷ that he told her all his heart, and said to her, "No razor has ever come upon my head, for I *have been* a Nazirite to God from my mother's womb. If I am shaven, then my strength will leave me, and I shall become weak, and be like any *other* man."

¹⁸ When Delilah saw that he had told her all his heart, she sent and called for the lords of the Philistines, saying, "Come up once more, for he has told me all his heart." So the lords of the Philistines came up to her and brought the money in their hand. ¹⁹ Then she lulled him to sleep on her knees, and called for a man and had him shave off the seven locks of his head. Then she began to torment him, and his strength left him. ²⁰ And she said, "The Philistines *are* upon you, Samson!" So he awoke from his sleep, and said, "I will go out as before, at other times, and shake myself free!" But he did not know that the LORD had departed from him.

²¹ Then the Philistines took him and put out his eyes, and brought him down to Gaza. They bound him with bronze fetters, and he became a grinder in the prison. ²² However, the hair of his head began to grow again after it had been shaven.

²³ Now the lords of the Philistines gathered together to offer a great sacrifice to Dagon their god, and to rejoice. And they said:

"Our god has delivered into our hands
Samson our enemy!"

²⁴ When the people saw him, they praised their god; for they said:

"Our god has delivered into our hands our enemy,
The destroyer of our land,
And the one who multiplied our dead."

²⁵ So it happened, when their hearts were merry, that they said, "Call for Samson, that he may perform for us." So they called for Samson from the prison, and he performed for them. And they stationed him between the pillars. ²⁶ Then Samson said to the lad who held him by the hand, "Let me feel the pillars which support the temple, so that I can lean on them." ²⁷ Now the temple was full of men and women. All the lords of the Philistines *were* there—about three thousand men and women on the roof watching while Samson performed.

²⁸ Then Samson called to the LORD, saying, "O Lord GOD, remember me, I pray! Strengthen me, I pray, just this once, O God, that I may with one *blow* take vengeance on the Philistines for my two eyes!" ²⁹ And Samson took hold of the two middle pillars which supported the temple, and he braced himself against them, one on his right and the other on his left. ³⁰ Then Samson said, "Let me die with the Philistines!" And he pushed with *all his* might, and the temple fell on the lords and all the people who *were* in it. So the dead that he killed at his death were more than he had killed in his life.

³¹ And his brothers and all his father's household came down and took him, and brought *him* up and buried him between Zorah and Eshtaol in the tomb of his father Manoah. He had judged Israel twenty years.

∼ PSALM 51:1–6 ∼

¹ Have mercy upon me, O God,
    According to Your lovingkindness;
    According to the multitude of Your tender mercies,
    Blot out my transgressions.
² Wash me thoroughly from my iniquity,
    And cleanse me from my sin.

³ For I acknowledge my transgressions,

And my sin *is* always before me.
4 Against You, You only, have I sinned,
And done *this* evil in Your sight—
That You may be found just when
   You speak,
And blameless when You judge.

5 Behold, I was brought forth in
   iniquity,
And in sin my mother conceived me.
6 Behold, You desire truth in the
   inward parts,
And in the hidden *part* You will
   make me to know wisdom.

~ PROVERBS 14:31, 32 ~

31 He who oppresses the poor
   reproaches his Maker,
But he who honors Him has mercy
   on the needy.

32 The wicked is banished in his
   wickedness,
But the righteous has a refuge in his
   death.

~ LUKE 18:1–23 ~

Then He spoke a parable to them, that
men always ought to pray and not lose
heart, 2 saying: "There was in a certain
city a judge who did not fear God nor
regard man. 3 Now there was a widow in
that city; and she came to him, saying,
'Get justice for me from my adversary.'
4 And he would not for a while; but afterward he said within himself, 'Though I
do not fear God nor regard man, 5 yet
because this widow troubles me I will
avenge her, lest by her continual coming
she weary me.' "
6 Then the Lord said, "Hear what the
unjust judge said. 7 And shall God not
avenge His own elect who cry out day
and night to Him, though He bears long
with them? 8 I tell you that He will avenge
them speedily. Nevertheless, when the Son

of Man comes, will He really find faith
on the earth?"
9 Also He spoke this parable to some
who trusted in themselves that they were
righteous, and despised others: 10 "Two
men went up to the temple to pray, one a
Pharisee and the other a tax collector.
11 The Pharisee stood and prayed thus with
himself, 'God, I thank You that I am not
like other men—extortioners, unjust,
adulterers, or even as this tax collector.
12 I fast twice a week; I give tithes of all
that I possess.' 13 And the tax collector,
standing afar off, would not so much as
raise *his* eyes to heaven, but beat his breast,
saying, 'God, be merciful to me a sinner!'
14 I tell you, this man went down to his
house justified *rather* than the other; for
everyone who exalts himself will be
humbled, and he who humbles himself
will be exalted."
15 Then they also brought infants to
Him that He might touch them; but when
the disciples saw *it,* they rebuked them.
16 But Jesus called them to *Him* and said,
"Let the little children come to Me, and
do not forbid them; for of such is the kingdom of God. 17 Assuredly, I say to you,
whoever does not receive the kingdom of
God as a little child will by no means
enter it."
18 Now a certain ruler asked Him, saying, "Good Teacher, what shall I do to
inherit eternal life?"
19 So Jesus said to him, "Why do
you call Me good? No one *is* good but
One, *that is,* God. 20 You know the commandments: 'Do not commit adultery,'
'Do not murder,' 'Do not steal,' 'Do not
bear false witness,' 'Honor your father and
your mother.' "
21 And he said, "All these things I have
kept from my youth."
22 So when Jesus heard these things, He
said to him, "You still lack one thing. Sell
all that you have and distribute to the
poor, and you will have treasure in
heaven; and come, follow Me."
23 But when he heard this, he became
very sorrowful, for he was very rich.

∼ JUDGES 17:1—19:30 ∼

Now there was a man from the mountains of Ephraim, whose name *was* Micah. ² And he said to his mother, "The eleven hundred *shekels* of silver that were taken from you, and on which you put a curse, even saying it in my ears—here *is* the silver with me; I took it."

And his mother said, "*May you be* blessed by the LORD, my son!" ³ So when he had returned the eleven hundred *shekels* of silver to his mother, his mother said, "I had wholly dedicated the silver from my hand to the LORD for my son, to make a carved image and a molded image; now therefore, I will return it to you." ⁴ Thus he returned the silver to his mother. Then his mother took two hundred *shekels* of silver and gave them to the silversmith, and he made it into a carved image and a molded image; and they were in the house of Micah.

⁵ The man Micah had a shrine, and made an ephod and household idols; and he consecrated one of his sons, who became his priest. ⁶ In those days *there was* no king in Israel; everyone did *what was* right in his own eyes.

⁷ Now there was a young man from Bethlehem in Judah, of the family of Judah; he *was* a Levite, and was staying there. ⁸ The man departed from the city of Bethlehem in Judah to stay wherever he could find *a place*. Then he came to the mountains of Ephraim, to the house of Micah, as he journeyed. ⁹ And Micah said to him, "Where do you come from?"

So he said to him, "I *am* a Levite from Bethlehem in Judah, and I am on my way to find *a place* to stay."

¹⁰ Micah said to him, "Dwell with me, and be a father and a priest to me, and I will give you ten *shekels* of silver per year, a suit of clothes, and your sustenance." So the Levite went in. ¹¹ Then the Levite was content to dwell with the man; and the young man became like one of his sons to him. ¹² So Micah consecrated the Levite, and the young man became his priest, and lived in the house of Micah. ¹³ Then Micah said, "Now I know that the LORD will be good to me, since I have a Levite as priest!"

18 In those days *there was* no king in Israel. And in those days the tribe of the Danites was seeking an inheritance for itself to dwell in; for until that day *their* inheritance among the tribes of Israel had not fallen to them. ² So the children of Dan sent five men of their family from their territory, men of valor from Zorah and Eshtaol, to spy out the land and search it. They said to them, "Go, search the land." So they went to the mountains of Ephraim, to the house of Micah, and lodged there. ³ While they *were* at the house of Micah, they recognized the voice of the young Levite. They turned aside and said to him, "Who brought you here? What are you doing in this *place*? What do you have here?"

⁴ He said to them, "Thus and so Micah did for me. He has hired me, and I have become his priest."

⁵ So they said to him, "Please inquire of God, that we may know whether the journey on which we go will be prosperous."

⁶ And the priest said to them, "Go in peace. The presence of the LORD *be* with you on your way."

⁷ So the five men departed and went to Laish. They saw the people who *were* there, how they dwelt safely, in the manner of the Sidonians, quiet and secure. *There were* no rulers in the land who might put *them* to shame for anything. They *were* far from the Sidonians, and they had no ties with anyone.

⁸ Then *the spies* came back to their brethren at Zorah and Eshtaol, and their brethren said to them, "What *is* your *report*?"

⁹ So they said, "Arise, let us go up against them. For we have seen the land, and indeed it *is* very good. *Would* you *do* nothing? Do not hesitate to go, *and* enter to possess the land. ¹⁰ When you go, you will come to a secure people and a large land. For God has given it into your hands, a place where *there is* no lack of anything that *is* on the earth."

World-changing Prayer

> But He said, "The things which are impossible with men are possible with God."
>
> *Luke 18:27*

Billy Graham had planned a meeting in Germany in 1992, but when the Berlin Wall came down in 1989, his plans were changed. On March 10, 1990, Graham spoke at the Platz der Republik, the great open area in front of the Reichstag, the historic site where Nazis once paraded by torchlight, preaching their doctrine of ethnic bitterness and hatred. In sharp contrast, Graham spoke of the good news of God's forgiveness and love. Just a few yards away, workers with saws and torches continued to rip out the bars that had supported the wall.

Graham told the large congregation, "God has answered our prayers." Members of the press corps asked if he truly believed the dismantling of the Iron Curtain was an answer to prayer. He told them yes. Christians in the East and the West had been praying for decades for the day the wall would be demolished. He told them the prospect of liberation, reunification, and the freedom to worship God made this the happiest hour for Germany.

Often, we mistakenly assume that major world events just happen. In nearly all cases however, you will find that those headlines which mark major changes for good have been birthed in prayer. God commands us to pray for all those in authority. Your prayers *do* make a difference in the world!

¹¹ And six hundred men of the family of the Danites went from there, from Zorah and Eshtaol, armed with weapons of war. ¹² Then they went up and encamped in Kirjath Jearim in Judah. (Therefore they call that place Mahaneh Dan to this day. There *it is,* west of Kirjath Jearim.) ¹³ And they passed from there to the mountains of Ephraim, and came to the house of Micah.

¹⁴ Then the five men who had gone to spy out the country of Laish answered and said to their brethren, "Do you know that there are in these houses an ephod, household idols, a carved image, and a molded image? Now therefore, consider what you should do." ¹⁵ So they turned aside there, and came to the house of the young Levite man—to the house of Micah—and greeted him. ¹⁶ The six hundred men armed with their weapons of war, who *were* of the children of Dan, stood by the entrance of the gate. ¹⁷ Then the five men who had gone to spy out the land went up. Entering there, they took the carved image, the ephod, the household idols, and the molded image. The priest stood at the entrance of the gate with the six hundred men *who were* armed with weapons of war.

¹⁸ When these went into Micah's house and took the carved image, the ephod, the household idols, and the molded image, the priest said to them, "What are you doing?"

¹⁹ And they said to him, "Be quiet, put your hand over your mouth, and come with us; be a father and a priest to us. *Is it* better for you to be a priest to the household of one man, or that you be a priest to a tribe and a family in Israel?" ²⁰ So the priest's heart was glad; and he took the ephod, the household idols, and the carved image, and took his place among the people.

²¹ Then they turned and departed, and put the little ones, the livestock, and the goods in front of them. ²² When they were a good way from the house of Micah, the men who *were* in the houses near Micah's house gathered together and overtook the children of Dan. ²³ And they called out to the children of Dan. So they turned around and said to Micah, "What ails you, that you have gathered such a company?"

²⁴ So he said, "You have taken away my gods which I made, and the priest, and you have gone away. Now what more do I have? How can you say to me, 'What ails you?'"

²⁵ And the children of Dan said to him, "Do not let your voice be heard among us, lest angry men fall upon you, and you lose your life, with the lives of your household!" ²⁶ Then the children of Dan went their way. And when Micah saw that they *were* too strong for him, he turned and went back to his house.

²⁷ So they took *the things* Micah had made, and the priest who had belonged to him, and went to Laish, to a people quiet and secure; and they struck them with the edge of the sword and burned the city with fire. ²⁸ *There was* no deliverer, because it *was* far from Sidon, and they had no ties with anyone. It was in the valley that belongs to Beth Rehob. So they rebuilt the city and dwelt there. ²⁹ And they called the name of the city Dan, after the name of Dan their father, who was born to Israel. However, the name of the city formerly *was* Laish.

³⁰ Then the children of Dan set up for themselves the carved image; and Jonathan the son of Gershom, the son of Manasseh, and his sons were priests to the tribe of Dan until the day of the captivity of the land. ³¹ So they set up for themselves Micah's carved image which he made, all the time that the house of God was in Shiloh.

19 And it came to pass in those days, when *there was* no king in Israel, that there was a certain Levite staying in the remote mountains of Ephraim. He took for himself a concubine from Bethlehem in Judah. ² But his concubine played the harlot against him, and went away from him to her father's house at Bethlehem in Judah, and was there four whole months. ³ Then her husband arose and went after her, to speak kindly to her *and* bring her back, having his servant and a couple of donkeys with him. So she brought him into her father's house; and when the father of the young woman saw him, he was glad to meet him. ⁴ Now his father-in-law, the young woman's father, detained him; and he stayed with him three days. So they ate and drank and lodged there.

⁵ Then it came to pass on the fourth day that they arose early in the morning, and he stood to depart; but the young woman's father said to his son-in-law, "Refresh your heart with a morsel of bread, and afterward go your way."

⁶ So they sat down, and the two of them ate and drank together. Then the young woman's father said to the man, "Please be content to stay all night, and let your heart be merry." ⁷ And when the man stood to depart, his father-in-law urged him; so he lodged there again. ⁸ Then he arose early in the morning on the fifth day to depart, but the young woman's father said, "Please refresh your heart." So they delayed until afternoon; and both of them ate.

⁹ And when the man stood to depart—he and his concubine and his servant—his father-in-law, the young woman's father, said to him, "Look, the day is now drawing toward evening; please spend the night. See, the day is coming to an end; lodge here, that your heart may be merry. Tomorrow go your way early, so that you may get home."

¹⁰ However, the man was not willing to spend that night; so he rose and departed, and came opposite Jebus (that *is,* Jerusalem). With him were the two saddled donkeys; his concubine *was* also with him. ¹¹ They *were* near Jebus, and the day was far spent; and the servant said to his master, "Come, please, and let us turn aside into this city of the Jebusites and lodge in it."

¹² But his master said to him, "We will not turn aside here into a city of foreigners, who *are* not of the children of Israel; we will go on to Gibeah." ¹³ So he said to his servant, "Come, let us draw near to one of these places, and spend the night in Gibeah or in Ramah." ¹⁴ And they passed by and went their way; and the sun went down on them near Gibeah, which belongs to Benjamin. ¹⁵ They turned aside there to go in to lodge in Gibeah. And when he went in, he sat down in the open square of the city, for no one would take them into *his* house to spend the night.

¹⁶ Just then an old man came in from his work in the field at evening, who also *was* from the mountains of Ephraim; he was staying in Gibeah, whereas the men of the place *were* Benjamites. ¹⁷ And when he raised his eyes, he saw the traveler in the open square of the city; and the old man said, "Where are you going, and where do you come from?"

¹⁸ So he said to him, "We *are* passing from Bethlehem in Judah toward the remote mountains of Ephraim; I *am* from there. I went to Bethlehem in Judah; *now* I am going to the house of the LORD. But there *is* no one who will take me into his house, ¹⁹ although we have both straw and fodder for our donkeys, and bread and wine for myself, for your female servant, and for the young man *who is* with your servant; *there is* no lack of anything."

²⁰ And the old man said, "Peace *be* with you! However, *let* all your needs *be* my responsibility; only do not spend the night in the open square." ²¹ So he brought him into his house, and gave fodder to the donkeys. And they washed their feet, and ate and drank.

²² As they were enjoying themselves, suddenly certain men of the city, perverted men, surrounded the house *and* beat on the door. They spoke to the master of the house, the old man, saying, "Bring out the man who came to your house, that we may know him *carnally!*"

²³ But the man, the master of the house, went out to them and said to them, "No, my brethren! I beg you, do not act *so* wickedly! Seeing this man has come into my house, do not commit this outrage. ²⁴ Look, *here is* my virgin daughter and *the man's* concubine; let me bring them out now. Humble them, and do with them as you please; but to this man do not do such a vile thing!" ²⁵ But the men would not heed him. So the man took his concubine and brought *her* out to them. And they knew her and abused her all night until morning; and when the day began to break, they let her go.

²⁶ Then the woman came as the day was dawning, and fell down at the door of the man's house where her master *was,* till it was light.

²⁷ When her master arose in the morning, and opened the doors of the house and went out to go his way, there was his

concubine, fallen *at* the door of the house with her hands on the threshold. ²⁸ And he said to her, "Get up and let us be going." But there was no answer. So the man lifted her onto the donkey; and the man got up and went to his place.

²⁹ When he entered his house he took a knife, laid hold of his concubine, and divided her into twelve pieces, limb by limb, and sent her throughout all the territory of Israel. ³⁰ And so it was that all who saw it said, "No such deed has been done or seen from the day that the children of Israel came up from the land of Egypt until this day. Consider it, confer, and speak up!"

∼ PSALM 51:7–11 ∼

⁷ Purge me with hyssop, and I shall be clean;
Wash me, and I shall be whiter than snow.
⁸ Make me hear joy and gladness,
That the bones You have broken may rejoice.
⁹ Hide Your face from my sins,
And blot out all my iniquities.

¹⁰ Create in me a clean heart, O God,
And renew a steadfast spirit within me.
¹¹ Do not cast me away from Your presence,
And do not take Your Holy Spirit from me.

∼ PROVERBS 14:33–35 ∼

³³ Wisdom rests in the heart of him who has understanding,
But *what is* in the heart of fools is made known.

³⁴ Righteousness exalts a nation,
But sin *is* a reproach to *any* people.

³⁵ The king's favor *is* toward a wise servant,
But his wrath *is against* him who causes shame.

∼ LUKE 18:24–43 ∼

And when Jesus saw that he became very sorrowful, He said, "How hard it is for those who have riches to enter the kingdom of God! ²⁵ For it is easier for a camel to go through the eye of a needle than for a rich man to enter the kingdom of God."

²⁶ And those who heard it said, "Who then can be saved?"

²⁷ But He said, "The things which are impossible with men are possible with God."

²⁸ Then Peter said, "See, we have left all and followed You."

²⁹ So He said to them, "Assuredly, I say to you, there is no one who has left house or parents or brothers or wife or children, for the sake of the kingdom of God, ³⁰ who shall not receive many times more in this present time, and in the age to come eternal life."

³¹ Then He took the twelve aside and said to them, "Behold, we are going up to Jerusalem, and all things that are written by the prophets concerning the Son of Man will be accomplished. ³² For He will be delivered to the Gentiles and will be mocked and insulted and spit upon. ³³ They will scourge *Him* and kill Him. And the third day He will rise again."

³⁴ But they understood none of these things; this saying was hidden from them, and they did not know the things which were spoken.

³⁵ Then it happened, as He was coming near Jericho, that a certain blind man sat by the road begging. ³⁶ And hearing a multitude passing by, he asked what it meant. ³⁷ So they told him that Jesus of Nazareth was passing by. ³⁸ And he cried out, saying, "Jesus, Son of David, have mercy on me!"

³⁹ Then those who went before warned him that he should be quiet; but he cried out all the more, "Son of David, have mercy on me!"

⁴⁰ So Jesus stood still and commanded him to be brought to Him. And when he had come near, He asked him, ⁴¹ saying, "What do you want Me to do for you?"

He said, "Lord, that I may receive my sight."

⁴² Then Jesus said to him, "Receive your sight; your faith has made you well." ⁴³ And immediately he received his sight, and followed Him, glorifying God. And all the people, when they saw *it,* gave praise to God.

~ JUDGES 20:1—21:25 ~

So all the children of Israel came out, from Dan to Beersheba, as well as from the land of Gilead, and the congregation gathered together as one man before the LORD at Mizpah. ² And the leaders of all the people, all the tribes of Israel, presented themselves in the assembly of the people of God, four hundred thousand foot soldiers who drew the sword. ³ (Now the children of Benjamin heard that the children of Israel had gone up to Mizpah.)

Then the children of Israel said, "Tell us, how did this wicked deed happen?"

⁴ So the Levite, the husband of the woman who was murdered, answered and said, "My concubine and I went into Gibeah, which belongs to Benjamin, to spend the night. ⁵ And the men of Gibeah rose against me, and surrounded the house at night because of me. They intended to kill me, but instead they ravished my concubine so that she died. ⁶ So I took hold of my concubine, cut her in pieces, and sent her throughout all the territory of the inheritance of Israel, because they committed lewdness and outrage in Israel. ⁷ Look! All of you are children of Israel; give your advice and counsel here and now!"

⁸ So all the people arose as one man, saying, "None of us will go to his tent, nor will any turn back to his house; ⁹ but now this is the thing which we will do to Gibeah: We will go up against it by lot. ¹⁰ We will take ten men out of every hundred throughout all the tribes of Israel, a hundred out of every thousand, and a thousand out of every ten thousand, to make provisions for the people, that when they come to Gibeah in Benjamin, they may repay all the vileness that they have done in Israel." ¹¹ So all the men of Israel were gathered against the city, united together as one man.

¹² Then the tribes of Israel sent men through all the tribe of Benjamin, saying, "What is this wickedness that has occurred among you? ¹³ Now therefore, deliver up the men, the perverted men who are in Gibeah, that we may put them to death and remove the evil from Israel!" But the children of Benjamin would not listen to the voice of their brethren, the children of Israel. ¹⁴ Instead, the children of Benjamin gathered together from their cities to Gibeah, to go to battle against the children of Israel. ¹⁵ And from their cities at that time the children of Benjamin numbered twenty-six thousand men who drew the sword, besides the inhabitants of Gibeah, who numbered seven hundred select men. ¹⁶ Among all this people were seven hundred select men who were left-handed; every one could sling a stone at a hair's breadth and not miss. ¹⁷ Now besides Benjamin, the men of Israel numbered four hundred thousand men who drew the sword; all of these were men of war.

¹⁸ Then the children of Israel arose and went up to the house of God to inquire of God. They said, "Which of us shall go up first to battle against the children of Benjamin?"

The LORD said, "Judah first!"

¹⁹ So the children of Israel rose in the morning and encamped against Gibeah. ²⁰ And the men of Israel went out to battle against Benjamin, and the men of Israel put themselves in battle array to fight against them at Gibeah. ²¹ Then the children of Benjamin came out of Gibeah, and on that day cut down to the ground twenty-two thousand men of the Israelites. ²² And the people, that is, the men of Israel, encouraged themselves and again formed the battle line at the place where they had put themselves in array on the first day. ²³ Then the children of Israel went up and wept before the LORD until evening, and asked counsel of the LORD, saying, "Shall I again draw near for battle against the children of my brother Benjamin?"

And the LORD said, "Go up against him."

²⁴ So the children of Israel approached the children of Benjamin on the second day. ²⁵ And Benjamin went out against them from Gibeah on the second day, and cut down to the ground eighteen thousand more of the children of Israel; all these drew the sword.

²⁶ Then all the children of Israel, that is, all the people, went up and came to the house of God and wept. They sat there before the LORD and fasted that day until evening; and they offered burnt offerings and peace offerings before the LORD. ²⁷ So the children of Israel inquired of the LORD (the ark of the covenant of God *was* there in those days, ²⁸ and Phinehas the son of Eleazar, the son of Aaron, stood before it in those days), saying, "Shall I yet again go out to battle against the children of my brother Benjamin, or shall I cease?"

And the LORD said, "Go up, for tomorrow I will deliver them into your hand."

²⁹ Then Israel set men in ambush all around Gibeah. ³⁰ And the children of Israel went up against the children of Benjamin on the third day, and put themselves in battle array against Gibeah as at the other times. ³¹ So the children of Benjamin went out against the people, *and* were drawn away from the city. They began to strike down *and* kill some of the people, as at the other times, in the highways (one of which goes up to Bethel and the other to Gibeah) and in the field, about thirty men of Israel. ³² And the children of Benjamin said, "They *are* defeated before us, as at first."

But the children of Israel said, "Let us flee and draw them away from the city to the highways." ³³ So all the men of Israel rose from their place and put themselves in battle array at Baal Tamar. Then Israel's men in ambush burst forth from their position in the plain of Geba. ³⁴ And ten thousand select men from all Israel came against Gibeah, and the battle was fierce. But *the Benjamites* did not know that disaster *was* upon them. ³⁵ The LORD defeated Benjamin before Israel. And the children of Israel destroyed that day twenty-five thousand one hundred Benjamites; all these drew the sword.

³⁶ So the children of Benjamin saw that they were defeated. The men of Israel had given ground to the Benjamites, because they relied on the men in ambush whom they had set against Gibeah. ³⁷ And the men in ambush quickly rushed upon Gibeah; the men in ambush spread out and struck the whole city with the edge of the sword. ³⁸ Now the appointed signal between the men of Israel and the men in ambush was that they would make a great cloud of smoke rise up from the city, ³⁹ whereupon the men of Israel would turn in battle. Now Benjamin had begun to strike *and* kill about thirty of the men of Israel. For they said, "Surely they are defeated before us, as *in* the first battle." ⁴⁰ But when the cloud began to rise from the city in a column of smoke, the Benjamites looked behind them, and there was the whole city going up *in smoke* to heaven. ⁴¹ And when the men of Israel turned back, the men of Benjamin panicked, for they saw that disaster had come upon them. ⁴² Therefore they turned *their backs* before the men of Israel in the direction of the wilderness; but the battle overtook them, and whoever *came* out of the cities they destroyed in their midst. ⁴³ They surrounded the Benjamites, chased them, *and* easily trampled them down as far as the front of Gibeah toward the east. ⁴⁴ And eighteen thousand men of Benjamin fell; all these *were* men of valor. ⁴⁵ Then they turned and fled toward the wilderness to the rock of Rimmon; and they cut down five thousand of them on the highways. Then they pursued them relentlessly up to Gidom, and killed two thousand of them. ⁴⁶ So all who fell of Benjamin that day were twenty-five thousand men who drew the sword; all these *were* men of valor.

⁴⁷ But six hundred men turned and fled toward the wilderness to the rock of Rimmon, and they stayed at the rock of Rimmon for four months. ⁴⁸ And the men of Israel turned back against the children of Benjamin, and struck them down with the edge of the sword—from *every* city, men and beasts, all who were found. They also set fire to all the cities they came to.

21 Now the men of Israel had sworn an oath at Mizpah, saying, "None of us shall give his daughter to Benjamin as a wife." ² Then the people came to the house of God, and remained there before God till evening. They lifted up their voices and wept bitterly, ³ and said, "O LORD God of Israel, why has this come to pass in Israel, that today there should be one tribe *missing* in Israel?"

⁴ So it was, on the next morning, that

Word Echoes

I shouted aloud and louder
While out on the plain one day;
The sound grew faint and fainter
Until it had died away.
My words had gone forever,
They left no trace or track,
But the hills nearby caught up the cry
And sent an echo back.
I spoke a word in anger
To one who was my friend,
Like a knife it cut him deeply,
A wound that was hard to mend.
That word, so thoughtlessly uttered,
I would we could both forget,
But its echo lives and memory gives
The recollection yet.
How many hearts are broken,
How many friends are lost
By some unkind word spoken
Before we count the cost!
But a word or deed of kindness
Will repay a hundred-fold,
For it echoes again in the hearts of men
And carries a joy untold.

— C. A. Lufburrow

the people rose early and built an altar there, and offered burnt offerings and peace offerings. [5] The children of Israel said, "Who *is there* among all the tribes of Israel who did not come up with the assembly to the LORD?" For they had made a great oath concerning anyone who had not come up to the LORD at Mizpah, saying, "He shall surely be put to death." [6] And the children of Israel grieved for Benjamin their brother, and said, "One tribe is cut off from Israel today. [7] What shall we do for wives for those who remain, seeing we have sworn by the LORD that we will not give them our daughters as wives?"

[8] And they said, "What one *is there* from the tribes of Israel who did not come up to Mizpah to the LORD?" And, in fact, no one had come to the camp from Jabesh Gilead to the assembly. [9] For when the people were counted, indeed, not one of the inhabitants of Jabesh Gilead *was* there. [10] So the congregation sent out there twelve thousand of their most valiant men, and commanded them, saying, "Go and strike the inhabitants of Jabesh Gilead with the edge of the sword, including the women and children. [11] And this *is* the thing that you shall do: You shall utterly destroy every male, and every woman who has known a man intimately." [12] So they found among the inhabitants of Jabesh Gilead four hundred young virgins who had not known a man intimately; and they brought them to the camp at Shiloh, which is in the land of Canaan.

[13] Then the whole congregation sent *word* to the children of Benjamin who *were* at the rock of Rimmon, and announced peace to them. [14] So Benjamin came back at that time, and they gave them the women whom they had saved alive of the women of Jabesh Gilead; and yet they had not found enough for them.

[15] And the people grieved for Benjamin, because the LORD had made a void in the tribes of Israel.

[16] Then the elders of the congregation said, "What shall we do for wives for those who remain, since the women of Benjamin have been destroyed?" [17] And they said, "*There must be* an inheritance for the survivors of Benjamin, that a tribe may not be destroyed from Israel. [18] However, we cannot give them wives from our daughters, for the children of Israel have sworn an oath, saying, 'Cursed *be* the one who gives a wife to Benjamin.' " [19] Then they said, "In fact, *there is* a yearly feast of the LORD in Shiloh, which *is* north of Bethel, on the east side of the highway that goes up from Bethel to Shechem, and south of Lebonah."

[20] Therefore they instructed the children of Benjamin, saying, "Go, lie in wait in the vineyards, [21] and watch; and just when the daughters of Shiloh come out to perform their dances, then come out from the vineyards, and every man catch a wife for himself from the daughters of Shiloh; then go to the land of Benjamin. [22] Then it shall be, when their fathers or their brothers come to us to complain, that we will say to them, 'Be kind to them for our sakes, because we did not take a wife for any of them in the war; for *it is* not *as though* you have given the *women* to them at this time, making yourselves guilty of your oath.' "

[23] And the children of Benjamin did so; they took enough wives for their number from those who danced, whom they caught. Then they went and returned to their inheritance, and they rebuilt the cities and dwelt in them. [24] So the children of Israel departed from there at that time, every man to his tribe and family; they went out from there, every man to his inheritance.

[25] In those days *there was* no king in Israel; everyone did *what was* right in his own eyes.

~ PSALM 51:12–19 ~

[12] Restore to me the joy of Your salvation,
And uphold me *by Your* generous Spirit.
[13] *Then* I will teach transgressors Your ways,
And sinners shall be converted to You.

[14] Deliver me from the guilt of bloodshed, O God,
The God of my salvation,
And my tongue shall sing aloud of Your righteousness.

15 O Lord, open my lips,
   And my mouth shall show forth Your
   praise.
16 For You do not desire sacrifice, or
   else I would give *it;*
   You do not delight in burnt offering.
17 The sacrifices of God *are* a broken
   spirit,
   A broken and a contrite heart—
   These, O God, You will not despise.

18 Do good in Your good pleasure to
   Zion;
   Build the walls of Jerusalem.
19 Then You shall be pleased with the
   sacrifices of righteousness,
   With burnt offering and whole burnt
   offering;
   Then they shall offer bulls on Your
   altar.

~ PROVERBS 15:1–3 ~

1 A soft answer turns away wrath,
  But a harsh word stirs up anger.
2 The tongue of the wise uses
  knowledge rightly,
  But the mouth of fools pours forth
  foolishness.

3 The eyes of the LORD *are* in every
  place,
  Keeping watch on the evil and the
  good.

~ LUKE 19:1–27 ~

Then *Jesus* entered and passed through
Jericho. 2 Now behold, *there was* a man
named Zacchaeus who was a chief tax
collector, and he was rich. 3 And he sought
to see who Jesus was, but could not because of the crowd, for he was of short
stature. 4 So he ran ahead and climbed up
into a sycamore tree to see Him, for He
was going to pass that *way.* 5 And when
Jesus came to the place, He looked up
and saw him, and said to him, "Zacchaeus,
make haste and come down, for today I
must stay at your house." 6 So he made
haste and came down, and received Him
joyfully. 7 But when they saw *it,* they all
complained, saying, "He has gone to be a
guest with a man who is a sinner."

8 Then Zacchaeus stood and said to the
Lord, "Look, Lord, I give half of my goods
to the poor; and if I have taken anything
from anyone by false accusation, I restore
fourfold."
9 And Jesus said to him, "Today salvation has come to this house, because he
also is a son of Abraham; 10 for the Son of
Man has come to seek and to save that
which was lost."
11 Now as they heard these things, He
spoke another parable, because He was
near Jerusalem and because they thought
the kingdom of God would appear
immediately. 12 Therefore He said: "A certain nobleman went into a far country to
receive for himself a kingdom and to return. 13 So he called ten of his servants,
delivered to them ten minas, and said to
them, 'Do business till I come.' 14 But his
citizens hated him, and sent a delegation
after him, saying, 'We will not have this
man to reign over us.'
15 "And so it was that when he returned,
having received the kingdom, he then
commanded these servants, to whom he
had given the money, to be called to him,
that he might know how much every man
had gained by trading. 16 Then came the
first, saying, 'Master, your mina has
earned ten minas.' 17 And he said to him,
'Well *done,* good servant; because you
were faithful in a very little, have authority over ten cities.' 18 And the second came,
saying, 'Master, your mina has earned five
minas.' 19 Likewise he said to him, 'You
also be over five cities.'
20 "Then another came, saying, 'Master, here is your mina, which I have kept
put away in a handkerchief. 21 For I feared
you, because you are an austere man. You
collect what you did not deposit, and reap
what you did not sow.' 22 And he said to
him, 'Out of your own mouth I will
judge you, *you* wicked servant. You knew
that I was an austere man, collecting
what I did not deposit and reaping what I
did not sow. 23 Why then did you not put
my money in the bank, that at my
coming I might have collected it with interest?'
24 "And he said to those who stood by,
'Take the mina from him, and give *it* to
him who has ten minas.' 25(But they said
to him, 'Master, he has ten minas.') 26 'For

I say to you, that to everyone who has will be given; and from him who does not have, even what he has will be taken away from him. ²⁷ But bring here those enemies of mine, who did not want me to reign over them, and slay *them* before me.' "

READING 118 · APRIL 28

~ RUTH 1:1—2:23 ~

Now it came to pass, in the days when the judges ruled, that there was a famine in the land. And a certain man of Bethlehem, Judah, went to dwell in the country of Moab, he and his wife and his two sons. ² The name of the man *was* Elimelech, the name of his wife *was* Naomi, and the names of his two sons *were* Mahlon and Chilion—Eph-rathites of Bethlehem, Judah. And they went to the country of Moab and re-mained there. ³ Then Elimelech, Naomi's husband, died; and she was left, and her two sons. ⁴ Now they took wives of the women of Moab: the name of the one *was* Orpah, and the name of the other Ruth. And they dwelt there about ten years. ⁵ Then both Mahlon and Chilion also died; so the woman survived her two sons and her husband.

⁶ Then she arose with her daughters-in-law that she might return from the country of Moab, for she had heard in the country of Moab that the LORD had visited His people by giving them bread. ⁷ Therefore she went out from the place where she was, and her two daughters-in-law with her; and they went on the way to return to the land of Judah. ⁸ And Naomi said to her two daughters-in-law, "Go, return each to her mother's house. The LORD deal kindly with you, as you have dealt with the dead and with me. ⁹ The LORD grant that you may find rest, each in the house of her husband."

So she kissed them, and they lifted up their voices and wept. ¹⁰ And they said to her, "Surely we will return with you to your people."

¹¹ But Naomi said, "Turn back, my daughters; why will you go with me? *Are* there still sons in my womb, that they may be your husbands? ¹² Turn back, my daughters, go—for I am too old to have a husband. If I should say I have hope, *if* I should have a husband tonight and should

also bear sons, ¹³ would you wait for them till they were grown? Would you restrain yourselves from having husbands? No, my daughters; for it grieves me very much for your sakes that the hand of the LORD has gone out against me!"

¹⁴ Then they lifted up their voices and wept again; and Orpah kissed her mother-in-law, but Ruth clung to her.

¹⁵ And she said, "Look, your sister-in-law has gone back to her people and to her gods; return after your sister-in-law."

¹⁶ But Ruth said:

"Entreat me not to leave you,
    Or to turn back from following
        after you;
    For wherever you go, I will go;
    And wherever you lodge, I will
        lodge;
    Your people *shall be* my people,
    And your God, my God.
¹⁷   Where you die, I will die,
    And there will I be buried.
    The LORD do so to me, and more
        also,
    If *anything but* death parts you
        and me."

¹⁸ When she saw that she was determined to go with her, she stopped speaking to her. ¹⁹ Now the two of them went until they came to Bethlehem. And it happened, when they had come to Bethlehem, that all the city was excited because of them; and the women said, "*Is* this Naomi?"

²⁰ But she said to them, "Do not call me Naomi; call me Mara, for the Almighty has dealt very bitterly with me. ²¹ I went out full, and the LORD has brought me home again empty. Why do you call me Naomi, since the LORD has testi-fied against me, and the Almighty has af-flicted me?"

²² So Naomi returned, and Ruth the

The Stepladder

A child once asked his father to draw a picture of a stepladder for him. The father did as he was asked. Then his son said, "No, Dad, you left out something." The father looked again at the double upside-down V he had drawn on the page and the lines he had drawn as the ladder's steps. "What did I leave out?" he asked. The little boy replied, "The part where you put the paint can."

The little boy may have been more interested in paint cans than a properly engineered ladder, but what the father later realized was that the crosspiece that extends to provide a resting place for paint cans is the one part of a stepladder that is truly indispensable! Without it, the inverted V shape of a ladder would collapse. The crosspiece is what makes a stepladder useful by allowing it to support weight.

If a couple is joined only by a recited vow, their marriage may quickly collapse. If Christ is the crosspiece that holds their lives in a sturdy triangle, they can withstand the pressures of life.

But Ruth said: "Entreat me not to leave you, or to turn back from following after you; for wherever you go, I will go; and wherever you lodge, I will lodge; your people shall be my people, and your God, my God."

Ruth 1:16

Moabitess her daughter-in-law with her, who returned from the country of Moab. Now they came to Bethlehem at the beginning of barley harvest.

2 There was a relative of Naomi's husband, a man of great wealth, of the family of Elimelech. His name *was* Boaz. [2] So Ruth the Moabitess said to Naomi, "Please let me go to the field, and glean heads of grain after *him* in whose sight I may find favor."

And she said to her, "Go, my daughter."

[3] Then she left, and went and gleaned in the field after the reapers. And she happened to come to the part of the field *belonging* to Boaz, who *was* of the family of Elimelech.

[4] Now behold, Boaz came from Bethlehem, and said to the reapers, "The LORD *be* with you!"

And they answered him, "The LORD bless you!"

[5] Then Boaz said to his servant who was in charge of the reapers, "Whose young woman *is* this?"

[6] So the servant who was in charge of the reapers answered and said, "It *is* the young Moabite woman who came back with Naomi from the country of Moab. [7] And she said, 'Please let me glean and gather the reapers among the sheaves.' So she came and has continued from morning until now, though she rested a little in the house."

[8] Then Boaz said to Ruth, "You will listen, my daughter, will you not? Do not go to glean in another field, nor go from here, but stay close by my young women. [9] *Let* your eyes *be* on the field which they reap, and go after them. Have I not commanded the young men not to touch you? And when you are thirsty, go to the vessels and drink from what the young men have drawn."

[10] So she fell on her face, bowed down to the ground, and said to him, "Why have I found favor in your eyes, that you should take notice of me, since I *am* a foreigner?"

[11] And Boaz answered and said to her, "It has been fully reported to me, all that you have done for your mother-in-law since the death of your husband, and *how* you have left your father and your mother and the land of your birth, and have come

to a people whom you did not know before. [12] The LORD repay your work, and a full reward be given you by the LORD God of Israel, under whose wings you have come for refuge."

[13] Then she said, "Let me find favor in your sight, my lord; for you have comforted me, and have spoken kindly to your maidservant, though I am not like one of your maidservants."

[14] Now Boaz said to her at mealtime, "Come here, and eat of the bread, and dip your piece of bread in the vinegar." So she sat beside the reapers, and he passed parched *grain* to her; and she ate and was satisfied, and kept some back. [15] And when she rose up to glean, Boaz commanded his young men, saying, "Let her glean even among the sheaves, and do not reproach her. [16] Also let *grain* from the bundles fall purposely for her; leave *it* that she may glean, and do not rebuke her."

[17] So she gleaned in the field until evening, and beat out what she had gleaned, and it was about an ephah of barley. [18] Then she took *it* up and went into the city, and her mother-in-law saw what she had gleaned. So she brought out and gave to her what she had kept back after she had been satisfied.

[19] And her mother-in-law said to her, "Where have you gleaned today? And where did you work? Blessed be the one who took notice of you."

So she told her mother-in-law with whom she had worked, and said, "The man's name with whom I worked today *is* Boaz."

[20] Then Naomi said to her daughter-in-law, "Blessed *be* he of the LORD, who has not forsaken His kindness to the living and the dead!" And Naomi said to her, "This man *is* a relation of ours, one of our close relatives."

[21] Ruth the Moabitess said, "He also said to me, 'You shall stay close by my young men until they have finished all my harvest.' "

[22] And Naomi said to Ruth her daughter-in-law, "*It is* good, my daughter, that you go out with his young women, and that people do not meet you in any other field." [23] So she stayed close by the young women of Boaz, to glean until the end of barley harvest and wheat

harvest; and she dwelt with her mother-in-law.

∼ PSALM 52:1–5 ∼

1 Why do you boast in evil, O mighty
    man?
    The goodness of God *endures*
    continually.
2 Your tongue devises destruction,
    Like a sharp razor, working
    deceitfully.
3 You love evil more than good,
    Lying rather than speaking
    righteousness.   Selah
4 You love all devouring words,
    You deceitful tongue.

5 God shall likewise destroy you
    forever;
    He shall take you away, and pluck
    you out of *your* dwelling place,
    And uproot you from the land of the
    living.   Selah

∼ PROVERBS 15:4, 5 ∼

4 A wholesome tongue *is* a tree of life,
    But perverseness in it breaks the
    spirit.

5 A fool despises his father's
    instruction,
    But he who receives correction is
    prudent.

∼ LUKE 19:28–48 ∼

When He had said this, He went on ahead,
going up to Jerusalem. ²⁹ And it came to
pass, when He drew near to Bethphage
and Bethany, at the mountain called
Olivet, *that* He sent two of His disciples,
³⁰ saying, "Go into the village opposite
you, where as you enter you will find a
colt tied, on which no one has ever sat.
Loose it and bring *it here.* ³¹ And if anyone asks you, 'Why are you loosing *it?*'
thus you shall say to him, 'Because the
Lord has need of it.'"
³² So those who were sent went their

way and found *it* just as He had said to
them. ³³ But as they were loosing the colt,
the owners of it said to them, "Why are
you loosing the colt?"
³⁴ And they said, "The Lord has need
of him." ³⁵ Then they brought him to
Jesus. And they threw their own clothes
on the colt, and they set Jesus on him.
³⁶ And as He went, *many* spread their
clothes on the road.
³⁷ Then, as He was now drawing near
the descent of the Mount of Olives, the
whole multitude of the disciples began to
rejoice and praise God with a loud voice
for all the mighty works they had seen,
³⁸ saying:

" 'Blessed *is* the King who comes in
    the name of the LORD!'
    Peace in heaven and glory in the
    highest!"

³⁹ And some of the Pharisees called to
Him from the crowd, "Teacher, rebuke
Your disciples."
⁴⁰ But He answered and said to them,
"I tell you that if these should keep silent,
the stones would immediately cry out."
⁴¹ Now as He drew near, He saw the
city and wept over it, ⁴² saying, "If you
had known, even you, especially in this
your day, the things *that make* for your
peace! But now they are hidden from
your eyes. ⁴³ For days will come upon you
when your enemies will build an embank-
ment around you, surround you and close
you in on every side, ⁴⁴ and level you, and
your children within you, to the ground;
and they will not leave in you one stone
upon another, because you did not know
the time of your visitation."
⁴⁵ Then He went into the temple and
began to drive out those who bought
and sold in it, ⁴⁶ saying to them, "It is written, 'My house is a house of prayer,' but
you have made it a 'den of thieves.'"
⁴⁷ And He was teaching daily in the
temple. But the chief priests, the scribes,
and the leaders of the people sought to
destroy Him, ⁴⁸ and were unable to do
anything; for all the people were very attentive to hear Him.

~ RUTH 3:1—4:22 ~

Then Naomi her mother-in-law said to her, "My daughter, shall I not seek security for you, that it may be well with you? ² Now Boaz, whose young women you were with, *is he* not our relative? In fact, he is winnowing barley tonight at the threshing floor. ³ Therefore wash yourself and anoint yourself, put on your *best* garment and go down to the threshing floor; *but* do not make yourself known to the man until he has finished eating and drinking. ⁴ Then it shall be, when he lies down, that you shall notice the place where he lies; and you shall go in, uncover his feet, and lie down; and he will tell you what you should do."

⁵ And she said to her, "All that you say to me I will do."

⁶ So she went down to the threshing floor and did according to all that her mother-in-law instructed her. ⁷ And after Boaz had eaten and drunk, and his heart was cheerful, he went to lie down at the end of the heap of grain; and she came softly, uncovered his feet, and lay down.

⁸ Now it happened at midnight that the man was startled, and turned himself; and there, a woman was lying at his feet. ⁹ And he said, "Who *are* you?"

So she answered, "I *am* Ruth, your maidservant. Take your maidservant under your wing, for you are a close relative."

¹⁰ Then he said, "Blessed *are* you of the LORD, my daughter! For you have shown more kindness at the end than at the beginning, in that you did not go after young men, whether poor or rich. ¹¹ And now, my daughter, do not fear. I will do for you all that you request, for all the people of my town know that you *are* a virtuous woman. ¹² Now it is true that I *am* a close relative; however, there is a relative closer than I. ¹³ Stay this night, and in the morning it shall be *that* if he will perform the duty of a close relative for you—good; let him do it. But if he does not want to perform the duty for you, then I will perform the duty for you, *as* the LORD lives! Lie down until morning."

¹⁴ So she lay at his feet until morning, and she arose before one could recognize another. Then he said, "Do not let it be known that the woman came to the threshing floor." ¹⁵ Also he said, "Bring the shawl that *is* on you and hold it." And when she held it, he measured six *ephahs* of barley, and laid *it* on her. Then she went into the city.

¹⁶ When she came to her mother-in-law, she said, "*Is* that you, my daughter?"

Then she told her all that the man had done for her. ¹⁷ And she said, "These six *ephahs* of barley he gave me; for he said to me, 'Do not go empty-handed to your mother-in-law.' "

¹⁸ Then she said, "Sit still, my daughter, until you know how the matter will turn out; for the man will not rest until he has concluded the matter this day."

4 Now Boaz went up to the gate and sat down there; and behold, the close relative of whom Boaz had spoken came by. So Boaz said, "Come aside, friend, sit down here." So he came aside and sat down. ² And he took ten men of the elders of the city, and said, "Sit down here." So they sat down. ³ Then he said to the close relative, "Naomi, who has come back from the country of Moab, sold the piece of land which *belonged* to our brother Elimelech. ⁴ And I thought to inform you, saying, 'Buy *it* back in the presence of the inhabitants and the elders of my people. If you will redeem *it,* redeem *it;* but if you will not redeem *it, then* tell me, that I may know; for *there* is no one but you to redeem *it,* and I *am* next after you.' "

And he said, "I will redeem *it.*"

⁵ Then Boaz said, "On the day you buy the field from the hand of Naomi, you must also buy *it* from Ruth the Moabitess, the wife of the dead, to perpetuate the name of the dead through his inheritance."

⁶ And the close relative said, "I cannot redeem *it* for myself, lest I ruin my own inheritance. You redeem my right of redemption for yourself, for I cannot redeem *it.*"

⁷ Now this *was the custom* in former

A Lonely Tree

When American poet and writer Edgar Guest was a young man, his first child died. He wrote about the experience: "There came a tragic night when our first baby was taken from us. I was lonely and defeated. There didn't seem to be anything in life ahead of me that mattered very much.

"I had to go to my neighbor's drugstore the next morning for something, and he motioned for me to step behind the counter with him. I followed him into his little office at the back of the store. He put both hands on my shoulders and said, 'Eddie, I can't really express what I want to say, the sympathy I have in my heart for you. All I can say is that I'm sorry, and I want you to know that if you need anything at all, come to me. What is mine is yours.'"

Guest recalls that this man was "just a neighbor across the way — a passing acquaintance." He says of the druggist that he "may long since have forgotten that moment when he gave me his hand and his sympathy, but I shall never forget it — never in all my life. To me it stands out like the silhouette of a lonely tree against a crimson sunset."

Is there someone who needs a kind word from you today?

> **Blessed are you of the Lord, my daughter! For you have shown more kindness at the end than at the beginning.**
>
> *Ruth 3:10*

times in Israel concerning redeeming and exchanging, to confirm anything: one man took off his sandal and gave *it* to the other, and this *was* a confirmation in Israel.

⁸ Therefore the close relative said to Boaz, "Buy *it* for yourself." So he took off his sandal. ⁹ And Boaz said to the elders and all the people, "You *are* witnesses this day that I have bought all that was Elimelech's, and all that *was* Chilion's and Mahlon's, from the hand of Naomi. ¹⁰ Moreover, Ruth the Moabitess, the widow of Mahlon, I have acquired as my wife, to perpetuate the name of the dead through his inheritance, that the name of the dead may not be cut off from among his brethren and from his position at the gate. You *are* witnesses this day."

¹¹ And all the people who *were* at the gate, and the elders, said, "*We are* witnesses. The LORD make the woman who is coming to your house like Rachel and Leah, the two who built the house of Israel; and may you prosper in Ephrathah and be famous in Bethlehem. ¹² May your house be like the house of Perez, whom Tamar bore to Judah, because of the offspring which the LORD will give you from this young woman."

¹³ So Boaz took Ruth and she became his wife; and when he went in to her, the LORD gave her conception, and she bore a son. ¹⁴ Then the women said to Naomi, "Blessed *be* the LORD, who has not left you this day without a close relative; and may his name be famous in Israel! ¹⁵ And may he be to you a restorer of life and a nourisher of your old age; for your daughter-in-law, who loves you, who is better to you than seven sons, has borne him." ¹⁶ Then Naomi took the child and laid him on her bosom, and became a nurse to him. ¹⁷ Also the neighbor women gave him a name, saying, "There is a son born to Naomi." And they called his name Obed. He *is* the father of Jesse, the father of David.

¹⁸ Now this *is* the genealogy of Perez: Perez begot Hezron; ¹⁹ Hezron begot Ram, and Ram begot Amminadab; ²⁰ Amminadab begot Nahshon, and Nahshon begot Salmon; ²¹ Salmon begot Boaz, and Boaz begot Obed; ²² Obed begot Jesse, and Jesse begot David.

∼ PSALM 52:6–9 ∼

⁶ The righteous also shall see and fear,
And shall laugh at him, *saying,*
⁷ "Here is the man *who* did not make God his strength,
But trusted in the abundance of his riches,
And strengthened himself in his wickedness."

⁸ But I *am* like a green olive tree in the house of God;
I trust in the mercy of God forever and ever.
⁹ I will praise You forever,
Because You have done *it;*
And in the presence of Your saints
I will wait on Your name, for *it is* good.

∼ PROVERBS 15:6, 7 ∼

⁶ *In* the house of the righteous *there is* much treasure,
But in the revenue of the wicked is trouble.

⁷ The lips of the wise disperse knowledge,
But the heart of the fool *does* not *do* so.

∼ LUKE 20:1–26 ∼

Now it happened on one of those days, as He taught the people in the temple and preached the gospel, *that* the chief priests and the scribes, together with the elders, confronted *Him* ² and spoke to Him, saying, "Tell us, by what authority are You doing these things? Or who is he who gave You this authority?"

³ But He answered and said to them, "I also will ask you one thing, and answer Me: ⁴ The baptism of John—was it from heaven or from men?"

⁵ And they reasoned among themselves, saying, "If we say, 'From heaven,' He will say, 'Why then did you not believe him?' ⁶ But if we say, 'From men,' all the people will stone us, for they are persuaded that

John was a prophet." ⁷ So they answered that they did not know where *it was* from.

⁸ And Jesus said to them, "Neither will I tell you by what authority I do these things."

⁹ Then He began to tell the people this parable: "A certain man planted a vineyard, leased it to vinedressers, and went into a far country for a long time. ¹⁰ Now at vintage-time he sent a servant to the vinedressers, that they might give him some of the fruit of the vineyard. But the vinedressers beat him and sent *him* away empty-handed. ¹¹ Again he sent another servant; and they beat him also, treated *him* shamefully, and sent *him* away empty-handed. ¹² And again he sent a third; and they wounded him also and cast *him* out.

¹³ "Then the owner of the vineyard said, 'What shall I do? I will send my beloved son. Probably they will respect *him* when they see him.' ¹⁴ But when the vinedressers saw him, they reasoned among themselves, saying, 'This is the heir. Come, let us kill him, that the inheritance may be ours.' ¹⁵ So they cast him out of the vineyard and killed *him*. Therefore what will the owner of the vineyard do to them? ¹⁶ He will come and destroy those vinedressers and give the vineyard to others."

And when they heard *it* they said, "Certainly not!"

¹⁷ Then He looked at them and said, "What then is this that is written:

'The stone which the builders rejected
Has become the chief cornerstone' ?

¹⁸ Whoever falls on that stone will be broken; but on whomever it falls, it will grind him to powder."

¹⁹ And the chief priests and the scribes that very hour sought to lay hands on Him, but they feared the people—for they knew He had spoken this parable against them.

²⁰ So they watched *Him,* and sent spies who pretended to be righteous, that they might seize on His words, in order to deliver Him to the power and the authority of the governor. ²¹ Then they asked Him, saying, "Teacher, we know that You say and teach rightly, and You do not show personal favoritism, but teach the way of God in truth: ²² Is it lawful for us to pay taxes to Caesar or not?"

²³ But He perceived their craftiness, and said to them, "Why do you test Me? ²⁴ Show Me a denarius. Whose image and inscription does it have?"

They answered and said, "Caesar's."

²⁵ And He said to them, "Render therefore to Caesar the things that are Caesar's, and to God the things that are God's."

²⁶ But they could not catch Him in His words in the presence of the people. And they marveled at His answer and kept silent.

READING 120 · APRIL 30

∼ 1 SAMUEL 1:1—3:21 ∼

Now there was a certain man of Ramathaim Zophim, of the mountains of Ephraim, and his name *was* Elkanah the son of Jeroham, the son of Elihu, the son of Tohu, the son of Zuph, an Ephraimite. ² And he had two wives: the name of one *was* Hannah, and the name of the other Peninnah. Peninnah had children, but Hannah had no children. ³ This man went up from his city yearly to worship and sacrifice to the LORD of hosts in Shiloh. Also the two sons of Eli, Hophni and Phinehas, the priests of the LORD, *were* there. ⁴ And whenever the time came for Elkanah to make an offering, he would give portions to Peninnah his wife and to all her sons and daughters. ⁵ But to Hannah he would give a double portion, for he loved Hannah, although the LORD had closed her womb. ⁶ And her rival also provoked her severely, to make her miserable, because the LORD had closed her womb. ⁷ So it was, year by year, when she went up to the house of the LORD, that she provoked her; therefore she wept and did not eat.

⁸ Then Elkanah her husband said to her, "Hannah, why do you weep? Why do you not eat? And why is your heart grieved? *Am* I not better to you than ten sons?"

⁹ So Hannah arose after they had finished eating and drinking in Shiloh. Now Eli the priest was sitting on the seat by the doorpost of the tabernacle of the LORD. ¹⁰ And she *was* in bitterness of soul, and prayed to the LORD and wept in anguish. ¹¹ Then she made a vow and said, "O LORD of hosts, if You will indeed look on the affliction of Your maidservant and remember me, and not forget Your maidservant, but will give Your maidservant a male child, then I will give him to the LORD all the days of his life, and no razor shall come upon his head."

¹² And it happened, as she continued praying before the LORD, that Eli watched her mouth. ¹³ Now Hannah spoke in her heart; only her lips moved, but her voice was not heard. Therefore Eli thought she was drunk. ¹⁴ So Eli said to her, "How long will you be drunk? Put your wine away from you!"

¹⁵ But Hannah answered and said, "No, my lord, I *am* a woman of sorrowful spirit. I have drunk neither wine nor intoxicating drink, but have poured out my soul before the LORD. ¹⁶ Do not consider your maidservant a wicked woman, for out of the abundance of my complaint and grief I have spoken until now."

¹⁷ Then Eli answered and said, "Go in peace, and the God of Israel grant your petition which you have asked of Him."

¹⁸ And she said, "Let your maidservant find favor in your sight." So the woman went her way and ate, and her face was no longer *sad*.

¹⁹ Then they rose early in the morning and worshiped before the LORD, and returned and came to their house at Ramah. And Elkanah knew Hannah his wife, and the LORD remembered her. ²⁰ So it came to pass in the process of time that Hannah conceived and bore a son, and called his name Samuel, *saying,* "Because I have asked for him from the LORD."

²¹ Now the man Elkanah and all his house went up to offer to the LORD the yearly sacrifice and his vow. ²² But Hannah did not go up, for she said to her husband, "*Not* until the child is weaned; then I will take him, that he may appear before the LORD and remain there forever."

²³ So Elkanah her husband said to her, "Do what seems best to you; wait until you have weaned him. Only let the LORD establish His word." Then the woman stayed and nursed her son until she had weaned him.

²⁴ Now when she had weaned him, she took him up with her, with three bulls, one ephah of flour, and a skin of wine, and brought him to the house of the LORD in Shiloh. And the child *was* young. ²⁵ Then they slaughtered a bull, and brought the child to Eli. ²⁶ And she said, "O my lord! As your soul lives, my lord, I *am* the woman who stood by you here, praying to the LORD. ²⁷ For this child I prayed, and the LORD has granted me my petition which I asked of Him. ²⁸ Therefore I also have lent him to the LORD; as long as he lives he shall be lent to the LORD." So they worshiped the LORD there.

2 And Hannah prayed and said:

"My heart rejoices in the LORD;
   My horn is exalted in the LORD.
   I smile at my enemies,
   Because I rejoice in Your salvation.

² "No one is holy like the LORD,
   For *there is* none besides You,
   Nor *is there* any rock like our
      God.

³ "Talk no more so very proudly;
   Let no arrogance come from your
      mouth,
   For the LORD *is* the God of
      knowledge;
   And by Him actions are weighed.

⁴ "The bows of the mighty men *are*
      broken,
   And those who stumbled are
      girded with strength.
⁵ *Those who were* full have hired
      themselves out for bread,
   And the hungry have ceased *to*
      hunger.
   Even the barren has borne seven,
   And she who has many children
      has become feeble.

Without Ransom

One night while Kao Er was attending a prayer meeting, his eight-year-old son and baby daughter were kidnapped. The kidnappers demanded 1,000 yuan in ransom. Mr. Er painted a large sign and posted it in front of his place of employment. It said, "I am not a wealthy man. I cannot pay 1,000 yuan ransom. I cannot pay 500 yuan. I cannot even pay 50 yuan. But I believe God. He is able to bring my children back without ransom."

The sign brought a great deal of ridicule from those who saw it. *No sane man could expect a kidnapped child to be returned alive without ransom!* Weeks passed. Finally, soldiers clashed with bandits in the Chinese countryside and the bandits were routed. In hot pursuit of the bandits, some soldiers heard a sound coming from a ditch beside the road. They found a skeleton-like child lying there, abandoned by the bandits. It was Mr. Er's son!

After a second battle between the bandits and soldiers, the wife of the bandit chief was captured. She was nursing two babies — one of whom was Mr. Er's daughter. Both children were returned home safely. God had done the impossible — returned kidnapped children *without ransom.*

God's answers to prayer are not dependent upon our ability to pray, but on His ability to answer.

6 "The LORD kills and makes alive;
  He brings down to the grave and
    brings up.
7 The LORD makes poor and makes
    rich;
  He brings low and lifts up.
8 He raises the poor from the dust
  And lifts the beggar from the ash
    heap,
  To set *them* among princes
  And make them inherit the throne
    of glory.

"For the pillars of the earth *are* the
    LORD's,
  And He has set the world upon
    them.
9 He will guard the feet of His
    saints,
  But the wicked shall be silent in
    darkness.

"For by strength no man shall
    prevail.
10 The adversaries of the LORD shall
    be broken in pieces;
  From heaven He will thunder
    against them.
  The LORD will judge the ends of
    the earth.

"He will give strength to His king,
  And exalt the horn of His
    anointed."

11 Then Elkanah went to his house at
Ramah. But the child ministered to the
LORD before Eli the priest.

12 Now the sons of Eli *were* corrupt;
they did not know the LORD. 13 And the
priests' custom with the people *was that*
when any man offered a sacrifice, the
priest's servant would come with a three-
pronged fleshhook in his hand while the
meat was boiling. 14 Then he would thrust
it into the pan, or kettle, or caldron, or
pot; and the priest would take for himself all that the fleshhook brought up. So
they did in Shiloh to all the Israelites who
came there. 15 Also, before they burned
the fat, the priest's servant would come
and say to the man who sacrificed, "Give
meat for roasting to the priest, for he will
not take boiled meat from you, but raw."
16 And *if* the man said to him, "They

should really burn the fat first; *then* you
may take *as much* as your heart desires,"
he would then answer him, "*No*, but you
must give *it* now; and if not, I will take *it*
by force."

17 Therefore the sin of the young men
was very great before the LORD, for
men abhorred the offering of the LORD.

18 But Samuel ministered before the
LORD, *even as* a child, wearing a linen
ephod. 19 Moreover his mother used to
make him a little robe, and bring *it* to him
year by year when she came up with her
husband to offer the yearly sacrifice.
20 And Eli would bless Elkanah and his
wife, and say, "The LORD give you descendants from this woman for the loan
that was given to the LORD." Then they
would go to their own home.

21 And the LORD visited Hannah, so that
she conceived and bore three sons and two
daughters. Meanwhile the child Samuel
grew before the LORD.

22 Now Eli was very old; and he heard
everything his sons did to all Israel, and
how they lay with the women who assembled at the door of the tabernacle of
meeting. 23 So he said to them, "Why do
you do such things? For I hear of your
evil dealings from all the people. 24 No,
my sons! For *it is* not a good report that I
hear. You make the LORD's people transgress. 25 If one man sins against another,
God will judge him. But if a man sins
against the LORD, who will intercede for
him?" Nevertheless they did not heed the
voice of their father, because the LORD
desired to kill them.

26 And the child Samuel grew in stature, and in favor both with the LORD and
men.

27 Then a man of God came to Eli and
said to him, "Thus says the LORD: 'Did I
not clearly reveal Myself to the house of
your father when they were in Egypt in
Pharaoh's house? 28 Did I not choose him
out of all the tribes of Israel *to be* My
priest, to offer upon My altar, to burn
incense, and to wear an ephod before Me?
And did I not give to the house of your
father all the offerings of the children of
Israel made by fire? 29 Why do you kick
at My sacrifice and My offering which I
have commanded *in My* dwelling place,
and honor your sons more than Me, to

make yourselves fat with the best of all the offerings of Israel My people?' ³⁰ Therefore the LORD God of Israel says: 'I said indeed *that* your house and the house of your father would walk before Me forever.' But now the LORD says: 'Far be it from Me; for those who honor Me I will honor, and those who despise Me shall be lightly esteemed. ³¹ Behold, the days are coming that I will cut off your arm and the arm of your father's house, so that there will not be an old man in your house. ³² And you will see an enemy *in My* dwelling place, *despite* all the good which God does for Israel. And there shall not be an old man in your house forever. ³³ But any of your men *whom* I do not cut off from My altar shall consume your eyes and grieve your heart. And all the descendants of your house shall die in the flower of their age. ³⁴ Now this *shall be* a sign to you that will come upon your two sons, on Hophni and Phinehas: in one day they shall die, both of them. ³⁵ Then I will raise up for Myself a faithful priest *who* shall do according to what *is* in My heart and in My mind. I will build him a sure house, and he shall walk before My anointed forever. ³⁶ And it shall come to pass that everyone who is left in your house will come *and* bow down to him for a piece of silver and a morsel of bread, and say, "Please, put me in one of the priestly positions, that I may eat a piece of bread." ' "

3 Now the boy Samuel ministered to the LORD before Eli. And the word of the LORD was rare in those days; *there was* no widespread revelation. ² And it came to pass at that time, while Eli *was* lying down in his place, and when his eyes had begun to grow so dim that he could not see, ³ and before the lamp of God went out in the tabernacle of the LORD where the ark of God *was,* and while Samuel was lying down, ⁴ that the LORD called Samuel. And he answered, "Here I am!" ⁵ So he ran to Eli and said, "Here I am, for you called me."

And he said, "I did not call; lie down again." And he went and lay down.

⁶ Then the LORD called yet again, "Samuel!"

So Samuel arose and went to Eli, and said, "Here I am, for you called me." He answered, "I did not call, my son; lie down again." ⁷(Now Samuel did not yet know the LORD, nor was the word of the LORD yet revealed to him.)

⁸ And the LORD called Samuel again the third time. So he arose and went to Eli, and said, "Here I am, for you did call me."

Then Eli perceived that the LORD had called the boy. ⁹ Therefore Eli said to Samuel, "Go, lie down; and it shall be, if He calls you, that you must say, 'Speak, LORD, for Your servant hears.' " So Samuel went and lay down in his place.

¹⁰ Now the LORD came and stood and called as at other times, "Samuel! Samuel!"

And Samuel answered, "Speak, for Your servant hears."

¹¹ Then the LORD said to Samuel: "Behold, I will do something in Israel at which both ears of everyone who hears it will tingle. ¹² In that day I will perform against Eli all that I have spoken concerning his house, from beginning to end. ¹³ For I have told him that I will judge his house forever for the iniquity which he knows, because his sons made themselves vile, and he did not restrain them. ¹⁴ And therefore I have sworn to the house of Eli that the iniquity of Eli's house shall not be atoned for by sacrifice or offering forever."

¹⁵ So Samuel lay down until morning, and opened the doors of the house of the LORD. And Samuel was afraid to tell Eli the vision. ¹⁶ Then Eli called Samuel and said, "Samuel, my son!"

He answered, "Here I am."

¹⁷ And he said, "What *is* the word that *the* LORD spoke to you? Please do not hide *it* from me. God do so to you, and more also, if you hide anything from me of all the things that He said to you." ¹⁸ Then Samuel told him everything, and hid nothing from him. And he said, "It *is* the LORD. Let Him do what seems good to Him."

¹⁹ So Samuel grew, and the LORD was with him and let none of his words fall to the ground. ²⁰ And all Israel from Dan to Beersheba knew that Samuel *had been* established as a prophet of the LORD. ²¹ Then the LORD appeared again in Shiloh. For the LORD revealed Himself to Samuel in Shiloh by the word of the LORD.

~ PSALM 53:1-6 ~

1 The fool has said in his heart,
   "*There is* no God."
   They are corrupt, and have done
      abominable iniquity;
   There is none who does good.

2 God looks down from heaven upon
      the children of men,
   To see if there are *any* who
      understand, who seek God.
3 Every one of them has turned aside;
   They have together become corrupt;
   There is none who does good,
   No, not one.

4 Have the workers of iniquity no
      knowledge,
   Who eat up my people *as* they eat
      bread,
   And do not call upon God?
5 There they are in great fear
   Where no fear was,
   For God has scattered the bones of
      him who encamps against you;
   You have put *them* to shame,
   Because God has despised them.

6 Oh, that the salvation of Israel
      would come out of Zion!
   When God brings back the captivity
      of His people,
   Let Jacob rejoice *and* Israel be glad.

~ PROVERBS 15:8-11 ~

8 The sacrifice of the wicked *is* an
      abomination to the LORD,
   But the prayer of the upright *is* His
      delight.
9 The way of the wicked *is* an
      abomination to the LORD,
   But He loves him who follows
      righteousness.

10 Harsh discipline *is* for him who
      forsakes the way,
   And he who hates correction will
      die.

11 Hell and Destruction *are* before the
      LORD;

So how much more the hearts of the
sons of men.

~ LUKE 20:27-47 ~

Then some of the Sadducees, who deny
that there is a resurrection, came to *Him*
and asked Him, 28 saying: "Teacher, Moses
wrote to us *that* if a man's brother dies,
having a wife, and he dies without children, his brother should take his wife and
raise up offspring for his brother. 29 Now
there were seven brothers. And the first
took a wife, and died without children.
30 And the second took her as wife, and
he died childless. 31 Then the third took
her, and in like manner the seven also;
and they left no children, and died. 32 Last
of all the woman died also. 33 Therefore,
in the resurrection, whose wife does she
become? For all seven had her as wife."
34 Jesus answered and said to them,
"The sons of this age marry and are given
in marriage. 35 But those who are counted
worthy to attain that age, and the resurrection from the dead, neither marry nor
are given in marriage; 36 nor can they die
anymore, for they are equal to the angels
and are sons of God, being sons of the
resurrection. 37 But even Moses showed
in the *burning* bush *passage* that the dead
are raised, when he called the Lord 'the
God of Abraham, the God of Isaac, and
the God of Jacob.' 38 For He is not the
God of the dead but of the living, for all
live to Him."
39 Then some of the scribes answered
and said, "Teacher, You have spoken well."
40 But after that they dared not question
Him anymore.
41 And He said to them, "How can they
say that the Christ is the Son of David?
42 Now David himself said in the Book of
Psalms:

'The LORD said to my Lord,
   "Sit at My right hand,
43   Till I make Your enemies Your
         footstool." '

44 Therefore David calls Him '*Lord*'; how
is He then his Son?"
45 Then, in the hearing of all the people,
He said to His disciples, 46 "Beware of the
scribes, who desire to go around in long

robes, love greetings in the marketplaces, the best seats in the synagogues, and the best places at feasts, [47] who devour widows' houses, and for a pretense make long prayers. These will receive greater condemnation."

~ 1 SAMUEL 4:1—5:12 ~

And the word of Samuel came to all Israel.

Now Israel went out to battle against the Philistines, and encamped beside Ebenezer; and the Philistines encamped in Aphek. [2] Then the Philistines put themselves in battle array against Israel. And when they joined battle, Israel was defeated by the Philistines, who killed about four thousand men of the army in the field. [3] And when the people had come into the camp, the elders of Israel said, "Why has the LORD defeated us today before the Philistines? Let us bring the ark of the covenant of the LORD from Shiloh to us, that when it comes among us it may save us from the hand of our enemies." [4] So the people sent to Shiloh, that they might bring from there the ark of the covenant of the LORD of hosts, who dwells *between* the cherubim. And the two sons of Eli, Hophni and Phinehas, *were* there with the ark of the covenant of God.

[5] And when the ark of the covenant of the LORD came into the camp, all Israel shouted so loudly that the earth shook. [6] Now when the Philistines heard the noise of the shout, they said, "What *does* the sound of this great shout in the camp of the Hebrews *mean?*" Then they understood that the ark of the LORD had come into the camp. [7] So the Philistines were afraid, for they said, "God has come into the camp!" And they said, "Woe to us! For such a thing has never happened before. [8] Woe to us! Who will deliver us from the hand of these mighty gods? These *are* the gods who struck the Egyptians with all the plagues in the wilderness. [9] Be strong and conduct yourselves like men, you Philistines, that you do not become servants of the Hebrews, as they have been to you. Conduct yourselves like men, and fight!"

[10] So the Philistines fought, and Israel was defeated, and every man fled to his tent. There was a very great slaughter, and there fell of Israel thirty thousand foot soldiers. [11] Also the ark of God was captured; and the two sons of Eli, Hophni and Phinehas, died.

[12] Then a man of Benjamin ran from the battle line the same day, and came to Shiloh with his clothes torn and dirt on his head. [13] Now when he came, there was Eli, sitting on a seat by the wayside watching, for his heart trembled for the ark of God. And when the man came into the city and told *it,* all the city cried out. [14] When Eli heard the noise of the outcry, he said, "What *does* the sound of this tumult *mean?*" And the man came quickly and told Eli. [15] Eli was ninety-eight years old, and his eyes were so dim that he could not see.

[16] Then the man said to Eli, "I *am* he who came from the battle. And I fled today from the battle line."

And he said, "What happened, my son?"

[17] So the messenger answered and said, "Israel has fled before the Philistines, and there has been a great slaughter among the people. Also your two sons, Hophni and Phinehas, are dead; and the ark of God has been captured."

[18] Then it happened, when he made mention of the ark of God, that Eli fell off the seat backward by the side of the gate; and his neck was broken and he died, for the man was old and heavy. And he had judged Israel forty years.

[19] Now his daughter-in-law, Phinehas' wife, was with child, *due* to be delivered; and when she heard the news that the ark of God was captured, and that her father-in-law and her husband were dead, she bowed herself and gave birth, for her labor pains came upon her. [20] And about the time of her death the women who stood by her said to her, "Do not fear, for you have borne a son." But she did not

answer, nor did she regard *it.* [21] Then she named the child Ichabod, saying, "The glory has departed from Israel!" because the ark of God had been captured and because of her father-in-law and her husband. [22] And she said, "The glory has departed from Israel, for the ark of God has been captured."

5 Then the Philistines took the ark of God and brought it from Ebenezer to Ashdod. [2] When the Philistines took the ark of God, they brought it into the house of Dagon and set it by Dagon. [3] And when the people of Ashdod arose early in the morning, there was Dagon, fallen on its face to the earth before the ark of the LORD. So they took Dagon and set it in its place again. [4] And when they arose early the next morning, there was Dagon, fallen on its face to the ground before the ark of the LORD. The head of Dagon and both the palms of its hands *were* broken off on the threshold; only Dagon's torso was left of it. [5] Therefore neither the priests of Dagon nor any who come into Dagon's house tread on the threshold of Dagon in Ashdod to this day.

[6] But the hand of the LORD was heavy on the people of Ashdod, and He ravaged them and struck them with tumors, *both* Ashdod and its territory. [7] And when the men of Ashdod saw how *it was,* they said, "The ark of the God of Israel must not remain with us, for His hand is harsh toward us and Dagon our god." [8] Therefore they sent and gathered to themselves all the lords of the Philistines, and said, "What shall we do with the ark of the God of Israel?"

And they answered, "Let the ark of the God of Israel be carried away to Gath." So they carried the ark of the God of Israel away. [9] So it was, after they had carried it away, that the hand of the LORD was against the city with a very great destruction; and He struck the men of the city, both small and great, and tumors broke out on them.

[10] Therefore they sent the ark of God to Ekron. So it was, as the ark of God came to Ekron, that the Ekronites cried out, saying, "They have brought the ark of the God of Israel to us, to kill us and our people!" [11] So they sent and gathered together all the lords of the Philistines, and said, "Send away the ark of the God of Israel, and let it go back to its own place, so that it does not kill us and our people." For there was a deadly destruction throughout all the city; the hand of God was very heavy there. [12] And the men who did not die were stricken with the tumors, and the cry of the city went up to heaven.

~ PSALM 54:1–7 ~

[1] Save me, O God, by Your name,
And vindicate me by Your strength.
[2] Hear my prayer, O God;
Give ear to the words of my mouth.
[3] For strangers have risen up against me,
And oppressors have sought after my life;
They have not set God before them.
Selah

[4] Behold, God *is* my helper;
The Lord *is* with those who uphold my life.
[5] He will repay my enemies for their evil.
Cut them off in Your truth.

[6] I will freely sacrifice to You;
I will praise Your name, O LORD, for *it is* good.
[7] For He has delivered me out of all trouble;
And my eye has seen *its desire* upon my enemies.

~ PROVERBS 15:12, 13 ~

[12] A scoffer does not love one who corrects him,
Nor will he go to the wise.

[13] A merry heart makes a cheerful countenance,
But by sorrow of the heart the spirit is broken.

~ LUKE 21:1–19 ~

And He looked up and saw the rich putting their gifts into the treasury, [2] and He saw also a certain poor widow putting in

Smile!

The practice of one particular church was to dismiss the children from the Sunday morning service just prior to the sermon. The children would all march forward in a make-shift processional and sing a song as they passed by the pulpit on their way to hear a sermon prepared just for them. The pastor enjoyed this part of the service. He made it a point to smile at each child and to receive a smile in return.

To his surprise, one morning a curly-headed four-year-old girl ran out of the procession and threw herself into her mother's arms, sobbing deeply. The pastor sought out the mother after the service to see what had happened. The child had told her, "I smiled at God, but He didn't smile back."

The pastor's heart sank. He had failed to smile and her joy had turned to torment.

We may not think our smiles represent God to another person, but they just might! Genuine smiles are a sign of affirmation, appreciation, and love.

Don't forget to smile! Your smile can bring hope and change someone's countenance today.

> A merry heart makes a cheerful countenance, but by sorrow of the heart the spirit is broken.
>
> *Proverbs 15:13*

two mites. ³ So He said, "Truly I say to you that this poor widow has put in more than all; ⁴ for all these out of their abundance have put in offerings for God, but she out of her poverty put in all the livelihood that she had."

⁵ Then, as some spoke of the temple, how it was adorned with beautiful stones and donations, He said, ⁶ "These things which you see—the days will come in which not *one* stone shall be left upon another that shall not be thrown down."

⁷ So they asked Him, saying, "Teacher, but when will these things be? And what sign *will there be* when these things are about to take place?"

⁸ And He said: "Take heed that you not be deceived. For many will come in My name, saying, 'I am *He*,' and, 'The time has drawn near.' Therefore do not go after them. ⁹ But when you hear of wars and commotions, do not be terrified; for these things must come to pass first, but the end *will not come* immediately."

¹⁰ Then He said to them, "Nation will rise against nation, and kingdom against kingdom. ¹¹ And there will be great earthquakes in various places, and famines and pestilences; and there will be fearful sights and great signs from heaven. ¹² But before all these things, they will lay their hands on you and persecute *you*, delivering *you* up to the synagogues and prisons. You will be brought before kings and rulers for My name's sake. ¹³ But it will turn out for you as an occasion for testimony. ¹⁴ Therefore settle *it* in your hearts not to meditate beforehand on what you will answer; ¹⁵ for I will give you a mouth and wisdom which all your adversaries will not be able to contradict or resist. ¹⁶ You will be betrayed even by parents and brothers, relatives and friends; and they will put *some* of you to death. ¹⁷ And you will be hated by all for My name's sake. ¹⁸ But not a hair of your head shall be lost. ¹⁹ By your patience possess your souls.

READING 122 · MAY 2

～ 1 SAMUEL 6:1—7:17 ～

Now the ark of the LORD was in the country of the Philistines seven months. ² And the Philistines called for the priests and the diviners, saying, "What shall we do with the ark of the LORD? Tell us how we should send it to its place."

³ So they said, "If you send away the ark of the God of Israel, do not send it empty; but by all means return *it* to Him *with* a trespass offering. Then you will be healed, and it will be known to you why His hand is not removed from you."

⁴ Then they said, "What *is* the trespass offering which we shall return to Him?"

They answered, "Five golden tumors and five golden rats, *according to* the number of the lords of the Philistines. For the same plague *was* on all of you and on your lords. ⁵ Therefore you shall make images of your tumors and images of your rats that ravage the land, and you shall give glory to the God of Israel; perhaps He will lighten His hand from you, from your gods, and from your land. ⁶ Why then do

you harden your hearts as the Egyptians and Pharaoh hardened their hearts? When He did mighty things among them, did they not let the people go, that they might depart? ⁷ Now therefore, make a new cart, take two milk cows which have never been yoked, and hitch the cows to the cart; and take their calves home, away from them. ⁸ Then take the ark of the LORD and set it on the cart; and put the articles of gold which you are returning to Him *as* a trespass offering in a chest by its side. Then send it away, and let it go. ⁹ And watch: if it goes up the road to its own territory, to Beth Shemesh, *then* He has done us this great evil. But if not, then we shall know that *it is* not His hand *that* struck us—it happened to us by chance."

¹⁰ Then the men did so; they took two milk cows and hitched them to the cart, and shut up their calves at home. ¹¹ And they set the ark of the LORD on the cart, and the chest with the gold rats and the images of their tumors. ¹² Then the cows headed straight for the road to Beth

Clear Away the Brambles

A man who owned a plot of land was about to leave the area on a journey that would take several years. Before he left, he leased his land to others. When he returned, he discovered his renters had been very careless and brambles had sprung up, turning his plot of land into a wilderness of thorns. Desiring to cultivate the land, he said to his son, "Your job is to go and clear that ground."

The son visited the acreage and quickly concluded, *It will take forever to get this land cleared!* Overwhelmed by the task, he lay on the ground and went to sleep. He did the same day after day. When his father came to see what had been done, he found his son asleep and the land untouched.

When his father woke him, the son complained that the job had looked so monumental, he could never make himself begin to tackle the project. His father replied, "Son, if you had only cleared the area on which you lay down for a nap each day, your work would have advanced and you would not have lost heart." After the father left, the son began to do what his father had advised. In a short time, the plot of land was cleared and cultivated.

Daily prayer clears away the brambles in our hearts. Don't give up! God is working something good in you — prayer by prayer!

> Do you see a man who excels in his work? He will stand before kings; he will not stand before unknown men.
>
> *Proverbs 22:29*

Shemesh, *and* went along the highway, lowing as they went, and did not turn aside to the right hand or the left. And the lords of the Philistines went after them to the border of Beth Shemesh.

¹³ Now *the people of* Beth Shemesh *were* reaping their wheat harvest in the valley; and they lifted their eyes and saw the ark, and rejoiced to see *it.* ¹⁴ Then the cart came into the field of Joshua of Beth Shemesh, and stood there; a large stone *was* there. So they split the wood of the cart and offered the cows as a burnt offering to the LORD. ¹⁵ The Levites took down the ark of the LORD and the chest that *was* with it, in which *were* the articles of gold, and put *them* on the large stone. Then the men of Beth Shemesh offered burnt offerings and made sacrifices the same day to the LORD. ¹⁶ So when the five lords of the Philistines had seen *it,* they returned to Ekron the same day.

¹⁷ These *are* the golden tumors which the Philistines returned *as* a trespass offering to the LORD: one for Ashdod, one for Gaza, one for Ashkelon, one for Gath, one for Ekron; ¹⁸ and the golden rats, *according to* the number of all the cities of the Philistines *belonging* to the five lords, *both* fortified cities and country villages, even as far as the large *stone of* Abel on which they set the ark of the LORD, *which stone remains* to this day in the field of Joshua of Beth Shemesh.

¹⁹ Then He struck the men of Beth Shemesh, because they had looked into the ark of the LORD. He struck fifty thousand and seventy men of the people, and the people lamented because the LORD had struck the people with a great slaughter.

²⁰ And the men of Beth Shemesh said, "Who is able to stand before this holy LORD God? And to whom shall it go up from us?" ²¹ So they sent messengers to the inhabitants of Kirjath Jearim, saying, "The Philistines have brought back the ark of the LORD; come down *and* take it up with you."

7 Then the men of Kirjath Jearim came and took the ark of the LORD, and brought it into the house of Abinadab on the hill, and consecrated Eleazar his son to keep the ark of the LORD.

² So it was that the ark remained in Kirjath Jearim a long time; it was there twenty years. And all the house of Israel lamented after the LORD.

³ Then Samuel spoke to all the house of Israel, saying, "If you return to the LORD with all your hearts, *then* put away the foreign gods and the Ashtoreths from among you, and prepare your hearts for the LORD, and serve Him only; and He will deliver you from the hand of the Philistines." ⁴ So the children of Israel put away the Baals and the Ashtoreths, and served the LORD only.

⁵ And Samuel said, "Gather all Israel to Mizpah, and I will pray to the LORD for you." ⁶ So they gathered together at Mizpah, drew water, and poured *it* out before the LORD. And they fasted that day, and said there, "We have sinned against the LORD." And Samuel judged the children of Israel at Mizpah.

⁷ Now when the Philistines heard that the children of Israel had gathered together at Mizpah, the lords of the Philistines went up against Israel. And when the children of Israel heard *of it,* they were afraid of the Philistines. ⁸ So the children of Israel said to Samuel, "Do not cease to cry out to the LORD our God for us, that He may save us from the hand of the Philistines."

⁹ And Samuel took a suckling lamb and offered *it as* a whole burnt offering to the LORD. Then Samuel cried out to the LORD for Israel, and the LORD answered him. ¹⁰ Now as Samuel was offering up the burnt offering, the Philistines drew near to battle against Israel. But the LORD thundered with a loud thunder upon the Philistines that day, and so confused them that they were overcome before Israel. ¹¹ And the men of Israel went out of Mizpah and pursued the Philistines, and drove them back as far as below Beth Car. ¹² Then Samuel took a stone and set *it* up between Mizpah and Shen, and called its name Ebenezer, saying, "Thus far the LORD has helped us."

¹³ So the Philistines were subdued, and they did not come anymore into the territory of Israel. And the hand of the LORD was against the Philistines all the days of Samuel. ¹⁴ Then the cities which the Philistines had taken from Israel were

restored to Israel, from Ekron to Gath; and Israel recovered its territory from the hands of the Philistines. Also there was peace between Israel and the Amorites. [15] And Samuel judged Israel all the days of his life. [16] He went from year to year on a circuit to Bethel, Gilgal, and Mizpah, and judged Israel in all those places. [17] But he always returned to Ramah, for his home *was* there. There he judged Israel, and there he built an altar to the LORD.

∼ PSALM 55:1–8 ∼

1   Give ear to my prayer, O God,
And do not hide Yourself from my
     supplication.
2   Attend to me, and hear me;
I am restless in my complaint, and
     moan noisily,
3   Because of the voice of the enemy,
Because of the oppression of the
     wicked;
For they bring down trouble upon
     me,
And in wrath they hate me.

4   My heart is severely pained within
     me,
And the terrors of death have fallen
     upon me.
5   Fearfulness and trembling have come
     upon me,
And horror has overwhelmed me.
6   So I said, "Oh, that I had wings like
     a dove!
I would fly away and be at rest.
7   Indeed, I would wander far off,
And remain in the wilderness.   Selah
8   I would hasten my escape
From the windy storm *and* tempest."

∼ PROVERBS 15:14 ∼

14   The heart of him who has
     understanding seeks knowledge,
But the mouth of fools feeds on
     foolishness.

∼ LUKE 21:20–38 ∼

"But when you see Jerusalem surrounded by armies, then know that its desolation is near. [21] Then let those who are in Judea flee to the mountains, let those who are in the midst of her depart, and let not those who are in the country enter her. [22] For these are the days of vengeance, that all things which are written may be fulfilled. [23] But woe to those who are pregnant and to those who are nursing babies in those days! For there will be great distress in the land and wrath upon this people. [24] And they will fall by the edge of the sword, and be led away captive into all nations. And Jerusalem will be trampled by Gentiles until the times of the Gentiles are fulfilled.

[25] "And there will be signs in the sun, in the moon, and in the stars; and on the earth distress of nations, with perplexity, the sea and the waves roaring; [26] men's hearts failing them from fear and the expectation of those things which are coming on the earth, for the powers of the heavens will be shaken. [27] Then they will see the Son of Man coming in a cloud with power and great glory. [28] Now when these things begin to happen, look up and lift up your heads, because your redemption draws near."

[29] Then He spoke to them a parable: "Look at the fig tree, and all the trees. [30] When they are already budding, you see and know for yourselves that summer is now near. [31] So you also, when you see these things happening, know that the kingdom of God is near. [32] Assuredly, I say to you, this generation will by no means pass away till all things take place. [33] Heaven and earth will pass away, but My words will by no means pass away.

[34] "But take heed to yourselves, lest your hearts be weighed down with carousing, drunkenness, and cares of this life, and that Day come on you unexpectedly. [35] For it will come as a snare on all those who dwell on the face of the whole earth. [36] Watch therefore, and pray always that you may be counted worthy to escape all these things that will come to pass, and to stand before the Son of Man."

[37] And in the daytime He was teaching in the temple, but at night He went out and stayed on the mountain called Olivet. [38] Then early in the morning all the people came to Him in the temple to hear Him.

~ 1 SAMUEL 8:1—9:27 ~

Now it came to pass when Samuel was old that he made his sons judges over Israel. ² The name of his firstborn was Joel, and the name of his second, Abijah; *they were* judges in Beersheba. ³ But his sons did not walk in his ways; they turned aside after dishonest gain, took bribes, and perverted justice.

⁴ Then all the elders of Israel gathered together and came to Samuel at Ramah, ⁵ and said to him, "Look, you are old, and your sons do not walk in your ways. Now make us a king to judge us like all the nations."

⁶ But the thing displeased Samuel when they said, "Give us a king to judge us." So Samuel prayed to the LORD. ⁷ And the LORD said to Samuel, "Heed the voice of the people in all that they say to you; for they have not rejected you, but they have rejected Me, that I should not reign over them. ⁸ According to all the works which they have done since the day that I brought them up out of Egypt, even to this day—with which they have forsaken Me and served other gods—so they are doing to you also. ⁹ Now therefore, heed their voice. However, you shall solemnly forewarn them, and show them the behavior of the king who will reign over them."

¹⁰ So Samuel told all the words of the LORD to the people who asked him for a king. ¹¹ And he said, "This will be the behavior of the king who will reign over you: He will take your sons and appoint *them* for his own chariots and *to be* his horsemen, and *some* will run before his chariots. ¹² He will appoint captains over his thousands and captains over his fifties, *will set some* to plow his ground and reap his harvest, and *some* to make his weapons of war and equipment for his chariots. ¹³ He will take your daughters *to be* perfumers, cooks, and bakers. ¹⁴ And he will take the best of your fields, your vineyards, and your olive groves, and give *them* to his servants. ¹⁵ He will take a tenth of your grain and your vintage, and give it to his officers and servants. ¹⁶ And he will take your male ser-

vants, your female servants, your finest young men, and your donkeys, and put *them* to his work. ¹⁷ He will take a tenth of your sheep. And you will be his servants. ¹⁸ And you will cry out in that day because of your king whom you have chosen for yourselves, and the LORD will not hear you in that day."

¹⁹ Nevertheless the people refused to obey the voice of Samuel; and they said, "No, but we will have a king over us, ²⁰ that we also may be like all the nations, and that our king may judge us and go out before us and fight our battles."

²¹ And Samuel heard all the words of the people, and he repeated them in the hearing of the LORD. ²² So the LORD said to Samuel, "Heed their voice, and make them a king."

And Samuel said to the men of Israel, "Every man go to his city."

9 There was a man of Benjamin whose name *was* Kish the son of Abiel, the son of Zeror, the son of Bechorath, the son of Aphiah, a Benjamite, a mighty man of power. ² And he had a choice and handsome son whose name *was* Saul. *There was* not a more handsome person than he among the children of Israel. From his shoulders upward *he was* taller than any of the people.

³ Now the donkeys of Kish, Saul's father, were lost. And Kish said to his son Saul, "Please take one of the servants with you, and arise, go and look for the donkeys." ⁴ So he passed through the mountains of Ephraim and through the land of Shalisha, but they did not find *them*. Then they passed through the land of Shaalim, and *they were* not *there*. Then he passed through the land of the Benjamites, but they did not find *them*. ⁵ When they had come to the land of Zuph, Saul said to his servant who *was* with him, "Come, let us return, lest my father cease *caring* about the donkeys and become worried about us."

⁶ And he said to him, "Look now, *there is* in this city a man of God, and *he is* an honorable man; all that he says surely comes to pass. So let us go there;

The Best Medicine

Standup comedian and author David Brenner was signing books in a San Francisco bookstore when a young man handed him a newly purchased copy to be signed and said softly, "I want to thank you for saving my life." Brenner replied flippantly, "That's okay." The young man stood his ground and said, "No, I really mean it."

Brenner stopped signing the book and looked at him. The man said, "My father died. He was my best friend. I loved him and couldn't stop crying for weeks. I decided to take my own life. The night I was going to do it, I happened to have the TV on. You were hosting The Tonight Show, and doing your monologue. Next thing I knew I was watching you and laughing. Then I started laughing hysterically. I realized then that if I was able to laugh, I was able to live. So I want to thank you for saving my life." Humbled and grateful, Brenner shook his hand and said, "No, I thank you."

Laughter does more than help us escape our problems. It sometimes gives us the courage to face them. As humorist Barbara Johnson has said: "Laughter is like changing a baby's diaper. It doesn't permanently solve any problems, but it makes things more acceptable for awhile."

perhaps he can show us the way that we should go."

⁷ Then Saul said to his servant, "But look, *if* we go, what shall we bring the man? For the bread in our vessels is all gone, and *there is* no present to bring to the man of God. What do we have?"

⁸ And the servant answered Saul again and said, "Look, I have here at hand one-fourth of a shekel of silver. I will give *that* to the man of God, to tell us our way." ⁹(Formerly in Israel, when a man went to inquire of God, he spoke thus: "Come, let us go to the seer"; for *he who is* now *called* a prophet was formerly called a seer.)

¹⁰ Then Saul said to his servant, "Well said; come, let us go." So they went to the city where the man of God *was*.

¹¹ As they went up the hill to the city, they met some young women going out to draw water, and said to them, "Is the seer here?"

¹² And they answered them and said, "Yes, there he is, just ahead of you. Hurry now; for today he came to this city, because there is a sacrifice of the people today on the high place. ¹³ As soon as you come into the city, you will surely find him before he goes up to the high place to eat. For the people will not eat until he comes, because he must bless the sacrifice; afterward those who are invited will eat. Now therefore, go up, for about this time you will find him." ¹⁴ So they went up to the city. As they were coming into the city, there was Samuel, coming out toward them on his way up to the high place.

¹⁵ Now the LORD had told Samuel in his ear the day before Saul came, saying, ¹⁶ "Tomorrow about this time I will send you a man from the land of Benjamin, and you shall anoint him commander over My people Israel, that he may save My people from the hand of the Philistines; for I have looked upon My people, because their cry has come to Me."

¹⁷ So when Samuel saw Saul, the LORD said to him, "There he is, the man of whom I spoke to you. This one shall reign over My people." ¹⁸ Then Saul drew near to Samuel in the gate, and said, "Please tell me, where *is* the seer's house?"

¹⁹ Samuel answered Saul and said, "I *am*

the seer. Go up before me to the high place, for you shall eat with me today; and tomorrow I will let you go and will tell you all that *is* in your heart. ²⁰ But as for your donkeys that were lost three days ago, do not be anxious about them, for they have been found. And on whom *is* all the desire of Israel? *Is it* not on you and on all your father's house?"

²¹ And Saul answered and said, "*Am* I not a Benjamite, of the smallest of the tribes of Israel, and my family the least of all the families of the tribe of Benjamin? Why then do you speak like this to me?"

²² Now Samuel took Saul and his servant and brought them into the hall, and had them sit in the place of honor among those who were invited; there *were* about thirty persons. ²³ And Samuel said to the cook, "Bring the portion which I gave you, of which I said to you, 'Set it apart.' " ²⁴ So the cook took up the thigh with its upper part and set *it* before Saul. And *Samuel* said, "Here it is, what was kept back. *It* was set apart for you. Eat; for until this time it has been kept for you, since I said I invited the people." So Saul ate with Samuel that day.

²⁵ When they had come down from the high place into the city, *Samuel* spoke with Saul on the top of the house. ²⁶ They arose early; and it was about the dawning of the day that Samuel called to Saul on the top of the house, saying, "Get up, that I may send you on your way." And Saul arose, and both of them went outside, he and Samuel.

²⁷ As they were going down to the outskirts of the city, Samuel said to Saul, "Tell the servant to go on ahead of us." And he went on. "But you stand here awhile, that I may announce to you the word of God."

~ PSALM 55:9–15 ~

⁹ Destroy, O Lord, *and* divide their
        tongues,
    For I have seen violence and strife in
        the city.
¹⁰ Day and night they go around it on
        its walls;
    Iniquity and trouble *are* also in the
        midst of it.
¹¹ Destruction *is* in its midst;

Oppression and deceit do not depart
from its streets.

¹² For *it is* not an enemy *who*
reproaches me;
Then I could bear *it*.
Nor *is it* one *who* hates me who has
exalted *himself* against me;
Then I could hide from him.
¹³ But *it was* you, a man my equal,
My companion and my
acquaintance.
¹⁴ We took sweet counsel together,
And walked to the house of God in
the throng.

¹⁵ Let death seize them;
Let them go down alive into hell,
For wickedness *is* in their dwellings
and among them.

~ PROVERBS 15:15–17 ~

¹⁵ All the days of the afflicted *are* evil,
But he who is of a merry heart *has* a
continual feast.

¹⁶ Better *is* a little with the fear of the
LORD,
Than great treasure with trouble.
¹⁷ Better *is* a dinner of herbs where
love is,
Than a fatted calf with hatred.

~ LUKE 22:1–23 ~

Now the Feast of Unleavened Bread drew
near, which is called Passover. ² And the
chief priests and the scribes sought how
they might kill Him, for they feared the
people.
³ Then Satan entered Judas, surnamed
Iscariot, who was numbered among the
twelve. ⁴ So he went his way and conferred
with the chief priests and captains, how
he might betray Him to them. ⁵ And they
were glad, and agreed to give him money.
⁶ So he promised and sought opportunity

to betray Him to them in the absence of
the multitude.
⁷ Then came the Day of Unleavened
Bread, when the Passover must be killed.
⁸ And He sent Peter and John, saying, "Go
and prepare the Passover for us, that we
may eat."
⁹ So they said to Him, "Where do You
want us to prepare?"
¹⁰ And He said to them, "Behold, when
you have entered the city, a man will
meet you carrying a pitcher of water; follow him into the house which he enters.
¹¹ Then you shall say to the master of the
house, 'The Teacher says to you, "Where
is the guest room where I may eat the
Passover with My disciples?" ' ¹² Then he
will show you a large, furnished upper
room; there make ready."
¹³ So they went and found it just as He
had said to them, and they prepared the
Passover.
¹⁴ When the hour had come, He sat
down, and the twelve apostles with Him.
¹⁵ Then He said to them, "With *fervent*
desire I have desired to eat this Passover
with you before I suffer; ¹⁶ for I say to
you, I will no longer eat of it until it is
fulfilled in the kingdom of God."
¹⁷ Then He took the cup, and gave
thanks, and said, "Take this and divide *it*
among yourselves; ¹⁸ for I say to you, I
will not drink of the fruit of the vine until
the kingdom of God comes."
¹⁹ And He took bread, gave thanks and
broke *it*, and gave *it* to them, saying, "This
is My body which is given for you; do
this in remembrance of Me."
²⁰ Likewise He also *took* the cup after
supper, saying, "This cup *is* the new covenant in My blood, which is shed for you.
²¹ But behold, the hand of My betrayer *is*
with Me on the table. ²² And truly the Son
of Man goes as it has been determined,
but woe to that man by whom He is betrayed!"
²³ Then they began to question among
themselves, which of them it was who
would do this thing.

~ 1 SAMUEL 10:1—11:15 ~

Then Samuel took a flask of oil and poured *it* on his head, and kissed him and said: "*Is it* not because the LORD has anointed you commander over His inheritance? ² When you have departed from me today, you will find two men by Rachel's tomb in the territory of Benjamin at Zelzah; and they will say to you, 'The donkeys which you went to look for have been found. And now your father has ceased caring about the donkeys and is worrying about you, saying, "What shall I do about my son?" ' ³ Then you shall go on forward from there and come to the terebinth tree of Tabor. There three men going up to God at Bethel will meet you, one carrying three young goats, another carrying three loaves of bread, and another carrying a skin of wine. ⁴ And they will greet you and give you two *loaves* of bread, which you shall receive from their hands. ⁵ After that you shall come to the hill of God where the Philistine garrison *is*. And it will happen, when you have come there to the city, that you will meet a group of prophets coming down from the high place with a stringed instrument, a tambourine, a flute, and a harp before them; and they will be prophesying. ⁶ Then the Spirit of the LORD will come upon you, and you will prophesy with them and be turned into another man. ⁷ And let it be, when these signs come to you, *that* you do as the occasion demands; for God *is* with you. ⁸ You shall go down before me to Gilgal; and surely I will come down to you to offer burnt offerings *and* make sacrifices of peace offerings. Seven days you shall wait, till I come to you and show you what you should do."

⁹ So it was, when he had turned his back to go from Samuel, that God gave him another heart; and all those signs came to pass that day. ¹⁰ When they came there to the hill, there was a group of prophets to meet him; then the Spirit of God came upon him, and he prophesied among them. ¹¹ And it happened, when all who knew him formerly saw that he indeed prophesied among the prophets, that the people said to one another, "What *is* this *that* has come upon the son of Kish? Is

Saul also among the prophets?" ¹² Then a man from there answered and said, "But who *is* their father?" Therefore it became a proverb: "*Is* Saul also among the prophets?" ¹³ And when he had finished prophesying, he went to the high place.

¹⁴ Then Saul's uncle said to him and his servant, "Where did you go?"

So he said, "To look for the donkeys. When we saw that *they were* nowhere *to be found,* we went to Samuel."

¹⁵ And Saul's uncle said, "Tell me, please, what Samuel said to you."

¹⁶ So Saul said to his uncle, "He told us plainly that the donkeys had been found." But about the matter of the kingdom, he did not tell him what Samuel had said.

¹⁷ Then Samuel called the people together to the LORD at Mizpah, ¹⁸ and said to the children of Israel, "Thus says the LORD God of Israel: 'I brought up Israel out of Egypt, and delivered you from the hand of the Egyptians *and* from the hand of all kingdoms and from those who oppressed you.' ¹⁹ But you have today rejected your God, who Himself saved you from all your adversities and your tribulations; and you have said to Him, 'No, set a king over us!' Now therefore, present yourselves before the LORD by your tribes and by your clans."

²⁰ And when Samuel had caused all the tribes of Israel to come near, the tribe of Benjamin was chosen. ²¹ When he had caused the tribe of Benjamin to come near by their families, the family of Matri was chosen. And Saul the son of Kish was chosen. But when they sought him, he could not be found. ²² Therefore they inquired of the LORD further, "Has the man come here yet?"

And the LORD answered, "There he is, hidden among the equipment."

²³ So they ran and brought him from there; and when he stood among the people, he was taller than any of the people from his shoulders upward. ²⁴ And Samuel said to all the people, "Do you see him whom the LORD has chosen, that *there is* no one like him among all the people?"

Praying on Your Fingers

Many children learn to count on their fingers, but a nurse once taught a child to pray "on his fingers."

This was her method:

Your thumb is the digit nearest to your heart, so pray first for those who are closest to you. Your own needs, of course, should be included, as well as those of your beloved family and friends.

The second finger is the one used for pointing. Pray for those who point you toward the truth, whether at church or school. Pray for your teachers, mentors, pastors, and those who inspire your faith.

The third finger is the tallest. Let it stand for the leaders in every sphere of life. Pray for those in authority — both within the body of Christ and those who hold office in various areas of government.

The fourth finger is the weakest, as every pianist knows. Let it stand for those who are in trouble and pain — the sick, injured, abused, wounded, or hurt.

The little finger is the smallest. Let it stand for those who often go unnoticed, including those who suffer abuse and deprivation.

What a great tool to use in teaching children how to pray for themselves and others. What a simple and wonderful reminder to use as we pray ourselves!

So all the people shouted and said, "Long live the king!"

²⁵ Then Samuel explained to the people the behavior of royalty, and wrote *it* in a book and laid *it* up before the LORD. And Samuel sent all the people away, every man to his house. ²⁶ And Saul also went home to Gibeah; and valiant *men* went with him, whose hearts God had touched. ²⁷ But some rebels said, "How can this man save us?" So they despised him, and brought him no presents. But he held his peace.

11 Then Nahash the Ammonite came up and encamped against Jabesh Gilead; and all the men of Jabesh said to Nahash, "Make a covenant with us, and we will serve you."

² And Nahash the Ammonite answered them, "On this *condition* I will make *a covenant* with you, that I may put out all your right eyes, and bring reproach on all Israel."

³ Then the elders of Jabesh said to him, "Hold off for seven days, that we may send messengers to all the territory of Israel. And then, if *there is* no one to save us, we will come out to you."

⁴ So the messengers came to Gibeah of Saul and told the news in the hearing of the people. And all the people lifted up their voices and wept. ⁵ Now there was Saul, coming behind the herd from the field; and Saul said, "What *troubles* the people, that they weep?" And they told him the words of the men of Jabesh. ⁶ Then the Spirit of God came upon Saul when he heard this news, and his anger was greatly aroused. ⁷ So he took a yoke of oxen and cut them in pieces, and sent *them* throughout all the territory of Israel by the hands of messengers, saying, "Whoever does not go out with Saul and Samuel to battle, so it shall be done to his oxen."

And the fear of the LORD fell on the people, and they came out with one consent. ⁸ When he numbered them in Bezek, the children of Israel were three hundred thousand, and the men of Judah thirty thousand. ⁹ And they said to the messengers who came, "Thus you shall say to the men of Jabesh Gilead: 'Tomorrow, by *the time* the sun is hot, you shall have help.' " Then the messengers came and reported *it* to the men of Jabesh, and they were glad. ¹⁰ Therefore the men of Jabesh said, "Tomorrow we will come out to you, and you may do with us whatever seems good to you."

¹¹ So it was, on the next day, that Saul put the people in three companies; and they came into the midst of the camp in the morning watch, and killed Ammonites until the heat of the day. And it happened that those who survived were scattered, so that no two of them were left together.

¹² Then the people said to Samuel, "Who *is* he who said, 'Shall Saul reign over us?' Bring the men, that we may put them to death."

¹³ But Saul said, "Not a man shall be put to death this day, for today the LORD has accomplished salvation in Israel."

¹⁴ Then Samuel said to the people, "Come, let us go to Gilgal and renew the kingdom there." ¹⁵ So all the people went to Gilgal, and there they made Saul king before the LORD in Gilgal. There they made sacrifices of peace offerings before the LORD, and there Saul and all the men of Israel rejoiced greatly.

∼ PSALM 55:16–23 ∼

¹⁶ As for me, I will call upon God,
And the LORD shall save me.
¹⁷ Evening and morning and at noon
I will pray, and cry aloud,
And He shall hear my voice.
¹⁸ He has redeemed my soul in peace
from the battle *that was* against me,
For there were many against me.
¹⁹ God will hear, and afflict them,
Even He who abides from of old. Selah
Because they do not change,
Therefore they do not fear God.

²⁰ He has put forth his hands against those who were at peace with him;
He has broken his covenant.
²¹ *The words* of his mouth were smoother than butter,
But war *was* in his heart;
His words were softer than oil,
Yet they *were* drawn swords.

²² Cast your burden on the LORD,
And He shall sustain you;
He shall never permit the righteous
   to be moved.

²³ But You, O God, shall bring them
   down to the pit of destruction;
Bloodthirsty and deceitful men shall
   not live out half their days;
But I will trust in You.

~ PROVERBS 15:18–20 ~

¹⁸ A wrathful man stirs up strife,
But *he who is* slow to anger allays
   contention.

¹⁹ The way of the lazy *man is* like a
   hedge of thorns,
But the way of the upright *is* a
   highway.

²⁰ A wise son makes a father glad,
But a foolish man despises his
   mother.

~ LUKE 22:24–46 ~

Now there was also a dispute among
them, as to which of them should be considered the greatest. ²⁵ And He said to
them, "The kings of the Gentiles exercise
lordship over them, and those who
exercise authority over them are called
'benefactors.' ²⁶ But not so *among* you;
on the contrary, he who is greatest among
you, let him be as the younger, and he
who governs as he who serves. ²⁷ For who
is greater, he who sits at the table, or he
who serves? *Is* it not he who sits at the
table? Yet I am among you as the One who
serves.

²⁸ "But you are those who have continued with Me in My trials. ²⁹ And I bestow
upon you a kingdom, just as My Father
bestowed *one* upon Me, ³⁰ that you may
eat and drink at My table in My kingdom, and sit on thrones judging the twelve
tribes of Israel."

³¹ And the Lord said, "Simon, Simon!
Indeed, Satan has asked for you, that he
may sift *you* as wheat. ³² But I have prayed
for you, that your faith should not fail;
and when you have returned to *Me*,
strengthen your brethren."

³³ But he said to Him, "Lord, I am ready
to go with You, both to prison and to
death."

³⁴ Then He said, "I tell you, Peter, the
rooster shall not crow this day before
you will deny three times that you know
Me."

³⁵ And He said to them, "When I sent
you without money bag, knapsack, and
sandals, did you lack anything?"

So they said, "Nothing."

³⁶ Then He said to them, "But now, he
who has a money bag, let him take *it,* and
likewise a knapsack; and he who has no
sword, let him sell his garment and buy
one. ³⁷ For I say to you that this which is
written must still be accomplished in Me:
'And He was numbered with the transgressors.' For the things concerning Me
have an end."

³⁸ So they said, "Lord, look, here *are*
two swords."

And He said to them, "It is enough."

³⁹ Coming out, He went to the Mount
of Olives, as He was accustomed, and His
disciples also followed Him. ⁴⁰ When He
came to the place, He said to them, "Pray
that you may not enter into temptation."

⁴¹ And He was withdrawn from them
about a stone's throw, and He knelt down
and prayed, ⁴² saying, "Father, if it is Your
will, take this cup away from Me; nevertheless not My will, but Yours, be done."
⁴³ Then an angel appeared to Him from
heaven, strengthening Him. ⁴⁴ And being
in agony, He prayed more earnestly. Then
His sweat became like great drops of
blood falling down to the ground.

⁴⁵ When He rose up from prayer, and
had come to His disciples, He found them
sleeping from sorrow. ⁴⁶ Then He said to
them, "Why do you sleep? Rise and pray,
lest you enter into temptation."

~ 1 SAMUEL 12:1—13:23 ~

Now Samuel said to all Israel: "Indeed I have heeded your voice in all that you said to me, and have made a king over you. ² And now here is the king, walking before you; and I am old and grayheaded, and look, my sons *are* with you. I have walked before you from my childhood to this day. ³ Here I am. Witness against me before the LORD and before His anointed: Whose ox have I taken, or whose donkey have I taken, or whom have I cheated? Whom have I oppressed, or from whose hand have I received *any* bribe with which to blind my eyes? I will restore *it* to you."

⁴ And they said, "You have not cheated us or oppressed us, nor have you taken anything from any man's hand."

⁵ Then he said to them, "The LORD *is* witness against you, and His anointed *is* witness this day, that you have not found anything in my hand."

And they answered, "*He is* witness."

⁶ Then Samuel said to the people, "*It is* the LORD who raised up Moses and Aaron, and who brought your fathers up from the land of Egypt. ⁷ Now therefore, stand still, that I may reason with you before the LORD concerning all the righteous acts of the LORD which He did to you and your fathers: ⁸ When Jacob had gone into Egypt, and your fathers cried out to the LORD, then the LORD sent Moses and Aaron, who brought your fathers out of Egypt and made them dwell in this place. ⁹ And when they forgot the LORD their God, He sold them into the hand of Sisera, commander of the army of Hazor, into the hand of the Philistines, and into the hand of the king of Moab; and they fought against them. ¹⁰ Then they cried out to the LORD, and said, 'We have sinned, because we have forsaken the LORD and served the Baals and Ashtoreths; but now deliver us from the hand of our enemies, and we will serve You.' ¹¹ And the LORD sent Jerubbaal, Bedan, Jephthah, and Samuel, and delivered you out of the hand of your enemies on every side; and you dwelt in safety. ¹² And when you saw that Nahash king of the Ammonites came against you, you said to me, 'No, but a king shall reign over us,' when the LORD your God *was* your king.

¹³ "Now therefore, here is the king whom you have chosen *and* whom you have desired. And take note, the LORD has set a king over you. ¹⁴ If you fear the LORD and serve Him and obey His voice, and do not rebel against the commandment of the LORD, then both you and the king who reigns over you will continue following the LORD your God. ¹⁵ However, if you do not obey the voice of the LORD, but rebel against the commandment of the LORD, then the hand of the LORD will be against you, as *it was* against your fathers.

¹⁶ "Now therefore, stand and see this great thing which the LORD will do before your eyes: ¹⁷ *Is* today not the wheat harvest? I will call to the LORD, and He will send thunder and rain, that you may perceive and see that your wickedness *is* great, which you have done in the sight of the LORD, in asking a king for yourselves."

¹⁸ So Samuel called to the LORD, and the LORD sent thunder and rain that day; and all the people greatly feared the LORD and Samuel.

¹⁹ And all the people said to Samuel, "Pray for your servants to the LORD your God, that we may not die; for we have added to all our sins the evil of asking a king for ourselves."

²⁰ Then Samuel said to the people, "Do not fear. You have done all this wickedness; yet do not turn aside from following the LORD, but serve the LORD with all your heart. ²¹ And do not turn aside; for *then you would go* after empty things which cannot profit or deliver, for they *are* nothing. ²² For the LORD will not forsake His people, for His great name's sake, because it has pleased the LORD to make you His people. ²³ Moreover, as for me, far be it from me that I should sin against the LORD in ceasing to pray for you; but I will teach you the good and the right way. ²⁴ Only fear the LORD, and serve Him in truth with all your heart; for consider what great things He has

Fixing Your Spouse

A demanding wife continually nagged her husband to conform to her very high standards: "This is how you should act, this is how you should dress, this is what you should say, this is where you should be seen, and this is how you should plan your career!" She insisted every aspect of his life be honed to perfection. Feeling thoroughly whipped, the man finally said, "Why don't you just write it all down? Then you won't have to tell me these things all the time." She gladly complied.

A short time later the wife died. Within the course of a year, the man met another woman and married. His new life seemed to be a perpetual honeymoon. He could hardly believe the great joy, and relief, he was experiencing with his new bride.

One day he came across the list of "do's and don'ts" his first wife had written. He read them and realized, to his amazement, he was following all of the instructions — even though his second wife had never mentioned them.

He thought about what might have happened and finally said to a friend, "My former wife began her statements, 'I hate it when...,' but my new wife says, 'I just love it when...'."

The most important thing we can do to help our husbands become the men God created them to be is to pray for them and always speak encouraging words to them and about them. When we trust in God to "fix" what we think is wrong with our spouse, we often find it is we who needed "fixing."

> A man has joy by the answer of his mouth, and a word spoken in due season, how good it is!
>
> *Proverbs 15:23*

done for you. 25 But if you still do wickedly, you shall be swept away, both you and your king."

13

Saul reigned one year; and when he had reigned two years over Israel, 2 Saul chose for himself three thousand *men* of Israel. Two thousand were with Saul in Michmash and in the mountains of Bethel, and a thousand were with Jonathan in Gibeah of Benjamin. The rest of the people he sent away, every man to his tent.

3 And Jonathan attacked the garrison of the Philistines that *was* in Geba, and the Philistines heard *of it*. Then Saul blew the trumpet throughout all the land, saying, "Let the Hebrews hear!" 4 Now all Israel heard it said *that* Saul had attacked a garrison of the Philistines, and *that* Israel had also become an abomination to the Philistines. And the people were called together to Saul at Gilgal.

5 Then the Philistines gathered together to fight with Israel, thirty thousand chariots and six thousand horsemen, and people as the sand which *is* on the seashore in multitude. And they came up and encamped in Michmash, to the east of Beth Aven. 6 When the men of Israel saw that they were in danger (for the people were distressed), then the people hid in caves, in thickets, in rocks, in holes, and in pits. 7 And *some of* the Hebrews crossed over the Jordan to the land of Gad and Gilead.

As for Saul, he *was* still in Gilgal, and all the people followed him trembling. 8 Then he waited seven days, according to the time set by Samuel. But Samuel did not come to Gilgal; and the people were scattered from him. 9 So Saul said, "Bring a burnt offering and peace offerings here to me." And he offered the burnt offering. 10 Now it happened, as soon as he had finished presenting the burnt offering, that Samuel came; and Saul went out to meet him, that he might greet him.

11 And Samuel said, "What have you done?"

Saul said, "When I saw that the people were scattered from me, and *that* you did not come within the days appointed, and *that* the Philistines gathered together at Michmash, 12 then I said, 'The Philistines will now come down on me at Gilgal, and

I have not made supplication to the LORD.' Therefore I felt compelled, and offered a burnt offering."

13 And Samuel said to Saul, "You have done foolishly. You have not kept the commandment of the LORD your God, which He commanded you. For now the LORD would have established your kingdom over Israel forever. 14 But now your kingdom shall not continue. The LORD has sought for Himself a man after His own heart, and the LORD has commanded him *to be* commander over His people, because you have not kept what the LORD commanded you."

15 Then Samuel arose and went up from Gilgal to Gibeah of Benjamin. And Saul numbered the people present with him, about six hundred men.

16 Saul, Jonathan his son, and the people present with them remained in Gibeah of Benjamin. But the Philistines encamped in Michmash. 17 Then raiders came out of the camp of the Philistines in three companies. One company turned onto the road to Ophrah, to the land of Shual, 18 another company turned to the road *to* Beth Horon, and another company turned *to* the road of the border that overlooks the Valley of Zeboim toward the wilderness.

19 Now there was no blacksmith to be found throughout all the land of Israel, for the Philistines said, "Lest the Hebrews make swords or spears." 20 But all the Israelites would go down to the Philistines to sharpen each man's plowshare, his mattock, his ax, and his sickle; 21 and the charge for a sharpening was a pim for the plowshares, the mattocks, the forks, and the axes, and to set the points of the goads. 22 So it came about, on the day of battle, that there was neither sword nor spear found in the hand of any of the people who *were* with Saul and Jonathan. But they were found with Saul and Jonathan his son.

23 And the garrison of the Philistines went out to the pass of Michmash.

~ PSALM 56:1–13 ~

1 Be merciful to me, O God, for man would swallow me up;

Fighting all day he oppresses me.
2 My enemies would hound *me* all
   day,
   For *there are* many who fight against
   me, O Most High.

3 Whenever I am afraid,
   I will trust in You.
4 In God (I will praise His word),
   In God I have put my trust;
   I will not fear.
   What can flesh do to me?

5 All day they twist my words;
   All their thoughts *are* against me for
   evil.
6 They gather together,
   They hide, they mark my steps,
   When they lie in wait for my life.
7 Shall they escape by iniquity?
   In anger cast down the peoples,
      O God!

8 You number my wanderings;
   Put my tears into Your bottle;
   Are they not in Your book?
9 When I cry out *to You,*
   Then my enemies will turn back;
   This I know, because God *is* for me.
10 In God (I will praise *His* word),
    In the LORD (I will praise *His* word),
11 In God I have put my trust;
    I will not be afraid.
    What can man do to me?

12 Vows *made* to You *are binding* upon
    me, O God;
    I will render praises to You,
13 For You have delivered my soul from
    death.
    Have You not *kept* my feet from
    falling,
    That I may walk before God
    In the light of the living?

~ PROVERBS 15:21–23 ~

21 Folly *is* joy *to him who is* destitute of
    discernment,
    But a man of understanding walks
    uprightly.

22 Without counsel, plans go awry,
    But in the multitude of counselors
    they are established.

23 A man has joy by the answer of his
    mouth,
    And a word *spoken* in due season,
    how good *it is!*

~ LUKE 22:47–71 ~

And while He was still speaking, behold,
a multitude; and he who was called Judas, one of the twelve, went before them
and drew near to Jesus to kiss Him. [48] But
Jesus said to him, "Judas, are you betraying the Son of Man with a kiss?"

[49] When those around Him saw
what was going to happen, they said to
Him, "Lord, shall we strike with the
sword?" [50] And one of them struck the
servant of the high priest and cut off his
right ear.

[51] But Jesus answered and said, "Permit
even this." And He touched his ear and
healed him.

[52] Then Jesus said to the chief priests,
captains of the temple, and the elders who
had come to Him, "Have you come out,
as against a robber, with swords and clubs?
[53] When I was with you daily in the
temple, you did not try to seize Me. But
this is your hour, and the power of darkness."

[54] Having arrested Him, they led *Him*
and brought Him into the high priest's
house. But Peter followed at a distance.
[55] Now when they had kindled a fire in
the midst of the courtyard and sat down
together, Peter sat among them. [56] And a
certain servant girl, seeing him as he sat
by the fire, looked intently at him and said,
"This man was also with Him."

[57] But he denied Him, saying, "Woman,
I do not know Him."

[58] And after a little while another saw
him and said, "You also are of them."

But Peter said, "Man, I am not!"

[59] Then after about an hour had passed,
another confidently affirmed, saying,
"Surely this *fellow* also was with Him, for
he is a Galilean."

[60] But Peter said, "Man, I do not know
what you are saying!"

Immediately, while he was still speaking, the rooster crowed. [61] And the Lord turned and looked at Peter. Then Peter remembered the word of the Lord, how He had said to him, "Before the rooster crows, you will deny Me three times." [62] So Peter went out and wept bitterly.

[63] Now the men who held Jesus mocked Him and beat Him. [64] And having blindfolded Him, they struck Him on the face and asked Him, saying, "Prophesy! Who is the one who struck You?" [65] And many other things they blasphemously spoke against Him.

[66] As soon as it was day, the elders of the people, both chief priests and scribes, came together and led Him into their council, saying, [67] "If You are the Christ, tell us."

But He said to them, "If I tell you, you will by no means believe. [68] And if I also ask *you,* you will by no means answer Me or let *Me* go. [69] Hereafter the Son of Man will sit on the right hand of the power of God."

[70] Then they all said, "Are You then the Son of God?"

So He said to them, "You *rightly* say that I am."

[71] And they said, "What further testimony do we need? For we have heard it ourselves from His own mouth."

READING 126 · MAY 6

～ 1 SAMUEL 14:1—15:35 ～

Now it happened one day that Jonathan the son of Saul said to the young man who bore his armor, "Come, let us go over to the Philistines' garrison that *is* on the other side." But he did not tell his father. [2] And Saul was sitting in the outskirts of Gibeah under a pomegranate tree which *is* in Migron. The people who *were* with him *were* about six hundred men. [3] Ahijah the son of Ahitub, Ichabod's brother, the son of Phinehas, the son of Eli, the LORD's priest in Shiloh, was wearing an ephod. But the people did not know that Jonathan had gone.

[4] Between the passes, by which Jonathan sought to go over to the Philistines' garrison, *there was* a sharp rock on one side and a sharp rock on the other side. And the name of one *was* Bozez, and the name of the other Seneh. [5] The front of one faced northward opposite Michmash, and the other southward opposite Gibeah.

[6] Then Jonathan said to the young man who bore his armor, "Come, let us go over to the garrison of these uncircumcised; it may be that the LORD will work for us. For nothing restrains the LORD from saving by many or by few."

[7] So his armorbearer said to him, "Do all that is in your heart. Go then; here I am with you, according to your heart."

[8] Then Jonathan said, "Very well, let us cross over to *these* men, and we will show ourselves to them. [9] If they say thus to us, 'Wait until we come to you,' then we will stand still in our place and not go up to them. [10] But if they say thus, 'Come up to us,' then we will go up. For the LORD has delivered them into our hand, and this *will be* a sign to us."

[11] So both of them showed themselves to the garrison of the Philistines. And the Philistines said, "Look, the Hebrews are coming out of the holes where they have hidden." [12] Then the men of the garrison called to Jonathan and his armorbearer, and said, "Come up to us, and we will show you something."

Jonathan said to his armorbearer, "Come up after me, for the LORD has delivered them into the hand of Israel." [13] And Jonathan climbed up on his hands and knees with his armorbearer after him; and they fell before Jonathan. And as he came after him, his armorbearer killed them. [14] That first slaughter which Jonathan and his armorbearer made was about twenty men within about half an acre of land.

[15] And there was trembling in the camp, in the field, and among all the people. The garrison and the raiders also trembled; and the earth quaked, so that it was a very great trembling. [16] Now the

Divert the Ice Cream Man

Whenever I am afraid, I will trust in You.

Psalm 56:3

Sally was trying desperately to save all the pennies she could for the doll carriage she wanted to buy. She was turning in aluminum cans, offering to do extra chores — anything to make a few more cents each week.

One night as she was saying her bedtime prayers, Sally's mother overheard her say in great earnest, "O Lord, please help me to save my money for the doll carriage in Mr. Brown's store window. It's so beautiful and I want it so much. It's just right for my doll. And I'd be sure to let my friends play with it too."

Pleased at her daughter's prayer, Sally's mother was startled to hear the final line of the prayer. "And please God, don't let the ice cream man come down our street this week!"

Just as we are each unique in our talents, abilities, and experiences, we are also unique in our temptations. What is tempting to one person may not be at all tempting to another.

Although the enemy of our souls knows our weaknesses, we know where to find our strength — in Jesus. As we stick close to Him, when temptation comes, we can draw on His strength to turn from it.

Always say "yes" to Jesus, and saying "no" to temptation becomes easier!

watchmen of Saul in Gibeah of Benjamin looked, and *there* was the multitude, melting away; and they went here and there. [17] Then Saul said to the people who *were* with him, "Now call the roll and see who has gone from us." And when they had called the roll, surprisingly, Jonathan and his armorbearer *were* not *there*. [18] And Saul said to Ahijah, "Bring the ark of God here" (for at that time the ark of God was with the children of Israel). [19] Now it happened, while Saul talked to the priest, that the noise which *was* in the camp of the Philistines continued to increase; so Saul said to the priest, "Withdraw your hand." [20] Then Saul and all the people who *were* with him assembled, and they went to the battle; and indeed every man's sword was against his neighbor, *and there was* very great confusion. [21] Moreover the Hebrews *who* were with the Philistines before that time, who went up with them into the camp *from the* surrounding *country,* they also joined the Israelites who *were* with Saul and Jonathan. [22] Likewise all the men of Israel who had hidden in the mountains of Ephraim, *when* they heard that the Philistines fled, they also followed hard after them in the battle. [23] So the LORD saved Israel that day, and the battle shifted to Beth Aven.

[24] And the men of Israel were distressed that day, for Saul had placed the people under oath, saying, "Cursed *is* the man who eats *any* food until evening, before I have taken vengeance on my enemies." So none of the people tasted food. [25] Now all *the people* of the land came to a forest; and there was honey on the ground. [26] And when the people had come into the woods, there was the honey, dripping; but no one put his hand to his mouth, for the people feared the oath. [27] But Jonathan had not heard his father charge the people with the oath; therefore he stretched out the end of the rod that *was* in his hand and dipped it in a honeycomb, and put his hand to his mouth; and his countenance brightened. [28] Then one of the people said, "Your father strictly charged the people with an oath, saying, 'Cursed *is* the man who eats food this day.' " And the people were faint.

[29] But Jonathan said, "My father has troubled the land. Look now, how my countenance has brightened because I tasted a little of this honey. [30] How much better if the people had eaten freely today of the spoil of their enemies which they found! For now would there not have been a much greater slaughter among the Philistines?"

[31] Now they had driven back the Philistines that day from Michmash to Aijalon. So the people were very faint. [32] And the people rushed on the spoil, and took sheep, oxen, and calves, and slaughtered *them* on the ground; and the people ate *them* with the blood. [33] Then they told Saul, saying, "Look, the people are sinning against the LORD by eating with the blood!"

So he said, "You have dealt treacherously; roll a large stone to me this day." [34] Then Saul said, "Disperse yourselves among the people, and say to them, 'Bring me here every man's ox and every man's sheep, slaughter *them* here, and eat; and do not sin against the LORD by eating with the blood.' " So every one of the people brought his ox with him that night, and slaughtered *it* there. [35] Then Saul built an altar to the LORD. This was the first altar that he built to the LORD.

[36] Now Saul said, "Let us go down after the Philistines by night, and plunder them until the morning light; and let us not leave a man of them."

And they said, "Do whatever seems good to you."

Then the priest said, "Let us draw near to God here."

[37] So Saul asked counsel of God, "Shall I go down after the Philistines? Will You deliver them into the hand of Israel?" But He did not answer him that day. [38] And Saul said, "Come over here, all you chiefs of the people, and know and see what this sin was today. [39] For *as* the LORD lives, who saves Israel, though it be in Jonathan my son, he shall surely die." But not a man among all the people answered him. [40] Then he said to all Israel, "You be on one side, and my son Jonathan and I will be on the other side."

And the people said to Saul, "Do what seems good to you."

[41] Therefore Saul said to the LORD God of Israel, "Give a perfect *lot*." So Saul and Jonathan were taken, but the people

escaped. ⁴² And Saul said, "Cast *lots* between my son Jonathan and me." So Jonathan was taken. ⁴³ Then Saul said to Jonathan, "Tell me what you have done."

And Jonathan told him, and said, "I only tasted a little honey with the end of the rod that *was* in my hand. So now I must die!"

⁴⁴ Saul answered, "God do so and more also; for you shall surely die, Jonathan."

⁴⁵ But the people said to Saul, "Shall Jonathan die, who has accomplished this great deliverance in Israel? Certainly not! *As* the LORD lives, not one hair of his head shall fall to the ground, for he has worked with God this day." So the people rescued Jonathan, and he did not die.

⁴⁶ Then Saul returned from pursuing the Philistines, and the Philistines went to their own place.

⁴⁷ So Saul established his sovereignty over Israel, and fought against all his enemies on every side, against Moab, against the people of Ammon, against Edom, against the kings of Zobah, and against the Philistines. Wherever he turned, he harassed *them*. ⁴⁸ And he gathered an army and attacked the Amalekites, and delivered Israel from the hands of those who plundered them.

⁴⁹ The sons of Saul were Jonathan, Jishui, and Malchishua. And the names of his two daughters *were these:* the name of the firstborn Merab, and the name of the younger Michal. ⁵⁰ The name of Saul's wife *was* Ahinoam the daughter of Ahimaaz. And the name of the commander of his army *was* Abner the son of Ner, Saul's uncle. ⁵¹ Kish *was* the father of Saul, and Ner the father of Abner *was* the son of Abiel.

⁵² Now there was fierce war with the Philistines all the days of Saul. And when Saul saw any strong man or any valiant man, he took him for himself.

15

Samuel also said to Saul, "The LORD sent me to anoint you king over His people, over Israel. Now therefore, heed the voice of the words of the LORD. ² Thus says the LORD of hosts: 'I will punish Amalek *for* what he did to Israel, how he ambushed him on the way when he came up from Egypt. ³ Now go and attack Amalek, and utterly destroy all that they have, and do not spare them. But kill both man and woman, infant and nursing child, ox and sheep, camel and donkey.' "

⁴ So Saul gathered the people together and numbered them in Telaim, two hundred thousand foot soldiers and ten thousand men of Judah. ⁵ And Saul came to a city of Amalek, and lay in wait in the valley.

⁶ Then Saul said to the Kenites, "Go, depart, get down from among the Amalekites, lest I destroy you with them. For you showed kindness to all the children of Israel when they came up out of Egypt." So the Kenites departed from among the Amalekites. ⁷ And Saul attacked the Amalekites, from Havilah all the way to Shur, which is east of Egypt. ⁸ He also took Agag king of the Amalekites alive, and utterly destroyed all the people with the edge of the sword. ⁹ But Saul and the people spared Agag and the best of the sheep, the oxen, the fatlings, the lambs, and all *that was* good, and were unwilling to utterly destroy them. But everything despised and worthless, that they utterly destroyed.

¹⁰ Now the word of the LORD came to Samuel, saying, ¹¹ "I greatly regret that I have set up Saul *as* king, for he has turned back from following Me, and has not performed My commandments." And it grieved Samuel, and he cried out to the LORD all night. ¹² So when Samuel rose early in the morning to meet Saul, it was told Samuel, saying, "Saul went to Carmel, and indeed, he set up a monument for himself; and he has gone on around, passed by, and gone down to Gilgal." ¹³ Then Samuel went to Saul, and Saul said to him, "Blessed *are* you of the LORD! I have performed the commandment of the LORD."

¹⁴ But Samuel said, "What then *is* this bleating of the sheep in my ears, and the lowing of the oxen which I hear?"

¹⁵ And Saul said, "They have brought them from the Amalekites; for the people spared the best of the sheep and the oxen, to sacrifice to the LORD your God; and the rest we have utterly destroyed."

¹⁶ Then Samuel said to Saul, "Be quiet! And I will tell you what the LORD said to me last night."

And he said to him, "Speak on."

17 So Samuel said, "When you *were* little in your own eyes, *were* you not head of the tribes of Israel? And did not the LORD anoint you king over Israel? 18 Now the LORD sent you on a mission, and said, 'Go, and utterly destroy the sinners, the Amalekites, and fight against them until they are consumed.' 19 Why then did you not obey the voice of the LORD? Why did you swoop down on the spoil, and do evil in the sight of the LORD?"

20 And Saul said to Samuel, "But I have obeyed the voice of the LORD, and gone on the mission on which the LORD sent me, and brought back Agag king of Amalek; I have utterly destroyed the Amalekites. 21 But the people took of the plunder, sheep and oxen, the best of the things which should have been utterly destroyed, to sacrifice to the LORD your God in Gilgal."

22 So Samuel said:

"Has the LORD *as great* delight in
      burnt offerings and sacrifices,
As in obeying the voice of the
      LORD?
Behold, to obey is better than
      sacrifice,
And to heed than the fat of rams.
23 For rebellion *is as* the sin of
      witchcraft,
And stubbornness *is as* iniquity
      and idolatry.
Because you have rejected the
      word of the LORD,
He also has rejected you from
      being king."

24 Then Saul said to Samuel, "I have sinned, for I have transgressed the commandment of the LORD and your words, because I feared the people and obeyed their voice. 25 Now therefore, please pardon my sin, and return with me, that I may worship the LORD." 26 But Samuel said to Saul, "I will not return with you, for you have rejected the word of the LORD, and the LORD has rejected you from being king over Israel." 27 And as Samuel turned around to go away, *Saul* seized the edge of his robe, and it tore. 28 So Samuel said to him, "The LORD has torn the kingdom of Israel from you today, and has given it to a neighbor

of yours, *who is* better than you. 29 And also the Strength of Israel will not lie nor relent. For He *is* not a man, that He should relent."

30 Then he said, "I have sinned; *yet* honor me now, please, before the elders of my people and before Israel, and return with me, that I may worship the LORD your God." 31 So Samuel turned back after Saul, and Saul worshiped the LORD.

32 Then Samuel said, "Bring Agag king of the Amalekites here to me." So Agag came to him cautiously.

And Agag said, "Surely the bitterness of death is past."

33 But Samuel said, "As your sword has made women childless, so shall your mother be childless among women." And Samuel hacked Agag in pieces before the LORD in Gilgal.

34 Then Samuel went to Ramah, and Saul went up to his house at Gibeah of Saul. 35 And Samuel went no more to see Saul until the day of his death. Nevertheless Samuel mourned for Saul, and the LORD regretted that He had made Saul king over Israel.

~ PSALM 57:1–3 ~

1 Be merciful to me, O God, be
      merciful to me!
For my soul trusts in You;
And in the shadow of Your wings I
      will make my refuge,
Until *these* calamities have passed by.

2 I will cry out to God Most High,
To God who performs *all things* for
      me.
3 He shall send from heaven and save
      me;
He reproaches the one who would
      swallow me up.   Selah
God shall send forth His mercy and
      His truth.

~ PROVERBS 15:24, 25 ~

24 The way of life *winds* upward for
      the wise,
That he may turn away from hell
      below.

²⁵ The LORD will destroy the house of
the proud,
But He will establish the boundary
of the widow.

∼ LUKE 23:1–25 ∼

Then the whole multitude of them arose
and led Him to Pilate. ² And they began
to accuse Him, saying, "We found this
fellow perverting the nation, and forbidding to pay taxes to Caesar, saying that
He Himself is Christ, a King."

³ Then Pilate asked Him, saying, "Are
You the King of the Jews?"

He answered him and said, "*It is as* you
say."

⁴ So Pilate said to the chief priests and
the crowd, "I find no fault in this Man."

⁵ But they were the more fierce, say-
ing, "He stirs up the people, teaching
throughout all Judea, beginning from
Galilee to this place."

⁶ When Pilate heard of Galilee, he asked
if the Man were a Galilean. ⁷ And as soon
as he knew that He belonged to Herod's
jurisdiction, he sent Him to Herod, who
was also in Jerusalem at that time. ⁸ Now
when Herod saw Jesus, he was exceed-
ingly glad; for he had desired for a long
time to see Him, because he had heard
many things about Him, and he hoped to
see some miracle done by Him. ⁹ Then he
questioned Him with many words, but
He answered him nothing. ¹⁰ And the chief
priests and scribes stood and vehemently
accused Him. ¹¹ Then Herod, with his
men of war, treated Him with contempt
and mocked *Him,* arrayed Him in a gor-
geous robe, and sent Him back to Pilate.

¹² That very day Pilate and Herod became
friends with each other, for previously
they had been at enmity with each other.

¹³ Then Pilate, when he had called to-
gether the chief priests, the rulers, and the
people, ¹⁴ said to them, "You have brought
this Man to me, as one who misleads the
people. And indeed, having examined
Him in your presence, I have found no
fault in this Man concerning those things
of which you accuse Him; ¹⁵ no, neither
did Herod, for I sent you back to him;
and indeed nothing deserving of death has
been done by Him. ¹⁶ I will therefore chastise Him and release *Him*" ¹⁷(for it was
necessary for him to release one to them
at the feast).

¹⁸ And they all cried out at once, say-
ing, "Away with this *Man,* and release to
us Barabbas"— ¹⁹ who had been thrown
into prison for a certain rebellion made
in the city, and for murder.

²⁰ Pilate, therefore, wishing to release
Jesus, again called out to them. ²¹ But they
shouted, saying, "Crucify *Him,* crucify
Him!"

²² Then he said to them the third time,
"Why, what evil has He done? I have
found no reason for death in Him. I
will therefore chastise Him and let *Him*
go."

²³ But they were insistent, demanding
with loud voices that He be crucified. And
the voices of these men and of the chief
priests prevailed. ²⁴ So Pilate gave sentence
that it should be as they requested. ²⁵ And
he released to them the one they re-
quested, who for rebellion and murder
had been thrown into prison; but he delivered Jesus to their will.

READING 127 · MAY 7

∼ 1 SAMUEL 16:1—17:58 ∼

Now the LORD said to Samuel,
"How long will you mourn for
Saul, seeing I have rejected him
from reigning over Israel? Fill your horn
with oil, and go; I am sending you to Jes-

se the Bethlehemite. For I have provided
Myself a king among his sons."

² And Samuel said, "How can I go? If
Saul hears *it,* he will kill me."

But the LORD said, "Take a heifer with

you, and say, 'I have come to sacrifice to the LORD.' ³ Then invite Jesse to the sacrifice, and I will show you what you shall do; you shall anoint for Me the one I name to you."

⁴ So Samuel did what the LORD said, and went to Bethlehem. And the elders of the town trembled at his coming, and said, "Do you come peaceably?"

⁵ And he said, "Peaceably; I have come to sacrifice to the LORD. Sanctify yourselves, and come with me to the sacrifice." Then he consecrated Jesse and his sons, and invited them to the sacrifice.

⁶ So it was, when they came, that he looked at Eliab and said, "Surely the LORD's anointed *is* before Him!"

⁷ But the LORD said to Samuel, "Do not look at his appearance or at his physical stature, because I have refused him. For *the LORD does* not *see* as man sees; for man looks at the outward appearance, but the LORD looks at the heart."

⁸ So Jesse called Abinadab, and made him pass before Samuel. And he said, "Neither has the LORD chosen this one." ⁹ Then Jesse made Shammah pass by. And he said, "Neither has the LORD chosen this one." ¹⁰ Thus Jesse made seven of his sons pass before Samuel. And Samuel said to Jesse, "The LORD has not chosen these." ¹¹ And Samuel said to Jesse, "Are all the young men here?" Then he said, "There remains yet the youngest, and there he is, keeping the sheep."

And Samuel said to Jesse, "Send and bring him. For we will not sit down till he comes here." ¹² So he sent and brought him in. Now he *was* ruddy, with bright eyes, and good-looking. And the LORD said, "Arise, anoint him; for this *is* the one!" ¹³ Then Samuel took the horn of oil and anointed him in the midst of his brothers; and the Spirit of the LORD came upon David from that day forward. So Samuel arose and went to Ramah.

¹⁴ But the Spirit of the LORD departed from Saul, and a distressing spirit from the LORD troubled him. ¹⁵ And Saul's servants said to him, "Surely, a distressing spirit from God is troubling you. ¹⁶ Let our master now command your servants, who *are* before you, to seek out a man *who is* a skillful player on the harp. And it shall be that he will play it with his

hand when the distressing spirit from God is upon you, and you shall be well."

¹⁷ So Saul said to his servants, "Provide me now a man who can play well, and bring *him* to me."

¹⁸ Then one of the servants answered and said, "Look, I have seen a son of Jesse the Bethlehemite, *who is* skillful in playing, a mighty man of valor, a man of war, prudent in speech, and a handsome person; and the LORD *is* with him."

¹⁹ Therefore Saul sent messengers to Jesse, and said, "Send me your son David, who *is* with the sheep." ²⁰ And Jesse took a donkey *loaded with* bread, a skin of wine, and a young goat, and sent *them* by his son David to Saul. ²¹ So David came to Saul and stood before him. And he loved him greatly, and he became his armorbearer. ²² Then Saul sent to Jesse, saying, "Please let David stand before me, for he has found favor in my sight." ²³ And so it was, whenever the spirit from God was upon Saul, that David would take a harp and play *it* with his hand. Then Saul would become refreshed and well, and the distressing spirit would depart from him.

17 Now the Philistines gathered their armies together to battle, and were gathered at Sochoh, which *belongs* to Judah; they encamped between Sochoh and Azekah, in Ephes Dammim. ² And Saul and the men of Israel were gathered together, and they encamped in the Valley of Elah, and drew up in battle array against the Philistines. ³ The Philistines stood on a mountain on one side, and Israel stood on a mountain on the other side, with a valley between them.

⁴ And a champion went out from the camp of the Philistines, named Goliath, from Gath, whose height *was* six cubits and a span. ⁵ *He had* a bronze helmet on his head, and he *was* armed with a coat of mail, and the weight of the coat *was* five thousand shekels of bronze. ⁶ And *he had* bronze armor on his legs and a bronze javelin between his shoulders. ⁷ Now the staff of his spear *was* like a weaver's beam, and his iron spearhead *weighed* six hundred shekels; and a shield-bearer went before him. ⁸ Then he stood and cried out to the armies of Israel, and said to them, "Why have you come out to line up for

Doing the Right Thing

During the Great Depression, Debbie and her family lived with her grandparents because her father couldn't find work. She slept in a bed with four other relatives and survived by eating jackrabbits caught on the Texas plains. When she was seven, her family moved to California and at age sixteen, she won the Miss Burbank contest, which led to a part in a movie.

As an adult, her first marriage ended in a bitter divorce, so she raised her two children alone. Her second marriage to a millionaire shoe manufacturer ended when his financial gambles brought an end to his business. He left her with millions of dollars of debt. Everything she owned was repossessed, including her home. Determined to pay back the debts and properly care for her family, she went on the road doing live theater. It took her more than ten years, working forty weeks a year, to pay back the debts of her ex-husband. But she did it.

Now out of debt and living in a home that is paid for, Debbie Reynolds has a satisfaction that only "doing the right thing" can produce.

Successful people accept responsibility for their mistakes, and learn from their experiences. And most importantly, they never give up.

> My heart is steadfast, O God, my heart is steadfast; I will sing and give praise.
>
> *Psalm* 57:7

battle? *Am* I not a Philistine, and you the servants of Saul? Choose a man for yourselves, and let him come down to me. [9] If he is able to fight with me and kill me, then we will be your servants. But if I prevail against him and kill him, then you shall be our servants and serve us." [10] And the Philistine said, "I defy the armies of Israel this day; give me a man, that we may fight together." [11] When Saul and all Israel heard these words of the Philistine, they were dismayed and greatly afraid.

[12] Now David *was* the son of that Ephrathite of Bethlehem Judah, whose name *was* Jesse, and who had eight sons. And the man was old, advanced *in years,* in the days of Saul. [13] The three oldest sons of Jesse had gone to follow Saul to the battle. The names of his three sons who went to the battle *were* Eliab the firstborn, next to him Abinadab, and the third Shammah. [14] David *was* the youngest. And the three oldest followed Saul. [15] But David occasionally went and returned from Saul to feed his father's sheep at Bethlehem.

[16] And the Philistine drew near and presented himself forty days, morning and evening.

[17] Then Jesse said to his son David, "Take now for your brothers an ephah of this dried *grain* and these ten loaves, and run to your brothers at the camp. [18] And carry these ten cheeses to the captain of *their* thousand, and see how your brothers fare, and bring back news of them." [19] Now Saul and they and all the men of Israel *were* in the Valley of Elah, fighting with the Philistines.

[20] So David rose early in the morning, left the sheep with a keeper, and took *the things* and went as Jesse had commanded him. And he came to the camp as the army was going out to the fight and shouting for the battle. [21] For Israel and the Philistines had drawn up in battle array, army against army. [22] And David left his supplies in the hand of the supply keeper, ran to the army, and came and greeted his brothers. [23] Then as he talked with them, there was the champion, the Philistine of Gath, Goliath by name, coming up from the armies of the Philistines; and he spoke according to the same words. So David heard *them.* [24] And all the men of Israel,

when they saw the man, fled from him and were dreadfully afraid. [25] So the men of Israel said, "Have you seen this man who has come up? Surely he has come up to defy Israel; and it shall be *that* the man who kills him the king will enrich with great riches, will give him his daughter, and give his father's house exemption *from taxes* in Israel."

[26] Then David spoke to the men who stood by him, saying, "What shall be done for the man who kills this Philistine and takes away the reproach from Israel? For who *is* this uncircumcised Philistine, that he should defy the armies of the living God?"

[27] And the people answered him in this manner, saying, "So shall it be done for the man who kills him."

[28] Now Eliab his oldest brother heard when he spoke to the men; and Eliab's anger was aroused against David, and he said, "Why did you come down here? And with whom have you left those few sheep in the wilderness? I know your pride and the insolence of your heart, for you have come down to see the battle."

[29] And David said, "What have I done now? *Is there* not a cause?" [30] Then he turned from him toward another and said the same thing; and these people answered him as the first ones *did.*

[31] Now when the words which David spoke were heard, they reported *them* to Saul; and he sent for him. [32] Then David said to Saul, "Let no man's heart fail because of him; your servant will go and fight with this Philistine."

[33] And Saul said to David, "You are not able to go against this Philistine to fight with him; for you *are* a youth, and he a man of war from his youth."

[34] But David said to Saul, "Your servant used to keep his father's sheep, and when a lion or a bear came and took a lamb out of the flock, [35] I went out after it and struck it, and delivered *the lamb* from its mouth; and when it arose against me, I caught *it* by its beard, and struck and killed it. [36] Your servant has killed both lion and bear; and this uncircumcised Philistine will be like one of them, seeing he has defied the armies of the living God." [37] Moreover David said, "The LORD, who delivered me from the paw of the lion and

from the paw of the bear, He will deliver me from the hand of this Philistine."

And Saul said to David, "Go, and the LORD be with you!"

³⁸ So Saul clothed David with his armor, and he put a bronze helmet on his head; he also clothed him with a coat of mail. ³⁹ David fastened his sword to his armor and tried to walk, for he had not tested *them*. And David said to Saul, "I cannot walk with these, for I have not tested *them*." So David took them off.

⁴⁰ Then he took his staff in his hand; and he chose for himself five smooth stones from the brook, and put them in a shepherd's bag, in a pouch which he had, and his sling was in his hand. And he drew near to the Philistine. ⁴¹ So the Philistine came, and began drawing near to David, and the man who bore the shield *went* before him. ⁴² And when the Philistine looked about and saw David, he disdained him; for he was *only* a youth, ruddy and good-looking. ⁴³ So the Philistine said to David, "*Am* I a dog, that you come to me with sticks?" And the Philistine cursed David by his gods. ⁴⁴ And the Philistine said to David, "Come to me, and I will give your flesh to the birds of the air and the beasts of the field!"

⁴⁵ Then David said to the Philistine, "You come to me with a sword, with a spear, and with a javelin. But I come to you in the name of the LORD of hosts, the God of the armies of Israel, whom you have defied. ⁴⁶ This day the LORD will deliver you into my hand, and I will strike you and take your head from you. And this day I will give the carcasses of the camp of the Philistines to the birds of the air and the wild beasts of the earth, that all the earth may know that there is a God in Israel. ⁴⁷ Then all this assembly shall know that the LORD does not save with sword and spear; for the battle *is* the LORD's, and He will give you into our hands."

⁴⁸ So it was, when the Philistine arose and came and drew near to meet David, that David hurried and ran toward the army to meet the Philistine. ⁴⁹ Then David put his hand in his bag and took out a stone; and he slung *it* and struck the Philistine in his forehead, so that the stone sank into his forehead, and he fell on his face to the earth. ⁵⁰ So David prevailed over the Philistine with a sling and a stone, and struck the Philistine and killed him. But *there was* no sword in the hand of David. ⁵¹ Therefore David ran and stood over the Philistine, took his sword and drew it out of its sheath and killed him, and cut off his head with it.

And when the Philistines saw that their champion was dead, they fled. ⁵² Now the men of Israel and Judah arose and shouted, and pursued the Philistines as far as the entrance of the valley and to the gates of Ekron. And the wounded of the Philistines fell along the road to Shaaraim, even as far as Gath and Ekron. ⁵³ Then the children of Israel returned from chasing the Philistines, and they plundered their tents. ⁵⁴ And David took the head of the Philistine and brought it to Jerusalem, but he put his armor in his tent.

⁵⁵ When Saul saw David going out against the Philistine, he said to Abner, the commander of the army, "Abner, whose son *is* this youth?"

And Abner said, "As your soul lives, O king, I do not know."

⁵⁶ So the king said, "Inquire whose son this young man *is*."

⁵⁷ Then, as David returned from the slaughter of the Philistine, Abner took him and brought him before Saul with the head of the Philistine in his hand. ⁵⁸ And Saul said to him, "Whose son *are* you, young man?"

So David answered, "*I am* the son of your servant Jesse the Bethlehemite."

∼ PSALM 57:4–11 ∼

⁴ My soul *is* among lions;
   I lie *among* the sons of men
   Who are set on fire,
   Whose teeth *are* spears and arrows,
   And their tongue a sharp sword.
⁵ Be exalted, O God, above the
      heavens;
   Let Your glory *be* above all the earth.

⁶ They have prepared a net for my
      steps;
   My soul is bowed down;
   They have dug a pit before me;

Into the midst of it they *themselves*
have fallen.   Selah

7 My heart is steadfast, O God, my
      heart is steadfast;
   I will sing and give praise.
8 Awake, my glory!
   Awake, lute and harp!
   I will awaken the dawn.

9 I will praise You, O Lord, among the
      peoples;
   I will sing to You among the nations.
10 For Your mercy reaches unto the
      heavens,
   And Your truth unto the clouds.

11 Be exalted, O God, above the
      heavens;
   Let Your glory *be* above all the earth.

~ PROVERBS 15:26 ~

26 The thoughts of the wicked *are* an
      abomination to the LORD,
   But *the words* of the pure *are*
      pleasant.

~ LUKE 23:26–56 ~

Now as they led Him away, they laid hold
of a certain man, Simon a Cyrenian, who
was coming from the country, and on him
they laid the cross that he might bear *it*
after Jesus.
   27 And a great multitude of the people
followed Him, and women who also
mourned and lamented Him. 28 But Jesus,
turning to them, said, "Daughters of
Jerusalem, do not weep for Me, but weep
for yourselves and for your children. 29 For
indeed the days are coming in which they
will say, 'Blessed *are* the barren, wombs
that never bore, and breasts which never
nursed!' 30 Then they will begin 'to say to
the mountains, "Fall on us!" and to the
hills, "Cover us!" ' 31 For if they do these
things in the green wood, what will be
done in the dry?"
   32 There were also two others, criminals, led with Him to be put to death.
33 And when they had come to the place
called Calvary, there they crucified Him,
and the criminals, one on the right
hand and the other on the left. 34 Then
Jesus said, "Father, forgive them, for they
do not know what they do."
   And they divided His garments and cast
lots. 35 And the people stood looking on.
But even the rulers with them sneered,
saying, "He saved others; let Him save
Himself if He is the Christ, the chosen of
God."
   36 The soldiers also mocked Him, coming and offering Him sour wine, 37 and
saying, "If You are the King of the Jews,
save Yourself."
   38 And an inscription also was written
over Him in letters of Greek, Latin, and
Hebrew:

THIS IS THE KING OF THE JEWS.

   39 Then one of the criminals who were
hanged blasphemed Him, saying, "If You
are the Christ, save Yourself and us."
   40 But the other, answering, rebuked
him, saying, "Do you not even fear God,
seeing you are under the same condemnation? 41 And we indeed justly, for we
receive the due reward of our deeds; but
this Man has done nothing wrong."
42 Then he said to Jesus, "Lord, remember me when You come into Your
kingdom."
   43 And Jesus said to him, "Assuredly, I
say to you, today you will be with Me in
Paradise."
   44 Now it was about the sixth hour, and
there was darkness over all the earth until the ninth hour. 45 Then the sun was
darkened, and the veil of the temple
was torn in two. 46 And when Jesus had
cried out with a loud voice, He said, "Father, 'into Your hands I commit My
spirit.' " Having said this, He breathed His
last.
   47 So when the centurion saw what had
happened, he glorified God, saying, "Certainly this was a righteous Man!"
   48 And the whole crowd who came together to that sight, seeing what had been
done, beat their breasts and returned.
49 But all His acquaintances, and the
women who followed Him from Galilee,
stood at a distance, watching these things.
   50 Now behold, *there was* a man named
Joseph, a council member, a good and just

man. ⁵¹ He had not consented to their decision and deed. *He was* from Arimathea, a city of the Jews, who himself was also waiting for the kingdom of God. ⁵² This man went to Pilate and asked for the body of Jesus. ⁵³ Then he took it down, wrapped it in linen, and laid it in a tomb *that was* hewn out of the rock, where no one had ever lain before. ⁵⁴ That day was the Preparation, and the Sabbath drew near.

⁵⁵ And the women who had come with Him from Galilee followed after, and they observed the tomb and how His body was laid. ⁵⁶ Then they returned and prepared spices and fragrant oils. And they rested on the Sabbath according to the commandment.

~ 1 Samuel 18:1—19:24 ~

Now when he had finished speaking to Saul, the soul of Jonathan was knit to the soul of David, and Jonathan loved him as his own soul. ² Saul took him that day, and would not let him go home to his father's house anymore. ³ Then Jonathan and David made a covenant, because he loved him as his own soul. ⁴ And Jonathan took off the robe that *was* on him and gave it to David, with his armor, even to his sword and his bow and his belt.

⁵ So David went out wherever Saul sent him, *and* behaved wisely. And Saul set him over the men of war, and he was accepted in the sight of all the people and also in the sight of Saul's servants. ⁶ Now it had happened as they were coming *home,* when David was returning from the slaughter of the Philistine, that the women had come out of all the cities of Israel, singing and dancing, to meet King Saul, with tambourines, with joy, and with musical instruments. ⁷ So the women sang as they danced, and said:

"Saul has slain his thousands,
And David his ten thousands."

⁸ Then Saul was very angry, and the saying displeased him; and he said, "They have ascribed to David ten thousands, and to me they have ascribed *only* thousands. Now *what* more can he have but the kingdom?" ⁹ So Saul eyed David from that day forward.

¹⁰ And it happened on the next day that the distressing spirit from God came upon Saul, and he prophesied inside the house. So David played *music* with his hand, as at other times; but *there was* a spear in Saul's hand. ¹¹ And Saul cast the spear, for he said, "I will pin David to the wall!" But David escaped his presence twice.

¹² Now Saul was afraid of David, because the LORD was with him, but had departed from Saul. ¹³ Therefore Saul removed him from his presence, and made him his captain over a thousand; and he went out and came in before the people. ¹⁴ And David behaved wisely in all his ways, and the LORD *was* with him. ¹⁵ Therefore, when Saul saw that he behaved very wisely, he was afraid of him. ¹⁶ But all Israel and Judah loved David, because he went out and came in before them.

¹⁷ Then Saul said to David, "Here is my older daughter Merab; I will give her to you as a wife. Only be valiant for me, and fight the LORD's battles." For Saul thought, "Let my hand not be against him, but let the hand of the Philistines be against him."

¹⁸ So David said to Saul, "Who *am* I, and what *is* my life or my father's family in Israel, that I should be son-in-law to the king?" ¹⁹ But it happened at the time when Merab, Saul's daughter, should have been given to David, that she was given to Adriel the Meholathite as a wife.

²⁰ Now Michal, Saul's daughter, loved David. And they told Saul, and the thing pleased him. ²¹ So Saul said, "I will give her to him, that she may be a snare to him, and that the hand of the Philistines may be against him." Therefore Saul said to David a second time, "You shall be my son-in-law today."

²² And Saul commanded his servants,

"Communicate with David secretly, and say, 'Look, the king has delight in you, and all his servants love you. Now therefore, become the king's son-in-law.' "

²³ So Saul's servants spoke those words in the hearing of David. And David said, "Does it seem to you *a* light *thing* to be a king's son-in-law, seeing I *am* a poor and lightly esteemed man?" ²⁴ And the servants of Saul told him, saying, "In this manner David spoke."

²⁵ Then Saul said, "Thus you shall say to David: 'The king does not desire any dowry but one hundred foreskins of the Philistines, to take vengeance on the king's enemies.' " But Saul thought to make David fall by the hand of the Philistines. ²⁶ So when his servants told David these words, it pleased David well to become the king's son-in-law. Now the days had not expired; ²⁷ therefore David arose and went, he and his men, and killed two hundred men of the Philistines. And David brought their foreskins, and they gave them in full count to the king, that he might become the king's son-in-law. Then Saul gave him Michal his daughter as a wife.

²⁸ Thus Saul saw and knew that the LORD *was* with David, and *that* Michal, Saul's daughter, loved him; ²⁹ and Saul was still more afraid of David. So Saul became David's enemy continually. ³⁰ Then the princes of the Philistines went out *to war.* And so it was, whenever they went out, *that* David behaved more wisely than all the servants of Saul, so that his name became highly esteemed.

19 Now Saul spoke to Jonathan his son and to all his servants, that they should kill David; but Jonathan, Saul's son, delighted greatly in David. ² So Jonathan told David, saying, "My father Saul seeks to kill you. Therefore please be on your guard until morning, and stay in a secret *place* and hide. ³ And I will go out and stand beside my father in the field where you *are,* and I will speak with my father about you. Then what I observe, I will tell you."

⁴ Thus Jonathan spoke well of David to Saul his father, and said to him, "Let not the king sin against his servant, against David, because he has not sinned against you, and because his works *have been* very good toward you. ⁵ For he took his life in his hands and killed the Philistine, and the LORD brought about a great deliverance for all Israel. You saw *it* and rejoiced. Why then will you sin against innocent blood, to kill David without a cause?"

⁶ So Saul heeded the voice of Jonathan, and Saul swore, "*As* the LORD lives, he shall not be killed." ⁷ Then Jonathan called David, and Jonathan told him all these things. So Jonathan brought David to Saul, and he was in his presence as in times past.

⁸ And there was war again; and David went out and fought with the Philistines, and struck them with a mighty blow, and they fled from him.

⁹ Now the distressing spirit from the LORD came upon Saul as he sat in his house with his spear in his hand. And David was playing *music* with *his* hand. ¹⁰ Then Saul sought to pin David to the wall with the spear, but he slipped away from Saul's presence; and he drove the spear into the wall. So David fled and escaped that night.

¹¹ Saul also sent messengers to David's house to watch him and to kill him in the morning. And Michal, David's wife, told him, saying, "If you do not save your life tonight, tomorrow you will be killed." ¹² So Michal let David down through a window. And he went and fled and escaped. ¹³ And Michal took an image and laid *it* in the bed, put a cover of goats' *hair* for his head, and covered *it* with clothes. ¹⁴ So when Saul sent messengers to take David, she said, "He *is* sick."

¹⁵ Then Saul sent the messengers *back* to see David, saying, "Bring him up to me in the bed, that I may kill him." ¹⁶ And when the messengers had come in, there was the image in the bed, with a cover of goats' *hair* for his head. ¹⁷ Then Saul said to Michal, "Why have you deceived me like this, and sent my enemy away, so that he has escaped?"

And Michal answered Saul, "He said to me, 'Let me go! Why should I kill you?' "

¹⁸ So David fled and escaped, and went to Samuel at Ramah, and told him all that Saul had done to him. And he and Samuel went and stayed in Naioth. ¹⁹ Now it was

A Reason to Laugh

Peggy was nervous about the upcoming dinner party she and her husband were hosting. It was their first time to have guests for dinner since the birth of their son, Pete. To top off Peggy's tension, one of the guests was her husband Bill's new supervisor.

Sensing the tension in his parents, the baby became irritable and "fussy," which only added to Peggy's frustration. In an attempt to comfort little Pete, Peggy picked him up, raised him high over her head, and kissed his bare tummy. To her surprise, he smiled and giggled — the first genuine laughter she had heard from her young son.

In an instant, the evening took on an entirely new tenor. Peggy became more relaxed, and Baby Pete relaxed as well. The dinner party was a great success.

Can the laughter of a small child change a day? Yes! So can laughter shared between adults, or a chuckle prompted by the memory of a funny event.

When you're feeling "stressed out," don't allow yourself to explode in anger. Get alone if you have to, but find a reason to laugh, and watch the stress melt away!

told Saul, saying, "Take note, David *is* at Naioth in Ramah!" 20 Then Saul sent messengers to take David. And when they saw the group of prophets prophesying, and Samuel standing *as* leader over them, the Spirit of God came upon the messengers of Saul, and they also prophesied. 21 And when Saul was told, he sent other messengers, and they prophesied likewise. Then Saul sent messengers again the third time, and they prophesied also. 22 Then he also went to Ramah, and came to the great well that *is* at Sechu. So he asked, and said, "Where *are* Samuel and David?"

And *someone* said, "Indeed *they are* at Naioth in Ramah." 23 So he went there to Naioth in Ramah. Then the Spirit of God was upon him also, and he went on and prophesied until he came to Naioth in Ramah. 24 And he also stripped off his clothes and prophesied before Samuel in like manner, and lay down naked all that day and all that night. Therefore they say, "*Is* Saul also among the prophets?"

~ PSALM 58:1–11 ~

1 Do you indeed speak righteousness, you silent ones?
Do you judge uprightly, you sons of men?
2 No, in heart you work wickedness;
You weigh out the violence of your hands in the earth.

3 The wicked are estranged from the womb;
They go astray as soon as they are born, speaking lies.
4 Their poison *is* like the poison of a serpent;
They are like the deaf cobra *that* stops its ear,
5 Which will not heed the voice of charmers,
Charming ever so skillfully.

6 Break their teeth in their mouth, O God!
Break out the fangs of the young lions, O LORD!
7 Let them flow away as waters *which* run continually;
When he bends *his bow,*
Let his arrows be as if cut in pieces.

8 *Let them be* like a snail which melts away as it goes,
Like a stillborn child of a woman, that they may not see the sun.

9 Before your pots can feel *the burning* thorns,
He shall take them away as with a whirlwind,
As in His living and burning wrath.
10 The righteous shall rejoice when he sees the vengeance;
He shall wash his feet in the blood of the wicked,
11 So that men will say,
"Surely *there is* a reward for the righteous;
Surely He is God who judges in the earth."

~ PROVERBS 15:27–30 ~

27 He who is greedy for gain troubles his own house,
But he who hates bribes will live.

28 The heart of the righteous studies how to answer,
But the mouth of the wicked pours forth evil.

29 The LORD *is* far from the wicked,
But He hears the prayer of the righteous.

30 The light of the eyes rejoices the heart,
And a good report makes the bones healthy.

~ LUKE 24:1–35 ~

Now on the first *day* of the week, very early in the morning, they, and certain *other women* with them, came to the tomb bringing the spices which they had prepared. 2 But they found the stone rolled away from the tomb. 3 Then they went in and did not find the body of the Lord Jesus. 4 And it happened, as they were greatly perplexed about this, that behold, two men stood by them in shining garments. 5 Then, as they were afraid and bowed *their* faces to the earth, they said to them, "Why do you seek the living among the dead? [6] He is not here, but is risen! Remember how He spoke to you when He was still in Galilee, [7] saying, 'The Son of Man must be delivered into the hands of sinful men, and be crucified, and the third day rise again.' "

[8] And they remembered His words. [9] Then they returned from the tomb and told all these things to the eleven and to all the rest. [10] It was Mary Magdalene, Joanna, Mary *the mother* of James, and the other *women* with them, who told these things to the apostles. [11] And their words seemed to them like idle tales, and they did not believe them. [12] But Peter arose and ran to the tomb; and stooping down, he saw the linen cloths lying by themselves; and he departed, marveling to himself at what had happened.

[13] Now behold, two of them were traveling that same day to a village called Emmaus, which was seven miles from Jerusalem. [14] And they talked together of all these things which had happened. [15] So it was, while they conversed and reasoned, that Jesus Himself drew near and went with them. [16] But their eyes were restrained, so that they did not know Him. [17] And He said to them, "What kind of conversation *is* this that you have with one another as you walk and are sad?"

[18] Then the one whose name was Cleopas answered and said to Him, "Are You the only stranger in Jerusalem, and have You not known the things which happened there in these days?"

[19] And He said to them, "What things?"

So they said to Him, "The things concerning Jesus of Nazareth, who was a Prophet mighty in deed and word before God and all the people, [20] and how the chief priests and our rulers delivered Him to be condemned to death, and crucified Him. [21] But we were hoping that it was

He who was going to redeem Israel. Indeed, besides all this, today is the third day since these things happened. [22] Yes, and certain women of our company, who arrived at the tomb early, astonished us. [23] When they did not find His body, they came saying that they had also seen a vision of angels who said He was alive. [24] And certain of those *who were* with us went to the tomb and found *it* just as the women had said; but Him they did not see."

[25] Then He said to them, "O foolish ones, and slow of heart to believe in all that the prophets have spoken! [26] Ought not the Christ to have suffered these things and to enter into His glory?" [27] And beginning at Moses and all the Prophets, He expounded to them in all the Scriptures the things concerning Himself.

[28] Then they drew near to the village where they were going, and He indicated that He would have gone farther. [29] But they constrained Him, saying, "Abide with us, for it is toward evening, and the day is far spent." And He went in to stay with them.

[30] Now it came to pass, as He sat at the table with them, that He took bread, blessed and broke *it*, and gave it to them. [31] Then their eyes were opened and they knew Him; and He vanished from their sight. [32] And they said to one another, "Did not our heart burn within us while He talked with us on the road, and while He opened the Scriptures to us?" [33] So they rose up that very hour and returned to Jerusalem, and found the eleven and those *who were* with them gathered together, [34] saying, "The Lord is risen indeed, and has appeared to Simon!" [35] And they told about the things *that had happened* on the road, and how He was known to them in the breaking of bread.

~ 1 SAMUEL 20:1—21:15 ~

Then David fled from Naioth in Ramah, and went and said to Jonathan, "What have I done?

What *is* my iniquity, and what *is* my sin before your father, that he seeks my life?"

[2] So Jonathan said to him, "By no

means! You shall not die! Indeed, my father will do nothing either great or small without first telling me. And why should my father hide this thing from me? It *is* not *so*!"

³ Then David took an oath again, and said, "Your father certainly knows that I have found favor in your eyes, and he has said, 'Do not let Jonathan know this, lest he be grieved.' But truly, *as* the LORD lives and *as* your soul lives, *there is* but a step between me and death."

⁴ So Jonathan said to David, "Whatever you yourself desire, I will do *it* for you."

⁵ And David said to Jonathan, "Indeed tomorrow *is* the New Moon, and I should not fail to sit with the king to eat. But let me go, that I may hide in the field until the third *day* at evening. ⁶ If your father misses me at all, then say, 'David earnestly asked *permission* of me that he might run over to Bethlehem, his city, for *there is* a yearly sacrifice there for all the family.' ⁷ If he says thus: '*It is* well,' your servant will be safe. But if he is very angry, be sure that evil is determined by him. ⁸ Therefore you shall deal kindly with your servant, for you have brought your servant into a covenant of the LORD with you. Nevertheless, if there is iniquity in me, kill me yourself, for why should you bring me to your father?"

⁹ But Jonathan said, "Far be it from you! For if I knew certainly that evil was determined by my father to come upon you, then would I not tell you?"

¹⁰ Then David said to Jonathan, "Who will tell me, or what *if* your father answers you roughly?"

¹¹ And Jonathan said to David, "Come, let us go out into the field." So both of them went out into the field. ¹² Then Jonathan said to David: "The LORD God of Israel *is witness*! When I have sounded out my father sometime tomorrow, *or* the third *day,* and indeed *there is* good toward David, and I do not send to you and tell you, ¹³ may the LORD do so and much more to Jonathan. But if it pleases my father *to do* you evil, then I will report it to you and send you away, that you may go in safety. And the LORD be with you as He has been with my father. ¹⁴ And you shall not only show me the kindness of the LORD while I still live, that I may not

die; ¹⁵ but you shall not cut off your kindness from my house forever, no, not when the LORD has cut off every one of the enemies of David from the face of the earth."

¹⁶ So Jonathan made *a covenant* with the house of David, *saying,* "Let the LORD require *it* at the hand of David's enemies."

¹⁷ Now Jonathan again caused David to vow, because he loved him; for he loved him as he loved his own soul. ¹⁸ Then Jonathan said to David, "Tomorrow *is* the New Moon; and you will be missed, because your seat will be empty. ¹⁹ And *when* you have stayed three days, go down quickly and come to the place where you hid on the day of the deed; and remain by the stone Ezel. ²⁰ Then I will shoot three arrows to the side, as though I shot at a target; ²¹ and there I will send a lad, *saying,* 'Go, find the arrows.' If I expressly say to the lad, 'Look, the arrows *are* on this side of you; get them and come'— then, as the LORD lives, *there is* safety for you and no harm. ²² But if I say thus to the young man, 'Look, the arrows *are* beyond you'—go your way, for the LORD has sent you away. ²³ And as for the matter which you and I have spoken of, indeed the LORD *be* between you and me forever."

²⁴ Then David hid in the field. And when the New Moon had come, the king sat down to eat the feast. ²⁵ Now the king sat on his seat, as at other times, on a seat by the wall. And Jonathan arose, and Abner sat by Saul's side, but David's place was empty. ²⁶ Nevertheless Saul did not say anything that day, for he thought, "Something has happened to him; he *is* unclean, surely he *is* unclean." ²⁷ And it happened the next day, the second *day* of the month, that David's place was empty. And Saul said to Jonathan his son, "Why has the son of Jesse not come to eat, either yesterday or today?"

²⁸ So Jonathan answered Saul, "David earnestly asked *permission* of me *to go* to Bethlehem. ²⁹ And he said, 'Please let me go, for our family has a sacrifice in the city, and my brother has commanded me *to be there.* And now, if I have found favor in your eyes, please let me get away and see my brothers.' Therefore he has not come to the king's table."

³⁰ Then Saul's anger was aroused against

You Are What You Think You Are

The story is told of a man who found an eagle's egg and put it into the nest of a barnyard chicken. The eaglet hatched with the brood of chicks and grew up with them. All his life, the eagle did what the chickens did. It scratched the dirt for seeds and insects to eat. It clucked and cackled. And it flew no more than a few feet off the ground, in a chicken-like thrashing of wings and flurry of feathers.

One day the eagle saw a magnificent bird far above him in the cloudless sky. He watched as the bird soared gracefully on the wind, gliding through the air with scarcely a beat of its powerful wings.

"What a beautiful bird," the young eagle said. "What is it called?"

The chicken next to him said, "Why, that's an eagle — the king of all birds. But don't give him any mind. You could never be like him."

So the young eagle returned to pecking the dirt for seeds, and it died thinking it was a chicken.

What you think of your own potential not only defines who you are today, but what you will be tomorrow.

Jonathan, and he said to him, "You son of a perverse, rebellious *woman*! Do I not know that you have chosen the son of Jesse to your own shame and to the shame of your mother's nakedness? [31] For as long as the son of Jesse lives on the earth, you shall not be established, nor your kingdom. Now therefore, send and bring him to me, for he shall surely die."

[32] And Jonathan answered Saul his father, and said to him, "Why should he be killed? What has he done?" [33] Then Saul cast a spear at him to kill him, by which Jonathan knew that it was determined by his father to kill David.

[34] So Jonathan arose from the table in fierce anger, and ate no food the second day of the month, for he was grieved for David, because his father had treated him shamefully.

[35] And so it was, in the morning, that Jonathan went out into the field at the time appointed with David, and a little lad *was* with him. [36] Then he said to his lad, "Now run, find the arrows which I shoot." As the lad ran, he shot an arrow beyond him. [37] When the lad had come to the place where the arrow was which Jonathan had shot, Jonathan cried out after the lad and said, "*Is* not the arrow beyond you?" [38] And Jonathan cried out after the lad, "Make haste, hurry, do not delay!" So Jonathan's lad gathered up the arrows and came back to his master. [39] But the lad did not know anything. Only Jonathan and David knew of the matter. [40] Then Jonathan gave his weapons to his lad, and said to him, "Go, carry *them* to the city."

[41] As soon as the lad had gone, David arose from *a place* toward the south, fell on his face to the ground, and bowed down three times. And they kissed one another; and they wept together, but David more so. [42] Then Jonathan said to David, "Go in peace, since we have both sworn in the name of the LORD, saying, 'May the LORD be between you and me, and between your descendants and my descendants, forever.' " So he arose and departed, and Jonathan went into the city.

21

Now David came to Nob, to Ahimelech the priest. And Ahimelech was afraid when he met David, and said to him, "Why *are* you alone, and no one is with you?"

[2] So David said to Ahimelech the priest, "The king has ordered me on some business, and said to me, 'Do not let anyone know anything about the business on which I send you, or what I have commanded you.' And I have directed *my* young men to such and such a place. [3] Now therefore, what have you on hand? Give *me* five *loaves of* bread in my hand, or whatever can be found."

[4] And the priest answered David and said, "*There is* no common bread on hand; but there is holy bread, if the young men have at least kept themselves from women."

[5] Then David answered the priest, and said to him, "Truly, women *have been* kept from us about three days since I came out. And the vessels of the young men are holy, and *the bread is* in effect common, even though it was consecrated in the vessel this day."

[6] So the priest gave him holy *bread;* for there was no bread there but the showbread which had been taken from before the LORD, in order to put hot bread *in its place* on the day when it was taken away.

[7] Now a certain man of the servants of Saul *was* there that day, detained before the LORD. And his name *was* Doeg, an Edomite, the chief of the herdsmen who *belonged* to Saul.

[8] And David said to Ahimelech, "Is there not here on hand a spear or a sword? For I have brought neither my sword nor my weapons with me, because the king's business required haste."

[9] So the priest said, "The sword of Goliath the Philistine, whom you killed in the Valley of Elah, there it is, wrapped in a cloth behind the ephod. If you will take that, take *it*. For *there is* no other except that one here."

And David said, "*There is* none like it; give it to me."

[10] Then David arose and fled that day from before Saul, and went to Achish the king of Gath. [11] And the servants of Achish said to him, "*Is* this not David the king of the land? Did they not sing of him to one another in dances, saying:

'Saul has slain his thousands,
And David his ten thousands'?"

¹² Now David took these words to heart, and was very much afraid of Achish the king of Gath. ¹³ So he changed his behavior before them, pretended madness in their hands, scratched on the doors of the gate, and let his saliva fall down on his beard. ¹⁴ Then Achish said to his servants, "Look, you see the man is insane. Why have you brought him to me? ¹⁵ Have I need of madmen, that you have brought this *fellow* to play the madman in my presence? Shall this *fellow* come into my house?"

~ PSALM 59:1–5 ~

¹ Deliver me from my enemies, O my God;
  Defend me from those who rise up against me.
² Deliver me from the workers of iniquity,
  And save me from bloodthirsty men.

³ For look, they lie in wait for my life;
  The mighty gather against me,
  Not *for* my transgression nor *for* my sin, O LORD.
⁴ They run and prepare themselves through no fault *of mine*.

  Awake to help me, and behold!
⁵ You therefore, O LORD God of hosts, the God of Israel,
  Awake to punish all the nations;
  Do not be merciful to any wicked transgressors.   Selah

~ PROVERBS 15:31–33 ~

³¹ The ear that hears the rebukes of life
  Will abide among the wise.
³² He who disdains instruction despises his own soul,
  But he who heeds rebuke gets understanding.

³³ The fear of the LORD *is* the instruction of wisdom,
  And before honor *is* humility.

~ LUKE 24:36–53 ~

Now as they said these things, Jesus Himself stood in the midst of them, and said to them, "Peace to you." ³⁷ But they were terrified and frightened, and supposed they had seen a spirit. ³⁸ And He said to them, "Why are you troubled? And why do doubts arise in your hearts? ³⁹ Behold My hands and My feet, that it is I Myself. Handle Me and see, for a spirit does not have flesh and bones as you see I have."

⁴⁰ When He had said this, He showed them His hands and His feet. ⁴¹ But while they still did not believe for joy, and marveled, He said to them, "Have you any food here?" ⁴² So they gave Him a piece of a broiled fish and some honeycomb. ⁴³ And He took *it* and ate in their presence.

⁴⁴ Then He said to them, "These *are* the words which I spoke to you while I was still with you, that all things must be fulfilled which were written in the Law of Moses and *the* Prophets and *the* Psalms concerning Me." ⁴⁵ And He opened their understanding, that they might comprehend the Scriptures.

⁴⁶ Then He said to them, "Thus it is written, and thus it was necessary for the Christ to suffer and to rise from the dead the third day, ⁴⁷ and that repentance and remission of sins should be preached in His name to all nations, beginning at Jerusalem. ⁴⁸ And you are witnesses of these things. ⁴⁹ Behold, I send the Promise of My Father upon you; but tarry in the city of Jerusalem until you are endued with power from on high."

⁵⁰ And He led them out as far as Bethany, and He lifted up His hands and blessed them. ⁵¹ Now it came to pass, while He blessed them, that He was parted from them and carried up into heaven. ⁵² And they worshiped Him, and returned to Jerusalem with great joy, ⁵³ and were continually in the temple praising and blessing God. Amen.

∼ 1 SAMUEL 22:1—23:29 ∼

David therefore departed from there and escaped to the cave of Adullam. So when his brothers and all his father's house heard *it,* they went down there to him. ² And everyone *who was* in distress, everyone who *was* in debt, and everyone *who was* discontented gathered to him. So he became captain over them. And there were about four hundred men with him.

³ Then David went from there to Mizpah of Moab; and he said to the king of Moab, "Please let my father and mother come here with you, till I know what God will do for me." ⁴ So he brought them before the king of Moab, and they dwelt with him all the time that David was in the stronghold.

⁵ Now the prophet Gad said to David, "Do not stay in the stronghold; depart, and go to the land of Judah." So David departed and went into the forest of Hereth.

⁶ When Saul heard that David and the men who *were* with him had been discovered—now Saul was staying in Gibeah under a tamarisk tree in Ramah, with his spear in his hand, and all his servants standing about him— ⁷ then Saul said to his servants who stood about him, "Hear now, you Benjamites! Will the son of Jesse give every one of you fields and vineyards, *and* make you all captains of thousands and captains of hundreds? ⁸ All of you have conspired against me, and *there is* no one who reveals to me that my son has made a covenant with the son of Jesse; and *there is* not one of you who is sorry for me or reveals to me that my son has stirred up my servant against me, to lie in wait, as *it is* this day."

⁹ Then answered Doeg the Edomite, who was set over the servants of Saul, and said, "I saw the son of Jesse going to Nob, to Ahimelech the son of Ahitub. ¹⁰ And he inquired of the LORD for him, gave him provisions, and gave him the sword of Goliath the Philistine."

¹¹ So the king sent to call Ahimelech the priest, the son of Ahitub, and all his father's house, the priests who *were* in Nob. And they all came to the king.

¹² And Saul said, "Hear now, son of Ahitub!"

He answered, "Here I am, my lord."

¹³ Then Saul said to him, "Why have you conspired against me, you and the son of Jesse, in that you have given him bread and a sword, and have inquired of God for him, that he should rise against me, to lie in wait, as it is this day?"

¹⁴ So Ahimelech answered the king and said, "And who among all your servants *is as* faithful as David, who is the king's son-in-law, who goes at your bidding, and is honorable in your house? ¹⁵ Did I then begin to inquire of God for him? Far be it from me! Let not the king impute anything to his servant, *or* to any in the house of my father. For your servant knew nothing of all this, little or much."

¹⁶ And the king said, "You shall surely die, Ahimelech, you and all your father's house!" ¹⁷ Then the king said to the guards who stood about him, "Turn and kill the priests of the LORD, because their hand also *is* with David, and because they knew when he fled and did not tell it to me." But the servants of the king would not lift their hands to strike the priests of the LORD. ¹⁸ And the king said to Doeg, "You turn and kill the priests!" So Doeg the Edomite turned and struck the priests, and killed on that day eighty-five men who wore a linen ephod. ¹⁹ Also Nob, the city of the priests, he struck with the edge of the sword, both men and women, children and nursing infants, oxen and donkeys and sheep—with the edge of the sword.

²⁰ Now one of the sons of Ahimelech the son of Ahitub, named Abiathar, escaped and fled after David. ²¹ And Abiathar told David that Saul had killed the LORD's priests. ²² So David said to Abiathar, "I knew that day, when Doeg the Edomite *was* there, that he would surely tell Saul. I have caused *the death* of all the persons of your father's house. ²³ Stay with me; do not fear. For he who seeks my life seeks your life, but with me you *shall be* safe."

23 Then they told David, saying, "Look, the Philistines are fighting against

Six Step Problem Solving

A man once recognized Norman Vincent Peale on an airplane and told him that he had read his books and benefited from them. He then told Peale that he was a training supervisor and had spent a great deal of time listening to the problems of employees. He said, "I worked out six practical points for handling a problem. Would you like to hear them?" Peale replied, "I sure would!" These are the six points he shared, which Peale in turn shared with millions of his readers:

1. When faced with a problem, pray about it, asking that God's will, rather than your own, be done.
2. Having prayed, believe that God will bring the matter out right.
3. Write the problem out in detail. This gives you a clearer view of it and prevents confusion.
4. Always ask yourself what is the right thing to do. Nothing that is wrong ever works out right. Ask yourself if you are being fair to everyone concerned.
5. Keep thinking and keep working at the problem. First try one thing, then another, until you find a solution.
6. When your problem is solved, thank God. Give one-tenth of your income to God's work. When you give, God's blessings will be released to flow into your life.

God has an answer for every problem you may face today, or will face in the future. He is ready to give you the solution and He is waiting to fill your life with blessings. Take it to God. He has an answer!

Keilah, and they are robbing the threshing floors."

² Therefore David inquired of the LORD, saying, "Shall I go and attack these Philistines?"

And the LORD said to David, "Go and attack the Philistines, and save Keilah."

³ But David's men said to him, "Look, we are afraid here in Judah. How much more then if we go to Keilah against the armies of the Philistines?" ⁴ Then David inquired of the LORD once again.

And the LORD answered him and said, "Arise, go down to Keilah. For I will deliver the Philistines into your hand." ⁵ And David and his men went to Keilah and fought with the Philistines, struck them with a mighty blow, and took away their livestock. So David saved the inhabitants of Keilah.

⁶ Now it happened, when Abiathar the son of Ahimelech fled to David at Keilah, *that* he went down *with* an ephod in his hand.

⁷ And Saul was told that David had gone to Keilah. So Saul said, "God has delivered him into my hand, for he has shut himself in by entering a town that has gates and bars." ⁸ Then Saul called all the people together for war, to go down to Keilah to besiege David and his men.

⁹ When David knew that Saul plotted evil against him, he said to Abiathar the priest, "Bring the ephod here." ¹⁰ Then David said, "O LORD God of Israel, Your servant has certainly heard that Saul seeks to come to Keilah to destroy the city for my sake. ¹¹ Will the men of Keilah deliver me into his hand? Will Saul come down, as Your servant has heard? O LORD God of Israel, I pray, tell Your servant."

And the LORD said, "He will come down."

¹² Then David said, "Will the men of Keilah deliver me and my men into the hand of Saul?"

And the LORD said, "They will deliver *you.*"

¹³ So David and his men, about six hundred, arose and departed from Keilah and went wherever they could go. Then it was told Saul that David had escaped from Keilah; so he halted the expedition.

¹⁴ And David stayed in strongholds in the wilderness, and remained in the mountains in the Wilderness of Ziph. Saul sought him every day, but God did not deliver him into his hand. ¹⁵ So David saw that Saul had come out to seek his life. And David *was* in the Wilderness of Ziph in a forest. ¹⁶ Then Jonathan, Saul's son, arose and went to David in the woods and strengthened his hand in God. ¹⁷ And he said to him, "Do not fear, for the hand of Saul my father shall not find you. You shall be king over Israel, and I shall be next to you. Even my father Saul knows that." ¹⁸ So the two of them made a covenant before the LORD. And David stayed in the woods, and Jonathan went to his own house.

¹⁹ Then the Ziphites came up to Saul at Gibeah, saying, "Is David not hiding with us in strongholds in the woods, in the hill of Hachilah, which *is* on the south of Jeshimon? ²⁰ Now therefore, O king, come down according to all the desire of your soul to come down; and our part *shall be* to deliver him into the king's hand."

²¹ And Saul said, "Blessed *are* you of the LORD, for you have compassion on me. ²² Please go and find out for sure, and see the place where his hideout is, *and* who has seen him there. For I am told he is very crafty. ²³ See therefore, and take knowledge of all the lurking places where he hides; and come back to me with certainty, and I will go with you. And it shall be, if he is in the land, that I will search for him throughout all the clans of Judah."

²⁴ So they arose and went to Ziph before Saul. But David and his men *were* in the Wilderness of Maon, in the plain on the south of Jeshimon. ²⁵ When Saul and his men went to seek *him,* they told David. Therefore he went down to the rock, and stayed in the Wilderness of Maon. And when Saul heard *that,* he pursued David in the Wilderness of Maon. ²⁶ Then Saul went on one side of the mountain, and David and his men on the other side of the mountain. So David made haste to get away from Saul, for Saul and his men were encircling David and his men to take them.

²⁷ But a messenger came to Saul, saying, "Hurry and come, for the Philistines have invaded the land!" ²⁸ Therefore Saul returned from pursuing David, and went

against the Philistines; so they called that place the Rock of Escape. ²⁹ Then David went up from there and dwelt in strongholds at En Gedi.

~ PSALM 59:6–17 ~

⁶ At evening they return,
They growl like a dog,
And go all around the city.
⁷ Indeed, they belch with their mouth;
Swords *are* in their lips;
For *they say,* "Who hears?"

⁸ But You, O LORD, shall laugh at them;
You shall have all the nations in derision.
⁹ I will wait for You, O You his Strength;
For God *is* my defense.
¹⁰ My God of mercy shall come to meet me;
God shall let me see *my desire* on my enemies.

¹¹ Do not slay them, lest my people forget;
Scatter them by Your power,
And bring them down,
O Lord our shield.
¹² *For* the sin of their mouth *and* the words of their lips,
Let them even be taken in their pride,
And for the cursing and lying *which* they speak.
¹³ Consume *them* in wrath, consume *them,*
That they *may* not *be;*
And let them know that God rules in Jacob
To the ends of the earth.   Selah

¹⁴ And at evening they return,
They growl like a dog,
And go all around the city.
¹⁵ They wander up and down for food,
And howl if they are not satisfied.

¹⁶ But I will sing of Your power;
Yes, I will sing aloud of Your mercy in the morning;
For You have been my defense
And refuge in the day of my trouble.

¹⁷ To You, O my Strength, I will sing praises;
For God *is* my defense,
My God of mercy.

~ PROVERBS 16:1, 2 ~

¹ The preparations of the heart *belong* to man,
But the answer of the tongue *is* from the LORD.

² All the ways of a man *are* pure in his own eyes,
But the LORD weighs the spirits.

~ JOHN 1:1–28 ~

In the beginning was the Word, and the Word was with God, and the Word was God. ² He was in the beginning with God. ³ All things were made through Him, and without Him nothing was made that was made. ⁴ In Him was life, and the life was the light of men. ⁵ And the light shines in the darkness, and the darkness did not comprehend it.

⁶ There was a man sent from God, whose name *was* John. ⁷ This man came for a witness, to bear witness of the Light, that all through him might believe. ⁸ He was not that Light, but *was sent* to bear witness of that Light. ⁹ That was the true Light which gives light to every man coming into the world.

¹⁰ He was in the world, and the world was made through Him, and the world did not know Him. ¹¹ He came to His own, and His own did not receive Him. ¹² But as many as received Him, to them He gave the right to become children of God, to those who believe in His name: ¹³ who were born, not of blood, nor of the will of the flesh, nor of the will of man, but of God.

¹⁴ And the Word became flesh and dwelt among us, and we beheld His glory, the glory as of the only begotten of the Father, full of grace and truth.

¹⁵ John bore witness of Him and cried out, saying, "This was He of whom I said, 'He who comes after me is preferred before me, for He was before me.' "

¹⁶ And of His fullness we have all received, and grace for grace. ¹⁷ For the law was given through Moses, *but* grace and truth came through Jesus Christ. ¹⁸ No one has seen God at any time. The only begotten Son, who is in the bosom of the Father, He has declared *Him*.

¹⁹ Now this is the testimony of John, when the Jews sent priests and Levites from Jerusalem to ask him, "Who are you?"

²⁰ He confessed, and did not deny, but confessed, "I am not the Christ."

²¹ And they asked him, "What then? Are you Elijah?"

He said, "I am not."

"Are you the Prophet?"

And he answered, "No."

²² Then they said to him, "Who are you, that we may give an answer to those who sent us? What do you say about yourself?"

²³ He said: "I *am*

'The voice of one crying in the
    wilderness:
"Make straight the way of the
    LORD," '

as the prophet Isaiah said."

²⁴ Now those who were sent were from the Pharisees. ²⁵ And they asked him, saying, "Why then do you baptize if you are not the Christ, nor Elijah, nor the Prophet?"

²⁶ John answered them, saying, "I baptize with water, but there stands One among you whom you do not know. ²⁷ It is He who, coming after me, is preferred before me, whose sandal strap I am not worthy to loose."

²⁸ These things were done in Bethabara beyond the Jordan, where John was baptizing.

READING 131 · MAY 11

~ 1 SAMUEL 24:1—25:44 ~

Now it happened, when Saul had returned from following the Philistines, that it was told him, saying, "Take note! David *is* in the Wilderness of En Gedi." ² Then Saul took three thousand chosen men from all Israel, and went to seek David and his men on the Rocks of the Wild Goats. ³ So he came to the sheepfolds by the road, where there *was* a cave; and Saul went in to attend to his needs. (David and his men were staying in the recesses of the cave.) ⁴ Then the men of David said to him, "This is the day of which the LORD said to you, 'Behold, I will deliver your enemy into your hand, that you may do to him as it seems good to you.' " And David arose and secretly cut off a corner of Saul's robe. ⁵ Now it happened afterward that David's heart troubled him because he had cut Saul's *robe*. ⁶ And he said to his men, "The LORD forbid that I should do this thing to my master, the LORD's anointed, to stretch out my hand against him, seeing he *is* the anointed of the LORD." ⁷ So David restrained his servants with *these* words, and

did not allow them to rise against Saul. And Saul got up from the cave and went on *his* way.

⁸ David also arose afterward, went out of the cave, and called out to Saul, saying, "My lord the king!" And when Saul looked behind him, David stooped with his face to the earth, and bowed down. ⁹ And David said to Saul: "Why do you listen to the words of men who say, 'Indeed David seeks your harm'? ¹⁰ Look, this day your eyes have seen that the LORD delivered you today into my hand in the cave, and *someone* urged *me* to kill you. But *my eye* spared you, and I said, 'I will not stretch out my hand against my lord, for he *is* the LORD's anointed.' ¹¹ Moreover, my father, see! Yes, see the corner of your robe in my hand! For in that I cut off the corner of your robe, and did not kill you, know and see that *there is* neither evil nor rebellion in my hand, and I have not sinned against you. Yet you hunt my life to take it. ¹² Let the LORD judge between you and me, and let the LORD avenge me on you. But my hand shall not

Hull House

Jane was only seven years old when she visited a shabby street in a nearby town, and seeing ragged children there, announced that she wanted to build a big house so poor children would have a place to play. As a young adult, Jane and a friend, Ellen Starr, visited Toynbee Hall in London, where they saw educated people helping the poor by living among them.

She and Ellen returned to the slums of Chicago, restored the old Hull mansion, and moved in! There they cared for children of working mothers, and held sewing and cooking classes. Older boys and girls had clubs at the mansion. An art gallery and playground and public music, reading, and craft rooms were created in the mansion. Her childhood dream came true!

Jane fought against child labor laws and campaigned for adult education, day nurseries, better housing, and women's suffrage. She was eventually awarded an honorary degree from Yale. President Theodore Roosevelt dubbed her, "America's most useful citizen" and she was awarded the Nobel Prize for Peace.

No matter how famous she became, however, Jane Addams remained a resident of Hull House. She died there, in the heart of the slum she had come to call home.

When we commit our dreams and plans to the Lord, He will see to it that they come to pass.

be against you. ¹³ As the proverb of the ancients says, 'Wickedness proceeds from the wicked.' But my hand shall not be against you. ¹⁴ After whom has the king of Israel come out? Whom do you pursue? A dead dog? A flea? ¹⁵ Therefore let the LORD be judge, and judge between you and me, and see and plead my case, and deliver me out of your hand."

¹⁶ So it was, when David had finished speaking these words to Saul, that Saul said, "*Is* this your voice, my son David?" And Saul lifted up his voice and wept. ¹⁷ Then he said to David: "You *are* more righteous than I; for you have rewarded me with good, whereas I have rewarded you with evil. ¹⁸ And you have shown this day how you have dealt well with me; for when the LORD delivered me into your hand, you did not kill me. ¹⁹ For if a man finds his enemy, will he let him get away safely? Therefore may the LORD reward you with good for what you have done to me this day. ²⁰ And now I know indeed that you shall surely be king, and that the kingdom of Israel shall be established in your hand. ²¹ Therefore swear now to me by the LORD that you will not cut off my descendants after me, and that you will not destroy my name from my father's house."

²² So David swore to Saul. And Saul went home, but David and his men went up to the stronghold.

25 Then Samuel died; and the Israelites gathered together and lamented for him, and buried him at his home in Ramah. And David arose and went down to the Wilderness of Paran.

² Now *there was* a man in Maon whose business *was* in Carmel, and the man *was* very rich. He had three thousand sheep and a thousand goats. And he was shearing his sheep in Carmel. ³ The name of the man *was* Nabal, and the name of his wife Abigail. And *she was* a woman of good understanding and beautiful appearance; but the man *was* harsh and evil in *his* doings. He *was of the house of* Caleb.

⁴ When David heard in the wilderness that Nabal was shearing his sheep, ⁵ David sent ten young men; and David said to the young men, "Go up to Carmel, go to Nabal, and greet him in my name. ⁶ And thus you shall say to him who lives *in prosperity:* 'Peace *be* to you, peace to your house, and peace to all that you have! ⁷ Now I have heard that you have shearers. Your shepherds were with us, and we did not hurt them, nor was there anything missing from them all the while they were in Carmel. ⁸ Ask your young men, and they will tell you. Therefore let *my* young men find favor in your eyes, for we come on a feast day. Please give whatever comes to your hand to your servants and to your son David.' "

⁹ So when David's young men came, they spoke to Nabal according to all these words in the name of David, and waited.

¹⁰ Then Nabal answered David's servants, and said, "Who *is* David, and who *is* the son of Jesse? There are many servants nowadays who break away each one from his master. ¹¹ Shall I then take my bread and my water and my meat that I have killed for my shearers, and give *it* to men when I do not know where they *are* from?"

¹² So David's young men turned on their heels and went back; and they came and told him all these words. ¹³ Then David said to his men, "Every man gird on his sword." So every man girded on his sword, and David also girded on his sword. And about four hundred men went with David, and two hundred stayed with the supplies.

¹⁴ Now one of the young men told Abigail, Nabal's wife, saying, "Look, David sent messengers from the wilderness to greet our master; and he reviled them. ¹⁵ But the men *were* very good to us, and we were not hurt, nor did we miss anything as long as we accompanied them, when we were in the fields. ¹⁶ They were a wall to us both by night and day, all the time we were with them keeping the sheep. ¹⁷ Now therefore, know and consider what you will do, for harm is determined against our master and against all his household. For he *is such* a scoundrel that *one* cannot speak to him."

¹⁸ Then Abigail made haste and took two hundred *loaves* of bread, two skins of wine, five sheep already dressed, five seahs of roasted *grain,* one hundred clusters of raisins, and two hundred cakes of figs, and loaded *them* on donkeys. ¹⁹ And

she said to her servants, "Go on before me; see, I am coming after you." But she did not tell her husband Nabal.

²⁰ So it was, *as* she rode on the donkey, that she went down under cover of the hill; and there were David and his men, coming down toward her, and she met them. ²¹ Now David had said, "Surely in vain I have protected all that this *fellow* has in the wilderness, so that nothing was missed of all that *belongs* to him. And he has repaid me evil for good. ²² May God do so, and more also, to the enemies of David, if I leave one male of all who *belong* to him by morning light."

²³ Now when Abigail saw David, she dismounted quickly from the donkey, fell on her face before David, and bowed down to the ground. ²⁴ So she fell at his feet and said: "On me, my lord, *on me let* this iniquity *be*! And please let your maidservant speak in your ears, and hear the words of your maidservant. ²⁵ Please, let not my lord regard this scoundrel Nabal. For as his name *is*, so *is* he: Nabal *is* his name, and folly *is* with him! But I, your maidservant, did not see the young men of my lord whom you sent. ²⁶ Now therefore, my lord, *as* the LORD lives and *as* your soul lives, since the LORD has held you back from coming to bloodshed and from avenging yourself with your own hand, now then, let your enemies and those who seek harm for my lord be as Nabal. ²⁷ And now this present which your maidservant has brought to my lord, let it be given to the young men who follow my lord. ²⁸ Please forgive the trespass of your maidservant. For the LORD will certainly make for my lord an enduring house, because my lord fights the battles of the LORD, and evil is not found in you throughout your days. ²⁹ Yet a man has risen to pursue you and seek your life, but the life of my lord shall be bound in the bundle of the living with the LORD your God; and the lives of your enemies He shall sling out, *as from* the pocket of a sling. ³⁰ And it shall come to pass, when the LORD has done for my lord according to all the good that He has spoken concerning you, and has appointed you ruler over Israel, ³¹ that this will be no grief to you, nor offense of heart to my lord, either that you have shed blood without

cause, or that my lord has avenged himself. But when the LORD has dealt well with my lord, then remember your maidservant."

³² Then David said to Abigail: "Blessed *is* the LORD God of Israel, who sent you this day to meet me! ³³ And blessed *is* your advice and blessed *are* you, because you have kept me this day from coming to bloodshed and from avenging myself with my own hand. ³⁴ For indeed, *as* the LORD God of Israel lives, who has kept me back from hurting you, unless you had hurried and come to meet me, surely by morning light no males would have been left to Nabal!" ³⁵ So David received from her hand what she had brought him, and said to her, "Go up in peace to your house. See, I have heeded your voice and respected your person."

³⁶ Now Abigail went to Nabal, and there he was, holding a feast in his house, like the feast of a king. And Nabal's heart *was* merry within him, for he *was* very drunk; therefore she told him nothing, little or much, until morning light. ³⁷ So it was, in the morning, when the wine had gone from Nabal, and his wife had told him these things, that his heart died within him, and he became *like* a stone. ³⁸ Then it happened, *after* about ten days, that the LORD struck Nabal, and he died.

³⁹ So when David heard that Nabal was dead, he said, "Blessed *be* the LORD, who has pleaded the cause of my reproach from the hand of Nabal, and has kept His servant from evil! For the LORD has returned the wickedness of Nabal on his own head."

And David sent and proposed to Abigail, to take her as his wife. ⁴⁰ When the servants of David had come to Abigail at Carmel, they spoke to her saying, "David sent us to you, to ask you to become his wife."

⁴¹ Then she arose, bowed her face to the earth, and said, "Here is your maidservant, a servant to wash the feet of the servants of my lord." ⁴² So Abigail rose in haste and rode on a donkey, attended by five of her maidens; and she followed the messengers of David, and became his wife. ⁴³ David also took Ahinoam of Jezreel, and so both of them were his wives. ⁴⁴ But Saul had given Michal his

daughter, David's wife, to Palti the son of Laish, who *was* from Gallim.

~ PSALM 60:1–5 ~

1 O God, You have cast us off;
  You have broken us down;
  You have been displeased;
  Oh, restore us again!
2 You have made the earth tremble;
  You have broken it;
  Heal its breaches, for it is shaking.
3 You have shown Your people hard
     things;
  You have made us drink the wine of
     confusion.

4 You have given a banner to those
     who fear You,
  That it may be displayed because of
     the truth.   Selah
5 That Your beloved may be delivered,
  Save *with* Your right hand, and hear
     me.

~ PROVERBS 16:3 ~

3 Commit your works to the LORD,
  And your thoughts will be
     established.

~ JOHN 1:29–51 ~

The next day John saw Jesus coming toward him, and said, "Behold! The Lamb of God who takes away the sin of the world! 30 This is He of whom I said, 'After me comes a Man who is preferred before me, for He was before me.' 31 I did not know Him; but that He should be revealed to Israel, therefore I came baptizing with water."

32 And John bore witness, saying, "I saw the Spirit descending from heaven like a dove, and He remained upon Him. 33 I did not know Him, but He who sent me to baptize with water said to me, 'Upon whom you see the Spirit descending, and remaining on Him, this is He who baptizes with the Holy Spirit.' 34 And I have seen and testified that this is the Son of God."

35 Again, the next day, John stood with two of his disciples. 36 And looking at Jesus as He walked, he said, "Behold the Lamb of God!"

37 The two disciples heard him speak, and they followed Jesus. 38 Then Jesus turned, and seeing them following, said to them, "What do you seek?"

They said to Him, "Rabbi" (which is to say, when translated, Teacher), "where are You staying?"

39 He said to them, "Come and see." They came and saw where He was staying, and remained with Him that day (now it was about the tenth hour).

40 One of the two who heard John *speak,* and followed Him, was Andrew, Simon Peter's brother. 41 He first found his own brother Simon, and said to him, "We have found the Messiah" (which is translated, the Christ). 42 And he brought him to Jesus.

Now when Jesus looked at him, He said, "You are Simon the son of Jonah. You shall be called Cephas" (which is translated, A Stone).

43 The following day Jesus wanted to go to Galilee, and He found Philip and said to him, "Follow Me." 44 Now Philip was from Bethsaida, the city of Andrew and Peter. 45 Philip found Nathanael and said to him, "We have found Him of whom Moses in the law, and also the prophets, wrote—Jesus of Nazareth, the son of Joseph."

46 And Nathanael said to him, "Can anything good come out of Nazareth?"

Philip said to him, "Come and see."

47 Jesus saw Nathanael coming toward Him, and said of him, "Behold, an Israelite indeed, in whom is no deceit!"

48 Nathanael said to Him, "How do You know me?"

Jesus answered and said to him, "Before Philip called you, when you were under the fig tree, I saw you."

49 Nathanael answered and said to Him, "Rabbi, You are the Son of God! You are the King of Israel!"

50 Jesus answered and said to him, "Because I said to you, 'I saw you under the fig tree,' do you believe? You will see greater things than these." 51 And He said to him, "Most assuredly, I say to you, hereafter you shall see heaven open, and the angels of God ascending and descending upon the Son of Man."

~ 1 Samuel 26:1—27:12 ~

Now the Ziphites came to Saul at Gibeah, saying, "Is David not hiding in the hill of Hachilah, opposite Jeshimon?" ² Then Saul arose and went down to the Wilderness of Ziph, having three thousand chosen men of Israel with him, to seek David in the Wilderness of Ziph. ³ And Saul encamped in the hill of Hachilah, which *is* opposite Jeshimon, by the road. But David stayed in the wilderness, and he saw that Saul came after him into the wilderness. ⁴ David therefore sent out spies, and understood that Saul had indeed come.

⁵ So David arose and came to the place where Saul had encamped. And David saw the place where Saul lay, and Abner the son of Ner, the commander of his army. Now Saul lay within the camp, with the people encamped all around him. ⁶ Then David answered, and said to Ahimelech the Hittite and to Abishai the son of Zeruiah, brother of Joab, saying, "Who will go down with me to Saul in the camp?"

And Abishai said, "I will go down with you."

⁷ So David and Abishai came to the people by night; and there Saul lay sleeping within the camp, with his spear stuck in the ground by his head. And Abner and the people lay all around him. ⁸ Then Abishai said to David, "God has delivered your enemy into your hand this day. Now therefore, please, let me strike him at once with the spear, right to the earth; and I will not *have to strike* him a second time!"

⁹ But David said to Abishai, "Do not destroy him; for who can stretch out his hand against the LORD's anointed, and be guiltless?" ¹⁰ David said furthermore, "*As* the LORD lives, the LORD shall strike him, or his day shall come to die, or he shall go out to battle and perish. ¹¹ The LORD forbid that I should stretch out my hand against the LORD's anointed. But please, take now the spear and the jug of water that *are* by his head, and let us go." ¹² So David took the spear and the jug of water *by* Saul's head, and they got away; and no man saw or knew *it* or awoke. For they

were all asleep, because a deep sleep from the LORD had fallen on them.

¹³ Now David went over to the other side, and stood on the top of a hill afar off, a great distance *being* between them. ¹⁴ And David called out to the people and to Abner the son of Ner, saying, "Do you not answer, Abner?"

Then Abner answered and said, "Who *are* you, calling out to the king?"

¹⁵ So David said to Abner, "*Are* you not a man? And who *is* like you in Israel? Why then have you not guarded your lord the king? For one of the people came in to destroy your lord the king. ¹⁶ This thing that you have done *is* not good. *As* the LORD lives, you deserve to die, because you have not guarded your master, the LORD's anointed. And now see where the king's spear *is,* and the jug of water that *was* by his head."

¹⁷ Then Saul knew David's voice, and said, "*Is* that your voice, my son David?"

David said, "*It is* my voice, my lord, O king." ¹⁸ And he said, "Why does my lord thus pursue his servant? For what have I done, or what evil *is* in my hand? ¹⁹ Now therefore, please, let my lord the king hear the words of his servant: If the LORD has stirred you up against me, let Him accept an offering. But if *it is* the children of men, *may* they *be* cursed before the LORD, for they have driven me out this day from sharing in the inheritance of the LORD, saying, 'Go, serve other gods.' ²⁰ So now, do not let my blood fall to the earth before the face of the LORD. For the king of Israel has come out to seek a flea, as when one hunts a partridge in the mountains."

²¹ Then Saul said, "I have sinned. Return, my son David. For I will harm you no more, because my life was precious in your eyes this day. Indeed I have played the fool and erred exceedingly."

²² And David answered and said, "Here is the king's spear. Let one of the young men come over and get it. ²³ May the LORD repay every man *for* his righteousness and his faithfulness; for the LORD delivered you into *my* hand today, but I would not stretch out my hand against the LORD's anointed. ²⁴ And indeed, as

your life was valued much this day in my eyes, so let my life be valued much in the eyes of the LORD, and let Him deliver me out of all tribulation."

²⁵ Then Saul said to David, "*May* you *be* blessed, my son David! You shall both do great things and also still prevail."

So David went on his way, and Saul returned to his place.

27 And David said in his heart, "Now I shall perish someday by the hand of Saul. *There is* nothing better for me than that I should speedily escape to the land of the Philistines; and Saul will despair of me, to seek me anymore in any part of Israel. So I shall escape out of his hand." ² Then David arose and went over with the six hundred men who *were* with him to Achish the son of Maoch, king of Gath. ³ So David dwelt with Achish at Gath, he and his men, each man with his household, *and* David with his two wives, Ahinoam the Jezreelitess, and Abigail the Carmelitess, Nabal's widow. ⁴ And it was told Saul that David had fled to Gath; so he sought him no more.

⁵ Then David said to Achish, "If I have now found favor in your eyes, let them give me a place in some town in the country, that I may dwell there. For why should your servant dwell in the royal city with you?" ⁶ So Achish gave him Ziklag that day. Therefore Ziklag has belonged to the kings of Judah to this day. ⁷ Now the time that David dwelt in the country of the Philistines was one full year and four months.

⁸ And David and his men went up and raided the Geshurites, the Girzites, and the Amalekites. For those nations were the inhabitants of the land from of old, as you go to Shur, even as far as the land of Egypt. ⁹ Whenever David attacked the land, he left neither man nor woman alive, but took away the sheep, the oxen, the donkeys, the camels, and the apparel, and returned and came to Achish. ¹⁰ Then Achish would say, "Where have you made a raid today?" And David would say, "Against the southern *area* of Judah, or against the southern *area* of the Jerahmeelites, or against the southern *area* of the Kenites." ¹¹ David would save neither man nor woman alive, to bring *news* to

Gath, saying, "Lest they should inform on us, saying, 'Thus David did.' " And thus *was* his behavior all the time he dwelt in the country of the Philistines. ¹² So Achish believed David, saying, "He has made his people Israel utterly abhor him; therefore he will be my servant forever."

∼ PSALM 60:6–12 ∼

⁶ God has spoken in His holiness:
   "I will rejoice;
   I will divide Shechem
   And measure out the Valley of
      Succoth.
⁷ Gilead *is* Mine, and Manasseh *is*
      Mine;
   Ephraim also *is* the helmet for My
      head;
   Judah *is* My lawgiver.
⁸ Moab *is* My washpot;
   Over Edom I will cast My shoe;
   Philistia, shout in triumph because of
      Me."

⁹ Who will bring me *to* the strong
      city?
   Who will lead me to Edom?
¹⁰ *Is it* not You, O God, *who* cast us
      off?
   And You, O God, *who* did not go
      out with our armies?
¹¹ Give us help from trouble,
   For the help of man *is* useless.
¹² Through God we will do valiantly,
   For *it is* He *who* shall tread down
      our enemies.

∼ PROVERBS 16:4, 5 ∼

⁴ The LORD has made all for Himself,
   Yes, even the wicked for the day of
      doom.

⁵ Everyone proud in heart *is* an
      abomination to the LORD;
   Though they join forces, none will go
      unpunished.

∼ JOHN 2:1–25 ∼

On the third day there was a wedding in Cana of Galilee, and the mother of Jesus was there. ² Now both Jesus and His

I Want It!

A man once went into a pastor's office and said, "I want what my wife has found." The pastor asked, "What do you think it is that she found?" "I'm not sure," the man replied, "but whatever it is, it sure has changed her disposition."

The man's wife had been a difficult, demanding person. She had found it excruciating to give without receiving twice as much in return. Her needs kept the family in constant turmoil. She could be extremely unpleasant when things didn't go as she had planned.

What had changed her? She started attending an Enabler's Group in her neighborhood. The women, all members of the same church, opened their hearts to this woman. One day, at the end of a meeting she stayed to talk with one of the women about her life. Facing the fact of her rotten disposition she prayed, almost as an experiment: "Jesus, if You are alive as these people say You are, help me to change." The result of that prayer came slowly but surely. She repeated the prayer each morning, and within just a few months, her husband had not only noticed the difference, but wanted the same Jesus in his own life!

The only way to effect real and lasting change in our lives is to invite Jesus to help us. He won't force us to change, or do all the work, but He will be with us every step of the way, pointing us toward the path of peace.

> The Lord has made all for Himself, yes, even the wicked for the day of doom.
>
> *Proverbs 16:4*

disciples were invited to the wedding. [3] And when they ran out of wine, the mother of Jesus said to Him, "They have no wine."

[4] Jesus said to her, "Woman, what does your concern have to do with Me? My hour has not yet come."

[5] His mother said to the servants, "Whatever He says to you, do *it.*"

[6] Now there were set there six waterpots of stone, according to the manner of purification of the Jews, containing twenty or thirty gallons apiece. [7] Jesus said to them, "Fill the waterpots with water." And they filled them up to the brim. [8] And He said to them, "Draw *some* out now, and take *it* to the master of the feast." And they took *it.* [9] When the master of the feast had tasted the water that was made wine, and did not know where it came from (but the servants who had drawn the water knew), the master of the feast called the bridegroom. [10] And he said to him, "Every man at the beginning sets out the good wine, and when the *guests* have well drunk, then the inferior. You have kept the good wine until now!"

[11] This beginning of signs Jesus did in Cana of Galilee, and manifested His glory; and His disciples believed in Him.

[12] After this He went down to Capernaum, He, His mother, His brothers, and His disciples; and they did not stay there many days.

[13] Now the Passover of the Jews was at hand, and Jesus went up to Jerusalem.

[14] And He found in the temple those who sold oxen and sheep and doves, and the money changers doing business. [15] When He had made a whip of cords, He drove them all out of the temple, with the sheep and the oxen, and poured out the changers' money and overturned the tables. [16] And He said to those who sold doves, "Take these things away! Do not make My Father's house a house of merchandise!" [17] Then His disciples remembered that it was written, "Zeal for Your house has eaten Me up."

[18] So the Jews answered and said to Him, "What sign do You show to us, since You do these things?"

[19] Jesus answered and said to them, "Destroy this temple, and in three days I will raise it up."

[20] Then the Jews said, "It has taken forty-six years to build this temple, and will You raise it up in three days?"

[21] But He was speaking of the temple of His body. [22] Therefore, when He had risen from the dead, His disciples remembered that He had said this to them; and they believed the Scripture and the word which Jesus had said.

[23] Now when He was in Jerusalem at the Passover, during the feast, many believed in His name when they saw the signs which He did. [24] But Jesus did not commit Himself to them, because He knew all *men,* [25] and had no need that anyone should testify of man, for He knew what was in man.

READING 133 · MAY 13

~ 1 SAMUEL 28:1–25 ~

Now it happened in those days that the Philistines gathered their armies together for war, to fight with Israel. And Achish said to David, "You assuredly know that you will go out with me to battle, you and your men."

[2] So David said to Achish, "Surely you know what your servant can do."

And Achish said to David, "Therefore I will make you one of my chief guardians forever."

[3] Now Samuel had died, and all Israel had lamented for him and buried him in

Ramah, in his own city. And Saul had put the mediums and the spiritists out of the land.

[4] Then the Philistines gathered together, and came and encamped at Shunem. So Saul gathered all Israel together, and they encamped at Gilboa. [5] When Saul saw the army of the Philistines, he was afraid, and his heart trembled greatly. [6] And when Saul inquired of the LORD, the LORD did not answer him, either by dreams or by Urim or by the prophets.

[7] Then Saul said to his servants, "Find

The Legend of David's Temple

Most authorities believe King David's Temple was built on Mount Moriah, the mount where Abraham was told to sacrifice Isaac. But there's another Hebrew legend that presents a different story.

The legend says that two brothers lived on adjoining farms which were divided from the peak to the base of the mountain. The younger brother lived alone, unmarried. The older brother had a large family.

One night during the grain harvest, the older brother awoke and thought, My brother is all alone. To cheer his heart, I will take some of my sheaves and lay them on his side of the field.

At the same hour, the younger brother awoke and thought, *My brother has a large family and greater needs than I do. As he sleeps, I'll put some of my sheaves on his side of the field*. Each brother went out carrying sheaves to the other's field and they met halfway. When they declared their intentions to one another, they dropped their sheaves and embraced. It is at that place, the legend claims, the Temple was built.

Whether this story is true or not, it exemplifies the highest expression of love — giving. Giving is one of life's best relationship-builders.

> For God so loved the world that He gave His only begotten Son, that whoever believes in Him should not perish but have everlasting life.
>
> *John 3:16*

me a woman who is a medium, that I may go to her and inquire of her."

And his servants said to him, "In fact, *there is* a woman who is a medium at En Dor."

⁸ So Saul disguised himself and put on other clothes, and he went, and two men with him; and they came to the woman by night. And he said, "Please conduct a séance for me, and bring up for me the one I shall name to you."

⁹ Then the woman said to him, "Look, you know what Saul has done, how he has cut off the mediums and the spiritists from the land. Why then do you lay a snare for my life, to cause me to die?"

¹⁰ And Saul swore to her by the LORD, saying, "*As* the LORD lives, no punishment shall come upon you for this thing."

¹¹ Then the woman said, "Whom shall I bring up for you?"

And he said, "Bring up Samuel for me."

¹² When the woman saw Samuel, she cried out with a loud voice. And the woman spoke to Saul, saying, "Why have you deceived me? For you *are* Saul!"

¹³ And the king said to her, "Do not be afraid. What did you see?"

And the woman said to Saul, "I saw a spirit ascending out of the earth."

¹⁴ So he said to her, "What *is* his form?"

And she said, "An old man is coming up, and he *is* covered with a mantle." And Saul perceived that it *was* Samuel, and he stooped with *his* face to the ground and bowed down.

¹⁵ Now Samuel said to Saul, "Why have you disturbed me by bringing me up?"

And Saul answered, "I am deeply distressed; for the Philistines make war against me, and God has departed from me and does not answer me anymore, neither by prophets nor by dreams. Therefore I have called you, that you may reveal to me what I should do."

¹⁶ Then Samuel said: "So why do you ask me, seeing the LORD has departed from you and has become your enemy? ¹⁷ And the LORD has done for Himself as He spoke by me. For the LORD has torn the kingdom out of your hand and given it to your neighbor, David. ¹⁸ Because you did not obey the voice of the LORD nor execute His fierce wrath upon Amalek, therefore the LORD has done this thing to

you this day. ¹⁹ Moreover the LORD will also deliver Israel with you into the hand of the Philistines. And tomorrow you and your sons *will be* with me. The LORD will also deliver the army of Israel into the hand of the Philistines."

²⁰ Immediately Saul fell full length on the ground, and was dreadfully afraid because of the words of Samuel. And there was no strength in him, for he had eaten no food all day or all night.

²¹ And the woman came to Saul and saw that he was severely troubled, and said to him, "Look, your maidservant has obeyed your voice, and I have put my life in my hands and heeded the words which you spoke to me. ²² Now therefore, please, heed also the voice of your maidservant, and let me set a piece of bread before you; and eat, that you may have strength when you go on *your* way."

²³ But he refused and said, "I will not eat."

So his servants, together with the woman, urged him; and he heeded their voice. Then he arose from the ground and sat on the bed. ²⁴ Now the woman had a fatted calf in the house, and she hastened to kill it. And she took flour and kneaded *it,* and baked unleavened bread from it. ²⁵ So she brought *it* before Saul and his servants, and they ate. Then they rose and went away that night.

∼ PSALM 61:1–4 ∼

¹ Hear my cry, O God;
   Attend to my prayer.
² From the end of the earth I will cry
      to You,
   When my heart is overwhelmed;
   Lead me to the rock that is higher
      than I.

³ For You have been a shelter for me,
   A strong tower from the enemy.
⁴ I will abide in Your tabernacle
      forever;
   I will trust in the shelter of Your
      wings.   Selah

∼ PROVERBS 16:6 ∼

⁶ In mercy and truth
   Atonement is provided for iniquity;

And by the fear of the LORD *one* departs from evil.

~ JOHN 3:1–18 ~

There was a man of the Pharisees named Nicodemus, a ruler of the Jews. ² This man came to Jesus by night and said to Him, "Rabbi, we know that You are a teacher come from God; for no one can do these signs that You do unless God is with him." ³ Jesus answered and said to him, "Most assuredly, I say to you, unless one is born again, he cannot see the kingdom of God." ⁴ Nicodemus said to Him, "How can a man be born when he is old? Can he enter a second time into his mother's womb and be born?" ⁵ Jesus answered, "Most assuredly, I say to you, unless one is born of water and the Spirit, he cannot enter the kingdom of God. ⁶ That which is born of the flesh is flesh, and that which is born of the Spirit is spirit. ⁷ Do not marvel that I said to you, 'You must be born again.' ⁸ The wind blows where it wishes, and you hear the sound of it, but cannot tell where it comes from and where it goes. So is everyone who is born of the Spirit."

⁹ Nicodemus answered and said to Him, "How can these things be?" ¹⁰ Jesus answered and said to him, "Are you the teacher of Israel, and do not know these things? ¹¹ Most assuredly, I say to you, We speak what We know and testify what We have seen, and you do not receive Our witness. ¹² If I have told you earthly things and you do not believe, how will you believe if I tell you heavenly things? ¹³ No one has ascended to heaven but He who came down from heaven, *that is,* the Son of Man who is in heaven. ¹⁴ And as Moses lifted up the serpent in the wilderness, even so must the Son of Man be lifted up, ¹⁵ that whoever believes in Him should not perish but have eternal life. ¹⁶ For God so loved the world that He gave His only begotten Son, that whoever believes in Him should not perish but have everlasting life. ¹⁷ For God did not send His Son into the world to condemn the world, but that the world through Him might be saved. ¹⁸ "He who believes in Him is not condemned; but he who does not believe is condemned already, because he has not believed in the name of the only begotten Son of God.

READING 134 · MAY 14

~ 1 SAMUEL 29:1—31:13 ~

Then the Philistines gathered together all their armies at Aphek, and the Israelites encamped by a fountain which *is* in Jezreel. ² And the lords of the Philistines passed in review by hundreds and by thousands, but David and his men passed in review at the rear with Achish. ³ Then the princes of the Philistines said, "What *are* these Hebrews *doing here?*"

And Achish said to the princes of the Philistines, "*Is* this not David, the servant of Saul king of Israel, who has been with me these days, or these years? And to this day I have found no fault in him since he defected *to me.*"

⁴ But the princes of the Philistines were angry with him; so the princes of the Philistines said to him, "Make this fellow return, that he may go back to the place which you have appointed for him, and do not let him go down with us to battle, lest in the battle he become our adversary. For with what could he reconcile himself to his master, if not with the heads of these men? ⁵ *Is* this not David, of whom they sang to one another in dances, saying:

'Saul has slain his thousands,
    And David his ten thousands'?"

⁶ Then Achish called David and said to him, "Surely, *as* the LORD lives, you have been upright, and your going out and your coming in with me in the army *is* good in my sight. For to this day I have not found evil in you since the day of your coming to me. Nevertheless the lords do not favor you. ⁷ Therefore return now, and go

in peace, that you may not displease the lords of the Philistines."

8 So David said to Achish, "But what have I done? And to this day what have you found in your servant as long as I have been with you, that I may not go and fight against the enemies of my lord the king?"

9 Then Achish answered and said to David, "I know that you *are* as good in my sight as an angel of God; nevertheless the princes of the Philistines have said, 'He shall not go up with us to the battle.' 10 Now therefore, rise early in the morning with your master's servants who have come with you. And as soon as you are up early in the morning and have light, depart."

11 So David and his men rose early to depart in the morning, to return to the land of the Philistines. And the Philistines went up to Jezreel.

30 Now it happened, when David and his men came to Ziklag, on the third day, that the Amalekites had invaded the South and Ziklag, attacked Ziklag and burned it with fire, 2 and had taken captive the women and those who *were* there, from small to great; they did not kill anyone, but carried *them* away and went their way. 3 So David and his men came to the city, and there it was, burned with fire; and their wives, their sons, and their daughters had been taken captive. 4 Then David and the people who *were* with him lifted up their voices and wept, until they had no more power to weep. 5 And David's two wives, Ahinoam the Jezreelitess, and Abigail the widow of Nabal the Carmelite, had been taken captive. 6 Now David was greatly distressed, for the people spoke of stoning him, because the soul of all the people was grieved, every man for his sons and his daughters. But David strengthened himself in the LORD his God.

7 Then David said to Abiathar the priest, Ahimelech's son, "Please bring the ephod here to me." And Abiathar brought the ephod to David. 8 So David inquired of the LORD, saying, "Shall I pursue this troop? Shall I overtake them?"

And He answered him, "Pursue, for you shall surely overtake *them* and without fail recover *all*."

9 So David went, he and the six hundred men who *were* with him, and came to the Brook Besor, where those stayed who were left behind. 10 But David pursued, he and four hundred men; for two hundred stayed *behind,* who were so weary that they could not cross the Brook Besor.

11 Then they found an Egyptian in the field, and brought him to David; and they gave him bread and he ate, and they let him drink water. 12 And they gave him a piece of a cake of figs and two clusters of raisins. So when he had eaten, his strength came back to him; for he had eaten no bread nor drunk water for three days and three nights. 13 Then David said to him, "To whom do you *belong,* and where *are* you from?"

And he said, "I *am* a young man from Egypt, servant of an Amalekite; and my master left me behind, because three days ago I fell sick. 14 We made an invasion of the southern *area* of the Cherethites, in the *territory* which *belongs* to Judah, and of the southern *area* of Caleb; and we burned Ziklag with fire."

15 And David said to him, "Can you take me down to this troop?"

So he said, "Swear to me by God that you will neither kill me nor deliver me into the hands of my master, and I will take you down to this troop."

16 And when he had brought him down, there they were, spread out over all the land, eating and drinking and dancing, because of all the great spoil which they had taken from the land of the Philistines and from the land of Judah. 17 Then David attacked them from twilight until the evening of the next day. Not a man of them escaped, except four hundred young men who rode on camels and fled. 18 So David recovered all that the Amalekites had carried away, and David rescued his two wives. 19 And nothing of theirs was lacking, either small or great, sons or daughters, spoil or anything which they had taken from them; David recovered all. 20 Then David took all the flocks and herds they had driven before those *other* livestock, and said, "This *is* David's spoil."

21 Now David came to the two hundred men who had been so weary that they could not follow David, whom they also had made to stay at the Brook Besor. So

Start with a Step

A comic strip created by Charles Schulz addresses the need for each of us to make the most of the present moment in our lives:

Charlie Brown is at bat. STRIKE THREE. He has struck out again. He slumps down on the players' bench. "Rats!" he exclaims. "I'll never be a big-league player. I just don't have it! All my life I've dreamed of playing in the big leagues, but I know I'll never make it."

Lucy turns to console him. "Charlie Brown," she says, "you're thinking too far ahead. What you need to do is set yourself more immediate goals."

Charlie Brown looks up and asks, "Immediate goals?"

Lucy responds, "Yes. Start with this next inning when you go out to pitch. See if you can walk out to the mound without falling down."

The first step toward walking into any future you can picture is the step that you take today. Make it a forward, positive, energetic, purposeful step. The steps you take today become the well-worn path of tomorrow.

A man's heart plans his way, but the Lord directs his steps.

Proverbs 16:9

they went out to meet David and to meet the people who *were* with him. And when David came near the people, he greeted them. ²² Then all the wicked and worthless men of those who went with David answered and said, "Because they did not go with us, we will not give them *any* of the spoil that we have recovered, except for every man's wife and children, that they may lead *them* away and depart."

²³ But David said, "My brethren, you shall not do so with what the LORD has given us, who has preserved us and delivered into our hand the troop that came against us. ²⁴ For who will heed you in this matter? But as his part *is* who goes down to the battle, so *shall* his part *be* who stays by the supplies; they shall share alike." ²⁵ So it was, from that day forward; he made it a statute and an ordinance for Israel to this day.

²⁶ Now when David came to Ziklag, he sent *some* of the spoil to the elders of Judah, to his friends, saying, "Here is a present for you from the spoil of the enemies of the LORD"— ²⁷ to *those* who *were* in Bethel, *those* who *were* in Ramoth of the South, *those* who *were* in Jattir, ²⁸ *those* who *were* in Aroer, *those* who *were* in Siphmoth, *those* who *were* in Eshtemoa, ²⁹ *those* who *were* in Rachal, *those* who *were* in the cities of the Jerahmeelites, *those* who *were* in the cities of the Kenites, ³⁰ *those* who *were* in Hormah, *those* who *were* in Chorashan, *those* who *were* in Athach, ³¹ *those* who *were* in Hebron, and to all the places where David himself and his men were accustomed to rove.

31 Now the Philistines fought against Israel; and the men of Israel fled from before the Philistines, and fell slain on Mount Gilboa. ² Then the Philistines followed hard after Saul and his sons. And the Philistines killed Jonathan, Abinadab, and Malchishua, Saul's sons. ³ The battle became fierce against Saul. The archers hit him, and he was severely wounded by the archers.

⁴ Then Saul said to his armorbearer, "Draw your sword, and thrust me through with it, lest these uncircumcised men come and thrust me through and abuse me."

But his armorbearer would not, for he was greatly afraid. Therefore Saul took a sword and fell on it. ⁵ And when his armorbearer saw that Saul was dead, he also fell on his sword, and died with him. ⁶ So Saul, his three sons, his armorbearer, and all his men died together that same day.

⁷ And when the men of Israel who *were* on the other side of the valley, and *those* who *were* on the other side of the Jordan, saw that the men of Israel had fled and that Saul and his sons were dead, they forsook the cities and fled; and the Philistines came and dwelt in them. ⁸ So it happened the next day, when the Philistines came to strip the slain, that they found Saul and his three sons fallen on Mount Gilboa. ⁹ And they cut off his head and stripped off his armor, and sent *word* throughout the land of the Philistines, to proclaim *it in* the temple of their idols and among the people. ¹⁰ Then they put his armor in the temple of the Ashtoreths, and they fastened his body to the wall of Beth Shan.

¹¹ Now when the inhabitants of Jabesh Gilead heard what the Philistines had done to Saul, ¹² all the valiant men arose and traveled all night, and took the body of Saul and the bodies of his sons from the wall of Beth Shan; and they came to Jabesh and burned them there. ¹³ Then they took their bones and buried *them* under the tamarisk tree at Jabesh, and fasted seven days.

∼ PSALM 61:5–8 ∼

⁵ For You, O God, have heard my
     vows;
  You have given *me* the heritage of
     those who fear Your name.
⁶ You will prolong the king's life,
  His years as many generations.
⁷ He shall abide before God forever.
  Oh, prepare mercy and truth, *which*
     may preserve him!

⁸ So I will sing praise to Your name
     forever,
  That I may daily perform my vows.

∼ PROVERBS 16:7–9 ∼

⁷ When a man's ways please the LORD,
  He makes even his enemies to be at
     peace with him.

8 Better *is* a little with righteousness,
   Than vast revenues without justice.

9 A man's heart plans his way,
   But the LORD directs his steps.

~ JOHN 3:19–36 ~

And this is the condemnation, that the light has come into the world, and men loved darkness rather than light, because their deeds were evil. ²⁰ For everyone practicing evil hates the light and does not come to the light, lest his deeds should be exposed. ²¹ But he who does the truth comes to the light, that his deeds may be clearly seen, that they have been done in God."

²²After these things Jesus and His disciples came into the land of Judea, and there He remained with them and baptized. ²³ Now John also was baptizing in Aenon near Salim, because there was much water there. And they came and were baptized. ²⁴ For John had not yet been thrown into prison.

²⁵ Then there arose a dispute between *some* of John's disciples and the Jews about purification. ²⁶ And they came to John and said to him, "Rabbi, He who was with you beyond the Jordan, to whom you have testified—behold, He is baptizing, and all are coming to Him!"

²⁷ John answered and said, "A man can receive nothing unless it has been given to him from heaven. ²⁸ You yourselves bear me witness, that I said, 'I am not the Christ,' but, 'I have been sent before Him.' ²⁹ He who has the bride is the bridegroom; but the friend of the bridegroom, who stands and hears him, rejoices greatly because of the bridegroom's voice. Therefore this joy of mine is fulfilled. ³⁰ He must increase, but I *must* decrease. ³¹ He who comes from above is above all; he who is of the earth is earthly and speaks of the earth. He who comes from heaven is above all. ³² And what He has seen and heard, that He testifies; and no one receives His testimony. ³³ He who has received His testimony has certified that God is true. ³⁴ For He whom God has sent speaks the words of God, for God does not give the Spirit by measure. ³⁵ The Father loves the Son, and has given all things into His hand. ³⁶ He who believes in the Son has everlasting life; and he who does not believe the Son shall not see life, but the wrath of God abides on him."

~ 2 SAMUEL 1:1—2:32 ~

Now it came to pass after the death of Saul, when David had returned from the slaughter of the Amalekites, and David had stayed two days in Ziklag, ² on the third day, behold, it happened that a man came from Saul's camp with his clothes torn and dust on his head. So it was, when he came to David, that he fell to the ground and prostrated himself.

³ And David said to him, "Where have you come from?"

So he said to him, "I have escaped from the camp of Israel."

⁴ Then David said to him, "How did the matter go? Please tell me."

And he answered, "The people have fled from the battle, many of the people are fallen and dead, and Saul and Jonathan his son are dead also."

⁵ So David said to the young man who told him, "How do you know that Saul and Jonathan his son are dead?"

⁶ Then the young man who told him said, "As I happened by chance *to be* on Mount Gilboa, there was Saul, leaning on his spear; and indeed the chariots and horsemen followed hard after him. ⁷ Now when he looked behind him, he saw me and called to me. And I answered, 'Here I am.' ⁸ And he said to me, 'Who *are* you?' So I answered him, 'I *am* an Amalekite.' ⁹ He said to me again, 'Please stand over me and kill me, for anguish has come upon me, but my life still *remains* in me.' ¹⁰ So I stood over him and killed him,

because I was sure that he could not live after he had fallen. And I took the crown that *was* on his head and the bracelet that *was* on his arm, and have brought them here to my lord."

[11] Therefore David took hold of his own clothes and tore them, and *so did* all the men who *were* with him. [12] And they mourned and wept and fasted until evening for Saul and for Jonathan his son, for the people of the LORD and for the house of Israel, because they had fallen by the sword.

[13] Then David said to the young man who told him, "Where *are* you from?"

And he answered, "I *am* the son of an alien, an Amalekite."

[14] So David said to him, "How was it you were not afraid to put forth your hand to destroy the LORD's anointed?" [15] Then David called one of the young men and said, "Go near, *and* execute him!" And he struck him so that he died. [16] So David said to him, "Your blood *is* on your own head, for your own mouth has testified against you, saying, 'I have killed the LORD's anointed.' "

[17] Then David lamented with this lamentation over Saul and over Jonathan his son, [18] and he told *them* to teach the children of Judah *the Song of* the Bow; indeed *it is* written in the Book of Jasher:

[19] "The beauty of Israel is slain on your high places!
How the mighty have fallen!
[20] Tell *it* not in Gath,
Proclaim *it* not in the streets of Ashkelon—
Lest the daughters of the Philistines rejoice,
Lest the daughters of the uncircumcised triumph.

[21] "O mountains of Gilboa,
Let there be no dew nor rain upon you,
Nor fields of offerings.
For the shield of the mighty is cast away there!
The shield of Saul, not anointed with oil.
[22] From the blood of the slain,
From the fat of the mighty,

The bow of Jonathan did not turn back,
And the sword of Saul did not return empty.

[23] "Saul and Jonathan *were* beloved and pleasant in their lives,
And in their death they were not divided;
They were swifter than eagles,
They were stronger than lions.

[24] "O daughters of Israel, weep over Saul,
Who clothed you in scarlet, with luxury;
Who put ornaments of gold on your apparel.

[25] "How the mighty have fallen in the midst of the battle!
Jonathan *was* slain in your high places.
[26] I am distressed for you, my brother Jonathan;
You have been very pleasant to me;
Your love to me was wonderful,
Surpassing the love of women.

[27] "How the mighty have fallen,
And the weapons of war perished!"

2 It happened after this that David inquired of the LORD, saying, "Shall I go up to any of the cities of Judah?"

And the LORD said to him, "Go up."

David said, "Where shall I go up?"

And He said, "To Hebron."

[2] So David went up there, and his two wives also, Ahinoam the Jezreelitess, and Abigail the widow of Nabal the Carmelite. [3] And David brought up the men who *were* with him, every man with his household. So they dwelt in the cities of Hebron. [4] Then the men of Judah came, and there they anointed David king over the house of Judah. And they told David, saying, "The men of Jabesh Gilead *were the ones* who buried Saul." [5] So David sent messengers to the men of Jabesh Gilead, and said to them, "You *are* blessed of the LORD, for you have shown this kindness to your lord, to Saul, and have buried him.

Always Useful to God

Truly my soul silently waits for God; from Him comes my salvation.

Psalm 62:1

In *Glorious Intruder*, Joni Eareckson Tada writes about Diane, who suffers from multiple sclerosis: "In her quiet sanctuary, Diane turns her head slightly on the pillow toward the corkboard on the wall. Her eyes scan each thumbtacked card and list. Each photo. Every torn piece of paper carefully pinned in a row. The stillness is broken as Diane begins to murmur. She is praying.

"Some would look at Diane — stiff and motionless — and shake their heads . . . 'What a shame. Her life has no meaning. She can't really do anything.' But Diane is confident, convinced her life is significant. Her labor of prayer counts. She moves mountains that block the paths of missionaries. She helps open the eyes of the spiritually blind in southeast Asia. She pushes back the kingdom of darkness that blackens the alleys and streets of the gangs in east LA. She aids homeless mothers, single parents, abused children, despondent teenagers, handicapped boys, and the dying and forgotten old people in the nursing home down the street from where she lives. Diane is on the front lines, advancing the gospel of Christ, holding up weak saints, inspiring doubting believers, energizing other prayer warriors, and delighting her Lord and Savior."

What a difference we can make, regardless of our situation in life, if we have the right attitude. God is willing and able to use us regardless of our ability or inability — He always has a plan!

---

⁶ And now may the LORD show kindness and truth to you. I also will repay you this kindness, because you have done this thing. ⁷ Now therefore, let your hands be strengthened, and be valiant; for your master Saul is dead, and also the house of Judah has anointed me king over them."

⁸ But Abner the son of Ner, commander of Saul's army, took Ishbosheth the son of Saul and brought him over to Mahanaim; ⁹ and he made him king over Gilead, over the Ashurites, over Jezreel, over Ephraim, over Benjamin, and over all Israel. ¹⁰ Ishbosheth, Saul's son, *was* forty years old when he began to reign over Israel, and he reigned two years. Only the house of Judah followed David. ¹¹ And the time that David was king in Hebron over the house of Judah was seven years and six months.

¹² Now Abner the son of Ner, and the servants of Ishbosheth the son of Saul, went out from Mahanaim to Gibeon. ¹³ And Joab the son of Zeruiah, and the servants of David, went out and met them by the pool of Gibeon. So they sat down, one on one side of the pool and the other on the other side of the pool. ¹⁴ Then Abner said to Joab, "Let the young men now arise and compete before us."

And Joab said, "Let them arise."

¹⁵ So they arose and went over by number, twelve from Benjamin, *followers* of Ishbosheth the son of Saul, and twelve from the servants of David. ¹⁶ And each one grasped his opponent by the head and *thrust* his sword in his opponent's side; so they fell down together. Therefore that place was called the Field of Sharp Swords, which *is* in Gibeon. ¹⁷ So there was a very fierce battle that day, and Abner and the men of Israel were beaten before the servants of David.

¹⁸ Now the three sons of Zeruiah were there: Joab and Abishai and Asahel. And Asahel *was as* fleet of foot as a wild gazelle. ¹⁹ So Asahel pursued Abner, and in going he did not turn to the right hand or to the left from following Abner. ²⁰ Then Abner looked behind him and said, "*Are* you Asahel?"

He answered, "I *am*."

²¹ And Abner said to him, "Turn aside to your right hand or to your left, and lay hold on one of the young men and take his armor for yourself." But Asahel would not turn aside from following him. ²² So Abner said again to Asahel, "Turn aside from following me. Why should I strike you to the ground? How then could I face your brother Joab?" ²³ However, he refused to turn aside. Therefore Abner struck him in the stomach with the blunt end of the spear, so that the spear came out of his back; and he fell down there and died on the spot. So it was *that* as many as came to the place where Asahel fell down and died, stood still.

²⁴ Joab and Abishai also pursued Abner. And the sun was going down when they came to the hill of Ammah, which *is* before Giah by the road to the Wilderness of Gibeon. ²⁵ Now the children of Benjamin gathered together behind Abner and became a unit, and took their stand on top of a hill. ²⁶ Then Abner called to Joab and said, "Shall the sword devour forever? Do you not know that it will be bitter in the latter end? How long will it be then until you tell the people to return from pursuing their brethren?"

²⁷ And Joab said, "*As* God lives, unless you had spoken, surely then by morning all the people would have given up pursuing their brethren." ²⁸ So Joab blew a trumpet; and all the people stood still and did not pursue Israel anymore, nor did they fight anymore. ²⁹ Then Abner and his men went on all that night through the plain, crossed over the Jordan, and went through all Bithron; and they came to Mahanaim.

³⁰ So Joab returned from pursuing Abner. And when he had gathered all the people together, there were missing of David's servants nineteen men and Asahel. ³¹ But the servants of David had struck down, of Benjamin and Abner's men, three hundred and sixty men who died. ³² Then they took up Asahel and buried him in his father's tomb, which *was in* Bethlehem. And Joab and his men went all night, and they came to Hebron at daybreak.

∼ PSALM 62:1–4 ∼

¹ Truly my soul silently *waits* for God;
   From Him *comes* my salvation.

2   He only *is* my rock and my
       salvation;
     He is my defense;
     I shall not be greatly moved.

3   How long will you attack a man?
     You shall be slain, all of you,
     Like a leaning wall and a tottering
       fence.
4   They only consult to cast *him* down
       from his high position;
     They delight in lies;
     They bless with their mouth,
     But they curse inwardly.   Selah

∼ PROVERBS 16:10–12 ∼

10   Divination *is* on the lips of the king;
     His mouth must not transgress in
       judgment.
11   Honest weights and scales *are* the
       LORD's;
     All the weights in the bag *are* His
       work.
12   *It is* an abomination for kings to
       commit wickedness,
     For a throne is established by
       righteousness.

∼ JOHN 4:1–30 ∼

Therefore, when the Lord knew that the
Pharisees had heard that Jesus made and
baptized more disciples than John
2(though Jesus Himself did not baptize,
but His disciples), 3 He left Judea and departed again to Galilee. 4 But He needed
to go through Samaria.
   5 So He came to a city of Samaria which
is called Sychar, near the plot of ground
that Jacob gave to his son Joseph. 6 Now
Jacob's well was there. Jesus therefore,
being wearied from *His* journey, sat thus
by the well. It was about the sixth hour.
   7 A woman of Samaria came to draw
water. Jesus said to her, "Give Me a
drink." 8 For His disciples had gone away
into the city to buy food.
   9 Then the woman of Samaria said to
Him, "How is it that You, being a Jew,
ask a drink from me, a Samaritan
woman?" For Jews have no dealings with
Samaritans.
   10 Jesus answered and said to her, "If
you knew the gift of God, and who it is

who says to you, 'Give Me a drink,' you
would have asked Him, and He would
have given you living water."
   11 The woman said to Him, "Sir, You
have nothing to draw with, and the well
is deep. Where then do You get that living water? 12 Are You greater than our
father Jacob, who gave us the well, and
drank from it himself, as well as his sons
and his livestock?"
   13 Jesus answered and said to her,
"Whoever drinks of this water will thirst
again, 14 but whoever drinks of the water
that I shall give him will never thirst. But
the water that I shall give him will become in him a fountain of water springing
up into everlasting life."
   15 The woman said to Him, "Sir, give
me this water, that I may not thirst, nor
come here to draw."
   16 Jesus said to her, "Go, call your husband, and come here."
   17 The woman answered and said, "I
have no husband."
   Jesus said to her, "You have well said,
'I have no husband,' 18 for you have had
five husbands, and the one whom you
now have is not your husband; in that
you spoke truly."
   19 The woman said to Him, "Sir, I perceive that You are a prophet. 20 Our fathers worshiped on this mountain, and
you *Jews* say that in Jerusalem is the place
where one ought to worship."
   21 Jesus said to her, "Woman, believe
Me, the hour is coming when you will
neither on this mountain, nor in Jerusalem, worship the Father. 22 You worship
what you do not know; we know what
we worship, for salvation is of the Jews.
23 But the hour is coming, and now is,
when the true worshipers will worship the
Father in spirit and truth; for the Father
is seeking such to worship Him. 24 God *is*
Spirit, and those who worship Him must
worship in spirit and truth."
   25 The woman said to Him, "I know
that Messiah is coming" (who is called
Christ). "When He comes, He will tell us
all things."
   26 Jesus said to her, "I who speak to you
am *He.*"
   27 And at this *point* His disciples came,
and they marveled that He talked with a
woman; yet no one said, "What do You

seek?" or, "Why are You talking with her?"

²⁸ The woman then left her waterpot, went her way into the city, and said to the men, ²⁹ "Come, see a Man who told me all things that I ever did. Could this be the Christ?" ³⁰ Then they went out of the city and came to Him.

READING 136 · MAY 16

～ 2 SAMUEL 3:1—4:12 ～

Now there was a long war between the house of Saul and the house of David. But David grew stronger and stronger, and the house of Saul grew weaker and weaker.

² Sons were born to David in Hebron: His firstborn was Amnon by Ahinoam the Jezreelitess; ³ his second, Chileab, by Abigail the widow of Nabal the Carmelite; the third, Absalom the son of Maacah, the daughter of Talmai, king of Geshur; ⁴ the fourth, Adonijah the son of Haggith; the fifth, Shephatiah the son of Abital; ⁵ and the sixth, Ithream, by David's wife Eglah. These were born to David in Hebron.

⁶ Now it was so, while there was war between the house of Saul and the house of David, that Abner was strengthening *his hold* on the house of Saul.

⁷ And Saul had a concubine, whose name *was* Rizpah, the daughter of Aiah. So *Ishbosheth* said to Abner, "Why have you gone in to my father's concubine?"

⁸ Then Abner became very angry at the words of Ishbosheth, and said, "*Am* I a dog's head that belongs to Judah? Today I show loyalty to the house of Saul your father, to his brothers, and to his friends, and have not delivered you into the hand of David; and you charge me today with a fault concerning this woman? ⁹ May God do so to Abner, and more also, if I do not do for David as the LORD has sworn to him— ¹⁰ to transfer the kingdom from the house of Saul, and set up the throne of David over Israel and over Judah, from Dan to Beersheba." ¹¹ And he could not answer Abner another word, because he feared him.

¹² Then Abner sent messengers on his behalf to David, saying, "Whose *is* the land?" saying *also,* "Make your covenant with me, and indeed my hand *shall be* with you to bring all Israel to you."

¹³ And *David* said, "Good, I will make a covenant with you. But one thing I require of you: you shall not see my face unless you first bring Michal, Saul's daughter, when you come to see my face."

¹⁴ So David sent messengers to Ishbosheth, Saul's son, saying, "Give *me* my wife Michal, whom I betrothed to myself for a hundred foreskins of the Philistines."

¹⁵ And Ishbosheth sent and took her from *her* husband, from Paltiel the son of Laish.

¹⁶ Then her husband went along with her to Bahurim, weeping behind her. So Abner said to him, "Go, return!" And he returned.

¹⁷ Now Abner had communicated with the elders of Israel, saying, "In time past you were seeking for David *to be* king over you. ¹⁸ Now then, do *it*! For the LORD has spoken of David, saying, 'By the hand of My servant David, I will save My people Israel from the hand of the Philistines and the hand of all their enemies.' "

¹⁹ And Abner also spoke in the hearing of Benjamin. Then Abner also went to speak in the hearing of David in Hebron all that seemed good to Israel and the whole house of Benjamin.

²⁰ So Abner and twenty men with him came to David at Hebron. And David made a feast for Abner and the men who *were* with him. ²¹ Then Abner said to David, "I will arise and go, and gather all Israel to my lord the king, that they may make a covenant with you, and that you may reign over all that your heart desires." So David sent Abner away, and he went in peace.

²² At that moment the servants of David and Joab came from a raid and brought much spoil with them. But Abner *was* not

Simplicity

One of the most influential and prominent people in the world is Pope John Paul II. Those who have known him through the years regard him as a man of simplicity and honor.

As a quarry worker in Poland in 1940, he endured bitterly cold temperatures dressed only in a sweat-soaked cap and blue cloth jacket and trousers. One day he arrived at work without his jacket — he had given it to someone he met on the road.

As a village cleric, he had a reputation as a "skinny priest in a threadbare cassock." He walked on an unpaved road to his first parish carrying all of his belongings in a battered briefcase. As a teacher of ethics at the Catholic University of Lublin, he often wore a black cassock frayed at the knees from the time he spent in prayer. As a cardinal at the Vatican, he owned practically nothing except his books, ecclesiastical robes, a few family mementos, skis, and hiking clothes.

Those who know him well have conjectured that it is because he has ties to so little in the way of family (most of whom died early in his life) or personal goods, that he is able to reach out so warmly to millions around the world who have very little to offer other than their faith.

The Bible says that whatever occupies your thoughts and time is what you truly value. Stop yourself today. What do you spend most of your time thinking about? You may find you need to simplify your life and cut back on some superfluous commitments, so that you can focus your attentions on those to whom God has called you to minister.

with David in Hebron, for he had sent him away, and he had gone in peace. ²³ When Joab and all the troops that *were* with him had come, they told Joab, saying, "Abner the son of Ner came to the king, and he sent him away, and he has gone in peace." ²⁴ Then Joab came to the king and said, "What have you done? Look, Abner came to you; why *is it that* you sent him away, and he has already gone? ²⁵ Surely you realize that Abner the son of Ner came to deceive you, to know your going out and your coming in, and to know all that you are doing."

²⁶ And when Joab had gone from David's presence, he sent messengers after Abner, who brought him back from the well of Sirah. But David did not know *it*. ²⁷ Now when Abner had returned to Hebron, Joab took him aside in the gate to speak with him privately, and there stabbed him in the stomach, so that he died for the blood of Asahel his brother.

²⁸ Afterward, when David heard *it*, he said, "My kingdom and I *are* guiltless before the LORD forever of the blood of Abner the son of Ner. ²⁹ Let it rest on the head of Joab and on all his father's house; and let there never fail to be in the house of Joab one who has a discharge or is a leper, who leans on a staff or falls by the sword, or who lacks bread." ³⁰ So Joab and Abishai his brother killed Abner, because he had killed their brother Asahel at Gibeon in the battle.

³¹ Then David said to Joab and to all the people who were with him, "Tear your clothes, gird yourselves with sackcloth, and mourn for Abner." And King David followed the coffin. ³² So they buried Abner in Hebron; and the king lifted up his voice and wept at the grave of Abner, and all the people wept. ³³ And the king sang *a lament* over Abner and said:

"Should Abner die as a fool dies?
³⁴ Your hands were not bound
    Nor your feet put into fetters;
    As a man falls before wicked men,
    so you fell."

Then all the people wept over him again. ³⁵ And when all the people came to persuade David to eat food while it was still day, David took an oath, saying, "God do so to me, and more also, if I taste bread or anything else till the sun goes down!" ³⁶ Now all the people took note *of it,* and it pleased them, since whatever the king did pleased all the people. ³⁷ For all the people and all Israel understood that day that it had not been the king's *intent* to kill Abner the son of Ner. ³⁸ Then the king said to his servants, "Do you not know that a prince and a great man has fallen this day in Israel? ³⁹ And I *am* weak today, though anointed king; and these men, the sons of Zeruiah, *are* too harsh for me. The LORD shall repay the evildoer according to his wickedness."

4 When Saul's son heard that Abner had died in Hebron, he lost heart, and all Israel was troubled. ² Now Saul's son *had* two men *who were* captains of troops. The name of one *was* Baanah and the name of the other Rechab, the sons of Rimmon the Beerothite, of the children of Benjamin. (For Beeroth also was *part* of Benjamin, ³ because the Beerothites fled to Gittaim and have been sojourners there until this day.)

⁴ Jonathan, Saul's son, had a son *who was* lame in *his* feet. He was five years old when the news about Saul and Jonathan came from Jezreel; and his nurse took him up and fled. And it happened, as she made haste to flee, that he fell and became lame. His name *was* Mephibosheth.

⁵ Then the sons of Rimmon the Beerothite, Rechab and Baanah, set out and came at about the heat of the day to the house of Ishbosheth, who was lying on his bed at noon. ⁶ And they came there, all the way into the house, *as though* to get wheat, and they stabbed him in the stomach. Then Rechab and Baanah his brother escaped. ⁷ For when they came into the house, he was lying on his bed in his bedroom; then they struck him and killed him, beheaded him and took his head, and were all night escaping through the plain. ⁸ And they brought the head of Ishbosheth to David at Hebron, and said to the king, "Here is the head of Ishbosheth, the son of Saul your enemy, who sought your life; and the LORD has avenged my lord the king this day of Saul and his descendants."

⁹ But David answered Rechab and Baanah his brother, the sons of Rimmon the Beerothite, and said to them, "As the LORD lives, who has redeemed my life from all adversity, ¹⁰ when someone told me, saying, 'Look, Saul is dead,' thinking to have brought good news, I arrested him and had him executed in Ziklag—the one who *thought* I would give him a reward for *his* news. ¹¹ How much more, when wicked men have killed a righteous person in his own house on his bed? Therefore, shall I not now require his blood at your hand and remove you from the earth?" ¹² So David commanded his young men, and they executed them, cut off their hands and feet, and hanged *them* by the pool in Hebron. But they took the head of Ishbosheth and buried *it* in the tomb of Abner in Hebron.

～ PSALM 62:5–12 ～

⁵ My soul, wait silently for God alone,
   For my expectation *is* from Him.
⁶ He only *is* my rock and my
      salvation;
   He is my defense;
   I shall not be moved.
⁷ In God *is* my salvation and my
      glory;
   The rock of my strength,
   And my refuge, *is* in God.

⁸ Trust in Him at all times, you
      people;
   Pour out your heart before Him;
   God *is* a refuge for us.   Selah

⁹ Surely men of low degree *are* a
      vapor,
   Men of high degree *are* a lie;
   If they are weighed on the scales,
   They *are* altogether *lighter* than
      vapor.
¹⁰ Do not trust in oppression,
   Nor vainly hope in robbery;
   If riches increase,
   Do not set *your* heart *on them.*

¹¹ God has spoken once,
   Twice I have heard this:
   That power *belongs* to God.

¹² Also to You, O Lord, *belongs* mercy;
   For You render to each one
      according to his work.

～ PROVERBS 16:13–15 ～

¹³ Righteous lips *are* the delight of
      kings,
   And they love him who speaks *what
   is* right.
¹⁴ As messengers of death *is* the king's
      wrath,
   But a wise man will appease it.
¹⁵ In the light of the king's face *is* life,
   And his favor *is* like a cloud of the
      latter rain.

～ JOHN 4:31–54 ～

In the meantime His disciples urged Him, saying, "Rabbi, eat."
³² But He said to them, "I have food to eat of which you do not know."
³³ Therefore the disciples said to one another, "Has anyone brought Him *anything* to eat?"
³⁴ Jesus said to them, "My food is to do the will of Him who sent Me, and to finish His work. ³⁵ Do you not say, 'There are still four months and *then* comes the harvest'? Behold, I say to you, lift up your eyes and look at the fields, for they are already white for harvest! ³⁶ And he who reaps receives wages, and gathers fruit for eternal life, that both he who sows and he who reaps may rejoice together. ³⁷ For in this the saying is true: 'One sows and another reaps.' ³⁸ I sent you to reap that for which you have not labored; others have labored, and you have entered into their labors."
³⁹ And many of the Samaritans of that city believed in Him because of the word of the woman who testified, "He told me all that I *ever* did." ⁴⁰ So when the Samaritans had come to Him, they urged Him to stay with them; and He stayed there two days. ⁴¹ And many more believed because of His own word.
⁴² Then they said to the woman, "Now we believe, not because of what you said, for we ourselves have heard *Him* and we know that this is indeed the Christ, the Savior of the world."
⁴³ Now after the two days He departed

from there and went to Galilee. ⁴⁴ For Jesus Himself testified that a prophet has no honor in his own country. ⁴⁵ So when He came to Galilee, the Galileans received Him, having seen all the things He did in Jerusalem at the feast; for they also had gone to the feast.

⁴⁶ So Jesus came again to Cana of Galilee where He had made the water wine. And there was a certain nobleman whose son was sick at Capernaum. ⁴⁷ When he heard that Jesus had come out of Judea into Galilee, he went to Him and implored Him to come down and heal his son, for he was at the point of death. ⁴⁸ Then Jesus said to him, "Unless you *people* see signs and wonders, you will by no means believe."

⁴⁹ The nobleman said to Him, "Sir, come down before my child dies!"

⁵⁰ Jesus said to him, "Go your way; your son lives." So the man believed the word that Jesus spoke to him, and he went his way. ⁵¹ And as he was now going down, his servants met him and told *him*, saying, "Your son lives!"

⁵² Then he inquired of them the hour when he got better. And they said to him, "Yesterday at the seventh hour the fever left him." ⁵³ So the father knew that *it was* at the same hour in which Jesus said to him, "Your son lives." And he himself believed, and his whole household.

⁵⁴ This again *is* the second sign Jesus did when He had come out of Judea into Galilee.

READING 137 · MAY 17

∼ 2 SAMUEL 5:1—6:23 ∼

Then all the tribes of Israel came to David at Hebron and spoke, saying, "Indeed we *are* your bone and your flesh. ² Also, in time past, when Saul was king over us, you were the one who led Israel out and brought them in; and the LORD said to you, 'You shall shepherd My people Israel, and be ruler over Israel.' " ³ Therefore all the elders of Israel came to the king at Hebron, and King David made a covenant with them at Hebron before the LORD. And they anointed David king over Israel. ⁴ David *was* thirty years old when he began to reign, *and* he reigned forty years. ⁵ In Hebron he reigned over Judah seven years and six months, and in Jerusalem he reigned thirty-three years over all Israel and Judah.

⁶ And the king and his men went to Jerusalem against the Jebusites, the inhabitants of the land, who spoke to David, saying, "You shall not come in here; but the blind and the lame will repel you," thinking, "David cannot come in here." ⁷ Nevertheless David took the stronghold of Zion (that *is*, the City of David).

⁸ Now David said on that day, "Whoever climbs up by way of the water shaft and defeats the Jebusites (the lame and the blind, *who are* hated by David's soul),

he shall be chief and captain." Therefore they say, "The blind and the lame shall not come into the house."

⁹ Then David dwelt in the stronghold, and called it the City of David. And David built all around from the Millo and inward. ¹⁰ So David went on and became great, and the LORD God of hosts *was* with him.

¹¹ Then Hiram king of Tyre sent messengers to David, and cedar trees, and carpenters and masons. And they built David a house. ¹² So David knew that the LORD had established him as king over Israel, and that He had exalted His kingdom for the sake of His people Israel.

¹³ And David took more concubines and wives from Jerusalem, after he had come from Hebron. Also more sons and daughters were born to David. ¹⁴ Now these *are* the names of those who were born to him in Jerusalem: Shammua, Shobab, Nathan, Solomon, ¹⁵ Ibhar, Elishua, Nepheg, Japhia, ¹⁶ Elishama, Eliada, and Eliphelet.

¹⁷ Now when the Philistines heard that they had anointed David king over Israel, all the Philistines went up to search for David. And David heard *of it* and went down to the stronghold. ¹⁸ The Philistines also went and deployed themselves in the Valley of Rephaim. ¹⁹ So David inquired

Time to Pray

How hollow our excuse sounds when we say, "I just didn't have time to spend with You today, Lord." Perhaps our not seeking Him is the reason so many of us have difficulty finding His answers.

I got up early one morning
And rushed right into the day;
I had so much to accomplish
I didn't have time to pray.

Troubles just tumbled about me
And heavier came each task.
Why doesn't God help me,
  I wondered.
He answered, "You didn't ask."

I tried to come into God's presence,
I used all my keys at the lock.
God gently and lovingly chided,
"Why child, you didn't knock."

I wanted to see joy and beauty,
But the day toiled on grey and bleak,
I called on the Lord for the reason —
He said, "You didn't seek."

I woke up early this morning
And paused before entering the day.
I had so much to accomplish
That I had to take time to pray.
                    — Unknown

O God, You are my God; early will I seek You; my soul thirsts for You; my flesh longs for You in a dry and thirsty land where there is no water.

Psalm 63:1

of the LORD, saying, "Shall I go up against the Philistines? Will You deliver them into my hand?"

And the LORD said to David, "Go up, for I will doubtless deliver the Philistines into your hand."

[20] So David went to Baal Perazim, and David defeated them there; and he said, "The LORD has broken through my enemies before me, like a breakthrough of water." Therefore he called the name of that place Baal Perazim. [21] And they left their images there, and David and his men carried them away.

[22] Then the Philistines went up once again and deployed themselves in the Valley of Rephaim. [23] Therefore David inquired of the LORD, and He said, "You shall not go up; circle around behind them, and come upon them in front of the mulberry trees. [24] And it shall be, when you hear the sound of marching in the tops of the mulberry trees, then you shall advance quickly. For then the LORD will go out before you to strike the camp of the Philistines." [25] And David did so, as the LORD commanded him; and he drove back the Philistines from Geba as far as Gezer.

6 Again David gathered all *the* choice *men* of Israel, thirty thousand. [2] And David arose and went with all the people who *were* with him from Baale Judah to bring up from there the ark of God, whose name is called by the Name, the LORD of Hosts, who dwells *between* the cherubim. [3] So they set the ark of God on a new cart, and brought it out of the house of Abinadab, which *was* on the hill; and Uzzah and Ahio, the sons of Abinadab, drove the new cart. [4] And they brought it out of the house of Abinadab, which *was* on the hill, accompanying the ark of God; and Ahio went before the ark. [5] Then David and all the house of Israel played *music* before the LORD on all kinds of *instruments of* fir wood, on harps, on stringed instruments, on tambourines, on sistrums, and on cymbals.

[6] And when they came to Nachon's threshing floor, Uzzah put out *his hand* to the ark of God and took hold of it, for the oxen stumbled. [7] Then the anger of the LORD was aroused against Uzzah,

and God struck him there for *his* error; and he died there by the ark of God. [8] And David became angry because of the LORD's outbreak against Uzzah; and he called the name of the place Perez Uzzah to this day.

[9] David was afraid of the LORD that day; and he said, "How can the ark of the LORD come to me?" [10] So David would not move the ark of the LORD with him into the City of David; but David took it aside into the house of Obed-Edom the Gittite. [11] The ark of the LORD remained in the house of Obed-Edom the Gittite three months. And the LORD blessed Obed-Edom and all his household.

[12] Now it was told King David, saying, "The LORD has blessed the house of Obed-Edom and all that *belongs* to him, because of the ark of God." So David went and brought up the ark of God from the house of Obed-Edom to the City of David with gladness. [13] And so it was, when those bearing the ark of the LORD had gone six paces, that he sacrificed oxen and fatted sheep. [14] Then David danced before the LORD with all *his* might; and David *was* wearing a linen ephod. [15] So David and all the house of Israel brought up the ark of the LORD with shouting and with the sound of the trumpet.

[16] Now as the ark of the LORD came into the City of David, Michal, Saul's daughter, looked through a window and saw King David leaping and whirling before the LORD; and she despised him in her heart. [17] So they brought the ark of the LORD, and set it in its place in the midst of the tabernacle that David had erected for it. Then David offered burnt offerings and peace offerings before the LORD. [18] And when David had finished offering burnt offerings and peace offerings, he blessed the people in the name of the LORD of hosts. [19] Then he distributed among all the people, among the whole multitude of Israel, both the women and the men, to everyone a loaf of bread, a piece *of meat,* and a cake of raisins. So all the people departed, everyone to his house.

[20] Then David returned to bless his household. And Michal the daughter of Saul came out to meet David, and said, "How glorious was the king of Israel

today, uncovering himself today in the eyes of the maids of his servants, as one of the base fellows shamelessly uncovers himself!"

²¹ So David said to Michal, "*It was* before the LORD, who chose me instead of your father and all his house, to appoint me ruler over the people of the LORD, over Israel. Therefore I will play *music* before the LORD. ²² And I will be even more undignified than this, and will be humble in my own sight. But as for the maidservants of whom you have spoken, by them I will be held in honor."

²³ Therefore Michal the daughter of Saul had no children to the day of her death.

∼ PSALM 63:1–11 ∼

¹ O God, You *are* my God;
Early will I seek You;
My soul thirsts for You;
My flesh longs for You
In a dry and thirsty land
Where there is no water.

² So I have looked for You in the sanctuary,
To see Your power and Your glory.

³ Because Your lovingkindness *is* better than life,
My lips shall praise You.

⁴ Thus I will bless You while I live;
I will lift up my hands in Your name.

⁵ My soul shall be satisfied as with marrow and fatness,
And my mouth shall praise You with joyful lips.

⁶ When I remember You on my bed,
I meditate on You in the *night* watches.

⁷ Because You have been my help,
Therefore in the shadow of Your wings I will rejoice.

⁸ My soul follows close behind You;
Your right hand upholds me.

⁹ But those *who* seek my life, to destroy *it*,
Shall go into the lower parts of the earth.

¹⁰ They shall fall by the sword;
They shall be a portion for jackals.

¹¹ But the king shall rejoice in God;
Everyone who swears by Him shall glory;
But the mouth of those who speak lies shall be stopped.

∼ PROVERBS 16:16, 17 ∼

¹⁶ How much better to get wisdom than gold!
And to get understanding is to be chosen rather than silver.

¹⁷ The highway of the upright *is* to depart from evil;
He who keeps his way preserves his soul.

∼ JOHN 5:1–23 ∼

After this there was a feast of the Jews, and Jesus went up to Jerusalem. ² Now there is in Jerusalem by the Sheep *Gate* a pool, which is called in Hebrew, Bethesda, having five porches. ³ In these lay a great multitude of sick people, blind, lame, paralyzed, waiting for the moving of the water. ⁴ For an angel went down at a certain time into the pool and stirred up the water; then whoever stepped in first, after the stirring of the water, was made well of whatever disease he had. ⁵ Now a certain man was there who had an infirmity thirty-eight years. ⁶ When Jesus saw him lying there, and knew that he already had been *in that condition* a long time, He said to him, "Do you want to be made well?"

⁷ The sick man answered Him, "Sir, I have no man to put me into the pool when the water is stirred up; but while I am coming, another steps down before me."

⁸ Jesus said to him, "Rise, take up your bed and walk." ⁹ And immediately the man was made well, took up his bed, and walked.

And that day was the Sabbath. ¹⁰ The Jews therefore said to him who was cured, "It is the Sabbath; it is not lawful for you to carry your bed."

¹¹ He answered them, "He who made me well said to me, 'Take up your bed and walk.' "

¹² Then they asked him, "Who is the Man who said to you, 'Take up your bed

and walk'?" [13] But the one who was healed did not know who it was, for Jesus had withdrawn, a multitude being in *that* place. [14] Afterward Jesus found him in the temple, and said to him, "See, you have been made well. Sin no more, lest a worse thing come upon you."

[15] The man departed and told the Jews that it was Jesus who had made him well.

[16] For this reason the Jews persecuted Jesus, and sought to kill Him, because He had done these things on the Sabbath. [17] But Jesus answered them, "My Father has been working until now, and I have been working."

[18] Therefore the Jews sought all the more to kill Him, because He not only broke the Sabbath, but also said that God was His Father, making Himself equal with God. [19] Then Jesus answered and said to them, "Most assuredly, I say to you, the Son can do nothing of Himself, but what He sees the Father do; for whatever He does, the Son also does in like manner. [20] For the Father loves the Son, and shows Him all things that He Himself does; and He will show Him greater works than these, that you may marvel. [21] For as the Father raises the dead and gives life to *them,* even so the Son gives life to whom He will. [22] For the Father judges no one, but has committed all judgment to the Son, [23] that all should honor the Son just as they honor the Father. He who does not honor the Son does not honor the Father who sent Him.

READING 138 · MAY 18

~ 2 SAMUEL 7:1—8:18 ~

Now it came to pass when the king was dwelling in his house, and the LORD had given him rest from all his enemies all around, [2] that the king said to Nathan the prophet, "See now, I dwell in a house of cedar, but the ark of God dwells inside tent curtains."

[3] Then Nathan said to the king, "Go, do all that *is* in your heart, for the LORD *is* with you."

[4] But it happened that night that the word of the LORD came to Nathan, saying, [5] "Go and tell My servant David, 'Thus says the LORD: "Would you build a house for Me to dwell in? [6] For I have not dwelt in a house since the time that I brought the children of Israel up from Egypt, even to this day, but have moved about in a tent and in a tabernacle. [7] Wherever I have moved about with all the children of Israel, have I ever spoken a word to anyone from the tribes of Israel, whom I commanded to shepherd My people Israel, saying, 'Why have you not built Me a house of cedar?' " ' [8] Now therefore, thus shall you say to My servant David, 'Thus says the LORD of hosts: "I took you from the sheepfold, from following the sheep, to be ruler over My people, over Israel. [9] And I have been with you wherever you have gone, and have cut off all your enemies from before you, and have made you a great name, like the name of the great men who *are* on the earth. [10] Moreover I will appoint a place for My people Israel, and will plant them, that they may dwell in a place of their own and move no more; nor shall the sons of wickedness oppress them anymore, as previously, [11] since the time that I commanded judges *to be* over My people Israel, and have caused you to rest from all your enemies. Also the LORD tells you that He will make you a house.

[12] "When your days are fulfilled and you rest with your fathers, I will set up your seed after you, who will come from your body, and I will establish his kingdom. [13] He shall build a house for My name, and I will establish the throne of his kingdom forever. [14] I will be his Father, and he shall be My son. If he commits iniquity, I will chasten him with the rod of men and with the blows of the sons of men. [15] But My mercy shall not depart from him, as I took *it* from Saul, whom I removed from before you. [16] And your house and your kingdom shall be

Handiwork

A carpenter had a brother who was a famous musician. When his brother came to visit the construction company where he worked, the foreman said, "You must be very proud to have a brother who is known around the world for his music." Then, feeling that he may have slighted his worker, he clumsily added, "Of course, not everyone in the same family can enjoy an equal amount of talent."

The carpenter responded, "You're right. My brother doesn't know the first thing about building a home. It's fortunate he could afford to hire others to build a house for him." The musician nodded in agreement and added, "My brother and I both work with our hands. I hold a musical instrument in mine, and he holds a hammer in his."

Not everybody is called to walk the same path through life. If that were true, we'd find our walk through life very crowded indeed! Booker T. Washington wrote in *Up From Slavery*: "There is as much dignity in tilling a field as in writing a poem." Dignity resides in a person's heart and attitude, not in their job description.

established forever before you. Your throne shall be established forever." ' "

[17] According to all these words and according to all this vision, so Nathan spoke to David.

[18] Then King David went in and sat before the LORD; and he said: "Who *am* I, O Lord GOD? And what is my house, that You have brought me this far? [19] And yet this was a small thing in Your sight, O Lord GOD; and You have also spoken of Your servant's house for a great while to come. *Is* this the manner of man, O Lord GOD? [20] Now what more can David say to You? For You, Lord GOD, know Your servant. [21] For Your word's sake, and according to Your own heart, You have done all these great things, to make Your servant know *them*. [22] Therefore You are great, O Lord GOD. For *there is* none like You, nor *is there any* God besides You, according to all that we have heard with our ears. [23] And who *is* like Your people, like Israel, the one nation on the earth whom God went to redeem for Himself as a people, to make for Himself a name—and to do for Yourself great and awesome deeds for Your land—before Your people whom You redeemed for Yourself from Egypt, the nations, and their gods? [24] For You have made Your people Israel Your very own people forever; and You, LORD, have become their God.

[25] "Now, O LORD God, the word which You have spoken concerning Your servant and concerning his house, establish *it* forever and do as You have said. [26] So let Your name be magnified forever, saying, 'The LORD of hosts *is* the God over Israel.' And let the house of Your servant David be established before You. [27] For You, O LORD of hosts, God of Israel, have revealed *this* to Your servant, saying, 'I will build you a house.' Therefore Your servant has found it in his heart to pray this prayer to You.

[28] "And now, O Lord GOD, You are God, and Your words are true, and You have promised this goodness to Your servant. [29] Now therefore, let it please You to bless the house of Your servant, that it may continue before You forever; for You, O Lord GOD, have spoken *it*, and with Your blessing let the house of Your servant be blessed forever."

8 After this it came to pass that David attacked the Philistines and subdued them. And David took Metheg Ammah from the hand of the Philistines.

[2] Then he defeated Moab. Forcing them down to the ground, he measured them off with a line. With two lines he measured off those to be put to death, and with one full line those to be kept alive. So the Moabites became David's servants, *and* brought tribute.

[3] David also defeated Hadadezer the son of Rehob, king of Zobah, as he went to recover his territory at the River Euphrates. [4] David took from him one thousand *chariots,* seven hundred horsemen, and twenty thousand foot soldiers. Also David hamstrung all the chariot horses, except that he spared *enough* of them for one hundred chariots.

[5] When the Syrians of Damascus came to help Hadadezer king of Zobah, David killed twenty-two thousand of the Syrians. [6] Then David put garrisons in Syria of Damascus; and the Syrians became David's servants, *and* brought tribute. So the LORD preserved David wherever he went. [7] And David took the shields of gold that had belonged to the servants of Hadadezer, and brought them to Jerusalem. [8] Also from Betah and from Berothai, cities of Hadadezer, King David took a large amount of bronze.

[9] When Toi king of Hamath heard that David had defeated all the army of Hadadezer, [10] then Toi sent Joram his son to King David, to greet him and bless him, because he had fought against Hadadezer and defeated him (for Hadadezer had been at war with Toi); and *Joram* brought with him articles of silver, articles of gold, and articles of bronze. [11] King David also dedicated these to the LORD, along with the silver and gold that he had dedicated from all the nations which he had subdued— [12] from Syria, from Moab, from the people of Ammon, from the Philistines, from Amalek, and from the spoil of Hadadezer the son of Rehob, king of Zobah.

[13] And David made *himself* a name when he returned from killing eighteen thousand Syrians in the Valley of Salt. [14] He also put garrisons in Edom;

throughout all Edom he put garrisons, and all the Edomites became David's servants. And the LORD preserved David wherever he went.

¹⁵ So David reigned over all Israel; and David administered judgment and justice to all his people. ¹⁶ Joab the son of Zeruiah *was* over the army; Jehoshaphat the son of Ahilud *was* recorder; ¹⁷ Zadok the son of Ahitub and Ahimelech the son of Abiathar *were* the priests; Seraiah *was* the scribe; ¹⁸ Benaiah the son of Jehoiada *was over* both the Cherethites and the Pelethites; and David's sons were chief ministers.

～ PSALM 64:1–10 ～

¹ Hear my voice, O God, in my meditation;
  Preserve my life from fear of the enemy.
² Hide me from the secret plots of the wicked,
  From the rebellion of the workers of iniquity,
³ Who sharpen their tongue like a sword,
  And bend *their bows to shoot* their arrows—bitter words,
⁴ That they may shoot in secret at the blameless;
  Suddenly they shoot at him and do not fear.

⁵ They encourage themselves *in* an evil matter;
  They talk of laying snares secretly;
  They say, "Who will see them?"
⁶ They devise iniquities:
  "We have perfected a shrewd scheme."
  Both the inward thought and the heart of man are deep.

⁷ But God shall shoot at them *with* an arrow;
  Suddenly they shall be wounded.
⁸ So He will make them stumble over their own tongue;
  All who see them shall flee away.
⁹ All men shall fear,
  And shall declare the work of God;
  For they shall wisely consider His doing.

¹⁰ The righteous shall be glad in the LORD, and trust in Him.
  And all the upright in heart shall glory.

～ PROVERBS 16:18, 19 ～

¹⁸ Pride *goes* before destruction,
  And a haughty spirit before a fall.
¹⁹ Better *to be* of a humble spirit with the lowly,
  Than to divide the spoil with the proud.

～ JOHN 5:24–47 ～

"Most assuredly, I say to you, he who hears My word and believes in Him who sent Me has everlasting life, and shall not come into judgment, but has passed from death into life. ²⁵ Most assuredly, I say to you, the hour is coming, and now is, when the dead will hear the voice of the Son of God; and those who hear will live. ²⁶ For as the Father has life in Himself, so He has granted the Son to have life in Himself, ²⁷ and has given Him authority to execute judgment also, because He is the Son of Man. ²⁸ Do not marvel at this; for the hour is coming in which all who are in the graves will hear His voice ²⁹ and come forth—those who have done good, to the resurrection of life, and those who have done evil, to the resurrection of condemnation. ³⁰ I can of Myself do nothing. As I hear, I judge; and My judgment is righteous, because I do not seek My own will but the will of the Father who sent Me.

³¹ "If I bear witness of Myself, My witness is not true. ³² There is another who bears witness of Me, and I know that the witness which He witnesses of Me is true. ³³ You have sent to John, and he has borne witness to the truth. ³⁴ Yet I do not receive testimony from man, but I say these things that you may be saved. ³⁵ He was the burning and shining lamp, and you were willing for a time to rejoice in his light. ³⁶ But I have a greater witness than John's; for the works which the Father has given Me to finish—the very works that I do—bear witness of Me, that the Father has sent Me. ³⁷ And the Father

Himself, who sent Me, has testified of Me. You have neither heard His voice at any time, nor seen His form. [38] But you do not have His word abiding in you, because whom He sent, Him you do not believe. [39] You search the Scriptures, for in them you think you have eternal life; and these are they which testify of Me. [40] But you are not willing to come to Me that you may have life.

[41] "I do not receive honor from men. [42] But I know you, that you do not have the love of God in you. [43] I have come in My Father's name, and you do not receive Me; if another comes in his own name, him you will receive. [44] How can you believe, who receive honor from one another, and do not seek the honor that *comes* from the only God? [45] Do not think that I shall accuse you to the Father; there is *one* who accuses you—Moses, in whom you trust. [46] For if you believed Moses, you would believe Me; for he wrote about Me. [47] But if you do not believe his writings, how will you believe My words?"

~ 2 SAMUEL 9:1—10:19 ~

Now David said, "Is there still anyone who is left of the house of Saul, that I may show him kindness for Jonathan's sake?"

[2] And *there was* a servant of the house of Saul whose name *was* Ziba. So when they had called him to David, the king said to him, "*Are* you Ziba?"

He said, "At your service!"

[3] Then the king said, "*Is* there not still someone of the house of Saul, to whom I may show the kindness of God?"

And Ziba said to the king, "There is still a son of Jonathan *who is* lame in *his* feet."

[4] So the king said to him, "Where *is* he?"

And Ziba said to the king, "Indeed he *is* in the house of Machir the son of Ammiel, in Lo Debar."

[5] Then King David sent and brought him out of the house of Machir the son of Ammiel, from Lo Debar.

[6] Now when Mephibosheth the son of Jonathan, the son of Saul, had come to David, he fell on his face and prostrated himself. Then David said, "Mephibosheth?"

And he answered, "Here is your servant!"

[7] So David said to him, "Do not fear, for I will surely show you kindness for Jonathan your father's sake, and will restore to you all the land of Saul your grandfather; and you shall eat bread at my table continually."

[8] Then he bowed himself, and said, "What *is* your servant, that you should look upon such a dead dog as I?"

[9] And the king called to Ziba, Saul's servant, and said to him, "I have given to your master's son all that belonged to Saul and to all his house. [10] You therefore, and your sons and your servants, shall work the land for him, and you shall bring in *the harvest,* that your master's son may have food to eat. But Mephibosheth your master's son shall eat bread at my table always." Now Ziba had fifteen sons and twenty servants.

[11] Then Ziba said to the king, "According to all that my lord the king has commanded his servant, so will your servant do."

"As for Mephibosheth," *said the king,* "he shall eat at my table like one of the king's sons." [12] Mephibosheth had a young son whose name *was* Micha. And all who dwelt in the house of Ziba *were* servants of Mephibosheth. [13] So Mephibosheth dwelt in Jerusalem, for he ate continually at the king's table. And he was lame in both his feet.

10 It happened after this that the king of the people of Ammon died, and Hanun his son reigned in his place. [2] Then David said, "I will show kindness to Hanun the son of Nahash, as his father showed kindness to me."

So David sent by the hand of his servants to comfort him concerning his father. And David's servants came into the

Vision, Risk, and Courage

In 1990, Bill and Gina Ellis were living a comfortable life in Los Angeles. Then just before Christmas, Bill was laid off from his job. To distract themselves from the loss during the holiday season, they reviewed sketches of a sofa Gina had seen in Spain. The style lent itself to washable slipcovers that could be changed with the seasons. They made slight variations in the design and had the sofa custom-built. Their friends raved.

Bill took a long hard look at drawings he had of other pieces of furniture. He said impulsively, "We could *sell* these." Gina agreed, and within a week they had launched Quatrine Washable Furniture. Using equity from their home, they leased a small shop and paid a craftsman to construct their first five sofas and chairs. Customers loved their furniture, but felt it was too expensive.

Three months later, a woman came into their shop, selected several pieces of furniture, and wrote a check for $14,000. With that profit, they were able to create a line of more reasonably priced furniture. By summer, the new pieces were ready. They moved their business to Detroit and eventually opened branches in Dallas, Chicago, and Denver. By 1996, their sales totaled more than $5 million a year.

Reward cannot be separated from vision, risk, and courage. If you want to grow and develop in any area of life, you have to pay the price. The benefits, however, far outweigh the cost.

land of the people of Ammon. ³ And the princes of the people of Ammon said to Hanun their lord, "Do you think that David really honors your father because he has sent comforters to you? Has David not *rather* sent his servants to you to search the city, to spy it out, and to overthrow it?"

⁴ Therefore Hanun took David's servants, shaved off half of their beards, cut off their garments in the middle, at their buttocks, and sent them away. ⁵ When they told David, he sent to meet them, because the men were greatly ashamed. And the king said, "Wait at Jericho until your beards have grown, and *then* return."

⁶ When the people of Ammon saw that they had made themselves repulsive to David, the people of Ammon sent and hired the Syrians of Beth Rehob and the Syrians of Zoba, twenty thousand foot soldiers; and from the king of Maacah one thousand men, and from Ish-Tob twelve thousand men. ⁷ Now when David heard *of it,* he sent Joab and all the army of the mighty men. ⁸ Then the people of Ammon came out and put themselves in battle array at the entrance of the gate. And the Syrians of Zoba, Beth Rehob, Ish-Tob, and Maacah *were* by themselves in the field.

⁹ When Joab saw that the battle line was against him before and behind, he chose some of Israel's best and put *them* in battle array against the Syrians. ¹⁰ And the rest of the people he put under the command of Abishai his brother, that he might set *them* in battle array against the people of Ammon. ¹¹ Then he said, "If the Syrians are too strong for me, then you shall help me; but if the people of Ammon are too strong for you, then I will come and help you. ¹² Be of good courage, and let us be strong for our people and for the cities of our God. And may the LORD do *what is* good in His sight."

¹³ So Joab and the people who *were* with him drew near for the battle against the Syrians, and they fled before him. ¹⁴ When the people of Ammon saw that the Syrians were fleeing, they also fled before Abishai, and entered the city. So Joab returned from the people of Ammon and went to Jerusalem.

¹⁵ When the Syrians saw that they had been defeated by Israel, they gathered together. ¹⁶ Then Hadadezer sent and brought out the Syrians who *were* beyond the River, and they came to Helam. And Shobach the commander of Hadadezer's army *went* before them. ¹⁷ When it was told David, he gathered all Israel, crossed over the Jordan, and came to Helam. And the Syrians set themselves in battle array against David and fought with him. ¹⁸ Then the Syrians fled before Israel; and David killed seven hundred charioteers and forty thousand horsemen of the Syrians, and struck Shobach the commander of their army, who died there. ¹⁹ And when all the kings *who were* servants to Hadadezer saw that they were defeated by Israel, they made peace with Israel and served them. So the Syrians were afraid to help the people of Ammon anymore.

∼ PSALM 65:1–8 ∼

¹ Praise is awaiting You, O God, in
    Zion;
  And to You the vow shall be
    performed.
² O You who hear prayer,
  To You all flesh will come.
³ Iniquities prevail against me;
  As for our transgressions,
  You will provide atonement for
    them.

⁴ Blessed *is the man* You choose,
  And cause to approach *You,*
  That he may dwell in Your courts.
  We shall be satisfied with the
    goodness of Your house,
  Of Your holy temple.

⁵ *By* awesome deeds in righteousness
    You will answer us,
  O God of our salvation,
  You who are the confidence of all the
    ends of the earth,
  And of the far-off seas;
⁶ Who established the mountains by
    His strength,
  Being clothed with power;
⁷ You who still the noise of the seas,
  The noise of their waves,
  And the tumult of the peoples.
⁸ They also who dwell in the farthest
    parts are afraid of Your signs;

You make the outgoings of the
morning and evening rejoice.

~ PROVERBS 16:20, 21 ~

20 He who heeds the word wisely will
find good,
And whoever trusts in the LORD,
happy *is* he.

21 The wise in heart will be called
prudent,
And sweetness of the lips increases
learning.

~ JOHN 6:1–21 ~

After these things Jesus went over the Sea
of Galilee, which is *the Sea* of Tiberias.
2 Then a great multitude followed Him,
because they saw His signs which He performed on those who were diseased. 3 And
Jesus went up on the mountain, and there
He sat with His disciples.

4 Now the Passover, a feast of the Jews,
was near. 5 Then Jesus lifted up *His* eyes,
and seeing a great multitude coming toward Him, He said to Philip, "Where shall
we buy bread, that these may eat?" 6 But
this He said to test him, for He Himself
knew what He would do.

7 Philip answered Him, "Two hundred
denarii worth of bread is not sufficient
for them, that every one of them may have
a little."

8 One of His disciples, Andrew, Simon
Peter's brother, said to Him, 9 "There is a
lad here who has five barley loaves and
two small fish, but what are they among
so many?"

10 Then Jesus said, "Make the people
sit down." Now there was much grass in
the place. So the men sat down, in number about five thousand. 11 And Jesus took
the loaves, and when He had given thanks
He distributed *them* to the disciples, and
the disciples to those sitting down;
and likewise of the fish, as much as they
wanted. 12 So when they were filled, He
said to His disciples, "Gather up the fragments that remain, so that nothing is lost."
13 Therefore they gathered *them* up, and
filled twelve baskets with the fragments
of the five barley loaves which were left
over by those who had eaten. 14 Then
those men, when they had seen the sign
that Jesus did, said, "This is truly the
Prophet who is to come into the world."

15 Therefore when Jesus perceived that
they were about to come and take Him
by force to make Him king, He departed
again to the mountain by Himself alone.

16 Now when evening came, His disciples went down to the sea, 17 got into
the boat, and went over the sea toward
Capernaum. And it was already dark, and
Jesus had not come to them. 18 Then the
sea arose because a great wind was blowing. 19 So when they had rowed about
three or four miles, they saw Jesus walking on the sea and drawing near the boat;
and they were afraid. 20 But He said to
them, "It is I; do not be afraid." 21 Then
they willingly received Him into the boat,
and immediately the boat was at the land
where they were going.

~ 2 SAMUEL 11:1—12:31 ~

It happened in the spring of the year,
at the time when kings go out *to battle,*
that David sent Joab and his servants
with him, and all Israel; and they destroyed the people of Ammon and
besieged Rabbah. But David remained at
Jerusalem.

2 Then it happened one evening that
David arose from his bed and walked
on the roof of the king's house. And from
the roof he saw a woman bathing, and
the woman *was* very beautiful to behold.
3 So David sent and inquired about the
woman. And *someone* said, "*Is* this not
Bathsheba, the daughter of Eliam, the wife
of Uriah the Hittite?" 4 Then David sent
messengers, and took her; and she came
to him, and he lay with her, for she was
cleansed from her impurity; and she
returned to her house. 5 And the woman
conceived; so she sent and told David, and
said, "I *am* with child."

⁶ Then David sent to Joab, *saying,* "Send me Uriah the Hittite." And Joab sent Uriah to David. ⁷ When Uriah had come to him, David asked how Joab was doing, and how the people were doing, and how the war prospered. ⁸ And David said to Uriah, "Go down to your house and wash your feet." So Uriah departed from the king's house, and a gift *of food* from the king followed him. ⁹ But Uriah slept at the door of the king's house with all the servants of his lord, and did not go down to his house. ¹⁰ So when they told David, saying, "Uriah did not go down to his house," David said to Uriah, "Did you not come from a journey? Why did you not go down to your house?"

¹¹ And Uriah said to David, "The ark and Israel and Judah are dwelling in tents, and my lord Joab and the servants of my lord are encamped in the open fields. Shall I then go to my house to eat and drink, and to lie with my wife? *As* you live, and *as* your soul lives, I will not do this thing."

¹² Then David said to Uriah, "Wait here today also, and tomorrow I will let you depart." So Uriah remained in Jerusalem that day and the next. ¹³ Now when David called him, he ate and drank before him; and he made him drunk. And at evening he went out to lie on his bed with the servants of his lord, but he did not go down to his house.

¹⁴ In the morning it happened that David wrote a letter to Joab and sent *it* by the hand of Uriah. ¹⁵ And he wrote in the letter, saying, "Set Uriah in the forefront of the hottest battle, and retreat from him, that he may be struck down and die." ¹⁶ So it was, while Joab besieged the city, that he assigned Uriah to a place where he knew there *were* valiant men. ¹⁷ Then the men of the city came out and fought with Joab. And *some* of the people of the servants of David fell; and Uriah the Hittite died also.

¹⁸ Then Joab sent and told David all the things concerning the war, ¹⁹ and charged the messenger, saying, "When you have finished telling the matters of the war to the king, ²⁰ if it happens that the king's wrath rises, and he says to you: 'Why did you approach so near to the city when you fought? Did you not know that they

would shoot from the wall? ²¹ Who struck Abimelech the son of Jerubbesheth? Was it not a woman who cast a piece of a millstone on him from the wall, so that he died in Thebez? Why did you go near the wall?'—then you shall say, 'Your servant Uriah the Hittite is dead also.' "

²² So the messenger went, and came and told David all that Joab had sent by him. ²³ And the messenger said to David, "Surely the men prevailed against us and came out to us in the field; then we drove them back as far as the entrance of the gate. ²⁴ The archers shot from the wall at your servants; and *some* of the king's servants are dead, and your servant Uriah the Hittite is dead also."

²⁵ Then David said to the messenger, "Thus you shall say to Joab: 'Do not let this thing displease you, for the sword devours one as well as another. Strengthen your attack against the city, and overthrow it.' So encourage him."

²⁶ When the wife of Uriah heard that Uriah her husband was dead, she mourned for her husband. ²⁷ And when her mourning was over, David sent and brought her to his house, and she became his wife and bore him a son. But the thing that David had done displeased the LORD.

12 Then the LORD sent Nathan to David. And he came to him, and said to him: "There were two men in one city, one rich and the other poor. ² The rich *man* had exceedingly many flocks and herds. ³ But the poor *man* had nothing, except one little ewe lamb which he had bought and nourished; and it grew up together with him and with his children. It ate of his own food and drank from his own cup and lay in his bosom; and it was like a daughter to him. ⁴ And a traveler came to the rich man, who refused to take from his own flock and from his own herd to prepare one for the wayfaring man who had come to him; but he took the poor man's lamb and prepared it for the man who had come to him."

⁵ So David's anger was greatly aroused against the man, and he said to Nathan, "*As* the LORD lives, the man who has done this shall surely die! ⁶ And he shall restore fourfold for the lamb, because he did this thing and because he had no pity."

A Trail of Kindness

The words of this poem are a good reminder that everything we say and do makes a difference — especially to those whom we love and live with daily:

Is anybody happier
    Because you passed his way?
Does anyone remember
    That you spoke to him today?
This day is almost over,
    And its toiling time is through;
Is there anyone to utter now
    A friendly word for you?
Can you say tonight in passing
    With the days that slipped so fast,
That you helped a single person,
    Of the many that you passed?
Is a single heart rejoicing
    Over what you did or said?
Does one whose hopes were fading
    Now with courage look ahead?
Did you waste the day, or lose it?
    Was it well or poorly spent?
Did you leave a trail of kindness
    Or a scar of discontent?

⁷ Then Nathan said to David, "You *are* the man! Thus says the LORD God of Israel: 'I anointed you king over Israel, and I delivered you from the hand of Saul. ⁸ I gave you your master's house and your master's wives into your keeping, and gave you the house of Israel and Judah. And if *that had been* too little, I also would have given you much more! ⁹ Why have you despised the commandment of the LORD, to do evil in His sight? You have killed Uriah the Hittite with the sword; you have taken his wife *to be* your wife, and have killed him with the sword of the people of Ammon. ¹⁰ Now therefore, the sword shall never depart from your house, because you have despised Me, and have taken the wife of Uriah the Hittite to be your wife.' ¹¹ Thus says the LORD: 'Behold, I will raise up adversity against you from your own house; and I will take your wives before your eyes and give *them* to your neighbor, and he shall lie with your wives in the sight of this sun. ¹² For you did *it* secretly, but I will do this thing before all Israel, before the sun.' "

¹³ So David said to Nathan, "I have sinned against the LORD."

And Nathan said to David, "The LORD also has put away your sin; you shall not die. ¹⁴ However, because by this deed you have given great occasion to the enemies of the LORD to blaspheme, the child also *who is* born to you shall surely die." ¹⁵ Then Nathan departed to his house.

And the LORD struck the child that Uriah's wife bore to David, and it became ill. ¹⁶ David therefore pleaded with God for the child, and David fasted and went in and lay all night on the ground. ¹⁷ So the elders of his house arose *and went* to him, to raise him up from the ground. But he would not, nor did he eat food with them. ¹⁸ Then on the seventh day it came to pass that the child died. And the servants of David were afraid to tell him that the child was dead. For they said, "Indeed, while the child was alive, we spoke to him, and he would not heed our voice. How can we tell him that the child is dead? He may do some harm!"

¹⁹ When David saw that his servants were whispering, David perceived that the child was dead. Therefore David said to his servants, "Is the child dead?"

And they said, "He is dead."

²⁰ So David arose from the ground, washed and anointed himself, and changed his clothes; and he went into the house of the LORD and worshiped. Then he went to his own house; and when he requested, they set food before him, and he ate. ²¹ Then his servants said to him, "What *is* this that you have done? You fasted and wept for the child *while he was* alive, but when the child died, you arose and ate food."

²² And he said, "While the child was alive, I fasted and wept; for I said, 'Who can tell *whether* the LORD will be gracious to me, that the child may live?' ²³ But now he is dead; why should I fast? Can I bring him back again? I shall go to him, but he shall not return to me."

²⁴ Then David comforted Bathsheba his wife, and went in to her and lay with her. So she bore a son, and he called his name Solomon. Now the LORD loved him, ²⁵ and He sent *word* by the hand of Nathan the prophet: So he called his name Jedidiah, because of the LORD.

²⁶ Now Joab fought against Rabbah of the people of Ammon, and took the royal city. ²⁷ And Joab sent messengers to David, and said, "I have fought against Rabbah, and I have taken the city's water *supply.* ²⁸ Now therefore, gather the rest of the people together and encamp against the city and take it, lest I take the city and it be called after my name." ²⁹ So David gathered all the people together and went to Rabbah, fought against it, and took it. ³⁰ Then he took their king's crown from his head. Its weight *was* a talent of gold, with precious stones. And it was *set* on David's head. Also he brought out the spoil of the city in great abundance. ³¹ And he brought out the people who *were* in it, and put *them to work* with saws and iron picks and iron axes, and made them cross over to the brick works. So he did to all the cities of the people of Ammon. Then David and all the people returned to Jerusalem.

～ PSALM 65:9–13 ～

⁹   You visit the earth and water it,
    You greatly enrich it;
    The river of God is full of water;

You provide their grain,
For so You have prepared it.
10 You water its ridges abundantly,
You settle its furrows;
You make it soft with showers,
You bless its growth.

11 You crown the year with Your
     goodness,
And Your paths drip *with*
     abundance.
12 They drop *on* the pastures of the
     wilderness,
And the little hills rejoice on every
     side.
13 The pastures are clothed with flocks;
The valleys also are covered with
     grain;
They shout for joy, they also sing.

~ PROVERBS 16:22–24 ~

22 Understanding *is* a wellspring of life
     to him who has it.
But the correction of fools *is* folly.

23 The heart of the wise teaches his
     mouth,
And adds learning to his lips.

24 Pleasant words *are like* a
     honeycomb,
Sweetness to the soul and health to
     the bones.

~ JOHN 6:22–51 ~

On the following day, when the people
who were standing on the other side of
the sea saw that there was no other boat
there, except that one which His disciples
had entered, and that Jesus had not entered the boat with His disciples, but His
disciples had gone away alone— 23 however, other boats came from Tiberias, near
the place where they ate bread after
the Lord had given thanks— 24 when the
people therefore saw that Jesus was not
there, nor His disciples, they also got into
boats and came to Capernaum, seeking
Jesus. 25 And when they found Him on
the other side of the sea, they said to Him,
"Rabbi, when did You come here?"
26 Jesus answered them and said, "Most
assuredly, I say to you, you seek Me, not

because you saw the signs, but because
you ate of the loaves and were filled. 27 Do
not labor for the food which perishes, but
for the food which endures to everlasting
life, which the Son of Man will give you,
because God the Father has set His seal
on Him."
28 Then they said to Him, "What shall
we do, that we may work the works of
God?"
29 Jesus answered and said to them,
"This is the work of God, that you believe in Him whom He sent."
30 Therefore they said to Him, "What
sign will You perform then, that we may
see it and believe You? What work will
You do? 31 Our fathers ate the manna in
the desert; as it is written, 'He gave them
bread from heaven to eat.' "
32 Then Jesus said to them, "Most assuredly, I say to you, Moses did not give
you the bread from heaven, but My Father gives you the true bread from heaven.
33 For the bread of God is He who comes
down from heaven and gives life to the
world."
34 Then they said to Him, "Lord, give
us this bread always."
35 And Jesus said to them, "I am the
bread of life. He who comes to Me shall
never hunger, and he who believes in Me
shall never thirst. 36 But I said to you that
you have seen Me and yet do not believe.
37 All that the Father gives Me will come
to Me, and the one who comes to Me I
will by no means cast out. 38 For I have
come down from heaven, not to do My
own will, but the will of Him who sent
Me. 39 This is the will of the Father who
sent Me, that of all He has given Me I
should lose nothing, but should raise it
up at the last day. 40 And this is the will of
Him who sent Me, that everyone who sees
the Son and believes in Him may have
everlasting life; and I will raise him up at
the last day."
41 The Jews then complained about
Him, because He said, "I am the bread
which came down from heaven." 42 And
they said, "Is not this Jesus, the son of
Joseph, whose father and mother we
know? How is it then that He says, 'I have
come down from heaven'?"
43 Jesus therefore answered and said
to them, "Do not murmur among

yourselves. [44] No one can come to Me unless the Father who sent Me draws him; and I will raise him up at the last day. [45] It is written in the prophets, 'And they shall all be taught by God.' Therefore everyone who has heard and learned from the Father comes to Me. [46] Not that anyone has seen the Father, except He who is from God; He has seen the Father. [47] Most assuredly, I say to you, he who believes in Me has everlasting life. [48] I am the bread of life. [49] Your fathers ate the manna in the wilderness, and are dead. [50] This is the bread which comes down from heaven, that one may eat of it and not die. [51] I am the living bread which came down from heaven. If anyone eats of this bread, he will live forever; and the bread that I shall give is My flesh, which I shall give for the life of the world."

<hr>

READING 141 · MAY 21

~ 2 SAMUEL 13:1—14:33 ~

After this Absalom the son of David had a lovely sister, whose name *was* Tamar; and Amnon the son of David loved her. [2] Amnon was so distressed over his sister Tamar that he became sick; for she *was* a virgin. And it was improper for Amnon to do anything to her. [3] But Amnon had a friend whose name *was* Jonadab the son of Shimeah, David's brother. Now Jonadab *was* a very crafty man. [4] And he said to him, "Why *are* you, the king's son, becoming thinner day after day? Will you not tell me?"

Amnon said to him, "I love Tamar, my brother Absalom's sister."

[5] So Jonadab said to him, "Lie down on your bed and pretend to be ill. And when your father comes to see you, say to him, 'Please let my sister Tamar come and give me food, and prepare the food in my sight, that I may see *it* and eat it from her hand.' " [6] Then Amnon lay down and pretended to be ill; and when the king came to see him, Amnon said to the king, "Please let Tamar my sister come and make a couple of cakes for me in my sight, that I may eat from her hand."

[7] And David sent home to Tamar, saying, "Now go to your brother Amnon's house, and prepare food for him." [8] So Tamar went to her brother Amnon's house; and he was lying down. Then she took flour and kneaded *it*, made cakes in his sight, and baked the cakes. [9] And she took the pan and placed *them* out before him, but he refused to eat. Then Amnon said, "Have everyone go out from me." And they all went out from him. [10] Then Amnon said to Tamar, "Bring the food into the bedroom, that I may eat from your hand." And Tamar took the cakes which she had made, and brought *them* to Amnon her brother in the bedroom. [11] Now when she had brought *them* to him to eat, he took hold of her and said to her, "Come, lie with me, my sister."

[12] But she answered him, "No, my brother, do not force me, for no such thing should be done in Israel. Do not do this disgraceful thing! [13] And I, where could I take my shame? And as for you, you would be like one of the fools in Israel. Now therefore, please speak to the king; for he will not withhold me from you." [14] However, he would not heed her voice; and being stronger than she, he forced her and lay with her.

[15] Then Amnon hated her exceedingly, so that the hatred with which he hated her *was* greater than the love with which he had loved her. And Amnon said to her, "Arise, be gone!"

[16] So she said to him, "No, indeed! This evil of sending me away *is* worse than the other that you did to me."

But he would not listen to her. [17] Then he called his servant who attended him, and said, "Here! Put this *woman* out, away from me, and bolt the door behind her." [18] Now she had on a robe of many colors, for the king's virgin daughters wore such apparel. And his servant put her out and bolted the door behind her.

[19] Then Tamar put ashes on her head, and tore her robe of many colors that *was* on her, and laid her hand on her head

The Big Picture

Earl Weaver, former manager of the Baltimore Orioles, had a rule that no one could steal a base unless he gave the steal sign. This upset Reggie Jackson, who felt he knew the pitchers and catchers well enough to judge when he could steal. One day, he decided to steal without the sign. He got a good jump off the pitcher and easily beat the throw to second base. As he shook the dirt from his uniform, he smiled with delight, feeling he had vindicated himself.

Later, Weaver took Jackson aside and explained why he hadn't given the steal sign. The next batter was Lee May, a major power hitter. Because first base was open, the opposing team intentionally walked May. The batter after May hadn't been strong against this pitcher, so Weaver had to send in a designated hitter. That left their team without the bench strength they might need later in the game.

Jackson had seen a stolen base as involving only the relationship between pitcher and catcher. Weaver was calling signals with the entire game in mind.

Don't put your trust in what you see immediately around you. Trust the One Who sees the "big picture" that spans all of time and eternity.

and went away crying bitterly. ²⁰ And Absalom her brother said to her, "Has Amnon your brother been with you? But now hold your peace, my sister. He *is* your brother; do not take this thing to heart." So Tamar remained desolate in her brother Absalom's house.

²¹ But when King David heard of all these things, he was very angry. ²² And Absalom spoke to his brother Amnon neither good nor bad. For Absalom hated Amnon, because he had forced his sister Tamar.

²³ And it came to pass, after two full years, that Absalom had sheepshearers in Baal Hazor, which *is* near Ephraim; so Absalom invited all the king's sons. ²⁴ Then Absalom came to the king and said, "Kindly note, your servant has sheepshearers; please, let the king and his servants go with your servant."

²⁵ But the king said to Absalom, "No, my son, let us not all go now, lest we be a burden to you." Then he urged him, but he would not go; and he blessed him.

²⁶ Then Absalom said, "If not, please let my brother Amnon go with us."

And the king said to him, "Why should he go with you?" ²⁷ But Absalom urged him; so he let Amnon and all the king's sons go with him.

²⁸ Now Absalom had commanded his servants, saying, "Watch now, when Amnon's heart is merry with wine, and when I say to you, 'Strike Amnon!' then kill him. Do not be afraid. Have I not commanded you? Be courageous and valiant." ²⁹ So the servants of Absalom did to Amnon as Absalom had commanded. Then all the king's sons arose, and each one got on his mule and fled.

³⁰ And it came to pass, while they were on the way, that news came to David, saying, "Absalom has killed all the king's sons, and not one of them is left!" ³¹ So the king arose and tore his garments and lay on the ground, and all his servants stood by with their clothes torn. ³² Then Jonadab the son of Shimeah, David's brother, answered and said, "Let not my lord suppose they have killed all the young men, the king's sons, for only Amnon is dead. For by the command of Absalom this has been determined from the day that he forced his sister Tamar. ³³ Now therefore,

let not my lord the king take the thing to his heart, to think that all the king's sons are dead. For only Amnon is dead."

³⁴ Then Absalom fled. And the young man who was keeping watch lifted his eyes and looked, and there, many people were coming from the road on the hillside behind him. ³⁵ And Jonadab said to the king, "Look, the king's sons are coming; as your servant said, so it is." ³⁶ So it was, as soon as he had finished speaking, that the king's sons indeed came, and they lifted up their voice and wept. Also the king and all his servants wept very bitterly.

³⁷ But Absalom fled and went to Talmai the son of Ammihud, king of Geshur. And *David* mourned for his son every day. ³⁸ So Absalom fled and went to Geshur, and was there three years. ³⁹ And King David longed to go to Absalom. For he had been comforted concerning Amnon, because he was dead.

14 So Joab the son of Zeruiah perceived that the king's heart *was* concerned about Absalom. ² And Joab sent to Tekoa and brought from there a wise woman, and said to her, "Please pretend to be a mourner, and put on mourning apparel; do not anoint yourself with oil, but act like a woman who has been mourning a long time for the dead. ³ Go to the king and speak to him in this manner." So Joab put the words in her mouth.

⁴ And when the woman of Tekoa spoke to the king, she fell on her face to the ground and prostrated herself, and said, "Help, O king!"

⁵ Then the king said to her, "What troubles you?"

And she answered, "Indeed I *am* a widow, my husband is dead. ⁶ Now your maidservant had two sons; and the two fought with each other in the field, and *there was* no one to part them, but the one struck the other and killed him. ⁷ And now the whole family has risen up against your maidservant, and they said, 'Deliver him who struck his brother, that we may execute him for the life of his brother whom he killed; and we will destroy the heir also.' So they would extinguish my ember that is left, and leave to my husband *neither* name nor remnant on the earth."

⁸ Then the king said to the woman, "Go to your house, and I will give orders concerning you."

⁹ And the woman of Tekoa said to the king, "My lord, O king, *let* the iniquity *be* on me and on my father's house, and the king and his throne *be* guiltless."

¹⁰ So the king said, "Whoever says *anything* to you, bring him to me, and he shall not touch you anymore."

¹¹ Then she said, "Please let the king remember the LORD your God, and do not permit the avenger of blood to destroy anymore, lest they destroy my son."

And he said, "*As* the LORD lives, not one hair of your son shall fall to the ground."

¹² Therefore the woman said, "Please, let your maidservant speak *another* word to my lord the king."

And he said, "Say on."

¹³ So the woman said: "Why then have you schemed such a thing against the people of God? For the king speaks this thing as one who is guilty, *in that* the king does not bring his banished one home again. ¹⁴ For we will surely die and *become* like water spilled on the ground, which cannot be gathered up again. Yet God does not take away a life; but He devises means, so that His banished ones are not expelled from Him. ¹⁵ Now therefore, I have come to speak of this thing to my lord the king because the people have made me afraid. And your maidservant said, 'I will now speak to the king; it may be that the king will perform the request of his maidservant. ¹⁶ For the king will hear and deliver his maidservant from the hand of the man *who would* destroy me and my son together from the inheritance of God.' ¹⁷ Your maidservant said, 'The word of my lord the king will now be comforting; for as the angel of God, so *is* my lord the king in discerning good and evil. And may the LORD your God be with you.' "

¹⁸ Then the king answered and said to the woman, "Please do not hide from me anything that I ask you."

And the woman said, "Please, let my lord the king speak."

¹⁹ So the king said, "*Is* the hand of Joab with you in all this?" And the woman answered and said, "*As* you live, my lord the king, no one can turn to the right hand or to the left from anything that my lord the king has spoken. For your servant Joab commanded me, and he put all these words in the mouth of your maidservant. ²⁰ To bring about this change of affairs your servant Joab has done this thing; but my lord *is* wise, according to the wisdom of the angel of God, to know everything that *is* in the earth."

²¹ And the king said to Joab, "All right, I have granted this thing. Go therefore, bring back the young man Absalom."

²² Then Joab fell to the ground on his face and bowed himself, and thanked the king. And Joab said, "Today your servant knows that I have found favor in your sight, my lord, O king, in that the king has fulfilled the request of his servant." ²³ So Joab arose and went to Geshur, and brought Absalom to Jerusalem. ²⁴ And the king said, "Let him return to his own house, but do not let him see my face." So Absalom returned to his own house, but did not see the king's face.

²⁵ Now in all Israel there was no one who was praised as much as Absalom for his good looks. From the sole of his foot to the crown of his head there was no blemish in him. ²⁶ And when he cut the hair of his head—at the end of every year he cut *it* because it was heavy on him—when he cut it, he weighed the hair of his head at two hundred shekels according to the king's standard. ²⁷ To Absalom were born three sons, and one daughter whose name *was* Tamar. She was a woman of beautiful appearance.

²⁸ And Absalom dwelt two full years in Jerusalem, but did not see the king's face. ²⁹ Therefore Absalom sent for Joab, to send him to the king, but he would not come to him. And when he sent again the second time, he would not come. ³⁰ So he said to his servants, "See, Joab's field is near mine, and he has barley there; go and set it on fire." And Absalom's servants set the field on fire.

³¹ Then Joab arose and came to Absalom's house, and said to him, "Why have your servants set my field on fire?"

³² And Absalom answered Joab, "Look, I sent to you, saying, 'Come here, so that I may send you to the king, to say, "Why have I come from Geshur? *It would be* better for me *to be* there still." ' Now

therefore, let me see the king's face; but if there is iniquity in me, let him execute me."

³³ So Joab went to the king and told him. And when he had called for Absalom, he came to the king and bowed himself on his face to the ground before the king. Then the king kissed Absalom.

~ PSALM 66:1–7 ~

¹ Make a joyful shout to God, all the earth!
² Sing out the honor of His name;
Make His praise glorious.
³ Say to God,
"How awesome are Your works!
Through the greatness of Your power
Your enemies shall submit themselves to You.
⁴ All the earth shall worship You
And sing praises to You;
They shall sing praises *to* Your name."   Selah

⁵ Come and see the works of God;
He is awesome *in His* doing toward the sons of men.
⁶ He turned the sea into dry *land;*
They went through the river on foot.
There we will rejoice in Him.
⁷ He rules by His power forever;
His eyes observe the nations;
Do not let the rebellious exalt themselves.   Selah

~ PROVERBS 16:25, 26 ~

²⁵ There is a way *that seems* right to a man,
But its end *is* the way of death.

²⁶ The person who labors, labors for himself,
For his *hungry* mouth drives him *on.*

~ JOHN 6:52–71 ~

The Jews therefore quarreled among themselves, saying, "How can this Man give us *His* flesh to eat?"

⁵³ Then Jesus said to them, "Most assuredly, I say to you, unless you eat the flesh of the Son of Man and drink His blood, you have no life in you. ⁵⁴ Whoever eats My flesh and drinks My blood has eternal life, and I will raise him up at the last day. ⁵⁵ For My flesh is food indeed, and My blood is drink indeed. ⁵⁶ He who eats My flesh and drinks My blood abides in Me, and I in him. ⁵⁷ As the living Father sent Me, and I live because of the Father, so he who feeds on Me will live because of Me. ⁵⁸ This is the bread which came down from heaven—not as your fathers ate the manna, and are dead. He who eats this bread will live forever."

⁵⁹ These things He said in the synagogue as He taught in Capernaum.

⁶⁰ Therefore many of His disciples, when they heard *this,* said, "This is a hard saying; who can understand it?"

⁶¹ When Jesus knew in Himself that His disciples complained about this, He said to them, "Does this offend you? ⁶² *What* then if you should see the Son of Man ascend where He was before? ⁶³ It is the Spirit who gives life; the flesh profits nothing. The words that I speak to you are spirit, and *they* are life. ⁶⁴ But there are some of you who do not believe." For Jesus knew from the beginning who they were who did not believe, and who would betray Him. ⁶⁵ And He said, "Therefore I have said to you that no one can come to Me unless it has been granted to him by My Father."

⁶⁶ From that *time* many of His disciples went back and walked with Him no more. ⁶⁷ Then Jesus said to the twelve, "Do you also want to go away?"

⁶⁸ But Simon Peter answered Him, "Lord, to whom shall we go? You have the words of eternal life. ⁶⁹ Also we have come to believe and know that You are the Christ, the Son of the living God."

⁷⁰ Jesus answered them, "Did I not choose you, the twelve, and one of you is a devil?" ⁷¹ He spoke of Judas Iscariot, *the son* of Simon, for it was he who would betray Him, being one of the twelve.

~ 2 SAMUEL 15:1—16:23 ~

After this it happened that Absalom provided himself with chariots and horses, and fifty men to run before him. [2] Now Absalom would rise early and stand beside the way to the gate. So it was, whenever anyone who had a lawsuit came to the king for a decision, that Absalom would call to him and say, "What city are you from?" And he would say, "Your servant is from such and such a tribe of Israel." [3] Then Absalom would say to him, "Look, your case is good and right; but there is no deputy of the king to hear you." [4] Moreover Absalom would say, "Oh, that I were made judge in the land, and everyone who has any suit or cause would come to me; then I would give him justice." [5] And so it was, whenever anyone came near to bow down to him, that he would put out his hand and take him and kiss him. [6] In this manner Absalom acted toward all Israel who came to the king for judgment. So Absalom stole the hearts of the men of Israel.

[7] Now it came to pass after forty years that Absalom said to the king, "Please, let me go to Hebron and pay the vow which I made to the LORD. [8] For your servant took a vow while I dwelt at Geshur in Syria, saying, 'If the LORD indeed brings me back to Jerusalem, then I will serve the LORD.' "

[9] And the king said to him, "Go in peace." So he arose and went to Hebron.

[10] Then Absalom sent spies throughout all the tribes of Israel, saying, "As soon as you hear the sound of the trumpet, then you shall say, 'Absalom reigns in Hebron!' " [11] And with Absalom went two hundred men invited from Jerusalem, and they went along innocently and did not know anything. [12] Then Absalom sent for Ahithophel the Gilonite, David's counselor, from his city—from Giloh—while he offered sacrifices. And the conspiracy grew strong, for the people with Absalom continually increased in number.

[13] Now a messenger came to David, saying, "The hearts of the men of Israel are with Absalom."

[14] So David said to all his servants who were with him at Jerusalem, "Arise, and let us flee, or we shall not escape from Absalom. Make haste to depart, lest he overtake us suddenly and bring disaster upon us, and strike the city with the edge of the sword."

[15] And the king's servants said to the king, "We are your servants, ready to do whatever my lord the king commands." [16] Then the king went out with all his household after him. But the king left ten women, concubines, to keep the house. [17] And the king went out with all the people after him, and stopped at the outskirts. [18] Then all his servants passed before him; and all the Cherethites, all the Pelethites, and all the Gittites, six hundred men who had followed him from Gath, passed before the king.

[19] Then the king said to Ittai the Gittite, "Why are you also going with us? Return and remain with the king. For you are a foreigner and also an exile from your own place. [20] In fact, you came only yesterday. Should I make you wander up and down with us today, since I go I know not where? Return, and take your brethren back. Mercy and truth be with you."

[21] But Ittai answered the king and said, "As the LORD lives, and as my lord the king lives, surely in whatever place my lord the king shall be, whether in death or life, even there also your servant will be."

[22] So David said to Ittai, "Go, and cross over." Then Ittai the Gittite and all his men and all the little ones who were with him crossed over. [23] And all the country wept with a loud voice, and all the people crossed over. The king himself also crossed over the Brook Kidron, and all the people crossed over toward the way of the wilderness.

[24] There was Zadok also, and all the Levites with him, bearing the ark of the covenant of God. And they set down the ark of God, and Abiathar went up until all the people had finished crossing over from the city. [25] Then the king said to Zadok, "Carry the ark of God back into the city. If I find favor in the eyes of the LORD, He will bring me back and show me both it and His dwelling place. [26] But

if He says thus: 'I have no delight in you,' here I am, let Him do to me as seems good to Him." [27] The king also said to Zadok the priest, "*Are* you *not* a seer? Return to the city in peace, and your two sons with you, Ahimaaz your son, and Jonathan the son of Abiathar. [28] See, I will wait in the plains of the wilderness until word comes from you to inform me." [29] Therefore Zadok and Abiathar carried the ark of God back to Jerusalem. And they remained there.

[30] So David went up by the Ascent of the *Mount of* Olives, and wept as he went up; and he had his head covered and went barefoot. And all the people who *were* with him covered their heads and went up, weeping as they went up. [31] Then *someone* told David, saying, "Ahithophel *is* among the conspirators with Absalom." And David said, "O LORD, I pray, turn the counsel of Ahithophel into foolishness!"

[32] Now it happened when David had come to the top *of the mountain,* where he worshiped God—there was Hushai the Archite coming to meet him with his robe torn and dust on his head. [33] David said to him, "If you go on with me, then you will become a burden to me. [34] But if you return to the city, and say to Absalom, 'I will be your servant, O king; *as* I *was* your father's servant previously, so I *will* now also *be* your servant,' then you may defeat the counsel of Ahithophel for me. [35] And *do* you not *have* Zadok and Abiathar the priests with you there? Therefore it will be *that* whatever you hear from the king's house, you shall tell to Zadok and Abiathar the priests. [36] Indeed *they have* there with them their two sons, Ahimaaz, Zadok's *son,* and Jonathan, Abiathar's *son;* and by them you shall send me everything you hear."

[37] So Hushai, David's friend, went into the city. And Absalom came into Jerusalem.

16 When David was a little past the top *of the mountain,* there was Ziba the servant of Mephibosheth, who met him with a couple of saddled donkeys, and on them two hundred *loaves* of bread, one hundred clusters of raisins, one hundred summer fruits, and a skin of wine. [2] And the king said to Ziba, "What do you mean to do with these?"

So Ziba said, "The donkeys *are* for the king's household to ride on, the bread and summer fruit for the young men to eat, and the wine for those who are faint in the wilderness to drink."

[3] Then the king said, "And where *is* your master's son?"

And Ziba said to the king, "Indeed he is staying in Jerusalem, for he said, 'Today the house of Israel will restore the kingdom of my father to me.' "

[4] So the king said to Ziba, "Here, all that *belongs* to Mephibosheth *is* yours."

And Ziba said, "I humbly bow before you, *that* I may find favor in your sight, my lord, O king!"

[5] Now when King David came to Bahurim, there was a man from the family of the house of Saul, whose name *was* Shimei the son of Gera, coming from there. He came out, cursing continuously as he came. [6] And he threw stones at David and at all the servants of King David. And all the people and all the mighty men *were* on his right hand and on his left. [7] Also Shimei said thus when he cursed: "Come out! Come out! You bloodthirsty man, you rogue! [8] The LORD has brought upon you all the blood of the house of Saul, in whose place you have reigned; and the LORD has delivered the kingdom into the hand of Absalom your son. So now you *are caught* in your own evil, because you are a bloodthirsty man!"

[9] Then Abishai the son of Zeruiah said to the king, "Why should this dead dog curse my lord the king? Please, let me go over and take off his head!"

[10] But the king said, "What have I to do with you, you sons of Zeruiah? So let him curse, because the LORD has said to him, 'Curse David.' Who then shall say, 'Why have you done so?' "

[11] And David said to Abishai and all his servants, "See how my son who came from my own body seeks my life. How much more now *may this* Benjamite? Let him alone, and let him curse; for so the LORD has ordered him. [12] It may be that the LORD will look on my affliction, and that the LORD will repay me with good for his cursing this day." [13] And as David and his men went along the road, Shimei

No Excuses

Some of the world's greatest achievers have been saddled with disabilities and adversities:

Sir Walter Scott — crippled.
John Bunyan — imprisoned.
George Washington — snowbound and freezing in Valley Forge.
Abraham Lincoln — raised in abject poverty.
Benjamin Disraeli — subject to bitter religious prejudice.
Franklin D. Roosevelt — struck with infantile paralysis.
Ludwig von Beethoven — deaf.
Glenn Cunningham, a world-record-holding sprinter — legs badly burned in a school fire.
Booker T. Washington,
Harriet Tubman,
Marian Anderson, and
George Washington Carver — all born into a society filled with racial discrimination.
Enrico Caruso — the first child to survive in a poor Italian family of eighteen children.
Itzhak Perlman, concert violinist — paralyzed from the waist down at age four.

There really are no good excuses for giving up!

⟨⟨⟨≡⟩⟩⟩

> Who keeps our soul among the living, and does not allow our feet to be moved. For You, O God, have tested us; You have refined us as silver is refined.
>
> *Psalm 66:9-10*

went along the hillside opposite him and cursed as he went, threw stones at him and kicked up dust. ¹⁴ Now the king and all the people who *were* with him became weary; so they refreshed themselves there.

¹⁵ Meanwhile Absalom and all the people, the men of Israel, came to Jerusalem; and Ahithophel *was* with him. ¹⁶ And so it was, when Hushai the Archite, David's friend, came to Absalom, that Hushai said to Absalom, "*Long* live the king! *Long* live the king!"

¹⁷ So Absalom said to Hushai, "*Is* this your loyalty to your friend? Why did you not go with your friend?"

¹⁸ And Hushai said to Absalom, "No, but whom the LORD and this people and all the men of Israel choose, his I will be, and with him I will remain. ¹⁹ "Furthermore, whom should I serve? *Should I* not *serve* in the presence of his son? As I have served in your father's presence, so will I be in your presence."

²⁰ Then Absalom said to Ahithophel, "Give advice as to what we should do."

²¹ And Ahithophel said to Absalom, "Go in to your father's concubines, whom he has left to keep the house; and all Israel will hear that you are abhorred by your father. Then the hands of all who are with you will be strong." ²² So they pitched a tent for Absalom on the top of the house, and Absalom went in to his father's concubines in the sight of all Israel.

²³ Now the advice of Ahithophel, which he gave in those days, *was* as if one had inquired at the oracle of God. So *was* all the advice of Ahithophel both with David and with Absalom.

∼ PSALM 66:8–15 ∼

⁸ Oh, bless our God, you peoples!
   And make the voice of His praise to be heard,
⁹ Who keeps our soul among the living,
   And does not allow our feet to be moved.
¹⁰ For You, O God, have tested us;
   You have refined us as silver is refined.
¹¹ You brought us into the net;
   You laid affliction on our backs.

¹² You have caused men to ride over our heads;
   We went through fire and through water;
   But You brought us out to rich *fulfillment.*

¹³ I will go into Your house with burnt offerings;
   I will pay You my vows,
¹⁴ Which my lips have uttered
   And my mouth has spoken when I was in trouble.
¹⁵ I will offer You burnt sacrifices of fat animals,
   With the sweet aroma of rams;
   I will offer bulls with goats.   Selah

∼ PROVERBS 16:27–30 ∼

²⁷ An ungodly man digs up evil,
   And *it is* on his lips like a burning fire.
²⁸ A perverse man sows strife,
   And a whisperer separates the best of friends.
²⁹ A violent man entices his neighbor,
   And leads him in a way *that is* not good.
³⁰ He winks his eye to devise perverse things;
   He purses his lips *and* brings about evil.

∼ JOHN 7:1–27 ∼

After these things Jesus walked in Galilee; for He did not want to walk in Judea, because the Jews sought to kill Him. ² Now the Jews' Feast of Tabernacles was at hand. ³ His brothers therefore said to Him, "Depart from here and go into Judea, that Your disciples also may see the works that You are doing. ⁴ For no one does anything in secret while he himself seeks to be known openly. If You do these things, show Yourself to the world." ⁵ For even His brothers did not believe in Him.

⁶ Then Jesus said to them, "My time has not yet come, but your time is always ready. ⁷ The world cannot hate you, but it hates Me because I testify of it that its works are evil. ⁸ You go up to this feast. I am not yet going up to this feast, for My time has not yet fully come." ⁹ When He

had said these things to them, He remained in Galilee.

¹⁰ But when His brothers had gone up, then He also went up to the feast, not openly, but as it were in secret. ¹¹ Then the Jews sought Him at the feast, and said, "Where is He?" ¹² And there was much complaining among the people concerning Him. Some said, "He is good"; others said, "No, on the contrary, He deceives the people." ¹³ However, no one spoke openly of Him for fear of the Jews.

¹⁴ Now about the middle of the feast Jesus went up into the temple and taught. ¹⁵ And the Jews marveled, saying, "How does this Man know letters, having never studied?"

¹⁶ Jesus answered them and said, "My doctrine is not Mine, but His who sent Me. ¹⁷ If anyone wills to do His will, he shall know concerning the doctrine, whether it is from God or *whether* I speak on My own *authority*. ¹⁸ He who speaks from himself seeks his own glory; but He who seeks the glory of the One who sent Him is true, and no unrighteousness is in

Him. ¹⁹ Did not Moses give you the law, yet none of you keeps the law? Why do you seek to kill Me?"

²⁰ The people answered and said, "You have a demon. Who is seeking to kill You?"

²¹ Jesus answered and said to them, "I did one work, and you all marvel. ²² Moses therefore gave you circumcision (not that it is from Moses, but from the fathers), and you circumcise a man on the Sabbath. ²³ If a man receives circumcision on the Sabbath, so that the law of Moses should not be broken, are you angry with Me because I made a man completely well on the Sabbath? ²⁴ Do not judge according to appearance, but judge with righteous judgment."

²⁵ Now some of them from Jerusalem said, "Is this not He whom they seek to kill? ²⁶ But look! He speaks boldly, and they say nothing to Him. Do the rulers know indeed that this is truly the Christ? ²⁷ However, we know where this Man is from; but when the Christ comes, no one knows where He is from."

READING 143 · MAY 23

～ 2 SAMUEL 17:1—18:33 ～

Moreover Ahithophel said to Absalom, "Now let me choose twelve thousand men, and I will arise and pursue David tonight. ² I will come upon him while he *is* weary and weak, and make him afraid. And all the people who *are* with him will flee, and I will strike only the king. ³ Then I will bring back all the people to you. When all return except the man whom you seek, all the people will be at peace." ⁴ And the saying pleased Absalom and all the elders of Israel.

⁵ Then Absalom said, "Now call Hushai the Archite also, and let us hear what he says too." ⁶ And when Hushai came to Absalom, Absalom spoke to him, saying, "Ahithophel has spoken in this manner. Shall we do as he says? If not, speak up."

⁷ So Hushai said to Absalom: "The advice that Ahithophel has given *is* not good at this time. ⁸ For," said Hushai, "you know your father and his men, that they

are mighty men, and they *are* enraged in their minds, like a bear robbed of her cubs in the field; and your father *is* a man of war, and will not camp with the people. ⁹ Surely by now he is hidden in some pit, or in some *other* place. And it will be, when some of them are overthrown at the first, that whoever hears *it* will say, 'There is a slaughter among the people who follow Absalom.' ¹⁰ And even he *who is* valiant, whose heart *is* like the heart of a lion, will melt completely. For all Israel knows that your father *is* a mighty man, and *those* who *are* with him *are* valiant men. ¹¹ Therefore I advise that all Israel be fully gathered to you, from Dan to Beersheba, like the sand that *is* by the sea for multitude, and that you go to battle in person. ¹² So we will come upon him in some place where he may be found, and we will fall on him as the dew falls on the ground. And of him and all the men who *are* with him there shall not be left so much as one. ¹³ Moreover, if he has withdrawn into a city, then all Israel shall bring ropes to that city; and we will pull it into the river, until there is not one small stone found there."

¹⁴ So Absalom and all the men of Israel said, "The advice of Hushai the Archite *is* better than the advice of Ahithophel." For the LORD had purposed to defeat the good advice of Ahithophel, to the intent that the LORD might bring disaster on Absalom.

¹⁵ Then Hushai said to Zadok and Abiathar the priests, "Thus and so Ahithophel advised Absalom and the elders of Israel, and thus and so I have advised. ¹⁶ Now therefore, send quickly and tell David, saying, 'Do not spend this night in the plains of the wilderness, but speedily cross over, lest the king and all the people who *are* with him be swallowed up.' " ¹⁷ Now Jonathan and Ahimaaz stayed at En Rogel, for they dared not be seen coming into the city; so a female servant would come and tell them, and they would go and tell King David. ¹⁸ Nevertheless a lad saw them, and told Absalom. But both of them went away quickly and came to a man's house in Bahurim, who had a well in his court; and they went down into it. ¹⁹ Then the woman took and spread a covering over the well's mouth, and spread ground grain on it; and the thing was not known. ²⁰ And when Absalom's servants came to the woman at the house, they said, "Where *are* Ahimaaz and Jonathan?"

So the woman said to them, "They have gone over the water brook."

And when they had searched and could not find *them,* they returned to Jerusalem. ²¹ Now it came to pass, after they had departed, that they came up out of the well and went and told King David, and said to David, "Arise and cross over the water quickly. For thus has Ahithophel advised against you." ²² So David and all the people who *were* with him arose and crossed over the Jordan. By morning light not one of them was left who had not gone over the Jordan.

²³ Now when Ahithophel saw that his advice was not followed, he saddled a donkey, and arose and went home to his house, to his city. Then he put his household in order, and hanged himself, and died; and he was buried in his father's tomb.

²⁴ Then David went to Mahanaim. And Absalom crossed over the Jordan, he and all the men of Israel with him. ²⁵ And Absalom made Amasa captain of the army instead of Joab. This Amasa *was* the son of a man whose name *was* Jithra, an Israelite, who had gone in to Abigail the daughter of Nahash, sister of Zeruiah, Joab's mother. ²⁶ So Israel and Absalom encamped in the land of Gilead.

²⁷ Now it happened, when David had come to Mahanaim, that Shobi the son of Nahash from Rabbah of the people of Ammon, Machir the son of Ammiel from Lo Debar, and Barzillai the Gileadite from Rogelim, ²⁸ brought beds and basins, earthen vessels and wheat, barley and flour, parched *grain* and beans, lentils and parched *seeds,* ²⁹ honey and curds, sheep and cheese of the herd, for David and the people who *were* with him to eat. For they said, "The people are hungry and weary and thirsty in the wilderness."

18 And David numbered the people who *were* with him, and set captains of thousands and captains of hundreds over them. ² Then David sent out one third of the people under the hand of Joab, one third under the hand of Abishai the son of Zeruiah, Joab's brother, and one third under the hand of Ittai the Gittite. And the king said to the people, "I also will surely go out with you myself."

³ But the people answered, "You shall not go out! For if we flee away, they will not care about us; nor if half of us die, will they care about us. But *you are* worth ten thousand of us now. For you are now more help to us in the city."

⁴ Then the king said to them, "Whatever seems best to you I will do." So the king stood beside the gate, and all the people went out by hundreds and by thousands. ⁵ Now the king had commanded Joab, Abishai, and Ittai, saying, "*Deal* gently for my sake with the young man Absalom." And all the people heard when the king gave all the captains orders concerning Absalom.

⁶ So the people went out into the field of battle against Israel. And the battle was

Pray High

Buddy's busy day was over. He was actually ready to kneel by his bed and join his father in bedtime prayers. He prayed about the many activities of his day, thanking God for the ability to catch a lizard and pass a spelling test. Then he listened as his father prayed for his health, safety, and protection from evil. The customary "amen" was said and Buddy was tucked into bed. Before his father left the room, however, he sat up to ask, "Daddy, how high did we pray tonight? Did our prayers get all the way to heaven?"

His father, accustomed to fielding such difficult questions, assured Buddy that God had heard their every word, since He always hears anything we pray. Buddy fell back onto his pillow and was asleep almost before his father left the room.

Daddy, however, pondered his son's question for some time. He was reminded that the Scriptures tell us we are not forgiven unless we first forgive others, and that Jesus once told a man to leave his offering at an altar and first go to make amends with a person he had offended.

The daddy realized there are some things that can hinder our prayers. His son's question was not really that far off.

How high did you pray today?

in the woods of Ephraim. [7] The people of Israel were overthrown there before the servants of David, and a great slaughter of twenty thousand took place there that day. [8] For the battle there was scattered over the face of the whole countryside, and the woods devoured more people that day than the sword devoured.

[9] Then Absalom met the servants of David. Absalom rode on a mule. The mule went under the thick boughs of a great terebinth tree, and his head caught in the terebinth; so he was left hanging between heaven and earth. And the mule which *was* under him went on. [10] Now a certain man saw *it* and told Joab, and said, "I just saw Absalom hanging in a terebinth tree!"

[11] So Joab said to the man who told him, "You just saw *him*! And why did you not strike him there to the ground? I would have given you ten *shekels* of silver and a belt."

[12] But the man said to Joab, "Though I were to receive a thousand *shekels* of silver in my hand, I would not raise my hand against the king's son. For in our hearing the king commanded you and Abishai and Ittai, saying, 'Beware lest anyone *touch* the young man Absalom!' [13] Otherwise I would have dealt falsely against my own life. For there is nothing hidden from the king, and you yourself would have set yourself against *me*."

[14] Then Joab said, "I cannot linger with you." And he took three spears in his hand and thrust them through Absalom's heart, while he was *still* alive in the midst of the terebinth tree. [15] And ten young men who bore Joab's armor surrounded Absalom, and struck and killed him.

[16] So Joab blew the trumpet, and the people returned from pursuing Israel. For Joab held back the people. [17] And they took Absalom and cast him into a large pit in the woods, and laid a very large heap of stones over him. Then all Israel fled, everyone to his tent.

[18] Now Absalom in his lifetime had taken and set up a pillar for himself, which *is* in the King's Valley. For he said, "I have no son to keep my name in remembrance." He called the pillar after his own name. And to this day it is called Absalom's Monument.

[19] Then Ahimaaz the son of Zadok said, "Let me run now and take the news to the king, how the LORD has avenged him of his enemies."

[20] And Joab said to him, "You shall not take the news this day, for you shall take the news another day. But today you shall take no news, because the king's son is dead." [21] Then Joab said to the Cushite, "Go, tell the king what you have seen." So the Cushite bowed himself to Joab and ran.

[22] And Ahimaaz the son of Zadok said again to Joab, "But whatever happens, please let me also run after the Cushite."

So Joab said, "Why will you run, my son, since you have no news ready?"

[23] "But whatever happens," *he said,* "let me run."

So he said to him, "Run." Then Ahimaaz ran by way of the plain, and outran the Cushite.

[24] Now David was sitting between the two gates. And the watchman went up to the roof over the gate, to the wall, lifted his eyes and looked, and there was a man, running alone. [25] Then the watchman cried out and told the king. And the king said, "If he *is* alone, *there is* news in his mouth." And he came rapidly and drew near.

[26] Then the watchman saw *another* man running, and the watchman called to the gatekeeper and said, "There is *another* man, running alone!"

And the king said, "He also brings news."

[27] So the watchman said, "I think the running of the first is like the running of Ahimaaz the son of Zadok."

And the king said, "He *is* a good man, and comes with good news."

[28] So Ahimaaz called out and said to the king, "All is well!" Then he bowed down with his face to the earth before the king, and said, "Blessed *be* the LORD your God, who has delivered up the men who raised their hand against my lord the king!"

[29] The king said, "Is the young man Absalom safe?"

Ahimaaz answered, "When Joab sent the king's servant and *me* your servant, I saw a great tumult, but I did not know what *it was about*."

³⁰ And the king said, "Turn aside *and* stand here." So he turned aside and stood still.

³¹ Just then the Cushite came, and the Cushite said, "There is good news, my lord the king! For the LORD has avenged you this day of all those who rose against you."

³² And the king said to the Cushite, "Is the young man Absalom safe?"

So the Cushite answered, "May the enemies of my lord the king, and all who rise against you to do harm, be like *that* young man!"

³³ Then the king was deeply moved, and went up to the chamber over the gate, and wept. And as he went, he said thus: "O my son Absalom—my son, my son Absalom—if only I had died in your place! O Absalom my son, my son!"

∼ PSALM 66:16–20 ∼

¹⁶ Come *and* hear, all you who fear God,
  And I will declare what He has done for my soul.
¹⁷ I cried to Him with my mouth,
  And He was extolled with my tongue.
¹⁸ If I regard iniquity in my heart,
  The Lord will not hear.
¹⁹ *But* certainly God has heard *me;*
  He has attended to the voice of my prayer.

²⁰ Blessed *be* God,
  Who has not turned away my prayer,
  Nor His mercy from me!

∼ PROVERBS 16:31, 32 ∼

³¹ The silver-haired head *is* a crown of glory,
  If it is found in the way of righteousness.

³² *He who is* slow to anger *is* better than the mighty,
  And he who rules his spirit than he who takes a city.

∼ JOHN 7:28–53 ∼

Then Jesus cried out, as He taught in the temple, saying, "You both know Me, and you know where I am from; and I have not come of Myself, but He who sent Me is true, whom you do not know. ²⁹ But I know Him, for I am from Him, and He sent Me."

³⁰ Therefore they sought to take Him; but no one laid a hand on Him, because His hour had not yet come. ³¹ And many of the people believed in Him, and said, "When the Christ comes, will He do more signs than these which this *Man* has done?"

³² The Pharisees heard the crowd murmuring these things concerning Him, and the Pharisees and the chief priests sent officers to take Him. ³³ Then Jesus said to them, "I shall be with you a little while longer, and *then* I go to Him who sent Me. ³⁴ You will seek Me and not find *Me,* and where I am you cannot come."

³⁵ Then the Jews said among themselves, "Where does He intend to go that we shall not find Him? Does He intend to go to the Dispersion among the Greeks and teach the Greeks? ³⁶ What is this thing that He said, 'You will seek Me and not find Me, and where I am you cannot come'?"

³⁷ On the last day, that great *day* of the feast, Jesus stood and cried out, saying, "If anyone thirsts, let him come to Me and drink. ³⁸ He who believes in Me, as the Scripture has said, out of his heart will flow rivers of living water." ³⁹ But this He spoke concerning the Spirit, whom those believing in Him would receive; for the Holy Spirit was not yet *given,* because Jesus was not yet glorified.

⁴⁰ Therefore many from the crowd, when they heard this saying, said, "Truly this is the Prophet." ⁴¹ Others said, "This is the Christ."

But some said, "Will the Christ come out of Galilee? ⁴² Has not the Scripture said that the Christ comes from the seed of David and from the town of Bethlehem, where David was?" ⁴³ So there was a division among the people because of Him. ⁴⁴ Now some of them wanted to take Him, but no one laid hands on Him.

45 Then the officers came to the chief priests and Pharisees, who said to them, "Why have you not brought Him?"

46 The officers answered, "No man ever spoke like this Man!"

47 Then the Pharisees answered them, "Are you also deceived? 48 Have any of the rulers or the Pharisees believed in Him? 49 But this crowd that does not know the law is accursed."

50 Nicodemus (he who came to Jesus by night, being one of them) said to them, 51 "Does our law judge a man before it hears him and knows what he is doing?"

52 They answered and said to him, "Are you also from Galilee? Search and look, for no prophet has arisen out of Galilee."

53 And everyone went to his *own* house.

READING 144 · MAY 24

～ 2 SAMUEL 19:1—20:26 ～

And Joab was told, "Behold, the king is weeping and mourning for Absalom." 2 So the victory that day was *turned* into mourning for all the people. For the people heard it said that day, "The king is grieved for his son." 3 And the people stole back into the city that day, as people who are ashamed steal away when they flee in battle. 4 But the king covered his face, and the king cried out with a loud voice, "O my son Absalom! O Absalom, my son, my son!"

5 Then Joab came into the house to the king, and said, "Today you have disgraced all your servants who today have saved your life, the lives of your sons and daughters, the lives of your wives and the lives of your concubines, 6 in that you love your enemies and hate your friends. For you have declared today that you regard neither princes nor servants; for today I perceive that if Absalom had lived and all of us had died today, then it would have pleased you well. 7 Now therefore, arise, go out and speak comfort to your servants. For I swear by the LORD, if you do not go out, not one will stay with you this night. And that will be worse for you than all the evil that has befallen you from your youth until now." 8 Then the king arose and sat in the gate. And they told all the people, saying, "There is the king, sitting in the gate." So all the people came before the king.

For everyone of Israel had fled to his tent.

9 Now all the people were in a dispute throughout all the tribes of Israel, saying, "The king saved us from the hand of our enemies, he delivered us from the hand of the Philistines, and now he has fled from the land because of Absalom. 10 But Absalom, whom we anointed over us, has died in battle. Now therefore, why do you say nothing about bringing back the king?"

11 So King David sent to Zadok and Abiathar the priests, saying, "Speak to the elders of Judah, saying, 'Why are you the last to bring the king back to his house, since the words of all Israel have come to the king, to his *very* house? 12 You *are* my brethren, you *are* my bone and my flesh. Why then are you the last to bring back the king?' 13 And say to Amasa, '*Are* you not my bone and my flesh? God do so to me, and more also, if you are not commander of the army before me continually in place of Joab.' " 14 So he swayed the hearts of all the men of Judah, just as *the heart of* one man, so that they sent *this word* to the king: "Return, you and all your servants!"

15 Then the king returned and came to the Jordan. And Judah came to Gilgal, to go to meet the king, to escort the king across the Jordan. 16 And Shimei the son of Gera, a Benjamite, who *was* from Bahurim, hurried and came down with the men of Judah to meet King David. 17 *There were* a thousand men of Benjamin with him, and Ziba the servant of the house of Saul, and his fifteen sons and his twenty servants with him; and they went over the Jordan before the king. 18 Then a ferryboat went across to carry over the king's household, and to do what he thought good.

A Picture-Perfect Christmas

During the Depression, many families could scarcely afford the bare essentials, much less Christmas presents. "But, I'll tell you what we can do," a father said to his six-year-old son, Pete. "We can use our imaginations and make pictures of the presents we would like to give each other."

For the next few days, each member of the family worked secretly, but joyfully. On Christmas morning, huddled around a scraggly tree decorated with a few pitiful decorations, the family gathered to exchange the presents they had created. And what gifts they were! Daddy got a shiny black limousine and a red motor boat. Mom received a diamond bracelet and a new hat. Little Pete had fun opening his gifts, a drawing of a swimming pool and pictures of toys cut from magazines.

Then it was Pete's turn to give his present to his parents. With great delight, he handed them a brightly colored crayon drawing of three people — man, woman, and little boy. They had their arms around one another and under the picture was one word: US. Even though other Christmases were far more prosperous for this family, no Christmas in the family's memory stands out as more precious!

Now Shimei the son of Gera fell down before the king when he had crossed the Jordan. ¹⁹ Then he said to the king, "Do not let my lord impute iniquity to me, or remember what wrong your servant did on the day that my lord the king left Jerusalem, that the king should take *it* to heart. ²⁰ For I, your servant, know that I have sinned. Therefore here I am, the first to come today of all the house of Joseph to go down to meet my lord the king."

²¹ But Abishai the son of Zeruiah answered and said, "Shall not Shimei be put to death for this, because he cursed the LORD's anointed?"

²² And David said, "What have I to do with you, you sons of Zeruiah, that you should be adversaries to me today? Shall any man be put to death today in Israel? For do I not know that today I *am* king over Israel?" ²³ Therefore the king said to Shimei, "You shall not die." And the king swore to him.

²⁴ Now Mephibosheth the son of Saul came down to meet the king. And he had not cared for his feet, nor trimmed his mustache, nor washed his clothes, from the day the king departed until the day he returned in peace. ²⁵ So it was, when he had come to Jerusalem to meet the king, that the king said to him, "Why did you not go with me, Mephibosheth?"

²⁶ And he answered, "My lord, O king, my servant deceived me. For your servant said, 'I will saddle a donkey for myself, that I may ride on it and go to the king,' because your servant *is* lame. ²⁷ And he has slandered your servant to my lord the king, but my lord the king *is* like the angel of God. Therefore do *what is* good in your eyes. ²⁸ For all my father's house were but dead men before my lord the king. Yet you set your servant among those who eat at your own table. Therefore what right have I still to cry out anymore to the king?"

²⁹ So the king said to him, "Why do you speak anymore of your matters? I have said, 'You and Ziba divide the land.' "

³⁰ Then Mephibosheth said to the king, "Rather, let him take it all, inasmuch as my lord the king has come back in peace to his own house."

³¹ And Barzillai the Gileadite came down from Rogelim and went across the Jordan with the king, to escort him across the Jordan. ³² Now Barzillai was a very aged man, eighty years old. And he had provided the king with supplies while he stayed at Mahanaim, for he *was* a very rich man. ³³ And the king said to Barzillai, "Come across with me, and I will provide for you while you are with me in Jerusalem."

³⁴ But Barzillai said to the king, "How long have I to live, that I should go up with the king to Jerusalem? ³⁵ I *am* today eighty years old. Can I discern between the good and bad? Can your servant taste what I eat or what I drink? Can I hear any longer the voice of singing men and singing women? Why then should your servant be a further burden to my lord the king? ³⁶ Your servant will go a little way across the Jordan with the king. And why should the king repay me *with* such a reward? ³⁷ Please let your servant turn back again, that I may die in my own city, near the grave of my father and mother. But here is your servant Chimham; let him cross over with my lord the king, and do for him what seems good to you."

³⁸ And the king answered, "Chimham shall cross over with me, and I will do for him what seems good to you. Now whatever you request of me, I will do for you." ³⁹ Then all the people went over the Jordan. And when the king had crossed over, the king kissed Barzillai and blessed him, and he returned to his own place.

⁴⁰ Now the king went on to Gilgal, and Chimham went on with him. And all the people of Judah escorted the king, and also half the people of Israel. ⁴¹ Just then all the men of Israel came to the king, and said to the king, "Why have our brethren, the men of Judah, stolen you away and brought the king, his household, and all David's men with him across the Jordan?"

⁴² So all the men of Judah answered the men of Israel, "Because the king *is* a close relative of ours. Why then are you angry over this matter? Have we ever eaten at the king's *expense?* Or has he given us any gift?"

⁴³ And the men of Israel answered the men of Judah, and said, "We have ten shares in the king; therefore we also have

more *right* to David than you. Why then do you despise us—were we not the first to advise bringing back our king?"

Yet the words of the men of Judah were fiercer than the words of the men of Israel.

20 And there happened to be there a rebel, whose name *was* Sheba the son of Bichri, a Benjamite. And he blew a trumpet, and said:

"We have no share in David,
Nor do we have inheritance in the
    son of Jesse;
Every man to his tents, O Israel!"

² So every man of Israel deserted David, *and* followed Sheba the son of Bichri. But the men of Judah, from the Jordan as far as Jerusalem, remained loyal to their king.

³ Now David came to his house at Jerusalem. And the king took the ten women, his concubines whom he had left to keep the house, and put them in seclusion and supported them, but did not go in to them. So they were shut up to the day of their death, living in widowhood.

⁴ And the king said to Amasa, "Assemble the men of Judah for me within three days, and be present here yourself." ⁵ So Amasa went to assemble *the men of* Judah. But he delayed longer than the set time which David had appointed him. ⁶ And David said to Abishai, "Now Sheba the son of Bichri will do us more harm than Absalom. Take your lord's servants and pursue him, lest he find for himself fortified cities, and escape us." ⁷ So Joab's men, with the Cherethites, the Pelethites, and all the mighty men, went out after him. And they went out of Jerusalem to pursue Sheba the son of Bichri. ⁸ When they *were* at the large stone which *is* in Gibeon, Amasa came before them. Now Joab was dressed in battle armor; on it was a belt *with* a sword fastened in its sheath at his hips; and as he was going forward, it fell out. ⁹ Then Joab said to Amasa, "*Are* you in health, my brother?" And Joab took Amasa by the beard with his right hand to kiss him. ¹⁰ But Amasa did not notice the sword that *was* in Joab's hand. And he struck him with it in the stomach, and his entrails poured out on the ground;

and he did not *strike* him again. Thus he died.

Then Joab and Abishai his brother pursued Sheba the son of Bichri. ¹¹ Meanwhile one of Joab's men stood near Amasa, and said, "Whoever favors Joab and whoever *is* for David—follow Joab!" ¹² But Amasa wallowed in *his* blood in the middle of the highway. And when the man saw that all the people stood still, he moved Amasa from the highway to the field and threw a garment over him, when he saw that everyone who came upon him halted. ¹³ When he was removed from the highway, all the people went on after Joab to pursue Sheba the son of Bichri.

¹⁴ And he went through all the tribes of Israel to Abel and Beth Maachah and all the Berites. So they were gathered together and also went after *Sheba*. ¹⁵ Then they came and besieged him in Abel of Beth Maachah; and they cast up a siege mound against the city, and it stood by the rampart. And all the people who *were* with Joab battered the wall to throw it down.

¹⁶ Then a wise woman cried out from the city, "Hear, hear! Please say to Joab, 'Come nearby, that I may speak with you.' " ¹⁷ When he had come near to her, the woman said, "*Are* you Joab?"

He answered, "I *am*."

Then she said to him, "Hear the words of your maidservant."

And he answered, "I am listening."

¹⁸ So she spoke, saying, "They used to talk in former times, saying, 'They shall surely seek *guidance* at Abel,' and so they would end *disputes*. ¹⁹ I *am among the* peaceable *and* faithful in Israel. You seek to destroy a city and a mother in Israel. Why would you swallow up the inheritance of the LORD?"

²⁰ And Joab answered and said, "Far be it, far be it from me, that I should swallow up or destroy! ²¹ That *is* not so. But a man from the mountains of Ephraim, Sheba the son of Bichri by name, has raised his hand against the king, against David. Deliver him only, and I will depart from the city."

So the woman said to Joab, "Watch, his head will be thrown to you over the wall." ²² Then the woman in her wisdom went to all the people. And they cut off the head of Sheba the son of Bichri, and threw *it* out to Joab. Then he blew a trumpet, and they withdrew from the city, every man to his tent. So Joab returned to the king at Jerusalem.

23 And Joab *was* over all the army of Israel; Benaiah the son of Jehoiada *was* over the Cherethites and the Pelethites; 24 Adoram *was* in charge of revenue; Jehoshaphat the son of Ahilud *was* recorder; 25 Sheva *was* scribe; Zadok and Abiathar *were* the priests; 26 and Ira the Jairite was a chief minister under David.

～ PSALM 67:1-7 ～

1   God be merciful to us and bless us,
    And cause His face to shine upon us,
                                    Selah
2   That Your way may be known on
       earth,
    Your salvation among all nations.

3   Let the peoples praise You, O God;
    Let all the peoples praise You.
4   Oh, let the nations be glad and sing
       for joy!
    For You shall judge the people
       righteously,
    And govern the nations on earth.
                                    Selah

5   Let the peoples praise You, O God;
    Let all the peoples praise You.
6   *Then* the earth shall yield her
       increase;
    God, our own God, shall bless us.
7   God shall bless us,
    And all the ends of the earth shall
       fear Him.

～ PROVERBS 16:33—17:1 ～

33 The lot is cast into the lap,
    But its every decision *is* from the
       LORD.

17 Better *is* a dry morsel with quietness,
    Than a house full of feasting *with*
       strife.

～ JOHN 8:1-27 ～

But Jesus went to the Mount of Olives. 2 Now early in the morning He came again into the temple, and all the people came to Him; and He sat down and taught them. 3 Then the scribes and Pharisees brought to Him a woman caught in adultery. And when they had set her in the midst, 4 they said to Him, "Teacher, this woman was caught in adultery, in the very act. 5 Now Moses, in the law, commanded us that such should be stoned. But what do You say?" 6 This they said, testing Him, that they might have *something* of which to accuse Him. But Jesus stooped down and wrote on the ground with *His* finger, as though He did not hear.

7 So when they continued asking Him, He raised Himself up and said to them, "He who is without sin among you, let him throw a stone at her first." 8 And again He stooped down and wrote on the ground. 9 Then those who heard *it,* being convicted by *their* conscience, went out one by one, beginning with the oldest *even* to the last. And Jesus was left alone, and the woman standing in the midst. 10 When Jesus had raised Himself up and saw no one but the woman, He said to her, "Woman, where are those accusers of yours? Has no one condemned you?"

11 She said, "No one, Lord."

And Jesus said to her, "Neither do I condemn you; go and sin no more."

12 Then Jesus spoke to them again, saying, "I am the light of the world. He who follows Me shall not walk in darkness, but have the light of life."

13 The Pharisees therefore said to Him, "You bear witness of Yourself; Your witness is not true."

14 Jesus answered and said to them, "Even if I bear witness of Myself, My witness is true, for I know where I came from and where I am going; but you do not know where I come from and where I am going. 15 You judge according to the flesh; I judge no one. 16 And yet if I do judge, My judgment is true; for I am not alone, but I *am* with the Father who sent Me. 17 It is also written in your law that the testimony of two men is true. 18 I am One who bears witness of Myself, and the Father who sent Me bears witness of Me."

19 Then they said to Him, "Where is Your Father?"

Jesus answered, "You know neither Me nor My Father. If you had known Me, you would have known My Father also."

²⁰ These words Jesus spoke in the treasury, as He taught in the temple; and no one laid hands on Him, for His hour had not yet come.

²¹ Then Jesus said to them again, "I am going away, and you will seek Me, and will die in your sin. Where I go you cannot come."

²² So the Jews said, "Will He kill Himself, because He says, 'Where I go you cannot come'?"

²³ And He said to them, "You are from beneath; I am from above. You are of this world; I am not of this world. ²⁴ Therefore I said to you that you will die in your sins; for if you do not believe that I am *He*, you will die in your sins."

²⁵ Then they said to Him, "Who are You?"

And Jesus said to them, "Just what I have been saying to you from the beginning. ²⁶ I have many things to say and to judge concerning you, but He who sent Me is true; and I speak to the world those things which I heard from Him."

²⁷ They did not understand that He spoke to them of the Father.

READING 145 · MAY 25

~ 2 SAMUEL 21:1—22:51 ~

Now there was a famine in the days of David for three years, year after year; and David inquired of the LORD. And the LORD answered, "*It is* because of Saul and *his* bloodthirsty house, because he killed the Gibeonites." ² So the king called the Gibeonites and spoke to them. Now the Gibeonites *were* not of the children of Israel, but of the remnant of the Amorites; the children of Israel had sworn protection to them, but Saul had sought to kill them in his zeal for the children of Israel and Judah. ³ Therefore David said to the Gibeonites, "What shall I do for you? And with what shall I make atonement, that you may bless the inheritance of the LORD?"

⁴ And the Gibeonites said to him, "We will have no silver or gold from Saul or from his house, nor shall you kill any man in Israel for us."

So he said, "Whatever you say, I will do for you."

⁵ Then they answered the king, "As for the man who consumed us and plotted against us, *that* we should be destroyed from remaining in any of the territories of Israel, ⁶ let seven men of his descendants be delivered to us, and we will hang them before the LORD in Gibeah of Saul, *whom* the LORD chose."

And the king said, "I will give *them*."

⁷ But the king spared Mephibosheth the son of Jonathan, the son of Saul, because of the LORD's oath that *was* between them, between David and Jonathan the son of Saul. ⁸ So the king took Armoni and Mephibosheth, the two sons of Rizpah the daughter of Aiah, whom she bore to Saul, and the five sons of Michal the daughter of Saul, whom she brought up for Adriel the son of Barzillai the Meholathite; ⁹ and he delivered them into the hands of the Gibeonites, and they hanged them on the hill before the LORD. So they fell, *all* seven together, and were put to death in the days of harvest, in the first *days*, in the beginning of barley harvest.

¹⁰ Now Rizpah the daughter of Aiah took sackcloth and spread it for herself on the rock, from the beginning of harvest until the late rains poured on them from heaven. And she did not allow the birds of the air to rest on them by day nor the beasts of the field by night.

¹¹ And David was told what Rizpah the daughter of Aiah, the concubine of Saul, had done. ¹² Then David went and took the bones of Saul, and the bones of Jonathan his son, from the men of Jabesh Gilead who had stolen them from the street of Beth Shan, where the Philistines had hung them up, after the Philistines had struck down Saul in Gilboa. ¹³ So he brought up the bones of Saul and the bones of Jonathan his son from there; and they gathered the bones of those who had been hanged. ¹⁴ They buried the bones

of Saul and Jonathan his son in the country of Benjamin in Zelah, in the tomb of Kish his father. So they performed all that the king commanded. And after that God heeded the prayer for the land.

¹⁵ When the Philistines were at war again with Israel, David and his servants with him went down and fought against the Philistines; and David grew faint. ¹⁶ Then Ishbi-Benob, who *was* one of the sons of the giant, the weight of whose bronze spear *was* three hundred *shekels,* who was bearing a new *sword,* thought he could kill David. ¹⁷ But Abishai the son of Zeruiah came to his aid, and struck the Philistine and killed him. Then the men of David swore to him, saying, "You shall go out no more with us to battle, lest you quench the lamp of Israel."

¹⁸ Now it happened afterward that there was again a battle with the Philistines at Gob. Then Sibbechai the Hushathite killed Saph, who *was* one of the sons of the giant. ¹⁹ Again there was war at Gob with the Philistines, where Elhanan the son of Jaare-Oregim the Bethlehemite killed *the brother of* Goliath the Gittite, the shaft of whose spear *was* like a weaver's beam.

²⁰ Yet again there was war at Gath, where there was a man of *great* stature, who had six fingers on each hand and six toes on each foot, twenty-four in number; and he also was born to the giant. ²¹ So when he defied Israel, Jonathan the son of Shimea, David's brother, killed him. ²² These four were born to the giant in Gath, and fell by the hand of David and by the hand of his servants.

22 Then David spoke to the LORD the words of this song, on the day when the LORD had delivered him from the hand of all his enemies, and from the hand of Saul. ² And he said:

"The LORD *is* my rock and my
    fortress and my deliverer;
³ The God of my strength, in whom
    I will trust;
  My shield and the horn of my
    salvation,
  My stronghold and my refuge;
  My Savior, You save me from
    violence.

⁴ I will call upon the LORD, *who is*
    worthy to be praised;
  So shall I be saved from my
    enemies.

⁵ "When the waves of death
    surrounded me,
  The floods of ungodliness made
    me afraid.
⁶ The sorrows of Sheol surrounded
    me;
  The snares of death confronted
    me.
⁷ In my distress I called upon the
    LORD,
  And cried out to my God;
  He heard my voice from His
    temple,
  And my cry *entered* His ears.

⁸ "Then the earth shook and
    trembled;
  The foundations of heaven quaked
    and were shaken,
  Because He was angry.
⁹ Smoke went up from His nostrils,
  And devouring fire from His
    mouth;
  Coals were kindled by it.
¹⁰ He bowed the heavens also, and
    came down
  With darkness under His feet.
¹¹ He rode upon a cherub, and flew;
  And He was seen upon the wings
    of the wind.
¹² He made darkness canopies
    around Him,
  Dark waters *and* thick clouds of
    the skies.
¹³ From the brightness before Him
  Coals of fire were kindled.

¹⁴ "The LORD thundered from
    heaven,
  And the Most High uttered His
    voice.
¹⁵ He sent out arrows and scattered
    them;
  Lightning bolts, and He
    vanquished them.
¹⁶ Then the channels of the sea were
    seen,
  The foundations of the world
    were uncovered,
  At the rebuke of the LORD,

Sticking with the Rules

The mother of three small children, each born only two years apart, often found herself exhausted by the end of a day. Along with the children's father, she had set strict rules that after a story time, prayers, one small drink of water, and a final trip to the bathroom, each child must go to bed and stay there.

One night, after a particularly trying day, all three children were finally tucked into bed and the two parents headed to the kitchen for some cookies and milk, and a little time alone together. They had just started to relax when they suddenly found themselves surrounded by three little people, all standing in silence as they watched Mom and Dad each bite into a delicious home-baked cookie. Turning to Dad, Mom asked, "Well, do we relent, or do we stick with the rules?"

Before Dad could answer, their three-year-old daughter piped up, "Stick with the rules, Mom!"

Knowing that her daughter didn't really want to be sent back to bed, Mom asked, "And what exactly are those rules, dear?"

Her daughter replied without hesitation, "Share with one another."

At the blast of the breath of His
    nostrils.

17 "He sent from above, He took me,
    He drew me out of many waters.
18 He delivered me from my strong
    enemy,
    From those who hated me;
    For they were too strong for me.
19 They confronted me in the day of
    my calamity,
    But the LORD was my support.
20 He also brought me out into a
    broad place;
    He delivered me because He
    delighted in me.

21 "The LORD rewarded me according
    to my righteousness;
    According to the cleanness of my
    hands
    He has recompensed me.
22 For I have kept the ways of the
    LORD,
    And have not wickedly departed
    from my God.
23 For all His judgments were before
    me;
    And as for His statutes, I did not
    depart from them.
24 I was also blameless before Him,
    And I kept myself from my
    iniquity.
25 Therefore the LORD has
    recompensed me according to
    my righteousness,
    According to my cleanness in His
    eyes.

26 "With the merciful You will show
    Yourself merciful;
    With a blameless man You will
    show Yourself blameless;
27 With the pure You will show
    Yourself pure;
    And with the devious You will
    show Yourself shrewd.
28 You will save the humble people;
    But Your eyes are on the haughty,
    that You may bring them down.

29 "For You are my lamp, O LORD;
    The LORD shall enlighten my
    darkness.

30 For by You I can run against a
    troop;
    By my God I can leap over a wall.
31 As for God, His way is perfect;
    The word of the LORD is proven;
    He is a shield to all who trust in
    Him.

32 "For who is God, except the LORD?
    And who is a rock, except our
    God?
33 God is my strength and power,
    And He makes my way perfect.
34 He makes my feet like the feet of
    deer,
    And sets me on my high places.
35 He teaches my hands to make war,
    So that my arms can bend a bow
    of bronze.

36 "You have also given me the shield
    of Your salvation;
    Your gentleness has made me
    great.
37 You enlarged my path under me;
    So my feet did not slip.

38 "I have pursued my enemies and
    destroyed them;
    Neither did I turn back again till
    they were destroyed.
39 And I have destroyed them and
    wounded them,
    So that they could not rise;
    They have fallen under my feet.
40 For You have armed me with
    strength for the battle;
    You have subdued under me those
    who rose against me.
41 You have also given me the necks
    of my enemies,
    So that I destroyed those who
    hated me.
42 They looked, but there was none
    to save;
    Even to the LORD, but He did not
    answer them.
43 Then I beat them as fine as the
    dust of the earth;
    I trod them like dirt in the streets,
    And I spread them out.

44 "You have also delivered me from
    the strivings of my people;

You have kept me as the head of
    the nations.
A people I have not known shall
    serve me.
45 The foreigners submit to me;
    As soon as they hear, they obey
    me.
46 The foreigners fade away,
    And come frightened from their
    hideouts.

47 "The LORD lives!
    Blessed *be* my Rock!
    Let God be exalted,
    The Rock of my salvation!
48 *It is* God who avenges me,
    And subdues the peoples under
    me;
49 He delivers me from my enemies.
    You also lift me up above those
    who rise against me;
    You have delivered me from the
    violent man.
50 Therefore I will give thanks to
    You, O LORD, among the
    Gentiles,
    And sing praises to Your name.

51 "*He is* the tower of salvation to His
    king,
    And shows mercy to His anointed,
    To David and his descendants
    forevermore."

～ PSALM 68:1–6 ～

1 Let God arise,
    Let His enemies be scattered;
    Let those also who hate Him flee
    before Him.
2 As smoke is driven away,
    So drive *them* away;
    As wax melts before the fire,
    So let the wicked perish at the
    presence of God.
3 But let the righteous be glad;
    Let them rejoice before God;
    Yes, let them rejoice exceedingly.

4 Sing to God, sing praises to His
    name;
    Extol Him who rides on the clouds,
    By His name YAH,
    And rejoice before Him.

5 A father of the fatherless, a defender
    of widows,
    Is God in His holy habitation.
6 God sets the solitary in families;
    He brings out those who are bound
    into prosperity;
    But the rebellious dwell in a dry
    land.

～ PROVERBS 17:2–4 ～

2 A wise servant will rule over a son
    who causes shame,
    And will share an inheritance among
    the brothers.

3 The refining pot *is* for silver and the
    furnace for gold,
    But the LORD tests the hearts.

4 An evildoer gives heed to false lips;
    A liar listens eagerly to a spiteful
    tongue.

～ JOHN 8:28–59 ～

Then Jesus said to them, "When you lift up the Son of Man, then you will know that I am *He,* and *that* I do nothing of Myself; but as My Father taught Me, I speak these things. 29 And He who sent Me is with Me. The Father has not left Me alone, for I always do those things that please Him." 30 As He spoke these words, many believed in Him.

31 Then Jesus said to those Jews who believed Him, "If you abide in My word, you are My disciples indeed. 32 And you shall know the truth, and the truth shall make you free."

33 They answered Him, "We are Abraham's descendants, and have never been in bondage to anyone. How *can* You say, 'You will be made free'?"

34 Jesus answered them, "Most assuredly, I say to you, whoever commits sin is a slave of sin. 35 And a slave does not abide in the house forever, *but* a son abides forever. 36 Therefore if the Son makes you free, you shall be free indeed.

37 "I know that you are Abraham's descendants, but you seek to kill Me, because My word has no place in you. 38 I

speak what I have seen with My Father, and you do what you have seen with your father."

³⁹ They answered and said to Him, "Abraham is our father."

Jesus said to them, "If you were Abraham's children, you would do the works of Abraham. ⁴⁰ But now you seek to kill Me, a Man who has told you the truth which I heard from God. Abraham did not do this. ⁴¹ You do the deeds of your father."

Then they said to Him, "We were not born of fornication; we have one Father—God."

⁴² Jesus said to them, "If God were your Father, you would love Me, for I proceeded forth and came from God; nor have I come of Myself, but He sent Me. ⁴³ Why do you not understand My speech? Because you are not able to listen to My word. ⁴⁴ You are of *your* father the devil, and the desires of your father you want to do. He was a murderer from the beginning, and does not stand in the truth, because there is no truth in him. When he speaks a lie, he speaks from his own *resources,* for he is a liar and the father of it. ⁴⁵ But because I tell the truth, you do not believe Me. ⁴⁶ Which of you convicts Me of sin? And if I tell the truth, why do you not believe Me? ⁴⁷ He who is of God hears God's words; therefore you do not hear, because you are not of God."

⁴⁸ Then the Jews answered and said to Him, "Do we not say rightly that You are a Samaritan and have a demon?"

⁴⁹ Jesus answered, "I do not have a demon; but I honor My Father, and you dishonor Me. ⁵⁰ And I do not seek My *own* glory; there is One who seeks and judges. ⁵¹ Most assuredly, I say to you, if anyone keeps My word he shall never see death."

⁵² Then the Jews said to Him, "Now we know that You have a demon! Abraham is dead, and the prophets; and You say, 'If anyone keeps My word he shall never taste death.' ⁵³ Are You greater than our father Abraham, who is dead? And the prophets are dead. Who do You make Yourself out to be?"

⁵⁴ Jesus answered, "If I honor Myself, My honor is nothing. It is My Father who honors Me, of whom you say that He is your God. ⁵⁵ Yet you have not known Him, but I know Him. And if I say, 'I do not know Him,' I shall be a liar like you; but I do know Him and keep His word. ⁵⁶ Your father Abraham rejoiced to see My day, and he saw *it* and was glad."

⁵⁷ Then the Jews said to Him, "You are not yet fifty years old, and have You seen Abraham?"

⁵⁸ Jesus said to them, "Most assuredly, I say to you, before Abraham was, I AM."

⁵⁹ Then they took up stones to throw at Him; but Jesus hid Himself and went out of the temple, going through the midst of them, and so passed by.

READING 146 · MAY 26

~ 2 SAMUEL 23:1—24:25 ~

Now these *are* the last words of David.

Thus says David the son of Jesse;
Thus says the man raised up on
    high,
The anointed of the God of Jacob,
And the sweet psalmist of Israel:

² "The Spirit of the LORD spoke by
    me,
And His word *was* on my tongue.
³ The God of Israel said,

The Rock of Israel spoke to me:
'He who rules over men *must be*
    just,
Ruling in the fear of God.
⁴ And *he shall be* like the light of
    the morning *when* the sun rises,
A morning without clouds,
Like the tender grass *springing* out
    of the earth,
By clear shining after rain.'

⁵ "Although my house *is* not so with
    God,

Kid-Care

Carol Porter, a registered nurse, is the co-founder of Kid-Care, Inc., a nonprofit group with a volunteer staff who deliver 500 free meals each day to poor neighborhoods. Each meal is prepared in Porter's cramped Houston home, where extra stoves and refrigerators have been installed in what used to be the family's living room and den. Kid-Care receives no public funding, and although Carol's efforts have resulted in help from some corporations, most of her $500,000 budget comes from individual donations.

Carol credits her late mother, Lula Doe, for giving her the idea for Kid-Care. In 1984, Lula persuaded a local supermarket not to discard its blemished produce, but to let her distribute it to the poor. Then, during Christmastime in 1989, Carol saw a group of children searching for food in a McDonalds' dumpster. She says, "I saw Third World conditions a stone's throw from where I live." Kid-Care was her response.

"People ask me what's in it for me. And I tell them to go on the route with me and see the kids' faces. That's what's in it for me." She sees the meals as "better than ice cream. It's hope."

Purpose in life comes when we purpose to lift the load of another — to show God's love by doing for them what they could not do for themselves.

Yet He has made with me an
everlasting covenant,
Ordered in all *things* and secure.
For *this is* all my salvation and all
my desire;
Will He not make *it* increase?

6 But *the sons* of rebellion *shall* all
be as thorns thrust away,
Because they cannot be taken with
hands.

7 But the man *who* touches them
Must be armed with iron and the
shaft of a spear,
And they shall be utterly burned
with fire in *their* place."

8 These *are* the names of the mighty
men whom David had: Josheb-Basshebeth
the Tachmonite, chief among the captains.
He was called Adino the Eznite, because
he had killed eight hundred men at one
time. 9 And after him *was* Eleazar the son
of Dodo, the Ahohite, *one* of the three
mighty men with David when they defied the Philistines *who* were gathered
there for battle, and the men of Israel had
retreated. 10 He arose and attacked the
Philistines until his hand was weary, and
his hand stuck to the sword. The LORD
brought about a great victory that day;
and the people returned after him only to
plunder. 11 And after him *was* Shammah
the son of Agee the Hararite. The Philistines had gathered together into a troop
where there was a piece of ground full of
lentils. So the people fled from the Philistines. 12 But he stationed himself in the
middle of the field, defended it, and killed
the Philistines. So the LORD brought about
a great victory.

13 Then three of the thirty chief men
went down at harvest time and came to
David at the cave of Adullam. And the
troop of Philistines encamped in the Valley of Rephaim. 14 David *was* then in the
stronghold, and the garrison of the Philistines *was* then *in* Bethlehem. 15 And
David said with longing, "Oh, that someone would give me a drink of the water
from the well of Bethlehem, which *is* by
the gate!" 16 So the three mighty men
broke through the camp of the Philistines,
drew water from the well of Bethlehem
that *was* by the gate, and took it and
brought *it* to David. Nevertheless he

would not drink it, but poured it out to
the LORD. 17 And he said, "Far be it from
me, O LORD, that I should do this! Is *this
not* the blood of the men who went in
jeopardy of their lives?" Therefore he
would not drink it.

These things were done by the three
mighty men.

18 Now Abishai the brother of Joab, the
son of Zeruiah, was chief of *another* three.
He lifted his spear against three hundred
men, killed *them,* and won a name among
these three. 19 Was he not the most honored of three? Therefore he became their
captain. However, he did not attain to the
first three.

20 Benaiah *was* the son of Jehoiada, the
son of a valiant man from Kabzeel, who
had done many deeds. He had killed two
lion-like heroes of Moab. He also had
gone down and killed a lion in the midst
of a pit on a snowy day. 21 And he killed
an Egyptian, a spectacular man. The Egyptian *had* a spear in his hand; so he went
down to him with a staff, wrested the spear
out of the Egyptian's hand, and killed him
with his own spear. 22 These *things*
Benaiah the son of Jehoiada did, and won
a name among three mighty men. 23 He
was more honored than the thirty, but
he did not attain to the *first* three. And
David appointed him over his guard.

24 Asahel the brother of Joab *was* one
of the thirty; Elhanan the son of Dodo of
Bethlehem, 25 Shammah the Harodite,
Elika the Harodite, 26 Helez the Paltite,
Ira the son of Ikkesh the Tekoite, 27 Abiezer
the Anathothite, Mebunnai the Hushathite, 28 Zalmon the Ahohite, Maharai the
Netophathite, 29 Heleb the son of Baanah
(the Netophathite), Ittai the son of Ribai
from Gibeah of the children of Benjamin,
30 Benaiah a Pirathonite, Hiddai from the
brooks of Gaash, 31 Abi-Albon the Arbathite, Azmaveth the Barhumite, 32 Eliahba the Shaalbonite (of the sons of Jashen),
Jonathan, 33 Shammah the Hararite, Ahiam the son of Sharar the Hararite, 34 Eliphelet the son of Ahasbai, the son of the
Maachathite, Eliam the son of Ahithophel the Gilonite, 35 Hezrai the Carmelite, Paarai the Arbite, 36 Igal the son of
Nathan of Zobah, Bani the Gadite, 37 Zelek the Ammonite, Naharai the Beerothite (armorbearer of Joab the son of

Zeruiah), [38] Ira the Ithrite, Gareb the Ithrite, [39] *and* Uriah the Hittite: thirty-seven in all.

24

Again the anger of the LORD was aroused against Israel, and He moved David against them to say, "Go, number Israel and Judah."

[2] So the king said to Joab the commander of the army who *was* with him, "Now go throughout all the tribes of Israel, from Dan to Beersheba, and count the people, that I may know the number of the people."

[3] And Joab said to the king, "Now may the LORD your God add to the people a hundred times more than there are, and may the eyes of my lord the king see *it*. But why does my lord the king desire this thing?" [4] Nevertheless the king's word prevailed against Joab and against the captains of the army. Therefore Joab and the captains of the army went out from the presence of the king to count the people of Israel.

[5] And they crossed over the Jordan and camped in Aroer, on the right side of the town which *is* in the midst of the ravine of Gad, and toward Jazer. [6] Then they came to Gilead and to the land of Tahtim Hodshi; they came to Dan Jaan and around to Sidon; [7] and they came to the stronghold of Tyre and to all the cities of the Hivites and the Canaanites. Then they went out to South Judah *as far as* Beersheba. [8] So when they had gone through all the land, they came to Jerusalem at the end of nine months and twenty days. [9] Then Joab gave the sum of the number of the people to the king. And there were in Israel eight hundred thousand valiant men who drew the sword, and the men of Judah were five hundred thousand men.

[10] And David's heart condemned him after he had numbered the people. So David said to the LORD, "I have sinned greatly in what I have done; but now, I pray, O LORD, take away the iniquity of Your servant, for I have done very foolishly."

[11] Now when David arose in the morning, the word of the LORD came to the prophet Gad, David's seer, saying, [12] "Go and tell David, 'Thus says the LORD: "I offer you three *things;* choose one of them for yourself, that I may do *it* to you." ' "

[13] So Gad came to David and told him; and he said to him, "Shall seven years of famine come to you in your land? Or shall you flee three months before your enemies, while they pursue you? Or shall there be three days' plague in your land? Now consider and see what answer I should take back to Him who sent me."

[14] And David said to Gad, "I am in great distress. Please let us fall into the hand of the LORD, for His mercies *are* great; but do not let me fall into the hand of man."

[15] So the LORD sent a plague upon Israel from the morning till the appointed time. From Dan to Beersheba seventy thousand men of the people died. [16] And when the angel stretched out His hand over Jerusalem to destroy it, the LORD relented from the destruction, and said to the angel who was destroying the people, "It is enough; now restrain your hand." And the angel of the LORD was by the threshing floor of Araunah the Jebusite.

[17] Then David spoke to the LORD when he saw the angel who was striking the people, and said, "Surely I have sinned, and I have done wickedly; but these sheep, what have they done? Let Your hand, I pray, be against me and against my father's house."

[18] And Gad came that day to David and said to him, "Go up, erect an altar to the LORD on the threshing floor of Araunah the Jebusite." [19] So David, according to the word of Gad, went up as the LORD commanded. [20] Now Araunah looked, and saw the king and his servants coming toward him. So Araunah went out and bowed before the king with his face to the ground.

[21] Then Araunah said, "Why has my lord the king come to his servant?"

And David said, "To buy the threshing floor from you, to build an altar to the LORD, that the plague may be withdrawn from the people."

[22] Now Araunah said to David, "Let my lord the king take and offer up whatever *seems* good to him. Look, *here are* oxen for burnt sacrifice, and threshing implements and the yokes of the oxen for wood.

²³ All these, O king, Araunah has given to the king."

And Araunah said to the king, "May the LORD your God accept you."

²⁴ Then the king said to Araunah, "No, but I will surely buy *it* from you for a price; nor will I offer burnt offerings to the LORD my God with that which costs me nothing." So David bought the threshing floor and the oxen for fifty shekels of silver. ²⁵ And David built there an altar to the LORD, and offered burnt offerings and peace offerings. So the LORD heeded the prayers for the land, and the plague was withdrawn from Israel.

∼ PSALM 68:7–10 ∼

7   O God, when You went out before
      Your people,
      When You marched through the
         wilderness,   Selah
8   The earth shook;
      The heavens also dropped *rain* at the
         presence of God;
      Sinai itself *was moved* at the
         presence of God, the God of
         Israel.
9   You, O God, sent a plentiful rain,
      Whereby You confirmed Your
         inheritance,
      When it was weary.
10 Your congregation dwelt in it;
      You, O God, provided from Your
         goodness for the poor.

∼ PROVERBS 17:5, 6 ∼

5   He who mocks the poor reproaches
      his Maker;
      He who is glad at calamity will not
         go unpunished.

6   Children's children *are* the crown of
      old men,
      And the glory of children *is* their
         father.

∼ JOHN 9:1–23 ∼

Now as *Jesus* passed by, He saw a man who was blind from birth. ² And His disciples asked Him, saying, "Rabbi, who sinned, this man or his parents, that he was born blind?"

³ Jesus answered, "Neither this man nor his parents sinned, but that the works of God should be revealed in him. ⁴ I must work the works of Him who sent Me while it is day; *the* night is coming when no one can work. ⁵ As long as I am in the world, I am the light of the world."

⁶ When He had said these things, He spat on the ground and made clay with the saliva; and He anointed the eyes of the blind man with the clay. ⁷ And He said to him, "Go, wash in the pool of Siloam" (which is translated, Sent). So he went and washed, and came back seeing.

⁸ Therefore the neighbors and those who previously had seen that he was blind said, "Is not this he who sat and begged?"

⁹ Some said, "This is he." Others *said,* "He is like him."

He said, "I am *he.*"

¹⁰ Therefore they said to him, "How were your eyes opened?"

¹¹ He answered and said, "A Man called Jesus made clay and anointed my eyes and said to me, 'Go to the pool of Siloam and wash.' So I went and washed, and I received sight."

¹² Then they said to him, "Where is He?"

He said, "I do not know."

¹³ They brought him who formerly was blind to the Pharisees. ¹⁴ Now it was a Sabbath when Jesus made the clay and opened his eyes. ¹⁵ Then the Pharisees also asked him again how he had received his sight. He said to them, "He put clay on my eyes, and I washed, and I see."

¹⁶ Therefore some of the Pharisees said, "This Man is not from God, because He does not keep the Sabbath."

Others said, "How can a man who is a sinner do such signs?" And there was a division among them.

¹⁷ They said to the blind man again, "What do you say about Him because He opened your eyes?"

He said, "He is a prophet."

¹⁸ But the Jews did not believe concerning him, that he had been blind and received his sight, until they called the parents of him who had received his sight. ¹⁹ And they asked them, saying, "Is this your son, who you say was born blind? How then does he now see?"

20 His parents answered them and said, "We know that this is our son, and that he was born blind; 21 but by what means he now sees we do not know, or who opened his eyes we do not know. He is of age; ask him. He will speak for himself." 22 His parents said these *things* because they feared the Jews, for the Jews had agreed already that if anyone confessed *that* He *was* Christ, he would be put out of the synagogue. 23 Therefore his parents said, "He is of age; ask him."

READING 147 · MAY 27

~ 1 KINGS 1:1—2:46 ~

Now King David was old, advanced in years; and they put covers on him, but he could not get warm. 2 Therefore his servants said to him, "Let a young woman, a virgin, be sought for our lord the king, and let her stand before the king, and let her care for him; and let her lie in your bosom, that our lord the king may be warm." 3 So they sought for a lovely young woman throughout all the territory of Israel, and found Abishag the Shunammite, and brought her to the king. 4 The young woman *was* very lovely; and she cared for the king, and served him; but the king did not know her.

5 Then Adonijah the son of Haggith exalted himself, saying, "I will be king"; and he prepared for himself chariots and horsemen, and fifty men to run before him. 6 (And his father had not rebuked him at any time by saying, "Why have you done so?" He *was* also very good-looking. *His mother* had borne him after Absalom.) 7 Then he conferred with Joab the son of Zeruiah and with Abiathar the priest, and they followed and helped Adonijah. 8 But Zadok the priest, Benaiah the son of Jehoiada, Nathan the prophet, Shimei, Rei, and the mighty men who *belonged* to David were not with Adonijah.

9 And Adonijah sacrificed sheep and oxen and fattened cattle by the stone of Zoheleth, which *is* by En Rogel; he also invited all his brothers, the king's sons, and all the men of Judah, the king's servants. 10 But he did not invite Nathan the prophet, Benaiah, the mighty men, or Solomon his brother.

11 So Nathan spoke to Bathsheba the mother of Solomon, saying, "Have you not heard that Adonijah the son of Haggith has become king, and David our lord does not know *it?* 12 Come, please, let me now give you advice, that you may save your own life and the life of your son Solomon. 13 Go immediately to King David and say to him, 'Did you not, my lord, O king, swear to your maidservant, saying, "Assuredly your son Solomon shall reign after me, and he shall sit on my throne"? Why then has Adonijah become king?' 14 Then, while you are still talking there with the king, I also will come in after you and confirm your words."

15 So Bathsheba went into the chamber to the king. (Now the king was very old, and Abishag the Shunammite was serving the king.) 16 And Bathsheba bowed and did homage to the king. Then the king said, "What is your wish?"

17 Then she said to him, "My lord, you swore by the LORD your God to your maidservant, *saying,* 'Assuredly Solomon your son shall reign after me, and he shall sit on my throne.' 18 So now, look! Adonijah has become king; and now, my lord the king, you do not know about *it.* 19 He has sacrificed oxen and fattened cattle and sheep in abundance, and has invited all the sons of the king, Abiathar the priest, and Joab the commander of the army; but Solomon your servant he has not invited. 20 And as for you, my lord, O king, the eyes of all Israel *are* on you, that you should tell them who will sit on the throne of my lord the king after him. 21 Otherwise it will happen, when my lord the king rests with his fathers, that I and my son Solomon will be counted as offenders."

22 And just then, while she was still talking with the king, Nathan the prophet also came in. 23 So they told the king, saying, "Here is Nathan the prophet." And when

he came in before the king, he bowed down before the king with his face to the ground. ²⁴ And Nathan said, "My lord, O king, have you said, 'Adonijah shall reign after me, and he shall sit on my throne'? ²⁵ For he has gone down today, and has sacrificed oxen and fattened cattle and sheep in abundance, and has invited all the king's sons, and the commanders of the army, and Abiathar the priest; and look! They are eating and drinking before him; and they say, '*Long* live King Adonijah!' ²⁶ But he has not invited me—me your servant—nor Zadok the priest, nor Benaiah the son of Jehoiada, nor your servant Solomon. ²⁷ Has this thing been done by my lord the king, and you have not told your servant who should sit on the throne of my lord the king after him?"

²⁸ Then King David answered and said, "Call Bathsheba to me." So she came into the king's presence and stood before the king. ²⁹ And the king took an oath and said, "*As* the LORD lives, who has redeemed my life from every distress, ³⁰ just as I swore to you by the LORD God of Israel, saying, 'Assuredly Solomon your son shall be king after me, and he shall sit on my throne in my place,' so I certainly will do this day."

³¹ Then Bathsheba bowed with *her* face to the earth, and paid homage to the king, and said, "Let my lord King David live forever!"

³² And King David said, "Call to me Zadok the priest, Nathan the prophet, and Benaiah the son of Jehoiada." So they came before the king. ³³ The king also said to them, "Take with you the servants of your lord, and have Solomon my son ride on my own mule, and take him down to Gihon. ³⁴ There let Zadok the priest and Nathan the prophet anoint him king over Israel; and blow the horn, and say, '*Long* live King Solomon!' ³⁵ Then you shall come up after him, and he shall come and sit on my throne, and he shall be king in my place. For I have appointed him to be ruler over Israel and Judah."

³⁶ Benaiah the son of Jehoiada answered the king and said, "Amen! May the LORD God of my lord the king say so *too*. ³⁷ As the LORD has been with my lord the king, even so may He be with Solomon, and make his throne greater than the throne of my lord King David."

³⁸ So Zadok the priest, Nathan the prophet, Benaiah the son of Jehoiada, the Cherethites, and the Pelethites went down and had Solomon ride on King David's mule, and took him to Gihon. ³⁹ Then Zadok the priest took a horn of oil from the tabernacle and anointed Solomon. And they blew the horn, and all the people said, "*Long* live King Solomon!" ⁴⁰ And all the people went up after him; and the people played the flutes and rejoiced with great joy, so that the earth *seemed to* split with their sound.

⁴¹ Now Adonijah and all the guests who *were* with him heard *it* as they finished eating. And when Joab heard the sound of the horn, he said, "Why *is* the city in such a noisy uproar?" ⁴² While he was still speaking, there came Jonathan, the son of Abiathar the priest. And Adonijah said to him, "Come in, for you *are* a prominent man, and bring good news."

⁴³ Then Jonathan answered and said to Adonijah, "No! Our lord King David has made Solomon king. ⁴⁴ The king has sent with him Zadok the priest, Nathan the prophet, Benaiah the son of Jehoiada, the Cherethites, and the Pelethites; and they have made him ride on the king's mule. ⁴⁵ So Zadok the priest and Nathan the prophet have anointed him king at Gihon; and they have gone up from there rejoicing, so that the city is in an uproar. This *is* the noise that you have heard. ⁴⁶ Also Solomon sits on the throne of the kingdom. ⁴⁷ And moreover the king's servants have gone to bless our lord King David, saying, 'May God make the name of Solomon better than your name, and may He make his throne greater than your throne.' Then the king bowed himself on the bed. ⁴⁸ Also the king said thus, 'Blessed *be* the LORD God of Israel, who has given *one* to sit on my throne this day, while my eyes see *it!*' "

⁴⁹ So all the guests who were with Adonijah were afraid, and arose, and each one went his way.

⁵⁰ Now Adonijah was afraid of Solomon; so he arose, and went and took hold of the horns of the altar. ⁵¹ And it was told Solomon, saying, "Indeed Adonijah is afraid of King Solomon; for

In All Things, Love

After he had been in the ministry for several years, a pastor was preparing a special sermon on love. When he went to his file cabinet to pull out the file of material he had collected on "Love" through the years, he was shocked to find that he didn't have such a file!

Thinking this to be virtually impossible, since he knew he had collected many anecdotes and quotes about love, he began searching through the cabinet folder by folder. He fully expected to find the Love folder stuck inside another folder. He searched among the folders on Faith and Fasting, Healing and Heaven, even Christology and Christian Education. But there was no folder on Love.

As he sat and pondered this, he began to think back over the sermons he had preached over the years. Then he suddenly realized that he had used bits and pieces of Love material in preparing dozens of other sermons. He quickly went back to the cabinet, and sure enough, he found parts of the Love file in the folders labeled Patience, Kindness, Humility, Trust, Hope, Loyalty, and Perseverance. The greatest amount of material on love, however, was found in his file labeled Forgiveness.

The Bible says that God's love is shed abroad in our hearts by the Holy Spirit. When we let it flow through, God's love can spill over into every area of our lives. The one area where that unconditional love is most vividly demonstrated is when we choose to overlook an offense and forgive someone who has wronged us.

look, he has taken hold of the horns of the altar, saying, 'Let King Solomon swear to me today that he will not put his servant to death with the sword.' "

⁵² Then Solomon said, "If he proves himself a worthy man, not one hair of him shall fall to the earth; but if wickedness is found in him, he shall die." ⁵³ So King Solomon sent them to bring him down from the altar. And he came and fell down before King Solomon; and Solomon said to him, "Go to your house."

2 Now the days of David drew near that he should die, and he charged Solomon his son, saying: ² "I go the way of all the earth; be strong, therefore, and prove yourself a man. ³ And keep the charge of the LORD your God: to walk in His ways, to keep His statutes, His commandments, His judgments, and His testimonies, as it is written in the Law of Moses, that you may prosper in all that you do and wherever you turn; ⁴ that the LORD may fulfill His word which He spoke concerning me, saying, 'If your sons take heed to their way, to walk before Me in truth with all their heart and with all their soul,' He said, 'you shall not lack a man on the throne of Israel.'

⁵ "Moreover you know also what Joab the son of Zeruiah did to me, *and* what he did to the two commanders of the armies of Israel, to Abner the son of Ner and Amasa the son of Jether, whom he killed. And he shed the blood of war in peacetime, and put the blood of war on his belt that *was* around his waist, and on his sandals that *were* on his feet. ⁶ Therefore do according to your wisdom, and do not let his gray hair go down to the grave in peace.

⁷ "But show kindness to the sons of Barzillai the Gileadite, and let them be among those who eat at your table, for so they came to me when I fled from Absalom your brother.

⁸ "And see, *you have* with you Shimei the son of Gera, a Benjamite from Bahurim, who cursed me with a malicious curse in the day when I went to Mahanaim. But he came down to meet me at the Jordan, and I swore to him by the LORD, saying, 'I will not put you to death with the sword.' ⁹ Now therefore, do not hold him

guiltless, for you *are* a wise man and know what you ought to do to him; but bring his gray hair down to the grave with blood."

¹⁰ So David rested with his fathers, and was buried in the City of David. ¹¹ The period that David reigned over Israel *was* forty years; seven years he reigned in Hebron, and in Jerusalem he reigned thirty-three years. ¹² Then Solomon sat on the throne of his father David; and his kingdom was firmly established.

¹³ Now Adonijah the son of Haggith came to Bathsheba the mother of Solomon. So she said, "Do you come peaceably?"

And he said, "Peaceably." ¹⁴ Moreover he said, "I have something *to say* to you."

And she said, "Say it."

¹⁵ Then he said, "You know that the kingdom was mine, and all Israel had set their expectations on me, that I should reign. However, the kingdom has been turned over, and has become my brother's; for it was his from the LORD. ¹⁶ Now I ask one petition of you; do not deny me."

And she said to him, "Say it."

¹⁷ Then he said, "Please speak to King Solomon, for he will not refuse you, that he may give me Abishag the Shunammite as wife."

¹⁸ So Bathsheba said, "Very well, I will speak for you to the king."

¹⁹ Bathsheba therefore went to King Solomon, to speak to him for Adonijah. And the king rose up to meet her and bowed down to her, and sat down on his throne and had a throne set for the king's mother; so she sat at his right hand. ²⁰ Then she said, "I desire one small petition of you; do not refuse me."

And the king said to her, "Ask it, my mother, for I will not refuse you."

²¹ So she said, "Let Abishag the Shunammite be given to Adonijah your brother as wife."

²² And King Solomon answered and said to his mother, "Now why do you ask Abishag the Shunammite for Adonijah? Ask for him the kingdom also—for he *is* my older brother—for him, and for Abiathar the priest, and for Joab the son of Zeruiah." ²³ Then King Solomon swore by the LORD, saying, "May God do so to

me, and more also, if Adonijah has not spoken this word against his own life! [24] Now therefore, *as* the LORD lives, who has confirmed me and set me on the throne of David my father, and who has established a house for me, as He promised, Adonijah shall be put to death today!"

[25] So King Solomon sent by the hand of Benaiah the son of Jehoiada; and he struck him down, and he died.

[26] And to Abiathar the priest the king said, "Go to Anathoth, to your own fields, for you *are* deserving of death; but I will not put you to death at this time, because you carried the ark of the Lord GOD before my father David, and because you were afflicted every time my father was afflicted." [27] So Solomon removed Abiathar from being priest to the LORD, that he might fulfill the word of the LORD which He spoke concerning the house of Eli at Shiloh.

[28] Then news came to Joab, for Joab had defected to Adonijah, though he had not defected to Absalom. So Joab fled to the tabernacle of the LORD, and took hold of the horns of the altar. [29] And King Solomon was told, "Joab has fled to the tabernacle of the LORD; there *he is,* by the altar." Then Solomon sent Benaiah the son of Jehoiada, saying, "Go, strike him down." [30] So Benaiah went to the tabernacle of the LORD, and said to him, "Thus says the king, 'Come out!' "

And he said, "No, but I will die here." And Benaiah brought back word to the king, saying, "Thus said Joab, and thus he answered me."

[31] Then the king said to him, "Do as he has said, and strike him down and bury him, that you may take away from me and from the house of my father the innocent blood which Joab shed. [32] So the LORD will return his blood on his head, because he struck down two men more righteous and better than he, and killed them with the sword—Abner the son of Ner, the commander of the army of Israel, and Amasa the son of Jether, the commander of the army of Judah—though my father David did not know *it.* [33] Their blood shall therefore return upon the head of Joab and upon the head of his descendants forever. But upon David and his descendants, upon his house and his throne, there shall be peace forever from the LORD."

[34] So Benaiah the son of Jehoiada went up and struck and killed him; and he was buried in his own house in the wilderness. [35] The king put Benaiah the son of Jehoiada in his place over the army, and the king put Zadok the priest in the place of Abiathar.

[36] Then the king sent and called for Shimei, and said to him, "Build yourself a house in Jerusalem and dwell there, and do not go out from there anywhere. [37] For it shall be, on the day you go out and cross the Brook Kidron, know for certain you shall surely die; your blood shall be on your own head."

[38] And Shimei said to the king, "The saying *is* good. As my lord the king has said, so your servant will do." So Shimei dwelt in Jerusalem many days.

[39] Now it happened at the end of three years, that two slaves of Shimei ran away to Achish the son of Maachah, king of Gath. And they told Shimei, saying, "Look, your slaves *are* in Gath!" [40] So Shimei arose, saddled his donkey, and went to Achish at Gath to seek his slaves. And Shimei went and brought his slaves from Gath. [41] And Solomon was told that Shimei had gone from Jerusalem to Gath and had come back. [42] Then the king sent and called for Shimei, and said to him, "Did I not make you swear by the LORD, and warn you, saying, 'Know for certain that on the day you go out and travel anywhere, you shall surely die'? And you said to me, 'The word I have heard *is* good.' [43] Why then have you not kept the oath of the LORD and the commandment that I gave you?" [44] The king said moreover to Shimei, "You know, as your heart acknowledges, all the wickedness that you did to my father David; therefore the LORD will return your wickedness on your own head. [45] But King Solomon *shall be* blessed, and the throne of David shall be established before the LORD forever."

[46] So the king commanded Benaiah the son of Jehoiada; and he went out and struck him down, and he died. Thus the kingdom was established in the hand of Solomon.

∼ Psalm 68:11–14 ∼

11 The Lord gave the word;
   Great *was* the company of those
      who proclaimed *it:*
12 "Kings of armies flee, they flee,
   And she who remains at home
      divides the spoil.
13 Though you lie down among the
      sheepfolds,
   You will be like the wings of a dove
      covered with silver,
   And her feathers with yellow gold."
14 When the Almighty scattered kings
      in it,
   It was *white* as snow in Zalmon.

∼ Proverbs 17:7–9 ∼

7 Excellent speech is not becoming to
      a fool,
   Much less lying lips to a prince.

8 A present *is* a precious stone in the
      eyes of its possessor;
   Wherever he turns, he prospers.

9 He who covers a transgression seeks
      love,
   But he who repeats a matter
      separates friends.

∼ John 9:24–41 ∼

So they again called the man who was
blind, and said to him, "Give God the
glory! We know that this Man is a sinner."

25 He answered and said, "Whether He
is a sinner *or not* I do not know. One thing
I know: that though I was blind, now I
see."

26 Then they said to him again, "What

did He do to you? How did He open your
eyes?"

27 He answered them, "I told you already, and you did not listen. Why do you
want to hear *it* again? Do you also want
to become His disciples?"

28 Then they reviled him and said, "You
are His disciple, but we are Moses' disciples. 29 We know that God spoke to
Moses; *as for* this *fellow,* we do not know
where He is from."

30 The man answered and said to them,
"Why, this is a marvelous thing, that you
do not know where He is from; yet He
has opened my eyes! 31 Now we know that
God does not hear sinners; but if anyone
is a worshiper of God and does His will,
He hears him. 32 Since the world began it
has been unheard of that anyone opened
the eyes of one who was born blind. 33 If
this Man were not from God, He could
do nothing."

34 They answered and said to him, "You
were completely born in sins, and are you
teaching us?" And they cast him out.

35 Jesus heard that they had cast him
out; and when He had found him, He
said to him, "Do you believe in the Son
of God?"

36 He answered and said, "Who is He,
Lord, that I may believe in Him?"

37 And Jesus said to him, "You have both
seen Him and it is He who is talking with
you."

38 Then he said, "Lord, I believe!" And
he worshiped Him.

39 And Jesus said, "For judgment I have
come into this world, that those who do
not see may see, and that those who see
may be made blind."

40 Then *some* of the Pharisees who were
with Him heard these words, and said to
Him, "Are we blind also?"

41 Jesus said to them, "If you were blind,
you would have no sin; but now you say,
'We see.' Therefore your sin remains.

∼ 1 Kings 3:1—4:34 ∼

Now Solomon made a treaty with
Pharaoh king of Egypt, and married Pharaoh's daughter; then he
brought her to the City of David until he
had finished building his own house, and
the house of the LORD, and the wall all

Shut Your Eyes and Hold Out Your Hand

Author Elisabeth Elliot writes in *A Lamp for My Feet*, about a game she played as a young girl. She writes, "My mother or father would say, 'Shut your eyes and hold out your hand.' That was the promise of some lovely surprise. I trusted them, so I shut my eyes instantly and held out my hand. Whatever they were going to give me I was ready to take." She continues, "So should it be in our trust of our heavenly Father. Faith is the willingness to receive whatever He wants to give, or the willingness not to have what He does not want to give."

If your prayers aren't answered in the way you expect them to be, there may be a good reason! Several months before Christmas, Jared begged his mother to buy him a new bicycle just like his friend's — and he had to have it now! His mother was a single mom, however, and there was no extra money for a new bicycle until Christmas.

Jared's friend generously lent him his bicycle to ride, and the longer Jared rode it, the more he realized it really wasn't the right bicycle for him. For one thing, it didn't have the racing brakes he wanted.

How often do we think God has forgotten us, when He's merely giving us time to understand what we really want so He can bring us His best?

around Jerusalem. ² Meanwhile the people sacrificed at the high places, because there was no house built for the name of the LORD until those days. ³ And Solomon loved the LORD, walking in the statutes of his father David, except that he sacrificed and burned incense at the high places.

⁴ Now the king went to Gibeon to sacrifice there, for that *was* the great high place: Solomon offered a thousand burnt offerings on that altar. ⁵ At Gibeon the LORD appeared to Solomon in a dream by night; and God said, "Ask! What shall I give you?"

⁶ And Solomon said: "You have shown great mercy to Your servant David my father, because he walked before You in truth, in righteousness, and in uprightness of heart with You; You have continued this great kindness for him, and You have given him a son to sit on his throne, as *it is* this day. ⁷ Now, O LORD my God, You have made Your servant king instead of my father David, but I *am* a little child; I do not know *how* to go out or come in. ⁸ And Your servant *is* in the midst of Your people whom You have chosen, a great people, too numerous to be numbered or counted. ⁹ Therefore give to Your servant an understanding heart to judge Your people, that I may discern between good and evil. For who is able to judge this great people of Yours?"

¹⁰ The speech pleased the LORD, that Solomon had asked this thing. ¹¹ Then God said to him: "Because you have asked this thing, and have not asked long life for yourself, nor have asked riches for yourself, nor have asked the life of your enemies, but have asked for yourself understanding to discern justice, ¹² behold, I have done according to your words; see, I have given you a wise and understanding heart, so that there has not been anyone like you before you, nor shall any like you arise after you. ¹³ And I have also given you what you have not asked: both riches and honor, so that there shall not be anyone like you among the kings all your days. ¹⁴ So if you walk in My ways, to keep My statutes and My commandments, as your father David walked, then I will lengthen your days."

¹⁵ Then Solomon awoke; and indeed it had been a dream. And he came to Jerusalem and stood before the ark of the covenant of the LORD, offered up burnt offerings, offered peace offerings, and made a feast for all his servants.

¹⁶ Now two women *who were* harlots came to the king, and stood before him. ¹⁷ And one woman said, "O my lord, this woman and I dwell in the same house; and I gave birth while she *was* in the house. ¹⁸ Then it happened, the third day after I had given birth, that this woman also gave birth. And we *were* together; no one *was* with us in the house, except the two of us in the house. ¹⁹ And this woman's son died in the night, because she lay on him. ²⁰ So she arose in the middle of the night and took my son from my side, while your maidservant slept, and laid him in her bosom, and laid her dead child in my bosom. ²¹ And when I rose in the morning to nurse my son, there he was, dead. But when I had examined him in the morning, indeed, he was not my son whom I had borne."

²² Then the other woman said, "No! But the living one *is* my son, and the dead one *is* your son."

And the first woman said, "No! But the dead one *is* your son, and the living one *is* my son."

Thus they spoke before the king.

²³ And the king said, "The one says, 'This *is* my son, who lives, and your son *is* the dead one'; and the other says, 'No! But your son *is* the dead one, and my son *is* the living one.' " ²⁴ Then the king said, "Bring me a sword." So they brought a sword before the king. ²⁵ And the king said, "Divide the living child in two, and give half to one, and half to the other."

²⁶ Then the woman whose son *was* living spoke to the king, for she yearned with compassion for her son; and she said, "O my lord, give her the living child, and by no means kill him!"

But the other said, "Let him be neither mine nor yours, *but* divide *him*."

²⁷ So the king answered and said, "Give the first woman the living child, and by no means kill him; she *is* his mother."

²⁸ And all Israel heard of the judgment which the king had rendered; and they feared the king, for they saw that the

wisdom of God *was* in him to administer justice.

4 So King Solomon was king over all Israel. [2] And these *were* his officials: Azariah the son of Zadok, the priest; [3] Elihoreph and Ahijah, the sons of Shisha, scribes; Jehoshaphat the son of Ahilud, the recorder; [4] Benaiah the son of Jehoiada, over the army; Zadok and Abiathar, the priests; [5] Azariah the son of Nathan, over the officers; Zabud the son of Nathan, a priest *and* the king's friend; [6] Ahishar, over the household; and Adoniram the son of Abda, over the labor force.

[7] And Solomon had twelve governors over all Israel, who provided food for the king and his household; each one made provision for one month of the year. [8] These *are* their names: Ben-Hur, in the mountains of Ephraim; [9] Ben-Deker, in Makaz, Shaalbim, Beth Shemesh, and Elon Beth Hanan; [10] Ben-Hesed, in Arubboth; to him *belonged* Sochoh and all the land of Hepher; [11] Ben-Abinadab, *in* all the regions of Dor; he had Taphath the daughter of Solomon as wife; [12] Baana the son of Ahilud, *in* Taanach, Megiddo, and all Beth Shean, which *is* beside Zaretan below Jezreel, from Beth Shean to Abel Meholah, as far as the other side of Jokneam; [13] Ben-Geber, in Ramoth Gilead; to him *belonged* the towns of Jair the son of Manasseh, in Gilead; to him *also belonged* the region of Argob in Bashan—sixty large cities with walls and bronze gate-bars; [14] Ahinadab the son of Iddo, *in* Mahanaim; [15] Ahimaaz, in Naphtali; he also took Basemath the daughter of Solomon as wife; [16] Baanah the son of Hushai, in Asher and Aloth; [17] Jehoshaphat the son of Paruah, in Issachar; [18] Shimei the son of Elah, in Benjamin; [19] Geber the son of Uri, in the land of Gilead, *in* the country of Sihon king of the Amorites, and of Og king of Bashan. *He was* the only governor who *was* in the land.

[20] Judah and Israel *were* as numerous as the sand by the sea in multitude, eating and drinking and rejoicing. [21] So Solomon reigned over all kingdoms from the River *to* the land of the Philistines, as far as the border of Egypt. *They* brought tribute and served Solomon all the days of his life.

[22] Now Solomon's provision for one day was thirty kors of fine flour, sixty kors of meal, [23] ten fatted oxen, twenty oxen from the pastures, and one hundred sheep, besides deer, gazelles, roebucks, and fatted fowl.

[24] For he had dominion over all *the region* on this side of the River from Tiphsah even to Gaza, namely over all the kings on this side of the River; and he had peace on every side all around him. [25] And Judah and Israel dwelt safely, each man under his vine and his fig tree, from Dan as far as Beersheba, all the days of Solomon.

[26] Solomon had forty thousand stalls of horses for his chariots, and twelve thousand horsemen. [27] And these governors, each man in his month, provided food for King Solomon and for all who came to King Solomon's table. There was no lack in their supply. [28] They also brought barley and straw to the proper place, for the horses and steeds, each man according to his charge.

[29] And God gave Solomon wisdom and exceedingly great understanding, and largeness of heart like the sand on the seashore. [30] Thus Solomon's wisdom excelled the wisdom of all the men of the East and all the wisdom of Egypt. [31] For he was wiser than all men—than Ethan the Ezrahite, and Heman, Chalcol, and Darda, the sons of Mahol; and his fame was in all the surrounding nations. [32] He spoke three thousand proverbs, and his songs were one thousand and five. [33] Also he spoke of trees, from the cedar tree of Lebanon even to the hyssop that springs out of the wall; he spoke also of animals, of birds, of creeping things, and of fish. [34] And men of all nations, from all the kings of the earth who had heard of his wisdom, came to hear the wisdom of Solomon.

~ PSALM 68:15–20 ~

[15] A mountain of God *is* the mountain of Bashan;
A mountain *of many* peaks *is* the mountain of Bashan.

[16] Why do you fume with envy, you mountains of *many* peaks?

This is the mountain *which* God
    desires to dwell in;
Yes, the LORD will dwell *in it* forever.

17 The chariots of God *are* twenty
    thousand,
Even thousands of thousands;
The Lord is among them *as in* Sinai,
    in the Holy *Place.*
18 You have ascended on high,
You have led captivity captive;
You have received gifts among men,
Even *from* the rebellious,
That the LORD God might dwell
    there.

19 Blessed *be* the Lord,
Who daily loads us *with benefits,*
The God of our salvation!   Selah
20 Our God *is* the God of salvation;
And to GOD the Lord *belong* escapes
    from death.

∼ PROVERBS 17:10–12 ∼

10 Rebuke is more effective for a wise
    man
Than a hundred blows on a fool.

11 An evil *man* seeks only rebellion;
Therefore a cruel messenger will be
    sent against him.

12 Let a man meet a bear robbed of her
    cubs,
Rather than a fool in his folly.

∼ JOHN 10:1–23 ∼

"Most assuredly, I say to you, he who does not enter the sheepfold by the door, but climbs up some other way, the same is a thief and a robber. 2 But he who enters by the door is the shepherd of the sheep. 3 To him the doorkeeper opens, and the sheep hear his voice; and he calls his own sheep by name and leads them out. 4 And when he brings out his own sheep, he goes before them; and the sheep follow him, for they know his voice. 5 Yet they will by no means follow a stranger, but will flee from him, for they do not know the voice of strangers." 6 Jesus used this illustration, but they did not understand the things which He spoke to them.

7 Then Jesus said to them again, "Most assuredly, I say to you, I am the door of the sheep. 8 All who *ever* came before Me are thieves and robbers, but the sheep did not hear them. 9 I am the door. If anyone enters by Me, he will be saved, and will go in and out and find pasture. 10 The thief does not come except to steal, and to kill, and to destroy. I have come that they may have life, and that they may have *it* more abundantly.

11 "I am the good shepherd. The good shepherd gives His life for the sheep. 12 But a hireling, *he who is* not the shepherd, one who does not own the sheep, sees the wolf coming and leaves the sheep and flees; and the wolf catches the sheep and scatters them. 13 The hireling flees because he is a hireling and does not care about the sheep. 14 I am the good shepherd; and I know My *sheep,* and am known by My own. 15 As the Father knows Me, even so I know the Father; and I lay down My life for the sheep. 16 And other sheep I have which are not of this fold; them also I must bring, and they will hear My voice; and there will be one flock *and* one shepherd.

17 "Therefore My Father loves Me, because I lay down My life that I may take it again. 18 No one takes it from Me, but I lay it down of Myself. I have power to lay it down, and I have power to take it again. This command I have received from My Father."

19 Therefore there was a division again among the Jews because of these sayings. 20 And many of them said, "He has a demon and is mad. Why do you listen to Him?"

21 Others said, "These are not the words of one who has a demon. Can a demon open the eyes of the blind?"

22 Now it was the Feast of Dedication in Jerusalem, and it was winter. 23 And Jesus walked in the temple, in Solomon's porch.

∼ 1 KINGS 5:1—6:38 ∼

Now Hiram king of Tyre sent his servants to Solomon, because he heard that they had anointed him king in place of his father, for Hiram had always loved David. ² Then Solomon sent to Hiram, saying:

3 You know how my father David could not build a house for the name of the LORD his God because of the wars which were fought against him on every side, until the LORD put *his foes* under the soles of his feet.

4 But now the LORD my God has given me rest on every side; *there is* neither adversary nor evil occurrence.

5 And behold, I propose to build a house for the name of the LORD my God, as the LORD spoke to my father David, saying, "Your son, whom I will set on your throne in your place, he shall build the house for My name."

6 Now therefore, command that they cut down cedars for me from Lebanon; and my servants will be with your servants, and I will pay you wages for your servants according to whatever you say. For you know *there is* none among us who has skill to cut timber like the Sidonians.

⁷ So it was, when Hiram heard the words of Solomon, that he rejoiced greatly and said,

Blessed *be* the LORD this day, for He has given David a wise son over this great people!

⁸ Then Hiram sent to Solomon, saying:

I have considered *the message* which you sent me, *and* I will do all you desire concerning the cedar and cypress logs.

9 My servants shall bring *them* down from Lebanon to the sea; I will float them in rafts by sea to the place you indicate to me, and will have them broken apart there; then you can take *them* away. And you shall fulfill my desire by giving food for my household.

¹⁰ Then Hiram gave Solomon cedar and cypress logs *according to* all his desire. ¹¹ And Solomon gave Hiram twenty thousand kors of wheat *as* food for his household, and twenty kors of pressed oil. Thus Solomon gave to Hiram year by year.

¹² So the LORD gave Solomon wisdom, as He had promised him; and there was peace between Hiram and Solomon, and the two of them made a treaty together.

¹³ Then King Solomon raised up a labor force out of all Israel; and the labor force was thirty thousand men. ¹⁴ And he sent them to Lebanon, ten thousand a month in shifts: they were one month in Lebanon *and* two months at home; Adoniram *was* in charge of the labor force. ¹⁵ Solomon had seventy thousand who carried burdens, and eighty thousand who quarried *stone* in the mountains, ¹⁶ besides three thousand three hundred from the chiefs of Solomon's deputies, who supervised the people who labored in the work. ¹⁷ And the king commanded them to quarry large stones, costly stones, *and* hewn stones, to lay the foundation of the temple. ¹⁸ So Solomon's builders, Hiram's builders, and the Gebalites quarried *them;* and they prepared timber and stones to build the temple.

6 And it came to pass in the four hundred and eightieth year after the children of Israel had come out of the land of Egypt, in the fourth year of Solomon's reign over Israel, in the month of Ziv, which *is* the second month, that he began to build the house of the LORD. ² Now the house which King Solomon built for the LORD, its length *was* sixty cubits, its width twenty, and its height thirty cubits. ³ The vestibule in front of the sanctuary of the house *was* twenty cubits long across the width of the house, *and* the width of *the vestibule extended* ten cubits

from the front of the house. [4] And he made for the house windows with beveled frames.

[5] Against the wall of the temple he built chambers all around, *against* the walls of the temple, all around the sanctuary and the inner sanctuary. Thus he made side chambers all around it. [6] The lowest chamber *was* five cubits wide, the middle *was* six cubits wide, and the third *was* seven cubits wide; for he made narrow ledges around the outside of the temple, so that *the support beams* would not be fastened into the walls of the temple. [7] And the temple, when it was being built, was built with stone finished at the quarry, so that no hammer or chisel *or* any iron tool was heard in the temple while it was being built. [8] The doorway for the middle story *was* on the right side of the temple. They went up by stairs to the middle *story,* and from the middle to the third.

[9] So he built the temple and finished it, and he paneled the temple with beams and boards of cedar. [10] And he built side chambers against the entire temple, each five cubits high; they were attached to the temple with cedar beams.

[11] Then the word of the LORD came to Solomon, saying: [12] "*Concerning* this temple which you are building, if you walk in My statutes, execute My judgments, keep all My commandments, and walk in them, then I will perform My word with you, which I spoke to your father David. [13] And I will dwell among the children of Israel, and will not forsake My people Israel."

[14] So Solomon built the temple and finished it. [15] And he built the inside walls of the temple with cedar boards; from the floor of the temple to the ceiling he paneled the inside with wood; and he covered the floor of the temple with planks of cypress. [16] Then he built the twenty-cubit room at the rear of the temple, from floor to ceiling, with cedar boards; he built *it* inside as the inner sanctuary, as the Most Holy *Place.* [17] And in front of it the temple sanctuary was forty cubits *long.* [18] The inside of the temple was cedar, carved with ornamental buds and open flowers. All *was* cedar; there was no stone *to be* seen.

[19] And he prepared the inner sanctuary inside the temple, to set the ark of the covenant of the LORD there. [20] The inner sanctuary *was* twenty cubits long, twenty cubits wide, and twenty cubits high. He overlaid it with pure gold, and overlaid the altar of cedar. [21] So Solomon overlaid the inside of the temple with pure gold. He stretched gold chains across the front of the inner sanctuary, and overlaid it with gold. [22] The whole temple he overlaid with gold, until he had finished all the temple; also he overlaid with gold the entire altar that *was* by the inner sanctuary.

[23] Inside the inner sanctuary he made two cherubim *of* olive wood, *each* ten cubits high. [24] One wing of the cherub *was* five cubits, and the other wing of the cherub five cubits: ten cubits from the tip of one wing to the tip of the other. [25] And the other cherub *was* ten cubits; both cherubim *were* of the same size and shape. [26] The height of one cherub *was* ten cubits, and so *was* the other cherub. [27] Then he set the cherubim inside the inner room; and they stretched out the wings of the cherubim so that the wing of the one touched *one* wall, and the wing of the other cherub touched the other wall. And their wings touched each other in the middle of the room. [28] Also he overlaid the cherubim with gold.

[29] Then he carved all the walls of the temple all around, both the inner and outer *sanctuaries,* with carved figures of cherubim, palm trees, and open flowers. [30] And the floor of the temple he overlaid with gold, both the inner and outer *sanctuaries.*

[31] For the entrance of the inner sanctuary he made doors *of* olive wood; the lintel *and* doorposts *were* one-fifth *of the wall.* [32] The two doors *were of* olive wood; and he carved on them figures of cherubim, palm trees, and open flowers, and overlaid *them* with gold; and he spread gold on the cherubim and on the palm trees. [33] So for the door of the sanctuary he also made doorposts *of* olive wood, one-fourth *of the wall.* [34] And the two doors *were of* cypress wood; two panels *comprised* one folding door, and two panels *comprised* the other folding door. [35] Then he carved cherubim, palm trees, and open flowers *on them,* and overlaid

Face Your Fear

In 1993, a deranged fan stabbed tennis star Monica Seles, narrowly missing her spinal cord. She recognized her assailant as a man she had seen loitering around her hotel but she had no idea why he had attacked her. At the hospital, she couldn't stop asking, *What if he comes back?* That night, her parents and brother all stayed in her hospital room with her. Monica was assured that her attacker was in custody. Even so, she had flashbacks of his face, the blood-stained knife, and her own screams.

Monica did her best to stick to her physical therapy regimen, but she found it difficult to concentrate. She broke into tears at odd moments, and nightmares haunted her. Six months after the attack, her assailant was given two years probation and set free. Her fear intensified, and she sought out a psychologist to help her. Encouraged by her peers, she made a decision to return to tennis. Then came yet another blow. A German judge upheld her assailant's suspended sentence, which had been appealed. She said to herself, "Monica, you have to move on." It was time for a showdown with her fear. Three months later, she played an exhibition match, and scored two wins — one on the court, and one in her mind and heart.

Are you facing an obstacle that seems insurmountable? Perhaps it's time to identify its source and face it head on. The God Who never leaves you or forsakes you will be with you, strengthening you every step of the way.

them with gold applied evenly on the carved work.

³⁶ And he built the inner court with three rows of hewn stone and a row of cedar beams.

³⁷ In the fourth year the foundation of the house of the LORD was laid, in the month of Ziv. ³⁸ And in the eleventh year, in the month of Bul, which is the eighth month, the house was finished in all its details and according to all its plans. So he was seven years in building it.

∼ PSALM 68:21–27 ∼

²¹ But God will wound the head of His
      enemies,
   The hairy scalp of the one who still
      goes on in his trespasses.
²² The Lord said, "I will bring back
      from Bashan,
   I will bring *them* back from the
      depths of the sea,
²³ That your foot may crush *them* in
      blood,
   And the tongues of your dogs *may
      have* their portion from *your*
      enemies."

²⁴ They have seen Your procession,
      O God,
   The procession of my God, my King,
      into the sanctuary.
²⁵ The singers went before, the players
      on instruments *followed* after;
   Among *them were* the maidens
      playing timbrels.
²⁶ Bless God in the congregations,
   The Lord, from the fountain of
      Israel.
²⁷ There *is* little Benjamin, their leader,
   The princes of Judah *and* their
      company,
   The princes of Zebulun *and* the
      princes of Naphtali.

∼ PROVERBS 17:13–15 ∼

¹³ Whoever rewards evil for good,
   Evil will not depart from his house.

¹⁴ The beginning of strife *is like*
      releasing water;
   Therefore stop contention before a
      quarrel starts.

¹⁵ He who justifies the wicked, and he
      who condemns the just,
   Both of them alike *are* an
      abomination to the LORD.

∼ JOHN 10:24–42 ∼

Then the Jews surrounded Him and said to Him, "How long do You keep us in doubt? If You are the Christ, tell us plainly."

²⁵ Jesus answered them, "I told you, and you do not believe. The works that I do in My Father's name, they bear witness of Me. ²⁶ But you do not believe, because you are not of My sheep, as I said to you. ²⁷ My sheep hear My voice, and I know them, and they follow Me. ²⁸ And I give them eternal life, and they shall never perish; neither shall anyone snatch them out of My hand. ²⁹ My Father, who has given *them* to Me, is greater than all; and no one is able to snatch *them* out of My Father's hand. ³⁰ I and *My* Father are one."

³¹ Then the Jews took up stones again to stone Him. ³² Jesus answered them, "Many good works I have shown you from My Father. For which of those works do you stone Me?"

³³ The Jews answered Him, saying, "For a good work we do not stone You, but for blasphemy, and because You, being a Man, make Yourself God."

³⁴ Jesus answered them, "Is it not written in your law, 'I said, "You are gods" '? ³⁵ If He called them gods, to whom the word of God came (and the Scripture cannot be broken), ³⁶ do you say of Him whom the Father sanctified and sent into the world, 'You are blaspheming,' because I said, 'I am the Son of God'? ³⁷ If I do not do the works of My Father, do not believe Me; ³⁸ but if I do, though you do not believe Me, believe the works, that you may know and believe that the Father *is* in Me, and I in Him." ³⁹ Therefore they sought again to seize Him, but He escaped out of their hand.

⁴⁰ And He went away again beyond the Jordan to the place where John was baptizing at first, and there He stayed. ⁴¹ Then many came to Him and said, "John performed no sign, but all the things that John spoke about this Man were true." ⁴² And many believed in Him there.

~ 1 KINGS 7:1—8:66 ~

But Solomon took thirteen years to build his own house; so he finished all his house.

² He also built the House of the Forest of Lebanon; its length *was* one hundred cubits, its width fifty cubits, and its height thirty cubits, with four rows of cedar pillars, and cedar beams on the pillars. ³ And *it was* paneled with cedar above the beams that *were* on forty-five pillars, fifteen *to* a row. ⁴ *There were* windows *with beveled frames in* three rows, and window *was* opposite window *in* three tiers. ⁵ And all the doorways and doorposts *had* rectangular frames; and window *was* opposite window *in* three tiers.

⁶ He also made the Hall of Pillars: its length *was* fifty cubits, and its width thirty cubits; and in front of them *was* a portico with pillars, and a canopy *was* in front of them.

⁷ Then he made a hall for the throne, the Hall of Judgment, where he might judge; and *it was* paneled with cedar from floor to ceiling.

⁸ And the house where he dwelt *had* another court inside the hall, of like workmanship. Solomon also made a house like this hall for Pharaoh's daughter, whom he had taken *as wife*.

⁹ All these *were* of costly stones cut to size, trimmed with saws, inside and out, from the foundation to the eaves, and also on the outside to the great court. ¹⁰ The foundation *was of* costly stones, large stones, some ten cubits and some eight cubits. ¹¹ And above *were* costly stones, hewn to size, and cedar wood. ¹² The great court *was* enclosed with three rows of hewn stones and a row of cedar beams. So were the inner court of the house of the LORD and the vestibule of the temple.

¹³ Now King Solomon sent and brought Huram from Tyre. ¹⁴ He *was* the son of a widow from the tribe of Naphtali, and his father *was* a man of Tyre, a bronze worker; he was filled with wisdom and understanding and skill in working with all kinds of bronze work. So he came to King Solomon and did all his work.

¹⁵ And he cast two pillars of bronze, each one eighteen cubits high, and a line of twelve cubits measured the circumference of each. ¹⁶ Then he made two capitals *of* cast bronze, to set on the tops of the pillars. The height of one capital *was* five cubits, and the height of the other capital *was* five cubits. ¹⁷ *He made* a lattice network, with wreaths of chainwork, for the capitals which *were* on top of the pillars: seven chains for one capital and seven for the other capital. ¹⁸ So he made the pillars, and two rows of pomegranates above the network all around to cover the capitals that *were* on top; and thus he did for the other capital.

¹⁹ The capitals which *were* on top of the pillars in the hall *were* in the shape of lilies, four cubits. ²⁰ The capitals on the two pillars also *had pomegranates* above, by the convex surface which *was* next to the network; and there *were* two hundred such pomegranates in rows on each of the capitals all around.

²¹ Then he set up the pillars by the vestibule of the temple; he set up the pillar on the right and called its name Jachin, and he set up the pillar on the left and called its name Boaz. ²² The tops of the pillars were in the shape of lilies. So the work of the pillars was finished.

²³ And he made the Sea of cast bronze, ten cubits from one brim to the other; *it was* completely round. Its height *was* five cubits, and a line of thirty cubits measured its circumference.

²⁴ Below its brim *were* ornamental buds encircling it all around, ten to a cubit, all the way around the Sea. The ornamental buds *were* cast in two rows when it was cast. ²⁵ It stood on twelve oxen: three looking toward the north, three looking toward the west, three looking toward the south, and three looking toward the east; the Sea *was set* upon them, and all their back parts *pointed* inward. ²⁶ It *was* a handbreadth thick; and its brim was shaped like the brim of a cup, *like* a lily blossom. It contained two thousand baths.

²⁷ He also made ten carts of bronze; four cubits *was* the length of each cart, four cubits its width, and three cubits its height. ²⁸ And this *was* the design of the carts: They had panels, and the

panels *were* between frames; ²⁹ on the panels that *were* between the frames *were* lions, oxen, and cherubim. And on the frames *was* a pedestal on top. Below the lions and oxen *were* wreaths of plaited work. ³⁰ Every cart had four bronze wheels and axles of bronze, and its four feet had supports. Under the laver *were* supports of cast *bronze* beside each wreath. ³¹ Its opening inside the crown at the top *was* one cubit in diameter; and the opening *was* round, shaped *like* a pedestal, one and a half cubits in outside diameter; and also on the opening *were* engravings, but the panels were square, not round. ³² Under the panels *were* the four wheels, and the axles of the wheels *were joined* to the cart. The height of a wheel *was* one and a half cubits. ³³ The workmanship of the wheels *was* like the workmanship of a chariot wheel; their axle pins, their rims, their spokes, and their hubs *were* all of cast *bronze.* ³⁴ And *there were* four supports at the four corners of each cart; its supports *were* part of the cart itself. ³⁵ On the top of the cart, at the height of half a cubit, *it was* perfectly round. And on the top of the cart, its flanges and its panels *were* of the same casting. ³⁶ On the plates of its flanges and on its panels he engraved cherubim, lions, and palm trees, wherever there was a clear space on each, with wreaths all around. ³⁷ Thus he made the ten carts. All of them were of the same mold, one measure, *and* one shape.

³⁸ Then he made ten lavers of bronze; each laver contained forty baths, *and* each laver *was* four cubits. On each of the ten carts *was* a laver. ³⁹ And he put five carts on the right side of the house, and five on the left side of the house. He set the Sea on the right side of the house, toward the southeast.

⁴⁰ Huram made the lavers and the shovels and the bowls. So Huram finished doing all the work that he was to do for King Solomon *for* the house of the LORD: ⁴¹ the two pillars, the *two* bowl-shaped capitals that *were* on top of the two pillars; the two networks covering the two bowl-shaped capitals which *were* on top of the pillars; ⁴² four hundred pomegranates for the two networks (two rows of pomegranates for each network, to cover the two bowl-shaped capitals that *were* on top of the pillars); ⁴³ the ten carts, and ten lavers on the carts; ⁴⁴ one Sea, and twelve oxen under the Sea; ⁴⁵ the pots, the shovels, and the bowls.

All these articles which Huram made for King Solomon *for* the house of the LORD *were of* burnished bronze. ⁴⁶ In the plain of Jordan the king had them cast in clay molds, between Succoth and Zaretan. ⁴⁷ And Solomon did not weigh all the articles, because *there were* so many; the weight of the bronze was not determined.

⁴⁸ Thus Solomon had all the furnishings made for the house of the LORD: the altar of gold, and the table of gold on which *was* the showbread; ⁴⁹ the lampstands of pure gold, five on the right *side* and five on the left in front of the inner sanctuary, with the flowers and the lamps and the wick-trimmers of gold; ⁵⁰ the basins, the trimmers, the bowls, the ladles, and the censers of pure gold; and the hinges of gold, *both* for the doors of the inner room (the Most Holy *Place*) *and* for the doors of the main hall of the temple.

⁵¹ So all the work that King Solomon had done for the house of the LORD was finished; and Solomon brought in the things which his father David had dedicated: the silver and the gold and the furnishings. He put them in the treasuries of the house of the LORD.

8 Now Solomon assembled the elders of Israel and all the heads of the tribes, the chief fathers of the children of Israel, to King Solomon in Jerusalem, that they might bring up the ark of the covenant of the LORD from the City of David, which *is* Zion. ² Therefore all the men of Israel assembled with King Solomon at the feast in the month of Ethanim, which *is* the seventh month. ³ So all the elders of Israel came, and the priests took up the ark. ⁴ Then they brought up the ark of the LORD, the tabernacle of meeting, and all the holy furnishings that *were* in the tabernacle. The priests and the Levites brought them up. ⁵ Also King Solomon, and all the congregation of Israel who were assembled with him, *were* with him before the ark, sacrificing sheep and oxen that could not be counted or numbered

On Being a "Sorrow-Carrier"

Although the North American Indians had no written alphabet before they met the white man, their language was anything but primitive. The vocabulary of many Indian languages was as large as that of their French and English conquerors. Often, their expressions were far more eloquent. In one Indian tongue, for example, the word "friend" is beautifully stated as "one-who-carries-my-sorrows-on-his-back."

A friend or family member who comes to you for solace, or even asking for advice, often wants nothing more than your presence, your listening ear, and your quiet caring. A young man discovered this shortly after his wedding. His new bride frequently came home from work and told him the woes of her day. His response was to offer suggestions and give solutions to her problems. His wife finally said to him, "I've already solved the problems of the day." The husband asked, perplexed, "Then why are you telling me about them?" She replied, "I don't need Mr. Fixit. I need a loving ear."

A friend who provides both physical and emotional shelter without always trying to fix things is a true haven, one who helps another weather the storms of life in safety.

for multitude. ⁶ Then the priests brought in the ark of the covenant of the LORD to its place, into the inner sanctuary of the temple, to the Most Holy *Place,* under the wings of the cherubim. ⁷ For the cherubim spread *their* two wings over the place of the ark, and the cherubim overshadowed the ark and its poles. ⁸ The poles extended so that the ends of the poles could be seen from the holy *place,* in front of the inner sanctuary; but they could not be seen from outside. And they are there to this day. ⁹ Nothing *was* in the ark except the two tablets of stone which Moses put there at Horeb, when the LORD made *a covenant* with the children of Israel, when they came out of the land of Egypt.

¹⁰ And it came to pass, when the priests came out of the holy *place,* that the cloud filled the house of the LORD, ¹¹ so that the priests could not continue ministering because of the cloud; for the glory of the LORD filled the house of the LORD.

¹² Then Solomon spoke:

"The LORD said He would dwell in the dark cloud.
¹³   I have surely built You an exalted house,
And a place for You to dwell in forever."

¹⁴ Then the king turned around and blessed the whole assembly of Israel, while all the assembly of Israel was standing. ¹⁵ And he said: "Blessed *be* the LORD God of Israel, who spoke with His mouth to my father David, and with His hand has fulfilled *it,* saying, ¹⁶ 'Since the day that I brought My people Israel out of Egypt, I have chosen no city from any tribe of Israel *in which* to build a house, that My name might be there; but I chose David to be over My people Israel.' ¹⁷ Now it was in the heart of my father David to build a temple for the name of the LORD God of Israel. ¹⁸ But the LORD said to my father David, 'Whereas it was in your heart to build a temple for My name, you did well that it was in your heart. ¹⁹ Nevertheless you shall not build the temple, but your son who will come from your body, he shall build the temple for My name.' ²⁰ So the LORD has fulfilled His word

which He spoke; and I have filled the position of my father David, and sit on the throne of Israel, as the LORD promised; and I have built a temple for the name of the LORD God of Israel. ²¹ And there I have made a place for the ark, in which *is* the covenant of the LORD which He made with our fathers, when He brought them out of the land of Egypt."

²² Then Solomon stood before the altar of the LORD in the presence of all the assembly of Israel, and spread out his hands toward heaven; ²³ and he said: "LORD God of Israel, *there is* no God in heaven above or on earth below like You, who keep *Your* covenant and mercy with Your servants who walk before You with all their hearts. ²⁴ You have kept what You promised Your servant David my father; You have both spoken with Your mouth and fulfilled *it* with Your hand, as *it is* this day. ²⁵ Therefore, LORD God of Israel, now keep what You promised Your servant David my father, saying, 'You shall not fail to have a man sit before Me on the throne of Israel, only if your sons take heed to their way, that they walk before Me as you have walked before Me.' ²⁶ And now I pray, O God of Israel, let Your word come true, which You have spoken to Your servant David my father.

²⁷ "But will God indeed dwell on the earth? Behold, heaven and the heaven of heavens cannot contain You. How much less this temple which I have built! ²⁸ Yet regard the prayer of Your servant and his supplication, O LORD my God, and listen to the cry and the prayer which Your servant is praying before You today: ²⁹ that Your eyes may be open toward this temple night and day, toward the place of which You said, 'My name shall be there,' that You may hear the prayer which Your servant makes toward this place. ³⁰ And may You hear the supplication of Your servant and of Your people Israel, when they pray toward this place. Hear in heaven Your dwelling place; and when You hear, forgive.

³¹ "When anyone sins against his neighbor, and is forced to take an oath, and comes *and* takes an oath before Your altar in this temple, ³² then hear in heaven, and act, and judge Your servants, condemning the wicked, bringing his way on his

head, and justifying the righteous by giving him according to his righteousness.

³³ "When Your people Israel are defeated before an enemy because they have sinned against You, and when they turn back to You and confess Your name, and pray and make supplication to You in this temple, ³⁴ then hear in heaven, and forgive the sin of Your people Israel, and bring them back to the land which You gave to their fathers.

³⁵ "When the heavens are shut up and there is no rain because they have sinned against You, when they pray toward this place and confess Your name, and turn from their sin because You afflict them, ³⁶ then hear in heaven, and forgive the sin of Your servants, Your people Israel, that You may teach them the good way in which they should walk; and send rain on Your land which You have given to Your people as an inheritance.

³⁷ "When there is famine in the land, pestilence *or* blight *or* mildew, locusts *or* grasshoppers; when their enemy besieges them in the land of their cities; whatever plague or whatever sickness *there is;* ³⁸ whatever prayer, whatever supplication is made by anyone, *or* by all Your people Israel, when each one knows the plague of his own heart, and spreads out his hands toward this temple: ³⁹ then hear in heaven Your dwelling place, and forgive, and act, and give to everyone according to all his ways, whose heart You know (for You alone know the hearts of all the sons of men), ⁴⁰ that they may fear You all the days that they live in the land which You gave to our fathers.

⁴¹ "Moreover, concerning a foreigner, who *is* not of Your people Israel, but has come from a far country for Your name's sake ⁴²(for they will hear of Your great name and Your strong hand and Your outstretched arm), when he comes and prays toward this temple, ⁴³ hear in heaven Your dwelling place, and do according to all for which the foreigner calls to You, that all peoples of the earth may know Your name and fear You, as *do* Your people Israel, and that they may know that this temple which I have built is called by Your name.

⁴⁴ "When Your people go out to battle against their enemy, wherever You send them, and when they pray to the LORD toward the city which You have chosen and the temple which I have built for Your name, ⁴⁵ then hear in heaven their prayer and their supplication, and maintain their cause.

⁴⁶ "When they sin against You (for *there is* no one who does not sin), and You become angry with them and deliver them to the enemy, and they take them captive to the land of the enemy, far or near; ⁴⁷ *yet* when they come to themselves in the land where they were carried captive, and repent, and make supplication to You in the land of those who took them captive, saying, 'We have sinned and done wrong, we have committed wickedness'; ⁴⁸ and *when* they return to You with all their heart and with all their soul in the land of their enemies who led them away captive, and pray to You toward their land which You gave to their fathers, the city which You have chosen and the temple which I have built for Your name: ⁴⁹ then hear in heaven Your dwelling place their prayer and their supplication, and maintain their cause, ⁵⁰ and forgive Your people who have sinned against You, and all their transgressions which they have transgressed against You; and grant them compassion before those who took them captive, that they may have compassion on them ⁵¹(for they *are* Your people and Your inheritance, whom You brought out of Egypt, out of the iron furnace), ⁵² that Your eyes may be open to the supplication of Your servant and the supplication of Your people Israel, to listen to them whenever they call to You. ⁵³ For You separated them from among all the peoples of the earth *to be* Your inheritance, as You spoke by Your servant Moses, when You brought our fathers out of Egypt, O Lord GOD."

⁵⁴ And so it was, when Solomon had finished praying all this prayer and supplication to the LORD, that he arose from before the altar of the LORD, from kneeling on his knees with his hands spread up to heaven. ⁵⁵ Then he stood and blessed all the assembly of Israel with a loud voice, saying: ⁵⁶ "Blessed *be* the LORD, who has given rest to His people Israel, according to all that He promised. There has not failed one word of all His good promise,

which He promised through His servant Moses. [57] May the LORD our God be with us, as He was with our fathers. May He not leave us nor forsake us, [58] that He may incline our hearts to Himself, to walk in all His ways, and to keep His commandments and His statutes and His judgments, which He commanded our fathers. [59] And may these words of mine, with which I have made supplication before the LORD, be near the LORD our God day and night, that He may maintain the cause of His servant and the cause of His people Israel, as each day may require, [60] that all the peoples of the earth may know that the LORD is God; there is no other. [61] Let your heart therefore be loyal to the LORD our God, to walk in His statutes and keep His commandments, as at this day."

[62] Then the king and all Israel with him offered sacrifices before the LORD. [63] And Solomon offered a sacrifice of peace offerings, which he offered to the LORD, twenty-two thousand bulls and one hundred and twenty thousand sheep. So the king and all the children of Israel dedicated the house of the LORD. [64] On the same day the king consecrated the middle of the court that was in front of the house of the LORD; for there he offered burnt offerings, grain offerings, and the fat of the peace offerings, because the bronze altar that was before the LORD was too small to receive the burnt offerings, the grain offerings, and the fat of the peace offerings.

[65] At that time Solomon held a feast, and all Israel with him, a great assembly from the entrance of Hamath to the Brook of Egypt, before the LORD our God, seven days and seven more days—fourteen days. [66] On the eighth day he sent the people away; and they blessed the king, and went to their tents joyful and glad of heart for all the good that the LORD had done for His servant David, and for Israel His people.

∼ PSALM 68:28–35 ∼

[28] Your God has commanded your strength;
Strengthen, O God, what You have done for us.

[29] Because of Your temple at Jerusalem, Kings will bring presents to You.
[30] Rebuke the beasts of the reeds,
The herd of bulls with the calves of the peoples,
Till everyone submits himself with pieces of silver.
Scatter the peoples who delight in war.
[31] Envoys will come out of Egypt;
Ethiopia will quickly stretch out her hands to God.

[32] Sing to God, you kingdoms of the earth;
Oh, sing praises to the Lord,   Selah
[33] To Him who rides on the heaven of heavens, which were of old!
Indeed, He sends out His voice, a mighty voice.
[34] Ascribe strength to God;
His excellence is over Israel,
And His strength is in the clouds.
[35] O God, You are more awesome than Your holy places.
The God of Israel is He who gives strength and power to His people.

Blessed be God!

∼ PROVERBS 17:16, 17 ∼

[16] Why is there in the hand of a fool the purchase price of wisdom,
Since he has no heart for it?

[17] A friend loves at all times,
And a brother is born for adversity.

∼ JOHN 11:1–29 ∼

Now a certain man was sick, Lazarus of Bethany, the town of Mary and her sister Martha. [2] It was that Mary who anointed the Lord with fragrant oil and wiped His feet with her hair, whose brother Lazarus was sick. [3] Therefore the sisters sent to Him, saying, "Lord, behold, he whom You love is sick."

[4] When Jesus heard that, He said, "This sickness is not unto death, but for the glory of God, that the Son of God may be glorified through it."

[5] Now Jesus loved Martha and her sister and Lazarus. [6] So, when He heard that

he was sick, He stayed two more days in the place where He was. [7] Then after this He said to *the* disciples, "Let us go to Judea again."

[8] *The* disciples said to Him, "Rabbi, lately the Jews sought to stone You, and are You going there again?"

[9] Jesus answered, "Are there not twelve hours in the day? If anyone walks in the day, he does not stumble, because he sees the light of this world. [10] But if one walks in the night, he stumbles, because the light is not in him." [11] These things He said, and after that He said to them, "Our friend Lazarus sleeps, but I go that I may wake him up."

[12] Then His disciples said, "Lord, if he sleeps he will get well." [13] However, Jesus spoke of his death, but they thought that He was speaking about taking rest in sleep.

[14] Then Jesus said to them plainly, "Lazarus is dead. [15] And I am glad for your sakes that I was not there, that you may believe. Nevertheless let us go to him."

[16] Then Thomas, who is called the Twin, said to his fellow disciples, "Let us also go, that we may die with Him."

[17] So when Jesus came, He found that he had already been in the tomb four days. [18] Now Bethany was near Jerusalem, about two miles away. [19] And many of the Jews had joined the women around Martha and Mary, to comfort them concerning their brother.

[20] Now Martha, as soon as she heard that Jesus was coming, went and met Him, but Mary was sitting in the house. [21] Now Martha said to Jesus, "Lord, if You had been here, my brother would not have died. [22] But even now I know that whatever You ask of God, God will give You." [23] Jesus said to her, "Your brother will rise again."

[24] Martha said to Him, "I know that he will rise again in the resurrection at the last day."

[25] Jesus said to her, "I am the resurrection and the life. He who believes in Me, though he may die, he shall live. [26] And whoever lives and believes in Me shall never die. Do you believe this?"

[27] She said to Him, "Yes, Lord, I believe that You are the Christ, the Son of God, who is to come into the world."

[28] And when she had said these things, she went her way and secretly called Mary her sister, saying, "The Teacher has come and is calling for you." [29] As soon as she heard *that,* she arose quickly and came to Him.

READING 151 · MAY 31

~ 1 KINGS 9:1—10:29 ~

And it came to pass, when Solomon had finished building the house of the LORD and the king's house, and all Solomon's desire which he wanted to do, [2] that the LORD appeared to Solomon the second time, as He had appeared to him at Gibeon. [3] And the LORD said to him: "I have heard your prayer and your supplication that you have made before Me; I have consecrated this house which you have built to put My name there forever, and My eyes and My heart will be there perpetually. [4] Now if you walk before Me as your father David walked, in integrity of heart and in uprightness, to do according to all that I have commanded you, *and* if you keep My statutes and My judgments, [5] then I will establish the throne of your kingdom over Israel forever, as I promised David your father, saying, 'You shall not fail to have a man on the throne of Israel.' [6] *But* if you or your sons at all turn from following Me, and do not keep My commandments *and* My statutes which I have set before you, but go and serve other gods and worship them, [7] then I will cut off Israel from the land which I have given them; and this house which I have consecrated for My name I will cast out of My sight. Israel will be a proverb and a byword among all peoples. [8] And *as for* this house, *which* is exalted, everyone who passes by it will be astonished and will hiss, and say, 'Why has the LORD done thus to this land and to this house?' [9] Then they will answer, 'Because they forsook the LORD their God, who brought their fathers out of the land of Egypt, and have embraced other gods, and worshiped them and served them; therefore the LORD has brought all this calamity on them.' "

¹⁰ Now it happened at the end of twenty years, when Solomon had built the two houses, the house of the LORD and the king's house ¹¹(Hiram the king of Tyre had supplied Solomon with cedar and cypress and gold, as much as he desired), *that* King Solomon then gave Hiram twenty cities in the land of Galilee. ¹² Then Hiram went from Tyre to see the cities which Solomon had given him, but they did not please him. ¹³ So he said, "What *kind of* cities *are* these which you have given me, my brother?" And he called them the land of Cabul, as they are to this day. ¹⁴ Then Hiram sent the king one hundred and twenty talents of gold.

¹⁵ And this *is* the reason for the labor force which King Solomon raised: to build the house of the LORD, his own house, the Millo, the wall of Jerusalem, Hazor, Megiddo, and Gezer. ¹⁶(Pharaoh king of Egypt had gone up and taken Gezer and burned it with fire, had killed the Canaanites who dwelt in the city, and had given it *as* a dowry to his daughter, Solomon's wife.) ¹⁷ And Solomon built Gezer, Lower Beth Horon, ¹⁸ Baalath, and Tadmor in the wilderness, in the land *of Judah,* ¹⁹ all the storage cities that Solomon had, cities for his chariots and cities for his cavalry, and whatever Solomon desired to build in Jerusalem, in Lebanon, and in all the land of his dominion.

²⁰ All the people *who were* left of the Amorites, Hittites, Perizzites, Hivites, and Jebusites, who *were* not of the children of Israel— ²¹ that is, their descendants who were left in the land after them, whom the children of Israel had not been able to destroy completely—from these Solomon raised forced labor, as it is to this day. ²² But of the children of Israel Solomon made no forced laborers, because they *were* men of war and his servants: his officers, his captains, commanders of his chariots, and his cavalry.

²³ Others *were* chiefs of the officials who *were* over Solomon's work: five hundred and fifty, who ruled over the people who did the work.

²⁴ But Pharaoh's daughter came up from the City of David to her house which *Solomon* had built for her. Then he built the Millo.

²⁵ Now three times a year Solomon offered burnt offerings and peace offerings on the altar which he had built for the LORD, and he burned incense with them *on the altar* that *was* before the LORD. So he finished the temple.

²⁶ King Solomon also built a fleet of ships at Ezion Geber, which *is* near Elath on the shore of the Red Sea, in the land of Edom. ²⁷ Then Hiram sent his servants with the fleet, seamen who knew the sea, to work with the servants of Solomon. ²⁸ And they went to Ophir, and acquired four hundred and twenty talents of gold from there, and brought *it* to King Solomon.

10 Now when the queen of Sheba heard of the fame of Solomon concerning the name of the LORD, she came to test him with hard questions. ² She came to Jerusalem with a very great retinue, with camels that bore spices, very much gold, and precious stones; and when she came to Solomon, she spoke with him about all that was in her heart. ³ So Solomon answered all her questions; there was nothing so difficult for the king that he could not explain *it* to her. ⁴ And when the queen of Sheba had seen all the wisdom of Solomon, the house that he had built, ⁵ the food on his table, the seating of his servants, the service of his waiters and their apparel, his cupbearers, and his entryway by which he went up to the house of the LORD, there was no more spirit in her. ⁶ Then she said to the king: "It was a true report which I heard in my own land about your words and your wisdom. ⁷ However I did not believe the words until I came and saw with my own eyes; and indeed the half was not told me. Your wisdom and prosperity exceed the fame of which I heard. ⁸ Happy *are* your men and happy *are* these your servants, who stand continually before you *and* hear your wisdom! ⁹ Blessed be the LORD your God, who delighted in you, setting you on the throne of Israel! Because the LORD has loved Israel forever, therefore He made you king, to do justice and righteousness."

Home Sweet Home

In *Secret Strength*, Joni Eareckson Tada writes a wonderful tribute to a genuine "home, sweet home":

"Not long ago I entered a friend's home and immediately sensed the glory of God. No, that impression was not based on some heebie-jeebie feeling or super-spiritual instinct. And it had nothing to do with several Christian plaques I spotted hanging in the hallway. Yet there was a peace and orderliness that pervaded that home. Joy and music hung in the air. Although the kids were normal, active youngsters, everyone's activity seemed to dovetail together, creating the impression that the home had direction, that the kids really cared about each other, that the parents put love into action.

"We didn't even spend that much time 'fellowshipping' in the usual sense of the word—talking about the Bible or praying together. Yet we laughed. And really heard each other. And opened our hearts like family members. After dinner I left that home refreshed. It was a place where God's essential being was on display. His kindness, His love, His justice. It was filled with God's glory."

The presence of the Lord makes any home sweet!

¹⁰ Then she gave the king one hundred and twenty talents of gold, spices in great quantity, and precious stones. There never again came such abundance of spices as the queen of Sheba gave to King Solomon. ¹¹ Also, the ships of Hiram, which brought gold from Ophir, brought great *quantities* of almug wood and precious stones from Ophir. ¹² And the king made steps of the almug wood for the house of the LORD and for the king's house, also harps and stringed instruments for singers. There never again came such almug wood, nor has the like been seen to this day.

¹³ Now King Solomon gave the queen of Sheba all she desired, whatever she asked, besides what Solomon had given her according to the royal generosity. So she turned and went to her own country, she and her servants.

¹⁴ The weight of gold that came to Solomon yearly was six hundred and sixty-six talents of gold, ¹⁵ besides *that* from the traveling merchants, from the income of traders, from all the kings of Arabia, and from the governors of the country.

¹⁶ And King Solomon made two hundred large shields *of* hammered gold; six hundred *shekels* of gold went into each shield. ¹⁷ He also *made* three hundred shields *of* hammered gold; three minas of gold went into each shield. The king put them in the House of the Forest of Lebanon.

¹⁸ Moreover the king made a great throne of ivory, and overlaid it with pure gold. ¹⁹ The throne had six steps, and the top of the throne *was* round at the back; *there were* armrests on either side of the place of the seat, and two lions stood beside the armrests. ²⁰ Twelve lions stood there, one on each side of the six steps; nothing like *this* had been made for any *other* kingdom.

²¹ All King Solomon's drinking vessels *were* gold, and all the vessels of the House of the Forest of Lebanon *were* pure gold. Not *one was* silver, for this was accounted as nothing in the days of Solomon. ²² For the king had merchant ships at sea with the fleet of Hiram. Once every three years the merchant ships came bringing gold, silver, ivory, apes, and monkeys.

²³ So King Solomon surpassed all the kings of the earth in riches and wisdom.

²⁴ Now all the earth sought the presence of Solomon to hear his wisdom, which God had put in his heart. ²⁵ Each man brought his present: articles of silver and gold, garments, armor, spices, horses, and mules, at a set rate year by year.

²⁶ And Solomon gathered chariots and horsemen; he had one thousand four hundred chariots and twelve thousand horsemen, whom he stationed in the chariot cities and with the king at Jerusalem. ²⁷ The king made silver *as common* in Jerusalem as stones, and he made cedar trees as abundant as the sycamores which *are* in the lowland.

²⁸ Also Solomon had horses imported from Egypt and Keveh; the king's merchants bought them in Keveh at the *current* price. ²⁹ Now a chariot that was imported from Egypt cost six hundred *shekels* of silver, and a horse one hundred and fifty; and thus, through their agents, they exported *them* to all the kings of the Hittites and the kings of Syria.

∼ PSALM 69:1–4 ∼

1 Save me, O God!
For the waters have come up to *my*
   neck.
2 I sink in deep mire,
Where *there is* no standing;
I have come into deep waters,
Where the floods overflow me.
3 I am weary with my crying;
My throat is dry;
My eyes fail while I wait for my
   God.

4 Those who hate me without a cause
Are more than the hairs of my head;
They are mighty who would destroy
   me,
Being my enemies wrongfully;
Though I have stolen nothing,
I *still* must restore *it*.

∼ PROVERBS 17:18, 19 ∼

18 A man devoid of understanding
   shakes hands in a pledge,
And becomes surety for his friend.

19 He who loves transgression loves
strife,
And he who exalts his gate seeks
destruction.

~ JOHN 11:30–57 ~

Now Jesus had not yet come into the
town, but was in the place where Martha
met Him. 31 Then the Jews who were with
her in the house, and comforting her,
when they saw that Mary rose up quickly
and went out, followed her, saying, "She
is going to the tomb to weep there."
32 Then, when Mary came where Jesus
was, and saw Him, she fell down at His
feet, saying to Him, "Lord, if You had been
here, my brother would not have died."
33 Therefore, when Jesus saw her weeping, and the Jews who came with her
weeping, He groaned in the spirit and was
troubled. 34 And He said, "Where have
you laid him?"
They said to Him, "Lord, come and
see."
35 Jesus wept. 36 Then the Jews said, "See
how He loved him!"
37 And some of them said, "Could not
this Man, who opened the eyes of the
blind, also have kept this man from
dying?"
38 Then Jesus, again groaning in Himself, came to the tomb. It was a cave, and
a stone lay against it. 39 Jesus said, "Take
away the stone."
Martha, the sister of him who was dead,
said to Him, "Lord, by this time there is a
stench, for he has been *dead* four days."
40 Jesus said to her, "Did I not say to
you that if you would believe you would
see the glory of God?" 41 Then they took
away the stone *from the place* where the
dead man was lying. And Jesus lifted up
His eyes and said, "Father, I thank
You that You have heard Me. 42 And I
know that You always hear Me, but because of the people who are standing by I
said *this*, that they may believe that You

sent Me." 43 Now when He had said these
things, He cried with a loud voice,
"Lazarus, come forth!" 44 And he who had
died came out bound hand and foot with
graveclothes, and his face was wrapped
with a cloth. Jesus said to them, "Loose
him, and let him go."
45 Then many of the Jews who had
come to Mary, and had seen the things
Jesus did, believed in Him. 46 But some of
them went away to the Pharisees and
told them the things Jesus did. 47 Then the
chief priests and the Pharisees gathered a
council and said, "What shall we do? For
this Man works many signs. 48 If we let
Him alone like this, everyone will believe
in Him, and the Romans will come and
take away both our place and nation."
49 And one of them, Caiaphas, being
high priest that year, said to them, "You
know nothing at all, 50 nor do you consider that it is expedient for us that one
man should die for the people, and not
that the whole nation should perish."
51 Now this he did not say on his own
authority; but being high priest that year
he prophesied that Jesus would die for
the nation, 52 and not for that nation only,
but also that He would gather together in
one the children of God who were scattered abroad.
53 Then, from that day on, they plotted
to put Him to death. 54 Therefore Jesus
no longer walked openly among the Jews,
but went from there into the country near
the wilderness, to a city called Ephraim,
and there remained with His disciples.
55 And the Passover of the Jews was
near, and many went from the country
up to Jerusalem before the Passover, to
purify themselves. 56 Then they sought
Jesus, and spoke among themselves as they
stood in the temple, "What do you
think—that He will not come to the
feast?" 57 Now both the chief priests and
the Pharisees had given a command, that
if anyone knew where He was, he should
report *it,* that they might seize Him.

~ 1 KINGS 11:1—12:33 ~

But King Solomon loved many foreign women, as well as the daughter of Pharaoh: women of the Moabites, Ammonites, Edomites, Sidonians, *and* Hittites— ² from the nations of whom the LORD had said to the children of Israel, "You shall not intermarry with them, nor they with you. Surely they will turn away your hearts after their gods." Solomon clung to these in love. ³ And he had seven hundred wives, princesses, and three hundred concubines; and his wives turned away his heart. ⁴ For it was so, when Solomon was old, that his wives turned his heart after other gods; and his heart was not loyal to the LORD his God, as *was* the heart of his father David. ⁵ For Solomon went after Ashtoreth the goddess of the Sidonians, and after Milcom the abomination of the Ammonites. ⁶ Solomon did evil in the sight of the LORD, and did not fully follow the LORD, as *did* his father David. ⁷ Then Solomon built a high place for Chemosh the abomination of Moab, on the hill that *is* east of Jerusalem, and for Molech the abomination of the people of Ammon. ⁸ And he did likewise for all his foreign wives, who burned incense and sacrificed to their gods.

⁹ So the LORD became angry with Solomon, because his heart had turned from the LORD God of Israel, who had appeared to him twice, ¹⁰ and had commanded him concerning this thing, that he should not go after other gods; but he did not keep what the LORD had commanded. ¹¹ Therefore the LORD said to Solomon, "Because you have done this, and have not kept My covenant and My statutes, which I have commanded you, I will surely tear the kingdom away from you and give it to your servant. ¹² Nevertheless I will not do it in your days, for the sake of your father David; I will tear it out of the hand of your son. ¹³ However I will not tear away the whole kingdom; I will give one tribe to your son for the sake of my servant David, and for the sake of Jerusalem which I have chosen."

¹⁴ Now the LORD raised up an adversary against Solomon, Hadad the Edom-

ite; he *was* a descendant of the king in Edom. ¹⁵ For it happened, when David was in Edom, and Joab the commander of the army had gone up to bury the slain, after he had killed every male in Edom ¹⁶ (because for six months Joab remained there with all Israel, until he had cut down every male in Edom), ¹⁷ that Hadad fled to go to Egypt, he and certain Edomites of his father's servants with him. Hadad *was* still a little child. ¹⁸ Then they arose from Midian and came to Paran; and they took men with them from Paran and came to Egypt, to Pharaoh king of Egypt, who gave him a house, apportioned food for him, and gave him land. ¹⁹ And Hadad found great favor in the sight of Pharaoh, so that he gave him as wife the sister of his own wife, that is, the sister of Queen Tahpenes. ²⁰ Then the sister of Tahpenes bore him Genubath his son, whom Tahpenes weaned in Pharaoh's house. And Genubath was in Pharaoh's household among the sons of Pharaoh.

²¹ So when Hadad heard in Egypt that David rested with his fathers, and that Joab the commander of the army was dead, Hadad said to Pharaoh, "Let me depart, that I may go to my own country."

²² Then Pharaoh said to him, "But what have you lacked with me, that suddenly you seek to go to your own country?"

So he answered, "Nothing, but do let me go anyway."

²³ And God raised up *another* adversary against him, Rezon the son of Eliadah, who had fled from his lord, Hadadezer king of Zobah. ²⁴ So he gathered men to him and became captain over a band *of raiders,* when David killed those *of Zobah.* And they went to Damascus and dwelt there, and reigned in Damascus. ²⁵ He was an adversary of Israel all the days of Solomon (besides the trouble that Hadad *caused*); and he abhorred Israel, and reigned over Syria.

²⁶ Then Solomon's servant, Jeroboam the son of Nebat, an Ephraimite from Zereda, whose mother's name *was* Zeruah, a widow, also rebelled against the king.

Foolproof Therapy

In *Growing Strong in the Seasons of Life*, Charles Swindoll writes: "Tonight was fun 'n' games night around the supper table in our house. It was wild. First of all, one of the kids snickered during the prayer (which isn't that unusual) and that tipped the first domino. Then a humorous incident from school was shared and the event (as well as how it was told) triggered havoc around the table. That was the beginning of twenty to thirty minutes of the loudest, silliest, most enjoyable laughter you can imagine. At one point I watched my oldest literally fall off his chair in hysterics, my youngest doubled over in his chair as his face wound up in his plate with corn chips stuck to his cheeks . . . and my two girls leaning back, lost and preoccupied in the most beautiful and beneficial therapy God ever granted humanity: laughter.

"What is so amazing is that everything seemed far less serious and heavy. Irritability and impatience were ignored like unwanted guests. For example, during the meal little Chuck spilled his drink twice . . . and even that brought the house down. If I remember correctly, that made six times during the day he accidentally spilled his drink, but nobody bothered to count."

What a treasure laughter is. It completely dissipates anxiety, erases stress, relieves fears. What a precious gift from God!

²⁷ And this *is* what caused him to rebel against the king: Solomon had built the Millo *and* repaired the damages to the City of David his father. ²⁸ The man Jeroboam *was* a mighty man of valor; and Solomon, seeing that the young man was industrious, made him the officer over all the labor force of the house of Joseph.

²⁹ Now it happened at that time, when Jeroboam went out of Jerusalem, that the prophet Ahijah the Shilonite met him on the way; and he had clothed himself with a new garment, and the two *were* alone in the field. ³⁰ Then Ahijah took hold of the new garment that *was* on him, and tore it *into* twelve pieces. ³¹ And he said to Jeroboam, "Take for yourself ten pieces, for thus says the LORD, the God of Israel: 'Behold, I will tear the kingdom out of the hand of Solomon and will give ten tribes to you ³²(but he shall have one tribe for the sake of My servant David, and for the sake of Jerusalem, the city which I have chosen out of all the tribes of Israel), ³³ because they have forsaken Me, and worshiped Ashtoreth the goddess of the Sidonians, Chemosh the god of the Moabites, and Milcom the god of the people of Ammon, and have not walked in My ways to do *what is* right in My eyes and *keep* My statutes and My judgments, as *did* his father David. ³⁴ However I will not take the whole kingdom out of his hand, because I have made him ruler all the days of his life for the sake of My servant David, whom I chose because he kept My commandments and My statutes. ³⁵ But I will take the kingdom out of his son's hand and give it to you— ten tribes. ³⁶ And to his son I will give one tribe, that My servant David may always have a lamp before Me in Jerusalem, the city which I have chosen for Myself, to put My name there. ³⁷ So I will take you, and you shall reign over all your heart desires, and you shall be king over Israel. ³⁸ Then it shall be, if you heed all that I command you, walk in My ways, and do *what is* right in My sight, to keep My statutes and My commandments, as My servant David did, then I will be with you and build for you an enduring house, as I built for David, and will give Israel to you. ³⁹ And I will afflict the de-

scendants of David because of this, but not forever.' "

⁴⁰ Solomon therefore sought to kill Jeroboam. But Jeroboam arose and fled to Egypt, to Shishak king of Egypt, and was in Egypt until the death of Solomon.

⁴¹ Now the rest of the acts of Solomon, all that he did, and his wisdom, *are* they not written in the book of the acts of Solomon? ⁴² And the period that Solomon reigned in Jerusalem over all Israel *was* forty years. ⁴³ Then Solomon rested with his fathers, and was buried in the City of David his father. And Rehoboam his son reigned in his place.

12 And Rehoboam went to Shechem, for all Israel had gone to Shechem to make him king. ² So it happened, when Jeroboam the son of Nebat heard *it* (he was still in Egypt, for he had fled from the presence of King Solomon and had been dwelling in Egypt), ³ that they sent and called him. Then Jeroboam and the whole assembly of Israel came and spoke to Rehoboam, saying, ⁴ "Your father made our yoke heavy; now therefore, lighten the burdensome service of your father, and his heavy yoke which he put on us, and we will serve you."

⁵ So he said to them, "Depart *for* three days, then come back to me." And the people departed.

⁶ Then King Rehoboam consulted the elders who stood before his father Solomon while he still lived, and he said, "How do you advise *me* to answer these people?"

⁷ And they spoke to him, saying, "If you will be a servant to these people today, and serve them, and answer them, and speak good words to them, then they will be your servants forever."

⁸ But he rejected the advice which the elders had given him, and consulted the young men who had grown up with him, who stood before him. ⁹ And he said to them, "What advice do you give? How should we answer this people who have spoken to me, saying, 'Lighten the yoke which your father put on us'?"

¹⁰ Then the young men who had grown up with him spoke to him, saying, "Thus you should speak to this people who have

spoken to you, saying, 'Your father made our yoke heavy, but you make *it* lighter on us'—thus you shall say to them: 'My little *finger* shall be thicker than my father's waist! [11] And now, whereas my father put a heavy yoke on you, I will add to your yoke; my father chastised you with whips, but I will chastise you with scourges!' "

[12] So Jeroboam and all the people came to Rehoboam the third day, as the king had directed, saying, "Come back to me the third day." [13] Then the king answered the people roughly, and rejected the advice which the elders had given him; [14] and he spoke to them according to the advice of the young men, saying, "My father made your yoke heavy, but I will add to your yoke; my father chastised you with whips, but I will chastise you with scourges!" [15] So the king did not listen to the people; for the turn *of events* was from the LORD, that He might fulfill His word, which the LORD had spoken by Ahijah the Shilonite to Jeroboam the son of Nebat.

[16] Now when all Israel saw that the king did not listen to them, the people answered the king, saying:

"What share have we in David?
We *have* no inheritance in the son of Jesse.
To your tents, O Israel!
Now, see to your own house, O David!"

So Israel departed to their tents. [17] But Rehoboam reigned over the children of Israel who dwelt in the cities of Judah.

[18] Then King Rehoboam sent Adoram, who *was* in charge of the revenue; but all Israel stoned him with stones, and he died. Therefore King Rehoboam mounted his chariot in haste to flee to Jerusalem. [19] So Israel has been in rebellion against the house of David to this day.

[20] Now it came to pass when all Israel heard that Jeroboam had come back, they sent for him and called him to the congregation, and made him king over all Israel. There was none who followed the house of David, but the tribe of Judah only.

[21] And when Rehoboam came to Jerusa- lem, he assembled all the house of Judah with the tribe of Benjamin, one hundred and eighty thousand chosen *men* who were warriors, to fight against the house of Israel, that he might restore the kingdom to Rehoboam the son of Solomon. [22] But the word of God came to Shemaiah the man of God, saying, [23] "Speak to Rehoboam the son of Solomon, king of Judah, to all the house of Judah and Benjamin, and to the rest of the people, saying, [24] 'Thus says the LORD: "You shall not go up nor fight against your brethren the children of Israel. Let every man return to his house, for this thing is from Me." ' " Therefore they obeyed the word of the LORD, and turned back, according to the word of the LORD.

[25] Then Jeroboam built Shechem in the mountains of Ephraim, and dwelt there. Also he went out from there and built Penuel. [26] And Jeroboam said in his heart, "Now the kingdom may return to the house of David: [27] If these people go up to offer sacrifices in the house of the LORD at Jerusalem, then the heart of this people will turn back to their lord, Rehoboam king of Judah, and they will kill me and go back to Rehoboam king of Judah." [28] Therefore the king asked advice, made two calves of gold, and said to the people, "It is too much for you to go up to Jerusalem. Here are your gods, O Israel, which brought you up from the land of Egypt!" [29] And he set up one in Bethel, and the other he put in Dan. [30] Now this thing became a sin, for the people went *to worship* before the one as far as Dan. [31] He made shrines on the high places, and made priests from every class of people, who were not of the sons of Levi.

[32] Jeroboam ordained a feast on the fifteenth day of the eighth month, like the feast that *was* in Judah, and offered sacrifices on the altar. So he did at Bethel, sacrificing to the calves that he had made. And at Bethel he installed the priests of the high places which he had made. [33] So he made offerings on the altar which he had made at Bethel on the fifteenth day of the eighth month, in the month which he had devised in his own heart. And he ordained a feast for the children of Israel, and offered sacrifices on the altar and burned incense.

~ PSALM 69:5–15 ~

5 O God, You know my foolishness;
  And my sins are not hidden from
  You.
6 Let not those who wait for You,
  O Lord GOD of hosts, be ashamed
  because of me;
  Let not those who seek You be
  confounded because of me,
  O God of Israel.
7 Because for Your sake I have borne
  reproach;
  Shame has covered my face.
8 I have become a stranger to my
  brothers,
  And an alien to my mother's
  children;
9 Because zeal for Your house has
  eaten me up,
  And the reproaches of those who
  reproach You have fallen on me.
10 When I wept *and chastened* my soul
   with fasting,
   That became my reproach.
11 I also made sackcloth my garment;
   I became a byword to them.
12 Those who sit in the gate speak
   against me,
   And I *am* the song of the
   drunkards.

13 But as for me, my prayer *is* to You,
   O LORD, *in* the acceptable time;
   O God, in the multitude of Your
   mercy,
   Hear me in the truth of Your
   salvation.
14 Deliver me out of the mire,
   And let me not sink;
   Let me be delivered from those who
   hate me,
   And out of the deep waters.
15 Let not the floodwater overflow me,
   Nor let the deep swallow me up;
   And let not the pit shut its mouth on
   me.

~ PROVERBS 17:20–22 ~

20 He who has a deceitful heart finds
   no good,
   And he who has a perverse tongue
   falls into evil.

21 He who begets a scoffer *does so* to
   his sorrow,
   And the father of a fool has no joy.

22 A merry heart does good, *like*
   medicine,
   But a broken spirit dries the bones.

~ JOHN 12:1–26 ~

Then, six days before the Passover, Jesus came to Bethany, where Lazarus was who had been dead, whom He had raised from the dead. ² There they made Him a supper; and Martha served, but Lazarus was one of those who sat at the table with Him. ³ Then Mary took a pound of very costly oil of spikenard, anointed the feet of Jesus, and wiped His feet with her hair. And the house was filled with the fragrance of the oil.

⁴ But one of His disciples, Judas Iscariot, Simon's *son*, who would betray Him, said, ⁵ "Why was this fragrant oil not sold for three hundred denarii and given to the poor?" ⁶ This he said, not that he cared for the poor, but because he was a thief, and had the money box; and he used to take what was put in it.

⁷ But Jesus said, "Let her alone; she has kept this for the day of My burial. ⁸ For the poor you have with you always, but Me you do not have always."

⁹ Now a great many of the Jews knew that He was there; and they came, not for Jesus' sake only, but that they might also see Lazarus, whom He had raised from the dead. ¹⁰ But the chief priests plotted to put Lazarus to death also, ¹¹ because on account of him many of the Jews went away and believed in Jesus.

¹² The next day a great multitude that had come to the feast, when they heard that Jesus was coming to Jerusalem, ¹³ took branches of palm trees and went out to meet Him, and cried out:

"Hosanna!
  'Blessed *is* He who comes in the
   name of the LORD!'
  The King of Israel!"

¹⁴ Then Jesus, when He had found a young donkey, sat on it; as it is written:

¹⁵ "Fear not, daughter of Zion;
    Behold, your King is coming,
    Sitting on a donkey's colt."

¹⁶ His disciples did not understand these things at first; but when Jesus was glorified, then they remembered that these things were written about Him and *that* they had done these things to Him. ¹⁷ Therefore the people, who were with Him when He called Lazarus out of his tomb and raised him from the dead, bore witness. ¹⁸ For this reason the people also met Him, because they heard that He had done this sign. ¹⁹ The Pharisees therefore said among themselves, "You see that you are accomplishing nothing. Look, the world has gone after Him!"

²⁰ Now there were certain Greeks among those who came up to worship at the feast. ²¹ Then they came to Philip, who was from Bethsaida of Galilee, and asked him, saying, "Sir, we wish to see Jesus."

²² Philip came and told Andrew, and in turn Andrew and Philip told Jesus.

²³ But Jesus answered them, saying, "The hour has come that the Son of Man should be glorified. ²⁴ Most assuredly, I say to you, unless a grain of wheat falls into the ground and dies, it remains alone; but if it dies, it produces much grain. ²⁵ He who loves his life will lose it, and he who hates his life in this world will keep it for eternal life. ²⁶ If anyone serves Me, let him follow Me; and where I am, there My servant will be also. If anyone serves Me, him *My* Father will honor.

∼ 1 KINGS 13:1—14:31 ∼

And behold, a man of God went from Judah to Bethel by the word of the LORD, and Jeroboam stood by the altar to burn incense. ² Then he cried out against the altar by the word of the LORD, and said, "O altar, altar! Thus says the LORD: 'Behold, a child, Josiah by name, shall be born to the house of David; and on you he shall sacrifice the priests of the high places who burn incense on you, and men's bones shall be burned on you.' " ³ And he gave a sign the same day, saying, "This *is* the sign which the LORD has spoken: Surely the altar shall split apart, and the ashes on it shall be poured out."

⁴ So it came to pass when King Jeroboam heard the saying of the man of God, who cried out against the altar in Bethel, that he stretched out his hand from the altar, saying, "Arrest him!" Then his hand, which he stretched out toward him, withered, so that he could not pull it back to himself. ⁵ The altar also was split apart, and the ashes poured out from the altar, according to the sign which the man of God had given by the word of the LORD. ⁶ Then the king answered and said to the man of God, "Please entreat the favor of the LORD your God, and pray for me, that my hand may be restored to me."

So the man of God entreated the LORD, and the king's hand was restored to him, and became as before. ⁷ Then the king said to the man of God, "Come home with me and refresh yourself, and I will give you a reward."

⁸ But the man of God said to the king, "If you were to give me half your house, I would not go in with you; nor would I eat bread nor drink water in this place. ⁹ For so it was commanded me by the word of the LORD, saying, 'You shall not eat bread, nor drink water, nor return by the same way you came.' " ¹⁰ So he went another way and did not return by the way he came to Bethel.

¹¹ Now an old prophet dwelt in Bethel, and his sons came and told him all the works that the man of God had done that day in Bethel; they also told their father the words which he had spoken to the king. ¹² And their father said to them, "Which way did he go?" For his sons had seen which way the man of God went who came from Judah. ¹³ Then he said to his

sons, "Saddle the donkey for me." So they saddled the donkey for him; and he rode on it, [14] and went after the man of God, and found him sitting under an oak. Then he said to him, "*Are* you the man of God who came from Judah?"

And he said, "I *am*."

[15] Then he said to him, "Come home with me and eat bread."

[16] And he said, "I cannot return with you nor go in with you; neither can I eat bread nor drink water with you in this place. [17] For I have been told by the word of the LORD, 'You shall not eat bread nor drink water there, nor return by going the way you came.' "

[18] He said to him, "I too *am* a prophet as you *are*, and an angel spoke to me by the word of the LORD, saying, 'Bring him back with you to your house, that he may eat bread and drink water.' " (He was lying to him.)

[19] So he went back with him, and ate bread in his house, and drank water.

[20] Now it happened, as they sat at the table, that the word of the LORD came to the prophet who had brought him back; [21] and he cried out to the man of God who came from Judah, saying, "Thus says the LORD: 'Because you have disobeyed the word of the LORD, and have not kept the commandment which the LORD your God commanded you, [22] but you came back, ate bread, and drank water in the place of which *the LORD* said to you, "Eat no bread and drink no water," your corpse shall not come to the tomb of your fathers.' "

[23] So it was, after he had eaten bread and after he had drunk, that he saddled the donkey for him, the prophet whom he had brought back. [24] When he was gone, a lion met him on the road and killed him. And his corpse was thrown on the road, and the donkey stood by it. The lion also stood by the corpse. [25] And there, men passed by and saw the corpse thrown on the road, and the lion standing by the corpse. Then they went and told *it* in the city where the old prophet dwelt.

[26] Now when the prophet who had brought him back from the way heard *it,* he said, "It *is* the man of God who was disobedient to the word of the LORD.

Therefore the LORD has delivered him to the lion, which has torn him and killed him, according to the word of the LORD which He spoke to him." [27] And he spoke to his sons, saying, "Saddle the donkey for me." So they saddled *it.* [28] Then he went and found his corpse thrown on the road, and the donkey and the lion standing by the corpse. The lion had not eaten the corpse nor torn the donkey. [29] And the prophet took up the corpse of the man of God, laid it on the donkey, and brought it back. So the old prophet came to the city to mourn, and to bury him. [30] Then he laid the corpse in his own tomb; and they mourned over him, *saying,* "Alas, my brother!" [31] So it was, after he had buried him, that he spoke to his sons, saying, "When I am dead, then bury me in the tomb where the man of God *is* buried; lay my bones beside his bones. [32] For the saying which he cried out by the word of the LORD against the altar in Bethel, and against all the shrines on the high places which *are* in the cities of Samaria, will surely come to pass."

[33] After this event Jeroboam did not turn from his evil way, but again he made priests from every class of people for the high places; whoever wished, he consecrated him, and he became *one* of the priests of the high places. [34] And this thing was the sin of the house of Jeroboam, so as to exterminate and destroy *it* from the face of the earth.

14 At that time Abijah the son of Jeroboam became sick. [2] And Jeroboam said to his wife, "Please arise, and disguise yourself, that they may not recognize you as the wife of Jeroboam, and go to Shiloh. Indeed, Ahijah the prophet *is* there, who told me that *I would be* king over this people. [3] Also take with you ten loaves, *some* cakes, and a jar of honey, and go to him; he will tell you what will become of the child." [4] And Jeroboam's wife did so; she arose and went to Shiloh, and came to the house of Ahijah. But Ahijah could not see, for his eyes were glazed by reason of his age.

[5] Now the LORD had said to Ahijah, "Here is the wife of Jeroboam, coming to ask you something about her son, for he *is* sick. Thus and thus you shall say to her;

Impatience

"Have you, perchance, found a diamond pendant? I feel certain I lost it last night in your theater," a woman phoned to ask the theater manager.

"Not that I know, madam," the manager said, "but let me ask some of my employees. Please hold the line for a minute while I make inquiry. If it hasn't been found, we certainly will make a diligent search for it."

Returning to the phone a few minutes later, the manager said, "I have good news for you! The diamond pendant has been found!"

There was no reply to his news however. "Hello! Hello!" he called into the phone, and then he heard the dial tone. The woman who made the inquiry about the lost diamond pendant had failed to wait for his answer. She had not given her name and attempts to trace her call were unsuccessful. The pendant was eventually sold to raise money for the theater.

We are often like this woman when we make our requests to God. We fail to wait on the Lord to hear His reply. Instead, we rush ahead impatiently, having no idea He has a great blessing to give us, if only we'd slow down long enough to receive it!

—

> Hear me, O Lord, for Your lovingkindness is good; turn to me according to the multitude of Your tender mercies. And do not hide Your face from Your servant, for I am in trouble; hear me speedily.
>
> *Psalm 69:16-17*

for it will be, when she comes in, that she will pretend *to be* another *woman.*"

⁶ And so it was, when Ahijah heard the sound of her footsteps as she came through the door, he said, "Come in, wife of Jeroboam. Why do you pretend *to be* another *person?* For I *have been* sent to you *with* bad *news.* ⁷ Go, tell Jeroboam, 'Thus says the LORD God of Israel: "Because I exalted you from among the people, and made you ruler over My people Israel, ⁸ and tore the kingdom away from the house of David, and gave it to you; and *yet* you have not been as My servant David, who kept My commandments and who followed Me with all his heart, to do only *what was* right in My eyes; ⁹ but you have done more evil than all who were before you, for you have gone and made for yourself other gods and molded images to provoke Me to anger, and have cast Me behind your back— ¹⁰ therefore behold! I will bring disaster on the house of Jeroboam, and will cut off from Jeroboam every male in Israel, bond and free; I will take away the remnant of the house of Jeroboam, as one takes away refuse until it is all gone. ¹¹ The dogs shall eat whoever belongs to Jeroboam and dies in the city, and the birds of the air shall eat whoever dies in the field; for the LORD has spoken!" '
¹² Arise therefore, go to your own house. When your feet enter the city, the child shall die. ¹³ And all Israel shall mourn for him and bury him, for he is the only one of Jeroboam who shall come to the grave, because in him there is found something good toward the LORD God of Israel in the house of Jeroboam.

¹⁴ "Moreover the LORD will raise up for Himself a king over Israel who shall cut off the house of Jeroboam; this is the day. What? Even now! ¹⁵ For the LORD will strike Israel, as a reed is shaken in the water. He will uproot Israel from this good land which He gave to their fathers, and will scatter them beyond the River, because they have made their wooden images, provoking the LORD to anger. ¹⁶ And He will give Israel up because of the sins of Jeroboam, who sinned and who made Israel sin."

¹⁷ Then Jeroboam's wife arose and departed, and came to Tirzah. When she came to the threshold of the house, the child died. ¹⁸ And they buried him; and all Israel mourned for him, according to the word of the LORD which He spoke through His servant Ahijah the prophet.

¹⁹ Now the rest of the acts of Jeroboam, how he made war and how he reigned, indeed they *are* written in the book of the chronicles of the kings of Israel. ²⁰ The period that Jeroboam reigned *was* twenty-two years. So he rested with his fathers. Then Nadab his son reigned in his place.

²¹ And Rehoboam the son of Solomon reigned in Judah. Rehoboam *was* forty-one years old when he became king. He reigned seventeen years in Jerusalem, the city which the LORD had chosen out of all the tribes of Israel, to put His name there. His mother's name *was* Naamah, an Ammonitess. ²² Now Judah did evil in the sight of the LORD, and they provoked Him to jealousy with their sins which they committed, more than all that their fathers had done. ²³ For they also built for themselves high places, *sacred* pillars, and wooden images on every high hill and under every green tree. ²⁴ And there were also perverted persons in the land. They did according to all the abominations of the nations which the LORD had cast out before the children of Israel.

²⁵ It happened in the fifth year of King Rehoboam *that* Shishak king of Egypt came up against Jerusalem. ²⁶ And he took away the treasures of the house of the LORD and the treasures of the king's house; he took away everything. He also took away all the gold shields which Solomon had made. ²⁷ Then King Rehoboam made bronze shields in their place, and committed *them* to the hands of the captains of the guard, who guarded the doorway of the king's house. ²⁸ And whenever the king entered the house of the LORD, the guards carried them, then brought them back into the guardroom.

²⁹ Now the rest of the acts of Rehoboam, and all that he did, *are* they not written in the book of the chronicles of the kings of Judah? ³⁰ And there was war between Rehoboam and Jeroboam all *their* days. ³¹ So Rehoboam rested with his fathers, and was buried with his fathers in the City of David. His mother's name *was*

Naamah, an Ammonitess. Then Abijam his son reigned in his place.

~ PSALM 69:16–21 ~

16 Hear me, O LORD, for Your
        lovingkindness *is* good;
   Turn to me according to the
        multitude of Your tender mercies.
17 And do not hide Your face from Your
        servant,
   For I am in trouble;
   Hear me speedily.
18 Draw near to my soul, *and* redeem
        it;
   Deliver me because of my enemies.

19 You know my reproach, my shame,
        and my dishonor;
   My adversaries *are* all before You.
20 Reproach has broken my heart,
   And I am full of heaviness;
   I looked *for someone* to take pity,
        but *there was* none;
   And for comforters, but I found
        none.
21 They also gave me gall for my food,
   And for my thirst they gave me
        vinegar to drink.

~ PROVERBS 17:23, 24 ~

23 A wicked *man* accepts a bribe behind
        the back
   To pervert the ways of justice.

24 Wisdom *is* in the sight of him who
        has understanding,
   But the eyes of a fool *are* on the ends
        of the earth.

~ JOHN 12:27–50 ~

"Now My soul is troubled, and what shall I say? 'Father, save Me from this hour'? But for this purpose I came to this hour. 28 Father, glorify Your name."

Then a voice came from heaven, *saying*, "I have both glorified *it* and will glorify *it* again."

29 Therefore the people who stood by and heard *it* said that it had thundered. Others said, "An angel has spoken to Him."

30 Jesus answered and said, "This voice did not come because of Me, but for your sake. 31 Now is the judgment of this world; now the ruler of this world will be cast out. 32 And I, if I am lifted up from the earth, will draw all *peoples* to Myself." 33 This He said, signifying by what death He would die.

34 The people answered Him, "We have heard from the law that the Christ remains forever; and how *can* You say, 'The Son of Man must be lifted up'? Who is this Son of Man?"

35 Then Jesus said to them, "A little while longer the light is with you. Walk while you have the light, lest darkness overtake you; he who walks in darkness does not know where he is going. 36 While you have the light, believe in the light, that you may become sons of light." These things Jesus spoke, and departed, and was hidden from them.

37 But although He had done so many signs before them, they did not believe in Him, 38 that the word of Isaiah the prophet might be fulfilled, which he spoke:

"Lord, who has believed our
        report?
   And to whom has the arm of the
        LORD been revealed?"

39 Therefore they could not believe, because Isaiah said again:

40 "He has blinded their eyes and
        hardened their hearts,
   Lest they should see with *their*
        eyes,
   Lest they should understand with
        their hearts and turn,
   So that I should heal them."

41 These things Isaiah said when he saw His glory and spoke of Him.

42 Nevertheless even among the rulers many believed in Him, but because of the Pharisees they did not confess Him, lest they should be put out of the synagogue; 43 for they loved the praise of men more than the praise of God.

44 Then Jesus cried out and said, "He who believes in Me, believes not in Me but in Him who sent Me. 45 And he who sees Me sees Him who sent Me. 46 I have

come *as* a light into the world, that whoever believes in Me should not abide in darkness. [47] And if anyone hears My words and does not believe, I do not judge him; for I did not come to judge the world but to save the world. [48] He who rejects Me, and does not receive My words, has that which judges him—the word that I have spoken will judge him in the last day. [49] For I have not spoken on My own *authority;* but the Father who sent Me gave Me a command, what I should say and what I should speak. [50] And I know that His command is everlasting life. Therefore, whatever I speak, just as the Father has told Me, so I speak."

READING 154 · JUNE 3

~ 1 KINGS 15:1—16:34 ~

In the eighteenth year of King Jeroboam the son of Nebat, Abijam became king over Judah. [2] He reigned three years in Jerusalem. His mother's name *was* Maachah the granddaughter of Abishalom. [3] And he walked in all the sins of his father, which he had done before him; his heart was not loyal to the LORD his God, as was the heart of his father David. [4] Nevertheless for David's sake the LORD his God gave him a lamp in Jerusalem, by setting up his son after him and by establishing Jerusalem; [5] because David did *what was* right in the eyes of the LORD, and had not turned aside from anything that He commanded him all the days of his life, except in the matter of Uriah the Hittite. [6] And there was war between Rehoboam and Jeroboam all the days of his life. [7] Now the rest of the acts of Abijam, and all that he did, *are* they not written in the book of the chronicles of the kings of Judah? And there was war between Abijam and Jeroboam.

[8] So Abijam rested with his fathers, and they buried him in the City of David. Then Asa his son reigned in his place.

[9] In the twentieth year of Jeroboam king of Israel, Asa became king over Judah. [10] And he reigned forty-one years in Jerusalem. His grandmother's name *was* Maachah the granddaughter of Abishalom. [11] Asa did *what was* right in the eyes of the LORD, as *did* his father David. [12] And he banished the perverted persons from the land, and removed all the idols that his fathers had made. [13] Also he removed Maachah his grandmother from *being* queen mother, because she had made an obscene image of Asherah. And Asa cut down her obscene image and burned *it* by the Brook Kidron. [14] But the high places were not removed. Nevertheless Asa's heart was loyal to the LORD all his days. [15] He also brought into the house of the LORD the things which his father had dedicated, and the things which he himself had dedicated: silver and gold and utensils.

[16] Now there was war between Asa and Baasha king of Israel all their days. [17] And Baasha king of Israel came up against Judah, and built Ramah, that he might let none go out or come in to Asa king of Judah. [18] Then Asa took all the silver and gold *that was* left in the treasuries of the house of the LORD and the treasuries of the king's house, and delivered them into the hand of his servants. And King Asa sent them to Ben-Hadad the son of Tabrimmon, the son of Hezion, king of Syria, who dwelt in Damascus, saying, [19] *"Let there be* a treaty between you and me, as there was between my father and your father. See, I have sent you a present of silver and gold. Come and break your treaty with Baasha king of Israel, so that he will withdraw from me."

[20] So Ben-Hadad heeded King Asa, and sent the captains of his armies against the cities of Israel. He attacked Ijon, Dan, Abel Beth Maachah, and all Chinneroth, with all the land of Naphtali. [21] Now it happened, when Baasha heard *it,* that he stopped building Ramah, and remained in Tirzah.

[22] Then King Asa made a proclamation throughout all Judah; none *was* exempted. And they took away the stones and timber of Ramah, which Baasha had used for building; and with them King Asa built Geba of Benjamin, and Mizpah.

Giving and Receiving

He received two degrees, including a master of science degree. He was elected a fellow of the Society for the Encouragement of Arts, Manufactures, and Commerce in London and won the Spingarn Medal. He received a $100,000-a-year job offer from Thomas A. Edison. He was visited by Presidents Calvin Coolidge and Franklin Roosevelt, and was invited by Joseph Stalin to superintend plantations in southern Russia. Yet for all he received, George Washington Carver is best known for what he gave.

He dedicated his life to making Tuskegee Institute an instrument of ministry to the needs of rural blacks — teaching them how to become skilled farmers and useful citizens. He taught better ways of tilling the soil, the importance of a balanced diet, and called upon black farmers to grow a variety of crops — including peanuts, sweet potatoes, and cowpeas — instead of only cotton. He led the way toward the development of more than 300 derivative food and industrial products from peanuts, and more than 100 products from sweet potatoes.

In the end, your résumé of accomplishments will mean little. Your gifts to others count the most!

> If I then, your Lord and Teacher, have washed your feet, you also ought to wash one another's feet.
>
> *John 13:14*

²³ The rest of all the acts of Asa, all his might, all that he did, and the cities which he built, *are* they not written in the book of the chronicles of the kings of Judah? But in the time of his old age he was diseased in his feet. ²⁴ So Asa rested with his fathers, and was buried with his fathers in the City of David his father. Then Jehoshaphat his son reigned in his place.

²⁵ Now Nadab the son of Jeroboam became king over Israel in the second year of Asa king of Judah, and he reigned over Israel two years. ²⁶ And he did evil in the sight of the LORD, and walked in the way of his father, and in his sin by which he had made Israel sin.

²⁷ Then Baasha the son of Ahijah, of the house of Issachar, conspired against him. And Baasha killed him at Gibbethon, which *belonged* to the Philistines, while Nadab and all Israel laid siege to Gibbethon. ²⁸ Baasha killed him in the third year of Asa king of Judah, and reigned in his place. ²⁹ And it was so, when he became king, *that* he killed all the house of Jeroboam. He did not leave to Jeroboam anyone that breathed, until he had destroyed him, according to the word of the LORD which He had spoken by His servant Ahijah the Shilonite, ³⁰ because of the sins of Jeroboam, which he had sinned and by which he had made Israel sin, because of his provocation with which he had provoked the LORD God of Israel to anger.

³¹ Now the rest of the acts of Nadab, and all that he did, *are* they not written in the book of the chronicles of the kings of Israel? ³² And there was war between Asa and Baasha king of Israel all their days.

³³ In the third year of Asa king of Judah, Baasha the son of Ahijah became king over all Israel in Tirzah, and *reigned* twenty-four years. ³⁴ He did evil in the sight of the LORD, and walked in the way of Jeroboam, and in his sin by which he had made Israel sin.

16 Then the word of the LORD came to Jehu the son of Hanani, against Baasha, saying: ² "Inasmuch as I lifted you out of the dust and made you ruler over My people Israel, and you have walked in the way of Jeroboam, and have made My people Israel sin, to provoke Me to anger with their sins, ³ surely I will take away the posterity of Baasha and the posterity of his house, and I will make your house like the house of Jeroboam the son of Nebat. ⁴ The dogs shall eat whoever belongs to Baasha and dies in the city, and the birds of the air shall eat whoever dies in the fields."

⁵ Now the rest of the acts of Baasha, what he did, and his might, *are* they not written in the book of the chronicles of the kings of Israel? ⁶ So Baasha rested with his fathers and was buried in Tirzah. Then Elah his son reigned in his place.

⁷ And also the word of the LORD came by the prophet Jehu the son of Hanani against Baasha and his house, because of all the evil that he did in the sight of the LORD in provoking Him to anger with the work of his hands, in being like the house of Jeroboam, and because he killed them.

⁸ In the twenty-sixth year of Asa king of Judah, Elah the son of Baasha became king over Israel, *and reigned* two years in Tirzah. ⁹ Now his servant Zimri, commander of half *his* chariots, conspired against him as he was in Tirzah drinking himself drunk in the house of Arza, steward of *his* house in Tirzah. ¹⁰ And Zimri went in and struck him and killed him in the twenty-seventh year of Asa king of Judah, and reigned in his place.

¹¹ Then it came to pass, when he began to reign, as soon as he was seated on his throne, *that* he killed all the household of Baasha; he did not leave him one male, neither of his relatives nor of his friends. ¹² Thus Zimri destroyed all the household of Baasha, according to the word of the LORD, which He spoke against Baasha by Jehu the prophet, ¹³ for all the sins of Baasha and the sins of Elah his son, by which they had sinned and by which they had made Israel sin, in provoking the LORD God of Israel to anger with their idols.

¹⁴ Now the rest of the acts of Elah, and all that he did, *are* they not written in the book of the chronicles of the kings of Israel?

¹⁵ In the twenty-seventh year of Asa king of Judah, Zimri had reigned in Tirzah seven days. And the people *were* encamped against Gibbethon, which

belonged to the Philistines. ¹⁶ Now the people *who were* encamped heard it said, "Zimri has conspired and also has killed the king." So all Israel made Omri, the commander of the army, king over Israel that day in the camp. ¹⁷ Then Omri and all Israel with him went up from Gibbethon, and they besieged Tirzah. ¹⁸ And it happened, when Zimri saw that the city was taken, that he went into the citadel of the king's house and burned the king's house down upon himself with fire, and died, ¹⁹ because of the sins which he had committed in doing evil in the sight of the LORD, in walking in the way of Jeroboam, and in his sin which he had committed to make Israel sin.

²⁰ Now the rest of the acts of Zimri, and the treason he committed, *are* they not written in the book of the chronicles of the kings of Israel?

²¹ Then the people of Israel were divided into two parts: half of the people followed Tibni the son of Ginath, to make him king, and half followed Omri. ²² But the people who followed Omri prevailed over the people who followed Tibni the son of Ginath. So Tibni died and Omri reigned. ²³ In the thirty-first year of Asa king of Judah, Omri became king over Israel, *and reigned* twelve years. Six years he reigned in Tirzah. ²⁴ And he bought the hill of Samaria from Shemer for two talents of silver; then he built on the hill, and called the name of the city which he built, Samaria, after the name of Shemer, owner of the hill. ²⁵ Omri did evil in the eyes of the LORD, and did worse than all who *were* before him. ²⁶ For he walked in all the ways of Jeroboam the son of Nebat, and in his sin by which he had made Israel sin, provoking the LORD God of Israel to anger with their idols.

²⁷ Now the rest of the acts of Omri which he did, and the might that he showed, *are* they not written in the book of the chronicles of the kings of Israel?

²⁸ So Omri rested with his fathers and was buried in Samaria. Then Ahab his son reigned in his place.

²⁹ In the thirty-eighth year of Asa king of Judah, Ahab the son of Omri became king over Israel; and Ahab the son of Omri reigned over Israel in Samaria twenty-two years. ³⁰ Now Ahab the son of Omri did evil in the sight of the LORD, more than all who *were* before him. ³¹ And it came to pass, as though it had been a trivial thing for him to walk in the sins of Jeroboam the son of Nebat, that he took as wife Jezebel the daughter of Ethbaal, king of the Sidonians; and he went and served Baal and worshiped him. ³² Then he set up an altar for Baal in the temple of Baal, which he had built in Samaria. ³³ And Ahab made a wooden image. Ahab did more to provoke the LORD God of Israel to anger than all the kings of Israel who were before him. ³⁴ In his days Hiel of Bethel built Jericho. He laid its foundation with Abiram his firstborn, and with his youngest *son* Segub he set up its gates, according to the word of the LORD, which He had spoken through Joshua the son of Nun.

∼ PSALM 69:22–28 ∼

²² Let their table become a snare before them,
   And their well-being a trap.
²³ Let their eyes be darkened, so that they do not see;
   And make their loins shake continually.
²⁴ Pour out Your indignation upon them,
   And let Your wrathful anger take hold of them.
²⁵ Let their dwelling place be desolate;
   Let no one live in their tents.
²⁶ For they persecute the *ones* You have struck,
   And talk of the grief of those You have wounded.
²⁷ Add iniquity to their iniquity,
   And let them not come into Your righteousness.
²⁸ Let them be blotted out of the book of the living,
   And not be written with the righteous.

∼ PROVERBS 17:25, 26 ∼

²⁵ A foolish son *is* a grief to his father,
   And bitterness to her who bore him.

²⁶ Also, to punish the righteous *is* not good,

Nor to strike princes for *their*
uprightness.

~ JOHN 13:1–20 ~

Now before the Feast of the Passover,
when Jesus knew that His hour had come
that He should depart from this world
to the Father, having loved His own
who were in the world, He loved them to
the end. ² And supper being ended, the devil
having already put it into the heart of Judas Iscariot, Simon's *son,* to betray Him,
³ Jesus, knowing that the Father had giv-
en all things into His hands, and that He
had come from God and was going to
God, ⁴ rose from supper and laid aside His
garments, took a towel and girded Himself. ⁵ After that, He poured water into a
basin and began to wash the disciples' feet,
and to wipe *them* with the towel with
which He was girded. ⁶ Then He came
to Simon Peter. And *Peter* said to Him,
"Lord, are You washing my feet?"

⁷ Jesus answered and said to him, "What
I am doing you do not understand now,
but you will know after this."

⁸ Peter said to Him, "You shall never
wash my feet!"

Jesus answered him, "If I do not wash
you, you have no part with Me."

⁹ Simon Peter said to Him, "Lord, not
my feet only, but also *my* hands and *my*
head!"

¹⁰ Jesus said to him, "He who is bathed
needs only to wash *his* feet, but is completely clean; and you are clean, but not
all of you." ¹¹ For He knew who would
betray Him; therefore He said, "You are
not all clean."

¹² So when He had washed their feet,
taken His garments, and sat down again,
He said to them, "Do you know what I
have done to you? ¹³ You call Me Teacher
and Lord, and you say well, for *so* I am.
¹⁴ If I then, *your* Lord and Teacher, have
washed your feet, you also ought to wash
one another's feet. ¹⁵ For I have given you
an example, that you should do as I have
done to you. ¹⁶ Most assuredly, I say to
you, a servant is not greater than his master; nor is he who is sent greater than he
who sent him. ¹⁷ If you know these things,
blessed are you if you do them.

¹⁸ "I do not speak concerning all of you.
I know whom I have chosen; but that
the Scripture may be fulfilled, 'He who
eats bread with Me has lifted up his
heel against Me.' ¹⁹ Now I tell you before
it comes, that when it does come to
pass, you may believe that I am *He.*
²⁰ Most assuredly, I say to you, he who
receives whomever I send receives Me;
and he who receives Me receives Him who
sent Me."

READING 155 · JUNE 4

~ 1 KINGS 17:1—18:46 ~

And Elijah the Tishbite, of the inhabitants of Gilead, said to Ahab, "*As*
the LORD God of Israel lives, before whom I stand, there shall not be dew
nor rain these years, except at my word."
² Then the word of the LORD came to
him, saying, ³ "Get away from here and
turn eastward, and hide by the Brook
Cherith, which flows into the Jordan.
⁴ And it will be *that* you shall drink from
the brook, and I have commanded the
ravens to feed you there."

⁵ So he went and did according to the
word of the LORD, for he went and stayed
by the Brook Cherith, which flows into
the Jordan. ⁶ The ravens brought him
bread and meat in the morning, and bread
and meat in the evening; and he drank
from the brook. ⁷ And it happened after a
while that the brook dried up, because
there had been no rain in the land.

⁸ Then the word of the LORD came to
him, saying, ⁹ "Arise, go to Zarephath,
which *belongs* to Sidon, and dwell there.
See, I have commanded a widow there to
provide for you." ¹⁰ So he arose and went
to Zarephath. And when he came to the
gate of the city, indeed a widow *was* there
gathering sticks. And he called to her and
said, "Please bring me a little water in a
cup, that I may drink." ¹¹ And as she was
going to get *it,* he called to her and said,

Love Believes the Best

One of the most noble friendships in literature is that of Melanie and Scarlett O'Hara in Margaret Mitchell's classic, *Gone with the Wind*. Melanie is characterized as a woman who "always saw the best in everyone and remarked kindly upon it." Even when Scarlett tries to confess her shameful behavior toward Ashley, Melanie's husband, Melanie says, "Darling, I don't want any explanation. . . . Do you think I could remember you walking in a furrow behind that Yankee's horse almost barefooted and with your hands blistered — just so the baby and I could have something to eat — and then believe such dreadful things about you? I don't want to hear a word."

Melanie's refusal to believe, or even hear, ill of Scarlett leads Scarlett to passionately desire to "keep Melanie's high opinion. She only knew that she did not care what the world thought of her or what Ashley or Rhett thought of her, but Melanie must not think her other than she had always thought her." It is as Melanie lays dying that Scarlett faces her deep need for Melanie's pure and generous friendship: "Panic clutching at her heart, she knew that Melanie had been her sword and her shield, her comfort and her strength." In two words, Melanie had been her true friend.

A true friend loves at all times and always believes the best. Is that the kind of friend you want to have? Is that the kind of friend you aspire to be?

> A new commandment I give to you, that you love one another; as I have loved you, that you also love one another.
>
> *John 13:34*

"Please bring me a morsel of bread in your hand."

[12] So she said, "As the LORD your God lives, I do not have bread, only a handful of flour in a bin, and a little oil in a jar; and see, I *am* gathering a couple of sticks that I may go in and prepare it for myself and my son, that we may eat it, and die."

[13] And Elijah said to her, "Do not fear; go *and* do as you have said, but make me a small cake from it first, and bring *it* to me; and afterward make *some* for yourself and your son. [14] For thus says the LORD God of Israel: 'The bin of flour shall not be used up, nor shall the jar of oil run dry, until the day the LORD sends rain on the earth.' "

[15] So she went away and did according to the word of Elijah; and she and he and her household ate for *many* days. [16] The bin of flour was not used up, nor did the jar of oil run dry, according to the word of the LORD which He spoke by Elijah.

[17] Now it happened after these things *that* the son of the woman who owned the house became sick. And his sickness was so serious that there was no breath left in him. [18] So she said to Elijah, "What have I to do with you, O man of God? Have you come to me to bring my sin to remembrance, and to kill my son?"

[19] And he said to her, "Give me your son." So he took him out of her arms and carried him to the upper room where he was staying, and laid him on his own bed. [20] Then he cried out to the LORD and said, "O LORD my God, have You also brought tragedy on the widow with whom I lodge, by killing her son?" [21] And he stretched himself out on the child three times, and cried out to the LORD and said, "O LORD my God, I pray, let this child's soul come back to him." [22] Then the LORD heard the voice of Elijah; and the soul of the child came back to him, and he revived.

[23] And Elijah took the child and brought him down from the upper room into the house, and gave him to his mother. And Elijah said, "See, your son lives!"

[24] Then the woman said to Elijah, "Now by this I know that you *are* a man of God, *and* that the word of the LORD in your mouth *is* the truth."

18 And it came to pass *after* many days that the word of the LORD came to Elijah, in the third year, saying, "Go, present yourself to Ahab, and I will send rain on the earth."

[2] So Elijah went to present himself to Ahab; and *there was* a severe famine in Samaria. [3] And Ahab had called Obadiah, who *was* in charge of *his* house. (Now Obadiah feared the LORD greatly. [4] For so it was, while Jezebel massacred the prophets of the LORD, that Obadiah had taken one hundred prophets and hidden them, fifty to a cave, and had fed them with bread and water.) [5] And Ahab had said to Obadiah, "Go into the land to all the springs of water and to all the brooks; perhaps we may find grass to keep the horses and mules alive, so that we will not have to kill any livestock." [6] So they divided the land between them to explore it; Ahab went one way by himself, and Obadiah went another way by himself.

[7] Now as Obadiah was on his way, suddenly Elijah met him; and he recognized him, and fell on his face, and said, "*Is* that you, my lord Elijah?"

[8] And he answered him, "*It is* I. Go, tell your master, 'Elijah *is here*.' "

[9] So he said, "How have I sinned, that you are delivering your servant into the hand of Ahab, to kill me? [10] *As* the LORD your God lives, there is no nation or kingdom where my master has not sent someone to hunt for you; and when they said, '*He is* not *here*,' he took an oath from the kingdom or nation that they could not find you. [11] And now you say, 'Go, tell your master, "Elijah *is here*" '! [12] And it shall come to pass, *as soon as* I am gone from you, that the Spirit of the LORD will carry you to a place I do not know; so when I go and tell Ahab, and he cannot find you, he will kill me. But I your servant have feared the LORD from my youth. [13] Was it not reported to my lord what I did when Jezebel killed the prophets of the LORD, how I hid one hundred men of the LORD's prophets, fifty to a cave, and fed them with bread and water? [14] And now you say, 'Go, tell your master, "Elijah *is here*." ' He will kill me!"

[15] Then Elijah said, "*As* the LORD of

hosts lives, before whom I stand, I will surely present myself to him today."

¹⁶ So Obadiah went to meet Ahab, and told him; and Ahab went to meet Elijah.

¹⁷ Then it happened, when Ahab saw Elijah, that Ahab said to him, "Is that you, O troubler of Israel?"

¹⁸ And he answered, "I have not troubled Israel, but you and your father's house have, in that you have forsaken the commandments of the LORD and have followed the Baals. ¹⁹ Now therefore, send and gather all Israel to me on Mount Carmel, the four hundred and fifty prophets of Baal, and the four hundred prophets of Asherah, who eat at Jezebel's table."

²⁰ So Ahab sent for all the children of Israel, and gathered the prophets together on Mount Carmel. ²¹ And Elijah came to all the people, and said, "How long will you falter between two opinions? If the LORD is God, follow Him; but if Baal, follow him." But the people answered him not a word. ²² Then Elijah said to the people, "I alone am left a prophet of the LORD; but Baal's prophets are four hundred and fifty men. ²³ Therefore let them give us two bulls; and let them choose one bull for themselves, cut it in pieces, and lay it on the wood, but put no fire under it; and I will prepare the other bull, and lay it on the wood, but put no fire under it. ²⁴ Then you call on the name of your gods, and I will call on the name of the LORD; and the God who answers by fire, He is God."

So all the people answered and said, "It is well spoken."

²⁵ Now Elijah said to the prophets of Baal, "Choose one bull for yourselves and prepare it first, for you are many; and call on the name of your god, but put no fire under it."

²⁶ So they took the bull which was given them, and they prepared it, and called on the name of Baal from morning even till noon, saying, "O Baal, hear us!" But there was no voice; no one answered. Then they leaped about the altar which they had made.

²⁷ And so it was, at noon, that Elijah mocked them and said, "Cry aloud, for he is a god; either he is meditating, or he is busy, or he is on a journey, or perhaps he is sleeping and must be awakened."

²⁸ So they cried aloud, and cut themselves, as was their custom, with knives and lances, until the blood gushed out on them. ²⁹ And when midday was past, they prophesied until the time of the offering of the evening sacrifice. But there was no voice; no one answered, no one paid attention.

³⁰ Then Elijah said to all the people, "Come near to me." So all the people came near to him. And he repaired the altar of the LORD that was broken down. ³¹ And Elijah took twelve stones, according to the number of the tribes of the sons of Jacob, to whom the word of the LORD had come, saying, "Israel shall be your name." ³² Then with the stones he built an altar in the name of the LORD; and he made a trench around the altar large enough to hold two seahs of seed. ³³ And he put the wood in order, cut the bull in pieces, and laid it on the wood, and said, "Fill four waterpots with water, and pour it on the burnt sacrifice and on the wood." ³⁴ Then he said, "Do it a second time," and they did it a second time; and he said, "Do it a third time," and they did it a third time. ³⁵ So the water ran all around the altar; and he also filled the trench with water.

³⁶ And it came to pass, at the time of the offering of the evening sacrifice, that Elijah the prophet came near and said, "LORD God of Abraham, Isaac, and Israel, let it be known this day that You are God in Israel and I am Your servant, and that I have done all these things at Your word. ³⁷ Hear me, O LORD, hear me, that this people may know that You are the LORD God, and that You have turned their hearts back to You again."

³⁸ Then the fire of the LORD fell and consumed the burnt sacrifice, and the wood and the stones and the dust, and it licked up the water that was in the trench. ³⁹ Now when all the people saw it, they fell on their faces; and they said, "The LORD, He is God! The LORD, He is God!"

⁴⁰ And Elijah said to them, "Seize the prophets of Baal! Do not let one of them escape!" So they seized them; and Elijah brought them down to the Brook Kishon and executed them there.

⁴¹ Then Elijah said to Ahab, "Go up, eat and drink; for there is the sound of

abundance of rain." [42] So Ahab went up to eat and drink. And Elijah went up to the top of Carmel; then he bowed down on the ground, and put his face between his knees, [43] and said to his servant, "Go up now, look toward the sea."

So he went up and looked, and said, "*There is* nothing." And seven times he said, "Go again."

[44] Then it came to pass the seventh *time*, that he said, "There is a cloud, as small as a man's hand, rising out of the sea!" So he said, "Go up, say to Ahab, 'Prepare *your chariot*, and go down before the rain stops you.' "

[45] Now it happened in the meantime that the sky became black with clouds and wind, and there was a heavy rain. So Ahab rode away and went to Jezreel. [46] Then the hand of the LORD came upon Elijah; and he girded up his loins and ran ahead of Ahab to the entrance of Jezreel.

~ PSALM 69:29–36 ~

[29] But I *am* poor and sorrowful;
   Let Your salvation, O God, set me up on high.
[30] I will praise the name of God with a song,
   And will magnify Him with thanksgiving.
[31] *This* also shall please the LORD better than an ox *or* bull,
   Which has horns and hooves.
[32] The humble shall see *this and* be glad;
   And you who seek God, your hearts shall live.
[33] For the LORD hears the poor,
   And does not despise His prisoners.
[34] Let heaven and earth praise Him,
   The seas and everything that moves in them.
[35] For God will save Zion
   And build the cities of Judah,
   That they may dwell there and possess it.
[36] Also, the descendants of His servants shall inherit it,
   And those who love His name shall dwell in it.

~ PROVERBS 17:27, 28 ~

[27] He who has knowledge spares his words,
   And a man of understanding is of a calm spirit.
[28] Even a fool is counted wise when he holds his peace;
   When he shuts his lips, *he is considered* perceptive.

~ JOHN 13:21–38 ~

When Jesus had said these things, He was troubled in spirit, and testified and said, "Most assuredly, I say to you, one of you will betray Me." [22] Then the disciples looked at one another, perplexed about whom He spoke.

[23] Now there was leaning on Jesus' bosom one of His disciples, whom Jesus loved. [24] Simon Peter therefore motioned to him to ask who it was of whom He spoke.

[25] Then, leaning back on Jesus' breast, he said to Him, "Lord, who is it?"

[26] Jesus answered, "It is he to whom I shall give a piece of bread when I have dipped *it*." And having dipped the bread, He gave *it* to Judas Iscariot, *the son* of Simon. [27] Now after the piece of bread, Satan entered him. Then Jesus said to him, "What you do, do quickly." [28] But no one at the table knew for what reason He said this to him. [29] For some thought, because Judas had the money box, that Jesus had said to him, "Buy *those things* we need for the feast," or that he should give something to the poor.

[30] Having received the piece of bread, he then went out immediately. And it was night.

[31] So, when he had gone out, Jesus said, "Now the Son of Man is glorified, and God is glorified in Him. [32] If God is glorified in Him, God will also glorify Him in Himself, and glorify Him immediately. [33] Little children, I shall be with you a little while longer. You will seek Me; and as I said to the Jews, 'Where I am going, you cannot come,' so now I say to you. [34] A new commandment I give to you, that you love one another; as I have loved you, that you also love one another. [35] By this all

will know that you are My disciples, if you have love for one another."

³⁶ Simon Peter said to Him, "Lord, where are You going?"

Jesus answered him, "Where I am going you cannot follow Me now, but you shall follow Me afterward."

³⁷ Peter said to Him, "Lord, why can I not follow You now? I will lay down my life for Your sake."

³⁸ Jesus answered him, "Will you lay down your life for My sake? Most assuredly, I say to you, the rooster shall not crow till you have denied Me three times.

∼ 1 KINGS 19:1—20:43 ∼

And Ahab told Jezebel all that Elijah had done, also how he had executed all the prophets with the sword. ² Then Jezebel sent a messenger to Elijah, saying, "So let the gods do *to me,* and more also, if I do not make your life as the life of one of them by tomorrow about this time." ³ And when he saw *that,* he arose and ran for his life, and went to Beersheba, which *belongs* to Judah, and left his servant there.

⁴ But he himself went a day's journey into the wilderness, and came and sat down under a broom tree. And he prayed that he might die, and said, "It is enough! Now, LORD, take my life, for I *am* no better than my fathers!"

⁵ Then as he lay and slept under a broom tree, suddenly an angel touched him, and said to him, "Arise *and* eat." ⁶ Then he looked, and there by his head *was* a cake baked on coals, and a jar of water. So he ate and drank, and lay down again. ⁷ And the angel of the LORD came back the second time, and touched him, and said, "Arise *and* eat, because the journey *is* too great for you." ⁸ So he arose, and ate and drank; and he went in the strength of that food forty days and forty nights as far as Horeb, the mountain of God.

⁹ And there he went into a cave, and spent the night in that place; and behold, the word of the LORD *came* to him, and He said to him, "What are you doing here, Elijah?"

¹⁰ So he said, "I have been very zealous for the LORD God of hosts; for the children of Israel have forsaken Your covenant, torn down Your altars, and killed Your prophets with the sword. I alone am left; and they seek to take my life."

¹¹ Then He said, "Go out, and stand on the mountain before the LORD." And behold, the LORD passed by, and a great and strong wind tore into the mountains and broke the rocks in pieces before the LORD, *but* the LORD *was* not in the wind; and after the wind an earthquake, *but* the LORD *was* not in the earthquake; ¹² and after the earthquake a fire, *but* the LORD *was* not in the fire; and after the fire a still small voice.

¹³ So it was, when Elijah heard *it,* that he wrapped his face in his mantle and went out and stood in the entrance of the cave. Suddenly a voice *came* to him, and said, "What are you doing here, Elijah?"

¹⁴ And he said, "I have been very zealous for the LORD God of hosts; because the children of Israel have forsaken Your covenant, torn down Your altars, and killed Your prophets with the sword. I alone am left; and they seek to take my life."

¹⁵ Then the LORD said to him: "Go, return on your way to the Wilderness of Damascus; and when you arrive, anoint Hazael *as* king over Syria. ¹⁶ Also you shall anoint Jehu the son of Nimshi *as* king over Israel. And Elisha the son of Shaphat of Abel Meholah you shall anoint *as* prophet in your place. ¹⁷ It shall be *that* whoever escapes the sword of Hazael, Jehu will kill; and whoever escapes the sword of Jehu, Elisha will kill. ¹⁸ Yet I have reserved seven thousand in Israel, all whose knees have not bowed to Baal, and every mouth that has not kissed him."

¹⁹ So he departed from there, and found Elisha the son of Shaphat, who *was* plowing *with* twelve yoke *of oxen* before him, and he was with the twelfth. Then Elijah passed by him and threw his mantle on

him. ²⁰ And he left the oxen and ran after Elijah, and said, "Please let me kiss my father and my mother, and *then* I will follow you."

And he said to him, "Go back again, for what have I done to you?"

²¹ So *Elisha* turned back from him, and took a yoke of oxen and slaughtered them and boiled their flesh, using the oxen's equipment, and gave it to the people, and they ate. Then he arose and followed Elijah, and became his servant.

20
Now Ben-Hadad the king of Syria gathered all his forces together; thirty-two kings *were* with him, with horses and chariots. And he went up and besieged Samaria, and made war against it. ² Then he sent messengers into the city to Ahab king of Israel, and said to him, "Thus says Ben-Hadad: ³ 'Your silver and your gold *are* mine; your loveliest wives and children *are* mine.' "

⁴ And the king of Israel answered and said, "My lord, O king, just as you say, I and all that I have *are* yours."

⁵ Then the messengers came back and said, "Thus speaks Ben-Hadad, saying, 'Indeed I have sent to you, saying, "You shall deliver to me your silver and your gold, your wives and your children"; ⁶ but I will send my servants to you tomorrow about this time, and they shall search your house and the houses of your servants. And it shall be, *that* whatever is pleasant in your eyes, they will put *it* in their hands and take *it*.' "

⁷ So the king of Israel called all the elders of the land, and said, "Notice, please, and see how this *man* seeks trouble, for he sent to me for my wives, my children, my silver, and my gold; and I did not deny him."

⁸ And all the elders and all the people said to him, "Do not listen or consent."

⁹ Therefore he said to the messengers of Ben-Hadad, "Tell my lord the king, 'All that you sent for to your servant the first time I will do, but this thing I cannot do.' "

And the messengers departed and brought back word to him.

¹⁰ Then Ben-Hadad sent to him and said, "The gods do so to me, and more also, if enough dust is left of Samaria for a handful for each of the people who follow me."

¹¹ So the king of Israel answered and said, "Tell *him*, 'Let not the one who puts on *his* armor boast like the one who takes *it off*.' "

¹² And it happened when *Ben-Hadad* heard this message, as he and the kings *were* drinking at the command post, that he said to his servants, "Get ready." And they got ready to attack the city.

¹³ Suddenly a prophet approached Ahab king of Israel, saying, "Thus says the LORD: 'Have you seen all this great multitude? Behold, I will deliver it into your hand today, and you shall know that I *am* the LORD.' "

¹⁴ So Ahab said, "By whom?"

And he said, "Thus says the LORD: 'By the young leaders of the provinces.' "

Then he said, "Who will set the battle in order?"

And he answered, "You."

¹⁵ Then he mustered the young leaders of the provinces, and there were two hundred and thirty-two; and after them he mustered all the people, all the children of Israel—seven thousand.

¹⁶ So they went out at noon. Meanwhile Ben-Hadad and the thirty-two kings helping him were getting drunk at the command post. ¹⁷ The young leaders of the provinces went out first. And Ben-Hadad sent out *a patrol*, and they told him, saying, "Men are coming out of Samaria!" ¹⁸ So he said, "If they have come out for peace, take them alive; and if they have come out for war, take them alive."

¹⁹ Then these young leaders of the provinces went out of the city with the army which followed them. ²⁰ And each one killed his man; so the Syrians fled, and Israel pursued them; and Ben-Hadad the king of Syria escaped on a horse with the cavalry. ²¹ Then the king of Israel went out and attacked the horses and chariots, and killed the Syrians with a great slaughter.

²² And the prophet came to the king of Israel and said to him, "Go, strengthen yourself; take note, and see what you should do, for in the spring of the year the king of Syria will come up against you."

²³ Then the servants of the king of Syria said to him, "Their gods *are* gods of the

Relax

Fay Angus has said about prayer: "Without circumventing scriptural directionals, encouragements and admonitions . . . the bottom line of prayer is to pray. When we do, the power of heaven picks up momentum to change our lives.

"Much as we try to put Him there, God is not on trial; the good news is that neither is man. Jesus Christ stood in the docket on our behalf.

"If the answers to our prayers depended upon our worth, they would never be answered — they would never even be heard. Through the righteousness of Christ, they are.

"We tend to stroke prayer like a lucky rabbit's foot, and seek God's fleece rather than His face.

"We try to manipulate His will to ours and sometimes call it faith. We push forward in the arrogance of our own stoic determination, limited by our finite vision, rather than pull back in the simple trust of His infinite plan.

"We expect Him to change the sovereignty of His omnipotent heart, instead of humbly asking Him to give us a heart willing to be changed.

"'Be still, and know that I am God' (Psalm 46:10 KJV) means, 'Relax, let God be God.'"

> And whatever you ask in My name, that I will do, that the Father may be glorified in the Son.
>
> *John 14:13*

hills. Therefore they were stronger than we; but if we fight against them in the plain, surely we will be stronger than they. ²⁴ So do this thing: Dismiss the kings, each from his position, and put captains in their places; ²⁵ and you shall muster an army like the army that you have lost, horse for horse and chariot for chariot. Then we will fight against them in the plain; surely we will be stronger than they."

And he listened to their voice and did so. ²⁶ So it was, in the spring of the year, that Ben-Hadad mustered the Syrians and went up to Aphek to fight against Israel. ²⁷ And the children of Israel were mustered and given provisions, and they went against them. Now the children of Israel encamped before them like two little flocks of goats, while the Syrians filled the countryside.

²⁸ Then a man of God came and spoke to the king of Israel, and said, "Thus says the LORD: 'Because the Syrians have said, "The LORD *is* God of the hills, but He *is* not God of the valleys," therefore I will deliver all this great multitude into your hand, and you shall know that I *am* the LORD.' " ²⁹ And they encamped opposite each other for seven days. So it was that on the seventh day the battle was joined; and the children of Israel killed one hundred thousand foot soldiers *of* the Syrians in one day. ³⁰ But the rest fled to Aphek, into the city; then a wall fell on twenty-seven thousand of the men *who were* left.

And Ben-Hadad fled and went into the city, into an inner chamber. ³¹ Then his servants said to him, "Look now, we have heard that the kings of the house of Israel *are* merciful kings. Please, let us put sackcloth around our waists and ropes around our heads, and go out to the king of Israel; perhaps he will spare your life." ³² So they wore sackcloth around their waists and *put* ropes around their heads, and came to the king of Israel and said, "Your servant Ben-Hadad says, 'Please let me live.' "

And he said, "*Is* he still alive? He *is* my brother."

³³ Now the men were watching closely to see whether *any sign of mercy would come* from him; and they quickly grasped *at this word* and said, "Your brother Ben-Hadad."

So he said, "Go, bring him." Then Ben-Hadad came out to him; and he had him come up into the chariot.

³⁴ So *Ben-Hadad* said to him, "The cities which my father took from your father I will restore; and you may set up marketplaces for yourself in Damascus, as my father did in Samaria."

Then *Ahab said,* "I will send you away with this treaty." So he made a treaty with him and sent him away.

³⁵ Now a certain man of the sons of the prophets said to his neighbor by the word of the LORD, "Strike me, please." And the man refused to strike him. ³⁶ Then he said to him, "Because you have not obeyed the voice of the LORD, surely, as soon as you depart from me, a lion shall kill you." And as soon as he left him, a lion found him and killed him.

³⁷ And he found another man, and said, "Strike me, please." So the man struck him, inflicting a wound. ³⁸ Then the prophet departed and waited for the king by the road, and disguised himself with a bandage over his eyes. ³⁹ Now as the king passed by, he cried out to the king and said, "Your servant went out into the midst of the battle; and there, a man came over and brought a man to me, and said, 'Guard this man; if by any means he is missing, your life shall be for his life, or else you shall pay a talent of silver.' ⁴⁰ While your servant was busy here and there, he was gone."

Then the king of Israel said to him, "So *shall* your judgment *be;* you yourself have decided *it.*"

⁴¹ And he hastened to take the bandage away from his eyes; and the king of Israel recognized him as one of the prophets. ⁴² Then he said to him, "Thus says the LORD: 'Because you have let slip out of *your* hand a man whom I appointed to utter destruction, therefore your life shall go for his life, and your people for his people.' "

⁴³ So the king of Israel went to his house sullen and displeased, and came to Samaria.

∼ PSALM 70:1–5 ∼

¹ *Make haste*, O God, to deliver me!
Make haste to help me, O LORD!

2 Let them be ashamed and
   confounded
   Who seek my life;
   Let them be turned back and
   confused
   Who desire my hurt.
3 Let them be turned back because of
   their shame,
   Who say, "Aha, aha!"

4 Let all those who seek You rejoice
   and be glad in You;
   And let those who love Your
   salvation say continually,
   "Let God be magnified!"

5 But I *am* poor and needy;
   Make haste to me, O God!
   You *are* my help and my deliverer;
   O LORD, do not delay.

~ PROVERBS 18:1, 2 ~

1 A man who isolates himself seeks his
   own desire;
   He rages against all wise judgment.

2 A fool has no delight in
   understanding,
   But in expressing his own heart.

~ JOHN 14:1–31 ~

"Let not your heart be troubled; you believe in God, believe also in Me. ² In My
Father's house are many mansions; if *it
were* not *so,* I would have told you. I go
to prepare a place for you. ³ And if I
go and prepare a place for you, I will come
again and receive you to Myself; that
where I am, *there* you may be also.
⁴ And where I go you know, and the way
you know."
⁵ Thomas said to Him, "Lord, we do
not know where You are going, and how
can we know the way?"
⁶ Jesus said to him, "I am the way, the
truth, and the life. No one comes to
the Father except through Me.
⁷ "If you had known Me, you would
have known My Father also; and from
now on you know Him and have seen
Him."
⁸ Philip said to Him, "Lord, show us
the Father, and it is sufficient for us."

⁹ Jesus said to him, "Have I been with
you so long, and yet you have not known
Me, Philip? He who has seen Me has seen
the Father; so how can you say, 'Show
us the Father'? ¹⁰ Do you not believe that
I am in the Father, and the Father in Me?
The words that I speak to you I do not
speak on My own *authority;* but the Father who dwells in Me does the works.
¹¹ Believe Me that I *am* in the Father and
the Father in Me, or else believe Me
for the sake of the works themselves.
¹² "Most assuredly, I say to you, he who
believes in Me, the works that I do he
will do also; and greater *works* than these
he will do, because I go to My Father.
¹³ And whatever you ask in My name, that
I will do, that the Father may be glorified
in the Son. ¹⁴ If you ask anything in My
name, I will do *it.*
¹⁵ "If you love Me, keep My commandments. ¹⁶ And I will pray the Father, and
He will give you another Helper, that He
may abide with you forever— ¹⁷ the Spirit
of truth, whom the world cannot receive,
because it neither sees Him nor knows
Him; but you know Him, for He dwells
with you and will be in you. ¹⁸ I will not
leave you orphans; I will come to you.
¹⁹ "A little while longer and the world
will see Me no more, but you will see Me.
Because I live, you will live also. ²⁰ At that
day you will know that I *am* in My Father, and you in Me, and I in you. ²¹ He
who has My commandments and keeps
them, it is he who loves Me. And he who
loves Me will be loved by My Father,
and I will love him and manifest Myself
to him."
²² Judas (not Iscariot) said to Him,
"Lord, how is it that You will manifest
Yourself to us, and not to the world?"
²³ Jesus answered and said to him, "If
anyone loves Me, he will keep My word;
and My Father will love him, and We will
come to him and make Our home with
him. ²⁴ He who does not love Me does
not keep My words; and the word which
you hear is not Mine but the Father's who
sent Me.
²⁵ "These things I have spoken to you
while being present with you. ²⁶ But the
Helper, the Holy Spirit, whom the Father
will send in My name, He will teach you
all things, and bring to your remembrance

all things that I said to you. ²⁷ Peace I leave with you, My peace I give to you; not as the world gives do I give to you. Let not your heart be troubled, neither let it be afraid. ²⁸ You have heard Me say to you, 'I am going away and coming *back* to you.' If you loved Me, you would rejoice because I said, 'I am going to the Father,' for My Father is greater than I.

²⁹ "And now I have told you before it comes, that when it does come to pass, you may believe. ³⁰ I will no longer talk much with you, for the ruler of this world is coming, and he has nothing in Me. ³¹ But that the world may know that I love the Father, and as the Father gave Me commandment, so I do. Arise, let us go from here.

READING 157 · JUNE 6

∼ 1 KINGS 21:1—22:53 ∼

And it came to pass after these things *that* Naboth the Jezreelite had a vineyard which *was* in Jezreel, next to the palace of Ahab king of Samaria. ² So Ahab spoke to Naboth, saying, "Give me your vineyard, that I may have it for a vegetable garden, because it *is* near, next to my house; and for it I will give you a vineyard better than it. *Or,* if it seems good to you, I will give you its worth in money."

³ But Naboth said to Ahab, "The LORD forbid that I should give the inheritance of my fathers to you!"

⁴ So Ahab went into his house sullen and displeased because of the word which Naboth the Jezreelite had spoken to him; for he had said, "I will not give you the inheritance of my fathers." And he lay down on his bed, and turned away his face, and would eat no food. ⁵ But Jezebel his wife came to him, and said to him, "Why is your spirit so sullen that you eat no food?"

⁶ He said to her, "Because I spoke to Naboth the Jezreelite, and said to him, 'Give me your vineyard for money; or else, if it pleases you, I will give you *another* vineyard for it.' And he answered, 'I will not give you my vineyard.' "

⁷ Then Jezebel his wife said to him, "You now exercise authority over Israel! Arise, eat food, and let your heart be cheerful; I will give you the vineyard of Naboth the Jezreelite."

⁸ And she wrote letters in Ahab's name, sealed *them* with his seal, and sent the letters to the elders and the nobles who *were* dwelling in the city with Naboth. ⁹ She wrote in the letters, saying,

Proclaim a fast, and seat Naboth with high honor among the people; ¹⁰ and seat two men, scoundrels, before him to bear witness against him, saying, You have blasphemed God and the king. *Then* take him out, and stone him, that he may die.

¹¹ So the men of his city, the elders and nobles who were inhabitants of his city, did as Jezebel had sent to them, as it *was* written in the letters which she had sent to them. ¹² They proclaimed a fast, and seated Naboth with high honor among the people. ¹³ And two men, scoundrels, came in and sat before him; and the scoundrels witnessed against him, against Naboth, in the presence of the people, saying, "Naboth has blasphemed God and the king!" Then they took him outside the city and stoned him with stones, so that he died. ¹⁴ Then they sent to Jezebel, saying, "Naboth has been stoned and is dead."

¹⁵ And it came to pass, when Jezebel heard that Naboth had been stoned and was dead, that Jezebel said to Ahab, "Arise, take possession of the vineyard of Naboth the Jezreelite, which he refused to give you for money; for Naboth is not alive, but dead." ¹⁶ So it was, when Ahab heard that Naboth was dead, that Ahab got up and went down to take possession of the vineyard of Naboth the Jezreelite.

¹⁷ Then the word of the LORD came to Elijah the Tishbite, saying, ¹⁸ "Arise, go down to meet Ahab king of Israel, who *lives* in Samaria. There *he is,* in the vineyard of Naboth, where he has gone down

Loving Sacrifice

A number of years ago, a young mother was making her way across the hills of South Wales on foot, carrying her tiny baby in her arms. The wintry winds were blowing stronger than she anticipated and her journey taking much longer than she had planned. Eventually, she was overtaken by a blinding blizzard.

The woman never reached her destination. When the blizzard had subsided, those expecting her arrival went in search of her. After hours of searching, they finally found her body underneath a mound of snow.

As they shoveled the snow away from her frozen corpse, they were amazed to see that she had taken off her outer clothing. When they finally lifted her body away from the ground, they discovered the reason why. This brave and self-sacrificing young mother had wrapped her own cloak and scarf around her baby and then huddled over her child. When the searchers unwrapped the child, they found to their great surprise and joy that he was alive and well!

Years later, that child, David Lloyd George, became prime minister of Great Britain, and is regarded as one of England's greatest statesmen.

Is any sacrifice too great?

to take possession of it. ¹⁹ You shall speak to him, saying, 'Thus says the LORD: "Have you murdered and also taken possession?" ' And you shall speak to him, saying, 'Thus says the LORD: "In the place where dogs licked the blood of Naboth, dogs shall lick your blood, even yours." ' "

²⁰ So Ahab said to Elijah, "Have you found me, O my enemy?"

And he answered, "I have found *you,* because you have sold yourself to do evil in the sight of the LORD: ²¹ 'Behold, I will bring calamity on you. I will take away your posterity, and will cut off from Ahab every male in Israel, both bond and free. ²² I will make your house like the house of Jeroboam the son of Nebat, and like the house of Baasha the son of Ahijah, because of the provocation with which you have provoked *Me* to anger, and made Israel sin.' ²³ And concerning Jezebel the LORD also spoke, saying, 'The dogs shall eat Jezebel by the wall of Jezreel.' ²⁴ The dogs shall eat whoever belongs to Ahab and dies in the city, and the birds of the air shall eat whoever dies in the field."

²⁵ But there was no one like Ahab who sold himself to do wickedness in the sight of the LORD, because Jezebel his wife stirred him up. ²⁶ And he behaved very abominably in following idols, according to all *that* the Amorites had done, whom the LORD had cast out before the children of Israel.

²⁷ So it was, when Ahab heard those words, that he tore his clothes and put sackcloth on his body, and fasted and lay in sackcloth, and went about mourning.

²⁸ And the word of the LORD came to Elijah the Tishbite, saying, ²⁹ "See how Ahab has humbled himself before Me? Because he has humbled himself before Me, I will not bring the calamity in his days. In the days of his son I will bring the calamity on his house."

22 Now three years passed without war between Syria and Israel. ² Then it came to pass, in the third year, that Jehoshaphat the king of Judah went down to *visit* the king of Israel.

³ And the king of Israel said to his servants, "Do you know that Ramoth in Gilead *is* ours, but we hesitate to take it out of the hand of the king of Syria?" ⁴ So he said to Jehoshaphat, "Will you go with me to fight at Ramoth Gilead?"

Jehoshaphat said to the king of Israel, "I *am* as you *are,* my people as your people, my horses as your horses." ⁵ Also Jehoshaphat said to the king of Israel, "Please inquire for the word of the LORD today."

⁶ Then the king of Israel gathered the prophets together, about four hundred men, and said to them, "Shall I go against Ramoth Gilead to fight, or shall I refrain?"

So they said, "Go up, for the Lord will deliver *it* into the hand of the king."

⁷ And Jehoshaphat said, "*Is there* not still a prophet of the LORD here, that we may inquire of Him?"

⁸ So the king of Israel said to Jehoshaphat, "*There is* still one man, Micaiah the son of Imlah, by whom we may inquire of the LORD; but I hate him, because he does not prophesy good concerning me, but evil."

And Jehoshaphat said, "Let not the king say such things!"

⁹ Then the king of Israel called an officer and said, "Bring Micaiah the son of Imlah quickly!"

¹⁰ The king of Israel and Jehoshaphat the king of Judah, having put on *their* robes, sat each on his throne, at a threshing floor at the entrance of the gate of Samaria; and all the prophets prophesied before them. ¹¹ Now Zedekiah the son of Chenaanah had made horns of iron for himself; and he said, "Thus says the LORD: 'With these you shall gore the Syrians until they are destroyed.' " ¹² And all the prophets prophesied so, saying, "Go up to Ramoth Gilead and prosper, for the LORD will deliver *it* into the king's hand."

¹³ Then the messenger who had gone to call Micaiah spoke to him, saying, "Now listen, the words of the prophets with one accord encourage the king. Please, let your word be like the word of one of them, and speak encouragement."

¹⁴ And Micaiah said, "*As* the LORD lives, whatever the LORD says to me, that I will speak."

¹⁵ Then he came to the king; and the king said to him, "Micaiah, shall we go to war against Ramoth Gilead, or shall we refrain?"

And he answered him, "Go and

prosper, for the LORD will deliver *it* into the hand of the king!"

¹⁶ So the king said to him, "How many times shall I make you swear that you tell me nothing but the truth in the name of the LORD?"

¹⁷ Then he said, "I saw all Israel scattered on the mountains, as sheep that have no shepherd. And the LORD said, 'These have no master. Let each return to his house in peace.' "

¹⁸ And the king of Israel said to Jehoshaphat, "Did I not tell you he would not prophesy good concerning me, but evil?"

¹⁹ Then *Micaiah* said, "Therefore hear the word of the LORD: I saw the LORD sitting on His throne, and all the host of heaven standing by, on His right hand and on His left. ²⁰ And the LORD said, 'Who will persuade Ahab to go up, that he may fall at Ramoth Gilead?' So one spoke in this manner, and another spoke in that manner. ²¹ Then a spirit came forward and stood before the LORD, and said, 'I will persuade him.' ²² The LORD said to him, 'In what way?' So he said, 'I will go out and be a lying spirit in the mouth of all his prophets.' And the LORD said, 'You shall persuade *him,* and also prevail. Go out and do so.' ²³ Therefore look! The LORD has put a lying spirit in the mouth of all these prophets of yours, and the LORD has declared disaster against you."

²⁴ Now Zedekiah the son of Chenaanah went near and struck Micaiah on the cheek, and said, "Which way did the spirit from the LORD go from me to speak to you?"

²⁵ And Micaiah said, "Indeed, you shall see on that day when you go into an inner chamber to hide!"

²⁶ So the king of Israel said, "Take Micaiah, and return him to Amon the governor of the city and to Joash the king's son; ²⁷ and say, 'Thus says the king: "Put this *fellow* in prison, and feed him with bread of affliction and water of affliction, until I come in peace." ' "

²⁸ But Micaiah said, "If you ever return in peace, the LORD has not spoken by me." And he said, "Take heed, all you people!"

²⁹ So the king of Israel and Jehoshaphat the king of Judah went up to Ramoth Gilead. ³⁰ And the king of Israel said to Jehoshaphat, "I will disguise myself and go into battle; but you put on your robes." So the king of Israel disguised himself and went into battle.

³¹ Now the king of Syria had commanded the thirty-two captains of his chariots, saying, "Fight with no one small or great, but only with the king of Israel." ³² So it was, when the captains of the chariots saw Jehoshaphat, that they said, "Surely it *is* the king of Israel!" Therefore they turned aside to fight against him, and Jehoshaphat cried out. ³³ And it happened, when the captains of the chariots saw that it *was* not the king of Israel, that they turned back from pursuing him. ³⁴ Now a *certain* man drew a bow at random, and struck the king of Israel between the joints of his armor. So he said to the driver of his chariot, "Turn around and take me out of the battle, for I am wounded."

³⁵ The battle increased that day; and the king was propped up in his chariot, facing the Syrians, and died at evening. The blood ran out from the wound onto the floor of the chariot. ³⁶ Then, as the sun was going down, a shout went throughout the army, saying, "Every man to his city, and every man to his own country!"

³⁷ So the king died, and was brought to Samaria. And they buried the king in Samaria. ³⁸ Then *someone* washed the chariot at a pool in Samaria, and the dogs licked up his blood while the harlots bathed, according to the word of the LORD which He had spoken.

³⁹ Now the rest of the acts of Ahab, and all that he did, the ivory house which he built and all the cities that he built, *are* they not written in the book of the chronicles of the kings of Israel? ⁴⁰ So Ahab rested with his fathers. Then Ahaziah his son reigned in his place.

⁴¹ Jehoshaphat the son of Asa had become king over Judah in the fourth year of Ahab king of Israel. ⁴² Jehoshaphat *was* thirty-five years old when he became king, and he reigned twenty-five years in Jerusalem. His mother's name *was* Azubah the daughter of Shilhi. ⁴³ And he walked in all the ways of his father Asa. He did not turn aside from them, doing *what was* right in the eyes of the LORD. Nevertheless the high places were not taken away,

for the people offered sacrifices and burned incense on the high places. ⁴⁴ Also Jehoshaphat made peace with the king of Israel.

⁴⁵ Now the rest of the acts of Jehoshaphat, the might that he showed, and how he made war, *are* they not written in the book of the chronicles of the kings of Judah? ⁴⁶ And the rest of the perverted persons, who remained in the days of his father Asa, he banished from the land. ⁴⁷ *There was* then no king in Edom, only a deputy of the king.

⁴⁸ Jehoshaphat made merchant ships to go to Ophir for gold; but they never sailed, for the ships were wrecked at Ezion Geber. ⁴⁹ Then Ahaziah the son of Ahab said to Jehoshaphat, "Let my servants go with your servants in the ships." But Jehoshaphat would not.

⁵⁰ And Jehoshaphat rested with his fathers, and was buried with his fathers in the City of David his father. Then Jehoram his son reigned in his place.

⁵¹ Ahaziah the son of Ahab became king over Israel in Samaria in the seventeenth year of Jehoshaphat king of Judah, and reigned two years over Israel. ⁵² He did evil in the sight of the LORD, and walked in the way of his father and in the way of his mother and in the way of Jeroboam the son of Nebat, who had made Israel sin; ⁵³ for he served Baal and worshiped him, and provoked the LORD God of Israel to anger, according to all that his father had done.

∼ PSALM 71:1–8 ∼

1 In You, O LORD, I put my trust;
    Let me never be put to shame.
2 Deliver me in Your righteousness,
        and cause me to escape;
    Incline Your ear to me, and save me.
3 Be my strong refuge,
    To which I may resort continually;
    You have given the commandment to
        save me,
    For You *are* my rock and my fortress.

4 Deliver me, O my God, out of the
        hand of the wicked,
    Out of the hand of the unrighteous
        and cruel man.
5 For You are my hope, O Lord GOD;

You are my trust from my youth.
6 By You I have been upheld from
        birth;
    You are He who took me out of my
        mother's womb.
    My praise *shall be* continually of
        You.

7 I have become as a wonder to many,
    But You *are* my strong refuge.
8 Let my mouth be filled *with* Your
        praise
    And with Your glory all the day.

∼ PROVERBS 18:3–5 ∼

3 When the wicked comes, contempt
        comes also;
    And with dishonor *comes* reproach.

4 The words of a man's mouth *are*
        deep waters;
    The wellspring of wisdom *is* a
        flowing brook.

5 *It is* not good to show partiality to
        the wicked,
    Or to overthrow the righteous in
        judgment.

∼ JOHN 15:1–27 ∼

"I am the true vine, and My Father is the vinedresser. ² Every branch in Me that does not bear fruit He takes away; and every *branch* that bears fruit He prunes, that it may bear more fruit. ³ You are already clean because of the word which I have spoken to you. ⁴ Abide in Me, and I in you. As the branch cannot bear fruit of itself, unless it abides in the vine, neither can you, unless you abide in Me.

⁵ "I am the vine, you *are* the branches. He who abides in Me, and I in him, bears much fruit; for without Me you can do nothing. ⁶ If anyone does not abide in Me, he is cast out as a branch and is withered; and they gather them and throw *them* into the fire, and they are burned. ⁷ If you abide in Me, and My words abide in you, you will ask what you desire, and it shall be done for you. ⁸ By this My Father is glorified, that you bear much fruit; so you will be My disciples.

⁹ "As the Father loved Me, I also have loved you; abide in My love. ¹⁰ If you keep My commandments, you will abide in My love, just as I have kept My Father's commandments and abide in His love.

¹¹ "These things I have spoken to you, that My joy may remain in you, and *that* your joy may be full. ¹² This is My commandment, that you love one another as I have loved you. ¹³ Greater love has no one than this, than to lay down one's life for his friends. ¹⁴ You are My friends if you do whatever I command you. ¹⁵ No longer do I call you servants, for a servant does not know what his master is doing; but I have called you friends, for all things that I heard from My Father I have made known to you. ¹⁶ You did not choose Me, but I chose you and appointed you that you should go and bear fruit, and *that* your fruit should remain, that whatever you ask the Father in My name He may give you. ¹⁷ These things I command you, that you love one another.

¹⁸ "If the world hates you, you know that it hated Me before *it hated* you. ¹⁹ If you were of the world, the world would love its own. Yet because you are not of the world, but I chose you out of the world, therefore the world hates you. ²⁰ Remember the word that I said to you, 'A servant is not greater than his master.' If they persecuted Me, they will also persecute you. If they kept My word, they will keep yours also. ²¹ But all these things they will do to you for My name's sake, because they do not know Him who sent Me. ²² If I had not come and spoken to them, they would have no sin, but now they have no excuse for their sin. ²³ He who hates Me hates My Father also. ²⁴ If I had not done among them the works which no one else did, they would have no sin; but now they have seen and also hated both Me and My Father. ²⁵ But *this happened* that the word might be fulfilled which is written in their law, 'They hated Me without a cause.'

²⁶ "But when the Helper comes, whom I shall send to you from the Father, the Spirit of truth who proceeds from the Father, He will testify of Me. ²⁷ And you also will bear witness, because you have been with Me from the beginning.

∼ 2 KINGS 1:1—2:25 ∼

Moab rebelled against Israel after the death of Ahab.

² Now Ahaziah fell through the lattice of his upper room in Samaria, and was injured; so he sent messengers and said to them, "Go, inquire of Baal-Zebub, the god of Ekron, whether I shall recover from this injury." ³ But the angel of the LORD said to Elijah the Tishbite, "Arise, go up to meet the messengers of the king of Samaria, and say to them, 'Is it because *there is* no God in Israel *that* you are going to inquire of Baal-Zebub, the god of Ekron?' ⁴ Now therefore, thus says the LORD: 'You shall not come down from the bed to which you have gone up, but you shall surely die.' " So Elijah departed.

⁵ And when the messengers returned to him, he said to them, "Why have you come back?"

⁶ So they said to him, "A man came up to meet us, and said to us, 'Go, return to the king who sent you, and say to him, "Thus says the LORD: 'Is it because *there* is no God in Israel *that* you are sending to inquire of Baal-Zebub, the god of Ekron? Therefore you shall not come down from the bed to which you have gone up, but you shall surely die.' " ' "

⁷ Then he said to them, "What kind of man *was it* who came up to meet you and told you these words?"

⁸ So they answered him, "A hairy man wearing a leather belt around his waist."

And he said, "It *is* Elijah the Tishbite."

⁹ Then the king sent to him a captain of fifty with his fifty men. So he went up to him; and there he was, sitting on the top of a hill. And he spoke to him: "Man of God, the king has said, 'Come down!' "

[10] So Elijah answered and said to the captain of fifty, "If I *am* a man of God, then let fire come down from heaven and consume you and your fifty men." And fire came down from heaven and consumed him and his fifty. [11] Then he sent to him another captain of fifty with his fifty men.

And he answered and said to him: "Man of God, thus has the king said, 'Come down quickly!' "

[12] So Elijah answered and said to them, "If I *am* a man of God, let fire come down from heaven and consume you and your fifty men." And the fire of God came down from heaven and consumed him and his fifty.

[13] Again, he sent a third captain of fifty with his fifty men. And the third captain of fifty went up, and came and fell on his knees before Elijah, and pleaded with him, and said to him: "Man of God, please let my life and the life of these fifty servants of yours be precious in your sight. [14] Look, fire has come down from heaven and burned up the first two captains of fifties with their fifties. But let my life now be precious in your sight."

[15] And the angel of the LORD said to Elijah, "Go down with him; do not be afraid of him." So he arose and went down with him to the king. [16] Then he said to him, "Thus says the LORD: 'Because you have sent messengers to inquire of Baal-Zebub, the god of Ekron, *is it* because *there is* no God in Israel to inquire of His word? Therefore you shall not come down from the bed to which you have gone up, but you shall surely die.' "

[17] So *Ahaziah* died according to the word of the LORD which Elijah had spoken. Because he had no son, Jehoram became king in his place, in the second year of Jehoram the son of Jehoshaphat, king of Judah.

[18] Now the rest of the acts of Ahaziah which he did, *are* they not written in the book of the chronicles of the kings of Israel?

2 And it came to pass, when the LORD was about to take up Elijah into heaven by a whirlwind, that Elijah went with Elisha from Gilgal. [2] Then Elijah said to Elisha, "Stay here, please, for the LORD has sent me on to Bethel."

But Elisha said, "*As* the LORD lives, and *as* your soul lives, I will not leave you!" So they went down to Bethel.

[3] Now the sons of the prophets who *were* at Bethel came out to Elisha, and said to him, "Do you know that the LORD will take away your master from over you today?"

And he said, "Yes, I know; keep silent!"

[4] Then Elijah said to him, "Elisha, stay here, please, for the LORD has sent me on to Jericho."

But he said, "*As* the LORD lives, and *as* your soul lives, I will not leave you!" So they came to Jericho.

[5] Now the sons of the prophets who *were* at Jericho came to Elisha and said to him, "Do you know that the LORD will take away your master from over you today?"

So he answered, "Yes, I know; keep silent!"

[6] Then Elijah said to him, "Stay here, please, for the LORD has sent me on to the Jordan."

But he said, "*As* the LORD lives, and *as* your soul lives, I will not leave you!" So the two of them went on. [7] And fifty men of the sons of the prophets went and stood facing *them* at a distance, while the two of them stood by the Jordan. [8] Now Elijah took his mantle, rolled *it* up, and struck the water; and it was divided this way and that, so that the two of them crossed over on dry ground.

[9] And so it was, when they had crossed over, that Elijah said to Elisha, "Ask! What may I do for you, before I am taken away from you?"

Elisha said, "Please let a double portion of your spirit be upon me."

[10] So he said, "You have asked a hard thing. *Nevertheless*, if you see me *when I am* taken from you, it shall be so for you; but if not, it shall not be *so*." [11] Then it happened, as they continued on and talked, that suddenly a chariot of fire *appeared* with horses of fire, and separated the two of them; and Elijah went up by a whirlwind into heaven.

[12] And Elisha saw *it*, and he cried out, "My father, my father, the chariot of Israel and its horsemen!" So he saw him no more. And he took hold of his own clothes and tore them into two pieces. [13] He also

Theodore?

What surely must have been one of the most frustrating conversations in history was reported in *Theatre Arts* magazine. A subscriber, desiring to report on a particular upcoming event in his community, dialed Information to get the magazine's telephone number.

The operator drawled, "Sorry, but there is nobody listed by the name of 'Theodore Arts.'"

The subscriber insisted: "It's not a person; it's a publication. I want Theatre Arts."

The operator responded, this time a little louder. "I told you, we have no listing for Theodore Arts in this city. Perhaps he lives in another city."

By now the subscriber was thoroughly peeved. "Confound it, the word is Theatre: T-H-E-A-T-R-E!"

The operator came back with certainty in her voice, "That — is not the way to spell Theodore."

Sometimes there's just no communicating with someone who refuses to hear you, who seems unwilling to understand your point of view, or who simply "doesn't get" what you are trying to say. Rather than give that person a real kick, however, it's better to hang up and try dialing someone who can hear you and understand!

took up the mantle of Elijah that had fallen from him, and went back and stood by the bank of the Jordan. [14] Then he took the mantle of Elijah that had fallen from him, and struck the water, and said, "Where *is* the LORD God of Elijah?" And when he also had struck the water, it was divided this way and that; and Elisha crossed over.

[15] Now when the sons of the prophets who *were* from Jericho saw him, they said, "The spirit of Elijah rests on Elisha." And they came to meet him, and bowed to the ground before him. [16] Then they said to him, "Look now, there are fifty strong men with your servants. Please let them go and search for your master, lest perhaps the Spirit of the LORD has taken him up and cast him upon some mountain or into some valley."

And he said, "You shall not send anyone."

[17] But when they urged him till he was ashamed, he said, "Send *them*!" Therefore they sent fifty men, and they searched for three days but did not find him. [18] And when they came back to him, for he had stayed in Jericho, he said to them, "Did I not say to you, 'Do not go'?"

[19] Then the men of the city said to Elisha, "Please notice, the situation of this city *is* pleasant, as my lord sees; but the water *is* bad, and the ground barren."

[20] And he said, "Bring me a new bowl, and put salt in it." So they brought *it* to him. [21] Then he went out to the source of the water, and cast in the salt there, and said, "Thus says the LORD: 'I have healed this water; from it there shall be no more death or barrenness.' " [22] So the water remains healed to this day, according to the word of Elisha which he spoke.

[23] Then he went up from there to Bethel; and as he was going up the road, some youths came from the city and mocked him, and said to him, "Go up, you baldhead! Go up, you baldhead!"

[24] So he turned around and looked at them, and pronounced a curse on them in the name of the LORD. And two female bears came out of the woods and mauled forty-two of the youths.

[25] Then he went from there to Mount Carmel, and from there he returned to Samaria.

~ PSALM 71:9–16 ~

[9] Do not cast me off in the time of old age;
Do not forsake me when my strength fails.
[10] For my enemies speak against me;
And those who lie in wait for my life take counsel together,
[11] Saying, "God has forsaken him;
Pursue and take him, for *there is* none to deliver *him.*"

[12] O God, do not be far from me;
O my God, make haste to help me!
[13] Let them be confounded *and* consumed
Who are adversaries of my life;
Let them be covered *with* reproach and dishonor
Who seek my hurt.

[14] But I will hope continually,
And will praise You yet more and more.
[15] My mouth shall tell of Your righteousness
And Your salvation all the day,
For I do not know *their* limits.
[16] I will go in the strength of the Lord GOD;
I will make mention of Your righteousness, of Yours only.

~ PROVERBS 18:6–8 ~

[6] A fool's lips enter into contention,
And his mouth calls for blows.
[7] A fool's mouth *is* his destruction,
And his lips *are* the snare of his soul.
[8] The words of a talebearer *are* like tasty trifles,
And they go down into the inmost body.

~ JOHN 16:1–33 ~

"These things I have spoken to you, that you should not be made to stumble. [2] They will put you out of the synagogues; yes, the time is coming that whoever kills you will think that he offers God service. [3] And these things they will do to you because they have not known the Father nor Me.

[4] But these things I have told you, that when the time comes, you may remember that I told you of them.

"And these things I did not say to you at the beginning, because I was with you.

[5] "But now I go away to Him who sent Me, and none of you asks Me, 'Where are You going?' [6] But because I have said these things to you, sorrow has filled your heart. [7] Nevertheless I tell you the truth. It is to your advantage that I go away; for if I do not go away, the Helper will not come to you; but if I depart, I will send Him to you. [8] And when He has come, He will convict the world of sin, and of righteousness, and of judgment: [9] of sin, because they do not believe in Me; [10] of righteousness, because I go to My Father and you see Me no more; [11] of judgment, because the ruler of this world is judged.

[12] "I still have many things to say to you, but you cannot bear *them* now. [13] However, when He, the Spirit of truth, has come, He will guide you into all truth; for He will not speak on His own *authority,* but whatever He hears He will speak; and He will tell you things to come. [14] He will glorify Me, for He will take of what is Mine and declare *it* to you. [15] All things that the Father has are Mine. Therefore I said that He will take of Mine and declare *it* to you.

[16] "A little while, and you will not see Me; and again a little while, and you will see Me, because I go to the Father."

[17] Then *some* of His disciples said among themselves, "What is this that He says to us, 'A little while, and you will not see Me; and again a little while, and you will see Me'; and, 'because I go to the Father'?" [18] They said therefore, "What is this that He says, 'A little while'? We do not know what He is saying."

[19] Now Jesus knew that they desired to ask Him, and He said to them, "Are you inquiring among yourselves about what I said, 'A little while, and you will not see Me; and again a little while, and you will see Me'? [20] Most assuredly, I say to you that you will weep and lament, but the world will rejoice; and you will be sorrowful, but your sorrow will be turned into joy. [21] A woman, when she is in labor, has sorrow because her hour has come; but as soon as she has given birth to the child, she no longer remembers the anguish, for joy that a human being has been born into the world. [22] Therefore you now have sorrow; but I will see you again and your heart will rejoice, and your joy no one will take from you.

[23] "And in that day you will ask Me nothing. Most assuredly, I say to you, whatever you ask the Father in My name He will give you. [24] Until now you have asked nothing in My name. Ask, and you will receive, that your joy may be full.

[25] "These things I have spoken to you in figurative language; but the time is coming when I will no longer speak to you in figurative language, but I will tell you plainly about the Father. [26] In that day you will ask in My name, and I do not say to you that I shall pray the Father for you; [27] for the Father Himself loves you, because you have loved Me, and have believed that I came forth from God. [28] I came forth from the Father and have come into the world. Again, I leave the world and go to the Father."

[29] His disciples said to Him, "See, now You are speaking plainly, and using no figure of speech! [30] Now we are sure that You know all things, and have no need that anyone should question You. By this we believe that You came forth from God."

[31] Jesus answered them, "Do you now believe? [32] Indeed the hour is coming, yes, has now come, that you will be scattered, each to his own, and will leave Me alone. And yet I am not alone, because the Father is with Me. [33] These things I have spoken to you, that in Me you may have peace. In the world you will have tribulation; but be of good cheer, I have overcome the world."

~ 2 KINGS 3:1—4:44 ~

Now Jehoram the son of Ahab became king over Israel at Samaria in the eighteenth year of Jehoshaphat king of Judah, and reigned twelve years. ² And he did evil in the sight of the LORD, but not like his father and mother; for he put away the *sacred* pillar of Baal that his father had made. ³ Nevertheless he persisted in the sins of Jeroboam the son of Nebat, who had made Israel sin; he did not depart from them.

⁴ Now Mesha king of Moab was a sheepbreeder, and he regularly paid the king of Israel one hundred thousand lambs and the wool of one hundred thousand rams. ⁵ But it happened, when Ahab died, that the king of Moab rebelled against the king of Israel.

⁶ So King Jehoram went out of Samaria at that time and mustered all Israel. ⁷ Then he went and sent to Jehoshaphat king of Judah, saying, "The king of Moab has rebelled against me. Will you go with me to fight against Moab?"

And he said, "I will go up; I *am* as you *are,* my people as your people, my horses as your horses." ⁸ Then he said, "Which way shall we go up?"

And he answered, "By way of the Wilderness of Edom."

⁹ So the king of Israel went with the king of Judah and the king of Edom, and they marched on that roundabout route seven days; and there was no water for the army, nor for the animals that followed them. ¹⁰ And the king of Israel said, "Alas! For the LORD has called these three kings together to deliver them into the hand of Moab."

¹¹ But Jehoshaphat said, "*Is there* no prophet of the LORD here, that we may inquire of the LORD by him?"

So one of the servants of the king of Israel answered and said, "Elisha the son of Shaphat *is* here, who poured water on the hands of Elijah."

¹² And Jehoshaphat said, "The word of the LORD is with him." So the king of Israel and Jehoshaphat and the king of Edom went down to him.

¹³ Then Elisha said to the king of Israel, "What have I to do with you? Go to the prophets of your father and the prophets of your mother."

But the king of Israel said to him, "No, for the LORD has called these three kings *together* to deliver them into the hand of Moab."

¹⁴ And Elisha said, "*As* the LORD of hosts lives, before whom I stand, surely were it not that I regard the presence of Jehoshaphat king of Judah, I would not look at you, nor see you. ¹⁵ But now bring me a musician."

Then it happened, when the musician played, that the hand of the LORD came upon him. ¹⁶ And he said, "Thus says the LORD: 'Make this valley full of ditches.' ¹⁷ For thus says the LORD: 'You shall not see wind, nor shall you see rain; yet that valley shall be filled with water, so that you, your cattle, and your animals may drink.' ¹⁸ And this is a simple matter in the sight of the LORD; He will also deliver the Moabites into your hand. ¹⁹ Also you shall attack every fortified city and every choice city, and shall cut down every good tree, and stop up every spring of water, and ruin every good piece of land with stones."

²⁰ Now it happened in the morning, when the grain offering was offered, that suddenly water came by way of Edom, and the land was filled with water.

²¹ And when all the Moabites heard that the kings had come up to fight against them, all who were able to bear arms and older were gathered; and they stood at the border. ²² Then they rose up early in the morning, and the sun was shining on the water; and the Moabites saw the water on the other side *as* red as blood. ²³ And they said, "This is blood; the kings have surely struck swords and have killed one another; now therefore, Moab, to the spoil!"

²⁴ So when they came to the camp of Israel, Israel rose up and attacked the Moabites, so that they fled before them; and they entered *their* land, killing the Moabites. ²⁵ Then they destroyed the cities, and each man threw a stone on every good piece of land and filled it; and they stopped up all the springs of water and

Freedom

Kari Torjesen Malcom, the daughter of missionaries, was interred in a Chinese prison camp during World War II. Only a teenager, she found herself a nameless prisoner, number "16." She was given a small space on a bare floor and reminded daily of her lack of freedom by a wall, a moat, and an electric barbed-wire fence. She met with other prisoners daily at noon to pray for freedom, but as time passed, the enemy seemed larger, and God smaller.

Kari desperately pleaded with God to reveal Himself to her. She said, "God answered my prayer and spoke to me as I searched the Bible. . . . Gradually it dawned on me that there was just one thing the enemy could not take from me. They had bombed our home, killed my father . . . but . . . they could not touch my relationship to my God."

With this revelation, Kari found it increasingly difficult to join her friends for prayer. There was more to life than just getting out of prison. The first day she missed the prayer meeting, a friend taunted her, "So we aren't good enough for you anymore, eh?" Even her peer group had been stripped away from her. Her last bit of security was peeled away. Kari said, "It was only then that I was able to pray the prayer that changed my life: 'Lord, I am willing to stay in this prison for the rest of my life if only I may know You.' At that moment I was free."

We can walk through life with tremendous freedom when we remember that relationship with God is paramount. His greatest desire is to be with us. The care of everything else melts away and joy and peace take its place when we truly know God.

> And this is eternal life, that they may know You, the only true God, and Jesus Christ whom You have sent.
>
> *John 17:3*

cut down all the good trees. But they left the stones of Kir Haraseth *intact*. However the slingers surrounded and attacked it.

26 And when the king of Moab saw that the battle was too fierce for him, he took with him seven hundred men who drew swords, to break through to the king of Edom, but they could not. 27 Then he took his eldest son who would have reigned in his place, and offered him *as* a burnt offering upon the wall; and there was great indignation against Israel. So they departed from him and returned to *their own* land.

4 A certain woman of the wives of the sons of the prophets cried out to Elisha, saying, "Your servant my husband is dead, and you know that your servant feared the LORD. And the creditor is coming to take my two sons to be his slaves."

2 So Elisha said to her, "What shall I do for you? Tell me, what do you have in the house?" And she said, "Your maidservant has nothing in the house but a jar of oil."

3 Then he said, "Go, borrow vessels from everywhere, from all your neighbors—empty vessels; do not gather just a few. 4 And when you have come in, you shall shut the door behind you and your sons; then pour it into all those vessels, and set aside the full ones."

5 So she went from him and shut the door behind her and her sons, who brought *the vessels* to her; and she poured *it* out. 6 Now it came to pass, when the vessels were full, that she said to her son, "Bring me another vessel."

And he said to her, "*There is* not another vessel." So the oil ceased. 7 Then she came and told the man of God. And he said, "Go, sell the oil and pay your debt; and you *and* your sons live on the rest."

8 Now it happened one day that Elisha went to Shunem, where there *was* a notable woman, and she persuaded him to eat some food. So it was, as often as he passed by, he would turn in there to eat some food. 9 And she said to her husband, "Look now, I know that this *is* a holy man of God, who passes by us regularly. 10 Please, let us make a small upper room on the wall; and let us put a bed for him there, and a table and a chair and a lampstand; so it will be, whenever he comes to us, he can turn in there."

11 And it happened one day that he came there, and he turned in to the upper room and lay down there. 12 Then he said to Gehazi his servant, "Call this Shunammite woman." When he had called her, she stood before him. 13 And he said to him, "Say now to her, 'Look, you have been concerned for us with all this care. What *can I* do for you? Do you want me to speak on your behalf to the king or to the commander of the army?'"

She answered, "I dwell among my own people."

14 So he said, "What then *is* to be done for her?"

And Gehazi answered, "Actually, she has no son, and her husband is old."

15 So he said, "Call her." When he had called her, she stood in the doorway. 16 Then he said, "About this time next year you shall embrace a son."

And she said, "No, my lord. Man of God, do not lie to your maidservant!"

17 But the woman conceived, and bore a son when the appointed time had come, of which Elisha had told her.

18 And the child grew. Now it happened one day that he went out to his father, to the reapers. 19 And he said to his father, "My head, my head!"

So he said to a servant, "Carry him to his mother." 20 When he had taken him and brought him to his mother, he sat on her knees till noon, and *then* died. 21 And she went up and laid him on the bed of the man of God, shut *the door* upon him, and went out. 22 Then she called to her husband, and said, "Please send me one of the young men and one of the donkeys, that I may run to the man of God and come back."

23 So he said, "Why are you going to him today? *It is* neither the New Moon nor the Sabbath."

And she said, "*It is* well." 24 Then she saddled a donkey, and said to her servant, "Drive, and go forward; do not slacken the pace for me unless I tell you." 25 And so she departed, and went to the man of God at Mount Carmel.

So it was, when the man of God saw her afar off, that he said to his servant Gehazi, "Look, the Shunammite woman!

²⁶ Please run now to meet her, and say to her, 'Is it well with you? Is it well with your husband? Is it well with the child?' "

And she answered, "It is well." ²⁷ Now when she came to the man of God at the hill, she caught him by the feet, but Gehazi came near to push her away. But the man of God said, "Let her alone; for her soul is in deep distress, and the LORD has hidden it from me, and has not told me."

²⁸ So she said, "Did I ask a son of my lord? Did I not say, 'Do not deceive me'?"

²⁹ Then he said to Gehazi, "Get yourself ready, and take my staff in your hand, and be on your way. If you meet anyone, do not greet him; and if anyone greets you, do not answer him; but lay my staff on the face of the child."

³⁰ And the mother of the child said, "As the LORD lives, and as your soul lives, I will not leave you." So he arose and followed her. ³¹ Now Gehazi went on ahead of them, and laid the staff on the face of the child; but there was neither voice nor hearing. Therefore he went back to meet him, and told him, saying, "The child has not awakened."

³² When Elisha came into the house, there was the child, lying dead on his bed. ³³ He went in therefore, shut the door behind the two of them, and prayed to the LORD. ³⁴ And he went up and lay on the child, and put his mouth on his mouth, his eyes on his eyes, and his hands on his hands; and he stretched himself out on the child, and the flesh of the child became warm. ³⁵ He returned and walked back and forth in the house, and again went up and stretched himself out on him; then the child sneezed seven times, and the child opened his eyes. ³⁶ And he called Gehazi and said, "Call this Shunammite woman." So he called her. And when she came in to him, he said, "Pick up your son." ³⁷ So she went in, fell at his feet, and bowed to the ground; then she picked up her son and went out.

³⁸ And Elisha returned to Gilgal, and there was a famine in the land. Now the sons of the prophets were sitting before him; and he said to his servant, "Put on the large pot, and boil stew for the sons of the prophets." ³⁹ So one went out into the field to gather herbs, and found a wild vine, and gathered from it a lapful of wild gourds, and came and sliced them into the pot of stew, though they did not know what they were. ⁴⁰ Then they served it to the men to eat. Now it happened, as they were eating the stew, that they cried out and said, "Man of God, there is death in the pot!" And they could not eat it.

⁴¹ So he said, "Then bring some flour." And he put it into the pot, and said, "Serve it to the people, that they may eat." And there was nothing harmful in the pot.

⁴² Then a man came from Baal Shalisha, and brought the man of God bread of the firstfruits, twenty loaves of barley bread, and newly ripened grain in his knapsack. And he said, "Give it to the people, that they may eat."

⁴³ But his servant said, "What? Shall I set this before one hundred men?"

He said again, "Give it to the people, that they may eat; for thus says the LORD: 'They shall eat and have some left over.' "
⁴⁴ So he set it before them; and they ate and had some left over, according to the word of the LORD.

～ PSALM 71:17–24 ～

¹⁷ O God, You have taught me from
    my youth;
And to this day I declare Your
    wondrous works.
¹⁸ Now also when I am old and
    grayheaded,
O God, do not forsake me,
Until I declare Your strength to this
    generation,
Your power to everyone who is to
    come.

¹⁹ Also Your righteousness, O God, is
    very high,
You who have done great things;
O God, who is like You?
²⁰ You, who have shown me great and
    severe troubles,
Shall revive me again,
And bring me up again from the
    depths of the earth.
²¹ You shall increase my greatness,
And comfort me on every side.

²² Also with the lute I will praise You—
And Your faithfulness, O my God!
To You I will sing with the harp,

O Holy One of Israel.
23 My lips shall greatly rejoice when I
    sing to You,
And my soul, which You have
    redeemed.
24 My tongue also shall talk of Your
    righteousness all the day long;
For they are confounded,
For they are brought to shame
Who seek my hurt.

~ PROVERBS 18:9 ~

9 He who is slothful in his work
   Is a brother to him who is a great
     destroyer.

~ JOHN 17:1–26 ~

Jesus spoke these words, lifted up His eyes
to heaven, and said: "Father, the hour has
come. Glorify Your Son, that Your Son
also may glorify You, 2 as You have given
Him authority over all flesh, that He
should give eternal life to as many as You
have given Him. 3 And this is eternal life,
that they may know You, the only true
God, and Jesus Christ whom You have
sent. 4 I have glorified You on the earth. I
have finished the work which You have
given Me to do. 5 And now, O Father, glorify Me together with Yourself, with
the glory which I had with You before the
world was.

6 "I have manifested Your name to the
men whom You have given Me out of
the world. They were Yours, You gave
them to Me, and they have kept Your
word. 7 Now they have known that all
things which You have given Me are from
You. 8 For I have given to them the words
which You have given Me; and they have
received *them,* and have known surely
that I came forth from You; and they have
believed that You sent Me.

9 "I pray for them. I do not pray for the
world but for those whom You have given
Me, for they are Yours. 10 And all Mine
are Yours, and Yours are Mine, and I am
glorified in them. 11 Now I am no longer

in the world, but these are in the world,
and I come to You. Holy Father, keep
through Your name those whom You have
given Me, that they may be one as We
are. 12 While I was with them in the world,
I kept them in Your name. Those whom
You gave Me I have kept; and none of
them is lost except the son of perdition,
that the Scripture might be fulfilled. 13 But
now I come to You, and these things I
speak in the world, that they may have
My joy fulfilled in themselves. 14 I
have given them Your word; and the
world has hated them because they are
not of the world, just as I am not of the
world. 15 I do not pray that You should
take them out of the world, but that You
should keep them from the evil one.
16 They are not of the world, just as I am
not of the world. 17 Sanctify them by Your
truth. Your word is truth. 18 As You sent
Me into the world, I also have sent them
into the world. 19 And for their sakes I
sanctify Myself, that they also may be sanctified by the truth.

20 "I do not pray for these alone, but
also for those who will believe in Me
through their word; 21 that they all may
be one, as You, Father, *are* in Me, and I in
You; that they also may be one in Us, that
the world may believe that You sent Me.
22 And the glory which You gave Me I have
given them, that they may be one just as
We are one: 23 I in them, and You in Me;
that they may be made perfect in one,
and that the world may know that You
have sent Me, and have loved them as
You have loved Me.

24 "Father, I desire that they also whom
You gave Me may be with Me where I
am, that they may behold My glory which
You have given Me; for You loved Me
before the foundation of the world. 25 O
righteous Father! The world has not
known You, but I have known You; and
these have known that You sent Me.
26 And I have declared to them Your name,
and will declare *it,* that the love with
which You loved Me may be in them, and
I in them."

~ 2 KINGS 5:1—6:33 ~

Now Naaman, commander of the army of the king of Syria, was a great and honorable man in the eyes of his master, because by him the LORD had given victory to Syria. He was also a mighty man of valor, *but* a leper. ² And the Syrians had gone out on raids, and had brought back captive a young girl from the land of Israel. She waited on Naaman's wife. ³ Then she said to her mistress, "If only my master *were* with the prophet who *is* in Samaria! For he would heal him of his leprosy." ⁴ And *Naaman* went in and told his master, saying, "Thus and thus said the girl who *is* from the land of Israel."

⁵ Then the king of Syria said, "Go now, and I will send a letter to the king of Israel."

So he departed and took with him ten talents of silver, six thousand *shekels* of gold, and ten changes of clothing. ⁶ Then he brought the letter to the king of Israel, which said,

Now be advised, when this letter comes to you, that I have sent Naaman my servant to you, that you may heal him of his leprosy.

⁷ And it happened, when the king of Israel read the letter, that he tore his clothes and said, "*Am* I God, to kill and make alive, that this man sends a man to me to heal him of his leprosy? Therefore please consider, and see how he seeks a quarrel with me."

⁸ So it was, when Elisha the man of God heard that the king of Israel had torn his clothes, that he sent to the king, saying, "Why have you torn your clothes? Please let him come to me, and he shall know that there is a prophet in Israel." ⁹ Then Naaman went with his horses and chariot, and he stood at the door of Elisha's house. ¹⁰ And Elisha sent a messenger to him, saying, "Go and wash in the Jordan seven times, and your flesh shall be restored to you, and *you shall* be clean." ¹¹ But Naaman became furious, and went away and said, "Indeed, I said to myself, 'He will surely come out *to me,*

and stand and call on the name of the LORD his God, and wave his hand over the place, and heal the leprosy.' ¹² *Are* not the Abanah and the Pharpar, the rivers of Damascus, better than all the waters of Israel? Could I not wash in them and be clean?" So he turned and went away in a rage. ¹³ And his servants came near and spoke to him, and said, "My father, *if* the prophet had told you *to do* something great, would you not have done *it*? How much more then, when he says to you, 'Wash, and be clean'?" ¹⁴ So he went down and dipped seven times in the Jordan, according to the saying of the man of God; and his flesh was restored like the flesh of a little child, and he was clean.

¹⁵ And he returned to the man of God, he and all his aides, and came and stood before him; and he said, "Indeed, now I know that *there is* no God in all the earth, except in Israel; now therefore, please take a gift from your servant."

¹⁶ But he said, "*As* the LORD lives, before whom I stand, I will receive nothing." And he urged him to take *it,* but he refused.

¹⁷ So Naaman said, "Then, if not, please let your servant be given two mule-loads of earth; for your servant will no longer offer either burnt offering or sacrifice to other gods, but to the LORD. ¹⁸ Yet in this thing may the LORD pardon your servant: when my master goes into the temple of Rimmon to worship there, and he leans on my hand, and I bow down in the temple of Rimmon—when I bow down in the temple of Rimmon, may the LORD please pardon your servant in this thing." ¹⁹ Then he said to him, "Go in peace." So he departed from him a short distance.

²⁰ But Gehazi, the servant of Elisha the man of God, said, "Look, my master has spared Naaman this Syrian, while not receiving from his hands what he brought; but *as* the LORD lives, I will run after him and take something from him." ²¹ So Gehazi pursued Naaman. When Naaman saw *him* running after him, he got down from the chariot to meet him, and said, "*Is* all well?"

²² And he said, "All *is* well. My master has sent me, saying, 'Indeed, just now two

young men of the sons of the prophets have come to me from the mountains of Ephraim. Please give them a talent of silver and two changes of garments.' "

²³ So Naaman said, "Please, take two talents." And he urged him, and bound two talents of silver in two bags, with two changes of garments, and handed *them* to two of his servants; and they carried *them* on ahead of him. ²⁴ When he came to the citadel, he took *them* from their hand, and stored *them* away in the house; then he let the men go, and they departed. ²⁵ Now he went in and stood before his master. Elisha said to him, "Where *did you* go, Gehazi?"

And he said, "Your servant did not go anywhere."

²⁶ Then he said to him, "Did not my heart go *with you* when the man turned back from his chariot to meet you? *Is it* time to receive money and to receive clothing, olive groves and vineyards, sheep and oxen, male and female servants? ²⁷ Therefore the leprosy of Naaman shall cling to you and your descendants forever." And he went out from his presence leprous, *as white* as snow.

6 And the sons of the prophets said to Elisha, "See now, the place where we dwell with you is too small for us. ² Please, let us go to the Jordan, and let every man take a beam from there, and let us make there a place where we may dwell."

So he answered, "Go."

³ Then one said, "Please consent to go with your servants."

And he answered, "I will go." ⁴ So he went with them. And when they came to the Jordan, they cut down trees. ⁵ But as one was cutting down a tree, the iron *ax head* fell into the water; and he cried out and said, "Alas, master! For it was borrowed."

⁶ So the man of God said, "Where did it fall?" And he showed him the place. So he cut off a stick, and threw *it* in there; and he made the iron float. ⁷ Therefore he said, "Pick *it* up for yourself." So he reached out his hand and took it.

⁸ Now the king of Syria was making war against Israel; and he consulted with his servants, saying, "My camp *will be* in such and such a place." ⁹ And the man of God

sent to the king of Israel, saying, "Beware that you do not pass this place, for the Syrians are coming down there." ¹⁰ Then the king of Israel sent *someone* to the place of which the man of God had told him. Thus he warned him, and he was watchful there, not just once or twice.

¹¹ Therefore the heart of the king of Syria was greatly troubled by this thing; and he called his servants and said to them, "Will you not show me which of us *is* for the king of Israel?"

¹² And one of his servants said, "None, my lord, O king; but Elisha, the prophet who *is* in Israel, tells the king of Israel the words that you speak in your bedroom."

¹³ So he said, "Go and see where he *is*, that I may send and get him."

And it was told him, saying, "Surely *he is* in Dothan."

¹⁴ Therefore he sent horses and chariots and a great army there, and they came by night and surrounded the city. ¹⁵ And when the servant of the man of God arose early and went out, there was an army, surrounding the city with horses and chariots. And his servant said to him, "Alas, my master! What shall we do?"

¹⁶ So he answered, "Do not fear, for those who *are* with us *are* more than those who *are* with them." ¹⁷ And Elisha prayed, and said, "LORD, I pray, open his eyes that he may see." Then the LORD opened the eyes of the young man, and he saw. And behold, the mountain *was* full of horses and chariots of fire all around Elisha. ¹⁸ So when *the Syrians* came down to him, Elisha prayed to the LORD, and said, "Strike this people, I pray, with blindness." And He struck them with blindness according to the word of Elisha.

¹⁹ Now Elisha said to them, "This *is* not the way, nor *is* this the city. Follow me, and I will bring you to the man whom you seek." But he led them to Samaria.

²⁰ So it was, when they had come to Samaria, that Elisha said, "LORD, open the eyes of these *men*, that they may see." And the LORD opened their eyes, and they saw; and there *they were*, inside Samaria!

²¹ Now when the king of Israel saw them, he said to Elisha, "My father, shall I kill *them*? Shall I kill *them*?"

²² But he answered, "You shall not kill *them*. Would you kill those whom you

Moving On

Withstanding 100-degree heat and tendinitis in her left knee, Monica Seles won her first tennis tournament in more than two years since she had been stabbed in the shoulder by a fanatical fan. She roared through the Canadian Open to defeat three Top 20 players en route to a finals match that lasted only fifty-one minutes. Her nightmare had truly come to an end.

To help in her recovery, Monica asked Olympic champion Jackie Joyner-Kersee and her coach/husband, Bob Kersee, to put her on a strict workout routine. While on this physical regimen she also worked to overcome the emotional problems that accompany such an attack.

Her father and coach, Karolj, who had been stricken by prostate and stomach cancer, was a continual source of inspiration. She said, "I was down and he came into my room and said he couldn't stand to see me that way. I decided then that I had to try and put it behind me and move on."

Have you ever felt "stabbed in the back" while doing good? Withdrawal is often our first temptation, but with a creative and loving God, Who continually inspires us, we just can't quit! Our critics will eventually always have to say about us what was said about Monica, "She's back!"

> So Jesus said to Peter, "Shall I not drink the cup which My Father has given Me?"
>
> *John 18:11*

have taken captive with your sword and your bow? Set food and water before them, that they may eat and drink and go to their master." [23] Then he prepared a great feast for them; and after they ate and drank, he sent them away and they went to their master. So the bands of Syrian *raiders* came no more into the land of Israel.

[24] And it happened after this that Ben-Hadad king of Syria gathered all his army, and went up and besieged Samaria. [25] And there was a great famine in Samaria; and indeed they besieged it until a donkey's head was *sold* for eighty *shekels* of silver, and one-fourth of a kab of dove droppings for five *shekels* of silver.

[26] Then, as the king of Israel was passing by on the wall, a woman cried out to him, saying, "Help, my lord, O king!"

[27] And he said, "If the LORD does not help you, where can I find help for you? From the threshing floor or from the winepress?" [28] Then the king said to her, "What is troubling you?"

And she answered, "This woman said to me, 'Give your son, that we may eat him today, and we will eat my son tomorrow.' [29] So we boiled my son, and ate him. And I said to her on the next day, 'Give your son, that we may eat him'; but she has hidden her son."

[30] Now it happened, when the king heard the words of the woman, that he tore his clothes; and as he passed by on the wall, the people looked, and there underneath *he had* sackcloth on his body. [31] Then he said, "God do so to me and more also, if the head of Elisha the son of Shaphat remains on him today!"

[32] But Elisha was sitting in his house, and the elders were sitting with him. And *the king* sent a man ahead of him, but before the messenger came to him, he said to the elders, "Do you see how this son of a murderer has sent someone to take away my head? Look, when the messenger comes, shut the door, and hold him fast at the door. *Is* not the sound of his master's feet behind him?" [33] And while he was still talking with them, there was the messenger, coming down to him; and then *the king* said, "Surely this calamity *is* from the LORD; why should I wait for the LORD any longer?"

∼ PSALM 72:1–7 ∼

[1] Give the king Your judgments,
 O God,
And Your righteousness to the king's
 Son.
[2] He will judge Your people with
 righteousness,
And Your poor with justice.
[3] The mountains will bring peace to
 the people,
And the little hills, by righteousness.
[4] He will bring justice to the poor of
 the people;
He will save the children of the
 needy,
And will break in pieces the
 oppressor.

[5] They shall fear You
As long as the sun and moon endure,
Throughout all generations.
[6] He shall come down like rain upon
 the grass before mowing,
Like showers *that* water the earth.
[7] In His days the righteous shall
 flourish,
And abundance of peace,
Until the moon is no more.

∼ PROVERBS 18:10, 11 ∼

[10] The name of the LORD *is* a strong
 tower;
The righteous run to it and are safe.
[11] The rich man's wealth *is* his strong
 city,
And like a high wall in his own
 esteem.

∼ JOHN 18:1–18 ∼

When Jesus had spoken these words, He went out with His disciples over the Brook Kidron, where there was a garden, which He and His disciples entered. [2] And Judas, who betrayed Him, also knew the place; for Jesus often met there with His disciples. [3] Then Judas, having received a detachment *of troops,* and officers from the chief priests and Pharisees, came there with lanterns, torches, and weapons. [4] Jesus therefore, knowing all things that would come upon Him, went forward and said to them, "Whom are you seeking?"

⁵ They answered Him, "Jesus of Nazareth."

Jesus said to them, "I am *He.*" And Judas, who betrayed Him, also stood with them. ⁶ Now when He said to them, "I am *He,*" they drew back and fell to the ground.

⁷ Then He asked them again, "Whom are you seeking?"

And they said, "Jesus of Nazareth."

⁸ Jesus answered, "I have told you that I am *He.* Therefore, if you seek Me, let these go their way," ⁹ that the saying might be fulfilled which He spoke, "Of those whom You gave Me I have lost none."

¹⁰ Then Simon Peter, having a sword, drew it and struck the high priest's servant, and cut off his right ear. The servant's name was Malchus.

¹¹ So Jesus said to Peter, "Put your sword into the sheath. Shall I not drink the cup which My Father has given Me?"

¹² Then the detachment *of troops* and the captain and the officers of the Jews arrested Jesus and bound Him. ¹³ And they led Him away to Annas first, for he was the father-in-law of Caiaphas who was high priest that year. ¹⁴ Now it was Caiaphas who advised the Jews that it was expedient that one man should die for the people.

¹⁵ And Simon Peter followed Jesus, and so *did* another disciple. Now that disciple was known to the high priest, and went with Jesus into the courtyard of the high priest. ¹⁶ But Peter stood at the door outside. Then the other disciple, who was known to the high priest, went out and spoke to her who kept the door, and brought Peter in. ¹⁷ Then the servant girl who kept the door said to Peter, "You are not also *one* of this Man's disciples, are you?"

He said, "I am not."

¹⁸ Now the servants and officers who had made a fire of coals stood there, for it was cold, and they warmed themselves. And Peter stood with them and warmed himself.

∼ 2 KINGS 7:1—8:29 ∼

Then Elisha said, "Hear the word of the LORD. Thus says the LORD: 'Tomorrow about this time a seah of fine flour *shall be sold* for a shekel, and two seahs of barley for a shekel, at the gate of Samaria.' "

² So an officer on whose hand the king leaned answered the man of God and said, "Look, *if* the LORD would make windows in heaven, could this thing be?"

And he said, "In fact, you shall see *it* with your eyes, but you shall not eat of it."

³ Now there were four leprous men at the entrance of the gate; and they said to one another, "Why are we sitting here until we die? ⁴ If we say, 'We will enter the city,' the famine *is* in the city, and we shall die there. And if we sit here, we die also. Now therefore, come, let us surrender to the army of the Syrians. If they keep us alive, we shall live; and if they kill us, we shall only die." ⁵ And they rose at twilight to go to the camp of the Syrians; and when they had come to the outskirts of the Syrian camp, to their surprise no one *was* there. ⁶ For the LORD had caused the army of the Syrians to hear the noise of chariots and the noise of horses—the noise of a great army; so they said to one another, "Look, the king of Israel has hired against us the kings of the Hittites and the kings of the Egyptians to attack us!" ⁷ Therefore they arose and fled at twilight, and left the camp intact—their tents, their horses, and their donkeys— and they fled for their lives. ⁸ And when these lepers came to the outskirts of the camp, they went into one tent and ate and drank, and carried from it silver and gold and clothing, and went and hid *them;* then they came back and entered another tent, and carried *some* from there *also,* and went and hid *it.*

⁹ Then they said to one another, "We are not doing right. This day *is* a day of good news, and we remain silent. If we wait until morning light, some

punishment will come upon us. Now therefore, come, let us go and tell the king's household." [10] So they went and called to the gatekeepers of the city, and told them, saying, "We went to the Syrian camp, and surprisingly no one *was* there, not a human sound—only horses and donkeys tied, and the tents intact." [11] And the gatekeepers called out, and they told *it* to the king's household inside.

[12] So the king arose in the night and said to his servants, "Let me now tell you what the Syrians have done to us. They know that we *are* hungry; therefore they have gone out of the camp to hide themselves in the field, saying, 'When they come out of the city, we shall catch them alive, and get into the city.' "

[13] And one of his servants answered and said, "Please, let several *men* take five of the remaining horses which are left in the city. Look, they *may either become* like all the multitude of Israel that are left in it; or indeed, *I say,* they *may become* like all the multitude of Israel left from those who are consumed; so let us send them and see." [14] Therefore they took two chariots with horses; and the king sent them in the direction of the Syrian army, saying, "Go and see." [15] And they went after them to the Jordan; and indeed all the road *was* full of garments and weapons which the Syrians had thrown away in their haste. So the messengers returned and told the king. [16] Then the people went out and plundered the tents of the Syrians. So a seah of fine flour was *sold* for a shekel, and two seahs of barley for a shekel, according to the word of the LORD.

[17] Now the king had appointed the officer on whose hand he leaned to have charge of the gate. But the people trampled him in the gate, and he died, just as the man of God had said, who spoke when the king came down to him. [18] So it happened just as the man of God had spoken to the king, saying, "Two seahs of barley for a shekel, and a seah of fine flour for a shekel, shall be *sold* tomorrow about this time in the gate of Samaria."

[19] Then that officer had answered the man of God, and said, "Now look, *if* the LORD would make windows in heaven, could such a thing be?"

And he had said, "In fact, you shall see *it* with your eyes, but you shall not eat of it." [20] And so it happened to him, for the people trampled him in the gate, and he died.

8 Then Elisha spoke to the woman whose son he had restored to life, saying, "Arise and go, you and your household, and stay wherever you can; for the LORD has called for a famine, and furthermore, it will come upon the land for seven years." [2] So the woman arose and did according to the saying of the man of God, and she went with her household and dwelt in the land of the Philistines seven years.

[3] It came to pass, at the end of seven years, that the woman returned from the land of the Philistines; and she went to make an appeal to the king for her house and for her land. [4] Then the king talked with Gehazi, the servant of the man of God, saying, "Tell me, please, all the great things Elisha has done." [5] Now it happened, as he was telling the king how he had restored the dead to life, that there was the woman whose son he had restored to life, appealing to the king for her house and for her land. And Gehazi said, "My lord, O king, this *is* the woman, and this *is* her son whom Elisha restored to life." [6] And when the king asked the woman, she told him.

So the king appointed a certain officer for her, saying, "Restore all that *was* hers, and all the proceeds of the field from the day that she left the land until now."

[7] Then Elisha went to Damascus, and Ben-Hadad king of Syria was sick; and it was told him, saying, "The man of God has come here." [8] And the king said to Hazael, "Take a present in your hand, and go to meet the man of God, and inquire of the LORD by him, saying, 'Shall I recover from this disease?' " [9] So Hazael went to meet him and took a present with him, of every good thing of Damascus, forty camel-loads; and he came and stood before him, and said, "Your son Ben-Hadad king of Syria has sent me to you, saying, 'Shall I recover from this disease?' "

[10] And Elisha said to him, "Go, say to him, 'You shall certainly recover.' However the LORD has shown me that he will

Too Close to See

A six-year-old boy was sent home from school one day with a note from his teacher. The note suggested that the boy be taken out of school since he was "too stupid to learn." That boy was Thomas A. Edison.

A grandfather once gave his grandson ten shillings for writing a eulogy about his grandmother. The grandfather said as he gave him the money, "There, that is the first money you ever earned for your poetry, and take my word for it, it will be the last." The lad was Alfred Tennyson.

A woman once hesitated in letting her daughter marry a printer who had asked for her hand in marriage. She wasn't sure if he could support her daughter because the United States already had two printing offices, and she feared the nation might not be able to support a third. That printer was Benjamin Franklin.

So often we fail to recognize the greatness in those with whom we live. It's almost as if we can't see the full length and breadth of the person's life because we are standing too close. Take a few steps back. Ask God to help you see the greatness He's placed in those around you, especially your children. It's your job to help them get there.

really die." ¹¹ Then he set his countenance in a stare until he was ashamed; and the man of God wept. ¹² And Hazael said, "Why is my lord weeping?"

He answered, "Because I know the evil that you will do to the children of Israel: Their strongholds you will set on fire, and their young men you will kill with the sword; and you will dash their children, and rip open their women with child."

¹³ So Hazael said, "But what *is* your servant—a dog, that he should do this gross thing?"

And Elisha answered, "The LORD has shown me that you *will become* king over Syria."

¹⁴ Then he departed from Elisha, and came to his master, who said to him, "What did Elisha say to you?" And he answered, "He told me you would surely recover." ¹⁵ But it happened on the next day that he took a thick cloth and dipped *it* in water, and spread *it* over his face so that he died; and Hazael reigned in his place.

¹⁶ Now in the fifth year of Joram the son of Ahab, king of Israel, Jehoshaphat *having been* king of Judah, Jehoram the son of Jehoshaphat began to reign as king of Judah. ¹⁷ He was thirty-two years old when he became king, and he reigned eight years in Jerusalem. ¹⁸ And he walked in the way of the kings of Israel, just as the house of Ahab had done, for the daughter of Ahab was his wife; and he did evil in the sight of the LORD. ¹⁹ Yet the LORD would not destroy Judah, for the sake of his servant David, as He promised him to give a lamp to him *and* his sons forever.

²⁰ In his days Edom revolted against Judah's authority, and made a king over themselves. ²¹ So Joram went to Zair, and all his chariots with him. Then he rose by night and attacked the Edomites who had surrounded him and the captains of the chariots; and the troops fled to their tents. ²² Thus Edom has been in revolt against Judah's authority to this day. And Libnah revolted at that time.

²³ Now the rest of the acts of Joram, and all that he did, *are* they not written in the book of the chronicles of the kings of Judah? ²⁴ So Joram rested with his fathers, and was buried with his fathers in the City of David. Then Ahaziah his son reigned in his place.

²⁵ In the twelfth year of Joram the son of Ahab, king of Israel, Ahaziah the son of Jehoram, king of Judah, began to reign. ²⁶ Ahaziah *was* twenty-two years old when he became king, and he reigned one year in Jerusalem. His mother's name *was* Athaliah the granddaughter of Omri, king of Israel. ²⁷ And he walked in the way of the house of Ahab, and did evil in the sight of the LORD, like the house of Ahab, for he *was* the son-in-law of the house of Ahab.

²⁸ Now he went with Joram the son of Ahab to war against Hazael king of Syria at Ramoth Gilead; and the Syrians wounded Joram. ²⁹ Then King Joram went back to Jezreel to recover from the wounds which the Syrians had inflicted on him at Ramah, when he fought against Hazael king of Syria. And Ahaziah the son of Jehoram, king of Judah, went down to see Joram the son of Ahab in Jezreel, because he was sick.

∼ PSALM 72:8–16 ∼

8   He shall have dominion also from
        sea to sea,
     And from the River to the ends of
        the earth.
9   Those who dwell in the wilderness
        will bow before Him,
     And His enemies will lick the dust.
10 The kings of Tarshish and of the isles
        Will bring presents;
     The kings of Sheba and Seba
        Will offer gifts.
11 Yes, all kings shall fall down before
        Him;
     All nations shall serve Him.

12 For He will deliver the needy when
        he cries,
     The poor also, and *him* who has no
        helper.
13 He will spare the poor and needy,
     And will save the souls of the needy.
14 He will redeem their life from
        oppression and violence;
     And precious shall be their blood in
        His sight.

15 And He shall live;

And the gold of Sheba will be given
   to Him;
Prayer also will be made for Him
   continually,
And daily He shall be praised.

16 There will be an abundance of grain
   in the earth,
On the top of the mountains;
Its fruit shall wave like Lebanon;
And *those* of the city shall flourish
   like grass of the earth.

~ PROVERBS 18:12, 13 ~

12 Before destruction the heart of a
   man is haughty,
And before honor *is* humility.

13 He who answers a matter before he
   hears *it,*
It *is* folly and shame to him.

~ JOHN 18:19–40 ~

The high priest then asked Jesus about His disciples and His doctrine.

20 Jesus answered him, "I spoke openly to the world. I always taught in synagogues and in the temple, where the Jews always meet, and in secret I have said nothing. 21 Why do you ask Me? Ask those who have heard Me what I said to them. Indeed they know what I said."

22 And when He had said these things, one of the officers who stood by struck Jesus with the palm of his hand, saying, "Do You answer the high priest like that?"

23 Jesus answered him, "If I have spoken evil, bear witness of the evil; but if well, why do you strike Me?"

24 Then Annas sent Him bound to Caiaphas the high priest.

25 Now Simon Peter stood and warmed himself. Therefore they said to him, "You are not also *one* of His disciples, are you?"

He denied *it* and said, "I am not!"

26 One of the servants of the high priest, a relative *of him* whose ear Peter cut off, said, "Did I not see you in the garden with Him?" 27 Peter then denied again; and immediately a rooster crowed.

28 Then they led Jesus from Caiaphas to the Praetorium, and it was early morning. But they themselves did not go into the Praetorium, lest they should be defiled, but that they might eat the Passover. 29 Pilate then went out to them and said, "What accusation do you bring against this Man?"

30 They answered and said to him, "If He were not an evildoer, we would not have delivered Him up to you."

31 Then Pilate said to them, "You take Him and judge Him according to your law."

Therefore the Jews said to him, "It is not lawful for us to put anyone to death," 32 that the saying of Jesus might be fulfilled which He spoke, signifying by what death He would die.

33 Then Pilate entered the Praetorium again, called Jesus, and said to Him, "Are You the King of the Jews?"

34 Jesus answered him, "Are you speaking for yourself about this, or did others tell you this concerning Me?"

35 Pilate answered, "Am I a Jew? Your own nation and the chief priests have delivered You to me. What have You done?"

36 Jesus answered, "My kingdom is not of this world. If My kingdom were of this world, My servants would fight, so that I should not be delivered to the Jews; but now My kingdom is not from here."

37 Pilate therefore said to Him, "Are You a king then?"

Jesus answered, "You say *rightly* that I am a king. For this cause I was born, and for this cause I have come into the world, that I should bear witness to the truth. Everyone who is of the truth hears My voice."

38 Pilate said to Him, "What is truth?" And when he had said this, he went out again to the Jews, and said to them, "I find no fault in Him at all.

39 "But you have a custom that I should release someone to you at the Passover. Do you therefore want me to release to you the King of the Jews?"

40 Then they all cried again, saying, "Not this Man, but Barabbas!" Now Barabbas was a robber.

~ 2 KINGS 9:1—10:36 ~

A nd Elisha the prophet called one of the sons of the prophets, and said to him, "Get yourself ready, take this flask of oil in your hand, and go to Ramoth Gilead. ² Now when you arrive at that place, look there for Jehu the son of Jehoshaphat, the son of Nimshi, and go in and make him rise up from among his associates, and take him to an inner room. ³ Then take the flask of oil, and pour *it* on his head, and say, 'Thus says the LORD: "I have anointed you king over Israel." ' Then open the door and flee, and do not delay."

⁴ So the young man, the servant of the prophet, went to Ramoth Gilead. ⁵ And when he arrived, there *were* the captains of the army sitting; and he said, "I have a message for you, Commander."

Jehu said, "For which *one* of us?"

And he said, "For you, Commander."

⁶ Then he arose and went into the house. And he poured the oil on his head, and said to him, "Thus says the LORD God of Israel: 'I have anointed you king over the people of the LORD, over Israel. ⁷ You shall strike down the house of Ahab your master, that I may avenge the blood of My servants the prophets, and the blood of all the servants of the LORD, at the hand of Jezebel. ⁸ For the whole house of Ahab shall perish; and I will cut off from Ahab all the males in Israel, both bond and free. ⁹ So I will make the house of Ahab like the house of Jeroboam the son of Nebat, and like the house of Baasha the son of Ahijah. ¹⁰ The dogs shall eat Jezebel on the plot *of ground* at Jezreel, and *there shall be* none to bury *her.*' " And he opened the door and fled.

¹¹ Then Jehu came out to the servants of his master, and *one* said to him, "*Is* all well? Why did this madman come to you?"

And he said to them, "You know the man and his babble."

¹² And they said, "A lie! Tell us now."

So he said, "Thus and thus he spoke to me, saying, 'Thus says the LORD: "I have anointed you king over Israel." ' "

¹³ Then each man hastened to take his garment and put *it* under him on the top of the steps; and they blew trumpets, saying, "Jehu is king!"

¹⁴ So Jehu the son of Jehoshaphat, the son of Nimshi, conspired against Joram. (Now Joram had been defending Ramoth Gilead, he and all Israel, against Hazael king of Syria. ¹⁵ But King Joram had returned to Jezreel to recover from the wounds which the Syrians had inflicted on him when he fought with Hazael king of Syria.) And Jehu said, "If you are so minded, let no one leave *or* escape from the city to go and tell *it* in Jezreel." ¹⁶ So Jehu rode in a chariot and went to Jezreel, for Joram was laid up there; and Ahaziah king of Judah had come down to see Joram.

¹⁷ Now a watchman stood on the tower in Jezreel, and he saw the company of Jehu as he came, and said, "I see a company of men."

And Joram said, "Get a horseman and send him to meet them, and let him say, '*Is it* peace?' "

¹⁸ So the horseman went to meet him, and said, "Thus says the king: '*Is it* peace?' "

And Jehu said, "What have you to do with peace? Turn around and follow me."

So the watchman reported, saying, "The messenger went to them, but is not coming back."

¹⁹ Then he sent out a second horseman who came to them, and said, "Thus says the king: '*Is it* peace?' "

And Jehu answered, "What have you to do with peace? Turn around and follow me."

²⁰ So the watchman reported, saying, "He went up to them and is not coming back; and the driving *is* like the driving of Jehu the son of Nimshi, for he drives furiously!"

²¹ Then Joram said, "Make ready." And his chariot was made ready. Then Joram king of Israel and Ahaziah king of Judah went out, each in his chariot; and they went out to meet Jehu, and met him on the property of Naboth the Jezreelite. ²² Now it happened, when Joram saw Jehu, that he said, "*Is it* peace, Jehu?"

So he answered, "What peace, as long

The Best is Yet to Come

John Erskine was one of the most versatile and well-educated men of his era — a true "Renaissance man."

He was an educator, considered one of the greatest teachers that Columbia University has ever had. He was a concert pianist, author of sixty books, the head of the Julliard School of Music, and a popular and witty lecturer to a wide variety of groups. He had a contagious excitement for learning.

Students flocked to Erskine's courses not because of his fame or his accomplished career, but because of what he believed about them. Erskine had a strong belief that the world did not belong to him, but to his students. He regularly told them, "The best books are yet to be written. The best paintings have not yet been painted. The best governments are yet to be formed. The best is yet to be done by you!"

It was this enthusiasm for life and optimism for tomorrow that became his greatest legacy.

Look forward and upward. Your greatest contributions in life — your best giving, your best caring, the best of your love — are yet to be given!

as the harlotries of your mother Jezebel and her witchcraft *are so* many?"

²³ Then Joram turned around and fled, and said to Ahaziah, "Treachery, Ahaziah!" ²⁴ Now Jehu drew his bow with full strength and shot Jehoram between his arms; and the arrow came out at his heart, and he sank down in his chariot. ²⁵ Then *Jehu* said to Bidkar his captain, "Pick *him* up, *and* throw him into the tract of the field of Naboth the Jezreelite; for remember, when you and I were riding together behind Ahab his father, that the LORD laid this burden upon him: ²⁶ 'Surely I saw yesterday the blood of Naboth and the blood of his sons,' says the LORD, 'and I will repay you in this plot,' says the LORD. Now therefore, take *and* throw him on the plot *of ground,* according to the word of the LORD."

²⁷ But when Ahaziah king of Judah saw *this,* he fled by the road to Beth Haggan. So Jehu pursued him, and said, "Shoot him also in the chariot." *And they shot him* at the Ascent of Gur, which is by Ibleam. Then he fled to Megiddo, and died there. ²⁸ And his servants carried him in the chariot to Jerusalem, and buried him in his tomb with his fathers in the City of David. ²⁹ In the eleventh year of Joram the son of Ahab, Ahaziah had become king over Judah.

³⁰ Now when Jehu had come to Jezreel, Jezebel heard *of it;* and she put paint on her eyes and adorned her head, and looked through a window. ³¹ Then, as Jehu entered at the gate, she said, "*Is it* peace, Zimri, murderer of your master?"

³² And he looked up at the window, and said, "Who *is* on my side? Who?" So two *or* three eunuchs looked out at him. ³³ Then he said, "Throw her down." So they threw her down, and *some* of her blood spattered on the wall and on the horses; and he trampled her underfoot. ³⁴ And when he had gone in, he ate and drank. Then he said, "Go now, see to this accursed *woman,* and bury her, for she was a king's daughter." ³⁵ So they went to bury her, but they found no more of her than the skull and the feet and the palms of *her* hands. ³⁶ Therefore they came back and told him. And he said, "This *is* the word of the LORD, which He spoke by His servant Elijah the Tishbite, saying, 'On the plot *of ground* at Jezreel dogs shall eat the flesh of Jezebel; ³⁷ and the corpse of Jezebel shall be as refuse on the surface of the field, in the plot at Jezreel, so that they shall not say, "Here *lies* Jezebel." ' "

10 Now Ahab had seventy sons in Samaria. And Jehu wrote and sent letters to Samaria, to the rulers of Jezreel, to the elders, and to those who reared Ahab's *sons,* saying:

² Now as soon as this letter comes to you, since your master's sons *are* with you, and you have chariots and horses, a fortified city also, and weapons, ³ choose the best qualified of your master's sons, set *him* on his father's throne, and fight for your master's house.

⁴ But they were exceedingly afraid, and said, "Look, two kings could not stand up to him; how then can we stand?" ⁵ And he who *was* in charge of the house, and he who *was* in charge of the city, the elders also, and those who reared *the sons,* sent to Jehu, saying, "We *are* your servants, we will do all you tell us; but we will not make anyone king. Do *what is* good in your sight." ⁶ Then he wrote a second letter to them, saying:

If you *are* for me and will obey my voice, take the heads of the men, your master's sons, and come to me at Jezreel by this time tomorrow.

Now the king's sons, seventy persons, *were* with the great men of the city, *who* were rearing them. ⁷ So it was, when the letter came to them, that they took the king's sons and slaughtered seventy persons, put their heads in baskets and sent *them* to him at Jezreel.

⁸ Then a messenger came and told him, saying, "They have brought the heads of the king's sons."

And he said, "Lay them in two heaps at the entrance of the gate until morning."

⁹ So it was, in the morning, that he went out and stood, and said to all the people, "You *are* righteous. Indeed I conspired

against my master and killed him; but who killed all these? [10] Know now that nothing shall fall to the earth of the word of the LORD which the LORD spoke concerning the house of Ahab; for the LORD has done what He spoke by His servant Elijah." [11] So Jehu killed all who remained of the house of Ahab in Jezreel, and all his great men and his close acquaintances and his priests, until he left him none remaining.

[12] And he arose and departed and went to Samaria. On the way, at Beth Eked of the Shepherds, [13] Jehu met with the brothers of Ahaziah king of Judah, and said, "Who *are* you?"

So they answered, "We *are* the brothers of Ahaziah; we have come down to greet the sons of the king and the sons of the queen mother."

[14] And he said, "Take them alive!" So they took them alive, and killed them at the well of Beth Eked, forty-two men; and he left none of them.

[15] Now when he departed from there, he met Jehonadab the son of Rechab, *coming* to meet him; and he greeted him and said to him, "Is your heart right, as my heart *is* toward your heart?"

And Jehonadab answered, "It is."

Jehu said, "If it is, give *me* your hand." So he gave *him* his hand, and he took him up to him into the chariot. [16] Then he said, "Come with me, and see my zeal for the LORD." So they had him ride in his chariot. [17] And when he came to Samaria, he killed all who remained to Ahab in Samaria, till he had destroyed them, according to the word of the LORD which He spoke to Elijah.

[18] Then Jehu gathered all the people together, and said to them, "Ahab served Baal a little, Jehu will serve him much. [19] Now therefore, call to me all the prophets of Baal, all his servants, and all his priests. Let no one be missing, for I have a great sacrifice for Baal. Whoever is missing shall not live." But Jehu acted deceptively, with the intent of destroying the worshipers of Baal. [20] And Jehu said, "Proclaim a solemn assembly for Baal." So they proclaimed *it.* [21] Then Jehu sent throughout all Israel; and all the worshipers of Baal came, so that there was not a man left who did not come. So they came into

the temple of Baal, and the temple of Baal was full from one end to the other. [22] And he said to the one in charge of the wardrobe, "Bring out vestments for all the worshipers of Baal." So he brought out vestments for them. [23] Then Jehu and Jehonadab the son of Rechab went into the temple of Baal, and said to the worshipers of Baal, "Search and see that no servants of the LORD are here with you, but only the worshipers of Baal." [24] So they went in to offer sacrifices and burnt offerings. Now Jehu had appointed for himself eighty men on the outside, and had said, "*If* any of the men whom I have brought into your hands escapes, *whoever lets him escape, it shall be* his life for the life of the other."

[25] Now it happened, as soon as he had made an end of offering the burnt offering, that Jehu said to the guard and to the captains, "Go in *and* kill them; let no one come out!" And they killed them with the edge of the sword; then the guards and the officers threw *them* out, and went into the inner room of the temple of Baal. [26] And they brought the *sacred* pillars out of the temple of Baal and burned them. [27] Then they broke down the *sacred* pillar of Baal, and tore down the temple of Baal and made it a refuse dump to this day. [28] Thus Jehu destroyed Baal from Israel.

[29] However Jehu did not turn away from the sins of Jeroboam the son of Nebat, who had made Israel sin, *that is,* from the golden calves that *were* at Bethel and Dan. [30] And the LORD said to Jehu, "Because you have done well in doing *what is* right in My sight, *and* have done to the house of Ahab all that *was* in My heart, your sons shall sit on the throne of Israel to the fourth *generation.*" [31] But Jehu took no heed to walk in the law of the LORD God of Israel with all his heart; for he did not depart from the sins of Jeroboam, who had made Israel sin.

[32] In those days the LORD began to cut off *parts* of Israel; and Hazael conquered them in all the territory of Israel [33] from the Jordan eastward: all the land of Gilead—Gad, Reuben, and Manasseh—from Aroer, which *is* by the River Arnon, including Gilead and Bashan. [34] Now the rest of the acts of Jehu, all that he did, and all his might, *are* they not

written in the book of the chronicles of the kings of Israel? [35] So Jehu rested with his fathers, and they buried him in Samaria. Then Jehoahaz his son reigned in his place. [36] And the period that Jehu reigned over Israel in Samaria *was* twenty-eight years.

~ PSALM 72:17–20 ~

[17] His name shall endure forever;
　　His name shall continue as long as
　　　the sun.
　　And *men* shall be blessed in Him;
　　All nations shall call Him blessed.

[18] Blessed *be* the LORD God, the God
　　　of Israel,
　　Who only does wondrous things!
[19] And blessed *be* His glorious name
　　　forever!
　　And let the whole earth be filled
　　　with His glory.
　　Amen and Amen.

[20] The prayers of David the son of Jesse
　　are ended.

~ PROVERBS 18:14, 15 ~

[14] The spirit of a man will sustain him
　　　in sickness,
　　But who can bear a broken spirit?

[15] The heart of the prudent acquires
　　　knowledge,
　　And the ear of the wise seeks
　　　knowledge.

~ JOHN 19:1–22 ~

So then Pilate took Jesus and scourged *Him*. [2] And the soldiers twisted a crown of thorns and put *it* on His head, and they put on Him a purple robe. [3] Then they said, "Hail, King of the Jews!" And they struck Him with their hands.

[4] Pilate then went out again, and said to them, "Behold, I am bringing Him out to you, that you may know that I find no fault in Him."

[5] Then Jesus came out, wearing the crown of thorns and the purple robe. And *Pilate* said to them, "Behold the Man!"

[6] Therefore, when the chief priests and officers saw Him, they cried out, saying, "Crucify *Him,* crucify *Him!*"

Pilate said to them, "You take Him and crucify *Him,* for I find no fault in Him."

[7] The Jews answered him, "We have a law, and according to our law He ought to die, because He made Himself the Son of God."

[8] Therefore, when Pilate heard that saying, he was the more afraid, [9] and went again into the Praetorium, and said to Jesus, "Where are You from?" But Jesus gave him no answer.

[10] Then Pilate said to Him, "Are You not speaking to me? Do You not know that I have power to crucify You, and power to release You?"

[11] Jesus answered, "You could have no power at all against Me unless it had been given you from above. Therefore the one who delivered Me to you has the greater sin."

[12] From then on Pilate sought to release Him, but the Jews cried out, saying, "If you let this Man go, you are not Caesar's friend. Whoever makes himself a king speaks against Caesar."

[13] When Pilate therefore heard that saying, he brought Jesus out and sat down in the judgment seat in a place that is called *The* Pavement, but in Hebrew, Gabbatha. [14] Now it was the Preparation Day of the Passover, and about the sixth hour. And he said to the Jews, "Behold your King!"

[15] But they cried out, "Away with *Him,* away with *Him!* Crucify Him!"

Pilate said to them, "Shall I crucify your King?"

The chief priests answered, "We have no king but Caesar!"

[16] Then he delivered Him to them to be crucified. Then they took Jesus and led *Him* away.

[17] And He, bearing His cross, went out to a place called *the Place* of a Skull, which is called in Hebrew, Golgotha, [18] where they crucified Him, and two others with Him, one on either side, and Jesus in the center. [19] Now Pilate wrote a title and put *it* on the cross. And the writing was:

JESUS OF NAZARETH,
THE KING OF THE JEWS.

²⁰ Then many of the Jews read this title, for the place where Jesus was crucified was near the city; and it was written in Hebrew, Greek, *and* Latin. ²¹ Therefore the chief priests of the Jews said to Pilate, "Do not write, 'The King of the Jews,' but, 'He said, "I am the King of the Jews." ' " ²² Pilate answered, "What I have written, I have written."

READING 163 · JUNE 12

~ 2 KINGS 11:1—13:25 ~

When Athaliah the mother of Ahaziah saw that her son was dead, she arose and destroyed all the royal heirs. ² But Jehosheba, the daughter of King Joram, sister of Ahaziah, took Joash the son of Ahaziah, and stole him away from among the king's sons *who were* being murdered; and they hid him and his nurse in the bedroom, from Athaliah, so that he was not killed. ³ So he was hidden with her in the house of the LORD for six years, while Athaliah reigned over the land.

⁴ In the seventh year Jehoiada sent and brought the captains of hundreds—of the bodyguards and the escorts—and brought them into the house of the LORD to him. And he made a covenant with them and took an oath from them in the house of the LORD, and showed them the king's son. ⁵ Then he commanded them, saying, "This *is* what you shall do: One-third of you who come on duty on the Sabbath shall be keeping watch over the king's house, ⁶ one-third *shall be* at the gate of Sur, and one-third at the gate behind the escorts. You shall keep the watch of the house, lest it be broken down. ⁷ The two contingents of you who go off duty on the Sabbath shall keep the watch of the house of the LORD for the king. ⁸ But you shall surround the king on all sides, every man with his weapons in his hand; and whoever comes within range, let him be put to death. You are to be with the king as he goes out and as he comes in."

⁹ So the captains of the hundreds did according to all that Jehoiada the priest commanded. Each of them took his men who were to be on duty on the Sabbath, with those who were going off duty on the Sabbath, and came to Jehoiada the priest. ¹⁰ And the priest gave the captains of hundreds the spears and shields which *had belonged* to King David, that were in the temple of the LORD. ¹¹ Then the escorts stood, every man with his weapons in his hand, all around the king, from the right side of the temple to the left side of the temple, by the altar and the house. ¹² And he brought out the king's son, put the crown on him, and *gave him* the Testimony; they made him king and anointed him, and they clapped their hands and said, "Long live the king!"

¹³ Now when Athaliah heard the noise of the escorts *and* the people, she came to the people *in* the temple of the LORD. ¹⁴ When she looked, there was the king standing by a pillar according to custom; and the leaders and the trumpeters were by the king. All the people of the land were rejoicing and blowing trumpets. So Athaliah tore her clothes and cried out, "Treason! Treason!"

¹⁵ And Jehoiada the priest commanded the captains of the hundreds, the officers of the army, and said to them, "Take her outside under guard, and slay with the sword whoever follows her." For the priest had said, "Do not let her be killed in the house of the LORD." ¹⁶ So they seized her; and she went by way of the horses' entrance *into* the king's house, and there she was killed.

¹⁷ Then Jehoiada made a covenant between the LORD, the king, and the people, that they should be the LORD's people, and *also* between the king and the people. ¹⁸ And all the people of the land went to the temple of Baal, and tore it down. They thoroughly broke in pieces its altars and images, and killed Mattan the priest of Baal before the altars. And the priest appointed officers over the house of the LORD. ¹⁹ Then he took the captains of hundreds, the bodyguards, the escorts, and all the people of

the land; and they brought the king down from the house of the LORD, and went by way of the gate of the escorts to the king's house. Then he sat on the throne of the kings. ²⁰ So all the people of the land rejoiced; and the city was quiet, for they had slain Athaliah with the sword *in* the king's house. ²¹ Jehoash *was* seven years old when he became king.

12 In the seventh year of Jehu, Jehoash became king, and he reigned forty years in Jerusalem. His mother's name *was* Zibiah of Beersheba. ² Jehoash did *what was* right in the sight of the LORD all the days in which Jehoiada the priest instructed him. ³ But the high places were not taken away; the people still sacrificed and burned incense on the high places.

⁴ And Jehoash said to the priests, "All the money of the dedicated gifts that are brought into the house of the LORD—each man's census money, each man's assessment money—*and* all the money that a man purposes in his heart to bring into the house of the LORD, ⁵ let the priests take *it* themselves, each from his constituency; and let them repair the damages of the temple, wherever any dilapidation is found."

⁶ Now it was so, by the twenty-third year of King Jehoash, *that* the priests had not repaired the damages of the temple. ⁷ So King Jehoash called Jehoiada the priest and the *other* priests, and said to them, "Why have you not repaired the damages of the temple? Now therefore, do not take *more* money from your constituency, but deliver it for repairing the damages of the temple." ⁸ And the priests agreed that they would neither receive *more* money from the people, nor repair the damages of the temple.

⁹ Then Jehoiada the priest took a chest, bored a hole in its lid, and set it beside the altar, on the right side as one comes into the house of the LORD; and the priests who kept the door put there all the money brought into the house of the LORD. ¹⁰ So it was, whenever they saw that *there was* much money in the chest, that the king's scribe and the high priest came up and put it in bags, and counted the money that was found in the house of the LORD. ¹¹ Then they gave the money, which had

been apportioned, into the hands of those who did the work, who had the oversight of the house of the LORD; and they paid it out to the carpenters and builders who worked on the house of the LORD, ¹² and to masons and stonecutters, and for buying timber and hewn stone, to repair the damage of the house of the LORD, and for all that was paid out to repair the temple. ¹³ However there were not made for the house of the LORD basins of silver, trimmers, sprinkling-bowls, trumpets, any articles of gold or articles of silver, from the money brought into the house of the LORD. ¹⁴ But they gave that to the workmen, and they repaired the house of the LORD with it. ¹⁵ Moreover they did not require an account from the men into whose hand they delivered the money to be paid to workmen, for they dealt faithfully. ¹⁶ The money from the trespass offerings and the money from the sin offerings was not brought into the house of the LORD. It belonged to the priests.

¹⁷ Hazael king of Syria went up and fought against Gath, and took it; then Hazael set his face to go up to Jerusalem. ¹⁸ And Jehoash king of Judah took all the sacred things that his fathers, Jehoshaphat and Jehoram and Ahaziah, kings of Judah, had dedicated, and his own sacred things, and all the gold found in the treasuries of the house of the LORD and in the king's house, and sent *them* to Hazael king of Syria. Then he went away from Jerusalem.

¹⁹ Now the rest of the acts of Joash, and all that he did, *are* they not written in the book of the chronicles of the kings of Judah?

²⁰ And his servants arose and formed a conspiracy, and killed Joash in the house of the Millo, which goes down to Silla. ²¹ For Jozachar the son of Shimeath and Jehozabad the son of Shomer, his servants, struck him. So he died, and they buried him with his fathers in the City of David. Then Amaziah his son reigned in his place.

13 In the twenty-third year of Joash the son of Ahaziah, king of Judah, Jehoahaz the son of Jehu became king over Israel in Samaria, *and reigned* seventeen years. ² And he did evil in the sight of the LORD, and followed the sins of Jeroboam the son

Giving While You're Living

A very rich man once moaned to a friend, "Why is it that everybody is always criticizing me for being miserly, when everyone knows I have made provisions to leave everything I possess to charity when I die?"

The friend paused for a moment and then said, "Well, I guess it's like the pig and the cow."

"What do you mean?" the rich man asked.

The friend said, "The story goes that a pig was lamenting to a cow one day about how unpopular he was. 'People are always talking about your gentleness and your kind brown eyes,' the pig said. 'They only speak of me in degrading terms. It seems grossly unfair. Sure, you give milk and cream, but I give even more. I give bacon and ham. I give bristles. Why, they even pickle my feet! Yet nobody likes me. Why is this?'

"The cow thought for a minute and then responded, 'Well, maybe it's because I give while I'm still living.'"

Reputations and generous acts of kindness toward others receive acclaim both during and after a person's lifetime, far more than bequests. Let people see your gifts as an extension of your life, not merely as a consequence of your death.

of Nebat, who had made Israel sin. He did not depart from them.

³ Then the anger of the LORD was aroused against Israel, and He delivered them into the hand of Hazael king of Syria, and into the hand of Ben-Hadad the son of Hazael, all *their* days. ⁴ So Jehoahaz pleaded with the LORD, and the LORD listened to him; for He saw the oppression of Israel, because the king of Syria oppressed them. ⁵ Then the LORD gave Israel a deliverer, so that they escaped from under the hand of the Syrians; and the children of Israel dwelt in their tents as before. ⁶ Nevertheless they did not depart from the sins of the house of Jeroboam, who had made Israel sin, *but* walked in them; and the wooden image also remained in Samaria. ⁷ For He left of the army of Jehoahaz only fifty horsemen, ten chariots, and ten thousand foot soldiers; for the king of Syria had destroyed them and made them like the dust at threshing.

⁸ Now the rest of the acts of Jehoahaz, all that he did, and his might, *are* they not written in the book of the chronicles of the kings of Israel? ⁹ So Jehoahaz rested with his fathers, and they buried him in Samaria. Then Joash his son reigned in his place.

¹⁰ In the thirty-seventh year of Joash king of Judah, Jehoash the son of Jehoahaz became king over Israel in Samaria, *and reigned* sixteen years. ¹¹ And he did evil in the sight of the LORD. He did not depart from all the sins of Jeroboam the son of Nebat, who made Israel sin, *but* walked in them.

¹² Now the rest of the acts of Joash, all that he did, and his might with which he fought against Amaziah king of Judah, *are* they not written in the book of the chronicles of the kings of Israel? ¹³ So Joash rested with his fathers. Then Jeroboam sat on his throne. And Joash was buried in Samaria with the kings of Israel.

¹⁴ Elisha had become sick with the illness of which he would die. Then Joash the king of Israel came down to him, and wept over his face, and said, "O my father, my father, the chariots of Israel and their horsemen!"

¹⁵ And Elisha said to him, "Take a bow and some arrows." So he took himself a bow and some arrows. ¹⁶ Then he said to the king of Israel, "Put your hand on the bow." So he put his hand *on it,* and Elisha put his hands on the king's hands. ¹⁷ And he said, "Open the east window"; and he opened *it.* Then Elisha said, "Shoot"; and he shot. And he said, "The arrow of the LORD's deliverance and the arrow of deliverance from Syria; for you must strike the Syrians at Aphek till you have destroyed *them.*" ¹⁸ Then he said, "Take the arrows"; so he took *them.* And he said to the king of Israel, "Strike the ground"; so he struck three times, and stopped. ¹⁹ And the man of God was angry with him, and said, "You should have struck five or six times; then you would have struck Syria till you had destroyed *it*! But now you will strike Syria *only* three times."

²⁰ Then Elisha died, and they buried him. And the *raiding* bands from Moab invaded the land in the spring of the year. ²¹ So it was, as they were burying a man, that suddenly they spied a band *of raiders;* and they put the man in the tomb of Elisha; and when the man was let down and touched the bones of Elisha, he revived and stood on his feet.

²² And Hazael king of Syria oppressed Israel all the days of Jehoahaz. ²³ But the LORD was gracious to them, had compassion on them, and regarded them, because of His covenant with Abraham, Isaac, and Jacob, and would not yet destroy them or cast them from His presence.

²⁴ Now Hazael king of Syria died. Then Ben-Hadad his son reigned in his place. ²⁵ And Jehoash the son of Jehoahaz recaptured from the hand of Ben-Hadad, the son of Hazael, the cities which he had taken out of the hand of Jehoahaz his father by war. Three times Joash defeated him and recaptured the cities of Israel.

∽ PSALM 73:1–9 ∽

1   Truly God *is* good to Israel,
    To such as are pure in heart.
2   But as for me, my feet had almost
       stumbled;
    My steps had nearly slipped.
3   For I *was* envious of the boastful,
    When I saw the prosperity of the
       wicked.

4 For *there are* no pangs in their death,
  But their strength *is* firm.
5 They *are* not in trouble *as other* men,
  Nor are they plagued like *other* men.
6 Therefore pride serves as their
    necklace;
  Violence covers them *like* a garment.
7 Their eyes bulge with abundance;
  They have more than heart could
    wish.
8 They scoff and speak wickedly
    concerning oppression;
  They speak loftily.
9 They set their mouth against the
    heavens,
  And their tongue walks through the
    earth.

~ PROVERBS 18:16, 17 ~

16 A man's gift makes room for him,
   And brings him before great men.

17 The first *one* to plead his cause
     seems right,
   Until his neighbor comes and
     examines him.

~ JOHN 19:23–42 ~

Then the soldiers, when they had crucified Jesus, took His garments and made
four parts, to each soldier a part, and also
the tunic. Now the tunic was without
seam, woven from the top in one piece.
24 They said therefore among themselves,
"Let us not tear it, but cast lots for it,
whose it shall be," that the Scripture might
be fulfilled which says:

> "They divided My garments among
>   them,
> And for My clothing they cast
>   lots."

Therefore the soldiers did these things.
25 Now there stood by the cross of Jesus
His mother, and His mother's sister, Mary
the *wife* of Clopas, and Mary Magdalene.
26 When Jesus therefore saw His mother,
and the disciple whom He loved standing
by, He said to His mother, "Woman, be-

hold your son!" 27 Then He said to the
disciple, "Behold your mother!" And from
that hour that disciple took her to his own
home.
  28 After this, Jesus, knowing that all
things were now accomplished, that
the Scripture might be fulfilled, said, "I
thirst!" 29 Now a vessel full of sour wine
was sitting there; and they filled a sponge
with sour wine, put *it* on hyssop, and put
it to His mouth. 30 So when Jesus had
received the sour wine, He said, "It is finished!" And bowing His head, He gave
up His spirit.
  31 Therefore, because it was the Preparation *Day,* that the bodies should not
remain on the cross on the Sabbath (for
that Sabbath was a high day), the Jews
asked Pilate that their legs might be broken, and *that* they might be taken away.
32 Then the soldiers came and broke the
legs of the first and of the other who was
crucified with Him. 33 But when they came
to Jesus and saw that He was already dead,
they did not break His legs. 34 But one of
the soldiers pierced His side with a spear,
and immediately blood and water came
out. 35 And he who has seen has testified,
and his testimony is true; and he knows
that he is telling the truth, so that you
may believe. 36 For these things were done
that the Scripture should be fulfilled, "Not
one of His bones shall be broken." 37 And
again another Scripture says, "They shall
look on Him whom they pierced."
  38 After this, Joseph of Arimathea, being a disciple of Jesus, but secretly, for fear
of the Jews, asked Pilate that he might
take away the body of Jesus; and Pilate
gave *him* permission. So he came and took
the body of Jesus. 39 And Nicodemus, who
at first came to Jesus by night, also came,
bringing a mixture of myrrh and aloes,
about a hundred pounds. 40 Then they
took the body of Jesus, and bound it in
strips of linen with the spices, as the custom of the Jews is to bury. 41 Now in the
place where He was crucified there was a
garden, and in the garden a new tomb in
which no one had yet been laid. 42 So there
they laid Jesus, because of the Jews' Preparation *Day,* for the tomb was nearby.

∼ 2 Kings 14:1–29 ∼

In the second year of Joash the son of Jehoahaz, king of Israel, Amaziah the son of Joash, king of Judah, became king. ² He was twenty-five years old when he became king, and he reigned twenty-nine years in Jerusalem. His mother's name was Jehoaddan of Jerusalem. ³ And he did *what was* right in the sight of the LORD, yet not like his father David; he did everything as his father Joash had done. ⁴ However the high places were not taken away, and the people still sacrificed and burned incense on the high places.

⁵ Now it happened, as soon as the kingdom was established in his hand, that he executed his servants who had murdered his father the king. ⁶ But the children of the murderers he did not execute, according to what is written in the Book of the Law of Moses, in which the LORD commanded, saying, "Fathers shall not be put to death for their children, nor shall children be put to death for their fathers; but a person shall be put to death for his own sin."

⁷ He killed ten thousand Edomites in the Valley of Salt, and took Sela by war, and called its name Joktheel to this day.

⁸ Then Amaziah sent messengers to Jehoash the son of Jehoahaz, the son of Jehu, king of Israel, saying, "Come, let us face one another *in battle.*" ⁹ And Jehoash king of Israel sent to Amaziah king of Judah, saying, "The thistle that *was* in Lebanon sent to the cedar that *was* in Lebanon, saying, 'Give your daughter to my son as wife'; and a wild beast that *was* in Lebanon passed by and trampled the thistle. ¹⁰ You have indeed defeated Edom, and your heart has lifted you up. Glory *in that,* and stay at home; for why should you meddle with trouble so that you fall—you and Judah with you?"

¹¹ But Amaziah would not heed. Therefore Jehoash king of Israel went out; so he and Amaziah king of Judah faced one another at Beth Shemesh, which *belongs* to Judah. ¹² And Judah was defeated by Israel, and every man fled to his tent. ¹³ Then Jehoash king of Israel captured Amaziah king of Judah, the son of Jehoash, the son of Ahaziah, at Beth Shemesh; and he went to Jerusalem, and broke down the wall of Jerusalem from the Gate of Ephraim to the Corner Gate—four hundred cubits. ¹⁴ And he took all the gold and silver, all the articles that were found in the house of the LORD and in the treasuries of the king's house, and hostages, and returned to Samaria.

¹⁵ Now the rest of the acts of Jehoash which he did—his might, and how he fought with Amaziah king of Judah—*are* they not written in the book of the chronicles of the kings of Israel? ¹⁶ So Jehoash rested with his fathers, and was buried in Samaria with the kings of Israel. Then Jeroboam his son reigned in his place.

¹⁷ Amaziah the son of Joash, king of Judah, lived fifteen years after the death of Jehoash the son of Jehoahaz, king of Israel. ¹⁸ Now the rest of the acts of Amaziah, *are* they not written in the book of the chronicles of the kings of Judah? ¹⁹ And they formed a conspiracy against him in Jerusalem, and he fled to Lachish; but they sent after him to Lachish and killed him there. ²⁰ Then they brought him on horses, and he was buried at Jerusalem with his fathers in the City of David.

²¹ And all the people of Judah took Azariah, who *was* sixteen years old, and made him king instead of his father Amaziah. ²² He built Elath and restored it to Judah, after the king rested with his fathers.

²³ In the fifteenth year of Amaziah the son of Joash, king of Judah, Jeroboam the son of Joash, king of Israel, became king in Samaria, *and reigned* forty-one years. ²⁴ And he did evil in the sight of the LORD; he did not depart from all the sins of Jeroboam the son of Nebat, who had made Israel sin. ²⁵ He restored the territory of Israel from the entrance of Hamath to the Sea of the Arabah, according to the word of the LORD God of Israel, which He had spoken through His servant Jonah the son of Amittai, the prophet who *was* from Gath Hepher. ²⁶ For the LORD saw *that* the affliction of Israel *was* very bitter; and whether bond or free, there was

The Spring of Forgiveness

> If you forgive the sins of any, they are forgiven them; if you retain the sins of any, they are retained.
>
> *John 20:23*

Many of us think of "springs" as emerging only high in the mountains, or as bubbling up in an arid desert, creating an oasis.

Some springs emerge from the earth very close to salt-water seas. The water gushes up from the beach sands just as sweet as any that might burst from the rocks in the high hills. When the sea is at low tide, one can dig into the spring and drink from its clear, refreshing water.

Once the tide rolls back in and covers the spring, one might assume it would "pollute" the spring and cause it to become salty. Not so. When the tide again is low, the spring continues to produce fresh, sparkling water, just as sweet as before.

So, too, is it with forgiveness born of love. No wrong, cruelty, or rejection can have an impact on genuine forgiveness. We forgive "no matter what" — first, because it is the nature of love to forgive. Second, because our forgiveness has tremendous potential to impact the hearts of those who wrong us. This is true even if we can see no evidence of it.

And finally, forgiveness keeps our own souls fresh and clear and sparkling. If we allow the brackish waters of unforgiveness to seep in, our spring becomes clogged and we begin to stagnate. All we have to do to release the spring once again is to forgive. When we choose to forgive, God gives us the grace necessary to do so.

no helper for Israel. ²⁷ And the LORD did not say that He would blot out the name of Israel from under heaven; but He saved them by the hand of Jeroboam the son of Joash.

²⁸ Now the rest of the acts of Jeroboam, and all that he did—his might, how he made war, and how he recaptured for Israel, from Damascus and Hamath, *what had belonged* to Judah—*are* they not written in the book of the chronicles of the kings of Israel? ²⁹ So Jeroboam rested with his fathers, the kings of Israel. Then Zechariah his son reigned in his place.

~ PSALM 73:10–20 ~

¹⁰ Therefore his people return here,
    And waters of a full *cup* are drained
        by them.
¹¹ And they say, "How does God
        know?
    And is there knowledge in the Most
        High?"
¹² Behold, these *are* the ungodly,
    Who are always at ease;
    They increase *in* riches.
¹³ Surely I have cleansed my heart *in*
        vain,
    And washed my hands in innocence.
¹⁴ For all day long I have been plagued,
    And chastened every morning.

¹⁵ If I had said, "I will speak thus,"
    Behold, I would have been untrue to
        the generation of Your children.
¹⁶ When I thought *how* to understand
        this,
    It *was* too painful for me—
¹⁷ Until I went into the sanctuary of
        God;
    Then I understood their end.

¹⁸ Surely You set them in slippery
        places;
    You cast them down to destruction.
¹⁹ Oh, how they are *brought* to
        desolation, as in a moment!
    They are utterly consumed with
        terrors.
²⁰ As a dream when *one* awakes,
    So, Lord, when You awake,
    You shall despise their image.

~ PROVERBS 18:18, 19 ~

¹⁸ Casting lots causes contentions to
        cease,
    And keeps the mighty apart.

¹⁹ A brother offended *is harder to win*
        than a strong city,
    And contentions *are* like the bars of
        a castle.

~ JOHN 20:1–31 ~

Now the first *day* of the week Mary Magdalene went to the tomb early, while it was still dark, and saw *that* the stone had been taken away from the tomb. ² Then she ran and came to Simon Peter, and to the other disciple, whom Jesus loved, and said to them, "They have taken away the Lord out of the tomb, and we do not know where they have laid Him."

³ Peter therefore went out, and the other disciple, and were going to the tomb. ⁴ So they both ran together, and the other disciple outran Peter and came to the tomb first. ⁵ And he, stooping down and looking in, saw the linen cloths lying *there;* yet he did not go in. ⁶ Then Simon Peter came, following him, and went into the tomb; and he saw the linen cloths lying *there,* ⁷ and the handkerchief that had been around His head, not lying with the linen cloths, but folded together in a place by itself. ⁸ Then the other disciple, who came to the tomb first, went in also; and he saw and believed. ⁹ For as yet they did not know the Scripture, that He must rise again from the dead. ¹⁰ Then the disciples went away again to their own homes.

¹¹ But Mary stood outside by the tomb weeping, and as she wept she stooped down *and looked* into the tomb. ¹² And she saw two angels in white sitting, one at the head and the other at the feet, where the body of Jesus had lain. ¹³ Then they said to her, "Woman, why are you weeping?"

She said to them, "Because they have taken away my Lord, and I do not know where they have laid Him."

¹⁴ Now when she had said this, she turned around and saw Jesus standing *there,* and did not know that it was Jesus.

¹⁵ Jesus said to her, "Woman, why are you weeping? Whom are you seeking?"

She, supposing Him to be the gardener, said to Him, "Sir, if You have carried Him away, tell me where You have laid Him, and I will take Him away."

¹⁶ Jesus said to her, "Mary!"

She turned and said to Him, "Rabboni!" (which is to say, Teacher).

¹⁷ Jesus said to her, "Do not cling to Me, for I have not yet ascended to My Father; but go to My brethren and say to them, 'I am ascending to My Father and your Father, and *to* My God and your God.' "

¹⁸ Mary Magdalene came and told the disciples that she had seen the Lord, and *that* He had spoken these things to her.

¹⁹ Then, the same day at evening, being the first *day* of the week, when the doors were shut where the disciples were assembled, for fear of the Jews, Jesus came and stood in the midst, and said to them, "Peace *be* with you." ²⁰ When He had said this, He showed them *His* hands and His side. Then the disciples were glad when they saw the Lord.

²¹ So Jesus said to them again, "Peace to you! As the Father has sent Me, I also send you." ²² And when He had said this, He breathed on *them,* and said to them, "Receive the Holy Spirit. ²³ If you forgive the sins of any, they are forgiven them; if you retain the *sins* of any, they are retained."

²⁴ Now Thomas, called the Twin, one of the twelve, was not with them when Jesus came. ²⁵ The other disciples therefore said to him, "We have seen the Lord."

So he said to them, "Unless I see in His hands the print of the nails, and put my finger into the print of the nails, and put my hand into His side, I will not believe."

²⁶ And after eight days His disciples were again inside, and Thomas with them. Jesus came, the doors being shut, and stood in the midst, and said, "Peace to you!" ²⁷ Then He said to Thomas, "Reach your finger here, and look at My hands; and reach your hand *here,* and put *it* into My side. Do not be unbelieving, but believing."

²⁸ And Thomas answered and said to Him, "My Lord and my God!"

²⁹ Jesus said to him, "Thomas, because you have seen Me, you have believed. Blessed *are* those who have not seen and *yet* have believed."

³⁰ And truly Jesus did many other signs in the presence of His disciples, which are not written in this book; ³¹ but these are written that you may believe that Jesus is the Christ, the Son of God, and that believing you may have life in His name.

~ 2 KINGS 15:1—16:20 ~

In the twenty-seventh year of Jeroboam king of Israel, Azariah the son of Amaziah, king of Judah, became king. ² He was sixteen years old when he became king, and he reigned fifty-two years in Jerusalem. His mother's name *was* Jecholiah of Jerusalem. ³ And he did *what was* right in the sight of the LORD, according to all that his father Amaziah had done, ⁴ except that the high places were not removed; the people still sacrificed and burned incense on the high places. ⁵ Then the LORD struck the king, so that he was a leper until the day of his death; so he dwelt in an isolated house. And Jotham the king's son *was* over the *royal* house, judging the people of the land.

⁶ Now the rest of the acts of Azariah, and all that he did, *are* they not written in the book of the chronicles of the kings of Judah? ⁷ So Azariah rested with his fathers, and they buried him with his fathers in the City of David. Then Jotham his son reigned in his place.

⁸ In the thirty-eighth year of Azariah king of Judah, Zechariah the son of Jeroboam reigned over Israel in Samaria six months. ⁹ And he did evil in the sight of the LORD, as his fathers had done; he did not depart from the sins of Jeroboam

the son of Nebat, who had made Israel sin. ¹⁰ Then Shallum the son of Jabesh conspired against him, and struck and killed him in front of the people; and he reigned in his place.

¹¹ Now the rest of the acts of Zechariah, indeed they *are* written in the book of the chronicles of the kings of Israel.

¹² This *was* the word of the LORD which He spoke to Jehu, saying, "Your sons shall sit on the throne of Israel to the fourth *generation*." And so it was.

¹³ Shallum the son of Jabesh became king in the thirty-ninth year of Uzziah king of Judah; and he reigned a full month in Samaria. ¹⁴ For Menahem the son of Gadi went up from Tirzah, came to Samaria, and struck Shallum the son of Jabesh in Samaria and killed him; and he reigned in his place.

¹⁵ Now the rest of the acts of Shallum, and the conspiracy which he led, indeed they *are* written in the book of the chronicles of the kings of Israel. ¹⁶ Then from Tirzah, Menahem attacked Tiphsah, all who *were* there, and its territory. Because they did not surrender, therefore he attacked *it*. All the women there who were with child he ripped open.

¹⁷ In the thirty-ninth year of Azariah king of Judah, Menahem the son of Gadi became king over Israel, *and reigned* ten years in Samaria. ¹⁸ And he did evil in the sight of the LORD; he did not depart all his days from the sins of Jeroboam the son of Nebat, who had made Israel sin. ¹⁹ Pul king of Assyria came against the land; and Menahem gave Pul a thousand talents of silver, that his hand might be with him to strengthen the kingdom under his control. ²⁰ And Menahem exacted the money from Israel, from all the very wealthy, from each man fifty shekels of silver, to give to the king of Assyria. So the king of Assyria turned back, and did not stay there in the land.

²¹ Now the rest of the acts of Menahem, and all that he did, *are* they not written in the book of the chronicles of the kings of Israel? ²² So Menahem rested with his fathers. Then Pekahiah his son reigned in his place.

²³ In the fiftieth year of Azariah king of Judah, Pekahiah the son of Menahem became king over Israel in Samaria, *and*

reigned two years. ²⁴ And he did evil in the sight of the LORD; he did not depart from the sins of Jeroboam the son of Nebat, who had made Israel sin. ²⁵ Then Pekah the son of Remaliah, an officer of his, conspired against him and killed him in Samaria, in the citadel of the king's house, along with Argob and Arieh; and with him were fifty men of Gilead. He killed him and reigned in his place.

²⁶ Now the rest of the acts of Pekahiah, and all that he did, indeed they *are* written in the book of the chronicles of the kings of Israel.

²⁷ In the fifty-second year of Azariah king of Judah, Pekah the son of Remaliah became king over Israel in Samaria, *and reigned* twenty years. ²⁸ And he did evil in the sight of the LORD; he did not depart from the sins of Jeroboam the son of Nebat, who had made Israel sin. ²⁹ In the days of Pekah king of Israel, Tiglath-Pileser king of Assyria came and took Ijon, Abel Beth Maachah, Janoah, Kedesh, Hazor, Gilead, and Galilee, all the land of Naphtali; and he carried them captive to Assyria. ³⁰ Then Hoshea the son of Elah led a conspiracy against Pekah the son of Remaliah, and struck and killed him; so he reigned in his place in the twentieth year of Jotham the son of Uzziah.

³¹ Now the rest of the acts of Pekah, and all that he did, indeed they *are* written in the book of the chronicles of the kings of Israel.

³² In the second year of Pekah the son of Remaliah, king of Israel, Jotham the son of Uzziah, king of Judah, began to reign. ³³ He was twenty-five years old when he became king, and he reigned sixteen years in Jerusalem. His mother's name *was* Jerusha the daughter of Zadok. ³⁴ And he did *what was* right in the sight of the LORD; he did according to all that his father Uzziah had done. ³⁵ However the high places were not removed; the people still sacrificed and burned incense on the high places. He built the Upper Gate of the house of the LORD.

³⁶ Now the rest of the acts of Jotham, and all that he did, *are* they not written in the book of the chronicles of the kings of Judah? ³⁷ In those days the LORD began to send Rezin king of Syria and Pekah the son of Remaliah against Judah. ³⁸ So

The Answer is Already Waiting

You will guide
me with
Your counsel,
and afterward
receive me
to glory.

Psalm 73:24

It was nearly 11 PM by the time two women left a parents'meeting at their children's school, which was located some 25 miles from their homes. As they neared their car, they noticed three youths running from the parking area, laughing. "It seems we got here just in time," the driver said, and was glad when her engine sputtered to life. "There's a shortcut my husband takes," she said, hoping to cut some time off of their drive, since it was so late.

Forty minutes later, they were lost. Then, their headlights began to flicker and the engine lost power. "Shall we walk and see if we can find a phone?" the driver asked. "Let's pray first," the other woman suggested. Together they prayed, "Lord, guide us to help."

They walked to a crossroad and saw a distant porch light. When a man answered their knock, they told him their problem. He said, "I'm a mechanic. Maybe I can help." When he checked the car, he said, "Some joker exchanged batteries with you. You have a golf-cart battery in your car! This may sound strange to you but just today I brought a new battery home from my garage. I'll put it in for you if you like." Before long, the car was repaired and the Lord had one more surprise. Friends visiting the man and his wife were from their home town. They were just about to leave, so the two women followed them home!

God is always available to lead us and guide us. He can see the road ahead and knows what we'll be needing. He prepares it, then when we ask, He leads us right to the answer we need. All we have to do is ask!

Jotham rested with his fathers, and was buried with his fathers in the City of David his father. Then Ahaz his son reigned in his place.

16 In the seventeenth year of Pekah the son of Remaliah, Ahaz the son of Jotham, king of Judah, began to reign. ² Ahaz *was* twenty years old when he became king, and he reigned sixteen years in Jerusalem; and he did not do *what was* right in the sight of the LORD his God, as his father David *had done.* ³ But he walked in the way of the kings of Israel; indeed he made his son pass through the fire, according to the abominations of the nations whom the LORD had cast out from before the children of Israel. ⁴ And he sacrificed and burned incense on the high places, on the hills, and under every green tree.

⁵ Then Rezin king of Syria and Pekah the son of Remaliah, king of Israel, came up to Jerusalem to *make* war; and they besieged Ahaz but could not overcome *him.* ⁶ At that time Rezin king of Syria captured Elath for Syria, and drove the men of Judah from Elath. Then the Edomites went to Elath, and dwell there to this day.

⁷ So Ahaz sent messengers to Tiglath-Pileser king of Assyria, saying, "I *am* your servant and your son. Come up and save me from the hand of the king of Syria and from the hand of the king of Israel, who rise up against me." ⁸ And Ahaz took the silver and gold that was found in the house of the LORD, and in the treasuries of the king's house, and sent *it as* a present to the king of Assyria. ⁹ So the king of Assyria heeded him; for the king of Assyria went up against Damascus and took it, carried *its people* captive to Kir, and killed Rezin.

¹⁰ Now King Ahaz went to Damascus to meet Tiglath-Pileser king of Assyria, and saw an altar that *was* at Damascus; and King Ahaz sent to Urijah the priest the design of the altar and its pattern, according to all its workmanship. ¹¹ Then Urijah the priest built an altar according to all that King Ahaz had sent from Damascus. So Urijah the priest made *it* before King Ahaz came back from Damascus. ¹² And when the king came

back from Damascus, the king saw the altar; and the king approached the altar and made offerings on it. ¹³ So he burned his burnt offering and his grain offering; and he poured his drink offering and sprinkled the blood of his peace offerings on the altar. ¹⁴ He also brought the bronze altar which *was* before the LORD, from the front of the temple—from between the *new* altar and the house of the LORD—and put it on the north side of the *new* altar. ¹⁵ Then King Ahaz commanded Urijah the priest, saying, "On the great *new* altar burn the morning burnt offering, the evening grain offering, the king's burnt sacrifice, and his grain offering, with the burnt offering of all the people of the land, their grain offering, and their drink offerings; and sprinkle on it all the blood of the burnt offering and all the blood of the sacrifice. And the bronze altar shall be for me to inquire *by.*" ¹⁶ Thus did Urijah the priest, according to all that King Ahaz commanded.

¹⁷ And King Ahaz cut off the panels of the carts, and removed the lavers from them; and he took down the Sea from the bronze oxen that *were* under it, and put it on a pavement of stones. ¹⁸ Also he removed the Sabbath pavilion which they had built in the temple, and he removed the king's outer entrance from the house of the LORD, on account of the king of Assyria.

¹⁹ Now the rest of the acts of Ahaz which he did, *are* they not written in the book of the chronicles of the kings of Judah? ²⁰ So Ahaz rested with his fathers, and was buried with his fathers in the City of David. Then Hezekiah his son reigned in his place.

~ PSALM 73:21–28 ~

²¹ Thus my heart was grieved,
   And I was vexed in my mind.
²² I *was* so foolish and ignorant;
   I was *like* a beast before You.
²³ Nevertheless I *am* continually with You;
   You hold *me* by my right hand.
²⁴ You will guide me with Your counsel,
   And afterward receive me *to* glory.

²⁵ Whom have I in heaven *but You?*
And *there is* none upon earth *that* I
  desire besides You.

²⁶ My flesh and my heart fail;
But God *is* the strength of my heart
  and my portion forever.

²⁷ For indeed, those who are far from
  You shall perish;
You have destroyed all those who
  desert You for harlotry.

²⁸ But *it is* good for me to draw near to
  God;
I have put my trust in the Lord GOD,
  That I may declare all Your works.

∼ PROVERBS 18:20, 21 ∼

²⁰ A man's stomach shall be satisfied
  from the fruit of his mouth;
From the produce of his lips he shall
  be filled.

²¹ Death and life *are* in the power of
  the tongue,
And those who love it will eat its fruit.

∼ JOHN 21:1–25 ∼

After these things Jesus showed Himself again to the disciples at the Sea of Tiberias, and in this way He showed *Himself:* ² Simon Peter, Thomas called the Twin, Nathanael of Cana in Galilee, the *sons* of Zebedee, and two others of His disciples were together. ³ Simon Peter said to them, "I am going fishing."

They said to him, "We are going with you also." They went out and immediately got into the boat, and that night they caught nothing. ⁴ But when the morning had now come, Jesus stood on the shore; yet the disciples did not know that it was Jesus. ⁵ Then Jesus said to them, "Children, have you any food?"

They answered Him, "No."

⁶ And He said to them, "Cast the net on the right side of the boat, and you will find *some.*" So they cast, and now they were not able to draw it in because of the multitude of fish.

⁷ Therefore that disciple whom Jesus loved said to Peter, "It is the Lord!" Now when Simon Peter heard that it was the Lord, he put on *his* outer garment (for he

had removed it), and plunged into the sea. ⁸ But the other disciples came in the little boat (for they were not far from land, but about two hundred cubits), dragging the net with fish. ⁹ Then, as soon as they had come to land, they saw a fire of coals there, and fish laid on it, and bread. ¹⁰ Jesus said to them, "Bring some of the fish which you have just caught."

¹¹ Simon Peter went up and dragged the net to land, full of large fish, one hundred and fifty-three; and although there were so many, the net was not broken. ¹² Jesus said to them, "Come *and* eat breakfast." Yet none of the disciples dared ask Him, "Who are You?"—knowing that it was the Lord. ¹³ Jesus then came and took the bread and gave it to them, and likewise the fish.

¹⁴ This *is* now the third time Jesus showed Himself to His disciples after He was raised from the dead.

¹⁵ So when they had eaten breakfast, Jesus said to Simon Peter, "Simon, *son* of Jonah, do you love Me more than these?"

He said to Him, "Yes, Lord; You know that I love You."

He said to him, "Feed My lambs."

¹⁶ He said to him again a second time, "Simon, *son* of Jonah, do you love Me?"

He said to Him, "Yes, Lord; You know that I love You."

He said to him, "Tend My sheep."

¹⁷ He said to him the third time, "Simon, *son* of Jonah, do you love Me?" Peter was grieved because He said to him the third time, "Do you love Me?"

And he said to Him, "Lord, You know all things; You know that I love You."

Jesus said to him, "Feed My sheep. ¹⁸ Most assuredly, I say to you, when you were younger, you girded yourself and walked where you wished; but when you are old, you will stretch out your hands, and another will gird you and carry *you* where you do not wish." ¹⁹ This He spoke, signifying by what death he would glorify God. And when He had spoken this, He said to him, "Follow Me."

²⁰ Then Peter, turning around, saw the disciple whom Jesus loved following, who also had leaned on His breast at the supper, and said, "Lord, who is the one who betrays You?" ²¹ Peter, seeing him, said to Jesus, "But Lord, what *about* this man?"

²² Jesus said to him, "If I will that he remain till I come, what *is that* to you? You follow Me."

²³ Then this saying went out among the brethren that this disciple would not die. Yet Jesus did not say to him that he would not die, but, "If I will that he remain till I come, what *is that* to you?"

²⁴ This is the disciple who testifies of these things, and wrote these things; and we know that his testimony is true.

²⁵ And there are also many other things that Jesus did, which if they were written one by one, I suppose that even the world itself could not contain the books that would be written. Amen.

READING 166 · JUNE 15

~ 2 KINGS 17:1—18:37 ~

In the twelfth year of Ahaz king of Judah, Hoshea the son of Elah became king of Israel in Samaria, *and he reigned* nine years. ² And he did evil in the sight of the LORD, but not as the kings of Israel who were before him. ³ Shalmaneser king of Assyria came up against him; and Hoshea became his vassal, and paid him tribute money. ⁴ And the king of Assyria uncovered a conspiracy by Hoshea; for he had sent messengers to So, king of Egypt, and brought no tribute to the king of Assyria, as *he had done* year by year. Therefore the king of Assyria shut him up, and bound him in prison.

⁵ Now the king of Assyria went throughout all the land, and went up to Samaria and besieged it for three years. ⁶ In the ninth year of Hoshea, the king of Assyria took Samaria and carried Israel away to Assyria, and placed them in Halah and by the Habor, the River of Gozan, and in the cities of the Medes.

⁷ For so it was that the children of Israel had sinned against the LORD their God, who had brought them up out of the land of Egypt, from under the hand of Pharaoh king of Egypt; and they had feared other gods, ⁸ and had walked in the statutes of the nations whom the LORD had cast out from before the children of Israel, and of the kings of Israel, which they had made. ⁹ Also the children of Israel secretly did against the LORD their God things that *were* not right, and they built for themselves high places in all their cities, from watchtower to fortified city. ¹⁰ They set up for themselves *sacred* pillars and wooden images on every high hill and under every green tree. ¹¹ There they burned incense on all the high places, like the nations whom the LORD had carried away before them; and they did wicked things to provoke the LORD to anger, ¹² for they served idols, of which the LORD had said to them, "You shall not do this thing."

¹³ Yet the LORD testified against Israel and against Judah, by all of His prophets, every seer, saying, "Turn from your evil ways, and keep My commandments *and* My statutes, according to all the law which I commanded your fathers, and which I sent to you by My servants the prophets." ¹⁴ Nevertheless they would not hear, but stiffened their necks, like the necks of their fathers, who did not believe in the LORD their God. ¹⁵ And they rejected His statutes and His covenant that He had made with their fathers, and His testimonies which He had testified against them; they followed idols, became idolaters, and *went* after the nations who *were* all around them, *concerning* whom the LORD had charged them that they should not do like them. ¹⁶ So they left all the commandments of the LORD their God, made for themselves a molded image *and* two calves, made a wooden image and worshiped all the host of heaven, and served Baal. ¹⁷ And they caused their sons and daughters to pass through the fire, practiced witchcraft and soothsaying, and sold themselves to do evil in the sight of the LORD, to provoke Him to anger. ¹⁸ Therefore the LORD was very angry with Israel, and removed them from His sight; there was none left but the tribe of Judah alone.

¹⁹ Also Judah did not keep the commandments of the LORD their God, but walked in the statutes of Israel which they made. ²⁰ And the LORD rejected all the

The Four C's

Is your spouse your best friend? How privileged you are if the answer is "yes." Perhaps an even more important question to ask is this: "Are you a good friend to your spouse?" In being a good friend, you very often gain a best friend!

A true friend is someone to whom you can empty your heart when it feels overloaded by stress, concern, or worry.

Francis Bacon once wrote: "We know diseases of stoppings and suffocations are the most dangerous in the body; and it is not much otherwise in the mind: you may take sarza to open the liver, steel to open the spleen, flower of sulphur for the lungs, castoreum for the brain; but no receipt openeth the heart but a true friend, to whom you may impart griefs, joys, fears, hopes, suspicions, counsels, and whatsoever lieth upon the heart to oppress it, in a kind of civil shrift or confusion."

One of the best gifts you can give to your spouse and your children is this: listening ears. Such ears are invariably connected to a kind and patient heart.

Be a friend of the four C's: compassion, caring, consideration, and comfort. Those four traits never grow old or fall out of fashion.

> A man who has friends must himself be friendly, but there is a friend who sticks closer than a brother.
>
> *Proverbs 18:24*

descendants of Israel, afflicted them, and delivered them into the hand of plunderers, until He had cast them from His sight. [21] For He tore Israel from the house of David, and they made Jeroboam the son of Nebat king. Then Jeroboam drove Israel from following the LORD, and made them commit a great sin. [22] For the children of Israel walked in all the sins of Jeroboam which he did; they did not depart from them, [23] until the LORD removed Israel out of His sight, as He had said by all His servants the prophets. So Israel was carried away from their own land to Assyria, *as it is* to this day.

[24] Then the king of Assyria brought *people* from Babylon, Cuthah, Ava, Hamath, and from Sepharvaim, and placed *them* in the cities of Samaria instead of the children of Israel; and they took possession of Samaria and dwelt in its cities. [25] And it was so, at the beginning of their dwelling there, *that* they did not fear the LORD; therefore the LORD sent lions among them, which killed *some* of them. [26] So they spoke to the king of Assyria, saying, "The nations whom you have removed and placed in the cities of Samaria do not know the rituals of the God of the land; therefore He has sent lions among them, and indeed, they are killing them because they do not know the rituals of the God of the land."

[27] Then the king of Assyria commanded, saying, "Send there one of the priests whom you brought from there; let him go and dwell there, and let him teach them the rituals of the God of the land." [28] Then one of the priests whom they had carried away from Samaria came and dwelt in Bethel, and taught them how they should fear the LORD.

[29] However every nation continued to make gods of its own, and put *them* in the shrines on the high places which the Samaritans had made, *every* nation in the cities where they dwelt. [30] The men of Babylon made Succoth Benoth, the men of Cuth made Nergal, the men of Hamath made Ashima, [31] and the Avites made Nibhaz and Tartak; and the Sepharvites burned their children in fire to Adrammelech and Anammelech, the gods of Sepharvaim. [32] So they feared the LORD, and from every class they appointed for

themselves priests of the high places, who sacrificed for them in the shrines of the high places. [33] They feared the LORD, yet served their own gods—according to the rituals of the nations from among whom they were carried away.

[34] To this day they continue practicing the former rituals; they do not fear the LORD, nor do they follow their statutes or their ordinances, or the law and commandment which the LORD had commanded the children of Jacob, whom He named Israel, [35] with whom the LORD had made a covenant and charged them, saying: "You shall not fear other gods, nor bow down to them nor serve them nor sacrifice to them; [36] but the LORD, who brought you up from the land of Egypt with great power and an outstretched arm, Him you shall fear, Him you shall worship, and to Him you shall offer sacrifice. [37] And the statutes, the ordinances, the law, and the commandment which He wrote for you, you shall be careful to observe forever; you shall not fear other gods. [38] And the covenant that I have made with you, you shall not forget, nor shall you fear other gods. [39] But the LORD your God you shall fear; and He will deliver you from the hand of all your enemies." [40] However they did not obey, but they followed their former rituals. [41] So these nations feared the LORD, yet served their carved images; also their children and their children's children have continued doing as their fathers did, even to this day.

18 Now it came to pass in the third year of Hoshea the son of Elah, king of Israel, *that* Hezekiah the son of Ahaz, king of Judah, began to reign. [2] He was twenty-five years old when he became king, and he reigned twenty-nine years in Jerusalem. His mother's name *was* Abi the daughter of Zechariah. [3] And he did *what was* right in the sight of the LORD, according to all that his father David had done.

[4] He removed the high places and broke the *sacred* pillars, cut down the wooden image and broke in pieces the bronze serpent that Moses had made; for until those days the children of Israel burned incense to it, and called it Nehushtan. [5] He trusted

in the LORD God of Israel, so that after him was none like him among all the kings of Judah, nor who were before him. ⁶ For he held fast to the LORD; he did not depart from following Him, but kept His commandments, which the LORD had commanded Moses. ⁷ The LORD was with him; he prospered wherever he went. And he rebelled against the king of Assyria and did not serve him. ⁸ He subdued the Philistines, as far as Gaza and its territory, from watchtower to fortified city.

⁹ Now it came to pass in the fourth year of King Hezekiah, which *was* the seventh year of Hoshea the son of Elah, king of Israel, *that* Shalmaneser king of Assyria came up against Samaria and besieged it. ¹⁰ And at the end of three years they took it. In the sixth year of Hezekiah, that *is,* the ninth year of Hoshea king of Israel, Samaria was taken. ¹¹ Then the king of Assyria carried Israel away captive to Assyria, and put them in Halah and by the Habor, the River of Gozan, and in the cities of the Medes, ¹² because they did not obey the voice of the LORD their God, but transgressed His covenant *and* all that Moses the servant of the LORD had commanded; and they would neither hear nor do *them.*

¹³ And in the fourteenth year of King Hezekiah, Sennacherib king of Assyria came up against all the fortified cities of Judah and took them. ¹⁴ Then Hezekiah king of Judah sent to the king of Assyria at Lachish, saying, "I have done wrong; turn away from me; whatever you impose on me I will pay." And the king of Assyria assessed Hezekiah king of Judah three hundred talents of silver and thirty talents of gold. ¹⁵ So Hezekiah gave *him* all the silver that was found in the house of the LORD and in the treasuries of the king's house. ¹⁶ At that time Hezekiah stripped *the gold from* the doors of the temple of the LORD, and *from* the pillars which Hezekiah king of Judah had overlaid, and gave it to the king of Assyria.

¹⁷ Then the king of Assyria sent *the* Tartan, *the* Rabsaris, *and the* Rabshakeh from Lachish, with a great army against Jerusalem, to King Hezekiah. And they went up and came to Jerusalem. When they had come up, they went and stood by the aqueduct from the upper pool, which *was* on the highway to the Fuller's Field. ¹⁸ And when they had called to the king, Eliakim the son of Hilkiah, who *was* over the household, Shebna the scribe, and Joah the son of Asaph, the recorder, came out to them. ¹⁹ Then *the* Rabshakeh said to them, "Say now to Hezekiah, 'Thus says the great king, the king of Assyria: "What confidence *is* this in which you trust? ²⁰ You speak of *having* plans and power for war; but *they are* mere words. And in whom do you trust, that you rebel against me? ²¹ Now look! You are trusting in the staff of this broken reed, Egypt, on which if a man leans, it will go into his hand and pierce it. So *is* Pharaoh king of Egypt to all who trust in him. ²² But if you say to me, 'We trust in the LORD our God,' *is* it not He whose high places and whose altars Hezekiah has taken away, and said to Judah and Jerusalem, 'You shall worship before this altar in Jerusalem'?" ' ²³ Now therefore, I urge you, give a pledge to my master the king of Assyria, and I will give you two thousand horses—if you are able on your part to put riders on them! ²⁴ How then will you repel one captain of the least of my master's servants, and put your trust in Egypt for chariots and horsemen? ²⁵ Have I now come up without the LORD against this place to destroy it? The LORD said to me, 'Go up against this land, and destroy it.' "

²⁶ Then Eliakim the son of Hilkiah, Shebna, and Joah said to *the* Rabshakeh, "Please speak to your servants in Aramaic, for we understand *it;* and do not speak to us in Hebrew in the hearing of the people who *are* on the wall."

²⁷ But *the* Rabshakeh said to them, "Has my master sent me to your master and to you to speak these words, and not to the men who sit on the wall, who will eat and drink their own waste with you?"

²⁸ Then *the* Rabshakeh stood and called out with a loud voice in Hebrew, and spoke, saying, "Hear the word of the great king, the king of Assyria! ²⁹ Thus says the king: 'Do not let Hezekiah deceive you, for he shall not be able to deliver you from his hand; ³⁰ nor let Hezekiah make you trust in the LORD, saying, "The LORD will surely deliver us; this city shall not be given into the hand of the

king of Assyria." ' 31 Do not listen to Hezekiah; for thus says the king of Assyria: 'Make *peace* with me by a present and come out to me; and every one of you eat from his own vine and every one from his own fig tree, and every one of you drink the waters of his own cistern; 32 until I come and take you away to a land like your own land, a land of grain and new wine, a land of bread and vineyards, a land of olive groves and honey, that you may live and not die. But do not listen to Hezekiah, lest he persuade you, saying, "The LORD will deliver us." 33 Has any of the gods of the nations at all delivered its land from the hand of the king of Assyria? 34 Where *are* the gods of Hamath and Arpad? Where *are* the gods of Sepharvaim and Hena and Ivah? Indeed, have they delivered Samaria from my hand? 35 Who among all the gods of the lands have delivered their countries from my hand, that the LORD should deliver Jerusalem from my hand?' "

36 But the people held their peace and answered him not a word; for the king's commandment was, "Do not answer him." 37 Then Eliakim the son of Hilkiah, who *was* over the household, Shebna the scribe, and Joah the son of Asaph, the recorder, came to Hezekiah with *their* clothes torn, and told him the words of *the* Rabshakeh.

~ PSALM 74:1–8 ~

1 O God, why have You cast *us* off forever?
   Why does Your anger smoke against the sheep of Your pasture?
2 Remember Your congregation, *which* You have purchased of old,
   The tribe of Your inheritance, *which* You have redeemed—
   This Mount Zion where You have dwelt.
3 Lift up Your feet to the perpetual desolations.
   The enemy has damaged everything in the sanctuary.
4 Your enemies roar in the midst of Your meeting place;
   They set up their banners *for* signs.
5 They seem like men who lift up Axes among the thick trees.

6 And now they break down its carved work, all at once,
   With axes and hammers.
7 They have set fire to Your sanctuary;
   They have defiled the dwelling place of Your name to the ground.
8 They said in their hearts,
   "Let us destroy them altogether."
   They have burned up all the meeting places of God in the land.

~ PROVERBS 18:22–24 ~

22 *He who* finds a wife finds a good *thing,*
   And obtains favor from the LORD.

23 The poor *man* uses entreaties,
   But the rich answers roughly.

24 A man *who has* friends must himself be friendly,
   But there is a friend *who* sticks closer than a brother.

~ ACTS 1:1–26 ~

The former account I made, O Theophilus, of all that Jesus began both to do and teach, 2 until the day in which He was taken up, after He through the Holy Spirit had given commandments to the apostles whom He had chosen, 3 to whom He also presented Himself alive after His suffering by many infallible proofs, being seen by them during forty days and speaking of the things pertaining to the kingdom of God.

4 And being assembled together with *them,* He commanded them not to depart from Jerusalem, but to wait for the Promise of the Father, "which," *He said,* "you have heard from Me; 5 for John truly baptized with water, but you shall be baptized with the Holy Spirit not many days from now." 6 Therefore, when they had come together, they asked Him, saying, "Lord, will You at this time restore the kingdom to Israel?" 7 And He said to them, "It is not for you to know times or seasons which the Father has put in His own authority. 8 But you shall receive power when the Holy Spirit has come upon you; and you shall be witnesses to

Me in Jerusalem, and in all Judea and Samaria, and to the end of the earth."

⁹ Now when He had spoken these things, while they watched, He was taken up, and a cloud received Him out of their sight. ¹⁰ And while they looked steadfastly toward heaven as He went up, behold, two men stood by them in white apparel, ¹¹ who also said, "Men of Galilee, why do you stand gazing up into heaven? This *same* Jesus, who was taken up from you into heaven, will so come in like manner as you saw Him go into heaven."

¹² Then they returned to Jerusalem from the mount called Olivet, which is near Jerusalem, a Sabbath day's journey. ¹³ And when they had entered, they went up into the upper room where they were staying: Peter, James, John, and Andrew; Philip and Thomas; Bartholomew and Matthew; James *the son* of Alphaeus and Simon the Zealot; and Judas *the son* of James. ¹⁴ These all continued with one accord in prayer and supplication, with the women and Mary the mother of Jesus, and with His brothers.

¹⁵ And in those days Peter stood up in the midst of the disciples (altogether the number of names was about a hundred and twenty), and said, ¹⁶ "Men *and* brethren, this Scripture had to be fulfilled, which the Holy Spirit spoke before by the mouth of David concerning Judas, who became a guide to those who arrested Jesus; ¹⁷ for he was numbered with us and obtained a part in this ministry."

¹⁸ (Now this man purchased a field with the wages of iniquity; and falling headlong, he burst open in the middle and all his entrails gushed out. ¹⁹ And it became known to all those dwelling in Jerusalem; so that field is called in their own language, Akel Dama, that is, Field of Blood.)

²⁰ "For it is written in the Book of Psalms:

'Let his dwelling place be desolate,
  And let no one live in it';

and,

'Let another take his office.'

²¹ "Therefore, of these men who have accompanied us all the time that the Lord Jesus went in and out among us, ²² beginning from the baptism of John to that day when He was taken up from us, one of these must become a witness with us of His resurrection."

²³ And they proposed two: Joseph called Barsabas, who was surnamed Justus, and Matthias. ²⁴ And they prayed and said, "You, O Lord, who know the hearts of all, show which of these two You have chosen ²⁵ to take part in this ministry and apostleship from which Judas by transgression fell, that he might go to his own place." ²⁶ And they cast their lots, and the lot fell on Matthias. And he was numbered with the eleven apostles.

READING 167 · JUNE 16

∼ 2 KINGS 19:1—21:26 ∼

And so it was, when King Hezekiah heard *it,* that he tore his clothes, covered himself with sackcloth, and went into the house of the LORD. ² Then he sent Eliakim, who *was* over the household, Shebna the scribe, and the elders of the priests, covered with sackcloth, to Isaiah the prophet, the son of Amoz. ³ And they said to him, "Thus says Hezekiah: 'This day *is* a day of trouble, and rebuke, and blasphemy; for the children have come to birth, but *there is* no strength to bring them forth. ⁴ It may be that the LORD your God will hear all the words of *the* Rabshakeh, whom his master the king of Assyria has sent to reproach the living God, and will rebuke the words which the LORD your God has heard. Therefore lift up *your* prayer for the remnant that is left.' "

⁵ So the servants of King Hezekiah came to Isaiah. ⁶ And Isaiah said to them, "Thus you shall say to your master, 'Thus says the LORD: "Do not be afraid of the words which you have heard, with which the servants of the king of Assyria have

blasphemed Me. [7] Surely I will send a spirit upon him, and he shall hear a rumor and return to his own land; and I will cause him to fall by the sword in his own land." ' "

[8] Then *the* Rabshakeh returned and found the king of Assyria warring against Libnah, for he heard that he had departed from Lachish. [9] And the king heard concerning Tirhakah king of Ethiopia, "Look, he has come out to make war with you." So he again sent messengers to Hezekiah, saying, [10] "Thus you shall speak to Hezekiah king of Judah, saying: 'Do not let your God in whom you trust deceive you, saying, "Jerusalem shall not be given into the hand of the king of Assyria." [11] Look! You have heard what the kings of Assyria have done to all lands by utterly destroying them; and shall you be delivered? [12] Have the gods of the nations delivered those whom my fathers have destroyed, Gozan and Haran and Rezeph, and the people of Eden who *were* in Telassar? [13] Where *is* the king of Hamath, the king of Arpad, and the king of the city of Sepharvaim, Hena, and Ivah?' "

[14] And Hezekiah received the letter from the hand of the messengers, and read it; and Hezekiah went up to the house of the LORD, and spread it before the LORD. [15] Then Hezekiah prayed before the LORD, and said: "O LORD God of Israel, *the One* who dwells *between* the cherubim, You are God, You alone, of all the kingdoms of the earth. You have made heaven and earth. [16] Incline Your ear, O LORD, and hear; open Your eyes, O LORD, and see; and hear the words of Sennacherib, which he has sent to reproach the living God. [17] Truly, LORD, the kings of Assyria have laid waste the nations and their lands, [18] and have cast their gods into the fire; for they *were* not gods, but the work of men's hands—wood and stone. Therefore they destroyed them. [19] Now therefore, O LORD our God, I pray, save us from his hand, that all the kingdoms of the earth may know that You *are* the LORD God, You alone."

[20] Then Isaiah the son of Amoz sent to Hezekiah, saying, "Thus says the LORD God of Israel: 'Because you have prayed to Me against Sennacherib king of Assyr-

ia, I have heard.' [21] This *is* the word which the LORD has spoken concerning him:

'The virgin, the daughter of Zion,
Has despised you, laughed you to
    scorn;
The daughter of Jerusalem
Has shaken *her* head behind your
    back!

[22] 'Whom have you reproached and
    blasphemed?
Against whom have you raised
    your voice,
And lifted up your eyes on high?
Against the Holy *One* of Israel.
[23] By your messengers you have
    reproached the Lord,
And said: "By the multitude of my
    chariots
I have come up to the height of
    the mountains,
To the limits of Lebanon;
I will cut down its tall cedars
And its choice cypress trees; .
I will enter the extremity of its
    borders,
To its fruitful forest.
[24] I have dug and drunk strange
    water,
And with the soles of my feet I
    have dried up
All the brooks of defense."

[25] 'Did you not hear long ago
How I made it,
From ancient times that I formed
    it?
Now I have brought it to pass,
That you should be
For crushing fortified cities *into*
    heaps of ruins.
[26] Therefore their inhabitants had
    little power;
They were dismayed and
    confounded;
They were *as* the grass of the field
And the green herb,
As the grass on the housetops
And *grain* blighted before it is
    grown.

[27] 'But I know your dwelling place,
Your going out and your coming
    in,

No Limit on Character

An elderly Southerner walked into his banker's office one day. The banker greeted him warmly and then asked, "What can I do for you?"

The Southerner, who was a true southern gentleman of the "old school" replied, "Well, about thirty-five years ago I loaned a man down South some money—not a very big sum. I told him that whenever I needed it I would let him know and he could repay me. The time has come when I need some money, so I would like to let him know. I would like to have you conduct the transaction for me."

The banker said, "My good friend, you have no claim on that money. The statute of limitations has run out against that loan years and years ago."

"Sir," the Southerner replied, "the man to whom I loaned that money is a gentleman. The statute of limitations never runs out for a gentleman."

Sure enough, when the banker made a formal request for the money, it came within a reasonable time. With it was a note: "Thank you. I hope I have the privilege of returning the favor some day."

True Christian character does not seek to escape from a promise. Rather, it reflects our Master whose Word to us is always reliable and never changing.

> Better is the poor who walks in his integrity than one who is perverse in his lips, and is a fool.
>
> *Proverbs 19:1*

And your rage against Me.
28 Because your rage against Me and
   your tumult
   Have come up to My ears,
   Therefore I will put My hook in
   your nose
   And My bridle in your lips,
   And I will turn you back
   By the way which you came.

29 'This *shall be* a sign to you:

   You shall eat this year such as
   grows of itself,
   And in the second year what
   springs from the same;
   Also in the third year sow and
   reap,
   Plant vineyards and eat the fruit of
   them.
30 And the remnant who have
   escaped of the house of Judah
   Shall again take root downward,
   And bear fruit upward.
31 For out of Jerusalem shall go a
   remnant,
   And those who escape from
   Mount Zion.
   The zeal of the LORD of hosts will
   do this.'

32 "Therefore thus says the LORD concerning the king of Assyria:

   'He shall not come into this city,
   Nor shoot an arrow there,
   Nor come before it with shield,
   Nor build a siege mound against
   it.
33 By the way that he came,
   By the same shall he return;
   And he shall not come into this
   city,'
   Says the LORD.
34 'For I will defend this city, to save
   it
   For My own sake and for My
   servant David's sake.' "

35 And it came to pass on a certain night
that the angel of the LORD went out, and
killed in the camp of the Assyrians one
hundred and eighty-five thousand; and
when *people* arose early in the morning,
there were the corpses—all dead. 36 So
Sennacherib king of Assyria departed and
went away, returned *home,* and remained
at Nineveh. 37 Now it came to pass, as he
was worshiping in the temple of Nisroch
his god, that his sons Adrammelech and
Sharezer struck him down with the sword;
and they escaped into the land of Ararat.
Then Esarhaddon his son reigned in his
place.

20 In those days Hezekiah was sick and
near death. And Isaiah the prophet, the
son of Amoz, went to him and said to him,
"Thus says the LORD: 'Set your house in
order, for you shall die, and not live.' "
2 Then he turned his face toward the
wall, and prayed to the LORD, saying,
3 "Remember now, O LORD, I pray, how I
have walked before You in truth and with
a loyal heart, and have done *what was*
good in Your sight." And Hezekiah wept
bitterly.
4 And it happened, before Isaiah had
gone out into the middle court, that the
word of the LORD came to him, saying,
5 "Return and tell Hezekiah the leader of
My people, 'Thus says the LORD, the God
of David your father: "I have heard your
prayer, I have seen your tears; surely I will
heal you. On the third day you shall go
up to the house of the LORD. 6 And I will
add to your days fifteen years. I will deliver you and this city from the hand of
the king of Assyria; and I will defend this
city for My own sake, and for the sake of
My servant David." ' "
7 Then Isaiah said, "Take a lump of figs."
So they took and laid *it* on the boil, and
he recovered.
8 And Hezekiah said to Isaiah, "What
is the sign that the LORD will heal me,
and that I shall go up to the house of the
LORD the third day?"
9 Then Isaiah said, "This is the sign to
you from the LORD, that the LORD will
do the thing which He has spoken: *shall*
the shadow go forward ten degrees or go
backward ten degrees?"
10 And Hezekiah answered, "It is an easy
thing for the shadow to go down ten degrees; no, but let the shadow go backward
ten degrees."
11 So Isaiah the prophet cried out to the
LORD, and He brought the shadow ten

degrees backward, by which it had gone down on the sundial of Ahaz.

¹² At that time Berodach-Baladan the son of Baladan, king of Babylon, sent letters and a present to Hezekiah, for he heard that Hezekiah had been sick. ¹³ And Hezekiah was attentive to them, and showed them all the house of his treasures—the silver and gold, the spices and precious ointment, and all his armory—all that was found among his treasures. There was nothing in his house or in all his dominion that Hezekiah did not show them.

¹⁴ Then Isaiah the prophet went to King Hezekiah, and said to him, "What did these men say, and from where did they come to you?"

So Hezekiah said, "They came from a far country, from Babylon."

¹⁵ And he said, "What have they seen in your house?"

So Hezekiah answered, "They have seen all that *is* in my house; there is nothing among my treasures that I have not shown them."

¹⁶ Then Isaiah said to Hezekiah, "Hear the word of the LORD: ¹⁷ 'Behold, the days are coming when all that *is* in your house, and what your fathers have accumulated until this day, shall be carried to Babylon; nothing shall be left,' says the LORD. ¹⁸ 'And they shall take away some of your sons who will descend from you, whom you will beget; and they shall be eunuchs in the palace of the king of Babylon.' "

¹⁹ So Hezekiah said to Isaiah, "The word of the LORD which you have spoken *is* good!" For he said, "Will there not be peace and truth at least in my days?"

²⁰ Now the rest of the acts of Hezekiah—all his might, and how he made a pool and a tunnel and brought water into the city—*are* they not written in the book of the chronicles of the kings of Judah? ²¹ So Hezekiah rested with his fathers. Then Manasseh his son reigned in his place.

21 Manasseh *was* twelve years old when he became king, and he reigned fifty-five years in Jerusalem. His mother's name *was* Hephzibah. ² And he did evil in the sight of the LORD, according to the abominations of the nations whom the LORD had cast out before the children of Israel. ³ For he rebuilt the high places which Hezekiah his father had destroyed; he raised up altars for Baal, and made a wooden image, as Ahab king of Israel had done; and he worshiped all the host of heaven and served them. ⁴ He also built altars in the house of the LORD, of which the LORD had said, "In Jerusalem I will put My name." ⁵ And he built altars for all the host of heaven in the two courts of the house of the LORD. ⁶ Also he made his son pass through the fire, practiced soothsaying, used witchcraft, and consulted spiritists and mediums. He did much evil in the sight of the LORD, to provoke *Him* to anger. ⁷ He even set a carved image of Asherah that he had made, in the house of which the LORD had said to David and to Solomon his son, "In this house and in Jerusalem, which I have chosen out of all the tribes of Israel, I will put My name forever; ⁸ and I will not make the feet of Israel wander anymore from the land which I gave their fathers—only if they are careful to do according to all that I have commanded them, and according to all the law that My servant Moses commanded them." ⁹ But they paid no attention, and Manasseh seduced them to do more evil than the nations whom the LORD had destroyed before the children of Israel.

¹⁰ And the LORD spoke by His servants the prophets, saying, ¹¹ "Because Manasseh king of Judah has done these abominations (he has acted more wickedly than all the Amorites who *were* before him, and has also made Judah sin with his idols), ¹² therefore thus says the LORD God of Israel: 'Behold, *I* am bringing *such* calamity upon Jerusalem and Judah, that whoever hears of it, both his ears will tingle. ¹³ And I will stretch over Jerusalem the measuring line of Samaria and the plummet of the house of Ahab; I will wipe Jerusalem as *one* wipes a dish, wiping *it* and turning *it* upside down. ¹⁴ So I will forsake the remnant of My inheritance and deliver them into the hand of their enemies; and they shall become victims of plunder to all their enemies, ¹⁵ because they have done evil in My sight, and have provoked Me to anger since the day their

fathers came out of Egypt, even to this day.' "

[16] Moreover Manasseh shed very much innocent blood, till he had filled Jerusalem from one end to another, besides his sin by which he made Judah sin, in doing evil in the sight of the LORD.

[17] Now the rest of the acts of Manasseh—all that he did, and the sin that he committed—*are* they not written in the book of the chronicles of the kings of Judah? [18] So Manasseh rested with his fathers, and was buried in the garden of his own house, in the garden of Uzza. Then his son Amon reigned in his place.

[19] Amon *was* twenty-two years old when he became king, and he reigned two years in Jerusalem. His mother's name *was* Meshullemeth the daughter of Haruz of Jotbah. [20] And he did evil in the sight of the LORD, as his father Manasseh had done. [21] So he walked in all the ways that his father had walked; and he served the idols that his father had served, and worshiped them. [22] He forsook the LORD God of his fathers, and did not walk in the way of the LORD.

[23] Then the servants of Amon conspired against him, and killed the king in his own house. [24] But the people of the land executed all those who had conspired against King Amon. Then the people of the land made his son Josiah king in his place.

[25] Now the rest of the acts of Amon which he did, *are* they not written in the book of the chronicles of the kings of Judah? [26] And he was buried in his tomb in the garden of Uzza. Then Josiah his son reigned in his place.

∼ PSALM 74:9–17 ∼

[9] We do not see our signs;
There is no longer any prophet;
Nor *is there* any among us who knows how long.
[10] O God, how long will the adversary reproach?
Will the enemy blaspheme Your name forever?
[11] Why do You withdraw Your hand, even Your right hand?
Take it out of Your bosom and destroy *them.*
[12] For God *is* my King from of old,

Working salvation in the midst of the earth.
[13] You divided the sea by Your strength;
You broke the heads of the sea serpents in the waters.
[14] You broke the heads of Leviathan in pieces,
And gave him *as* food to the people inhabiting the wilderness.
[15] You broke open the fountain and the flood;
You dried up mighty rivers.
[16] The day *is* Yours, the night also *is* Yours;
You have prepared the light and the sun.
[17] You have set all the borders of the earth;
You have made summer and winter.

∼ PROVERBS 19:1, 2 ∼

[1] Better *is* the poor who walks in his integrity
Than *one who is* perverse in his lips, and is a fool.

[2] Also it is not good *for* a soul *to be* without knowledge,
And he sins who hastens with *his* feet.

∼ ACTS 2:1–21 ∼

When the Day of Pentecost had fully come, they were all with one accord in one place. [2] And suddenly there came a sound from heaven, as of a rushing mighty wind, and it filled the whole house where they were sitting. [3] Then there appeared to them divided tongues, as of fire, and *one* sat upon each of them. [4] And they were all filled with the Holy Spirit and began to speak with other tongues, as the Spirit gave them utterance.

[5] And there were dwelling in Jerusalem Jews, devout men, from every nation under heaven. [6] And when this sound occurred, the multitude came together, and were confused, because everyone heard them speak in his own language. [7] Then they were all amazed and marveled, saying to one another, "Look, are not all these who speak Galileans? [8] And how *is it that* we hear, each in our own language in

which we were born? ⁹ Parthians and Medes and Elamites, those dwelling in Mesopotamia, Judea and Cappadocia, Pontus and Asia, ¹⁰ Phrygia and Pamphylia, Egypt and the parts of Libya adjoining Cyrene, visitors from Rome, both Jews and proselytes, ¹¹ Cretans and Arabs—we hear them speaking in our own tongues the wonderful works of God." ¹² So they were all amazed and perplexed, saying to one another, "Whatever could this mean?"

¹³ Others mocking said, "They are full of new wine."

¹⁴ But Peter, standing up with the eleven, raised his voice and said to them, "Men of Judea and all who dwell in Jerusalem, let this be known to you, and heed my words. ¹⁵ For these are not drunk, as you suppose, since it is *only* the third hour of the day. ¹⁶ But this is what was spoken by the prophet Joel:

¹⁷ 'And it shall come to pass in the
     last days, says God,

That I will pour out of My Spirit
     on all flesh;
Your sons and your daughters shall
     prophesy,
Your young men shall see visions,
Your old men shall dream dreams.
¹⁸ And on My menservants and on
     My maidservants
I will pour out My Spirit in those
     days;
And they shall prophesy.
¹⁹ I will show wonders in heaven
     above
And signs in the earth beneath:
Blood and fire and vapor of
     smoke.
²⁰ The sun shall be turned into
     darkness,
And the moon into blood,
Before the coming of the great
     and awesome day of the LORD.
²¹ And it shall come to pass
That whoever calls on the name of
     the LORD
Shall be saved.'

~ 2 KINGS 22:1—24:20 ~

Josiah *was* eight years old when he became king, and he reigned thirty-one years in Jerusalem. His mother's name *was* Jedidah the daughter of Adaiah of Bozkath. ² And he did *what was* right in the sight of the LORD, and walked in all the ways of his father David; he did not turn aside to the right hand or to the left.

³ Now it came to pass, in the eighteenth year of King Josiah, *that* the king sent Shaphan the scribe, the son of Azaliah, the son of Meshullam, to the house of the LORD, saying: ⁴ "Go up to Hilkiah the high priest, that he may count the money which has been brought into the house of the LORD, which the doorkeepers have gathered from the people. ⁵ And let them deliver it into the hand of those doing the work, who are the overseers in the house of the LORD; let them give it to those who *are* in the house of the LORD doing the work, to repair the damages of the house— ⁶ to carpenters and builders and masons—and to buy timber and hewn stone to repair the house. ⁷ However there need be no accounting made with them of the money delivered into their hand, because they deal faithfully."

⁸ Then Hilkiah the high priest said to Shaphan the scribe, "I have found the Book of the Law in the house of the LORD." And Hilkiah gave the book to Shaphan, and he read it. ⁹ So Shaphan the scribe went to the king, bringing the king word, saying, "Your servants have gathered the money that was found in the house, and have delivered it into the hand of those who do the work, who oversee the house of the LORD." ¹⁰ Then Shaphan the scribe showed the king, saying, "Hilkiah the priest has given me a book." And Shaphan read it before the king.

¹¹ Now it happened, when the king heard the words of the Book of the Law, that he tore his clothes. ¹² Then the king commanded Hilkiah the priest, Ahikam the son of Shaphan, Achbor the son of Michaiah, Shaphan the scribe, and Asaiah

a servant of the king, saying, [13] "Go, inquire of the LORD for me, for the people and for all Judah, concerning the words of this book that has been found; for great *is* the wrath of the LORD that is aroused against us, because our fathers have not obeyed the words of this book, to do according to all that is written concerning us."

[14] So Hilkiah the priest, Ahikam, Achbor, Shaphan, and Asaiah went to Huldah the prophetess, the wife of Shallum the son of Tikvah, the son of Harhas, keeper of the wardrobe. (She dwelt in Jerusalem in the Second Quarter.) And they spoke with her. [15] Then she said to them, "Thus says the LORD God of Israel, 'Tell the man who sent you to Me, [16] "Thus says the LORD: 'Behold, I will bring calamity on this place and on its inhabitants—all the words of the book which the king of Judah has read— [17] because they have forsaken Me and burned incense to other gods, that they might provoke Me to anger with all the works of their hands. Therefore My wrath shall be aroused against this place and shall not be quenched.' " ' [18] But as for the king of Judah, who sent you to inquire of the LORD, in this manner you shall speak to him, 'Thus says the LORD God of Israel: "*Concerning* the words which you have heard— [19] because your heart was tender, and you humbled yourself before the LORD when you heard what I spoke against this place and against its inhabitants, that they would become a desolation and a curse, and you tore your clothes and wept before Me, I also have heard *you*," says the LORD. [20] Surely, therefore, I will gather you to your fathers, and you shall be gathered to your grave in peace; and your eyes shall not see all the calamity which I will bring on this place." ' " So they brought back word to the king.

23 Now the king sent them to gather all the elders of Judah and Jerusalem to him. [2] The king went up to the house of the LORD with all the men of Judah, and with him all the inhabitants of Jerusalem—the priests and the prophets and all the people, both small and great. And he read in their hearing all the words of the

Book of the Covenant which had been found in the house of the LORD.

[3] Then the king stood by a pillar and made a covenant before the LORD, to follow the LORD and to keep His commandments and His testimonies and His statutes, with all *his* heart and all *his* soul, to perform the words of this covenant that were written in this book. And all the people took a stand for the covenant. [4] And the king commanded Hilkiah the high priest, the priests of the second order, and the doorkeepers, to bring out of the temple of the LORD all the articles that were made for Baal, for Asherah, and for all the host of heaven; and he burned them outside Jerusalem in the fields of Kidron, and carried their ashes to Bethel. [5] Then he removed the idolatrous priests whom the kings of Judah had ordained to burn incense on the high places in the cities of Judah and in the places all around Jerusalem, and those who burned incense to Baal, to the sun, to the moon, to the constellations, and to all the host of heaven. [6] And he brought out the wooden image from the house of the LORD, to the Brook Kidron outside Jerusalem, burned it at the Brook Kidron and ground *it* to ashes, and threw its ashes on the graves of the common people. [7] Then he tore down the *ritual* booths of the perverted persons that *were* in the house of the LORD, where the women wove hangings for the wooden image. [8] And he brought all the priests from the cities of Judah, and defiled the high places where the priests had burned incense, from Geba to Beersheba; also he broke down the high places at the gates which *were* at the entrance of the Gate of Joshua the governor of the city, which *were* to the left of the city gate. [9] Nevertheless the priests of the high places did not come up to the altar of the LORD in Jerusalem, but they ate unleavened bread among their brethren.

[10] And he defiled Topheth, which *is* in the Valley of the Son of Hinnom, that no man might make his son or his daughter pass through the fire to Molech. [11] Then he removed the horses that the kings of Judah had dedicated to the sun, at the entrance to the house of the LORD, by the chamber of Nathan-Melech, the officer who *was* in the court; and he burned the

God's Presence

Dr. George Washington Carver had this to say about prayer, "My prayers seem to be more of an attitude than anything else. I indulge in no lip service, but ask the great God silently, daily, and often many times a day, to permit me to speak to Him. I ask Him to give me wisdom, understanding, and bodily strength to do His will. Hence, I am asking and receiving all the time."

One of the most magnificent truths about God is that He meets us in every moment of prayer with all the fullness of His being. He reveals Himself to us as I AM, ever-present and available. He brings the totality of who He is to each moment of our lives. He brings not just a part of Himself, but all of Himself — His undiminished majesty, power, wisdom, and love.

Our best and highest response to such marvelous access to the fullness of the holy, omnipotent, infinite King of the universe must surely be one of awe. It matters very little what we *say*. Just to be in His presence, and to be aware of His presence, is to be put into a position of humility, need, and provision.

Rousseau once noted, "To write a good love letter, you will begin without knowing what you are going to say, and end without knowing what you have said." The same is true for prayer. To be in God's presence and to have a relationship with Him is all that matters.

> You have made known to me the ways of life; You will make me full of joy in Your presence.
>
> *Acts 2:28*

chariots of the sun with fire. ¹² The altars that *were* on the roof, the upper chamber of Ahaz, which the kings of Judah had made, and the altars which Manasseh had made in the two courts of the house of the LORD, the king broke down and pulverized there, and threw their dust into the Brook Kidron. ¹³ Then the king defiled the high places that *were* east of Jerusalem, which *were* on the south of the Mount of Corruption, which Solomon king of Israel had built for Ashtoreth the abomination of the Sidonians, for Chemosh the abomination of the Moabites, and for Milcom the abomination of the people of Ammon. ¹⁴ And he broke in pieces the *sacred* pillars and cut down the wooden images, and filled their places with the bones of men.

¹⁵ Moreover the altar that *was* at Bethel, *and* the high place which Jeroboam the son of Nebat, who made Israel sin, had made, both that altar and the high place he broke down; and he burned the high place *and* crushed *it* to powder, and burned the wooden image. ¹⁶ As Josiah turned, he saw the tombs that *were* there on the mountain. And he sent and took the bones out of the tombs and burned *them* on the altar, and defiled it according to the word of the LORD which the man of God proclaimed, who proclaimed these words. ¹⁷ Then he said, "What gravestone *is* this that I see?"

So the men of the city told him, "*It is* the tomb of the man of God who came from Judah and proclaimed these things which you have done against the altar of Bethel."

¹⁸ And he said, "Let him alone; let no one move his bones." So they let his bones alone, with the bones of the prophet who came from Samaria.

¹⁹ Now Josiah also took away all the shrines of the high places that *were* in the cities of Samaria, which the kings of Israel had made to provoke the LORD to anger; and he did to them according to all the deeds he had done in Bethel. ²⁰ He executed all the priests of the high places who *were* there, on the altars, and burned men's bones on them; and he returned to Jerusalem.

²¹ Then the king commanded all the people, saying, "Keep the Passover to the LORD your God, as *it is* written in this Book of the Covenant." ²² Such a Passover surely had never been held since the days of the judges who judged Israel, nor in all the days of the kings of Israel and the kings of Judah. ²³ But in the eighteenth year of King Josiah this Passover was held before the LORD in Jerusalem. ²⁴ Moreover Josiah put away those who consulted mediums and spiritists, the household gods and idols, all the abominations that were seen in the land of Judah and in Jerusalem, that he might perform the words of the law which were written in the book that Hilkiah the priest found in the house of the LORD. ²⁵ Now before him there was no king like him, who turned to the LORD with all his heart, with all his soul, and with all his might, according to all the Law of Moses; nor after him did *any* arise like him.

²⁶ Nevertheless the LORD did not turn from the fierceness of His great wrath, with which His anger was aroused against Judah, because of all the provocations with which Manasseh had provoked Him. ²⁷ And the LORD said, "I will also remove Judah from My sight, as I have removed Israel, and will cast off this city Jerusalem which I have chosen, and the house of which I said, 'My name shall be there.' "

²⁸ Now the rest of the acts of Josiah, and all that he did, *are* they not written in the book of the chronicles of the kings of Judah? ²⁹ In his days Pharaoh Necho king of Egypt went to the aid of the king of Assyria, to the River Euphrates; and King Josiah went against him. And *Pharaoh Necho* killed him at Megiddo when he confronted him. ³⁰ Then his servants moved his body in a chariot from Megiddo, brought him to Jerusalem, and buried him in his own tomb. And the people of the land took Jehoahaz the son of Josiah, anointed him, and made him king in his father's place.

³¹ Jehoahaz *was* twenty-three years old when he became king, and he reigned three months in Jerusalem. His mother's name *was* Hamutal the daughter of Jeremiah of Libnah. ³² And he did evil in the sight of the LORD, according to all that his fathers had done. ³³ Now Pharaoh Necho put him in prison at Riblah in the land of Hamath, that he might not reign

in Jerusalem; and he imposed on the land a tribute of one hundred talents of silver and a talent of gold. ³⁴ Then Pharaoh Necho made Eliakim the son of Josiah king in place of his father Josiah, and changed his name to Jehoiakim. And *Pharaoh* took Jehoahaz and went to Egypt, and he died there.

³⁵ So Jehoiakim gave the silver and gold to Pharaoh; but he taxed the land to give money according to the command of Pharaoh; he exacted the silver and gold from the people of the land, from every one according to his assessment, to give *it* to Pharaoh Necho. ³⁶ Jehoiakim *was* twenty-five years old when he became king, and he reigned eleven years in Jerusalem. His mother's name *was* Zebudah the daughter of Pedaiah of Rumah. ³⁷ And he did evil in the sight of the LORD, according to all that his fathers had done.

24 In his days Nebuchadnezzar king of Babylon came up, and Jehoiakim became his vassal *for* three years. Then he turned and rebelled against him. ² And the LORD sent against him *raiding* bands of Chaldeans, bands of Syrians, bands of Moabites, and bands of the people of Ammon; He sent them against Judah to destroy it, according to the word of the LORD which He had spoken by His servants the prophets. ³ Surely at the commandment of the LORD *this* came upon Judah, to remove *them* from His sight because of the sins of Manasseh, according to all that he had done, ⁴ and also because of the innocent blood that he had shed; for he had filled Jerusalem with innocent blood, which the LORD would not pardon.

⁵ Now the rest of the acts of Jehoiakim, and all that he did, *are* they not written in the book of the chronicles of the kings of Judah? ⁶ So Jehoiakim rested with his fathers. Then Jehoiachin his son reigned in his place.

⁷ And the king of Egypt did not come out of his land anymore, for the king of Babylon had taken all that belonged to the king of Egypt from the Brook of Egypt to the River Euphrates.

⁸ Jehoiachin *was* eighteen years old when he became king, and he reigned in Jerusalem three months. His mother's name *was* Nehushta the daughter of Elnathan of Jerusalem. ⁹ And he did evil in the sight of the LORD, according to all that his father had done.

¹⁰ At that time the servants of Nebuchadnezzar king of Babylon came up against Jerusalem, and the city was besieged. ¹¹ And Nebuchadnezzar king of Babylon came against the city, as his servants were besieging it. ¹² Then Jehoiachin king of Judah, his mother, his servants, his princes, and his officers went out to the king of Babylon; and the king of Babylon, in the eighth year of his reign, took him prisoner.

¹³ And he carried out from there all the treasures of the house of the LORD and the treasures of the king's house, and he cut in pieces all the articles of gold which Solomon king of Israel had made in the temple of the LORD, as the LORD had said. ¹⁴ Also he carried into captivity all Jerusalem: all the captains and all the mighty men of valor, ten thousand captives, and all the craftsmen and smiths. None remained except the poorest people of the land. ¹⁵ And he carried Jehoiachin captive to Babylon. The king's mother, the king's wives, his officers, and the mighty of the land he carried into captivity from Jerusalem to Babylon. ¹⁶ All the valiant men, seven thousand, and craftsmen and smiths, one thousand, all *who were* strong *and* fit for war, these the king of Babylon brought captive to Babylon.

¹⁷ Then the king of Babylon made Mattaniah, *Jehoiachin's* uncle, king in his place, and changed his name to Zedekiah.

¹⁸ Zedekiah *was* twenty-one years old when he became king, and he reigned eleven years in Jerusalem. His mother's name *was* Hamutal the daughter of Jeremiah of Libnah. ¹⁹ He also did evil in the sight of the LORD, according to all that Jehoiakim had done. ²⁰ For because of the anger of the LORD *this* happened in Jerusalem and Judah, that He finally cast them out from His presence. Then Zedekiah rebelled against the king of Babylon.

~ PSALM 74:18–23 ~

¹⁸ Remember this, *that* the enemy has reproached, O LORD,

And *that* a foolish people has blasphemed Your name.

19 Oh, do not deliver the life of Your turtledove to the wild beast!
Do not forget the life of Your poor forever.

20 Have respect to the covenant;
For the dark places of the earth are full of the haunts of cruelty.

21 Oh, do not let the oppressed return ashamed!
Let the poor and needy praise Your name.

22 Arise, O God, plead Your own cause;
Remember how the foolish man reproaches You daily.

23 Do not forget the voice of Your enemies;
The tumult of those who rise up against You increases continually.

∼ PROVERBS 19:3 ∼

3 The foolishness of a man twists his way,
And his heart frets against the LORD.

∼ ACTS 2:22–47 ∼

"Men of Israel, hear these words: Jesus of Nazareth, a Man attested by God to you by miracles, wonders, and signs which God did through Him in your midst, as you yourselves also know— 23 Him, being delivered by the determined purpose and foreknowledge of God, you have taken by lawless hands, have crucified, and put to death; 24 whom God raised up, having loosed the pains of death, because it was not possible that He should be held by it. 25 For David says concerning Him:

'I foresaw the LORD always before my face,
For He is at my right hand, that I may not be shaken.
26 Therefore my heart rejoiced, and my tongue was glad;
Moreover my flesh also will rest in hope.
27 For You will not leave my soul in Hades,
Nor will You allow Your Holy One to see corruption.
28 You have made known to me the ways of life;
You will make me full of joy in Your presence.'

29 "Men *and* brethren, let *me* speak freely to you of the patriarch David, that he is both dead and buried, and his tomb is with us to this day. 30 Therefore, being a prophet, and knowing that God had sworn with an oath to him that of the fruit of his body, according to the flesh, He would raise up the Christ to sit on his throne, 31 he, foreseeing this, spoke concerning the resurrection of the Christ, that His soul was not left in Hades, nor did His flesh see corruption. 32 This Jesus God has raised up, of which we are all witnesses. 33 Therefore being exalted to the right hand of God, and having received from the Father the promise of the Holy Spirit, He poured out this which you now see and hear.

34 "For David did not ascend into the heavens, but he says himself:

'The LORD said to my Lord,
"Sit at My right hand,
35 Till I make Your enemies Your footstool."'

36 "Therefore let all the house of Israel know assuredly that God has made this Jesus, whom you crucified, both Lord and Christ."

37 Now when they heard *this,* they were cut to the heart, and said to Peter and the rest of the apostles, "Men *and* brethren, what shall we do?"

38 Then Peter said to them, "Repent, and let every one of you be baptized in the name of Jesus Christ for the remission of sins; and you shall receive the gift of the Holy Spirit. 39 For the promise is to you and to your children, and to all who are afar off, as many as the Lord our God will call."

40 And with many other words he testified and exhorted them, saying, "Be saved from this perverse generation." 41 Then those who gladly received his word were baptized; and that day about three thousand souls were added *to them.* 42 And they continued steadfastly in the apostles' doctrine and fellowship, in the breaking

of bread, and in prayers. ⁴³ Then fear came upon every soul, and many wonders and signs were done through the apostles. ⁴⁴ Now all who believed were together, and had all things in common, ⁴⁵ and sold their possessions and goods, and divided them among all, as anyone had need.

⁴⁶ So continuing daily with one accord in the temple, and breaking bread from house to house, they ate their food with gladness and simplicity of heart, ⁴⁷ praising God and having favor with all the people. And the Lord added to the church daily those who were being saved.

READING 169 · JUNE 18

∼ 2 Kings 25:1–30 ∼

Now it came to pass in the ninth year of his reign, in the tenth month, on the tenth *day* of the month, *that* Nebuchadnezzar king of Babylon and all his army came against Jerusalem and encamped against it; and they built a siege wall against it all around. ² So the city was besieged until the eleventh year of King Zedekiah. ³ By the ninth *day* of the *fourth* month the famine had become so severe in the city that there was no food for the people of the land.

⁴ Then the city wall was broken through, and all the men of war *fled* at night by way of the gate between two walls, which was by the king's garden, even though the Chaldeans *were* still encamped all around against the city. And *the king* went by way of the plain. ⁵ But the army of the Chaldeans pursued the king, and they overtook him in the plains of Jericho. All his army was scattered from him. ⁶ So they took the king and brought him up to the king of Babylon at Riblah, and they pronounced judgment on him. ⁷ Then they killed the sons of Zedekiah before his eyes, put out the eyes of Zedekiah, bound him with bronze fetters, and took him to Babylon.

⁸ And in the fifth month, on the seventh *day* of the month (which *was* the nineteenth year of King Nebuchadnezzar king of Babylon), Nebuzaradan the captain of the guard, a servant of the king of Babylon, came to Jerusalem. ⁹ He burned the house of the LORD and the king's house; all the houses of Jerusalem, that is, all the houses of the great, he burned with fire. ¹⁰ And all the army of the Chaldeans who *were with* the captain of the guard broke down the walls of Jerusalem all around.

¹¹ Then Nebuzaradan the captain of the guard carried away captive the rest of the people *who* remained in the city and the defectors who had deserted to the king of Babylon, with the rest of the multitude. ¹² But the captain of the guard left *some* of the poor of the land as vinedressers and farmers. ¹³ The bronze pillars that *were* in the house of the LORD, and the carts and the bronze Sea that *were* in the house of the LORD, the Chaldeans broke in pieces, and carried their bronze to Babylon. ¹⁴ They also took away the pots, the shovels, the trimmers, the spoons, and all the bronze utensils with which the priests ministered. ¹⁵ The firepans and the basins, the things of solid gold and solid silver, the captain of the guard took away. ¹⁶ The two pillars, one Sea, and the carts, which Solomon had made for the house of the LORD, the bronze of all these articles was beyond measure. ¹⁷ The height of one pillar *was* eighteen cubits, and the capital on it *was* of bronze. The height of the capital was three cubits, and the network and pomegranates all around the capital were all of bronze. The second pillar was the same, with a network.

¹⁸ And the captain of the guard took Seraiah the chief priest, Zephaniah the second priest, and the three doorkeepers. ¹⁹ He also took out of the city an officer who had charge of the men of war, five men of the king's close associates who were found in the city, the chief recruiting officer of the army, who mustered the people of the land, and sixty men of the people of the land *who were* found in the city. ²⁰ So Nebuzaradan, captain of the guard, took these and brought them to the king of Babylon at Riblah. ²¹ Then

the king of Babylon struck them and put them to death at Riblah in the land of Hamath. Thus Judah was carried away captive from its own land.

²² Then he made Gedaliah the son of Ahikam, the son of Shaphan, governor over the people who remained in the land of Judah, whom Nebuchadnezzar king of Babylon had left. ²³ Now when all the captains of the armies, they and *their* men, heard that the king of Babylon had made Gedaliah governor, they came to Gedaliah at Mizpah—Ishmael the son of Nethaniah, Johanan the son of Careah, Seraiah the son of Tanhumeth the Netophathite, and Jaazaniah the son of a Maachathite, they and their men. ²⁴ And Gedaliah took an oath before them and their men, and said to them, "Do not be afraid of the servants of the Chaldeans. Dwell in the land and serve the king of Babylon, and it shall be well with you."

²⁵ But it happened in the seventh month that Ishmael the son of Nethaniah, the son of Elishama, of the royal family, came with ten men and struck and killed Gedaliah, the Jews, as well as the Chaldeans who were with him at Mizpah. ²⁶ And all the people, small and great, and the captains of the armies, arose and went to Egypt; for they were afraid of the Chaldeans.

²⁷ Now it came to pass in the thirty-seventh year of the captivity of Jehoiachin king of Judah, in the twelfth month, on the twenty-seventh *day* of the month, *that* Evil-Merodach king of Babylon, in the year that he began to reign, released Jehoiachin king of Judah from prison. ²⁸ He spoke kindly to him, and gave him a more prominent seat than those of the kings who *were* with him in Babylon. ²⁹ So Jehoiachin changed from his prison garments, and he ate bread regularly before the king all the days of his life. ³⁰ And as for his provisions, *there was* a regular ration given him by the king, a portion for each day, all the days of his life.

~ PSALM 75:1–10 ~

¹ We give thanks to You, O God, we
    give thanks!
For Your wondrous works declare
    that Your name is near.

² "When I choose the proper time,
    I will judge uprightly.
³ The earth and all its inhabitants are
        dissolved;
I set up its pillars firmly.   Selah

⁴ "I said to the boastful, 'Do not deal
        boastfully,'
And to the wicked, 'Do not lift up
    the horn.
⁵ Do not lift up your horn on high;
Do *not* speak with a stiff neck.' "

⁶ For exaltation *comes* neither from
        the east
Nor from the west nor from the
    south.
⁷ But God *is* the Judge:
He puts down one,
And exalts another.
⁸ For in the hand of the LORD *there is*
    a cup,
And the wine is red;
It is fully mixed, and He pours it
    out;
Surely its dregs shall all the wicked
    of the earth
Drain *and* drink down.

⁹ But I will declare forever,
I will sing praises to the God of
    Jacob.

¹⁰ "All the horns of the wicked I will
    also cut off,
But the horns of the righteous shall
    be exalted."

~ PROVERBS 19:4, 5 ~

⁴ Wealth makes many friends,
But the poor is separated from his
    friend.

⁵ A false witness will not go
    unpunished,
And *he who* speaks lies will not
    escape.

~ ACTS 3:1–26 ~

Now Peter and John went up together to the temple at the hour of prayer, the ninth *hour.* ² And a certain man lame from his

How to Spend an Hour

A time management expert once asked a seminar group to "brainstorm" a list of all the things they could do in one hour. Among the many answers written on the blackboard were these:

Walk the dog
Mow the lawn
Have a relaxed conversation with
   my spouse
Visit a sick or elderly friend
Take a nap
Jog through the park
Play ball with my son
Write a long-overdue letter
Pay the monthly bills
Listen to an entire CD
Clean the fish tank
Play a set of tennis

The group laughed at some of their ideas and were serious about others. At the end of a two-minute session, they had listed more than a hundred ideas. When the expert asked them to identify the one activity that would have the greatest long-term impact on their lives, the great majority chose an idea that could be explained in only one word: Pray.

Repent therefore and be converted, that your sins may be blotted out, so that times of refreshing may come from the presence of the Lord.

Acts 3:19

mother's womb was carried, whom they laid daily at the gate of the temple which is called Beautiful, to ask alms from those who entered the temple; ³ who, seeing Peter and John about to go into the temple, asked for alms. ⁴ And fixing his eyes on him, with John, Peter said, "Look at us." ⁵ So he gave them his attention, expecting to receive something from them. ⁶ Then Peter said, "Silver and gold I do not have, but what I do have I give you: In the name of Jesus Christ of Nazareth, rise up and walk." ⁷ And he took him by the right hand and lifted *him* up, and immediately his feet and ankle bones received strength. ⁸ So he, leaping up, stood and walked and entered the temple with them—walking, leaping, and praising God. ⁹ And all the people saw him walking and praising God. ¹⁰ Then they knew that it was he who sat begging alms at the Beautiful Gate of the temple; and they were filled with wonder and amazement at what had happened to him.

¹¹ Now as the lame man who was healed held on to Peter and John, all the people ran together to them in the porch which is called Solomon's, greatly amazed. ¹² So when Peter saw *it*, he responded to the people: "Men of Israel, why do you marvel at this? Or why look so intently at us, as though by our own power or godliness we had made this man walk? ¹³ The God of Abraham, Isaac, and Jacob, the God of our fathers, glorified His Servant Jesus, whom you delivered up and denied in the presence of Pilate, when he was determined to let *Him* go. ¹⁴ But you denied the Holy One and the Just, and asked for a murderer to be granted to you, ¹⁵ and

killed the Prince of life, whom God raised from the dead, of which we are witnesses. ¹⁶ And His name, through faith in His name, has made this man strong, whom you see and know. Yes, the faith which *comes* through Him has given him this perfect soundness in the presence of you all.

¹⁷ "Yet now, brethren, I know that you did *it* in ignorance, as *did* also your rulers. ¹⁸ But those things which God foretold by the mouth of all His prophets, that the Christ would suffer, He has thus fulfilled. ¹⁹ Repent therefore and be converted, that your sins may be blotted out, so that times of refreshing may come from the presence of the Lord, ²⁰ and that He may send Jesus Christ, who was preached to you before, ²¹ whom heaven must receive until the times of restoration of all things, which God has spoken by the mouth of all His holy prophets since the world began. ²² For Moses truly said to the fathers, 'The LORD your God will raise up for you a Prophet like me from your brethren. Him you shall hear in all things, whatever He says to you. ²³ And it shall be that every soul who will not hear that Prophet shall be utterly destroyed from among the people.' ²⁴ Yes, and all the prophets, from Samuel and those who follow, as many as have spoken, have also foretold these days. ²⁵ You are sons of the prophets, and of the covenant which God made with our fathers, saying to Abraham, 'And in your seed all the families of the earth shall be blessed.' ²⁶ To you first, God, having raised up His Servant Jesus, sent Him to bless you, in turning away every one *of you* from your iniquities."

READING 170 · JUNE 19

~ 1 CHRONICLES 1:1—2:55 ~

Adam, Seth, Enosh, ² Cainan, Mahalalel, Jared, ³ Enoch , Methuselah, Lamech, ⁴ Noah, Shem, Ham, and Japheth.
⁵ The sons of Japheth *were* Gomer, Magog, Madai, Javan, Tubal, Meshech, and Tiras. ⁶ The sons of Gomer *were* Ashkenaz, Diphath, and Togarmah. ⁷ The

sons of Javan *were* Elishah, Tarshishah, Kittim, and Rodanim.
⁸ The sons of Ham *were* Cush, Mizraim, Put, and Canaan. ⁹ The sons of Cush *were* Seba, Havilah, Sabta, Raama, and Sabtecha. The sons of Raama *were* Sheba and Dedan. ¹⁰ Cush begot Nimrod; he began to be a mighty one on the earth.

A Legacy of Prayer

In the early days of the formation of the United States, a stranger once asked how he might identify George Washington among those present at Congress. He was told, "You can easily distinguish him when Congress goes to prayer. Washington is the gentleman who kneels."

Washington had a long-standing reputation as a man of prayer. At Valley Forge, he frequently found rest and relief in prayer. One day a farmer approaching the military camp heard an earnest voice. When he drew nearer, he saw Washington on his knees, his cheeks wet with tears. The farmer returned home and said to his wife: "George Washington will succeed! George Washington will succeed! The Americans will secure their independence!"

"What makes you think so, Isaac?" his wife asked. The farmer replied, "I heard him pray, Hannah, out in the woods today, and the Lord will surely hear his prayer. He will, Hannah; thee may rest assured He will."

One person, willing to humble himself and pray can leave a legacy of faith and hope, giving courage to future generations.

Now when they saw the boldness of Peter and John, and perceived that they were uneducated and untrained men, they marveled. And they realized that they had been with Jesus.

Acts 4:13

¹¹ Mizraim begot Ludim, Anamim, Lehabim, Naphtuhim, ¹² Pathrusim, Casluhim (from whom came the Philistines and the Caphtorim). ¹³ Canaan begot Sidon, his firstborn, and Heth; ¹⁴ the Jebusite, the Amorite, and the Girgashite; ¹⁵ the Hivite, the Arkite, and the Sinite; ¹⁶ the Arvadite, the Zemarite, and the Hamathite.

¹⁷ The sons of Shem were Elam, Asshur, Arphaxad, Lud, Aram, Uz, Hul, Gether, and Meshech. ¹⁸ Arphaxad begot Shelah, and Shelah begot Eber. ¹⁹ To Eber were born two sons: the name of one was Peleg, for in his days the earth was divided; and his brother's name was Joktan. ²⁰ Joktan begot Almodad, Sheleph, Hazarmaveth, Jerah, ²¹ Hadoram, Uzal, Diklah, ²² Ebal, Abimael, Sheba, ²³ Ophir, Havilah, and Jobab. All these were the sons of Joktan.

²⁴ Shem, Arphaxad, Shelah, ²⁵ Eber, Peleg, Reu, ²⁶ Serug, Nahor, Terah, ²⁷ and Abram, who is Abraham. ²⁸ The sons of Abraham were Isaac and Ishmael.

²⁹ These are their genealogies: The firstborn of Ishmael was Nebajoth; then Kedar, Adbeel, Mibsam, ³⁰ Mishma, Dumah, Massa, Hadad, Tema, ³¹ Jetur, Naphish, and Kedemah. These were the sons of Ishmael.

³² Now the sons born to Keturah, Abraham's concubine, were Zimran, Jokshan, Medan, Midian, Ishbak, and Shuah. The sons of Jokshan were Sheba and Dedan. ³³ The sons of Midian were Ephah, Epher, Hanoch, Abida, and Eldaah. All these were the children of Keturah.

³⁴ And Abraham begot Isaac. The sons of Isaac were Esau and Israel. ³⁵ The sons of Esau were Eliphaz, Reuel, Jeush, Jaalam, and Korah. ³⁶ And the sons of Eliphaz were Teman, Omar, Zephi, Gatam, and Kenaz; and by Timna, Amalek. ³⁷ The sons of Reuel were Nahath, Zerah, Shammah, and Mizzah.

³⁸ The sons of Seir were Lotan, Shobal, Zibeon, Anah, Dishon, Ezer, and Dishan. ³⁹ And the sons of Lotan were Hori and Homam; Lotan's sister was Timna. ⁴⁰ The sons of Shobal were Alian, Manahath, Ebal, Shephi, and Onam. The sons of Zibeon were Ajah and Anah. ⁴¹ The son of Anah was Dishon. The sons of Dishon were Hamran, Eshban, Ithran, and Cheran. ⁴² The sons of Ezer were Bilhan, Zaavan, and Jaakan. The sons of Dishan were Uz and Aran.

⁴³ Now these were the kings who reigned in the land of Edom before a king reigned over the children of Israel: Bela the son of Beor, and the name of his city was Dinhabah. ⁴⁴ And when Bela died, Jobab the son of Zerah of Bozrah reigned in his place. ⁴⁵ When Jobab died, Husham of the land of the Temanites reigned in his place. ⁴⁶ And when Husham died, Hadad the son of Bedad, who attacked Midian in the field of Moab, reigned in his place. The name of his city was Avith. ⁴⁷ When Hadad died, Samlah of Masrekah reigned in his place. ⁴⁸ And when Samlah died, Saul of Rehoboth-by-the-River reigned in his place. ⁴⁹ When Saul died, Baal-Hanan the son of Achbor reigned in his place. ⁵⁰ And when Baal-Hanan died, Hadad reigned in his place; and the name of his city was Pai. His wife's name was Mehetabel the daughter of Matred, the daughter of Mezahab. ⁵¹ Hadad died also. And the chiefs of Edom were Chief Timnah, Chief Aliah, Chief Jetheth, ⁵² Chief Aholibamah, Chief Elah, Chief Pinon, ⁵³ Chief Kenaz, Chief Teman, Chief Mibzar, ⁵⁴ Chief Magdiel, and Chief Iram. These were the chiefs of Edom.

2 These were the sons of Israel: Reuben, Simeon, Levi, Judah, Issachar, Zebulun, ² Dan, Joseph, Benjamin, Naphtali, Gad, and Asher.

³ The sons of Judah were Er, Onan, and Shelah. These three were born to him by the daughter of Shua, the Canaanitess. Er, the firstborn of Judah, was wicked in the sight of the LORD; so He killed him. ⁴ And Tamar, his daughter-in-law, bore him Perez and Zerah. All the sons of Judah were five.

⁵ The sons of Perez were Hezron and Hamul. ⁶ The sons of Zerah were Zimri, Ethan, Heman, Calcol, and Dara—five of them in all.

⁷ The son of Carmi was Achar, the troubler of Israel, who transgressed in the accursed thing.

⁸ The son of Ethan was Azariah.

⁹ Also the sons of Hezron who were born to him were Jerahmeel, Ram, and

Chelubai. [10] Ram begot Amminadab, and Amminadab begot Nahshon, leader of the children of Judah; [11] Nahshon begot Salma, and Salma begot Boaz; [12] Boaz begot Obed, and Obed begot Jesse; [13] Jesse begot Eliab his firstborn, Abinadab the second, Shimea the third, [14] Nethanel the fourth, Raddai the fifth, [15] Ozem the sixth, *and* David the seventh.

[16] Now their sisters *were* Zeruiah and Abigail. And the sons of Zeruiah *were* Abishai, Joab, and Asahel—three. [17] Abigail bore Amasa; and the father of Amasa *was* Jether the Ishmaelite.

[18] Caleb the son of Hezron had children by Azubah, *his* wife, and by Jerioth. Now these were her sons: Jesher, Shobab, and Ardon. [19] When Azubah died, Caleb took Ephrath as his wife, who bore him Hur. [20] And Hur begot Uri, and Uri begot Bezalel.

[21] Now afterward Hezron went in to the daughter of Machir the father of Gilead, whom he married when he *was* sixty years old; and she bore him Segub. [22] Segub begot Jair, who had twenty-three cities in the land of Gilead. [23] (Geshur and Syria took from them the towns of Jair, with Kenath and its towns—sixty towns.) All these *belonged to* the sons of Machir the father of Gilead. [24] After Hezron died in Caleb Ephrathah, Hezron's wife Abijah bore him Ashhur the father of Tekoa.

[25] The sons of Jerahmeel, the firstborn of Hezron, *were* Ram, the firstborn, and Bunah, Oren, Ozem, *and* Ahijah. [26] Jerahmeel had another wife, whose name was Atarah; she was the mother of Onam. [27] The sons of Ram, the firstborn of Jerahmeel, were Maaz, Jamin, and Eker. [28] The sons of Onam were Shammai and Jada. The sons of Shammai *were* Nadab and Abishur.

[29] And the name of the wife of Abishur *was* Abihail, and she bore him Ahban and Molid. [30] The sons of Nadab *were* Seled and Appaim; Seled died without children. [31] The son of Appaim *was* Ishi, the son of Ishi *was* Sheshan, and Sheshan's son *was* Ahlai. [32] The sons of Jada, the brother of Shammai, *were* Jether and Jonathan; Jether died without children. [33] The sons of Jonathan *were* Peleth and Zaza. These were the sons of Jerahmeel.

[34] Now Sheshan had no sons, only daughters. And Sheshan had an Egyptian servant whose name *was* Jarha. [35] Sheshan gave his daughter to Jarha his servant as wife, and she bore him Attai. [36] Attai begot Nathan, and Nathan begot Zabad; [37] Zabad begot Ephlal, and Ephlal begot Obed; [38] Obed begot Jehu, and Jehu begot Azariah; [39] Azariah begot Helez, and Helez begot Eleasah; [40] Eleasah begot Sismai, and Sismai begot Shallum; [41] Shallum begot Jekamiah, and Jekamiah begot Elishama.

[42] The descendants of Caleb the brother of Jerahmeel *were* Mesha, his firstborn, who was the father of Ziph, and the sons of Mareshah the father of Hebron. [43] The sons of Hebron *were* Korah, Tappuah, Rekem, and Shema. [44] Shema begot Raham the father of Jorkoam, and Rekem begot Shammai. [45] And the son of Shammai *was* Maon, and Maon *was* the father of Beth Zur.

[46] Ephah, Caleb's concubine, bore Haran, Moza, and Gazez; and Haran begot Gazez. [47] And the sons of Jahdai *were* Regem, Jotham, Geshan, Pelet, Ephah, and Shaaph.

[48] Maachah, Caleb's concubine, bore Sheber and Tirhanah. [49] She also bore Shaaph the father of Madmannah, Sheva the father of Machbenah and the father of Gibea. And the daughter of Caleb *was* Achsah.

[50] These were the descendants of Caleb: The sons of Hur, the firstborn of Ephrathah, *were* Shobal the father of Kirjath Jearim, [51] Salma the father of Bethlehem, *and* Hareph the father of Beth Gader.

[52] And Shobal the father of Kirjath Jearim had descendants: Haroeh, *and* half of the families of Manuhoth. [53] The families of Kirjath Jearim *were* the Ithrites, the Puthites, the Shumathites, and the Mishraites. From these came the Zorathites and the Eshtaolites.

[54] The sons of Salma *were* Bethlehem, the Netophathites, Atroth Beth Joab, half of the Manahethites, and the Zorites. [55] And the families of the scribes who dwelt at Jabez *were* the Tirathites, the Shimeathites, *and* the Suchathites. These *were* the Kenites who came from Hammath, the father of the house of Rechab.

~ PSALM 76:1-6 ~

1 In Judah God *is* known;
    His name *is* great in Israel.
2 In Salem also is His tabernacle,
    And His dwelling place in Zion.
3 There He broke the arrows of the
        bow,
    The shield and sword of battle. Selah

4 You *are* more glorious and excellent
    Than the mountains of prey.
5 The stouthearted were plundered;
    They have sunk into their sleep;
    And none of the mighty men have
        found the use of their hands.
6 At Your rebuke, O God of Jacob,
    Both the chariot and horse were cast
        into a dead sleep.

~ PROVERBS 19:6, 7 ~

6 Many entreat the favor of the
        nobility,
    And every man *is* a friend to one
        who gives gifts.
7 All the brothers of the poor hate
        him;
    How much more do his friends go
        far from him!
    He may pursue *them with* words,
        yet they abandon *him*.

~ ACTS 4:1-22 ~

Now as they spoke to the people, the priests, the captain of the temple, and the Sadducees came upon them, 2 being greatly disturbed that they taught the people and preached in Jesus the resurrection from the dead. 3 And they laid hands on them, and put *them* in custody until the next day, for it was already evening. 4 However, many of those who heard the word believed; and the number of the men came to be about five thousand.

5 And it came to pass, on the next day, that their rulers, elders, and scribes, 6 as well as Annas the high priest, Caiaphas, John, and Alexander, and as many as were of the family of the high priest, were gathered together at Jerusalem. 7 And when they had set them in the midst, they asked, "By what power or by what name have you done this?"

8 Then Peter, filled with the Holy Spirit, said to them, "Rulers of the people and elders of Israel: 9 If we this day are judged for a good deed *done* to a helpless man, by what means he has been made well, 10 let it be known to you all, and to all the people of Israel, that by the name of Jesus Christ of Nazareth, whom you crucified, whom God raised from the dead, by Him this man stands here before you whole. 11 This is the 'stone which was rejected by you builders, which has become the chief cornerstone.' 12 Nor is there salvation in any other, for there is no other name under heaven given among men by which we must be saved."

13 Now when they saw the boldness of Peter and John, and perceived that they were uneducated and untrained men, they marveled. And they realized that they had been with Jesus. 14 And seeing the man who had been healed standing with them, they could say nothing against it. 15 But when they had commanded them to go aside out of the council, they conferred among themselves, 16 saying, "What shall we do to these men? For, indeed, that a notable miracle has been done through them *is* evident to all who dwell in Jerusalem, and we cannot deny *it*. 17 But so that it spreads no further among the people, let us severely threaten them, that from now on they speak to no man in this name."

18 So they called them and commanded them not to speak at all nor teach in the name of Jesus. 19 But Peter and John answered and said to them, "Whether it is right in the sight of God to listen to you more than to God, you judge. 20 For we cannot but speak the things which we have seen and heard." 21 So when they had further threatened them, they let them go, finding no way of punishing them, because of the people, since they all glorified God for what had been done. 22 For the man was over forty years old on whom this miracle of healing had been performed.

∼ 1 CHRONICLES 3:1—4:43 ∼

Now these were the sons of David who were born to him in Hebron: The firstborn *was* Amnon, by Ahinoam the Jezreelitess; the second, Daniel, by Abigail the Carmelitess; ² the third, Absalom the son of Maacah, the daughter of Talmai, king of Geshur; the fourth, Adonijah the son of Haggith; ³ the fifth, Shephatiah, by Abital; the sixth, Ithream, by his wife Eglah.

⁴ *These* six were born to him in Hebron. There he reigned seven years and six months, and in Jerusalem he reigned thirty-three years. ⁵ And these were born to him in Jerusalem: Shimea, Shobab, Nathan, and Solomon—four by Bathshua the daughter of Ammiel. ⁶ Also *there* were Ibhar, Elishama, Eliphelet, ⁷ Nogah, Nepheg, Japhia, ⁸ Elishama, Eliada, and Eliphelet—nine *in all.* ⁹ *These were* all the sons of David, besides the sons of the concubines, and Tamar their sister.

¹⁰ Solomon's son *was* Rehoboam; Abijah *was* his son, Asa his son, Jehoshaphat his son, ¹¹ Joram his son, Ahaziah his son, Joash his son, ¹² Amaziah his son, Azariah his son, Jotham his son, ¹³ Ahaz his son, Hezekiah his son, Manasseh his son, ¹⁴ Amon his son, *and* Josiah his son. ¹⁵ The sons of Josiah *were* Johanan the firstborn, the second Jehoiakim, the third Zedekiah, and the fourth Shallum. ¹⁶ The sons of Jehoiakim *were* Jeconiah his son *and* Zedekiah his son.

¹⁷ And the sons of Jeconiah *were* Assir, Shealtiel his son, ¹⁸ *and* Malchiram, Pedaiah, Shenazzar, Jecamiah, Hoshama, and Nedabiah. ¹⁹ The sons of Pedaiah *were* Zerubbabel and Shimei. The sons of Zerubbabel *were* Meshullam, Hananiah, Shelomith their sister, ²⁰ and Hashubah, Ohel, Berechiah, Hasadiah, and Jushab-Hesed—five *in all.* ²¹ The sons of Hananiah *were* Pelatiah and Jeshaiah, the sons of Rephaiah, the sons of Arnan, the sons of Obadiah, and the sons of Shechaniah. ²² The son of Shechaniah was Shemaiah. The sons of Shemaiah *were* Hattush, Igal, Bariah, Neariah, and Shaphat—six *in all.* ²³ The sons of Neariah *were* Elioenai, Hezekiah, and Azrikam—three *in all.* ²⁴ The sons of

Elioenai *were* Hodaviah, Eliashib, Pelaiah, Akkub, Johanan, Delaiah, and Anani—seven *in all.*

4 The sons of Judah *were* Perez, Hezron, Carmi, Hur, and Shobal. ² And Reaiah the son of Shobal begot Jahath, and Jahath begot Ahumai and Lahad. These *were* the families of the Zorathites. ³ These *were* the sons *of the father* of Etam: Jezreel, Ishma, and Idbash; and the name of their sister *was* Hazelelponi; ⁴ and Penuel *was* the father of Gedor, and Ezer *was the* father of Hushah.

These *were* the sons of Hur, the firstborn of Ephrathah the father of Bethlehem.

⁵ And Ashhur the father of Tekoa had two wives, Helah and Naarah. ⁶ Naarah bore him Ahuzzam, Hepher, Temeni, and Haahashtari. These *were* the sons of Naarah. ⁷ The sons of Helah *were* Zereth, Zohar, and Ethnan; ⁸ and Koz begot Anub, Zobebah, and the families of Aharhel the son of Harum.

⁹ Now Jabez was more honorable than his brothers, and his mother called his name Jabez, saying, "Because I bore *him* in pain." ¹⁰ And Jabez called on the God of Israel saying, "Oh, that You would bless me indeed, and enlarge my territory, that Your hand would be with me, and that You would keep *me* from evil, that I may not cause pain!" So God granted him what he requested.

¹¹ Chelub the brother of Shuhah begot Mehir, who *was* the father of Eshton. ¹² And Eshton begot Beth-Rapha, Paseah, and Tehinnah the father of Ir-Nahash. These *were* the men of Rechah.

¹³ The sons of Kenaz *were* Othniel and Seraiah. The sons of Othniel *were* Hathath, ¹⁴ and Meonothai *who* begot Ophrah. Seraiah begot Joab the father of Ge Harashim, for they were craftsmen. ¹⁵ The sons of Caleb the son of Jephunneh *were* Iru, Elah, and Naam. The son of Elah *was* Kenaz. ¹⁶ The sons of Jehallelel *were* Ziph, Ziphah, Tiria, and Asarel. ¹⁷ The sons of Ezrah *were* Jether, Mered, Epher, and Jalon. And *Mered's wife bore* Miriam, Shammai, and Ishbah the father

of Eshtemoa. ¹⁸(His wife Jehudijah bore Jered the father of Gedor, Heber the father of Sochoh, and Jekuthiel the father of Zanoah.) And these were the sons of Bithiah the daughter of Pharaoh, whom Mered took.

¹⁹ The sons of Hodiah's wife, the sister of Naham, *were* the fathers of Keilah the Garmite and of Eshtemoa the Maachathite. ²⁰ And the sons of Shimon *were* Amnon, Rinnah, Ben-Hanan, and Tilon. And the sons of Ishi *were* Zoheth and Ben-Zoheth.

²¹ The sons of Shelah the son of Judah *were* Er the father of Lecah, Laadah the father of Mareshah, and the families of the house of the linen workers of the house of Ashbea; ²² also Jokim, the men of Chozeba, and Joash; Saraph, who ruled in Moab, and Jashubi-Lehem. Now the records are ancient. ²³ These *were* the potters and those who dwell at Netaim and Gederah; there they dwelt with the king for his work.

²⁴ The sons of Simeon *were* Nemuel, Jamin, Jarib, Zerah, *and* Shaul, ²⁵ Shallum his son, Mibsam his son, and Mishma his son. ²⁶ And the sons of Mishma *were* Hamuel his son, Zacchur his son, and Shimei his son. ²⁷ Shimei had sixteen sons and six daughters; but his brothers did not have many children, nor did any of their families multiply as much as the children of Judah.

²⁸ They dwelt at Beersheba, Moladah, Hazar Shual, ²⁹ Bilhah, Ezem, Tolad, ³⁰ Bethuel, Hormah, Ziklag, ³¹ Beth Marcaboth, Hazar Susim, Beth Biri, and at Shaaraim. These *were* their cities until the reign of David. ³² And their villages *were* Etam, Ain, Rimmon, Tochen, and Ashan—five cities— ³³ and all the villages that *were* around these cities as far as Baal. These *were* their dwelling places, and they maintained their genealogy: ³⁴ Meshobab, Jamlech, and Joshah the son of Amaziah; ³⁵ Joel, and Jehu the son of Joshibiah, the son of Seraiah, the son of Asiel; ³⁶ Elioenai, Jaakobah, Jeshohaiah, Asaiah, Adiel, Jesimiel, and Benaiah; ³⁷ Ziza the son of Shiphi, the son of Allon, the son of Jedaiah, the son of Shimri, the son of Shemaiah— ³⁸ these mentioned by name *were* leaders in their families, and their father's house increased greatly.

³⁹ So they went to the entrance of Gedor, as far as the east side of the valley, to seek pasture for their flocks. ⁴⁰ And they found rich, good pasture, and the land *was* broad, quiet, and peaceful; for some Hamites formerly lived there.

⁴¹ These recorded by name came in the days of Hezekiah king of Judah; and they attacked their tents and the Meunites who were found there, and utterly destroyed them, as it is to this day. So they dwelt in their place, because *there was* pasture for their flocks there. ⁴² Now *some of* them, five hundred men of the sons of Simeon, went to Mount Seir, having as their captains Pelatiah, Neariah, Rephaiah, and Uzziel, the sons of Ishi. ⁴³ And they defeated the rest of the Amalekites who had escaped. They have dwelt there to this day.

∼ PSALM 76:7–12 ∼

⁷ You, Yourself, *are* to be feared;
   And who may stand in Your presence
   When once You are angry?
⁸ You caused judgment to be heard
      from heaven;
   The earth feared and was still,
⁹ When God arose to judgment,
   To deliver all the oppressed of the
      earth.   Selah

¹⁰ Surely the wrath of man shall praise
      You;
   With the remainder of wrath You
      shall gird Yourself.

¹¹ Make vows to the LORD your God,
      and pay *them;*
   Let all who are around Him bring
      presents to Him who ought to be
      feared.
¹² He shall cut off the spirit of princes;
   He is awesome to the kings of the
      earth.

∼ PROVERBS 19:8, 9 ∼

⁸ He who gets wisdom loves his own
      soul;
   He who keeps understanding will
      find good.

Bless Those Who Curse You

The story is told that General Robert E. Lee was asked by Confederate President Jefferson Davis to give his opinion about a certain officer. Lee gave the officer a glowing report.

One of the officers in attendance was greatly astonished by his words and said to Lee, "General, do you not know that the man of whom you speak so highly to the President is one of your bitterest enemies, and misses no opportunity to malign you?"

"Yes," said Lee, "but the President asked my opinion of him; he did not ask for his opinion of me."

When we speak well of our enemies, we are doing three things: First, we increase our own value. We show that we are able to rise above cheap criticism and bestow costly praise on another.

Second, we diffuse our enemy's criticism. Any person hearing both our praise of an enemy and our enemy's disdain for us is likely to conclude that we are nothing like we have been described!

Third, we reveal to others that we are diligent investigators. It takes an effort to find something good to say about someone who hates you; it takes very little effort or intelligence to respond with hate or hurtful ridicule.

The truth will always reveal itself — God will see to it!

⁹ A false witness will not go
    unpunished,
And *he who* speaks lies shall perish.

∼ ACTS 4:23–37 ∼

And being let go, they went to their own *companions* and reported all that the chief priests and elders had said to them. ²⁴ So when they heard that, they raised their voice to God with one accord and said: "Lord, You *are* God, who made heaven and earth and the sea, and all that is in them, ²⁵ who by the mouth of Your servant David have said:

'Why did the nations rage,
    And the people plot vain things?
²⁶ The kings of the earth took their
    stand,
    And the rulers were gathered
        together
    Against the LORD and against His
        Christ.'

²⁷ "For truly against Your holy Servant Jesus, whom You anointed, both Herod and Pontius Pilate, with the Gentiles and the people of Israel, were gathered together ²⁸ to do whatever Your hand and Your purpose determined before to be done. ²⁹ Now, Lord, look on their threats, and grant to Your servants that with all boldness they may speak Your word, ³⁰ by stretching out Your hand to heal, and that signs and wonders may be done through the name of Your holy Servant Jesus."

³¹ And when they had prayed, the place where they were assembled together was shaken; and they were all filled with the Holy Spirit, and they spoke the word of God with boldness.

³² Now the multitude of those who believed were of one heart and one soul; neither did anyone say that any of the things he possessed was his own, but they had all things in common. ³³ And with great power the apostles gave witness to the resurrection of the Lord Jesus. And great grace was upon them all. ³⁴ Nor was there anyone among them who lacked; for all who were possessors of lands or houses sold them, and brought the proceeds of the things that were sold, ³⁵ and laid *them* at the apostles' feet; and they distributed to each as anyone had need.

³⁶ And Joses, who was also named Barnabas by the apostles (which is translated Son of Encouragement), a Levite of the country of Cyprus, ³⁷ having land, sold *it,* and brought the money and laid *it* at the apostles' feet.

READING 172 · JUNE 21

∼ 1 CHRONICLES 5:1—6:81 ∼

Now the sons of Reuben the first-born of Israel—he *was* indeed the firstborn, but because he defiled his father's bed, his birthright was given to the sons of Joseph, the son of Israel, so that the genealogy is not listed according to the birthright; ² yet Judah prevailed over his brothers, and from him *came* a ruler, although the birthright was Joseph's— ³ the sons of Reuben the first-born of Israel were Hanoch, Pallu, Hezron, and Carmi.

⁴ The sons of Joel *were* Shemaiah his son, Gog his son, Shimei his son, ⁵ Micah his son, Reaiah his son, Baal his son, ⁶ and Beerah his son, whom Tiglath-Pileser king of Assyria carried into captivity. He *was* leader of the Reubenites. ⁷ And his brethren by their families, when the genealogy of their generations was registered: the chief, Jeiel, and Zechariah, ⁸ and Bela the son of Azaz, the son of Shema, the son of Joel, who dwelt in Aroer, as far as Nebo and Baal Meon. ⁹ Eastward they settled as far as the entrance of the wilderness this side of the River Euphrates, because their cattle had multiplied in the land of Gilead.

¹⁰ Now in the days of Saul they made war with the Hagrites, who fell by their hand; and they dwelt in their tents throughout the entire *area* east of Gilead.

¹¹ And the children of Gad dwelt next to them in the land of Bashan as far as Salcah: ¹² Joel *was* the chief, Shapham the next, then Jaanai and Shaphat in Bashan,

Overlooking Faults

The story is told of a couple at their golden wedding anniversary celebration. Surrounded by her children, grandchildren, and great grandchildren, the wife was asked the secret to a long and happy marriage. With a loving glance toward her husband, she answered: "On my wedding day, I decided to make a list of ten of my husband's faults which, for the sake of our marriage, I would overlook. I figured I could live with at least ten faults."

A guest asked her to identify some of the faults she had chosen to overlook. Her husband looked a bit troubled at the thought of having his foibles and flaws revealed to the assembled group. However, his wife sweetly replied, "To tell you the truth, dear, I never did get around to listing them. Instead, every time my husband did something that made me hopping mad, I would simply say to myself, *Lucky for him that's one of the ten!*"

Even the most devoted friends and spouses will experience storms in their relationships from time to time. Some problems are worth addressing in order to resolve them. Others are best left unspoken. With time, those issues which are truly of little importance tend to blow past without any need for a "blowup."

[13] and their brethren of their father's house: Michael, Meshullam, Sheba, Jorai, Jachan, Zia, and Eber—seven *in all.* [14] These *were* the children of Abihail the son of Huri, the son of Jaroah, the son of Gilead, the son of Michael, the son of Jeshishai, the son of Jahdo, the son of Buz; [15] Ahi the son of Abdiel, the son of Guni, *was* chief of their father's house. [16] And *the Gadites* dwelt in Gilead, in Bashan and in its villages, and in all the commonlands of Sharon within their borders. [17] All these were registered by genealogies in the days of Jotham king of Judah, and in the days of Jeroboam king of Israel.

[18] The sons of Reuben, the Gadites, and half the tribe of Manasseh *had* forty-four thousand seven hundred and sixty valiant men, men able to bear shield and sword, to shoot with the bow, and skillful in war, who went to war. [19] They made war with the Hagrites, Jetur, Naphish, and Nodab. [20] And they were helped against them, and the Hagrites were delivered into their hand, and all who *were* with them, for they cried out to God in the battle. He heeded their prayer, because they put their trust in Him. [21] Then they took away their livestock—fifty thousand of their camels, two hundred and fifty thousand of their sheep, and two thousand of their donkeys—also one hundred thousand of their men; [22] for many fell dead, because the war *was* God's. And they dwelt in their place until the captivity.

[23] So the children of the half-tribe of Manasseh dwelt in the land. Their *numbers* increased from Bashan to Baal Hermon, that is, to Senir, or Mount Hermon. [24] These *were* the heads of their fathers' houses: Epher, Ishi, Eliel, Azriel, Jeremiah, Hodaviah, and Jahdiel. They were mighty men of valor, famous men, *and* heads of their fathers' houses.

[25] And they were unfaithful to the God of their fathers, and played the harlot after the gods of the peoples of the land, whom God had destroyed before them. [26] So the God of Israel stirred up the spirit of Pul king of Assyria, that is, Tiglath-Pileser king of Assyria. He carried the Reubenites, the Gadites, and the half-tribe of Manasseh into captivity. He took them to Halah, Habor, Hara, and the river of Gozan to this day.

6 The sons of Levi *were* Gershon, Kohath, and Merari. [2] The sons of Kohath *were* Amram, Izhar, Hebron, and Uzziel. [3] The children of Amram *were* Aaron, Moses, and Miriam. And the sons of Aaron *were* Nadab, Abihu, Eleazar, and Ithamar. [4] Eleazar begot Phinehas, *and* Phinehas begot Abishua; [5] Abishua begot Bukki, and Bukki begot Uzzi; [6] Uzzi begot Zerahiah, and Zerahiah begot Meraioth; [7] Meraioth begot Amariah, and Amariah begot Ahitub; [8] Ahitub begot Zadok, and Zadok begot Ahimaaz; [9] Ahimaaz begot Azariah, and Azariah begot Johanan; [10] Johanan begot Azariah (it was he who ministered as priest in the temple that Solomon built in Jerusalem); [11] Azariah begot Amariah, and Amariah begot Ahitub; [12] Ahitub begot Zadok, and Zadok begot Shallum; [13] Shallum begot Hilkiah, and Hilkiah begot Azariah; [14] Azariah begot Seraiah, and Seraiah begot Jehozadak. [15] Jehozadak went *into captivity* when the LORD carried Judah and Jerusalem into captivity by the hand of Nebuchadnezzar.

[16] The sons of Levi *were* Gershon, Kohath, and Merari. [17] These are the names of the sons of Gershon: Libni and Shimei. [18] The sons of Kohath *were* Amram, Izhar, Hebron, and Uzziel. [19] The sons of Merari *were* Mahli and Mushi. Now these *are* the families of the Levites according to their fathers: [20] Of Gershon *were* Libni his son, Jahath his son, Zimmah his son, [21] Joah his son, Iddo his son, Zerah his son, *and* Jeatherai his son. [22] The sons of Kohath *were* Amminadab his son, Korah his son, Assir his son, [23] Elkanah his son, Ebiasaph his son, Assir his son, [24] Tahath his son, Uriel his son, Uzziah his son, and Shaul his son. [25] The sons of Elkanah *were* Amasai and Ahimoth. [26] *As for* Elkanah, the sons of Elkanah *were* Zophai his son, Nahath his son, [27] Eliab his son, Jeroham his son, *and* Elkanah his son. [28] The sons of Samuel *were* Joel the firstborn, and Abijah the second. [29] The sons of Merari *were* Mahli, Libni his son, Shimei his son, Uzzah his son, [30] Shimea his son, Haggiah his son, *and* Asaiah his son.

[31] Now these are the men whom David appointed over the service of song in the house of the LORD, after the ark came to

rest. ³² They were ministering with music before the dwelling place of the tabernacle of meeting, until Solomon had built the house of the LORD in Jerusalem, and they served in their office according to their order.

³³ And these *are* the ones who ministered with their sons: Of the sons of the Kohathites *were* Heman the singer, the son of Joel, the son of Samuel, ³⁴ the son of Elkanah, the son of Jeroham, the son of Eliel, the son of Toah, ³⁵ the son of Zuph, the son of Elkanah, the son of Mahath, the son of Amasai, ³⁶ the son of Elkanah, the son of Joel, the son of Azariah, the son of Zephaniah, ³⁷ the son of Tahath, the son of Assir, the son of Ebiasaph, the son of Korah, ³⁸ the son of Izhar, the son of Kohath, the son of Levi, the son of Israel. ³⁹ And his brother Asaph, who stood at his right hand, *was* Asaph the son of Berachiah, the son of Shimea, ⁴⁰ the son of Michael, the son of Baaseiah, the son of Malchijah, ⁴¹ the son of Ethni, the son of Zerah, the son of Adaiah, ⁴² the son of Ethan, the son of Zimmah, the son of Shimei, ⁴³ the son of Jahath, the son of Gershon, the son of Levi.

⁴⁴ Their brethren, the sons of Merari, on the left hand, *were* Ethan the son of Kishi, the son of Abdi, the son of Malluch, ⁴⁵ the son of Hashabiah, the son of Amaziah, the son of Hilkiah, ⁴⁶ the son of Amzi, the son of Bani, the son of Shamer, ⁴⁷ the son of Mahli, the son of Mushi, the son of Merari, the son of Levi.

⁴⁸ And their brethren, the Levites, *were* appointed to every kind of service of the tabernacle of the house of God.

⁴⁹ But Aaron and his sons offered sacrifices on the altar of burnt offering and on the altar of incense, for all the work of the Most Holy *Place,* and to make atonement for Israel, according to all that Moses the servant of God had commanded. ⁵⁰ Now these *are* the sons of Aaron: Eleazar his son, Phinehas his son, Abishua his son, ⁵¹ Bukki his son, Uzzi his son, Zerahiah his son, ⁵² Meraioth his son, Amariah his son, Ahitub his son, ⁵³ Zadok his son, *and* Ahimaaz his son.

⁵⁴ Now these *are* their dwelling places throughout their settlements in their territory, for they were *given* by lot to the sons of Aaron, of the family of the Kohathites: ⁵⁵ They gave them Hebron in the land of Judah, with its surrounding common-lands. ⁵⁶ But the fields of the city and its villages they gave to Caleb the son of Jephunneh. ⁵⁷ And to the sons of Aaron they gave *one of* the cities of refuge, Hebron; also Libnah with its common-lands, Jattir, Eshtemoa with its common-lands, ⁵⁸ Hilen with its common-lands, Debir with its common-lands, ⁵⁹ Ashan with its common-lands, and Beth Shemesh with its common-lands. ⁶⁰ And from the tribe of Benjamin: Geba with its common-lands, Alemeth with its common-lands, and Anathoth with its common-lands. All their cities among their families *were* thirteen.

⁶¹ To the rest of the family of the tribe of the Kohathites *they gave* by lot ten cities from half the tribe of Manasseh. ⁶² And to the sons of Gershon, throughout their families, *they gave* thirteen cities from the tribe of Issachar, from the tribe of Asher, from the tribe of Naphtali, and from the tribe of Manasseh in Bashan. ⁶³ To the sons of Merari, throughout their families, *they gave* twelve cities from the tribe of Reuben, from the tribe of Gad, and from the tribe of Zebulun. ⁶⁴ So the children of Israel gave *these* cities with their common-lands to the Levites. ⁶⁵ And they gave by lot from the tribe of the children of Judah, from the tribe of the children of Simeon, and from the tribe of the children of Benjamin these cities which are called by *their* names.

⁶⁶ Now some of the families of the sons of Kohath *were given* cities as their territory from the tribe of Ephraim. ⁶⁷ And they gave them *one of* the cities of refuge, Shechem with its common-lands, in the mountains of Ephraim, also Gezer with its common-lands, ⁶⁸ Jokmeam with its common-lands, Beth Horon with its common-lands, ⁶⁹ Aijalon with its common-lands, and Gath Rimmon with its common-lands. ⁷⁰ And from the half-tribe of Manasseh: Aner with its common-lands and Bileam with its common-lands, for the rest of the family of the sons of Kohath.

⁷¹ From the family of the half-tribe of Manasseh the sons of Gershon *were given* Golan in Bashan with its common-lands

and Ashtaroth with its common-lands. 72 And from the tribe of Issachar: Kedesh with its common-lands, Daberath with its common-lands, 73 Ramoth with its common-lands, and Anem with its common-lands. 74 And from the tribe of Asher: Mashal with its common-lands, Abdon with its common-lands, 75 Hukok with its common-lands, and Rehob with its common-lands. 76 And from the tribe of Naphtali: Kedesh in Galilee with its common-lands, Hammon with its common-lands, and Kirjathaim with its common-lands.

77 From the tribe of Zebulun the rest of the children of Merari *were given* Rimmon with its common-lands and Tabor with its common-lands. 78 And on the other side of the Jordan, across from Jericho, on the east side of the Jordan, *they were given* from the tribe of Reuben: Bezer in the wilderness with its common-lands, Jahzah with its common-lands, 79 Kedemoth with its common-lands, and Mephaath with its common-lands. 80 And from the tribe of Gad: Ramoth in Gilead with its common-lands, Mahanaim with its common-lands, 81 Heshbon with its common-lands, and Jazer with its common-lands.

∼ PSALM 77:1–3 ∼

1 I cried out to God with my voice—
   To God with my voice;
   And He gave ear to me.
2 In the day of my trouble I sought the
      Lord;
   My hand was stretched out in the
      night without ceasing;
   My soul refused to be comforted.
3 I remembered God, and was
      troubled;
   I complained, and my spirit was
      overwhelmed.   Selah

∼ PROVERBS 19:10–12 ∼

10 Luxury is not fitting for a fool,
   Much less for a servant to rule over
      princes.

11 The discretion of a man makes him
      slow to anger,

And his glory *is* to overlook a
   transgression.

12 The king's wrath *is* like the roaring
      of a lion,
   But his favor *is* like dew on the grass.

∼ ACTS 5:1–21 ∼

But a certain man named Ananias, with Sapphira his wife, sold a possession. 2 And he kept back *part* of the proceeds, his wife also being aware *of it,* and brought a certain part and laid *it* at the apostles' feet. 3 But Peter said, "Ananias, why has Satan filled your heart to lie to the Holy Spirit and keep back *part* of the price of the land for yourself? 4 While it remained, was it not your own? And after it was sold, was it not in your own control? Why have you conceived this thing in your heart? You have not lied to men but to God."

5 Then Ananias, hearing these words, fell down and breathed his last. So great fear came upon all those who heard these things. 6 And the young men arose and wrapped him up, carried *him* out, and buried *him.*

7 Now it was about three hours later when his wife came in, not knowing what had happened. 8 And Peter answered her, "Tell me whether you sold the land for so much?"

She said, "Yes, for so much."

9 Then Peter said to her, "How is it that you have agreed together to test the Spirit of the Lord? Look, the feet of those who have buried your husband *are* at the door, and they will carry you out." 10 Then immediately she fell down at his feet and breathed her last. And the young men came in and found her dead, and carrying *her* out, buried *her* by her husband. 11 So great fear came upon all the church and upon all who heard these things.

12 And through the hands of the apostles many signs and wonders were done among the people. And they were all with one accord in Solomon's Porch. 13 Yet none of the rest dared join them, but the people esteemed them highly. 14 And believers were increasingly added to the Lord, multitudes of both men and women, 15 so that they brought the sick out into

the streets and laid *them* on beds and couches, that at least the shadow of Peter passing by might fall on some of them. [16] Also a multitude gathered from the surrounding cities to Jerusalem, bringing sick people and those who were tormented by unclean spirits, and they were all healed.

[17] Then the high priest rose up, and all those who *were* with him (which is the sect of the Sadducees), and they were filled with indignation, [18] and laid their hands on the apostles and put them in the com-mon prison. [19] But at night an angel of the Lord opened the prison doors and brought them out, and said, [20] "Go, stand in the temple and speak to the people all the words of this life."

[21] And when they heard *that,* they entered the temple early in the morning and taught. But the high priest and those with him came and called the council together, with all the elders of the children of Israel, and sent to the prison to have them brought.

~ 1 Chronicles 7:1—8:40 ~

The sons of Issachar *were* Tola, Puah, Jashub, and Shimron—four *in all.* [2] The sons of Tola *were* Uzzi, Rephaiah, Jeriel, Jahmai, Jibsam, and Shemuel, heads of their father's house. *The sons* of Tola *were* mighty men of valor in their generations; their number in the days of David *was* twenty-two thousand six hundred. [3] The son of Uzzi *was* Izrahiah, and the sons of Izrahiah *were* Michael, Obadiah, Joel, and Ishiah. All five of them *were* chief men. [4] And with them, by their generations, according to their fathers' houses, *were* thirty-six thousand troops ready for war; for they had many wives and sons.

[5] Now their brethren among all the families of Issachar *were* mighty men of valor, listed by their genealogies, eighty-seven thousand in all.

[6] *The sons* of Benjamin *were* Bela, Becher, and Jediael—three *in all.* [7] The sons of Bela were Ezbon, Uzzi, Uzziel, Jerimoth, and Iri—five *in all.* They *were* heads of *their* fathers' houses, and they were listed by their genealogies, twenty-two thousand and thirty-four mighty men of valor.

[8] The sons of Becher *were* Zemirah, Joash, Eliezer, Elioenai, Omri, Jerimoth, Abijah, Anathoth, and Alemeth. All these *are* the sons of Becher. [9] And they were recorded by genealogy according to their generations, heads of their fathers' houses, twenty thousand two hundred mighty men of valor. [10] The son of Jediael *was* Bilhan, and the sons of Bilhan *were* Jeush, Benjamin, Ehud, Chenaanah, Zethan, Tharshish, and Ahishahar.

[11] All these sons of Jediael *were* heads of their fathers' houses; *there were* seventeen thousand two hundred mighty men of valor fit to go out for war *and* battle. [12] Shuppim and Huppim *were* the sons of Ir, *and* Hushim *was* the son of Aher.

[13] The sons of Naphtali *were* Jahziel, Guni, Jezer, and Shallum, the sons of Bilhah.

[14] The descendants of Manasseh: his Syrian concubine bore him Machir the father of Gilead, the father of Asriel. [15] Machir took as his wife *the sister* of Huppim and Shuppim, whose name *was* Maachah. The name of *Gilead's* grandson *was* Zelophehad, but Zelophehad begot only daughters. [16] (Maachah the wife of Machir bore a son, and she called his name Peresh. The name of his brother *was* Sheresh, and his sons *were* Ulam and Rakem. [17] The son of Ulam *was* Bedan.) These *were* the descendants of Gilead the son of Machir, the son of Manasseh.

[18] His sister Hammoleketh bore Ishhod, Abiezer, and Mahlah.

[19] And the sons of Shemida were Ahian, Shechem, Likhi, and Aniam.

[20] The sons of Ephraim *were* Shuthelah, Bered his son, Tahath his son, Eladah his son, Tahath his son, [21] Zabad his son, Shuthelah his son, and Ezer and Elead. The men of Gath who were born in *that* land killed *them* because they came down

to take away their cattle. ²² Then Ephraim their father mourned many days, and his brethren came to comfort him.

²³ And when he went in to his wife, she conceived and bore a son; and he called his name Beriah, because tragedy had come upon his house. ²⁴ Now his daughter *was* Sheerah, who built Lower and Upper Beth Horon and Uzzen Sheerah; ²⁵ and Rephah *was* his son, *as well* as Resheph, and Telah his son, Tahan his son, ²⁶ Laadan his son, Ammihud his son, Elishama his son, ²⁷ Nun his son, and Joshua his son.

²⁸ Now their possessions and dwelling places *were* Bethel and its towns: to the east Naaran, to the west Gezer and its towns, and Shechem and its towns, as far as Ayyah and its towns; ²⁹ and by the borders of the children of Manasseh *were* Beth Shean and its towns, Taanach and its towns, Megiddo and its towns, Dor and its towns. In these dwelt the children of Joseph, the son of Israel.

³⁰ The sons of Asher *were* Imnah, Ishvah, Ishvi, Beriah, and their sister Serah. ³¹ The sons of Beriah *were* Heber and Malchiel, who was the father of Birzaith. ³² And Heber begot Japhlet, Shomer, Hotham, and their sister Shua. ³³ The sons of Japhlet *were* Pasach, Bimhal, and Ashvath. These *were* the children of Japhlet. ³⁴ The sons of Shemer *were* Ahi, Rohgah, Jehubbah, and Aram. ³⁵ And the sons of his brother Helem *were* Zophah, Imna, Shelesh, and Amal. ³⁶ The sons of Zophah *were* Suah, Harnepher, Shual, Beri, Imrah, ³⁷ Bezer, Hod, Shamma, Shilshah, Jithran, and Beera. ³⁸ The sons of Jether *were* Jephunneh, Pispah, and Ara. ³⁹ The sons of Ulla *were* Arah, Haniel, and Rizia.

⁴⁰ All these *were* the children of Asher, heads of *their* fathers' houses, choice men, mighty men of valor, chief leaders. And they were recorded by genealogies among the army fit for battle; their number *was* twenty-six thousand.

8 Now Benjamin begot Bela his firstborn, Ashbel the second, Aharah the third, ² Nohah the fourth, and Rapha the fifth. ³ The sons of Bela *were* Addar, Gera, Abihud, ⁴ Abishua, Naaman, Ahoah, ⁵ Gera, Shephuphan, and Huram.

⁶ These *are* the sons of Ehud, who were the heads of the fathers' *houses* of the inhabitants of Geba, and who forced them to move to Manahath: ⁷ Naaman, Ahijah, and Gera who forced them to move. He begot Uzza and Ahihud.

⁸ Also Shaharaim had children in the country of Moab, after he had sent away Hushim and Baara his wives. ⁹ By Hodesh his wife he begot Jobab, Zibia, Mesha, Malcam, ¹⁰ Jeuz, Sachiah, and Mirmah. These *were* his sons, heads of their fathers' *houses.*

¹¹ And by Hushim he begot Abitub and Elpaal. ¹² The sons of Elpaal *were* Eber, Misham, and Shemed, who built Ono and Lod with its towns; ¹³ and Beriah and Shema, who *were* heads of their fathers' *houses* of the inhabitants of Aijalon, who drove out the inhabitants of Gath. ¹⁴ Ahio, Shashak, Jeremoth, ¹⁵ Zebadiah, Arad, Eder, ¹⁶ Michael, Ispah, and Joha *were* the sons of Beriah. ¹⁷ Zebadiah, Meshullam, Hizki, Heber, ¹⁸ Ishmerai, Jizliah, and Jobab *were* the sons of Elpaal. ¹⁹ Jakim, Zichri, Zabdi, ²⁰ Elienai, Zillethai, Eliel, ²¹ Adaiah, Beraiah, and Shimrath *were* the sons of Shimei. ²² Ishpan, Eber, Eliel, ²³ Abdon, Zichri, Hanan, ²⁴ Hananiah, Elam, Antothijah, ²⁵ Iphdeiah, and Penuel *were* the sons of Shashak. ²⁶ Shamsherai, Shehariah, Athaliah, ²⁷ Jaareshiah, Elijah, and Zichri *were* the sons of Jeroham.

²⁸ These *were* heads of the fathers' *houses* by their generations, chief men. These dwelt in Jerusalem.

²⁹ Now the father of Gibeon, whose wife's name *was* Maacah, dwelt at Gibeon. ³⁰ And his firstborn son *was* Abdon, then Zur, Kish, Baal, Nadab, ³¹ Gedor, Ahio, Zecher, ³² and Mikloth, *who* begot Shimeah. They also dwelt alongside their relatives in Jerusalem, with their brethren. ³³ Ner begot Kish, Kish begot Saul, and Saul begot Jonathan, Malchishua, Abinadab, and Esh-Baal. ³⁴ The son of Jonathan *was* Merib-Baal, and Merib-Baal begot Micah. ³⁵ The sons of Micah *were* Pithon, Melech, Tarea, and Ahaz. ³⁶ And Ahaz begot Jehoaddah; Jehoaddah begot Alemeth, Azmaveth, and Zimri; and Zimri begot Moza. ³⁷ Moza begot Binea, Raphah his son, Eleasah his son, *and* Azel his son.

³⁸ Azel had six sons whose names *were*

Communing with God

Dr. Wilbur Chapman wrote the following letter to a friend, telling him about a great lesson he had learned concerning prayer:

"At one of our missions in England the audiences were exceedingly small; but I received a note saying that an American missionary was going to pray God's blessing down on our work. He was known as Praying Hyde. Almost instantly the tide turned. The hall became packed, and at my first invitation fifty men accepted Christ as their Savior. As we were leaving I said, 'Mr. Hyde, I want you to pray for me.' He came to my room, turned the key in the door, dropped on his knees, and waited five minutes without a single syllable coming from his lips. I could hear my own heart thumping, and his beating. I felt hot tears running down my face. I knew I was with God. Then, with upturned face, down which the tears were streaming, he said, 'O God.' Then for five minutes at least he was still again; and then, when he knew that he was talking with God there came from the depths of his heart such petitions for me as I had never heard before. I rose from my knees to know what real prayer was."

True prayer is communion with God, not a one-way conversation. When we wait on God and listen to what He has to say, He will even give us the words to pray so that our prayers can be most effective. God is speaking. Are you listening?

> I call to remembrance my song in the night; I meditate within my heart, and my spirit makes diligent search.
>
> *Psalm 77:6*

these: Azrikam, Bocheru, Ishmael, Shea-riah, Obadiah, and Hanan. All these *were* the sons of Azel. [39] And the sons of Eshek his brother *were* Ulam his firstborn, Je-ush the second, and Eliphelet the third.

[40] The sons of Ulam were mighty men of valor—archers. *They* had many sons and grandsons, one hundred and fifty *in all*. These *were* all sons of Benjamin.

~ PSALM 77:4–9 ~

[4] You hold my eyelids *open;*
    I am so troubled that I cannot speak.
[5] I have considered the days of old,
    The years of ancient times.
[6] I call to remembrance my song in the night;
    I meditate within my heart,
    And my spirit makes diligent search.

[7] Will the Lord cast off forever?
    And will He be favorable no more?
[8] Has His mercy ceased forever?
    Has *His* promise failed forevermore?
[9] Has God forgotten to be gracious?
    Has He in anger shut up His tender mercies?   Selah

~ PROVERBS 19:13, 14 ~

[13] A foolish son *is* the ruin of his father,
    And the contentions of a wife *are* a continual dripping.

[14] Houses and riches *are* an inheritance from fathers,
    But a prudent wife *is* from the LORD.

~ ACTS 5:22–42 ~

But when the officers came and did not find them in the prison, they returned and reported, [23] saying, "Indeed we found the prison shut securely, and the guards stand-ing outside before the doors; but when we opened them, we found no one in-side!" [24] Now when the high priest, the captain of the temple, and the chief priests heard these things, they wondered what the outcome would be. [25] So one came and told them, saying, "Look, the men whom you put in prison are standing in the temple and teaching the people!"

[26] Then the captain went with the of-ficers and brought them without violence, for they feared the people, lest they should be stoned. [27] And when they had brought them, they set *them* before the council. And the high priest asked them, [28] saying, "Did we not strictly command you not to teach in this name? And look, you have filled Jerusalem with your doctrine, and intend to bring this Man's blood on us!"

[29] But Peter and the *other* apostles an-swered and said: "We ought to obey God rather than men. [30] The God of our fa-thers raised up Jesus whom you murdered by hanging on a tree. [31] Him God has ex-alted to His right hand *to be* Prince and Savior, to give repentance to Israel and forgiveness of sins. [32] And we are His witnesses to these things, and *so* also *is* the Holy Spirit whom God has given to those who obey Him."

[33] When they heard *this,* they were fu-rious and plotted to kill them. [34] Then one in the council stood up, a Pharisee named Gamaliel, a teacher of the law held in re-spect by all the people, and commanded them to put the apostles outside for a little while. [35] And he said to them: "Men of Israel, take heed to yourselves what you intend to do regarding these men. [36] For some time ago Theudas rose up, claiming to be somebody. A number of men, about four hundred, joined him. He was slain, and all who obeyed him were scattered and came to nothing. [37] After this man, Judas of Galilee rose up in the days of the census, and drew away many people af-ter him. He also perished, and all who obeyed him were dispersed. [38] And now I say to you, keep away from these men and let them alone; for if this plan or this work is of men, it will come to nothing; [39] but if it is of God, you cannot overthrow it—lest you even be found to fight against God."

[40] And they agreed with him, and when they had called for the apostles and beaten *them,* they commanded that they should not speak in the name of Jesus, and let them go. [41] So they departed from the presence of the council, rejoicing that they were counted worthy to suffer shame for His name. [42] And daily in the temple, and in every house, they did not cease teach-ing and preaching Jesus *as* the Christ.

~ 1 CHRONICLES 9:1—10:14 ~

So all Israel was recorded by genealogies, and indeed, they *were* inscribed in the book of the kings of Israel. But Judah was carried away captive to Babylon because of their unfaithfulness. ² And the first inhabitants who *dwelt* in their possessions in their cities *were* Israelites, priests, Levites, and the Nethinim.

³ Now in Jerusalem the children of Judah dwelt, and some of the children of Benjamin, and of the children of Ephraim and Manasseh: ⁴ Uthai the son of Ammihud, the son of Omri, the son of Imri, the son of Bani, of the descendants of Perez, the son of Judah. ⁵ Of the Shilonites: Asaiah the firstborn and his sons. ⁶ Of the sons of Zerah: Jeuel, and their brethren—six hundred and ninety. ⁷ Of the sons of Benjamin: Sallu the son of Meshullam, the son of Hodaviah, the son of Hassenuah; ⁸ Ibneiah the son of Jeroham; Elah the son of Uzzi, the son of Michri; Meshullam the son of Shephatiah, the son of Reuel, the son of Ibnijah; ⁹ and their brethren, according to their generations—nine hundred and fifty-six. All these men *were* heads of a father's *house* in their fathers' houses.

¹⁰ Of the priests: Jedaiah, Jehoiarib, and Jachin; ¹¹ Azariah the son of Hilkiah, the son of Meshullam, the son of Zadok, the son of Meraioth, the son of Ahitub, the officer over the house of God; ¹² Adaiah the son of Jeroham, the son of Pashur, the son of Malchijah; Maasai the son of Adiel, the son of Jahzerah, the son of Meshullam, the son of Meshillemith, the son of Immer; ¹³ and their brethren, heads of their fathers' *houses*—one thousand seven hundred and sixty. *They were* very able men for the work of the service of the house of God.

¹⁴ Of the Levites: Shemaiah the son of Hasshub, the son of Azrikam, the son of Hashabiah, of the sons of Merari; ¹⁵ Bakbakkar, Heresh, Galal, and Mattaniah the son of Micah, the son of Zichri, the son of Asaph; ¹⁶ Obadiah the son of Shemaiah, the son of Galal, the son of Jeduthun; and Berechiah the son of Asa, the son of Elkanah, who lived in the villages of the Netophathites.

¹⁷ And the gatekeepers *were* Shallum, Akkub, Talmon, Ahiman, and their brethren. Shallum *was* the chief. ¹⁸ Until then *they had been* gatekeepers for the camps of the children of Levi at the King's Gate on the east.

¹⁹ Shallum the son of Kore, the son of Ebiasaph, the son of Korah, and his brethren, from his father's house, the Korahites, *were* in charge of the work of the service, gatekeepers of the tabernacle. Their fathers had been keepers of the entrance to the camp of the LORD. ²⁰ And Phinehas the son of Eleazar had been the officer over them in time past; the LORD *was* with him. ²¹ Zechariah the son of Meshelemiah *was* keeper of the door of the tabernacle of meeting.

²² All those chosen as gatekeepers *were* two hundred and twelve. They were recorded by their genealogy, in their villages. David and Samuel the seer had appointed them to their trusted office. ²³ So they and their children *were* in charge of the gates of the house of the LORD, the house of the tabernacle, by assignment. ²⁴ The gatekeepers were assigned to the four directions: the east, west, north, and south. ²⁵ And their brethren in their villages *had* to come with them from time to time for seven days. ²⁶ For in this trusted office *were* four chief gatekeepers; they were Levites. And they had charge over the chambers and treasuries of the house of God. ²⁷ And they lodged *all* around the house of God because they *had* the responsibility, and they *were* in charge of opening *it* every morning.

²⁸ Now *some* of them were in charge of the serving vessels, for they brought them in and took them out by count. ²⁹ *Some* of them *were* appointed over the furnishings and over all the implements of the sanctuary, and over the fine flour and the wine and the oil and the incense and the spices. ³⁰ And *some* of the sons of the priests made the ointment of the spices.

³¹ Mattithiah of the Levites, the firstborn of Shallum the Korahite, had the trusted office over the things that were baked in the pans. ³² And some of their

brethren of the sons of the Kohathites *were* in charge of preparing the showbread for every Sabbath.

³³ These are the singers, heads of the fathers' *houses* of the Levites, *who lodged* in the chambers, *and were* free *from other duties;* for they were employed in *that* work day and night. ³⁴ These heads of the fathers' *houses* of the Levites *were* heads throughout their generations. They dwelt at Jerusalem.

³⁵ Jeiel the father of Gibeon, whose wife's name *was* Maacah, dwelt at Gibeon. ³⁶ His firstborn son *was* Abdon, then Zur, Kish, Baal, Ner, Nadab, ³⁷ Gedor, Ahio, Zechariah, and Mikloth. ³⁸ And Mikloth begot Shimeam. They also dwelt alongside their relatives in Jerusalem, with their brethren. ³⁹ Ner begot Kish, Kish begot Saul, and Saul begot Jonathan, Malchishua, Abinadab, and Esh-Baal. ⁴⁰ The son of Jonathan *was* Merib-Baal, and Merib-Baal begot Micah. ⁴¹ The sons of Micah *were* Pithon, Melech, Tahrea, *and Ahaz.* ⁴² And Ahaz begot Jarah; Jarah begot Alemeth, Azmaveth, and Zimri; and Zimri begot Moza; ⁴³ Moza begot Binea, Rephaiah his son, Eleasah his son, and Azel his son.

⁴⁴ And Azel had six sons whose names *were* these: Azrikam, Bocheru, Ishmael, Sheariah, Obadiah, and Hanan; these *were* the sons of Azel.

10 Now the Philistines fought against Israel; and the men of Israel fled from before the Philistines, and fell slain on Mount Gilboa. ² Then the Philistines followed hard after Saul and his sons. And the Philistines killed Jonathan, Abinadab, and Malchishua, Saul's sons. ³ The battle became fierce against Saul. The archers hit him, and he was wounded by the archers. ⁴ Then Saul said to his armorbearer, "Draw your sword, and thrust me through with it, lest these uncircumcised men come and abuse me." But his armorbearer would not, for he was greatly afraid. Therefore Saul took a sword and fell on it. ⁵ And when his armorbearer saw that Saul was dead, he also fell on his sword and died. ⁶ So Saul and his three sons died, and all his house died together. ⁷ And when all the men of Israel who *were* in the valley saw that they had fled and that

Saul and his sons were dead, they forsook their cities and fled; then the Philistines came and dwelt in them.

⁸ So it happened the next day, when the Philistines came to strip the slain, that they found Saul and his sons fallen on Mount Gilboa. ⁹ And they stripped him and took his head and his armor, and sent word *throughout* the land of the Philistines to proclaim the news *in the temple* of their idols and among the people. ¹⁰ Then they put his armor in the temple of their gods, and fastened his head in the temple of Dagon.

¹¹ And when all Jabesh Gilead heard all that the Philistines had done to Saul, ¹² all the valiant men arose and took the body of Saul and the bodies of his sons; and they brought them to Jabesh, and buried their bones under the tamarisk tree at Jabesh, and fasted seven days.

¹³ So Saul died for his unfaithfulness which he had committed against the LORD, because he did not keep the word of the LORD, and also because he consulted a medium for guidance. ¹⁴ But *he* did not inquire of the LORD; therefore He killed him, and turned the kingdom over to David the son of Jesse.

∼ PSALM 77:10–15 ∼

¹⁰ And I said, "This *is* my anguish;
  But I will remember the years of the
    right hand of the Most High."
¹¹ I will remember the works of the
    LORD;
  Surely I will remember Your
    wonders of old.
¹² I will also meditate on all Your work,
  And talk of Your deeds.
¹³ Your way, O God, *is* in the sanctuary;
  Who *is* so great a God as *our* God?
¹⁴ You *are* the God who does wonders;
  You have declared Your strength
    among the peoples.
¹⁵ You have with *Your* arm redeemed
    Your people,
  The sons of Jacob and Joseph. Selah

∼ PROVERBS 19:15, 16 ∼

¹⁵ Laziness casts *one* into a deep
    sleep,

Making a House a Home

In *Little House in the Ozarks*, Laura Ingalls Wilder writes, "I spent an afternoon a short time ago with a friend in her new home. The house was beautiful and well-furnished with new furniture, but it seemed bare and empty to me. I wondered why this was until I remembered my experience with my new house. I could not make the living room seem homelike. I would move the chairs here and there and change the pictures on the wall, but something was lacking. Nothing seemed to change the feeling of coldness and vacancy that displeased me whenever I entered the room.

"Then, as I stood in the middle of the room one day wondering what I could possibly do to improve it, it came to me that all that was needed was for someone to live in it and furnish it with the everyday, pleasant thoughts of friendship and cheerfulness and hospitality."

A homey atmosphere is not a matter of the right decorations; it emanates from the thoughts and feelings of the people who live there. Feelings of warmth and welcome can be created only by people who are kind, generous, and even-tempered. Why not determine to "warm-up" the atmosphere where you live today?

And an idle person will suffer
   hunger.

16 He who keeps the commandment
   keeps his soul,
But he who is careless of his ways
   will die.

∼ ACTS 6:1–15 ∼

Now in those days, when *the number of* the disciples was multiplying, there arose a complaint against the Hebrews by the Hellenists, because their widows were neglected in the daily distribution. 2 Then the twelve summoned the multitude of the disciples and said, "It is not desirable that we should leave the word of God and serve tables. 3 Therefore, brethren, seek out from among you seven men of *good* reputation, full of the Holy Spirit and wisdom, whom we may appoint over this business; 4 but we will give ourselves continually to prayer and to the ministry of the word."

5 And the saying pleased the whole multitude. And they chose Stephen, a man full of faith and the Holy Spirit, and Philip, Prochorus, Nicanor, Timon, Parmenas, and Nicolas, a proselyte from Antioch,

6 whom they set before the apostles; and when they had prayed, they laid hands on them.

7 Then the word of God spread, and the number of the disciples multiplied greatly in Jerusalem, and a great many of the priests were obedient to the faith.

8 And Stephen, full of faith and power, did great wonders and signs among the people. 9 Then there arose some from what is called the Synagogue of the Freedmen (Cyrenians, Alexandrians, and those from Cilicia and Asia), disputing with Stephen. 10 And they were not able to resist the wisdom and the Spirit by which he spoke. 11 Then they secretly induced men to say, "We have heard him speak blasphemous words against Moses and God." 12 And they stirred up the people, the elders, and the scribes; and they came upon *him,* seized him, and brought *him* to the council. 13 They also set up false witnesses who said, "This man does not cease to speak blasphemous words against this holy place and the law; 14 for we have heard him say that this Jesus of Nazareth will destroy this place and change the customs which Moses delivered to us." 15 And all who sat in the council, looking steadfastly at him, saw his face as the face of an angel.

READING 175 · JUNE 24

∼ 1 CHRONICLES 11:1—12:40 ∼

Then all Israel came together to David at Hebron, saying, "Indeed we *are* your bone and your flesh. 2 Also, in time past, even when Saul was king, you *were* the one who led Israel out and brought them in; and the LORD your God said to you, 'You shall shepherd My people Israel, and be ruler over My people Israel.' " 3 Therefore all the elders of Israel came to the king at Hebron, and David made a covenant with them at Hebron before the LORD. And they anointed David king over Israel, according to the word of the LORD by Samuel.

4 And David and all Israel went to Jerusalem, which is Jebus, where the Jebusites *were,* the inhabitants of the land.

5 But the inhabitants of Jebus said to David, "You shall not come in here!" Nevertheless David took the stronghold of Zion (that is, the City of David). 6 Now David said, "Whoever attacks the Jebusites first shall be chief and captain." And Joab the son of Zeruiah went up first, and became chief. 7 Then David dwelt in the stronghold; therefore they called it the City of David. 8 And he built the city around it, from the Millo to the surrounding area. Joab repaired the rest of the city. 9 So David went on and became great, and the LORD of hosts *was* with him.

10 Now these *were* the heads of the mighty men whom David had, who strengthened themselves with him in his

Ambassadors of Peace

> Peace, peace to you, and peace to your helpers! For your God helps you.
>
> *1 Chronicles 12:18*

Some years ago, a boy in a small Florida town heard that the Russians were our enemies. He began to wonder about the Russian children, finding it hard to believe they were his enemies, too. He wrote a short note: "Dear Comrade in Russia, I am seven years old and I believe that we can live in peace. I want to be your friend, not your enemy. Will you become my friend and write to me?"

He closed the letter "Love and Peace" and signed his name. He then neatly folded the note, put it into an empty bottle, and threw it into an inland lake near his home. Several days later, the bottle and note were retrieved on a nearby beach. A story about the note appeared in a local newspaper and a wire service picked up the story and sent it nationwide. A group of people from New Hampshire who were taking children to the Soviet Union as ambassadors of peace read the article, contacted the boy and his family, and invited them to go with them. In the end, the little boy and his father traveled to Moscow as peacemakers!

One boy decided he could make a difference and acted on it. Jesus told us to have faith like a little child. When we have that kind of faith, nothing is impossible to us!

kingdom, with all Israel, to make him king, according to the word of the LORD concerning Israel.

[11] And this *is* the number of the mighty men whom David had: Jashobeam the son of a Hachmonite, chief of the captains; he had lifted up his spear against three hundred, killed *by him* at one time.

[12] After him *was* Eleazar the son of Dodo, the Ahohite, who *was one* of the three mighty men. [13] He was with David at Pasdammim. Now there the Philistines were gathered for battle, and there was a piece of ground full of barley. So the people fled from the Philistines. [14] But they stationed themselves in the middle of *that* field, defended it, and killed the Philistines. So the LORD brought about a great victory.

[15] Now three of the thirty chief men went down to the rock to David, into the cave of Adullam; and the army of the Philistines encamped in the Valley of Rephaim. [16] David *was* then in the stronghold, and the garrison of the Philistines *was* then in Bethlehem. [17] And David said with longing, "Oh, that someone would give me a drink of water from the well of Bethlehem, which is by the gate!" [18] So the three broke through the camp of the Philistines, drew water from the well of Bethlehem that *was* by the gate, and took *it* and brought *it* to David. Nevertheless David would not drink it, but poured it out to the LORD. [19] And he said, "Far be it from me, O my God, that I should do this! Shall I drink the blood of these men *who have put* their lives *in jeopardy?* For at the risk of their lives they brought it." Therefore he would not drink it. These things were done by the three mighty men.

[20] Abishai the brother of Joab was chief of *another* three. He had lifted up his spear against three hundred *men,* killed *them,* and won a name among *these* three. [21] Of the three he was more honored than the other two men. Therefore he became their captain. However he did not attain to the *first* three.

[22] Benaiah was the son of Jehoiada, the son of a valiant man from Kabzeel, who had done many deeds. He had killed two lion-like heroes of Moab. He also had gone down and killed a lion in the midst of a pit on a snowy day. [23] And he killed an Egyptian, a man of *great* height, five cubits tall. In the Egyptian's hand *there was* a spear like a weaver's beam; and he went down to him with a staff, wrested the spear out of the Egyptian's hand, and killed him with his own spear. [24] These *things* Benaiah the son of Jehoiada did, and won a name among three mighty men. [25] Indeed he was more honored than the thirty, but he did not attain to the *first* three. And David appointed him over his guard.

[26] Also the mighty warriors *were* Asahel the brother of Joab, Elhanan the son of Dodo of Bethlehem, [27] Shammoth the Harorite, Helez the Pelonite, [28] Ira the son of Ikkesh the Tekoite, Abiezer the Anathothite, [29] Sibbechai the Hushathite, Ilai the Ahohite, [30] Maharai the Netophathite, Heled the son of Baanah the Netophathite, [31] Ithai the son of Ribai of Gibeah, of the sons of Benjamin, Benaiah the Pirathonite, [32] Hurai of the brooks of Gaash, Abiel the Arbathite, [33] Azmaveth the Baharumite, Eliahba the Shaalbonite, [34] the sons of Hashem the Gizonite, Jonathan the son of Shageh the Hararite, [35] Ahiam the son of Sacar the Hararite, Eliphal the son of Ur, [36] Hepher the Mecherathite, Ahijah the Pelonite, [37] Hezro the Carmelite, Naarai the son of Ezbai, [38] Joel the brother of Nathan, Mibhar the son of Hagri, [39] Zelek the Ammonite, Naharai the Berothite (the armorbearer of Joab the son of Zeruiah), [40] Ira the Ithrite, Gareb the Ithrite, [41] Uriah the Hittite, Zabad the son of Ahlai, [42] Adina the son of Shiza the Reubenite (a chief of the Reubenites) and thirty with him, [43] Hanan the son of Maachah, Joshaphat the Mithnite, [44] Uzzia the Ashterathite, Shama and Jeiel the sons of Hotham the Aroerite, [45] Jediael the son of Shimri, and Joha his brother, the Tizite, [46] Eliel the Mahavite, Jeribai and Joshaviah the sons of Elnaam, Ithmah the Moabite, [47] Eliel, Obed, and Jaasiel the Mezobaite.

12 Now these *were* the men who came to David at Ziklag while he was still a fugitive from Saul the son of Kish; and they *were* among the mighty men, helpers in the war, [2] armed with bows, using both the right hand and the left in *hurling* stones and *shooting* arrows with the bow. *They were* of Benjamin, Saul's brethren.

³ The chief *was* Ahiezer, then Joash, the sons of Shemaah the Gibeathite; Jeziel and Pelet the sons of Azmaveth; Berachah, and Jehu the Anathothite; ⁴ Ishmaiah the Gibeonite, a mighty man among the thirty, and over the thirty; Jeremiah, Jahaziel, Johanan, and Jozabad the Gederathite; ⁵ Eluzai, Jerimoth, Bealiah, Shemariah, and Shephatiah the Haruphite; ⁶ Elkanah, Jisshiah, Azarel, Joezer, and Jashobeam, the Korahites; ⁷ and Joelah and Zebadiah the sons of Jeroham of Gedor.

⁸ *Some* Gadites joined David at the stronghold in the wilderness, mighty men of valor, men trained for battle, who could handle shield and spear, whose faces *were like* the faces of lions, and *were* as swift as gazelles on the mountains: ⁹ Ezer the first, Obadiah the second, Eliab the third, ¹⁰ Mishmannah the fourth, Jeremiah the fifth, ¹¹ Attai the sixth, Eliel the seventh, ¹² Johanan the eighth, Elzabad the ninth, ¹³ Jeremiah the tenth, and Machbanai the eleventh. ¹⁴ These *were* from the sons of Gad, captains of the army; the least was over a hundred, and the greatest was over a thousand. ¹⁵ These *are* the ones who crossed the Jordan in the first month, when it had overflowed all its banks; and they put to flight all *those* in the valleys, to the east and to the west.

¹⁶ Then some of the sons of Benjamin and Judah came to David at the stronghold. ¹⁷ And David went out to meet them, and answered and said to them, "If you have come peaceably to me to help me, my heart will be united with you; but if to betray me to my enemies, since *there is* no wrong in my hands, may the God of our fathers look and bring judgment." ¹⁸ Then the Spirit came upon Amasai, chief of the captains, *and he said:*

> "*We are* yours, O David;
> We *are* on your side, O son of
>   Jesse!
> Peace, peace to you,
> And peace to your helpers!
> For your God helps you."

So David received them, and made them captains of the troop.

¹⁹ And *some* from Manasseh defected to David when he was going with the Philistines to battle against Saul; but they did not help them, for the lords of the Philistines sent him away by agreement, saying, "He may defect to his master Saul *and endanger* our heads." ²⁰ When he went to Ziklag, those of Manasseh who defected to him were Adnah, Jozabad, Jediael, Michael, Jozabad, Elihu, and Zillethai, captains of the thousands who *were* from Manasseh. ²¹ And they helped David against the bands *of raiders,* for they *were* all mighty men of valor, and they were captains in the army. ²² For at *that* time they came to David day by day to help him, until *it was* a great army, like the army of God.

²³ Now these *were* the numbers of the divisions *that were* equipped for war, *and* came to David at Hebron to turn *over* the kingdom of Saul to him, according to the word of the LORD: ²⁴ of the sons of Judah bearing shield and spear, six thousand eight hundred armed for war; ²⁵ of the sons of Simeon, mighty men of valor fit for war, seven thousand one hundred; ²⁶ of the sons of Levi four thousand six hundred; ²⁷ Jehoiada, the leader of the Aaronites, and with him three thousand seven hundred; ²⁸ Zadok, a young man, a valiant warrior, and from his father's house twenty-two captains; ²⁹ of the sons of Benjamin, relatives of Saul, three thousand (until then the greatest part of them had remained loyal to the house of Saul); ³⁰ of the sons of Ephraim twenty thousand eight hundred, mighty men of valor, famous men throughout their father's house; ³¹ of the half-tribe of Manasseh eighteen thousand, who were designated by name to come and make David king; ³² of the sons of Issachar who had understanding of the times, to know what Israel ought to do, their chiefs were two hundred; and all their brethren were at their command; ³³ of Zebulun there were fifty thousand who went out to battle, expert in war with all weapons of war, stouthearted men who could keep ranks; ³⁴ of Naphtali one thousand captains, and with them thirty-seven thousand with shield and spear; ³⁵ of the Danites who could keep battle formation, twenty-eight thousand six hundred; ³⁶ of Asher, those who could go out to war, able to keep battle

formation, forty thousand; ³⁷ of the Reubenites and the Gadites and the half-tribe of Manasseh, from the other side of the Jordan, one hundred and twenty thousand armed for battle with every *kind* of weapon of war.

³⁸ All these men of war, who could keep ranks, came to Hebron with a loyal heart, to make David king over all Israel; and all the rest of Israel *were* of one mind to make David king. ³⁹ And they were there with David three days, eating and drinking, for their brethren had prepared for them. ⁴⁰ Moreover those who were near to them, from as far away as Issachar and Zebulun and Naphtali, were bringing food on donkeys and camels, on mules and oxen—provisions of flour and cakes of figs and cakes of raisins, wine and oil and oxen and sheep abundantly, for *there was* joy in Israel.

~ PSALM 77:16–20 ~

¹⁶ The waters saw You, O God;
    The waters saw You, they were afraid;
    The depths also trembled.
¹⁷ The clouds poured out water;
    The skies sent out a sound;
    Your arrows also flashed about.
¹⁸ The voice of Your thunder *was* in the whirlwind;
    The lightnings lit up the world;
    The earth trembled and shook.
¹⁹ Your way *was* in the sea,
    Your path in the great waters,
    And Your footsteps were not known.
²⁰ You led Your people like a flock
    By the hand of Moses and Aaron.

~ PROVERBS 19:17–19 ~

¹⁷ He who has pity on the poor lends to the LORD,
    And He will pay back what he has given.

¹⁸ Chasten your son while there is hope,
    And do not set your heart on his destruction.

¹⁹ *A man of* great wrath will suffer punishment;

For if you rescue *him,* you will have to do it again.

~ ACTS 7:1–21 ~

Then the high priest said, "Are these things so?"

² And he said, "Brethren and fathers, listen: The God of glory appeared to our father Abraham when he was in Mesopotamia, before he dwelt in Haran, ³ and said to him, 'Get out of your country and from your relatives, and come to a land that I will show you.' ⁴ Then he came out of the land of the Chaldeans and dwelt in Haran. And from there, when his father was dead, He moved him to this land in which you now dwell. ⁵ And *God* gave him no inheritance in it, not even *enough* to set his foot on. But even when *Abraham* had no child, He promised to give it to him for a possession, and to his descendants after him. ⁶ But God spoke in this way: that his descendants would dwell in a foreign land, and that they would bring them into bondage and oppress *them* four hundred years. ⁷ 'And the nation to whom they will be in bondage I will judge,' said God, 'and after that they shall come out and serve Me in this place.' ⁸ Then He gave him the covenant of circumcision; and so *Abraham* begot Isaac and circumcised him on the eighth day; and Isaac *begot* Jacob, and Jacob *begot* the twelve patriarchs.

⁹ "And the patriarchs, becoming envious, sold Joseph into Egypt. But God was with him ¹⁰ and delivered him out of all his troubles, and gave him favor and wisdom in the presence of Pharaoh, king of Egypt; and he made him governor over Egypt and all his house. ¹¹ Now a famine and great trouble came over all the land of Egypt and Canaan, and our fathers found no sustenance. ¹² But when Jacob heard that there was grain in Egypt, he sent out our fathers first. ¹³ And the second *time* Joseph was made known to his brothers, and Joseph's family became known to the Pharaoh. ¹⁴ Then Joseph sent and called his father Jacob and all his relatives to *him,* seventy-five people. ¹⁵ So Jacob went down to Egypt; and he died, he and our fathers. ¹⁶ And they were

carried back to Shechem and laid in the tomb that Abraham bought for a sum of money from the sons of Hamor, *the father* of Shechem.

¹⁷ "But when the time of the promise drew near which God had sworn to Abraham, the people grew and multiplied in Egypt ¹⁸ till another king arose who did not know Joseph. ¹⁹ This man dealt treach-erously with our people, and oppressed our forefathers, making them expose their babies, so that they might not live. ²⁰ At this time Moses was born, and was well pleasing to God; and he was brought up in his father's house for three months. ²¹ But when he was set out, Pharaoh's daughter took him away and brought him up as her own son.

READING 176 · JUNE 25

~ 1 Chronicles 13:1—14:17 ~

Then David consulted with the captains of thousands and hundreds, *and* with every leader. ² And David said to all the assembly of Israel, "If *it seems* good to you, and if it is of the LORD our God, let us send out to our brethren everywhere *who are* left in all the land of Israel, and with them to the priests and Levites *who are* in their cities *and* their common-lands, that they may gather together to us; ³ and let us bring the ark of our God back to us, for we have not inquired at it since the days of Saul." ⁴ Then all the assembly said that they would do so, for the thing was right in the eyes of all the people.

⁵ So David gathered all Israel together, from Shihor in Egypt to as far as the entrance of Hamath, to bring the ark of God from Kirjath Jearim. ⁶ And David and all Israel went up to Baalah, to Kirjath Jearim, which belonged to Judah, to bring up from there the ark of God the LORD, who dwells *between* the cherubim, where *His* name is proclaimed. ⁷ So they carried the ark of God on a new cart from the house of Abinadab, and Uzza and Ahio drove the cart. ⁸ Then David and all Israel played *music* before God with all *their* might, with singing, on harps, on stringed instruments, on tambourines, on cymbals, and with trumpets.

⁹ And when they came to Chidon's threshing floor, Uzza put out his hand to hold the ark, for the oxen stumbled. ¹⁰ Then the anger of the LORD was aroused against Uzza, and He struck him because he put his hand to the ark; and he died there before God. ¹¹ And David became angry because of the LORD's outbreak against Uzza; therefore that place is called Perez Uzza to this day. ¹² David was afraid of God that day, saying, "How can I bring the ark of God to me?"

¹³ So David would not move the ark with him into the City of David, but took it aside into the house of Obed-Edom the Gittite. ¹⁴ The ark of God remained with the family of Obed-Edom in his house three months. And the LORD blessed the house of Obed-Edom and all that he had.

14 Now Hiram king of Tyre sent messengers to David, and cedar trees, with masons and carpenters, to build him a house. ² So David knew that the LORD had established him as king over Israel, for his kingdom was highly exalted for the sake of His people Israel.

³ Then David took more wives in Jerusalem, and David begot more sons and daughters. ⁴ And these are the names of his children whom he had in Jerusalem: Shammua, Shobab, Nathan, Solomon, ⁵ Ibhar, Elishua, Elpelet, ⁶ Nogah, Nepheg, Japhia, ⁷ Elishama, Beeliada, and Eliphelet.

⁸ Now when the Philistines heard that David had been anointed king over all Israel, all the Philistines went up to search for David. And David heard *of it* and went out against them. ⁹ Then the Philistines went and made a raid on the Valley of Rephaim. ¹⁰ And David inquired of God, saying, "Shall I go up against the Philistines? Will You deliver them into my hand?"

The LORD said to him, "Go up, for I will deliver them into your hand."

¹¹ So they went up to Baal Perazim, and

David defeated them there. Then David said, "God has broken through my enemies by my hand like a breakthrough of water." Therefore they called the name of that place Baal Perazim. [12] And when they left their gods there, David gave a commandment, and they were burned with fire.

[13] Then the Philistines once again made a raid on the valley. [14] Therefore David inquired again of God, and God said to him, "You shall not go up after them; circle around them, and come upon them in front of the mulberry trees. [15] And it shall be, when you hear a sound of marching in the tops of the mulberry trees, then you shall go out to battle, for God has gone out before you to strike the camp of the Philistines." [16] So David did as God commanded him, and they drove back the army of the Philistines from Gibeon as far as Gezer. [17] Then the fame of David went out into all lands, and the LORD brought the fear of him upon all nations.

~ PSALM 78:1–11 ~

[1] Give ear, O my people, *to* my law;
  Incline your ears to the words of my mouth.
[2] I will open my mouth in a parable;
  I will utter dark sayings of old,
[3] Which we have heard and known,
  And our fathers have told us.
[4] We will not hide *them* from their children,
  Telling to the generation to come the praises of the LORD,
  And His strength and His wonderful works that He has done.

[5] For He established a testimony in Jacob,
  And appointed a law in Israel,
  Which He commanded our fathers,
  That they should make them known to their children;
[6] That the generation to come might know *them,*
  The children *who* would be born,
  That they may arise and declare *them* to their children,
[7] That they may set their hope in God,
  And not forget the works of God,
  But keep His commandments;

[8] And may not be like their fathers,
  A stubborn and rebellious generation,
  A generation *that* did not set its heart aright,
  And whose spirit was not faithful to God.

[9] The children of Ephraim, *being* armed *and* carrying bows,
  Turned back in the day of battle.
[10] They did not keep the covenant of God;
  They refused to walk in His law,
[11] And forgot His works
  And His wonders that He had shown them.

~ PROVERBS 19:20, 21 ~

[20] Listen to counsel and receive instruction,
  That you may be wise in your latter days.

[21] There are many plans in a man's heart,
  Nevertheless the LORD's counsel— that will stand.

~ ACTS 7:22–43 ~

And Moses was learned in all the wisdom of the Egyptians, and was mighty in words and deeds.

[23] "Now when he was forty years old, it came into his heart to visit his brethren, the children of Israel. [24] And seeing one of *them* suffer wrong, he defended and avenged him who was oppressed, and struck down the Egyptian. [25] For he supposed that his brethren would have understood that God would deliver them by his hand, but they did not understand. [26] And the next day he appeared to two of them as they were fighting, and *tried to* reconcile them, saying, 'Men, you are brethren; why do you wrong one another?' [27] But he who did his neighbor wrong pushed him away, saying, 'Who made you a ruler and a judge over us? [28] Do you want to kill me as you did the Egyptian yesterday?' [29] Then, at this saying, Moses fled and became a dweller in the land of Midian, where he had two sons.

The Desert Fox

His teachers considered him a lazy student. One teacher said he was convinced he would never amount to anything. Another said, "If Rommel ever hands in a dictation without a mistake we'll hire a band and go off for a day in the country."

That was all the incentive young Rommel needed. He immediately sat up, paid attention, and turned in a dictation without one single error. He obviously could do the work if he wanted to and if there was sufficient motivation to make the effort! When the promised award was not forthcoming, however, Rommel fell back into his old ways.

Later in life, however, Rommel did find a cause that motivated him. It fired his ambition to the extent that he was filled with driving energy, rose above the ranks, and eventually gained a reputation as one of the ablest military men in the world. Marshal Rommel became known as "the Desert Fox," one of Britain's foremost heroes of World War II.

Each person is motivated in different ways. For most people, their deepest motivation lies in their faith. However, the outcome of motivation is universal: It sparks the actions which will change your dreams into reality.

30 "And when forty years had passed, an Angel of the Lord appeared to him in a flame of fire in a bush, in the wilderness of Mount Sinai. 31 When Moses saw *it,* he marveled at the sight; and as he drew near to observe, the voice of the Lord came to him, 32 *saying,* 'I am the God of your fathers—the God of Abraham, the God of Isaac, and the God of Jacob.' And Moses trembled and dared not look. 33 'Then the LORD said to him, "Take your sandals off your feet, for the place where you stand is holy ground. 34 I have surely seen the oppression of My people who are in Egypt; I have heard their groaning and have come down to deliver them. And now come, I will send you to Egypt." '

35 "This Moses whom they rejected, saying, 'Who made you a ruler and a judge?' is the one God sent *to be* a ruler and a deliverer by the hand of the Angel who appeared to him in the bush. 36 He brought them out, after he had shown wonders and signs in the land of Egypt, and in the Red Sea, and in the wilderness forty years.

37 "This is that Moses who said to the children of Israel, 'The LORD your God will raise up for you a Prophet like me from your brethren. Him you shall hear.'

38 "This is he who was in the congregation in the wilderness with the Angel who spoke to him on Mount Sinai, and *with* our fathers, the one who received the living oracles to give to us, 39 whom our fathers would not obey, but rejected. And in their hearts they turned back to Egypt, 40 saying to Aaron, 'Make us gods to go before us; *as for* this Moses who brought us out of the land of Egypt, we do not know what has become of him.' 41 And they made a calf in those days, offered sacrifices to the idol, and rejoiced in the works of their own hands. 42 Then God turned and gave them up to worship the host of heaven, as it is written in the book of the Prophets:

'Did you offer Me slaughtered
    animals and sacrifices *during*
    forty years in the wilderness,
O house of Israel?
43 You also took up the tabernacle of
    Moloch,
And the star of your god
    Remphan,
Images which you made to
    worship;
And I will carry you away beyond
    Babylon.'

READING 177 · JUNE 26

∼ 1 CHRONICLES 15:1—16:43 ∼

David built houses for himself in the City of David; and he prepared a place for the ark of God, and pitched a tent for it. 2 Then David said, "No one may carry the ark of God but the Levites, for the LORD has chosen them to carry the ark of God and to minister before Him forever." 3 And David gathered all Israel together at Jerusalem, to bring up the ark of the LORD to its place, which he had prepared for it. 4 Then David assembled the children of Aaron and the Levites: 5 of the sons of Kohath, Uriel the chief, and one hundred and twenty of his brethren; 6 of the sons of Merari, Asaiah the chief, and two hundred and twenty of his brethren; 7 of the sons of Gershom, Joel the chief, and one hundred and thirty of his brethren; 8 of the sons of Elizaphan, Shemaiah the chief, and two hundred of his brethren; 9 of the sons of Hebron, Eliel the chief, and eighty of his brethren; 10 of the sons of Uzziel, Amminadab the chief, and one hundred and twelve of his brethren.

11 And David called for Zadok and Abiathar the priests, and for the Levites: for Uriel, Asaiah, Joel, Shemaiah, Eliel, and Amminadab. 12 He said to them, "You are the heads of the fathers' houses of the Levites; sanctify yourselves, you and your brethren, that you may bring up the ark of the LORD God of Israel to *the place* I have prepared for it. 13 For because you *did* not *do it the first time,* the LORD our God broke out against us, because we did not consult Him about the proper order."

14 So the priests and the Levites sanctified

Shelter

Have you ever explored a tidal pool? Low tide is the perfect time to find a myriad of creatures that have temporarily washed ashore from the depths of the sea.

Children are often amazed that they can pick up these shelled creatures and stare at them eyeball to eyeball. The creatures rarely exhibit any form of overt fear, such as moving to attack or attempting to scurry away. Usually, the children are the ones who squeal in fear, thinking themselves exposed and vulnerable to the possibility of the creatures' bites, pinches, or stings. The creatures simply withdraw into their shells, instinctively knowing they are safe as long as they remain in their nice, strong shelters.

Likewise, we are safe when we remain in Christ. We are protected from the hassles of life, the unknowns, the bites and stings of temptation and sin. Those things will come against us, much like the fingers of a brave and curious child try to invade the sea creature's shell, but they have no power to harm us when we retreat into the shelter of Christ.

The Lord commanded us to learn to *abide* in Him and to *remain* steadfast in our faith. He tells us to *trust* in Him absolutely, and to *shelter* ourselves under His strong wings, and in the cleft of His rock-like presence. He delights when we *retreat* into His arms for comfort and tender expressions of love.

themselves to bring up the ark of the LORD God of Israel. ¹⁵ And the children of the Levites bore the ark of God on their shoulders, by its poles, as Moses had commanded according to the word of the LORD.

¹⁶ Then David spoke to the leaders of the Levites to appoint their brethren *to be* the singers accompanied by instruments of music, stringed instruments, harps, and cymbals, by raising the voice with resounding joy. ¹⁷ So the Levites appointed Heman the son of Joel; and of his brethren, Asaph the son of Berechiah; and of their brethren, the sons of Merari, Ethan the son of Kushaiah; ¹⁸ and with them their brethren of the second *rank:* Zechariah, Ben, Jaaziel, Shemiramoth, Jehiel, Unni, Eliab, Benaiah, Maaseiah, Mattithiah, Elipheleh, Mikneiah, Obed-Edom, and Jeiel, the gatekeepers; ¹⁹ the singers, Heman, Asaph, and Ethan, *were* to sound the cymbals of bronze; ²⁰ Zechariah, Aziel, Shemiramoth, Jehiel, Unni, Eliab, Maaseiah, and Benaiah, with strings according to Alamoth; ²¹ Mattithiah, Elipheleh, Mikneiah, Obed-Edom, Jeiel, and Azaziah, to direct with harps on the Sheminith; ²² Chenaniah, leader of the Levites, was instructor *in charge of* the music, because he *was* skillful; ²³ Berechiah and Elkanah *were* doorkeepers for the ark; ²⁴ Shebaniah, Joshaphat, Nethanel, Amasai, Zechariah, Benaiah, and Eliezer, the priests, were to blow the trumpets before the ark of God; and Obed-Edom and Jehiah, doorkeepers for the ark.

²⁵ So David, the elders of Israel, and the captains over thousands went to bring up the ark of the covenant of the LORD from the house of Obed-Edom with joy. ²⁶ And so it was, when God helped the Levites who bore the ark of the covenant of the LORD, that they offered seven bulls and seven rams. ²⁷ David was clothed with a robe of fine linen, as were all the Levites who bore the ark, the singers, and Chenaniah the music master with the singers. David also wore a linen ephod. ²⁸ Thus all Israel brought up the ark of the covenant of the LORD with shouting and with the sound of the horn, with trumpets and with cymbals, making music with stringed instruments and harps.

²⁹ And it happened, *as* the ark of the covenant of the LORD came to the City of David, that Michal, Saul's daughter, looked through a window and saw King David whirling and playing music; and she despised him in her heart.

16 So they brought the ark of God, and set it in the midst of the tabernacle that David had erected for it. Then they offered burnt offerings and peace offerings before God. ² And when David had finished offering the burnt offerings and the peace offerings, he blessed the people in the name of the LORD. ³ Then he distributed to everyone of Israel, both man and woman, to everyone a loaf of bread, a piece *of meat,* and a cake of raisins.

⁴ And he appointed some of the Levites to minister before the ark of the LORD, to commemorate, to thank, and to praise the LORD God of Israel: ⁵ Asaph the chief, and next to him Zechariah, *then* Jeiel, Shemiramoth, Jehiel, Mattithiah, Eliab, Benaiah, and Obed-Edom: Jeiel with stringed instruments and harps, but Asaph made music with cymbals; ⁶ Benaiah and Jahaziel the priests regularly *blew* the trumpets before the ark of the covenant of God.

⁷ On that day David first delivered *this psalm* into the hand of Asaph and his brethren, to thank the LORD:

⁸   Oh, give thanks to the LORD!
    Call upon His name;
    Make known His deeds among
      the peoples!
⁹   Sing to Him, sing psalms to Him;
    Talk of all His wondrous works!
¹⁰   Glory in His holy name;
    Let the hearts of those rejoice who
      seek the LORD!
¹¹   Seek the LORD and His strength;
    Seek His face evermore!
¹²   Remember His marvelous works
      which He has done,
    His wonders, and the judgments
      of His mouth,
¹³   O seed of Israel His servant,
    You children of Jacob, His chosen
      ones!

¹⁴   He *is* the LORD our God;
    His judgments are in all the earth.

15 Remember His covenant forever,
The word which He commanded,
for a thousand generations,
16 *The covenant which* He made
with Abraham,
And His oath to Isaac,
17 And confirmed it to Jacob for a
statute,
To Israel *for* an everlasting
covenant,
18 Saying, "To you I will give the
land of Canaan
As the allotment of your
inheritance,"
19 When you were few in number,
Indeed very few, and strangers in
it.

20 When they went from one nation
to another,
And from *one* kingdom to another
people,
21 He permitted no man to do them
wrong;
Yes, He rebuked kings for their
sakes,
22 *Saying*, "Do not touch My
anointed ones,
And do My prophets no harm."

23 Sing to the LORD, all the earth;
Proclaim the good news of His
salvation from day to day.
24 Declare His glory among the
nations,
His wonders among all peoples.

25 For the LORD *is* great and greatly
to be praised;
He *is* also to be feared above all
gods.
26 For all the gods of the peoples *are*
idols,
But the LORD made the heavens.
27 Honor and majesty *are* before
Him;
Strength and gladness are in His
place.

28 Give to the LORD, O families of
the peoples,
Give to the LORD glory and
strength.
29 Give to the LORD the glory *due*
His name;

Bring an offering, and come
before Him.
Oh, worship the LORD in the
beauty of holiness!
30 Tremble before Him, all the earth.
The world also is firmly
established,
It shall not be moved.

31 Let the heavens rejoice, and let the
earth be glad;
And let them say among the
nations, "The LORD reigns."
32 Let the sea roar, and all its
fullness;
Let the field rejoice, and all that *is*
in it.
33 Then the trees of the woods shall
rejoice before the LORD,
For He is coming to judge the
earth.

34 Oh, give thanks to the LORD, for
He is good!
For His mercy *endures* forever.
35 And say, "Save us, O God of our
salvation;
Gather us together, and deliver us
from the Gentiles,
To give thanks to Your holy name,
To triumph in Your praise."

36 Blessed *be* the LORD God of Israel
From everlasting to everlasting!

And all the people said, "Amen!" and
praised the LORD.

37 So he left Asaph and his brothers
there before the ark of the covenant of
the LORD to minister before the ark regularly, as every day's work required; 38 and
Obed-Edom with his sixty-eight brethren,
including Obed-Edom the son of Jeduthun, and Hosah, *to be* gatekeepers; 39 and
Zadok the priest and his brethren the
priests, before the tabernacle of the LORD
at the high place that *was* at Gibeon, 40 to
offer burnt offerings to the LORD on
the altar of burnt offering regularly morning and evening, and *to do* according to
all that is written in the Law of the LORD
which He commanded Israel; 41 and with
them Heman and Jeduthun and the rest
who were chosen, who were designated
by name, to give thanks to the LORD,

because His mercy *endures* forever; [42] and with them Heman and Jeduthun, to sound aloud with trumpets and cymbals and the musical instruments of God. Now the sons of Jeduthun *were* gatekeepers.

[43] Then all the people departed, every man to his house; and David returned to bless his house.

~ PSALM 78:12–16 ~

[12] Marvelous things He did in the sight of their fathers,
In the land of Egypt, *in* the field of Zoan.
[13] He divided the sea and caused them to pass through;
And He made the waters stand up like a heap.
[14] In the daytime also He led them with the cloud,
And all the night with a light of fire.
[15] He split the rocks in the wilderness,
And gave *them* drink in abundance like the depths.
[16] He also brought streams out of the rock,
And caused waters to run down like rivers.

~ PROVERBS 19:22–24 ~

[22] What is desired in a man is kindness,
And a poor man is better than a liar.

[23] The fear of the LORD *leads* to life,
And *he who has it* will abide in satisfaction;
He will not be visited with evil.

[24] A lazy *man* buries his hand in the bowl,
And will not so much as bring it to his mouth again.

~ ACTS 7:44–60 ~

"Our fathers had the tabernacle of witness in the wilderness, as He appointed, instructing Moses to make it according to the pattern that he had seen, [45] which our fathers, having received it in turn, also brought with Joshua into the land possessed by the Gentiles, whom God drove out before the face of our fathers until the days of David, [46] who found favor before God and asked to find a dwelling for the God of Jacob. [47] But Solomon built Him a house.

[48] "However, the Most High does not dwell in temples made with hands, as the prophet says:

[49] 'Heaven *is* My throne,
And earth *is* My footstool.
What house will you build for Me? says the LORD,
Or what *is* the place of My rest?
[50] Has My hand not made all these things?'

[51] "*You* stiff-necked and uncircumcised in heart and ears! You always resist the Holy Spirit; as your fathers *did*, so *do* you. [52] Which of the prophets did your fathers not persecute? And they killed those who foretold the coming of the Just One, of whom you now have become the betrayers and murderers, [53] who have received the law by the direction of angels and have not kept *it*."

[54] When they heard these things they were cut to the heart, and they gnashed at him with *their* teeth. [55] But he, being full of the Holy Spirit, gazed into heaven and saw the glory of God, and Jesus standing at the right hand of God, [56] and said, "Look! I see the heavens opened and the Son of Man standing at the right hand of God!"

[57] Then they cried out with a loud voice, stopped their ears, and ran at him with one accord; [58] and they cast *him* out of the city and stoned *him*. And the witnesses laid down their clothes at the feet of a young man named Saul. [59] And they stoned Stephen as he was calling on *God* and saying, "Lord Jesus, receive my spirit." [60] Then he knelt down and cried out with a loud voice, "Lord, do not charge them with this sin." And when he had said this, he fell asleep.

~ 1 Chronicles 17:1—18:17 ~

Now it came to pass, when David was dwelling in his house, that David said to Nathan the prophet, "See now, I dwell in a house of cedar, but the ark of the covenant of the LORD is under tent curtains."

² Then Nathan said to David, "Do all that is in your heart, for God is with you."

³ But it happened that night that the word of God came to Nathan, saying, ⁴ "Go and tell My servant David, 'Thus says the LORD: "You shall not build Me a house to dwell in. ⁵ For I have not dwelt in a house since the time that I brought up Israel, even to this day, but have gone from tent to tent, and from one tabernacle to another. ⁶ Wherever I have moved about with all Israel, have I ever spoken a word to any of the judges of Israel, whom I commanded to shepherd My people, saying, 'Why have you not built Me a house of cedar?' " ' ⁷ Now therefore, thus shall you say to My servant David, 'Thus says the LORD of hosts: "I took you from the sheepfold, from following the sheep, to be ruler over My people Israel. ⁸ And I have been with you wherever you have gone, and have cut off all your enemies from before you, and have made you a name like the name of the great men who are on the earth. ⁹ Moreover I will appoint a place for My people Israel, and will plant them, that they may dwell in a place of their own and move no more; nor shall the sons of wickedness oppress them anymore, as previously, ¹⁰ since the time that I commanded judges to be over My people Israel. Also I will subdue all your enemies. Furthermore I tell you that the LORD will build you a house. ¹¹ And it shall be, when your days are fulfilled, when you must go to be with your fathers, that I will set up your seed after you, who will be of your sons; and I will establish his kingdom. ¹² He shall build Me a house, and I will establish his throne forever. ¹³ I will be his Father, and he shall be My son; and I will not take My mercy away from him, as I took it from him who was before you. ¹⁴ And I will establish him in My house and in My kingdom forever;

and his throne shall be established forever." ' "

¹⁵ According to all these words and according to all this vision, so Nathan spoke to David.

¹⁶ Then King David went in and sat before the LORD; and he said: "Who am I, O LORD God? And what is my house, that You have brought me this far? ¹⁷ And yet this was a small thing in Your sight, O God; and You have also spoken of Your servant's house for a great while to come, and have regarded me according to the rank of a man of high degree, O LORD God. ¹⁸ What more can David say to You for the honor of Your servant? For You know Your servant. ¹⁹ O LORD, for Your servant's sake, and according to Your own heart, You have done all this greatness, in making known all these great things. ²⁰ O LORD, there is none like You, nor is there any God besides You, according to all that we have heard with our ears. ²¹ And who is like Your people Israel, the one nation on the earth whom God went to redeem for Himself as a people—to make for Yourself a name by great and awesome deeds, by driving out nations from before Your people whom You redeemed from Egypt? ²² For You have made Your people Israel Your very own people forever; and You, LORD, have become their God.

²³ "And now, O LORD, the word which You have spoken concerning Your servant and concerning his house, let it be established forever, and do as You have said. ²⁴ So let it be established, that Your name may be magnified forever, saying, 'The LORD of hosts, the God of Israel, is Israel's God.' And let the house of Your servant David be established before You. ²⁵ For You, O my God, have revealed to Your servant that You will build him a house. Therefore Your servant has found it in his heart to pray before You. ²⁶ And now, LORD, You are God, and have promised this goodness to Your servant. ²⁷ Now You have been pleased to bless the house of Your servant, that it may continue before You forever; for You have blessed it, O LORD, and it shall be blessed forever."

18 After this it came to pass that David attacked the Philistines, subdued them, and took Gath and its towns from the hand of the Philistines. ² Then he defeated Moab, and the Moabites became David's servants, *and* brought tribute.

³ And David defeated Hadadezer king of Zobah *as far as* Hamath, as he went to establish his power by the River Euphrates. ⁴ David took from him one thousand chariots, seven thousand horsemen, and twenty thousand foot soldiers. Also David hamstrung all the chariot horses, except that he spared enough of them for one hundred chariots.

⁵ When the Syrians of Damascus came to help Hadadezer king of Zobah, David killed twenty-two thousand of the Syrians. ⁶ Then David put *garrisons* in Syria of Damascus; and the Syrians became David's servants, *and* brought tribute. So the LORD preserved David wherever he went. ⁷ And David took the shields of gold that were on the servants of Hadadezer, and brought them to Jerusalem. ⁸ Also from Tibhath and from Chun, cities of Hadadezer, David brought a large amount of bronze, with which Solomon made the bronze Sea, the pillars, and the articles of bronze.

⁹ Now when Tou king of Hamath heard that David had defeated all the army of Hadadezer king of Zobah, ¹⁰ he sent Hadoram his son to King David, to greet him and bless him, because he had fought against Hadadezer and defeated him (for Hadadezer had been at war with Tou); and *Hadoram brought with him* all kinds of articles of gold, silver, and bronze. ¹¹ King David also dedicated these to the LORD, along with the silver and gold that he had brought from all *these* nations— from Edom, from Moab, from the people of Ammon, from the Philistines, and from Amalek.

¹² Moreover Abishai the son of Zeruiah killed eighteen thousand Edomites in the Valley of Salt. ¹³ He also put garrisons in Edom, and all the Edomites became David's servants. And the LORD preserved David wherever he went.

¹⁴ So David reigned over all Israel, and administered judgment and justice to all his people. ¹⁵ Joab the son of Zeruiah *was* over the army; Jehoshaphat the son of Ahilud *was* recorder; ¹⁶ Zadok the son of Ahitub and Abimelech the son of Abiathar *were* the priests; Shavsha *was* the scribe; ¹⁷ Benaiah the son of Jehoiada *was* over the Cherethites and the Pelethites; and David's sons *were* chief ministers at the king's side.

∼ PSALM 78:17–25 ∼

¹⁷ But they sinned even more against Him
By rebelling against the Most High in the wilderness.
¹⁸ And they tested God in their heart
By asking for the food of their fancy.
¹⁹ Yes, they spoke against God:
They said, "Can God prepare a table in the wilderness?
²⁰ Behold, He struck the rock,
So that the waters gushed out,
And the streams overflowed.
Can He give bread also?
Can He provide meat for His people?"

²¹ Therefore the LORD heard *this* and was furious;
So a fire was kindled against Jacob,
And anger also came up against Israel,
²² Because they did not believe in God,
And did not trust in His salvation.
²³ Yet He had commanded the clouds above,
And opened the doors of heaven,
²⁴ Had rained down manna on them to eat,
And given them of the bread of heaven.
²⁵ Men ate angels' food;
He sent them food to the full.

∼ PROVERBS 19:25, 26 ∼

²⁵ Strike a scoffer, and the simple will become wary;
Rebuke one who has understanding, *and* he will discern knowledge.

²⁶ He who mistreats *his* father *and* chases away *his* mother
Is a son who causes shame and brings reproach.

Money, Money, Money

In 1923, eight of the most powerful money magnates in the world gathered for a meeting at the Edgewater Beach Hotel in Chicago, Illinois. The combined resources and assets of these eight men tallied more than the U.S. Treasury that year. In the group were: Charles Schwab, president of a steel company; Richard Whitney, president of the New York Stock Exchange; and Arthur Cutton, a wheat speculator. Albert Fall was a presidential cabinet member, a personally wealthy man. Jesse Livermore was the greatest Wall Street "bear" in his generation. Leon Fraser was the president of the International Bank of Settlements, and Ivan Krueger headed the largest monopoly in the nation. An impressive gathering of financial eagles!

What happened to these men in later years? Schwab died penniless. Whitney served a life sentence in Sing Sing Prison. Cutton became insolvent. Fall was pardoned from a federal prison so he might die at home. Fraser, Livermore, and Krueger committed suicide. Seven of these eight extremely rich men ended their lives with nothing.

Money is certainly not the answer to life's ills! Only God can give us peace, happiness, and joy. When we focus on God and His goodness in our lives whether we have money or not, we can live content, knowing that God will meet all our needs.

> But Peter said to him, "Your money perish with you, because you thought that the gift of God could be purchased with money!"
>
> *Acts 8:20*

～ ACTS 8:1–25 ～

Now Saul was consenting to his death.

At that time a great persecution arose against the church which was at Jerusalem; and they were all scattered throughout the regions of Judea and Samaria, except the apostles. ² And devout men carried Stephen *to his burial*, and made great lamentation over him.

³ As for Saul, he made havoc of the church, entering every house, and dragging off men and women, committing *them* to prison.

⁴ Therefore those who were scattered went everywhere preaching the word. ⁵ Then Philip went down to the city of Samaria and preached Christ to them. ⁶ And the multitudes with one accord heeded the things spoken by Philip, hearing and seeing the miracles which he did. ⁷ For unclean spirits, crying with a loud voice, came out of many who were possessed; and many who were paralyzed and lame were healed. ⁸ And there was great joy in that city.

⁹ But there was a certain man called Simon, who previously practiced sorcery in the city and astonished the people of Samaria, claiming that he was someone great, ¹⁰ to whom they all gave heed, from the least to the greatest, saying, "This man is the great power of God." ¹¹ And they heeded him because he had astonished them with his sorceries for a long time. ¹² But when they believed Philip as he preached the things concerning the kingdom of God and the name of Jesus Christ, both men and women were baptized.

¹³ Then Simon himself also believed; and when he was baptized he continued with Philip, and was amazed, seeing the miracles and signs which were done.

¹⁴ Now when the apostles who were at Jerusalem heard that Samaria had received the word of God, they sent Peter and John to them, ¹⁵ who, when they had come down, prayed for them that they might receive the Holy Spirit. ¹⁶ For as yet He had fallen upon none of them. They had only been baptized in the name of the Lord Jesus. ¹⁷ Then they laid hands on them, and they received the Holy Spirit.

¹⁸ And when Simon saw that through the laying on of the apostles' hands the Holy Spirit was given, he offered them money, ¹⁹ saying, "Give me this power also, that anyone on whom I lay hands may receive the Holy Spirit."

²⁰ But Peter said to him, "Your money perish with you, because you thought that the gift of God could be purchased with money! ²¹ You have neither part nor portion in this matter, for your heart is not right in the sight of God. ²² Repent therefore of this your wickedness, and pray God if perhaps the thought of your heart may be forgiven you. ²³ For I see that you are poisoned by bitterness and bound by iniquity."

²⁴ Then Simon answered and said, "Pray to the Lord for me, that none of the things which you have spoken may come upon me."

²⁵ So when they had testified and preached the word of the Lord, they returned to Jerusalem, preaching the gospel in many villages of the Samaritans.

READING 179 · JUNE 28

～ 1 CHRONICLES 19:1—20:8 ～

It happened after this that Nahash the king of the people of Ammon died, and his son reigned in his place. ² Then David said, "I will show kindness to Hanun the son of Nahash, because his father showed kindness to me." So David sent messengers to comfort him concerning his father. And David's servants came to Hanun in the land of the people of Ammon to comfort him.

³ And the princes of the people of Ammon said to Hanun, "Do you think that David really honors your father because he has sent comforters to you? Did

Know What You Believe

During the Revolutionary War at age thirty-four, "Mad Anthony" Wayne became a Brigadier General. Theodore Roosevelt spoke of him as "the greatest field general America ever produced."

When the British encamped at Germantown, George Washington held a "council of war" with his advisors. Wayne was all for attacking immediately and openly stated his views from the outset. Virtually all of the other officers sat around the table to deliberate the issue, offering innumerable excuses for holding back. After all the dissenting arguments had been made, Washington turned again to Wayne, who had been sitting quietly in a corner reading a book while the other military officers debated the issue. "What would you say, General?" Washington asked. Wayne slammed the book shut, rose slowly to his feet, and with a glare at the group of distinguished officers, declared, "I'd say nothing, Sir. I'd fight."

Wayne was not a warmonger. Rather, he was a patriot. His values about the importance of individual freedoms were rock solid, and he was willing to defend his position with his life.

Know what you believe, and you will know what to do.

And [Israel] did not believe in His wondrous works. Therefore their days He consumed in futility, and their years in fear.

Psalm 78:32-33

his servants not come to you to search and to overthrow and to spy out the land?"

⁴ Therefore Hanun took David's servants, shaved them, and cut off their garments in the middle, at their buttocks, and sent them away. ⁵ Then *some* went and told David about the men; and he sent to meet them, because the men were greatly ashamed. And the king said, "Wait at Jericho until your beards have grown, and *then* return."

⁶ When the people of Ammon saw that they had made themselves repulsive to David, Hanun and the people of Ammon sent a thousand talents of silver to hire for themselves chariots and horsemen from Mesopotamia, from Syrian Maacah, and from Zobah. ⁷ So they hired for themselves thirty-two thousand chariots, with the king of Maacah and his people, who came and encamped before Medeba. Also the people of Ammon gathered together from their cities, and came to battle.

⁸ Now when David heard *of it,* he sent Joab and all the army of the mighty men. ⁹ Then the people of Ammon came out and put themselves in battle array before the gate of the city, and the kings who had come *were* by themselves in the field. ¹⁰ When Joab saw that the battle line was against him before and behind, he chose some of Israel's best, and put *them* in battle array against the Syrians. ¹¹ And the rest of the people he put under the command of Abishai his brother, and they set *themselves* in battle array against the people of Ammon. ¹² Then he said, "If the Syrians are too strong for me, then you shall help me; but if the people of Ammon are too strong for you, then I will help you. ¹³ Be of good courage, and let us be strong for our people and for the cities of our God. And may the LORD do *what is* good in His sight."

¹⁴ So Joab and the people who *were* with him drew near for the battle against the Syrians, and they fled before him. ¹⁵ When the people of Ammon saw that the Syrians were fleeing, they also fled before Abishai his brother, and entered the city. So Joab went to Jerusalem.

¹⁶ Now when the Syrians saw that they had been defeated by Israel, they sent messengers and brought the Syrians who were beyond the River, and Shophach the commander of Hadadezer's army *went* before them. ¹⁷ When it was told David, he gathered all Israel, crossed over the Jordan and came upon them, and set up in battle array against them. So when David had set up in *battle* array against the Syrians, they fought with him. ¹⁸ Then the Syrians fled before Israel; and David killed seven thousand charioteers and forty thousand foot soldiers of the Syrians, and killed Shophach the commander of the army. ¹⁹ And when the servants of Hadadezer saw that they were defeated by Israel, they made peace with David and became his servants. So the Syrians were not willing to help the people of Ammon anymore.

20 It happened in the spring of the year, at the time kings go out *to battle,* that Joab led out the armed forces and ravaged the country of the people of Ammon, and came and besieged Rabbah. But David stayed at Jerusalem. And Joab defeated Rabbah and overthrew it. ² Then David took their king's crown from his head, and found it to weigh a talent of gold, and *there were* precious stones in it. And it was set on David's head. Also he brought out the spoil of the city in great abundance. ³ And he brought out the people who *were* in it, and put *them* to work with saws, with iron picks, and with axes. So David did to all the cities of the people of Ammon. Then David and all the people returned to Jerusalem.

⁴ Now it happened afterward that war broke out at Gezer with the Philistines, at which time Sibbechai the Hushathite killed Sippai, *who was one* of the sons of the giant. And they were subdued.

⁵ Again there was war with the Philistines, and Elhanan the son of Jair killed Lahmi the brother of Goliath the Gittite, the shaft of whose spear *was* like a weaver's beam.

⁶ Yet again there was war at Gath, where there was a man of *great* stature, with twenty-four fingers and toes, six *on each hand* and six *on each foot;* and he also was born to the giant. ⁷ So when he defied Israel, Jonathan the son of Shimea, David's brother, killed him.

⁸ These were born to the giant in Gath,

and they fell by the hand of David and by the hand of his servants.

∼ PSALM 78:26–33 ∼

26 He caused an east wind to blow in the heavens;
And by His power He brought in the south wind.
27 He also rained meat on them like the dust,
Feathered fowl like the sand of the seas;
28 And He let *them* fall in the midst of their camp,
All around their dwellings.
29 So they ate and were well filled,
For He gave them their own desire.
30 They were not deprived of their craving;
But while their food *was* still in their mouths,
31 The wrath of God came against them,
And slew the stoutest of them,
And struck down the choice *men* of Israel.
32 In spite of this they still sinned,
And did not believe in His wondrous works.
33 Therefore their days He consumed in futility,
And their years in fear.

∼ PROVERBS 19:27–29 ∼

27 Cease listening to instruction, my son,
And you will stray from the words of knowledge.

28 A disreputable witness scorns justice,
And the mouth of the wicked devours iniquity.

29 Judgments are prepared for scoffers,
And beatings for the backs of fools.

∼ ACTS 8:26–40 ∼

Now an angel of the Lord spoke to Philip, saying, "Arise and go toward the south along the road which goes down from Jerusalem to Gaza." This is desert. 27 So he arose and went. And behold, a man of Ethiopia, a eunuch of great authority under Candace the queen of the Ethiopians, who had charge of all her treasury, and had come to Jerusalem to worship, 28 was returning. And sitting in his chariot, he was reading Isaiah the prophet. 29 Then the Spirit said to Philip, "Go near and overtake this chariot."

30 So Philip ran to him, and heard him reading the prophet Isaiah, and said, "Do you understand what you are reading?"

31 And he said, "How can I, unless someone guides me?" And he asked Philip to come up and sit with him. 32 The place in the Scripture which he read was this:

"He was led as a sheep to the slaughter;
And as a lamb before its shearer *is* silent,
So He opened not His mouth.
33 In His humiliation His justice was taken away,
And who will declare His generation?
For His life is taken from the earth."

34 So the eunuch answered Philip and said, "I ask you, of whom does the prophet say this, of himself or of some other man?" 35 Then Philip opened his mouth, and beginning at this Scripture, preached Jesus to him. 36 Now as they went down the road, they came to some water. And the eunuch said, "See, *here is* water. What hinders me from being baptized?"

37 Then Philip said, "If you believe with all your heart, you may."

And he answered and said, "I believe that Jesus Christ is the Son of God."

38 So he commanded the chariot to stand still. And both Philip and the eunuch went down into the water, and he baptized him. 39 Now when they came up out of the water, the Spirit of the Lord caught Philip away, so that the eunuch saw him no more; and he went on his way rejoicing. 40 But Philip was found at Azotus. And passing through, he preached in all the cities till he came to Caesarea.

~ 1 Chronicles 21:1—22:19 ~

Now Satan stood up against Israel, and moved David to number Israel. ² So David said to Joab and to the leaders of the people, "Go, number Israel from Beersheba to Dan, and bring the number of them to me that I may know *it*."

³ And Joab answered, "May the LORD make His people a hundred times more than they are. But, my lord the king, *are* they not all my lord's servants? Why then does my lord require this thing? Why should he be a cause of guilt in Israel?"

⁴ Nevertheless the king's word prevailed against Joab. Therefore Joab departed and went throughout all Israel and came to Jerusalem. ⁵ Then Joab gave the sum of the number of the people to David. All Israel *had* one million one hundred thousand men who drew the sword, and Judah *had* four hundred and seventy thousand men who drew the sword. ⁶ But he did not count Levi and Benjamin among them, for the king's word was abominable to Joab.

⁷ And God was displeased with this thing; therefore He struck Israel. ⁸ So David said to God, "I have sinned greatly, because I have done this thing; but now, I pray, take away the iniquity of Your servant, for I have done very foolishly."

⁹ Then the LORD spoke to Gad, David's seer, saying, ¹⁰ "Go and tell David, saying, 'Thus says the LORD: "I offer you three *things;* choose one of them for yourself, that I may do *it* to you." ' "

¹¹ So Gad came to David and said to him, "Thus says the LORD: 'Choose for yourself, ¹² either three years of famine, or three months to be defeated by your foes with the sword of your enemies overtaking *you*, or else for three days the sword of the LORD—the plague in the land, with the angel of the LORD destroying throughout all the territory of Israel.' Now consider what answer I should take back to Him who sent me."

¹³ And David said to Gad, "I am in great distress. Please let me fall into the hand of the LORD, for His mercies *are* very great; but do not let me fall into the hand of man."

¹⁴ So the LORD sent a plague upon Israel, and seventy thousand men of Israel fell. ¹⁵ And God sent an angel to Jerusalem to destroy it. As he was destroying, the LORD looked and relented of the disaster, and said to the angel who was destroying, "It is enough; now restrain your hand." And the angel of the LORD stood by the threshing floor of Ornan the Jebusite.

¹⁶ Then David lifted his eyes and saw the angel of the LORD standing between earth and heaven, having in his hand a drawn sword stretched out over Jerusalem. So David and the elders, clothed in sackcloth, fell on their faces. ¹⁷ And David said to God, "Was it not I who commanded the people to be numbered? I am the one who has sinned and done evil indeed; but these sheep, what have they done? Let Your hand, I pray, O LORD my God, be against me and my father's house, but not against Your people that they should be plagued."

¹⁸ Therefore, the angel of the LORD commanded Gad to say to David that David should go and erect an altar to the LORD on the threshing floor of Ornan the Jebusite. ¹⁹ So David went up at the word of Gad, which he had spoken in the name of the LORD. ²⁰ Now Ornan turned and saw the angel; and his four sons *who were* with him hid themselves, but Ornan continued threshing wheat. ²¹ So David came to Ornan, and Ornan looked and saw David. And he went out from the threshing floor, and bowed before David with *his* face to the ground. ²² Then David said to Ornan, "Grant me the place of *this* threshing floor, that I may build an altar on it to the LORD. You shall grant it to me at the full price, that the plague may be withdrawn from the people."

²³ But Ornan said to David, "Take *it* to yourself, and let my lord the king do *what is* good in his eyes. Look, I *also* give *you* the oxen for burnt offerings, the threshing implements for wood, and the wheat for the grain offering; I give *it* all."

²⁴ Then King David said to Ornan, "No, but I will surely buy *it* for the full price, for I will not take what is yours for the

Living Prayer

George Whitefield, the famous English evangelist, said, "O Lord, give me souls, or take my soul!"

Missionary Henry Martyn knelt on India's coral strands and cried out, "Here let me burn out for God."

David Brainerd, a missionary to the North American Indians prayed, "Lord, to Thee I dedicate myself. O accept of me, and let me be Thine forever. Lord, I desire nothing else, I desire nothing more."

Thomas á Kempis prayed, "Give what Thou wilt, and how much Thou wilt, and when Thou wilt. Set me where Thou wilt and deal with me in all things, just as Thou wilt."

Dwight L. Moody prayed, "Use me then, my Savior, for whatever purpose and in whatever way Thou mayest require. Here is my poor heart, an empty vessel; fill it with Thy grace."

John McKenzie prayed as a young missionary candidate, "O Lord, send me to the darkest spot on earth!"

John Hunt, a missionary to the Fiji Islands, prayed upon his deathbed, "Lord, save Fiji, save Fiji; save these people, O Lord; have mercy upon Fiji; save Fiji."

What you pray today will determine how you live when you rise from your knees.

> And when Paul had laid hands on them, the Holy Spirit came upon them, and they spoke with tongues and prophesied.
>
> *Acts 19:6*

LORD, nor offer burnt offerings with *that which* costs *me* nothing." ²⁵ So David gave Ornan six hundred shekels of gold by weight for the place. ²⁶ And David built there an altar to the LORD, and offered burnt offerings and peace offerings, and called on the LORD; and He answered him from heaven by fire on the altar of burnt offering.

²⁷ So the LORD commanded the angel, and he returned his sword to its sheath.

²⁸ At that time, when David saw that the LORD had answered him on the threshing floor of Ornan the Jebusite, he sacrificed there. ²⁹ For the tabernacle of the LORD and the altar of the burnt offering, which Moses had made in the wilderness, *were* at that time at the high place in Gibeon. ³⁰ But David could not go before it to inquire of God, for he was afraid of the sword of the angel of the LORD.

22 Then David said, "This *is* the house of the LORD God, and this *is* the altar of burnt offering for Israel." ² So David commanded to gather the aliens who *were* in the land of Israel; and he appointed masons to cut hewn stones to build the house of God. ³ And David prepared iron in abundance for the nails of the doors of the gates and for the joints, and bronze in abundance beyond measure, ⁴ and cedar trees in abundance; for the Sidonians and those from Tyre brought much cedar wood to David.

⁵ Now David said, "Solomon my son *is* young and inexperienced, and the house to be built for the LORD *must be* exceedingly magnificent, famous and glorious throughout all countries. I will now make preparation for it." So David made abundant preparations before his death.

⁶ Then he called for his son Solomon, and charged him to build a house for the LORD God of Israel. ⁷ And David said to Solomon: "My son, as for me, it was in my mind to build a house to the name of the LORD my God; ⁸ but the word of the LORD came to me, saying, 'You have shed much blood and have made great wars; you shall not build a house for My name, because you have shed much blood on the earth in My sight. ⁹ Behold, a son shall be born to you, who shall be a man of rest;

and I will give him rest from all his enemies all around. His name shall be Solomon, for I will give peace and quietness to Israel in his days. ¹⁰ He shall build a house for My name, and he shall be My son, and I *will be* his Father; and I will establish the throne of his kingdom over Israel forever.' ¹¹ Now, my son, may the LORD be with you; and may you prosper, and build the house of the LORD your God, as He has said to you. ¹² Only may the LORD give you wisdom and understanding, and give you charge concerning Israel, that you may keep the law of the LORD your God. ¹³ Then you will prosper, if you take care to fulfill the statutes and judgments with which the LORD charged Moses concerning Israel. Be strong and of good courage; do not fear nor be dismayed. ¹⁴ Indeed I have taken much trouble to prepare for the house of the LORD one hundred thousand talents of gold and one million talents of silver, and bronze and iron beyond measure, for it is so abundant. I have prepared timber and stone also, and you may add to them. ¹⁵ Moreover *there are* workmen with you in abundance: woodsmen and stonecutters, and all types of skillful men for every kind of work. ¹⁶ Of gold and silver and bronze and iron *there is* no limit. Arise and begin working, and the LORD be with you."

¹⁷ David also commanded all the leaders of Israel to help Solomon his son, *saying,* ¹⁸ "*Is* not the LORD your God with you? And has He *not* given you rest on every side? For He has given the inhabitants of the land into my hand, and the land is subdued before the LORD and before His people. ¹⁹ Now set your heart and your soul to seek the LORD your God. Therefore arise and build the sanctuary of the LORD God, to bring the ark of the covenant of the LORD and the holy articles of God into the house that is to be built for the name of the LORD."

~ PSALM 78:34–39 ~

³⁴ When He slew them, then they
  sought Him;
And they returned and sought
  earnestly for God.

35 Then they remembered that God
    was their rock,
  And the Most High God their
    Redeemer.
36 Nevertheless they flattered Him with
    their mouth,
  And they lied to Him with their
    tongue;
37 For their heart was not steadfast
    with Him,
  Nor were they faithful in His
    covenant.
38 But He, *being* full of compassion,
    forgave *their* iniquity,
  And did not destroy *them*.
  Yes, many a time He turned His
    anger away,
  And did not stir up all His wrath;
39 For He remembered that they *were*
    but flesh,
  A breath that passes away and does
    not come again.

∼ PROVERBS 20:1, 2 ∼

1 Wine *is* a mocker,
  Strong drink *is* a brawler,
  And whoever is led astray by it is not
    wise.

2 The wrath of a king *is* like the
    roaring of a lion;
  Whoever provokes him to anger sins
    against his own life.

∼ ACTS 9:1–21 ∼

Then Saul, still breathing threats and murder against the disciples of the Lord, went to the high priest 2 and asked letters from him to the synagogues of Damascus, so that if he found any who were of the Way, whether men or women, he might bring them bound to Jerusalem.
3 As he journeyed he came near Damascus, and suddenly a light shone around him from heaven. 4 Then he fell to the ground, and heard a voice saying to him, "Saul, Saul, why are you persecuting Me?"
5 And he said, "Who are You, Lord?"
Then the Lord said, "I am Jesus, whom you are persecuting. It *is* hard for you to kick against the goads."
6 So he, trembling and astonished, said, "Lord, what do You want me to do?"

Then the Lord *said* to him, "Arise and go into the city, and you will be told what you must do."
7 And the men who journeyed with him stood speechless, hearing a voice but seeing no one. 8 Then Saul arose from the ground, and when his eyes were opened he saw no one. But they led him by the hand and brought *him* into Damascus. 9 And he was three days without sight, and neither ate nor drank.
10 Now there was a certain disciple at Damascus named Ananias; and to him the Lord said in a vision, "Ananias."
And he said, "Here I am, Lord."
11 So the Lord *said* to him, "Arise and go to the street called Straight, and inquire at the house of Judas for *one* called Saul of Tarsus, for behold, he is praying. 12 And in a vision he has seen a man named Ananias coming in and putting *his* hand on him, so that he might receive his sight."
13 Then Ananias answered, "Lord, I have heard from many about this man, how much harm he has done to Your saints in Jerusalem. 14 And here he has authority from the chief priests to bind all who call on Your name."
15 But the Lord said to him, "Go, for he is a chosen vessel of Mine to bear My name before Gentiles, kings, and the children of Israel. 16 For I will show him how many things he must suffer for My name's sake."
17 And Ananias went his way and entered the house; and laying his hands on him he said, "Brother Saul, the Lord Jesus, who appeared to you on the road as you came, has sent me that you may receive your sight and be filled with the Holy Spirit." 18 Immediately there fell from his eyes *something* like scales, and he received his sight at once; and he arose and was baptized.
19 So when he had received food, he was strengthened. Then Saul spent some days with the disciples at Damascus.
20 Immediately he preached the Christ in the synagogues, that He is the Son of God.
21 Then all who heard were amazed, and said, "Is this not he who destroyed those who called on this name in Jerusalem, and has come here for that purpose, so that he might bring them bound to the chief priests?"

~ 1 CHRONICLES 23:1—25:31 ~

So when David was old and full of days, he made his son Solomon king over Israel. ² And he gathered together all the leaders of Israel, with the priests and the Levites. ³ Now the Levites were numbered from the age of thirty years and above; and the number of individual males was thirty-eight thousand. ⁴ Of these, twenty-four thousand *were* to look after the work of the house of the LORD, six thousand *were* officers and judges, ⁵ four thousand *were* gatekeepers, and four thousand praised the LORD with *musical instruments,* "which I made," *said David,* "for giving praise."

⁶ Also David separated them into divisions among the sons of Levi: Gershon, Kohath, and Merari.

⁷ Of the Gershonites: Laadan and Shimei. ⁸ The sons of Laadan: the first Jehiel, then Zetham and Joel—three *in all.* ⁹ The sons of Shimei: Shelomith, Haziel, and Haran—three *in all.* These were the heads of the fathers' *houses* of Laadan. ¹⁰ And the sons of Shimei: Jahath, Zina, Jeush, and Beriah. These *were* the four sons of Shimei. ¹¹ Jahath was the first and Zizah the second. But Jeush and Beriah did not have many sons; therefore they were assigned as one father's house.

¹² The sons of Kohath: Amram, Izhar, Hebron, and Uzziel—four *in all.* ¹³ The sons of Amram: Aaron and Moses; and Aaron was set apart, he and his sons forever, that he should sanctify the most holy things, to burn incense before the LORD, to minister to Him, and to give the blessing in His name forever. ¹⁴ Now the sons of Moses the man of God were reckoned to the tribe of Levi. ¹⁵ The sons of Moses *were* Gershon and Eliezer. ¹⁶ Of the sons of Gershon, Shebuel *was* the first. ¹⁷ Of the descendants of Eliezer, Rehabiah was the first. And Eliezer had no other sons, but the sons of Rehabiah were very many. ¹⁸ Of the sons of Izhar, Shelomith *was* the first. ¹⁹ Of the sons of Hebron, Jeriah *was* the first, Amariah the second, Jahaziel the third, and Jekameam the fourth. ²⁰ Of the sons of Uzziel, Michah *was* the first and Jesshiah the second.

²¹ The sons of Merari *were* Mahli and Mushi. The sons of Mahli *were* Eleazar and Kish. ²² And Eleazar died, and had no sons, but only daughters; and their brethren, the sons of Kish, took them *as wives.* ²³ The sons of Mushi *were* Mahli, Eder, and Jeremoth—three *in all.*

²⁴ These *were* the sons of Levi by their fathers' houses—the heads of the fathers' *houses* as they were counted individually by the number of their names, who did the work for the service of the house of the LORD, from the age of twenty years and above.

²⁵ For David said, "The LORD God of Israel has given rest to His people, that they may dwell in Jerusalem forever"; ²⁶ and also to the Levites, "They shall no longer carry the tabernacle, or any of the articles for its service." ²⁷ For by the last words of David the Levites *were* numbered from twenty years old and above; ²⁸ because their duty *was* to help the sons of Aaron in the service of the house of the LORD, in the courts and in the chambers, in the purifying of all holy things and the work of the service of the house of God, ²⁹ both with the showbread and the fine flour for the grain offering, with the unleavened cakes and *what is baked in* the pan, with what is mixed and with all kinds of measures and sizes; ³⁰ to stand every morning to thank and praise the LORD, and likewise at evening; ³¹ and at every presentation of a burnt offering to the LORD on the Sabbaths and on the New Moons and on the set feasts, by number according to the ordinance governing them, regularly before the LORD; ³² and that they should attend to the needs of the tabernacle of meeting, the needs of the holy *place,* and the needs of the sons of Aaron their brethren in the work of the house of the LORD.

24 Now *these are* the divisions of the sons of Aaron. The sons of Aaron *were* Nadab, Abihu, Eleazar, and Ithamar. ² And Nadab and Abihu died before their father, and had no children; therefore Eleazar and Ithamar ministered as priests. ³ Then David with Zadok of the

"Can-Do" Potential

Author Phyllis Theroux writes about her father, "If there was any one thing that my father did for me when I was growing up it was to give me the promise that ahead of me was dry land — a bright, marshless territory, without chuckholes or traps, where one day I would walk easily and as befitting my talents. . . .

"Thus it was, when he came upon me one afternoon sobbing out my unsuccesses into a wet pillow, that he sat down on the bed and . . . assured me that my grief was only a temporary setback. Oh, very temporary! Why he couldn't think of any other little girl who was so talented, so predestined to succeed in every department as I was. 'And don't forget,' he added with a smile, 'that we can trace our ancestry right back to Pepin the Stupid!'

"By the time he had finished talking I really did understand that someday I would live among rational beings, and walk with kind, unvindictive people who, by virtue of their maturity and mine, would take no pleasure in cruelty and would welcome my presence among them. . . . There are some people who carry the flint that lights other people's torches. They get them all excited about . . . the 'can-do' potential of one's own being. That was my father's gift to me."

Determine today to give your child the same gift. The gift of knowing they were created by God for a purpose and they have the potential to be anything they want to be.

sons of Eleazar, and Ahimelech of the sons of Ithamar, divided them according to the schedule of their service.

⁴ There were more leaders found of the sons of Eleazar than of the sons of Ithamar, and *thus* they were divided. Among the sons of Eleazar *were* sixteen heads of *their* fathers' houses, and eight heads of their fathers' houses among the sons of Ithamar. ⁵ Thus they were divided by lot, one group as another, for there were officials of the sanctuary and officials *of the house* of God, from the sons of Eleazar and from the sons of Ithamar. ⁶ And the scribe, Shemaiah the son of Nethanel, *one of* the Levites, wrote them down before the king, the leaders, Zadok the priest, Ahimelech the son of Abiathar, and the heads of the fathers' *houses* of the priests and Levites, one father's house taken for Eleazar and *one* for Ithamar.

⁷ Now the first lot fell to Jehoiarib, the second to Jedaiah, ⁸ the third to Harim, the fourth to Seorim, ⁹ the fifth to Malchijah, the sixth to Mijamin, ¹⁰ the seventh to Hakkoz, the eighth to Abijah, ¹¹ the ninth to Jeshua, the tenth to Shecaniah, ¹² the eleventh to Eliashib, the twelfth to Jakim, ¹³ the thirteenth to Huppah, the fourteenth to Jeshebeab, ¹⁴ the fifteenth to Bilgah, the sixteenth to Immer, ¹⁵ the seventeenth to Hezir, the eighteenth to Happizzez, ¹⁶ the nineteenth to Pethahiah, the twentieth to Jehezekel, ¹⁷ the twenty-first to Jachin, the twenty-second to Gamul, ¹⁸ the twenty-third to Delaiah, the twenty-fourth to Maaziah.

¹⁹ This *was* the schedule of their service for coming into the house of the LORD according to their ordinance by the hand of Aaron their father, as the LORD God of Israel had commanded him.

²⁰ And the rest of the sons of Levi: of the sons of Amram, Shubael; of the sons of Shubael, Jehdeiah. ²¹ Concerning Rehabiah, of the sons of Rehabiah, the first *was* Isshiah. ²² Of the Izharites, Shelomoth; of the sons of Shelomoth, Jahath. ²³ Of the sons *of Hebron*, Jeriah *was the first*, Amariah the second, Jahaziel the third, *and* Jekameam the fourth. ²⁴ *Of* the sons of Uzziel, Michah; of the sons of Michah, Shamir. ²⁵ The brother of Michah, Isshiah; of the sons of Isshiah, Zechariah. ²⁶ The sons of Merari *were* Mahli and Mushi; the son of Jaaziah, Beno. ²⁷ The sons of Merari by Jaaziah *were* Beno, Shoham, Zaccur, and Ibri. ²⁸ Of Mahli: Eleazar, who had no sons. ²⁹ Of Kish: the son of Kish, Jerahmeel. ³⁰ Also the sons of Mushi *were* Mahli, Eder, and Jerimoth. These *were* the sons of the Levites according to their fathers' houses.

³¹ These also cast lots just as their brothers the sons of Aaron did, in the presence of King David, Zadok, Ahimelech, and the heads of the fathers' *houses* of the priests and Levites. The chief fathers *did* just as their younger brethren.

25 Moreover David and the captains of the army separated for the service *some* of the sons of Asaph, of Heman, and of Jeduthun, who *should* prophesy with harps, stringed instruments, and cymbals. And the number of the skilled men performing their service was: ² Of the sons of Asaph: Zaccur, Joseph, Nethaniah, and Asharelah; the sons of Asaph *were* under the direction of Asaph, who prophesied according to the order of the king. ³ Of Jeduthun, the sons of Jeduthun: Gedaliah, Zeri, Jeshaiah, Shimei, Hashabiah, and Mattithiah, six, under the direction of their father Jeduthun, who prophesied with a harp to give thanks and to praise the LORD. ⁴ Of Heman, the sons of Heman: Bukkiah, Mattaniah, Uzziel, Shebuel, Jerimoth, Hananiah, Hanani, Eliathah, Giddalti, Romamti-Ezer, Joshbekashah, Mallothi, Hothir, *and* Mahazioth. ⁵ All these *were* the sons of Heman the king's seer in the words of God, to exalt his horn. For God gave Heman fourteen sons and three daughters.

⁶ All these *were* under the direction of their father for the music *in* the house of the LORD, with cymbals, stringed instruments, and harps, for the service of the house of God. Asaph, Jeduthun, and Heman *were* under the authority of the king. ⁷ So the number of them, with their brethren who were instructed in the songs of the LORD, all who were skillful, *was* two hundred and eighty-eight.

⁸ And they cast lots for their duty, the small as well as the great, the teacher with the student.

9 Now the first lot for Asaph came out for Joseph; the second for Gedaliah, him with his brethren and sons, twelve; 10 the third for Zaccur, his sons and his brethren, twelve; 11 the fourth for Jizri, his sons and his brethren, twelve; 12 the fifth for Nethaniah, his sons and his brethren, twelve; 13 the sixth for Bukkiah, his sons and his brethren, twelve; 14 the seventh for Jesharelah, his sons and his brethren, twelve; 15 the eighth for Jeshaiah, his sons and his brethren, twelve; 16 the ninth for Mattaniah, his sons and his brethren, twelve; 17 the tenth for Shimei, his sons and his brethren, twelve; 18 the eleventh for Azarel, his sons and his brethren, twelve; 19 the twelfth for Hashabiah, his sons and his brethren, twelve; 20 the thirteenth for Shubael, his sons and his brethren, twelve; 21 the fourteenth for Mattithiah, his sons and his brethren, twelve; 22 the fifteenth for Jeremoth, his sons and his brethren, twelve; 23 the sixteenth for Hananiah, his sons and his brethren, twelve; 24 the seventeenth for Joshbekashah, his sons and his brethren, twelve; 25 the eighteenth for Hanani, his sons and his brethren, twelve; 26 the nineteenth for Mallothi, his sons and his brethren, twelve; 27 the twentieth for Eliathah, his sons and his brethren, twelve; 28 the twenty-first for Hothir, his sons and his brethren, twelve; 29 the twenty-second for Giddalti, his sons and his brethren, twelve; 30 the twenty-third for Mahazioth, his sons and his brethren, twelve; 31 the twenty-fourth for Romamti-Ezer, his sons and his brethren, twelve.

∼ PSALM 78:40–55 ∼

40 How often they provoked Him in the wilderness,
And grieved Him in the desert!
41 Yes, again and again they tempted God,
And limited the Holy One of Israel.
42 They did not remember His power:
The day when He redeemed them from the enemy,
43 When He worked His signs in Egypt,
And His wonders in the field of Zoan;
44 Turned their rivers into blood,

And their streams, that they could not drink.
45 He sent swarms of flies among them, which devoured them,
And frogs, which destroyed them.
46 He also gave their crops to the caterpillar,
And their labor to the locust.
47 He destroyed their vines with hail,
And their sycamore trees with frost.
48 He also gave up their cattle to the hail,
And their flocks to fiery lightning.
49 He cast on them the fierceness of His anger,
Wrath, indignation, and trouble,
By sending angels of destruction among them.
50 He made a path for His anger;
He did not spare their soul from death,
But gave their life over to the plague,
51 And destroyed all the firstborn in Egypt,
The first of their strength in the tents of Ham.
52 But He made His own people go forth like sheep,
And guided them in the wilderness like a flock;
53 And He led them on safely, so that they did not fear;
But the sea overwhelmed their enemies.
54 And He brought them to His holy border,
This mountain which His right hand had acquired.
55 He also drove out the nations before them,
Allotted them an inheritance by survey,
And made the tribes of Israel dwell in their tents.

∼ PROVERBS 20:3 ∼

3 It is honorable for a man to stop striving,
Since any fool can start a quarrel.

∼ ACTS 9:22–43 ∼

But Saul increased all the more in strength, and confounded the Jews who dwelt in

Damascus, proving that this *Jesus* is the Christ.

²³ Now after many days were past, the Jews plotted to kill him. ²⁴ But their plot became known to Saul. And they watched the gates day and night, to kill him. ²⁵ Then the disciples took him by night and let *him* down through the wall in a large basket.

²⁶ And when Saul had come to Jerusalem, he tried to join the disciples; but they were all afraid of him, and did not believe that he was a disciple. ²⁷ But Barnabas took him and brought *him* to the apostles. And he declared to them how he had seen the Lord on the road, and that He had spoken to him, and how he had preached boldly at Damascus in the name of Jesus. ²⁸ So he was with them at Jerusalem, coming in and going out. ²⁹ And he spoke boldly in the name of the Lord Jesus and disputed against the Hellenists, but they attempted to kill him. ³⁰ When the brethren found out, they brought him down to Caesarea and sent him out to Tarsus.

³¹ Then the churches throughout all Judea, Galilee, and Samaria had peace and were edified. And walking in the fear of the Lord and in the comfort of the Holy Spirit, they were multiplied.

³² Now it came to pass, as Peter went through all *parts of the country,* that he also came down to the saints who dwelt in Lydda. ³³ There he found a certain man named Aeneas, who had been bedridden eight years and was paralyzed. ³⁴ And Peter said to him, "Aeneas, Jesus the Christ heals you. Arise and make your bed." Then he arose immediately. ³⁵ So all who dwelt at Lydda and Sharon saw him and turned to the Lord.

³⁶ At Joppa there was a certain disciple named Tabitha, which is translated Dorcas. This woman was full of good works and charitable deeds which she did. ³⁷ But it happened in those days that she became sick and died. When they had washed her, they laid *her* in an upper room. ³⁸ And since Lydda was near Joppa, and the disciples had heard that Peter was there, they sent two men to him, imploring *him* not to delay in coming to them. ³⁹ Then Peter arose and went with them. When he had come, they brought *him* to the upper room. And all the widows stood by him weeping, showing the tunics and garments which Dorcas had made while she was with them. ⁴⁰ But Peter put them all out, and knelt down and prayed. And turning to the body he said, "Tabitha, arise." And she opened her eyes, and when she saw Peter she sat up. ⁴¹ Then he gave her *his* hand and lifted her up; and when he had called the saints and widows, he presented her alive. ⁴² And it became known throughout all Joppa, and many believed on the Lord. ⁴³ So it was that he stayed many days in Joppa with Simon, a tanner.

READING 182 · JULY 1

~ 1 CHRONICLES 26:1—27:34 ~

Concerning the divisions of the gatekeepers: of the Korahites, Meshelemiah the son of Kore, of the sons of Asaph. ² And the sons of Meshelemiah *were* Zechariah the firstborn, Jediael the second, Zebadiah the third, Jathniel the fourth, ³ Elam the fifth, Jehohanan the sixth, Eliehoenai the seventh.

⁴ Moreover the sons of Obed-Edom *were* Shemaiah the firstborn, Jehozabad the second, Joah the third, Sacar the fourth, Nethanel the fifth, ⁵ Ammiel the sixth, Issachar the seventh, Peulthai the eighth; for God blessed him.

⁶ Also to Shemaiah his son were sons born who governed their fathers' houses, because they *were* men of great ability. ⁷ The sons of Shemaiah *were* Othni, Rephael, Obed, and Elzabad, whose brothers Elihu and Semachiah *were* able men.

⁸ All these *were* of the sons of Obed-Edom, they and their sons and their brethren, able men with strength for the work: sixty-two of Obed-Edom.

Your Reputation Precedes You

Roger was a good employee — not spectacular — but reliable, punctual, even-tempered, and always willing to go the extra mile.

Brian also did good work, but he didn't mind cutting a few corners to finish a job, or taking off work a few minutes early to attend to his personal needs.

When Mr. Jones, their supervisor, announced that one of the two men would be promoted, Roger counted on his record and his reputation to win him the post. Brian lobbied hard for the job in an underhanded fashion by telling several of his coworkers that Roger had stolen credit for his innovative cost-saving measures, had misappropriated supplies, and was known to overextend his lunch hour. He was careful, of course, to preface all of his remarks by saying, "Just between the two of us. . . ."

The following week, when Mr. Jones announced that Roger had received the promotion, he received a rousing applause from his fellow employees. No one was surprised — except Brian, of course. After all, Roger's reputation had preceded him.

So had Brian's.

And they said, "Cornelius the centurion, a just man, one who fears God and has a good reputation among all the nation of the Jews, was divinely instructed by a holy angel to summon you to his house, and to hear words from you."

Acts 10:22

⁹ And Meshelemiah had sons and brethren, eighteen able men.

¹⁰ Also Hosah, of the children of Merari, had sons: Shimri the first (for *though* he was not the firstborn, his father made him the first), ¹¹ Hilkiah the second, Tebaliah the third, Zechariah the fourth; all the sons and brethren of Hosah *were* thirteen.

¹² Among these *were* the divisions of the gatekeepers, among the chief men, *having* duties just like their brethren, to serve in the house of the LORD. ¹³ And they cast lots for each gate, the small as well as the great, according to their father's house. ¹⁴ The lot for the East *Gate* fell to Shelemiah. Then they cast lots *for* his son Zechariah, a wise counselor, and his lot came out for the North Gate; ¹⁵ to Obed-Edom the South Gate, and to his sons the storehouse. ¹⁶ To Shuppim and Hosah *the lot came out* for the West Gate, with the Shallecheth Gate on the ascending highway—watchman opposite watchman. ¹⁷ On the east were *six* Levites, on the north four each day, on the south four each day, and for the storehouse two by two. ¹⁸ As for the Parbar on the west, *there were* four on the highway *and* two at the Parbar. ¹⁹ These were the divisions of the gatekeepers among the sons of Korah and among the sons of Merari.

²⁰ Of the Levites, Ahijah *was* over the treasuries of the house of God and over the treasuries of the dedicated things. ²¹ The sons of Laadan, the descendants of the Gershonites of Laadan, heads of their fathers' *houses,* of Laadan the Gershonite: Jehieli. ²² The sons of Jehieli, Zetham and Joel his brother, *were* over the treasuries of the house of the LORD. ²³ Of the Amramites, the Izharites, the Hebronites, and the Uzzielites: ²⁴ Shebuel the son of Gershom, the son of Moses, *was* overseer of the treasuries. ²⁵ And his brethren by Eliezer *were* Rehabiah his son, Jeshaiah his son, Joram his son, Zichri his son, and Shelomith his son.

²⁶ This Shelomith and his brethren *were* over all the treasuries of the dedicated things which King David and the heads of fathers' *houses,* the captains over thousands and hundreds, and the captains of the army, had dedicated. ²⁷ Some of the spoils won in battles they dedicated to maintain the house of the LORD. ²⁸ And all that Samuel the seer, Saul the son of Kish, Abner the son of Ner, and Joab the son of Zeruiah had dedicated, every dedicated *thing,* was under the hand of Shelomith and his brethren.

²⁹ Of the Izharites, Chenaniah and his sons *performed* duties as officials and judges over Israel outside Jerusalem.

³⁰ Of the Hebronites, Hashabiah and his brethren, one thousand seven hundred able men, had the oversight of Israel on the west side of the Jordan for all the business of the LORD, and in the service of the king. ³¹ Among the Hebronites, Jerijah *was* head of the Hebronites according to his genealogy of the fathers. In the fortieth year of the reign of David they were sought, and there were found among them capable men at Jazer of Gilead. ³² And his brethren *were* two thousand seven hundred able men, heads of fathers' *houses,* whom King David made officials over the Reubenites, the Gadites, and the half-tribe of Manasseh, for every matter pertaining to God and the affairs of the king.

27

And the children of Israel, according to their number, the heads of fathers' *houses,* the captains of thousands and hundreds and their officers, served the king in every matter of the *military* divisions. *These divisions* came in and went out month by month throughout all the months of the year, each division *having* twenty-four thousand.

² Over the first division for the first month *was* Jashobeam the son of Zabdiel, and in his division *were* twenty-four thousand; ³ he *was* of the children of Perez, and the chief of all the captains of the army for the first month. ⁴ Over the division of the second month *was* Dodai an Ahohite, and of his division Mikloth also *was* the leader; in his division *were* twenty-four thousand. ⁵ The third captain of the army for the third month *was* Benaiah, the son of Jehoiada the priest, who was chief; in his division *were* twenty-four thousand. ⁶ This was the Benaiah *who was* mighty *among* the thirty, and was over the thirty; in his division *was* Ammizabad his son. ⁷ The fourth *captain* for the fourth month *was* Asahel the brother of Joab, and Zebadiah his son after him; in his

division *were* twenty-four thousand. ⁸ The fifth *captain* for the fifth month *was* Shamhuth the Izrahite; in his division were twenty-four thousand. ⁹ The sixth *captain* for the sixth month *was* Ira the son of Ikkesh the Tekoite; in his division *were* twenty-four thousand. ¹⁰ The seventh *captain* for the seventh month *was* Helez the Pelonite, of the children of Ephraim; in his division *were* twenty-four thousand. ¹¹ The eighth *captain* for the eighth month *was* Sibbechai the Hushathite, of the Zarhites; in his division *were* twenty-four thousand. ¹² The ninth *captain* for the ninth month *was* Abiezer the Anathothite, of the Benjamites; in his division *were* twenty-four thousand. ¹³ The tenth *captain* for the tenth month *was* Maharai the Netophathite, of the Zarhites; in his division *were* twenty-four thousand. ¹⁴ The eleventh *captain* for the eleventh month *was* Benaiah the Pirathonite, of the children of Ephraim; in his division *were* twenty-four thousand. ¹⁵ The twelfth *captain* for the twelfth month *was* Heldai the Netophathite, of Othniel; in his division *were* twenty-four thousand.

¹⁶ Furthermore, over the tribes of Israel: the officer over the Reubenites *was* Eliezer the son of Zichri; over the Simeonites, Shephatiah the son of Maachah; ¹⁷ *over* the Levites, Hashabiah the son of Kemuel; over the Aaronites, Zadok; ¹⁸ *over* Judah, Elihu, *one* of David's brothers; *over* Issachar, Omri the son of Michael; ¹⁹ *over* Zebulun, Ishmaiah the son of Obadiah; *over* Naphtali, Jerimoth the son of Azriel; ²⁰ *over* the children of Ephraim, Hoshea the son of Azaziah; *over* the half-tribe of Manasseh, Joel the son of Pedaiah; ²¹ *over* the half-*tribe* of Manasseh in Gilead, Iddo the son of Zechariah; *over* Benjamin, Jaasiel the son of Abner; ²² *over* Dan, Azarel the son of Jeroham. These *were* the leaders of the tribes of Israel.

²³ But David did not take the number of those twenty years old and under, because the LORD had said He would multiply Israel like the stars of the heavens. ²⁴ Joab the son of Zeruiah began a census, but he did not finish, for wrath came upon Israel because of this census; nor was the number recorded in the account of the chronicles of King David.

²⁵ And Azmaveth the son of Adiel *was* over the king's treasuries; and Jehonathan the son of Uzziah was over the storehouses in the field, in the cities, in the villages, and in the fortresses. ²⁶ Ezri the son of Chelub was over those who did the work of the field for tilling the ground. ²⁷ And Shimei the Ramathite *was* over the vineyards, and Zabdi the Shiphmite was over the produce of the vineyards for the supply of wine. ²⁸ Baal-Hanan the Gederite was over the olive trees and the sycamore trees that *were* in the lowlands, and Joash *was* over the store of oil. ²⁹ And Shitrai the Sharonite *was* over the herds that fed in Sharon, and Shaphat the son of Adlai was over the herds *that were* in the valleys. ³⁰ Obil the Ishmaelite *was* over the camels, Jehdeiah the Meronothite *was* over the donkeys, ³¹ and Jaziz the Hagrite *was* over the flocks. All these *were* the officials over King David's property.

³² Also Jehonathan, David's uncle, *was* a counselor, a wise man, and a scribe; and Jehiel the son of Hachmoni *was* with the king's sons. ³³ Ahithophel *was* the king's counselor, and Hushai the Archite *was* the king's companion. ³⁴ After Ahithophel *was* Jehoiada the son of Benaiah, then Abiathar. And the general of the king's army *was* Joab.

～ PSALM 78:56–66 ～

⁵⁶ Yet they tested and provoked the
   Most High God,
   And did not keep His testimonies,
⁵⁷ But turned back and acted
   unfaithfully like their fathers;
   They were turned aside like a
   deceitful bow.
⁵⁸ For they provoked Him to anger
   with their high places,
   And moved Him to jealousy with
   their carved images.
⁵⁹ When God heard *this,* He was
   furious,
   And greatly abhorred Israel,
⁶⁰ So that He forsook the tabernacle of
   Shiloh,
   The tent He had placed among men,
⁶¹ And delivered His strength into
   captivity,
   And His glory into the enemy's
   hand.

⁶² He also gave His people over to the
    sword,
    And was furious with His
    inheritance.
⁶³ The fire consumed their young men,
    And their maidens were not given in
    marriage.
⁶⁴ Their priests fell by the sword,
    And their widows made no
    lamentation.

⁶⁵ Then the Lord awoke as *from* sleep,
    Like a mighty man who shouts
    because of wine.
⁶⁶ And He beat back His enemies;
    He put them to a perpetual
    reproach.

∼ PROVERBS 20:4, 5 ∼

⁴ The lazy *man* will not plow because
    of winter;
    He will beg during harvest and *have*
    nothing.

⁵ Counsel in the heart of man *is like*
    deep water,
    But a man of understanding will
    draw it out.

∼ ACTS 10:1–23 ∼

There was a certain man in Caesarea called
Cornelius, a centurion of what was
called the Italian Regiment, ² a devout
man and one who feared God with all his
household, who gave alms generously to
the people, and prayed to God always.
³ About the ninth hour of the day he saw
clearly in a vision an angel of God coming in and saying to him, "Cornelius!"

⁴ And when he observed him, he was
afraid, and said, "What is it, lord?"

So he said to him, "Your prayers and
your alms have come up for a memorial
before God. ⁵ Now send men to Joppa,
and send for Simon whose surname is
Peter. ⁶ He is lodging with Simon, a tanner, whose house is by the sea. He will
tell you what you must do." ⁷ And when
the angel who spoke to him had departed,
Cornelius called two of his household

servants and a devout soldier from among
those who waited on him continually. ⁸ So
when he had explained all *these* things to
them, he sent them to Joppa.

⁹ The next day, as they went on their
journey and drew near the city, Peter went
up on the housetop to pray, about the sixth
hour. ¹⁰ Then he became very hungry and
wanted to eat; but while they made ready,
he fell into a trance ¹¹ and saw heaven
opened and an object like a great sheet
bound at the four corners, descending to
him and let down to the earth. ¹² In it were
all kinds of four-footed animals of the
earth, wild beasts, creeping things, and
birds of the air. ¹³ And a voice came to
him, "Rise, Peter; kill and eat."

¹⁴ But Peter said, "Not so, Lord! For I
have never eaten anything common or
unclean."

¹⁵ And a voice *spoke* to him again the
second time, "What God has cleansed you
must not call common." ¹⁶ This was done
three times. And the object was taken up
into heaven again.

¹⁷ Now while Peter wondered within
himself what this vision which he had seen
meant, behold, the men who had been
sent from Cornelius had made inquiry for
Simon's house, and stood before the gate.
¹⁸ And they called and asked whether
Simon, whose surname was Peter, was
lodging there.

¹⁹ While Peter thought about the vision,
the Spirit said to him, "Behold, three men
are seeking you. ²⁰ Arise therefore, go
down and go with them, doubting nothing; for I have sent them."

²¹ Then Peter went down to the men
who had been sent to him from Cornelius,
and said, "Yes, I am he whom you seek.
For what reason have you come?"

²² And they said, "Cornelius *the* centurion, a just man, one who fears God and
has a good reputation among all the nation of the Jews, was divinely instructed
by a holy angel to summon you to his
house, and to hear words from you."
²³ Then he invited them in and lodged
them.

On the next day Peter went away with
them, and some brethren from Joppa accompanied him.

～ 1 Chronicles 28:1—29:30 ～

Now David assembled at Jerusalem all the leaders of Israel: the officers of the tribes and the captains of the divisions who served the king, the captains over thousands and captains over hundreds, and the stewards over all the substance and possessions of the king and of his sons, with the officials, the valiant men, and all the mighty men of valor. ² Then King David rose to his feet and said, "Hear me, my brethren and my people: I *had* it in my heart to build a house of rest for the ark of the covenant of the LORD, and for the footstool of our God, and had made preparations to build it. ³ But God said to me, 'You shall not build a house for My name, because you *have been* a man of war and have shed blood.' ⁴ However the LORD God of Israel chose me above all the house of my father to be king over Israel forever, for He has chosen Judah *to be* the ruler. And of the house of Judah, the house of my father, and among the sons of my father, He was pleased with me to make *me* king over all Israel. ⁵ And of all my sons (for the LORD has given me many sons) He has chosen my son Solomon to sit on the throne of the kingdom of the LORD over Israel. ⁶ Now He said to me, 'It is your son Solomon *who* shall build My house and My courts; for I have chosen him *to be* My son, and I will be his Father. ⁷ Moreover I will establish his kingdom forever, if he is steadfast to observe My commandments and My judgments, as it is this day.' ⁸ Now therefore, in the sight of all Israel, the assembly of the LORD, and in the hearing of our God, be careful to seek out all the commandments of the LORD your God, that you may possess this good land, and leave *it* as an inheritance for your children after you forever. ⁹ "As for you, my son Solomon, know the God of your father, and serve Him with a loyal heart and with a willing mind; for the LORD searches all hearts and understands all the intent of the thoughts. If you seek Him, He will be found by you; but if you forsake Him, He will cast you off forever. ¹⁰ Consider now, for the

LORD has chosen you to build a house for the sanctuary; be strong, and do it."

¹¹ Then David gave his son Solomon the plans for the vestibule, its houses, its treasuries, its upper chambers, its inner chambers, and the place of the mercy seat; ¹² and the plans for all that he had by the Spirit, of the courts of the house of the LORD, of all the chambers all around, of the treasuries of the house of God, and of the treasuries for the dedicated things; ¹³ also for the division of the priests and the Levites, for all the work of the service of the house of the LORD, and for all the articles of service in the house of the LORD. ¹⁴ *He gave* gold by weight for *things* of gold, for all articles used in every kind of service; also *silver* for all articles of silver by weight, for all articles used in every kind of service; ¹⁵ the weight for the lampstands of gold, and their lamps of gold, by weight for each lampstand and its lamps; for the lampstands of silver by weight, for the lampstand and its lamps, according to the use of each lampstand. ¹⁶ And by weight *he gave* gold for the tables of the showbread, for each table, and silver for the tables of silver; ¹⁷ also pure gold for the forks, the basins, the pitchers of pure gold, and the golden bowls—*he gave gold* by weight for every bowl; and for the silver bowls, *silver* by weight for every bowl; ¹⁸ and refined gold by weight for the altar of incense, and for the construction of the chariot, that is, the gold cherubim that spread *their wings* and overshadowed the ark of the covenant of the LORD. ¹⁹ "All *this,*" *said David,* "the LORD made me understand in writing, by *His* hand upon me, all the works of these plans."

²⁰ And David said to his son Solomon, "Be strong and of good courage, and do *it;* do not fear nor be dismayed, for the LORD God—my God—*will be* with you. He will not leave you nor forsake you, until you have finished all the work for the service of the house of the LORD. ²¹ *Here are* the divisions of the priests and the Levites for all the service of the house of God; and every willing craftsman *will be* with you for all manner of

workmanship, for every kind of service; also the leaders and all the people *will be* completely at your command."

29 Furthermore King David said to all the assembly: "My son Solomon, whom alone God has chosen, *is* young and inexperienced; and the work *is* great, because the temple *is* not for man but for the LORD God. ²Now for the house of my God I have prepared with all my might: gold for *things to be made of* gold, silver for *things of* silver, bronze for *things of* bronze, iron for *things of* iron, wood for *things of* wood, onyx stones, *stones* to be set, glistening stones of various colors, all kinds of precious stones, and marble slabs in abundance. ³Moreover, because I have set my affection on the house of my God, I have given to the house of my God, over and above all that I have prepared for the holy house, my own special treasure of gold and silver: ⁴three thousand talents of gold, of the gold of Ophir, and seven thousand talents of refined silver, to overlay the walls of the houses; ⁵the gold for *things of* gold and the silver for *things of* silver, and for all kinds of work *to be done* by the hands of craftsmen. Who *then* is willing to consecrate himself this day to the LORD?"

⁶Then the leaders of the fathers' *houses,* leaders of the tribes of Israel, the captains of thousands and of hundreds, with the officers over the king's work, offered willingly. ⁷They gave for the work of the house of God five thousand talents and ten thousand darics of gold, ten thousand talents of silver, eighteen thousand talents of bronze, and one hundred thousand talents of iron. ⁸And whoever had *precious* stones gave *them* to the treasury of the house of the LORD, into the hand of Jehiel the Gershonite. ⁹Then the people rejoiced, for they had offered willingly, because with a loyal heart they had offered willingly to the LORD; and King David also rejoiced greatly.

¹⁰Therefore David blessed the LORD before all the assembly; and David said:

"Blessed are You, LORD God of
    Israel, our Father, forever and
    ever.
¹¹ Yours, O LORD, *is* the greatness,

The power and the glory,
The victory and the majesty;
For all *that is* in heaven and in
    earth *is Yours;*
Yours *is* the kingdom, O LORD,
And You are exalted as head over
    all.
¹² Both riches and honor *come* from
    You,
And You reign over all.
In Your hand *is* power and might;
In Your hand *it is* to make great
And to give strength to all.

¹³ "Now therefore, our God,
We thank You
And praise Your glorious name.
¹⁴ But who *am* I, and who *are* my
    people,
That we should be able to offer so
    willingly as this?
For all things *come* from You,
And of Your own we have given
    You.
¹⁵ For we *are* aliens and pilgrims
    before You,
As *were* all our fathers;
Our days on earth *are* as a shadow,
And without hope.

¹⁶ "O LORD our God, all this abundance that we have prepared to build You a house for Your holy name is from Your hand, and *is* all Your own. ¹⁷I know also, my God, that You test the heart and have pleasure in uprightness. As for me, in the uprightness of my heart I have willingly offered all these *things;* and now with joy I have seen Your people, who are present here to offer willingly to You. ¹⁸O LORD God of Abraham, Isaac, and Israel, our fathers, keep this forever in the intent of the thoughts of the heart of Your people, and fix their heart toward You. ¹⁹And give my son Solomon a loyal heart to keep Your commandments and Your testimonies and Your statutes, to do all *these things,* and to build the temple for which I have made provision."

²⁰Then David said to all the assembly, "Now bless the LORD your God." So all the assembly blessed the LORD God of their fathers, and bowed their heads and prostrated themselves before the LORD and the king.

Traits of a Champion

Sports psychologists have identified six traits which are common among gold-medal athletes. These "traits of a champion" apply to both men and women, and are also dominant factors in the lives of those who succeed in non-athletic vocations:

1. *Self-analysis*. The successful athlete knows her strengths and weaknesses, and engages in critical appraisal that is honest, but never negative.
2. *Self-competition*. A winner knows she can only control her own performance, so she competes against her own best effort, not others.
3. *Focus*. The champion is always "in the present," concentrating on the task at hand.
4. *Confidence*. Successful athletes control anxiety by setting tough but reasonable goals. As goals are reached, confidence increases.
5. *Toughness*. This is a mental trait that involves accepting risk and trying to win, rather than trying not to lose. A winner sees change as opportunity and accepts responsibility for her own destiny.
6. *Having a game plan*. Even elite athletes know talent is not enough. They have a game plan.

You don't have to be an Olympic athlete to develop these skills, they can be beneficial to every area of your life. Whether it's on the job, in the home, or at the gym, these traits can build excellence into your everyday life.

> Be strong and of good courage, and do it; do not fear nor be dismayed, for the Lord God… will be with you. He will not leave you nor forsake you.
>
> *1 Chronicles 28:20*

²¹ And they made sacrifices to the LORD and offered burnt offerings to the LORD on the next day: a thousand bulls, a thousand rams, a thousand lambs, with their drink offerings, and sacrifices in abundance for all Israel. ²² So they ate and drank before the LORD with great gladness on that day. And they made Solomon the son of David king the second time, and anointed *him* before the LORD *to be* the leader, and Zadok *to be* priest. ²³ Then Solomon sat on the throne of the LORD as king instead of David his father, and prospered; and all Israel obeyed him. ²⁴ All the leaders and the mighty men, and also all the sons of King David, submitted themselves to King Solomon. ²⁵ So the LORD exalted Solomon exceedingly in the sight of all Israel, and bestowed on him *such* royal majesty as had not been on any king before him in Israel.

²⁶ Thus David the son of Jesse reigned over all Israel. ²⁷ And the period that he reigned over Israel *was* forty years; seven years he reigned in Hebron, and thirty-three *years* he reigned in Jerusalem. ²⁸ So he died in a good old age, full of days and riches and honor; and Solomon his son reigned in his place. ²⁹ Now the acts of King David, first and last, indeed they *are* written in the book of Samuel the seer, in the book of Nathan the prophet, and in the book of Gad the seer, ³⁰ with all his reign and his might, and the events that happened to him, to Israel, and to all the kingdoms of the lands.

~ PSALM 78:67–72 ~

⁶⁷ Moreover He rejected the tent of Joseph,
  And did not choose the tribe of Ephraim,
⁶⁸ But chose the tribe of Judah,
  Mount Zion which He loved.
⁶⁹ And He built His sanctuary like the heights,
  Like the earth which He has established forever.
⁷⁰ He also chose David His servant,
  And took him from the sheepfolds;
⁷¹ From following the ewes that had young He brought him,
  To shepherd Jacob His people,
  And Israel His inheritance.

⁷² So he shepherded them according to the integrity of his heart,
  And guided them by the skillfulness of his hands.

~ PROVERBS 20:6, 7 ~

⁶ Most men will proclaim each his own goodness,
  But who can find a faithful man?

⁷ The righteous *man* walks in his integrity;
  His children *are* blessed after him.

~ ACTS 10:24–48 ~

And the following day they entered Caesarea. Now Cornelius was waiting for them, and had called together his relatives and close friends. ²⁵ As Peter was coming in, Cornelius met him and fell down at his feet and worshiped *him*. ²⁶ But Peter lifted him up, saying, "Stand up; I myself am also a man." ²⁷ And as he talked with him, he went in and found many who had come together. ²⁸ Then he said to them, "You know how unlawful it is for a Jewish man to keep company with or go to one of another nation. But God has shown me that I should not call any man common or unclean. ²⁹ Therefore I came without objection as soon as I was sent for. I ask, then, for what reason have you sent for me?"

³⁰ So Cornelius said, "Four days ago I was fasting until this hour; and at the ninth hour I prayed in my house, and behold, a man stood before me in bright clothing, ³¹ and said, 'Cornelius, your prayer has been heard, and your alms are remembered in the sight of God. ³² Send therefore to Joppa and call Simon here, whose surname is Peter. He is lodging in the house of Simon, a tanner, by the sea. When he comes, he will speak to you.' ³³ So I sent to you immediately, and you have done well to come. Now therefore, we are all present before God, to hear all the things commanded you by God."

³⁴ Then Peter opened *his* mouth and said: "In truth I perceive that God shows no partiality. ³⁵ But in every nation whoever fears Him and works righteousness is accepted by Him. ³⁶ The word which

God sent to the children of Israel, preaching peace through Jesus Christ—He is Lord of all— [37] that word you know, which was proclaimed throughout all Judea, and began from Galilee after the baptism which John preached: [38] how God anointed Jesus of Nazareth with the Holy Spirit and with power, who went about doing good and healing all who were oppressed by the devil, for God was with Him. [39] And we are witnesses of all things which He did both in the land of the Jews and in Jerusalem, whom they killed by hanging on a tree. [40] Him God raised up on the third day, and showed Him openly, [41] not to all the people, but to witnesses chosen before by God, *even* to us who ate and drank with Him after He arose from the dead. [42] And He commanded us to preach to the people, and to testify that it is He who was ordained by God *to be* Judge of the living and the dead. [43] To Him all the prophets witness that, through His name, whoever believes in Him will receive remission of sins."

[44] While Peter was still speaking these words, the Holy Spirit fell upon all those who heard the word. [45] And those of the circumcision who believed were astonished, as many as came with Peter, because the gift of the Holy Spirit had been poured out on the Gentiles also. [46] For they heard them speak with tongues and magnify God.

Then Peter answered, [47] "Can anyone forbid water, that these should not be baptized who have received the Holy Spirit just as we *have?*" [48] And he commanded them to be baptized in the name of the Lord. Then they asked him to stay a few days.

～ 2 CHRONICLES 1:1—2:18 ～

Now Solomon the son of David was strengthened in his kingdom, and the LORD his God *was* with him and exalted him exceedingly.

[2] And Solomon spoke to all Israel, to the captains of thousands and of hundreds, to the judges, and to every leader in all Israel, the heads of the fathers' *houses.* [3] Then Solomon, and all the assembly with him, went to the high place that *was* at Gibeon; for the tabernacle of meeting with God was there, which Moses the servant of the LORD had made in the wilderness. [4] But David had brought up the ark of God from Kirjath Jearim to *the place* David had prepared for it, for he had pitched a tent for it at Jerusalem. [5] Now the bronze altar that Bezalel the son of Uri, the son of Hur, had made, he put before the tabernacle of the LORD; Solomon and the assembly sought Him *there.* [6] And Solomon went up there to the bronze altar before the LORD, which *was* at the tabernacle of meeting, and offered a thousand burnt offerings on it.

[7] On that night God appeared to Solomon, and said to him, "Ask! What shall I give you?"

[8] And Solomon said to God: "You have shown great mercy to David my father, and have made me king in his place. [9] Now, O LORD God, let Your promise to David my father be established, for You have made me king over a people like the dust of the earth in multitude. [10] Now give me wisdom and knowledge, that I may go out and come in before this people; for who can judge this great people of Yours?"

[11] Then God said to Solomon: "Because this was in your heart, and you have not asked riches or wealth or honor or the life of your enemies, nor have you asked long life—but have asked wisdom and knowledge for yourself, that you may judge My people over whom I have made you king— [12] wisdom and knowledge *are* granted to you; and I will give you riches and wealth and honor, such as none of the kings have had who *were* before you, nor shall any after you have the like."

[13] So Solomon came to Jerusalem from the high place that *was* at Gibeon, from before the tabernacle of meeting, and reigned over Israel. [14] And Solomon gathered chariots and horsemen; he had

one thousand four hundred chariots and twelve thousand horsemen, whom he stationed in the chariot cities and with the king in Jerusalem. ¹⁵ Also the king made silver and gold as common in Jerusalem as stones, and he made cedars as abundant as the sycamores which *are* in the lowland. ¹⁶ And Solomon had horses imported from Egypt and Keveh; the king's merchants bought them in Keveh at the *current* price. ¹⁷ They also acquired and imported from Egypt a chariot for six hundred *shekels* of silver, and a horse for one hundred and fifty; thus, through their agents, they exported them to all the kings of the Hittites and the kings of Syria.

2 Then Solomon determined to build a temple for the name of the LORD, and a royal house for himself. ² Solomon selected seventy thousand men to bear burdens, eighty thousand to quarry *stone* in the mountains, and three thousand six hundred to oversee them.

³ Then Solomon sent to Hiram king of Tyre, saying:

> As you have dealt with David my father, and sent him cedars to build himself a house to dwell in, *so deal with me.* ⁴ Behold, I am building a temple for the name of the LORD my God, to dedicate *it* to Him, to burn before Him sweet incense, for the continual showbread, for the burnt offerings morning and evening, on the Sabbaths, on the New Moons, and on the set feasts of the LORD our God. This *is an ordinance* forever to Israel.

⁵ And the temple which I build *will be* great, for our God is greater than all gods. ⁶ But who is able to build Him a temple, since heaven and the heaven of heavens cannot contain Him? Who *am* I then, that I should build Him a temple, except to burn sacrifice before Him?

⁷ Therefore send me at once a man skillful to work in gold and silver, in bronze and iron, in purple and crimson and blue, who has skill to engrave with the skillful men who are with me in Judah and Jerusalem, whom David my father provided. ⁸ Also send me cedar and cypress and algum logs from Lebanon, for I know that your servants have skill to cut timber in Lebanon; and indeed my servants *will be* with your servants, ⁹ to prepare timber for me in abundance, for the temple which I am about to build *shall be* great and wonderful.

¹⁰ And indeed I will give to your servants, the woodsmen who cut timber, twenty thousand kors of ground wheat, twenty thousand kors of barley, twenty thousand baths of wine, and twenty thousand baths of oil.

¹¹ Then Hiram king of Tyre answered in writing, which he sent to Solomon:

> Because the LORD loves His people, He has made you king over them.

¹² Hiram also said:

> Blessed *be* the LORD God of Israel, who made heaven and earth, for He has given King David a wise son, endowed with prudence and understanding, who will build a temple for the LORD and a royal house for himself!

¹³ And now I have sent a skillful man, endowed with understanding, Huram my master *craftsman* ¹⁴(the son of a woman of the daughters of Dan, and his father was a man of Tyre), skilled to work in gold and silver, bronze and iron, stone and wood, purple and blue, fine linen and crimson, and to make any engraving and to accomplish any plan which may be given to him, with your skillful men and with the skillful men of my lord David your father.

¹⁵ Now therefore, the wheat, the barley, the oil, and the wine which

The Joy of Little Cranberry Island

When he came
and had seen
the grace
of God,
he was glad,
and encouraged
them all that
with purpose
of heart they
should continue
with the Lord.

Acts 11:23

Joy Sprague knows how to brighten the days of her customers. As the postmaster for Little Cranberry Island, Maine, she actually has customers competing to get their pictures on her post-office wall. Every 25th customer to use the U.S. Postal Service's Express Mail has a "mug shot" taken which is hung on the wall (which is actually a portion of the general store), and then receives a plate of Joy's home-baked cream puffs!

That's not all Joy does to make Little Cranberry, population 90, a friendlier place. She operates a mail-order stamp business that is so popular her tiny post office ranks fourth in sales out of 450 outlets in Maine. Why? Most of Joy's customers are summer visitors who want to stay in contact with the island. Joy sends a snapshot of an island scene and a handwritten note about island events along with each order.

One of the residents has said, "She invents ways to bring pleasure to others." Joy has received praise from the U.S. Postmaster General and has the warm affection not only of the local residents, but friends across America who delight in corresponding with her.

Why not ask the Lord to give you creative ideas which will brighten someone's life today? Perhaps a brief telephone call or post card will remind them how important they really are to you and to God, their Heavenly Father.

my lord has spoken of, let him send to his servants. ¹⁶ And we will cut wood from Lebanon, as much as you need; we will bring it to you in rafts by sea to Joppa, and you will carry it up to Jerusalem.

¹⁷ Then Solomon numbered all the aliens who *were* in the land of Israel, after the census in which David his father had numbered them; and there were found to be one hundred and fifty-three thousand six hundred. ¹⁸ And he made seventy thousand of them bearers of burdens, eighty thousand stonecutters in the mountain, and three thousand six hundred overseers to make the people work.

∼ PSALM 79:1–4 ∼

1   O God, the nations have come into
        Your inheritance;
    Your holy temple they have defiled;
    They have laid Jerusalem in heaps.
2   The dead bodies of Your servants
    They have given *as* food for the
        birds of the heavens,
    The flesh of Your saints to the beasts
        of the earth.
3   Their blood they have shed like
        water all around Jerusalem,
    And *there was* no one to bury *them*.
4   We have become a reproach to our
        neighbors,
    A scorn and derision to those who
        are around us.

∼ PROVERBS 20:8, 9 ∼

8   A king who sits on the throne of
        judgment
    Scatters all evil with his eyes.

9   Who can say, "I have made my heart
        clean,
    I am pure from my sin"?

∼ ACTS 11:1–30 ∼

Now the apostles and brethren who were in Judea heard that the Gentiles had also received the word of God. ² And when Peter came up to Jerusalem, those of the circumcision contended with him, ³ saying, "You went in to uncircumcised men and ate with them!"

⁴ But Peter explained *it* to them in order from the beginning, saying: ⁵ "I was in the city of Joppa praying; and in a trance I saw a vision, an object descending like a great sheet, let down from heaven by four corners; and it came to me. ⁶ When I observed it intently and considered, I saw four-footed animals of the earth, wild beasts, creeping things, and birds of the air. ⁷ And I heard a voice saying to me, 'Rise, Peter; kill and eat.' ⁸ But I said, 'Not so, Lord! For nothing common or unclean has at any time entered my mouth.' ⁹ But the voice answered me again from heaven, 'What God has cleansed you must not call common.' ¹⁰ Now this was done three times, and all were drawn up again into heaven. ¹¹ At that very moment, three men stood before the house where I was, having been sent to me from Caesarea. ¹² Then the Spirit told me to go with them, doubting nothing. Moreover these six brethren accompanied me, and we entered the man's house. ¹³ And he told us how he had seen an angel standing in his house, who said to him, 'Send men to Joppa, and call for Simon whose surname is Peter, ¹⁴ who will tell you words by which you and all your household will be saved.' ¹⁵ And as I began to speak, the Holy Spirit fell upon them, as upon us at the beginning. ¹⁶ Then I remembered the word of the Lord, how He said, 'John indeed baptized with water, but you shall be baptized with the Holy Spirit.' ¹⁷ If therefore God gave them the same gift as *He gave* us when we believed on the Lord Jesus Christ, who was I that I could withstand God?"

¹⁸ When they heard these things they became silent; and they glorified God, saying, "Then God has also granted to the Gentiles repentance to life."

¹⁹ Now those who were scattered after the persecution that arose over Stephen traveled as far as Phoenicia, Cyprus, and Antioch, preaching the word to no one but the Jews only. ²⁰ But some of them were men from Cyprus and Cyrene, who, when they had come to Antioch, spoke to the Hellenists, preaching the Lord

Jesus. ²¹ And the hand of the Lord was with them, and a great number believed and turned to the Lord.

²² Then news of these things came to the ears of the church in Jerusalem, and they sent out Barnabas to go as far as Antioch. ²³ When he came and had seen the grace of God, he was glad, and encouraged them all that with purpose of heart they should continue with the Lord. ²⁴ For he was a good man, full of the Holy Spirit and of faith. And a great many people were added to the Lord.

²⁵ Then Barnabas departed for Tarsus to seek Saul. ²⁶ And when he had found him, he brought him to Antioch. So it was

that for a whole year they assembled with the church and taught a great many people. And the disciples were first called Christians in Antioch.

²⁷ And in these days prophets came from Jerusalem to Antioch. ²⁸ Then one of them, named Agabus, stood up and showed by the Spirit that there was going to be a great famine throughout all the world, which also happened in the days of Claudius Caesar. ²⁹ Then the disciples, each according to his ability, determined to send relief to the brethren dwelling in Judea. ³⁰ This they also did, and sent it to the elders by the hands of Barnabas and Saul.

~ 2 CHRONICLES 3:1—4:22 ~

Now Solomon began to build the house of the LORD at Jerusalem on Mount Moriah, where the LORD had appeared to his father David, at the place that David had prepared on the threshing floor of Ornan the Jebusite. ² And he began to build on the second *day* of the second month in the fourth year of his reign.

³ This is the foundation which Solomon laid for building the house of God: The length *was* sixty cubits (by cubits according to the former measure) and the width twenty cubits. ⁴ And the vestibule that *was* in front *of the sanctuary* was twenty cubits long across the width of the house, and the height *was* one hundred and twenty. He overlaid the inside with pure gold. ⁵ The larger room he paneled with cypress which he overlaid with fine gold, and he carved palm trees and chainwork on it. ⁶ And he decorated the house with precious stones for beauty, and the gold *was* gold from Parvaim. ⁷ He also overlaid the house—the beams and doorposts, its walls and doors—with gold; and he carved cherubim on the walls.

⁸ And he made the Most Holy Place. Its length was according to the width of the house, twenty cubits, and its width twenty cubits. He overlaid it with six hun-

dred talents of fine gold. ⁹ The weight of the nails *was* fifty shekels of gold; and he overlaid the upper area with gold. ¹⁰ In the Most Holy Place he made two cherubim, fashioned by carving, and overlaid them with gold. ¹¹ The wings of the cherubim *were* twenty cubits in *overall* length: one wing *of the one cherub was* five cubits, touching the wall of the room, and the other wing *was* five cubits, touching the wing of the other cherub; ¹² *one* wing of the other cherub *was* five cubits, touching the wall of the room, and the other wing *also was* five cubits, touching the wing of the other cherub. ¹³ The wings of these cherubim spanned twenty cubits overall. They stood on their feet, and they faced inward. ¹⁴ And he made the veil of blue, purple, crimson, and fine linen, and wove cherubim into it.

¹⁵ Also he made in front of the temple two pillars thirty-five cubits high, and the capital that *was* on the top of each of *them* was five cubits. ¹⁶ He made wreaths of chainwork, as in the inner sanctuary, and put *them* on top of the pillars; and he made one hundred pomegranates, and put *them* on the wreaths of chainwork. ¹⁷ Then he set up the pillars before the temple, one on the right hand and the other on the left; he called the name

of the one on the right hand Jachin, and the name of the one on the left Boaz.

4 Moreover he made a bronze altar: twenty cubits was its length, twenty cubits its width, and ten cubits its height.

² Then he made the Sea of cast *bronze,* ten cubits from one brim to the other; *it was* completely round. Its height *was* five cubits, and a line of thirty cubits measured its circumference. ³ And under it *was* the likeness of oxen encircling it all around, ten to a cubit, all the way around the Sea. The oxen *were* cast in two rows, when it was cast. ⁴ It stood on twelve oxen: three looking toward the north, three looking toward the west, three looking toward the south, and three looking toward the east; the Sea *was set* upon them, and all their back parts *pointed* inward. ⁵ It *was* a handbreadth thick; and its brim was shaped like the brim of a cup, *like* a lily blossom. It contained three thousand baths.

⁶ He also made ten lavers, and put five on the right side and five on the left, to wash in them; such things as they offered for the burnt offering they would wash in them, but the Sea *was* for the priests to wash in. ⁷ And he made ten lampstands of gold according to their design, and set *them* in the temple, five on the right side and five on the left. ⁸ He also made ten tables, and placed *them* in the temple, five on the right side and five on the left. And he made one hundred bowls of gold.

⁹ Furthermore he made the court of the priests, and the great court and doors for the court; and he overlaid these doors with bronze. ¹⁰ He set the Sea on the right side, toward the southeast.

¹¹ Then Huram made the pots and the shovels and the bowls. So Huram finished doing the work that he was to do for King Solomon for the house of God: ¹² the two pillars and the bowl-shaped capitals *that were* on top of the two pillars; the two networks covering the two bowl-shaped capitals which *were* on top of the pillars; ¹³ four hundred pomegranates for the two networks (two rows of pomegranates for each network, to cover the two bowl-shaped capitals that *were* on the pillars); ¹⁴ he also made carts and the lavers on the carts; ¹⁵ one Sea and twelve oxen under

it; ¹⁶ also the pots, the shovels, the forks— and all their articles Huram his master *craftsman* made of burnished bronze for King Solomon for the house of the LORD.

¹⁷ In the plain of Jordan the king had them cast in clay molds, between Succoth and Zeredah. ¹⁸ And Solomon had all these articles made in such great abundance that the weight of the bronze was not determined.

¹⁹ Thus Solomon had all the furnishings made for the house of God: the altar of gold and the tables on which *was* the showbread; ²⁰ the lampstands with their lamps of pure gold, to burn in the prescribed manner in front of the inner sanctuary, ²¹ with the flowers and the lamps and the wick-trimmers of gold, of purest gold; ²² the trimmers, the bowls, the ladles, and the censers of pure gold. As for the entry of the sanctuary, its inner doors to the Most Holy *Place,* and the doors of the main hall of the temple, *were* gold.

∼ PSALM 79:5–10 ∼

⁵ How long, LORD?
  Will You be angry forever?
  Will Your jealousy burn like fire?
⁶ Pour out Your wrath on the nations
    that do not know You,
  And on the kingdoms that do not
    call on Your name.
⁷ For they have devoured Jacob,
  And laid waste his dwelling
    place.

⁸ Oh, do not remember former
    iniquities against us!
  Let Your tender mercies come
    speedily to meet us,
  For we have been brought very
    low.
⁹ Help us, O God of our salvation,
  For the glory of Your name;
  And deliver us, and provide
    atonement for our sins,
  For Your name's sake!
¹⁰ Why should the nations say,
  "Where *is* their God?"
  Let there be known among the
    nations in our sight

The Language of the Heart

Rabbi Harold S. Kushner writes in *When All You've Ever Wanted Isn't Enough*:

"A business associate of my father's died under particularly tragic circumstances, and I accompanied my father to the funeral. The man's widow and children were surrounded by clergy and psychiatrists trying to ease their grief and make them feel better. They knew all the right words, but nothing helped. They were beyond being comforted. The widow kept saying, 'You're right, I know you're right, but it doesn't make any difference.'

"Then a man walked in, a big burly man in his eighties who was a legend in the toy and game industry. He had come to this country illiterate and penniless and had built up an immensely successful company. He was known as a hard bargainer, a ruthless competitor. Despite his success, he had never learned to read or write. . . . He had been sick recently, and his face and his walking showed it. But he walked over to the widow and started to cry, and she cried with him, and you could feel the atmosphere in the room change. This man who had never read a book in his life spoke the language of the heart and held the key that opened the gates of solace where learned doctors and clergy could not."

The Bible tells us to mourn with those who mourn and rejoice with those who rejoice. As women, we often feel the need to "fix" whatever is wrong, to somehow make the problem go away. What hurting people need most is a listening ear, a comforting shoulder, a sympathizing hug — unconditional love.

The avenging of the blood of Your
servants *which has been* shed.

~ PROVERBS 20:10–12 ~

10 Diverse weights *and* diverse
    measures,
    They *are* both alike, an abomination
    to the LORD.

11 Even a child is known by his deeds,
    Whether what he does *is* pure and
    right.

12 The hearing ear and the seeing eye,
    The LORD has made them both.

~ ACTS 12:1–25 ~

Now about that time Herod the king
stretched out *his* hand to harass some from
the church. ² Then he killed James the
brother of John with the sword. ³ And
because he saw that it pleased the Jews,
he proceeded further to seize Peter also.
Now it was *during* the Days of Unleavened Bread. ⁴ So when he had arrested
him, he put *him* in prison, and delivered
him to four squads of soldiers to keep him,
intending to bring him before the people
after Passover.

⁵ Peter was therefore kept in prison, but
constant prayer was offered to God for
him by the church. ⁶ And when Herod was
about to bring him out, that night Peter
was sleeping, bound with two chains
between two soldiers; and the guards before the door were keeping the prison.
⁷ Now behold, an angel of the Lord stood
by *him,* and a light shone in the prison;
and he struck Peter on the side and raised
him up, saying, "Arise quickly!" And his
chains fell off *his* hands. ⁸ Then the angel
said to him, "Gird yourself and tie on your
sandals"; and so he did. And he said to
him, "Put on your garment and follow
me." ⁹ So he went out and followed him,
and did not know that what was done by
the angel was real, but thought he was
seeing a vision. ¹⁰ When they were past
the first and the second guard posts, they
came to the iron gate that leads to the
city, which opened to them of its own

accord; and they went out and went down
one street, and immediately the angel departed from him.

¹¹ And when Peter had come to himself, he said, "Now I know for certain that
the Lord has sent His angel, and has delivered me from the hand of Herod and
from all the expectation of the Jewish
people."

¹² So, when he had considered *this,* he
came to the house of Mary, the mother of
John whose surname was Mark, where
many were gathered together praying.
¹³ And as Peter knocked at the door of the
gate, a girl named Rhoda came to answer.
¹⁴ When she recognized Peter's voice, because of *her* gladness she did not open the
gate, but ran in and announced that Peter
stood before the gate. ¹⁵ But they said to
her, "You are beside yourself!" Yet she kept
insisting that it was so. So they said, "It is
his angel."

¹⁶ Now Peter continued knocking; and
when they opened *the door* and saw him,
they were astonished. ¹⁷ But motioning to
them with his hand to keep silent, he declared to them how the Lord had brought
him out of the prison. And he said, "Go,
tell these things to James and to the
brethren." And he departed and went to
another place.

¹⁸ Then, as soon as it was day, there was
no small stir among the soldiers about
what had become of Peter. ¹⁹ But when
Herod had searched for him and not
found him, he examined the guards and
commanded that *they* should be put to
death.

And he went down from Judea to
Caesarea, and stayed *there.*

²⁰ Now Herod had been very angry with
the people of Tyre and Sidon; but they
came to him with one accord, and having
made Blastus the king's personal aide their
friend, they asked for peace, because
their country was supplied with food by
the king's *country.*

²¹ So on a set day Herod, arrayed in
royal apparel, sat on his throne and gave
an oration to them. ²² And the people kept
shouting, "The voice of a god and not of
a man!" ²³ Then immediately an angel
of the Lord struck him, because he did
not give glory to God. And he was eaten
by worms and died.

²⁴ But the word of God grew and multiplied.

²⁵ And Barnabas and Saul returned from Jerusalem when they had fulfilled *their* ministry, and they also took with them John whose surname was Mark.

~ 2 CHRONICLES 5:1—6:42 ~

So all the work that Solomon had done for the house of the LORD was finished; and Solomon brought in the things which his father David had dedicated: the silver and the gold and all the furnishings. And he put *them* in the treasuries of the house of God.

² Now Solomon assembled the elders of Israel and all the heads of the tribes, the chief fathers of the children of Israel, in Jerusalem, that they might bring the ark of the covenant of the LORD up from the City of David, which *is* Zion. ³ Therefore all the men of Israel assembled with the king at the feast, which *was* in the seventh month. ⁴ So all the elders of Israel came, and the Levites took up the ark. ⁵ Then they brought up the ark, the tabernacle of meeting, and all the holy furnishings that *were* in the tabernacle. The priests and the Levites brought them up. ⁶ Also King Solomon, and all the congregation of Israel who were assembled with him before the ark, *were* sacrificing sheep and oxen that could not be counted or numbered for multitude. ⁷ Then the priests brought in the ark of the covenant of the LORD to its place, into the inner sanctuary of the temple, to the Most Holy *Place*, under the wings of the cherubim. ⁸ For the cherubim spread *their* wings over the place of the ark, and the cherubim overshadowed the ark and its poles. ⁹ The poles extended so that the ends of the poles of the ark could be seen from *the holy place,* in front of the inner sanctuary; but they could not be seen from outside. And they are there to this day. ¹⁰ Nothing *was* in the ark except the two tablets which Moses put *there* at Horeb, when the LORD made *a covenant* with the children of Israel, when they had come out of Egypt.

¹¹ And it came to pass when the priests came out of the *Most* Holy *Place* (for all the priests who *were* present had sancti-

fied themselves, without keeping to their divisions), ¹² and the Levites *who were* the singers, all those of Asaph and Heman and Jeduthun, with their sons and their brethren, stood at the east end of the altar, clothed in white linen, having cymbals, stringed instruments and harps, and with them one hundred and twenty priests sounding with trumpets— ¹³ indeed it came to pass, when the trumpeters and singers *were* as one, to make one sound to be heard in praising and thanking the LORD, and when they lifted up their voice with the trumpets and cymbals and instruments of music, and praised the LORD, *saying:*

> "*For He is* good,
> For His mercy *endures* forever,"

that the house, the house of the LORD, was filled with a cloud, ¹⁴ so that the priests could not continue ministering because of the cloud; for the glory of the LORD filled the house of God.

6 Then Solomon spoke:

> "The LORD said He would dwell in the dark cloud.
> ²   I have surely built You an exalted house,
>   And a place for You to dwell in forever."

³ Then the king turned around and blessed the whole assembly of Israel, while all the assembly of Israel was standing. ⁴ And he said: "Blessed *be* the LORD God of Israel, who has fulfilled with His hands *what* He spoke with His mouth to my father David, saying, ⁵ 'Since the day that I brought My people out of the land of Egypt, I have chosen no city from any tribe of Israel *in which* to build a house, that My name might be there, nor did I choose

any man to be a ruler over My people Israel. [6] Yet I have chosen Jerusalem, that My name may be there, and I have chosen David to be over My people Israel.' [7] Now it was in the heart of my father David to build a temple for the name of the LORD God of Israel. [8] But the LORD said to my father David, 'Whereas it was in your heart to build a temple for My name, you did well in that it was in your heart. [9] Nevertheless you shall not build the temple, but your son who will come from your body, he shall build the temple for My name.' [10] So the LORD has fulfilled His word which He spoke, and I have filled the position of my father David, and sit on the throne of Israel, as the LORD promised; and I have built the temple for the name of the LORD God of Israel. [11] And there I have put the ark, in which *is* the covenant of the LORD which He made with the children of Israel."

[12] Then *Solomon* stood before the altar of the LORD in the presence of all the assembly of Israel, and spread out his hands [13](for Solomon had made a bronze platform five cubits long, five cubits wide, and three cubits high, and had set it in the midst of the court; and he stood on it, knelt down on his knees before all the assembly of Israel, and spread out his hands toward heaven); [14] and he said: "LORD God of Israel, *there is* no God in heaven or on earth like You, who keep *Your* covenant and mercy with Your servants who walk before You with all their hearts. [15] You have kept what You promised Your servant David my father; You have both spoken with Your mouth and fulfilled *it* with Your hand, as *it is* this day. [16] Therefore, LORD God of Israel, now keep what You promised Your servant David my father, saying, 'You shall not fail to have a man sit before Me on the throne of Israel, only if your sons take heed to their way, that they walk in My law as you have walked before Me.' [17] And now, O LORD God of Israel, let Your word come true, which You have spoken to Your servant David.

[18] "But will God indeed dwell with men on the earth? Behold, heaven and the heaven of heavens cannot contain You. How much less this temple which I have built! [19] Yet regard the prayer of Your ser-

vant and his supplication, O LORD my God, and listen to the cry and the prayer which Your servant is praying before You: [20] that Your eyes may be open toward this temple day and night, toward the place where *You* said *You would* put Your name, that You may hear the prayer which Your servant makes toward this place. [21] And may You hear the supplications of Your servant and of Your people Israel, when they pray toward this place. Hear from heaven Your dwelling place, and when You hear, forgive.

[22] "If anyone sins against his neighbor, and is forced to take an oath, and comes *and* takes an oath before Your altar in this temple, [23] then hear from heaven, and act, and judge Your servants, bringing retribution on the wicked by bringing his way on his own head, and justifying the righteous by giving him according to his righteousness.

[24] "Or if Your people Israel are defeated before an enemy because they have sinned against You, and return and confess Your name, and pray and make supplication before You in this temple, [25] then hear from heaven and forgive the sin of Your people Israel, and bring them back to the land which You gave to them and their fathers.

[26] "When the heavens are shut up and there is no rain because they have sinned against You, when they pray toward this place and confess Your name, and turn from their sin because You afflict them, [27] then hear *in* heaven, and forgive the sin of Your servants, Your people Israel, that You may teach them the good way in which they should walk; and send rain on Your land which You have given to Your people as an inheritance.

[28] "When there is famine in the land, pestilence or blight or mildew, locusts or grasshoppers; when their enemies besiege them in the land of their cities; whatever plague or whatever sickness *there is;* [29] whatever prayer, whatever supplication is *made* by anyone, or by all Your people Israel, when each one knows his own burden and his own grief, and spreads out his hands to this temple: [30] then hear from heaven Your dwelling place, and forgive, and give to everyone according to all his ways, whose heart You know (for You

Changing Course

Admiral Sir Thomas Williams was in command of a ship that routinely crossed the Atlantic. His course brought him in sight of Ascension Island, which was uninhabited most of the time. It was visited only once a year for the purpose of collecting turtles.

During one crossing, the island was barely visible on the horizon when Sir Thomas felt a great urge to steer his vessel toward it. The closer he came to the island, the greater the urgency grew. When he gave the order to head for the island, his lieutenant officer respectfully pointed out that such a course change would greatly delay them. Even so, the admiral remained intent. The inner urging, which he had come to recognize as God's Spirit inside him, was very strong.

As the ship neared the island, his crew spotted a white flag. "It must be a signal!" Williams concluded. Sure enough, as the ship neared the beach they found sixteen men who had wrecked on the coast many days before. They were starving and had nearly given up hope of rescue.

In prayer, we are called upon to yield the rudder of our soul to God, so that He might steer us toward opportunities to bless or help others.

> Lord God of Israel, there is no God in heaven or on earth like You, who keep Your covenant and mercy with Your servants who walk before You with all their hearts.
>
> *2 Chronicles 6:14*

alone know the hearts of the sons of men), [31] that they may fear You, to walk in Your ways as long as they live in the land which You gave to our fathers.

[32] "Moreover, concerning a foreigner, who is not of Your people Israel, but has come from a far country for the sake of Your great name and Your mighty hand and Your outstretched arm, when they come and pray in this temple; [33] then hear from heaven Your dwelling place, and do according to all for which the foreigner calls to You, that all peoples of the earth may know Your name and fear You, as *do* Your people Israel, and that they may know that this temple which I have built is called by Your name.

[34] "When Your people go out to battle against their enemies, wherever You send them, and when they pray to You toward this city which You have chosen and the temple which I have built for Your name, [35] then hear from heaven their prayer and their supplication, and maintain their cause.

[36] "When they sin against You (for *there is* no one who does not sin), and You become angry with them and deliver them to the enemy, and they take them captive to a land far or near; [37] *yet* when they come to themselves in the land where they were carried captive, and repent, and make supplication to You in the land of their captivity, saying, 'We have sinned, we have done wrong, and have committed wickedness'; [38] and *when* they return to You with all their heart and with all their soul in the land of their captivity, where they have been carried captive, and pray toward their land which You gave to their fathers, the city which You have chosen, and toward the temple which I have built for Your name: [39] then hear from heaven Your dwelling place their prayer and their supplications, and maintain their cause, and forgive Your people who have sinned against You. [40] Now, my God, I pray, let Your eyes be open and *let* Your ears *be* attentive to the prayer *made* in this place.

[41] "Now therefore,
Arise, O LORD God, to Your
resting place,
You and the ark of Your strength.

Let Your priests, O LORD God, be
clothed with salvation,
And let Your saints rejoice in
goodness.

[42] "O LORD God, do not turn away
the face of Your Anointed;
Remember the mercies of Your
servant David."

∼ PSALM 79:11–13 ∼

[11] Let the groaning of the prisoner
come before You;
According to the greatness of Your
power
Preserve those who are appointed to
die;
[12] And return to our neighbors
sevenfold into their bosom
Their reproach with which they have
reproached You, O Lord.

[13] So we, Your people and sheep of
Your pasture,
Will give You thanks forever;
We will show forth Your praise to all
generations.

∼ PROVERBS 20:13, 14 ∼

[13] Do not love sleep, lest you come to
poverty;
Open your eyes, *and* you will be
satisfied with bread.

[14] "*It is* good for nothing," cries the
buyer;
But when he has gone his way, then
he boasts.

∼ ACTS 13:1–25 ∼

Now in the church that was at Antioch there were certain prophets and teachers: Barnabas, Simeon who was called Niger, Lucius of Cyrene, Manaen who had been brought up with Herod the tetrarch, and Saul. [2] As they ministered to the Lord and fasted, the Holy Spirit said, "Now separate to Me Barnabas and Saul for the work to which I have called them." [3] Then, having fasted and prayed, and laid hands on them, they sent *them* away.

⁴ So, being sent out by the Holy Spirit, they went down to Seleucia, and from there they sailed to Cyprus. ⁵ And when they arrived in Salamis, they preached the word of God in the synagogues of the Jews. They also had John as *their* assistant.

⁶ Now when they had gone through the island to Paphos, they found a certain sorcerer, a false prophet, a Jew whose name *was* Bar-Jesus, ⁷ who was with the proconsul, Sergius Paulus, an intelligent man. This man called for Barnabas and Saul and sought to hear the word of God. ⁸ But Elymas the sorcerer (for so his name is translated) withstood them, seeking to turn the proconsul away from the faith. ⁹ Then Saul, who also *is called* Paul, filled with the Holy Spirit, looked intently at him ¹⁰ and said, "O full of all deceit and all fraud, *you* son of the devil, *you* enemy of all righteousness, will you not cease perverting the straight ways of the Lord? ¹¹ And now, indeed, the hand of the Lord *is* upon you, and you shall be blind, not seeing the sun for a time."

And immediately a dark mist fell on him, and he went around seeking someone to lead him by the hand. ¹² Then the proconsul believed, when he saw what had been done, being astonished at the teaching of the Lord.

¹³ Now when Paul and his party set sail from Paphos, they came to Perga in Pamphylia; and John, departing from them, returned to Jerusalem. ¹⁴ But when they departed from Perga, they came to Antioch in Pisidia, and went into the synagogue on the Sabbath day and sat down. ¹⁵ And after the reading of the Law and the Prophets, the rulers of the synagogue sent to them, saying, "Men *and* brethren, if you have any word of exhortation for the people, say on."

¹⁶ Then Paul stood up, and motioning with *his* hand said, "Men of Israel, and you who fear God, listen: ¹⁷ The God of this people Israel chose our fathers, and exalted the people when they dwelt as strangers in the land of Egypt, and with an uplifted arm He brought them out of it. ¹⁸ Now for a time of about forty years He put up with their ways in the wilderness. ¹⁹ And when He had destroyed seven nations in the land of Canaan, He distributed their land to them by allotment.

²⁰ "After that He gave *them* judges for about four hundred and fifty years, until Samuel the prophet. ²¹ And afterward they asked for a king; so God gave them Saul the son of Kish, a man of the tribe of Benjamin, for forty years. ²² And when He had removed him, He raised up for them David as king, to whom also He gave testimony and said, 'I have found David the *son* of Jesse, a man after My *own* heart, who will do all My will.' ²³ From this man's seed, according to *the* promise, God raised up for Israel a Savior—Jesus— ²⁴ after John had first preached, before His coming, the baptism of repentance to all the people of Israel. ²⁵ And as John was finishing his course, he said, 'Who do you think I am? I am not *He*. But behold, there comes One after me, the sandals of whose feet I am not worthy to loose.'

READING 187 · JULY 6

∼ 2 CHRONICLES 7:1—8:18 ∼

When Solomon had finished praying, fire came down from heaven and consumed the burnt offering and the sacrifices; and the glory of the LORD filled the temple. ² And the priests could not enter the house of the LORD, because the glory of the LORD had filled the LORD's house. ³ When all the children of Israel saw how the fire came down, and the glory of the LORD on the temple, they bowed their faces to the ground on the pavement, and worshiped and praised the LORD, *saying:*

"For *He is* good,
For His mercy *endures* forever."

⁴ Then the king and all the people offered sacrifices before the LORD. ⁵ King Solomon offered a sacrifice of twenty-two thousand bulls and one hundred and twenty thousand sheep. So the king

and all the people dedicated the house of God. [6] And the priests attended to their services; the Levites also with instruments of the music of the LORD, which King David had made to praise the LORD, saying, "For His mercy *endures* forever," whenever David offered praise by their ministry. The priests sounded trumpets opposite them, while all Israel stood.

[7] Furthermore Solomon consecrated the middle of the court that *was* in front of the house of the LORD; for there he offered burnt offerings and the fat of the peace offerings, because the bronze altar which Solomon had made was not able to receive the burnt offerings, the grain offerings, and the fat.

[8] At that time Solomon kept the feast seven days, and all Israel with him, a very great assembly from the entrance of Hamath to the Brook of Egypt. [9] And on the eighth day they held a sacred assembly, for they observed the dedication of the altar seven days, and the feast seven days. [10] On the twenty-third day of the seventh month he sent the people away to their tents, joyful and glad of heart for the good that the LORD had done for David, for Solomon, and for His people Israel. [11] Thus Solomon finished the house of the LORD and the king's house; and Solomon successfully accomplished all that came into his heart to make in the house of the LORD and in his own house.

[12] Then the LORD appeared to Solomon by night, and said to him: "I have heard your prayer, and have chosen this place for Myself as a house of sacrifice. [13] When I shut up heaven and there is no rain, or command the locusts to devour the land, or send pestilence among My people, [14] if My people who are called by My name will humble themselves, and pray and seek My face, and turn from their wicked ways, then I will hear from heaven, and will forgive their sin and heal their land. [15] Now My eyes will be open and My ears attentive to prayer *made* in this place. [16] For now I have chosen and sanctified this house, that My name may be there forever; and My eyes and My heart will be there perpetually. [17] As for you, if you walk before Me as your father David walked, and do according to all that I have commanded you, and if you keep My statutes

and My judgments, [18] then I will establish the throne of your kingdom, as I covenanted with David your father, saying, 'You shall not fail *to have* a man as ruler in Israel.'

[19] "But if you turn away and forsake My statutes and My commandments which I have set before you, and go and serve other gods, and worship them, [20] then I will uproot them from My land which I have given them; and this house which I have sanctified for My name I will cast out of My sight, and will make it a proverb and a byword among all peoples.

[21] "And *as for* this house, which is exalted, everyone who passes by it will be astonished and say, 'Why has the LORD done thus to this land and this house?' [22] Then they will answer, 'Because they forsook the LORD God of their fathers, who brought them out of the land of Egypt, and embraced other gods, and worshiped them and served them; therefore He has brought all this calamity on them.' "

8 It came to pass at the end of twenty years, when Solomon had built the house of the LORD and his own house, [2] that the cities which Hiram had given to Solomon, Solomon built them; and he settled the children of Israel there. [3] And Solomon went to Hamath Zobah and seized it. [4] He also built Tadmor in the wilderness, and all the storage cities which he built in Hamath. [5] He built Upper Beth Horon and Lower Beth Horon, fortified cities *with* walls, gates, and bars, [6] also Baalath and all the storage cities that Solomon had, and all the chariot cities and the cities of the cavalry, and all that Solomon desired to build in Jerusalem, in Lebanon, and in all the land of his dominion.

[7] All the people *who were* left of the Hittites, Amorites, Perizzites, Hivites, and Jebusites, who *were* not of Israel— [8] that is, their descendants who were left in the land after them, whom the children of Israel did not destroy—from these Solomon raised forced labor, as it is to this day. [9] But Solomon did not make the children of Israel servants for his work. Some *were* men of war, captains of his officers, captains of his chariots, and his cavalry. [10] And others *were* chiefs of

Bearing Fruit

An Arab proverb illustrates the concept that as the tares and wheat grow, they show which God has blessed. The stalks of wheat bow their heads because God has blessed them with abundant grain. The more fruitful they are, the lower their heads. The tares lift their heads up high above the wheat, for they are empty of grain.

D. L. Moody once said, "I have a pear tree on my farm that is very beautiful; it appears to be one of the most beautiful trees on my place. Every branch seems to be reaching up to the light and stands almost like a wax candle, but I never get any fruit from it. I have another tree, which was so full of fruit last year that the branches almost touched the ground. If we only get down low enough, my friends, God will use every one of us to His glory. . . . The holiest Christians are the humblest."

When our prayers focus only on ourselves and our needs, they bear little fruit. When our prayers are focused on the Lord and *His* desires, they produce a great harvest. To yield what *we* want to what *He* wants is not only the key to prayer, but the key to success in every area of our lives.

> If My people who are called by My name will humble themselves, and pray and seek My face, and turn from their wicked ways, then I will hear from heaven, and will forgive their sin and heal their land.
>
> *2 Chronicles 7:14*

the officials of King Solomon: two hundred and fifty, who ruled over the people.

[11] Now Solomon brought the daughter of Pharaoh up from the City of David to the house he had built for her, for he said, "My wife shall not dwell in the house of David king of Israel, because *the places* to which the ark of the LORD has come are holy."

[12] Then Solomon offered burnt offerings to the LORD on the altar of the LORD which he had built before the vestibule, [13] according to the daily rate, offering according to the commandment of Moses, for the Sabbaths, the New Moons, and the three appointed yearly feasts—the Feast of Unleavened Bread, the Feast of Weeks, and the Feast of Tabernacles. [14] And, according to the order of David his father, he appointed the divisions of the priests for their service, the Levites for their duties (to praise and serve before the priests) as the duty of each day required, and the gatekeepers by their divisions at each gate; for so David the man of God had commanded. [15] They did not depart from the command of the king to the priests and Levites concerning any matter or concerning the treasuries.

[16] Now all the work of Solomon was well-ordered from the day of the foundation of the house of the LORD until it was finished. So the house of the LORD was completed.

[17] Then Solomon went to Ezion Geber and Elath on the seacoast, in the land of Edom. [18] And Hiram sent him ships by the hand of his servants, and servants who knew the sea. They went with the servants of Solomon to Ophir, and acquired four hundred and fifty talents of gold from there, and brought it to King Solomon.

~ PSALM 80:1–6 ~

[1]   Give ear, O Shepherd of Israel,
      You who lead Joseph like a flock;
      You who dwell *between* the
          cherubim, shine forth!
[2]   Before Ephraim, Benjamin, and
          Manasseh,
      Stir up Your strength,
      And come *and* save us!

[3]   Restore us, O God;
      Cause Your face to shine,
      And we shall be saved!

[4]   O LORD God of hosts,
      How long will You be angry
      Against the prayer of Your people?
[5]   You have fed them with the bread of
          tears,
      And given them tears to drink in
          great measure.
[6]   You have made us a strife to our
          neighbors,
      And our enemies laugh among
          themselves.

~ PROVERBS 20:15 ~

[15] There is gold and a multitude of
          rubies,
      But the lips of knowledge *are* a
          precious jewel.

~ ACTS 13:26–52 ~

"Men *and* brethren, sons of the family of Abraham, and those among you who fear God, to you the word of this salvation has been sent. [27] For those who dwell in Jerusalem, and their rulers, because they did not know Him, nor even the voices of the Prophets which are read every Sabbath, have fulfilled *them* in condemning *Him.* [28] And though they found no cause for death *in Him,* they asked Pilate that He should be put to death. [29] Now when they had fulfilled all that was written concerning Him, they took *Him* down from the tree and laid *Him* in a tomb. [30] But God raised Him from the dead. [31] He was seen for many days by those who came up with Him from Galilee to Jerusalem, who are His witnesses to the people. [32] And we declare to you glad tidings— that promise which was made to the fathers. [33] God has fulfilled this for us their children, in that He has raised up Jesus. As it is also written in the second Psalm:

> 'You are My Son,
> Today I have begotten You.'

[34] And that He raised Him from the dead, no more to return to corruption, He has spoken thus:

'I will give you the sure mercies of David.'

[35] Therefore He also says in another *Psalm:*

'You will not allow Your Holy One to see corruption.'

[36] "For David, after he had served his own generation by the will of God, fell asleep, was buried with his fathers, and saw corruption; [37] but He whom God raised up saw no corruption. [38] Therefore let it be known to you, brethren, that through this Man is preached to you the forgiveness of sins; [39] and by Him everyone who believes is justified from all things from which you could not be justified by the law of Moses. [40] Beware therefore, lest what has been spoken in the prophets come upon you:

[41] ' Behold, you despisers,
Marvel and perish!
For I work a work in your days,
A work which you will by no
means believe,
Though one were to declare it to
you.' "

[42] So when the Jews went out of the synagogue, the Gentiles begged that these words might be preached to them the next Sabbath. [43] Now when the congregation had broken up, many of the Jews and devout proselytes followed Paul and Barnabas, who, speaking to them, persuaded them to continue in the grace of God.

[44] On the next Sabbath almost the whole city came together to hear the word of God. [45] But when the Jews saw the multitudes, they were filled with envy; and contradicting and blaspheming, they opposed the things spoken by Paul. [46] Then Paul and Barnabas grew bold and said, "It was necessary that the word of God should be spoken to you first; but since you reject it, and judge yourselves unworthy of everlasting life, behold, we turn to the Gentiles. [47] For so the Lord has commanded us:

'I have set you as a light to the Gentiles,
That you should be for salvation to the ends of the earth.' "

[48] Now when the Gentiles heard this, they were glad and glorified the word of the Lord. And as many as had been appointed to eternal life believed.
[49] And the word of the Lord was being spread throughout all the region. [50] But the Jews stirred up the devout and prominent women and the chief men of the city, raised up persecution against Paul and Barnabas, and expelled them from their region. [51] But they shook off the dust from their feet against them, and came to Iconium. [52] And the disciples were filled with joy and with the Holy Spirit.

READING 188 · JULY 7

~ 2 CHRONICLES 9:1—10:19 ~

Now when the queen of Sheba heard of the fame of Solomon, she came to Jerusalem to test Solomon with hard questions, *having* a very great retinue, camels that bore spices, gold in abundance, and precious stones; and when she came to Solomon, she spoke with him about all that was in her heart. [2] So Solomon answered all her questions; there was nothing so difficult for Solomon that he could not explain it to her. [3] And when the queen of Sheba had seen the wisdom of Solomon, the house that he had built, [4] the food on his table, the seating of his servants, the service of his waiters and their apparel, his cupbearers and their apparel, and his entryway by which he went up to the house of the LORD, there was no more spirit in her.
[5] Then she said to the king: "*It was* a true report which I heard in my own land about your words and your wisdom. [6] However I did not believe their words until I came and saw with my own eyes;

and indeed the half of the greatness of your wisdom was not told me. You exceed the fame of which I heard. [7] Happy *are* your men and happy *are* these your servants, who stand continually before you and hear your wisdom! [8] Blessed be the LORD your God, who delighted in you, setting you on His throne *to be* king for the LORD your God! Because your God has loved Israel, to establish them forever, therefore He made you king over them, to do justice and righteousness."

[9] And she gave the king one hundred and twenty talents of gold, spices in great abundance, and precious stones; there never were any spices such as those the queen of Sheba gave to King Solomon.

[10] Also, the servants of Hiram and the servants of Solomon, who brought gold from Ophir, brought algum wood and precious stones. [11] And the king made walkways *of* the algum wood for the house of the LORD and for the king's house, also harps and stringed instruments for singers; and there were none such *as these* seen before in the land of Judah.

[12] Now King Solomon gave to the queen of Sheba all she desired, whatever she asked, *much more* than she had brought to the king. So she turned and went to her own country, she and her servants.

[13] The weight of gold that came to Solomon yearly was six hundred and sixty-six talents of gold, [14] besides *what* the traveling merchants and traders brought. And all the kings of Arabia and governors of the country brought gold and silver to Solomon. [15] And King Solomon made two hundred large shields of hammered gold; six hundred *shekels* of hammered gold went into each shield. [16] *He* also *made* three hundred shields of hammered gold; three hundred *shekels* of gold went into each shield. The king put them in the House of the Forest of Lebanon.

[17] Moreover the king made a great throne of ivory, and overlaid it with pure gold. [18] The throne *had* six steps, with a footstool of gold, *which were* fastened to the throne; there were armrests on either side of the place of the seat, and two lions stood beside the armrests. [19] Twelve lions stood there, one on each side of the six steps; nothing like *this* had been made for any *other* kingdom.

[20] All King Solomon's drinking vessels *were* gold, and all the vessels of the House of the Forest of Lebanon *were* pure gold. Not *one was* silver, for this was accounted as nothing in the days of Solomon. [21] For the king's ships went to Tarshish with the servants of Hiram. Once every three years the merchant ships came, bringing gold, silver, ivory, apes, and monkeys.

[22] So King Solomon surpassed all the kings of the earth in riches and wisdom. [23] And all the kings of the earth sought the presence of Solomon to hear his wisdom, which God had put in his heart. [24] Each man brought his present: articles of silver and gold, garments, armor, spices, horses, and mules, at a set rate year by year.

[25] Solomon had four thousand stalls for horses and chariots, and twelve thousand horsemen whom he stationed in the chariot cities and with the king at Jerusalem. [26] So he reigned over all the kings from the River to the land of the Philistines, as far as the border of Egypt. [27] The king made silver *as common* in Jerusalem as stones, and he made cedar trees as abundant as the sycamores which *are* in the lowland. [28] And they brought horses to Solomon from Egypt and from all lands.

[29] Now the rest of the acts of Solomon, first and last, *are* they not written in the book of Nathan the prophet, in the prophecy of Ahijah the Shilonite, and in the visions of Iddo the seer concerning Jeroboam the son of Nebat? [30] Solomon reigned in Jerusalem over all Israel forty years. [31] Then Solomon rested with his fathers, and was buried in the City of David his father. And Rehoboam his son reigned in his place.

10 And Rehoboam went to Shechem, for all Israel had gone to Shechem to make him king. [2] So it happened, when Jeroboam the son of Nebat heard *it* (he was in Egypt, where he had fled from the presence of King Solomon), that Jeroboam returned from Egypt. [3] Then they sent for him and called him. And Jeroboam and all Israel came and spoke to Rehoboam, saying, [4] "Your father made

Taking Action

In the winter of 1995, a fishing boat began to sink in the rough, cold waters off Vancouver Island, west of British Columbia, Canada. The two men on board quickly moved to a life raft that was tied to the sinking boat by a nylon rope. Unfortunately, the rope was tied so tightly, they could not untie it.

As the fishing vessel began to take on more and more water, the men knew they couldn't reboard it. Neither of them had brought a knife onto the life raft with which to cut the raft free from the sinking ship. Both men knew that if the boat went down, it would pull the life raft under — and them along with it! They were in severe danger of drowning unless they could find a way to cut the rope.

The two men began to chew the rope, taking turns as each man's jaw became exhausted. One man lost a tooth in the process. They worked steadily and feverishly for more than an hour, and minutes before the fishing boat sank, they chewed through the rope! They survived and were later rescued by another fishing vessel.

Don't let panic keep you from taking action in an adverse situation. Do whatever you find at hand to do!

They stoned Paul and dragged him out of the city, supposing him to be dead. However, when the disciples gathered around him, he rose up and went into the city. And the next day he departed with Barnabas to Derbe.

Acts 14:19-20

our yoke heavy; now therefore, lighten the burdensome service of your father and his heavy yoke which he put on us, and we will serve you."

[5] So he said to them, "Come back to me after three days." And the people departed.

[6] Then King Rehoboam consulted the elders who stood before his father Solomon while he still lived, saying, "How do you advise *me* to answer these people?"

[7] And they spoke to him, saying, "If you are kind to these people, and please them, and speak good words to them, they will be your servants forever."

[8] But he rejected the advice which the elders had given him, and consulted the young men who had grown up with him, who stood before him. [9] And he said to them, "What advice do you give? How should we answer this people who have spoken to me, saying, 'Lighten the yoke which your father put on us'?"

[10] Then the young men who had grown up with him spoke to him, saying, "Thus you should speak to the people who have spoken to you, saying, 'Your father made our yoke heavy, but you make *it* lighter on us'—thus you shall say to them: 'My little *finger* shall be thicker than my father's waist! [11] And now, whereas my father put a heavy yoke on you, I will add to your yoke; my father chastised you with whips, but I *will chastise you* with scourges!' "

[12] So Jeroboam and all the people came to Rehoboam on the third day, as the king had directed, saying, "Come back to me the third day." [13] Then the king answered them roughly. King Rehoboam rejected the advice of the elders, [14] and he spoke to them according to the advice of the young men, saying, "My father made your yoke heavy, but I will add to it; my father chastised you with whips, but I *will chastise you* with scourges!" [15] So the king did not listen to the people; for the turn *of events* was from God, that the LORD might fulfill His word, which He had spoken by the hand of Ahijah the Shilonite to Jeroboam the son of Nebat.

[16] Now when all Israel *saw* that the king did not listen to them, the people answered the king, saying:

"What share have we in David?
    We have no inheritance in the son
        of Jesse.
Every man to your tents, O Israel!
Now see to your own house,
    O David!"

So all Israel departed to their tents. [17] But Rehoboam reigned over the children of Israel who dwelt in the cities of Judah. [18] Then King Rehoboam sent Hadoram, who *was* in charge of revenue; but the children of Israel stoned him with stones, and he died. Therefore King Rehoboam mounted *his* chariot in haste to flee to Jerusalem. [19] So Israel has been in rebellion against the house of David to this day.

~ PSALM 80:7–13 ~

[7] Restore us, O God of hosts;
    Cause Your face to shine,
    And we shall be saved!

[8] You have brought a vine out of
        Egypt;
    You have cast out the nations, and
        planted it.
[9] You prepared *room* for it,
    And caused it to take deep root,
    And it filled the land.
[10] The hills were covered with its
        shadow,
    And the mighty cedars with its
        boughs.
[11] She sent out her boughs to the Sea,
    And her branches to the River.

[12] Why have You broken down her
        hedges,
    So that all who pass by the way
        pluck her *fruit?*
[13] The boar out of the woods uproots
        it,
    And the wild beast of the field
        devours it.

~ PROVERBS 20:16–18 ~

[16] Take the garment of one who is
        surety *for* a stranger,
    And hold it as a pledge *when it* is for
        a seductress.

¹⁷ Bread gained by deceit *is* sweet to a
man,
But afterward his mouth will be
filled with gravel.

¹⁸ Plans are established by counsel;
By wise counsel wage war.

～ ACTS 14:1–28 ～

Now it happened in Iconium that they
went together to the synagogue of the
Jews, and so spoke that a great multitude
both of the Jews and of the Greeks believed. ² But the unbelieving Jews stirred
up the Gentiles and poisoned their minds
against the brethren. ³ Therefore they
stayed there a long time, speaking boldly
in the Lord, who was bearing witness to
the word of His grace, granting signs and
wonders to be done by their hands.
⁴ But the multitude of the city was di-
vided: part sided with the Jews, and part
with the apostles. ⁵ And when a violent
attempt was made by both the Gentiles
and Jews, with their rulers, to abuse and
stone them, ⁶ they became aware of it
and fled to Lystra and Derbe, cities of
Lycaonia, and to the surrounding region.
⁷ And they were preaching the gospel
there.
⁸ And in Lystra a certain man without
strength in his feet was sitting, a cripple
from his mother's womb, who had never
walked. ⁹ *This* man heard Paul speaking.
Paul, observing him intently and seeing
that he had faith to be healed, ¹⁰ said with
a loud voice, "Stand up straight on your
feet!" And he leaped and walked. ¹¹ Now
when the people saw what Paul had done,
they raised their voices, saying in the
Lycaonian *language*, "The gods have come
down to us in the likeness of men!" ¹² And
Barnabas they called Zeus, and Paul,
Hermes, because he was the chief speaker.
¹³ Then the priest of Zeus, whose temple
was in front of their city, brought oxen
and garlands to the gates, intending to
sacrifice with the multitudes.

¹⁴ But when the apostles Barnabas and
Paul heard this, they tore their clothes and
ran in among the multitude, crying out
¹⁵ and saying, "Men, why are you doing
these things? We also are men with the
same nature as you, and preach to you
that you should turn from these useless
things to the living God, who made the
heaven, the earth, the sea, and all things
that are in them, ¹⁶ who in bygone generations allowed all nations to walk in
their own ways. ¹⁷ Nevertheless He did
not leave Himself without witness, in that
He did good, gave us rain from heaven
and fruitful seasons, filling our hearts with
food and gladness." ¹⁸ And with these sayings they could scarcely restrain the
multitudes from sacrificing to them.
¹⁹ Then Jews from Antioch and Iconium
came there; and having persuaded the
multitudes, they stoned Paul *and* dragged
him out of the city, supposing him to be
dead. ²⁰ However, when the disciples gathered around him, he rose up and went
into the city. And the next day he departed
with Barnabas to Derbe.
²¹ And when they had preached the
gospel to that city and made many disciples, they returned to Lystra, Iconium,
and Antioch, ²² strengthening the souls of
the disciples, exhorting *them* to continue
in the faith, and *saying,* "We must through
many tribulations enter the kingdom of
God." ²³ So when they had appointed
elders in every church, and prayed with
fasting, they commended them to the
Lord in whom they had believed. ²⁴ And
after they had passed through Pisidia, they
came to Pamphylia. ²⁵ Now when they had
preached the word in Perga, they went
down to Attalia. ²⁶ From there they sailed
to Antioch, where they had been com-
mended to the grace of God for the work
which they had completed.
²⁷ Now when they had come and gath-
ered the church together, they reported
all that God had done with them, and that
He had opened the door of faith to the
Gentiles. ²⁸ So they stayed there a long
time with the disciples.

~ 2 CHRONICLES 11:1—12:16 ~

Now when Rehoboam came to Jerusalem, he assembled from the house of Judah and Benjamin one hundred and eighty thousand chosen *men* who were warriors, to fight against Israel, that he might restore the kingdom to Rehoboam.

2 But the word of the LORD came to Shemaiah the man of God, saying, 3 "Speak to Rehoboam the son of Solomon, king of Judah, and to all Israel in Judah and Benjamin, saying, 4 'Thus says the LORD: "You shall not go up or fight against your brethren! Let every man return to his house, for this thing is from Me." ' " Therefore they obeyed the words of the LORD, and turned back from attacking Jeroboam.

5 So Rehoboam dwelt in Jerusalem, and built cities for defense in Judah. 6 And he built Bethlehem, Etam, Tekoa, 7 Beth Zur, Sochoh, Adullam, 8 Gath, Mareshah, Ziph, 9 Adoraim, Lachish, Azekah, 10 Zorah, Aijalon, and Hebron, which are in Judah and Benjamin, fortified cities. 11 And he fortified the strongholds, and put captains in them, and stores of food, oil, and wine. 12 Also in every city *he put* shields and spears, and made them very strong, having Judah and Benjamin on his side.

13 And from all their territories the priests and the Levites who *were* in all Israel took their stand with him. 14 For the Levites left their common-lands and their possessions and came to Judah and Jerusalem, for Jeroboam and his sons had rejected them from serving as priests to the LORD. 15 Then he appointed for himself priests for the high places, for the demons, and the calf idols which he had made. 16 And after *the Levites left,* those from all the tribes of Israel, such as set their heart to seek the LORD God of Israel, came to Jerusalem to sacrifice to the LORD God of their fathers. 17 So they strengthened the kingdom of Judah, and made Rehoboam the son of Solomon strong for three years, because they walked in the way of David and Solomon for three years.

18 Then Rehoboam took for himself as wife Mahalath the daughter of Jerimoth the son of David, *and of* Abihail the daughter of Eliab the son of Jesse. 19 And she bore him children: Jeush, Shamariah, and Zaham. 20 After her he took Maachah the granddaughter of Absalom; and she bore him Abijah, Attai, Ziza, and Shelomith. 21 Now Rehoboam loved Maachah the granddaughter of Absalom more than all his wives and his concubines; for he took eighteen wives and sixty concubines, and begot twenty-eight sons and sixty daughters. 22 And Rehoboam appointed Abijah the son of Maachah as chief, *to be* leader among his brothers; for he *intended* to make him king. 23 He dealt wisely, and dispersed some of his sons throughout all the territories of Judah and Benjamin, to every fortified city; and he gave them provisions in abundance. He also sought many wives *for them.*

12 Now it came to pass, when Rehoboam had established the kingdom and had strengthened himself, that he forsook the law of the LORD, and all Israel along with him. 2 And it happened in the fifth year of King Rehoboam *that* Shishak king of Egypt came up against Jerusalem, because they had transgressed against the LORD, 3 with twelve hundred chariots, sixty thousand horsemen, and people without number who came with him out of Egypt—the Lubim and the Sukkiim and the Ethiopians. 4 And he took the fortified cities of Judah and came to Jerusalem.

5 Then Shemaiah the prophet came to Rehoboam and the leaders of Judah, who were gathered together in Jerusalem because of Shishak, and said to them, "Thus says the LORD: 'You have forsaken Me, and therefore I also have left you in the hand of Shishak.' "

6 So the leaders of Israel and the king humbled themselves; and they said, "The LORD *is* righteous."

7 Now when the LORD saw that they humbled themselves, the word of the LORD came to Shemaiah, saying, "They have humbled themselves; *therefore* I will not destroy them, but I will grant them

Different, but the Same

At the height of the segregation storm in the United States, a six-year-old girl headed out for her first day of school. Her elementary school was one that had been integrated recently and the community was still full of tension. After school her mother met her anxiously at the door, eager to hear how the day had gone. "Did everything go alright, honey?" she asked.

"Oh, Mother! You know what?" the little girl said eagerly, "A little black girl sat next to me."

With growing apprehension the mother asked, "And what happened?"

The little girl replied, "We were both so scared about our first day at school that we held hands all day."

Often, jealousy and hate are born out of a lack of information — we simply don't know a person or an individual member of a group. Once we discover the many things that we share in common with another person — including our fears, our hopes, our concerns, our desires — our differences simply enhance our relationships.

When we allow one another our unique differences, love grows.

> So God, who knows the heart, acknowledged them by giving them the Holy Spirit, just as He did to us, and made no distinction between us and them, purifying their hearts by faith.
>
> *Acts 15:8-9*

some deliverance. My wrath shall not be poured out on Jerusalem by the hand of Shishak. ⁸ Nevertheless they will be his servants, that they may distinguish My service from the service of the kingdoms of the nations."

⁹ So Shishak king of Egypt came up against Jerusalem, and took away the treasures of the house of the LORD and the treasures of the king's house; he took everything. He also carried away the gold shields which Solomon had made. ¹⁰ Then King Rehoboam made bronze shields in their place, and committed *them* to the hands of the captains of the guard, who guarded the doorway of the king's house. ¹¹ And whenever the king entered the house of the LORD, the guard would go and bring them out; then they would take them back into the guardroom. ¹² When he humbled himself, the wrath of the LORD turned from him, so as not to destroy *him* completely; and things also went well in Judah.

¹³ Thus King Rehoboam strengthened himself in Jerusalem and reigned. Now Rehoboam *was* forty-one years old when he became king; and he reigned seventeen years in Jerusalem, the city which the LORD had chosen out of all the tribes of Israel, to put His name there. His mother's name *was* Naamah, an Ammonitess. ¹⁴ And he did evil, because he did not prepare his heart to seek the LORD.

¹⁵ The acts of Rehoboam, first and last, *are* they not written in the book of Shemaiah the prophet, and of Iddo the seer concerning genealogies? And *there were* wars between Rehoboam and Jeroboam all their days. ¹⁶ So Rehoboam rested with his fathers, and was buried in the City of David. Then Abijah his son reigned in his place.

∼ PSALM 80:14–19 ∼

¹⁴ Return, we beseech You, O God of hosts;
Look down from heaven and see,
And visit this vine
¹⁵ And the vineyard which Your right hand has planted,
And the branch *that* You made strong for Yourself.
¹⁶ *It is* burned with fire, *it is* cut down;

They perish at the rebuke of Your countenance.
¹⁷ Let Your hand be upon the man of Your right hand,
Upon the son of man *whom* You made strong for Yourself.
¹⁸ Then we will not turn back from You;
Revive us, and we will call upon Your name.

¹⁹ Restore us, O LORD God of hosts;
Cause Your face to shine,
And we shall be saved!

∼ PROVERBS 20:19–21 ∼

¹⁹ He who goes about *as* a talebearer reveals secrets;
Therefore do not associate with one who flatters with his lips.

²⁰ Whoever curses his father or his mother,
His lamp will be put out in deep darkness.

²¹ An inheritance gained hastily at the beginning
Will not be blessed at the end.

∼ ACTS 15:1–21 ∼

And certain *men* came down from Judea and taught the brethren, "Unless you are circumcised according to the custom of Moses, you cannot be saved." ² Therefore, when Paul and Barnabas had no small dissension and dispute with them, they determined that Paul and Barnabas and certain others of them should go up to Jerusalem, to the apostles and elders, about this question.

³ So, being sent on their way by the church, they passed through Phoenicia and Samaria, describing the conversion of the Gentiles; and they caused great joy to all the brethren. ⁴ And when they had come to Jerusalem, they were received by the church and the apostles and the elders; and they reported all things that God had done with them. ⁵ But some of the sect of the Pharisees who believed rose up, saying, "It is necessary to circumcise

them, and to command *them* to keep the law of Moses."

⁶ Now the apostles and elders came together to consider this matter. ⁷ And when there had been much dispute, Peter rose up and said to them: "Men and brethren, you know that a good while ago God chose among us, that by my mouth the Gentiles should hear the word of the gospel and believe. ⁸ So God, who knows the heart, acknowledged them by giving them the Holy Spirit, just as *He did* to us, ⁹ and made no distinction between us and them, purifying their hearts by faith. ¹⁰ Now therefore, why do you test God by putting a yoke on the neck of the disciples which neither our fathers nor we were able to bear? ¹¹ But we believe that through the grace of the Lord Jesus Christ we shall be saved in the same manner as they."

¹² Then all the multitude kept silent and listened to Barnabas and Paul declaring how many miracles and wonders God had worked through them among the Gentiles. ¹³ And after they had become silent, James answered, saying, "Men *and* brethren, listen to me: ¹⁴ Simon has declared how God at the first visited the Gentiles to take out of them a people for His name. ¹⁵ And with this the words of the prophets agree, just as it is written:

¹⁶ ' After this I will return
　　And will rebuild the tabernacle of
　　　David, which has fallen down;
　　I will rebuild its ruins,
　　And I will set it up;
¹⁷ 　So that the rest of mankind may
　　　seek the LORD,
　　Even all the Gentiles who are
　　　called by My name,
　　Says the LORD who does all these
　　　things.'

¹⁸ "Known to God from eternity are all His works. ¹⁹ Therefore I judge that we should not trouble those from among the Gentiles who are turning to God, ²⁰ but that we write to them to abstain from things polluted by idols, *from* sexual immorality, *from* things strangled, and *from* blood. ²¹ For Moses has had throughout many generations those who preach him in every city, being read in the synagogues every Sabbath."

READING 190 · JULY 9

~ 2 CHRONICLES 13:1—14:15 ~

In the eighteenth year of King Jeroboam, Abijah became king over Judah. ² He reigned three years in Jerusalem. His mother's name *was* Michaiah the daughter of Uriel of Gibeah.

And there was war between Abijah and Jeroboam. ³ Abijah set the battle in order with an army of valiant warriors, four hundred thousand choice men. Jeroboam also drew up in battle formation against him with eight hundred thousand choice men, mighty men of valor.

⁴ Then Abijah stood on Mount Zemaraim, which *is* in the mountains of Ephraim, and said, "Hear me, Jeroboam and all Israel: ⁵ Should you not know that the LORD God of Israel gave the dominion over Israel to David forever, to him and his sons, by a covenant of salt? ⁶ Yet Jeroboam the son of Nebat, the servant of Solomon the son of David, rose up and rebelled against his lord. ⁷ Then worthless rogues gathered to him, and strengthened themselves against Rehoboam the son of Solomon, when Rehoboam was young and inexperienced and could not withstand them. ⁸ And now you think to withstand the kingdom of the LORD, which is in the hand of the sons of David; and you *are* a great multitude, and with you are the gold calves which Jeroboam made for you as gods. ⁹ Have you not cast out the priests of the LORD, the sons of Aaron, and the Levites, and made for yourselves priests, like the peoples of *other* lands, so that whoever comes to consecrate himself with a young bull and seven rams may be a priest of *things that are* not gods? ¹⁰ But as for us, the LORD *is* our God, and we have not forsaken Him;

and the priests who minister to the LORD *are* the sons of Aaron, and the Levites *attend to their* duties. [11] And they burn to the LORD every morning and every evening burnt sacrifices and sweet incense; *they* also *set* the showbread *in order on* the pure *gold* table, and the lampstand of gold with its lamps to burn every evening; for we keep the command of the LORD our God, but you have forsaken Him. [12] Now look, God Himself is with us as *our* head, and His priests with sounding trumpets to sound the alarm against you. O children of Israel, do not fight against the LORD God of your fathers, for you shall not prosper!"

[13] But Jeroboam caused an ambush to go around behind them; so they were in front of Judah, and the ambush *was* behind them. [14] And when Judah looked around, to their surprise the battle line *was* at both front and rear; and they cried out to the LORD, and the priests sounded the trumpets. [15] Then the men of Judah gave a shout; and as the men of Judah shouted, it happened that God struck Jeroboam and all Israel before Abijah and Judah. [16] And the children of Israel fled before Judah, and God delivered them into their hand. [17] Then Abijah and his people struck them with a great slaughter; so five hundred thousand choice men of Israel fell slain. [18] Thus the children of Israel were subdued at that time; and the children of Judah prevailed, because they relied on the LORD God of their fathers.

[19] And Abijah pursued Jeroboam and took cities from him: Bethel with its villages, Jeshanah with its villages, and Ephrain with its villages. [20] So Jeroboam did not recover strength again in the days of Abijah; and the LORD struck him, and he died.

[21] But Abijah grew mighty, married fourteen wives, and begot twenty-two sons and sixteen daughters. [22] Now the rest of the acts of Abijah, his ways, and his sayings *are* written in the annals of the prophet Iddo.

14 So Abijah rested with his fathers, and they buried him in the City of David. Then Asa his son reigned in his place. In his days the land was quiet for ten years.

[2] Asa did *what was* good and right in the eyes of the LORD his God, [3] for he removed the altars of the foreign *gods* and the high places, and broke down the *sacred* pillars and cut down the wooden images. [4] He commanded Judah to seek the LORD God of their fathers, and to observe the law and the commandment. [5] He also removed the high places and the incense altars from all the cities of Judah, and the kingdom was quiet under him. [6] And he built fortified cities in Judah, for the land had rest; he had no war in those years, because the LORD had given him rest. [7] Therefore he said to Judah, "Let us build these cities and make walls around *them,* and towers, gates, and bars, *while* the land *is* yet before us, because we have sought the LORD our God; we have sought *Him,* and He has given us rest on every side." So they built and prospered. [8] And Asa had an army of three hundred thousand from Judah who carried shields and spears, and from Benjamin two hundred and eighty thousand men who carried shields and drew bows; all these *were* mighty men of valor.

[9] Then Zerah the Ethiopian came out against them with an army of a million men and three hundred chariots, and he came to Mareshah. [10] So Asa went out against him, and they set the troops in battle array in the Valley of Zephathah at Mareshah. [11] And Asa cried out to the LORD his God, and said, "LORD, *it is* nothing for You to help, whether with many or with those who have no power; help us, O LORD our God, for we rest on You, and in Your name we go against this multitude. O LORD, You *are* our God; do not let man prevail against You!"

[12] So the LORD struck the Ethiopians before Asa and Judah, and the Ethiopians fled. [13] And Asa and the people who *were* with him pursued them to Gerar. So the Ethiopians were overthrown, and they could not recover, for they were broken before the LORD and His army. And they carried away very much spoil. [14] Then they defeated all the cities around Gerar, for the fear of the LORD came upon them; and they plundered all the cities, for there was exceedingly much spoil in them. [15] They also attacked the livestock enclosures, and carried off sheep and

Express Lane?

A woman once visited a friend in Cambridge, Massachusetts, the home of several well-known institutions of higher learning. She accompanied the friend to a supermarket on Saturday afternoon, finding it crammed with shoppers and long checkout lines.

While the two of them stood patiently in line, they noticed a young college-age man wheel an obviously full shopping cart into the cash register lane that was clearly marked, "Express Lane — 8 Items Or Less."

The checkout girl looked at the loaded cart and then at the young man. He was trying to ignore her exasperated expression by fumbling in his knapsack for his checkbook.

Realizing she was stuck with a stubborn and inconsiderate customer, the girl said loudly to the high school student who was helping her bag groceries, "This guy either goes to Harvard and can't count, or he goes to MIT and can't read!"

Although we don't always think of it in these terms, our impatience reveals a selfish and often mean spirit, while patience is really a simple act of kindness.

camels in abundance, and returned to Jerusalem.

~ PSALM 81:1–5 ~

1 Sing aloud to God our strength;
  Make a joyful shout to the God of
  Jacob.
2 Raise a song and strike the timbrel,
  The pleasant harp with the lute.

3 Blow the trumpet at the time of the
  New Moon,
  At the full moon, on our solemn
  feast day.
4 For this *is* a statute for Israel,
  A law of the God of Jacob.
5 This He established in Joseph *as* a
  testimony,
  When He went throughout the land
  of Egypt,
  Where I heard a language I did not
  understand.

~ PROVERBS 20:22, 23 ~

22 Do not say, "I will recompense evil";
   Wait for the LORD, and He will save
   you.

23 Diverse weights *are* an abomination
   to the LORD,
   And dishonest scales *are* not good.

~ ACTS 15:22–41 ~

Then it pleased the apostles and elders, with the whole church, to send chosen men of their own company to Antioch with Paul and Barnabas, *namely,* Judas who was also named Barsabas, and Silas, leading men among the brethren. 23 They wrote this *letter* by them:

The apostles, the elders, and the brethren,

To the brethren who are of the Gentiles in Antioch, Syria, and Cilicia:

Greetings.

24 Since we have heard that some who went out from us have troubled you with words, unsettling your souls, saying, "You *must* be circumcised and keep the law"—to whom we gave no *such* commandment— 25 it seemed good to us, being assembled with one accord, to send chosen men to you with our beloved Barnabas and Paul, 26 men who have risked their lives for the name of our Lord Jesus Christ. 27 We have therefore sent Judas and Silas, who will also report the same things by word of mouth. 28 For it seemed good to the Holy Spirit, and to us, to lay upon you no greater burden than these necessary things: 29 that you abstain from things offered to idols, from blood, from things strangled, and from sexual immorality. If you keep yourselves from these, you will do well.

Farewell.

30 So when they were sent off, they came to Antioch; and when they had gathered the multitude together, they delivered the letter. 31 When they had read it, they rejoiced over its encouragement. 32 Now Judas and Silas, themselves being prophets also, exhorted and strengthened the brethren with many words. 33 And after they had stayed *there* for a time, they were sent back with greetings from the brethren to the apostles.
34 However, it seemed good to Silas to remain there. 35 Paul and Barnabas also remained in Antioch, teaching and preaching the word of the Lord, with many others also.
36 Then after some days Paul said to Barnabas, "Let us now go back and visit our brethren in every city where we have preached the word of the Lord, *and see* how they are doing." 37 Now Barnabas was determined to take with them John called Mark. 38 But Paul insisted that they should not take with them the one who had departed from them in Pamphylia, and had not gone with them to the work. 39 Then the contention became so sharp that they parted from one another. And

so Barnabas took Mark and sailed to Cyprus; [40] but Paul chose Silas and departed, being commended by the brethren to the grace of God. [41] And he went through Syria and Cilicia, strengthening the churches.

READING 191 · JULY 10

~ 2 CHRONICLES 15:1—16:14 ~

Now the Spirit of God came upon Azariah the son of Oded. [2] And he went out to meet Asa, and said to him: "Hear me, Asa, and all Judah and Benjamin. The LORD *is* with you while you are with Him. If you seek Him, He will be found by you; but if you forsake Him, He will forsake you. [3] For a long time Israel *has been* without the true God, without a teaching priest, and without law; [4] but when in their trouble they turned to the LORD God of Israel, and sought Him, He was found by them. [5] And in those times *there was* no peace to the one who went out, nor to the one who came in, but great turmoil *was* on all the inhabitants of the lands. [6] So nation was destroyed by nation, and city by city, for God troubled them with every adversity. [7] But you, be strong and do not let your hands be weak, for your work shall be rewarded!"

[8] And when Asa heard these words and the prophecy of Oded the prophet, he took courage, and removed the abominable idols from all the land of Judah and Benjamin and from the cities which he had taken in the mountains of Ephraim; and he restored the altar of the LORD that *was* before the vestibule of the LORD. [9] Then he gathered all Judah and Benjamin, and those who dwelt with them from Ephraim, Manasseh, and Simeon, for they came over to him in great numbers from Israel when they saw that the LORD his God was with him.

[10] So they gathered together at Jerusalem in the third month, in the fifteenth year of the reign of Asa. [11] And they offered to the LORD at that time seven hundred bulls and seven thousand sheep from the spoil they had brought. [12] Then they entered into a covenant to seek the LORD God of their fathers with all their heart and with all their soul; [13] and whoever would not seek the LORD God of Israel was to be put to death, whether small or great, whether man or woman. [14] Then they took an oath before the LORD with a loud voice, with shouting and trumpets and rams' horns. [15] And all Judah rejoiced at the oath, for they had sworn with all their heart and sought Him with all their soul; and He was found by them, and the LORD gave them rest all around.

[16] Also he removed Maachah, the mother of Asa the king, from *being* queen mother, because she had made an obscene image of Asherah; and Asa cut down her obscene image, then crushed and burned *it* by the Brook Kidron. [17] But the high places were not removed from Israel. Nevertheless the heart of Asa was loyal all his days.

[18] He also brought into the house of God the things that his father had dedicated and that he himself had dedicated: silver and gold and utensils. [19] And there was no war until the thirty-fifth year of the reign of Asa.

16 In the thirty-sixth year of the reign of Asa, Baasha king of Israel came up against Judah and built Ramah, that he might let none go out or come in to Asa king of Judah. [2] Then Asa brought silver and gold from the treasuries of the house of the LORD and of the king's house, and sent to Ben-Hadad king of Syria, who dwelt in Damascus, saying, [3] "*Let there be* a treaty between you and me, as there was between my father and your father. See, I have sent you silver and gold; come, break your treaty with Baasha king of Israel, so that he will withdraw from me."

[4] So Ben-Hadad heeded King Asa, and sent the captains of his armies against the cities of Israel. They attacked Ijon, Dan, Abel Maim, and all the storage cities of Naphtali. [5] Now it happened, when Baasha heard *it*, that he stopped building Ramah and ceased his work. [6] Then King

Asa took all Judah, and they carried away the stones and timber of Ramah, which Baasha had used for building; and with them he built Geba and Mizpah.

⁷ And at that time Hanani the seer came to Asa king of Judah, and said to him: "Because you have relied on the king of Syria, and have not relied on the LORD your God, therefore the army of the king of Syria has escaped from your hand. ⁸ Were the Ethiopians and the Lubim not a huge army with very many chariots and horsemen? Yet, because you relied on the LORD, He delivered them into your hand. ⁹ For the eyes of the LORD run to and fro throughout the whole earth, to show Himself strong on behalf of *those* whose heart *is* loyal to Him. In this you have done foolishly; therefore from now on you shall have wars." ¹⁰ Then Asa was angry with the seer, and put him in prison, for *he was* enraged at him because of this. And Asa oppressed *some* of the people at that time.

¹¹ Note that the acts of Asa, first and last, are indeed written in the book of the kings of Judah and Israel. ¹² And in the thirty-ninth year of his reign, Asa became diseased in his feet, and his malady was severe; yet in his disease he did not seek the LORD, but the physicians.

¹³ So Asa rested with his fathers; he died in the forty-first year of his reign. ¹⁴ They buried him in his own tomb, which he had made for himself in the City of David; and they laid him in the bed which was filled with spices and various ingredients prepared in a mixture of ointments. They made a very great burning for him.

∼ PSALM 81:6–10 ∼

⁶ "I removed his shoulder from the burden;
His hands were freed from the baskets.
⁷ You called in trouble, and I delivered you;
I answered you in the secret place of thunder;
I tested you at the waters of Meribah.   Selah

⁸ "Hear, O My people, and I will admonish you!

O Israel, if you will listen to Me!
⁹ There shall be no foreign god among you;
Nor shall you worship any foreign god.
¹⁰ I *am* the LORD your God,
Who brought you out of the land of Egypt;
Open your mouth wide, and I will fill it.

∼ PROVERBS 20:24, 25 ∼

²⁴ A man's steps *are* of the LORD;
How then can a man understand his own way?

²⁵ *It is* a snare for a man to devote rashly *something as* holy,
And afterward to reconsider *his* vows.

∼ ACTS 16:1–21 ∼

Then he came to Derbe and Lystra. And behold, a certain disciple was there, named Timothy, *the* son of a certain Jewish woman who believed, but his father *was* Greek. ² He was well spoken of by the brethren who were at Lystra and Iconium. ³ Paul wanted to have him go on with him. And he took *him* and circumcised him because of the Jews who were in that region, for they all knew that his father was Greek. ⁴ And as they went through the cities, they delivered to them the decrees to keep, which were determined by the apostles and elders at Jerusalem. ⁵ So the churches were strengthened in the faith, and increased in number daily.

⁶ Now when they had gone through Phrygia and the region of Galatia, they were forbidden by the Holy Spirit to preach the word in Asia. ⁷ After they had come to Mysia, they tried to go into Bithynia, but the Spirit did not permit them. ⁸ So passing by Mysia, they came down to Troas. ⁹ And a vision appeared to Paul in the night. A man of Macedonia stood and pleaded with him, saying, "Come over to Macedonia and help us." ¹⁰ Now after he had seen the vision, immediately we sought to go to Macedonia, concluding that the Lord had called us to preach the gospel to them.

Bound by Your Word

In *Up from Slavery*, Booker T. Washington tells of an ex-slave from Virginia: "I found that this man had made a contract with his master, two or three years previous to the Emancipation Proclamation, to the effect that the slave was to be permitted to buy himself, by paying so much per year for his body; and while he was paying for himself, he was to be permitted to labor where and for whom he pleased.

> It is a snare for a man to devote rashly something as holy, and afterward to reconsider his vows.
>
> *Proverbs 20:25*

"Finding that he could secure better wages in Ohio, he went there. When freedom came, he was still in debt to his master some three hundred dollars. Notwithstanding that the Emancipation Proclamation freed him from any obligation to his master, this black man walked the greater portion of the distance back to where his old master lived in Virginia and placed the last dollar, with interest, in his hands.

"In talking to me about this, the man told me that he knew that he did not have to pay his debt, but that he had given his word to his master, and his word he had never broken. He felt that he could not enjoy his freedom till he had fulfilled his promise."

Your word is the highest valued currency you can carry, no matter what your wallet may hold.

[11] Therefore, sailing from Troas, we ran a straight course to Samothrace, and the next *day* came to Neapolis, [12] and from there to Philippi, which is the foremost city of that part of Macedonia, a colony. And we were staying in that city for some days. [13] And on the Sabbath day we went out of the city to the riverside, where prayer was customarily made; and we sat down and spoke to the women who met *there*. [14] Now a certain woman named Lydia heard *us*. She was a seller of purple from the city of Thyatira, who worshiped God. The Lord opened her heart to heed the things spoken by Paul. [15] And when she and her household were baptized, she begged *us*, saying, "If you have judged me to be faithful to the Lord, come to my house and stay." So she persuaded us.

[16] Now it happened, as we went to prayer, that a certain slave girl possessed with a spirit of divination met us, who brought her masters much profit by fortune-telling. [17] This girl followed Paul and us, and cried out, saying, "These men are the servants of the Most High God, who proclaim to us the way of salvation." [18] And this she did for many days.

But Paul, greatly annoyed, turned and said to the spirit, "I command you in the name of Jesus Christ to come out of her." And he came out that very hour. [19] But when her masters saw that their hope of profit was gone, they seized Paul and Silas and dragged *them* into the marketplace to the authorities.

[20] And they brought them to the magistrates, and said, "These men, being Jews, exceedingly trouble our city; [21] and they teach customs which are not lawful for us, being Romans, to receive or observe."

READING 192 · JULY 11

~ 2 CHRONICLES 17:1—18:34 ~

Then Jehoshaphat his son reigned in his place, and strengthened himself against Israel. [2] And he placed troops in all the fortified cities of Judah, and set garrisons in the land of Judah and in the cities of Ephraim which Asa his father had taken. [3] Now the LORD was with Jehoshaphat, because he walked in the former ways of his father David; he did not seek the Baals, [4] but sought the God of his father, and walked in His commandments and not according to the acts of Israel. [5] Therefore the LORD established the kingdom in his hand; and all Judah gave presents to Jehoshaphat, and he had riches and honor in abundance. [6] And his heart took delight in the ways of the LORD; moreover he removed the high places and wooden images from Judah.

[7] Also in the third year of his reign he sent his leaders, Ben-Hail, Obadiah, Zechariah, Nethanel, and Michaiah, to teach in the cities of Judah. [8] And with them *he sent* Levites: Shemaiah, Nethaniah, Zebadiah, Asahel, Shemiramoth, Jehonathan, Adonijah, Tobijah, and Tobadonijah—the Levites; and with them Elishama and Jehoram, the priests. [9] So they taught in Judah, and *had* the Book of the Law of the LORD with them; they went throughout all the cities of Judah and taught the people.

[10] And the fear of the LORD fell on all the kingdoms of the lands that *were* around Judah, so that they did not make war against Jehoshaphat. [11] Also *some* of the Philistines brought Jehoshaphat presents and silver as tribute; and the Arabians brought him flocks, seven thousand seven hundred rams and seven thousand seven hundred male goats.

[12] So Jehoshaphat became increasingly powerful, and he built fortresses and storage cities in Judah. [13] He had much property in the cities of Judah; and the men of war, mighty men of valor, *were* in Jerusalem.

[14] These *are* their numbers, according to their fathers' houses. Of Judah, the captains of thousands: Adnah the captain, and with him three hundred thousand mighty men of valor; [15] and next to him *was* Jehohanan the captain, and with him two hundred and eighty thousand; [16] and next to him *was* Amasiah the son of Zichri, who willingly offered himself

The Tondelayo

In *The Fall of Fortresses*, Elmer Bendiner tells of a miracle that happened to him and a few others aboard their B-17 bomber "The Tondelayo." During a run over Kassel, Germany, the plane was barraged by flack from Nazi antiaircraft guns. That in itself was not unusual, but on this particular flight the fuel tanks of the plane were hit. The crew was amazed that the 20-millimeter shell piercing the tank didn't cause an explosion. The following morning, the pilot, Bohn Fawkes, asked the crew chief for the shell as a souvenir of their unbelievable luck.

Bohn was told that not just one shell had been found in the gas tanks, but eleven! Eleven unexploded shells—it truly seemed to be a miracle.

The shells were sent to the armorers to be defused, and there Intelligence picked them up. Later they informed the Tondelayo crew that when they opened the shells, they found no explosive charge in any of them. They were clean and harmless. One of the shells, however, was not completely empty. It contained a carefully rolled piece of paper. On it was scrawled in the Czech language: "This is all we can do for you now." The miracle had not been one of misfired shells, but of peace-loving hearts.

When we want peace in our homes, we must disarm our weapons — hurtful words, prideful looks, hurtful attitudes. We must do all we can, for when we do, God does all He can — flood our home with His peace and love.

And the Lord said, "These have no master. Let each return to his house in peace."

2 Chronicles 18:16

to the LORD, and with him two hundred thousand mighty men of valor. [17] Of Benjamin: Eliada a mighty man of valor, and with him two hundred thousand men armed with bow and shield; [18] and next to him *was* Jehozabad, and with him one hundred and eighty thousand prepared for war. [19] These served the king, besides those the king put in the fortified cities throughout all Judah.

18 Jehoshaphat had riches and honor in abundance; and by marriage he allied himself with Ahab. [2] After some years he went down to *visit* Ahab in Samaria; and Ahab killed sheep and oxen in abundance for him and the people who were with him, and persuaded him to go up *with him* to Ramoth Gilead. [3] So Ahab king of Israel said to Jehoshaphat king of Judah, "Will you go with me *against* Ramoth Gilead?"

And he answered him, "I *am* as you *are,* and my people as your people; *we will be* with you in the war."

[4] Also Jehoshaphat said to the king of Israel, "Please inquire for the word of the LORD today."

[5] Then the king of Israel gathered the prophets together, four hundred men, and said to them, "Shall we go to war against Ramoth Gilead, or shall I refrain?"

So they said, "Go up, for God will deliver it into the king's hand."

[6] But Jehoshaphat said, "*Is there* not still a prophet of the LORD here, that we may inquire of Him?"

[7] So the king of Israel said to Jehoshaphat, "*There is* still one man by whom we may inquire of the LORD; but I hate him, because he never prophesies good concerning me, but always evil. He *is* Micaiah the son of Imla."

And Jehoshaphat said, "Let not the king say such things!"

[8] Then the king of Israel called one *of his* officers and said, "Bring Micaiah the son of Imla quickly!"

[9] The king of Israel and Jehoshaphat king of Judah, clothed in *their* robes, sat each on his throne; and they sat at a threshing floor at the entrance of the gate of Samaria; and all the prophets prophesied before them. [10] Now Zedekiah the son of Chenaanah had made horns of iron

for himself; and he said, "Thus says the LORD: 'With these you shall gore the Syrians until they are destroyed.' "

[11] And all the prophets prophesied so, saying, "Go up to Ramoth Gilead and prosper, for the LORD will deliver *it* into the king's hand."

[12] Then the messenger who had gone to call Micaiah spoke to him, saying, "Now listen, the words of the prophets with one accord encourage the king. Therefore please let your word be like *the word of* one of them, and speak encouragement."

[13] And Micaiah said, "*As* the LORD lives, whatever my God says, that I will speak."

[14] Then he came to the king; and the king said to him, "Micaiah, shall we go to war against Ramoth Gilead, or shall I refrain?"

And he said, "Go and prosper, and they shall be delivered into your hand!"

[15] So the king said to him, "How many times shall I make you swear that you tell me nothing but the truth in the name of the LORD?"

[16] Then he said, "I saw all Israel scattered on the mountains, as sheep that have no shepherd. And the LORD said, 'These have no master. Let each return to his house in peace.' "

[17] And the king of Israel said to Jehoshaphat, "Did I not tell you he would not prophesy good concerning me, but evil?"

[18] Then *Micaiah* said, "Therefore hear the word of the LORD: I saw the LORD sitting on His throne, and all the host of heaven standing on His right hand and His left. [19] And the LORD said, 'Who will persuade Ahab king of Israel to go up, that he may fall at Ramoth Gilead?' So one spoke in this manner, and another spoke in that manner. [20] Then a spirit came forward and stood before the LORD, and said, 'I will persuade him.' The LORD said to him, 'In what way?' [21] So he said, 'I will go out and be a lying spirit in the mouth of all his prophets.' And *the* LORD said, 'You shall persuade *him* and also prevail; go out and do so.' [22] Therefore look! The LORD has put a lying spirit in the mouth of these prophets of yours, and the LORD has declared disaster against you."

[23] Then Zedekiah the son of Chenaanah

went near and struck Micaiah on the cheek, and said, "Which way did the spirit from the LORD go from me to speak to you?"

²⁴ And Micaiah said, "Indeed you shall see on that day when you go into an inner chamber to hide!"

²⁵ Then the king of Israel said, "Take Micaiah, and return him to Amon the governor of the city and to Joash the king's son; ²⁶ and say, 'Thus says the king: "Put this *fellow* in prison, and feed him with bread of affliction and water of affliction, until I return in peace." ' "

²⁷ But Micaiah said, "If you ever return in peace, the LORD has not spoken by me." And he said, "Take heed, all you people!"

²⁸ So the king of Israel and Jehoshaphat the king of Judah went up to Ramoth Gilead. ²⁹ And the king of Israel said to Jehoshaphat, "I will disguise myself and go into battle; but you put on your robes." So the king of Israel disguised himself, and they went into battle.

³⁰ Now the king of Syria had commanded the captains of the chariots who *were* with him, saying, "Fight with no one small or great, but only with the king of Israel."

³¹ So it was, when the captains of the chariots saw Jehoshaphat, that they said, "It *is* the king of Israel!" Therefore they surrounded him to attack; but Jehoshaphat cried out, and the LORD helped him, and God diverted them from him. ³² For so it was, when the captains of the chariots saw that it was not the king of Israel, that they turned back from pursuing him. ³³ Now a certain man drew a bow at random, and struck the king of Israel between the joints of his armor. So he said to the driver of his chariot, "Turn around and take me out of the battle, for I am wounded." ³⁴ The battle increased that day, and the king of Israel propped *himself* up in *his* chariot facing the Syrians until evening; and about the time of sunset he died.

～ PSALM 81:11–16 ～

¹¹ "But My people would not heed My voice,
And Israel would *have* none of Me.

¹² So I gave them over to their own stubborn heart,
To walk in their own counsels.

¹³ "Oh, that My people would listen to Me,
That Israel would walk in My ways!

¹⁴ I would soon subdue their enemies,
And turn My hand against their adversaries.

¹⁵ The haters of the LORD would pretend submission to Him,
But their fate would endure forever.

¹⁶ He would have fed them also with the finest of wheat;
And with honey from the rock I would have satisfied you."

～ PROVERBS 20:26–28 ～

²⁶ A wise king sifts out the wicked,
And brings the threshing wheel over them.

²⁷ The spirit of a man *is* the lamp of the LORD,
Searching all the inner depths of his heart.

²⁸ Mercy and truth preserve the king,
And by lovingkindness he upholds his throne.

～ ACTS 16:22–40 ～

Then the multitude rose up together against them; and the magistrates tore off their clothes and commanded *them* to be beaten with rods. ²³ And when they had laid many stripes on them, they threw *them* into prison, commanding the jailer to keep them securely. ²⁴ Having received such a charge, he put them into the inner prison and fastened their feet in the stocks.

²⁵ But at midnight Paul and Silas were praying and singing hymns to God, and the prisoners were listening to them. ²⁶ Suddenly there was a great earthquake, so that the foundations of the prison were shaken; and immediately all the doors were opened and everyone's chains were loosed. ²⁷ And the keeper of the prison, awaking from sleep and seeing the prison doors open, supposing the prisoners had fled, drew his sword and was about

to kill himself. ²⁸ But Paul called with a loud voice, saying, "Do yourself no harm, for we are all here."

²⁹ Then he called for a light, ran in, and fell down trembling before Paul and Silas. ³⁰ And he brought them out and said, "Sirs, what must I do to be saved?"

³¹ So they said, "Believe on the Lord Jesus Christ, and you will be saved, you and your household." ³² Then they spoke the word of the Lord to him and to all who were in his house. ³³ And he took them the same hour of the night and washed *their* stripes. And immediately he and all his family were baptized. ³⁴ Now when he had brought them into his house, he set food before them; and he rejoiced, having believed in God with all his household.

³⁵ And when it was day, the magis-trates sent the officers, saying, "Let those men go."

³⁶ So the keeper of the prison reported these words to Paul, saying, "The magis-trates have sent to let you go. Now therefore depart, and go in peace."

³⁷ But Paul said to them, "They have beaten us openly, uncondemned Romans, *and* have thrown *us* into prison. And now do they put us out secretly? No indeed! Let them come themselves and get us out."

³⁸ And the officers told these words to the magistrates, and they were afraid when they heard that they were Romans. ³⁹ Then they came and pleaded with them and brought *them* out, and asked *them* to depart from the city. ⁴⁰ So they went out of the prison and entered *the house of Lydia;* and when they had seen the breth-ren, they encouraged them and departed.

READING 193 · JULY 12

～ 2 CHRONICLES 19:1—20:37 ～

Then Jehoshaphat the king of Judah returned safely to his house in Jerusalem. ² And Jehu the son of Hanani the seer went out to meet him, and said to King Jehoshaphat, "Should you help the wicked and love those who hate the LORD? Therefore the wrath of the LORD *is* upon you. ³ Nevertheless good things are found in you, in that you have removed the wooden images from the land, and have prepared your heart to seek God."

⁴ So Jehoshaphat dwelt at Jerusalem; and he went out again among the people from Beersheba to the mountains of Ephraim, and brought them back to the LORD God of their fathers. ⁵ Then he set judges in the land throughout all the for-tified cities of Judah, city by city, ⁶ and said to the judges, "Take heed to what you are doing, for you do not judge for man but for the LORD, who *is* with you in the judgment. ⁷ Now therefore, let the fear of the LORD be upon you; take care and do *it,* for *there is* no iniquity with the LORD our God, no partiality, nor taking of bribes."

⁸ Moreover in Jerusalem, for the judg-ment of the LORD and for controversies, Jehoshaphat appointed some of the Le-vites and priests, and some of the chief fathers of Israel, when they returned to Jerusalem. ⁹ And he commanded them, saying, "Thus you shall act in the fear of the LORD, faithfully and with a loyal heart: ¹⁰ Whatever case comes to you from your brethren who dwell in their cities, whether of bloodshed or offenses against law or commandment, against statutes or ordi-nances, you shall warn them, lest they trespass against the LORD and wrath come upon you and your brethren. Do this, and you will not be guilty. ¹¹ And take notice: Amariah the chief priest *is* over you in all matters of the LORD; and Zebadiah the son of Ishmael, the ruler of the house of Judah, for all the king's matters; also the Levites *will be* officials before you. Be-have courageously, and the LORD will be with the good."

20 It happened after this *that* the people of Moab with the people of Ammon, and *others* with them besides the Ammonites, came to battle against Je-hoshaphat. ² Then some came and told Jehoshaphat, saying, "A great multitude is coming against you from beyond the

Step-by-Step

Several years ago, the world watched in awe as media attention was focused on three gray whales that were ice-bound off Point Barrow, Alaska. The battered whales floated listlessly as they gasped for breath through a small hole in the ice. They had somehow become trapped in an ice pack before they could begin their annual migration. Their only hope for survival was to be transported five miles past the ice pack to the open sea.

Rescuers began cutting a string of breathing holes about twenty yards apart in the six-inch-thick ice. Then for eight days, they coaxed the whales from hole to hole, mile after mile. Along the way, one of the whales vanished, but the other two eventually swam to freedom.

Are you feeling trapped under a heavy load today? Do you fear it may suffocate you? Do you seem to be far from the "open seas," or the free schedule you desire?

Identify where you want to be and then chart your course in a series of small steps or short-term goals. Take time for a breather as you reach each goal. God will lead you and help you toward any destination that is in keeping with His good desire for you, but you must make the effort to follow. Remember, God leads us step-by-step, not leap-by-leap!

And he said, "Listen, all you of Judah and you inhabitants of Jerusalem, and you, King Jehoshaphat! Thus says the Lord to you: 'Do not be afraid nor dismayed because of this great multitude, for the battle is not yours, but God's.'"

2 Chronicles 20:15

sea, from Syria; and they are in Hazazon Tamar" (which *is* En Gedi). ³ And Jehoshaphat feared, and set himself to seek the LORD, and proclaimed a fast throughout all Judah. ⁴ So Judah gathered together to ask *help* from the LORD; and from all the cities of Judah they came to seek the LORD.

⁵ Then Jehoshaphat stood in the assembly of Judah and Jerusalem, in the house of the LORD, before the new court, ⁶ and said: "O LORD God of our fathers, *are* You not God in heaven, and do You *not* rule over all the kingdoms of the nations, and in Your hand *is there not* power and might, so that no one is able to withstand You? ⁷ *Are* You not our God, *who* drove out the inhabitants of this land before Your people Israel, and gave it to the descendants of Abraham Your friend forever? ⁸ And they dwell in it, and have built You a sanctuary in it for Your name, saying, ⁹ 'If disaster comes upon us—sword, judgment, pestilence, or famine—we will stand before this temple and in Your presence (for Your name *is* in this temple), and cry out to You in our affliction, and You will hear and save.' ¹⁰ And now, here are the people of Ammon, Moab, and Mount Seir—whom You would not let Israel invade when they came out of the land of Egypt, but they turned from them and did not destroy them— ¹¹ here they are, rewarding us by coming to throw us out of Your possession which You have given us to inherit. ¹² O our God, will You not judge them? For we have no power against this great multitude that is coming against us; nor do we know what to do, but our eyes *are* upon You."

¹³ Now all Judah, with their little ones, their wives, and their children, stood before the LORD.

¹⁴ Then the Spirit of the LORD came upon Jahaziel the son of Zechariah, the son of Benaiah, the son of Jeiel, the son of Mattaniah, a Levite of the sons of Asaph, in the midst of the assembly. ¹⁵ And he said, "Listen, all you of Judah and you inhabitants of Jerusalem, and you, King Jehoshaphat! Thus says the LORD to you: 'Do not be afraid nor dismayed because of this great multitude, for the battle *is* not yours, but God's. ¹⁶ Tomorrow go down against them. They will surely come

up by the Ascent of Ziz, and you will find them at the end of the brook before the Wilderness of Jeruel. ¹⁷ You will not *need* to fight in this *battle*. Position yourselves, stand still and see the salvation of the LORD, who is with you, O Judah and Jerusalem!' Do not fear or be dismayed; tomorrow go out against them, for the LORD *is* with you."

¹⁸ And Jehoshaphat bowed his head with *his* face to the ground, and all Judah and the inhabitants of Jerusalem bowed before the LORD, worshiping the LORD. ¹⁹ Then the Levites of the children of the Kohathites and of the children of the Korahites stood up to praise the LORD God of Israel with voices loud and high.

²⁰ So they rose early in the morning and went out into the Wilderness of Tekoa; and as they went out, Jehoshaphat stood and said, "Hear me, O Judah and you inhabitants of Jerusalem: Believe in the LORD your God, and you shall be established; believe His prophets, and you shall prosper." ²¹ And when he had consulted with the people, he appointed those who should sing to the LORD, and who should praise the beauty of holiness, as they went out before the army and were saying:

"Praise the LORD,
  For His mercy *endures* forever."

²² Now when they began to sing and to praise, the LORD set ambushes against the people of Ammon, Moab, and Mount Seir, who had come against Judah; and they were defeated. ²³ For the people of Ammon and Moab stood up against the inhabitants of Mount Seir to utterly kill and destroy *them*. And when they had made an end of the inhabitants of Seir, they helped to destroy one another.

²⁴ So when Judah came to a place overlooking the wilderness, they looked toward the multitude; and there *were* their dead bodies, fallen on the earth. No one had escaped.

²⁵ When Jehoshaphat and his people came to take away their spoil, they found among them an abundance of valuables on the dead bodies, and precious jewelry, which they stripped off for themselves, more than they could carry away; and they

were three days gathering the spoil because there was so much. ²⁶ And on the fourth day they assembled in the Valley of Berachah, for there they blessed the LORD; therefore the name of that place was called The Valley of Berachah until this day. ²⁷ Then they returned, every man of Judah and Jerusalem, with Jehoshaphat in front of them, to go back to Jerusalem with joy, for the LORD had made them rejoice over their enemies. ²⁸ So they came to Jerusalem, with stringed instruments and harps and trumpets, to the house of the LORD. ²⁹ And the fear of God was on all the kingdoms of *those* countries when they heard that the LORD had fought against the enemies of Israel. ³⁰ Then the realm of Jehoshaphat was quiet, for his God gave him rest all around.

³¹ So Jehoshaphat was king over Judah. *He was* thirty-five years old when he became king, and he reigned twenty-five years in Jerusalem. His mother's name *was* Azubah the daughter of Shilhi. ³² And he walked in the way of his father Asa, and did not turn aside from it, doing *what was* right in the sight of the LORD. ³³ Nevertheless the high places were not taken away, for as yet the people had not directed their hearts to the God of their fathers.

³⁴ Now the rest of the acts of Jehoshaphat, first and last, indeed they *are* written in the book of Jehu the son of Hanani, which *is* mentioned in the book of the kings of Israel.

³⁵ After this Jehoshaphat king of Judah allied himself with Ahaziah king of Israel, who acted very wickedly. ³⁶ And he allied himself with him to make ships to go to Tarshish, and they made the ships in Ezion Geber. ³⁷ But Eliezer the son of Dodavah of Mareshah prophesied against Jehoshaphat, saying, "Because you have allied yourself with Ahaziah, the LORD has destroyed your works." Then the ships were wrecked, so that they were not able to go to Tarshish.

~ PSALM 82:1-8 ~

¹ God stands in the congregation of the mighty;
He judges among the gods.

² How long will you judge unjustly,
And show partiality to the wicked?
                              Selah
³ Defend the poor and fatherless;
Do justice to the afflicted and needy.
⁴ Deliver the poor and needy;
Free *them* from the hand of the wicked.

⁵ They do not know, nor do they understand;
They walk about in darkness;
All the foundations of the earth are unstable.

⁶ I said, "You *are* gods,
And all of you *are* children of the Most High.
⁷ But you shall die like men,
And fall like one of the princes."

⁸ Arise, O God, judge the earth;
For You shall inherit all nations.

~ PROVERBS 20:29, 30 ~

²⁹ The glory of young men *is* their strength,
And the splendor of old men *is* their gray head.

³⁰ Blows that hurt cleanse away evil,
As *do* stripes the inner depths of the heart.

~ ACTS 17:1-15 ~

Now when they had passed through Amphipolis and Apollonia, they came to Thessalonica, where there was a synagogue of the Jews. ² Then Paul, as his custom was, went in to them, and for three Sabbaths reasoned with them from the Scriptures, ³ explaining and demonstrating that the Christ had to suffer and rise again from the dead, and *saying,* "This Jesus whom I preach to you is the Christ." ⁴ And some of them were persuaded; and a great multitude of the devout Greeks, and not a few of the leading women, joined Paul and Silas.

⁵ But the Jews who were not persuaded, becoming envious, took some of the evil men from the marketplace, and

gathering a mob, set all the city in an uproar and attacked the house of Jason, and sought to bring them out to the people. ⁶ But when they did not find them, they dragged Jason and some brethren to the rulers of the city, crying out, "These who have turned the world upside down have come here too. ⁷ Jason has harbored them, and these are all acting contrary to the decrees of Caesar, saying there is another king—Jesus." ⁸ And they troubled the crowd and the rulers of the city when they heard these things. ⁹ So when they had taken security from Jason and the rest, they let them go.

¹⁰ Then the brethren immediately sent Paul and Silas away by night to Berea. When they arrived, they went into the synagogue of the Jews. ¹¹ These were more fair-minded than those in Thessalonica, in that they received the word with all readiness, and searched the Scriptures daily *to find out* whether these things were so. ¹² Therefore many of them believed, and also not a few of the Greeks, prominent women as well as men. ¹³ But when the Jews from Thessalonica learned that the word of God was preached by Paul at Berea, they came there also and stirred up the crowds. ¹⁴ Then immediately the brethren sent Paul away, to go to the sea; but both Silas and Timothy remained there. ¹⁵ So those who conducted Paul brought him to Athens; and receiving a command for Silas and Timothy to come to him with all speed, they departed.

READING 194 · JULY 13

~ 2 CHRONICLES 21:1—22:12 ~

And Jehoshaphat rested with his fathers, and was buried with his fathers in the City of David. Then Jehoram his son reigned in his place. ² He had brothers, the sons of Jehoshaphat: Azariah, Jehiel, Zechariah, Azaryahu, Michael, and Shephatiah; all these *were* the sons of Jehoshaphat king of Israel. ³ Their father gave them great gifts of silver and gold and precious things, with fortified cities in Judah; but he gave the kingdom to Jehoram, because he *was* the firstborn.

⁴ Now when Jehoram was established over the kingdom of his father, he strengthened himself and killed all his brothers with the sword, and also *others* of the princes of Israel.

⁵ Jehoram *was* thirty-two years old when he became king, and he reigned eight years in Jerusalem. ⁶ And he walked in the way of the kings of Israel, just as the house of Ahab had done, for he had the daughter of Ahab as a wife; and he did evil in the sight of the LORD. ⁷ Yet the LORD would not destroy the house of David, because of the covenant that He had made with David, and since He had promised to give a lamp to him and to his sons forever.

⁸ In his days Edom revolted against Judah's authority, and made a king over themselves. ⁹ So Jehoram went out with his officers, and all his chariots with him. And he rose by night and attacked the Edomites who had surrounded him and the captains of the chariots. ¹⁰ Thus Edom has been in revolt against Judah's authority to this day. At that time Libnah revolted against his rule, because he had forsaken the LORD God of his fathers. ¹¹ Moreover he made high places in the mountains of Judah, and caused the inhabitants of Jerusalem to commit harlotry, and led Judah astray.

¹² And a letter came to him from Elijah the prophet, saying,

Thus says the LORD God of your
father David:
Because you have not walked in
the ways of Jehoshaphat your
father, or in the ways of Asa king
of Judah, ¹³ but have walked in the
way of the kings of Israel, and have
made Judah and the inhabitants of
Jerusalem to play the harlot like
the harlotry of the house of Ahab,
and also have killed your brothers,
those of your father's household,
who were better than yourself,
¹⁴ behold, the LORD will strike your

Soar with the Eagles

A farmer once caught a young eagle in the forest, brought it home, and raised it among his ducks and turkeys. Five years later, a naturalist came to visit him and saw the bird. "That's an eagle, not a chicken!" he said. "Yes," said the farmer, "but I've raised it to be a chicken." "Still," said the naturalist, "it has a wing span of fifteen feet. It's an eagle!" "It will never fly," said the farmer. The naturalist disagreed and they decided to put their argument to the test.

First, the naturalist picked up the eagle and said, "Eagle, thou art an eagle; thou dost belong to the sky and not to this earth; stretch forth thy wings and fly." The eagle saw the chickens and jumped down. The next day the naturalist took the eagle to the top of the house, said the same thing, and let the eagle go. Again, it spotted the chickens below and fluttered down to join them in feeding.

"One more try," said the naturalist. He took the eagle up a mountain. The trembling bird looked around, and then the naturalist made it look into the sun. Suddenly, the eagle stretched out its wings, gave a mighty screech, and flew away, never to return.

People may say you are a nobody, just a hunk of flesh. But deep inside, you have a spirit created in God's image. Look to Him and you can fly!

> For in Him we live and move and have our being, as also some of your own poets have said, "For we are also His offspring."
>
> *Acts 17:28*

people with a serious affliction—your children, your wives, and all your possessions; ¹⁵ and you *will become* very sick with a disease of your intestines, until your intestines come out by reason of the sickness, day by day.

¹⁶ Moreover the LORD stirred up against Jehoram the spirit of the Philistines and the Arabians who *were* near the Ethiopians. ¹⁷ And they came up into Judah and invaded it, and carried away all the possessions that were found in the king's house, and also his sons and his wives, so that there was not a son left to him except Jehoahaz, the youngest of his sons. ¹⁸ After all this the LORD struck him in his intestines with an incurable disease. ¹⁹ Then it happened in the course of time, after the end of two years, that his intestines came out because of his sickness; so he died in severe pain. And his people made no burning for him, like the burning for his fathers.

²⁰ He was thirty-two years old when he became king. He reigned in Jerusalem eight years and, to no one's sorrow, departed. However they buried him in the City of David, but not in the tombs of the kings.

22 Then the inhabitants of Jerusalem made Ahaziah his youngest son king in his place, for the raiders who came with the Arabians into the camp had killed all the older *sons.* So Ahaziah the son of Jehoram, king of Judah, reigned. ² Ahaziah *was* forty-two years old when he became king, and he reigned one year in Jerusalem. His mother's name *was* Athaliah the granddaughter of Omri. ³ He also walked in the ways of the house of Ahab, for his mother advised him to do wickedly. ⁴ Therefore he did evil in the sight of the LORD, like the house of Ahab; for they were his counselors after the death of his father, to his destruction. ⁵ He also followed their advice, and went with Jehoram the son of Ahab king of Israel to war against Hazael king of Syria at Ramoth Gilead; and the Syrians wounded Joram. ⁶ Then he returned to Jezreel to recover from the wounds which he had received at Ramah, when he fought against Haza-

el king of Syria. And Azariah the son of Jehoram, king of Judah, went down to see Jehoram the son of Ahab in Jezreel, because he was sick.

⁷ His going to Joram was God's occasion for Ahaziah's downfall; for when he arrived, he went out with Jehoram against Jehu the son of Nimshi, whom the LORD had anointed to cut off the house of Ahab. ⁸ And it happened, when Jehu was executing judgment on the house of Ahab, and found the princes of Judah and the sons of Ahaziah's brothers who served Ahaziah, that he killed them. ⁹ Then he searched for Ahaziah; and they caught him (he was hiding in Samaria), and brought him to Jehu. When they had killed him, they buried him, "because," they said, "he is the son of Jehoshaphat, who sought the LORD with all his heart."

So the house of Ahaziah had no one to assume power over the kingdom.

¹⁰ Now when Athaliah the mother of Ahaziah saw that her son was dead, she arose and destroyed all the royal heirs of the house of Judah. ¹¹ But Jehoshabeath, the daughter of the king, took Joash the son of Ahaziah, and stole him away from among the king's sons who were being murdered, and put him and his nurse in a bedroom. So Jehoshabeath, the daughter of King Jehoram, the wife of Jehoiada the priest (for she was the sister of Ahaziah), hid him from Athaliah so that she did not kill him. ¹² And he was hidden with them in the house of God for six years, while Athaliah reigned over the land.

~ PSALM 83:1–8 ~

¹   Do not keep silent, O God!
    Do not hold Your peace,
    And do not be still, O God!
²   For behold, Your enemies make a
        tumult;
    And those who hate You have lifted
        up their head.
³   They have taken crafty counsel
        against Your people,
    And consulted together against Your
        sheltered ones.
⁴   They have said, "Come, and let us
        cut them off from *being* a nation,
    That the name of Israel may be
        remembered no more."

⁵ For they have consulted together
   with one consent;
   They form a confederacy against
   You:
⁶ The tents of Edom and the
   Ishmaelites;
   Moab and the Hagrites;
⁷ Gebal, Ammon, and Amalek;
   Philistia with the inhabitants of Tyre;
⁸ Assyria also has joined with them;
   They have helped the children of
   Lot.   Selah

∼ PROVERBS 21:1 ∼

¹ The king's heart *is* in the hand of the
   LORD,
   Like the rivers of water; He turns it
   wherever He wishes.

∼ ACTS 17:16–34 ∼

Now while Paul waited for them at Athens, his spirit was provoked within him when he saw that the city was given over to idols. ¹⁷ Therefore he reasoned in the synagogue with the Jews and with the *Gentile* worshipers, and in the marketplace daily with those who happened to be there. ¹⁸ Then certain Epicurean and Stoic philosophers encountered him. And some said, "What does this babbler want to say?"

Others said, "He seems to be a proclaimer of foreign gods," because he preached to them Jesus and the resurrection.

¹⁹ And they took him and brought him to the Areopagus, saying, "May we know what this new doctrine *is* of which you speak? ²⁰ For you are bringing some strange things to our ears. Therefore we want to know what these things mean." ²¹ For all the Athenians and the foreigners who were there spent their time in nothing else but either to tell or to hear some new thing.

²² Then Paul stood in the midst of the Areopagus and said, "Men of Athens, I perceive that in all things you are very religious; ²³ for as I was passing through and considering the objects of your worship, I even found an altar with this inscription:

TO THE UNKNOWN GOD.

Therefore, the One whom you worship without knowing, Him I proclaim to you: ²⁴ God, who made the world and everything in it, since He is Lord of heaven and earth, does not dwell in temples made with hands. ²⁵ Nor is He worshiped with men's hands, as though He needed anything, since He gives to all life, breath, and all things. ²⁶ And He has made from one blood every nation of men to dwell on all the face of the earth, and has determined their preappointed times and the boundaries of their dwellings, ²⁷ so that they should seek the Lord, in the hope that they might grope for Him and find Him, though He is not far from each one of us; ²⁸ for in Him we live and move and have our being, as also some of your own poets have said, 'For we are also His offspring.' ²⁹ Therefore, since we are the offspring of God, we ought not to think that the Divine Nature is like gold or silver or stone, something shaped by art and man's devising. ³⁰ Truly, these times of ignorance God overlooked, but now commands all men everywhere to repent, ³¹ because He has appointed a day on which He will judge the world in righteousness by the Man whom He has ordained. He has given assurance of this to all by raising Him from the dead."

³² And when they heard of the resurrection of the dead, some mocked, while others said, "We will hear you again on this *matter*." ³³ So Paul departed from among them. ³⁴ However, some men joined him and believed, among them Dionysius the Areopagite, a woman named Damaris, and others with them.

~ 2 CHRONICLES 23:1—24:27 ~

In the seventh year Jehoiada strengthened himself, *and made a* covenant with the captains of hundreds: Azariah the son of Jeroham, Ishmael the son of Jehohanan, Azariah the son of Obed, Maaseiah the son of Adaiah, and Elishaphat the son of Zichri. ² And they went throughout Judah and gathered the Levites from all the cities of Judah, and the chief fathers of Israel, and they came to Jerusalem.

³ Then all the assembly made a covenant with the king in the house of God. And he said to them, "Behold, the king's son shall reign, as the LORD has said of the sons of David. ⁴ This *is* what you shall do: One-third of you entering on the Sabbath, of the priests and the Levites, *shall be* keeping watch over the doors; ⁵ one-third *shall be* at the king's house; and one-third at the Gate of the Foundation. All the people *shall be* in the courts of the house of the LORD. ⁶ But let no one come into the house of the LORD except the priests and those of the Levites who serve. They may go in, for they *are* holy; but all the people shall keep the watch of the LORD. ⁷ And the Levites shall surround the king on all sides, every man with his weapons in his hand; and whoever comes into the house, let him be put to death. You are to be with the king when he comes in and when he goes out."

⁸ So the Levites and all Judah did according to all that Jehoiada the priest commanded. And each man took his men who were to be on duty on the Sabbath, with those who were going *off duty* on the Sabbath; for Jehoiada the priest had not dismissed the divisions. ⁹ And Jehoiada the priest gave to the captains of hundreds the spears and the large and small shields which *had belonged* to King David, that *were* in the temple of God. ¹⁰ Then he set all the people, every man with his weapon in his hand, from the right side of the temple to the left side of the temple, along by the altar and by the temple, all around the king. ¹¹ And they brought out the king's son, put the crown on him, *gave him* the Testimony, and made him king. Then Jehoiada and his sons anointed him, and said, "*Long* live the king!"

¹² Now when Athaliah heard the noise of the people running and praising the king, she came to the people *in* the temple of the LORD. ¹³ *When* she looked, there was the king standing by his pillar at the entrance; and the leaders and the trumpeters *were* by the king. All the people of the land were rejoicing and blowing trumpets, also the singers with musical instruments, and those who led in praise. So Athaliah tore her clothes and said, "Treason! Treason!"

¹⁴ And Jehoiada the priest brought out the captains of hundreds who were set over the army, and said to them, "Take her outside under guard, and slay with the sword whoever follows her." For the priest had said, "Do not kill her in the house of the LORD."

¹⁵ So they seized her; and she went by way of the entrance of the Horse Gate *into* the king's house, and they killed her there.

¹⁶ Then Jehoiada made a covenant between himself, the people, and the king, that they should be the LORD's people. ¹⁷ And all the people went to the temple of Baal, and tore it down. They broke in pieces its altars and images, and killed Mattan the priest of Baal before the altars. ¹⁸ Also Jehoiada appointed the oversight of the house of the LORD to the hand of the priests, the Levites, whom David had assigned in the house of the LORD, to offer the burnt offerings of the LORD, as *it is* written in the Law of Moses, with rejoicing and with singing, *as it was established* by David. ¹⁹ And he set the gatekeepers at the gates of the house of the LORD, so that no one *who was* in any way unclean should enter.

²⁰ Then he took the captains of hundreds, the nobles, the governors of the people, and all the people of the land, and brought the king down from the house of the LORD; and they went through the Upper Gate to the king's house, and set the king on the throne of the kingdom. ²¹ So all the people of the land rejoiced; and the city was quiet, for they had slain Athaliah with the sword.

An Honorable Title

Horace Mann is considered one of America's greatest educators. In 1837 as a lawyer, not a teacher, he entered politics and became president of the Massachusetts State Senate. A visionary, he saw vast possibilities for developing the public education system of the nation, and he pushed for improvements in education wherever he had an opportunity to speak.

> To do righteousness and justice is more acceptable to the Lord than sacrifice.
>
> *Proverbs 21:3*

Mann's pleas for education resulted in Massachusetts creating a State Board of Education as an "experiment." The leadership position of the board was offered to Mann. His friends, who truly believed that his political career might culminate in the presidency of the United States, urged him to decline. But Mann accepted the position. His statement to his downcast friends became a classic: "If the title is not sufficiently honorable, then it is clearly left to me to elevate it."

Not only did the position have little prestige, but the $1,500 salary was only a fraction of what Mann had earned as a lawyer. About this Mann noted, "One thing is certain — if I live and have good health, I will do more than $1,500 worth of good." And he did. From his position he gave Massachusetts a public school system that many other states adopted, to the benefit of millions of children through the years.

The title of "Mom," or "Wife," may not seem very honorable, but as women, we make it honorable by the attitude with which we approach the job. The pay is next to nothing, but benefits are out of this world!

24 Joash *was* seven years old when he became king, and he reigned forty years in Jerusalem. His mother's name *was* Zibiah of Beersheba. ² Joash did *what was* right in the sight of the LORD all the days of Jehoiada the priest. ³ And Jehoiada took two wives for him, and he had sons and daughters.

⁴ Now it happened after this *that* Joash set his heart on repairing the house of the LORD. ⁵ Then he gathered the priests and the Levites, and said to them, "Go out to the cities of Judah, and gather from all Israel money to repair the house of your God from year to year, and see that you do it quickly."

However the Levites did not do it quickly. ⁶ So the king called Jehoiada the chief *priest,* and said to him, "Why have you not required the Levites to bring in from Judah and from Jerusalem the collection, *according to the commandment* of Moses the servant of the LORD and of the assembly of Israel, for the tabernacle of witness?" ⁷ For the sons of Athaliah, that wicked woman, had broken into the house of God, and had also presented all the dedicated things of the house of the LORD to the Baals.

⁸ Then at the king's command they made a chest, and set it outside at the gate of the house of the LORD. ⁹ And they made a proclamation throughout Judah and Jerusalem to bring to the LORD the collection *that* Moses the servant of God *had imposed* on Israel in the wilderness. ¹⁰ Then all the leaders and all the people rejoiced, brought their contributions, and put *them* into the chest until all had given. ¹¹ So it was, at that time, when the chest was brought to the king's official by the hand of the Levites, and when they saw that *there was* much money, that the king's scribe and the high priest's officer came and emptied the chest, and took it and returned it to its place. Thus they did day by day, and gathered money in abundance. ¹² The king and Jehoiada gave it to those who did the work of the service of the house of the LORD; and they hired masons and carpenters to repair the house of the LORD, and also those who worked in iron and bronze to restore the house of the LORD. ¹³ So the workmen labored, and

the work was completed by them; they restored the house of God to its original condition and reinforced it. ¹⁴ When they had finished, they brought the rest of the money before the king and Jehoiada; they made from it articles for the house of the LORD, articles for serving and offering, spoons and vessels of gold and silver. And they offered burnt offerings in the house of the LORD continually all the days of Jehoiada.

¹⁵ But Jehoiada grew old and was full of days, and he died; *he was* one hundred and thirty years old when he died. ¹⁶ And they buried him in the City of David among the kings, because he had done good in Israel, both toward God and His house.

¹⁷ Now after the death of Jehoiada the leaders of Judah came and bowed down to the king. And the king listened to them. ¹⁸ Therefore they left the house of the LORD God of their fathers, and served wooden images and idols; and wrath came upon Judah and Jerusalem because of their trespass. ¹⁹ Yet He sent prophets to them, to bring them back to the LORD; and they testified against them, but they would not listen.

²⁰ Then the Spirit of God came upon Zechariah the son of Jehoiada the priest, who stood above the people, and said to them, "Thus says God: 'Why do you transgress the commandments of the LORD, so that you cannot prosper? Because you have forsaken the LORD, He also has forsaken you.' " ²¹ So they conspired against him, and at the command of the king they stoned him with stones in the court of the house of the LORD. ²² Thus Joash the king did not remember the kindness which Jehoiada his father had done to him, but killed his son; and as he died, he said, "The LORD look on *it,* and repay!"

²³ So it happened in the spring of the year *that* the army of Syria came up against him; and they came to Judah and Jerusalem, and destroyed all the leaders of the people from among the people, and sent all their spoil to the king of Damascus. ²⁴ For the army of the Syrians came with a small company of men; but the LORD delivered a very great army into their hand, because they had forsaken the LORD God of their fathers. So they

executed judgment against Joash. ²⁵ And when they had withdrawn from him (for they left him severely wounded), his own servants conspired against him because of the blood of the sons of Jehoiada the priest, and killed him on his bed. So he died. And they buried him in the City of David, but they did not bury him in the tombs of the kings.

²⁶ These are the ones who conspired against him: Zabad the son of Shimeath the Ammonitess, and Jehozabad the son of Shimrith the Moabitess. ²⁷ Now *concerning* his sons, and the many oracles about him, and the repairing of the house of God, indeed they *are* written in the annals of the book of the kings. Then Amaziah his son reigned in his place.

~ PSALM 83:9–18 ~

⁹ Deal with them as *with* Midian,
  As *with* Sisera,
  As *with* Jabin at the Brook Kishon,
¹⁰ Who perished at En Dor,
  Who became *as* refuse on the earth.
¹¹ Make their nobles like Oreb and like Zeeb,
  Yes, all their princes like Zebah and Zalmunna,
¹² Who said, "Let us take for ourselves
  The pastures of God for a possession."

¹³ O my God, make them like the whirling dust,
  Like the chaff before the wind!
¹⁴ As the fire burns the woods,
  And as the flame sets the mountains on fire,
¹⁵ So pursue them with Your tempest,
  And frighten them with Your storm.
¹⁶ Fill their faces with shame,
  That they may seek Your name, O LORD.
¹⁷ Let them be confounded and dismayed forever;
  Yes, let them be put to shame and perish,
¹⁸ That they may know that You, whose name alone *is* the LORD,
  Are the Most High over all the earth.

~ PROVERBS 21:2, 3 ~

² Every way of a man *is* right in his own eyes,
  But the LORD weighs the hearts.

³ To do righteousness and justice
  Is more acceptable to the LORD than sacrifice.

~ ACTS 18:1–28 ~

After these things Paul departed from Athens and went to Corinth. ² And he found a certain Jew named Aquila, born in Pontus, who had recently come from Italy with his wife Priscilla (because Claudius had commanded all the Jews to depart from Rome); and he came to them. ³ So, because he was of the same trade, he stayed with them and worked; for by occupation they were tentmakers. ⁴ And he reasoned in the synagogue every Sabbath, and persuaded both Jews and Greeks.

⁵ When Silas and Timothy had come from Macedonia, Paul was compelled by the Spirit, and testified to the Jews *that* Jesus *is* the Christ. ⁶ But when they opposed him and blasphemed, he shook *his* garments and said to them, "Your blood *be* upon your *own* heads; I *am* clean. From now on I will go to the Gentiles." ⁷ And he departed from there and entered the house of a certain *man* named Justus, *one* who worshiped God, whose house was next door to the synagogue. ⁸ Then Crispus, the ruler of the synagogue, believed on the Lord with all his household. And many of the Corinthians, hearing, believed and were baptized.

⁹ Now the Lord spoke to Paul in the night by a vision, "Do not be afraid, but speak, and do not keep silent; ¹⁰ for I am with you, and no one will attack you to hurt you; for I have many people in this city." ¹¹ And he continued *there* a year and six months, teaching the word of God among them.

¹² When Gallio was proconsul of Achaia, the Jews with one accord rose up against Paul and brought him to the

judgment seat, [13] saying, "This *fellow* persuades men to worship God contrary to the law."

[14] And when Paul was about to open *his* mouth, Gallio said to the Jews, "If it were a matter of wrongdoing or wicked crimes, O Jews, there would be reason why I should bear with you. [15] But if it is a question of words and names and your own law, look *to it* yourselves; for I do not want to be a judge of such *matters.*" [16] And he drove them from the judgment seat. [17] Then all the Greeks took Sosthenes, the ruler of the synagogue, and beat *him* before the judgment seat. But Gallio took no notice of these things.

[18] So Paul still remained a good while. Then he took leave of the brethren and sailed for Syria, and Priscilla and Aquila *were* with him. He had *his* hair cut off at Cenchrea, for he had taken a vow. [19] And he came to Ephesus, and left them there; but he himself entered the synagogue and reasoned with the Jews. [20] When they asked *him* to stay a longer time with them, he did not consent, [21] but took leave of them, saying, "I must by all means keep this coming feast in Jerusalem; but I will return again to you, God willing." And he sailed from Ephesus.

[22] And when he had landed at Caesarea, and gone up and greeted the church, he went down to Antioch. [23] After he had spent some time *there*, he departed and went over the region of Galatia and Phrygia in order, strengthening all the disciples.

[24] Now a certain Jew named Apollos, born at Alexandria, an eloquent man *and* mighty in the Scriptures, came to Ephesus. [25] This man had been instructed in the way of the Lord; and being fervent in spirit, he spoke and taught accurately the things of the Lord, though he knew only the baptism of John. [26] So he began to speak boldly in the synagogue. When Aquila and Priscilla heard him, they took him aside and explained to him the way of God more accurately. [27] And when he desired to cross to Achaia, the brethren wrote, exhorting the disciples to receive him; and when he arrived, he greatly helped those who had believed through grace; [28] for he vigorously refuted the Jews publicly, showing from the Scriptures that Jesus is the Christ.

READING 196 · JULY 15

～ 2 CHRONICLES 25:1—27:9 ～

Amaziah *was* twenty-five years old *when* he became king, and he reigned twenty-nine years in Jerusalem. His mother's name *was* Jehoaddan of Jerusalem. [2] And he did *what was* right in the sight of the LORD, but not with a loyal heart.

[3] Now it happened, as soon as the kingdom was established for him, that he executed his servants who had murdered his father the king. [4] However he did not execute their children, but *did* as *it is* written in the Law in the Book of Moses, where the LORD commanded, saying, "The fathers shall not be put to death for their children, nor shall the children be put to death for their fathers; but a person shall die for his own sin."

[5] Moreover Amaziah gathered Judah together and set over them captains of thousands and captains of hundreds, according to *their* fathers' houses, throughout all Judah and Benjamin; and he numbered them from twenty years old and above, and found them to be three hundred thousand choice *men, able* to go to war, who could handle spear and shield. [6] He also hired one hundred thousand mighty men of valor from Israel for one hundred talents of silver. [7] But a man of God came to him, saying, "O king, do not let the army of Israel go with you, for the LORD *is* not with Israel—*not with* any of the children of Ephraim. [8] But if you go, be gone! Be strong in battle! *Even so,* God shall make you fall before the enemy; for God has power to help and to overthrow."

[9] Then Amaziah said to the man of God, "But what *shall we* do about the hundred talents which I have given to the troops of Israel?"

The Kid Who Couldn't Sit Still

> **For you have need of endurance, so that after you have done the will of God, you may receive the promise.**
>
> *Hebrews 10:36*

Nelson Diebel, a hyperactive and delinquent child, was enrolled in The Peddie School. There he met swimming coach Chris Martin, who believed the more one practices, the better one performs. Within a month, he had Nelson swimming 30 to 40 hours a week, even though Nelson could not sit still in a classroom for 15 minutes. Martin saw potential in Nelson. He constantly put new goals in front of him, trying to get him to focus and turn his anger into strength. Nelson eventually qualified for the Junior Nationals, where his times qualified him for the Olympic Trials.

However, Nelson broke both hands and arms in a diving accident and doctors warned he probably would never regain his winning form. Martin said to him, "You're coming all the way back. . . . If you're not committed to that, we're going to stop right now." Nelson agreed and within weeks after his casts were off, he was swimming again. In 1992, he won Olympic gold. As he accepted his medal, he recalls thinking, *I planned and dreamed and worked so hard . . . and I did it! The kid who once couldn't sit still and who had no ambition . . . had learned to make a plan, pursue it, and achieve it.* He had become a winner in far more than swimming!

And the man of God answered, "The LORD is able to give you much more than this." [10] So Amaziah discharged the troops that had come to him from Ephraim, to go back home. Therefore their anger was greatly aroused against Judah, and they returned home in great anger.

[11] Then Amaziah strengthened himself, and leading his people, he went to the Valley of Salt and killed ten thousand of the people of Seir. [12] Also the children of Judah took captive ten thousand alive, brought them to the top of the rock, and cast them down from the top of the rock, so that they all were dashed in pieces.

[13] But as for the soldiers of the army which Amaziah had discharged, so that they would not go with him to battle, they raided the cities of Judah from Samaria to Beth Horon, killed three thousand in them, and took much spoil.

[14] Now it was so, after Amaziah came from the slaughter of the Edomites, that he brought the gods of the people of Seir, set them up *to be* his gods, and bowed down before them and burned incense to them. [15] Therefore the anger of the LORD was aroused against Amaziah, and He sent him a prophet who said to him, "Why have you sought the gods of the people, which could not rescue their own people from your hand?"

[16] So it was, as he talked with him, that *the king* said to him, "Have we made you the king's counselor? Cease! Why should you be killed?"

Then the prophet ceased, and said, "I know that God has determined to destroy you, because you have done this and have not heeded my advice."

[17] Now Amaziah king of Judah asked advice and sent to Joash the son of Jehoahaz, the son of Jehu, king of Israel, saying, "Come, let us face one another *in battle.*"

[18] And Joash king of Israel sent to Amaziah king of Judah, saying, "The thistle that *was* in Lebanon sent to the cedar that was in Lebanon, saying, 'Give your daughter to my son as wife'; and a wild beast that *was* in Lebanon passed by and trampled the thistle. [19] Indeed you say that you have defeated the Edomites, and your heart is lifted up to boast. Stay at home now; why should you

meddle with trouble, that you should fall—you and Judah with you?"

[20] But Amaziah would not heed, for it *came* from God, that He might give them into the hand *of their enemies,* because they sought the gods of Edom. [21] So Joash king of Israel went out; and he and Amaziah king of Judah faced one another at Beth Shemesh, which *belongs* to Judah. [22] And Judah was defeated by Israel, and every man fled to his tent. [23] Then Joash the king of Israel captured Amaziah king of Judah, the son of Joash, the son of Jehoahaz, at Beth Shemesh; and he brought him to Jerusalem, and broke down the wall of Jerusalem from the Gate of Ephraim to the Corner Gate—four hundred cubits. [24] And *he took* all the gold and silver, all the articles that were found in the house of God with Obed-Edom, the treasures of the king's house, and hostages, and returned to Samaria.

[25] Amaziah the son of Joash, king of Judah, lived fifteen years after the death of Joash the son of Jehoahaz, king of Israel. [26] Now the rest of the acts of Amaziah, from first to last, indeed *are* they not written in the book of the kings of Judah and Israel? [27] After the time that Amaziah turned away from following the LORD, they made a conspiracy against him in Jerusalem, and he fled to Lachish; but they sent after him to Lachish and killed him there. [28] Then they brought him on horses and buried him with his fathers in the City of Judah.

26 Now all the people of Judah took Uzziah, who *was* sixteen years old, and made him king instead of his father Amaziah. [2] He built Elath and restored it to Judah, after the king rested with his fathers.

[3] Uzziah *was* sixteen years old when he became king, and he reigned fifty-two years in Jerusalem. His mother's name was Jecholiah of Jerusalem. [4] And he did *what was* right in the sight of the LORD, according to all that his father Amaziah had done. [5] He sought God in the days of Zechariah, who had understanding in the visions of God; and as long as he sought the LORD, God made him prosper.

[6] Now he went out and made war against the Philistines, and broke down

the wall of Gath, the wall of Jabneh, and the wall of Ashdod; and he built cities *around* Ashdod and among the Philistines. [7] God helped him against the Philistines, against the Arabians who lived in Gur Baal, and against the Meunites. [8] Also the Ammonites brought tribute to Uzziah. His fame spread as far as the entrance of Egypt, for he became exceedingly strong.

[9] And Uzziah built towers in Jerusalem at the Corner Gate, at the Valley Gate, and at the corner buttress of the wall; then he fortified them. [10] Also he built towers in the desert. He dug many wells, for he had much livestock, both in the lowlands and in the plains; *he also had* farmers and vinedressers in the mountains and in Carmel, for he loved the soil.

[11] Moreover Uzziah had an army of fighting men who went out to war by companies, according to the number on their roll as prepared by Jeiel the scribe and Maaseiah the officer, under the hand of Hananiah, *one* of the king's captains. [12] The total number of chief officers of the mighty men of valor *was* two thousand six hundred. [13] And under their authority *was* an army of three hundred and seven thousand five hundred, that made war with mighty power, to help the king against the enemy. [14] Then Uzziah prepared for them, for the entire army, shields, spears, helmets, body armor, bows, and slings *to cast* stones. [15] And he made devices in Jerusalem, invented by skillful men, to be on the towers and the corners, to shoot arrows and large stones. So his fame spread far and wide, for he was marvelously helped till he became strong.

[16] But when he was strong his heart was lifted up, to *his* destruction, for he transgressed against the LORD his God by entering the temple of the LORD to burn incense on the altar of incense. [17] So Azariah the priest went in after him, and with him were eighty priests of the LORD—valiant men. [18] And they withstood King Uzziah, and said to him, "*It is* not for you, Uzziah, to burn incense to the LORD, but for the priests, the sons of Aaron, who are consecrated to burn incense. Get out of the sanctuary, for you have trespassed! You *shall have* no honor from the LORD God."

[19] Then Uzziah became furious; and he *had* a censer in his hand to burn incense. And while he was angry with the priests, leprosy broke out on his forehead, before the priests in the house of the LORD, beside the incense altar. [20] And Azariah the chief priest and all the priests looked at him, and there, on his forehead, he *was* leprous; so they thrust him out of that place. Indeed he also hurried to get out, because the LORD had struck him.

[21] King Uzziah was a leper until the day of his death. He dwelt in an isolated house, because he was a leper; for he was cut off from the house of the LORD. Then Jotham his son *was* over the king's house, judging the people of the land.

[22] Now the rest of the acts of Uzziah, from first to last, the prophet Isaiah the son of Amoz wrote. [23] So Uzziah rested with his fathers, and they buried him with his fathers in the field of burial which *belonged* to the kings, for they said, "He is a leper." Then Jotham his son reigned in his place.

27 Jotham *was* twenty-five years old when he became king, and he reigned sixteen years in Jerusalem. His mother's name *was* Jerushah the daughter of Zadok. [2] And he did *what was* right in the sight of the LORD, according to all that his father Uzziah had done (although he did not enter the temple of the LORD). But still the people acted corruptly.

[3] He built the Upper Gate of the house of the LORD, and he built extensively on the wall of Ophel. [4] Moreover he built cities in the mountains of Judah, and in the forests he built fortresses and towers. [5] He also fought with the king of the Ammonites and defeated them. And the people of Ammon gave him in that year one hundred talents of silver, ten thousand kors of wheat, and ten thousand of barley. The people of Ammon paid this to him in the second and third years also. [6] So Jotham became mighty, because he prepared his ways before the LORD his God.

[7] Now the rest of the acts of Jotham, and all his wars and his ways, indeed they *are* written in the book of the kings of Israel and Judah. [8] He was twenty-five years old when he became king, and he

reigned sixteen years in Jerusalem. ⁹ So Jotham rested with his fathers, and they buried him in the City of David. Then Ahaz his son reigned in his place.

∼ PSALM 84:1-7 ∼

1 How lovely *is* Your tabernacle,
   O LORD of hosts!
2 My soul longs, yes, even faints
   For the courts of the LORD;
   My heart and my flesh cry out for
      the living God.

3 Even the sparrow has found a home,
   And the swallow a nest for herself,
   Where she may lay her young—
   Even Your altars, O LORD of hosts,
   My King and my God.
4 Blessed *are* those who dwell in Your
      house;
   They will still be praising You.   Selah

5 Blessed *is* the man whose strength *is*
      in You,
   Whose heart *is* set on pilgrimage.
6 *As they* pass through the Valley of
      Baca,
   They make it a spring;
   The rain also covers it with pools.
7 They go from strength to strength;
   Each one appears before God in
      Zion.

∼ PROVERBS 21:4, 5 ∼

4 A haughty look, a proud heart,
   And the plowing of the wicked *are*
      sin.

5 The plans of the diligent *lead* surely
      to plenty,
   But *those of* everyone *who is* hasty,
      surely to poverty.

∼ ACTS 19:1-20 ∼

And it happened, while Apollos was at Corinth, that Paul, having passed through the upper regions, came to Ephesus. And finding some disciples ² he said to them, "Did you receive the Holy Spirit when you believed?"

So they said to him, "We have not so much as heard whether there is a Holy Spirit."

³ And he said to them, "Into what then were you baptized?"

So they said, "Into John's baptism."

⁴ Then Paul said, "John indeed baptized with a baptism of repentance, saying to the people that they should believe on Him who would come after him, that is, on Christ Jesus."

⁵ When they heard *this,* they were baptized in the name of the Lord Jesus. ⁶ And when Paul had laid hands on them, the Holy Spirit came upon them, and they spoke with tongues and prophesied. ⁷ Now the men were about twelve in all.

⁸ And he went into the synagogue and spoke boldly for three months, reasoning and persuading concerning the things of the kingdom of God. ⁹ But when some were hardened and did not believe, but spoke evil of the Way before the multitude, he departed from them and withdrew the disciples, reasoning daily in the school of Tyrannus. ¹⁰ And this continued for two years, so that all who dwelt in Asia heard the word of the Lord Jesus, both Jews and Greeks.

¹¹ Now God worked unusual miracles by the hands of Paul, ¹² so that even handkerchiefs or aprons were brought from his body to the sick, and the diseases left them and the evil spirits went out of them. ¹³ Then some of the itinerant Jewish exorcists took it upon themselves to call the name of the Lord Jesus over those who had evil spirits, saying, "We exorcise you by the Jesus whom Paul preaches." ¹⁴ Also there were seven sons of Sceva, a Jewish chief priest, who did so.

¹⁵ And the evil spirit answered and said, "Jesus I know, and Paul I know; but who are you?"

¹⁶ Then the man in whom the evil spirit was leaped on them, overpowered them, and prevailed against them, so that they fled out of that house naked and wounded. ¹⁷ This became known both to all Jews and Greeks dwelling in Ephesus; and fear fell on them all, and the name of the Lord Jesus was magnified. ¹⁸ And many who had believed came confessing and telling their deeds. ¹⁹ Also, many of

those who had practiced magic brought their books together and burned *them* in the sight of all. And they counted up the value of them, and *it* totaled fifty thousand *pieces* of silver. [20] So the word of the Lord grew mightily and prevailed.

~ 2 CHRONICLES 28:1—29:36 ~

Ahaz *was* twenty years old when he became king, and he reigned sixteen years in Jerusalem; and he did not do *what was* right in the sight of the LORD, as his father David *had done.* [2] For he walked in the ways of the kings of Israel, and made molded images for the Baals. [3] He burned incense in the Valley of the Son of Hinnom, and burned his children in the fire, according to the abominations of the nations whom the LORD had cast out before the children of Israel. [4] And he sacrificed and burned incense on the high places, on the hills, and under every green tree.

[5] Therefore the LORD his God delivered him into the hand of the king of Syria. They defeated him, and carried away a great multitude of them as captives, and brought *them* to Damascus. Then he was also delivered into the hand of the king of Israel, who defeated him with a great slaughter. [6] For Pekah the son of Remaliah killed one hundred and twenty thousand in Judah in one day, all valiant men, because they had forsaken the LORD God of their fathers. [7] Zichri, a mighty man of Ephraim, killed Maaseiah the king's son, Azrikam the officer over the house, and Elkanah *who was* second to the king. [8] And the children of Israel carried away captive of their brethren two hundred thousand women, sons, and daughters; and they also took away much spoil from them, and brought the spoil to Samaria.

[9] But a prophet of the LORD was there, whose name *was* Oded; and he went out before the army that came to Samaria, and said to them: "Look, because the LORD God of your fathers was angry with Judah, He has delivered them into your hand; but you have killed them in a rage *that* reaches up to heaven. [10] And now you propose to force the children of Judah and Jerusalem to be your male and female slaves; *but are* you not also guilty before the LORD your God? [11] Now hear me, therefore, and return the captives, whom you have taken captive from your brethren, for the fierce wrath of the LORD *is* upon you."

[12] Then some of the heads of the children of Ephraim, Azariah the son of Johanan, Berechiah the son of Meshillemoth, Jehizkiah the son of Shallum, and Amasa the son of Hadlai, stood up against those who came from the war, [13] and said to them, "You shall not bring the captives here, for we *already* have offended the LORD. You intend to add to our sins and to our guilt; for our guilt is great, and *there is* fierce wrath against Israel." [14] So the armed men left the captives and the spoil before the leaders and all the assembly. [15] Then the men who were designated by name rose up and took the captives, and from the spoil they clothed all who were naked among them, dressed them and gave them sandals, gave them food and drink, and anointed them; and they let all the feeble ones ride on donkeys. So they brought them to their brethren at Jericho, the city of palm trees. Then they returned to Samaria.

[16] At the same time King Ahaz sent to the kings of Assyria to help him. [17] For again the Edomites had come, attacked Judah, and carried away captives. [18] The Philistines also had invaded the cities of the lowland and of the South of Judah, and had taken Beth Shemesh, Aijalon, Gederoth, Sochoh with its villages, Timnah with its villages, and Gimzo with its villages; and they dwelt there. [19] For the LORD brought Judah low because of Ahaz king of Israel, for he had encouraged moral decline in Judah and had been continually unfaithful to the LORD. [20] Also Tiglath-Pileser king of Assyria came to him and distressed him, and did not assist him. [21] For Ahaz took part *of the treasures* from the house of the LORD, from the

house of the king, and from the leaders, and he gave *it* to the king of Assyria; but he did not help him.

²² Now in the time of his distress King Ahaz became increasingly unfaithful to the LORD. This *is that* King Ahaz. ²³ For he sacrificed to the gods of Damascus which had defeated him, saying, "Because the gods of the kings of Syria help them, I will sacrifice to them that they may help me." But they were the ruin of him and of all Israel. ²⁴ So Ahaz gathered the articles of the house of God, cut in pieces the articles of the house of God, shut up the doors of the house of the LORD, and made for himself altars in every corner of Jerusalem. ²⁵ And in every single city of Judah he made high places to burn incense to other gods, and provoked to anger the LORD God of his fathers.

²⁶ Now the rest of his acts and all his ways, from first to last, indeed they *are* written in the book of the kings of Judah and Israel. ²⁷ So Ahaz rested with his fathers, and they buried him in the city, in Jerusalem; but they did not bring him into the tombs of the kings of Israel. Then Hezekiah his son reigned in his place.

29 Hezekiah became king *when he was* twenty-five years old, and he reigned twenty-nine years in Jerusalem. His mother's name *was* Abijah the daughter of Zechariah. ² And he did *what was* right in the sight of the LORD, according to all that his father David had done.

³ In the first year of his reign, in the first month, he opened the doors of the house of the LORD and repaired them. ⁴ Then he brought in the priests and the Levites, and gathered them in the East Square, ⁵ and said to them: "Hear me, Levites! Now sanctify yourselves, sanctify the house of the LORD God of your fathers, and carry out the rubbish from the holy *place*. ⁶ For our fathers have trespassed and done evil in the eyes of the LORD our God; they have forsaken Him, have turned their faces away from the dwelling place of the LORD, and turned *their* backs *on Him*. ⁷ They have also shut up the doors of the vestibule, put out the lamps, and have not burned incense or offered burnt offerings in the holy *place* to the God of Israel. ⁸ Therefore the wrath

of the LORD fell upon Judah and Jerusalem, and He has given them up to trouble, to desolation, and to jeering, as you see with your eyes. ⁹ For indeed, because of this our fathers have fallen by the sword; and our sons, our daughters, and our wives *are* in captivity.

¹⁰ "Now *it is* in my heart to make a covenant with the LORD God of Israel, that His fierce wrath may turn away from us. ¹¹ My sons, do not be negligent now, for the LORD has chosen you to stand before Him, to serve Him, and that you should minister to Him and burn incense."

¹² Then these Levites arose: Mahath the son of Amasai and Joel the son of Azariah, of the sons of the Kohathites; of the sons of Merari, Kish the son of Abdi and Azariah the son of Jehallelel; of the Gershonites, Joah the son of Zimmah and Eden the son of Joah; ¹³ of the sons of Elizaphan, Shimri and Jeiel; of the sons of Asaph, Zechariah and Mattaniah; ¹⁴ of the sons of Heman, Jehiel and Shimei; and of the sons of Jeduthun, Shemaiah and Uzziel.

¹⁵ And they gathered their brethren, sanctified themselves, and went according to the commandment of the king, at the words of the LORD, to cleanse the house of the LORD. ¹⁶ Then the priests went into the inner part of the house of the LORD to cleanse *it*, and brought out all the debris that they found in the temple of the LORD to the court of the house of the LORD. And the Levites took *it* out and carried *it* to the Brook Kidron.

¹⁷ Now they began to sanctify on the first *day* of the first month, and on the eighth day of the month they came to the vestibule of the LORD. So they sanctified the house of the LORD in eight days, and on the sixteenth day of the first month they finished.

¹⁸ Then they went in to King Hezekiah and said, "We have cleansed all the house of the LORD, the altar of burnt offerings with all its articles, and the table of the showbread with all its articles. ¹⁹ Moreover all the articles which King Ahaz in his reign had cast aside in his transgression we have prepared and sanctified; and there they *are*, before the altar of the LORD."

²⁰ Then King Hezekiah rose early,

Defying the Odds

Lord of hosts, blessed is the man who trusts in You!

Psalm 84:12

Joseph Strauss, the engineer responsible for building the Golden Gate Bridge, took great pride in his achievement, not only because the bridge was one of the most beautiful in the world but because it was the safest. Strauss had heard all his life that "a bridge demands its life." At that time, it was normal to expect one death for every million dollars when building a bridge. Strauss was determined to beat that expectation.

Joseph took to heart the problems experienced by the Oakland Bay Bridge builders who were working at the same time. He kept a doctor and nurse on the construction wharf. When his suspicions about lead poisoning were confirmed, he switched from lead to iron oxide paint on the tower splices. He insisted on safety belts, hard hats, and goggles. He even put his "bridge monkeys" on special diets in hopes of helping them counteract dizziness and vertigo. He fired men who drank on the job or were reckless showoffs. And, he spent $82,000 on a safety net that eventually saved the lives of nineteen men.

Although unavoidable accidents did claim lives, Strauss' bridge construction went for forty-four months with no deaths — a phenomenal record — all because he rejected negative expectations and became a wise example.

gathered the rulers of the city, and went up to the house of the LORD. [21] And they brought seven bulls, seven rams, seven lambs, and seven male goats for a sin offering for the kingdom, for the sanctuary, and for Judah. Then he commanded the priests, the sons of Aaron, to offer *them* on the altar of the LORD. [22] So they killed the bulls, and the priests received the blood and sprinkled *it* on the altar. Likewise they killed the rams and sprinkled the blood on the altar. They also killed the lambs and sprinkled the blood on the altar. [23] Then they brought out the male goats *for* the sin offering before the king and the assembly, and they laid their hands on them. [24] And the priests killed them; and they presented their blood on the altar as a sin offering to make an atonement for all Israel, for the king commanded *that* the burnt offering and the sin offering *be made* for all Israel.

[25] And he stationed the Levites in the house of the LORD with cymbals, with stringed instruments, and with harps, according to the commandment of David, of Gad the king's seer, and of Nathan the prophet; for thus *was* the commandment of the LORD by his prophets. [26] The Levites stood with the instruments of David, and the priests with the trumpets. [27] Then Hezekiah commanded *them* to offer the burnt offering on the altar. And when the burnt offering began, the song of the LORD *also* began, with the trumpets and with the instruments of David king of Israel. [28] So all the assembly worshiped, the singers sang, and the trumpeters sounded; all *this continued* until the burnt offering was finished. [29] And when they had finished offering, the king and all who were present with him bowed and worshiped. [30] Moreover King Hezekiah and the leaders commanded the Levites to sing praise to the LORD with the words of David and of Asaph the seer. So they sang praises with gladness, and they bowed their heads and worshiped.

[31] Then Hezekiah answered and said, "Now *that* you have consecrated yourselves to the LORD, come near, and bring sacrifices and thank offerings into the house of the LORD." So the assembly brought in sacrifices and thank offerings, and as many as were of a willing heart *brought* burnt offerings. [32] And the number of the burnt offerings which the assembly brought was seventy bulls, one hundred rams, *and* two hundred lambs; all these *were* for a burnt offering to the LORD. [33] The consecrated things *were* six hundred bulls and three thousand sheep. [34] But the priests were too few, so that they could not skin all the burnt offerings; therefore their brethren the Levites helped them until the work was ended and until the *other* priests had sanctified themselves, for the Levites were more diligent in sanctifying themselves than the priests. [35] Also the burnt offerings *were* in abundance, with the fat of the peace offerings and *with* the drink offerings for *every* burnt offering.

So the service of the house of the LORD was set in order. [36] Then Hezekiah and all the people rejoiced that God had prepared the people, since the events took place so suddenly.

～ PSALM 84:8–12 ～

[8] O LORD God of hosts, hear my prayer;
Give ear, O God of Jacob!   Selah
[9] O God, behold our shield,
And look upon the face of Your anointed.

[10] For a day in Your courts *is* better than a thousand.
I would rather be a doorkeeper in the house of my God
Than dwell in the tents of wickedness.
[11] For the LORD God *is* a sun and shield;
The LORD will give grace and glory;
No good *thing* will He withhold
From those who walk uprightly.

[12] O LORD of hosts,
Blessed *is* the man who trusts in You!

～ PROVERBS 21:6–8 ～

[6] Getting treasures by a lying tongue
Is the fleeting fantasy of those who seek death.

7 The violence of the wicked will
      destroy them,
   Because they refuse to do justice.

8 The way of a guilty man *is* perverse;
   But *as for* the pure, his work *is* right.

~ ACTS 19:21–41 ~

When these things were accomplished, Paul purposed in the Spirit, when he had passed through Macedonia and Achaia, to go to Jerusalem, saying, "After I have been there, I must also see Rome." ²² So he sent into Macedonia two of those who ministered to him, Timothy and Erastus, but he himself stayed in Asia for a time.

²³ And about that time there arose a great commotion about the Way. ²⁴ For a certain man named Demetrius, a silver-smith, who made silver shrines of Diana, brought no small profit to the craftsmen. ²⁵ He called them together with the work-ers of similar occupation, and said: "Men, you know that we have our prosperity by this trade. ²⁶ Moreover you see and hear that not only at Ephesus, but throughout almost all Asia, this Paul has persuaded and turned away many people, saying that they are not gods which are made with hands. ²⁷ So not only is this trade of ours in danger of falling into disrepute, but also the temple of the great goddess Diana may be despised and her magnificence de-stroyed, whom all Asia and the world worship."

²⁸ Now when they heard *this,* they were full of wrath and cried out, saying, "Great *is* Diana of the Ephesians!" ²⁹ So the whole city was filled with confusion, and rushed into the theater with one accord, having

seized Gaius and Aristarchus, Mace-donians, Paul's travel companions. ³⁰ And when Paul wanted to go in to the people, the disciples would not allow him. ³¹ Then some of the officials of Asia, who were his friends, sent to him pleading that he would not venture into the theater. ³² Some therefore cried one thing and some another, for the assembly was con-fused, and most of them did not know why they had come together. ³³ And they drew Alexander out of the multitude, the Jews putting him forward. And Alexander motioned with his hand, and wanted to make his defense to the people. ³⁴ But when they found out that he was a Jew, all with one voice cried out for about two hours, "Great *is* Diana of the Ephesians!"

³⁵ And when the city clerk had quieted the crowd, he said: "Men of Ephesus, what man is there who does not know that the city of the Ephesians is temple guardian of the great goddess Diana, and of the *image* which fell down from Zeus? ³⁶ Therefore, since these things cannot be denied, you ought to be quiet and do noth-ing rashly. ³⁷ For you have brought these men here who are neither robbers of temples nor blasphemers of your goddess. ³⁸ Therefore, if Demetrius and his fellow craftsmen have a case against anyone, the courts are open and there are proconsuls. Let them bring charges against one an-other. ³⁹ But if you have any other inquiry to make, it shall be determined in the law-ful assembly. ⁴⁰ For we are in danger of being called in question for today's up-roar, there being no reason which we may give to account for this disorderly gather-ing." ⁴¹ And when he had said these things, he dismissed the assembly.

~ 2 CHRONICLES 30:1—31:21 ~

And Hezekiah sent to all Israel and Judah, and also wrote letters to Ephraim and Manasseh, that they should come to the house of the LORD at Jerusalem, to keep the Passover to the LORD God of Israel. ² For the king and his leaders and all the assembly in Jerusa-

lem had agreed to keep the Passover in the second month. ³ For they could not keep it at the regular time, because a sufficient number of priests had not con-secrated themselves, nor had the people gathered together at Jerusalem. ⁴ And the matter pleased the king and all the assembly. ⁵ So they resolved to make a proclamation throughout all Israel, from Beersheba to Dan, that they should come to keep the Passover to the LORD God of Israel at Jerusalem, since they had not done it for a long time in the prescribed manner.

⁶ Then the runners went throughout all Israel and Judah with the letters from the king and his leaders, and spoke according to the command of the king: "Children of Israel, return to the LORD God of Abraham, Isaac, and Israel; then He will return to the remnant of you who have escaped from the hand of the kings of Assyria. ⁷ And do not be like your fathers and your brethren, who trespassed against the LORD God of their fathers, so that He gave them up to desolation, as you see. ⁸ Now do not be stiff-necked, as your fathers were, but yield yourselves to the LORD; and enter His sanctuary, which He has sanctified forever, and serve the LORD your God, that the fierceness of His wrath may turn away from you. ⁹ For if you return to the LORD, your brethren and your children will be treated with compassion by those who lead them captive, so that they may come back to this land; for the LORD your God is gracious and merciful, and will not turn His face from you if you return to Him."

¹⁰ So the runners passed from city to city through the country of Ephraim and Manasseh, as far as Zebulun; but they laughed at them and mocked them. ¹¹ Nevertheless some from Asher, Manasseh, and Zebulun humbled themselves and came to Jerusalem. ¹² Also the hand of God was on Judah to give them singleness of heart to obey the command of the king and the leaders, at the word of the LORD.

¹³ Now many people, a very great assembly, gathered at Jerusalem to keep the Feast of Unleavened Bread in the second month. ¹⁴ They arose and took away the altars that were in Jerusalem, and they took away all the incense altars and cast them into the Brook Kidron. ¹⁵ Then they slaughtered the Passover lambs on the fourteenth day of the second month. The priests and the Levites were ashamed, and sanctified themselves, and brought the burnt offerings to the house of the LORD. ¹⁶ They stood in their place according to their custom, according to the Law of Moses the man of God; the priests sprinkled the blood received from the hand of the Levites. ¹⁷ For there were many in the assembly who had not sanctified themselves; therefore the Levites had charge of the slaughter of the Passover lambs for everyone who was not clean, to sanctify them to the LORD. ¹⁸ For a multitude of the people, many from Ephraim, Manasseh, Issachar, and Zebulun, had not cleansed themselves, yet they ate the Passover contrary to what was written. But Hezekiah prayed for them, saying, "May the good LORD provide atonement for everyone ¹⁹ who prepares his heart to seek God, the LORD God of his fathers, though he is not cleansed according to the purification of the sanctuary." ²⁰ And the LORD listened to Hezekiah and healed the people.

²¹ So the children of Israel who were present at Jerusalem kept the Feast of Unleavened Bread seven days with great gladness; and the Levites and the priests praised the LORD day by day, singing to the LORD, accompanied by loud instruments. ²² And Hezekiah gave encouragement to all the Levites who taught the good knowledge of the LORD; and they ate throughout the feast seven days, offering peace offerings and making confession to the LORD God of their fathers.

²³ Then the whole assembly agreed to keep the feast another seven days, and they kept it another seven days with gladness. ²⁴ For Hezekiah king of Judah gave to the assembly a thousand bulls and seven thousand sheep, and the leaders gave to the assembly a thousand bulls and ten thousand sheep; and a great number of priests sanctified themselves. ²⁵ The whole assembly of Judah rejoiced, also the priests and Levites, all the assembly that came from Israel, the sojourners who came from the land of Israel, and those who dwelt in Judah. ²⁶ So there was great joy in Jerusalem, for since the time of Solomon the son of David, king of Israel, there had been nothing like this in Jerusalem. ²⁷ Then the priests, the Levites, arose and blessed the people, and their voice was heard; and

Shoot for the Goal

> For the Lord your God is gracious and merciful, and will not turn His face from you if you return to Him.
>
> *2 Chronicles 30:9*

When Michigan played Wisconsin in basketball early in the 1989 season, Michigan's Rumeal Robinson found himself at the foul line with just seconds left in the fourth quarter. His team was trailing by one point, and Rumeal knew that if he could sink both shots, Michigan would win. Sadly, Rumeal missed both shots. Wisconsin upset the favored Michigan, and Rumeal went to the locker room feeling devastated and embarrassed.

His dejection, however, led to a positive move on his part. He determined that for the rest of the season at the end of each practice, he was going to shoot 100 extra foul shots. And shoot 'em he did!

The moment came when Rumeal stepped to the foul line in yet another game, again with the opportunity to make two shots. This time there were only three seconds left in overtime, and the game was the NCAA finals! Swish went the first shot — and swish went the second. Those two points gave Michigan the victory and the collegiate national championship.

Have you just failed at something? Don't give up. Instead, work harder. Success is possible!

their prayer came *up* to His holy dwelling place, to heaven.

31 Now when all this was finished, all Israel who were present went out to the cities of Judah and broke the sacred pillars in pieces, cut down the wooden images, and threw down the high places and the altars—from all Judah, Benjamin, Ephraim, and Manasseh—until they had utterly destroyed them all. Then all the children of Israel returned to their own cities, every man to his possession.

² And Hezekiah appointed the divisions of the priests and the Levites according to their divisions, each man according to his service, the priests and Levites for burnt offerings and peace offerings, to serve, to give thanks, and to praise in the gates of the camp of the LORD. ³ The king also *appointed* a portion of his possessions for the burnt offerings: for the morning and evening burnt offerings, the burnt offerings for the Sabbaths and the New Moons and the set feasts, as *it is* written in the Law of the LORD.

⁴ Moreover he commanded the people who dwelt in Jerusalem to contribute support for the priests and the Levites, that they might devote themselves to the Law of the LORD.

⁵ As soon as the commandment was circulated, the children of Israel brought in abundance the firstfruits of grain and wine, oil and honey, and of all the produce of the field; and they brought in abundantly the tithe of everything. ⁶ And the children of Israel and Judah, who dwelt in the cities of Judah, brought the tithe of oxen and sheep; also the tithe of holy things which were consecrated to the LORD their God they laid in heaps.

⁷ In the third month they began laying them in heaps, and they finished in the seventh month. ⁸ And when Hezekiah and the leaders came and saw the heaps, they blessed the LORD and His people Israel. ⁹ Then Hezekiah questioned the priests and the Levites concerning the heaps. ¹⁰ And Azariah the chief priest, from the house of Zadok, answered him and said, "Since *the people* began to bring the offerings into the house of the LORD, we have had enough to eat and have plenty left, for the LORD has blessed His

people; and what is left *is* this great abundance."

¹¹ Now Hezekiah commanded *them* to prepare rooms in the house of the LORD, and they prepared them. ¹² Then they faithfully brought in the offerings, the tithes, and the dedicated things; Cononiah the Levite had charge of them, and Shimei his brother *was* the next. ¹³ Jehiel, Azaziah, Nahath, Asahel, Jerimoth, Jozabad, Eliel, Ismachiah, Mahath, and Benaiah *were* overseers under the hand of Cononiah and Shimei his brother, at the commandment of Hezekiah the king and Azariah the ruler of the house of God. ¹⁴ Kore the son of Imnah the Levite, the keeper of the East Gate, *was* over the freewill offerings to God, to distribute the offerings of the LORD and the most holy things. ¹⁵ And under him *were* Eden, Miniamin, Jeshua, Shemaiah, Amariah, and Shecaniah, *his* faithful assistants in the cities of the priests, to distribute allotments to their brethren by divisions, to the great as well as the small.

¹⁶ Besides those males from three years old and up who were written in the genealogy, they distributed to everyone who entered the house of the LORD his daily portion for the work of his service, by his division, ¹⁷ and to the priests who were written in the genealogy according to their father's house, and to the Levites from twenty years old and up according to their work, by their divisions, ¹⁸ and to all who were written in the genealogy—their little ones and their wives, their sons and daughters, the whole company of them— for in their faithfulness they sanctified themselves in holiness.

¹⁹ Also for the sons of Aaron the priests, *who were* in the fields of the commonlands of their cities, in every single city, *there were* men who were designated by name to distribute portions to all the males among the priests and to all who were listed by genealogies among the Levites.

²⁰ Thus Hezekiah did throughout all Judah, and he did what *was* good and right and true before the LORD his God. ²¹ And in every work that he began in the service of the house of God, in the law and in the commandment, to seek his God, he did *it* with all his heart. So he prospered.

~ PSALM 85:1–7 ~

¹ LORD, You have been favorable to
    Your land;
  You have brought back the captivity
    of Jacob.
² You have forgiven the iniquity of
    Your people;
  You have covered all their sin.   Selah
³ You have taken away all Your wrath;
  You have turned from the fierceness
    of Your anger.

⁴ Restore us, O God of our salvation,
  And cause Your anger toward us to
    cease.
⁵ Will You be angry with us forever?
  Will You prolong Your anger to all
    generations?
⁶ Will You not revive us again,
  That Your people may rejoice in
    You?
⁷ Show us Your mercy, LORD,
  And grant us Your salvation.

~ PROVERBS 21:9–11 ~

⁹ Better to dwell in a corner of a
    housetop,
  Than in a house shared with a
    contentious woman.

¹⁰ The soul of the wicked desires evil;
   His neighbor finds no favor in his
     eyes.

¹¹ When the scoffer is punished, the
     simple is made wise;
   But when the wise is instructed, he
     receives knowledge.

~ ACTS 20:1–16 ~

After the uproar had ceased, Paul called
the disciples to *himself,* embraced *them,*
and departed to go to Macedonia. ² Now
when he had gone over that region and

encouraged them with many words, he
came to Greece ³ and stayed three months.
And when the Jews plotted against him
as he was about to sail to Syria, he decided to return through Macedonia. ⁴ And
Sopater of Berea accompanied him to
Asia—also Aristarchus and Secundus of
the Thessalonians, and Gaius of Derbe,
and Timothy, and Tychicus and Trophimus
of Asia. ⁵ These men, going ahead, waited
for us at Troas. ⁶ But we sailed away from
Philippi after the Days of Unleavened
Bread, and in five days joined them at
Troas, where we stayed seven days.

⁷ Now on the first *day* of the week,
when the disciples came together to break
bread, Paul, ready to depart the next day,
spoke to them and continued his message
until midnight. ⁸ There were many lamps
in the upper room where they were gathered together. ⁹ And in a window sat a
certain young man named Eutychus, who
was sinking into a deep sleep. He was
overcome by sleep; and as Paul continued speaking, he fell down from the third
story and was taken up dead. ¹⁰ But Paul
went down, fell on him, and embracing
him said, "Do not trouble yourselves, for
his life is in him." ¹¹ Now when he had
come up, had broken bread and eaten,
and talked a long while, even till daybreak,
he departed. ¹² And they brought the
young man in alive, and they were not a
little comforted.

¹³ Then we went ahead to the ship and
sailed to Assos, there intending to take
Paul on board; for so he had given orders, intending himself to go on foot.
¹⁴ And when he met us at Assos, we took
him on board and came to Mitylene. ¹⁵ We
sailed from there, and the next *day* came
opposite Chios. The following *day* we
arrived at Samos and stayed at Trogyllium.
The next *day* we came to Miletus. ¹⁶ For
Paul had decided to sail past Ephesus, so
that he would not have to spend time in
Asia; for he was hurrying to be at Jerusalem, if possible, on the Day of Pentecost.

~ 2 CHRONICLES 32:1—33:25 ~

After these deeds of faithfulness, Sennacherib king of Assyria came and entered Judah; he encamped against the fortified cities, thinking to win them over to himself. ² And when Hezekiah saw that Sennacherib had come, and that his purpose was to make war against Jerusalem, ³ he consulted with his leaders and commanders to stop the water from the springs which *were* outside the city; and they helped him. ⁴ Thus many people gathered together who stopped all the springs and the brook that ran through the land, saying, "Why should the kings of Assyria come and find much water?" ⁵ And he strengthened himself, built up all the wall that was broken, raised *it* up to the towers, and *built* another wall outside; also he repaired the Millo *in* the City of David, and made weapons and shields in abundance. ⁶ Then he set military captains over the people, gathered them together to him in the open square of the city gate, and gave them encouragement, saying, ⁷ "Be strong and courageous; do not be afraid nor dismayed before the king of Assyria, nor before all the multitude that *is* with him; for *there are* more with us than with him. ⁸ With him *is* an arm of flesh; but with us *is* the LORD our God, to help us and to fight our battles." And the people were strengthened by the words of Hezekiah king of Judah.

⁹ After this Sennacherib king of Assyria sent his servants to Jerusalem (but he and all the forces with him *laid siege* against Lachish), to Hezekiah king of Judah, and to all Judah who *were* in Jerusalem, saying, ¹⁰ "Thus says Sennacherib king of Assyria: 'In what do you trust, that you remain under siege in Jerusalem? ¹¹ Does not Hezekiah persuade you to give yourselves over to die by famine and by thirst, saying, "The LORD our God will deliver us from the hand of the king of Assyria"? ¹² Has not the same Hezekiah taken away His high places and His altars, and commanded Judah and Jerusalem, saying, "You shall worship before one altar and burn incense on it"? ¹³ Do you not know what I and my fathers have done to all

the peoples of *other* lands? Were the gods of the nations of those lands in any way able to deliver their lands out of my hand? ¹⁴ Who *was there* among all the gods of those nations that my fathers utterly destroyed that could deliver his people from my hand, that your God should be able to deliver you from my hand? ¹⁵ Now therefore, do not let Hezekiah deceive you or persuade you like this, and do not believe him; for no god of any nation or kingdom was able to deliver his people from my hand or the hand of my fathers. How much less will your God deliver you from my hand?' "

¹⁶ Furthermore, his servants spoke against the LORD God and against His servant Hezekiah.

¹⁷ He also wrote letters to revile the LORD God of Israel, and to speak against Him, saying, "As the gods of the nations of *other* lands have not delivered their people from my hand, so the God of Hezekiah will not deliver His people from my hand." ¹⁸ Then they called out with a loud voice in Hebrew to the people of Jerusalem who *were* on the wall, to frighten them and trouble them, that they might take the city. ¹⁹ And they spoke against the God of Jerusalem, as against the gods of the people of the earth—the work of men's hands.

²⁰ Now because of this King Hezekiah and the prophet Isaiah, the son of Amoz, prayed and cried out to heaven. ²¹ Then the LORD sent an angel who cut down every mighty man of valor, leader, and captain in the camp of the king of Assyria. So he returned shamefaced to his own land. And when he had gone into the temple of his god, some of his own offspring struck him down with the sword there.

²² Thus the LORD saved Hezekiah and the inhabitants of Jerusalem from the hand of Sennacherib the king of Assyria, and from the hand of all *others*, and guided them on every side. ²³ And many brought gifts to the LORD at Jerusalem, and presents to Hezekiah king of Judah, so that he was exalted in the sight of all nations thereafter.

What Money Can't Buy

J. C. Macaulay once took a group of his college students who were preparing for Christian service on the mission field to the famous Biltmore Estate near Asheville, North Carolina. He was eager to see their response to the vast wealth of the grounds, and he was hopeful that his students would confront any materialistic desires they might have before going abroad.

He watched as the students viewed the fabulous treasures on display, moving from one luxurious room to another. Several of the students commented on the value of various items. Others remarked about the exquisite perfection of various artifacts and pieces of furniture. All demonstrated a great appreciation for the upkeep of the spacious and beautiful grounds.

His heart was warmed, though, when, as they returned from the trip, the students spontaneously began to sing the words of an old hymn:

> *When you look at others with their lands and gold,*
> *Think that Christ has promised you His wealth untold;*
> *Count your blessings — money cannot buy*
> *Your reward in Heaven nor your home on high.*

When the allure of materialism threatens to pull you in, recount to yourself the marvelous blessings God has given you. Blessings that cannot be bought or sold, lost or stolen, broken or used up. God's blessings are eternal.

> I have shown you in every way, by laboring like this, that you must support the weak. And remember the words of the Lord Jesus, that He said, "It is more blessed to give than to receive."
>
> *Acts 20:35*

24 In those days Hezekiah was sick and near death, and he prayed to the LORD; and He spoke to him and gave him a sign. 25 But Hezekiah did not repay according to the favor *shown* him, for his heart was lifted up; therefore wrath was looming over him and over Judah and Jerusalem. 26 Then Hezekiah humbled himself for the pride of his heart, he and the inhabitants of Jerusalem, so that the wrath of the LORD did not come upon them in the days of Hezekiah.

27 Hezekiah had very great riches and honor. And he made himself treasuries for silver, for gold, for precious stones, for spices, for shields, and for all kinds of desirable items; 28 storehouses for the harvest of grain, wine, and oil; and stalls for all kinds of livestock, and folds for flocks. 29 Moreover he provided cities for himself, and possessions of flocks and herds in abundance; for God had given him very much property. 30 This same Hezekiah also stopped the water outlet of Upper Gihon, and brought the water by tunnel to the west side of the City of David. Hezekiah prospered in all his works.

31 However, *regarding* the ambassadors of the princes of Babylon, whom they sent to him to inquire about the wonder that was *done* in the land, God withdrew from him, in order to test him, that He might know all *that was* in his heart.

32 Now the rest of the acts of Hezekiah, and his goodness, indeed they *are* written in the vision of Isaiah the prophet, the son of Amoz, *and* in the book of the kings of Judah and Israel. 33 So Hezekiah rested with his fathers, and they buried him in the upper tombs of the sons of David; and all Judah and the inhabitants of Jerusalem honored him at his death. Then Manasseh his son reigned in his place.

33 Manasseh *was* twelve years old when he became king, and he reigned fifty-five years in Jerusalem. 2 But he did evil in the sight of the LORD, according to the abominations of the nations whom the LORD had cast out before the children of Israel. 3 For he rebuilt the high places which Hezekiah his father had broken down; he raised up altars for the Baals, and made wooden images; and he worshiped all the host of heaven and served

them. 4 He also built altars in the house of the LORD, of which the LORD had said, "In Jerusalem shall My name be forever." 5 And he built altars for all the host of heaven in the two courts of the house of the LORD. 6 Also he caused his sons to pass through the fire in the Valley of the Son of Hinnom; he practiced soothsaying, used witchcraft and sorcery, and consulted mediums and spiritists. He did much evil in the sight of the LORD, to provoke Him to anger. 7 He even set a carved image, the idol which he had made, in the house of God, of which God had said to David and to Solomon his son, "In this house and in Jerusalem, which I have chosen out of all the tribes of Israel, I will put My name forever; 8 and I will not again remove the foot of Israel from the land which I have appointed for your fathers— only if they are careful to do all that I have commanded them, according to the whole law and the statutes and the ordinances by the hand of Moses." 9 So Manasseh seduced Judah and the inhabitants of Jerusalem to do more evil than the nations whom the LORD had destroyed before the children of Israel.

10 And the LORD spoke to Manasseh and his people, but they would not listen. 11 Therefore the LORD brought upon them the captains of the army of the king of Assyria, who took Manasseh with hooks, bound him with bronze *fetters,* and carried him off to Babylon. 12 Now when he was in affliction, he implored the LORD his God, and humbled himself greatly before the God of his fathers, 13 and prayed to Him; and He received his entreaty, heard his supplication, and brought him back to Jerusalem into his kingdom. Then Manasseh knew that the LORD *was* God.

14 After this he built a wall outside the City of David on the west side of Gihon, in the valley, as far as the entrance of the Fish Gate; and *it* enclosed Ophel, and he raised it to a very great height. Then he put military captains in all the fortified cities of Judah. 15 He took away the foreign gods and the idol from the house of the LORD, and all the altars that he had built in the mount of the house of the LORD and in Jerusalem; and he cast *them* out of the city. 16 He also repaired the altar

of the LORD, sacrificed peace offerings and thank offerings on it, and commanded Judah to serve the LORD God of Israel. [17] Nevertheless the people still sacrificed on the high places, *but* only to the LORD their God.

[18] Now the rest of the acts of Manasseh, his prayer to his God, and the words of the seers who spoke to him in the name of the LORD God of Israel, indeed they *are written* in the book of the kings of Israel. [19] Also his prayer and *how God* received his entreaty, and all his sin and trespass, and the sites where he built high places and set up wooden images and carved images, before he was humbled, indeed they *are* written among the sayings of Hozai. [20] So Manasseh rested with his fathers, and they buried him in his own house. Then his son Amon reigned in his place.

[21] Amon *was* twenty-two years old when he became king, and he reigned two years in Jerusalem. [22] But he did evil in the sight of the LORD, as his father Manasseh had done; for Amon sacrificed to all the carved images which his father Manasseh had made, and served them. [23] And he did not humble himself before the LORD, as his father Manasseh had humbled himself; but Amon trespassed more and more.

[24] Then his servants conspired against him, and killed him in his own house. [25] But the people of the land executed all those who had conspired against King Amon. Then the people of the land made his son Josiah king in his place.

~ PSALM 85:8–13 ~

[8] I will hear what God the LORD will speak,
   For He will speak peace
   To His people and to His saints;
   But let them not turn back to folly.
[9] Surely His salvation *is* near to those who fear Him,
   That glory may dwell in our land.

[10] Mercy and truth have met together;
   Righteousness and peace have kissed.
[11] Truth shall spring out of the earth,
   And righteousness shall look down from heaven.

[12] Yes, the LORD will give *what is* good;
   And our land will yield its increase.
[13] Righteousness will go before Him,
   And shall make His footsteps *our* pathway.

~ PROVERBS 21:12 ~

[12] The righteous *God* wisely considers the house of the wicked,
   Overthrowing the wicked for *their* wickedness.

~ ACTS 20:17–38 ~

From Miletus he sent to Ephesus and called for the elders of the church. [18] And when they had come to him, he said to them: "You know, from the first day that I came to Asia, in what manner I always lived among you, [19] serving the Lord with all humility, with many tears and trials which happened to me by the plotting of the Jews; [20] how I kept back nothing that was helpful, but proclaimed it to you, and taught you publicly and from house to house, [21] testifying to Jews, and also to Greeks, repentance toward God and faith toward our Lord Jesus Christ. [22] And see, now I go bound in the spirit to Jerusalem, not knowing the things that will happen to me there, [23] except that the Holy Spirit testifies in every city, saying that chains and tribulations await me. [24] But none of these things move me; nor do I count my life dear to myself, so that I may finish my race with joy, and the ministry which I received from the Lord Jesus, to testify to the gospel of the grace of God.

[25] "And indeed, now I know that you all, among whom I have gone preaching the kingdom of God, will see my face no more. [26] Therefore I testify to you this day that I *am* innocent of the blood of all *men*. [27] For I have not shunned to declare to you the whole counsel of God. [28] Therefore take heed to yourselves and to all the flock, among which the Holy Spirit has made you overseers, to shepherd the church of God which He purchased with His own blood. [29] For I know this, that after my departure savage wolves will come in among you, not sparing the flock. [30] Also from among yourselves men will

rise up, speaking perverse things, to draw away the disciples after themselves. [31] Therefore watch, and remember that for three years I did not cease to warn everyone night and day with tears.

[32] "So now, brethren, I commend you to God and to the word of His grace, which is able to build you up and give you an inheritance among all those who are sanctified. [33] I have coveted no one's silver or gold or apparel. [34] Yes, you yourselves know that these hands have provided for my necessities, and for those who were with me. [35] I have shown you in every way, by laboring like this, that you must support the weak. And remember the words of the Lord Jesus, that He said, 'It is more blessed to give than to receive.' "

[36] And when he had said these things, he knelt down and prayed with them all. [37] Then they all wept freely, and fell on Paul's neck and kissed him, [38] sorrowing most of all for the words which he spoke, that they would see his face no more. And they accompanied him to the ship.

READING 200 · JULY 19

～ 2 CHRONICLES 34:1—36:23 ～

Josiah *was* eight years old when he became king, and he reigned thirty-one years in Jerusalem. [2] And he did *what was* right in the sight of the LORD, and walked in the ways of his father David; *he* did *not* turn aside to the right hand or to the left.

[3] For in the eighth year of his reign, while he was still young, he began to seek the God of his father David; and in the twelfth year he began to purge Judah and Jerusalem of the high places, the wooden images, the carved images, and the molded images. [4] They broke down the altars of the Baals in his presence, and the incense altars which *were* above them he cut down; and the wooden images, the carved images, and the molded images he broke in pieces, and made dust of them and scattered *it* on the graves of those who had sacrificed to them. [5] He also burned the bones of the priests on their altars, and cleansed Judah and Jerusalem. [6] And *so he did* in the cities of Manasseh, Ephraim, and Simeon, as far as Naphtali and all around, with axes. [7] When he had broken down the altars and the wooden images, had beaten the carved images into powder, and cut down all the incense altars throughout all the land of Israel, he returned to Jerusalem.

[8] In the eighteenth year of his reign, when he had purged the land and the temple, he sent Shaphan the son of Azaliah, Maaseiah the governor of the city, and Joah the son of Joahaz the recorder, to repair the house of the LORD his God. [9] When they came to Hilkiah the high priest, they delivered the money that was brought into the house of God, which the Levites who kept the doors had gathered from the hand of Manasseh and Ephraim, from all the remnant of Israel, from all Judah and Benjamin, and *which* they had brought back to Jerusalem. [10] Then they put *it* in the hand of the foremen who had the oversight of the house of the LORD; and they gave it to the workmen who worked in the house of the LORD, to repair and restore the house. [11] They gave *it* to the craftsmen and builders to buy hewn stone and timber for beams, and to floor the houses which the kings of Judah had destroyed. [12] And the men did the work faithfully. Their overseers *were* Jahath and Obadiah the Levites, of the sons of Merari, and Zechariah and Meshullam, of the sons of the Kohathites, to supervise. *Others of* the Levites, all of whom were skillful with instruments of music, [13] *were* over the burden bearers and *were* overseers of all who did work in any kind of service. And *some* of the Levites *were* scribes, officers, and gatekeepers.

[14] Now when they brought out the money that was brought into the house of the LORD, Hilkiah the priest found the Book of the Law of the LORD *given* by Moses. [15] Then Hilkiah answered and said to Shaphan the scribe, "I have found the Book of the Law in the house of the

Help Me!

In an article written for *America* magazine entitled, "Praying in a Time of Depression," Jane Redmont wrote:

"On a quick trip to New York for a consulting job, a week or two into the anti-depressant drug and feeling no relief, I fell into a seven-hour anxiety attack with recurring suicidal ideations. On the morning after my arrival I found I could not focus my attention; yet focus was crucial in the job I was contracted to do for 24 hours, as recorder and process observer at a conference of urban activists that was beginning later that day. I felt as if I were about to jump out of my skin — or throw myself under a truck.

"An hour away from the beginning of the conference, walking uptown on a noisy Manhattan street in the afternoon, I prayed . . . perhaps out loud, I am not sure. I said with all my strength, 'Jesus, I don't usually ask you for much, but I am asking you now, in the name of all those people whom you healed, in the name of the man born blind and the bent-over woman and the woman who bled for years, in the name of the man with the demons and the little girl whom you raised up, *help me*.'

"Within an hour, I was calm again."

God is our high tower, a refuge in times of trouble. We can pray in the midst of anxiety and depression and God will fill us with His peace that passes understanding, sheltering us from the torment of our worry and restoring us to wholeness once again.

LORD." And Hilkiah gave the book to Shaphan. [16] So Shaphan carried the book to the king, bringing the king word, saying, "All that was committed to your servants they are doing. [17] And they have gathered the money that was found in the house of the LORD, and have delivered it into the hand of the overseers and the workmen." [18] Then Shaphan the scribe told the king, saying, "Hilkiah the priest has given me a book." And Shaphan read it before the king.

[19] Thus it happened, when the king heard the words of the Law, that he tore his clothes. [20] Then the king commanded Hilkiah, Ahikam the son of Shaphan, Abdon the son of Micah, Shaphan the scribe, and Asaiah a servant of the king, saying, [21] "Go, inquire of the LORD for me, and for those who are left in Israel and Judah, concerning the words of the book that is found; for great *is* the wrath of the LORD that is poured out on us, because our fathers have not kept the word of the LORD, to do according to all that is written in this book."

[22] So Hilkiah and those the king *had appointed* went to Huldah the prophetess, the wife of Shallum the son of Tokhath, the son of Hasrah, keeper of the wardrobe. (She dwelt in Jerusalem in the Second Quarter.) And they spoke to her to that *effect*.

[23] Then she answered them, "Thus says the LORD God of Israel, 'Tell the man who sent you to Me, [24] "Thus says the LORD: 'Behold, I will bring calamity on this place and on its inhabitants, all the curses that are written in the book which they have read before the king of Judah, [25] because they have forsaken Me and burned incense to other gods, that they might provoke Me to anger with all the works of their hands. Therefore My wrath will be poured out on this place, and not be quenched.' " ' [26] But as for the king of Judah, who sent you to inquire of the LORD, in this manner you shall speak to him, 'Thus says the LORD God of Israel: "*Concerning* the words which you have heard— [27] because your heart was tender, and you humbled yourself before God when you heard His words against this place and against its inhabitants, and you humbled yourself before Me, and you tore

your clothes and wept before Me, I also have heard *you*," says the LORD. [28] "Surely I will gather you to your fathers, and you shall be gathered to your grave in peace; and your eyes shall not see all the calamity which I will bring on this place and its inhabitants." ' " So they brought back word to the king.

[29] Then the king sent and gathered all the elders of Judah and Jerusalem. [30] The king went up to the house of the LORD, with all the men of Judah and the inhabitants of Jerusalem—the priests and the Levites, and all the people, great and small. And he read in their hearing all the words of the Book of the Covenant which had been found in the house of the LORD. [31] Then the king stood in his place and made a covenant before the LORD, to follow the LORD, and to keep His commandments and His testimonies and His statutes with all his heart and all his soul, to perform the words of the covenant that were written in this book. [32] And he made all who were present in Jerusalem and Benjamin take a stand. So the inhabitants of Jerusalem did according to the covenant of God, the God of their fathers. [33] Thus Josiah removed all the abominations from all the country that *belonged* to the children of Israel, and made all who were present in Israel diligently serve the LORD their God. All his days they did not depart from following the LORD God of their fathers.

35

Now Josiah kept a Passover to the LORD in Jerusalem, and they slaughtered the Passover *lambs* on the fourteenth *day* of the first month. [2] And he set the priests in their duties and encouraged them for the service of the house of the LORD. [3] Then he said to the Levites who taught all Israel, who were holy to the LORD: "Put the holy ark in the house which Solomon the son of David, king of Israel, built. *It shall* no longer *be* a burden on *your* shoulders. Now serve the LORD your God and His people Israel. [4] Prepare *yourselves* according to your fathers' houses, according to your divisions, following the written instruction of David king of Israel and the written instruction of Solomon his son. [5] And stand in the holy *place* according to the divisions of the fathers' houses of your brethren the *lay* people, and *according to* the division of the father's house of the Levites. ⁶ So slaughter the Passover *offerings,* consecrate yourselves, and prepare *them* for your brethren, that *they* may do according to the word of the LORD by the hand of Moses."

⁷ Then Josiah gave the *lay* people lambs and young goats from the flock, all for Passover *offerings* for all who were present, to the number of thirty thousand, as well as three thousand cattle; these *were* from the king's possessions. ⁸ And his leaders gave willingly to the people, to the priests, and to the Levites. Hilkiah, Zechariah, and Jehiel, rulers of the house of God, gave to the priests for the Passover *offerings* two thousand six hundred *from the flock,* and three hundred cattle. ⁹ Also Conaniah, his brothers Shemaiah and Nethanel, and Hashabiah and Jeiel and Jozabad, chief of the Levites, gave to the Levites for Passover *offerings* five thousand *from the flock* and five hundred cattle.

¹⁰ So the service was prepared, and the priests stood in their places, and the Levites in their divisions, according to the king's command. ¹¹ And they slaughtered the Passover *offerings;* and the priests sprinkled *the blood* with their hands, while the Levites skinned *the animals.* ¹² Then they removed the burnt offerings that *they* might give them to the divisions of the fathers' houses of the *lay* people, to offer to the LORD, as *it is* written in the Book of Moses. And so *they did* with the cattle. ¹³ Also they roasted the Passover *offerings* with fire according to the ordinance; but the *other* holy *offerings* they boiled in pots, in caldrons, and in pans, and divided *them* quickly among all the *lay* people. ¹⁴ Then afterward they prepared portions for themselves and for the priests, because the priests, the sons of Aaron, *were busy* in offering burnt offerings and fat until night; therefore the Levites prepared portions for themselves and for the priests, the sons of Aaron. ¹⁵ And the singers, the sons of Asaph, *were* in their places, according to the command of David, Asaph, Heman, and Jeduthun the king's seer. Also the gatekeepers were at each gate; they

did not have to leave their position, because their brethren the Levites prepared portions for them.

¹⁶ So all the service of the LORD was prepared the same day, to keep the Passover and to offer burnt offerings on the altar of the LORD, according to the command of King Josiah. ¹⁷ And the children of Israel who were present kept the Passover at that time, and the Feast of Unleavened Bread for seven days. ¹⁸ There had been no Passover kept in Israel like that since the days of Samuel the prophet; and none of the kings of Israel had kept such a Passover as Josiah kept, with the priests and the Levites, all Judah and Israel who were present, and the inhabitants of Jerusalem. ¹⁹ In the eighteenth year of the reign of Josiah this Passover was kept.

²⁰ After all this, when Josiah had prepared the temple, Necho king of Egypt came up to fight against Carchemish by the Euphrates; and Josiah went out against him. ²¹ But he sent messengers to him, saying, "What have I to do with you, king of Judah? *I have* not *come* against you this day, but against the house with which I have war; for God commanded me to make haste. Refrain *from meddling with* God, who *is* with me, lest He destroy you." ²² Nevertheless Josiah would not turn his face from him, but disguised himself so that he might fight with him, and did not heed the words of Necho from the mouth of God. So he came to fight in the Valley of Megiddo.

²³ And the archers shot King Josiah; and the king said to his servants, "Take me away, for I am severely wounded." ²⁴ His servants therefore took him out of that chariot and put him in the second chariot that he had, and they brought him to Jerusalem. So he died, and was buried in *one of* the tombs of his fathers. And all Judah and Jerusalem mourned for Josiah.

²⁵ Jeremiah also lamented for Josiah. And to this day all the singing men and the singing women speak of Josiah in their lamentations. They made it a custom in Israel; and indeed they *are* written in the Laments.

²⁶ Now the rest of the acts of Josiah and his goodness, according to *what was* written in the Law of the LORD, ²⁷ and his

deeds from first to last, indeed they *are* written in the book of the kings of Israel and Judah.

36 Then the people of the land took Jehoahaz the son of Josiah, and made him king in his father's place in Jerusalem. ² Jehoahaz *was* twenty-three years old when he became king, and he reigned three months in Jerusalem. ³ Now the king of Egypt deposed him at Jerusalem; and he imposed on the land a tribute of one hundred talents of silver and a talent of gold. ⁴ Then the king of Egypt made *Jehoahaz's* brother Eliakim king over Judah and Jerusalem, and changed his name to Jehoiakim. And Necho took Jehoahaz his brother and carried him off to Egypt.

⁵ Jehoiakim *was* twenty-five years old when he became king, and he reigned eleven years in Jerusalem. And he did evil in the sight of the LORD his God. ⁶ Nebuchadnezzar king of Babylon came up against him, and bound him in bronze *fetters* to carry him off to Babylon. ⁷ Nebuchadnezzar also carried off *some* of the articles from the house of the LORD to Babylon, and put them in his temple at Babylon. ⁸ Now the rest of the acts of Jehoiakim, the abominations which he did, and what was found against him, indeed they *are* written in the book of the kings of Israel and Judah. Then Jehoiachin his son reigned in his place.

⁹ Jehoiachin *was* eight years old when he became king, and he reigned in Jerusalem three months and ten days. And he did evil in the sight of the LORD. ¹⁰ At the turn of the year King Nebuchadnezzar summoned *him* and took him to Babylon, with the costly articles from the house of the LORD, and made Zedekiah, *Jehoiakim's* brother, king over Judah and Jerusalem.

¹¹ Zedekiah *was* twenty-one years old when he became king, and he reigned eleven years in Jerusalem. ¹² He did evil in the sight of the LORD his God, *and* did not humble himself before Jeremiah the prophet, *who spoke* from the mouth of the LORD. ¹³ And he also rebelled against King Nebuchadnezzar, who had made him swear *an oath* by God; but he stiffened his neck and hardened his heart against turning to the LORD God of Is-

rael. ¹⁴ Moreover all the leaders of the priests and the people transgressed more and more, *according* to all the abominations of the nations, and defiled the house of the LORD which He had consecrated in Jerusalem.

¹⁵ And the LORD God of their fathers sent *warnings* to them by His messengers, rising up early and sending *them,* because He had compassion on His people and on His dwelling place. ¹⁶ But they mocked the messengers of God, despised His words, and scoffed at His prophets, until the wrath of the LORD arose against His people, till *there was* no remedy.

¹⁷ Therefore He brought against them the king of the Chaldeans, who killed their young men with the sword in the house of their sanctuary, and had no compassion on young man or virgin, on the aged or the weak; He gave *them* all into his hand. ¹⁸ And all the articles from the house of God, great and small, the treasures of the house of the LORD, and the treasures of the king and of his leaders, all *these* he took to Babylon. ¹⁹ Then they burned the house of God, broke down the wall of Jerusalem, burned all its palaces with fire, and destroyed all its precious possessions. ²⁰ And those who escaped from the sword he carried away to Babylon, where they became servants to him and his sons until the rule of the kingdom of Persia, ²¹ to fulfill the word of the LORD by the mouth of Jeremiah, until the land had enjoyed her Sabbaths. As long as she lay desolate she kept Sabbath, to fulfill seventy years.

²² Now in the first year of Cyrus king of Persia, that the word of the LORD by the mouth of Jeremiah might be fulfilled, the LORD stirred up the spirit of Cyrus king of Persia, so that he made a proclamation throughout all his kingdom, and also *put it* in writing, saying,

²³ Thus says Cyrus king of Persia:
All the kingdoms of the earth the LORD God of heaven has given me. And He has commanded me to build Him a house at Jerusalem which is in Judah. Who *is* among you of all His people? May the LORD his God *be* with him, and let him go up!

~ Psalm 86:1–5 ~

1 Bow down Your ear, O LORD, hear
      me;
   For I *am* poor and needy.
2 Preserve my life, for I *am* holy;
   You are my God;
   Save Your servant who trusts in You!
3 Be merciful to me, O Lord,
   For I cry to You all day long.
4 Rejoice the soul of Your servant,
   For to You, O Lord, I lift up my soul.
5 For You, Lord, *are* good, and ready
      to forgive,
   And abundant in mercy to all those
      who call upon You.

~ Proverbs 21:13, 14 ~

13 Whoever shuts his ears to the cry of
      the poor
   Will also cry himself and not be
      heard.

14 A gift in secret pacifies anger,
   And a bribe behind the back, strong
      wrath.

~ Acts 21:1–17 ~

Now it came to pass, that when we had
departed from them and set sail, running
a straight course we came to Cos, the following *day* to Rhodes, and from there to
Patara. 2 And finding a ship sailing over
to Phoenicia, we went aboard and set sail.
3 When we had sighted Cyprus, we passed
it on the left, sailed to Syria, and landed
at Tyre; for there the ship was to unload
her cargo. 4 And finding disciples, we
stayed there seven days. They told Paul
through the Spirit not to go up to Jerusalem. 5 When we had come to the end of
those days, we departed and went on our
way; and they all accompanied us, with
wives and children, till *we were* out of the
city. And we knelt down on the shore and
prayed. 6 When we had taken our leave
of one another, we boarded the ship, and
they returned home.

7 And when we had finished *our* voyage from Tyre, we came to Ptolemais,
greeted the brethren, and stayed with
them one day. 8 On the next *day* we who
were Paul's companions departed and
came to Caesarea, and entered the house
of Philip the evangelist, who was *one* of
the seven, and stayed with him. 9 Now this
man had four virgin daughters who
prophesied. 10 And as we stayed many
days, a certain prophet named Agabus
came down from Judea. 11 When he had
come to us, he took Paul's belt, bound his
own hands and feet, and said, "Thus says
the Holy Spirit, 'So shall the Jews at
Jerusalem bind the man who owns this
belt, and deliver *him* into the hands of
the Gentiles.'"

12 Now when we heard these things,
both we and those from that place pleaded
with him not to go up to Jerusalem.
13 Then Paul answered, "What do you
mean by weeping and breaking my heart?
For I am ready not only to be bound, but
also to die at Jerusalem for the name of
the Lord Jesus."

14 So when he would not be persuaded,
we ceased, saying, "The will of the Lord
be done."

15 And after those days we packed and
went up to Jerusalem. 16 Also some of the
disciples from Caesarea went with us and
brought with them a certain Mnason of
Cyprus, an early disciple, with whom we
were to lodge.

17 And when we had come to Jerusalem, the brethren received us gladly.

~ Ezra 1:1—2:70 ~

Now in the first year of Cyrus king
of Persia, that the word of the
LORD by the mouth of Jeremiah
might be fulfilled, the LORD stirred up the
spirit of Cyrus king of Persia, so that he
made a proclamation throughout all his
kingdom, and also *put it* in writing, saying,

2   Thus says Cyrus king of Persia:
     All the kingdoms of the earth the

LORD God of heaven has given me. And He has commanded me to build Him a house at Jerusalem which *is* in Judah. ³ Who *is* among you of all His people? May his God be with him, and let him go up to Jerusalem which *is* in Judah, and build the house of the LORD God of Israel (He *is* God), which *is* in Jerusalem. ⁴ And whoever is left in any place where he dwells, let the men of his place help him with silver and gold, with goods and livestock, besides the freewill offerings for the house of God which *is* in Jerusalem.

⁵ Then the heads of the fathers' *houses* of Judah and Benjamin, and the priests and the Levites, with all whose spirits God had moved, arose to go up and build the house of the LORD which *is* in Jerusalem. ⁶ And all those who *were* around them encouraged them with articles of silver and gold, with goods and livestock, and with precious things, besides all *that* was willingly offered.

⁷ King Cyrus also brought out the articles of the house of the LORD, which Nebuchadnezzar had taken from Jerusalem and put in the temple of his gods; ⁸ and Cyrus king of Persia brought them out by the hand of Mithredath the treasurer, and counted them out to Sheshbazzar the prince of Judah. ⁹ This *is* the number of them: thirty gold platters, one thousand silver platters, twenty-nine knives, ¹⁰ thirty gold basins, four hundred and ten silver basins of a similar *kind, and* one thousand other articles. ¹¹ All the articles of gold and silver *were* five thousand four hundred. All *these* Sheshbazzar took with the captives who were brought from Babylon to Jerusalem.

2 Now these *are* the people of the province who came back from the captivity, of those who had been carried away, whom Nebuchadnezzar the king of Babylon had carried away to Babylon, and who returned to Jerusalem and Judah, everyone to his *own* city. ² *Those* who came with Zerubbabel *were* Jeshua, Nehemiah, Seraiah, Reelaiah, Mordecai, Bilshan, Mispar, Bigvai, Re-

hum, *and* Baanah. The number of the men of the people of Israel: ³ the people of Parosh, two thousand one hundred and seventy-two; ⁴ the people of Shephatiah, three hundred and seventy-two; ⁵ the people of Arah, seven hundred and seventy-five; ⁶ the people of Pahath-Moab, of the people of Jeshua *and* Joab, two thousand eight hundred and twelve; ⁷ the people of Elam, one thousand two hundred and fifty-four; ⁸ the people of Zattu, nine hundred and forty-five; ⁹ the people of Zaccai, seven hundred and sixty; ¹⁰ the people of Bani, six hundred and forty-two; ¹¹ the people of Bebai, six hundred and twenty-three; ¹² the people of Azgad, one thousand two hundred and twenty-two; ¹³ the people of Adonikam, six hundred and sixty-six; ¹⁴ the people of Bigvai, two thousand and fifty-six; ¹⁵ the people of Adin, four hundred and fifty-four; ¹⁶ the people of Ater of Hezekiah, ninety-eight; ¹⁷ the people of Bezai, three hundred and twenty-three; ¹⁸ the people of Jorah, one hundred and twelve; ¹⁹ the people of Hashum, two hundred and twenty-three; ²⁰ the people of Gibbar, ninety-five; ²¹ the people of Bethlehem, one hundred and twenty-three; ²² the men of Netophah, fifty-six; ²³ the men of Anathoth, one hundred and twenty-eight; ²⁴ the people of Azmaveth, forty-two; ²⁵ the people of Kirjath Arim, Chephirah, and Beeroth, seven hundred and forty-three; ²⁶ the people of Ramah and Geba, six hundred and twenty-one; ²⁷ the men of Michmas, one hundred and twenty-two; ²⁸ the men of Bethel and Ai, two hundred and twenty-three; ²⁹ the people of Nebo, fifty-two; ³⁰ the people of Magbish, one hundred and fifty-six; ³¹ the people of the other Elam, one thousand two hundred and fifty-four; ³² the people of Harim, three hundred and twenty; ³³ the people of Lod, Hadid, and Ono, seven hundred and twenty-five; ³⁴ the people of Jericho, three hundred and forty-five; ³⁵ the people of Senaah, three thousand six hundred and thirty.

³⁶ The priests: the sons of Jedaiah, of the house of Jeshua, nine hundred and seventy-three; ³⁷ the sons of Immer, one thousand and fifty-two; ³⁸ the sons of Pashhur, one thousand two hundred and forty-seven; ³⁹ the sons of Harim, one thousand and seventeen.

Begin With Prayer

Pope John Paul II has made no secret of his daily schedule in the Vatican. He begins his day at 5:30 AM, while most of Rome is still asleep. By 6:15 he is in his private chapel, meditating and praying before its altar, over which hangs a large bronze crucifix. Also within sight is a copy of Poland's most cherished Catholic icon, the Black Virgin of Czestochowa.

Those who have seen the Pope in prayer state that at times he prostrates himself before the altar. At other times he sits or kneels, and with closed eyes cradles his forehead in his hands.

This early-morning prayer session is his time to bring before God his prayer requests for others. It is not uncommon for the stack of intentions to have more than 200 sheets, with many names written on each one.

The Pope considers prayer, more than liquid or food, to be the sustaining force of his life. Says Monsignor Diarmuid Martin, secretary of the Vatican's Justice and Peace Commission, the Pope makes all his decisions "on his knees."

Prayer — there's no better way to start a day, or to begin and end the decision-making process.

> Give ear, O Lord, to my prayer; and attend to the voice of my supplications. In the day of my trouble I will call upon You, for You will answer me.
>
> *Psalm 86:6-7*

⁴⁰ The Levites: the sons of Jeshua and Kadmiel, of the sons of Hodaviah, seventy-four.

⁴¹ The singers: the sons of Asaph, one hundred and twenty-eight.

⁴² The sons of the gatekeepers: the sons of Shallum, the sons of Ater, the sons of Talmon, the sons of Akkub, the sons of Hatita, and the sons of Shobai, one hundred and thirty-nine *in* all.

⁴³ The Nethinim: the sons of Ziha, the sons of Hasupha, the sons of Tabbaoth, ⁴⁴ the sons of Keros, the sons of Siaha, the sons of Padon, ⁴⁵ the sons of Lebanah, the sons of Hagabah, the sons of Akkub, ⁴⁶ the sons of Hagab, the sons of Shalmai, the sons of Hanan, ⁴⁷ the sons of Giddel, the sons of Gahar, the sons of Reaiah, ⁴⁸ the sons of Rezin, the sons of Nekoda, the sons of Gazzam, ⁴⁹ the sons of Uzza, the sons of Paseah, the sons of Besai, ⁵⁰ the sons of Asnah, the sons of Meunim, the sons of Nephusim, ⁵¹ the sons of Bakbuk, the sons of Hakupha, the sons of Harhur, ⁵² the sons of Bazluth, the sons of Mehida, the sons of Harsha, ⁵³ the sons of Barkos, the sons of Sisera, the sons of Tamah, ⁵⁴ the sons of Neziah, and the sons of Hatipha.

⁵⁵ The sons of Solomon's servants: the sons of Sotai, the sons of Sophereth, the sons of Peruda, ⁵⁶ the sons of Jaala, the sons of Darkon, the sons of Giddel, ⁵⁷ the sons of Shephatiah, the sons of Hattil, the sons of Pochereth of Zebaim, and the sons of Ami. ⁵⁸ All the Nethinim and the children of Solomon's servants were three hundred and ninety-two.

⁵⁹ And these *were* the ones who came up from Tel Melah, Tel Harsha, Cherub, Addan, and Immer; but they could not identify their father's house or their genealogy, whether they *were* of Israel: ⁶⁰ the sons of Delaiah, the sons of Tobiah, and the sons of Nekoda, six hundred and fifty-two; ⁶¹ and of the sons of the priests: the sons of Habaiah, the sons of Koz, and the sons of Barzillai, who took a wife of the daughters of Barzillai the Gileadite, and was called by their name. ⁶² These sought their listing *among* those who were registered by genealogy, but they were not found; therefore they *were excluded* from the priesthood as defiled. ⁶³ And the governor said to them that they should not eat of the most holy things till a priest could consult with the Urim and Thummim.

⁶⁴ The whole assembly together *was* forty-two thousand three hundred *and* sixty, ⁶⁵ besides their male and female servants, of whom *there were* seven thousand three hundred and thirty-seven; and they had two hundred men and women singers. ⁶⁶ Their horses *were* seven hundred and thirty-six, their mules two hundred and forty-five, ⁶⁷ their camels four hundred and thirty-five, and *their* donkeys six thousand seven hundred and twenty.

⁶⁸ *Some* of the heads of the fathers' *houses,* when they came to the house of the LORD which *is* in Jerusalem, offered freely for the house of God, to erect it in its place: ⁶⁹ According to their ability, they gave to the treasury for the work sixty-one thousand gold drachmas, five thousand minas of silver, and one hundred priestly garments.

⁷⁰ So the priests and the Levites, *some* of the people, the singers, the gatekeepers, and the Nethinim, dwelt in their cities, and all Israel in their cities.

～ PSALM 86:6-10 ～

6 Give ear, O LORD, to my prayer;
   And attend to the voice of my
      supplications.
7 In the day of my trouble I will call
      upon You,
   For You will answer me.

8 Among the gods *there is* none like
      You, O Lord;
   Nor *are there any works* like Your
      works.
9 All nations whom You have made
   Shall come and worship before You,
      O Lord,
   And shall glorify Your name.
10 For You *are* great, and do wondrous
      things;
   You alone *are* God.

～ PROVERBS 21:15, 16 ～

15 *It is* a joy for the just to do justice,
   But destruction *will come* to the
      workers of iniquity.

¹⁶ A man who wanders from the way
    of understanding
  Will rest in the assembly of the dead.

~ ACTS 21:18–40 ~

On the following *day* Paul went in with
us to James, and all the elders were
present. ¹⁹ When he had greeted them, he
told in detail those things which God had
done among the Gentiles through his ministry. ²⁰ And when they heard *it*, they
glorified the Lord. And they said to him,
"You see, brother, how many myriads of
Jews there are who have believed, and
they are all zealous for the law; ²¹ but they
have been informed about you that you
teach all the Jews who are among the
Gentiles to forsake Moses, saying that they
ought not to circumcise *their* children nor
to walk according to the customs. ²² What
then? The assembly must certainly meet,
for they will hear that you have come.
²³ Therefore do what we tell you: We have
four men who have taken a vow. ²⁴ Take
them and be purified with them, and pay
their expenses so that they may shave *their*
heads, and that all may know that those
things of which they were informed concerning you are nothing, but *that* you
yourself also walk orderly and keep the
law. ²⁵ But concerning the Gentiles who
believe, we have written *and* decided that
they should observe no such thing, except that they should keep themselves
from *things* offered to idols, from
blood, from things strangled, and from
sexual immorality."
²⁶ Then Paul took the men, and the next
day, having been purified with them,
entered the temple to announce the expi-
ration of the days of purification, at which
time an offering should be made for each
one of them.
²⁷ Now when the seven days were al-
most ended, the Jews from Asia, seeing
him in the temple, stirred up the whole
crowd and laid hands on him, ²⁸ crying
out, "Men of Israel, help! This is the man

who teaches all *men* everywhere against
the people, the law, and this place; and
furthermore he also brought Greeks into
the temple and has defiled this holy place."
²⁹(For they had previously seen Trophimus
the Ephesian with him in the city, whom
they supposed that Paul had brought into
the temple.)
³⁰ And all the city was disturbed; and
the people ran together, seized Paul,
and dragged him out of the temple; and
immediately the doors were shut. ³¹ Now
as they were seeking to kill him, news
came to the commander of the garrison
that all Jerusalem was in an uproar. ³² He
immediately took soldiers and centurions,
and ran down to them. And when they
saw the commander and the soldiers,
they stopped beating Paul. ³³ Then the
commander came near and took him, and
commanded *him* to be bound with two
chains; and he asked who he was and what
he had done. ³⁴ And some among the
multitude cried one thing and some another.
So when he could not ascertain the
truth because of the tumult, he commanded him to be taken into the barracks.
³⁵ When he reached the stairs, he had to
be carried by the soldiers because of the
violence of the mob. ³⁶ For the multitude
of the people followed after, crying out,
"Away with him!"
³⁷ Then as Paul was about to be led into
the barracks, he said to the commander,
"May I speak to you?"
He replied, "Can you speak Greek?
³⁸ Are you not the Egyptian who some
time ago stirred up a rebellion and led
the four thousand assassins out into the
wilderness?"
³⁹ But Paul said, "I am a Jew from Tar-
sus, in Cilicia, a citizen of no mean city;
and I implore you, permit me to speak to
the people."
⁴⁰ So when he had given him permis-
sion, Paul stood on the stairs and motioned with his hand to the people. And
when there was a great silence, he spoke
to *them* in the Hebrew language, saying,

~ EZRA 3:1—4:24 ~

And when the seventh month had come, and the children of Israel *were* in the cities, the people gathered together as one man to Jerusalem. ² Then Jeshua the son of Jozadak and his brethren the priests, and Zerubbabel the son of Shealtiel and his brethren, arose and built the altar of the God of Israel, to offer burnt offerings on it, as *it is* written in the Law of Moses the man of God. ³ Though fear *had come* upon them because of the people of those countries, they set the altar on its bases; and they offered burnt offerings on it to the LORD, *both* the morning and evening burnt offerings. ⁴ They also kept the Feast of Tabernacles, as *it is* written, and *offered* the daily burnt offerings in the number required by ordinance for each day. ⁵ Afterwards *they offered* the regular burnt offering, and *those* for New Moons and for all the appointed feasts of the LORD that were consecrated, and *those* of everyone who willingly offered a freewill offering to the LORD. ⁶ From the first day of the seventh month they began to offer burnt offerings to the LORD, although the foundation of the temple of the LORD had not been laid. ⁷ They also gave money to the masons and the carpenters, and food, drink, and oil to the people of Sidon and Tyre to bring cedar logs from Lebanon to the sea, to Joppa, according to the permission which they had from Cyrus king of Persia.

⁸ Now in the second month of the second year of their coming to the house of God at Jerusalem, Zerubbabel the son of Shealtiel, Jeshua the son of Jozadak, and the rest of their brethren the priests and the Levites, and all those who had come out of the captivity to Jerusalem, began *work* and appointed the Levites from twenty years old and above to oversee the work of the house of the LORD. ⁹ Then Jeshua *with* his sons and brothers, Kadmiel *with* his sons, and the sons of Judah, arose as one to oversee those working on the house of God: the sons of Henadad *with* their sons and their brethren the Levites.

¹⁰ When the builders laid the foundation of the temple of the LORD, the priests stood in their apparel with trumpets, and the Levites, the sons of Asaph, with cymbals, to praise the LORD, according to the ordinance of David king of Israel. ¹¹ And they sang responsively, praising and giving thanks to the LORD:

> "For *He is* good,
>   For His mercy *endures* forever
>   toward Israel."

Then all the people shouted with a great shout, when they praised the LORD, because the foundation of the house of the LORD was laid.

¹² But many of the priests and Levites and heads of the fathers' *houses,* old men who had seen the first temple, wept with a loud voice when the foundation of this temple was laid before their eyes. Yet many shouted aloud for joy, ¹³ so that the people could not discern the noise of the shout of joy from the noise of the weeping of the people, for the people shouted with a loud shout, and the sound was heard afar off.

4 Now when the adversaries of Judah and Benjamin heard that the descendants of the captivity were building the temple of the LORD God of Israel, ² they came to Zerubbabel and the heads of the fathers' *houses,* and said to them, "Let us build with you, for we seek your God as you *do;* and we have sacrificed to Him since the days of Esarhaddon king of Assyria, who brought us here." ³ But Zerubbabel and Jeshua and the rest of the heads of the fathers' *houses* of Israel said to them, "You may do nothing with us to build a house for our God; but we alone will build to the LORD God of Israel, as King Cyrus the king of Persia has commanded us." ⁴ Then the people of the land tried to discourage the people of Judah. They troubled them in building, ⁵ and hired counselors against them to frustrate their purpose all the days of Cyrus king of Persia, even until the reign of Darius king of Persia.

Age Doesn't Matter

One of the marks of maturity is the ability to accept the responsibility for a talent — to diligently develop the inherent, God-given abilities and to make the most of them with joy and thanksgiving. A person who does this can become a success at any age:

Victor Hugo wrote his first tragedy at age fifteen.

John de Medecci was fifteen when he became a cardinal.

Raphael painted his masterpieces before he died at age thirty-seven.

Tennyson wrote his first volume of poetry at age eighteen.

Pascal wrote his great works between the ages of sixteen and his death at thirty-seven.

Joan of Arc was burned at the stake at nineteen.

Romulus founded Rome at twenty.

Calvin joined the Reformation at age twenty-one and wrote his famous Institutes at age twenty-seven.

Alexander the Great had conquered his world by the time he was twenty-three.

Isaac Newton was twenty-four when he introduced the Law of Gravity.

McCormick was twenty-three when he invented the reaper.

Charles Dickens wrote Oliver Twist at twenty-five.

Age had nothing to do with the genius of these great people. They merely took full responsibility for their God-given gifts and wasted no time as they maximized every opportunity to its fullest potential.

> The God of our fathers has chosen you that you should know His will, and see the Just One, and hear the voice of His mouth.
>
> *Acts 22:14*

⁶ In the reign of Ahasuerus, in the beginning of his reign, they wrote an accusation against the inhabitants of Judah and Jerusalem.

⁷ In the days of Artaxerxes also, Bishlam, Mithredath, Tabel, and the rest of their companions wrote to Artaxerxes king of Persia; and the letter *was* written in Aramaic script, and translated into the Aramaic language. ⁸ Rehum the commander and Shimshai the scribe wrote a letter against Jerusalem to King Artaxerxes in this fashion:

⁹ From Rehum the commander, Shimshai the scribe, and the rest of their companions—*representatives* of the Dinaites, the Apharsathchites, the Tarpelites, the people of Persia and Erech and Babylon and Shushan, the Dehavites, the Elamites, ¹⁰ and the rest of the nations whom the great and noble Osnapper took captive and settled in the cities of Samaria and the remainder beyond the River—and so forth.

¹¹ (This *is* a copy of the letter that they sent him)

To King Artaxerxes from your servants, the men *of the region* beyond the River, and so forth:

¹² Let it be known to the king that the Jews who came up from you have come to us at Jerusalem, and are building the rebellious and evil city, and are finishing *its* walls and repairing the foundations. ¹³ Let it now be known to the king that, if this city is built and the walls completed, they will not pay tax, tribute, or custom, and the king's treasury will be diminished. ¹⁴ Now because we receive support from the palace, it was not proper for us to see the king's dishonor; therefore we have sent and informed the king, ¹⁵ that search may be made in the book of the records of your fathers. And you will find in the book of the records and know that this city *is* a rebellious city, harmful to kings and provinces, and that they have incited sedition within the city in former times, for which cause this city was destroyed.

¹⁶ We inform the king that if this city is rebuilt and its walls are completed, the result will be that you will have no dominion beyond the River.

¹⁷ The king sent an answer:

To Rehum the commander, *to* Shimshai the scribe, *to* the rest of their companions who dwell in Samaria, and *to* the remainder beyond the River:

Peace, and so forth.

¹⁸ The letter which you sent to us has been clearly read before me. ¹⁹ And I gave the command, and a search has been made, and it was found that this city in former times has revolted against kings, and rebellion and sedition have been fostered in it. ²⁰ There have also been mighty kings over Jerusalem, who have ruled over all *the region* beyond the River; and tax, tribute, and custom were paid to them. ²¹ Now give the command to make these men cease, that this city may not be built until the command is given by me.

²² Take heed now that you do not fail to do this. Why should damage increase to the hurt of the kings?

²³ Now when the copy of King Artaxerxes' letter *was* read before Rehum, Shimshai the scribe, and their companions, they went up in haste to Jerusalem against the Jews, and by force of arms made them cease. ²⁴ Thus the work of the house of God which *is* at Jerusalem ceased, and it was discontinued until the second year of the reign of Darius king of Persia.

~ PSALM 86:11–17 ~

11 Teach me Your way, O LORD;
   I will walk in Your truth;
   Unite my heart to fear Your name.
12 I will praise You, O Lord my God,
   with all my heart,
   And I will glorify Your name
      forevermore.
13 For great *is* Your mercy toward me,
   And You have delivered my soul
   from the depths of Sheol.

14 O God, the proud have risen against
   me,
   And a mob of violent *men* have
   sought my life,
   And have not set You before them.
15 But You, O Lord, *are* a God full of
   compassion, and gracious,
   Longsuffering and abundant in
   mercy and truth.

16 Oh, turn to me, and have mercy on
   me!
   Give Your strength to Your servant,
   And save the son of Your
   maidservant.
17 Show me a sign for good,
   That those who hate me may see *it*
   and be ashamed,
   Because You, LORD, have helped me
   and comforted me.

~ PROVERBS 21:17, 18 ~

17 He who loves pleasure *will be* a poor
   man;
   He who loves wine and oil will not
   be rich.

18 The wicked *shall be* a ransom for the
   righteous,
   And the unfaithful for the upright.

~ ACTS 22:1–30 ~

"Brethren and fathers, hear my defense
before you now." 2 And when they heard
that he spoke to them in the Hebrew language, they kept all the more silent.
   Then he said: 3 "I am indeed a Jew, born
in Tarsus of Cilicia, but brought up in this
city at the feet of Gamaliel, taught according to the strictness of our fathers' law,
and was zealous toward God as you all
are today. 4 I persecuted this Way to the
death, binding and delivering into prisons both men and women, 5 as also the
high priest bears me witness, and all
the council of the elders, from whom I
also received letters to the brethren, and
went to Damascus to bring in chains even
those who were there to Jerusalem to be
punished.

6 "Now it happened, as I journeyed and
came near Damascus at about noon, suddenly a great light from heaven shone
around me. 7 And I fell to the ground and
heard a voice saying to me, 'Saul, Saul,
why are you persecuting Me?' 8 So I answered, 'Who are You, Lord?' And He said
to me, 'I am Jesus of Nazareth, whom you
are persecuting.'

9 "And those who were with me indeed
saw the light and were afraid, but they
did not hear the voice of Him who spoke
to me. 10 So I said, 'What shall I do, Lord?'
And the Lord said to me, 'Arise and go
into Damascus, and there you will be told
all things which are appointed for you to
do.' 11 And since I could not see for the
glory of that light, being led by the hand
of those who were with me, I came into
Damascus.

12 "Then a certain Ananias, a devout
man according to the law, having a good
testimony with all the Jews who dwelt
there, 13 came to me; and he stood and
said to me, 'Brother Saul, receive your
sight.' And at that same hour I looked up
at him. 14 Then he said, 'The God of our
fathers has chosen you that you should
know His will, and see the Just One, and
hear the voice of His mouth. 15 For you
will be His witness to all men of what
you have seen and heard. 16 And now why
are you waiting? Arise and be baptized,
and wash away your sins, calling on the
name of the Lord.'

17 "Now it happened, when I returned
to Jerusalem and was praying in the
temple, that I was in a trance 18 and saw
Him saying to me, 'Make haste and get
out of Jerusalem quickly, for they will not
receive your testimony concerning Me.'
19 So I said, 'Lord, they know that in every synagogue I imprisoned and beat those

who believe on You. ²⁰ And when the blood of Your martyr Stephen was shed, I also was standing by consenting to his death, and guarding the clothes of those who were killing him.' ²¹ Then He said to me, 'Depart, for I will send you far from here to the Gentiles.' "

²² And they listened to him until this word, and *then* they raised their voices and said, "Away with such a *fellow* from the earth, for he is not fit to live!" ²³ Then, as they cried out and tore off *their* clothes and threw dust into the air, ²⁴ the commander ordered him to be brought into the barracks, and said that he should be examined under scourging, so that he might know why they shouted so against him. ²⁵ And as they bound him with thongs, Paul said to the centurion who stood by, "Is it lawful for you to scourge a man who is a Roman, and uncondemned?"

²⁶ When the centurion heard *that,* he went and told the commander, saying, "Take care what you do, for this man is a Roman."

²⁷ Then the commander came and said to him, "Tell me, are you a Roman?"

He said, "Yes."

²⁸ The commander answered, "With a large sum I obtained this citizenship."

And Paul said, "But I was born *a citizen.*"

²⁹ Then immediately those who were about to examine him withdrew from him; and the commander was also afraid after he found out that he was a Roman, and because he had bound him.

³⁰ The next day, because he wanted to know for certain why he was accused by the Jews, he released him from *his* bonds, and commanded the chief priests and all their council to appear, and brought Paul down and set him before them.

READING 203 · JULY 22

~ EZRA 5:1—6:22 ~

Then the prophet Haggai and Zechariah the son of Iddo, prophets, prophesied to the Jews who *were* in Judah and Jerusalem, in the name of the God of Israel, *who was* over them. ² So Zerubbabel the son of Shealtiel and Jeshua the son of Jozadak rose up and began to build the house of God which *is* in Jerusalem; and the prophets of God *were* with them, helping them.

³ At the same time Tattenai the governor of *the region* beyond the River and Shethar-Boznai and their companions came to them and spoke thus to them: "Who has commanded you to build this temple and finish this wall?" ⁴ Then, accordingly, we told them the names of the men who were constructing this building. ⁵ But the eye of their God was upon the elders of the Jews, so that they could not make them cease till a report could go to Darius. Then a written answer was returned concerning this *matter.* ⁶ This is a copy of the letter that Tattenai sent:

The governor of *the region* beyond the River, and Shethar-Boznai, and

his companions, the Persians who *were in the region* beyond the River, to Darius the king.

⁷ (They sent a letter to him, in which was written thus)

To Darius the king:

All peace.

⁸ Let it be known to the king that we went into the province of Judea, to the temple of the great God, which is being built with heavy stones, and timber is being laid in the walls; and this work goes on diligently and prospers in their hands.

⁹ Then we asked those elders, *and* spoke thus to them: "Who commanded you to build this temple and to finish these walls?" ¹⁰ We also asked them their names to inform you, that we might write

The Smile Parade

A pastor tells the story of how during the twelve years of his pastorate at one particular church, he had a custom of calling the children forward just before his Sunday morning sermon so that they could go to "children's church" and hear a sermon geared especially for them. During their processional to their assembly hall, the children marched past the pulpit and the pastor made it a point to smile at each child. He always received their smiles in return. "It was one of the high points of the service," he recalled.

One day, however, the pastor apparently missed smiling at one child. A curly-headed four-year-old ran out of the procession and threw herself into the arms of her mother, sobbing as if her heart was broken.

After the service the pastor sought out the mother to find out what had happened. The mother explained that after her child had quieted, she asked what caused the tears. The child had said, "I smiled at God, but he didn't smile back!" The pastor reflected, "To that child, I stood for God. I had failed with my smile, and the world went dark."

Smile at each person you meet today. You may never know how much you have brightened a life!

⸻⹈⹈⸻

But the following night the Lord stood by him and said, "Be of good cheer, Paul; for as you have testified for Me in Jerusalem, so you must also bear witness at Rome."

Acts 23:11

the names of the men who *were* chief among them.

11 And thus they returned us an answer, saying: "We are the servants of the God of heaven and earth, and we are rebuilding the temple that was built many years ago, which a great king of Israel built and completed. 12 But because our fathers provoked the God of heaven to wrath, He gave them into the hand of Nebuchadnezzar king of Babylon, the Chaldean, *who* destroyed this temple and carried the people away to Babylon. 13 However, in the first year of Cyrus king of Babylon, King Cyrus issued a decree to build this house of God. 14 Also, the gold and silver articles of the house of God, which Nebuchadnezzar had taken from the temple that *was* in Jerusalem and carried into the temple of Babylon—those King Cyrus took from the temple of Babylon, and they were given to one named Sheshbazzar, whom he had made governor. 15 And he said to him, 'Take these articles; go, carry them to the temple *site* that *is* in Jerusalem, and let the house of God be rebuilt on its former site.' 16 Then the same Sheshbazzar came *and* laid the foundation of the house of God which *is* in Jerusalem; but from that time even until now it has been under construction, and it is not finished."

17 Now therefore, if *it seems* good to the king, let a search be made in the king's treasure house, which *is* there in Babylon, whether it is *so* that a decree was issued by King Cyrus to build this house of God at Jerusalem, and let the king send us his pleasure concerning this *matter.*

6 Then King Darius issued a decree, and a search was made in the archives, where the treasures were stored in Babylon. 2 And at Achmetha, in the palace that *is* in the province of Media, a scroll was found, and in it a record *was* written thus:

3 In the first year of King Cyrus, King Cyrus issued a decree *concerning* the house of God at Jerusalem: "Let the house be rebuilt, the place where they offered sacrifices; and let the foundations of it be firmly laid, its height sixty cubits *and* its width sixty cubits, 4 *with* three rows of heavy stones and one row of new timber. Let the expenses be paid from the king's treasury. 5 Also let the gold and silver articles of the house of God, which Nebuchadnezzar took from the temple which *is* in Jerusalem and brought to Babylon, be restored and taken back to the temple which *is* in Jerusalem, *each* to its place; and deposit *them* in the house of God"—

6 Now *therefore,* Tattenai, governor of *the region* beyond the River, and Shethar-Boznai, and your companions the Persians who *are* beyond the River, keep yourselves far from there. 7 Let the work of this house of God alone; let the governor of the Jews and the elders of the Jews build this house of God on its site.

8 Moreover I issue a decree *as to* what you shall do for the elders of these Jews, for the building of this house of God: Let the cost be paid at the king's expense from taxes *on the region* beyond the River; this is to be given immediately to these men, so that they are not hindered. 9 And whatever they need—young bulls, rams, and lambs for the burnt offerings of the God of heaven, wheat, salt, wine, and oil, according to the request of the priests who *are* in Jerusalem—let it be given them day by day without fail, 10 that they may offer sacrifices of sweet aroma to the God of heaven, and pray for the life of the king and his sons.

11 Also I issue a decree that whoever alters this edict, let a timber be pulled from his house and erected,

and let him be hanged on it; and let his house be made a refuse heap because of this. ¹² And may the God who causes His name to dwell there destroy any king or people who put their hand to alter it, or to destroy this house of God which is in Jerusalem. I Darius issue a decree; let it be done diligently.

¹³ Then Tattenai, governor of *the region* beyond the River, Shethar-Boznai, and their companions diligently did according to what King Darius had sent. ¹⁴ So the elders of the Jews built, and they prospered through the prophesying of Haggai the prophet and Zechariah the son of Iddo. And they built and finished *it,* according to the commandment of the God of Israel, and according to the command of Cyrus, Darius, and Artaxerxes king of Persia. ¹⁵ Now the temple was finished on the third day of the month of Adar, which was in the sixth year of the reign of King Darius. ¹⁶ Then the children of Israel, the priests and the Levites and the rest of the descendants of the captivity, celebrated the dedication of this house of God with joy. ¹⁷ And they offered sacrifices at the dedication of this house of God, one hundred bulls, two hundred rams, four hundred lambs, and as a sin offering for all Israel twelve male goats, according to the number of the tribes of Israel. ¹⁸ They assigned the priests to their divisions and the Levites to their divisions, over the service of God in Jerusalem, as it is written in the Book of Moses.

¹⁹ And the descendants of the captivity kept the Passover on the fourteenth *day* of the first month. ²⁰ For the priests and the Levites had purified themselves; all of them *were ritually* clean. And they slaughtered the Passover *lambs* for all the descendants of the captivity, for their brethren the priests, and for themselves. ²¹ Then the children of Israel who had returned from the captivity ate together with all who had separated themselves from the filth of the nations of the land in order to seek the LORD God of Israel. ²² And they kept the Feast of Unleavened Bread seven days with joy; for the LORD made them joyful, and turned the heart of the king of Assyria toward them, to strengthen their hands in the work of the house of God, the God of Israel.

∼ PSALM 87:1–7 ∼

1   His foundation *is* in the holy
    mountains.
2   The LORD loves the gates of Zion
    More than all the dwellings of Jacob.
3   Glorious things are spoken of you,
    O city of God!   Selah

4   "I will make mention of Rahab and
    Babylon to those who know Me;
  Behold, O Philistia and Tyre, with
    Ethiopia:
  'This *one* was born there.' "

5   And of Zion it will be said,
  "This *one* and that *one* were born in
    her;
  And the Most High Himself shall
    establish her."
6   The LORD will record,
  When He registers the peoples:
  "This *one* was born there."   Selah

7   Both the singers and the players on
    instruments *say,*
  "All my springs *are* in you."

∼ PROVERBS 21:19, 20 ∼

19 Better to dwell in the wilderness,
   Than with a contentious and angry
    woman.

20 *There is* desirable treasure,
   And oil in the dwelling of the wise,
   But a foolish man squanders it.

∼ ACTS 23:1–15 ∼

Then Paul, looking earnestly at the council, said, "Men *and* brethren, I have lived in all good conscience before God until this day." ² And the high priest Ananias commanded those who stood by him to strike him on the mouth. ³ Then Paul said to him, "God will strike you, *you* whitewashed wall! For you sit to judge me according to the law, and do you command me to be struck contrary to the law?"

⁴ And those who stood by said, "Do you revile God's high priest?"

⁵ Then Paul said, "I did not know, brethren, that he was the high priest; for it is written, 'You shall not speak evil of a ruler of your people.' "

⁶ But when Paul perceived that one part were Sadducees and the other Pharisees, he cried out in the council, "Men *and* brethren, I am a Pharisee, the son of a Pharisee; concerning the hope and resurrection of the dead I am being judged!"

⁷ And when he had said this, a dissension arose between the Pharisees and the Sadducees; and the assembly was divided. ⁸ For Sadducees say that there is no resurrection—and no angel or spirit; but the Pharisees confess both. ⁹ Then there arose a loud outcry. And the scribes of the Pharisees' party arose and protested, saying, "We find no evil in this man; but if a spirit or an angel has spoken to him, let us not fight against God."

¹⁰ Now when there arose a great dissension, the commander, fearing lest Paul might be pulled to pieces by them, commanded the soldiers to go down and take him by force from among them, and bring *him* into the barracks.

¹¹ But the following night the Lord stood by him and said, "Be of good cheer, Paul; for as you have testified for Me in Jerusalem, so you must also bear witness at Rome."

¹² And when it was day, some of the Jews banded together and bound themselves under an oath, saying that they would neither eat nor drink till they had killed Paul. ¹³ Now there were more than forty who had formed this conspiracy. ¹⁴ They came to the chief priests and elders, and said, "We have bound ourselves under a great oath that we will eat nothing until we have killed Paul. ¹⁵ Now you, therefore, together with the council, suggest to the commander that he be brought down to you tomorrow, as though you were going to make further inquiries concerning him; but we are ready to kill him before he comes near."

READING 204 · JULY 23

~ EZRA 7:1—8:36 ~

Now after these things, in the reign of Artaxerxes king of Persia, Ezra the son of Seraiah, the son of Azariah, the son of Hilkiah, ² the son of Shallum, the son of Zadok, the son of Ahitub, ³ the son of Amariah, the son of Azariah, the son of Meraioth, ⁴ the son of Zerahiah, the son of Uzzi, the son of Bukki, ⁵ the son of Abishua, the son of Phinehas, the son of Eleazar, the son of Aaron the chief priest— ⁶ this Ezra came up from Babylon; and he *was* a skilled scribe in the Law of Moses, which the LORD God of Israel had given. The king granted him all his request, according to the hand of the LORD his God upon him. ⁷ *Some* of the children of Israel, the priests, the Levites, the singers, the gatekeepers, and the Nethinim came up to Jerusalem in the seventh year of King Artaxerxes. ⁸ And Ezra came to Jerusalem in the fifth month, which *was* in the seventh year of the king. ⁹ On the first *day* of the first month he began *his* journey from Babylon, and on the first *day* of the fifth month he came to Jerusalem, according to the good hand of his God upon him. ¹⁰ For Ezra had prepared his heart to seek the Law of the LORD, and to do *it,* and to teach statutes and ordinances in Israel.

¹¹ This *is* a copy of the letter that King Artaxerxes gave Ezra the priest, the scribe, expert in the words of the commandments of the LORD, and of His statutes to Israel:

¹²   Artaxerxes, king of kings,

       To Ezra the priest, a scribe of the Law of the God of heaven:

       Perfect *peace,* and so forth.

¹³   I issue a decree that all those of the people of Israel and the priests and Levites in my realm, who volunteer to go up to Jerusalem, may go with you. ¹⁴ And whereas you are being sent by the king and his seven

Measure of Success

Steve's father was passed over for promotion after promotion because he wasn't willing to play political games and use other people to get ahead. As a teenager, Steve promised himself that when he grew up he would make it to the top, and that is exactly what he did. By the time he was thirty-five Steve was second in command in a large corporation with a significant salary and a generous yearly bonus.

Steve once asked his dad, "Does it bother you that you have worked hard all your life and have so little to show for it? I mean, you've lived in the same house all your life. You've never gotten away for more than a week at a time. Your pension isn't going to let you really enjoy your retirement. Do you ever regret not getting ahead more?"

After some silence the elderly man responded, "Steve, maybe I use a different measure than you do. There's never been a night in my life that I couldn't put my head down and go to sleep knowing I have lived my life with honor. I raised a son who is successful, and I have a wife whom I love. I have what I need and what makes me happy. How much farther ahead should I be?"

His dad's answer made Steve realize the wealth he had been given by a man who he thought had nothing.

> He who pursues righteousness and love finds life, prosperity and honor.
>
> *Proverbs 21:21*

counselors to inquire concerning Judah and Jerusalem, with regard to the Law of your God which *is* in your hand; ¹⁵ and *whereas you are* to carry the silver and gold which the king and his counselors have freely offered to the God of Israel, whose dwelling *is* in Jerusalem; ¹⁶ and *whereas* all the silver and gold that you may find in all the province of Babylon, along with the freewill offering of the people and the priests, *are to be* freely offered for the house of their God in Jerusalem— ¹⁷ now therefore, be careful to buy with this money bulls, rams, and lambs, with their grain offerings and their drink offerings, and offer them on the altar of the house of your God in Jerusalem.

¹⁸ And whatever seems good to you and your brethren to do with the rest of the silver and the gold, do it according to the will of your God. ¹⁹ Also the articles that are given to you for the service of the house of your God, deliver in full before the God of Jerusalem. ²⁰ And whatever more may be needed for the house of your God, which you may have occasion to provide, pay *for it* from the king's treasury.

²¹ And I, *even* I, Artaxerxes the king, issue a decree to all the treasurers who *are in the region* beyond the River, that whatever Ezra the priest, the scribe of the Law of the God of heaven, may require of you, let it be done diligently, ²² up to one hundred talents of silver, one hundred kors of wheat, one hundred baths of wine, one hundred baths of oil, and salt without prescribed limit. ²³ Whatever is commanded by the God of heaven, let it diligently be done for the house of the God of heaven. For why should there be wrath against the realm of the king and his sons?

²⁴ Also we inform you that it shall not be lawful to impose tax, tribute, or custom *on* any of the priests, Levites, singers, gatekeepers, Nethinim, or servants of this house of God. ²⁵ And you, Ezra, according to your God-given wisdom, set magistrates and judges who may judge all the people who *are in the region* beyond the River, all such as know the laws of your God; and teach those who do not know *them.* ²⁶ Whoever will not observe the law of your God and the law of the king, let judgment be executed speedily on him, whether *it be* death, or banishment, or confiscation of goods, or imprisonment.

²⁷ Blessed *be* the LORD God of our fathers, who has put *such a thing* as this in the king's heart, to beautify the house of the LORD which *is* in Jerusalem, ²⁸ and has extended mercy to me before the king and his counselors, and before all the king's mighty princes.

So I was encouraged, as the hand of the LORD my God *was* upon me; and I gathered leading men of Israel to go up with me.

8 These *are* the heads of their fathers' *houses,* and *this is* the genealogy of those who went up with me from Babylon, in the reign of King Artaxerxes: ² of the sons of Phinehas, Gershom; of the sons of Ithamar, Daniel; of the sons of David, Hattush; ³ of the sons of Shecaniah, of the sons of Parosh, Zechariah; and registered with him *were* one hundred and fifty males; ⁴ of the sons of Pahath-Moab, Eliehoenai the son of Zerahiah, and with him two hundred males; ⁵ of the sons of Shechaniah, Ben-Jahaziel, and with him three hundred males; ⁶ of the sons of Adin, Ebed the son of Jonathan, and with him fifty males; ⁷ of the sons of Elam, Jeshaiah the son of Athaliah, and with him seventy males; ⁸ of the sons of Shephatiah, Zebadiah the son of Michael, and with him eighty males; ⁹ of the sons of Joab, Obadiah the son of Jehiel, and with him two hundred and eighteen males; ¹⁰ of the sons of Shelomith, Ben-Josiphiah, and with him one hundred and sixty males; [11] of the sons of Bebai, Zechariah the son of Bebai, and with him twenty-eight males; [12] of the sons of Azgad, Johanan the son of Hakkatan, and with him one hundred and ten males; [13] of the last sons of Adonikam, whose names *are* these— Eliphelet, Jeiel, and Shemaiah—and with them sixty males; [14] also of the sons of Bigvai, Uthai and Zabbud, and with them seventy males.

[15] Now I gathered them by the river that flows to Ahava, and we camped there three days. And I looked among the people and the priests, and found none of the sons of Levi there. [16] Then I sent for Eliezer, Ariel, Shemaiah, Elnathan, Jarib, Elnathan, Nathan, Zechariah, and Meshullam, leaders; also for Joiarib and Elnathan, men of understanding. [17] And I gave them a command for Iddo the chief man at the place Casiphia, and I told them what they should say to Iddo *and* his brethren the Nethinim at the place Casiphia—that they should bring us servants for the house of our God. [18] Then, by the good hand of our God upon us, they brought us a man of understanding, of the sons of Mahli the son of Levi, the son of Israel, namely Sherebiah, with his sons and brothers, eighteen men; [19] and Hashabiah, and with him Jeshaiah of the sons of Merari, his brothers and their sons, twenty men; [20] also of the Nethinim, whom David and the leaders had appointed for the service of the Levites, two hundred and twenty Nethinim. All of them were designated by name.

[21] Then I proclaimed a fast there at the river of Ahava, that we might humble ourselves before our God, to seek from Him the right way for us and our little ones and all our possessions. [22] For I was ashamed to request of the king an escort of soldiers and horsemen to help us against the enemy on the road, because we had spoken to the king, saying, "The hand of our God *is* upon all those for good who seek Him, but His power and His wrath *are* against all those who forsake Him." [23] So we fasted and entreated our God for this, and He answered our prayer.

[24] And I separated twelve of the leaders of the priests—Sherebiah, Hashabiah, and ten of their brethren with them— [25] and weighed out to them the silver, the gold, and the articles, the offering for the house of our God which the king and his counselors and his princes, and all Israel *who were* present, had offered. [26] I weighed into their hand six hundred and fifty talents of silver, silver articles *weighing* one hundred talents, one hundred talents of gold, [27] twenty gold basins *worth* a thousand drachmas, and two vessels of fine polished bronze, precious as gold. [28] And I said to them, "You *are* holy to the LORD; the articles *are* holy also; and the silver and the gold *are* a freewill offering to the LORD God of your fathers. [29] Watch and keep *them* until you weigh *them* before the leaders of the priests and the Levites and heads of the fathers' *houses* of Israel in Jerusalem, *in* the chambers of the house of the LORD." [30] So the priests and the Levites received the silver and the gold and the articles by weight, to bring *them* to Jerusalem to the house of our God.

[31] Then we departed from the river of Ahava on the twelfth *day* of the first month, to go to Jerusalem. And the hand of our God was upon us, and He delivered us from the hand of the enemy and from ambush along the road. [32] So we came to Jerusalem, and stayed there three days.

[33] Now on the fourth day the silver and the gold and the articles were weighed in the house of our God by the hand of Meremoth the son of Uriah the priest, and with him *was* Eleazar the son of Phinehas; with them *were* the Levites, Jozabad the son of Jeshua and Noadiah the son of Binnui, [34] with the number *and* weight of everything. All the weight was written down at that time.

[35] The children of those who had been carried away captive, who had come from the captivity, offered burnt offerings to the God of Israel: twelve bulls for all Israel, ninety-six rams, seventy-seven lambs, and twelve male goats *as* a sin offering. All *this was* a burnt offering to the LORD.

[36] And they delivered the king's orders to the king's satraps and the governors *in the region* beyond the River. So they gave support to the people and the house of God.

~ PSALM 88:1–5 ~

1   O LORD, God of my salvation,
    I have cried out day and night before
        You.
2   Let my prayer come before You;
    Incline Your ear to my cry.

3   For my soul is full of troubles,
    And my life draws near to the grave.
4   I am counted with those who go
        down to the pit;
    I am like a man *who has* no strength,
5   Adrift among the dead,
    Like the slain who lie in the grave,
    Whom You remember no more,
    And who are cut off from Your
        hand.

~ PROVERBS 21:21, 22 ~

21 He who follows righteousness and
        mercy
    Finds life, righteousness and honor.

22 A wise *man* scales the city of the
        mighty,
    And brings down the trusted
        stronghold.

~ ACTS 23:16–35 ~

So when Paul's sister's son heard of their
ambush, he went and entered the barracks
and told Paul. 17 Then Paul called one of
the centurions to *him* and said, "Take this
young man to the commander, for he has
something to tell him." 18 So he took him
and brought *him* to the commander and
said, "Paul the prisoner called me to *him*
and asked *me* to bring this young man to
you. He has something to say to you."
19 Then the commander took him by
the hand, went aside, and asked privately,
"What is it that you have to tell me?"
20 And he said, "The Jews have agreed
to ask that you bring Paul down to the
council tomorrow, as though they were
going to inquire more fully about him.
21 But do not yield to them, for more than
forty of them lie in wait for him, men who
have bound themselves by an oath that
they will neither eat nor drink till they
have killed him; and now they are ready,
waiting for the promise from you."
22 So the commander let the young man
depart, and commanded *him*, "Tell no one
that you have revealed these things to me."
23 And he called for two centurions,
saying, "Prepare two hundred soldiers,
seventy horsemen, and two hundred
spearmen to go to Caesarea at the third
hour of the night; 24 and provide mounts
to set Paul on, and bring *him* safely to
Felix the governor." 25 He wrote a letter
in the following manner:

26   Claudius Lysias,

     To the most excellent governor
     Felix:

     Greetings.

27   This man was seized by the Jews
     and was about to be killed by them.
     Coming with the troops I rescued
     him, having learned that he was a
     Roman. 28 And when I wanted to
     know the reason they accused him,
     I brought him before their council.
     29 I found out that he was accused
     concerning questions of their law,
     but had nothing charged against
     him deserving of death or chains.
     30 And when it was told me that the
     Jews lay in wait for the man, I sent
     him immediately to you, and also
     commanded his accusers to state
     before you the charges against him.

     Farewell.

31 Then the soldiers, as they were commanded, took Paul and brought *him* by
night to Antipatris. 32 The next day they
left the horsemen to go on with him, and
returned to the barracks. 33 When they
came to Caesarea and had delivered the
letter to the governor, they also presented
Paul to him. 34 And when the governor
had read *it,* he asked what province he
was from. And when he understood that
he was from Cilicia, 35 he said, "I will hear
you when your accusers also have come."
And he commanded him to be kept in
Herod's Praetorium.

~ EZRA 9:1—10:44 ~

When these things were done, the leaders came to me, saying, "The people of Israel and the priests and the Levites have not separated themselves from the peoples of the lands, with respect to the abominations of the Canaanites, the Hittites, the Perizzites, the Jebusites, the Ammonites, the Moabites, the Egyptians, and the Amorites. ² For they have taken some of their daughters *as wives* for themselves and their sons, so that the holy seed is mixed with the peoples of *those* lands. Indeed, the hand of the leaders and rulers has been foremost in this trespass." ³ So when I heard this thing, I tore my garment and my robe, and plucked out some of the hair of my head and beard, and sat down astonished. ⁴ Then everyone who trembled at the words of the God of Israel assembled to me, because of the transgression of those who had been carried away captive, and I sat astonished until the evening sacrifice.

⁵ At the evening sacrifice I arose from my fasting; and having torn my garment and my robe, I fell on my knees and spread out my hands to the LORD my God. ⁶ And I said: "O my God, I am too ashamed and humiliated to lift up my face to You, my God; for our iniquities have risen higher than *our* heads, and our guilt has grown up to the heavens. ⁷ Since the days of our fathers to this day we *have been* very guilty, and for our iniquities we, our kings, *and* our priests have been delivered into the hand of the kings of the lands, to the sword, to captivity, to plunder, and to humiliation, as *it is* this day. ⁸ And now for a little while grace has been *shown* from the LORD our God, to leave us a remnant to escape, and to give us a peg in His holy place, that our God may enlighten our eyes and give us a measure of revival in our bondage. ⁹ For we *were* slaves. Yet our God did not forsake us in our bondage; but He extended mercy to us in the sight of the kings of Persia, to revive us, to repair the house of our God, to rebuild its ruins, and to give us a wall in Judah and Jerusalem. ¹⁰ And now, O our God, what shall we say after this? For we have forsaken Your commandments,

¹¹ which You commanded by Your servants the prophets, saying, 'The land which you are entering to possess is an unclean land, with the uncleanness of the peoples of the lands, with their abominations which have filled it from one end to another with their impurity. ¹² Now therefore, do not give your daughters as wives for their sons, nor take their daughters to your sons; and never seek their peace or prosperity, that you may be strong and eat the good of the land, and leave *it* as an inheritance to your children forever.' ¹³ And after all that has come upon us for our evil deeds and for our great guilt, since You our God have punished us less than our iniquities *deserve,* and have given us *such* deliverance as this, ¹⁴ should we again break Your commandments, and join in marriage with the people *committing* these abominations? Would You not be angry with us until You had consumed *us,* so that *there would be* no remnant or survivor? ¹⁵ O LORD God of Israel, You *are* righteous, for we are left as a remnant, as *it is* this day. Here we *are* before You, in our guilt, though no one can stand before You because of this!"

10 Now while Ezra was praying, and while he was confessing, weeping, and bowing down before the house of God, a very large assembly of men, women, and children gathered to him from Israel; for the people wept very bitterly. ² And Shechaniah the son of Jehiel, *one* of the sons of Elam, spoke up and said to Ezra, "We have trespassed against our God, and have taken pagan wives from the peoples of the land; yet now there is hope in Israel in spite of this. ³ Now therefore, let us make a covenant with our God to put away all these wives and those who have been born to them, according to the advice of my master and of those who tremble at the commandment of our God; and let it be done according to the law. ⁴ Arise, for *this* matter *is* your *responsibility.* We also *are* with you. Be of good courage, and do *it.*"

⁵ Then Ezra arose, and made the leaders of the priests, the Levites, and all Israel

swear an oath that they would do according to this word. So they swore an oath. [6] Then Ezra rose up from before the house of God, and went into the chamber of Jehohanan the son of Eliashib; and *when* he came there, he ate no bread and drank no water, for he mourned because of the guilt of those from the captivity.

[7] And they issued a proclamation throughout Judah and Jerusalem to all the descendants of the captivity, that they must gather at Jerusalem, [8] and that whoever would not come within three days, according to the instructions of the leaders and elders, all his property would be confiscated, and he himself would be separated from the assembly of those from the captivity.

[9] So all the men of Judah and Benjamin gathered at Jerusalem within three days. It *was* the ninth month, on the twentieth of the month; and all the people sat in the open square of the house of God, trembling because of *this* matter and because of heavy rain. [10] Then Ezra the priest stood up and said to them, "You have transgressed and have taken pagan wives, adding to the guilt of Israel. [11] Now therefore, make confession to the LORD God of your fathers, and do His will; separate yourselves from the peoples of the land, and from the pagan wives."

[12] Then all the assembly answered and said with a loud voice, "Yes! As you have said, so we must do. [13] But *there are* many people; *it is* the season for heavy rain, and we are not able to stand outside. Nor *is this* the work of one or two days, for *there are* many of us who have transgressed in this matter. [14] Please, let the leaders of our entire assembly stand; and let all those in our cities who have taken pagan wives come at appointed times, together with the elders and judges of their cities, until the fierce wrath of our God is turned away from us in this matter." [15] Only Jonathan the son of Asahel and Jahaziah the son of Tikvah opposed this, and Meshullam and Shabbethai the Levite gave them support.

[16] Then the descendants of the captivity did so. And Ezra the priest, *with* certain heads of the fathers' *households*, were set apart by the fathers' *households*, each of them by name; and they sat down on the first day of the tenth month to examine the matter. [17] By the first day of the first month they finished *questioning* all the men who had taken pagan wives.

[18] And among the sons of the priests who had taken pagan wives *the following* were found of the sons of Jeshua the son of Jozadak, and his brothers: Maaseiah, Eliezer, Jarib, and Gedaliah. [19] And they gave their promise that they would put away their wives; and *being* guilty, *they presented* a ram of the flock as their trespass offering.

[20] Also of the sons of Immer: Hanani and Zebadiah; [21] of the sons of Harim: Maaseiah, Elijah, Shemaiah, Jehiel, and Uzziah; [22] of the sons of Pashhur: Elioenai, Maaseiah, Ishmael, Nethanel, Jozabad, and Elasah.

[23] Also of the Levites: Jozabad, Shimei, Kelaiah (the same *is* Kelita), Pethahiah, Judah, and Eliezer.

[24] Also of the singers: Eliashib; and of the gatekeepers: Shallum, Telem, and Uri.

[25] And others of Israel: of the sons of Parosh: Ramiah, Jeziah, Malchiah, Mijamin, Eleazar, Malchijah, and Benaiah; [26] of the sons of Elam: Mattaniah, Zechariah, Jehiel, Abdi, Jeremoth, and Eliah; [27] of the sons of Zattu: Elioenai, Eliashib, Mattaniah, Jeremoth, Zabad, and Aziza; [28] of the sons of Bebai: Jehohanan, Hananiah, Zabbai, *and* Athlai; [29] of the sons of Bani: Meshullam, Malluch, Adaiah, Jashub, Sheal, *and* Ramoth; [30] of the sons of Pahath-Moab: Adna, Chelal, Benaiah, Maaseiah, Mattaniah, Bezalel, Binnui, and Manasseh; [31] *of* the sons of Harim: Eliezer, Ishijah, Malchijah, Shemaiah, Shimeon, [32] Benjamin, Malluch, *and* Shemariah; [33] of the sons of Hashum: Mattenai, Mattattah, Zabad, Eliphelet, Jeremai, Manasseh, *and* Shimei; [34] of the sons of Bani: Maadai, Amram, Uel, [35] Benaiah, Bedeiah, Cheluh, [36] Vaniah, Meremoth, Eliashib, [37] Mattaniah, Mattenai, Jaasai, [38] Bani, Binnui, Shimei, [39] Shelemiah, Nathan, Adaiah, [40] Machnadebai, Shashai, Sharai, [41] Azarel, Shelemiah, Shemariah, [42] Shallum, Amariah, *and* Joseph; [43] of the sons of Nebo: Jeiel, Mattithiah, Zabad, Zebina, Jaddai, Joel, *and* Benaiah.

[44] All these had taken pagan wives, and

Found: Black Derby

In the 1890s a man drove by the farm of Mrs. John R. McDonald. A sudden gust of wind caught his black derby hat and whirled it onto the McDonald property. He searched in vain for the hat and finally drove off bareheaded.

Mrs. McDonald retrieved the hat, and for the next forty-five years various members of her family wore it. Finally the old derby was completely worn-out, beyond repair. At long last, Mrs. McDonald went to the local newspaper and advertised for the owner of the hat. She noted in her ad that while the hat had been on the heads of the menfolk in her family, it had been on her conscience!

Is something nagging your heart today — an awareness that you have committed a wrong against another person, or a feeling that something has gone amiss in a relationship? Don't ignore those feelings. Seek to make amends.

A guilty conscience is a very heavy load to carry through life. Jesus died on the cross so you wouldn't have to bear that burden. He did His part; now you do yours. Strive to obtain and maintain the freedom and peace He purchased for you!

some of them had wives *by whom* they had children.

～ PSALM 88:6–10 ～

6 You have laid me in the lowest pit,
  In darkness, in the depths.
7 Your wrath lies heavy upon me,
  And You have afflicted *me* with all
      Your waves.   Selah
8 You have put away my acquaintances
      far from me;
  You have made me an abomination
      to them;
  I am shut up, and I cannot get out;
9 My eye wastes away because of
      affliction.

  LORD, I have called daily upon You;
  I have stretched out my hands to
      You.
10 Will You work wonders for the
      dead?
  Shall the dead arise *and* praise You?
                                   Selah

～ PROVERBS 21:23, 24 ～

23 Whoever guards his mouth and
      tongue
  Keeps his soul from troubles.

24 A proud *and* haughty *man*—
      "Scoffer" *is* his name;
  He acts with arrogant pride.

～ ACTS 24:1–27 ～

Now after five days Ananias the high priest came down with the elders and a certain orator *named* Tertullus. These gave evidence to the governor against Paul.

2 And when he was called upon, Tertullus began his accusation, saying: "Seeing that through you we enjoy great peace, and prosperity is being brought to this nation by your foresight, 3 we accept *it* always and in all places, most noble Felix, with all thankfulness. 4 Nevertheless, not to be tedious to you any further, I beg you to hear, by your courtesy, a few words from us. 5 For we have found this man a plague, a creator of dissension among all the Jews throughout the world, and a ringleader of the sect of the Nazarenes. 6 He even tried to profane the temple, and we seized him, and wanted to judge him according to our law. 7 But the commander Lysias came by and with great violence took *him* out of our hands, 8 commanding his accusers to come to you. By examining him yourself you may ascertain all these things of which we accuse him." 9 And the Jews also assented, maintaining that these things were so.

10 Then Paul, after the governor had nodded to him to speak, answered: "Inasmuch as I know that you have been for many years a judge of this nation, I do the more cheerfully answer for myself, 11 because you may ascertain that it is no more than twelve days since I went up to Jerusalem to worship. 12 And they neither found me in the temple disputing with anyone nor inciting the crowd, either in the synagogues or in the city. 13 Nor can they prove the things of which they now accuse me. 14 But this I confess to you, that according to the Way which they call a sect, so I worship the God of my fathers, believing all things which are written in the Law and in the Prophets. 15 I have hope in God, which they themselves also accept, that there will be a resurrection of *the* dead, both of *the* just and *the* unjust. 16 This *being* so, I myself always strive to have a conscience without offense toward God and men.

17 "Now after many years I came to bring alms and offerings to my nation, 18 in the midst of which some Jews from Asia found me purified in the temple, neither with a mob nor with tumult. 19 They ought to have been here before you to object if they had anything against me. 20 Or else let those who are *here* themselves say if they found any wrongdoing in me while I stood before the council, 21 unless *it is* for this one statement which I cried out, standing among them, 'Concerning the resurrection of the dead I am being judged by you this day.' "

22 But when Felix heard these things, having more accurate knowledge of *the* Way, he adjourned the proceedings and said, "When Lysias the commander comes down, I will make a decision on your case." 23 So he commanded the centurion to keep Paul and to let *him* have liberty,

and told him not to forbid any of his friends to provide for or visit him.

²⁴ And after some days, when Felix came with his wife Drusilla, who was Jewish, he sent for Paul and heard him concerning the faith in Christ. ²⁵ Now as he reasoned about righteousness, self-control, and the judgment to come, Felix was afraid and answered, "Go away for now; when I have a convenient time I will call for you." ²⁶ Meanwhile he also hoped that money would be given him by Paul, that he might release him. Therefore he sent for him more often and conversed with him.

²⁷ But after two years Porcius Festus succeeded Felix; and Felix, wanting to do the Jews a favor, left Paul bound.

~ NEHEMIAH 1:1—2:20 ~

The words of Nehemiah the son of Hachaliah.

It came to pass in the month of Chislev, *in* the twentieth year, as I was in Shushan the citadel, ² that Hanani one of my brethren came with men from Judah; and I asked them concerning the Jews who had escaped, who had survived the captivity, and concerning Jerusalem. ³ And they said to me, "The survivors who are left from the captivity in the province *are* there in great distress and reproach. The wall of Jerusalem *is* also broken down, and its gates *are* burned with fire."

⁴ So it was, when I heard these words, that I sat down and wept, and mourned *for many* days; I was fasting and praying before the God of heaven.

⁵ And I said: "I pray, LORD God of heaven, O great and awesome God, *You* who keep *Your* covenant and mercy with those who love You and observe Your commandments, ⁶ please let Your ear be attentive and Your eyes open, that You may hear the prayer of Your servant which I pray before You now, day and night, for the children of Israel Your servants, and confess the sins of the children of Israel which we have sinned against You. Both my father's house and I have sinned. ⁷ We have acted very corruptly against You, and have not kept the commandments, the statutes, nor the ordinances which You commanded Your servant Moses. ⁸ Remember, I pray, the word that You commanded Your servant Moses, saying, 'If you are unfaithful, I will scatter you among the nations; ⁹ but *if* you return to Me, and keep My commandments and do them, though some of you were cast out to the farthest part of the heavens, *yet* I will gather them from there, and bring them to the place which I have chosen as a dwelling for My name.' ¹⁰ Now these *are* Your servants and Your people, whom You have redeemed by Your great power, and by Your strong hand. ¹¹ O Lord, I pray, please let Your ear be attentive to the prayer of Your servant, and to the prayer of Your servants who desire to fear Your name; and let Your servant prosper this day, I pray, and grant him mercy in the sight of this man."

For I was the king's cupbearer.

2 And it came to pass in the month of Nisan, in the twentieth year of King Artaxerxes, *when* wine *was* before him, that I took the wine and gave it to the king. Now I had never been sad in his presence before. ² Therefore the king said to me, "Why *is* your face sad, since you *are* not sick? This *is* nothing but sorrow of heart."

So I became dreadfully afraid, ³ and said to the king, "May the king live forever! Why should my face not be sad, when the city, the place of my fathers' tombs, *lies* waste, and its gates are burned with fire?"

⁴ Then the king said to me, "What do you request?"

So I prayed to the God of heaven. ⁵ And I said to the king, "If it pleases the king, and if your servant has found favor in your sight, I ask that you send me to Judah, to the city of my fathers' tombs, that I may rebuild it."

⁶ Then the king said to me (the queen also sitting beside him), "How long will your journey be? And when will you

return?" So it pleased the king to send me; and I set him a time.

7 Furthermore I said to the king, "If it pleases the king, let letters be given to me for the governors *of the region* beyond the River, that they must permit me to pass through till I come to Judah, 8 and a letter to Asaph the keeper of the king's forest, that he must give me timber to make beams for the gates of the citadel which *pertains* to the temple, for the city wall, and for the house that I will occupy." And the king granted *them* to me according to the good hand of my God upon me.

9 Then I went to the governors *in the region* beyond the River, and gave them the king's letters. Now the king had sent captains of the army and horsemen with me. 10 When Sanballat the Horonite and Tobiah the Ammonite official heard *of it,* they were deeply disturbed that a man had come to seek the well-being of the children of Israel.

11 So I came to Jerusalem and was there three days. 12 Then I arose in the night, I and a few men with me; I told no one what my God had put in my heart to do at Jerusalem; nor was there any animal with me, except the one on which I rode. 13 And I went out by night through the Valley Gate to the Serpent Well and the Refuse Gate, and viewed the walls of Jerusalem which were broken down and its gates which were burned with fire. 14 Then I went on to the Fountain Gate and to the King's Pool, but *there was* no room for the animal under me to pass. 15 So I went up in the night by the valley, and viewed the wall; then I turned back and entered by the Valley Gate, and so returned. 16 And the officials did not know where I had gone or what I had done; I had not yet told the Jews, the priests, the nobles, the officials, or the others who did the work.

17 Then I said to them, "You see the distress that we *are* in, how Jerusalem *lies* waste, and its gates are burned with fire. Come and let us build the wall of Jerusalem, that we may no longer be a reproach." 18 And I told them of the hand of my God which had been good upon me, and also of the king's words that he had spoken to me.

So they said, "Let us rise up and build."

Then they set their hands to *this* good *work.*

19 But when Sanballat the Horonite, Tobiah the Ammonite official, and Geshem the Arab heard *of it,* they laughed at us and despised us, and said, "What *is* this thing that you are doing? Will you rebel against the king?"

20 So I answered them, and said to them, "The God of heaven Himself will prosper us; therefore we His servants will arise and build, but you have no heritage or right or memorial in Jerusalem."

～ PSALM 88:11–18 ～

11 Shall Your lovingkindness be
declared in the grave?
Or Your faithfulness in the place of
destruction?
12 Shall Your wonders be known in the
dark?
And Your righteousness in the land
of forgetfulness?

13 But to You I have cried out, O LORD,
And in the morning my prayer
comes before You.
14 LORD, why do You cast off my soul?
Why do You hide Your face from
me?
15 I *have been* afflicted and ready to die
from *my* youth;
I suffer Your terrors;
I am distraught.
16 Your fierce wrath has gone over me;
Your terrors have cut me off.
17 They came around me all day long
like water;
They engulfed me altogether.
18 Loved one and friend You have put
far from me,
And my acquaintances into
darkness.

～ PROVERBS 21:25, 26 ～

25 The desire of the lazy *man* kills him,
For his hands refuse to labor.
26 He covets greedily all day long,
But the righteous gives and does not
spare.

Dedication

As coach of the St. Anthony Friars basketball team, Bob Hurley has a stunning record — 517 wins, only 60 losses, 15 state championships, 5 Top Ten rankings, and 1 national championship. More important to Hurley, however, are the following records: nearly half of his varsity players routinely make the high school's honor roll, all but one of his players have gone on to college, and approximately 60 percent have graduated from college.

Hurley has a reputation for helping his players choose a college based on academics first, and athletics second. He declares players ineligible if their grades suffer: "If you're not committed to your education, how committed can you be to this team?" On the court, he is tough, impatient, and noisy. On the other hand, players who honestly struggle in their studies are often treated to dinner and private tutoring at Hurley's home.

Hurley has been offered numerous opportunities to leave his high school position in Jersey City, but for him, that's home. It's the place where he has invested his life. In 1992, he was honored by his city with a major banquet and rousing accolades. The next day he was back to work, out hunting summer work for his players.

If you're truly dedicated to what you do, accolades or the lack thereof, don't change anything. You enjoy them for the moment, then go on doing what you do best.

> He covets greedily all day long, but the righteous gives and does not spare.
>
> *Proverbs 21:26*

~ ACTS 25:1-27 ~

Now when Festus had come to the province, after three days he went up from Caesarea to Jerusalem. ² Then the high priest and the chief men of the Jews informed him against Paul; and they petitioned him, ³ asking a favor against him, that he would summon him to Jerusalem—while *they* lay in ambush along the road to kill him. ⁴ But Festus answered that Paul should be kept at Caesarea, and that he himself was going *there* shortly. ⁵ "Therefore," he said, "let those who have authority among you go down with *me* and accuse this man, to see if there is any fault in him."

⁶ And when he had remained among them more than ten days, he went down to Caesarea. And the next day, sitting on the judgment seat, he commanded Paul to be brought. ⁷ When he had come, the Jews who had come down from Jerusalem stood about and laid many serious complaints against Paul, which they could not prove, ⁸ while he answered for himself, "Neither against the law of the Jews, nor against the temple, nor against Caesar have I offended in anything at all."

⁹ But Festus, wanting to do the Jews a favor, answered Paul and said, "Are you willing to go up to Jerusalem and there be judged before me concerning these things?"

¹⁰ So Paul said, "I stand at Caesar's judgment seat, where I ought to be judged. To the Jews I have done no wrong, as you very well know. ¹¹ For if I am an offender, or have committed anything deserving of death, I do not object to dying; but if there is nothing in these things of which these men accuse me, no one can deliver me to them. I appeal to Caesar."

¹² Then Festus, when he had conferred with the council, answered, "You have appealed to Caesar? To Caesar you shall go!"

¹³ And after some days King Agrippa and Bernice came to Caesarea to greet Festus. ¹⁴ When they had been there many days, Festus laid Paul's case before the king, saying: "There is a certain man left a prisoner by Felix, ¹⁵ about whom the chief priests and the elders of the Jews informed *me,* when I was in Jerusalem, asking for a judgment against him. ¹⁶ To them I answered, 'It is not the custom of the Romans to deliver any man to destruction before the accused meets the accusers face to face, and has opportunity to answer for himself concerning the charge against him.' ¹⁷ Therefore when they had come together, without any delay, the next day I sat on the judgment seat and commanded the man to be brought in. ¹⁸ When the accusers stood up, they brought no accusation against him of such things as I supposed, ¹⁹ but had some questions against him about their own religion and about a certain Jesus, who had died, whom Paul affirmed to be alive. ²⁰ And because I was uncertain of such questions, I asked whether he was willing to go to Jerusalem and there be judged concerning these matters. ²¹ But when Paul appealed to be reserved for the decision of Augustus, I commanded him to be kept till I could send him to Caesar."

²² Then Agrippa said to Festus, "I also would like to hear the man myself."

"Tomorrow," he said, "you shall hear him."

²³ So the next day, when Agrippa and Bernice had come with great pomp, and had entered the auditorium with the commanders and the prominent men of the city, at Festus' command Paul was brought in. ²⁴ And Festus said: "King Agrippa and all the men who are here present with us, you see this man about whom the whole assembly of the Jews petitioned me, both at Jerusalem and here, crying out that he was not fit to live any longer. ²⁵ But when I found that he had committed nothing deserving of death, and that he himself had appealed to Augustus, I decided to send him. ²⁶ I have nothing certain to write to my lord concerning him. Therefore I have brought him out before you, and especially before you, King Agrippa, so that after the examination has taken place I may have something to write. ²⁷ For it seems to me unreasonable to send a prisoner and not to specify the charges against him."

~ NEHEMIAH 3:1—5:19 ~

Then Eliashib the high priest rose up with his brethren the priests and built the Sheep Gate; they consecrated it and hung its doors. They built as far as the Tower of the Hundred, *and* consecrated it, then as far as the Tower of Hananel. ² Next to *Eliashib* the men of Jericho built. And next to them Zaccur the son of Imri built.

³ Also the sons of Hassenaah built the Fish Gate; they laid its beams and hung its doors with its bolts and bars. ⁴ And next to them Meremoth the son of Urijah, the son of Koz, made repairs. Next to them Meshullam the son of Berechiah, the son of Meshezabel, made repairs. Next to them Zadok the son of Baana made repairs. ⁵ Next to them the Tekoites made repairs; but their nobles did not put their shoulders to the work of their Lord.

⁶ Moreover Jehoiada the son of Paseah and Meshullam the son of Besodeiah repaired the Old Gate; they laid its beams and hung its doors, with its bolts and bars. ⁷ And next to them Melatiah the Gibeonite, Jadon the Meronothite, the men of Gibeon and Mizpah, repaired the residence of the governor *of the region* beyond the River. ⁸ Next to him Uzziel the son of Harhaiah, one of the goldsmiths, made repairs. Also next to him Hananiah, one of the perfumers, made repairs; and they fortified Jerusalem as far as the Broad Wall. ⁹ And next to them Rephaiah the son of Hur, leader of half the district of Jerusalem, made repairs. ¹⁰ Next to them Jedaiah the son of Harumaph made repairs in front of his house. And next to him Hattush the son of Hashabniah made repairs.

¹¹ Malchijah the son of Harim and Hashub the son of Pahath-Moab repaired another section, as well as the Tower of the Ovens. ¹² And next to him was Shallum the son of Hallohesh, leader of half the district of Jerusalem; he and his daughters made repairs.

¹³ Hanun and the inhabitants of Zanoah repaired the Valley Gate. They built it, hung its doors with its bolts and bars, and *repaired* a thousand cubits of the wall as far as the Refuse Gate.

¹⁴ Malchijah the son of Rechab, leader of the district of Beth Haccerem, repaired the Refuse Gate; he built it and hung its doors with its bolts and bars.

¹⁵ Shallun the son of Col-Hozeh, leader of the district of Mizpah, repaired the Fountain Gate; he built it, covered it, hung its doors with its bolts and bars, and repaired the wall of the Pool of Shelah by the King's Garden, as far as the stairs that go down from the City of David. ¹⁶ After him Nehemiah the son of Azbuk, leader of half the district of Beth Zur, made repairs as far as *the place* in front of the tombs of David, to the man-made pool, and as far as the House of the Mighty.

¹⁷ After him the Levites, *under* Rehum the son of Bani, made repairs. Next to him Hashabiah, leader of half the district of Keilah, made repairs for his district. ¹⁸ After him their brethren, *under* Bavai the son of Henadad, leader of the *other* half of the district of Keilah, made repairs. ¹⁹ And next to him Ezer the son of Jeshua, the leader of Mizpah, repaired another section in front of the Ascent to the Armory at the buttress. ²⁰ After him Baruch the son of Zabbai carefully repaired the other section, from the buttress to the door of the house of Eliashib the high priest. ²¹ After him Meremoth the son of Urijah, the son of Koz, repaired another section, from the door of the house of Eliashib to the end of the house of Eliashib.

²² And after him the priests, the men of the plain, made repairs. ²³ After him Benjamin and Hasshub made repairs opposite their house. After them Azariah the son of Maaseiah, the son of Ananiah, made repairs by his house. ²⁴ After him Binnui the son of Henadad repaired another section, from the house of Azariah to the buttress, even as far as the corner. ²⁵ Palal the son of Uzai *made repairs* opposite the buttress, and on the tower which projects from the king's upper house that *was* by the court of the prison. After him Pedaiah the son of Parosh *made repairs*.

²⁶ Moreover the Nethinim who dwelt in Ophel *made repairs* as far as *the place*

in front of the Water Gate toward the east, and on the projecting tower. ²⁷ After them the Tekoites repaired another section, next to the great projecting tower, and as far as the wall of Ophel.

²⁸ Beyond the Horse Gate the priests made repairs, each in front of his *own* house. ²⁹ After them Zadok the son of Immer made repairs in front of his *own* house. After him Shemaiah the son of Shechaniah, the keeper of the East Gate, made repairs. ³⁰ After him Hananiah the son of Shelemiah, and Hanun, the sixth son of Zalaph, repaired another section. After him Meshullam the son of Berechiah made repairs in front of his dwelling. ³¹ After him Malchijah, one of the goldsmiths, made repairs as far as the house of the Nethinim and of the merchants, in front of the Miphkad Gate, and as far as the upper room at the corner. ³² And between the upper room and the corner, as far as the Sheep Gate, the goldsmiths and the merchants made repairs.

4 But it so happened, when Sanballat heard that we were rebuilding the wall, that he was furious and very indignant, and mocked the Jews. ² And he spoke before his brethren and the army of Samaria, and said, "What are these feeble Jews doing? Will they fortify themselves? Will they offer sacrifices? Will they complete it in a day? Will they revive the stones from the heaps of rubbish—*stones* that are burned?"

³ Now Tobiah the Ammonite *was* beside him, and he said, "Whatever they build, if even a fox goes up *on it,* he will break down their stone wall."

⁴ Hear, O our God, for we are despised; turn their reproach on their own heads, and give them as plunder to a land of captivity! ⁵ Do not cover their iniquity, and do not let their sin be blotted out from before You; for they have provoked *You* to anger before the builders.

⁶ So we built the wall, and the entire wall was joined together up to half its *height,* for the people had a mind to work.

⁷ Now it happened, when Sanballat, Tobiah, the Arabs, the Ammonites, and the Ashdodites heard that the walls of Jerusalem were being restored and the gaps were beginning to be closed, that they

became very angry, ⁸ and all of them conspired together to come *and* attack Jerusalem and create confusion. ⁹ Nevertheless we made our prayer to our God, and because of them we set a watch against them day and night.

¹⁰ Then Judah said, "The strength of the laborers is failing, and *there is* so much rubbish that we are not able to build the wall."

¹¹ And our adversaries said, "They will neither know nor see anything, till we come into their midst and kill them and cause the work to cease."

¹² So it was, when the Jews who dwelt near them came, that they told us ten times, "From whatever place you turn, *they will be* upon us."

¹³ Therefore I positioned *men* behind the lower parts of the wall, at the openings; and I set the people according to their families, with their swords, their spears, and their bows. ¹⁴ And I looked, and arose and said to the nobles, to the leaders, and to the rest of the people, "Do not be afraid of them. Remember the Lord, great and awesome, and fight for your brethren, your sons, your daughters, your wives, and your houses."

¹⁵ And it happened, when our enemies heard that it was known to us, and *that* God had brought their plot to nothing, that all of us returned to the wall, everyone to his work. ¹⁶ So it was, from that time on, *that* half of my servants worked at construction, while the other half held the spears, the shields, the bows, and *wore* armor; and the leaders *were* behind all the house of Judah. ¹⁷ Those who built on the wall, and those who carried burdens, loaded themselves so that with one hand they worked at construction, and with the other held a weapon. ¹⁸ Every one of the builders had his sword girded at his side as he built. And the one who sounded the trumpet *was* beside me.

¹⁹ Then I said to the nobles, the rulers, and the rest of the people, "The work *is* great and extensive, and we are separated far from one another on the wall. ²⁰ Wherever you hear the sound of the trumpet, rally to us there. Our God will fight for us."

²¹ So we labored in the work, and half of *the men* held the spears from daybreak

The World Won't Make You Happy

> ### The sacrifice of the wicked is an abomination; how much more when he brings it with wicked intent!
>
> *Proverbs 21:27*

When the great golfer Babe Didrikson Zaharias was dying of cancer, her husband, George Zaharias, came to her bedside. Although he desired to be strong for her sake, he found he was unable to control his emotions and began to cry. Babe said to him gently, "Now honey, don't take on so. While I've been in the hospital, I have learned one thing. A moment of happiness is a lifetime, and I have had a lot of happiness."

Happiness does not come wrapped in brightly colored packages as a "gift" given to us by others. Happiness comes when we uncover the gifts that lie within us and begin to use them to please God and bless others.

Happiness flows from within. It is found in the moments of life we label as "quality" rather than quantity. It rises up in life's greatest tragedies when we choose to smile at what we know to be good and lasting, rather than to cry at what temporarily hurts us. George Bernard Shaw once said, "This is the true joy in life: Being used for a purpose recognized by yourself as a mighty one . . . being a force of nature instead of a feverish, selfish, little clod of ailments and grievances, complaining that the world will not devote itself to making you happy."

The only person who can truly make you happy is yourself. You simply have to decide to be.

until the stars appeared. ²² At the same time I also said to the people, "Let each man and his servant stay at night in Jerusalem, that they may be our guard by night and a working party by day." ²³ So neither I, my brethren, my servants, nor the men of the guard who followed me took off our clothes, *except* that everyone took them off for washing.

5 And there was a great outcry of the people and their wives against their Jewish brethren. ² For there were those who said, "We, our sons, and our daughters *are* many; therefore let us get grain, that we may eat and live."

³ There were also *some* who said, "We have mortgaged our lands and vineyards and houses, that we might buy grain because of the famine."

⁴ There were also those who said, "We have borrowed money for the king's tax *on* our lands and vineyards. ⁵ Yet now our flesh *is* as the flesh of our brethren, our children as their children; and indeed we are forcing our sons and our daughters to be slaves, and *some* of our daughters have been brought into slavery. *It is* not in our power *to redeem them*, for other men have our lands and vineyards."

⁶ And I became very angry when I heard their outcry and these words. ⁷ After serious thought, I rebuked the nobles and rulers, and said to them, "Each of you is exacting usury from his brother." So I called a great assembly against them. ⁸ And I said to them, "According to our ability we have redeemed our Jewish brethren who were sold to the nations. Now indeed, will you even sell your brethren? Or should they be sold to us?"

Then they were silenced and found nothing *to say.* ⁹ Then I said, "What you are doing *is* not good. Should you not walk in the fear of our God because of the reproach of the nations, our enemies? ¹⁰ I also, *with* my brethren and my servants, am lending them money and grain. Please, let us stop this usury! ¹¹ Restore now to them, even this day, their lands, their vineyards, their olive groves, and their houses, also a hundredth of the money and the grain, the new wine and the oil, that you have charged them."

¹² So they said, "We will restore *it,* and will require nothing from them; we will do as you say."

Then I called the priests, and required an oath from them that they would do according to this promise. ¹³ Then I shook out the fold of my garment and said, "So may God shake out each man from his house, and from his property, who does not perform this promise. Even thus may he be shaken out and emptied."

And all the assembly said, "Amen!" and praised the LORD. Then the people did according to this promise.

¹⁴ Moreover, from the time that I was appointed to be their governor in the land of Judah, from the twentieth year until the thirty-second year of King Artaxerxes, twelve years, neither I nor my brothers ate the governor's provisions. ¹⁵ But the former governors who *were* before me laid burdens on the people, and took from them bread and wine, besides forty shekels of silver. Yes, even their servants bore rule over the people, but I did not do so, because of the fear of God. ¹⁶ Indeed, I also continued the work on this wall, and we did not buy any land. All my servants *were* gathered there for the work.

¹⁷ And at my table *were* one hundred and fifty Jews and rulers, besides those who came to us from the nations around us. ¹⁸ Now *that* which was prepared daily *was* one ox *and* six choice sheep. Also fowl were prepared for me, and once every ten days an abundance of all kinds of wine. Yet in spite of this I did not demand the governor's provisions, because the bondage was heavy on this people.

¹⁹ Remember me, my God, for good, *according to* all that I have done for this people.

~ PSALM 89:1–4 ~

1   I will sing of the mercies of the LORD
       forever;
     With my mouth will I make known
       Your faithfulness to all
       generations.
2   For I have said, "Mercy shall be built
       up forever;
     Your faithfulness You shall establish
       in the very heavens."

3 "I have made a covenant with My
        chosen,
    I have sworn to My servant David:
4 'Your seed I will establish forever,
        And build up your throne to all
        generations.' "   Selah

∼ PROVERBS 21:27 ∼

27 The sacrifice of the wicked *is* an
        abomination;
    How much more *when* he brings it
        with wicked intent!

∼ ACTS 26:1–32 ∼

Then Agrippa said to Paul, "You are permitted to speak for yourself."

So Paul stretched out his hand and answered for himself: 2 "I think myself
happy, King Agrippa, because today I shall
answer for myself before you concerning
all the things of which I am accused by
the Jews, 3 especially because you are expert in all customs and questions which
have to do with the Jews. Therefore I beg
you to hear me patiently.

4 "My manner of life from my youth,
which was spent from the beginning
among my own nation at Jerusalem, all
the Jews know. 5 They knew me from the
first, if they were willing to testify, that
according to the strictest sect of our religion I lived a Pharisee. 6 And now I stand
and am judged for the hope of the promise made by God to our fathers. 7 To this
promise our twelve tribes, earnestly serving *God* night and day, hope to attain. For
this hope's sake, King Agrippa, I am accused by the Jews. 8 Why should it be
thought incredible by you that God raises
the dead?

9 "Indeed, I myself thought I must do
many things contrary to the name of Jesus
of Nazareth. 10 This I also did in Jerusalem, and many of the saints I shut up in
prison, having received authority from the
chief priests; and when they were put to
death, I cast my vote against *them*. 11 And
I punished them often in every synagogue
and compelled *them* to blaspheme; and
being exceedingly enraged against them,
I persecuted *them* even to foreign cities.
12 "While thus occupied, as I journeyed
to Damascus with authority and commis-

sion from the chief priests, 13 at midday,
O king, along the road I saw a light from
heaven, brighter than the sun, shining
around me and those who journeyed with
me. 14 And when we all had fallen to the
ground, I heard a voice speaking to me
and saying in the Hebrew language, 'Saul,
Saul, why are you persecuting Me? *It is*
hard for you to kick against the goads.'
15 So I said, 'Who are You, Lord?' And He
said, 'I am Jesus, whom you are persecuting. 16 But rise and stand on your feet; for
I have appeared to you for this purpose,
to make you a minister and a witness both
of the things which you have seen and of
the things which I will yet reveal to you.
17 I will deliver you from the *Jewish*
people, as well as *from* the Gentiles, to
whom I now send you, 18 to open their
eyes, *in order* to turn *them* from darkness
to light, and *from* the power of Satan to
God, that they may receive forgiveness of
sins and an inheritance among those who
are sanctified by faith in Me.'

19 "Therefore, King Agrippa, I was not
disobedient to the heavenly vision, 20 but
declared first to those in Damascus and
in Jerusalem, and throughout all the region of Judea, and *then* to the Gentiles,
that they should repent, turn to God, and
do works befitting repentance. 21 For these
reasons the Jews seized me in the temple
and tried to kill *me*. 22 Therefore, having
obtained help from God, to this day I
stand, witnessing both to small and great,
saying no other things than those which
the prophets and Moses said would
come— 23 that the Christ would suffer,
that He would be the first to rise from
the dead, and would proclaim light to the
Jewish people and to the Gentiles."

24 Now as he thus made his defense,
Festus said with a loud voice, "Paul, you
are beside yourself! Much learning is driving you mad!"

25 But he said, "I am not mad, most
noble Festus, but speak the words of truth
and reason. 26 For the king, before whom
I also speak freely, knows these things;
for I am convinced that none of these
things escapes his attention, since this
thing was not done in a corner. 27 King
Agrippa, do you believe the prophets? I
know that you do believe."

28 Then Agrippa said to Paul, "You

almost persuade me to become a Christian."

²⁹ And Paul said, "I would to God that not only you, but also all who hear me today, might become both almost and altogether such as I am, except for these chains."

³⁰ When he had said these things, the king stood up, as well as the governor and Bernice and those who sat with them; ³¹ and when they had gone aside, they talked among themselves, saying, "This man is doing nothing deserving of death or chains."

³² Then Agrippa said to Festus, "This man might have been set free if he had not appealed to Caesar."

～ NEHEMIAH 6:1—7:73 ～

Now it happened when Sanballat, Tobiah, Geshem the Arab, and the rest of our enemies heard that I had rebuilt the wall, and *that* there were no breaks left in it (though at that time I had not hung the doors in the gates), ² that Sanballat and Geshem sent to me, saying, "Come, let us meet together among the villages in the plain of Ono." But they thought to do me harm.

³ So I sent messengers to them, saying, "I *am* doing a great work, so that I cannot come down. Why should the work cease while I leave it and go down to you?"

⁴ But they sent me this message four times, and I answered them in the same manner.

⁵ Then Sanballat sent his servant to me as before, the fifth time, with an open letter in his hand. ⁶ In it *was* written:

It is reported among the nations, and Geshem says, *that* you and the Jews plan to rebel; therefore, according to these rumors, you are rebuilding the wall, that you may be their king. ⁷ And you have also appointed prophets to proclaim concerning you at Jerusalem, saying, "*There is* a king in Judah!" Now these matters will be reported to the king. So come, therefore, and let us consult together.

⁸ Then I sent to him, saying, "No such things as you say are being done, but you invent them in your own heart."

⁹ For they all *were trying to* make us afraid, saying, "Their hands will be weakened in the work, and it will not be done."

Now therefore, *O God,* strengthen my hands.

¹⁰ Afterward I came to the house of Shemaiah the son of Delaiah, the son of Mehetabel, who *was* a secret informer; and he said, "Let us meet together in the house of God, within the temple, and let us close the doors of the temple, for they are coming to kill you; indeed, at night they will come to kill you."

¹¹ And I said, "Should such a man as I flee? And who *is there* such as I who would go into the temple to save his life? I will not go in!" ¹² Then I perceived that God had not sent him at all, but that he pronounced *this* prophecy against me because Tobiah and Sanballat had hired him. ¹³ For this reason he *was* hired, that I should be afraid and act that way and sin, so *that* they might have *cause* for an evil report, that they might reproach me.

¹⁴ My God, remember Tobiah and Sanballat, according to these their works, and the prophetess Noadiah and the rest of the prophets who would have made me afraid.

¹⁵ So the wall was finished on the twenty-fifth *day* of Elul, in fifty-two days. ¹⁶ And it happened, when all our enemies heard *of it,* and all the nations around us saw *these things,* that they were very disheartened in their own eyes; for they perceived that this work was done by our God.

¹⁷ Also in those days the nobles of Judah sent many letters to Tobiah, and *the letters of* Tobiah came to them. ¹⁸ For many in Judah were pledged to him, because he was the son-in-law of Shechaniah the son of Arah, and his son Jehohanan had married the daughter of Meshullam

Keep Swimming!

The pessimist sees a glass filled half way with water as being half empty, the optimist sees it as half full. The optimistically creative person will see it as a vase for a rosebud, the optimistic pragmatist as a means of quenching thirst, the optimistic priest as holy baptismal water!

Consider the benefits of choosing the optimistic route as described in this poem:

> Two frogs fell into a deep cream bowl,
> One was an optimistic soul;
> But the other took the gloomy view,
> "I shall drown," he cried, "and so will you."
> So with a last despairing cry,
> He closed his eyes and said, "Good-bye."
> But the other frog, with a merry grin
> Said, "I can't get out, but I won't give in!
> I'll swim around till my strength is spent.
> For having tried, I'll die content."
> Bravely he swam until it would seem
> His struggles began to churn the cream.
> On the top of the butter at last he stopped
> And out of the bowl he happily hopped.
> What is the moral? It's easily found.
> If you can't get out — keep swimming around!

For they all were trying to make us afraid, saying, "Their hands will be weakened in the work, and it will not be done." Now therefore, O God, strengthen my hands.

Proverbs 21:26

the son of Berechiah. ¹⁹ Also they reported his good deeds before me, and reported my words to him. Tobiah sent letters
to frighten me.

7 Then it was, when the wall was built
and I had hung the doors, when the
gatekeepers, the singers, and the Levites
had been appointed, ² that I gave the
charge of Jerusalem to my brother
Hanani, and Hananiah the leader of the
citadel, for he *was* a faithful man and
feared God more than many.

³ And I said to them, "Do not let the
gates of Jerusalem be opened until the sun
is hot; and while they stand *guard,* let them
shut and bar the doors; and appoint
guards from among the inhabitants of
Jerusalem, one at his watch station and
another in front of his own house."

⁴ Now the city *was* large and spacious,
but the people in it *were* few, and the
houses *were* not rebuilt. ⁵ Then my God
put it into my heart to gather the nobles,
the rulers, and the people, that they might
be registered by genealogy. And I found a
register of the genealogy of those who had
come up in the first *return,* and found
written in it:

6 These *are* the people of the
   province who came back from the
   captivity, of those who had been
   carried away, whom
   Nebuchadnezzar the king of
   Babylon had carried away, and who
   returned to Jerusalem and Judah,
   everyone to his city.

7 Those who came with Zerubbabel
   were Jeshua, Nehemiah, Azariah,
   Raamiah, Nahamani, Mordecai,
   Bilshan, Mispereth, Bigvai,
   Nehum, and Baanah.

   The number of the men of the
   people of Israel: ⁸ the sons of
   Parosh, two thousand one hundred
   and seventy-two;
⁹ the sons of Shephatiah, three
hundred and seventy-two;
¹⁰ the sons of Arah, six hundred
and fifty-two;
¹¹ the sons of Pahath-Moab, of the
sons of Jeshua and Joab, two

thousand eight hundred and
eighteen;
¹² the sons of Elam, one thousand
two hundred and fifty-four;
¹³ the sons of Zattu, eight hundred
and forty-five;
¹⁴ the sons of Zaccai, seven
hundred and sixty;
¹⁵ the sons of Binnui, six hundred
and forty-eight;
¹⁶ the sons of Bebai, six hundred
and twenty-eight;
¹⁷ the sons of Azgad, two thousand
three hundred and twenty-two;
¹⁸ the sons of Adonikam, six
hundred and sixty-seven;
¹⁹ the sons of Bigvai, two thousand
and sixty-seven;
²⁰ the sons of Adin, six hundred
and fifty-five;
²¹ the sons of Ater of Hezekiah,
ninety-eight;
²² the sons of Hashum, three
hundred and twenty-eight;
²³ the sons of Bezai, three hundred
and twenty-four;
²⁴ the sons of Hariph, one hundred
and twelve;
²⁵ the sons of Gibeon, ninety-five;
²⁶ the men of Bethlehem and
Netophah, one hundred and
eighty-eight;
²⁷ the men of Anathoth, one
hundred and twenty-eight;
²⁸ the men of Beth Azmaveth, forty-
two;
²⁹ the men of Kirjath Jearim,
Chephirah, and Beeroth, seven
hundred and forty-three;
³⁰ the men of Ramah and Geba, six
hundred and twenty-one;
³¹ the men of Michmas, one
hundred and twenty-two;
³² the men of Bethel and Ai, one
hundred and twenty-three;
³³ the men of the other Nebo, fifty-
two;
³⁴ the sons of the other Elam, one
thousand two hundred and fifty-
four;
³⁵ the sons of Harim, three hundred
and twenty;
³⁶ the sons of Jericho, three
hundred and forty-five;
³⁷ the sons of Lod, Hadid, and

Ono, seven hundred and twenty-one;

³⁸ the sons of Senaah, three thousand nine hundred and thirty.

³⁹ The priests: the sons of Jedaiah, of the house of Jeshua, nine hundred and seventy-three;
⁴⁰ the sons of Immer, one thousand and fifty-two;
⁴¹ the sons of Pashhur, one thousand two hundred and forty-seven;
⁴² the sons of Harim, one thousand and seventeen.

⁴³ The Levites: the sons of Jeshua, of Kadmiel,
and of the sons of Hodevah, seventy-four.

⁴⁴ The singers: the sons of Asaph, one hundred and forty-eight.

⁴⁵ The gatekeepers: the sons of Shallum,
the sons of Ater,
the sons of Talmon,
the sons of Akkub,
the sons of Hatita,
the sons of Shobai, one hundred and thirty-eight.

⁴⁶ The Nethinim: the sons of Ziha,
the sons of Hasupha,
the sons of Tabbaoth,
⁴⁷ the sons of Keros,
the sons of Sia,
the sons of Padon,
⁴⁸ the sons of Lebana,
the sons of Hagaba,
the sons of Salmai,
⁴⁹ the sons of Hanan,
the sons of Giddel,
the sons of Gahar,
⁵⁰ the sons of Reaiah,
the sons of Rezin,
the sons of Nekoda,
⁵¹ the sons of Gazzam,
the sons of Uzza,
the sons of Paseah,
⁵² the sons of Besai,
the sons of Meunim,
the sons of Nephishesim,
⁵³ the sons of Bakbuk,

the sons of Hakupha,
the sons of Harhur,
⁵⁴ the sons of Bazlith,
the sons of Mehida,
the sons of Harsha,
⁵⁵ the sons of Barkos,
the sons of Sisera,
the sons of Tamah,
⁵⁶ the sons of Neziah,
and the sons of Hatipha.

⁵⁷ The sons of Solomon's servants:
the sons of Sotai,
the sons of Sophereth,
the sons of Perida,
⁵⁸ the sons of Jaala,
the sons of Darkon,
the sons of Giddel,
⁵⁹ the sons of Shephatiah,
the sons of Hattil,
the sons of Pochereth of Zebaim,
and the children of Amon.
⁶⁰ All the Nethinim, and the sons of Solomon's servants, *were* three hundred and ninety-two.

⁶¹ And these *were* the ones who came up from Tel Melah, Tel Harsha, Cherub, Addon, and Immer, but they could not identify their father's house nor their lineage, whether they *were* of Israel: ⁶² the sons of Delaiah,
the sons of Tobiah,
the sons of Nekoda, six hundred and forty-two;
⁶³ and of the priests: the sons of Habaiah,
the sons of Koz,
the sons of Barzillai, who took a wife of the daughters of Barzillai the Gileadite, and was called by their name.
⁶⁴ These sought their listing *among* those who were registered by genealogy, but it was not found; therefore they were excluded from the priesthood as defiled. ⁶⁵ And the governor said to them that they should not eat of the most holy things till a priest could consult with the Urim and Thummim.

⁶⁶ Altogether the whole assembly *was* forty-two thousand three hundred

and sixty, 67 besides their male and female servants, of whom *there were* seven thousand three hundred and thirty-seven; and they had two hundred and forty-five men and women singers. 68 Their horses were seven hundred and thirty-six, their mules two hundred and forty-five, 69 *their* camels four hundred and thirty-five, *and* donkeys six thousand seven hundred and twenty.

70 And some of the heads of the fathers' houses gave to the work. The governor gave to the treasury one thousand gold drachmas, fifty basins, and five hundred and thirty priestly garments. 71 Some of the heads of the fathers' *houses* gave to the treasury of the work twenty thousand gold drachmas, and two thousand two hundred silver minas. 72 And that which the rest of the people gave *was* twenty thousand gold drachmas, two thousand silver minas, and sixty-seven priestly garments.

73 So the priests, the Levites, the gatekeepers, the singers, *some* of the people, the Nethinim, and all Israel dwelt in their cities.

When the seventh month came, the children of Israel *were* in their cities.

~ PSALM 89:5–10 ~

5 And the heavens will praise Your
     wonders, O LORD;
   Your faithfulness also in the assembly
     of the saints.

6 For who in the heavens can be
     compared to the LORD?
   Who among the sons of the mighty
     can be likened to the LORD?

7 God is greatly to be feared in the
     assembly of the saints,
   And to be held in reverence by all
     those around Him.

8 O LORD God of hosts,
   Who *is* mighty like You, O LORD?
   Your faithfulness also surrounds You.

9 You rule the raging of the sea;
   When its waves rise, You still them.

10 You have broken Rahab in pieces, as
     one who is slain;
   You have scattered Your enemies
     with Your mighty arm.

~ PROVERBS 21:28 ~

28 A false witness shall perish,
   But the man who hears *him* will
     speak endlessly.

~ ACTS 27:1–26 ~

And when it was decided that we should sail to Italy, they delivered Paul and some other prisoners to *one* named Julius, a centurion of the Augustan Regiment. 2 So, entering a ship of Adramyttium, we put to sea, meaning to sail along the coasts of Asia. Aristarchus, a Macedonian of Thessalonica, was with us. 3 And the next *day* we landed at Sidon. And Julius treated Paul kindly and gave *him* liberty to go to his friends and receive care. 4 When we had put to sea from there, we sailed under *the shelter of* Cyprus, because the winds were contrary. 5 And when we had sailed over the sea which is off Cilicia and Pamphylia, we came to Myra, *a city* of Lycia. 6 There the centurion found an Alexandrian ship sailing to Italy, and he put us on board.

7 When we had sailed slowly many days, and arrived with difficulty off Cnidus, the wind not permitting us to proceed, we sailed under *the shelter of* Crete off Salmone. 8 Passing it with difficulty, we came to a place called Fair Havens, near the city *of* Lasea.

9 Now when much time had been spent, and sailing was now dangerous because the Fast was already over, Paul advised them, 10 saying, "Men, I perceive that this voyage will end with disaster and much loss, not only of the cargo and ship, but also our lives." 11 Nevertheless the centurion was more persuaded by the helmsman and the owner of the ship than by the things spoken by Paul. 12 And because the harbor was not suitable to winter in, the majority advised to set sail from there also, if by any means they could reach Phoenix, a harbor of Crete opening toward the southwest and northwest, *and* winter *there*.

¹³ When the south wind blew softly, supposing that they had obtained *their* desire, putting out to sea, they sailed close by Crete. ¹⁴ But not long after, a tempestuous head wind arose, called Euroclydon. ¹⁵ So when the ship was caught, and could not head into the wind, we let *her* drive. ¹⁶ And running under *the shelter of* an island called Clauda, we secured the skiff with difficulty. ¹⁷ When they had taken it on board, they used cables to undergird the ship; and fearing lest they should run aground on the Syrtis *Sands,* they struck sail and so were driven. ¹⁸ And because we were exceedingly tempest-tossed, the next *day* they lightened the ship. ¹⁹ On the third *day* we threw the ship's tackle overboard with our own hands. ²⁰ Now when neither sun nor stars appeared for many days, and no small tempest beat on *us,* all hope that we would be saved was finally given up.

²¹ But after long abstinence from food, then Paul stood in the midst of them and said, "Men, you should have listened to me, and not have sailed from Crete and incurred this disaster and loss. ²² And now I urge you to take heart, for there will be no loss of life among you, but only of the ship. ²³ For there stood by me this night an angel of the God to whom I belong and whom I serve, ²⁴ saying, 'Do not be afraid, Paul; you must be brought before Caesar; and indeed God has granted you all those who sail with you.' ²⁵ Therefore take heart, men, for I believe God that it will be just as it was told me. ²⁶ However, we must run aground on a certain island."

～ NEHEMIAH 8:1—9:38 ～

Now all the people gathered together as one man in the open square that *was* in front of the Water Gate; and they told Ezra the scribe to bring the Book of the Law of Moses, which the LORD had commanded Israel. ² So Ezra the priest brought the Law before the assembly of men and women and all who *could* hear with understanding on the first day of the seventh month. ³ Then he read from it in the open square that *was* in front of the Water Gate from morning until midday, before the men and women and those who could understand; and the ears of all the people *were attentive* to the Book of the Law.

⁴ So Ezra the scribe stood on a platform of wood which they had made for the purpose; and beside him, at his right hand, stood Mattithiah, Shema, Anaiah, Urijah, Hilkiah, and Maaseiah; and at his left hand Pedaiah, Mishael, Malchijah, Hashum, Hashbadana, Zechariah, *and* Meshullam. ⁵ And Ezra opened the book in the sight of all the people, for he was *standing* above all the people; and when he opened it, all the people stood up. ⁶ And Ezra blessed the LORD, the great God.

Then all the people answered, "Amen, Amen!" while lifting up their hands. And they bowed their heads and worshiped the LORD with *their* faces to the ground.

⁷ Also Jeshua, Bani, Sherebiah, Jamin, Akkub, Shabbethai, Hodijah, Maaseiah, Kelita, Azariah, Jozabad, Hanan, Pelaiah, and the Levites, helped the people to understand the Law; and the people *stood* in their place. ⁸ So they read distinctly from the book, in the Law of God; and they gave the sense, and helped *them* to understand the reading.

⁹ And Nehemiah, who *was* the governor, Ezra the priest *and* scribe, and the Levites who taught the people said to all the people, "This day *is* holy to the LORD your God; do not mourn nor weep." For all the people wept, when they heard the words of the Law.

¹⁰ Then he said to them, "Go your way, eat the fat, drink the sweet, and send portions to those for whom nothing is prepared; for *this* day *is* holy to our Lord. Do not sorrow, for the joy of the LORD is your strength."

¹¹ So the Levites quieted all the people, saying, "Be still, for the day *is* holy; do not be grieved." ¹² And all the people went their way to eat and drink, to send portions and rejoice greatly, because they

understood the words that were declared to them.

¹³ Now on the second day the heads of the fathers' *houses* of all the people, with the priests and Levites, were gathered to Ezra the scribe, in order to understand the words of the Law. ¹⁴ And they found written in the Law, which the LORD had commanded by Moses, that the children of Israel should dwell in booths during the feast of the seventh month, ¹⁵ and that they should announce and proclaim in all their cities and in Jerusalem, saying, "Go out to the mountain, and bring olive branches, branches of oil trees, myrtle branches, palm branches, and branches of leafy trees, to make booths, as *it is* written."

¹⁶ Then the people went out and brought *them* and made themselves booths, each one on the roof of his house, or in their courtyards or in the courts of the house of God, and in the open square of the Water Gate and in the open square of the Gate of Ephraim. ¹⁷ So the whole assembly of those who had returned from the captivity made booths and sat under the booths; for since the days of Joshua the son of Nun until that day the children of Israel had not done so. And there was very great gladness. ¹⁸ Also day by day, from the first day until the last day, he read from the Book of the Law of God. And they kept the feast seven days; and on the eighth day *there was* a sacred assembly, according to the *prescribed* manner.

9 Now on the twenty-fourth day of this month the children of Israel were assembled with fasting, in sackcloth, and with dust on their heads. ² Then those of Israelite lineage separated themselves from all foreigners; and they stood and confessed their sins and the iniquities of their fathers. ³ And they stood up in their place and read from the Book of the Law of the LORD their God *for one*-fourth of the day; and *for another* fourth they confessed and worshiped the LORD their God.

⁴ Then Jeshua, Bani, Kadmiel, Shebaniah, Bunni, Sherebiah, Bani, *and* Chenani stood on the stairs of the Levites and cried out with a loud voice to the LORD their God. ⁵ And the Levites, Jeshua,

Kadmiel, Bani, Hashabniah, Sherebiah, Hodijah, Shebaniah, *and* Pethahiah, said:

"Stand up *and* bless the LORD your God
Forever and ever!

"Blessed be Your glorious name,
Which is exalted above all blessing and praise!
⁶ You alone *are* the LORD;
You have made heaven,
The heaven of heavens, with all their host,
The earth and everything on it,
The seas and all that is in them,
And You preserve them all.
The host of heaven worships You.

⁷ "You *are* the LORD God,
Who chose Abram,
And brought him out of Ur of the Chaldeans,
And gave him the name Abraham;
⁸ You found his heart faithful before You,
And made a covenant with him
To give the land of the Canaanites,
The Hittites, the Amorites,
The Perizzites, the Jebusites,
And the Girgashites—
To give *it* to his descendants.
You have performed Your words,
For You *are* righteous.

⁹ "You saw the affliction of our fathers in Egypt,
And heard their cry by the Red Sea.
¹⁰ You showed signs and wonders against Pharaoh,
Against all his servants,
And against all the people of his land.
For You knew that they acted proudly against them.
So You made a name for Yourself, as *it is* this day.
¹¹ And You divided the sea before them,
So that they went through the midst of the sea on the dry land;
And their persecutors You threw into the deep,

Is the Door Really Locked?

Do not sorrow, for the joy of the Lord is your strength.

Nehemiah 8:10

Harry Houdini, the early twentieth century escape artist, issued a challenge wherever he went. He claimed he could be locked in any jail cell in the country and set himself free within minutes. He had a long track record of proving himself!

One time, however, something seemed to go wrong. Houdini entered a jail cell in his street clothes. The heavy metal doors clanged shut behind him, and he took from his belt a concealed piece of strong, but flexible metal. He set to work on the lock to his cell, but something seemed different about this particular lock. He worked for thirty minutes without results. An hour passed. This was long after the time that Houdini normally freed himself and he began to sweat and pant in exasperation. Still, he could not pick the lock.

Finally, after laboring for two hours, Houdini — feeling a sense of failure close in around him — leaned against the door in frustration. To his amazement, as he collapsed against the door, it swung open! It had not been locked in the first place!

How many times are challenges impossible — or doors locked — only because we think they are? When we put our minds and energy toward them, we often find impossible tasks turn into achievements.

As a stone into the mighty waters.

12 Moreover You led them by day
   with a cloudy pillar,
And by night with a pillar of fire,
To give them light on the road
Which they should travel.

13 "You came down also on Mount
   Sinai,
And spoke with them from
   heaven,
And gave them just ordinances
   and true laws,
Good statutes and
   commandments.

14 You made known to them Your
   holy Sabbath,
And commanded them precepts,
   statutes and laws,
By the hand of Moses Your
   servant.

15 You gave them bread from heaven
   for their hunger,
And brought them water out of
   the rock for their thirst,
And told them to go in to possess
   the land
Which You had sworn to give
   them.

16 "But they and our fathers acted
   proudly,
Hardened their necks,
And did not heed Your
   commandments.

17 They refused to obey,
And they were not mindful of
   Your wonders
That You did among them.
But they hardened their necks,
And in their rebellion
They appointed a leader
To return to their bondage.
But You *are* God,
Ready to pardon,
Gracious and merciful,
Slow to anger,
Abundant in kindness,
And did not forsake them.

18 "Even when they made a molded
   calf for themselves,
And said, 'This *is* your god
That brought you up out of
   Egypt,'

And worked great
   provocations,

19 Yet in Your manifold mercies
You did not forsake them in the
   wilderness.
The pillar of the cloud did not
   depart from them by day,
To lead them on the road;
Nor the pillar of fire by night,
To show them light,
And the way they should go.

20 You also gave Your good Spirit to
   instruct them,
And did not withhold Your manna
   from their mouth,
And gave them water for their
   thirst.

21 Forty years You sustained them in
   the wilderness;
They lacked nothing;
Their clothes did not wear out
And their feet did not swell.

22 "Moreover You gave them
   kingdoms and nations,
And divided them into districts.
So they took possession of the
   land of Sihon,
The land of the king of Heshbon,
And the land of Og king of
   Bashan.

23 You also multiplied their children
   as the stars of heaven,
And brought them into the land
Which You had told their fathers
To go in and possess.

24 So the people went in
And possessed the land;
You subdued before them the
   inhabitants of the land,
The Canaanites,
And gave them into their hands,
With their kings
And the people of the land,
That they might do with them as
   they wished.

25 And they took strong cities and a
   rich land,
And possessed houses full of all
   goods,
Cisterns *already* dug, vineyards,
   olive groves,
And fruit trees in abundance.
So they ate and were filled and
   grew fat,

And delighted themselves in Your
great goodness.

26 "Nevertheless they were
disobedient
And rebelled against You,
Cast Your law behind their backs
And killed Your prophets, who
testified against them
To turn them to Yourself;
And they worked great
provocations.
27 Therefore You delivered them into
the hand of their enemies,
Who oppressed them;
And in the time of their trouble,
When they cried to You,
You heard from heaven;
And according to Your abundant
mercies
You gave them deliverers who
saved them
From the hand of their enemies.

28 "But after they had rest,
They again did evil before You.
Therefore You left them in the
hand of their enemies,
So that they had dominion over
them;
Yet when they returned and cried
out to You,
You heard from heaven;
And many times You delivered
them according to Your mercies,
29 And testified against them,
That You might bring them back
to Your law.
Yet they acted proudly,
And did not heed Your
commandments,
But sinned against Your
judgments,
'Which if a man does, he shall live
by them.'
And they shrugged their
shoulders,
Stiffened their necks,
And would not hear.
30 Yet for many years You had
patience with them,
And testified against them by Your
Spirit in Your prophets.
Yet they would not listen;

Therefore You gave them into the
hand of the peoples of the
lands.
31 Nevertheless in Your great mercy
You did not utterly consume them
nor forsake them;
For You *are* God, gracious and
merciful.

32 "Now therefore, our God,
The great, the mighty, and
awesome God,
Who keeps covenant and mercy:
Do not let all the trouble seem
small before You
That has come upon us,
Our kings and our princes,
Our priests and our prophets,
Our fathers and on all Your
people,
From the days of the kings of
Assyria until this day.
33 However You *are* just in all that
has befallen us;
For You have dealt faithfully,
But we have done wickedly.
34 Neither our kings nor our
princes,
Our priests nor our fathers,
Have kept Your law,
Nor heeded Your commandments
and Your testimonies,
With which You testified against
them.
35 For they have not served You in
their kingdom,
Or in the many good *things* that
You gave them,
Or in the large and rich land
which You set before them;
Nor did they turn from their
wicked works.

36 "Here we *are*, servants today!
And the land that You gave to our
fathers,
To eat its fruit and its bounty,
Here we *are*, servants in it!
37 And it yields much increase to the
kings
You have set over us,
Because of our sins;
Also they have dominion over our
bodies and our cattle

At their pleasure;
And we *are* in great distress.

38 "And because of all this,
We make a sure *covenant* and
write *it;*
Our leaders, our Levites, *and* our
priests seal *it.*"

~ PSALM 89:11–18 ~

11 The heavens *are* Yours, the earth also
is Yours;
The world and all its fullness, You
have founded them.
12 The north and the south, You have
created them;
Tabor and Hermon rejoice in Your
name.
13 You have a mighty arm;
Strong is Your hand, *and* high is Your
right hand.
14 Righteousness and justice *are* the
foundation of Your throne;
Mercy and truth go before Your face.
15 Blessed *are* the people who know the
joyful sound!
They walk, O LORD, in the light of
Your countenance.
16 In Your name they rejoice all day
long,
And in Your righteousness they are
exalted.
17 For You *are* the glory of their
strength,
And in Your favor our horn is
exalted.
18 For our shield *belongs* to the LORD,
And our king to the Holy One of
Israel.

~ PROVERBS 21:29–31 ~

29 A wicked man hardens his face,
But *as for* the upright, he establishes
his way.

30 *There is* no wisdom or understanding
Or counsel against the LORD.

31 The horse *is* prepared for the day of
battle,
But deliverance *is* of the LORD.

~ ACTS 27:27–44 ~

Now when the fourteenth night had
come, as we were driven up and down in
the Adriatic *Sea,* about midnight the sailors sensed that they were drawing near
some land. 28 And they took soundings and
found *it* to be twenty fathoms; and when
they had gone a little farther, they took
soundings again and found *it* to be fifteen
fathoms. 29 Then, fearing lest we should
run aground on the rocks, they dropped
four anchors from the stern, and prayed
for day to come. 30 And as the sailors were
seeking to escape from the ship, when they
had let down the skiff into the sea, under
pretense of putting out anchors from the
prow, 31 Paul said to the centurion and
the soldiers, "Unless these men stay in the
ship, you cannot be saved." 32 Then the
soldiers cut away the ropes of the skiff
and let it fall off.

33 And as day was about to dawn, Paul
implored *them* all to take food, saying,
"Today is the fourteenth day you have
waited and continued without food, and
eaten nothing. 34 Therefore I urge you to
take nourishment, for this is for your survival, since not a hair will fall from the
head of any of you." 35 And when he had
said these things, he took bread and gave
thanks to God in the presence of them
all; and when he had broken *it* he began
to eat. 36 Then they were all encouraged,
and also took food themselves. 37 And in
all we were two hundred and seventy-six
persons on the ship. 38 So when they had
eaten enough, they lightened the ship and
threw out the wheat into the sea.

39 When it was day, they did not recognize the land; but they observed a bay with
a beach, onto which they planned to run
the ship if possible. 40 And they let go the
anchors and left *them* in the sea, meanwhile loosing the rudder ropes; and they
hoisted the mainsail to the wind and made
for shore. 41 But striking a place where two
seas met, they ran the ship aground; and
the prow stuck fast and remained immovable, but the stern was being broken up
by the violence of the waves.

42 And the soldiers' plan was to kill the
prisoners, lest any of them should swim
away and escape. 43 But the centurion,

wanting to save Paul, kept them from *their* purpose, and commanded that those who could swim should jump *overboard* first and get to land, ⁴⁴ and the rest, some on boards and some on *parts* of the ship. And so it was that they all escaped safely to land.

∾ NEHEMIAH 10:1—11:36 ∾

Now those who placed *their* seal on *the document were:*
Nehemiah the governor, the son of Hacaliah, and Zedekiah, ² Seraiah, Azariah, Jeremiah, ³ Pashhur, Amariah, Malchijah, ⁴ Hattush, Shebaniah, Malluch, ⁵ Harim, Meremoth, Obadiah, ⁶ Daniel, Ginnethon, Baruch, ⁷ Meshullam, Abijah, Mijamin, ⁸ Maaziah, Bilgai, *and* Shemaiah. These *were* the priests.

⁹ The Levites: Jeshua the son of Azaniah, Binnui of the sons of Henadad, *and* Kadmiel. ¹⁰ Their brethren: Shebaniah, Hodijah, Kelita, Pelaiah, Hanan, ¹¹ Micha, Rehob, Hashabiah, ¹² Zaccur, Sherebiah, Shebaniah, ¹³ Hodijah, Bani, *and* Beninu.

¹⁴ The leaders of the people: Parosh, Pahath-Moab, Elam, Zattu, Bani, ¹⁵ Bunni, Azgad, Bebai, ¹⁶ Adonijah, Bigvai, Adin, ¹⁷ Ater, Hezekiah, Azzur, ¹⁸ Hodijah, Hashum, Bezai, ¹⁹ Hariph, Anathoth, Nebai, ²⁰ Magpiash, Meshullam, Hezir, ²¹ Meshezabel, Zadok, Jaddua, ²² Pelatiah, Hanan, Anaiah, ²³ Hoshea, Hananiah, Hasshub, ²⁴ Hallohesh, Pilha, Shobek, ²⁵ Rehum, Hashabnah, Maaseiah, ²⁶ Ahijah, Hanan, Anan, ²⁷ Malluch, Harim, *and* Baanah.

²⁸ Now the rest of the people—the priests, the Levites, the gatekeepers, the singers, the Nethinim, and all those who had separated themselves from the peoples of the lands to the Law of God, their wives, their sons, and their daughters, everyone who had knowledge and understanding— ²⁹ these joined with their brethren, their nobles, and entered into a curse and an oath to walk in God's Law, which was given by Moses the servant of

God, and to observe and do all the commandments of the LORD our Lord, and His ordinances and His statutes: ³⁰ We would not give our daughters as wives to the peoples of the land, nor take their daughters for our sons; ³¹ *if* the peoples of the land brought wares or any grain to sell on the Sabbath day, we would not buy it from them on the Sabbath, or on a holy day; and we would forego the seventh year's *produce* and the exacting of every debt.

³² Also we made ordinances for ourselves, to exact from ourselves yearly one-third of a shekel for the service of the house of our God: ³³ for the showbread, for the regular grain offering, for the regular burnt offering of the Sabbaths, the New Moons, and the set feasts; for the holy things, for the sin offerings to make atonement for Israel, and all the work of the house of our God. ³⁴ We cast lots among the priests, the Levites, and the people, for *bringing* the wood offering into the house of our God, according to our fathers' houses, at the appointed times year by year, to burn on the altar of the LORD our God as *it is* written in the Law.

³⁵ And *we made ordinances* to bring the firstfruits of our ground and the firstfruits of all fruit of all trees, year by year, to the house of the LORD; ³⁶ to bring the firstborn of our sons and our cattle, as *it is* written in the Law, and the firstborn of our herds and our flocks, to the house of our God, to the priests who minister in the house of our God; ³⁷ to bring the firstfruits of our dough, our offerings, the fruit from all kinds of trees, *the* new wine and oil, to the priests, to the storerooms of the house of our God; and to bring the tithes of our land to the Levites, for the Levites should receive the tithes in all our farming communities. ³⁸ And the priest, the descendant of Aaron, shall be

with the Levites when the Levites receive tithes; and the Levites shall bring up a tenth of the tithes to the house of our God, to the rooms of the storehouse.

³⁹ For the children of Israel and the children of Levi shall bring the offering of the grain, of the new wine and the oil, to the storerooms where the articles of the sanctuary *are, where* the priests who minister and the gatekeepers and the singers *are;* and we will not neglect the house of our God.

11 Now the leaders of the people dwelt at Jerusalem; the rest of the people cast lots to bring one out of ten to dwell in Jerusalem, the holy city, and nine-tenths *were to dwell* in *other* cities. ² And the people blessed all the men who willingly offered themselves to dwell at Jerusalem.

³ These *are* the heads of the province who dwelt in Jerusalem. (But in the cities of Judah everyone dwelt in his own possession in their cities—Israelites, priests, Levites, Nethinim, and descendants of Solomon's servants.) ⁴ Also in Jerusalem dwelt *some* of the children of Judah and of the children of Benjamin.

The children of Judah: Athaiah the son of Uzziah, the son of Zechariah, the son of Amariah, the son of Shephatiah, the son of Mahalalel, of the children of Perez; ⁵ and Maaseiah the son of Baruch, the son of Col-Hozeh, the son of Hazaiah, the son of Adaiah, the son of Joiarib, the son of Zechariah, the son of Shiloni. ⁶ All the sons of Perez who dwelt at Jerusalem *were* four hundred and sixty-eight valiant men.

⁷ And these are the sons of Benjamin: Sallu the son of Meshullam, the son of Joed, the son of Pedaiah, the son of Kolaiah, the son of Maaseiah, the son of Ithiel, the son of Jeshaiah; ⁸ and after him Gabbai *and* Sallai, nine hundred and twenty-eight. ⁹ Joel the son of Zichri *was* their overseer, and Judah the son of Senuah *was* second over the city.

¹⁰ Of the priests: Jedaiah the son of Joiarib, and Jachin; ¹¹ Seraiah the son of Hilkiah, the son of Meshullam, the son of Zadok, the son of Meraioth, the son of Ahitub, *was* the leader of the house of God. ¹² Their brethren who did the work of the house *were* eight hundred

and twenty-two; and Adaiah the son of Jeroham, the son of Pelaliah, the son of Amzi, the son of Zechariah, the son of Pashhur, the son of Malchijah, ¹³ and his brethren, heads of the fathers' *houses, were* two hundred and forty-two; and Amashai the son of Azarel, the son of Ahzai, the son of Meshillemoth, the son of Immer, ¹⁴ and their brethren, mighty men of valor, *were* one hundred and twenty-eight. Their overseer *was* Zabdiel the son of *one of* the great men.

¹⁵ Also of the Levites: Shemaiah the son of Hasshub, the son of Azrikam, the son of Hashabiah, the son of Bunni; ¹⁶ Shabbethai and Jozabad, of the heads of the Levites, *had* the oversight of the business outside of the house of God; ¹⁷ Mattaniah the son of Micha, the son of Zabdi, the son of Asaph, the leader *who* began the thanksgiving with prayer; Bakbukiah, the second among his brethren; and Abda the son of Shammua, the son of Galal, the son of Jeduthun. ¹⁸ All the Levites in the holy city *were* two hundred and eighty-four.

¹⁹ Moreover the gatekeepers, Akkub, Talmon, and their brethren who kept the gates, *were* one hundred and seventy-two.

²⁰ And the rest of Israel, of the priests *and* Levites, *were* in all the cities of Judah, everyone in his inheritance. ²¹ But the Nethinim dwelt in Ophel. And Ziha and Gishpa *were* over the Nethinim.

²² Also the overseer of the Levites at Jerusalem *was* Uzzi the son of Bani, the son of Hashabiah, the son of Mattaniah, the son of Micha, of the sons of Asaph, the singers in charge of the service of the house of God. ²³ For *it was* the king's command concerning them that a certain portion should be for the singers, a quota day by day. ²⁴ Pethahiah the son of Meshezabel, of the children of Zerah the son of Judah, *was* the king's deputy in all matters concerning the people.

²⁵ And as for the villages with their fields, *some* of the children of Judah dwelt in Kirjath Arba and its villages, Dibon and its villages, Jekabzeel and its villages; ²⁶ in Jeshua, Moladah, Beth Pelet, ²⁷ Hazar Shual, and Beersheba and its villages; ²⁸ in Ziklag and Meconah and its villages; ²⁹ in En Rimmon, Zorah, Jarmuth, ³⁰ Zanoah, Adullam, and their villages; in Lachish and

Taking the First Step

In Montgomery, Alabama, in 1955 the city buses were segregated, by law. White people and black people were not allowed to sit together.

On December 1 of that year, Mrs. Rosa Parks was riding the bus home from her job at a tailor shop. As the section for whites filled up, the black people were ordered to move to the back to make room for the white passengers who were boarding. Three blacks in Mrs. Parks' row moved, but she remained in her seat. Later she said, "Our mistreatment was just not right, and I was tired of it. I knew someone had to take the first step. So I made up my mind not to move."

The bus driver asked her if she was going to stand up. "No, I am not," she answered him. Mrs. Parks was arrested and taken to jail. Four days later sympathizers, black and white, organized a boycott of the city bus line that lasted until a year later, when the Supreme Court declared the segregation ordinance unconstitutional.

Today, Mrs. Parks is known as the "mother of the modern-day civil rights movement." Her name inspires others to take courage and continue taking steps toward justice despite the often overwhelming opposition. She made a name for herself, not because of her great talent, or wisdom, or education. Rosa Parks is remembered for standing her ground for righteousness' sake — something you can do every day, everywhere you go.

> A good name is to be chosen rather than great riches, loving favor rather than silver and gold.
>
> *Proverbs 22:1*

its fields; in Azekah and its villages. They dwelt from Beersheba to the Valley of Hinnom.

³¹ Also the children of Benjamin from Geba *dwelt* in Michmash, Aija, and Bethel, and their villages; ³² in Anathoth, Nob, Ananiah; ³³ in Hazor, Ramah, Gittaim; ³⁴ in Hadid, Zeboim, Neballat; ³⁵ in Lod, Ono, *and* the Valley of Craftsmen. ³⁶ Some of the Judean divisions of Levites *were* in Benjamin.

~ PSALM 89:19–29 ~

¹⁹ Then You spoke in a vision to Your holy one,
     And said: "I have given help to *one who is* mighty;
     I have exalted one chosen from the people.
²⁰ I have found My servant David;
     With My holy oil I have anointed him,
²¹ With whom My hand shall be established;
     Also My arm shall strengthen him.
²² The enemy shall not outwit him,
     Nor the son of wickedness afflict him.
²³ I will beat down his foes before his face,
     And plague those who hate him.

²⁴ "But My faithfulness and My mercy *shall be* with him,
     And in My name his horn shall be exalted.
²⁵ Also I will set his hand over the sea,
     And his right hand over the rivers.
²⁶ He shall cry to Me, 'You *are* my Father,
     My God, and the rock of my salvation.'
²⁷ Also I will make him *My* firstborn,
     The highest of the kings of the earth.
²⁸ My mercy I will keep for him forever,
     And My covenant shall stand firm with him.
²⁹ His seed also I will make *to endure* forever,
     And his throne as the days of heaven.

~ PROVERBS 22:1, 2 ~

¹ A *good* name is to be chosen rather than great riches,
     Loving favor rather than silver and gold.

² The rich and the poor have this in common,
     The LORD *is* the maker of them all.

~ ACTS 28:1–31 ~

Now when they had escaped, they then found out that the island was called Malta. ² And the natives showed us unusual kindness; for they kindled a fire and made us all welcome, because of the rain that was falling and because of the cold. ³ But when Paul had gathered a bundle of sticks and laid *them* on the fire, a viper came out because of the heat, and fastened on his hand. ⁴ So when the natives saw the creature hanging from his hand, they said to one another, "No doubt this man is a murderer, whom, though he has escaped the sea, yet justice does not allow to live." ⁵ But he shook off the creature into the fire and suffered no harm. ⁶ However, they were expecting that he would swell up or suddenly fall down dead. But after they had looked for a long time and saw no harm come to him, they changed their minds and said that he was a god.

⁷ In that region there was an estate of the leading citizen of the island, whose name was Publius, who received us and entertained us courteously for three days. ⁸ And it happened that the father of Publius lay sick of a fever and dysentery. Paul went in to him and prayed, and he laid his hands on him and healed him. ⁹ So when this was done, the rest of those on the island who had diseases also came and were healed. ¹⁰ They also honored us in many ways; and when we departed, they provided such things as were necessary.

¹¹ After three months we sailed in an Alexandrian ship whose figurehead was the Twin Brothers, which had wintered at the island. ¹² And landing at Syracuse, we stayed three days. ¹³ From there we circled round and reached Rhegium. And after one day the south wind blew;

and the next day we came to Puteoli, [14] where we found brethren, and were invited to stay with them seven days. And so we went toward Rome. [15] And from there, when the brethren heard about us, they came to meet us as far as Appii Forum and Three Inns. When Paul saw them, he thanked God and took courage.

[16] Now when we came to Rome, the centurion delivered the prisoners to the captain of the guard; but Paul was permitted to dwell by himself with the soldier who guarded him.

[17] And it came to pass after three days that Paul called the leaders of the Jews together. So when they had come together, he said to them: "Men *and* brethren, though I have done nothing against our people or the customs of our fathers, yet I was delivered as a prisoner from Jerusalem into the hands of the Romans, [18] who, when they had examined me, wanted to let *me* go, because there was no cause for putting me to death. [19] But when the Jews spoke against *it,* I was compelled to appeal to Caesar, not that I had anything of which to accuse my nation. [20] For this reason therefore I have called for you, to see *you* and speak with *you,* because for the hope of Israel I am bound with this chain."

[21] Then they said to him, "We neither received letters from Judea concerning you, nor have any of the brethren who came reported or spoken any evil of you. [22] But we desire to hear from you what you think; for concerning this sect, we know that it is spoken against everywhere."

[23] So when they had appointed him a day, many came to him at *his* lodging, to whom he explained and solemnly testified of the kingdom of God, persuading them concerning Jesus from both the Law of Moses and the Prophets, from morning till evening. [24] And some were persuaded by the things which were spoken, and some disbelieved. [25] So when they did not agree among themselves, they departed after Paul had said one word: "The Holy Spirit spoke rightly through Isaiah the prophet to our fathers, [26] saying,

'Go to this people and say:
"Hearing you will hear, and shall
  not understand;
And seeing you will see, and not
  perceive;
[27] For the hearts of this people have
  grown dull.
Their ears are hard of hearing,
And their eyes they have closed,
Lest they should see with *their*
  eyes and hear with *their* ears,
Lest they should understand with
  their hearts and turn,
So that I should heal them." '

[28] "Therefore let it be known to you that the salvation of God has been sent to the Gentiles, and they will hear it!" [29] And when he had said these words, the Jews departed and had a great dispute among themselves.

[30] Then Paul dwelt two whole years in his own rented house, and received all who came to him, [31] preaching the kingdom of God and teaching the things which concern the Lord Jesus Christ with all confidence, no one forbidding him.

READING 211 · JULY 30

∽ NEHEMIAH 12:1—13:31 ∽

Now these *are* the priests and the Levites who came up with Zerubbabel the son of Shealtiel, and Jeshua: Seraiah, Jeremiah, Ezra, [2] Amariah, Malluch, Hattush, [3] Shechaniah, Rehum, Meremoth, [4] Iddo, Ginnethoi, Abijah, [5] Mijamin, Maadiah, Bilgah, [6] She-maiah, Joiarib, Jedaiah, [7] Sallu, Amok, Hilkiah, *and* Jedaiah.

These *were* the heads of the priests and their brethren in the days of Jeshua.

[8] Moreover the Levites *were* Jeshua, Binnui, Kadmiel, Sherebiah, Judah, *and* Mattaniah *who led* the thanksgiving

psalms, he and his brethren. [9] Also Bakbukiah and Unni, their brethren, *stood* across from them in *their* duties.

[10] Jeshua begot Joiakim, Joiakim begot Eliashib, Eliashib begot Joiada, [11] Joiada begot Jonathan, and Jonathan begot Jaddua.

[12] Now in the days of Joiakim, the priests, the heads of the fathers' *houses were:* of Seraiah, Meraiah; of Jeremiah, Hananiah; [13] of Ezra, Meshullam; of Amariah, Jehohanan; [14] of Melichu, Jonathan; of Shebaniah, Joseph; [15] of Harim, Adna; of Meraioth, Helkai; [16] of Iddo, Zechariah; of Ginnethon, Meshullam; [17] of Abijah, Zichri; *the son* of Minjamin; of Moadiah, Piltai; [18] of Bilgah, Shammua; of Shemaiah, Jehonathan; [19] of Joiarib, Mattenai; of Jedaiah, Uzzi; [20] of Sallai, Kallai; of Amok, Eber; [21] of Hilkiah, Hashabiah; *and* of Jedaiah, Nethanel.

[22] During the reign of Darius the Persian, a record *was also kept* of the Levites and priests *who had been* heads of their fathers' *houses* in the days of Eliashib, Joiada, Johanan, and Jaddua. [23] The sons of Levi, the heads of the fathers' *houses* until the days of Johanan the son of Eliashib, *were* written in the book of the chronicles.

[24] And the heads of the Levites *were* Hashabiah, Sherebiah, and Jeshua the son of Kadmiel, with their brothers across from them, to praise *and* give thanks, group alternating with group, according to the command of David the man of God. [25] Mattaniah, Bakbukiah, Obadiah, Meshullam, Talmon, and Akkub *were* gatekeepers keeping the watch at the storerooms of the gates. [26] These *lived* in the days of Joiakim the son of Jeshua, the son of Jozadak, and in the days of Nehemiah the governor, and of Ezra the priest, the scribe.

[27] Now at the dedication of the wall of Jerusalem they sought out the Levites in all their places, to bring them to Jerusalem to celebrate the dedication with gladness, both with thanksgivings and singing, *with* cymbals and stringed instruments and harps. [28] And the sons of the singers gathered together from the countryside around Jerusalem, from the villages of the Netophathites, [29] from the house of Gilgal, and from the fields of Geba and Azmaveth; for the singers had built themselves villages all around Jerusalem. [30] Then the priests and Levites purified themselves, and purified the people, the gates, and the wall.

[31] So I brought the leaders of Judah up on the wall, and appointed two large thanksgiving choirs. *One* went to the right hand on the wall toward the Refuse Gate. [32] After them went Hoshaiah and half of the leaders of Judah, [33] and Azariah, Ezra, Meshullam, [34] Judah, Benjamin, Shemaiah, Jeremiah, [35] and some of the priests' sons with trumpets—Zechariah the son of Jonathan, the son of Shemaiah, the son of Mattaniah, the son of Michaiah, the son of Zaccur, the son of Asaph, [36] and his brethren, Shemaiah, Azarel, Milalai, Gilalai, Maai, Nethanel, Judah, *and* Hanani, with the musical instruments of David the man of God. And Ezra the scribe *went* before them. [37] By the Fountain Gate, in front of them, they went up the stairs of the City of David, on the stairway of the wall, beyond the house of David, as far as the Water Gate eastward.

[38] The other thanksgiving choir went the opposite *way,* and I *was* behind them with half of the people on the wall, going past the Tower of the Ovens as far as the Broad Wall, [39] and above the Gate of Ephraim, above the Old Gate, above the Fish Gate, the Tower of Hananel, the Tower of the Hundred, as far as the Sheep Gate; and they stopped by the Gate of the Prison.

[40] So the two thanksgiving choirs stood in the house of God, likewise I and the half of the rulers with me; [41] and the priests, Eliakim, Maaseiah, Minjamin, Michaiah, Elioenai, Zechariah, *and* Hananiah, with trumpets; [42] also Maaseiah, Shemaiah, Eleazar, Uzzi, Jehohanan, Malchijah, Elam, and Ezer. The singers sang loudly with Jezrahiah the director.

[43] Also that day they offered great sacrifices, and rejoiced, for God had made them rejoice with great joy; the women and the children also rejoiced, so that the joy of Jerusalem was heard afar off.

[44] And at the same time some were appointed over the rooms of the storehouse for the offerings, the firstfruits, and the tithes, to gather into them from the fields

Carrying our Precious Possessions

> For God is my witness, whom I serve with my spirit in the gospel of His Son, that without ceasing I make mention of you always in my prayers.
>
> *Romans 1:9*

Before the surrender of Weinsberg, the women of that besieged city asked the enemy to allow them to leave the city carrying their most precious possessions with them. Permission was granted. To their astonishment, the women of Weinsberg, displaying both shrewdness and love, came plodding through the city gates with their husbands, sons, and brothers on their shoulders!

How wise we are to carry our dear ones out of sin, away from evil, and far from the carnal world on the shoulders of our prayers. During one of D. L. Moody's services in London, this was demonstrated in a profound way. A father and mother voiced great distress about their son, who had given up God's ways and run away to the bush of Australia. They asked the vast congregation to pray for their son. That night, some 20,000 believers voiced prayers on his behalf.

Later, the parents learned that at the very hour of that prayer, their son had been riding through the Australian bush into town, a day's ride from his camp. As he rode, the Spirit of the Lord convicted him of his sin. Dismounting, he knelt and asked God for forgiveness. When he reached town, he wired the news of his repentance to his mother and asked her if he might come home. Her reply was cabled immediately, "Come home at once!"

of the cities the portions specified by the Law for the priests and Levites; for Judah rejoiced over the priests and Levites who ministered. [45] Both the singers and the gatekeepers kept the charge of their God and the charge of the purification, according to the command of David *and* Solomon his son. [46] For in the days of David and Asaph of old *there were* chiefs of the singers, and songs of praise and thanksgiving to God. [47] In the days of Zerubbabel and in the days of Nehemiah all Israel gave the portions for the singers and the gatekeepers, a portion for each day. They also consecrated *holy things* for the Levites, and the Levites consecrated *them* for the children of Aaron.

13 On that day they read from the Book of Moses in the hearing of the people, and in it was found written that no Ammonite or Moabite should ever come into the assembly of God, [2] because they had not met the children of Israel with bread and water, but hired Balaam against them to curse them. However, our God turned the curse into a blessing. [3] So it was, when they had heard the Law, that they separated all the mixed multitude from Israel.

[4] Now before this, Eliashib the priest, having authority over the storerooms of the house of our God, *was* allied with Tobiah. [5] And he had prepared for him a large room, where previously they had stored the grain offerings, the frankincense, the articles, the tithes of grain, the new wine and oil, which were commanded *to be given* to the Levites and singers and gatekeepers, and the offerings for the priests. [6] But during all this I was not in Jerusalem, for in the thirty-second year of Artaxerxes king of Babylon I had returned to the king. Then after certain days I obtained leave from the king, [7] and I came to Jerusalem and discovered the evil that Eliashib had done for Tobiah, in preparing a room for him in the courts of the house of God. [8] And it grieved me bitterly; therefore I threw all the household goods of Tobiah out of the room. [9] Then I commanded them to cleanse the rooms; and I brought back into them the articles of the house of God, with the grain offering and the frankincense.

[10] I also realized that the portions for the Levites had not been given *them;* for each of the Levites and the singers who did the work had gone back to his field. [11] So I contended with the rulers, and said, "Why is the house of God forsaken?" And I gathered them together and set them in their place. [12] Then all Judah brought the tithe of the grain and the new wine and the oil to the storehouse. [13] And I appointed as treasurers over the storehouse Shelemiah the priest and Zadok the scribe, and of the Levites, Pedaiah; and next to them *was* Hanan the son of Zaccur, the son of Mattaniah; for they were considered faithful, and their task *was* to distribute to their brethren.

[14] Remember me, O my God, concerning this, and do not wipe out my good deeds that I have done for the house of my God, and for its services!

[15] In those days I saw *people* in Judah treading wine presses on the Sabbath, and bringing in sheaves, and loading donkeys with wine, grapes, figs, and all *kinds of* burdens, which they brought into Jerusalem on the Sabbath day. And I warned *them* about the day on which they were selling provisions. [16] Men of Tyre dwelt there also, who brought in fish and all kinds of goods, and sold *them* on the Sabbath to the children of Judah, and in Jerusalem.

[17] Then I contended with the nobles of Judah, and said to them, "What evil thing *is* this that you do, by which you profane the Sabbath day? [18] Did not your fathers do thus, and did not our God bring all this disaster on us and on this city? Yet you bring added wrath on Israel by profaning the Sabbath."

[19] So it was, at the gates of Jerusalem, as it began to be dark before the Sabbath, that I commanded the gates to be shut, and charged that they must not be opened till after the Sabbath. Then I posted *some* of my servants at the gates, *so that* no burdens would be brought in on the Sabbath day. [20] Now the merchants and sellers of all kinds of wares lodged outside Jerusalem once or twice.

[21] Then I warned them, and said to them, "Why do you spend the night around the wall? If you do *so* again, I will lay hands on you!" From that time on they

came no *more* on the Sabbath. ²² And I commanded the Levites that they should cleanse themselves, and that they should go and guard the gates, to sanctify the Sabbath day.

Remember me, O my God, *concerning* this also, and spare me according to the greatness of Your mercy!

²³ In those days I also saw Jews *who* had married women of Ashdod, Ammon, *and* Moab. ²⁴ And half of their children spoke the language of Ashdod, and could not speak the language of Judah, but spoke according to the language of one or the other people.

²⁵ So I contended with them and cursed them, struck some of them and pulled out their hair, and made them swear by God, *saying,* "You shall not give your daughters as wives to their sons, nor take their daughters for your sons or yourselves. ²⁶ Did not Solomon king of Israel sin by these things? Yet among many nations there was no king like him, who was beloved of his God; and God made him king over all Israel. Nevertheless pagan women caused even him to sin. ²⁷ Should we then hear of your doing all this great evil, transgressing against our God by marrying pagan women?"

²⁸ And *one* of the sons of Joiada, the son of Eliashib the high priest, *was* a son-in-law of Sanballat the Horonite; therefore I drove him from me.

²⁹ Remember them, O my God, because they have defiled the priesthood and the covenant of the priesthood and the Levites.

³⁰ Thus I cleansed them of everything pagan. I also assigned duties to the priests and the Levites, each to his service, ³¹ and *to bringing* the wood offering and the firstfruits at appointed times.

Remember me, O my God, for good!

~ PSALM 89:30–37 ~

³⁰ "If his sons forsake My law
And do not walk in My judgments,
³¹ If they break My statutes
And do not keep My
commandments,
³² Then I will punish their
transgression with the rod,
And their iniquity with stripes.

³³ Nevertheless My lovingkindness I
will not utterly take from him,
Nor allow My faithfulness to fail.
³⁴ My covenant I will not break,
Nor alter the word that has gone out
of My lips.
³⁵ Once I have sworn by My holiness;
I will not lie to David:
³⁶ His seed shall endure forever,
And his throne as the sun before Me;
³⁷ It shall be established forever like the
moon,
Even *like* the faithful witness in the
sky."   Selah

~ PROVERBS 22:3, 4 ~

³ A prudent *man* foresees evil and
hides himself,
But the simple pass on and are
punished.

⁴ By humility *and* the fear of the LORD
Are riches and honor and life.

~ ROMANS 1:1–32 ~

Paul, a bondservant of Jesus Christ, called *to be* an apostle, separated to the gospel of God ² which He promised before through His prophets in the Holy Scriptures, ³ concerning His Son Jesus Christ our Lord, who was born of the seed of David according to the flesh, ⁴ *and* declared *to be* the Son of God with power according to the Spirit of holiness, by the resurrection from the dead. ⁵ Through Him we have received grace and apostleship for obedience to the faith among all nations for His name, ⁶ among whom you also are the called of Jesus Christ;

⁷ To all who are in Rome, beloved of God, called *to be* saints:

Grace to you and peace from God our Father and the Lord Jesus Christ.

⁸ First, I thank my God through Jesus Christ for you all, that your faith is spoken of throughout the whole world. ⁹ For God is my witness, whom I serve with my spirit in the gospel of His Son, that without ceasing I make mention of you always in my prayers, ¹⁰ making request if, by

some means, now at last I may find a way in the will of God to come to you. ¹¹ For I long to see you, that I may impart to you some spiritual gift, so that you may be established— ¹² that is, that I may be encouraged together with you by the mutual faith both of you and me.

¹³ Now I do not want you to be unaware, brethren, that I often planned to come to you (but was hindered until now), that I might have some fruit among you also, just as among the other Gentiles. ¹⁴ I am a debtor both to Greeks and to barbarians, both to wise and to unwise. ¹⁵ So, as much as is in me, *I am* ready to preach the gospel to you who are in Rome also.

¹⁶ For I am not ashamed of the gospel of Christ, for it is the power of God to salvation for everyone who believes, for the Jew first and also for the Greek. ¹⁷ For in it the righteousness of God is revealed from faith to faith; as it is written, "The just shall live by faith."

¹⁸ For the wrath of God is revealed from heaven against all ungodliness and unrighteousness of men, who suppress the truth in unrighteousness, ¹⁹ because what may be known of God is manifest in them, for God has shown *it* to them. ²⁰ For since the creation of the world His invisible *attributes* are clearly seen, being understood by the things that are made, *even* His eternal power and Godhead, so that they are without excuse, ²¹ because, although they knew God, they did not glorify *Him* as God, nor were thankful, but became futile in their thoughts, and their foolish hearts were darkened. ²² Pro-fessing to be wise, they became fools, ²³ and changed the glory of the incorruptible God into an image made like corruptible man—and birds and four-footed animals and creeping things.

²⁴ Therefore God also gave them up to uncleanness, in the lusts of their hearts, to dishonor their bodies among themselves, ²⁵ who exchanged the truth of God for the lie, and worshiped and served the creature rather than the Creator, who is blessed forever. Amen.

²⁶ For this reason God gave them up to vile passions. For even their women exchanged the natural use for what is against nature. ²⁷ Likewise also the men, leaving the natural use of the woman, burned in their lust for one another, men with men committing what is shameful, and receiving in themselves the penalty of their error which was due.

²⁸ And even as they did not like to retain God in *their* knowledge, God gave them over to a debased mind, to do those things which are not fitting; ²⁹ being filled with all unrighteousness, sexual immorality, wickedness, covetousness, maliciousness; full of envy, murder, strife, deceit, evil-mindedness; *they are* whisperers, ³⁰ backbiters, haters of God, violent, proud, boasters, inventors of evil things, disobedient to parents, ³¹ undiscerning, untrustworthy, unloving, unforgiving, unmerciful; ³² who, knowing the righteous judgment of God, that those who practice such things are deserving of death, not only do the same but also approve of those who practice them.

READING 212 · JULY 31

~ ESTHER 1:1—2:23 ~

Now it came to pass in the days of Ahasuerus (this *was* the Ahasuerus who reigned over one hundred and twenty-seven provinces, from India to Ethiopia), ² in those days when King Ahasuerus sat on the throne of his kingdom, which *was* in Shushan the citadel, ³ *that* in the third year of his reign he made a feast for all his officials and servants—the powers of Persia and Media, the nobles, and the princes of the prov-inces *being* before him— ⁴ when he showed the riches of his glorious kingdom and the splendor of his excellent majesty for many days, one hundred and eighty days *in all.*

⁵ And when these days were completed, the king made a feast lasting seven days for all the people who were present in Shushan the citadel, from great to small, in the court of the garden of the king's palace. ⁶ *There were* white and blue linen

The Attitude Diet

Train up a child in the way he should go, and when he is old he will not depart from it.

Proverbs 22:6

Several years ago, a man was asked to give a commencement address. After he had given his speech, he sat on the platform watching the graduates receive their college degrees. Suddenly, the entire audience began applauding for a student who had earned a perfect 4.0 grade point average. During the applause, a faculty member seated next to the speaker leaned over and said to him, "She may be Miss Genius, but her attitude stinks." The speaker later said, "Without even thinking, my hands stopped clapping in mid-air. I couldn't help but think, *How sad.*"

No matter how beautiful, intelligent, talented, or athletic a child may be, there's no substitute for a positive, loving attitude toward others! The foremost architects of that attitude is not a child's teacher or pastor, but the parents.

Be cognizant of the attitudes you "feed" your children every day. They are the diet of your child's mind, just as food is the diet of your child's body. Don't feed your children junky ideas, sour opinions, rotten theology, poisoned feelings, or wilted enthusiasm. Instead, feed your children with the best and most positive ideas, emotional expressions, and thoughtful opinions you have!

curtains fastened with cords of fine linen and purple on silver rods and marble pillars; *and the* couches *were* of gold and silver on a *mosaic* pavement of alabaster, turquoise, and white and black marble. [7] And they served drinks in golden vessels, each vessel being different from the other, with royal wine in abundance, according to the generosity of the king. [8] In accordance with the law, the drinking was not compulsory; for so the king had ordered all the officers of his household, that they should do according to each man's pleasure.

[9] Queen Vashti also made a feast for the women *in* the royal palace which *belonged* to King Ahasuerus.

[10] On the seventh day, when the heart of the king was merry with wine, he commanded Mehuman, Biztha, Harbona, Bigtha, Abagtha, Zethar, and Carcas, seven eunuchs who served in the presence of King Ahasuerus, [11] to bring Queen Vashti before the king, *wearing* her royal crown, in order to show her beauty to the people and the officials, for she *was* beautiful to behold. [12] But Queen Vashti refused to come at the king's command *brought* by *his* eunuchs; therefore the king was furious, and his anger burned within him.

[13] Then the king said to the wise men who understood the times (for this *was* the king's manner toward all who knew law and justice, [14] those closest to him *being* Carshena, Shethar, Admatha, Tarshish, Meres, Marsena, and Memucan, the seven princes of Persia and Media, who had access to the king's presence, *and* who ranked highest in the kingdom): [15] "What *shall we* do to Queen Vashti, according to law, because she did not obey the command of King Ahasuerus *brought to her* by the eunuchs?"

[16] And Memucan answered before the king and the princes: "Queen Vashti has not only wronged the king, but also all the princes, and all the people who *are* in all the provinces of King Ahasuerus. [17] For the queen's behavior will become known to all women, so that they will despise their husbands in their eyes, when they report, 'King Ahasuerus commanded Queen Vashti to be brought in before him, but she did not come.' [18] This very day the *noble* ladies of Persia and Media will say to all the king's officials that they have heard of the behavior of the queen. Thus *there will be* excessive contempt and wrath. [19] If it pleases the king, let a royal decree go out from him, and let it be recorded in the laws of the Persians and the Medes, so that it will not be altered, that Vashti shall come no more before King Ahasuerus; and let the king give her royal position to another who is better than she. [20] When the king's decree which he will make is proclaimed throughout all his empire (for it is great), all wives will honor their husbands, both great and small."

[21] And the reply pleased the king and the princes, and the king did according to the word of Memucan. [22] Then he sent letters to all the king's provinces, to each province in its own script, and to every people in their own language, that each man should be master in his own house, and speak in the language of his own people.

2 After these things, when the wrath of King Ahasuerus subsided, he remembered Vashti, what she had done, and what had been decreed against her. [2] Then the king's servants who attended him said: "Let beautiful young virgins be sought for the king; [3] and let the king appoint officers in all the provinces of his kingdom, that they may gather all the beautiful young virgins to Shushan the citadel, into the women's quarters, under the custody of Hegai the king's eunuch, custodian of the women. And let beauty preparations be given *them.* [4] Then let the young woman who pleases the king be queen instead of Vashti."

This thing pleased the king, and he did so.

[5] In Shushan the citadel there was a certain Jew whose name *was* Mordecai the son of Jair, the son of Shimei, the son of Kish, a Benjamite. [6] *Kish* had been carried away from Jerusalem with the captives who had been captured with Jeconiah king of Judah, whom Nebuchadnezzar the king of Babylon had carried away. [7] And *Mordecai* had brought up Hadassah, that *is,* Esther, his uncle's daughter, for she had neither father nor mother. The young woman *was* lovely and beautiful.

When her father and mother died, Mordecai took her as his own daughter.

[8] So it was, when the king's command and decree were heard, and when many young women were gathered at Shushan the citadel, *under* the custody of Hegai, that Esther also was taken to the king's palace, into the care of Hegai the custodian of the women. [9] Now the young woman pleased him, and she obtained his favor; so he readily gave beauty preparations to her, besides her allowance. Then seven choice maidservants were provided for her from the king's palace, and he moved her and her maidservants to the best *place* in the house of the women.

[10] Esther had not revealed her people or family, for Mordecai had charged her not to reveal *it*. [11] And every day Mordecai paced in front of the court of the women's quarters, to learn of Esther's welfare and what was happening to her.

[12] Each young woman's turn came to go in to King Ahasuerus after she had completed twelve months' preparation, according to the regulations for the women, for thus were the days of their preparation apportioned: six months with oil of myrrh, and six months with perfumes and preparations for beautifying women. [13] Thus *prepared, each* young woman went to the king, and she was given whatever she desired to take with her from the women's quarters to the king's palace. [14] In the evening she went, and in the morning she returned to the second house of the women, to the custody of Shaashgaz, the king's eunuch who kept the concubines. She would not go in to the king again unless the king delighted in her and called for her by name.

[15] Now when the turn came for Esther the daughter of Abihail the uncle of Mordecai, who had taken her as his daughter, to go in to the king, she requested nothing but what Hegai the king's eunuch, the custodian of the women, advised. And Esther obtained favor in the sight of all who saw her. [16] So Esther was taken to King Ahasuerus, into his royal palace, in the tenth month, which *is* the month of Tebeth, in the seventh year of his reign. [17] The king loved Esther more than all the *other* women, and she obtained grace and favor in his sight more than all the virgins; so he set the royal crown upon her head and made her queen instead of Vashti. [18] Then the king made a great feast, the Feast of Esther, for all his officials and servants; and he proclaimed a holiday in the provinces and gave gifts according to the generosity of a king.

[19] When virgins were gathered together a second time, Mordecai sat within the king's gate. [20] *Now* Esther had not revealed her family and her people, just as Mordecai had charged her, for Esther obeyed the command of Mordecai as when she was brought up by him.

[21] In those days, while Mordecai sat within the king's gate, two of the king's eunuchs, Bigthan and Teresh, doorkeepers, became furious and sought to lay hands on King Ahasuerus. [22] So the matter became known to Mordecai, who told Queen Esther, and Esther informed the king in Mordecai's name. [23] And when an inquiry was made into the matter, it was confirmed, and both were hanged on a gallows; and it was written in the book of the chronicles in the presence of the king.

~ PSALM 89:38–45 ~

[38] But You have cast off and abhorred,
You have been furious with Your
anointed.
[39] You have renounced the covenant of
Your servant;
You have profaned his crown *by*
casting it to the ground.
[40] You have broken down all his
hedges;
You have brought his strongholds to
ruin.
[41] All who pass by the way plunder
him;
He is a reproach to his neighbors.
[42] You have exalted the right hand of
his adversaries;
You have made all his enemies
rejoice.
[43] You have also turned back the edge
of his sword,
And have not sustained him in the
battle.
[44] You have made his glory cease,
And cast his throne down to the
ground.

[45] The days of his youth You have
    shortened;
    You have covered him with shame.
                                    Selah

~ PROVERBS 22:5, 6 ~

[5] Thorns *and* snares *are* in the way of
    the perverse;
    He who guards his soul will be far
    from them.

[6] Train up a child in the way he should
    go,
    And when he is old he will not
    depart from it.

~ ROMANS 2:1–29 ~

Therefore you are inexcusable, O man,
whoever you are who judge, for in whatever you judge another you condemn
yourself; for you who judge practice the
same things. [2] But we know that the judgment of God is according to truth against
those who practice such things. [3] And do
you think this, O man, you who judge
those practicing such things, and doing
the same, that you will escape the judgment of God? [4] Or do you despise the
riches of His goodness, forbearance, and
longsuffering, not knowing that the goodness of God leads you to repentance? [5] But
in accordance with your hardness and
your impenitent heart you are treasuring
up for yourself wrath in the day of wrath
and revelation of the righteous judgment
of God, [6] who "will render to each one
according to his deeds": [7] eternal life to
those who by patient continuance in doing
good seek for glory, honor, and immortality; [8] but to those who are self-seeking
and do not obey the truth, but obey
unrighteousness—indignation and wrath,
[9] tribulation and anguish, on every soul
of man who does evil, of the Jew first
and also of the Greek; [10] but glory, hon-
or, and peace to everyone who works
what is good, to the Jew first and also to
the Greek. [11] For there is no partiality
with God.
    [12] For as many as have sinned without

law will also perish without law, and as
many as have sinned in the law will be
judged by the law [13](for not the hearers
of the law *are* just in the sight of God, but
the doers of the law will be justified; [14] for
when Gentiles, who do not have the law,
by nature do the things in the law, these,
although not having the law, are a law to
themselves, [15] who show the work of the
law written in their hearts, their conscience also bearing witness, and between
themselves *their* thoughts accusing or else
excusing *them*) [16] in the day when God
will judge the secrets of men by Jesus
Christ, according to my gospel.
    [17] Indeed you are called a Jew, and rest
on the law, and make your boast in God,
[18] and know *His* will, and approve the
things that are excellent, being instructed
out of the law, [19] and are confident that
you yourself are a guide to the blind, a
light to those who are in darkness, [20] an
instructor of the foolish, a teacher of
babes, having the form of knowledge and
truth in the law. [21] You, therefore, who
teach another, do you not teach yourself?
You who preach that a man should not
steal, do you steal? [22] You who say, "Do
not commit adultery," do you commit
adultery? You who abhor idols, do you
rob temples? [23] You who make your boast
in the law, do you dishonor God through
breaking the law? [24] For "the name of God
is blasphemed among the Gentiles because
of you," as it is written.
    [25] For circumcision is indeed profitable
if you keep the law; but if you are a breaker
of the law, your circumcision has become
uncircumcision. [26] Therefore, if an uncircumcised man keeps the righteous
requirements of the law, will not his
uncircumcision be counted as circumcision? [27] And will not the physically uncircumcised, if he fulfills the law, judge you
who, *even* with *your* written *code* and circumcision, *are* a transgressor of the law?
[28] For he is not a Jew who *is one* outwardly,
nor *is* circumcision that which *is* outward
in the flesh; [29] but *he is* a Jew who *is one*
inwardly; and circumcision *is that* of the
heart, in the Spirit, not in the letter; whose
praise *is* not from men but from God.

~ ESTHER 3:1—4:17 ~

After these things King Ahasuerus promoted Haman, the son of Hammedatha the Agagite, and advanced him and set his seat above all the princes who *were* with him. ² And all the king's servants who *were* within the king's gate bowed and paid homage to Haman, for so the king had commanded concerning him. But Mordecai would not bow or pay homage. ³ Then the king's servants who *were* within the king's gate said to Mordecai, "Why do you transgress the king's command?" ⁴ Now it happened, when they spoke to him daily and he would not listen to them, that they told *it* to Haman, to see whether Mordecai's words would stand; for *Mordecai* had told them that he *was* a Jew. ⁵ When Haman saw that Mordecai did not bow or pay him homage, Haman was filled with wrath. ⁶ But he disdained to lay hands on Mordecai alone, for they had told him of the people of Mordecai. Instead, Haman sought to destroy all the Jews who *were* throughout the whole kingdom of Ahasuerus—the people of Mordecai.

⁷ In the first month, which is the month of Nisan, in the twelfth year of King Ahasuerus, they cast Pur (that *is*, the lot), before Haman to determine the day and the month, until *it fell on the* twelfth *month,* which *is* the month of Adar.

⁸ Then Haman said to King Ahasuerus, "There is a certain people scattered and dispersed among the people in all the provinces of your kingdom; their laws *are* different from all *other* people's, and they do not keep the king's laws. Therefore it *is* not fitting for the king to let them remain. ⁹ If it pleases the king, let *a decree* be written that they be destroyed, and I will pay ten thousand talents of silver into the hands of those who do the work, to bring *it* into the king's treasuries."

¹⁰ So the king took his signet ring from his hand and gave it to Haman, the son of Hammedatha the Agagite, the enemy of the Jews. ¹¹ And the king said to Haman, "The money and the people *are* given to you, to do with them as seems good to you."

¹² Then the king's scribes were called on the thirteenth day of the first month, and *a decree* was written according to all that Haman commanded—to the king's satraps, to the governors who *were* over each province, to the officials of all people, to every province according to its script, and to every people in their language. In the name of King Ahasuerus it was written, and sealed with the king's signet ring. ¹³ And the letters were sent by couriers into all the king's provinces, to destroy, to kill, and to annihilate all the Jews, both young and old, little children and women, in one day, on the thirteenth *day* of the twelfth *month,* which *is* the month of Adar, and to plunder their possessions. ¹⁴ A copy of the document was to be issued as law in every province, being published for all people, that they should be ready for that day. ¹⁵ The couriers went out, hastened by the king's command; and the decree was proclaimed in Shushan the citadel. So the king and Haman sat down to drink, but the city of Shushan was perplexed.

4 When Mordecai learned all that had happened, he tore his clothes and put on sackcloth and ashes, and went out into the midst of the city. He cried out with a loud and bitter cry. ² He went as far as the front of the king's gate, for no one *might* enter the king's gate clothed with sackcloth. ³ And in every province where the king's command and decree arrived, *there was* great mourning among the Jews, with fasting, weeping, and wailing; and many lay in sackcloth and ashes.

⁴ So Esther's maids and eunuchs came and told her, and the queen was deeply distressed. Then she sent garments to clothe Mordecai and take his sackcloth away from him, but he would not accept *them.* ⁵ Then Esther called Hathach, *one* of the king's eunuchs whom he had appointed to attend her, and she gave him a command concerning Mordecai, to learn what and why this *was.* ⁶ So Hathach went out to Mordecai in the city square that *was* in front of the king's gate. ⁷ And Mordecai told him all that had happened to him, and the sum of money that Haman

had promised to pay into the king's treasuries to destroy the Jews. [8] He also gave him a copy of the written decree for their destruction, which was given at Shushan, that he might show it to Esther and explain it to her, and that he might command her to go in to the king to make supplication to him and plead before him for her people. [9] So Hathach returned and told Esther the words of Mordecai.

[10] Then Esther spoke to Hathach, and gave him a command for Mordecai: [11] "All the king's servants and the people of the king's provinces know that any man or woman who goes into the inner court to the king, who has not been called, *he has* but one law: put *all* to death, except the one to whom the king holds out the golden scepter, that he may live. Yet I myself have not been called to go in to the king these thirty days." [12] So they told Mordecai Esther's words.

[13] And Mordecai told *them* to answer Esther: "Do not think in your heart that you will escape in the king's palace any more than all the other Jews. [14] For if you remain completely silent at this time, relief and deliverance will arise for the Jews from another place, but you and your father's house will perish. Yet who knows whether you have come to the kingdom for *such* a time as this?"

[15] Then Esther told *them* to reply to Mordecai: [16] "Go, gather all the Jews who are present in Shushan, and fast for me; neither eat nor drink for three days, night or day. My maids and I will fast likewise. And so I will go to the king, which *is* against the law; and if I perish, I perish!"

[17] So Mordecai went his way and did according to all that Esther commanded him.

～ PSALM 89:46–52 ～

[46] How long, LORD?
Will You hide Yourself forever?
Will Your wrath burn like fire?

[47] Remember how short my time is;
For what futility have You created all
the children of men?

[48] What man can live and not see
death?
Can he deliver his life from the
power of the grave?   Selah

[49] Lord, where *are* Your former
lovingkindnesses,
Which You swore to David in Your
truth?

[50] Remember, Lord, the reproach of
Your servants—
How I bear in my bosom *the
reproach of* all the many peoples,

[51] With which Your enemies have
reproached, O LORD,
With which they have reproached
the footsteps of Your anointed.

[52] Blessed *be* the LORD forevermore!
Amen and Amen.

～ PROVERBS 22:7, 8 ～

[7] The rich rules over the poor,
And the borrower *is* servant to the
lender.

[8] He who sows iniquity will reap
sorrow,
And the rod of his anger will fail.

～ ROMANS 3:1–31 ～

What advantage then has the Jew, or what *is* the profit of circumcision? [2] Much in every way! Chiefly because to them were committed the oracles of God. [3] For what if some did not believe? Will their unbelief make the faithfulness of God without effect? [4] Certainly not! Indeed, let God be true but every man a liar. As it is written:

"That You may be justified in Your
words,
And may overcome when You are
judged."

[5] But if our unrighteousness demonstrates the righteousness of God, what shall we say? *Is* God unjust who inflicts wrath? (I speak as a man.) [6] Certainly not! For then how will God judge the world? [7] For if the truth of God has increased through my lie to His glory, why am I also still judged as a sinner? [8] And *why* not *say,* "Let us do evil that good may come"?— as we are slanderously reported and as some affirm that we say. Their condemnation is just.

Daily Deposit

A woman once had a dream that an angel was giving her this message: "As a reward for your virtues, the sum of $1,440 will be deposited into your bank account every morning. There is only one condition. At the close of each business day, any balance that has not been used will be canceled. It won't carry over to the next day or accrue interest. Each morning, a new $1,440 will be credited to you."

The dream was so vivid, she asked the Lord to show her what it meant. He led her to realize she was receiving 1,440 minutes every morning, the total number of minutes in a 24-hour day. What she did with this deposit of time was important, because 1,440 minutes per day was all she would ever receive!

Each of us has a similar account. At the close of each day, we should be able to look over our ledger and see that these golden minutes were spent wisely.

Time is God's gift to you. What you do with your time is your gift to God.

Remember how short my time is; for what futility have You created all the children of men?

Psalm 89:47

[9] What then? Are we better *than they?* Not at all. For we have previously charged both Jews and Greeks that they are all under sin.

[10] As it is written:

"There is none righteous, no, not one;
[11] There is none who understands;
    There is none who seeks after God.
[12] They have all turned aside;
    They have together become unprofitable;
    There is none who does good, no, not one."
[13] "Their throat *is* an open tomb;
    With their tongues they have practiced deceit";
    "The poison of asps *is* under their lips";
[14] "Whose mouth *is* full of cursing and bitterness."
[15] "Their feet *are* swift to shed blood;
[16] Destruction and misery *are* in their ways;
[17] And the way of peace they have not known."
[18] "There is no fear of God before their eyes."

[19] Now we know that whatever the law says, it says to those who are under the law, that every mouth may be stopped, and all the world may become guilty before God. [20] Therefore by the deeds of the law no flesh will be justified in His sight, for by the law *is* the knowledge of sin.

[21] But now the righteousness of God apart from the law is revealed, being witnessed by the Law and the Prophets, [22] even the righteousness of God, through faith in Jesus Christ, to all and on all who believe. For there is no difference; [23] for all have sinned and fall short of the glory of God, [24] being justified freely by His grace through the redemption that is in Christ Jesus, [25] whom God set forth *as* a propitiation by His blood, through faith, to demonstrate His righteousness, because in His forbearance God had passed over the sins that were previously committed, [26] to demonstrate at the present time His righteousness, that He might be just and the justifier of the one who has faith in Jesus.

[27] Where *is* boasting then? It is excluded. By what law? Of works? No, but by the law of faith. [28] Therefore we conclude that a man is justified by faith apart from the deeds of the law. [29] Or *is He* the God of the Jews only? *Is He* not also the God of the Gentiles? Yes, of the Gentiles also, [30] since *there is* one God who will justify the circumcised by faith and the uncircumcised through faith. [31] Do we then make void the law through faith? Certainly not! On the contrary, we establish the law.

READING 214 · AUGUST 2

~ ESTHER 5:1—6:14 ~

Now it happened on the third day that Esther put on *her* royal *robes* and stood in the inner court of the king's palace, across from the king's house, while the king sat on his royal throne in the royal house, facing the entrance of the house. [2] So it was, when the king saw Queen Esther standing in the court, *that* she found favor in his sight, and the king held out to Esther the golden scepter that *was* in his hand. Then Esther went near and touched the top of the scepter.

[3] And the king said to her, "What do you wish, Queen Esther? What *is* your request? It shall be given to you—up to half the kingdom!"

[4] So Esther answered, "If it pleases the king, let the king and Haman come today to the banquet that I have prepared for him."

[5] Then the king said, "Bring Haman

The Lady with the Lamp

> He who has a generous eye will be blessed, for he gives of his bread to the poor.
>
> *Proverbs 22:9*

One night in 1837, she believed she heard the voice of God telling her that she had a mission. Nine years later, that mission began to take shape when a friend sent her information about the Institution of Protestant Deaconesses in Germany. She later entered the institution to learn how to care for the sick. In 1853, she became superintendent of a "women's hospital" in London. But then in 1854, the Crimean War broke out and she volunteered at once to care for British soldiers, leaving for Constantinople almost immediately.

Once in Turkey, she was put in charge of nursing at the military hospital. Even though doctors were hostile toward her and the hospital itself was deplorably filthy, she dug in her heels and began caring for her patients. She first used the provisions she had brought with her, then undertook a correspondence campaign to restock the hospital. She spent many hours each day in the wards, touching virtually every man who ever entered the hospital. The comfort she gave on night rounds earned her the nickname, "The Lady with the Lamp."

Her selfless giving eventually made her name, Florence Nightingale, synonymous with compassionate nursing care.

quickly, that he may do as Esther has said."
So the king and Haman went to the banquet that Esther had prepared.

⁶ At the banquet of wine the king said to Esther, "What *is* your petition? It shall be granted you. What *is* your request, up to half the kingdom? It shall be done!"

⁷ Then Esther answered and said, "My petition and request *is this:* ⁸ If I have found favor in the sight of the king, and if it pleases the king to grant my petition and fulfill my request, then let the king and Haman come to the banquet which I will prepare for them, and tomorrow I will do as the king has said."

⁹ So Haman went out that day joyful and with a glad heart; but when Haman saw Mordecai in the king's gate, and that he did not stand or tremble before him, he was filled with indignation against Mordecai. ¹⁰ Nevertheless Haman restrained himself and went home, and he sent and called for his friends and his wife Zeresh. ¹¹ Then Haman told them of his great riches, the multitude of his children, everything in which the king had promoted him, and how he had advanced him above the officials and servants of the king. ¹² Moreover Haman said, "Besides, Queen Esther invited no one but me to come in with the king to the banquet that she prepared; and tomorrow I am again invited by her, along with the king. ¹³ Yet all this avails me nothing, so long as I see Mordecai the Jew sitting at the king's gate."

¹⁴ Then his wife Zeresh and all his friends said to him, "Let a gallows be made, fifty cubits high, and in the morning suggest to the king that Mordecai be hanged on it; then go merrily with the king to the banquet."

And the thing pleased Haman; so he had the gallows made.

6

That night the king could not sleep. So one was commanded to bring the book of the records of the chronicles; and they were read before the king. ² And it was found written that Mordecai had told of Bigthana and Teresh, two of the king's eunuchs, the doorkeepers who had sought to lay hands on King Ahasuerus. ³ Then the king said, "What honor or dignity has been bestowed on Mordecai for this?"

And the king's servants who attended him said, "Nothing has been done for him."

⁴ So the king said, "Who *is* in the court?" Now Haman had *just* entered the outer court of the king's palace to suggest that the king hang Mordecai on the gallows that he had prepared for him.

⁵ The king's servants said to him, "Haman is there, standing in the court."

And the king said, "Let him come in."

⁶ So Haman came in, and the king asked him, "What shall be done for the man whom the king delights to honor?"

Now Haman thought in his heart, "Whom would the king delight to honor more than me?" ⁷ And Haman answered the king, "*For* the man whom the king delights to honor, ⁸ let a royal robe be brought which the king has worn, and a horse on which the king has ridden, which has a royal crest placed on its head. ⁹ Then let this robe and horse be delivered to the hand of one of the king's most noble princes, that he may array the man whom the king delights to honor. Then parade him on horseback through the city square, and proclaim before him: 'Thus shall it be done to the man whom the king delights to honor!' "

¹⁰ Then the king said to Haman, "Hurry, take the robe and the horse, as you have suggested, and do so for Mordecai the Jew who sits within the king's gate! Leave nothing undone of all that you have spoken."

¹¹ So Haman took the robe and the horse, arrayed Mordecai and led him on horseback through the city square, and proclaimed before him, "Thus shall it be done to the man whom the king delights to honor!"

¹² Afterward Mordecai went back to the king's gate. But Haman hurried to his house, mourning and with his head covered. ¹³ When Haman told his wife Zeresh and all his friends everything that had happened to him, his wise men and his wife Zeresh said to him, "If Mordecai, before whom you have begun to fall, is of Jewish descent, you will not prevail against him but will surely fall before him."

¹⁴ While they *were* still talking with him, the king's eunuchs came, and hastened to

bring Haman to the banquet which Esther had prepared.

~ PSALM 90:1–6 ~

1 LORD, You have been our dwelling place in all generations.
2 Before the mountains were brought forth,
Or ever You had formed the earth and the world,
Even from everlasting to everlasting, You *are* God.

3 You turn man to destruction,
And say, "Return, O children of men."
4 For a thousand years in Your sight
Are like yesterday when it is past,
And *like* a watch in the night.
5 You carry them away *like* a flood;
They are like a sleep.
In the morning they are like grass *which* grows up:
6 In the morning it flourishes and grows up;
In the evening it is cut down and withers.

~ PROVERBS 22:9 ~

9 He who has a generous eye will be blessed,
For he gives of his bread to the poor.

~ ROMANS 4:1–25 ~

What then shall we say that Abraham our father has found according to the flesh? 2 For if Abraham was justified by works, he has *something* to boast about, but not before God. 3 For what does the Scripture say? "Abraham believed God, and it was accounted to him for righteousness." 4 Now to him who works, the wages are not counted as grace but as debt. 5 But to him who does not work but believes on Him who justifies the ungodly, his faith is accounted for righteousness, 6 just as David also describes the blessedness of the man to whom God imputes righteousness apart from works:

7 "Blessed *are those* whose lawless deeds are forgiven,
And whose sins are covered;
8 Blessed *is the* man to whom the LORD shall not impute sin."

9 *Does* this blessedness then *come* upon the circumcised *only,* or upon the uncircumcised also? For we say that faith was accounted to Abraham for righteousness. 10 How then was it accounted? While he was circumcised, or uncircumcised? Not while circumcised, but while uncircumcised. 11 And he received the sign of circumcision, a seal of the righteousness of the faith which *he had while still* uncircumcised, that he might be the father of all those who believe, though they are uncircumcised, that righteousness might be imputed to them also, 12 and the father of circumcision to those who not only *are* of the circumcision, but who also walk in the steps of the faith which our father Abraham *had while still* uncircumcised.

13 For the promise that he would be the heir of the world *was* not to Abraham or to his seed through the law, but through the righteousness of faith. 14 For if those who are of the law *are* heirs, faith is made void and the promise made of no effect, 15 because the law brings about wrath; for where there is no law *there is* no transgression.

16 Therefore *it is* of faith that *it might be* according to grace, so that the promise might be sure to all the seed, not only to those who are of the law, but also to those who are of the faith of Abraham, who is the father of us all 17 (as it is written, "I have made you a father of many nations") in the presence of Him whom he believed—God, who gives life to the dead and calls those things which do not exist as though they did; 18 who, contrary to hope, in hope believed, so that he became the father of many nations, according to what was spoken, "So shall your descendants be." 19 And not being weak in faith, he did not consider his own body, already dead (since he was about a hundred years old), and the deadness of Sarah's womb. 20 He did not waver at the promise of God through unbelief, but was strengthened in faith, giving glory to God, 21 and being fully convinced that what He

had promised He was also able to perform. [22] And therefore "it was accounted to him for righteousness."

[23] Now it was not written for his sake alone that it was imputed to him, [24] but also for us. It shall be imputed to us who believe in Him who raised up Jesus our Lord from the dead, [25] who was delivered up because of our offenses, and was raised because of our justification.

～ ESTHER 7:1—8:17 ～

So the king and Haman went to dine with Queen Esther. [2] And on the second day, at the banquet of wine, the king again said to Esther, "What *is* your petition, Queen Esther? It shall be granted you. And what *is* your request, up to half the kingdom? It shall be done!"

[3] Then Queen Esther answered and said, "If I have found favor in your sight, O king, and if it pleases the king, let my life be given me at my petition, and my people at my request. [4] For we have been sold, my people and I, to be destroyed, to be killed, and to be annihilated. Had we been sold as male and female slaves, I would have held my tongue, although the enemy could never compensate for the king's loss."

[5] So King Ahasuerus answered and said to Queen Esther, "Who is he, and where is he, who would dare presume in his heart to do such a thing?"

[6] And Esther said, "The adversary and enemy *is* this wicked Haman!"

So Haman was terrified before the king and queen.

[7] Then the king arose in his wrath from the banquet of wine *and went* into the palace garden; but Haman stood before Queen Esther, pleading for his life, for he saw that evil was determined against him by the king. [8] When the king returned from the palace garden to the place of the banquet of wine, Haman had fallen across the couch where Esther *was*. Then the king said, "Will he also assault the queen while I *am* in the house?"

As the word left the king's mouth, they covered Haman's face. [9] Now Harbonah, one of the eunuchs, said to the king, "Look! The gallows, fifty cubits high, which Haman made for Mordecai, who spoke good on the king's behalf, is standing at the house of Haman."

Then the king said, "Hang him on it!" [10] So they hanged Haman on the gallows that he had prepared for Mordecai. Then the king's wrath subsided.

8 On that day King Ahasuerus gave Queen Esther the house of Haman, the enemy of the Jews. And Mordecai came before the king, for Esther had told how he *was related* to her. [2] So the king took off his signet ring, which he had taken from Haman, and gave it to Mordecai; and Esther appointed Mordecai over the house of Haman.

[3] Now Esther spoke again to the king, fell down at his feet, and implored him with tears to counteract the evil of Haman the Agagite, and the scheme which he had devised against the Jews. [4] And the king held out the golden scepter toward Esther. So Esther arose and stood before the king, [5] and said, "If it pleases the king, and if I have found favor in his sight and the thing *seems* right to the king and I am pleasing in his eyes, let it be written to revoke the letters devised by Haman, the son of Hammedatha the Agagite, which he wrote to annihilate the Jews who *are* in all the king's provinces. [6] For how can I endure to see the evil that will come to my people? Or how can I endure to see the destruction of my countrymen?"

[7] Then King Ahasuerus said to Queen Esther and Mordecai the Jew, "Indeed, I have given Esther the house of Haman, and they have hanged him on the gallows because he *tried to* lay his hand on the Jews. [8] You yourselves write *a decree* concerning the Jews, as you please, in the king's name, and seal *it* with the king's signet ring; for whatever is written in the king's name and sealed with the king's signet ring no one can revoke."

[9] So the king's scribes were called at that

Even Cockroaches?

A pastor's wife was accustomed to uninvited guests and was usually delighted to have them — but *not* when the guests were cockroaches. She was appalled when they made their appearance in her new parsonage. The very word, "cockroaches," sounded dirty to her. She immediately sought a way to get rid of them. Spraying pesticides in the house was impossible due to the physical condition of one of her children. The only solution seemed to be the use of roach traps — a safe, but slow process. It took almost a year before the house was free of the dirty insects.

During that year, the pastor's wife encountered Romans 8:28 — "We know that all things work together for good to those who love God." She laughed and said, "Well, Lord, if you say so!" She couldn't imagine what good might come of battling cockroaches month after month, but she trusted God.

Several weeks after the disappearance of the last cockroach, she received a letter from her daughter, who had gone to Paraguay as a missionary. She wrote: "Mom, do you remember all those awful cockroaches we had? Well, we have huge, flying ones here! I'm glad I was able to get used to them at home before coming to Paraguay!"

God is in the process of perfecting you. His greatest aim is to build His character in you. He doesn't send the "cockroaches" into our lives, but He will use them for our benefit. He always has your ultimate good in mind!

> And not only that, but we also glory in tribulations, knowing that tribulation produces perseverance; and perseverance, character; and character, hope.
>
> *Romans 5:3-4*

time, in the third month, which *is* the month of Sivan, on the twenty-third *day;* and it was written, according to all that Mordecai commanded, to the Jews, the satraps, the governors, and the princes of the provinces from India to Ethiopia, one hundred and twenty-seven provinces *in all,* to every province in its own script, to every people in their own language, and to the Jews in their own script and language. ¹⁰ And he wrote in the name of King Ahasuerus, sealed *it* with the king's signet ring, and sent letters by couriers on horseback, riding on royal horses bred from swift steeds.

¹¹ By these letters the king permitted the Jews who *were* in every city to gather together and protect their lives—to destroy, kill, and annihilate all the forces of any people or province that would assault them, *both* little children and women, and to plunder their possessions, ¹² on one day in all the provinces of King Ahasuerus, on the thirteenth *day* of the twelfth month, which *is* the month of Adar. ¹³ A copy of the document was to be issued as a decree in every province and published for all people, so that the Jews would be ready on that day to avenge themselves on their enemies. ¹⁴ The couriers who rode on royal horses went out, hastened and pressed on by the king's command. And the decree was issued in Shushan the citadel.

¹⁵ So Mordecai went out from the presence of the king in royal apparel of blue and white, with a great crown of gold and a garment of fine linen and purple; and the city of Shushan rejoiced and was glad. ¹⁶ The Jews had light and gladness, joy and honor. ¹⁷ And in every province and city, wherever the king's command and decree came, the Jews had joy and gladness, a feast and a holiday. Then many of the people of the land became Jews, because fear of the Jews fell upon them.

~ PSALM 90:7–17 ~

⁷ For we have been consumed by Your anger,
  And by Your wrath we are terrified.
⁸ You have set our iniquities before You,

Our secret *sins* in the light of Your countenance.
⁹ For all our days have passed away in Your wrath;
  We finish our years like a sigh.
¹⁰ The days of our lives *are* seventy years;
  And if by reason of strength *they are* eighty years,
  Yet their boast *is* only labor and sorrow;
  For it is soon cut off, and we fly away.
¹¹ Who knows the power of Your anger?
  For as the fear of You, *so is* Your wrath.
¹² So teach *us* to number our days,
  That we may gain a heart of wisdom.

¹³ Return, O LORD!
  How long?
  And have compassion on Your servants.
¹⁴ Oh, satisfy us early with Your mercy,
  That we may rejoice and be glad all our days!
¹⁵ Make us glad according to the days *in which* You have afflicted us,
  The years *in which* we have seen evil.
¹⁶ Let Your work appear to Your servants,
  And Your glory to their children.
¹⁷ And let the beauty of the LORD our God be upon us,
  And establish the work of our hands for us;
  Yes, establish the work of our hands.

~ PROVERBS 22:10, 11 ~

¹⁰ Cast out the scoffer, and contention will leave;
  Yes, strife and reproach will cease.

¹¹ He who loves purity of heart
  And has grace on his lips,
  The king *will be* his friend.

~ ROMANS 5:1–21 ~

Therefore, having been justified by faith, we have peace with God through our Lord

Jesus Christ, [2] through whom also we have access by faith into this grace in which we stand, and rejoice in hope of the glory of God. [3] And not only *that,* but we also glory in tribulations, knowing that tribulation produces perseverance; [4] and perseverance, character; and character, hope. [5] Now hope does not disappoint, because the love of God has been poured out in our hearts by the Holy Spirit who was given to us.

[6] For when we were still without strength, in due time Christ died for the ungodly. [7] For scarcely for a righteous man will one die; yet perhaps for a good man someone would even dare to die. [8] But God demonstrates His own love toward us, in that while we were still sinners, Christ died for us. [9] Much more then, having now been justified by His blood, we shall be saved from wrath through Him. [10] For if when we were enemies we were reconciled to God through the death of His Son, much more, having been reconciled, we shall be saved by His life. [11] And not only *that,* but we also rejoice in God through our Lord Jesus Christ, through whom we have now received the reconciliation.

[12] Therefore, just as through one man sin entered the world, and death through sin, and thus death spread to all men, because all sinned— [13](For until the law sin was in the world, but sin is not imputed when there is no law. [14] Never-

theless death reigned from Adam to Moses, even over those who had not sinned according to the likeness of the transgression of Adam, who is a type of Him who was to come. [15] But the free gift *is* not like the offense. For if by the one man's offense many died, much more the grace of God and the gift by the grace of the one Man, Jesus Christ, abounded to many. [16] And the gift *is* not like *that which came* through the one who sinned. For the judgment *which came* from one *offense resulted* in condemnation, but the free gift *which came* from many offenses *resulted* in justification. [17] For if by the one man's offense death reigned through the one, much more those who receive abundance of grace and of the gift of righteousness will reign in life through the One, Jesus Christ.)

[18] Therefore, as through one man's offense *judgment* came to all men, resulting in condemnation, even so through one Man's righteous act *the free gift came* to all men, resulting in justification of life. [19] For as by one man's disobedience many were made sinners, so also by one Man's obedience many will be made righteous.

[20] Moreover the law entered that the offense might abound. But where sin abounded, grace abounded much more, [21] so that as sin reigned in death, even so grace might reign through righteousness to eternal life through Jesus Christ our Lord.

READING 216 · AUGUST 4

~ ESTHER 9:1—10:3 ~

Now in the twelfth month, that *is,* the month of Adar, on the thirteenth day, *the time* came for the king's command and his decree to be executed. On the day that the enemies of the Jews had hoped to overpower them, the opposite occurred, in that the Jews themselves overpowered those who hated them. [2] The Jews gathered together in their cities throughout all the provinces of King Ahasuerus to lay hands on those who sought their harm. And no one could withstand them, because fear of them fell

upon all people. [3] And all the officials of the provinces, the satraps, the governors, and all those doing the king's work, helped the Jews, because the fear of Mordecai fell upon them. [4] For Mordecai *was* great in the king's palace, and his fame spread throughout all the provinces; for this man Mordecai became increasingly prominent. [5] Thus the Jews defeated all their enemies with the stroke of the sword, with slaughter and destruction, and did what they pleased with those who hated them.

[6] And in Shushan the citadel the Jews

killed and destroyed five hundred men. [7] Also Parshandatha, Dalphon, Aspatha, [8] Poratha, Adalia, Aridatha, [9] Parmashta, Arisai, Aridai, and Vajezatha— [10] the ten sons of Haman the son of Hammedatha, the enemy of the Jews—they killed; but they did not lay a hand on the plunder.

[11] On that day the number of those who were killed in Shushan the citadel was brought to the king. [12] And the king said to Queen Esther, "The Jews have killed and destroyed five hundred men in Shushan the citadel, and the ten sons of Haman. What have they done in the rest of the king's provinces? Now what *is* your petition? It shall be granted to you. Or what *is* your further request? It shall be done."

[13] Then Esther said, "If it pleases the king, let it be granted to the Jews who *are* in Shushan to do again tomorrow according to today's decree, and let Haman's ten sons be hanged on the gallows."

[14] So the king commanded this to be done; the decree was issued in Shushan, and they hanged Haman's ten sons.

[15] And the Jews who *were* in Shushan gathered together again on the fourteenth day of the month of Adar and killed three hundred men at Shushan; but they did not lay a hand on the plunder.

[16] The remainder of the Jews in the king's provinces gathered together and protected their lives, had rest from their enemies, and killed seventy-five thousand of their enemies; but they did not lay a hand on the plunder. [17] *This was* on the thirteenth day of the month of Adar. And on the fourteenth of *the month* they rested and made it a day of feasting and gladness.

[18] But the Jews who *were* at Shushan assembled together on the thirteenth *day,* as well as on the fourteenth; and on the fifteenth of *the month* they rested, and made it a day of feasting and gladness. [19] Therefore the Jews of the villages who dwelt in the unwalled towns celebrated the fourteenth day of the month of Adar *with* gladness and feasting, as a holiday, and for sending presents to one another.

[20] And Mordecai wrote these things and sent letters to all the Jews, near and far, who *were* in all the provinces of King Ahasuerus, [21] to establish among them that they should celebrate yearly the fourteenth and fifteenth days of the month of Adar, [22] as the days on which the Jews had rest from their enemies, as the month which was turned from sorrow to joy for them, and from mourning to a holiday; that they should make them days of feasting and joy, of sending presents to one another and gifts to the poor. [23] So the Jews accepted the custom which they had begun, as Mordecai had written to them, [24] because Haman, the son of Hammedatha the Agagite, the enemy of all the Jews, had plotted against the Jews to annihilate them, and had cast Pur (that *is,* the lot), to consume them and destroy them; [25] but when *Esther* came before the king, he commanded by letter that this wicked plot which *Haman* had devised against the Jews should return on his own head, and that he and his sons should be hanged on the gallows.

[26] So they called these days Purim, after the name Pur. Therefore, because of all the words of this letter, what they had seen concerning this matter, and what had happened to them, [27] the Jews established and imposed it upon themselves and their descendants and all who would join them, that without fail they should celebrate these two days every year, according to the written *instructions* and according to the *prescribed* time, [28] *that* these days *should be* remembered and kept throughout every generation, every family, every province, and every city, that these days of Purim should not fail *to be observed* among the Jews, and *that* the memory of them should not perish among their descendants.

[29] Then Queen Esther, the daughter of Abihail, with Mordecai the Jew, wrote with full authority to confirm this second letter about Purim. [30] And *Mordecai* sent letters to all the Jews, to the one hundred and twenty-seven provinces of the kingdom of Ahasuerus, *with* words of peace and truth, [31] to confirm these days of Purim at their *appointed* time, as Mordecai the Jew and Queen Esther had prescribed for them, and as they had decreed for themselves and their descendants concerning matters of their fasting and lamenting. [32] So the decree of Esther confirmed

Inside Information

He who dwells in the secret place of the Most High shall abide under the shadow of the Almighty.

Psalm 91:1

Down through the years, a number of famous quotes about character have focused on one attribute: The hidden nature of character.

Character is what you are in the dark.

The measure of someone's real character is what he would do if he knew he never would be found out.

The difference between personality and character: Personality is what you are when lots of people are around; character is what you are when everybody goes home.

Ultimately, you are the only person who truly knows the nature of your character. It's like the little boy who once came crying to his mother with the pronouncement, "Mommy, eating too many green apples can make a person sick." His mother tried to comfort him and asked, "Where did you learn this?" The little boy replied, "I have inside information."

Only you know what you would do in any given situation. As you formulate the could's, should's, and would's of your life in accordance with God's Word, your character grows. Look within, and see what kind of person you find!

these matters of Purim, and it was written in the book.

10 And King Ahasuerus imposed tribute on the land and *on* the islands of the sea. [2] Now all the acts of his power and his might, and the account of the greatness of Mordecai, to which the king advanced him, *are* they not written in the book of the chronicles of the kings of Media and Persia? [3] For Mordecai the Jew *was* second to King Ahasuerus, and was great among the Jews and well received by the multitude of his brethren, seeking the good of his people and speaking peace to all his countrymen.

~ PSALM 91:1–6 ~

[1] He who dwells in the secret place of the Most High
Shall abide under the shadow of the Almighty.
[2] I will say of the LORD, "*He is* my refuge and my fortress;
My God, in Him I will trust."

[3] Surely He shall deliver you from the snare of the fowler
And from the perilous pestilence.
[4] He shall cover you with His feathers,
And under His wings you shall take refuge;
His truth *shall be your* shield and buckler.
[5] You shall not be afraid of the terror by night,
Nor of the arrow *that* flies by day,
[6] *Nor* of the pestilence *that* walks in darkness,
Nor of the destruction *that* lays waste at noonday.

~ PROVERBS 22:12 ~

[12] The eyes of the LORD preserve knowledge,
But He overthrows the words of the faithless.

~ ROMANS 6:1–23 ~

What shall we say then? Shall we continue in sin that grace may abound? [2] Certainly not! How shall we who died to sin live any longer in it? [3] Or do you not know that as many of us as were baptized into Christ Jesus were baptized into His death? [4] Therefore we were buried with Him through baptism into death, that just as Christ was raised from the dead by the glory of the Father, even so we also should walk in newness of life.

[5] For if we have been united together in the likeness of His death, certainly we also shall be *in the likeness* of His resurrection, [6] knowing this, that our old man was crucified with *Him*, that the body of sin might be done away with, that we should no longer be slaves of sin. [7] For he who has died has been freed from sin. [8] Now if we died with Christ, we believe that we shall also live with Him, [9] knowing that Christ, having been raised from the dead, dies no more. Death no longer has dominion over Him. [10] For *the death* that He died, He died to sin once for all; but *the life* that He lives, He lives to God. [11] Likewise you also, reckon yourselves to be dead indeed to sin, but alive to God in Christ Jesus our Lord.

[12] Therefore do not let sin reign in your mortal body, that you should obey it in its lusts. [13] And do not present your members *as* instruments of unrighteousness to sin, but present yourselves to God as being alive from the dead, and your members *as* instruments of righteousness to God. [14] For sin shall not have dominion over you, for you are not under law but under grace.

[15] What then? Shall we sin because we are not under law but under grace? Certainly not! [16] Do you not know that to whom you present yourselves slaves to obey, you are that one's slaves whom you obey, whether of sin *leading* to death, or of obedience *leading* to righteousness? [17] But God be thanked that *though* you were slaves of sin, yet you obeyed from the heart that form of doctrine to which you were delivered. [18] And having been set free from sin, you became slaves of righteousness. [19] I speak in human *terms* because of the weakness of your flesh. For just as you presented your members *as* slaves of uncleanness, and of lawlessness *leading* to *more* lawlessness, so now present your members *as* slaves *of* righteousness for holiness.

[20] For when you were slaves of sin, you

were free in regard to righteousness. ²¹ What fruit did you have then in the things of which you are now ashamed? For the end of those things *is* death. ²² But now having been set free from sin, and having become slaves of God, you have your fruit to holiness, and the end, everlasting life. ²³ For the wages of sin *is* death, but the gift of God *is* eternal life in Christ Jesus our Lord.

READING 217 · AUGUST 5

~ JOB 1:1—2:13 ~

There was a man in the land of Uz, whose name *was* Job; and that man was blameless and upright, and one who feared God and shunned evil. ² And seven sons and three daughters were born to him. ³ Also, his possessions were seven thousand sheep, three thousand camels, five hundred yoke of oxen, five hundred female donkeys, and a very large household, so that this man was the greatest of all the people of the East.

⁴ And his sons would go and feast *in their* houses, each on his *appointed* day, and would send and invite their three sisters to eat and drink with them. ⁵ So it was, when the days of feasting had run their course, that Job would send and sanctify them, and he would rise early in the morning and offer burnt offerings *according to* the number of them all. For Job said, "It may be that my sons have sinned and cursed God in their hearts." Thus Job did regularly.

⁶ Now there was a day when the sons of God came to present themselves before the LORD, and Satan also came among them. ⁷ And the LORD said to Satan, "From where do you come?"

So Satan answered the LORD and said, "From going to and fro on the earth, and from walking back and forth on it."

⁸ Then the LORD said to Satan, "Have you considered My servant Job, that *there is* none like him on the earth, a blameless and upright man, one who fears God and shuns evil?"

⁹ So Satan answered the LORD and said, "Does Job fear God for nothing? ¹⁰ Have You not made a hedge around him, around his household, and around all that he has on every side? You have blessed the work of his hands, and his possessions have increased in the land. ¹¹ But now, stretch out Your hand and touch all that he has, and he will surely curse You to Your face!"

¹² And the LORD said to Satan, "Behold, all that he has *is* in your power; only do not lay a hand on his *person.*"

So Satan went out from the presence of the LORD.

¹³ Now there was a day when his sons and daughters *were* eating and drinking wine in their oldest brother's house; ¹⁴ and a messenger came to Job and said, "The oxen were plowing and the donkeys feeding beside them, ¹⁵ when the Sabeans raided *them* and took them away—indeed they have killed the servants with the edge of the sword; and I alone have escaped to tell you!"

¹⁶ While he *was* still speaking, another also came and said, "The fire of God fell from heaven and burned up the sheep and the servants, and consumed them; and I alone have escaped to tell you!"

¹⁷ While he *was* still speaking, another also came and said, "The Chaldeans formed three bands, raided the camels and took them away, yes, and killed the servants with the edge of the sword; and I alone have escaped to tell you!"

¹⁸ While he *was* still speaking, another also came and said, "Your sons and daughters *were* eating and drinking wine in their oldest brother's house, ¹⁹ and suddenly a great wind came from across the wilderness and struck the four corners of the house, and it fell on the young people, and they are dead; and I alone have escaped to tell you!"

²⁰ Then Job arose, tore his robe, and shaved his head; and he fell to the ground and worshiped. ²¹ And he said:

"Naked I came from my mother's womb,

And naked shall I return there.
The LORD gave, and the LORD has
   taken away;
Blessed be the name of the LORD."

22 In all this Job did not sin nor charge
God with wrong.

2 Again there was a day when the sons
of God came to present themselves before the LORD, and Satan came also among
them to present himself before the LORD.
2 And the LORD said to Satan, "From
where do you come?"

Satan answered the LORD and said,
"From going to and fro on the earth, and
from walking back and forth on it."

3 Then the LORD said to Satan, "Have
you considered My servant Job, that *there
is* none like him on the earth, a blameless
and upright man, one who fears God and
shuns evil? And still he holds fast to his
integrity, although you incited Me against
him, to destroy him without cause."

4 So Satan answered the LORD and said,
"Skin for skin! Yes, all that a man has he
will give for his life. 5 But stretch out Your
hand now, and touch his bone and his
flesh, and he will surely curse You to Your
face!"

6 And the LORD said to Satan, "Behold,
he *is* in your hand, but spare his life."

7 So Satan went out from the presence
of the LORD, and struck Job with painful
boils from the sole of his foot to the crown
of his head. 8 And he took for himself a
potsherd with which to scrape himself
while he sat in the midst of the ashes.

9 Then his wife said to him, "Do you
still hold fast to your integrity? Curse God
and die!"

10 But he said to her, "You speak as one
of the foolish women speaks. Shall we
indeed accept good from God, and shall
we not accept adversity?" In all this Job
did not sin with his lips.

11 Now when Job's three friends heard
of all this adversity that had come upon
him, each one came from his own place—
Eliphaz the Temanite, Bildad the Shuhite,
and Zophar the Naamathite. For they had
made an appointment together to come
and mourn with him, and to comfort him.
12 And when they raised their eyes from
afar, and did not recognize him, they lifted

their voices and wept; and each one tore
his robe and sprinkled dust on his head
toward heaven. 13 So they sat down with
him on the ground seven days and seven
nights, and no one spoke a word to him,
for they saw that *his* grief was very great.

~ PSALM 91:7–13 ~

7 A thousand may fall at your side,
   And ten thousand at your right
     hand;
   But it shall not come near you.
8 Only with your eyes shall you look,
   And see the reward of the wicked.

9 Because you have made the LORD,
   who is my refuge,
   Even the Most High, your dwelling
     place,
10 No evil shall befall you,
   Nor shall any plague come near your
     dwelling;
11 For He shall give His angels charge
     over you,
   To keep you in all your ways.
12 In *their* hands they shall bear you up,
   Lest you dash your foot against a
     stone.
13 You shall tread upon the lion and the
     cobra,
   The young lion and the serpent you
     shall trample underfoot.

~ PROVERBS 22:13, 14 ~

13 The lazy *man* says, "*There is* a lion
     outside!
   I shall be slain in the streets!"

14 The mouth of an immoral woman *is*
     a deep pit;
   He who is abhorred by the LORD
     will fall there.

~ ROMANS 7:1–25 ~

Or do you not know, brethren (for I speak
to those who know the law), that the law
has dominion over a man as long as he
lives? 2 For the woman who has a husband
is bound by the law to *her* husband as long
as he lives. But if the husband dies, she
is released from the law of *her* husband.
3 So then if, while *her* husband lives, she

Lasting Treasures

Paula doesn't have any dolls from her childhood. The quilts her grandmother made are nowhere to be found. The boxes in her attic are few, mostly seasonal things she packs back up with each holiday. There are no heirlooms, no hand-me-downs, no furniture from a previous generation.

If you ask her why, Paula will tell you about a fire that destroyed her home when she was a teenager. She'll tell you about walking through the blackened outline of her bedroom and weeping over the hope chest that was charred — the contents destroyed.

Paula doesn't hold tightly to her possessions since the fire. Instead, she holds tightly to the people in her life and to each moment as it comes.

She says, "We embrace our belongings as if they are ours forever. But one day we'll be gone and nothing will be like we once knew it. I'm glad to have nice things in my house, but I don't think of them as 'mine' anymore. They are toys I get to borrow for this life. All that is really mine is the love I've received and the love I've given. That can never be destroyed or taken away."

> "Naked I came from my mother's womb, and naked I will depart. The LORD gave and the LORD has taken away; may the name of the LORD be praised."
>
> *Job 1:21*

marries another man, she will be called an adulteress; but if her husband dies, she is free from that law, so that she is no adulteress, though she has married another man. ⁴ Therefore, my brethren, you also have become dead to the law through the body of Christ, that you may be married to another—to Him who was raised from the dead, that we should bear fruit to God. ⁵ For when we were in the flesh, the sinful passions which were aroused by the law were at work in our members to bear fruit to death. ⁶ But now we have been delivered from the law, having died to what we were held by, so that we should serve in the newness of the Spirit and not *in* the oldness of the letter.

⁷ What shall we say then? *Is* the law sin? Certainly not! On the contrary, I would not have known sin except through the law. For I would not have known covetousness unless the law had said, "You shall not covet." ⁸ But sin, taking opportunity by the commandment, produced in me all *manner of evil* desire. For apart from the law sin *was* dead. ⁹ I was alive once without the law, but when the commandment came, sin revived and I died. ¹⁰ And the commandment, which *was* to *bring* life, I found to *bring* death. ¹¹ For sin, taking occasion by the commandment, deceived me, and by it killed *me.* ¹² Therefore the law *is* holy, and the commandment holy and just and good.

¹³ Has then what is good become death to me? Certainly not! But sin, that it might appear sin, was producing death in me through what is good, so that sin through the commandment might become exceedingly sinful. ¹⁴ For we know that the law is spiritual, but I am carnal, sold under sin. ¹⁵ For what I am doing, I do not understand. For what I will to do, that I do not practice; but what I hate, that I do. ¹⁶ If, then, I do what I will not to do, I agree with the law that *it is* good. ¹⁷ But now, *it is* no longer I who do it, but sin that dwells in me. ¹⁸ For I know that in me (that is, in my flesh) nothing good dwells; for to will is present with me, but *how* to perform what is good I do not find. ¹⁹ For the good that I will *to do,* I do not do; but the evil I will not *to do,* that I practice. ²⁰ Now if I do what I will not *to do,* it is no longer I who do it, but sin that dwells in me.

²¹ I find then a law, that evil is present with me, the one who wills to do good. ²² For I delight in the law of God according to the inward man. ²³ But I see another law in my members, warring against the law of my mind, and bringing me into captivity to the law of sin which is in my members. ²⁴ O wretched man that I am! Who will deliver me from this body of death? ²⁵ I thank God—through Jesus Christ our Lord!

So then, with the mind I myself serve the law of God, but with the flesh the law of sin.

～ JOB 3:1—4:21 ～

After this Job opened his mouth and cursed the day of his *birth.* ² And Job spoke, and said:

³ "May the day perish on which I
      was born,
   And the night *in which* it was said,
   'A male child is conceived.'
⁴   May that day be darkness;
   May God above not seek it,
   Nor the light shine upon it.
⁵   May darkness and the shadow of
      death claim it;
   May a cloud settle on it;

   May the blackness of the day
      terrify it.
⁶   *As for* that night, may darkness
      seize it;
   May it not rejoice among the days
      of the year,
   May it not come into the number
      of the months.
⁷   Oh, may that night be barren!
   May no joyful shout come into it!
⁸   May those curse it who curse the
      day,
   Those who are ready to arouse
      Leviathan.

Hand of Comfort

On the first of June, John Alexander spent the evening playing basketball at the gym. When his wife was late picking him up, he began to worry. Within an hour he had some horrible news. On their way to the gym his wife and daughter had been killed in a collision with a drunken driver.

John's life became a tailspin of grief and anger. After a few weeks he began to exude a calmness that baffled those closest to him.

When he returned to work the team members he led were uncomfortable and afraid of doing or saying the wrong thing. In order to dispel the awkwardness, John called a meeting on a Friday afternoon. He reviewed the facts of the accident, then before closing the meeting gave an opportunity for questions. Their question: What had enabled him to move from intense grief to the calm they sensed from him now?

"Well, first of all, don't mistake my calm for a lack of grief. I will miss my family everyday for the rest of my life. But about two weeks after their deaths I woke up one morning with the distinct sensation of a hand on my shoulder. I couldn't escape the feeling. It became a comfort. I felt less alone. As crazy as it sounds, I think it is God's presence with me, helping me through. It's been there ever since. It gives me hope that I will get through this and God won't leave me alone."

9 May the stars of its morning be
dark;
May it look for light, but *have*
none,
And not see the dawning of the
day;
10 Because it did not shut up the
doors of my *mother's* womb,
Nor hide sorrow from my eyes.

11 "Why did I not die at birth?
Why did I *not* perish when I came
from the womb?
12 Why did the knees receive me?
Or why the breasts, that I should
nurse?
13 For now I would have lain still
and been quiet,
I would have been asleep;
Then I would have been at rest
14 With kings and counselors of the
earth,
Who built ruins for themselves,
15 Or with princes who had gold,
Who filled their houses *with*
silver;
16 Or *why* was I not hidden like a
stillborn child,
Like infants who never saw light?
17 There the wicked cease *from*
troubling,
And there the weary are at rest.
18 *There* the prisoners rest together;
They do not hear the voice of the
oppressor.
19 The small and great are there,
And the servant *is* free from his
master.

20 "Why is light given to him who is
in misery,
And life to the bitter of soul,
21 Who long for death, but it does
not *come,*
And search for it more than
hidden treasures;
22 Who rejoice exceedingly,
And are glad when they can find
the grave?
23 *Why is light given* to a man whose
way is hidden,
And whom God has hedged in?
24 For my sighing comes before I eat,
And my groanings pour out like
water.

25 For the thing I greatly feared has
come upon me,
And what I dreaded has happened
to me.
26 I am not at ease, nor am I quiet;
I have no rest, for trouble comes."

4 Then Eliphaz the Temanite answered
and said:

2 "*If* one attempts a word with you,
will you become weary?
But who can withhold himself
from speaking?
3 Surely you have instructed many,
And you have strengthened weak
hands.
4 Your words have upheld him who
was stumbling,
And you have strengthened the
feeble knees;
5 But now it comes upon you, and
you are weary;
It touches you, and you are
troubled.
6 *Is* not your reverence your
confidence?
And the integrity of your ways
your hope?

7 "Remember now, who *ever*
perished being innocent?
Or where were the upright *ever*
cut off?
8 Even as I have seen,
Those who plow iniquity
And sow trouble reap the same.
9 By the blast of God they perish,
And by the breath of His anger
they are consumed.
10 The roaring of the lion,
The voice of the fierce lion,
And the teeth of the young lions
are broken.
11 The old lion perishes for lack of
prey,
And the cubs of the lioness are
scattered.

12 "Now a word was secretly brought
to me,
And my ear received a whisper of
it.

13 In disquieting thoughts from the
      visions of the night,
    When deep sleep falls on men,
14 Fear came upon me, and
      trembling,
    Which made all my bones shake.
15 Then a spirit passed before my
      face;
    The hair on my body stood up.
16 It stood still,
    But I could not discern its
      appearance.
    A form *was* before my eyes;
    There was silence;
    Then I heard a voice *saying:*
17 'Can a mortal be more righteous
      than God?
    Can a man be more pure than his
      Maker?
18 If He puts no trust in His servants,
    If He charges His angels with
      error,
19 How much more those who dwell
      in houses of clay,
    Whose foundation is in the dust,
    Who are crushed before a moth?
20 They are broken in pieces from
      morning till evening;
    They perish forever, with no one
      regarding.
21 Does not their own excellence go
      away?
    They die, even without wisdom.'

∼ PSALM 91:14–16 ∼

14 "Because he has set his love upon Me,
      therefore I will deliver him;
    I will set him on high, because he has
      known My name.
15 He shall call upon Me, and I will
      answer him;
    I *will be* with him in trouble;
    I will deliver him and honor him.
16 With long life I will satisfy him,
    And show him My salvation."

∼ PROVERBS 22:15 ∼

15 Foolishness *is* bound up in the heart
      of a child;
    The rod of correction will drive it far
      from him.

∼ ROMANS 8:1–21 ∼

There is therefore now no condemnation
to those who are in Christ Jesus, who do
not walk according to the flesh, but according to the Spirit. 2 For the law of the
Spirit of life in Christ Jesus has made me
free from the law of sin and death. 3 For
what the law could not do in that it was
weak through the flesh, God *did* by sending His own Son in the likeness of sinful
flesh, on account of sin: He condemned
sin in the flesh, 4 that the righteous requirement of the law might be fulfilled in
us who do not walk according to the flesh
but according to the Spirit. 5 For those
who live according to the flesh set their
minds on the things of the flesh, but those
who live according to the Spirit, the things
of the Spirit. 6 For to be carnally minded
is death, but to be spiritually minded *is*
life and peace. 7 Because the carnal mind
is enmity against God; for it is not subject
to the law of God, nor indeed can be. 8 So
then, those who are in the flesh cannot
please God.

9 But you are not in the flesh but in the
Spirit, if indeed the Spirit of God dwells
in you. Now if anyone does not have the
Spirit of Christ, he is not His. 10 And if
Christ *is* in you, the body *is* dead because
of sin, but the Spirit *is* life because of
righteousness. 11 But if the Spirit of Him
who raised Jesus from the dead dwells
in you, He who raised Christ from the
dead will also give life to your mortal
bodies through His Spirit who dwells in
you.

12 Therefore, brethren, we are debtors—not to the flesh, to live according to
the flesh. 13 For if you live according
to the flesh you will die; but if by the Spirit
you put to death the deeds of the
body, you will live. 14 For as many as are
led by the Spirit of God, these are sons of
God. 15 For you did not receive the spirit
of bondage again to fear, but you received
the Spirit of adoption by whom we cry
out, "Abba, Father." 16 The Spirit Himself
bears witness with our spirit that we are
children of God, 17 and if children, then
heirs—heirs of God and joint heirs with
Christ, if indeed we suffer with *Him,* that
we may also be glorified together.

18 For I consider that the sufferings of this present time are not worthy *to be compared* with the glory which shall be revealed in us. 19 For the earnest expectation of the creation eagerly waits for the revealing of the sons of God. 20 For the creation was subjected to futility, not willingly, but because of Him who subjected *it* in hope; 21 because the creation itself also will be delivered from the bondage of corruption into the glorious liberty of the children of God.

READING 219 · AUGUST 7

~ JOB 5:1—6:30 ~

1 "Call out now;
    Is there anyone who will answer you?
    And to which of the holy ones will you turn?
2 For wrath kills a foolish man,
    And envy slays a simple one.
3 I have seen the foolish taking root,
    But suddenly I cursed his dwelling place.
4 His sons are far from safety,
    They are crushed in the gate,
    And *there is* no deliverer.
5 Because the hungry eat up his harvest,
    Taking it even from the thorns,
    And a snare snatches their substance.
6 For affliction does not come from the dust,
    Nor does trouble spring from the ground;
7 Yet man is born to trouble,
    As the sparks fly upward.

8 "But as for me, I would seek God,
    And to God I would commit my cause—
9 Who does great things, and unsearchable,
    Marvelous things without number.
10 He gives rain on the earth,
    And sends waters on the fields.
11 He sets on high those who are lowly,
    And those who mourn are lifted to safety.
12 He frustrates the devices of the crafty,
    So that their hands cannot carry out their plans.

13 He catches the wise in their own craftiness,
    And the counsel of the cunning comes quickly upon them.
14 They meet with darkness in the daytime,
    And grope at noontime as in the night.
15 But He saves the needy from the sword,
    From the mouth of the mighty,
    And from their hand.
16 So the poor have hope,
    And injustice shuts her mouth.

17 "Behold, happy *is* the man whom God corrects;
    Therefore do not despise the chastening of the Almighty.
18 For He bruises, but He binds up;
    He wounds, but His hands make whole.
19 He shall deliver you in six troubles,
    Yes, in seven no evil shall touch you.
20 In famine He shall redeem you from death,
    And in war from the power of the sword.
21 You shall be hidden from the scourge of the tongue,
    And you shall not be afraid of destruction when it comes.
22 You shall laugh at destruction and famine,
    And you shall not be afraid of the beasts of the earth.
23 For you shall have a covenant with the stones of the field,
    And the beasts of the field shall be at peace with you.

Expressions of Divine Exactness

What then shall we say to these things? If God is for us, who can be against us?

Romans 8:31

Cardinal von Faulhaber of Munich is reported once to have had a conversation with the famed physicist, Albert Einstein.

"Cardinal von Faulhaber," Einstein said, "I respect religion, but I believe in mathematics. Probably it is the other way around with you."

"You are mistaken," replied the Cardinal. "To me, both are merely different expressions of the same divine exactness."

"But, your Eminence, what would you say if mathematical science should someday come to conclusions directly contradictory to religious beliefs?"

"Oh," the Cardinal answered with ease, "I have the highest respect for the competence of mathematicians. I am sure they would never rest until they discovered their mistake."

Regardless of how ardently some people try to suppress it, God's truth will always prevail!

24 You shall know that your tent *is* in
    peace;
    You shall visit your dwelling and
    find nothing amiss.
25 You shall also know that your
    descendants *shall be* many,
    And your offspring like the grass
    of the earth.
26 You shall come to the grave at a
    full age,
    As a sheaf of grain ripens in its
    season.
27 Behold, this we have searched out;
    It *is* true.
    Hear it, and know for yourself."

6 Then Job answered and said:

2 "Oh, that my grief were fully
    weighed,
    And my calamity laid with it on
    the scales!
3 For then it would be heavier than
    the sand of the sea—
    Therefore my words have been
    rash.
4 For the arrows of the Almighty *are*
    within me;
    My spirit drinks in their poison;
    The terrors of God are arrayed
    against me.
5 Does the wild donkey bray when
    it has grass,
    Or does the ox low over its
    fodder?
6 Can flavorless food be eaten
    without salt?
    Or is there *any* taste in the white
    of an egg?
7 My soul refuses to touch them;
    They *are* as loathsome food to me.

8 "Oh, that I might have my request,
    That God would grant *me* the
    thing that I long for!
9 That it would please God to crush
    me,
    That He would loose His hand
    and cut me off!
10 Then I would still have comfort;
    Though in anguish I would exult,
    He will not spare;
    For I have not concealed the
    words of the Holy One.

11 "What strength do I have, that I
    should hope?
    And what *is* my end, that I should
    prolong my life?
12 *Is* my strength the strength of
    stones?
    Or is my flesh bronze?
13 *Is* my help not within me?
    And is success driven from me?

14 "To him who is afflicted, kindness
    should be shown by his friend,
    Even though he forsakes the fear
    of the Almighty.
15 My brothers have dealt deceitfully
    like a brook,
    Like the streams of the brooks
    that pass away,
16 Which are dark because of the ice,
    And into which the snow vanishes.
17 When it is warm, they cease to
    flow;
    When it is hot, they vanish from
    their place.
18 The paths of their way turn aside,
    They go nowhere and perish.
19 The caravans of Tema look,
    The travelers of Sheba hope for
    them.
20 They are disappointed because
    they were confident;
    They come there and are
    confused.
21 For now you are nothing,
    You see terror and are afraid.
22 Did I ever say, 'Bring *something* to
    me'?
    Or, 'Offer a bribe for me from
    your wealth'?
23 Or, 'Deliver me from the enemy's
    hand'?
    Or, 'Redeem me from the hand of
    oppressors'?

24 "Teach me, and I will hold my
    tongue;
    Cause me to understand wherein I
    have erred.
25 How forceful are right words!
    But what does your arguing
    prove?
26 Do you intend to rebuke *my*
    words,
    And the speeches of a desperate
    one, *which are* as wind?

²⁷ Yes, you overwhelm the fatherless,
And you undermine your friend.
²⁸ Now therefore, be pleased to look
at me;
For I would never lie to your face.
²⁹ Yield now, let there be no
injustice!
Yes, concede, my righteousness
still stands!
³⁰ Is there injustice on my tongue?
Cannot my taste discern the
unsavory?

~ PSALM 92:1–7 ~

¹ It is good to give thanks to the
LORD,
And to sing praises to Your name,
O Most High;
² To declare Your lovingkindness in
the morning,
And Your faithfulness every night,
³ On an instrument of ten strings,
On the lute,
And on the harp,
With harmonious sound.
⁴ For You, LORD, have made me glad
through Your work;
I will triumph in the works of Your
hands.

⁵ O LORD, how great are Your works!
Your thoughts are very deep.
⁶ A senseless man does not know,
Nor does a fool understand this.
⁷ When the wicked spring up like
grass,
And when all the workers of iniquity
flourish,
It is that they may be destroyed
forever.

~ PROVERBS 22:16 ~

¹⁶ He who oppresses the poor to
increase his riches,
And he who gives to the rich, will
surely come to poverty.

~ ROMANS 8:22–39 ~

For we know that the whole creation
groans and labors with birth pangs together until now. ²³ Not only that, but we
also who have the firstfruits of the Spirit,
even we ourselves groan within ourselves,
eagerly waiting for the adoption, the redemption of our body. ²⁴ For we were
saved in this hope, but hope that is seen is
not hope; for why does one still hope for
what he sees? ²⁵ But if we hope for what
we do not see, we eagerly wait for it with
perseverance.

²⁶ Likewise the Spirit also helps in our
weaknesses. For we do not know what
we should pray for as we ought, but the
Spirit Himself makes intercession for us
with groanings which cannot be uttered.
²⁷ Now He who searches the hearts knows
what the mind of the Spirit is, because
He makes intercession for the saints according to the will of God.

²⁸ And we know that all things work
together for good to those who love God,
to those who are the called according to
His purpose. ²⁹ For whom He foreknew,
He also predestined to be conformed to
the image of His Son, that He might
be the firstborn among many brethren.
³⁰ Moreover whom He predestined, these
He also called; whom He called, these He
also justified; and whom He justified,
these He also glorified.

³¹ What then shall we say to these
things? If God is for us, who can be against
us? ³² He who did not spare His own Son,
but delivered Him up for us all, how shall
He not with Him also freely give us all
things? ³³ Who shall bring a charge against
God's elect? It is God who justifies. ³⁴ Who
is he who condemns? It is Christ who died,
and furthermore is also risen, who is even
at the right hand of God, who also makes
intercession for us. ³⁵ Who shall separate
us from the love of Christ? Shall tribulation, or distress, or persecution, or famine,
or nakedness, or peril, or sword? ³⁶ As it
is written:

"For Your sake we are killed all day
long;
We are accounted as sheep for the
slaughter."

³⁷ Yet in all these things we are more
than conquerors through Him who loved
us. ³⁸ For I am persuaded that neither

death nor life, nor angels nor principalities nor powers, nor things present nor things to come, [39] nor height nor depth, nor any other created thing, shall be able to separate us from the love of God which is in Christ Jesus our Lord.

READING 220 · AUGUST 8

~ JOB 7:1—8:22 ~

[1] "*Is there* not a time of hard service
for man on earth?
Are not his days also like the days
of a hired man?
[2] Like a servant who earnestly
desires the shade,
And like a hired man who eagerly
looks for his wages,
[3] So I have been allotted months of
futility,
And wearisome nights have been
appointed to me.
[4] When I lie down, I say, 'When
shall I arise,
And the night be ended?'
For I have had my fill of tossing
till dawn.
[5] My flesh is caked with worms and
dust,
My skin is cracked and breaks out
afresh.

[6] "My days are swifter than a
weaver's shuttle,
And are spent without hope.
[7] Oh, remember that my life *is* a
breath!
My eye will never again see good.
[8] The eye of him who sees me will
see me no *more;*
While your *eyes* are upon me, I
shall no longer *be.*
[9] *As* the cloud disappears and
vanishes away,
So he who goes down to the grave
does not come up.
[10] He shall never return to his house,
Nor shall his place know him
anymore.

[11] "Therefore I will not restrain my
mouth;
I will speak in the anguish of my
spirit;
I will complain in the bitterness of
my soul.

[12] *Am* I a sea, or a sea serpent,
That You set a guard over me?
[13] When I say, 'My bed will comfort
me,
My couch will ease my
complaint,'
[14] Then You scare me with dreams
And terrify me with visions,
[15] So that my soul chooses strangling
And death rather than my body.
[16] I loathe *my life;*
I would not live forever.
Let me alone,
For my days *are but* a breath.

[17] "What *is* man, that You should
exalt him,
That You should set Your heart on
him,
[18] That You should visit him every
morning,
And test him every moment?
[19] How long?
Will You not look away from me,
And let me alone till I swallow my
saliva?
[20] Have I sinned?
What have I done to You,
O watcher of men?
Why have You set me as Your
target,
So that I am a burden to myself?
[21] Why then do You not pardon my
transgression,
And take away my iniquity?
For now I will lie down in the
dust,
And You will seek me diligently,
But I *will* no longer *be.*"

8 Then Bildad the Shuhite answered and
said:

[2] "How long will you speak these
things,

Finish Big

Scott McGregor worked for a company that rented cellular phones to business travelers. The phones were not designed to produce itemized bills, however, and some corporations refused to reimburse their employees without one. Each phone needed a computer chip to keep a billing record of calls made.

> Though your beginning was small, yet your latter end would increase abundantly.
>
> *Job 8:7*

McGregor quit his job and began to pursue the idea full-time. He felt sure it was a winner. But despite two years of effort, he met with very little success and faced being evicted from his home. At the eleventh hour, he found an investor willing to help him turn his idea into a reality.

McGregor used part of the money to hire a consulting engineer, but after several months the engineer said the system McGregor wanted was impossible. He already had an appointment to demonstrate a prototype to BellSouth, so he called his twenty-two-year-old son, Greg, who was a computer science major. Greg began working up to eighteen hours a day to create an automated circuit that would defy the experts. He and his dad flew to Atlanta to meet with BellSouth and his solution worked.

Today, the McGregor family firm, Telemac Cellular Corporation, is an industry leader worth millions of dollars.

A slow start diligently pursued can result in a big finish.

And the words of your mouth *be
like* a strong wind?
3 Does God subvert judgment?
Or does the Almighty pervert
justice?
4 If your sons have sinned against
Him,
He has cast them away for their
transgression.
5 If you would earnestly seek God
And make your supplication to the
Almighty,
6 If you *were* pure and upright,
Surely now He would awake for
you,
And prosper your rightful
dwelling place.
7 Though your beginning was small,
Yet your latter end would increase
abundantly.

8 "For inquire, please, of the former
age,
And consider the things
discovered by their fathers;
9 For we *were born* yesterday, and
know nothing,
Because our days on earth *are* a
shadow.
10 Will they not teach you and tell
you,
And utter words from their heart?

11 "Can the papyrus grow up without
a marsh?
Can the reeds flourish without
water?
12 While it *is* yet green *and* not cut
down,
It withers before any *other* plant.
13 So *are* the paths of all who forget
God;
And the hope of the hypocrite
shall perish,
14 Whose confidence shall be cut
off,
And whose trust *is* a spider's web.
15 He leans on his house, but it does
not stand.
He holds it fast, but it does not
endure.
16 He grows green in the sun,
And his branches spread out in his
garden.

17 His roots wrap around the rock
heap,
And look for a place in the stones.
18 If he is destroyed from his place,
Then *it* will deny him, *saying*, 'I
have not seen you.'

19 "Behold, this is the joy of His way,
And out of the earth others will
grow.
20 Behold, God will not cast away
the blameless,
Nor will He uphold the evildoers.
21 He will yet fill your mouth with
laughing,
And your lips with rejoicing.
22 Those who hate you will be
clothed with shame,
And the dwelling place of the
wicked will come to nothing."

∼ PSALM 92:8–15 ∼

8 But You, LORD, *are* on high
forevermore.
9 For behold, Your enemies, O LORD,
For behold, Your enemies shall
perish;
All the workers of iniquity shall be
scattered.

10 But my horn You have exalted like a
wild ox;
I have been anointed with fresh oil.
11 My eye also has seen *my desire* on
my enemies;
My ears hear *my desire* on the
wicked
Who rise up against me.

12 The righteous shall flourish like a
palm tree,
He shall grow like a cedar in
Lebanon.
13 Those who are planted in the house
of the LORD
Shall flourish in the courts of our
God.
14 They shall still bear fruit in old age;
They shall be fresh and flourishing,
15 To declare that the LORD is upright;
He is my rock, and *there is* no
unrighteousness in Him.

∼ PROVERBS 22:17–21 ∼

¹⁷ Incline your ear and hear the words
of the wise,
And apply your heart to my
knowledge;
¹⁸ For *it is* a pleasant thing if you keep
them within you;
Let them all be fixed upon your lips,
¹⁹ So that your trust may be in the
LORD;
I have instructed you today, even
you.
²⁰ Have I not written to you excellent
things
Of counsels and knowledge,
²¹ That I may make you know the
certainty of the words of truth,
That you may answer words of truth
To those who send to you?

∼ ROMANS 9:1–15 ∼

I tell the truth in Christ, I am not lying,
my conscience also bearing me witness in
the Holy Spirit, ² that I have great sorrow
and continual grief in my heart. ³ For I
could wish that I myself were accursed
from Christ for my brethren, my countrymen according to the flesh, ⁴ who are Israelites, to whom *pertain* the adoption,
the glory, the covenants, the giving of the
law, the service *of God,* and the promises; ⁵ of whom *are* the fathers and from
whom, according to the flesh, Christ
came, who is over all, *the* eternally blessed
God. Amen.
⁶ But it is not that the word of God has
taken no effect. For they *are* not all Israel
who *are* of Israel, ⁷ nor *are they* all children because they are the seed of
Abraham; but, "In Isaac your seed shall
be called." ⁸ That is, those who *are* the
children of the flesh, these *are* not
the children of God; but the children
of the promise are counted as the seed.
⁹ For this *is* the word of promise: "At this
time I will come and Sarah shall have
a son."
¹⁰ And not only *this,* but when Rebecca
also had conceived by one man, *even* by
our father Isaac ¹¹(for *the children* not yet
being born, nor having done any good or
evil, that the purpose of God according
to election might stand, not of works but
of Him who calls), ¹² it was said to her,
"The older shall serve the younger." ¹³ As
it is written, "Jacob I have loved, but Esau
I have hated."
¹⁴ What shall we say then? *Is there*
unrighteousness with God? Certainly not!
¹⁵ For He says to Moses, "I will have mercy
on whomever I will have mercy, and I will
have compassion on whomever I will have
compassion."

∼ JOB 9:1—10:22 ∼

Then Job answered and said:

² "Truly I know *it is* so,
But how can a man be righteous
before God?
³ If one wished to contend with
Him,
He could not answer Him one
time out of a thousand.
⁴ *God is* wise in heart and mighty in
strength.
Who has hardened *himself* against
Him and prospered?

⁵ He removes the mountains, and
they do not know
When He overturns them in His
anger;
⁶ He shakes the earth out of its
place,
And its pillars tremble;
⁷ He commands the sun, and it does
not rise;
He seals off the stars;
⁸ He alone spreads out the heavens,
And treads on the waves of the
sea;

9   He made the Bear, Orion, and the
      Pleiades,
    And the chambers of the south;
10 He does great things past finding
      out,
    Yes, wonders without number.
11 If He goes by me, I do not see
      Him;
    If He moves past, I do not
      perceive Him;
12 If He takes away, who can hinder
      Him?
    Who can say to Him, 'What are
      You doing?'
13 God will not withdraw His anger,
    The allies of the proud lie
      prostrate beneath Him.

14 "How then can I answer Him,
    And choose my words to reason
      with Him?
15 For though I were righteous, I
      could not answer Him;
    I would beg mercy of my Judge.
16 If I called and He answered me,
    I would not believe that He was
      listening to my voice.
17 For He crushes me with a
      tempest,
    And multiplies my wounds
      without cause.
18 He will not allow me to catch my
      breath,
    But fills me with bitterness.
19 If it is a matter of strength, indeed
      He is strong;
    And if of justice, who will appoint
      my day in court?
20 Though I were righteous, my own
      mouth would condemn me;
    Though I were blameless, it would
      prove me perverse.

21 "I am blameless, yet I do not know
      myself;
    I despise my life.
22 It is all one thing;
    Therefore I say, 'He destroys the
      blameless and the wicked.'
23 If the scourge slays suddenly,
    He laughs at the plight of the
      innocent.
24 The earth is given into the hand of
      the wicked.
    He covers the faces of its judges.

If it is not He, who else could it
  be?

25 "Now my days are swifter than a
      runner;
    They flee away, they see no good.
26 They pass by like swift ships,
    Like an eagle swooping on its
      prey.
27 If I say, 'I will forget my
      complaint,
    I will put off my sad face and wear
      a smile,'
28 I am afraid of all my sufferings;
    I know that You will not hold me
      innocent.
29 If I am condemned,
    Why then do I labor in vain?
30 If I wash myself with snow water,
    And cleanse my hands with soap,
31 Yet You will plunge me into the
      pit,
    And my own clothes will abhor
      me.

32 "For He is not a man, as I am,
    That I may answer Him,
    And that we should go to court
      together.
33 Nor is there any mediator
      between us,
    Who may lay his hand on us both.
34 Let Him take His rod away from
      me,
    And do not let dread of Him
      terrify me.
35 Then I would speak and not fear
      Him,
    But it is not so with me.

10 "My soul loathes my life;
     I will give free course to my
       complaint,
     I will speak in the bitterness of my
       soul.
2   I will say to God, 'Do not
      condemn me;
    Show me why You contend with
      me.
3   Does it seem good to You that You
      should oppress,
    That You should despise the work
      of Your hands,
    And smile on the counsel of the
      wicked?

Cattle for Sale

Soon after Dallas Theological Seminary opened in 1924, it faced a major financial crisis. Creditors banded together and announced that they intended to foreclose. On the morning of the threatened foreclosure, the leadership of the seminary met in the president's office to pray that God would meet their need. One of the men present was Harry Ironside, who prayed in his characteristic style, "Lord, the cattle on a thousand hills are Thine. Please sell some of them and send us the money."

While they were praying, a tall Texan walked into the outer office and said to the secretary, "I just sold two carloads of cattle. I've been trying to make a business deal but it fell through, and I feel compelled to give the money to the seminary. I don't know if you need it, but here's the check."

Knowing the financial need, the secretary took the check and timidly tapped on the door of the office where the prayer meeting was being held. When Dr. Chafer saw the check, he was amazed. The gift was *exactly* the amount of the debt! Recognizing the name on the check as that of a prominent Ft. Worth cattleman, he announced with joy, "Harry, God sold the cattle!"

⁴ Do You have eyes of flesh?
Or do You see as man sees?
⁵ *Are* Your days like the days of a
mortal man,
Are Your years like the days of a
mighty man,
⁶ That You should seek for my
iniquity
And search out my sin,
⁷ Although You know that I am not
wicked,
And *there is* no one who can
deliver from Your hand?

⁸ 'Your hands have made me and
fashioned me,
An intricate unity;
Yet You would destroy me.
⁹ Remember, I pray, that You have
made me like clay.
And will You turn me into dust
again?
¹⁰ Did You not pour me out like
milk,
And curdle me like cheese,
¹¹ Clothe me with skin and flesh,
And knit me together with bones
and sinews?
¹² You have granted me life and
favor,
And Your care has preserved my
spirit.

¹³ 'And these *things* You have hidden
in Your heart;
I know that this *was* with You:
¹⁴ If I sin, then You mark me,
And will not acquit me of my
iniquity.
¹⁵ If I am wicked, woe to me;
Even *if* I am righteous, I cannot
lift up my head.
I am full of disgrace!
See my misery!
¹⁶ If *my head* is exalted,
You hunt me like a fierce lion,
And again You show Yourself
awesome against me.
¹⁷ You renew Your witnesses against
me,
And increase Your indignation
toward me;
Changes and war are *ever* with
me.

¹⁸ 'Why then have You brought me
out of the womb?
Oh, that I had perished and no eye
had seen me!
¹⁹ I would have been as though I had
not been.
I would have been carried from
the womb to the grave.
²⁰ Are not my days few?
Cease! Leave me alone, that I may
take a little comfort,
²¹ Before I go *to the place from
which* I shall not return,
To the land of darkness and the
shadow of death,
²² A land as dark as darkness *itself,*
As the shadow of death, without
any order,
Where even the light *is* like
darkness.' "

～ PSALM 93:1–5 ～

¹ The LORD reigns, He is clothed with
majesty;
The LORD is clothed,
He has girded Himself with strength.
Surely the world is established, so
that it cannot be moved.
² Your throne *is* established from of
old;
You *are* from everlasting.

³ The floods have lifted up, O LORD,
The floods have lifted up their voice;
The floods lift up their waves.
⁴ The LORD on high *is* mightier
Than the noise of many waters,
Than the mighty waves of the sea.

⁵ Your testimonies are very sure;
Holiness adorns Your house,
O LORD, forever.

～ PROVERBS 22:22, 23 ～

²² Do not rob the poor because he *is*
poor,
Nor oppress the afflicted at the gate;
²³ For the LORD will plead their cause,
And plunder the soul of those who
plunder them.

~ ROMANS 9:16–33 ~

So then *it is* not of him who wills, nor of him who runs, but of God who shows mercy. [17] For the Scripture says to the Pharaoh, "For this very purpose I have raised you up, that I may show My power in you, and that My name may be declared in all the earth." [18] Therefore He has mercy on whom He wills, and whom He wills He hardens.

[19] You will say to me then, "Why does He still find fault? For who has resisted His will?" [20] But indeed, O man, who are you to reply against God? Will the thing formed say to him who formed *it*, "Why have you made me like this?" [21] Does not the potter have power over the clay, from the same lump to make one vessel for honor and another for dishonor?

[22] *What* if God, wanting to show *His* wrath and to make His power known, endured with much longsuffering the vessels of wrath prepared for destruction, [23] and that He might make known the riches of His glory on the vessels of mercy, which He had prepared beforehand for glory, [24] *even* us whom He called, not of the Jews only, but also of the Gentiles? [25] As He says also in Hosea:

"I will call them My people, who
    were not My people,
And her beloved, who was not
    beloved."
[26] "And it shall come to pass in the
    place where it was said to them,
'You are not My people,'

There they shall be called sons of
    the living God."

[27] Isaiah also cries out concerning Israel:

"Though the number of the
    children of Israel be as the sand
    of the sea,
The remnant will be saved.
[28]   For He will finish the work and
    cut *it* short in righteousness,
Because the LORD will make a
    short work upon the earth."

[29] And as Isaiah said before:

"Unless the LORD of Sabaoth had
    left us a seed,
We would have become like
    Sodom,
And we would have been made
    like Gomorrah."

[30] What shall we say then? That Gentiles, who did not pursue righteousness, have attained to righteousness, even the righteousness of faith; [31] but Israel, pursuing the law of righteousness, has not attained to the law of righteousness. [32] Why? Because *they did* not *seek it* by faith, but as it were, by the works of the law. For they stumbled at that stumbling stone. [33] As it is written:

"Behold, I lay in Zion a stumbling
    stone and rock of offense,
And whoever believes on Him will
    not be put to shame."

~ JOB 11:1—12:25 ~

Then Zophar the Naamathite answered and said:
[2] "Should not the multitude of words
    be answered?
And should a man full of talk be
    vindicated?
[3] Should your empty talk make men
    hold their peace?

And when you mock, should no
    one rebuke you?
[4]   For you have said,
'My doctrine *is* pure,
And I am clean in your eyes.'
[5]   But oh, that God would speak,
And open His lips against you,
[6]   That He would show you the
    secrets of wisdom!

For *they would* double *your*
prudence.
Know therefore that God exacts
from you
Less than your iniquity *deserves.*

7 "Can you search out the deep
things of God?
Can you find out the limits of the
Almighty?
8 *They are* higher than heaven—
what can you do?
Deeper than Sheol—what can you
know?
9 Their measure *is* longer than the
earth
And broader than the sea.

10 "If He passes by, imprisons, and
gathers *to judgment,*
Then who can hinder Him?
11 For He knows deceitful men;
He sees wickedness also.
Will He not then consider *it?*
12 For an empty-headed man will be
wise,
When a wild donkey's colt is born
a man.

13 "If you would prepare your heart,
And stretch out your hands
toward Him;
14 If iniquity *were* in your hand, *and
you* put it far away,
And would not let wickedness
dwell in your tents;
15 Then surely you could lift up your
face without spot;
Yes, you could be steadfast, and
not fear;
16 Because you would forget *your*
misery,
And remember *it* as waters *that
have* passed away,
17 And *your* life would be brighter
than noonday.
Though you were dark, you would
be like the morning.
18 And you would be secure, because
there is hope;
Yes, you would dig *around you,
and* take your rest in safety.
19 You would also lie down,
and no one would make *you*
afraid;

Yes, many would court your
favor.
20 But the eyes of the wicked will
fail,
And they shall not escape,
And their hope—loss of life!"

12 Then Job answered and said:

2 "No doubt you *are* the people,
And wisdom will die with you!
3 But I have understanding as well
as you;
I *am* not inferior to you.
Indeed, who does not *know* such
things as these?

4 "I am one mocked by his friends,
Who called on God, and He
answered him,
The just and blameless *who is*
ridiculed.
5 A lamp is despised in the thought
of one who is at ease;
It is made ready for those whose
feet slip.
6 The tents of robbers prosper,
And those who provoke God are
secure—
In what God provides by His
hand.

7 "But now ask the beasts, and they
will teach you;
And the birds of the air, and they
will tell you;
8 Or speak to the earth, and it will
teach you;
And the fish of the sea will explain
to you.
9 Who among all these does not
know
That the hand of the LORD has
done this,
10 In whose hand *is* the life of every
living thing,
And the breath of all mankind?
11 Does not the ear test words
And the mouth taste its food?
12 Wisdom *is* with aged men,
And with length of days,
understanding.

13 "With Him *are* wisdom and
strength,

Level Ground

Amy can tell you the exact moment she fell in love with Brian. One cold, rainy night they were on a date, and Brian's car stalled. When they couldn't get it started Brian asked her to steer while he pushed the car off the road. Amy was an inexperienced driver and began to steer the car toward a rising incline which would have been impossible to climb with a dead motor and one man pushing.

"Amy, if you'll turn the wheel to the right we'll be on level ground," was all she heard from Brian at the rear of the automobile.

For someone like Amy who had been berated for the smallest of mistakes, the moment was monumental. When all she expected was anger and impatience, and all she received was gentle instruction, she knew she'd found a man who she could spend the rest of her life with.

Times of inconvenience and adversity give us a window into our truest selves. It is in those times we show our truest colors. Brian showed Amy she could depend on him for more than a hot-tempered response when the going got rough. That simple window into his soul let love shine through.

> Do not make friends with a hot-tempered man, do not associate with one easily angered, or you may learn his ways and get yourself ensnared.
>
> *Proverbs 22:24-25*

He has counsel and
understanding.
14 If He breaks *a thing* down, it
cannot be rebuilt;
If He imprisons a man, there can
be no release.
15 If He withholds the waters, they
dry up;
If He sends them out, they
overwhelm the earth.
16 With Him *are* strength and
prudence.
The deceived and the deceiver *are*
His.
17 He leads counselors away
plundered,
And makes fools of the judges.
18 He loosens the bonds of kings,
And binds their waist with a belt.
19 He leads princes away plundered,
And overthrows the mighty.
20 He deprives the trusted ones of
speech,
And takes away the discernment
of the elders.
21 He pours contempt on princes,
And disarms the mighty.
22 He uncovers deep things out of
darkness,
And brings the shadow of death to
light.
23 He makes nations great, and
destroys them;
He enlarges nations, and guides
them.
24 He takes away the understanding
of the chiefs of the people of
the earth,
And makes them wander in a
pathless wilderness.
25 They grope in the dark without
light,
And He makes them stagger like a
drunken *man.*

~ PSALM 94:1–11 ~

1 O LORD God, to whom vengeance
belongs—
O God, to whom vengeance belongs,
shine forth!
2 Rise up, O Judge of the earth;
Render punishment to the proud.
3 LORD, how long will the wicked,
How long will the wicked triumph?

4 They utter speech, *and* speak
insolent things;
All the workers of iniquity boast in
themselves.
5 They break in pieces Your people,
O LORD,
And afflict Your heritage.
6 They slay the widow and the
stranger,
And murder the fatherless.
7 Yet they say, "The LORD does not
see,
Nor does the God of Jacob
understand."

8 Understand, you senseless among the
people;
And *you* fools, when will you be
wise?
9 He who planted the ear, shall He not
hear?
He who formed the eye, shall He
not see?
10 He who instructs the nations, shall
He not correct,
He who teaches man knowledge?
11 The LORD knows the thoughts of
man,
That they *are* futile.

~ PROVERBS 22:24, 25 ~

24 Make no friendship with an angry
man,
And with a furious man do not go,
25 Lest you learn his ways
And set a snare for your soul.

~ ROMANS 10:1–21 ~

Brethren, my heart's desire and prayer to
God for Israel is that they may be saved.
2 For I bear them witness that they have a
zeal for God, but not according to knowledge. 3 For they being ignorant of God's
righteousness, and seeking to establish
their own righteousness, have not submitted to the righteousness of God. 4 For
Christ *is* the end of the law for righteousness to everyone who believes.

5 For Moses writes about the righteousness which is of the law, "The man who
does those things shall live by them." 6 But
the righteousness of faith speaks in this

way, "Do not say in your heart, 'Who will ascend into heaven?' " (that is, to bring Christ down *from above*) [7] or, " 'Who will descend into the abyss?' " (that is, to bring Christ up from the dead). [8] But what does it say? "The word is near you, in your mouth and in your heart" (that is, the word of faith which we preach): [9] that if you confess with your mouth the Lord Jesus and believe in your heart that God has raised Him from the dead, you will be saved. [10] For with the heart one believes unto righteousness, and with the mouth confession is made unto salvation. [11] For the Scripture says, "Whoever believes on Him will not be put to shame." [12] For there is no distinction between Jew and Greek, for the same Lord over all is rich to all who call upon Him. [13] For "whoever calls on the name of the LORD shall be saved."

[14] How then shall they call on Him in whom they have not believed? And how shall they believe in Him of whom they have not heard? And how shall they hear without a preacher? [15] And how shall they preach unless they are sent? As it is written:

> "How beautiful are the feet of
>   those who preach the gospel of
>   peace,
>   Who bring glad tidings of good
>   things!"

[16] But they have not all obeyed the gospel. For Isaiah says, "LORD, who has believed our report?" [17] So then faith *comes* by hearing, and hearing by the word of God.

[18] But I say, have they not heard? Yes indeed:

> "Their sound has gone out to all
>   the earth,
>   And their words to the ends of the
>   world."

[19] But I say, did Israel not know? First Moses says:

> "I will provoke you to jealousy by
>   *those who are* not a nation,
>   I will move you to anger by a
>   foolish nation."

[20] But Isaiah is very bold and says:

> "I was found by those who did not
>   seek Me;
>   I was made manifest to those who
>   did not ask for Me."

[21] But to Israel he says:

> "All day long I have stretched out
>   My hands
>   To a disobedient and contrary
>   people."

READING 223 · AUGUST 11

～ JOB 13:1—14:22 ～

[1] "Behold, my eye has seen all *this,*
    My ear has heard and understood
      it.
[2] What you know, I also know;
    I *am* not inferior to you.
[3] But I would speak to the Almighty,
    And I desire to reason with God.
[4] But you forgers of lies,
    You *are* all worthless physicians.
[5] Oh, that you would be silent,
    And it would be your wisdom!
[6] Now hear my reasoning,
    And heed the pleadings of my lips.
[7] Will you speak wickedly for God,
    And talk deceitfully for Him?

[8] Will you show partiality for Him?
    Will you contend for God?
[9] Will it be well when He searches
      you out?
    Or can you mock Him as one
      mocks a man?
[10] He will surely rebuke you
    If you secretly show partiality.
[11] Will not His excellence make you
      afraid,
    And the dread of Him fall upon
      you?
[12] Your platitudes *are* proverbs of
      ashes,
    Your defenses are defenses of clay.

13 "Hold your peace with me, and let
   me speak,
   Then let come on me what *may*!
14 Why do I take my flesh in my
   teeth,
   And put my life in my hands?
15 Though He slay me, yet will I
   trust Him.
   Even so, I will defend my own
   ways before Him.
16 He also *shall* be my salvation,
   For a hypocrite could not come
   before Him.
17 Listen carefully to my speech,
   And to my declaration with your
   ears.
18 See now, I have prepared *my* case,
   I know that I shall be vindicated.
19 Who *is* he *who* will contend with
   me?
   If now I hold my tongue, I perish.

20 "Only two *things* do not do to me,
   Then I will not hide myself from
   You:
21 Withdraw Your hand far from me,
   And let not the dread of You make
   me afraid.
22 Then call, and I will answer;
   Or let me speak, then You respond
   to me.
23 How many *are* my iniquities and
   sins?
   Make me know my transgression
   and my sin.
24 Why do You hide Your face,
   And regard me as Your enemy?
25 Will You frighten a leaf driven to
   and fro?
   And will You pursue dry stubble?
26 For You write bitter things against
   me,
   And make me inherit the iniquities
   of my youth.
27 You put my feet in the stocks,
   And watch closely all my paths.
   You set a limit for the soles of my
   feet.

28 "*Man* decays like a rotten thing,
   Like a garment that is moth-eaten.

14 "Man *who is* born of woman
   Is of few days and full of trouble.

2 He comes forth like a flower and
   fades away;
   He flees like a shadow and does
   not continue.
3 And do You open Your eyes on
   such a one,
   And bring me to judgment with
   Yourself?
4 Who can bring a clean *thing* out
   of an unclean?
   No one!
5 Since his days *are* determined,
   The number of his months *is* with
   You;
   You have appointed his limits, so
   that he cannot pass.
6 Look away from him that he may
   rest,
   Till like a hired man he finishes his
   day.

7 "For there is hope for a tree,
   If it is cut down, that it will sprout
   again,
   And that its tender shoots will not
   cease.
8 Though its root may grow old in
   the earth,
   And its stump may die in the
   ground,
9 *Yet* at the scent of water it will bud
   And bring forth branches like a
   plant.
10 But man dies and is laid away;
   Indeed he breathes his last
   And where *is* he?
11 *As* water disappears from the sea,
   And a river becomes parched and
   dries up,
12 So man lies down and does not
   rise.
   Till the heavens *are* no more,
   They will not awake
   Nor be roused from their sleep.

13 "Oh, that You would hide me in the
   grave,
   That You would conceal me until
   Your wrath is past,
   That You would appoint me a set
   time, and remember me!
14 If a man dies, shall he live *again*?
   All the days of my hard service I
   will wait,
   Till my change comes.

Quiet Communication

Author and pastor's wife Colleen Townsend Evans has written, "Silence need not be awkward or embarrassing, for to be with one you love, without the need for words, is a beautiful and satisfying form of communication.

"I remember times when our children used to come running to me, all of them chattering at once about the events of their day — and it was wonderful to have them share their feelings with me. But there were also the times when they came to me wanting only to be held, to have me stroke their heads and caress them into sleep. And so it is, sometimes, with us and with God our Father."

Don't force your child to talk to you. Give him the respect and "space" to remain silent. Sometimes children need to work out their own ideas and opinions in quiet before voicing them. On the other hand, when he does talk, take time to listen intently, carefully, and kindly. In so doing, your child will know that he can talk to you whenever he wants or needs to, and you can rest assured that his silence is not rooted in suspicion or fear.

Communication goes far beyond words. We communicate to our children, and others, through our attitudes and actions as well.

15 You shall call, and I will answer
　　　You;
　　　You shall desire the work of Your
　　　　hands.
16 For now You number my steps,
　　　But do not watch over my sin.
17 My transgression *is* sealed up in a
　　　bag,
　　　And You cover my iniquity.

18 "But *as* a mountain falls *and*
　　　crumbles away,
　　　And *as* a rock is moved from its
　　　　place;
19 *As* water wears away stones,
　　　And as torrents wash away the soil
　　　　of the earth;
　　　So You destroy the hope of man.
20 You prevail forever against him,
　　　and he passes on;
　　　You change his countenance and
　　　　send him away.
21 His sons come to honor, and he
　　　does not know *it;*
　　　They are brought low, and he does
　　　　not perceive *it.*
22 But his flesh will be in pain over it,
　　　And his soul will mourn over it."

～ PSALM 94:12–19 ～

12 Blessed *is* the man whom You
　　　instruct, O LORD,
　　　And teach out of Your law,
13 That You may give him rest from the
　　　days of adversity,
　　　Until the pit is dug for the wicked.
14 For the LORD will not cast off His
　　　people,
　　　Nor will He forsake His inheritance.
15 But judgment will return to
　　　righteousness,
　　　And all the upright in heart will
　　　　follow it.
16 Who will rise up for me against the
　　　evildoers?
　　　Who will stand up for me against the
　　　　workers of iniquity?
17 Unless the LORD *had been* my help,
　　　My soul would soon have settled in
　　　　silence.
18 If I say, "My foot slips,"
　　　Your mercy, O LORD, will hold me
　　　　up.

19 In the multitude of my anxieties
　　　within me,
　　　Your comforts delight my soul.

～ PROVERBS 22:26, 27 ～

26 Do not be one of those who shakes
　　　hands in a pledge,
　　　One of those who is surety for debts;
27 If you have nothing *with which* to
　　　pay,
　　　Why should he take away your bed
　　　　from under you?

～ ROMANS 11:1–18 ～

I say then, has God cast away His people?
Certainly not! For I also am an Israelite,
of the seed of Abraham, *of* the tribe of
Benjamin. 2 God has not cast away His
people whom He foreknew. Or do you
not know what the Scripture says of Elijah, how he pleads with God against Israel, saying, 3 "LORD, they have killed Your
prophets and torn down Your altars, and
I alone am left, and they seek my life"?
4 But what does the divine response say
to him? "I have reserved for Myself seven
thousand men who have not bowed the
knee to Baal." 5 Even so then, at this
present time there is a remnant according
to the election of grace. 6 And if by grace,
then *it is* no longer of works; otherwise
grace is no longer grace. But if *it is* of
works, it is no longer grace; otherwise
work is no longer work.
7 What then? Israel has not obtained
what it seeks; but the elect have obtained
it, and the rest were blinded. 8 Just as it is
written:

　　　"God has given them a spirit of
　　　　stupor,
　　　Eyes that they should not see
　　　And ears that they should not
　　　　hear,
　　　To this very day."

9 And David says:

　　　"Let their table become a snare and
　　　　a trap,
　　　A stumbling block and a
　　　　recompense to them.

¹⁰ Let their eyes be darkened, so that
    they do not see,
    And bow down their back
    always."

¹¹ I say then, have they stumbled that they should fall? Certainly not! But through their fall, to provoke them to jealousy, salvation *has come* to the Gentiles. ¹² Now if their fall *is* riches for the world, and their failure riches for the Gentiles, how much more their fullness!

¹³ For I speak to you Gentiles; inasmuch as I am an apostle to the Gentiles, I magnify my ministry, ¹⁴ if by any means I may provoke to jealousy *those who are* my flesh and save some of them. ¹⁵ For if their being cast away *is* the reconciling of the world, what *will* their acceptance *be* but life from the dead?

¹⁶ For if the firstfruit *is* holy, the lump *is* also *holy;* and if the root *is* holy, so *are* the branches. ¹⁷ And if some of the branches were broken off, and you, being a wild olive tree, were grafted in among them, and with them became a partaker of the root and fatness of the olive tree, ¹⁸ do not boast against the branches. But if you do boast, *remember that* you do not support the root, but the root supports you.

∼ JOB 15:1—16:22 ∼

Then Eliphaz the Temanite answered and said:

² "Should a wise man answer with
    empty knowledge,
    And fill himself with the east
    wind?
³ Should he reason with
    unprofitable talk,
    Or by speeches with which he can
    do no good?
⁴ Yes, you cast off fear,
    And restrain prayer before God.
⁵ For your iniquity teaches your
    mouth,
    And you choose the tongue of the
    crafty.
⁶ Your own mouth condemns you,
    and not I;
    Yes, your own lips testify against
    you.

⁷ "Are you the first man *who* was
    born?
    Or were you made before the
    hills?
⁸ Have you heard the counsel of
    God?
    Do you limit wisdom to yourself?
⁹ What do you know that we do not
    know?

What do you understand that *is*
    not in us?
¹⁰ Both the gray-haired and the aged
    are among us,
    Much older than your father.
¹¹ *Are* the consolations of God too
    small for you,
    And the word *spoken* gently with
    you?
¹² Why does your heart carry you
    away,
    And what do your eyes wink at,
¹³ That you turn your spirit against
    God,
    And let *such* words go out of your
    mouth?

¹⁴ "What *is* man, that he could be
    pure?
    And *he who is* born of a woman,
    that he could be righteous?
¹⁵ If *God* puts no trust in His saints,
    And the heavens are not pure in
    His sight,
¹⁶ How much less man, *who is*
    abominable and filthy,
    Who drinks iniquity like water!

¹⁷ "I will tell you, hear me;
    What I have seen I will declare,
¹⁸ What wise men have told,

Not hiding *anything received* from
their fathers,

¹⁹ To whom alone the land was
given,
And no alien passed among them:

²⁰ The wicked man writhes with pain
all *his* days,
And the number of years is hidden
from the oppressor.

²¹ Dreadful sounds *are* in his ears;
In prosperity the destroyer comes
upon him.

²² He does not believe that he will
return from darkness,
For a sword is waiting for him.

²³ He wanders about for bread,
saying, 'Where *is it?'*
He knows that a day of darkness is
ready at his hand.

²⁴ Trouble and anguish make him
afraid;
They overpower him, like a king
ready for battle.

²⁵ For he stretches out his hand
against God,
And acts defiantly against the
Almighty,

²⁶ Running stubbornly against Him
With his strong, embossed shield.

²⁷ "Though he has covered his face
with his fatness,
And made *his* waist heavy with
fat,

²⁸ He dwells in desolate cities,
In houses which no one inhabits,
Which are destined to become
ruins.

²⁹ He will not be rich,
Nor will his wealth continue,
Nor will his possessions
overspread the earth.

³⁰ He will not depart from darkness;
The flame will dry out his
branches,
And by the breath of His mouth
he will go away.

³¹ Let him not trust in futile *things,*
deceiving himself,
For futility will be his reward.

³² It will be accomplished before his
time,
And his branch will not be green.

³³ He will shake off his unripe grape
like a vine,

And cast off his blossom like an
olive tree.

³⁴ For the company of hypocrites
will be barren,
And fire will consume the tents of
bribery.

³⁵ They conceive trouble and bring
forth futility;
Their womb prepares deceit."

16

Then Job answered and said:

² "I have heard many such things;
Miserable comforters *are* you all!

³ Shall words of wind have
an end?
Or what provokes you that you
answer?

⁴ I also could speak as you *do,*
If your soul were in my soul's
place.
I could heap up words against
you,
And shake my head at you;

⁵ *But* I would strengthen you with
my mouth,
And the comfort of my lips would
relieve *your grief.*

⁶ "Though I speak, my grief is not
relieved;
And *if* I remain silent, how am I
eased?

⁷ But now He has worn me out;
You have made desolate all my
company.

⁸ You have shriveled me up,
And it is a witness *against me;*
My leanness rises up against me
And bears witness to my face.

⁹ He tears *me* in His wrath, and
hates me;
He gnashes at me with His
teeth;
My adversary sharpens His gaze
on me.

¹⁰ They gape at me with their
mouth,
They strike me reproachfully on
the cheek,
They gather together against me.

¹¹ God has delivered me to the
ungodly,
And turned me over to the hands
of the wicked.

Entrance Exam

The order from the head teacher was abrupt: "The classroom needs sweeping. Take the broom and sweep it."

Young Booker T. Washington knew this was his chance. He swept the room three times, and then dusted the furniture four times. When the head teacher came back to evaluate his work, she inspected the floor closely and then used her handkerchief to rub the woodwork around the walls, the table, and the students' benches. When she could not find one speck of dust anywhere in the room, she said quietly, "I guess you will do to enter this institution."

Cleaning a classroom was Booker T. Washington's entrance examination to Hampton Institute in Virginia. In later years, he would recall this as the turning point in his life. He wrote in his autobiography, *Up From Slavery,* "I have passed several examinations since then, but I have always felt that this was the best one I ever passed."

Slacking off, goofing off, and dozing off rarely open doors of opportunity. Those doors are best opened and entered into by consistent, excellent effort. Give your family, your job, your world, your God your best effort today!

¹² I was at ease, but He has shattered
   me;
   He also has taken *me* by my neck,
      and shaken me to pieces;
   He has set me up for His target,
¹³ His archers surround me.
   He pierces my heart and does not
      pity;
   He pours out my gall on the
      ground.
¹⁴ He breaks me with wound upon
      wound;
   He runs at me like a warrior.

¹⁵ "I have sewn sackcloth over my
      skin,
   And laid my head in the dust.
¹⁶ My face is flushed from weeping,
   And on my eyelids *is* the shadow
      of death;
¹⁷ Although no violence *is* in my
      hands,
   And my prayer *is* pure.

¹⁸ "O earth, do not cover my blood,
   And let my cry have no *resting*
      place!
¹⁹ Surely even now my witness *is* in
      heaven,
   And my evidence *is* on high.
²⁰ My friends scorn me;
   My eyes pour out *tears* to God.
²¹ Oh, that one might plead for a
      man with God,
   As a man *pleads* for his neighbor!
²² For when a few years are finished,
   I shall go the way of no return.

∼ PSALM 94:20–23 ∼

²⁰ Shall the throne of iniquity, which
      devises evil by law,
   Have fellowship with You?
²¹ They gather together against the life
      of the righteous,
   And condemn innocent blood.
²² But the LORD has been my defense,
   And my God the rock of my refuge.
²³ He has brought on them their own
      iniquity,
   And shall cut them off in their own
      wickedness;
   The LORD our God shall cut them
      off.

∼ PROVERBS 22:28, 29 ∼

²⁸ Do not remove the ancient
      landmark
   Which your fathers have set.

²⁹ Do you see a man *who* excels in his
      work?
   He will stand before kings;
   He will not stand before unknown
   men.

∼ ROMANS 11:19–36 ∼

You will say then, "Branches were broken off that I might be grafted in." ²⁰ Well *said.* Because of unbelief they were broken off, and you stand by faith. Do not be haughty, but fear. ²¹ For if God did not spare the natural branches, He may not spare you either. ²² Therefore consider the goodness and severity of God: on those who fell, severity; but toward you, goodness, if you continue in *His* goodness. Otherwise you also will be cut off. ²³ And they also, if they do not continue in unbelief, will be grafted in, for God is able to graft them in again. ²⁴ For if you were cut out of the olive tree which is wild by nature, and were grafted contrary to nature into a cultivated olive tree, how much more will these, who *are* natural *branches,* be grafted into their own olive tree?

²⁵ For I do not desire, brethren, that you should be ignorant of this mystery, lest you should be wise in your own opinion, that blindness in part has happened to Israel until the fullness of the Gentiles has come in. ²⁶ And so all Israel will be saved, as it is written:

   "The Deliverer will come out of
      Zion,
   And He will turn away
      ungodliness from Jacob;
²⁷ For this *is* My covenant with
      them,
   When I take away their sins."

²⁸ Concerning the gospel *they are* enemies for your sake, but concerning the

election *they are* beloved for the sake of the fathers. ²⁹ For the gifts and the calling of God *are* irrevocable. ³⁰ For as you were once disobedient to God, yet have now obtained mercy through their disobedience, ³¹ even so these also have now been disobedient, that through the mercy shown you they also may obtain mercy. ³² For God has committed them all to disobedience, that He might have mercy on all.

³³ Oh, the depth of the riches both of the wisdom and knowledge of God! How unsearchable *are* His judgments and His ways past finding out!

³⁴ "For who has known the mind of
    the LORD?
    Or who has become His
        counselor?"
³⁵ "Or who has first given to Him
    And it shall be repaid to him?"

³⁶ For of Him and through Him and to Him *are* all things, to whom *be* glory forever. Amen.

READING 225 · AUGUST 13

～ JOB 17:1—18:21 ～

¹ "My spirit is broken,
    My days are extinguished,
    The grave *is ready* for me.
² *Are* not mockers with me?
    And does not my eye dwell on
        their provocation?

³ "Now put down a pledge for me
        with Yourself.
    Who *is* he *who* will shake hands
        with me?
⁴ For You have hidden their heart
        from understanding;
    Therefore You will not exalt *them.*
⁵ He who speaks flattery to *his*
        friends,
    Even the eyes of his children will
        fail.

⁶ "But He has made me a byword of
        the people,
    And I have become one in whose
        face men spit.
⁷ My eye has also grown dim
        because of sorrow,
    And all my members *are* like
        shadows.
⁸ Upright *men* are astonished at
        this,
    And the innocent stirs himself up
        against the hypocrite.
⁹ Yet the righteous will hold to his
        way,
    And he who has clean hands will
        be stronger and stronger.

¹⁰ "But please, come back again, all of
        you,
    For I shall not find *one* wise *man*
        among you.
¹¹ My days are past,
    My purposes are broken off,
    Even the thoughts of my heart.
¹² They change the night into day;
    'The light *is* near,' *they say,* in the
        face of darkness.
¹³ If I wait *for* the grave *as* my house,
    If I make my bed in the darkness,
¹⁴ If I say to corruption, 'You *are* my
        father,'
    And to the worm, 'You *are* my
        mother and my sister,'
¹⁵ Where then *is* my hope?
    As for my hope, who can see it?
¹⁶ *Will* they go down to the gates of
        Sheol?
    Shall *we have* rest together in the
        dust?"

18 Then Bildad the Shuhite answered and said:

² "How long *till* you put an end to
        words?
    Gain understanding, and
        afterward we will speak.
³ Why are we counted as beasts,
    And regarded as stupid in your
        sight?
⁴ You who tear yourself in anger,
    Shall the earth be forsaken for
        you?

Or shall the rock be removed
   from its place?

5 "The light of the wicked indeed
      goes out,
   And the flame of his fire does not
      shine.
6 The light is dark in his tent,
   And his lamp beside him is put
      out.
7 The steps of his strength are
      shortened,
   And his own counsel casts him
      down.
8 For he is cast into a net by his own
      feet,
   And he walks into a snare.
9 The net takes *him* by the heel,
   And a snare lays hold of him.
10 A noose *is* hidden for him on the
      ground,
   And a trap for him in the road.
11 Terrors frighten him on
      every side,
   And drive him to his feet.
12 His strength is starved,
   And destruction *is* ready at his
      side.
13 It devours patches of his skin;
   The firstborn of death devours his
      limbs.
14 He is uprooted from the shelter of
      his tent,
   And they parade him before the
      king of terrors.
15 They dwell in his tent *who are*
      none of his;
   Brimstone is scattered on his
      dwelling.
16 His roots are dried out below,
   And his branch withers above.
17 The memory of him perishes from
      the earth,
   And he has no name among the
      renowned.
18 He is driven from light into
      darkness,
   And chased out of the world.
19 He has neither son nor posterity
      among his people,
   Nor any remaining in his
      dwellings.
20 Those in the west are astonished
      at his day,
   As those in the east are frightened.

21 Surely such *are* the dwellings of
      the wicked,
   And this *is* the place *of him who*
      does not know God."

∼ PSALM 95:1–5 ∼

1 Oh come, let us sing to the LORD!
   Let us shout joyfully to the Rock of
      our salvation.
2 Let us come before His presence
      with thanksgiving;
   Let us shout joyfully to Him with
      psalms.
3 For the LORD *is* the great God,
   And the great King above all gods.
4 In His hand *are* the deep places of
      the earth;
   The heights of the hills *are* His also.
5 The sea *is* His, for He made it;
   And His hands formed the dry *land*.

∼ PROVERBS 23:1–3 ∼

1 When you sit down to eat with a
      ruler,
   Consider carefully what *is* before
      you;
2 And put a knife to your throat
   If you *are* a man given to appetite.
3 Do not desire his delicacies,
   For they *are* deceptive food.

∼ ROMANS 12:1–21 ∼

I beseech you therefore, brethren, by the
mercies of God, that you present your
bodies a living sacrifice, holy, acceptable
to God, *which is* your reasonable service.
2 And do not be conformed to this world,
but be transformed by the renewing of
your mind, that you may prove what *is*
that good and acceptable and perfect will
of God.

3 For I say, through the grace given to
me, to everyone who is among you, not
to think *of himself* more highly than he
ought to think, but to think soberly, as
God has dealt to each one a measure of
faith. 4 For as we have many members in
one body, but all the members do not have
the same function, 5 so we, *being* many,
are one body in Christ, and individually
members of one another. 6 Having then

Saints in Circulation

During the reign of Oliver Cromwell, the British government ran low on the silver they used to make their coins. Lord Cromwell sent his men to a local cathedral in search of silver. They reported, "The only silver we could find is in the statues of the saints standing in the corners." "Good!" Cromwell replied, "We'll melt down the saints and put them into circulation."

Circulating melted-down saints? It's an unusual metaphor, but good theology! The Lord never intended for us to be silver-plated, highly polished ornaments solely for liturgical use. He intends for us to give our all — our very life's blood, talent, sweat, resources, time, and yes, silver — to wage war against evil out in the trenches of life.

A man once prayed, "Lord, I want to be Your man, so I give You my money, my car, and my home." Then he added, "I bet it's been a while since someone gave so much." The Lord replied, "No. Not really."

The Lord wants far more than our material possessions. He wants our hearts, our prayers, our tears. He wants to be the object of our desire. The blood of Jesus can't be bought. It can only be received — by giving nothing less than our all.

> I beseech you therefore, brethren, by the mercies of God, that you present your bodies a living sacrifice, holy, acceptable to God, which is your reasonable service.
>
> *Romans 12:1*

gifts differing according to the grace that is given to us, *let us use them:* if prophecy, *let us prophesy* in proportion to our faith; [7] or ministry, *let us use it* in *our* ministering; he who teaches, in teaching; [8] he who exhorts, in exhortation; he who gives, with liberality; he who leads, with diligence; he who shows mercy, with cheerfulness.

[9] *Let* love *be* without hypocrisy. Abhor what is evil. Cling to what is good. [10] *Be* kindly affectionate to one another with brotherly love, in honor giving preference to one another; [11] not lagging in diligence, fervent in spirit, serving the Lord; [12] rejoicing in hope, patient in tribulation, continuing steadfastly in prayer; [13] distributing to the needs of the saints, given to hospitality.

[14] Bless those who persecute you; bless and do not curse. [15] Rejoice with those who rejoice, and weep with those who weep. [16] Be of the same mind toward one another. Do not set your mind on high things, but associate with the humble. Do not be wise in your own opinion.

[17] Repay no one evil for evil. Have regard for good things in the sight of all men. [18] If it is possible, as much as depends on you, live peaceably with all men. [19] Beloved, do not avenge yourselves, but *rather* give place to wrath; for it is written, "Vengeance *is* Mine, I will repay," says the Lord. [20] Therefore

"If your enemy is hungry, feed him;
If he is thirsty, give him a drink;
For in so doing you will heap coals
of fire on his head."

[21] Do not be overcome by evil, but overcome evil with good.

READING 226 · AUGUST 14

～ JOB 19:1—20:29 ～

Then Job answered and said:

[2] "How long will you torment my soul,
And break me in pieces with words?
[3] These ten times you have reproached me;
You are not ashamed *that* you have wronged me.
[4] And if indeed I have erred,
My error remains with me.
[5] If indeed you exalt *yourselves* against me,
And plead my disgrace against me,
[6] Know then that God has wronged me,
And has surrounded me with His net.

[7] "If I cry out concerning wrong, I am not heard.
If I cry aloud, *there is* no justice.
[8] He has fenced up my way, so that I cannot pass;
And He has set darkness in my paths.

[9] He has stripped me of my glory,
And taken the crown *from* my head.
[10] He breaks me down on every side,
And I am gone;
My hope He has uprooted like a tree.
[11] He has also kindled His wrath against me,
And He counts me as *one of* His enemies.
[12] His troops come together
And build up their road against me;
They encamp all around my tent.

[13] "He has removed my brothers far from me,
And my acquaintances are completely estranged from me.
[14] My relatives have failed,
And my close friends have forgotten me.
[15] Those who dwell in my house, and my maidservants,
Count me as a stranger;

The Secret of His Happiness

A fable is told of a young orphan boy who had no family and no one to love him. Feeling sad and lonely, he was walking through a meadow one day when he saw a small butterfly caught in a thorn bush. The more the butterfly struggled to free itself, the deeper the thorns cut into its fragile body. The boy carefully released the butterfly, but instead of flying away, right before his eyes the butterfly transformed into an angel.

The boy rubbed his eyes in disbelief as the angel said, "For your wonderful kindness, I will do whatever you would like." The little boy thought for a moment and then said, "I want to be happy!" The angel replied, "Very well," and then leaned toward him, whispered in his ear, and vanished.

As the little boy grew up, there was no one in the land as happy as he. When people asked him the secret of his happiness, he would only smile and say, "I listened to an angel when I was a little boy."

On his deathbed, his neighbors rallied around him and asked him to divulge the key to his happiness before he died. The old man finally told them: "The angel told me that everyone, no matter how secure they seemed, no matter how old or young, how rich or poor, had need of me."

You have something to give to everyone you come in contact with today. It may be as simple as a friendly smile or a kind word. Whatever it may be, know that you are needed by God to spread His love. There's not a person in the world who doesn't need it.

I am an alien in their sight.

16 I call my servant, but he gives no answer;
I beg him with my mouth.

17 My breath is offensive to my wife,
And I am repulsive to the children of my own body.

18 Even young children despise me;
I arise, and they speak against me.

19 All my close friends abhor me,
And those whom I love have turned against me.

20 My bone clings to my skin and to my flesh,
And I have escaped by the skin of my teeth.

21 "Have pity on me, have pity on me, O you my friends,
For the hand of God has struck me!

22 Why do you persecute me as God *does,*
And are not satisfied with my flesh?

23 "Oh, that my words were written!
Oh, that they were inscribed in a book!

24 That they were engraved on a rock
With an iron pen and lead, forever!

25 For I know *that* my Redeemer lives,
And He shall stand at last on the earth;

26 And after my skin is destroyed, this *I know,*
That in my flesh I shall see God,

27 Whom I shall see for myself,
And my eyes shall behold, and not another.
How my heart yearns within me!

28 If you should say, 'How shall we persecute him?'—
Since the root of the matter is found in me,

29 Be afraid of the sword for yourselves;
For wrath *brings* the punishment of the sword,

That you may know *there is* a judgment."

20 Then Zophar the Naamathite answered and said:

2 "Therefore my anxious thoughts make me answer,
Because of the turmoil within me.

3 I have heard the rebuke that reproaches me,
And the spirit of my understanding causes me to answer.

4 "Do you *not* know this of old,
Since man was placed on earth,

5 That the triumphing of the wicked is short,
And the joy of the hypocrite is *but* for a moment?

6 Though his haughtiness mounts up to the heavens,
And his head reaches to the clouds,

7 *Yet* he will perish forever like his own refuse;
Those who have seen him will say, 'Where is he?'

8 He will fly away like a dream, and not be found;
Yes, he will be chased away like a vision of the night.

9 The eye *that* saw him will *see him* no more,
Nor will his place behold him anymore.

10 His children will seek the favor of the poor,
And his hands will restore his wealth.

11 His bones are full of his youthful vigor,
But it will lie down with him in the dust.

12 "Though evil is sweet in his mouth,
And he hides it under his tongue,

13 *Though* he spares it and does not forsake it,
But still keeps it in his mouth,

14 *Yet* his food in his stomach turns sour;
It becomes cobra venom within him.

15 He swallows down riches
And vomits them up again;
God casts them out of his belly.
16 He will suck the poison
of cobras;
The viper's tongue will slay him.
17 He will not see the streams,
The rivers flowing with honey and
cream.
18 He will restore that for which he
labored,
And will not swallow *it* down;
From the proceeds of business
He will get no enjoyment.
19 For he has oppressed *and* forsaken
the poor,
He has violently seized a house
which he did not build.

20 "Because he knows no quietness in
his heart,
He will not save anything he
desires.
21 Nothing is left for him to eat;
Therefore his well-being will not
last.
22 In his self-sufficiency he will be in
distress;
Every hand of misery will come
against him.
23 *When* he is about to fill his
stomach,
God will cast on him the fury of
His wrath,
And will rain *it* on him while he is
eating.
24 He will flee from the iron
weapon;
A bronze bow will pierce him
through.
25 It is drawn, and comes out of the
body;
Yes, the glittering *point comes* out
of his gall.
Terrors *come* upon him;
26 Total darkness *is* reserved for his
treasures.
An unfanned fire will consume
him;
It shall go ill with him who is left
in his tent.
27 The heavens will reveal his
iniquity,
And the earth will rise up against
him.

28 The increase of his house will
depart,
And his goods will flow away in
the day of His wrath.
29 This *is* the portion from God for a
wicked man,
The heritage appointed to him by
God."

~ PSALM 95:6–11 ~

6 Oh come, let us worship and bow
down;
Let us kneel before the LORD our
Maker.
7 For He *is* our God,
And we *are* the people of His
pasture,
And the sheep of His hand.

Today, if you will hear His voice:
8 "Do not harden your hearts, as in the
rebellion,
As *in* the day of trial in the
wilderness,
9 When your fathers tested Me;
They tried Me, though they saw My
work.
10 For forty years I was grieved with
that generation,
And said, 'It *is* a people who go
astray in their hearts,
And they do not know My ways.'
11 So I swore in My wrath,
'They shall not enter My rest.' "

~ PROVERBS 23:4, 5 ~

4 Do not overwork to be rich;
Because of your own understanding,
cease!
5 Will you set your eyes on that which
is not?
For *riches* certainly make themselves
wings;
They fly away like an eagle *toward*
heaven.

~ ROMANS 13:1–14 ~

Let every soul be subject to the governing
authorities. For there is no authority except from God, and the authorities that
exist are appointed by God. 2 Therefore

whoever resists the authority resists the ordinance of God, and those who resist will bring judgment on themselves. ³ For rulers are not a terror to good works, but to evil. Do you want to be unafraid of the authority? Do what is good, and you will have praise from the same. ⁴ For he is God's minister to you for good. But if you do evil, be afraid; for he does not bear the sword in vain; for he is God's minister, an avenger to *execute* wrath on him who practices evil. ⁵ Therefore *you* must be subject, not only because of wrath but also for conscience' sake. ⁶ For because of this you also pay taxes, for they are God's ministers attending continually to this very thing. ⁷ Render therefore to all their due: taxes to whom taxes *are due,* customs to whom customs, fear to whom fear, honor to whom honor.

⁸ Owe no one anything except to love one another, for he who loves another has fulfilled the law. ⁹ For the commandments, "You shall not commit adultery," "You shall not murder," "You shall not steal," "You shall not bear false witness," "You shall not covet," and if *there is* any other commandment, are *all* summed up in this saying, namely, "You shall love your neighbor as yourself." ¹⁰ Love does no harm to a neighbor; therefore love *is* the fulfillment of the law.

¹¹ And *do* this, knowing the time, that now *it is* high time to awake out of sleep; for now our salvation *is* nearer than when we *first* believed. ¹² The night is far spent, the day is at hand. Therefore let us cast off the works of darkness, and let us put on the armor of light. ¹³ Let us walk properly, as in the day, not in revelry and drunkenness, not in lewdness and lust, not in strife and envy. ¹⁴ But put on the Lord Jesus Christ, and make no provision for the flesh, to *fulfill its* lusts.

READING 227 · AUGUST 15

∼ JOB 21:1—22:30 ∼

Then Job answered and said:

² "Listen carefully to my speech,
And let this be your consolation.
³ Bear with me that I may speak,
And after I have spoken, keep
mocking.

⁴ "As for me, *is* my complaint against
man?
And if *it were,* why should I not be
impatient?
⁵ Look at me and be astonished;
Put *your* hand over *your* mouth.
⁶ Even when I remember I am
terrified,
And trembling takes hold of my
flesh.
⁷ Why do the wicked live *and*
become old,
Yes, become mighty in power?
⁸ Their descendants are established
with them in their sight,
And their offspring before their
eyes.
⁹ Their houses *are* safe from fear,

Neither *is* the rod of God upon
them.
¹⁰ Their bull breeds without
failure;
Their cow calves without
miscarriage.
¹¹ They send forth their little ones
like a flock,
And their children dance.
¹² They sing to the tambourine and
harp,
And rejoice to the sound of the
flute.
¹³ They spend their days in wealth,
And in a moment go down to the
grave.
¹⁴ Yet they say to God, 'Depart from
us,
For we do not desire the
knowledge of Your ways.
¹⁵ Who *is* the Almighty, that we
should serve Him?
And what profit do we have if we
pray to Him?'
¹⁶ Indeed their prosperity *is* not in
their hand;

Little Annie

For as he thinks
in his heart,
so is he.
"Eat and drink!"
he says to you,
but his heart is
not with you.

Proverbs 23:7

A number of years ago, a young girl known as "Little Annie" was locked in the dungeon of a mental institution outside Boston — the only place, said the doctors, for the hopelessly insane. At times, Annie behaved like an animal, attacking anyone who came close to her cage. At other times, she just sat in a daze.

An elderly nurse held hope for all God's children and she began taking her lunch break in the dungeon, just outside Little Annie's cage. She hoped to somehow communicate love to her. One day she left her dessert — a brownie — next to Annie's cage. There was no response from Annie, but the next day, the nurse found the brownie had been eaten. Every Thursday thereafter, she brought a brownie to Annie.

As the weeks passed, doctors noticed a change in Little Annie. After several months, they moved her upstairs. And eventually, the day came when this "hopeless case" was told she could return home. By that time, Annie was an adult, however, and she chose to stay at the institution to help others. One of those she cared for, taught, and nurtured was Helen Keller. Little Annie's full and proper name was Anne Sullivan.

Your children become the embodiment of the love you pour into them. Pour generously!

The counsel of the wicked is far
   from me.

17 "How often is the lamp of the
   wicked put out?
   How often does their destruction
     come upon them,
   The sorrows *God* distributes in
     His anger?
18 They are like straw before the
   wind,
   And like chaff that a storm carries
     away.
19 *They say,* 'God lays up one's
   iniquity for his children';
   Let Him recompense him, that he
     may know *it*.
20 Let his eyes see his destruction,
   And let him drink of the wrath of
     the Almighty.
21 For what does he care about his
   household after him,
   When the number of his months is
     cut in half?

22 "Can *anyone* teach God
   knowledge,
   Since He judges those on high?
23 One dies in his full strength,
   Being wholly at ease and secure;
24 His pails are full of milk,
   And the marrow of his bones is
     moist.
25 Another man dies in the bitterness
   of his soul,
   Never having eaten with pleasure.
26 They lie down alike in the dust,
   And worms cover them.

27 "Look, I know your thoughts,
   And the schemes *with which* you
     would wrong me.
28 For you say,
   'Where *is* the house of the prince?
   And where *is* the tent,
   The dwelling place of the wicked?'
29 Have you not asked those who
   travel the road?
   And do you not know their signs?
30 For the wicked are reserved for
   the day of doom;
   They shall be brought out on the
     day of wrath.
31 Who condemns his way to his
   face?

And who repays him *for what* he
   has done?
32 Yet he shall be brought to the
   grave,
   And a vigil kept over the tomb.
33 The clods of the valley shall be
   sweet to him;
   Everyone shall follow him,
   As countless *have gone* before
     him.
34 How then can you comfort me
   with empty words,
   Since falsehood remains in your
     answers?"

22 Then Eliphaz the Temanite answered and said:

2 "Can a man be profitable to God,
   Though he who is wise may be
     profitable to himself?
3 *Is it* any pleasure to the Almighty
   that you are righteous?
   Or *is it* gain *to Him* that you make
     your ways blameless?

4 "Is it because of your fear of Him
   that He corrects you,
   And enters into judgment with
     you?
5 *Is* not your wickedness great,
   And your iniquity without end?
6 For you have taken pledges from
   your brother for no reason,
   And stripped the naked of their
     clothing.
7 You have not given the weary
   water to drink,
   And you have withheld bread
     from the hungry.
8 But the mighty man possessed the
   land,
   And the honorable man dwelt in
     it.
9 You have sent widows away
   empty,
   And the strength of the fatherless
     was crushed.
10 Therefore snares *are* all around
   you,
   And sudden fear troubles you,
11 Or darkness *so that* you cannot
   see;
   And an abundance of water covers
     you.

12 "Is not God in the height of
       heaven?
   And see the highest stars, how
       lofty they are!
13 And you say, 'What does God
       know?
   Can He judge through the deep
       darkness?
14 Thick clouds cover Him, so that
       He cannot see,
   And He walks above the circle of
       heaven.'
15 Will you keep to the old way
   Which wicked men have trod,
16 Who were cut down before their
       time,
   Whose foundations were swept
       away by a flood?
17 They said to God, 'Depart from
       us!
   What can the Almighty do to
       them?'
18 Yet He filled their houses with
       good *things*;
   But the counsel of the wicked is
       far from me.

19 "The righteous see *it* and are glad,
   And the innocent laugh at them:
20 'Surely our adversaries are cut
       down,
   And the fire consumes their
       remnant.'

21 "Now acquaint yourself with Him,
       and be at peace;
   Thereby good will come to you.
22 Receive, please, instruction from
       His mouth,
   And lay up His words in your
       heart.
23 If you return to the Almighty, you
       will be built up;
   You will remove iniquity far from
       your tents.
24 Then you will lay your gold in the
       dust,
   And the *gold* of Ophir among the
       stones of the brooks.
25 Yes, the Almighty will be your
       gold
   And your precious silver;
26 For then you will have your
       delight in the Almighty,
   And lift up your face to God.

27 You will make your prayer to
       Him,
   He will hear you,
   And you will pay your vows.
28 You will also declare a thing,
   And it will be established for you;
   So light will shine on your ways.
29 When they cast *you* down, and
       you say, 'Exaltation *will come!*'
   Then He will save the humble
       person.
30 He will *even* deliver one who is
       not innocent;
   Yes, he will be delivered by the
       purity of your hands."

∼ PSALM 96:1–6 ∼

1 Oh, sing to the LORD a new song!
   Sing to the LORD, all the earth.
2 Sing to the LORD, bless His name;
   Proclaim the good news of His
       salvation from day to day.
3 Declare His glory among the
       nations,
   His wonders among all peoples.

4 For the LORD *is* great and greatly to
       be praised;
   He *is* to be feared above all gods.
5 For all the gods of the peoples *are*
       idols,
   But the LORD made the heavens.
6 Honor and majesty *are* before Him;
   Strength and beauty *are* in His
       sanctuary.

∼ PROVERBS 23:6–8 ∼

6 Do not eat the bread of a miser,
   Nor desire his delicacies;
7 For as he thinks in his heart, so *is* he.
   "Eat and drink!" he says to you,
   But his heart is not with you.
8 The morsel you have eaten, you will
       vomit up,
   And waste your pleasant words.

∼ ROMANS 14:1–23 ∼

Receive one who is weak in the faith, *but*
not to disputes over doubtful things. 2 For
one believes he may eat all things, but he
who is weak eats *only* vegetables. 3 Let not
him who eats despise him who does not

eat, and let not him who does not eat judge him who eats; for God has received him. ⁴ Who are you to judge another's servant? To his own master he stands or falls. Indeed, he will be made to stand, for God is able to make him stand.

⁵ One person esteems *one* day above another; another esteems every day *alike*. Let each be fully convinced in his own mind. ⁶ He who observes the day, observes *it* to the Lord; and he who does not observe the day, to the Lord he does not observe *it*. He who eats, eats to the Lord, for he gives God thanks; and he who does not eat, to the Lord he does not eat, and gives God thanks. ⁷ For none of us lives to himself, and no one dies to himself. ⁸ For if we live, we live to the Lord; and if we die, we die to the Lord. Therefore, whether we live or die, we are the Lord's. ⁹ For to this end Christ died and rose and lived again, that He might be Lord of both the dead and the living. ¹⁰ But why do you judge your brother? Or why do you show contempt for your brother? For we shall all stand before the judgment seat of Christ. ¹¹ For it is written:

"As I live, says the LORD,
Every knee shall bow to Me,
And every tongue shall confess to
    God."

¹² So then each of us shall give account of himself to God. ¹³ Therefore let us not judge one another anymore, but rather resolve this, not to put a stumbling block or a cause to fall in *our* brother's way.

¹⁴ I know and am convinced by the Lord Jesus that *there is* nothing unclean of itself; but to him who considers anything to be unclean, to him *it is* unclean. ¹⁵ Yet if your brother is grieved because of *your* food, you are no longer walking in love. Do not destroy with your food the one for whom Christ died. ¹⁶ Therefore do not let your good be spoken of as evil; ¹⁷ for the kingdom of God is not eating and drinking, but righteousness and peace and joy in the Holy Spirit. ¹⁸ For he who serves Christ in these things *is* acceptable to God and approved by men.

¹⁹ Therefore let us pursue the things *which make* for peace and the things by which one may edify another. ²⁰ Do not destroy the work of God for the sake of food. All things indeed *are* pure, but *it is* evil for the man who eats with offense. ²¹ *It is* good neither to eat meat nor drink wine nor *do anything* by which your brother stumbles or is offended or is made weak. ²² Do you have faith? Have *it* to yourself before God. Happy *is* he who does not condemn himself in what he approves. ²³ But he who doubts is condemned if he eats, because *he does* not *eat* from faith; for whatever *is* not from faith is sin.

<hr>

READING 228 · AUGUST 16

~ JOB 23:1—25:6 ~

Then Job answered and said:

² "Even today my complaint is
    bitter;
My hand is listless because of my
    groaning.
³   Oh, that I knew where I might
    find Him,
That I might come to His seat!
⁴   I would present *my* case before
    Him,
And fill my mouth with
    arguments.
⁵   I would know the words *which*
    He would answer me,

And understand what He would
    say to me.
⁶   Would He contend with me in His
    great power?
No! But He would take *note* of
    me.
⁷   There the upright could reason
    with Him,
And I would be delivered forever
    from my Judge.

⁸   "Look, I go forward, but He is not
    there,
And backward, but I cannot
    perceive Him;

Listen

One day, an old woman went to Anthony Bloom and told him that while she had recited the prayer of Jesus for many years, she had never really experienced the presence of God.

Bloom replied, "How can God get a word in edgeways if you never stop talking? Give him a chance. Keep quiet."

"How can I do that?" she asked. He then gave her this advice, which he subsequently gave to many others. He advised her to tidy her room each day after breakfast, making it as pleasant as possible. Then, to sit down in a position where she could see the entire room, including the window that looked out on the garden. "When you have sat down, rest for a quarter of an hour in the presence of God, but take care not to pray," Bloom said. "Be as quiet as you can and as you obviously can't do *nothing*, knit before the Lord and tell me what happens." She returned several days later, happy to report that at long last she had felt the presence of God!

The Lord most often speaks gently — in a still, small voice — therefore, it takes a still, quiet heart to hear Him.

> I would know the words which He would answer me, and understand what He would say to me.
>
> *Job 23:5*

9 When He works on the left hand,
  I cannot behold *Him;*
  When He turns to the right hand,
  I cannot see *Him.*
10 But He knows the way that
  I take;
  When He has tested me, I shall
  come forth as gold.
11 My foot has held fast to His steps;
  I have kept His way and not
  turned aside.
12 I have not departed from the
  commandment of His lips;
  I have treasured the words of His
  mouth
  More than my necessary *food.*

13 "But He *is* unique, and who can
  make Him change?
  And *whatever* His soul desires,
  that He does.
14 For He performs *what is*
  appointed for me,
  And many such *things are* with
  Him.
15 Therefore I am terrified at His
  presence;
  When I consider *this,* I am afraid
  of Him.
16 For God made my heart weak,
  And the Almighty terrifies me;
17 Because I was not cut off from the
  presence of darkness,
  And He did *not* hide deep
  darkness from my face.

24 "*Since* times are not hidden from
  the Almighty,
  Why do those who know Him see
  not His days?

2 "*Some* remove landmarks;
  They seize flocks violently and
  feed *on them;*
3 They drive away the donkey of
  the fatherless;
  They take the widow's ox as a
  pledge.
4 They push the needy off the road;
  All the poor of the land are forced
  to hide.
5 Indeed, *like* wild donkeys in the
  desert,
  They go out to their work,
  searching for food.

The wilderness *yields* food for
  them *and* for *their* children.
6 They gather their fodder in the
  field
  And glean in the vineyard of the
  wicked.
7 They spend the night naked,
  without clothing,
  And have no covering in the cold.
8 They are wet with the showers of
  the mountains,
  And huddle around the rock for
  want of shelter.

9 "*Some* snatch the fatherless from
  the breast,
  And take a pledge from the poor.
10 They cause *the poor* to go naked,
  without clothing;
  And they take away the sheaves
  from the hungry.
11 They press out oil within their
  walls,
  And tread winepresses, yet suffer
  thirst.
12 The dying groan in the city,
  And the souls of the wounded cry
  out;
  Yet God does not charge *them*
  with wrong.

13 "There are those who rebel against
  the light;
  They do not know its ways
  Nor abide in its paths.
14 The murderer rises with the light;
  He kills the poor and needy;
  And in the night he is like
  a thief.
15 The eye of the adulterer waits for
  the twilight,
  Saying, 'No eye will see me';
  And he disguises *his* face.
16 In the dark they break into houses
  Which they marked for themselves
  in the daytime;
  They do not know the light.
17 For the morning is the same to
  them as the shadow of death;
  If *someone* recognizes *them,*
  They are in the terrors of the
  shadow of death.

18 "They *should be* swift on the face
  of the waters,

Their portion *should be* cursed in
the earth,
So *that* no *one would* turn into the
way of their vineyards.
19 As drought and heat consume the
snow waters,
So the grave *consumes those who*
have sinned.
20 The womb *should* forget him,
The worm *should* feed sweetly on
him;
He *should* be remembered no
more,
And wickedness *should* be broken
like a tree.
21 For he preys on the barren *who* do
not bear,
And does no good for the widow.

22 "But *God* draws the mighty away
with His power;
He rises up, but no *man* is sure of
life.
23 He gives them security, and they
rely *on it;*
Yet His eyes *are* on their ways.
24 They are exalted for a little while,
Then they are gone.
They are brought low;
They are taken out of the way like
all *others;*
They dry out like the heads of
grain.

25 "Now if *it is* not *so,* who will prove
me a liar,
And make my speech worth
nothing?"

25 Then Bildad the Shuhite answered
and said:

2 "Dominion and fear *belong* to
Him;
He makes peace in His high
places.
3 Is there any number to His
armies?
Upon whom does His light not
rise?
4 How then can man be righteous
before God?
Or how can he be pure *who is*
born of a woman?
5 If even the moon does not shine,

And the stars are not pure in His
sight,
6 How much less man, *who is* a
maggot,
And a son of man, *who is* a
worm?"

∼ PSALM 96:7–10 ∼

7 Give to the LORD, O families of the
peoples,
Give to the LORD glory and strength.
8 Give to the LORD the glory *due* His
name;
Bring an offering, and come into His
courts.
9 Oh, worship the LORD in the beauty
of holiness!
Tremble before Him, all the earth.

10 Say among the nations, "The LORD
reigns;
The world also is firmly established,
It shall not be moved;
He shall judge the peoples
righteously."

∼ PROVERBS 23:9 ∼

9 Do not speak in the hearing of a
fool,
For he will despise the wisdom of
your words.

∼ ROMANS 15:1–24 ∼

We then who are strong ought to bear with
the scruples of the weak, and not to please
ourselves. 2 Let each of us please *his* neighbor for *his* good, leading to edification.
3 For even Christ did not please Himself;
but as it is written, "The reproaches of
those who reproached You fell on Me."
4 For whatever things were written before
were written for our learning, that we
through the patience and comfort of the
Scriptures might have hope. 5 Now may
the God of patience and comfort grant
you to be like-minded toward one another, according to Christ Jesus, 6 that you
may with one mind *and* one mouth glorify the God and Father of our Lord Jesus
Christ.
7 Therefore receive one another, just as
Christ also received us, to the glory of

God. ⁸ Now I say that Jesus Christ has become a servant to the circumcision for the truth of God, to confirm the promises *made* to the fathers, ⁹ and that the Gentiles might glorify God for *His* mercy, as it is written:

"For this reason I will confess to
  You among the Gentiles,
  And sing to Your name."

¹⁰ And again he says:

"Rejoice, O Gentiles, with His
  people!"

¹¹ And again:

"Praise the LORD, all you
  Gentiles!
  Laud Him, all you peoples!"

¹² And again, Isaiah says:

"There shall be a root of Jesse;
  And He who shall rise to reign
    over the Gentiles,
  In Him the Gentiles shall hope."

¹³ Now may the God of hope fill you with all joy and peace in believing, that you may abound in hope by the power of the Holy Spirit.
¹⁴ Now I myself am confident concerning you, my brethren, that you also are full of goodness, filled with all knowledge, able also to admonish one another.

¹⁵ Nevertheless, brethren, I have written more boldly to you on *some* points, as reminding you, because of the grace given to me by God, ¹⁶ that I might be a minister of Jesus Christ to the Gentiles, ministering the gospel of God, that the offering of the Gentiles might be acceptable, sanctified by the Holy Spirit. ¹⁷ Therefore I have reason to glory in Christ Jesus in the things *which pertain* to God. ¹⁸ For I will not dare to speak of any of those things which Christ has not accomplished through me, in word and deed, to make the Gentiles obedient— ¹⁹ in mighty signs and wonders, by the power of the Spirit of God, so that from Jerusalem and round about to Illyricum I have fully preached the gospel of Christ. ²⁰ And so I have made it my aim to preach the gospel, not where Christ was named, lest I should build on another man's foundation, ²¹ but as it is written:

"To whom He was not announced,
  they shall see;
  And those who have not heard
  shall understand."

²² For this reason I also have been much hindered from coming to you. ²³ But now no longer having a place in these parts, and having a great desire these many years to come to you, ²⁴ whenever I journey to Spain, I shall come to you. For I hope to see you on my journey, and to be helped on my way there by you, if first I may enjoy your *company* for a while.

∼ JOB 26:1–14 ∼

But Job answered and said:

² "How have you helped *him*
    who is without power?
  How have you saved the arm *that*
    has no strength?
³ How have you counseled *one who*
    has no wisdom?
  And *how* have you declared sound
    advice to many?

⁴ To whom have you uttered words?
  And whose spirit came from you?

⁵ "The dead tremble,
  Those under the waters and those
    inhabiting them.
⁶ Sheol *is* naked before Him,
  And Destruction has no covering.
⁷ He stretches out the north over
    empty space;

Pea Soup Prayers

Apply your heart to instruction, and your ears to words of knowledge.

Proverbs 23:12

Many of us show up for prayer times with a long list of things we want God to do for us. In addition, we often include instructions about *how* we want Him to accomplish these things.

Ruby Johnson has referred to such prayers as "pea soup prayers." She has said, "Curt taught us about 'pea soup prayers.' When he was in grade school, he walked home for lunch every day. As he walked, he would pray something like, 'Please Lord, don't let Mom fix pea soup today.'

"Why did he pray like that? The answer is probably obvious: he hated pea soup. No matter how hungry he was, a bowl of that 'green goop' just didn't appeal to him at all. He knew it was nutritious and good for him, but that did not change his view in the least. Nutritious or not, he wanted no part of pea soup."

According to Johnson, a pea soup prayer is when, "instead of allowing Him to intervene and solve the problem in His own way . . . we tell Him how to provide the solution. . . . [Curt] recognized God's superior abilities, but on the other hand he played the superior role by advising God. Absurd, isn't it?"

If we are praying for God's will to be done, we must first dismiss our own will from the room.

He hangs the earth on nothing.
8 He binds up the water in His thick
   clouds,
   Yet the clouds are not broken
   under it.
9 He covers the face of *His* throne,
   And spreads His cloud over it.
10 He drew a circular horizon on the
   face of the waters,
   At the boundary of light and
   darkness.
11 The pillars of heaven tremble,
   And are astonished at His rebuke.
12 He stirs up the sea with His
   power,
   And by His understanding He
   breaks up the storm.
13 By His Spirit He adorned the
   heavens;
   His hand pierced the fleeing
   serpent.
14 Indeed these *are* the mere edges of
   His ways,
   And how small a whisper we hear
   of Him!
   But the thunder of His power who
   can understand?"

~ PSALM 96:11-13 ~

11 Let the heavens rejoice, and let the
   earth be glad;
   Let the sea roar, and all its fullness;
12 Let the field be joyful, and all that *is*
   in it.
   Then all the trees of the woods will
   rejoice before the LORD.
13 For He is coming, for He is coming
   to judge the earth.
   He shall judge the world with
   righteousness,
   And the peoples with His truth.

~ PROVERBS 23:10-12 ~

10 Do not remove the ancient
   landmark,
   Nor enter the fields of the fatherless;
11 For their Redeemer *is* mighty;
   He will plead their cause against
   you.

12 Apply your heart to instruction,
   And your ears to words of
   knowledge.

~ ROMANS 15:25-33 ~

But now I am going to Jerusalem to minister to the saints. 26 For it pleased those
from Macedonia and Achaia to make a
certain contribution for the poor among
the saints who are in Jerusalem. 27 It
pleased them indeed, and they are their
debtors. For if the Gentiles have been partakers of their spiritual things, their duty
is also to minister to them in material
things. 28 Therefore, when I have performed this and have sealed to them this
fruit, I shall go by way of you to Spain.
29 But I know that when I come to you, I
shall come in the fullness of the blessing
of the gospel of Christ.
   30 Now I beg you, brethren, through the
Lord Jesus Christ, and through the love
of the Spirit, that you strive together with
me in prayers to God for me, 31 that I may
be delivered from those in Judea who do
not believe, and that my service for Jerusalem may be acceptable to the saints, 32 that
I may come to you with joy by the will of
God, and may be refreshed together with
you. 33 Now the God of peace *be* with you
all. Amen.

READING 230 · AUGUST 18

~ JOB 27:1-28:28 ~

Moreover Job continued his discourse, and said:

2 "*As* God lives, *who* has taken away
   my justice,
   And the Almighty, *who* has made
   my soul bitter,

3 As long as my breath *is* in me,
   And the breath of God in my
   nostrils,
4 My lips will not speak wickedness,
   Nor my tongue utter deceit.
5 Far be it from me
   That I should say you are right;

True Beauty

Many years ago, a boy was born in Russia who thought himself to be so ugly, he was certain there would be no happiness for him in life. He bemoaned the fact that he had a wide nose, thick lips, small gray eyes, and big hands and feet. He was so distraught about his ugliness, he asked God to work a miracle and turn him into a handsome man. He vowed that if God would do this, he would give Him all he possessed, as well as all he might possess in the future.

That Russian boy was Count Leo Tolstoy, one of the world's foremost twentieth century authors, perhaps best known for his epic *War and Peace*. In one of his books, Tolstoy admits that through the years he discovered that the beauty of physical appearance he had once sought was not the only beauty in life. Indeed, it was not the best beauty. Instead, Tolstoy came to regard the beauty of a strong character as the greatest beauty.

Today, so many people spend enormous sums of money on their physical appearance. Character, in contrast, is not a matter of money or beauty. It is a matter of doing what is right in spite of money, and of standing up for what is right in spite of appearances.

It's still true, and always will be: True beauty comes from the inside.

Till I die I will not put away my
integrity from me.

6 My righteousness I hold fast, and
will not let it go;
My heart shall not reproach *me* as
long as I live.

7 "May my enemy be like the
wicked,
And he who rises up against me
like the unrighteous.

8 For what is the hope of the
hypocrite,
Though he may gain *much,*
If God takes away his life?

9 Will God hear his cry
When trouble comes upon him?

10 Will he delight himself in the
Almighty?
Will he always call on God?

11 "I will teach you about the hand of
God;
What *is* with the Almighty I will
not conceal.

12 Surely all of you have seen *it;*
Why then do you behave with
complete nonsense?

13 "This is the portion of a wicked
man with God,
And the heritage of oppressors,
received from the Almighty:

14 If his children are multiplied, *it is*
for the sword;
And his offspring shall not be
satisfied with bread.

15 Those who survive him shall be
buried in death,
And their widows shall not weep,

16 Though he heaps up silver like
dust,
And piles up clothing like clay—

17 He may pile *it* up, but the just will
wear *it,*
And the innocent will divide the
silver.

18 He builds his house like a moth,
Like a booth *which* a watchman
makes.

19 The rich man will lie down,
But not be gathered *up;*
He opens his eyes,
And he *is* no more.

20 Terrors overtake him like a flood;

A tempest steals him away in the
night.

21 The east wind carries him away,
and he is gone;
It sweeps him out of his place.

22 It hurls against him and does not
spare;
He flees desperately from its
power.

23 *Men* shall clap their hands at him,
And shall hiss him out of his
place.

28 "Surely there is a mine for silver,
And a place *where* gold is refined.

2 Iron is taken from the earth,
And copper *is* smelted *from* ore.

3 *Man* puts an end to darkness,
And searches every recess
For ore in the darkness and the
shadow of death.

4 He breaks open a shaft away from
people;
In places forgotten by feet
They hang far away from men;
They swing to and fro.

5 *As for* the earth, from it comes
bread,
But underneath it is turned up as
by fire;

6 Its stones *are* the source of
sapphires,
And it contains gold dust.

7 *That* path no bird knows,
Nor has the falcon's eye seen it.

8 The proud lions have not trodden
it,
Nor has the fierce lion passed over
it.

9 He puts his hand on the flint;
He overturns the mountains at the
roots.

10 He cuts out channels in the rocks,
And his eye sees every precious
thing.

11 He dams up the streams from
trickling;
What is hidden he brings forth to
light.

12 "But where can wisdom be found?
And where *is* the place of
understanding?

13 Man does not know its value,

Nor is it found in the land of the living.

14 The deep says, 'It is not in me';
And the sea says, 'It is not with me.'

15 It cannot be purchased for gold,
Nor can silver be weighed for its price.

16 It cannot be valued in the gold of Ophir,
In precious onyx or sapphire.

17 Neither gold nor crystal can equal it,
Nor can it be exchanged for jewelry of fine gold.

18 No mention shall be made of coral or quartz,
For the price of wisdom is above rubies.

19 The topaz of Ethiopia cannot equal it,
Nor can it be valued in pure gold.

20 "From where then does wisdom come?
And where is the place of understanding?

21 It is hidden from the eyes of all living,
And concealed from the birds of the air.

22 Destruction and Death say,
'We have heard a report about it with our ears.'

23 God understands its way,
And He knows its place.

24 For He looks to the ends of the earth,
And sees under the whole heavens,

25 To establish a weight for the wind,
And apportion the waters by measure.

26 When He made a law for the rain,
And a path for the thunderbolt,

27 Then He saw wisdom and declared it;
He prepared it, indeed, He searched it out.

28 And to man He said,
'Behold, the fear of the Lord, that is wisdom,
And to depart from evil is understanding.' "

∽ PSALM 97:1–6 ∽

1 The LORD reigns;
Let the earth rejoice;
Let the multitude of isles be glad!

2 Clouds and darkness surround Him;
Righteousness and justice are the foundation of His throne.

3 A fire goes before Him,
And burns up His enemies round about.

4 His lightnings light the world;
The earth sees and trembles.

5 The mountains melt like wax at the presence of the LORD,
At the presence of the Lord of the whole earth.

6 The heavens declare His righteousness,
And all the peoples see His glory.

∽ PROVERBS 23:13, 14 ∽

13 Do not withhold correction from a child,
For if you beat him with a rod, he will not die.

14 You shall beat him with a rod,
And deliver his soul from hell.

∽ ROMANS 16:1–27 ∽

I commend to you Phoebe our sister, who is a servant of the church in Cenchrea, 2 that you may receive her in the Lord in a manner worthy of the saints, and assist her in whatever business she has need of you; for indeed she has been a helper of many and of myself also.

3 Greet Priscilla and Aquila, my fellow workers in Christ Jesus, 4 who risked their own necks for my life, to whom not only I give thanks, but also all the churches of the Gentiles. 5 Likewise greet the church that is in their house.

Greet my beloved Epaenetus, who is the firstfruits of Achaia to Christ. 6 Greet Mary, who labored much for us. 7 Greet Andronicus and Junia, my countrymen and my fellow prisoners, who are of note among the apostles, who also were in Christ before me.

⁸ Greet Amplias, my beloved in the Lord. ⁹ Greet Urbanus, our fellow worker in Christ, and Stachys, my beloved. ¹⁰ Greet Apelles, approved in Christ. Greet those who are of the *household* of Aristobulus. ¹¹ Greet Herodion, my countryman. Greet those who are of the *household* of Narcissus who are in the Lord.

¹² Greet Tryphena and Tryphosa, who have labored in the Lord. Greet the beloved Persis, who labored much in the Lord. ¹³ Greet Rufus, chosen in the Lord, and his mother and mine. ¹⁴ Greet Asyncritus, Phlegon, Hermas, Patrobas, Hermes, and the brethren who are with them. ¹⁵ Greet Philologus and Julia, Nereus and his sister, and Olympas, and all the saints who are with them.

¹⁶ Greet one another with a holy kiss. The churches of Christ greet you.

¹⁷ Now I urge you, brethren, note those who cause divisions and offenses, contrary to the doctrine which you learned, and avoid them. ¹⁸ For those who are such do not serve our Lord Jesus Christ, but their own belly, and by smooth words and flattering speech deceive the hearts of the simple. ¹⁹ For your obedience has become known to all. Therefore I am glad on your behalf; but I want you to be wise in what is good, and simple concerning evil. ²⁰ And the God of peace will crush Satan under your feet shortly.

The grace of our Lord Jesus Christ *be* with you. Amen.

²¹ Timothy, my fellow worker, and Lucius, Jason, and Sosipater, my countrymen, greet you.

²² I, Tertius, who wrote *this* epistle, greet you in the Lord.

²³ Gaius, my host and *the host* of the whole church, greets you. Erastus, the treasurer of the city, greets you, and Quartus, a brother. ²⁴ The grace of our Lord Jesus Christ *be* with you all. Amen.

²⁵ Now to Him who is able to establish you according to my gospel and the preaching of Jesus Christ, according to the revelation of the mystery kept secret since the world began ²⁶ but now made manifest, and by the prophetic Scriptures made known to all nations, according to the commandment of the everlasting God, for obedience to the faith— ²⁷ to God, alone wise, *be* glory through Jesus Christ forever. Amen.

READING 231 · AUGUST 19

~ JOB 29:1—30:31 ~

Job further continued his discourse, and said:

² "Oh, that I were as *in* months past,
  As *in* the days *when* God watched over me;
³   When His lamp shone upon my head,
  And when by His light I walked *through* darkness;
⁴   Just as I was in the days of my prime,
  When the friendly counsel of God *was* over my tent;
⁵   When the Almighty *was* yet with me,
  When my children *were* around me;
⁶   When my steps were bathed with cream,

And the rock poured out rivers of oil for me!

⁷ "When I went out to the gate by the city,
  When I took my seat in the open square,
⁸   The young men saw me and hid,
  And the aged arose *and* stood;
⁹   The princes refrained from talking,
  And put *their* hand on their mouth;
¹⁰   The voice of nobles was hushed,
  And their tongue stuck to the roof of their mouth.
¹¹   When the ear heard, then it blessed me,
  And when the eye saw, then it approved me;

Father Knows Best

A little girl watched with envy as her older brother and his friends worked a gumball machine outside the local hardware store. When she asked her brother for a gumball, he told her he didn't have any more quarters for the machine and she would have to use her own allowance for such treats.

When her father arrived at home that evening, the little girl approached him to make her request, "Daddy, can I have a quarter?" Feeling generous, the father pulled out his wallet and offered his daughter a crisp new twenty-dollar bill.

Not realizing what the bill was, the little girl refused the paper money. As far as she was concerned, it was useless — it wouldn't fit into the gumball machine. She said, "No, I don't want that. I want a *quarter*."

Are there times when we deal with our Heavenly Father as this little girl dealt with her father? Do we sometimes ask for some small favor, refusing His offer of a blessing that is a hundred times more valuable?

God may not answer our prayers precisely as we would desire, but we can always know He will answer our prayers in the way that is best for us.

> Because the foolishness of God is wiser than men, and the weakness of God is stronger than men.
>
> *1 Corinthians 1:25*

12 Because I delivered the poor who cried out,
The fatherless and *the one who* had no helper.
13 The blessing of a perishing *man* came upon me,
And I caused the widow's heart to sing for joy.
14 I put on righteousness, and it clothed me;
My justice *was* like a robe and a turban.
15 I *was* eyes to the blind,
And I *was* feet to the lame.
16 I *was* a father to the poor,
And I searched out the case *that* I did not know.
17 I broke the fangs of the wicked,
And plucked the victim from his teeth.

18 "Then I said, 'I shall die in my nest,
And multiply *my* days as the sand.
19 My root *is* spread out to the waters,
And the dew lies all night on my branch.
20 My glory *is* fresh within me,
And my bow is renewed in my hand.'

21 "*Men* listened to me and waited,
And kept silence for my counsel.
22 After my words they did not speak again,
And my speech settled on them *as* dew.
23 They waited for me *as* for the rain,
And they opened their mouth wide *as* for the spring rain.
24 *If* I mocked at them, they did not believe *it*,
And the light of my countenance they did not cast down.
25 I chose the way for them, and sat as chief;
So I dwelt as a king in the army,
As one *who* comforts mourners.

30 "But now they mock at me, *men* younger than I,
Whose fathers I disdained to put with the dogs of my flock.

2 Indeed, what *profit* is the strength of their hands to me?
Their vigor has perished.
3 *They are* gaunt from want and famine,
Fleeing late to the wilderness, desolate and waste,
4 Who pluck mallow by the bushes,
And broom tree roots *for* their food.
5 They were driven out from among *men*,
They shouted at them as *at* a thief.
6 *They had* to live in the clefts of the valleys,
In caves of the earth and the rocks.
7 Among the bushes they brayed,
Under the nettles they nestled.
8 *They were* sons of fools,
Yes, sons of vile men;
They were scourged from the land.

9 "And now I am their taunting song;
Yes, I am their byword.
10 They abhor me, they keep far from me;
They do not hesitate to spit in my face.
11 Because He has loosed my bowstring and afflicted me,
They have cast off restraint before me.
12 At *my* right *hand* the rabble arises;
They push away my feet,
And they raise against me their ways of destruction.
13 They break up my path,
They promote my calamity;
They have no helper.
14 They come as broad breakers;
Under the ruinous storm they roll along.
15 Terrors are turned upon me;
They pursue my honor as the wind,
And my prosperity has passed like a cloud.

16 "And now my soul is poured out because of my *plight;*
The days of affliction take hold of me.

17 My bones are pierced in me at
    night,
    And my gnawing pains take no
    rest.
18 By great force my garment is
    disfigured;
    It binds me about as the collar of
    my coat.
19 He has cast me into the mire,
    And I have become like dust and
    ashes.

20 "I cry out to You, but You do not
    answer me;
    I stand up, and You regard me.
21 *But* You have become cruel to me;
    With the strength of Your hand
    You oppose me.
22 You lift me up to the wind and
    cause me to ride *on it;*
    You spoil my success.
23 For I know *that* You will bring me
    to death,
    And *to* the house appointed for all
    living.

24 "Surely He would not stretch out
    His hand against a heap of
    ruins,
    If they cry out when He destroys
    it.
25 Have I not wept for him who was
    in trouble?
    Has *not* my soul grieved for the
    poor?
26 But when I looked for good, evil
    came *to me;*
    And when I waited for light, then
    came darkness.
27 My heart is in turmoil and cannot
    rest;
    Days of affliction confront me.
28 I go about mourning, but not in
    the sun;
    I stand up in the assembly *and* cry
    out for help.
29 I am a brother of jackals,
    And a companion of ostriches.
30 My skin grows black and falls
    from me;
    My bones burn with fever.
31 My harp is *turned* to mourning,
    And my flute to the voice of those
    who weep.

∼ PSALM 97:7–12 ∼

7   Let all be put to shame who serve
    carved images,
    Who boast of idols.
    Worship Him, all *you* gods.
8   Zion hears and is glad,
    And the daughters of Judah rejoice
    Because of Your judgments, O LORD.
9   For You, LORD, *are* most high above
    all the earth;
    You are exalted far above all gods.

10 You who love the LORD, hate evil!
    He preserves the souls of His saints;
    He delivers them out of the hand of
    the wicked.
11 Light is sown for the righteous,
    And gladness for the upright in
    heart.
12 Rejoice in the LORD, you righteous,
    And give thanks at the remembrance
    of His holy name.

∼ PROVERBS 23:15, 16 ∼

15 My son, if your heart is wise,
    My heart will rejoice—indeed, I
    myself;
16 Yes, my inmost being will rejoice
    When your lips speak right things.

∼ 1 CORINTHIANS 1:1–31 ∼

Paul, called *to be* an apostle of Jesus Christ
through the will of God, and Sosthenes
our brother,

2 To the church of God which is at
Corinth, to those who are sanctified in
Christ Jesus, called *to be* saints, with all
who in every place call on the name of
Jesus Christ our Lord, both theirs and
ours:

3 Grace to you and peace from God our
Father and the Lord Jesus Christ.
4 I thank my God always concerning
you for the grace of God which was given
to you by Christ Jesus, 5 that you were
enriched in everything by Him in all utterance and all knowledge, 6 even as the
testimony of Christ was confirmed in
you, 7 so that you come short in no gift,

eagerly waiting for the revelation of our Lord Jesus Christ, ⁸ who will also confirm you to the end, *that you may be* blameless in the day of our Lord Jesus Christ. ⁹ God *is* faithful, by whom you were called into the fellowship of His Son, Jesus Christ our Lord.

¹⁰ Now I plead with you, brethren, by the name of our Lord Jesus Christ, that you all speak the same thing, and *that* there be no divisions among you, but *that* you be perfectly joined together in the same mind and in the same judgment. ¹¹ For it has been declared to me concerning you, my brethren, by those of Chloe's *household,* that there are contentions among you. ¹² Now I say this, that each of you says, "I am of Paul," or "I am of Apollos," or "I am of Cephas," or "I am of Christ." ¹³ Is Christ divided? Was Paul crucified for you? Or were you baptized in the name of Paul?

¹⁴ I thank God that I baptized none of you except Crispus and Gaius, ¹⁵ lest anyone should say that I had baptized in my own name. ¹⁶ Yes, I also baptized the household of Stephanas. Besides, I do not know whether I baptized any other. ¹⁷ For Christ did not send me to baptize, but to preach the gospel, not with wisdom of words, lest the cross of Christ should be made of no effect.

¹⁸ For the message of the cross is foolishness to those who are perishing, but to us who are being saved it is the power of God. ¹⁹ For it is written:

"I will destroy the wisdom of the wise,

And bring to nothing the understanding of the prudent."

²⁰ Where *is* the wise? Where *is* the scribe? Where *is* the disputer of this age? Has not God made foolish the wisdom of this world? ²¹ For since, in the wisdom of God, the world through wisdom did not know God, it pleased God through the foolishness of the message preached to save those who believe. ²² For Jews request a sign, and Greeks seek after wisdom; ²³ but we preach Christ crucified, to the Jews a stumbling block and to the Greeks foolishness, ²⁴ but to those who are called, both Jews and Greeks, Christ the power of God and the wisdom of God. ²⁵ Because the foolishness of God is wiser than men, and the weakness of God is stronger than men.

²⁶ For you see your calling, brethren, that not many wise according to the flesh, not many mighty, not many noble, *are called.* ²⁷ But God has chosen the foolish things of the world to put to shame the wise, and God has chosen the weak things of the world to put to shame the things which are mighty; ²⁸ and the base things of the world and the things which are despised God has chosen, and the things which are not, to bring to nothing the things that are, ²⁹ that no flesh should glory in His presence. ³⁰ But of Him you are in Christ Jesus, who became for us wisdom from God—and righteousness and sanctification and redemption— ³¹ that, as it is written, "He who glories, let him glory in the LORD."

READING 232 · AUGUST 20

~ JOB 31:1—32:22 ~

¹ "I have made a covenant with my eyes;
Why then should I look upon a young woman?
² For what *is* the allotment of God from above,
And the inheritance of the Almighty from on high?
³ *Is* it not destruction for the wicked,

And disaster for the workers of iniquity?
⁴ Does He not see my ways,
And count all my steps?

⁵ "If I have walked with falsehood,
Or if my foot has hastened to deceit,
⁶ Let me be weighed on honest scales,

Trust Your Instruments

Richard E. Byrd spent the winter of 1934 at Bolling Advance Weather Base in Antarctica, where the temperature ranged from -58° to -76° F. By the time he was rescued, he was suffering from frostbite and carbon-monoxide poisoning. He wrote in his book, *Alone*: "I had hardly strength to move. I clung to the sleeping bag, which was the only source of comfort and warmth left to me and mournfully debated the little that might be done.

"Two facts stood clear. One was that my chances of recovering were slim. The other was that in my weakness I was incapable of taking care of myself. *But you must have faith — you must have faith in the outcome*, I whispered to myself. It is like a flight . . . into another unknown. You start and you cannot turn back. You must go on . . . trusting your instruments, the course you have plotted."

With faith as his only guidance tool, Byrd forced himself to do the necessary things for survival very slowly and with great deliberation. At times he felt as if he was living a thousand years any given minute. But at each day's end, he could say he was still alive. And that was enough.

Sometimes the only thing left to do in an impossible situation is to press on in faith. God still makes the impossible possible!

That God may know my integrity.
7 If my step has turned from the way,
Or my heart walked after my eyes,
Or if any spot adheres to my hands,
8 *Then* let me sow, and another eat;
Yes, let my harvest be rooted out.

9 "If my heart has been enticed by a woman,
Or *if* I have lurked at my neighbor's door,
10 *Then* let my wife grind for another,
And let others bow down over her.
11 For that *would be* wickedness;
Yes, it *would be* iniquity *deserving* of judgment.
12 For that *would be* a fire *that* consumes to destruction,
And would root out all my increase.

13 "If I have despised the cause of my male or female servant
When they complained against me,
14 What then shall I do when God rises up?
When He punishes, how shall I answer Him?
15 Did not He who made me in the womb make them?
Did not the same One fashion us in the womb?

16 "If I have kept the poor from *their* desire,
Or caused the eyes of the widow to fail,
17 Or eaten my morsel by myself,
So that the fatherless could not eat of it
18 (But from my youth I reared him as a father,
And from my mother's womb I guided *the widow*);
19 If I have seen anyone perish for lack of clothing,
Or any poor *man* without covering;
20 If his heart has not blessed me,

And *if* he was *not* warmed with the fleece of my sheep;
21 If I have raised my hand against the fatherless,
When I saw I had help in the gate;
22 *Then* let my arm fall from my shoulder,
Let my arm be torn from the socket.
23 For destruction *from* God *is* a terror to me,
And because of His magnificence I cannot endure.

24 "If I have made gold my hope,
Or said to fine gold, 'You *are* my confidence';
25 If I have rejoiced because my wealth *was* great,
And because my hand had gained much;
26 If I have observed the sun when it shines,
Or the moon moving *in* brightness,
27 So that my heart has been secretly enticed,
And my mouth has kissed my hand;
28 This also *would be* an iniquity *deserving* of judgment,
For I would have denied God *who is* above.

29 "If I have rejoiced at the destruction of him who hated me,
Or lifted myself up when evil found him
30 (Indeed I have not allowed my mouth to sin
By asking for a curse on his soul);
31 If the men of my tent have not said,
'Who is there that has not been satisfied with his meat?'
32 (*But* no sojourner had to lodge in the street,
For I have opened my doors to the traveler);
33 If I have covered my transgressions as Adam,
By hiding my iniquity in my bosom,

³⁴ Because I feared the great
multitude,
And dreaded the contempt of
families,
So that I kept silence
And did not go out of the door—
³⁵ Oh, that I had one to hear me!
Here is my mark.
Oh, that the Almighty would
answer me,
That my Prosecutor had written a
book!
³⁶ Surely I would carry it on my
shoulder,
And bind it on me *like* a crown;
³⁷ I would declare to Him the
number of my steps;
Like a prince I would approach
Him.

³⁸ "If my land cries out against me,
And its furrows weep together;
³⁹ If I have eaten its fruit without
money,
Or caused its owners to lose their
lives;
⁴⁰ *Then* let thistles grow instead of
wheat,
And weeds instead of barley."

The words of Job are ended.

32 So these three men ceased answering Job, because he *was* righteous in his own eyes. ² Then the wrath of Elihu, the son of Barachel the Buzite, of the family of Ram, was aroused against Job; his wrath was aroused because he justified himself rather than God. ³ Also against his three friends his wrath was aroused, because they had found no answer, and *yet* had condemned Job.

⁴ Now because they *were* years older than he, Elihu had waited to speak to Job. ⁵ When Elihu saw that *there was* no answer in the mouth of these three men, his wrath was aroused.

⁶ So Elihu, the son of Barachel the Buzite, answered and said:

"I *am* young in years, and you *are*
very old;
Therefore I was afraid,

And dared not declare my opinion
to you.
⁷ I said, 'Age should speak,
And multitude of years should
teach wisdom.'
⁸ But *there is* a spirit in man,
And the breath of the Almighty
gives him understanding.
⁹ Great men are not *always* wise,
Nor do the aged *always*
understand justice.

¹⁰ "Therefore I say, 'Listen to me,
I also will declare my opinion.'
¹¹ Indeed I waited for your words,
I listened to your reasonings,
while you searched out what to
say.
¹² I paid close attention to you;
And surely not one of you
convinced Job,
Or answered his words—
¹³ Lest you say,
'We have found wisdom';
God will vanquish him, not man.
¹⁴ Now he has not directed *his*
words against me;
So I will not answer him with
your words.

¹⁵ "They are dismayed and answer no
more;
Words escape them.
¹⁶ And I have waited, because they
did not speak,
Because they stood still *and*
answered no more.
¹⁷ I also will answer my part,
I too will declare my opinion.
¹⁸ For I am full of words;
The spirit within me compels me.
¹⁹ Indeed my belly *is* like wine *that*
has no vent;
It is ready to burst like new
wineskins.
²⁰ I will speak, that I may find
relief;
I must open my lips and answer.
²¹ Let me not, I pray, show partiality
to anyone;
Nor let me flatter any man.
²² For I do not know how to flatter,
Else my Maker would soon take
me away.

~ PSALM 98:1-3 ~

1 Oh, sing to the LORD a new song!
   For He has done marvelous things;
   His right hand and His holy arm
      have gained Him the victory.
2 The LORD has made known His
      salvation;
   His righteousness He has revealed in
      the sight of the nations.
3 He has remembered His mercy and
      His faithfulness to the house of
      Israel;
   All the ends of the earth have seen
      the salvation of our God.

~ PROVERBS 23:17, 18 ~

17 Do not let your heart envy sinners,
    But *be zealous* for the fear of the
       LORD all the day;
18 For surely there is a hereafter,
    And your hope will not be cut off.

~ 1 CORINTHIANS 2:1–16 ~

And I, brethren, when I came to you, did
not come with excellence of speech or of
wisdom declaring to you the testimony
of God. ² For I determined not to know
anything among you except Jesus Christ
and Him crucified. ³ I was with you in
weakness, in fear, and in much trembling.
⁴ And my speech and my preaching *were*
not with persuasive words of human wisdom, but in demonstration of the Spirit
and of power, ⁵ that your faith should not
be in the wisdom of men but in the power
of God.

⁶ However, we speak wisdom among
those who are mature, yet not the wisdom of this age, nor of the rulers of this
age, who are coming to nothing. ⁷ But we
speak the wisdom of God in a mystery,
the hidden *wisdom* which God ordained
before the ages for our glory, ⁸ which none
of the rulers of this age knew; for had they
known, they would not have crucified the
Lord of glory.

⁹ But as it is written:

"Eye has not seen, nor ear heard,
   Nor have entered into the heart of
      man
   The things which God has
      prepared for those who love
      Him."

¹⁰ But God has revealed *them* to us
through His Spirit. For the Spirit searches
all things, yes, the deep things of God.
¹¹ For what man knows the things of a man
except the spirit of the man which is in
him? Even so no one knows the things of
God except the Spirit of God. ¹² Now we
have received, not the spirit of the world,
but the Spirit who is from God, that we
might know the things that have been freely given to us by God.

¹³ These things we also speak, not in
words which man's wisdom teaches but
which the Holy Spirit teaches, compar-
ing spiritual things with spiritual. ¹⁴ But
the natural man does not receive the
things of the Spirit of God, for they are
foolishness to him; nor can he know *them*,
because they are spiritually discerned.
¹⁵ But he who is spiritual judges all things,
yet he himself is *rightly* judged by no one.
¹⁶ For "who has known the mind of the
LORD that he may instruct Him?" But we
have the mind of Christ.

READING 233 · AUGUST 21

~ JOB 33:1—34:37 ~

1 "But please, Job, hear my speech,
   And listen to all my words.
2 Now, I open my mouth;
   My tongue speaks in my mouth.
3 My words *come* from my upright
      heart;
   My lips utter pure knowledge.

4 The Spirit of God has made me,
   And the breath of the Almighty
      gives me life.
5 If you can answer me,
   Set *your words* in order before
      me;
   Take your stand.

Dial 911

In recent years, nearly every community in the United States has been equipped with a 911 emergency phone system. The newest versions of this system are state of the art. All a person has to do is dial those three numbers and he is instantly connected to a dispatcher.

The dispatcher's computer screen identifies the number from which the call is being made, the address, and the name by which the telephone number is listed. The system is simultaneously connected to the police department, fire department, and paramedics. A person using the 911 system doesn't even need to utter a word in order for help to be activated and dispatched to the scene.

God has long had His own 911 system — a system more foolproof, fail-proof, and faithful than anything man can ever hope to design. When we "dial" 911 prayers, we are sometimes hysterical, or we don't know the right words to convey the deep need we feel. But God hears. He already knows our name and all about our circumstances. He knows the precise answer to our need even before we voice it. His help is on the way the very moment we turn to Him.

> So that they caused the cry of the poor to come to Him; for He hears the cry of the afflicted.
>
> *Job 34:28*

6 Truly I *am* as your spokesman
    before God;
  I also have been formed out of
    clay.
7 Surely no fear of me will terrify
    you,
  Nor will my hand be heavy on you.

8 "Surely you have spoken in my
    hearing,
  And I have heard the sound of
    your words, *saying,*
9 'I *am* pure, without transgression;
  I *am* innocent, and *there is* no
    iniquity in me.
10 Yet He finds occasions against me,
  He counts me as His enemy;
11 He puts my feet in the stocks,
  He watches all my paths.'

12 "Look, *in* this you are not
    righteous.
  I will answer you,
  For God is greater than man.
13 Why do you contend with Him?
  For He does not give an
    accounting of any of His words.
14 For God may speak in one way, or
    in another,
  Yet man does not perceive it.
15 In a dream, in a vision of the
    night,
  When deep sleep falls upon men,
  While slumbering on their beds,
16 Then He opens the ears of men,
  And seals their instruction.
17 In order to turn man *from his*
    deed,
  And conceal pride from man,
18 He keeps back his soul from the
    Pit,
  And his life from perishing by the
    sword.

19 "*Man* is also chastened with pain
    on his bed,
  And with strong *pain* in many of
    his bones,
20 So that his life abhors bread,
  And his soul succulent food.
21 His flesh wastes away from sight,
  And his bones stick out *which
    once* were not seen.
22 Yes, his soul draws near the Pit,
  And his life to the executioners.

23 "If there is a messenger for him,
  A mediator, one among a
    thousand,
  To show man His uprightness,
24 Then He is gracious to him, and
    says,
  'Deliver him from going down to
    the Pit;
  I have found a ransom';
25 His flesh shall be young like a
    child's,
  He shall return to the days of his
    youth.
26 He shall pray to God, and He will
    delight in him,
  He shall see His face with joy,
  For He restores to man His
    righteousness.
27 Then he looks at men and says,
  'I have sinned, and perverted *what
    was* right,
  And it did not profit me.'
28 He will redeem his soul from
    going down to the Pit,
  And his life shall see the light.

29 "Behold, God works all these
    things,
  Twice, *in fact,* three *times* with a
    man,
30 To bring back his soul from the
    Pit,
  That he may be enlightened with
    the light of life.

31 "Give ear, Job, listen to me;
  Hold your peace, and I will speak.
32 If you have anything to say,
    answer me;
  Speak, for I desire to justify you.
33 If not, listen to me;
  Hold your peace, and I will teach
    you wisdom."

34 Elihu further answered and said:

2 "Hear my words, you wise *men;*
  Give ear to me, you who have
    knowledge.
3 For the ear tests words
  As the palate tastes food.
4 Let us choose justice for ourselves;
  Let us know among ourselves
    what *is* good.

5 "For Job has said, 'I am righteous,
But God has taken away my
justice;
6 Should I lie concerning my right?
My wound *is* incurable, *though I
am* without transgression.'
7 What man *is* like Job,
Who drinks scorn like water,
8 Who goes in company with the
workers of iniquity,
And walks with wicked men?
9 For he has said, 'It profits a man
nothing
That he should delight in God.'

10 "Therefore listen to me, you men
of understanding:
Far be it from God *to do*
wickedness,
And *from* the Almighty to *commit*
iniquity.
11 For He repays man *according to*
his work,
And makes man to find a reward
according to *his* way.
12 Surely God will never do
wickedly,
Nor will the Almighty pervert
justice.
13 Who gave Him charge over the
earth?
Or who appointed *Him over* the
whole world?
14 If He should set His heart on it,
If He should gather to Himself
His Spirit and His breath,
15 All flesh would perish together,
And man would return to dust.

16 "If *you have* understanding, hear
this;
Listen to the sound of my words:
17 Should one who hates justice
govern?
Will you condemn *Him who is*
most just?
18 *Is it fitting* to say to a king, '*You
are* worthless,'
And to nobles, '*You are* wicked'?
19 Yet He is not partial to princes,
Nor does He regard the rich more
than the poor;
For they *are* all the work of His
hands.

20 In a moment they die, in the
middle of the night;
The people are shaken and pass
away;
The mighty are taken away
without a hand.

21 "For His eyes *are* on the ways of
man,
And He sees all his steps.
22 There is no darkness nor shadow
of death
Where the workers of iniquity
may hide themselves.
23 For He need not further consider
a man,
That he should go before God in
judgment.
24 He breaks in pieces mighty men
without inquiry,
And sets others in their place.
25 Therefore He knows their
works;
He overthrows *them* in the night,
And they are crushed.
26 He strikes them as wicked *men*
In the open sight of others,
27 Because they turned back from
Him,
And would not consider any of
His ways,
28 So that they caused the cry of the
poor to come to Him;
For He hears the cry of the
afflicted.
29 When He gives quietness, who
then can make trouble?
And when He hides *His* face, who
then can see Him,
Whether *it is* against a nation or a
man alone?—
30 That the hypocrite should not
reign,
Lest the people be ensnared.

31 "For has *anyone* said to God,
'I have borne *chastening*;
I will offend no more;
32 Teach me *what* I do not see;
If I have done iniquity, I will do no
more'?
33 Should He repay *it* according to
your *terms*,
Just because you disavow it?

You must choose, and not I;
Therefore speak what you know.

34 "Men of understanding say to
me,
Wise men who listen to me:
35 'Job speaks without knowledge,
His words *are* without wisdom.'
36 Oh, that Job were tried to the
utmost,
Because *his* answers *are like* those
of wicked men!
37 For he adds rebellion to his sin;
He claps *his hands* among us,
And multiplies his words against
God."

∼ PSALM 98:4–9 ∼

4 Shout joyfully to the LORD, all the
earth;
Break forth in song, rejoice, and sing
praises.
5 Sing to the LORD with the harp,
With the harp and the sound of a
psalm,
6 With trumpets and the sound of a
horn;
Shout joyfully before the LORD, the
King.

7 Let the sea roar, and all its fullness,
The world and those who dwell in
it;
8 Let the rivers clap *their* hands;
Let the hills be joyful together before
the LORD,
9 For He is coming to judge the earth.
With righteousness He shall judge
the world,
And the peoples with equity.

∼ PROVERBS 23:19–21 ∼

19 Hear, my son, and be wise;
And guide your heart in the way.
20 Do not mix with winebibbers,
Or with gluttonous eaters of meat;
21 For the drunkard and the glutton
will come to poverty,
And drowsiness will clothe *a man*
with rags.

∼ 1 CORINTHIANS 3:1–23 ∼

And I, brethren, could not speak to you
as to spiritual *people* but as to carnal, as
to babes in Christ. 2 I fed you with milk
and not with solid food; for until now
you were not able *to receive it,* and even
now you are still not able; 3 for you are
still carnal. For where *there are* envy, strife,
and divisions among you, are you not carnal and behaving like *mere* men? 4 For
when one says, "I am of Paul," and another, "I *am* of Apollos," are you not
carnal?

5 Who then is Paul, and who *is* Apollos,
but ministers through whom you believed,
as the Lord gave to each one? 6 I planted,
Apollos watered, but God gave the increase. 7 So then neither he who plants is
anything, nor he who waters, but God
who gives the increase. 8 Now he who
plants and he who waters are one, and
each one will receive his own reward according to his own labor.

9 For we are God's fellow workers; you
are God's field, *you are* God's building.
10 According to the grace of God which
was given to me, as a wise master builder
I have laid the foundation, and another
builds on it. But let each one take heed
how he builds on it. 11 For no other foundation can anyone lay than that which is
laid, which is Jesus Christ. 12 Now if anyone builds on this foundation *with*
gold, silver, precious stones, wood, hay,
straw, 13 each one's work will become
clear; for the Day will declare it, because
it will be revealed by fire; and the fire will
test each one's work, of what sort it is.
14 If anyone's work which he has built on
it endures, he will receive a reward. 15 If
anyone's work is burned, he will suffer
loss; but he himself will be saved, yet so
as through fire.

16 Do you not know that you are the
temple of God and *that* the Spirit of God
dwells in you? 17 If anyone defiles the
temple of God, God will destroy him. For
the temple of God is holy, which *temple*
you are.

18 Let no one deceive himself. If anyone among you seems to be wise in this
age, let him become a fool that he may
become wise. 19 For the wisdom of this

world is foolishness with God. For it is written, "He catches the wise in their *own* craftiness"; [20] and again, "The LORD knows the thoughts of the wise, that they are futile." [21] Therefore let no one boast in men. For all things are yours: [22] whether Paul or Apollos or Cephas, or the world or life or death, or things present or things to come—all are yours. [23] And you *are* Christ's, and Christ *is* God's.

READING 234 · AUGUST 22

~ JOB 35:1—36:33 ~

Moreover Elihu answered and said:

[2] "Do you think this is right?
Do you say,
'My righteousness is more than God's'?
[3] For you say,
'What advantage will it be to You?
What profit shall I have, more than *if* I had sinned?'

[4] "I will answer you,
And your companions with you.
[5] Look to the heavens and see;
And behold the clouds—
They are higher than you.
[6] If you sin, what do you accomplish against Him?
Or, *if* your transgressions are multiplied, what do you do to Him?
[7] If you are righteous, what do you give Him?
Or what does He receive from your hand?
[8] Your wickedness affects a man such as you,
And your righteousness a son of man.

[9] "Because of the multitude of oppressions they cry out;
They cry out for help because of the arm of the mighty.
[10] But no one says, 'Where *is* God my Maker,
Who gives songs in the night,
[11] Who teaches us more than the beasts of the earth,
And makes us wiser than the birds of heaven?'

[12] There they cry out, but He does not answer,
Because of the pride of evil men.
[13] Surely God will not listen to empty *talk*,
Nor will the Almighty regard it.
[14] Although you say you do not see Him,
Yet justice *is* before Him, and you must wait for Him.
[15] And now, because He has not punished in His anger,
Nor taken much notice of folly,
[16] Therefore Job opens his mouth in vain;
He multiplies words without knowledge."

36 Elihu also proceeded and said:

[2] "Bear with me a little, and I will show you
That *there are* yet words to speak on God's behalf.
[3] I will fetch my knowledge from afar;
I will ascribe righteousness to my Maker.
[4] For truly my words *are* not false;
One who is perfect in knowledge *is* with you.

[5] "Behold, God *is* mighty, but despises *no one*;
He is mighty in strength of understanding.
[6] He does not preserve the life of the wicked,
But gives justice to the oppressed.
[7] He does not withdraw His eyes from the righteous;
But *they are* on the throne with kings,

For He has seated them forever,
And they are exalted.

8 And if *they are* bound in fetters,
Held in the cords of affliction,

9 Then He tells them their work
and their transgressions—
That they have acted defiantly.

10 He also opens their ear to
instruction,
And commands that they turn
from iniquity.

11 If they obey and serve *Him,*
They shall spend their days in
prosperity,
And their years in pleasures.

12 But if they do not obey,
They shall perish by the sword,
And they shall die without
knowledge.

13 "But the hypocrites in heart store
up wrath;
They do not cry for help when He
binds them.

14 They die in youth,
And their life *ends* among the
perverted persons.

15 He delivers the poor in their
affliction,
And opens their ears in
oppression.

16 "Indeed He would have brought
you out of dire distress,
Into a broad place where *there is*
no restraint;
And what is set on your table
would be full of richness.

17 But you are filled with the
judgment due the wicked;
Judgment and justice take hold *of*
you.

18 Because *there is* wrath, *beware* lest
He take you away with *one*
blow;
For a large ransom would not help
you avoid *it.*

19 Will your riches,
Or all the mighty forces,
Keep you from distress?

20 Do not desire the night,
When people are cut off in their
place.

21 Take heed, do not turn to iniquity,

For you have chosen this rather
than affliction.

22 "Behold, God is exalted by His
power;
Who teaches like Him?

23 Who has assigned Him His way,
Or who has said, 'You have done
wrong'?

24 "Remember to magnify His work,
Of which men have sung.

25 Everyone has seen it;
Man looks on *it* from afar.

26 "Behold, God *is* great, and we do
not know *Him;*
Nor can the number of His years
be discovered.

27 For He draws up drops of water,
Which distill as rain from the mist,

28 Which the clouds drop down
And pour abundantly on man.

29 Indeed, can *anyone* understand
the spreading of clouds,
The thunder from His canopy?

30 Look, He scatters His light upon
it,
And covers the depths of the sea.

31 For by these He judges the
peoples;
He gives food in abundance.

32 He covers *His* hands with
lightning,
And commands it to strike.

33 His thunder declares it,
The cattle also, concerning the
rising *storm.*

～ PSALM 99:1–9 ～

1 The LORD reigns;
Let the peoples tremble!
He dwells *between* the cherubim;
Let the earth be moved!

2 The LORD *is* great in Zion,
And He *is* high above all the peoples.

3 Let them praise Your great and
awesome name—
He *is* holy.

4 The King's strength also loves
justice;
You have established equity;

Life is a Gift, Not a Right

At age fourteen, Andrea Jaeger won her first professional tennis tournament. At eighteen, she reached the finals at Wimbledon. Then at nineteen, a bad shoulder all but ended her career. Many a world-class athlete may have become bitter or discontented with life at that point. Jaeger, however, turned her competitive spirit to a new endeavor, a nonprofit organization called Kids' Stuff Foundation that attempts to bring joy to children suffering from cancer and other life-threatening illnesses. Her work there has also inspired her to take correspondence courses in nursing and child psychology.

Jaeger not only created the program, but runs it full-time, year-round, unpaid. "I'm inspired by these brave kids, and humbled," she has said. "They lose their health, their friends, and sometimes their lives. And yet their spirit never wavers. They look at life as a gift. The rest of us sometimes look at ourselves as a gift to life."

"You get very spoiled on the tour," she adds with a twinkle in her eye. "The courtesy cars, the five-star hotels, the thousands of people clapping for you when you hit a good shot. It's easy to forget what's important in life. . . . I forget it a lot less lately."

Today, remember that your life is a gift. Your children are a gift. Your spouse is a gift. Your extended family and friends are a gift. And don't miss the other gifts God sends your way — those in need. The opportunity to make a difference in a life, that's truly a gift from God.

> If they obey and serve Him, they shall spend their days in prosperity, and their years in pleasures.
>
> *Job 36:11*

You have executed justice and
    righteousness in Jacob.
5 Exalt the LORD our God,
    And worship at His footstool—
    He *is* holy.

6 Moses and Aaron were among His
       priests,
    And Samuel was among those who
       called upon His name;
    They called upon the LORD, and He
       answered them.
7 He spoke to them in the cloudy
       pillar;
    They kept His testimonies and the
       ordinance He gave them.

8 You answered them, O LORD our
       God;
    You were to them God-Who-
       Forgives,
    Though You took vengeance on their
       deeds.
9 Exalt the LORD our God,
    And worship at His holy hill;
    For the LORD our God *is* holy.

∼ PROVERBS 23:22–25 ∼

22 Listen to your father who begot you,
    And do not despise your mother
       when she is old.

23 Buy the truth, and do not sell *it,*
    Also wisdom and instruction and
       understanding.

24 The father of the righteous will
       greatly rejoice,
    And he who begets a wise *child* will
       delight in him.
25 Let your father and your mother be
       glad,
    And let her who bore you rejoice.

∼ 1 CORINTHIANS 4:1–21 ∼

Let a man so consider us, as servants
of Christ and stewards of the mysteries of
God. ² Moreover it is required in stewards that one be found faithful. ³ But with
me it is a very small thing that I should be
judged by you or by a human court. In
fact, I do not even judge myself. ⁴ For I
know of nothing against myself, yet I am
not justified by this; but He who judges
me is the Lord. ⁵ Therefore judge nothing before the time, until the Lord comes,
who will both bring to light the hidden
things of darkness and reveal the counsels of the hearts. Then each one's praise
will come from God.

⁶ Now these things, brethren, I have
figuratively transferred to myself and
Apollos for your sakes, that you may learn
in us not to think beyond what is written,
that none of you may be puffed up on
behalf of one against the other. ⁷ For who
makes you differ *from another?* And what
do you have that you did not receive?
Now if you did indeed receive *it,* why do
you boast as if you had not received *it?*

⁸ You are already full! You are already
rich! You have reigned as kings without
us—and indeed I could wish you did reign,
that we also might reign with you! ⁹ For I
think that God has displayed us, the apostles, last, as men condemned to death; for
we have been made a spectacle to the
world, both to angels and to men. ¹⁰ We
are fools for Christ's sake, but you *are* wise
in Christ! We *are* weak, but you *are*
strong! You *are* distinguished, but we *are*
dishonored! ¹¹ To the present hour we
both hunger and thirst, and we are poorly
clothed, and beaten, and homeless. ¹² And
we labor, working with our own hands.
Being reviled, we bless; being persecuted, we endure; ¹³ being defamed, we entreat. We have been made as the filth of
the world, the offscouring of all things
until now.

¹⁴ I do not write these things to shame
you, but as my beloved children I warn
you. ¹⁵ For though you might have ten
thousand instructors in Christ, yet *you do*
not *have* many fathers; for in Christ Jesus
I have begotten you through the gospel.
¹⁶ Therefore I urge you, imitate me. ¹⁷ For
this reason I have sent Timothy to you,
who is my beloved and faithful son in the
Lord, who will remind you of my ways in
Christ, as I teach everywhere in every
church.

¹⁸ Now some are puffed up, as though
I were not coming to you. ¹⁹ But I will
come to you shortly, if the Lord wills, and

I will know, not the word of those who are puffed up, but the power. [20] For the kingdom of God *is* not in word but in power. [21] What do you want? Shall I come to you with a rod, or in love and a spirit of gentleness?

READING 235 · AUGUST 23

~ JOB 37:1—38:41 ~

[1] "At this also my heart trembles,
And leaps from its place.
[2] Hear attentively the thunder of
His voice,
And the rumbling *that* comes from
His mouth.
[3] He sends it forth under the whole
heaven,
His lightning to the ends of the
earth.
[4] After it a voice roars;
He thunders with His majestic
voice,
And He does not restrain them
when His voice is heard.
[5] God thunders marvelously with
His voice;
He does great things which we
cannot comprehend.
[6] For He says to the snow, 'Fall *on*
the earth';
Likewise to the gentle rain and the
heavy rain of His strength.
[7] He seals the hand of every man,
That all men may know His work.
[8] The beasts go into dens,
And remain in their lairs.
[9] From the chamber *of the south*
comes the whirlwind,
And cold from the scattering
winds *of the north.*
[10] By the breath of God ice is given,
And the broad waters are frozen.
[11] Also with moisture He saturates
the thick clouds;
He scatters His bright clouds.
[12] And they swirl about, being
turned by His guidance,
That they may do whatever He
commands them
On the face of the whole earth.
[13] He causes it to come,
Whether for correction,
Or for His land,
Or for mercy.

[14] "Listen to this, O Job;
Stand still and consider the
wondrous works of God.
[15] Do you know when God
dispatches them,
And causes the light of His cloud
to shine?
[16] Do you know how the clouds are
balanced,
Those wondrous works of Him
who is perfect in knowledge?
[17] Why *are* your garments hot,
When He quiets the earth by the
south *wind?*
[18] With Him, have you spread out
the skies,
Strong as a cast metal mirror?

[19] "Teach us what we should say to
Him,
For we can prepare nothing
because of the darkness.
[20] Should He be told that I *wish to*
speak?
If a man were to speak, surely he
would be swallowed up.
[21] Even now *men* cannot look at the
light *when it is* bright in the
skies,
When the wind has passed and
cleared them.
[22] He comes from the north *as*
golden *splendor;*
With God *is* awesome majesty.
[23] *As for* the Almighty, we cannot
find Him;
He is excellent in power,
In judgment and abundant justice;
He does not oppress.
[24] Therefore men fear Him;
He shows no partiality to any *who*
are wise of heart."

38 Then the LORD answered Job out
of the whirlwind, and said:

2 "Who *is* this who darkens counsel
By words without knowledge?
3 Now prepare yourself like a man;
I will question you, and you shall
answer Me.

4 "Where were you when I laid the
foundations of the earth?
Tell *Me,* if you have
understanding.
5 Who determined its
measurements?
Surely you know!
Or who stretched the line upon it?
6 To what were its foundations
fastened?
Or who laid its cornerstone,
7 When the morning stars sang
together,
And all the sons of God shouted
for joy?

8 "Or *who* shut in the sea with doors,
When it burst forth *and* issued
from the womb;
9 When I made the clouds its
garment,
And thick darkness its swaddling
band;
10 When I fixed My limit for it,
And set bars and doors;
11 When I said,
'This far you may come, but no
farther,
And here your proud waves must
stop!'

12 "Have you commanded the
morning since your days *began,*
And caused the dawn to know its
place,
13 That it might take hold of the
ends of the earth,
And the wicked be shaken out of
it?
14 It takes on form like clay *under* a
seal,
And stands out like a garment.
15 From the wicked their light is
withheld,
And the upraised arm is broken.

16 "Have you entered the springs of
the sea?

Or have you walked in search of
the depths?
17 Have the gates of death been
revealed to you?
Or have you seen the doors of the
shadow of death?
18 Have you comprehended the
breadth of the earth?
Tell *Me,* if you know all this.

19 "Where *is* the way *to* the dwelling
of light?
And darkness, where *is* its place,
20 That you may take it to its
territory,
That you may know the paths *to*
its home?
21 Do you know *it,* because you were
born then,
Or *because* the number of your
days *is* great?

22 "Have you entered the treasury of
snow,
Or have you seen the treasury of
hail,
23 Which I have reserved for the time
of trouble,
For the day of battle and war?
24 By what way is light diffused,
Or the east wind scattered over
the earth?

25 "Who has divided a channel for the
overflowing *water,*
Or a path for the thunderbolt,
26 To cause it to rain on a land *where*
there is no one,
A wilderness in which *there is* no
man;
27 To satisfy the desolate waste,
And cause to spring forth the
growth of tender grass?
28 Has the rain a father?
Or who has begotten the drops of
dew?
29 From whose womb comes the ice?
And the frost of heaven, who gives
it birth?
30 The waters harden like stone,
And the surface of the deep is
frozen.

31 "Can you bind the cluster of the
Pleiades,

Maintaining Love

> Serve the LORD with gladness; Come before His presence with singing.
>
> *Psalm 100:2*

A woman once went away on a long weekend retreat with a group of women from her church. About halfway through the final session, she suddenly jumped to her feet and left the room. Concerned, a friend followed her to see what had caused her to leave the meeting so abruptly. She found her friend just as she was hanging up a telephone in the lobby.

"Is everything all right?" she asked urgently.

"Oh, yes," the woman responded. "I didn't mean to cause you alarm." A bit sheepishly, she added, "I suddenly remembered that it's Monday morning — trash day."

"Trash day? Your husband is still at home. Surely..."

"Yes," the woman interrupted, "but it takes two of us to put out the trash. I can't carry it. And he can't remember it."

Marriages are meant to be complementary — two pulling together as one, not in competition, but in mutual association. Learning how to work together and how to live together is the "maintenance" of love.

Or loose the belt of Orion?

32 Can you bring out Mazzaroth in
its season?
Or can you guide the Great Bear
with its cubs?

33 Do you know the ordinances of
the heavens?
Can you set their dominion over
the earth?

34 "Can you lift up your voice to the
clouds,
That an abundance of water may
cover you?

35 Can you send out lightnings, that
they may go,
And say to you, 'Here we *are*!'?

36 Who has put wisdom in the mind?
Or who has given understanding
to the heart?

37 Who can number the clouds by
wisdom?
Or who can pour out the bottles
of heaven,

38 When the dust hardens in clumps,
And the clods cling together?

39 "Can you hunt the prey for the
lion,
Or satisfy the appetite of the
young lions,

40 When they crouch in *their* dens,
Or lurk in their lairs to lie in wait?

41 Who provides food for the raven,
When its young ones cry to God,
And wander about for lack of
food?

∼ PSALM 100:1–5 ∼

1 Make a joyful shout to the LORD, all
you lands!

2 Serve the LORD with gladness;
Come before His presence with
singing.

3 Know that the LORD, He *is* God;
It is He *who* has made us, and not
we ourselves;
We are His people and the sheep of
His pasture.

4 Enter into His gates with
thanksgiving,
And into His courts with praise.

Be thankful to Him, *and* bless His
name.

5 For the LORD *is* good;
His mercy *is* everlasting,
And His truth *endures* to all
generations.

∼ PROVERBS 23:26–28 ∼

26 My son, give me your heart,
And let your eyes observe my ways.

27 For a harlot *is* a deep pit,
And a seductress *is* a narrow well.

28 She also lies in wait as *for* a victim,
And increases the unfaithful among
men.

∼ 1 CORINTHIANS 5:1–13 ∼

It is actually reported *that there is* sexual
immorality among you, and such
sexual immorality as is not even named
among the Gentiles—that a man has his
father's wife! 2 And you are puffed up, and
have not rather mourned, that he who has
done this deed might be taken away from
among you. 3 For I indeed, as absent in
body but present in spirit, have already
judged (as though I were present) him who
has so done this deed. 4 In the name of
our Lord Jesus Christ, when you are gathered together, along with my spirit, with
the power of our Lord Jesus Christ, 5 deliver such a one to Satan for the destruction of the flesh, that his spirit may be
saved in the day of the Lord Jesus.

6 Your glorying *is* not good. Do you not
know that a little leaven leavens the whole
lump? 7 Therefore purge out the old
leaven, that you may be a new lump, since
you truly are unleavened. For indeed
Christ, our Passover, was sacrificed for us.
8 Therefore let us keep the feast, not with
old leaven, nor with the leaven of malice
and wickedness, but with the unleavened
bread of sincerity and truth.

9 I wrote to you in my epistle not to
keep company with sexually immoral
people. 10 Yet I certainly *did* not *mean* with
the sexually immoral people of this world,
or with the covetous, or extortioners, or
idolaters, since then you would need to
go out of the world. 11 But now I have
written to you not to keep company with

anyone named a brother, who is sexually immoral, or covetous, or an idolater, or a reviler, or a drunkard, or an extortioner— not even to eat with such a person. ¹² For what *have* I *to do* with judging those also who are outside? Do you not judge those who are inside? ¹³ But those who are outside God judges. Therefore "put away from yourselves the evil person."

∼ JOB 39:1—40:24 ∼

¹ "Do you know the time when the
wild mountain goats bear
young?
Or can you mark when the deer
gives birth?
² Can you number the months *that*
they fulfill?
Or do you know the time when
they bear young?
³ They bow down,
They bring forth their young,
They deliver their offspring.
⁴ Their young ones are healthy,
They grow strong with grain;
They depart and do not return to
them.

⁵ "Who set the wild donkey free?
Who loosed the bonds of the
onager,
⁶ Whose home I have made the
wilderness,
And the barren land his dwelling?
⁷ He scorns the tumult of the city;
He does not heed the shouts of
the driver.
⁸ The range of the mountains *is* his
pasture,
And he searches after every green
thing.

⁹ "Will the wild ox be willing to
serve you?
Will he bed by your manger?
¹⁰ Can you bind the wild ox in the
furrow with ropes?
Or will he plow the valleys behind
you?
¹¹ Will you trust him because his
strength *is* great?
Or will you leave your labor to
him?
¹² Will you trust him to bring home
your grain,
And gather it to your threshing
floor?

¹³ "The wings of the ostrich wave
proudly,
But are her wings and pinions *like*
the kindly stork's?
¹⁴ For she leaves her eggs on the
ground,
And warms them in the dust;
¹⁵ She forgets that a foot may crush
them,
Or that a wild beast may break
them.
¹⁶ She treats her young harshly, as
though *they were* not hers;
Her labor is in vain, without
concern,
¹⁷ Because God deprived her of
wisdom,
And did not endow her with
understanding.
¹⁸ When she lifts herself on high,
She scorns the horse and its rider.

¹⁹ "Have you given the horse
strength?
Have you clothed his neck with
thunder?
²⁰ Can you frighten him like a
locust?
His majestic snorting strikes
terror.
²¹ He paws in the valley, and rejoices
in *his* strength;
He gallops into the clash of arms.
²² He mocks at fear, and is not
frightened;
Nor does he turn back from the
sword.
²³ The quiver rattles against him,
The glittering spear and javelin.
²⁴ He devours the distance with
fierceness and rage;

Nor does he come to a halt
  because the trumpet *has*
  sounded.
25 At *the blast of* the trumpet he says,
  'Aha!'
  He smells the battle from afar,
  The thunder of captains and
  shouting.

26 "Does the hawk fly by your
  wisdom,
  And spread its wings toward the
  south?
27 Does the eagle mount up at your
  command,
  And make its nest on high?
28 On the rock it dwells and resides,
  On the crag of the rock and the
  stronghold.
29 From there it spies out the prey;
  Its eyes observe from afar.
30 Its young ones suck up blood;
  And where the slain *are,* there it
  is."

40 Moreover the LORD answered Job, and said:

2 "Shall the one who contends with
  the Almighty correct *Him?*
  He who rebukes God, let him
  answer it."

3 Then Job answered the LORD and
said:

4 "Behold, I am vile;
  What shall I answer You?
  I lay my hand over my mouth.
5 Once I have spoken, but I will not
  answer;
  Yes, twice, but I will proceed no
  further."

6 Then the LORD answered Job out of
the whirlwind, and said:

7 "Now prepare yourself like a man;
  I will question you, and you shall
  answer Me:

8 "Would you indeed annul My
  judgment?

Would you condemn Me that you
  may be justified?
9 Have you an arm like God?
  Or can you thunder with a voice
  like His?
10 Then adorn yourself *with* majesty
  and splendor,
  And array yourself with glory and
  beauty.
11 Disperse the rage of your wrath;
  Look on everyone *who is* proud,
  and humble him.
12 Look on everyone *who is* proud,
  and bring him low;
  Tread down the wicked in their
  place.
13 Hide them in the dust together,
  Bind their faces in hidden
  darkness.
14 Then I will also confess to you
  That your own right hand can
  save you.

15 "Look now at the behemoth, which
  I made *along* with you;
  He eats grass like an ox.
16 See now, his strength *is* in his hips,
  And his power *is* in his stomach
  muscles.
17 He moves his tail like a cedar;
  The sinews of his thighs are tightly
  knit.
18 His bones *are like* beams of
  bronze,
  His ribs like bars of iron.
19 He *is* the first of the ways of God;
  Only He who made him can bring
  near His sword.
20 Surely the mountains yield food
  for him,
  And all the beasts of the field play
  there.
21 He lies under the lotus trees,
  In a covert of reeds and marsh.
22 The lotus trees cover him *with*
  their shade;
  The willows by the brook
  surround him.
23 Indeed the river may rage,
  Yet he is not disturbed;
  He is confident, though the
  Jordan gushes into his mouth,
24 *Though* he takes it in his eyes,
  Or one pierces *his* nose with a
  snare.

Seeds of Self-Respect

A businessman hurriedly plunked a dollar into the cup of a man who was selling flowers on a street corner and rushed away. Half a block down the street, he suddenly whirled about and made his way back to the beggar. "I'm sorry," he said, picking out a flower from the bunch that the beggar had in a canister beside him. "In my haste I failed to make my purchase. After all, you are a businessman just like me. Your merchandise is fairly priced and of good quality. I trust you won't be upset with my failure to take more care in my purchase." And with that, the businessman smiled and walked away, flower in hand.

At lunch a few weeks later, the businessman was approached by a neatly dressed, well-groomed man who introduced himself and then said, "I'm sure you don't remember me, and I don't even know your name, but your face is one I will never forget. You are the man who inspired me to make something of myself. I was a vagrant selling wilted flowers until you gave me back my self-respect. Now I believe I am a businessman."

Self-respect is vital to every person. Purpose in your heart to build up the respect and self-esteem of others. In so doing, you'll be building more respect for yourself!

> Or do you not know that your body is the temple of the Holy Spirit who is in you?
>
> *1 Corinthians 6:19*

◆

~ Psalm 101:1–4 ~

1 I will sing of mercy and justice;
   To You, O Lord, I will sing praises.

2 I will behave wisely in a perfect way.
   Oh, when will You come to me?
   I will walk within my house with a
     perfect heart.

3 I will set nothing wicked before my
     eyes;
   I hate the work of those who fall
     away;
   It shall not cling to me.
4 A perverse heart shall depart from
     me;
   I will not know wickedness.

~ Proverbs 23:29, 30 ~

29 Who has woe?
   Who has sorrow?
   Who has contentions?
   Who has complaints?
   Who has wounds without cause?
   Who has redness of eyes?
30 Those who linger long at the wine,
   Those who go in search of mixed
     wine.

~ 1 Corinthians 6:1–20 ~

Dare any of you, having a matter against another, go to law before the unrighteous, and not before the saints? 2 Do you not know that the saints will judge the world? And if the world will be judged by you, are you unworthy to judge the smallest matters? 3 Do you not know that we shall judge angels? How much more, things that pertain to this life? 4 If then you have judgments concerning things pertaining to this life, do you appoint those who are least esteemed by the church to judge? 5 I say this to your shame. Is it so, that there is not a wise man among you, not even one, who will be able to judge between his brethren? 6 But brother goes to law against brother, and that before unbelievers!

7 Now therefore, it is already an utter failure for you that you go to law against one another. Why do you not rather accept wrong? Why do you not rather *let yourselves* be cheated? 8 No, you yourselves do wrong and cheat, and *you do* these things *to your* brethren! 9 Do you not know that the unrighteous will not inherit the kingdom of God? Do not be deceived. Neither fornicators, nor idolaters, nor adulterers, nor homosexuals, nor sodomites, 10 nor thieves, nor covetous, nor drunkards, nor revilers, nor extortioners will inherit the kingdom of God. 11 And such were some of you. But you were washed, but you were sanctified, but you were justified in the name of the Lord Jesus and by the Spirit of our God.

12 All things are lawful for me, but all things are not helpful. All things are lawful for me, but I will not be brought under the power of any. 13 Foods for the stomach and the stomach for foods, but God will destroy both it and them. Now the body *is* not for sexual immorality but for the Lord, and the Lord for the body. 14 And God both raised up the Lord and will also raise us up by His power.

15 Do you not know that your bodies are members of Christ? Shall I then take the members of Christ and make *them* members of a harlot? Certainly not! 16 Or do you not know that he who is joined to a harlot is one body *with her*? For "the two," He says, "shall become one flesh." 17 But he who is joined to the Lord is one spirit *with Him*.

18 Flee sexual immorality. Every sin that a man does is outside the body, but he who commits sexual immorality sins against his own body. 19 Or do you not know that your body is the temple of the Holy Spirit *who is* in you, whom you have from God, and you are not your own? 20 For you were bought at a price; therefore glorify God in your body and in your spirit, which are God's.

~ JOB 41:1—42:17 ~

1 "Can you draw out Leviathan with
   a hook,
   Or *snare* his tongue with a line
   which you lower?
2 Can you put a reed through his
   nose,
   Or pierce his jaw with a hook?
3 Will he make many supplications
   to you?
   Will he speak softly to you?
4 Will he make a covenant with
   you?
   Will you take him as a servant
   forever?
5 Will you play with him as *with* a
   bird,
   Or will you leash him for your
   maidens?
6 Will *your* companions make a
   banquet of him?
   Will they apportion him among
   the merchants?
7 Can you fill his skin with
   harpoons,
   Or his head with fishing spears?
8 Lay your hand on him;
   Remember the battle—
   Never do it again!
9 Indeed, *any* hope of *overcoming*
   him is false;
   Shall *one not* be overwhelmed at
   the sight of him?
10 No one *is so* fierce that he would
   dare stir him up.
   Who then is able to stand against
   Me?
11 Who has preceded Me, that I
   should pay *him*?
   Everything under heaven is Mine.

12 "I will not conceal his limbs,
   His mighty power, or his graceful
   proportions.
13 Who can remove his outer coat?
   Who can approach *him* with a
   double bridle?
14 Who can open the doors of his
   face,
   With his terrible teeth all around?
15 *His* rows of scales are *his* pride,
   Shut up tightly *as with* a seal;
16 One is so near another

That no air can come between
   them;
17 They are joined one to another,
   They stick together and cannot be
   parted.
18 His sneezings flash forth light,
   And his eyes *are* like the eyelids of
   the morning.
19 Out of his mouth go burning
   lights;
   Sparks of fire shoot out.
20 Smoke goes out of his nostrils,
   As *from* a boiling pot and burning
   rushes.
21 His breath kindles coals,
   And a flame goes out of his
   mouth.
22 Strength dwells in his neck,
   And sorrow dances before him.
23 The folds of his flesh are joined
   together;
   They are firm on him and cannot
   be moved.
24 His heart is as hard as stone,
   Even as hard as the lower
   millstone.
25 When he raises himself up, the
   mighty are afraid;
   Because of his crashings they are
   beside themselves.
26 *Though* the sword reaches him, it
   cannot avail;
   Nor does spear, dart, or javelin.
27 He regards iron as straw,
   And bronze as rotten wood.
28 The arrow cannot make him flee;
   Slingstones become like stubble to
   him.
29 Darts are regarded as straw;
   He laughs at the threat of javelins.
30 His undersides *are* like sharp
   potsherds;
   He spreads pointed *marks* in the
   mire.
31 He makes the deep boil like a pot;
   He makes the sea like a pot of
   ointment.
32 He leaves a shining wake behind
   him;
   One would think the deep had
   white hair.
33 On earth there is nothing like him,

Which is made without fear.
³⁴ He beholds every high *thing*;
   He *is* king over all the children of
   pride."

42 Then Job answered the LORD and said:

² "I know that You can do
   everything,
   And that no purpose *of Yours* can
   be withheld from You.
³ *You asked,* 'Who *is* this who hides
   counsel without knowledge?'
   Therefore I have uttered what I
   did not understand,
   Things too wonderful for me,
   which I did not know.
⁴ Listen, please, and let me speak;
   You said, 'I will question you, and
   you shall answer Me.'

⁵ "I have heard of You by the hearing
   of the ear,
   But now my eye sees You.
⁶ Therefore I abhor *myself,*
   And repent in dust and ashes."

⁷ And so it was, after the LORD had spoken these words to Job, that the LORD said to Eliphaz the Temanite, "My wrath is aroused against you and your two friends, for you have not spoken of Me *what is* right, as My servant Job *has.* ⁸ Now therefore, take for yourselves seven bulls and seven rams, go to My servant Job, and offer up for yourselves a burnt offering; and My servant Job shall pray for you. For I will accept him, lest I deal with you *according to your* folly; because you have not spoken of Me *what is* right, as My servant Job *has.*" ⁹ So Eliphaz the Temanite and Bildad the Shuhite *and* Zophar the Naamathite went and did as the LORD commanded them; for the LORD had accepted Job. ¹⁰ And the LORD restored Job's losses when he prayed for his friends. Indeed the LORD gave Job twice as much as he had before. ¹¹ Then all his brothers, all his sisters, and all those who had been his acquaintances before, came to him and ate food with him in his house; and they consoled him and comforted him for all the adversity that the LORD had brought upon

him. Each one gave him a piece of silver and each a ring of gold.
¹² Now the LORD blessed the latter *days* of Job more than his beginning; for he had fourteen thousand sheep, six thousand camels, one thousand yoke of oxen, and one thousand female donkeys. ¹³ He also had seven sons and three daughters. ¹⁴ And he called the name of the first Jemimah, the name of the second Keziah, and the name of the third Keren-Happuch. ¹⁵ In all the land were found no women *so* beautiful as the daughters of Job; and their father gave them an inheritance among their brothers.
¹⁶ After this Job lived one hundred and forty years, and saw his children and grandchildren *for* four generations. ¹⁷ So Job died, old and full of days.

∼ PSALM 101:5–8 ∼

⁵ Whoever secretly slanders his
   neighbor,
   Him I will destroy;
   The one who has a haughty look and
   a proud heart,
   Him I will not endure.

⁶ My eyes *shall be* on the faithful of
   the land,
   That they may dwell with me;
   He who walks in a perfect way,
   He shall serve me.
⁷ He who works deceit shall not dwell
   within my house;
   He who tells lies shall not continue
   in my presence.
⁸ Early I will destroy all the wicked of
   the land,
   That I may cut off all the evildoers
   from the city of the LORD.

∼ PROVERBS 23:31–35 ∼

³¹ Do not look on the wine when it is
   red,
   When it sparkles in the cup,
   When it swirls around smoothly;
³² At the last it bites like a serpent,
   And stings like a viper.
³³ Your eyes will see strange things,
   And your heart will utter perverse
   things.

Standing in the Gap

A young woman lay in a hospital, far from home and family, drifting in and out of consciousness. Several times she became aware of a woman's voice praying for her salvation, as well as for her physical healing. At one point, a physician described her condition as critical, warning those present in the room that she might not survive. She heard all of this as if she were in a stupor, unable to respond. Then she heard a second voice, one that spoke in faith: "Doctor, I respect what you say, but I cannot accept it. I've been praying and I believe she will not only recover, but she will walk out of here and live for God."

Before long, the young woman did walk out of that hospital and return to work. It was then she learned that it had been her boss' wife (whom she had met only twice) who had stood in the gap, interceding for her at her hospital bed. When she attempted to thank this woman for her prayers, she replied, "Don't thank me, thank God. Others have prayed for me. Their prayers changed my life. I believe God has great plans for you."

It was five more years before she gave her life to Christ, but all the while, she never forgot how a faithful woman of God had believed He would answer prayer.

Have someone's prayers for you brought a change in your life? Be assured, your prayers for others will too!

> And the Lord restored Job's losses when he prayed for his friends. Indeed the Lord gave Job twice as much as he had before.
>
> *Job 42:10*

³⁴ Yes, you will be like one who lies
down in the midst of the sea,
Or like one who lies at the top of the
mast, *saying:*
³⁵ "They have struck me, *but* I was not
hurt;
They have beaten me, but I did not
feel *it*.
When shall I awake, that I may seek
another *drink?*"

~ 1 CORINTHIANS 7:1–19 ~

Now concerning the things of which you
wrote to me:

It is good for a man not to touch a
woman. ² Nevertheless, because of sexual
immorality, let each man have his own
wife, and let each woman have her
own husband. ³ Let the husband render
to his wife the affection due her, and likewise also the wife to her husband. ⁴ The
wife does not have authority over her own
body, but the husband *does*. And likewise
the husband does not have authority over
his own body, but the wife *does*. ⁵ Do not
deprive one another except with consent
for a time, that you may give yourselves
to fasting and prayer; and come together
again so that Satan does not tempt you
because of your lack of self-control. ⁶ But
I say this as a concession, not as a commandment. ⁷ For I wish that all men were
even as I myself. But each one has his own
gift from God, one in this manner and
another in that.

⁸ But I say to the unmarried and to the
widows: It is good for them if they remain even as I am; ⁹ but if they cannot
exercise self-control, let them marry. For
it is better to marry than to burn *with
passion.*

¹⁰ Now to the married I command, *yet*
not I but the Lord: A wife is not to depart
from *her* husband. ¹¹ But even if she does
depart, let her remain unmarried or be
reconciled to *her* husband. And a husband
is not to divorce *his* wife.

¹² But to the rest I, not the Lord, say: If
any brother has a wife who does not be-
lieve, and she is willing to live with him,
let him not divorce her. ¹³ And a woman
who has a husband who does not believe,
if he is willing to live with her, let her not
divorce him. ¹⁴ For the unbelieving husband is sanctified by the wife, and the
unbelieving wife is sanctified by the husband; otherwise your children would be
unclean, but now they are holy. ¹⁵ But if
the unbeliever departs, let him depart; a
brother or a sister is not under bondage
in such *cases*. But God has called us to
peace. ¹⁶ For how do you know, O wife,
whether you will save *your* husband? Or
how do you know, O husband, whether
you will save *your* wife?

¹⁷ But as God has distributed to each
one, as the Lord has called each one, so
let him walk. And so I ordain in all the
churches. ¹⁸ Was anyone called while
circumcised? Let him not become uncircumcised. Was anyone called while
uncircumcised? Let him not be circumcised. ¹⁹ Circumcision is nothing and
uncircumcision is nothing, but keeping the
commandments of God *is what matters.*

READING 238 · AUGUST 26

~ ECCLESIASTES 1:1—2:26 ~

The words of the Preacher, the son
of David, king in Jerusalem.

² "Vanity of vanities," says the
Preacher;
"Vanity of vanities, all *is* vanity."

³ What profit has a man from all his
labor
In which he toils under the sun?

⁴ *One* generation passes away, and
another generation comes;
But the earth abides forever.
⁵ The sun also rises, and the sun
goes down,
And hastens to the place where it
arose.
⁶ The wind goes toward the south,
And turns around to the north;
The wind whirls about
continually,

Search Me, O God

One day during her morning devotions, Jeannie found herself weeping as she read Psalm 139:23, "Search me, O God, and know my heart." She cried out to the Lord to cleanse her of several bad attitudes she had been harboring. Later that morning as she boarded an airplane, she sensed God asking her, "Are you ready?" She had a strong feeling that God was confirming to her that He had forgiven her and could now use her for a special assignment. She whispered a prayer. "Lord, help me to stay awake."

Jeannie usually took motion-sickness medication before flying, and therefore, often slept from take-off to landing. On this flight, however, she forced herself to stay awake. A woman took the seat next to her on the flight and as they began to talk, the woman asked, "Why do you have so much joy?" Jeannie replied, "Because of Jesus." And for the next three hours, she had a wonderful opportunity to witness to the woman. Later, she sent her a Bible and they exchanged letters. Then late one evening, the woman called and Jeannie led her to the Lord over the phone.

The Lord will not only hear your heart's cry today, but His answer will bring a blessing to your life that you will be able to share with others.

And comes again on its circuit.
7 All the rivers run into the sea,
Yet the sea *is* not full;
To the place from which the rivers
come,
There they return again.
8 All things *are* full of labor;
Man cannot express *it*.
The eye is not satisfied with
seeing,
Nor the ear filled with hearing.

9 That which has been *is* what will
be,
That which *is* done is what will be
done,
And *there is* nothing new under
the sun.
10 Is there anything of which it may
be said,
"See, this *is* new"?
It has already been in ancient
times before us.
11 *There is* no remembrance of
former *things,*
Nor will there be any
remembrance of *things* that are
to come
By *those* who will come after.

12 I, the Preacher, was king over Israel
in Jerusalem. 13 And I set my heart to seek
and search out by wisdom concerning all
that is done under heaven; this burdensome task God has given to the sons of
man, by which they may be exercised. 14 I
have seen all the works that are done under the sun; and indeed, all *is* vanity and
grasping for the wind.

15 *What is* crooked cannot be made
straight,
And what is lacking cannot be
numbered.

16 I communed with my heart, saying,
"Look, I have attained greatness, and have
gained more wisdom than all who were
before me in Jerusalem. My heart has
understood great wisdom and knowledge." 17 And I set my heart to know
wisdom and to know madness and folly. I
perceived that this also is grasping for the
wind.

18 For in much wisdom *is* much grief,
And he who increases knowledge
increases sorrow.

2 I said in my heart, "Come now, I will
test you with mirth; therefore enjoy pleasure"; but surely, this also *was* vanity. 2 I
said of laughter—"Madness!"; and of
mirth, "What does it accomplish?" 3 I
searched in my heart *how* to gratify my
flesh with wine, while guiding my heart
with wisdom, and how to lay hold on folly,
till I might see what *was* good for the sons
of men to do under heaven all the days of
their lives.
4 I made my works great, I built myself
houses, and planted myself vineyards. 5 I
made myself gardens and orchards, and
I planted all *kinds* of fruit trees in them.
6 I made myself water pools from which
to water the growing trees of the grove.
7 I acquired male and female servants, and
had servants born in my house. Yes, I had
greater possessions of herds and flocks
than all who were in Jerusalem before me.
8 I also gathered for myself silver and gold
and the special treasures of kings and of
the provinces. I acquired male and female
singers, the delights of the sons of men,
and musical instruments of all kinds.
9 So I became great and excelled more
than all who were before me in Jerusalem. Also my wisdom remained with me.

10 Whatever my eyes desired I did
not keep from them.
I did not withhold my heart from
any pleasure,
For my heart rejoiced in all my
labor;
And this was my reward from all
my labor.
11 Then I looked on all the works
that my hands had done
And on the labor in which I had
toiled;
And indeed all *was* vanity and
grasping for the wind.
There was no profit under the sun.

12 Then I turned myself to consider
wisdom and madness and folly;
For what *can* the man *do* who
succeeds the king?—
Only what he has already done.

13 Then I saw that wisdom excels
       folly
     As light excels darkness.
14 The wise man's eyes *are* in his
       head,
     But the fool walks in darkness.
     Yet I myself perceived
     That the same event happens to
       them all.

15 So I said in my heart,
     "As it happens to the fool,
     It also happens to me,
     And why was I then more wise?"
     Then I said in my heart,
     "This also *is* vanity."
16 For *there is* no more remembrance
       of the wise than of the fool
       forever,
     Since all that now *is* will be
       forgotten in the days to come.
     And how does a wise *man* die?
     As the fool!

17 Therefore I hated life because the work that was done under the sun *was* distressing to me, for all *is* vanity and grasping for the wind. 18 Then I hated all my labor in which I had toiled under the sun, because I must leave it to the man who will come after me. 19 And who knows whether he will be wise or a fool? Yet he will rule over all my labor in which I toiled and in which I have shown myself wise under the sun. This also *is* vanity. 20 Therefore I turned my heart and despaired of all the labor in which I had toiled under the sun. 21 For there is a man whose labor *is* with wisdom, knowledge, and skill; yet he must leave his heritage to a man who has not labored for it. This also *is* vanity and a great evil. 22 For what has man for all his labor, and for the striving of his heart with which he has toiled under the sun? 23 For all his days *are* sorrowful, and his work burdensome; even in the night his heart takes no rest. This also is vanity.

24 Nothing *is* better for a man *than* that he should eat and drink, and *that* his soul should enjoy good in his labor. This also, I saw, was from the hand of God. 25 For who can eat, or who can have enjoyment, more than I? 26 For *God* gives wisdom and knowledge and joy to a man who *is* good

in His sight; but to the sinner He gives the work of gathering and collecting, that he may give to *him who is* good before God. This also *is* vanity and grasping for the wind.

∽ PSALM 102:1–11 ∽

1 Hear my prayer, O LORD,
     And let my cry come to You.
2 Do not hide Your face from me in
       the day of my trouble;
     Incline Your ear to me;
     In the day that I call, answer me
       speedily.

3 For my days are consumed like
       smoke,
     And my bones are burned like a
       hearth.
4 My heart is stricken and withered
       like grass,
     So that I forget to eat my bread.
5 Because of the sound of my groaning
     My bones cling to my skin.
6 I am like a pelican of the wilderness;
     I am like an owl of the desert.
7 I lie awake,
     And am like a sparrow alone on the
       housetop.

8 My enemies reproach me all day
       long;
     Those who deride me swear an oath
       against me.
9 For I have eaten ashes like bread,
     And mingled my drink with
       weeping,
10 Because of Your indignation and
       Your wrath;
     For You have lifted me up and cast
       me away.
11 My days *are* like a shadow that
       lengthens,
     And I wither away like grass.

∽ PROVERBS 24:1, 2 ∽

1 Do not be envious of evil men,
     Nor desire to be with them;
2 For their heart devises violence,
     And their lips talk of troublemaking.

~ 1 CORINTHIANS 7:20–40 ~

Let each one remain in the same calling in which he was called. ²¹ Were you called *while* a slave? Do not be concerned about it; but if you can be made free, rather use *it.* ²² For he who is called in the Lord *while* a slave is the Lord's freedman. Likewise he who is called *while* free is Christ's slave. ²³ You were bought at a price; do not become slaves of men. ²⁴ Brethren, let each one remain with God in that *state* in which he was called.

²⁵ Now concerning virgins: I have no commandment from the Lord; yet I give judgment as one whom the Lord in His mercy *has made* trustworthy. ²⁶ I suppose therefore that this is good because of the present distress—that *it is* good for a man to remain as he is: ²⁷ Are you bound to a wife? Do not seek to be loosed. Are you loosed from a wife? Do not seek a wife. ²⁸ But even if you do marry, you have not sinned; and if a virgin marries, she has not sinned. Nevertheless such will have trouble in the flesh, but I would spare you.

²⁹ But this I say, brethren, the time *is* short, so that from now on even those who have wives should be as though they had none, ³⁰ those who weep as though they did not weep, those who rejoice as though they did not rejoice, those who buy as though they did not possess, ³¹ and those who use this world as not misusing *it.* For the form of this world is passing away.

³² But I want you to be without care. He who is unmarried cares for the things of the Lord—how he may please the Lord. ³³ But he who is married cares about the things of the world—how he may please *his* wife. ³⁴ There is a difference between a wife and a virgin. The unmarried woman cares about the things of the Lord, that she may be holy both in body and in spirit. But she who is married cares about the things of the world—how she may please *her* husband. ³⁵ And this I say for your own profit, not that I may put a leash on you, but for what is proper, and that you may serve the Lord without distraction.

³⁶ But if any man thinks he is behaving improperly toward his virgin, if she is past the flower of youth, and thus it must be, let him do what he wishes. He does not sin; let them marry. ³⁷ Nevertheless he who stands steadfast in his heart, having no necessity, but has power over his own will, and has so determined in his heart that he will keep his virgin, does well. ³⁸ So then he who gives *her* in marriage does well, but he who does not give *her* in marriage does better.

³⁹ A wife is bound by law as long as her husband lives; but if her husband dies, she is at liberty to be married to whom she wishes, only in the Lord. ⁴⁰ But she is happier if she remains as she is, according to my judgment—and I think I also have the Spirit of God.

READING 239 · AUGUST 27

~ ECCLESIASTES 3:1–22 ~

¹ To everything *there is* a season,
  A time for every purpose under
    heaven:

² A time to be born,
    And a time to die;
  A time to plant,
    And a time to pluck *what is*
      planted;

³ A time to kill,
    And a time to heal;

  A time to break down,
    And a time to build up;

⁴ A time to weep,
    And a time to laugh;
  A time to mourn,
    And a time to dance;

⁵ A time to cast away stones,
    And a time to gather stones;
  A time to embrace,
    And a time to refrain from
      embracing;

Unexpected Beauty

Karen had been *volunteered* to take some Christmas gifts to a home for mentally handicapped children. Her plan was to drop the presents at the door and be on her way. Places "like that" made her uncomfortable.

Before she could make her get-away, a voice called out behind her, "Oh thank you so much!" Karen looked back to see a middle aged woman in nurse-type shoes standing at the door. Seeing the name Lily on her name tag, Karen introduced herself. She explained why she was bringing the gifts, keeping one eye on the clock and the other on the door.

Lily seemed unaware of Karen's exaggerated hurry. She invited Karen to take part in giving the children their gifts. Karen wasn't sure she could bear to witness such a heartbreaking situation in the midst of such a festive season but was unable to resist Lily's sincere offer.

The fear in Karen's heart subsided as she went from room to room. She saw shining eyes and grateful hearts as she placed her gifts in eager hands.

On her way out she noticed the sign by the door, "God makes everything beautiful in its time" and said, "I wouldn't have believed this sign before. I thought of handicapped children as miserable and even, I'm ashamed to say, unsightly. But now that I've spent time with them I know I have truly seen the beauty only God can create."

Lily just smiled, for Karen was not the first to discover, in these children, God's unexpected beauty.

> He has made everything beautiful in its time. Also He has put eternity in their hearts, except that no one can find out the work that God does from beginning to end.
>
> *Ecclesiastes 3:11*

6 A time to gain,
   And a time to lose;
   A time to keep,
   And a time to throw away;
7 A time to tear,
   And a time to sew;
   A time to keep silence,
   And a time to speak;
8 A time to love,
   And a time to hate;
   A time of war,
   And a time of peace.

9 What profit has the worker from that in which he labors? 10 I have seen the God-given task with which the sons of men are to be occupied. 11 He has made everything beautiful in its time. Also He has put eternity in their hearts, except that no one can find out the work that God does from beginning to end.

12 I know that nothing *is* better for them than to rejoice, and to do good in their lives, 13 and also that every man should eat and drink and enjoy the good of all his labor—it *is* the gift of God.

14 I know that whatever God does,
   It shall be forever.
   Nothing can be added to it,
   And nothing taken from it.
   God does *it,* that men should fear
      before Him.
15 That which is has already been,
   And what is to be has already
      been;
   And God requires an account of
      what is past.

16 Moreover I saw under the sun:

   In the place of judgment,
   Wickedness *was* there;
   And *in* the place of righteousness,
   Iniquity *was* there.

17 I said in my heart,

   "God shall judge the righteous and
      the wicked,
   For *there is* a time there for every
      purpose and for every work."

18 I said in my heart, "Concerning the condition of the sons of men, God tests

them, that they may see that they themselves are *like* animals." 19 For what happens to the sons of men also happens to animals; one thing befalls them: as one dies, so dies the other. Surely, they all have one breath; man has no advantage over animals, for all *is* vanity. 20 All go to one place: all are from the dust, and all return to dust. 21 Who knows the spirit of the sons of men, which goes upward, and the spirit of the animal, which goes down to the earth? 22 So I perceived that nothing *is* better than that a man should rejoice in his own works, for that *is* his heritage. For who can bring him to see what will happen after him?

~ PSALM 102:12–17 ~

12 But You, O LORD, shall endure
      forever,
   And the remembrance of Your name
      to all generations.
13 You will arise *and* have mercy on
      Zion;
   For the time to favor her,
   Yes, the set time, has come.
14 For Your servants take pleasure in
      her stones,
   And show favor to her dust.
15 So the nations shall fear the name of
      the LORD,
   And all the kings of the earth Your
      glory.
16 For the LORD shall build up Zion;
   He shall appear in His glory.
17 He shall regard the prayer of the
      destitute,
   And shall not despise their prayer.

~ PROVERBS 24:3, 4 ~

3 Through wisdom a house is built,
   And by understanding it is
      established;
4 By knowledge the rooms are filled
   With all precious and pleasant riches.

~ 1 CORINTHIANS 8:1–13 ~

Now concerning things offered to idols: We know that we all have knowledge. Knowledge puffs up, but love edifies. 2 And if anyone thinks that he knows anything, he knows nothing yet as he ought to know. ³ But if anyone loves God, this one is known by Him.

⁴ Therefore concerning the eating of things offered to idols, we know that an idol *is* nothing in the world, and that *there is* no other God but one. ⁵ For even if there are so-called gods, whether in heaven or on earth (as there are many gods and many lords), ⁶ yet for us *there is* one God, the Father, of whom *are* all things, and we for Him; and one Lord Jesus Christ, through whom *are* all things, and through whom we *live*.

⁷ However, *there is* not in everyone that knowledge; for some, with consciousness of the idol, until now eat *it* as a thing offered to an idol; and their conscience, being weak, is defiled. ⁸ But food does not commend us to God; for neither if we eat are we the better, nor if we do not eat are we the worse.

⁹ But beware lest somehow this liberty of yours become a stumbling block to those who are weak. ¹⁰ For if anyone sees you who have knowledge eating in an idol's temple, will not the conscience of him who is weak be emboldened to eat those things offered to idols? ¹¹ And because of your knowledge shall the weak brother perish, for whom Christ died? ¹² But when you thus sin against the brethren, and wound their weak conscience, you sin against Christ. ¹³ Therefore, if food makes my brother stumble, I will never again eat meat, lest I make my brother stumble.

READING 240 · AUGUST 28

~ ECCLESIASTES 4:1—6:12 ~

Then I returned and considered all the oppression that is done under the sun:

> And look! The tears of the oppressed,
> But they have no comforter—
> On the side of their oppressors
> *there is* power,
> But they have no comforter.

² Therefore I praised the dead who were already dead,
More than the living who are still alive.
³ Yet, better than both *is he* who has never existed,
Who has not seen the evil work that is done under the sun.

⁴ Again, I saw that for all toil and every skillful work a man is envied by his neighbor. This also *is* vanity and grasping for the wind.

⁵ The fool folds his hands
And consumes his own flesh.
⁶ Better a handful *with* quietness
Than both hands full, *together with* toil and grasping for the wind.

⁷ Then I returned, and I saw vanity under the sun:

⁸ There is one alone, without companion:
He has neither son nor brother.
Yet *there is* no end to all his labors,
Nor is his eye satisfied with riches.
But he never asks,
"For whom do I toil and deprive myself of good?"
This also *is* vanity and a grave misfortune.

⁹ Two *are* better than one,
Because they have a good reward for their labor.
¹⁰ For if they fall, one will lift up his companion.
But woe to him *who is* alone when he falls,
For *he has* no one to help him up.
¹¹ Again, if two lie down together, they will keep warm;
But how can one be warm *alone*?
¹² Though one may be overpowered by another, two can withstand him.
And a threefold cord is not quickly broken.

13 Better a poor and wise youth
   Than an old and foolish king who
      will be admonished no more.
14 For he comes out of prison to be
      king,
   Although he was born poor in his
      kingdom.
15 I saw all the living who walk
      under the sun;
   They were with the second youth
      who stands in his place.
16 *There was* no end of all the people
      over whom he was made king;
   Yet those who come afterward will
      not rejoice in him.
   Surely this also *is* vanity and
      grasping for the wind.

5 Walk prudently when you go to the
house of God; and draw near to hear
rather than to give the sacrifice of fools,
for they do not know that they do evil.

2 Do not be rash with your mouth,
   And let not your heart utter
      anything hastily before God.
   For God *is* in heaven, and you on
      earth;
   Therefore let your words be few.
3 For a dream comes through much
      activity,
   And a fool's voice *is known* by *his*
      many words.

4 When you make a vow to God, do
      not delay to pay it;
   For *He has* no pleasure in fools.
   Pay what you have vowed—
5 Better not to vow than to vow and
      not pay.

6 Do not let your mouth cause your flesh
to sin, nor say before the messenger *of
God* that it *was* an error. Why should God
be angry at your excuse and destroy the
work of your hands? 7 For in the multitude of dreams and many words *there is*
also vanity. But fear God.
   8 If you see the oppression of the poor,
and the violent perversion of justice and
righteousness in a province, do not marvel at the matter; for high official watches
over high official, and higher officials
are over them.

9 Moreover the profit of the land is for
all; *even* the king is served from the field.

10 He who loves silver will not be
      satisfied with silver;
   Nor he who loves abundance,
      with increase.
   This also *is* vanity.

11 When goods increase,
   They increase who eat them;
   So what profit have the owners
   Except to see *them* with their
      eyes?

12 The sleep of a laboring man *is*
      sweet,
   Whether he eats little or much;
   But the abundance of the rich will
      not permit him to sleep.

13 There is a severe evil *which* I have
      seen under the sun:
   Riches kept for their owner to his
      hurt.
14 But those riches perish through
      misfortune;
   When he begets a son, *there is*
      nothing in his hand.
15 As he came from his mother's
      womb, naked shall he return,
   To go as he came;
   And he shall take nothing from his
      labor
   Which he may carry away in his
      hand.

16 And this also *is* a severe evil—
   Just exactly as he came, so shall he
      go.
   And what profit has he who has
      labored for the wind?
17 All his days he also eats in
      darkness,
   And *he has* much sorrow and
      sickness and anger.

18 Here is what I have seen: *It is* good
and fitting *for one* to eat and drink, and
to enjoy the good of all his labor in which
he toils under the sun all the days of his
life which God gives him; for it *is* his heritage. 19 As for every man to whom God
has given riches and wealth, and given him

The Common Law of Life

The tree that never had to fight
For sun and sky and air and light,
That stood out in the open plain
And always got its share of rain,
Never became a forest king,
But lived and died a common thing.
The man who never had to toil,
Who never had to win his share
Of sun and sky and light and air,
Never became a manly man,
But lived and died as he began.
Good timber does not grow on ease
The stronger wind, the tougher trees,
The farther sky, the greater length,
By sun and cold, by rain and snows,
In tree or man good timber grows.
Where thickest stands the forest growth,
We find the patriarchs of both,
And they hold converse with the stars
Whose broken branches show the scars
Of many winds and much of strife,
This is the common law of life.

Do you not know that those who run in a race all run, but one receives the prize? Run in such a way that you may obtain it.

1 Corinthians 9:24

power to eat of it, to receive his heritage and rejoice in his labor—this *is* the gift of God. ²⁰ For he will not dwell unduly on the days of his life, because God keeps *him* busy with the joy of his heart.

6 There is an evil which I have seen under the sun, and it *is* common among men: ² A man to whom God has given riches and wealth and honor, so that he lacks nothing for himself of all he desires; yet God does not give him power to eat of it, but a foreigner consumes it. This *is* vanity, and it *is* an evil affliction. ³ If a man begets a hundred *children* and lives many years, so that the days of his years are many, but his soul is not satisfied with goodness, or indeed he has no burial, I say *that* a stillborn child *is* better than he— ⁴ for it comes in vanity and departs in darkness, and its name is covered with darkness. ⁵ Though it has not seen the sun or known *anything*, this has more rest than that man, ⁶ even if he lives a thousand years twice—but has not seen goodness. Do not all go to one place?

7   All the labor of man *is* for his
     mouth,
  And yet the soul is not satisfied.
8   For what more has the wise *man*
     than the fool?
  What does the poor man have,
  Who knows *how* to walk before
     the living?
9   Better *is* the sight of the eyes than
     the wandering of desire.
  This also *is* vanity and grasping for
     the wind.

10   Whatever one is, he has been
     named already,
  For it is known that he *is* man;
  And he cannot contend with Him
     who is mightier than he.
11   Since there are many things that
     increase vanity,
  How *is* man the better?

¹² For who knows what *is* good for man in life, all the days of his vain life which he passes like a shadow? Who can tell a man what will happen after him under the sun?

~ PSALM 102:18–28 ~

18   This will be written for the
     generation to come,
  That a people yet to be created may
     praise the LORD.
19   For He looked down from the
     height of His sanctuary;
  From heaven the LORD viewed the
     earth,
20   To hear the groaning of the prisoner,
  To release those appointed to death,
21   To declare the name of the LORD in
     Zion,
  And His praise in Jerusalem,
22   When the peoples are gathered
     together,
  And the kingdoms, to serve the
     LORD.

23   He weakened my strength in the
     way;
  He shortened my days.
24   I said, "O my God,
  Do not take me away in the midst of
     my days;
  Your years *are* throughout all
     generations.
25   Of old You laid the foundation of
     the earth,
  And the heavens *are* the work of
     Your hands.
26   They will perish, but You will
     endure;
  Yes, they will all grow old like a
     garment;
  Like a cloak You will change them,
  And they will be changed.
27   But You *are* the same,
  And Your years will have no end.
28   The children of Your servants will
     continue,
  And their descendants will be
     established before You."

~ PROVERBS 24:5, 6 ~

5   A wise man *is* strong,
  Yes, a man of knowledge increases
     strength;
6   For by wise counsel you will wage
     your own war,

And in a multitude of counselors
there is safety.

~ 1 CORINTHIANS 9:1–27 ~

Am I not an apostle? Am I not free? Have I not seen Jesus Christ our Lord? Are you not my work in the Lord? ² If I am not an apostle to others, yet doubtless I am to you. For you are the seal of my apostleship in the Lord.

³ My defense to those who examine me is this: ⁴ Do we have no right to eat and drink? ⁵ Do we have no right to take along a believing wife, as *do* also the other apostles, the brothers of the Lord, and Cephas? ⁶ Or *is it* only Barnabas and I *who* have no right to refrain from working? ⁷ Who ever goes to war at his own expense? Who plants a vineyard and does not eat of its fruit? Or who tends a flock and does not drink of the milk of the flock?

⁸ Do I say these things as a *mere* man? Or does not the law say the same also? ⁹ For it is written in the law of Moses, "You shall not muzzle an ox while it treads out the grain." Is it oxen God is concerned about? ¹⁰ Or does He say *it* altogether for our sakes? For our sakes, no doubt, *this* is written, that he who plows should plow in hope, and he who threshes in hope should be partaker of his hope. ¹¹ If we have sown spiritual things for you, *is it* a great thing if we reap your material things? ¹² If others are partakers of *this* right over you, *are* we not even more?

Nevertheless we have not used this right, but endure all things lest we hinder the gospel of Christ. ¹³ Do you not know that those who minister the holy things eat *of the things* of the temple, and those who serve at the altar partake of *the offerings of* the altar? ¹⁴ Even so the Lord

has commanded that those who preach the gospel should live from the gospel. ¹⁵ But I have used none of these things, nor have I written these things that it should be done so to me; for it *would be* better for me to die than that anyone should make my boasting void. ¹⁶ For if I preach the gospel, I have nothing to boast of, for necessity is laid upon me; yes, woe is me if I do not preach the gospel! ¹⁷ For if I do this willingly, I have a reward; but if against my will, I have been entrusted with a stewardship. ¹⁸ What is my reward then? That when I preach the gospel, I may present the gospel of Christ without charge, that I may not abuse my authority in the gospel.

¹⁹ For though I am free from all *men,* I have made myself a servant to all, that I might win the more; ²⁰ and to the Jews I became as a Jew, that I might win Jews; to those *who are* under the law, as under the law, that I might win those *who are* under the law; ²¹ to those *who are* without law, as without law (not being without law toward God, but under law toward Christ), that I might win those *who are* without law; ²² to the weak I became as weak, that I might win the weak. I have become all things to all *men,* that I might by all means save some. ²³ Now this I do for the gospel's sake, that I may be partaker of it with *you.*

²⁴ Do you not know that those who run in a race all run, but one receives the prize? Run in such a way that you may obtain *it.* ²⁵ And everyone who competes *for the prize* is temperate in all things. Now they *do it* to obtain a perishable crown, but we *for* an imperishable *crown.* ²⁶ Therefore I run thus: not with uncertainty. Thus I fight: not as *one who* beats the air. ²⁷ But I discipline my body and bring *it* into subjection, lest, when I have preached to others, I myself should become disqualified.

~ ECCLESIASTES 7:1–29 ~

¹ A good name *is* better than
precious ointment,
And the day of death than the day
of one's birth;

² Better to go to the house of
mourning
Than to go to the house of
feasting,

For that *is* the end of all men;
And the living will take *it* to heart.

3 Sorrow *is* better than laughter,
For by a sad countenance the
heart is made better.

4 The heart of the wise *is* in the
house of mourning,
But the heart of fools *is* in the
house of mirth.

5 *It is* better to hear the rebuke of
the wise
Than for a man to hear the song
of fools.

6 For like the crackling of thorns
under a pot,
So *is* the laughter of the fool.
This also is vanity.

7 Surely oppression destroys a wise
man's reason,
And a bribe debases the heart.

8 The end of a thing *is* better than
its beginning;
The patient in spirit *is* better than
the proud in spirit.

9 Do not hasten in your spirit to be
angry,
For anger rests in the bosom of
fools.

10 Do not say,
"Why were the former days better
than these?"
For you do not inquire wisely
concerning this.

11 Wisdom *is* good with an
inheritance,
And profitable to those who see
the sun.

12 For wisdom *is* a defense *as* money
is a defense,
But the excellence of knowledge *is*
that wisdom gives life to those
who have it.

13 Consider the work of God;
For who can make straight what
He has made crooked?

14 In the day of prosperity be joyful,
But in the day of adversity
consider:
Surely God has appointed the one
as well as the other,

So that man can find out nothing
that will come after him.

15 I have seen everything in my days of
vanity:

There is a just *man* who perishes
in his righteousness,
And there is a wicked *man* who
prolongs *life* in his wickedness.

16 Do not be overly righteous,
Nor be overly wise:
Why should you destroy yourself?

17 Do not be overly wicked,
Nor be foolish:
Why should you die before your
time?

18 *It is* good that you grasp this,
And also not remove your hand
from the other;
For he who fears God will escape
them all.

19 Wisdom strengthens the wise
More than ten rulers of the city.

20 For *there is* not a just man on
earth who does good
And does not sin.

21 Also do not take to heart
everything people say,
Lest you hear your servant cursing
you.

22 For many times, also, your own
heart has known
That even you have cursed others.

23 All this I have proved by wisdom.
I said, "I will be wise";
But it *was* far from me.

24 As for that which is far off and
exceedingly deep,
Who can find it out?

25 I applied my heart to know,
To search and seek out wisdom
and the reason *of things,*
To know the wickedness of folly,
Even of foolishness *and* madness.

26 And I find more bitter than death
The woman whose heart *is* snares
and nets,
Whose hands *are* fetters.

Visualization

Major James Nesmeth, an average weekend golfer shooting in the mid- to low-nineties, dreamed of improving his golf game. But for seven years, he never touched a club nor set foot on a fairway. During those years however, he developed an amazingly effective technique for improving his game. The first time he returned to a course, he shot an astonishing 74! He had cut 20 strokes off his average.

What was his secret? Visualization. For seven years, Major Nesmeth was a prisoner of war in North Vietnam. He was imprisoned in a cage four-and-a-half feet high and five feet long. Most of those years, he saw no one, talked to no one, and had no physical activity. He knew he had to find some way to occupy his mind or he would lose his sanity, so he began to visualize playing golf. Each day, he played a full 18 holes at the imaginary country club of his dreams. He imagined every detail, every shot. And not once did he miss a shot or putt. Seven days a week, four hours a day, he played eighteen holes in his mind.

Your dreams for the future will be much more likely to come true if you visualize your goals and imagine reaching them. You will be training your mind to produce successful thoughts and ideas.

I applied my heart to know, to search and seek out wisdom and the reason of things, to know the wickedness of folly, even of foolishness and madness.

Ecclesiastes 7:25

He who pleases God shall escape
from her,
But the sinner shall be trapped by
her.

27 "Here is what I have found," says
the Preacher,
  "*Adding* one thing to the other to
find out the reason,
28 Which my soul still seeks but I
cannot find:
One man among a thousand I
have found,
But a woman among all these I
have not found.
29 Truly, this only I have found:
That God made man upright,
But they have sought out many
schemes."

~ PSALM 103:1–5 ~

1 Bless the LORD, O my soul;
And all that is within me, *bless* His
holy name!
2 Bless the LORD, O my soul,
And forget not all His benefits:
3 Who forgives all your iniquities,
Who heals all your diseases,
4 Who redeems your life from
destruction,
Who crowns you with
lovingkindness and tender
mercies,
5 Who satisfies your mouth with good
things,
So that your youth is renewed like
the eagle's.

~ PROVERBS 24:7–9 ~

7 Wisdom *is* too lofty for a fool;
He does not open his mouth in the
gate.

8 He who plots to do evil
Will be called a schemer.
9 The devising of foolishness *is* sin,
And the scoffer *is* an abomination to
men.

~ 1 CORINTHIANS 10:1–18 ~

Moreover, brethren, I do not want you
to be unaware that all our fathers were
under the cloud, all passed through the
sea, 2 all were baptized into Moses in
the cloud and in the sea, 3 all ate the same
spiritual food, 4 and all drank the same
spiritual drink. For they drank of that
spiritual Rock that followed them, and
that Rock was Christ. 5 But with most
of them God was not well pleased, for
their bodies were scattered in the wilderness.
6 Now these things became our examples, to the intent that we should not
lust after evil things as they also lusted.
7 And do not become idolaters as *were*
some of them. As it is written, "The people
sat down to eat and drink, and rose up to
play." 8 Nor let us commit sexual immorality, as some of them did, and in one
day twenty-three thousand fell; 9 nor let
us tempt Christ, as some of them also
tempted, and were destroyed by serpents;
10 nor complain, as some of them also
complained, and were destroyed by the
destroyer. 11 Now all these things happened to them as examples, and they were
written for our admonition, upon whom
the ends of the ages have come.
12 Therefore let him who thinks he
stands take heed lest he fall. 13 No temptation has overtaken you except such as is
common to man; but God *is* faithful, who
will not allow you to be tempted beyond
what you are able, but with the temptation will also make the way of escape, that
you may be able to bear *it.*
14 Therefore, my beloved, flee from
idolatry. 15 I speak as to wise men; judge
for yourselves what I say. 16 The cup of
blessing which we bless, is it not the communion of the blood of Christ? The bread
which we break, is it not the communion
of the body of Christ? 17 For we, *though*
many, are one bread *and* one body; for
we all partake of that one bread.
18 Observe Israel after the flesh: Are not
those who eat of the sacrifices partakers
of the altar?

~ ECCLESIASTES 8:1—10:20 ~

1 Who *is* like a wise *man*?
   And who knows the interpretation
      of a thing?
   A man's wisdom makes his face
      shine,
   And the sternness of his face is
      changed.

2 I *say,* "Keep the king's commandment
for the sake of your oath to God. 3 Do
not be hasty to go from his presence. Do
not take your stand for an evil thing, for
he does whatever pleases him."

4 Where the word of a king *is, there
      is* power;
   And who may say to him, "What
      are you doing?"
5 He who keeps his command will
      experience nothing harmful;
   And a wise man's heart discerns
      both time and judgment,
6 Because for every matter there is a
      time and judgment,
   Though the misery of man
      increases greatly.
7 For he does not know what will
      happen;
   So who can tell him when it will
      occur?
8 No one has power over the spirit
      to retain the spirit,
   And no one has power in the day
      of death.
   There is no release from that war,
   And wickedness will not deliver
      those who are given to it.

9 All this I have seen, and applied my
heart to every work that is done under
the sun: *There is* a time in which one man
rules over another to his own hurt.
10 Then I saw the wicked buried, who
had come and gone from the place of
holiness, and they were forgotten in the
city where they had so done. This also *is*
vanity. 11 Because the sentence against an
evil work is not executed speedily, therefore the heart of the sons of men is fully
set in them to do evil. 12 Though a sinner
does evil a hundred *times,* and his *days*
are prolonged, yet I surely know that it

will be well with those who fear God, who
fear before Him. 13 But it will not be well
with the wicked; nor will he prolong *his*
days, *which are* as a shadow, because he
does not fear before God.

14 There is a vanity which occurs on
earth, that there are just *men* to whom it
happens according to the work of the
wicked; again, there are wicked *men* to
whom it happens according to the work
of the righteous. I said that this also *is*
vanity.

15 So I commended enjoyment, because
a man has nothing better under the sun
than to eat, drink, and be merry; for this
will remain with him in his labor *all* the
days of his life which God gives him under the sun.

16 When I applied my heart to know
wisdom and to see the business that is
done on earth, even though one sees no
sleep day or night, 17 then I saw all the
work of God, that a man cannot find out
the work that is done under the sun. For
though a man labors to discover *it,* yet he
will not find *it;* moreover, though a wise
man attempts to know *it,* he will not be
able to find *it.*

9 For I considered all this in my heart,
so that I could declare it all: that the righteous and the wise and their works *are* in
the hand of God. People know neither
love nor hatred *by* anything *they see* before them. 2 All things *come* alike to all:

   One event *happens* to the
      righteous and the wicked;
   To the good, the clean, and the
      unclean;
   To him who sacrifices and him
      who does not sacrifice.
   As is the good, so *is* the sinner;
   He who takes an oath as *he* who
      fears an oath.

3 This *is* an evil in all that is done under
the sun: that one thing *happens* to all.
Truly the hearts of the sons of men are
full of evil; madness *is* in their hearts while
they live, and after that *they go* to the
dead. 4 But for him who is joined to all

the living there is hope, for a living dog is better than a dead lion.

5 For the living know that they will die;
But the dead know nothing,
And they have no more reward,
For the memory of them is forgotten.
6 Also their love, their hatred, and their envy have now perished;
Nevermore will they have a share
In anything done under the sun.

7 Go, eat your bread with joy,
And drink your wine with a merry heart;
For God has already accepted your works.
8 Let your garments always be white,
And let your head lack no oil.

9 Live joyfully with the wife whom you love all the days of your vain life which He has given you under the sun, all your days of vanity; for that *is* your portion in life, and in the labor which you perform under the sun. 10 Whatever your hand finds to do, do *it* with your might; for *there is* no work or device or knowledge or wisdom in the grave where you are going.

11 I returned and saw under the sun that—

The race *is* not to the swift,
Nor the battle to the strong,
Nor bread to the wise,
Nor riches to men of understanding,
Nor favor to men of skill;
But time and chance happen to them all.
12 For man also does not know his time:
Like fish taken in a cruel net,
Like birds caught in a snare,
So the sons of men *are* snared in an evil time,
When it falls suddenly upon them.

13 This wisdom I have also seen under the sun, and it *seemed* great to me: 14 *There was* a little city with few men in it; and a great king came against it, besieged it, and built great snares around it. 15 Now there was found in it a poor wise man, and he by his wisdom delivered the city. Yet no one remembered that same poor man. 16 Then I said:

"Wisdom *is* better than strength.
Nevertheless the poor man's wisdom *is* despised,
And his words are not heard.
17 Words of the wise, *spoken* quietly, *should be* heard
Rather than the shout of a ruler of fools.
18 Wisdom *is* better than weapons of war;
But one sinner destroys much good."

10 Dead flies putrefy the perfumer's ointment,
And cause it to give off a foul odor;
So does a little folly to one respected for wisdom *and* honor.
2 A wise man's heart *is* at his right hand,
But a fool's heart at his left.
3 Even when a fool walks along the way,
He lacks wisdom,
And he shows everyone *that* he *is* a fool.
4 If the spirit of the ruler rises against you,
Do not leave your post;
For conciliation pacifies great offenses.

5 There is an evil I have seen under the sun,
As an error proceeding from the ruler:
6 Folly is set in great dignity,
While the rich sit in a lowly place.
7 I have seen servants on horses,
While princes walk on the ground like servants.

8 He who digs a pit will fall into it,
And whoever breaks through a wall will be bitten by a serpent.

Investing the Best

On a December evening in 1995, the employees of Malden Mills in Lawrence, Massachusetts, thought their jobs had gone up in smoke. The mill had been destroyed by fire. But when morning came, the company leader, Aaron Feuerstein, told his 3,000-plus employees that he had decided to rebuild — immediately. Not only that, he intended to keep everyone on the payroll for thirty days. That decision cost him millions of dollars a week.

It was not the first time Feuerstein had disregarded the obvious. When other textile mills in the area moved south to take advantage of lower taxes and cheaper labor, Feuerstein felt he had a responsibility to the people he employed, and stayed put.

When paychecks were handed out two days after the fire, each employee received a Christmas bonus and a note from the boss that read, "Do not despair. God bless each of you."

By January 2, the mill had reopened and within ninety days, seventy-five percent of the workers were back on the job. Experts had said it could never be done. The mill was able to fill eighty percent of its orders in spite of the fire. Feuerstein's investment in his employees had been returned to him in miracle-working effort and loyalty.

When we give our best to others, we inspire them to give their best in return.

> Whatever your hand finds to do, do it with your might; for there is no work or device or knowledge or wisdom in the grave where you are going.
>
> *Ecclesiastes 9:10*

9   He who quarries stones may be
        hurt by them,
    And he who splits wood may be
        endangered by it.
10 If the ax is dull,
    And one does not sharpen the
        edge,
    Then he must use more strength;
    But wisdom brings success.

11 A serpent may bite when *it is* not
        charmed;
    The babbler is no different.
12 The words of a wise man's mouth
        are gracious,
    But the lips of a fool shall swallow
        him up;
13 The words of his mouth begin
        with foolishness,
    And the end of his talk *is* raving
        madness.
14 A fool also multiplies words.
    No man knows what is to be;
    Who can tell him what will be
        after him?
15 The labor of fools wearies them,
    For they do not even know how
        to go to the city!

16 Woe to you, O land, when your
        king *is* a child,
    And your princes feast in the
        morning!
17 Blessed *are* you, O land, when
        your king *is* the son of nobles,
    And your princes feast at the
        proper time—
    For strength and not for
        drunkenness!
18 Because of laziness the building
        decays,
    And through idleness of hands the
        house leaks.
19 A feast is made for laughter,
    And wine makes merry;
    But money answers everything.

20 Do not curse the king, even in
        your thought;
    Do not curse the rich, even in
        your bedroom;
    For a bird of the air may carry
        your voice,
    And a bird in flight may tell the
        matter.

~ PSALM 103:6–14 ~

6   The LORD executes righteousness
    And justice for all who are
        oppressed.
7   He made known His ways to Moses,
    His acts to the children of Israel.
8   The LORD *is* merciful and gracious,
    Slow to anger, and abounding in
        mercy.
9   He will not always strive *with us,*
    Nor will He keep *His anger* forever.
10 He has not dealt with us according
        to our sins,
    Nor punished us according to our
        iniquities.

11 For as the heavens are high above
        the earth,
    So great is His mercy toward those
        who fear Him;
12 As far as the east is from the west,
    So far has He removed our
        transgressions from us.
13 As a father pities *his* children,
    So the LORD pities those who fear
        Him.
14 For He knows our frame;
    He remembers that we *are* dust.

~ PROVERBS 24:10–12 ~

10 *If* you faint in the day of adversity,
    Your strength *is* small.

11 Deliver *those who* are drawn toward
        death,
    And hold back *those* stumbling to
        the slaughter.
12 If you say, "Surely we did not know
        this,"
    Does not He who weighs the hearts
        consider *it?*
    He who keeps your soul, does He
        not know *it?*
    And will He *not* render to *each* man
        according to his deeds?

~ 1 CORINTHIANS 10:19–33 ~

What am I saying then? That an idol
is anything, or what is offered to idols is
anything? 20 Rather, that the things which

the Gentiles sacrifice they sacrifice to demons and not to God, and I do not want
you to have fellowship with demons.
²¹ You cannot drink the cup of the Lord
and the cup of demons; you cannot partake of the Lord's table and of the table
of demons. ²² Or do we provoke the Lord
to jealousy? Are we stronger than He?

²³ All things are lawful for me, but not
all things are helpful; all things are lawful
for me, but not all things edify. ²⁴ Let no
one seek his own, but each one the other's
well-being.

²⁵ Eat whatever is sold in the meat market, asking no questions for conscience'
sake; ²⁶ for "the earth *is* the LORD's, and
all its fullness."

²⁷ If any of those who do not believe
invites you *to dinner,* and you desire to
go, eat whatever is set before you, asking
no question for conscience' sake. ²⁸ But if
anyone says to you, "This was offered to
idols," do not eat it for the sake of the
one who told you, and for conscience'
sake; for "the earth *is* the LORD's, and all
its fullness." ²⁹ "Conscience," I say, not
your own, but that of the other. For why
is my liberty judged by another *man's*
conscience? ³⁰ But if I partake with thanks,
why am I evil spoken of for *the food* over
which I give thanks?

³¹ Therefore, whether you eat or drink,
or whatever you do, do all to the glory of
God. ³² Give no offense, either to the Jews
or to the Greeks or to the church of God,
³³ just as I also please all *men* in all *things,*
not seeking my own profit, but the *profit*
of many, that they may be saved.

~ ECCLESIASTES 11:1—12:14 ~

¹ Cast your bread upon the waters,
For you will find it after many
days.
² Give a serving to seven, and also
to eight,
For you do not know what evil
will be on the earth.

³ If the clouds are full of rain,
They empty *themselves* upon the
earth;
And if a tree falls to the south or
the north,
In the place where the tree falls,
there it shall lie.
⁴ He who observes the wind will
not sow,
And he who regards the clouds
will not reap.

⁵ As you do not know what *is* the
way of the wind,
Or how the bones *grow* in the
womb of her who is with child,
So you do not know the works of
God who makes everything.
⁶ In the morning sow your seed,
And in the evening do not
withhold your hand;
For you do not know which will
prosper,
Either this or that,
Or whether both alike *will be*
good.

⁷ Truly the light is sweet,
And *it is* pleasant for the eyes to
behold the sun;
⁸ But if a man lives many years
And rejoices in them all,
Yet let him remember the days of
darkness,
For they will be many.
All that is coming *is* vanity.

⁹ Rejoice, O young man, in your
youth,
And let your heart cheer you in
the days of your youth;
Walk in the ways of your heart,
And in the sight of your eyes;
But know that for all these
God will bring you into judgment.
¹⁰ Therefore remove sorrow from
your heart,
And put away evil from your flesh,
For childhood and youth *are*
vanity.

12 Remember now your Creator in
the days of your youth,
Before the difficult days come,
And the years draw near when
you say,
"I have no pleasure in them":
² While the sun and the light,
The moon and the stars,
Are not darkened,
And the clouds do not return after
the rain;
³ In the day when the keepers of the
house tremble,
And the strong men bow down;
When the grinders cease because
they are few,
And those that look through the
windows grow dim;
⁴ When the doors are shut in the
streets,
And the sound of grinding is low;
When one rises up at the sound of
a bird,
And all the daughters of music are
brought low.
⁵ Also they are afraid of height,
And of terrors in the way;
When the almond tree blossoms,
The grasshopper is a burden,
And desire fails.
For man goes to his eternal home,
And the mourners go about the
streets.

⁶ *Remember your Creator* before the
silver cord is loosed,
Or the golden bowl is broken,
Or the pitcher shattered at the
fountain,
Or the wheel broken at the well.
⁷ Then the dust will return to the
earth as it was,
And the spirit will return to God
who gave it.

⁸ "Vanity of vanities," says the
Preacher,
"All *is* vanity."

⁹ And moreover, because the Preacher
was wise, he still taught the people knowledge; yes, he pondered and sought out
and set in order many proverbs. ¹⁰ The

Preacher sought to find acceptable words;
and *what was* written *was* upright—
words of truth. ¹¹ The words of the
wise are like goads, and the words of
scholars are like well-driven nails, given
by one Shepherd. ¹² And further, my son,
be admonished by these. Of making many
books *there is* no end, and much study *is*
wearisome to the flesh.

¹³ Let us hear the conclusion of the
whole matter:

Fear God and keep His
commandments,
For this is man's all.
¹⁴ For God will bring every work
into judgment,
Including every secret thing,
Whether good or evil.

~ PSALM 103:15–22 ~

¹⁵ *As for* man, his days *are* like grass;
As a flower of the field, so he
flourishes.
¹⁶ For the wind passes over it, and it is
gone,
And its place remembers it no more.
¹⁷ But the mercy of the LORD *is* from
everlasting to everlasting
On those who fear Him,
And His righteousness to children's
children,
¹⁸ To such as keep His covenant,
And to those who remember His
commandments to do them.

¹⁹ The LORD has established His throne
in heaven,
And His kingdom rules over all.

²⁰ Bless the LORD, you His angels,
Who excel in strength, who do His
word,
Heeding the voice of His word.
²¹ Bless the LORD, all *you* His hosts,
You ministers of His, who do His
pleasure.
²² Bless the LORD, all His works,
In all places of His dominion.

Bless the LORD, O my soul!

Experiencing Leadership

Earl Reum has written these thought-inspiring words about experience:

"I wish you could know how it feels 'to run' with all your heart and lose — horribly!

"I wish that you could achieve some great good for mankind, but have nobody know about it except for you.

"I wish you could find something so worthwhile that you deem it worthy of investing your life within it.

"I hope you become frustrated and challenged enough to begin to push back the very barriers of your own personal limitations.

"I hope you make a stupid mistake and get caught red-handed and are big enough to say those magic words: 'I was wrong.'

"I hope you give so much of yourself that some days you wonder if it's worth all the effort.

"I wish for you a magnificent obsession that will give you reason for living and purpose and direction and life.

"I wish for you the worst kind of everything you do, because that makes you fight to achieve beyond what you normally would.

"I wish you the experience of leadership."

My son, eat honey because it is good, and the honeycomb which is sweet to your taste. So shall the knowledge of wisdom be to your soul; if you have found it, there is a prospect, and your hope will not be cut off.

Proverbs 24:13-14

~ PROVERBS 24:13, 14 ~

13 My son, eat honey because *it is*
    good,
  And the honeycomb *which is* sweet
    to your taste;
14 So *shall* the knowledge of wisdom
    be to your soul;
  If you have found *it*, there is a
    prospect,
  And your hope will not be cut
    off.

~ 1 CORINTHIANS 11:1–16 ~

Imitate me, just as I also *imitate* Christ.

2 Now I praise you, brethren, that you remember me in all things and keep the traditions just as I delivered *them* to you. 3 But I want you to know that the head of every man is Christ, the head of woman *is* man, and the head of Christ *is* God. 4 Every man praying or prophesying, having *his* head covered, dishonors his head. 5 But every woman who prays or prophesies with *her* head uncovered dishonors her head, for that is one and the same as if her head were shaved. 6 For if a woman is not covered, let her also be shorn. But if it is shameful for a woman to be shorn or shaved, let her be covered. 7 For a man indeed ought not to cover *his* head, since he is the image and glory of God; but woman is the glory of man. 8 For man is not from woman, but woman from man. 9 Nor was man created for the woman, but woman for the man. 10 For this reason the woman ought to have *a symbol of* authority on *her* head, because of the angels. 11 Nevertheless, neither *is* man independent of woman, nor woman independent of man, in the Lord. 12 For as woman *came* from man, even so man also *comes* through woman; but all things are from God.

13 Judge among yourselves. Is it proper for a woman to pray to God with her head uncovered? 14 Does not even nature itself teach you that if a man has long hair, it is a dishonor to him? 15 But if a woman has long hair, it is a glory to her; for *her* hair is given to her for a covering. 16 But if anyone seems to be contentious, we have no such custom, nor *do* the churches of God.

READING 244 · SEPTEMBER 1

~ SONG OF SOLOMON 1:1—2:17 ~

The song of songs, which *is* Solomon's.

2 Let him kiss me with the kisses of
    his mouth—
  For your love *is* better than wine.
3 Because of the fragrance of your
    good ointments,
  Your name *is* ointment poured
    forth;
  Therefore the virgins love you.
4 Draw me away!

We will run after you.

The king has brought me into his
  chambers.

We will be glad and rejoice in you.

We will remember your love more
  than wine.

Rightly do they love you.

5 I *am* dark, but lovely,
  O daughters of Jerusalem,
  Like the tents of Kedar,
  Like the curtains of Solomon.
6 Do not look upon me, because I
    am dark,
  Because the sun has tanned me.
  My mother's sons were angry with
    me;
  They made me the keeper of the
    vineyards,
  But my own vineyard I have not
    kept.

7 Tell me, O you whom I love,

Starting Over

In 1991, Anne Busquet was General Manager of the Optima Card division for American Express. When five of her 2,000 employees were found to have hidden $24 million in losses, she was held accountable. Busquet had to face the fact that, because she was an intense perfectionist, she apparently came across as intimidating and confrontational to her subordinates — so much so, they were more willing to lie than to report bad news to her!

Busquet lost her Optima job, but was given a second chance by American Express: An opportunity to salvage one of its smaller businesses. Her self-esteem shaken, she nearly turned down the offer. However, she decided this was her chance to improve the way she related to others. She took on the new job as a personal challenge to change.

Realizing she had to be much more understanding, she began to work on being more patient and listening more carefully and intently. She learned to solicit bad news in a reassuring way.

Four years after she was removed from her previous position, Anne Busquet was promoted to an executive vice-president position at American Express.

Failure is not the end; it is a teacher for a new beginning and a better life!

Where you feed *your flock,*
Where you make *it* rest at noon.
For why should I be as one who
    veils herself
By the flocks of your companions?

8 If you do not know, O fairest
        among women,
    Follow in the footsteps of the
        flock,
    And feed your little goats
    Beside the shepherds' tents.
9 I have compared you, my love,
    To my filly among Pharaoh's
        chariots.
10 Your cheeks are lovely with
        ornaments,
    Your neck with chains *of gold.*

11 We will make you ornaments of
        gold
    With studs of silver.

12 While the king *is* at his table,
    My spikenard sends forth its
        fragrance.
13 A bundle of myrrh *is* my beloved
        to me,
    That lies all night between my
        breasts.
14 My beloved *is* to me a cluster of
        henna *blooms*
    In the vineyards of En Gedi.

15 Behold, you *are* fair, my love!
    Behold, you *are* fair!
    You *have* dove's eyes.

16 Behold, you *are* handsome, my
        beloved!
    Yes, pleasant!
    Also our bed *is* green.
17 The beams of our houses *are*
        cedar,
    And our rafters of fir.

2 I *am* the rose of Sharon,
    And the lily of the valleys.

2 Like a lily among thorns,
    So is my love among the
        daughters.

3 Like an apple tree among the trees
        of the woods,

So *is* my beloved among the sons.
I sat down in his shade with great
    delight,
And his fruit *was* sweet to my
    taste.

4 He brought me to the banqueting
        house,
    And his banner over me *was* love.
5 Sustain me with cakes of raisins,
    Refresh me with apples,
    For I *am* lovesick.

6 His left hand *is* under my head,
    And his right hand embraces me.
7 I charge you, O daughters of
        Jerusalem,
    By the gazelles or by the does of
        the field,
    Do not stir up nor awaken love
    Until it pleases.

8 The voice of my beloved!
    Behold, he comes
    Leaping upon the mountains,
    Skipping upon the hills.
9 My beloved is like a gazelle or a
        young stag.
    Behold, he stands behind our wall;
    He is looking through the
        windows,
    Gazing through the lattice.

10 My beloved spoke, and said to
        me:
    "Rise up, my love, my fair one,
        And come away.
11 For lo, the winter is past,
    The rain is over *and* gone.
12 The flowers appear on the earth;
    The time of singing has come,
    And the voice of the turtledove
    Is heard in our land.
13 The fig tree puts forth her green
        figs,
    And the vines *with* the tender
        grapes
    Give a good smell.
    Rise up, my love, my fair one,
    And come away!

14 "O my dove, in the clefts of the
        rock,
    In the secret *places* of the cliff,
    Let me see your face,

Let me hear your voice;
For your voice *is* sweet,
And your face *is* lovely."

15 Catch us the foxes,
The little foxes that spoil the
vines,
For our vines *have* tender grapes.

16 My beloved *is* mine, and I *am* his.
He feeds *his flock* among the lilies.

17 Until the day breaks
And the shadows flee away,
Turn, my beloved,
And be like a gazelle
Or a young stag
Upon the mountains of Bether.

∼ PSALM 104:1–9 ∼

1 Bless the LORD, O my soul!

O LORD my God, You are very great:
You are clothed with honor and
majesty,
2 Who cover *Yourself* with light as
with a garment,
Who stretch out the heavens like a
curtain.

3 He lays the beams of His upper
chambers in the waters,
Who makes the clouds His chariot,
Who walks on the wings of the
wind,
4 Who makes His angels spirits,
His ministers a flame of fire.

5 *You who* laid the foundations of the
earth,
So *that* it should not be moved
forever,
6 You covered it with the deep as *with*
a garment;
The waters stood above the
mountains.
7 At Your rebuke they fled;
At the voice of Your thunder they
hastened away.
8 They went up over the mountains;
They went down into the valleys,
To the place which You founded for
them.

9 You have set a boundary that they
may not pass over,
That they may not return to cover
the earth.

∼ PROVERBS 24:15, 16 ∼

15 Do not lie in wait, O wicked *man,*
against the dwelling of the
righteous;
Do not plunder his resting place;
16 For a righteous *man* may fall seven
times
And rise again,
But the wicked shall fall by calamity.

∼ 1 CORINTHIANS 11:17–34 ∼

Now in giving these instructions I do not
praise *you,* since you come together
not for the better but for the worse. 18 For
first of all, when you come together as a
church, I hear that there are divisions
among you, and in part I believe it. 19 For
there must also be factions among you,
that those who are approved may be recognized among you. 20 Therefore when
you come together in one place, it is not
to eat the Lord's Supper. 21 For in eating,
each one takes his own supper ahead of
others; and one is hungry and another is
drunk. 22 What! Do you not have houses
to eat and drink in? Or do you despise
the church of God and shame those
who have nothing? What shall I say to
you? Shall I praise you in this? I do not
praise *you.*

23 For I received from the Lord that
which I also delivered to you: that the
Lord Jesus on the *same* night in which
He was betrayed took bread; 24 and
when He had given thanks, He broke *it*
and said, "Take, eat; this is My body which
is broken for you; do this in remembrance
of Me." 25 In the same manner *He* also
took the cup after supper, saying, "This
cup is the new covenant in My blood.
This do, as often as you drink *it,* in remembrance of Me."

26 For as often as you eat this bread and
drink this cup, you proclaim the Lord's
death till He comes.

27 Therefore whoever eats this bread or
drinks *this* cup of the Lord in an unworthy manner will be guilty of the body and

blood of the Lord. ²⁸ But let a man examine himself, and so let him eat of the bread and drink of the cup. ²⁹ For he who eats and drinks in an unworthy manner eats and drinks judgment to himself, not discerning the Lord's body. ³⁰ For this reason many *are* weak and sick among you, and many sleep. ³¹ For if we would judge ourselves, we would not be judged. ³² But when we are judged, we are chastened by the Lord, that we may not be condemned with the world.

³³ Therefore, my brethren, when you come together to eat, wait for one another. ³⁴ But if anyone is hungry, let him eat at home, lest you come together for judgment. And the rest I will set in order when I come.

<hr>

READING 245 · SEPTEMBER 2

~ Song of Solomon 3:1—4:16 ~

¹ By night on my bed I sought the
　　one I love;
　I sought him, but I did not find
　　him.
² "I will rise now," *I said,*
　"And go about the city;
　In the streets and in the squares
　I will seek the one I love."
　I sought him, but I did not find
　　him.
³ The watchmen who go about the
　　city found me;
　I said,
　"Have you seen the one I love?"

⁴ Scarcely had I passed by them,
　When I found the one I love.
　I held him and would not let him
　　go,
　Until I had brought him to the
　　house of my mother,
　And into the chamber of her who
　　conceived me.

⁵ I charge you, O daughters of
　　Jerusalem,
　By the gazelles or by the does of
　　the field,
　Do not stir up nor awaken love
　Until it pleases.

⁶ Who *is* this coming out of the
　　wilderness
　Like pillars of smoke,
　Perfumed with myrrh and
　　frankincense,
　With all the merchant's fragrant
　　powders?
⁷ Behold, it *is* Solomon's couch,

With sixty valiant men around it,
　Of the valiant of Israel.
⁸ They all hold swords,
　Being expert in war.
　Every man *has* his sword on his
　　thigh
　Because of fear in the night.

⁹ Of the wood of Lebanon
　Solomon the King
　Made himself a palanquin:
¹⁰ He made its pillars *of* silver,
　Its support *of* gold,
　Its seat *of* purple,
　Its interior paved *with* love
　By the daughters of Jerusalem.
¹¹ Go forth, O daughters of Zion,
　And see King Solomon with the
　　crown
　With which his mother crowned
　　him
　On the day of his wedding,
　The day of the gladness of his
　　heart.

4 Behold, you *are* fair, my love!
　Behold, you *are* fair!
　You *have* dove's eyes behind your
　　veil.
　Your hair *is* like a flock of goats,
　Going down from Mount Gilead.
² Your teeth *are* like a flock of shorn
　　sheep
　Which have come up from the
　　washing,
　Every one of which bears twins,
　And none *is* barren among them.
³ Your lips *are* like a strand of
　　scarlet,

The Power of a Hug

> Scarcely had I passed by them, when I found the one I love.
>
> *Song of Solomon 3:4*

Our ability to become emotionally involved with and vulnerable to others is directly related to our having been stroked, caressed, and cuddled as children. We learn how to give and receive affection from the tender models in our lives. We learn security from the warmth of being held close.

Before birth, a baby is enveloped in the soft, warm embrace of the womb. After birth, a child who is not touched and cuddled will form a bond with anything it can touch, even a stuffed toy. If all human contact is denied, the baby will die.

Our need for touch continues throughout our lifetime. In fact, our body chemistry changes when we are physically close to another person. When a person is touched, the amount of hemoglobin in the blood — which carries oxygen and helps prevent disease and speed recovery from illness — increases significantly. In one animal study, rabbits that were held close and stroked often developed less hardening of the arteries than those rabbits which were deprived of touch.

You've heard the question a thousand times, but it bears repeating: Have you hugged your child today?

And your mouth is lovely.
Your temples behind your veil
Are like a piece of pomegranate.
⁴ Your neck *is* like the tower of
    David,
Built for an armory,
On which hang a thousand
    bucklers,
All shields of mighty men.
⁵ Your two breasts *are* like two
    fawns,
Twins of a gazelle,
Which feed among the lilies.

⁶ Until the day breaks
And the shadows flee away,
I will go my way to the mountain
    of myrrh
And to the hill of frankincense.

⁷ You *are* all fair, my love,
And *there is* no spot in you.
⁸ Come with me from Lebanon, *my*
    spouse,
With me from Lebanon.
Look from the top of Amana,
From the top of Senir and
    Hermon,
From the lions' dens,
From the mountains of the
    leopards.

⁹ You have ravished my heart,
My sister, *my* spouse;
You have ravished my heart
With one *look* of your eyes,
With one link of your necklace.
¹⁰ How fair is your love,
My sister, *my* spouse!
How much better than wine is
    your love,
And the scent of your perfumes
Than all spices!
¹¹ Your lips, O *my* spouse,
Drip as the honeycomb;
Honey and milk *are* under your
    tongue;
And the fragrance of your
    garments
Is like the fragrance of Lebanon.

¹² A garden enclosed
Is my sister, *my* spouse,
A spring shut up,
A fountain sealed.

¹³ Your plants *are* an orchard of
    pomegranates
With pleasant fruits,
Fragrant henna with spikenard,
¹⁴ Spikenard and saffron,
Calamus and cinnamon,
With all trees of frankincense,
Myrrh and aloes,
With all the chief spices—
¹⁵ A fountain of gardens,
A well of living waters,
And streams from Lebanon.

¹⁶ Awake, O north *wind,*
And come, O south!
Blow upon my garden,
That its spices may flow out.
Let my beloved come to his
    garden
And eat its pleasant fruits.

∼ PSALM 104:10–23 ∼

¹⁰ He sends the springs into the valleys;
They flow among the hills.
¹¹ They give drink to every beast of the
    field;
The wild donkeys quench their
    thirst.
¹² By them the birds of the heavens
    have their home;
They sing among the branches.
¹³ He waters the hills from His upper
    chambers;
The earth is satisfied with the fruit of
    Your works.
¹⁴ He causes the grass to grow for the
    cattle,
And vegetation for the service of
    man,
That he may bring forth food from
    the earth,
¹⁵ And wine *that* makes glad the heart
    of man,
Oil to make *his* face shine,
And bread *which* strengthens man's
    heart.
¹⁶ The trees of the LORD are full *of sap,*
The cedars of Lebanon which He
    planted,
¹⁷ Where the birds make their nests;
The stork has her home in the fir
    trees.
¹⁸ The high hills *are* for the wild goats;

The cliffs are a refuge for the rock
  badgers.

19 He appointed the moon for seasons;
  The sun knows its going down.
20 You make darkness, and it is night,
  In which all the beasts of the forest
    creep about.
21 The young lions roar after their prey,
  And seek their food from God.
22 *When* the sun rises, they gather
    together
  And lie down in their dens.
23 Man goes out to his work
  And to his labor until the evening.

~ PROVERBS 24:17, 18 ~

17 Do not rejoice when your enemy
    falls,
  And do not let your heart be glad
    when he stumbles;
18 Lest the LORD see *it,* and it displease
    Him,
  And He turn away His wrath from
    him.

~ 1 CORINTHIANS 12:1–31 ~

Now concerning spiritual *gifts,* brethren,
I do not want you to be ignorant: 2 You
know that you were Gentiles, carried
away to these dumb idols, however you
were led. 3 Therefore I make known to
you that no one speaking by the Spirit of
God calls Jesus accursed, and no one can
say that Jesus is Lord except by the Holy
Spirit.

4 There are diversities of gifts, but the
same Spirit. 5 There are differences of
ministries, but the same Lord. 6 And there
are diversities of activities, but it is the
same God who works all in all. 7 But
the manifestation of the Spirit is given to
each one for the profit *of all:* 8 for to one
is given the word of wisdom through the
Spirit, to another the word of knowledge
through the same Spirit, 9 to another faith
by the same Spirit, to another gifts
of healings by the same Spirit, 10 to another the working of miracles, to another
prophecy, to another discerning of spirits, to another *different* kinds of tongues,
to another the interpretation of tongues.
11 But one and the same Spirit works all

these things, distributing to each one individually as He wills.

12 For as the body is one and has many
members, but all the members of that one
body, being many, are one body, so also *is*
Christ. 13 For by one Spirit we were all
baptized into one body—whether Jews or
Greeks, whether slaves or free—and have
all been made to drink into one Spirit.
14 For in fact the body is not one member
but many.

15 If the foot should say, "Because I am
not a hand, I am not of the body," is it
therefore not of the body? 16 And if the
ear should say, "Because I am not an eye,
I am not of the body," is it therefore not
of the body? 17 If the whole body *were* an
eye, where *would be* the hearing? If the
whole *were* hearing, where *would be*
the smelling? 18 But now God has set the
members, each one of them, in the body
just as He pleased. 19 And if they *were* all
one member, where *would* the body *be?*

20 But now indeed *there are* many members, yet one body. 21 And the eye cannot
say to the hand, "I have no need of you";
nor again the head to the feet, "I have no
need of you." 22 No, much rather, those
members of the body which seem to be
weaker are necessary. 23 And those *members* of the body which we think to be less
honorable, on these we bestow greater
honor; and our unpresentable *parts* have
greater modesty, 24 but our presentable
parts have no need. But God composed
the body, having given greater honor to
that *part* which lacks it, 25 that there
should be no schism in the body, but *that*
the members should have the same care
for one another. 26 And if one member
suffers, all the members suffer with *it;* or
if one member is honored, all the members rejoice with *it.*

27 Now you are the body of Christ, and
members individually. 28 And God has
appointed these in the church: first
apostles, second prophets, third teachers,
after that miracles, then gifts of healings, helps, administrations, varieties of
tongues. 29 *Are* all apostles? *Are* all prophets? *Are* all teachers? *Are* all workers of
miracles? 30 Do all have gifts of healings?
Do all speak with tongues? Do all interpret? 31 But earnestly desire the best gifts.
And yet I show you a more excellent way.

∼ Song of Solomon 5:1—6:13 ∼

1 I have come to my garden, my
sister, *my* spouse;
I have gathered my myrrh with my
spice;
I have eaten my honeycomb with
my honey;
I have drunk my wine with my
milk.

Eat, O friends!
Drink, yes, drink deeply,
O beloved ones!

2 I sleep, but my heart is awake;
It is the voice of my beloved!
He knocks, *saying,*
"Open for me, my sister, my love,
My dove, my perfect one;
For my head is covered with dew,
My locks with the drops of the
night."

3 I have taken off my robe;
How can I put it on *again?*
I have washed my feet;
How can I defile them?
4 My beloved put his hand
By the latch *of the door,*
And my heart yearned for him.
5 I arose to open for my beloved,
And my hands dripped *with*
myrrh,
My fingers with liquid myrrh,
On the handles of the lock.

6 I opened for my beloved,
But my beloved had turned away
and was gone.
My heart leaped up when he
spoke.
I sought him, but I could not find
him;
I called him, but he gave me no
answer.
7 The watchmen who went about
the city found me.
They struck me, they wounded
me;
The keepers of the walls
Took my veil away from me.
8 I charge you, O daughters of
Jerusalem,

If you find my beloved,
That you tell him I *am* lovesick!

9 What *is* your beloved
More than *another* beloved,
O fairest among women?
What *is* your beloved
More than *another* beloved,
That you so charge us?

10 My beloved *is* white and ruddy,
Chief among ten thousand.
11 His head *is like* the finest gold;
His locks *are* wavy,
And black as a raven.
12 His eyes *are* like doves
By the rivers of waters,
Washed with milk,
And fitly set.
13 His cheeks *are* like a bed of spices,
Banks of scented herbs.
His lips *are* lilies,
Dripping liquid myrrh.

14 His hands *are* rods of gold
Set with beryl.
His body *is* carved ivory
Inlaid *with* sapphires.
15 His legs *are* pillars of marble
Set on bases of fine gold.
His countenance *is* like Lebanon,
Excellent as the cedars.
16 His mouth *is* most sweet,
Yes, he *is* altogether lovely.
This *is* my beloved,
And this *is* my friend,
O daughters of Jerusalem!

6 Where has your beloved gone,
O fairest among women?
Where has your beloved turned
aside,
That we may seek him with you?

2 My beloved has gone to his
garden,
To the beds of spices,
To feed *his flock* in the gardens,
And to gather lilies.
3 I *am* my beloved's,
And my beloved *is* mine.
He feeds *his flock* among the lilies.

Love Never Fails

> [Love] bears all things, believes all things, hopes all things, endures all things. Love never fails.
>
> *1 Corinthians 13:7*

Napoleon went to school in Brienne with a young man named Demasis, who greatly admired him. After Napoleon quelled the mob in Paris and served at Toulon, his authority was stripped from him and he became penniless. We rarely think of Napoleon as struggling through hard times. However, with thoughts of suicide, he proceeded toward a bridge to throw himself into the waters below. On the way he met his old friend Demasis, who asked him what was troubling him.

Napoleon told him bluntly he was without money, his mother was in need, and he despaired of his situation ever changing. "Oh, if that is all," Demasis said, "take this; it will supply your wants." He put a pouch of gold into his hands and walked away. Normally Napoleon would have never taken such a handout, but that night he did and his hope was renewed.

When Napoleon came to power, he sought far and wide to thank his friend and promote him, but he never found him. It was rumored that Demasis lived and served in one of Napoleon's own armies, but never revealed his true identity. He was content to quietly serve in support of the leader he admired.

Sometimes our simple words or deeds can make all the difference in the world to someone who doesn't know where to turn. Sometimes the opportunities God sends your way are so simple, they could easily be missed. Today, keep your eyes, your ears, and your heart open.

⁴ O my love, you *are as* beautiful as
   Tirzah,
   Lovely as Jerusalem,
   Awesome as *an army* with
   banners!
⁵ Turn your eyes away from me,
   For they have overcome me.
   Your hair *is* like a flock of goats
   Going down from Gilead.
⁶ Your teeth *are* like a flock of sheep
   Which have come up from the
   washing;
   Every one bears twins,
   And none *is* barren among them.
⁷ Like a piece of pomegranate
   Are your temples behind your veil.

⁸ There are sixty queens
   And eighty concubines,
   And virgins without number.
⁹ My dove, my perfect one,
   Is the only one,
   The only one of her mother,
   The favorite of the one who bore
   her.
   The daughters saw her
   And called her blessed,
   The queens and the concubines,
   And they praised her.

¹⁰ Who is she who looks forth as the
   morning,
   Fair as the moon,
   Clear as the sun,
   Awesome as *an army* with
   banners?

¹¹ I went down to the garden of nuts
   To see the verdure of the valley,
   To see whether the vine had
   budded
   And the pomegranates had
   bloomed.
¹² Before I was even aware,
   My soul had made me
   As the chariots of my noble
   people.

¹³ Return, return, O Shulamite;
   Return, return, that we may look
   upon you!
   What would you see in the
   Shulamite—
   As it were, the dance of the two
   camps?

∼ PSALM 104:24–30 ∼

²⁴ O LORD, how manifold are Your
   works!
   In wisdom You have made them all.
   The earth is full of Your
   possessions—
²⁵ This great and wide sea,
   In which *are* innumerable teeming
   things,
   Living things both small and great.
²⁶ There the ships sail about;
   There is that Leviathan
   Which You have made to play there.

²⁷ These all wait for You,
   That You may give *them* their food
   in due season.
²⁸ *What* You give them they gather in;
   You open Your hand, they are filled
   with good.
²⁹ You hide Your face, they are
   troubled;
   You take away their breath, they die
   and return to their dust.
³⁰ You send forth Your Spirit, they are
   created;
   And You renew the face of the earth.

∼ PROVERBS 24:19, 20 ∼

¹⁹ Do not fret because of evildoers,
   Nor be envious of the wicked;
²⁰ For there will be no prospect for the
   evil *man;*
   The lamp of the wicked will be put
   out.

∼ 1 CORINTHIANS 13:1–13 ∼

Though I speak with the tongues of men
and of angels, but have not love, I have
become sounding brass or a clanging
cymbal. ² And though I have *the gift of*
prophecy, and understand all mysteries
and all knowledge, and though I have all
faith, so that I could remove mountains,
but have not love, I am nothing. ³ And
though I bestow all my goods to feed *the
poor,* and though I give my body to be
burned, but have not love, it profits me
nothing.
   ⁴ Love suffers long *and* is kind; love
does not envy; love does not parade

itself, is not puffed up; [5] does not behave rudely, does not seek its own, is not provoked, thinks no evil; [6] does not rejoice in iniquity, but rejoices in the truth; [7] bears all things, believes all things, hopes all things, endures all things.

[8] Love never fails. But whether *there are* prophecies, they will fail; whether *there are* tongues, they will cease; whether *there is* knowledge, it will vanish away. [9] For we know in part and we prophesy in part. [10] But when that which is perfect has come, then that which is in part will be done away.

[11] When I was a child, I spoke as a child, I understood as a child, I thought as a child; but when I became a man, I put away childish things. [12] For now we see in a mirror, dimly, but then face to face. Now I know in part, but then I shall know just as I also am known.

[13] And now abide faith, hope, love, these three; but the greatest of these *is* love.

~ SONG OF SOLOMON 7:1—8:14 ~

1 How beautiful are your feet in sandals,
O prince's daughter!
The curves of your thighs *are* like jewels,
The work of the hands of a skillful workman.

2 Your navel *is* a rounded goblet;
It lacks no blended beverage.
Your waist *is* a heap of wheat
Set about with lilies.

3 Your two breasts *are* like two fawns,
Twins of a gazelle.

4 Your neck *is* like an ivory tower,
Your eyes *like* the pools in Heshbon
By the gate of Bath Rabbim.
Your nose *is* like the tower of Lebanon
Which looks toward Damascus.

5 Your head *crowns* you like *Mount* Carmel,
And the hair of your head *is* like purple;
A king *is* held captive by *your* tresses.

6 How fair and how pleasant you are,
O love, with your delights!

7 This stature of yours is like a palm tree,
And your breasts *like* its clusters.

8 I said, "I will go up to the palm tree,
I will take hold of its branches."

Let now your breasts be like clusters of the vine,
The fragrance of your breath like apples,

9 And the roof of your mouth like the best wine.

The wine goes *down* smoothly for my beloved,
Moving gently the lips of sleepers.

10 I *am* my beloved's,
And his desire *is* toward me.

11 Come, my beloved,
Let us go forth to the field;
Let us lodge in the villages.

12 Let us get up early to the vineyards;
Let us see if the vine has budded,
Whether the grape blossoms are open,
And the pomegranates are in bloom.
There I will give you my love.

13 The mandrakes give off a fragrance,
And at our gates *are* pleasant *fruits,*
All manner, new and old,
Which I have laid up for you, my beloved.

8 Oh, that you were like my brother,
Who nursed at my mother's breasts!
If I should find you outside,

I would kiss you;
I would not be despised.
2 I would lead you *and* bring you
Into the house of my mother,
She *who* used to instruct me.
I would cause you to drink of
 spiced wine,
Of the juice of my pomegranate.

3 His left hand *is* under my head,
And his right hand embraces me.
4 I charge you, O daughters of
 Jerusalem,
Do not stir up nor awaken love
Until it pleases.

5 Who *is* this coming up from the
 wilderness,
Leaning upon her beloved?

I awakened you under the apple
 tree.
There your mother brought you
 forth;
There she *who* bore you brought
 you forth.

6 Set me as a seal upon your heart,
As a seal upon your arm;
For love *is as* strong as death,
Jealousy *as* cruel as the grave;
Its flames *are* flames of fire,
A most vehement flame.

7 Many waters cannot quench love,
Nor can the floods drown it.
If a man would give for love
All the wealth of his house,
It would be utterly despised.

8 We have a little sister,
And she has no breasts.
What shall we do for our sister
In the day when she is spoken for?
9 If she *is* a wall,
We will build upon her
A battlement of silver;
And if she *is* a door,
We will enclose her
With boards of cedar.

10 I *am* a wall,
And my breasts like towers;
Then I became in his eyes
As one who found peace.

11 Solomon had a vineyard at Baal
 Hamon;
He leased the vineyard to keepers;
Everyone was to bring for its fruit
A thousand silver coins.

12 My own vineyard *is* before me.
You, O Solomon, *may have* a
 thousand,
And those who tend its fruit two
 hundred.

13 You who dwell in the gardens,
The companions listen for your
 voice—
Let me hear it!

14 Make haste, my beloved,
And be like a gazelle
Or a young stag
On the mountains of spices.

~ PSALM 104:31–35 ~

31 May the glory of the LORD endure
 forever;
May the LORD rejoice in His works.
32 He looks on the earth, and it
 trembles;
He touches the hills, and they
 smoke.
33 I will sing to the LORD as long as I
 live;
I will sing praise to my God while I
 have my being.
34 May my meditation be sweet to
 Him;
I will be glad in the LORD.
35 May sinners be consumed from the
 earth,
And the wicked be no more.

Bless the LORD, O my soul!
Praise the LORD!

~ PROVERBS 24:21, 22 ~

21 My son, fear the LORD and the king;
Do not associate with those given to
 change;
22 For their calamity will rise suddenly,

Show Me How to Live

Joni Eareckson Tada lives such an inspirational life of ministry today, it is often difficult for others to accept the fact that in the wake of her paralyzing accident, Joni experienced nearly three years of depression and suicidal despair. She finally reached the point where she prayed, "God, if I can't die, show me how to live, please!"

Things didn't change for Joni overnight, but they did begin to change. Very little about her *situation* changed, but her outlook — her attitude, her mind, her perspective, her spirit — began to change and grow. She knew with an increasing assurance that God would help her learn how to do what seemed to be impossible: handle life in a wheelchair.

Are you facing a seemingly impossible situation today? Do you feel as if any option you might have is really no option at all? Perhaps it's time to pray: "God, show me how to live in the midst of this situation." Accepting God's help in coping with the despair and hopelessness of a situation is very often the first step God uses in preparing us to live a new way — a way that is far beyond mere coping. His way is always one of true fulfillment and joy.

> What is the conclusion then? I will pray with the spirit, and I will also pray with the understanding. I will sing with the spirit, and I will also sing with the understanding.
>
> *1 Corinthians 14:15*

And who knows the ruin those two can bring?

~ 1 CORINTHIANS 14:1–20 ~

Pursue love, and desire spiritual *gifts,* but especially that you may prophesy. ² For he who speaks in a tongue does not speak to men but to God, for no one understands *him;* however, in the spirit he speaks mysteries. ³ But he who prophesies speaks edification and exhortation and comfort to men. ⁴ He who speaks in a tongue edifies himself, but he who prophesies edifies the church. ⁵ I wish you all spoke with tongues, but even more that you prophesied; for he who prophesies *is* greater than he who speaks with tongues, unless indeed he interprets, that the church may receive edification.

⁶ But now, brethren, if I come to you speaking with tongues, what shall I profit you unless I speak to you either by revelation, by knowledge, by prophesying, or by teaching? ⁷ Even things without life, whether flute or harp, when they make a sound, unless they make a distinction in the sounds, how will it be known what is piped or played? ⁸ For if the trumpet makes an uncertain sound, who will prepare for battle? ⁹ So likewise you, unless you utter by the tongue words easy to understand, how will it be known what is spoken? For you will be speaking into the air. ¹⁰ There are, it may be, so many kinds of languages in the world, and none of them *is* without significance. ¹¹ Therefore, if I do not know the meaning of the language, I shall be a foreigner to him who speaks, and he who speaks *will be* a foreigner to me. ¹² Even so you, since you are zealous for spiritual *gifts, let it be* for the edification of the church *that* you seek to excel.

¹³ Therefore let him who speaks in a tongue pray that he may interpret. ¹⁴ For if I pray in a tongue, my spirit prays, but my understanding is unfruitful. ¹⁵ What is *the conclusion* then? I will pray with the spirit, and I will also pray with the understanding. I will sing with the spirit, and I will also sing with the understanding. ¹⁶ Otherwise, if you bless with the spirit, how will he who occupies the place of the uninformed say "Amen" at your giving of thanks, since he does not understand what you say? ¹⁷ For you indeed give thanks well, but the other is not edified.

¹⁸ I thank my God I speak with tongues more than you all; ¹⁹ yet in the church I would rather speak five words with my understanding, that I may teach others also, than ten thousand words in a tongue.

²⁰ Brethren, do not be children in understanding; however, in malice be babes, but in understanding be mature.

READING 248 · SEPTEMBER 5

~ ISAIAH 1:1–2:22 ~

The vision of Isaiah the son of Amoz, which he saw concerning Judah and Jerusalem in the days of Uzziah, Jotham, Ahaz, *and* Hezekiah, kings of Judah.

² Hear, O heavens, and give ear,
O earth!
For the LORD has spoken:
"I have nourished and brought up
children,
And they have rebelled against
Me;
³ The ox knows its owner
And the donkey its master's crib;

But Israel does not know,
My people do not consider."

⁴ Alas, sinful nation,
A people laden with iniquity,
A brood of evildoers,
Children who are corrupters!
They have forsaken the LORD,
They have provoked to anger
The Holy One of Israel,
They have turned away backward.

⁵ Why should you be stricken again?
You will revolt more and more.
The whole head is sick,

Knowing God

At times, we are tempted to think that because we are Christians, read our Bibles, and know a great deal *about* God, that we *know* God. Nothing could be more wrong. The only way we can know God is by experiencing Him. Many of those experiences come in prayer, as we listen quietly, so that we can truly hear God's whispering in our hearts.

Soren Kierkegäard noted that most of us are "so busy," we are unwilling to wait patiently for God. We might consider an appointment with a hairdresser to be inviolable, but when God lays claim to our time, we balk. Rather than spend time with God and allow ourselves to bask in His presence and soak up His love, we manufacture substitutes: things to *do* to take the place of simply *being* with Him. We offer praise, do good works, memorize Bible verses — all good activities, but unequal to resting quietly before Him.

The highest value of prayer is found in developing a relationship with God. That takes both our time and our willingness to receive from Him. There is no substitute for either.

> "Come now, and let us reason together," says the Lord, "though your sins are like scarlet, they shall be as white as snow; though they are red like crimson, they shall be as wool."
>
> *Isaiah 1:18*

And the whole heart faints.

6 From the sole of the foot even to
the head,
There is no soundness in it,
But wounds and bruises and
putrefying sores;
They have not been closed or
bound up,
Or soothed with ointment.

7 Your country *is* desolate,
Your cities *are* burned with fire;
Strangers devour your land in
your presence;
And *it is* desolate, as overthrown
by strangers.

8 So the daughter of Zion is left as a
booth in a vineyard,
As a hut in a garden of cucumbers,
As a besieged city.

9 Unless the LORD of hosts
Had left to us a very small
remnant,
We would have become like
Sodom,
We would have been made like
Gomorrah.

10 Hear the word of the LORD,
You rulers of Sodom;
Give ear to the law of our God,
You people of Gomorrah:

11 "To what purpose *is* the multitude
of your sacrifices to Me?"
Says the LORD.
"I have had enough of burnt
offerings of rams
And the fat of fed cattle.
I do not delight in the blood of
bulls,
Or of lambs or goats.

12 "When you come to appear before
Me,
Who has required this from your
hand,
To trample My courts?

13 Bring no more futile sacrifices;
Incense is an abomination to Me.
The New Moons, the Sabbaths,
and the calling of assemblies—
I cannot endure iniquity and the
sacred meeting.

14 Your New Moons and your
appointed feasts

My soul hates;
They are a trouble to Me,
I am weary of bearing *them.*

15 When you spread out your hands,
I will hide My eyes from you;
Even though you make many
prayers,
I will not hear.
Your hands are full of blood.

16 "Wash yourselves, make yourselves
clean;
Put away the evil of your doings
from before My eyes.
Cease to do evil,

17 Learn to do good;
Seek justice,
Rebuke the oppressor;
Defend the fatherless,
Plead for the widow.

18 "Come now, and let us reason
together,"
Says the LORD,
"Though your sins are like scarlet,
They shall be as white as snow;
Though they are red like crimson,
They shall be as wool.

19 If you are willing and obedient,
You shall eat the good of the land;

20 But if you refuse and rebel,
You shall be devoured by the
sword";
For the mouth of the LORD has
spoken.

21 How the faithful city has become
a harlot!
It was full of justice;
Righteousness lodged in it,
But now murderers.

22 Your silver has become dross,
Your wine mixed with water.

23 Your princes *are* rebellious,
And companions of thieves;
Everyone loves bribes,
And follows after rewards.
They do not defend the fatherless,
Nor does the cause of the widow
come before them.

24 Therefore the Lord says,
The LORD of hosts, the Mighty
One of Israel,

"Ah, I will rid Myself of My
   adversaries,
And take vengeance on My
   enemies.
25 I will turn My hand against you,
And thoroughly purge away your
   dross,
And take away all your alloy.
26 I will restore your judges as at the
   first,
And your counselors as at the
   beginning.
Afterward you shall be called the
   city of righteousness, the
   faithful city."

27 Zion shall be redeemed with
   justice,
And her penitents with
   righteousness.
28 The destruction of transgressors
   and of sinners *shall be* together,
And those who forsake the LORD
   shall be consumed.
29 For they shall be ashamed of the
   terebinth trees
Which you have desired;
And you shall be embarrassed
   because of the gardens
Which you have chosen.
30 For you shall be as a terebinth
   whose leaf fades,
And as a garden that has no
   water.
31 The strong shall be as tinder,
And the work of it as a spark;
Both will burn together,
And no one shall quench *them*.

2 The word that Isaiah the son of Amoz
saw concerning Judah and Jerusalem.

2 Now it shall come to pass in the
   latter days
That the mountain of the LORD's
   house
Shall be established on the top of
   the mountains,
And shall be exalted above the
   hills;
And all nations shall flow to it.
3 Many people shall come and say,
"Come, and let us go up to the
   mountain of the LORD,

To the house of the God of
   Jacob;
He will teach us His ways,
And we shall walk in His paths."
For out of Zion shall go forth the
   law,
And the word of the LORD from
   Jerusalem.
4 He shall judge between the
   nations,
And rebuke many people;
They shall beat their swords into
   plowshares,
And their spears into pruning
   hooks;
Nation shall not lift up sword
   against nation,
Neither shall they learn war
   anymore.

5 O house of Jacob, come and let us
   walk
In the light of the LORD.

6 For You have forsaken Your
   people, the house of Jacob,
Because they are filled with
   eastern ways;
They *are* soothsayers like the
   Philistines,
And they are pleased with the
   children of foreigners.
7 Their land is also full of silver and
   gold,
And there is no end to their
   treasures;
Their land is also full of horses,
And there is no end to their
   chariots.
8 Their land is also full of idols;
They worship the work of their
   own hands,
That which their own fingers have
   made.
9 People bow down,
And each man humbles himself;
Therefore do not forgive them.

10 Enter into the rock, and hide in
   the dust,
From the terror of the LORD
And the glory of His majesty.
11 The lofty looks of man shall be
   humbled,

The haughtiness of men shall be
    bowed down,
And the LORD alone shall be
    exalted in that day.

12 For the day of the LORD of hosts
    Shall come upon everything proud
      and lofty,
    Upon everything lifted up—
    And it shall be brought low—
13 Upon all the cedars of Lebanon
    that are high and lifted up,
    And upon all the oaks of Bashan;
14 Upon all the high mountains,
    And upon all the hills *that are*
      lifted up;
15 Upon every high tower,
    And upon every fortified wall;
16 Upon all the ships of Tarshish,
    And upon all the beautiful sloops.
17 The loftiness of man shall be
    bowed down,
    And the haughtiness of men shall
      be brought low;
    The LORD alone will be exalted in
      that day,
18 But the idols He shall utterly
    abolish.

19 They shall go into the holes of the
    rocks,
    And into the caves of the earth,
    From the terror of the LORD
    And the glory of His majesty,
    When He arises to shake the earth
      mightily.

20 In that day a man will cast away
    his idols of silver
    And his idols of gold,
    Which they made, *each* for
      himself to worship,
    To the moles and bats,
21 To go into the clefts of the rocks,
    And into the crags of the rugged
      rocks,
    From the terror of the LORD
    And the glory of His majesty,
    When He arises to shake the earth
      mightily.

22 Sever yourselves from such a man,
    Whose breath *is* in his nostrils;
    For of what account is he?

~ PSALM 105:1–6 ~

1 Oh, give thanks to the LORD!
    Call upon His name;
    Make known His deeds among the
      peoples!
2 Sing to Him, sing psalms to Him;
    Talk of all His wondrous works!
3 Glory in His holy name;
    Let the hearts of those rejoice who
      seek the LORD!
4 Seek the LORD and His strength;
    Seek His face evermore!
5 Remember His marvelous works
      which He has done,
    His wonders, and the judgments of
      His mouth,
6 O seed of Abraham His servant,
    You children of Jacob, His chosen
      ones!

~ PROVERBS 24:23–25 ~

23These *things* also *belong* to the wise:

    It is not good to show partiality in
      judgment.
24 He who says to the wicked, "You *are*
    righteous,"
    Him the people will curse;
    Nations will abhor him.
25 But those who rebuke *the wicked*
    will have delight,
    And a good blessing will come upon
    them.

~ 1 CORINTHIANS 14:21–40 ~

In the law it is written:

    "With *men of* other tongues and
      other lips
    I will speak to this people;
    And yet, for all that, they will not
      hear Me,"

says the Lord. 22 Therefore tongues are for a sign, not to those who believe but to unbelievers; but prophesying is not for unbelievers but for those who believe. 23 Therefore if the whole church comes together in one place, and all speak with tongues, and there come in *those who are* uninformed or unbelievers, will they not say that you are out of your mind? [24] But if all prophesy, and an unbeliever or an uninformed person comes in, he is convinced by all, he is convicted by all. [25] And thus the secrets of his heart are revealed; and so, falling down on *his* face, he will worship God and report that God is truly among you.

[26] How is it then, brethren? Whenever you come together, each of you has a psalm, has a teaching, has a tongue, has a revelation, has an interpretation. Let all things be done for edification. [27] If anyone speaks in a tongue, *let there be* two or at the most three, *each* in turn, and let one interpret. [28] But if there is no interpreter, let him keep silent in church, and let him speak to himself and to God. [29] Let two or three prophets speak, and let the others judge. [30] But if *anything* is revealed to another who sits by, let the first keep silent. [31] For you can all prophesy one by one, that all may learn and all may be encouraged. [32] And the spirits of the prophets are subject to the prophets. [33] For God is not *the author* of confusion but of peace, as in all the churches of the saints.

[34] Let your women keep silent in the churches, for they are not permitted to speak; but *they are* to be submissive, as the law also says. [35] And if they want to learn something, let them ask their own husbands at home; for it is shameful for women to speak in church.

[36] Or did the word of God come *originally* from you? Or *was it* you only that it reached? [37] If anyone thinks himself to be a prophet or spiritual, let him acknowledge that the things which I write to you are the commandments of the Lord. [38] But if anyone is ignorant, let him be ignorant.

[39] Therefore, brethren, desire earnestly to prophesy, and do not forbid to speak with tongues. [40] Let all things be done decently and in order.

READING 249 · SEPTEMBER 6

~ ISAIAH 3:1—4:6 ~

[1] For behold, the Lord, the LORD of hosts,
Takes away from Jerusalem and from Judah
The stock and the store,
The whole supply of bread and the whole supply of water;
[2] The mighty man and the man of war,
The judge and the prophet,
And the diviner and the elder;
[3] The captain of fifty and the honorable man,
The counselor and the skillful artisan,
And the expert enchanter.

[4] "I will give children *to be* their princes,
And babes shall rule over them.
[5] The people will be oppressed,
Every one by another and every one by his neighbor;
The child will be insolent toward the elder,

And the base toward the honorable."

[6] When a man takes hold of his brother
In the house of his father, *saying,*
"You have clothing;
You be our ruler,
And *let* these ruins *be* under your power,"
[7] In that day he will protest, saying,
"I cannot cure *your* ills,
For in my house *is* neither food nor clothing;
Do not make me a ruler of the people."

[8] For Jerusalem stumbled,
And Judah is fallen,
Because their tongue and their doings
Are against the LORD,
To provoke the eyes of His glory.
[9] The look on their countenance witnesses against them,

And they declare their sin as
    Sodom;
They do not hide *it*.
Woe to their soul!
For they have brought evil upon
    themselves.

10 "Say to the righteous that *it shall be*
    well *with them*,
For they shall eat the fruit of their
    doings.
11 Woe to the wicked! *It shall be* ill
    with him,
For the reward of his hands shall
    be given him.
12 *As for* My people, children *are*
    their oppressors,
And women rule over them.
O My people! Those who lead
    you cause *you* to err,
And destroy the way of your
    paths."

13 The LORD stands up to plead,
    And stands to judge the people.
14 The LORD will enter into
    judgment
With the elders of His people
And His princes:
"For you have eaten up the
    vineyard;
The plunder of the poor *is* in your
    houses.
15 What do you mean by crushing
    My people
And grinding the faces of the
    poor?"
Says the Lord GOD of hosts.

16 Moreover the LORD says:

"Because the daughters of Zion are
    haughty,
And walk with outstretched necks
And wanton eyes,
Walking and mincing *as* they go,
Making a jingling with their feet,
17 Therefore the Lord will strike
    with a scab
The crown of the head of the
    daughters of Zion,
And the LORD will uncover their
    secret parts."

18 In that day the Lord will take
    away the finery:
The jingling anklets, the scarves,
    and the crescents;
19 The pendants, the bracelets, and
    the veils;
20 The headdresses, the leg
    ornaments, and the headbands;
The perfume boxes, the charms,
21   and the rings;
The nose jewels,
22   the festal apparel, and the
    mantles;
The outer garments, the purses,
23   and the mirrors;
The fine linen, the turbans, and
    the robes.

24 And so it shall be:

Instead of a sweet smell there will
    be a stench;
Instead of a sash, a rope;
Instead of well-set hair, baldness;
Instead of a rich robe, a girding of
    sackcloth;
And branding instead of beauty.
25 Your men shall fall by the sword,
    And your mighty in the war.

26 Her gates shall lament and mourn,
    And she *being* desolate shall sit on
    the ground.

4 And in that day seven women shall
    take hold of one man, saying,
"We will eat our own food and
    wear our own apparel;
Only let us be called by your
    name,
To take away our reproach."
2 In that day the Branch of the
    LORD shall be beautiful and
    glorious;
And the fruit of the earth *shall be*
    excellent and appealing
For those of Israel who have
    escaped.

3 And it shall come to pass that *he who
is* left in Zion and remains in Jerusalem
will be called holy—everyone who is recorded among the living in Jerusalem.
4 When the Lord has washed away the filth
of the daughters of Zion, and purged the

Old Friends

All of their lives Mary and Walt worked hard. One would have thought they'd be ready to relax when they hit retirement years. They had good health, sufficient income, a home and cars that were paid for, and children who were happily married and self-sufficient. "You ought to travel some," their friends advised them. But Mary's response was always, "What would our old friends do?"

Mary and Walt's "old friends" were several elderly neighbors who lived nearby. Mary was in the habit of getting up at five in the morning and making her rounds — helping these neighbors with their showers and breakfasts. Then in the afternoon, she and Walt would return to help them with laundry, housework, and grocery shopping. In the evenings, Mary would bake bread and make casseroles to take to her neighbors. "Old people need someone to help them so they can stay in their own homes," Mary would tell her concerned friends. "Mother always said to me, 'Go see if Mrs. So-and-so needs anything.' And that's still what I'm doing! I'd feel bad if something happened to one of these old people because I failed to help them."

"But Mary," her friends protested, "your 'old' people are in their late seventies. You're eighty-three!"

You're never too old (or too young) to help someone. Teach your children this principle by modeling it for them, like Mary's mother did. There's nothing so rewarding in life as helping someone else — give the gift of compassion to your children and they will pass it to their children.

blood of Jerusalem from her midst, by the spirit of judgment and by the spirit of burning, [5] then the LORD will create above every dwelling place of Mount Zion, and above her assemblies, a cloud and smoke by day and the shining of a flaming fire by night. For over all the glory there *will be* a covering. [6] And there will be a tabernacle for shade in the daytime from the heat, for a place of refuge, and for a shelter from storm and rain.

~ PSALM 105:7–22 ~

[7] He *is* the LORD our God;
  His judgments *are* in all the earth.
[8] He remembers His covenant forever,
  The word *which* He commanded,
    for a thousand generations,
[9] *The covenant* which He made with
    Abraham,
  And His oath to Isaac,
[10] And confirmed it to Jacob for a
    statute,
  To Israel *as* an everlasting covenant,
[11] Saying, "To you I will give the land
    of Canaan
  As the allotment of your
    inheritance,"
[12] When they were few in number,
  Indeed very few, and strangers in it.

[13] When they went from one nation to
    another,
  From *one* kingdom to another
    people,
[14] He permitted no one to do them
    wrong;
  Yes, He rebuked kings for their
    sakes,
[15] *Saying,* "Do not touch My anointed
    ones,
  And do My prophets no harm."

[16] Moreover He called for a famine in
    the land;
  He destroyed all the provision of
    bread.
[17] He sent a man before them—
  Joseph—*who* was sold as a slave.
[18] They hurt his feet with fetters,
  He was laid in irons.
[19] Until the time that his word came to
    pass,
  The word of the LORD tested him.

[20] The king sent and released him,
  The ruler of the people let him go
    free.
[21] He made him lord of his house,
  And ruler of all his possessions,
[22] To bind his princes at his pleasure,
  And teach his elders wisdom.

~ PROVERBS 24:26, 27 ~

[26] He who gives a right answer kisses
    the lips.

[27] Prepare your outside work,
  Make it fit for yourself in the field;
  And afterward build your house.

~ 1 CORINTHIANS 15:1–28 ~

Moreover, brethren, I declare to you the gospel which I preached to you, which also you received and in which you stand, [2] by which also you are saved, if you hold fast that word which I preached to you— unless you believed in vain.

[3] For I delivered to you first of all that which I also received: that Christ died for our sins according to the Scriptures, [4] and that He was buried, and that He rose again the third day according to the Scriptures, [5] and that He was seen by Cephas, then by the twelve. [6] After that He was seen by over five hundred brethren at once, of whom the greater part remain to the present, but some have fallen asleep. [7] After that He was seen by James, then by all the apostles. [8] Then last of all He was seen by me also, as by one born out of due time.

[9] For I am the least of the apostles, who am not worthy to be called an apostle, because I persecuted the church of God. [10] But by the grace of God I am what I am, and His grace toward me was not in vain; but I labored more abundantly than they all, yet not I, but the grace of God *which was* with me. [11] Therefore, whether *it was* I or they, so we preach and so you believed.

[12] Now if Christ is preached that He has been raised from the dead, how do some among you say that there is no resurrection of the dead? [13] But if there is no resurrection of the dead, then Christ is not risen. [14] And if Christ is not risen, then

our preaching *is* empty and your faith *is* also empty. [15] Yes, and we are found false witnesses of God, because we have testified of God that He raised up Christ, whom He did not raise up—if in fact the dead do not rise. [16] For if *the* dead do not rise, then Christ is not risen. [17] And if Christ is not risen, your faith *is* futile; you are still in your sins! [18] Then also those who have fallen asleep in Christ have perished. [19] If in this life only we have hope in Christ, we are of all men the most pitiable.

[20] But now Christ is risen from the dead, *and* has become the firstfruits of those who have fallen asleep. [21] For since by man *came* death, by Man also *came* the resurrection of the dead. [22] For as in Adam all die, even so in Christ all shall be made alive. [23] But each one in his own order: Christ the firstfruits, afterward those *who are* Christ's at His coming. [24] Then *comes* the end, when He delivers the kingdom to God the Father, when He puts an end to all rule and all authority and power. [25] For He must reign till He has put all enemies under His feet. [26] The last enemy *that* will be destroyed *is* death. [27] For "He has put all things under His feet." But when He says "all things are put under *Him*," *it is* evident that He who put all things under Him is excepted. [28] Now when all things are made subject to Him, then the Son Himself will also be subject to Him who put all things under Him, that God may be all in all.

∼ ISAIAH 5:1—6:13 ∼

1 Now let me sing to my Well-
   beloved
   A song of my Beloved regarding
   His vineyard:

   My Well-beloved has a vineyard
   On a very fruitful hill.
2 He dug it up and cleared out its
   stones,
   And planted it with the choicest
   vine.
   He built a tower in its midst,
   And also made a winepress in it;
   So He expected *it* to bring forth
   good grapes,
   But it brought forth wild grapes.

3 "And now, O inhabitants of
   Jerusalem and men of Judah,
   Judge, please, between Me and
   My vineyard.
4 What more could have been done
   to My vineyard
   That I have not done in it?
   Why then, when I expected *it* to
   bring forth *good* grapes,
   Did it bring forth wild grapes?
5 And now, please let Me tell you
   what I will do to My vineyard:
   I will take away its hedge, and it
   shall be burned;

   And break down its wall, and it
   shall be trampled down.
6 I will lay it waste;
   It shall not be pruned or dug,
   But there shall come up briers and
   thorns.
   I will also command the clouds
   That they rain no rain on it."

7 For the vineyard of the LORD of
   hosts *is* the house of Israel,
   And the men of Judah are His
   pleasant plant.
   He looked for justice, but behold,
   oppression;
   For righteousness, but behold, a
   cry *for help.*

8 Woe to those who join house to
   house;
   They add field to field,
   Till *there is* no place
   Where they may dwell alone in
   the midst of the land!
9 In my hearing the LORD of hosts
   said,

   "Truly, many houses shall be
   desolate,
   Great and beautiful ones, without
   inhabitant.

10 For ten acres of vineyard shall
   yield one bath,
   And a homer of seed shall yield
   one ephah."

11 Woe to those who rise early in the
   morning,
   That they may follow intoxicating
   drink;
   Who continue until night, *till*
   wine inflames them!
12 The harp and the strings,
   The tambourine and flute,
   And wine are in their feasts;
   But they do not regard the work
   of the LORD,
   Nor consider the operation of His
   hands.

13 Therefore my people have gone
   into captivity,
   Because *they have* no knowledge;
   Their honorable men *are*
   famished,
   And their multitude dried up with
   thirst.
14 Therefore Sheol has enlarged
   itself
   And opened its mouth beyond
   measure;
   Their glory and their multitude
   and their pomp,
   And he who is jubilant, shall
   descend into it.
15 People shall be brought down,
   Each man shall be humbled,
   And the eyes of the lofty shall be
   humbled.
16 But the LORD of hosts shall be
   exalted in judgment,
   And God who is holy shall be
   hallowed in righteousness.
17 Then the lambs shall feed in their
   pasture,
   And in the waste places of the fat
   ones strangers shall eat.

18 Woe to those who draw iniquity
   with cords of vanity,
   And sin as if with a cart rope;
19 That say, "Let Him make speed
   and hasten His work,
   That we may see *it;*
   And let the counsel of the Holy

One of Israel draw near and
come,
That we may know *it.*"

20 Woe to those who call evil good,
   and good evil;
   Who put darkness for light, and
   light for darkness;
   Who put bitter for sweet, and
   sweet for bitter!

21 Woe to *those who are* wise in their
   own eyes,
   And prudent in their own sight!

22 Woe to men mighty at drinking
   wine,
   Woe to men valiant for mixing
   intoxicating drink,
23 Who justify the wicked for a bribe,
   And take away justice from the
   righteous man!

24 Therefore, as the fire devours the
   stubble,
   And the flame consumes the chaff,
   So their root will be as rottenness,
   And their blossom will ascend like
   dust;
   Because they have rejected the law
   of the LORD of hosts,
   And despised the word of the
   Holy One of Israel.
25 Therefore the anger of the LORD
   is aroused against His people;
   He has stretched out His hand
   against them
   And stricken them,
   And the hills trembled.
   Their carcasses *were* as refuse in
   the midst of the streets.

   For all this His anger is not turned
   away,
   But His hand *is* stretched out still.

26 He will lift up a banner to the
   nations from afar,
   And will whistle to them from the
   end of the earth;
   Surely they shall come with speed,
   swiftly.
27 No one will be weary or stumble
   among them,
   No one will slumber or sleep;

Working for Your Dreams

All her life, Veronica worked in jobs that served other people but gave her little personal satisfaction. As a young girl, she missed a lot of school to take care of her younger siblings and help with the family business. Consequently, she never learned to read.

After getting married, she worked as a cook in a restaurant, memorizing ingredient labels and recipes to conceal her illiteracy. Every day she lived in fear of making a mistake, while dreaming of one day being able to read.

Then, a serious illness put Veronica in the hospital and then at home for a long recovery. Her health improved some, but not enough for her to go back to work. She saw this time as her opportunity to learn to read and enrolled in an adult reading program.

Veronica's new reading skills boosted her self-confidence and she became involved in her church and in organizing community activities. Eventually, she wrote a prize-winning cookbook and became a local celebrity.

While working hard wherever she found herself, Veronica never let go of her dream. In the end, her dreams were realized far beyond her imagination!

Where you are may not be where you want to be, but the Bible says if we're faithful in the small things, God will make us rulers over bigger things. It has been said, "Diligence is the mother of all good fortune."

> Therefore, my beloved brethren, be steadfast, immovable, always abounding in the work of the Lord, knowing that your labor is not in vain.
>
> *1 Corinthians 15:58*

Nor will the belt on their loins be
loosed,
Nor the strap of their sandals be
broken;
28 Whose arrows *are* sharp,
And all their bows bent;
Their horses' hooves will seem
like flint,
And their wheels like a whirlwind.
29 Their roaring *will be* like a lion,
They will roar like young lions;
Yes, they will roar
And lay hold of the prey;
They will carry *it* away safely,
And no one will deliver.
30 In that day they will roar against
them
Like the roaring of the sea.
And if *one* looks to the land,
Behold, darkness *and* sorrow;
And the light is darkened by the
clouds.

6 In the year that King Uzziah died, I
saw the Lord sitting on a throne, high and
lifted up, and the train of His *robe* filled
the temple. 2 Above it stood seraphim;
each one had six wings: with two he covered his face, with two he covered his feet,
and with two he flew. 3 And one cried to
another and said:

"Holy, holy, holy *is* the LORD of
hosts;
The whole earth *is* full of His
glory!"

4 And the posts of the door were shaken
by the voice of him who cried out, and
the house was filled with smoke.
5 So I said:

"Woe *is* me, for I am undone!
Because I *am* a man of unclean
lips,
And I dwell in the midst of a
people of unclean lips;
For my eyes have seen the King,
The LORD of hosts."

6 Then one of the seraphim flew to me,
having in his hand a live coal *which* he
had taken with the tongs from the altar.
7 And he touched my mouth *with it,* and
said:

"Behold, this has touched your lips;
Your iniquity is taken away,
And your sin purged."

8 Also I heard the voice of the Lord,
saying:

"Whom shall I send,
And who will go for Us?"

Then I said, "Here *am* I! Send me."
9 And He said, "Go, and tell this people:

'Keep on hearing, but do not
understand;
Keep on seeing, but do not
perceive.'

10 "Make the heart of this people dull,
And their ears heavy,
And shut their eyes;
Lest they see with their eyes,
And hear with their ears,
And understand with their heart,
And return and be healed."

11 Then I said, "Lord, how long?"
And He answered:

"Until the cities are laid waste and
without inhabitant,
The houses are without a man,
The land is utterly desolate,
12 The LORD has removed men far
away,
And the forsaken places *are* many
in the midst of the land.
13 But yet a tenth *will be* in it,
And will return and be for
consuming,
As a terebinth tree or as an oak,
Whose stump *remains* when it is
cut down.
So the holy seed *shall be* its
stump."

~ PSALM 105:23–36 ~

23 Israel also came into Egypt,
And Jacob dwelt in the land of Ham.
24 He increased His people greatly,
And made them stronger than their
enemies.

25 He turned their heart to hate His
     people,
   To deal craftily with His servants.

26 He sent Moses His servant,
   And Aaron whom He had chosen.
27 They performed His signs among
     them,
   And wonders in the land of Ham.
28 He sent darkness, and made *it* dark;
   And they did not rebel against His
     word.
29 He turned their waters into blood,
   And killed their fish.
30 Their land abounded with frogs,
   Even in the chambers of their kings.
31 He spoke, and there came swarms of
     flies,
   And lice in all their territory.
32 He gave them hail for rain,
   And flaming fire in their land.
33 He struck their vines also, and their
     fig trees,
   And splintered the trees of their
     territory.
34 He spoke, and locusts came,
   Young locusts without number,
35 And ate up all the vegetation in their
     land,
   And devoured the fruit of their
     ground.
36 He also destroyed all the firstborn in
     their land,
   The first of all their strength.

∼ PROVERBS 24:28, 29 ∼

28 Do not be a witness against your
     neighbor without cause,
   For would you deceive with your
     lips?
29 Do not say, "I will do to him just as
     he has done to me;
   I will render to the man according to
     his work."

∼ 1 CORINTHIANS 15:29–58 ∼

Otherwise, what will they do who are
baptized for the dead, if the dead do not
rise at all? Why then are they baptized
for the dead? 30 And why do we stand in
jeopardy every hour? 31 I affirm, by the
boasting in you which I have in Christ
Jesus our Lord, I die daily. 32 If, in the
manner of men, I have fought with beasts
at Ephesus, what advantage *is it* to me? If
the dead do not rise, "Let us eat and drink,
for tomorrow we die!"

33 Do not be deceived: "Evil company
corrupts good habits." 34 Awake to righteousness, and do not sin; for some do
not have the knowledge of God. I speak
this to your shame.

35 But someone will say, "How are the
dead raised up? And with what body do
they come?" 36 Foolish one, what you sow
is not made alive unless it dies. 37 And what
you sow, you do not sow that body that
shall be, but mere grain—perhaps wheat
or some other *grain.* 38 But God gives it a
body as He pleases, and to each seed its
own body.

39 All flesh *is* not the same flesh, but
there is one *kind of* flesh of men, another
flesh of animals, another of fish, *and* another of birds.

40 *There are* also celestial bodies and terrestrial bodies; but the glory of the celestial *is* one, and the *glory* of the terrestrial
is another. 41 *There is* one glory of the sun,
another glory of the moon, and another
glory of the stars; for *one* star differs from
another star in glory.

42 So also *is* the resurrection of the dead.
The body is sown in corruption, it is raised
in incorruption. 43 It is sown in dishonor,
it is raised in glory. It is sown in weakness, it is raised in power. 44 It is sown a
natural body, it is raised a spiritual body.
There is a natural body, and there is a spiritual body. 45 And so it is written, "The first
man Adam became a living being." The
last Adam *became* a life-giving spirit.

46 However, the spiritual is not first, but
the natural, and afterward the spiritual.
47 The first man *was* of the earth, *made* of
dust; the second Man *is* the Lord from
heaven. 48 As *was* the *man* of dust, so also
are those *who are made* of dust; and as *is*
the heavenly *Man,* so also *are* those *who
are* heavenly. 49 And as we have borne the
image of the *man* of dust, we shall also
bear the image of the heavenly *Man.*

50 Now this I say, brethren, that flesh
and blood cannot inherit the kingdom of
God; nor does corruption inherit incorruption. 51 Behold, I tell you a mystery:
We shall not all sleep, but we shall all be

changed— [52] in a moment, in the twinkling of an eye, at the last trumpet. For the trumpet will sound, and the dead will be raised incorruptible, and we shall be changed. [53] For this corruptible must put on incorruption, and this mortal *must* put on immortality. [54] So when this corruptible has put on incorruption, and this mortal has put on immortality, then shall be brought to pass the saying that is written: "Death is swallowed up in victory."

[55] "O Death, where *is* your sting?
O Hades, where *is* your victory?"

[56] The sting of death *is* sin, and the strength of sin *is* the law. [57] But thanks *be* to God, who gives us the victory through our Lord Jesus Christ.
[58] Therefore, my beloved brethren, be steadfast, immovable, always abounding in the work of the Lord, knowing that your labor is not in vain in the Lord.

READING 251 · SEPTEMBER 8

~ ISAIAH 7:1—8:22 ~

Now it came to pass in the days of Ahaz the son of Jotham, the son of Uzziah, king of Judah, *that* Rezin king of Syria and Pekah the son of Remaliah, king of Israel, went up to Jerusalem to *make* war against it, but could not prevail against it. [2] And it was told to the house of David, saying, "Syria's forces are deployed in Ephraim." So his heart and the heart of his people were moved as the trees of the woods are moved with the wind.

[3] Then the LORD said to Isaiah, "Go out now to meet Ahaz, you and Shear-Jashub your son, at the end of the aqueduct from the upper pool, on the highway to the Fuller's Field, [4] and say to him: 'Take heed, and be quiet; do not fear or be fainthearted for these two stubs of smoking firebrands, for the fierce anger of Rezin and Syria, and the son of Remaliah. [5] Because Syria, Ephraim, and the son of Remaliah have plotted evil against you, saying, [6] "Let us go up against Judah and trouble it, and let us make a gap in its wall for ourselves, and set a king over them, the son of Tabel"— [7] thus says the Lord GOD:

"It shall not stand,
Nor shall it come to pass.
[8] For the head of Syria *is* Damascus,
And the head of Damascus *is* Rezin.
Within sixty-five years Ephraim will be broken,
So that it will not *be* a people.

[9] The head of Ephraim *is* Samaria,
And the head of Samaria *is* Remaliah's son.
If you will not believe,
Surely you shall not be established." ' "

[10] Moreover the LORD spoke again to Ahaz, saying, [11] "Ask a sign for yourself from the LORD your God; ask it either in the depth or in the height above."
[12] But Ahaz said, "I will not ask, nor will I test the LORD!"
[13] Then he said, "Hear now, O house of David! *Is it* a small thing for you to weary men, but will you weary my God also? [14] Therefore the Lord Himself will give you a sign: Behold, the virgin shall conceive and bear a Son, and shall call His name Immanuel. [15] Curds and honey He shall eat, that He may know to refuse the evil and choose the good. [16] For before the Child shall know to refuse the evil and choose the good, the land that you dread will be forsaken by both her kings. [17] The LORD will bring the king of Assyria upon you and your people and your father's house—days that have not come since the day that Ephraim departed from Judah."

[18] And it shall come to pass in that day
That the LORD will whistle for the fly
That *is* in the farthest part of the rivers of Egypt,

Success Takes Wisdom

> Curds and honey He shall eat, that He may know to refuse the evil and choose the good.
>
> *Isaiah 7:15*

Charles Goodyear had no formal education. At the age of twenty-one, he went into partnership with his father in a hardware business that soon failed. It was the first of many losses. Failure and poverty characterized much of his life and more than once, he spent time in debtor's prison. His family frequently existed on the charity of neighbors. Six of his twelve children died in infancy. By the time he was forty, his health was very poor. He could not get around without the aid of crutches.

Most of Goodyear's troubles stemmed from his obsession with rubber. He had a fanatic determination to transform raw rubber into a useful material. To pursue his experiments, he sold his watch, the living room furniture, even the dishes off the table. Even while in jail, he experimented with rubber, trying to discover its unique properties and mold it to his satisfaction.

Quite by accident, he stumbled upon the process of vulcanizing rubber when he dropped a piece of the material that had been treated with sulfur on a hot stove. He refined this process, which opened the development of an entire industry. While he might have amassed a fortune, his own bad judgment resulted in his dying in poverty.

It takes more than effort and goals to gain *and keep* success. It also takes wisdom.

And for the bee that *is* in the land of Assyria.

¹⁹ They will come, and all of them will rest
In the desolate valleys and in the clefts of the rocks,
And on all thorns and in all pastures.

²⁰ In the same day the Lord will shave with a hired razor,
With those from beyond the River, with the king of Assyria,
The head and the hair of the legs,
And will also remove the beard.

²¹ It shall be in that day
That a man will keep alive a young cow and two sheep;
²² So it shall be, from the abundance of milk they give,
That he will eat curds;
For curds and honey everyone will eat who is left in the land.

²³ It shall happen in that day,
That wherever there could be a thousand vines
Worth a thousand *shekels* of silver,
It will be for briers and thorns.
²⁴ With arrows and bows men will come there,
Because all the land will become briers and thorns.

²⁵ And to any hill which could be dug with the hoe,
You will not go there for fear of briers and thorns;
But it will become a range for oxen
And a place for sheep to roam.

8 Moreover the LORD said to me, "Take a large scroll, and write on it with a man's pen concerning Maher-Shalal-Hash-Baz. ² And I will take for Myself faithful witnesses to record, Uriah the priest and Zechariah the son of Jeberechiah."

³ Then I went to the prophetess, and she conceived and bore a son. Then the LORD said to me, "Call his name Maher-Shalal-Hash-Baz; ⁴ for before the child shall have knowledge to cry 'My father' and 'My mother,' the riches of Damascus

and the spoil of Samaria will be taken away before the king of Assyria."

⁵ The LORD also spoke to me again, saying:

⁶ "Inasmuch as these people refused
The waters of Shiloah that flow softly,
And rejoice in Rezin and in Remaliah's son;
⁷ Now therefore, behold, the Lord brings up over them
The waters of the River, strong and mighty—
The king of Assyria and all his glory;
He will go up over all his channels
And go over all his banks.
⁸ He will pass through Judah,
He will overflow and pass over,
He will reach up to the neck;
And the stretching out of his wings
Will fill the breadth of Your land, O Immanuel.

⁹ "Be shattered, O you peoples, and be broken in pieces!
Give ear, all you from far countries.
Gird yourselves, but be broken in pieces;
Gird yourselves, but be broken in pieces.
¹⁰ Take counsel together, but it will come to nothing;
Speak the word, but it will not stand,
For God *is* with us."

¹¹ For the LORD spoke thus to me with a strong hand, and instructed me that I should not walk in the way of this people, saying:

¹² "Do not say, 'A conspiracy,'
Concerning all that this people call a conspiracy,
Nor be afraid of their threats, nor be troubled.
¹³ The LORD of hosts, Him you shall hallow;
Let Him *be* your fear,
And *let* Him *be* your dread.
¹⁴ He will be as a sanctuary,

But a stone of stumbling and a
     rock of offense
To both the houses of Israel,
As a trap and a snare to the
     inhabitants of Jerusalem.
15 And many among them shall
     stumble;
They shall fall and be broken,
Be snared and taken."

16 Bind up the testimony,
Seal the law among my disciples.
17 And I will wait on the LORD,
Who hides His face from the
     house of Jacob;
And I will hope in Him.
18 Here am I and the children whom
     the LORD has given me!
We are for signs and wonders in
     Israel
From the LORD of hosts,
Who dwells in Mount Zion.

19 And when they say to you, "Seek
those who are mediums and wizards, who
whisper and mutter," should not a people
seek their God? *Should they seek* the dead
on behalf of the living? 20 To the law and
to the testimony! If they do not speak according to this word, *it is* because *there is*
no light in them. 21 They will pass through it hard-
pressed and hungry; and it shall happen,
when they are hungry, that they will be
enraged and curse their king and their
God, and look upward. 22 Then they will
look to the earth, and see trouble and
darkness, gloom of anguish; and *they will
be* driven into darkness.

~ PSALM 105:37–45 ~

37 He also brought them out with silver
     and gold,
And *there was* none feeble among
     His tribes.
38 Egypt was glad when they departed,
For the fear of them had fallen upon
     them.
39 He spread a cloud for a covering,
And fire to give light in the night.
40 *The people* asked, and He brought
     quail,
And satisfied them with the bread of
     heaven.

41 He opened the rock, and water
     gushed out;
It ran in the dry places *like* a river.
42 For He remembered His holy
     promise,
And Abraham His servant.
43 He brought out His people with joy,
His chosen ones with gladness.
44 He gave them the lands of the
     Gentiles,
And they inherited the labor of the
     nations,
45 That they might observe His statutes
And keep His laws.

Praise the LORD!

~ PROVERBS 24:30–34 ~

30 I went by the field of the lazy *man,*
And by the vineyard of the man
     devoid of understanding;
31 And there it was, all overgrown with
     thorns;
Its surface was covered with nettles;
Its stone wall was broken down.
32 When I saw *it,* I considered *it* well;
I looked on *it and* received
     instruction:
33 A little sleep, a little slumber,
A little folding of the hands to rest;
34 So shall your poverty come *like* a
     prowler,
And your need like an armed man.

~ 1 CORINTHIANS 16:1–24 ~

Now concerning the collection for
the saints, as I have given orders to the
churches of Galatia, so you must do also:
2 On the first *day* of the week let each one
of you lay something aside, storing up as
he may prosper, that there be no collec-
tions when I come. 3 And when I come,
whomever you approve by *your* letters I
will send to bear your gift to Jerusalem.
4 But if it is fitting that I go also, they will
go with me.
    5 Now I will come to you when I pass
through Macedonia (for I am passing
through Macedonia). 6 And it may be that
I will remain, or even spend the winter
with you, that you may send me on my
journey, wherever I go. 7 For I do not wish

to see you now on the way; but I hope to stay a while with you, if the Lord permits.

⁸ But I will tarry in Ephesus until Pentecost. ⁹ For a great and effective door has opened to me, and *there are* many adversaries.

¹⁰ And if Timothy comes, see that he may be with you without fear; for he does the work of the Lord, as I also *do*. ¹¹ Therefore let no one despise him. But send him on his journey in peace, that he may come to me; for I am waiting for him with the brethren.

¹² Now concerning *our* brother Apollos, I strongly urged him to come to you with the brethren, but he was quite unwilling to come at this time; however, he will come when he has a convenient time.

¹³ Watch, stand fast in the faith, be brave, be strong. ¹⁴ Let all *that* you *do* be done with love.

¹⁵ I urge you, brethren—you know the household of Stephanas, that it is the firstfruits of Achaia, and *that* they have devoted themselves to the ministry of the saints— ¹⁶ that you also submit to such, and to everyone who works and labors with *us*.

¹⁷ I am glad about the coming of Stephanas, Fortunatus, and Achaicus, for what was lacking on your part they supplied. ¹⁸ For they refreshed my spirit and yours. Therefore acknowledge such men.

¹⁹ The churches of Asia greet you. Aquila and Priscilla greet you heartily in the Lord, with the church that is in their house. ²⁰ All the brethren greet you.

Greet one another with a holy kiss.

²¹ The salutation with my own hand—Paul's.

²² If anyone does not love the Lord Jesus Christ, let him be accursed. O Lord, come!

²³ The grace of our Lord Jesus Christ *be* with you. ²⁴ My love *be* with you all in Christ Jesus. Amen.

READING 252 · SEPTEMBER 9

∼ ISAIAH 9:1—10:34 ∼

¹ Nevertheless the gloom *will* not *be* upon her who *is* distressed,
  As when at first He lightly esteemed
The land of Zebulun and the land of Naphtali,
And afterward more heavily oppressed *her,*
  By the way of the sea, beyond the Jordan,
In Galilee of the Gentiles.

² The people who walked in darkness
Have seen a great light;
Those who dwelt in the land of the shadow of death,
Upon them a light has shined.

³ You have multiplied the nation
And increased its joy;
They rejoice before You
According to the joy of harvest,
As *men* rejoice when they divide the spoil.

⁴ For You have broken the yoke of his burden
And the staff of his shoulder,
The rod of his oppressor,
As in the day of Midian.

⁵ For every warrior's sandal from the noisy battle,
And garments rolled in blood,
Will be used for burning *and* fuel of fire.

⁶ For unto us a Child is born,
Unto us a Son is given;
And the government will be upon His shoulder.
And His name will be called Wonderful, Counselor, Mighty God,
Everlasting Father, Prince of Peace.

⁷ Of the increase of *His* government and peace
There will be no end,
Upon the throne of David and over His kingdom,
To order it and establish it with judgment and justice

Why to Live

Victor Frankl was stripped of everything he owned when he was arrested by the Nazis in World War II. He arrived at Auschwitz with only his manuscript — a book he had been researching and writing for years — sewn into the lining of his coat. Upon arrival, even that was taken from him. He later wrote, "I had to undergo and overcome the loss of my spiritual child. . . . It seemed as if nothing and no one would survive me. I found myself confronted with the question of whether under such circumstances my life was ultimately void of any meaning."

Days later, the Nazis forced the prisoners to give up their clothes. In return Frankl was given the rags of an inmate who had been sent to the gas chamber. In the pocket of the garment he found a torn piece of paper — a page from a Hebrew prayer book. On it was the foremost Jewish prayer, "Shema Yisrael" which begins, "Hear, O Israel! The Lord our God is one God."

Frankl says, "How should I have interpreted such a 'coincidence' other than as a challenge to live my thoughts instead of merely putting them on paper?" He later wrote in his classic masterpiece, *Man's Search for Meaning*, "He who has a why to live for can bear almost any how."

From that time forward, even
forever.
The zeal of the LORD of hosts will
perform this.

8 The Lord sent a word against
Jacob,
And it has fallen on Israel.
9 All the people will know—
Ephraim and the inhabitant of
Samaria—
Who say in pride and arrogance of
heart:
10 "The bricks have fallen down,
But we will rebuild with hewn
stones;
The sycamores are cut down,
But we will replace *them* with
cedars."
11 Therefore the LORD shall set up
The adversaries of Rezin against
him,
And spur his enemies on,
12 The Syrians before and the
Philistines behind;
And they shall devour Israel with
an open mouth.

For all this His anger is not turned
away,
But His hand *is* stretched out still.

13 For the people do not turn to Him
who strikes them,
Nor do they seek the LORD of
hosts.
14 Therefore the LORD will cut off
head and tail from Israel,
Palm branch and bulrush in one
day.
15 The elder and honorable, he *is* the
head;
The prophet who teaches lies, he
is the tail.
16 For the leaders of this people
cause *them* to err,
And *those who are* led by them are
destroyed.
17 Therefore the Lord will have no
joy in their young men,
Nor have mercy on their fatherless
and widows;
For everyone *is* a hypocrite and an
evildoer,
And every mouth speaks folly.

For all this His anger is not turned
away,
But His hand *is* stretched out still.

18 For wickedness burns as the fire;
It shall devour the briers and
thorns,
And kindle in the thickets of the
forest;
They shall mount up *like* rising
smoke.
19 Through the wrath of the LORD of
hosts
The land is burned up,
And the people shall be as fuel for
the fire;
No man shall spare his brother.
20 And he shall snatch on the right
hand
And be hungry;
He shall devour on the left hand
And not be satisfied;
Every man shall eat the flesh of his
own arm.
21 Manasseh *shall devour* Ephraim,
and Ephraim Manasseh;
Together they *shall be* against
Judah.

For all this His anger is not turned
away,
But His hand *is* stretched out still.

10 "Woe to those who decree
unrighteous decrees,
Who write misfortune,
Which they have prescribed
2 To rob the needy of justice,
And to take what is right from the
poor of My people,
That widows may be their prey,
And *that* they may rob the
fatherless.
3 What will you do in the day of
punishment,
And in the desolation *which* will
come from afar?
To whom will you flee for help?
And where will you leave your
glory?
4 Without Me they shall bow down
among the prisoners,
And they shall fall among the
slain."

For all this His anger is not turned
away,
But His hand *is* stretched out still.

5 "Woe to Assyria, the rod of My
anger
And the staff in whose hand is My
indignation.
6 I will send him against an ungodly
nation,
And against the people of My
wrath
I will give him charge,
To seize the spoil, to take the prey,
And to tread them down like the
mire of the streets.
7 Yet he does not mean so,
Nor does his heart think so;
But *it is* in his heart to destroy,
And cut off not a few nations.
8 For he says,
'*Are* not my princes altogether
kings?
9 *Is* not Calno like Carchemish?
Is not Hamath like Arpad?
Is not Samaria like Damascus?
10 As my hand has found the
kingdoms of the idols,
Whose carved images excelled
those of Jerusalem and Samaria,
11 As I have done to Samaria and her
idols,
Shall I not do also to Jerusalem
and her idols?' "

12 Therefore it shall come to pass, when
the Lord has performed all His work on
Mount Zion and on Jerusalem, *that He
will say,* "I will punish the fruit of the arrogant heart of the king of Assyria, and
the glory of his haughty looks."
13 For he says:

"By the strength of my hand I have
done *it,*
And by my wisdom, for I am
prudent;
Also I have removed the
boundaries of the people,
And have robbed their treasuries;
So I have put down the
inhabitants like a valiant *man.*
14 My hand has found like a nest the
riches of the people,

And as one gathers eggs *that are*
left,
I have gathered all the earth;
And there was no one who moved
his wing,
Nor opened *his* mouth with even
a peep."

15 Shall the ax boast itself against
him who chops with it?
Or shall the saw exalt itself against
him who saws with it?
As if a rod could wield *itself*
against those who lift it up,
Or as if a staff could lift up, *as if it
were* not wood!
16 Therefore the Lord, the Lord of
hosts,
Will send leanness among his fat
ones;
And under his glory
He will kindle a burning
Like the burning of a fire.
17 So the Light of Israel will be for a
fire,
And his Holy One for a flame;
It will burn and devour
His thorns and his briers in one
day.
18 And it will consume the glory of
his forest and of his fruitful
field,
Both soul and body;
And they will be as when a sick
man wastes away.
19 Then the rest of the trees of his
forest
Will be so few in number
That a child may write them.

20 And it shall come to pass in that
day
That the remnant of Israel,
And such as have escaped of the
house of Jacob,
Will never again depend on him
who defeated them,
But will depend on the LORD, the
Holy One of Israel, in truth.
21 The remnant will return, the
remnant of Jacob,
To the Mighty God.
22 For though your people, O Israel,
be as the sand of the sea,
A remnant of them will return;

The destruction decreed shall
overflow with righteousness.
²³ For the Lord GOD of hosts
Will make a determined end
In the midst of all the land.

²⁴ Therefore thus says the Lord GOD of hosts: "O My people, who dwell in Zion, do not be afraid of the Assyrian. He shall strike you with a rod and lift up his staff against you, in the manner of Egypt. ²⁵ For yet a very little while and the indignation will cease, as will My anger in their destruction." ²⁶ And the LORD of hosts will stir up a scourge for him like the slaughter of Midian at the rock of Oreb; *as* His rod was on the sea, so will He lift it up in the manner of Egypt.

²⁷ It shall come to pass in that day
That his burden will be taken
away from your shoulder,
And his yoke from your neck,
And the yoke will be destroyed
because of the anointing oil.

²⁸ He has come to Aiath,
He has passed Migron;
At Michmash he has attended to
his equipment.
²⁹ They have gone along the ridge,
They have taken up lodging at
Geba.
Ramah is afraid,
Gibeah of Saul has fled.
³⁰ Lift up your voice,
O daughter of Gallim!
Cause it to be heard as far as
Laish—
O poor Anathoth!
³¹ Madmenah has fled,
The inhabitants of Gebim seek
refuge.
³² As yet he will remain at Nob that
day;
He will shake his fist at the mount
of the daughter of Zion,
The hill of Jerusalem.

³³ Behold, the Lord,
The LORD of hosts,
Will lop off the bough with terror;
Those of high stature *will be* hewn
down,
And the haughty will be humbled.

³⁴ He will cut down the thickets of
the forest with iron,
And Lebanon will fall by the
Mighty One.

~ PSALM 106:1–5 ~

¹ Praise the LORD!

Oh, give thanks to the LORD, for *He
is* good!
For His mercy *endures* forever.

² Who can utter the mighty acts of the
LORD?
Who can declare all His praise?
³ Blessed *are* those who keep justice,
And he who does righteousness at all
times!

⁴ Remember me, O LORD, with the
favor *You have toward* Your
people.
Oh, visit me with Your salvation,
⁵ That I may see the benefit of Your
chosen ones,
That I may rejoice in the gladness of
Your nation,
That I may glory with Your
inheritance.

~ PROVERBS 25:1, 2 ~

These also *are* proverbs of Solomon which the men of Hezekiah king of Judah copied:

² *It is* the glory of God to conceal a
matter,
But the glory of kings *is* to search
out a matter.

~ 2 CORINTHIANS 1:1–24 ~

Paul, an apostle of Jesus Christ by the will of God, and Timothy *our* brother,

To the church of God which is at Corinth, with all the saints who are in all Achaia:

² Grace to you and peace from God our Father and the Lord Jesus Christ.
³ Blessed *be* the God and Father of our

Lord Jesus Christ, the Father of mercies and God of all comfort, [4] who comforts us in all our tribulation, that we may be able to comfort those who are in any trouble, with the comfort with which we ourselves are comforted by God. [5] For as the sufferings of Christ abound in us, so our consolation also abounds through Christ. [6] Now if we are afflicted, *it is* for your consolation and salvation, which is effective for enduring the same sufferings which we also suffer. Or if we are comforted, *it is* for your consolation and salvation. [7] And our hope for you *is* steadfast, because we know that as you are partakers of the sufferings, so also *you will partake* of the consolation.

[8] For we do not want you to be ignorant, brethren, of our trouble which came to us in Asia: that we were burdened beyond measure, above strength, so that we despaired even of life. [9] Yes, we had the sentence of death in ourselves, that we should not trust in ourselves but in God who raises the dead, [10] who delivered us from so great a death, and does deliver us; in whom we trust that He will still deliver *us,* [11] you also helping together in prayer for us, that thanks may be given by many persons on our behalf for the gift *granted* to us through many.

[12] For our boasting is this: the testimony of our conscience that we conducted ourselves in the world in simplicity and godly sincerity, not with fleshly wisdom but by the grace of God, and more abundantly toward you. [13] For we are not writing any other things to you than what you read or understand. Now I trust you will understand, even to the end [14](as also you have understood us in part), that we are your boast as you also *are* ours, in the day of the Lord Jesus.

[15] And in this confidence I intended to come to you before, that you might have a second benefit— [16] to pass by way of you to Macedonia, to come again from Macedonia to you, and be helped by you on my way to Judea. [17] Therefore, when I was planning this, did I do it lightly? Or the things I plan, do I plan according to the flesh, that with me there should be Yes, Yes, and No, No? [18] But *as* God *is* faithful, our word to you was not Yes and No. [19] For the Son of God, Jesus Christ, who was preached among you by us—by me, Silvanus, and Timothy—was not Yes and No, but in Him was Yes. [20] For all the promises of God in Him *are* Yes, and in Him Amen, to the glory of God through us. [21] Now He who establishes us with you in Christ and has anointed us *is* God, [22] who also has sealed us and given us the Spirit in our hearts as a guarantee.

[23] Moreover I call God as witness against my soul, that to spare you I came no more to Corinth. [24] Not that we have dominion over your faith, but are fellow workers for your joy; for by faith you stand.

READING 253 · SEPTEMBER 10

~ ISAIAH 11:1—12:6 ~

[1] There shall come forth a Rod
    from the stem of Jesse,
And a Branch shall grow out of his
    roots.
[2] The Spirit of the LORD shall rest
    upon Him,
The Spirit of wisdom and
    understanding,
The Spirit of counsel and
    might,
The Spirit of knowledge and of
    the fear of the LORD.

[3] His delight *is* in the fear of the
    LORD,
And He shall not judge by the
    sight of His eyes,
Nor decide by the hearing of His
    ears;
[4] But with righteousness He shall
    judge the poor,
And decide with equity for the
    meek of the earth;
He shall strike the earth with the
    rod of His mouth,

And with the breath of His lips He
shall slay the wicked.
5 Righteousness shall be the belt of
His loins,
And faithfulness the belt of His
waist.

6 "The wolf also shall dwell with the
lamb,
The leopard shall lie down with
the young goat,
The calf and the young lion and
the fatling together;
And a little child shall lead them.
7 The cow and the bear shall graze;
Their young ones shall lie down
together;
And the lion shall eat straw like
the ox.
8 The nursing child shall play by the
cobra's hole,
And the weaned child shall put his
hand in the viper's den.
9 They shall not hurt nor destroy in
all My holy mountain,
For the earth shall be full of the
knowledge of the LORD
As the waters cover the sea.

10 "And in that day there shall be a
Root of Jesse,
Who shall stand as a banner to the
people;
For the Gentiles shall seek Him,
And His resting place shall be
glorious."

11 It shall come to pass in that day
That the Lord shall set His hand
again the second time
To recover the remnant of His
people who are left,
From Assyria and Egypt,
From Pathros and Cush,
From Elam and Shinar,
From Hamath and the islands of
the sea.

12 He will set up a banner for the
nations,
And will assemble the outcasts of
Israel,
And gather together the dispersed
of Judah

From the four corners of the
earth.
13 Also the envy of Ephraim shall
depart,
And the adversaries of Judah shall
be cut off;
Ephraim shall not envy Judah,
And Judah shall not harass
Ephraim.
14 But they shall fly down upon the
shoulder of the Philistines
toward the west;
Together they shall plunder the
people of the East;
They shall lay their hand on Edom
and Moab;
And the people of Ammon shall
obey them.
15 The LORD will utterly destroy the
tongue of the Sea of Egypt;
With His mighty wind He will
shake His fist over the River,
And strike it in the seven streams,
And make *men* cross over
dryshod.
16 There will be a highway for the
remnant of His people
Who will be left from Assyria,
As it was for Israel
In the day that he came up from
the land of Egypt.

12 And in that day you will say:

"O LORD, I will praise You;
Though You were angry with me,
Your anger is turned away, and
You comfort me.
2 Behold, God *is* my salvation,
I will trust and not be afraid;
'For YAH, the LORD, *is* my strength
and song;
He also has become my
salvation.' "

3 Therefore with joy you will draw
water
From the wells of salvation.

4 And in that day you will say:

"Praise the LORD, call upon His
name;
Declare His deeds among the
peoples,

No Limits

As a senior in high school, Jim batted .427 and led his team in home runs. He also quarterbacked the football team to the state semifinals. Later, Jim went on to pitch professionally for the New York Yankees.

That's a remarkable achievement for any athlete. But it's an almost unbeliev-able one for Jim, because he was born without a right hand.

A little boy who had only parts of two fingers on one of his hands once came to Jim in the clubhouse after a Yankees game and said, "They call me crab at camp. Did kids ever tease you?"

"Yeah," Jim replied. "Kids used to tell me that my hand looked like a foot." And then he asked the boy an all-important question, "Is there anything you can't do?" The boy wisely answered, "No."

"Well, I don't think so either," Jim responded.

What others see as your "limitation" is only a limitation if you think it is. God certainly doesn't see you as limited — He sees you as having unlimited potential. When we begin to see ourselves the way God sees us, there truly are no limits to what we can do!

Behold, God is my salvation, I will trust and not be afraid; "For Yah, the Lord, is my strength and song; He also has become my salvation."

Isaiah 12:2

Make mention that His name is
exalted.
5 Sing to the LORD,
For He has done excellent things;
This *is* known in all the earth.
6 Cry out and shout, O inhabitant
of Zion,
For great *is* the Holy One of Israel
in your midst!"

∽ PSALM 106:6–18 ∽

6 We have sinned with our fathers,
We have committed iniquity,
We have done wickedly.
7 Our fathers in Egypt did not
understand Your wonders;
They did not remember the
multitude of Your mercies,
But rebelled by the sea—the Red
Sea.

8 Nevertheless He saved them for His
name's sake,
That He might make His mighty
power known.
9 He rebuked the Red Sea also, and it
dried up;
So He led them through the depths,
As through the wilderness.
10 He saved them from the hand of him
who hated *them,*
And redeemed them from the hand
of the enemy.
11 The waters covered their enemies;
There was not one of them left.
12 Then they believed His words;
They sang His praise.

13 They soon forgot His works;
They did not wait for His counsel,
14 But lusted exceedingly in the
wilderness,
And tested God in the desert.
15 And He gave them their request,
But sent leanness into their soul.

16 When they envied Moses in the
camp,
And Aaron the saint of the LORD,
17 The earth opened up and swallowed
Dathan,
And covered the faction of Abiram.
18 A fire was kindled in their company;
The flame burned up the wicked.

∽ PROVERBS 25:3–5 ∽

3 *As* the heavens for height and the
earth for depth,
So the heart of kings *is* unsearchable.

4 Take away the dross from silver,
And it will go to the silversmith *for*
jewelry.
5 Take away the wicked from before
the king,
And his throne will be established in
righteousness.

∽ 2 CORINTHIANS 2:1–17 ∽

But I determined this within myself, that
I would not come again to you in sorrow.
2 For if I make you sorrowful, then who
is he who makes me glad but the one
who is made sorrowful by me? 3 And I wrote this very thing to you,
lest, when I came, I should have sorrow
over those from whom I ought to have
joy, having confidence in you all that
my joy is *the joy* of you all. 4 For out of
much affliction and anguish of heart I
wrote to you, with many tears, not that
you should be grieved, but that you might
know the love which I have so abundantly
for you.
5 But if anyone has caused grief, he has
not grieved me, but all of you to some
extent—not to be too severe. 6 This punishment which *was inflicted* by the
majority *is* sufficient for such a man, 7 so
that, on the contrary, you *ought* rather to
forgive and comfort *him,* lest perhaps such
a one be swallowed up with too much sorrow. 8 Therefore I urge you to reaffirm
your love to him. 9 For to this end I also
wrote, that I might put you to the test,
whether you are obedient in all things.
10 Now whom you forgive anything, I also
forgive. For if indeed I have forgiven anything, I have forgiven that one for your
sakes in the presence of Christ, 11 lest Satan should take advantage of us; for we
are not ignorant of his devices.
12 Furthermore, when I came to Troas
to *preach* Christ's gospel, and a door was
opened to me by the Lord, 13 I had no rest
in my spirit, because I did not find Titus

my brother; but taking my leave of them, I departed for Macedonia.

¹⁴ Now thanks *be* to God who always leads us in triumph in Christ, and through us diffuses the fragrance of His knowledge in every place. ¹⁵ For we are to God the fragrance of Christ among those who are being saved and among those who are perishing. ¹⁶ To the one *we are* the aroma of death *leading* to death, and to the other the aroma of life *leading* to life. And who *is* sufficient for these things? ¹⁷ For we are not, as so many, peddling the word of God; but as of sincerity, but as from God, we speak in the sight of God in Christ.

∼ ISAIAH 13:1—14:32 ∼

The burden against Babylon which Isaiah the son of Amoz saw.

2 "Lift up a banner on the high
     mountain,
   Raise your voice to them;
   Wave your hand, that they may
     enter the gates of the nobles.
3 I have commanded My sanctified
     ones;
   I have also called My mighty ones
     for My anger—
   Those who rejoice in My
     exaltation."

4 The noise of a multitude in the
     mountains,
   Like that of many people!
   A tumultuous noise of the
     kingdoms of nations gathered
     together!
   The LORD of hosts musters
   The army for battle.
5 They come from a far country,
   From the end of heaven—
   The LORD and His weapons of
     indignation,
   To destroy the whole land.

6 Wail, for the day of the LORD *is* at
     hand!
   It will come as destruction from
     the Almighty.
7 Therefore all hands will be limp,
   Every man's heart will melt,
8 And they will be afraid.
   Pangs and sorrows will take hold
     of *them;*
   They will be in pain as a woman
     in childbirth;
   They will be amazed at one
     another;
   Their faces *will be like* flames.

9 Behold, the day of the LORD
     comes,
   Cruel, with both wrath and fierce
     anger,
   To lay the land desolate;
   And He will destroy its sinners
     from it.
10 For the stars of heaven and their
     constellations
   Will not give their light;
   The sun will be darkened in its
     going forth,
   And the moon will not cause its
     light to shine.

11 "I will punish the world for *its* evil,
   And the wicked for their iniquity;
   I will halt the arrogance of the
     proud,
   And will lay low the haughtiness
     of the terrible.
12 I will make a mortal more rare
     than fine gold,
   A man more than the golden
     wedge of Ophir.
13 Therefore I will shake the
     heavens,
   And the earth will move out of
     her place,
   In the wrath of the LORD of hosts
   And in the day of His fierce anger.
14 It shall be as the hunted gazelle,
   And as a sheep that no man takes
     up;
   Every man will turn to his own
     people,

And everyone will flee to his own land.

15 Everyone who is found will be thrust through,
And everyone who is captured will fall by the sword.

16 Their children also will be dashed to pieces before their eyes;
Their houses will be plundered
And their wives ravished.

17 "Behold, I will stir up the Medes against them,
Who will not regard silver;
And *as for* gold, they will not delight in it.

18 Also *their* bows will dash the young men to pieces,
And they will have no pity on the fruit of the womb;
Their eye will not spare children.

19 And Babylon, the glory of kingdoms,
The beauty of the Chaldeans' pride,
Will be as when God overthrew Sodom and Gomorrah.

20 It will never be inhabited,
Nor will it be settled from generation to generation;
Nor will the Arabian pitch tents there,
Nor will the shepherds make their sheepfolds there.

21 But wild beasts of the desert will lie there,
And their houses will be full of owls;
Ostriches will dwell there,
And wild goats will caper there.

22 The hyenas will howl in their citadels,
And jackals in their pleasant palaces.
Her time *is* near to come,
And her days will not be prolonged."

14 For the LORD will have mercy on Jacob, and will still choose Israel, and settle them in their own land. The strangers will be joined with them, and they will cling to the house of Jacob. 2 Then people will take them and bring them to their place, and the house of Israel will possess them for servants and maids in the land of the LORD; they will take them captive whose captives they were, and rule over their oppressors.

3 It shall come to pass in the day the LORD gives you rest from your sorrow, and from your fear and the hard bondage in which you were made to serve, 4 that you will take up this proverb against the king of Babylon, and say:

"How the oppressor has ceased,
The golden city ceased!

5 The LORD has broken the staff of the wicked,
The scepter of the rulers;

6 He who struck the people in wrath with a continual stroke,
He who ruled the nations in anger,
Is persecuted *and* no one hinders.

7 The whole earth is at rest *and* quiet;
They break forth into singing.

8 Indeed the cypress trees rejoice over you,
And the cedars of Lebanon,
Saying, 'Since you were cut down,
No woodsman has come up against us.'

9 "Hell from beneath is excited about you,
To meet *you* at your coming;
It stirs up the dead for you,
All the chief ones of the earth;
It has raised up from their thrones
All the kings of the nations.

10 They all shall speak and say to you:
'Have you also become as weak as we?
Have you become like us?

11 Your pomp is brought down to Sheol,
And the sound of your stringed instruments;
The maggot is spread under you,
And worms cover you.'

12 "How you are fallen from heaven,
O Lucifer, son of the morning!
How you are cut down to the ground,
You who weakened the nations!

Transformation

Two friends who were in love with men who had deep-seated problems, decided to meet weekly to fast and pray. Over the weeks and months that followed, they prayed for every possible "angle" related to the difficulties their loved ones were experiencing — from physiology to prenatal memories, from early-childhood experiences to spiritual conversion, from lack of ability to communicate to physical healing from addictions. One of the women said, "We were praying for a *total* healing in their lives. Looking back, I realize we were also asking God to transform them into the men *we* thought they should be, and which we genuinely thought God wanted them to be."

After nearly a year, both of the women thought they had prayed all they could and must now trust God. "Nothing happened to improve our relationships," one of the women said. "Both men went their own way and we know of no change in their attitudes or behavior. What *did* happen was that my friend and I were transformed. *We* were healed of broken hearts and shattered dreams. *We* had our faith renewed and our hope restored. God surely will work in their lives, but the real miracle happened in us!"

When we pray for change in others, we may not get what we expect. As a result of spending time with God and caring for others enough to spend time praying on their behalf, we are changed.

> But we all, with unveiled face, beholding as in a mirror the glory of the Lord, are being transformed into the same image from glory to glory, just as by the Spirit of the Lord.
>
> *2 Corinthians 3:18*

13 For you have said in your heart:
   "I will ascend into heaven,
      I will exalt my throne above the
         stars of God;
      I will also sit on the mount of the
         congregation
      On the farthest sides of the north;
14 I will ascend above the heights of
      the clouds,
   I will be like the Most High.'
15 Yet you shall be brought down to
      Sheol,
   To the lowest depths of the Pit.

16 "Those who see you will gaze at
      you,
   And consider you, *saying*:
   '*Is* this the man who made the
      earth tremble,
   Who shook kingdoms,
17 Who made the world as a
      wilderness
   And destroyed its cities,
   Who did not open the house of his
      prisoners?'

18 "All the kings of the nations,
   All of them, sleep in glory,
   Everyone in his own house;
19 But you are cast out of your grave
   Like an abominable branch,
   Like the garment of those who are
      slain,
   Thrust through with a sword,
   Who go down to the stones of the
      pit,
   Like a corpse trodden underfoot.
20 You will not be joined with them
      in burial,
   Because you have destroyed your
      land
   And slain your people.
   The brood of evildoers shall never
      be named.
21 Prepare slaughter for his children
   Because of the iniquity of their
      fathers,
   Lest they rise up and possess the
      land,
   And fill the face of the world with
      cities."

22 "For I will rise up against them,"
      says the LORD of hosts,

"And cut off from Babylon the
      name and remnant,
   And offspring and posterity," says
      the LORD.
23 "I will also make it a possession for
      the porcupine,
   And marshes of muddy water;
   I will sweep it with the broom of
      destruction," says the LORD of
      hosts.

24 The LORD of hosts has sworn,
      saying,
"Surely, as I have thought, so it
      shall come to pass,
   And as I have purposed, *so* it shall
      stand:
25 That I will break the Assyrian in
      My land,
   And on My mountains tread him
      underfoot.
   Then his yoke shall be removed
      from them,
   And his burden removed from
      their shoulders.
26 This *is* the purpose that is
      purposed against the whole
      earth,
   And this *is* the hand that is
      stretched out over all the
      nations.
27 For the LORD of hosts has
      purposed,
   And who will annul *it*?
   His hand *is* stretched out,
   And who will turn it back?"

28 This is the burden which came in the
year that King Ahaz died.

29 "Do not rejoice, all you of Philistia,
   Because the rod that struck you is
      broken;
   For out of the serpent's roots will
      come forth a viper,
   And its offspring *will be* a fiery
      flying serpent.
30 The firstborn of the poor will
      feed,
   And the needy will lie down in
      safety;
   I will kill your roots with famine,
   And it will slay your remnant.
31 Wail, O gate! Cry, O city!
   All you of Philistia *are* dissolved;

For smoke will come from the
north,
And no one *will be* alone in his
appointed times."

32 What will they answer the
messengers of the nation?
That the LORD has founded Zion,
And the poor of His people shall
take refuge in it.

~ PSALM 106:19-23 ~

19 They made a calf in Horeb,
And worshiped the molded image.
20 Thus they changed their glory
Into the image of an ox that eats
grass.
21 They forgot God their Savior,
Who had done great things in Egypt,
22 Wondrous works in the land of
Ham,
Awesome things by the Red Sea.
23 Therefore He said that He would
destroy them,
Had not Moses His chosen one
stood before Him in the breach,
To turn away His wrath, lest He
destroy *them.*

~ PROVERBS 25:6, 7 ~

6 Do not exalt yourself in the presence
of the king,
And do not stand in the place of the
great;
7 For *it is* better that he say to you,
"Come up here,"
Than that you should be put lower
in the presence of the prince,
Whom your eyes have seen.

~ 2 CORINTHIANS 3:1-18 ~

Do we begin again to commend ourselves?
Or do we need, as some *others,* epistles
of commendation to you or *letters* of commendation from you? 2 You are our epistle
written in our hearts, known and read by
all men; 3 clearly *you are* an epistle of
Christ, ministered by us, written not with
ink but by the Spirit of the living God,
not on tablets of stone but on tablets of
flesh, *that is,* of the heart.

4 And we have such trust through Christ
toward God. 5 Not that we are sufficient
of ourselves to think of anything as *being*
from ourselves, but our sufficiency *is* from
God, 6 who also made us sufficient as ministers of the new covenant, not of the letter
but of the Spirit; for the letter kills, but
the Spirit gives life.

7 But if the ministry of death, written
and engraved on stones, was glorious, so
that the children of Israel could not look
steadily at the face of Moses because of
the glory of his countenance, which *glory*
was passing away, 8 how will the ministry
of the Spirit not be more glorious? 9 For
if the ministry of condemnation *had* glory,
the ministry of righteousness exceeds
much more in glory. 10 For even what was
made glorious had no glory in this respect,
because of the glory that excels. 11 For if
what is passing away *was* glorious, what
remains *is* much more glorious.

12 Therefore, since we have such hope,
we use great boldness of speech— 13 unlike Moses, *who* put a veil over his face so
that the children of Israel could not look
steadily at the end of what was passing
away. 14 But their minds were blinded. For
until this day the same veil remains
unlifted in the reading of the Old Testament, because the *veil* is taken away in
Christ. 15 But even to this day, when Moses
is read, a veil lies on their heart. 16 Nevertheless when one turns to the Lord, the
veil is taken away. 17 Now the Lord is
the Spirit; and where the Spirit of the Lord
is, there *is* liberty. 18 But we all, with un-
veiled face, beholding as in a mirror the
glory of the Lord, are being transformed
into the same image from glory to glory,
just as by the Spirit of the Lord.

~ ISAIAH 15:1—16:14 ~

The burden against Moab.

Because in the night Ar of Moab is
  laid waste
And destroyed,
Because in the night Kir of Moab
  is laid waste
And destroyed,

2 He has gone up to the temple and
    Dibon,
To the high places to weep.
Moab will wail over Nebo and
  over Medeba;
On all their heads *will be*
  baldness,
And every beard cut off.

3 In their streets they will clothe
    themselves with sackcloth;
On the tops of their houses
And in their streets
Everyone will wail, weeping
  bitterly.

4 Heshbon and Elealeh will cry out,
Their voice shall be heard as far as
  Jahaz;
Therefore the armed soldiers of
  Moab will cry out;
His life will be burdensome to
  him.

5 "My heart will cry out for Moab;
His fugitives *shall flee* to Zoar,
Like a three-year-old heifer.
For by the Ascent of Luhith
They will go up with weeping;
For in the way of Horonaim
They will raise up a cry of
  destruction,

6 For the waters of Nimrim will be
    desolate,
For the green grass has withered
  away;
The grass fails, there is nothing
  green.

7 Therefore the abundance they
    have gained,
And what they have laid up,
They will carry away to the Brook
  of the Willows.

8 For the cry has gone all around
    the borders of Moab,
Its wailing to Eglaim

And its wailing to Beer Elim.

9 For the waters of Dimon will be
    full of blood;
Because I will bring more upon
  Dimon,
Lions upon him who escapes from
  Moab,
And on the remnant of the land."

16 Send the lamb to the ruler of the
    land,
From Sela to the wilderness,
To the mount of the daughter of
  Zion.

2 For it shall be as a wandering bird
    thrown out of the nest;
So shall be the daughters of Moab
  at the fords of the Arnon.

3 "Take counsel, execute judgment;
Make your shadow like the night
  in the middle of the day;
Hide the outcasts,
Do not betray him who escapes.

4 Let My outcasts dwell with you,
  O Moab;
Be a shelter to them from the face
  of the spoiler.
For the extortioner is at an end,
Devastation ceases,
The oppressors are consumed out
  of the land.

5 In mercy the throne will be
    established;
And One will sit on it in truth, in
  the tabernacle of David,
Judging and seeking justice and
  hastening righteousness."

6 We have heard of the pride of
    Moab—
He is very proud—
Of his haughtiness and his pride
  and his wrath;
But his lies *shall* not *be* so.

7 Therefore Moab shall wail for
    Moab;
Everyone shall wail.
For the foundations of Kir
  Hareseth you shall mourn;
Surely *they are* stricken.

Preparing for Eternity

> For our light affliction, which is but for a moment, is working for us a far more exceeding and eternal weight of glory.
>
> *2 Corinthians 4:17*

A shipwrecked sailor was found by natives on the beach of a South Sea island. They seized him, hoisted him to their shoulders, and carried him to their village. When they arrived in the village, they set him upon a crudely fashioned throne. It was apparent to him that they were having a coronation ceremony, but he understood little else. Over time, as he learned their language, he discovered that the natives had a custom of choosing a new man to be king each year. Once the period of kingship was over, however, the man was banished to a nearby island where he starved to death.

Not particularly looking forward to this outcome, the sailor decided to take full advantage of his position as king. Rather than sitting around idle and being waited upon, he put his carpenters to work making boats, his farmers to work transplanting trees and growing crops, and his masons to work building houses on the nearby island. When the year was over and he was exiled, the formerly barren island had become an abundant paradise.

As we live our lives here on earth, we must never lose sight of eternity. Remember that with each trial or affliction you walk through with God's grace, you are adding to your future glory.

8 For the fields of Heshbon
    languish,
  And the vine of Sibmah;
  The lords of the nations have
    broken down its choice plants,
  Which have reached to Jazer
  And wandered through the
    wilderness.
  Her branches are stretched out,
  They are gone over the sea.
9 Therefore I will bewail the vine of
    Sibmah,
  With the weeping of Jazer;
  I will drench you with my tears,
  O Heshbon and Elealeh;
  For battle cries have fallen
  Over your summer fruits and your
    harvest.

10 Gladness is taken away,
   And joy from the plentiful field;
   In the vineyards there will be no
     singing,
   Nor will there be shouting;
   No treaders will tread out wine in
     the presses;
   I have made their shouting cease.
11 Therefore my heart shall resound
     like a harp for Moab,
   And my inner being for Kir Heres.

12 And it shall come to pass,
   When it is seen that Moab is
     weary on the high place,
   That he will come to his sanctuary
     to pray;
   But he will not prevail.

13 This *is* the word which the LORD has
spoken concerning Moab since that time.
14 But now the LORD has spoken, saying,
"Within three years, as the years of a hired
man, the glory of Moab will be despised
with all that great multitude, and the remnant *will be* very small *and* feeble."

∽ PSALM 106:24–31 ∽

24 Then they despised the pleasant
     land;
   They did not believe His word,
25 But complained in their tents,
   And did not heed the voice of the
     LORD.

26 Therefore He raised His hand *in an
     oath* against them,
   To overthrow them in the
     wilderness,
27 To overthrow their descendants
     among the nations,
   And to scatter them in the lands.

28 They joined themselves also to Baal
     of Peor,
   And ate sacrifices made to the dead.
29 Thus they provoked *Him* to anger
     with their deeds,
   And the plague broke out among
     them.
30 Then Phinehas stood up and
     intervened,
   And the plague was stopped.
31 And that was accounted to him for
     righteousness
   To all generations forevermore.

∽ PROVERBS 25:8–10 ∽

8 Do not go hastily to court;
  For what will you do in the end,
  When your neighbor has put you to
    shame?
9 Debate your case with your
    neighbor,
  And do not disclose the secret to
    another;
10 Lest he who hears *it* expose your
     shame,
   And your reputation be ruined.

∽ 2 CORINTHIANS 4:1–18 ∽

Therefore, since we have this ministry,
as we have received mercy, we do not lose
heart. 2 But we have renounced the hidden
things of shame, not walking in craftiness
nor handling the word of God deceitfully, but by manifestation of the truth
commending ourselves to every man's
conscience in the sight of God. 3 But even
if our gospel is veiled, it is veiled to those
who are perishing, 4 whose minds the god
of this age has blinded, who do not believe, lest the light of the gospel of the
glory of Christ, who is the image of God,
should shine on them. 5 For we do not
preach ourselves, but Christ Jesus the
Lord, and ourselves your bondservants
for Jesus' sake. 6 For it is the God who

commanded light to shine out of darkness, who has shone in our hearts to *give* the light of the knowledge of the glory of God in the face of Jesus Christ.

[7] But we have this treasure in earthen vessels, that the excellence of the power may be of God and not of us. [8] *We are* hard-pressed on every side, yet not crushed; *we are* perplexed, but not in despair; [9] persecuted, but not forsaken; struck down, but not destroyed— [10] always carrying about in the body the dying of the Lord Jesus, that the life of Jesus also may be manifested in our body. [11] For we who live are always delivered to death for Jesus' sake, that the life of Jesus also may be manifested in our mortal flesh. [12] So then death is working in us, but life in you.

[13] And since we have the same spirit of faith, according to what is written, "I believed and therefore I spoke," we also believe and therefore speak, [14] knowing that He who raised up the Lord Jesus will also raise us up with Jesus, and will present *us* with you. [15] For all things *are* for your sakes, that grace, having spread through the many, may cause thanksgiving to abound to the glory of God.

[16] Therefore we do not lose heart. Even though our outward man is perishing, yet the inward *man* is being renewed day by day. [17] For our light affliction, which is but for a moment, is working for us a far more exceeding *and* eternal weight of glory, [18] while we do not look at the things which are seen, but at the things which are not seen. For the things which are seen *are* temporary, but the things which are not seen *are* eternal.

READING 256 · SEPTEMBER 13

~ ISAIAH 17:1—18:7 ~

The burden against Damascus.

"Behold, Damascus will cease from
   being a city,
And it will be a ruinous heap.
[2] The cities of Aroer *are* forsaken;
   They will be for flocks
Which lie down, and no one will
   make *them* afraid.
[3] The fortress also will cease from
   Ephraim,
The kingdom from Damascus,
And the remnant of Syria;
They will be as the glory of the
   children of Israel,"
Says the LORD of hosts.

[4] "In that day it shall come to pass
   That the glory of Jacob will
     wane,
And the fatness of his flesh grow
     lean.
[5] It shall be as when the harvester
   gathers the grain,
And reaps the heads with his
     arm;
It shall be as he who gathers heads
   of grain

In the Valley of Rephaim.
[6] Yet gleaning grapes will be left in
   it,
Like the shaking of an olive tree,
Two *or* three olives at the top of
   the uppermost bough,
Four *or* five in its most fruitful
   branches,"
Says the LORD God of Israel.

[7] In that day a man will look to his
   Maker,
And his eyes will have respect for
   the Holy One of Israel.
[8] He will not look to the altars,
The work of his hands;
He will not respect what his
   fingers have made,
Nor the wooden images nor the
   incense altars.

[9] In that day his strong cities will be
   as a forsaken bough
And an uppermost branch,
Which they left because of the
   children of Israel;
And there will be desolation.

10 Because you have forgotten the
   God of your salvation,
   And have not been mindful of the
   Rock of your stronghold,
   Therefore you will plant pleasant
   plants
   And set out foreign seedlings;
11 In the day you will make your
   plant to grow,
   And in the morning you will make
   your seed to flourish;
   But the harvest *will be* a heap of
   ruins
   In the day of grief and desperate
   sorrow.

12 Woe to the multitude of many
   people
   Who make a noise like the roar of
   the seas,
   And to the rushing of nations
   That make a rushing like the
   rushing of mighty waters!
13 The nations will rush like the
   rushing of many waters;
   But *God* will rebuke them and
   they will flee far away,
   And be chased like the chaff of the
   mountains before the wind,
   Like a rolling thing before the
   whirlwind.
14 Then behold, at eventide, trouble!
   And before the morning, he *is* no
   more.
   This *is* the portion of those who
   plunder us,
   And the lot of those who rob us.

18 Woe to the land shadowed with
   buzzing wings,
   Which *is* beyond the rivers of
   Ethiopia,
2 Which sends ambassadors by sea,
   Even in vessels of reed on the
   waters, *saying,*
   "Go, swift messengers, to a nation
   tall and smooth *of skin,*
   To a people terrible from their
   beginning onward,
   A nation powerful and treading
   down,
   Whose land the rivers divide."

3 All inhabitants of the world and
   dwellers on the earth:

When he lifts up a banner on the
   mountains, you see *it;*
   And when he blows a trumpet,
   you hear *it.*
4 For so the LORD said to me,
   "I will take My rest,
   And I will look from My dwelling
   place
   Like clear heat in sunshine,
   Like a cloud of dew in the heat of
   harvest."
5 For before the harvest, when the
   bud is perfect
   And the sour grape is ripening in
   the flower,
   He will both cut off the sprigs
   with pruning hooks
   And take away *and* cut down the
   branches.
6 They will be left together for the
   mountain birds of prey
   And for the beasts of the earth;
   The birds of prey will summer on
   them,
   And all the beasts of the earth will
   winter on them.

7 In that time a present will be
   brought to the LORD of hosts
   From a people tall and smooth *of
   skin,*
   And from a people terrible from
   their beginning onward,
   A nation powerful and treading
   down,
   Whose land the rivers divide—
   To the place of the name of the
   LORD of hosts,
   To Mount Zion.

~ PSALM 106:32–39 ~

32 They angered *Him* also at the waters
   of strife,
   So that it went ill with Moses on
   account of them;
33 Because they rebelled against His
   Spirit,
   So that he spoke rashly with his lips.

34 They did not destroy the peoples,
   Concerning whom the LORD had
   commanded them,
35 But they mingled with the Gentiles
   And learned their works;

Buzzards and Bees

Buzzards and bees have a major difference in their feeding habits. Buzzards fly overhead searching for dead animals. When they spy a decaying carcass, they swoop down to gorge themselves on it, stripping it to the bare bones. Honey bees, by comparison, look for the sweetest nectar. They are very discriminating as they search through the flowers in a garden.

Buzzards produce nothing, except fear in those who behold them at work. Honey bees produce honeycombs, dripping with honey, for the health and delight of others.

Just as the bees and buzzards always find what they are seeking, so a spouse can generally find what he or she is looking for. If you focus on your partner's faults and mistakes, you'll find them. Your relationship will become one to be avoided, not cherished. On the other hand, if you seek out the goodness in your spouse, you can find that, too! And you may be surprised at how sweet your relationship can become.

Unlike buzzards and bees, creatures that cannot choose their own instincts and behavior, we have a choice in what we elect to perceive and comment upon. Choose affirmation and virtue.

36 They served their idols,
   Which became a snare to them.
37 They even sacrificed their sons
   And their daughters to demons,
38 And shed innocent blood,
   The blood of their sons and
      daughters,
   Whom they sacrificed to the idols of
      Canaan;
   And the land was polluted with
      blood.
39 Thus they were defiled by their own
      works,
   And played the harlot by their own
      deeds.

~ PROVERBS 25:11, 12 ~

11 A word fitly spoken *is like* apples of
      gold
   In settings of silver.
12 *Like* an earring of gold and an
      ornament of fine gold
   Is a wise rebuker to an obedient ear.

~ 2 CORINTHIANS 5:1–21 ~

For we know that if our earthly house,
this tent, is destroyed, we have a building
from God, a house not made with hands,
eternal in the heavens. ² For in this we
groan, earnestly desiring to be clothed
with our habitation which is from heaven,
³ if indeed, having been clothed, we shall
not be found naked. ⁴ For we who are in
this tent groan, being burdened, not
because we want to be unclothed, but
further clothed, that mortality may be
swallowed up by life. ⁵ Now He who has
prepared us for this very thing *is* God,
who also has given us the Spirit as a guarantee.

⁶ So *we are* always confident, knowing
that while we are at home in the body we
are absent from the Lord. ⁷ For we walk
by faith, not by sight. ⁸ We are confident,
yes, well pleased rather to be absent from

the body and to be present with the Lord.
⁹ Therefore we make it our aim,
whether present or absent, to be well
pleasing to Him. ¹⁰ For we must all appear before the judgment seat of Christ,
that each one may receive the things *done*
in the body, according to what he has
done, whether good or bad. ¹¹ Knowing,
therefore, the terror of the Lord, we persuade men; but we are well known to
God, and I also trust are well known in
your consciences.

¹² For we do not commend ourselves
again to you, but give you opportunity to
boast on our behalf, that you may have
an answer for those who boast in appearance and not in heart. ¹³ For if we are
beside ourselves, *it is* for God; or if we
are of sound mind, *it is* for you. ¹⁴ For the
love of Christ compels us, because we
judge thus: that if One died for all, then
all died; ¹⁵ and He died for all, that those
who live should live no longer for themselves, but for Him who died for them
and rose again.

¹⁶ Therefore, from now on, we regard
no one according to the flesh. Even
though we have known Christ according
to the flesh, yet now we know *Him thus*
no longer. ¹⁷ Therefore, if anyone *is* in
Christ, *he is* a new creation; old things
have passed away; behold, all things have
become new. ¹⁸ Now all things *are* of God,
who has reconciled us to Himself through
Jesus Christ, and has given us the ministry of reconciliation, ¹⁹ that is, that God
was in Christ reconciling the world to
Himself, not imputing their trespasses
to them, and has committed to us the
word of reconciliation.

²⁰ Now then, we are ambassadors for
Christ, as though God were pleading
through us: we implore *you* on Christ's
behalf, be reconciled to God. ²¹ For He
made Him who knew no sin *to be* sin for
us, that we might become the righteousness of God in Him.

~ ISAIAH 19:1—20:6 ~

The burden against Egypt.

Behold, the LORD rides on a swift cloud,
And will come into Egypt;
The idols of Egypt will totter at His presence,
And the heart of Egypt will melt in its midst.

2 "I will set Egyptians against Egyptians;
Everyone will fight against his brother,
And everyone against his neighbor,
City against city, kingdom against kingdom.
3 The spirit of Egypt will fail in its midst;
I will destroy their counsel,
And they will consult the idols and the charmers,
The mediums and the sorcerers.
4 And the Egyptians I will give
Into the hand of a cruel master,
And a fierce king will rule over them,"
Says the Lord, the LORD of hosts.

5 The waters will fail from the sea,
And the river will be wasted and dried up.
6 The rivers will turn foul;
The brooks of defense will be emptied and dried up;
The reeds and rushes will wither.
7 The papyrus reeds by the River, by the mouth of the River,
And everything sown by the River,
Will wither, be driven away, and be no more.
8 The fishermen also will mourn;
All those will lament who cast hooks into the River,
And they will languish who spread nets on the waters.
9 Moreover those who work in fine flax
And those who weave fine fabric will be ashamed;

10 And its foundations will be broken.
All who make wages *will be* troubled of soul.

11 Surely the princes of Zoan *are* fools;
Pharaoh's wise counselors give foolish counsel.
How do you say to Pharaoh, "I *am* the son of the wise,
The son of ancient kings?"
12 Where *are* they?
Where are your wise men?
Let them tell you now,
And let them know what the LORD of hosts has purposed against Egypt.
13 The princes of Zoan have become fools;
The princes of Noph are deceived;
They have also deluded Egypt,
Those who are the mainstay of its tribes.
14 The LORD has mingled a perverse spirit in her midst;
And they have caused Egypt to err in all her work,
As a drunken man staggers in his vomit.
15 Neither will there be *any* work for Egypt,
Which the head or tail,
Palm branch or bulrush, may do.

16 In that day Egypt will be like women, and will be afraid and fear because of the waving of the hand of the LORD of hosts, which He waves over it. 17 And the land of Judah will be a terror to Egypt; everyone who makes mention of it will be afraid in himself, because of the counsel of the LORD of hosts which He has determined against it.
18 In that day five cities in the land of Egypt will speak the language of Canaan and swear by the LORD of hosts; one will be called the City of Destruction.
19 In that day there will be an altar to the LORD in the midst of the land of Egypt, and a pillar to the LORD at its border. 20 And it will be for a sign and for a

witness to the LORD of hosts in the land of Egypt; for they will cry to the LORD because of the oppressors, and He will send them a Savior and a Mighty One, and He will deliver them. ²¹ Then the LORD will be known to Egypt, and the Egyptians will know the LORD in that day, and will make sacrifice and offering; yes, they will make a vow to the LORD and perform *it*. ²² And the LORD will strike Egypt, He will strike and heal *it;* they will return to the LORD, and He will be entreated by them and heal them.

²³ In that day there will be a highway from Egypt to Assyria, and the Assyrian will come into Egypt and the Egyptian into Assyria, and the Egyptians will serve with the Assyrians.

²⁴ In that day Israel will be one of three with Egypt and Assyria—a blessing in the midst of the land, ²⁵ whom the LORD of hosts shall bless, saying, "Blessed *is* Egypt My people, and Assyria the work of My hands, and Israel My inheritance."

20 In the year that Tartan came to Ashdod, when Sargon the king of Assyria sent him, and he fought against Ashdod and took it, ² at the same time the LORD spoke by Isaiah the son of Amoz, saying, "Go, and remove the sackcloth from your body, and take your sandals off your feet." And he did so, walking naked and barefoot.

³ Then the LORD said, "Just as My servant Isaiah has walked naked and barefoot three years *for* a sign and a wonder against Egypt and Ethiopia, ⁴ so shall the king of Assyria lead away the Egyptians as prisoners and the Ethiopians as captives, young and old, naked and barefoot, with their buttocks uncovered, to the shame of Egypt. ⁵ Then they shall be afraid and ashamed of Ethiopia their expectation and Egypt their glory. ⁶ And the inhabitant of this territory will say in that day, 'Surely such *is* our expectation, wherever we flee for help to be delivered from the king of Assyria; and how shall we escape?'"

∼ PSALM 106:40–48 ∼

⁴⁰ Therefore the wrath of the LORD was kindled against His people,

So that He abhorred His own inheritance.
⁴¹ And He gave them into the hand of the Gentiles,
And those who hated them ruled over them.
⁴² Their enemies also oppressed them, And they were brought into subjection under their hand.
⁴³ Many times He delivered them; But they rebelled in their counsel, And were brought low for their iniquity.

⁴⁴ Nevertheless He regarded their affliction,
When He heard their cry;
⁴⁵ And for their sake He remembered His covenant,
And relented according to the multitude of His mercies.
⁴⁶ He also made them to be pitied By all those who carried them away captive.

⁴⁷ Save us, O LORD our God,
And gather us from among the Gentiles,
To give thanks to Your holy name,
To triumph in Your praise.

⁴⁸ Blessed *be* the LORD God of Israel From everlasting to everlasting! And let all the people say, "Amen!"

Praise the LORD!

∼ PROVERBS 25:13 ∼

¹³ Like the cold of snow in time of harvest
Is a faithful messenger to those who send him,
For he refreshes the soul of his masters.

∼ 2 CORINTHIANS 6:1–18 ∼

We then, *as* workers together *with Him* also plead with *you* not to receive the grace of God in vain. ² For He says:

"In an acceptable time I have heard you,

By Kindness

After two years of marriage, Pete no longer saw his wife as interesting, fun, or attractive. In his mind, he regarded her as an overweight, sloppy housekeeper with a fault-finding personality. He visited a divorce attorney, who advised him: "Pete, if you really want to get even with your wife, start treating her like a queen! Do everything in your power to serve her, please her, and make her feel special. Then, after a couple of months of this royal treatment, pack your bags and leave. That way you'll disappoint her as much as she has disappointed you." Pete could hardly wait to enact the plan! He picked up a dozen roses on his way home, helped his wife with the dinner dishes, brought her breakfast in bed, and began complimenting her on her clothes, cooking, and house-keeping. He even treated her to an out-of-town trip.

After three months, the attorney called and said, "Well, I have the divorce papers ready for you to sign. In a matter of minutes, you can be a happy bachelor."

"Are you crazy?" Pete said. "My wife has made so many changes. I wouldn't think of divorcing her now!"

Kindness extended toward another person may or may not change the other person, but it certainly changes the perspective of the kindness-giver!

> By purity,
> by knowledge,
> by longsuffering,
> by kindness,
> by the
> Holy Spirit,
> by sincere love.
>
> *2 Corinthians 6:6*

And in the day of salvation I have helped you."

Behold, now *is* the accepted time; behold, now *is* the day of salvation. [3] We give no offense in anything, that our ministry may not be blamed. [4] But in all *things* we commend ourselves as ministers of God: in much patience, in tribulations, in needs, in distresses, [5] in stripes, in imprisonments, in tumults, in labors, in sleeplessness, in fastings; [6] by purity, by knowledge, by longsuffering, by kindness, by the Holy Spirit, by sincere love, [7] by the word of truth, by the power of God, by the armor of righteousness on the right hand and on the left, [8] by honor and dishonor, by evil report and good report; as deceivers, and *yet* true; [9] as unknown, and *yet* well known; as dying, and behold we live; as chastened, and *yet* not killed; [10] as sorrowful, yet always rejoicing; as poor, yet making many rich; as having nothing, and *yet* possessing all things.

[11] O Corinthians! We have spoken openly to you, our heart is wide open. [12] You are not restricted by us, but you are restricted by your *own* affections.

[13] Now in return for the same (I speak as to children), you also be open.

[14] Do not be unequally yoked together with unbelievers. For what fellowship has righteousness with lawlessness? And what communion has light with darkness? [15] And what accord has Christ with Belial? Or what part has a believer with an unbeliever? [16] And what agreement has the temple of God with idols? For you are the temple of the living God. As God has said:

> "I will dwell in them
> And walk among them.
> I will be their God,
> And they shall be My people."

[17] Therefore

> "Come out from among them
> And be separate, says the Lord.
> Do not touch what is unclean,
> And I will receive you."

[18] "I will be a Father to you,
> And you shall be My sons and
> daughters,
> Says the LORD Almighty."

READING 258 · SEPTEMBER 15

~ ISAIAH 21:1—22:25 ~

The burden against the Wilderness of the Sea.

> As whirlwinds in the South pass
> through,
> *So* it comes from the desert, from
> a terrible land.

[2] A distressing vision is declared to
> me;
> The treacherous dealer deals
> treacherously,
> And the plunderer plunders.
> Go up, O Elam!
> Besiege, O Media!
> All its sighing I have made to
> cease.

[3] Therefore my loins are filled with
> pain;
> Pangs have taken hold of me, like
> the pangs of a woman in labor.

> I was distressed when *I* heard *it;*
> I was dismayed when *I* saw *it.*

[4] My heart wavered, fearfulness
> frightened me;
> The night for which I longed He
> turned into fear for me.

[5] Prepare the table,
> Set a watchman in the tower,
> Eat and drink.
> Arise, you princes,
> Anoint the shield!

[6] For thus has the Lord said to me:
> "Go, set a watchman,
> Let him declare what he sees."

[7] And he saw a chariot *with* a pair
> of horsemen,
> A chariot of donkeys, *and* a
> chariot of camels,
> And he listened earnestly with
> great care.

Tool of Togetherness

Eleven years ago, Sheila watched from her window as her neighbor tried to train her new pup to walk on a leash. Pulling and pushing and straining to run, that pup had no idea of what walking on a leash was all about. Through the days and weeks that followed, slowly the pup learned what was expected of him. Sheila's neighbor spent time each day with the dog to practice his skills.

More recently, Sheila has watched her neighbor bring out the leash and the now aging adult dog. The leash seemed almost a redundancy. It seemed now that the dog was pleased and happy to stay by his master's side and walk together. What had once been a restriction of obedience had become a tool of togetherness.

That is how it is with us as we obey God. We feel restricted at first to adhere our will to his own. After years of trusting and trying, though, our obedience becomes our sense of presence and togetherness. As we learn to obey we sense God's closeness and rejoice as he leads us along.

> Since we have these promises, dear friends, let us purify ourselves from everything that contaminates body and spirit, perfecting holiness out of reverence for God.
>
> *2 Corinthians 7:1*

8 Then he cried, "A lion, my Lord!
I stand continually on the
watchtower in the daytime;
I have sat at my post every night.
9 And look, here comes a chariot of
men *with* a pair of horsemen!"
Then he answered and said,
"Babylon is fallen, is fallen!
And all the carved images of her
gods
He has broken to the ground."

10 Oh, my threshing and the grain of
my floor!
That which I have heard from the
LORD of hosts,
The God of Israel,
I have declared to you.

11 The burden against Dumah.

He calls to me out of Seir,
"Watchman, what of the night?
Watchman, what of the night?"
12 The watchman said,
"The morning comes, and also the
night.
If you will inquire, inquire;
Return! Come back!"

13 The burden against Arabia.

In the forest in Arabia you will
lodge,
O you traveling companies of
Dedanites.
14 O inhabitants of the land of Tema,
Bring water to him who is thirsty;
With their bread they met him
who fled.
15 For they fled from the swords,
from the drawn sword,
From the bent bow, and from the
distress of war.

16 For thus the LORD has said to me:
"Within a year, according to the year of a
hired man, all the glory of Kedar will fail;
17 and the remainder of the number of
archers, the mighty men of the people of
Kedar, will be diminished; for the LORD
God of Israel has spoken it."

22 The burden against the Valley of
Vision.

What ails you now, that you have
all gone up to the housetops,
2 You who are full of noise,
A tumultuous city, a joyous city?
Your slain *men are* not slain with
the sword,
Nor dead in battle.
3 All your rulers have fled together;
They are captured by the archers.
All who are found in you are
bound together;
They have fled from afar.
4 Therefore I said, "Look away
from me,
I will weep bitterly;
Do not labor to comfort me
Because of the plundering of the
daughter of my people."

5 For *it is* a day of trouble and
treading down and perplexity
By the Lord GOD of hosts
In the Valley of Vision—
Breaking down the walls
And of crying to the mountain.
6 Elam bore the quiver
With chariots of men *and*
horsemen,
And Kir uncovered the shield.
7 It shall come to pass *that* your
choicest valleys
Shall be full of chariots,
And the horsemen shall set
themselves in array at the gate.

8 He removed the protection of
Judah.
You looked in that day to the
armor of the House of the
Forest;
9 You also saw the damage to the
city of David,
That it was great;
And you gathered together the
waters of the lower pool.
10 You numbered the houses of
Jerusalem,
And the houses you broke down
To fortify the wall.
11 You also made a reservoir between
the two walls
For the water of the old pool.
But you did not look to its Maker,
Nor did you have respect for Him
who fashioned it long ago.

¹² And in that day the Lord GOD of
      hosts
   Called for weeping and for
      mourning,
   For baldness and for girding with
      sackcloth.
¹³ But instead, joy and gladness,
   Slaying oxen and killing sheep,
   Eating meat and drinking wine:
   "Let us eat and drink, for
      tomorrow we die!"

¹⁴ Then it was revealed in my
      hearing by the LORD of hosts,
   "Surely for this iniquity there will
      be no atonement for you,
   Even to your death," says the Lord
      GOD of hosts.

¹⁵ Thus says the Lord GOD of hosts:

   "Go, proceed to this steward,
   To Shebna, who *is* over the house,
      and say:
¹⁶ 'What have you here, and whom
      have you here,
   That you have hewn a sepulcher
      here,
   As he who hews himself a
      sepulcher on high,
   Who carves a tomb for himself in
      a rock?
¹⁷ Indeed, the LORD will throw you
      away violently,
   O mighty man,
   And will surely seize you.
¹⁸ He will surely turn violently and
      toss you like a ball
   Into a large country;
   There you shall die, and there
      your glorious chariots
   Shall be the shame of your
      master's house.
¹⁹ So I will drive you out of your
      office,
   And from your position he will
      pull you down.

²⁰ 'Then it shall be in that day,
   That I will call My servant Eliakim
      the son of Hilkiah;
²¹ I will clothe him with your robe
   And strengthen him with your
      belt;

I will commit your responsibility
   into his hand.
He shall be a father to the
   inhabitants of Jerusalem
And to the house of Judah.
²² The key of the house of David
   I will lay on his shoulder;
   So he shall open, and no one shall
      shut;
   And he shall shut, and no one
      shall open.
²³ I will fasten him *as* a peg in a
      secure place,
   And he will become a glorious
      throne to his father's house.

²⁴ 'They will hang on him all the glory
of his father's house, the offspring and
the posterity, all vessels of small quantity,
from the cups to all the pitchers. ²⁵ In that
day,' says the LORD of hosts, 'the peg that
is fastened in the secure place will be removed and be cut down and fall, and the
burden that *was* on it will be cut off; for
the LORD has spoken.' "

~ PSALM 107:1–9 ~

¹ Oh, give thanks to the LORD, for *He
      is* good!
   For His mercy *endures* forever.
² Let the redeemed of the LORD say
      so,
   Whom He has redeemed from the
      hand of the enemy,
³ And gathered out of the lands,
   From the east and from the west,
   From the north and from the south.

⁴ They wandered in the wilderness in
      a desolate way;
   They found no city to dwell in.
⁵ Hungry and thirsty,
   Their soul fainted in them.
⁶ Then they cried out to the LORD in
      their trouble,
   And He delivered them out of their
      distresses.
⁷ And He led them forth by the right
      way,
   That they might go to a city for a
      dwelling place.
⁸ Oh, that *men* would give thanks to
      the LORD *for* His goodness,

And *for* His wonderful works to the children of men!

9 For He satisfies the longing soul,
And fills the hungry soul with goodness.

∾ PROVERBS 25:14–16 ∾

14 Whoever falsely boasts of giving
Is like clouds and wind without rain.

15 By long forbearance a ruler is persuaded,
And a gentle tongue breaks a bone.

16 Have you found honey?
Eat only as much as you need,
Lest you be filled with it and vomit.

∾ 2 CORINTHIANS 7:1–16 ∾

Therefore, having these promises, beloved, let us cleanse ourselves from all filthiness of the flesh and spirit, perfecting holiness in the fear of God.

2 Open *your hearts* to us. We have wronged no one, we have corrupted no one, we have cheated no one. 3 I do not say *this* to condemn; for I have said before that you are in our hearts, to die together and to live together. 4 Great *is* my boldness of speech toward you, great *is* my boasting on your behalf. I am filled with comfort. I am exceedingly joyful in all our tribulation.

5 For indeed, when we came to Macedonia, our bodies had no rest, but we were troubled on every side. Outside *were* conflicts, inside *were* fears. 6 Nevertheless God, who comforts the downcast, comforted us by the coming of Titus, 7 and not only by his coming, but also by the consolation with which he was comforted in you, when he told us of your earnest desire, your mourning, your zeal for me, so that I rejoiced even more.

8 For even if I made you sorry with my letter, I do not regret it; though I did regret it. For I perceive that the same epistle made you sorry, though only for a while. 9 Now I rejoice, not that you were made sorry, but that your sorrow led to repentance. For you were made sorry in a godly manner, that you might suffer loss from us in nothing. 10 For godly sorrow produces repentance *leading* to salvation, not to be regretted; but the sorrow of the world produces death. 11 For observe this very thing, that you sorrowed in a godly manner: What diligence it produced in you, *what* clearing *of yourselves, what* indignation, *what* fear, *what* vehement desire, *what* zeal, *what* vindication! In all *things* you proved yourselves to be clear in this matter. 12 Therefore, although I wrote to you, *I did* not *do it* for the sake of him who had done the wrong, nor for the sake of him who suffered wrong, but that our care for you in the sight of God might appear to you.

13 Therefore we have been comforted in your comfort. And we rejoiced exceedingly more for the joy of Titus, because his spirit has been refreshed by you all. 14 For if in anything I have boasted to him about you, I am not ashamed. But as we spoke all things to you in truth, even so our boasting to Titus was found true. 15 And his affections are greater for you as he remembers the obedience of you all, how with fear and trembling you received him. 16 Therefore I rejoice that I have confidence in you in everything.

READING 259 · SEPTEMBER 16

∾ ISAIAH 23:1—24:23 ∾

The burden against Tyre.

Wail, you ships of Tarshish!
For it is laid waste,
So that there is no house, no harbor;

From the land of Cyprus it is revealed to them.

2 Be still, you inhabitants of the coastland,
You merchants of Sidon,

Winning Friends

Dale Carnegie, author of *How To Win Friends and Influence People*, is considered one of the greatest "friend winners" of the century. He taught, "You can make more friends in two months by becoming interested in other people than you can in two years by trying to get other people interested in you."

To illustrate his point, Carnegie would tell how dogs have learned the fine art of making friends better than most people. When you get within ten feet of a friendly dog, he will begin to wag his tail, a visible sign that he welcomes and enjoys your presence. If you take time to pet the dog, he will become excited, lick you, and jump all over you to show how much he appreciates you. The dog became man's best friend by being genuinely interested in people!

One of the foremost ways, of course, in which we show our interest in others is to listen to them — to ask questions, intently listen to their answers, and ask further questions based upon what they say. The person who feels "heard" is likely to seek out his friendly listener again and again, and to count that person as a great friend.

If you feel alone and in need of friendship, learn to be a listener. If you sow the seeds of friendship by listening, you'll reap a harvest of friendship and an available ear when you really need it.

Whom those who cross the sea
   have filled.
³ And on great waters the grain of
   Shihor,
The harvest of the River, *is* her
   revenue;
And she is a marketplace for the
   nations.

⁴ Be ashamed, O Sidon;
For the sea has spoken,
The strength of the sea, saying,
"I do not labor, nor bring forth
   children;
Neither do I rear young men,
Nor bring up virgins."
⁵ When the report *reaches* Egypt,
They also will be in agony at the
   report of Tyre.

⁶ Cross over to Tarshish;
Wail, you inhabitants of the
   coastland!
⁷ *Is* this your joyous *city,*
Whose antiquity *is* from ancient
   days,
Whose feet carried her far off to
   dwell?
⁸ Who has taken this counsel
   against Tyre, the crowning *city,*
Whose merchants *are* princes,
Whose traders *are* the honorable
   of the earth?
⁹ The LORD of hosts has purposed
   it,
To bring to dishonor the pride of
   all glory,
To bring into contempt all the
   honorable of the earth.

¹⁰ Overflow through your land like
   the River,
O daughter of Tarshish;
There is no more strength.
¹¹ He stretched out His hand over
   the sea,
He shook the kingdoms;
The LORD has given a
   commandment against Canaan
To destroy its strongholds.
¹² And He said, "You will rejoice no
   more,
O you oppressed virgin daughter
   of Sidon.

Arise, cross over to Cyprus;
There also you will have no rest."

¹³ Behold, the land of the Chaldeans,
This people *which* was not;
Assyria founded it for wild beasts
   of the desert.
They set up its towers,
They raised up its palaces,
And brought it to ruin.

¹⁴ Wail, you ships of Tarshish!
For your strength is laid waste.

¹⁵ Now it shall come to pass in that day
that Tyre will be forgotten seventy years,
according to the days of one king. At the
end of seventy years it will happen to Tyre
as *in* the song of the harlot:

¹⁶ "Take a harp, go about the city,
   You forgotten harlot;
Make sweet melody, sing many
   songs,
That you may be remembered."

¹⁷ And it shall be, at the end of seventy
years, that the LORD will deal with Tyre.
She will return to her hire, and commit
fornication with all the kingdoms of the
world on the face of the earth. ¹⁸ Her gain
and her pay will be set apart for the LORD;
it will not be treasured nor laid up, for
her gain will be for those who dwell before the LORD, to eat sufficiently, and for
fine clothing.

24 Behold, the LORD makes the earth
   empty and makes it waste,
Distorts its surface
And scatters abroad its
   inhabitants.
² And it shall be:
As with the people, so with the
   priest;
As with the servant, so with his
   master;
As with the maid, so with her
   mistress;
As with the buyer, so with the
   seller;
As with the lender, so with the
   borrower;
As with the creditor, so with the
   debtor.

3   The land shall be entirely emptied
    and utterly plundered,
    For the LORD has spoken this
    word.

4   The earth mourns *and* fades away,
    The world languishes *and* fades
    away;
    The haughty people of the earth
    languish.

5   The earth is also defiled under its
    inhabitants,
    Because they have transgressed the
    laws,
    Changed the ordinance,
    Broken the everlasting covenant.

6   Therefore the curse has devoured
    the earth,
    And those who dwell in it are
    desolate.
    Therefore the inhabitants of the
    earth are burned,
    And few men *are* left.

7   The new wine fails, the vine
    languishes,
    All the merry-hearted sigh.

8   The mirth of the tambourine
    ceases,
    The noise of the jubilant ends,
    The joy of the harp ceases.

9   They shall not drink wine with a
    song;
    Strong drink is bitter to those who
    drink it.

10 The city of confusion is broken
    down;
    Every house is shut up, so that
    none may go in.

11 *There is* a cry for wine in the
    streets,
    All joy is darkened,
    The mirth of the land is gone.

12 In the city desolation is left,
    And the gate is stricken with
    destruction.

13 When it shall be thus in the midst
    of the land among the people,
    It shall be like the shaking of an
    olive tree,
    Like the gleaning of grapes when
    the vintage is done.

14 They shall lift up their voice, they
    shall sing;
    For the majesty of the LORD
    They shall cry aloud from the
    sea.

15 Therefore glorify the LORD in the
    dawning light,
    The name of the LORD God of
    Israel in the coastlands of the
    sea.

16 From the ends of the earth we
    have heard songs:
    "Glory to the righteous!"
    But I said, "I am ruined, ruined!
    Woe to me!
    The treacherous dealers have dealt
    treacherously,
    Indeed, the treacherous dealers
    have dealt very treacherously."

17 Fear and the pit and the snare
    Are upon you, O inhabitant of the
    earth.

18 And it shall be
    That he who flees from the noise
    of the fear
    Shall fall into the pit,
    And he who comes up from the
    midst of the pit
    Shall be caught in the snare;
    For the windows from on high are
    open,
    And the foundations of the earth
    are shaken.

19 The earth is violently broken,
    The earth is split open,
    The earth is shaken exceedingly.

20 The earth shall reel to and fro like
    a drunkard,
    And shall totter like a hut;
    Its transgression shall be heavy
    upon it,
    And it will fall, and not rise again.

21 It shall come to pass in that day
    That the LORD will punish on high
    the host of exalted ones,
    And on the earth the kings of the
    earth.

22 They will be gathered together,
    As prisoners are gathered in the
    pit,
    And will be shut up in the prison;
    After many days they will be
    punished.

23 Then the moon will be disgraced
And the sun ashamed;
For the LORD of hosts will reign
On Mount Zion and in Jerusalem
And before His elders, gloriously.

~ PSALM 107:10–22 ~

10 Those who sat in darkness and in the
shadow of death,
Bound in affliction and irons—
11 Because they rebelled against the
words of God,
And despised the counsel of the
Most High,
12 Therefore He brought down their
heart with labor;
They fell down, and *there was* none
to help.
13 Then they cried out to the LORD in
their trouble,
And He saved them out of their
distresses.
14 He brought them out of darkness
and the shadow of death,
And broke their chains in pieces.
15 Oh, that *men* would give thanks to
the LORD *for* His goodness,
And *for* His wonderful works to the
children of men!
16 For He has broken the gates of
bronze,
And cut the bars of iron in two.

17 Fools, because of their transgression,
And because of their iniquities, were
afflicted.
18 Their soul abhorred all manner of
food,
And they drew near to the gates of
death.
19 Then they cried out to the LORD in
their trouble,
And He saved them out of their
distresses.
20 He sent His word and healed them,
And delivered *them* from their
destructions.
21 Oh, that *men* would give thanks to
the LORD *for* His goodness,
And *for* His wonderful works to the
children of men!
22 Let them sacrifice the sacrifices of
thanksgiving,

And declare His works with
rejoicing.

~ PROVERBS 25:17 ~

17 Seldom set foot in your neighbor's
house,
Lest he become weary of you and
hate you.

~ 2 CORINTHIANS 8:1–24 ~

Moreover, brethren, we make known to
you the grace of God bestowed on the
churches of Macedonia: 2 that in a great
trial of affliction the abundance of their
joy and their deep poverty abounded in
the riches of their liberality. 3 For I bear
witness that according to *their* ability, yes,
and beyond *their* ability, *they were* freely
willing, 4 imploring us with much urgency
that we would receive the gift and the fellowship of the ministering to the saints.
5 And not *only* as we had hoped, but they
first gave themselves to the Lord, and *then*
to us by the will of God. 6 So we urged
Titus, that as he had begun, so he would
also complete this grace in you as well.
7 But as you abound in everything—in
faith, in speech, in knowledge, in all diligence, and in your love for us—*see* that
you abound in this grace also.

8 I speak not by commandment, but I
am testing the sincerity of your love
by the diligence of others. 9 For you know
the grace of our Lord Jesus Christ, that
though He was rich, yet for your sakes
He became poor, that you through His
poverty might become rich.

10 And in this I give advice: It is to your
advantage not only to be doing what you
began and were desiring to do a year ago;
11 but now you also must complete the
doing *of it;* that as *there was* a readiness
to desire *it,* so *there* also *may be* a completion out of what *you* have. 12 For if there
is first a willing mind, *it is* accepted
according to what one has, *and* not according to what he does not have.

13 For *I do not mean* that others should
be eased and you burdened; 14 but by an
equality, *that* now at this time your abundance *may supply* their lack, that their
abundance also may supply your lack—
that there may be equality. 15 As it is

written, "He who *gathered* much had nothing left over, and he who *gathered* little had no lack."

¹⁶ But thanks *be* to God who puts the same earnest care for you into the heart of Titus. ¹⁷ For he not only accepted the exhortation, but being more diligent, he went to you of his own accord. ¹⁸ And we have sent with him the brother whose praise *is* in the gospel throughout all the churches, ¹⁹ and not only *that,* but who was also chosen by the churches to travel with us with this gift, which is administered by us to the glory of the Lord Himself and *to show* your ready mind, ²⁰ avoiding this: that anyone should blame us in this lavish gift which is administered by us— ²¹ providing honorable things, not only in the sight of the Lord, but also in the sight of men.

²² And we have sent with them our brother whom we have often proved diligent in many things, but now much more diligent, because of the great confidence which *we have* in you. ²³ If *anyone inquires* about Titus, *he is* my partner and fellow worker concerning you. Or if our brethren *are inquired about, they are* messengers of the churches, the glory of Christ. ²⁴ Therefore show to them, and before the churches the proof of your love and of our boasting on your behalf.

~ ISAIAH 25:1—26:21 ~

¹ O LORD, You *are* my God.
I will exalt You,
I will praise Your name,
For You have done wonderful
    things;
Your counsels of old *are*
    faithfulness *and* truth.
² For You have made a city a ruin,
A fortified city a ruin,
A palace of foreigners to be a city
    no more;
It will never be rebuilt.
³ Therefore the strong people will
    glorify You;
The city of the terrible nations will
    fear You.
⁴ For You have been a strength to
    the poor,
A strength to the needy in his
    distress,
A refuge from the storm,
A shade from the heat;
For the blast of the terrible ones *is*
    as a storm *against* the wall.
⁵ You will reduce the noise of aliens,
As heat in a dry place;
As heat in the shadow of a cloud,
The song of the terrible ones will
    be diminished.

⁶ And in this mountain
The LORD of hosts will make for
    all people
A feast of choice pieces,
A feast of wines on the lees,
Of fat things full of marrow,
Of well-refined wines on the lees.
⁷ And He will destroy on this
    mountain
The surface of the covering cast
    over all people,
And the veil that is spread over all
    nations.
⁸ He will swallow up death forever,
And the Lord GOD will wipe away
    tears from all faces;
The rebuke of His people
He will take away from all the
    earth;
For the LORD has spoken.

⁹ And it will be said in that day:
"Behold, this *is* our God;
We have waited for Him, and He
    will save us.
This *is* the LORD;
We have waited for Him;
We will be glad and rejoice in His
    salvation."

¹⁰ For on this mountain the hand of
    the LORD will rest,
And Moab shall be trampled
    down under Him,
As straw is trampled down for the
    refuse heap.

¹¹ And He will spread out His hands
in their midst
As a swimmer reaches out to
swim,
And He will bring down their
pride
Together with the trickery of their
hands.
¹² The fortress of the high fort of
your walls
He will bring down, lay low,
And bring to the ground, down to
the dust.

26 In that day this song will be sung in
the land of Judah:

"We have a strong city;
God will appoint salvation *for*
walls and bulwarks.
² Open the gates,
That the righteous nation which
keeps the truth may enter in.
³ You will keep *him* in perfect
peace,
Whose mind *is* stayed *on You,*
Because he trusts in You.
⁴ Trust in the LORD forever,
For in YAH, the LORD, *is*
everlasting strength.
⁵ For He brings down those who
dwell on high,
The lofty city;
He lays it low,
He lays it low to the ground,
He brings it down to the dust.
⁶ The foot shall tread it down—
The feet of the poor
And the steps of the needy."

⁷ The way of the just *is* uprightness;
O Most Upright,
You weigh the path of the just.
⁸ Yes, in the way of Your judgments,
O LORD, we have waited for You;
The desire of *our* soul *is* for Your
name
And for the remembrance of You.
⁹ With my soul I have desired You in
the night,
Yes, by my spirit within me I will
seek You early;
For when Your judgments *are* in
the earth,

The inhabitants of the world will
learn righteousness.
¹⁰ Let grace be shown to the wicked,
Yet he will not learn righteousness;
In the land of uprightness he will
deal unjustly,
And will not behold the majesty of
the LORD.
¹¹ LORD, *when* Your hand is lifted
up, they will not see.
But they will see and be ashamed
For *their* envy of people;
Yes, the fire of Your enemies shall
devour them.

¹² LORD, You will establish peace for
us,
For You have also done all our
works in us.
¹³ O LORD our God, masters besides
You
Have had dominion over us;
But by You only we make mention
of Your name.
¹⁴ *They are* dead, they will not live;
They are deceased, they will not
rise.
Therefore You have punished and
destroyed them,
And made all their memory to
perish.
¹⁵ You have increased the nation,
O LORD,
You have increased the nation;
You are glorified;
You have expanded all the borders
of the land.
¹⁶ LORD, in trouble they have visited
You,
They poured out a prayer *when*
Your chastening *was* upon
them.
¹⁷ As a woman with child
Is in pain and cries out in her
pangs,
When she draws near the time of
her delivery,
So have we been in Your sight,
O LORD.
¹⁸ We have been with child, we have
been in pain;
We have, as it were, brought forth
wind;

He'll Catch You

When Walter Wangerin was a boy, he told all of his friends that his father was the strongest man alive. Then came the day when Wally climbed to the top of the backyard cherry tree. A storm blew up suddenly and Wally was trapped. Wind ripped through the tree with such velocity that it was all Wally could do to hang onto a branch about ten feet above the ground. "Daddy!" he shouted, and instantly, his father appeared. "Jump," he yelled. "Jump, and I'll catch you."

Wally was frozen in fear. His big, strong dad looked quite small and frail down there on the ground, two skinny arms reaching out to catch him. Wally thought, *If I jump and Dad doesn't catch me, I'll hit the ground and die!* "No!" he screamed back. At that very moment the limb Wally was clinging to cracked at the trunk. Wally surrendered. He didn't jump — he *fell* — straight into Dad's ready arms. Crying and trembling, Wally wrapped his arms and legs around his father. Dad *was* strong after all. Up to that point, it had only been a theory. Now, it was a reality; it was *experience*.

Prayer is about surrendering our will to God's will, yielding our strength to God's strength, giving up our desires to take on God's desires, and surrendering when He asks us to jump into His waiting arms.

> And God is able to make all grace abound toward you, that you, always having all sufficiency in all things, may have an abundance for every good work.
>
> *2 Corinthians 9:8*

We have not accomplished any
deliverance in the earth,
Nor have the inhabitants of the
world fallen.

19 Your dead shall live;
Together with my dead body they
shall arise.
Awake and sing, you who dwell in
dust;
For your dew *is like* the dew of
herbs,
And the earth shall cast out the
dead.

20 Come, my people, enter your
chambers,
And shut your doors behind you;
Hide yourself, as it were, for a
little moment,
Until the indignation is past.
21 For behold, the LORD comes out
of His place
To punish the inhabitants of the
earth for their iniquity;
The earth will also disclose her
blood,
And will no more cover her slain.

~ PSALM 107:23–32 ~

23 Those who go down to the sea in
ships,
Who do business on great waters,
24 They see the works of the LORD,
And His wonders in the deep.
25 For He commands and raises the
stormy wind,
Which lifts up the waves of the sea.
26 They mount up to the heavens,
They go down again to the depths;
Their soul melts because of trouble.
27 They reel to and fro, and stagger like
a drunken man,
And are at their wits' end.
28 Then they cry out to the LORD in
their trouble,
And He brings them out of their
distresses.
29 He calms the storm,
So that its waves are still.
30 Then they are glad because they are
quiet;
So He guides them to their desired
haven.

31 Oh, that *men* would give thanks to
the LORD *for* His goodness,
And *for* His wonderful works to the
children of men!
32 Let them exalt Him also in the
assembly of the people,
And praise Him in the company of
the elders.

~ PROVERBS 25:18, 19 ~

18 A man who bears false witness
against his neighbor
Is like a club, a sword, and a sharp
arrow.

19 Confidence in an unfaithful *man* in
time of trouble
Is like a bad tooth and a foot out of
joint.

~ 2 CORINTHIANS 9:1–15 ~

Now concerning the ministering to the
saints, it is superfluous for me to write to
you; ² for I know your willingness, about
which I boast of you to the Macedonians,
that Achaia was ready a year ago; and your
zeal has stirred up the majority. ³ Yet I have
sent the brethren, lest our boasting of you
should be in vain in this respect, that, as I
said, you may be ready; ⁴ lest if *some*
Macedonians come with me and find you
unprepared, we (not to mention you!)
should be ashamed of this confident boasting. ⁵ Therefore I thought it necessary to
exhort the brethren to go to you ahead of
time, and prepare your generous gift beforehand, which *you had* previously promised, that it may be ready as *a matter of*
generosity and not as a grudging obligation.

⁶ But this *I say:* He who sows sparingly
will also reap sparingly, and he who sows
bountifully will also reap bountifully. ⁷ *So
let* each one *give* as he purposes in his
heart, not grudgingly or of necessity; for
God loves a cheerful giver. ⁸ And God *is*
able to make all grace abound toward you,
that you, always having all sufficiency in
all *things,* may have an abundance for
every good work. ⁹ As it is written:

"He has dispersed abroad,
He has given to the poor;
His righteousness endures forever."

[10] Now may He who supplies seed to the sower, and bread for food, supply and multiply the seed you have *sown* and increase the fruits of your righteousness, [11] while *you are* enriched in everything for all liberality, which causes thanksgiving through us to God. [12] For the administration of this service not only supplies the needs of the saints, but also is abounding through many thanksgivings to God, [13] while, through the proof of this ministry, they glorify God for the obedience of your confession to the gospel of Christ, and for *your* liberal sharing with them and all *men*, [14] and by their prayer for you, who long for you because of the exceeding grace of God in you. [15] Thanks *be* to God for His indescribable gift!

~ ISAIAH 27:1—28:29 ~

[1] In that day the LORD with His
　　severe sword, great and strong,
　Will punish Leviathan the fleeing
　　serpent,
　Leviathan that twisted serpent;
　And He will slay the reptile that *is*
　　in the sea.

[2] In that day sing to her,
　"A vineyard of red wine!
[3] I, the LORD, keep it,
　I water it every moment;
　Lest any hurt it,
　I keep it night and day.
[4] Fury *is* not in Me.
　Who would set briers *and* thorns
　Against Me in battle?
　I would go through them,
　I would burn them together.
[5] Or let him take hold of My
　　strength,
　That he may make peace with Me;
　And he shall make peace with
　　Me."

[6] Those who come He shall cause to
　　take root in Jacob;
　Israel shall blossom and bud,
　And fill the face of the world with
　　fruit.

[7] Has He struck Israel as He struck
　　those who struck him?
　Or has He been slain according to
　　the slaughter of those who were
　　slain by Him?
[8] In measure, by sending it away,
　You contended with it.

He removes *it* by His rough wind
　In the day of the east wind.
[9] Therefore by this the iniquity of
　　Jacob will be covered;
　And this *is* all the fruit of taking
　　away his sin:
　When he makes all the stones of
　　the altar
　Like chalkstones that are beaten to
　　dust,
　Wooden images and incense altars
　　shall not stand.

[10] Yet the fortified city *will be*
　　desolate,
　The habitation forsaken and left
　　like a wilderness;
　There the calf will feed, and there
　　it will lie down
　And consume its branches.
[11] When its boughs are withered,
　　they will be broken off;
　The women come *and* set them on
　　fire.
　For it *is* a people of no
　　understanding;
　Therefore He who made them
　　will not have mercy on them,
　And He who formed them will
　　show them no favor.

[12] And it shall come to pass in that day
　That the LORD will thresh,
　From the channel of the River to
　　the Brook of Egypt;
　And you will be gathered one by
　　one,
　O you children of Israel.

13 So it shall be in that day:
The great trumpet will be blown;
They will come, who are about to
    perish in the land of Assyria,
And they who are outcasts in the
    land of Egypt,
And shall worship the LORD in the
    holy mount at Jerusalem.

28 Woe to the crown of pride, to the
    drunkards of Ephraim,
Whose glorious beauty *is* a fading
    flower
Which *is* at the head of the
    verdant valleys,
To those who are overcome with
    wine!

2 Behold, the Lord has a mighty and
    strong one,
Like a tempest of hail and a
    destroying storm,
Like a flood of mighty waters
    overflowing,
Who will bring *them* down to the
    earth with *His* hand.

3 The crown of pride, the drunkards
    of Ephraim,
Will be trampled underfoot;

4 And the glorious beauty is a fading
    flower
Which *is* at the head of the
    verdant valley,
Like the first fruit before the
    summer,
Which an observer sees;
He eats it up while it is still in his
    hand.

5 In that day the LORD of hosts will
    be
For a crown of glory and a diadem
    of beauty
To the remnant of His people,

6 For a spirit of justice to him who
    sits in judgment,
And for strength to those who
    turn back the battle at the gate.

7 But they also have erred through
    wine,
And through intoxicating drink
    are out of the way;
The priest and the prophet have
    erred through intoxicating
    drink,

They are swallowed up by wine,
They are out of the way through
    intoxicating drink;
They err in vision, they stumble *in*
    judgment.

8 For all tables are full of vomit *and*
    filth;
No place *is clean.*

9 "Whom will he teach knowledge?
And whom will he make to
    understand the message?
Those *just* weaned from milk?
Those *just* drawn from the
    breasts?

10 For precept *must be* upon precept,
    precept upon precept,
Line upon line, line upon line,
Here a little, there a little."

11 For with stammering lips and
    another tongue
He will speak to this people,

12 To whom He said, "This *is* the rest
    with which
You may cause the weary to rest,"
And, "This *is* the refreshing";
Yet they would not hear.

13 But the word of the LORD was to
    them,
"Precept upon precept, precept
    upon precept,
Line upon line, line upon line,
Here a little, there a little,"
That they might go and fall
    backward, and be broken
And snared and caught.

14 Therefore hear the word of the
    LORD, you scornful men,
Who rule this people who *are* in
    Jerusalem,

15 Because you have said, "We have
    made a covenant with death,
And with Sheol we are in
    agreement.
When the overflowing scourge
    passes through,
It will not come to us,
For we have made lies our refuge,
And under falsehood we have
    hidden ourselves."

16 Therefore thus says the Lord GOD:

The Thundering Legion

The Militine Legion was one of the two most famous legions in the Roman army. It was also known as the Thundering Legion. The nickname was given by the philosopher-emperor, Marcus Aurelius in 176 A.D., during a military campaign against the Germans.

In their march northward, the Romans were encircled by precipitous mountains which were occupied by their enemies. In addition, due to a drought, they were tormented by great thirst. Then a member of the Praetorian Guard informed the emperor that the Militine Legion was made up of Christians who believed in the power of prayer. Although he himself had been a great persecutor of the Church, the emperor said, "Let them pray then." The soldiers bowed on the ground and earnestly sought God to deliver them in the name of Jesus Christ.

They had scarcely risen from their knees when a great thunderstorm arose. The storm drove their enemies from their strongholds and into their arms, where they pleaded for mercy. The storm also provided water to drink and ended the drought. The emperor renamed them the "Thundering Legion," and subsequently abated some of his persecution of the Christians in Rome.

Let prayer be your first resort, instead of your last. Prayer and deliverance go hand in hand!

"Behold, I lay in Zion a stone for a
  foundation,
A tried stone, a precious
  cornerstone, a sure foundation;
Whoever believes will not act
  hastily.
17 Also I will make justice the
  measuring line,
And righteousness the plummet;
The hail will sweep away the
  refuge of lies,
And the waters will overflow the
  hiding place.
18 Your covenant with death will be
  annulled,
And your agreement with Sheol
  will not stand;
When the overflowing scourge
  passes through,
Then you will be trampled down
  by it.
19 As often as it goes out it will take
  you;
For morning by morning it will
  pass over,
And by day and by night;
It will be a terror just to
  understand the report."

20 For the bed is too short to stretch
  out *on,*
And the covering so narrow that
  one cannot wrap himself *in it.*
21 For the LORD will rise up as *at*
  Mount Perazim,
He will be angry as in the Valley
  of Gibeon—
That He may do His work, His
  awesome work,
And bring to pass His act, His
  unusual act.
22 Now therefore, do not be
  mockers,
Lest your bonds be made strong;
For I have heard from the Lord
  GOD of hosts,
A destruction determined even
  upon the whole earth.

23 Give ear and hear my voice,
Listen and hear my speech.
24 Does the plowman keep plowing
  all day to sow?
Does he keep turning his soil and
  breaking the clods?

25 When he has leveled its surface,
Does he not sow the black
  cummin
And scatter the cummin,
Plant the wheat in rows,
The barley in the appointed place,
And the spelt in its place?
26 For He instructs him in right
  judgment,
His God teaches him.

27 For the black cummin is not
  threshed with a threshing
  sledge,
Nor is a cartwheel rolled over the
  cummin;
But the black cummin is beaten
  out with a stick,
And the cummin with a rod.
28 Bread *flour* must be ground;
Therefore he does not thresh it
  forever,
Break *it with* his cartwheel,
Or crush *it with* his horsemen.
29 This also comes from the LORD of
  hosts,
Who is wonderful in counsel *and*
  excellent in guidance.

~ PSALM 107:33–43 ~

33 He turns rivers into a wilderness,
And the watersprings into dry
  ground;
34 A fruitful land into barrenness,
For the wickedness of those who
  dwell in it.
35 He turns a wilderness into pools of
  water,
And dry land into watersprings.
36 There He makes the hungry dwell,
That they may establish a city for a
  dwelling place;
37 And sow fields and plant vineyards,
That they may yield a fruitful
  harvest.
38 He also blesses them, and they
  multiply greatly;
And He does not let their cattle
  decrease.

39 When they are diminished and
  brought low
Through oppression, affliction and
  sorrow,

40 He pours contempt on princes,
And causes them to wander in the
wilderness *where there is* no way;
41 Yet He sets the poor on high, far
from affliction,
And makes *their* families like a
flock.
42 The righteous see *it* and rejoice,
And all iniquity stops its mouth.

43 Whoever *is* wise will observe these
things,
And they will understand the
lovingkindness of the LORD.

~ PROVERBS 25:20 ~

20 *Like* one who takes away a garment
in cold weather,
And like vinegar on soda,
Is one who sings songs to a heavy
heart.

~ 2 CORINTHIANS 10:1–18 ~

Now I, Paul, myself am pleading with you
by the meekness and gentleness of
Christ—who in presence *am* lowly among
you, but being absent am bold toward you.
2 But I beg *you* that when I am present I
may not be bold with that confidence by
which I intend to be bold against some,
who think of us as if we walked according to the flesh. 3 For though we walk in
the flesh, we do not war according to the
flesh. 4 For the weapons of our warfare
are not carnal but mighty in God for
pulling down strongholds, 5 casting down
arguments and every high thing that exalts itself against the knowledge of God,
bringing every thought into captivity to
the obedience of Christ, 6 and being ready
to punish all disobedience when your obedience is fulfilled.
7 Do you look at things according to
the outward appearance? If anyone is convinced in himself that he is Christ's, let
him again consider this in himself, that
just as he *is* Christ's, even so we *are*
Christ's. 8 For even if I should boast some-
what more about our authority, which the
Lord gave us for edification and not for
your destruction, I shall not be ashamed—
9 lest I seem to terrify you by letters. 10 "For
his letters," they say, "*are* weighty and
powerful, but *his* bodily presence *is* weak,
and *his* speech contemptible." 11 Let such
a person consider this, that what we are
in word by letters when we are absent,
such *we will* also *be* in deed when we are
present.
12 For we dare not class ourselves or
compare ourselves with those who
commend themselves. But they, measuring themselves by themselves, and com-
paring themselves among themselves, are
not wise. 13 We, however, will not boast
beyond measure, but within the limits of
the sphere which God appointed us—a
sphere which especially includes you.
14 For we are not overextending ourselves
(as though *our authority* did not extend
to you), for it was to you that we came
with the gospel of Christ; 15 not boasting
of things beyond measure, *that is,* in other
men's labors, but having hope, *that* as your
faith is increased, we shall be greatly enlarged by you in our sphere, 16 to preach
the gospel in the *regions* beyond you, *and*
not to boast in another man's sphere of
accomplishment.
17 But "he who glories, let him glory in
the LORD." 18 For not he who commends
himself is approved, but whom the Lord
commends.

~ ISAIAH 29:1–24 ~

1 "Woe to Ariel, to Ariel, the city
where David dwelt!
Add year to year;
Let feasts come around.
2 Yet I will distress Ariel;
There shall be heaviness and
sorrow,
And it shall be to Me as Ariel.
3 I will encamp against you all
around,

I will lay siege against you with a
  mound,
And I will raise siegeworks against
  you.
4 You shall be brought down,
You shall speak out of the ground;
Your speech shall be low, out of
  the dust;
Your voice shall be like a
  medium's, out of the ground;
And your speech shall whisper out
  of the dust.

5 "Moreover the multitude of your
  foes
Shall be like fine dust,
And the multitude of the terrible
  ones
Like chaff that passes away;
Yes, it shall be in an instant,
  suddenly.
6 You will be punished by the LORD
  of hosts
With thunder and earthquake and
  great noise,
With storm and tempest
And the flame of devouring fire.
7 The multitude of all the nations
  who fight against Ariel,
Even all who fight against her and
  her fortress,
And distress her,
Shall be as a dream of a night
  vision.
8 It shall even be as when a hungry
  man dreams,
And look—he eats;
But he awakes, and his soul is still
  empty;
Or as when a thirsty man dreams,
And look—he drinks;
But he awakes, and indeed *he is*
  faint,
And his soul still craves:
So the multitude of all the nations
  shall be,
Who fight against Mount Zion."

9 Pause and wonder!
Blind yourselves and be blind!
They are drunk, but not with wine;
They stagger, but not with
  intoxicating drink.
10 For the LORD has poured out on
  you

The spirit of deep sleep,
And has closed your eyes, namely,
  the prophets;
And He has covered your heads,
  namely, the seers.

11 The whole vision has become to you
like the words of a book that is sealed,
which *men* deliver to one who is literate,
saying, "Read this, please."
And he says, "I cannot, for it *is* sealed."
12 Then the book is delivered to one
who is illiterate, saying, "Read this,
please."
And he says, "I am not literate."
13 Therefore the Lord said:

"Inasmuch as these people draw
  near with their mouths
And honor Me with their lips,
But have removed their hearts far
  from Me,
And their fear toward Me is
  taught by the commandment of
  men,
14 Therefore, behold, I will again do
  a marvelous work
Among this people,
A marvelous work and a wonder;
For the wisdom of their wise *men*
  shall perish,
And the understanding of their
  prudent *men* shall be hidden."

15 Woe to those who seek deep to
  hide their counsel far from the
  LORD,
And their works are in the dark;
They say, "Who sees us?" and,
  "Who knows us?"
16 Surely you have things turned
  around!
Shall the potter be esteemed as the
  clay;
For shall the thing made say of
  him who made it,
"He did not make me"?
Or shall the thing formed say of
  him who formed it,
"He has no understanding"?

17 *Is* it not yet a very little while
Till Lebanon shall be turned into a
  fruitful field,

My Left Foot

Christy Brown was born in Ireland in 1932 and raised in a Dublin slum. Born with a severe form of cerebral palsy, he could not walk, talk, eat, or drink without help. He never went to school.

One day, one of his siblings was on the floor drawing letters on a piece of paper with crayons. Christy suddenly moved his left foot, managed to pick up and hold the crayon with his toes, and tried to copy the letters. From that day until his death in 1981, he was able to write using his left foot, typing with his little toe. That was enough, however, for him to be able to write his autobiography, *My Left Foot*, which became a major motion picture. He also wrote two works of fiction. It took him fifteen years to type one of them, *Down All the Days*, but his effort resulted in his being hailed "a man of genius" by the New York Times.

Christy Brown never moved from the slums. He eventually fell in love and married. He was a man who first learned to accept his limitations and then rise above them!

Accept who you are and what you have today. Then use what you have. You will find it's enough to bring you to a place of fulfillment in life.

> "He did not make me"? Or shall the thing formed say of him who formed it, "He has no understanding"?
>
> *Isaiah 29:16*

And the fruitful field be esteemed as a forest?

18 In that day the deaf shall hear the words of the book,
And the eyes of the blind shall see out of obscurity and out of darkness.

19 The humble also shall increase *their* joy in the LORD,
And the poor among men shall rejoice
In the Holy One of Israel.

20 For the terrible one is brought to nothing,
The scornful one is consumed,
And all who watch for iniquity are cut off—

21 Who make a man an offender by a word,
And lay a snare for him who reproves in the gate,
And turn aside the just by empty words.

22 Therefore thus says the LORD, who redeemed Abraham, concerning the house of Jacob:

"Jacob shall not now be ashamed,
Nor shall his face now grow pale;

23 But when he sees his children,
The work of My hands, in his midst,
They will hallow My name,
And hallow the Holy One of Jacob,
And fear the God of Israel.

24 These also who erred in spirit will come to understanding,
And those who complained will learn doctrine."

~ PSALM 108:1-6 ~

1 O God, my heart is steadfast;
I will sing and give praise, even with my glory.

2 Awake, lute and harp!
I will awaken the dawn.

3 I will praise You, O LORD, among the peoples,
And I will sing praises to You among the nations.

4 For Your mercy *is* great above the heavens,
And Your truth *reaches* to the clouds.

5 Be exalted, O God, above the heavens,
And Your glory above all the earth;

6 That Your beloved may be delivered,
Save *with* Your right hand, and hear me.

~ PROVERBS 25:21, 22 ~

21 If your enemy is hungry, give him bread to eat;
And if he is thirsty, give him water to drink;

22 For *so* you will heap coals of fire on his head,
And the LORD will reward you.

~ 2 CORINTHIANS 11:1-15 ~

Oh, that you would bear with me in a little folly—and indeed you do bear with me. 2 For I am jealous for you with godly jealousy. For I have betrothed you to one husband, that I may present *you as* a chaste virgin to Christ. 3 But I fear, lest somehow, as the serpent deceived Eve by his craftiness, so your minds may be corrupted from the simplicity that is in Christ. 4 For if he who comes preaches another Jesus whom we have not preached, or *if* you receive a different spirit which you have not received, or a different gospel which you have not accepted—you may well put up with it!

5 For I consider that I am not at all inferior to the most eminent apostles. 6 Even though *I am* untrained in speech, yet *I am* not in knowledge. But we have been thoroughly manifested among you in all things.

7 Did I commit sin in humbling myself that you might be exalted, because I preached the gospel of God to you free of charge? 8 I robbed other churches, taking wages *from them* to minister to you. 9 And when I was present with you, and in need, I was a burden to no one, for what I lacked the brethren who came from Macedonia supplied. And in everything I kept myself from being burdensome to you, and so I will keep *myself*. 10 As the truth of Christ is in me, no one shall stop

me from this boasting in the regions of Achaia. [11] Why? Because I do not love you? God knows!

[12] But what I do, I will also continue to do, that I may cut off the opportunity from those who desire an opportunity to be regarded just as we are in the things of which they boast. [13] For such *are* false apostles, deceitful workers, transforming themselves into apostles of Christ. [14] And no wonder! For Satan himself transforms himself into an angel of light. [15] Therefore *it is* no great thing if his ministers also transform themselves into ministers of righteousness, whose end will be according to their works.

READING 263 · SEPTEMBER 20

~ ISAIAH 30:1—32:20 ~

[1] "Woe to the rebellious children,"
   says the LORD,
"Who take counsel, but not of Me,
   And who devise plans, but not of
      My Spirit,
   That they may add sin to sin;
[2] Who walk to go down to Egypt,
   And have not asked My advice,
   To strengthen themselves in the
      strength of Pharaoh,
   And to trust in the shadow of
      Egypt!
[3] Therefore the strength of Pharaoh
   Shall be your shame,
   And trust in the shadow of Egypt
   Shall be *your* humiliation.
[4] For his princes were at Zoan,
   And his ambassadors came to
      Hanes.
[5] They were all ashamed of a people
   who could not benefit them,
   Or be help or benefit,
   But a shame and also a reproach."

[6] The burden against the beasts of the South.

   Through a land of trouble and
      anguish,
   From which *came* the lioness and
      lion,
   The viper and fiery flying serpent,
   They will carry their riches on the
      backs of young donkeys,
   And their treasures on the humps
      of camels,
   To a people *who* shall not profit;
[7] For the Egyptians shall help in
      vain and to no purpose.
   Therefore I have called her
   Rahab-Hem-Shebeth.

[8] Now go, write it before them on a
      tablet,
   And note it on a scroll,
   That it may be for time to come,
   Forever and ever:
[9] That this *is* a rebellious people,
   Lying children,
   Children *who* will not hear the
      law of the LORD;
[10] Who say to the seers, "Do not
      see,"
   And to the prophets, "Do not
      prophesy to us right things;
   Speak to us smooth things,
      prophesy deceits.
[11] Get out of the way,
   Turn aside from the path,
   Cause the Holy One of Israel
   To cease from before us."

[12] Therefore thus says the Holy One of Israel:

   "Because you despise this word,
   And trust in oppression and
      perversity,
   And rely on them,
[13] Therefore this iniquity shall be to
      you
   Like a breach ready to fall,
   A bulge in a high wall,
   Whose breaking comes suddenly,
      in an instant.
[14] And He shall break it like the
      breaking of the potter's vessel,
   Which is broken in pieces;
   He shall not spare.
   So there shall not be found among
      its fragments
   A shard to take fire from the
      hearth,

Or to take water from the
cistern."

¹⁵ For thus says the Lord GOD, the Holy
One of Israel:

"In returning and rest you shall be
saved;
In quietness and confidence shall
be your strength."
But you would not,
¹⁶ And you said, "No, for we will
flee on horses"—
Therefore you shall flee!
And, "We will ride on swift
horses"—
Therefore those who pursue you
shall be swift!

¹⁷ One thousand *shall flee* at the
threat of one,
At the threat of five you shall flee,
Till you are left as a pole on top of
a mountain
And as a banner on a hill.

¹⁸ Therefore the LORD will wait, that
He may be gracious to you;
And therefore He will be exalted,
that He may have mercy on
you.
For the LORD *is* a God of justice;
Blessed *are* all those who wait for
Him.

¹⁹ For the people shall dwell in Zion
at Jerusalem;
You shall weep no more.
He will be very gracious to you at
the sound of your cry;
When He hears it, He will answer
you.
²⁰ And *though* the Lord gives you
The bread of adversity and the
water of affliction,
Yet your teachers will not be
moved into a corner anymore,
But your eyes shall see your
teachers.
²¹ Your ears shall hear a word behind
you, saying,
"This *is* the way, walk in it,"
Whenever you turn to the right
hand
Or whenever you turn to the left.

²² You will also defile the covering of
your images of silver,
And the ornament of your molded
images of gold.
You will throw them away as an
unclean thing;
You will say to them, "Get away!"

²³ Then He will give the rain for
your seed
With which you sow the ground,
And bread of the increase of the
earth;
It will be fat and plentiful.
In that day your cattle will feed
In large pastures.
²⁴ Likewise the oxen and the young
donkeys that work the ground
Will eat cured fodder,
Which has been winnowed with
the shovel and fan.
²⁵ There will be on every high
mountain
And on every high hill
Rivers *and* streams of waters,
In the day of the great slaughter,
When the towers fall.
²⁶ Moreover the light of the moon
will be as the light of the sun,
And the light of the sun will be
sevenfold,
As the light of seven days,
In the day that the LORD binds up
the bruise of His people
And heals the stroke of their wound.

²⁷ Behold, the name of the LORD
comes from afar,
Burning *with* His anger,
And *His* burden *is* heavy;
His lips are full of indignation,
And *His* tongue like a devouring
fire.
²⁸ His breath is like an overflowing
stream,
Which reaches up to the neck,
To sift the nations with the sieve
of futility;
And *there shall be* a bridle in the
jaws of the people,
Causing *them* to err.

²⁹ You shall have a song
As in the night *when* a holy
festival is kept,

Start Somewhere

Sue had fairly serious health problems. An invalid since childhood, she had a birth defect that left a hole in one of the chambers of her heart. The births of five children, a number of surgeries, and weight gain all took their toll. She lived in almost constant pain. Then she decided that one of the things she wanted to do most in life was to run a marathon, a feat her friends and husband thought was totally unrealistic. She became committed to her goal, however, and began running — very slowly — in the subdivision where they lived. Each day she ran just a little further. Soon she was running one mile, then three, then five. Finally, Sue registered to run her first marathon.

Sue ran a smart race — stopping regularly to stretch, drinking plenty of water, and pacing herself. The race was run mostly in the rain, however, and when no more runners were seen crossing the finish line, Sue's family became concerned. Her husband went in search of her. He found her a couple of miles from the finish, encouraging a group of friends with whom she was running. She crossed the finish line five-and-a-half hours after starting the race, but she finished! Her goal had been reached!

Having goals changes us. Working toward them develops us. Reaching them establishes us.

And gladness of heart as when one
      goes with a flute,
To come into the mountain of the
      LORD,
To the Mighty One of Israel.
30   The LORD will cause His glorious
      voice to be heard,
And show the descent of His arm,
With the indignation of *His* anger
And the flame of a devouring fire,
With scattering, tempest, and
      hailstones.
31   For through the voice of the LORD
Assyria will be beaten down,
As He strikes with the rod.
32   And *in* every place where the staff
      of punishment passes,
Which the LORD lays on him,
It will be with tambourines and
      harps;
And in battles of brandishing He
      will fight with it.
33   For Tophet *was* established of
      old,
Yes, for the king it is prepared.
He has made *it* deep and large;
Its pyre *is* fire with much wood;
The breath of the LORD, like a
      stream of brimstone,
Kindles it.

31 Woe to those who go down to
      Egypt for help,
And rely on horses,
Who trust in chariots because *they
      are* many,
And in horsemen because they are
      very strong,
But who do not look to the Holy
      One of Israel,
Nor seek the LORD!
2   Yet He also *is* wise and will bring
      disaster,
And will not call back His words,
But will arise against the house of
      evildoers,
And against the help of those who
      work iniquity.
3   Now the Egyptians *are* men, and
      not God;
And their horses are flesh, and not
      spirit.
When the LORD stretches out His
      hand,
Both he who helps will fall,

And he who is helped will fall
      down;
They all will perish together.

4 For thus the LORD has spoken to me:

"As a lion roars,
And a young lion over his prey
(When a multitude of shepherds is
      summoned against him,
He will not be afraid of their
      voice
Nor be disturbed by their noise),
So the LORD of hosts will come
      down
To fight for Mount Zion and for
      its hill.
5   Like birds flying about,
So will the LORD of hosts defend
      Jerusalem.
Defending, He will also deliver *it;*
Passing over, He will preserve *it.*"

6 Return *to Him* against whom the children of Israel have deeply revolted. 7 For
in that day every man shall throw away
his idols of silver and his idols of gold—
sin, which your own hands have made for
yourselves.

8   "Then Assyria shall fall by a sword
      not of man,
And a sword not of mankind shall
      devour him.
But he shall flee from the sword,
And his young men shall become
      forced labor.
9   He shall cross over to his
      stronghold for fear,
And his princes shall be afraid of
      the banner,"
Says the LORD,
Whose fire *is* in Zion
And whose furnace *is* in
      Jerusalem.

32 Behold, a king will reign in
      righteousness,
And princes will rule with justice.
2   A man will be as a hiding place
      from the wind,
And a cover from the tempest,
As rivers of water in a dry place,
As the shadow of a great rock in a
      weary land.

3   The eyes of those who see will not
be dim,
And the ears of those who hear
will listen.
4   Also the heart of the rash will
understand knowledge,
And the tongue of the stammerers
will be ready to speak plainly.

5   The foolish person will no longer
be called generous,
Nor the miser said *to be* bountiful;
6   For the foolish person will speak
foolishness,
And his heart will work iniquity:
To practice ungodliness,
To utter error against the LORD,
To keep the hungry unsatisfied,
And he will cause the drink of the
thirsty to fail.
7   Also the schemes of the schemer
are evil;
He devises wicked plans
To destroy the poor with lying
words,
Even when the needy speaks
justice.
8   But a generous man devises
generous things,
And by generosity he shall stand.

9   Rise up, you women who are at
ease,
Hear my voice;
You complacent daughters,
Give ear to my speech.
10 In a year and *some* days
You will be troubled, you
complacent women;
For the vintage will fail,
The gathering will not come.
11 Tremble, you *women* who are at
ease;
Be troubled, you complacent ones;
Strip yourselves, make yourselves
bare,
And gird *sackcloth* on *your* waists.

12 People shall mourn upon their
breasts
For the pleasant fields, for the
fruitful vine.
13 On the land of my people will
come up thorns *and* briers,

Yes, on all the happy homes *in* the
joyous city;
14 Because the palaces will be
forsaken,
The bustling city will be deserted.
The forts and towers will become
lairs forever,
A joy of wild donkeys, a pasture of
flocks—
15 Until the Spirit is poured upon us
from on high,
And the wilderness becomes a
fruitful field,
And the fruitful field is counted as
a forest.

16 Then justice will dwell in the
wilderness,
And righteousness remain in the
fruitful field.
17 The work of righteousness will be
peace,
And the effect of righteousness,
quietness and assurance forever.
18 My people will dwell in a peaceful
habitation,
In secure dwellings, and in quiet
resting places,
19 Though hail comes down on the
forest,
And the city is brought low in
humiliation.

20 Blessed *are* you who sow beside all
waters,
Who send out freely the feet of
the ox and the donkey.

∼ PSALM 108:7–13 ∼

7   God has spoken in His holiness:
"I will rejoice;
I will divide Shechem
And measure out the Valley of
Succoth.
8   Gilead *is* Mine; Manasseh *is* Mine;
Ephraim also *is* the helmet for My
head;
Judah *is* My lawgiver.
9   Moab *is* My washpot;
Over Edom I will cast My shoe;
Over Philistia I will triumph."

10 Who will bring me *into* the strong
city?

Who will lead me to Edom?
11 *Is it* not *You,* O God, *who* cast us
   off?
   And *You,* O God, *who* did not go
   out with our armies?
12 Give us help from trouble,
   For the help of man is useless.
13 Through God we will do valiantly,
   For *it is* He *who* shall tread down
   our enemies.

~ PROVERBS 25:23, 24 ~

23 The north wind brings forth rain,
   And a backbiting tongue an angry
   countenance.

24 *It is* better to dwell in a corner of a
   housetop,
   Than in a house shared with a
   contentious woman.

~ 2 CORINTHIANS 11:16–33 ~

I say again, let no one think me a fool. If
otherwise, at least receive me as a fool,
that I also may boast a little. 17 What I
speak, I speak not according to the Lord,
but as it were, foolishly, in this confidence
of boasting. 18 Seeing that many boast according to the flesh, I also will boast. 19 For
you put up with fools gladly, since you
yourselves are wise! 20 For you put up with
it if one brings you into bondage, if one
devours *you,* if one takes *from you,* if
one exalts himself, if one strikes you
on the face. 21 To *our* shame I say that we

were too weak for that! But in whatever
anyone is bold—I speak foolishly—I am
bold also.
22 Are they Hebrews? So *am* I. Are they
Israelites? So *am* I. Are they the seed
of Abraham? So *am* I. 23 Are they ministers of Christ?—I speak as a fool—I *am*
more: in labors more abundant, in stripes
above measure, in prisons more frequently, in deaths often. 24 From the Jews
five times I received forty *stripes* minus
one. 25 Three times I was beaten with rods;
once I was stoned; three times I was shipwrecked; a night and a day I have been in
the deep; 26 *in* journeys often, *in* perils
of waters, *in* perils of robbers, *in* perils of
my own countrymen, *in* perils of the Gentiles, *in* perils in the city, *in* perils in the
wilderness, *in* perils in the sea, *in* perils
among false brethren; 27 in weariness and
toil, in sleeplessness often, in hunger
and thirst, in fastings often, in cold and
nakedness— 28 besides the other things,
what comes upon me daily: my deep concern for all the churches. 29 Who is weak,
and I am not weak? Who is made to
stumble, and I do not burn *with indignation?*
30 If I must boast, I will boast in the
things which concern my infirmity.
31 The God and Father of our Lord Jesus
Christ, who is blessed forever, knows that
I am not lying. 32 In Damascus the governor, under Aretas the king, was guarding
the city of the Damascenes with a garrison, desiring to arrest me; 33 but I was let
down in a basket through a window in
the wall, and escaped from his hands.

READING 264 · SEPTEMBER 21

~ ISAIAH 33:1—34:17 ~

1 Woe to you who plunder, though
   you *have* not *been* plundered;
   And you who deal treacherously,
      though they have not dealt
      treacherously with you!
   When you cease plundering,
   You will be plundered;
   When you make an end of dealing
      treacherously,
   They will deal treacherously with
      you.

2 O LORD, be gracious to us;
   We have waited for You.
   Be their arm every morning,
   Our salvation also in the time of
      trouble.
3 At the noise of the tumult the
      people shall flee;
   When You lift Yourself up, the
      nations shall be scattered;
4 And Your plunder shall be
      gathered

In the Thick of It

Does it seem to you that the only stories you hear about miracles occur in remote African villages or obscure Chinese provinces? Do you wonder if God is visibly active only on the mission field? Steven Mosley, author of *If Only God Would Answer*, believes the reason we hear more stories from missionary ventures than local churches is, "God is most active when we are reaching out most. He stretches out when we stretch out.

"Consider the life of George Müeller. He wrote an entire book of answers to specific prayer requests he made while living in complacent Victorian England. Müeller was stretched — he was seeking to meet the needs of two thousand orphans. In remote China, Hudson Taylor was given needed funds or had personal needs met without ever making an appeal to any human being. Taylor was stretched —sharing the Gospel where it had not been preached before. Brother Andrew, 'God's Smuggler,' had an abundance of answered prayers. He, too, was stretched — devoting his life to taking Bibles behind the iron curtain."

Mosley has concluded, "God is most active in the thick of it."

Are you asking God to help you meet your heart's desires today, or are you asking Him how you might help Him meet *His* heart's desires?

> O Lord, be gracious to us; we have waited for You. Be their arm every morning, our salvation also in the time of trouble.
>
> *Isaiah 33:2*

Like the gathering of the
caterpillar;
As the running to and fro of
locusts,
He shall run upon them.

5 The LORD is exalted, for He
dwells on high;
He has filled Zion with justice and
righteousness.
6 Wisdom and knowledge will be
the stability of your times,
And the strength of salvation;
The fear of the LORD *is* His
treasure.

7 Surely their valiant ones shall cry
outside,
The ambassadors of peace shall
weep bitterly.
8 The highways lie waste,
The traveling man ceases.
He has broken the covenant,
He has despised the cities,
He regards no man.
9 The earth mourns *and* languishes,
Lebanon is shamed *and* shriveled;
Sharon is like a wilderness,
And Bashan and Carmel shake off
their fruits.

10 "Now I will rise," says the LORD;
"Now I will be exalted,
Now I will lift Myself up.
11 You shall conceive chaff,
You shall bring forth stubble;
Your breath, *as* fire, shall devour
you.
12 And the people shall be *like* the
burnings of lime;
Like thorns cut up they shall be
burned in the fire.
13 Hear, you *who are* afar off, what I
have done;
And you *who are* near,
acknowledge My might."

14 The sinners in Zion are afraid;
Fearfulness has seized the
hypocrites:
"Who among us shall dwell with
the devouring fire?
Who among us shall dwell with
everlasting burnings?"

15 He who walks righteously and
speaks uprightly,
He who despises the gain of
oppressions,
Who gestures with his hands,
refusing bribes,
Who stops his ears from hearing
of bloodshed,
And shuts his eyes from seeing evil:
16 He will dwell on high;
His place of defense *will be* the
fortress of rocks;
Bread will be given him,
His water *will be* sure.

17 Your eyes will see the King in His
beauty;
They will see the land that is very
far off.
18 Your heart will meditate on terror:
"Where *is* the scribe?
Where *is* he who weighs?
Where *is* he who counts the
towers?"
19 You will not see a fierce people,
A people of obscure speech,
beyond perception,
Of a stammering tongue *that you*
cannot understand.

20 Look upon Zion, the city of our
appointed feasts;
Your eyes will see Jerusalem, a
quiet home,
A tabernacle *that* will not be taken
down;
Not one of its stakes will ever be
removed,
Nor will any of its cords be
broken.
21 But there the majestic LORD *will
be* for us
A place of broad rivers *and*
streams,
In which no galley with oars will
sail,
Nor majestic ships pass by
22 (For the LORD *is* our Judge,
The LORD *is* our Lawgiver,
The LORD *is* our King;
He will save us);
23 Your tackle is loosed,
They could not strengthen their
mast,
They could not spread the sail.

Then the prey of great plunder is
　　divided;
The lame take the prey.
24 And the inhabitant will not say, "I
　　am sick";
The people who dwell in it *will be*
　　forgiven *their* iniquity.

34 Come near, you nations, to hear;
　　And heed, you people!
Let the earth hear, and all that is
　　in it,
The world and all things that
　　come forth from it.
2 For the indignation of the LORD *is*
　　against all nations,
And *His* fury against all their
　　armies;
He has utterly destroyed them,
He has given them over to the
　　slaughter.
3 Also their slain shall be thrown
　　out;
Their stench shall rise from their
　　corpses,
And the mountains shall be melted
　　with their blood.
4 All the host of heaven shall be
　　dissolved,
And the heavens shall be rolled up
　　like a scroll;
All their host shall fall down
As the leaf falls from the vine,
And as *fruit* falling from a fig tree.

5 "For My sword shall be bathed in
　　heaven;
Indeed it shall come down on
　　Edom,
And on the people of My curse,
　　for judgment.
6 The sword of the LORD is filled
　　with blood,
It is made overflowing with
　　fatness,
With the blood of lambs and
　　goats,
With the fat of the kidneys of
　　rams.
For the LORD has a sacrifice in
　　Bozrah,
And a great slaughter in the land
　　of Edom.
7 The wild oxen shall come down
　　with them,

And the young bulls with the
　　mighty bulls;
Their land shall be soaked with
　　blood,
And their dust saturated with
　　fatness."

8 For *it is* the day of the LORD's
　　vengeance,
The year of recompense for the
　　cause of Zion.
9 Its streams shall be turned into
　　pitch,
And its dust into brimstone;
Its land shall become burning
　　pitch.
10 It shall not be quenched night or
　　day;
Its smoke shall ascend forever.
From generation to generation it
　　shall lie waste;
No one shall pass through it
　　forever and ever.
11 But the pelican and the porcupine
　　shall possess it,
Also the owl and the raven shall
　　dwell in it.
And He shall stretch out over it
The line of confusion and the
　　stones of emptiness.
12 They shall call its nobles to the
　　kingdom,
But none *shall be* there, and all its
　　princes shall be nothing.

13 And thorns shall come up in its
　　palaces,
Nettles and brambles in its
　　fortresses;
It shall be a habitation of jackals,
A courtyard for ostriches.
14 The wild beasts of the desert shall
　　also meet with the jackals,
And the wild goat shall bleat to its
　　companion;
Also the night creature shall rest
　　there,
And find for herself a place of rest.
15 There the arrow snake shall make
　　her nest and lay *eggs*
And hatch, and gather *them* under
　　her shadow;
There also shall the hawks be
　　gathered,
Every one with her mate.

16 "Search from the book of the
     LORD, and read:
   Not one of these shall fail;
   Not one shall lack her mate.
   For My mouth has commanded it,
     and His Spirit has gathered
     them.
17 He has cast the lot for them,
   And His hand has divided it
     among them with a measuring
     line.
   They shall possess it forever;
   From generation to generation
     they shall dwell in it."

～ PSALM 109:1–5 ～

1 Do not keep silent,
  O God of my praise!
2 For the mouth of the wicked and the
    mouth of the deceitful
  Have opened against me;
  They have spoken against me with a
    lying tongue.
3 They have also surrounded me with
    words of hatred,
  And fought against me without a
    cause.
4 In return for my love they are my
    accusers,
  But I *give myself to* prayer.
5 Thus they have rewarded me evil for
    good,
  And hatred for my love.

～ PROVERBS 25:25, 26 ～

25 *As* cold water to a weary soul,
   So *is* good news from a far country.

26 A righteous *man* who falters before
     the wicked
   Is like a murky spring and a polluted
     well.

～ 2 CORINTHIANS 12:1–21 ～

It is doubtless not profitable for me to
boast. I will come to visions and revela-
tions of the Lord: 2 I know a man in Christ
who fourteen years ago—whether in the
body I do not know, or whether out of
the body I do not know, God knows—

such a one was caught up to the third
heaven. 3 And I know such a man—
whether in the body or out of the body I
do not know, God knows— 4 how he was
caught up into Paradise and heard inexpressible words, which it is not lawful for
a man to utter. 5 Of such a one I will boast;
yet of myself I will not boast, except in
my infirmities. 6 For though I might desire to boast, I will not be a fool; for I will
speak the truth. But I refrain, lest anyone
should think of me above what he sees
me *to be* or hears from me.

7 And lest I should be exalted above
measure by the abundance of the revela-
tions, a thorn in the flesh was given to
me, a messenger of Satan to buffet me,
lest I be exalted above measure. 8 Concerning this thing I pleaded with the Lord
three times that it might depart from me.
9 And He said to me, "My grace is sufficient for you, for My strength is made
perfect in weakness." Therefore most
gladly I will rather boast in my infirmities, that the power of Christ may rest
upon me. 10 Therefore I take pleasure
in infirmities, in reproaches, in needs, in
persecutions, in distresses, for Christ's
sake. For when I am weak, then I am
strong.

11 I have become a fool in boasting; you
have compelled me. For I ought to have
been commended by you; for in nothing
was I behind the most eminent apostles,
though I am nothing. 12 Truly the signs of
an apostle were accomplished among you
with all perseverance, in signs and wonders and mighty deeds. 13 For what is it in
which you were inferior to other churches,
except that I myself was not burdensome
to you? Forgive me this wrong!

14 Now *for* the third time I am ready to
come to you. And I will not be burdensome to you; for I do not seek yours, but
you. For the children ought not to lay up
for the parents, but the parents for the
children. 15 And I will very gladly spend
and be spent for your souls; though the
more abundantly I love you, the less I am
loved.

16 But be that *as it may,* I did not burden you. Nevertheless, being crafty, I
caught you by cunning! 17 Did I take advantage of you by any of those whom I
sent to you? 18 I urged Titus, and sent our

brother with *him*. Did Titus take advantage of you? Did we not walk in the same spirit? Did *we* not *walk* in the same steps? ¹⁹ Again, do you think that we excuse ourselves to you? We speak before God in Christ. But *we do* all things, beloved, for your edification. ²⁰ For I fear lest, when I come, I shall not find you such as I wish, and *that* I shall be found by you such as you do not wish; lest *there be* contentions, jealousies, outbursts of wrath, selfish ambitions, backbitings, whisperings, conceits, tumults; ²¹ lest, when I come again, my God will humble me among you, and I shall mourn for many who have sinned before and have not repented of the uncleanness, fornication, and lewdness which they have practiced.

READING 265 · SEPTEMBER 22

~ ISAIAH 35:1—36:22 ~

¹ The wilderness and the wasteland
  shall be glad for them,
  And the desert shall rejoice and
  blossom as the rose;
² It shall blossom abundantly and
  rejoice,
  Even with joy and singing.
  The glory of Lebanon shall be
  given to it,
  The excellence of Carmel and
  Sharon.
  They shall see the glory of the
  LORD,
  The excellency of our God.

³ Strengthen the weak hands,
  And make firm the feeble knees.
⁴ Say to those *who are* fearful-
  hearted,
  "Be strong, do not fear!
  Behold, your God will come *with*
  vengeance,
  With the recompense of God;
  He will come and save you."

⁵ Then the eyes of the blind shall be
  opened,
  And the ears of the deaf shall be
  unstopped.
⁶ Then the lame shall leap like a
  deer,
  And the tongue of the dumb sing.
  For waters shall burst forth in the
  wilderness,
  And streams in the desert.
⁷ The parched ground shall become
  a pool,
  And the thirsty land springs of
  water;
  In the habitation of jackals, where
  each lay,
  There shall be grass with reeds and
  rushes.

⁸ A highway shall be there, and a
  road,
  And it shall be called the Highway
  of Holiness.
  The unclean shall not pass over it,
  But it *shall be* for others.
  Whoever walks the road, although
  a fool,
  Shall not go astray.
⁹ No lion shall be there,
  Nor shall *any* ravenous beast go
  up on it;
  It shall not be found there.
  But the redeemed shall walk *there,*
¹⁰ And the ransomed of the LORD
  shall return,
  And come to Zion with singing,
  With everlasting joy on their
  heads.
  They shall obtain joy and gladness,
  And sorrow and sighing shall flee
  away.

36 Now it came to pass in the four-teenth year of King Hezekiah *that* Sennacherib king of Assyria came up against all the fortified cities of Judah and took them. ² Then the king of Assyria sent *the* Rabshakeh with a great army from Lachish to King Hezekiah at Jerusalem. And he stood by the aqueduct from the upper pool, on the highway to the Fuller's Field. ³ And Eliakim the son of Hilkiah, who was over the household, Shebna the scribe, and Joah the son of Asaph, the recorder, came out to him.

⁴ Then *the* Rabshakeh said to them, "Say now to Hezekiah, 'Thus says the great king, the king of Assyria: "What confidence is this in which you trust? ⁵ I say you speak of having plans and power for war; but *they are* mere words. Now in whom do you trust, that you rebel against me? ⁶ Look! You are trusting in the staff of this broken reed, Egypt, on which if a man leans, it will go into his hand and pierce it. So *is* Pharaoh king of Egypt to all who trust in him.

⁷ "But if you say to me, 'We trust in the LORD our God,' *is it* not He whose high places and whose altars Hezekiah has taken away, and said to Judah and Jerusalem, 'You shall worship before this altar'?' ' ⁸ Now therefore, I urge you, give a pledge to my master the king of Assyria, and I will give you two thousand horses— if you are able on your part to put riders on them! ⁹ How then will you repel one captain of the least of my master's servants, and put your trust in Egypt for chariots and horsemen? ¹⁰ Have I now come up without the LORD against this land to destroy it? The LORD said to me, 'Go up against this land, and destroy it.' "

¹¹ Then Eliakim, Shebna, and Joah said to *the* Rabshakeh, "Please speak to your servants in Aramaic, for we understand *it;* and do not speak to us in Hebrew in the hearing of the people who *are* on the wall."

¹² But *the* Rabshakeh said, "Has my master sent me to your master and to you to speak these words, and not to the men who sit on the wall, who will eat and drink their own waste with you?"

¹³ Then *the* Rabshakeh stood and called out with a loud voice in Hebrew, and said, "Hear the words of the great king, the king of Assyria! ¹⁴ Thus says the king: 'Do not let Hezekiah deceive you, for he will not be able to deliver you; ¹⁵ nor let Hezekiah make you trust in the LORD, saying, "The LORD will surely deliver us; this city will not be given into the hand of the king of Assyria." ' ¹⁶ Do not listen to Hezekiah; for thus says the king of Assyria: 'Make *peace* with me *by a* present and come out to me; and every one of you eat from his own vine and every one from his own fig tree, and every one of you drink the waters of his own cistern; ¹⁷ until I come and take you away to a land like your own land, a land of grain and new wine, a land of bread and vineyards. ¹⁸ *Beware* lest Hezekiah persuade you, saying, "The LORD will deliver us." Has any one of the gods of the nations delivered its land from the hand of the king of Assyria? ¹⁹ Where *are* the gods of Hamath and Arpad? Where *are* the gods of Sepharvaim? Indeed, have they delivered Samaria from my hand? ²⁰ Who among all the gods of these lands have delivered their countries from my hand, that the LORD should deliver Jerusalem from my hand?' "

²¹ But they held their peace and answered him not a word; for the king's commandment was, "Do not answer him." ²² Then Eliakim the son of Hilkiah, who *was* over the household, Shebna the scribe, and Joah the son of Asaph, the recorder, came to Hezekiah with *their* clothes torn, and told him the words of *the* Rabshakeh.

~ PSALM 109:6–13 ~

⁶ Set a wicked man over him,
And let an accuser stand at his right hand.
⁷ When he is judged, let him be found guilty,
And let his prayer become sin.
⁸ Let his days be few,
And let another take his office.
⁹ Let his children be fatherless,
And his wife a widow.
¹⁰ Let his children continually be vagabonds, and beg;
Let them seek *their bread* also from their desolate places.
¹¹ Let the creditor seize all that he has,
And let strangers plunder his labor.
¹² Let there be none to extend mercy to him,
Nor let there be any to favor his fatherless children.
¹³ Let his posterity be cut off,

Pressed, but not Crushed

> For we also are weak in Him, but we shall live with Him by the power of God toward you.
>
> *2 Corinthians 13:4*

Bathyspheres are amazing inventions. Operating like a miniature submarine, they have been used to explore the ocean in places so deep the water pressure would crush a conventional submarine as easily as if it were an aluminum can. Bathyspheres compensate for the intense water pressure with plates of steel several inches thick. The steel keeps the water out, but it also makes a bathysphere very heavy and difficult to maneuver. The space inside is cramped, allowing for only one or two people to survey the ocean floor by looking through a tiny plate-glass window.

What divers invariably find at every depth of the ocean are fish and other sea creatures. Some of these creatures are quite small and appear to have fairly normal skin. They look flexible and supple as they swim through the inky waters. How can they live at these depths without steel plating? They compensate for the outside pressure through equal and opposite pressure on the inside.

Spiritual fortitude works in the same way. The more negative the circumstances around us, the more we need to allow God's power to work within us to exert an equal and opposite pressure from the inside. With God on the inside, no pressure on earth can crush us!

And in the generation following let
their name be blotted out.

～ PROVERBS 25:27, 28 ～

27 *It is* not good to eat much honey;
So to seek one's own glory *is not*
glory.

28 Whoever *has* no rule over his own
spirit
Is like a city broken down, without
walls.

～ 2 CORINTHIANS 13:1-14 ～

This *will be* the third *time* I am coming to
you. "By the mouth of two or three witnesses every word shall be established."
² I have told you before, and foretell as if
I were present the second time, and now
being absent I write to those who have
sinned before, and to all the rest, that if I
come again I will not spare— ³ since you
seek a proof of Christ speaking in me, who
is not weak toward you, but mighty
in you. ⁴ For though He was crucified in
weakness, yet He lives by the power of
God. For we also are weak in Him, but
we shall live with Him by the power of
God toward you.

⁵ Examine yourselves *as to* whether you
are in the faith. Test yourselves. Do
you not know yourselves, that Jesus Christ
is in you?—unless indeed you are disqualified. ⁶ But I trust that you will know that
we are not disqualified.

⁷ Now I pray to God that you do no
evil, not that we should appear approved,
but that you should do what is honorable,
though we may seem disqualified. ⁸ For
we can do nothing against the truth, but
for the truth. ⁹ For we are glad when we
are weak and you are strong. And this also
we pray, that you may be made complete.
¹⁰ Therefore I write these things being
absent, lest being present I should use
sharpness, according to the authority
which the Lord has given me for edification and not for destruction.

¹¹ Finally, brethren, farewell. Become
complete. Be of good comfort, be of one
mind, live in peace; and the God of love
and peace will be with you.

¹² Greet one another with a holy kiss.

¹³ All the saints greet you.

¹⁴ The grace of the Lord Jesus Christ,
and the love of God, and the communion
of the Holy Spirit *be* with you all. Amen.

READING 266 · SEPTEMBER 23

～ ISAIAH 37:1—38:22 ～

And so it was, when King Hezekiah
heard *it,* that he tore his clothes,
covered himself with sackcloth,
and went into the house of the LORD.
² Then he sent Eliakim, who *was* over the
household, Shebna the scribe, and the elders of the priests, covered with sackcloth,
to Isaiah the prophet, the son of Amoz.
³ And they said to him, "Thus says Hezekiah: 'This day *is* a day of trouble and
rebuke and blasphemy; for the children
have come to birth, but *there is* no strength
to bring them forth. ⁴ It may be that the
LORD your God will hear the words of
the Rabshakeh, whom his master the king
of Assyria has sent to reproach the living
God, and will rebuke the words which
the LORD your God has heard. Therefore
lift up *your* prayer for the remnant that is
left.' "

⁵ So the servants of King Hezekiah came
to Isaiah. ⁶ And Isaiah said to them, "Thus
you shall say to your master, 'Thus says
the LORD: "Do not be afraid of the words
which you have heard, with which the
servants of the king of Assyria have blasphemed Me. ⁷ Surely I will send a spirit
upon him, and he shall hear a rumor and
return to his own land; and I will cause
him to fall by the sword in his own
land." ' "

⁸ Then *the* Rabshakeh returned, and
found the king of Assyria warring against
Libnah, for he heard that he had departed
from Lachish. ⁹ And the king heard concerning Tirhakah king of Ethiopia, "He

Being a Great Mom

When Rose Kennedy died at age 104, the world lost one of the most dedicated and famous mothers of this century. She was mother to nine children, among them a former United States President, an Attorney General, and a current United States Senator.

In spite of her own marital challenges, the birth of a mentally challenged child, and the early deaths of four of her children, Rose Kennedy lived a life of faith and strength before her children and grandchildren. At her funeral, her son Ted put into perspective the considerable impact she had on the lives of her family members — with actions both great and small — conveying to her children her love and care, and God's love and care: "She sustained us in the saddest times. . . . Her faith in God was the greatest gift she gave us. . . . She was ambitious not only for our success but for our souls. From our youth we remember how, with effortless ease, she could bandage a cut, dry a tear, recite from memory 'The Midnight Ride of Paul Revere,' and spot a hole in a sock from a hundred yards away."

Great mothers don't always bear children who achieve greatness in the eyes of the world, but great mothers always convey great love.

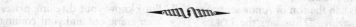

has come out to make war with you." So when he heard *it*, he sent messengers to Hezekiah, saying, [10] "Thus you shall speak to Hezekiah king of Judah, saying: 'Do not let your God in whom you trust deceive you, saying, "Jerusalem shall not be given into the hand of the king of Assyria." [11] Look! You have heard what the kings of Assyria have done to all lands by utterly destroying them; and shall you be delivered? [12] Have the gods of the nations delivered those whom my fathers have destroyed, Gozan and Haran and Rezeph, and the people of Eden who *were* in Telassar? [13] Where *is* the king of Hamath, the king of Arpad, and the king of the city of Sepharvaim, Hena, and Ivah?' "

[14] And Hezekiah received the letter from the hand of the messengers, and read it; and Hezekiah went up to the house of the LORD, and spread it before the LORD. [15] Then Hezekiah prayed to the LORD, saying: [16] "O LORD of hosts, God of Israel, *the One* who dwells *between* the cherubim, You *are* God, You alone, of all the kingdoms of the earth. You have made heaven and earth. [17] Incline Your ear, O LORD, and hear; open Your eyes, O LORD, and see; and hear all the words of Sennacherib, which he has sent to reproach the living God. [18] Truly, LORD, the kings of Assyria have laid waste all the nations and their lands, [19] and have cast their gods into the fire; for they *were* not gods, but the work of men's hands—wood and stone. Therefore they destroyed them. [20] Now therefore, O LORD our God, save us from his hand, that all the kingdoms of the earth may know that You *are* the LORD, You alone."

[21] Then Isaiah the son of Amoz sent to Hezekiah, saying, "Thus says the LORD God of Israel, 'Because you have prayed to Me against Sennacherib king of Assyria, [22] this *is* the word which the LORD has spoken concerning him:

> "The virgin, the daughter of Zion,
>> Has despised you, laughed you to scorn;
> The daughter of Jerusalem
>> Has shaken *her* head behind your back!

[23] "Whom have you reproached and blasphemed?
> Against whom have you raised *your* voice,
> And lifted up your eyes on high?
> Against the Holy One of Israel.
[24] By your servants you have reproached the Lord,
> And said, 'By the multitude of my chariots
> I have come up to the height of the mountains,
> To the limits of Lebanon;
> I will cut down its tall cedars
> *And* its choice cypress trees;
> I will enter its farthest height,
> To its fruitful forest.
[25] I have dug and drunk water,
> And with the soles of my feet I have dried up
> All the brooks of defense.'

[26] "Did you not hear long ago
> *How* I made it,
> From ancient times that I formed it?
> Now I have brought it to pass,
> That you should be
> For crushing fortified cities *into* heaps of ruins.
[27] Therefore their inhabitants *had* little power;
> They were dismayed and confounded;
> They were *as* the grass of the field
> And the green herb,
> *As* the grass on the housetops
> And grain blighted before it is grown.

[28] "But I know your dwelling place,
> Your going out and your coming in,
> And your rage against Me.
[29] Because your rage against Me and your tumult
> Have come up to My ears,
> Therefore I will put My hook in your nose
> And My bridle in your lips,
> And I will turn you back
> By the way which you came." '

[30] "This *shall be* a sign to you:

You shall eat this year such as
  grows of itself,
And the second year what springs
  from the same;
Also in the third year sow and
  reap,
Plant vineyards and eat the fruit of
  them.
³¹ And the remnant who have
  escaped of the house of Judah
Shall again take root downward,
And bear fruit upward.
³² For out of Jerusalem shall go a
  remnant,
And those who escape from
  Mount Zion.
The zeal of the LORD of hosts will
  do this.

³³ "Therefore thus says the LORD concerning the king of Assyria:

'He shall not come into this city,
Nor shoot an arrow there,
Nor come before it with shield,
Nor build a siege mound against
  it.
³⁴ By the way that he came,
By the same shall he return;
And he shall not come into this
  city,'
Says the LORD.
³⁵ 'For I will defend this city, to save
  it
For My own sake and for My
  servant David's sake.' "

³⁶ Then the angel of the LORD went out,
and killed in the camp of the Assyrians
one hundred and eighty-five thousand;
and when *people* arose early in the morning, there were the corpses—all dead. ³⁷ So
Sennacherib king of Assyria departed and
went away, returned *home,* and remained
at Nineveh. ³⁸ Now it came to pass, as he
was worshiping in the house of Nisroch
his god, that his sons Adrammelech and
Sharezer struck him down with the sword;
and they escaped into the land of Ararat.
Then Esarhaddon his son reigned in his
place.

38 In those days Hezekiah was sick
and near death. And Isaiah the prophet,
the son of Amoz, went to him and said to
him, "Thus says the LORD: 'Set your house
in order, for you shall die and not live.' "

² Then Hezekiah turned his face toward
the wall, and prayed to the LORD, ³ and
said, "Remember now, O LORD, I pray,
how I have walked before You in truth
and with a loyal heart, and have done
what is good in Your sight." And Hezekiah
wept bitterly.

⁴ And the word of the LORD came to
Isaiah, saying, ⁵ "Go and tell Hezekiah,
'Thus says the LORD, the God of David
your father: "I have heard your prayer, I
have seen your tears; surely I will add to
your days fifteen years. ⁶ I will deliver you
and this city from the hand of the king of
Assyria, and I will defend this city." ' ⁷ And
this *is* the sign to you from the LORD, that
the LORD will do this thing which He has
spoken: ⁸ Behold, I will bring the shadow
on the sundial, which has gone down with
the sun on the sundial of Ahaz, ten degrees backward." So the sun returned ten
degrees on the dial by which it had gone
down.

⁹ This is the writing of Hezekiah king
of Judah, when he had been sick and had
recovered from his sickness:

¹⁰ I said,
  "In the prime of my life
  I shall go to the gates of Sheol;
  I am deprived of the remainder of
    my years."
¹¹ I said,
  "I shall not see YAH,
  The Lord in the land of the living;
  I shall observe man no more
    among the inhabitants of the
    world.
¹² My life span is gone,
  Taken from me like a shepherd's
    tent;
  I have cut off my life like a
    weaver.
  He cuts me off from the loom;
  From day until night You make an
    end of me.
¹³ I have considered until morning—
  Like a lion,
  So He breaks all my bones;
  From day until night You make an
    end of me.
¹⁴ Like a crane *or* a swallow, so I
    chattered;

I mourned like a dove;
My eyes fail *from looking* upward.
O LORD, I am oppressed;
Undertake for me!

15 "What shall I say?
He has both spoken to me,
And He Himself has done *it*.
I shall walk carefully all my years
In the bitterness of my soul.
16 O Lord, by these *things men* live;
And in all these *things is* the life of
my spirit;
So You will restore me and make
me live.
17 Indeed *it was* for *my own* peace
That I had great bitterness;
But You have lovingly *delivered*
my soul from the pit of
corruption,
For You have cast all my sins
behind Your back.
18 For Sheol cannot thank You,
Death cannot praise You;
Those who go down to the pit
cannot hope for Your truth.
19 The living, the living man, he shall
praise You,
As I *do* this day;
The father shall make known Your
truth to the children.

20 "The LORD *was ready* to save me;
Therefore we will sing my songs
with stringed instruments
All the days of our life, in the
house of the LORD."

21 Now Isaiah had said, "Let them take
a lump of figs, and apply *it* as a poultice
on the boil, and he shall recover."
22 And Hezekiah had said, "What *is* the
sign that I shall go up to the house of the
LORD?"

∼ PSALM 109:14–20 ∼

14 Let the iniquity of his fathers be
remembered before the LORD,
And let not the sin of his mother be
blotted out.
15 Let them be continually before the
LORD,
That He may cut off the memory of
them from the earth;

16 Because he did not remember to
show mercy,
But persecuted the poor and needy
man,
That he might even slay the broken
in heart.
17 As he loved cursing, so let it come to
him;
As he did not delight in blessing, so
let it be far from him.
18 As he clothed himself with cursing as
with his garment,
So let it enter his body like water,
And like oil into his bones.
19 Let it be to him like the garment
which covers him,
And for a belt with which he girds
himself continually.
20 *Let* this *be* the LORD's reward to my
accusers,
And to those who speak evil against
my person.

∼ PROVERBS 26:1 ∼

1 As snow in summer and rain in
harvest,
So honor is not fitting for a fool.

∼ GALATIANS 1:1–24 ∼

Paul, an apostle (not from men nor
through man, but through Jesus Christ
and God the Father who raised Him from
the dead), 2 and all the brethren who are
with me,

To the churches of Galatia:

3 Grace to you and peace from God the
Father and our Lord Jesus Christ, 4 who
gave Himself for our sins, that He might
deliver us from this present evil age, according to the will of our God and Father,
5 to whom *be* glory forever and ever.
Amen.
6 I marvel that you are turning away so
soon from Him who called you in the
grace of Christ, to a different gospel,
7 which is not another; but there are some
who trouble you and want to pervert the
gospel of Christ. 8 But even if we, or an
angel from heaven, preach any other gospel to you than what we have preached
to you, let him be accursed. 9 As we have

said before, so now I say again, if anyone preaches any other gospel to you than what you have received, let him be accursed.

[10] For do I now persuade men, or God? Or do I seek to please men? For if I still pleased men, I would not be a bondservant of Christ.

[11] But I make known to you, brethren, that the gospel which was preached by me is not according to man. [12] For I neither received it from man, nor was I taught *it*, but *it came* through the revelation of Jesus Christ.

[13] For you have heard of my former conduct in Judaism, how I persecuted the church of God beyond measure and *tried to* destroy it. [14] And I advanced in Judaism beyond many of my contemporaries in my own nation, being more exceedingly zealous for the traditions of my fathers.

[15] But when it pleased God, who separated me from my mother's womb and called *me* through His grace, [16] to reveal His Son in me, that I might preach Him among the Gentiles, I did not immediately confer with flesh and blood, [17] nor did I go up to Jerusalem to those *who were* apostles before me; but I went to Arabia, and returned again to Damascus.

[18] Then after three years I went up to Jerusalem to see Peter, and remained with him fifteen days. [19] But I saw none of the other apostles except James, the Lord's brother. [20] (Now *concerning* the things which I write to you, indeed, before God, I do not lie.)

[21] Afterward I went into the regions of Syria and Cilicia. [22] And I was unknown by face to the churches of Judea which *were* in Christ. [23] But they were hearing only, "He who formerly persecuted us now preaches the faith which he once *tried to* destroy." [24] And they glorified God in me.

～ ISAIAH 39:1—40:31 ～

At that time Merodach-Baladan the son of Baladan, king of Babylon, sent letters and a present to Hezekiah, for he heard that he had been sick and had recovered. [2] And Hezekiah was pleased with them, and showed them the house of his treasures—the silver and gold, the spices and precious ointment, and all his armory—all that was found among his treasures. There was nothing in his house or in all his dominion that Hezekiah did not show them.

[3] Then Isaiah the prophet went to King Hezekiah, and said to him, "What did these men say, and from where did they come to you?"

So Hezekiah said, "They came to me from a far country, from Babylon."

[4] And he said, "What have they seen in your house?"

So Hezekiah answered, "They have seen all that *is* in my house; there is nothing among my treasures that I have not shown them."

[5] Then Isaiah said to Hezekiah, "Hear the word of the LORD of hosts: [6] 'Behold, the days are coming when all that *is* in your house, and what your fathers have accumulated until this day, shall be carried to Babylon; nothing shall be left,' says the LORD. [7] 'And they shall take away *some* of your sons who will descend from you, whom you will beget; and they shall be eunuchs in the palace of the king of Babylon.' "

[8] So Hezekiah said to Isaiah, "The word of the LORD which you have spoken *is* good!" For he said, "At least there will be peace and truth in my days."

40 "Comfort, yes, comfort My people!"
     Says your God.
[2] "Speak comfort to Jerusalem, and
     cry out to her,
That her warfare is ended,
That her iniquity is pardoned;
For she has received from the
     LORD's hand
Double for all her sins."

3 The voice of one crying in the
wilderness:
"Prepare the way of the LORD;
Make straight in the desert
A highway for our God.
4 Every valley shall be exalted
And every mountain and hill
brought low;
The crooked places shall be made
straight
And the rough places smooth;
5 The glory of the LORD shall be
revealed,
And all flesh shall see *it* together;
For the mouth of the LORD has
spoken."

6 The voice said, "Cry out!"
And he said, "What shall I cry?"

"All flesh *is* grass,
And all its loveliness *is* like the
flower of the field.
7 The grass withers, the flower
fades,
Because the breath of the LORD
blows upon it;
Surely the people *are* grass.
8 The grass withers, the flower
fades,
But the word of our God stands
forever."

9 O Zion,
You who bring good tidings,
Get up into the high mountain;
O Jerusalem,
You who bring good tidings,
Lift up your voice with strength,
Lift *it* up, be not afraid;
Say to the cities of Judah, "Behold
your God!"

10 Behold, the Lord GOD shall come
with a strong *hand*,
And His arm shall rule for Him;
Behold, His reward *is* with Him,
And His work before Him.
11 He will feed His flock like a
shepherd;
He will gather the lambs with His
arm,
And carry *them* in His bosom,
And gently lead those who are
with young.

12 Who has measured the waters in
the hollow of His hand,
Measured heaven with a span
And calculated the dust of the
earth in a measure?
Weighed the mountains in scales
And the hills in a balance?
13 Who has directed the Spirit of the
LORD,
Or *as* His counselor has taught
Him?
14 With whom did He take counsel,
and *who* instructed Him,
And taught Him in the path of
justice?
Who taught Him knowledge,
And showed Him the way of
understanding?

15 Behold, the nations *are* as a drop
in a bucket,
And are counted as the small dust
on the scales;
Look, He lifts up the isles as a very
little thing.
16 And Lebanon *is* not sufficient to
burn,
Nor its beasts sufficient for a burnt
offering.
17 All nations before Him *are* as
nothing,
And they are counted by Him less
than nothing and worthless.

18 To whom then will you liken
God?
Or what likeness will you compare
to Him?
19 The workman molds an image,
The goldsmith overspreads it with
gold,
And the silversmith casts silver
chains.
20 Whoever *is* too impoverished for
such a contribution
Chooses a tree *that* will not rot;
He seeks for himself a skillful
workman
To prepare a carved image *that*
will not totter.

21 Have you not known?
Have you not heard?
Has it not been told you from the
beginning?

The Harvest is Ripe

When Martin Luther began the work that became the Great Reformation, his friend Myconius said, "I can best help where I am. I will remain and pray while you toil."

Then, one night Myconius dreamed that Jesus approached him and showed him His hands and feet, wounded by His crucifixion. He looked into the eyes of his Savior and heard Jesus say to him, "Follow Me." Jesus led him to a mountaintop and pointed eastward. Myconius looked and saw a plain stretching away to the horizon. It was dotted with thousands and thousands of white sheep. One man was trying to shepherd the great flock. Myconius recognized him as his friend, Luther. The Savior then pointed westward and Myconius saw a great field of standing corn. Only one reaper was trying to harvest it all. The lonely laborer was obviously exhausted, but he persisted. Myconius recognized the solitary reaper. Again, it was Luther.

"It is not enough that I should pray," said Myconius when he awoke. "The sheep must be shepherded; the field must be reaped. Here am I; send me." He immediately sought out Luther and volunteered to serve in whatever capacity Luther desired.

Today, are you praying to help, or to be of help?

> But those who wait on the Lord shall renew their strength; they shall mount up with wings like eagles, they shall run and not be weary, they shall walk and not faint.
>
> *Isaiah 40:31*

Have you not understood from
the foundations of the earth?
22 *It is* He who sits above the circle
of the earth,
And its inhabitants *are* like
grasshoppers,
Who stretches out the heavens like
a curtain,
And spreads them out like a tent
to dwell in.
23 He brings the princes to nothing;
He makes the judges of the earth
useless.

24 Scarcely shall they be planted,
Scarcely shall they be sown,
Scarcely shall their stock take root
in the earth,
When He will also blow on them,
And they will wither,
And the whirlwind will take them
away like stubble.

25 "To whom then will you liken Me,
Or *to whom* shall I be equal?" says
the Holy One.
26 Lift up your eyes on high,
And see who has created these
things,
Who brings out their host by
number;
He calls them all by name,
By the greatness of His might
And the strength of *His* power;
Not one is missing.

27 Why do you say, O Jacob,
And speak, O Israel:
"My way is hidden from the LORD,
And my just claim is passed over
by my God"?
28 Have you not known?
Have you not heard?
The everlasting God, the LORD,
The Creator of the ends of the
earth,
Neither faints nor is weary.
His understanding is unsearchable.
29 He gives power to the weak,
And to *those who have* no might
He increases strength.
30 Even the youths shall faint and be
weary,
And the young men shall utterly
fall,

31 But those who wait on the LORD
Shall renew *their* strength;
They shall mount up with wings
like eagles,
They shall run and not be weary,
They shall walk and not faint.

~ PSALM 109:21–25 ~

21 But You, O GOD the Lord,
Deal with me for Your name's sake;
Because Your mercy *is* good, deliver
me.
22 For I *am* poor and needy,
And my heart is wounded within me.
23 I am gone like a shadow when it
lengthens;
I am shaken off like a locust.
24 My knees are weak through fasting,
And my flesh is feeble from lack of
fatness.
25 I also have become a reproach to
them;
When they look at me, they shake
their heads.

~ PROVERBS 26:2 ~

2 Like a flitting sparrow, like a flying
swallow,
So a curse without cause shall not
alight.

~ GALATIANS 2:1–21 ~

Then after fourteen years I went up again
to Jerusalem with Barnabas, and also took
Titus with *me.* 2 And I went up by revelation, and communicated to them that
gospel which I preach among the Gentiles, but privately to those who were of
reputation, lest by any means I might run,
or had run, in vain. 3 Yet not even Titus
who *was* with me, being a Greek, was
compelled to be circumcised. 4 And *this
occurred* because of false brethren secretly
brought in (who came in by stealth to spy
out our liberty which we have in Christ
Jesus, that they might bring us into
bondage), 5 to whom we did not yield submission even for an hour, that the truth
of the gospel might continue with you.

6 But from those who seemed to be
something—whatever they were, it makes

no difference to me; God shows personal favoritism to no man—for those who seemed *to be something* added nothing to me. [7] But on the contrary, when they saw that the gospel for the uncircumcised had been committed to me, as *the gospel* for the circumcised *was* to Peter [8](for He who worked effectively in Peter for the apostleship to the circumcised also worked effectively in me toward the Gentiles), [9] and when James, Cephas, and John, who seemed to be pillars, perceived the grace that had been given to me, they gave me and Barnabas the right hand of fellowship, that we *should go* to the Gentiles and they to the circumcised. [10] *They desired* only that we should remember the poor, the very thing which I also was eager to do.

[11] Now when Peter had come to Antioch, I withstood him to his face, because he was to be blamed; [12] for before certain men came from James, he would eat with the Gentiles; but when they came, he withdrew and separated himself, fearing those who were of the circumcision. [13] And the rest of the Jews also played the hypocrite with him, so that even Barnabas was carried away with their hypocrisy.

[14] But when I saw that they were not straightforward about the truth of the gospel, I said to Peter before *them* all, "If you, being a Jew, live in the manner of Gentiles and not as the Jews, why do you compel Gentiles to live as Jews? [15] We *who are* Jews by nature, and not sinners of the Gentiles, [16] knowing that a man is not justified by the works of the law but by faith in Jesus Christ, even we have believed in Christ Jesus, that we might be justified by faith in Christ and not by the works of the law; for by the works of the law no flesh shall be justified.

[17] "But if, while we seek to be justified by Christ, we ourselves also are found sinners, *is* Christ therefore a minister of sin? Certainly not! [18] For if I build again those things which I destroyed, I make myself a transgressor. [19] For I through the law died to the law that I might live to God. [20] I have been crucified with Christ; it is no longer I who live, but Christ lives in me; and the *life* which I now live in the flesh I live by faith in the Son of God, who loved me and gave Himself for me. [21] I do not set aside the grace of God; for if righteousness *comes* through the law, then Christ died in vain."

READING 268 · SEPTEMBER 25

~ ISAIAH 41:1—42:25 ~

[1] "Keep silence before Me,
  O coastlands,
And let the people renew *their* strength!
Let them come near, then let them speak;
Let us come near together for judgment.

[2] "Who raised up one from the east?
Who in righteousness called him to His feet?
Who gave the nations before him,
And made *him* rule over kings?
Who gave *them* as the dust *to* his sword,
As driven stubble to his bow?
[3] Who pursued them, *and* passed safely

By the way *that* he had not gone with his feet?
[4] Who has performed and done *it*,
Calling the generations from the beginning?
'I, the LORD, am the first;
And with the last I *am* He.' "

[5] The coastlands saw *it* and feared,
The ends of the earth were afraid;
They drew near and came.
[6] Everyone helped his neighbor,
And said to his brother,
"Be of good courage!"
[7] So the craftsman encouraged the goldsmith;
He who smooths *with* the hammer *inspired* him who strikes the anvil,

Saying, "It *is* ready for the
soldering";
Then he fastened it with pegs,
That it might not totter.

8 "But you, Israel, *are* My servant,
Jacob whom I have chosen,
The descendants of Abraham My
friend.
9 *You* whom I have taken from the
ends of the earth,
And called from its farthest
regions,
And said to you,
'You *are* My servant,
I have chosen you and have not
cast you away:
10 Fear not, for I *am* with you;
Be not dismayed, for I *am* your
God.
I will strengthen you,
Yes, I will help you,
I will uphold you with My
righteous right hand.'

11 "Behold, all those who were
incensed against you
Shall be ashamed and disgraced;
They shall be as nothing,
And those who strive with you
shall perish.
12 You shall seek them and not find
them—
Those who contended with you.
Those who war against you
Shall be as nothing,
As a nonexistent thing.
13 For I, the LORD your God, will
hold your right hand,
Saying to you, 'Fear not, I will
help you.'

14 "Fear not, you worm Jacob,
You men of Israel!
I will help you," says the LORD
And your Redeemer, the Holy
One of Israel.
15 "Behold, I will make you into a
new threshing sledge with sharp
teeth;
You shall thresh the mountains
and beat *them* small,
And make the hills like chaff.
16 You shall winnow them, the wind
shall carry them away,

And the whirlwind shall scatter
them;
You shall rejoice in the LORD,
And glory in the Holy One of
Israel.

17 "The poor and needy seek water,
but *there is* none,
Their tongues fail for thirst.
I, the LORD, will hear them;
I, the God of Israel, will not
forsake them.
18 I will open rivers in desolate
heights,
And fountains in the midst of the
valleys;
I will make the wilderness a pool
of water,
And the dry land springs of water.
19 I will plant in the wilderness the
cedar and the acacia tree,
The myrtle and the oil tree;
I will set in the desert the cypress
tree *and* the pine
And the box tree together,
20 That they may see and know,
And consider and understand
together,
That the hand of the LORD has
done this,
And the Holy One of Israel has
created it.

21 "Present your case," says the LORD.
"Bring forth your strong *reasons*,"
says the King of Jacob.
22 "Let them bring forth and show us
what will happen;
Let them show the former things,
what they *were*,
That we may consider them,
And know the latter end of them;
Or declare to us things to come.
23 Show the things that are to come
hereafter,
That we may know that you *are*
gods;
Yes, do good or do evil,
That we may be dismayed and see
it together.
24 Indeed you *are* nothing,
And your work *is* nothing;
He who chooses you *is* an
abomination.

Set an Extra Place

A businessman called his wife one day to ask if he might bring home a visiting foreigner as a dinner guest that night. At the time, the wife had three children in school and one preschooler at home, so she had a full workload on any given day, apart from entertaining strangers. Still, she agreed and the meal she prepared was both delicious and graciously served. The foreigner, an important official in Spain, had a delightful time and thanked the couple repeatedly for inviting him into their home and treating him to a home-cooked meal and an evening of family warmth and fellowship.

Years later, friends of this family went to Spain as missionaries. However, their work was brought to a standstill by government regulations. This particular Spanish official got word that the missionaries were friends of the couple who had hosted him in such a loving manner, and he used his influence to clear away the restrictions on their behalf. Today in that province of Spain a church exists, due in part to the setting of one extra place at the dinner table!

As busy as you may be today, take time for the people God may bring across your path. Only God knows what His plan may be for the future.

25 "I have raised up one from the
     north,
   And he shall come;
   From the rising of the sun he shall
     call on My name;
   And he shall come against princes
     as *though* mortar,
   As the potter treads clay.
26 Who has declared from the
     beginning, that we may know?
   And former times, that we may
     say, 'He is righteous'?
   Surely *there is* no one who shows,
   Surely *there is* no one who
     declares,
   Surely *there is* no one who hears
     your words.
27 The first time I *said* to Zion,
   'Look, there they are!'
   And I will give to Jerusalem one
     who brings good tidings.
28 For I looked, and *there was* no
     man;
   I looked among them, but *there
     was* no counselor,
   Who, when I asked of them, could
     answer a word.
29 Indeed they *are* all worthless;
   Their works *are* nothing;
   Their molded images *are* wind and
     confusion.

42 "Behold! My Servant whom I
     uphold,
   My Elect One *in whom* My soul
     delights!
   I have put My Spirit upon Him;
   He will bring forth justice to the
     Gentiles.
2 He will not cry out, nor raise *His
     voice*,
   Nor cause His voice to be heard in
     the street.
3 A bruised reed He will not break,
   And smoking flax He will not
     quench;
   He will bring forth justice for
     truth.
4 He will not fail nor be
     discouraged,
   Till He has established justice in
     the earth;
   And the coastlands shall wait for
     His law."

5 Thus says God the LORD,
   Who created the heavens and
     stretched them out,
   Who spread forth the earth and
     that which comes from it,
   Who gives breath to the people on
     it,
   And spirit to those who walk on it:
6 "I, the LORD, have called You in
     righteousness,
   And will hold Your hand;
   I will keep You and give You as a
     covenant to the people,
   As a light to the Gentiles,
7 To open blind eyes,
   To bring out prisoners from the
     prison,
   Those who sit in darkness from
     the prison house.
8 I *am* the LORD, that *is* My name;
   And My glory I will not give to
     another,
   Nor My praise to carved images.
9 Behold, the former things have
     come to pass,
   And new things I declare;
   Before they spring forth I tell you
     of them."

10 Sing to the LORD a new song,
   And His praise from the ends of
     the earth,
   You who go down to the sea, and
     all that is in it,
   You coastlands and you
     inhabitants of them!
11 Let the wilderness and its cities lift
     up *their voice*,
   The villages *that* Kedar inhabits.
   Let the inhabitants of Sela sing,
   Let them shout from the top of
     the mountains.
12 Let them give glory to the LORD,
   And declare His praise in the
     coastlands.
13 The LORD shall go forth like a
     mighty man;
   He shall stir up *His* zeal like a man
     of war.
   He shall cry out, yes, shout aloud;
   He shall prevail against His enemies.

14 "I have held My peace a long time,
   I have been still and restrained
     Myself.

Now I will cry like a woman in
   labor,
I will pant and gasp at once.
15 I will lay waste the mountains and
   hills,
And dry up all their vegetation;
I will make the rivers coastlands,
And I will dry up the pools.
16 I will bring the blind by a way
   they did not know;
I will lead them in paths they have
   not known.
I will make darkness light before
   them,
And crooked places straight.
These things I will do for them,
And not forsake them.
17 They shall be turned back,
They shall be greatly ashamed,
Who trust in carved images,
Who say to the molded images,
'You *are* our gods.'

18 "Hear, you deaf;
And look, you blind, that you may
   see.
19 Who *is* blind but My servant,
Or deaf as My messenger *whom* I
   send?
Who *is* blind as *he who is* perfect,
And blind as the LORD's servant?
20 Seeing many things, but you do
   not observe;
Opening the ears, but he does not
   hear."

21 The LORD is well pleased for His
   righteousness' sake;
He will exalt the law and make *it*
   honorable.
22 But this *is* a people robbed and
   plundered;
All of them are snared in holes,
And they are hidden in prison
   houses;
They are for prey, and no one
   delivers;
For plunder, and no one says,
   "Restore!"

23 Who among you will give ear to
   this?
Who will listen and hear for the
   time to come?

24 Who gave Jacob for plunder, and
   Israel to the robbers?
Was it not the LORD,
He against whom we have
   sinned?
For they would not walk in His
   ways,
Nor were they obedient to His
   law.
25 Therefore He has poured on him
   the fury of His anger
And the strength of battle;
It has set him on fire all around,
Yet he did not know;
And it burned him,
Yet he did not take *it* to heart.

～ PSALM 109:26–31 ～

26 Help me, O LORD my God!
Oh, save me according to Your
   mercy,
27 That they may know that this *is* Your
   hand—
That You, LORD, have done it!
28 Let them curse, but You bless;
When they arise, let them be
   ashamed,
But let Your servant rejoice.
29 Let my accusers be clothed with
   shame,
And let them cover themselves with
   their own disgrace as with a
   mantle.

30 I will greatly praise the LORD with
   my mouth;
Yes, I will praise Him among the
   multitude.
31 For He shall stand at the right hand
   of the poor,
To save *him* from those who
   condemn him.

～ PROVERBS 26:3, 4 ～

3 A whip for the horse,
A bridle for the donkey,
And a rod for the fool's back.
4 Do not answer a fool according to
   his folly,
Lest you also be like him.

~ GALATIANS 3:1–29 ~

O foolish Galatians! Who has bewitched you that you should not obey the truth, before whose eyes Jesus Christ was clearly portrayed among you as crucified? ² This only I want to learn from you: Did you receive the Spirit by the works of the law, or by the hearing of faith? ³ Are you so foolish? Having begun in the Spirit, are you now being made perfect by the flesh? ⁴ Have you suffered so many things in vain—if indeed it *was* in vain?

⁵ Therefore He who supplies the Spirit to you and works miracles among you, *does He do it* by the works of the law, or by the hearing of faith?— ⁶ just as Abraham "believed God, and it was accounted to him for righteousness." ⁷ Therefore know that *only* those who are of faith are sons of Abraham. ⁸ And the Scripture, foreseeing that God would justify the Gentiles by faith, preached the gospel to Abraham beforehand, *saying,* "In you all the nations shall be blessed." ⁹ So then those who *are* of faith are blessed with believing Abraham.

¹⁰ For as many as are of the works of the law are under the curse; for it is written, "Cursed *is* everyone who does not continue in all things which are written in the book of the law, to do them." ¹¹ But that no one is justified by the law in the sight of God *is* evident, for "the just shall live by faith." ¹² Yet the law is not of faith, but "the man who does them shall live by them."

¹³ Christ has redeemed us from the curse of the law, having become a curse for us (for it is written, "Cursed *is* everyone who hangs on a tree"), ¹⁴ that the blessing of Abraham might come upon the Gentiles in Christ Jesus, that we might receive the promise of the Spirit through faith.

¹⁵ Brethren, I speak in the manner of men: Though *it is* only a man's covenant, yet *if it is* confirmed, no one annuls or adds to it. ¹⁶ Now to Abraham and his Seed were the promises made. He does not say, "And to seeds," as of many, but as of one, "And to your Seed," who is Christ. ¹⁷ And this I say, *that* the law, which was four hundred and thirty years later, cannot annul the covenant that was confirmed before by God in Christ, that it should make the promise of no effect. ¹⁸ For if the inheritance *is* of the law, *it is* no longer of promise; but God gave *it* to Abraham by promise.

¹⁹ What purpose then *does* the law *serve?* It was added because of transgressions, till the Seed should come to whom the promise was made; *and it was* appointed through angels by the hand of a mediator. ²⁰ Now a mediator does not *mediate* for one *only,* but God is one.

²¹ *Is* the law then against the promises of God? Certainly not! For if there had been a law given which could have given life, truly righteousness would have been by the law. ²² But the Scripture has confined all under sin, that the promise by faith in Jesus Christ might be given to those who believe. ²³ But before faith came, we were kept under guard by the law, kept for the faith which would afterward be revealed. ²⁴ Therefore the law was our tutor *to bring us* to Christ, that we might be justified by faith. ²⁵ But after faith has come, we are no longer under a tutor.

²⁶ For you are all sons of God through faith in Christ Jesus. ²⁷ For as many of you as were baptized into Christ have put on Christ. ²⁸ There is neither Jew nor Greek, there is neither slave nor free, there is neither male nor female; for you are all one in Christ Jesus. ²⁹ And if you *are* Christ's, then you are Abraham's seed, and heirs according to the promise.

~ ISAIAH 43:1—44:28 ~

1 But now, thus says the LORD, who
   created you, O Jacob,
   And He who formed you,
   O Israel:
   "Fear not, for I have redeemed you;
   I have called *you* by your name;
   You *are* Mine.
2 When you pass through the
   waters, I *will be* with you;
   And through the rivers, they shall
   not overflow you.
   When you walk through the fire,
   you shall not be burned,
   Nor shall the flame scorch you.
3 For I *am* the LORD your God,
   The Holy One of Israel, your
   Savior;
   I gave Egypt for your ransom,
   Ethiopia and Seba in your place.
4 Since you were precious in My
   sight,
   You have been honored,
   And I have loved you;
   Therefore I will give men for you,
   And people for your life.
5 Fear not, for I *am* with you;
   I will bring your descendants from
   the east,
   And gather you from the west;
6 I will say to the north, 'Give them
   up!'
   And to the south, 'Do not keep
   them back!'
   Bring My sons from afar,
   And My daughters from the ends
   of the earth—
7 Everyone who is called by My
   name,
   Whom I have created for My
   glory;
   I have formed him, yes, I have
   made him."

8 Bring out the blind people who
   have eyes,
   And the deaf who have ears.
9 Let all the nations be gathered
   together,
   And let the people be assembled.
   Who among them can declare
   this,
   And show us former things?

Let them bring out their witnesses,
   that they may be justified;
   Or let them hear and say, "*It is*
   truth."
10 "You *are* My witnesses," says the
   LORD,
   "And My servant whom I have
   chosen,
   That you may know and believe
   Me,
   And understand that I *am* He.
   Before Me there was no God
   formed,
   Nor shall there be after Me.
11 I, *even* I, *am* the LORD,
   And besides Me *there is* no savior.
12 I have declared and saved,
   I have proclaimed,
   And *there was* no foreign *god*
   among you;
   Therefore you *are* My witnesses,"
   Says the LORD, "that I *am* God.
13 Indeed before the day *was,* I *am*
   He;
   And *there is* no one who can
   deliver out of My hand;
   I work, and who will reverse it?"

14 Thus says the LORD, your
   Redeemer,
   The Holy One of Israel:
   "For your sake I will send to
   Babylon,
   And bring them all down as
   fugitives—
   The Chaldeans, who rejoice in
   their ships.
15 I *am* the LORD, your Holy One,
   The Creator of Israel, your King."

16 Thus says the LORD, who makes a
   way in the sea
   And a path through the mighty
   waters,
17 Who brings forth the chariot and
   horse,
   The army and the power
   (They shall lie down together, they
   shall not rise;
   They are extinguished, they are
   quenched like a wick):

¹⁸ "Do not remember the former
    things,
    Nor consider the things of old.
¹⁹ Behold, I will do a new thing,
    Now it shall spring forth;
    Shall you not know it?
    I will even make a road in the
    wilderness
    And rivers in the desert.
²⁰ The beast of the field will honor
    Me,
    The jackals and the ostriches,
    Because I give waters in the
    wilderness
    And rivers in the desert,
    To give drink to My people, My
    chosen.
²¹ This people I have formed for
    Myself;
    They shall declare My praise.

²² "But you have not called upon Me,
    O Jacob;
    And you have been weary of Me,
    O Israel.
²³ You have not brought Me the
    sheep for your burnt offerings,
    Nor have you honored Me with
    your sacrifices.
    I have not caused you to serve
    with grain offerings,
    Nor wearied you with incense.
²⁴ You have bought Me no sweet
    cane with money,
    Nor have you satisfied Me with
    the fat of your sacrifices;
    But you have burdened Me with
    your sins,
    You have wearied Me with your
    iniquities.

²⁵ "I, *even* I, *am* He who blots out
    your transgressions for My own
    sake;
    And I will not remember your
    sins.
²⁶ Put Me in remembrance;
    Let us contend together;
    State your *case,* that you may be
    acquitted.
²⁷ Your first father sinned,
    And your mediators have
    transgressed against Me.
²⁸ Therefore I will profane the
    princes of the sanctuary;

I will give Jacob to the curse,
    And Israel to reproaches.

44 "Yet hear me now, O Jacob My
    servant,
    And Israel whom I have chosen.
² Thus says the LORD who made
    you
    And formed you from the womb,
    who will help you:
    'Fear not, O Jacob My servant;
    And you, Jeshurun, whom I have
    chosen.
³ For I will pour water on him who
    is thirsty,
    And floods on the dry ground;
    I will pour My Spirit on your
    descendants,
    And My blessing on your
    offspring;
⁴ They will spring up among the
    grass
    Like willows by the watercourses.'
⁵ One will say, 'I *am* the LORD's';
    Another will call *himself* by the
    name of Jacob;
    Another will write *with* his hand,
    'The LORD's,'
    And name *himself* by the name of
    Israel.

⁶ "Thus says the LORD, the King of
    Israel,
    And his Redeemer, the LORD of
    hosts:
    'I *am* the First and I *am* the Last;
    Besides Me *there is* no God.
⁷ And who can proclaim as I do?
    Then let him declare it and set it
    in order for Me,
    Since I appointed the ancient
    people.
    And the things that are coming
    and shall come,
    Let them show these to them.
⁸ Do not fear, nor be afraid;
    Have I not told you from that
    time, and declared *it?*
    You *are* My witnesses.
    Is there a God besides Me?
    Indeed *there is* no other Rock;
    I know not *one.*' "

⁹ Those who make an image, all of
    them *are* useless,

A Way in the Sea

Thus says
the Lord,
who makes a
way in the sea
and a path
through the
mighty waters.

Isaiah 43:16

Don played the tambourine in junior high, and that seemed about the extent of his musical ability — at least in the opinion of his peers. They recall that he couldn't carry a tune in a bucket. However, Don considered himself a musician.

When his friends graduated and went on to college, Don packed his things and moved to Nashville. He bought a used car and slept in it, took a job working nights so he could visit record companies during the day, and learned to play the guitar. For years, he practiced, wrote songs, and knocked on doors, with virtually no breaks. Then one day, his old friends heard a song on the radio. It was a good song by a good singer, who was rising on the country charts. It was Don Schlitz singing a song he had written and recorded.

A short time later, Kenny Rogers recorded one of Don's songs. "The Gambler" became the title song for one of the best-selling country-music albums of the 80s. Don has since written twenty-three number-one hits.

Don didn't wait for fame and fortune to come to him. He went in search of them.

There's an old saying among business planners that can apply to virtually every area of your life: Plan your work, then work your plan. Go for your goals. Don't expect them to arrive on your doorstep in a neatly packaged bundle. God will direct your steps, but He can't take them for you.

And their precious things shall not
profit;
They *are* their own witnesses;
They neither see nor know, that
they may be ashamed.

10 Who would form a god or mold
an image
That profits him nothing?

11 Surely all his companions would
be ashamed;
And the workmen, they *are* mere
men.
Let them all be gathered together,
Let them stand up;
Yet they shall fear,
They shall be ashamed together.

12 The blacksmith with the tongs
works one in the coals,
Fashions it with hammers,
And works it with the strength of
his arms.
Even so, he is hungry, and his
strength fails;
He drinks no water and is faint.

13 The craftsman stretches out *his*
rule,
He marks one out with chalk;
He fashions it with a plane,
He marks it out with the compass,
And makes it like the figure of a
man,
According to the beauty of a man,
that it may remain in the house.

14 He cuts down cedars for himself,
And takes the cypress and the oak;
He secures *it* for himself among
the trees of the forest.
He plants a pine, and the rain
nourishes *it*.

15 Then it shall be for a man to burn,
For he will take some of it and
warm himself;
Yes, he kindles *it* and bakes bread;
Indeed he makes a god and
worships *it*;
He makes it a carved image, and
falls down to it.

16 He burns half of it in the fire;
With this half he eats meat;
He roasts a roast, and is satisfied.
He even warms *himself* and says,
"Ah! I am warm,

I have seen the fire."

17 And the rest of it he makes into a
god,
His carved image.
He falls down before it and
worships *it*,
Prays to it and says,
"Deliver me, for you *are* my god!"

18 They do not know nor
understand;
For He has shut their eyes, so that
they cannot see,
And their hearts, so that they
cannot understand.

19 And no one considers in his heart,
Nor *is there* knowledge nor
understanding to say,
"I have burned half of it in the fire,
Yes, I have also baked bread on its
coals;
I have roasted meat and eaten *it;*
And shall I make the rest of it an
abomination?
Shall I fall down before a block of
wood?"

20 He feeds on ashes;
A deceived heart has turned him
aside;
And he cannot deliver his soul,
Nor say, "*Is there* not a lie in my
right hand?"

21 "Remember these, O Jacob,
And Israel, for you *are* My
servant;
I have formed you, you *are* My
servant;
O Israel, you will not be forgotten
by Me!

22 I have blotted out, like a thick
cloud, your transgressions,
And like a cloud, your sins.
Return to Me, for I have
redeemed you."

23 Sing, O heavens, for the LORD has
done *it!*
Shout, you lower parts of the
earth;
Break forth into singing, you
mountains,
O forest, and every tree in it!
For the LORD has redeemed Jacob,
And glorified Himself in Israel.

²⁴ Thus says the LORD, your
    Redeemer,
  And He who formed you from the
    womb:
  "I *am* the LORD, who makes all
    things,
  Who stretches out the heavens all
    alone,
  Who spreads abroad the earth by
    Myself;
²⁵ Who frustrates the signs of the
    babblers,
  And drives diviners mad;
  Who turns wise men backward,
  And makes their knowledge
    foolishness;
²⁶ Who confirms the word of His
    servant,
  And performs the counsel of His
    messengers;
  Who says to Jerusalem, 'You shall
    be inhabited,'
  To the cities of Judah, 'You shall
    be built,'
  And I will raise up her waste
    places;
²⁷ Who says to the deep, 'Be dry!
  And I will dry up your rivers';
²⁸ Who says of Cyrus, '*He is* My
    shepherd,
  And he shall perform all My
    pleasure,
  Saying to Jerusalem, "You shall be
    built,"
  And to the temple, "Your
    foundation shall be laid." ' '

∼ PSALM 110:1–7 ∼

¹ The LORD said to my Lord,
  "Sit at My right hand,
  Till I make Your enemies Your
    footstool."
² The LORD shall send the rod of Your
    strength out of Zion.
  Rule in the midst of Your enemies!

³ Your people *shall be* volunteers
  In the day of Your power;
  In the beauties of holiness, from the
    womb of the morning,
  You have the dew of Your youth.
⁴ The LORD has sworn
  And will not relent,
  "You *are* a priest forever

According to the order of
    Melchizedek."
⁵ The Lord *is* at Your right hand;
  He shall execute kings in the day of
    His wrath.
⁶ He shall judge among the nations,
  He shall fill *the places* with dead
    bodies,
  He shall execute the heads of many
    countries.
⁷ He shall drink of the brook by the
    wayside;
  Therefore He shall lift up the head.

∼ PROVERBS 26:5–9 ∼

⁵ Answer a fool according to his folly,
  Lest he be wise in his own eyes.
⁶ He who sends a message by the hand
    of a fool
  Cuts off *his own* feet *and* drinks
    violence.
⁷ *Like* the legs of the lame that hang
    limp
  Is a proverb in the mouth of fools.
⁸ Like one who binds a stone in a sling
  Is he who gives honor to a fool.
⁹ *Like* a thorn *that* goes into the hand
    of a drunkard
  Is a proverb in the mouth of fools.

∼ GALATIANS 4:1–31 ∼

Now I say *that* the heir, as long as he is a
child, does not differ at all from a slave,
though he is master of all, ² but is under
guardians and stewards until the time appointed by the father. ³ Even so we, when
we were children, were in bondage under the elements of the world. ⁴ But when
the fullness of the time had come, God
sent forth His Son, born of a woman, born
under the law, ⁵ to redeem those who
were under the law, that we might receive
the adoption as sons.

⁶ And because you are sons, God
has sent forth the Spirit of His Son into
your hearts, crying out, "Abba, Father!"
⁷ Therefore you are no longer a slave but
a son, and if a son, then an heir of God
through Christ.

⁸ But then, indeed, when you did not
know God, you served those which by
nature are not gods. ⁹ But now after you

have known God, or rather are known by God, how *is it that* you turn again to the weak and beggarly elements, to which you desire again to be in bondage? ¹⁰ You observe days and months and seasons and years. ¹¹ I am afraid for you, lest I have labored for you in vain.

¹² Brethren, I urge you to become like me, for I *became* like you. You have not injured me at all. ¹³ You know that because of physical infirmity I preached the gospel to you at the first. ¹⁴ And my trial which was in my flesh you did not despise or reject, but you received me as an angel of God, *even* as Christ Jesus. ¹⁵ What then was the blessing you *enjoyed*? For I bear you witness that, if possible, you would have plucked out your own eyes and given them to me. ¹⁶ Have I therefore become your enemy because I tell you the truth?

¹⁷ They zealously court you, *but* for no good; yes, they want to exclude you, that you may be zealous for them. ¹⁸ But it is good to be zealous in a good thing always, and not only when I am present with you. ¹⁹ My little children, for whom I labor in birth again until Christ is formed in you, ²⁰ I would like to be present with you now and to change my tone; for I have doubts about you.

²¹ Tell me, you who desire to be under the law, do you not hear the law? ²² For it is written that Abraham had two sons: the one by a bondwoman, the other by a freewoman. ²³ But he *who was* of the bondwoman was born according to the flesh, and he of the freewoman through promise, ²⁴ which things are symbolic. For these are the two covenants: the one from Mount Sinai which gives birth to bondage, which is Hagar— ²⁵ for this Hagar is Mount Sinai in Arabia, and corresponds to Jerusalem which now is, and is in bondage with her children— ²⁶ but the Jerusalem above is free, which is the mother of us all. ²⁷ For it is written:

"Rejoice, O barren,
You who do not bear!
Break forth and shout,
You who are not in labor!
For the desolate has many more children
Than she who has a husband."

²⁸ Now we, brethren, as Isaac *was,* are children of promise. ²⁹ But, as he who was born according to the flesh then persecuted him *who was born* according to the Spirit, even so *it is* now. ³⁰ Nevertheless what does the Scripture say? "Cast out the bondwoman and her son, for the son of the bondwoman shall not be heir with the son of the freewoman." ³¹ So then, brethren, we are not children of the bondwoman but of the free.

READING 270 · SEPTEMBER 27

~ ISAIAH 45:1—46:13 ~

¹ "Thus says the LORD to His anointed,
To Cyrus, whose right hand I have held—
To subdue nations before him
And loose the armor of kings,
To open before him the double doors,
So that the gates will not be shut:
² 'I will go before you
And make the crooked places straight;
I will break in pieces the gates of bronze
And cut the bars of iron.

³ I will give you the treasures of darkness
And hidden riches of secret places,
That you may know that I, the LORD,
Who call *you* by your name,
Am the God of Israel.
⁴ For Jacob My servant's sake,
And Israel My elect,
I have even called you by your name;
I have named you, though you have not known Me.
⁵ I *am* the LORD, and *there is* no other;

Gentleness

George Washington and General Lafayette were walking together one morning when they were greeted on their path by a slave. The old man paused, tipped his hat, and said, "Good mo'nin', Gen'l Washin'ton."

Immediately George Washington removed his hat, bowed, and answered, "Good morning to you, and I hope you have a pleasant day."

General Lafayette was shocked, but when he recovered his composure he exclaimed, "Why did you bow to a slave?"

Washington smiled and replied, "I would not allow him to be a better gentleman than I."

Gentleness is a character trait that results from the indwelling Spirit of God in our lives. Consider this approach in evaluating yourself as a gentle person:

G — Gracious and good
E — Engaging, willing to listen
N — Nice to others, regardless of who they are
T — Taking the time to move at another's pace
L — Loving
E — Endearing by acts of kindness and goodwill

> But the fruit of the Spirit is love, joy, peace, longsuffering, kindness, goodness, faithfulness, gentleness, self-control.
>
> *Galatians 5:22-23*

There is no God besides Me.
I will gird you, though you have
    not known Me,
6 That they may know from the
    rising of the sun to its setting
That *there is* none besides Me.
I *am* the LORD, and *there is* no
    other;
7 I form the light and create
    darkness,
I make peace and create calamity;
I, the LORD, do all these *things.'*

8 "Rain down, you heavens, from
    above,
And let the skies pour down
    righteousness;
Let the earth open, let them bring
    forth salvation,
And let righteousness spring up
    together.
I, the LORD, have created it.

9 "Woe to him who strives with his
    Maker!
Let the potsherd *strive* with the
    potsherds of the earth!
Shall the clay say to him who
    forms it, 'What are you
    making?'
Or shall your handiwork *say,* 'He
    has no hands'?
10 Woe to him who says to *his* father,
    'What are you begetting?'
Or to the woman, 'What have you
    brought forth?' "

11 Thus says the LORD,
The Holy One of Israel, and his
    Maker:
"Ask Me of things to come
    concerning My sons;
And concerning the work of My
    hands, you command Me.
12 I have made the earth,
And created man on it.
I—My hands—stretched out the
    heavens,
And all their host I have
    commanded.
13 I have raised him up in
    righteousness,
And I will direct all his ways;
He shall build My city
And let My exiles go free,

Not for price nor reward,"
Says the LORD of hosts.

14 Thus says the LORD:

"The labor of Egypt and
    merchandise of Cush
And of the Sabeans, men of
    stature,
Shall come over to you, and they
    shall be yours;
They shall walk behind you,
They shall come over in chains;
And they shall bow down to you.
They will make supplication to
    you, *saying,* 'Surely God *is* in
    you,
And *there is* no other;
There is no other God.' "

15 Truly You *are* God, who hide
    Yourself,
O God of Israel, the Savior!
16 They shall be ashamed
And also disgraced, all of them;
They shall go in confusion
    together,
Who are makers of idols.
17 *But* Israel shall be saved by the
    LORD
With an everlasting salvation;
You shall not be ashamed or
    disgraced
Forever and ever.

18 For thus says the LORD,
Who created the heavens,
Who is God,
Who formed the earth and made
    it,
Who has established it,
Who did not create it in vain,
Who formed it to be inhabited:
"I *am* the LORD, and *there is* no
    other.
19 I have not spoken in secret,
In a dark place of the earth;
I did not say to the seed of Jacob,
'Seek Me in vain';
I, the LORD, speak righteousness,
I declare things that are right.

20 "Assemble yourselves and come;
Draw near together,

You *who have* escaped from the nations.
They have no knowledge,
Who carry the wood of their carved image,
And pray to a god *that* cannot save.

21 Tell and bring forth *your case;*
Yes, let them take counsel together.
Who has declared this from ancient time?
Who has told it from that time?
Have not I, the LORD?
And *there is* no other God besides Me,
A just God and a Savior;
There is none besides Me.

22 "Look to Me, and be saved,
All you ends of the earth!
For I *am* God, and *there is* no other.

23 I have sworn by Myself;
The word has gone out of My mouth *in* righteousness,
And shall not return,
That to Me every knee shall bow,
Every tongue shall take an oath.

24 He shall say,
'Surely in the LORD I have righteousness and strength.
To Him *men* shall come,
And all shall be ashamed
Who are incensed against Him.

25 In the LORD all the descendants of Israel
Shall be justified, and shall glory.' "

46 Bel bows down, Nebo stoops;
Their idols were on the beasts and on the cattle.
Your carriages *were* heavily loaded,
A burden to the weary *beast.*

2 They stoop, they bow down together;
They could not deliver the burden,
But have themselves gone into captivity.

3 "Listen to Me, O house of Jacob,
And all the remnant of the house of Israel,

Who have been upheld *by Me* from birth,
Who have been carried from the womb:

4 Even to *your* old age, I *am* He,
And *even* to gray hairs I will carry *you!*
I have made, and I will bear;
Even I will carry, and will deliver *you.*

5 "To whom will you liken Me, and make *Me* equal
And compare Me, that we should be alike?

6 They lavish gold out of the bag,
And weigh silver on the scales;
They hire a goldsmith, and he makes it a god;
They prostrate themselves, yes, they worship.

7 They bear it on the shoulder, they carry it
And set it in its place, and it stands;
From its place it shall not move.
Though *one* cries out to it, yet it cannot answer
Nor save him out of his trouble.

8 "Remember this, and show yourselves men;
Recall to mind, O you transgressors.

9 Remember the former things of old,
For I *am* God, and *there is* no other;
I am God, and *there is* none like Me,

10 Declaring the end from the beginning,
And from ancient times *things* that are not *yet* done,
Saying, 'My counsel shall stand,
And I will do all My pleasure,'

11 Calling a bird of prey from the east,
The man who executes My counsel, from a far country.
Indeed I have spoken *it;*
I will also bring it to pass.
I have purposed *it;*
I will also do it.

[12] "Listen to Me, you stubborn-
hearted,
Who *are* far from righteousness:
[13] I bring My righteousness near, it
shall not be far off;
My salvation shall not linger.
And I will place salvation in Zion,
For Israel My glory.

~ PSALM 111:1–6 ~

[1] Praise the LORD!

I will praise the LORD with *my*
whole heart,
In the assembly of the upright and *in*
the congregation.

[2] The works of the LORD *are* great,
Studied by all who have pleasure in
them.
[3] His work *is* honorable and
glorious,
And His righteousness endures
forever.
[4] He has made His wonderful works
to be remembered;
The LORD *is* gracious and full of
compassion.
[5] He has given food to those who fear
Him;
He will ever be mindful of His
covenant.
[6] He has declared to His people the
power of His works,
In giving them the heritage of the
nations.

~ PROVERBS 26:10 ~

[10] The great *God* who formed
everything
Gives the fool *his* hire and the
transgressor *his* wages.

~ GALATIANS 5:1–26 ~

Stand fast therefore in the liberty by which
Christ has made us free, and do not be
entangled again with a yoke of bondage.
[2] Indeed I, Paul, say to you that if you become circumcised, Christ will profit you
nothing. [3] And I testify again to every man
who becomes circumcised that he is a
debtor to keep the whole law. [4] You have
become estranged from Christ, you who
attempt to be justified by law; you have
fallen from grace. [5] For we through the
Spirit eagerly wait for the hope of righteousness by faith. [6] For in Christ Jesus
neither circumcision nor uncircumcision
avails anything, but faith working through
love.

[7] You ran well. Who hindered you from
obeying the truth? [8] This persuasion does
not *come* from Him who calls you. [9] A
little leaven leavens the whole lump. [10] I
have confidence in you, in the Lord, that
you will have no other mind; but he
who troubles you shall bear his judgment,
whoever he is.

[11] And I, brethren, if I still preach
circumcision, why do I still suffer persecution? Then the offense of the cross has
ceased. [12] I could wish that those who
trouble you would even cut themselves
off!

[13] For you, brethren, have been called
to liberty; only do not *use* liberty as an
opportunity for the flesh, but through
love serve one another. [14] For all the law
is fulfilled in one word, *even* in this: "You
shall love your neighbor as yourself."
[15] But if you bite and devour one another,
beware lest you be consumed by one another!

[16] I say then: Walk in the Spirit, and you
shall not fulfill the lust of the flesh. [17] For
the flesh lusts against the Spirit, and the
Spirit against the flesh; and these are contrary to one another, so that you do not
do the things that you wish. [18] But if you
are led by the Spirit, you are not under
the law.

[19] Now the works of the flesh are evident, which are: adultery, fornication,
uncleanness, lewdness, [20] idolatry, sorcery,
hatred, contentions, jealousies, outbursts
of wrath, selfish ambitions, dissensions,
heresies, [21] envy, murders, drunkenness,
revelries, and the like; of which I tell
you beforehand, just as I also told *you* in
time past, that those who practice such
things will not inherit the kingdom of
God.

[22] But the fruit of the Spirit is love, joy,
peace, longsuffering, kindness, goodness,
faithfulness, [23] gentleness, self-control.

Against such there is no law. ²⁴ And those
who are Christ's have crucified the flesh
with its passions and desires. ²⁵ If we live
in the Spirit, let us also walk in the Spirit.
²⁶ Let us not become conceited, provoking one another, envying one another.

READING 271 · SEPTEMBER 28

~ ISAIAH 47:1—48:22 ~

¹ "Come down and sit in the dust,
  O virgin daughter of Babylon;
  Sit on the ground without a
    throne,
  O daughter of the Chaldeans!
  For you shall no more be called
  Tender and delicate.
² Take the millstones and grind
    meal.
  Remove your veil,
  Take off the skirt,
  Uncover the thigh,
  Pass through the rivers.
³ Your nakedness shall be
    uncovered,
  Yes, your shame will be seen;
  I will take vengeance,
  And I will not arbitrate with a
    man."

⁴ As for our Redeemer, the LORD of
    hosts is His name,
  The Holy One of Israel.

⁵ "Sit in silence, and go into
    darkness,
  O daughter of the Chaldeans;
  For you shall no longer be called
  The Lady of Kingdoms.
⁶ I was angry with My people;
  I have profaned My inheritance,
  And given them into your hand.
  You showed them no mercy;
  On the elderly you laid your yoke
    very heavily.
⁷ And you said, 'I shall be a lady
    forever,'
  So that you did not take these
    things to heart,
  Nor remember the latter end of
    them.

⁸ "Therefore hear this now, you who
    are given to pleasures,
  Who dwell securely,

  Who say in your heart, 'I am, and
    there is no one else besides me;
  I shall not sit as a widow,
  Nor shall I know the loss of
    children';
⁹ But these two things shall come to
    you
  In a moment, in one day:
  The loss of children, and
    widowhood.
  They shall come upon you in their
    fullness
  Because of the multitude of your
    sorceries,
  For the great abundance of your
    enchantments.

¹⁰ "For you have trusted in your
    wickedness;
  You have said, 'No one sees me';
  Your wisdom and your knowledge
    have warped you;
  And you have said in your heart,
  'I am, and there is no one else
    besides me.'
¹¹ Therefore evil shall come upon
    you;
  You shall not know from where it
    arises.
  And trouble shall fall upon you;
  You will not be able to put it off.
  And desolation shall come upon
    you suddenly,
  Which you shall not know.

¹² "Stand now with your
    enchantments
  And the multitude of your
    sorceries,
  In which you have labored from
    your youth—
  Perhaps you will be able to profit,
  Perhaps you will prevail.
¹³ You are wearied in the multitude
    of your counsels;

Let now the astrologers, the
   stargazers,
And the monthly prognosticators
Stand up and save you
From what shall come upon you.
14 Behold, they shall be as stubble,
The fire shall burn them;
They shall not deliver themselves
From the power of the flame;
It shall not *be* a coal to be warmed
   by,
Nor a fire to sit before!
15 Thus shall they be to you
With whom you have labored,
Your merchants from your youth;
They shall wander each one to his
   quarter.
No one shall save you.

48 "Hear this, O house of Jacob,
Who are called by the name of
   Israel,
And have come forth from the
   wellsprings of Judah;
Who swear by the name of the
   LORD,
And make mention of the God of
   Israel,
But not in truth or in
   righteousness;
2 For they call themselves after the
   holy city,
And lean on the God of Israel;
The LORD of hosts *is* His name:

3 "I have declared the former things
   from the beginning;
They went forth from My mouth,
   and I caused them to hear it.
Suddenly I did *them,* and they
   came to pass.
4 Because I knew that you *were*
   obstinate,
And your neck *was* an iron sinew,
And your brow bronze,
5 Even from the beginning I have
   declared *it* to you;
Before it came to pass I
   proclaimed *it* to you,
Lest you should say, 'My idol has
   done them,
And my carved image and my
   molded image
Have commanded them.'
6 "You have heard;

See all this.
And will you not declare *it?*
I have made you hear new things
   from this time,
Even hidden things, and you did
   not know them.
7 They are created now and not
   from the beginning;
And before this day you have not
   heard them,
Lest you should say, 'Of course I
   knew them.'
8 Surely you did not hear,
Surely you did not know;
Surely from long ago your ear was
   not opened.
For I knew that you would deal
   very treacherously,
And were called a transgressor
   from the womb.

9 "For My name's sake I will defer
   My anger,
And *for* My praise I will restrain it
   from you,
So that I do not cut you off.
10 Behold, I have refined you, but
   not as silver;
I have tested you in the furnace of
   affliction.
11 For My own sake, for My own
   sake, I will do *it;*
For how should *My name* be
   profaned?
And I will not give My glory to
   another.

12 "Listen to Me, O Jacob,
And Israel, My called:
I *am* He, I *am* the First,
I *am* also the Last.
13 Indeed My hand has laid the
   foundation of the earth,
And My right hand has stretched
   out the heavens;
When I call to them,
They stand up together.

14 "All of you, assemble yourselves,
   and hear!
Who among them has declared
   these *things?*
The LORD loves him;
He shall do His pleasure on
   Babylon,

It Can't Be Done

Somebody said that it couldn't be done,
But he with a chuckle replied,
That "maybe it couldn't" but he would
    be one
Who wouldn't say so till he'd tried.

So he buckled right in with the trace of
    a grin
On his face. If he worried, he hid it.
He started to sing as he tackled the thing
That couldn't be done. And he did it.

Somebody scoffed: "Oh, you'll never do that,
At least no one ever has done it."
But he took off his coat and took off his hat
And the first thing he knew he'd begun it.

With the lift of his chin and a bit of a grin,
If any doubt rose he forbid it;
He started to sing as he tackled the thing
That couldn't be done, and he did it.

There are thousands to tell you it cannot be done,
There are thousands to prophesy failure;
There are thousands to point out to you, one by one,
The dangers that wait to assail you,

But just buckle right in with a bit of a grin,
Then take off your coat and go to it.
Just start in to sing as you tackle the thing
That cannot be done, and you'll do it.
                        — Unknown

And let us not grow weary while doing good, for in due season we shall reap if we do not lose heart.

Galatians 6:9

And His arm *shall be against* the Chaldeans.

15 I, *even* I, have spoken;
Yes, I have called him,
I have brought him, and his way will prosper.

16 "Come near to Me, hear this:
I have not spoken in secret from the beginning;
From the time that it was, I *was* there.
And now the Lord GOD and His Spirit
Have sent Me."

17 Thus says the LORD, your Redeemer,
The Holy One of Israel:
"I *am* the LORD your God,
Who teaches you to profit,
Who leads you by the way you should go.

18 Oh, that you had heeded My commandments!
Then your peace would have been like a river,
And your righteousness like the waves of the sea.

19 Your descendants also would have been like the sand,
And the offspring of your body like the grains of sand;
His name would not have been cut off
Nor destroyed from before Me."

20 Go forth from Babylon!
Flee from the Chaldeans!
With a voice of singing,
Declare, proclaim this,
Utter it to the end of the earth;
Say, "The LORD has redeemed His servant Jacob!"

21 And they did not thirst
When He led them through the deserts;
He caused the waters to flow from the rock for them;
He also split the rock, and the waters gushed out.

22 "*There is* no peace," says the LORD, "for the wicked."

∼ PSALM 111:7–10 ∼

7 The works of His hands *are* verity and justice;
All His precepts *are* sure.

8 They stand fast forever and ever,
And are done in truth and uprightness.

9 He has sent redemption to His people;
He has commanded His covenant forever:
Holy and awesome *is* His name.

10 The fear of the LORD *is* the beginning of wisdom;
A good understanding have all those who do *His commandments*.
His praise endures forever.

∼ PROVERBS 26:11, 12 ∼

11 As a dog returns to his own vomit,
So a fool repeats his folly.

12 Do you see a man wise in his own eyes?
There is more hope for a fool than for him.

∼ GALATIANS 6:1–18 ∼

Brethren, if a man is overtaken in any trespass, you who *are* spiritual restore such a one in a spirit of gentleness, considering yourself lest you also be tempted. 2 Bear one another's burdens, and so fulfill the law of Christ. 3 For if anyone thinks himself to be something, when he is nothing, he deceives himself. 4 But let each one examine his own work, and then he will have rejoicing in himself alone, and not in another. 5 For each one shall bear his own load.

6 Let him who is taught the word share in all good things with him who teaches.

7 Do not be deceived, God is not mocked; for whatever a man sows, that he will also reap. 8 For he who sows to his flesh will of the flesh reap corruption, but he who sows to the Spirit will of the Spirit reap everlasting life. 9 And let us not grow weary while doing good, for in due season we shall reap if we do not lose heart. 10 Therefore, as we have opportunity, let

us do good to all, especially to those who are of the household of faith.

[11] See with what large letters I have written to you with my own hand! [12] As many as desire to make a good showing in the flesh, these *would* compel you to be circumcised, only that they may not suffer persecution for the cross of Christ. [13] For not even those who are circumcised keep the law, but they desire to have you circumcised that they may boast in your flesh. [14] But God forbid that I should boast except in the cross of our Lord Jesus Christ, by whom the world has been crucified to me, and I to the world. [15] For in Christ Jesus neither circumcision nor uncircumcision avails anything, but a new creation.

[16] And as many as walk according to this rule, peace and mercy *be* upon them, and upon the Israel of God.

[17] From now on let no one trouble me, for I bear in my body the marks of the Lord Jesus.

[18] Brethren, the grace of our Lord Jesus Christ *be* with your spirit. Amen.

READING 272 · SEPTEMBER 29

~ ISAIAH 49:1—50:11 ~

[1] "Listen, O coastlands, to Me,
    And take heed, you peoples from afar!
    The LORD has called Me from the womb;
    From the matrix of My mother He has made mention of My name.
[2] And He has made My mouth like a sharp sword;
    In the shadow of His hand He has hidden Me,
    And made Me a polished shaft;
    In His quiver He has hidden Me."

[3] "And He said to me,
    'You *are* My servant, O Israel,
    In whom I will be glorified.'
[4] Then I said, 'I have labored in vain,
    I have spent my strength for nothing and in vain;
    Yet surely my just reward *is* with the LORD,
    And my work with my God.' "

[5] "And now the LORD says,
    Who formed Me from the womb *to be* His Servant,
    To bring Jacob back to Him,
    So that Israel is gathered to Him
    (For I shall be glorious in the eyes of the LORD,
    And My God shall be My strength),

[6] Indeed He says,
    'It is too small a thing that You should be My Servant
    To raise up the tribes of Jacob,
    And to restore the preserved ones of Israel;
    I will also give You as a light to the Gentiles,
    That You should be My salvation to the ends of the earth.' "

[7] Thus says the LORD,
    The Redeemer of Israel, their Holy One,
    To Him whom man despises,
    To Him whom the nation abhors,
    To the Servant of rulers:
"Kings shall see and arise,
    Princes also shall worship,
    Because of the LORD who is faithful,
    The Holy One of Israel;
    And He has chosen You."

[8] Thus says the LORD:

"In an acceptable time I have heard You,
    And in the day of salvation I have helped You;
    I will preserve You and give You As a covenant to the people,
    To restore the earth,
    To cause them to inherit the desolate heritages;

⁹ That You may say to the prisoners,
  'Go forth,'
To those who *are* in darkness,
  'Show yourselves.'

"They shall feed along the roads,
  And their pastures *shall be* on all
    desolate heights.
¹⁰ They shall neither hunger nor
    thirst,
  Neither heat nor sun shall strike
    them;
  For He who has mercy on them
    will lead them,
  Even by the springs of water He
    will guide them.
¹¹ I will make each of My mountains
    a road,
  And My highways shall be
    elevated.
¹² Surely these shall come from afar;
  Look! Those from the north and
    the west,
  And these from the land of
    Sinim."

¹³ Sing, O heavens!
  Be joyful, O earth!
  And break out in singing,
    O mountains!
  For the LORD has comforted His
    people,
  And will have mercy on His
    afflicted.

¹⁴ But Zion said, "The LORD has
    forsaken me,
  And my Lord has forgotten me."

¹⁵ "Can a woman forget her nursing
    child,
  And not have compassion on the
    son of her womb?
  Surely they may forget,
  Yet I will not forget you.
¹⁶ See, I have inscribed you on the
    palms *of My hands;*
  Your walls *are* continually before
    Me.
¹⁷ Your sons shall make haste;
  Your destroyers and those who
    laid you waste
  Shall go away from you.

¹⁸ Lift up your eyes, look around and
    see;
  All these gather together *and*
    come to you.
  As I live," says the LORD,
  "You shall surely clothe yourselves
    with them all as an ornament,
  And bind them *on you* as a bride
    does.

¹⁹ "For your waste and desolate
    places,
  And the land of your destruction,
  Will even now be too small for the
    inhabitants;
  And those who swallowed you up
    will be far away.
²⁰ The children you will have,
  After you have lost the others,
  Will say again in your ears,
  'The place *is* too small for me;
  Give me a place where I may
    dwell.'
²¹ Then you will say in your heart,
  'Who has begotten these for me,
  Since I have lost my children and
    am desolate,
  A captive, and wandering to and
    fro?
  And who has brought these up?
  There I was, left alone;
  But these, where *were* they?' "

²² Thus says the Lord GOD:

"Behold, I will lift My hand in an
    oath to the nations,
  And set up My standard for the
    peoples;
  They shall bring your sons in *their*
    arms,
  And your daughters shall be
    carried on *their* shoulders;
²³ Kings shall be your foster fathers,
  And their queens your nursing
    mothers;
  They shall bow down to you with
    their faces to the earth,
  And lick up the dust of your feet.
  Then you will know that I *am* the
    LORD,
  For they shall not be ashamed
    who wait for Me."

Mother Hen

Hard work means nothing to a hen. Regardless of what business prognosticators say about the price of eggs, regardless of what others expect of her, regardless of fluctuations in the commodities market, she keeps on digging worms and laying eggs.

If the ground is hard, she scratches harder.

If it's dry, she digs deeper.

If it's wet, she digs where it is dry.

If she strikes a rock, she digs around it.

If she gets a few more hours of daylight in the barnyard, she digs a few more hours.

Have you ever seen a pessimistic hen?

Have you ever seen a hen cackle in disgust at the prospect of her job?

Did you ever hear one cluck because the work was hard, the conditions were poor, and some of her eggs were taken from her before they hatched?

No.

Hens save their breath for digging and their cackles for the eggs that are hatched!

²⁴ Shall the prey be taken from the mighty,
  Or the captives of the righteous be delivered?

²⁵ But thus says the LORD:

"Even the captives of the mighty
  shall be taken away,
And the prey of the terrible be delivered;
For I will contend with him who contends with you,
And I will save your children.
²⁶ I will feed those who oppress you
  with their own flesh,
And they shall be drunk with their own blood as with sweet wine.
All flesh shall know
That I, the LORD, *am* your Savior,
And your Redeemer, the Mighty One of Jacob."

50 Thus says the LORD:

"Where *is* the certificate of your mother's divorce,
Whom I have put away?
Or which of My creditors *is it* to whom I have sold you?
For your iniquities you have sold yourselves,
And for your transgressions your mother has been put away.
² Why, when I came, *was there* no man?
Why, when I called, *was there* none to answer?
Is My hand shortened at all that it cannot redeem?
Or have I no power to deliver?
Indeed with My rebuke I dry up the sea,
I make the rivers a wilderness;
Their fish stink because *there is* no water,
And die of thirst.
³ I clothe the heavens with blackness,
And I make sackcloth their covering."

⁴ "The Lord GOD has given Me
The tongue of the learned,
That I should know how to speak
A word in season to *him who is* weary.
He awakens Me morning by morning,
He awakens My ear
To hear as the learned.
⁵ The Lord GOD has opened My ear;
And I was not rebellious,
Nor did I turn away.
⁶ I gave My back to those who struck *Me,*
And My cheeks to those who plucked out the beard;
I did not hide My face from shame and spitting.

⁷ "For the Lord GOD will help Me;
Therefore I will not be disgraced;
Therefore I have set My face like a flint,
And I know that I will not be ashamed.
⁸ *He is* near who justifies Me;
Who will contend with Me?
Let us stand together.
Who *is* My adversary?
Let him come near Me.
⁹ Surely the Lord GOD will help Me;
Who *is* he *who* will condemn Me?
Indeed they will all grow old like a garment;
The moth will eat them up.

¹⁰ "Who among you fears the LORD?
Who obeys the voice of His Servant?
Who walks in darkness
And has no light?
Let him trust in the name of the LORD
And rely upon his God.
¹¹ Look, all you who kindle a fire,
Who encircle *yourselves* with sparks:
Walk in the light of your fire and in the sparks you have kindled—
This you shall have from My hand:
You shall lie down in torment.

～ PSALM 112:1–4 ～

1 Praise the LORD!

Blessed *is* the man *who* fears the
  LORD,
Who delights greatly in His
  commandments.

2 His descendants will be mighty on
  earth;
The generation of the upright will be
  blessed.
3 Wealth and riches *will be* in his
  house,
And his righteousness endures
  forever.
4 Unto the upright there arises light in
  the darkness;
He is gracious, and full of
  compassion, and righteous.

～ PROVERBS 26:13–15 ～

13 The lazy *man* says, "*There is* a lion in
  the road!
A fierce lion *is* in the streets!"
14 *As* a door turns on its hinges,
So *does* the lazy *man* on his bed.
15 The lazy *man* buries his hand in the
  bowl;
It wearies him to bring it back to his
  mouth.

～ EPHESIANS 1:1–23 ～

Paul, an apostle of Jesus Christ by the will
of God,

To the saints who are in Ephesus, and
faithful in Christ Jesus:

2 Grace to you and peace from God our
Father and the Lord Jesus Christ.
3 Blessed *be* the God and Father of our
Lord Jesus Christ, who has blessed us with
every spiritual blessing in the heavenly
places in Christ, 4 just as He chose us in
Him before the foundation of the world,
that we should be holy and without blame
before Him in love, 5 having predestined
us to adoption as sons by Jesus Christ to
Himself, according to the good pleasure
of His will, 6 to the praise of the glory of
His grace, by which He made us accepted
in the Beloved.
7 In Him we have redemption through
His blood, the forgiveness of sins, according to the riches of His grace 8 which He
made to abound toward us in all wisdom
and prudence, 9 having made known to
us the mystery of His will, according
to His good pleasure which He purposed
in Himself, 10 that in the dispensation of
the fullness of the times He might gather
together in one all things in Christ, both
which are in heaven and which are on
earth—in Him. 11 In Him also we have
obtained an inheritance, being predestined
according to the purpose of Him who
works all things according to the counsel
of His will, 12 that we who first trusted in
Christ should be to the praise of His glory.
13 In Him you also *trusted*, after you
heard the word of truth, the gospel of your
salvation; in whom also, having believed,
you were sealed with the Holy Spirit of
promise, 14 who is the guarantee of our
inheritance until the redemption of
the purchased possession, to the praise
of His glory.
15 Therefore I also, after I heard of your
faith in the Lord Jesus and your love for
all the saints, 16 do not cease to give thanks
for you, making mention of you in my
prayers: 17 that the God of our Lord Jesus
Christ, the Father of glory, may give to
you the spirit of wisdom and revelation
in the knowledge of Him, 18 the eyes of
your understanding being enlightened;
that you may know what is the hope of
His calling, what are the riches of the glory
of His inheritance in the saints, 19 and what
is the exceeding greatness of His power
toward us who believe, according to the
working of His mighty power 20 which He
worked in Christ when He raised Him
from the dead and seated *Him* at His right
hand in the heavenly *places,* 21 far above
all principality and power and might and
dominion, and every name that is named,
not only in this age but also in that which
is to come.
22 And He put all *things* under His feet,
and gave Him *to be* head over all *things*
to the church, 23 which is His body, the
fullness of Him who fills all in all.

~ ISAIAH 51:1—52:15 ~

1 "Listen to Me, you who follow
   after righteousness,
   You who seek the LORD:
   Look to the rock *from which* you
   were hewn,
   And to the hole of the pit *from
   which* you were dug.
2 Look to Abraham your father,
   And to Sarah *who* bore you;
   For I called him alone,
   And blessed him and increased
   him."

3 For the LORD will comfort Zion,
   He will comfort all her waste
   places;
   He will make her wilderness like
   Eden,
   And her desert like the garden of
   the LORD;
   Joy and gladness will be found in
   it,
   Thanksgiving and the voice of
   melody.

4 "Listen to Me, My people;
   And give ear to Me, O My nation:
   For law will proceed from Me,
   And I will make My justice rest
   As a light of the peoples.
5 My righteousness *is* near,
   My salvation has gone forth,
   And My arms will judge the
   peoples;
   The coastlands will wait upon Me,
   And on My arm they will trust.
6 Lift up your eyes to the heavens,
   And look on the earth beneath.
   For the heavens will vanish away
   like smoke,
   The earth will grow old like a
   garment,
   And those who dwell in it will die
   in like manner;
   But My salvation will be forever,
   And My righteousness will not be
   abolished.

7 "Listen to Me, you who know
   righteousness,
   You people in whose heart *is* My
   law:

Do not fear the reproach of men,
   Nor be afraid of their insults.
8 For the moth will eat them up like
   a garment,
   And the worm will eat them like
   wool;
   But My righteousness will be
   forever,
   And My salvation from generation
   to generation."

9 Awake, awake, put on strength,
   O arm of the LORD!
   Awake as in the ancient days,
   In the generations of old.
   Are You not *the arm* that cut
   Rahab apart,
   And wounded the serpent?

10 *Are* You not *the One* who dried up
   the sea,
   The waters of the great deep;
   That made the depths of the sea a
   road
   For the redeemed to cross over?
11 So the ransomed of the LORD shall
   return,
   And come to Zion with singing,
   With everlasting joy on their
   heads.
   They shall obtain joy and
   gladness;
   Sorrow and sighing shall flee
   away.

12 "I, *even* I, *am* He who comforts
   you.
   Who *are* you that you should be
   afraid
   Of a man *who* will die,
   And of the son of a man *who* will
   be made like grass?
13 And you forget the LORD your
   Maker,
   Who stretched out the heavens
   And laid the foundations of the
   earth;
   You have feared continually every
   day
   Because of the fury of the
   oppressor,
   When *he has* prepared to destroy.

Tea Party

In the mid-nineteenth century, tea cost about a dollar a pound, making it an expensive staple. George Hartford and George Gilman came up with a simple but revolutionary plan to lower the price. They bought tea directly from the ships in New York Harbor. Then, taking a low-percentage profit, they worked for high-volume sales. Their tactics worked. They soon turned their mail-order business into a chain of stores called the Great Atlantic and Pacific Tea Co. — A&P.

From the outset, even with a family of five children, Hartford generously gave thousands of dollars a year to charitable causes, ranging from the Pius X Mission in Skagway, Alaska, to the First Methodist Church in Urbana, Illinois. As his fortune increased, he established a foundation as a conduit for his giving. Hartford's desire was that his contributions benefit people such as those whose purchases at A&P stores had built his fortune. Later, he reorganized the foundation to receive his estate, so that by the time he died, bequests to individuals totaled $500,000, with $55 million going to the foundation, including $40 million in A&P stock. Thus, a portion of every dollar spent at an A&P store would eventually be donated.

In many ways, Hartford is still giving his fortune away!

And where *is* the fury of the oppressor?

14 The captive exile hastens, that he may be loosed,
That he should not die in the pit,
And that his bread should not fail.
15 But I *am* the LORD your God,
Who divided the sea whose waves roared—
The LORD of hosts *is* His name.
16 And I have put My words in your mouth;
I have covered you with the shadow of My hand,
That I may plant the heavens,
Lay the foundations of the earth,
And say to Zion, 'You *are* My people.' "

17 Awake, awake!
Stand up, O Jerusalem,
You who have drunk at the hand of the LORD
The cup of His fury;
You have drunk the dregs of the cup of trembling,
And drained *it* out.
18 *There is* no one to guide her
Among all the sons she has brought forth;
Nor *is there any* who takes her by the hand
Among all the sons she has brought up.
19 These two *things* have come to you;
Who will be sorry for you?—
Desolation and destruction,
famine and sword—
By whom will I comfort you?
20 Your sons have fainted,
They lie at the head of all the streets,
Like an antelope in a net;
They are full of the fury of the LORD,
The rebuke of your God.

21 Therefore please hear this, you afflicted,
And drunk but not with wine.
22 Thus says your Lord,
The LORD and your God,
Who pleads the cause of His people:

"See, I have taken out of your hand
The cup of trembling,
The dregs of the cup of My fury;
You shall no longer drink it.
23 But I will put it into the hand of those who afflict you,
Who have said to you,
'Lie down, that we may walk over you.'
And you have laid your body like the ground,
And as the street, for those who walk over."

52 Awake, awake!
Put on your strength, O Zion;
Put on your beautiful garments,
O Jerusalem, the holy city!
For the uncircumcised and the unclean
Shall no longer come to you.
2 Shake yourself from the dust, arise;
Sit down, O Jerusalem!
Loose yourself from the bonds of your neck,
O captive daughter of Zion!

3 For thus says the LORD:

"You have sold yourselves for nothing,
And you shall be redeemed without money."

4 For thus says the Lord GOD:

"My people went down at first
Into Egypt to dwell there;
Then the Assyrian oppressed them without cause.
5 Now therefore, what have I here," says the LORD,
"That My people are taken away for nothing?
Those who rule over them
Make them wail," says the LORD,
"And My name *is* blasphemed continually every day.
6 Therefore My people shall know My name;
Therefore *they shall know* in that day
That I *am* He who speaks:
'Behold, *it is* I.' "

7 How beautiful upon the
mountains
Are the feet of him who brings
good news,
Who proclaims peace,
Who brings glad tidings of good
things,
Who proclaims salvation,
Who says to Zion,
"Your God reigns!"

8 Your watchmen shall lift up *their*
voices,
With their voices they shall sing
together;
For they shall see eye to eye
When the LORD brings back Zion.

9 Break forth into joy, sing together,
You waste places of Jerusalem!
For the LORD has comforted His
people,
He has redeemed Jerusalem.

10 The LORD has made bare His holy
arm
In the eyes of all the nations;
And all the ends of the earth shall
see
The salvation of our God.

11 Depart! Depart! Go out from
there,
Touch no unclean *thing;*
Go out from the midst of her,
Be clean,
You who bear the vessels of the
LORD.

12 For you shall not go out with
haste,
Nor go by flight;
For the LORD will go before you,
And the God of Israel *will be* your
rear guard.

13 Behold, My Servant shall deal
prudently;
He shall be exalted and extolled
and be very high.

14 Just as many were astonished at
you,
So His visage was marred more
than any man,
And His form more than the sons
of men;

15 So shall He sprinkle many nations.
Kings shall shut their mouths at
Him;

For what had not been told them
they shall see,
And what they had not heard they
shall consider.

～ PSALM 112:5–10 ～

5 A good man deals graciously and
lends;
He will guide his affairs with
discretion.

6 Surely he will never be shaken;
The righteous will be in everlasting
remembrance.

7 He will not be afraid of evil tidings;
His heart is steadfast, trusting in the
LORD.

8 His heart *is* established;
He will not be afraid,
Until he sees *his desire* upon his
enemies.

9 He has dispersed abroad,
He has given to the poor;
His righteousness endures forever;
His horn will be exalted with honor.

10 The wicked will see *it* and be
grieved;
He will gnash his teeth and melt
away;
The desire of the wicked shall perish.

～ PROVERBS 26:16 ～

16 The lazy *man is* wiser in his own
eyes
Than seven men who can answer
sensibly.

～ EPHESIANS 2:1–22 ～

And you *He made alive,* who were dead
in trespasses and sins, ² in which you once
walked according to the course of this
world, according to the prince of the
power of the air, the spirit who now works
in the sons of disobedience, ³ among
whom also we all once conducted ourselves in the lusts of our flesh, fulfilling
the desires of the flesh and of the mind,
and were by nature children of wrath, just
as the others.

4 But God, who is rich in mercy, because of His great love with which He loved us, 5 even when we were dead in trespasses, made us alive together with Christ (by grace you have been saved), 6 and raised *us* up together, and made *us* sit together in the heavenly *places* in Christ Jesus, 7 that in the ages to come He might show the exceeding riches of His grace in *His* kindness toward us in Christ Jesus. 8 For by grace you have been saved through faith, and that not of yourselves; *it is* the gift of God, 9 not of works, lest anyone should boast. 10 For we are His workmanship, created in Christ Jesus for good works, which God prepared beforehand that we should walk in them.

11 Therefore remember that you, once Gentiles in the flesh—who are called Uncircumcision by what is called the Circumcision made in the flesh by hands— 12 that at that time you were without Christ, being aliens from the commonwealth of Israel and strangers from the covenants of promise, having no hope and without God in the world. 13 But now in Christ Jesus you who once were far off have been brought near by the blood of Christ.

14 For He Himself is our peace, who has made both one, and has broken down the middle wall of separation, 15 having abolished in His flesh the enmity, *that is,* the law of commandments *contained* in ordinances, so as to create in Himself one new man *from* the two, *thus* making peace, 16 and that He might reconcile them both to God in one body through the cross, thereby putting to death the enmity. 17 And He came and preached peace to you who were afar off and to those who were near. 18 For through Him we both have access by one Spirit to the Father.

19 Now, therefore, you are no longer strangers and foreigners, but fellow citizens with the saints and members of the household of God, 20 having been built on the foundation of the apostles and prophets, Jesus Christ Himself being the chief corner*stone,* 21 in whom the whole building, being fitted together, grows into a holy temple in the Lord, 22 in whom you also are being built together for a dwelling place of God in the Spirit.

READING 274 · OCTOBER 1

~ ISAIAH 53:1—54:17 ~

1 Who has believed our report?
And to whom has the arm of the LORD been revealed?
2 For He shall grow up before Him as a tender plant,
And as a root out of dry ground.
He has no form or comeliness;
And when we see Him,
There is no beauty that we should desire Him.
3 He is despised and rejected by men,
A Man of sorrows and acquainted with grief.
And we hid, as it were, *our* faces from Him;
He was despised, and we did not esteem Him.

4 Surely He has borne our griefs
And carried our sorrows;
Yet we esteemed Him stricken,
Smitten by God, and afflicted.
5 But He *was* wounded for our transgressions,
He was bruised for our iniquities;
The chastisement for our peace *was* upon Him,
And by His stripes we are healed.
6 All we like sheep have gone astray;
We have turned, every one, to his own way;
And the LORD has laid on Him the iniquity of us all.

7 He was oppressed and He was afflicted,
Yet He opened not His mouth;
He was led as a lamb to the slaughter,
And as a sheep before its shearers is silent,

Barbed Wire Fences

Tom has been angry most of his life. You can tell it from his conversation, his actions, and his words. When he first comes into a new group he is the jokester, the loudmouth, but then as you get to know him you find out that being the loudmouth is the only way he knows to communicate. While his manner of speaking is that of a joke, his words often cut like a knife.

> Like a madman shooting firebrands or deadly arrows is a man who deceives his neighbor and says, "I was only joking!"
>
> *Proverbs 26:18-19*

The puzzling thing about Tom is how lonely he is. He is constantly keeping himself from being close to anyone with his verbal barbs and fences, yet he longs for companionship and connection. That is why Tom is angry.

The sad thing is, Tom is like a lot of us. We protect ourselves to the point of hurting ourselves, and too often we hurt each other as well.

Tom needs people. He needs friends. But he pushes them away with his words and his demeanor. We are all Tom sometimes. But there is hope for us yet within God's grace.

So He opened not His mouth.
8 He was taken from prison and
      from judgment,
    And who will declare His
      generation?
    For He was cut off from the land
      of the living;
    For the transgressions of My
      people He was stricken.
9 And they made His grave with the
      wicked—
    But with the rich at His death,
    Because He had done no violence,
    Nor *was any* deceit in His mouth.

10 Yet it pleased the LORD to bruise
      Him;
    He has put *Him* to grief.
    When You make His soul an
      offering for sin,
    He shall see *His* seed, He shall
      prolong *His* days,
    And the pleasure of the LORD shall
      prosper in His hand.
11 He shall see the labor of His soul,
      and be satisfied.
    By His knowledge My righteous
      Servant shall justify many,
    For He shall bear their iniquities.
12 Therefore I will divide Him a
      portion with the great,
    And He shall divide the spoil with
      the strong,
    Because He poured out His soul
      unto death,
    And He was numbered with the
      transgressors,
    And He bore the sin of many,
    And made intercession for the
      transgressors.

54 "Sing, O barren,
    You *who* have not borne!
    Break forth into singing, and cry
      aloud,
    You *who* have not labored with
      child!
    For more *are* the children of the
      desolate
    Than the children of the married
      woman," says the LORD.
2 "Enlarge the place of your tent,
    And let them stretch out the
      curtains of your dwellings;
    Do not spare;

Lengthen your cords,
    And strengthen your stakes.
3 For you shall expand to the right
      and to the left,
    And your descendants will inherit
      the nations,
    And make the desolate cities
      inhabited.

4 "Do not fear, for you will not be
      ashamed;
    Neither be disgraced, for you will
      not be put to shame;
    For you will forget the shame of
      your youth,
    And will not remember the
      reproach of your widowhood
      anymore.
5 For your Maker *is* your husband,
    The LORD of hosts *is* His name;
    And your Redeemer *is* the Holy
      One of Israel;
    He is called the God of the whole
      earth.
6 For the LORD has called you
    Like a woman forsaken and
      grieved in spirit,
    Like a youthful wife when you
      were refused,"
    Says your God.
7 "For a mere moment I have
      forsaken you,
    But with great mercies I will
      gather you.
8 With a little wrath I hid My face
      from you for a moment;
    But with everlasting kindness I
      will have mercy on you,"
    Says the LORD, your Redeemer.

9 "For this *is* like the waters of Noah
      to Me;
    For as I have sworn
    That the waters of Noah would no
      longer cover the earth,
    So have I sworn
    That I would not be angry with
      you, nor rebuke you.
10 For the mountains shall depart
    And the hills be removed,
    But My kindness shall not depart
      from you,
    Nor shall My covenant of peace
      be removed,"

Says the LORD, who has mercy on you.

11 "O you afflicted one,
Tossed with tempest, *and* not comforted,
Behold, I will lay your stones with colorful gems,
And lay your foundations with sapphires.
12 I will make your pinnacles of rubies,
Your gates of crystal,
And all your walls of precious stones.
13 All your children *shall be* taught by the LORD,
And great *shall be* the peace of your children.
14 In righteousness you shall be established;
You shall be far from oppression, for you shall not fear;
And from terror, for it shall not come near you.
15 Indeed they shall surely assemble, *but* not because of Me.
Whoever assembles against you shall fall for your sake.

16 "Behold, I have created the blacksmith
Who blows the coals in the fire,
Who brings forth an instrument for his work;
And I have created the spoiler to destroy.
17 No weapon formed against you shall prosper,
And every tongue *which* rises against you in judgment
You shall condemn.
This *is* the heritage of the servants of the LORD,
And their righteousness *is* from Me,"
Says the LORD.

∼ PSALM 113:1–4 ∼

1 Praise the LORD!

Praise, O servants of the LORD,
Praise the name of the LORD!
2 Blessed be the name of the LORD

From this time forth and forevermore!
3 From the rising of the sun to its going down
The LORD's name *is* to be praised.

4 The LORD *is* high above all nations,
His glory above the heavens.

∼ PROVERBS 26:17–19 ∼

17 He who passes by *and* meddles in a quarrel not his own
Is like one who takes a dog by the ears.

18 Like a madman who throws firebrands, arrows, and death,
19 *Is* the man *who* deceives his neighbor,
And says, "I was only joking!"

∼ EPHESIANS 3:1–21 ∼

For this reason I, Paul, the prisoner of Christ Jesus for you Gentiles— 2 if indeed you have heard of the dispensation of the grace of God which was given to me for you, 3 how that by revelation He made known to me the mystery (as I have briefly written already, 4 by which, when you read, you may understand my knowledge in the mystery of Christ), 5 which in other ages was not made known to the sons of men, as it has now been revealed by the Spirit to His holy apostles and prophets: 6 that the Gentiles should be fellow heirs, of the same body, and partakers of His promise in Christ through the gospel, 7 of which I became a minister according to the gift of the grace of God given to me by the effective working of His power.

8 To me, who am less than the least of all the saints, this grace was given, that I should preach among the Gentiles the unsearchable riches of Christ, 9 and to make all see what *is* the fellowship of the mystery, which from the beginning of the ages has been hidden in God who created all things through Jesus Christ; 10 to the intent that now the manifold wisdom of God might be made known by the church to the principalities and powers in the heavenly *places,* 11 according to the eternal purpose which He accomplished

in Christ Jesus our Lord, [12] in whom we have boldness and access with confidence through faith in Him. [13] Therefore I ask that you do not lose heart at my tribulations for you, which is your glory.

[14] For this reason I bow my knees to the Father of our Lord Jesus Christ, [15] from whom the whole family in heaven and earth is named, [16] that He would grant you, according to the riches of His glory, to be strengthened with might through His Spirit in the inner man, [17] that Christ may dwell in your hearts through faith;

that you, being rooted and grounded in love, [18] may be able to comprehend with all the saints what *is* the width and length and depth and height— [19] to know the love of Christ which passes knowledge; that you may be filled with all the fullness of God.

[20] Now to Him who is able to do exceedingly abundantly above all that we ask or think, according to the power that works in us, [21] to Him *be* glory in the church by Christ Jesus to all generations, forever and ever. Amen.

READING 275 · OCTOBER 2

~ ISAIAH 55:1—56:12 ~

[1] "Ho! Everyone who thirsts,
  Come to the waters;
  And you who have no money,
  Come, buy and eat.
  Yes, come, buy wine and milk
  Without money and without price.
[2] Why do you spend money for
    what is not bread,
  And your wages for *what* does not
    satisfy?
  Listen carefully to Me, and eat
    what is good,
  And let your soul delight itself in
    abundance.
[3] Incline your ear, and come to Me.
  Hear, and your soul shall live;
  And I will make an everlasting
    covenant with you—
  The sure mercies of David.
[4] Indeed I have given him *as* a
    witness to the people,
  A leader and commander for the
    people.
[5] Surely you shall call a nation you
    do not know,
  And nations *who* do not know
    you shall run to you,
  Because of the LORD your God,
  And the Holy One of Israel;
  For He has glorified you."

[6] Seek the LORD while He may be
    found,
  Call upon Him while He is near.
[7] Let the wicked forsake his way,

And the unrighteous man his
    thoughts;
  Let him return to the LORD,
  And He will have mercy on him;
  And to our God,
  For He will abundantly pardon.

[8] "For My thoughts *are* not your
    thoughts,
  Nor *are* your ways My ways," says
    the LORD.
[9] "For *as* the heavens are higher than
    the earth,
  So are My ways higher than your
    ways,
  And My thoughts than your
    thoughts.

[10] "For as the rain comes down, and
    the snow from heaven,
  And do not return there,
  But water the earth,
  And make it bring forth and bud,
  That it may give seed to the sower
  And bread to the eater,
[11] So shall My word be that goes
    forth from My mouth;
  It shall not return to Me void,
  But it shall accomplish what I
    please,
  And it shall prosper *in the thing*
    for which I sent it.

[12] "For you shall go out with joy,
  And be led out with peace;

Forgive and Forget

A man once had too much to drink at a party. First, he made a foolish spectacle of himself — even to the point of wearing the proverbial lampshade as a hat — and then he passed out. Friends helped his wife take him home and put him to bed. The next morning he was very remorseful and asked his wife to forgive him. She agreed to "forgive and forget" the incident.

As the months went by, however, the wife referred to the incident from time to time, always with a hint of ridicule and shame in her voice. Finally, the man grew weary of being reminded of his bad behavior and said, "I thought you were going to forgive and forget."

"I have forgiven and forgotten," the wife argued, "but I just don't want you to forget that I have forgiven and forgotten."

Once we have confronted an offender, we must remember nothing is gained from harboring unforgiveness in our hearts. True forgiveness releases a healing process inside us — to the point where eventually, the memory of what the other person did or said to injure us no longer causes pain.

We have "forgotten" when we no longer hurt! When you make a commitment to forgive another person, ask the Lord to heal you of the impact of that person's behavior on your life. Forgive, forget, and go on living in peace.

> And be kind to one another, tenderhearted, forgiving one another, even as God in Christ forgave you.
>
> *Ephesians 4:32*

The mountains and the hills
Shall break forth into singing
  before you,
And all the trees of the field shall
  clap *their* hands.
¹³ Instead of the thorn shall come up
  the cypress tree,
And instead of the brier shall
  come up the myrtle tree;
And it shall be to the LORD for a
  name,
For an everlasting sign *that* shall
  not be cut off."

56 Thus says the LORD:

"Keep justice, and do righteousness,
For My salvation *is* about to
  come,
And My righteousness to be
  revealed.
² Blessed *is* the man *who* does this,
And the son of man *who* lays hold
  on it;
Who keeps from defiling the
  Sabbath,
And keeps his hand from doing
  any evil."

³ Do not let the son of the foreigner
Who has joined himself to the
  LORD
Speak, saying,
"The LORD has utterly separated
  me from His people";
Nor let the eunuch say,
"Here I am, a dry tree."
⁴ For thus says the LORD:
"To the eunuchs who keep My
  Sabbaths,
And choose what pleases Me,
And hold fast My covenant,
⁵ Even to them I will give in My
  house
And within My walls a place and a
  name
Better than that of sons and
  daughters;
I will give them an everlasting
  name
That shall not be cut off.

⁶ "Also the sons of the foreigner
Who join themselves to the LORD,
  to serve Him,

And to love the name of the
  LORD, to be His servants—
Everyone who keeps from defiling
  the Sabbath,
And holds fast My covenant—
⁷ Even them I will bring to My holy
  mountain,
And make them joyful in My
  house of prayer.
Their burnt offerings and their
  sacrifices
Will be accepted on My altar;
For My house shall be called a
  house of prayer for all nations."
⁸ The Lord GOD, who gathers the
  outcasts of Israel, says,
"Yet I will gather to him
Others besides those who are
  gathered to him."

⁹ All you beasts of the field, come to
  devour,
All you beasts in the forest.
¹⁰ His watchmen *are* blind,
They are all ignorant;
They *are* all dumb dogs,
They cannot bark;
Sleeping, lying down, loving to
  slumber.
¹¹ Yes, *they are* greedy dogs
Which never have enough.
And they *are* shepherds
Who cannot understand;
They all look to their own way,
Every one for his own gain,
From his *own* territory.
¹² "Come," one says, "I will bring
  wine,
And we will fill ourselves with
  intoxicating drink;
Tomorrow will be as today,
And much more abundant."

~ PSALM 113:5–9 ~

⁵ Who *is* like the LORD our God,
Who dwells on high,
⁶ Who humbles Himself to behold
The things that are in the heavens
  and in the earth?

⁷ He raises the poor out of the dust,
And lifts the needy out of the ash
  heap,

8 That He may seat *him* with
    princes—
  With the princes of His people.
9 He grants the barren woman a
    home,
  Like a joyful mother of children.

  Praise the LORD!

∼ PROVERBS 26:20, 21 ∼

20 Where *there is* no wood, the fire
     goes out;
   And where *there is* no talebearer,
     strife ceases.
21 As charcoal *is* to burning coals, and
     wood to fire,
   So *is* a contentious man to kindle
     strife.

∼ EPHESIANS 4:1-32 ∼

I, therefore, the prisoner of the Lord, beseech you to walk worthy of the calling
with which you were called, 2 with all lowliness and gentleness, with longsuffering,
bearing with one another in love, 3 en-
deavoring to keep the unity of the Spirit
in the bond of peace. 4 *There is* one body
and one Spirit, just as you were called in
one hope of your calling; 5 one Lord, one
faith, one baptism; 6 one God and Father
of all, who *is* above all, and through all,
and in you all.

7 But to each one of us grace was given
according to the measure of Christ's gift.
8 Therefore He says:

  "When He ascended on high,
   He led captivity captive,
   And gave gifts to men."

9 (Now this, "He ascended"—what does
it mean but that He also first descended
into the lower parts of the earth? 10 He
who descended is also the One who ascended far above all the heavens, that He
might fill all things.)
11 And He Himself gave some *to be*
apostles, some prophets, some evangelists,
and some pastors and teachers, 12 for the
equipping of the saints for the work of
ministry, for the edifying of the body
of Christ, 13 till we all come to the unity

of the faith and of the knowledge of the
Son of God, to a perfect man, to the measure of the stature of the fullness of Christ;
14 that we should no longer be children,
tossed to and fro and carried about with
every wind of doctrine, by the trickery of
men, in the cunning craftiness of deceitful plotting, 15 but, speaking the truth in
love, may grow up in all things into Him
who is the head—Christ— 16 from whom
the whole body, joined and knit together
by what every joint supplies, according
to the effective working by which every
part does its share, causes growth of the
body for the edifying of itself in love.

17 This I say, therefore, and testify in the
Lord, that you should no longer walk as
the rest of the Gentiles walk, in the futility of their mind, 18 having their understanding darkened, being alienated from
the life of God, because of the ignorance
that is in them, because of the blindness
of their heart; 19 who, being past feeling,
have given themselves over to lewdness,
to work all uncleanness with greediness.

20 But you have not so learned Christ,
21 if indeed you have heard Him and have
been taught by Him, as the truth is in
Jesus: 22 that you put off, concerning your
former conduct, the old man which grows
corrupt according to the deceitful lusts,
23 and be renewed in the spirit of your
mind, 24 and that you put on the new man
which was created according to God, in
true righteousness and holiness.

25 Therefore, putting away lying, "*Let
each one of you* speak truth with his neighbor," for we are members of one another.
26 "Be angry, and do not sin": do not let
the sun go down on your wrath, 27 nor
give place to the devil. 28 Let him who stole
steal no longer, but rather let him labor,
working with *his* hands what is good, that
he may have something to give him who
has need. 29 Let no corrupt word proceed
out of your mouth, but what is good for
necessary edification, that it may impart
grace to the hearers. 30 And do not grieve
the Holy Spirit of God, by whom you
were sealed for the day of redemption.
31 Let all bitterness, wrath, anger, clamor,
and evil speaking be put away from you,
with all malice. 32 And be kind to one
another, tenderhearted, forgiving one another, even as God in Christ forgave you.

～ ISAIAH 57:1—58:14 ～

1 The righteous perishes,
 And no man takes *it* to heart;
 Merciful men *are* taken away,
 While no one considers
 That the righteous is taken away
  from evil.
2 He shall enter into peace;
 They shall rest in their beds,
 Each one walking *in* his
  uprightness.

3 "But come here,
 You sons of the sorceress,
 You offspring of the adulterer and
  the harlot!
4 Whom do you ridicule?
 Against whom do you make a
  wide mouth
 And stick out the tongue?
 Are you not children of
  transgression,
 Offspring of falsehood,
5 Inflaming yourselves with gods
  under every green tree,
 Slaying the children in the valleys,
 Under the clefts of the rocks?
6 Among the smooth *stones* of the
  stream
 Is your portion;
 They, they, *are* your lot!
 Even to them you have poured a
  drink offering,
 You have offered a grain offering.
 Should I receive comfort in these?

7 "On a lofty and high mountain
 You have set your bed;
 Even there you went up
 To offer sacrifice.
8 Also behind the doors and their
  posts
 You have set up your
  remembrance;
 For you have uncovered yourself
  to those other than Me,
 And have gone up to them;
 You have enlarged your bed
 And made *a covenant* with them;
 You have loved their bed,
 Where you saw *their* nudity.
9 You went to the king with
  ointment,

 And increased your perfumes;
 You sent your messengers far off,
 And *even* descended to Sheol.
10 You are wearied in the length of
  your way;
 Yet you did not say, 'There is no
  hope.'
 You have found the life of your
  hand;
 Therefore you were not grieved.

11 "And of whom have you been
  afraid, or feared,
 That you have lied
 And not remembered Me,
 Nor taken *it* to your heart?
 Is it not because I have held My
  peace from of old
 That you do not fear Me?
12 I will declare your righteousness
 And your works,
 For they will not profit you.
13 When you cry out,
 Let your collection *of idols* deliver
  you.
 But the wind will carry them all
  away,
 A breath will take *them*.
 But he who puts his trust in Me
  shall possess the land,
 And shall inherit My holy
  mountain."

14 And one shall say,
 "Heap it up! Heap it up!
 Prepare the way,
 Take the stumbling block out of
  the way of My people."

15 For thus says the High and Lofty
  One
 Who inhabits eternity, whose
  name *is* Holy:
 "I dwell in the high and holy *place*,
 With him *who* has a contrite and
  humble spirit,
 To revive the spirit of the humble,
 And to revive the heart of the
  contrite ones.
16 For I will not contend forever,
 Nor will I always be angry;

A Matter of Perspective

Mary Smith went to church one Sunday morning and winced when she heard the organist play a wrong note during the processional. She noticed a teenager talking during the opening prayer. She also couldn't help but notice that the altar bouquets were looking wilted. She felt the usher passing the offering plate was scrutinizing what every person put in, which made her angry. To top it all off, the preacher made at least five grammatical errors in his sermon. After the closing hymn, as she left the church through the side door she thought, *What a careless group of people*!

Amy Jones went to church one Sunday morning and was thrilled by the arrangement of "A Mighty Fortress" that was performed. Her heart was touched at hearing a teenager read the morning Scripture lesson. She was delighted to see the church take up an offering to help hungry children in Nigeria. In addition, the preacher's sermon answered a question that had been bothering her for some time. During the recessional, she felt radiant joy from the choir members. She left the church thinking, *What a wonderful place to worship God*!

Mary and Amy went to the same church, on the same Sunday morning. Which service would you have attended?

For the spirit would fail before
Me,
And the souls *which* I have made.
17 For the iniquity of his
covetousness
I was angry and struck him;
I hid and was angry,
And he went on backsliding in the
way of his heart.
18 I have seen his ways, and will heal
him;
I will also lead him,
And restore comforts to him
And to his mourners.

19 "I create the fruit of the lips:
Peace, peace to *him who is* far off
and to *him who is* near,"
Says the LORD,
"And I will heal him."
20 But the wicked *are* like the
troubled sea,
When it cannot rest,
Whose waters cast up mire and
dirt.

21 "*There is* no peace,"
Says my God, "for the wicked."

58 "Cry aloud, spare not;
Lift up your voice like a trumpet;
Tell My people their transgression,
And the house of Jacob their sins.
2 Yet they seek Me daily,
And delight to know My ways,
As a nation that did righteousness,
And did not forsake the ordinance
of their God.
They ask of Me the ordinances of
justice;
They take delight in approaching
God.
3 'Why have we fasted,' *they say,*
'and You have not seen?
Why have we afflicted our souls,
and You take no notice?'

"In fact, in the day of your fast you
find pleasure,
And exploit all your laborers.
4 Indeed you fast for strife and
debate,
And to strike with the fist of
wickedness.

You will not fast as *you do* this
day,
To make your voice heard on
high.
5 Is it a fast that I have chosen,
A day for a man to afflict his soul?
Is it to bow down his head like a
bulrush,
And to spread out sackcloth and
ashes?
Would you call this a fast,
And an acceptable day to the
LORD?

6 "*Is* this not the fast that I have
chosen:
To loose the bonds of wickedness,
To undo the heavy burdens,
To let the oppressed go free,
And that you break every yoke?
7 *Is it* not to share your bread with
the hungry,
And that you bring to your house
the poor who are cast out;
When you see the naked, that you
cover him,
And not hide yourself from your
own flesh?
8 Then your light shall break forth
like the morning,
Your healing shall spring forth
speedily,
And your righteousness shall go
before you;
The glory of the LORD shall be
your rear guard.
9 Then you shall call, and the LORD
will answer;
You shall cry, and He will say,
'Here I *am*.'

"If you take away the yoke from
your midst,
The pointing of the finger, and
speaking wickedness,
10 *If* you extend your soul to the
hungry
And satisfy the afflicted soul,
Then your light shall dawn in the
darkness,
And your darkness shall *be* as the
noonday.
11 The LORD will guide you
continually,
And satisfy your soul in drought,

And strengthen your bones;
You shall be like a watered garden,
And like a spring of water, whose
   waters do not fail.
12 Those from among you
Shall build the old waste places;
You shall raise up the foundations
   of many generations;
And you shall be called the
   Repairer of the Breach,
The Restorer of Streets to Dwell
   In.

13 "If you turn away your foot from
   the Sabbath,
From doing your pleasure on My
   holy day,
And call the Sabbath a delight,
The holy *day* of the LORD
   honorable,
And shall honor Him, not doing
   your own ways,
Nor finding your own pleasure,
Nor speaking *your own* words,
14 Then you shall delight yourself in
   the LORD;
And I will cause you to ride on the
   high hills of the earth,
And feed you with the heritage of
   Jacob your father.
The mouth of the LORD has
   spoken."

∾ PSALM 114:1–8 ∾

1 When Israel went out of Egypt,
The house of Jacob from a people of
   strange language,
2 Judah became His sanctuary,
And Israel His dominion.

3 The sea saw *it* and fled;
Jordan turned back.
4 The mountains skipped like rams,
The little hills like lambs.
5 What ails you, O sea, that you fled?
O Jordan, *that* you turned back?
6 O mountains, *that* you skipped like
   rams?
O little hills, like lambs?

7 Tremble, O earth, at the presence of
   the Lord,

At the presence of the God of Jacob,
8 Who turned the rock *into* a pool of
   water,
The flint into a fountain of waters.

∾ PROVERBS 26:22 ∾

22 The words of a talebearer *are* like
   tasty trifles,
And they go down into the inmost
   body.

∾ EPHESIANS 5:1–16 ∾

Therefore be imitators of God as dear children. 2 And walk in love, as Christ also has loved us and given Himself for us, an offering and a sacrifice to God for a sweet-smelling aroma.

3 But fornication and all uncleanness or covetousness, let it not even be named among you, as is fitting for saints; 4 neither filthiness, nor foolish talking, nor coarse jesting, which are not fitting, but rather giving of thanks. 5 For this you know, that no fornicator, unclean person, nor covetous man, who is an idolater, has any inheritance in the kingdom of Christ and God. 6 Let no one deceive you with empty words, for because of these things the wrath of God comes upon the sons of disobedience. 7 Therefore do not be partakers with them.

8 For you were once darkness, but now *you are* light in the Lord. Walk as children of light 9(for the fruit of the Spirit *is* in all goodness, righteousness, and truth), 10 finding out what is acceptable to the Lord. 11 And have no fellowship with the unfruitful works of darkness, but rather expose *them*. 12 For it is shameful even to speak of those things which are done by them in secret. 13 But all things that are exposed are made manifest by the light, for whatever makes manifest is light. 14 Therefore He says:

   "Awake, you who sleep,
     Arise from the dead,
     And Christ will give you light."

15 See then that you walk circumspectly, not as fools but as wise, 16 redeeming the time, because the days are evil.

~ ISAIAH 59:1—60:22 ~

1 Behold, the LORD's hand is not
     shortened,
   That it cannot save;
   Nor His ear heavy,
   That it cannot hear.
2 But your iniquities have separated
     you from your God;
   And your sins have hidden *His*
     face from you,
   So that He will not hear.
3 For your hands are defiled with
     blood,
   And your fingers with iniquity;
   Your lips have spoken lies,
   Your tongue has muttered
     perversity.

4 No one calls for justice,
   Nor does *any* plead for truth.
   They trust in empty words and
     speak lies;
   They conceive evil and bring forth
     iniquity.
5 They hatch vipers' eggs and weave
     the spider's web;
   He who eats of their eggs dies,
   And *from* that which is crushed a
     viper breaks out.

6 Their webs will not become
     garments,
   Nor will they cover themselves
     with their works;
   Their works *are* works of iniquity,
   And the act of violence *is* in their
     hands.
7 Their feet run to evil,
   And they make haste to shed
     innocent blood;
   Their thoughts *are* thoughts of
     iniquity;
   Wasting and destruction *are* in
     their paths.
8 The way of peace they have not
     known,
   And *there is* no justice in their
     ways;
   They have made themselves
     crooked paths;
   Whoever takes that way shall not
     know peace.

9 Therefore justice is far from us,
   Nor does righteousness overtake
     us;
   We look for light, but there is
     darkness!
   For brightness, *but* we walk in
     blackness!
10 We grope for the wall like the
     blind,
   And we grope as if *we had* no
     eyes;
   We stumble at noonday as at
     twilight;
   We are as dead *men* in desolate
     places.
11 We all growl like bears,
   And moan sadly like doves;
   We look for justice, but *there is*
     none;
   For salvation, *but* it is far from us.
12 For our transgressions are
     multiplied before You,
   And our sins testify against us;
   For our transgressions *are* with us,
   And *as for* our iniquities, we know
     them:
13 In transgressing and lying against
     the LORD,
   And departing from our God,
   Speaking oppression and revolt,
   Conceiving and uttering from the
     heart words of falsehood.
14 Justice is turned back,
   And righteousness stands afar off;
   For truth is fallen in the street,
   And equity cannot enter.
15 So truth fails,
   And he *who* departs from evil
     makes himself a prey.

   Then the LORD saw *it*, and it
     displeased Him
   That *there was* no justice.
16 He saw that *there was* no man,
   And wondered that *there was* no
     intercessor;
   Therefore His own arm brought
     salvation for Him;
   And His own righteousness, it
     sustained Him.
17 For He put on righteousness as a
     breastplate,

Digging Ditches

Richard Foster has written: "I had come to Kotzebue on the adventure of helping to 'build the first high school above the Arctic Circle,' but the work itself was far from an adventure. It was hard, backbreaking labor.

"One day I was trying to dig a trench for a sewer line — no small task in a world of frozen tundra. An Eskimo man whose face and hands displayed the leathery toughness of many winters came by and watched me for a while. Finally he said simply and profoundly, 'You are digging a ditch to the glory of God.'

"He said it to encourage me, I know. And I have never forgotten his words. Beyond my Eskimo friend no human being ever knew or cared whether I dug that ditch well or poorly. In time it was to be covered up and forgotten. But because of my friend's words, I dug with all my might, for every shovelful of dirt was a prayer to God.

"Even though I did not know it at the time, I was attempting in my small and unsophisticated way to do what the great artisans of the Middle Ages did when they carved the back of a piece of art, knowing that God alone would see it."

When life gets tough and all our hard work seems to be for naught, our tendency is to ask the Lord to change our circumstances. Perhaps we should ask Him to change our outlook instead.

And a helmet of salvation on His
  head;
He put on the garments of
  vengeance for clothing,
And was clad with zeal as a cloak.
18 According to *their* deeds,
  accordingly He will repay,
Fury to His adversaries,
Recompense to His enemies;
The coastlands He will fully repay.
19 So shall they fear
The name of the LORD from the
  west,
And His glory from the rising of
  the sun;
When the enemy comes in like a
  flood,
The Spirit of the LORD will lift up
  a standard against him.

20 "The Redeemer will come to Zion,
And to those who turn from
  transgression in Jacob,"
Says the LORD.

21 "As for Me," says the LORD, "this *is*
My covenant with them: My Spirit who
is upon you, and My words which I have
put in your mouth, shall not depart from
your mouth, nor from the mouth of your
descendants, nor from the mouth of your
descendants' descendants," says the LORD,
"from this time and forevermore."

60 Arise, shine;
  For your light has come!
  And the glory of the LORD is risen
    upon you.
2 For behold, the darkness shall
    cover the earth,
  And deep darkness the people;
  But the LORD will arise over you,
  And His glory will be seen upon
    you.
3 The Gentiles shall come to your
    light,
  And kings to the brightness of
    your rising.

4 "Lift up your eyes all around, and
    see:
  They all gather together, they
    come to you;
  Your sons shall come from afar,

And your daughters shall be
  nursed at *your* side.
5 Then you shall see and become
  radiant,
And your heart shall swell with
  joy;
Because the abundance of the sea
  shall be turned to you,
The wealth of the Gentiles shall
  come to you.
6 The multitude of camels shall
  cover your *land*,
The dromedaries of Midian and
  Ephah;
All those from Sheba shall come;
They shall bring gold and incense,
And they shall proclaim the
  praises of the LORD.
7 All the flocks of Kedar shall be
  gathered together to you,
The rams of Nebaioth shall
  minister to you;
They shall ascend with acceptance
  on My altar,
And I will glorify the house of My
  glory.

8 "Who *are* these *who* fly like a
  cloud,
And like doves to their roosts?
9 Surely the coastlands shall wait for
  Me;
And the ships of Tarshish *will*
  come first,
To bring your sons from afar,
Their silver and their gold with
  them,
To the name of the LORD your
  God,
And to the Holy One of Israel,
Because He has glorified you.
10 "The sons of foreigners shall build
  up your walls,
And their kings shall minister to
  you;
For in My wrath I struck you,
But in My favor I have had mercy
  on you.
11 Therefore your gates shall be open
  continually;
They shall not be shut day or
  night,
That *men* may bring to you the
  wealth of the Gentiles,

And their kings in procession.

12 For the nation and kingdom
which will not serve you shall
perish,
And *those* nations shall be utterly
ruined.

13 "The glory of Lebanon shall come
to you,
The cypress, the pine, and the box
tree together,
To beautify the place of My
sanctuary;
And I will make the place of My
feet glorious.

14 Also the sons of those who
afflicted you
Shall come bowing to you,
And all those who despised you
shall fall prostrate at the soles of
your feet;
And they shall call you The City
of the LORD,
Zion of the Holy One of Israel.

15 "Whereas you have been forsaken
and hated,
So that no one went through *you,*
I will make you an eternal
excellence,
A joy of many generations.

16 You shall drink the milk of the
Gentiles,
And milk the breast of kings;
You shall know that I, the LORD,
am your Savior
And your Redeemer, the Mighty
One of Jacob.

17 "Instead of bronze I will bring gold,
Instead of iron I will bring silver,
Instead of wood, bronze,
And instead of stones, iron.
I will also make your officers
peace,
And your magistrates
righteousness.

18 Violence shall no longer be heard
in your land,
Neither wasting nor destruction
within your borders;
But you shall call your walls
Salvation,
And your gates Praise.

19 "The sun shall no longer be your
light by day,
Nor for brightness shall the moon
give light to you;
But the LORD will be to you an
everlasting light,
And your God your glory.

20 Your sun shall no longer go down,
Nor shall your moon withdraw
itself;
For the LORD will be your
everlasting light,
And the days of your mourning
shall be ended.

21 Also your people *shall* all *be*
righteous;
They shall inherit the land forever,
The branch of My planting,
The work of My hands,
That I may be glorified.

22 A little one shall become a
thousand,
And a small one a strong nation.
I, the LORD, will hasten it in its
time."

∼ PSALM 115:1–8 ∼

1   Not unto us, O LORD, not unto us,
But to Your name give glory,
Because of Your mercy,
Because of Your truth.
2   Why should the Gentiles say,
"So where *is* their God?"

3   But our God *is* in heaven;
He does whatever He pleases.
4   Their idols *are* silver and gold,
The work of men's hands.
5   They have mouths, but they do not
speak;
Eyes they have, but they do not see;
6   They have ears, but they do not
hear;
Noses they have, but they do not
smell;
7   They have hands, but they do not
handle;
Feet they have, but they do not
walk;
Nor do they mutter through their
throat.
8   Those who make them are like
them;
So is everyone who trusts in them.

~ PROVERBS 26:23 ~

²³ Fervent lips with a wicked heart
   Are like earthenware covered with
   silver dross.

~ EPHESIANS 5:17–33 ~

Therefore do not be unwise, but understand what the will of the Lord *is*. ¹⁸ And do not be drunk with wine, in which is dissipation; but be filled with the Spirit, ¹⁹ speaking to one another in psalms and hymns and spiritual songs, singing and making melody in your heart to the Lord, ²⁰ giving thanks always for all things to God the Father in the name of our Lord Jesus Christ, ²¹ submitting to one another in the fear of God.

²² Wives, submit to your own husbands, as to the Lord. ²³ For the husband is head of the wife, as also Christ is head of the church; and He is the Savior of the body. ²⁴ Therefore, just as the church is subject to Christ, so *let* the wives *be* to their own husbands in everything.

²⁵ Husbands, love your wives, just as Christ also loved the church and gave Himself for her, ²⁶ that He might sanctify and cleanse her with the washing of water by the word, ²⁷ that He might present her to Himself a glorious church, not having spot or wrinkle or any such thing, but that she should be holy and without blemish. ²⁸ So husbands ought to love their own wives as their own bodies; he who loves his wife loves himself. ²⁹ For no one ever hated his own flesh, but nourishes and cherishes it, just as the Lord *does* the church. ³⁰ For we are members of His body, of His flesh and of His bones. ³¹ "For this reason a man shall leave his father and mother and be joined to his wife, and the two shall become one flesh." ³² This is a great mystery, but I speak concerning Christ and the church. ³³ Nevertheless let each one of you in particular so love his own wife as himself, and let the wife *see* that she respects *her* husband.

READING 278 · OCTOBER 5

~ ISAIAH 61:1—62:12 ~

¹ "The Spirit of the Lord GOD *is*
      upon Me,
   Because the LORD has anointed
      Me
   To preach good tidings to the
      poor;
   He has sent Me to heal the
      brokenhearted,
   To proclaim liberty to the captives,
   And the opening of the prison to
      those who are bound;
² To proclaim the acceptable year of
      the LORD,
   And the day of vengeance of our
      God;
   To comfort all who mourn,
³ To console those who mourn in
      Zion,
   To give them beauty for ashes,
   The oil of joy for mourning,
   The garment of praise for the
      spirit of heaviness;
   That they may be called trees of
      righteousness,

   The planting of the LORD, that He
      may be glorified."

⁴ And they shall rebuild the old
      ruins,
   They shall raise up the former
      desolations,
   And they shall repair the ruined
      cities,
   The desolations of many
      generations.
⁵ Strangers shall stand and feed your
      flocks,
   And the sons of the foreigner
   Shall be your plowmen and your
      vinedressers.
⁶ But you shall be named the priests
      of the LORD,
   They shall call you the servants of
      our God.
   You shall eat the riches of the
      Gentiles,
   And in their glory you shall boast.

Be Strong and Courageous

Napoleon called Marshall Ney the bravest man he had ever known. Yet Ney's knees trembled so badly one morning before a battle, he had difficulty mounting his horse. When he was finally in the saddle, he shouted contemptuously down at his limbs, "Shake away, knees. You would shake worse than that if you knew where I am going to take you."

Courage is not a matter of not being afraid. It is a matter of taking action even when you are afraid!

Courage is more than sheer bravado — shouting, "I can do this!" and launching out with a do-or-die attitude over some reckless dare.

True courage is manifest when a person chooses to take a difficult or even dangerous course of action, simply because it is the right thing to do. Courage is looking beyond yourself to what is best for another.

The source of all courage is the Holy Spirit, our Comforter. It is His very nature to remain at our side, helping us. When we welcome Him into our lives and He compels us to do something, we can confidently trust He will be right there helping us accomplish whatever task He has called us to.

> Therefore take up the whole armor of God, that you may be able to withstand in the evil day, and having done all, to stand. Stand therefore, having girded your waist with truth, having put on the breastplate of righteousness.
>
> *Ephesians 6:13-14*

7 Instead of your shame *you shall
       have* double *honor*,
   And *instead of* confusion they
       shall rejoice in their portion.
   Therefore in their land they shall
       possess double;
   Everlasting joy shall be theirs.

8 "For I, the LORD, love justice;
   I hate robbery for burnt offering;
   I will direct their work in truth,
   And will make with them an
       everlasting covenant.
9 Their descendants shall be known
       among the Gentiles,
   And their offspring among the
       people.
   All who see them shall
       acknowledge them,
   That they *are* the posterity *whom*
       the LORD has blessed."

10 I will greatly rejoice in the LORD,
   My soul shall be joyful in my God;
   For He has clothed me with the
       garments of salvation,
   He has covered me with the robe
       of righteousness,
   As a bridegroom decks *himself*
       with ornaments,
   And as a bride adorns *herself* with
       her jewels.
11 For as the earth brings forth its
       bud,
   As the garden causes the things
       that are sown in it to spring
       forth,
   So the Lord GOD will cause
       righteousness and praise to
       spring forth before all the
       nations.

62 For Zion's sake I will not hold
       My peace,
   And for Jerusalem's sake I will not
       rest,
   Until her righteousness goes forth
       as brightness,
   And her salvation as a lamp *that*
       burns.
2 The Gentiles shall see your
       righteousness,
   And all kings your glory.
   You shall be called by a new name,

Which the mouth of the LORD
    will name.
3 You shall also be a crown of glory
   In the hand of the LORD,
   And a royal diadem
   In the hand of your God.
4 You shall no longer be termed
       Forsaken,
   Nor shall your land any more be
       termed Desolate;
   But you shall be called Hephzibah,
       and your land Beulah;
   For the LORD delights in you,
   And your land shall be married.
5 For *as* a young man marries a
       virgin,
   So shall your sons marry you;
   And *as* the bridegroom rejoices
       over the bride,
   So shall your God rejoice over you.

6 I have set watchmen on your
       walls, O Jerusalem;
   They shall never hold their peace
       day or night.
   You who make mention of the
       LORD, do not keep silent,
7 And give Him no rest till He
       establishes
   And till He makes Jerusalem a
       praise in the earth.

8 The LORD has sworn by His right
       hand
   And by the arm of His strength:
   "Surely I will no longer give your
       grain
   As food for your enemies;
   And the sons of the foreigner shall
       not drink your new wine,
   For which you have labored.
9 But those who have gathered it
       shall eat it,
   And praise the LORD;
   Those who have brought it
       together shall drink it in My
       holy courts."

10 Go through,
   Go through the gates!
   Prepare the way for the people;
   Build up,
   Build up the highway!
   Take out the stones,
   Lift up a banner for the peoples!

¹¹ Indeed the LORD has proclaimed
   To the end of the world:
   "Say to the daughter of Zion,
   'Surely your salvation is coming;
   Behold, His reward *is* with Him,
   And His work before Him.' "
¹² And they shall call them The Holy
   People,
   The Redeemed of the LORD;
   And you shall be called Sought
   Out,
   A City Not Forsaken.

～ PSALM 115:9–13 ～

⁹ O Israel, trust in the LORD;
   He *is* their help and their shield.
¹⁰ O house of Aaron, trust in the
   LORD;
   He *is* their help and their shield.
¹¹ You who fear the LORD, trust in the
   LORD;
   He *is* their help and their shield.

¹² The LORD has been mindful of *us;*
   He will bless us;
   He will bless the house of Israel;
   He will bless the house of Aaron.
¹³ He will bless those who fear the
   LORD,
   Both small and great.

～ PROVERBS 26:24–26 ～

²⁴ He who hates, disguises *it* with his
   lips,
   And lays up deceit within himself;
²⁵ When he speaks kindly, do not
   believe him,
   For *there are* seven abominations in
   his heart;
²⁶ *Though his* hatred is covered by
   deceit,
   His wickedness will be revealed
   before the assembly.

～ EPHESIANS 6:1–24 ～

Children, obey your parents in the Lord,
for this is right. ² "Honor your father and
mother," which is the first commandment
with promise: ³ "that it may be well with
you and you may live long on the earth."

⁴ And you, fathers, do not provoke your
children to wrath, but bring them up in
the training and admonition of the Lord.
⁵ Bondservants, be obedient to those
who are your masters according to the
flesh, with fear and trembling, in sincerity of heart, as to Christ; ⁶ not with
eyeservice, as men-pleasers, but as
bondservants of Christ, doing the will of
God from the heart, ⁷ with goodwill doing service, as to the Lord, and not to men,
⁸ knowing that whatever good anyone
does, he will receive the same from the
Lord, whether *he is* a slave or free.
⁹ And you, masters, do the same things
to them, giving up threatening, knowing
that your own Master also is in heaven,
and there is no partiality with Him.
¹⁰ Finally, my brethren, be strong in the
Lord and in the power of His might. ¹¹ Put
on the whole armor of God, that you may
be able to stand against the wiles of the
devil. ¹² For we do not wrestle against flesh
and blood, but against principalities,
against powers, against the rulers of the
darkness of this age, against spiritual *hosts*
of wickedness in the heavenly *places*.
¹³ Therefore take up the whole armor of
God, that you may be able to withstand
in the evil day, and having done all, to
stand.
¹⁴ Stand therefore, having girded your
waist with truth, having put on the breastplate of righteousness, ¹⁵ and having shod
your feet with the preparation of the gospel of peace; ¹⁶ above all, taking the shield
of faith with which you will be able to
quench all the fiery darts of the wicked
one. ¹⁷ And take the helmet of salvation,
and the sword of the Spirit, which is the
word of God; ¹⁸ praying always with all
prayer and supplication in the Spirit, being
watchful to this end with all perseverance
and supplication for all the saints— ¹⁹ and
for me, that utterance may be given to
me, that I may open my mouth boldly
to make known the mystery of the gospel, ²⁰ for which I am an ambassador in
chains; that in it I may speak boldly, as I
ought to speak.
²¹ But that you also may know my
affairs *and* how I am doing, Tychicus, a
beloved brother and faithful minister in
the Lord, will make all things known to
you; ²² whom I have sent to you for

this very purpose, that you may know our affairs, and *that* he may comfort your hearts.

²³ Peace to the brethren, and love with faith, from God the Father and the Lord Jesus Christ. ²⁴ Grace *be* with all those who love our Lord Jesus Christ in sincerity. Amen.

READING 279 · OCTOBER 6

∼ ISAIAH 63:1—64:12 ∼

1 Who *is* this who comes from Edom,
With dyed garments from Bozrah,
This *One who is* glorious in His apparel,
Traveling in the greatness of His strength?—

"I who speak in righteousness,
mighty to save."

2 Why *is* Your apparel red,
And Your garments like one who treads in the winepress?

3 "I have trodden the winepress alone,
And from the peoples no one *was* with Me.
For I have trodden them in My anger,
And trampled them in My fury;
Their blood is sprinkled upon My garments,
And I have stained all My robes.
4 For the day of vengeance *is* in My heart,
And the year of My redeemed has come.
5 I looked, but *there was* no one to help,
And I wondered
That *there was* no one to uphold;
Therefore My own arm brought salvation for Me;
And My own fury, it sustained Me.
6 I have trodden down the peoples in My anger,
Made them drunk in My fury,
And brought down their strength to the earth."

7 I will mention the lovingkindnesses of the LORD

And the praises of the LORD,
According to all that the LORD has bestowed on us,
And the great goodness toward the house of Israel,
Which He has bestowed on them according to His mercies,
According to the multitude of His lovingkindnesses.
8 For He said, "Surely they *are* My people,
Children *who* will not lie."
So He became their Savior.
9 In all their affliction He was afflicted,
And the Angel of His Presence saved them;
In His love and in His pity He redeemed them;
And He bore them and carried them
All the days of old.
10 But they rebelled and grieved His Holy Spirit;
So He turned Himself against them as an enemy,
And He fought against them.

11 Then he remembered the days of old,
Moses *and* his people, *saying:*
"Where *is* He who brought them up out of the sea
With the shepherd of His flock?
Where *is* He who put His Holy Spirit within them,
12 Who led *them* by the right hand of Moses,
With His glorious arm,
Dividing the water before them
To make for Himself an everlasting name,
13 Who led them through the deep,
As a horse in the wilderness,
That they might not stumble?"

Positioned for Prayer

Three ministers were talking about prayer one day, and they began debating among themselves the most appropriate and effective positions for prayer. As they talked, they were totally oblivious of a telephone repairman working on the phone system in a corner of the room where they were sitting.

One minister contended that the key to prayer was in the hands. He always held his hands together to show a firmness of commitment and then pointed his hands upward as a symbolic form of worship. The second minister countered, real prayer could only be made if a person was on his knees. That, to him, was the proper position for submission to God. The third suggested that the very best position for prayer was to pray while stretched out flat on one's face, the position of supreme surrender.

By this time, the telephone repairman could no longer refrain from adding his opinion: "Well, I have found that the most powerful prayer I ever made was while I was suspended forty feet above the ground dangling upside down by my heels from a telephone pole."

The real power of prayer lies in the One Who hears our prayers, not in the form of the prayer.

> For I know that this will turn out for my deliverance through your prayer and the supply of the Spirit of Jesus Christ.
>
> *Philippians 1:19*

14 As a beast goes down into the
    valley,
    And the Spirit of the LORD causes
    him to rest,
    So You lead Your people,
    To make Yourself a glorious name.

15 Look down from heaven,
    And see from Your habitation,
    holy and glorious.
    Where *are* Your zeal and Your
    strength,
    The yearning of Your heart and
    Your mercies toward me?
    Are they restrained?

16 Doubtless You *are* our Father,
    Though Abraham was ignorant of
    us,
    And Israel does not acknowledge
    us.
    You, O LORD, *are* our Father;
    Our Redeemer from Everlasting *is*
    Your name.

17 O LORD, why have You made us
    stray from Your ways,
    And hardened our heart from Your
    fear?
    Return for Your servants' sake,
    The tribes of Your inheritance.

18 Your holy people have possessed *it*
    but a little while;
    Our adversaries have trodden
    down Your sanctuary.

19 We have become *like* those of old,
    over whom You never ruled,
    Those who were never called by
    Your name.

64 Oh, that You would rend the
    heavens!
    That You would come down!
    That the mountains might shake
    at Your presence—

2 As fire burns brushwood,
    As fire causes water to boil—
    To make Your name known to
    Your adversaries,
    That the nations may tremble at
    Your presence!

3 When You did awesome things *for
    which* we did not look,
    You came down,
    The mountains shook at Your
    presence.

4 For since the beginning of the
    world
    Men have not heard nor perceived
    by the ear,
    Nor has the eye seen any God
    besides You,
    Who acts for the one who waits
    for Him.

5 You meet him who rejoices and
    does righteousness,
    Who remembers You in Your ways.
    You are indeed angry, for we have
    sinned—
    In these ways we continue;
    And we need to be saved.

6 But we are all like an unclean
    thing,
    And all our righteousnesses *are*
    like filthy rags;
    We all fade as a leaf,
    And our iniquities, like the wind,
    Have taken us away.

7 And *there is* no one who calls on
    Your name,
    Who stirs himself up to take hold
    of You;
    For You have hidden Your face
    from us,
    And have consumed us because of
    our iniquities.

8 But now, O LORD,
    You *are* our Father;
    We *are* the clay, and You our
    potter;
    And all we *are* the work of Your
    hand.

9 Do not be furious, O LORD,
    Nor remember iniquity forever;
    Indeed, please look—we all *are*
    Your people!

10 Your holy cities are a wilderness,
    Zion is a wilderness,
    Jerusalem a desolation.

11 Our holy and beautiful temple,
    Where our fathers praised You,
    Is burned up with fire;
    And all our pleasant things are laid
    waste.

12 Will You restrain Yourself because
    of these *things,* O LORD?
    Will You hold Your peace, and
    afflict us very severely?

∼ Psalm 115:14–18 ∼

14 May the LORD give you increase
more and more,
You and your children.
15 *May* you *be* blessed by the LORD,
Who made heaven and earth.

16 The heaven, *even* the heavens, *are*
the LORD's;
But the earth He has given to the
children of men.
17 The dead do not praise the LORD,
Nor any who go down into silence.
18 But we will bless the LORD
From this time forth and
forevermore.

Praise the LORD!

∼ Proverbs 26:27 ∼

27 Whoever digs a pit will fall into it,
And he who rolls a stone will have it
roll back on him.

∼ Philippians 1:1–30 ∼

Paul and Timothy, bondservants of Jesus
Christ,

To all the saints in Christ Jesus who are
in Philippi, with the bishops and deacons:

2 Grace to you and peace from God our
Father and the Lord Jesus Christ.
3 I thank my God upon every remembrance of you, 4 always in every prayer of
mine making request for you all with joy,
5 for your fellowship in the gospel from
the first day until now, 6 being confident
of this very thing, that He who has begun
a good work in you will complete *it* until
the day of Jesus Christ; 7 just as it is right
for me to think this of you all, because I
have you in my heart, inasmuch as both
in my chains and in the defense and
confirmation of the gospel, you all are partakers with me of grace. 8 For God is my
witness, how greatly I long for you all with
the affection of Jesus Christ.
9 And this I pray, that your love may
abound still more and more in knowledge

and all discernment, 10 that you may approve the things that are excellent, that
you may be sincere and without offense
till the day of Christ, 11 being filled with
the fruits of righteousness which *are* by
Jesus Christ, to the glory and praise of
God.
12 But I want you to know, brethren,
that the things *which happened* to me have
actually turned out for the furtherance of
the gospel, 13 so that it has become evident to the whole palace guard, and to all
the rest, that my chains are in Christ;
14 and most of the brethren in the Lord,
having become confident by my chains,
are much more bold to speak the word
without fear.
15 Some indeed preach Christ even from
envy and strife, and some also from goodwill: 16 The former preach Christ from
selfish ambition, not sincerely, supposing
to add affliction to my chains; 17 but the
latter out of love, knowing that I am appointed for the defense of the gospel.
18 What then? Only *that* in every way,
whether in pretense or in truth, Christ is
preached; and in this I rejoice, yes, and
will rejoice.
19 For I know that this will turn out for
my deliverance through your prayer and
the supply of the Spirit of Jesus Christ,
20 according to my earnest expectation and
hope that in nothing I shall be ashamed,
but with all boldness, as always, so now
also Christ will be magnified in my body,
whether by life or by death. 21 For to me,
to live *is* Christ, and to die *is* gain. 22 But
if *I* live on in the flesh, this *will mean* fruit
from *my* labor; yet what I shall choose I
cannot tell. 23 For I am hard-pressed between the two, having a desire to depart
and be with Christ, *which is* far better.
24 Nevertheless to remain in the flesh *is*
more needful for you. 25 And being confident of this, I know that I shall remain
and continue with you all for your
progress and joy of faith, 26 that your rejoicing for me may be more abundant in
Jesus Christ by my coming to you again.
27 Only let your conduct be worthy of
the gospel of Christ, so that whether I
come and see you or am absent, I may
hear of your affairs, that you stand fast in
one spirit, with one mind striving together
for the faith of the gospel, 28 and not in

any way terrified by your adversaries, which is to them a proof of perdition, but to you of salvation, and that from God. ²⁹ For to you it has been granted on behalf of Christ, not only to believe in Him, but also to suffer for His sake, ³⁰ having the same conflict which you saw in me and now hear *is* in me.

READING 280 · OCTOBER 7

∽ ISAIAH 65:1—66:24 ∽

¹ "I was sought by *those who* did not
    ask *for Me;*
  I was found by *those who* did not
    seek Me.
  I said, 'Here I am, here I am,'
  To a nation *that* was not called by
    My name.
² I have stretched out My hands all
    day long to a rebellious people,
  Who walk in a way *that is* not
    good,
  According to their own thoughts;
³ A people who provoke Me to
    anger continually to My face;
  Who sacrifice in gardens,
  And burn incense on altars of
    brick;
⁴ Who sit among the graves,
  And spend the night in the tombs;
  Who eat swine's flesh,
  And the broth of abominable
    things is *in* their vessels;
⁵ Who say, 'Keep to yourself,
  Do not come near me,
  For I am holier than you!'
  These *are* smoke in My nostrils,
  A fire that burns all the day.

⁶ "Behold, *it is* written before Me:
  I will not keep silence, but will
    repay—
  Even repay into their bosom—
⁷ Your iniquities and the iniquities
    of your fathers together,"
  Says the LORD,
  "Who have burned incense on the
    mountains
  And blasphemed Me on the hills;
  Therefore I will measure their
    former work into their bosom."

⁸ Thus says the LORD:

  "As the new wine is found in the
    cluster,

And *one* says, 'Do not destroy it,
  For a blessing *is* in it,'
  So will I do for My servants' sake,
  That I may not destroy them all.
⁹ I will bring forth descendants
    from Jacob,
  And from Judah an heir of My
    mountains;
  My elect shall inherit it,
  And My servants shall dwell there.
¹⁰ Sharon shall be a fold of flocks,
  And the Valley of Achor a place
    for herds to lie down,
  For My people who have sought
    Me.

¹¹ "But you *are* those who forsake the
    LORD,
  Who forget My holy mountain,
  Who prepare a table for Gad,
  And who furnish a drink offering
    for Meni.
¹² Therefore I will number you for
    the sword,
  And you shall all bow down to the
    slaughter;
  Because, when I called, you did
    not answer;
  When I spoke, you did not hear,
  But did evil before My eyes,
  And chose *that* in which I do not
    delight."

¹³ Therefore thus says the Lord GOD:

  "Behold, My servants shall eat,
  But you shall be hungry;
  Behold, My servants shall drink,
  But you shall be thirsty;
  Behold, My servants shall rejoice,
  But you shall be ashamed;
¹⁴ Behold, My servants shall sing for
    joy of heart,
  But you shall cry for sorrow of
    heart,

Thou Shalt Not Whine

> **Do all things without complaining and disputing.**
>
> *Philippians 2:14*

Rather than whining because we don't have certain things in our lives or because we think something is wrong, we should take positive action.

Here are four steps for turning whining into thanksgiving:

1. *Give something away.* When you give, you create both a physical and a mental space for something new and better to come into your life. Although you may think you are "lacking" something in life, when you give you demonstrate the abundance in your life.

2. *Narrow your goals.* Don't expect everything good to come into your life all at once. When you focus your expectations toward specific, attainable goals, you are more apt to direct your time and energy toward reaching them.

3. *Change your vocabulary from "I need" to "I want."* Most of the things we think we *need* are actually things we *want.* When you receive them, you will be thankful for even small luxuries, rather than seeing them as necessities you can't live without.

4. *Choose to be thankful for what you already have.* Thanksgiving is a choice. Every one of us has more things to be thankful for than we could even begin to recount in a single day.

Each time you catch yourself whining about something, apply one or more of these steps to the situation. As you put these into practice, you will find yourself whining less, and thanking God more. Living a life of gratitude and thanksgiving to God is the best antidote for stress there is!

And wail for grief of spirit.

15 You shall leave your name as a
curse to My chosen;
For the Lord GOD will slay you,
And call His servants by another
name;

16 So that he who blesses himself in
the earth
Shall bless himself in the God of
truth;
And he who swears in the earth
Shall swear by the God of truth;
Because the former troubles are
forgotten,
And because they are hidden from
My eyes.

17 "For behold, I create new heavens
and a new earth;
And the former shall not be
remembered or come to mind.

18 But be glad and rejoice forever in
what I create;
For behold, I create Jerusalem *as a*
rejoicing,
And her people a joy.

19 I will rejoice in Jerusalem,
And joy in My people;
The voice of weeping shall no
longer be heard in her,
Nor the voice of crying.

20 "No more shall an infant from
there *live but a few* days,
Nor an old man who has not
fulfilled his days;
For the child shall die one
hundred years old,
But the sinner *being* one hundred
years old shall be accursed.

21 They shall build houses and
inhabit *them;*
They shall plant vineyards and eat
their fruit.

22 They shall not build and another
inhabit;
They shall not plant and another
eat;
For as the days of a tree, *so shall
be* the days of My people,
And My elect shall long enjoy the
work of their hands.

23 They shall not labor in vain,
Nor bring forth children for
trouble;

For they *shall be* the descendants
of the blessed of the LORD,
And their offspring with them.

24 "It shall come to pass
That before they call, I will
answer;
And while they are still speaking, I
will hear.

25 The wolf and the lamb shall feed
together,
The lion shall eat straw like the
ox,
And dust *shall be* the serpent's
food.
They shall not hurt nor destroy in
all My holy mountain,"
Says the LORD.

66 Thus says the LORD:

"Heaven *is* My throne,
And earth *is* My footstool.
Where *is* the house that you will
build Me?
And where *is* the place of My rest?

2 For all those *things* My hand has
made,
And all those *things* exist,"
Says the LORD.
"But on this *one* will I look:
On *him who is* poor and of a
contrite spirit,
And who trembles at My word.

3 "He who kills a bull *is as if* he slays
a man;
He who sacrifices a lamb, *as if* he
breaks a dog's neck;
He who offers a grain offering, *as
if he offers* swine's blood;
He who burns incense, *as if* he
blesses an idol.
Just as they have chosen their own
ways,
And their soul delights in their
abominations,

4 So will I choose their delusions,
And bring their fears on them;
Because, when I called, no one
answered,
When I spoke they did not hear;
But they did evil before My eyes,
And chose *that* in which I do not
delight."

5 Hear the word of the LORD,
 You who tremble at His word:
 "Your brethren who hated you,
 Who cast you out for My name's
  sake, said,
 'Let the LORD be glorified,
 That we may see your joy.'
 But they shall be ashamed."

6 The sound of noise from the city!
 A voice from the temple!
 The voice of the LORD,
 Who fully repays His enemies!

7 "Before she was in labor, she gave
  birth;
 Before her pain came,
 She delivered a male child.
8 Who has heard such a thing?
 Who has seen such things?
 Shall the earth be made to give
  birth in one day?
 Or shall a nation be born at once?
 For as soon as Zion was in labor,
 She gave birth to her children.
9 Shall I bring to the time of birth,
  and not cause delivery?" says
  the LORD.
 "Shall I who cause delivery shut up
  the womb?" says your God.
10 "Rejoice with Jerusalem,
 And be glad with her, all you who
  love her;
 Rejoice for joy with her, all you
  who mourn for her;
11 That you may feed and be satisfied
 With the consolation of her
  bosom,
 That you may drink deeply and be
  delighted
 With the abundance of her glory."

12 For thus says the LORD:

 "Behold, I will extend peace to her
  like a river,
 And the glory of the Gentiles like
  a flowing stream.
 Then you shall feed;
 On *her* sides shall you be carried,
 And be dandled on *her* knees.
13 As one whom his mother
  comforts,
 So I will comfort you;

And you shall be comforted in
 Jerusalem."

14 When you see *this*, your heart
  shall rejoice,
 And your bones shall flourish like
  grass;
 The hand of the LORD shall be
  known to His servants,
 And *His* indignation to His
  enemies.
15 For behold, the LORD will come
  with fire
 And with His chariots, like a
  whirlwind,
 To render His anger with fury,
 And His rebuke with flames of
  fire.
16 For by fire and by His sword
 The LORD will judge all flesh;
 And the slain of the LORD shall be
  many.

17 "Those who sanctify themselves
  and purify themselves,
 To go to the gardens
 After an *idol* in the midst,
 Eating swine's flesh and the
  abomination and the mouse,
 Shall be consumed together," says
  the LORD.

18 "For I *know* their works and their
thoughts. It shall be that I will gather all
nations and tongues; and they shall come
and see My glory. 19 I will set a sign among
them; and those among them who escape
I will send to the nations: *to* Tarshish and
Pul and Lud, who draw the bow, and Tubal and Javan, *to* the coastlands afar off
who have not heard My fame nor seen
My glory. And they shall declare My glory
among the Gentiles. 20 Then they shall
bring all your brethren for an offering to
the LORD out of all nations, on horses and
in chariots and in litters, on mules and on
camels, to My holy mountain Jerusalem,"
says the LORD, "as the children of Israel
bring an offering in a clean vessel into the
house of the LORD. 21 And I will also take
some of them for priests *and* Levites," says
the LORD.

22 "For as the new heavens and the
  new earth

Which I will make shall remain before Me," says the LORD, "So shall your descendants and your name remain.

23 And it shall come to pass
That from one New Moon to another,
And from one Sabbath to another,
All flesh shall come to worship before Me," says the LORD.

24 "And they shall go forth and look
Upon the corpses of the men
Who have transgressed against Me.
For their worm does not die,
And their fire is not quenched.
They shall be an abhorrence to all flesh."

∼ PSALM 116:1–4 ∼

1 I love the LORD, because He has heard
My voice *and* my supplications.

2 Because He has inclined His ear to me,
Therefore I will call *upon Him* as long as I live.

3 The pains of death surrounded me,
And the pangs of Sheol laid hold of me;
I found trouble and sorrow.

4 Then I called upon the name of the LORD:
"O LORD, I implore You, deliver my soul!"

∼ PROVERBS 26:28 ∼

28 A lying tongue hates *those who are* crushed by it,
And a flattering mouth works ruin.

∼ PHILIPPIANS 2:1–30 ∼

Therefore if *there is* any consolation in Christ, if any comfort of love, if any fellowship of the Spirit, if any affection and mercy, 2 fulfill my joy by being likeminded, having the same love, *being* of one accord, of one mind. 3 *Let* nothing *be done* through selfish ambition or conceit, but in lowliness of mind let each esteem others better than himself. 4 Let each of you look out not only for his own interests, but also for the interests of others.

5 Let this mind be in you which was also in Christ Jesus, 6 who, being in the form of God, did not consider it robbery to be equal with God, 7 but made Himself of no reputation, taking the form of a bondservant, *and* coming in the likeness of men. 8 And being found in appearance as a man, He humbled Himself and became obedient to *the point of* death, even the death of the cross. 9 Therefore God also has highly exalted Him and given Him the name which is above every name, 10 that at the name of Jesus every knee should bow, of those in heaven, and of those on earth, and of those under the earth, 11 and *that* every tongue should confess that Jesus Christ *is* Lord, to the glory of God the Father.

12 Therefore, my beloved, as you have always obeyed, not as in my presence only, but now much more in my absence, work out your own salvation with fear and trembling; 13 for it is God who works in you both to will and to do for *His* good pleasure.

14 Do all things without complaining and disputing, 15 that you may become blameless and harmless, children of God without fault in the midst of a crooked and perverse generation, among whom you shine as lights in the world, 16 holding fast the word of life, so that I may rejoice in the day of Christ that I have not run in vain or labored in vain.

17 Yes, and if I am being poured out *as a drink offering* on the sacrifice and service of your faith, I am glad and rejoice with you all. 18 For the same reason you also be glad and rejoice with me.

19 But I trust in the Lord Jesus to send Timothy to you shortly, that I also may be encouraged when I know your state. 20 For I have no one like-minded, who will sincerely care for your state. 21 For all seek their own, not the things which are of Christ Jesus. 22 But you know his proven character, that as a son with *his* father he served with me in the gospel. 23 Therefore I hope to send him at once, as soon

as I see how it goes with me. ²⁴ But I trust in the Lord that I myself shall also come shortly.

²⁵ Yet I considered it necessary to send to you Epaphroditus, my brother, fellow worker, and fellow soldier, but your messenger and the one who ministered to my need; ²⁶ since he was longing for you all, and was distressed because you had heard that he was sick. ²⁷ For indeed he was sick almost unto death; but God had mercy on him, and not only on him but on me also, lest I should have sorrow upon sorrow. ²⁸ Therefore I sent him the more eagerly, that when you see him again you may rejoice, and I may be less sorrowful. ²⁹ Receive him therefore in the Lord with all gladness, and hold such men in esteem; ³⁰ because for the work of Christ he came close to death, not regarding his life, to supply what was lacking in your service toward me.

READING 281 · OCTOBER 8

~ JEREMIAH 1:1—2:37 ~

The words of Jeremiah the son of Hilkiah, of the priests who *were* in Anathoth in the land of Benjamin, ² to whom the word of the LORD came in the days of Josiah the son of Amon, king of Judah, in the thirteenth year of his reign. ³ It came also in the days of Jehoiakim the son of Josiah, king of Judah, until the end of the eleventh year of Zedekiah the son of Josiah, king of Judah, until the carrying away of Jerusalem captive in the fifth month.

⁴ Then the word of the LORD came to me, saying:

⁵ "Before I formed you in the womb
    I knew you;
Before you were born I sanctified
    you;
I ordained you a prophet to the
    nations."

⁶ Then said I:

"Ah, Lord GOD!
Behold, I cannot speak, for I *am* a
    youth."

⁷ But the LORD said to me:

"Do not say, 'I *am* a youth,'
For you shall go to all to whom I
    send you,
And whatever I command you,
    you shall speak.
⁸ Do not be afraid of their faces,
For I *am* with you to deliver you,"
    says the LORD.

⁹ Then the LORD put forth His hand and touched my mouth, and the LORD said to me:

"Behold, I have put My words in
    your mouth.
¹⁰ See, I have this day set you over
    the nations and over the
    kingdoms,
To root out and to pull down,
To destroy and to throw down,
To build and to plant."

¹¹ Moreover the word of the LORD came to me, saying, "Jeremiah, what do you see?"
And I said, "I see a branch of an almond tree."
¹² Then the LORD said to me, "You have seen well, for I am ready to perform My word."
¹³ And the word of the LORD came to me the second time, saying, "What do you see?"
And I said, "I see a boiling pot, and it is facing away from the north."
¹⁴ Then the LORD said to me:

"Out of the north calamity shall
        break forth
On all the inhabitants of the land.
¹⁵ For behold, I am calling
All the families of the kingdoms of
    the north," says the LORD;
"They shall come and each one set
    his throne
At the entrance of the gates of
    Jerusalem,

Against all its walls all around,
And against all the cities
    of Judah.
16 I will utter My judgments
    Against them concerning all their
        wickedness,
    Because they have forsaken Me,
    Burned incense to other gods,
    And worshiped the works of their
        own hands.

17 "Therefore prepare yourself and
        arise,
    And speak to them all that I
        command you.
    Do not be dismayed before their
        faces,
    Lest I dismay you before them.
18 For behold, I have made you this
        day
    A fortified city and an iron pillar,
    And bronze walls against the
        whole land—
    Against the kings of Judah,
    Against its princes,
    Against its priests,
    And against the people of the
        land.
19 They will fight against you,
    But they shall not prevail against
        you.
    For I *am* with you," says the
    LORD, "to deliver you."

2 Moreover the word of the LORD came
to me, saying, ² "Go and cry in the hearing of Jerusalem, saying, 'Thus says the
LORD:

    "I remember you,
        The kindness of your youth,
        The love of your betrothal,
        When you went after Me in the
            wilderness,
        In a land not sown.
3   Israel *was* holiness to the LORD,
        The firstfruits of His increase.
        All that devour him will offend;
        Disaster will come upon them,"
        says the LORD.' "

⁴ Hear the word of the LORD, O house
of Jacob and all the families of the house
of Israel. ⁵ Thus says the LORD:

"What injustice have your fathers
        found in Me,
    That they have gone far from Me,
    Have followed idols,
    And have become idolaters?
6   Neither did they say, 'Where *is* the
        LORD,
    Who brought us up out of the
        land of Egypt,
    Who led us through the
        wilderness,
    Through a land of deserts and
        pits,
    Through a land of drought and
        the shadow of death,
    Through a land that no one
        crossed
    And where no one dwelt?'
7   I brought you into a bountiful
        country,
    To eat its fruit and its goodness.
    But when you entered, you defiled
        My land
    And made My heritage an
        abomination.
8   The priests did not say, 'Where *is*
        the LORD?'
    And those who handle the law did
        not know Me;
    The rulers also transgressed
        against Me;
    The prophets prophesied by Baal,
    And walked after *things that* do
        not profit.

9   "Therefore I will yet bring charges
        against you," says the LORD,
    "And against your children's
        children I will bring charges.
10 For pass beyond the coasts of
        Cyprus and see,
    Send to Kedar and consider
        diligently,
    And see if there has been such *a*
        thing.
11 Has a nation changed *its* gods,
    Which *are* not gods?
    But My people have changed their
        Glory
    For *what* does not profit.
12 Be astonished, O heavens, at this,
    And be horribly afraid;
    Be very desolate," says the LORD.
13 "For My people have committed
        two evils:

Only the Strong

Many people are good starters but poor finishers. When things start getting tough they listen to the little imp on their shoulder who whispers, "You can't do it" and "You'll never make it." Others don't even start.

We must realize that while "doing something" requires taking a risk, so does "doing nothing." The risk of action may be failure, but the risks of a failure to act can be stagnation, dissatisfaction, and frustration.

The story of the covered wagon crossing the plains toward the Golden West began with a song:

> The Coward never started;
> The Weak died on the way;
> Only the Strong came through!

Brethren, I do not count myself to have apprehended; but one thing I do, forgetting those things which are behind and reaching forward to those things which are ahead.

Philippians 3:13

That's the way it is in life. Being strong does not refer only to physical strength. True strength flows from a strong spirit — a spirit made powerful by a close relationship with God. He gives us the will to succeed, dreams that will not die, and wisdom to turn evil into blessing.

Lean on God for direction, and keep leaning on Him for the wisdom and courage to finish what you've begun.

They have forsaken Me, the
   fountain of living waters,
And hewn themselves cisterns—
   broken cisterns that can hold no
   water.

14 "*Is* Israel a servant?
   Is he a homeborn *slave?*
   Why is he plundered?
15 The young lions roared at him,
   and growled;
   They made his land waste;
   His cities are burned, without
   inhabitant.
16 Also the people of Noph and
   Tahpanhes
   Have broken the crown of your
   head.
17 Have you not brought this on
   yourself,
   In that you have forsaken the
   LORD your God
   When He led you in the way?
18 And now why take the road to
   Egypt,
   To drink the waters of Sihor?
   Or why take the road to Assyria,
   To drink the waters of the River?
19 Your own wickedness will correct
   you,
   And your backslidings will rebuke
   you.
   Know therefore and see that *it is*
   an evil and bitter *thing*
   That you have forsaken the LORD
   your God,
   And the fear of Me *is* not in you,"
   Says the Lord GOD of hosts.

20 "For of old I have broken your
   yoke *and* burst your bonds;
   And you said, 'I will not
   transgress,'
   When on every high hill and
   under every green tree
   You lay down, playing the harlot.
21 Yet I had planted you a noble vine,
   a seed of highest quality.
   How then have you turned before
   Me
   Into the degenerate plant of an
   alien vine?
22 For though you wash yourself
   with lye, and use much soap,

Yet your iniquity is marked before
   Me," says the Lord GOD.

23 "How can you say, 'I am not
   polluted,
   I have not gone after the Baals'?
   See your way in the valley;
   Know what you have done:
   You are a swift dromedary
   breaking loose in her ways,
24 A wild donkey used to the
   wilderness,
   That sniffs at the wind in her
   desire;
   In her time of mating, who can
   turn her away?
   All those who seek her will not
   weary themselves;
   In her month they will find her.
25 Withhold your foot from being
   unshod, and your throat from
   thirst.
   But you said, 'There is no hope.
   No! For I have loved aliens, and
   after them I will go.'

26 "As the thief is ashamed when he is
   found out,
   So is the house of Israel ashamed;
   They and their kings and their
   princes, and their priests and
   their prophets.
27 Saying to a tree, 'You *are* my
   father,'
   And to a stone, 'You gave birth to
   me.'
   For they have turned *their* back to
   Me, and not *their* face.
   But in the time of their trouble
   They will say, 'Arise and save us.'
28 But where *are* your gods that you
   have made for yourselves?
   Let them arise,
   If they can save you in the time of
   your trouble;
   For *according to* the number of
   your cities
   Are your gods, O Judah.

29 "Why will you plead with Me?
   You all have transgressed against
   Me," says the LORD.
30 "In vain I have chastened your
   children;
   They received no correction.

Your sword has devoured your
   prophets
Like a destroying lion.

31 "O generation, see the word of the
   LORD!
   Have I been a wilderness to Israel,
   Or a land of darkness?
   Why do My people say, 'We are
   lords;
   We will come no more to You'?
32 Can a virgin forget her ornaments,
   Or a bride her attire?
   Yet My people have forgotten Me
   days without number.

33 "Why do you beautify your way to
   seek love?
   Therefore you have also taught
   The wicked women your ways.
34 Also on your skirts is found
   The blood of the lives of the poor
   innocents.
   I have not found it by secret
   search,
   But plainly on all these things.
35 Yet you say, 'Because I am
   innocent,
   Surely His anger shall turn from
   me.'
   Behold, I will plead My case
   against you,
   Because you say, 'I have not
   sinned.'
36 Why do you gad about so much to
   change your way?
   Also you shall be ashamed of
   Egypt as you were ashamed of
   Assyria.
37 Indeed you will go forth from him
   With your hands on your head;
   For the LORD has rejected your
   trusted allies,
   And you will not prosper by them.

~ PSALM 116:5–14 ~

5 Gracious is the LORD, and righteous;
   Yes, our God is merciful.
6 The LORD preserves the simple;
   I was brought low, and He saved me.
7 Return to your rest, O my soul,
   For the LORD has dealt bountifully
   with you.

8 For You have delivered my soul from
   death,
   My eyes from tears,
   And my feet from falling.
9 I will walk before the LORD
   In the land of the living.
10 I believed, therefore I spoke,
   "I am greatly afflicted."
11 I said in my haste,
   "All men are liars."

12 What shall I render to the LORD
   For all His benefits toward me?
13 I will take up the cup of salvation,
   And call upon the name of the
   LORD.
14 I will pay my vows to the LORD
   Now in the presence of all His
   people.

~ PROVERBS 27:1 ~

1 Do not boast about tomorrow,
   For you do not know what a day
   may bring forth.

~ PHILIPPIANS 3:1–21 ~

Finally, my brethren, rejoice in the Lord.
For me to write the same things to you is
not tedious, but for you it is safe.
² Beware of dogs, beware of evil workers, beware of the mutilation! ³ For we are
the circumcision, who worship God in the
Spirit, rejoice in Christ Jesus, and have
no confidence in the flesh, ⁴ though I also
might have confidence in the flesh. If anyone else thinks he may have confidence
in the flesh, I more so: ⁵ circumcised the
eighth day, of the stock of Israel, of the
tribe of Benjamin, a Hebrew of the Hebrews; concerning the law, a Pharisee;
⁶ concerning zeal, persecuting the church;
concerning the righteousness which is in
the law, blameless.
⁷ But what things were gain to me, these
I have counted loss for Christ. ⁸ Yet indeed I also count all things loss for the
excellence of the knowledge of Christ
Jesus my Lord, for whom I have suffered
the loss of all things, and count them as
rubbish, that I may gain Christ ⁹ and be
found in Him, not having my own righteousness, which is from the law, but
that which is through faith in Christ, the

righteousness which is from God by faith; [10] that I may know Him and the power of His resurrection, and the fellowship of His sufferings, being conformed to His death, [11] if, by any means, I may attain to the resurrection from the dead.

[12] Not that I have already attained, or am already perfected; but I press on, that I may lay hold of that for which Christ Jesus has also laid hold of me. [13] Brethren, I do not count myself to have apprehended; but one thing I do, forgetting those things which are behind and reaching forward to those things which are ahead, [14] I press toward the goal for the prize of the upward call of God in Christ Jesus.

[15] Therefore let us, as many as are mature, have this mind; and if in anything you think otherwise, God will reveal even this to you. [16] Nevertheless, to the degree that we have already attained, let us walk by the same rule, let us be of the same mind.

[17] Brethren, join in following my example, and note those who so walk, as you have us for a pattern. [18] For many walk, of whom I have told you often, and now tell you even weeping, that they are the enemies of the cross of Christ: [19] whose end is destruction, whose god is their belly, and whose glory is in their shame—who set their mind on earthly things. [20] For our citizenship is in heaven, from which we also eagerly wait for the Savior, the Lord Jesus Christ, [21] who will transform our lowly body that it may be conformed to His glorious body, according to the working by which He is able even to subdue all things to Himself.

READING 282 · OCTOBER 9

~ JEREMIAH 3:1—4:31 ~

[1] "They say, 'If a man divorces his wife,
And she goes from him
And becomes another man's,
May he return to her again?'
Would not that land be greatly polluted?
But you have played the harlot with many lovers;
Yet return to Me," says the LORD.

[2] "Lift up your eyes to the desolate heights and see:
Where have you not lain with men?
By the road you have sat for them
Like an Arabian in the wilderness;
And you have polluted the land
With your harlotries and your wickedness.

[3] Therefore the showers have been withheld,
And there has been no latter rain.
You have had a harlot's forehead;
You refuse to be ashamed.

[4] Will you not from this time cry to Me,
'My Father, You are the guide of my youth?

[5] Will He remain angry forever?
Will He keep it to the end?'
Behold, you have spoken and done evil things,
As you were able."

[6] The LORD said also to me in the days of Josiah the king: "Have you seen what backsliding Israel has done? She has gone up on every high mountain and under every green tree, and there played the harlot. [7] And I said, after she had done all these things, 'Return to Me.' But she did not return. And her treacherous sister Judah saw it. [8] Then I saw that for all the causes for which backsliding Israel had committed adultery, I had put her away and given her a certificate of divorce; yet her treacherous sister Judah did not fear, but went and played the harlot also. [9] So it came to pass, through her casual harlotry, that she defiled the land and committed adultery with stones and trees. [10] And yet for all this her treacherous sister Judah has not turned to Me with her whole heart, but in pretense," says the LORD.

[11] Then the LORD said to me, "Backsliding Israel has shown herself more

The Wind Blows

And the peace of God, which surpasses all understanding, will guard your hearts and minds through Christ Jesus.

Philippians 4:7

Tom Dooley was a young doctor who gave up an easy, prosperous career in the States to organize hospitals in Southeast Asia and to pour out his life in service to the afflicted people there. As he lay dying of cancer at age thirty-four, Dooley wrote to the president of Notre Dame, his alma mater:

"Dear Father Hesburgh: They've got me down. Flat on the back, with plaster, sand bags, and hot water bottles. I've contrived a way of pumping the bed up a bit so that, with a long reach, I can get to my typewriter. . . . Two things prompt this note to you. The first is that whenever my cancer acts up a bit . . . I turn inward. Less do I think of my hospitals around the world, or of 94 doctors, fund-raisers, and the like. More do I think of one Divine Doctor and my personal fund of grace. . . . I have monstrous phantoms; all men do. And inside and outside the wind blows. But when the time comes, like now, then the storm around me does not matter. The winds within me do not matter. Nothing human or earthly can touch me. A peace gathers in my heart. What seems unpossessable, I can possess. What seems unfathomable, I can fathom. What is unutterable, I can utter. Because I can pray. I can communicate. How do people endure anything on earth if they cannot have God?"

The storms of life will come and go, vary in their intensity, and hit us at our worst moments, but the peace of God remains the same — constant, enduring, comforting. When we choose His peace over worry, fear, and anxiety, our hearts and minds abide secure therein.

righteous than treacherous Judah. ¹² Go and proclaim these words toward the north, and say:

'Return, backsliding Israel,' says
    the LORD;
'I will not cause My anger to fall
    on you.
For I *am* merciful,' says the LORD;
'I will not remain angry forever.
¹³ Only acknowledge your iniquity,
    That you have transgressed against
        the LORD your God,
    And have scattered your charms
    To alien deities under every green
        tree,
    And you have not obeyed My
        voice,' says the LORD.

¹⁴ "Return, O backsliding children," says the LORD; "for I am married to you. I will take you, one from a city and two from a family, and I will bring you to Zion. ¹⁵ And I will give you shepherds according to My heart, who will feed you with knowledge and understanding.

¹⁶ "Then it shall come to pass, when you are multiplied and increased in the land in those days," says the LORD, "that they will say no more, 'The ark of the covenant of the LORD.' It shall not come to mind, nor shall they remember it, nor shall they visit *it*, nor shall it be made anymore. ¹⁷ "At that time Jerusalem shall be called The Throne of the LORD, and all the nations shall be gathered to it, to the name of the LORD, to Jerusalem. No more shall they follow the dictates of their evil hearts. ¹⁸ "In those days the house of Judah shall walk with the house of Israel, and they shall come together out of the land of the north to the land that I have given as an inheritance to your fathers.

¹⁹ "But I said:

'How can I put you among the
    children
And give you a pleasant land,
A beautiful heritage of the hosts of
    nations?'

"And I said:

'You shall call Me, "My Father,"
And not turn away from Me.'

²⁰ Surely, *as* a wife treacherously
    departs from her husband,
So have you dealt treacherously
    with Me,
O house of Israel," says the LORD.

²¹ A voice was heard on the desolate
    heights,
Weeping *and* supplications of the
    children of Israel.
For they have perverted their way;
They have forgotten the LORD
    their God.

²² "Return, you backsliding children,
And I will heal your backslidings."

"Indeed we do come to You,
    For You are the LORD our God.
²³ Truly, in vain *is salvation hoped for*
    from the hills,
And from the multitude of
    mountains;
Truly, in the LORD our God
Is the salvation of Israel.
²⁴ For shame has devoured
    The labor of our fathers from our
        youth—
    Their flocks and their herds,
    Their sons and their daughters.
²⁵ We lie down in our shame,
    And our reproach covers us.
For we have sinned against the
    LORD our God,
We and our fathers,
From our youth even to this day,
And have not obeyed the voice of
    the LORD our God."

4 "If you will return, O Israel," says
    the LORD,
"Return to Me;
And if you will put away your
    abominations out of My sight,
Then you shall not be moved.
² And you shall swear, 'The LORD
    lives,'
In truth, in judgment, and in
    righteousness;
The nations shall bless themselves
    in Him,
And in Him they shall glory."

³ For thus says the LORD to the men of Judah and Jerusalem:

"Break up your fallow ground,
And do not sow among thorns.
4 Circumcise yourselves to the
LORD,
And take away the foreskins of
your hearts,
You men of Judah and inhabitants
of Jerusalem,
Lest My fury come forth like fire,
And burn so that no one can
quench *it,*
Because of the evil of your
doings."

5 Declare in Judah and proclaim in
Jerusalem, and say:

"Blow the trumpet in the land;
Cry, 'Gather together,'
And say, 'Assemble yourselves,
And let us go into the fortified
cities.'
6 Set up the standard toward Zion.
Take refuge! Do not delay!
For I will bring disaster from the
north,
And great destruction."

7 The lion has come up from his
thicket,
And the destroyer of nations is on
his way.
He has gone forth from his place
To make your land desolate.
Your cities will be laid waste,
Without inhabitant.
8 For this, clothe yourself with
sackcloth,
Lament and wail.
For the fierce anger of the LORD
Has not turned back from us.

9 "And it shall come to pass in that
day," says the LORD,
"*That* the heart of the king shall
perish,
And the heart of the princes;
The priests shall be astonished,
And the prophets shall wonder."

10 Then I said, "Ah, Lord GOD!
Surely You have greatly deceived
this people and Jerusalem,
Saying, 'You shall have peace,'

Whereas the sword reaches to the
heart."

11 At that time it will be said
To this people and to Jerusalem,
"A dry wind of the desolate heights
blows in the wilderness
Toward the daughter of My
people—
Not to fan or to cleanse—
12 A wind too strong for these will
come for Me;
Now I will also speak judgment
against them."

13 "Behold, he shall come up like
clouds,
And his chariots like a whirlwind.
His horses are swifter
than eagles.
Woe to us, for we are plundered!"

14 O Jerusalem, wash your heart
from wickedness,
That you may be saved.
How long shall your evil thoughts
lodge within you?
15 For a voice declares from Dan
And proclaims affliction from
Mount Ephraim:
16 "Make mention to the nations,
Yes, proclaim against Jerusalem,
That watchers come from a far
country
And raise their voice against the
cities of Judah.
17 Like keepers of a field they are
against her all around,
Because she has been rebellious
against Me," says the LORD.
18 "Your ways and your doings
Have procured these *things* for
you.
This *is* your wickedness,
Because it is bitter,
Because it reaches to your
heart."

19 O my soul, my soul!
I am pained in my very heart!
My heart makes a noise in me;
I cannot hold my peace,
Because you have heard, O my
soul,
The sound of the trumpet,

The alarm of war.

20 Destruction upon destruction is
   cried,
   For the whole land is plundered.
   Suddenly my tents are plundered,
   And my curtains in a moment.

21 How long will I see the standard,
   And hear the sound of the
   trumpet?

22 "For My people *are* foolish,
   They have not known Me.
   They *are* silly children,
   And they have no understanding.
   They *are* wise to do evil,
   But to do good they have no
   knowledge."

23 I beheld the earth, and indeed *it
   was* without form, and void;
   And the heavens, they *had* no
   light.

24 I beheld the mountains, and
   indeed they trembled,
   And all the hills moved back and
   forth.

25 I beheld, and indeed *there was* no
   man,
   And all the birds of the heavens
   had fled.

26 I beheld, and indeed the fruitful
   land *was* a wilderness,
   And all its cities were broken
   down
   At the presence of the LORD,
   By His fierce anger.

27 For thus says the LORD:

   "The whole land shall be
   desolate;
   Yet I will not make a full end.

28 For this shall the earth mourn,
   And the heavens above be black,
   Because I have spoken.
   I have purposed and will not
   relent,
   Nor will I turn back from it.

29 The whole city shall flee from the
   noise of the horsemen and
   bowmen.
   They shall go into thickets and
   climb up on the rocks.
   Every city *shall be* forsaken,
   And not a man shall dwell in it.

30 "And *when* you *are* plundered,
   What will you do?
   Though you clothe yourself with
   crimson,
   Though you adorn *yourself* with
   ornaments of gold,
   Though you enlarge your eyes
   with paint,
   In vain you will make yourself
   fair;
   Your lovers will despise you;
   They will seek your life.

31 "For I have heard a voice as of a
   woman in labor,
   The anguish as of her who brings
   forth her first child,
   The voice of the daughter of Zion
   bewailing herself;
   She spreads her hands, *saying,*
   'Woe *is* me now, for my soul is
   weary
   Because of murderers!'

～ PSALM 116:15–19 ～

15 Precious in the sight of the LORD
   Is the death of His saints.

16 O LORD, truly I *am* Your servant;
   I *am* Your servant, the son of Your
   maidservant;
   You have loosed my bonds.

17 I will offer to You the sacrifice of
   thanksgiving,
   And will call upon the name of the
   LORD.

18 I will pay my vows to the LORD
   Now in the presence of all His
   people,

19 In the courts of the LORD's house,
   In the midst of you, O Jerusalem.

   Praise the LORD!

～ PROVERBS 27:2 ～

2 Let another man praise you, and not
   your own mouth;
   A stranger, and not your own lips.

~ PHILIPPIANS 4:1–23 ~

Therefore, my beloved and longed-for brethren, my joy and crown, so stand fast in the Lord, beloved.

[2] I implore Euodia and I implore Syntyche to be of the same mind in the Lord. [3] And I urge you also, true companion, help these women who labored with me in the gospel, with Clement also, and the rest of my fellow workers, whose names *are* in the Book of Life.

[4] Rejoice in the Lord always. Again I will say, rejoice!

[5] Let your gentleness be known to all men. The Lord *is* at hand.

[6] Be anxious for nothing, but in everything by prayer and supplication, with thanksgiving, let your requests be made known to God; [7] and the peace of God, which surpasses all understanding, will guard your hearts and minds through Christ Jesus.

[8] Finally, brethren, whatever things are true, whatever things *are* noble, whatever things *are* just, whatever things *are* pure, whatever things *are* lovely, whatever things *are* of good report, if *there is* any virtue and if *there is* anything praiseworthy—meditate on these things. [9] The things which you learned and received and heard and saw in me, these do, and the God of peace will be with you.

[10] But I rejoiced in the Lord greatly that now at last your care for me has flourished again; though you surely did care, but you lacked opportunity. [11] Not that I speak in regard to need, for I have learned in whatever state I am, to be content: [12] I know how to be abased, and I know how to abound. Everywhere and in all things I have learned both to be full and to be hungry, both to abound and to suffer need. [13] I can do all things through Christ who strengthens me.

[14] Nevertheless you have done well that you shared in my distress. [15] Now you Philippians know also that in the beginning of the gospel, when I departed from Macedonia, no church shared with me concerning giving and receiving but you only. [16] For even in Thessalonica you sent *aid* once and again for my necessities. [17] Not that I seek the gift, but I seek the fruit that abounds to your account. [18] Indeed I have all and abound. I am full, having received from Epaphroditus the things *sent* from you, a sweet-smelling aroma, an acceptable sacrifice, well pleasing to God. [19] And my God shall supply all your need according to His riches in glory by Christ Jesus. [20] Now to our God and Father *be* glory forever and ever. Amen.

[21] Greet every saint in Christ Jesus. The brethren who are with me greet you. [22] All the saints greet you, but especially those who are of Caesar's household.

[23] The grace of our Lord Jesus Christ be with you all. Amen.

~ JEREMIAH 5:1—6:30 ~

[1] "Run to and fro through the streets
　　of Jerusalem;
　See now and know;
　And seek in her open places
　If you can find a man,
　If there is *anyone* who executes
　　judgment,
　Who seeks the truth,
　And I will pardon her.

[2] Though they say, '*As* the LORD
　　lives,'
　Surely they swear falsely."

[3] O LORD, *are* not Your eyes on the
　　truth?
　You have stricken them,
　But they have not grieved;
　You have consumed them,

But they have refused to receive correction.
They have made their faces harder than rock;
They have refused to return.

4 Therefore I said, "Surely these *are* poor.
They are foolish;
For they do not know the way of the LORD,
The judgment of their God.
5 I will go to the great men and speak to them,
For they have known the way of the LORD,
The judgment of their God."

But these have altogether broken the yoke
And burst the bonds.
6 Therefore a lion from the forest shall slay them,
A wolf of the deserts shall destroy them;
A leopard will watch over their cities.
Everyone who goes out from there shall be torn in pieces,
Because their transgressions are many;
Their backslidings have increased.

7 "How shall I pardon you for this?
Your children have forsaken Me
And sworn by *those that are* not gods.
When I had fed them to the full,
Then they committed adultery
And assembled themselves by troops in the harlots' houses.
8 They were *like* well-fed lusty stallions;
Every one neighed after his neighbor's wife.
9 Shall I not punish *them* for these *things?*" says the LORD.
"And shall I not avenge Myself on such a nation as this?

10 "Go up on her walls and destroy,
But do not make a complete end.
Take away her branches,
For they *are* not the LORD's.

11 For the house of Israel and the house of Judah
Have dealt very treacherously with Me," says the LORD.

12 They have lied about the LORD,
And said, "*It is* not He.
Neither will evil come upon us,
Nor shall we see sword or famine.
13 And the prophets become wind,
For the word *is* not in them.
Thus shall it be done to them."

14 Therefore thus says the LORD God of hosts:

"Because you speak this word,
Behold, I will make My words in your mouth fire,
And this people wood,
And it shall devour them.
15 Behold, I will bring a nation against you from afar,
O house of Israel," says the LORD.
"It *is* a mighty nation,
It *is* an ancient nation,
A nation whose language you do not know,
Nor can you understand what they say.
16 Their quiver *is* like an open tomb;
They *are* all mighty men.
17 And they shall eat up your harvest and your bread,
Which your sons and daughters should eat.
They shall eat up your flocks and your herds;
They shall eat up your vines and your fig trees;
They shall destroy your fortified cities,
In which you trust, with the sword.

18 "Nevertheless in those days," says the LORD, "I will not make a complete end of you. 19 And it will be when you say, 'Why does the LORD our God do all these *things* to us?' then you shall answer them, ' Just as you have forsaken Me and served foreign gods in your land, so you shall serve aliens in a land *that is* not yours.'

20 "Declare this in the house of Jacob
And proclaim it in Judah, saying,

An Old-Fashioned Working

> For His merciful kindness is great toward us, and the truth of the Lord endures forever. Praise the Lord!
>
> *Psalm 117:2*

"I often have thought that we are a little old-fashioned here in the Ozark hills," writes Laura Ingalls Wilder in *Little House in the Ozarks*. "Now I know we are, because we had a 'working' in our neighborhood this winter. That is a blessed, old-fashioned way of helping out a neighbor.

"While the winter was warm, still it has been much too cold to be without firewood; and this neighbor, badly crippled with rheumatism, was not able to get up his winter's wood. . . . So the men of the neighborhood gathered together one morning and dropped in on him. With cross-cut saws and axes, they took possession of his wood lot. . . . By night there was enough wood ready . . . to last the rest of the winter.

"The women did their part, too. All morning they kept arriving with well-filled baskets, and at noon a long table was filled with a country neighborhood dinner. . . . When the dishes were washed, they sewed, knit, crocheted, and talked for the rest of the afternoon. It was a regular old-fashioned good time, and we all went home with the feeling expressed by a newcomer when he said, 'Don't you know I'm proud to live in a neighborhood like this where they turn out and help one another when it's needed.' "

21 'Hear this now, O foolish people,
    Without understanding,
    Who have eyes and see not,
    And who have ears and hear not:
22 Do you not fear Me?' says the
    LORD.
    'Will you not tremble at My
        presence,
    Who have placed the sand as the
        bound of the sea,
    By a perpetual decree, that it
        cannot pass beyond it?
    And though its waves toss to and
        fro,
    Yet they cannot prevail;
    Though they roar, yet they cannot
        pass over it.
23 But this people has a defiant and
        rebellious heart;
    They have revolted and departed.
24 They do not say in their heart,
    "Let us now fear the LORD our
        God,
    Who gives rain, both the former
        and the latter, in its season.
    He reserves for us the appointed
        weeks of the harvest."
25 Your iniquities have turned these
        things away,
    And your sins have withheld good
        from you.

26 'For among My people are found
        wicked *men;*
    They lie in wait as one who sets
        snares;
    They set a trap;
    They catch men.
27 As a cage is full of birds,
    So their houses *are* full of deceit.
    Therefore they have become great
        and grown rich.
28 They have grown fat, they are
        sleek;
    Yes, they surpass the deeds of the
        wicked;
    They do not plead the cause,
    The cause of the fatherless;
    Yet they prosper,
    And the right of the needy they do
        not defend.
29 Shall I not punish *them* for these
        things?' says the LORD.
    'Shall I not avenge Myself on such
        a nation as this?'

30 "An astonishing and horrible thing
    Has been committed in the land:
31 The prophets prophesy falsely,
    And the priests rule by their *own*
        power;
    And My people love *to have it* so.
    But what will you do in the end?

6 "O you children of Benjamin,
    Gather yourselves to flee from the
        midst of Jerusalem!
    Blow the trumpet in Tekoa,
    And set up a signal-fire in Beth
        Haccerem;
    For disaster appears out of the
        north,
    And great destruction.
2 I have likened the daughter of
        Zion
    To a lovely and delicate woman.
3 The shepherds with their flocks
        shall come to her.
    They shall pitch *their* tents against
        her all around.
    Each one shall pasture in his own
        place."

4 "Prepare war against her;
    Arise, and let us go up at noon.
    Woe to us, for the day goes away,
    For the shadows of the evening
        are lengthening.
5 Arise, and let us go by night,
    And let us destroy her palaces."

6 For thus has the LORD of hosts said:

    "Cut down trees,
    And build a mound against
        Jerusalem.
    This *is* the city to be punished.
    She *is* full of oppression in her
        midst.
7 As a fountain wells up with water,
    So she wells up with her
        wickedness.
    Violence and plundering are heard
        in her.
    Before Me continually *are* grief
        and wounds.
8 Be instructed, O Jerusalem,
    Lest My soul depart from you;
    Lest I make you desolate,
    A land not inhabited."

9 Thus says the LORD of hosts:

"They shall thoroughly glean as a
vine the remnant of Israel;
As a grape-gatherer, put your hand
back into the branches."

10 To whom shall I speak and give
warning,
That they may hear?
Indeed their ear is uncircumcised,
And they cannot give heed.
Behold, the word of the LORD is a
reproach to them;
They have no delight in it.

11 Therefore I am full of the fury of
the LORD.
I am weary of holding it in.
"I will pour it out on the children
outside,
And on the assembly of young
men together;
For even the husband shall be
taken with the wife,
The aged with him who is full of
days.

12 And their houses shall be turned
over to others,
Fields and wives together;
For I will stretch out My hand
Against the inhabitants of the
land," says the LORD.

13 "Because from the least of them
even to the greatest of them,
Everyone is given to
covetousness;
And from the prophet even to the
priest,
Everyone deals falsely.

14 They have also healed the hurt of
My people slightly,
Saying, 'Peace, peace!'
When there is no peace.

15 Were they ashamed when they had
committed abomination?
No! They were not at all
ashamed;
Nor did they know how to blush.
Therefore they shall fall among
those who fall;
At the time I punish them,
They shall be cast down," says the
LORD.

16 Thus says the LORD:

"Stand in the ways and see,
And ask for the old paths, where
the good way is,
And walk in it;
Then you will find rest for your
souls.
But they said, 'We will not walk in
it.'

17 Also, I set watchmen over you,
saying,
'Listen to the sound of the
trumpet!'
But they said, 'We will not listen.'

18 Therefore hear, you nations,
And know, O congregation, what
is among them.

19 Hear, O earth!
Behold, I will certainly bring
calamity on this people—
The fruit of their thoughts,
Because they have not heeded My
words
Nor My law, but rejected it.

20 For what purpose to Me
Comes frankincense from Sheba,
And sweet cane from a far
country?
Your burnt offerings are not
acceptable,
Nor your sacrifices sweet to Me."

21 Therefore thus says the LORD:

"Behold, I will lay stumbling blocks
before this people,
And the fathers and the sons
together shall fall on them.
The neighbor and his friend shall
perish."

22 Thus says the LORD:

"Behold, a people comes from the
north country,
And a great nation will be raised
from the farthest parts of the
earth.

23 They will lay hold on bow and
spear;
They are cruel and have no
mercy;
Their voice roars like the sea;
And they ride on horses,
As men of war set in array against
you, O daughter of Zion."

24 We have heard the report of it;
   Our hands grow feeble.
   Anguish has taken hold of us,
   Pain as of a woman in labor.
25 Do not go out into the field,
   Nor walk by the way.
   Because of the sword of the
      enemy,
   Fear *is* on every side.
26 O daughter of my people,
   Dress in sackcloth
   And roll about in ashes!
   Make mourning *as for* an only
      son, most bitter lamentation;
   For the plunderer will suddenly
      come upon us.

27 "I have set you *as* an assayer *and* a
      fortress among My people,
   That you may know and test their
      way.
28 They *are* all stubborn rebels,
      walking as slanderers.
   They are bronze and iron,
   They *are* all corrupters;
29 The bellows blow fiercely,
   The lead is consumed by the fire;
   The smelter refines in vain,
   For the wicked are not drawn off.
30 *People* will call them rejected
      silver,
   Because the LORD has rejected
      them."

~ PSALM 117:1, 2 ~

1 Praise the LORD, all you Gentiles!
   Laud Him, all you peoples!
2 For His merciful kindness is great
      toward us,
   And the truth of the LORD *endures*
      forever.

   Praise the LORD!

~ PROVERBS 27:3, 4 ~

3 A stone *is* heavy and sand *is* weighty,
   But a fool's wrath *is* heavier than
      both of them.

4 Wrath *is* cruel and anger a torrent,
   But who *is* able to stand before
      jealousy?

~ COLOSSIANS 1:1–29 ~

Paul, an apostle of Jesus Christ by the will of God, and Timothy our brother,

2 To the saints and faithful brethren in Christ *who are* in Colosse:

Grace to you and peace from God our Father and the Lord Jesus Christ.
3 We give thanks to the God and Father of our Lord Jesus Christ, praying always for you, 4 since we heard of your faith in Christ Jesus and of your love for all the saints; 5 because of the hope which is laid up for you in heaven, of which you heard before in the word of the truth of the gospel, 6 which has come to you, as *it has* also in all the world, and is bringing forth fruit, as *it is* also among you since the day you heard and knew the grace of God in truth; 7 as you also learned from Epaphras, our dear fellow servant, who is a faithful minister of Christ on your behalf, 8 who also declared to us your love in the Spirit.
9 For this reason we also, since the day we heard it, do not cease to pray for you, and to ask that you may be filled with the knowledge of His will in all wisdom and spiritual understanding; 10 that you may walk worthy of the Lord, fully pleasing *Him,* being fruitful in every good work and increasing in the knowledge of God; 11 strengthened with all might, according to His glorious power, for all patience and longsuffering with joy; 12 giving thanks to the Father who has qualified us to be partakers of the inheritance of the saints in the light. 13 He has delivered us from the power of darkness and conveyed *us* into the kingdom of the Son of His love, 14 in whom we have redemption through His blood, the forgiveness of sins.
15 He is the image of the invisible God, the firstborn over all creation. 16 For by Him all things were created that are in heaven and that are on earth, visible and invisible, whether thrones or dominions or principalities or powers. All things were created through Him and for Him. 17 And He is before all things, and in Him all things consist. 18 And He is the head of the body, the church, who is the beginning, the firstborn from the dead, that in

all things He may have the preeminence. ¹⁹ For it pleased *the Father that* in Him all the fullness should dwell, ²⁰ and by Him to reconcile all things to Himself, by Him, whether things on earth or things in heaven, having made peace through the blood of His cross.

²¹ And you, who once were alienated and enemies in your mind by wicked works, yet now He has reconciled ²² in the body of His flesh through death, to present you holy, and blameless, and above reproach in His sight— ²³ if indeed you continue in the faith, grounded and steadfast, and are not moved away from the hope of the gospel which you heard, which was preached to every creature under heaven, of which I, Paul, became a minister.

²⁴ I now rejoice in my sufferings for you, and fill up in my flesh what is lacking in the afflictions of Christ, for the sake of His body, which is the church, ²⁵ of which I became a minister according to the stewardship from God which was given to me for you, to fulfill the word of God, ²⁶ the mystery which has been hidden from ages and from generations, but now has been revealed to His saints. ²⁷ To them God willed to make known what are the riches of the glory of this mystery among the Gentiles: which is Christ in you, the hope of glory. ²⁸ Him we preach, warning every man and teaching every man in all wisdom, that we may present every man perfect in Christ Jesus. ²⁹ To this *end* I also labor, striving according to His working which works in me mightily.

~ JEREMIAH 7:1—8:22 ~

The word that came to Jeremiah from the LORD, saying, ² "Stand in the gate of the LORD's house, and proclaim there this word, and say, 'Hear the word of the LORD, all *you of* Judah who enter in at these gates to worship the LORD!' " ³ Thus says the LORD of hosts, the God of Israel: "Amend your ways and your doings, and I will cause you to dwell in this place. ⁴ Do not trust in these lying words, saying, 'The temple of the LORD, the temple of the LORD, the temple of the LORD *are* these.'

⁵ "For if you thoroughly amend your ways and your doings, if you thoroughly execute judgment between a man and his neighbor, ⁶ *if* you do not oppress the stranger, the fatherless, and the widow, and do not shed innocent blood in this place, or walk after other gods to your hurt, ⁷ then I will cause you to dwell in this place, in the land that I gave to your fathers forever and ever.

⁸ "Behold, you trust in lying words that cannot profit. ⁹ Will you steal, murder, commit adultery, swear falsely, burn incense to Baal, and walk after other gods whom you do not know, ¹⁰ and *then* come and stand before Me in this house which is called by My name, and say, 'We are delivered to do all these abominations'? ¹¹ Has this house, which is called by My name, become a den of thieves in your eyes? Behold, I, even I, have seen *it*," says the LORD.

¹² "But go now to My place which *was* in Shiloh, where I set My name at the first, and see what I did to it because of the wickedness of My people Israel. ¹³ And now, because you have done all these works," says the LORD, "and I spoke to you, rising up early and speaking, but you did not hear, and I called you, but you did not answer, ¹⁴ therefore I will do to the house which is called by My name, in which you trust, and to this place which I gave to you and your fathers, as I have done to Shiloh. ¹⁵ And I will cast you out of My sight, as I have cast out all your brethren—the whole posterity of Ephraim.

¹⁶ "Therefore do not pray for this people, nor lift up a cry or prayer for them, nor make intercession to Me; for I will not hear you. ¹⁷ Do you not see what they do in the cities of Judah and in the streets of Jerusalem? ¹⁸ The children gather wood, the fathers kindle the fire, and the women knead dough, to make cakes for the queen of heaven; and *they* pour out

drink offerings to other gods, that they may provoke Me to anger. [19] Do they provoke Me to anger?" says the LORD. "*Do they* not *provoke* themselves, to the shame of their own faces?"

[20] Therefore thus says the Lord GOD: "Behold, My anger and My fury will be poured out on this place—on man and on beast, on the trees of the field and on the fruit of the ground. And it will burn and not be quenched."

[21] Thus says the LORD of hosts, the God of Israel: "Add your burnt offerings to your sacrifices and eat meat. [22] For I did not speak to your fathers, or command them in the day that I brought them out of the land of Egypt, concerning burnt offerings or sacrifices. [23] But this is what I commanded them, saying, 'Obey My voice, and I will be your God, and you shall be My people. And walk in all the ways that I have commanded you, that it may be well with you.' [24] Yet they did not obey or incline their ear, but followed the counsels *and* the dictates of their evil hearts, and went backward and not forward. [25] Since the day that your fathers came out of the land of Egypt until this day, I have even sent to you all My servants the prophets, daily rising up early and sending *them*. [26] Yet they did not obey Me or incline their ear, but stiffened their neck. They did worse than their fathers.

[27] "Therefore you shall speak all these words to them, but they will not obey you. You shall also call to them, but they will not answer you.

[28] "So you shall say to them, 'This *is* a nation that does not obey the voice of the LORD their God nor receive correction. Truth has perished and has been cut off from their mouth. [29] Cut off your hair and cast *it* away, and take up a lamentation on the desolate heights; for the LORD has rejected and forsaken the generation of His wrath.' [30] For the children of Judah have done evil in My sight," says the LORD. "They have set their abominations in the house which is called by My name, to pollute it. [31] And they have built the high places of Tophet, which *is* in the Valley of the Son of Hinnom, to burn their sons and their daughters in the fire, which I did not command, nor did it come into My heart.

[32] "Therefore behold, the days are coming," says the LORD, "when it will no more be called Tophet, or the Valley of the Son of Hinnom, but the Valley of Slaughter; for they will bury in Tophet until there is no room. [33] The corpses of this people will be food for the birds of the heaven and for the beasts of the earth. And no one will frighten *them away.* [34] Then I will cause to cease from the cities of Judah and from the streets of Jerusalem the voice of mirth and the voice of gladness, the voice of the bridegroom and the voice of the bride. For the land shall be desolate.

8 "At that time," says the LORD, "they shall bring out the bones of the kings of Judah, and the bones of its princes, and the bones of the priests, and the bones of the prophets, and the bones of the inhabitants of Jerusalem, out of their graves. [2] They shall spread them before the sun and the moon and all the host of heaven, which they have loved and which they have served and after which they have walked, which they have sought and which they have worshiped. They shall not be gathered nor buried; they shall be like refuse on the face of the earth. [3] Then death shall be chosen rather than life by all the residue of those who remain of this evil family, who remain in all the places where I have driven them," says the LORD of hosts.

[4] "Moreover you shall say to them, 'Thus says the LORD:

"Will they fall and not rise?
Will one turn away and not
 return?
[5] Why has this people slidden back,
Jerusalem, in a perpetual
 backsliding?
They hold fast to deceit,
They refuse to return.
[6] I listened and heard,
But they do not speak aright.
No man repented of his
 wickedness,
Saying, 'What have I done?'
Everyone turned to his own
 course,
As the horse rushes into the
 battle.

Friend in Need

The Moores and the Lamberts have been friends for years. They went to some of the same schools. They had children about the same time. They've known each other through the important times and the everydays. They've served on PTA and played on softball leagues together.

It was Brenda Moore that let Coleen Lambert know her oldest son was taking drugs. It was Ben Lambert that let Bob Moore know that his daughter was in trouble at school. They wouldn't have trusted it from anyone else. They might not have believed it from anyone else. They saw the pain in each other's eyes and knew that they could trust the wounds of their friend.

Many people have come and gone in their town, but these families have remained friends and probably always will. They have stood by each other in every circumstance and they have grieved their losses together.

That's the kind of friends we all need to have. That's the kind of friends we all need to be: Friends who can be trusted in any kind of weather and with any kind of message.

Be that kind of friend today.

7 "Even the stork in the heavens
　　Knows her appointed times;
　　And the turtledove, the swift, and
　　　the swallow
　　Observe the time of their coming.
　　But My people do not know the
　　　judgment of the LORD.

8 "How can you say, 'We *are* wise,
　　And the law of the LORD *is* with
　　　us'?
　　Look, the false pen of the scribe
　　　certainly works falsehood.

9 The wise men are ashamed,
　　They are dismayed and taken.
　　Behold, they have rejected the
　　　word of the LORD;
　　So what wisdom do they have?

10 Therefore I will give their wives to
　　　others,
　　And their fields to those who will
　　　inherit *them;*
　　Because from the least even to the
　　　greatest
　　Everyone is given to covetousness;
　　From the prophet even to the
　　　priest
　　Everyone deals falsely.

11 For they have healed the hurt of
　　　the daughter of My people
　　　slightly,
　　Saying, 'Peace, peace!'
　　When *there is* no peace.

12 Were they ashamed when they had
　　　committed abomination?
　　No! They were not at all ashamed,
　　Nor did they know how to blush.
　　Therefore they shall fall among
　　　those who fall;
　　In the time of their punishment
　　They shall be cast down," says the
　　　LORD.

13 "I will surely consume them," says
　　　the LORD.
　　"No grapes *shall be* on the vine,
　　Nor figs on the fig tree,
　　And the leaf shall fade;
　　And *the things* I have given them
　　　shall pass away from them." ' "

14 "Why do we sit still?
　　Assemble yourselves,
　　And let us enter the fortified cities,
　　And let us be silent there.

For the LORD our God has put us
　　to silence
And given us water of gall to
　　drink,
Because we have sinned against
　　the LORD.

15 "We looked for peace, but no good
　　came;
　　And for a time of health, and
　　　there was trouble!

16 The snorting of His horses was
　　　heard from Dan.
　　The whole land trembled at the
　　　sound of the neighing of His
　　　strong ones;
　　For they have come and devoured
　　　the land and all that is in it,
　　The city and those who dwell in
　　　it."

17 "For behold, I will send serpents
　　　among you,
　　Vipers which cannot be charmed,
　　And they shall bite you," says the
　　　LORD.

18 I would comfort myself in sorrow;
　　My heart *is* faint in me.

19 Listen! The voice,
　　The cry of the daughter of my
　　　people
　　From a far country:
　　"Is not the LORD in Zion?
　　Is not her King in her?"

　　"Why have they provoked Me to
　　　anger
　　With their carved images—
　　With foreign idols?"

20 "The harvest is past,
　　The summer is ended,
　　And we are not saved!"

21 For the hurt of the daughter of my
　　　people I am hurt.
　　I am mourning;
　　Astonishment has taken hold of
　　　me.

22 *Is there* no balm in Gilead,
　　Is there no physician there?
　　Why then is there no recovery
　　For the health of the daughter of
　　　my people?

∼ PSALM 118:1-4 ∼

1 Oh, give thanks to the LORD, for *He is* good!
   For His mercy *endures* forever.

2 Let Israel now say,
   "His mercy *endures* forever."
3 Let the house of Aaron now say,
   "His mercy *endures* forever."
4 Let those who fear the LORD now say,
   "His mercy *endures* forever."

∼ PROVERBS 27:5, 6 ∼

5 Open rebuke *is* better
   Than love carefully concealed.

6 Faithful *are* the wounds of a friend,
   But the kisses of an enemy *are* deceitful.

∼ COLOSSIANS 2:1-23 ∼

For I want you to know what a great conflict I have for you and those in Laodicea, and *for* as many as have not seen my face in the flesh, [2] that their hearts may be encouraged, being knit together in love, and *attaining* to all riches of the full assurance of understanding, to the knowledge of the mystery of God, both of the Father and of Christ, [3] in whom are hidden all the treasures of wisdom and knowledge.

[4] Now this I say lest anyone should deceive you with persuasive words. [5] For though I am absent in the flesh, yet I am with you in spirit, rejoicing to see your *good* order and the steadfastness of your faith in Christ.

[6] As you therefore have received Christ Jesus the Lord, so walk in Him, [7] rooted and built up in Him and established in the faith, as you have been taught, abounding in it with thanksgiving.

[8] Beware lest anyone cheat you through philosophy and empty deceit, according to the tradition of men, according to the basic principles of the world, and not according to Christ. [9] For in Him dwells all the fullness of the Godhead bodily; [10] and you are complete in Him, who is the head of all principality and power.

[11] In Him you were also circumcised with the circumcision made without hands, by putting off the body of the sins of the flesh, by the circumcision of Christ, [12] buried with Him in baptism, in which you also were raised with *Him* through faith in the working of God, who raised Him from the dead. [13] And you, being dead in your trespasses and the uncircumcision of your flesh, He has made alive together with Him, having forgiven you all trespasses, [14] having wiped out the handwriting of requirements that was against us, which was contrary to us. And He has taken it out of the way, having nailed it to the cross. [15] Having disarmed principalities and powers, He made a public spectacle of them, triumphing over them in it.

[16] So let no one judge you in food or in drink, or regarding a festival or a new moon or sabbaths, [17] which are a shadow of things to come, but the substance is of Christ. [18] Let no one cheat you of your reward, taking delight in *false* humility and worship of angels, intruding into those things which he has not seen, vainly puffed up by his fleshly mind, [19] and not holding fast to the Head, from whom all the body, nourished and knit together by joints and ligaments, grows with the increase *that is* from God.

[20] Therefore, if you died with Christ from the basic principles of the world, why, as *though* living in the world, do you subject yourselves to regulations— [21] "Do not touch, do not taste, do not handle," [22] which all concern things which perish with the using—according to the commandments and doctrines of men? [23] These things indeed have an appearance of wisdom in self-imposed religion, *false* humility, and neglect of the body, *but are* of no value against the indulgence of the flesh.

1 Oh, that my head were waters,
And my eyes a fountain of tears,
That I might weep day and night
For the slain of the daughter of
my people!
2 Oh, that I had in the wilderness
A lodging place for travelers;
That I might leave my people,
And go from them!
For they *are* all adulterers,
An assembly of treacherous men.

3 "And *like* their bow they have bent
their tongues *for* lies.
They are not valiant for the truth
on the earth.
For they proceed from evil to evil,
And they do not know Me," says
the LORD.
4 "Everyone take heed to his
neighbor,
And do not trust any brother;
For every brother will utterly
supplant,
And every neighbor will walk with
slanderers.
5 Everyone will deceive his
neighbor,
And will not speak the truth;
They have taught their tongue to
speak lies;
They weary themselves to commit
iniquity.
6 Your dwelling place *is* in the midst
of deceit;
Through deceit they refuse to
know Me," says the LORD.

7 Therefore thus says the LORD of hosts:

"Behold, I will refine them and try
them;
For how shall I deal with the
daughter of My people?
8 Their tongue *is* an arrow shot
out;
It speaks deceit;
One speaks peaceably to his
neighbor with his mouth,
But in his heart he lies in wait.
9 Shall I not punish them for these
things?" says the LORD.

"Shall I not avenge Myself on such
a nation as this?"

10 I will take up a weeping and
wailing for the mountains,
And for the dwelling places of the
wilderness a lamentation,
Because they are burned up,
So that no one can pass through;
Nor can *men* hear the voice of the
cattle.
Both the birds of the heavens and
the beasts have fled;
They are gone.

11 "I will make Jerusalem a heap of
ruins, a den of jackals.
I will make the cities of Judah
desolate, without an
inhabitant."

12 Who *is* the wise man who may understand this? And *who is he* to whom
the mouth of the LORD has spoken, that
he may declare it? Why does the land
perish *and* burn up like a wilderness, so
that no one can pass through?
13 And the LORD said, "Because they
have forsaken My law which I set before
them, and have not obeyed My voice, nor
walked according to it, 14 but they have
walked according to the dictates of their
own hearts and after the Baals, which their
fathers taught them," 15 therefore thus says
the LORD of hosts, the God of Israel: "Behold, I will feed them, this people, with
wormwood, and give them water of gall
to drink. 16 I will scatter them also among
the Gentiles, whom neither they nor their
fathers have known. And I will send a
sword after them until I have consumed
them."
17 Thus says the LORD of hosts:

"Consider and call for the
mourning women,
That they may come;
And send for skillful wailing
women,
That they may come.
18 Let them make haste
And take up a wailing for us,

Slides, Swings, and Monkey Bars

> And whatever you do, do it heartily, as to the Lord and not to men.
>
> *Colossians 3:23*

A man once dreamed of building a playground in a ghetto neighborhood. He approached the owners of an apartment complex who gave him permission to build, but offered no help. As he walked through the complex one day, he met a little girl. He shared his dream of a playground with her and she immediately ran to her apartment. She returned with a thick stack of crayon sketches. She already shared his vision! Her drawings showed him the playground she wanted — one with two slides, lots of swings, and monkey bars. She showed him the exact spot where she wanted it built, and then she said, "I've been praying for this a long time!"

The man told her he would need lots of help to turn the dream into a reality, and the little girl nodded in agreement. In the coming weeks, she tirelessly slipped flyers under doors and made appointments for the man to speak to parents and teachers. Word of the project quickly spread. Several companies donated materials. The little girl convinced architects and fund-raisers to help. When construction began, hundreds of volunteers showed up to help. In no time at all, the playground the man and the young girl had dreamed of was a reality!

Are you willing to work for what you desire? It may be the very key to receiving God's best.

That our eyes may run with tears,
And our eyelids gush with water.

19 For a voice of wailing is heard
     from Zion:
'How we are plundered!
We are greatly ashamed,
Because we have forsaken the
     land,
Because we have been cast out of
     our dwellings.' "

20 Yet hear the word of the LORD,
     O women,
And let your ear receive the word
     of His mouth;
Teach your daughters wailing,
And everyone her neighbor a
     lamentation.

21 For death has come through our
     windows,
Has entered our palaces,
To kill off the children—*no longer
     to be* outside!
And the young men—*no longer* on
     the streets!

22 Speak, "Thus says the LORD:

'Even the carcasses of men shall fall
     as refuse on the open field,
Like cuttings after the harvester,
And no one shall gather *them*.' "

23 Thus says the LORD:

"Let not the wise *man* glory in his
     wisdom,
Let not the mighty *man* glory in
     his might,
Nor let the rich *man* glory in his
     riches;

24 But let him who glories glory in
     this,
That he understands and knows
     Me,
That I *am* the LORD, exercising
     lovingkindness, judgment, and
     righteousness in the earth.
For in these I delight," says the
     LORD.

25 "Behold, the days are coming," says
the LORD, "that I will punish all *who are*
circumcised with the uncircumcised—
26 Egypt, Judah, Edom, the people of Am-

mon, Moab, and all *who are* in the
farthest corners, who dwell in the wilderness. For all *these* nations *are* uncircumcised, and all the house of Israel *are*
uncircumcised in the heart."

10

Hear the word which the LORD
speaks to you, O house of Israel.
2 Thus says the LORD:

"Do not learn the way of the
     Gentiles;
Do not be dismayed at the signs of
     heaven,
For the Gentiles are dismayed at
     them.

3 For the customs of the peoples *are*
     futile;
For *one* cuts a tree from the
     forest,
The work of the hands of the
     workman, with the ax.

4 They decorate it with silver and
     gold;
They fasten it with nails and
     hammers
So that it will not topple.

5 They *are* upright, like a palm tree,
And they cannot speak;
They must be carried,
Because they cannot go *by
     themselves*.
Do not be afraid of them,
For they cannot do evil,
Nor can they do any good."

6 Inasmuch as *there is* none like You,
     O LORD
(You *are* great, and Your name *is*
     great in might),

7 Who would not fear You, O King
     of the nations?
For this is Your rightful due.
For among all the wise *men* of the
     nations,
And in all their kingdoms,
There is none like You.

8 But they are altogether dull-
     hearted and foolish;
A wooden idol *is* a worthless
     doctrine.

9 Silver is beaten into plates;
It is brought from Tarshish,
And gold from Uphaz,
The work of the craftsman

And of the hands of the
metalsmith;
Blue and purple *are* their clothing;
They *are* all the work of skillful
men.

10 But the LORD *is* the true God;
He *is* the living God and the
everlasting King.
At His wrath the earth will
tremble,
And the nations will not be able to
endure His indignation.

11 Thus you shall say to them: "The gods
that have not made the heavens and the
earth shall perish from the earth and from
under these heavens."

12 He has made the earth by His
power,
He has established the world by
His wisdom,
And has stretched out the heavens
at His discretion.

13 When He utters His voice,
There is a multitude of waters in
the heavens:
"And He causes the vapors to
ascend from the ends of the
earth.
He makes lightning for the rain,
He brings the wind out of His
treasuries."

14 Everyone is dull-hearted, without
knowledge;
Every metalsmith is put to shame
by an image;
For his molded image *is* falsehood,
And *there is* no breath in them.

15 They *are* futile, a work of errors;
In the time of their punishment
they shall perish.

16 The Portion of Jacob *is* not like
them,
For He *is* the Maker of all *things,*
And Israel *is* the tribe of His
inheritance;
The LORD of hosts *is* His name.

17 Gather up your wares from the
land,
O inhabitant of the fortress!

18 For thus says the LORD:

"Behold, I will throw out at this
time
The inhabitants of the land,
And will distress them,
That they may find *it so.*"

19 Woe is me for my hurt!
My wound is severe.
But I say, "Truly this *is* an
infirmity,
And I must bear it."

20 My tent is plundered,
And all my cords are broken;
My children have gone from me,
And they *are* no more.
There is no one to pitch my tent
anymore,
Or set up my curtains.

21 For the shepherds have become
dull-hearted,
And have not sought the LORD;
Therefore they shall not prosper,
And all their flocks shall be
scattered.

22 Behold, the noise of the report has
come,
And a great commotion out of the
north country,
To make the cities of Judah
desolate, a den of jackals.

23 O LORD, I know the way of man
is not in himself;
It is not in man who walks to
direct his own steps.

24 O LORD, correct me, but with
justice;
Not in Your anger, lest You bring
me to nothing.

25 Pour out Your fury on the
Gentiles, who do not know You,
And on the families who do not
call on Your name;
For they have eaten up Jacob,
Devoured him and consumed him,
And made his dwelling place
desolate.

~ PSALM 118:5-9 ~

5 I called on the LORD in distress;
The LORD answered me *and set me*
in a broad place.
6 The LORD *is* on my side;

I will not fear.
What can man do to me?
7 The LORD is for me among those
who help me;
Therefore I shall see *my desire* on
those who hate me.
8 *It is* better to trust in the LORD
Than to put confidence in man.
9 *It is* better to trust in the LORD
Than to put confidence in princes.

~ PROVERBS 27:7 ~

7 A satisfied soul loathes the
honeycomb,
But to a hungry soul every bitter
thing *is* sweet.

~ COLOSSIANS 3:1–25 ~

If then you were raised with Christ, seek those things which are above, where Christ is, sitting at the right hand of God. 2 Set your mind on things above, not on things on the earth. 3 For you died, and your life is hidden with Christ in God. 4 When Christ *who is* our life appears, then you also will appear with Him in glory.

5 Therefore put to death your members which are on the earth: fornication, uncleanness, passion, evil desire, and covetousness, which is idolatry. 6 Because of these things the wrath of God is coming upon the sons of disobedience, 7 in which you yourselves once walked when you lived in them.

8 But now you yourselves are to put off all these: anger, wrath, malice, blasphemy, filthy language out of your mouth. 9 Do not lie to one another, since you have put off the old man with his deeds, 10 and have put on the new *man* who is renewed in knowledge according to the image of Him who created him, 11 where there is neither Greek nor Jew, circumcised nor uncircumcised, barbarian, Scythian, slave *nor* free, but Christ *is* all and in all.

12 Therefore, as *the* elect of God, holy and beloved, put on tender mercies, kindness, humility, meekness, longsuffering; 13 bearing with one another, and forgiving one another, if anyone has a complaint against another; even as Christ forgave you, so you also *must do.* 14 But above all these things put on love, which is the bond of perfection. 15 And let the peace of God rule in your hearts, to which also you were called in one body; and be thankful. 16 Let the word of Christ dwell in you richly in all wisdom, teaching and admonishing one another in psalms and hymns and spiritual songs, singing with grace in your hearts to the Lord. 17 And *whatever* you do in word or deed, *do* all in the name of the Lord Jesus, giving thanks to God the Father through Him.

18 Wives, submit to your own husbands, as is fitting in the Lord.

19 Husbands, love your wives and do not be bitter toward them.

20 Children, obey your parents in all things, for this is well pleasing to the Lord.

21 Fathers, do not provoke your children, lest they become discouraged.

22 Bondservants, obey in all things your masters according to the flesh, not with eyeservice, as men-pleasers, but in sincerity of heart, fearing God. 23 And whatever you do, do it heartily, as to the Lord and not to men, 24 knowing that from the Lord you will receive the reward of the inheritance; for you serve the Lord Christ. 25 But he who does wrong will be repaid for what he has done, and there is no partiality.

READING 286 · OCTOBER 13

~ JEREMIAH 11:1—12:17 ~

The word that came to Jeremiah from the LORD, saying, 2 "Hear the words of this covenant, and speak to the men of Judah and to the inhabitants of Jerusalem; 3 and say to them, 'Thus says the LORD God of Israel: "Cursed *is* the man who does not obey the words of this covenant 4 which I commanded your fathers in the day I brought them out of the land of Egypt, from the iron furnace, saying, 'Obey My voice, and do according to all that I command you;

The Grand Adventure

In *A Closer Walk*, Catherine Marshall writes about a neighbor, "Cynthia felt she was losing her identity in an endless procession of social events and chauffeuring of children. During one cocktail party, Cynthia decided to limit herself to ginger ale and made some discoveries — not especially pleasant: 'I saw our crowd through new eyes,' she told me. 'No one was really saying anything. . . . All at once I began to ask questions about what we call "the good life." '

"In a search for answers, Cynthia set aside an hour each day for meditation. As she did this over a period of weeks there came to her the realization that she was being met in this quiet hour by something more than her own thoughts and psyche. . . . By Someone Who loved her and insisted this love be passed on to her family and friends."

Cynthia made changes in her life as the result of her "hour with God." She turned meal times into a time for family sharing. Family Game Night became a substitute for television once a week. She and her husband joined a Bible study that met twice a month. In all, Cynthia concluded, "God . . . the Author of creativity, is ready to make a dull life adventuresome the moment we allow His Holy Spirit to go to work."

Does your life seem dull and monotonous? Join the grand adventure. It's as simple as letting God lead you.

so shall you be My people, and I will be your God,' ⁵ that I may establish the oath which I have sworn to your fathers, to give them 'a land flowing with milk and honey,' as *it is* this day." ' "

And I answered and said, "So be it, LORD."

⁶ Then the LORD said to me, "Proclaim all these words in the cities of Judah and in the streets of Jerusalem, saying: 'Hear the words of this covenant and do them. ⁷ For I earnestly exhorted your fathers in the day I brought them up out of the land of Egypt, until this day, rising early and exhorting, saying, "Obey My voice." ⁸ Yet they did not obey or incline their ear, but everyone followed the dictates of his evil heart; therefore I will bring upon them all the words of this covenant, which I commanded *them* to do, but *which* they have not done.' "

⁹ And the LORD said to me, "A conspiracy has been found among the men of Judah and among the inhabitants of Jerusalem. ¹⁰ They have turned back to the iniquities of their forefathers who refused to hear My words, and they have gone after other gods to serve them; the house of Israel and the house of Judah have broken My covenant which I made with their fathers."

¹¹ Therefore thus says the LORD: "Behold, I will surely bring calamity on them which they will not be able to escape; and though they cry out to Me, I will not listen to them. ¹² Then the cities of Judah and the inhabitants of Jerusalem will go and cry out to the gods to whom they offer incense, but they will not save them at all in the time of their trouble. ¹³ For *according to* the number of your cities were your gods, O Judah; and *according to* the number of the streets of Jerusalem you have set up altars to *that* shameful thing, altars to burn incense to Baal.

¹⁴ "So do not pray for this people, or lift up a cry or prayer for them; for I will not hear *them* in the time that they cry out to Me because of their trouble.

¹⁵ "What has My beloved to do in My house,
  Having done lewd deeds with many?

And the holy flesh has passed from you.
When you do evil, then you rejoice.
¹⁶ The LORD called your name,
  Green Olive Tree, Lovely *and* of Good Fruit.
With the noise of a great tumult
He has kindled fire on it,
And its branches are broken.

¹⁷ "For the LORD of hosts, who planted you, has pronounced doom against you for the evil of the house of Israel and of the house of Judah, which they have done against themselves to provoke Me to anger in offering incense to Baal."

¹⁸ Now the LORD gave me knowledge *of it,* and I know *it;* for You showed me their doings. ¹⁹ But I *was* like a docile lamb brought to the slaughter; and I did not know that they had devised schemes against me, *saying,* "Let us destroy the tree with its fruit, and let us cut him off from the land of the living, that his name may be remembered no more."

²⁰ But, O LORD of hosts,
  You who judge righteously,
  Testing the mind and the heart,
  Let me see Your vengeance on them,
  For to You I have revealed my cause.

²¹ "Therefore thus says the LORD concerning the men of Anathoth who seek your life, saying, 'Do not prophesy in the name of the LORD, lest you die by our hand'— ²² therefore thus says the LORD of hosts: 'Behold, I will punish them. The young men shall die by the sword, their sons and their daughters shall die by famine; ²³ and there shall be no remnant of them, for I will bring catastrophe on the men of Anathoth, *even* the year of their punishment.' "

12 Righteous *are* You, O LORD,
  when I plead with You;
  Yet let me talk with You about *Your* judgments.
  Why does the way of the wicked prosper?

Why are those happy who deal so
   treacherously?
2   You have planted them, yes, they
   have taken root;
They grow, yes, they bear fruit.
You *are* near in their mouth
But far from their mind.

3   But You, O LORD, know me;
You have seen me,
And You have tested my heart
   toward You.
Pull them out like sheep for the
   slaughter,
And prepare them for the day of
   slaughter.
4   How long will the land mourn,
And the herbs of every field
   wither?
The beasts and birds are
   consumed,
For the wickedness of those who
   dwell there,
Because they said, "He will not see
   our final end."

5   "If you have run with the
   footmen, and they have wearied
   you,
Then how can you contend with
   horses?
And *if* in the land of peace,
In which you trusted, *they wearied
   you,*
Then how will you do in the
   floodplain of the Jordan?
6   For even your brothers, the house
   of your father,
Even they have dealt treacherously
   with you;
Yes, they have called a multitude
   after you.
Do not believe them,
Even though they speak smooth
   words to you.

7   "I have forsaken My house, I have
   left My heritage;
I have given the dearly beloved of
   My soul into the hand of her
   enemies.
8   My heritage is to Me like a lion in
   the forest;
It cries out against Me;

Therefore I have hated it.
9   My heritage *is* to Me *like* a
   speckled vulture;
The vultures all around *are* against
   her.
Come, assemble all the beasts of
   the field,
Bring them to devour!

10   "Many rulers have destroyed My
   vineyard,
They have trodden My portion
   underfoot;
They have made My pleasant
   portion a desolate wilderness.
11   They have made it desolate;
Desolate, it mourns to Me;
The whole land is made
   desolate,
Because no one takes *it* to heart.
12   The plunderers have come
On all the desolate heights in the
   wilderness,
For the sword of the LORD shall
   devour
From *one* end of the land to the
   other end of the land;
No flesh shall have peace.
13   They have sown wheat but reaped
   thorns;
They have put themselves to pain
   but do not profit.
But be ashamed of your harvest
Because of the fierce anger of the
   LORD."

14 Thus says the LORD: "Against all My
evil neighbors who touch the inheritance
which I have caused My people Israel to
inherit—behold, I will pluck them out
of their land and pluck out the house of
Judah from among them. 15 Then it shall
be, after I have plucked them out, that I
will return and have compassion on them
and bring them back, everyone to his heritage and everyone to his land. 16 And it
shall be, if they will learn carefully the
ways of My people, to swear by My name,
'As the LORD lives,' as they taught My
people to swear by Baal, then they shall
be established in the midst of My people.
17 But if they do not obey, I will utterly
pluck up and destroy that nation," says
the LORD.

~ PSALM 118:10–14 ~

10 All nations surrounded me,
But in the name of the LORD I will
destroy them.
11 They surrounded me,
Yes, they surrounded me;
But in the name of the LORD I will
destroy them.
12 They surrounded me like bees;
They were quenched like a fire of
thorns;
For in the name of the LORD I will
destroy them.
13 You pushed me violently, that I
might fall,
But the LORD helped me.
14 The LORD *is* my strength and song,
And He has become my salvation.

~ PROVERBS 27:8 ~

8 Like a bird that wanders from its
nest
Is a man who wanders from his
place.

~ COLOSSIANS 4:1–18 ~

Masters, give your bondservants what is
just and fair, knowing that you also have
a Master in heaven.
2 Continue earnestly in prayer, being
vigilant in it with thanksgiving; 3 meanwhile praying also for us, that God would
open to us a door for the word, to speak
the mystery of Christ, for which I am also
in chains, 4 that I may make it manifest,
as I ought to speak.
5 Walk in wisdom toward those *who are*
outside, redeeming the time. 6 *Let* your
speech always *be* with grace, seasoned
with salt, that you may know how you
ought to answer each one.
7 Tychicus, a beloved brother, faithful
minister, and fellow servant in the Lord,
will tell you all the news about me. 8 I am
sending him to you for this very purpose,
that he may know your circumstances and
comfort your hearts, 9 with Onesimus, a
faithful and beloved brother, who is *one*
of you. They will make known to you all
things which *are happening* here.
10 Aristarchus my fellow prisoner greets
you, with Mark the cousin of Barnabas
(about whom you received instructions:
if he comes to you, welcome him), 11 and
Jesus who is called Justus. These *are my*
only fellow workers for the kingdom of
God who are of the circumcision; they
have proved to be a comfort to me.
12 Epaphras, who is *one* of you, a
bondservant of Christ, greets you, always
laboring fervently for you in prayers, that
you may stand perfect and complete in
all the will of God. 13 For I bear him witness that he has a great zeal for you, and
those who are in Laodicea, and those in
Hierapolis. 14 Luke the beloved physician
and Demas greet you. 15 Greet the brethren who are in Laodicea, and Nymphas
and the church that *is* in his house.
16 Now when this epistle is read among
you, see that it is read also in the church
of the Laodiceans, and that you likewise
read the epistle from Laodicea. 17 And say
to Archippus, "Take heed to the ministry
which you have received in the Lord, that
you may fulfill it."
18 This salutation by my own hand—
Paul. Remember my chains. Grace *be* with
you. Amen.

READING 287 · OCTOBER 14

~ JEREMIAH 13:1—14:22 ~

Thus the LORD said to me: "Go and
get yourself a linen sash, and put it
around your waist, but do not put
it in water." 2 So I got a sash according to
the word of the LORD, and put *it* around
my waist.
3 And the word of the LORD came to
me the second time, saying, 4 "Take the
sash that you acquired, which *is* around
your waist, and arise, go to the Euphrates,
and hide it there in a hole in the rock."
5 So I went and hid it by the Euphrates, as
the LORD commanded me.
6 Now it came to pass after many days

Offspring Day

On the fourth Sunday of July, the descendants of Roberto and Raquel Beaumont celebrate "Offspring Day." They have been doing this since 1956, when Raquel gathered her five preteen children around the dinner table at their home in Lima, Peru. She placed a rose by the napkin of each daughter and a carnation by the napkin of each son.

Knowing in a few years her children would be going their separate ways, she told her children that the gifts she gave them on Offspring Day were not mere flowers, but a token of her true gifts to them — time and love. Furthermore, she expected them to pass on those same gifts to their children. Through the years, Raquel was the best example of her message: She always had time and love for each of her children, who regularly sought her advice and encouragement.

On Offspring Day each year, the elders who gather offer words of wisdom to their children. The young are encouraged to pick one thing about themselves they hope to improve in the coming year. It is a time for the generations to hear from one another and to set new goals for relationships. They do it all in the spirit of Raquel's example.

that the LORD said to me, "Arise, go to the Euphrates, and take from there the sash which I commanded you to hide there." [7] Then I went to the Euphrates and dug, and I took the sash from the place where I had hidden it; and there was the sash, ruined. It was profitable for nothing.

[8] Then the word of the LORD came to me, saying, [9] "Thus says the LORD: 'In this manner I will ruin the pride of Judah and the great pride of Jerusalem. [10] This evil people, who refuse to hear My words, who follow the dictates of their hearts, and walk after other gods to serve them and worship them, shall be just like this sash which is profitable for nothing. [11] For as the sash clings to the waist of a man, so I have caused the whole house of Israel and the whole house of Judah to cling to Me,' says the LORD, 'that they may become My people, for renown, for praise, and for glory; but they would not hear.'

[12] "Therefore you shall speak to them this word: 'Thus says the LORD God of Israel: "Every bottle shall be filled with wine." '

"And they will say to you, 'Do we not certainly know that every bottle will be filled with wine?'

[13] "Then you shall say to them, 'Thus says the LORD: "Behold, I will fill all the inhabitants of this land—even the kings who sit on David's throne, the priests, the prophets, and all the inhabitants of Jerusalem—with drunkenness! [14] And I will dash them one against another, even the fathers and the sons together," says the LORD. "I will not pity nor spare nor have mercy, but will destroy them." ' "

[15] Hear and give ear:
Do not be proud,
For the LORD has spoken.
[16] Give glory to the LORD your God
Before He causes darkness,
And before your feet stumble
On the dark mountains,
And while you are looking for
    light,
He turns it into the shadow of
    death
And makes *it* dense darkness.
[17] But if you will not hear it,

My soul will weep in secret for
    your pride;
My eyes will weep bitterly
And run down with tears,
Because the LORD's flock has been
    taken captive.

[18] Say to the king and to the queen
    mother,
"Humble yourselves;
Sit down,
For your rule shall collapse, the
    crown of your glory."
[19] The cities of the South shall be
    shut up,
And no one shall open *them;*
Judah shall be carried away
    captive, all of it;
It shall be wholly carried away
    captive.

[20] Lift up your eyes and see
Those who come from the north.
Where *is* the flock *that* was given
    to you,
Your beautiful sheep?
[21] What will you say when He
    punishes you?
For you have taught them
To be chieftains, to be head over
    you.
Will not pangs seize you,
Like a woman in labor?
[22] And if you say in your heart,
"Why have these things come upon
    me?"
For the greatness of your iniquity
Your skirts have been uncovered,
Your heels made bare.
[23] Can the Ethiopian change his skin
    or the leopard its spots?
Then may you also do good who
    are accustomed to do evil.

[24] "Therefore I will scatter them like
    stubble
That passes away by the wind of
    the wilderness.
[25] This is your lot,
The portion of your measures
    from Me," says the LORD,
"Because you have forgotten Me
And trusted in falsehood.
[26] Therefore I will uncover your
    skirts over your face,

That your shame may appear.
27 I have seen your adulteries
And your *lustful* neighings,
The lewdness of your harlotry,
Your abominations on the hills in
the fields.
Woe to you, O Jerusalem!
Will you still not be made clean?"

14 The word of the LORD that came to Jeremiah concerning the droughts.

2 "Judah mourns,
And her gates languish;
They mourn for the land,
And the cry of Jerusalem has gone
up.
3 Their nobles have sent their lads
for water;
They went to the cisterns *and*
found no water.
They returned with their vessels
empty;
They were ashamed and
confounded
And covered their heads.
4 Because the ground is parched,
For there was no rain in the land,
The plowmen were ashamed;
They covered their heads.
5 Yes, the deer also gave birth in the
field,
But left because there was no
grass.
6 And the wild donkeys stood in the
desolate heights;
They sniffed at the wind like
jackals;
Their eyes failed because *there was*
no grass."

7 O LORD, though our iniquities
testify against us,
Do it for Your name's sake;
For our backslidings are many,
We have sinned against You.
8 O the Hope of Israel, his Savior in
time of trouble,
Why should You be like a stranger
in the land,
And like a traveler *who* turns aside
to tarry for a night?
9 Why should You be like a man
astonished,

Like a mighty one *who* cannot
save?
Yet You, O LORD, *are* in our midst,
And we are called by Your name;
Do not leave us!

10 Thus says the LORD to this people:

"Thus they have loved to wander;
They have not restrained their
feet.
Therefore the LORD does not
accept them;
He will remember their iniquity
now,
And punish their sins."

11 Then the LORD said to me, "Do not pray for this people, for *their* good. 12 When they fast, I will not hear their cry; and when they offer burnt offering and grain offering, I will not accept them. But I will consume them by the sword, by the famine, and by the pestilence." 13 Then I said, "Ah, Lord GOD! Behold, the prophets say to them, 'You shall not see the sword, nor shall you have famine, but I will give you assured peace in this place.' " 14 And the LORD said to me, "The prophets prophesy lies in My name. I have not sent them, commanded them, nor spoken to them; they prophesy to you a false vision, divination, a worthless thing, and the deceit of their heart. 15 Therefore thus says the LORD concerning the prophets who prophesy in My name, whom I did not send, and who say, 'Sword and famine shall not be in this land'—'By sword and famine those prophets shall be consumed! 16 And the people to whom they prophesy shall be cast out in the streets of Jerusalem because of the famine and the sword; they will have no one to bury them—them nor their wives, their sons nor their daughters—for I will pour their wickedness on them.' 17 "Therefore you shall say this word to them:

'Let my eyes flow with tears night
and day,
And let them not cease;
For the virgin daughter of my
people

Has been broken with a mighty stroke, with a very severe blow.

18 If I go out to the field,
Then behold, those slain with the sword!
And if I enter the city,
Then behold, those sick from famine!
Yes, both prophet and priest go about in a land they do not know.' "

19 Have You utterly rejected Judah?
Has Your soul loathed Zion?
Why have You stricken us so that there is no healing for us?
We looked for peace, but there was no good;
And for the time of healing, and there was trouble.

20 We acknowledge, O LORD, our wickedness
And the iniquity of our fathers,
For we have sinned against You.

21 Do not abhor us, for Your name's sake;
Do not disgrace the throne of Your glory.
Remember, do not break Your covenant with us.

22 Are there any among the idols of the nations that can cause rain?
Or can the heavens give showers?
Are You not He, O LORD our God?
Therefore we will wait for You,
Since You have made all these.

~ PSALM 118:15-20 ~

15 The voice of rejoicing and salvation
Is in the tents of the righteous;
The right hand of the LORD does valiantly.

16 The right hand of the LORD is exalted;
The right hand of the LORD does valiantly.

17 I shall not die, but live,
And declare the works of the LORD.

18 The LORD has chastened me severely,
But He has not given me over to death.

19 Open to me the gates of righteousness;
I will go through them,
And I will praise the LORD.

20 This is the gate of the LORD,
Through which the righteous shall enter.

~ PROVERBS 27:9 ~

9 Ointment and perfume delight the heart,
And the sweetness of a man's friend gives delight by hearty counsel.

~ 1 THESSALONIANS 1:1-10 ~

Paul, Silvanus, and Timothy,

To the church of the Thessalonians in God the Father and the Lord Jesus Christ:

Grace to you and peace from God our Father and the Lord Jesus Christ.

2 We give thanks to God always for you all, making mention of you in our prayers, 3 remembering without ceasing your work of faith, labor of love, and patience of hope in our Lord Jesus Christ in the sight of our God and Father, 4 knowing, beloved brethren, your election by God. 5 For our gospel did not come to you in word only, but also in power, and in the Holy Spirit and in much assurance, as you know what kind of men we were among you for your sake.

6 And you became followers of us and of the Lord, having received the word in much affliction, with joy of the Holy Spirit, 7 so that you became examples to all in Macedonia and Achaia who believe. 8 For from you the word of the Lord has sounded forth, not only in Macedonia and Achaia, but also in every place. Your faith toward God has gone out, so that we do not need to say anything. 9 For they themselves declare concerning us what manner of entry we had to you, and how you turned to God from idols to serve the living and true God, 10 and to wait for His Son from heaven, whom He raised from the dead, even Jesus who delivers us from the wrath to come.

~ JEREMIAH 15:1—16:21 ~

Then the LORD said to me, "*Even* if Moses and Samuel stood before Me, My mind *would* not *be* favorable toward this people. Cast *them* out of My sight, and let them go forth. ² And it shall be, if they say to you, 'Where should we go?' then you shall tell them, 'Thus says the LORD:

"Such as *are* for death, to death;
And such as *are* for the sword, to
the sword;
And such as *are* for the famine, to
the famine;
And such as *are* for the captivity,
to the captivity." '

³ "And I will appoint over them four forms *of destruction*," says the LORD: "the sword to slay, the dogs to drag, the birds of the heavens and the beasts of the earth to devour and destroy. ⁴ I will hand them over to trouble, to all kingdoms of the earth, because of Manasseh the son of Hezekiah, king of Judah, for what he did in Jerusalem.

⁵ "For who will have pity on you,
O Jerusalem?
Or who will bemoan you?
Or who will turn aside to ask how
you are doing?
⁶ You have forsaken Me," says the
LORD,
"You have gone backward.
Therefore I will stretch out My
hand against you and destroy
you;
I am weary of relenting!
⁷ And I will winnow them with a
winnowing fan in the gates of
the land;
I will bereave *them* of children;
I will destroy My people,
Since they do not return from
their ways.
⁸ Their widows will be increased to
Me more than the sand of the
seas;
I will bring against them,
Against the mother of the young
men,

A plunderer at noonday;
I will cause anguish and terror to
fall on them suddenly.

⁹ "She languishes who has borne
seven;
She has breathed her last;
Her sun has gone down
While *it was* yet day;
She has been ashamed and
confounded.
And the remnant of them I will
deliver to the sword
Before their enemies," says the
LORD.

¹⁰ Woe is me, my mother,
That you have borne me,
A man of strife and a man of
contention to the whole earth!
I have neither lent for interest,
Nor have men lent to me for
interest.
Every one of them curses me.

¹¹ The LORD said:

"Surely it will be well with your
remnant;
Surely I will cause the enemy to
intercede with you
In the time of adversity and in the
time of affliction.
¹² Can anyone break iron,
The northern iron and the
bronze?
¹³ Your wealth and your treasures
I will give as plunder without
price,
Because of all your sins,
Throughout your territories.
¹⁴ And I will make *you* cross over
with your enemies
Into a land *which* you do not
know;
For a fire is kindled in My anger,
Which shall burn upon you."

¹⁵ O LORD, You know;
Remember me and visit me,
And take vengeance for me on my
persecutors.

In Your enduring patience, do not
take me away.
Know that for Your sake I have
suffered rebuke.
16 Your words were found, and I ate
them,
And Your word was to me the joy
and rejoicing of my heart;
For I am called by Your name,
O LORD God of hosts.
17 I did not sit in the assembly of the
mockers,
Nor did I rejoice;
I sat alone because of Your hand,
For You have filled me with
indignation.
18 Why is my pain perpetual
And my wound incurable,
Which refuses to be healed?
Will You surely be to me like an
unreliable stream,
As waters *that* fail?

19 Therefore thus says the LORD:

"If you return,
Then I will bring you back;
You shall stand before Me;
If you take out the precious from
the vile,
You shall be as My mouth.
Let them return to you,
But you must not return to them.
20 And I will make you to this people
a fortified bronze wall;
And they will fight against you,
But they shall not prevail against
you;
For I *am* with you to save you
And deliver you," says the LORD.
21 "I will deliver you from the hand of
the wicked,
And I will redeem you from the
grip of the terrible."

16 The word of the LORD also came to
me, saying, 2 "You shall not take a wife,
nor shall you have sons or daughters in
this place." 3 For thus says the LORD concerning the sons and daughters who are
born in this place, and concerning their
mothers who bore them and their fathers
who begot them in this land: 4 "They shall
die gruesome deaths; they shall not be
lamented nor shall they be buried, *but* they

shall be like refuse on the face of the earth.
They shall be consumed by the sword and
by famine, and their corpses shall be meat
for the birds of heaven and for the beasts
of the earth."
5 For thus says the LORD: "Do not enter
the house of mourning, nor go to lament
or bemoan them; for I have taken away
My peace from this people," says the
LORD, "lovingkindness and mercies.
6 Both the great and the small shall die in
this land. They shall not be buried; neither shall men lament for them, cut
themselves, nor make themselves bald for
them. 7 Nor shall *men* break *bread* in
mourning for them, to comfort them for
the dead; nor shall *men* give them the cup
of consolation to drink for their father or
their mother. 8 Also you shall not go into
the house of feasting to sit with them, to
eat and drink.
9 For thus says the LORD of hosts, the
God of Israel: "Behold, I will cause to
cease from this place, before your eyes and
in your days, the voice of mirth and the
voice of gladness, the voice of the bridegroom and the voice of the bride.
10 "And it shall be, when you show this
people all these words, and they say to
you, 'Why has the LORD pronounced all
this great disaster against us? Or what *is*
our iniquity? Or what *is* our sin that we
have committed against the LORD our
God?' 11 then you shall say to them, 'Because your fathers have forsaken Me,' says
the LORD; 'they have walked after other
gods and have served them and worshiped
them, and have forsaken Me and not kept
My law. 12 And you have done worse than
your fathers, for behold, each one follows
the dictates of his own evil heart, so that
no one listens to Me. 13 Therefore I will
cast you out of this land into a land that
you do not know, neither you nor your
fathers; and there you shall serve other
gods day and night, where I will not show
you favor.'
14 "Therefore behold, the days are coming," says the LORD, "that it shall no more
be said, 'The LORD lives who brought up
the children of Israel from the land of
Egypt,' 15 but, 'The LORD lives who
brought up the children of Israel from the
land of the north and from all the lands
where He had driven them.' For I will

The Flowers

The fictional character Sherlock Holmes is known for his keen powers of observation in solving crimes. But Holmes also used his skills for renewing his faith. In *The Adventure of the Naval Treaty*, Dr. Watson says of Holmes: "He walked past the couch to an open window and held up the drooping stalk of a moss rose, looking down at the dainty blend of crimson and green. It was a new phase of his character to me, for I had never before seen him show an interest in natural objects.

"'There is nothing in which deduction is so necessary as in religion,' said he, leaning with his back against the shutters. . . . 'Our highest assurance of the goodness of Providence seems to me to rest in the flowers. All other things, our powers, our desires, our food, are really necessary for our existence in the first instance. But this rose is an extra. Its smell and its color are an embellishment of life, not a condition of it. It is only goodness which gives extras, and so I say again that we have much to hope from the flowers.'"

Life is filled with these "extras"— gifts from a loving God that embellish and enrich our lives. Take time to notice them today!

bring them back into their land which I gave to their fathers.

[16] "Behold, I will send for many fishermen," says the LORD, "and they shall fish them; and afterward I will send for many hunters, and they shall hunt them from every mountain and every hill, and out of the holes of the rocks. [17] For My eyes *are* on all their ways; they are not hidden from My face, nor is their iniquity hidden from My eyes. [18] And first I will repay double for their iniquity and their sin, because they have defiled My land; they have filled My inheritance with the carcasses of their detestable and abominable idols."

[19] O LORD, my strength and my
    fortress,
My refuge in the day of affliction,
The Gentiles shall come to You
From the ends of the earth and
    say,
"Surely our fathers have inherited
    lies,
Worthlessness and unprofitable
    things."
[20] Will a man make gods for himself,
Which *are* not gods?

[21] "Therefore behold, I will this once
    cause them to know,
I will cause them to know
My hand and My might;
And they shall know that My
    name *is* the LORD.

～ PSALM 118:21–24 ～

[21] I will praise You,
For You have answered me,
And have become my salvation.

[22] The stone *which* the builders
    rejected
Has become the chief cornerstone.
[23] This was the LORD's doing;
It *is* marvelous in our eyes.
[24] This *is* the day the LORD has made;
We will rejoice and be glad in it.

～ PROVERBS 27:10 ～

[10] Do not forsake your own friend or
    your father's friend,

Nor go to your brother's house in
    the day of your calamity;
Better *is* a neighbor nearby than a
    brother far away.

～ 1 THESSALONIANS 2:1–20 ～

For you yourselves know, brethren, that our coming to you was not in vain. [2] But even after we had suffered before and were spitefully treated at Philippi, as you know, we were bold in our God to speak to you the gospel of God in much conflict. [3] For our exhortation *did* not *come* from error or uncleanness, nor *was it* in deceit.

[4] But as we have been approved by God to be entrusted with the gospel, even so we speak, not as pleasing men, but God who tests our hearts. [5] For neither at any time did we use flattering words, as you know, nor a cloak for covetousness—God *is* witness. [6] Nor did we seek glory from men, either from you or from others, when we might have made demands as apostles of Christ. [7] But we were gentle among you, just as a nursing *mother* cherishes her own children. [8] So, affectionately longing for you, we were well pleased to impart to you not only the gospel of God, but also our own lives, because you had become dear to us. [9] For you remember, brethren, our labor and toil; for laboring night and day, that we might not be a burden to any of you, we preached to you the gospel of God.

[10] You *are* witnesses, and God *also*, how devoutly and justly and blamelessly we behaved ourselves among you who believe; [11] as you know how we exhorted, and comforted, and charged every one of you, as a father *does* his own children, [12] that you would walk worthy of God who calls you into His own kingdom and glory.

[13] For this reason we also thank God without ceasing, because when you received the word of God which you heard from us, you welcomed *it* not *as* the word of men, but as it is in truth, the word of God, which also effectively works in you who believe. [14] For you, brethren, became imitators of the churches of God which are in Judea in Christ Jesus. For you also suffered the same things from your own

countrymen, just as they *did* from the Judeans, ¹⁵ who killed both the Lord Jesus and their own prophets, and have persecuted us; and they do not please God and are contrary to all men, ¹⁶ forbidding us to speak to the Gentiles that they may be saved, so as always to fill up *the measure of* their sins; but wrath has come upon them to the uttermost.

¹⁷ But we, brethren, having been taken away from you for a short time in presence, not in heart, endeavored more eagerly to see your face with great desire. ¹⁸ Therefore we wanted to come to you— even I, Paul, time and again—but Satan hindered us. ¹⁹ For what *is* our hope, or joy, or crown of rejoicing? *Is it* not even you in the presence of our Lord Jesus Christ at His coming? ²⁰ For you are our glory and joy.

READING 289 · OCTOBER 16

~ JEREMIAH 17:1—18:23 ~

¹ "The sin of Judah *is* written with a
    pen of iron;
With the point of a diamond *it is*
    engraved
On the tablet of their heart,
And on the horns of your altars,
² While their children remember
Their altars and their wooden
    images
By the green trees on the high
    hills.
³ O My mountain in the field,
I will give as plunder your wealth,
    all your treasures,
And your high places of sin within
    all your borders.
⁴ And you, even yourself,
Shall let go of your heritage which
    I gave you;
And I will cause you to serve your
    enemies
In the land which you do not
    know;
For you have kindled a fire in My
    anger *which* shall burn forever."

⁵ Thus says the LORD:

"Cursed *is* the man who trusts in
    man
And makes flesh his strength,
Whose heart departs from the
    LORD.
⁶ For he shall be like a shrub in the
    desert,
And shall not see when good
    comes,

But shall inhabit the parched
    places in the wilderness,
In a salt land *which is* not
    inhabited.

⁷ "Blessed *is* the man who trusts in
    the LORD,
And whose hope is the LORD.
⁸ For he shall be like a tree planted
    by the waters,
Which spreads out its roots by the
    river,
And will not fear when heat
    comes;
But its leaf will be green,
And will not be anxious in the
    year of drought,
Nor will cease from yielding fruit.

⁹ "The heart *is* deceitful above all
    things,
And desperately wicked;
Who can know it?
¹⁰ I, the LORD, search the heart,
I test the mind,
Even to give every man according
    to his ways,
According to the fruit of his
    doings.

¹¹ "*As* a partridge that broods but
    does not hatch,
So is he who gets riches, but not
    by right;
It will leave him in the midst of his
    days,
And at his end he will be a fool."

12 A glorious high throne from the
    beginning
    Is the place of our sanctuary.
13 O LORD, the hope of Israel,
    All who forsake You shall be
    ashamed.

"Those who depart from Me
Shall be written in the earth,
Because they have forsaken the
    LORD,
The fountain of living waters."

14 Heal me, O LORD, and I shall be
    healed;
    Save me, and I shall be saved,
    For You *are* my praise.
15 Indeed they say to me,
    "Where *is* the word of the LORD?
    Let it come now!"
16 As for me, I have not hurried
    away from *being* a shepherd
    who follows You,
    Nor have I desired the woeful day;
    You know what came out of my
    lips;
    It was right there before You.
17 Do not be a terror to me;
    You *are* my hope in the day of
    doom.
18 Let them be ashamed who
    persecute me,
    But do not let me be put to
    shame;
    Let them be dismayed,
    But do not let me be dismayed.
    Bring on them the day of doom,
    And destroy them with double
    destruction!

19 Thus the LORD said to me: "Go and
stand in the gate of the children of the
people, by which the kings of Judah come
in and by which they go out, and in all
the gates of Jerusalem; 20 and say to them,
'Hear the word of the LORD, you kings of
Judah, and all Judah, and all the inhabitants of Jerusalem, who enter by these
gates. 21 Thus says the LORD: "Take heed
to yourselves, and bear no burden on the
Sabbath day, nor bring *it* in by the gates
of Jerusalem; 22 nor carry a burden out of
your houses on the Sabbath day, nor do
any work, but hallow the Sabbath day, as
I commanded your fathers. 23 But they did

not obey nor incline their ear, but made
their neck stiff, that they might not hear
nor receive instruction.

24 "And it shall be, if you heed Me carefully," says the LORD, "to bring no burden
through the gates of this city on the Sabbath day, but hallow the Sabbath day, to
do no work in it, 25 then shall enter the
gates of this city kings and princes sitting
on the throne of David, riding in chariots
and on horses, they and their princes, accompanied by the men of Judah and the
inhabitants of Jerusalem; and this city shall
remain forever. 26 And they shall come
from the cities of Judah and from the
places around Jerusalem, from the land
of Benjamin and from the lowland, from
the mountains and from the South, bringing burnt offerings and sacrifices, grain
offerings and incense, bringing sacrifices
of praise to the house of the LORD.
27 "But if you will not heed Me to hallow the Sabbath day, such as not carrying
a burden when entering the gates of
Jerusalem on the Sabbath day, then I will
kindle a fire in its gates, and it shall devour the palaces of Jerusalem, and it shall
not be quenched." ' "

18 The word which came to Jeremiah
from the LORD, saying: 2 "Arise and go
down to the potter's house, and there I
will cause you to hear My words." 3 Then
I went down to the potter's house, and
there he was, making something at the
wheel. 4 And the vessel that he made
of clay was marred in the hand of the
potter; so he made it again into another
vessel, as it seemed good to the potter to
make.
5 Then the word of the LORD came to
me, saying: 6 "O house of Israel, can I not
do with you as this potter?" says the LORD.
"Look, as the clay *is* in the potter's hand,
so *are* you in My hand, O house of Israel!
7 The instant I speak concerning a nation
and concerning a kingdom, to pluck up,
to pull down, and to destroy *it*, 8 if that
nation against whom I have spoken turns
from its evil, I will relent of the disaster
that I thought to bring upon it. 9 And the
instant I speak concerning a nation and
concerning a kingdom, to build and to
plant *it*, 10 if it does evil in My sight so
that it does not obey My voice, then I will

Rah! Rah! Rah!

Part of our role as family members is to be a "fan" of those with whom we live. We are to be the number-one cheerleader for our spouse and children. In return, our children and spouse root us on in every area of our own life.

E-N-C-O-U-R-A-G-E-M-E-N-T is perhaps the best cheer you can learn!

E   is for enthusiasm and energy in supporting causes important to your family members.

N   is for saying, "Next time you'll succeed."

C   is for compassion.

O   is for open lines of communication.

U   is for understanding.

R   is for rooting on the team.

A   is for arranging your schedule to make time for others in your family.

G   is for going the second mile.

E   is for entertaining your children's friends.

M   is for modeling a positive attitude.

E   is for empowering your child with God's Word.

N   is for never giving up.

T   is for taking time out for hugs and praise.

"E-N-C-O-U-R-A-G-E" your family today, and let them know you "M-E-N-T" it!

relent concerning the good with which I said I would benefit it.

11 "Now therefore, speak to the men of Judah and to the inhabitants of Jerusalem, saying, 'Thus says the LORD: "Behold, I am fashioning a disaster and devising a plan against you. Return now every one from his evil way, and make your ways and your doings good." ' "

12 And they said, "That is hopeless! So we will walk according to our own plans, and we will every one obey the dictates of his evil heart."

13 Therefore thus says the LORD:

"Ask now among the Gentiles,
Who has heard such things?
The virgin of Israel has done a
    very horrible thing.
14 Will *a man* leave the snow water
    of Lebanon,
Which comes from the rock of the
    field?
Will the cold flowing waters be
    forsaken for strange waters?

15 "Because My people have forgotten
    Me,
They have burned incense to
    worthless idols.
And they have caused themselves
    to stumble in their ways,
From the ancient paths,
To walk in pathways and not on a
    highway,
16 To make their land desolate *and* a
    perpetual hissing;
Everyone who passes by it will be
    astonished
And shake his head.
17 I will scatter them as with an east
    wind before the enemy;
I will show them the back and not
    the face
In the day of their calamity."

18 Then they said, "Come and let us devise plans against Jeremiah; for the law shall not perish from the priest, nor counsel from the wise, nor the word from the prophet. Come and let us attack him with the tongue, and let us not give heed to any of his words."

19 Give heed to me, O LORD,
And listen to the voice of those
    who contend with me!
20 Shall evil be repaid for good?
For they have dug a pit for my
    life.
Remember that I stood before
    You
To speak good for them,
To turn away Your wrath from
    them.
21 Therefore deliver up their children
    to the famine,
And pour out their *blood*
By the force of the sword;
Let their wives *become* widows
And bereaved of their children.
Let their men be put to death,
Their young men *be* slain
By the sword in battle.
22 Let a cry be heard from their
    houses,
When You bring a troop suddenly
    upon them;
For they have dug a pit to take
    me,
And hidden snares for my feet.
23 Yet, LORD, You know all their
    counsel
Which is against me, to slay *me*.
Provide no atonement for their
    iniquity,
Nor blot out their sin from Your
    sight;
But let them be overthrown before
    You.
Deal *thus* with them
In the time of Your anger.

~ PSALM 118:25–29 ~

25 Save now, I pray, O LORD;
O LORD, I pray, send now prosperity.
26 Blessed *is* he who comes in the name
    of the LORD!
We have blessed you from the house
    of the LORD.
27 God *is* the LORD,
And He has given us light;
Bind the sacrifice with cords to the
    horns of the altar.
28 You *are* my God, and I will praise
    You;
You are my God, I will exalt You.

²⁹ Oh, give thanks to the LORD, for *He is* good!
For His mercy *endures* forever.

~ PROVERBS 27:11, 12 ~

¹¹ My son, be wise, and make my heart glad,
That I may answer him who reproaches me.

¹² A prudent *man* foresees evil *and* hides himself;
The simple pass on *and* are punished.

~ 1 THESSALONIANS 3:1–13 ~

Therefore, when we could no longer endure it, we thought it good to be left in Athens alone, ² and sent Timothy, our brother and minister of God, and our fellow laborer in the gospel of Christ, to establish you and encourage you concerning your faith, ³ that no one should be shaken by these afflictions; for you yourselves know that we are appointed to this. ⁴ For, in fact, we told you before when we were with you that we would suffer tribulation, just as it happened, and you know. ⁵ For this reason, when I could no longer endure it, I sent to know your faith, lest by some means the tempter had tempted you, and our labor might be in vain.

⁶ But now that Timothy has come to us from you, and brought us good news of your faith and love, and that you always have good remembrance of us, greatly desiring to see us, as we also *to see* you— ⁷ therefore, brethren, in all our affliction and distress we were comforted concerning you by your faith. ⁸ For now we live, if you stand fast in the Lord. ⁹ For what thanks can we render to God for you, for all the joy with which we rejoice for your sake before our God, ¹⁰ night and day praying exceedingly that we may see your face and perfect what is lacking in your faith?

¹¹ Now may our God and Father Himself, and our Lord Jesus Christ, direct our way to you. ¹² And may the Lord make you increase and abound in love to one another and to all, just as we *do* to you, ¹³ so that He may establish your hearts blameless in holiness before our God and Father at the coming of our Lord Jesus Christ with all His saints.

~ JEREMIAH 19:1—20:18 ~

Thus says the LORD: "Go and get a potter's earthen flask, and *take* some of the elders of the people and some of the elders of the priests. ² And go out to the Valley of the Son of Hinnom, which *is* by the entry of the Potsherd Gate; and proclaim there the words that I will tell you, ³ and say, 'Hear the word of the LORD, O kings of Judah and inhabitants of Jerusalem. Thus says the LORD of hosts, the God of Israel: "Behold, I will bring such a catastrophe on this place, that whoever hears of it, his ears will tingle.

⁴ "Because they have forsaken Me and made this an alien place, because they have burned incense in it to other gods whom neither they, their fathers, nor the kings of Judah have known, and have filled this place with the blood of the innocents ⁵ (they have also built the high places of Baal, to burn their sons with fire *for* burnt offerings to Baal, which I did not command or speak, nor did it come into My mind), ⁶ therefore behold, the days are coming," says the LORD, "that this place shall no more be called Tophet or the Valley of the Son of Hinnom, but the Valley of Slaughter. ⁷ And I will make void the counsel of Judah and Jerusalem in this place, and I will cause them to fall by the sword before their enemies and by the hands of those who seek their lives; their corpses I will give as meat for the birds of the heaven and for the beasts of the earth. ⁸ I will make this city desolate and a hissing; everyone who passes by it will be astonished and hiss because of all its plagues. ⁹ And I will cause them to eat the flesh of their sons and the flesh of their daughters, and everyone shall eat the flesh

of his friend in the siege and in the desperation with which their enemies and those who seek their lives shall drive them to despair." '

¹⁰ "Then you shall break the flask in the sight of the men who go with you, ¹¹ and say to them, 'Thus says the LORD of hosts: "Even so I will break this people and this city, as *one* breaks a potter's vessel, which cannot be made whole again; and they shall bury *them* in Tophet till *there is* no place to bury. ¹² Thus I will do to this place," says the LORD, "and to its inhabitants, and make this city like Tophet. ¹³ And the houses of Jerusalem and the houses of the kings of Judah shall be defiled like the place of Tophet, because of all the houses on whose roofs they have burned incense to all the host of heaven, and poured out drink offerings to other gods." ' "

¹⁴ Then Jeremiah came from Tophet, where the LORD had sent him to prophesy; and he stood in the court of the Lord's house and said to all the people, ¹⁵ "Thus says the LORD of hosts, the God of Israel: 'Behold, I will bring on this city and on all her towns all the doom that I have pronounced against it, because they have stiffened their necks that they might not hear My words.' "

20

Now Pashhur the son of Immer, the priest who *was* also chief governor in the house of the LORD, heard that Jeremiah prophesied these things. ² Then Pashhur struck Jeremiah the prophet, and put him in the stocks that *were* in the high gate of Benjamin, which *was* by the house of the LORD.

³ And it happened on the next day that Pashhur brought Jeremiah out of the stocks. Then Jeremiah said to him, "The LORD has not called your name Pashhur, but Magor-Missabib. ⁴ For thus says the LORD: 'Behold, I will make you a terror to yourself and to all your friends; and they shall fall by the sword of their enemies, and your eyes shall see *it*. I will give all Judah into the hand of the king of Babylon, and he shall carry them captive to Babylon and slay them with the sword. ⁵ Moreover I will deliver all the wealth of this city, all its produce, and all its precious things; all the treasures of the kings

of Judah I will give into the hand of their enemies, who will plunder them, seize them, and carry them to Babylon. ⁶ And you, Pashhur, and all who dwell in your house, shall go into captivity. You shall go to Babylon, and there you shall die, and be buried there, you and all your friends, to whom you have prophesied lies.' "

⁷ O LORD, You induced me, and I
        was persuaded;
    You are stronger than I, and have
        prevailed.
    I am in derision daily;
    Everyone mocks me.
⁸ For when I spoke, I cried out;
    I shouted, "Violence and
        plunder!"
    Because the word of the LORD was
        made to me
    A reproach and a derision daily.
⁹ Then I said, "I will not make
        mention of Him,
    Nor speak anymore in His name."
    But *His word* was in my heart like
        a burning fire
    Shut up in my bones;
    I was weary of holding *it* back,
    And I could not.
¹⁰ For I heard many mocking:
    "Fear on every side!"
    "Report," *they say,* "and we will
        report it!"
    All my acquaintances watched for
        my stumbling, *saying,*
    "Perhaps he can be induced;
    Then we will prevail against him,
    And we will take our revenge on
        him."

¹¹ But the LORD *is* with me as a
        mighty, awesome One.
    Therefore my persecutors will
        stumble, and will not prevail.
    They will be greatly ashamed, for
        they will not prosper.
    Their everlasting confusion will
        never be forgotten.
¹² But, O LORD of hosts,
    You who test the righteous,
    And see the mind and heart,
    Let me see Your vengeance on
        them;
    For I have pleaded my cause
        before You.

For Love

Perhaps the most famous "mother" in the world was Mother Teresa. In 1948 as Sister Teresa, she was given permission to leave her order of nearly twenty years and travel to India. On her first day in Calcutta, Teresa picked up five abandoned children and brought them to her "school." Before the year ended, she had forty-one students learning about hygiene in her classroom in a public park. Shortly thereafter, a new congregation was approved. Mother Teresa quickly named it "Missionaries of Charity." Within two years, their attention had become focused on the care of the dying.

Once, a poor beggar was picked up as he was dying in a pile of rubbish. Reduced by suffering and hunger to a mere specter, Mother Teresa took him to the Home for the Dying and put him in bed. When she began to wash him, she discovered his body was covered with worms. Pieces of skin came off as she washed him. For a brief moment, the man revived. In his semi-conscious state, he asked, "Why do you do it?" Mother Teresa responded with the two words that became her hallmark: "For love."

Ask any mother why she does what she does and you are likely to receive the same answer. Love is both a mother's work — and a mother's reward.

> For you yourselves are taught by God to love one another.
>
> *1 Thessalonians 4:9*

13 Sing to the LORD! Praise the
   LORD!
   For He has delivered the life of
      the poor
   From the hand of evildoers.

14 Cursed *be* the day in which I was
      born!
   Let the day not be blessed in
      which my mother bore me!
15 Let the man *be* cursed
   Who brought news to my father,
      saying,
   "A male child has been born to
      you!"
   Making him very glad.
16 And let that man be like the cities
   Which the LORD overthrew, and
      did not relent;
   Let him hear the cry in the
      morning
   And the shouting at noon,
17 Because he did not kill me from
      the womb,
   That my mother might have been
      my grave,
   And her womb always enlarged
      with me.
18 Why did I come forth from the
      womb to see labor and sorrow,
   That my days should be consumed
      with shame?

～ PSALM 119:1–8 ～

1 Blessed *are* the undefiled in the way,
   Who walk in the law of the LORD!
2 Blessed *are* those who keep His
      testimonies,
   Who seek Him with the whole
      heart!
3 They also do no iniquity;
   They walk in His ways.
4 You have commanded *us*
   To keep Your precepts diligently.
5 Oh, that my ways were directed
   To keep Your statutes!
6 Then I would not be ashamed,
   When I look into all Your
      commandments.
7 I will praise You with uprightness of
      heart,
   When I learn Your righteous
      judgments.

8 I will keep Your statutes;
   Oh, do not forsake me utterly!

～ PROVERBS 27:13 ～

13 Take the garment of him who is
      surety for a stranger,
   And hold it in pledge *when* he is
      surety for a seductress.

～ 1 THESSALONIANS 4:1–18 ～

Finally then, brethren, we urge and exhort in the Lord Jesus that you should
abound more and more, just as you received from us how you ought to walk
and to please God; ² for you know what
commandments we gave you through the
Lord Jesus.

³ For this is the will of God, your sanctification: that you should abstain from
sexual immorality; ⁴ that each of you
should know how to possess his own vessel in sanctification and honor, ⁵ not in
passion of lust, like the Gentiles who do
not know God; ⁶ that no one should take
advantage of and defraud his brother in
this matter, because the Lord *is* the
avenger of all such, as we also forewarned
you and testified. ⁷ For God did not call
us to uncleanness, but in holiness. ⁸ Therefore he who rejects *this* does not reject
man, but God, who has also given us His
Holy Spirit.

⁹ But concerning brotherly love you
have no need that I should write to
you, for you yourselves are taught by God
to love one another; ¹⁰ and indeed you
do so toward all the brethren who are in
all Macedonia. But we urge you, brethren, that you increase more and more;
¹¹ that you also aspire to lead a quiet life,
to mind your own business, and to work
with your own hands, as we commanded
you, ¹² that you may walk properly toward
those who are outside, and *that* you may
lack nothing.

¹³ But I do not want you to be ignorant, brethren, concerning those who have
fallen asleep, lest you sorrow as others
who have no hope. ¹⁴ For if we believe
that Jesus died and rose again, even so
God will bring with Him those who sleep
in Jesus.

15 For this we say to you by the word of the Lord, that we who are alive *and* remain until the coming of the Lord will by no means precede those who are asleep. 16 For the Lord Himself will descend from heaven with a shout, with the voice of an archangel, and with the trumpet of God. And the dead in Christ will rise first. 17 Then we who are alive *and* remain shall be caught up together with them in the clouds to meet the Lord in the air. And thus we shall always be with the Lord. 18 Therefore comfort one another with these words.

READING 291 · OCTOBER 18

~ JEREMIAH 21:1—22:30 ~

The word which came to Jeremiah from the LORD when King Zedekiah sent to him Pashhur the son of Melchiah, and Zephaniah the son of Maaseiah, the priest, saying, 2 "Please inquire of the LORD for us, for Nebuchadnezzar king of Babylon makes war against us. Perhaps the LORD will deal with us according to all His wonderful works, that *the king* may go away from us."

3 Then Jeremiah said to them, "Thus you shall say to Zedekiah, 4 'Thus says the LORD God of Israel: "Behold, I will turn back the weapons of war that *are* in your hands, with which you fight against the king of Babylon and the Chaldeans who besiege you outside the walls; and I will assemble them in the midst of this city. 5 I Myself will fight against you with an outstretched hand and with a strong arm, even in anger and fury and great wrath. 6 I will strike the inhabitants of this city, both man and beast; they shall die of a great pestilence. 7 And afterward," says the LORD, "I will deliver Zedekiah king of Judah, his servants and the people, and such as are left in this city from the pestilence and the sword and the famine, into the hand of Nebuchadnezzar king of Babylon, into the hand of their enemies, and into the hand of those who seek their life; and he shall strike them with the edge of the sword. He shall not spare them, or have pity or mercy." '

8 "Now you shall say to this people, 'Thus says the LORD: "Behold, I set before you the way of life and the way of death. 9 He who remains in this city shall die by the sword, by famine, and by pestilence; but he who goes out and defects to the Chaldeans who besiege you, he shall live, and his life shall be as a prize to him. 10 For I have set My face against this city for adversity and not for good," says the LORD. "It shall be given into the hand of the king of Babylon, and he shall burn it with fire." '

11 "And concerning the house of the king of Judah, *say,* 'Hear the word of the LORD, 12 O house of David! Thus says the LORD:

> "Execute judgment in the morning;
> And deliver *him who is* plundered
> Out of the hand of the oppressor,
> Lest My fury go forth like fire
> And burn so that no one can
>   quench *it,*
> Because of the evil of your doings.

13 "Behold, I *am* against you,
> O inhabitant of the valley,
> *And* rock of the plain," says the
>   LORD,
> "Who say, 'Who shall come down
>   against us?
> Or who shall enter our dwellings?'
14 But I will punish you according to
>   the fruit of your doings," says
>   the LORD;
> "I will kindle a fire in its forest,
> And it shall devour all things
>   around it." ' "

22 Thus says the LORD: "Go down to the house of the king of Judah, and there speak this word, 2 and say, 'Hear the word of the LORD, O king of Judah, you who sit on the throne of David, you and your servants and your people who enter these gates! 3 Thus says the LORD: "Execute judgment and righteousness, and deliver

the plundered out of the hand of the oppressor. Do no wrong and do no violence to the stranger, the fatherless, or the widow, nor shed innocent blood in this place. ⁴ For if you indeed do this thing, then shall enter the gates of this house, riding on horses and in chariots, accompanied by servants and people, kings who sit on the throne of David. ⁵ But if you will not hear these words, I swear by Myself," says the LORD, "that this house shall become a desolation." ' "

⁶ For thus says the LORD to the house of the king of Judah:

> "You *are* Gilead to Me,
> The head of Lebanon;
> *Yet* I surely will make you a
>   wilderness,
> Cities *which* are not inhabited.
> ⁷ I will prepare destroyers against
>   you,
> Everyone with his weapons;
> They shall cut down your choice
>   cedars
> And cast *them* into the fire.

⁸ And many nations will pass by this city; and everyone will say to his neighbor, 'Why has the LORD done so to this great city?' ⁹ Then they will answer, 'Because they have forsaken the covenant of the LORD their God, and worshiped other gods and served them.' "

> ¹⁰ Weep not for the dead, nor
>   bemoan him;
> Weep bitterly for him who goes
>   away,
> For he shall return no more,
> Nor see his native country.

¹¹ For thus says the LORD concerning Shallum the son of Josiah, king of Judah, who reigned instead of Josiah his father, who went from this place: "He shall not return here anymore, ¹² but he shall die in the place where they have led him captive, and shall see this land no more.

> ¹³ "Woe to him who builds his house
>   by unrighteousness
> And his chambers by injustice,
> *Who* uses his neighbor's service
>   without wages

> And gives him nothing for his
>   work,
> ¹⁴ Who says, 'I will build myself a
>   wide house with spacious
>   chambers,
> And cut out windows for it,
> Paneling *it* with cedar
> And painting *it* with vermilion.'

> ¹⁵ "Shall you reign because you
>   enclose *yourself* in cedar?
> Did not your father eat and drink,
> And do justice and righteousness?
> Then *it was* well with him.
> ¹⁶ He judged the cause of the poor
>   and needy;
> Then *it was* well.
> *Was* not this knowing Me?" says
>   the LORD.
> ¹⁷ "Yet your eyes and your heart *are*
>   for nothing but your
>   covetousness,
> For shedding innocent blood,
> And practicing oppression and
>   violence."

¹⁸ Therefore thus says the LORD concerning Jehoiakim the son of Josiah, king of Judah:

> "They shall not lament for him,
> *Saying,* 'Alas, my brother!' or 'Alas,
>   my sister!'
> They shall not lament for him,
> *Saying,* 'Alas, master!' or 'Alas, his
>   glory!'
> ¹⁹ He shall be buried with the burial
>   of a donkey,
> Dragged and cast out beyond the
>   gates of Jerusalem.

> ²⁰ "Go up to Lebanon, and cry out,
> And lift up your voice in Bashan;
> Cry from Abarim,
> For all your lovers are destroyed.
> ²¹ I spoke to you in your prosperity,
> *But* you said, 'I will not hear.'
> This *has been* your manner from
>   your youth,
> That you did not obey My voice.
> ²² The wind shall eat up all your
>   rulers,
> And your lovers shall go into
>   captivity;

All Things Are for the Best

Bernard Gilpin was accused of heresy before Bishop Bonner, and shortly thereafter was sent to London for trial. Gilpin's favorite saying was, "All things are for the best." He set out on his journey with that attitude, but on his way fell from his horse and broke his leg.

"Is all for the best now?" a mocker said, scorning Gilpin for his optimism. "I still believe so," he replied.

He turned out to be right. During the time he was convalescing from the accident and unable to resume his journey, Queen Mary died. Consequently, the case against him was dropped. Instead of being burned at the stake, Gilpin returned home in triumph.

While God never leads us into accidents or causes illness, He can take those things our enemy intends for evil and use them for our ultimate good. Therefore, rather than spending our energy railing against bad times, perhaps we should direct our efforts toward praising the One Who promises to work all things together for our good.

Surely then you will be ashamed
and humiliated
For all your wickedness.
23 O inhabitant of Lebanon,
Making your nest in the cedars,
How gracious will you be when
pangs come upon you,
Like the pain of a woman in
labor?

24 "As I live," says the LORD, "though
Coniah the son of Jehoiakim, king of
Judah, were the signet on My right hand,
yet I would pluck you off; 25 and I will
give you into the hand of those who seek
your life, and into the hand *of those* whose
face you fear—the hand of Nebuchadnezzar king of Babylon and the hand of the
Chaldeans. 26 So I will cast you out, and
your mother who bore you, into another
country where you were not born; and
there you shall die. 27 But to the land to
which they desire to return, there they
shall not return.

28 "Is this man Coniah a despised,
broken idol—
A vessel in which *is* no pleasure?
Why are they cast out, he and his
descendants,
And cast into a land which they do
not know?
29 O earth, earth, earth,
Hear the word of the LORD!
30 Thus says the LORD:
'Write this man down as childless,
A man *who* shall not prosper in
his days;
For none of his descendants shall
prosper,
Sitting on the throne of David,
And ruling anymore in Judah.' "

~ PSALM 119:9–16 ~

9 How can a young man cleanse his
way?
By taking heed according to Your
word.
10 With my whole heart I have sought
You;
Oh, let me not wander from Your
commandments!
11 Your word I have hidden in my
heart,

That I might not sin against You.
12 Blessed *are* You, O LORD!
Teach me Your statutes.
13 With my lips I have declared
All the judgments of Your mouth.
14 I have rejoiced in the way of Your
testimonies,
As *much as* in all riches.
15 I will meditate on Your precepts,
And contemplate Your ways.
16 I will delight myself in Your statutes;
I will not forget Your word.

~ PROVERBS 27:14 ~

14 He who blesses his friend with a
loud voice, rising early in the
morning,
It will be counted a curse to him.

~ 1 THESSALONIANS 5:1–28 ~

But concerning the times and the seasons,
brethren, you have no need that I should
write to you. 2 For you yourselves know
perfectly that the day of the Lord so comes
as a thief in the night. 3 For when they
say, "Peace and safety!" then sudden destruction comes upon them, as labor pains
upon a pregnant woman. And they shall
not escape. 4 But you, brethren, are not
in darkness, so that this Day should overtake you as a thief. 5 You are all sons of
light and sons of the day. We are not
of the night nor of darkness. 6 Therefore
let us not sleep, as others *do,* but let us
watch and be sober. 7 For those who sleep,
sleep at night, and those who get drunk
are drunk at night. 8 But let us who are of
the day be sober, putting on the breastplate of faith and love, and *as* a helmet
the hope of salvation. 9 For God did not
appoint us to wrath, but to obtain salvation through our Lord Jesus Christ, 10 who
died for us, that whether we wake or sleep,
we should live together with Him.
11 Therefore comfort each other and
edify one another, just as you also are
doing.
12 And we urge you, brethren, to recognize those who labor among you, and
are over you in the Lord and admonish
you, 13 and to esteem them very highly in
love for their work's sake. Be at peace
among yourselves.

¹⁴ Now we exhort you, brethren, warn those who are unruly, comfort the fainthearted, uphold the weak, be patient with all. ¹⁵ See that no one renders evil for evil to anyone, but always pursue what is good both for yourselves and for all.

¹⁶ Rejoice always, ¹⁷ pray without ceasing, ¹⁸ in everything give thanks; for this is the will of God in Christ Jesus for you.

¹⁹ Do not quench the Spirit. ²⁰ Do not despise prophecies. ²¹ Test all things; hold fast what is good. ²² Abstain from every form of evil.

²³ Now may the God of peace Himself sanctify you completely; and may your whole spirit, soul, and body be preserved blameless at the coming of our Lord Jesus Christ. ²⁴ He who calls you *is* faithful, who also will do *it*.

²⁵ Brethren, pray for us.

²⁶ Greet all the brethren with a holy kiss.

²⁷ I charge you by the Lord that this epistle be read to all the holy brethren.

²⁸ The grace of our Lord Jesus Christ *be* with you. Amen.

READING 292 · OCTOBER 19

~ JEREMIAH 23:1—24:10 ~

"Woe to the shepherds who destroy and scatter the sheep of My pasture!" says the LORD. ² Therefore thus says the LORD God of Israel against the shepherds who feed My people: "You have scattered My flock, driven them away, and not attended to them. Behold, I will attend to you for the evil of your doings," says the LORD. ³ "But I will gather the remnant of My flock out of all countries where I have driven them, and bring them back to their folds; and they shall be fruitful and increase. ⁴ I will set up shepherds over them who will feed them; and they shall fear no more, nor be dismayed, nor shall they be lacking," says the LORD.

⁵ "Behold, *the* days are coming," says the LORD,
"That I will raise to David a Branch of righteousness;
A King shall reign and prosper,
And execute judgment and righteousness in the earth.
⁶ In His days Judah will be saved,
And Israel will dwell safely;
Now this *is* His name by which He will be called:

THE LORD OUR RIGHTEOUSNESS.

⁷ "Therefore, behold, *the* days are coming," says the LORD, "that they shall no longer say, 'As the LORD lives who brought up the children of Israel from the land of Egypt,' ⁸ but, 'As the LORD lives who brought up and led the descendants of the house of Israel from the north country and from all the countries where I had driven them.' And they shall dwell in their own land."

⁹ My heart within me is broken Because of the prophets;
All my bones shake.
I am like a drunken man,
And like a man whom wine has overcome,
Because of the LORD,
And because of His holy words.
¹⁰ For the land is full of adulterers;
For because of a curse the land mourns.
The pleasant places of the wilderness are dried up.
Their course of life is evil,
And their might *is* not right.

¹¹ "For both prophet and priest are profane;
Yes, in My house I have found their wickedness," says the LORD.
¹² "Therefore their way shall be to them
Like slippery *ways;*
In the darkness they shall be driven on
And fall in them;
For I will bring disaster on them,

The year of their punishment,"
   says the LORD.
13 "And I have seen folly in the
   prophets of Samaria:
They prophesied by Baal
And caused My people Israel to
   err.
14 Also I have seen a horrible thing in
   the prophets of Jerusalem:
They commit adultery and walk in
   lies;
They also strengthen the hands of
   evildoers,
So that no one turns back from his
   wickedness.
All of them are like Sodom to Me,
And her inhabitants like
   Gomorrah.

15 "Therefore thus says the LORD of
hosts concerning the prophets:

'Behold, I will feed them with
   wormwood,
And make them drink the water of
   gall;
For from the prophets of
   Jerusalem
Profaneness has gone out into all
   the land.' "

16 Thus says the LORD of hosts:

"Do not listen to the words of the
   prophets who prophesy to you.
They make you worthless;
They speak a vision of their own
   heart,
Not from the mouth of the LORD.
17 They continually say to those who
   despise Me,
'The LORD has said, "You shall
   have peace" ';
And to everyone who walks
   according to the dictates of his
   own heart, they say,
'No evil shall come upon you.' "

18 For who has stood in the counsel
   of the LORD,
And has perceived and heard His
   word?
Who has marked His word and
   heard it?

19 Behold, a whirlwind of the LORD
   has gone forth in fury—
A violent whirlwind!
It will fall violently on the head of
   the wicked.
20 The anger of the LORD will not
   turn back
Until He has executed and
   performed the thoughts of His
   heart.
In the latter days you will
   understand it perfectly.

21 "I have not sent these prophets, yet
   they ran.
I have not spoken to them, yet
   they prophesied.
22 But if they had stood in My
   counsel,
And had caused My people to
   hear My words,
Then they would have turned
   them from their evil way
And from the evil of their doings.

23 "Am I a God near at hand," says
   the LORD,
"And not a God afar off?
24 Can anyone hide himself in secret
   places,
So I shall not see him?" says the
   LORD;
"Do I not fill heaven and earth?"
   says the LORD.

25 "I have heard what the prophets have
said who prophesy lies in My name, saying, 'I have dreamed, I have dreamed!'
26 How long will this be in the heart of
the prophets who prophesy lies? Indeed
they are prophets of the deceit of their
own heart, 27 who try to make My people
forget My name by their dreams which
everyone tells his neighbor, as their fathers
forgot My name for Baal.

28 "The prophet who has a dream, let
   him tell a dream;
And he who has My word, let him
   speak My word faithfully.
What is the chaff to the wheat?"
   says the LORD.
29 "Is not My word like a fire?" says
   the LORD,

One Thing at a Time

Charles Schwab, one of the first presidents of Bethlehem Steel Company, once told efficiency expert Ivy Lee, "If you can give us something to pep us up to do the things we ought to do, I'll gladly pay you anything you ask within reason."

"Fine," Lee said, "I can give you something in twenty minutes that will step up your 'doing' by at least fifty percent." He then handed Schwab a piece of paper and said, "Write down the six most important tasks you have to do tomorrow and number them in the order of their importance." Then Lee said, "Now put this paper in your pocket and first thing tomorrow morning look at item one and start working on it until it is finished. Then tackle item two in the same way; then item three and so on. Do this until quitting time. . . . Do this every working day. After you've convinced yourself of the value of this system, have your men try it . . . and then send me a check for what you think it is worth." A few weeks later Schwab sent Lee a check for $25,000, calling his advice the most profitable lesson he had ever learned.

In just five years, Lee's plan was largely responsible for turning Bethlehem Steel Company into the biggest independent steel producer in the world.

What are the six most important tasks you have to do?

"And like a hammer *that* breaks the rock in pieces?

[30] "Therefore behold, I *am* against the prophets," says the LORD, "who steal My words every one from his neighbor. [31] Behold, I *am* against the prophets," says the LORD, "who use their tongues and say, 'He says.' [32] Behold, I *am* against those who prophesy false dreams," says the LORD, "and tell them, and cause My people to err by their lies and by their recklessness. Yet I did not send them or command them; therefore they shall not profit this people at all," says the LORD.

[33] "So when these people or the prophet or the priest ask you, saying, 'What is the oracle of the LORD?' you shall then say to them, 'What oracle?' I will even forsake you," says the LORD. [34] "And *as for* the prophet and the priest and the people who say, 'The oracle of the LORD!' I will even punish that man and his house. [35] Thus every one of you shall say to his neighbor, and every one to his brother, 'What has the LORD answered?' and, 'What has the LORD spoken?' [36] And the oracle of the LORD you shall mention no more. For every man's word will be his oracle, for you have perverted the words of the living God, the LORD of hosts, our God. [37] Thus you shall say to the prophet, 'What has the LORD answered you?' and, 'What has the LORD spoken?' [38] But since you say, 'The oracle of the LORD!' therefore thus says the LORD: 'Because you say this word, "The oracle of the LORD!" and I have sent to you, saying, "Do not say, 'The oracle of the LORD!' " [39] therefore behold, I, even I, will utterly forget you and forsake you, and the city that I gave you and your fathers, and *will cast you* out of My presence. [40] And I will bring an everlasting reproach upon you, and a perpetual shame, which shall not be forgotten.' "

24 The LORD showed me, and there were two baskets of figs set before the temple of the LORD, after Nebuchadnezzar king of Babylon had carried away captive Jeconiah the son of Jehoiakim, king of Judah, and the princes of Judah with the craftsmen and smiths, from Jerusalem, and had brought them to Babylon. [2] One basket *had* very good figs, like the figs *that are* first ripe; and the other basket *had* very bad figs which could not be eaten, they were so bad. [3] Then the LORD said to me, "What do you see, Jeremiah?"

And I said, "Figs, the good figs, very good; and the bad, very bad, which cannot be eaten, they are so bad."

[4] Again the word of the LORD came to me, saying, [5] "Thus says the LORD, the God of Israel: 'Like these good figs, so will I acknowledge those who are carried away captive from Judah, whom I have sent out of this place for *their own* good, into the land of the Chaldeans. [6] For I will set My eyes on them for good, and I will bring them back to this land; I will build them and not pull *them* down, and I will plant them and not pluck *them* up. [7] Then I will give them a heart to know Me, that I *am* the LORD; and they shall be My people, and I will be their God, for they shall return to Me with their whole heart.

[8] 'And as the bad figs which cannot be eaten, they are so bad'—surely thus says the LORD—'so will I give up Zedekiah the king of Judah, his princes, the residue of Jerusalem who remain in this land, and those who dwell in the land of Egypt. [9] I will deliver them to trouble into all the kingdoms of the earth, for *their* harm, *to be* a reproach and a byword, a taunt and a curse, in all places where I shall drive them. [10] And I will send the sword, the famine, and the pestilence among them, till they are consumed from the land that I gave to them and their fathers.' "

~ PSALM 119:17–24 ~

[17] Deal bountifully with Your servant,
That I may live and keep Your word.
[18] Open my eyes, that I may see
Wondrous things from Your law.
[19] I *am* a stranger in the earth;
Do not hide Your commandments
from me.
[20] My soul breaks with longing
For Your judgments at all times.
[21] You rebuke the proud—the cursed,
Who stray from Your
commandments.

22 Remove from me reproach and
     contempt,
     For I have kept Your testimonies.
23 Princes also sit *and* speak against me,
     But Your servant meditates on Your
     statutes.
24 Your testimonies also *are* my delight
     And my counselors.

~ PROVERBS 27:15, 16 ~

15 A continual dripping on a very rainy
     day
     And a contentious woman are alike;
16 Whoever restrains her restrains the
     wind,
     And grasps oil with his right hand.

~ 2 THESSALONIANS 1:1–12 ~

Paul, Silvanus, and Timothy,

To the church of the Thessalonians in
God our Father and the Lord Jesus Christ:

2 Grace to you and peace from God our
Father and the Lord Jesus Christ.
3 We are bound to thank God always
for you, brethren, as it is fitting, because
your faith grows exceedingly, and the love
of every one of you all abounds toward
each other, 4 so that we ourselves boast of
you among the churches of God for your
patience and faith in all your persecutions
and tribulations that you endure, 5 *which
is* manifest evidence of the righteous judgment of God, that you may be counted
worthy of the kingdom of God, for which
you also suffer; 6 since *it is* a righteous
thing with God to repay with tribulation
those who trouble you, 7 and to *give* you
who are troubled rest with us when the
Lord Jesus is revealed from heaven with
His mighty angels, 8 in flaming fire taking
vengeance on those who do not know
God, and on those who do not obey the
gospel of our Lord Jesus Christ. 9 These
shall be punished with everlasting destruction from the presence of the Lord and
from the glory of His power, 10 when He
comes, in that Day, to be glorified in His
saints and to be admired among all those
who believe, because our testimony
among you was believed.
11 Therefore we also pray always for you
that our God would count you worthy of
this calling, and fulfill all the good pleasure of *His* goodness and the work of faith
with power, 12 that the name of our Lord
Jesus Christ may be glorified in you, and
you in Him, according to the grace of our
God and the Lord Jesus Christ.

~ JEREMIAH 25:1—26:24 ~

The word that came to Jeremiah
concerning all the people of Judah,
in the fourth year of Jehoiakim the
son of Josiah, king of Judah (which *was*
the first year of Nebuchadnezzar king of
Babylon), 2 which Jeremiah the prophet
spoke to all the people of Judah and to all
the inhabitants of Jerusalem, saying:
3 "From the thirteenth year of Josiah the
son of Amon, king of Judah, even to this
day, this *is* the twenty-third year in which
the word of the LORD has come to me;
and I have spoken to you, rising early and
speaking, but you have not listened.
4 And the LORD has sent to you all His
servants the prophets, rising early and
sending *them*, but you have not listened
nor inclined your ear to hear. 5 They said,
'Repent now everyone of his evil way and
his evil doings, and dwell in the land that
the LORD has given to you and your fathers forever and ever. 6 Do not go after
other gods to serve them and worship
them, and do not provoke Me to anger
with the works of your hands; and I will
not harm you.' 7 Yet you have not listened
to Me," says the LORD, "that you might
provoke Me to anger with the works of
your hands to your own hurt.
8 "Therefore thus says the LORD of
hosts: 'Because you have not heard My
words, 9 behold, I will send and take all
the families of the north,' says the LORD,
'and Nebuchadnezzar the king of Babylon,

My servant, and will bring them against this land, against its inhabitants, and against these nations all around, and will utterly destroy them, and make them an astonishment, a hissing, and perpetual desolations. ¹⁰ Moreover I will take from them the voice of mirth and the voice of gladness, the voice of the bridegroom and the voice of the bride, the sound of the millstones and the light of the lamp. ¹¹ And this whole land shall be a desolation *and* an astonishment, and these nations shall serve the king of Babylon seventy years.

¹² 'Then it will come to pass, when seventy years are completed, *that* I will punish the king of Babylon and that nation, the land of the Chaldeans, for their iniquity,' says the LORD; 'and I will make it a perpetual desolation. ¹³ So I will bring on that land all My words which I have pronounced against it, all that is written in this book, which Jeremiah has prophesied concerning all the nations. ¹⁴(For many nations and great kings shall be served by them also; and I will repay them according to their deeds and according to the works of their own hands.)' "

¹⁵ For thus says the LORD God of Israel to me: "Take this wine cup of fury from My hand, and cause all the nations, to whom I send you, to drink it. ¹⁶ And they will drink and stagger and go mad because of the sword that I will send among them."

¹⁷ Then I took the cup from the LORD's hand, and made all the nations drink, to whom the LORD had sent me: ¹⁸ Jerusalem and the cities of Judah, its kings and its princes, to make them a desolation, an astonishment, a hissing, and a curse, as *it is* this day; ¹⁹ Pharaoh king of Egypt, his servants, his princes, and all his people; ²⁰ all the mixed multitude, all the kings of the land of Uz, all the kings of the land of the Philistines (namely, Ashkelon, Gaza, Ekron, and the remnant of Ashdod); ²¹ Edom, Moab, and the people of Ammon; ²² all the kings of Tyre, all the kings of Sidon, and the kings of the coastlands which *are* across the sea; ²³ Dedan, Tema, Buz, and all *who are* in the farthest corners; ²⁴ all the kings of Arabia and all the kings of the mixed multitude who dwell in the desert; ²⁵ all the kings of Zimri, all the kings of Elam, and all the kings of the Medes; ²⁶ all the kings of the north, far and near, one with another; and all the kingdoms of the world which *are* on the face of the earth. Also the king of Sheshach shall drink after them.

²⁷ "Therefore you shall say to them, 'Thus says the LORD of hosts, the God of Israel: "Drink, be drunk, and vomit! Fall and rise no more, because of the sword which I will send among you." ' ²⁸ And it shall be, if they refuse to take the cup from your hand to drink, then you shall say to them, 'Thus says the LORD of hosts: "You shall certainly drink! ²⁹ For behold, I begin to bring calamity on the city which is called by My name, and should you be utterly unpunished? You shall not be unpunished, for I will call for a sword on all the inhabitants of the earth," says the LORD of hosts.'

³⁰ "Therefore prophesy against them all these words, and say to them:

'The LORD will roar from on high,
And utter His voice from His holy habitation;
He will roar mightily against His fold.
He will give a shout, as those who tread *the grapes,*
Against all the inhabitants of the earth.
³¹ A noise will come to the ends of the earth—
For the LORD has a controversy with the nations;
He will plead His case with all flesh.
He will give those *who are* wicked to the sword,' says the LORD."

³² Thus says the LORD of hosts:

"Behold, disaster shall go forth
From nation to nation,
And a great whirlwind shall be raised up
From the farthest parts of the earth.

³³ "And at that day the slain of the LORD shall be from *one* end of the earth even to the *other* end of the earth. They shall not

Playing in Harmony

Leonard Bernstein, the famous orchestra conductor, was once asked by an admirer, "What is the hardest instrument to play?"

Bernstein responded without hesitation, "Second fiddle. I can always get plenty of first violinists, but to find one who plays second violin with as much enthusiasm or second French horn or second flute, now that's a problem. And yet if no one plays second, we have no harmony."

Leaders cannot lead without followers, contributors, supporters; those willing to help without fanfare. Without leadership, an institution or organization of any size fails to move forward. Without those who follow enthusiastically, an institution has no strength. Envy can kill both progress and stability!

A true friend chooses to rejoice with those who succeed rather than envy them. This can be difficult at times, but when the glow of the success or blessing grows dim, the friendship remains brighter and more satisfying than ever.

be lamented, or gathered, or buried; they shall become refuse on the ground.

³⁴ "Wail, shepherds, and cry!
Roll about *in the ashes*,
You leaders of the flock!
For the days of your slaughter and
    your dispersions are fulfilled;
You shall fall like a precious vessel.
³⁵ And the shepherds will have no
    way to flee,
Nor the leaders of the flock to
    escape.
³⁶ A voice of the cry of the
    shepherds,
And a wailing of the leaders to the
    flock *will be heard.*
For the LORD has plundered their
    pasture,
³⁷ And the peaceful dwellings are cut
    down
Because of the fierce anger of the
    LORD.
³⁸ He has left His lair like the lion;
For their land is desolate
Because of the fierceness of the
    Oppressor,
And because of His fierce anger."

26

In the beginning of the reign of Jehoiakim the son of Josiah, king of Judah, this word came from the LORD, saying, ² "Thus says the LORD: 'Stand in the court of the LORD's house, and speak to all the cities of Judah, which come to worship *in* the LORD's house, all the words that I command you to speak to them. Do not diminish a word. ³ Perhaps everyone will listen and turn from his evil way, that I may relent concerning the calamity which I purpose to bring on them because of the evil of their doings.' ⁴ And you shall say to them, 'Thus says the LORD: "If you will not listen to Me, to walk in My law which I have set before you, ⁵ to heed the words of My servants the prophets whom I sent to you, both rising up early and sending *them* (but you have not heeded), ⁶ then I will make this house like Shiloh, and will make this city a curse to all the nations of the earth." ' "

⁷ So the priests and the prophets and all the people heard Jeremiah speaking these words in the house of the LORD. ⁸ Now it happened, when Jeremiah had made an end of speaking all that the LORD had commanded *him* to speak to all the people, that the priests and the prophets and all the people seized him, saying, "You will surely die! ⁹ Why have you prophesied in the name of the LORD, saying, 'This house shall be like Shiloh, and this city shall be desolate, without an inhabitant'?" And all the people were gathered against Jeremiah in the house of the LORD.

¹⁰ When the princes of Judah heard these things, they came up from the king's house to the house of the LORD and sat down in the entry of the New Gate of the LORD's *house.* ¹¹ And the priests and the prophets spoke to the princes and all the people, saying, "This man deserves to die! For he has prophesied against this city, as you have heard with your ears."
¹² Then Jeremiah spoke to all the princes and all the people, saying: "The LORD sent me to prophesy against this house and against this city with all the words that you have heard. ¹³ Now therefore, amend your ways and your doings, and obey the voice of the LORD your God; then the LORD will relent concerning the doom that He has pronounced against you. ¹⁴ As for me, here I am, in your hand; do with me as seems good and proper to you. ¹⁵ But know for certain that if you put me to death, you will surely bring innocent blood on yourselves, on this city, and on its inhabitants; for truly the LORD has sent me to you to speak all these words in your hearing."

¹⁶ So the princes and all the people said to the priests and the prophets, "This man does not deserve to die. For he has spoken to us in the name of the LORD our God."

¹⁷ Then certain of the elders of the land rose up and spoke to all the assembly of the people, saying: ¹⁸ "Micah of Moresheth prophesied in the days of Hezekiah king of Judah, and spoke to all the people of Judah, saying, 'Thus says the LORD of hosts:

"Zion shall be plowed *like* a field,
    Jerusalem shall become heaps of
        ruins,
    And the mountain of the temple
    Like the bare hills of the forest." '

¹⁹ Did Hezekiah king of Judah and all Judah ever put him to death? Did he not fear the LORD and seek the LORD's favor? And the LORD relented concerning the doom which He had pronounced against them. But we are doing great evil against ourselves."

²⁰ Now there was also a man who prophesied in the name of the LORD, Urijah the son of Shemaiah of Kirjath Jearim, who prophesied against this city and against this land according to all the words of Jeremiah. ²¹ And when Jehoiakim the king, with all his mighty men and all the princes, heard his words, the king sought to put him to death; but when Urijah heard *it,* he was afraid and fled, and went to Egypt. ²² Then Jehoiakim the king sent men to Egypt: Elnathan the son of Achbor, and *other* men *who went* with him to Egypt. ²³ And they brought Urijah from Egypt and brought him to Jehoiakim the king, who killed him with the sword and cast his dead body into the graves of the common people.

²⁴ Nevertheless the hand of Ahikam the son of Shaphan was with Jeremiah, so that they should not give him into the hand of the people to put him to death.

∼ PSALM 119:25–32 ∼

²⁵ My soul clings to the dust;
    Revive me according to Your
        word.
²⁶ I have declared my ways, and You
        answered me;
    Teach me Your statutes.
²⁷ Make me understand the way of
        Your precepts;
    So shall I meditate on Your
        wonderful works.
²⁸ My soul melts from heaviness;
    Strengthen me according to Your
        word.
²⁹ Remove from me the way of lying,
    And grant me Your law graciously.
³⁰ I have chosen the way of truth;
    Your judgments I have laid *before
        me.*
³¹ I cling to Your testimonies;
    O LORD, do not put me to shame!
³² I will run the course of Your
        commandments,
    For You shall enlarge my heart.

∼ PROVERBS 27:17 ∼

¹⁷ *As* iron sharpens iron,
    So a man sharpens the countenance
        of his friend.

∼ 2 THESSALONIANS 2:1–17 ∼

Now, brethren, concerning the coming of our Lord Jesus Christ and our gathering together to Him, we ask you, ² not to be soon shaken in mind or troubled, either by spirit or by word or by letter, as if from us, as though the day of Christ had come. ³ Let no one deceive you by any means; for *that Day will not come* unless the falling away comes first, and the man of sin is revealed, the son of perdition, ⁴ who opposes and exalts himself above all that is called God or that is worshiped, so that he sits as God in the temple of God, showing himself that he is God.

⁵ Do you not remember that when I was still with you I told you these things? ⁶ And now you know what is restraining, that he may be revealed in his own time. ⁷ For the mystery of lawlessness is already at work; only He who now restrains *will do so* until He is taken out of the way. ⁸ And then the lawless one will be revealed, whom the Lord will consume with the breath of His mouth and destroy with the brightness of His coming. ⁹ The coming of the *lawless one* is according to the working of Satan, with all power, signs, and lying wonders, ¹⁰ and with all unrighteous deception among those who perish, because they did not receive the love of the truth, that they might be saved. ¹¹ And for this reason God will send them strong delusion, that they should believe the lie, ¹² that they all may be condemned who did not believe the truth but had pleasure in unrighteousness.

¹³ But we are bound to give thanks to God always for you, brethren beloved by the Lord, because God from the beginning chose you for salvation through sanctification by the Spirit and belief in the truth, ¹⁴ to which He called you by our gospel, for the obtaining of the glory of our Lord Jesus Christ. ¹⁵ Therefore, brethren, stand fast and hold the

traditions which you were taught, whether by word or our epistle.

¹⁶ Now may our Lord Jesus Christ Himself, and our God and Father, who has loved us and given *us* everlasting consolation and good hope by grace, ¹⁷ comfort your hearts and establish you in every good word and work.

READING 294 · OCTOBER 21

～ JEREMIAH 27:1—28:17 ～

In the beginning of the reign of Jehoiakim the son of Josiah, king of Judah, this word came to Jeremiah from the LORD, saying, ² "Thus says the LORD to me: 'Make for yourselves bonds and yokes, and put them on your neck, ³ and send them to the king of Edom, the king of Moab, the king of the Ammonites, the king of Tyre, and the king of Sidon, by the hand of the messengers who come to Jerusalem to Zedekiah king of Judah. ⁴ And command them to say to their masters, "Thus says the LORD of hosts, the God of Israel—thus you shall say to your masters: ⁵ 'I have made the earth, the man and the beast that *are* on the ground, by My great power and by My outstretched arm, and have given it to whom it seemed proper to Me. ⁶ And now I have given all these lands into the hand of Nebuchadnezzar the king of Babylon, My servant; and the beasts of the field I have also given him to serve him. ⁷ So all nations shall serve him and his son and his son's son, until the time of his land comes; and then many nations and great kings shall make him serve them. ⁸ And it shall be, *that* the nation and kingdom which will not serve Nebuchadnezzar the king of Babylon, and which will not put its neck under the yoke of the king of Babylon, that nation I will punish,' says the LORD, 'with the sword, the famine, and the pestilence, until I have consumed them by his hand. ⁹ Therefore do not listen to your prophets, your diviners, your dreamers, your soothsayers, or your sorcerers, who speak to you, saying, "You shall not serve the king of Babylon." ¹⁰ For they prophesy a lie to you, to remove you far from your land; and I will drive you out, and you will perish. ¹¹ But the nations that bring their necks under the yoke of the king of Babylon and serve him, I will let them remain in their own land,' says the LORD, 'and they shall till it and dwell in it.' " ' "

¹² I also spoke to Zedekiah king of Judah according to all these words, saying, "Bring your necks under the yoke of the king of Babylon, and serve him and his people, and live! ¹³ Why will you die, you and your people, by the sword, by the famine, and by the pestilence, as the LORD has spoken against the nation that will not serve the king of Babylon? ¹⁴ Therefore do not listen to the words of the prophets who speak to you, saying, 'You shall not serve the king of Babylon,' for they prophesy a lie to you; ¹⁵ for I have not sent them," says the LORD, "yet they prophesy a lie in My name, that I may drive you out, and that you may perish, you and the prophets who prophesy to you."

¹⁶ Also I spoke to the priests and to all this people, saying, "Thus says the LORD: 'Do not listen to the words of your prophets who prophesy to you, saying, "Behold, the vessels of the LORD's house will now shortly be brought back from Babylon"; for they prophesy a lie to you. ¹⁷ Do not listen to them; serve the king of Babylon, and live! Why should this city be laid waste? ¹⁸ But if they *are* prophets, and if the word of the LORD is with them, let them now make intercession to the LORD of hosts, that the vessels which are left in the house of the LORD, *in* the house of the king of Judah, and at Jerusalem, do not go to Babylon.'

¹⁹ "For thus says the LORD of hosts concerning the pillars, concerning the Sea, concerning the carts, and concerning the remainder of the vessels that remain in this city, ²⁰ which Nebuchadnezzar king of Babylon did not take, when he carried away captive Jeconiah the son of Jehoiakim, king of Judah, from Jerusalem

Then Comes the Harvest

In *Traveling Hopefully*, Stan Mooneyham writes, "Early on I learned that it is a lot more fun to harvest than to hoe. Or, for that matter to plant. Few rewards can compare with that of plucking the bounty of the earth which represents the fruit of your labor. Harvesting is dramatic, fulfilling. You see what you get and you get what you see.

"Not that harvesting isn't hard work, too; but it's different. That's the payoff. The sense of reward represented by autumn's harvest can cause you to forget the less satisfying work of spring and summer. . . .

"Of course, it goes without saying that there would be no autumn harvest if there was no drudgery of spring and summer. Full barns require soil preparation, planting, and hoeing. The 'winning run' in baseball may top off all the prior runs, but the first was as necessary as the final one, even if the crowds didn't leap to their feet and tear the stadium apart early in the game."

If you find yourself feeling that your marriage has turned into drudgery and work, remember that life has a wonderful reward ahead. You may not see it today, but the harvest is growing!

to Babylon, and all the nobles of Judah and Jerusalem— 21 yes, thus says the LORD of hosts, the God of Israel, concerning the vessels that remain in the house of the LORD, and in the house of the king of Judah and of Jerusalem: 22 'They shall be carried to Babylon, and there they shall be until the day that I visit them,' says the LORD. 'Then I will bring them up and restore them to this place.' "

28 And it happened in the same year, at the beginning of the reign of Zedekiah king of Judah, in the fourth year *and* in the fifth month, *that* Hananiah the son of Azur the prophet, who *was* from Gibeon, spoke to me in the house of the LORD in the presence of the priests and of all the people, saying, 2 "Thus speaks the LORD of hosts, the God of Israel, saying: 'I have broken the yoke of the king of Babylon. 3 Within two full years I will bring back to this place all the vessels of the LORD's house, that Nebuchadnezzar king of Babylon took away from this place and carried to Babylon. 4 And I will bring back to this place Jeconiah the son of Jehoiakim, king of Judah, with all the captives of Judah who went to Babylon,' says the LORD, 'for I will break the yoke of the king of Babylon.' "

5 Then the prophet Jeremiah spoke to the prophet Hananiah in the presence of the priests and in the presence of all the people who stood in the house of the LORD, 6 and the prophet Jeremiah said, "Amen! The LORD do so; the LORD perform your words which you have prophesied, to bring back the vessels of the LORD's house and all who were carried away captive, from Babylon to this place. 7 Nevertheless hear now this word that I speak in your hearing and in the hearing of all the people: 8 The prophets who have been before me and before you of old prophesied against many countries and great kingdoms—of war and disaster and pestilence. 9 As for the prophet who prophesies of peace, when the word of the prophet comes to pass, the prophet will be known *as* one whom the LORD has truly sent."

10 Then Hananiah the prophet took the yoke off the prophet Jeremiah's neck and broke it. 11 And Hananiah spoke in the presence of all the people, saying, "Thus says the LORD: 'Even so I will break the yoke of Nebuchadnezzar king of Babylon from the neck of all nations within the space of two full years.' " And the prophet Jeremiah went his way.

12 Now the word of the LORD came to Jeremiah, after Hananiah the prophet had broken the yoke from the neck of the prophet Jeremiah, saying, 13 "Go and tell Hananiah, saying, 'Thus says the LORD: "You have broken the yokes of wood, but you have made in their place yokes of iron." 14 For thus says the LORD of hosts, the God of Israel: "I have put a yoke of iron on the neck of all these nations, that they may serve Nebuchadnezzar king of Babylon; and they shall serve him. I have given him the beasts of the field also." ' "

15 Then the prophet Jeremiah said to Hananiah the prophet, "Hear now, Hananiah, the LORD has not sent you, but you make this people trust in a lie. 16 Therefore thus says the LORD: 'Behold, I will cast you from the face of the earth. This year you shall die, because you have taught rebellion against the LORD.' "

17 So Hananiah the prophet died the same year in the seventh month.

∼ PSALM 119:33–40 ∼

33 Teach me, O LORD, the way of Your statutes,
And I shall keep it *to* the end.
34 Give me understanding, and I shall keep Your law;
Indeed, I shall observe it with *my* whole heart.
35 Make me walk in the path of Your commandments,
For I delight in it.
36 Incline my heart to Your testimonies,
And not to covetousness.
37 Turn away my eyes from looking at worthless things,
And revive me in Your way.
38 Establish Your word to Your servant,
Who *is devoted* to fearing You.
39 Turn away my reproach which I dread,
For Your judgments *are* good.
40 Behold, I long for Your precepts;
Revive me in Your righteousness.

～ PROVERBS 27:18 ～

18 Whoever keeps the fig tree will eat
    its fruit;
    So he who waits on his master will
    be honored.

～ 2 THESSALONIANS 3:1–18 ～

Finally, brethren, pray for us, that the
word of the Lord may run *swiftly* and be
glorified, just as *it is* with you, ² and that
we may be delivered from unreasonable
and wicked men; for not all have faith.
³ But the Lord is faithful, who will establish you and guard *you* from the evil
one. ⁴ And we have confidence in the Lord
concerning you, both that you do and will
do the things we command you.
⁵ Now may the Lord direct your hearts
into the love of God and into the patience
of Christ.
⁶ But we command you, brethren, in the
name of our Lord Jesus Christ, that you
withdraw from every brother who walks
disorderly and not according to the tradition which he received from us. ⁷ For you
yourselves know how you ought to follow us, for we were not disorderly among

you; ⁸ nor did we eat anyone's bread free
of charge, but worked with labor and toil
night and day, that we might not be a burden to any of you, ⁹ not because we do
not have authority, but to make ourselves
an example of how you should follow us.
¹⁰ For even when we were with you, we
commanded you this: If anyone will not
work, neither shall he eat. ¹¹ For we hear
that there are some who walk among you
in a disorderly manner, not working at
all, but are busybodies. ¹² Now those who
are such we command and exhort through
our Lord Jesus Christ that they work in
quietness and eat their own bread.
¹³ But *as for* you, brethren, do not grow
weary *in* doing good. ¹⁴ And if anyone
does not obey our word in this epistle,
note that person and do not keep company with him, that he may be ashamed.
¹⁵ Yet do not count *him* as an enemy, but
admonish *him* as a brother.
¹⁶ Now may the Lord of peace Himself
give you peace always in every way. The
Lord *be* with you all.
¹⁷ The salutation of Paul with my own
hand, which is a sign in every epistle; so I
write.
¹⁸ The grace of our Lord Jesus Christ
be with you all. Amen.

～ JEREMIAH 29:1—30:24 ～

Now these *are* the words of the letter that Jeremiah the prophet sent
from Jerusalem to the remainder
of the elders who were carried away captive—to the priests, the prophets, and all
the people whom Nebuchadnezzar had
carried away captive from Jerusalem to
Babylon. ²(This happened after Jeconiah
the king, the queen mother, the eunuchs,
the princes of Judah and Jerusalem, the
craftsmen, and the smiths had departed
from Jerusalem.) ³ *The letter was sent* by
the hand of Elasah the son of Shaphan,
and Gemariah the son of Hilkiah, whom
Zedekiah king of Judah sent to Babylon,
to Nebuchadnezzar king of Babylon,
saying,

⁴   Thus says the LORD of hosts, the
    God of Israel, to all who were
    carried away captive, whom I have
    caused to be carried away from
    Jerusalem to Babylon:

⁵   Build houses and dwell *in them;*
    plant gardens and eat their fruit.
    ⁶ Take wives and beget sons and
    daughters; and take wives for your
    sons and give your daughters to
    husbands, so that they may bear
    sons and daughters—that you may
    be increased there, and not
    diminished. ⁷ And seek the peace of
    the city where I have caused you to
    be carried away captive, and pray

to the LORD for it; for in its peace you will have peace. ⁸ For thus says the LORD of hosts, the God of Israel: Do not let your prophets and your diviners who are in your midst deceive you, nor listen to your dreams which you cause to be dreamed. ⁹ For they prophesy falsely to you in My name; I have not sent them, says the LORD.

¹⁰ For thus says the LORD: After seventy years are completed at Babylon, I will visit you and perform My good word toward you, and cause you to return to this place. ¹¹ For I know the thoughts that I think toward you, says the LORD, thoughts of peace and not of evil, to give you a future and a hope. ¹² Then you will call upon Me and go and pray to Me, and I will listen to you. ¹³ And you will seek Me and find *Me,* when you search for Me with all your heart. ¹⁴ I will be found by you, says the LORD, and I will bring you back from your captivity; I will gather you from all the nations and from all the places where I have driven you, says the LORD, and I will bring you to the place from which I cause you to be carried away captive.

¹⁵ Because you have said, "The LORD has raised up prophets for us in Babylon"— ¹⁶ therefore thus says the LORD concerning the king who sits on the throne of David, concerning all the people who dwell in this city, and concerning your brethren who have not gone out with you into captivity— ¹⁷ thus says the LORD of hosts: Behold, I will send on them the sword, the famine, and the pestilence, and will make them like rotten figs that cannot be eaten, they are so bad. ¹⁸ And I will pursue them with the sword, with famine, and with pestilence; and I will deliver them to trouble among all the kingdoms of the earth—to be a curse, an astonishment, a

hissing, and a reproach among all the nations where I have driven them, ¹⁹ because they have not heeded My words, says the LORD, which I sent to them by My servants the prophets, rising up early and sending *them;* neither would you heed, says the LORD. ²⁰ Therefore hear the word of the LORD, all you of the captivity, whom I have sent from Jerusalem to Babylon.

²¹ Thus says the LORD of hosts, the God of Israel, concerning Ahab the son of Kolaiah, and Zedekiah the son of Maaseiah, who prophesy a lie to you in My name: Behold, I will deliver them into the hand of Nebuchadnezzar king of Babylon, and he shall slay them before your eyes. ²² And because of them a curse shall be taken up by all the captivity of Judah who *are* in Babylon, saying, "The LORD make you like Zedekiah and Ahab, whom the king of Babylon roasted in the fire"; ²³ because they have done disgraceful things in Israel, have committed adultery with their neighbors' wives, and have spoken lying words in My name, which I have not commanded them. Indeed I know, and *am* a witness, says the LORD.

²⁴ You shall also speak to Shemaiah the Nehelamite, saying, ²⁵ Thus speaks the LORD of hosts, the God of Israel, saying: You have sent letters in your name to all the people who *are* at Jerusalem, to Zephaniah the son of Maaseiah the priest, and to all the priests, saying, ²⁶ "The LORD has made you priest instead of Jehoiada the priest, so that there should be officers *in* the house of the LORD over every man *who* is demented and considers himself a prophet, that you should put him in prison and in the stocks. ²⁷ Now therefore, why have you not rebuked Jeremiah of Anathoth who makes himself a prophet to you? ²⁸ For he has sent to us *in*

On Her Knees

Fanny Crosby, the eminent hymn writer, said she never attempted to write a hymn without first kneeling in prayer. Given the fact that she wrote more than 8,000 songs, she was obviously a woman of considerable prayer!

Like many creative people, Miss Crosby was often under pressure to meet deadlines. One such time came in 1869 as she tried to write lyrics for a tune composer, W. H. Doane. She couldn't seem to find the words, and then she remembered she had forgotten to pray. As she rose from her knees, she dictated — as fast as her assistant could write — the words for the famous hymn, "Jesus, Keep Me Near the Cross."

Another time, she had run short of money and needed exactly five dollars for a particular purpose. There was no time to call upon her publishers, so she simply prayed for the money. As she ended her prayer, she began to pace back and forth in her room, trying to get in the mood to write. Just at that time, an admirer called upon her. The two chatted briefly, and in parting, the woman pressed something into her hand. It was a five-dollar bill! Fanny fell to her knees in a prayer of thanksgiving, and upon rising, wrote, "All the Way My Saviour Leads Me."

Jesus does not just give us answers, He gives us Himself — He is The Answer.

> Then you will call upon Me and go and pray to Me, and I will listen to you. And you will seek Me and find Me, when you search for Me with all your heart.
>
> *Jeremiah 29:12-13*

Babylon, saying, 'This *captivity is* long; build houses and dwell *in them,* and plant gardens and eat their fruit.' "

29 Now Zephaniah the priest read this letter in the hearing of Jeremiah the prophet. 30 Then the word of the LORD came to Jeremiah, saying: 31 Send to all those in captivity, saying, Thus says the LORD concerning Shemaiah the Nehelamite: Because Shemaiah has prophesied to you, and I have not sent him, and he has caused you to trust in a lie— 32 therefore thus says the LORD: Behold, I will punish Shemaiah the Nehelamite and his family: he shall not have anyone to dwell among this people, nor shall he see the good that I will do for My people, says the LORD, because he has taught rebellion against the LORD.

30 The word that came to Jeremiah from the LORD, saying, 2 "Thus speaks the LORD God of Israel, saying: 'Write in a book for yourself all the words that I have spoken to you. 3 For behold, the days are coming,' says the LORD, 'that I will bring back from captivity My people Israel and Judah,' says the LORD. 'And I will cause them to return to the land that I gave to their fathers, and they shall possess it.' "

4 Now these *are* the words that the LORD spoke concerning Israel and Judah. 5 "For thus says the LORD:

'We have heard a voice of trembling,
Of fear, and not of peace.
6 Ask now, and see,
Whether a man is ever in labor with child?
So why do I see every man *with* his hands on his loins
Like a woman in labor,
And all faces turned pale?
7 Alas! For that day *is* great,
So that none *is* like it;
And it *is* the time of Jacob's trouble,
But he shall be saved out of it.

8 'For it shall come to pass in that day,'
Says the LORD of hosts,
'That I will break his yoke from your neck,
And will burst your bonds;
Foreigners shall no more enslave them.
9 But they shall serve the LORD their God,
And David their king,
Whom I will raise up for them.

10 'Therefore do not fear, O My servant Jacob,' says the LORD,
'Nor be dismayed, O Israel;
For behold, I will save you from afar,
And your seed from the land of their captivity.
Jacob shall return, have rest and be quiet,
And no one shall make *him* afraid.
11 For I *am* with you,' says the LORD,
'to save you;
Though I make a full end of all nations where I have scattered you,
Yet I will not make a complete end of you.
But I will correct you in justice,
And will not let you go altogether unpunished.'

12 "For thus says the LORD:

'Your affliction *is* incurable,
Your wound *is* severe.
13 *There is* no one to plead your cause,
That you may be bound up;
You have no healing medicines.
14 All your lovers have forgotten you;
They do not seek you;
For I have wounded you with the wound of an enemy,
With the chastisement of a cruel one,
For the multitude of your iniquities,
Because your sins have increased.
15 Why do you cry about your affliction?
Your sorrow *is* incurable.

Because of the multitude of your
   iniquities,
Because your sins have increased,
I have done these things to you.

16 'Therefore all those who devour
   you shall be devoured;
And all your adversaries, every
   one of them, shall go into
   captivity;
Those who plunder you shall
   become plunder,
And all who prey upon you I will
   make a prey.
17 For I will restore health to you
And heal you of your wounds,'
   says the LORD,
'Because they called you an outcast
   saying:
"This *is* Zion;
No one seeks her." '

18 "Thus says the LORD:

'Behold, I will bring back the
   captivity of Jacob's tents,
And have mercy on his dwelling
   places;
The city shall be built upon its
   own mound,
And the palace shall remain
   according to its own plan.
19 Then out of them shall proceed
   thanksgiving
And the voice of those who make
   merry;
I will multiply them, and they
   shall not diminish;
I will also glorify them, and they
   shall not be small.
20 Their children also shall be as
   before,
And their congregation shall be
   established before Me;
And I will punish all who oppress
   them.
21 Their nobles shall be from among
   them,
And their governor shall come
   from their midst;
Then I will cause him to draw
   near,
And he shall approach Me;

For who *is* this who pledged his
   heart to approach Me?' says the
   LORD.
22 'You shall be My people,
And I will be your God.' "

23 Behold, the whirlwind of the
   LORD
Goes forth with fury,
A continuing whirlwind;
It will fall violently on the head of
   the wicked.
24 The fierce anger of the LORD will
   not return until He has done it,
And until He has performed the
   intents of His heart.

In the latter days you will consider
   it.

∼ PSALM 119:41–48 ∼

41 Let Your mercies come also to me,
   O LORD—
Your salvation according to Your
   word.
42 So shall I have an answer for him
   who reproaches me,
For I trust in Your word.
43 And take not the word of truth
   utterly out of my mouth,
For I have hoped in Your
   ordinances.
44 So shall I keep Your law continually,
Forever and ever.
45 And I will walk at liberty,
For I seek Your precepts.
46 I will speak of Your testimonies also
   before kings,
And will not be ashamed.
47 And I will delight myself in Your
   commandments,
Which I love.
48 My hands also I will lift up to Your
   commandments,
Which I love,
And I will meditate on Your
   statutes.

∼ PROVERBS 27:19 ∼

19 As in water face *reflects* face,
So a man's heart *reveals* the man.

~ 1 TIMOTHY 1:1–20 ~

Paul, an apostle of Jesus Christ, by the commandment of God our Savior and the Lord Jesus Christ, our hope,

² To Timothy, a true son in the faith:

Grace, mercy, *and* peace from God our Father and Jesus Christ our Lord. ³ As I urged you when I went into Macedonia—remain in Ephesus that you may charge some that they teach no other doctrine, ⁴ nor give heed to fables and endless genealogies, which cause disputes rather than godly edification which is in faith. ⁵ Now the purpose of the commandment is love from a pure heart, *from* a good conscience, and *from* sincere faith, ⁶ from which some, having strayed, have turned aside to idle talk, ⁷ desiring to be teachers of the law, understanding neither what they say nor the things which they affirm.

⁸ But we know that the law *is* good if one uses it lawfully, ⁹ knowing this: that the law is not made for a righteous person, but for *the* lawless and insubordinate, for *the* ungodly and for sinners, for *the* unholy and profane, for murderers of fathers and murderers of mothers, for manslayers, ¹⁰ for fornicators, for sodomites, for kidnappers, for liars, for perjurers, and if there is any other thing that is contrary to sound doctrine, ¹¹ according to the glorious gospel of the blessed God which was committed to my trust.

¹² And I thank Christ Jesus our Lord who has enabled me, because He counted me faithful, putting *me* into the ministry, ¹³ although I was formerly a blasphemer, a persecutor, and an insolent man; but I obtained mercy because I did *it* ignorantly in unbelief. ¹⁴ And the grace of our Lord was exceedingly abundant, with faith and love which are in Christ Jesus. ¹⁵ This *is* a faithful saying and worthy of all acceptance, that Christ Jesus came into the world to save sinners, of whom I am chief. ¹⁶ However, for this reason I obtained mercy, that in me first Jesus Christ might show all longsuffering, as a pattern to those who are going to believe on Him for everlasting life. ¹⁷ Now to the King eternal, immortal, invisible, to God who alone is wise, *be* honor and glory forever and ever. Amen.

¹⁸ This charge I commit to you, son Timothy, according to the prophecies previously made concerning you, that by them you may wage the good warfare, ¹⁹ having faith and a good conscience, which some having rejected, concerning the faith have suffered shipwreck, ²⁰ of whom are Hymenaeus and Alexander, whom I delivered to Satan that they may learn not to blaspheme.

READING 296 · OCTOBER 23

~ JEREMIAH 31:1—32:44 ~

"At the same time," says the LORD, "I will be the God of all the families of Israel, and they shall be My people."
² Thus says the LORD:

"The people who survived the sword
Found grace in the wilderness—

Israel, when I went to give him rest."

³   The LORD has appeared of old to me, *saying:*
"Yes, I have loved you with an everlasting love;
Therefore with lovingkindness I have drawn you.

Boulders and Pebbles

In *He Still Moves Stones*, Max Lucado writes: "What matters to you matters to God. You probably think that's true when it comes to the big stuff. When it comes to the major-league difficulties like death, disease, sin, and disaster — you know that God cares. But what about the smaller things? What about grouchy bosses or flat tires or lost dogs? What about broken dishes, late flights, toothaches, or a crashed hard drive? Do these matter to God?

"I mean, he's got a universe to run. He's got the planets to keep balanced and presidents and kings to watch over. He's got wars to worry with and famines to fix. Who am I to tell him about my ingrown toenail? I'm glad you asked. Let me tell you who you are . . . you are God's child. . . . As a result, if something is important to you, it's important to God."

In labeling something as a "big" problem, we are implying that it will take God more effort to resolve it. To say something is a "little" problem implies less effort. The fact is, there are no degrees of difficulty to One Who is omnipotent. God is all-powerful, and therefore, all-capable. He knows all the solutions, even as He knows all the problems. No problem, big or small, is beyond His love, concern, and ability. He removes the boulders from our path and the pebbles from our shoe.

> Ah, Lord God! Behold, You have made the heavens and the earth by Your great power and outstretched arm. There is nothing too hard for You.
>
> *Jeremiah 32:17*

4 Again I will build you, and you
    shall be rebuilt,
  O virgin of Israel!
  You shall again be adorned with
    your tambourines,
  And shall go forth in the dances of
    those who rejoice.
5 You shall yet plant vines on the
    mountains of Samaria;
  The planters shall plant and eat
    them as ordinary food.
6 For there shall be a day
  When the watchmen will cry on
    Mount Ephraim,
  'Arise, and let us go up *to* Zion,
  To the LORD our God.' "

7 For thus says the LORD:

  "Sing with gladness for Jacob,
  And shout among the chief of the
    nations;
  Proclaim, give praise, and say,
  'O LORD, save Your people,
  The remnant of Israel!'
8 Behold, I will bring them from the
    north country,
  And gather them from the ends of
    the earth,
  Among them the blind and the
    lame,
  The woman with child
  And the one who labors with
    child, together;
  A great throng shall return there.
9 They shall come with weeping,
  And with supplications I will lead
    them.
  I will cause them to walk by the
    rivers of waters,
  In a straight way in which they
    shall not stumble;
  For I am a Father to Israel,
  And Ephraim *is* My firstborn.

10 "Hear the word of the LORD,
    O nations,
  And declare *it* in the isles afar off,
    and say,
  'He who scattered Israel will
    gather him,
  And keep him as a shepherd *does*
    his flock.'
11 For the LORD has redeemed Jacob,

  And ransomed him from the hand
    of one stronger than he.
12 Therefore they shall come and
    sing in the height of Zion,
  Streaming to the goodness of the
    LORD—
  For wheat and new wine and oil,
  For the young of the flock and the
    herd;
  Their souls shall be like a well-
    watered garden,
  And they shall sorrow no more at
    all.
13 "Then shall the virgin rejoice in the
    dance,
  And the young men and the old,
    together;
  For I will turn their mourning to
    joy,
  Will comfort them,
  And make them rejoice rather
    than sorrow.
14 I will satiate the soul of the priests
    with abundance,
  And My people shall be satisfied
    with My goodness, says the
    LORD."

15 Thus says the LORD:

  "A voice was heard in Ramah,
  Lamentation *and* bitter weeping,
  Rachel weeping for her children,
  Refusing to be comforted for her
    children,
  Because they *are* no more."

16 Thus says the LORD:

  "Refrain your voice from weeping,
  And your eyes from tears;
  For your work shall be rewarded,
    says the LORD,
  And they shall come back from
    the land of the enemy.
17 There is hope in your future, says
    the LORD,
  That *your* children shall come
    back to their own border.

18 "I have surely heard Ephraim
    bemoaning himself:
  'You have chastised me, and I was
    chastised,

Like an untrained bull;
Restore me, and I will return,
For You *are* the LORD my God.
¹⁹ Surely, after my turning, I
    repented;
And after I was instructed, I struck
    myself on the thigh;
I was ashamed, yes, even
    humiliated,
Because I bore the reproach of my
    youth.'
²⁰ *Is* Ephraim My dear son?
Is he a pleasant child?
For though I spoke against him,
I earnestly remember him still;
Therefore My heart yearns for
    him;
I will surely have mercy on him,
    says the LORD.

²¹ "Set up signposts,
Make landmarks;
Set your heart toward the
    highway,
The way in *which* you went.
Turn back, O virgin of Israel,
Turn back to these your cities.
²² How long will you gad about,
O you backsliding daughter?
For the LORD has created a new
    thing in the earth—
A woman shall encompass a man."

²³ Thus says the LORD of hosts, the God
of Israel: "They shall again use this speech
in the land of Judah and in its cities, when
I bring back their captivity: 'The LORD
bless you, O home of justice, *and* mountain of holiness!' ²⁴ And there shall dwell
in Judah itself, and in all its cities together,
farmers and those going out with flocks.
²⁵ For I have satiated the weary soul, and
I have replenished every sorrowful soul."
²⁶ After this I awoke and looked around,
and my sleep was sweet to me.

²⁷ "Behold, the days are coming, says
the LORD, that I will sow the house of
Israel and the house of Judah with the seed
of man and the seed of beast. ²⁸ And it
shall come to pass, *that* as I have watched
over them to pluck up, to break down, to
throw down, to destroy, and to afflict, so
I will watch over them to build and to
plant, says the LORD. ²⁹ In those days they
shall say no more:

'The fathers have eaten sour
    grapes,
And the children's teeth are set on
    edge.'

³⁰ But every one shall die for his own iniquity; every man who eats the sour
grapes, his teeth shall be set on edge.

³¹ "Behold, the days are coming, says
the LORD, when I will make a new covenant with the house of Israel and with
the house of Judah— ³² not according
to the covenant that I made with their fathers in the day *that* I took them by the
hand to lead them out of the land of
Egypt, My covenant which they broke,
though I was a husband to them, says the
LORD. ³³ But this *is* the covenant that I
will make with the house of Israel after
those days, says the LORD: I will put My
law in their minds, and write it on their
hearts; and I will be their God, and they
shall be My people. ³⁴ No more shall every man teach his neighbor, and every man
his brother, saying, 'Know the LORD,' for
they all shall know Me, from the least of
them to the greatest of them, says the
LORD. For I will forgive their iniquity, and
their sin I will remember no more."

³⁵ Thus says the LORD,
Who gives the sun for a light by
    day,
The ordinances of the moon and
    the stars for a light by night,
Who disturbs the sea,
And its waves roar
(The LORD of hosts *is* His name):

³⁶ "If those ordinances depart
From before Me, says the LORD,
Then the seed of Israel shall also
    cease
From being a nation before Me
    forever."

³⁷ Thus says the LORD:

"If heaven above can be measured,
And the foundations of the earth
    searched out beneath,
I will also cast off all the seed of
    Israel
For all that they have done, says
    the LORD.

38 "Behold, the days are coming, says the LORD, that the city shall be built for the LORD from the Tower of Hananel to the Corner Gate. 39 The surveyor's line shall again extend straight forward over the hill Gareb; then it shall turn toward Goath. 40 And the whole valley of the dead bodies and of the ashes, and all the fields as far as the Brook Kidron, to the corner of the Horse Gate toward the east, *shall be* holy to the LORD. It shall not be plucked up or thrown down anymore forever."

32 The word that came to Jeremiah from the LORD in the tenth year of Zedekiah king of Judah, which was the eighteenth year of Nebuchadnezzar. 2 For then the king of Babylon's army besieged Jerusalem, and Jeremiah the prophet was shut up in the court of the prison, which *was in* the king of Judah's house. 3 For Zedekiah king of Judah had shut him up, saying, "Why do you prophesy and say, 'Thus says the LORD: "Behold, I will give this city into the hand of the king of Babylon, and he shall take it; 4 and Zedekiah king of Judah shall not escape from the hand of the Chaldeans, but shall surely be delivered into the hand of the king of Babylon, and shall speak with him face to face, and see him eye to eye; 5 then he shall lead Zedekiah to Babylon, and there he shall be until I visit him," says the LORD; "though you fight with the Chaldeans, you shall not succeed" '?"

6 And Jeremiah said, "The word of the LORD came to me, saying, 7 'Behold, Hanamel the son of Shallum your uncle will come to you, saying, "Buy my field which *is* in Anathoth, for the right of redemption *is* yours to buy *it*." ' 8 Then Hanamel my uncle's son came to me in the court of the prison according to the word of the LORD, and said to me, 'Please buy my field that *is* in Anathoth, which *is* in the country of Benjamin; for the right of inheritance *is* yours, and the redemption yours; buy *it* for yourself.' Then I knew that this was the word of the LORD. 9 So I bought the field from Hanamel, the son of my uncle who *was* in Anathoth, and weighed *out to* him the money—seventeen shekels of silver. 10 And I signed the deed and sealed *it*, took witnesses, and

weighed the money on the scales. 11 So I took the purchase deed, *both* that which was sealed *according* to the law and custom, and that which was open; 12 and I gave the purchase deed to Baruch the son of Neriah, son of Mahseiah, in the presence of Hanamel my uncle's *son,* and in the presence of the witnesses who signed the purchase deed, before all the Jews who sat in the court of the prison.

13 "Then I charged Baruch before them, saying, 14 'Thus says the LORD of hosts, the God of Israel: "Take these deeds, both this purchase deed which is sealed and this deed which is open, and put them in an earthen vessel, that they may last many days." 15 For thus says the LORD of hosts, the God of Israel: "Houses and fields and vineyards shall be possessed again in this land." '

16 "Now when I had delivered the purchase deed to Baruch the son of Neriah, I prayed to the LORD, saying: 17 'Ah, Lord GOD! Behold, You have made the heavens and the earth by Your great power and outstretched arm. There is nothing too hard for You. 18 *You* show lovingkindness to thousands, and repay the iniquity of the fathers into the bosom of their children after them—the Great, the Mighty God, whose name *is* the LORD of hosts. 19 *You are* great in counsel and mighty in work, for your eyes *are* open to all the ways of the sons of men, to give everyone according to his ways and according to the fruit of his doings. 20 You have set signs and wonders in the land of Egypt, to this day, and in Israel and among *other* men; and You have made Yourself a name, as it is this day. 21 You have brought Your people Israel out of the land of Egypt with signs and wonders, with a strong hand and an outstretched arm, and with great terror; 22 You have given them this land, of which You swore to their fathers to give them—"a land flowing with milk and honey." 23 And they came in and took possession of it, but they have not obeyed Your voice or walked in Your law. They have done nothing of all that You commanded them to do; therefore You have caused all this calamity to come upon them.

24 'Look, the siege mounds! They have come to the city to take it; and the city

has been given into the hand of the Chaldeans who fight against it, because of the sword and famine and pestilence. What You have spoken has happened; there You see *it!* ²⁵ And You have said to me, O Lord GOD, "Buy the field for money, and take witnesses"!—yet the city has been given into the hand of the Chaldeans.' "

²⁶ Then the word of the LORD came to Jeremiah, saying, ²⁷ "Behold, I *am* the LORD, the God of all flesh. Is there anything too hard for Me? ²⁸ Therefore thus says the LORD: 'Behold, I will give this city into the hand of the Chaldeans, into the hand of Nebuchadnezzar king of Babylon, and he shall take it. ²⁹ And the Chaldeans who fight against this city shall come and set fire to this city and burn it, with the houses on whose roofs they have offered incense to Baal and poured out drink offerings to other gods, to provoke Me to anger; ³⁰ because the children of Israel and the children of Judah have done only evil before Me from their youth. For the children of Israel have provoked Me only to anger with the work of their hands,' says the LORD. ³¹ 'For this city has been to Me *a provocation of* My anger and My fury from the day that they built it, even to this day; so I will remove it from before My face ³² because of all the evil of the children of Israel and the children of Judah, which they have done to provoke Me to anger—they, their kings, their princes, their priests, their prophets, the men of Judah, and the inhabitants of Jerusalem. ³³ And they have turned to Me the back, and not the face; though I taught them, rising up early and teaching *them,* yet they have not listened to receive instruction. ³⁴ But they set their abominations in the house which is called by My name, to defile it. ³⁵ And they built the high places of Baal which *are* in the Valley of the Son of Hinnom, to cause their sons and their daughters to pass through *the fire* to Molech, which I did not command them, nor did it come into My mind that they should do this abomination, to cause Judah to sin.'

³⁶ "Now therefore, thus says the LORD, the God of Israel, concerning this city of which you say, 'It shall be delivered into the hand of the king of Babylon by the sword, by the famine, and by the pestilence: ³⁷ Behold, I will gather them out of all countries where I have driven them in My anger, in My fury, and in great wrath; I will bring them back to this place, and I will cause them to dwell safely. ³⁸ They shall be My people, and I will be their God; ³⁹ then I will give them one heart and one way, that they may fear Me forever, for the good of them and their children after them. ⁴⁰ And I will make an everlasting covenant with them, that I will not turn away from doing them good; but I will put My fear in their hearts so that they will not depart from Me. ⁴¹ Yes, I will rejoice over them to do them good, and I will assuredly plant them in this land, with all My heart and with all My soul.'

⁴² "For thus says the LORD: 'Just as I have brought all this great calamity on this people, so I will bring on them all the good that I have promised them. ⁴³ And fields will be bought in this land of which you say, "It is desolate, without man or beast; it has been given into the hand of the Chaldeans." ⁴⁴ Men will buy fields for money, sign deeds and seal *them,* and take witnesses, in the land of Benjamin, in the places around Jerusalem, in the cities of Judah, in the cities of the mountains, in the cities of the lowland, and in the cities of the South; for I will cause their captives to return,' says the LORD."

∼ PSALM 119:49–56 ∼

⁴⁹ Remember the word to Your servant,
Upon which You have caused me to hope.
⁵⁰ This *is* my comfort in my affliction,
For Your word has given me life.
⁵¹ The proud have me in great derision,
Yet I do not turn aside from Your law.
⁵² I remembered Your judgments of old, O LORD,
And have comforted myself.
⁵³ Indignation has taken hold of me
Because of the wicked, who forsake Your law.
⁵⁴ Your statutes have been my songs
In the house of my pilgrimage.
⁵⁵ I remember Your name in the night, O LORD,
And I keep Your law.

56 This has become mine,
Because I kept Your precepts.

~ PROVERBS 27:20 ~

20 Hell and Destruction are never full;
So the eyes of man are never
satisfied.

~ 1 TIMOTHY 2:1–15 ~

Therefore I exhort first of all that supplications, prayers, intercessions, *and* giving of thanks be made for all men, 2 for kings and all who are in authority, that we may lead a quiet and peaceable life in all godliness and reverence. 3 For this *is* good and acceptable in the sight of God our Savior, 4 who desires all men to be saved and to come to the knowledge of the truth. 5 For *there is* one God and one Mediator between God and men, *the* Man Christ Jesus, 6 who gave Himself a ransom for all, to be testified in due time, 7 for which I was appointed a preacher and an apostle—I am speaking the truth in Christ *and* not lying—a teacher of the Gentiles in faith and truth.

8 I desire therefore that the men pray everywhere, lifting up holy hands, without wrath and doubting; 9 in like manner also, that the women adorn themselves in modest apparel, with propriety and moderation, not with braided hair or gold or pearls or costly clothing, 10 but, which is proper for women professing godliness, with good works. 11 Let a woman learn in silence with all submission. 12 And I do not permit a woman to teach or to have authority over a man, but to be in silence. 13 For Adam was formed first, then Eve. 14 And Adam was not deceived, but the woman being deceived, fell into transgression. 15 Nevertheless she will be saved in childbearing if they continue in faith, love, and holiness, with self-control.

READING 297 · OCTOBER 24

~ JEREMIAH 33:1—34:22 ~

Moreover the word of the LORD came to Jeremiah a second time, while he was still shut up in the court of the prison, saying, 2 "Thus says the LORD who made it, the LORD who formed it to establish it (the LORD *is* His name): 3 'Call to Me, and I will answer you, and show you great and mighty things, which you do not know.'

4 "For thus says the LORD, the God of Israel, concerning the houses of this city and the houses of the kings of Judah, which have been pulled down *to fortify* against the siege mounds and the sword: 5 'They come to fight with the Chaldeans, but *only* to fill their places with the dead bodies of men whom I will slay in My anger and My fury, all for whose wickedness I have hidden My face from this city. 6 Behold, I will bring it health and healing; I will heal them and reveal to them the abundance of peace and truth. 7 And I will cause the captives of Judah and the captives of Israel to return, and will rebuild those places as at the first. 8 I will cleanse them from all their iniquity by which they have sinned against Me, and I will pardon all their iniquities by which they have sinned and by which they have transgressed against Me. 9 Then it shall be to Me a name of joy, a praise, and an honor before all nations of the earth, who shall hear all the good that I do to them; they shall fear and tremble for all the goodness and all the prosperity that I provide for it.'

10 "Thus says the LORD: 'Again there shall be heard in this place—of which you say, "It *is* desolate, without man and without beast"—in the cities of Judah, in the streets of Jerusalem that are desolate, without man and without inhabitant and without beast, 11 the voice of joy and the voice of gladness, the voice of the bridegroom and the voice of the bride, the voice of those who will say:

"Praise the LORD of hosts,
For the LORD *is* good,
For His mercy *endures* forever"—

The Gasoline is Prayer

> Call to Me, and I will answer you, and show you great and mighty things, which you do not know.
>
> *Jeremiah 33:3*

Mother Teresa once said, "Prayer feeds the soul — as blood is to the body, prayer is to the soul — and it brings you closer to God. It also gives you a clean and pure heart. A clean heart can see God, can speak to God, and can see the love of God in others."

This view has been echoed by Sister Kateri, who is affiliated with the Sisters of Charity (the order founded by Mother Teresa) in the Bronx, New York. She has said:

"The most important thing that a human being can do is pray, because we've been made for God and our hearts are restless until we rest with Him. And it's in prayer that we come into contact with God. . . .

"I used to share this with the men at the prison I visited. I'd give them the example: If you had to go on a trip, what would you need? And the men would say, 'You'd need a car and you'd need gasoline.' We used to have a good time because we usually decided that the gasoline was prayer, the car was our life, the journey was to heaven, you had to have a map, you had to know where you were going, and so on. My point really is that the gasoline of our life is prayer and without that we won't reach our destination, and we won't reach the fulfillment of our being."

Is your tank running on empty today? Maybe it's time to get off the expressway and stop for a fill-up.

and of those *who will* bring the sacrifice of praise into the house of the LORD. For I will cause the captives of the land to return as at the first,' says the LORD.

¹² "Thus says the LORD of hosts: 'In this place which is desolate, without man and without beast, and in all its cities, there shall again be a dwelling place of shepherds causing *their* flocks to lie down. ¹³ In the cities of the mountains, in the cities of the lowland, in the cities of the South, in the land of Benjamin, in the places around Jerusalem, and in the cities of Judah, the flocks shall again pass under the hands of him who counts *them*,' says the LORD.

¹⁴ 'Behold, the days are coming,' says the LORD, 'that I will perform that good thing which I have promised to the house of Israel and to the house of Judah:

¹⁵ 'In those days and at that time
  I will cause to grow up to David
  A Branch of righteousness;
  He shall execute judgment and
    righteousness in the earth.
¹⁶ In those days Judah will be saved,
  And Jerusalem will dwell safely.
  And this *is the name* by which she
    will be called:

THE LORD OUR RIGHTEOUSNESS.'

¹⁷ "For thus says the LORD: 'David shall never lack a man to sit on the throne of the house of Israel; ¹⁸ nor shall the priests, the Levites, lack a man to offer burnt offerings before Me, to kindle grain offerings, and to sacrifice continually.' "

¹⁹ And the word of the LORD came to Jeremiah, saying, ²⁰ "Thus says the LORD: 'If you can break My covenant with the day and My covenant with the night, so that there will not be day and night in their season, ²¹ then My covenant may also be broken with David My servant, so that he shall not have a son to reign on his throne, and with the Levites, the priests, My ministers. ²² As the host of heaven cannot be numbered, nor the sand of the sea measured, so will I multiply the descendants of David My servant and the Levites who minister to Me.' "

²³ Moreover the word of the LORD came to Jeremiah, saying, ²⁴ "Have you not considered what these people have spoken, saying, 'The two families which the LORD has chosen, He has also cast them off'? Thus they have despised My people, as if they should no more be a nation before them.

²⁵ "Thus says the LORD: 'If My covenant *is* not with day and night, *and if* I have not appointed the ordinances of heaven and earth, ²⁶ then I will cast away the descendants of Jacob and David My servant, so that I will not take *any* of his descendants *to be* rulers over the descendants of Abraham, Isaac, and Jacob. For I will cause their captives to return, and will have mercy on them.' "

34 The word which came to Jeremiah from the LORD, when Nebuchadnezzar king of Babylon and all his army, all the kingdoms of the earth under his dominion, and all the people, fought against Jerusalem and all its cities, saying, ² "Thus says the LORD, the God of Israel: 'Go and speak to Zedekiah king of Judah and tell him, "Thus says the LORD: 'Behold, I will give this city into the hand of the king of Babylon, and he shall burn it with fire. ³ And you shall not escape from his hand, but shall surely be taken and delivered into his hand; your eyes shall see the eyes of the king of Babylon, he shall speak with you face to face, and you shall go to Babylon.' " ' ⁴ Yet hear the word of the LORD, O Zedekiah king of Judah! Thus says the LORD concerning you: 'You shall not die by the sword. ⁵ You shall die in peace; as in the ceremonies of your fathers, the former kings who were before you, so they shall burn incense for you and lament for you, *saying,* "Alas, lord!" For I have pronounced the word, says the LORD.' "

⁶ Then Jeremiah the prophet spoke all these words to Zedekiah king of Judah in Jerusalem, ⁷ when the king of Babylon's army fought against Jerusalem and all the cities of Judah that were left, against Lachish and Azekah; for *only* these fortified cities remained of the cities of Judah.

⁸ *This is* the word that came to Jeremiah from the LORD, after King Zedekiah had made a covenant with all the people who *were* at Jerusalem to proclaim liberty to them: ⁹ that every man should set free his

male and female slave—a Hebrew man or woman—that no one should keep a Jewish brother in bondage. ¹⁰ Now when all the princes and all the people, who had entered into the covenant, heard that everyone should set free his male and female slaves, that no one should keep them in bondage anymore, they obeyed and let *them* go. ¹¹ But afterward they changed their minds and made the male and female slaves return, whom they had set free, and brought them into subjection as male and female slaves.

¹² Therefore the word of the LORD came to Jeremiah from the LORD, saying, ¹³ "Thus says the LORD, the God of Israel: 'I made a covenant with your fathers in the day that I brought them out of the land of Egypt, out of the house of bondage, saying, ¹⁴ "At the end of seven years let every man set free his Hebrew brother, who has been sold to him; and when he has served you six years, you shall let him go free from you." But your fathers did not obey Me nor incline their ear. ¹⁵ Then you recently turned and did what was right in My sight—every man proclaiming liberty to his neighbor; and you made a covenant before Me in the house which is called by My name. ¹⁶ Then you turned around and profaned My name, and every one of you brought back his male and female slaves, whom he had set at liberty, at their pleasure, and brought them back into subjection, to be your male and female slaves.'

¹⁷ "Therefore thus says the LORD: 'You have not obeyed Me in proclaiming liberty, every one to his brother and every one to his neighbor. Behold, I proclaim liberty to you,' says the LORD—'to the sword, to pestilence, and to famine! And I will deliver you to trouble among all the kingdoms of the earth. ¹⁸ And I will give the men who have transgressed My covenant, who have not performed the words of the covenant which they made before Me, when they cut the calf in two and passed between the parts of it— ¹⁹ the princes of Judah, the princes of Jerusalem, the eunuchs, the priests, and all the people of the land who passed between the parts of the calf— ²⁰ I will give them into the hand of their enemies and into the hand of those who seek their life. Their dead bodies shall be for meat for the birds of the heaven and the beasts of the earth. ²¹ And I will give Zedekiah king of Judah and his princes into the hand of their enemies, into the hand of those who seek their life, and into the hand of the king of Babylon's army which has gone back from you. ²² Behold, I will command,' says the LORD, 'and cause them to return to this city. They will fight against it and take it and burn it with fire; and I will make the cities of Judah a desolation without inhabitant.' "

∼ PSALM 119:57–64 ∼

⁵⁷ *You are* my portion, O LORD;
    I have said that I would keep Your
        words.
⁵⁸ I entreated Your favor with *my*
        whole heart;
    Be merciful to me according to Your
        word.
⁵⁹ I thought about my ways,
    And turned my feet to Your
        testimonies.
⁶⁰ I made haste, and did not delay
    To keep Your commandments.
⁶¹ The cords of the wicked have bound
        me,
    But I have not forgotten Your law.
⁶² At midnight I will rise to give thanks
        to You,
    Because of Your righteous
        judgments.
⁶³ I *am* a companion of all who fear
        You,
    And of those who keep Your
        precepts.
⁶⁴ The earth, O LORD, is full of Your
        mercy;
    Teach me Your statutes.

∼ PROVERBS 27:21 ∼

²¹ The refining pot *is* for silver and the
        furnace for gold,
    And a man *is valued* by what others
        say of him.

∼ 1 TIMOTHY 3:1–16 ∼

This *is* a faithful saying: If a man desires the position of a bishop, he desires a good work. ² A bishop then must be blameless, the husband of one wife, temperate, sober-minded, of good behavior, hospitable, able to teach; ³ not given to wine, not violent, not greedy for money, but gentle, not quarrelsome, not covetous; ⁴ one who rules his own house well, having *his* children in submission with all reverence ⁵(for if a man does not know how to rule his own house, how will he take care of the church of God?); ⁶ not a novice, lest being puffed up with pride he fall into the *same* condemnation as the devil. ⁷ Moreover he must have a good testimony among those who are outside, lest he fall into reproach and the snare of the devil.

⁸ Likewise deacons *must be* reverent, not double-tongued, not given to much wine, not greedy for money, ⁹ holding the mystery of the faith with a pure conscience. ¹⁰ But let these also first be tested; then let them serve as deacons, being *found* blameless. ¹¹ Likewise, *their* wives *must be* reverent, not slanderers, temperate, faithful in all things. ¹² Let deacons be the husbands of one wife, ruling *their* children and their own houses well. ¹³ For those who have served well as deacons obtain for themselves a good standing and great boldness in the faith which is in Christ Jesus.

¹⁴ These things I write to you, though I hope to come to you shortly; ¹⁵ but if I am delayed, *I write* so that you may know how you ought to conduct yourself in the house of God, which is the church of the living God, the pillar and ground of the truth. ¹⁶ And without controversy great is the mystery of godliness:

> God was manifested in the flesh,
> Justified in the Spirit,
> Seen by angels,
> Preached among the Gentiles,
> Believed on in the world,
> Received up in glory.

READING 298 · OCTOBER 25

~ JEREMIAH 35:1—36:32 ~

The word which came to Jeremiah from the LORD in the days of Jehoiakim the son of Josiah, king of Judah, saying, ² "Go to the house of the Rechabites, speak to them, and bring them into the house of the LORD, into one of the chambers, and give them wine to drink."

³ Then I took Jaazaniah the son of Jeremiah, the son of Habazziniah, his brothers and all his sons, and the whole house of the Rechabites, ⁴ and I brought them into the house of the LORD, into the chamber of the sons of Hanan the son of Igdaliah, a man of God, which *was* by the chamber of the princes, above the chamber of Maaseiah the son of Shallum, the keeper of the door. ⁵ Then I set before the sons of the house of the Rechabites bowls full of wine, and cups; and I said to them, "Drink wine."

⁶ But they said, "We will drink no wine, for Jonadab the son of Rechab, our father, commanded us, saying, 'You shall drink no wine, you nor your sons, forever. ⁷ You shall not build a house, sow seed, plant a vineyard, nor have *any of these;* but all your days you shall dwell in tents, that you may live many days in the land where you are sojourners.' ⁸ Thus we have obeyed the voice of Jonadab the son of Rechab, our father, in all that he charged us, to drink no wine all our days, we, our wives, our sons, or our daughters, ⁹ nor to build ourselves houses to dwell in; nor do we have vineyard, field, or seed. ¹⁰ But we have dwelt in tents, and have obeyed and done according to all that Jonadab our father commanded us. ¹¹ But it came to pass, when Nebuchadnezzar king of Babylon came up into the land, that we said, 'Come, let us go to Jerusalem for fear of the army of the Chaldeans and for fear of the army of the Syrians.' So we dwell at Jerusalem."

¹² Then came the word of the LORD to Jeremiah, saying, ¹³ "Thus says the LORD of hosts, the God of Israel: 'Go and tell the men of Judah and the inhabitants of Jerusalem, "Will you not receive instruction to obey My words?" says the LORD. ¹⁴ "The words of Jonadab the son of

A Close Family

The daughter of missionaries to India, Wendy resented being held to the high expectations of others. As a teenager in boarding school, she rebelled against those expectations. Her parents returned to Canada so the family might be together, but Wendy continued to rebel. Her mother and father, however, didn't judge or condemn her. She says, "They just kept on loving me. I discovered that I could fight rules and people who criticized me, but I couldn't put up walls against love. Because of my parents' patient love for me, I stopped rebelling, and . . . I recommitted my life to Christ."

As a young adult, Wendy herself became a missionary to India! One of her students, Anne, had a very negative attitude toward Christianity. Wendy said, "I prayed diligently for Anne, and decided that I would treat her with the same lovingkindness with which my parents had treated me. I accepted Anne as she was, without placing spiritual expectations on her. When Anne realized that I didn't intend to judge her . . . she began opening up to me." Finally, Anne accepted Christ into her life. Wendy concludes, "A 'close family' has little to do with geography and being together physically. But [it] has everything to do with loving . . . supporting . . . and communicating with each other."

> Let no one despise your youth, but be an example to the believers in word, in conduct, in love, in spirit, in faith, in purity.
>
> *1 Timothy 4:12*

Rechab, which he commanded his sons, not to drink wine, are performed; for to this day they drink none, and obey their father's commandment. But although I have spoken to you, rising early and speaking, you did not obey Me. [15] I have also sent to you all My servants the prophets, rising up early and sending *them,* saying, 'Turn now everyone from his evil way, amend your doings, and do not go after other gods to serve them; then you will dwell in the land which I have given you and your fathers.' But you have not inclined your ear, nor obeyed Me. [16] Surely the sons of Jonadab the son of Rechab have performed the commandment of their father, which he commanded them, but this people has not obeyed Me." '

[17] "Therefore thus says the LORD God of hosts, the God of Israel: 'Behold, I will bring on Judah and on all the inhabitants of Jerusalem all the doom that I have pronounced against them; because I have spoken to them but they have not heard, and I have called to them but they have not answered.' "

[18] And Jeremiah said to the house of the Rechabites, "Thus says the LORD of hosts, the God of Israel: 'Because you have obeyed the commandment of Jonadab your father, and kept all his precepts and done according to all that he commanded you, [19] therefore thus says the LORD of hosts, the God of Israel: "Jonadab the son of Rechab shall not lack a man to stand before Me forever." ' "

36 Now it came to pass in the fourth year of Jehoiakim the son of Josiah, king of Judah, *that* this word came to Jeremiah from the LORD, saying: [2] "Take a scroll of a book and write on it all the words that I have spoken to you against Israel, against Judah, and against all the nations, from the day I spoke to you, from the days of Josiah even to this day. [3] It may be that the house of Judah will hear all the adversities which I purpose to bring upon them, that everyone may turn from his evil way, that I may forgive their iniquity and their sin."

[4] Then Jeremiah called Baruch the son of Neriah; and Baruch wrote on a scroll of a book, at the instruction of Jeremiah, all the words of the LORD which

He had spoken to him. [5] And Jeremiah commanded Baruch, saying, "I *am* confined, I cannot go into the house of the LORD. [6] You go, therefore, and read from the scroll which you have written at my instruction, the words of the LORD, in the hearing of the people in the LORD's house on the day of fasting. And you shall also read them in the hearing of all Judah who come from their cities. [7] It may be that they will present their supplication before the LORD, and everyone will turn from his evil way. For great *is* the anger and the fury that the LORD has pronounced against this people." [8] And Baruch the son of Neriah did according to all that Jeremiah the prophet commanded him, reading from the book the words of the LORD in the LORD's house.

[9] Now it came to pass in the fifth year of Jehoiakim the son of Josiah, king of Judah, in the ninth month, *that* they proclaimed a fast before the LORD to all the people in Jerusalem, and to all the people who came from the cities of Judah to Jerusalem. [10] Then Baruch read from the book the words of Jeremiah in the house of the LORD, in the chamber of Gemariah the son of Shaphan the scribe, in the upper court at the entry of the New Gate of the LORD's house, in the hearing of all the people.

[11] When Michaiah the son of Gemariah, the son of Shaphan, heard all the words of the LORD from the book, [12] he then went down to the king's house, into the scribe's chamber; and there all the princes were sitting—Elishama the scribe, Delaiah the son of Shemaiah, Elnathan the son of Achbor, Gemariah the son of Shaphan, Zedekiah the son of Hananiah, and all the princes. [13] Then Michaiah declared to them all the words that he had heard when Baruch read the book in the hearing of the people. [14] Therefore all the princes sent Jehudi the son of Nethaniah, the son of Shelemiah, the son of Cushi, to Baruch, saying, "Take in your hand the scroll from which you have read in the hearing of the people, and come." So Baruch the son of Neriah took the scroll in his hand and came to them. [15] And they said to him, "Sit down now, and read it in our hearing." So Baruch read *it* in their hearing.

¹⁶ Now it happened, when they had heard all the words, that they looked in fear from one to another, and said to Baruch, "We will surely tell the king of all these words." ¹⁷ And they asked Baruch, saying, "Tell us now, how did you write all these words—at his instruction?"

¹⁸ So Baruch answered them, "He proclaimed with his mouth all these words to me, and I wrote *them* with ink in the book."

¹⁹ Then the princes said to Baruch, "Go and hide, you and Jeremiah; and let no one know where you are."

²⁰ And they went to the king, into the court; but they stored the scroll in the chamber of Elishama the scribe, and told all the words in the hearing of the king. ²¹ So the king sent Jehudi to bring the scroll, and he took it from Elishama the scribe's chamber. And Jehudi read it in the hearing of the king and in the hearing of all the princes who stood beside the king. ²² Now the king was sitting in the winter house in the ninth month, with *a fire* burning on the hearth before him. ²³ And it happened, when Jehudi had read three or four columns, *that the king* cut it with the scribe's knife and cast *it* into the fire that *was* on the hearth, until all the scroll was consumed in the fire that *was* on the hearth. ²⁴ Yet they were not afraid, nor did they tear their garments, the king nor any of his servants who heard all these words. ²⁵ Nevertheless Elnathan, Delaiah, and Gemariah implored the king not to burn the scroll; but he would not listen to them. ²⁶ And the king commanded Jerahmeel the king's son, Seraiah the son of Azriel, and Shelemiah the son of Abdeel, to seize Baruch the scribe and Jeremiah the prophet, but the LORD hid them.

²⁷ Now after the king had burned the scroll with the words which Baruch had written at the instruction of Jeremiah, the word of the LORD came to Jeremiah, saying: ²⁸ "Take yet another scroll, and write on it all the former words that were in the first scroll which Jehoiakim the king of Judah has burned. ²⁹ And you shall say to Jehoiakim king of Judah, 'Thus says the LORD: "You have burned this scroll, saying, 'Why have you written in it that the king of Babylon will certainly come

and destroy this land, and cause man and beast to cease from here?' " ³⁰ Therefore thus says the LORD concerning Jehoiakim king of Judah: "He shall have no one to sit on the throne of David, and his dead body shall be cast out to the heat of the day and the frost of the night. ³¹ I will punish him, his family, and his servants for their iniquity; and I will bring on them, on the inhabitants of Jerusalem, and on the men of Judah all the doom that I have pronounced against them; but they did not heed." ' "

³² Then Jeremiah took another scroll and gave it to Baruch the scribe, the son of Neriah, who wrote on it at the instruction of Jeremiah all the words of the book which Jehoiakim king of Judah had burned in the fire. And besides, there were added to them many similar words.

~ PSALM 119:65–72 ~

⁶⁵ You have dealt well with Your
    servant,
  O LORD, according to Your word.
⁶⁶ Teach me good judgment and
    knowledge,
  For I believe Your commandments.
⁶⁷ Before I was afflicted I went
    astray,
  But now I keep Your word.
⁶⁸ You *are* good, and do good;
  Teach me Your statutes.
⁶⁹ The proud have forged a lie against
    me,
  But I will keep Your precepts with
    my whole heart.
⁷⁰ Their heart is as fat as grease,
  But I delight in Your law.
⁷¹ *It is* good for me that I have been
    afflicted,
  That I may learn Your statutes.
⁷² The law of Your mouth *is* better to
    me
  Than thousands of *coins of* gold and
    silver.

~ PROVERBS 27:22 ~

²² Though you grind a fool in a mortar
    with a pestle along with crushed
    grain,

Yet his foolishness will not depart from him.

~ 1 TIMOTHY 4:1–16 ~

Now the Spirit expressly says that in latter times some will depart from the faith, giving heed to deceiving spirits and doctrines of demons, ² speaking lies in hypocrisy, having their own conscience seared with a hot iron, ³ forbidding to marry, *and commanding* to abstain from foods which God created to be received with thanksgiving by those who believe and know the truth. ⁴ For every creature of God *is* good, and nothing is to be refused if it is received with thanksgiving; ⁵ for it is sanctified by the word of God and prayer.

⁶ If you instruct the brethren in these things, you will be a good minister of Jesus Christ, nourished in the words of faith and of the good doctrine which you have carefully followed. ⁷ But reject profane and old wives' fables, and exercise yourself toward godliness. ⁸ For bodily exercise profits a little, but godliness is profitable for all things, having promise of the life that now is and of that which is to come. ⁹ This *is* a faithful saying and worthy of all acceptance. ¹⁰ For to this *end* we both labor and suffer reproach, because we trust in the living God, who is *the* Savior of all men, especially of those who believe. ¹¹ These things command and teach.

¹² Let no one despise your youth, but be an example to the believers in word, in conduct, in love, in spirit, in faith, in purity. ¹³ Till I come, give attention to reading, to exhortation, to doctrine. ¹⁴ Do not neglect the gift that is in you, which was given to you by prophecy with the laying on of the hands of the eldership. ¹⁵ Meditate on these things; give yourself entirely to them, that your progress may be evident to all. ¹⁶ Take heed to yourself and to the doctrine. Continue in them, for in doing this you will save both yourself and those who hear you.

READING 299 · OCTOBER 26

~ JEREMIAH 37:1—38:28 ~

Now King Zedekiah the son of Josiah reigned instead of Coniah the son of Jehoiakim, whom Nebuchadnezzar king of Babylon made king in the land of Judah. ² But neither he nor his servants nor the people of the land gave heed to the words of the LORD which He spoke by the prophet Jeremiah.

³ And Zedekiah the king sent Jehucal the son of Shelemiah, and Zephaniah the son of Maaseiah, the priest, to the prophet Jeremiah, saying, "Pray now to the LORD our God for us." ⁴ Now Jeremiah was coming and going among the people, for they had not *yet* put him in prison. ⁵ Then Pharaoh's army came up from Egypt; and when the Chaldeans who were besieging Jerusalem heard news of them, they departed from Jerusalem.

⁶ Then the word of the LORD came to the prophet Jeremiah, saying, ⁷ "Thus says the LORD, the God of Israel, 'Thus you shall say to the king of Judah, who sent you to Me to inquire of Me: "Behold, Pharaoh's army which has come up to help you will return to Egypt, to their own land. ⁸ And the Chaldeans shall come back and fight against this city, and take it and burn it with fire." ' ⁹ Thus says the LORD: 'Do not deceive yourselves, saying, "The Chaldeans will surely depart from us," for they will not depart. ¹⁰ For though you had defeated the whole army of the Chaldeans who fight against you, and there remained *only* wounded men among them, they would rise up, every man in his tent, and burn the city with fire.' "

¹¹ And it happened, when the army of the Chaldeans left *the siege* of Jerusalem for fear of Pharaoh's army, ¹² that Jeremiah went out of Jerusalem to go into the land of Benjamin to claim his property there among the people. ¹³ And when he was in the Gate of Benjamin, a captain of the guard *was* there whose name *was* Irijah

Seed Money

It was almost planting season and a farmer found himself without any money to buy seed. He had prepared his fields for planting, assuming that the bank would lend him money for seed as they had for several years. This year, however, the bank had changed its policy — no more seed money.

The farmer didn't know what to do, except to talk to God about the problem. As he prayed, the idea came to him, *Perhaps the co-op will advance me the seed*. He knew the co-op rule: credit for fertilizer, chemicals, and fuel — but seed had to be paid for in cash. Even so, he decided to go talk to the co-op manager. Upon arriving at the office, the secretary greeted him warmly and handed him an envelope as she ushered him into the manager's office. "What's this?" he asked. "Your payment for last year's crop," the manager replied.

"I didn't think it was due for several months," the farmer said as he opened the envelope. The manager smiled and said, "This year we decided to do it earlier."

"Thank you!" the farmer blurted out as he saw the amount of the check — it was $10,000 *more* than he needed for seed. "Now, what did you want to talk to me about this morning?" the manager asked. "Not a thing," the farmer replied thinking, *Talking to God has already taken care of it.*

the son of Shelemiah, the son of Hananiah; and he seized Jeremiah the prophet, saying, "You are defecting to the Chaldeans!"

[14] Then Jeremiah said, "False! I am not defecting to the Chaldeans." But he did not listen to him.

So Irijah seized Jeremiah and brought him to the princes. [15] Therefore the princes were angry with Jeremiah, and they struck him and put him in prison in the house of Jonathan the scribe. For they had made that the prison.

[16] When Jeremiah entered the dungeon and the cells, and Jeremiah had remained there many days, [17] then Zedekiah the king sent and took him *out*. The king asked him secretly in his house, and said, "Is there *any* word from the LORD?"

And Jeremiah said, "There is." Then he said, "You shall be delivered into the hand of the king of Babylon!"

[18] Moreover Jeremiah said to King Zedekiah, "What offense have I committed against you, against your servants, or against this people, that you have put me in prison? [19] Where now *are* your prophets who prophesied to you, saying, 'The king of Babylon will not come against you or against this land?' [20] Therefore please hear now, O my lord the king. Please, let my petition be accepted before you, and do not make me return to the house of Jonathan the scribe, lest I die there."

[21] Then Zedekiah the king commanded that they should commit Jeremiah to the court of the prison, and that they should give him daily a piece of bread from the bakers' street, until all the bread in the city was gone. Thus Jeremiah remained in the court of the prison.

38

Now Shephatiah the son of Mattan, Gedaliah the son of Pashhur, Jucal the son of Shelemiah, and Pashhur the son of Malchiah heard the words that Jeremiah had spoken to all the people, saying, [2] "Thus says the LORD: 'He who remains in this city shall die by the sword, by famine, and by pestilence; but he who goes over to the Chaldeans shall live; his life shall be as a prize to him, and he shall live.' [3] Thus says the LORD: 'This city shall surely be given into the hand of the king of Babylon's army, which shall take it.' "

[4] Therefore the princes said to the king, "Please, let this man be put to death, for thus he weakens the hands of the men of war who remain in this city, and the hands of all the people, by speaking such words to them. For this man does not seek the welfare of this people, but their harm."

[5] Then Zedekiah the king said, "Look, he *is* in your hand. For the king can *do* nothing against you." [6] So they took Jeremiah and cast him into the dungeon of Malchiah the king's son, which *was* in the court of the prison, and they let Jeremiah down with ropes. And in the dungeon *there was* no water, but mire. So Jeremiah sank in the mire.

[7] Now Ebed-Melech the Ethiopian, one of the eunuchs, who was in the king's house, heard that they had put Jeremiah in the dungeon. When the king was sitting at the Gate of Benjamin, [8] Ebed-Melech went out of the king's house and spoke to the king, saying: [9] "My lord the king, these men have done evil in all that they have done to Jeremiah the prophet, whom they have cast into the dungeon, and he is likely to die from hunger in the place where he is. For *there is* no more bread in the city." [10] Then the king commanded Ebed-Melech the Ethiopian, saying, "Take from here thirty men with you, and lift Jeremiah the prophet out of the dungeon before he dies." [11] So Ebed-Melech took the men with him and went into the house of the king under the treasury, and took from there old clothes and old rags, and let them down by ropes into the dungeon to Jeremiah. [12] Then Ebed-Melech the Ethiopian said to Jeremiah, "Please put these old clothes and rags under your armpits, under the ropes." And Jeremiah did so. [13] So they pulled Jeremiah up with ropes and lifted him out of the dungeon. And Jeremiah remained in the court of the prison.

[14] Then Zedekiah the king sent and had Jeremiah the prophet brought to him at the third entrance of the house of the LORD. And the king said to Jeremiah, "I will ask you something. Hide nothing from me."

[15] Jeremiah said to Zedekiah, "If I declare *it* to you, will you not surely put me to death? And if I give you advice, you will not listen to me."

¹⁶ So Zedekiah the king swore secretly to Jeremiah, saying, "As the LORD lives, who made our very souls, I will not put you to death, nor will I give you into the hand of these men who seek your life."

¹⁷ Then Jeremiah said to Zedekiah, "Thus says the LORD, the God of hosts, the God of Israel: 'If you surely surrender to the king of Babylon's princes, then your soul shall live; this city shall not be burned with fire, and you and your house shall live. ¹⁸ But if you do not surrender to the king of Babylon's princes, then this city shall be given into the hand of the Chaldeans; they shall burn it with fire, and you shall not escape from their hand.' "

¹⁹ And Zedekiah the king said to Jeremiah, "I am afraid of the Jews who have defected to the Chaldeans, lest they deliver me into their hand, and they abuse me."

²⁰ But Jeremiah said, "They shall not deliver *you*. Please, obey the voice of the LORD which I speak to you. So it shall be well with you, and your soul shall live. ²¹ But if you refuse to surrender, this *is* the word that the LORD has shown me: ²² 'Now behold, all the women who are left in the king of Judah's house *shall be* surrendered to the king of Babylon's princes, and those *women* shall say:

"Your close friends have set upon you
And prevailed against you;
Your feet have sunk in the mire,
And they have turned away again."

²³ 'So they shall surrender all your wives and children to the Chaldeans. You shall not escape from their hand, but shall be taken by the hand of the king of Babylon. And you shall cause this city to be burned with fire.' "

²⁴ Then Zedekiah said to Jeremiah, "Let no one know of these words, and you shall not die. ²⁵ But if the princes hear that I have talked with you, and they come to you and say to you, 'Declare to us now what you have said to the king, and also what the king said to you; do not hide *it* from us, and we will not put you to death,' ²⁶ then you shall say to them, 'I presented my request before the king, that he would not make me return to Jonathan's house to die there.' "

²⁷ Then all the princes came to Jeremiah and asked him. And he told them according to all these words that the king had commanded. So they stopped speaking with him, for the conversation had not been heard. ²⁸ Now Jeremiah remained in the court of the prison until the day that Jerusalem was taken. And he was *there* when Jerusalem was taken.

~ PSALM 119:73–80 ~

⁷³ Your hands have made me and
    fashioned me;
Give me understanding, that I may
    learn Your commandments.
⁷⁴ Those who fear You will be glad
    when they see me,
Because I have hoped in Your word.
⁷⁵ I know, O LORD, that Your
    judgments *are* right,
And *that* in faithfulness You have
    afflicted me.
⁷⁶ Let, I pray, Your merciful kindness be
    for my comfort,
According to Your word to Your
    servant.
⁷⁷ Let Your tender mercies come to me,
    that I may live;
For Your law *is* my delight.
⁷⁸ Let the proud be ashamed,
For they treated me wrongfully with
    falsehood;
But I will meditate on Your precepts.
⁷⁹ Let those who fear You turn to me,
Those who know Your testimonies.
⁸⁰ Let my heart be blameless regarding
    Your statutes,
That I may not be ashamed.

~ PROVERBS 27:23–27 ~

²³ Be diligent to know the state of your
    flocks,
And attend to your herds;
²⁴ For riches *are* not forever,
Nor does a crown *endure* to all
    generations.
²⁵ *When* the hay is removed, and the
    tender grass shows itself,
And the herbs of the mountains are
    gathered in,

²⁶ The lambs *will provide* your
    clothing,
And the goats the price of a field;
²⁷ *You shall have* enough goats' milk
    for your food,
For the food of your household,
And the nourishment of your
    maidservants.

~ 1 TIMOTHY 5:1–25 ~

Do not rebuke an older man, but exhort *him* as a father, younger men as brothers, ² older women as mothers, younger women as sisters, with all purity.

³ Honor widows who are really widows. ⁴ But if any widow has children or grandchildren, let them first learn to show piety at home and to repay their parents; for this is good and acceptable before God. ⁵ Now she who is really a widow, and left alone, trusts in God and continues in supplications and prayers night and day. ⁶ But she who lives in pleasure is dead while she lives. ⁷ And these things command, that they may be blameless. ⁸ But if anyone does not provide for his own, and especially for those of his household, he has denied the faith and is worse than an unbeliever.

⁹ Do not let a widow under sixty years old be taken into the number, *and not unless* she has been the wife of one man, ¹⁰ well reported for good works: if she has brought up children, if she has lodged strangers, if she has washed the saints' feet, if she has relieved the afflicted, if she has diligently followed every good work.

¹¹ But refuse *the* younger widows; for when they have begun to grow wanton against Christ, they desire to marry, ¹² hav-ing condemnation because they have cast off their first faith. ¹³ And besides they learn *to be* idle, wandering about from house to house, and not only idle but also gossips and busybodies, saying things which they ought not. ¹⁴ Therefore I desire that *the* younger *widows* marry, bear children, manage the house, give no opportunity to the adversary to speak reproachfully. ¹⁵ For some have already turned aside after Satan. ¹⁶ If any believing man or woman has widows, let them relieve them, and do not let the church be burdened, that it may relieve those who are really widows.

¹⁷ Let the elders who rule well be counted worthy of double honor, especially those who labor in the word and doctrine. ¹⁸ For the Scripture says, "You shall not muzzle an ox while it treads out the grain," and, "The laborer *is* worthy of his wages." ¹⁹ Do not receive an accusation against an elder except from two or three witnesses. ²⁰ Those who are sinning rebuke in the presence of all, that the rest also may fear.

²¹ I charge *you* before God and the Lord Jesus Christ and the elect angels that you observe these things without prejudice, doing nothing with partiality. ²² Do not lay hands on anyone hastily, nor share in other people's sins; keep yourself pure.

²³ No longer drink only water, but use a little wine for your stomach's sake and your frequent infirmities.

²⁴ Some men's sins are clearly evident, preceding *them* to judgment, but those of some *men* follow later. ²⁵ Likewise, the good works *of some* are clearly evident, and those that are otherwise cannot be hidden.

READING 300 · OCTOBER 27

~ JEREMIAH 39:1—40:16 ~

In the ninth year of Zedekiah king of Judah, in the tenth month, Nebuchadnezzar king of Babylon and all his army came against Jerusalem, and besieged it. ² In the eleventh year of Zedekiah, in the fourth month, on the ninth *day* of the month, the city was penetrated. ³ Then all the princes of the king of Babylon came in and sat in the Middle Gate: Nergal-Sharezer, Samgar-Nebo, Sarsechim, Rabsaris, Nergal-Sarezer, Rabmag, with the rest of the princes of the king of Babylon. ⁴ So it was, when Zedekiah the king of Judah and all the men of war saw them, that they fled and went out of the city by

The Gift of Life

Once a nationally syndicated columnist and now an author, Anna Quindlen seems to have enjoyed success at everything she has attempted. However, in taking a fellow commentator to task after he made light of teenage problems, Anna was reminded of the two attempts she had made to end her own life at age sixteen. She writes, "I was really driven through my high school years. I always had to be perfect in every way, ranging from how I looked to how my grades were. It was too much pressure."

In the early 1970s, Anna's mother died from ovarian cancer. This tragedy cured Anna from any desire to commit suicide. Her attitude toward life changed. "I could never look at life as anything but a great gift. I realized I didn't have any business taking it for granted."

When we are faced with the realization that life is "temporary," we can finally come to grips with what is important. When we face our own immortality, our priorities quickly come into focus.

Consider your life as God's gift to you. Every moment is precious, so cherish them all. In doing so, you'll find purpose and meaning for each day.

night, by way of the king's garden, by the gate between the two walls. And he went out by way of the plain. ⁵ But the Chaldean army pursued them and overtook Zedekiah in the plains of Jericho. And when they had captured him, they brought him up to Nebuchadnezzar king of Babylon, to Riblah in the land of Hamath, where he pronounced judgment on him. ⁶ Then the king of Babylon killed the sons of Zedekiah before his eyes in Riblah; the king of Babylon also killed all the nobles of Judah. ⁷ Moreover he put out Zedekiah's eyes, and bound him with bronze fetters to carry him off to Babylon. ⁸ And the Chaldeans burned the king's house and the houses of the people with fire, and broke down the walls of Jerusalem. ⁹ Then Nebuzaradan the captain of the guard carried away captive to Babylon the remnant of the people who remained in the city and those who defected to him, with the rest of the people who remained. ¹⁰ But Nebuzaradan the captain of the guard left in the land of Judah the poor people, who had nothing, and gave them vineyards and fields at the same time.

¹¹ Now Nebuchadnezzar king of Babylon gave charge concerning Jeremiah to Nebuzaradan the captain of the guard, saying, ¹² "Take him and look after him, and do him no harm; but do to him just as he says to you." ¹³ So Nebuzaradan the captain of the guard sent Nebushasban, Rabsaris, Nergal-Sharezer, Rabmag, and all the king of Babylon's chief officers; ¹⁴ then they sent *someone* to take Jeremiah from the court of the prison, and committed him to Gedaliah the son of Ahikam, the son of Shaphan, that he should take him home. So he dwelt among the people.

¹⁵ Meanwhile the word of the LORD had come to Jeremiah while he was shut up in the court of the prison, saying, ¹⁶ "Go and speak to Ebed-Melech the Ethiopian, saying, 'Thus says the LORD of hosts, the God of Israel: "Behold, I will bring My words upon this city for adversity and not for good, and they shall be *performed* in that day before you. ¹⁷ But I will deliver you in that day," says the LORD, "and you shall not be given into the hand of the men of whom you *are* afraid. ¹⁸ For I will surely deliver you, and you shall not fall by the sword; but your life shall be as a prize to you, because you have put your trust in Me," says the LORD.' "

40 The word that came to Jeremiah from the LORD after Nebuzaradan the captain of the guard had let him go from Ramah, when he had taken him bound in chains among all who were carried away captive from Jerusalem and Judah, who were carried away captive to Babylon.

² And the captain of the guard took Jeremiah and said to him: "The LORD your God has pronounced this doom on this place. ³ Now the LORD has brought *it,* and has done just as He said. Because you *people* have sinned against the LORD, and not obeyed His voice, therefore this thing has come upon you. ⁴ And now look, I free you this day from the chains that *were* on your hand. If it seems good to you to come with me to Babylon, come, and I will look after you. But if it seems wrong for you to come with me to Babylon, remain here. See, all the land *is* before you; wherever it seems good and convenient for you to go, go there." ⁵ Now while Jeremiah had not yet gone back, *Nebuzaradan said,* "Go back to Gedaliah the son of Ahikam, the son of Shaphan, whom the king of Babylon has made governor over the cities of Judah, and dwell with him among the people. Or go wherever it seems convenient for you to go." So the captain of the guard gave him rations and a gift and let him go. ⁶ Then Jeremiah went to Gedaliah the son of Ahikam, to Mizpah, and dwelt with him among the people who were left in the land.

⁷ And when all the captains of the armies who *were* in the fields, they and their men, heard that the king of Babylon had made Gedaliah the son of Ahikam governor in the land, and had committed to him men, women, children, and the poorest of the land who had not been carried away captive to Babylon, ⁸ then they came to Gedaliah at Mizpah— Ishmael the son of Nethaniah, Johanan and Jonathan the sons of Kareah, Seraiah the son of Tanhumeth, the sons of Ephai the Netophathite, and Jezaniah the son of a Maachathite, they and their men.

⁹ And Gedaliah the son of Ahikam, the son of Shaphan, took an oath before them and their men, saying, "Do not be afraid to serve the Chaldeans. Dwell in the land and serve the king of Babylon, and it shall be well with you. ¹⁰ As for me, I will indeed dwell at Mizpah and serve the Chaldeans who come to us. But you, gather wine and summer fruit and oil, put *them* in your vessels, and dwell in your cities that you have taken." ¹¹ Likewise, when all the Jews who *were* in Moab, among the Ammonites, in Edom, and who *were* in all the countries, heard that the king of Babylon had left a remnant of Judah, and that he had set over them Gedaliah the son of Ahikam, the son of Shaphan, ¹² then all the Jews returned out of all places where they had been driven, and came to the land of Judah, to Gedaliah at Mizpah, and gathered wine and summer fruit in abundance.

¹³ Moreover Johanan the son of Kareah and all the captains of the forces that *were* in the fields came to Gedaliah at Mizpah, ¹⁴ and said to him, "Do you certainly know that Baalis the king of the Ammonites has sent Ishmael the son of Nethaniah to murder you?" But Gedaliah the son of Ahikam did not believe them.

¹⁵ Then Johanan the son of Kareah spoke secretly to Gedaliah in Mizpah, saying, "Let me go, please, and I will kill Ishmael the son of Nethaniah, and no one will know *it*. Why should he murder you, so that all the Jews who are gathered to you would be scattered, and the remnant in Judah perish?"

¹⁶ But Gedaliah the son of Ahikam said to Johanan the son of Kareah, "You shall not do this thing, for you speak falsely concerning Ishmael."

~ PSALM 119:81–88 ~

⁸¹ My soul faints for Your salvation,
But I hope in Your word.
⁸² My eyes fail *from searching* Your word,
Saying, "When will You comfort me?"
⁸³ For I have become like a wineskin in smoke,
Yet I do not forget Your statutes.

⁸⁴ How many *are* the days of Your servant?
When will You execute judgment on those who persecute me?
⁸⁵ The proud have dug pits for me,
Which *is* not according to Your law.
⁸⁶ All Your commandments *are* faithful;
They persecute me wrongfully;
Help me!
⁸⁷ They almost made an end of me on earth,
But I did not forsake Your precepts.
⁸⁸ Revive me according to Your lovingkindness,
So that I may keep the testimony of Your mouth.

~ PROVERBS 28:1 ~

¹ The wicked flee when no one pursues,
But the righteous are bold as a lion.

~ 1 TIMOTHY 6:1–21 ~

Let as many bondservants as are under the yoke count their own masters worthy of all honor, so that the name of God and *His* doctrine may not be blasphemed. ² And those who have believing masters, let them not despise *them* because they are brethren, but rather serve *them* because those who are benefited are believers and beloved. Teach and exhort these things.

³ If anyone teaches otherwise and does not consent to wholesome words, *even* the words of our Lord Jesus Christ, and to the doctrine which accords with godliness, ⁴ he is proud, knowing nothing, but is obsessed with disputes and arguments over words, from which come envy, strife, reviling, evil suspicions, ⁵ useless wranglings of men of corrupt minds and destitute of the truth, who suppose that godliness is a *means of* gain. From such withdraw yourself.

⁶ Now godliness with contentment is great gain. ⁷ For we brought nothing into *this* world, *and it is* certain we can carry nothing out. ⁸ And having food and clothing, with these we shall be content. ⁹ But those who desire to be rich fall into temptation and a snare, and *into* many foolish

and harmful lusts which drown men in destruction and perdition. ¹⁰ For the love of money is a root of all *kinds of* evil, for which some have strayed from the faith in their greediness, and pierced themselves through with many sorrows.

¹¹ But you, O man of God, flee these things and pursue righteousness, godliness, faith, love, patience, gentleness. ¹² Fight the good fight of faith, lay hold on eternal life, to which you were also called and have confessed the good confession in the presence of many witnesses. ¹³ I urge you in the sight of God who gives life to all things, and *before* Christ Jesus who witnessed the good confession before Pontius Pilate, ¹⁴ that you keep *this* commandment without spot, blameless until our Lord Jesus Christ's appearing, ¹⁵ which He will manifest in His own time, *He who is* the blessed and only Potentate,

the King of kings and Lord of lords, ¹⁶ who alone has immortality, dwelling in unapproachable light, whom no man has seen or can see, to whom *be* honor and everlasting power. Amen.

¹⁷ Command those who are rich in this present age not to be haughty, nor to trust in uncertain riches but in the living God, who gives us richly all things to enjoy. ¹⁸ *Let them* do good, that they be rich in good works, ready to give, willing to share, ¹⁹ storing up for themselves a good foundation for the time to come, that they may lay hold on eternal life.

²⁰ O Timothy! Guard what was committed to your trust, avoiding the profane *and* idle babblings and contradictions of what is falsely called knowledge— ²¹ by professing it some have strayed concerning the faith.

Grace *be* with you. Amen.

READING 301 · OCTOBER 28

~ JEREMIAH 41:1—42:22 ~

Now it came to pass in the seventh month *that* Ishmael the son of Nethaniah, the son of Elishama, of the royal family and of the officers of the king, came with ten men to Gedaliah the son of Ahikam, at Mizpah. And there they ate bread together in Mizpah. ² Then Ishmael the son of Nethaniah, and the ten men who were with him, arose and struck Gedaliah the son of Ahikam, the son of Shaphan, with the sword, and killed him whom the king of Babylon had made governor over the land. ³ Ishmael also struck down all the Jews who were with him, *that is,* with Gedaliah at Mizpah, and the Chaldeans who were found there, the men of war.

⁴ And it happened, on the second day after he had killed Gedaliah, when as yet no one knew *it,* ⁵ that certain men came from Shechem, from Shiloh, and from Samaria, eighty men with their beards shaved and their clothes torn, having cut themselves, with offerings and incense in their hand, to bring *them* to the house of the LORD. ⁶ Now Ishmael the son of Nethaniah went out from Mizpah to meet them, weeping as he went along; and it

happened as he met them that he said to them, "Come to Gedaliah the son of Ahikam!" ⁷ So it was, when they came into the midst of the city, that Ishmael the son of Nethaniah killed them *and cast them* into the midst of a pit, he and the men who were with him. ⁸ But ten men were found among them who said to Ishmael, "Do not kill us, for we have treasures of wheat, barley, oil, and honey in the field." So he desisted and did not kill them among their brethren. ⁹ Now the pit into which Ishmael had cast all the dead bodies of the men whom he had slain, because of Gedaliah, *was* the same one Asa the king had made for fear of Baasha king of Israel. Ishmael the son of Nethaniah filled it with *the* slain. ¹⁰ Then Ishmael carried away captive all the rest of the people who *were* in Mizpah, the king's daughters and all the people who remained in Mizpah, whom Nebuzaradan the captain of the guard had committed to Gedaliah the son of Ahikam. And Ishmael the son of Nethaniah carried them away captive and departed to go over to the Ammonites.

¹¹ But when Johanan the son of Kareah and all the captains of the forces that *were*

Go

From childhood, two sisters had desired to one day go to the mission field together. As they approached mid-life, they realized they were both well established in their professions, and they began to investigate where they might go to serve God. After several months of talking to various missionary agencies, one of the sisters quit her job and moved to South America, where she became involved in pioneering churches.

The other sister, however, decided the hazards of the mission field were too great. She would remain at home and make even more money. "I'll go later," she said as she bid her sister good-bye. Two years later she died in an accident on the job. She had "saved" her life, only to lose it.

Apart from God, safety is an illusion. Many people trust in their jobs — unaware that their companies are on the brink of bankruptcy. Others trust in the government — unaware that funds are diminishing and laws are subject to change. Still others trust in their own abilities — never considering the possibility of accident or illness.

If the Lord has spoken to your heart to "Go," be swift to respond when He opens the door for you to do so. The safest place to be is in the shelter of His will.

> For I know whom I have believed and am persuaded that He is able to keep what I have committed to Him until that Day.
>
> *2 Timothy 1:12*

with him heard of all the evil that Ishmael the son of Nethaniah had done, ¹² they took all the men and went to fight with Ishmael the son of Nethaniah; and they found him by the great pool that *is* in Gibeon. ¹³ So it was, when all the people who *were* with Ishmael saw Johanan the son of Kareah, and all the captains of the forces who *were* with him, that they were glad. ¹⁴ Then all the people whom Ishmael had carried away captive from Mizpah turned around and came back, and went to Johanan the son of Kareah. ¹⁵ But Ishmael the son of Nethaniah escaped from Johanan with eight men and went to the Ammonites.

¹⁶ Then Johanan the son of Kareah, and all the captains of the forces that were with him, took from Mizpah all the rest of the people whom he had recovered from Ishmael the son of Nethaniah after he had murdered Gedaliah the son of Ahikam— the mighty men of war and the women and the children and the eunuchs, whom he had brought back from Gibeon. ¹⁷ And they departed and dwelt in the habitation of Chimham, which is near Bethlehem, as they went on their way to Egypt, ¹⁸ because of the Chaldeans; for they were afraid of them, because Ishmael the son of Nethaniah had murdered Gedaliah the son of Ahikam, whom the king of Babylon had made governor in the land.

42 Now all the captains of the forces, Johanan the son of Kareah, Jezaniah the son of Hoshaiah, and all the people, from the least to the greatest, came near ² and said to Jeremiah the prophet, "Please, let our petition be acceptable to you, and pray for us to the LORD your God, for all this remnant (since we are left *but* a few of many, as you can see), ³ that the LORD your God may show us the way in which we should walk and the thing we should do."

⁴ Then Jeremiah the prophet said to them, "I have heard. Indeed, I will pray to the LORD your God according to your words, and it shall be, *that* whatever the LORD answers you, I will declare *it* to you. I will keep nothing back from you."

⁵ So they said to Jeremiah, "Let the LORD be a true and faithful witness between us, if we do not do according to everything which the LORD your God sends us by you. ⁶ Whether *it is* pleasing or displeasing, we will obey the voice of the LORD our God to whom we send you, that it may be well with us when we obey the voice of the LORD our God."

⁷ And it happened after ten days that the word of the LORD came to Jeremiah. ⁸ Then he called Johanan the son of Kareah, all the captains of the forces which *were* with him, and all the people from the least even to the greatest, ⁹ and said to them, "Thus says the LORD, the God of Israel, to whom you sent me to present your petition before Him: ¹⁰ 'If you will still remain in this land, then I will build you and not pull *you* down, and I will plant you and not pluck *you* up. For I relent concerning the disaster that I have brought upon you. ¹¹ Do not be afraid of the king of Babylon, of whom you are afraid; do not be afraid of him,' says the LORD, 'for I *am* with you, to save you and deliver you from his hand. ¹² And I will show you mercy, that he may have mercy on you and cause you to return to your own land.'

¹³ "But if you say, 'We will not dwell in this land,' disobeying the voice of the LORD your God, ¹⁴ saying, 'No, but we will go to the land of Egypt where we shall see no war, nor hear the sound of the trumpet, nor be hungry for bread, and there we will dwell'— ¹⁵ Then hear now the word of the LORD, O remnant of Judah! Thus says the LORD of hosts, the God of Israel: 'If you wholly set your faces to enter Egypt, and go to dwell there, ¹⁶ then it shall be *that* the sword which you feared shall overtake you there in the land of Egypt; the famine of which you were afraid shall follow close after you there *in* Egypt; and there you shall die. ¹⁷ So shall it be with all the men who set their faces to go to Egypt to dwell there. They shall die by the sword, by famine, and by pestilence. And none of them shall remain or escape from the disaster that I will bring upon them.'

¹⁸ "For thus says the LORD of hosts, the God of Israel: 'As My anger and My fury have been poured out on the inhabitants of Jerusalem, so will My fury be poured out on you when you enter Egypt. And you shall be an oath, an astonishment, a

curse, and a reproach; and you shall see this place no more.'

¹⁹ "The LORD has said concerning you, O remnant of Judah, 'Do not go to Egypt!' Know certainly that I have admonished you this day. ²⁰ For you were hypocrites in your hearts when you sent me to the LORD your God, saying, 'Pray for us to the LORD our God, and according to all that the LORD your God says, so declare to us and we will do it.' ²¹ And I have this day declared it to you, but you have not obeyed the voice of the LORD your God, or anything which He has sent you by me. ²² Now therefore, know certainly that you shall die by the sword, by famine, and by pestilence in the place where you desire to go to dwell."

~ PSALM 119:89–96 ~

⁸⁹ Forever, O LORD,
Your word is settled in heaven.
⁹⁰ Your faithfulness *endures* to all generations;
You established the earth, and it abides.
⁹¹ They continue this day according to Your ordinances,
For all *are* Your servants.
⁹² Unless Your law *had been* my delight,
I would then have perished in my affliction.
⁹³ I will never forget Your precepts,
For by them You have given me life.
⁹⁴ I *am* Yours, save me;
For I have sought Your precepts.
⁹⁵ The wicked wait for me to destroy me,
But I will consider Your testimonies.
⁹⁶ I have seen the consummation of all perfection,
But Your commandment *is* exceedingly broad.

~ PROVERBS 28:2 ~

² Because of the transgression of a land, many *are* its princes;
But by a man of understanding *and* knowledge
Right will be prolonged.

~ 2 TIMOTHY 1:1–18 ~

Paul, an apostle of Jesus Christ by the will of God, according to the promise of life which is in Christ Jesus,

² To Timothy, a beloved son:

Grace, mercy, *and* peace from God the Father and Christ Jesus our Lord.

³ I thank God, whom I serve with a pure conscience, as *my* forefathers *did,* as without ceasing I remember you in my prayers night and day, ⁴ greatly desiring to see you, being mindful of your tears, that I may be filled with joy, ⁵ when I call to remembrance the genuine faith that is in you, which dwelt first in your grandmother Lois and your mother Eunice, and I am persuaded is in you also. ⁶ Therefore I remind you to stir up the gift of God which is in you through the laying on of my hands. ⁷ For God has not given us a spirit of fear, but of power and of love and of a sound mind.

⁸ Therefore do not be ashamed of the testimony of our Lord, nor of me His prisoner, but share with me in the sufferings for the gospel according to the power of God, ⁹ who has saved us and called *us* with a holy calling, not according to our works, but according to His own purpose and grace which was given to us in Christ Jesus before time began, ¹⁰ but has now been revealed by the appearing of our Savior Jesus Christ, *who* has abolished death and brought life and immortality to light through the gospel, ¹¹ to which I was appointed a preacher, an apostle, and a teacher of the Gentiles. ¹² For this reason I also suffer these things; nevertheless I am not ashamed, for I know whom I have believed and am persuaded that He is able to keep what I have committed to Him until that Day.

¹³ Hold fast the pattern of sound words which you have heard from me, in faith and love which are in Christ Jesus. ¹⁴ That good thing which was committed to you, keep by the Holy Spirit who dwells in us. ¹⁵ This you know, that all those in Asia have turned away from me, among whom are Phygellus and Hermogenes. ¹⁶ The Lord grant mercy to the household of

Onesiphorus, for he often refreshed me, and was not ashamed of my chain; [17] but when he arrived in Rome, he sought me out very zealously and found *me*. [18] The

Lord grant to him that he may find mercy from the Lord in that Day—and you know very well how many ways he ministered *to me* at Ephesus.

READING 302 · OCTOBER 29

~ JEREMIAH 43:1—44:30 ~

Now it happened, when Jeremiah had stopped speaking to all the people all the words of the LORD their God, for which the LORD their God had sent him to them, all these words, [2] that Azariah the son of Hoshaiah, Johanan the son of Kareah, and all the proud men spoke, saying to Jeremiah, "You speak falsely! The LORD our God has not sent you to say, 'Do not go to Egypt to dwell there.' [3] But Baruch the son of Neriah has set you against us, to deliver us into the hand of the Chaldeans, that they may put us to death or carry us away captive to Babylon." [4] So Johanan the son of Kareah, all the captains of the forces, and all the people would not obey the voice of the LORD, to remain in the land of Judah. [5] But Johanan the son of Kareah and all the captains of the forces took all the remnant of Judah who had returned to dwell in the land of Judah, from all nations where they had been driven— [6] men, women, children, the king's daughters, and every person whom Nebuzaradan the captain of the guard had left with Gedaliah the son of Ahikam, the son of Shaphan, and Jeremiah the prophet and Baruch the son of Neriah. [7] So they went to the land of Egypt, for they did not obey the voice of the LORD. And they went as far as Tahpanhes.

[8] Then the word of the LORD came to Jeremiah in Tahpanhes, saying, [9] "Take large stones in your hand, and hide them in the sight of the men of Judah, in the clay in the brick courtyard which *is* at the entrance to Pharaoh's house in Tahpanhes; [10] and say to them, 'Thus says the LORD of hosts, the God of Israel: "Behold, I will send and bring Nebuchadnezzar the king of Babylon, My servant, and will set his throne above these stones that I have hidden. And he will spread his royal pavilion over them. [11] When he comes, he

shall strike the land of Egypt *and deliver* to death *those appointed* for death, and to captivity *those appointed* for captivity, and to the sword *those appointed* for the sword. [12] I will kindle a fire in the houses of the gods of Egypt, and he shall burn them and carry them away captive. And he shall array himself with the land of Egypt, as a shepherd puts on his garment, and he shall go out from there in peace. [13] He shall also break the sacred pillars of Beth Shemesh that *are* in the land of Egypt; and the houses of the gods of the Egyptians he shall burn with fire." ' "

44 The word that came to Jeremiah concerning all the Jews who dwell in the land of Egypt, who dwell at Migdol, at Tahpanhes, at Noph, and in the country of Pathros, saying, [2] "Thus says the LORD of hosts, the God of Israel: 'You have seen all the calamity that I have brought on Jerusalem and on all the cities of Judah; and behold, this day they *are* a desolation, and no one dwells in them, [3] because of their wickedness which they have committed to provoke Me to anger, in that they went to burn incense *and* to serve other gods whom they did not know, they nor you nor your fathers. [4] However I have sent to you all My servants the prophets, rising early and sending *them,* saying, "Oh, do not do this abominable thing that I hate!" [5] But they did not listen or incline their ear to turn from their wickedness, to burn no incense to other gods. [6] So My fury and My anger were poured out and kindled in the cities of Judah and in the streets of Jerusalem; and they are wasted *and* desolate, as it is this day.'

[7] "Now therefore, thus says the LORD, the God of hosts, the God of Israel: 'Why do you commit *this* great evil against yourselves, to cut off from you man and

Wars and Rumors of Wars

A little girl once asked her father how wars got started.

"Well," said her father, "suppose America persisted in quarreling with England, and. . . ."

"But," interrupted her mother, "America must never quarrel with England."

"I know," said the father, "but I am only using a hypothetical instance."

"But you are misleading the child," protested Mom.

"No, I am not," replied the father indignantly, with an edge of anger in his tone.

"Never mind, Daddy," the little girl interjected, "I think I know how wars get started."

Most major arguments don't begin major, but are rooted in small annoyances, breaches, or trespasses. It's like the mighty oak that stood on the skyline of the Rocky Mountains. The tree had survived hail, heavy snows, bitter cold, and ferocious storms for more than a century. It was finally felled not by a great lightning strike or an avalanche, but by an attack of tiny beetles.

A little hurt, neglect, or insult can be the beginning of the end for virtually any relationship. Therefore, take care what you say, check your attitude, and be quick to ask for forgiveness when you've been wrong.

woman, child and infant, out of Judah, leaving none to remain, [8] in that you provoke Me to wrath with the works of your hands, burning incense to other gods in the land of Egypt where you have gone to dwell, that you may cut yourselves off and be a curse and a reproach among all the nations of the earth? [9] Have you forgotten the wickedness of your fathers, the wickedness of the kings of Judah, the wickedness of their wives, your own wickedness, and the wickedness of your wives, which they committed in the land of Judah and in the streets of Jerusalem? [10] They have not been humbled, to this day, nor have they feared; they have not walked in My law or in My statutes that I set before you and your fathers.'

[11] "Therefore thus says the LORD of hosts, the God of Israel: 'Behold, I will set My face against you for catastrophe and for cutting off all Judah. [12] And I will take the remnant of Judah who have set their faces to go into the land of Egypt to dwell there, and they shall all be consumed *and* fall in the land of Egypt. They shall be consumed by the sword *and* by famine. They shall die, from the least to the greatest, by the sword and by famine; and they shall be an oath, an astonishment, a curse and a reproach! [13] For I will punish those who dwell in the land of Egypt, as I have punished Jerusalem, by the sword, by famine, and by pestilence, [14] so that none of the remnant of Judah who have gone into the land of Egypt to dwell there shall escape or survive, lest they return to the land of Judah, to which they desire to return and dwell. For none shall return except those who escape.' "

[15] Then all the men who knew that their wives had burned incense to other gods, with all the women who stood by, a great multitude, and all the people who dwelt in the land of Egypt, in Pathros, answered Jeremiah, saying: [16] "*As for* the word that you have spoken to us in the name of the LORD, we will not listen to you! [17] But we will certainly do whatever has gone out of our own mouth, to burn incense to the queen of heaven and pour out drink offerings to her, as we have done, we and our fathers, our kings and our princes, in the cities of Judah and in the streets of Jerusalem. For *then* we had plenty of food, were well-off, and saw no trouble. [18] But since we stopped burning incense to the queen of heaven and pouring out drink offerings to her, we have lacked everything and have been consumed by the sword and by famine."

[19] *The women also said,* "And when we burned incense to the queen of heaven and poured out drink offerings to her, did we make cakes for her, to worship her, and pour out drink offerings to her without our husbands' *permission?*"

[20] Then Jeremiah spoke to all the people—the men, the women, and all the people who had given him *that* answer—saying: [21] "The incense that you burned in the cities of Judah and in the streets of Jerusalem, you and your fathers, your kings and your princes, and the people of the land, did not the LORD remember them, and did it *not* come into His mind? [22] So the LORD could no longer bear *it,* because of the evil of your doings *and* because of the abominations which you committed. Therefore your land is a desolation, an astonishment, a curse, and without an inhabitant, as *it is* this day. [23] Because you have burned incense and because you have sinned against the LORD, and have not obeyed the voice of the LORD or walked in His law, in His statutes or in His testimonies, therefore this calamity has happened to you, as *at* this day."

[24] Moreover Jeremiah said to all the people and to all the women, "Hear the word of the LORD, all Judah who *are* in the land of Egypt! [25] Thus says the LORD of hosts, the God of Israel, saying: 'You and your wives have spoken with your mouths and fulfilled with your hands, saying, "We will surely keep our vows that we have made, to burn incense to the queen of heaven and pour out drink offerings to her." You will surely keep your vows and perform your vows!' [26] Therefore hear the word of the LORD, all Judah who dwell in the land of Egypt: 'Behold, I have sworn by My great name,' says the LORD, 'that My name shall no more be named in the mouth of any man of Judah in all the land of Egypt, saying, "The Lord GOD lives." [27] Behold, I will watch over them for adversity and not for good. And all the men of Judah who *are* in the land of Egypt shall be consumed by the sword

and by famine, until there is an end to them. ²⁸ Yet a small number who escape the sword shall return from the land of Egypt to the land of Judah; and all the remnant of Judah, who have gone to the land of Egypt to dwell there, shall know whose words will stand, Mine or theirs. ²⁹ And this *shall be* a sign to you,' says the LORD, 'that I will punish you in this place, that you may know that My words will surely stand against you for adversity.'

³⁰ "Thus says the LORD: 'Behold, I will give Pharaoh Hophra king of Egypt into the hand of his enemies and into the hand of those who seek his life, as I gave Zedekiah king of Judah into the hand of Nebuchadnezzar king of Babylon, his enemy who sought his life.' "

∼ PSALM 119:97–104 ∼

⁹⁷ Oh, how I love Your law!
It *is* my meditation all the day.
⁹⁸ You, through Your commandments,
make me wiser than my enemies;
For they *are* ever with me.
⁹⁹ I have more understanding than all
my teachers,
For Your testimonies *are* my
meditation.
¹⁰⁰ I understand more than the
ancients,
Because I keep Your precepts.
¹⁰¹ I have restrained my feet from every
evil way,
That I may keep Your word.
¹⁰² I have not departed from Your
judgments,
For You Yourself have taught me.
¹⁰³ How sweet are Your words to my
taste,
Sweeter than honey to my
mouth!
¹⁰⁴ Through Your precepts I get
understanding;
Therefore I hate every false way.

∼ PROVERBS 28:3 ∼

³ A poor man who oppresses the poor
Is like a driving rain which leaves no
food.

∼ 2 TIMOTHY 2:1–26 ∼

You therefore, my son, be strong in the grace that is in Christ Jesus. ² And the things that you have heard from me among many witnesses, commit these to faithful men who will be able to teach others also. ³ You therefore must endure hardship as a good soldier of Jesus Christ. ⁴ No one engaged in warfare entangles himself with the affairs of *this* life, that he may please him who enlisted him as a soldier. ⁵ And also if anyone competes in athletics, he is not crowned unless he competes according to the rules. ⁶ The hardworking farmer must be first to partake of the crops. ⁷ Consider what I say, and may the Lord give you understanding in all things.

⁸ Remember that Jesus Christ, of the seed of David, was raised from the dead according to my gospel, ⁹ for which I suffer trouble as an evildoer, *even* to the point of chains; but the word of God is not chained. ¹⁰ Therefore I endure all things for the sake of the elect, that they also may obtain the salvation which is in Christ Jesus with eternal glory.

¹¹ *This is* a faithful saying:

For if we died with *Him,*
We shall also live with *Him.*
¹² If we endure,
We shall also reign with *Him.*
If we deny *Him,*
He also will deny us.
¹³ If we are faithless,
He remains faithful;
He cannot deny Himself.

¹⁴ Remind *them* of these things, charging *them* before the Lord not to strive about words to no profit, to the ruin of the hearers. ¹⁵ Be diligent to present yourself approved to God, a worker who does not need to be ashamed, rightly dividing the word of truth. ¹⁶ But shun profane *and* idle babblings, for they will increase to more ungodliness. ¹⁷ And their message will spread like cancer. Hymenaeus and Philetus are of this sort, ¹⁸ who have strayed concerning the truth, saying that the resurrection is already past; and they overthrow the faith of some.

[19] Nevertheless the solid foundation of God stands, having this seal: "The Lord knows those who are His," and, "Let everyone who names the name of Christ depart from iniquity."

[20] But in a great house there are not only vessels of gold and silver, but also of wood and clay, some for honor and some for dishonor. [21] Therefore if anyone cleanses himself from the latter, he will be a vessel for honor, sanctified and useful for the Master, prepared for every good work. [22] Flee also youthful lusts; but pursue righ-teousness, faith, love, peace with those who call on the Lord out of a pure heart. [23] But avoid foolish and ignorant disputes, knowing that they generate strife. [24] And a servant of the Lord must not quarrel but be gentle to all, able to teach, patient, [25] in humility correcting those who are in opposition, if God perhaps will grant them repentance, so that they may know the truth, [26] and *that* they may come to their senses *and escape* the snare of the devil, having been taken captive by him to *do* his will.

READING 303 · OCTOBER 30

~ JEREMIAH 45:1—46:28 ~

The word that Jeremiah the prophet spoke to Baruch the son of Neriah, when he had written these words in a book at the instruction of Jeremiah, in the fourth year of Jehoiakim the son of Josiah, king of Judah, saying, [2] "Thus says the LORD, the God of Israel, to you, O Baruch: [3] 'You said, "Woe is me now! For the LORD has added grief to my sorrow. I fainted in my sighing, and I find no rest." '

[4] "Thus you shall say to him, 'Thus says the LORD: "Behold, what I have built I will break down, and what I have planted I will pluck up, that is, this whole land. [5] And do you seek great things for yourself? Do not seek *them;* for behold, I will bring adversity on all flesh," says the LORD. "But I will give your life to you as a prize in all places, wherever you go." ' "

46 The word of the LORD which came to Jeremiah the prophet against the nations. [2] Against Egypt.

Concerning the army of Pharaoh Necho, king of Egypt, which was by the River Euphrates in Carchemish, and which Nebuchadnezzar king of Babylon defeated in the fourth year of Jehoiakim the son of Josiah, king of Judah:

[3] "Order the buckler and shield,
    And draw near to battle!
[4] Harness the horses,
    And mount up, you horsemen!
    Stand forth with *your* helmets,
    Polish the spears,
    Put on the armor!
[5] Why have I seen them dismayed
    and turned back?
    Their mighty ones are beaten
      down;
    They have speedily fled,
    And did not look back,
    For fear *was* all around," says the
      LORD.
[6] "Do not let the swift flee away,
    Nor the mighty man escape;
    They will stumble and fall
    Toward the north, by the River
      Euphrates.

[7] "Who *is* this coming up like a
      flood,
    Whose waters move like the
      rivers?
[8] Egypt rises up like a flood,
    And *its* waters move like the
      rivers;
    And he says, 'I will go up *and*
      cover the earth,
    I will destroy the city and its
      inhabitants.'
[9] Come up, O horses, and rage,
      O chariots!
    And let the mighty men come
      forth:
    The Ethiopians and the Libyans
      who handle the shield,
    And the Lydians who handle *and*
      bend the bow.

Plan B

In the 1984 Olympics, heavyweight boxer Henry Tillman planned out a very careful strategy. He decided he would fight defensively, simply warding off his opponent's blows, until he saw an opening for a strike of his own. Minutes into the fight, it became obvious to Tillman that his opponent had planned the same strategy! After the bell sounded ending the first round, Tillman stepped back, dropped his hands, and mentally shifted gears. He recognized that his initial game plan might not work, but he had come prepared with a second plan. He switched to a take-the-offensive mode of fighting, won the match, and ultimately won a gold medal.

Figure skater Kristi Yamaguchi also had a "plan B" for her Olympic bid. Originally, she had planned to perform her most difficult jump — three revolutions in the air and a graceful single-skate landing known as the triple salchow. A slight stumble in the early portion of her routine led her to make a change. She cut the triple salchow to a double, regained her balance, caught up with her music, and then went on to perform another triple jump — the lutz.

No matter how much we rehearse or plan, things don't always go as we desire. True champions are those who are prepared to adapt if necessary and switch to what works. Be flexible. You'll have much more peace and a lot less stress if you don't expect things to always go the way you planned.

10 For this *is* the day of the Lord
   GOD of hosts,
   A day of vengeance,
   That He may avenge Himself on
   His adversaries.
   The sword shall devour;
   It shall be satiated and made
   drunk with their blood;
   For the Lord GOD of hosts has a
   sacrifice
   In the north country by the River
   Euphrates.

11 "Go up to Gilead and take balm,
   O virgin, the daughter of Egypt;
   In vain you will use many
   medicines;
   You shall not be cured.
12 The nations have heard of your
   shame,
   And your cry has filled the land;
   For the mighty man has stumbled
   against the mighty;
   They both have fallen together."

13 The word that the LORD spoke to
Jeremiah the prophet, how Nebuchadnezzar king of Babylon would come *and*
strike the land of Egypt.

14 "Declare in Egypt, and proclaim in
   Migdol;
   Proclaim in Noph and in
   Tahpanhes;
   Say, 'Stand fast and prepare
   yourselves,
   For the sword devours all around
   you.'
15 Why are your valiant *men* swept
   away?
   They did not stand
   Because the LORD drove them
   away.
16 He made many fall;
   Yes, one fell upon another.
   And they said, 'Arise!
   Let us go back to our own people
   And to the land of our nativity
   From the oppressing sword.'
17 They cried there,
   'Pharaoh, king of Egypt, *is but* a
   noise.
   He has passed by the appointed
   time!'

18 "*As* I live," says the King,
   Whose name *is* the LORD of hosts,
   "Surely as Tabor *is* among the
   mountains
   And as Carmel by the sea, *so* he
   shall come.
19 O you daughter dwelling in Egypt,
   Prepare yourself to go into
   captivity!
   For Noph shall be waste and
   desolate, without inhabitant.

20 "Egypt *is* a very pretty heifer,
   But destruction comes, it comes
   from the north.
21 Also her mercenaries are in her
   midst like fat bulls,
   For they also are turned back,
   They have fled away together.
   They did not stand,
   For the day of their calamity had
   come upon them,
   The time of their punishment.
22 Her noise shall go like a serpent,
   For they shall march with an army
   And come against her with axes,
   Like those who chop wood.

23 "They shall cut down her forest,"
   says the LORD,
   "Though it cannot be searched,
   Because they *are* innumerable,
   And more numerous than
   grasshoppers.
24 The daughter of Egypt shall be
   ashamed;
   She shall be delivered into the
   hand
   Of the people of the north."

25 The LORD of hosts, the God of Israel,
says: "Behold, I will bring punishment on
Amon of No, and Pharaoh and Egypt,
with their gods and their kings—Pharaoh
and those who trust in him. 26 And I will
deliver them into the hand of those who
seek their lives, into the hand of Nebuchadnezzar king of Babylon and the hand
of his servants. Afterward it shall be inhabited as in the days of old," says the
LORD.

27 "But do not fear, O My servant
   Jacob,
   And do not be dismayed, O Israel!

For behold, I will save you from
afar,
And your offspring from the land
of their captivity;
Jacob shall return, have rest and
be at ease;
No one shall make *him* afraid.
28 Do not fear, O Jacob My servant,"
says the LORD,
"For I *am* with you;
For I will make a complete end of
all the nations
To which I have driven you,
But I will not make a complete
end of you.
I will rightly correct you,
For I will not leave you wholly
unpunished."

~ PSALM 119:105–112 ~

105 Your word *is* a lamp to my feet
And a light to my path.
106 I have sworn and confirmed
That I will keep Your righteous
judgments.
107 I am afflicted very much;
Revive me, O LORD, according to
Your word.
108 Accept, I pray, the freewill offerings
of my mouth, O LORD,
And teach me Your judgments.
109 My life *is* continually in my hand,
Yet I do not forget Your law.
110 The wicked have laid a snare for
me,
Yet I have not strayed from Your
precepts.
111 Your testimonies I have taken as a
heritage forever,
For they *are* the rejoicing of my
heart.
112 I have inclined my heart to perform
Your statutes
Forever, to the very end.

~ PROVERBS 28:4 ~

4 Those who forsake the law praise
the wicked,

But such as keep the law contend
with them.

~ 2 TIMOTHY 3:1–17 ~

But know this, that in the last days perilous times will come: 2 For men will be
lovers of themselves, lovers of money,
boasters, proud, blasphemers, disobedient
to parents, unthankful, unholy, 3 unloving, unforgiving, slanderers, without self-
control, brutal, despisers of good,
4 traitors, headstrong, haughty, lovers of
pleasure rather than lovers of God, 5 having a form of godliness but denying its
power. And from such people turn away!
6 For of this sort are those who creep into
households and make captives of gullible
women loaded down with sins, led away
by various lusts, 7 always learning and
never able to come to the knowledge of
the truth. 8 Now as Jannes and Jambres
resisted Moses, so do these also resist the
truth: men of corrupt minds, disapproved
concerning the faith; 9 but they will progress no further, for their folly will be
manifest to all, as theirs also was.

10 But you have carefully followed my
doctrine, manner of life, purpose, faith,
longsuffering, love, perseverance, 11 persecutions, afflictions, which happened to
me at Antioch, at Iconium, at Lystra—
what persecutions I endured. And out of
them all the Lord delivered me. 12 Yes, and
all who desire to live godly in Christ Jesus
will suffer persecution. 13 But evil men and
impostors will grow worse and worse,
deceiving and being deceived. 14 But you
must continue in the things which you
have learned and been assured of, knowing from whom you have learned *them,*
15 and that from childhood you have
known the Holy Scriptures, which are able
to make you wise for salvation through
faith which is in Christ Jesus.

16 All Scripture *is* given by inspiration
of God, and *is* profitable for doctrine, for
reproof, for correction, for instruction in
righteousness, 17 that the man of God may
be complete, thoroughly equipped for
every good work.

~ JEREMIAH 47:1—48:47 ~

The word of the LORD that came to Jeremiah the prophet against the Philistines, before Pharaoh attacked Gaza.
² Thus says the LORD:

"Behold, waters rise out of the
    north,
And shall be an overflowing flood;
They shall overflow the land and
    all that is in it,
The city and those who dwell
    within;
Then the men shall cry,
And all the inhabitants of the land
    shall wail.
³ At the noise of the stamping
        hooves of his strong horses,
    At the rushing of his chariots,
    At the rumbling of his wheels,
    The fathers will not look back for
        their children,
    Lacking courage,
⁴ Because of the day that comes to
        plunder all the Philistines,
    To cut off from Tyre and Sidon
        every helper who remains;
    For the LORD shall plunder the
        Philistines,
    The remnant of the country of
        Caphtor.
⁵ Baldness has come upon Gaza,
    Ashkelon is cut off
    With the remnant of their valley.
    How long will you cut yourself?

⁶ "O you sword of the LORD,
    How long until you are quiet?
    Put yourself up into your
        scabbard,
    Rest and be still!
⁷ How can it be quiet,
    Seeing the LORD has given it a
        charge
    Against Ashkelon and against the
        seashore?
    There He has appointed it."

48 Against Moab.
Thus says the LORD of hosts, the God of Israel:

"Woe to Nebo!
For it is plundered,
Kirjathaim is shamed *and* taken;
The high stronghold is shamed
    and dismayed—
² No more praise of Moab.
    In Heshbon they have devised evil
        against her:
    'Come, and let us cut her off as a
        nation.'
    You also shall be cut down,
        O Madmen!
    The sword shall pursue you;
³ A voice of crying *shall be* from
        Horonaim:
    'Plundering and great destruction!'

⁴ "Moab is destroyed;
    Her little ones have caused a cry
        to be heard;
⁵ For in the Ascent of Luhith they
        ascend with continual weeping;
    For in the descent of Horonaim
        the enemies have heard a cry of
        destruction.

⁶ "Flee, save your lives!
    And be like the juniper in the
        wilderness.
⁷ For because you have trusted in
        your works and your treasures,
    You also shall be taken.
    And Chemosh shall go forth into
        captivity,
    His priests and his princes
        together.
⁸ And the plunderer shall come
        against every city;
    No one shall escape.
    The valley also shall perish,
    And the plain shall be destroyed,
    As the LORD has spoken.

⁹ "Give wings to Moab,
    That she may flee and get away;
    For her cities shall be desolate,
    Without any to dwell in them.
¹⁰ Cursed *is* he who does the work
        of the LORD deceitfully,
    And cursed *is* he who keeps back
        his sword from blood.

They Shall Take Up Serpents

A woman was sitting in her den one day when a small black snake suddenly appeared, slithered across the floor, and made its way under the couch. Being deathly afraid of snakes, the woman promptly ran to the bathroom to get her husband, who was taking a shower. He came running from the shower wearing only a towel, grabbed an old broom handle from the closet, and began poking under the couch.

At this point, the sleeping family dog woke up. Curious to see what was happening, he came up behind the husband and touched his cold nose to the back of the man's heel. The man, surmising that the snake had outmaneuvered him and had bitten him on the heel, fainted dead away. The wife concluded that her husband had overexerted and collapsed with a heart attack. She ran from the house to a hospital just one block away. The ambulance drivers promptly returned to the house with her and placed the man on a stretcher. As they were carrying him out of the house, the snake reappeared from beneath the couch. One of the drivers became so excited that he dropped his end of the stretcher and broke the husband's leg. Seeing her husband's twisted leg, the wife passed out.

Meanwhile, the snake slithered quietly away!

When you face a frightening situation, don't lose your cool. Keep your wits about you. God is there with you in the midst, and He will deliver you!

11 "Moab has been at ease from his
        youth;
    He has settled on his dregs,
    And has not been emptied from
        vessel to vessel,
    Nor has he gone into captivity.
    Therefore his taste remained in
        him,
    And his scent has not changed.

12 "Therefore behold, the days are
        coming," says the LORD,
    "That I shall send him wine
        workers
    Who will tip him over
    And empty his vessels
    And break the bottles.
13 Moab shall be ashamed of
        Chemosh,
    As the house of Israel was
        ashamed of Bethel, their
        confidence.

14 "How can you say, 'We *are* mighty
    And strong men for the war'?
15 Moab is plundered and gone up
    from her cities;
    Her chosen young men have gone
        down to the slaughter," says the
        King,
    Whose name *is* the LORD of hosts.

16 "The calamity of Moab *is* near at
        hand,
    And his affliction comes quickly.
17 Bemoan him, all you who are
        around him;
    And all you who know his name,
    Say, 'How the strong staff is
        broken,
    The beautiful rod!'

18 "O daughter inhabiting Dibon,
    Come down from *your* glory,
    And sit in thirst;
    For the plunderer of Moab has
        come against you,
    He has destroyed your
        strongholds.
19 O inhabitant of Aroer,
    Stand by the way and watch;
    Ask him who flees
    And her who escapes;
    Say, 'What has happened?'

20 Moab is shamed, for he is broken
        down.
    Wail and cry!
    Tell it in Arnon, that Moab is
        plundered.

21 "And judgment has come on the
        plain country:
    On Holon and Jahzah and
        Mephaath,
22 On Dibon and Nebo and Beth
        Diblathaim,
23 On Kirjathaim and Beth Gamul
        and Beth Meon,
24 On Kerioth and Bozrah,
    On all the cities of the land of
        Moab,
    Far or near.
25 The horn of Moab is cut off,
    And his arm is broken," says the
        LORD.

26 "Make him drunk,
    Because he exalted *himself* against
        the LORD.
    Moab shall wallow in his vomit,
    And he shall also be in derision.
27 For was not Israel a derision to
        you?
    Was he found among thieves?
    For whenever you speak of him,
    You shake *your head in scorn*.
28 You who dwell in Moab,
    Leave the cities and dwell in the
        rock,
    And be like the dove *which* makes
        her nest
    In the sides of the cave's mouth.

29 "We have heard the pride of Moab
    (He *is* exceedingly proud),
    Of his loftiness and arrogance and
        pride,
    And of the haughtiness of his
        heart."

30 "I know his wrath," says the LORD,
    "But it *is* not right;
    His lies have made nothing right.
31 Therefore I will wail for Moab,
    And I will cry out for all Moab;
    I will mourn for the men of Kir
        Heres.
32 O vine of Sibmah! I will weep for
        you with the weeping of Jazer.

Your plants have gone over the
    sea,
They reach to the sea of Jazer.
The plunderer has fallen on your
    summer fruit and your vintage.
33 Joy and gladness are taken
From the plentiful field
And from the land of Moab;
I have caused wine to fail from the
    winepresses;
No one will tread with joyous
    shouting—
Not joyous shouting!

34 "From the cry of Heshbon to
    Elealeh and to Jahaz
They have uttered their voice,
From Zoar to Horonaim,
Like a three-year-old heifer;
For the waters of Nimrim also
    shall be desolate.

35 "Moreover," says the LORD,
"I will cause to cease in Moab
    The one who offers *sacrifices* in
    the high places
And burns incense to his gods.
36 Therefore My heart shall wail like
    flutes for Moab,
And like flutes My heart shall wail
For the men of Kir Heres.
Therefore the riches they have
    acquired have perished.

37 "For every head *shall be* bald, and
    every beard clipped;
On all the hands *shall be* cuts, and
    on the loins sackcloth—
38 A general lamentation
On all the housetops of Moab,
And in its streets;
For I have broken Moab like a
    vessel in which *is* no pleasure,"
    says the LORD.
39 "They shall wail:
'How she is broken down!
How Moab has turned her back
    with shame!'
So Moab shall be a derision
And a dismay to all those about
    her."

40 For thus says the LORD:

"Behold, one shall fly like an eagle,
And spread his wings over Moab.
41 Kerioth is taken,
And the strongholds are surprised;
The mighty men's hearts in Moab
    on that day shall be
Like the heart of a woman in birth
    pangs.
42 And Moab shall be destroyed as a
    people,
Because he exalted *himself* against
    the LORD.
43 Fear and the pit and the snare
    shall be upon you,
O inhabitant of Moab," says the
    LORD.
44 "He who flees from the fear shall
    fall into the pit,
And he who gets out of the pit
    shall be caught in the snare.
For upon Moab, upon it I will
    bring
The year of their punishment,"
    says the LORD.

45 "Those who fled stood under the
    shadow of Heshbon
Because of exhaustion.
But a fire shall come out of
    Heshbon,
A flame from the midst of Sihon,
And shall devour the brow of
    Moab,
The crown of the head of the sons
    of tumult.
46 Woe to you, O Moab!
The people of Chemosh perish;
For your sons have been taken
    captive,
And your daughters captive.

47 "Yet I will bring back the captives
    of Moab
In the latter days," says the LORD.

Thus far *is* the judgment of Moab.

~ PSALM 119:113–120 ~

113 I hate the double-minded,
But I love Your law.
114 You *are* my hiding place and my
    shield;
I hope in Your word.
115 Depart from me, you evildoers,

For I will keep the commandments
of my God!

116 Uphold me according to Your word,
that I may live;
And do not let me be ashamed of my
hope.

117 Hold me up, and I shall be safe,
And I shall observe Your statutes
continually.

118 You reject all those who stray from
Your statutes,
For their deceit *is* falsehood.

119 You put away all the wicked of the
earth *like* dross;
Therefore I love Your testimonies.

120 My flesh trembles for fear of You,
And I am afraid of Your judgments.

~ PROVERBS 28:5 ~

5 Evil men do not understand justice,
But those who seek the LORD
understand all.

~ 2 TIMOTHY 4:1–22 ~

I charge *you* therefore before God and
the Lord Jesus Christ, who will judge the
living and the dead at His appearing and
His kingdom: 2 Preach the word! Be ready
in season *and* out of season. Convince,
rebuke, exhort, with all longsuffering and
teaching. 3 For the time will come when
they will not endure sound doctrine, but
according to their own desires, *because*
they have itching ears, they will heap up
for themselves teachers; 4 and they will
turn *their* ears away from the truth, and
be turned aside to fables. 5 But you be
watchful in all things, endure afflictions,
do the work of an evangelist, fulfill your
ministry.

6 For I am already being poured out as
a drink offering, and the time of my departure is at hand. 7 I have fought the good
fight, I have finished the race, I have kept
the faith. 8 Finally, there is laid up for
me the crown of righteousness, which the
Lord, the righteous Judge, will give to me
on that Day, and not to me only but also
to all who have loved His appearing.

9 Be diligent to come to me quickly;
10 for Demas has forsaken me, having
loved this present world, and has departed
for Thessalonica—Crescens for Galatia,
Titus for Dalmatia. 11 Only Luke is with
me. Get Mark and bring him with you,
for he is useful to me for ministry. 12 And
Tychicus I have sent to Ephesus. 13 Bring
the cloak that I left with Carpus at Troas
when you come—and the books, especially the parchments.

14 Alexander the coppersmith did me
much harm. May the Lord repay him according to his works. 15 You also must
beware of him, for he has greatly resisted
our words.

16 At my first defense no one stood with
me, but all forsook me. May it not be
charged against them.

17 But the Lord stood with me and
strengthened me, so that the message
might be preached fully through me, and
that all the Gentiles might hear. Also I was
delivered out of the mouth of the lion.
18 And the Lord will deliver me from every evil work and preserve *me* for His
heavenly kingdom. To Him *be* glory forever and ever. Amen!

19 Greet Prisca and Aquila, and the
household of Onesiphorus. 20 Erastus
stayed in Corinth, but Trophimus I have
left in Miletus sick.

21 Do your utmost to come before
winter.

Eubulus greets you, as well as Pudens,
Linus, Claudia, and all the brethren.

22 The Lord Jesus Christ be with your
spirit. Grace be with you. Amen.

~ JEREMIAH 49:1—50:46 ~

Against the Ammonites.
Thus says the LORD:

"Has Israel no sons?
Has he no heir?
Why *then* does Milcom inherit
Gad,
And his people dwell in its cities?
2 Therefore behold, the days are
coming," says the LORD,
"That I will cause to be heard an
alarm of war
In Rabbah of the Ammonites;
It shall be a desolate mound,
And her villages shall be burned
with fire.
Then Israel shall take possession
of his inheritance," says the
LORD.

3 "Wail, O Heshbon, for Ai is
plundered!
Cry, you daughters of Rabbah,
Gird yourselves with sackcloth!
Lament and run to and fro by the
walls;
For Milcom shall go into
captivity
With his priests and his princes
together.
4 Why do you boast in the valleys,
Your flowing valley, O backsliding
daughter?
Who trusted in her treasures,
saying,
'Who will come against me?'
5 Behold, I will bring fear upon
you,"
Says the Lord GOD of hosts,
"From all those who are around
you;
You shall be driven out, everyone
headlong,
And no one will gather those who
wander off.
6 But afterward I will bring back
The captives of the people of
Ammon," says the LORD.

7 Against Edom.
Thus says the LORD of hosts:

"*Is* wisdom no more in Teman?
Has counsel perished from the
prudent?
Has their wisdom vanished?
8 Flee, turn back, dwell in the
depths, O inhabitants of Dedan!
For I will bring the calamity of
Esau upon him,
The time *that* I will punish him.
9 If grape-gatherers came to you,
Would they not leave *some*
gleaning grapes?
If thieves by night,
Would they not destroy until they
have enough?
10 But I have made Esau bare;
I have uncovered his secret places,
And he shall not be able to hide
himself.
His descendants are plundered,
His brethren and his neighbors,
And he *is* no more.
11 Leave your fatherless children,
I will preserve *them* alive;
And let your widows trust in Me."

12 For thus says the LORD: "Behold,
those whose judgment *was* not to drink
of the cup have assuredly drunk. And *are*
you the one who will altogether go unpunished? You shall not go unpunished,
but you shall surely drink *of it.* 13 For I
have sworn by Myself," says the LORD,
"that Bozrah shall become a desolation, a
reproach, a waste, and a curse. And all its
cities shall be perpetual wastes."

14 I have heard a message from the
LORD,
And an ambassador has been sent
to the nations:
"Gather together, come against her,
And rise up to battle!

15 "For indeed, I will make you small
among nations,
Despised among men.
16 Your fierceness has deceived you,
The pride of your heart,
O you who dwell in the clefts of
the rock,
Who hold the height of the hill!

Though you make your nest as
   high as the eagle,
I will bring you down from there,"
   says the LORD.

17 "Edom also shall be an
      astonishment;
   Everyone who goes by it will be
      astonished
   And will hiss at all its plagues.
18 As in the overthrow of Sodom and
      Gomorrah
   And their neighbors," says the
      LORD,
   "No one shall remain there,
   Nor shall a son of man dwell in it.

19 "Behold, he shall come up like a
      lion from the floodplain of the
      Jordan
   Against the dwelling place of the
      strong;
   But I will suddenly make him run
      away from her.
   And who is a chosen man that I
      may appoint over her?
   For who is like Me?
   Who will arraign Me?
   And who is that shepherd
   Who will withstand Me?"

20 Therefore hear the counsel of the
      LORD that He has taken against
      Edom,
   And His purposes that He has
      proposed against the inhabitants
      of Teman:
   Surely the least of the flock shall
      draw them out;
   Surely He shall make their
      dwelling places desolate with
      them.
21 The earth shakes at the noise of
      their fall;
   At the cry its noise is heard at the
      Red Sea.
22 Behold, He shall come up and fly
      like the eagle,
   And spread His wings over
      Bozrah;
   The heart of the mighty men of
      Edom in that day shall be
   Like the heart of a woman in birth
      pangs.

23 Against Damascus.

   "Hamath and Arpad are shamed,
      For they have heard bad news.
   They are fainthearted;
   There is trouble on the sea;
   It cannot be quiet.
24 Damascus has grown feeble;
      She turns to flee,
   And fear has seized her.
   Anguish and sorrows have taken
      her like a woman in labor.
25 Why is the city of praise not
      deserted, the city of My joy?
26 Therefore her young men shall fall
      in her streets,
   And all the men of war shall be
      cut off in that day," says the
      LORD of hosts.
27 "I will kindle a fire in the wall of
      Damascus,
   And it shall consume the palaces
      of Ben-Hadad."

28 Against Kedar and against the kingdoms of Hazor, which Nebuchadnezzar
king of Babylon shall strike.
   Thus says the LORD:

   "Arise, go up to Kedar,
      And devastate the men of the East!
29 Their tents and their flocks they
      shall take away.
   They shall take for themselves
      their curtains,
   All their vessels and their camels;
   And they shall cry out to them,
   'Fear is on every side!'

30 "Flee, get far away! Dwell in the
      depths,
   O inhabitants of Hazor!" says the
      LORD.
   "For Nebuchadnezzar king of
      Babylon has taken counsel
      against you,
   And has conceived a plan against
      you.

31 "Arise, go up to the wealthy nation
      that dwells securely," says the
      LORD,
   "Which has neither gates nor bars,
   Dwelling alone.

The Hallmark of Integrity

Dwight L. Moody's father died when Dwight was only four. A month later, Mrs. Moody gave birth to twins. With nine mouths to feed and no income, the widow Moody was dogged by creditors. In response to such a dire and impoverished situation, the eldest son ran away from home. Few would have criticized Mrs. Moody for seeking institutional assistance or letting others help raise her children. However, she was determined to keep her family together.

On a nightly basis, Mrs. Moody placed a light in the window, certain her son would return home. Dwight wrote of those days, "When the wind was very high and the house would tremble at every gust, the voice of my mother was raised in prayer." In time, her prayers were answered. Moody recalls that no one recognized his older brother when he came to the door, a great beard flowed down his chest. It was only as the tears began to soak his beard that Mrs. Moody recognized her son and invited him in. He said, "No, Mother, I will not come in until I hear first that you have forgiven me." She was only too willing to forgive, of course, and threw her arms around her son in a warm embrace.

Mrs. Moody didn't change just because her circumstances did. That is the hallmark of integrity.

32 Their camels shall be for booty,
   And the multitude of their cattle
      for plunder.
   I will scatter to all winds those in
      the farthest corners,
   And I will bring their calamity
      from all its sides," says the
      LORD.
33 "Hazor shall be a dwelling for
      jackals, a desolation forever;
   No one shall reside there,
   Nor son of man dwell in it."

34 The word of the LORD that came to
Jeremiah the prophet against Elam, in the
beginning of the reign of Zedekiah king
of Judah, saying, 35 "Thus says the LORD
of hosts:

   'Behold, I will break the bow of
      Elam,
   The foremost of their might.
36 Against Elam I will bring the four
      winds
   From the four quarters of heaven,
   And scatter them toward all those
      winds;
   There shall be no nations where
      the outcasts of Elam will not go.
37 For I will cause Elam to be
      dismayed before their enemies
   And before those who seek their
      life.
   I will bring disaster upon them,
   My fierce anger,' says the LORD;
   'And I will send the sword after
      them
   Until I have consumed them.
38 I will set My throne in Elam,
   And will destroy from there the
      king and the princes,' says the
      LORD.

39 'But it shall come to pass in the
      latter days:
   I will bring back the captives of
      Elam,' says the LORD."

50 The word that the LORD spoke
against Babylon and against the land of
the Chaldeans by Jeremiah the prophet.

2 "Declare among the nations,
   Proclaim, and set up a standard;
   Proclaim—do not conceal it—

Say, 'Babylon is taken, Bel is
   shamed.
Merodach is broken in pieces;
Her idols are humiliated,
Her images are broken in pieces.'
3 For out of the north a nation
   comes up against her,
Which shall make her land
   desolate,
And no one shall dwell therein.
They shall move, they shall depart,
Both man and beast.

4 "In those days and in that time,"
      says the LORD,
"The children of Israel shall come,
They and the children of Judah
   together;
With continual weeping they shall
   come,
And seek the LORD their God.
5 They shall ask the way to Zion,
With their faces toward it, saying,
'Come and let us join ourselves to
   the LORD
In a perpetual covenant
That will not be forgotten.'

6 "My people have been lost sheep.
Their shepherds have led them
   astray;
They have turned them away on
   the mountains.
They have gone from mountain to
   hill;
They have forgotten their resting
   place.
7 All who found them have
   devoured them;
And their adversaries said, 'We
   have not offended,
Because they have sinned against
   the LORD, the habitation of
   justice,
The LORD, the hope of their
   fathers.'

8 "Move from the midst of Babylon,
Go out of the land of the
   Chaldeans;
And be like the rams before the
   flocks.
9 For behold, I will raise and cause
   to come up against Babylon

An assembly of great nations from
the north country,
And they shall array themselves
against her;
From there she shall be captured.
Their arrows *shall be* like *those* of
an expert warrior;
None shall return in vain.
10 And Chaldea shall become
plunder;
All who plunder her shall be
satisfied," says the LORD.

11 "Because you were glad, because
you rejoiced,
You destroyers of My heritage,
Because you have grown fat like a
heifer threshing grain,
And you bellow like bulls,
12 Your mother shall be deeply
ashamed;
She who bore you shall be
ashamed.
Behold, the least of the nations
shall be a wilderness,
A dry land and a desert.
13 Because of the wrath of the LORD
She shall not be inhabited,
But she shall be wholly desolate.
Everyone who goes by Babylon
shall be horrified
And hiss at all her plagues.

14 "Put yourselves in array against
Babylon all around,
All you who bend the bow;
Shoot at her, spare no arrows,
For she has sinned against the
LORD.
15 Shout against her all around;
She has given her hand,
Her foundations have fallen,
Her walls are thrown down;
For it *is* the vengeance of the
LORD.
Take vengeance on her.
As she has done, so do to her.
16 Cut off the sower from Babylon,
And him who handles the sickle at
harvest time.
For fear of the oppressing sword
Everyone shall turn to his own
people,
And everyone shall flee to his own
land.

17 "Israel *is* like scattered sheep;
The lions have driven *him* away.
First the king of Assyria devoured
him;
Now at last this Nebuchadnezzar
king of Babylon has broken his
bones."

18 Therefore thus says the LORD of
hosts, the God of Israel:

"Behold, I will punish the king of
Babylon and his land,
As I have punished the king of
Assyria.
19 But I will bring back Israel to his
home,
And he shall feed on Carmel and
Bashan;
His soul shall be satisfied on
Mount Ephraim and Gilead.
20 In those days and in that time,"
says the LORD,
"The iniquity of Israel shall be
sought, but *there shall be* none;
And the sins of Judah, but they
shall not be found;
For I will pardon those whom I
preserve.

21 "Go up against the land of
Merathaim, against it,
And against the inhabitants of
Pekod.
Waste and utterly destroy them,"
says the LORD,
"And do according to all that I have
commanded you.
22 A sound of battle *is* in the land,
And of great destruction.
23 How the hammer of the whole
earth has been cut apart and
broken!
How Babylon has become a
desolation among the nations!
I have laid a snare for you;
24 You have indeed been trapped,
O Babylon,
And you were not aware;
You have been found and also
caught,
Because you have contended
against the LORD.
25 The LORD has opened His armory,

And has brought out the weapons
    of His indignation;
For this *is* the work of the Lord
    GOD of hosts
In the land of the Chaldeans.
26 Come against her from the
    farthest border;
Open her storehouses;
Cast her up as heaps of ruins,
And destroy her utterly;
Let nothing of her be left.
27 Slay all her bulls,
    Let them go down to the
    slaughter.
Woe to them!
For their day has come, the time
    of their punishment.
28 The voice of those who flee and
    escape from the land of Babylon
Declares in Zion the vengeance of
    the LORD our God,
The vengeance of His temple.

29 "Call together the archers against
    Babylon.
All you who bend the bow,
    encamp against it all around;
Let none of them escape.
Repay her according to her work;
According to all she has done, do
    to her;
For she has been proud against the
    LORD,
Against the Holy One of Israel.
30 Therefore her young men shall fall
    in the streets,
And all her men of war shall be
    cut off in that day," says the
    LORD.
31 "Behold, I *am* against you,
    O most haughty one!" says the
    Lord GOD of hosts;
"For your day has come,
    The time *that* I will punish you.
32 The most proud shall stumble and
    fall,
And no one will raise him up;
I will kindle a fire in his cities,
And it will devour all around
    him."

33 Thus says the LORD of hosts:

"The children of Israel *were*
    oppressed,

Along with the children of Judah;
All who took them captive have
    held them fast;
They have refused to let them go.
34 Their Redeemer *is* strong;
    The LORD of hosts *is* His name.
He will thoroughly plead their
    case,
That He may give rest to the land,
And disquiet the inhabitants of
    Babylon.

35 "A sword *is* against the Chaldeans,"
    says the LORD,
  "Against the inhabitants of
    Babylon,
And against her princes and her
    wise men.
36 A sword *is* against the soothsayers,
    and they will be fools.
A sword *is* against her mighty
    men, and they will be dismayed.
37 A sword *is* against their horses,
    Against their chariots,
And against all the mixed peoples
    who *are* in her midst;
And they will become like women.
A sword *is* against her treasures,
    and they will be robbed.
38 A drought *is* against her waters,
    and they will be dried up.
For it *is* the land of carved images,
And they are insane with *their*
    idols.

39 "Therefore the wild desert beasts
    shall dwell *there* with the
    jackals,
And the ostriches shall dwell in it.
It shall be inhabited no more
    forever,
Nor shall it be dwelt in from
    generation to generation.
40 As God overthrew Sodom and
    Gomorrah
And their neighbors," says the
    LORD,
"*So* no one shall reside there,
Nor son of man dwell in it.

41 "Behold, a people shall come from
    the north,
And a great nation and many
    kings

Shall be raised up from the ends of
   the earth.
42 They shall hold the bow and the
   lance;
They *are* cruel and shall not show
   mercy.
Their voice shall roar like the sea;
They shall ride on horses,
Set in array, like a man for the
   battle,
Against you, O daughter of
   Babylon.

43 "The king of Babylon has heard the
   report about them,
And his hands grow feeble;
Anguish has taken hold of him,
Pangs as of a woman in childbirth.

44 "Behold, he shall come up like a
   lion from the floodplain of the
   Jordan
Against the dwelling place of the
   strong;
But I will make them suddenly run
   away from her.
And who *is* a chosen *man that* I
   may appoint over her?
For who *is* like Me?
Who will arraign Me?
And who *is* that shepherd
Who will withstand Me?"

45 Therefore hear the counsel of the
   LORD that He has taken against
   Babylon,
And His purposes that He has
   proposed against the land of the
   Chaldeans:
Surely the least of the flock shall
   draw them out;
Surely He will make their dwelling
   place desolate with them.
46 At the noise of the taking of
   Babylon
The earth trembles,
And the cry is heard among the
   nations.

~ PSALM 119:121–128 ~

121 I have done justice and
   righteousness;
Do not leave me to my oppressors.
122 Be surety for Your servant for good;

Do not let the proud oppress me.
123 My eyes fail *from seeking* Your
   salvation
And Your righteous word.
124 Deal with Your servant according to
   Your mercy,
And teach me Your statutes.
125 I *am* Your servant;
Give me understanding,
That I may know Your testimonies.
126 *It is* time for *You* to act, O LORD,
For they have regarded Your law as
   void.
127 Therefore I love Your
   commandments
More than gold, yes, than fine gold!
128 Therefore all *Your* precepts
   concerning all *things*
I consider *to be* right;
I hate every false way.

~ PROVERBS 28:6 ~

6 Better *is* the poor who walks in his
   integrity
Than one perverse *in his* ways,
   though he *be* rich.

~ TITUS 1:1–16 ~

Paul, a bondservant of God and an apostle
of Jesus Christ, according to the faith of
God's elect and the acknowledgment
of the truth which accords with godliness,
2 in hope of eternal life which God, who
cannot lie, promised before time began,
3 but has in due time manifested His word
through preaching, which was committed to me according to the commandment
of God our Savior;

4 To Titus, a true son in *our* common
faith:

Grace, mercy, *and* peace from God
the Father and the Lord Jesus Christ our
Savior.
5 For this reason I left you in Crete, that
you should set in order the things
that are lacking, and appoint elders in
every city as I commanded you— 6 if a
man is blameless, the husband of one wife,
having faithful children not accused of dissipation or insubordination. 7 For a bishop
must be blameless, as a steward of God,

not self-willed, not quick-tempered, not given to wine, not violent, not greedy for money, [8] but hospitable, a lover of what is good, sober-minded, just, holy, self-controlled, [9] holding fast the faithful word as he has been taught, that he may be able, by sound doctrine, both to exhort and convict those who contradict.

[10] For there are many insubordinate, both idle talkers and deceivers, especially those of the circumcision, [11] whose mouths must be stopped, who subvert whole households, teaching things which they ought not, for the sake of dishonest gain. [12] One of them, a prophet of their own, said, "Cretans *are* always liars, evil beasts, lazy gluttons." [13] This testimony is true. Therefore rebuke them sharply, that they may be sound in the faith, [14] not giving heed to Jewish fables and commandments of men who turn from the truth. [15] To the pure all things are pure, but to those who are defiled and unbelieving nothing is pure; but even their mind and conscience are defiled. [16] They profess to know God, but in works they deny Him, being abominable, disobedient, and disqualified for every good work.

READING 306 · NOVEMBER 2

~ JEREMIAH 51:1—52:34 ~

Thus says the LORD:

"Behold, I will raise up against Babylon,
Against those who dwell in Leb Kamai,
A destroying wind.
[2] And I will send winnowers to Babylon,
Who shall winnow her and empty her land.
For in the day of doom
They shall be against her all around.
[3] Against *her* let the archer bend his bow,
And lift himself up against *her* in his armor.
Do not spare her young men;
Utterly destroy all her army.
[4] Thus the slain shall fall in the land of the Chaldeans,
And *those* thrust through in her streets.
[5] For Israel is not forsaken, nor Judah,
By his God, the LORD of hosts,
Though their land was filled with sin against the Holy One of Israel."

[6] Flee from the midst of Babylon,
And every one save his life!
Do not be cut off in her iniquity,
For this *is* the time of the LORD's vengeance;
He shall recompense her.
[7] Babylon *was* a golden cup in the LORD's hand,
That made all the earth drunk.
The nations drank her wine;
Therefore the nations are deranged.
[8] Babylon has suddenly fallen and been destroyed.
Wail for her!
Take balm for her pain;
Perhaps she may be healed.
[9] We would have healed Babylon,
But she is not healed.
Forsake her, and let us go everyone to his own country;
For her judgment reaches to heaven and is lifted up to the skies.
[10] The LORD has revealed our righteousness.
Come and let us declare in Zion the work of the LORD our God.

[11] Make the arrows bright!
Gather the shields!
The LORD has raised up the spirit of the kings of the Medes.
For His plan *is* against Babylon to destroy it,
Because it *is* the vengeance of the LORD,

In Every Circumstance

> In all things showing yourself to be a pattern of good works; in doctrine showing integrity, reverence, incorruptibility.
>
> *Titus 2:7*

Max had one of the worst jobs in the camp — carrying stones and planks through the mud to build a crematorium. Daily, he was under the lash of the camp's infamous guard, "Bloody Krott." Yet all the while, Father Maximillian Kolbe kept smiling. One prisoner recalled, "Because they were trying to survive at any cost, all the prisoners had wildly roving eyes watching in every direction for trouble or the ready clubs. Kolbe, alone, had a calm straightforward look, the look of a thoughtful man. . . . In spite of his physical suffering, he was completely healthy, serene . . . extraordinary in character." Another said, "Those eyes of his were always strangely penetrating. The SS men couldn't stand his glance, and used to yell at him, 'Look at the ground, not at us!'"

Kolbe often let others take his food ration. He said to those who questioned this, "Every man has an aim in life. Most of you men want to return to your wives . . . your families. My part is to give my life for the good of all men." Kolbe encouraged others to keep hope, to lift their voices in songs of praise. One recalled, "He made us see that our souls were not dead."

Good circumstances don't create great people. Great people create good in every circumstance.

The vengeance for His temple.

12 Set up the standard on the walls of
      Babylon;
   Make the guard strong,
   Set up the watchmen,
   Prepare the ambushes.
   For the LORD has both devised
      and done
   What He spoke against the
      inhabitants of Babylon.

13 O you who dwell by many waters,
   Abundant in treasures,
   Your end has come,
   The measure of your
      covetousness.

14 The LORD of hosts has sworn by
      Himself:
   "Surely I will fill you with men, as
      with locusts,
   And they shall lift up a shout
      against you."

15 He has made the earth by His
      power;
   He has established the world by
      His wisdom,
   And stretched out the heaven by
      His understanding.

16 When He utters *His* voice—
   There is a multitude of waters in
      the heavens:
   "He causes the vapors to ascend
      from the ends of the earth;
   He makes lightnings for the rain;
   He brings the wind out of His
      treasuries."

17 Everyone is dull-hearted, without
      knowledge;
   Every metalsmith is put to shame
      by the carved image;
   For his molded image *is* falsehood,
   And *there is* no breath in them.

18 They *are* futile, a work of errors;
   In the time of their punishment
      they shall perish.

19 The Portion of Jacob *is* not like
      them,
   For He *is* the Maker of all things;
   And *Israel is* the tribe of His
      inheritance.
   The LORD of hosts *is* His name.

20 "You *are* My battle-ax *and* weapons
      of war:

For with you I will break the
      nation in pieces;
   With you I will destroy kingdoms;

21 With you I will break in pieces the
      horse and its rider;
   With you I will break in pieces the
      chariot and its rider;

22 With you also I will break in
      pieces man and woman;
   With you I will break in pieces old
      and young;
   With you I will break in pieces the
      young man and the maiden;

23 With you also I will break in
      pieces the shepherd and his
      flock;
   With you I will break in pieces the
      farmer and his yoke of oxen;
   And with you I will break in pieces
      governors and rulers.

24 "And I will repay Babylon
   And all the inhabitants of Chaldea
   For all the evil they have done
   In Zion in your sight," says the
      LORD.

25 "Behold, I *am* against you,
      O destroying mountain,
   Who destroys all the earth," says
      the LORD.
   "And I will stretch out My hand
      against you,
   Roll you down from the rocks,
   And make you a burnt mountain.

26 They shall not take from you a
      stone for a corner
   Nor a stone for a foundation,
   But you shall be desolate forever,"
      says the LORD.

27 Set up a banner in the land,
   Blow the trumpet among the
      nations!
   Prepare the nations against her,
   Call the kingdoms together against
      her:
   Ararat, Minni, and Ashkenaz.
   Appoint a general against her;
   Cause the horses to come up like
      the bristling locusts.

28 Prepare against her the nations,
   With the kings of the Medes,
   Its governors and all its rulers,
   All the land of his dominion.

²⁹ And the land will tremble and
  sorrow;
  For every purpose of the LORD
  shall be performed against
  Babylon,
  To make the land of Babylon a
  desolation without inhabitant.
³⁰ The mighty men of Babylon have
  ceased fighting,
  They have remained in their
  strongholds;
  Their might has failed,
  They became *like* women;
  They have burned her dwelling
  places,
  The bars of her *gate* are broken.
³¹ One runner will run to meet
  another,
  And one messenger to meet
  another,
  To show the king of Babylon that
  his city is taken on *all* sides;
³² The passages are blocked,
  The reeds they have burned with
  fire,
  And the men of war are terrified.

³³ For thus says the LORD of hosts, the
God of Israel:

  "The daughter of Babylon *is* like a
  threshing floor
  When it is time to thresh her;
  Yet a little while
  And the time of her harvest will
  come."

³⁴ "Nebuchadnezzar the king of
  Babylon
  Has devoured me, he has crushed
  me;
  He has made me an empty vessel,
  He has swallowed me up like a
  monster;
  He has filled his stomach with my
  delicacies,
  He has spit me out.
³⁵ Let the violence *done* to me and
  my flesh *be* upon Babylon,"
  The inhabitant of Zion will say;
  "And my blood be upon the
  inhabitants of Chaldea!"
  Jerusalem will say.

³⁶ Therefore thus says the LORD:

"Behold, I will plead your case and
  take vengeance for you.
  I will dry up her sea and make her
  springs dry.
³⁷ Babylon shall become a heap,
  A dwelling place for jackals,
  An astonishment and a hissing,
  Without an inhabitant.
³⁸ They shall roar together like lions,
  They shall growl like lions'
  whelps.
³⁹ In their excitement I will prepare
  their feasts;
  I will make them drunk,
  That they may rejoice,
  And sleep a perpetual sleep
  And not awake," says the LORD.
⁴⁰ "I will bring them down
  Like lambs to the slaughter,
  Like rams with male goats.

⁴¹ "Oh, how Sheshach is taken!
  Oh, how the praise of the whole
  earth is seized!
  How Babylon has become
  desolate among the nations!
⁴² The sea has come up over
  Babylon;
  She is covered with the multitude
  of its waves.
⁴³ Her cities are a desolation,
  A dry land and a wilderness,
  A land where no one dwells,
  Through which no son of man
  passes.
⁴⁴ I will punish Bel in Babylon,
  And I will bring out of his mouth
  what he has swallowed;
  And the nations shall not stream
  to him anymore.
  Yes, the wall of Babylon shall fall.

⁴⁵ "My people, go out of the midst of
  her!
  And let everyone deliver himself
  from the fierce anger of the
  LORD.
⁴⁶ And lest your heart faint,
  And you fear for the rumor that
  will be heard in the land
  (A rumor will come *one* year,
  And after that, in *another* year
  A rumor *will come,*
  And violence in the land,
  Ruler against ruler),

47 Therefore behold, the days are coming
That I will bring judgment on the carved images of Babylon;
Her whole land shall be ashamed,
And all her slain shall fall in her midst.

48 Then the heavens and the earth and all that *is* in them
Shall sing joyously over Babylon;
For the plunderers shall come to her from the north," says the LORD.

49 As Babylon *has caused* the slain of Israel to fall,
So at Babylon the slain of all the earth shall fall.

50 You who have escaped the sword,
Get away! Do not stand still!
Remember the LORD afar off,
And let Jerusalem come to your mind.

51 We are ashamed because we have heard reproach.
Shame has covered our faces,
For strangers have come into the sanctuaries of the LORD's house.

52 "Therefore behold, the days are coming," says the LORD,
"That I will bring judgment on her carved images,
And throughout all her land the wounded shall groan.

53 Though Babylon were to mount up to heaven,
And though she were to fortify the height of her strength,
Yet from Me plunderers would come to her," says the LORD.

54 The sound of a cry *comes* from Babylon,
And great destruction from the land of the Chaldeans,

55 Because the LORD is plundering Babylon
And silencing her loud voice,
Though her waves roar like great waters,
And the noise of their voice is uttered,

56 Because the plunderer comes against her, against Babylon,
And her mighty men are taken.
Every one of their bows is broken;
For the LORD *is* the God of recompense,
He will surely repay.

57 "And I will make drunk
Her princes and wise men,
Her governors, her deputies, and her mighty men.
And they shall sleep a perpetual sleep
And not awake," says the King,
Whose name *is* the LORD of hosts.

58 Thus says the LORD of hosts:

"The broad walls of Babylon shall be utterly broken,
And her high gates shall be burned with fire;
The people will labor in vain,
And the nations, because of the fire;
And they shall be weary."

59 The word which Jeremiah the prophet commanded Seraiah the son of Neriah, the son of Mahseiah, when he went with Zedekiah the king of Judah to Babylon in the fourth year of his reign. And Seraiah *was* the quartermaster. 60 So Jeremiah wrote in a book all the evil that would come upon Babylon, all these words that are written against Babylon. 61 And Jeremiah said to Seraiah, "When you arrive in Babylon and see it, and read all these words, 62 then you shall say, 'O LORD, You have spoken against this place to cut it off, so that none shall remain in it, neither man nor beast, but it shall be desolate forever.' 63 Now it shall be, when you have finished reading this book, *that* you shall tie a stone to it and throw it out into the Euphrates. 64 Then you shall say, 'Thus Babylon shall sink and not rise from the catastrophe that I will bring upon her. And they shall be weary.' "
Thus far *are* the words of Jeremiah.

52 Zedekiah *was* twenty-one years old when he became king, and he reigned eleven years in Jerusalem. His mother's

name *was* Hamutal the daughter of Jeremiah of Libnah. ² He also did evil in the sight of the LORD, according to all that Jehoiakim had done. ³ For because of the anger of the LORD *this* happened in Jerusalem and Judah, till He finally cast them out from His presence. Then Zedekiah rebelled against the king of Babylon.

⁴ Now it came to pass in the ninth year of his reign, in the tenth month, on the tenth *day* of the month, *that* Nebuchadnezzar king of Babylon and all his army came against Jerusalem and encamped against it; and *they* built a siege wall against it all around. ⁵ So the city was besieged until the eleventh year of King Zedekiah. ⁶ By the fourth month, on the ninth day of the month, the famine had become so severe in the city that there was no food for the people of the land. ⁷ Then the city wall was broken through, and all the men of war fled and went out of the city at night by way of the gate between the two walls, which *was* by the king's garden, even though the Chaldeans *were* near the city all around. And they went by way of the plain.

⁸ But the army of the Chaldeans pursued the king, and they overtook Zedekiah in the plains of Jericho. All his army was scattered from him. ⁹ So they took the king and brought him up to the king of Babylon at Riblah in the land of Hamath, and he pronounced judgment on him. ¹⁰ Then the king of Babylon killed the sons of Zedekiah before his eyes. And he killed all the princes of Judah in Riblah. ¹¹ He also put out the eyes of Zedekiah; and the king of Babylon bound him in bronze fetters, took him to Babylon, and put him in prison till the day of his death.

¹² Now in the fifth month, on the tenth *day* of the month (which *was* the nineteenth year of King Nebuchadnezzar king of Babylon), Nebuzaradan, the captain of the guard, *who* served the king of Babylon, came to Jerusalem. ¹³ He burned the house of the LORD and the king's house; all the houses of Jerusalem, that is, all the houses of the great, he burned with fire. ¹⁴ And all the army of the Chaldeans who *were* with the captain of the guard broke down all the walls of Jerusalem all around.

¹⁵ Then Nebuzaradan the captain of the guard carried away captive *some* of the poor people, the rest of the people who remained in the city, the defectors who had deserted to the king of Babylon, and the rest of the craftsmen. ¹⁶ But Nebuzaradan the captain of the guard left *some* of the poor of the land as vinedressers and farmers.

¹⁷ The bronze pillars that *were* in the house of the LORD, and the carts and the bronze Sea that *were* in the house of the LORD, the Chaldeans broke in pieces, and carried all their bronze to Babylon. ¹⁸ They also took away the pots, the shovels, the trimmers, the bowls, the spoons, and all the bronze utensils with which the priests ministered. ¹⁹ The basins, the firepans, the bowls, the pots, the lampstands, the spoons, and the cups, whatever *was* solid gold and whatever *was* solid silver, the captain of the guard took away. ²⁰ The two pillars, one Sea, the twelve bronze bulls which *were* under *it, and* the carts, which King Solomon had made for the house of the LORD—the bronze of all these articles was beyond measure. ²¹ Now *concerning* the pillars: the height of one pillar *was* eighteen cubits, a measuring line of twelve cubits could measure its circumference, and its thickness *was* four fingers; *it was* hollow. ²² A capital of bronze *was* on it; and the height of one capital *was* five cubits, with a network and pomegranates all around the capital, all of bronze. The second pillar, with pomegranates was the same. ²³ There were ninety-six pomegranates on the sides; all the pomegranates, all around on the network, *were* one hundred.

²⁴ The captain of the guard took Seraiah the chief priest, Zephaniah the second priest, and the three doorkeepers. ²⁵ He also took out of the city an officer who had charge of the men of war, seven men of the king's close associates who were found in the city, the principal scribe of the army who mustered the people of the land, and sixty men of the people of the land who were found in the midst of the city. ²⁶ And Nebuzaradan the captain of the guard took these and brought them to the king of Babylon at Riblah. ²⁷ Then the king of Babylon struck them and put them to death at Riblah in the

land of Hamath. Thus Judah was carried away captive from its own land.

²⁸ These *are* the people whom Nebuchadnezzar carried away captive: in the seventh year, three thousand and twenty-three Jews; ²⁹ in the eighteenth year of Nebuchadnezzar he carried away captive from Jerusalem eight hundred and thirty-two persons; ³⁰ in the twenty-third year of Nebuchadnezzar, Nebuzaradan the captain of the guard carried away captive of the Jews seven hundred and forty-five persons. All the persons *were* four thousand six hundred.

³¹ Now it came to pass in the thirty-seventh year of the captivity of Jehoiachin king of Judah, in the twelfth month, on the twenty-fifth *day* of the month, *that* Evil-Merodach king of Babylon, in the first *year* of his reign, lifted up the head of Jehoiachin king of Judah and brought him out of prison. ³² And he spoke kindly to him and gave him a more prominent seat than those of the kings who *were* with him in Babylon. ³³ So Jehoiachin changed from his prison garments, and he ate bread regularly before the king all the days of his life. ³⁴ And as for his provisions, there was a regular ration given him by the king of Babylon, a portion for each day until the day of his death, all the days of his life.

∼ PSALM 119:129–136 ∼

¹²⁹ Your testimonies are wonderful;
    Therefore my soul keeps them.
¹³⁰ The entrance of Your words gives
    light;
    It gives understanding to the simple.
¹³¹ I opened my mouth and panted,
    For I longed for Your
    commandments.
¹³² Look upon me and be merciful to
    me,
    As Your custom *is* toward those who
    love Your name.
¹³³ Direct my steps by Your word,
    And let no iniquity have dominion
    over me.
¹³⁴ Redeem me from the oppression of
    man,
    That I may keep Your precepts.
¹³⁵ Make Your face shine upon Your
    servant,

And teach me Your statutes.
¹³⁶ Rivers of water run down from my
    eyes,
    Because *men* do not keep Your law.

∼ PROVERBS 28:7, 8 ∼

⁷ Whoever keeps the law *is* a
    discerning son,
    But a companion of gluttons shames
    his father.

⁸ One who increases his possessions by
    usury and extortion
    Gathers it for him who will pity the
    poor.

∼ TITUS 2:1–15 ∼

But as for you, speak the things which are proper for sound doctrine: ² that the older men be sober, reverent, temperate, sound in faith, in love, in patience; ³ the older women likewise, that they be reverent in behavior, not slanderers, not given to much wine, teachers of good things— ⁴ that they admonish the young women to love their husbands, to love their children, ⁵ to be discreet, chaste, homemakers, good, obedient to their own husbands, that the word of God may not be blasphemed.

⁶ Likewise, exhort the young men to be sober-minded, ⁷ in all things showing yourself *to be* a pattern of good works; in doctrine *showing* integrity, reverence, incorruptibility, ⁸ sound speech that cannot be condemned, that one who is an opponent may be ashamed, having nothing evil to say of you.

⁹ *Exhort* bondservants to be obedient to their own masters, to be well pleasing in all *things,* not answering back, ¹⁰ not pilfering, but showing all good fidelity, that they may adorn the doctrine of God our Savior in all things.

¹¹ For the grace of God that brings salvation has appeared to all men, ¹² teaching us that, denying ungodliness and worldly lusts, we should live soberly, righteously, and godly in the present age, ¹³ looking for the blessed hope and glorious appearing of our great God and Savior Jesus Christ, ¹⁴ who gave Himself for us,

that He might redeem us from every lawless deed and purify for Himself *His* own
special people, zealous for good works.

15 Speak these things, exhort, and rebuke with all authority. Let no one despise
you.

READING 307 · NOVEMBER 3

~ LAMENTATIONS 1:1—2:22 ~

1 How lonely sits the city
  That was full of people!
  How like a widow is she,
  Who *was* great among the
    nations!
  The princess among the provinces
  Has become a slave!

2 She weeps bitterly in the night,
  Her tears *are* on her cheeks;
  Among all her lovers
  She has none to comfort *her.*
  All her friends have dealt
    treacherously with her;
  They have become her enemies.

3 Judah has gone into captivity,
  Under affliction and hard
    servitude;
  She dwells among the nations,
  She finds no rest;
  All her persecutors overtake her in
    dire straits.

4 The roads to Zion mourn
  Because no one comes to the set
    feasts.
  All her gates are desolate;
  Her priests sigh,
  Her virgins are afflicted,
  And she *is* in bitterness.

5 Her adversaries have become the
    master,
  Her enemies prosper;
  For the LORD has afflicted her
  Because of the multitude of her
    transgressions.
  Her children have gone into
    captivity before the enemy.

6 And from the daughter of Zion
  All her splendor has departed.
  Her princes have become like deer
  That find no pasture,

That flee without strength
Before the pursuer.

7 In the days of her affliction and
    roaming,
  Jerusalem remembers all her
    pleasant things
  That she had in the days of old.
  When her people fell into the
    hand of the enemy,
  With no one to help her,
  The adversaries saw her
  And mocked at her downfall.

8 Jerusalem has sinned gravely,
  Therefore she has become vile.
  All who honored her despise her
  Because they have seen her
    nakedness;
  Yes, she sighs and turns away.

9 Her uncleanness *is* in her skirts;
  She did not consider her destiny;
  Therefore her collapse was
    awesome;
  She had no comforter.
  "O LORD, behold my affliction,
  For *the* enemy is exalted!"

10 The adversary has spread his hand
   Over all her pleasant things;
   For she has seen the nations enter
     her sanctuary,
   Those whom You commanded
   Not to enter Your assembly.

11 All her people sigh,
   They seek bread;
   They have given their valuables
     for food to restore life.
   "See, O LORD, and consider,
   For I am scorned."

12 "*Is it* nothing to you, all you who
     pass by?

Behold and see
If there is any sorrow like my
    sorrow,
Which has been brought on me,
Which the LORD has inflicted
In the day of His fierce anger.

13 "From above He has sent fire into
        my bones,
    And it overpowered them;
    He has spread a net for my feet
    And turned me back;
    He has made me desolate
    And faint all the day.

14 "The yoke of my transgressions was
        bound;
    They were woven together by His
        hands,
    And thrust upon my neck.
    He made my strength fail;
    The Lord delivered me into the
        hands of *those whom* I am not
        able to withstand.

15 "The Lord has trampled underfoot
        all my mighty *men* in my midst;
    He has called an assembly against
        me
    To crush my young men;
    The Lord trampled *as* in a
        winepress
    The virgin daughter of Judah.

16 "For these *things* I weep;
    My eye, my eye overflows with
        water;
    Because the comforter, who
        should restore my life,
    Is far from me.
    My children are desolate
    Because the enemy prevailed."

17 Zion spreads out her hands,
    But no one comforts her;
    The LORD has commanded
        concerning Jacob
    That those around him *become* his
        adversaries;
    Jerusalem has become an unclean
        thing among them.

18 "The LORD is righteous,
    For I rebelled against His
        commandment.

Hear now, all peoples,
And behold my sorrow;
My virgins and my young men
Have gone into captivity.

19 "I called for my lovers,
    But they deceived me;
    My priests and my elders
    Breathed their last in the city,
    While they sought food
    To restore their life.

20 "See, O LORD, that I *am* in distress;
    My soul is troubled;
    My heart is overturned within me,
    For I have been very rebellious.
    Outside the sword bereaves,
    At home *it is* like death.

21 "They have heard that I sigh,
    But no one comforts me.
    All my enemies have heard of my
        trouble;
    They are glad that You have done
        it.
    Bring on the day You have
        announced,
    That they may become like me.

22 "Let all their wickedness come
        before You,
    And do to them as You have done
        to me
    For all my transgressions;
    For my sighs *are* many,
    And my heart *is* faint."

2   How the Lord has covered the
        daughter of Zion
    With a cloud in His anger!
    He cast down from heaven to the
        earth
    The beauty of Israel,
    And did not remember His
        footstool
    In the day of His anger.

2   The Lord has swallowed up and
        has not pitied
    All the dwelling places of Jacob.
    He has thrown down in His wrath
    The strongholds of the daughter
        of Judah;
    He has brought *them* down to the
        ground;

Imprisoned by Hatred

On February 9, 1960, Adolph Coors III was kidnapped and held for ransom. His body was found seven months later on a remote hillside. He had been shot to death. Adolph Coors IV, who was fifteen years old at the time, lost not only his father but his best friend. For years, young Coors hated Joseph Corbett, the man who was sentenced to life for the slaying.

Then in 1975, Adolph Coors IV became a Christian. He knew his hatred for Corbett impeded his growth in faith and also alienated him from other people. Still, resentment seethed within him. He asked God to help him stop hating Corbett.

Coors eventually felt led to visit Corbett in the maximum security unit of Colorado's Canon City penitentiary. Corbett refused to see him, but Coors left a Bible with this inscription: "I'm here to see you today and I'm sorry that we could not meet. As a Christian I am summoned by our Lord and Savior, Jesus Christ, to forgive. I do forgive you, and I ask you to forgive me for the hatred I've held in my heart for you." Coors later confessed, "I have a love for that man that only Jesus Christ could have put in my heart." Coors' heart, imprisoned by hatred, was at last set free.

Today, check your heart. Is there anyone you need to forgive?

> For we ourselves were also once foolish, disobedient, deceived, serving various lusts and pleasures, living in malice and envy, hateful and hating one another.
>
> *Titus 3:3*

He has profaned the kingdom and
its princes.

3 He has cut off in fierce anger
Every horn of Israel;
He has drawn back His right hand
From before the enemy.
He has blazed against Jacob like a
flaming fire
Devouring all around.

4 Standing like an enemy, He has
bent His bow;
With His right hand, like an
adversary,
He has slain all *who were* pleasing
to His eye;
On the tent of the daughter of
Zion,
He has poured out His fury like
fire.

5 The Lord was like an enemy.
He has swallowed up Israel,
He has swallowed up all her
palaces;
He has destroyed her strongholds,
And has increased mourning and
lamentation
In the daughter of Judah.

6 He has done violence to His
tabernacle,
As if it were a garden;
He has destroyed His place of
assembly;
The LORD has caused
The appointed feasts and Sabbaths
to be forgotten in Zion.
In His burning indignation He has
spurned the king and the priest.

7 The Lord has spurned His altar,
He has abandoned His sanctuary;
He has given up the walls of her
palaces
Into the hand of the enemy.
They have made a noise in the
house of the LORD
As on the day of a set feast.

8 The LORD has purposed to destroy
The wall of the daughter of Zion.
He has stretched out a line;

He has not withdrawn His hand
from destroying;
Therefore He has caused the
rampart and wall to lament;
They languished together.

9 Her gates have sunk into the
ground;
He has destroyed and broken her
bars.
Her king and her princes *are*
among the nations;
The Law *is no more,*
And her prophets find no vision
from the LORD.

10 The elders of the daughter of Zion
Sit on the ground *and* keep
silence;
They throw dust on their heads
And gird themselves with
sackcloth.
The virgins of Jerusalem
Bow their heads to the ground.

11 My eyes fail with tears,
My heart is troubled;
My bile is poured on the ground
Because of the destruction of the
daughter of my people,
Because the children and the
infants
Faint in the streets of the city.

12 They say to their mothers,
"Where *is* grain and wine?"
As they swoon like the wounded
In the streets of the city,
As their life is poured out
In their mothers' bosom.

13 How shall I console you?
To what shall I liken you,
O daughter of Jerusalem?
What shall I compare with you,
that I may comfort you,
O virgin daughter of Zion?
For your ruin *is* spread wide as the
sea;
Who can heal you?

14 Your prophets have seen for you
False and deceptive visions;
They have not uncovered your
iniquity,

To bring back your captives,
But have envisioned for you false
   prophecies and delusions.

¹⁵ All who pass by clap *their* hands at
   you;
They hiss and shake their heads
At the daughter of Jerusalem:
"*Is* this the city that is called
'The perfection of beauty,
The joy of the whole earth'?"

¹⁶ All your enemies have opened
   their mouth against you;
They hiss and gnash *their* teeth.
They say, "We have swallowed *her*
   up!
Surely this *is* the day we have
   waited for;
We have found *it*, we have seen
   it!"

¹⁷ The LORD has done what He
   purposed;
He has fulfilled His word
Which He commanded in days of
   old.
He has thrown down and has not
   pitied,
And He has caused an enemy to
   rejoice over you;
He has exalted the horn of your
   adversaries.

¹⁸ Their heart cried out to the Lord,
"O wall of the daughter of Zion,
Let tears run down like a river day
   and night;
Give yourself no relief;
Give your eyes no rest.

¹⁹ "Arise, cry out in the night,
At the beginning of the watches;
Pour out your heart like water
   before the face of the Lord.
Lift your hands toward Him
For the life of your young
   children,
Who faint from hunger at the
   head of every street."

²⁰ "See, O LORD, and consider!
To whom have You done this?
Should the women eat their
   offspring,

The children they have cuddled?
Should the priest and prophet be
   slain
In the sanctuary of the Lord?

²¹ "Young and old lie
On the ground in the streets;
My virgins and my young men
Have fallen by the sword;
You have slain *them* in the day of
   Your anger,
You have slaughtered *and* not
   pitied.

²² "You have invited as to a feast day
The terrors that surround me.
In the day of the LORD's anger
There was no refugee or survivor.
Those whom I have borne and
   brought up
My enemies have destroyed."

~ PSALM 119:137–144 ~

¹³⁷ Righteous *are* You, O LORD,
And upright *are* Your judgments.
¹³⁸ Your testimonies, *which* You have
   commanded,
Are righteous and very faithful.
¹³⁹ My zeal has consumed me,
Because my enemies have forgotten
   Your words.
¹⁴⁰ Your word *is* very pure;
Therefore Your servant loves it.
¹⁴¹ I *am* small and despised,
Yet I do not forget Your precepts.
¹⁴² Your righteousness *is* an everlasting
   righteousness,
And Your law *is* truth.
¹⁴³ Trouble and anguish have overtaken
   me,
Yet Your commandments *are* my
   delights.
¹⁴⁴ The righteousness of Your
   testimonies *is* everlasting;
Give me understanding, and I shall
   live.

~ PROVERBS 28:9, 10 ~

⁹ One who turns away his ear from
   hearing the law,
Even his prayer *is* an abomination.

¹⁰ Whoever causes the upright to go
    astray in an evil way,
He himself will fall into his own
    pit;
But the blameless will inherit good.

~ TITUS 3:1–15 ~

Remind them to be subject to rulers and authorities, to obey, to be ready for every good work, ² to speak evil of no one, to be peaceable, gentle, showing all humility to all men. ³ For we ourselves were also once foolish, disobedient, deceived, serving various lusts and pleasures, living in malice and envy, hateful and hating one another. ⁴ But when the kindness and the love of God our Savior toward man appeared, ⁵ not by works of righteousness which we have done, but according to His mercy He saved us, through the washing of regeneration and renewing of the Holy Spirit, ⁶ whom He poured out on us abundantly through Jesus Christ our Savior, ⁷ that having been justified by His grace we should become heirs according to the hope of eternal life.

⁸ This is a faithful saying, and these things I want you to affirm constantly, that those who have believed in God should be careful to maintain good works. These things are good and profitable to men. ⁹ But avoid foolish disputes, genealogies, contentions, and strivings about the law; for they are unprofitable and useless. ¹⁰ Reject a divisive man after the first and second admonition, ¹¹ knowing that such a person is warped and sinning, being self-condemned.

¹² When I send Artemas to you, or Tychicus, be diligent to come to me at Nicopolis, for I have decided to spend the winter there. ¹³ Send Zenas the lawyer and Apollos on their journey with haste, that they may lack nothing. ¹⁴ And let our *people* also learn to maintain good works, to *meet* urgent needs, that they may not be unfruitful.

¹⁵ All who *are* with me greet you. Greet those who love us in the faith.

Grace *be* with you all. Amen.

READING 308 · NOVEMBER 4

~ LAMENTATIONS 3:1—5:22 ~

¹ I *am* the man *who* has seen
    affliction by the rod of His
    wrath.
² He has led me and made *me* walk
    In darkness and not *in* light.
³ Surely He has turned His hand
    against me
Time and time again throughout
    the day.

⁴ He has aged my flesh and my skin,
    And broken my bones.
⁵ He has besieged me
    And surrounded *me* with
    bitterness and woe.
⁶ He has set me in dark places
    Like the dead of long ago.

⁷ He has hedged me in so that I
    cannot get out;
He has made my chain heavy.
⁸ Even when I cry and shout,
    He shuts out my prayer.

⁹ He has blocked my ways with
    hewn stone;
He has made my paths crooked.
¹⁰ He *has been* to me a bear lying in
    wait,
Like a lion in ambush.
¹¹ He has turned aside my ways and
    torn me in pieces;
He has made me desolate.
¹² He has bent His bow
And set me up as a target for the
    arrow.

¹³ He has caused the arrows of His
    quiver
To pierce my loins.
¹⁴ I have become the ridicule of all
    my people—
Their taunting song all the day.
¹⁵ He has filled me with bitterness,
He has made me drink
    wormwood.

The Lord is My Pacesetter

Not one of us automatically has time to pray. We have to make time for prayer — carving a time out of our day and setting it aside as a sacred appointment that cannot be changed, and must not be delayed. As you set aside your prayer time for today, consider this Japanese version of the 23rd Psalm:

The Lord is my pacesetter . . . I shall not rush
He makes me stop for quiet intervals
He provides me with images of stillness which restore
my serenity
He leads me in the way of efficiency through calmness of
mind and His guidance is peace
Even though I have a great many things to accomplish each
day, I will not fret, for His presence is here
His timelessness, His all importance will keep me
in balance
He prepares refreshment and renewal in the midst of
my activity by anointing my mind with the oils of
tranquillity
My cup of joyous energy overflows
Truly harmony and effectiveness shall be the fruits of my
hours for I shall walk in the pace of my Lord and dwell
in his house for ever.

> I rise before the dawning of the morning, and cry for help; I hope in Your word.
>
> *Psalm 119:147*

16 He has also broken my teeth with
   gravel,
   And covered me with ashes.
17 You have moved my soul far from
   peace;
   I have forgotten prosperity.
18 And I said, "My strength and my
   hope
   Have perished from the LORD."

19 Remember my affliction and
   roaming,
   The wormwood and the gall.
20 My soul still remembers
   And sinks within me.
21 This I recall to my mind,
   Therefore I have hope.

22 *Through* the LORD's mercies we
   are not consumed,
   Because His compassions fail not.
23 *They are* new every morning;
   Great *is* Your faithfulness.
24 "The LORD *is* my portion," says my
   soul,
   "Therefore I hope in Him!"

25 The LORD *is* good to those who
   wait for Him,
   To the soul *who* seeks Him.
26 *It is* good that *one* should hope
   and wait quietly
   For the salvation of the LORD.
27 *It is* good for a man to bear
   The yoke in his youth.

28 Let him sit alone and keep silent,
   Because *God* has laid *it* on him;
29 Let him put his mouth in the
   dust—
   There may yet be hope.
30 Let him give *his* cheek to the one
   who strikes him,
   And be full of reproach.

31 For the Lord will not cast off
   forever.
32 Though He causes grief,
   Yet He will show compassion
   According to the multitude of His
   mercies.
33 For He does not afflict willingly,
   Nor grieve the children of men.

34 To crush under one's feet
   All the prisoners of the earth,
35 To turn aside the justice *due* a man
   Before the face of the Most High,
36 Or subvert a man in his cause—
   The Lord does not approve.

37 Who *is* he *who* speaks and it
   comes to pass,
   When the Lord has not
   commanded *it?*
38 *Is it* not from the mouth of the
   Most High
   That woe and well-being proceed?
39 Why should a living man
   complain,
   A man for the punishment of his
   sins?

40 Let us search out and examine our
   ways,
   And turn back to the LORD;
41 Let us lift our hearts and hands
   To God in heaven.
42 We have transgressed and
   rebelled;
   You have not pardoned.

43 You have covered *Yourself* with
   anger
   And pursued us;
   You have slain *and* not pitied.
44 You have covered Yourself with a
   cloud,
   That prayer should not pass
   through.
45 You have made us an offscouring
   and refuse
   In the midst of the peoples.

46 All our enemies
   Have opened their mouths against
   us.
47 Fear and a snare have come upon
   us,
   Desolation and destruction.
48 My eyes overflow with rivers of
   water
   For the destruction of the
   daughter of my people.

49 My eyes flow and do not cease,
   Without interruption,
50 Till the LORD from heaven
   Looks down and sees.

⁵¹ My eyes bring suffering to my soul
   Because of all the daughters of my
      city.

⁵² My enemies without cause
   Hunted me down like a bird.
⁵³ They silenced my life in the pit
   And threw stones at me.
⁵⁴ The waters flowed over my head;
   I said, "I am cut off!"

⁵⁵ I called on Your name, O LORD,
   From the lowest pit.
⁵⁶ You have heard my voice:
   "Do not hide Your ear
   From my sighing, from my cry for
      help."
⁵⁷ You drew near on the day I called
      on You,
   And said, "Do not fear!"

⁵⁸ O Lord, You have pleaded the case
      for my soul;
   You have redeemed my life.
⁵⁹ O LORD, You have seen *how* I am
      wronged;
   Judge my case.
⁶⁰ You have seen all their vengeance,
   All their schemes against me.

⁶¹ You have heard their reproach,
      O LORD,
   All their schemes against me,
⁶² The lips of my enemies
   And their whispering against me
      all the day.
⁶³ Look at their sitting down and
      their rising up;
   I *am* their taunting song.

⁶⁴ Repay them, O LORD,
   According to the work of their
      hands.
⁶⁵ Give them a veiled heart;
   Your curse *be* upon them!
⁶⁶ In Your anger,
   Pursue and destroy them
   From under the heavens of the
      LORD.

4 How the gold has become dim!
   How changed the fine gold!

The stones of the sanctuary are
      scattered
   At the head of every street.

² The precious sons of Zion,
   Valuable as fine gold,
   How they are regarded as clay
      pots,
   The work of the hands of the
      potter!

³ Even the jackals present their
      breasts
   To nurse their young;
   But the daughter of my people *is*
      cruel,
   Like ostriches in the wilderness.

⁴ The tongue of the infant clings
   To the roof of its mouth for thirst;
   The young children ask for bread,
   But no one breaks *it* for them.

⁵ Those who ate delicacies
   Are desolate in the streets;
   Those who were brought up in
      scarlet
   Embrace ash heaps.

⁶ The punishment of the iniquity of
      the daughter of my people
   Is greater than the punishment of
      the sin of Sodom,
   Which was overthrown in a
      moment,
   With no hand to help her!

⁷ Her Nazirites were brighter than
      snow
   And whiter than milk;
   They were more ruddy in body
      than rubies,
   Like sapphire in their appearance.

⁸ *Now* their appearance is blacker
      than soot;
   They go unrecognized in the
      streets;
   Their skin clings to their bones,
   It has become as dry as wood.

⁹ *Those* slain by the sword are better
      off
   Than *those* who die of hunger;
   For these pine away,

Stricken *for lack* of the fruits of
the field.

10 The hands of the compassionate
women
Have cooked their own children;
They became food for them
In the destruction of the daughter
of my people.

11 The LORD has fulfilled His fury,
He has poured out His fierce
anger.
He kindled a fire in Zion,
And it has devoured its
foundations.

12 The kings of the earth,
And all inhabitants of the world,
Would not have believed
That the adversary and the enemy
Could enter the gates of
Jerusalem—

13 Because of the sins of her prophets
And the iniquities of her priests,
Who shed in her midst
The blood of the just.

14 They wandered blind in the
streets;
They have defiled themselves with
blood,
So that no one would touch their
garments.

15 They cried out to them,
"Go away, unclean!
Go away, go away,
Do not touch us!"
When they fled and wandered,
Those among the nations said,
"They shall no longer dwell *here.*"

16 The face of the LORD scattered
them;
He no longer regards them.
The people do not respect the
priests
Nor show favor to the elders.

17 Still our eyes failed us,
Watching vainly for our help;
In our watching we watched

For a nation *that* could not save
us.

18 They tracked our steps
So that we could not walk in our
streets.
Our end was near;
Our days were over,
For our end had come.

19 Our pursuers were swifter
Than the eagles of the heavens.
They pursued us on the mountains
And lay in wait for us in the
wilderness.

20 The breath of our nostrils, the
anointed of the LORD,
Was caught in their pits,
Of whom we said, "Under his
shadow
We shall live among the nations."

21 Rejoice and be glad, O daughter
of Edom,
You who dwell in the land of Uz!
The cup shall also pass over to you
And you shall become drunk and
make yourself naked.

22 *The punishment of* your iniquity is
accomplished,
O daughter of Zion;
He will no longer send you into
captivity.
He will punish your iniquity,
O daughter of Edom;
He will uncover your sins!

5 Remember, O LORD, what has
come upon us;
Look, and behold our reproach!
2 Our inheritance has been turned
over to aliens,
And our houses to foreigners.
3 We have become orphans and
waifs,
Our mothers *are* like widows.

4 We pay for the water we drink,
And our wood comes at a price.
5 *They* pursue at our heels;
We labor *and* have no rest.
6 We have given our hand *to* the
Egyptians

And the Assyrians, to be satisfied
with bread.

7 Our fathers sinned *and are* no
more,
But we bear their iniquities.
8 Servants rule over us;
There is none to deliver *us* from
their hand.
9 We get our bread *at the risk* of our
lives,
Because of the sword in the
wilderness.

10 Our skin is hot as an oven,
Because of the fever of famine.
11 They ravished the women in Zion,
The maidens in the cities of Judah.
12 Princes were hung up by their
hands,
And elders were not respected.
13 Young men ground at the
millstones;
Boys staggered under *loads of*
wood.
14 The elders have ceased *gathering*
at the gate,
And the young men from their
music.

15 The joy of our heart has ceased;
Our dance has turned into
mourning.
16 The crown has fallen *from* our
head.
Woe to us, for we have sinned!
17 Because of this our heart is faint;
Because of these *things* our eyes
grow dim;
18 Because of Mount Zion which is
desolate,
With foxes walking about on it.

19 You, O LORD, remain forever;
Your throne from generation to
generation.
20 Why do You forget us forever,
And forsake us for so long a time?
21 Turn us back to You, O LORD, and
we will be restored;
Renew our days as of old,
22 Unless You have utterly rejected
us,
And are very angry with us!

～ PSALM 119:145–152 ～

145 I cry out with *my* whole heart;
Hear me, O LORD!
I will keep Your statutes.
146 I cry out to You;
Save me, and I will keep Your
testimonies.
147 I rise before the dawning of the
morning,
And cry for help;
I hope in Your word.
148 My eyes are awake through the *night*
watches,
That I may meditate on Your word.
149 Hear my voice according to Your
lovingkindness;
O LORD, revive me according to
Your justice.
150 They draw near who follow after
wickedness;
They are far from Your law.
151 You *are* near, O LORD,
And all Your commandments *are*
truth.
152 Concerning Your testimonies,
I have known of old that You have
founded them forever.

～ PROVERBS 28:11 ～

11 The rich man *is* wise in his own eyes,
But the poor who has understanding
searches him out.

～ PHILEMON 1–25 ～

Paul, a prisoner of Christ Jesus, and Timothy *our* brother,

To Philemon our beloved *friend* and
fellow laborer, 2 to the beloved Apphia,
Archippus our fellow soldier, and to the
church in your house:

3 Grace to you and peace from God our
Father and the Lord Jesus Christ.
4 I thank my God, making mention
of you always in my prayers, 5 hearing of
your love and faith which you have toward the Lord Jesus and toward all the
saints, 6 that the sharing of your faith may
become effective by the acknowledgment
of every good thing which is in you in

Christ Jesus. [7] For we have great joy and consolation in your love, because the hearts of the saints have been refreshed by you, brother.

[8] Therefore, though I might be very bold in Christ to command you what is fitting, [9] yet for love's sake I rather appeal to you—being such a one as Paul, the aged, and now also a prisoner of Jesus Christ— [10] I appeal to you for my son Onesimus, whom I have begotten while in my chains, [11] who once was unprofitable to you, but now is profitable to you and to me.

[12] I am sending him back. You therefore receive him, that is, my own heart, [13] whom I wished to keep with me, that on your behalf he might minister to me in my chains for the gospel. [14] But without your consent I wanted to do nothing, that your good deed might not be by compulsion, as it were, but voluntary.

[15] For perhaps he departed for a while for this purpose, that you might receive him forever, [16] no longer as a slave but more than a slave—a beloved brother, especially to me but how much more to you, both in the flesh and in the Lord.

[17] If then you count me as a partner, receive him as you would me. [18] But if he has wronged you or owes anything, put that on my account. [19] I, Paul, am writing with my own hand. I will repay—not to mention to you that you owe me even your own self besides. [20] Yes, brother, let me have joy from you in the Lord; refresh my heart in the Lord.

[21] Having confidence in your obedience, I write to you, knowing that you will do even more than I say. [22] But, meanwhile, also prepare a guest room for me, for I trust that through your prayers I shall be granted to you.

[23] Epaphras, my fellow prisoner in Christ Jesus, greets you, [24] as do Mark, Aristarchus, Demas, Luke, my fellow laborers.

[25] The grace of our Lord Jesus Christ be with your spirit. Amen.

READING 309 · NOVEMBER 5

~ EZEKIEL 1:1—2:10 ~

Now it came to pass in the thirtieth year, in the fourth month, on the fifth day of the month, as I was among the captives by the River Chebar, that the heavens were opened and I saw visions of God. [2] On the fifth day of the month, which was in the fifth year of King Jehoiachin's captivity, [3] the word of the LORD came expressly to Ezekiel the priest, the son of Buzi, in the land of the Chaldeans by the River Chebar; and the hand of the LORD was upon him there.

[4] Then I looked, and behold, a whirlwind was coming out of the north, a great cloud with raging fire engulfing itself; and brightness was all around it and radiating out of its midst like the color of amber, out of the midst of the fire. [5] Also from within it came the likeness of four living creatures. And this was their appearance: they had the likeness of a man. [6] Each one had four faces, and each one had four wings. [7] Their legs were straight, and the soles of their feet were like the soles of calves' feet. They sparkled like the color of burnished bronze. [8] The hands of a man were under their wings on their four sides; and each of the four had faces and wings. [9] Their wings touched one another. The creatures did not turn when they went, but each one went straight forward.

[10] As for the likeness of their faces, each had the face of a man; each of the four had the face of a lion on the right side, each of the four had the face of an ox on the left side, and each of the four had the face of an eagle. [11] Thus were their faces. Their wings stretched upward; two wings of each one touched one another, and two covered their bodies. [12] And each one went straight forward; they went wherever the spirit wanted to go, and they did not turn when they went.

[13] As for the likeness of the living creatures, their appearance was like burning coals of fire, like the appearance of torches going back and forth among the living creatures. The fire was bright, and out of the fire went lightning. [14] And the living

The Passions of Life

In his autobiography, Bertrand Russell identified the passions which he believed had fueled his long life. He wrote: "Three passions, simple but overwhelmingly strong, have governed my life: the longing for love, the search for knowledge, and unbearable pity for the sufferings of mankind. These passions, like great winds, have blown me hither and thither, in a wayward course, over a deep ocean of anguish, reaching to the very verge of despair."

Oh, to be a person of passion — to care so deeply that you put all personal need aside in the pursuit of the goal you desire. The passionate way may not be easy or without inner pain, as Russell eloquently stated, but intense passion is rich in the intangible jewels of satisfaction, fulfillment, and deep joy.

creatures ran back and forth, in appearance like a flash of lightning.

[15] Now as I looked at the living creatures, behold, a wheel *was* on the earth beside each living creature with its four faces. [16] The appearance of the wheels and their workings *was* like the color of beryl, and all four had the same likeness. The appearance of their workings *was*, as it were, a wheel in the middle of a wheel. [17] When they moved, they went toward any one of four directions; they did not turn aside when they went. [18] As for their rims, they were so high they were awesome; and their rims *were* full of eyes, all around the four of them. [19] When the living creatures went, the wheels went beside them; and when the living creatures were lifted up from the earth, the wheels were lifted up. [20] Wherever the spirit wanted to go, they went, *because* there the spirit went; and the wheels were lifted together with them, for the spirit of the living creatures *was* in the wheels. [21] When those went, *these* went; when those stood, *these* stood; and when those were lifted up from the earth, the wheels were lifted up together with them, for the spirit of the living creatures *was* in the wheels.

[22] The likeness of the firmament above the heads of the living creatures *was* like the color of an awesome crystal, stretched out over their heads. [23] And under the firmament their wings *spread out* straight, one toward another. Each one had two which covered one side, and each one had two which covered the other side of the body. [24] When they went, I heard the noise of their wings, like the noise of many waters, like the voice of the Almighty, a tumult like the noise of an army; and when they stood still, they let down their wings. [25] A voice came from above the firmament that *was* over their heads; whenever they stood, they let down their wings.

[26] And above the firmament over their heads *was* the likeness of a throne, in appearance like a sapphire stone; on the likeness of the throne *was* a likeness with the appearance of a man high above it. [27] Also from the appearance of His waist and upward I saw, as it were, the color of amber with the appearance of fire all around within it; and from the appearance of His waist and downward I saw, as it were, the appearance of fire with brightness all around. [28] Like the appearance of a rainbow in a cloud on a rainy day, so *was* the appearance of the brightness all around it. This *was* the appearance of the likeness of the glory of the LORD.

So when I saw *it,* I fell on my face, and I heard a voice of One speaking.

2 And He said to me, "Son of man, stand on your feet, and I will speak to you." [2] Then the Spirit entered me when He spoke to me, and set me on my feet; and I heard Him who spoke to me. [3] And He said to me: "Son of man, I am sending you to the children of Israel, to a rebellious nation that has rebelled against Me; they and their fathers have transgressed against Me to this very day. [4] For *they are* impudent and stubborn children. I am sending you to them, and you shall say to them, 'Thus says the Lord GOD.' [5] As for them, whether they hear or whether they refuse—for they *are* a rebellious house—yet they will know that a prophet has been among them.

[6] "And you, son of man, do not be afraid of them nor be afraid of their words, though briers and thorns *are* with you and you dwell among scorpions; do not be afraid of their words or dismayed by their looks, though they *are* a rebellious house. [7] You shall speak My words to them, whether they hear or whether they refuse, for they *are* rebellious. [8] But you, son of man, hear what I say to you. Do not be rebellious like that rebellious house; open your mouth and eat what I give you."

[9] Now when I looked, there was a hand stretched out to me; and behold, a scroll of a book *was* in it. [10] Then He spread it before me; and *there was* writing on the inside and on the outside, and written on it *were* lamentations and mourning and woe.

∼ PSALM 119:153–160 ∼

[153] Consider my affliction and deliver me,
For I do not forget Your law.
[154] Plead my cause and redeem me;
Revive me according to Your word.
[155] Salvation *is* far from the wicked,

For they do not seek Your statutes.
156 Great *are* Your tender mercies,
    O LORD;
Revive me according to Your
    judgments.
157 Many *are* my persecutors and my
    enemies,
Yet I do not turn from Your
    testimonies.
158 I see the treacherous, and am
    disgusted,
Because they do not keep Your
    word.
159 Consider how I love Your precepts;
Revive me, O LORD, according to
    Your lovingkindness.
160 The entirety of Your word *is* truth,
And every one of Your righteous
    judgments *endures* forever.

～ PROVERBS 28:12 ～

12 When the righteous rejoice, *there is*
    great glory;
But when the wicked arise, men hide
    themselves.

～ HEBREWS 1:1–14 ～

God, who at various times and in various
ways spoke in time past to the fathers by
the prophets, ² has in these last days
spoken to us by *His* Son, whom He has
appointed heir of all things, through
whom also He made the worlds; ³ who
being the brightness of *His* glory and the
express image of His person, and uphold-
ing all things by the word of His power,
when He had by Himself purged our
sins, sat down at the right hand of the
Majesty on high, ⁴ having become so much
better than the angels, as He has by inheritance obtained a more excellent name
than they.
    ⁵ For to which of the angels did He ever
say:

    "You are My Son,
    Today I have begotten You"?

And again:

    "I will be to Him a Father,
    And He shall be to Me a Son"?

    ⁶ But when He again brings the first-
born into the world, He says:

    "Let all the angels of God worship
    Him."

⁷ And of the angels He says:

    "Who makes His angels spirits
    And His ministers a flame of fire."

⁸ But to the Son *He says:*

    "Your throne, O God, is forever
    and ever;
    A scepter of righteousness *is* the
    scepter of Your kingdom.
9   You have loved righteousness and
    hated lawlessness;
    Therefore God, Your God, has
    anointed You
    With the oil of gladness more than
    Your companions."

10 And:

    "You, LORD, in the beginning laid
    the foundation of the earth,
    And the heavens are the work of
    Your hands.
11   They will perish, but You remain;
    And they will all grow old like a
    garment;
12   Like a cloak You will fold them
    up,
    And they will be changed.
    But You are the same,
    And Your years will not fail."

13 But to which of the angels has He
ever said:

    "Sit at My right hand,
    Till I make Your enemies Your
    footstool"?

14 Are they not all ministering spirits sent
forth to minister for those who will inherit salvation?

~ EZEKIEL 3:1—4:17 ~

Moreover He said to me, "Son of man, eat what you find; eat this scroll, and go, speak to the house of Israel." ² So I opened my mouth, and He caused me to eat that scroll.

³ And He said to me, "Son of man, feed your belly, and fill your stomach with this scroll that I give you." So I ate, and it was in my mouth like honey in sweetness.

⁴ Then He said to me: "Son of man, go to the house of Israel and speak with My words to them. ⁵ For you *are* not sent to a people of unfamiliar speech and of hard language, *but* to the house of Israel, ⁶ not to many people of unfamiliar speech and of hard language, whose words you cannot understand. Surely, had I sent you to them, they would have listened to you. ⁷ But the house of Israel will not listen to you, because they will not listen to Me; for all the house of Israel *are* impudent and hard-hearted. ⁸ Behold, I have made your face strong against their faces, and your forehead strong against their foreheads. ⁹ Like adamant stone, harder than flint, I have made your forehead; do not be afraid of them, nor be dismayed at their looks, though they *are* a rebellious house."

¹⁰ Moreover He said to me: "Son of man, receive into your heart all My words that I speak to you, and hear with your ears. ¹¹ And go, get to the captives, to the children of your people, and speak to them and tell them, 'Thus says the Lord GOD,' whether they hear, or whether they refuse."

¹² Then the Spirit lifted me up, and I heard behind me a great thunderous voice: "Blessed *is* the glory of the LORD from His place!" ¹³ I also *heard* the noise of the wings of the living creatures that touched one another, and the noise of the wheels beside them, and a great thunderous noise. ¹⁴ So the Spirit lifted me up and took me away, and I went in bitterness, in the heat of my spirit; but the hand of the LORD was strong upon me. ¹⁵ Then I came to the captives at Tel Abib, who dwelt by the River Chebar; and I sat where they sat, and remained there astonished among them seven days.

¹⁶ Now it came to pass at the end of seven days that the word of the LORD came to me, saying, ¹⁷ "Son of man, I have made you a watchman for the house of Israel; therefore hear a word from My mouth, and give them warning from Me: ¹⁸ When I say to the wicked, 'You shall surely die,' and you give him no warning, nor speak to warn the wicked from his wicked way, to save his life, that same wicked *man* shall die in his iniquity; but his blood I will require at your hand. ¹⁹ Yet, if you warn the wicked, and he does not turn from his wickedness, nor from his wicked way, he shall die in his iniquity; but you have delivered your soul.

²⁰ "Again, when a righteous *man* turns from his righteousness and commits iniquity, and I lay a stumbling block before him, he shall die; because you did not give him warning, he shall die in his sin, and his righteousness which he has done shall not be remembered; but his blood I will require at your hand. ²¹ Nevertheless if you warn the righteous *man* that the righteous should not sin, and he does not sin, he shall surely live because he took warning; also you will have delivered your soul."

²² Then the hand of the LORD was upon me there, and He said to me, "Arise, go out into the plain, and there I shall talk with you."

²³ So I arose and went out into the plain, and behold, the glory of the LORD stood there, like the glory which I saw by the River Chebar; and I fell on my face. ²⁴ Then the Spirit entered me and set me on my feet, and spoke with me and said to me: "Go, shut yourself inside your house. ²⁵ And you, O son of man, surely they will put ropes on you and bind you with them, so that you cannot go out among them. ²⁶ I will make your tongue cling to the roof of your mouth, so that you shall be mute and not be one to rebuke them, for they *are* a rebellious house. ²⁷ But when I speak with you, I will open your mouth, and you shall say to them, 'Thus says the Lord GOD.' He who hears, let him hear; and he who refuses, let him refuse; for they *are* a rebellious house.

The Discovery of Comet Hale-Bopp

For astronomer Alan Hale, there's no line between vocation and avocation, between profession and passion. Astronomy is his life. "A lot of this is hobby," he has said. "I'm an amateur astronomer who also decided to make a professional career out of it."

Hale graduated from New Mexico State University with a doctorate in astronomy, but then searched unsuccessfully for a research position. He finally formed the nonprofit Southwest Institute for Space Research, which does other research and education work as well as stargazing. Looking through his high-powered telescope continues to be Hale's great love, however. A concrete driveway doubles as his observatory and a basketball court.

Hale's approach is simple: "As long as the telescope is out, I might as well point it at something." One night while aiming at a cluster of stars known as M70, he saw a fuzzy blob where no fuzzy blob should have been. He checked his star charts, then sent an e-mail message to the International Astronomical Union. His find became known as the Hale-Bopp comet, a comet some say may become "the comet of the century."

Discover what it is you love to do, and then do it with your whole heart. Who knows what you may find!

4 "You also, son of man, take a clay tablet and lay it before you, and portray on it a city, Jerusalem. ² Lay siege against it, build a siege wall against it, and heap up a mound against it; set camps against it also, and place battering rams against it all around. ³ Moreover take for yourself an iron plate, and set it *as* an iron wall between you and the city. Set your face against it, and it shall be besieged, and you shall lay siege against it. This *will be* a sign to the house of Israel.

⁴ "Lie also on your left side, and lay the iniquity of the house of Israel upon it. *According* to the number of the days that you lie on it, you shall bear their iniquity. ⁵ For I have laid on you the years of their iniquity, according to the number of the days, three hundred and ninety days; so you shall bear the iniquity of the house of Israel. ⁶ And when you have completed them, lie again on your right side; then you shall bear the iniquity of the house of Judah forty days. I have laid on you a day for each year.

⁷ "Therefore you shall set your face toward the siege of Jerusalem; your arm *shall be* uncovered, and you shall prophesy against it. ⁸ And surely I will restrain you so that you cannot turn from one side to another till you have ended the days of your siege.

⁹ "Also take for yourself wheat, barley, beans, lentils, millet, and spelt; put them into one vessel, and make bread of them for yourself. *During* the number of days that you lie on your side, three hundred and ninety days, you shall eat it. ¹⁰ And your food which you eat *shall be* by weight, twenty shekels a day; from time to time you shall eat it. ¹¹ You shall also drink water by measure, one-sixth of a hin; from time to time you shall drink. ¹² And you shall eat it *as* barley cakes; and bake it using fuel of human waste in their sight."

¹³ Then the LORD said, "So shall the children of Israel eat their defiled bread among the Gentiles, where I will drive them."

¹⁴ So I said, "Ah, Lord GOD! Indeed I have never defiled myself from my youth till now; I have never eaten what died of itself or was torn by beasts, nor has abominable flesh ever come into my mouth."

¹⁵ Then He said to me, "See, I am giving you cow dung instead of human waste, and you shall prepare your bread over it."

¹⁶ Moreover He said to me, "Son of man, surely I will cut off the supply of bread in Jerusalem; they shall eat bread by weight and with anxiety, and shall drink water by measure and with dread, ¹⁷ that they may lack bread and water, and be dismayed with one another, and waste away because of their iniquity.

∼ PSALM 119:161–168 ∼

¹⁶¹ Princes persecute me without a
cause,
But my heart stands in awe of Your
word.
¹⁶² I rejoice at Your word
As one who finds great treasure.
¹⁶³ I hate and abhor lying,
But I love Your law.
¹⁶⁴ Seven times a day I praise You,
Because of Your righteous
judgments.
¹⁶⁵ Great peace have those who love
Your law,
And nothing causes them to stumble.
¹⁶⁶ LORD, I hope for Your salvation,
And I do Your commandments.
¹⁶⁷ My soul keeps Your testimonies,
And I love them exceedingly.
¹⁶⁸ I keep Your precepts and Your
testimonies,
For all my ways *are* before You.

∼ PROVERBS 28:13 ∼

¹³ He who covers his sins will not
prosper,
But whoever confesses and forsakes
them will have mercy.

∼ HEBREWS 2:1–18 ∼

Therefore we must give the more earnest heed to the things we have heard, lest we drift away. ² For if the word spoken through angels proved steadfast, and every transgression and disobedience received a just reward, ³ how shall we escape if we neglect so great a salvation, which at the first began to be spoken by the Lord, and was confirmed to us by those who heard

Him, [4] God also bearing witness both with signs and wonders, with various miracles, and gifts of the Holy Spirit, according to His own will?

[5] For He has not put the world to come, of which we speak, in subjection to angels. [6] But one testified in a certain place, saying:

"What is man that You are mindful of him,
Or the son of man that You take care of him?
[7] You have made him a little lower than the angels;
You have crowned him with glory and honor,
And set him over the works of Your hands.
[8] You have put all things in subjection under his feet."

For in that He put all in subjection under him, He left nothing *that is* not put under him. But now we do not yet see all things put under him. [9] But we see Jesus, who was made a little lower than the angels, for the suffering of death crowned with glory and honor, that He, by the grace of God, might taste death for everyone.

[10] For it was fitting for Him, for whom *are* all things and by whom *are* all things, in bringing many sons to glory, to make the captain of their salvation perfect through sufferings. [11] For both He who sanctifies and those who are being sanctified *are* all of one, for which reason He is not ashamed to call them brethren, [12] saying:

"I will declare Your name to My brethren;
In the midst of the assembly I will sing praise to You."

[13] And again:

"I will put My trust in Him."

And again:

"Here am I and the children whom God has given Me."

[14] Inasmuch then as the children have partaken of flesh and blood, He Himself likewise shared in the same, that through death He might destroy him who had the power of death, that is, the devil, [15] and release those who through fear of death were all their lifetime subject to bondage. [16] For indeed He does not give aid to angels, but He does give aid to the seed of Abraham. [17] Therefore, in all things He had to be made like *His* brethren, that He might be a merciful and faithful High Priest in things *pertaining* to God, to make propitiation for the sins of the people. [18] For in that He Himself has suffered, being tempted, He is able to aid those who are tempted.

READING 311 · NOVEMBER 7

~ EZEKIEL 5:1—6:14 ~

"And you, son of man, take a sharp sword, take it as a barber's razor, and pass *it* over your head and your beard; then take scales to weigh and divide the hair. [2] You shall burn with fire one-third in the midst of the city, when the days of the siege are finished; then you shall take one-third and strike around *it* with the sword, and one-third you shall scatter in the wind: I will draw out a sword after them. [3] You shall also take a small number of them and bind them in the edge of your *garment.* [4] Then take some of them again and throw them into the midst of the fire, and burn them in the fire. From there a fire will go out into all the house of Israel.

[5] "Thus says the Lord GOD: 'This *is* Jerusalem; I have set her in the midst of the nations and the countries all around her. [6] She has rebelled against My judgments by doing wickedness more than the

nations, and against My statutes more than the countries that *are* all around her; for they have refused My judgments, and they have not walked in My statutes.' [7] Therefore thus says the Lord GOD: 'Because you have multiplied *disobedience* more than the nations that *are* all around you, have not walked in My statutes nor kept My judgments, nor even done according to the judgments of the nations that *are* all around you'— [8] therefore thus says the Lord GOD: 'Indeed I, even I, *am* against you and will execute judgments in your midst in the sight of the nations. [9] And I will do among you what I have never done, and the like of which I will never do again, because of all your abominations. [10] Therefore fathers shall eat *their* sons in your midst, and sons shall eat their fathers; and I will execute judgments among you, and all of you who remain I will scatter to all the winds.

[11] 'Therefore, *as* I live,' says the Lord GOD, 'surely, because you have defiled My sanctuary with all your detestable things and with all your abominations, therefore I will also diminish *you;* My eye will not spare, nor will I have any pity. [12] One-third of you shall die of the pestilence, and be consumed with famine in your midst; and one-third shall fall by the sword all around you; and I will scatter another third to all the winds, and I will draw out a sword after them.

[13] 'Thus shall My anger be spent, and I will cause My fury to rest upon them, and I will be avenged; and they shall know that I, the LORD, have spoken *it* in My zeal, when I have spent My fury upon them. [14] Moreover I will make you a waste and a reproach among the nations that *are* all around you, in the sight of all who pass by.

[15] 'So it shall be a reproach, a taunt, a lesson, and an astonishment to the nations that *are* all around you, when I execute judgments among you in anger and in fury and in furious rebukes. I, the LORD, have spoken. [16] When I send against them the terrible arrows of famine which shall be for destruction, which I will send to destroy you, I will increase the famine upon you and cut off your supply of bread. [17] So I will send against you famine and wild beasts, and they will bereave you. Pestilence and blood shall pass through you, and I will bring the sword against you. I, the LORD, have spoken.' "

6 Now the word of the LORD came to me, saying: [2] "Son of man, set your face toward the mountains of Israel, and prophesy against them, [3] and say, 'O mountains of Israel, hear the word of the Lord GOD! Thus says the Lord GOD to the mountains, to the hills, to the ravines, and to the valleys: "Indeed I, *even* I, will bring a sword against you, and I will destroy your high places. [4] Then your altars shall be desolate, your incense altars shall be broken, and I will cast down your slain *men* before your idols. [5] And I will lay the corpses of the children of Israel before their idols, and I will scatter your bones all around your altars. [6] In all your dwelling places the cities shall be laid waste, and the high places shall be desolate, so that your altars may be laid waste and made desolate, your idols may be broken and made to cease, your incense altars may be cut down, and your works may be abolished. [7] The slain shall fall in your midst, and you shall know that I *am* the LORD.

[8] "Yet I will leave a remnant, so that you may have *some* who escape the sword among the nations, when you are scattered through the countries. [9] Then those of you who escape will remember Me among the nations where they are carried captive, because I was crushed by their adulterous heart which has departed from Me, and by their eyes which play the harlot after their idols; they will loathe themselves for the evils which they committed in all their abominations. [10] And they shall know that I *am* the LORD; I have not said in vain that I would bring this calamity upon them."

[11] 'Thus says the Lord GOD: "Pound your fists and stamp your feet, and say, 'Alas, for all the evil abominations of the house of Israel! For they shall fall by the sword, by famine, and by pestilence. [12] He who is far off shall die by the pestilence, he who is near shall fall by the sword, and he who remains and is besieged shall die by the famine. Thus will I spend My fury upon them. [13] Then you shall know that I *am* the LORD, when their slain are among their idols all around

Are You a Spy?

For many years, it has been as common for Christians to give thanks before meals as it has been for them to eat.

During the Thirty Years' War, several Protestant officers were hiding together in a cave. Every day, a little girl from the nearest farm was sent to bring them provisions.

One day a stranger who happened to be walking through the woods joined the officers. Naturally they were suspicious of him, but he talked so much like one of them that their doubts were overcome.

When the little farm girl came with their supplies, they offered to share their food with the stranger. To their surprise he began to eat without giving thanks. That single omission revealed the true character of the man. He was what they had suspected at the first — a spy! They barely escaped him and his comrades.

When we fail to pray, we cheat ourselves of our identity with Christ, and deny ourselves the reputation of a faithful follower. A Christian who doesn't pray is like a spy who gets all his information second-hand, rather than from the source — the Commander in Chief.

> Happy is the man who is always reverent, but he who hardens his heart will fall into calamity.
>
> *Proverbs 28:14*

their altars, on every high hill, on all the mountaintops, under every green tree, and under every thick oak, wherever they offered sweet incense to all their idols. ¹⁴ So I will stretch out My hand against them and make the land desolate, yes, more desolate than the wilderness toward Diblah, in all their dwelling places. Then they shall know that I *am* the LORD.' " ' "

∼ PSALM 119:169–176 ∼

¹⁶⁹ Let my cry come before You,
    O LORD;
  Give me understanding according to
    Your word.
¹⁷⁰ Let my supplication come before
    You;
  Deliver me according to Your word.
¹⁷¹ My lips shall utter praise,
  For You teach me Your statutes.
¹⁷² My tongue shall speak of Your word,
  For all Your commandments *are*
    righteousness.
¹⁷³ Let Your hand become my help,
  For I have chosen Your precepts.
¹⁷⁴ I long for Your salvation, O LORD,
  And Your law *is* my delight.
¹⁷⁵ Let my soul live, and it shall praise
    You;
  And let Your judgments help me.
¹⁷⁶ I have gone astray like a lost sheep;
  Seek Your servant,
  For I do not forget Your
    commandments.

∼ PROVERBS 28:14 ∼

¹⁴ Happy *is* the man who is always
    reverent,
  But he who hardens his heart will
    fall into calamity.

∼ HEBREWS 3:1–19 ∼

Therefore, holy brethren, partakers of the heavenly calling, consider the Apostle and High Priest of our confession, Christ Jesus, ² who was faithful to Him who appointed Him, as Moses also *was faithful* in all His house. ³ For this One has been counted worthy of more glory than Moses, inas-

much as He who built the house has more honor than the house. ⁴ For every house is built by someone, but He who built all things *is* God. ⁵ And Moses indeed *was* faithful in all His house as a servant, for a testimony of those things which would be spoken *afterward,* ⁶ but Christ as a Son over His own house, whose house we are if we hold fast the confidence and the rejoicing of the hope firm to the end.

⁷ Therefore, as the Holy Spirit says:

  "Today, if you will hear His voice,
⁸   Do not harden your hearts as in
      the rebellion,
    In the day of trial in the
      wilderness,
⁹   Where your fathers tested Me,
      tried Me,
    And saw My works forty years.
¹⁰   Therefore I was angry with that
      generation,
    And said, 'They always go astray
      in *their* heart,
    And they have not known My
      ways.'
¹¹   So I swore in My wrath,
    'They shall not enter My rest.' "

¹² Beware, brethren, lest there be in any of you an evil heart of unbelief in departing from the living God; ¹³ but exhort one another daily, while it is called "Today," lest any of you be hardened through the deceitfulness of sin. ¹⁴ For we have become partakers of Christ if we hold the beginning of our confidence steadfast to the end, ¹⁵ while it is said:

  "Today, if you will hear His voice,
    Do not harden your hearts as in
      the rebellion."

¹⁶ For who, having heard, rebelled? Indeed, *was it* not all who came out of Egypt, *led* by Moses? ¹⁷ Now with whom was He angry forty years? *Was it* not with those who sinned, whose corpses fell in the wilderness? ¹⁸ And to whom did He swear that they would not enter His rest, but to those who did not obey? ¹⁹ So we see that they could not enter in because of unbelief.

~ EZEKIEL 7:1—8:18 ~

Moreover the word of the LORD came to me, saying, [2] "And you, son of man, thus says the Lord GOD to the land of Israel:

'An end! The end has come upon the four corners of the land.
[3] Now the end *has come* upon you, And I will send My anger against you;
I will judge you according to your ways,
And I will repay you for all your abominations.
[4] My eye will not spare you, Nor will I have pity;
But I will repay your ways, And your abominations will be in your midst;
Then you shall know that I *am* the LORD!'

[5] "Thus says the Lord GOD:

'A disaster, a singular disaster; Behold, it has come!
[6] An end has come, The end has come;
It has dawned for you; Behold, it has come!
[7] Doom has come to you, you who dwell in the land;
The time has come, A day of trouble *is* near,
And not of rejoicing in the mountains.
[8] Now upon you I will soon pour out My fury,
And spend My anger upon you; I will judge you according to your ways,
And I will repay you for all your abominations.

[9] 'My eye will not spare, Nor will I have pity;
I will repay you according to your ways,
And your abominations will be in your midst.
Then you shall know that I *am* the LORD who strikes.

[10] 'Behold, the day! Behold, it has come!
Doom has gone out; The rod has blossomed, Pride has budded.
[11] Violence has risen up into a rod of wickedness;
None of them *shall remain,* None of their multitude, None of them;
Nor *shall there be* wailing for them.
[12] The time has come, The day draws near.

'Let not the buyer rejoice, Nor the seller mourn,
For wrath *is* on their whole multitude.
[13] For the seller shall not return to what has been sold,
Though he may still be alive; For the vision concerns the whole multitude,
And it shall not turn back; No one will strengthen himself Who lives in iniquity.

[14] 'They have blown the trumpet and made everyone ready,
But no one goes to battle; For My wrath *is* on all their multitude.
[15] The sword *is* outside, And the pestilence and famine within.
Whoever *is* in the field Will die by the sword;
And whoever *is* in the city, Famine and pestilence will devour him.

[16] 'Those who survive will escape and be on the mountains
Like doves of the valleys, All of them mourning, Each for his iniquity.
[17] Every hand will be feeble, And every knee will be *as* weak *as* water.
[18] They will also be girded with sackcloth;

Horror will cover them;
Shame *will be* on every face,
Baldness on all their heads.

19 'They will throw their silver into
      the streets,
And their gold will be like refuse;
Their silver and their gold will not
      be able to deliver them
In the day of the wrath of the
      LORD;
They will not satisfy their souls,
Nor fill their stomachs,
Because it became their stumbling
      block of iniquity.

20 'As for the beauty of his
      ornaments,
He set it in majesty;
But they made from it
The images of their
      abominations—
Their detestable things;
Therefore I have made it
Like refuse to them.
21 I will give it as plunder
Into the hands of strangers,
And to the wicked of the earth as
      spoil;
And they shall defile it.
22 I will turn My face from them,
And they will defile My secret
      place;
For robbers shall enter it and
      defile it.

23 'Make a chain,
For the land is filled with crimes
      of blood,
And the city is full of violence.
24 Therefore I will bring the worst of
      the Gentiles,
And they will possess their houses;
I will cause the pomp of the strong
      to cease,
And their holy places shall be
      defiled.
25 Destruction comes;
They will seek peace, but *there
      shall be* none.
26 Disaster will come upon disaster,
And rumor will be upon rumor.
Then they will seek a vision from
      a prophet;

But the law will perish from the
      priest,
And counsel from the elders.

27 'The king will mourn,
The prince will be clothed with
      desolation,
And the hands of the common
      people will tremble.
I will do to them according to
      their way,
And according to what they
      deserve I will judge them;
Then they shall know that I *am*
      the LORD!' "

8 And it came to pass in the sixth year, in the sixth *month,* on the fifth *day* of the month, as I sat in my house with the elders of Judah sitting before me, that the hand of the Lord GOD fell upon me there. 2 Then I looked, and there was a likeness, like the appearance of fire—from the appearance of His waist and downward, fire; and from His waist and upward, like the appearance of brightness, like the color of amber. 3 He stretched out the form of a hand, and took me by a lock of my hair; and the Spirit lifted me up between earth and heaven, and brought me in visions of God to Jerusalem, to the door of the north gate of the inner *court,* where the seat of the image of jealousy *was,* which provokes to jealousy. 4 And behold, the glory of the God of Israel *was* there, like the vision that I saw in the plain.

5 Then He said to me, "Son of man, lift your eyes now toward the north." So I lifted my eyes toward the north, and there, north of the altar gate, was this image of jealousy in the entrance.

6 Furthermore He said to me, "Son of man, do you see what they are doing, the great abominations that the house of Israel commits here, to make Me go far away from My sanctuary? Now turn again, you will see greater abominations." 7 So He brought me to the door of the court; and when I looked, there was a hole in the wall. 8 Then He said to me, "Son of man, dig into the wall"; and when I dug into the wall, there was a door.

9 And He said to me, "Go in, and see the wicked abominations which they are doing there." 10 So I went in and saw, and

What is Prayer For?

A physician once went to the home of one of his patients who was dying of lung cancer. The doctor spent time sitting at the patient's bedside, with the man's wife and children. The dying man knew that he had little time left and he chose his words carefully, speaking to the physician in a hoarse whisper. Although he had not been a very religious person, he revealed to his doctor that he had recently begun to pray frequently.

"What do you pray for?" the physician asked.

"I don't pray for anything," the dying man responded. "How would I know what to ask for?" The physician found this surprising. Surely this dying man could think of *some* request.

"If prayer is not for asking, what is it *for*?" the physician asked.

"It isn't *for* anything," the man said after a few moments of silent thought. "It mainly reminds me I am not alone."

God desires to have a relationship with each one of us — that relationship is the very reason for our creation. Relationship with God is what gives our life meaning and purpose. Relationship is what Jesus embodied, and what the Holy Spirit establishes. Relationship is *why* we pray, and why we have the privilege of praying.

there—every sort of creeping thing, abominable beasts, and all the idols of the house of Israel, portrayed all around on the walls. ¹¹ And there stood before them seventy men of the elders of the house of Israel, and in their midst stood Jaazaniah the son of Shaphan. Each man had a censer in his hand, and a thick cloud of incense went up. ¹² Then He said to me, "Son of man, have you seen what the elders of the house of Israel do in the dark, every man in the room of his idols? For they say, 'The LORD does not see us, the LORD has forsaken the land.' "

¹³ And He said to me, "Turn again, *and* you will see greater abominations that they are doing." ¹⁴ So He brought me to the door of the north gate of the LORD's house; and to my dismay, women were sitting there weeping for Tammuz.

¹⁵ Then He said to me, "Have you seen *this,* O son of man? Turn again, you will see greater abominations than these." ¹⁶ So He brought me into the inner court of the LORD's house; and there, at the door of the temple of the LORD, between the porch and the altar, *were* about twenty-five men with their backs toward the temple of the LORD and their faces toward the east, and they were worshiping the sun toward the east.

¹⁷ And He said to me, "Have you seen *this,* O son of man? Is it a trivial thing to the house of Judah to commit the abominations which they commit here? For they have filled the land with violence; then they have returned to provoke Me to anger. Indeed they put the branch to their nose. ¹⁸ Therefore I also will act in fury. My eye will not spare nor will I have pity; and though they cry in My ears with a loud voice, I will not hear them."

～ PSALM 120:1-7 ～

¹ In my distress I cried to the LORD,
    And He heard me.
² Deliver my soul, O LORD, from lying
    lips
    And from a deceitful tongue.

³ What shall be given to you,
    Or what shall be done to you,
    You false tongue?

⁴ Sharp arrows of the warrior,
    With coals of the broom tree!

⁵ Woe is me, that I dwell in Meshech,
    That I dwell among the tents of
    Kedar!
⁶ My soul has dwelt too long
    With one who hates peace.
⁷ I *am for* peace;
    But when I speak, they *are* for war.

～ PROVERBS 28:15 ～

¹⁵ *Like* a roaring lion and a charging
    bear
    Is a wicked ruler over poor people.

～ HEBREWS 4:1-16 ～

Therefore, since a promise remains of entering His rest, let us fear lest any of you seem to have come short of it. ² For indeed the gospel was preached to us as well as to them; but the word which they heard did not profit them, not being mixed with faith in those who heard *it.* ³ For we who have believed do enter that rest, as He has said:

"So I swore in My wrath,
'They shall not enter My rest,' "

although the works were finished from the foundation of the world. ⁴ For He has spoken in a certain place of the seventh *day* in this way: "And God rested on the seventh day from all His works"; ⁵ and again in this *place:* "They shall not enter My rest."

⁶ Since therefore it remains that some *must* enter it, and those to whom it was first preached did not enter because of disobedience, ⁷ again He designates a certain day, saying in David, "Today," after such a long time, as it has been said:

"Today, if you will hear His voice,
Do not harden your hearts."

⁸ For if Joshua had given them rest, then He would not afterward have spoken of another day. ⁹ There remains therefore a rest for the people of God. ¹⁰ For he who

has entered His rest has himself also ceased from his works as God *did* from His. ¹¹ Let us therefore be diligent to enter that rest, lest anyone fall according to the same example of disobedience. ¹² For the word of God *is* living and powerful, and sharper than any two-edged sword, piercing even to the division of soul and spirit, and of joints and marrow, and is a discerner of the thoughts and intents of the heart. ¹³ And there is no creature hidden from His sight, but all things *are* naked and open to the eyes of Him to whom we *must give* account.

¹⁴ Seeing then that we have a great High Priest who has passed through the heavens, Jesus the Son of God, let us hold fast *our* confession. ¹⁵ For we do not have a High Priest who cannot sympathize with our weaknesses, but was in all *points* tempted as *we are, yet* without sin. ¹⁶ Let us therefore come boldly to the throne of grace, that we may obtain mercy and find grace to help in time of need.

READING 313 · NOVEMBER 9

~ EZEKIEL 9:1—10:22 ~

Then He called out in my hearing with a loud voice, saying, "Let those who have charge over the city draw near, each *with* a deadly weapon in his hand." ² And suddenly six men came from the direction of the upper gate, which faces north, each with his battle-ax in his hand. One man among them *was* clothed with linen and had a writer's inkhorn at his side. They went in and stood beside the bronze altar.

³ Now the glory of the God of Israel had gone up from the cherub, where it had been, to the threshold of the temple. And He called to the man clothed with linen, who *had* the writer's inkhorn at his side; ⁴ and the LORD said to him, "Go through the midst of the city, through the midst of Jerusalem, and put a mark on the foreheads of the men who sigh and cry over all the abominations that are done within it."

⁵ To the others He said in my hearing, "Go after him through the city and kill; do not let your eye spare, nor have any pity. ⁶ Utterly slay old *and* young men, maidens and little children and women; but do not come near anyone on whom *is* the mark; and begin at My sanctuary." So they began with the elders who *were* before the temple. ⁷ Then He said to them, "Defile the temple, and fill the courts with the slain. Go out!" And they went out and killed in the city.

⁸ So it was, that while they were killing them, I was left *alone;* and I fell on my face and cried out, and said, "Ah, Lord GOD! Will You destroy all the remnant of Israel in pouring out Your fury on Jerusalem?"

⁹ Then He said to me, "The iniquity of the house of Israel and Judah *is* exceedingly great, and the land is full of bloodshed, and the city full of perversity; for they say, 'The LORD has forsaken the land, and the LORD does not see!' ¹⁰ And as for Me also, My eye will neither spare, nor will I have pity, *but* I will recompense their deeds on their own head."

¹¹ Just then, the man clothed with linen, who *had* the inkhorn at his side, reported back and said, "I have done as You commanded me."

10 And I looked, and there in the firmament that was above the head of the cherubim, there appeared something like a sapphire stone, having the appearance of the likeness of a throne. ² Then He spoke to the man clothed with linen, and said, "Go in among the wheels, under the cherub, fill your hands with coals of fire from among the cherubim, and scatter *them* over the city." And he went in as I watched.

³ Now the cherubim were standing on the south side of the temple when the man went in, and the cloud filled the inner court. ⁴ Then the glory of the LORD went up from the cherub, *and paused* over the threshold of the temple; and the house was filled with the cloud, and the

court was full of the brightness of the LORD's glory. ⁵ And the sound of the wings of the cherubim was heard *even* in the outer court, like the voice of Almighty God when He speaks.

⁶ Then it happened, when He commanded the man clothed in linen, saying, "Take fire from among the wheels, from among the cherubim," that he went in and stood beside the wheels. ⁷ And the cherub stretched out his hand from among the cherubim to the fire that *was* among the cherubim, and took *some of it* and put *it* into the hands of the *man* clothed with linen, who took *it* and went out. ⁸ The cherubim appeared to have the form of a man's hand under their wings.

⁹ And when I looked, there were four wheels by the cherubim, one wheel by one cherub and another wheel by each other cherub; the wheels appeared *to have* the color of a beryl stone. ¹⁰ *As for* their appearance, all four looked alike—as it were, a wheel in the middle of a wheel. ¹¹ When they went, they went toward *any of* their four directions; they did not turn aside when they went, but followed in the direction the head was facing. They did not turn aside when they went. ¹² And their whole body, with their back, their hands, their wings, and the wheels that the four had, *were* full of eyes all around. ¹³ As for the wheels, they were called in my hearing, "Wheel."

¹⁴ Each one had four faces: the first face *was* the face of a cherub, the second face the face of a man, the third the face of a lion, and the fourth the face of an eagle. ¹⁵ And the cherubim were lifted up. This *was* the living creature I saw by the River Chebar. ¹⁶ When the cherubim went, the wheels went beside them; and when the cherubim lifted their wings to mount up from the earth, the same wheels also did not turn from beside them. ¹⁷ When *the cherubim* stood still, *the wheels* stood still, and when *one* was lifted up, *the other* lifted itself up, for the spirit of the living creature *was* in them.

¹⁸ Then the glory of the LORD departed from the threshold of the temple and stood over the cherubim. ¹⁹ And the cherubim lifted their wings and mounted up from the earth in my sight. When they went out, the wheels *were* beside them; and they stood at the door of the east gate of the LORD's house, and the glory of the God of Israel *was* above them.

²⁰ This *is* the living creature I saw under the God of Israel by the River Chebar, and I knew they *were* cherubim. ²¹ Each one had four faces and each one four wings, and the likeness of the hands of a man *was* under their wings. ²² And the likeness of their faces *was* the same *as* the faces which I had seen by the River Chebar, their appearance and their persons. They each went straight forward.

～ PSALM 121:1–8 ～

1 I will lift up my eyes to the hills—
   From whence comes my help?
2 My help *comes* from the LORD,
   Who made heaven and earth.

3 He will not allow your foot to be
      moved;
   He who keeps you will not slumber.
4 Behold, He who keeps Israel
   Shall neither slumber nor sleep.

5 The LORD *is* your keeper;
   The LORD *is* your shade at your right
      hand.
6 The sun shall not strike you by day,
   Nor the moon by night.

7 The LORD shall preserve you from
      all evil;
   He shall preserve your soul.
8 The LORD shall preserve your going
      out and your coming in
   From this time forth, and even
      forevermore.

～ PROVERBS 28:16 ～

16 A ruler who lacks understanding *is* a
       great oppressor,
    But he who hates covetousness will
       prolong *his* days.

～ HEBREWS 5:1–14 ～

For every high priest taken from among men is appointed for men in things *pertaining* to God, that he may offer both gifts and sacrifices for sins. ² He can have compassion on those who are ignorant

Knowing the Shepherd

A house party once was held in an English manor. As was customary, the after-dinner entertainment featured recitations and songs from the guests. A famous actor was present, and when it came his turn to perform, he recited the Twenty-third Psalm. His rendition of the familiar psalm was magnificent and received with much applause.

Later in the evening, the hostess noticed her little old great-aunt dozing in the corner of the room. She was almost completely deaf and had missed most of the evening's entertainment. Still, the other guests urged her to recite something. Since most people of that era knew many poems by memory, the hostess felt sure she would recite a poem. To everyone's surprise, she stood up, her voice quivering, and recited the Twenty-third Psalm! When she finished there were tears in most eyes, including those of the famous actor. One of the guests later approached the actor and said, "You recited that psalm absolutely superbly. It was incomparable. So why were we so moved by that funny, little old lady?"

He replied, "I know the psalm. She knows the Shepherd."

Prayer is our foremost way of getting better acquainted with Him.

> I will lift up my eyes to the hills — from whence comes my help?
> My help comes from the Lord, Who made heaven and earth.
>
> *Psalm 121:1-2*

and going astray, since he himself is also subject to weakness. ³ Because of this he is required as for the people, so also for himself, to offer *sacrifices* for sins. ⁴ And no man takes this honor to himself, but he who is called by God, just as Aaron *was.*

⁵ So also Christ did not glorify Himself to become High Priest, *but it* was He who said to Him:

"You are My Son,
Today I have begotten You."

⁶ As *He* also *says* in another *place:*

"You are a priest forever
According to the order of
Melchizedek";

⁷ who, in the days of His flesh, when He had offered up prayers and supplications, with vehement cries and tears to Him who was able to save Him from death, and was heard because of His godly fear, ⁸ though He was a Son, yet He learned obedience by the things which He suffered. ⁹ And having been perfected, He became the author of eternal salvation to all who obey Him, ¹⁰ called by God as High Priest "according to the order of Melchizedek," ¹¹ of whom we have much to say, and hard to explain, since you have become dull of hearing.

¹² For though by this time you ought to be teachers, you need *someone* to teach you again the first principles of the oracles of God; and you have come to need milk and not solid food. ¹³ For everyone who partakes *only* of milk *is* unskilled in the word of righteousness, for he is a babe. ¹⁴ But solid food belongs to those who are of full age, *that is,* those who by reason of use have their senses exercised to discern both good and evil.

READING 314 · NOVEMBER 10

~ EZEKIEL 11:1—12:28 ~

Then the Spirit lifted me up and brought me to the East Gate of the LORD's house, which faces eastward; and there at the door of the gate were twenty-five men, among whom I saw Jaazaniah the son of Azzur, and Pelatiah the son of Benaiah, princes of the people. ² And He said to me: "Son of man, these *are* the men who devise iniquity and give wicked counsel in this city, ³ who say, 'The time is not near to build houses; this city is the caldron, and we are the meat.' ⁴ Therefore prophesy against them, prophesy, O son of man!"

⁵ Then the Spirit of the LORD fell upon me, and said to me, "Speak! 'Thus says the LORD: "Thus you have said, O house of Israel; for I know the things that come into your mind. ⁶ You have multiplied your slain in this city, and you have filled its streets with the slain." ⁷ Therefore thus says the Lord GOD: "Your slain whom you have laid in its midst, they *are* the meat, and this *city is* the caldron; but I shall bring you out of the midst of it. ⁸ You have feared the sword; and I will bring a sword upon you," says the Lord GOD. ⁹ "And I will bring you out of its midst, and deliver you into the hands of strangers, and execute judgments on you. ¹⁰ You shall fall by the sword. I will judge you at the border of Israel. Then you shall know that I *am* the LORD. ¹¹ This *city* shall not be your caldron, nor shall you be the meat in its midst. I will judge you at the border of Israel. ¹² And you shall know that I *am* the LORD; for you have not walked in My statutes nor executed My judgments, but have done according to the customs of the Gentiles which *are* all around you." ' "

¹³ Now it happened, while I was prophesying, that Pelatiah the son of Benaiah died. Then I fell on my face and cried with a loud voice, and said, "Ah, Lord GOD! Will You make a complete end of the remnant of Israel?"

¹⁴ Again the word of the LORD came to me, saying, ¹⁵ "Son of man, your brethren, your relatives, your countrymen, and all the house of Israel in its entirety, *are* those about whom the inhabitants of Jerusalem have said, 'Get far away from

A Better Recipe

During World War II, Marie Callender was making potato salad and cole slaw in a Los Angeles delicatessen. Then one day her boss asked her to make pies for the lunch crowd. It was the start of a new career!

At first she baked her pies at home, dragging hundred-pound flour sacks into her kitchen. Then in 1948, she and her husband sold their car and bought a Quonset hut, an oven, and a refrigerator — her first commercial kitchen.

She baked the pies, then her husband delivered them to restaurants in the area. She began by baking about ten pies a day. Two years later, she was baking more than two hundred pies a day. Sixteen years later, several thousand were coming out of the oven each day.

Marie and her husband opened their first pie shop in Orange County in 1964. They barely broke even that year. Over time her husband, and later her son, guided the business to a soaring success. Other items were added to the menu, and by 1986, Ramada Inns, Inc. bought the family business — 115 restaurants at that time — from Marie and her son for $90 million.

If a young mother with a rolling pin and sack of flour could give rise to an empire, think what other opportunities await those who will respond with hard work and a "better recipe."

> And we desire that each one of you show the same diligence to the full assurance of hope until the end.
>
> *Hebrews 6:11*

———⚓———

the LORD; this land has been given to us as a possession.' ¹⁶ Therefore say, 'Thus says the Lord GOD: "Although I have cast them far off among the Gentiles, and although I have scattered them among the countries, yet I shall be a little sanctuary for them in the countries where they have gone." ' ¹⁷ Therefore say, 'Thus says the Lord GOD: "I will gather you from the peoples, assemble you from the countries where you have been scattered, and I will give you the land of Israel." ' ¹⁸ And they will go there, and they will take away all its detestable things and all its abominations from there. ¹⁹ Then I will give them one heart, and I will put a new spirit within them, and take the stony heart out of their flesh, and give them a heart of flesh, ²⁰ that they may walk in My statutes and keep My judgments and do them; and they shall be My people, and I will be their God. ²¹ But *as for those* whose hearts follow the desire for their detestable things and their abominations, I will recompense their deeds on their own heads," says the Lord GOD.

²² So the cherubim lifted up their wings, with the wheels beside them, and the glory of the God of Israel *was* high above them. ²³ And the glory of the LORD went up from the midst of the city and stood on the mountain, which *is* on the east side of the city.

²⁴ Then the Spirit took me up and brought me in a vision by the Spirit of God into Chaldea, to those in captivity. And the vision that I had seen went up from me. ²⁵ So I spoke to those in captivity of all the things the LORD had shown me.

12 Now the word of the LORD came to me, saying: ² "Son of man, you dwell in the midst of a rebellious house, which has eyes to see but does not see, and ears to hear but does not hear; for they *are* a rebellious house.

³ "Therefore, son of man, prepare your belongings for captivity, and go into captivity by day in their sight. You shall go from your place into captivity to another place in their sight. It may be that they will consider, though they *are* a rebellious house. ⁴ By day you shall bring out your belongings in their sight, as though going

into captivity; and at evening you shall go in their sight, like those who go into captivity. ⁵ Dig through the wall in their sight, and carry your belongings out through it. ⁶ In their sight you shall bear *them* on *your* shoulders *and* carry *them* out at twilight; you shall cover your face, so that you cannot see the ground, for I have made you a sign to the house of Israel."

⁷ So I did as I was commanded. I brought out my belongings by day, as though going into captivity, and at evening I dug through the wall with my hand. I brought *them* out at twilight, *and* I bore *them* on *my* shoulder in their sight.

⁸ And in the morning the word of the LORD came to me, saying, ⁹ "Son of man, has not the house of Israel, the rebellious house, said to you, 'What are you doing?' ¹⁰ Say to them, 'Thus says the Lord GOD: "This burden *concerns* the prince in Jerusalem and all the house of Israel who are among them." ' ¹¹ Say, 'I *am* a sign to you. As I have done, so shall it be done to them; they shall be carried away into captivity.' ¹² And the prince who *is* among them shall bear *his* belongings on *his* shoulder at twilight and go out. They shall dig through the wall to carry *them* out through it. He shall cover his face, so that he cannot see the ground with *his* eyes. ¹³ I will also spread My net over him, and he shall be caught in My snare. I will bring him to Babylon, *to* the land of the Chaldeans; yet he shall not see it, though he shall die there. ¹⁴ I will scatter to every wind all who *are* around him to help him, and all his troops; and I will draw out the sword after them.

¹⁵ "Then they shall know that I *am* the LORD, when I scatter them among the nations and disperse them throughout the countries. ¹⁶ But I will spare a few of their men from the sword, from famine, and from pestilence, that they may declare all their abominations among the Gentiles wherever they go. Then they shall know that I *am* the LORD."

¹⁷ Moreover the word of the LORD came to me, saying, ¹⁸ "Son of man, eat your bread with quaking, and drink your water with trembling and anxiety. ¹⁹ And say to the people of the land, 'Thus says the Lord GOD to the inhabitants of Jerusalem *and* to the land of Israel: "They shall

eat their bread with anxiety, and drink their water with dread, so that her land may be emptied of all who are in it, because of the violence of all those who dwell in it. [20] Then the cities that are inhabited shall be laid waste, and the land shall become desolate; and you shall know that I *am* the LORD." ' "

[21] And the word of the LORD came to me, saying, [22] "Son of man, what *is* this proverb *that* you *people* have about the land of Israel, which says, 'The days are prolonged, and every vision fails'? [23] Tell them therefore, 'Thus says the Lord GOD: "I will lay this proverb to rest, and they shall no more use it as a proverb in Israel." But say to them, "The days are at hand, and the fulfillment of every vision. [24] For no more shall there be any false vision or flattering divination within the house of Israel. [25] For I *am* the LORD. I speak, and the word which I speak will come to pass; it will no more be postponed; for in your days, O rebellious house, I will say the word and perform it," says the Lord GOD.' "

[26] Again the word of the LORD came to me, saying, [27] "Son of man, look, the house of Israel is saying, 'The vision that he sees *is* for many days *from now,* and he prophesies of times far off.' [28] Therefore say to them, 'Thus says the Lord GOD: "None of My words will be postponed any more, but the word which I speak will be done," says the Lord GOD.' "

~ PSALM 122:1–5 ~

[1] I was glad when they said to me,
    "Let us go into the house of the
        LORD."
[2] Our feet have been standing
    Within your gates, O Jerusalem!

[3] Jerusalem is built
    As a city that is compact together,
[4] Where the tribes go up,
    The tribes of the LORD,
    To the Testimony of Israel,
    To give thanks to the name of the
        LORD.
[5] For thrones are set there for
        judgment,
    The thrones of the house of David.

~ PROVERBS 28:17, 18 ~

[17] A man burdened with bloodshed will
        flee into a pit;
    Let no one help him.

[18] Whoever walks blamelessly will be
        saved,
    But *he who is* perverse *in his* ways
        will suddenly fall.

~ HEBREWS 6:1–20 ~

Therefore, leaving the discussion of the elementary *principles* of Christ, let us go on to perfection, not laying again the foundation of repentance from dead works and of faith toward God, [2] of the doctrine of baptisms, of laying on of hands, of resurrection of the dead, and of eternal judgment. [3] And this we will do if God permits.

[4] For *it is* impossible for those who were once enlightened, and have tasted the heavenly gift, and have become partakers of the Holy Spirit, [5] and have tasted the good word of God and the powers of the age to come, [6] if they fall away, to renew them again to repentance, since they crucify again for themselves the Son of God, and put *Him* to an open shame.

[7] For the earth which drinks in the rain that often comes upon it, and bears herbs useful for those by whom it is cultivated, receives blessing from God; [8] but if it bears thorns and briers, *it is* rejected and near to being cursed, whose end *is* to be burned.

[9] But, beloved, we are confident of better things concerning you, yes, things that accompany salvation, though we speak in this manner. [10] For God *is* not unjust to forget your work and labor of love which you have shown toward His name, *in that* you have ministered to the saints, and do minister. [11] And we desire that each one of you show the same diligence to the full assurance of hope until the end, [12] that you do not become sluggish, but imitate those who through faith and patience inherit the promises.

[13] For when God made a promise to Abraham, because He could swear by no

one greater, He swore by Himself, ¹⁴ saying, "Surely blessing I will bless you, and multiplying I will multiply you." ¹⁵ And so, after he had patiently endured, he obtained the promise. ¹⁶ For men indeed swear by the greater, and an oath for confirmation *is* for them an end of all dispute. ¹⁷ Thus God, determining to show more abundantly to the heirs of promise the immutability of His counsel, confirmed *it* by an oath, ¹⁸ that by two immutable things, in which it *is* impossible for God to lie, we might have strong consolation, who have fled for refuge to lay hold of the hope set before *us*.

¹⁹ This *hope* we have as an anchor of the soul, both sure and steadfast, and which enters the Presence *behind* the veil, ²⁰ where the forerunner has entered for us, *even* Jesus, having become High Priest forever according to the order of Melchizedek.

READING 315 · NOVEMBER 11

~ EZEKIEL 13:1—14:23 ~

And the word of the LORD came to me, saying, ² "Son of man, prophesy against the prophets of Israel who prophesy, and say to those who prophesy out of their own heart, 'Hear the word of the LORD!' "

³ Thus says the Lord GOD: "Woe to the foolish prophets, who follow their own spirit and have seen nothing! ⁴ O Israel, your prophets are like foxes in the deserts. ⁵ You have not gone up into the gaps to build a wall for the house of Israel to stand in battle on the day of the LORD. ⁶ They have envisioned futility and false divination, saying, 'Thus says the LORD!' But the LORD has not sent them; yet they hope that the word may be confirmed. ⁷ Have you not seen a futile vision, and have you not spoken false divination? You say, 'The LORD says,' but I have not spoken."

⁸ Therefore thus says the Lord GOD: "Because you have spoken nonsense and envisioned lies, therefore I *am* indeed against you," says the Lord GOD. ⁹ "My hand will be against the prophets who envision futility and who divine lies; they shall not be in the assembly of My people, nor be written in the record of the house of Israel, nor shall they enter into the land of Israel. Then you shall know that I *am* the Lord GOD.

¹⁰ "Because, indeed, because they have seduced My people, saying, 'Peace!' when *there is* no peace—and one builds a wall, and they plaster it with untempered *mortar*— ¹¹ say to those who plaster *it* with untempered *mortar,* that it will fall. There will be flooding rain, and you, O great

hailstones, shall fall; and a stormy wind shall tear *it* down. ¹² Surely, when the wall has fallen, will it not be said to you, 'Where *is* the mortar with which you plastered *it?*' "

¹³ Therefore thus says the Lord GOD: "I will cause a stormy wind to break forth in My fury; and there shall be a flooding rain in My anger, and great hailstones in fury to consume *it*. ¹⁴ So I will break down the wall you have plastered with untempered *mortar,* and bring it down to the ground, so that its foundation will be uncovered; it will fall, and you shall be consumed in the midst of it. Then you shall know that I *am* the LORD.

¹⁵ "Thus will I accomplish My wrath on the wall and on those who have plastered it with untempered *mortar;* and I will say to you, 'The wall *is* no *more,* nor those who plastered it, ¹⁶ *that is,* the prophets of Israel who prophesy concerning Jerusalem, and who see visions of peace for her when *there is* no peace,' " says the Lord GOD.

¹⁷ "Likewise, son of man, set your face against the daughters of your people, who prophesy out of their own heart; prophesy against them, ¹⁸ and say, 'Thus says the Lord GOD: "Woe to the *women* who sew *magic* charms on their sleeves and make veils for the heads of people of every height to hunt souls! Will you hunt the souls of My people, and keep yourselves alive? ¹⁹ And will you profane Me among My people for handfuls of barley and for pieces of bread, killing people who should not die, and keeping people alive who

The Source of Power

One day in Lucerne, Switzerland, a man rode to the summit of Mount Pilatus in a hydraulically-powered cable car. As the car rose along the side of the mountain, he marveled at the wonders of modern engineering. A little more than halfway to the summit, he noticed a beautiful waterfall splashing down the mountainside.

What a contrast! he thought. In one glance, he had a comparison of the primitive power of nature and the advanced power of technology. Then it occurred to him. The waterfall was not in contrast to the cable car. Rather, it was a complement. It was the source of the hydraulic power — it was the force of that very water that was driving the cable car.

So it is with prayer. The power that takes us up to God is the same power that comes from God. He is the One Who:
- calls us to pray,
- enables us to pray,
- energizes our prayers with His Spirit,
- and gives us the capacity to receive His answers.

When we pray in the name of Jesus, the Lord is in our prayers as much as He is in the answers.

> Therefore He is also able to save to the uttermost those who come to God through Him, since He always lives to make intercession for them.
>
> *Hebrews 7:25*

should not live, by your lying to My people who listen to lies?"

²⁰ 'Therefore thus says the Lord GOD: "Behold, I *am* against your *magic* charms by which you hunt souls there like birds. I will tear them from your arms, and let the souls go, the souls you hunt like birds. ²¹ I will also tear off your veils and deliver My people out of your hand, and they shall no longer be as prey in your hand. Then you shall know that I *am* the LORD. ²² "Because with lies you have made the heart of the righteous sad, whom I have not made sad; and you have strengthened the hands of the wicked, so that he does not turn from his wicked way to save his life. ²³ Therefore you shall no longer envision futility nor practice divination; for I will deliver My people out of your hand, and you shall know that I *am* the LORD." ' "

14 Now some of the elders of Israel came to me and sat before me. ² And the word of the LORD came to me, saying, ³ "Son of man, these men have set up their idols in their hearts, and put before them that which causes them to stumble into iniquity. Should I let Myself be inquired of at all by them?

⁴ "Therefore speak to them, and say to them, 'Thus says the Lord GOD: "Everyone of the house of Israel who sets up his idols in his heart, and puts before him what causes him to stumble into iniquity, and then comes to the prophet, I the LORD will answer him who comes, according to the multitude of his idols, ⁵ that I may seize the house of Israel by their heart, because they are all estranged from Me by their idols." '

⁶ "Therefore say to the house of Israel, 'Thus says the Lord GOD: "Repent, turn away from your idols, and turn your faces away from all your abominations. ⁷ For anyone of the house of Israel, or of the strangers who dwell in Israel, who separates himself from Me and sets up his idols in his heart and puts before him what causes him to stumble into iniquity, then comes to a prophet to inquire of him concerning Me, I the LORD will answer him by Myself. ⁸ I will set My face against that man and make him a sign and a proverb, and I will cut him off from the midst of

My people. Then you shall know that I *am* the LORD.

⁹ "And if the prophet is induced to speak anything, I the LORD have induced that prophet, and I will stretch out My hand against him and destroy him from among My people Israel. ¹⁰ And they shall bear their iniquity; the punishment of the prophet shall be the same as the punishment of the one who inquired, ¹¹ that the house of Israel may no longer stray from Me, nor be profaned anymore with all their transgressions, but that they may be My people and I may be their God," says the Lord GOD.' "

¹² The word of the LORD came again to me, saying: ¹³ "Son of man, when a land sins against Me by persistent unfaithfulness, I will stretch out My hand against it; I will cut off its supply of bread, send famine on it, and cut off man and beast from it. ¹⁴ Even *if* these three men, Noah, Daniel, and Job, were in it, they would deliver *only* themselves by their righteousness," says the Lord GOD.

¹⁵ "If I cause wild beasts to pass through the land, and they empty it, and make it so desolate that no man may pass through because of the beasts, ¹⁶ *even though* these three men *were* in it, *as* I live," says the Lord GOD, "they would deliver neither sons nor daughters; only they would be delivered, and the land would be desolate.

¹⁷ "Or *if* I bring a sword on that land, and say, 'Sword, go through the land,' and I cut off man and beast from it, ¹⁸ even *though* these three men *were* in it, *as* I live," says the Lord GOD, "they would deliver neither sons nor daughters, but only they themselves would be delivered.

¹⁹ "Or *if* I send a pestilence into that land and pour out My fury on it in blood, and cut off from it man and beast, ²⁰ even *though* Noah, Daniel, and Job *were* in it, *as* I live," says the Lord GOD, "they would deliver neither son nor daughter; they would deliver *only* themselves by their righteousness."

²¹ For thus says the Lord GOD: "How much more it shall be when I send My four severe judgments on Jerusalem—the sword and famine and wild beasts and pestilence—to cut off man and beast from it? ²² Yet behold, there shall be left in it a

remnant who will be brought out, *both* sons and daughters; surely they will come out to you, and you will see their ways and their doings. Then you will be comforted concerning the disaster that I have brought upon Jerusalem, all that I have brought upon it. 23 And they will comfort you, when you see their ways and their doings; and you shall know that I have done nothing without cause that I have done in it," says the Lord GOD.

～ PSALM 122:6–9 ～

6 Pray for the peace of Jerusalem:
"May they prosper who love you.
7 Peace be within your walls,
Prosperity within your palaces."
8 For the sake of my brethren and companions,
I will now say, "Peace *be* within you."
9 Because of the house of the LORD our God
I will seek your good.

～ PROVERBS 28:19 ～

19 He who tills his land will have plenty of bread,
But he who follows frivolity will have poverty enough!

～ HEBREWS 7:1–28 ～

For this Melchizedek, king of Salem, priest of the Most High God, who met Abraham returning from the slaughter of the kings and blessed him, 2 to whom also Abraham gave a tenth part of all, first being translated "king of righteousness," and then also king of Salem, meaning "king of peace," 3 without father, without mother, without genealogy, having neither beginning of days nor end of life, but made like the Son of God, remains a priest continually.

4 Now consider how great this man *was,* to whom even the patriarch Abraham gave a tenth of the spoils. 5 And indeed those who are of the sons of Levi, who receive the priesthood, have a commandment to receive tithes from the people according to the law, that is, from their brethren, though they have come from the loins of Abraham; 6 but he whose genealogy is not derived from them received tithes from Abraham and blessed him who had the promises. 7 Now beyond all contradiction the lesser is blessed by the better. 8 Here mortal men receive tithes, but there he *receives them,* of whom it is witnessed that he lives. 9 Even Levi, who receives tithes, paid tithes through Abraham, so to speak, 10 for he was still in the loins of his father when Melchizedek met him.

11 Therefore, if perfection were through the Levitical priesthood (for under it the people received the law), what further need *was there* that another priest should rise according to the order of Melchizedek, and not be called according to the order of Aaron? 12 For the priesthood being changed, of necessity there is also a change of the law. 13 For He of whom these things are spoken belongs to another tribe, from which no man has officiated at the altar.

14 For *it is* evident that our Lord arose from Judah, of which tribe Moses spoke nothing concerning priesthood. 15 And it is yet far more evident if, in the likeness of Melchizedek, there arises another priest 16 who has come, not according to the law of a fleshly commandment, but according to the power of an endless life. 17 For He testifies:

"You *are* a priest forever
According to the order of
Melchizedek."

18 For on the one hand there is an annulling of the former commandment because of its weakness and unprofitableness, 19 for the law made nothing perfect; on the other hand, there is the bringing in of a better hope, through which we draw near to God.

20 And inasmuch as He was not made priest without an oath 21(for they have become priests without an oath, but He with an oath by Him who said to Him:

"The LORD has sworn
And will not relent,
'You *are* a priest forever
According to the order of
Melchizedek' "),

²² by so much more Jesus has become a surety of a better covenant.

²³ Also there were many priests, because they were prevented by death from continuing. ²⁴ But He, because He continues forever, has an unchangeable priesthood. ²⁵ Therefore He is also able to save to the uttermost those who come to God through Him, since He always lives to make intercession for them.

²⁶ For such a High Priest was fitting for us, *who is* holy, harmless, undefiled, separate from sinners, and has become higher than the heavens; ²⁷ who does not need daily, as those high priests, to offer up sacrifices, first for His own sins and then for the people's, for this He did once for all when He offered up Himself. ²⁸ For the law appoints as high priests men who have weakness, but the word of the oath, which came after the law, *appoints* the Son who has been perfected forever.

READING 316 · NOVEMBER 12

~ EZEKIEL 15:1—16:63 ~

Then the word of the LORD came to me, saying: ² "Son of man, how is the wood of the vine *better* than any other wood, the vine branch which is among the trees of the forest? ³ Is wood taken from it to make any object? Or can *men* make a peg from it to hang any vessel on? ⁴ Instead, it is thrown into the fire for fuel; the fire devours both ends of it, and its middle is burned. Is it useful for *any* work? ⁵ Indeed, when it was whole, no object could be made from it. How much less will it be useful for *any* work when the fire has devoured it, and it is burned?

⁶ "Therefore thus says the Lord GOD: 'Like the wood of the vine among the trees of the forest, which I have given to the fire for fuel, so I will give up the inhabitants of Jerusalem; ⁷ and I will set My face against them. They will go out from *one* fire, but *another* fire shall devour them. Then you shall know that I *am* the LORD, when I set My face against them. ⁸ Thus I will make the land desolate, because they have persisted in unfaithfulness,' says the Lord GOD."

16 Again the word of the LORD came to me, saying, ² "Son of man, cause Jerusalem to know her abominations, ³ and say, 'Thus says the Lord GOD to Jerusalem: "Your birth and your nativity *are* from the land of Canaan; your father *was* an Amorite and your mother a Hittite. ⁴ *As for* your nativity, on the day you were born your navel cord was not cut, nor were you washed in water to cleanse *you*; you were not rubbed with salt nor wrapped in swaddling cloths. ⁵ No eye pitied you, to do any of these things for you, to have compassion on you; but you were thrown out into the open field, when you yourself were loathed on the day you were born.

⁶ "And when I passed by you and saw you struggling in your own blood, I said to you in your blood, 'Live!' Yes, I said to you in your blood, 'Live!' ⁷ I made you thrive like a plant in the field; and you grew, matured, and became very beautiful. *Your* breasts were formed, *your* hair grew, but you *were* naked and bare.

⁸ "When I passed by you again and looked upon you, indeed your time *was* the time of love; so I spread My wing over you and covered your nakedness. Yes, I swore an oath to you and entered into a covenant with you, and you became Mine," says the Lord GOD.

⁹ "Then I washed you in water; yes, I thoroughly washed off your blood, and I anointed you with oil. ¹⁰ I clothed you in embroidered cloth and gave you sandals of badger skin; I clothed you with fine linen and covered you with silk. ¹¹ I adorned you with ornaments, put bracelets on your wrists, and a chain on your neck. ¹² And I put a jewel in your nose, earrings in your ears, and a beautiful crown on your head. ¹³ Thus you were adorned with gold and silver, and your clothing *was of* fine linen, silk, and embroidered cloth. You ate *pastry of* fine flour, honey, and oil. You were exceedingly beautiful, and succeeded to royalty.

Going the Extra Mile

An insurance salesman in Nova Scotia was told by his boss that he and other agents were not assertive enough — that they were not as outgoing as they needed to be in order to score sales. Moments after this pep talk, when he returned to his office the insurance salesman glanced out his window and had an idea.

Outside his 17th-floor window he saw some window washers working from a scaffold. He quickly wrote a note and held it up to the window for them to see. The note asked them if they'd be interested in life, accident, or disability insurance.

The men responded, jokingly, that they couldn't stop what they were doing to talk to him, but if he wanted to join them out on the scaffold, they'd be willing to listen to him while they worked. The insurance salesman took them up on their offer! Using an extra cable on the roof, he lowered himself onto their scaffold. During the course of their conversation, he sold one of the men fifty thousand dollars worth of life insurance!

Sometimes you have to go to tough places and into tough situations — the "extra mile" — to succeed. Challenge yourself today. Don't let a good opportunity pass you by, even if it seems extraordinarily difficult. With God, all things are possible!

¹⁴ Your fame went out among the nations because of your beauty, for it *was* perfect through My splendor which I had bestowed on you," says the Lord GOD.

¹⁵ "But you trusted in your own beauty, played the harlot because of your fame, and poured out your harlotry on everyone passing by who *would have* it. ¹⁶ You took some of your garments and adorned multicolored high places for yourself, and played the harlot on them. *Such* things should not happen, nor be. ¹⁷ You have also taken your beautiful jewelry from My gold and My silver, which I had given you, and made for yourself male images and played the harlot with them. ¹⁸ You took your embroidered garments and covered them, and you set My oil and My incense before them. ¹⁹ Also My food which I gave you—the pastry of fine flour, oil, and honey *which* I fed you—you set it before them as sweet incense; and *so* it was," says the Lord GOD.

²⁰ "Moreover you took your sons and your daughters, whom you bore to Me, and these you sacrificed to them to be devoured. *Were* your *acts* of harlotry a small matter, ²¹ that you have slain My children and offered them up to them by causing them to pass through *the fire?* ²² And in all your abominations and acts of harlotry you did not remember the days of your youth, when you were naked and bare, struggling in your blood.

²³ "Then it was so, after all your wickedness—'Woe, woe to you!' says the Lord GOD— ²⁴ *that* you also built for yourself a shrine, and made a high place for yourself in every street. ²⁵ You built your high places at the head of every road, and made your beauty to be abhorred. You offered yourself to everyone who passed by, and multiplied your acts of harlotry. ²⁶ You also committed harlotry with the Egyptians, your very fleshly neighbors, and increased your acts of harlotry to provoke Me to anger.

²⁷ "Behold, therefore, I stretched out My hand against you, diminished your allotment, and gave you up to the will of those who hate you, the daughters of the Philistines, who were ashamed of your lewd behavior. ²⁸ You also played the harlot with the Assyrians, because you were insatiable; indeed you played the harlot with them and still were not satisfied. ²⁹ Moreover you multiplied your acts of harlotry as far as the land of the trader, Chaldea; and even then you were not satisfied.

³⁰ "How degenerate is your heart!" says the Lord GOD, "seeing you do all these *things,* the deeds of a brazen harlot. ³¹ "You erected your shrine at the head of every road, and built your high place in every street. Yet you were not like a harlot, because you scorned payment. ³² *You are* an adulterous wife, *who* takes strangers instead of her husband. ³³ Men make payment to all harlots, but you made your payments to all your lovers, and hired them to come to you from all around for your harlotry. ³⁴ You are the opposite of *other* women in your harlotry, because no one solicited you to be a harlot. In that you gave payment but no payment was given you, therefore you are the opposite."

³⁵ 'Now then, O harlot, hear the word of the LORD! ³⁶ Thus says the Lord GOD: "Because your filthiness was poured out and your nakedness uncovered in your harlotry with your lovers, and with all your abominable idols, and because of the blood of your children which you gave to them, ³⁷ surely, therefore, I will gather all your lovers with whom you took pleasure, all those you loved, *and* all those you hated; I will gather them from all around against you and will uncover your nakedness to them, that they may see all your nakedness. ³⁸ And I will judge you as women who break wedlock or shed blood are judged; I will bring blood upon you in fury and jealousy. ³⁹ I will also give you into their hand, and they shall throw down your shrines and break down your high places. They shall also strip you of your clothes, take your beautiful jewelry, and leave you naked and bare.

⁴⁰ "They shall also bring up an assembly against you, and they shall stone you with stones and thrust you through with their swords. ⁴¹ They shall burn your houses with fire, and execute judgments on you in the sight of many women; and I will make you cease playing the harlot, and you shall no longer hire lovers. ⁴² So I will lay to rest My fury toward you, and My jealousy shall depart from you. I will

be quiet, and be angry no more. ⁴³ Because you did not remember the days of your youth, but agitated Me with all these *things,* surely I will also recompense your deeds on *your own* head," says the Lord GOD. "And you shall not commit lewdness in addition to all your abominations.

⁴⁴ "Indeed everyone who quotes proverbs will use *this* proverb against you: 'Like mother, like daughter!' ⁴⁵ You *are* your mother's daughter, loathing husband and children; and you *are* the sister of your sisters, who loathed their husbands and children; your mother *was* a Hittite and your father an Amorite.

⁴⁶ "Your elder sister *is* Samaria, who dwells with her daughters to the north of you; and your younger sister, who dwells to the south of you, *is* Sodom and her daughters. ⁴⁷ You did not walk in their ways nor act according to their abominations; but, as *if that were* too little, you became more corrupt than they in all your ways.

⁴⁸ "*As* I live," says the Lord GOD, "neither your sister Sodom nor her daughters have done as you and your daughters have done. ⁴⁹ Look, this was the iniquity of your sister Sodom: She and her daughter had pride, fullness of food, and abundance of idleness; neither did she strengthen the hand of the poor and needy. ⁵⁰ And they were haughty and committed abomination before Me; therefore I took them away as I saw *fit.*

⁵¹ "Samaria did not commit half of your sins; but you have multiplied your abominations more than they, and have justified your sisters by all the abominations which you have done. ⁵² You who judged your sisters, bear your own shame also, because the sins which you committed were more abominable than theirs; they are more righteous than you. Yes, be disgraced also, and bear your own shame, because you justified your sisters.

⁵³ "When I bring back their captives, the captives of Sodom and her daughters, and the captives of Samaria and her daughters, then *I will also bring back* the captives of your captivity among them, ⁵⁴ that you may bear your own shame and be disgraced by all that you did when you comforted them. ⁵⁵ When your sisters, Sodom and her daughters, return to their former state, and Samaria and her daughters return to their former state, then you and your daughters will return to your former state. ⁵⁶ For your sister Sodom was not a byword in your mouth in the days of your pride, ⁵⁷ before your wickedness was uncovered. It was like the time of the reproach of the daughters of Syria and all *those* around her, and of the daughters of the Philistines, who despise you everywhere. ⁵⁸ You have paid for your lewdness and your abominations," says the LORD. ⁵⁹ For thus says the Lord GOD: "I will deal with you as you have done, who despised the oath by breaking the covenant.

⁶⁰ "Nevertheless I will remember My covenant with you in the days of your youth, and I will establish an everlasting covenant with you. ⁶¹ Then you will remember your ways and be ashamed, when you receive your older and your younger sisters; for I will give them to you for daughters, but not because of My covenant with you. ⁶² And I will establish My covenant with you. Then you shall know that I *am* the LORD, ⁶³ that you may remember and be ashamed, and never open your mouth anymore because of your shame, when I provide you an atonement for all you have done," says the Lord GOD.' "

～ PSALM 123:1–4 ～

1 Unto You I lift up my eyes,
   O You who dwell in the heavens.
2 Behold, as the eyes of servants *look*
      to the hand of their masters,
   As the eyes of a maid to the hand of
      her mistress,
   So our eyes *look* to the LORD our
      God,
   Until He has mercy on us.

3 Have mercy on us, O LORD, have
      mercy on us!
   For we are exceedingly filled with
      contempt.
4 Our soul is exceedingly filled
   With the scorn of those who are at
      ease,
   With the contempt of the proud.

~ PROVERBS 28:20 ~

20 A faithful man will abound with
    blessings,
    But he who hastens to be rich will
      not go unpunished.

~ HEBREWS 8:1–13 ~

Now *this is* the main point of the things
we are saying: We have such a High Priest,
who is seated at the right hand of the
throne of the Majesty in the heavens, ² a
Minister of the sanctuary and of the true
tabernacle which the Lord erected, and
not man.

³ For every high priest is appointed to
offer both gifts and sacrifices. Therefore
it is necessary that this One also have
something to offer. ⁴ For if He were on
earth, He would not be a priest, since there
are priests who offer the gifts according
to the law; ⁵ who serve the copy and
shadow of the heavenly things, as Moses
was divinely instructed when he was about
to make the tabernacle. For He said, "See
that you make all things according to the
pattern shown you on the mountain."
⁶ But now He has obtained a more excellent ministry, inasmuch as He is also

Mediator of a better covenant, which was
established on better promises.

⁷ For if that first *covenant* had been
faultless, then no place would have
been sought for a second. ⁸ Because finding fault with them, He says: "Behold, the
days are coming, says the LORD, when I
will make a new covenant with the house
of Israel and with the house of Judah—
⁹ not according to the covenant that I
made with their fathers in the day when
I took them by the hand to lead them out
of the land of Egypt; because they did not
continue in My covenant, and I disregarded them, says the LORD. ¹⁰ For this *is*
the covenant that I will make with the
house of Israel after those days, says
the LORD: I will put My laws in their mind
and write them on their hearts; and I will
be their God, and they shall be My people.
¹¹ None of them shall teach his neighbor,
and none his brother, saying, 'Know the
LORD,' for all shall know Me, from the
least of them to the greatest of them. ¹² For
I will be merciful to their unrighteousness,
and their sins and their lawless deeds I
will remember no more."

¹³ In that He says, "A new *covenant,*"
He has made the first obsolete. Now what
is becoming obsolete and growing old is
ready to vanish away.

READING 317 · NOVEMBER 13

~ EZEKIEL 17:1—18:32 ~

And the word of the LORD came to
me, saying, ² "Son of man, pose a
riddle, and speak a parable to the
house of Israel, ³ and say, 'Thus says
the Lord GOD:

"A great eagle with large wings and
    long pinions,
  Full of feathers of various colors,
  Came to Lebanon
  And took from the cedar the
    highest branch.
⁴ He cropped off its topmost young
    twig
  And carried it to a land of trade;
  He set it in a city of merchants.
⁵ Then he took some of the seed of
    the land

  And planted it in a fertile field;
  He placed *it* by abundant waters
  And set it like a willow tree.
⁶ And it grew and became a
    spreading vine of low stature;
  Its branches turned toward him,
  But its roots were under it.
  So it became a vine,
  Brought forth branches,
  And put forth shoots.

⁷ "But there was another great eagle
    with large wings and many
    feathers;
  And behold, this vine bent its
    roots toward him,
  And stretched its branches toward
    him,

No One to Applaud

Bill Galston was at the peak of his career when he resigned as a domestic policy adviser to President Clinton to return to teaching at the University of Maryland. Galston's reason: "To strike a new balance between work and family."

Galston had worked more than a decade on the ideas he hoped to see come to pass. At the White House, he helped in forming the National Campaign Against Teen Pregnancy, planning the National Service Program, and working on education reform and Head Start legislation. He consulted widely with administration officials, had an excellent reputation, and loved his job. He tried integrating time with his son, Ezra, into his schedule — even bringing him to his White House office in the evening — but Galston was continually hounded by the fact that he often came home too tired to spend quality time with his son. He struggled with the contradiction between his "Putting Children First" theme for welfare and the reality in his own home. What triggered his resignation? His son Ezra sent him a note: "Baseball's not fun when there's no one there to applaud you."

The choices you make not only impact your future, but the future of your children. Make sure you have their best in mind in your decisions today.

From the garden terrace where it
    had been planted,
That he might water it.
8   It was planted in good soil by
    many waters,
To bring forth branches, bear fruit,
And become a majestic vine." '

9 "Say, 'Thus says the Lord GOD:

"Will it thrive?
Will he not pull up its roots,
Cut off its fruit,
And leave it to wither?
All of its spring leaves will wither,
And no great power or many
    people
Will be needed to pluck it up by
    its roots.
10 Behold, *it is* planted,
Will it thrive?
Will it not utterly wither when the
    east wind touches it?
It will wither in the garden terrace
    where it grew." ' "

11 Moreover the word of the LORD
came to me, saying, 12 "Say now to the
rebellious house: 'Do you not know what
these *things mean?*' Tell *them,* 'Indeed the
king of Babylon went to Jerusalem and
took its king and princes, and led them
with him to Babylon. 13 And he took the
king's offspring, made a covenant with
him, and put him under oath. He also
took away the mighty of the land, 14 that
the kingdom might be brought low and
not lift itself up, *but* that by keeping his
covenant it might stand. 15 But he rebelled
against him by sending his ambassadors
to Egypt, that they might give him horses
and many people. Will he prosper? Will
he who does such *things* escape? Can he
break a covenant and still be delivered?
16 '*As* I live,' says the Lord GOD, 'surely
in the place *where* the king *dwells* who
made him king, whose oath he despised
and whose covenant he broke—with him
in the midst of Babylon he shall die. 17 Nor
will Pharaoh with *his* mighty army and
great company do anything in the war,
when they heap up a siege mound and
build a wall to cut off many persons.
18 Since he despised the oath by breaking
the covenant, and in fact gave his hand

and still did all these *things,* he shall not
escape.' "
19 Therefore thus says the Lord GOD:
"*As* I live, surely My oath which he despised, and My covenant which he broke,
I will recompense on his own head. 20 I
will spread My net over him, and he shall
be taken in My snare. I will bring him to
Babylon and try him there for the treason
which he committed against Me. 21 All his
fugitives with all his troops shall fall by
the sword, and those who remain shall be
scattered to every wind; and you shall
know that I, the LORD, have spoken."
22 Thus says the Lord GOD: "I will take
also *one* of the highest branches of the
high cedar and set *it* out. I will crop off
from the topmost of its young twigs a tender one, and will plant *it* on a high and
prominent mountain. 23 On the mountain
height of Israel I will plant it; and it will
bring forth boughs, and bear fruit, and be
a majestic cedar. Under it will dwell birds
of every sort; in the shadow of its branches
they will dwell. 24 And all the trees of the
field shall know that I, the LORD, have
brought down the high tree and exalted
the low tree, dried up the green tree and
made the dry tree flourish; I, the LORD,
have spoken and have done *it.*"

18

The word of the LORD came to me
again, saying, 2 "What do you mean when
you use this proverb concerning the land
of Israel, saying:

'The fathers have eaten sour
    grapes,
And the children's teeth are set on
    edge'?

3 "*As* I live," says the Lord GOD, "you
shall no longer use this proverb in Israel.

4 "Behold, all souls are Mine;
The soul of the father
As well as the soul of the son is
    Mine;
The soul who sins shall die.
5 But if a man is just
And does what is lawful and right;
6 If he has not eaten on the
    mountains,
Nor lifted up his eyes to the idols
    of the house of Israel,

Nor defiled his neighbor's wife,
Nor approached a woman during
   her impurity;
7 If he has not oppressed anyone,
But has restored to the debtor his
   pledge;
Has robbed no one by violence,
But has given his bread to the
   hungry
And covered the naked with
   clothing;
8 If he has not exacted usury
Nor taken any increase,
But has withdrawn his hand from
   iniquity
And executed true judgment
   between man and man;
9 *If* he has walked in My statutes
And kept My judgments
   faithfully—
He *is* just;
He shall surely live!"
Says the Lord GOD.

10 "If he begets a son *who is* a robber
Or a shedder of blood,
Who does any of these things
11 And does none of those *duties,*
But has eaten on the mountains
Or defiled his neighbor's wife;
12 If he has oppressed the poor and
   needy,
Robbed by violence,
Not restored the pledge,
Lifted his eyes to the idols,
Or committed abomination;
13 If he has exacted usury
Or taken increase—
Shall he then live?
He shall not live!
If he has done any of these
   abominations,
He shall surely die;
His blood shall be upon him.

14 "*If,* however, he begets a son
Who sees all the sins which his
   father has done,
And considers but does not do
   likewise;
15 *Who* has not eaten on the
   mountains,
Nor lifted his eyes to the idols of
   the house of Israel,
Nor defiled his neighbor's wife;

16 Has not oppressed anyone,
Nor withheld a pledge,
Nor robbed by violence,
But has given his bread to the
   hungry
And covered the naked with
   clothing;
17 *Who* has withdrawn his hand from
   the poor
And not received usury or
   increase,
But has executed My judgments
And walked in My statutes—
He shall not die for the iniquity of
   his father;
He shall surely live!

18 "*As for* his father,
Because he cruelly oppressed,
Robbed his brother by violence,
And did what *is* not good among
   his people,
Behold, he shall die for his
   iniquity.

19 "Yet you say, 'Why should the son not bear the guilt of the father?' Because the son has done what is lawful and right, and has kept all My statutes and observed them, he shall surely live. 20 The soul who sins shall die. The son shall not bear the guilt of the father, nor the father bear the guilt of the son. The righteousness of the righteous shall be upon himself, and the wickedness of the wicked shall be upon himself.

21 "But if a wicked man turns from all his sins which he has committed, keeps all My statutes, and does what is lawful and right, he shall surely live; he shall not die. 22 None of the transgressions which he has committed shall be remembered against him; because of the righteousness which he has done, he shall live. 23 Do I have any pleasure at all that the wicked should die?" says the Lord GOD, "*and* not that he should turn from his ways and live?

24 "But when a righteous man turns away from his righteousness and commits iniquity, and does according to all the abominations that the wicked *man* does, shall he live? All the righteousness which he has done shall not be remembered; because of the unfaithfulness of which he is guilty and the sin which he has

committed, because of them he shall die.
²⁵ "Yet you say, 'The way of the Lord is not fair.' Hear now, O house of Israel, is it not My way which is fair, and your ways which are not fair? ²⁶ When a righteous *man* turns away from his righteousness, commits iniquity, and dies in it, it is because of the iniquity which he has done that he dies. ²⁷ Again, when a wicked *man* turns away from the wickedness which he committed, and does what is lawful and right, he preserves himself alive. ²⁸ Because he considers and turns away from all the transgressions which he committed, he shall surely live; he shall not die. ²⁹ Yet the house of Israel says, 'The way of the Lord is not fair.' O house of Israel, is it not My ways which are fair, and your ways which are not fair?

³⁰ "Therefore I will judge you, O house of Israel, every one according to his ways," says the Lord GOD. "Repent, and turn from all your transgressions, so that iniquity will not be your ruin. ³¹ Cast away from you all the transgressions which you have committed, and get yourselves a new heart and a new spirit. For why should you die, O house of Israel? ³² For I have no pleasure in the death of one who dies," says the Lord GOD. "Therefore turn and live!"

~ PSALM 124:1–8 ~

¹ "If it had not been the LORD who was on our side,"
　　Let Israel now say—
² "If it had not been the LORD who was on our side,
　　When men rose up against us,
³ Then they would have swallowed us alive,
　　When their wrath was kindled against us;
⁴ Then the waters would have overwhelmed us,
　　The stream would have gone over our soul;
⁵ Then the swollen waters
　　Would have gone over our soul."

⁶ Blessed *be* the LORD,
　　Who has not given us *as* prey to their teeth.
⁷ Our soul has escaped as a bird from the snare of the fowlers;
　　The snare is broken, and we have escaped.
⁸ Our help *is* in the name of the LORD,
　　Who made heaven and earth.

~ PROVERBS 28:21 ~

²¹ To show partiality *is* not good,
　　Because for a piece of bread a man will transgress.

~ HEBREWS 9:1–28 ~

Then indeed, even the first *covenant* had ordinances of divine service and the earthly sanctuary. ² For a tabernacle was prepared: the first *part,* in which *was* the lampstand, the table, and the showbread, which is called the sanctuary; ³ and behind the second veil, the part of the tabernacle which is called the Holiest of All, ⁴ which had the golden censer and the ark of the covenant overlaid on all sides with gold, in which *were* the golden pot that had the manna, Aaron's rod that budded, and the tablets of the covenant; ⁵ and above it were the cherubim of glory overshadowing the mercy seat. Of these things we cannot now speak in detail.

⁶ Now when these things had been thus prepared, the priests always went into the first part of the tabernacle, performing *the services.* ⁷ But into the second part the high priest *went* alone once a year, not without blood, which he offered for himself and *for* the people's sins *committed* in ignorance; ⁸ the Holy Spirit indicating this, that the way into the Holiest of All was not yet made manifest while the first tabernacle was still standing. ⁹ It *was* symbolic for the present time in which both gifts and sacrifices are offered which cannot make him who performed the service perfect in regard to the conscience— ¹⁰ *concerned* only with foods and drinks, various washings, and fleshly ordinances imposed until the time of reformation.

¹¹ But Christ came *as* High Priest of the good things to come, with the greater and more perfect tabernacle not made with hands, that is, not of this creation. ¹² Not with the blood of goats and calves,

but with His own blood He entered the Most Holy Place once for all, having obtained eternal redemption. ¹³ For if the blood of bulls and goats and the ashes of a heifer, sprinkling the unclean, sanctifies for the purifying of the flesh, ¹⁴ how much more shall the blood of Christ, who through the eternal Spirit offered Himself without spot to God, cleanse your conscience from dead works to serve the living God? ¹⁵ And for this reason He is the Mediator of the new covenant, by means of death, for the redemption of the transgressions under the first covenant, that those who are called may receive the promise of the eternal inheritance.

¹⁶ For where there *is* a testament, there must also of necessity be the death of the testator. ¹⁷ For a testament *is* in force after men are dead, since it has no power at all while the testator lives. ¹⁸ Therefore not even the first *covenant* was dedicated without blood. ¹⁹ For when Moses had spoken every precept to all the people according to the law, he took the blood of calves and goats, with water, scarlet wool, and hyssop, and sprinkled both the book itself and all the people, ²⁰ saying, "This *is* the blood of the covenant which

God has commanded you." ²¹ Then likewise he sprinkled with blood both the tabernacle and all the vessels of the ministry. ²² And according to the law almost all things are purified with blood, and without shedding of blood there is no remission.

²³ Therefore *it was* necessary that the copies of the things in the heavens should be purified with these, but the heavenly things themselves with better sacrifices than these. ²⁴ For Christ has not entered the holy places made with hands, *which are* copies of the true, but into heaven itself, now to appear in the presence of God for us; ²⁵ not that He should offer Himself often, as the high priest enters the Most Holy Place every year with blood of another— ²⁶ He then would have had to suffer often since the foundation of the world; but now, once at the end of the ages, He has appeared to put away sin by the sacrifice of Himself. ²⁷ And as it is appointed for men to die once, but after this the judgment, ²⁸ so Christ was offered once to bear the sins of many. To those who eagerly wait for Him He will appear a second time, apart from sin, for salvation.

READING 318 · NOVEMBER 14

~ EZEKIEL 19:1—20:49 ~

"Moreover take up a lamentation for the princes of Israel, ² and say:

'What *is* your mother? A lioness:
She lay down among the lions;
Among the young lions she
    nourished her cubs.
³ She brought up one of her cubs,
And he became a young lion;
He learned to catch prey,
And he devoured men.
⁴ The nations also heard of him;
He was trapped in their pit,
And they brought him with chains
    to the land of Egypt.

⁵ 'When she saw that she waited,
    that her hope was lost,

She took another of her cubs *and*
    made him a young lion.
⁶ He roved among the lions,
And became a young lion;
He learned to catch prey;
He devoured men.
⁷ He knew their desolate places,
And laid waste their cities;
The land with its fullness was
    desolated
By the noise of his roaring.
⁸ Then the nations set against him
    from the provinces on every
    side,
And spread their net over him;
He was trapped in their pit.
⁹ They put him in a cage with
    chains,
And brought him to the king of
    Babylon;

They brought him in nets,
That his voice should no longer be
    heard on the mountains of
    Israel.

10 'Your mother *was* like a vine in
    your bloodline,
    Planted by the waters,
    Fruitful and full of branches
    Because of many waters.
11 She had strong branches for
    scepters of rulers.
    She towered in stature above the
    thick branches,
    And was seen in her height amid
    the dense foliage.
12 But she was plucked up in fury,
    She was cast down to the ground,
    And the east wind dried her fruit.
    Her strong branches were broken
    and withered;
    The fire consumed them.
13 And now she *is* planted in the
    wilderness,
    In a dry and thirsty land.
14 Fire has come out from a rod of
    her branches
    And devoured her fruit,
    So that she has no strong
    branch— a scepter for ruling.' "

This *is* a lamentation, and has become
a lamentation.

20 It came to pass in the seventh year,
in the fifth *month,* on the tenth *day* of
the month, *that* certain of the elders
of Israel came to inquire of the LORD, and
sat before me. ² Then the word of the
LORD came to me, saying, ³ "Son of man,
speak to the elders of Israel, and say to
them, 'Thus says the Lord GOD: "Have
you come to inquire of Me? *As* I live,"
says the Lord GOD, "I will not be inquired
of by you." ' ⁴ Will you judge them,
son of man, will you judge *them?* Then
make known to them the abominations
of their fathers.

⁵ "Say to them, 'Thus says the Lord
GOD: "On the day when I chose Israel
and raised My hand in an oath to the descendants of the house of Jacob, and made
Myself known to them in the land of
Egypt, I raised My hand in an oath to
them, saying, 'I *am* the LORD your God.'

⁶ On that day I raised My hand in an oath
to them, to bring them out of the land of
Egypt into a land that I had searched out
for them, 'flowing with milk and honey,'
the glory of all lands. ⁷ Then I said to them,
'Each of you, throw away the abominations which are before his eyes, and do
not defile yourselves with the idols of
Egypt. I *am* the LORD your God.' ⁸ But
they rebelled against Me and would not
obey Me. They did not all cast away the
abominations which were before their
eyes, nor did they forsake the idols of
Egypt. Then I said, 'I will pour out My
fury on them and fulfill My anger against
them in the midst of the land of Egypt.'
⁹ But I acted for My name's sake, that it
should not be profaned before the Gentiles among whom they *were,* in whose
sight I had made Myself known to them,
to bring them out of the land of Egypt.
¹⁰ "Therefore I made them go out of
the land of Egypt and brought them into
the wilderness. ¹¹ And I gave them My statutes and showed them My judgments,
'which, *if* a man does, he shall live by
them.' ¹² Moreover I also gave them My
Sabbaths, to be a sign between them and
Me, that they might know that I *am* the
LORD who sanctifies them. ¹³ Yet the house
of Israel rebelled against Me in the wilderness; they did not walk in My statutes;
they despised My judgments, 'which, *if* a
man does, he shall live by them'; and they
greatly defiled My Sabbaths. Then I said I
would pour out My fury on them in the
wilderness, to consume them. ¹⁴ But I
acted for My name's sake, that it should
not be profaned before the Gentiles, in
whose sight I had brought them out. ¹⁵ So
I also raised My hand in an oath to them
in the wilderness, that I would not bring
them into the land which I had given
them, 'flowing with milk and honey,' the
glory of all lands, ¹⁶ because they despised
My judgments and did not walk in My
statutes, but profaned My Sabbaths; for
their heart went after their idols. ¹⁷ Nevertheless My eye spared them from
destruction. I did not make an end of them
in the wilderness.

¹⁸ "But I said to their children in the
wilderness, 'Do not walk in the statutes
of your fathers, nor observe their judgments, nor defile yourselves with their

The Wind Beneath Their Wings

When John was just a boy, he journeyed with his family across the American continent. It took the family a full year to make their way from coast to coast. As each sunset and sunrise glorified the sky, the Scotsman would take his children out to show them the sky and speak to them about how the cloud formations were surely "the robes of God."

Who can fathom the full impact this trip had on young John? Or how deeply rooted became his reverence for nature on this year-long journey? What we do know is that John Muir became one of America's greatest naturalists. His love for nature led him to the mountains, the glacial meadows, and eventually to the icebound bays of Alaska. The lovely Muir Woods in northern California are named in his honor.

What are you "showing" to your children today? What "wind" are you putting under their wings? What examples, what encouragement, what insights are you giving to your child?

As the song declares so poignantly: "You are the wind beneath my wings" — so is a parent's influence upon a child.

idols. ¹⁹ I *am* the LORD your God: Walk in My statutes, keep My judgments, and do them; ²⁰ hallow My Sabbaths, and they will be a sign between Me and you, that you may know that I *am* the LORD your God.'

²¹ "Notwithstanding, the children rebelled against Me; they did not walk in My statutes, and were not careful to observe My judgments, 'which, *if* a man does, he shall live by them'; but they profaned My Sabbaths. Then I said I would pour out My fury on them and fulfill My anger against them in the wilderness. ²² Nevertheless I withdrew My hand and acted for My name's sake, that it should not be profaned in the sight of the Gentiles, in whose sight I had brought them out. ²³ Also I raised My hand in an oath to those in the wilderness, that I would scatter them among the Gentiles and disperse them throughout the countries, ²⁴ because they had not executed My judgments, but had despised My statutes, profaned My Sabbaths, and their eyes were fixed on their fathers' idols.

²⁵ "Therefore I also gave them up to statutes *that were* not good, and judgments by which they could not live; ²⁶ and I pronounced them unclean because of their ritual gifts, in that they caused all their firstborn to pass through *the fire*, that I might make them desolate and that they might know that I am the LORD." '

²⁷ "Therefore, son of man, speak to the house of Israel, and say to them, 'Thus says the Lord GOD: "In this too your fathers have blasphemed Me, by being unfaithful to Me. ²⁸ When I brought them into the land *concerning* which I had raised My hand in an oath to give them, and they saw all the high hills and all the thick trees, there they offered their sacrifices and provoked Me with their offerings. There they also sent up their sweet aroma and poured out their drink offerings. ²⁹ Then I said to them, 'What *is* this high place to which you go?' So its name is called Bamah to this day." '

³⁰ Therefore say to the house of Israel, 'Thus says the Lord GOD: "Are you defiling yourselves in the manner of your fathers, and committing harlotry according to their abominations? ³¹ For when you offer your gifts and make your sons

pass through the fire, you defile yourselves with all your idols, even to this day. So shall I be inquired of by you, O house of Israel? *As* I live," says the Lord GOD, "I will not be inquired of by you. ³² What you have in your mind shall never be, when you say, 'We will be like the Gentiles, like the families in other countries, serving wood and stone.'

³³ "*As* I live," says the Lord GOD, "surely with a mighty hand, with an outstretched arm, and with fury poured out, I will rule over you. ³⁴ I will bring you out from the peoples and gather you out of the countries where you are scattered, with a mighty hand, with an outstretched arm, and with fury poured out. ³⁵ And I will bring you into the wilderness of the peoples, and there I will plead My case with you face to face. ³⁶ Just as I pleaded My case with your fathers in the wilderness of the land of Egypt, so I will plead My case with you," says the Lord GOD.

³⁷ "I will make you pass under the rod, and I will bring you into the bond of the covenant; ³⁸ I will purge the rebels from among you, and those who transgress against Me; I will bring them out of the country where they dwell, but they shall not enter the land of Israel. Then you will know that I *am* the LORD.

³⁹ "As for you, O house of Israel," thus says the Lord GOD: "Go, serve every one of you his idols—and hereafter—if you will not obey Me; but profane My holy name no more with your gifts and your idols. ⁴⁰ For on My holy mountain, on the mountain height of Israel," says the Lord GOD, "there all the house of Israel, all of them in the land, shall serve Me; there I will accept them, and there I will require your offerings and the firstfruits of your sacrifices, together with all your holy things. ⁴¹ I will accept you as a sweet aroma when I bring you out from the peoples and gather you out of the countries where you have been scattered; and I will be hallowed in you before the Gentiles. ⁴² Then you shall know that I *am* the LORD, when I bring you into the land of Israel, into the country *for* which I raised My hand in an oath to give to your fathers. ⁴³ And there you shall remember your ways and all your doings with which you were defiled; and you shall loathe

yourselves in your own sight because of all the evils that you have committed. ⁴⁴ Then you shall know that I *am* the LORD, when I have dealt with you for My name's sake, not according to your wicked ways nor according to your corrupt doings, O house of Israel," says the Lord GOD.' "

⁴⁵ Furthermore the word of the LORD came to me, saying, ⁴⁶ "Son of man, set your face toward the south; preach against the south and prophesy against the forest land, the South, ⁴⁷ and say to the forest of the South, 'Hear the word of the LORD! Thus says the Lord GOD: "Behold, I will kindle a fire in you, and it shall devour every green tree and every dry tree in you; the blazing flame shall not be quenched, and all faces from the south to the north shall be scorched by it. ⁴⁸ All flesh shall see that I, the LORD, have kindled it; it shall not be quenched." ' "

⁴⁹ Then I said, "Ah, Lord GOD! They say of me, 'Does he not speak parables?' "

∼ PSALM 125:1–5 ∼

¹ Those who trust in the LORD
     Are like Mount Zion,
     Which cannot be moved, *but* abides
        forever.
² As the mountains surround
        Jerusalem,
     So the LORD surrounds His people
     From this time forth and forever.

³ For the scepter of wickedness shall
        not rest
     On the land allotted to the
        righteous,
     Lest the righteous reach out their
        hands to iniquity.

⁴ Do good, O LORD, to *those who are*
        good,
     And to *those who are* upright in their
        hearts.

⁵ As for such as turn aside to their
        crooked ways,
     The LORD shall lead them away
     With the workers of iniquity.

     Peace *be* upon Israel!

∼ PROVERBS 28:22 ∼

²² A man with an evil eye hastens after
        riches,
      And does not consider that poverty
        will come upon him.

∼ HEBREWS 10:1–18 ∼

For the law, having a shadow of the good things to come, *and* not the very image of the things, can never with these same sacrifices, which they offer continually year by year, make those who approach perfect. ² For then would they not have ceased to be offered? For the worshipers, once purified, would have had no more consciousness of sins. ³ But in those *sacrifices there is* a reminder of sins every year. ⁴ For *it is* not possible that the blood of bulls and goats could take away sins.

⁵ Therefore, when He came into the world, He said:

     "Sacrifice and offering You did not
        desire,
      But a body You have prepared for
        Me.
⁶   In burnt offerings and *sacrifices*
        for sin
      You had no pleasure.
⁷   Then I said, 'Behold, I have
        come—
      In the volume of the book it is
        written of Me—
      To do Your will, O God.' "

⁸ Previously saying, "Sacrifice and offering, burnt offerings, and *offerings* for sin You did not desire, nor had pleasure *in them*" (which are offered according to the law), ⁹ then He said, "Behold, I have come to do Your will, O God." He takes away the first that He may establish the second. ¹⁰ By that will we have been sanctified through the offering of the body of Jesus Christ once *for all*.

¹¹ And every priest stands ministering daily and offering repeatedly the same sacrifices, which can never take away sins. ¹² But this Man, after He had offered one sacrifice for sins forever, sat down at the right hand of God, ¹³ from that time

waiting till His enemies are made His footstool. ¹⁴ For by one offering He has perfected forever those who are being sanctified.

¹⁵ But the Holy Spirit also witnesses to us; for after He had said before,

¹⁶ "This *is* the covenant that I will make with them after those days, says the LORD: I will put My laws into their hearts, and in their minds I will write them," ¹⁷ *then He adds,* "Their sins and their lawless deeds I will remember no more." ¹⁸ Now where there is remission of these, *there is* no longer an offering for sin.

READING 319 · NOVEMBER 15

~ EZEKIEL 21:1—22:31 ~

And the word of the LORD came to me, saying, ² "Son of man, set your face toward Jerusalem, preach against the holy places, and prophesy against the land of Israel; ³ and say to the land of Israel, 'Thus says the LORD: "Behold, I *am* against you, and I will draw My sword out of its sheath and cut off both righteous and wicked from you. ⁴ Because I will cut off both righteous and wicked from you, therefore My sword shall go out of its sheath against all flesh from south *to* north, ⁵ that all flesh may know that I, the LORD, have drawn My sword out of its sheath; it shall not return anymore." ' ⁶ Sigh therefore, son of man, with a breaking heart, and sigh with bitterness before their eyes. ⁷ And it shall be when they say to you, 'Why are you sighing?' that you shall answer, 'Because of the news; when it comes, every heart will melt, all hands will be feeble, every spirit will faint, and all knees will be weak *as* water. Behold, it is coming and shall be brought to pass,' says the Lord GOD."

⁸ Again the word of the LORD came to me, saying, ⁹ "Son of man, prophesy and say, 'Thus says the LORD!' Say:

'A sword, a sword is sharpened
  And also polished!
¹⁰ Sharpened to make a dreadful
    slaughter,
  Polished to flash like lightning!
  Should we then make mirth?
  It despises the scepter of My son,
  As it does all wood.
¹¹ And He has given it to be
    polished,
  That it may be handled;

This sword is sharpened, and it is
    polished
  To be given into the hand of the
    slayer.'

¹² "Cry and wail, son of man;
  For it will be against My people,
  Against all the princes of Israel.
  Terrors including the sword will
    be against My people;
  Therefore strike *your* thigh.

¹³ "Because *it is* a testing,
  And what if *the sword* despises
    even the scepter?
  The scepter shall be no *more*,"

says the Lord GOD.

¹⁴ "You therefore, son of man,
    prophesy,
  And strike *your* hands together.
  The third time let the sword do
    double *damage*.
  It *is* the sword *that* slays,
  The sword that slays the great
    men,
  That enters their private
    chambers.
¹⁵ I have set the point of the sword
    against all their gates,
  That the heart may melt and many
    may stumble.
  Ah! *It is* made bright;
  It is grasped for slaughter:

¹⁶ "Swords at the ready!
  Thrust right!
  Set your blade!

Being Rooted

The next time you visit a very dense forest, try to imagine what is taking place under your feet. Scientists now know when the roots of trees come into contact with one another, a substance is released which encourages the growth of a particular kind of fungus. This fungus helps link roots of different trees — even those of dissimilar species. If one tree has access to water, another to nutrients, and a third to sunlight, the fungus enables the transfer of these items to trees that may be in need. Thus, the trees have the means of sharing with one another to preserve them all.

Our culture today applauds individualism. However, it tends to isolate people from one another and cut them off from the mainstream of life. With more and more people working at home or in walled offices and with schedules crammed tighter than ever with work and activities, feelings of loneliness are more likely to increase than decrease. Don't allow isolation to overcome you!

Reach out to others. Begin to give where you can. Learn to receive when others give to you. Build a network of friends, not just colleagues. And above all, root yourself into a group that nourishes and builds you up spiritually — your church.

> Not forsaking the assembling of ourselves together, as is the manner of some, but exhorting one another, and so much the more as you see the Day approaching.
>
> *Hebrews 10:25*

Thrust left—
Wherever your edge is ordered!

¹⁷ "I also will beat My fists together,
And I will cause My fury to rest;
I, the LORD, have spoken."

¹⁸ The word of the LORD came to me again, saying: ¹⁹ "And son of man, appoint for yourself two ways for the sword of the king of Babylon to go; both of them shall go from the same land. Make a sign; put *it* at the head of the road to the city. ²⁰ Appoint a road for the sword to go to Rabbah of the Ammonites, and to Judah, into fortified Jerusalem. ²¹ For the king of Babylon stands at the parting of the road, at the fork of the two roads, to use divination: he shakes the arrows, he consults the images, he looks at the liver. ²² In his right hand is the divination for Jerusalem: to set up battering rams, to call for a slaughter, to lift the voice with shouting, to set battering rams against the gates, to heap up a *siege* mound, and to build a wall. ²³ And it will be to them like a false divination in the eyes of those who have sworn oaths with them; but he will bring their iniquity to remembrance, that they may be taken.

²⁴ "Therefore thus says the Lord GOD: 'Because you have made your iniquity to be remembered, in that your transgressions are uncovered, so that in all your doings your sins appear—because you have come to remembrance, you shall be taken in hand.

²⁵ 'Now to you, O profane, wicked prince of Israel, whose day has come, whose iniquity *shall* end, ²⁶ thus says the Lord GOD:

"Remove the turban, and take off the crown;
Nothing *shall remain* the same.
Exalt the humble, and humble the exalted.
²⁷ Overthrown, overthrown,
I will make it overthrown!
It shall be no *longer,*
Until He comes whose right it is,
And I will give it *to Him.*" '

²⁸ "And you, son of man, prophesy and say, 'Thus says the Lord GOD concerning the Ammonites and concerning their reproach,' and say:

'A sword, a sword *is* drawn,
Polished for slaughter,
For consuming, for flashing—
²⁹ While they see false visions for you,
While they divine a lie to you,
To bring you on the necks of the wicked, the slain
Whose day has come,
Whose iniquity *shall* end.

³⁰ 'Return *it* to its sheath.
I will judge you
In the place where you were created,
In the land of your nativity.
³¹ I will pour out My indignation on you;
I will blow against you with the fire of My wrath,
And deliver you into the hands of brutal men *who are* skillful to destroy.
³² You shall be fuel for the fire;
Your blood shall be in the midst of the land.
You shall not be remembered,
For I the LORD have spoken.' "

22 Moreover the word of the LORD came to me, saying, ² "Now, son of man, will you judge, will you judge the bloody city? Yes, show her all her abominations! ³ Then say, 'Thus says the Lord GOD: "The city sheds blood in her own midst, that her time may come; and she makes idols within herself to defile herself. ⁴ You have become guilty by the blood which you have shed, and have defiled yourself with the idols which you have made. You have caused your days to draw near, and have come to *the end of* your years; therefore I have made you a reproach to the nations, and a mockery to all countries. ⁵ *Those* near and *those* far from you will mock you as infamous *and* full of tumult.

⁶ "Look, the princes of Israel: each one has used his power to shed blood in you. ⁷ In you they have made light of father and mother; in your midst they have oppressed the stranger; in you they have mistreated the fatherless and the widow.

⁸ You have despised My holy things and profaned My Sabbaths. ⁹ In you are men who slander to cause bloodshed; in you are those who eat on the mountains; in your midst they commit lewdness. ¹⁰ In you men uncover their fathers' nakedness; in you they violate women who are set apart during their impurity. ¹¹ One commits abomination with his neighbor's wife; another lewdly defiles his daughter-in-law; and another in you violates his sister, his father's daughter. ¹² In you they take bribes to shed blood; you take usury and increase; you have made profit from your neighbors by extortion, and have forgotten Me," says the Lord GOD.

¹³ "Behold, therefore, I beat My fists at the dishonest profit which you have made, and at the bloodshed which has been in your midst. ¹⁴ Can your heart endure, or can your hands remain strong, in the days when I shall deal with you? I, the LORD, have spoken, and will do *it*. ¹⁵ I will scatter you among the nations, disperse you throughout the countries, and remove your filthiness completely from you. ¹⁶ You shall defile yourself in the sight of the nations; then you shall know that I *am* the LORD." ' "

¹⁷ The word of the LORD came to me, saying, ¹⁸ "Son of man, the house of Israel has become dross to Me; they *are* all bronze, tin, iron, and lead, in the midst of a furnace; they have become dross from silver. ¹⁹ Therefore thus says the Lord GOD: 'Because you have all become dross, therefore behold, I will gather you into the midst of Jerusalem. ²⁰ *As men* gather silver, bronze, iron, lead, and tin into the midst of a furnace, to blow fire on it, to melt *it;* so I will gather *you* in My anger and in My fury, and I will leave *you there* and melt you. ²¹ Yes, I will gather you and blow on you with the fire of My wrath, and you shall be melted in its midst. ²² As silver is melted in the midst of a furnace, so shall you be melted in its midst; then you shall know that I, the LORD, have poured out My fury on you.' "

²³ And the word of the LORD came to me, saying, ²⁴ "Son of man, say to her: 'You *are* a land that is not cleansed or rained on in the day of indignation.' ²⁵ The conspiracy of her prophets in her midst is like a roaring lion tearing the prey; they have devoured people; they have taken treasure and precious things; they have made many widows in her midst. ²⁶ Her priests have violated My law and profaned My holy things; they have not distinguished between the holy and unholy, nor have they made known *the difference* between the unclean and the clean; and they have hidden their eyes from My Sabbaths, so that I am profaned among them. ²⁷ Her princes in her midst *are* like wolves tearing the prey, to shed blood, to destroy people, and to get dishonest gain. ²⁸ Her prophets plastered them with untempered *mortar,* seeing false visions, and divining lies for them, saying, 'Thus says the Lord GOD,' when the LORD had not spoken. ²⁹ The people of the land have used oppressions, committed robbery, and mistreated the poor and needy; and they wrongfully oppress the stranger. ³⁰ So I sought for a man among them who would make a wall, and stand in the gap before Me on behalf of the land, that I should not destroy it; but I found no one. ³¹ Therefore I have poured out My indignation on them; I have consumed them with the fire of My wrath; and I have recompensed their deeds on their own heads," says the Lord GOD.

∼ PSALM 126:1–6 ∼

1   When the LORD brought back the
       captivity of Zion,
     We were like those who dream.
2   Then our mouth was filled with
       laughter,
     And our tongue with singing.
     Then they said among the nations,
     "The LORD has done great things for
       them."
3   The LORD has done great things for
       us,
     And we are glad.

4   Bring back our captivity, O LORD,
     As the streams in the South.

5   Those who sow in tears
     Shall reap in joy.
6   He who continually goes forth
       weeping,
     Bearing seed for sowing,

Shall doubtless come again with
  rejoicing,
Bringing his sheaves *with him.*

～ PROVERBS 28:23 ～

23 He who rebukes a man will find
    more favor afterward
  Than he who flatters with the
    tongue.

～ HEBREWS 10:19–39 ～

Therefore, brethren, having boldness to
enter the Holiest by the blood of Jesus,
20 by a new and living way which He consecrated for us, through the veil, that is,
His flesh, 21 and *having* a High Priest over
the house of God, 22 let us draw near with
a true heart in full assurance of faith, having our hearts sprinkled from an evil
conscience and our bodies washed with
pure water. 23 Let us hold fast the confession of *our* hope without wavering, for
He who promised *is* faithful. 24 And let us
consider one another in order to stir up
love and good works, 25 not forsaking the
assembling of ourselves together, as *is* the
manner of some, but exhorting *one another*, and so much the more as you see
the Day approaching.

26 For if we sin willfully after we have
received the knowledge of the truth, there
no longer remains a sacrifice for sins, 27 but
a certain fearful expectation of judgment,
and fiery indignation which will devour
the adversaries. 28 Anyone who has rejected Moses' law dies without mercy on

the testimony of two or three witnesses.
29 Of how much worse punishment, do
you suppose, will he be thought worthy
who has trampled the Son of God underfoot, counted the blood of the covenant
by which he was sanctified a common
thing, and insulted the Spirit of grace?
30 For we know Him who said, "Vengeance is Mine, I will repay," says the
Lord. And again, "The LORD will judge
His people." 31 It is a fearful thing to fall
into the hands of the living God.

32 But recall the former days in which,
after you were illuminated, you endured
a great struggle with sufferings: 33 partly
while you were made a spectacle both by
reproaches and tribulations, and partly
while you became companions of those
who were so treated; 34 for you had compassion on me in my chains, and joyfully
accepted the plundering of your goods,
knowing that you have a better and an
enduring possession for yourselves in
heaven. 35 Therefore do not cast away
your confidence, which has great reward.
36 For you have need of endurance, so that
after you have done the will of God, you
may receive the promise:

37 "For yet a little while,
    And He who is coming will come
      and will not tarry.
38   Now the just shall live by faith;
    But if *anyone* draws back,
    My soul has no pleasure in him."

39 But we are not of those who draw back
to perdition, but of those who believe to
the saving of the soul.

READING 320 · NOVEMBER 16

～ EZEKIEL 23:1—24:27 ～

The word of the LORD came again
  to me, saying:

2 "Son of man, there were two
    women,
  The daughters of one mother.
3 They committed harlotry in
    Egypt,

They committed harlotry in their
    youth;
  Their breasts were there
    embraced,
  Their virgin bosom was there
    pressed.
4 Their names: Oholah the elder
    and Oholibah her sister;

Getting Your Zzzzz's

Medical researchers have come to what may seem to be a common-sense conclusion: a missing ingredient in many people's health may be "vitamin Zzzzzzzz."

When participants in one study were cheated out of four hours of sleep for four consecutive nights, they had on average a 30 percent drop in their immune systems. Such a drop can tremendously increase a person's susceptibility to colds and flu, and perhaps to other serious diseases. Says sleep researcher Michael Irwin, MD, "Many people just need a regular-length sleep to get their natural killer cells revved up again."

While a steady diet of sufficient sleep may not completely prevent disease, it can improve the body's defense system and help a person combat disease more efficiently and effectively.

Sleep is the cheapest health aid a person can "take." Sleep is God's own means of restoring health to the body, as well as providing rest to the mind. Often, after a good night's sleep people report a new outlook on life or a change of heart.

Ask God to renew your strength as you sleep tonight. Then, get to bed on time so He can give you what you requested!

They were Mine,
And they bore sons and daughters.
As for their names,
Samaria *is* Oholah, and Jerusalem
  is Oholibah.

5 "Oholah played the harlot even
    though she was Mine;
And she lusted for her lovers, the
    neighboring Assyrians,
6 *Who were* clothed in purple,
  Captains and rulers,
  All of them desirable young men,
  Horsemen riding on horses.
7 Thus she committed her harlotry
    with them,
  All of them choice men of Assyria;
  And with all for whom she lusted,
  With all their idols, she defiled
    herself.
8 She has never given up her
    harlotry *brought* from Egypt,
  For in her youth they had lain
    with her,
  Pressed her virgin bosom,
  And poured out their immorality
    upon her.

9 "Therefore I have delivered her
  Into the hand of her lovers,
  Into the hand of the Assyrians,
  For whom she lusted.
10 They uncovered her nakedness,
   Took away her sons and
     daughters,
   And slew her with the sword;
   She became a byword among
     women,
   For they had executed judgment
     on her.

11 "Now although her sister Oholibah
saw *this*, she became more corrupt in her
lust than she, and in her harlotry more
corrupt than her sister's harlotry.

12 "She lusted for the neighboring
     Assyrians,
   Captains and rulers,
   Clothed most gorgeously,
   Horsemen riding on horses,
   All of them desirable young men.
13 Then I saw that she was defiled;
   Both *took* the same way.
14 But she increased her harlotry;

She looked at men portrayed on
  the wall,
Images of Chaldeans portrayed in
  vermilion,
15 Girded with belts around their
     waists,
   Flowing turbans on their heads,
   All of them looking like captains,
   In the manner of the Babylonians
     of Chaldea,
   The land of their nativity.
16 As soon as her eyes saw them,
   She lusted for them
   And sent messengers to them in
     Chaldea.

17 "Then the Babylonians came to her,
     into the bed of love,
   And they defiled her with their
     immorality;
   So she was defiled by them, and
     alienated herself from them.
18 She revealed her harlotry and
     uncovered her nakedness.
   Then I alienated Myself from her,
   As I had alienated Myself from her
     sister.

19 "Yet she multiplied her harlotry
   In calling to remembrance the
     days of her youth,
   When she had played the harlot in
     the land of Egypt.
20 For she lusted for her paramours,
   Whose flesh *is like* the flesh of
     donkeys,
   And whose issue *is like* the issue of
     horses.
21 Thus you called to remembrance
     the lewdness of your youth,
   When the Egyptians pressed your
     bosom
   Because of your youthful breasts.

22 "Therefore, Oholibah, thus says the
Lord GOD:

   'Behold, I will stir up your lovers
     against you,
   From whom you have alienated
     yourself,
   And I will bring them against you
     from every side:
23 The Babylonians,
   All the Chaldeans,

Pekod, Shoa, Koa,
All the Assyrians with them,
All of them desirable young men,
Governors and rulers,
Captains and men of renown,
All of them riding on horses.
24 And they shall come against you
With chariots, wagons, and war-
horses,
With a horde of people.
They shall array against you
Buckler, shield, and helmet all
around.

'I will delegate judgment to them,
And they shall judge you
according to their judgments.
25 I will set My jealousy against you,
And they shall deal furiously with
you;
They shall remove your nose and
your ears,
And your remnant shall fall by the
sword;
They shall take your sons and
your daughters,
And your remnant shall be
devoured by fire.
26 They shall also strip you of your
clothes
And take away your beautiful
jewelry.

27 'Thus I will make you cease your
lewdness and your harlotry
Brought from the land of Egypt,
So that you will not lift your eyes
to them,
Nor remember Egypt anymore.'

28 "For thus says the Lord GOD: 'Surely I will deliver you into the hand of those you hate, into the hand *of those* from whom you alienated yourself. 29 They will deal hatefully with you, take away all you have worked for, and leave you naked and bare. The nakedness of your harlotry shall be uncovered, both your lewdness and your harlotry. 30 I will do these *things* to you because you have gone as a harlot after the Gentiles, because you have become defiled by their idols. 31 You have walked in the way of your sister; therefore I will put her cup in your hand.'
32 "Thus says the Lord GOD:

'You shall drink of your sister's
cup,
The deep and wide one;
You shall be laughed to scorn
And held in derision;
It contains much.
33 You will be filled with
drunkenness and sorrow,
The cup of horror and desolation,
The cup of your sister Samaria.
34 You shall drink and drain it,
You shall break its shards,
And tear at your own breasts;
For I have spoken,'
Says the Lord GOD.

35 "Therefore thus says the Lord GOD:

'Because you have forgotten Me
and cast Me behind your back,
Therefore you shall bear the
penalty
Of your lewdness and your
harlotry.' "

36 The LORD also said to me: "Son of man, will you judge Oholah and Oholibah? Then declare to them their abominations. 37 For they have committed adultery, and blood *is* on their hands. They have committed adultery with their idols, and even sacrificed their sons whom they bore to Me, passing them through *the fire,* to devour *them.* 38 Moreover they have done this to Me: They have defiled My sanctuary on the same day and profaned My Sabbaths. 39 For after they had slain their children for their idols, on the same day they came into My sanctuary to profane it; and indeed thus they have done in the midst of My house.

40 "Furthermore you sent for men to come from afar, to whom a messenger *was* sent; and there they came. And you washed yourself for them, painted your eyes, and adorned yourself with ornaments. 41 You sat on a stately couch, with a table prepared before it, on which you had set My incense and My oil. 42 The sound of a carefree multitude *was* with her, and Sabeans *were* brought from the wilderness with men of the common sort, who put bracelets on their wrists and beautiful crowns on their heads. 43 Then I said concerning *her who had grown* old

in adulteries, 'Will they commit harlotry with her now, and she *with them?*' ⁴⁴ Yet they went in to her, as men go in to a woman who plays the harlot; thus they went in to Oholah and Oholibah, the lewd women. ⁴⁵ But righteous men will judge them after the manner of adulteresses, and after the manner of women who shed blood, because they *are* adulteresses, and blood *is* on their hands.

⁴⁶ "For thus says the Lord GOD: 'Bring up an assembly against them, give them up to trouble and plunder. ⁴⁷ The assembly shall stone them with stones and execute them with their swords; they shall slay their sons and their daughters, and burn their houses with fire. ⁴⁸ Thus I will cause lewdness to cease from the land, that all women may be taught not to practice your lewdness. ⁴⁹ They shall repay you for your lewdness, and you shall pay for your idolatrous sins. Then you shall know that I *am* the Lord GOD.' "

24 Again, in the ninth year, in the tenth month, on the tenth *day* of the month, the word of the LORD came to me, saying, ² "Son of man, write down the name of the day, this very day—the king of Babylon started his siege against Jerusalem this very day. ³ And utter a parable to the rebellious house, and say to them, 'Thus says the Lord GOD:

"Put on a pot, set *it* on,
    And also pour water into it.
⁴ Gather pieces *of meat* in it,
    Every good piece,
    The thigh and the shoulder.
    Fill *it* with choice cuts;
⁵ Take the choice of the flock.
    Also pile *fuel* bones under it,
    Make it boil well,
    And let the cuts simmer in it."

⁶ 'Therefore thus says the Lord GOD:

"Woe to the bloody city,
    To the pot whose scum *is* in it,
    And whose scum is not gone from it!
    Bring it out piece by piece,
    On which no lot has fallen.
⁷ For her blood is in her midst;
    She set it on top of a rock;

She did not pour it on the ground,
    To cover it with dust.
⁸ That it may raise up fury and take vengeance,
    I have set her blood on top of a rock,
    That it may not be covered."

⁹ 'Therefore thus says the Lord GOD:

"Woe to the bloody city!
    I too will make the pyre great.
¹⁰ Heap on the wood,
    Kindle the fire;
    Cook the meat well,
    Mix in the spices,
    And let the cuts be burned up.

¹¹ "Then set the pot empty on the coals,
    That it may become hot and its bronze may burn,
    That its filthiness may be melted in it,
    That its scum may be consumed.
¹² She has grown weary with lies,
    And her great scum has not gone from her.
    Let her scum *be* in the fire!
¹³ In your filthiness *is* lewdness.
    Because I have cleansed you, and you were not cleansed,
    You will not be cleansed of your filthiness anymore,
    Till I have caused My fury to rest upon you.
¹⁴ I, the LORD, have spoken *it;*
    It shall come to pass, and I will do *it;*
    I will not hold back,
    Nor will I spare,
    Nor will I relent;
    According to your ways
    And according to your deeds
    They will judge you,"
    Says the Lord GOD.' "

¹⁵ Also the word of the LORD came to me, saying, ¹⁶ "Son of man, behold, I take away from you the desire of your eyes with one stroke; yet you shall neither mourn nor weep, nor shall your tears run down. ¹⁷ Sigh in silence, make no mourning for the dead; bind your turban on your head, and put your sandals on your feet;

do not cover *your* lips, and do not eat man's bread *of sorrow.*"

¹⁸ So I spoke to the people in the morning, and at evening my wife died; and the next morning I did as I was commanded. ¹⁹ And the people said to me, "Will you not tell us what these *things signify* to us, that you behave so?"

²⁰ Then I answered them, "The word of the LORD came to me, saying, ²¹ 'Speak to the house of Israel, "Thus says the Lord GOD: 'Behold, I will profane My sanctuary, your arrogant boast, the desire of your eyes, the delight of your soul; and your sons and daughters whom you left behind shall fall by the sword. ²² And you shall do as I have done; you shall not cover *your* lips nor eat man's bread *of sorrow.* ²³ Your turbans shall be on your heads and your sandals on your feet; you shall neither mourn nor weep, but you shall pine away in your iniquities and mourn with one another. ²⁴ Thus Ezekiel is a sign to you; according to all that he has done you shall do; and when this comes, you shall know that I *am* the Lord GOD.' "

²⁵ 'And you, son of man—*will it* not *be* in the day when I take from them their stronghold, their joy and their glory, the desire of their eyes, and that on which they set their minds, their sons and their daughters: ²⁶ on that day one who escapes will come to you to let *you* hear *it* with *your* ears; ²⁷ on that day your mouth will be opened to him who has escaped; you shall speak and no longer be mute. Thus you will be a sign to them, and they shall know that I *am* the LORD.' "

∼ PSALM 127:1–5 ∼

¹ Unless the LORD builds the house,
They labor in vain who build it;
Unless the LORD guards the city,
The watchman stays awake in vain.
² *It is* vain for you to rise up early,
To sit up late,
To eat the bread of sorrows;
For so He gives His beloved sleep.

³ Behold, children *are* a heritage from
the LORD,
The fruit of the womb *is* a reward.
⁴ Like arrows in the hand of a warrior,
So *are* the children of one's youth.

⁵ Happy *is* the man who has his quiver
full of them;
They shall not be ashamed,
But shall speak with their enemies in
the gate.

∼ PROVERBS 28:24 ∼

²⁴ Whoever robs his father or his
mother,
And says, "*It is* no transgression,"
The same *is* companion to a
destroyer.

∼ HEBREWS 11:1–16 ∼

Now faith is the substance of things hoped for, the evidence of things not seen. ² For by it the elders obtained a *good* testimony.

³ By faith we understand that the worlds were framed by the word of God, so that the things which are seen were not made of things which are visible.

⁴ By faith Abel offered to God a more excellent sacrifice than Cain, through which he obtained witness that he was righteous, God testifying of his gifts; and through it he being dead still speaks.

⁵ By faith Enoch was taken away so that he did not see death, "and was not found, because God had taken him"; for before he was taken he had this testimony, that he pleased God. ⁶ But without faith *it is* impossible to please *Him,* for he who comes to God must believe that He is, and *that* He is a rewarder of those who diligently seek Him.

⁷ By faith Noah, being divinely warned of things not yet seen, moved with godly fear, prepared an ark for the saving of his household, by which he condemned the world and became heir of the righteousness which is according to faith.

⁸ By faith Abraham obeyed when he was called to go out to the place which he would receive as an inheritance. And he went out, not knowing where he was going. ⁹ By faith he dwelt in the land of promise as *in* a foreign country, dwelling in tents with Isaac and Jacob, the heirs with him of the same promise; ¹⁰ for he waited for the city which has foundations, whose builder and maker *is* God.

¹¹ By faith Sarah herself also received

strength to conceive seed, and she bore a child when she was past the age, because she judged Him faithful who had promised. ¹² Therefore from one man, and him as good as dead, were born *as many* as the stars of the sky in multitude—innumerable as the sand which is by the seashore.

¹³ These all died in faith, not having received the promises, but having seen them afar off were assured of them, embraced *them* and confessed that they were strangers and pilgrims on the earth. ¹⁴ For those who say such things declare plainly that they seek a homeland. ¹⁵ And truly if they had called to mind that *country* from which they had come out, they would have had opportunity to return. ¹⁶ But now they desire a better, that is, a heavenly *country*. Therefore God is not ashamed to be called their God, for He has prepared a city for them.

READING 321 · NOVEMBER 17

~ EZEKIEL 25:1—26:21 ~

The word of the LORD came to me, saying, ² "Son of man, set your face against the Ammonites, and prophesy against them. ³ Say to the Ammonites, 'Hear the word of the Lord GOD! Thus says the Lord GOD: "Because you said, 'Aha!' against My sanctuary when it was profaned, and against the land of Israel when it was desolate, and against the house of Judah when they went into captivity, ⁴ indeed, therefore, I will deliver you as a possession to the men of the East, and they shall set their encampments among you and make their dwellings among you; they shall eat your fruit, and they shall drink your milk. ⁵ And I will make Rabbah a stable for camels and Ammon a resting place for flocks. Then you shall know that I *am* the LORD."

⁶ 'For thus says the Lord GOD: "Because you clapped *your* hands, stamped your feet, and rejoiced in heart with all your disdain for the land of Israel, ⁷ indeed, therefore, I will stretch out My hand against you, and give you as plunder to the nations; I will cut you off from the peoples, and I will cause you to perish from the countries; I will destroy you, and you shall know that I *am* the LORD."

⁸ 'Thus says the Lord GOD: "Because Moab and Seir say, 'Look! The house of Judah *is* like all the nations,' ⁹ therefore, behold, I will clear the territory of Moab of cities, of the cities on its frontier, the glory of the country, Beth Jeshimoth, Baal Meon, and Kirjathaim. ¹⁰ To the men of the East I will give it as a possession, together with the Ammonites, that the Ammonites may not be remembered among the nations. ¹¹ And I will execute judgments upon Moab, and they shall know that I *am* the LORD."

¹² 'Thus says the Lord GOD: "Because of what Edom did against the house of Judah by taking vengeance, and has greatly offended by avenging itself on them," ¹³ therefore thus says the Lord GOD: "I will also stretch out My hand against Edom, cut off man and beast from it, and make it desolate from Teman; Dedan shall fall by the sword. ¹⁴ I will lay My vengeance on Edom by the hand of My people Israel, that they may do in Edom according to My anger and according to My fury; and they shall know My vengeance," says the Lord GOD.

¹⁵ 'Thus says the Lord GOD: "Because the Philistines dealt vengefully and took vengeance with a spiteful heart, to destroy because of the old hatred," ¹⁶ therefore thus says the Lord GOD: "I will stretch out My hand against the Philistines, and I will cut off the Cherethites and destroy the remnant of the seacoast. ¹⁷ I will execute great vengeance on them with furious rebukes; and they shall know that I *am* the LORD, when I lay My vengeance upon them." ' "

26 And it came to pass in the eleventh year, on the first *day* of the month, *that* the word of the LORD came to me, saying, ² "Son of man, because Tyre has said against Jerusalem, 'Aha! She is broken who

The Happiest People on Earth

A newspaper in England once asked this question of its readers, "Who are the happiest people on the earth?"

The four prize-winning answers were:

A little child building sand castles.
A craftsman or artist whistling over a job well done.
A mother, bathing her baby after a busy day.
A doctor who has finished a difficult and dangerous operation that saved a human life.

The paper's editors were surprised to find virtually no one submitted kings, emperors, millionaires, or others of wealth and rank as the happiest people on earth.

W. Beran Wolfe once said, "If you observe a really happy man you will find him building a boat, writing a symphony, educating his son, growing double dahlias in his garden, or looking for dinosaur eggs in the Gobi desert. He will not be searching for happiness as if it were a collar button that has rolled under the radiator. He will not be striving for it as a goal in itself. He will have become aware that he is happy in the course of living life twenty-four crowded hours of the day."

> When you eat the labor of your hands, you shall be happy, and it shall be well with you.
>
> *Psalm 128:2*

was the gateway of the peoples; now she is turned over to me; I shall be filled; she is laid waste.'

3 "Therefore thus says the Lord GOD: 'Behold, I *am* against you, O Tyre, and will cause many nations to come up against you, as the sea causes its waves to come up. 4 And they shall destroy the walls of Tyre and break down her towers; I will also scrape her dust from her, and make her like the top of a rock. 5 It shall be *a place for* spreading nets in the midst of the sea, for I have spoken,' says the Lord GOD; 'it shall become plunder for the nations. 6 Also her daughter *villages* which *are* in the fields shall be slain by the sword. Then they shall know that I am the LORD.'

7 "For thus says the Lord GOD: 'Behold, I will bring against Tyre from the north Nebuchadnezzar king of Babylon, king of kings, with horses, with chariots, and with horsemen, and an army with many people. 8 He will slay with the sword your daughter *villages* in the fields; he will heap up a siege mound against you, build a wall against you, and raise a defense against you. 9 He will direct his battering rams against your walls, and with his axes he will break down your towers. 10 Because of the abundance of his horses, their dust will cover you; your walls will shake at the noise of the horsemen, the wagons, and the chariots, when he enters your gates, as men enter a city that has been breached. 11 With the hooves of his horses he will trample all your streets; he will slay your people by the sword, and your strong pillars will fall to the ground. 12 They will plunder your riches and pillage your merchandise; they will break down your walls and destroy your pleasant houses; they will lay your stones, your timber, and your soil in the midst of the water. 13 I will put an end to the sound of your songs, and the sound of your harps shall be heard no more. 14 I will make you like the top of a rock; you shall be *a place for* spreading nets, and you shall never be rebuilt, for I the LORD have spoken,' says the Lord GOD.

15 "Thus says the Lord GOD to Tyre: 'Will the coastlands not shake at the sound of your fall, when the wounded cry, when slaughter is made in the midst of you? 16 Then all the princes of the sea will come down from their thrones, lay aside their robes, and take off their embroidered garments; they will clothe themselves with trembling; they will sit on the ground, tremble *every* moment, and be astonished at you. 17 And they will take up a lamentation for you, and say to you:

"How you have perished,
  O one inhabited by seafaring men,
  O renowned city,
  Who was strong at sea,
  She and her inhabitants,
  Who caused their terror *to be* on
    all her inhabitants!
18 Now the coastlands tremble on
    the day of your fall;
  Yes, the coastlands by the sea are
    troubled at your departure." '

19 "For thus says the Lord GOD: 'When I make you a desolate city, like cities that are not inhabited, when I bring the deep upon you, and great waters cover you, 20 then I will bring you down with those who descend into the Pit, to the people of old, and I will make you dwell in the lowest part of the earth, in places desolate from antiquity, with those who go down to the Pit, so that you may never be inhabited; and I shall establish glory in the land of the living. 21 I will make you a terror, and you *shall be* no *more;* though you are sought for, you will never be found again,' says the Lord GOD."

∼ PSALM 128:1–6 ∼

1 Blessed *is* every one who fears the
    LORD,
  Who walks in His ways.

2 When you eat the labor of your
    hands,
  You *shall be* happy, and *it shall be*
    well with you.
3 Your wife *shall be* like a fruitful vine
  In the very heart of your house,
  Your children like olive plants
  All around your table.
4 Behold, thus shall the man be blessed
  Who fears the LORD.

5 The LORD bless you out of Zion,
  And may you see the good of
      Jerusalem
  All the days of your life.
6 Yes, may you see your children's
  children.

Peace *be* upon Israel!

~ PROVERBS 28:25 ~

25 He who is of a proud heart stirs up
      strife,
   But he who trusts in the LORD will
      be prospered.

~ HEBREWS 11:17-40 ~

By faith Abraham, when he was tested,
offered up Isaac, and he who had received
the promises offered up his only begotten *son*, 18 of whom it was said, "In Isaac
your seed shall be called," 19 concluding
that God *was* able to raise *him* up, even
from the dead, from which he also received him in a figurative sense.

20 By faith Isaac blessed Jacob and Esau
concerning things to come.

21 By faith Jacob, when he was dying,
blessed each of the sons of Joseph, and
worshiped, *leaning* on the top of his staff.

22 By faith Joseph, when he was dying,
made mention of the departure of the
children of Israel, and gave instructions
concerning his bones.

23 By faith Moses, when he was born,
was hidden three months by his parents,
because they saw *he was* a beautiful child;
and they were not afraid of the king's
command.

24 By faith Moses, when he became
of age, refused to be called the son of
Pharaoh's daughter, 25 choosing rather to
suffer affliction with the people of God
than to enjoy the passing pleasures of sin,

26 esteeming the reproach of Christ greater
riches than the treasures in Egypt; for he
looked to the reward.

27 By faith he forsook Egypt, not fearing the wrath of the king; for he endured
as seeing Him who is invisible. 28 By faith
he kept the Passover and the sprinkling
of blood, lest he who destroyed the firstborn should touch them.

29 By faith they passed through the Red
Sea as by dry *land, whereas* the Egyptians,
attempting *to do* so, were drowned.

30 By faith the walls of Jericho fell down
after they were encircled for seven days.
31 By faith the harlot Rahab did not perish with those who did not believe, when
she had received the spies with peace.

32 And what more shall I say? For the
time would fail me to tell of Gideon and
Barak and Samson and Jephthah, also *of*
David and Samuel and the prophets:
33 who through faith subdued kingdoms,
worked righteousness, obtained promises,
stopped the mouths of lions, 34 quenched
the violence of fire, escaped the edge
of the sword, out of weakness were made
strong, became valiant in battle, turned
to flight the armies of the aliens. 35 Women
received their dead raised to life again.

Others were tortured, not accepting
deliverance, that they might obtain a better resurrection. 36 Still others had trial
of mockings and scourgings, yes, and
of chains and imprisonment. 37 They
were stoned, they were sawn in two, were
tempted, were slain with the sword. They
wandered about in sheepskins and
goatskins, being destitute, afflicted, tormented— 38 of whom the world was not
worthy. They wandered in deserts and
mountains, *in* dens and caves of the earth.

39 And all these, having obtained a good
testimony through faith, did not receive
the promise, 40 God having provided
something better for us, that they should
not be made perfect apart from us.

~ EZEKIEL 27:1—28:26 ~

The word of the LORD came again to me, saying, [2] "Now, son of man, take up a lamentation for Tyre, [3] and say to Tyre, 'You who are situated at the entrance of the sea, merchant of the peoples on many coastlands, thus says the Lord GOD:

"O Tyre, you have said,
 'I *am* perfect in beauty.'
[4]   Your borders *are* in the midst of
        the seas.
     Your builders have perfected your
        beauty.
[5]   They made all *your* planks of fir
        trees from Senir;
     They took a cedar from Lebanon
        to make you a mast.
[6]   *Of* oaks from Bashan they made
        your oars;
     The company of Ashurites have
        inlaid your planks
     With ivory from the coasts of
        Cyprus.
[7]   Fine embroidered linen from
        Egypt was what you spread for
        your sail;
     Blue and purple from the coasts of
        Elishah was what covered you.

[8] "Inhabitants of Sidon and Arvad
        were your oarsmen;
     Your wise men, O Tyre, were in
        you;
     They became your pilots.
[9]   Elders of Gebal and its wise men
     Were in you to caulk your seams;
     All the ships of the sea
     And their oarsmen were in you
     To market your merchandise.

[10] "Those from Persia, Lydia, and
        Libya
     Were in your army as men of war;
     They hung shield and helmet in
        you;
     They gave splendor to you.
[11] Men of Arvad with your army
        were on your walls *all* around,
     And the men of Gammad were in
        your towers;

     They hung their shields on your
        walls *all* around;
     They made your beauty perfect.

[12] "Tarshish *was* your merchant because of your many luxury goods. They gave you silver, iron, tin, and lead for your goods. [13] Javan, Tubal, and Meshech *were* your traders. They bartered human lives and vessels of bronze for your merchandise. [14] Those from the house of Togarmah traded for your wares with horses, steeds, and mules. [15] The men of Dedan *were* your traders; many isles *were* the market of your hand. They brought you ivory tusks and ebony as payment. [16] Syria *was* your merchant because of the abundance of goods you made. They gave you for your wares emeralds, purple, embroidery, fine linen, corals, and rubies. [17] Judah and the land of Israel *were* your traders. They traded for your merchandise wheat of Minnith, millet, honey, oil, and balm. [18] Damascus *was* your merchant because of the abundance of goods you made, because of your many luxury items, with the wine of Helbon and with white wool. [19] Dan and Javan paid for your wares, traversing back and forth. Wrought iron, cassia, and cane were among your merchandise. [20] Dedan *was* your merchant in saddlecloths for riding. [21] Arabia and all the princes of Kedar *were* your regular merchants. They traded with you in lambs, rams, and goats. [22] The merchants of Sheba and Raamah *were* your merchants. They traded for your wares the choicest spices, all kinds of precious stones, and gold. [23] Haran, Canneh, Eden, the merchants of Sheba, Assyria, *and* Chilmad *were* your merchants. [24] These *were* your merchants in choice items—in purple clothes, in embroidered garments, in chests of multicolored apparel, in sturdy woven cords, which were in your marketplace.

[25] "The ships of Tarshish were carriers
        of your merchandise.
     You were filled and very glorious
        in the midst of the seas.

Help of the Helpless

After two long days of lying on the ocean floor in a disabled submarine, the sub's crew members received orders from their commanding officer to sing the following hymn:

Abide with me! Fast falls the eventide.
The darkness deepens — Lord, with
  me abide!
When other helpers fail and
  comforts flee,
Help of the helpless, oh, abide with me!

After the hymn had been sung, the commander explained to his men that the hymn was his prayer for them, and that he hoped it would hold the same meaning for them as it did for him. He then explained that based upon the best information he had, they did not have long to live. There was little to no hope of outside aid, because any searchers who may be on the surface did not know the vessel's position.

Sedatives were distributed to the men to quiet their nerves. One sailor, overcome at the commander's news, fainted. As he swooned, he fell against a piece of equipment, setting in motion the surfacing mechanism that had been jammed! The submarine rose to the surface safely and soon made port.

When we hit bottom in life, prayer is our best resort, for only God knows how to constrain the forces that are keeping His blessings from reaching us!

Looking unto Jesus, the author and finisher of our faith, who for the joy that was set before Him endured the cross... for consider Him who endured... lest you become weary and discouraged in your souls.

Hebrews 12:2-3

26 Your oarsmen brought you into
        many waters,
    But the east wind broke you in the
        midst of the seas.

27 "Your riches, wares, and
        merchandise,
    Your mariners and pilots,
    Your caulkers and merchandisers,
    All your men of war who *are* in
        you,
    And the entire company which *is*
        in your midst,
    Will fall into the midst of the seas
        on the day of your ruin.
28 The common-land will shake at
        the sound of the cry of your
        pilots.

29 "All who handle the oar,
    The mariners,
    All the pilots of the sea
    Will come down from their ships
        and stand on the shore.
30 They will make their voice heard
        because of you;
    They will cry bitterly and cast dust
        on their heads;
    They will roll about in ashes;
31 They will shave themselves
        completely bald because of you,
    Gird themselves with sackcloth,
    And weep for you
    With bitterness of heart *and* bitter
        wailing.
32 In their wailing for you
    They will take up a lamentation,
    And lament for you:
    'What *city is* like Tyre,
    Destroyed in the midst of the sea?

33 'When your wares went out by sea,
    You satisfied many people;
    You enriched the kings of the
        earth
    With your many luxury goods and
        your merchandise.
34 But you are broken by the seas in
        the depths of the waters;
    Your merchandise and the entire
        company will fall in your midst.
35 All the inhabitants of the isles will
        be astonished at you;
    Their kings will be greatly afraid,

And *their* countenance will be
    troubled.
36 The merchants among the peoples
    will hiss at you;
    You will become a horror, and *be*
        no more forever.' " ' "

28

The word of the LORD came to me
again, saying, 2 "Son of man, say to the
prince of Tyre, 'Thus says the Lord GOD:

"Because your heart *is* lifted up,
    And you say, 'I *am* a god,
    I sit *in* the seat of gods,
    In the midst of the seas,'
    Yet you *are* a man, and not a god,
    Though you set your heart as the
        heart of a god
3   (Behold, you *are* wiser than
        Daniel!
    There is no secret that can be
        hidden from you!
4   With your wisdom and your
        understanding
    You have gained riches for
        yourself,
    And gathered gold and silver into
        your treasuries;
5   By your great wisdom in trade you
        have increased your riches,
    And your heart is lifted up because
        of your riches),"

6 'Therefore thus says the Lord GOD:

"Because you have set your heart as
        the heart of a god,
7   Behold, therefore, I will bring
        strangers against you,
    The most terrible of the nations;
    And they shall draw their swords
        against the beauty of your
        wisdom,
    And defile your splendor.
8   They shall throw you down into
        the Pit,
    And you shall die the death of the
        slain
    In the midst of the seas.

9 "Will you still say before him who
        slays you,
    'I *am* a god'?
    But you *shall be* a man, and not a
        god,

In the hand of him who slays you.
¹⁰ You shall die the death of the
uncircumcised
By the hand of aliens;
For I have spoken," says the Lord
GOD.' "

¹¹ Moreover the word of the LORD
came to me, saying, ¹² "Son of man, take
up a lamentation for the king of Tyre, and
say to him, 'Thus says the Lord GOD:

"You *were* the seal of perfection,
Full of wisdom and perfect in
beauty.
¹³ You were in Eden, the garden of
God;
Every precious stone *was* your
covering:
The sardius, topaz, and diamond,
Beryl, onyx, and jasper,
Sapphire, turquoise, and emerald
with gold.
The workmanship of your
timbrels and pipes
Was prepared for you on the day
you were created.

¹⁴ "You *were* the anointed cherub who
covers;
I established you;
You were on the holy mountain of
God;
You walked back and forth in the
midst of fiery stones.
¹⁵ You *were* perfect in your ways
from the day you were created,
Till iniquity was found in you.

¹⁶ "By the abundance of your trading
You became filled with violence
within,
And you sinned;
Therefore I cast you as a profane
thing
Out of the mountain of God;
And I destroyed you, O covering
cherub,
From the midst of the fiery stones.

¹⁷ "Your heart was lifted up because
of your beauty;
You corrupted your wisdom for
the sake of your splendor;
I cast you to the ground,

I laid you before kings,
That they might gaze at you.

¹⁸ "You defiled your sanctuaries
By the multitude of your
iniquities,
By the iniquity of your trading;
Therefore I brought fire from
your midst;
It devoured you,
And I turned you to ashes upon
the earth
In the sight of all who saw you.
¹⁹ All who knew you among the
peoples are astonished at you;
You have become a horror,
And *shall be* no more forever." ' "

²⁰ Then the word of the LORD came to
me, saying, ²¹ "Son of man, set your face
toward Sidon, and prophesy against her,
²² and say, 'Thus says the Lord GOD:

"Behold, I *am* against you,
O Sidon;
I will be glorified in your midst;
And they shall know that I *am* the
LORD,
When I execute judgments in her
and am hallowed in her.
²³ For I will send pestilence upon
her,
And blood in her streets;
The wounded shall be judged in
her midst
By the sword against her on every
side;
Then they shall know that I *am*
the LORD.

²⁴ "And there shall no longer be a prick-
ing brier or a painful thorn for the house
of Israel from among all *who are* around
them, who despise them. Then they shall
know that I *am* the Lord GOD."
²⁵ 'Thus says the Lord GOD: "When
I have gathered the house of Israel from
the peoples among whom they are scattered, and am hallowed in them in the
sight of the Gentiles, then they will dwell
in their own land which I gave to My servant Jacob. ²⁶ And they will dwell safely
there, build houses, and plant vineyards;
yes, they will dwell securely, when I execute judgments on all those around them

who despise them. Then they shall know that I *am* the LORD their God." ' "

~ PSALM 129:1–4 ~

1 "Many a time they have afflicted me
    from my youth,"
Let Israel now say—
2 "Many a time they have afflicted me
    from my youth;
Yet they have not prevailed against
    me.
3 The plowers plowed on my back;
They made their furrows long."
4 The LORD *is* righteous;
He has cut in pieces the cords of the
    wicked.

~ PROVERBS 28:26 ~

26 He who trusts in his own heart is a
    fool,
But whoever walks wisely will be
    delivered.

~ HEBREWS 12:1–29 ~

Therefore we also, since we are surrounded by so great a cloud of witnesses, let us lay aside every weight, and the sin which so easily ensnares *us,* and let us run with endurance the race that is set before us, 2 looking unto Jesus, the author and finisher of *our* faith, who for the joy that was set before Him endured the cross, despising the shame, and has sat down at the right hand of the throne of God.

3 For consider Him who endured such hostility from sinners against Himself, lest you become weary and discouraged in your souls. 4 You have not yet resisted to bloodshed, striving against sin. 5 And you have forgotten the exhortation which speaks to you as to sons:

"My son, do not despise the
    chastening of the LORD,
Nor be discouraged when you are
    rebuked by Him;
6 For whom the LORD loves He
    chastens,
And scourges every son whom He
    receives."

7 If you endure chastening, God deals with you as with sons; for what son is there whom a father does not chasten? 8 But if you are without chastening, of which all have become partakers, then you are illegitimate and not sons. 9 Furthermore, we have had human fathers who corrected *us,* and we paid *them* respect. Shall we not much more readily be in subjection to the Father of spirits and live? 10 For they indeed for a few days chastened *us* as seemed *best* to them, but He for *our* profit, that *we* may be partakers of His holiness. 11 Now no chastening seems to be joyful for the present, but painful; nevertheless, afterward it yields the peaceable fruit of righteousness to those who have been trained by it.

12 Therefore strengthen the hands which hang down, and the feeble knees, 13 and make straight paths for your feet, so that what is lame may not be *dislocated,* but rather be healed.

14 Pursue peace with all *people,* and holiness, without which no one will see the Lord: 15 looking carefully lest anyone fall short of the grace of God; lest any root of bitterness springing up cause trouble, and by this many become defiled; 16 lest there *be* any fornicator or profane person like Esau, who for one morsel of food sold his birthright. 17 For you know that afterward, when he wanted to inherit the blessing, he was rejected, for he found no place for repentance, though he sought it diligently with tears.

18 For you have not come to the mountain that may be touched and that burned with fire, and to blackness and darkness and tempest, 19 and the sound of a trumpet and the voice of words, so that those who heard *it* begged that the word should not be spoken to them anymore. 20 (For they could not endure what was commanded: "And if so much as a beast touches the mountain, it shall be stoned or shot with an arrow." 21 And so terrifying was the sight *that* Moses said, "I am exceedingly afraid and trembling.")

22 But you have come to Mount Zion and to the city of the living God, the heavenly Jerusalem, to an innumerable company of angels, 23 to the general assembly and church of the firstborn *who are* registered in heaven, to God the Judge

of all, to the spirits of just men made perfect, [24] to Jesus the Mediator of the new covenant, and to the blood of sprinkling that speaks better things than *that of* Abel.

[25] See that you do not refuse Him who speaks. For if they did not escape who refused Him who spoke on earth, much more *shall we not escape* if we turn away from Him who *speaks* from heaven, [26] whose voice then shook the earth; but now He has promised, saying, "Yet once

more I shake not only the earth, but also heaven." [27] Now this, "Yet once more," indicates the removal of those things that are being shaken, as of things that are made, that the things which cannot be shaken may remain.

[28] Therefore, since we are receiving a kingdom which cannot be shaken, let us have grace, by which we may serve God acceptably with reverence and godly fear. [29] For our God *is* a consuming fire.

~ EZEKIEL 29:1—30:26 ~

In the tenth year, in the tenth *month,* on the twelfth *day* of the month, the word of the LORD came to me, saying, [2] "Son of man, set your face against Pharaoh king of Egypt, and prophesy against him, and against all Egypt. [3] Speak, and say, 'Thus says the Lord GOD:

"Behold, I *am* against you,
   O Pharaoh king of Egypt,
   O great monster who lies in the
      midst of his rivers,
   Who has said, 'My River *is* my
      own;
   I have made *it* for myself.'
[4]   But I will put hooks in your jaws,
   And cause the fish of your rivers
      to stick to your scales;
   I will bring you up out of the
      midst of your rivers,
   And all the fish in your rivers will
      stick to your scales.
[5]   I will leave you in the wilderness,
   You and all the fish of your rivers;
   You shall fall on the open field;
   You shall not be picked up or
      gathered.
   I have given you as food
   To the beasts of the field
   And to the birds of the heavens.

[6]   "Then all the inhabitants of Egypt
   Shall know that I *am* the LORD,
   Because they have been a staff of
      reed to the house of Israel.
[7]   When they took hold of you with
      the hand,

You broke and tore all their
      shoulders;
   When they leaned on you,
   You broke and made all their
      backs quiver."

[8] 'Therefore thus says the Lord GOD: "Surely I will bring a sword upon you and cut off from you man and beast. [9] And the land of Egypt shall become desolate and waste; then they will know that I *am* the LORD, because he said, 'The River *is* mine, and I have made *it*.' [10] Indeed, therefore, I *am* against you and against your rivers, and I will make the land of Egypt utterly waste and desolate, from Migdol *to* Syene, as far as the border of Ethiopia. [11] Neither foot of man shall pass through it nor foot of beast pass through it, and it shall be uninhabited forty years. [12] I will make the land of Egypt desolate in the midst of the countries *that are* desolate; and among the cities *that are* laid waste, her cities shall be desolate forty years; and I will scatter the Egyptians among the nations and disperse them throughout the countries."

[13] 'Yet, thus says the Lord GOD: "At the end of forty years I will gather the Egyptians from the peoples among whom they were scattered. [14] I will bring back the captives of Egypt and cause them to return to the land of Pathros, to the land of their origin, and there they shall be a lowly kingdom. [15] It shall be the lowliest of kingdoms; it shall never again exalt itself above the nations, for I will diminish them so

that they will not rule over the nations anymore. [16] No longer shall it be the confidence of the house of Israel, but will remind them of *their* iniquity when they turned to follow them. Then they shall know that I *am* the Lord GOD." ' "

[17] And it came to pass in the twenty-seventh year, in the first *month,* on the first *day* of the month, that the word of the LORD came to me, saying, [18] "Son of man, Nebuchadnezzar king of Babylon caused his army to labor strenuously against Tyre; every head *was* made bald, and every shoulder rubbed raw; yet neither he nor his army received wages from Tyre, for the labor which they expended on it. [19] Therefore thus says the Lord GOD: 'Surely I will give the land of Egypt to Nebuchadnezzar king of Babylon; he shall take away her wealth, carry off her spoil, and remove her pillage; and that will be the wages for his army. [20] I have given him the land of Egypt *for* his labor, because they worked for Me,' says the Lord GOD.

[21] 'In that day I will cause the horn of the house of Israel to spring forth, and I will open your mouth to speak in their midst. Then they shall know that I *am* the LORD.' "

30

The word of the LORD came to me again, saying, [2] "Son of man, prophesy and say, 'Thus says the Lord GOD:

"Wail, 'Woe to the day!'
[3]   For the day *is* near,
        Even the day of the LORD *is*
            near;
        It will be a day of clouds, the time
            of the Gentiles.
[4]   The sword shall come upon
            Egypt,
        And great anguish shall be in
            Ethiopia,
        When the slain fall in Egypt,
        And they take away her wealth,
        And her foundations are broken
            down.

[5] "Ethiopia, Libya, Lydia, all the mingled people, Chub, and the men of the lands who are allied, shall fall with them by the sword."

[6] 'Thus says the LORD:

"Those who uphold Egypt shall
    fall,
And the pride of her power shall
    come down.
From Migdol *to* Syene
Those within her shall fall by the
    sword,"
Says the Lord GOD.

[7]   "They shall be desolate in the midst
            of the desolate countries,
        And her cities shall be in the midst
            of the cities *that are* laid waste.
[8]   Then they will know that I *am* the
            LORD,
        When I have set a fire in Egypt
        And all her helpers are destroyed.
[9]   On that day messengers shall go
            forth from Me in ships
        To make the careless Ethiopians
            afraid,
        And great anguish shall come
            upon them,
        As on the day of Egypt;
        For indeed it is coming!"

[10] 'Thus says the Lord GOD:

"I will also make a multitude of
    Egypt to cease
By the hand of Nebuchadnezzar
    king of Babylon.
[11]   He and his people with him, the
            most terrible of the nations,
        Shall be brought to destroy the
            land;
        They shall draw their swords
            against Egypt,
        And fill the land with the slain.
[12]   I will make the rivers dry,
        And sell the land into the hand of
            the wicked;
        I will make the land waste, and all
            that is in it,
        By the hand of aliens.
        I, the LORD, have spoken."

[13] 'Thus says the Lord GOD:

"I will also destroy the idols,
And cause the images to cease
    from Noph;
There shall no longer be princes
    from the land of Egypt;
I will put fear in the land of Egypt.

Become a World-Traveler

In *Diamonds in the Dust*, Joni Eareckson Tada reveals that her bed is the place she prays best. Because of her paralysis, she is forced to lie down early each evening. Sometimes, a friend comes over to sit on the edge of her bed and pray with her. One night, her friend "sprang a surprise and brought a small shortwave radio. . . . She flicked it on and tuned in Trans World Radio from the Caribbean. Another jiggle of the knob and we picked up someone leading a Bible study over station HCJB in Ecuador. A little more fiddling and we pulled in the BBC from Hong Kong. Together, my friend and I tuned in to the world."

They used the radio as a springboard for prayer. Tada says, "We covered the planet, yet didn't budge beyond my bed. . . . Just as the voices of people around the world reached us through shortwave, my prayers, immediate and instant, were touching others. That very second, godly grace was being applied as I prayed, and I didn't even have to leave my room."

Where will you travel in prayer today? What spiritual battles will you wage in faraway places? As you pray, remember these words of Bernard of Clairvaux: "However great may be the temptation, if we know how to use the weapon of prayer well we shall come off conquerors at last, for prayer is more powerful than all the devils."

> Pray for us; for we are confident that we have a good conscience, in all things desiring to live honorably.
>
> *Hebrews 13:18*

¹⁴ I will make Pathros desolate,
Set fire to Zoan,
And execute judgments in No.
¹⁵ I will pour My fury on Sin, the
strength of Egypt;
I will cut off the multitude of No,
¹⁶ And set a fire in Egypt;
Sin shall have great pain,
No shall be split open,
And Noph *shall be in* distress
daily.
¹⁷ The young men of Aven and Pi
Beseth shall fall by the sword,
And these *cities* shall go into
captivity.
¹⁸ At Tehaphnehes the day shall also
be darkened,
When I break the yokes of Egypt
there.
And her arrogant strength shall
cease in her;
As for her, a cloud shall cover her,
And her daughters shall go into
captivity.
¹⁹ Thus I will execute judgments on
Egypt,
Then they shall know that I *am*
the LORD.' ' "

²⁰ And it came to pass in the eleventh
year, in the first *month,* on the seventh
day of the month, *that* the word of the
LORD came to me, saying, ²¹ "Son of man,
I have broken the arm of Pharaoh king of
Egypt; and see, it has not been bandaged
for healing, nor a splint put on to bind it,
to make it strong enough to hold a sword.
²² Therefore thus says the Lord GOD:
'Surely I *am* against Pharaoh king of
Egypt, and will break his arms, both the
strong one and the one that was broken;
and I will make the sword fall out of his
hand. ²³ I will scatter the Egyptians among
the nations, and disperse them through-
out the countries. ²⁴ I will strengthen the
arms of the king of Babylon and put My
sword in his hand; but I will break
Pharaoh's arms, and he will groan before
him with the groanings of a mortally
wounded *man.* ²⁵ Thus I will strengthen
the arms of the king of Babylon, but the
arms of Pharaoh shall fall down; they shall
know that I *am* the LORD, when I put My
sword into the hand of the king of
Babylon and he stretches it out against the

land of Egypt. ²⁶ I will scatter the Egyptians among the nations and disperse them
throughout the countries. Then they shall
know that I *am* the LORD.' "

~ PSALM 129:5–8 ~

⁵ Let all those who hate Zion
Be put to shame and turned back.
⁶ Let them be as the grass *on* the
housetops,
Which withers before it grows up,
⁷ With which the reaper does not fill
his hand,
Nor he who binds sheaves, his arms.
⁸ Neither let those who pass by them
say,
"The blessing of the LORD *be* upon
you;
We bless you in the name of the
LORD!"

~ PROVERBS 28:27 ~

²⁷ He who gives to the poor will not
lack,
But he who hides his eyes will have
many curses.

~ HEBREWS 13:1–25 ~

Let brotherly love continue. ² Do not forget to entertain strangers, for by so *doing*
some have unwittingly entertained angels.
³ Remember the prisoners as if chained
with them—those who are mistreated—
since you yourselves are in the body also.

⁴ Marriage *is* honorable among all,
and the bed undefiled; but fornicators and
adulterers God will judge.

⁵ *Let your* conduct *be* without covet-
ousness; *be* content with such things as
you have. For He Himself has said, "I will
never leave you nor forsake you." ⁶ So we
may boldly say:

"The LORD *is* my helper;
I will not fear.
What can man do to me?"

⁷ Remember those who rule over you,
who have spoken the word of God to
you, whose faith follow, considering the
outcome of *their* conduct. ⁸ Jesus Christ

is the same yesterday, today, and forever. [9] Do not be carried about with various and strange doctrines. For *it is* good that the heart be established by grace, not with foods which have not profited those who have been occupied with them.

[10] We have an altar from which those who serve the tabernacle have no right to eat. [11] For the bodies of those animals, whose blood is brought into the sanctuary by the high priest for sin, are burned outside the camp. [12] Therefore Jesus also, that He might sanctify the people with His own blood, suffered outside the gate. [13] Therefore let us go forth to Him, outside the camp, bearing His reproach. [14] For here we have no continuing city, but we seek the one to come. [15] Therefore by Him let us continually offer the sacrifice of praise to God, that is, the fruit of *our* lips, giving thanks to His name. [16] But do not forget to do good and to share, for with such sacrifices God is well pleased.

[17] Obey those who rule over you, and be submissive, for they watch out for your souls, as those who must give account. Let them do so with joy and not with grief, for that would be unprofitable for you.

[18] Pray for us; for we are confident that we have a good conscience, in all things desiring to live honorably. [19] But I especially urge *you* to do this, that I may be restored to you the sooner.

[20] Now may the God of peace who brought up our Lord Jesus from the dead, that great Shepherd of the sheep, through the blood of the everlasting covenant, [21] make you complete in every good work to do His will, working in you what is well pleasing in His sight, through Jesus Christ, to whom *be* glory forever and ever. Amen.

[22] And I appeal to you, brethren, bear with the word of exhortation, for I have written to you in few words. [23] Know that *our* brother Timothy has been set free, with whom I shall see you if he comes shortly.

[24] Greet all those who rule over you, and all the saints. Those from Italy greet you.

[25] Grace *be* with you all. Amen.

READING 324 · NOVEMBER 20

~ EZEKIEL 31:1—32:32 ~

Now it came to pass in the eleventh year, in the third *month,* on the first *day* of the month, *that* the word of the LORD came to me, saying, [2] "Son of man, say to Pharaoh king of Egypt and to his multitude:

'Whom are you like in your greatness?
[3] Indeed Assyria *was* a cedar in Lebanon,
With fine branches that shaded the forest,
And of high stature;
And its top was among the thick boughs.
[4] The waters made it grow;
Underground waters gave it height,
With their rivers running around the place where it was planted,
And sent out rivulets to all the trees of the field.

[5] 'Therefore its height was exalted above all the trees of the field;
Its boughs were multiplied,
And its branches became long because of the abundance of water,
As it sent them out.
[6] All the birds of the heavens made their nests in its boughs;
Under its branches all the beasts of the field brought forth their young;
And in its shadow all great nations made their home.

[7] 'Thus it was beautiful in greatness and in the length of its branches,
Because its roots reached to abundant waters.
[8] The cedars in the garden of God could not hide it;

The fir trees were not like its
boughs,
And the chestnut trees were not
like its branches;
No tree in the garden of God was
like it in beauty.
9 I made it beautiful with a
multitude of branches,
So that all the trees of Eden envied
it,
That *were* in the garden of God.'

10 "Therefore thus says the Lord GOD: 'Because you have increased in height, and it set its top among the thick boughs, and its heart was lifted up in its height, 11 therefore I will deliver it into the hand of the mighty one of the nations, and he shall surely deal with it; I have driven it out for its wickedness. 12 And aliens, the most terrible of the nations, have cut it down and left it; its branches have fallen on the mountains and in all the valleys; its boughs lie broken by all the rivers of the land; and all the peoples of the earth have gone from under its shadow and left it.

13 'On its ruin will remain all the
birds of the heavens,
And all the beasts of the field will
come to its branches—

14 'So that no trees by the waters may ever again exalt themselves for their height, nor set their tops among the thick boughs, that no tree which drinks water may ever be high enough to reach up to them.

'For they have all been delivered to
death,
To the depths of the earth,
Among the children of men who
go down to the Pit.'

15 "Thus says the Lord GOD: 'In the day when it went down to hell, I caused mourning. I covered the deep because of it. I restrained its rivers, and the great waters were held back. I caused Lebanon to mourn for it, and all the trees of the field wilted because of it. 16 I made the nations shake at the sound of its fall, when I cast it down to hell together with those who descend into the Pit; and all

the trees of Eden, the choice and best of Lebanon, all that drink water, were comforted in the depths of the earth. 17 They also went down to hell with it, with those *slain* by the sword; and *those who were* its *strong* arm dwelt in its shadows among the nations.

18 'To which of the trees in Eden will you then be likened in glory and greatness? Yet you shall be brought down with the trees of Eden to the depths of the earth; you shall lie in the midst of the uncircumcised, with *those* slain by the sword. This *is* Pharaoh and all his multitude,' says the Lord GOD."

32 And it came to pass in the twelfth year, in the twelfth *month,* on the first *day* of the month, *that* the word of the LORD came to me, saying, 2 "Son of man, take up a lamentation for Pharaoh king of Egypt, and say to him:

'You are like a young lion among
the nations,
And you *are* like a monster in the
seas,
Bursting forth in your rivers,
Troubling the waters with your
feet,
And fouling their rivers.'

3 "Thus says the Lord GOD:

'I will therefore spread My net
over you with a company of
many people,
And they will draw you up in My
net.
4 Then I will leave you on the land;
I will cast you out on the open
fields,
And cause to settle on you all the
birds of the heavens.
And with you I will fill the beasts
of the whole earth.
5 I will lay your flesh on the
mountains,
And fill the valleys with your
carcass.

6 'I will also water the land with the
flow of your blood,
Even to the mountains;

A Pound of Prayer

Just after World War I, a woman went into a store and asked the grocer for food to make a Christmas dinner for her children. He asked her how much she had to spend. She answered, "My husband was killed in the war. I have nothing to offer but a prayer."

The grocer said gruffly, "Write it down," and turned to go about his business. To his surprise however, the woman took a slip of paper from her purse and handed it to him. "I wrote it down during the night while I was watching over my sick baby," she said. The grocer took the paper and callously placed it on the weight side of his old-fashioned scales. He said, "I'll give you food equal to the weight of this prayer."

To his great astonishment, when he put a loaf of bread on the other side of the scale it didn't budge. Startled, he added a brick of cheese, and then a turkey, but it still didn't move. Finally, he had loaded so much food on the scale it couldn't hold any more. He handed the woman a bag and said, "You'll have to sack it all yourself," then turned away. It was only after the woman left, tears of joy streaming down her face, that the grocer discovered his scale had broken at the precise moment he placed her prayer on it. For the first time, he looked down to read what the woman had written: "Please, Lord, give us this day our daily bread."

And the riverbeds will be full of
     you.
7 When *I* put out your light,
     I will cover the heavens, and make
        its stars dark;
     I will cover the sun with a cloud,
     And the moon shall not give her
        light.
8 All the bright lights of the heavens
        I will make dark over you,
     And bring darkness upon your
        land,'
   Says the Lord GOD.

9 'I will also trouble the hearts of many
peoples, when I bring your destruction
among the nations, into the countries
which you have not known. 10 Yes, I will
make many peoples astonished at you, and
their kings shall be horribly afraid of you
when I brandish My sword before them;
and they shall tremble *every* moment,
every man for his own life, in the day of
your fall.'
   11 "For thus says the Lord GOD: 'The
sword of the king of Babylon shall come
upon you. 12 By the swords of the mighty
warriors, all of them the most terrible of
the nations, I will cause your multitude
to fall.

   'They shall plunder the pomp of
     Egypt,
     And all its multitude shall be
        destroyed.
13 Also I will destroy all its animals
     From beside its great waters;
     The foot of man shall muddy
        them no more,
     Nor shall the hooves of animals
        muddy them.
14 Then I will make their waters
        clear,
     And make their rivers run like oil,'
   Says the Lord GOD.

15 'When I make the land of Egypt
        desolate,
     And the country is destitute of all
        that once filled it,
     When I strike all who dwell in it,
     Then they shall know that I *am*
        the LORD.

16 'This *is* the lamentation
     With which they shall lament her;
     The daughters of the nations shall
        lament her;
     They shall lament for her, for
        Egypt,
     And for all her multitude,'
   Says the Lord GOD."

17 It came to pass also in the twelfth year,
on the fifteenth *day* of the month, that
the word of the LORD came to me, saying:

18 "Son of man, wail over the
        multitude of Egypt,
     And cast them down to the depths
        of the earth,
     Her and the daughters of the
        famous nations,
     With those who go down to the
        Pit:
19 'Whom do you surpass in beauty?
     Go down, be placed with the
        uncircumcised.'

20 "They shall fall in the midst of
        those slain by the sword;
     She is delivered to the sword,
     Drawing her and all her
        multitudes.
21 The strong among the mighty
     Shall speak to him out of the
        midst of hell
     With those who help him:
     'They have gone down,
     They lie with the uncircumcised,
        slain by the sword.'

22 "Assyria *is* there, and all her
        company,
     With their graves all around her,
     All of them slain, fallen by the
        sword.
23 Her graves are set in the recesses
        of the Pit,
     And her company is all around her
        grave,
     All of them slain, fallen by the
        sword,
     Who caused terror in the land of
        the living.

24 "There *is* Elam and all her
        multitude,

All around her grave,
All of them slain, fallen by the
    sword,
Who have gone down
    uncircumcised to the lower
    parts of the earth,
Who caused their terror in the
    land of the living;
Now they bear their shame with
    those who go down to the Pit.

25 They have set her bed in the midst
    of the slain,
With all her multitude,
With her graves all around it,
All of them uncircumcised, slain
    by the sword;
Though their terror was caused
In the land of the living,
Yet they bear their shame
With those who go down to the
    Pit;
It was put in the midst of the slain.

26 "There *are* Meshech and Tubal and
    all their multitudes,
With all their graves around it,
All of them uncircumcised, slain
    by the sword,
Though they caused their terror in
    the land of the living.

27 They do not lie with the mighty
Who are fallen of the
    uncircumcised,
Who have gone down to hell with
    their weapons of war;
They have laid their swords under
    their heads,
But their iniquities will be on their
    bones,
Because of the terror of the
    mighty in the land of the living.

28 Yes, you shall be broken in the
    midst of the uncircumcised,
And lie with *those* slain by the
    sword.

29 "There *is* Edom,
Her kings and all her princes,
Who despite their might
Are laid beside *those* slain by the
    sword;
They shall lie with the
    uncircumcised,
And with those who go down to
    the Pit.

30 There *are* the princes of the north,
All of them, and all the Sidonians,
Who have gone down with the
    slain
In shame at the terror which they
    caused by their might;
They lie uncircumcised with *those*
    slain by the sword,
And bear their shame with those
    who go down to the Pit.

31 "Pharaoh will see them
And be comforted over all his
    multitude,
Pharaoh and all his army,
Slain by the sword,"
Says the Lord GOD.

32 "For I have caused My terror in the
    land of the living;
And he shall be placed in the
    midst of the uncircumcised
With *those* slain by the sword,
Pharaoh and all his multitude,"
Says the Lord GOD.

~ PSALM 130:1–4 ~

1 Out of the depths I have cried to
    You, O LORD;
2 Lord, hear my voice!
Let Your ears be attentive
To the voice of my supplications.

3 If You, LORD, should mark iniquities,
    O Lord, who could stand?
4 But *there is* forgiveness with You,
That You may be feared.

~ PROVERBS 28:28 ~

28 When the wicked arise, men hide
    themselves;
But when they perish, the righteous
    increase.

~ JAMES 1:1–27 ~

James, a bondservant of God and of the
Lord Jesus Christ,

To the twelve tribes which are scattered
abroad:

Greetings.

² My brethren, count it all joy when you fall into various trials, ³ knowing that the testing of your faith produces patience. ⁴ But let patience have *its* perfect work, that you may be perfect and complete, lacking nothing. ⁵ If any of you lacks wisdom, let him ask of God, who gives to all liberally and without reproach, and it will be given to him. ⁶ But let him ask in faith, with no doubting, for he who doubts is like a wave of the sea driven and tossed by the wind. ⁷ For let not that man suppose that he will receive anything from the Lord; ⁸ *he is* a double-minded man, unstable in all his ways.

⁹ Let the lowly brother glory in his exaltation, ¹⁰ but the rich in his humiliation, because as a flower of the field he will pass away. ¹¹ For no sooner has the sun risen with a burning heat than it withers the grass; its flower falls, and its beautiful appearance perishes. So the rich man also will fade away in his pursuits.

¹² Blessed *is* the man who endures temptation; for when he has been approved, he will receive the crown of life which the Lord has promised to those who love Him. ¹³ Let no one say when he is tempted, "I am tempted by God"; for God cannot be tempted by evil, nor does He Himself tempt anyone. ¹⁴ But each one is tempted when he is drawn away by his own desires and enticed. ¹⁵ Then, when desire has conceived, it gives birth to sin; and sin, when it is full-grown, brings forth death.

¹⁶ Do not be deceived, my beloved brethren. ¹⁷ Every good gift and every perfect gift is from above, and comes down from the Father of lights, with whom there is no variation or shadow of turning. ¹⁸ Of His own will He brought us forth by the word of truth, that we might be a kind of firstfruits of His creatures.

¹⁹ So then, my beloved brethren, let every man be swift to hear, slow to speak, slow to wrath; ²⁰ for the wrath of man does not produce the righteousness of God.

²¹ Therefore lay aside all filthiness and overflow of wickedness, and receive with meekness the implanted word, which is able to save your souls.

²² But be doers of the word, and not hearers only, deceiving yourselves. ²³ For if anyone is a hearer of the word and not a doer, he is like a man observing his natural face in a mirror; ²⁴ for he observes himself, goes away, and immediately forgets what kind of man he was. ²⁵ But he who looks into the perfect law of liberty and continues *in it,* and is not a forgetful hearer but a doer of the work, this one will be blessed in what he does.

²⁶ If anyone among you thinks he is religious, and does not bridle his tongue but deceives his own heart, this one's religion *is* useless. ²⁷ Pure and undefiled religion before God and the Father is this: to visit orphans and widows in their trouble, *and* to keep oneself unspotted from the world.

READING 325 · NOVEMBER 21

~ EZEKIEL 33:1—34:31 ~

A gain the word of the LORD came to me, saying, ² "Son of man, speak to the children of your people, and say to them: 'When I bring the sword upon a land, and the people of the land take a man from their territory and make him their watchman, ³ when he sees the sword coming upon the land, if he blows the trumpet and warns the people, ⁴ then whoever hears the sound of the trumpet and does not take warning, if the sword comes and takes him away, his blood shall be on his *own* head. ⁵ He heard the sound of the trumpet, but did not take warning; his blood shall be upon himself. But he who takes warning will save his life. ⁶ But if the watchman sees the sword coming and does not blow the trumpet, and the people are not warned, and the sword comes and takes *any* person from among them, he is taken away in his iniquity; but his blood I will require at the watchman's hand.'

⁷ "So you, son of man: I have made you

In Need of Mercy

For judgment is without mercy to the one who has shown no mercy. Mercy triumphs over judgment.

James 2:13

According to a traditional Hebrew legend, Abraham was sitting by his tent one evening when he saw an old man walking toward him. He could tell long before the man arrived that he was weary from age and travel. Abraham rushed out to greet him, and then invited him into his tent. He washed the old man's feet and gave him something to drink and eat.

The old man immediately began eating without saying a prayer or invoking a blessing. Abraham asked him, "Don't you worship God?" The old traveler replied, "I worship fire only and reverence no other god." Upon hearing this, Abraham grabbed the old man by the shoulders and with indignation, threw him out of his tent into the cold night air.

The old man walked off into the night and after he had gone, God called to His friend Abraham and asked where the stranger was. Abraham replied, "I forced him out of my tent because he did not worship You." The Lord responded, "I have suffered him these eighty years although he dishonors Me. Could you not endure him one night?"

Do you know someone who needs to experience your mercy as a tangible expression of the mercy God is extending to him or her? Don't turn them away, take them in.

———⌘———

a watchman for the house of Israel; therefore you shall hear a word from My mouth and warn them for Me. [8] When I say to the wicked, 'O wicked *man*, you shall surely die!' and you do not speak to warn the wicked from his way, that wicked *man* shall die in his iniquity; but his blood I will require at your hand. [9] Nevertheless if you warn the wicked to turn from his way, and he does not turn from his way, he shall die in his iniquity; but you have delivered your soul.

[10] "Therefore you, O son of man, say to the house of Israel: 'Thus you say, "If our transgressions and our sins *lie* upon us, and we pine away in them, how can we then live?" ' [11] Say to them: '*As* I live,' says the Lord GOD, 'I have no pleasure in the death of the wicked, but that the wicked turn from his way and live. Turn, turn from your evil ways! For why should you die, O house of Israel?'

[12] "Therefore you, O son of man, say to the children of your people: 'The righteousness of the righteous man shall not deliver him in the day of his transgression; as for the wickedness of the wicked, he shall not fall because of it in the day that he turns from his wickedness; nor shall the righteous be able to live because of *his righteousness* in the day that he sins.' [13] When I say to the righteous *that* he shall surely live, but he trusts in his own righteousness and commits iniquity, none of his righteous works shall be remembered; but because of the iniquity that he has committed, he shall die. [14] Again, when I say to the wicked, 'You shall surely die,' if he turns from his sin and does what is lawful and right, [15] *if* the wicked restores the pledge, gives back what he has stolen, and walks in the statutes of life without committing iniquity, he shall surely live; he shall not die. [16] None of his sins which he has committed shall be remembered against him; he has done what is lawful and right; he shall surely live.

[17] "Yet the children of your people say, 'The way of the LORD is not fair.' But it is their way which is not fair! [18] When the righteous turns from his righteousness and commits iniquity, he shall die because of it. [19] But when the wicked turns from his wickedness and does what is lawful and right, he shall live because of it. [20] Yet you say, 'The way of the LORD is not fair.' O house of Israel, I will judge every one of you according to his own ways."

[21] And it came to pass in the twelfth year of our captivity, in the tenth *month*, on the fifth *day* of the month, *that* one who had escaped from Jerusalem came to me and said, "The city has been captured!" [22] Now the hand of the LORD had been upon me the evening before the man came who had escaped. And He had opened my mouth; so when he came to me in the morning, my mouth was opened, and I was no longer mute.

[23] Then the word of the LORD came to me, saying: [24] "Son of man, they who inhabit those ruins in the land of Israel are saying, 'Abraham was only one, and he inherited the land. But we *are* many; the land has been given to us as a possession.' [25] "Therefore say to them, 'Thus says the Lord GOD: "You eat *meat* with blood, you lift up your eyes toward your idols, and shed blood. Should you then possess the land? [26] You rely on your sword, you commit abominations, and you defile one another's wives. Should you then possess the land?" '

[27] "Say thus to them, 'Thus says the Lord GOD: "*As* I live, surely those who *are* in the ruins shall fall by the sword, and the one who *is* in the open field I will give to the beasts to be devoured, and those who *are* in the strongholds and caves shall die of the pestilence. [28] For I will make the land most desolate, her arrogant strength shall cease, and the mountains of Israel shall be so desolate that no one will pass through. [29] Then they shall know that I *am* the LORD, when I have made the land most desolate because of all their abominations which they have committed." '

[30] "As for you, son of man, the children of your people are talking about you beside the walls and in the doors of the houses; and they speak to one another, everyone saying to his brother, 'Please come and hear what the word is that comes from the LORD.' [31] So they come to you as people do, they sit before you *as* My people, and they hear your words, but they do not do them; for with their mouth they show much love, *but* their hearts pursue their *own* gain.

32 Indeed you *are* to them as a very lovely song of one who has a pleasant voice and can play well on an instrument; for they hear your words, but they do not do them. 33 And when this comes to pass—surely it will come—then they will know that a prophet has been among them.

34 And the word of the LORD came to me, saying, 2 "Son of man, prophesy against the shepherds of Israel, prophesy and say to them, 'Thus says the Lord GOD to the shepherds: "Woe to the shepherds of Israel who feed themselves! Should not the shepherds feed the flocks? 3 You eat the fat and clothe yourselves with the wool; you slaughter the fatlings, *but* you do not feed the flock. 4 The weak you have not strengthened, nor have you healed those who were sick, nor bound up the broken, nor brought back what was driven away, nor sought what was lost; but with force and cruelty you have ruled them. 5 So they were scattered because *there was* no shepherd; and they became food for all the beasts of the field when they were scattered. 6 My sheep wandered through all the mountains, and on every high hill; yes, My flock was scattered over the whole face of the earth, and no one was seeking or searching *for them*."

7 'Therefore, you shepherds, hear the word of the LORD: 8 "*As* I live," says the Lord GOD, "surely because My flock became a prey, and My flock became food for every beast of the field, because *there was* no shepherd, nor did My shepherds search for My flock, but the shepherds fed themselves and did not feed My flock"— 9 therefore, O shepherds, hear the word of the LORD! 10 Thus says the Lord GOD: "Behold, I *am* against the shepherds, and I will require My flock at their hand; I will cause them to cease feeding the sheep, and the shepherds shall feed themselves no more; for I will deliver My flock from their mouths, that they may no longer be food for them."

11 'For thus says the Lord GOD: "Indeed I Myself will search for My sheep and seek them out. 12 As a shepherd seeks out his flock on the day he is among his scattered sheep, so will I seek out My sheep and deliver them from all the places where they were scattered on a cloudy and dark day. 13 And I will bring them out from the peoples and gather them from the countries, and will bring them to their own land; I will feed them on the mountains of Israel, in the valleys and in all the inhabited places of the country. 14 I will feed them in good pasture, and their fold shall be on the high mountains of Israel. There they shall lie down in a good fold and feed in rich pasture on the mountains of Israel. 15 I will feed My flock, and I will make them lie down," says the Lord GOD. 16 "I will seek what was lost and bring back what was driven away, bind up the broken and strengthen what was sick; but I will destroy the fat and the strong, and feed them in judgment."

17 'And *as for* you, O My flock, thus says the Lord GOD: "Behold, I shall judge between sheep and sheep, between rams and goats. 18 *Is it* too little for you to have eaten up the good pasture, that you must tread down with your feet the residue of your pasture—and to have drunk of the clear waters, that you must foul the residue with your feet? 19 And *as for* My flock, they eat what you have trampled with your feet, and they drink what you have fouled with your feet."

20 'Therefore thus says the Lord GOD to them: "Behold, I Myself will judge between the fat and the lean sheep. 21 Because you have pushed with side and shoulder, butted all the weak ones with your horns, and scattered them abroad, 22 therefore I will save My flock, and they shall no longer be a prey; and I will judge between sheep and sheep. 23 I will establish one shepherd over them, and he shall feed them—My servant David. He shall feed them and be their shepherd. 24 And I, the LORD, will be their God, and My servant David a prince among them; I, the LORD, have spoken.

25 "I will make a covenant of peace with them, and cause wild beasts to cease from the land; and they will dwell safely in the wilderness and sleep in the woods. 26 I will make them and the places all around My hill a blessing; and I will cause showers to come down in their season; there shall be showers of blessing. 27 Then the trees of the field shall yield their fruit, and the earth shall yield her increase. They shall be safe in their land; and they shall know

that I *am* the LORD, when I have broken the bands of their yoke and delivered them from the hand of those who enslaved them. 28 And they shall no longer be a prey for the nations, nor shall beasts of the land devour them; but they shall dwell safely, and no one shall make *them* afraid. 29 I will raise up for them a garden of renown, and they shall no longer be consumed with hunger in the land, nor bear the shame of the Gentiles anymore. 30 Thus they shall know that I, the LORD their God, *am* with them, and they, the house of Israel, *are* My people," says the Lord GOD.' "

31 "You are My flock, the flock of My pasture; you *are* men, *and* I *am* your God," says the Lord GOD.

∼ PSALM 130:5–8 ∼

5 I wait for the LORD, my soul waits,
And in His word I do hope.
6 My soul *waits* for the Lord
More than those who watch for the morning—
Yes, more than those who watch for the morning.

7 O Israel, hope in the LORD;
For with the LORD *there is* mercy,
And with Him *is* abundant redemption.
8 And He shall redeem Israel
From all his iniquities.

∼ PROVERBS 29:1 ∼

1 He who is often rebuked, *and* hardens *his* neck,
Will suddenly be destroyed, and that without remedy.

∼ JAMES 2:1–26 ∼

My brethren, do not hold the faith of our Lord Jesus Christ, *the Lord* of glory, with partiality. 2 For if there should come into your assembly a man with gold rings, in fine apparel, and there should also come in a poor man in filthy clothes, 3 and you pay attention to the one wearing the fine clothes and say to him, "You sit here in a good place," and say to the poor man,

"You stand there," or, "Sit here at my footstool," 4 have you not shown partiality among yourselves, and become judges with evil thoughts?

5 Listen, my beloved brethren: Has God not chosen the poor of this world *to be* rich in faith and heirs of the kingdom which He promised to those who love Him? 6 But you have dishonored the poor man. Do not the rich oppress you and drag you into the courts? 7 Do they not blaspheme that noble name by which you are called?

8 If you really fulfill *the* royal law according to the Scripture, "You shall love your neighbor as yourself," you do well; 9 but if you show partiality, you commit sin, and are convicted by the law as transgressors. 10 For whoever shall keep the whole law, and yet stumble in one *point,* he is guilty of all. 11 For He who said, "Do not commit adultery," also said, "Do not murder." Now if you do not commit adultery, but you do murder, you have become a transgressor of the law. 12 So speak and so do as those who will be judged by the law of liberty. 13 For judgment is without mercy to the one who has shown no mercy. Mercy triumphs over judgment.

14 What *does it* profit, my brethren, if someone says he has faith but does not have works? Can faith save him? 15 If a brother or sister is naked and destitute of daily food, 16 and one of you says to them, "Depart in peace, be warmed and filled," but you do not give them the things which are needed for the body, what *does it* profit? 17 Thus also faith by itself, if it does not have works, is dead.

18 But someone will say, "You have faith, and I have works." Show me your faith without your works, and I will show you my faith by my works. 19 You believe that there is one God. You do well. Even the demons believe—and tremble! 20 But do you want to know, O foolish man, that faith without works is dead? 21 Was not Abraham our father justified by works when he offered Isaac his son on the altar? 22 Do you see that faith was working together with his works, and by works faith was made perfect? 23 And the Scripture was fulfilled which says, "Abraham believed God, and it was accounted to him for righteousness." And he was called the

friend of God. ²⁴ You see then that a man is justified by works, and not by faith only.

²⁵ Likewise, was not Rahab the harlot also justified by works when she received the messengers and sent *them* out another way?

²⁶ For as the body without the spirit is dead, so faith without works is dead also.

READING 326 · NOVEMBER 22

~ EZEKIEL 35:1—36:38 ~

Moreover the word of the LORD came to me, saying, ² "Son of man, set your face against Mount Seir and prophesy against it, ³ and say to it, 'Thus says the Lord GOD:

"Behold, O Mount Seir, I *am*
     against you;
I will stretch out My hand against
     you,
And make you most desolate;
⁴   I shall lay your cities waste,
And you shall be desolate.
Then you shall know that I *am* the
     LORD.

⁵ "Because you have had an ancient hatred, and have shed *the blood of* the children of Israel by the power of the sword at the time of their calamity, *when* their iniquity *came to an* end, ⁶ therefore, *as* I live," says the Lord GOD, "I will prepare you for blood, and blood shall pursue you; since you have not hated blood, therefore blood shall pursue you. ⁷ Thus I will make Mount Seir most desolate, and cut off from it the one who leaves and the one who returns. ⁸ And I will fill its mountains with the slain; on your hills and in your valleys and in all your ravines those who are slain by the sword shall fall. ⁹ I will make you perpetually desolate, and your cities shall be uninhabited; then you shall know that I *am* the LORD.

¹⁰ "Because you have said, 'These two nations and these two countries shall be mine, and we will possess them,' although the LORD was there, ¹¹ therefore, *as* I live," says the Lord GOD, "I will do according to your anger and according to the envy which you showed in your hatred against them; and I will make Myself known among them when I judge you. ¹² Then you shall know that I *am* the LORD. I have heard all your blasphemies which you have spoken against the mountains of Israel, saying, 'They are desolate; they are given to us to consume.' ¹³ Thus with your mouth you have boasted against Me and multiplied your words against Me; I have heard *them*."

¹⁴ 'Thus says the Lord GOD: "The whole earth will rejoice when I make you desolate. ¹⁵ As you rejoiced because the inheritance of the house of Israel was desolate, so I will do to you; you shall be desolate, O Mount Seir, as well as all of Edom—all of it! Then they shall know that I *am* the LORD." '

36 "And you, son of man, prophesy to the mountains of Israel, and say, 'O mountains of Israel, hear the word of the LORD! ² Thus says the Lord GOD: "Because the enemy has said of you, 'Aha! The ancient heights have become our possession,' " ' ³ therefore prophesy, and say, 'Thus says the Lord GOD: "Because they made *you* desolate and swallowed you up on every side, so that you became the possession of the rest of the nations, and you are taken up by the lips of talkers and slandered by the people"— ⁴ therefore, O mountains of Israel, hear the word of the Lord GOD! Thus says the Lord GOD to the mountains, the hills, the rivers, the valleys, the desolate wastes, and the cities that have been forsaken, which became plunder and mockery to the rest of the nations all around— ⁵ therefore thus says the Lord GOD: "Surely I have spoken in My burning jealousy against the rest of the nations and against all Edom, who gave My land to themselves as a possession, with wholehearted joy *and* spiteful minds, in order to plunder its open country." '

⁶ "Therefore prophesy concerning the land of Israel, and say to the mountains,

the hills, the rivers, and the valleys, 'Thus says the Lord GOD: "Behold, I have spoken in My jealousy and My fury, because you have borne the shame of the nations." [7] Therefore thus says the Lord GOD: "I have raised My hand in an oath that surely the nations that *are* around you shall bear their own shame. [8] But you, O mountains of Israel, you shall shoot forth your branches and yield your fruit to My people Israel, for they are about to come. [9] For indeed I *am* for you, and I will turn to you, and you shall be tilled and sown. [10] I will multiply men upon you, all the house of Israel, all of it; and the cities shall be inhabited and the ruins rebuilt. [11] I will multiply upon you man and beast; and they shall increase and bear young; I will make you inhabited as in former times, and do better *for you* than at your beginnings. Then you shall know that I *am* the LORD. [12] Yes, I will cause men to walk on you, My people Israel; they shall take possession of you, and you shall be their inheritance; no more shall you bereave them *of children*."

[13] 'Thus says the Lord GOD: "Because they say to you, 'You devour men and bereave your nation *of children*,' [14] therefore you shall devour men no more, nor bereave your nation anymore," says the Lord GOD. [15] Nor will I let you hear the taunts of the nations anymore, nor bear the reproach of the peoples anymore, nor shall you cause your nation to stumble anymore," says the Lord GOD.' "

[16] Moreover the word of the LORD came to me, saying: [17] "Son of man, when the house of Israel dwelt in their own land, they defiled it by their own ways and deeds; to Me their way was like the uncleanness of a woman in her customary impurity. [18] Therefore I poured out My fury on them for the blood they had shed on the land, and for their idols *with which* they had defiled it. [19] So I scattered them among the nations, and they were dispersed throughout the countries; I judged them according to their ways and their deeds. [20] When they came to the nations, wherever they went, they profaned My holy name—when they said of them, 'These *are* the people of the LORD, *and* yet they have gone out of His land.' [21] But I had concern for My holy name, which the house of Israel had profaned among the nations wherever they went.

[22] "Therefore say to the house of Israel, 'Thus says the Lord GOD: "I do not do *this* for your sake, O house of Israel, but for My holy name's sake, which you have profaned among the nations wherever you went. [23] And I will sanctify My great name, which has been profaned among the nations, which you have profaned in their midst; and the nations shall know that I *am* the LORD," says the Lord GOD, "when I am hallowed in you before their eyes. [24] For I will take you from among the nations, gather you out of all countries, and bring you into your own land. [25] Then I will sprinkle clean water on you, and you shall be clean; I will cleanse you from all your filthiness and from all your idols. [26] I will give you a new heart and put a new spirit within you; I will take the heart of stone out of your flesh and give you a heart of flesh. [27] I will put My Spirit within you and cause you to walk in My statutes, and you will keep My judgments and do *them*. [28] Then you shall dwell in the land that I gave to your fathers; you shall be My people, and I will be your God. [29] I will deliver you from all your uncleannesses. I will call for the grain and multiply it, and bring no famine upon you. [30] And I will multiply the fruit of your trees and the increase of your fields, so that you need never again bear the reproach of famine among the nations. [31] Then you will remember your evil ways and your deeds that *were* not good; and you will loathe yourselves in your own sight, for your iniquities and your abominations. [32] Not for your sake do I do *this*," says the Lord GOD, "let it be known to you. Be ashamed and confounded for your own ways, O house of Israel!"

[33] 'Thus says the Lord GOD: "On the day that I cleanse you from all your iniquities, I will also enable *you* to dwell in the cities, and the ruins shall be rebuilt. [34] The desolate land shall be tilled instead of lying desolate in the sight of all who pass by. [35] So they will say, 'This land that was desolate has become like the garden of Eden; and the wasted, desolate, and ruined cities *are now* fortified *and* inhabited.' [36] Then the nations which are left all around you shall know that I, the

The River Flows to the Sea

Two men once made small talk at a party: "You and your wife seem to get along very well," one man said. "Don't you ever have differences?" "Sure," said the other. "We often have differences, but we get over them quickly."

"How do you do that?" the first man asked. "Simple," said the second. "I don't tell her we have them."

In *Letters to Philip*, Charles Shedd describes a slightly different situation — harmony that comes after love has conquered conflict. He writes: "In one town where I lived two rivers met. There was a bluff high above them where you could sit and watch their coming together. . . . Those two nice streams came at each other like fury. I have actually seen them on days when it was almost frightening to watch. They clashed in a wild commotion of frenzy and confusion. . . . Then, as you watched, you could almost see the angry white caps pair off, bow in respect to each other, and join forces as if to say, 'Let us get along now. Ahead of us there is something better.' Sure enough, on downstream, at some distance, the river swept steadily on once more."

Don't avoid the conflicts in your marriage. Choose to apply God's love in order to overcome them. Unresolved conflicts weaken a marriage, but conflicts resolved with love help make two small streams into one large river, flowing on to something better.

LORD, have rebuilt the ruined places *and* planted what was desolate. I, the LORD, have spoken *it,* and I will do *it.*"

[37] 'Thus says the Lord GOD: "I will also let the house of Israel inquire of Me to do this for them: I will increase their men like a flock. [38] Like a flock *offered as* holy *sacrifices,* like the flock at Jerusalem on its feast days, so shall the ruined cities be filled with flocks of men. Then they shall know that I *am* the LORD." ' "

∼ PSALM 131:1-3 ∼

[1]   LORD, my heart is not haughty,
      Nor my eyes lofty.
      Neither do I concern myself with
         great matters,
      Nor with things too profound for
         me.

[2]   Surely I have calmed and quieted my
         soul,
      Like a weaned child with his mother;
      Like a weaned child *is* my soul
         within me.

[3]   O Israel, hope in the LORD
      From this time forth and forever.

∼ PROVERBS 29:2, 3 ∼

[2]   When the righteous are in authority,
         the people rejoice;
      But when a wicked *man* rules, the
         people groan.

[3]   Whoever loves wisdom makes his
         father rejoice,
      But a companion of harlots wastes
         his wealth.

∼ JAMES 3:1-18 ∼

My brethren, let not many of you become teachers, knowing that we shall receive a stricter judgment. [2] For we all stumble in many things. If anyone does not stumble in word, he *is* a perfect man, able also to bridle the whole body. [3] Indeed, we put bits in horses' mouths that they may obey us, and we turn their whole body. [4] Look also at ships: although they are so large and are driven by fierce winds, they are turned by a very small rudder wherever the pilot desires. [5] Even so the tongue is a little member and boasts great things.

See how great a forest a little fire kindles! [6] And the tongue *is* a fire, a world of iniquity. The tongue is so set among our members that it defiles the whole body, and sets on fire the course of nature; and it is set on fire by hell. [7] For every kind of beast and bird, of reptile and creature of the sea, is tamed and has been tamed by mankind. [8] But no man can tame the tongue. *It is* an unruly evil, full of deadly poison. [9] With it we bless our God and Father, and with it we curse men, who have been made in the similitude of God. [10] Out of the same mouth proceed blessing and cursing. My brethren, these things ought not to be so. [11] Does a spring send forth fresh *water* and bitter from the same opening? [12] Can a fig tree, my brethren, bear olives, or a grapevine bear figs? Thus no spring yields both salt water and fresh.

[13] Who *is* wise and understanding among you? Let him show by good conduct *that* his works *are done* in the meekness of wisdom. [14] But if you have bitter envy and self-seeking in your hearts, do not boast and lie against the truth. [15] This wisdom does not descend from above, but *is* earthly, sensual, demonic. [16] For where envy and self-seeking *exist,* confusion and every evil thing *are* there. [17] But the wisdom that is from above is first pure, then peaceable, gentle, willing to yield, full of mercy and good fruits, without partiality and without hypocrisy. [18] Now the fruit of righteousness is sown in peace by those who make peace.

~ EZEKIEL 37:1—38:23 ~

The hand of the LORD came upon me and brought me out in the Spirit of the LORD, and set me down in the midst of the valley; and it *was* full of bones. ² Then He caused me to pass by them all around, and behold, *there were* very many in the open valley; and indeed *they were* very dry. ³ And He said to me, "Son of man, can these bones live?"

So I answered, "O Lord GOD, You know."

⁴ Again He said to me, "Prophesy to these bones, and say to them, 'O dry bones, hear the word of the LORD! ⁵ Thus says the Lord GOD to these bones: "Surely I will cause breath to enter into you, and you shall live. ⁶ I will put sinews on you and bring flesh upon you, cover you with skin and put breath in you; and you shall live. Then you shall know that I *am* the LORD." ' "

⁷ So I prophesied as I was commanded; and as I prophesied, there was a noise, and suddenly a rattling; and the bones came together, bone to bone. ⁸ Indeed, as I looked, the sinews and the flesh came upon them, and the skin covered them over; but *there was* no breath in them.

⁹ Also He said to me, "Prophesy to the breath, prophesy, son of man, and say to the breath, 'Thus says the Lord GOD: "Come from the four winds, O breath, and breathe on these slain, that they may live." ' " ¹⁰ So I prophesied as He commanded me, and breath came into them, and they lived, and stood upon their feet, an exceedingly great army.

¹¹ Then He said to me, "Son of man, these bones are the whole house of Israel. They indeed say, 'Our bones are dry, our hope is lost, and we ourselves are cut off!' ¹² Therefore prophesy and say to them, 'Thus says the Lord GOD: "Behold, O My people, I will open your graves and cause you to come up from your graves, and bring you into the land of Israel. ¹³ Then you shall know that I *am* the LORD, when I have opened your graves, O My people, and brought you up from your graves. ¹⁴ I will put My Spirit in you, and you shall live, and I will place you in your own land.

Then you shall know that I, the LORD, have spoken *it* and performed *it*," says the LORD.' "

¹⁵ Again the word of the LORD came to me, saying, ¹⁶ "As for you, son of man, take a stick for yourself and write on it: 'For Judah and for the children of Israel, his companions.' Then take another stick and write on it, 'For Joseph, the stick of Ephraim, and *for* all the house of Israel, his companions.' ¹⁷ Then join them one to another for yourself into one stick, and they will become one in your hand.

¹⁸ "And when the children of your people speak to you, saying, 'Will you not show us what you *mean* by these?'— ¹⁹ say to them, 'Thus says the Lord GOD: "Surely I will take the stick of Joseph, which *is* in the hand of Ephraim, and the tribes of Israel, his companions; and I will join them with it, with the stick of Judah, and make them one stick, and they will be one in My hand." ' ²⁰ And the sticks on which you write will be in your hand before their eyes.

²¹ "Then say to them, 'Thus says the Lord GOD: "Surely I will take the children of Israel from among the nations, wherever they have gone, and will gather them from every side and bring them into their own land; ²² and I will make them one nation in the land, on the mountains of Israel; and one king shall be king over them all; they shall no longer be two nations, nor shall they ever be divided into two kingdoms again. ²³ They shall not defile themselves anymore with their idols, nor with their detestable things, nor with any of their transgressions; but I will deliver them from all their dwelling places in which they have sinned, and will cleanse them. Then they shall be My people, and I will be their God.

²⁴ "David My servant *shall be* king over them, and they shall all have one shepherd; they shall also walk in My judgments and observe My statutes, and do them. ²⁵ Then they shall dwell in the land that I have given to Jacob My servant, where your fathers dwelt; and they shall dwell there, they, their children, and their children's children, forever; and My

servant David *shall be* their prince forever. [26] Moreover I will make a covenant of peace with them, and it shall be an everlasting covenant with them; I will establish them and multiply them, and I will set My sanctuary in their midst forevermore. [27] My tabernacle also shall be with them; indeed I will be their God, and they shall be My people. [28] The nations also will know that I, the LORD, sanctify Israel, when My sanctuary is in their midst forevermore." ' "

38 Now the word of the LORD came to me, saying, [2] "Son of man, set your face against Gog, of the land of Magog, the prince of Rosh, Meshech, and Tubal, and prophesy against him, [3] and say, 'Thus says the Lord GOD: "Behold, I *am* against you, O Gog, the prince of Rosh, Meshech, and Tubal. [4] I will turn you around, put hooks into your jaws, and lead you out, with all your army, horses, and horsemen, all splendidly clothed, a great company *with* bucklers and shields, all of them handling swords. [5] Persia, Ethiopia, and Libya are with them, all of them *with* shield and helmet; [6] Gomer and all its troops; the house of Togarmah *from* the far north and all its troops—many people *are* with you.

[7] "Prepare yourself and be ready, you and all your companies that are gathered about you; and be a guard for them. [8] After many days you will be visited. In the latter years you will come into the land of those brought back from the sword *and* gathered from many people on the mountains of Israel, which had long been desolate; they were brought out of the nations, and now all of them dwell safely. [9] You will ascend, coming like a storm, covering the land like a cloud, you and all your troops and many peoples with you.'

[10] 'Thus says the Lord GOD: "On that day it shall come to pass *that* thoughts will arise in your mind, and you will make an evil plan: [11] You will say, 'I will go up against a land of unwalled villages; I will go to a peaceful people, who dwell safely, all of them dwelling without walls, and having neither bars nor gates'— [12] to take plunder and to take booty, to stretch out your hand against the waste places *that are again* inhabited, and against a people

gathered from the nations, who have acquired livestock and goods, who dwell in the midst of the land. [13] Sheba, Dedan, the merchants of Tarshish, and all their young lions will say to you, 'Have you come to take plunder? Have you gathered your army to take booty, to carry away silver and gold, to take away livestock and goods, to take great plunder?' " '

[14] "Therefore, son of man, prophesy and say to Gog, 'Thus says the Lord GOD: "On that day when My people Israel dwell safely, will you not know *it*? [15] Then you will come from your place out of the far north, you and many peoples with you, all of them riding on horses, a great company and a mighty army. [16] You will come up against My people Israel like a cloud, to cover the land. It will be in the latter days that I will bring you against My land, so that the nations may know Me, when I am hallowed in you, O Gog, before their eyes." [17] Thus says the Lord GOD: "Are *you* he of whom I have spoken in former days by My servants the prophets of Israel, who prophesied for years in those days that I would bring you against them?

[18] "And it will come to pass at the same time, when Gog comes against the land of Israel," says the Lord GOD, "*that* My fury will show in My face. [19] For in My jealousy *and* in the fire of My wrath I have spoken: 'Surely in that day there shall be a great earthquake in the land of Israel, [20] so that the fish of the sea, the birds of the heavens, the beasts of the field, all creeping things that creep on the earth, and all men who *are* on the face of the earth shall shake at My presence. The mountains shall be thrown down, the steep places shall fall, and every wall shall fall to the ground.' [21] I will call for a sword against Gog throughout all My mountains," says the Lord GOD. "Every man's sword will be against his brother. [22] And I will bring him to judgment with pestilence and bloodshed; I will rain down on him, on his troops, and on the many peoples who *are* with him, flooding rain, great hailstones, fire, and brimstone. [23] Thus I will magnify Myself and sanctify Myself, and I will be known in the eyes of many nations. Then they shall know that I *am* the LORD." '

In the Blink of an Eye

We've only a moment here. It just seems like a lifetime. Ask any ninety-year-old and she'll tell you, it flies by like a magic carpet.

Our lives are that moment when the perfume hangs in the air before dissipating. We've only a mist of a lifetime, then it will be spent. While our souls will live eternally, our opportunities on this earth to love and laugh with people will be gone before we can fully appreciate it.

That is why we must breathe deeply and live fully and thank wholeheartedly and kiss passionately and hug warmly and love without reserve. That's why we must have babies and train pets and smell good food and laugh with friends. That's why we must cry freely and dance sometimes and sing whenever we have the chance.

We've only a moment here and then it is gone. Looking ahead it seems like a lifetime but looking back, like the blink of an eye.

> Why, you do not even know what will happen tomorrow. What is your life? You are a mist that appears for a little while and then vanishes.
>
> *James 4:14*

～ PSALM 132:1–9 ～

1 LORD, remember David
   And all his afflictions;
2 How he swore to the LORD,
   And vowed to the Mighty One of
      Jacob:
3 "Surely I will not go into the chamber
      of my house,
   Or go up to the comfort of my bed;
4 I will not give sleep to my eyes
   Or slumber to my eyelids,
5 Until I find a place for the LORD,
   A dwelling place for the Mighty One
      of Jacob."

6 Behold, we heard of it in Ephrathah;
   We found it in the fields of the
      woods.
7 Let us go into His tabernacle;
   Let us worship at His footstool.
8 Arise, O LORD, to Your resting place,
   You and the ark of Your strength.
9 Let Your priests be clothed with
      righteousness,
   And let Your saints shout for joy.

～ PROVERBS 29:4 ～

4 The king establishes the land by
      justice,
   But he who receives bribes
      overthrows it.

～ JAMES 4:1–17 ～

Where do wars and fights *come* from among you? Do *they* not *come* from your *desires for* pleasure that war in your members? ² You lust and do not have. You murder and covet and cannot obtain. You fight and war. Yet you do not have because you do not ask. ³ You ask and do not receive, because you ask amiss, that you may spend *it* on your pleasures. ⁴ Adulterers and adulteresses! Do you not know that friendship with the world is enmity with God? Whoever therefore wants to be a friend of the world makes himself an enemy of God. ⁵ Or do you think that the Scripture says in vain, "The Spirit who dwells in us yearns jealously"?

⁶ But He gives more grace. Therefore He says:

"God resists the proud,
   But gives grace to the humble."

⁷ Therefore submit to God. Resist the devil and he will flee from you. ⁸ Draw near to God and He will draw near to you. Cleanse *your* hands, *you* sinners; and purify *your* hearts, *you* double-minded. ⁹ Lament and mourn and weep! Let your laughter be turned to mourning and *your* joy to gloom. ¹⁰ Humble yourselves in the sight of the Lord, and He will lift you up.

¹¹ Do not speak evil of one another, brethren. He who speaks evil of a brother and judges his brother, speaks evil of the law and judges the law. But if you judge the law, you are not a doer of the law but a judge. ¹² There is one Lawgiver, who is able to save and to destroy. Who are you to judge another?

¹³ Come now, you who say, "Today or tomorrow we will go to such and such a city, spend a year there, buy and sell, and make a profit"; ¹⁴ whereas you do not know what *will happen* tomorrow. For what *is* your life? It is even a vapor that appears for a little time and then vanishes away. ¹⁵ Instead you *ought* to say, "If the Lord wills, we shall live and do this or that." ¹⁶ But now you boast in your arrogance. All such boasting is evil. ¹⁷ Therefore, to him who knows to do good and does not do *it*, to him it is sin.

READING 328 · NOVEMBER 24

～ EZEKIEL 39:1—40:49 ～

"And you, son of man, prophesy against Gog, and say, 'Thus says the Lord GOD: "Behold, I *am* against you, O Gog, the prince of Rosh, Meshech, and Tubal; ² and I will turn you around and lead you on, bringing you up from the far north, and bring you against the mountains of Israel. ³ Then I will

As White as Soapsuds

An old woman with a halo of silvered hair — the hot tears flowing down her furrowed cheeks — her worn hands busy over a washboard in a room of poverty — praying — for her son John — John who ran away from home in his teens to become a sailor — John of whom it was now reported that he had become a very wicked man — praying, praying always, that her son might be of service to God. The mother believed in two things, the power of prayer and the reformation of her son.

God answered the prayer by working a miracle in the heart of John Newton. John Newton, the drunken sailor became John Newton, the sailor-preacher [who wrote the words to "Amazing Grace."] Among the thousands of men and women he brought to Christ was Thomas Scott . . . [who] used both his pen and voice to lead thousands of unbelieving hearts to Christ, among them William Cowper . . . [who] in a moment of inspiration wrote "There Is a Fountain Filled with Blood," a song which has brought countless thousands to the Man Who died on Calvary.

All this resulted because a mother took God at His Word and prayed that her son's heart might become as white as the soapsuds in the washtub.

— Springs in the Valley
by Mrs. Charles E. Cowman

> Confess your trespasses to one another, and pray for one another, that you may be healed. The effective, fervent prayer of a righteous man avails much.
>
> *James 5:16*

knock the bow out of your left hand, and cause the arrows to fall out of your right hand. ⁴ You shall fall upon the mountains of Israel, you and all your troops and the peoples who *are* with you; I will give you to birds of prey of every sort and *to* the beasts of the field to be devoured. ⁵ You shall fall on the open field; for I have spoken," says the Lord GOD. ⁶ "And I will send fire on Magog and on those who live in security in the coastlands. Then they shall know that I *am* the LORD. ⁷ So I will make My holy name known in the midst of My people Israel, and I will not *let them* profane My holy name anymore. Then the nations shall know that *I am* the LORD, the Holy One in Israel. ⁸ Surely it is coming, and it shall be done," says the Lord GOD. "This *is* the day of which I have spoken.

⁹ "Then those who dwell in the cities of Israel will go out and set on fire and burn the weapons, both the shields and bucklers, the bows and arrows, the javelins and spears; and they will make fires with them for seven years. ¹⁰ They will not take wood from the field nor cut down *any* from the forests, because they will make fires with the weapons; and they will plunder those who plundered them, and pillage those who pillaged them," says the Lord GOD.

¹¹ "It will come to pass in that day *that* I will give Gog a burial place there in Israel, the valley of those who pass by east of the sea; and it will obstruct travelers, because there they will bury Gog and all his multitude. Therefore they will call *it* the Valley of Hamon Gog. ¹² For seven months the house of Israel will be burying them, in order to cleanse the land. ¹³ Indeed all the people of the land will be burying, and they will gain renown for it on the day that I am glorified," says the Lord GOD. ¹⁴ "They will set apart men regularly employed, with the help of a search party, to pass through the land and bury those bodies remaining on the ground, in order to cleanse it. At the end of seven months they will make a search. ¹⁵ The search party will pass through the land; and *when anyone* sees a man's bone, he shall set up a marker by it, till the buriers have buried it in the Valley of Hamon Gog. ¹⁶ *The* name of *the* city *will*

also *be* Hamonah. Thus they shall cleanse the land." '

¹⁷ "And as for you, son of man, thus says the Lord GOD, 'Speak to every sort of bird and to every beast of the field:

"Assemble yourselves and come;
    Gather together from all sides to
        My sacrificial meal
    Which I am sacrificing for you,
    A great sacrificial meal on the
        mountains of Israel,
    That you may eat flesh and drink
        blood.
¹⁸ You shall eat the flesh of the
        mighty,
    Drink the blood of the princes of
        the earth,
    Of rams and lambs,
    Of goats and bulls,
    All of them fatlings of Bashan.
¹⁹ You shall eat fat till you are full,
    And drink blood till you are
        drunk,
    At My sacrificial meal
    Which I am sacrificing for you.
²⁰ You shall be filled at My table
    With horses and riders,
    With mighty men
    And with all the men of war," says
        the Lord GOD.

²¹ "I will set My glory among the nations; all the nations shall see My judgment which I have executed, and My hand which I have laid on them. ²² So the house of Israel shall know that I *am* the LORD their God from that day forward. ²³ The Gentiles shall know that the house of Israel went into captivity for their iniquity; because they were unfaithful to Me, therefore I hid My face from them. I gave them into the hand of their enemies, and they all fell by the sword. ²⁴ According to their uncleanness and according to their transgressions I have dealt with them, and hidden My face from them." '

²⁵ "Therefore thus says the Lord GOD: 'Now I will bring back the captives of Jacob, and have mercy on the whole house of Israel; and I will be jealous for My holy name— ²⁶ after they have borne their shame, and all their unfaithfulness in which they were unfaithful to Me, when they dwelt safely in their *own* land and

no one made *them* afraid. ²⁷ When I have brought them back from the peoples and gathered them out of their enemies' lands, and I am hallowed in them in the sight of many nations, ²⁸ then they shall know that I *am* the LORD their God, who sent them into captivity among the nations, but also brought them back to their land, and left none of them captive any longer. ²⁹ And I will not hide My face from them anymore; for I shall have poured out My Spirit on the house of Israel,' says the Lord GOD."

40 In the twenty-fifth year of our captivity, at the beginning of the year, on the tenth *day* of the month, in the fourteenth year after the city was captured, on the very same day the hand of the LORD was upon me; and He took me there. ² In the visions of God He took me into the land of Israel and set me on a very high mountain; on it toward the south *was* something like the structure of a city. ³ He took me there, and behold, *there was* a man whose appearance *was* like the appearance of bronze. He had a line of flax and a measuring rod in his hand, and he stood in the gateway.

⁴ And the man said to me, "Son of man, look with your eyes and hear with your ears, and fix your mind on everything I show you; for you *were* brought here so that I might show *them* to you. Declare to the house of Israel everything you see." ⁵ Now there was a wall all around the outside of the temple. In the man's hand was a measuring rod six cubits *long, each being a* cubit and a handbreadth; and he measured the width of the wall structure, one rod; and the height, one rod.

⁶ Then he went to the gateway which faced east; and he went up its stairs and measured the threshold of the gateway, *which was* one rod wide, and the other threshold *was* one rod wide. ⁷ Each gate chamber *was* one rod long and one rod wide; between the gate chambers *was a space of* five cubits; and the threshold of the gateway by the vestibule of the inside gate *was* one rod. ⁸ He also measured the vestibule of the inside gate, one rod. ⁹ Then he measured the vestibule of the gateway, eight cubits; and the gateposts, two cubits. The vestibule of the gate *was* on the inside. ¹⁰ In the eastern gateway *were* three gate chambers on one side and three on the other; the three *were* all the same size; also the gateposts were of the same size on this side and that side.

¹¹ He measured the width of the entrance to the gateway, ten cubits; *and* the length of the gate, thirteen cubits. ¹² *There was* a space in front of the gate chambers, one cubit *on this side* and one cubit on that side; the gate chambers *were* six cubits on this side and six cubits on that side. ¹³ Then he measured the gateway from the roof of *one* gate chamber to the roof of the other; the width *was* twenty-five cubits, as door faces door. ¹⁴ He measured the gateposts, sixty cubits high, and the court all around the gateway *extended* to the gatepost. ¹⁵ *From* the front of the entrance gate to the front of the vestibule of the inner gate *was* fifty cubits. ¹⁶ *There were* beveled window *frames* in the gate chambers and in their intervening archways on the inside of the gateway all around, and likewise in the vestibules. *There were* windows all around on the inside. And on each gatepost *were* palm trees.

¹⁷ Then he brought me into the outer court; and *there were* chambers and a pavement made all around the court; thirty chambers faced the pavement. ¹⁸ The pavement was by the side of the gateways, corresponding to the length of the gateways; *this was* the lower pavement. ¹⁹ Then he measured the width from the front of the lower gateway to the front of the inner court exterior, one hundred cubits toward the east and the north.

²⁰ On the outer court was also a gateway facing north, and he measured its length and its width. ²¹ Its gate chambers, three on this side and three on that side, its gateposts and its archways, had the same measurements as the first gate; its length *was* fifty cubits and its width twenty-five cubits. ²² Its windows and those of its archways, and also its palm trees, *had* the same measurements as the gateway facing east; it was ascended by seven steps, and its archway *was* in front of it. ²³ A gate of the inner court was opposite the northern gateway, just as the eastern *gateway;* and he measured from gateway to gateway, one hundred cubits.

²⁴ After that he brought me toward

the south, and there a gateway was facing south; and he measured its gateposts and archways according to these same measurements. ²⁵ There were windows in it and in its archways all around like those windows; its length was fifty cubits and its width twenty-five cubits. ²⁶ Seven steps led up to it, and its archway was in front of them; and it had palm trees on its gateposts, one on this side and one on that side. ²⁷ There was also a gateway on the inner court, facing south; and he measured from gateway to gateway toward the south, one hundred cubits.

²⁸ Then he brought me to the inner court through the southern gateway; he measured the southern gateway according to these same measurements. ²⁹ Also its gate chambers, its gateposts, and its archways were according to these same measurements; there were windows in it and in its archways all around; it was fifty cubits long and twenty-five cubits wide. ³⁰ There were archways all around, twenty-five cubits long and five cubits wide. ³¹ Its archways faced the outer court, palm trees were on its gateposts, and going up to it were eight steps.

³² And he brought me into the inner court facing east; he measured the gateway according to these same measurements. ³³ Also its gate chambers, its gateposts, and its archways were according to these same measurements; and there were windows in it and in its archways all around; it was fifty cubits long and twenty-five cubits wide. ³⁴ Its archways faced the outer court, and palm trees were on its gateposts on this side and on that side; and going up to it were eight steps.

³⁵ Then he brought me to the north gateway and measured it according to these same measurements— ³⁶ also its gate chambers, its gateposts, and its archways. It had windows all around; its length was fifty cubits and its width twenty-five cubits. ³⁷ Its gateposts faced the outer court, palm trees were on its gateposts on this side and on that side, and going up to it were eight steps.

³⁸ There was a chamber and its entrance by the gateposts of the gateway, where they washed the burnt offering. ³⁹ In the vestibule of the gateway were two tables on this side and two tables on that side,

on which to slay the burnt offering, the sin offering, and the trespass offering. ⁴⁰ At the outer side of the vestibule, as one goes up to the entrance of the northern gateway, were two tables; and on the other side of the vestibule of the gateway were two tables. ⁴¹ Four tables were on this side and four tables on that side, by the side of the gateway, eight tables on which they slaughtered the sacrifices. ⁴² There were also four tables of hewn stone for the burnt offering, one cubit and a half long, one cubit and a half wide, and one cubit high; on these they laid the instruments with which they slaughtered the burnt offering and the sacrifice. ⁴³ Inside were hooks, a handbreadth wide, fastened all around; and the flesh of the sacrifices was on the tables.

⁴⁴ Outside the inner gate were the chambers for the singers in the inner court, one facing south at the side of the northern gateway, and the other facing north at the side of the southern gateway. ⁴⁵ Then he said to me, "This chamber which faces south is for the priests who have charge of the temple. ⁴⁶ The chamber which faces north is for the priests who have charge of the altar; these are the sons of Zadok, from the sons of Levi, who come near the LORD to minister to Him."

⁴⁷ And he measured the court, one hundred cubits long and one hundred cubits wide, foursquare. The altar was in front of the temple. ⁴⁸ Then he brought me to the vestibule of the temple and measured the doorposts of the vestibule, five cubits on this side and five cubits on that side; and the width of the gateway was three cubits on this side and three cubits on that side. ⁴⁹ The length of the vestibule was twenty cubits, and the width eleven cubits; and by the steps which led up to it there were pillars by the doorposts, one on this side and another on that side.

∼ PSALM 132:10–18 ∼

¹⁰ For Your servant David's sake,
   Do not turn away the face of Your
   Anointed.

¹¹ The LORD has sworn in truth to
   David;
   He will not turn from it:

"I will set upon your throne the fruit
of your body.

12 If your sons will keep My covenant
And My testimony which I shall
teach them,
Their sons also shall sit upon your
throne forevermore."

13 For the LORD has chosen Zion;
He has desired *it* for His dwelling
place:

14 "This *is* My resting place forever;
Here I will dwell, for I have desired
it.

15 I will abundantly bless her provision;
I will satisfy her poor with bread.

16 I will also clothe her priests with
salvation,
And her saints shall shout aloud for
joy.

17 There I will make the horn of David
grow;
I will prepare a lamp for My
Anointed.

18 His enemies I will clothe with
shame,
But upon Himself His crown shall
flourish."

∼ PROVERBS 29:5 ∼

5 A man who flatters his neighbor
Spreads a net for his feet.

∼ JAMES 5:1–20 ∼

Come now, *you* rich, weep and howl for
your miseries that are coming upon *you*!
2 Your riches are corrupted, and your garments are moth-eaten. 3 Your gold and silver are corroded, and their corrosion will
be a witness against you and will eat your
flesh like fire. You have heaped up treasure in the last days. 4 Indeed the wages
of the laborers who mowed your fields,
which you kept back by fraud, cry out;
and the cries of the reapers have reached
the ears of the Lord of Sabaoth. 5 You have
lived on the earth in pleasure and luxury;
you have fattened your hearts as in a day
of slaughter. 6 You have condemned, you
have murdered the just; he does not resist you.

7 Therefore be patient, brethren, until
the coming of the Lord. See *how* the
farmer waits for the precious fruit of
the earth, waiting patiently for it until it
receives the early and latter rain. 8 You also
be patient. Establish your hearts, for the
coming of the Lord is at hand.

9 Do not grumble against one another,
brethren, lest you be condemned. Behold,
the Judge is standing at the door! 10 My
brethren, take the prophets, who spoke
in the name of the Lord, as an example of
suffering and patience. 11 Indeed we count
them blessed who endure. You have heard
of the perseverance of Job and seen the
end *intended by* the Lord—that the Lord
is very compassionate and merciful.

12 But above all, my brethren, do not
swear, either by heaven or by earth or with
any other oath. But let your "Yes" be
"Yes," and *your* "No," "No," lest you fall
into judgment.

13 Is anyone among you suffering? Let
him pray. Is anyone cheerful? Let him sing
psalms. 14 Is anyone among you sick? Let
him call for the elders of the church, and
let them pray over him, anointing him
with oil in the name of the Lord. 15 And
the prayer of faith will save the sick,
and the Lord will raise him up. And if he
has committed sins, he will be forgiven.
16 Confess *your* trespasses to one another,
and pray for one another, that you may
be healed. The effective, fervent prayer
of a righteous man avails much. 17 Elijah
was a man with a nature like ours, and he
prayed earnestly that it would not rain;
and it did not rain on the land for three
years and six months. 18 And he prayed
again, and the heaven gave rain, and the
earth produced its fruit.

19 Brethren, if anyone among you wanders from the truth, and someone turns
him back, 20 let him know that he who
turns a sinner from the error of his way
will save a soul from death and cover a
multitude of sins.

~ EZEKIEL 41:1—42:20 ~

Then he brought me into the sanctuary and measured the doorposts, six cubits wide on one side and six cubits wide on the other side—the width of the tabernacle. ² The width of the entryway *was* ten cubits, and the side walls of the entrance *were* five cubits on this side and five cubits on the other side; and he measured its length, forty cubits, and its width, twenty cubits.

³ Also he went inside and measured the doorposts, two cubits; and the entrance, six cubits *high;* and the width of the entrance, seven cubits. ⁴ He measured the length, twenty cubits; and the width, twenty cubits, beyond the sanctuary; and he said to me, "This *is* the Most Holy *Place.*"

⁵ Next, he measured the wall of the temple, six cubits. The width of each side chamber all around the temple *was* four cubits on every side. ⁶ The side chambers *were* in three stories, one above the other, thirty chambers in each story; they rested on ledges which *were* for the side chambers all around, that they might be supported, but not fastened to the wall of the temple. ⁷ As one went up from story to story, the side chambers became wider all around, because their supporting ledges in the wall of the temple ascended like steps; therefore the width of the structure increased as one went up *from* the lowest *story* to the highest by way of the middle one. ⁸ I also saw an elevation all around the temple; it was the foundation of the side chambers, a full rod, *that is,* six cubits *high.* ⁹ The thickness of the outer wall of the side chambers *was* five cubits, and so also the remaining terrace by the place of the side chambers of the temple. ¹⁰ And between *it and the wall* chambers was a width of twenty cubits all around the temple on every side. ¹¹ The doors of the side chambers opened on the terrace, one door toward the north and another toward the south; and the width of the terrace *was* five cubits all around.

¹² The building that faced the separating courtyard at its western end *was* seventy cubits wide; the wall of the building *was* five cubits thick all around, and its length ninety cubits.

¹³ So he measured the temple, one hundred cubits long; and the separating courtyard with the building and its walls *was* one hundred cubits long; ¹⁴ also the width of the eastern face of the temple, including the separating courtyard, *was* one hundred cubits. ¹⁵ He measured the length of the building behind it, facing the separating courtyard, with its galleries on the one side and on the other side, one hundred cubits, as well as the inner temple and the porches of the court, ¹⁶ their doorposts and the beveled window frames. And the galleries all around their three stories opposite the threshold were paneled with wood from the ground to the windows—the windows were covered— ¹⁷ from the space above the door, even to the inner room, as well as outside, and on every wall all around, inside and outside, by measure.

¹⁸ And *it was* made with cherubim and palm trees, a palm tree between cherub and cherub. *Each* cherub had two faces, ¹⁹ so that the face of a man *was* toward a palm tree on one side, and the face of a young lion toward a palm tree on the other side; thus *it was* made throughout the temple all around. ²⁰ From the floor to the space above the door, and on the wall of the sanctuary, cherubim and palm trees *were* carved.

²¹ The doorposts of the temple *were* square, *as was* the front of the sanctuary; their appearance was similar. ²² The altar *was* of wood, three cubits high, and its length two cubits. Its corners, its length, and its sides *were* of wood; and he said to me, "This *is* the table that *is* before the LORD."

²³ The temple and the sanctuary had two doors. ²⁴ The doors had two panels *apiece,* two folding panels: two *panels* for one door and two panels for the other *door.* ²⁵ Cherubim and palm trees *were* carved on the doors of the temple just as they *were* carved on the walls. A wooden canopy *was* on the front of the vestibule outside. ²⁶ *There were* beveled window *frames* and palm trees on one side and on the other, on the sides of the vestibule— also on the side chambers of the temple and on the canopies.

I Will Rejoice in the Lord

> **Though now you do not see Him, yet believing, you rejoice with joy inexpressible and full of glory.**
>
> *1 Peter 1:8*

A woman was very fearful about the outcome of the surgery she faced. Doctors had not been able to discover the reason for her symptoms, and cancer seemed an undeniable possibility. To add to her concern she had little in savings, and being self-employed, she had no insurance or paid sick leave.

As the day of her surgery drew closer, she found herself reading her Bible more and more frequently. A passage in Habakkuk puzzled her. The prophet obviously knew his nation was about to be invaded and ravaged, but he said, "Though the fig tree may not blossom, nor fruit be on the vines; though the labor of the olive may fail, and the fields yield no food; though the flock may be cut off from the fold, and there be no herd in the stalls — Yet I will rejoice in the LORD" (Habakkuk 3:17-18). She began to reflect on the fact that God was always with her and always loved her. Instead of asking for healing, finances, or peace, her prayer became simply, "I love You, too! I love You, too!"

As it turned out, the surgeons removed a benign cyst. Her recovery passed quickly. Friends helped with meals, laundry, housecleaning, errands, and even a mortgage payment. She reflected later, "This experience made my love for God grow deeper. And that was far more meaningful than a good medical report."

If you are facing a burdensome situation today, reflect on God's love for you. Remember His faithfulness in the past. Then, with joy in your heart, tell God how much you love Him. As you express your love to Him, it will grow.

42 Then he brought me out into the outer court, by the way toward the north; and he brought me into the chamber which *was* opposite the separating courtyard, and which *was* opposite the building toward the north. [2] Facing the length, *which was* one hundred cubits (the width was fifty cubits), was the north door. [3] Opposite the inner court of twenty *cubits,* and opposite the pavement of the outer court, *was* gallery against gallery in three *stories.* [4] In front of the chambers, toward the inside, *was* a walk ten cubits wide, at a distance of one cubit; and their doors faced north. [5] Now the upper chambers *were* shorter, because the galleries took away *space* from them more than from the lower and middle stories of the building. [6] For they *were* in three *stories* and did not have pillars like the pillars of the courts; therefore *the upper level* was shortened more than the lower and middle levels from the ground up. [7] And a wall which *was* outside ran parallel to the chambers, at the front of the chambers, toward the outer court; its length *was* fifty cubits. [8] The length of the chambers toward the outer court *was* fifty cubits, whereas that facing the temple *was* one hundred cubits. [9] At the lower chambers *was* the entrance on the east side, as one goes into them from the outer court.

[10] Also *there were* chambers in the thickness of the wall of the court toward the east, opposite the separating courtyard and opposite the building. [11] *There was* a walk in front of them also, and their appearance *was* like the chambers which *were* toward the north; they *were* as long and as wide as the others, and all their exits and entrances *were* according to plan. [12] And corresponding to the doors of the chambers that *were* facing south, as one enters them, *there was* a door in front of the walk, the way directly in front of the wall toward the east.

[13] Then he said to me, "The north chambers *and* the south chambers, which *are* opposite the separating courtyard, *are* the holy chambers where the priests who approach the LORD shall eat the most holy offerings. There they shall lay the most holy offerings—the grain offering, the sin offering, and the trespass offer-

ing—for the place *is* holy. [14] When the priests enter them, they shall not go out of the holy *chamber* into the outer court; but there they shall leave their garments in which they minister, for they *are* holy. They shall put on other garments; then they may approach *that* which *is* for the people."

[15] Now when he had finished measuring the inner temple, he brought me out through the gateway that faces toward the east, and measured it all around. [16] He measured the east side with the measuring rod, five hundred rods by the measuring rod all around. [17] He measured the north side, five hundred rods by the measuring rod all around. [18] He measured the south side, five hundred rods by the measuring rod. [19] He came around to the west side *and* measured five hundred rods by the measuring rod. [20] He measured it on the four sides; it had a wall all around, five hundred *cubits* long and five hundred wide, to separate the holy areas from the common.

~ PSALM 133:1–3 ~

[1] Behold, how good and how pleasant
   it is
   For brethren to dwell together in
      unity!

[2] *It is* like the precious oil upon the
      head,
   Running down on the beard,
   The beard of Aaron,
   Running down on the edge of his
      garments.
[3] *It is* like the dew of Hermon,
   Descending upon the mountains of
      Zion;
   For there the LORD commanded the
      blessing—
   Life forevermore.

~ PROVERBS 29:6 ~

[6] By transgression an evil man is
      snared,
   But the righteous sings and
      rejoices.

～ 1 PETER 1:1–25 ～

Peter, an apostle of Jesus Christ,

To the pilgrims of the Dispersion in Pontus, Galatia, Cappadocia, Asia, and Bithynia, ² elect according to the foreknowledge of God the Father, in sanctification of the Spirit, for obedience and sprinkling of the blood of Jesus Christ:

Grace to you and peace be multiplied.
³ Blessed *be* the God and Father of our Lord Jesus Christ, who according to His abundant mercy has begotten us again to a living hope through the resurrection of Jesus Christ from the dead, ⁴ to an inheritance incorruptible and undefiled and that does not fade away, reserved in heaven for you, ⁵ who are kept by the power of God through faith for salvation ready to be revealed in the last time.
⁶ In this you greatly rejoice, though now for a little while, if need be, you have been grieved by various trials, ⁷ that the genuineness of your faith, *being* much more precious than gold that perishes, though it is tested by fire, may be found to praise, honor, and glory at the revelation of Jesus Christ, ⁸ whom having not seen you love. Though now you do not see *Him,* yet believing, you rejoice with joy inexpressible and full of glory, ⁹ receiving the end of your faith—the salvation of *your* souls.
¹⁰ Of this salvation the prophets have inquired and searched carefully, who prophesied of the grace *that would come* to you, ¹¹ searching what, or what manner of time, the Spirit of Christ who was in them was indicating when He testified beforehand the sufferings of Christ and the glories that would follow. ¹² To them it was revealed that, not to themselves, but to us they were ministering the things which now have been reported to you through those who have preached the gospel to you by the Holy Spirit sent from heaven—things which angels desire to look into.

¹³ Therefore gird up the loins of your mind, be sober, and rest *your* hope fully upon the grace that is to be brought to you at the revelation of Jesus Christ; ¹⁴ as obedient children, not conforming yourselves to the former lusts, *as* in your ignorance; ¹⁵ but as He who called you *is* holy, you also be holy in all *your* conduct, ¹⁶ because it is written, "Be holy, for I am holy."
¹⁷ And if you call on the Father, who without partiality judges according to each one's work, conduct yourselves throughout the time of your stay *here* in fear; ¹⁸ knowing that you were not redeemed with corruptible things, *like* silver or gold, from your aimless conduct *received* by tradition from your fathers, ¹⁹ but with the precious blood of Christ, as of a lamb without blemish and without spot. ²⁰ He indeed was foreordained before the foundation of the world, but was manifest in these last times for you ²¹ who through Him believe in God, who raised Him from the dead and gave Him glory, so that your faith and hope are in God.
²² Since you have purified your souls in obeying the truth through the Spirit in sincere love of the brethren, love one another fervently with a pure heart, ²³ having been born again, not of corruptible seed but incorruptible, through the word of God which lives and abides forever, ²⁴ because

"All flesh *is* as grass,
  And all the glory of man as the
    flower of the grass.
The grass withers,
  And its flower falls away,
²⁵ But the word of the LORD endures
    forever."

Now this is the word which by the gospel was preached to you.

~ EZEKIEL 43:1—44:31 ~

Afterward he brought me to the gate, the gate that faces toward the east. [2] And behold, the glory of the God of Israel came from the way of the east. His voice *was* like the sound of many waters; and the earth shone with His glory. [3] *It was* like the appearance of the vision which I saw—like the vision which I saw when I came to destroy the city. The visions *were* like the vision which I saw by the River Chebar; and I fell on my face. [4] And the glory of the LORD came into the temple by way of the gate which faces toward the east. [5] The Spirit lifted me up and brought me into the inner court; and behold, the glory of the LORD filled the temple.

[6] Then I heard *Him* speaking to me from the temple, while a man stood beside me. [7] And He said to me, "Son of man, *this is* the place of My throne and the place of the soles of My feet, where I will dwell in the midst of the children of Israel forever. No more shall the house of Israel defile My holy name, they nor their kings, by their harlotry or with the carcasses of their kings on their high places. [8] When they set their threshold by My threshold, and their doorpost by My doorpost, with a wall between them and Me, they defiled My holy name by the abominations which they committed; therefore I have consumed them in My anger. [9] Now let them put their harlotry and the carcasses of their kings far away from Me, and I will dwell in their midst forever.

[10] "Son of man, describe the temple to the house of Israel, that they may be ashamed of their iniquities; and let them measure the pattern. [11] And if they are ashamed of all that they have done, make known to them the design of the temple and its arrangement, its exits and its entrances, its entire design and all its ordinances, all its forms and all its laws. Write *it* down in their sight, so that they may keep its whole design and all its ordinances, and perform them. [12] This *is* the law of the temple: The whole area surrounding the mountaintop *is* most holy. Behold, this *is* the law of the temple.

[13] "These are the measurements of the altar in cubits (the *cubit is* one cubit and a handbreadth): the base one cubit high and one cubit wide, with a rim all around its edge of one span. This *is* the height of the altar: [14] from the base on the ground to the lower ledge, two cubits; the width of the ledge, one cubit; from the smaller ledge to the larger ledge, four cubits; and the width of the ledge, *one* cubit. [15] The altar hearth *is* four cubits high, with four horns extending upward from the hearth. [16] The altar hearth *is* twelve cubits long, twelve wide, square at its four corners; [17] the ledge, fourteen *cubits* long and fourteen wide on its four sides, with a rim of half a cubit around it; its base, one cubit all around; and its steps face toward the east."

[18] And He said to me, "Son of man, thus says the Lord GOD: 'These *are* the ordinances for the altar on the day when it is made, for sacrificing burnt offerings on it, and for sprinkling blood on it. [19] You shall give a young bull for a sin offering to the priests, the Levites, who are of the seed of Zadok, who approach Me to minister to Me,' says the Lord GOD. [20] You shall take some of its blood and put *it* on the four horns of the altar, on the four corners of the ledge, and on the rim around it; thus you shall cleanse it and make atonement for it. [21] Then you shall also take the bull of the sin offering, and burn it in the appointed place of the temple, outside the sanctuary. [22] On the second day you shall offer a kid of the goats without blemish for a sin offering; and they shall cleanse the altar, as they cleansed *it* with the bull. [23] When you have finished cleansing *it,* you shall offer a young bull without blemish, and a ram from the flock without blemish. [24] When you offer them before the LORD, the priests shall throw salt on them, and they will offer them up *as* a burnt offering to the LORD. [25] Every day for seven days you shall prepare a goat *for* a sin offering; they shall also prepare a young bull and a ram from the flock, both without blemish. [26] Seven days they shall make atonement for the altar and purify it, and so

How to Fight Fair

Author Charlie W. Shedd shares "Our Seven Official Rules for a Good, Clean Fight" in the book he wrote to his daughter, *Letters to Karen*. They are:

1. Before we begin we must both agree that the time is right.
2. We will remember that our only aim is deeper understanding.
3. We will check our weapons often to be sure they're not deadly.
4. We will lower our voices one notch instead of raising them two.
5. We will never quarrel or reveal private matters in public.
6. We will discuss an armistice whenever either of us calls "halt."
7. When we have come to terms, we will put it away till we both agree it needs more discussing.

Says Shedd, "No small part of the zest in a good marriage comes from working through differences. Learning to zig and zag with the entanglements; studying each other's reactions under pressure; handling one another's emotions intelligently — all these offer a challenge that simply can't be beat for sheer fun and excitement."

> Therefore, laying aside all malice, all deceit, hypocrisy, envy, and all evil speaking.
>
> *1 Peter 2:1*

consecrate *it*. [27] When these days are over it shall be, on the eighth day and thereafter, that the priests shall offer your burnt offerings and your peace offerings on the altar; and I will accept you,' says the Lord GOD."

44 Then He brought me back to the outer gate of the sanctuary which faces toward the east, but it *was* shut. [2] And the LORD said to me, "This gate shall be shut; it shall not be opened, and no man shall enter by it, because the LORD God of Israel has entered by it; therefore it shall be shut. [3] *As for* the prince, *because* he *is* the prince, he may sit in it to eat bread before the LORD; he shall enter by way of the vestibule of the gateway, and go out the same way."

[4] Also He brought me by way of the north gate to the front of the temple; so I looked, and behold, the glory of the LORD filled the house of the LORD; and I fell on my face. [5] And the LORD said to me, "Son of man, mark well, see with your eyes and hear with your ears, all that I say to you concerning all the ordinances of the house of the LORD and all its laws. Mark well who may enter the house and all who go out from the sanctuary.

[6] "Now say to the rebellious, to the house of Israel, 'Thus says the Lord GOD: "O house of Israel, let Us have no more of all your abominations. [7] When you brought in foreigners, uncircumcised in heart and uncircumcised in flesh, to be in My sanctuary to defile it—My house—and when you offered My food, the fat and the blood, then they broke My covenant because of all your abominations. [8] And you have not kept charge of My holy things, but you have set *others* to keep charge of My sanctuary for you." [9] Thus says the Lord GOD: "No foreigner, uncircumcised in heart or uncircumcised in flesh, shall enter My sanctuary, including any foreigner who *is* among the children of Israel.

[10] "And the Levites who went far from Me, when Israel went astray, who strayed away from Me after their idols, they shall bear their iniquity. [11] Yet they shall be ministers in My sanctuary, *as* gatekeepers of the house and ministers of the house; they shall slay the burnt offering and the sacrifice for the people, and they shall stand before them to minister to them. [12] Because they ministered to them before their idols and caused the house of Israel to fall into iniquity, therefore I have raised My hand in an oath against them," says the Lord GOD, "that they shall bear their iniquity. [13] And they shall not come near Me to minister to Me as priest, nor come near any of My holy things, nor into the Most Holy *Place;* but they shall bear their shame and their abominations which they have committed. [14] Nevertheless I will make them keep charge of the temple, for all its work, and for all that has to be done in it.

[15] "But the priests, the Levites, the sons of Zadok, who kept charge of My sanctuary when the children of Israel went astray from Me, they shall come near Me to minister to Me; and they shall stand before Me to offer to Me the fat and the blood," says the Lord GOD. [16] "They shall enter My sanctuary, and they shall come near My table to minister to Me, and they shall keep My charge. [17] And it shall be, whenever they enter the gates of the inner court, that they shall put on linen garments; no wool shall come upon them while they minister within the gates of the inner court or within the house. [18] They shall have linen turbans on their heads and linen trousers on their bodies; they shall not clothe themselves with *anything that causes* sweat. [19] When they go out to the outer court, to the *outer* court to the people, they shall take off their garments in which they have ministered, leave them in the holy chambers, and put on other garments; and in their holy garments they shall not sanctify the people.

[20] "They shall neither shave their heads, nor let their hair grow long, but they shall keep their hair well trimmed. [21] No priest shall drink wine when he enters the inner court. [22] They shall not take as wife a widow or a divorced woman, but take virgins of the descendants of the house of Israel, or widows of priests.

[23] "And they shall teach My people *the difference* between the holy and the unholy, and cause them to discern between the unclean and the clean. [24] In controversy they shall stand as judges, *and* judge it according to My judgments. They shall keep My laws and My statutes in all My

appointed meetings, and they shall hallow My Sabbaths.

²⁵ "They shall not defile *themselves* by coming near a dead person. Only for father or mother, for son or daughter, for brother or unmarried sister may they defile themselves. ²⁶ After he is cleansed, they shall count seven days for him. ²⁷ And on the day that he goes to the sanctuary to minister in the sanctuary, he must offer his sin offering in the inner court," says the Lord GOD.

²⁸ "It shall be, in regard to their inheritance, *that* I *am* their inheritance. You shall give them no possession in Israel, for I *am* their possession. ²⁹ They shall eat the grain offering, the sin offering, and the trespass offering; every dedicated thing in Israel shall be theirs. ³⁰ The best of all firstfruits of any kind, and every sacrifice of any kind from all your sacrifices, shall be the priest's; also you shall give to the priest the first of your ground meal, to cause a blessing to rest on your house. ³¹ The priests shall not eat anything, bird or beast, that died naturally or was torn *by wild beasts.*

∼ PSALM 134:1–3 ∼

¹ Behold, bless the LORD,
All *you* servants of the LORD,
Who by night stand in the house of
    the LORD!
² Lift up your hands *in* the sanctuary,
And bless the LORD.

³ The LORD who made heaven and
    earth
Bless you from Zion!

∼ PROVERBS 29:7 ∼

⁷ The righteous considers the cause of
    the poor,
But the wicked does not understand
such knowledge.

∼ 1 PETER 2:1–25 ∼

Therefore, laying aside all malice, all deceit, hypocrisy, envy, and all evil speaking, ² as newborn babes, desire the pure milk of the word, that you may grow

thereby, ³ if indeed you have tasted that the Lord *is* gracious.

⁴ Coming to Him *as to* a living stone, rejected indeed by men, but chosen by God *and* precious, ⁵ you also, as living stones, are being built up a spiritual house, a holy priesthood, to offer up spiritual sacrifices acceptable to God through Jesus Christ. ⁶ Therefore it is also contained in the Scripture,

> "Behold, I lay in Zion
>   A chief cornerstone, elect,
>   precious,
>   And he who believes on Him will
>   by no means be put to shame."

⁷ Therefore, to you who believe, *He is* precious; but to those who are disobedient,

> "The stone which the builders
>   rejected
> Has become the chief
>   cornerstone,"

⁸ and

> "A stone of stumbling
>   And a rock of offense."

They stumble, being disobedient to the word, to which they also were appointed.

⁹ But you *are* a chosen generation, a royal priesthood, a holy nation, His own special people, that you may proclaim the praises of Him who called you out of darkness into His marvelous light; ¹⁰ who once *were* not a people but *are* now the people of God, who had not obtained mercy but now have obtained mercy.

¹¹ Beloved, I beg *you* as sojourners and pilgrims, abstain from fleshly lusts which war against the soul, ¹² having your conduct honorable among the Gentiles, that when they speak against you as evildoers, they may, by *your* good works which they observe, glorify God in the day of visitation.

¹³ Therefore submit yourselves to every ordinance of man for the Lord's sake, whether to the king as supreme, ¹⁴ or to governors, as to those who are sent by him for the punishment of evildoers and

for the praise of those who do good. ¹⁵ For this is the will of God, that by doing good you may put to silence the ignorance of foolish men— ¹⁶ as free, yet not using liberty as a cloak for vice, but as bondservants of God. ¹⁷ Honor all *people*. Love the brotherhood. Fear God. Honor the king.

¹⁸ Servants, *be* submissive to *your* masters with all fear, not only to the good and gentle, but also to the harsh. ¹⁹ For this *is* commendable, if because of conscience toward God one endures grief, suffering wrongfully. ²⁰ For what credit *is it* if, when you are beaten for your faults, you take it patiently? But when you do good and suffer, if you take it patiently, this *is* commendable before God. ²¹ For to this you were called, because Christ also suffered for us, leaving us an example, that you should follow His steps:

²² "Who committed no sin,
    Nor was deceit found in His
      mouth";

²³ who, when He was reviled, did not revile in return; when He suffered, He did not threaten, but committed *Himself* to Him who judges righteously; ²⁴ who Himself bore our sins in His own body on the tree, that we, having died to sins, might live for righteousness—by whose stripes you were healed. ²⁵ For you were like sheep going astray, but have now returned to the Shepherd and Overseer of your souls.

READING 331 · NOVEMBER 27

~ EZEKIEL 45:1—46:24 ~

"Moreover, when you divide the land by lot into inheritance, you shall set apart a district for the LORD, a holy section of the land; its length *shall be* twenty-five thousand *cubits*, and the width ten thousand. It *shall be* holy throughout its territory all around. ² Of this there shall be a square plot for the sanctuary, five hundred by five hundred *rods,* with fifty cubits around it for an open space. ³ So this is the district you shall measure: twenty-five thousand *cubits* long and ten thousand wide; in it shall be the sanctuary, the Most Holy *Place*. ⁴ It shall be a holy *section* of the land, belonging to the priests, the ministers of the sanctuary, who come near to minister to the LORD; it shall be a place for their houses and a holy place for the sanctuary. ⁵ *An area* twenty-five thousand *cubits* long and ten thousand wide shall belong to the Levites, the ministers of the temple; they shall have twenty chambers as a possession.

⁶ "You shall appoint as the property of the city *an area* five thousand *cubits* wide and twenty-five thousand long, adjacent to the district of the holy *section;* it shall belong to the whole house of Israel.

⁷ "The prince shall have *a section* on one side and the other of the holy district and the city's property; and bordering on the holy district and the city's property, extending westward on the west side and eastward on the east side, the length *shall be* side by side with one of the *tribal* portions, from the west border to the east border. ⁸ The land shall be his possession in Israel; and My princes shall no more oppress My people, but they shall give *the rest of* the land to the house of Israel, according to their tribes."

⁹ 'Thus says the Lord GOD: "Enough, O princes of Israel! Remove violence and plundering, execute justice and righteousness, and stop dispossessing My people," says the Lord GOD. ¹⁰ "You shall have honest scales, an honest ephah, and an honest bath. ¹¹ The ephah and the bath shall be of the same measure, so that the bath contains one-tenth of a homer, and the ephah one-tenth of a homer; their measure shall be according to the homer. ¹² The shekel *shall be* twenty gerahs; twenty shekels, twenty-five shekels, *and* fifteen shekels shall be your mina.

¹³ "This *is* the offering which you shall offer: you shall give one-sixth of an ephah from a homer of wheat, and one-sixth of an ephah from a homer of barley. ¹⁴ The ordinance concerning oil, the bath of oil, *is* one-tenth of a bath from a kor. A kor *is*

Patience and Kindness

Firmin Abautiz was known as a man of serene disposition. Nobody in his town could recall his having ever lost his temper during his 87 years. One man, who doubted the possibility that a person could be so unflappable, made a deal with a housekeeper, offering her money if she could provoke him.

The housekeeper knew that Abautiz was very fond of a comfortable, orderly bed, so she neglected to make his bed one day. The next morning, Abautiz kindly reminded her of the undone chore. The next night, Abautiz again found an unmade bed and the following morning, he again called it to her attention. She made a lame excuse, which he kindly accepted.

> **Husbands, likewise, dwell with them with understanding, giving honor to the wife…being heirs together of the grace of life, that your prayers may not be hindered.**
>
> *1 Peter 3:7*

On the third morning, Abautiz said, "You still have not made my bed; it is evident you are determined not to do it. Well, I suppose you find the job troublesome; but it is of little consequence, for I begin to be used to it already." Moved by such kindness, the woman called off the deal and never again failed to make his bed as comfortable as possible!

Not everything can be the way we like it all the time, but criticism and harsh words rarely bring about a lasting and peaceful cooperation or fulfillment of our desires. Patience and kindness, on the other hand, do.

a homer or ten baths, for ten baths *are* a homer. ¹⁵ And one lamb shall be given from a flock of two hundred, from the rich pastures of Israel. These shall be for grain offerings, burnt offerings, and peace offerings, to make atonement for them," says the Lord GOD. ¹⁶ "All the people of the land shall give this offering for the prince in Israel. ¹⁷ Then it shall be the prince's part *to give* burnt offerings, grain offerings, and drink offerings, at the feasts, the New Moons, the Sabbaths, and at all the appointed seasons of the house of Israel. He shall prepare the sin offering, the grain offering, the burnt offering, and the peace offerings to make atonement for the house of Israel."

¹⁸ 'Thus says the Lord GOD: "In the first *month,* on the first *day* of the month, you shall take a young bull without blemish and cleanse the sanctuary. ¹⁹ The priest shall take some of the blood of the sin offering and put *it* on the doorposts of the temple, on the four corners of the ledge of the altar, and on the gateposts of the gate of the inner court. ²⁰ And so you shall do on the seventh *day* of the month for everyone who has sinned unintentionally or in ignorance. Thus you shall make atonement for the temple.

²¹ "In the first *month,* on the fourteenth day of the month, you shall observe the Passover, a feast of seven days; unleavened bread shall be eaten. ²² And on that day the prince shall prepare for himself and for all the people of the land a bull *for* a sin offering. ²³ On the seven days of the feast he shall prepare a burnt offering to the LORD, seven bulls and seven rams without blemish, daily for seven days, and a kid of the goats daily *for* a sin offering. ²⁴ And he shall prepare a grain offering of one ephah for each bull and one ephah for each ram, together with a hin of oil for each ephah.

²⁵ "In the seventh *month,* on the fifteenth day of the month, at the feast, he shall do likewise for seven days, according to the sin offering, the burnt offering, the grain offering, and the oil."

46
'Thus says the Lord GOD: "The gateway of the inner court that faces toward the east shall be shut the six working days; but on the Sabbath it shall be opened, and on the day of the New Moon it shall be opened. ² The prince shall enter by way of the vestibule of the gateway from the outside, and stand by the gatepost. The priests shall prepare his burnt offering and his peace offerings. He shall worship at the threshold of the gate. Then he shall go out, but the gate shall not be shut until evening. ³ Likewise the people of the land shall worship at the entrance to this gateway before the LORD on the Sabbaths and the New Moons. ⁴ The burnt offering that the prince offers to the LORD on the Sabbath day *shall be* six lambs without blemish, and a ram without blemish; ⁵ and the grain offering *shall be one* ephah for a ram, and the grain offering for the lambs, as much as he wants to give, as well as a hin of oil with every ephah. ⁶ On the day of the New Moon *it shall be* a young bull without blemish, six lambs, and a ram; they shall be without blemish. ⁷ He shall prepare a grain offering of an ephah for a bull, an ephah for a ram, as much as he wants to give for the lambs, and a hin of oil with every ephah. ⁸ When the prince enters, he shall go in by way of the vestibule of the gateway, and go out the same way.

⁹ "But when the people of the land come before the LORD on the appointed feast days, whoever enters by way of the north gate to worship shall go out by way of the south gate; and whoever enters by way of the south gate shall go out by way of the north gate. He shall not return by way of the gate through which he came, but shall go out through the opposite gate. ¹⁰ The prince shall then be in their midst. When they go in, he shall go in; and when they go out, he shall go out. ¹¹ At the festivals and the appointed feast days the grain offering shall be an ephah for a bull, an ephah for a ram, as much as he wants to give for the lambs, and a hin of oil with every ephah.

¹² "Now when the prince makes a voluntary burnt offering or voluntary peace offering to the LORD, the gate that faces toward the east shall then be opened for him; and he shall prepare his burnt offering and his peace offerings as he did on the Sabbath day. Then he shall go out, and after he goes out the gate shall be shut.

¹³ "You shall daily make a burnt offering to the LORD *of* a lamb of the first year without blemish; you shall prepare it every morning. ¹⁴ And you shall prepare a grain offering with it every morning, a sixth of an ephah, and a third of a hin of oil to moisten the fine flour. This grain offering is a perpetual ordinance, to be made regularly to the LORD. ¹⁵ Thus they shall prepare the lamb, the grain offering, and the oil, *as* a regular burnt offering every morning."

¹⁶ 'Thus says the Lord GOD: "If the prince gives a gift *of some* of his inheritance to any of his sons, it shall belong to his sons; it is their possession by inheritance. ¹⁷ But if he gives a gift of some of his inheritance to one of his servants, it shall be his until the year of liberty, after which it shall return to the prince. But his inheritance shall belong to his sons; it shall become theirs. ¹⁸ Moreover the prince shall not take any of the people's inheritance by evicting them from their property; he shall provide an inheritance for his sons from his own property, so that none of My people may be scattered from his property." ' "

¹⁹ Now he brought me through the entrance, which *was* at the side of the gate, into the holy chambers of the priests which face toward the north; and there a place *was* situated at their extreme western end. ²⁰ And he said to me, "This *is* the place where the priests shall boil the trespass offering and the sin offering, *and* where they shall bake the grain offering, so that they do not bring *them* out into the outer court to sanctify the people."

²¹ Then he brought me out into the outer court and caused me to pass by the four corners of the court; and in fact, in every corner of the court *there was another* court. ²² In the four corners of the court *were* enclosed courts, forty *cubits* long and thirty wide; all four corners *were* the same size. ²³ *There was* a row *of building stones* all around in them, all around the four of them; and cooking hearths were made under the rows of stones all around. ²⁴ And he said to me, "These *are* the kitchens where the ministers of the temple shall boil the sacrifices of the people."

~ PSALM 135:1–7 ~

¹ Praise the LORD!

Praise the name of the LORD;
Praise *Him*, O you servants of the LORD!
² You who stand in the house of the LORD,
In the courts of the house of our God,
³ Praise the LORD, for the LORD *is* good;
Sing praises to His name, for *it is* pleasant.
⁴ For the LORD has chosen Jacob for Himself,
Israel for His special treasure.

⁵ For I know that the LORD *is* great,
And our Lord *is* above all gods.
⁶ Whatever the LORD pleases He does,
In heaven and in earth,
In the seas and in all deep places.
⁷ He causes the vapors to ascend from the ends of the earth;
He makes lightning for the rain;
He brings the wind out of His treasuries.

~ PROVERBS 29:8 ~

⁸ Scoffers set a city aflame,
But wise *men* turn away wrath.

~ 1 PETER 3:1–22 ~

Wives, likewise, *be* submissive to your own husbands, that even if some do not obey the word, they, without a word, may be won by the conduct of their wives, ² when they observe your chaste conduct *accompanied* by fear. ³ Do not let your adornment be *merely* outward—arranging the hair, wearing gold, or putting on *fine* apparel— ⁴ rather *let it be* the hidden person of the heart, with the incorruptible *beauty* of a gentle and quiet spirit, which is very precious in the sight of God. ⁵ For in this manner, in former times, the holy women who trusted in God also adorned themselves, being submissive to their own husbands, ⁶ as Sarah obeyed Abraham, calling him lord, whose daughters you are if you do good and are not afraid with any terror.

⁷ Husbands, likewise, dwell with *them* with understanding, giving honor to the wife, as to the weaker vessel, and as *being* heirs together of the grace of life, that your prayers may not be hindered.

⁸ Finally, all *of you be* of one mind, having compassion for one another; love as brothers, *be* tenderhearted, *be* courteous; ⁹ not returning evil for evil or reviling for reviling, but on the contrary blessing, knowing that you were called to this, that you may inherit a blessing. ¹⁰ For

"He who would love life
And see good days,
Let him refrain his tongue from
  evil,
And his lips from speaking
  deceit.
¹¹ Let him turn away from evil and
  do good;
Let him seek peace and pursue it.
¹² For the eyes of the LORD *are* on
  the righteous,
And His ears *are open* to their
  prayers;
But the face of the LORD *is* against
  those who do evil."

¹³ And who *is* he who will harm you if you become followers of what is good? ¹⁴ But even if you should suffer for righteousness' sake, *you are* blessed. "And do not be afraid of their threats, nor be troubled." ¹⁵ But sanctify the Lord God in your hearts, and always *be* ready to *give* a defense to everyone who asks you a reason for the hope that is in you, with meekness and fear; ¹⁶ having a good conscience, that when they defame you as evildoers, those who revile your good conduct in Christ may be ashamed. ¹⁷ For *it is* better, if it is the will of God, to suffer for doing good than for doing evil.

¹⁸ For Christ also suffered once for sins, the just for the unjust, that He might bring us to God, being put to death in the flesh but made alive by the Spirit, ¹⁹ by whom also He went and preached to the spirits in prison, ²⁰ who formerly were disobedient, when once the Divine longsuffering waited in the days of Noah, while *the* ark was being prepared, in which a few, that is, eight souls, were saved through water. ²¹ There is also an antitype which now saves us—baptism (not the removal of the filth of the flesh, but the answer of a good conscience toward God), through the resurrection of Jesus Christ, ²² who has gone into heaven and is at the right hand of God, angels and authorities and powers having been made subject to Him.

READING 332 · NOVEMBER 28

~ EZEKIEL 47:1—48:35 ~

Then he brought me back to the door of the temple; and there was water, flowing from under the threshold of the temple toward the east, for the front of the temple faced east; the water was flowing from under the right side of the temple, south of the altar. ² He brought me out by way of the north gate, and led me around on the outside to the outer gateway that faces east; and there was water, running out on the right side.

³ And when the man went out to the east with the line in his hand, he measured one thousand cubits, and he brought me through the waters; the water came up to my ankles. ⁴ Again he measured one thousand and brought me through the waters; the water *came up to my* knees. Again he measured one thousand and brought me through; the water *came up to my* waist. ⁵ Again he measured one thousand, *and it was* a river that I could not cross; for the water was too deep, water in which one must swim, a river that could not be crossed. ⁶ He said to me, "Son of man, have you seen *this?*" Then he brought me and returned me to the bank of the river.

⁷ When I returned, there, along the bank of the river, *were* very many trees on one side and the other. ⁸ Then he said to me: "This water flows toward the eastern

When the Shoe's on the Other Foot

Have you ever noticed . . .

When others are set in their ways, they're obstinate — but you are firm and resolved.

When your neighbor doesn't like your friend, she's prejudiced — but when you don't like her friend, you're a good judge of human nature.

When she tries to treat someone especially well, she's buttering up the person — but when you do so, you're being thoughtful.

When she takes time to do things well, she's lazy — but when you do so, you're meticulous.

When she spends a lot, she's a spendthrift — but when you overdo, you're generous.

When she picks flaws in things, she's critical — but when you do, you are perceptive.

When she is mild-mannered, you call her weak — but when you are, you're gracious.

When she dresses well, she is extravagant — but when you do, you're tastefully in style.

When she says what she thinks, she's spiteful — but when you do, you're being honest.

When she takes great risks, she's foolhardy — but when you do, you're brave.

> And above all things have fervent love for one another, for "love will cover a multitude of sins."
>
> *1 Peter 4:8*

region, goes down into the valley, and enters the sea. *When it* reaches the sea, *its* waters are healed. [9] And it shall be *that* every living thing that moves, wherever the rivers go, will live. There will be a very great multitude of fish, because these waters go there; for they will be healed, and everything will live wherever the river goes. [10] It shall be *that* fishermen will stand by it from En Gedi to En Eglaim; they will be *places* for spreading their nets. Their fish will be of the same kinds as the fish of the Great Sea, exceedingly many. [11] But its swamps and marshes will not be healed; they will be given over to salt. [12] Along the bank of the river, on this side and that, will grow all *kinds of* trees used for food; their leaves will not wither, and their fruit will not fail. They will bear fruit every month, because their water flows from the sanctuary. Their fruit will be for food, and their leaves for medicine."

[13] Thus says the Lord GOD: "These *are* the borders by which you shall divide the land as an inheritance among the twelve tribes of Israel. Joseph *shall have two* portions. [14] You shall inherit it equally with one another; for I raised My hand in an oath to give it to your fathers, and this land shall fall to you as your inheritance.

[15] "This *shall be* the border of the land on the north: from the Great Sea, *by* the road to Hethlon, as one goes to Zedad, [16] Hamath, Berothah, Sibraim (which *is* between the border of Damascus and the border of Hamath), to Hazar Hatticon (which *is* on the border of Hauran). [17] Thus the boundary shall be from the Sea to Hazar Enan, the border of Damascus; and as for the north, northward, it is the border of Hamath. *This is* the north side.

[18] "On the east side you shall mark out the border from between Hauran and Damascus, and between Gilead and the land of Israel, along the Jordan, and along the eastern side of the sea. *This is* the east side.

[19] "The south side, toward the South, *shall be* from Tamar to the waters of Meribah by Kadesh, along the brook to the Great Sea. *This is* the south side, toward the South.

[20] "The west side *shall be* the Great Sea, from the *southern* boundary until one comes to a point opposite Hamath. This *is* the west side.

[21] "Thus you shall divide this land among yourselves according to the tribes of Israel. [22] It shall be that you will divide it by lot as an inheritance for yourselves, and for the strangers who dwell among you and who bear children among you. They shall be to you as native-born among the children of Israel; they shall have an inheritance with you among the tribes of Israel. [23] And it shall be *that* in whatever tribe the stranger dwells, there you shall give *him* his inheritance," says the Lord GOD.

48 "Now these *are* the names of the tribes: From the northern border along the road to Hethlon at the entrance of Hamath, to Hazar Enan, the border of Damascus northward, in the direction of Hamath, *there shall be* one *section for* Dan from its east to its west side; [2] by the border of Dan, from the east side to the west, one *section for* Asher; [3] by the border of Asher, from the east side to the west, one *section for* Naphtali; [4] by the border of Naphtali, from the east side to the west, one *section for* Manasseh; [5] by the border of Manasseh, from the east side to the west, one *section for* Ephraim; [6] by the border of Ephraim, from the east side to the west, one *section for* Reuben; [7] by the border of Reuben, from the east side to the west, one *section for* Judah; [8] by the border of Judah, from the east side to the west, shall be the district which you shall set apart, twenty-five thousand *cubits* in width, and *in* length the same as one of the *other* portions, from the east side to the west, with the sanctuary in the center.

[9] "The district that you shall set apart for the LORD *shall be* twenty-five thousand *cubits* in length and ten thousand in width. [10] To these—to the priests—the holy district shall belong: on the north twenty-five thousand *cubits in length,* on the west ten thousand in width, on the east ten thousand in width, and on the south twenty-five thousand in length. The sanctuary of the LORD shall be in the center. [11] *It shall be* for the priests of the sons of Zadok, who are sanctified, who have kept My charge, who did not

go astray when the children of Israel went astray, as the Levites went astray. ¹² And *this* district of land that is set apart shall be to them a thing most holy by the border of the Levites.

¹³ "Opposite the border of the priests, the Levites *shall have an area* twenty-five thousand *cubits* in length and ten thousand in width; its entire length *shall be* twenty-five thousand and its width ten thousand. ¹⁴ And they shall not sell or exchange any of it; they may not alienate this best *part* of the land, for *it is* holy to the LORD.

¹⁵ "The five thousand *cubits* in width that remain, along the edge of the twenty-five thousand, shall be for general use by the city, for dwellings and common-land; and the city shall be in the center. ¹⁶ These *shall be* its measurements: the north side four thousand five hundred *cubits,* the south side four thousand five hundred, the east side four thousand five hundred, and the west side four thousand five hundred. ¹⁷ The common-land of the city shall be: to the north two hundred and fifty *cubits,* to the south two hundred and fifty, to the east two hundred and fifty, and to the west two hundred and fifty. ¹⁸ The rest of the length, alongside the district of the holy *section, shall be* ten thousand *cubits* to the east and ten thousand to the west. It shall be adjacent to the district of the holy *section,* and its produce shall be food for the workers of the city. ¹⁹ The workers of the city, from all the tribes of Israel, shall cultivate it. ²⁰ The entire district *shall be* twenty-five thousand *cubits* by twenty-five thousand *cubits,* foursquare. You shall set apart the holy district with the property of the city.

²¹ "The rest *shall belong* to the prince, on one side and on the other of the holy district and of the city's property, next to the twenty-five thousand *cubits* of the *holy* district as far as the eastern border, and westward next to the twenty-five thousand as far as the western border, adjacent to the *tribal* portions; *it shall belong* to the prince. It shall be the holy district, and the sanctuary of the temple *shall be* in the center. ²² Moreover, apart from the possession of the Levites and the possession of the city *which are* in the midst of what *belongs* to the prince, *the area* be-

tween the border of Judah and the border of Benjamin shall belong to the prince.

²³ "As for the rest of the tribes, from the east side to the west, Benjamin *shall have* one *section;* ²⁴ by the border of Benjamin, from the east side to the west, Simeon *shall have* one *section;* ²⁵ by the border of Simeon, from the east side to the west, Issachar *shall have* one *section;* ²⁶ by the border of Issachar, from the east side to the west, Zebulun *shall have* one *section;* ²⁷ by the border of Zebulun, from the east side to the west, Gad *shall have* one *section;* ²⁸ by the border of Gad, on the south side, toward the South, the border shall be from Tamar *to* the waters of Meribah *by* Kadesh, along the brook to the Great Sea. ²⁹ This *is* the land which you shall divide by lot as an inheritance among the tribes of Israel, and these *are* their portions," says the Lord GOD.

³⁰ "These *are* the exits of the city. On the north side, measuring four thousand five hundred *cubits* ³¹(the gates of the city *shall be* named after the tribes of Israel), the three gates northward: one gate for Reuben, one gate for Judah, and one gate for Levi; ³² on the east side, four thousand five hundred *cubits,* three gates: one gate for Joseph, one gate for Benjamin, and one gate for Dan; ³³ on the south side, measuring four thousand five hundred *cubits,* three gates: one gate for Simeon, one gate for Issachar, and one gate for Zebulun; ³⁴ on the west side, four thousand five hundred *cubits* with their three gates: one gate for Gad, one gate for Asher, and one gate for Naphtali. ³⁵ All the way around *shall be* eighteen thousand *cubits;* and the name of the city from *that* day *shall be:* THE LORD *IS* THERE."

~ PSALM 135:8–14 ~

⁸ He destroyed the firstborn of Egypt,
   Both of man and beast.
⁹ He sent signs and wonders into the
      midst of you, O Egypt,
   Upon Pharaoh and all his servants.
¹⁰ He defeated many nations
   And slew mighty kings—
¹¹ Sihon king of the Amorites,
   Og king of Bashan,
   And all the kingdoms of Canaan—

¹² And gave their land *as* a heritage,
    A heritage to Israel His people.

¹³ Your name, O LORD, *endures*
    forever,
    Your fame, O LORD, throughout all
    generations.

¹⁴ For the LORD will judge His people,
    And He will have compassion on His
    servants.

～ PROVERBS 29:9 ～

⁹ *If* a wise man contends with a foolish
    man,
    Whether *the fool* rages or laughs,
    there is no peace.

～ 1 PETER 4:1–19 ～

Therefore, since Christ suffered for us in the flesh, arm yourselves also with the same mind, for he who has suffered in the flesh has ceased from sin, ² that he no longer should live the rest of *his* time in the flesh for the lusts of men, but for the will of God. ³ For we *have spent* enough of our past lifetime in doing the will of the Gentiles—when we walked in lewdness, lusts, drunkenness, revelries, drinking parties, and abominable idolatries. ⁴ In regard to these, they think it strange that you do not run with *them* in the same flood of dissipation, speaking evil of *you*. ⁵ They will give an account to Him who is ready to judge the living and the dead. ⁶ For this reason the gospel was preached also to those who are dead, that they might be judged according to men in the flesh, but live according to God in the spirit.

⁷ But the end of all things is at hand; therefore be serious and watchful in your prayers. ⁸ And above all things have fervent love for one another, for "love will cover a multitude of sins." ⁹ *Be* hospitable to one another without grumbling. ¹⁰ As each one has received a gift, minister it to one another, as good stewards of the manifold grace of God. ¹¹ If anyone speaks, *let him speak* as the oracles of God. If anyone ministers, *let him do it* as with the ability which God supplies, that in all things God may be glorified through Jesus Christ, to whom belong the glory and the dominion forever and ever. Amen.

¹² Beloved, do not think it strange concerning the fiery trial which is to try you, as though some strange thing happened to you; ¹³ but rejoice to the extent that you partake of Christ's sufferings, that when His glory is revealed, you may also be glad with exceeding joy. ¹⁴ If you are reproached for the name of Christ, blessed *are you*, for the Spirit of glory and of God rests upon you. On their part He is blasphemed, but on your part He is glorified. ¹⁵ But let none of you suffer as a murderer, a thief, an evildoer, or as a busybody in other people's matters. ¹⁶ Yet if *anyone suffers* as a Christian, let him not be ashamed, but let him glorify God in this matter.

¹⁷ For the time *has come* for judgment to begin at the house of God; and if *it begins* with us first, what will *be* the end of those who do not obey the gospel of God? ¹⁸ Now

> "If the righteous one is scarcely
>   saved,
>   Where will the ungodly and the
>   sinner appear?"

¹⁹ Therefore let those who suffer according to the will of God commit their souls *to Him* in doing good, as to a faithful Creator.

READING 333 · NOVEMBER 29

～ DANIEL 1:1—2:49 ～

In the third year of the reign of Jehoiakim king of Judah, Nebuchadnezzar king of Babylon came to Jerusalem and besieged it. ² And the Lord gave Jehoiakim king of Judah into his hand, with some of the articles of the house of God, which he carried into the land of Shinar to the house of his god; and he

Worry, Worry, Worry

People who continually worry about every detail of their lives are like this patient in a mental hospital who stood with her ear pressed against the wall:

"What are you doing?" asked a curious attendant.

"Shhhh," the woman whispered, beckoning to the attendant to join her at the wall.

The attendant pressed her ear to the wall and stood there for several moments listening intently. "I can't hear anything," she said.

"No," the patient replied with a furrowed brow. "It's been like that all day!"

Some worry about what might be said. Others worry about what hasn't been said. Some worry about what might happen. Others worry about what hasn't happened, but should have happened by now. Others worry about their future while others fret over the consequences of their past.

We were created for abundant life — mind, body, and spirit. Like a flower, we were meant to blossom, not to wither on the vine. Turn your worries over to Jesus today and walk in peace — mind, body, and spirit.

brought the articles into the treasure house of his god.

³ Then the king instructed Ashpenaz, the master of his eunuchs, to bring some of the children of Israel and some of the king's descendants and some of the nobles, ⁴ young men in whom *there was* no blemish, but good-looking, gifted in all wisdom, possessing knowledge and quick to understand, who *had* ability to serve in the king's palace, and whom they might teach the language and literature of the Chaldeans. ⁵ And the king appointed for them a daily provision of the king's delicacies and of the wine which he drank, and three years of training for them, so that at the end of *that time* they might serve before the king. ⁶ Now from among those of the sons of Judah were Daniel, Hananiah, Mishael, and Azariah. ⁷ To them the chief of the eunuchs gave names: he gave Daniel *the name* Belteshazzar; to Hananiah, Shadrach; to Mishael, Meshach; and to Azariah, Abed-Nego.

⁸ But Daniel purposed in his heart that he would not defile himself with the portion of the king's delicacies, nor with the wine which he drank; therefore he requested of the chief of the eunuchs that he might not defile himself. ⁹ Now God had brought Daniel into the favor and goodwill of the chief of the eunuchs. ¹⁰ And the chief of the eunuchs said to Daniel, "I fear my lord the king, who has appointed your food and drink. For why should he see your faces looking worse than the young men who *are* your age? Then you would endanger my head before the king."

¹¹ So Daniel said to the steward whom the chief of the eunuchs had set over Daniel, Hananiah, Mishael, and Azariah, ¹² "Please test your servants for ten days, and let them give us vegetables to eat and water to drink. ¹³ Then let our appearance be examined before you, and the appearance of the young men who eat the portion of the king's delicacies; and as you see fit, *so* deal with your servants." ¹⁴ So he consented with them in this matter, and tested them ten days.

¹⁵ And at the end of ten days their features appeared better and fatter in flesh than all the young men who ate the portion of the king's delicacies. ¹⁶ Thus the steward took away their portion of delicacies and the wine that they were to drink, and gave them vegetables.

¹⁷ As for these four young men, God gave them knowledge and skill in all literature and wisdom; and Daniel had understanding in all visions and dreams.

¹⁸ Now at the end of the days, when the king had said that they should be brought in, the chief of the eunuchs brought them in before Nebuchadnezzar. ¹⁹ Then the king interviewed them, and among them all none was found like Daniel, Hananiah, Mishael, and Azariah; therefore they served before the king. ²⁰ And in all matters of wisdom *and* understanding about which the king examined them, he found them ten times better than all the magicians *and* astrologers who *were* in all his realm. ²¹ Thus Daniel continued until the first year of King Cyrus.

2 Now in the second year of Nebuchadnezzar's reign, Nebuchadnezzar had dreams; and his spirit was *so* troubled that his sleep left him. ² Then the king gave the command to call the magicians, the astrologers, the sorcerers, and the Chaldeans to tell the king his dreams. So they came and stood before the king. ³ And the king said to them, "I have had a dream, and my spirit is anxious to know the dream."

⁴ Then the Chaldeans spoke to the king in Aramaic, "O king, live forever! Tell your servants the dream, and we will give the interpretation."

⁵ The king answered and said to the Chaldeans, "My decision is firm: if you do not make known the dream to me, and its interpretation, you shall be cut in pieces, and your houses shall be made an ash heap. ⁶ However, if you tell the dream and its interpretation, you shall receive from me gifts, rewards, and great honor. Therefore tell me the dream and its interpretation."

⁷ They answered again and said, "Let the king tell his servants the dream, and we will give its interpretation."

⁸ The king answered and said, "I know for certain that you would gain time, because you see that my decision is firm: ⁹ if you do not make known the dream to me,

there is only one decree for you! For you have agreed to speak lying and corrupt words before me till the time has changed. Therefore tell me the dream, and I shall know that you can give me its interpretation."

¹⁰ The Chaldeans answered the king, and said, "There is not a man on earth who can tell the king's matter; therefore no king, lord, or ruler has *ever* asked such things of any magician, astrologer, or Chaldean. ¹¹ *It is* a difficult thing that the king requests, and there is no other who can tell it to the king except the gods, whose dwelling is not with flesh."

¹² For this reason the king was angry and very furious, and gave the command to destroy all the wise *men* of Babylon. ¹³ So the decree went out, and they began killing the wise *men;* and they sought Daniel and his companions, to kill *them.*

¹⁴ Then with counsel and wisdom Daniel answered Arioch, the captain of the king's guard, who had gone out to kill the wise *men* of Babylon; ¹⁵ he answered and said to Arioch the king's captain, "Why is the decree from the king so urgent?" Then Arioch made the decision known to Daniel.

¹⁶ So Daniel went in and asked the king to give him time, that he might tell the king the interpretation. ¹⁷ Then Daniel went to his house, and made the decision known to Hananiah, Mishael, and Azariah, his companions, ¹⁸ that they might seek mercies from the God of heaven concerning this secret, so that Daniel and his companions might not perish with the rest of the wise *men* of Babylon. ¹⁹ Then the secret was revealed to Daniel in a night vision. So Daniel blessed the God of heaven.

²⁰ Daniel answered and said:

"Blessed be the name of God
    forever and ever,
For wisdom and might are His.
²¹ And He changes the times and the
    seasons;
He removes kings and raises up
    kings;
He gives wisdom to the wise
And knowledge to those who have
    understanding.
²² He reveals deep and secret things;

He knows what *is* in the darkness,
And light dwells with Him.

²³ "I thank You and praise You,
    O God of my fathers;
You have given me wisdom and
    might,
And have now made known to me
    what we asked of You,
For You have made known to us
    the king's demand."

²⁴ Therefore Daniel went to Arioch, whom the king had appointed to destroy the wise *men* of Babylon. He went and said thus to him: "Do not destroy the wise *men* of Babylon; take me before the king, and I will tell the king the interpretation."

²⁵ Then Arioch quickly brought Daniel before the king, and said thus to him, "I have found a man of the captives of Judah, who will make known to the king the interpretation."

²⁶ The king answered and said to Daniel, whose name *was* Belteshazzar, "Are you able to make known to me the dream which I have seen, and its interpretation?"

²⁷ Daniel answered in the presence of the king, and said, "The secret which the king has demanded, the wise *men*, the astrologers, the magicians, and the soothsayers cannot declare to the king. ²⁸ But there is a God in heaven who reveals secrets, and He has made known to King Nebuchadnezzar what will be in the latter days. Your dream, and the visions of your head upon your bed, were these: ²⁹ As for you, O king, thoughts came *to* your *mind while* on your bed, *about* what would come to pass after this; and He who reveals secrets has made known to you what will be. ³⁰ But as for me, this secret has not been revealed to me because I have more wisdom than anyone living, but for *our* sakes who make known the interpretation to the king, and that you may know the thoughts of your heart.

³¹ "You, O king, were watching; and behold, a great image! This great image, whose splendor *was* excellent, stood before you; and its form *was* awesome. ³² This image's head *was* of fine gold, its chest and arms of silver, its belly and thighs of bronze, ³³ its legs of iron, its feet partly of iron and partly of clay. ³⁴ You watched

while a stone was cut out without hands, which struck the image on its feet of iron and clay, and broke them in pieces. [35] Then the iron, the clay, the bronze, the silver, and the gold were crushed together, and became like chaff from the summer threshing floors; the wind carried them away so that no trace of them was found. And the stone that struck the image became a great mountain and filled the whole earth.

[36] "This *is* the dream. Now we will tell the interpretation of it before the king. [37] You, O king, *are* a king of kings. For the God of heaven has given you a kingdom, power, strength, and glory; [38] and wherever the children of men dwell, or the beasts of the field and the birds of the heaven, He has given *them* into your hand, and has made you ruler over them all—you *are* this head of gold. [39] But after you shall arise another kingdom inferior to yours; then another, a third kingdom of bronze, which shall rule over all the earth. [40] And the fourth kingdom shall be as strong as iron, inasmuch as iron breaks in pieces and shatters everything; and like iron that crushes, *that kingdom* will break in pieces and crush all the others. [41] Whereas you saw the feet and toes, partly of potter's clay and partly of iron, the kingdom shall be divided; yet the strength of the iron shall be in it, just as you saw the iron mixed with ceramic clay. [42] And *as* the toes of the feet *were* partly of iron and partly of clay, *so* the kingdom shall be partly strong and partly fragile. [43] As you saw iron mixed with ceramic clay, they will mingle with the seed of men; but they will not adhere to one another, just as iron does not mix with clay. [44] And in the days of these kings the God of heaven will set up a kingdom which shall never be destroyed; and the kingdom shall not be left to other people; it shall break in pieces and consume all these kingdoms, and it shall stand forever. [45] Inasmuch as you saw that the stone was cut out of the mountain without hands, and that it broke in pieces the iron, the bronze, the clay, the silver, and the gold—the great God has made known to the king what will come to pass after this. The dream is certain, and its interpretation is sure."

[46] Then King Nebuchadnezzar fell on his face, prostrate before Daniel, and commanded that they should present an offering and incense to him. [47] The king answered Daniel, and said, "Truly your God *is* the God of gods, the Lord of kings, and a revealer of secrets, since you could reveal this secret." [48] Then the king promoted Daniel and gave him many great gifts; and he made him ruler over the whole province of Babylon, and chief administrator over all the wise *men* of Babylon. [49] Also Daniel petitioned the king, and he set Shadrach, Meshach, and Abed-Nego over the affairs of the province of Babylon; but Daniel *sat* in the gate of the king.

∼ PSALM 135:15–21 ∼

[15] The idols of the nations *are* silver and gold,
  The work of men's hands.
[16] They have mouths, but they do not speak;
  Eyes they have, but they do not see;
[17] They have ears, but they do not hear;
  Nor is there *any* breath in their mouths.
[18] Those who make them are like them;
  So is everyone who trusts in them.

[19] Bless the LORD, O house of Israel!
  Bless the LORD, O house of Aaron!
[20] Bless the LORD, O house of Levi!
  You who fear the LORD, bless the LORD!
[21] Blessed be the LORD out of Zion,
  Who dwells in Jerusalem!

  Praise the LORD!

∼ PROVERBS 29:10 ∼

[10] The bloodthirsty hate the blameless,
  But the upright seek his well-being.

∼ 1 PETER 5:1–14 ∼

The elders who are among you I exhort, I who am a fellow elder and a witness of the sufferings of Christ, and also a partaker of the glory that will be revealed: [2] Shepherd the flock of God which is among you, serving as overseers, not by compulsion but willingly, not for dishonest gain but eagerly; [3] nor as being lords over those entrusted to you, but being examples to the flock; [4] and when the Chief Shepherd appears, you will receive the crown of glory that does not fade away.

[5] Likewise you younger people, submit yourselves to *your* elders. Yes, all of *you* be submissive to one another, and be clothed with humility, for

"God resists the proud,
But gives grace to the humble."

[6] Therefore humble yourselves under the mighty hand of God, that He may exalt you in due time, [7] casting all your care upon Him, for He cares for you.

[8] Be sober, be vigilant; because your adversary the devil walks about like a roaring lion, seeking whom he may devour. [9] Resist him, steadfast in the faith, knowing that the same sufferings are experienced by your brotherhood in the world. [10] But may the God of all grace, who called us to His eternal glory by Christ Jesus, after you have suffered a while, perfect, establish, strengthen, and settle *you.* [11] To Him *be* the glory and the dominion forever and ever. Amen.

[12] By Silvanus, our faithful brother as I consider him, I have written to you briefly, exhorting and testifying that this is the true grace of God in which you stand.

[13] She who is in Babylon, elect together with *you,* greets you; and *so does* Mark my son. [14] Greet one another with a kiss of love.

Peace to you all who are in Christ Jesus. Amen.

~ DANIEL 3:1—4:37 ~

Nebuchadnezzar the king made an image of gold, whose height *was* sixty cubits *and* its width six cubits. He set it up in the plain of Dura, in the province of Babylon. [2] And King Nebuchadnezzar sent *word* to gather together the satraps, the administrators, the governors, the counselors, the treasurers, the judges, the magistrates, and all the officials of the provinces, to come to the dedication of the image which King Nebuchadnezzar had set up. [3] So the satraps, the administrators, the governors, the counselors, the treasurers, the judges, the magistrates, and all the officials of the provinces gathered together for the dedication of the image that King Nebuchadnezzar had set up; and they stood before the image that Nebuchadnezzar had set up. [4] Then a herald cried aloud: "To you it is commanded, O peoples, nations, and languages, [5] *that* at the time you hear the sound of the horn, flute, harp, lyre, *and* psaltery, in symphony with all kinds of music, you shall fall down and worship the gold image that King Nebuchadnez-

zar has set up; [6] and whoever does not fall down and worship shall be cast immediately into the midst of a burning fiery furnace."

[7] So at that time, when all the people heard the sound of the horn, flute, harp, *and* lyre, in symphony with all kinds of music, all the people, nations, and languages fell down *and* worshiped the gold image which King Nebuchadnezzar had set up.

[8] Therefore at that time certain Chaldeans came forward and accused the Jews. [9] They spoke and said to King Nebuchadnezzar, "O king, live forever! [10] You, O king, have made a decree that everyone who hears the sound of the horn, flute, harp, lyre, *and* psaltery, in symphony with all kinds of music, shall fall down and worship the gold image; [11] and whoever does not fall down and worship shall be cast into the midst of a burning fiery furnace. [12] There are certain Jews whom you have set over the affairs of the province of Babylon: Shadrach, Meshach, and Abed-Nego; these men, O king, have not

paid due regard to you. They do not serve your gods or worship the gold image which you have set up."

¹³ Then Nebuchadnezzar, in rage and fury, gave the command to bring Shadrach, Meshach, and Abed-Nego. So they brought these men before the king. ¹⁴ Nebuchadnezzar spoke, saying to them, "*Is it true*, Shadrach, Meshach, and Abed-Nego, *that* you do not serve my gods or worship the gold image which I have set up? ¹⁵ Now if you are ready at the time you hear the sound of the horn, flute, harp, lyre, *and* psaltery, in symphony with all kinds of music, and you fall down and worship the image which I have made, *good*! But if you do not worship, you shall be cast immediately into the midst of a burning fiery furnace. And who *is* the god who will deliver you from my hands?"

¹⁶ Shadrach, Meshach, and Abed-Nego answered and said to the king, "O Nebuchadnezzar, we have no need to answer you in this matter. ¹⁷ If that *is the case*, our God whom we serve is able to deliver us from the burning fiery furnace, and He will deliver *us* from your hand, O king. ¹⁸ But if not, let it be known to you, O king, that we do not serve your gods, nor will we worship the gold image which you have set up."

¹⁹ Then Nebuchadnezzar was full of fury, and the expression on his face changed toward Shadrach, Meshach, and Abed-Nego. He spoke and commanded that they heat the furnace seven times more than it was usually heated. ²⁰ And he commanded certain mighty men of valor who *were* in his army to bind Shadrach, Meshach, and Abed-Nego, *and* cast *them* into the burning fiery furnace. ²¹ Then these men were bound in their coats, their trousers, their turbans, and their *other* garments, and were cast into the midst of the burning fiery furnace. ²² Therefore, because the king's command was urgent, and the furnace exceedingly hot, the flame of the fire killed those men who took up Shadrach, Meshach, and Abed-Nego. ²³ And these three men, Shadrach, Meshach, and Abed-Nego, fell down bound into the midst of the burning fiery furnace.

²⁴ Then King Nebuchadnezzar was astonished; and he rose in haste *and* spoke, saying to his counselors, "Did we not cast three men bound into the midst of the fire?"

They answered and said to the king, "True, O king."

²⁵ "Look!" he answered, "I see four men loose, walking in the midst of the fire; and they are not hurt, and the form of the fourth is like the Son of God."

²⁶ Then Nebuchadnezzar went near the mouth of the burning fiery furnace *and* spoke, saying, "Shadrach, Meshach, and Abed-Nego, servants of the Most High God, come out, and come *here*." Then Shadrach, Meshach, and Abed-Nego came from the midst of the fire. ²⁷ And the satraps, administrators, governors, and the king's counselors gathered together, and they saw these men on whose bodies the fire had no power; the hair of their head was not singed nor were their garments affected, and the smell of fire was not on them.

²⁸ Nebuchadnezzar spoke, saying, "Blessed be the God of Shadrach, Meshach, and Abed-Nego, who sent His Angel and delivered His servants who trusted in Him, and they have frustrated the king's word, and yielded their bodies, that they should not serve nor worship any god except their own God! ²⁹ Therefore I make a decree that any people, nation, or language which speaks anything amiss against the God of Shadrach, Meshach, and Abed-Nego shall be cut in pieces, and their houses shall be made an ash heap; because there is no other God who can deliver like this."

³⁰ Then the king promoted Shadrach, Meshach, and Abed-Nego in the province of Babylon.

4 Nebuchadnezzar the king,

To all peoples, nations, and languages that dwell in all the earth:

Peace be multiplied to you.

² I thought it good to declare the signs and wonders that the Most High God has worked for me.

Make an Honest Soap

When William was only sixteen years old, he tied all his possessions into a small bundle and left home to seek his fortune. He told an old canal-boat captain that his father was too poor to keep him and the only trade he knew was soap and candle making.

The old captain knelt and earnestly prayed for the boy, then advised him, "Soon, someone will be the leading soap-maker in New York. It can be you as well as someone else. Be a good man, give your heart to Christ, pay the Lord all that belongs to Him, make an honest soap; give a full pound, and I'm certain you'll be a prosperous and rich man."

When he arrived in the city, William remembered the captain's words and although poor and lonely, he joined a church and gave one-tenth of his first dollar, just as the captain had exhorted him. Once he gained regular employment, he soon became a partner in the business, then later, the sole owner. He made an honest soap, and as he became more successful, he increased his giving from 10 percent to 50 percent — eventually to 100 percent of his income. In all, William Colgate gave millions.

The marks of success are not only know-how and diligence, but humility and generosity.

But also for this very reason, giving all diligence, add to your faith virtue, to virtue knowledge, to knowledge self-control, to self-control perseverance, to perseverance godliness, to godliness brotherly kindness, and to brotherly kindness love. Therefore, brethren, be even more diligent to make your call and election sure, for if you do these things you will never stumble.

2 Peter 1:5-7,10

3   How great *are* His signs,
      And how mighty His wonders!
      His kingdom *is* an everlasting
          kingdom,
      And His dominion *is* from
          generation to generation.

4 I, Nebuchadnezzar, was at rest in
my house, and flourishing in my
palace. [5] I saw a dream which made
me afraid, and the thoughts on my
bed and the visions of my head
troubled me. [6] Therefore I issued a
decree to bring in all the wise *men*
of Babylon before me, that they
might make known to me the
interpretation of the dream. [7] Then
the magicians, the astrologers, the
Chaldeans, and the soothsayers
came in, and I told them the
dream; but they did not make
known to me its interpretation.
[8] But at last Daniel came before me
(his name *is* Belteshazzar, according
to the name of my god; in him *is*
the Spirit of the Holy God), and I
told the dream before him, *saying:*
[9] "Belteshazzar, chief of the
magicians, because I know that the
Spirit of the Holy God *is* in you,
and no secret troubles you, explain
to me the visions of my dream that
I have seen, and its interpretation.

10   "These *were* the visions of my head
      while on my bed:

      I was looking, and behold,
      A tree in the midst of the earth,
      And its height was great.
11   The tree grew and became strong;
      Its height reached to the heavens,
      And it could be seen to the ends of
          all the earth.
12   Its leaves *were* lovely,
      Its fruit abundant,
      And in it *was* food for all.
      The beasts of the field found
          shade under it,
      The birds of the heavens dwelt in
          its branches,
      And all flesh was fed from it.

13   "I saw in the visions of my head
      while on my bed, and there was a

watcher, a holy one, coming down
from heaven. [14] He cried aloud and
said thus:

      'Chop down the tree and cut off its
          branches,
      Strip off its leaves and scatter its
          fruit.
      Let the beasts get out from under
          it,
      And the birds from its branches.
15   Nevertheless leave the stump and
          roots in the earth,
      Bound with a band of iron and
          bronze,
      In the tender grass of the field.
      Let it be wet with the dew of
          heaven,
      And *let* him graze with the beasts
      On the grass of the earth.
16   Let his heart be changed from *that*
          of a man,
      Let him be given the heart of a
          beast,
      And let seven times pass over him.

17   'This decision *is* by the decree of
          the watchers,
      And the sentence by the word of
          the holy ones,
      In order that the living may know
      That the Most High rules in the
          kingdom of men,
      Gives it to whomever He will,
      And sets over it the lowest of men.'

18   "This dream I, King
Nebuchadnezzar, have seen.
Now you, Belteshazzar, declare
its interpretation, since all the
wise *men* of my kingdom are
not able to make known to me
the interpretation; but you *are*
able, for the Spirit of the
Holy God *is* in you."

19   Then Daniel, whose name was
Belteshazzar, was astonished for a
time, and his thoughts troubled
him. *So* the king spoke, and said,
"Belteshazzar, do not let the dream
or its interpretation trouble you."
      Belteshazzar answered and said,
"My lord, *may* the dream concern
those who hate you, and its

interpretation concern your enemies!

20 "The tree that you saw, which grew and became strong, whose height reached to the heavens and which *could be seen* by all the earth, 21 whose leaves *were* lovely and its fruit abundant, in which *was* food for all, under which the beasts of the field dwelt, and in whose branches the birds of the heaven had their home— 22 it *is* you, O king, who have grown and become strong; for your greatness has grown and reaches to the heavens, and your dominion to the end of the earth.

23 "And inasmuch as the king saw a watcher, a holy one, coming down from heaven and saying, 'Chop down the tree and destroy it, but leave its stump and roots in the earth, *bound* with a band of iron and bronze in the tender grass of the field; let it be wet with the dew of heaven, and let him graze with the beasts of the field, till seven times pass over him'; 24 this is the interpretation, O king, and this is the decree of the Most High, which has come upon my lord the king: 25 They shall drive you from men, your dwelling shall be with the beasts of the field, and they shall make you eat grass like oxen. They shall wet you with the dew of heaven, and seven times shall pass over you, till you know that the Most High rules in the kingdom of men, and gives it to whomever He chooses.

26 "And inasmuch as they gave the command to leave the stump *and* roots of the tree, your kingdom shall be assured to you, after you come to know that Heaven rules. 27 Therefore, O king, let my advice be acceptable to you; break off your sins by *being* righteous, and your iniquities by showing mercy to *the* poor. Perhaps there may be a lengthening of your prosperity."

28 All *this* came upon King Nebuchadnezzar. 29 At the end of the twelve months he was walking about the royal palace of Babylon. 30 The king spoke, saying, "Is not this great Babylon, that I have built for a royal dwelling by my mighty power and for the honor of my majesty?"

31 While the word *was still* in the king's mouth, a voice fell from heaven: "King Nebuchadnezzar, to you it is spoken: the kingdom has departed from you! 32 And they shall drive you from men, and your dwelling *shall be* with the beasts of the field. They shall make you eat grass like oxen; and seven times shall pass over you, until you know that the Most High rules in the kingdom of men, and gives it to whomever He chooses."

33 That very hour the word was fulfilled concerning Nebuchadnezzar; he was driven from men and ate grass like oxen; his body was wet with the dew of heaven till his hair had grown like eagles' *feathers* and his nails like birds' *claws*.

34 And at the end of the time I, Nebuchadnezzar, lifted my eyes to heaven, and my understanding returned to me; and I blessed the Most High and praised and honored Him who lives forever:

For His dominion *is* an everlasting dominion,
And His kingdom *is* from generation to generation.
35 All the inhabitants of the earth *are* reputed as nothing;
He does according to His will in the army of heaven
And *among* the inhabitants of the earth.
No one can restrain His hand
Or say to Him, "What have You done?"

36 At the same time my reason returned to me, and for the glory of my kingdom, my honor and splendor returned to me. My counselors and nobles resorted to me, I was restored to my kingdom, and excellent majesty was added to me. 37 Now I, Nebuchadnezzar, praise and extol and honor the King of heaven, all of whose works *are* truth, and His ways justice. And those who walk in pride He is able to put down.

∼ PSALM 136:1–9 ∼

1 Oh, give thanks to the LORD, for *He is* good!
    For His mercy *endures* forever.
2 Oh, give thanks to the God of gods!
    For His mercy *endures* forever.
3 Oh, give thanks to the Lord of lords!
    For His mercy *endures* forever:

4 To Him who alone does great wonders,
    For His mercy *endures* forever;
5 To Him who by wisdom made the heavens,
    For His mercy *endures* forever;
6 To Him who laid out the earth above the waters,
    For His mercy *endures* forever;
7 To Him who made great lights,
    For His mercy *endures* forever—
8 The sun to rule by day,
    For His mercy *endures* forever;
9 The moon and stars to rule by night,
    For His mercy *endures* forever.

∼ PROVERBS 29:11 ∼

11 A fool vents all his feelings,
    But a wise *man* holds them back.

∼ 2 PETER 1:1–21 ∼

Simon Peter, a bondservant and apostle of Jesus Christ,

To those who have obtained like precious faith with us by the righteousness of our God and Savior Jesus Christ:

2 Grace and peace be multiplied to you in the knowledge of God and of Jesus our Lord, 3 as His divine power has given to us all things that *pertain* to life and godliness, through the knowledge of Him who called us by glory and virtue, 4 by which have been given to us exceedingly great and precious promises, that through these you may be partakers of the divine nature, having escaped the corruption *that is* in the world through lust.

5 But also for this very reason, giving all diligence, add to your faith virtue, to virtue knowledge, 6 to knowledge self-control, to self-control perseverance, to perseverance godliness, 7 to godliness brotherly kindness, and to brotherly kindness love. 8 For if these things are yours and abound, *you will be* neither barren nor unfruitful in the knowledge of our Lord Jesus Christ. 9 For he who lacks these things is shortsighted, even to blindness, and has forgotten that he was cleansed from his old sins.

10 Therefore, brethren, be even more diligent to make your call and election sure, for if you do these things you will never stumble; 11 for so an entrance will be supplied to you abundantly into the everlasting kingdom of our Lord and Savior Jesus Christ.

12 For this reason I will not be negligent to remind you always of these things, though you know and are established in the present truth. 13 Yes, I think it is right, as long as I am in this tent, to stir you up by reminding *you,* 14 knowing that shortly I *must* put off my tent, just as our Lord Jesus Christ showed me. 15 Moreover I will be careful to ensure that you always have a reminder of these things after my decease.

16 For we did not follow cunningly devised fables when we made known to you the power and coming of our Lord Jesus Christ, but were eyewitnesses of His majesty. 17 For He received from God the Father honor and glory when such a voice came to Him from the Excellent Glory: "This is My beloved Son, in whom I am well pleased." 18 And we heard this voice which came from heaven when we were with Him on the holy mountain.

19 And so we have the prophetic word confirmed, which you do well to heed as

a light that shines in a dark place, until the day dawns and the morning star rises in your hearts; [20] knowing this first, that no prophecy of Scripture is of any private interpretation, [21] for prophecy never came by the will of man, but holy men of God spoke *as they were* moved by the Holy Spirit.

READING 335 · DECEMBER 1

~ DANIEL 5:1—6:28 ~

Belshazzar the king made a great feast for a thousand of his lords, and drank wine in the presence of the thousand. [2] While he tasted the wine, Belshazzar gave the command to bring the gold and silver vessels which his father Nebuchadnezzar had taken from the temple which *had been* in Jerusalem, that the king and his lords, his wives, and his concubines might drink from them. [3] Then they brought the gold vessels that had been taken from the temple of the house of God which *had been* in Jerusalem; and the king and his lords, his wives, and his concubines drank from them. [4] They drank wine, and praised the gods of gold and silver, bronze and iron, wood and stone.

[5] In the same hour the fingers of a man's hand appeared and wrote opposite the lampstand on the plaster of the wall of the king's palace; and the king saw the part of the hand that wrote. [6] Then the king's countenance changed, and his thoughts troubled him, so that the joints of his hips were loosened and his knees knocked against each other. [7] The king cried aloud to bring in the astrologers, the Chaldeans, and the soothsayers. The king spoke, saying to the wise *men* of Babylon, "Whoever reads this writing, and tells me its interpretation, shall be clothed with purple and *have* a chain of gold around his neck; and he shall be the third ruler in the kingdom." [8] Now all the king's wise *men* came, but they could not read the writing, or make known to the king its interpretation. [9] Then King Belshazzar was greatly troubled, his countenance was changed, and his lords were astonished.

[10] The queen, because of the words of the king and his lords, came to the banquet hall. The queen spoke, saying, "O king, live forever! Do not let your thoughts trouble you, nor let your countenance change. [11] There is a man in your kingdom in whom *is* the Spirit of the Holy God. And in the days of your father, light and understanding and wisdom, like the wisdom of the gods, were found in him; and King Nebuchadnezzar your father— your father the king—made him chief of the magicians, astrologers, Chaldeans, *and* soothsayers. [12] Inasmuch as an excellent spirit, knowledge, understanding, interpreting dreams, solving riddles, and explaining enigmas were found in this Daniel, whom the king named Belteshazzar, now let Daniel be called, and he will give the interpretation."

[13] Then Daniel was brought in before the king. The king spoke, and said to Daniel, "*Are* you that Daniel who is one of the captives from Judah, whom my father the king brought from Judah? [14] I have heard of you, that the Spirit of God *is* in you, and *that* light and understanding and excellent wisdom are found in you. [15] Now the wise *men,* the astrologers, have been brought in before me, that they should read this writing and make known to me its interpretation, but they could not give the interpretation of the thing. [16] And I have heard of you, that you can give interpretations and explain enigmas. Now if you can read the writing and make known to me its interpretation, you shall be clothed with purple and *have* a chain of gold around your neck, and shall be the third ruler in the kingdom."

[17] Then Daniel answered, and said before the king, "Let your gifts be for yourself, and give your rewards to another; yet I will read the writing to the king, and make known to him the interpretation. [18] O king, the Most High God gave Nebuchadnezzar your father a kingdom and majesty, glory and honor. [19] And because of the majesty that He gave him, all peoples, nations, and languages trembled

and feared before him. Whomever he wished, he executed; whomever he wished, he kept alive; whomever he wished, he set up; and whomever he wished, he put down. [20] But when his heart was lifted up, and his spirit was hardened in pride, he was deposed from his kingly throne, and they took his glory from him. [21] Then he was driven from the sons of men, his heart was made like the beasts, and his dwelling *was* with the wild donkeys. They fed him with grass like oxen, and his body was wet with the dew of heaven, till he knew that the Most High God rules in the kingdom of men, and appoints over it whomever He chooses.

[22] "But you his son, Belshazzar, have not humbled your heart, although you knew all this. [23] And you have lifted yourself up against the Lord of heaven. They have brought the vessels of His house before you, and you and your lords, your wives and your concubines, have drunk wine from them. And you have praised the gods of silver and gold, bronze and iron, wood and stone, which do not see or hear or know; and the God who *holds* your breath in His hand and owns all your ways, you have not glorified. [24] Then the fingers of the hand were sent from Him, and this writing was written.

[25] "And this is the inscription that was written:

MENE, MENE, TEKEL, UPHARSIN.

[26] This *is* the interpretation of *each* word. MENE: God has numbered your kingdom, and finished it; [27]TEKEL: You have been weighed in the balances, and found wanting; [28]PERES: Your kingdom has been divided, and given to the Medes and Persians." [29] Then Belshazzar gave the command, and they clothed Daniel with purple and *put* a chain of gold around his neck, and made a proclamation concerning him that he should be the third ruler in the kingdom.

[30] That very night Belshazzar, king of the Chaldeans, was slain. [31] And Darius the Mede received the kingdom, *being* about sixty-two years old.

6 It pleased Darius to set over the kingdom one hundred and twenty satraps, to be over the whole kingdom; [2] and over these, three governors, of whom Daniel *was* one, that the satraps might give account to them, so that the king would suffer no loss. [3] Then this Daniel distinguished himself above the governors and satraps, because an excellent spirit *was* in him; and the king gave thought to setting him over the whole realm. [4] So the governors and satraps sought to find *some* charge against Daniel concerning the kingdom; but they could find no charge or fault, because he *was* faithful; nor was there any error or fault found in him. [5] Then these men said, "We shall not find any charge against this Daniel unless we find *it* against him concerning the law of his God."

[6] So these governors and satraps thronged before the king, and said thus to him: "King Darius, live forever! [7] All the governors of the kingdom, the administrators and satraps, the counselors and advisors, have consulted together to establish a royal statute and to make a firm decree, that whoever petitions any god or man for thirty days, except you, O king, shall be cast into the den of lions. [8] Now, O king, establish the decree and sign the writing, so that it cannot be changed, according to the law of the Medes and Persians, which does not alter." [9] Therefore King Darius signed the written decree.

[10] Now when Daniel knew that the writing was signed, he went home. And in his upper room, with his windows open toward Jerusalem, he knelt down on his knees three times that day, and prayed and gave thanks before his God, as was his custom since early days.

[11] Then these men assembled and found Daniel praying and making supplication before his God. [12] And they went before the king, and spoke concerning the king's decree: "Have you not signed a decree that every man who petitions any god or man within thirty days, except you, O king, shall be cast into the den of lions?"

The king answered and said, "The thing *is* true, according to the law of the Medes and Persians, which does not alter."

[13] So they answered and said before the king, "That Daniel, who is one of the captives from Judah, does not show due regard for you, O king, or for the decree

Breathe Without Ceasing

On a trip across the Atlantic, Dwight L. Moody had an opportunity to help the crew and other volunteers put out a fire in the hold of the ship. As they stood in the bucket line a friend said to Moody, "Let's go up to the other end of the ship and pray."

Moody, a commonsense evangelist, said, "No, sir, we will stand right here, pass buckets, and pray hard all the time we are doing so!"

To be a praying Christian does not mean we pray occasionally, but that we pray continually — wherever we are, whatever we are doing. We must put our faith into action. Just as:

- no one can live by taking a breath only once in a while, or survive by taking only a sip of water once a week . . .
- no person can read by a light that flickers on and off . . .
- no sailor can steer his course with only an occasional puff of wind . . .

So too, with prayer and the Christian life. We must pray always, in all things, in spite of all circumstances.

> Now when Daniel knew that the writing was signed, he went home… knelt down on his knees three times that day, and prayed and gave thanks before his God, as was his custom since early days.
>
> *Daniel 6:10*

that you have signed, but makes his petition three times a day."

¹⁴ And the king, when he heard *these* words, was greatly displeased with himself, and set *his* heart on Daniel to deliver him; and he labored till the going down of the sun to deliver him. ¹⁵ Then these men approached the king, and said to the king, "Know, O king, that *it is* the law of the Medes and Persians that no decree or statute which the king establishes may be changed."

¹⁶ So the king gave the command, and they brought Daniel and cast *him* into the den of lions. *But* the king spoke, saying to Daniel, "Your God, whom you serve continually, He will deliver you." ¹⁷ Then a stone was brought and laid on the mouth of the den, and the king sealed it with his own signet ring and with the signets of his lords, that the purpose concerning Daniel might not be changed.

¹⁸ Now the king went to his palace and spent the night fasting; and no musicians were brought before him. Also his sleep went from him. ¹⁹ Then the king arose very early in the morning and went in haste to the den of lions. ²⁰ And when he came to the den, he cried out with a lamenting voice to Daniel. The king spoke, saying to Daniel, "Daniel, servant of the living God, has your God, whom you serve continually, been able to deliver you from the lions?"

²¹ Then Daniel said to the king, "O king, live forever! ²² My God sent His angel and shut the lions' mouths, so that they have not hurt me, because I was found innocent before Him; and also, O king, I have done no wrong before you."

²³ Now the king was exceedingly glad for him, and commanded that they should take Daniel up out of the den. So Daniel was taken up out of the den, and no injury whatever was found on him, because he believed in his God.

²⁴ And the king gave the command, and they brought those men who had accused Daniel, and they cast *them* into the den of lions—them, their children, and their wives; and the lions overpowered them, and broke all their bones in pieces before they ever came to the bottom of the den.

²⁵ Then King Darius wrote:

To all peoples, nations, and languages that dwell in all the earth:

Peace be multiplied to you.

²⁶ I make a decree that in every dominion of my kingdom *men must* tremble and fear before the God of Daniel.

For He *is* the living God,
And steadfast forever;
His kingdom *is the one* which
shall not be destroyed,
And His dominion *shall endure* to
the end.
²⁷ He delivers and rescues,
And He works signs and wonders
In heaven and on earth,
Who has delivered Daniel from
the power of the lions.

²⁸ So this Daniel prospered in the reign of Darius and in the reign of Cyrus the Persian.

∼ PSALM 136:10–26 ∼

¹⁰ To Him who struck Egypt in their
firstborn,
For His mercy *endures* forever;
¹¹ And brought out Israel from among
them,
For His mercy *endures* forever;
¹² With a strong hand, and with an
outstretched arm,
For His mercy *endures* forever;
¹³ To Him who divided the Red Sea in
two,
For His mercy *endures* forever;
¹⁴ And made Israel pass through the
midst of it,
For His mercy *endures* forever;
¹⁵ But overthrew Pharaoh and his army
in the Red Sea,
For His mercy *endures* forever;
¹⁶ To Him who led His people through
the wilderness,
For His mercy *endures* forever;
¹⁷ To Him who struck down great
kings,
For His mercy *endures* forever;
¹⁸ And slew famous kings,
For His mercy *endures* forever—

19 Sihon king of the Amorites,
    For His mercy *endures* forever;
20 And Og king of Bashan,
    For His mercy *endures* forever—
21 And gave their land as a heritage,
    For His mercy *endures* forever;
22 A heritage to Israel His servant,
    For His mercy *endures* forever.

23 Who remembered us in our lowly
    state,
    For His mercy *endures* forever;
24 And rescued us from our enemies,
    For His mercy *endures* forever;
25 Who gives food to all flesh,
    For His mercy *endures* forever.

26 Oh, give thanks to the God of
    heaven!
    For His mercy *endures* forever.

～ PROVERBS 29:12, 13 ～

12 If a ruler pays attention to lies,
    All his servants *become* wicked.

13 The poor *man* and the oppressor
    have this in common:
    The LORD gives light to the eyes of
    both.

～ 2 PETER 2:1–22 ～

But there were also false prophets
among the people, even as there will
be false teachers among you, who will secretly bring in destructive heresies, even
denying the Lord who bought them, *and*
bring on themselves swift destruction.
2 And many will follow their destructive
ways, because of whom the way of truth
will be blasphemed. 3 By covetousness
they will exploit you with deceptive
words; for a long time their judgment has
not been idle, and their destruction does
not slumber.
  4 For if God did not spare the angels
who sinned, but cast *them* down to hell
and delivered *them* into chains of darkness, to be reserved for judgment; 5 and
did not spare the ancient world, but saved
Noah, *one of* eight *people,* a preacher of
righteousness, bringing in the flood on the
world of the ungodly; 6 and turning the

cities of Sodom and Gomorrah into ashes,
condemned *them* to destruction, making
them an example to those who afterward
would live ungodly; 7 and delivered righteous Lot, *who was* oppressed by the filthy
conduct of the wicked 8(for that righteous
man, dwelling among them, tormented
his righteous soul from day to day by seeing and hearing *their* lawless deeds)—
9 *then* the Lord knows how to deliver the
godly out of temptations and to reserve
the unjust under punishment for the day
of judgment, 10 and especially those who
walk according to the flesh in the lust of
uncleanness and despise authority. *They
are* presumptuous, self-willed. They are
not afraid to speak evil of dignitaries,
11 whereas angels, who are greater in
power and might, do not bring a reviling
accusation against them before the Lord.
  12 But these, like natural brute beasts
made to be caught and destroyed, speak
evil of the things they do not understand,
and will utterly perish in their own corruption, 13 *and* will receive the wages of
unrighteousness, *as* those who count it
pleasure to carouse in the daytime. *They
are* spots and blemishes, carousing in their
own deceptions while they feast with you,
14 having eyes full of adultery and that
cannot cease from sin, enticing unstable
souls. *They have* a heart trained in covetous practices, *and are* accursed children.
15 They have forsaken the right way and
gone astray, following the way of Balaam
the *son* of Beor, who loved the wages of
unrighteousness; 16 but he was rebuked for
his iniquity: a dumb donkey speaking with
a man's voice restrained the madness of
the prophet.
  17 These are wells without water, clouds
carried by a tempest, for whom is reserved
the blackness of darkness forever.
  18 For when they speak great swelling
words of emptiness, they allure through
the lusts of the flesh, through lewdness,
the ones who have actually escaped from
those who live in error. 19 While they
promise them liberty, they themselves are
slaves of corruption; for by whom a person is overcome, by him also he is brought
into bondage. 20 For if, after they have escaped the pollutions of the world through
the knowledge of the Lord and Savior
Jesus Christ, they are again entangled in

them and overcome, the latter end is worse for them than the beginning. ²¹ For it would have been better for them not to have known the way of righteousness, than having known *it*, to turn from the holy commandment delivered to them. ²² But it has happened to them according to the true proverb: "A dog returns to his own vomit," and, "a sow, having washed, to her wallowing in the mire."

READING 336 · DECEMBER 2

∼ DANIEL 7:1—8:27 ∼

In the first year of Belshazzar king of Babylon, Daniel had a dream and visions of his head *while* on his bed. Then he wrote down the dream, telling the main facts.

² Daniel spoke, saying, "I saw in my vision by night, and behold, the four winds of heaven were stirring up the Great Sea. ³ And four great beasts came up from the sea, each different from the other. ⁴ The first *was* like a lion, and had eagle's wings. I watched till its wings were plucked off; and it was lifted up from the earth and made to stand on two feet like a man, and a man's heart was given to it.

⁵ "And suddenly another beast, a second, like a bear. It was raised up on one side, and *had* three ribs in its mouth between its teeth. And they said thus to it: 'Arise, devour much flesh!'

⁶ "After this I looked, and there was another, like a leopard, which had on its back four wings of a bird. The beast also had four heads, and dominion was given to it.

⁷ "After this I saw in the night visions, and behold, a fourth beast, dreadful and terrible, exceedingly strong. It had huge iron teeth; it was devouring, breaking in pieces, and trampling the residue with its feet. It *was* different from all the beasts that *were* before it, and it had ten horns. ⁸ I was considering the horns, and there was another horn, a little one, coming up among them, before whom three of the first horns were plucked out by the roots. And there, in this horn, *were* eyes like the eyes of a man, and a mouth speaking pompous words.

⁹ "I watched till thrones were put in place,
And the Ancient of Days was seated;

His garment *was* white as snow,
And the hair of His head *was* like pure wool.
His throne *was* a fiery flame,
Its wheels a burning fire;
¹⁰ A fiery stream issued
And came forth from before Him.
A thousand thousands ministered to Him;
Ten thousand times ten thousand stood before Him.
The court was seated,
And the books were opened.

¹¹ "I watched then because of the sound of the pompous words which the horn was speaking; I watched till the beast was slain, and its body destroyed and given to the burning flame. ¹² As for the rest of the beasts, they had their dominion taken away, yet their lives were prolonged for a season and a time.

¹³ "I was watching in the night visions,
And behold, *One* like the Son of Man,
Coming with the clouds of heaven!
He came to the Ancient of Days,
And they brought Him near before Him.
¹⁴ Then to Him was given dominion and glory and a kingdom,
That all peoples, nations, and languages should serve Him.
His dominion *is* an everlasting dominion,
Which shall not pass away,
And His kingdom *the one*
Which shall not be destroyed.

¹⁵ "I, Daniel, was grieved in my spirit within *my* body, and the visions of my

Grow in Grace

> But grow in the grace and knowledge of our Lord and Savior Jesus Christ. To Him be the glory both now and forever. Amen.
>
> *2 Peter 3:18*

The story is told of a king who owned a valuable diamond, one of the rarest and most perfect in the world. One day the diamond fell and a deep scratch marred its face. The king summoned the best diamond experts in the land to correct the blemish, but they all agreed they could not remove the scratch without cutting away a good part of the surface, thus reducing the weight and value of the diamond.

Finally one expert appeared and assured him that he could fix the diamond without reducing its value. His confidence was convincing and the king gave the diamond to the man. In a few days, the artisan returned the diamond to the king, who was amazed to find that the ugly scratch was gone, and in its place a beautiful rose was etched. The former scratch had become the stem of an exquisite flower!

Any mistake we make in life may temporarily mar our reputation. But if we stick to what we know is right and continue to attempt to conform our will to that of God, we can trust Him to turn the "scratches" on our souls into part of His signature — that's what it means to grow in God's grace.

head troubled me. ¹⁶ I came near to one of those who stood by, and asked him the truth of all this. So he told me and made known to me the interpretation of these things: ¹⁷ 'Those great beasts, which are four, *are* four kings *which* arise out of the earth. ¹⁸ But the saints of the Most High shall receive the kingdom, and possess the kingdom forever, even forever and ever.'

¹⁹ "Then I wished to know the truth about the fourth beast, which was different from all the others, exceedingly dreadful, *with* its teeth of iron and its nails of bronze, *which* devoured, broke in pieces, and trampled the residue with its feet; ²⁰ and the ten horns that *were* on its head, and the other *horn* which came up, before which three fell, namely, that horn which had eyes and a mouth which spoke pompous words, whose appearance *was* greater than his fellows.

²¹ "I was watching; and the same horn was making war against the saints, and prevailing against them, ²² until the Ancient of Days came, and a judgment was made *in favor* of the saints of the Most High, and the time came for the saints to possess the kingdom.

²³ "Thus he said:

'The fourth beast shall be
A fourth kingdom on earth,
Which shall be different from all
    other kingdoms,
And shall devour the whole earth,
Trample it and break it in pieces.
²⁴ The ten horns *are* ten kings
Who shall arise from this
    kingdom.
And another shall rise after them;
He shall be different from the first
    ones,
And shall subdue three kings.
²⁵ He shall speak *pompous* words
    against the Most High,
Shall persecute the saints of the
    Most High,
And shall intend to change times
    and law.
Then *the saints* shall be given into
    his hand
For a time and times and half a
    time.

²⁶ 'But the court shall be seated,
And they shall take away his
    dominion,
To consume and destroy *it* forever.
²⁷ Then the kingdom and dominion,
And the greatness of the kingdoms
    under the whole heaven,
Shall be given to the people, the
    saints of the Most High.
His kingdom *is* an everlasting
    kingdom,
And all dominions shall serve and
    obey Him.'

²⁸ "This *is* the end of the account. As for me, Daniel, my thoughts greatly troubled me, and my countenance changed; but I kept the matter in my heart."

8 In the third year of the reign of King Belshazzar a vision appeared *to* me—to me, Daniel—after the one that appeared to me the first time. ² I saw in the vision, and it so happened while I was looking, that I *was* in Shushan, the citadel, which *is* in the province of Elam; and I saw in the vision that I was by the River Ulai. ³ Then I lifted my eyes and saw, and there, standing beside the river, was a ram which had two horns, and the two horns *were* high; but one *was* higher than the other, and the higher *one* came up last. ⁴ I saw the ram pushing westward, northward, and southward, so that no animal could withstand him; nor *was there any* that could deliver from his hand, but he did according to his will and became great.

⁵ And as I was considering, suddenly a male goat came from the west, across the surface of the whole earth, without touching the ground; and the goat *had* a notable horn between his eyes. ⁶ Then he came to the ram that had two horns, which I had seen standing beside the river, and ran at him with furious power. ⁷ And I saw him confronting the ram; he was moved with rage against him, attacked the ram, and broke his two horns. There was no power in the ram to withstand him, but he cast him down to the ground and trampled him; and there was no one that could deliver the ram from his hand. ⁸ Therefore the male goat grew very

great; but when he became strong, the large horn was broken, and in place of it four notable ones came up toward the four winds of heaven. ⁹ And out of one of them came a little horn which grew exceedingly great toward the south, toward the east, and toward the Glorious *Land.* ¹⁰ And it grew up to the host of heaven; and it cast down *some* of the host and *some* of the stars to the ground, and trampled them. ¹¹ He even exalted *himself* as high as the Prince of the host; and by him the daily *sacrifices* were taken away, and the place of His sanctuary was cast down. ¹² Because of transgression, an army was given over *to the horn* to oppose the daily *sacrifices;* and he cast truth down to the ground. He did *all this* and prospered.

¹³ Then I heard a holy one speaking; and *another* holy one said to that certain *one* who was speaking, "How long *will* the vision *be, concerning* the daily *sacrifices* and the transgression of desolation, the giving of both the sanctuary and the host to be trampled underfoot?"

¹⁴ And he said to me, "For two thousand three hundred days; then the sanctuary shall be cleansed."

¹⁵ Then it happened, when I, Daniel, had seen the vision and was seeking the meaning, that suddenly there stood before me one having the appearance of a man. ¹⁶ And I heard a man's voice between *the banks of* the Ulai, who called, and said, "Gabriel, make this *man* understand the vision." ¹⁷ So he came near where I stood, and when he came I was afraid and fell on my face; but he said to me, "Understand, son of man, that the vision *refers* to the time of the end."

¹⁸ Now, as he was speaking with me, I was in a deep sleep with my face to the ground; but he touched me, and stood me upright. ¹⁹ And he said, "Look, I am making known to you what shall happen in the latter time of the indignation; for at the appointed time the end *shall be.* ²⁰ The ram which you saw, having the two horns—*they are* the kings of Media and Persia. ²¹ And the male goat *is* the kingdom of Greece. The large horn that *is* between its eyes *is* the first king. ²² As for the broken *horn* and the four that stood up in its place, four kingdoms shall arise out of that nation, but not with its power.

²³ "And in the latter time of their kingdom,
When the transgressors have reached their fullness,
A king shall arise,
Having fierce features,
Who understands sinister schemes.
²⁴ His power shall be mighty, but not by his own power;
He shall destroy fearfully,
And shall prosper and thrive;
He shall destroy the mighty, and *also* the holy people.

²⁵ "Through his cunning
He shall cause deceit to prosper under his rule;
And he shall exalt *himself* in his heart.
He shall destroy many in *their* prosperity.
He shall even rise against the Prince of princes;
But he shall be broken without *human* means.

²⁶ "And the vision of the evenings and mornings
Which was told is true;
Therefore seal up the vision,
For *it refers* to many days *in the future.*"

²⁷ And I, Daniel, fainted and was sick for days; afterward I arose and went about the king's business. I was astonished by the vision, but no one understood it.

∼ PSALM 137:1-6 ∼

¹ By the rivers of Babylon,
There we sat down, yea, we wept
When we remembered Zion.
² We hung our harps
Upon the willows in the midst of it.
³ For there those who carried us away captive asked of us a song,
And those who plundered us *requested* mirth,
Saying, "Sing us *one* of the songs of Zion!"

4 How shall we sing the LORD's song
In a foreign land?
5 If I forget you, O Jerusalem,
Let my right hand forget *its skill!*
6 If I do not remember you,
Let my tongue cling to the roof of
my mouth—
If I do not exalt Jerusalem
Above my chief joy.

～ PROVERBS 29:14 ～

14 The king who judges the poor with
truth,
His throne will be established
forever.

～ 2 PETER 3:1–18 ～

Beloved, I now write to you this second epistle (in *both of* which I stir up your pure minds by way of reminder), 2 that you may be mindful of the words which were spoken before by the holy prophets, and of the commandment of us, the apostles of the Lord and Savior, 3 knowing this first: that scoffers will come in the last days, walking according to their own lusts, 4 and saying, "Where is the promise of His coming? For since the fathers fell asleep, all things continue as *they were* from the beginning of creation." 5 For this they willfully forget: that by the word of God the heavens were of old, and the earth standing out of water and in the water, 6 by which the world *that* then existed perished, being flooded with water. 7 But the heavens and the earth *which* are now preserved by the same word, are reserved for fire until the day of judgment and perdition of ungodly men.

8 But, beloved, do not forget this one thing, that with the Lord one day *is* as a thousand years, and a thousand years as one day. 9 The Lord is not slack concerning *His* promise, as some count slackness, but is longsuffering toward us, not willing that any should perish but that all should come to repentance.

10 But the day of the Lord will come as a thief in the night, in which the heavens will pass away with a great noise, and the elements will melt with fervent heat; both the earth and the works that are in it will be burned up. 11 Therefore, since all these things will be dissolved, what manner *of persons* ought you to be in holy conduct and godliness, 12 looking for and hastening the coming of the day of God, because of which the heavens will be dissolved, being on fire, and the elements will melt with fervent heat? 13 Nevertheless we, according to His promise, look for new heavens and a new earth in which righteousness dwells.

14 Therefore, beloved, looking forward to these things, be diligent to be found by Him in peace, without spot and blameless; 15 and consider *that* the longsuffering of our Lord *is* salvation—as also our beloved brother Paul, according to the wisdom given to him, has written to you, 16 as also in all his epistles, speaking in them of these things, in which are some things hard to understand, which untaught and unstable *people* twist to their own destruction, as *they do* also the rest of the Scriptures.

17 You therefore, beloved, since you know *this* beforehand, beware lest you also fall from your own steadfastness, being led away with the error of the wicked; 18 but grow in the grace and knowledge of our Lord and Savior Jesus Christ.

To Him *be* the glory both now and forever. Amen.

READING 337 · DECEMBER 3

～ DANIEL 9:1—10:21 ～

In the first year of Darius the son of Ahasuerus, of the lineage of the Medes, who was made king over the realm of the Chaldeans— 2 in the first year of his reign I, Daniel, understood by the books the number of the years *specified* by the word of the LORD through Jeremiah the prophet, that He would accomplish seventy years in the desolations of Jerusalem.

Wholeness

When Helen Keller was about six years old, her aunt made her a doll out of towels. It was a gangly, misshapen creation. The first thing Helen noticed when she picked up the doll, however, was not its shape, but that it had no eyes. She tugged at a string of beads her aunt was wearing and placed them approximately where the doll's eyes should have been. Her aunt touched Helen's eyes and then with Helen's hand in hers, touched the doll's head. Helen nodded, "Yes!"

Immediately, her aunt found two buttons and sewed them onto the doll. Not being able to see herself, Helen insisted that her aunt make her doll better than she was. She wanted her doll to be whole.

Each of us instinctively desires to be whole. In the recesses of our hearts we know that we are not complete, in spite of what others tell us or what we try to tell ourselves. True wholeness comes when our entire identity is with the Lord. He alone is completion.

Our prayers take on new intensity and meaning when we have a hunger to become like Christ. It is then that prayer becomes a path to genuine health and wholeness. In becoming Christ-like we become whole.

> If we confess our sins, He is faithful and just to forgive us our sins and to cleanse us from all unrighteousness.
>
> *1 John 1:9*

³ Then I set my face toward the Lord God to make request by prayer and supplications, with fasting, sackcloth, and ashes. ⁴ And I prayed to the LORD my God, and made confession, and said, "O Lord, great and awesome God, who keeps His covenant and mercy with those who love Him, and with those who keep His commandments, ⁵ we have sinned and committed iniquity, we have done wickedly and rebelled, even by departing from Your precepts and Your judgments. ⁶ Neither have we heeded Your servants the prophets, who spoke in Your name to our kings and our princes, to our fathers and all the people of the land. ⁷ O Lord, righteousness *belongs* to You, but to us shame of face, as *it is* this day—to the men of Judah, to the inhabitants of Jerusalem and all Israel, those near and those far off in all the countries to which You have driven them, because of the unfaithfulness which they have committed against You.

⁸ "O Lord, to us *belongs* shame of face, to our kings, our princes, and our fathers, because we have sinned against You. ⁹ To the Lord our God *belong* mercy and forgiveness, though we have rebelled against Him. ¹⁰ We have not obeyed the voice of the LORD our God, to walk in His laws, which He set before us by His servants the prophets. ¹¹ Yes, all Israel has transgressed Your law, and has departed so as not to obey Your voice; therefore the curse and the oath written in the Law of Moses the servant of God have been poured out on us, because we have sinned against Him. ¹² And He has confirmed His words, which He spoke against us and against our judges who judged us, by bringing upon us a great disaster; for under the whole heaven such has never been done as what has been done to Jerusalem. ¹³ "As *it is* written in the Law of Moses, all this disaster has come upon us; yet we have not made our prayer before the LORD our God, that we might turn from our iniquities and understand Your truth. ¹⁴ Therefore the LORD has kept the disaster in mind, and brought it upon us; for the LORD our God *is* righteous in all the works which He does, though we have not obeyed His voice. ¹⁵ And now, O Lord our God, who brought Your people out of the land of Egypt with a mighty hand, and made Yourself a name, as *it is* this day—we have sinned, we have done wickedly!

¹⁶ "O Lord, according to all Your righteousness, I pray, let Your anger and Your fury be turned away from Your city Jerusalem, Your holy mountain; because for our sins, and for the iniquities of our fathers, Jerusalem and Your people *are* a reproach to all *those* around us. ¹⁷ Now therefore, our God, hear the prayer of Your servant, and his supplications, and for the Lord's sake cause Your face to shine on Your sanctuary, which is desolate. ¹⁸ O my God, incline Your ear and hear; open Your eyes and see our desolations, and the city which is called by Your name; for we do not present our supplications before You because of our righteous deeds, but because of Your great mercies. ¹⁹ O Lord, hear! O Lord, forgive! O Lord, listen and act! Do not delay for Your own sake, my God, for Your city and Your people are called by Your name."

²⁰ Now while I *was* speaking, praying, and confessing my sin and the sin of my people Israel, and presenting my supplication before the LORD my God for the holy mountain of my God, ²¹ yes, while I *was* speaking in prayer, the man Gabriel, whom I had seen in the vision at the beginning, being caused to fly swiftly, reached me about the time of the evening offering. ²² And he informed *me,* and talked with me, and said, "O Daniel, I have now come forth to give you skill to understand. ²³ At the beginning of your supplications the command went out, and I have come to tell *you,* for you *are* greatly beloved; therefore consider the matter, and understand the vision:

²⁴ "Seventy weeks are determined
For your people and for your holy
    city,
To finish the transgression,
To make an end of sins,
To make reconciliation for
    iniquity,
To bring in everlasting
    righteousness,
To seal up vision and
    prophecy,
And to anoint the Most Holy.

25 "Know therefore and understand,
 That from the going forth of the
   command
 To restore and build Jerusalem
 Until Messiah the Prince,
 There shall be seven weeks and
   sixty-two weeks;
 The street shall be built again, and
   the wall,
 Even in troublesome times.

26 "And after the sixty-two weeks
 Messiah shall be cut off, but not
   for Himself;
 And the people of the prince who
   is to come
 Shall destroy the city and the
   sanctuary.
 The end of it *shall be* with a
   flood,
 And till the end of the war
   desolations are determined.
27 Then he shall confirm a covenant
   with many for one week;
 But in the middle of the week
 He shall bring an end to sacrifice
   and offering.
 And on the wing of abominations
   shall be one who makes
   desolate,
 Even until the consummation,
   which is determined,
 Is poured out on the desolate."

10 In the third year of Cyrus king of Persia a message was revealed to Daniel, whose name was called Belteshazzar. The message *was* true, but the appointed time *was* long; and he understood the message, and had understanding of the vision. ² In those days I, Daniel, was mourning three full weeks. ³ I ate no pleasant food, no meat or wine came into my mouth, nor did I anoint myself at all, till three whole weeks were fulfilled.

⁴ Now on the twenty-fourth day of the first month, as I was by the side of the great river, that *is,* the Tigris, ⁵ I lifted my eyes and looked, and behold, a certain man clothed in linen, whose waist *was* girded with gold of Uphaz! ⁶ His body *was* like beryl, his face like the appearance of lightning, his eyes like torches of fire, his arms and feet like burnished bronze in color, and the sound of his words like the voice of a multitude.

⁷ And I, Daniel, alone saw the vision, for the men who were with me did not see the vision; but a great terror fell upon them, so that they fled to hide themselves. ⁸ Therefore I was left alone when I saw this great vision, and no strength remained in me; for my vigor was turned to frailty in me, and I retained no strength. ⁹ Yet I heard the sound of his words; and while I heard the sound of his words I was in a deep sleep on my face, with my face to the ground.

¹⁰ Suddenly, a hand touched me, which made me tremble on my knees and *on* the palms of my hands. ¹¹ And he said to me, "O Daniel, man greatly beloved, understand the words that I speak to you, and stand upright, for I have now been sent to you." While he was speaking this word to me, I stood trembling.

¹² Then he said to me, "Do not fear, Daniel, for from the first day that you set your heart to understand, and to humble yourself before your God, your words were heard; and I have come because of your words. ¹³ But the prince of the kingdom of Persia withstood me twenty-one days; and behold, Michael, one of the chief princes, came to help me, for I had been left alone there with the kings of Persia. ¹⁴ Now I have come to make you understand what will happen to your people in the latter days, for the vision *refers* to *many* days yet *to come.*"

¹⁵ When he had spoken such words to me, I turned my face toward the ground and became speechless. ¹⁶ And suddenly, *one* having the likeness of the sons of men touched my lips; then I opened my mouth and spoke, saying to him who stood before me, "My lord, because of the vision my sorrows have overwhelmed me, and I have retained no strength. ¹⁷ For how can this servant of my lord talk with you, my lord? As for me, no strength remains in me now, nor is any breath left in me."

¹⁸ Then again, *the one* having the likeness of a man touched me and strengthened me. ¹⁹ And he said, "O man greatly beloved, fear not! Peace *be* to you; be strong, yes, be strong!"

So when he spoke to me I was

strengthened, and said, "Let my lord speak, for you have strengthened me."

²⁰ Then he said, "Do you know why I have come to you? And now I must return to fight with the prince of Persia; and when I have gone forth, indeed the prince of Greece will come. ²¹ But I will tell you what is noted in the Scripture of Truth. (No one upholds me against these, except Michael your prince.

~ PSALM 137:7–9 ~

⁷ Remember, O LORD, against the sons of Edom
The day of Jerusalem,
Who said, "Raze *it*, raze *it*,
To its very foundation!"

⁸ O daughter of Babylon, who are to be destroyed,
Happy the one who repays you as you have served us!
⁹ Happy the one who takes and dashes
Your little ones against the rock!

~ PROVERBS 29:15 ~

¹⁵ The rod and rebuke give wisdom,
But a child left *to himself* brings shame to his mother.

~ 1 JOHN 1:1–10 ~

That which was from the beginning, which we have heard, which we have seen with our eyes, which we have looked upon, and our hands have handled, concerning the Word of life— ² the life was manifested, and we have seen, and bear witness, and declare to you that eternal life which was with the Father and was manifested to us— ³ that which we have seen and heard we declare to you, that you also may have fellowship with us; and truly our fellowship *is* with the Father and with His Son Jesus Christ. ⁴ And these things we write to you that your joy may be full.

⁵ This is the message which we have heard from Him and declare to you, that God is light and in Him is no darkness at all. ⁶ If we say that we have fellowship with Him, and walk in darkness, we lie and do not practice the truth. ⁷ But if we walk in the light as He is in the light, we have fellowship with one another, and the blood of Jesus Christ His Son cleanses us from all sin.

⁸ If we say that we have no sin, we deceive ourselves, and the truth is not in us. ⁹ If we confess our sins, He is faithful and just to forgive us *our* sins and to cleanse us from all unrighteousness. ¹⁰ If we say that we have not sinned, we make Him a liar, and His word is not in us.

READING 338 · DECEMBER 4

~ DANIEL 11:1—12:13 ~

"Also in the first year of Darius the Mede, I, *even* I, stood up to confirm and strengthen him.) ² And now I will tell you the truth: Behold, three more kings will arise in Persia, and the fourth shall be far richer than *them* all; by his strength, through his riches, he shall stir up all against the realm of Greece. ³ Then a mighty king shall arise, who shall rule with great dominion, and do according to his will. ⁴ And when he has arisen, his kingdom shall be broken up and divided toward the four winds of heaven, but not among his posterity nor according to his dominion with which he ruled; for his kingdom shall be uprooted, even for others besides these.

⁵ "Also the king of the South shall become strong, as well as *one* of his princes; and he shall gain power over him and have dominion. His dominion *shall be* a great dominion. ⁶ And at the end of *some* years they shall join forces, for the daughter of the king of the South shall go to the king of the North to make an agreement; but she shall not retain the power of her authority, and neither he nor his authority shall stand; but she shall be given up,

Down in the Mire

   D. L. Moody told the story of a Chinese convert who gave this testimony: "I was down in a deep pit, half sunk in the mire, crying for someone to help me out. As I looked up I saw a venerable, gray-haired man looking down at me. I said, 'Can you help me out?' 'My son,' he replied, 'I am Confucius. If you had read my books and followed what I taught, you would never have fallen into this dreadful pit.'

   "Then he was gone. Soon I saw another man coming. He bent over me with closed eyes and folded arms. 'My son,' Buddha said, 'forget about yourself. Get into a state of rest. Then, my child, you will be in a delicious state just as I am.' 'Yes,' I said, 'I will do that when I am above this mire. Can you help me out?' I looked and he was gone.

   "I was beginning to sink into despair when I saw another figure above me. There were marks of suffering on His face. 'My child,' He said, 'what is the matter?' But before I could reply, He was down in the mire by my side. He folded His arms about me and lifted me up and then fed and rested me. When I was well He did not say, 'Shame on you for falling into that pit.' Instead He said, 'We will walk on together now.' And we have been walking together until this day."

   No one can pray for you with greater insight or compassion than Jesus — and the Bible says He is continually making intercession to the Father on your behalf. He doesn't condemn you when you've failed, He climbs right into your failure with you and pulls you out. He is the Friend Who sticks closer than a brother.

with those who brought her, and with him who begot her, and with him who strengthened her in *those* times. [7] But from a branch of her roots *one* shall arise in his place, who shall come with an army, enter the fortress of the king of the North, and deal with them and prevail. [8] And he shall also carry their gods captive to Egypt, with their princes *and* their precious articles of silver and gold; and he shall continue *more* years than the king of the North.

[9] "Also *the king of the North* shall come to the kingdom of the king of the South, but shall return to his own land. [10] However his sons shall stir up strife, and assemble a multitude of great forces; and *one* shall certainly come and overwhelm and pass through; then he shall return to his fortress and stir up strife.

[11] "And the king of the South shall be moved with rage, and go out and fight with him, with the king of the North, who shall muster a great multitude; but the multitude shall be given into the hand of his *enemy*. [12] When he has taken away the multitude, his heart will be lifted up; and he will cast down tens of thousands, but he will not prevail. [13] For the king of the North will return and muster a multitude greater than the former, and shall certainly come at the end of some years with a great army and much equipment.

[14] "Now in those times many shall rise up against the king of the South. Also, violent men of your people shall exalt themselves in fulfillment of the vision, but they shall fall. [15] So the king of the North shall come and build a siege mound, and take a fortified city; and the forces of the South shall not withstand *him*. Even his choice troops *shall have* no strength to resist. [16] But he who comes against him shall do according to his own will, and no one shall stand against him. He shall stand in the Glorious Land with destruction in his power.

[17] "He shall also set his face to enter with the strength of his whole kingdom, and upright ones with him; thus shall he do. And he shall give him the daughter of women to destroy it; but she shall not stand *with him*, or be for him. [18] After this he shall turn his face to the coastlands, and shall take many. But a ruler shall bring the reproach against them to an end; and with the reproach removed, he shall turn back on him. [19] Then he shall turn his face toward the fortress of his own land; but he shall stumble and fall, and not be found.

[20] "There shall arise in his place one who imposes taxes *on* the glorious kingdom; but within a few days he shall be destroyed, but not in anger or in battle. [21] And in his place shall arise a vile person, to whom they will not give the honor of royalty; but he shall come in peaceably, and seize the kingdom by intrigue. [22] With the force of a flood they shall be swept away from before him and be broken, and also the prince of the covenant. [23] And after the league *is made* with him he shall act deceitfully, for he shall come up and become strong with a small *number of* people. [24] He shall enter peaceably, even into the richest places of the province; and he shall do *what* his fathers have not done, nor his forefathers: he shall disperse among them the plunder, spoil, and riches; and he shall devise his plans against the strongholds, but *only* for a time.

[25] "He shall stir up his power and his courage against the king of the South with a great army. And the king of the South shall be stirred up to battle with a very great and mighty army; but he shall not stand, for they shall devise plans against him. [26] Yes, those who eat of the portion of his delicacies shall destroy him; his army shall be swept away, and many shall fall down slain. [27] Both these kings' hearts *shall be* bent on evil, and they shall speak lies at the same table; but it shall not prosper, for the end *will* still *be* at the appointed time. [28] While returning to his land with great riches, his heart shall be *moved* against the holy covenant; so he shall do *damage* and return to his own land.

[29] "At the appointed time he shall return and go toward the south; but it shall not be like the former or the latter. [30] For ships from Cyprus shall come against him; therefore he shall be grieved, and return in rage against the holy covenant, and do *damage*.

"So he shall return and show regard for those who forsake the holy covenant. [31] And forces shall be mustered by him, and they shall defile the sanctuary fortress; then they shall take away the daily *sacrifices,* and place *there* the abomination of desolation. [32] Those who do wickedly against the covenant he shall corrupt with flattery; but the people who know their God shall be strong, and carry out *great exploits.* [33] And those of the people who understand shall instruct many; yet *for many* days they shall fall by sword and flame, by captivity and plundering. [34] Now when they fall, they shall be aided with a little help; but many shall join with them by intrigue. [35] And *some* of those of understanding shall fall, to refine them, purify *them,* and make *them* white, *until* the time of the end; because *it is* still for the appointed time.

[36] "Then the king shall do according to his own will: he shall exalt and magnify himself above every god, shall speak blasphemies against the God of gods, and shall prosper till the wrath has been accomplished; for what has been determined shall be done. [37] He shall regard neither the God of his fathers nor the desire of women, nor regard any god; for he shall exalt himself above *them* all. [38] But in their place he shall honor a god of fortresses; and a god which his fathers did not know he shall honor with gold and silver, with precious stones and pleasant things. [39] Thus he shall act against the strongest fortresses with a foreign god, which he shall acknowledge, *and* advance *its* glory; and he shall cause them to rule over many, and divide the land for gain.

[40] "At the time of the end the king of the South shall attack him; and the king of the North shall come against him like a whirlwind, with chariots, horsemen, and with many ships; and he shall enter the countries, overwhelm *them,* and pass through. [41] He shall also enter the Glorious Land, and many *countries* shall be overthrown; but these shall escape from his hand: Edom, Moab, and the prominent people of Ammon. [42] He shall stretch out his hand against the countries, and the land of Egypt shall not escape. [43] He shall have power over the treasures of gold and silver, and over all the precious things of Egypt; also the Libyans and Ethiopians *shall follow* at his heels. [44] But news from the east and the north shall trouble

him; therefore he shall go out with great fury to destroy and annihilate many. [45] And he shall plant the tents of his palace between the seas and the glorious holy mountain; yet he shall come to his end, and no one will help him.

12 "At that time Michael shall stand up,
The great prince who stands *watch* over the sons of your people;
And there shall be a time of trouble,
Such as never was since there was a nation,
Even to that time.
And at that time your people shall be delivered,
Every one who is found written in the book.
[2] And many of those who sleep in the dust of the earth shall awake,
Some to everlasting life,
Some to shame *and* everlasting contempt.
[3] Those who are wise shall shine
Like the brightness of the firmament,
And those who turn many to righteousness
Like the stars forever and ever.

[4] "But you, Daniel, shut up the words, and seal the book until the time of the end; many shall run to and fro, and knowledge shall increase."

[5] Then I, Daniel, looked; and there stood two others, one on this riverbank and the other on that riverbank. [6] And *one* said to the man clothed in linen, who *was* above the waters of the river, "How long shall the fulfillment of these wonders *be?*"

[7] Then I heard the man clothed in linen, who *was* above the waters of the river, when he held up his right hand and his left hand to heaven, and swore by Him who lives forever, that *it shall be* for a time, times, and half *a time;* and when the power of the holy people has been completely shattered, all these *things* shall be finished.

[8] Although I heard, I did not understand.

Then I said, "My lord, what *shall be* the end of these *things?*"

⁹ And he said, "Go *your way*, Daniel, for the words *are* closed up and sealed till the time of the end. ¹⁰ Many shall be purified, made white, and refined, but the wicked shall do wickedly; and none of the wicked shall understand, but the wise shall understand.

¹¹ "And from the time *that* the daily *sacrifice* is taken away, and the abomination of desolation is set up, *there shall be* one thousand two hundred and ninety days. ¹² Blessed *is* he who waits, and comes to the one thousand three hundred and thirty-five days.

¹³ "But you, go *your way* till the end; for you shall rest, and will arise to your inheritance at the end of the days."

∼ PSALM 138:1–3 ∼

1   I will praise You with my whole
      heart;
      Before the gods I will sing praises to
      You.
2   I will worship toward Your holy
      temple,
      And praise Your name
      For Your lovingkindness and Your
      truth;
      For You have magnified Your word
      above all Your name.
3   In the day when I cried out, You
      answered me,
      And made me bold *with* strength in
      my soul.

∼ PROVERBS 29:16 ∼

16 When the wicked are multiplied,
      transgression increases;
      But the righteous will see their fall.

∼ 1 JOHN 2:1–29 ∼

My little children, these things I write to you, so that you may not sin. And if anyone sins, we have an Advocate with the Father, Jesus Christ the righteous. ² And He Himself is the propitiation for our sins, and not for ours only but also for the whole world.

³ Now by this we know that we know Him, if we keep His commandments. ⁴ He who says, "I know Him," and does not keep His commandments, is a liar, and the truth is not in him. ⁵ But whoever keeps His word, truly the love of God is perfected in him. By this we know that we are in Him. ⁶ He who says he abides in Him ought himself also to walk just as He walked.

⁷ Brethren, I write no new commandment to you, but an old commandment which you have had from the beginning. The old commandment is the word which you heard from the beginning. ⁸ Again, a new commandment I write to you, which thing is true in Him and in you, because the darkness is passing away, and the true light is already shining.

⁹ He who says he is in the light, and hates his brother, is in darkness until now. ¹⁰ He who loves his brother abides in the light, and there is no cause for stumbling in him. ¹¹ But he who hates his brother is in darkness and walks in darkness, and does not know where he is going, because the darkness has blinded his eyes.

¹² I write to you, little children,
        Because your sins are forgiven
        you for His name's sake.
¹³ I write to you, fathers,
        Because you have known Him
        who is from the beginning.
     I write to you, young men,
        Because you have overcome the
        wicked one.
     I write to you, little children,
        Because you have known the
        Father.
¹⁴ I have written to you, fathers,
        Because you have known Him
        who is from the beginning.
     I have written to you, young
        men,
        Because you are strong, and the
        word of God abides in you,
     And you have overcome the
        wicked one.

¹⁵ Do not love the world or the things in the world. If anyone loves the world, the love of the Father is not in him. ¹⁶ For all that *is* in the world—the lust of the

flesh, the lust of the eyes, and the pride of life—is not of the Father but is of the world. ¹⁷ And the world is passing away, and the lust of it; but he who does the will of God abides forever.

¹⁸ Little children, it is the last hour; and as you have heard that the Antichrist is coming, even now many antichrists have come, by which we know that it is the last hour. ¹⁹ They went out from us, but they were not of us; for if they had been of us, they would have continued with us; but *they went out* that they might be made manifest, that none of them were of us.

²⁰ But you have an anointing from the Holy One, and you know all things. ²¹ I have not written to you because you do not know the truth, but because you know it, and that no lie is of the truth.

²² Who is a liar but he who denies that Jesus is the Christ? He is antichrist who denies the Father and the Son. ²³ Whoever denies the Son does not have the Father either; he who acknowledges the Son has the Father also.

²⁴ Therefore let that abide in you which you heard from the beginning. If what you heard from the beginning abides in you, you also will abide in the Son and in the Father. ²⁵ And this is the promise that He has promised us—eternal life.

²⁶ These things I have written to you concerning those who *try to* deceive you. ²⁷ But the anointing which you have received from Him abides in you, and you do not need that anyone teach you; but as the same anointing teaches you concerning all things, and is true, and is not a lie, and just as it has taught you, you will abide in Him.

²⁸ And now, little children, abide in Him, that when He appears, we may have confidence and not be ashamed before Him at His coming. ²⁹ If you know that He is righteous, you know that everyone who practices righteousness is born of Him.

READING 339 · DECEMBER 5

~ HOSEA 1:1—2:23 ~

The word of the LORD that came to Hosea the son of Beeri, in the days of Uzziah, Jotham, Ahaz, *and* Hezekiah, kings of Judah, and in the days of Jeroboam the son of Joash, king of Israel. ² When the LORD began to speak by Hosea, the LORD said to Hosea:

"Go, take yourself a wife of
　　harlotry
And children of harlotry,
For the land has committed great
　　harlotry
By departing from the LORD."

³ So he went and took Gomer the daughter of Diblaim, and she conceived and bore him a son. ⁴ Then the LORD said to him:

"Call his name Jezreel,
　For in a little *while*
I will avenge the bloodshed of
　　Jezreel on the house of Jehu,

And bring an end to the kingdom
　　of the house of Israel.
⁵　It shall come to pass in that day
　That I will break the bow of Israel
　　in the Valley of Jezreel."

⁶ And she conceived again and bore a daughter. Then *God* said to him:

"Call her name Lo-Ruhamah,
　For I will no longer have mercy on
　　the house of Israel,
　But I will utterly take them away.
⁷　Yet I will have mercy on the house
　　of Judah,
　Will save them by the LORD their
　　God,
　And will not save them by bow,
　Nor by sword or battle,
　By horses or horsemen."

⁸ Now when she had weaned Lo-Ruhamah, she conceived and bore a son. ⁹ Then *God* said:

"Call his name Lo-Ammi,
   For you *are* not My people,
   And I will not be your *God*.

10 "Yet the number of the children of
      Israel
   Shall be as the sand of the sea,
   Which cannot be measured or
      numbered.
   And it shall come to pass
   In the place where it was said to
      them,
   'You *are* not My people,'
   There it shall be said to them,
   'You are sons of the living God.'
11 Then the children of Judah and
      the children of Israel
   Shall be gathered together,
   And appoint for themselves one
      head;
   And they shall come up out of the
      land,
   For great *will be* the day of
      Jezreel!

2 Say to your brethren, 'My people,'
   And to your sisters, 'Mercy *is*
      shown.'

2 "Bring charges against your mother,
      bring charges;
   For she *is* not My wife, nor *am* I
      her Husband!
   Let her put away her harlotries
      from her sight,
   And her adulteries from between
      her breasts;
3 Lest I strip her naked
   And expose her, as in the day she
      was born,
   And make her like a wilderness,
   And set her like a dry land,
   And slay her with thirst.

4 "I will not have mercy on her
      children,
   For they *are* the children of
      harlotry.
5 For their mother has played the
      harlot;
   She who conceived them has
      behaved shamefully.
   For she said, 'I will go after my
      lovers,

Who give *me* my bread and my
   water,
My wool and my linen,
My oil and my drink.'

6 "Therefore, behold,
   I will hedge up your way with
      thorns,
   And wall her in,
   So that she cannot find her paths.
7 She will chase her lovers,
   But not overtake them;
   Yes, she will seek them, but not
      find *them*.
   Then she will say,
   'I will go and return to my first
      husband,
   For then *it was* better for me than
      now.'
8 For she did not know
   That I gave her grain, new wine,
      and oil,
   And multiplied her silver and
      gold—
   Which they prepared for Baal.

9 "Therefore I will return and take
      away
   My grain in its time
   And My new wine in its season,
   And will take back My wool and
      My linen,
   Given to cover her nakedness.
10 Now I will uncover her lewdness
      in the sight of her lovers,
   And no one shall deliver her from
      My hand.
11 I will also cause all her mirth to
      cease,
   Her feast days,
   Her New Moons,
   Her Sabbaths—
   All her appointed feasts.

12 "And I will destroy her vines and
      her fig trees,
   Of which she has said,
   'These *are* my wages that my lovers
      have given me.'
   So I will make them a forest,
   And the beasts of the field shall eat
      them.
13 I will punish her
   For the days of the Baals to which
      she burned incense.

Small Deeds

A missionary was sailing home on furlough when she heard a cry one night — a cry that is perhaps the most frightening to hear when at sea: "Man overboard!" She quickly arose from her berth, lit her cabin lamp, and then held it at the window of her cabin in hopes of seeing some sign of life in the murky dark waters outside.

Seeing nothing, she hung the lamp back on its bracket, snuffed it out, and returned to her berth to pray for the man lost at sea. In the morning, she discovered the man had been rescued. Not only that, but she learned it was the flash of her lamp through the porthole that showed the rescuers the location of the missing man, who was desperately clinging to a rope still attached to the deck. He was pulled from the cold waters in the nick of time. Her small deed of shining a lamp at the right time had saved a man's life.

It isn't the size of the deeds you do that counts. It's the fact that you do them for good and not for evil, trusting that God can take every deed we perform and use it for His purpose — in our lives and in the lives of others.

She decked herself with her
earrings and jewelry,
And went after her lovers;
But Me she forgot," says the
LORD.

14 "Therefore, behold, I will allure
her,
Will bring her into the wilderness,
And speak comfort to her.
15 I will give her her vineyards from
there,
And the Valley of Achor as a door
of hope;
She shall sing there,
As in the days of her youth,
As in the day when she came up
from the land of Egypt.

16 "And it shall be, in that day,"
Says the LORD,
"That you will call Me 'My
Husband,'
And no longer call Me 'My
Master,'
17 For I will take from her mouth the
names of the Baals,
And they shall be remembered by
their name no more.
18 In that day I will make a covenant
for them
With the beasts of the field,
With the birds of the air,
And with the creeping things of
the ground.
Bow and sword of battle I will
shatter from the earth,
To make them lie down safely.

19 "I will betroth you to Me forever;
Yes, I will betroth you to Me
In righteousness and justice,
In lovingkindness and mercy;
20 I will betroth you to Me in
faithfulness,
And you shall know the LORD.

21 "It shall come to pass in that day
That I will answer," says the
LORD;
"I will answer the heavens,
And they shall answer the earth.
22 The earth shall answer
With grain,
With new wine,

And with oil;
They shall answer Jezreel.
23 Then I will sow her for Myself in
the earth,
And I will have mercy on *her who
had* not obtained mercy;
Then I will say to *those who were*
not My people,
'You *are* My people!'
And they shall say, '*You are* my
God!' "

∼ PSALM 138:4–6 ∼

4 All the kings of the earth shall praise
You, O LORD,
When they hear the words of Your
mouth.
5 Yes, they shall sing of the ways of the
LORD,
For great *is* the glory of the LORD.
6 Though the LORD *is* on high,
Yet He regards the lowly;
But the proud He knows from afar.

∼ PROVERBS 29:17 ∼

17 Correct your son, and he will give
you rest;
Yes, he will give delight to your soul.

∼ 1 JOHN 3:1–24 ∼

Behold what manner of love the Father
has bestowed on us, that we should be
called children of God! Therefore the
world does not know us, because it did
not know Him. 2 Beloved, now we are
children of God; and it has not yet been
revealed what we shall be, but we know
that when He is revealed, we shall be like
Him, for we shall see Him as He is. 3 And
everyone who has this hope in Him puri-
fies himself, just as He is pure.

4 Whoever commits sin also commits
lawlessness, and sin is lawlessness. 5 And
you know that He was manifested to take
away our sins, and in Him there is no sin.
6 Whoever abides in Him does not
sin. Whoever sins has neither seen Him
nor known Him.

7 Little children, let no one deceive you.
He who practices righteousness is righteous, just as He is righteous. 8 He who
sins is of the devil, for the devil has sinned

from the beginning. For this purpose the Son of God was manifested, that He might destroy the works of the devil. [9] Whoever has been born of God does not sin, for His seed remains in him; and he cannot sin, because he has been born of God.

[10] In this the children of God and the children of the devil are manifest: Whoever does not practice righteousness is not of God, nor *is* he who does not love his brother. [11] For this is the message that you heard from the beginning, that we should love one another, [12] not as Cain *who* was of the wicked one and murdered his brother. And why did he murder him? Because his works were evil and his brother's righteous.

[13] Do not marvel, my brethren, if the world hates you. [14] We know that we have passed from death to life, because we love the brethren. He who does not love *his* brother abides in death. [15] Whoever hates his brother is a murderer, and you know that no murderer has eternal life abiding in him.

[16] By this we know love, because He laid down His life for us. And we also ought to lay down *our* lives for the brethren. [17] But whoever has this world's goods, and sees his brother in need, and shuts up his heart from him, how does the love of God abide in him?

[18] My little children, let us not love in word or in tongue, but in deed and in truth. [19] And by this we know that we are of the truth, and shall assure our hearts before Him. [20] For if our heart condemns us, God is greater than our heart, and knows all things. [21] Beloved, if our heart does not condemn us, we have confidence toward God. [22] And whatever we ask we receive from Him, because we keep His commandments and do those things that are pleasing in His sight. [23] And this is His commandment: that we should believe on the name of His Son Jesus Christ and love one another, as He gave us commandment.

[24] Now he who keeps His commandments abides in Him, and He in him. And by this we know that He abides in us, by the Spirit whom He has given us.

READING 340 · DECEMBER 6

~ HOSEA 3:1—4:19 ~

Then the LORD said to me, "Go again, love a woman *who is* loved by a lover and is committing adultery, just like the love of the LORD for the children of Israel, who look to other gods and love *the* raisin cakes *of the pagans.*"

[2] So I bought her for myself for fifteen *shekels* of silver, and one and one-half *homers* of barley. [3] And I said to her, "You shall stay with me many days; you shall not play the harlot, nor shall you have a man—so, too, *will* I *be* toward you."

[4] For the children of Israel shall abide many days without king or prince, without sacrifice or sacred pillar, without ephod or teraphim. [5] Afterward the children of Israel shall return and seek the LORD their God and David their king. They shall fear the LORD and His goodness in the latter days.

4 Hear the word of the LORD,
　　You children of Israel,

For the LORD *brings* a charge
　　against the inhabitants of the
　　land:

　"There is no truth or mercy
　　Or knowledge of God in the land.
[2]　*By* swearing and lying,
　　Killing and stealing and
　　　committing adultery,
　　They break all restraint,
　　With bloodshed upon bloodshed.
[3]　Therefore the land will mourn;
　　And everyone who dwells there
　　　will waste away
　　With the beasts of the field
　　And the birds of the air;
　　Even the fish of the sea will be
　　　taken away.

[4]　"Now let no man contend, or
　　　rebuke another;
　　For your people *are* like those
　　　who contend with the priest.

5 Therefore you shall stumble in the day;
The prophet also shall stumble with you in the night;
And I will destroy your mother.

6 My people are destroyed for lack of knowledge.
Because you have rejected knowledge,
I also will reject you from being priest for Me;
Because you have forgotten the law of your God,
I also will forget your children.

7 "The more they increased,
The more they sinned against Me;
I will change their glory into shame.

8 They eat up the sin of My people;
They set their heart on their iniquity.

9 And it shall be: like people, like priest.
So I will punish them for their ways,
And reward them for their deeds.

10 For they shall eat, but not have enough;
They shall commit harlotry, but not increase;
Because they have ceased obeying the LORD.

11 "Harlotry, wine, and new wine enslave the heart.

12 My people ask counsel from their wooden *idols,*
And their staff informs them.
For the spirit of harlotry has caused *them* to stray,
And they have played the harlot against their God.

13 They offer sacrifices on the mountaintops,
And burn incense on the hills,
Under oaks, poplars, and terebinths,
Because their shade *is* good.
Therefore your daughters commit harlotry,
And your brides commit adultery.

14 "I will not punish your daughters when they commit harlotry,

Nor your brides when they commit adultery;
For *the men* themselves go apart with harlots,
And offer sacrifices with a ritual harlot.
Therefore people *who* do not understand will be trampled.

15 "Though you, Israel, play the harlot,
Let not Judah offend.
Do not come up to Gilgal,
Nor go up to Beth Aven,
Nor swear an oath, *saying,* 'As the LORD lives'—

16 "For Israel is stubborn
Like a stubborn calf;
Now the LORD will let them forage
Like a lamb in open country.

17 "Ephraim *is* joined to idols,
Let him alone.

18 Their drink is rebellion,
They commit harlotry continually.
Her rulers dearly love dishonor.

19 The wind has wrapped her up in its wings,
And they shall be ashamed because of their sacrifices.

～ PSALM 138:7, 8 ～

7 Though I walk in the midst of trouble, You will revive me;
You will stretch out Your hand
Against the wrath of my enemies,
And Your right hand will save me.

8 The LORD will perfect *that which* concerns me;
Your mercy, O LORD, *endures* forever;
Do not forsake the works of Your hands.

～ PROVERBS 29:18 ～

18 Where *there is* no revelation, the people cast off restraint;
But happy *is* he who keeps the law.

Only Temporary

In *My Mother Worked and I Turned Out Okay*, Katherine Wyse Goldman tells about Margaret, one of five children in a family during the 1930s and 1940s.

Margaret's mother left her alcoholic husband and took her children to live in a three-room apartment, which was all she could afford. To make ends meet, she worked two jobs. Her night job, from 10 PM to 7:30 AM, was editing the company newspaper for the Pennsylvania Railroad. The children would greet their mother by the curb when her trolley pulled up in the morning, and she'd get them ready for school. After only a couple of hours of sleep, she'd go to her day job at 10 AM. A little after 4 PM, her children would greet her at the same curb. After a light supper, the children did their homework as quietly as possible so their mother could get a few more hours of sleep. Margaret said of her mother: "Mother never had a day off both jobs at the same time. My grandmother wanted to put us in foster homes, but my mother said no, that she could do it. She'd tell us the way we lived was temporary."

What wonderful wisdom to apply to any of the hardships we experience as mothers. Remember: This, too, is only temporary!

> In this is love, not that we loved God, but that He loved us and sent His Son to be the propitiation for our sins.
>
> *1 John 4:10*

~ 1 John 4:1–21 ~

Beloved, do not believe every spirit, but test the spirits, whether they are of God; because many false prophets have gone out into the world. ² By this you know the Spirit of God: Every spirit that confesses that Jesus Christ has come in the flesh is of God, ³ and every spirit that does not confess that Jesus Christ has come in the flesh is not of God. And this is the *spirit* of the Antichrist, which you have heard was coming, and is now already in the world.

⁴ You are of God, little children, and have overcome them, because He who is in you is greater than he who is in the world. ⁵ They are of the world. Therefore they speak *as* of the world, and the world hears them. ⁶ We are of God. He who knows God hears us; he who is not of God does not hear us. By this we know the spirit of truth and the spirit of error.

⁷ Beloved, let us love one another, for love is of God; and everyone who loves is born of God and knows God. ⁸ He who does not love does not know God, for God is love. ⁹ In this the love of God was manifested toward us, that God has sent His only begotten Son into the world, that we might live through Him. ¹⁰ In this is love, not that we loved God, but that He loved us and sent His Son *to be* the propitiation for our sins. ¹¹ Beloved, if God so loved us, we also ought to love one another.

¹² No one has seen God at any time. If we love one another, God abides in us, and His love has been perfected in us. ¹³ By this we know that we abide in Him, and He in us, because He has given us of His Spirit. ¹⁴ And we have seen and testify that the Father has sent the Son *as* Savior of the world. ¹⁵ Whoever confesses that Jesus is the Son of God, God abides in him, and he in God. ¹⁶ And we have known and believed the love that God has for us. God is love, and he who abides in love abides in God, and God in him.

¹⁷ Love has been perfected among us in this: that we may have boldness in the day of judgment; because as He is, so are we in this world. ¹⁸ There is no fear in love; but perfect love casts out fear, because fear involves torment. But he who fears has not been made perfect in love. ¹⁹ We love Him because He first loved us.

²⁰ If someone says, "I love God," and hates his brother, he is a liar; for he who does not love his brother whom he has seen, how can he love God whom he has not seen? ²¹ And this commandment we have from Him: that he who loves God *must* love his brother also.

READING 341 · DECEMBER 7

~ Hosea 5:1—6:11 ~

¹ "Hear this, O priests!
Take heed, O house of Israel!
Give ear, O house of the king!
For yours *is* the judgment,
Because you have been a snare to Mizpah
And a net spread on Tabor.
² The revolters are deeply involved in slaughter,
Though I rebuke them all.
³ I know Ephraim,
And Israel is not hidden from Me;
For now, O Ephraim, you commit harlotry;
Israel is defiled.

⁴ "They do not direct their deeds
Toward turning to their God,
For the spirit of harlotry is in their midst,
And they do not know the LORD.
⁵ The pride of Israel testifies to his face;
Therefore Israel and Ephraim stumble in their iniquity;
Judah also stumbles with them.

⁶ "With their flocks and herds
They shall go to seek the LORD,
But they will not find *Him*;

Nobody's Perfect

While teaching a Bible class, a woman lost her place in her notes as she was speaking. As she continued to speak, she tried to find where she had gotten off course, but when she realized she was hopelessly lost in her own muddle of words, she apologized to the group and paused to search for the missing page. The pause grew agonizingly long and at last, she gave up the search and ad-libbed her way through the rest of the lesson. She couldn't remember the applications she had planned to make, forgot part of her main illustration, and knew her conclusion was weak. As she left the lectern, she was on the verge of tears, feeling like an abysmal failure.

To her great surprise, a woman came to her to say that she thought this had been the best Bible class so far. Later, another woman called to thank her for a specific word that was just what she needed to hear.

The teacher called a friend and said, "I don't understand what happened. I had prepared the best I could." Her friend laughed and said, "Do you remember what you said last week — that you were praying these women would be able to relate to you and you to them? Perhaps that's precisely what happened. They aren't perfect, either!"

God's answers to prayer may not always be what we expect, but they are always fruitful.

> Now this is the confidence that we have in Him, that if we ask anything according to His will, He hears us. And if we know that He hears us, whatever we ask, we know that we have the petitions that we have asked of Him.
>
> *1 John 5:14-15*

He has withdrawn Himself from
them.

7 They have dealt treacherously
with the LORD,
For they have begotten pagan
children.
Now a New Moon shall devour
them and their heritage.

8 "Blow the ram's horn in Gibeah,
The trumpet in Ramah!
Cry aloud *at* Beth Aven,
'*Look* behind you, O Benjamin!'

9 Ephraim shall be desolate in the
day of rebuke;
Among the tribes of Israel I make
known what is sure.

10 "The princes of Judah are like those
who remove a landmark;
I will pour out my wrath on them
like water.

11 Ephraim is oppressed *and* broken
in judgment,
Because he willingly walked by
human precept.

12 Therefore I *will be* to Ephraim
like a moth,
And to the house of Judah like
rottenness.

13 "When Ephraim saw his sickness,
And Judah *saw* his wound,
Then Ephraim went to Assyria
And sent to King Jareb;
Yet he cannot cure you,
Nor heal you of your wound.

14 For I *will be* like a lion to
Ephraim,
And like a young lion to the house
of Judah.
I, *even* I, will tear *them* and go
away;
I will take *them* away, and no one
shall rescue.

15 I will return again to My place
Till they acknowledge their
offense.
Then they will seek My face;
In their affliction they will
earnestly seek Me."

6 Come, and let us return to the
LORD;

For He has torn, but He will heal
us;
He has stricken, but He will bind
us up.

2 After two days He will revive us;
On the third day He will raise us
up,
That we may live in His sight.

3 Let us know,
Let us pursue the knowledge of
the LORD.
His going forth is established as
the morning;
He will come to us like the rain,
Like the latter *and* former rain to
the earth.

4 "O Ephraim, what shall I do to
you?
O Judah, what shall I do to you?
For your faithfulness is like a
morning cloud,
And like the early dew it goes
away.

5 Therefore I have hewn *them* by
the prophets,
I have slain them by the words of
My mouth;
And your judgments *are like* light
that goes forth.

6 For I desire mercy and not
sacrifice,
And the knowledge of God more
than burnt offerings.

7 "But like men they transgressed the
covenant;
There they dealt treacherously
with Me.

8 Gilead *is* a city of evildoers
And defiled with blood.

9 As bands of robbers lie in wait for
a man,
So the company of priests murder
on the way to Shechem;
Surely they commit lewdness.

10 I have seen a horrible thing in the
house of Israel:
There *is* the harlotry of Ephraim;
Israel is defiled.

11 Also, O Judah, a harvest is
appointed for you,
When I return the captives of My
people.

~ PSALM 139:1–6 ~

1 O LORD, You have searched me and
known *me.*

2 You know my sitting down and my
rising up;
You understand my thought afar off.

3 You comprehend my path and my
lying down,
And are acquainted with all my
ways.

4 For *there is* not a word on my
tongue,
But behold, O LORD, You know it
altogether.

5 You have hedged me behind and
before,
And laid Your hand upon me.

6 *Such* knowledge *is* too wonderful for
me;
It is high, I cannot *attain* it.

~ PROVERBS 29:19 ~

19 A servant will not be corrected by
mere words;
For though he understands, he will
not respond.

~ 1 JOHN 5:1–21 ~

Whoever believes that Jesus is the Christ
is born of God, and everyone who loves
Him who begot also loves him who is
begotten of Him. 2 By this we know that
we love the children of God, when we
love God and keep His commandments.
3 For this is the love of God, that we keep
His commandments. And His commandments are not burdensome. 4 For whatever is born of God overcomes the world.
And this is the victory that has overcome
the world—our faith. 5 Who is he who
overcomes the world, but he who believes
that Jesus is the Son of God?

6 This is He who came by water and
blood—Jesus Christ; not only by water,
but by water and blood. And it is the Spirit
who bears witness, because the Spirit is
truth. 7 For there are three that bear witness in heaven: the Father, the Word, and
the Holy Spirit; and these three are one.
8 And there are three that bear witness on
earth: the Spirit, the water, and the blood;
and these three agree as one.

9 If we receive the witness of men, the
witness of God is greater; for this is
the witness of God which He has testified of His Son. 10 He who believes in
the Son of God has the witness in himself; he who does not believe God has
made Him a liar, because he has not believed the testimony that God has given
of His Son. 11 And this is the testimony:
that God has given us eternal life, and this
life is in His Son. 12 He who has the Son
has life; he who does not have the Son of
God does not have life. 13 These things I
have written to you who believe in the
name of the Son of God, that you may
know that you have eternal life, and that
you may *continue to* believe in the name
of the Son of God.

14 Now this is the confidence that we
have in Him, that if we ask anything according to His will, He hears us. 15 And if
we know that He hears us, whatever we
ask, we know that we have the petitions
that we have asked of Him.

16 If anyone sees his brother sinning a
sin *which does* not *lead* to death, he will
ask, and He will give him life for those
who commit sin not *leading* to death.
There is sin *leading* to death. I do not say
that he should pray about that. 17 All
unrighteousness is sin, and there is sin not
leading to death.

18 We know that whoever is born of
God does not sin; but he who has been
born of God keeps himself, and the wicked
one does not touch him.

19 We know that we are of God, and
the whole world lies *under the sway
of* the wicked one.

20 And we know that the Son of God
has come and has given us an understanding, that we may know Him who is true;
and we are in Him who is true, in His
Son Jesus Christ. This is the true God and
eternal life.

21 Little children, keep yourselves from
idols. Amen.

~ HOSEA 7:1—8:14 ~

1 "When I would have healed Israel,
Then the iniquity of Ephraim was
uncovered,
And the wickedness of Samaria.
For they have committed fraud;
A thief comes in;
A band of robbers takes spoil
outside.
2 They do not consider in their
hearts
That I remember all their
wickedness;
Now their own deeds have
surrounded them;
They are before My face.
3 They make a king glad with their
wickedness,
And princes with their lies.

4 "They *are* all adulterers.
Like an oven heated by a
baker—
He ceases stirring *the fire* after
kneading the dough,
Until it is leavened.
5 In the day of our king
Princes have made *him* sick,
inflamed with wine;
He stretched out his hand with
scoffers.
6 They prepare their heart like an
oven,
While they lie in wait;
Their baker sleeps all night;
In the morning it burns like a
flaming fire.
7 They are all hot, like an oven,
And have devoured their judges;
All their kings have fallen.
None among them calls
upon Me.

8 "Ephraim has mixed himself among
the peoples;
Ephraim is a cake unturned.
9 Aliens have devoured his strength,
But he does not know *it;*
Yes, gray hairs are here and there
on him,
Yet he does not know *it.*
10 And the pride of Israel testifies to
his face,

But they do not return to the
LORD their God,
Nor seek Him for all this.

11 "Ephraim also is like a silly dove,
without sense—
They call to Egypt,
They go to Assyria.
12 Wherever they go, I will spread
My net on them;
I will bring them down like birds
of the air;
I will chastise them
According to what their
congregation has heard.

13 "Woe to them, for they have fled
from Me!
Destruction to them,
Because they have transgressed
against Me!
Though I redeemed them,
Yet they have spoken lies against
Me.
14 They did not cry out to Me with
their heart
When they wailed upon their
beds.

"They assemble together for grain
and new wine,
They rebel against Me;
15 Though I disciplined *and*
strengthened their arms,
Yet they devise evil against Me;
16 They return, *but* not to the Most
High;
They are like a treacherous bow.
Their princes shall fall by the
sword
For the cursings of their tongue.
This *shall be* their derision in the
land of Egypt.

8 "*Set* the trumpet to your mouth!
He shall come like an eagle against
the house of the LORD,
Because they have transgressed
My covenant
And rebelled against My law.
2 Israel will cry to Me,
'My God, we know You!'

Simple Decision-making

When reporters bombarded Cardinal Francis Spellman with a barrage of questions during a surprise interview, he finally pointed to a mounted fish on the wall behind his desk. Under the fish was inscribed: "If I had kept my mouth shut, I wouldn't be here."

Perhaps the most potent words in any language are a simple "Yes" or "No," without explanation or elaboration. Most decisions eventually become that simple.

To reach the point of answering yes or no, we do well to ask ourselves these questions:

1) Is there anyone else who must take part in this decision? If you are either the sole decision-maker or the final decision-maker, then you alone must make a decision!
2) What will happen if I wait? In most cases, things will either get better or worse. Weigh your decision in the balances, realizing that your decision is likely to lean in favor of the heavier weight of the argument, then decide.
3) Does the decision have a moral dimension? If so, hold to your values and make your decision based upon them.

In every decision, lean on the One Who knows the beginning from the end of every situation — your Father God!

3 Israel has rejected the good;
The enemy will pursue him.

4 "They set up kings, but not by Me;
They made princes, but I did not
acknowledge *them*.
From their silver and gold
They made idols for themselves—
That they might be cut off.

5 Your calf is rejected, O Samaria!
My anger is aroused against
them—
How long until they attain to
innocence?

6 For from Israel *is* even this:
A workman made it, and it *is* not
God;
But the calf of Samaria shall be
broken to pieces.

7 "They sow the wind,
And reap the whirlwind.
The stalk has no bud;
It shall never produce meal.
If it should produce,
Aliens would swallow it up.

8 Israel is swallowed up;
Now they are among the Gentiles
Like a vessel in which *is* no
pleasure.

9 For they have gone up to Assyria,
Like a wild donkey alone by itself;
Ephraim has hired lovers.

10 Yes, though they have hired
among the nations,
Now I will gather them;
And they shall sorrow a little,
Because of the burden of the king
of princes.

11 "Because Ephraim has made many
altars for sin,
They have become for him altars
for sinning.

12 I have written for him the great
things of My law,
But they were considered a
strange thing.

13 *For* the sacrifices of My offerings
they sacrifice flesh and eat *it,*
But the LORD does not accept
them.
Now He will remember their
iniquity and punish their sins.
They shall return to Egypt.

14 "For Israel has forgotten his Maker,
And has built temples;
Judah also has multiplied fortified
cities;
But I will send fire upon his cities,
And it shall devour his palaces."

∼ PSALM 139:7–12 ∼

7 Where can I go from Your Spirit?
Or where can I flee from Your
presence?

8 If I ascend into heaven, You *are*
there;
If I make my bed in hell, behold, You
are there.

9 *If* I take the wings of the morning,
And dwell in the uttermost parts of
the sea,

10 Even there Your hand shall lead me,
And Your right hand shall hold me.

11 If I say, "Surely the darkness shall fall
on me,"
Even the night shall be light about
me;

12 Indeed, the darkness shall not hide
from You,
But the night shines as the day;
The darkness and the light *are* both
alike *to You.*

∼ PROVERBS 29:20 ∼

20 Do you see a man hasty in his
words?
There is more hope for a fool than
for him.

∼ 2 JOHN 1–13 ∼

The Elder,

To the elect lady and her children,
whom I love in truth, and not only I, but
also all those who have known the truth,
2 because of the truth which abides in us
and will be with us forever:

3 Grace, mercy, *and* peace will be with
you from God the Father and from the
Lord Jesus Christ, the Son of the Father,
in truth and love.

4 I rejoiced greatly that I have found

some of your children walking in truth, as we received commandment from the Father. ⁵ And now I plead with you, lady, not as though I wrote a new commandment to you, but that which we have had from the beginning: that we love one another. ⁶ This is love, that we walk according to His commandments. This is the commandment, that as you have heard from the beginning, you should walk in it.

⁷ For many deceivers have gone out into the world who do not confess Jesus Christ *as* coming in the flesh. This is a deceiver and an antichrist. ⁸ Look to yourselves, that we do not lose those things we worked for, but *that* we may receive a full reward.

⁹ Whoever transgresses and does not abide in the doctrine of Christ does not have God. He who abides in the doctrine of Christ has both the Father and the Son. ¹⁰ If anyone comes to you and does not bring this doctrine, do not receive him into your house nor greet him; ¹¹ for he who greets him shares in his evil deeds.

¹² Having many things to write to you, I did not wish *to do so* with paper and ink; but I hope to come to you and speak face to face, that our joy may be full.

¹³ The children of your elect sister greet you. Amen.

∼ HOSEA 9:1—10:15 ∼

¹ Do not rejoice, O Israel, with joy
  like *other* peoples,
For you have played the harlot
  against your God.
You have made love *for* hire on
  every threshing floor.

² The threshing floor and the
  winepress
Shall not feed them,
And the new wine shall fail in her.

³ They shall not dwell in the LORD's
  land,
But Ephraim shall return to Egypt,
And shall eat unclean *things* in
  Assyria.

⁴ They shall not offer wine *offerings*
  to the LORD,
Nor shall their sacrifices be
  pleasing to Him.
It shall be like bread of mourners
  to them;
All who eat it shall be defiled.
For their bread *shall be* for their
  own life;
It shall not come into the house of
  the LORD.

⁵ What will you do in the appointed
  day,
And in the day of the feast of the
  LORD?

⁶ For indeed they are gone because
  of destruction.
Egypt shall gather them up;
Memphis shall bury them.
Nettles shall possess their
  valuables of silver;
Thorns *shall be* in their tents.

⁷ The days of punishment have
  come;
The days of recompense have
  come.
Israel knows!
The prophet *is* a fool,
The spiritual man *is* insane,
Because of the greatness of your
  iniquity and great enmity.

⁸ The watchman of Ephraim *is* with
  my God;
But the prophet *is* a fowler's snare
  in all his ways—
Enmity in the house of his God.

⁹ They are deeply corrupted,
As in the days of Gibeah.
He will remember their iniquity;
He will punish their sins.

¹⁰ "I found Israel
Like grapes in the wilderness;
I saw your fathers
As the firstfruits on the fig tree in
  its first season.

But they went to Baal Peor,
And separated themselves *to that*
    shame;
They became an abomination like
    the thing they loved.

11 *As for* Ephraim, their glory shall
    fly away like a bird—
No birth, no pregnancy, and no
    conception!

12 Though they bring up their
    children,
Yet I will bereave them to the last
    man.
Yes, woe to them when I depart
    from them!

13 Just as I saw Ephraim like Tyre,
    planted in a pleasant place,
So Ephraim will bring out his
    children to the murderer."

14 Give them, O LORD—
What will You give?
Give them a miscarrying womb
And dry breasts!

15 "All their wickedness *is* in Gilgal,
For there I hated them.
Because of the evil of their deeds
I will drive them from My house;
I will love them no more.
All their princes *are* rebellious.

16 Ephraim is stricken,
Their root is dried up;
They shall bear no fruit.
Yes, were they to bear children,
I would kill the darlings of their
    womb."

17 My God will cast them away,
Because they did not obey Him;
And they shall be wanderers
    among the nations.

10 Israel empties *his* vine;
He brings forth fruit for himself.
According to the multitude of his
    fruit
He has increased the altars;
According to the bounty of his
    land
They have embellished *his* sacred
    pillars.

2 Their heart is divided;
Now they are held guilty.

He will break down their altars;
He will ruin their sacred pillars.

3 For now they say,
"We have no king,
Because we did not fear
    the LORD.
And as for a king, what would he
    do for us?"

4 They have spoken words,
Swearing falsely in making a
    covenant.
Thus judgment springs up like
    hemlock in the furrows of the
    field.

5 The inhabitants of Samaria fear
Because of the calf of
    Beth Aven.
For its people mourn for it,
And its priests shriek for it—
Because its glory has departed
    from it.

6 *The idol* also shall be carried to
    Assyria
As a present for King Jareb.
Ephraim shall receive shame,
And Israel shall be ashamed of his
    own counsel.

7 *As for* Samaria, her king is cut off
Like a twig on the water.

8 Also the high places of Aven, the
    sin of Israel,
Shall be destroyed.
The thorn and thistle shall grow
    on their altars;
They shall say to the mountains,
    "Cover us!"
And to the hills, "Fall on us!"

9 "O Israel, you have sinned from the
    days of Gibeah;
There they stood.
The battle in Gibeah against the
    children of iniquity
Did not overtake them.

10 When *it is* My desire, I will
    chasten them.
Peoples shall be gathered against
    them
When I bind them for their two
    transgressions.

11 Ephraim *is* a trained heifer
That loves to thresh *grain*;

More Than Enough

A poor young artist called her aunt one day to let her know that she was leaving on a trip. She was going to try to sell her wood carvings of sea birds to the owner of the gift shop at a fashionable resort. She asked her aunt to pray that her venture would be successful. Her aunt assured her that she would pray for the largest order she had ever received!

That evening, the young artist called her aunt back. With great exuberance she told her aunt what had happened. Not only had the gift-shop owner purchased all of her carvings, but the owner of a chain of gift shops had ordered as many carvings as she could make! She was filled with wonder at how abundantly God had answered prayer. "Now," she said to her aunt, "pray that I can fill his order!"

Her aunt wisely replied, "The Lord doesn't open a door for us unless He expects us to walk through it successfully. When you pray for rain, don't be surprised when you get a cloudburst!"

Are you praying for God to meet a need in your life today? Are you expecting a bare-minimum, meager-but-satisfactory answer? Or, are you expecting an abundant, more-than-enough supply? Our God is a generous Giver!

But I harnessed her fair neck,
I will make Ephraim pull *a plow.*
Judah shall plow;
Jacob shall break his clods."

12 Sow for yourselves righteousness;
Reap in mercy;
Break up your fallow ground,
For *it is* time to seek the LORD,
Till He comes and rains
righteousness on you.

13 You have plowed wickedness;
You have reaped iniquity.
You have eaten the fruit of lies,
Because you trusted in your own
way,
In the multitude of your mighty
men.
14 Therefore tumult shall arise
among your people,
And all your fortresses shall be
plundered
As Shalman plundered Beth Arbel
in the day of battle—
A mother dashed in pieces upon
her children.
15 Thus it shall be done to you,
O Bethel,
Because of your great wickedness.
At dawn the king of Israel
Shall be cut off utterly.

～ PSALM 139:13–16 ～

13 For You formed my inward parts;
You covered me in my mother's
womb.
14 I will praise You, for I am fearfully
and wonderfully made;
Marvelous are Your works,
And *that* my soul knows very well.
15 My frame was not hidden from You,
When I was made in secret,
And skillfully wrought in the lowest
parts of the earth.
16 Your eyes saw my substance, being
yet unformed.
And in Your book they all were
written,
The days fashioned for me,
When *as yet there were* none of
them.

～ PROVERBS 29:21 ～

21 He who pampers his servant from
childhood
Will have him as a son in the end.

～ 3 JOHN 1–14 ～

The Elder,

To the beloved Gaius, whom I love in
truth:

2 Beloved, I pray that you may prosper
in all things and be in health, just as your
soul prospers. 3 For I rejoiced greatly when
brethren came and testified of the truth
that is in you, just as you walk in the
truth. 4 I have no greater joy than to hear
that my children walk in truth.

5 Beloved, you do faithfully whatever
you do for the brethren and for strangers, 6 who have borne witness of your love
before the church. *If* you send them forward on their journey in a manner
worthy of God, you will do well, 7 because
they went forth for His name's sake,
taking nothing from the Gentiles. 8 We
therefore ought to receive such, that we
may become fellow workers for the truth.

9 I wrote to the church, but Diotrephes,
who loves to have the preeminence among
them, does not receive us. 10 Therefore, if
I come, I will call to mind his deeds which
he does, prating against us with malicious
words. And not content with that, he himself does not receive the brethren, and
forbids those who wish to, putting *them*
out of the church.

11 Beloved, do not imitate what is evil,
but what is good. He who does good is
of God, but he who does evil has not seen
God.

12 Demetrius has a *good* testimony from
all, and from the truth itself. And we also
bear witness, and you know that our testimony is true.

13 I had many things to write, but I do
not wish to write to you with pen and
ink; 14 but I hope to see you shortly,
and we shall speak face to face.

Peace to you. Our friends greet you.
Greet the friends by name.

～ HOSEA 11:1—12:14 ～

1 "When Israel was a child, I loved him,
And out of Egypt I called My son.
2 *As* they called them,
So they went from them;
They sacrificed to the Baals,
And burned incense to carved images.

3 "I taught Ephraim to walk,
Taking them by their arms;
But they did not know that I healed them.
4 I drew them with gentle cords,
With bands of love,
And I was to them as those who take the yoke from their neck.
I stooped *and* fed them.

5 "He shall not return to the land of Egypt;
But the Assyrian shall be his king,
Because they refused to repent.
6 And the sword shall slash in his cities,
Devour his districts,
And consume *them,*
Because of their own counsels.
7 My people are bent on backsliding from Me.
Though they call to the Most High,
None at all exalt *Him.*

8 "How can I give you up, Ephraim?
How can I hand you over, Israel?
How can I make you like Admah?
How can I set you like Zeboiim?
My heart churns within Me;
My sympathy is stirred.
9 I will not execute the fierceness of My anger;
I will not again destroy Ephraim.
For I *am* God, and not man,
The Holy One in your midst;
And I will not come with terror.

10 "They shall walk after the LORD.
He will roar like a lion.
When He roars,
Then *His* sons shall come trembling from the west;

11 They shall come trembling like a bird from Egypt,
Like a dove from the land of Assyria.
And I will let them dwell in their houses,"
Says the LORD.

12 "Ephraim has encircled Me with lies,
And the house of Israel with deceit;
But Judah still walks with God,
Even with the Holy One *who is* faithful.

12 "Ephraim feeds on the wind,
And pursues the east wind;
He daily increases lies and desolation.
Also they make a covenant with the Assyrians,
And oil is carried to Egypt.

2 "The LORD also *brings* a charge against Judah,
And will punish Jacob according to his ways;
According to his deeds He will recompense him.
3 He took his brother by the heel in the womb,
And in his strength he struggled with God.
4 Yes, he struggled with the Angel and prevailed;
He wept, and sought favor from Him.
He found Him *in* Bethel,
And there He spoke to us—
5 That is, the LORD God of hosts.
The LORD *is* His memorable name.
6 So you, by *the help of* your God, return;
Observe mercy and justice,
And wait on your God continually.

7 "A cunning Canaanite!
Deceitful scales *are* in his hand;
He loves to oppress.

8 And Ephraim said,
  'Surely I have become rich,
  I have found wealth for myself;
  In all my labors
  They shall find in me no iniquity
    that *is* sin.'

9 "But I *am* the LORD your God,
  Ever since the land of Egypt;
  I will again make you dwell in
    tents,
  As in the days of the appointed
    feast.
10 I have also spoken by the
    prophets,
  And have multiplied visions;
  I have given symbols through the
    witness of the prophets."

11 Though Gilead *has* idols—
  Surely they are vanity—
  Though they sacrifice bulls in
    Gilgal,
  Indeed their altars *shall be* heaps
    in the furrows of the field.

12 Jacob fled to the country of Syria;
  Israel served for a spouse,
  And for a wife he tended *sheep*.
13 By a prophet the LORD brought
    Israel out of Egypt,
  And by a prophet he was
    preserved.
14 Ephraim provoked *Him* to anger
    most bitterly;
  Therefore his Lord will leave the
    guilt of his bloodshed upon
    him,
  And return his reproach upon
    him.

∼ PSALM 139:17–24 ∼

17 How precious also are Your thoughts
    to me, O God!
  How great is the sum of them!
18 *If* I should count them, they would
    be more in number than the sand;
  When I awake, I am still with You.

19 Oh, that You would slay the wicked,
    O God!
  Depart from me, therefore, you
    bloodthirsty men.
20 For they speak against You wickedly;

Your enemies take *Your name* in
  vain.
21 Do I not hate them, O LORD, who
    hate You?
  And do I not loathe those who rise
    up against You?
22 I hate them with perfect hatred;
  I count them my enemies.

23 Search me, O God, and know my
    heart;
  Try me, and know my anxieties;
24 And see if *there is any* wicked way in
    me,
  And lead me in the way everlasting.

∼ PROVERBS 29:22 ∼

22 An angry man stirs up strife,
  And a furious man abounds in
    transgression.

∼ JUDE 1–25 ∼

Jude, a bondservant of Jesus Christ, and
brother of James,

To those who are called, sanctified by
God the Father, and preserved in Jesus
Christ:

2 Mercy, peace, and love be multiplied
to you.
3 Beloved, while I was very diligent to
write to you concerning our common salvation, I found it necessary to write to
you exhorting you to contend earnestly
for the faith which was once for all delivered to the saints. 4 For certain men have
crept in unnoticed, who long ago were
marked out for this condemnation, ungodly men, who turn the grace of our God
into lewdness and deny the only Lord
God and our Lord Jesus Christ.
5 But I want to remind you, though you
once knew this, that the Lord, having
saved the people out of the land of Egypt,
afterward destroyed those who did not
believe. 6 And the angels who did not keep
their proper domain, but left their own
abode, He has reserved in everlasting
chains under darkness for the judgment
of the great day; 7 as Sodom and Gomorrah, and the cities around them in a
similar manner to these, having given

Lord, Be My Strength

Dr. A. B. Simpson, a New York preacher, was plagued by poor health. Two nervous breakdowns and a heart condition led a well-known New York physician to tell him — at the age of thirty-eight — that he would never live to be forty. The physician's diagnosis was no surprise to Simpson. Preaching was agonizing for him; even climbing a slight elevation left him breathless.

In desperation, Simpson went to the Bible to find out what Jesus had to say about disease. He became convinced that Jesus always meant for healing to be a part of redemption. One Friday afternoon shortly after Simpson came to this conclusion, he went for a walk in the country. Coming to a pine woods, he sat down on a log to rest and pray. He asked Christ to enter him and to become his physical strength until his life's work was accomplished. He later said, "Every fiber in me was tingling with the sense of God's presence."

Days later, Simpson climbed a 3,000-foot mountain. He said, "When I reached the top, the world of weakness and fear was lying at my feet. From that time on I literally had a new heart." He went on to preach 3,000 sermons in the next three years, holding as many as twenty meetings a week. He amassed an amazing volume of work before he died — at the age of seventy-six.

Whatever you may be facing that leaves you feeling weak and fearful — illness, injury, stress, anxiety — God will take your strength, which is weakness, and replace it with His strength. His strength is more than enough to see you through every trial or temptation and it's always available. All you need to do is ask.

themselves over to sexual immorality and gone after strange flesh, are set forth as an example, suffering the vengeance of eternal fire.

8 Likewise also these dreamers defile the flesh, reject authority, and speak evil of dignitaries. 9 Yet Michael the archangel, in contending with the devil, when he disputed about the body of Moses, dared not bring against him a reviling accusation, but said, "The Lord rebuke you!" 10 But these speak evil of whatever they do not know; and whatever they know naturally, like brute beasts, in these things they corrupt themselves. 11 Woe to them! For they have gone in the way of Cain, have run greedily in the error of Balaam for profit, and perished in the rebellion of Korah.

12 These are spots in your love feasts, while they feast with you without fear, serving *only* themselves. *They are* clouds without water, carried about by the winds; late autumn trees without fruit, twice dead, pulled up by the roots; 13 raging waves of the sea, foaming up their own shame; wandering stars for whom is reserved the blackness of darkness forever.

14 Now Enoch, the seventh from Adam, prophesied about these men also, saying, "Behold, the Lord comes with ten thousands of His saints, 15 to execute judgment on all, to convict all who are ungodly among them of all their ungodly deeds which they have committed in an ungodly way, and of all the harsh things which ungodly sinners have spoken against Him."

16 These are grumblers, complainers, walking according to their own lusts; and they mouth great swelling *words,* flattering people to gain advantage. 17 But you, beloved, remember the words which were spoken before by the apostles of our Lord Jesus Christ: 18 how they told you that there would be mockers in the last time who would walk according to their own ungodly lusts. 19 These are sensual persons, who cause divisions, not having the Spirit.

20 But you, beloved, building yourselves up on your most holy faith, praying in the Holy Spirit, 21 keep yourselves in the love of God, looking for the mercy of our Lord Jesus Christ unto eternal life.

22 And on some have compassion, making a distinction; 23 but others save with fear, pulling *them* out of the fire, hating even the garment defiled by the flesh.

24 Now to Him who is able to keep
   you from stumbling,
  And to present *you* faultless
  Before the presence of His glory
   with exceeding joy,
25 To God our Savior,
  Who alone is wise,
  Be glory and majesty,
  Dominion and power,
  Both now and forever.
  Amen.

READING 345 · DECEMBER 11

~ HOSEA 13:1—14:9 ~

1 When Ephraim spoke, trembling,
  He exalted *himself* in Israel;
  But when he offended through
   Baal *worship,* he died.
2 Now they sin more and more,
  And have made for themselves
   molded images,
  Idols of their silver, according to
   their skill;
  All of it *is* the work of craftsmen.
  They say of them,
  "Let the men who sacrifice kiss the
   calves!"

3 Therefore they shall be like the
   morning cloud
  And like the early dew that passes
   away,
  Like chaff blown off from a
   threshing floor
  And like smoke from a chimney.

4 "Yet I *am* the LORD your God
  Ever since the land of Egypt,
  And you shall know no God but
   Me;
  For *there is* no savior besides Me.

5 I knew you in the wilderness,
In the land of great drought.
6 When they had pasture, they were filled;
They were filled and their heart was exalted;
Therefore they forgot Me.

7 "So I will be to them like a lion;
Like a leopard by the road I will lurk;
8 I will meet them like a bear deprived *of her cubs;*
I will tear open their rib cage,
And there I will devour them like a lion.
The wild beast shall tear them.

9 "O Israel, you are destroyed,
But your help *is* from Me.
10 I will be your King;
Where *is any other,*
That he may save you in all your cities?
And your judges to whom you said,
'Give me a king and princes'?
11 I gave you a king in My anger,
And took *him* away in My wrath.

12 "The iniquity of Ephraim *is* bound up;
His sin *is* stored up.
13 The sorrows of a woman in childbirth shall come upon him.
He *is* an unwise son,
For he should not stay long where children are born.

14 "I will ransom them from the power of the grave;
I will redeem them from death.
O Death, I will be your plagues!
O Grave, I will be your destruction!
Pity is hidden from My eyes."

15 Though he is fruitful among *his* brethren,
An east wind shall come;
The wind of the LORD shall come up from the wilderness.
Then his spring shall become dry,
And his fountain shall be dried up.

He shall plunder the treasury of every desirable prize.
16 Samaria is held guilty,
For she has rebelled against her God.
They shall fall by the sword,
Their infants shall be dashed in pieces,
And their women with child ripped open.

14 O Israel, return to the LORD your God,
For you have stumbled because of your iniquity;
2 Take words with you,
And return to the LORD.
Say to Him,
"Take away all iniquity;
Receive *us* graciously,
For we will offer the sacrifices of our lips.
3 Assyria shall not save us,
We will not ride on horses,
Nor will we say anymore to the work of our hands, '*You are* our gods.'
For in You the fatherless finds mercy."

4 "I will heal their backsliding,
I will love them freely,
For My anger has turned away from him.
5 I will be like the dew to Israel;
He shall grow like the lily,
And lengthen his roots like Lebanon.
6 His branches shall spread;
His beauty shall be like an olive tree,
And his fragrance like Lebanon.
7 Those who dwell under his shadow shall return;
They shall be revived *like* grain,
And grow like a vine.
Their scent *shall be* like the wine of Lebanon.

8 "Ephraim *shall say,* 'What have I to do anymore with idols?'
I have heard and observed him.
I *am* like a green cypress tree;
Your fruit is found in Me."

⁹ Who *is* wise?
  Let him understand these things.
Who is prudent?
  Let him know them.
For the ways of the LORD *are*
  right;
The righteous walk in them,
But transgressors stumble in them.

～ PSALM 140:1–5 ～

¹ Deliver me, O LORD, from evil men;
  Preserve me from violent men,
² Who plan evil things in *their* hearts;
  They continually gather together *for*
  war.
³ They sharpen their tongues like a
  serpent;
  The poison of asps *is* under their
  lips.   Selah

⁴ Keep me, O LORD, from the hands
  of the wicked;
  Preserve me from violent men,
  Who have purposed to make my
  steps stumble.
⁵ The proud have hidden a snare for
  me, and cords;
  They have spread a net by the
  wayside;
  They have set traps for me.   Selah

～ PROVERBS 29:23 ～

²³ A man's pride will bring him low,
  But the humble in spirit will retain
  honor.

～ REVELATION 1:1–20 ～

The Revelation of Jesus Christ, which God gave Him to show His servants—things which must shortly take place. And He sent and signified *it* by His angel to His servant John, ² who bore witness to the word of God, and to the testimony of Jesus Christ, to all things that he saw. ³ Blessed *is* he who reads and those who hear the words of this prophecy, and keep those things which are written in it; for the time *is* near.

⁴ John, to the seven churches which are in Asia:

Grace to you and peace from Him who is and who was and who is to come, and from the seven Spirits who are before His throne, ⁵ and from Jesus Christ, the faithful witness, the firstborn from the dead, and the ruler over the kings of the earth.

To Him who loved us and washed us from our sins in His own blood, ⁶ and has made us kings and priests to His God and Father, to Him *be* glory and dominion forever and ever. Amen.

⁷ Behold, He is coming with clouds, and every eye will see Him, even they who pierced Him. And all the tribes of the earth will mourn because of Him. Even so, Amen.

⁸ "I am the Alpha and the Omega, *the* Beginning and *the* End," says the Lord, "who is and who was and who is to come, the Almighty."

⁹ I, John, both your brother and companion in the tribulation and kingdom and patience of Jesus Christ, was on the island that is called Patmos for the word of God and for the testimony of Jesus Christ. ¹⁰ I was in the Spirit on the Lord's Day, and I heard behind me a loud voice, as of a trumpet, ¹¹ saying, "I am the Alpha and the Omega, the First and the Last," and, "What you see, write in a book and send *it* to the seven churches which are in Asia: to Ephesus, to Smyrna, to Pergamos, to Thyatira, to Sardis, to Philadelphia, and to Laodicea."

¹² Then I turned to see the voice that spoke with me. And having turned I saw seven golden lampstands, ¹³ and in the midst of the seven lampstands *One* like the Son of Man, clothed with a garment down to the feet and girded about the chest with a golden band. ¹⁴ His head and hair *were* white like wool, as white as snow, and His eyes like a flame of fire; ¹⁵ His feet *were* like fine brass, as if refined in a furnace, and His voice as the sound of many waters; ¹⁶ He had in His right hand seven stars, out of His mouth went a sharp two-edged sword, and His countenance *was* like the sun shining in its strength. ¹⁷ And when I saw Him, I fell at His feet as dead. But He laid His right hand on me, saying to me, "Do not be afraid; I am the First and the Last. ¹⁸ I *am* He who lives, and was dead, and behold, I am alive forevermore. Amen. And I

Overflowing Blessings

Until the time Jane learned she needed an operation, the question, "Who will take care of me if I get sick?" had only been hypothetical. As a single woman, she hadn't given much thought to how she would survive a major illness or operation. As it turned out, she found that she had a "loving menagerie of friends" who "cobbled together a schedule of ministry and then passed the baton from one to the next while I marveled at my good fortune."

Stephanie was the ringmaster, the one by her side at the hospital, who also helped her check her incision and take showers. Bob drove up from Los Angeles with his dog to stay for a few days after she returned home. Peggy brought over Thai take-out food. Ann arrived with a bread machine and bags of groceries. She also made soup, mopped the kitchen floor, and did the laundry. Michelle brought mail from the office and drove her to doctors' appointments.

It was amazing to Jane that these various people hardly knew each other when they first began helping her, but by the time she recovered, they had all become friends.

God's provision in your life is always beneficial for you. However, He often provides in such wonderful abundance that even those who carry the blessing to you are blessed themselves.

have the keys of Hades and of Death. [19] Write the things which you have seen, and the things which are, and the things which will take place after this. [20] The mystery of the seven stars which you saw in My right hand, and the seven golden lampstands: The seven stars are the angels of the seven churches, and the seven lampstands which you saw are the seven churches.

READING 346 · DECEMBER 12

～ JOEL 1:1—3:21 ～

The word of the LORD that came to Joel the son of Pethuel.

[2] Hear this, you elders,
And give ear, all you inhabitants of the land!
Has *anything like* this happened in your days,
Or even in the days of your fathers?

[3] Tell your children about it,
Let your children *tell* their children,
And their children another generation.

[4] What the chewing locust left, the swarming locust has eaten;
What the swarming locust left, the crawling locust has eaten;
And what the crawling locust left, the consuming locust has eaten.

[5] Awake, you drunkards, and weep;
And wail, all you drinkers of wine,
Because of the new wine,
For it has been cut off from your mouth.

[6] For a nation has come up against My land,
Strong, and without number;
His teeth *are* the teeth of a lion,
And he has the fangs of a fierce lion.

[7] He has laid waste My vine,
And ruined My fig tree;
He has stripped it bare and thrown *it* away;
Its branches are made white.

[8] Lament like a virgin girded with sackcloth

For the husband of her youth.

[9] The grain offering and the drink offering
Have been cut off from the house of the LORD;
The priests mourn, who minister to the LORD.

[10] The field is wasted,
The land mourns;
For the grain is ruined,
The new wine is dried up,
The oil fails.

[11] Be ashamed, you farmers,
Wail, you vinedressers,
For the wheat and the barley;
Because the harvest of the field has perished.

[12] The vine has dried up,
And the fig tree has withered;
The pomegranate tree,
The palm tree also,
And the apple tree—
All the trees of the field are withered;
Surely joy has withered away from the sons of men.

[13] Gird yourselves and lament, you priests;
Wail, you who minister before the altar;
Come, lie all night in sackcloth,
You who minister to my God;
For the grain offering and the drink offering
Are withheld from the house of your God.

[14] Consecrate a fast,
Call a sacred assembly;
Gather the elders
And all the inhabitants of the land

Into the house of the LORD your
God,
And cry out to the LORD.

15 Alas for the day!
For the day of the LORD *is* at
hand;
It shall come as destruction from
the Almighty.
16 Is not the food cut off before our
eyes,
Joy and gladness from the house
of our God?
17 The seed shrivels under the clods,
Storehouses are in shambles;
Barns are broken down,
For the grain has withered.
18 How the animals groan!
The herds of cattle are restless,
Because they have no pasture;
Even the flocks of sheep suffer
punishment.

19 O LORD, to You I cry out;
For fire has devoured the open
pastures,
And a flame has burned all the
trees of the field.
20 The beasts of the field also cry out
to You,
For the water brooks are dried up,
And fire has devoured the open
pastures.

2 Blow the trumpet in Zion,
And sound an alarm in My holy
mountain!
Let all the inhabitants of the land
tremble;
For the day of the LORD is
coming,
For it is at hand:
2 A day of darkness and
gloominess,
A day of clouds and thick
darkness,
Like the morning *clouds* spread
over the mountains.
A people *come,* great and strong,
The like of whom has never been;
Nor will there ever be any *such*
after them,
Even for many successive
generations.

3 A fire devours before them,
And behind them a flame burns;
The land *is* like the Garden of
Eden before them,
And behind them a desolate
wilderness;
Surely nothing shall escape them.
4 Their appearance is like the
appearance of horses;
And like swift steeds, so they run.
5 With a noise like chariots
Over mountaintops they leap,
Like the noise of a flaming fire
that devours the stubble,
Like a strong people set in battle
array.

6 Before them the people writhe in
pain;
All faces are drained of color.
7 They run like mighty men,
They climb the wall like men of
war;
Every one marches in formation,
And they do not break ranks.
8 They do not push one another;
Every one marches in his own
column.
Though they lunge between the
weapons,
They are not cut down.
9 They run to and fro in the city,
They run on the wall;
They climb into the houses,
They enter at the windows like a
thief.

10 The earth quakes before them,
The heavens tremble;
The sun and moon grow dark,
And the stars diminish their
brightness.
11 The LORD gives voice before His
army,
For His camp is very great;
For strong *is the One* who
executes His word.
For the day of the LORD *is* great
and very terrible;
Who can endure it?

12 "Now, therefore," says the LORD,
"Turn to Me with all your heart,
With fasting, with weeping, and
with mourning."

13 So rend your heart, and not your
    garments;
Return to the LORD your God,
For He *is* gracious and merciful,
Slow to anger, and of great
    kindness;
And He relents from doing harm.
14 Who knows *if* He will turn and
    relent,
And leave a blessing behind
    Him—
A grain offering and a drink
    offering
For the LORD your God?

15 Blow the trumpet in Zion,
Consecrate a fast,
Call a sacred assembly;
16 Gather the people,
Sanctify the congregation,
Assemble the elders,
Gather the children and nursing
    babes;
Let the bridegroom go out from
    his chamber,
And the bride from her dressing
    room.
17 Let the priests, who minister to
    the LORD,
Weep between the porch and the
    altar;
Let them say, "Spare Your people,
    O LORD,
And do not give Your heritage to
    reproach,
That the nations should rule over
    them.
Why should they say among the
    peoples,
'Where *is* their God?' "

18 Then the LORD will be zealous for
    His land,
And pity His people.
19 The LORD will answer and say to
    His people,
"Behold, I will send you grain and
    new wine and oil,
And you will be satisfied by them;
I will no longer make you a
    reproach among the nations.

20 "But I will remove far from you the
    northern *army*,

And will drive him away into a
    barren and desolate land,
With his face toward the eastern
    sea
And his back toward the western
    sea;
His stench will come up,
And his foul odor will rise,
Because he has done monstrous
    things."

21 Fear not, O land;
Be glad and rejoice,
For the LORD has done marvelous
    things!
22 Do not be afraid, you beasts of the
    field;
For the open pastures are
    springing up,
And the tree bears its fruit;
The fig tree and the vine yield
    their strength.
23 Be glad then, you children of
    Zion,
And rejoice in the LORD your
    God;
For He has given you the former
    rain faithfully,
And He will cause the rain to
    come down for you—
The former rain,
And the latter rain in the first
    month.
24 The threshing floors shall be full
    of wheat,
And the vats shall overflow with
    new wine and oil.

25 "So I will restore to you the years
    that the swarming locust has
    eaten,
The crawling locust,
The consuming locust,
And the chewing locust,
My great army which I sent
    among you.
26 You shall eat in plenty and be
    satisfied,
And praise the name of the LORD
    your God,
Who has dealt wondrously with
    you;
And My people shall never be put
    to shame.

Reaping a Harvest

The late Spencer Penrose, whose brother was a major political leader in Philadelphia in the late nineteenth century, was considered the "black sheep" of the family. He chose to live in the West, instead of the East. In 1891, fresh out of Harvard, he made his way to Colorado Springs. Not long after his move, he wired his brother for $1500 so that he might go into a mining venture. His brother telegraphed him $150 instead — enough for train fare home — and warned him against the deal.

Years later, Spencer returned to Philadelphia and handed his brother $75,000 in gold coins — payment, he said, for his "investment" in his mining operation. His brother was stunned. He had qualms about accepting the money, however, and reminded his brother that he had advised against the venture and had only given him $150. "That," replied Spencer, "is why I'm only giving you $75,000. If you had sent me the full $1500 I requested, I would be giving you three-quarters of a million dollars."

Nothing invested, nothing gained. Every harvest requires an initial seed. Be generous in your seed-sowing. Plant in good ground and you can anticipate a good return.

> Put in the sickle, for the harvest is ripe. Come, go down; for the winepress is full, the vats overflow — for their wickedness is great.
>
> Joel 3:13

————◦⊐▬◌▬⊏◦————

27 Then you shall know that I *am* in
    the midst of Israel:
I *am* the LORD your God
And there is no other.
My people shall never be put to
    shame.

28 "And it shall come to pass
    afterward
That I will pour out My Spirit on
    all flesh;
Your sons and your daughters shall
    prophesy,
Your old men shall dream dreams,
Your young men shall see visions.
29 And also on *My* menservants and
    on *My* maidservants
I will pour out My Spirit in those
    days.

30 "And I will show wonders in the
    heavens and in the earth:
Blood and fire and pillars of
    smoke.
31 The sun shall be turned into
    darkness,
And the moon into blood,
Before the coming of the great
    and awesome day of the LORD.
32 And it shall come to pass
That whoever calls on the name of
    the LORD
Shall be saved.
For in Mount Zion and in
    Jerusalem there shall be
    deliverance,
As the LORD has said,
Among the remnant whom the
    LORD calls.

3 "For behold, in those days and at
    that time,
When I bring back the captives of
    Judah and Jerusalem,
2 I will also gather all nations,
And bring them down to the
    Valley of Jehoshaphat;
And I will enter into judgment
    with them there
On account of My people, My
    heritage Israel,
Whom they have scattered among
    the nations;
They have also divided up My
    land.

3 They have cast lots for My
    people,
Have given a boy *as payment* for a
    harlot,
And sold a girl for wine, that they
    may drink.

4 "Indeed, what have you to do with
    Me,
O Tyre and Sidon, and all the
    coasts of Philistia?
Will you retaliate against Me?
But if you retaliate against Me,
Swiftly and speedily I will return
    your retaliation upon your own
    head;
5 Because you have taken My silver
    and My gold,
And have carried into your
    temples My prized possessions.
6 Also the people of Judah and the
    people of Jerusalem
You have sold to the Greeks,
That you may remove them far
    from their borders.

7 "Behold, I will raise them
Out of the place to which you
    have sold them,
And will return your retaliation
    upon your own head.
8 I will sell your sons and your
    daughters
Into the hand of the people of
    Judah,
And they will sell them to the
    Sabeans,
To a people far off;
For the LORD has spoken."

9 Proclaim this among the nations:
"Prepare for war!
Wake up the mighty men,
Let all the men of war draw near,
Let them come up.
10 Beat your plowshares into
    swords
And your pruning hooks into
    spears;
Let the weak say, 'I *am* strong.' "
11 Assemble and come, all you
    nations,
And gather together all around.
Cause Your mighty ones to go
    down there, O LORD.

12 "Let the nations be wakened, and
come up to the Valley of
Jehoshaphat;
For there I will sit to judge all the
surrounding nations.
13 Put in the sickle, for the harvest is
ripe.
Come, go down;
For the winepress is full,
The vats overflow—
For their wickedness *is* great."

14 Multitudes, multitudes in the
valley of decision!
For the day of the LORD *is* near in
the valley of decision.
15 The sun and moon will grow dark,
And the stars will diminish their
brightness.
16 The LORD also will roar from
Zion,
And utter His voice from
Jerusalem;
The heavens and earth will shake;
But the LORD will be a shelter for
His people,
And the strength of the children of
Israel.

17 "So you shall know that I *am* the
LORD your God,
Dwelling in Zion My holy
mountain.
Then Jerusalem shall be holy,
And no aliens shall ever pass
through her again."

18 And it will come to pass in that
day
That the mountains shall drip with
new wine,
The hills shall flow with milk,
And all the brooks of Judah shall
be flooded with water;
A fountain shall flow from the
house of the LORD
And water the Valley of Acacias.

19 "Egypt shall be a desolation,
And Edom a desolate wilderness,
Because of violence *against* the
people of Judah,
For they have shed innocent blood
in their land.
20 But Judah shall abide forever,

And Jerusalem from generation to
generation.
21 For I will acquit them of the guilt
of bloodshed, whom I had not
acquitted;
For the LORD dwells in Zion."

~ PSALM 140:6–13 ~

6 I said to the LORD: "You *are* my
God;
Hear the voice of my supplications,
O LORD.
7 O GOD the Lord, the strength of my
salvation,
You have covered my head in the day
of battle.
8 Do not grant, O LORD, the desires of
the wicked;
Do not further his *wicked* scheme,
Lest they be exalted.   Selah

9 "As for the head of those who
surround me,
Let the evil of their lips cover them;
10 Let burning coals fall upon them;
Let them be cast into the fire,
Into deep pits, that they rise not up
again.
11 Let not a slanderer be established in
the earth;
Let evil hunt the violent man to
overthrow *him*."

12 I know that the LORD will maintain
The cause of the afflicted,
And justice for the poor.
13 Surely the righteous shall give thanks
to Your name;
The upright shall dwell in Your
presence.

~ PROVERBS 29:24 ~

24 Whoever is a partner with a thief
hates his own life;
He swears to tell the truth, but
reveals nothing.

~ REVELATION 2:1–29 ~

"To the angel of the church of Ephesus
write,
'These things says He who holds the
seven stars in His right hand, who walks

in the midst of the seven golden lamp-stands: [2] "I know your works, your labor, your patience, and that you cannot bear those who are evil. And you have tested those who say they are apostles and are not, and have found them liars; [3] and you have persevered and have patience, and have labored for My name's sake and have not become weary. [4] Nevertheless I have *this* against you, that you have left your first love. [5] Remember therefore from where you have fallen; repent and do the first works, or else I will come to you quickly and remove your lampstand from its place—unless you repent. [6] But this you have, that you hate the deeds of the Nicolaitans, which I also hate.

[7] "He who has an ear, let him hear what the Spirit says to the churches. To him who overcomes I will give to eat from the tree of life, which is in the midst of the Paradise of God." '

[8] "And to the angel of the church in Smyrna write,

'These things says the First and the Last, who was dead, and came to life: [9] "I know your works, tribulation, and poverty (but you are rich); and *I know* the blasphemy of those who say they are Jews and are not, but *are* a synagogue of Satan. [10] Do not fear any of those things which you are about to suffer. Indeed, the devil is about to throw *some* of you into prison, that you may be tested, and you will have tribulation ten days. Be faithful until death, and I will give you the crown of life.

[11] "He who has an ear, let him hear what the Spirit says to the churches. He who overcomes shall not be hurt by the second death." '

[12] "And to the angel of the church in Pergamos write,

'These things says He who has the sharp two-edged sword: [13] "I know your works, and where you dwell, where Satan's throne *is*. And you hold fast to My name, and did not deny My faith even in the days in which Antipas *was* My faithful martyr, who was killed among you, where Satan dwells. [14] But I have a few things against you, because you have there those who hold the doctrine of Balaam, who taught Balak to put a stumbling block before the children of Israel, to eat things

sacrificed to idols, and to commit sexual immorality. [15] Thus you also have those who hold the doctrine of the Nicolaitans, which thing I hate. [16] Repent, or else I will come to you quickly and will fight against them with the sword of My mouth.

[17] "He who has an ear, let him hear what the Spirit says to the churches. To him who overcomes I will give some of the hidden manna to eat. And I will give him a white stone, and on the stone a new name written which no one knows except him who receives *it*." '

[18] "And to the angel of the church in Thyatira write,

'These things says the Son of God, who has eyes like a flame of fire, and His feet like fine brass: [19] "I know your works, love, service, faith, and your patience; and *as* for your works, the last *are* more than the first. [20] Nevertheless I have a few things against you, because you allow that woman Jezebel, who calls herself a prophetess, to teach and seduce My servants to commit sexual immorality and eat things sacrificed to idols. [21] And I gave her time to repent of her sexual immorality, and she did not repent. [22] Indeed I will cast her into a sickbed, and those who commit adultery with her into great tribulation, unless they repent of their deeds. [23] I will kill her children with death, and all the churches shall know that I am He who searches the minds and hearts. And I will give to each one of you according to your works.

[24] "Now to you I say, and to the rest in Thyatira, as many as do not have this doctrine, who have not known the depths of Satan, as they say, I will put on you no other burden. [25] But hold fast what you have till I come. [26] And he who overcomes, and keeps My works until the end, to him I will give power over the nations—

[27] 'He shall rule them with a rod of iron;
They shall be dashed to pieces like the potter's vessels'—

as I also have received from My Father; [28] and I will give him the morning star. [29] "He who has an ear, let him hear what the Spirit says to the churches." '

∼ Amos 1:1—3:15 ∼

The words of Amos, who was among the sheepbreeders of Tekoa, which he saw concerning Israel in the days of Uzziah king of Judah, and in the days of Jeroboam the son of Joash, king of Israel, two years before the earthquake.

2 And he said:

"The LORD roars from Zion,
And utters His voice from
Jerusalem;
The pastures of the shepherds
mourn,
And the top of Carmel withers."

3 Thus says the LORD:

"For three transgressions of
Damascus, and for four,
I will not turn away its
punishment,
Because they have threshed Gilead
with implements of iron.
4 But I will send a fire into the
house of Hazael,
Which shall devour the palaces of
Ben-Hadad.
5 I will also break the *gate* bar of
Damascus,
And cut off the inhabitant from
the Valley of Aven,
And the one who holds the scepter
from Beth Eden.
The people of Syria shall go
captive to Kir,"
Says the LORD.

6 Thus says the LORD:

"For three transgressions of Gaza,
and for four,
I will not turn away its
punishment,
Because they took captive the
whole captivity
To deliver *them* up to Edom.
7 But I will send a fire upon the wall
of Gaza,
Which shall devour its palaces.
8 I will cut off the inhabitant from
Ashdod,

And the one who holds the scepter
from Ashkelon;
I will turn My hand against Ekron,
And the remnant of the Philistines
shall perish,"
Says the Lord GOD.

9 Thus says the LORD:

"For three transgressions of Tyre,
and for four,
I will not turn away its
punishment,
Because they delivered up the
whole captivity to Edom,
And did not remember the
covenant of brotherhood.
10 But I will send a fire upon the wall
of Tyre,
Which shall devour its palaces."

11 Thus says the LORD:

"For three transgressions of Edom,
and for four,
I will not turn away its
punishment,
Because he pursued his brother
with the sword,
And cast off all pity;
His anger tore perpetually,
And he kept his wrath forever.
12 But I will send a fire upon Teman,
Which shall devour the palaces of
Bozrah."

13 Thus says the LORD:

"For three transgressions of the
people of Ammon, and for four,
I will not turn away its
punishment,
Because they ripped open the
women with child in Gilead,
That they might enlarge their
territory.
14 But I will kindle a fire in the wall
of Rabbah,
And it shall devour its palaces,
Amid shouting in the day of battle,
And a tempest in the day of the
whirlwind.

¹⁵ Their king shall go into captivity,
He and his princes together,"
Says the LORD.

2 Thus says the LORD:

"For three transgressions of Moab,
and for four,
I will not turn away its
punishment,
Because he burned the bones of
the king of Edom to lime.
² But I will send a fire upon Moab,
And it shall devour the palaces of
Kerioth;
Moab shall die with tumult,
With shouting *and* trumpet
sound.
³ And I will cut off the judge from
its midst,
And slay all its princes with him,"
Says the LORD.

⁴ Thus says the LORD:

"For three transgressions of Judah,
and for four,
I will not turn away its
punishment,
Because they have despised the
law of the LORD,
And have not kept His
commandments.
Their lies lead them astray,
Lies which their fathers followed.
⁵ But I will send a fire upon Judah,
And it shall devour the palaces of
Jerusalem."

⁶ Thus says the LORD:

"For three transgressions of Israel,
and for four,
I will not turn away its
punishment,
Because they sell the righteous for
silver,
And the poor for a pair of sandals.
⁷ They pant after the dust of the
earth *which is* on the head of
the poor,
And pervert the way of the
humble.
A man and his father go in to the
same girl,

To defile My holy name.
⁸ They lie down by every altar on
clothes taken in pledge,
And drink the wine of the
condemned *in* the house of
their god.

⁹ "Yet *it was* I *who* destroyed the
Amorite before them,
Whose height *was* like the height
of the cedars,
And he *was as* strong as the oaks;
Yet I destroyed his fruit above
And his roots beneath.
¹⁰ Also *it was* I *who* brought you up
from the land of Egypt,
And led you forty years through
the wilderness,
To possess the land of the
Amorite.
¹¹ I raised up some of your sons as
prophets,
And some of your young men as
Nazirites.
Is it not so, O you children of
Israel?"
Says the LORD.
¹² "But you gave the Nazirites wine to
drink,
And commanded the prophets
saying,
'Do not prophesy!'

¹³ "Behold, I am weighed down by
you,
As a cart full of sheaves is weighed
down.
¹⁴ Therefore flight shall perish from
the swift,
The strong shall not strengthen his
power,
Nor shall the mighty deliver
himself;
¹⁵ He shall not stand who handles
the bow,
The swift of foot shall not escape,
Nor shall he who rides a horse
deliver himself.
¹⁶ The most courageous men of
might
Shall flee naked in that day,"
Says the LORD.

3 Hear this word that the LORD has spoken against you, O children of Israel,

Starve Your Anger

General Horace Porter once wrote about a conversation he had with General Ulysses Grant one evening while they were sitting by a campfire. Porter noted, "General, it seems singular that you should have gone through all the rough and tumble of army service and frontier life, and have never been provoked into swearing. I have never heard you utter an oath."

Grant replied, "Well, somehow or other, I never learned to swear. When a boy, I seemed to have an aversion to it, and when I became a man I saw the folly of it. I have always noticed, too, that swearing helps to arouse a man's anger; and when a man flies into a passion his adversary who keeps cool always gets the better of him. In fact, I could never see the value of swearing. I think it is the case with many people who swear excessively that it is a mere habit . . . they do not mean to be profane; to say the least, it is a great waste of time."

Not only does anger give rise to harsh words, but harsh words feed anger. The seething soul uses up valuable inner energy, leaving far less for the normal healthy functioning of spirit, mind, and body. To rid yourself of feelings of anger and frustration, perhaps the first step is to watch your tongue!

against the whole family which I brought up from the land of Egypt, saying:

2 "You only have I known of all the
     families of the earth;
   Therefore I will punish you for all
     your iniquities."

3 Can two walk together, unless
     they are agreed?
4 Will a lion roar in the forest, when
     he has no prey?
   Will a young lion cry out of his
     den, if he has caught nothing?
5 Will a bird fall into a snare on the
     earth, where there is no trap for
     it?
   Will a snare spring up from the
     earth, if it has caught nothing at
     all?
6 If a trumpet is blown in a city, will
     not the people be afraid?
   If there is calamity in a city, will
     not the LORD have done *it?*

7 Surely the Lord GOD does
     nothing,
   Unless He reveals His secret to His
     servants the prophets.
8 A lion has roared!
   Who will not fear?
   The Lord GOD has spoken!
   Who can but prophesy?

9 "Proclaim in the palaces at
     Ashdod,
   And in the palaces in the land of
     Egypt, and say:
   'Assemble on the mountains of
     Samaria;
   See great tumults in her midst,
   And the oppressed within her.
10 For they do not know to do right,'
   Says the LORD,
   'Who store up violence and
     robbery in their palaces.' "

11 Therefore thus says the Lord GOD:

   "An adversary *shall be* all around
     the land;
   He shall sap your strength from
     you,
   And your palaces shall be
     plundered."

12 Thus says the LORD:

   "As a shepherd takes from the
     mouth of a lion
   Two legs or a piece of an ear,
   So shall the children of Israel be
     taken out
   Who dwell in Samaria—
   In the corner of a bed and on the
     edge of a couch!
13 Hear and testify against the house
     of Jacob,"
   Says the Lord GOD, the God of
     hosts,
14 "That in the day I punish Israel for
     their transgressions,
   I will also visit *destruction* on the
     altars of Bethel;
   And the horns of the altar shall be
     cut off
   And fall to the ground.
15 I will destroy the winter house
     along with the summer house;
   The houses of ivory shall perish,
   And the great houses shall have an
     end,"
   Says the LORD.

∼ PSALM 141:1–4 ∼

1 LORD, I cry out to You;
   Make haste to me!
   Give ear to my voice when I cry out
     to You.
2 Let my prayer be set before You *as*
     incense,
   The lifting up of my hands *as* the
     evening sacrifice.

3 Set a guard, O LORD, over my
     mouth;
   Keep watch over the door of my lips.
4 Do not incline my heart to any evil
     thing,
   To practice wicked works
   With men who work iniquity;
   And do not let me eat of their
     delicacies.

∼ PROVERBS 29:25 ∼

25 The fear of man brings a snare,
   But whoever trusts in the LORD shall
     be safe.

～ REVELATION 3:1–22 ～

"And to the angel of the church in Sardis write,

'These things says He who has the seven Spirits of God and the seven stars: "I know your works, that you have a name that you are alive, but you are dead. ² Be watchful, and strengthen the things which remain, that are ready to die, for I have not found your works perfect before God. ³ Remember therefore how you have received and heard; hold fast and repent. Therefore if you will not watch, I will come upon you as a thief, and you will not know what hour I will come upon you. ⁴ You have a few names even in Sardis who have not defiled their garments; and they shall walk with Me in white, for they are worthy. ⁵ He who overcomes shall be clothed in white garments, and I will not blot out his name from the Book of Life; but I will confess his name before My Father and before His angels.

⁶ "He who has an ear, let him hear what the Spirit says to the churches." '

⁷ "And to the angel of the church in Philadelphia write,

'These things says He who is holy, He who is true, "He who has the key of David, He who opens and no one shuts, and shuts and no one opens": ⁸ I know your works. See, I have set before you an open door, and no one can shut it; for you have a little strength, have kept My word, and have not denied My name. ⁹ Indeed I will make *those* of the synagogue of Satan, who say they are Jews and are not, but lie—indeed I will make them come and worship before your feet, and to know that I have loved you. ¹⁰ Because you have kept My command to persevere, I also will keep you from the hour of trial which shall come upon the whole world, to test those who dwell on the earth. ¹¹ Behold, I am coming quickly! Hold fast what you have, that no one may take your crown. ¹² He who overcomes, I will make him a pillar in the temple of My God, and he shall go out no more. I will write on him the name of My God and the name of the city of My God, the New Jerusalem, which comes down out of heaven from My God. And *I will write on him My new name.*

¹³ "He who has an ear, let him hear what the Spirit says to the churches." '

¹⁴ "And to the angel of the church of the Laodiceans write,

'These things says the Amen, the Faithful and True Witness, the Beginning of the creation of God: ¹⁵ "I know your works, that you are neither cold nor hot. I could wish you were cold or hot. ¹⁶ So then, because you are lukewarm, and neither cold nor hot, I will vomit you out of My mouth. ¹⁷ Because you say, 'I am rich, have become wealthy, and have need of nothing'—and do not know that you are wretched, miserable, poor, blind, and naked— ¹⁸ I counsel you to buy from Me gold refined in the fire, that you may be rich; and white garments, that you may be clothed, *that* the shame of your nakedness may not be revealed; and anoint your eyes with eye salve, that you may see. ¹⁹ As many as I love, I rebuke and chasten. Therefore be zealous and repent. ²⁰ Behold, I stand at the door and knock. If anyone hears My voice and opens the door, I will come in to him and dine with him, and he with Me. ²¹ To him who overcomes I will grant to sit with Me on My throne, as I also overcame and sat down with My Father on His throne.

²² "He who has an ear, let him hear what the Spirit says to the churches." ' "

∼ AMOS 4:1—5:27 ∼

1 Hear this word, you cows of
Bashan, who *are* on the
mountain of Samaria,
Who oppress the poor,
Who crush the needy,
Who say to your husbands, "Bring
wine, let us drink!"
2 The Lord GOD has sworn by His
holiness:
"Behold, the days shall come upon
you
When He will take you away with
fishhooks,
And your posterity with
fishhooks.
3 You will go out *through* broken
walls,
Each one straight ahead of her,
And you will be cast into
Harmon,"
Says the LORD.

4 "Come to Bethel and transgress,
At Gilgal multiply transgression;
Bring your sacrifices every
morning,
Your tithes every three days.
5 Offer a sacrifice of thanksgiving
with leaven,
Proclaim *and* announce the
freewill offerings;
For this you love,
You children of Israel!"
Says the Lord GOD.
6 "Also I gave you cleanness of teeth
in all your cities.
And lack of bread in all your
places;
Yet you have not returned to Me,"
Says the LORD.

7 "I also withheld rain from you,
When *there were* still three
months to the harvest.
I made it rain on one city,
I withheld rain from another city.
One part was rained upon,
And where it did not rain the part
withered.
8 So two *or* three cities wandered to
another city to drink water,
But they were not satisfied;

Yet you have not returned to Me,"
Says the LORD.

9 "I blasted you with blight and
mildew.
When your gardens increased,
Your vineyards,
Your fig trees,
And your olive trees,
The locust devoured *them;*
Yet you have not returned to Me,"
Says the LORD.

10 "I sent among you a plague after
the manner of Egypt;
Your young men I killed with a
sword,
Along with your captive horses;
I made the stench of your camps
come up into your nostrils;
Yet you have not returned
to Me,"
Says the LORD.

11 "I overthrew *some* of you,
As God overthrew Sodom and
Gomorrah,
And you were like a firebrand
plucked from the burning;
Yet you have not returned
to Me,"
Says the LORD.

12 "Therefore thus will I do to you,
O Israel;
Because I will do this to you,
Prepare to meet your God,
O Israel!"

13 For behold,
He who forms mountains,
And creates the wind,
Who declares to man what his
thought *is,*
And makes the morning darkness,
Who treads the high places of the
earth—
The LORD God of hosts *is* His
name.

5 Hear this word which I take up against
you, a lamentation, O house of Israel:

Twelve Dollars and Eighty-Two Cents

A young boy was walking along a road one day when he spotted a copper penny shining in the dust. He picked it up and clutched it with excitement. The penny was his, and it had cost him nothing!

From that day on wherever he walked he kept his head down, his eyes closely surveying the ground for more pennies — and perhaps even greater treasure. During his lifetime, he found more money to be sure. In fact, he collected 302 pennies, 24 nickels, 41 dimes, 8 quarters, 3 half-dollar pieces, and 1 worn-out paper dollar — a total of $12.82. He kept his treasure safe, protecting it as a "free legacy" of wealth. He delighted in the fact that the money had cost him nothing.

Or had it? In the course of scouting out his treasure, he had missed seeing the full beauty of 35,127 sunsets, the splendor of 327 rainbows, the beauty of white clouds floating overhead in crystal blue skies, birds soaring, squirrels hopping from branch to branch in the trees above the paths on which he walked, and the brilliance of autumn leaves fluttering against a backdrop of autumn sunshine.

What he had acquired — all $12.82 — certainly wasn't equal to what he had missed.

² The virgin of Israel has fallen;
  She will rise no more.
  She lies forsaken on her land;
  There is no one to raise her up.

³ For thus says the Lord GOD:

  "The city that goes out by a
    thousand
  Shall have a hundred left,
  And that which goes out by a
    hundred
  Shall have ten left to the house of
    Israel."

⁴ For thus says the LORD to the house
of Israel:

  "Seek Me and live;
⁵   But do not seek Bethel,
  Nor enter Gilgal,
  Nor pass over to Beersheba;
  For Gilgal shall surely go into
    captivity,
  And Bethel shall come to nothing.
⁶   Seek the LORD and live,
  Lest He break out like fire *in* the
    house of Joseph,
  And devour *it*,
  With no one to quench *it* in
    Bethel—
⁷   You who turn justice to
    wormwood,
  And lay righteousness to rest in
    the earth!"

⁸ He made the Pleiades and Orion;
  He turns the shadow of death into
    morning
  And makes the day dark as night;
  He calls for the waters of the sea
  And pours them out on the face of
    the earth;
  The LORD *is* His name.
⁹ He rains ruin upon the strong,
  So that fury comes upon the
    fortress.

¹⁰ They hate the one who rebukes in
    the gate,
  And they abhor the one who
    speaks uprightly.
¹¹ Therefore, because you tread
    down the poor
  And take grain taxes from him,

Though you have built houses of
    hewn stone,
  Yet you shall not dwell in them;
  You have planted pleasant
    vineyards,
  But you shall not drink wine from
    them.
¹² For I know your manifold
    transgressions
  And your mighty sins:
  Afflicting the just *and* taking
    bribes;
  Diverting the poor *from justice* at
    the gate.
¹³ Therefore the prudent keep silent
    at that time,
  For it *is* an evil time.

¹⁴ Seek good and not evil,
  That you may live;
  So the LORD God of hosts will be
    with you,
  As you have spoken.
¹⁵ Hate evil, love good;
  Establish justice in the gate.
  It may be that the LORD God of
    hosts
  Will be gracious to the remnant of
    Joseph.

¹⁶ Therefore the LORD God of hosts, the
Lord, says this:

  "*There shall be* wailing in all streets,
  And they shall say in all the
    highways,
  'Alas! Alas!'
  They shall call the farmer to
    mourning,
  And skillful lamenters to wailing.
¹⁷ In all vineyards *there shall be*
    wailing,
  For I will pass through you,"
  Says the LORD.

¹⁸ Woe to you who desire the day of
    the LORD!
  For what good *is* the day of the
    LORD to you?
  It *will be* darkness, and not light.
¹⁹ It *will be* as though a man fled
    from a lion,
  And a bear met him!
  Or *as though* he went into the
    house,

Leaned his hand on the wall,
And a serpent bit him!
20 *Is* not the day of the LORD
    darkness, and not light?
    Is it not very dark, with no
    brightness in it?

21 "I hate, I despise your feast days,
    And I do not savor your sacred
        assemblies.
22 Though you offer Me burnt
        offerings and your grain
        offerings,
    I will not accept *them,*
    Nor will I regard your fattened
        peace offerings.
23 Take away from Me the noise of
        your songs,
    For I will not hear the melody of
        your stringed instruments.
24 But let justice run down like
        water,
    And righteousness like a mighty
        stream.

25 "Did you offer Me sacrifices and
        offerings
    In the wilderness forty years,
        O house of Israel?
26 You also carried Sikkuth your king
    And Chiun, your idols,
    The star of your gods,
    Which you made for yourselves.
27 Therefore I will send you into
        captivity beyond Damascus,"
    Says the LORD, whose name *is* the
        God of hosts.

∼ PSALM 141:5–10 ∼

5 Let the righteous strike me;
    It shall be a kindness.
    And let him rebuke me;
    It shall be as excellent oil;
    Let my head not refuse it.

    For still my prayer *is* against the
        deeds of the wicked.
6 Their judges are overthrown by the
        sides of the cliff,
    And they hear my words, for they
        are sweet.
7 Our bones are scattered at the
        mouth of the grave,

As when one plows and breaks up
    the earth.

8 But my eyes *are* upon You, O GOD
    the Lord;
    In You I take refuge;
    Do not leave my soul destitute.
9 Keep me from the snares they have
        laid for me,
    And from the traps of the workers of
        iniquity.
10 Let the wicked fall into their own
        nets,
    While I escape safely.

∼ PROVERBS 29:26 ∼

26 Many seek the ruler's favor,
    But justice for man *comes* from the
        LORD.

∼ REVELATION 4:1–11 ∼

After these things I looked, and behold, a
door *standing* open in heaven. And the
first voice which I heard *was* like a trumpet speaking with me, saying, "Come up
here, and I will show you things which
must take place after this."

2 Immediately I was in the Spirit; and
behold, a throne set in heaven, and *One*
sat on the throne. 3 And He who sat there
was like a jasper and a sardius stone in
appearance; and *there was* a rainbow
around the throne, in appearance like an
emerald. 4 Around the throne *were*
twenty-four thrones, and on the thrones
I saw twenty-four elders sitting, clothed
in white robes; and they had crowns of
gold on their heads. 5 And from the throne
proceeded lightnings, thunderings, and
voices. Seven lamps of fire *were* burning
before the throne, which are the seven
Spirits of God.

6 Before the throne *there was* a sea of
glass, like crystal. And in the midst of the
throne, and around the throne, *were* four
living creatures full of eyes in front and in
back. 7 The first living creature *was* like a
lion, the second living creature like a calf,
the third living creature had a face like a
man, and the fourth living creature *was*
like a flying eagle. 8 *The* four living creatures, each having six wings, were full of

eyes around and within. And they do not rest day or night, saying:

> "Holy, holy, holy,
> Lord God Almighty,
> Who was and is and is to come!"

[9] Whenever the living creatures give glory and honor and thanks to Him who sits on the throne, who lives forever and ever, [10] the twenty-four elders fall down before Him who sits on the throne and worship Him who lives forever and ever, and cast their crowns before the throne, saying:

> [11] "You are worthy, O Lord,
> To receive glory and honor and
>   power;
> For You created all things,
> And by Your will they exist and
>   were created."

∼ Amos 6:1—7:17 ∼

[1] Woe to you *who are* at ease in
>   Zion,
>   And trust in Mount Samaria,
>   Notable persons in the chief
>   nation,
>   To whom the house of Israel
>   comes!
[2] Go over to Calneh and see;
>   And from there go to Hamath the
>   great;
>   Then go down to Gath of the
>   Philistines.
>   *Are you* better than these
>   kingdoms?
>   Or is their territory greater than
>   your territory?

[3] *Woe to* you who put far off the
>   day of doom,
>   Who cause the seat of violence to
>   come near;
[4] Who lie on beds of ivory,
>   Stretch out on your couches,
>   Eat lambs from the flock
>   And calves from the midst of the
>   stall;
[5] Who sing idly to the sound of
>   stringed instruments,
>   *And* invent for yourselves musical
>   instruments like David;
[6] Who drink wine from bowls,
>   And anoint yourselves with the
>   best ointments,
>   But are not grieved for the
>   affliction of Joseph.
[7] Therefore they shall now go
>   captive as the first of the
>   captives,

>   And those who recline at banquets
>   shall be removed.

[8] The Lord GOD has sworn by
>   Himself,
>   The LORD God of hosts says:
>   "I abhor the pride of Jacob,
>   And hate his palaces;
>   Therefore I will deliver up
>   *the* city
>   And all that is in it."

[9] Then it shall come to pass, that if ten men remain in one house, they shall die. [10] And when a relative *of the dead,* with one who will burn *the bodies,* picks up the bodies to take them out of the house, he will say to one inside the house, *"Are there* any more with you?"

Then someone will say, "None."

And he will say, "Hold your tongue! For we dare not mention the name of the LORD."

[11] For behold, the LORD gives a
>   command:
>   He will break the great house into
>   bits,
>   And the little house into pieces.

[12] Do horses run on rocks?
>   Does *one* plow *there* with oxen?
>   Yet you have turned justice into
>   gall,
>   And the fruit of righteousness into
>   wormwood,
[13] You who rejoice over Lo Debar,

Finding Yourself

One of the central characters of the 1960s TV show, "Dobie Gillis," was Maynard, a "beatnik" with beads, sandals, and goatee who avoided work at all cost. He was more comical than intelligent. In one show, Maynard informed Dobie that he was planning to do what many rock stars were doing during that era — make a pilgrimage to the Far East to consult with a guru about the meaning of life. Maynard did his best to explain to Dobie why he felt he needed to speak with an ancient wise man and find out who he really was.

Dobie finally said to him with candor, "Maynard, you will never find yourself on a mountain in Tibet."

"Why not?" Maynard asked.

"Because you didn't lose yourself on a mountain in Tibet!"

The real "you" isn't to be found on a mountain somewhere, or in any other change of physical location. We find ourselves not by searching outside ourselves, but through the Spirit of God within. When we ask God to reveal to us who He's created us to be, we can rejoice in His loving grace and mercy. He will gently point out our weaknesses and failings and graciously forgive us when we ask Him to. The One Who created you is the One Who knows you — you will only find yourself in Him.

> When my spirit was overwhelmed within me, then You knew my path. In the way in which I walk they have secretly set a snare for me.
>
> *Psalm 142:3*

Who say, "Have we not taken
　　Karnaim for ourselves
　　By our own strength?"

14 "But, behold, I will raise up a
　　　nation against you,
　　O house of Israel,"
　　Says the LORD God of hosts;
　　"And they will afflict you from the
　　　entrance of Hamath
　　To the Valley of the Arabah."

7 Thus the Lord GOD showed me: Behold, He formed locust swarms at the beginning of the late crop; indeed *it was* the late crop after the king's mowings. 2 And so it was, when they had finished eating the grass of the land, that I said:

　　"O Lord GOD, forgive, I pray!
　　　Oh, that Jacob may stand,
　　　For he *is* small!"
3 　　So the LORD relented concerning
　　　this.
　　"It shall not be," said the LORD.

4 Thus the Lord GOD showed me: Behold, the Lord GOD called for conflict by fire, and it consumed the great deep and devoured the territory. 5 Then I said:

　　"O Lord GOD, cease, I pray!
　　　Oh, that Jacob may stand,
　　　For he *is* small!"
6 　　So the LORD relented concerning
　　　this.
　　"This also shall not be," said the
　　　Lord GOD.

7 Thus He showed me: Behold, the Lord stood on a wall *made* with a plumb line, with a plumb line in His hand. 8 And the LORD said to me, "Amos, what do you see?"
　　And I said, "A plumb line."
　　Then the Lord said:

　　"Behold, I am setting a plumb line
　　　In the midst of My people Israel;
　　　I will not pass by them anymore.
9 　　The high places of Isaac shall be
　　　desolate,
　　　And the sanctuaries of Israel shall
　　　be laid waste.

I will rise with the sword against
　　the house of Jeroboam."

10 Then Amaziah the priest of Bethel sent to Jeroboam king of Israel, saying, "Amos has conspired against you in the midst of the house of Israel. The land is not able to bear all his words. 11 For thus Amos has said:

　　'Jeroboam shall die by the sword,
　　　And Israel shall surely be led away
　　　captive
　　From their own land.' "

12 Then Amaziah said to Amos:

　　"Go, you seer!
　　　Flee to the land of Judah.
　　　There eat bread,
　　　And there prophesy.
13 　　But never again prophesy at
　　　Bethel,
　　　For it *is* the king's sanctuary,
　　　And it *is* the royal residence."

14 Then Amos answered, and said to Amaziah:

　　"I *was* no prophet,
　　　Nor *was* I a son of a prophet,
　　　But I *was* a sheepbreeder
　　　And a tender of sycamore fruit.
15 　　Then the LORD took me as I
　　　followed the flock,
　　　And the LORD said to me,
　　　'Go, prophesy to My people
　　　Israel.'
16 　　Now therefore, hear the word of
　　　the LORD:
　　You say, 'Do not prophesy against
　　　Israel,
　　　And do not spout against the
　　　house of Isaac.'

17 "Therefore thus says the LORD:

　　'Your wife shall be a harlot in the
　　　city;
　　　Your sons and daughters shall fall
　　　by the sword;
　　　Your land shall be divided by
　　　survey line;
　　　You shall die in a defiled land;

And Israel shall surely be led away
 captive
From his own land.' "

~ PSALM 142:1–7 ~

1 I cry out to the LORD with my voice;
 With my voice to the LORD I make
  my supplication.
2 I pour out my complaint before
  Him;
 I declare before Him my trouble.

3 When my spirit was overwhelmed
  within me,
 Then You knew my path.
 In the way in which I walk
 They have secretly set a snare for
  me.

4 Look on *my* right hand and see,
 For *there is* no one who
  acknowledges me;
 Refuge has failed me;
 No one cares for my soul.

5 I cried out to You, O LORD:
 I said, "You *are* my refuge,
 My portion in the land of the living.
6 Attend to my cry,
 For I am brought very low;
 Deliver me from my persecutors,
 For they are stronger than I.
7 Bring my soul out of prison,
 That I may praise Your name;
 The righteous shall surround me,
 For You shall deal bountifully with
  me."

~ PROVERBS 29:27 ~

27 An unjust man *is* an abomination to
 the righteous,
 And *he who is* upright in the way *is*
 an abomination to the wicked.

~ REVELATION 5:1–14 ~

And I saw in the right *hand* of Him who
sat on the throne a scroll written inside
and on the back, sealed with seven seals.
2 Then I saw a strong angel proclaiming
with a loud voice, "Who is worthy to open
the scroll and to loose its seals?" 3 And no
one in heaven or on the earth or under
the earth was able to open the scroll, or
to look at it.

4 So I wept much, because no one was
found worthy to open and read the scroll,
or to look at it. 5 But one of the elders
said to me, "Do not weep. Behold, the
Lion of the tribe of Judah, the Root of
David, has prevailed to open the scroll
and to loose its seven seals."

6 And I looked, and behold, in the midst
of the throne and of the four living creatures, and in the midst of the elders, stood
a Lamb as though it had been slain, having seven horns and seven eyes, which are
the seven Spirits of God sent out into
all the earth. 7 Then He came and took
the scroll out of the right hand of Him
who sat on the throne.

8 Now when He had taken the scroll,
the four living creatures and the twenty-
four elders fell down before the Lamb,
each having a harp, and golden bowls
full of incense, which are the prayers of
the saints. 9 And they sang a new song,
saying:

"You are worthy to take
 the scroll,
 And to open its seals;
 For You were slain,
 And have redeemed us to God by
  Your blood
 Out of every tribe and tongue and
  people and nation,
10 And have made us kings and
  priests to our God;
 And we shall reign on the earth."

11 Then I looked, and I heard the voice
of many angels around the throne, the living creatures, and the elders; and the number of them was ten thousand times ten
thousand, and thousands of thousands,
12 saying with a loud voice:

"Worthy is the Lamb who was slain
 To receive power and riches and
  wisdom,
 And strength and honor and glory
  and blessing!"

13 And every creature which is in heaven
and on the earth and under the earth and
such as are in the sea, and all that are in
them, I heard saying:

"Blessing and honor and glory and
      power
   Be to Him who sits on the throne,
   And to the Lamb, forever and ever!"

[14] Then the four living creatures said,
"Amen!" And the twenty-four elders fell
down and worshiped Him who lives forever and ever.

~ AMOS 8:1—9:15 ~

Thus the Lord GOD showed me:
Behold, a basket of summer fruit.
[2] And He said, "Amos, what do
you see?"

So I said, "A basket of summer fruit."

Then the LORD said to me:

"The end has come upon My
      people Israel;
   I will not pass by them anymore.
[3] And the songs of the temple
   Shall be wailing in that day,"
   Says the Lord GOD—
   "Many dead bodies everywhere,
   They shall be thrown out in
      silence."

[4] Hear this, you who swallow up
      the needy,
   And make the poor of the land
      fail,

[5] Saying:

"When will the New Moon be past,
   That we may sell grain?
   And the Sabbath,
   That we may trade wheat?
   Making the ephah small and the
      shekel large,
   Falsifying the scales by deceit,
[6] That we may buy the poor for
      silver,
   And the needy for a pair of
      sandals—
   Even sell the bad wheat?"

[7] The LORD has sworn by the pride
      of Jacob:
   "Surely I will never forget any of
      their works.
[8] Shall the land not tremble for this,

And everyone mourn who dwells
      in it?
   All of it shall swell like the River,
   Heave and subside
   Like the River of Egypt.

[9] "And it shall come to pass in that
      day," says the Lord GOD,
   "That I will make the sun go down
      at noon,
   And I will darken the earth in
      broad daylight;
[10] I will turn your feasts into
      mourning,
   And all your songs into
      lamentation;
   I will bring sackcloth on every
      waist,
   And baldness on every head;
   I will make it like mourning for an
      only *son*,
   And its end like a bitter day.

[11] "Behold, the days are coming," says
      the Lord GOD,
   "That I will send a famine on the
      land,
   Not a famine of bread,
   Nor a thirst for water,
   But of hearing the words of the
      LORD.
[12] They shall wander from sea to sea,
   And from north to east;
   They shall run to and fro, seeking
      the word of the LORD,
   But shall not find *it*.

[13] "In that day the fair virgins
   And strong young men
   Shall faint from thirst.
[14] Those who swear by the sin of
      Samaria,

Find No Excuse for Mediocrity

Someone once asked Al Jolson, a popular musical comedy star of the twenties, what he did to warm up a cold audience. Jolson answered, "Whenever I go out before an audience and don't get the response I feel that I ought to get . . . I don't go back behind the scenes and say to myself, 'That audience is dead from the neck up — it's a bunch of wooden nutmegs.' No, instead I say to myself, 'Look here, Al, what is wrong with you tonight? The audience is all right, but you're all wrong, Al.'"

Many a performer has blamed a poor showing on an audience. Al Jolson took a different approach. He tried to give the best performance of his career to his coldest, most unresponsive audiences, and the result was that before an evening was over, he had them applauding and begging for more.

You'll always be able to find excuses for mediocrity. In fact, a person intent on justifying a bad performance usually has their excuses lined up before the final curtain falls. Choose instead to put your full energy into your performance. Your extra effort will turn an average performance into something outstanding.

Who say,
'As your god lives, O Dan!'
And, 'As the way of Beersheba
lives!'
They shall fall and never rise
again."

9 I saw the Lord standing by the altar,
and He said:

"Strike the doorposts, that the
thresholds may shake,
And break them on the heads of
them all.
I will slay the last of them with the
sword.
He who flees from them shall not
get away,
And he who escapes from them
shall not be delivered.

2 "Though they dig into hell,
From there My hand shall take
them;
Though they climb up to heaven,
From there I will bring them
down;
3 And though they hide themselves
on top of Carmel,
From there I will search and take
them;
Though they hide from My sight
at the bottom of the sea,
From there I will command the
serpent, and it shall bite them;
4 Though they go into captivity
before their enemies,
From there I will command the
sword,
And it shall slay them.
I will set My eyes on them for
harm and not for good."

5 The Lord GOD of hosts,
He who touches the earth and it
melts,
And all who dwell there mourn;
All of it shall swell like the River,
And subside like the River of
Egypt.
6 He who builds His layers in the
sky,
And has founded His strata in the
earth;

Who calls for the waters of the
sea,
And pours them out on the face of
the earth—
The LORD *is* His name.

7 "*Are* you not like the people of
Ethiopia to Me,
O children of Israel?" says the
LORD.
"Did I not bring up Israel from the
land of Egypt,
The Philistines from Caphtor,
And the Syrians from Kir?

8 "Behold, the eyes of the Lord GOD
are on the sinful kingdom,
And I will destroy it from the face
of the earth;
Yet I will not utterly destroy the
house of Jacob,"
Says the LORD.

9 "For surely I will command,
And will sift the house of Israel
among all nations,
As *grain* is sifted in a sieve;
Yet not the smallest grain shall fall
to the ground.
10 All the sinners of My people shall
die by the sword,
Who say, 'The calamity shall not
overtake nor confront us.'

11 "On that day I will raise up
The tabernacle of David, which
has fallen down,
And repair its damages;
I will raise up its ruins,
And rebuild it as in the days of old;
12 That they may possess the
remnant of Edom,
And all the Gentiles who are
called by My name,"
Says the LORD who does this
thing.

13 "Behold, the days are coming," says
the LORD,
"When the plowman shall overtake
the reaper,
And the treader of grapes him
who sows seed;
The mountains shall drip with
sweet wine,

And all the hills shall flow *with it*.
14 I will bring back the captives of
   My people Israel;
   They shall build the waste cities
   and inhabit *them;*
   They shall plant vineyards and
   drink wine from them;
   They shall also make gardens and
   eat fruit from them.
15 I will plant them in their land,
   And no longer shall they be pulled
   up
   From the land I have given them,"
   Says the LORD your God.

~ PSALM 143:1–6 ~

1 Hear my prayer, O LORD,
   Give ear to my supplications!
   In Your faithfulness answer me,
   And in Your righteousness.
2 Do not enter into judgment with
   Your servant,
   For in Your sight no one living is
   righteous.

3 For the enemy has persecuted my
   soul;
   He has crushed my life to the
   ground;
   He has made me dwell in darkness,
   Like those who have long been dead.
4 Therefore my spirit is overwhelmed
   within me;
   My heart within me is distressed.

5 I remember the days of old;
   I meditate on all Your works;
   I muse on the work of Your hands.
6 I spread out my hands to You;
   My soul *longs* for You like a thirsty
   land.   Selah

~ PROVERBS 30:1–4 ~

The words of Agur the son of Jakeh,
his utterance. This man declared to
Ithiel—to Ithiel and Ucal:

2 Surely I *am* more stupid than *any*
   man,
   And do not have the understanding
   of a man.
3 I neither learned wisdom

Nor have knowledge of the Holy
   One.

4 Who has ascended into heaven, or
   descended?
   Who has gathered the wind in His
   fists?
   Who has bound the waters in a
   garment?
   Who has established all the ends of
   the earth?
   What *is* His name, and what *is* His
   Son's name,
   If you know?

~ REVELATION 6:1–17 ~

Now I saw when the Lamb opened one
of the seals; and I heard one of the four
living creatures saying with a voice like
thunder, "Come and see." 2 And I looked,
and behold, a white horse. He who sat on
it had a bow; and a crown was given to
him, and he went out conquering and
to conquer.

3 When He opened the second seal, I
heard the second living creature saying,
"Come and see." 4 Another horse, fiery
red, went out. And it was granted to the
one who sat on it to take peace from
the earth, and that *people* should kill one
another; and there was given to him a
great sword.

5 When He opened the third seal, I
heard the third living creature say, "Come
and see." So I looked, and behold, a black
horse, and he who sat on it had a pair of
scales in his hand. 6 And I heard a voice in
the midst of the four living creatures saying, "A quart of wheat for a denarius, and
three quarts of barley for a denarius;
and do not harm the oil and the wine."

7 When He opened the fourth seal, I
heard the voice of the fourth living creature saying, "Come and see." 8 So I
looked, and behold, a pale horse. And the
name of him who sat on it was Death,
and Hades followed with him. And power
was given to them over a fourth of the
earth, to kill with sword, with hunger,
with death, and by the beasts of the earth.

9 When He opened the fifth seal, I saw
under the altar the souls of those who had
been slain for the word of God and for
the testimony which they held. 10 And they

cried with a loud voice, saying, "How long, O Lord, holy and true, until You judge and avenge our blood on those who dwell on the earth?" [11] Then a white robe was given to each of them; and it was said to them that they should rest a little while longer, until both *the number of* their fellow servants and their brethren, who would be killed as they *were,* was completed.

[12] I looked when He opened the sixth seal, and behold, there was a great earthquake; and the sun became black as sackcloth of hair, and the moon became like blood. [13] And the stars of heaven fell to the earth, as a fig tree drops its late figs when it is shaken by a mighty wind. [14] Then the sky receded as a scroll when it is rolled up, and every mountain and island was moved out of its place. [15] And the kings of the earth, the great men, the rich men, the commanders, the mighty men, every slave and every free man, hid themselves in the caves and in the rocks of the mountains, [16] and said to the mountains and rocks, "Fall on us and hide us from the face of Him who sits on the throne and from the wrath of the Lamb! [17] For the great day of His wrath has come, and who is able to stand?"

READING 351 · DECEMBER 17

~ OBADIAH 1–21 ~

The vision of Obadiah.

Thus says the Lord GOD
  concerning Edom
(We have heard a report from the
  LORD,
And a messenger has been sent
  among the nations, *saying,*
"Arise, and let us rise up against her
  for battle"):

[2] "Behold, I will make you small
  among the nations;
You shall be greatly despised.
[3] The pride of your heart has
  deceived you,
You who dwell in the clefts of the
  rock,
Whose habitation is high;
You who say in your heart, 'Who
  will bring me down to the
  ground?'
[4] Though you ascend *as* high as the
  eagle,
And though you set your nest
  among the stars,
From there I will bring you
  down," says the LORD.

[5] "If thieves had come to you,
If robbers by night—
Oh, how you will be cut off!—
Would they not have stolen till
  they had enough?
If grape-gatherers had come to
  you,
Would they not have left *some*
  gleanings?

[6] "Oh, how Esau shall be searched
  out!
How his hidden treasures shall be
  sought after!
[7] All the men in your
  confederacy
Shall force you to the border;
The men at peace with you
Shall deceive you *and* prevail
  against you.
Those who eat your bread shall lay
  a trap for you.
No one is aware of it.

[8] "Will I not in that day," says the
  LORD,
"Even destroy the wise *men* from
  Edom,
And understanding from the
  mountains of Esau?
[9] Then your mighty men, O Teman,
  shall be dismayed,
To the end that everyone from the
  mountains of Esau
May be cut off by slaughter.

Pray Without Ceasing

> Cause me to know the way in which I should walk, for I lift up my soul to You.
>
> *Psalm 143:8*

The wife of a dairy farmer habitually rose at 4:30 each morning to milk the cows. When she recognized the need to begin each morning with prayer, she began rising thirty minutes earlier to pray before going to the barn. "Just made a startling discovery!" she wrote in her journal shortly after starting this practice. "The time on my knees each morning is the *preparation* for prayer. The rest of the day then *becomes* the prayer."

The great Christian doctor Paul Tournier had a similar experience with prayer. Determined to have a time of prayer before his early rounds, he went to his study, took out his pocket watch, and sat down. He planned to commit an hour to prayer. After a few minutes, he opened his eyes and discovered only a few minutes had elapsed! The next time he looked at his watch, it had been only a few more minutes.

Finally, the hour was over. He was disappointed that he had felt nothing during his prayer time. As he prepared to rise from his desk, he had an impulse to remain seated for a few more moments. He said it was in those moments, that God visited his heart. He was convinced that God had used the hour to test his obedience; the reward came in the brief time that followed.

The Bible tells us to "pray without ceasing." On the surface, that admonition seems impossible. How can we carry out our responsibilities if we are locked in a prayer closet? However, if you begin the day in prayer and maintain the attitude of prayer in your heart, your entire day can be spent in communion with God, dwelling in His presence.

10 "For violence against your brother
    Jacob,
    Shame shall cover you,
    And you shall be cut off forever.
11 In the day that you stood on the
    other side—
    In the day that strangers carried
    captive his forces,
    When foreigners entered his gates
    And cast lots for Jerusalem—
    Even you *were* as one of them.

12 "But you should not have gazed on
    the day of your brother
    In the day of his captivity;
    Nor should you have rejoiced over
    the children of Judah
    In the day of their destruction;
    Nor should you have spoken
    proudly
    In the day of distress.
13 You should not have entered the
    gate of My people
    In the day of their calamity.
    Indeed, you should not have gazed
    on their affliction
    In the day of their calamity,
    Nor laid *hands* on their substance
    In the day of their calamity.
14 You should not have stood at the
    crossroads
    To cut off those among them who
    escaped;
    Nor should you have delivered up
    those among them who
    remained
    In the day of distress.

15 "For the day of the LORD upon all
    the nations *is* near;
    As you have done, it shall be done
    to you;
    Your reprisal shall return upon
    your own head.
16 For as you drank on My holy
    mountain,
    So shall all the nations drink
    continually;
    Yes, they shall drink, and swallow,
    And they shall be as though they
    had never been.

17 "But on Mount Zion there shall be
    deliverance,
    And there shall be holiness;

The house of Jacob shall possess
    their possessions.
18 The house of Jacob shall be a fire,
    And the house of Joseph a flame;
    But the house of Esau *shall be*
    stubble;
    They shall kindle them and
    devour them,
    And no survivor shall *remain* of
    the house of Esau,"
    For the LORD has spoken.

19 The South shall possess the
    mountains of Esau,
    And the Lowland shall possess
    Philistia.
    They shall possess the fields of
    Ephraim
    And the fields of Samaria.
    Benjamin *shall possess* Gilead.
20 And the captives of this host of the
    children of Israel
    Shall possess the land of the
    Canaanites
    As far as Zarephath.
    The captives of Jerusalem who are
    in Sepharad
    Shall possess the cities of the
    South.
21 Then saviors shall come to Mount
    Zion
    To judge the mountains of Esau,
    And the kingdom shall be the
    LORD's.

~ PSALM 143:7–12 ~

7 Answer me speedily, O LORD;
    My spirit fails!
    Do not hide Your face from me,
    Lest I be like those who go down
    into the pit.
8 Cause me to hear Your
    lovingkindness in the morning,
    For in You do I trust;
    Cause me to know the way in which
    I should walk,
    For I lift up my soul to You.

9 Deliver me, O LORD, from my
    enemies;
    In You I take shelter.
10 Teach me to do Your will,
    For You *are* my God;

Your Spirit *is* good.
Lead me in the land of uprightness.

¹¹ Revive me, O LORD, for Your name's
sake!
For Your righteousness' sake bring
my soul out of trouble.
¹² In Your mercy cut off my enemies,
And destroy all those who afflict my
soul;
For I *am* Your servant.

~ PROVERBS 30:5 ~

⁵ Every word of God *is* pure;
He *is* a shield to those who put their
trust in Him.

~ REVELATION 7:1–17 ~

After these things I saw four angels
standing at the four corners of the earth,
holding the four winds of the earth, that
the wind should not blow on the earth,
on the sea, or on any tree. ² Then I saw
another angel ascending from the east,
having the seal of the living God. And he
cried with a loud voice to the four angels
to whom it was granted to harm the earth
and the sea, ³ saying, "Do not harm the
earth, the sea, or the trees till we have
sealed the servants of our God on their
foreheads." ⁴ And I heard the number of
those who were sealed. One hundred *and*
forty-four thousand of all the tribes of the
children of Israel *were* sealed:

⁵ of the tribe of Judah twelve
thousand *were* sealed;
of the tribe of Reuben twelve
thousand *were* sealed;
of the tribe of Gad twelve
thousand *were* sealed;
⁶ of the tribe of Asher twelve
thousand *were* sealed;
of the tribe of Naphtali twelve
thousand *were* sealed;
of the tribe of Manasseh twelve
thousand *were* sealed;
⁷ of the tribe of Simeon twelve
thousand *were* sealed;

of the tribe of Levi twelve
thousand *were* sealed;
of the tribe of Issachar twelve
thousand *were* sealed;
⁸ of the tribe of Zebulun twelve
thousand *were* sealed;
of the tribe of Joseph twelve
thousand *were* sealed;
of the tribe of Benjamin twelve
thousand *were* sealed.

⁹ After these things I looked, and be-
hold, a great multitude which no one
could number, of all nations, tribes,
peoples, and tongues, standing before the
throne and before the Lamb, clothed with
white robes, with palm branches in their
hands, ¹⁰ and crying out with a loud voice,
saying, "Salvation *belongs* to our God who
sits on the throne, and to the Lamb!" ¹¹ All
the angels stood around the throne
and the elders and the four living creatures, and fell on their faces before the
throne and worshiped God, ¹² saying:

"Amen! Blessing and glory and
wisdom,
Thanksgiving and honor and
power and might,
Be to our God forever and ever.
Amen."

¹³ Then one of the elders answered,
saying to me, "Who are these arrayed in
white robes, and where did they come
from?"
¹⁴ And I said to him, "Sir, you know."
So he said to me, "These are the ones
who come out of the great tribulation, and
washed their robes and made them white
in the blood of the Lamb. ¹⁵ Therefore
they are before the throne of God, and
serve Him day and night in His temple.
And He who sits on the throne will dwell
among them. ¹⁶ They shall neither hunger anymore nor thirst anymore; the sun
shall not strike them, nor any heat; ¹⁷ for
the Lamb who is in the midst of the throne
will shepherd them and lead them to living fountains of waters. And God will
wipe away every tear from their eyes."

~ JONAH 1:1—4:11 ~

Now the word of the LORD came to Jonah the son of Amittai, saying, ² "Arise, go to Nineveh, that great city, and cry out against it; for their wickedness has come up before Me." ³ But Jonah arose to flee to Tarshish from the presence of the LORD. He went down to Joppa, and found a ship going to Tarshish; so he paid the fare, and went down into it, to go with them to Tarshish from the presence of the LORD.

⁴ But the LORD sent out a great wind on the sea, and there was a mighty tempest on the sea, so that the ship was about to be broken up.

⁵ Then the mariners were afraid; and every man cried out to his god, and threw the cargo that *was* in the ship into the sea, to lighten the load. But Jonah had gone down into the lowest parts of the ship, had lain down, and was fast asleep.

⁶ So the captain came to him, and said to him, "What do you mean, sleeper? Arise, call on your God; perhaps your God will consider us, so that we may not perish."

⁷ And they said to one another, "Come, let us cast lots, that we may know for whose cause this trouble *has come* upon us." So they cast lots, and the lot fell on Jonah. ⁸ Then they said to him, "Please tell us! For whose cause *is* this trouble upon us? What is your occupation? And where do you come from? What is your country? And of what people are you?"

⁹ So he said to them, "I *am* a Hebrew; and I fear the LORD, the God of heaven, who made the sea and the dry *land*."

¹⁰ Then the men were exceedingly afraid, and said to him, "Why have you done this?" For the men knew that he fled from the presence of the LORD, because he had told them. ¹¹ Then they said to him, "What shall we do to you that the sea may be calm for us?"—for the sea was growing more tempestuous.

¹² And he said to them, "Pick me up and throw me into the sea; then the sea will become calm for you. For I know that this great tempest *is* because of me."

¹³ Nevertheless the men rowed hard to return to land, but they could not, for the sea continued to grow more tempestuous against them. ¹⁴ Therefore they cried out to the LORD and said, "We pray, O LORD, please do not let us perish for this man's life, and do not charge us with innocent blood; for You, O LORD, have done as it pleased You." ¹⁵ So they picked up Jonah and threw him into the sea, and the sea ceased from its raging. ¹⁶ Then the men feared the LORD exceedingly, and offered a sacrifice to the LORD and took vows.

¹⁷ Now the LORD had prepared a great fish to swallow Jonah. And Jonah was in the belly of the fish three days and three nights.

2 Then Jonah prayed to the LORD his God from the fish's belly. ² And he said:

"I cried out to the LORD because of
    my affliction,
And He answered me.

"Out of the belly of Sheol I cried,
    And You heard my voice.
³   For You cast me into the deep,
    Into the heart of the seas,
    And the floods surrounded me;
    All Your billows and Your waves
        passed over me.
⁴   Then I said, 'I have been cast out
        of Your sight;
    Yet I will look again toward Your
        holy temple.'
⁵   The waters surrounded me, *even*
        to my soul;
    The deep closed around me;
    Weeds were wrapped around my
        head.
⁶   I went down to the moorings of
        the mountains;
    The earth with its bars *closed*
        behind me forever;
    Yet You have brought up my life
        from the pit,
    O LORD, my God.

⁷   "When my soul fainted within me,
    I remembered the LORD;
    And my prayer went *up* to You,
    Into Your holy temple.

Giving Up Control

I cried out to the Lord because of my affliction, and He answered me. Out of the belly of Sheol I cried, and You heard my voice.

Jonah 2:2

After two failed attempts at landing, the balloonist panicked. He frantically searched for a third spot to attempt a touchdown, but all he could see for miles was thick woods. He had only half of one tank of fuel left. Nevertheless, he felt his only option was to hit the burners and try to find a clearing. Nearly paralyzed with fear, he cried out to God, "Help me. Take control of this situation. Lord, find me a safe place to land!" With that prayer, a feeling of calm came over him. His fists unclenched and he felt a wave of peace.

Even so, the landscape below sped by and he had no idea where his ground crew might be. Then he spotted a small clearing directly ahead — and in it, two of the biggest bulls he had ever seen. "Lord, I trusted you to find me a safe place to land, and I trust you completely with those bulls!" He held on tightly as the basket hit the ground roughly, tipped over, and was dragged along the ground for about fifty yards.

To his amazement, the bulls seemed oblivious to all the commotion. Almost instantly, his ground crew came racing toward him. One of them said, "You got caught in some nasty wind shear. It's a miracle you kept control." The balloonist knew the true miracle. *The true miracle was that he had given up control.*

God may not always answer our prayers the way we think they ought to be answered. When we give up all control, and simply trust Him, he will handle any obstacle that gets in our way.

8 "Those who regard worthless idols
　Forsake their own Mercy.
9 But I will sacrifice to You
　With the voice of thanksgiving;
　I will pay what I have vowed.
　Salvation *is* of the LORD."

10 So the LORD spoke to the fish, and it vomited Jonah onto dry *land.*

3 Now the word of the LORD came to Jonah the second time, saying, 2 "Arise, go to Nineveh, that great city, and preach to it the message that I tell you." 3 So Jonah arose and went to Nineveh, according to the word of the LORD. Now Nineveh was an exceedingly great city, a three-day journey *in extent.* 4 And Jonah began to enter the city on the first day's walk. Then he cried out and said, "Yet forty days, and Nineveh shall be overthrown!"

5 So the people of Nineveh believed God, proclaimed a fast, and put on sackcloth, from the greatest to the least of them. 6 Then word came to the king of Nineveh; and he arose from his throne and laid aside his robe, covered *himself* with sackcloth and sat in ashes. 7 And he caused *it* to be proclaimed and published throughout Nineveh by the decree of the king and his nobles, saying,

Let neither man nor beast, herd nor flock, taste anything; do not let them eat, or drink water. 8 But let man and beast be covered with sackcloth, and cry mightily to God; yes, let every one turn from his evil way and from the violence that is in his hands. 9 Who can tell *if* God will turn and relent, and turn away from His fierce anger, so that we may not perish?

10 Then God saw their works, that they turned from their evil way; and God relented from the disaster that He had said He would bring upon them, and He did not do it.

4 But it displeased Jonah exceedingly, and he became angry. 2 So he prayed to the LORD, and said, "Ah, LORD, was not this what I said when I was still in my country? Therefore I fled previously to Tarshish; for I know that You *are* a gracious and merciful God, slow to anger and abundant in lovingkindness, One who relents from doing harm. 3 Therefore now, O LORD, please take my life from me, for *it is* better for me to die than to live!"

4 Then the LORD said, "*Is it* right for you to be angry?"

5 So Jonah went out of the city and sat on the east side of the city. There he made himself a shelter and sat under it in the shade, till he might see what would become of the city. 6 And the LORD God prepared a plant and made it come up over Jonah, that it might be shade for his head to deliver him from his misery. So Jonah was very grateful for the plant. 7 But as morning dawned the next day God prepared a worm, and it *so* damaged the plant that it withered. 8 And it happened, when the sun arose, that God prepared a vehement east wind; and the sun beat on Jonah's head, so that he grew faint. Then he wished death for himself, and said, "*It is* better for me to die than to live."

9 Then God said to Jonah, "*Is it* right for you to be angry about the plant?"

And he said, "*It is* right for me to be angry, even to death!"

10 But the LORD said, "You have had pity on the plant for which you have not labored, nor made it grow, which came up in a night and perished in a night. 11 And should I not pity Nineveh, that great city, in which are more than one hundred and twenty thousand persons who cannot discern between their right hand and their left—and much livestock?"

～ PSALM 144:1–8 ～

1 Blessed *be* the LORD my Rock,
　Who trains my hands for war,
　And my fingers for battle—
2 My lovingkindness and my fortress,
　My high tower and my deliverer,
　My shield and *the One* in whom I
　take refuge,
　Who subdues my people under me.

3 LORD, what *is* man, that You take
　knowledge of him?
　Or the son of man, that You are
　mindful of him?

4 Man is like a breath;
His days *are* like a passing shadow.

5 Bow down Your heavens, O LORD,
and come down;
Touch the mountains, and they shall
smoke.
6 Flash forth lightning and scatter
them;
Shoot out Your arrows and destroy
them.
7 Stretch out Your hand from above;
Rescue me and deliver me out of
great waters,
From the hand of foreigners,
8 Whose mouth speaks lying words,
And whose right hand *is* a right hand
of falsehood.

∼ PROVERBS 30:6–9 ∼

6 Do not add to His words,
Lest He rebuke you, and you be
found a liar.

7 Two *things* I request of You
(Deprive me not before I die):
8 Remove falsehood and lies far from
me;
Give me neither poverty nor
riches—
Feed me with the food allotted to
me;
9 Lest I be full and deny *You,*
And say, "Who *is* the LORD?"
Or lest I be poor and steal,
And profane the name of my God.

∼ REVELATION 8:1–13 ∼

When He opened the seventh seal, there
was silence in heaven for about half an
hour. 2 And I saw the seven angels who
stand before God, and to them were given
seven trumpets. 3 Then another angel,
having a golden censer, came and stood
at the altar. He was given much incense,
that he should offer *it* with the prayers of
all the saints upon the golden altar which
was before the throne. 4 And the smoke
of the incense, with the prayers of
the saints, ascended before God from the
angel's hand. 5 Then the angel took the
censer, filled it with fire from the altar,
and threw *it* to the earth. And there were
noises, thunderings, lightnings, and an
earthquake.

6 So the seven angels who had the seven
trumpets prepared themselves to sound.

7 The first angel sounded: And hail and
fire followed, mingled with blood,
and they were thrown to the earth. And a
third of the trees were burned up, and all
green grass was burned up.

8 Then the second angel sounded: And
something like a great mountain burning
with fire was thrown into the sea, and
a third of the sea became blood. 9 And a
third of the living creatures in the sea died,
and a third of the ships were destroyed.

10 Then the third angel sounded: And a
great star fell from heaven, burning like
a torch, and it fell on a third of the rivers
and on the springs of water. 11 The name
of the star is Wormwood. A third of the
waters became wormwood, and many
men died from the water, because it was
made bitter.

12 Then the fourth angel sounded: And
a third of the sun was struck, a third of
the moon, and a third of the stars, so that
a third of them were darkened. A third of
the day did not shine, and likewise the
night.

13 And I looked, and I heard an angel
flying through the midst of heaven, saying with a loud voice, "Woe, woe, woe
to the inhabitants of the earth, because of
the remaining blasts of the trumpet of the
three angels who are about to sound!"

∽ MICAH 1:1—3:12 ∽

The word of the LORD that came to Micah of Moresheth in the days of Jotham, Ahaz, *and* Hezekiah, kings of Judah, which he saw concerning Samaria and Jerusalem.

2 Hear, all you peoples!
Listen, O earth, and all that is in it!
Let the Lord GOD be a witness against you,
The Lord from His holy temple.

3 For behold, the LORD is coming out of His place;
He will come down
And tread on the high places of the earth.
4 The mountains will melt under Him,
And the valleys will split
Like wax before the fire,
Like waters poured down a steep place.
5 All this is for the transgression of Jacob
And for the sins of the house of Israel.
What *is* the transgression of Jacob?
Is it not Samaria?
And what *are* the high places of Judah?
Are they not Jerusalem?

6 "Therefore I will make Samaria a heap of ruins in the field,
Places for planting a vineyard;
I will pour down her stones into the valley,
And I will uncover her foundations.
7 All her carved images shall be beaten to pieces,
And all her pay as a harlot shall be burned with the fire;
All her idols I will lay desolate,
For she gathered *it* from the pay of a harlot,
And they shall return to the pay of a harlot."

8 Therefore I will wail and howl,
I will go stripped and naked;
I will make a wailing like the jackals
And a mourning like the ostriches,
9 For her wounds *are* incurable.
For it has come to Judah;
It has come to the gate of My people—
To Jerusalem.

10 Tell *it* not in Gath,
Weep not at all;
In Beth Aphrah
Roll yourself in the dust.
11 Pass by in naked shame, you inhabitant of Shaphir;
The inhabitant of Zaanan does not go out.
Beth Ezel mourns;
Its place to stand is taken away from you.

12 For the inhabitant of Maroth pined for good,
But disaster came down from the LORD
To the gate of Jerusalem.
13 O inhabitant of Lachish,
Harness the chariot to the swift steeds
(She *was* the beginning of sin to the daughter of Zion),
For the transgressions of Israel were found in you.

14 Therefore you shall give presents to Moresheth Gath;
The houses of Achzib *shall be* a lie to the kings of Israel.
15 I will yet bring an heir to you, O inhabitant of Mareshah;
The glory of Israel shall come to Adullam.
16 Make yourself bald and cut off your hair,
Because of your precious children;
Enlarge your baldness like an eagle,
For they shall go from you into captivity.

Look for the Beauty

One rainy day a woman overheard someone say, "What miserable weather!" She looked out her office window to see a big fat robin using a nearby puddle of water for a bathtub. He was splashing and fluttering, thoroughly enjoying himself. She couldn't help but think, Miserable for whom? It's all a matter of perspective.

That's a lesson that Lincoln Steffens learned as a young boy. He was watching an artist paint a picture of a muddy river. He told the artist he didn't like the picture because there was so much "mud" in it. The artist admitted there was mud in the picture, but what he saw was the beautiful colors and contrasts of the light against the dark.

Steffens later preached in a sermon, "Mud or beauty — which do we look for as we journey through life? If we look for mud and ugliness, we find them — they are there. Just as the artist found beauty in the muddy river, because that is what he was looking for, we will find, in the stream of life, those things which we desire to see. To look for the best and see the beautiful is the way to get the best out of life each day."

> Happy are the people who are in such a state; happy are the people whose God is the Lord!
>
> *Psalm 144:15*

2 Woe to those who devise iniquity,
And work out evil on their beds!
At morning light they practice it,
Because it is in the power of their
hand.
2 They covet fields and take *them*
by violence,
Also houses, and seize *them*.
So they oppress a man and his
house,
A man and his inheritance.

3 Therefore thus says the LORD:

"Behold, against this family I am
devising disaster,
From which you cannot remove
your necks;
Nor shall you walk haughtily,
For this *is* an evil time.
4 In that day *one* shall take up a
proverb against you,
And lament with a bitter
lamentation, saying:
'We are utterly destroyed!
He has changed the heritage of my
people;
How He has removed *it* from me!
To a turncoat He has divided our
fields.' "

5 Therefore you will have no one to
determine boundaries by lot
In the assembly of the LORD.

6 "Do not prattle," *you say to those*
who prophesy.
So they shall not prophesy to you;
They shall not return insult for
insult.
7 *You who are* named the house of
Jacob:
"Is the Spirit of the LORD
restricted?
Are these His doings?
Do not My words do good
To him who walks uprightly?

8 "Lately My people have risen up as
an enemy—
You pull off the robe with the
garment
From those who trust *you*, as they
pass by,
Like men returned from war.
9 The women of My people you
cast out
From their pleasant houses;
From their children
You have taken away My glory
forever.

10 "Arise and depart,
For this *is* not *your* rest;
Because it is defiled, it shall
destroy,
Yes, with utter destruction.
11 If a man should walk in a false
spirit
And speak a lie, *saying,*
'I will prophesy to you of wine and
drink,'
Even he would be the prattler of
this people.

12 "I will surely assemble all of you,
O Jacob,
I will surely gather the remnant of
Israel;
I will put them together like sheep
of the fold,
Like a flock in the midst of their
pasture;
They shall make a loud noise
because of *so many* people.
13 The one who breaks open will
come up before them;
They will break out,
Pass through the gate,
And go out by it;
Their king will pass before them,
With the LORD at their head."

3 And I said:

"Hear now, O heads of Jacob,
And you rulers of the house of
Israel:
Is it not for you to know justice?
2 You who hate good and love evil;
Who strip the skin from My
people,
And the flesh from their bones;
3 Who also eat the flesh of My
people,
Flay their skin from them,
Break their bones,
And chop *them* in pieces

Like *meat* for the pot,
Like flesh in the caldron."

4 Then they will cry to the LORD,
But He will not hear them;
He will even hide His face from
them at that time,
Because they have been evil in
their deeds.

5 Thus says the LORD concerning
the prophets
Who make my people stray;
Who chant "Peace"
While they chew with their teeth,
But who prepare war against him
Who puts nothing into their
mouths:
6 "Therefore you shall have night
without vision,
And you shall have darkness
without divination;
The sun shall go down on the
prophets,
And the day shall be dark for
them.
7 So the seers shall be ashamed,
And the diviners abashed;
Indeed they shall all cover their
lips;
For *there is* no answer from God."

8 But truly I am full of power by the
Spirit of the LORD,
And of justice and might,
To declare to Jacob his
transgression
And to Israel his sin.
9 Now hear this,
You heads of the house of Jacob
And rulers of the house of Israel,
Who abhor justice
And pervert all equity,
10 Who build up Zion with
bloodshed
And Jerusalem with iniquity:
11 Her heads judge for a bribe,
Her priests teach for pay,
And her prophets divine for
money.
Yet they lean on the LORD, and
say,
"Is not the LORD among us?
No harm can come upon us."
12 Therefore because of you

Zion shall be plowed *like* a field,
Jerusalem shall become heaps of
ruins,
And the mountain of the temple
Like the bare hills of the forest.

～ PSALM 144:9–15 ～

9 I will sing a new song to You,
O God;
On a harp of ten strings I will sing
praises to You,
10 *The One* who gives salvation to
kings,
Who delivers David His servant
From the deadly sword.

11 Rescue me and deliver me from the
hand of foreigners,
Whose mouth speaks lying words,
And whose right hand *is* a right hand
of falsehood—
12 That our sons *may be* as plants
grown up in their youth;
That our daughters *may be* as pillars,
Sculptured in palace style;
13 *That* our barns *may be* full,
Supplying all kinds of produce;
That our sheep may bring forth
thousands
And ten thousands in our fields;
14 *That* our oxen *may be* well laden;
That there be no breaking in or going
out;
That there be no outcry in our
streets.
15 Happy *are* the people who are in
such a state;
Happy *are* the people whose God *is*
the LORD!

～ PROVERBS 30:10 ～

10 Do not malign a servant to his
master,
Lest he curse you, and you be found
guilty.

～ REVELATION 9:1–21 ～

Then the fifth angel sounded: And I saw
a star fallen from heaven to the earth. To
him was given the key to the bottomless
pit. 2 And he opened the bottomless pit,

and smoke arose out of the pit like the smoke of a great furnace. So the sun and the air were darkened because of the smoke of the pit. ³ Then out of the smoke locusts came upon the earth. And to them was given power, as the scorpions of the earth have power. ⁴ They were commanded not to harm the grass of the earth, or any green thing, or any tree, but only those men who do not have the seal of God on their foreheads. ⁵ And they were not given *authority* to kill them, but to torment them *for* five months. Their torment *was* like the torment of a scorpion when it strikes a man. ⁶ In those days men will seek death and will not find it; they will desire to die, and death will flee from them.

⁷ The shape of the locusts was like horses prepared for battle. On their heads were crowns of something like gold, and their faces *were* like the faces of men. ⁸ They had hair like women's hair, and their teeth were like lions' *teeth*. ⁹ And they had breastplates like breastplates of iron, and the sound of their wings *was* like the sound of chariots with many horses running into battle. ¹⁰ They had tails like scorpions, and there were stings in their tails. Their power *was* to hurt men five months. ¹¹ And they had as king over them the angel of the bottomless pit, whose name in Hebrew *is* Abaddon, but in Greek he has the name Apollyon.

¹² One woe is past. Behold, still two more woes are coming after these things.

¹³ Then the sixth angel sounded: And I heard a voice from the four horns of the golden altar which is before God, ¹⁴ saying to the sixth angel who had the trumpet, "Release the four angels who are bound at the great river Euphrates." ¹⁵ So the four angels, who had been prepared for the hour and day and month and year, were released to kill a third of mankind. ¹⁶ Now the number of the army of the horsemen *was* two hundred million; I heard the number of them. ¹⁷ And thus I saw the horses in the vision: those who sat on them had breastplates of fiery red, hyacinth blue, and sulfur yellow; and the heads of the horses *were* like the heads of lions; and out of their mouths came fire, smoke, and brimstone. ¹⁸ By these three *plagues* a third of mankind was killed— by the fire and the smoke and the brimstone which came out of their mouths. ¹⁹ For their power is in their mouth and in their tails; for their tails *are* like serpents, having heads; and with them they do harm.

²⁰ But the rest of mankind, who were not killed by these plagues, did not repent of the works of their hands, that they should not worship demons, and idols of gold, silver, brass, stone, and wood, which can neither see nor hear nor walk. ²¹ And they did not repent of their murders or their sorceries or their sexual immorality or their thefts.

READING 354 · DECEMBER 20

~ MICAH 4:1—5:15 ~

1   Now it shall come to pass in the latter days
    That the mountain of the LORD's house
    Shall be established on the top of the mountains,
    And shall be exalted above the hills;
    And peoples shall flow to it.
2   Many nations shall come and say,
    "Come, and let us go up to the mountain of the LORD,
    To the house of the God of Jacob;
    He will teach us His ways,
    And we shall walk in His paths."
    For out of Zion the law shall go forth,
    And the word of the LORD from Jerusalem.
3   He shall judge between many peoples,
    And rebuke strong nations afar off;

It's All About Relationship

Imagine for a moment that someone you love comes to you and asks to borrow a small sum of money. You no doubt would lend it gladly, in part because of the close relationship you share.

Now imagine that this same person continues to come to you, asking for loans, food, clothing, the use of your car, a place to stay, and to borrow tools and appliances. While you do love this person, you would probably begin to feel that something was wrong. It's not the asking, but the attitude.

What causes the dilemma in this type of situation? The person who is coming with requests no longer sees his friend as someone with thoughts and feelings, but as a source of goods and services. From the perspective of the one who is giving, the friend with whom dreams and innermost thoughts have been shared is now perceived as being concerned only with getting his own needs met.

So often we come to God in prayer with our request list in hand — "God, please do this. . . ." or "God, I want. . . ." We are wise to reconsider our relationship with God in prayer. Who is this One to Whom we pray? How good has He been to us? Doesn't He deserve our praise and thanksgiving?

We are missing out on the incredible benefits of an intimate relationship with God when we always come to Him with an empty hand, instead of a heart full of praise and thanksgiving.

> I will extol You, my God… I will bless You, and I will praise Your name forever and ever. Great is the Lord, and greatly to be praised.
>
> *Psalm 145:1-3*

They shall beat their swords into
    plowshares,
And their spears into pruning
    hooks;
Nation shall not lift up sword
    against nation,
Neither shall they learn war
    anymore.

4 But everyone shall sit under his
    vine and under his fig tree,
And no one shall make *them*
    afraid;
For the mouth of the LORD of
    hosts has spoken.
5 For all people walk each in the
    name of his god,
But we will walk in the name of
    the LORD our God
Forever and ever.

6 "In that day," says the LORD,
"I will assemble the lame,
I will gather the outcast
And those whom I have afflicted;
7 I will make the lame a remnant,
And the outcast a strong nation;
So the LORD will reign over them
    in Mount Zion
From now on, even forever.
8 And you, O tower of the flock,
The stronghold of the daughter of
    Zion,
To you shall it come,
Even the former dominion shall
    come,
The kingdom of the daughter of
    Jerusalem."

9 Now why do you cry aloud?
Is there no king in your midst?
Has your counselor perished?
For pangs have seized you like a
    woman in labor.
10 Be in pain, and labor to bring
    forth,
O daughter of Zion,
Like a woman in birth pangs.
For now you shall go forth from
    the city,
You shall dwell in the field,
And to Babylon you shall go.
There you shall be delivered;
There the LORD will redeem you
From the hand of your enemies.

11 Now also many nations have
    gathered against you,
Who say, "Let her be defiled,
And let our eye look upon Zion."
12 But they do not know the
    thoughts of the LORD,
Nor do they understand His
    counsel;
For He will gather them like
    sheaves to the threshing floor.

13 "Arise and thresh, O daughter of
    Zion;
For I will make your horn iron,
And I will make your hooves
    bronze;
You shall beat in pieces many
    peoples;
I will consecrate their gain to the
    LORD,
And their substance to the Lord of
    the whole earth."

5 Now gather yourself in troops,
O daughter of troops;
He has laid siege against us;
They will strike the judge of Israel
    with a rod on the cheek.
2 "But you, Bethlehem Ephrathah,
Though you are little among the
    thousands of Judah,
Yet out of you shall come forth to
    Me
The One to be Ruler in Israel,
Whose goings forth *are* from of
    old,
From everlasting."

3 Therefore He shall give them up,
Until the time *that* she who is in
    labor has given birth;
Then the remnant of His
    brethren
Shall return to the children of
    Israel.
4 And He shall stand and feed *His*
    flock
In the strength of the LORD,
In the majesty of the name of the
    LORD His God;
And they shall abide,
For now He shall be great
To the ends of the earth;
5 And this *One* shall be peace.

When the Assyrian comes into our
   land,
And when he treads in our
   palaces,
Then we will raise against him
Seven shepherds and eight
   princely men.
6 They shall waste with the sword
   the land of Assyria,
And the land of Nimrod at its
   entrances;
Thus He shall deliver *us* from the
   Assyrian,
When he comes into our land
And when he treads within our
   borders.

7 Then the remnant of Jacob
Shall be in the midst of many
   peoples,
Like dew from the LORD,
Like showers on the grass,
That tarry for no man
Nor wait for the sons of men.
8 And the remnant of Jacob
Shall be among the Gentiles,
In the midst of many peoples,
Like a lion among the beasts of
   the forest,
Like a young lion among flocks of
   sheep,
Who, if he passes through,
Both treads down and tears in
   pieces,
And none can deliver.
9 Your hand shall be lifted against
   your adversaries,
And all your enemies shall be cut
   off.

10 "And it shall be in that day," says
   the LORD,
"That I will cut off your horses
   from your midst
And destroy your chariots.
11 I will cut off the cities of your
   land
And throw down all your
   strongholds.
12 I will cut off sorceries from your
   hand,
And you shall have no
   soothsayers.
13 Your carved images I will also cut
   off,

And your sacred pillars from your
   midst;
You shall no more worship the
   work of your hands;
14 I will pluck your wooden images
   from your midst;
Thus I will destroy your cities.
15 And I will execute vengeance in
   anger and fury
On the nations that have not
   heard."

∼ PSALM 145:1–9 ∼

1 I will extol You, my God, O King;
And I will bless Your name forever
   and ever.
2 Every day I will bless You,
And I will praise Your name forever
   and ever.
3 Great *is* the LORD, and greatly to be
   praised;
And His greatness *is* unsearchable.

4 One generation shall praise Your
   works to another,
And shall declare Your mighty acts.
5 I will meditate on the glorious
   splendor of Your majesty,
And on Your wondrous works.
6 *Men* shall speak of the might of Your
   awesome acts,
And I will declare Your greatness.
7 They shall utter the memory of Your
   great goodness,
And shall sing of Your righteousness.

8 The LORD *is* gracious and full of
   compassion,
Slow to anger and great in mercy.
9 The LORD *is* good to all,
And His tender mercies *are* over all
   His works.

∼ PROVERBS 30:11–14 ∼

11 *There is* a generation *that* curses its
   father,
And does not bless its mother.
12 *There is* a generation *that is* pure in
   its own eyes,
Yet is not washed from its filthiness.
13 *There is* a generation— oh, how lofty
   are their eyes!
And their eyelids are lifted up.

14 *There is* a generation whose teeth *are* like swords,
And whose fangs *are like* knives,
To devour the poor from off the earth,
And the needy from *among* men.

~ REVELATION 10:1–11 ~

I saw still another mighty angel coming down from heaven, clothed with a cloud. And a rainbow *was* on his head, his face *was* like the sun, and his feet like pillars of fire. ² He had a little book open in his hand. And he set his right foot on the sea and *his* left *foot* on the land, ³ and cried with a loud voice, as *when* a lion roars. When he cried out, seven thunders uttered their voices. ⁴ Now when the seven thunders uttered their voices, I was about to write; but I heard a voice from heaven saying to me, "Seal up the things which the seven thunders uttered, and do not write them."

⁵ The angel whom I saw standing on the sea and on the land raised up his hand to heaven ⁶ and swore by Him who lives forever and ever, who created heaven and the things that are in it, the earth and the things that are in it, and the sea and the things that are in it, that there should be delay no longer, ⁷ but in the days of the sounding of the seventh angel, when he is about to sound, the mystery of God would be finished, as He declared to His servants the prophets.

⁸ Then the voice which I heard from heaven spoke to me again and said, "Go, take the little book which is open in the hand of the angel who stands on the sea and on the earth."

⁹ So I went to the angel and said to him, "Give me the little book."

And he said to me, "Take and eat it; and it will make your stomach bitter, but it will be as sweet as honey in your mouth."

¹⁰ Then I took the little book out of the angel's hand and ate it, and it was as sweet as honey in my mouth. But when I had eaten it, my stomach became bitter. ¹¹ And he said to me, "You must prophesy again about many peoples, nations, tongues, and kings."

READING 355 · DECEMBER 21

~ MICAH 6:1—7:20 ~

Hear now what the LORD says:
"Arise, plead your case before the mountains,
And let the hills hear your voice.
² Hear, O you mountains, the LORD's complaint,
And you strong foundations of the earth;
For the LORD has a complaint against His people,
And He will contend with Israel.

³ "O My people, what have I done to you?
And how have I wearied you?
Testify against Me.
⁴ For I brought you up from the land of Egypt,
I redeemed you from the house of bondage;
And I sent before you Moses, Aaron, and Miriam.
⁵ O My people, remember now
What Balak king of Moab counseled,
And what Balaam the son of Beor answered him,
From Acacia Grove to Gilgal,
That you may know the righteousness of the LORD."

⁶ With what shall I come before the LORD,
And bow myself before the High God?
Shall I come before Him with burnt offerings,
With calves a year old?
⁷ Will the LORD be pleased with thousands of rams,
Ten thousand rivers of oil?

Escaping the Sirens

As the ancient myth goes, when Ulysses sailed out to meet the Sirens, he stopped his ears with wax and had himself bound to the mast of his ship. He was apparently unaware that every traveler before him had done the same thing and that wax and chains were no match for the Sirens. Their alluring song could pierce through anything, causing sailors to break all manner of bonds.

However, the Sirens had an even more fatal weapon than their song. Silence. As Ulysses approached, the Sirens chose to employ that weapon. Rather than be seduced into straining to hear their song though, Ulysses concluded that he must be the only person who could not hear their song and that he must be immune to their powers. Strengthened in that confidence, he set his gaze on the distant horizon and escaped the Sirens as no man before him.

Temptation always begins in what we see and what we hear. Choose carefully what your eyes see and what your ears hear. When you choose to look God's way, He will show you what is good.

> He has shown you, O man, what is good; and what does the Lord require of you but to do justly, to love mercy, and to walk humbly with your God?
>
> *Micah 6:8*

Shall I give my firstborn *for* my
   transgression,
The fruit of my body *for* the sin of
   my soul?

8 He has shown you, O man, what
   is good;
And what does the LORD require
   of you
But to do justly,
To love mercy,
And to walk humbly with your
   God?

9 The LORD's voice cries to the
   city—
Wisdom shall see Your name:

"Hear the rod!
Who has appointed it?
10 Are there yet the treasures of
   wickedness
In the house of the wicked,
And the short measure *that is* an
   abomination?
11 Shall I count pure *those* with the
   wicked scales,
And with the bag of deceitful
   weights?
12 For her rich men are full of
   violence,
Her inhabitants have spoken lies,
And their tongue is deceitful in
   their mouth.

13 "Therefore I will also make *you*
   sick by striking you,
By making *you* desolate because of
   your sins.
14 You shall eat, but not be satisfied;
Hunger *shall be* in your midst.
You may carry *some* away, but
   shall not save *them;*
And what you do rescue I will give
   over to the sword.

15 "You shall sow, but not reap;
You shall tread the olives, but not
   anoint yourselves with oil;
And *make* sweet wine, but not
   drink wine.
16 For the statutes of Omri are kept;
All the works of Ahab's house *are*
   done;
And you walk in their counsels,

That I may make you a desolation,
And your inhabitants a hissing.
Therefore you shall bear the
   reproach of My people."

7 Woe is me!
For I am like those who gather
   summer fruits,
Like those who glean vintage
   grapes;
There is no cluster to eat
Of the first-ripe fruit *which* my
   soul desires.
2 The faithful *man* has perished
   from the earth,
And *there is* no one upright
   among men.
They all lie in wait for blood;
Every man hunts his brother with
   a net.

3 That they may successfully do evil
   with both hands—
The prince asks *for gifts,*
The judge *seeks* a bribe,
And the great *man* utters his evil
   desire;
So they scheme together.
4 The best of them *is* like a brier;
The most upright *is sharper* than a
   thorn hedge;
The day of your watchman and
   your punishment comes;
Now shall be their perplexity.

5 Do not trust in a friend;
Do not put your confidence in a
   companion;
Guard the doors of your mouth
From her who lies in your bosom.
6 For son dishonors father,
Daughter rises against her mother,
Daughter-in-law against her
   mother-in-law;
A man's enemies *are* the men of
   his own household.
7 Therefore I will look to the LORD;
I will wait for the God of my
   salvation;
My God will hear me.

8 Do not rejoice over me, my
   enemy;
When I fall, I will arise;
When I sit in darkness,

The LORD *will be* a light to me.

9 I will bear the indignation of the
LORD,
Because I have sinned against
Him,
Until He pleads my case
And executes justice for me.
He will bring me forth to the
light;
I will see His righteousness.

10 Then *she who is* my enemy will
see,
And shame will cover her who
said to me,
"Where is the LORD your God?"
My eyes will see her;
Now she will be trampled down
Like mud in the streets.

11 *In* the day when your walls are to
be built,
In that day the decree shall go far
and wide.

12 *In* that day they shall come
to you
From Assyria and the fortified
cities,
From the fortress to the River,
From sea to sea,
And mountain *to* mountain.

13 Yet the land shall be desolate
Because of those who dwell in it,
And for the fruit of their deeds.

14 Shepherd Your people with Your
staff,
The flock of Your heritage,
Who dwell solitarily *in* a
woodland,
In the midst of Carmel;
Let them feed *in* Bashan and
Gilead,
As in days of old.

15 "As in the days when you came out
of the land of Egypt,
I will show them wonders."

16 The nations shall see and be
ashamed of all their might;
They shall put *their* hand over
their mouth;
Their ears shall be deaf.

17 They shall lick the dust like a
serpent;
They shall crawl from their holes
like snakes of the earth.
They shall be afraid of the LORD
our God,
And shall fear because of You.

18 Who *is* a God like You,
Pardoning iniquity
And passing over the transgression
of the remnant of His heritage?

He does not retain His anger
forever,
Because He delights *in* mercy.

19 He will again have compassion on
us,
And will subdue our iniquities.

You will cast all our sins
Into the depths of the sea.

20 You will give truth to Jacob
And mercy to Abraham,
Which You have sworn to our
fathers
From days of old.

～ PSALM 145:10–16 ～

10 All Your works shall praise You,
O LORD,
And Your saints shall bless You.

11 They shall speak of the glory of Your
kingdom,
And talk of Your power,

12 To make known to the sons of men
His mighty acts,
And the glorious majesty of His
kingdom.

13 Your kingdom *is* an everlasting
kingdom,
And Your dominion *endures*
throughout all generations.

14 The LORD upholds all who fall,
And raises up all *who are* bowed
down.

15 The eyes of all look expectantly to
You,
And You give them their food in due
season.

16 You open Your hand
And satisfy the desire of every living
thing.

∼ PROVERBS 30:15 ∼

15 The leech has two daughters—
Give *and* Give!

There are three *things that* are never
    satisfied,
Four never say, "Enough!":

∼ REVELATION 11:1–19 ∼

Then I was given a reed like a measuring
rod. And the angel stood, saying, "Rise
and measure the temple of God, the altar, and those who worship there. ² But
leave out the court which is outside the
temple, and do not measure it, for it has
been given to the Gentiles. And they will
tread the holy city underfoot *for* forty-
two months. ³ And I will give *power* to
my two witnesses, and they will prophesy one thousand two hundred and sixty
days, clothed in sackcloth."

⁴ These are the two olive trees and the
two lampstands standing before the God
of the earth. ⁵ And if anyone wants to
harm them, fire proceeds from their
mouth and devours their enemies. And if
anyone wants to harm them, he must be
killed in this manner. ⁶ These have power
to shut heaven, so that no rain falls in the
days of their prophecy; and they have
power over waters to turn them to blood,
and to strike the earth with all plagues, as
often as they desire.

⁷ When they finish their testimony, the
beast that ascends out of the bottomless
pit will make war against them, overcome
them, and kill them. ⁸ And their dead bodies *will lie* in the street of the great city
which spiritually is called Sodom and
Egypt, where also our Lord was crucified.
⁹ Then *those* from the peoples, tribes,
tongues, and nations will see their dead
bodies three-and-a-half days, and not allow their dead bodies to be put into graves.
¹⁰ And those who dwell on the earth will
rejoice over them, make merry, and send
gifts to one another, because these two
prophets tormented those who dwell on
the earth.

¹¹ Now after the three-and-a-half days
the breath of life from God entered them,
and they stood on their feet, and great
fear fell on those who saw them. ¹² And
they heard a loud voice from heaven saying to them, "Come up here." And they
ascended to heaven in a cloud, and their
enemies saw them. ¹³ In the same hour
there was a great earthquake, and a tenth
of the city fell. In the earthquake seven
thousand people were killed, and the rest
were afraid and gave glory to the God of
heaven.

¹⁴ The second woe is past. Behold, the
third woe is coming quickly.

¹⁵ Then the seventh angel sounded: And
there were loud voices in heaven, saying,
"The kingdoms of this world have become
the kingdoms of our Lord and of His
Christ, and He shall reign forever and
ever!" ¹⁶ And the twenty-four elders who
sat before God on their thrones fell on
their faces and worshiped God, ¹⁷ saying:

"We give You thanks, O Lord God
    Almighty,
The One who is and who was and
    who is to come,
Because You have taken Your great
    power and reigned.
¹⁸ The nations were angry, and Your
    wrath has come,
And the time of the dead, that
    they should be judged,
And that You should reward Your
    servants the prophets and the
    saints,
And those who fear Your name,
    small and great,
And should destroy those who
    destroy the earth."

¹⁹ Then the temple of God was opened
in heaven, and the ark of His covenant
was seen in His temple. And there were
lightnings, noises, thunderings, an earthquake, and great hail.

∼ NAHUM 1:1—3:19 ∼

The burden against Nineveh. The book of the vision of Nahum the Elkoshite.

2 God *is* jealous, and the LORD avenges;
The LORD avenges and *is* furious.
The LORD will take vengeance on His adversaries,
And He reserves *wrath* for His enemies;
3 The LORD *is* slow to anger and great in power,
And will not at all acquit *the wicked.*

The LORD has His way
In the whirlwind and in the storm,
And the clouds *are* the dust of His feet.
4 He rebukes the sea and makes it dry,
And dries up all the rivers.
Bashan and Carmel wither,
And the flower of Lebanon wilts.
5 The mountains quake before Him,
The hills melt,
And the earth heaves at His presence,
Yes, the world and all who dwell in it.

6 Who can stand before His indignation?
And who can endure the fierceness of His anger?
His fury is poured out like fire,
And the rocks are thrown down by Him.

7 The LORD *is* good,
A stronghold in the day of trouble;
And He knows those who trust in Him.
8 But with an overflowing flood
He will make an utter end of its place,
And darkness will pursue His enemies.

9 What do you conspire against the LORD?
He will make an utter end *of it.*
Affliction will not rise up a second time.
10 For while tangled *like* thorns,
And while drunken *like* drunkards,
They shall be devoured like stubble fully dried.
11 From you comes forth *one*
Who plots evil against the LORD,
A wicked counselor.

12 Thus says the LORD:

"Though *they are* safe, and likewise many,
Yet in this manner they will be cut down
When he passes through.
Though I have afflicted you,
I will afflict you no more;
13 For now I will break off his yoke from you,
And burst your bonds apart."

14 The LORD has given a command concerning you:
"Your name shall be perpetuated no longer.
Out of the house of your gods
I will cut off the carved image and the molded image.
I will dig your grave,
For you are vile."

15 Behold, on the mountains
The feet of him who brings good tidings,
Who proclaims peace!
O Judah, keep your appointed feasts,
Perform your vows.
For the wicked one shall no more pass through you;
He is utterly cut off.

2 He who scatters has come up before your face.
Man the fort!
Watch the road!

Strengthen *your* flanks!
Fortify *your* power mightily.

2   For the LORD will restore the
      excellence of Jacob
    Like the excellence of Israel,
    For the emptiers have emptied
      them out
    And ruined their vine branches.

3   The shields of his mighty men *are*
      made red,
    The valiant men *are* in scarlet.
    The chariots *come* with flaming
      torches
    In the day of his preparation,
    And the spears are brandished.
4   The chariots rage in the streets,
    They jostle one another in the
      broad roads;
    They seem like torches,
    They run like lightning.

5   He remembers his nobles;
    They stumble in their walk;
    They make haste to her walls,
    And the defense is prepared.
6   The gates of the rivers are opened,
    And the palace is dissolved.
7   It is decreed:
    She shall be led away captive,
    She shall be brought up;
    And her maidservants shall lead
      her as with the voice of doves,
    Beating their breasts.

8   Though Nineveh of old *was* like a
      pool of water,
    Now they flee away.
    "Halt! Halt!" *they cry;*
    But no one turns back.
9   Take spoil of silver!
    Take spoil of gold!
    There is no end of treasure,
    Or wealth of every desirable prize.
10 She is empty, desolate, and waste!
    The heart melts, and the knees
      shake;
    Much pain *is* in every side,
    And all their faces are drained of
      color.

11 Where *is* the dwelling of the lions,
    And the feeding place of the
      young lions,

Where the lion walked, the lioness
  and lion's cub,
And no one made *them* afraid?
12 The lion tore in pieces enough for
      his cubs,
    Killed for his lionesses,
    Filled his caves with prey,
    And his dens with flesh.

13 "Behold, I *am* against you," says the
LORD of hosts, "I will burn your chariots
in smoke, and the sword shall devour your
young lions; I will cut off your prey from
the earth, and the voice of your messengers shall be heard no more."

3   Woe to the bloody city!
    It *is* all full of lies *and* robbery.
    Its victim never departs.
2   The noise of a whip
    And the noise of rattling wheels,
    Of galloping horses,
    Of clattering chariots!
3   Horsemen charge with bright
      sword and glittering spear.
    There is a multitude of slain,
    A great number of bodies,
    Countless corpses—
    They stumble over the corpses—
4   Because of the multitude of
      harlotries of the seductive
      harlot,
    The mistress of sorceries,
    Who sells nations through her
      harlotries,
    And families through her
      sorceries.

5   "Behold, I *am* against you," says
      the LORD of hosts;
    "I will lift your skirts over your
      face,
    I will show the nations your
      nakedness,
    And the kingdoms your shame.
6   I will cast abominable filth upon
      you,
    Make you vile,
    And make you a spectacle.
7   It shall come to pass *that* all who
      look upon you
    Will flee from you, and say,
    'Nineveh is laid waste!
    Who will bemoan her?'

It Wasn't Luck At All

On a remote farm in California, a young mother was alone with her three children. The children had been swimming in the family pool, when the mother suddenly noticed that her two-and-a-half-year-old son was at the bottom of it. She dove in and pulled him out as quickly as she could.

Just at that moment, a neighboring farmer came by. He immediately began careful mouth-to-mouth resuscitation. After several minutes, the child stirred. The mother and the farmer took him to the nearest hospital for examination, and the doctors assured them that the little boy had suffered no brain damage.

In the days following, as people heard of the child's rescue, several commented to the mother and father, "You sure were lucky!" The father said to his pastor, "When people said that to me, I replied, 'It wasn't luck at all. My wife and daughter were on their knees praying while the farmer was working on my son.'"

Those who pray can always be assured that God is at work in their particular circumstance — for their eternal benefit.

> The Lord is righteous in all His ways, gracious in all His works. He will fulfill the desire of those who fear Him; he also will hear their cry and save them.
>
> *Psalm 145:17, 19*

Where shall I seek comforters for
you?"

8   Are you better than No Amon
     That was situated by the River,
     That had the waters around her,
     Whose rampart *was* the sea,
     Whose wall *was* the sea?
9   Ethiopia and Egypt *were* her
     strength,
     And *it was* boundless;
     Put and Lubim were your helpers.
10   Yet she *was* carried away,
     She went into captivity;
     Her young children also were
     dashed to pieces
     At the head of every street;
     They cast lots for her honorable
     men,
     And all her great men were bound
     in chains.
11   You also will be drunk;
     You will be hidden;
     You also will seek refuge from the
     enemy.

12   All your strongholds *are* fig trees
     with ripened figs:
     If they are shaken,
     They fall into the mouth of the
     eater.
13   Surely, your people in your midst
     are women!
     The gates of your land are wide
     open for your enemies;
     Fire shall devour the bars of your
     gates.

14   Draw your water for the siege!
     Fortify your strongholds!
     Go into the clay and tread the
     mortar!
     Make strong the brick kiln!
15   There the fire will devour you,
     The sword will cut you off;
     It will eat you up like a locust.

     Make yourself many—like the
     locust!
     Make yourself many— like the
     swarming locusts!
16   You have multiplied your
     merchants more than the stars
     of heaven.
     The locust plunders and flies away.

17   Your commanders *are* like
     swarming locusts,
     And your generals like great
     grasshoppers,
     Which camp in the hedges on a
     cold day;
     When the sun rises they flee
     away,
     And the place where they *are* is
     not known.
18   Your shepherds slumber, O king of
     Assyria;
     Your nobles rest *in the dust*.
     Your people are scattered on the
     mountains,
     And no one gathers them.
19   Your injury *has* no healing,
     Your wound is severe.
     All who hear news of you
     Will clap *their* hands over you,
     For upon whom has not your
     wickedness passed continually?

∼ PSALM 145:17–21 ∼

17   The LORD *is* righteous in all His
     ways,
     Gracious in all His works.
18   The LORD *is* near to all who call
     upon Him,
     To all who call upon Him in truth.
19   He will fulfill the desire of those
     who fear Him;
     He also will hear their cry and save
     them.
20   The LORD preserves all who love
     Him,
     But all the wicked He will destroy.
21   My mouth shall speak the praise of
     the LORD,
     And all flesh shall bless His holy
     name
     Forever and ever.

∼ PROVERBS 30:16 ∼

16   The grave,
     The barren womb,
     The earth *that* is not satisfied with
     water—
     And the fire never says,
     "Enough!"

~ REVELATION 12:1–17 ~

Now a great sign appeared in heaven: a woman clothed with the sun, with the moon under her feet, and on her head a garland of twelve stars. ² Then being with child, she cried out in labor and in pain to give birth.

³ And another sign appeared in heaven: behold, a great, fiery red dragon having seven heads and ten horns, and seven diadems on his heads. ⁴ His tail drew a third of the stars of heaven and threw them to the earth. And the dragon stood before the woman who was ready to give birth, to devour her Child as soon as it was born. ⁵ She bore a male Child who was to rule all nations with a rod of iron. And her Child was caught up to God and His throne. ⁶ Then the woman fled into the wilderness, where she has a place prepared by God, that they should feed her there one thousand two hundred and sixty days.

⁷ And war broke out in heaven: Michael and his angels fought with the dragon; and the dragon and his angels fought, ⁸ but they did not prevail, nor was a place found for them in heaven any longer. ⁹ So the great dragon was cast out, that serpent of old, called the Devil and Satan, who deceives the whole world; he was cast to the earth, and his angels were cast out with him.

¹⁰ Then I heard a loud voice saying in heaven, "Now salvation, and strength, and the kingdom of our God, and the power of His Christ have come, for the accuser of our brethren, who accused them before our God day and night, has been cast down. ¹¹ And they overcame him by the blood of the Lamb and by the word of their testimony, and they did not love their lives to the death. ¹² Therefore rejoice, O heavens, and you who dwell in them! Woe to the inhabitants of the earth and the sea! For the devil has come down to you, having great wrath, because he knows that he has a short time."

¹³ Now when the dragon saw that he had been cast to the earth, he persecuted the woman who gave birth to the male *Child.* ¹⁴ But the woman was given two wings of a great eagle, that she might fly into the wilderness to her place, where she is nourished for a time and times and half a time, from the presence of the serpent. ¹⁵ So the serpent spewed water out of his mouth like a flood after the woman, that he might cause her to be carried away by the flood. ¹⁶ But the earth helped the woman, and the earth opened its mouth and swallowed up the flood which the dragon had spewed out of his mouth. ¹⁷ And the dragon was enraged with the woman, and he went to make war with the rest of her offspring, who keep the commandments of God and have the testimony of Jesus Christ.

READING 357 · DECEMBER 23

~ HABAKKUK 1:1—3:19 ~

The burden which the prophet Habakkuk saw.

² O LORD, how long shall I cry,
And You will not hear?
Even cry out to You,
"Violence!"
And You will not save.
³ Why do You show me iniquity,
And cause *me* to see trouble?
For plundering and violence *are*
before me;
There is strife, and contention
arises.

⁴ Therefore the law is powerless,
And justice never goes forth.
For the wicked surround the
righteous;
Therefore perverse judgment
proceeds.

⁵ "Look among the nations and
watch—
Be utterly astounded!
For *I will* work a work in your
days
Which you would not believe,
though it were told *you.*

6 For indeed I am raising up the
 Chaldeans,
 A bitter and hasty nation
 Which marches through the
  breadth of the earth,
 To possess dwelling places *that are*
  not theirs.
7 They are terrible and dreadful;
 Their judgment and their dignity
  proceed from themselves.
8 Their horses also are swifter than
  leopards,
 And more fierce than evening
  wolves.
 Their chargers charge ahead;
 Their cavalry comes from afar;
 They fly as the eagle *that* hastens
  to eat.

9 "They all come for violence;
 Their faces are set *like* the east
  wind.
 They gather captives like sand.
10 They scoff at kings,
 And princes are scorned by them.
 They deride every stronghold,
 For they heap up earthen *mounds*
  and seize it.
11 Then *his* mind changes, and he
  transgresses;
 He commits offense,
 Ascribing this power to his god."

12 Are You not from everlasting,
 O LORD my God, my Holy One?
 We shall not die.
 O LORD, You have appointed
  them for judgment;
 O Rock, You have marked them
  for correction.
13 *You are* of purer eyes than to
  behold evil,
 And cannot look on wickedness.
 Why do You look on those who
  deal treacherously,
 And hold Your tongue when the
  wicked devours
 A *person* more righteous than he?
14 *Why* do You make men like fish of
  the sea,
 Like creeping things *that have* no
  ruler over them?

15 They take up all of them with a
  hook,

They catch them in their net,
 And gather them in their dragnet.
 Therefore they rejoice and are
  glad.
16 Therefore they sacrifice to their
  net,
 And burn incense to their dragnet;
 Because by them their share *is*
  sumptuous
 And their food plentiful.
17 Shall they therefore empty their
  net,
 And continue to slay nations
  without pity?

2 I will stand my watch
 And set myself on the rampart,
 And watch to see what He will say
  to me,
 And what I will answer when I am
  corrected.

2 Then the LORD answered me and said:

 "Write the vision
 And make *it* plain on tablets,
 That he may run who reads it.
3 For the vision *is* yet for an
  appointed time;
 But at the end it will speak, and it
  will not lie.
 Though it tarries, wait for it;
 Because it will surely come,
 It will not tarry.

4 "Behold the proud,
 His soul is not upright in him;
 But the just shall live by his faith.

5 "Indeed, because he transgresses by
  wine,
 He is a proud man,
 And he does not stay at home.
 Because he enlarges his desire as
  hell,
 And he *is* like death, and cannot
  be satisfied,
 He gathers to himself all nations
 And heaps up for himself all
  peoples.

6 "Will not all these take up a
  proverb against him,
 And a taunting riddle against him,
  and say,

Propelled by a Dream

At the young age of sixteen, Romana was deserted by her husband and left to raise her two children alone. Living in Mexico, she was poverty-stricken, untrained, and unable to speak English, but she dreamed of a better life. With only a few dollars to fuel that dream, she headed for Los Angeles, where she used her last seven dollars to take a taxi to the home of a distant relative.

Romana refused to live on the charity of others. She immediately found a job washing dishes, followed by a job making tortillas from midnight to 6 AM. From her two jobs she was able to save $500, which she used to invest in her own tortilla machine. Over time, and with a great deal of hard work, Romana became the manager of the largest Mexican wholesale food business in the world.

Eventually, Romana Banuelos was hand-picked by Dwight D. Eisenhower to become the 37th United States Treasurer. She exemplified what Eisenhower proclaimed about dreams propelling our future: "We succeed only as we identify in life, or in war, or in anything else, a single overriding objective, and make all other considerations bend to that one objective."

God also bearing witness both with signs and wonders, with various miracles, and gifts of the Holy Spirit, according to His own will?

Hebrews 2:4

'Woe to him who increases
What is not his—how long?
And to him who loads himself
    with many pledges'?
7 Will not your creditors rise up
    suddenly?
Will they not awaken who oppress
    you?
And you will become their booty.
8 Because you have plundered many
    nations,
All the remnant of the people shall
    plunder you,
Because of men's blood
And the violence of the land *and*
    the city,
And of all who dwell in it.

9 "Woe to him who covets evil gain
    for his house,
That he may set his nest on high,
That he may be delivered from the
    power of disaster!
10 You give shameful counsel to your
    house,
Cutting off many peoples,
And sin *against* your soul.
11 For the stone will cry out from the
    wall,
And the beam from the timbers
    will answer it.

12 "Woe to him who builds a town
    with bloodshed,
Who establishes a city by iniquity!
13 Behold, *is it* not of the LORD of
    hosts
That the peoples labor to feed the
    fire,
And nations weary themselves in
    vain?
14 For the earth will be filled
With the knowledge of the glory
    of the LORD,
As the waters cover the sea.

15 "Woe to him who gives drink to his
    neighbor,
Pressing *him to* your bottle,
Even to make *him* drunk,
That you may look on his
    nakedness!
16 You are filled with shame instead
    of glory.
You also—drink!

And be exposed as uncircumcised!
The cup of the LORD's right hand
    will be turned against you,
And utter shame *will be* on your
    glory.
17 For the violence *done to* Lebanon
    will cover you,
And the plunder of beasts *which*
    made them afraid,
Because of men's blood
And the violence of the land *and*
    the city,
And of all who dwell in it.

18 "What profit is the image, that its
    maker should carve it,
The molded image, a teacher of
    lies,
That the maker of its mold should
    trust in it,
To make mute idols?
19 Woe to him who says to wood,
    'Awake!'
To silent stone, 'Arise! It shall
    teach!'
Behold, it is overlaid with gold
    and silver,
Yet in it there is no breath at all.

20 "But the LORD is in His holy
    temple.
Let all the earth keep silence
    before Him."

3 A prayer of Habakkuk the prophet,
on Shigionoth.

2 O LORD, I have heard Your speech
    and was afraid;
O LORD, revive Your work in the
    midst of the years!
In the midst of the years make *it*
    known;
In wrath remember mercy.

3 God came from Teman,
The Holy One from Mount Paran.
                                    Selah

His glory covered the heavens,
And the earth was full of His
    praise.
4 *His* brightness was like the light;
He had rays *flashing* from His
    hand,

And there His power *was* hidden.
5 Before Him went pestilence,
And fever followed at His feet.

6 He stood and measured the earth;
He looked and startled the
nations.
And the everlasting mountains
were scattered,
The perpetual hills bowed.
His ways *are* everlasting.
7 I saw the tents of Cushan in
affliction;
The curtains of the land of Midian
trembled.

8 O LORD, were *You* displeased with
the rivers,
Was Your anger against the rivers,
Was Your wrath against the sea,
That You rode on Your horses,
Your chariots of salvation?
9 Your bow was made quite ready;
Oaths were sworn over *Your*
arrows.   Selah

You divided the earth with rivers.
10 The mountains saw You *and*
trembled;
The overflowing of the water
passed by.
The deep uttered its voice,
And lifted its hands on high.
11 The sun and moon stood still in
their habitation;
At the light of Your arrows they
went,
At the shining of Your glittering
spear.

12 You marched through the land in
indignation;
You trampled the nations
in anger.
13 You went forth for the salvation of
Your people,
For salvation with Your Anointed.
You struck the head from the
house of the wicked,
By laying bare from foundation to
neck.   Selah

14 You thrust through with his own
arrows
The head of his villages.

They came out like a whirlwind to
scatter me;
Their rejoicing was like feasting
on the poor in secret.
15 You walked through the sea with
Your horses,
Through the heap of great waters.

16 When I heard, my body
trembled;
My lips quivered at *the* voice;
Rottenness entered my bones;
And I trembled in myself,
That I might rest in the day of
trouble.
When he comes up to the people,
He will invade them with his
troops.

17 Though the fig tree may not
blossom,
Nor fruit be on the vines;
Though the labor of the olive may
fail,
And the fields yield no food;
Though the flock may be cut off
from the fold,
And there be no herd in the
stalls—
18 Yet I will rejoice in the LORD,
I will joy in the God of my
salvation.

19 The LORD God is my strength;
He will make my feet like deer's
feet,
And He will make me walk on my
high hills.

To the Chief Musician. With my
stringed instruments.

∼ PSALM 146:1–10 ∼

1 Praise the LORD!

Praise the LORD, O my soul!
2 While I live I will praise the LORD;
I will sing praises to my God while I
have my being.

3 Do not put your trust in princes,
Nor in a son of man, in whom *there
is* no help.

4 His spirit departs, he returns to his
   earth;
   In that very day his plans perish.

5 Happy *is he* who *has* the God of
   Jacob for his help,
   Whose hope *is* in the LORD his God,
6 Who made heaven and earth,
   The sea, and all that *is* in them;
   Who keeps truth forever,
7 Who executes justice for the
   oppressed,
   Who gives food to the hungry.
   The LORD gives freedom to the
   prisoners.

8 The LORD opens *the eyes of* the
   blind;
   The LORD raises those who are
   bowed down;
   The LORD loves the righteous.
9 The LORD watches over the
   strangers;
   He relieves the fatherless and
   widow;
   But the way of the wicked He turns
   upside down.

10 The LORD shall reign forever—
   Your God, O Zion, to all
   generations.

   Praise the LORD!

~ PROVERBS 30:17 ~

17 The eye *that* mocks *his* father,
   And scorns obedience to *his* mother,
   The ravens of the valley will pick it
   out,
   And the young eagles will eat it.

~ REVELATION 13:1–18 ~

Then I stood on the sand of the sea. And
I saw a beast rising up out of the sea,
having seven heads and ten horns, and on
his horns ten crowns, and on his heads a
blasphemous name. ² Now the beast
which I saw was like a leopard, his feet
were like *the feet of* a bear, and his mouth
like the mouth of a lion. The dragon gave
him his power, his throne, and great authority. ³ And *I saw* one of his heads as if
it had been mortally wounded, and his
deadly wound was healed. And all the
world marveled and followed the beast.
⁴ So they worshiped the dragon who gave
authority to the beast; and they worshiped
the beast, saying, "Who *is* like the beast?
Who is able to make war with him?"

⁵ And he was given a mouth speaking
great things and blasphemies, and he was
given authority to continue for forty-two
months. ⁶ Then he opened his mouth in
blasphemy against God, to blaspheme His
name, His tabernacle, and those who
dwell in heaven. ⁷ It was granted to him
to make war with the saints and to overcome them. And authority was given him
over every tribe, tongue, and nation. ⁸ All
who dwell on the earth will worship him,
whose names have not been written in the
Book of Life of the Lamb slain from
the foundation of the world.

⁹ If anyone has an ear, let him hear. ¹⁰ He
who leads into captivity shall go into captivity; he who kills with the sword must
be killed with the sword. Here is the patience and the faith of the saints.

¹¹ Then I saw another beast coming up
out of the earth, and he had two horns
like a lamb and spoke like a dragon. ¹² And
he exercises all the authority of the first
beast in his presence, and causes the earth
and those who dwell in it to worship the
first beast, whose deadly wound was
healed. ¹³ He performs great signs, so that
he even makes fire come down from heav-
en on the earth in the sight of men. ¹⁴ And
he deceives those who dwell on the earth
by those signs which he was granted to
do in the sight of the beast, telling those
who dwell on the earth to make an image
to the beast who was wounded by the
sword and lived. ¹⁵ He was granted *power* to give breath to the image of the beast,
that the image of the beast should both
speak and cause as many as would not
worship the image of the beast to be killed.
¹⁶ He causes all, both small and great, rich
and poor, free and slave, to receive a mark
on their right hand or on their foreheads,
¹⁷ and that no one may buy or sell except
one who has the mark or the name of the
beast, or the number of his name.

¹⁸ Here is wisdom. Let him who has
understanding calculate the number of the
beast, for it is the number of a man: His
number *is* 666.

~ ZEPHANIAH 1:1—3:20 ~

The word of the LORD which came to Zephaniah the son of Cushi, the son of Gedaliah, the son of Amariah, the son of Hezekiah, in the days of Josiah the son of Amon, king of Judah.

2 "I will utterly consume everything
From the face of the land,"
Says the LORD;
3 "I will consume man and beast;
I will consume the birds of the heavens,
The fish of the sea,
And the stumbling blocks along with the wicked.
I will cut off man from the face of the land,"
Says the LORD.

4 "I will stretch out My hand against Judah,
And against all the inhabitants of Jerusalem.
I will cut off every trace of Baal from this place,
The names of the idolatrous priests with the *pagan* priests—
5 Those who worship the host of heaven on the housetops;
Those who worship and swear *oaths* by the LORD,
But who *also* swear by Milcom;
6 Those who have turned back from *following* the LORD,
And have not sought the LORD, nor inquired of Him."

7 Be silent in the presence of the Lord GOD;
For the day of the LORD *is* at hand,
For the LORD has prepared a sacrifice;
He has invited His guests.

8 "And it shall be,
In the day of the LORD's sacrifice,
That I will punish the princes and the king's children,
And all such as are clothed with foreign apparel.
9 In the same day I will punish All those who leap over the threshold,
Who fill their masters' houses with violence and deceit.

10 "And there shall be on that day," says the LORD,
"The sound of a mournful cry from the Fish Gate,
A wailing from the Second Quarter,
And a loud crashing from the hills.
11 Wail, you inhabitants of Maktesh!
For all the merchant people are cut down;
All those who handle money are cut off.

12 "And it shall come to pass at that time
That I will search Jerusalem with lamps,
And punish the men
Who are settled in complacency,
Who say in their heart,
'The LORD will not do good,
Nor will He do evil.'
13 Therefore their goods shall become booty,
And their houses a desolation;
They shall build houses, but not inhabit *them;*
They shall plant vineyards, but not drink their wine."

14 The great day of the LORD *is* near;
It is near and hastens quickly.
The noise of the day of the LORD is bitter;
There the mighty men shall cry out.
15 That day *is* a day of wrath,
A day of trouble and distress,
A day of devastation and desolation,
A day of darkness and gloominess,
A day of clouds and thick darkness,
16 A day of trumpet and alarm
Against the fortified cities
And against the high towers.

17 "I will bring distress upon men,
   And they shall walk like blind
      men,
   Because they have sinned against
      the LORD;
   Their blood shall be poured out
      like dust,
   And their flesh like refuse."

18 Neither their silver nor their gold
   Shall be able to deliver them
   In the day of the LORD's wrath;
   But the whole land shall be
      devoured
   By the fire of His jealousy,
   For He will make speedy riddance
   Of all those who dwell in the land.

2 Gather yourselves together, yes,
      gather together,
   O undesirable nation,
2 Before the decree is issued,
   Or the day passes like chaff,
   Before the LORD's fierce anger
      comes upon you,
   Before the day of the LORD's
      anger comes upon you!
3 Seek the LORD, all you meek of
      the earth,
   Who have upheld His justice.
   Seek righteousness, seek
      humility.
   It may be that you will be hidden
   In the day of the LORD's anger.

4 For Gaza shall be forsaken,
   And Ashkelon desolate;
   They shall drive out Ashdod at
      noonday,
   And Ekron shall be uprooted.
5 Woe to the inhabitants of the
      seacoast,
   The nation of the Cherethites!
   The word of the LORD *is* against
      you,
   O Canaan, land of the Philistines:
   "I will destroy you;
   So there shall be no inhabitant."

6 The seacoast shall be pastures,
   With shelters for shepherds and
      folds for flocks.
7 The coast shall be for the remnant
      of the house of Judah;
   They shall feed *their* flocks there;

In the houses of Ashkelon they
      shall lie down at evening.
   For the LORD their God will
      intervene for them,
   And return their captives.

8 "I have heard the reproach of
      Moab,
   And the insults of the people of
      Ammon,
   With which they have reproached
      My people,
   And made arrogant threats against
      their borders.
9 Therefore, *as* I live,"
   Says the LORD of hosts, the God
      of Israel,
   "Surely Moab shall be like Sodom,
   And the people of Ammon like
      Gomorrah—
   Overrun with weeds and
      saltpits,
   And a perpetual desolation.
   The residue of My people shall
      plunder them,
   And the remnant of My people
      shall possess them."

10 This they shall have for their
      pride,
   Because they have reproached and
      made arrogant threats
   Against the people of the LORD of
      hosts.
11 The LORD *will be* awesome to
      them,
   For He will reduce to nothing all
      the gods of the earth;
   People shall worship Him,
   Each one from his place,
   Indeed all the shores of the
      nations.

12 "You Ethiopians also,
   You shall be slain by My sword."

13 And He will stretch out His hand
      against the north,
   Destroy Assyria,
   And make Nineveh a desolation,
   As dry as the wilderness.
14 The herds shall lie down in her
      midst,
   Every beast of the nation.
   Both the pelican and the bittern

The Art of Listening

Be silent in the presence of the Lord God; for the day of the Lord is at hand.

Zephaniah 1:7

A woman complained that she was coming down with the flu, so her husband took her to the doctor. Immediately, the doctor thrust a thermometer in her mouth and said, "Sit there quietly for five minutes." The woman did as she was told.

The husband was astonished and fascinated. When the doctor returned to the examining room, he pointed with enthusiasm to the thermometer and said, "Doc, how much will you take for that thing?"

Listening is truly a fine art, a great personal trait to cultivate. Those who have the ability to listen are truly valuable.

A man was considered an expert in staging sales seminars. As his new assistant was helping him set up the stage for a presentation, he gave him this advice: "One temptation I must warn you against is this: As you are conducting a meeting you will often find people disagree with some of your ideas. You may see someone shaking his head negatively as you speak. Now, the natural thing for you to do is to take out after that person and try to convince him further that you are right. Don't do it. The chances are he is the only person listening to you!"

Shall lodge on the capitals *of* her
   pillars;
Their voice shall sing in the
   windows;
Desolation *shall be* at the
   threshold;
For He will lay bare the cedar
   work.

15 This is the rejoicing city
That dwelt securely,
That said in her heart,
"I *am it,* and *there is* none besides
   me."
How has she become a desolation,
A place for beasts to lie down!
Everyone who passes by her
Shall hiss and shake his fist.

3   Woe to her who is rebellious and
   polluted,
To the oppressing city!

2 She has not obeyed *His* voice,
She has not received correction;
She has not trusted in the LORD,
She has not drawn near to her
   God.

3 Her princes in her midst *are*
   roaring lions;
Her judges *are* evening wolves
That leave not a bone till
   morning.

4 Her prophets are insolent,
   treacherous people;
Her priests have polluted the
   sanctuary,
They have done violence to the
   law.

5 The LORD *is* righteous in her
   midst,
He will do no unrighteousness.
Every morning He brings His
   justice to light;
He never fails,
But the unjust knows no shame.

6 "I have cut off nations,
Their fortresses are devastated;
I have made their streets
   desolate,
With none passing by.
Their cities are destroyed;
There is no one, no inhabitant.

7 I said, 'Surely you will fear Me,
You will receive instruction'—

So that her dwelling would not be
   cut off,
Despite everything for which I
   punished her.
But they rose early and corrupted
   all their deeds.

8 "Therefore wait for Me," says the
   LORD,
"Until the day I rise up for plunder;
My determination *is* to gather the
   nations
To My assembly of kingdoms,
To pour on them My indignation,
All My fierce anger;
All the earth shall be devoured
With the fire of My jealousy.

9 "For then I will restore to the
   peoples a pure language,
That they all may call on the name
   of the LORD,
To serve Him with one accord.

10 From beyond the rivers of
   Ethiopia
My worshipers,
The daughter of My dispersed
   ones,
Shall bring My offering.

11 In that day you shall not be
   shamed for any of your deeds
In which you transgress against
   Me;
For then I will take away from
   your midst
Those who rejoice in your pride,
And you shall no longer be
   haughty
In My holy mountain.

12 I will leave in your midst
A meek and humble people,
And they shall trust in the name of
   the LORD.

13 The remnant of Israel shall do no
   unrighteousness
And speak no lies,
Nor shall a deceitful tongue be
   found in their mouth;
For they shall feed *their* flocks and
   lie down,
And no one shall make *them*
   afraid."

14 Sing, O daughter of Zion!
Shout, O Israel!

Be glad and rejoice with all *your* heart,
O daughter of Jerusalem!

15 The LORD has taken away your judgments,
He has cast out your enemy.
The King of Israel, the LORD, *is* in your midst;
You shall see disaster no more.

16 In that day it shall be said to Jerusalem:
"Do not fear;
Zion, let not your hands be weak.

17 The LORD your God in your midst,
The Mighty One, will save;
He will rejoice over you with gladness,
He will quiet *you* with His love,
He will rejoice over you with singing."

18 "I will gather those who sorrow over the appointed assembly,
Who are among you,
To whom its reproach *is* a burden.

19 Behold, at that time
I will deal with all who afflict you;
I will save the lame,
And gather those who were driven out;
I will appoint them for praise and fame
In every land where they were put to shame.

20 At that time I will bring you back,
Even at the time I gather you;
For I will give you fame and praise
Among all the peoples of the earth,
When I return your captives before your eyes,"
Says the LORD.

∼ PSALM 147:1–6 ∼

1 Praise the LORD!
For *it is* good to sing praises to our God;
For *it is* pleasant, *and* praise is beautiful.

2 The LORD builds up Jerusalem;
He gathers together the outcasts of Israel.

3 He heals the brokenhearted
And binds up their wounds.

4 He counts the number of the stars;
He calls them all by name.

5 Great *is* our Lord, and mighty in power;
His understanding *is* infinite.

6 The LORD lifts up the humble;
He casts the wicked down to the ground.

∼ PROVERBS 30:18, 19 ∼

18 There are three *things which* are too wonderful for me,
Yes, four *which* I do not understand:

19 The way of an eagle in the air,
The way of a serpent on a rock,
The way of a ship in the midst of the sea,
And the way of a man with a virgin.

∼ REVELATION 14:1–20 ∼

Then I looked, and behold, a Lamb standing on Mount Zion, and with Him one hundred *and* forty-four thousand, having His Father's name written on their foreheads. 2 And I heard a voice from heaven, like the voice of many waters, and like the voice of loud thunder. And I heard the sound of harpists playing their harps. 3 They sang as it were a new song before the throne, before the four living creatures, and the elders; and no one could learn that song except the hundred *and* forty-four thousand who were redeemed from the earth. 4 These are the ones who were not defiled with women, for they are virgins. These are the ones who follow the Lamb wherever He goes. These were redeemed from *among* men, *being* firstfruits to God and to the Lamb. 5 And in their mouth was found no deceit, for they are without fault before the throne of God.

6 Then I saw another angel flying in the midst of heaven, having the everlasting gospel to preach to those who dwell on the earth—to every nation, tribe, tongue,

and people— [7] saying with a loud voice, "Fear God and give glory to Him, for the hour of His judgment has come; and worship Him who made heaven and earth, the sea and springs of water."

[8] And another angel followed, saying, "Babylon is fallen, is fallen, that great city, because she has made all nations drink of the wine of the wrath of her fornication."

[9] Then a third angel followed them, saying with a loud voice, "If anyone worships the beast and his image, and receives *his* mark on his forehead or on his hand, [10] he himself shall also drink of the wine of the wrath of God, which is poured out full strength into the cup of His indignation. He shall be tormented with fire and brimstone in the presence of the holy angels and in the presence of the Lamb. [11] And the smoke of their torment ascends forever and ever; and they have no rest day or night, who worship the beast and his image, and whoever receives the mark of his name."

[12] Here is the patience of the saints; here *are* those who keep the commandments of God and the faith of Jesus.

[13] Then I heard a voice from heaven saying to me, "Write: 'Blessed *are* the dead who die in the Lord from now on.' "

"Yes," says the Spirit, "that they may rest from their labors, and their works follow them."

[14] Then I looked, and behold, a white cloud, and on the cloud sat *One* like the Son of Man, having on His head a golden crown, and in His hand a sharp sickle. [15] And another angel came out of the temple, crying with a loud voice to Him who sat on the cloud, "Thrust in Your sickle and reap, for the time has come for You to reap, for the harvest of the earth is ripe." [16] So He who sat on the cloud thrust in His sickle on the earth, and the earth was reaped.

[17] Then another angel came out of the temple which is in heaven, he also having a sharp sickle.

[18] And another angel came out from the altar, who had power over fire, and he cried with a loud cry to him who had the sharp sickle, saying, "Thrust in your sharp sickle and gather the clusters of the vine of the earth, for her grapes are fully ripe." [19] So the angel thrust his sickle into the earth and gathered the vine of the earth, and threw *it* into the great winepress of the wrath of God. [20] And the winepress was trampled outside the city, and blood came out of the winepress, up to the horses' bridles, for one thousand six hundred furlongs.

READING 359 · DECEMBER 25

～ HAGGAI 1:1—2:23 ～

In the second year of King Darius, in the sixth month, on the first day of the month, the word of the LORD came by Haggai the prophet to Zerubbabel the son of Shealtiel, governor of Judah, and to Joshua the son of Jehozadak, the high priest, saying, [2] "Thus speaks the LORD of hosts, saying: 'This people says, "The time has not come, the time that the LORD's house should be built." ' "

[3] Then the word of the LORD came by Haggai the prophet, saying, [4] "*Is it* time for you yourselves to dwell in your paneled houses, and this temple *to lie* in ruins?" [5] Now therefore, thus says the LORD of hosts: "Consider your ways!

[6] "You have sown much, and bring in little;
You eat, but do not have enough;
You drink, but you are not filled with drink;
You clothe yourselves, but no one is warm;
And he who earns wages,
Earns wages *to put* into a bag with holes."

[7] Thus says the LORD of hosts: "Consider your ways! [8] Go up to the mountains and bring wood and build the temple, that I may take pleasure in it and be glorified," says the LORD. [9] "*You* looked

Only Love Lasts

H. Ross Perot, internationally famous billionaire, entrepreneur, and politician, was once quoted as saying, "Guys, just remember, if you get real lucky, if you make a lot of money, if you go out and buy a lot of stuff — it's gonna break. You got your biggest, fanciest mansion in the world. It has air-conditioning. It's got a pool. Just think of all the pumps that are going to go out. Or go to a yacht basin any place in the world. Nobody is smiling, and I'll tell you why. Something broke that morning. The generator's out; the microwave oven doesn't work. . . . Things just don't mean happiness."

When you look around today at the things you possess, ask yourself a question, "What is likely to be in existence 200 years from now?"

Very likely, nothing you currently own, occupy, or consider to be yours will still have any value, and virtually everything you have may be considered garbage one day. The "things" of life simply aren't permanent. What is lasting is the love we share and pass on to the next generation.

He does not delight in the strength of the horse; He takes no pleasure in the legs of a man. The Lord takes pleasure in those who fear Him, in those who hope in His mercy.

Psalm 147:10-11

for much, but indeed *it came to* little; and when you brought it home, I blew it away. Why?" says the LORD of hosts. "Because of My house that *is in* ruins, while every one of you runs to his own house. ¹⁰ Therefore the heavens above you withhold the dew, and the earth withholds its fruit. ¹¹ For I called for a drought on the land and the mountains, on the grain and the new wine and the oil, on whatever the ground brings forth, on men and livestock, and on all the labor of *your* hands."

¹² Then Zerubbabel the son of Shealtiel, and Joshua the son of Jehozadak, the high priest, with all the remnant of the people, obeyed the voice of the LORD their God, and the words of Haggai the prophet, as the LORD their God had sent him; and the people feared the presence of the LORD. ¹³ Then Haggai, the LORD's messenger, spoke the LORD's message to the people, saying, "I *am* with you, says the LORD." ¹⁴ So the LORD stirred up the spirit of Zerubbabel the son of Shealtiel, governor of Judah, and the spirit of Joshua the son of Jehozadak, the high priest, and the spirit of all the remnant of the people; and they came and worked on the house of the LORD of hosts, their God, ¹⁵ on the twenty-fourth day of the sixth month, in the second year of King Darius.

2 In the seventh *month,* on the twenty-first of the month, the word of the LORD came by Haggai the prophet, saying: ² "Speak now to Zerubbabel the son of Shealtiel, governor of Judah, and to Joshua the son of Jehozadak, the high priest, and to the remnant of the people, saying: ³ 'Who is left among you who saw this temple in its former glory? And how do you see it now? In comparison with it, *is this* not in your eyes as nothing? ⁴ Yet now be strong, Zerubbabel,' says the LORD; 'and be strong, Joshua, son of Jehozadak, the high priest; and be strong, all you people of the land,' says the LORD, 'and work; for I *am* with you,' says the LORD of hosts. ⁵ '*According to* the word that I covenanted with you when you came out of Egypt, so My Spirit remains among you; do not fear!'

⁶ "For thus says the LORD of hosts: 'Once more (it *is* a little while) I will shake heaven and earth, the sea and dry land; ⁷ and I will shake all nations, and they shall come to the Desire of All Nations, and I will fill this temple with glory,' says the LORD of hosts. ⁸ 'The silver *is* Mine, and the gold *is* Mine,' says the LORD of hosts. ⁹ 'The glory of this latter temple shall be greater than the former,' says the LORD of hosts. 'And in this place I will give peace,' says the LORD of hosts."

¹⁰ On the twenty-fourth *day* of the ninth *month,* in the second year of Darius, the word of the LORD came by Haggai the prophet, saying, ¹¹ "Thus says the LORD of hosts: 'Now, ask the priests *concerning the* law, saying, ¹² "If one carries holy meat in the fold of his garment, and with the edge he touches bread or stew, wine or oil, or any food, will it become holy?" ' "

Then the priests answered and said, "No."

¹³ And Haggai said, "If *one who is* unclean *because* of a dead body touches any of these, will it be unclean?"

So the priests answered and said, "It shall be unclean."

¹⁴ Then Haggai answered and said, " 'So is this people, and so is this nation before Me,' says the LORD, 'and so is every work of their hands; and what they offer there is unclean.

¹⁵ 'And now, carefully consider from this day forward: from before stone was laid upon stone in the temple of the LORD— ¹⁶ since those *days,* when *one* came to a heap of twenty ephahs, there were *but* ten; when *one* came to the wine vat to draw out fifty baths from the press, there were *but* twenty. ¹⁷ I struck you with blight and mildew and hail in all the labors of your hands; yet you did not *turn* to Me,' says the LORD. ¹⁸ 'Consider now from this day forward, from the twenty-fourth day of the ninth month, from the day that the foundation of the LORD's temple was laid—consider it: ¹⁹ Is the seed still in the barn? As yet the vine, the fig tree, the pomegranate, and the olive tree have not yielded *fruit. But* from this day I will bless *you.* ' "

²⁰ And again the word of the LORD came to Haggai on the twenty-fourth day of the month, saying, ²¹ "Speak to Zerubbabel, governor of Judah, saying:

'I will shake heaven and earth.
22 I will overthrow the throne of
    kingdoms;
I will destroy the strength of the
    Gentile kingdoms.
I will overthrow the chariots
And those who ride in them;
The horses and their riders shall
    come down,
Every one by the sword of his
    brother.

23 'In that day,' says the LORD of hosts,
'I will take you, Zerubbabel My servant,
the son of Shealtiel,' says the LORD, 'and
will make you like a signet *ring;* for I have
chosen you,' says the LORD of hosts."

∼ PSALM 147:7–11 ∼

7 Sing to the LORD with thanksgiving;
    Sing praises on the harp to our God,
8 Who covers the heavens with clouds,
    Who prepares rain for the earth,
    Who makes grass to grow on the
       mountains.
9 He gives to the beast its food,
    And to the young ravens that cry.

10 He does not delight in the strength
       of the horse;
    He takes no pleasure in the legs of a
       man.
11 The LORD takes pleasure in those
       who fear Him,
    In those who hope in His mercy.

∼ PROVERBS 30:20 ∼

20 This *is* the way of an adulterous
       woman:
    She eats and wipes her mouth,
    And says, "I have done no
       wickedness."

∼ REVELATION 15:1–8 ∼

Then I saw another sign in heaven, great
and marvelous: seven angels having the
seven last plagues, for in them the wrath
of God is complete.
2 And I saw *something* like a sea of glass
mingled with fire, and those who have
the victory over the beast, over his image
and over his mark *and* over the number
of his name, standing on the sea of glass,
having harps of God. 3 They sing the song
of Moses, the servant of God, and the
song of the Lamb, saying:

"Great and marvelous *are* Your
    works,
Lord God Almighty!
Just and true *are* Your ways,
O King of the saints!
4 Who shall not fear You, O Lord,
    and glorify Your name?
For *You* alone *are* holy.
For all nations shall come and
    worship before You,
For Your judgments have been
    manifested."

5 After these things I looked, and behold, the temple of the tabernacle of the
testimony in heaven was opened. 6 And
out of the temple came the seven angels
having the seven plagues, clothed in pure
bright linen, and having their chests girded
with golden bands. 7 Then one of the four
living creatures gave to the seven angels
seven golden bowls full of the wrath of
God who lives forever and ever. 8 The
temple was filled with smoke from the
glory of God and from His power, and
no one was able to enter the temple till
the seven plagues of the seven angels were
completed.

∼ ZECHARIAH 1:1—3:10 ∼

In the eighth month of the second year
of Darius, the word of the LORD came
to Zechariah the son of Berechiah,
the son of Iddo the prophet, saying, 2 "The
LORD has been very angry with your fathers. 3 Therefore say to them, 'Thus says
the LORD of hosts: "Return to Me," '
says the LORD of hosts, "and I will return

to you," says the LORD of hosts. ⁴ "Do not be like your fathers, to whom the former prophets preached, saying, 'Thus says the LORD of hosts: "Turn now from your evil ways and your evil deeds." ' But they did not hear nor heed Me," says the LORD.

⁵ "Your fathers, where *are* they?
  And the prophets, do they live
    forever?
⁶ Yet surely My words and My
    statutes,
  Which I commanded My servants
    the prophets,
  Did they not overtake your
    fathers?

"So they returned and said:

'Just as the LORD of hosts
    determined to do to us,
  According to our ways and
    according to our deeds,
  So He has dealt with us.' " ' "

⁷ On the twenty-fourth day of the eleventh month, which is the month Shebat, in the second year of Darius, the word of the LORD came to Zechariah the son of Berechiah, the son of Iddo the prophet: ⁸ I saw by night, and behold, a man riding on a red horse, and it stood among the myrtle trees in the hollow; and behind him *were* horses: red, sorrel, and white. ⁹ Then I said, "My lord, what *are* these?" So the angel who talked with me said to me, "I will show you what they *are*."

¹⁰ And the man who stood among the myrtle trees answered and said, "These *are the ones* whom the LORD has sent to walk to and fro throughout the earth."

¹¹ So they answered the Angel of the LORD, who stood among the myrtle trees, and said, "We have walked to and fro throughout the earth, and behold, all the earth is resting quietly."

¹² Then the Angel of the LORD answered and said, "O LORD of hosts, how long will You not have mercy on Jerusalem and on the cities of Judah, against which You were angry these seventy years?"

¹³ And the LORD answered the angel who talked to me, *with* good *and* comforting words. ¹⁴ So the angel who spoke with me said to me, "Proclaim, saying, 'Thus says the LORD of hosts:

"I am zealous for Jerusalem
  And for Zion with great zeal.
¹⁵ I am exceedingly angry with the
    nations at ease;
  For I was a little angry,
  And they helped—*but* with evil
    intent."

¹⁶ 'Therefore thus says the LORD:

"I am returning to Jerusalem with
    mercy;
  My house shall be built in it," says
    the LORD of hosts,
"And a *surveyor's* line shall be
    stretched out over Jerusalem." '

¹⁷ "Again proclaim, saying, 'Thus says the LORD of hosts:

"My cities shall again spread out
    through prosperity;
  The LORD will again comfort
    Zion,
  And will again choose
    Jerusalem." ' "

¹⁸ Then I raised my eyes and looked, and there *were* four horns. ¹⁹ And I said to the angel who talked with me, "What *are* these?"

So he answered me, "These *are* the horns that have scattered Judah, Israel, and Jerusalem."

²⁰ Then the LORD showed me four craftsmen. ²¹ And I said, "What are these coming to do?"

So he said, "These *are* the horns that scattered Judah, so that no one could lift up his head; but the craftsmen are coming to terrify them, to cast out the horns of the nations that lifted up *their* horn against the land of Judah to scatter it."

2 Then I raised my eyes and looked, and behold, a man with a measuring line in his hand. ² So I said, "Where are you going?"

And he said to me, "To measure Jerusalem, to see what *is* its width and what *is* its length."

³ And there *was* the angel who talked

Straight Talk about Spending Time with Your Kids

Lee Iacocca, former president of Ford Motor Company and former CEO of Chrysler Corporation, writes in his book, *Straight Talk*:

"My parents spent a lot of time with me, and I wanted my kids to be treated with as much love and care as I got. Well, that's a noble objective . . . but to translate it into daily life, you really have to work at it.

"I spent all my weekends with the kids and all my vacations. Kathi was on the swim team for seven years, and I never missed a meet. Then there were tennis matches . . . and piano recitals. I made all of them too. I was always afraid that if I missed one, Kathi might finish first or finish last and I would . . . not be there to congratulate — or console — her.

"The same with Lia. . . . Once I picked up Lia at Brownie camp. She was six years old and came running out to the car in her new khaki uniform with an orange bandana around her neck and a little beanie on her head. She had just made it into the Potawatami Tribe. She had hoped to join the Nava-joes, as she called them, but she was turned down. Still, she was excited, and so was I. Funny thing, I missed an important meeting that day, but for the life of me I have no recollection of what it was."

with me, going out; and another angel was coming out to meet him, ⁴ who said to him, "Run, speak to this young man, saying: 'Jerusalem shall be inhabited *as* towns without walls, because of the multitude of men and livestock in it. ⁵ For I,' says the LORD, 'will be a wall of fire all around her, and I will be the glory in her midst.' "

⁶ "Up, up! Flee from the land of the north," says the LORD; "for I have spread you abroad like the four winds of heaven," says the LORD. ⁷ Up, Zion! Escape, you who dwell with the daughter of Babylon."

⁸ For thus says the LORD of hosts: "He sent Me after glory, to the nations which plunder you; for he who touches you touches the apple of His eye. ⁹ For surely I will shake My hand against them, and they shall become spoil for their servants. Then you will know that the LORD of hosts has sent Me.

¹⁰ "Sing and rejoice, O daughter of Zion! For behold, I am coming and I will dwell in your midst," says the LORD. ¹¹ "Many nations shall be joined to the LORD in that day, and they shall become My people. And I will dwell in your midst. Then you will know that the LORD of hosts has sent Me to you. ¹² And the LORD will take possession of Judah as His inheritance in the Holy Land, and will again choose Jerusalem. ¹³ Be silent, all flesh, before the LORD, for He is aroused from His holy habitation!"

3 Then he showed me Joshua the high priest standing before the Angel of the LORD, and Satan standing at his right hand to oppose him. ² And the LORD said to Satan, "The LORD rebuke you, Satan! The LORD who has chosen Jerusalem rebuke you! *Is* this not a brand plucked from the fire?"

³ Now Joshua was clothed with filthy garments, and was standing before the Angel. ⁴ Then He answered and spoke to those who stood before Him, saying, "Take away the filthy garments from him." And to him He said, "See, I have removed your iniquity from you, and I will clothe you with rich robes."

⁵ And I said, "Let them put a clean turban on his head."

So they put a clean turban on his head, and they put the clothes on him. And the Angel of the LORD stood by.

⁶ Then the Angel of the LORD admonished Joshua, saying, ⁷ "Thus says the LORD of hosts:

'If you will walk in My ways,
And if you will keep My
    command,
Then you shall also judge My
    house,
And likewise have charge of My
    courts;
I will give you places to walk
Among these who stand here.

⁸ 'Hear, O Joshua, the high priest,
You and your companions who sit
    before you,
For they are a wondrous sign;
For behold, I am bringing forth
    My Servant the BRANCH.
⁹ For behold, the stone
That I have laid before Joshua:
Upon the stone *are* seven eyes.
Behold, I will engrave its
    inscription,'
Says the LORD of hosts,
'And I will remove the iniquity of
    that land in one day.
¹⁰ In that day,' says the LORD of
    hosts,
'Everyone will invite his neighbor
Under his vine and under his fig
    tree.' "

∼ PSALM 147:12–20 ∼

¹² Praise the LORD, O Jerusalem!
Praise your God, O Zion!
¹³ For He has strengthened the bars of
    your gates;
He has blessed your children within
    you.
¹⁴ He makes peace *in* your borders,
And fills you with the finest wheat.

¹⁵ He sends out His command *to the*
    earth;
His word runs very swiftly.
¹⁶ He gives snow like wool;
He scatters the frost like ashes;
¹⁷ He casts out His hail like morsels;
Who can stand before His cold?

18 He sends out His word and melts
    them;
    He causes His wind to blow, *and* the
    waters flow.

19 He declares His word to Jacob,
    His statutes and His judgments to
    Israel.
20 He has not dealt thus with any
    nation;
    And *as for His* judgments, they have
    not known them.

    Praise the LORD!

∼ PROVERBS 30:21–23 ∼

21 For three *things* the earth is
    perturbed,
    Yes, for four it cannot bear up:
22 For a servant when he reigns,
    A fool when he is filled with food,
23 A hateful *woman* when she is
    married,
    And a maidservant who succeeds her
    mistress.

∼ REVELATION 16:1–21 ∼

Then I heard a loud voice from the temple saying to the seven angels, "Go and
pour out the bowls of the wrath of God
on the earth."

2 So the first went and poured out his
bowl upon the earth, and a foul and loathsome sore came upon the men who had
the mark of the beast and those who worshiped his image.

3 Then the second angel poured out his
bowl on the sea, and it became blood as
of a dead *man;* and every living creature
in the sea died.

4 Then the third angel poured out his
bowl on the rivers and springs of water,
and they became blood. 5 And I heard the
angel of the waters saying:

    "You are righteous, O Lord,
    The One who is and who was and
    who is to be,
    Because You have judged these
    things.

6 For they have shed the blood of
    saints and prophets,
    And You have given them blood to
    drink.
    For it is their just due."

7 And I heard another from the altar
saying, "Even so, Lord God Almighty, true
and righteous *are* Your judgments."

8 Then the fourth angel poured out his
bowl on the sun, and power was given to
him to scorch men with fire. 9 And men
were scorched with great heat, and they
blasphemed the name of God who has
power over these plagues; and they did
not repent and give Him glory.

10 Then the fifth angel poured out his
bowl on the throne of the beast, and his
kingdom became full of darkness; and
they gnawed their tongues because of the
pain. 11 They blasphemed the God of heav-
en because of their pains and their sores,
and did not repent of their deeds.

12 Then the sixth angel poured out his
bowl on the great river Euphrates, and its
water was dried up, so that the way of
the kings from the east might be prepared.
13 And I saw three unclean spirits like frogs
coming out of the mouth of the dragon,
out of the mouth of the beast, and out of
the mouth of the false prophet. 14 For they
are spirits of demons, performing signs,
which go out to the kings of the earth and
of the whole world, to gather them to the
battle of that great day of God Almighty.

15 "Behold, I am coming as a thief.
Blessed *is* he who watches, and keeps his
garments, lest he walk naked and they see
his shame."

16 And they gathered them together to
the place called in Hebrew, Armageddon.

17 Then the seventh angel poured out
his bowl into the air, and a loud voice came
out of the temple of heaven, from the
throne, saying, "It is done!" 18 And there
were noises and thunderings and lightnings; and there was a great earthquake,
such a mighty and great earthquake as had
not occurred since men were on the earth.
19 Now the great city was divided into
three parts, and the cities of the nations
fell. And great Babylon was remembered
before God, to give her the cup of the
wine of the fierceness of His wrath.
20 Then every island fled away, and the

mountains were not found. ²¹ And great hail from heaven fell upon men, *each hailstone* about the weight of a talent. Men blasphemed God because of the plague of the hail, since that plague was exceedingly great.

~ ZECHARIAH 4:1—6:15 ~

Now the angel who talked with me came back and wakened me, as a man who is wakened out of his sleep. ² And he said to me, "What do you see?"

So I said, "I am looking, and there *is* a lampstand of solid gold with a bowl on top of it, and on the *stand* seven lamps with seven pipes to the seven lamps. ³ Two olive trees *are* by it, one at the right of the bowl and the other at its left." ⁴ So I answered and spoke to the angel who talked with me, saying, "What *are* these, my lord?"

⁵ Then the angel who talked with me answered and said to me, "Do you not know what these are?"

And I said, "No, my lord."

⁶ So he answered and said to me:

"This *is* the word of the LORD to
      Zerubbabel:
'Not by might nor by power, but
      by My Spirit,'
Says the LORD of hosts.
⁷ 'Who *are* you, O great mountain?
Before Zerubbabel *you shall
      become* a plain!
And he shall bring forth the
      capstone
With shouts of "Grace, grace to
      it!" ' "

⁸ Moreover the word of the LORD came to me, saying:

⁹ "The hands of Zerubbabel
Have laid the foundation of this
      temple;
His hands shall also finish *it*.
Then you will know
That the LORD of hosts has sent
      Me to you.
¹⁰ For who has despised the day of
      small things?
For these seven rejoice to see

The plumb line in the hand of
      Zerubbabel.
They are the eyes of the LORD,
Which scan to and fro throughout
      the whole earth."

¹¹ Then I answered and said to him, "What *are* these two olive trees—at the right of the lampstand and at its left?" ¹² And I further answered and said to him, "What *are these* two olive branches that *drip* into the receptacles of the two gold pipes from which the golden *oil* drains?"

¹³ Then he answered me and said, "Do you not know what these *are?*"

And I said, "No, my lord."

¹⁴ So he said, "These *are* the two anointed ones, who stand beside the Lord of the whole earth."

5 Then I turned and raised my eyes, and saw there a flying scroll.

² And he said to me, "What do you see?"

So I answered, "I see a flying scroll. Its length *is* twenty cubits and its width ten cubits."

³ Then he said to me, "This *is* the curse that goes out over the face of the whole earth: 'Every thief shall be expelled,' according *to* this side of *the scroll;* and, 'Every perjurer shall be expelled,' according *to* that side of it."

⁴ "I will send out *the curse,*" says the
      LORD of hosts;
"It shall enter the house of the
      thief
And the house of the one who
      swears falsely by My name.
It shall remain in the midst of his
      house
And consume it, with its timber
      and stones."

Family Traditions

The story is told of a devout Christian who was faithful in his daily devotions. He read portions of Scripture and a devotional book, meditated silently for awhile, and then prayed. As time went by, his prayers became longer and more intense. He came to cherish this quiet time in his bedroom. And his cat liked it, too! She would snuggle against him, purring loudly. This interrupted the man so he put a collar around the cat's neck and tied her to the bedpost whenever he wanted undisturbed devotional time.

The daughter of this man noticed how much his devotional time meant to him, and she adopted the practice. She dutifully tied her cat to the bedpost and proceeded to read and pray. Her prayer time was shorter, however. The day came when her son grew up. He desired also to keep some of the family traditions, but by his generation, the pace of life had quickened greatly. He felt he had no time for elaborate devotions, so he eliminated the time for meditation, Bible reading, and prayer. Still, in order to carry on the tradition, while dressing each morning, he tied his cat to the bedpost!

Explain to your children why you keep certain rituals, lest they follow them blindly, without meaning or purpose.

5 Then the angel who talked with me came out and said to me, "Lift your eyes now, and see what this *is* that goes forth."

6 So I asked, "What *is* it?" And he said, "It *is* a basket that is going forth."

He also said, "This *is* their resemblance throughout the earth: 7 Here *is* a lead disc lifted up, and this *is* a woman sitting inside the basket"; 8 then he said, "This *is* Wickedness!" And he thrust her down into the basket, and threw the lead cover over its mouth. 9 Then I raised my eyes and looked, and there *were* two women, coming with the wind in their wings; for they had wings like the wings of a stork, and they lifted up the basket between earth and heaven.

10 So I said to the angel who talked with me, "Where are they carrying the basket?"

11 And he said to me, "To build a house for it in the land of Shinar; when it is ready, *the basket* will be set there on its base."

6 Then I turned and raised my eyes and looked, and behold, four chariots *were* coming from between two mountains, and the mountains *were* mountains of bronze. 2 With the first chariot *were* red horses, with the second chariot black horses, 3 with the third chariot white horses, and with the fourth chariot dappled horses— strong *steeds*. 4 Then I answered and said to the angel who talked with me, "What *are* these, my lord?"

5 And the angel answered and said to me, "These *are* four spirits of heaven, who go out from *their* station before the Lord of all the earth. 6 The one with the black horses is going to the north country, the white are going after them, and the dappled are going toward the south country." 7 Then the strong *steeds* went out, eager to go, that they might walk to and fro throughout the earth. And He said, "Go, walk to and fro throughout the earth." So they walked to and fro throughout the earth. 8 And He called to me, and spoke to me, saying, "See, those who go toward the north country have given rest to My Spirit in the north country."

9 Then the word of the LORD came to me, saying: 10 "Receive *the gift* from the captives—from Heldai, Tobijah, and Jedaiah, who have come from Babylon— and go the same day and enter the house of Josiah the son of Zephaniah. 11 Take the silver and gold, make an elaborate crown, and set *it* on the head of Joshua the son of Jehozadak, the high priest. 12 Then speak to him, saying, 'Thus says the LORD of hosts, saying:

"Behold, the Man whose name *is* the BRANCH!
From His place He shall branch out,
And He shall build the temple of the LORD;
13 Yes, He shall build the temple of the LORD.
He shall bear the glory,
And shall sit and rule on His throne;
So He shall be a priest on His throne,
And the counsel of peace shall be between them both." '

14 "Now the elaborate crown shall be for a memorial in the temple of the LORD for Helem, Tobijah, Jedaiah, and Hen the son of Zephaniah. 15 Even those from afar shall come and build the temple of the LORD. Then you shall know that the LORD of hosts has sent Me to you. And *this* shall come to pass if you diligently obey the voice of the LORD your God."

～ PSALM 148:1–6 ～

1 Praise the LORD!

Praise the LORD from the heavens;
Praise Him in the heights!
2 Praise Him, all His angels;
Praise Him, all His hosts!
3 Praise Him, sun and moon;
Praise Him, all you stars of light!
4 Praise Him, you heavens of heavens,
And you waters above the heavens!

5 Let them praise the name of the LORD,
For He commanded and they were created.
6 He also established them forever and ever;

He made a decree which shall not
pass away.

～ PROVERBS 30:24–28 ～

²⁴ There are four *things which* are little
on the earth,
But they *are* exceedingly wise:
²⁵ The ants *are* a people not strong,
Yet they prepare their food in the
summer;
²⁶ The rock badgers are a feeble
folk,
Yet they make their homes in the
crags;
²⁷ The locusts have no king,
Yet they all advance in ranks;
²⁸ The spider skillfully grasps with its
hands,
And it is in kings' palaces.

～ REVELATION 17:1–18 ～

Then one of the seven angels who had
the seven bowls came and talked with me,
saying to me, "Come, I will show you the
judgment of the great harlot who sits on
many waters, ² with whom the kings of
the earth committed fornication, and the
inhabitants of the earth were made drunk
with the wine of her fornication."

³ So he carried me away in the Spirit
into the wilderness. And I saw a woman
sitting on a scarlet beast *which was* full of
names of blasphemy, having seven heads
and ten horns. ⁴ The woman was arrayed
in purple and scarlet, and adorned with
gold and precious stones and pearls,
having in her hand a golden cup full of
abominations and the filthiness of her fornication. ⁵ And on her forehead a name
was written:

MYSTERY, BABYLON THE GREAT,
THE MOTHER OF HARLOTS AND
OF THE ABOMINATIONS OF THE
EARTH.

⁶ I saw the woman, drunk with the blood
of the saints and with the blood of the
martyrs of Jesus. And when I saw her, I
marveled with great amazement.

⁷ But the angel said to me, "Why did
you marvel? I will tell you the mystery of
the woman and of the beast that carries
her, which has the seven heads and the
ten horns. ⁸ The beast that you saw was,
and is not, and will ascend out of the bottomless pit and go to perdition. And those
who dwell on the earth will marvel, whose
names are not written in the Book of Life
from the foundation of the world, when
they see the beast that was, and is not,
and yet is.

⁹ "Here *is* the mind which has wisdom:
The seven heads are seven mountains on
which the woman sits. ¹⁰ There are also
seven kings. Five have fallen, one is, *and*
the other has not yet come. And when he
comes, he must continue a short time.
¹¹ The beast that was, and is not, is himself also the eighth, and is of the seven,
and is going to perdition.

¹² "The ten horns which you saw are
ten kings who have received no kingdom
as yet, but they receive authority for one
hour as kings with the beast. ¹³ These are
of one mind, and they will give their
power and authority to the beast. ¹⁴ These
will make war with the Lamb, and the
Lamb will overcome them, for He is Lord
of lords and King of kings; and those
who are with Him *are* called, chosen, and
faithful."

¹⁵ Then he said to me, "The waters
which you saw, where the harlot sits, are
peoples, multitudes, nations, and tongues.
¹⁶ And the ten horns which you saw on
the beast, these will hate the harlot, make
her desolate and naked, eat her flesh and
burn her with fire. ¹⁷ For God has put it
into their hearts to fulfill His purpose, to
be of one mind, and to give their kingdom to the beast, until the words of God
are fulfilled. ¹⁸ And the woman whom you
saw is that great city which reigns over
the kings of the earth."

~ ZECHARIAH 7:1—9:17 ~

Now in the fourth year of King Darius it came to pass *that* the word of the LORD came to Zechariah, on the fourth day of the ninth month, Chislev, ² when *the people* sent Sherezer, with Regem-Melech and his men, *to* the house of God, to pray before the LORD, ³ *and* to ask the priests who *were* in the house of the LORD of hosts, and the prophets, saying, "Should I weep in the fifth month and fast as I have done for so many years?"

⁴ Then the word of the LORD of hosts came to me, saying, ⁵ "Say to all the people of the land, and to the priests: 'When you fasted and mourned in the fifth and seventh *months* during those seventy years, did you really fast for Me—for Me? ⁶ When you eat and when you drink, do you not eat and drink *for yourselves?* ⁷ *Should you* not *have obeyed* the words which the LORD proclaimed through the former prophets when Jerusalem and the cities around it were inhabited and prosperous, and the South and the Lowland were inhabited?' "

⁸ Then the word of the LORD came to Zechariah, saying, ⁹ "Thus says the LORD of hosts:

'Execute true justice,
    Show mercy and compassion
    Everyone to his brother.
¹⁰ Do not oppress the widow or the
        fatherless,
    The alien or the poor.
    Let none of you plan evil in his
        heart
    Against his brother.'

¹¹ But they refused to heed, shrugged their shoulders, and stopped their ears so that they could not hear. ¹² Yes, they made their hearts like flint, refusing to hear the law and the words which the LORD of hosts had sent by His Spirit through the former prophets. Thus great wrath came from the LORD of hosts. ¹³ Therefore it happened, *that* just as He proclaimed and they would not hear, so they called out and I would not listen," says the LORD of hosts. ¹⁴ "But I scattered them with a whirlwind among all the nations which they had not known. Thus the land became desolate after them, so that no one passed through or returned; for they made the pleasant land desolate."

8 Again the word of the LORD of hosts came, saying, ² "Thus says the LORD of hosts:

'I am zealous for Zion with great
        zeal;
    With great fervor I am zealous for
        her.'

³ "Thus says the LORD:

'I will return to Zion,
    And dwell in the midst of
        Jerusalem.
    Jerusalem shall be called the City
        of Truth,
    The Mountain of the LORD of
        hosts,
    The Holy Mountain.'

⁴ "Thus says the LORD of hosts:

'Old men and old women shall
        again sit
    In the streets of Jerusalem,
    Each one with his staff in his hand
    Because of great age.
⁵   The streets of the city
    Shall be full of boys and girls
    Playing in its streets.'

⁶ "Thus says the LORD of hosts:

'If it is marvelous in the eyes of the
        remnant of this people in these
        days,
    Will it also be marvelous in My
        eyes?'
    Says the LORD of hosts.

⁷ "Thus says the LORD of hosts:

'Behold, I will save My people
        from the land of the east
    And from the land of the west;
⁸   I will bring them *back,*

Honest Communication

These are the things you shall do: speak each man the truth to his neighbor; give judgment in your gates for truth, justice, and peace.

Zechariah 8:16

Bill and Lynne Hybels write in *Fit to Be Tied*: "Picture this: It is midnight. The full moon is postcard perfect and the breeze is warm. Lynne and I are sitting on a park bench at a wooded camp in Wisconsin. Twenty years old. Dating seriously. No one around . . . I wrap my arms around her. This is what it's all about, I think. Lynne lifts her head and looks deeply into my eyes. 'Bill, I just don't feel close to you right now.' . . . 'For heaven's sake, honey, what do you want?' I hug her a little tighter, laugh off her comment, and dismiss it from my mind.

"Big mistake! If I could play that scene over, I would do it this way. I would take her hands off my shoulders, slide about a foot away, look her straight in the eye and say, 'Why don't you feel close to me? . . . If you don't know exactly why you said it, just start talking about how you feel. Maybe we can figure it out.'

"A response like that would have set a precedent for honest communication that could have made our marriage much easier. Instead we set a precedent for evasiveness, for burying feelings, for dismissing uncomfortable thoughts."

Never dismiss what your spouse says. There's a grain of truth in every joke, every sigh, every whim. Don't let those opportunities for honest communication pass by. Seize the moment to grow closer to one another.

And they shall dwell in the midst
   of Jerusalem.
They shall be My people
And I will be their God,
In truth and righteousness.'

9 "Thus says the LORD of hosts:

'Let your hands be strong,
You who have been hearing in
   these days
These words by the mouth of the
   prophets,
Who *spoke* in the day the
   foundation was laid
For the house of the LORD of
   hosts,
That the temple might be built.
10 For before these days
There were no wages for man nor
   any hire for beast;
There was no peace from the
   enemy for whoever went out or
   came in;
For I set all men, everyone, against
   his neighbor.

11 But now I *will* not *treat* the remnant of
this people as in the former days,' says
the LORD of hosts.

12 'For the seed *shall be* prosperous,
The vine shall give its fruit,
The ground shall give her increase,
And the heavens shall give their
   dew—
I will cause the remnant of this
   people
To possess all these.
13 And it shall come to pass
That just as you were a curse
   among the nations,
O house of Judah and house of
   Israel,
So I will save you, and you shall
   be a blessing.
Do not fear,
Let your hands be strong.'

14 "For thus says the LORD of hosts:

'Just as I determined to punish you
When your fathers provoked Me
   to wrath,'
Says the LORD of hosts,

'And I would not relent,
15 So again in these days
I am determined to do good
To Jerusalem and to the house of
   Judah.
Do not fear.
16 These *are* the things you shall do:
Speak each man the truth to his
   neighbor;
Give judgment in your gates for
   truth, justice, and peace;
17 Let none of you think evil in your
   heart against your neighbor;
And do not love a false oath.
For all these *are things* that I hate,'
Says the LORD."

18 Then the word of the LORD of hosts
came to me, saying, 19 "Thus says the
LORD of hosts:

'The fast of the fourth *month,*
The fast of the fifth,
The fast of the seventh,
And the fast of the tenth,
Shall be joy and gladness and
   cheerful feasts
For the house of Judah.
Therefore love truth and peace.'

20 "Thus says the LORD of hosts:

'Peoples shall yet come,
Inhabitants of many cities;
21 The inhabitants of one *city* shall
   go to another, saying,
"Let us continue to go and pray
   before the LORD,
And seek the LORD of hosts.
I myself will go also."
22 Yes, many peoples and strong
   nations
Shall come to seek the LORD of
   hosts in Jerusalem,
And to pray before the LORD.'

23 "Thus says the LORD of hosts: 'In
those days ten men from every language
of the nations shall grasp the sleeve of a
Jewish man, saying, "Let us go with you,
for we have heard *that* God *is* with
you." ' "

9   The burden of the word of the
       LORD

Against the land of Hadrach,
And Damascus its resting place
(For the eyes of men
And all the tribes of Israel
Are on the LORD);
2 Also *against* Hamath, *which*
    borders on it,
And *against* Tyre and Sidon,
    though they are very wise.

3 For Tyre built herself a tower,
Heaped up silver like the dust,
And gold like the mire of the
    streets.
4 Behold, the LORD will cast her
    out;
He will destroy her power in the
    sea,
And she will be devoured by fire.

5 Ashkelon shall see *it* and fear;
Gaza also shall be very sorrowful;
And Ekron, for He dried up her
    expectation.
The king shall perish from Gaza,
And Ashkelon shall not be
    inhabited.

6 "A mixed race shall settle in
    Ashdod,
And I will cut off the pride of the
    Philistines.
7 I will take away the blood from
    his mouth,
And the abominations from
    between his teeth.
But he who remains, even he *shall
    be* for our God,
And shall be like a leader
    in Judah,
And Ekron like a Jebusite.
8 I will camp around My house
Because of the army,
Because of him who passes by and
    him who returns.
No more shall an oppressor pass
    through them,
For now I have seen with My eyes.

9 "Rejoice greatly, O daughter of
    Zion!
Shout, O daughter of Jerusalem!
Behold, your King is coming to
    you;
He *is* just and having salvation,

Lowly and riding on a donkey,
A colt, the foal of a donkey.
10 I will cut off the chariot from
    Ephraim
And the horse from Jerusalem;
The battle bow shall be cut off.
He shall speak peace to the
    nations;
His dominion *shall be* 'from sea to
    sea,
And from the River to the ends of
    the earth.'

11 "As for you also,
Because of the blood of your
    covenant,
I will set your prisoners free from
    the waterless pit.
12 Return to the stronghold,
You prisoners of hope.
Even today I declare
That I will restore double to you.
13 For I have bent Judah, My *bow*,
Fitted the bow with Ephraim,
And raised up your sons, O Zion,
Against your sons, O Greece,
And made you like the sword of a
    mighty man."

14 Then the LORD will be seen over
    them,
And His arrow will go forth like
    lightning.
The Lord GOD will blow the
    trumpet,
And go with whirlwinds from the
    south.
15 The LORD of hosts will defend
    them;
They shall devour and subdue
    with slingstones.
They shall drink *and* roar as if
    with wine;
They shall be filled *with blood* like
    basins,
Like the corners of the altar.
16 The LORD their God will save
    them in that day,
As the flock of His people.
For they *shall be like* the jewels of
    a crown,
Lifted like a banner over His
    land—
17 For how great is its goodness
And how great its beauty!

Grain shall make the young men
thrive,
And new wine the young women.

~ PSALM 148:7–14 ~

7 Praise the LORD from the earth,
You great sea creatures and all the
depths;
8 Fire and hail, snow and clouds;
Stormy wind, fulfilling His word;
9 Mountains and all hills;
Fruitful trees and all cedars;
10 Beasts and all cattle;
Creeping things and flying fowl;
11 Kings of the earth and all peoples;
Princes and all judges of the earth;
12 Both young men and maidens;
Old men and children.

13 Let them praise the name of the
LORD,
For His name alone is exalted;
His glory is above the earth and
heaven.
14 And He has exalted the horn of His
people,
The praise of all His saints—
Of the children of Israel,
A people near to Him.

Praise the LORD!

~ PROVERBS 30:29–31 ~

29 There are three things which are
majestic in pace,
Yes, four which are stately in walk:
30 A lion, which is mighty among beasts
And does not turn away from any;
31 A greyhound,
A male goat also,
And a king whose troops are with
him.

~ REVELATION 18:1–24 ~

After these things I saw another angel
coming down from heaven, having great
authority, and the earth was illuminated
with his glory. 2 And he cried mightily with
a loud voice, saying, "Babylon the great
is fallen, is fallen, and has become a dwelling place of demons, a prison for every
foul spirit, and a cage for every unclean
and hated bird! 3 For all the nations have
drunk of the wine of the wrath of her fornication, the kings of the earth have committed fornication with her, and the
merchants of the earth have become rich
through the abundance of her luxury."

4 And I heard another voice from heav-
en saying, "Come out of her, my people,
lest you share in her sins, and lest you receive of her plagues. 5 For her sins have
reached to heaven, and God has remembered her iniquities. 6 Render to her just
as she rendered to you, and repay her
double according to her works; in the cup
which she has mixed, mix double for her.
7 In the measure that she glorified herself
and lived luxuriously, in the same measure give her torment and sorrow; for
she says in her heart, 'I sit as queen, and
am no widow, and will not see sorrow.'
8 Therefore her plagues will come in one
day—death and mourning and famine.
And she will be utterly burned with
fire, for strong is the Lord God who
judges her.

9 "The kings of the earth who committed fornication and lived luxuriously
with her will weep and lament for her,
when they see the smoke of her burning,
10 standing at a distance for fear of her
torment, saying, 'Alas, alas, that great city
Babylon, that mighty city! For in one hour
your judgment has come.'

11 "And the merchants of the earth will
weep and mourn over her, for no one buys
their merchandise anymore: 12 merchandise of gold and silver, precious stones and
pearls, fine linen and purple, silk and scarlet, every kind of citron wood, every kind
of object of ivory, every kind of object of
most precious wood, bronze, iron, and
marble; 13 and cinnamon and incense, fragrant oil and frankincense, wine and oil,
fine flour and wheat, cattle and sheep,
horses and chariots, and bodies and souls
of men. 14 The fruit that your soul longed
for has gone from you, and all the things
which are rich and splendid have gone
from you, and you shall find them no
more at all. 15 The merchants of these
things, who became rich by her, will stand
at a distance for fear of her torment, weeping and wailing, 16 and saying, 'Alas, alas,
that great city that was clothed in fine

linen, purple, and scarlet, and adorned with gold and precious stones and pearls! [17] For in one hour such great riches came to nothing.' Every shipmaster, all who travel by ship, sailors, and as many as trade on the sea, stood at a distance [18] and cried out when they saw the smoke of her burning, saying, 'What *is* like this great city?'

[19] "They threw dust on their heads and cried out, weeping and wailing, and saying, 'Alas, alas, that great city, in which all who had ships on the sea became rich by her wealth! For in one hour she is made desolate.'

[20] "Rejoice over her, O heaven, and *you* holy apostles and prophets, for God has avenged you on her!"

[21] Then a mighty angel took up a stone like a great millstone and threw *it* into the sea, saying, "Thus with violence the great city Babylon shall be thrown down, and shall not be found anymore. [22] The sound of harpists, musicians, flutists, and trumpeters shall not be heard in you anymore. No craftsman of any craft shall be found in you anymore, and the sound of a millstone shall not be heard in you anymore. [23] The light of a lamp shall not shine in you anymore, and the voice of bridegroom and bride shall not be heard in you anymore. For your merchants were the great men of the earth, for by your sorcery all the nations were deceived. [24] And in her was found the blood of prophets and saints, and of all who were slain on the earth."

～ ZECHARIAH 10:1—12:14 ～

[1] Ask the LORD for rain
In the time of the latter rain.
The LORD will make flashing clouds;
He will give them showers of rain,
Grass in the field for everyone.

[2] For the idols speak delusion;
The diviners envision lies,
And tell false dreams;
They comfort in vain.
Therefore *the people* wend their way like sheep;
They are in trouble because *there is* no shepherd.

[3] "My anger is kindled against the shepherds,
And I will punish the goatherds.
For the LORD of hosts will visit His flock,
The house of Judah,
And will make them as His royal horse in the battle.
[4] From him comes the cornerstone,
From him the tent peg,
From him the battle bow,
From him every ruler together.
[5] They shall be like mighty men,
Who tread down *their enemies*
In the mire of the streets in the battle.
They shall fight because the LORD is with them,
And the riders on horses shall be put to shame.

[6] "I will strengthen the house of Judah,
And I will save the house of Joseph.
I will bring them back,
Because I have mercy on them.
They shall be as though I had not cast them aside;
For I *am* the LORD their God,
And I will hear them.
[7] *Those of* Ephraim shall be like a mighty man,
And their heart shall rejoice as if with wine.
Yes, their children shall see *it* and be glad;
Their heart shall rejoice in the LORD.
[8] I will whistle for them and gather them,
For I will redeem them;
And they shall increase as they once increased.

9 "I will sow them among the
    peoples,
  And they shall remember Me in
    far countries;
  They shall live, together with their
    children,
  And they shall return.
10 I will also bring them back from
    the land of Egypt,
  And gather them from Assyria.
  I will bring them into the land of
    Gilead and Lebanon,
  Until no *more room* is found for
    them.
11 He shall pass through the sea with
    affliction,
  And strike the waves of the sea:
  All the depths of the River shall
    dry up.
  Then the pride of Assyria shall be
    brought down,
  And the scepter of Egypt shall
    depart.

12 "So I will strengthen them in the
    LORD,
  And they shall walk up and down
    in His name,"
  Says the LORD.

11 Open your doors, O Lebanon,
  That fire may devour your cedars.
2 Wail, O cypress, for the cedar has
    fallen,
  Because the mighty *trees* are
    ruined.
  Wail, O oaks of Bashan,
  For the thick forest has come
    down.
3 *There is* the sound of wailing
    shepherds!
  For their glory is in ruins.
  There is the sound of roaring
    lions!
  For the pride of the Jordan is in
    ruins.

4 Thus says the LORD my God, "Feed
the flock for slaughter, 5 whose owners
slaughter them and feel no guilt; those
who sell them say, 'Blessed be the LORD,
for I am rich'; and their shepherds do not
pity them. 6 For I will no longer pity the
inhabitants of the land," says the LORD.

"But indeed I will give everyone into his
neighbor's hand and into the hand of
his king. They shall attack the land, and I
will not deliver *them* from their hand."
7 So I fed the flock for slaughter, in particular the poor of the flock. I took for
myself two staffs: the one I called Beauty,
and the other I called Bonds; and I fed
the flock. 8 I dismissed the three shepherds
in one month. My soul loathed them, and
their soul also abhorred me. 9 Then I said,
"I will not feed you. Let what is dying
die, and what is perishing perish. Let those
that are left eat each other's flesh." 10 And
I took my staff, Beauty, and cut it in two,
that I might break the covenant which I
had made with all the peoples. 11 So it was
broken on that day. Thus the poor of the
flock, who were watching me, knew that
it *was* the word of the LORD. 12 Then I
said to them, "If it is agreeable to you,
give *me* my wages; and if not, refrain."
So they weighed out for my wages thirty
pieces of silver.
13 And the LORD said to me, "Throw it
to the potter"—that princely price they
set on me. So I took the thirty *pieces* of
silver and threw them into the house
of the LORD for the potter. 14 Then I cut
in two my other staff, Bonds, that I might
break the brotherhood between Judah and
Israel.
15 And the LORD said to me, "Next, take
for yourself the implements of a foolish
shepherd. 16 For indeed I will raise up
a shepherd in the land *who* will not care
for those who are cut off, nor seek the
young, nor heal those that are broken, nor
feed those that still stand. But he will eat
the flesh of the fat and tear their hooves
in pieces.

17 "Woe to the worthless shepherd,
    Who leaves the flock!
  A sword *shall be* against his arm
  And against his right eye;
  His arm shall completely wither,
  And his right eye shall be totally
    blinded."

12 The burden of the word of the LORD
against Israel. Thus says the LORD, who
stretches out the heavens, lays the foundation of the earth, and forms the spirit
of man within him: 2 "Behold, I will make

Good Humor

A missionary from Sweden was once urged by his friends to give up his idea of returning to India because it was so hot there. "Man," the fellow Swede urged, as if telling his friend something he didn't already know, "It's 120 degrees in the shade in that country!" The Swedish missionary replied, "Vell, ve don't always have to stay in the shade, do ve?"

Humor is not a sin. It is a God-given escape hatch. Being able to see the lighter side of life is a virtue. And indeed, every vocation and behavior in life has a lighter side, if we are only willing to see it. Wholesome humor can do a great deal to help defuse a tense, heated situation.

In developing a good sense of humor, we must be able to laugh at our own mistakes; accept justified criticism — and recover from it; and learn to avoid using statements that are unsuitable — even though they may be funny.

James M. Gray and William Houghton — two godly men — were praying together one day and the elderly Dr. Gray concluded his prayer by saying: "Lord, keep me cheerful. Keep me from becoming a cranky, old man." Keeping a sense of humor is a great way to avoid becoming a bitter, impatient, critical person.

> Let Israel rejoice in their Maker; let the children of Zion be joyful in their King.
>
> *Psalm 149:2*

Jerusalem a cup of drunkenness to all the surrounding peoples, when they lay siege against Judah and Jerusalem. ³ And it shall happen in that day that I will make Jerusalem a very heavy stone for all peoples; all who would heave it away will surely be cut in pieces, though all nations of the earth are gathered against it. ⁴ In that day," says the LORD, "I will strike every horse with confusion, and its rider with madness; I will open My eyes on the house of Judah, and will strike every horse of the peoples with blindness. ⁵ And the governors of Judah shall say in their heart, 'The inhabitants of Jerusalem *are* my strength in the LORD of hosts, their God.' ⁶ In that day I will make the governors of Judah like a firepan in the woodpile, and like a fiery torch in the sheaves; they shall devour all the surrounding peoples on the right hand and on the left, but Jerusalem shall be inhabited again in her own place—Jerusalem.

⁷ "The LORD will save the tents of Judah first, so that the glory of the house of David and the glory of the inhabitants of Jerusalem shall not become greater than that of Judah. ⁸ In that day the LORD will defend the inhabitants of Jerusalem; the one who is feeble among them in that day shall be like David, and the house of David *shall be* like God, like the Angel of the LORD before them. ⁹ It shall be in that day *that* I will seek to destroy all the nations that come against Jerusalem.

¹⁰ "And I will pour on the house of David and on the inhabitants of Jerusalem the Spirit of grace and supplication; then they will look on Me whom they pierced. Yes, they will mourn for Him as one mourns for *his* only *son*, and grieve for Him as one grieves for a firstborn. ¹¹ In that day there shall be a great mourning in Jerusalem, like the mourning at Hadad Rimmon in the plain of Megiddo. ¹² And the land shall mourn, every family by itself: the family of the house of David by itself, and their wives by themselves; the family of the house of Nathan by itself, and their wives by themselves; ¹³ the family of the house of Levi by itself, and their wives by themselves; the family of Shimei by itself, and their wives by themselves; ¹⁴ all the families that remain, every family by itself, and their wives by themselves.

~ PSALM 149:1–4 ~

1   Praise the LORD!

Sing to the LORD a new song,
And His praise in the assembly of
saints.

2   Let Israel rejoice in their Maker;
Let the children of Zion be joyful in
their King.
3   Let them praise His name with the
dance;
Let them sing praises to Him with
the timbrel and harp.
4   For the LORD takes pleasure in His
people;
He will beautify the humble with
salvation.

~ PROVERBS 30:32, 33 ~

32 If you have been foolish in exalting
yourself,
Or if you have devised evil, *put your*
hand on *your* mouth.
33 For *as* the churning of milk produces
butter,
And wringing the nose produces
blood,
So the forcing of wrath produces
strife.

~ REVELATION 19:1–21 ~

After these things I heard a loud voice of a great multitude in heaven, saying, "Alleluia! Salvation and glory and honor and power *belong* to the Lord our God! ² For true and righteous *are* His judgments, because He has judged the great harlot who corrupted the earth with her fornication; and He has avenged on her the blood of His servants *shed* by her." ³ Again they said, "Alleluia! Her smoke rises up forever and ever!" ⁴ And the twenty-four elders and the four living creatures fell down and worshiped God who sat on the throne, saying, "Amen! Alleluia!" ⁵ Then a voice came from the throne, saying, "Praise our God, all you His servants and those who fear Him, both small and great!"

⁶ And I heard, as it were, the voice of a

great multitude, as the sound of many waters and as the sound of mighty thunderings, saying, "Alleluia! For the Lord God Omnipotent reigns! ⁷ Let us be glad and rejoice and give Him glory, for the marriage of the Lamb has come, and His wife has made herself ready." ⁸ And to her it was granted to be arrayed in fine linen, clean and bright, for the fine linen is the righteous acts of the saints.

⁹ Then he said to me, "Write: 'Blessed *are* those who are called to the marriage supper of the Lamb!' " And he said to me, "These are the true sayings of God." ¹⁰ And I fell at his feet to worship him. But he said to me, "See *that you do* not *do that*! I am your fellow servant, and of your brethren who have the testimony of Jesus. Worship God! For the testimony of Jesus is the spirit of prophecy."

¹¹ Now I saw heaven opened, and behold, a white horse. And He who sat on him *was* called Faithful and True, and in righteousness He judges and makes war. ¹² His eyes *were* like a flame of fire, and on His head *were* many crowns. He had a name written that no one knew except Himself. ¹³ He *was* clothed with a robe dipped in blood, and His name is called The Word of God. ¹⁴ And the armies in heaven, clothed in fine linen, white and clean, followed Him on white horses. ¹⁵ Now out of His mouth goes a sharp sword, that with it He should strike the nations. And He Himself will rule them with a rod of iron. He Himself treads the winepress of the fierceness and wrath of Almighty God. ¹⁶ And He has on *His* robe and on His thigh a name written:

KING OF KINGS
AND LORD OF LORDS.

¹⁷ Then I saw an angel standing in the sun; and he cried with a loud voice, saying to all the birds that fly in the midst of heaven, "Come and gather together for the supper of the great God, ¹⁸ that you may eat the flesh of kings, the flesh of captains, the flesh of mighty men, the flesh of horses and of those who sit on them, and the flesh of all *people,* free and slave, both small and great."

¹⁹ And I saw the beast, the kings of the earth, and their armies, gathered together to make war against Him who sat on the horse and against His army. ²⁰ Then the beast was captured, and with him the false prophet who worked signs in his presence, by which he deceived those who received the mark of the beast and those who worshiped his image. These two were cast alive into the lake of fire burning with brimstone. ²¹ And the rest were killed with the sword which proceeded from the mouth of Him who sat on the horse. And all the birds were filled with their flesh.

READING 364 · DECEMBER 30

~ ZECHARIAH 13:1—14:21 ~

In that day a fountain shall be opened for the house of David and for the inhabitants of Jerusalem, for sin and for uncleanness.

² "It shall be in that day," says the LORD of hosts, "*that* I will cut off the names of the idols from the land, and they shall no longer be remembered. I will also cause the prophets and the unclean spirit to depart from the land. ³ It shall come to pass *that* if anyone still prophesies, then his father and mother who begot him will say to him, 'You shall not live, because you have spoken lies in the name of the LORD.' And his father and mother who begot him shall thrust him through when he prophesies.

⁴ "And it shall be in that day *that* every prophet will be ashamed of his vision when he prophesies; they will not wear a robe of coarse hair to deceive. ⁵ But he will say, 'I *am* no prophet, I *am* a farmer; for a man taught me to keep cattle from my youth.' ⁶ And *one* will say to him, 'What are these wounds between your arms?' Then he will answer, '*Those* with which I was wounded in the house of my friends.'

7 "Awake, O sword, against My
    Shepherd,
    Against the Man who is My
       Companion,"
    Says the LORD of hosts.
    "Strike the Shepherd,
    And the sheep will be scattered;
    Then I will turn My hand against
       the little ones.
8 And it shall come to pass in all the
    land,"
    Says the LORD,
    "*That* two-thirds in it shall be cut
       off *and* die,
    But *one*-third shall be left in it:
9 I will bring the *one*-third through
    the fire,
    Will refine them as silver is
       refined,
    And test them as gold is tested.
    They will call on My name,
    And I will answer them.
    I will say, 'This *is* My people';
    And each one will say, 'The LORD
    is my God.' "

14 Behold, the day of the LORD is
    coming,
    And your spoil will be divided in
       your midst.
2 For I will gather all the nations to
    battle against Jerusalem;
    The city shall be taken,
    The houses rifled,
    And the women ravished.
    Half of the city shall go into
       captivity,
    But the remnant of the people
       shall not be cut off from the
       city.

3 Then the LORD will go forth
    And fight against those nations,
    As He fights in the day of battle.
4 And in that day His feet will stand
    on the Mount of Olives,
    Which faces Jerusalem
       on the east.
    And the Mount of Olives shall be
       split in two,
    From east to west,
    Making a very large valley;
    Half of the mountain shall move
       toward the north
    And half of it toward the south.

5 Then you shall flee *through* My
    mountain valley,
    For the mountain valley shall
       reach to Azal.
    Yes, you shall flee
    As you fled from the earthquake
    In the days of Uzziah king of
       Judah.

    Thus the LORD my God will
       come,
    And all the saints with You.

6 It shall come to pass in that day
    That there will be no light;
    The lights will diminish.
7 It shall be one day
    Which is known to the LORD—
    Neither day nor night.
    But at evening time it shall
       happen
    That it will be light.

8 And in that day it shall be
    That living waters shall flow from
       Jerusalem,
    Half of them toward the eastern
       sea
    And half of them toward the
       western sea;
    In both summer and winter it shall
       occur.
9 And the LORD shall be King over
    all the earth.
    In that day it shall be—
    "The LORD *is* one,"
    And His name one.

10 All the land shall be turned into a
plain from Geba to Rimmon south of Jerusalem. *Jerusalem* shall be raised up and
inhabited in her place from Benjamin's
Gate to the place of the First Gate and
the Corner Gate, and *from* the Tower of
Hananel to the king's winepresses.

11 *The people* shall dwell in it;
    And no longer shall there be utter
       destruction,
    But Jerusalem shall be safely
       inhabited.

12 And this shall be the plague with
which the LORD will strike all the people
who fought against Jerusalem:

Gossip Golden?

Laura Ingalls Wilder writes in *Little House in the Ozarks*: "I know a little band of friends that calls itself a women's club. The avowed purpose of this club is study, but there is an undercurrent of deeper, truer things than even culture and self-improvement. There is no obligation, and there are no promises; but in forming the club and in selecting new members, only those are chosen who are kindhearted and dependable as well as the possessors of a certain degree of intelligence and a small amount of that genius which is the capacity for careful work. In short, those who are taken into membership are those who will make good friends, and so they are a little band who are each for all and all for each. . . .

"They are getting so in the habit of speaking good words that I expect to see them all develop into Golden Gossips.

"Ever hear of golden gossip? I read of it some years ago. A woman who was always talking about her friends and neighbors made it her business to talk of them, in fact, never said anything but good of them. She was a gossip, but it was 'golden gossip.' This women's club seems to be working in the same way."

Who wouldn't enjoy belonging to such a club?

Their flesh shall dissolve while
they stand on their feet,
Their eyes shall dissolve in their
sockets,
And their tongues shall dissolve in
their mouths.

13 It shall come to pass in that day
That a great panic from the LORD
will be among them.
Everyone will seize the hand of his
neighbor,
And raise his hand against his
neighbor's hand;

14 Judah also will fight at Jerusalem.
And the wealth of all the
surrounding nations
Shall be gathered together:
Gold, silver, and apparel in great
abundance.

15 Such also shall be the plague
On the horse *and* the mule,
On the camel and the donkey,
And on all the cattle that will be in
those camps.
So *shall* this plague *be*.

16 And it shall come to pass *that* everyone who is left of all the nations which
came against Jerusalem shall go up from
year to year to worship the King, the LORD
of hosts, and to keep the Feast of Tabernacles. 17 And it shall be *that* whichever
of the families of the earth do not come
up to Jerusalem to worship the King, the
LORD of hosts, on them there will be no
rain. 18 If the family of Egypt will not come
up and enter in, they *shall have* no *rain;*
they shall receive the plague with which
the LORD strikes the nations who do not
come up to keep the Feast of Tabernacles.
19 This shall be the punishment of Egypt
and the punishment of all the nations that
do not come up to keep the Feast of Tabernacles.
20 In that day "HOLINESS TO THE
LORD" shall be *engraved* on the bells of
the horses. The pots in the LORD's house
shall be like the bowls before the altar.
21 Yes, every pot in Jerusalem and Judah
shall be holiness to the LORD of hosts.
Everyone who sacrifices shall come and
take them and cook in them. In that day

there shall no longer be a Canaanite in
the house of the LORD of hosts.

∼ PSALM 149:5–9 ∼

5 Let the saints be joyful in glory;
Let them sing aloud on their beds.
6 *Let* the high praises of God *be* in
their mouth,
And a two-edged sword in their
hand,
7 To execute vengeance on the
nations,
And punishments on the peoples;
8 To bind their kings with chains,
And their nobles with fetters
of iron;
9 To execute on them the written
judgment—
This honor have all His saints.

Praise the LORD!

∼ PROVERBS 31:1–9 ∼

The words of King Lemuel, the utterance
which his mother taught him:

2 What, my son?
And what, son of my womb?
And what, son of my vows?
3 Do not give your strength to
women,
Nor your ways to that which
destroys kings.

4 *It is* not for kings, O Lemuel,
It is not for kings to drink wine,
Nor for princes intoxicating drink;
5 Lest they drink and forget the law,
And pervert the justice of all the
afflicted.
6 Give strong drink to him who is
perishing,
And wine to those who are bitter of
heart.
7 Let him drink and forget his poverty,
And remember his misery no more.

8 Open your mouth for the speechless,
In the cause of all *who are* appointed
to die.
9 Open your mouth, judge righteously,

And plead the cause of the poor and needy.

∼ REVELATION 20:1–15 ∼

Then I saw an angel coming down from heaven, having the key to the bottomless pit and a great chain in his hand. ² He laid hold of the dragon, that serpent of old, who is *the* Devil and Satan, and bound him for a thousand years; ³ and he cast him into the bottomless pit, and shut him up, and set a seal on him, so that he should deceive the nations no more till the thousand years were finished. But after these things he must be released for a little while.

⁴ And I saw thrones, and they sat on them, and judgment was committed to them. Then *I saw* the souls of those who had been beheaded for their witness to Jesus and for the word of God, who had not worshiped the beast or his image, and had not received *his* mark on their foreheads or on their hands. And they lived and reigned with Christ for a thousand years. ⁵ But the rest of the dead did not live again until the thousand years were finished. This *is* the first resurrection. ⁶ Blessed and holy *is* he who has part in the first resurrection. Over such the second death has no power, but they shall be priests of God and of Christ, and shall reign with Him a thousand years.

⁷ Now when the thousand years have expired, Satan will be released from his prison ⁸ and will go out to deceive the nations which are in the four corners of the earth, Gog and Magog, to gather them together to battle, whose number *is* as the sand of the sea. ⁹ They went up on the breadth of the earth and surrounded the camp of the saints and the beloved city. And fire came down from God out of heaven and devoured them. ¹⁰ The devil, who deceived them, was cast into the lake of fire and brimstone where the beast and the false prophet *are.* And they will be tormented day and night forever and ever.

¹¹ Then I saw a great white throne and Him who sat on it, from whose face the earth and the heaven fled away. And there was found no place for them. ¹² And I saw the dead, small and great, standing before God, and books were opened. And another book was opened, which is *the Book* of Life. And the dead were judged according to their works, by the things which were written in the books. ¹³ The sea gave up the dead who were in it, and Death and Hades delivered up the dead who were in them. And they were judged, each one according to his works. ¹⁴ Then Death and Hades were cast into the lake of fire. This is the second death. ¹⁵ And anyone not found written in the Book of Life was cast into the lake of fire.

∼ MALACHI 1:1—4:6 ∼

The burden of the word of the LORD to Israel by Malachi.

² "I have loved you," says the LORD.
  "Yet you say, 'In what way have You loved us?'
  Was not Esau Jacob's brother?"
  Says the LORD.
  "Yet Jacob I have loved;
³ But Esau I have hated,

And laid waste his mountains and his heritage
For the jackals of the wilderness."

⁴ Even though Edom has said,
  "We have been impoverished,
  But we will return and build the desolate places,"

Thus says the LORD of hosts:

"They may build, but I will throw
      down;
   They shall be called the Territory
      of Wickedness,
   And the people against whom the
      LORD will have indignation
      forever.
5   Your eyes shall see,
   And you shall say,
   'The LORD is magnified beyond the
      border of Israel.'

6   "A son honors *his* father,
   And a servant *his* master.
   If then I am the Father,
   Where *is* My honor?
   And if I *am* a Master,
   Where *is* My reverence?
   Says the LORD of hosts
   To you priests who despise My
      name.
   Yet you say, 'In what way have we
      despised Your name?'

7   "You offer defiled food on My
      altar,
   But say,
   'In what way have we defiled
      You?'
   By saying,
   'The table of the LORD is
      contemptible.'
8   And when you offer the blind as a
      sacrifice,
   Is it not evil?
   And when you offer the lame and
      sick,
   Is it not evil?
   Offer it then to your governor!
   Would he be pleased with you?
   Would he accept you favorably?"
   Says the LORD of hosts.

9   "But now entreat God's favor,
   That He may be gracious to us.
   While this is being *done* by your
      hands,
   Will He accept you favorably?"
   Says the LORD of hosts.
10 "Who *is there* even among you who
      would shut the doors,
   So that you would not kindle fire
      on My altar in vain?
   I have no pleasure in you,"
   Says the LORD of hosts,

"Nor will I accept an offering from
      your hands.
11 For from the rising of the sun,
      even to its going down,
   My name *shall be* great among the
      Gentiles;
   In every place incense *shall be*
      offered to My name,
   And a pure offering;
   For My name shall be great among
      the nations,"
   Says the LORD of hosts.

12 "But you profane it,
   In that you say,
   'The table of the LORD is defiled;
   And its fruit, its food, *is*
      contemptible.'
13 You also say,
   'Oh, what a weariness!'
   And you sneer at it,"
   Says the LORD of hosts.
   "And you bring the stolen, the
      lame, and the sick;
   Thus you bring an offering!
   Should I accept this from your
      hand?"
   Says the LORD.
14 "But cursed *be* the deceiver
   Who has in his flock a male,
   And takes a vow,
   But sacrifices to the Lord what is
      blemished—
   For I *am* a great King,"
   Says the LORD of hosts,
   "And My name *is to be* feared
      among the nations.

2   "And now, O priests, this
      commandment is for you.
2   If you will not hear,
   And if you will not take *it* to
      heart,
   To give glory to My name,"
   Says the LORD of hosts,
   "I will send a curse upon you,
   And I will curse your blessings.
   Yes, I have cursed them already,
   Because you do not take *it* to
      heart.

3   "Behold, I will rebuke your
      descendants
   And spread refuse on your faces,
   The refuse of your solemn feasts;

I Think You Are Wonderful

Many years ago, a famous singer was booked to perform at a Paris opera house. The event was sold out in a matter of days. The entire city was abuzz with anticipation. The night of the performance, the hall was packed with stately dressed men and women eager to hear the much-admired musician. The house manager took the stage and announced, "Ladies and gentlemen, thank you for your enthusiastic support. I am afraid that due to illness, the woman whom you've all come to hear will not be performing tonight. However, we have found a suitable substitute we hope will provide you with comparable entertainment."

The crowd groaned so loudly in its disappointment that few heard the singer's name. Their excitement fizzled into frustration. The stand-in singer gave everything she had, but when her performance was over she was met with an uncomfortable silence rather than applause. Then, from the balcony, a child stood up and shouted, "Mommy, I think you are wonderful!"

The crowd instantly responded with a thunderous ovation.

Once in a while we all need to hear someone say, "I think you are wonderful." Today, be the person who gives that kind word of encouragement to someone in need. God will reward you.

And *one* will take you away with
  it.
4 Then you shall know that I have
    sent this commandment to you,
  That My covenant with Levi may
    continue,"
  Says the LORD of hosts.
5 "My covenant was with him, *one* of
    life and peace,
  And I gave them to him *that he
    might* fear Me;
  So he feared Me
  And was reverent before My
    name.
6 The law of truth was in his
    mouth,
  And injustice was not found on his
    lips.
  He walked with Me in peace and
    equity,
  And turned many away from
    iniquity.

7 "For the lips of a priest should keep
    knowledge,
  And *people* should seek the law
    from his mouth;
  For he is the messenger of the
    LORD of hosts.
8 But you have departed from the
    way;
  You have caused many to stumble
    at the law.
  You have corrupted the covenant
    of Levi,"
  Says the LORD of hosts.
9 "Therefore I also have made you
    contemptible and base
  Before all the people,
  Because you have not kept My
    ways
  But have shown partiality in the
    law."

10 Have we not all one Father?
  Has not one God created us?
  Why do we deal treacherously
    with one another
  By profaning the covenant of the
    fathers?
11 Judah has dealt treacherously,
  And an abomination has been
    committed in Israel and in
    Jerusalem,
  For Judah has profaned

The LORD's holy *institution* which
    He loves:
  He has married the daughter of a
    foreign god.
12 May the LORD cut off from the
    tents of Jacob
  The man who does this, being
    awake and aware,
  Yet who brings an offering to the
    LORD of hosts!

13 And this is the second thing you
    do:
  You cover the altar of the LORD
    with tears,
  With weeping and crying;
  So He does not regard the offering
    anymore,
  Nor receive *it* with goodwill from
    your hands.
14 Yet you say, "For what reason?"
  Because the LORD has been
    witness
  Between you and the wife of your
    youth,
  With whom you have dealt
    treacherously;
  Yet she is your companion
  And your wife by covenant.
15 But did He not make *them* one,
  Having a remnant of the Spirit?
  And why one?
  He seeks godly offspring.
  Therefore take heed to your
    spirit,
  And let none deal treacherously
    with the wife of his youth.

16 "For the LORD God of Israel says
  That He hates divorce,
  For it covers one's garment with
    violence,"
  Says the LORD of hosts.
  "Therefore take heed to your spirit,
  That you do not deal
    treacherously."

17 You have wearied the LORD with
    your words;
  Yet you say,
  "In what way have we wearied
    Him?"
  In that you say,
  "Everyone who does evil
  Is good in the sight of the LORD,

And He delights in them,"
Or, "Where *is* the God of justice?"

3 "Behold, I send My messenger,
  And he will prepare the way
    before Me.
  And the Lord, whom you seek,
  Will suddenly come to His
    temple,
  Even the Messenger of the
    covenant,
  In whom you delight.
  Behold, He is coming,"
  Says the LORD of hosts.

2 "But who can endure the day of
    His coming?
  And who can stand when He
    appears?
  For He *is* like a refiner's fire
  And like launderers' soap.
3 He will sit as a refiner and a
    purifier of silver;
  He will purify the sons of Levi,
  And purge them as gold and
    silver,
  That they may offer to the LORD
  An offering in righteousness.

4 "Then the offering of Judah and
    Jerusalem
  Will be pleasant to the LORD,
  As in the days of old,
  As in former years.
5 And I will come near you for
    judgment;
  I will be a swift witness
  Against sorcerers,
  Against adulterers,
  Against perjurers,
  Against those who exploit wage
    earners and widows and
    orphans,
  And against those who turn away
    an alien—
  Because they do not fear Me,"
  Says the LORD of hosts.

6 "For I *am* the LORD, I do not
    change;
  Therefore you are not consumed,
  O sons of Jacob.
7 Yet from the days of your fathers
  You have gone away from My
    ordinances

And have not kept *them*.
  Return to Me, and I will return to
    you,"
  Says the LORD of hosts.
  "But you said,
  'In what way shall we return?'

8 "Will a man rob God?
  Yet you have robbed Me!
  But you say,
  'In what way have we robbed You?'
  In tithes and offerings.
9 You are cursed with a curse,
  For you have robbed Me,
  Even this whole nation.
10 Bring all the tithes into the
    storehouse,
  That there may be food in My
    house,
  And try Me now in this,"
  Says the LORD of hosts,
  "If I will not open for you the
    windows of heaven
  And pour out for you *such*
    blessing
  That *there will* not *be room*
    enough *to receive it.*

11 "And I will rebuke the devourer for
    your sakes,
  So that he will not destroy the
    fruit of your ground,
  Nor shall the vine fail to bear fruit
    for you in the field,"
  Says the LORD of hosts;
12 And all nations will call you
    blessed,
  For you will be a delightful land,"
  Says the LORD of hosts.
13 "Your words have been harsh
    against Me,"
  Says the LORD,
  "Yet you say,
  'What have we spoken against
    You?'
14 You have said,
  'It is useless to serve God;
  What profit *is it* that we have kept
    His ordinance,
  And that we have walked as
    mourners
  Before the LORD of hosts?
15 So now we call the proud blessed,
  For those who do wickedness are
    raised up;

They even tempt God and go
free.' "

16 Then those who feared the LORD
spoke to one another,
And the LORD listened and heard
them;
So a book of remembrance was
written before Him
For those who fear the LORD
And who meditate on His name.

17 "They shall be Mine," says the
LORD of hosts,
"On the day that I make them My
jewels.
And I will spare them
As a man spares his own son who
serves him."

18 Then you shall again discern
Between the righteous and the
wicked,
Between one who serves God
And one who does not serve Him.

4 "For behold, the day is coming,
Burning like an oven,
And all the proud, yes, all who do
wickedly will be stubble.
And the day which is coming shall
burn them up,"
Says the LORD of hosts,
"That will leave them neither root
nor branch.

2 But to you who fear My name
The Sun of Righteousness shall
arise
With healing in His wings;
And you shall go out
And grow fat like stall-fed calves.

3 You shall trample the wicked,
For they shall be ashes under the
soles of your feet
On the day that I do *this*,"
Says the LORD of hosts.

4 "Remember the Law of Moses, My
servant,
Which I commanded him in
Horeb for all Israel,
With the statutes and judgments.

5 Behold, I will send you Elijah the
prophet
Before the coming of the great
and dreadful day of the LORD.

6 And he will turn
The hearts of the fathers to the
children,
And the hearts of the children to
their fathers,
Lest I come and strike the earth
with a curse."

～ PSALM 150:1–6 ～

1 Praise the LORD!

Praise God in His sanctuary;
Praise Him in His mighty firmament!

2 Praise Him for His mighty acts;
Praise Him according to His
excellent greatness!

3 Praise Him with the sound of the
trumpet;
Praise Him with the lute and harp!

4 Praise Him with the timbrel and
dance;
Praise Him with stringed instruments
and flutes!

5 Praise Him with loud cymbals;
Praise Him with clashing cymbals!

6 Let everything that has breath praise
the LORD.

Praise the LORD!

～ PROVERBS 31:10–31 ～

10 Who can find a virtuous wife?
For her worth *is* far above rubies.

11 The heart of her husband safely
trusts her;
So he will have no lack of gain.

12 She does him good and not evil
All the days of her life.

13 She seeks wool and flax,
And willingly works with her hands.

14 She is like the merchant ships,
She brings her food from afar.

15 She also rises while it is yet night,
And provides food for her
household,
And a portion for her maidservants.

16 She considers a field and buys it;
From her profits she plants a
vineyard.

17 She girds herself with strength,

And strengthens her arms.
18 She perceives that her merchandise *is* good,
And her lamp does not go out by night.
19 She stretches out her hands to the distaff,
And her hand holds the spindle.
20 She extends her hand to the poor,
Yes, she reaches out her hands to the needy.
21 She is not afraid of snow for her household,
For all her household *is* clothed with scarlet.
22 She makes tapestry for herself;
Her clothing *is* fine linen and purple.
23 Her husband is known in the gates,
When he sits among the elders of the land.
24 She makes linen garments and sells *them*,
And supplies sashes for the merchants.
25 Strength and honor *are* her clothing;
She shall rejoice in time to come.
26 She opens her mouth with wisdom,
And on her tongue *is* the law of kindness.
27 She watches over the ways of her household,
And does not eat the bread of idleness.
28 Her children rise up and call her blessed;
Her husband *also,* and he praises her:
29 "Many daughters have done well,
But you excel them all."
30 Charm *is* deceitful and beauty *is* passing,
But a woman *who* fears the LORD, she shall be praised.
31 Give her of the fruit of her hands,
And let her own works praise her in the gates.

～ REVELATION 21:1—22:21 ～

Now I saw a new heaven and a new earth, for the first heaven and the first earth had passed away. Also there was no more sea. 2 Then I, John, saw the holy city, New Jerusalem, coming down out of heaven from God, prepared as a bride adorned for her husband. 3 And I heard a loud voice from heaven saying, "Behold, the tabernacle of God *is* with men, and He will dwell with them, and they shall be His people. God Himself will be with them *and be* their God. 4 And God will wipe away every tear from their eyes; there shall be no more death, nor sorrow, nor crying. There shall be no more pain, for the former things have passed away."

5 Then He who sat on the throne said, "Behold, I make all things new." And He said to me, "Write, for these words are true and faithful."

6 And He said to me, "It is done! I am the Alpha and the Omega, the Beginning and the End. I will give of the fountain of the water of life freely to him who thirsts. 7 He who overcomes shall inherit all things, and I will be his God and he shall be My son. 8 But the cowardly, unbelieving, abominable, murderers, sexually immoral, sorcerers, idolaters, and all liars shall have their part in the lake which burns with fire and brimstone, which is the second death."

9 Then one of the seven angels who had the seven bowls filled with the seven last plagues came to me and talked with me, saying, "Come, I will show you the bride, the Lamb's wife." 10 And he carried me away in the Spirit to a great and high mountain, and showed me the great city, the holy Jerusalem, descending out of heaven from God, 11 having the glory of God. Her light *was* like a most precious stone, like a jasper stone, clear as crystal. 12 Also she had a great and high wall with twelve gates, and twelve angels at the gates, and names written on them, which are *the names* of the twelve tribes of the children of Israel: 13 three gates on the east, three gates on the north, three gates on the south, and three gates on the west. 14 Now the wall of the city had twelve foundations, and on them were the names of the twelve apostles of the Lamb. 15 And he who talked with me had a gold reed to measure the city, its gates, and its wall. 16 The city is laid out as a square; its length is as great as its breadth. And he measured the city with the reed: twelve thousand furlongs. Its length, breadth, and height are equal. 17 Then he measured its wall: one hundred *and* forty-four cubits,

according to the measure of a man, that is, of an angel. ¹⁸ The construction of its wall was *of* jasper; and the city *was* pure gold, like clear glass. ¹⁹ The foundations of the wall of the city *were* adorned with all kinds of precious stones: the first foundation *was* jasper, the second sapphire, the third chalcedony, the fourth emerald, ²⁰ the fifth sardonyx, the sixth sardius, the seventh chrysolite, the eighth beryl, the ninth topaz, the tenth chrysoprase, the eleventh jacinth, and the twelfth amethyst. ²¹ The twelve gates *were* twelve pearls: each individual gate was of one pearl. And the street of the city *was* pure gold, like transparent glass.

²² But I saw no temple in it, for the Lord God Almighty and the Lamb are its temple. ²³ The city had no need of the sun or of the moon to shine in it, for the glory of God illuminated it. The Lamb *is* its light. ²⁴ And the nations of those who are saved shall walk in its light, and the kings of the earth bring their glory and honor into it. ²⁵ Its gates shall not be shut at all by day (there shall be no night there). ²⁶ And they shall bring the glory and the honor of the nations into it. ²⁷ But there shall by no means enter it anything that defiles, or causes an abomination or a lie, but only those who are written in the Lamb's Book of Life.

22 And he showed me a pure river of water of life, clear as crystal, proceeding from the throne of God and of the Lamb. ² In the middle of its street, and on either side of the river, *was* the tree of life, which bore twelve fruits, each *tree* yielding its fruit every month. The leaves of the tree *were* for the healing of the nations. ³ And there shall be no more curse, but the throne of God and of the Lamb shall be in it, and His servants shall serve Him. ⁴ They shall see His face, and His name *shall be* on their foreheads. ⁵ There shall be no night there: They need no lamp nor light of the sun, for the Lord God gives them light. And they shall reign forever and ever.

⁶ Then he said to me, "These words *are* faithful and true." And the Lord God of the holy prophets sent His angel to show His servants the things which must shortly take place.

⁷ "Behold, I am coming quickly! Blessed *is* he who keeps the words of the prophecy of this book."

⁸ Now I, John, saw and heard these things. And when I heard and saw, I fell down to worship before the feet of the angel who showed me these things. ⁹ Then he said to me, "See *that you do not do that.* For I am your fellow servant, and of your brethren the prophets, and of those who keep the words of this book. Worship God." ¹⁰ And he said to me, "Do not seal the words of the prophecy of this book, for the time is at hand. ¹¹ He who is unjust, let him be unjust still; he who is filthy, let him be filthy still; he who is righteous, let him be righteous still; he who is holy, let him be holy still."

¹² "And behold, I am coming quickly, and My reward *is* with Me, to give to every one according to his work. ¹³ I am the Alpha and the Omega, *the* Beginning and *the* End, the First and the Last."

¹⁴ Blessed *are* those who do His commandments, that they may have the right to the tree of life, and may enter through the gates into the city. ¹⁵ But outside *are* dogs and sorcerers and sexually immoral and murderers and idolaters, and whoever loves and practices a lie.

¹⁶ "I, Jesus, have sent My angel to testify to you these things in the churches. I am the Root and the Offspring of David, the Bright and Morning Star."

¹⁷ And the Spirit and the bride say, "Come!" And let him who hears say, "Come!" And let him who thirsts come. Whoever desires, let him take the water of life freely.

¹⁸ For I testify to everyone who hears the words of the prophecy of this book: If anyone adds to these things, God will add to him the plagues that are written in this book; ¹⁹ and if anyone takes away from the words of the book of this prophecy, God shall take away his part from the Book of Life, from the holy city, and *from* the things which are written in this book.

²⁰ He who testifies to these things says, "Surely I am coming quickly."

Amen. Even so, come, Lord Jesus!

²¹ The grace of our Lord Jesus Christ *be* with you all. Amen.

INDEX
TO
THE DEVOTIONS

INDEX TO THE DEVOTIONS